ὁ δὲ κολλώμενος τῷ κυρίῳ
ἓν πνεῦμά ἐστιν.

Ra Ward

THE EXPOSITOR'S

GREEK TESTAMENT

EDITED BY THE REV.

W. ROBERTSON NICOLL, M.A., LL.D.

EDITOR OF " THE EXPOSITOR," " THE EXPOSITOR'S BIBLE," ETC.

VOLUME II.

LONDON
HODDER AND STOUGHTON
27 PATERNOSTER ROW
1900

ABERDEEN UNIVERSITY PRESS

THE EXPOSITOR'S
GREEK TESTAMENT

I
THE ACTS OF THE APOSTLES

BY THE REV.

R. J. KNOWLING, D.D.

PROFESSOR OF NEW TESTAMENT EXEGESIS, KING'S COLLEGE, LONDON

II
ST. PAUL'S EPISTLE TO THE ROMANS

BY THE REV.

JAMES DENNEY, D.D.

PROFESSOR OF SYSTEMATIC AND PASTORAL THEOLOGY, FREE CHURCH COLLEGE, GLASGOW

III
ST. PAUL'S FIRST EPISTLE TO THE CORINTHIANS

BY THE REV.

G. G. FINDLAY, B.A.

PROFESSOR OF BIBLICAL LITERATURE, EXEGESIS AND CLASSICS, HEADINGLEY COLLEGE

LONDON

HODDER AND STOUGHTON

27 PATERNOSTER ROW

1900

THE ACTS

OF THE

APOSTLES.

INTRODUCTION.

THE AUTHOR OF THE BOOK. Whoever wrote the Acts wrote also the Gospel which bears the name of St. Luke. We find writers far removed in standpoint from each other, *e.g.*, H. Holtzmann, *Einleitung*³, p. 391, and Zöckler, *Greifswalder Studien*, p. 128, agreeing in this conviction, and appealing to the same work, Friedrich's *Das Lukas Evangelium und die Apostelgeschichte, Werke desselben Verfassers* (1890; see commentary), in support of it. In recent years the philologist Gercke seems to be almost the only convert to the opposite view who, with Sorof, regards the author of Acts as the reviser of the δεύτερος λόγος of Luke; but his efforts in promulgating his views cannot be said to have met with any success (see Zöckler, *u. s.; Theologische Rundschau*, pp. 50, 129: 1899; and Wendt, *Apostelgeschichte*, p. 4, 1899).

Friedrich's pamphlet, which contains a useful summary of the whole evidence on the subject, much of which had been previously collected by Zeller and Lekebusch (although their readings, like those too of Friedrich, sometimes require careful testing), gives instances of language, style, and treatment of various subjects which place the identity of authorship beyond reasonable doubt (see instances noted in commentary).[1] At the same time it would be misleading to say that recent critics have been unmindful of the linguistic *differences* which the two books present, although a candid examination shows that these differences are comparatively slight (*cf.* Hawkins, *Horæ Synopticæ*, p. 140; Zahn, *Einleitung*, ii., p. 381, 1899). In earlier days Zeller had not lost sight of those peculiarities which are entirely linguistic, and he maintains that they are not of a nature to prove anything against the same origin of the two writings, *Acts*, vol. ii., p. 243, E.T.

---

[1] Amongst recent writers, Blass, in his Index ii., *Acta Apostolorum*, marks fifty-six words as peculiar to St. Luke's Gospel and the Acts; *cf.* also the list in Plummer's *St. Luke*, lii., liii. The instances of words and phrases characteristic of St. Luke's Gospel in Sir J. Hawkins' *Horæ Synopticæ*, 1899, pp. 29-41, will enable any one to see at a glance by the references how far such words and phrases are also characteristic of, or peculiar to, Acts; see also in commentary.

Who is the early Christian writer thus able to give us not only such an account of the Life of our Lord that Renan could describe it as the most beautiful book in the world (*Les Evangiles*, p. 283), but also an account of the *origines* of the Christian Church which Jülicher regards as an ideal Church history, *Einleitung*, p. 270, and of which Blass could write "hunc libellum non modo inter omnes Novi T. optima compositione uti, sed etiam eam artem monstrare, quæ Græco Romanove scriptore rerum non indigna sit"? One thing seems certain, that the writer, whoever he was, represents himself in four passages, xvi. 10-17, xx. 5-15, xxi. 1-18, xxvii. 1-xxviii. 16 inclusive, *cf.* also Acts xi. 28, Codex D (on which see below, and *in loco*), as a companion of St. Paul. If we examine the phraseology of these sections (ninety-seven verses in all), we find that it is in many respects common to that employed in the rest of the book (Klostermann, *Vindiciæ Lucanæ*, p. 46 ff.; Nösgen, *Apostelgeschichte*, pp. 15, 16; Blass, *Acta Apostolorum*, p. 10; Vogel, *Zur Charakteristik des Lukas nach Sprache und Stil*, p. 41; Hawkins, *u. s.*, p. 149; Spitta, *Apostelgeschichte*, pp. 235, 257).[1]

Those who deny this identity of authorship are not only obliged to face the difficulty of accounting for this similarity of style and language, but also to account for the introduction of the "We" sections at all. If the writer of the rest of the book had wished to palm himself off at a later period as a companion of St. Paul, he would scarcely have sought to accomplish this on the strength of the insertion of these sections alone, as they stand. It may be fairly urged that he would at least have adopted one of the unmistakable

---

[1] Sir J. Hawkins not only gives us, p. 151, seventeen words and phrases found only in the "We" sections and in the rest of Acts; twenty-seven words and phrases found in the "We" sections and Luke, with or without the rest of Acts also; thirty-seven words and phrases found in the "We" sections, and also used predominantly, though not exclusively, in the rest of Acts or Luke or either of them; but he remarks that out of the eighty-six Matthæan words and phrases, ten, or rather less than *one eighth* occur in the "We" sections; out of the thirty-seven Marcan words and phrases, six, or about *one sixth;* out of the 140 Lucan words and phrases, less than *one third*, p. 14, ff.: "Is it not utterly impossible," he asks, p. 150, "that the language of the original writer of the 'We' sections should have chanced to have so very many more correspondences with the language of the subsequent compiler than with that of Matthew or Mark?" The expressions peculiar to the "We" sections are for the most part fairly accounted for by the subject-matter, p. 153, *e.g.*, εὐθυδρομέω, κατάγεσθαι, παραλέγομαι, πλόος, ὑποπλέω. Part iii., C, Section iv., of the same book should also be consulted where the identity of the third Synoptist with a friend and companion of St. Paul is further confirmed by the similarities between his Gospel and St. Paul's Epistles.

methods of which a Thucydides, a Polybius, a Josephus availed themselves to make their personal relation to the facts narrated known to their readers (Zahn, *Einleitung*, ii., pp. 387, 426, 435).

This unknown author of Acts, moreover, whoever he was, was a man of such literary skill that he was able to assimilate the " We " sections to the rest of his book, and to introduce cross references from them to other parts of his work, *e.g.*, xxi. 8 and vi. 5 ; and yet, with all this, he is so deficient in literary taste as to allow the first person plural in the " We " sections to remain, a blunder avoidable by a stroke of his pen.

The German philologist, Vogel, who cannot be accused of speaking with a theological bias, states the common-sense view of the matter in pointing out that when an author of such literary skill as the author of Acts undoubtedly possessed passes without a break from the third to the first person in his narrative, every unprejudiced reader will explain it on the ground that the author thus wished modestly to intimate his own personal presence during certain events. This is the one natural explanation, and to this Vogel determines to adhere, until it is shown to be untenable ; and he justly pours ridicule upon the notion that the author of Acts would have interwoven into a work written in such a delicate and finished style the travel-diary of some other person without altering the pronouns (*Charakteristik des Lukas nach Sprache und Stil*, pp. 12, 13).

If we are asked to believe that this first person plural was introduced from time to time merely for the purpose of giving an air of verisimilitude to the narrative (or in imitation of certain passages in Ezra and Nehemiah, or Tobit),[1] why should we not find it in the account, *e.g.*, of St. Peter's escape from prison, chap. xii., where Wendt maintains that the author probably had possession of a narrative full of details, derived probably from John Mark himself ? There can be no doubt that the " We " sections are introduced for the definite purpose of marking the writer's presence with St. Paul ; we cannot, *e.g.*, conclude that there is any other reason for the circumstance that the " We " section of chap. xvi. breaks off at Philippi, and that the following " We " section, chap. xx., commences again at Philippi. But if this is so, how again could a later unknown writer have gained possession of a document of such high value as that comprising or embodying these " We " sections ? A day-journal

---

[1] See Weiss, *Einleitung*, p. 583, and Overbeck (De Wette, 4th edition), p. xliv., who both point out that the cases are not analogous, although, on the other hand, Hilgenfeld and Wendt have recently pressed them into service.

left behind by an intimate companion of St. Paul must have been preserved long enough for this unknown writer to have incorporated it, or at least some of it, into his own work, and it must then have vanished altogether out of sight, although one would have supposed that a treasure so valuable would have been preserved and guarded in some Christian circle with the greatest care.[1]

But if we further ask who amongst the companions of St. Paul speaks to us in these "We" sections, the testimony of critics of various schools—of critics who draw a distinction between the authorship of the "We" sections and the rest of the book—may be quoted in favour of St. Luke as the author of the former, if not, as we believe, of the latter also. Thus Holtzmann, *Einleitung*[3], pp. 394, 395, examines the question, and decides in favour of St. Luke as against the claims of Timothy, Silas, or Titus (so Overbeck (De Wette, 4th edit.), pp. l., li.; Mangold, *Einleitung* (Bleek), p. 445; Spitta, *u. s.*, p. 312). Acts xx. 5, 6 may be fairly quoted as decisive against Timothy, to say nothing of the impossibility that the author of Acts should assume the character of a person in the "We" sections, and by naming this same person elsewhere should thus distinguish him from himself (Overbeck). For Silas nothing can be said, and the advocacy of his claims is the most groundless of any of the three. He appears nowhere in the third missionary journey, an absence which would be fatally inconsistent with his presence in the "We" sections, and he is nowhere named in any of the letters of the First Imprisonment, whereas the narrator of xxvii. 1-xxviii. 16 would naturally be found amongst the companions of the Apostle during that period (of course, if xi. 27, 28 in β-text be taken into account, both Timothy and Silas are thereby excluded, Zahn, *Einleitung*, ii., p. 425). The same objection may be made to Titus, since there is no hint that he was with St. Paul at Rome (even if we allow that he may have been included in the ἡμεῖς at Antioch, xi. 27, and that, as he is not mentioned at all in Acts, the difficulties which are presented by the names of Timothy and Silas do not occur in his case). Moreover, the travel-journey of Silas would have commenced rather with xv. 1, as Holtzmann urges; nor is there any reason to suppose that Silas was at Philippi during the time required (Holtz-

---

[1] This, no doubt, presents less difficulty to advanced critics who find it apparently easy to credit that the Pastoral Epistles contain fragments of genuine letters of St. Paul, and that these letters having supplied the fragments to the Pastorals were themselves no longer cared for or regarded (McGiffert, *Apostolic Age*, pp. 407, 408, and, on the other hand, Dr. Salmon, *Introd.*, p. 408).

mann, *u. s.*, p. 395). See further Zahn, *u. s.*, pp. 351, 388, 425 ; Lightfoot, B.D.², i., 32.

But if the author of these sections is to be found amongst the intimate companions of St. Paul, and amongst those who were with him in Rome, no one fulfils the conditions better than St. Luke. Even Jülicher, who declines to decide positively which of the four companions, Silas, Timothy, Titus, Luke, was the author, considers that if it was St. Luke, we have in that fact the best explanation that his name remained attached to the Third Gospel and Acts alike, *Einleitung*, p. 269. The writer of Acts xxvii. 1-xxviii. 16 evidently accompanied St. Paul to Rome, and that St. Luke was with the Apostle at the time of his first captivity we learn on the authority of two Epistles which very few of the best critics would now care to dispute, Col. iv. 14, Philem. ver. 24.

But the writer of Acts has not felt the need of using the Epistles of St. Paul as sources for his work, although they were the most weighty documents for the history which he professes to describe. There are numbers of undesigned coincidences between the letters and the history, and Paley, in his *Horæ Paulinæ*, has done invaluable service in drawing attention to them. But still Acts is written independently of the Epistles, and it cannot be said that any one letter in particular is employed by the writer. Yet this would be inconceivable if the former work was composed 100-120 A.D., especially when we remember the knowledge of the Epistles displayed by the writer of the Epistle of Barnabas, by St. Ignatius or St. Polycarp (Harnack, *Chron.*, i., 249). Moreover the writer, whoever he was, was beyond all doubt intensely interested in St. Paul, and it is strange that he should not have made use of his letters, when we remember the impression which they made upon those contemporary with the great Apostle, *cf.* 2 Cor. x. 10, 2 Pet. iii. 15 (Zahn, *u. s.*, p. 412).

But this relation between Acts and the Pauline Epistles not only shows that the former was written before the close of the first century, but that the author stood sufficiently near to St. Paul to be able to write without enriching his knowledge by references to the Apostle's letters. This, however, becomes natural enough on the supposition that the writer was a Timothy, or a Titus, or a Luke. If, however, the two former are excluded, probabilities again point to Luke (Zahn). (For recent writers who deny the acquaintance of the author of Acts with St. Paul's Epistles we may refer to Wendt, Felten, McGiffert, Harnack, Zahn, Jülicher, Rackham.) And we thus come into line with early Church tradition which referred the third

Gospel and the Acts to Luke, the beloved physician, the friend of St. Paul, *cf. Frag. Murator.*, and Iren., *Adv. Hær.*, iii., 14.

But Luke, we have been recently reminded, was not an uncommon name, and many Christians may have borne it in the latter part of the first century (McGiffert, *Apostolic Age*, p. 435). But not only is the above tradition precise in its mention of Luke as a physician; the writings attributed to him bear upon the face of them indications of the hand of a medical man. No reference, however, to the possibility of this is made by Dr. McGiffert. He tells us, p. 239, that nowhere is the source used by the author of Acts marked by anything like the vividness, preciseness, and fulness of detail that characterise the "We" sections.[1] The writer of these sections was not Silas or Timothy, but "the unknown author of the 'We' passages," p. 239. This unknown author was evidently the intimate companion of St. Paul, and of his other companions in Rome none is more likely to have written the personal notes of travel than Luke, who seems indeed to have been the nearest and dearest to the Apostle of all his friends (pp. 434, 435). The inference from all this, coupled with the tradition of

---

[1] "If there is one narrative of the N.T. which more than another contains internal proof of having been related by an eye-witness, it is the account of the voyage and shipwreck of St. Paul," Salmon, *Introd.*, p. 5, and this judgment based upon the valuable monograph of James Smith (himself a Fellow of the Royal Society) of Jordan Hill, *Voyage and Shipwreck of St. Paul*, 4th edit., revised and corrected, 1880, has received fresh and remarkable confirmation, not only from English but from German and French sources of a technical and professional kind: *e.g.*, Dr. Breusing, Director of the Seefahrtschule in Bremen, published in 1886 his *Die Nautik der Alten* with a close examination verse by verse of the narrative in Acts xxvii., and he has been followed precisely on the same lines by J. Vars, Professor in the Lycée of Brest in his *L'Art Nautique dans l'antiquité*, 1887. Both writers make constant reference to Smith's work, although they often differ from him in *technical* details, and references to Breusing will be found in Blass and Wendt (1899). The latter writer also refers to a thoughtful article with a similar testimony to St. Luke's accuracy by Von Goerne in the *Neue Kirchliche Zeitschrift*, p. 352, 1898, and allusions will be found to this, as to the above-mentioned works, in the commentary. Breusing's testimony is very striking, p. xiii.: "The most valuable nautical document of antiquity which has come down to us is the account of the voyage and shipwreck of the Apostle Paul. Every one can see at a glance that it could only have been composed by an eye-witness." The strangest exception perhaps to this almost universal recognition of the value of the narrative in Acts xxvii. (*cf.*, *e.g.*, the remarkable testimony in its favour by Weizsäcker, *Apostolic Age*, ii., p. 126 ff., E.T.) is Mommsen's attack upon it in *Sitzungsber. d. berl. Ak.*, 1895, p. 503; but, as Zahn justly remarks, Mommsen has not increased his reputation by alleging that "Luke speaks of the Adriatic Sea by Crete and of the barbarians of Malta"; see answers to these objections in Zahn, *Einleitung*, ii., p. 421, and also in commentary, Acts xxvii. 27, and xxviii. 2.

the Church, would seem to be quite plain, but Dr. McGiffert declines to draw it, and falls back upon the belief that some other person named Luke was the writer of the third Gospel and Acts, p. 433. But if there had been such a person there would have been no need for tradition to identify him with Luke the beloved physician, since his own intrinsic merits as an author and historian would have been amply sufficient to secure him an undying recognition.

Here comes in the value of the argument from the medical language employed in the third Gospel and the Acts. The Church in identifying the writer with St. Paul's beloved friend was not following some fanciful or unreliable tradition, but a tradition amply supported by an examination of the language of the books in question; language which not only witnesses to the truth of the tradition, but also to the unity of Acts, since this medical phraseology may be traced in every part, and not in the "We" sections alone. The present Introduction, which must of necessity be brief, does not allow of any lengthy examination of this important subject (to which the writer hopes to return), but in a large number of passages in the commentary notes are given with special reference to indications of medical phraseology. But one or two remarks may be added here. In the first place, it is well to bear in mind that St. Luke's medical phraseology was fully recognised before Dr. Hobart's interesting and valuable book, *The Medical Language of St. Luke*, 1882 (*cf., e.g.,* Dr. Belcher's *Our Lord's Miracles of Healing*, 1st edit., with Preface by Archbishop Trench, 1871, 2nd edit., 1890). The *Gentleman's Magazine*, June, 1841, containing a short article of some two and a half pages, pp. 585-587, is often referred to as a kind of starting-point for this inquiry, but it should not be forgotten that the great names of Wetstein and Bengel may be quoted as fully recognising the hand of a medical writer; thus in commenting not only on Luke xiv. 2, but also on Acts xxviii. 8, Wetstein makes the same remark: "Lucas qui medicus fuerat morbos accuratius describere solet," *cf.* Bengel on Acts iii. 7, "Proprie locutus est *medicus* Lucas," and Luke viii. 43, where the disputed reading does not interfere with the force of the comment: "Lucas medicus ingenue scribit". Indeed it is not too much to say that the main position taken up by Hobart has been abundantly recognised both in France and Germany, and not always in quarters where such a recognition might have been anticipated, *cf., e.g.,* Renan, *Saint Paul*, p. 133, 12th edit.; J. Weiss, *Evangelium des Lukas*, 1892, with reference to Dr. Hobart's book, and with quotations from it, although with the qualification that many of the instances require careful sifting,

p. 274 ff. More recently the German philologist Vogel, 1897, *Zur Charakteristik des Lukas nach Sprache und Stil*, p. 17, draws attention to the fact that a large number of words peculiar to the Acts are found in Luke's contemporary, the physician Dioscorides of Anazarbus in Cilicia, not far from Antioch, and he speaks of the use of Dioscorides by the Evangelist as highly probable. But the fullest recognition of Dr. Hobart's work comes to us even more recently by Zahn: " Dr. Hobart has proved for every one for whom anything can be proved, that the author of the Lucan work (by which Zahn means both the third Gospel and Acts) is a Greek physician, acquainted with the technical terms of the medical art," *Einleitung*, ii., pp. 427, 435 (1899). The language is strong, and it may perhaps be fairly contended that some of the instances cited by Dr. Zahn may well have been subjected to the cross-examination instituted so carefully and fully by Dr. Plummer, *St. Luke*, pp. lii., lxiii.-lxvi., in his inquiry into the validity of Dr. Hobart's position.[1] The evidence in favour of this position must be cumulative, but it depends not merely upon the occurrence of technical medical terms in St. Luke's writings, but also upon his *tendency* to employ medical language more frequently than the other Evangelists, upon the passages in his Gospel in which we come across medical terms which are wanting in the parallel passages in St. Matthew and St. Mark, upon the account which he gives of miracles of healing not only in comparison with the other Evangelists, but also of the miracles peculiar to his own narratives; upon the way in which he *abstains from using* in a medical sense words which medical writers abstain from so using, although employed in this sense elsewhere in the Gospels; upon the frequency with which he uses medical language and phraseology in a secondary sense. Illustrations of some of these characteristic peculiarities are noted in the commentary, and a passing reference (space allows this only) may be made to two others. Each of the Synoptists gives our Lord's comparison between the passage of a camel through the eye of a needle and the entrance of a rich man into the kingdom of heaven, St. Matt. xix. 24, St. Mark x. 25, St. Luke xviii. 25. St. Matthew and St. Mark have the same word for

---

[1] Whatever strictures may be passed upon Dr. Hobart's book, it must not be forgotten that the following authorities amongst others are persuaded that the author's main thesis has been abundantly proved: Bishop Lightfoot, " Acts," B.D.[2], i., p. 31; Dr. Salmon, *Introd.*, p. 129; Professor Ramsay, *St. Paul*, p. 205; Dr. Plummer, *St. Luke, u. s.* (*cf.* Sir J. Hawkins, *Horæ Synopticæ*, p. 154, 1899); and it is significant that Dr. B. Weiss in the 3rd edit. of his *Einleitung* refers to the book, and no longer speaks of the argument as mere " trifling ".

needle ῥαφίδος: διὰ τρυπήματος ῥαφίδος, Matt., T.R.; but W.H. τρήματος in text, τρυπήματος in margin, διὰ (τῆς) τρυμαλιᾶς (τῆς) ῥαφίδος, Mark. But when we turn to St. Luke, he introduces at least one different word (if we adopt W.H. for St. Matt.), and a combination peculiar to himself, διὰ τρήματος βελόνης (W.H. and R.V.). It cannot be said that the words used by St. Luke occur in LXX, since neither of them is found there (although St. Mark's τρυμαλία occurs in LXX possibly six and at least three times). But both words used by St. Luke were in technical medical use, τρῆμα being the great medical word for a perforation of any kind, βελόνη being the surgical needle; and not only so but the two words are found combined as here by Galen: διὰ τοῦ κατὰ τὴν βελόνην τρήματος and again τοῦ διατρήματος τῆς βελόνης (cf. Hobart, p. 60, J. Weiss, u. s., p. 567, Zahn, u. s., p. 436, and Nestle, Einführung in das G. N. T., p. 228).

Dr. Plummer points out that τρῆμα is not peculiar to St. Luke (see W.H. above), but the *combination* is peculiar to St. Luke, and the force of this fact and of the combination of undoubted medical terms is not lessened by Grimm's description of βελόνη as a more classical word than ῥαφίς.

Once again: St. Luke's characteristic medical style shows itself in abstention as well as in employment. In three passages, *e.g.*, μαλακία is used by St. Matthew to denote disease, but in medical language it is used as in its primary classical sense of delicacy, effeminacy, and St. Luke never uses it in St. Matthew's sense, although he employs the cognate adjective μαλακός of " soft " raiment in vii. 25. But this non-usage of the noun by the medical Luke is all the more significant, since in the LXX it is found at least a dozen times to denote sickness and disease.

In St. Matt. iv. 24, viii. 6, both βασανίζειν and βάσανος are used of bodily sickness, but in medical writers the words are not employed in this sense, and St. Luke refrains from so employing them (Hobart, p. 63, and Zahn, u. s., p. 435). But here again significance is added to this non-usage by St. Luke when we remember that βάσανος is not only used of the torments after death in Wisd. iii. 1, 4 Macc. iii. 15, cf. Luke xvi. 23, 28, but also of the pain of bodily disease, 1 Macc. ix. 56.

THE AIM OF THE BOOK. Not only the aim but the purpose and contents of the book are set forth, according to Lightfoot, in the Preface, chap. i. 1-8. The prophetic words of the Lord in ver. 8 implicitly involve a table of contents: " Ye shall receive power when the Holy Ghost," etc., ii. 1-13; " witnesses unto me " (1) " in Jerusalem," ii. 14-viii. 1, and (2) " in all Judæa and Samaria," viii. 2-xi. 18, (3) " and to the uttermost part of the earth," xi. 19-xxviii.

31 (on the latter expression see comment. *in loco* and reference to *Psalms of Solomon*, viii. 16). The writer closes with the event which his aim required, the preaching of the Gospel in Rome, the capital of the world, the metropolis of the human race, without hindrance ; and the fulfilment of the third section mentioned above is thus given, not actually, but potentially, while an earnest is afforded of its ultimate accomplishment ; *Philippians*, p. 3 ; B.D.[2], i., p. 26 ; *cf.* also Weiss, *Einleitung*, p. 562, Blass, *Acta Apost.*, Proleg., p. 3 : " At hic liber non est imperfectus, cum longi cursus evangelii Roma terminus sit ". But starting from the distinction which Lightfoot himself thus draws between the potential and actual, is it not quite possible that there may thus be room for the τρίτος λόγος for which Lightfoot, it is true, saw no conceivable place, *cf.* Harnack, *Chron.*, i., p. 248, but for the purpose of which Professor Ramsay, *St. Paul*, p. 380, and others, notably Zahn, *Einleitung*, ii., p. 380, have so strongly argued (see list of earlier advocates in Bleek-Mangold, *Einleitung*, p. 462, and note in comment. on xxviii. 31)? It is perhaps worth noting that Bengel, to whom we owe the oft-quoted words, *Victoria verbi Dei, Paulus Romæ, apex evangelii, Actorum Finis,* reminds us on the same page of the words of Estius : " Fortasse Lucas meditabatur *tertium librum*, in quo repeteret acta illius biennii ; sicut, *Act.* i., quædam exposuit tacita ultimo capite evangelii ". Moreover, if we take Acts i. 8 as giving us in outline the programme of the book, it seems that its purpose would have been fulfilled not so much in the triumph of the Gospel, but in the bearing witness to Christ in Jerusalem, Samaria, and to the end of the earth : the Apostles were to be witnesses, i. 8 ; St. Paul was told that he was " to bear witness " in Rome, μαρτυρῆσαι xxiii. 11, *cf.* xxviii. 23 ; the triumph would succeed the witness, and the keynote of victory is struck in the word ἀκωλύτως.

Nothing, it is true, is said in Acts of the beginnings of Christianity in Rome, or as to how the Church was first founded in that city ; but when we consider the importance that St. Paul plainly attached to his seeing for himself the metropolis of the world, *cf.* xix. 21, and when his Epistle addressed to the Roman Church indicates how clearly he foresaw the importance which that Church would have for Gentile Christianity in the future, it is quite conceivable that the universalist Luke would draw his second treatise to a fitting close by showing that blindness in part had happened to Israel that the fulness of the Gentiles might come in. " We are not told," says Holtzmann, quoting Overbeck, " how the Gospel came to Rome, but how Paul came to Rome " : but this objection, which

Overbeck considered the greatest against the view that the contents of Acts were summed up in chap. i. 8, is obviated by the above considerations; St. Paul was to bear witness in Rome as he had at Jerusalem, but the result of his final witness in Jerusalem, xxiii. 1 ff., resulted in a division among the Jews, and a similar result followed his first testimony in Rome. The Gospel had come to Rome already, but those who accepted it were only a sect everywhere spoken against; now its foremost representative gains it a hearing from the Gentiles, and that too without interruption or prohibition.

But this recognition of the importance of St. Paul's witness and work in Rome, and of their subsequent development, by no means excludes other purposes which may have been present to the mind of St. Luke. "No other N.T. writer," says Zahn, "mentions a Roman emperor by name," and he proceeds to point out the significance of this fact in connection with the whole design of St. Luke to show that Christianity was an historical religion; how the edicts of Augustus, Luke ii. 1, and of Claudius, Acts xviii. 2, had their influence on the new faith (*cf.* Luke iii. 1), how in comparison with the other Evangelists St. Luke constantly introduces the names of those who were connected indirectly as well as directly with political events (*Einleitung*, ii., p. 375, and *cf.* Ramsay, *St. Paul*, p. 385, Friedrich, *u. s.*, p. 53 ff.). Not only would notices of this kind impress a reader of the type of Theophilus with a sense of the certainty of those things in which he had been instructed, but they are also of importance in that they indicate that a writer, who thus took pains to gain accurate information with regard to events in the Roman world, would naturally be interested in tracing carefully the relations between the empire and the infant Church, and all the more so if it was important to show his readers that Christianity stood in no hostile relationship to the imperial government (*cf.* Zahn, *u. s.*, p. 379).

But it is one thing to describe one of the objects of the book in this way, *viz.*, as an attempt to reassure those who had been already instructed in the *origines* of the Christian Faith, and to emphasise its evident power and rectitude at the bar of the rulers of this world, and to maintain that all this was done with a political-apologetic aim, regardless of truthfulness to fact, and only concerned with representing Christianity in a favourable light before magistrates and kings. No doubt we are repeatedly told how St. Paul took shelter in an appeal to Roman law and Roman authority, and how much more justly and calmly the Roman authorities judged of his case than the fanatical and insensate Jews; "but," says Wendt with admirable candour (*Apostelgeschichte*, p. 17), "there is no reason to doubt that this representation simply corresponded to historical truth" (see the whole paragraph in Wendt, 1899, and *cf.* Weiss, *u. s.*, p. 569, as against Overbeck and Mangold, *u. s.*, p. 427, following Schnecken-burger and Zeller). Moreover, when we remember that the writer of Acts deliberately enters upon a field of history "where perhaps beyond all others there was room for mistake and blunder, the administration of the Roman Empire and its provinces," nothing is more surprising than the way in which his accuracy is confirmed by every fresh and searching investigation.[1]

But if there is no reason to attribute a political tendency (see further below) to the writer, still less is there room for the attribu-tion of a doctrinal tendency. The earlier representatives of this latter view of the book, Baur and Zeller, started with insisting upon the fundamental opposition which prevailed between the view of the relationship of St. Paul with the primitive Apostles as set forth in those Epistles which these critics accepted, and in the Acts : to St. Paul a Judaising tendency was ascribed in the latter which was not in harmony with his statements in his own writings, whilst, on the other hand, to St. Peter especially a liberal stand-point was ascribed, which was not to be expected in view of the utterances of St. Paul in his Epistles, a standpoint which would make Peter, not Paul, the originator of Gentile Christianity. On the whole the Acts represented an idealised and harmonising view of the relation of parties in the primitive Church, and its object as the work of a Pauline Christian was to reconcile the Jewish and Pauline parties. Schneckenburger had previously emphasised the supposed parallel in Acts between Peter and Paul (see further below), and had represented the book as written with the apologetie aim of defending Paul against the misrepresentation of the Juda-isers ; but it must always be remembered that Schneckenburger, although emphasising the apologetic tendency of St. Luke, never denied

---

[1] *Cf., e.g.*, the notes on xvii. 6, xxviii. 7, etc., the references to the invaluable and epoch-making works of Professor Ramsay, and Vogel, *Zur Charakteristik des Lukas nach Sprache und Stil*, p. 28, 1897, on the remarkable degree of confidence with which military, political, and judicial terms are employed in Acts. Professor Schmiedel in his review of Professor Ramsay's *St. Paul* describes it as the work on the whole not of the historian or archæologist, but of the narrow apologist, *Theolo-gische Literaturzeitung*, 1897, No. 23, and more recently, Professor H. Holtzmann, characterises Professor Ramsay's description and illustration of the scene, Acts xvi. 25-34, as "humbug"! *Theologische Literaturzeitung*, 1899, No. 7 ; such remarks are ill calculated to promote candid and respectful criticism.

his historical truthfulness, whilst Baur fastened upon Schnecken-burger's view, and further developed his own previous attack on the historical character of Acts (Zahn, *u. s.*, p. 393, Lightfoot, B.D.², i., 41). But Baur's theory in its extreme form could not maintain its ground, and various modifications of it took place within his own school. Certainly, to take an illustration, it must always remain a strange fact that, if Acts was written with the conciliatory tendency alluded to, only one indirect mention in it is found, xxiv. 17, of the collection for the poor Saints at Jerusalem, which played so promi-nent a part in St. Paul's work and writings, and which was in itself such a palpable proof of the Apostle's love for his Jewish brethren. The tendency view adopted by some of the writers succeeding Baur, *e.g.*, Reuss, Keim, Weizsäcker, regards the author of Acts as not intentionally departing from the historical relations between the two parties, but as forming his judgment of the relations between them from the standpoint of his own time. One of the most recent attempts to represent the conciliatory tendency of Acts as an apo-logy for the Christian religion before Gentiles, *i.e.*, before a heathen public, against the charges of the Jews, and to show how Judaism, through Christianity, broke up into its world-wide mission, is that of J. Weiss, *Über die Absicht und den literar. Charakter der A. G.*, 1897 (see further below); but whatever amount of correctness there may be in this view we may frankly adopt, without committing ourselves to the very precarious explanations and deductions of the writer; St. Luke's own prologue, and the dedication of his two writings to the Gentile Theophilus, are in themselves sufficient to lead us to expect that the design accentuated by J. Weiss would not be alto-gether absent from his mind in composing his history (see the remarks of Zahn, *u. s.*, ii., p. 393).

But if there is no satisfaction in the more recent attempts to represent Acts as written mainly with a conciliatory " tendency," still less can satisfaction be found in the view, older in its origin, of a supposed *parallelism* between St. Peter and St. Paul, drawn out by a writer who wished in this way to reconcile the Petrine and Pauline parties in the Church, by placing the leaders of each in a position of equal authority. That there are points of similarity in the life and work of the two Apostles may be readily admitted, but these likenesses are of the most general kind, and only such as we might expect in cases where two men work in the same calling at the same period and under the same conditions, *cf.* to this effect Clemen, *Die Chronologie der Paulinischen Briefe*, pp. 17, 18, and Feine, *Eine vorkanonische Überlieferung des Lukas*, p. 214. The parallel can only be extended to a few instances such as the healing of the lame man by Peter at Jerusalem, iii. 2, and by Paul at Lystra, xiv. 8, but there is no real ground for the institution of a parallel between the worship paid to Peter by Cornelius, x. 25, and by the inhabitants of Lystra to St. Paul, xiv. 11, or between the judgment inflicted on Ananias and Sapphira by Peter, v. 1, and on Elymas by St. Paul, xiii. 6.   The position thus advocated by Clemen is taken up by B. Weiss, *Einleitung*, p. 540, 3rd edit., 1897, no less than by earlier writers like Lekebusch and Nösgen (*cf.* too Sanday, *Bampton Lectures*, p. 327, and Salmon, *Introduction*, p. 310).   But whether we consider that the parallel was instituted to place Paul on an equality with Peter, or, as Van Manen has recently urged, *Paulus I.: De handelingen der Apostelen*, p. 126, 1890, that the writer wished to represent Peter in accordance with the delineation of Paul, there is one fact fatal to both points of view, *viz.*, that if either of these purposes had been in the mind of the author of Acts, we cannot account for his omission of the crowning point to the parallel between the two Apostles, *viz.*, their martyrdom in the same city, and in the same persecution.   An already discredited theory can scarcely survive the ridicule of Dr. Blass, *Proleg.*, p. 8, and of Dr. Salmon, *u. s.*, pp. 310, 311 : in all true history we may expect to find parallelisms, and these parallels exist in the lives of nations no less than of individuals. When we consider the various attempts which have been made to describe the aim of Acts, it is something to find that a critic who does not hesitate to regard the book as written to some extent with an idealising and harmonising purpose, should nevertheless be constrained to reckon it, on account of its many trustworthy traditions, as an historical work of invaluable worth, see Wendt, *Apostelgeschichte*, p. 33, 1899.

Sources.   If St. Luke is acknowledged as the writer of Acts, we can understand the remark of Blass that in this case the question of sources for the greater part of the book need not be raised, Blass, *Acta Apost.*, Proleg., p. 10; *cf.* Zahn, *u. s.*, pp. 404, 412; Knabenbauer, *Actus Apostolorum*, p. 8, 1899.   It is plain from the narrative that a man in St. Luke's position would be brought into contact with many persons from whom he could have obtained rich and varied information, and in many cases the details of his narrative point unmistakably to the origin of the information.   A good example may be seen in chap. xii. (see commentary), in which the vivid and circumstantial details of St. Peter's escape from prison are best accounted for on the supposition that the narrative comes from John Mark : to the house of the mother of Mark St. Peter makes his way, ver. 12, and not only does later history associate St. Mark with St. Peter, but also with St. Luke and St. Paul, inasmuch as he is with the latter in Rome, Col. iv. 10, Philem., ver. 24 (*cf.* 2 Tim. iv. 11), to say nothing of an earlier association, *cf.* Acts xiii. (Ramsay, *St. Paul*, p. 385 ; Blass, *u. s.*, p. 11 ; Belser, *Theologische Quartalschrift*, p. 62, 1895) ; and even Wendt, p. 31 (1899), sees no other way of accounting for the contrast between the brief notice of the death of St. James, xii. 1, and the lengthy account of the liberation of St. Peter than the probability that the latter was derived from John Mark, whilst more exact information was wanting for the former.

But John Mark was not the only member of the Jerusalem Church from whom, or through whom, St. Luke could have obtained information as to the origin of the Christian community.   Barnabas, the cousin of John Mark, was in a position to know accurately the same events, in some of which he had shared, iv. 36, and if St. Luke was a member of the Church at Antioch when Barnabas settled there (*cf.* note on xi. 28) he would have learnt from the lips of Barnabas the early history of the Jerusalem Church ; and it would have been strange if amongst the men of Cyprus and Cyrene who fled from Judæa to Antioch, xi. 19, there had been none who were baptised at the first Christian Pentecost, *cf.* ii. 10, 41 (Zahn, *u. s.*, p. 414).

For the same series of events St. Luke had access also to the information preserved by Mnason, a disciple ἀρχαῖος, *i.e.*, from the first Pentecost, *cf.* xi. 15, xxi. 16, from whom likewise he may have learnt the account given in ix. 31-43.   In chap. xxi. we are also told how Luke was a guest for several days in the house of Philip the Evangelist, vv. 8-12, an intercourse which could have furnished him with the information narrated not only in viii. 4-40, but in vi. 1-viii. 3, x. 1-xi. 18.   And from Jerusalem itself, no less than from Cæsarea, information might have been acquired, for Luke, xxi. 18, had intercourse not only with the elders but with no less a person than St. James, the head of the Church at Jerusalem, and at an earlier period he must have shared at Philippi, xvi. 19 ff., the company of Silas, who is mentioned as one of the chief among the brethren of the mother city, xv. 22.   In this connection we may note that St. Luke alone gives us two incidents connected with Herod Antipas, Luke xiii. 31-33, xxiii. 6-12, 15, *cf.* Acts iv. 27, which are not narrated by the other Evangelists, but this intimate acquaintance of St. Luke with the court of Herod is in strict harmony with the notice of Manaen the foster-brother of Herod, Acts xiii. 1, *cf.* Luke viii. 3, a teacher of the Church at Antioch when St. Luke may himself have been there, and from whom the Evangelist may at all events have learnt much of the information about other members of the Herodian family which comes to us from him only (Plumptre, Zahn, Belser, Feine). It may no doubt be contended, with considerable plausibility, that St. Luke must have had at his command written documents as well, *e.g.*, in his account of the speeches of St. Peter and St. Stephen, and it is quite possible that he might have obtained such documents from the Church at Jerusalem. One thing is quite certain, that these addresses like all others throughout the book are in striking harmony with the circumstances and crises to which they relate (see further below): "quo intentius has orationes inspexeris," writes Blass, "eo plura in eis reperies, quæ cum sint temporibus personisque egregie accommodata, ad rhetoricam licentiam scriptoris referri se vetent" (*Proleg.*, p. 11). But at the same time it requires no great stretch of imagination to conclude with Zahn (ii., p. 412) that such a man as Luke required no other sources of information for the composition of Acts, or at least for a great portion of that work, than his own recollections, partly of the narratives of St. Paul, partly of the events in which he himself had shared, *cf.* vi. 8-viii. 3, ix. 1-30, xiii.-xxviii. There is abundant proof in St. Paul's Epistles that the Apostle must have constantly referred to his earlier experiences in way of conversation, or in the delivery of his discourses, *cf.* 2 Cor. i. 8-10, xi. 22, xii. 9, Gal. i. 11-ii. 14, Phil. iii. 3-7, Rom. xv. 16-32, xvi. 7, and during periods of enforced inactivity, while Luke was with him at Cæsarea, or during the winter months at Malta, or later in Rome, nothing was more natural, as Zahn urges, than that the great missionary should communicate to his beloved friend the records of his work and experience in great heathen centres of commercial or intellectual life, like Corinth, Ephesus, Athens. After his return from his travels, and on many other occasions, Zahn points out that it was St. Paul's habit to relate minutely καθ᾽ ἓν ἕκαστον, xxi. 19, what God had wrought by him, xiv. 27, xv. 3, 12, 26, Gal. ii. 2, 7-9, and there is no reason whatever to suppose that such recitals were withheld from St. Luke. No doubt it may be urged that the style in the second part of the book is less Hebraistic than in chaps. i.-xii., but this may be fairly accounted for if we remember that St. Luke would often obtain his information for the earlier events from Jewish Christians, and on the soil of Palestine, and that he may have purposely retained the Hebraistic colouring in his embodiment of these narratives, *cf.* Plummer, *St. Luke*, p. xlix.; Zahn, *u. s.*, ii.,

pp. 414, 423; Dalman, *Die Worte Jesu*, p. 31, 1898.[1] If it be maintained that the earlier chapters of Acts, i.-v., were incorporated from
some earlier document, it is admitted that this was of Jewish-
Christian origin, derived from the Jewish Church through an
eye-witness (*cf.* B. Weiss, *Einleitung*, p. 549, 3rd edit.; Feine, *u.
s.*, p. 233). Thus in these chapters, *e.g.*, the Sadducees appear
as the chief opponents of the new faith, *cf.* note on iv. 1, and the
members of the hierarchy are represented as in the main members
of the same sect, a fact which strikes us as strange, but which is
in strict accordance with the testimony of Josephus. A careful consideration of the speeches and of their appropriateness to their
various occasions tends more and more surely to refute the notion
that they are fictitious addresses, the work of a writer of the second
century. The testimony of Dr. McGiffert may be cited as bearing
witness to the primitive character of the reports of the speeches of
St. Peter in the early chapters of Acts, and for the truthful manner
in which they represent a very early type of Christian teaching (see
comment., p. 119), and *cf.* also the remarks of Schmiedel, *Enc.
Bibl.*, i., 48, 1899.

At the delivery of St. Stephen's speech Paul himself was present,
xxvi. 10, *cf.* vi. 12, and there is good reason for thinking that the
speech made a deep impression upon him (see, *e.g.*, Felten, *Apostelgeschichte*, p. 31), while the many Lucan expressions and turns
of thought which it contains (*cf.* Zeller, *Acts*, ii., p. 313, E.T.,
and Overbeck, *Apostelgeschichte*, p. 93) are natural enough if the
address comes to us through the medium of a translation (see
commentary for the speech and its meaning).

For the second part of the book we perceive that St. Luke might
have easily obtained accurate reports of the speeches even in cases
where he was not present; *e.g.*, the speech at the Pisidian Antioch,
chap. xiii., gives us what we may well regard as a familiar example
of St. Paul's teaching on many similar occasions (*cf.* also in commentary the striking resemblances recently noted by Professor
Ramsay between this speech and the Galatian Epistle). The addresses at Lystra and at Athens delivered to heathen, so wonderfully adapted to the audience in each place, in the one instance
appealing to a more popular and ruder, in the latter to a more
learned and philosophic class of hearers ("ita sunt omnia et loco et

---

[1] Dr. Dalman's sharp distinction between Aramaisms and Hebraisms should be
noted, p. 16 ff., whilst he allows that the pure Hebraisms in the Gospels are almost
exclusively peculiar to that of St. Luke, and that by these peculiarities of diction
Acts is also marked, p. 29; see further in commentary.

audientibus accommodata," says Blass); in both cases starting
from truths which some of the Greek philosophers might themselves
have pressed home, but in each case leading up to and insisting
upon the need and necessity of repentance for wise and simple
alike; were eminently characteristic of a man who became as a
Jew to the Jews, as without law to those without law, as a Greek
to the Greeks, and such discourses in the brief form in which they
have reached us in Acts may well have expressed the actual teaching delivered by St. Paul in Lystra and in Athens (see for these
speeches especially Ramsay, *St. Paul*, p. 146 ff., and for the speech
at Athens, Curtius, "Paulus in Athen," *Gesammelte Abhandlungen*,
ii., pp. 527-543, and references in commentary [1]): "there is no
reason," writes McGiffert, "for questioning the trustworthiness of
the discourse at Athens as a whole . . . in fact such a discourse
as that ascribed to Paul is exactly what we should expect from him
under the circumstances" (*u. s.*, p. 260).

The speech to the Ephesian elders at Miletus, xx. 18-35, is
constantly marked by St. Paul's characteristic words and phrases,
and its teaching is strikingly connected with that of the Ephesian
Epistle (see notes in commentary, and *cf.* Page, *Acts*, p. xxxvi.;
Lock, "Ephesians," Hastings' B.D.; Cook, *Speaker's Commentary*,
p. 342, and also Lekebusch, *Apostelgeschichte*, pp. 336-339; Nösgen,
u. s., p. 53; Felten, *u. s.*, p. 33). No one has affirmed the historical
truthfulness of this address more strongly than Spitta, and in this
instance also we may again conclude with McGiffert, p. 339, that
"we shall be safe in assuming that the account of Paul's meeting
with the elder brethren of Ephesus, and the report of the words
which he uttered are substantially accurate". We may well feel
this security when we recall that St. Luke would be himself a hearer
of St. Paul's pathetic farewell.

The three remaining speeches contain three ἀπολογίαι of St.
Paul, one before the Jews and the chiliarch in Jerusalem, xxii.
1-21, the second before Felix, xxiv. 10-21, and the third before
Festus and Agrippa, xxvi. The first reaches us through the
medium of a Greek translation, and it is noticeable that the
speech in this form contains no Pauline words or expressions,
although some words remind us of him, *e.g.*, ἀπολογία, ἀπολούειν, παρα-

---

[1] Hilgenfeld blames Curtius because he has not explained the source of information for St. Paul's address, since the Apostle was at Athens alone, but Knabenbauer writes, *Actus Apostolorum*, p. 308, "Probabilissime is cum aliis id plane
superfluum reputavit, quia Paulus post eam orationem neque memoriam neque
loquelam amisit; unde ipse potuit narrare quid Athenis egerit".

δέχομαι, ἐπικαλεῖσθαι and τὸ ὄνομα (Nösgen, Felten), while it contains several peculiar to St. Luke. But if the Evangelist was present at the delivery of the defence, he would have been able to reproduce the speech himself, or at least its substance, and we have an explanation of the fact just mentioned (see Salmon, *Introd.*, pp. 317, 318 ; Page, *Acts*, p. xxxvi. ; Alford, *Proleg.*, pp. 13-15).

The vivid description, xxi. 30-40, and especially the local details, vv. 34, 35, point to the presence of an eye-witness, who was in possession of information which he could use with accuracy, and at the same time with discrimination, limiting himself to the re-quisites of his narrative (Bethge, *Die Paulinischen Reden*, p. 174). It is difficult to understand why Blass should say that although Luke may have heard the speech, it is doubtful if he understood it. In his *Præf.* to his *Evangelium secundum Lucam*, pp. xxi.-xxiii., he not only adopts Nestle's theory that an Aramaic document underlies the first part of Acts, i.-xii., but amongst the few Aramaisms from chap. xiii. onwards he notes especially, p. xxi., two from the chapter before us, xxii., *viz.*, ver. 19, ἤμην φυλακίζων " periphrasis illa aramaica imperfecti futurique, quæ fit per participium et verbum ἤμην (ἔσομαι)," and ver. 14, φωνὴν ἐκ τοῦ στόματος αὐτοῦ, *cf.* i. 16, iii. 18, 21 for στόμα. We must also bear in mind the strictures of Dalman upon Blass in this connection : *cf. Die Worte Jesu*, p. 28, 1898.

In the apology before Felix, xxiv. 10-21, we have traces of St. Paul's diction (see commentary, and *cf.* Nösgen, *u. s.*, p. 54, Felten, *u. s.*, p. 34), and although it would be rash to affirm that St. Luke was present at the delivery of this defence, yet, if he was with St. Paul during any of the time of the Apostle's imprisonment at Cæsarea, it is surely not difficult to suppose that he would have received from the prisoner's own lips a summary of his ἀπολογία before Felix. The same remark might account for St. Luke's information as to the longer ἀπολογία before Agrippa, chap. xxvi., and it is specially noteworthy that in this speech, which may easily have been repro-duced exactly as it was delivered, *cf.* Blass, *Grammatik*, p. 5, and *Proleg.*, p. 13, we have Greek phrases and words of a more cultured and literary style, such as would be more suited to the most distin-guished audience before which the Apostle had yet pleaded (see commentary). At the same time we may note that while the speech has many points of contact with St. Paul's peculiar language and favourite words, there are other expressions which may be described as Lucan, to which we may appeal as justifying the belief that if St. Luke was present at the hearing, he reproduced the speech not immediately, but after an interval, when it had passed through his

own mind, Bethge, *Die Paulinischen Reden*, pp. 259, 260. That
the speeches in Acts bear the impress of St. Luke's own style and
revising hand is freely admitted by conservative critics (*cf.* Lightfoot,
B.D.², i., p. 36; Headlam, "Acts," Hastings' B.D., i., p. 34; Salmon,
Introd., p. 317), and we may thus unhesitatingly account for the
combination in them of peculiar Pauline expressions with those
which may be classed as Lucan or Lucan-Pauline. These linguistic
phenomena by no means destroy the substantial accuracy of the
report; rather they are exactly what we should expect to find. It
is admitted on all sides that by comparing the language of St.
Paul's speeches in Acts with the language of his Epistles a striking
amount of similarity is evident. But if the writer of Acts was not
acquainted with St. Paul's Epistles, we cannot account for this
similarity of diction on the ground of literary dependence. If,
however, the writer of Acts was a constant and frequent companion
of St. Paul the explanation is easy enough, and we can readily
believe that whilst in his report or revision of a speech words of
the disciple might sometimes be found side by side with those of
the master, yet the influence of the latter would nevertheless make
itself felt in the disciple's thoughts and language (*cf.* Salmon, *u. s.*,
p. 315 ff., and Felten, *u. s.*, p. 32). In many cases it is perfectly obvious that the account of the speeches in Acts is an abridged account
—the longest of them would not take more than some five or six
minutes in delivery—and therefore, as a matter of necessity, such an
abridgment would bear upon it, in a sense, the impress of St. Luke's
own style. Blass, *Acta Apostolorum*, p. 191, in speaking of St. Paul's
address at Athens expresses the belief that it has come down to us
"fideliter etsi brevissime: ita sunt omnia et loco et audientibus
accommodata," and he adds a remark applicable to all the Apostle's
speeches: "Tum quilibet qui paullo recentiore ætate orationes Pauli
confcturus esset, usurus erat Pauli epistolis; quarum in hac non
magis quam in ceteris orationibus (*c.* 13, 20, 22, 24, 26) ullus usus
comparet".

It cannot be said that the recent and frequent attempts to
multiply and differentiate sources in Acts, to assign them to various
revisers or redactors, have met with any degree of real success.
If Holtzmann and Wendt (see also a description of these attempts
in *Theologische Rundschau*, Feb., March, April, 1899) contend that
they have done so, and that with regard to the first few chapters of
Acts some consensus of opinion has been gained, we may set against
such contentions not only the opinion of Zahn, *Einleitung*, ii.,
pp. 414, 424, who maintains that none of these repeated attempts

has attained any measure of probability (so too Zöckler, *Apostel-geschichte*, p. 154, 2nd edit., and Knabenbauer, *Actus Apostolorum*, p. 9 ff., 1899), but also the opinion of Wendt, who, after a careful and on the whole sympathetic review, is obliged to confess that one must limit oneself in any attempt to discover the sources of the book to what is attainable and provable in the circumstances, and that the more complicated the hypothesis suggested, the more difficult it is to make it intelligible to others, *Apostelgeschichte*, p. 17, 1899.   In his own examination of the problem he limits himself to one great source, p. 30, and plainly declares that it does not seem to be possible to discover others, although he enumerates various passages in which old and trustworthy traditions were combined; but whether these were derived from written documents or from one and the same source he declines to say, and he is evidently inclined to admit that in many cases oral tradition may also have been at work.   Thus whilst iv. 1-22, v. 17-42, are regarded as parallel pieces of information of what was in reality the same event, or whilst again the liberation of St. Peter in chap. xii. is a parallel to the release of the Apostle in chap. v. 18-20, the work of St. Philip and the death of St. James rest upon good and trustworthy tradition.   The source to which Wendt attaches such importance includes the "We" sections, and the whole of the book from xiii. onwards, with the exception of xv. 1-33, the source continuing with ver. 35, whilst it can be traced further back to xi. 19, 27, and to viii. 1-4.   But this large source is full of traces of revision and redaction, which mark not only the narratives but also the addresses.   Its interest centred chiefly in the person of St. Paul and in his work, and it gave no history of the *origines* of the Church or of the missionary journeys of the other Apostles, although it introduced its account of St. Paul by tracing the foundation of the Church in Antioch from the mother Church in Jerusalem as a result of the death of St. Stephen and the subsequent persecution, and by showing how that same Church of Antioch became the starting-point for St. Paul's missionary labours.

This view of the sources adopted by Wendt contrasts favourably with some of the extraordinary and complicated theories which from time to time have been advocated in Germany, more especially during the last few years.

As early as 1845 Schleiermacher's published lectures referred the authorship of the "We" sections not to Luke but to Timothy, and some two years before this E. M. Mayerhoff had suggested that the same hypothesis might be extended to all parts of Acts, not however without the opposition of Bleek and Ulrich, the former of whom supported Schleiermacher. But Schleiermacher's view of the part played by Timothy had already met with the strong opposition of Schneckenburger, 1841, and Swanbeck, 1847, attacked it by means of his own more complicated and more hazardous attempt to solve the sources of Acts. According to Swanbeck, the book is made up of a biography of Peter, a source containing the death of Stephen, a biography of Barnabas, the memoirs of Silas including the "We" sections. But the theory gained no acceptance, and most critics will probably agree with Lekebusch (*Apostelgeschichte*, p. 188) that Swanbeck in his attempt to avoid the misleading theory as to Timothy involved himself in a still greater error by his advocacy of Silas.

For the Tübingen school the question of sources occupied a less important place than the question of "tendency," and more weight was attached to the imaginative power of the author than to the possibility of his possession of any reliable tradition; and consequently for a time the attempts to discriminate and estimate various sources sank into abeyance. It was, however, supposed by some critics that in the first part of Acts either a pentateuch source or an Hellenistic history of Stephen had been worked up (Zeller, Overbeck), or that some old πράξεις Παύλου formed a foundation for the narrative. Hilgenfeld (see also below) maintained the probable existence of this latter document, and Holsten thought that he could discover traces of a Judaistic source in the speeches of the first part of the book. B. Weiss, as long ago as 1854, had referred the speeches of St. Peter to a written source, but the speeches were closely connected with the historical episodes, and so in his *Einleitung*, 2nd and 3rd editions, Weiss has attempted to trace throughout the whole first part of the book, *i.e.*, from i. 15-xv., a Jewish-Christian source, whilst Feine, 1891, has maintained that the Jewish-Christian source already employed in the third Gospel was also the source of the history of the Jerusalem Church in Acts i.-xii., and he gives, *u. s.*, p. 236 ff., many verbal likenesses between this source in St. Luke's Gospel and in the earlier portion of Acts. Feine's handling of the whole question is much more conservative than that of the other attempts to which allusion will be made, especially as he regards St. Luke as the author of the third Gospel and the Acts, and claims a high historical value for the episodes and speeches in the source.

But the interest in the hypothesis of a source or sources chiefly centres around the second rather than the first part of Acts. For here the "We" sections are concerned, and when the view was once started that these sections, although not the work of St. Luke, were the work of an eye-witness (since their vividness and circumstantiality could not otherwise be accounted for), and so derived from a source, the whole question of the authorship of this source was revived, and the claims of Timothy, Silas, Titus, again found advocates; and not only so, but the further question was debated as to how far this source extended. Was it limited to the "We" sections only? But the view which prevailed (and which still prevails, cf., e.g., Holtzmann, *Einleitung*[3], p. 393, and see above) makes Luke the author of the "We" sections, although not of the whole book, which was referred to the close of the first, and even to the second century. This latter date (amongst the supporters of which may be included H. Holtzmann, Pfleiderer, Jülicher (100-105), Weizsäcker, to say nothing of earlier critics, or of those mentioned below) finds no support in the general character of the book, and it depends upon other very precarious arguments, e.g., the dependency of the author upon Josephus. But if it cannot be substantiated, it is in itself fatal to the partition theories put forward by Van Manen (125-150), Clemen (60-140), and Jüngst (110-125).

With Van Manen we mark one of the earliest of the many complicated attempts, to which reference has been already made, in proof of the use of sources throughout the whole of Acts. According to him, *Acta Petri* and *Acta Pauli* form the two sources, of which the final redactor, writing about the middle of the second century, availed himself. In the *Acta Pauli*, H. Pa., which fill the second half of the canonical book of Acts, with the exception of xv. 1-33 and some other passages due to the reviser (although some of the incidents of these *Acta* which refer to Barnabas, Stephen, Paul, find a place in the first half of the book), a Gentile Christian, the first redactor, writing at the end of the first, or beginning of the second century, has embodied the Lucan Travel-Document, probably written by Luke himself, consisting of the "We" sections and the bare recital of one of Paul's voyages from Jerusalem to Rome. This document is, however, much revised, and according to it the Apostle travels to Rome not as a prisoner, but as a free man. The final redactor, moreover, seems to have forgotten that such a document had ever existed, and to have depended upon the Epistles of St. Paul and the notices of Josephus. The second source, *Acta Petri*, H. Pe., chaps. i.-xii., is of very small historical value; it was composed later than the *Acta Pauli*, and aimed at placing Peter on a level with Paul. It is not perhaps to be wondered at that Van Manen himself seems to hesitate about the exact details of his partitions, that even Heitmüller cannot give anything but modified commendation to his theory, *Theol. Rundschau*, p. 87, 1899, and that a still severer condemnation is inflicted by Zöckler, *Greifswalder Studien*, p. 114, *cf.* Knabenbauer, p. 11.

In the same year, 1890, Sorof published his *Die Entstehung der Apostelgeschichte*. He too has his two written sources. Of the first the physician Luke was the author; this source runs through the book, and has for its purpose to represent the missionary spread of Christianity from Jerusalem to Rome, making prominent the figure of Paul. But this source was revised by another disciple of Paul, Timothy, who as the son of a Jewish mother stood nearer than Luke to Jewish-Christian interests. Timothy, to magnify Peter, introduced much legendary matter relating to him in the first portion of St. Luke's account, and also revised and corrected the record of St. Paul's missionary activity on the strength of his authorship of the "We" sections and his own eye-witness. (It is no wonder that Heitmüller, *u. s.*, p. 85, again welcomes this theory with qualified praise, and considers the division of the parts of the book assigned to Luke and Timothy as improbable, if not impossible.) Another attempt in the succeeding year by Spitta gained much more notice than that of Sorof. He also has his two sources—A, an older source including the "We" sections, probably the work of Paul's companion, Luke: a very valuable and erudite source containing the speeches of the book (see references in commentary); and B, a secondary source, unhistorical, depending on popular traditions, with a great tendency to introduce miraculous embellishments. B is the work of a Jewish Christian who writes with a desire to magnify Peter by miracles which equal those of the great Gentile Apostle. Spitta has further to suppose that these two sources, the one Pauline-Lucan and the other Jewish-Christian, were combined by a Catholic-Christian redactor R, with some additions of his own. Here again Heitmüller, p. 91, sees no hope of a satisfactory solution of the problem under investigation, and can only wonder at the manner in which two sources of a directly opposite tendency can be so simply interwoven by the redactor; the part played by the latter is altogether unsatisfactory, as he does little else than effect this combination of the two sources, with an occasional interpolation of his own. Spitta's attempt was also sharply criticised by Jülicher, *Einleitung*, p. 270, and by Von Soden, *Theologische Literaturzeitung*, 26, 1892, and its value will be seen by references in the commentary.

The most complicated of all these recent attempts at the

reconstruction of Acts is that of Dr. C. Clemen. His three chief sources (with which he closely connects other shorter sources, *e.g.*, a source for vi. 1-6) are named (1) Historia Hellenistarum, H.H., vi. 9, 10, vii. 1-36, 35-58[a], 59[b], viii. 1[b], xi. 19-21, 24[a], 26 : this source Clemen regards as very old and trustworthy ; (2) Historia Petri, H.Pe., consisting chiefly of i.-v., and of some passages inserted in H.H., *viz.*, vi. 7, 8, 11-15, vii. 37, 60, viii. 2, viii. 4-13, 18-24, the account of Simon Magus ; viii. 26-40, the conversion of the Ethiopian ; (3) Historia Pauli, H.Pa., xiii. 1-xxviii. 30, 31, a source which may have originated in a diary kept by Luke on a journey to Rome called (4) Itinerarium Pauli, I.Pa., containing the " We " sections, and combined with (3) by the first of the three redactors. The first redactor is simply R., and to him are attributed other additions besides the " We " sections to the Historia Pauli, although no " tendency " can be assigned to him, *cf.*, *e.g.*, xiv. 8-18, xvi. 23[b]-34, xvii. 19-33, the Athenian discourse, etc. The two other redactors are much more pronounced : one, Redactor Judaicus, R.J., writing 93-117 A.D., compiled and revised the above sources, making many additions, *e.g.*, the miracles at Lydda and Joppa, ix. 23-43, and for the most part the Cornelius history, x. 1-xi. 18 ; xvi. 1-3, xxi. 20[b]-26, etc. ; and finally, the third redactor, Redactor Antijudaicus, R.A., writing probably in the time of Hadrian, with the object of counterbalancing the wrong tendencies of his predecessor ; to him we owe, before all, ix. 1-31, Paul's conversion, xii. 1-25, xv. 5-12, 19, 23-33, 41, and additions to the speech at Miletus, xx. 19[b], 25-35, 38[a]. Other instances will be found in the commentary of the manner in which the additions of " these two antipodes," R.J. and R.A., are given precisely by Clemen, even to parts of verses, and it is no unfriendly critic (Heitmüller, *u. s.*, p. 128) who points out that of the five journeys of Paul to Jerusalem mentioned in Acts no less than four are referred by Clemen to his redactors, which is fatal to the historical character of these visits : ix. 26, R.A. ; xi. 30, R.A. ; xv. 1-33, R.J. and R.A. ; and xviii. 22[b], R. ; the last journey, xxi., is found in the source H.Pa., and this according to Clemen is a journey identical with Gal. ii. 1. There is indeed no occasion to look to a conservative critic like Zöckler for a sharp criticism of the ingenious but purely subjective theory of Clemen ; the latter's immediate successor in the same attempt to split up Acts into its component parts not only describes Clemen's theory as over-ingenious, but speaks of the somewhat mechanical way in which his Redactor Judaicus brings Paul into the synagogue, only to allow the Apostle to be at once expelled therefrom by the

Redactor Antijudaicus, Jüngst, *Die Quellen der Apostelgeschichte*, p. 9. Whether we view it from its critical or from its chronological standpoint, Clemen's theory has not gained favour in England; for the former, see Ramsay, *St. Paul*, p. 11, and for the latter, Sanday and Headlam, *Romans*, p. xxxviii. But further, it cannot be said that Jüngst's own theory is likely to find wider acceptance than that of his predecessor. To say nothing of the difficulties of the date which he proposes, and his advocacy of St. Luke's dependence on Josephus, in which he is at one with Clemen (see further below), we find ourselves, as in dealing with Spitta's theory, face to face with two sources, A and B. The Paulinist of the second half of Acts is A, and the simplest and most natural view, according to Jüngst himself, is to identify this A with the beloved physician Luke, Col. iv. 14, Philem. ver. 24, 2 Tim. iv. 11, who was with Paul during his imprisonment at Cæsarea and Rome; B represents the Petrine-Jewish Christian mainly of the first half, but whose hand may be seen in xiii. 40 f., xv. ver. 13 ἀπεκρίθη to ver. 19 κρίνω, and in ver. 20 ἐπιστεῖλαι to αἵματος, whose name and date remain unknown, and whose narrative is full of miraculous events and legendary stories. Jüngst's redactor has an important part to play, and whilst on the one hand he advocates the abrogation of the Mosaic law (Jüngst does not hesitate to attribute to him ver. 39, xiii.), on the other hand he allows Paul to circumcise Timothy, xvi. 2, to undertake a Nazarite vow, xxi. 20b-26, and to acknowledge himself a Pharisee, xxiii. 6. The redactor's aim was to represent Christianity as a *religio licita*, and he thus endeavours to bring it by a conciliatory process into close connection with the Jewish religion. It would be difficult to find in the range of criticism anything more purely arbitrary than Jüngst's arrangement of his sections chronologically, see Table, p. 225, at the end of his book (and notes in commentary), and the instances given above are sufficient to show how he does not hesitate to split up a verse amongst his various sources: we cannot be surprised that Clemen retorted upon him the charge of over-ingeniousness with which Jüngst had greeted Clemen's own subtle endeavours.

In the same year as Jüngst's publication, the veteran Hilgenfeld explained his own views of the sources of Acts, *Zeitschrift für wissenschaftliche Theologie*, 1895, 1896, following partly the lines upon which he had previously worked twenty years before in his *Einleitung*, but also taking into account either adversely or with different degrees of agreement, the theories since propounded. According to him the sources are three in number : (1) πράξεις Πέτρου,

A, a Jewish-Christian source, i. 15-v. 42, describing the origin and development of the mother-Church; from it were also derived ix. 31-42, xi. 2, Cod. D, a passage relating a missionary circuit, xii. 1-23; (2) πράξεις τῶν ἑπτά, a Jewish-Christian document hellenised, commencing with vi. 1, and continuing to viii. 40, including the choice of the Seven, and describing what was known of two of them, St. Stephen and St. Philip; (3) πράξεις Παύλου: this C source commences with (vii. 58ᵇ, viii. 1ᵃ, 3) ix., and includes nearly the whole of that chapter, xi. 27-29, and the greater portion of xiii.- xxviii., with the "We" sections. But it will be noticed that, according to Hilgenfeld, we owe this source C probably to one of the early Christians of Antioch (xi. 28 D), and that it affords us a trust- worthy account, and partly that of an eye-witness, of the missionary work of St. Paul begun at Antioch and spread over the heathen world. Each of the three sources is revised and added to by the "author to Theophilus," who as a unionist-Pauline makes it his chief aim to represent the origin of the Gentile Church as essentially dependent upon the mother-Church of Jerusalem, and Paul as in full agreement with the primitive Apostles, and as acting after the precedent of St. Peter; thus to C is referred the whole episode of Cornelius and the account of the Church in Antioch, x. 1-xi. 18 (except xi. 2 β text), xi. 19-26, 30, xii. 24, 25. Hilgenfeld is not only often greatly dependent upon the Western text (see below and in commentary), but it will be seen that the reference of large sections to his "author to Theophilus" is often quite arbitrary (cf. notes in comment.).

One more well-known name follows that of Hilgenfeld—the name of J. Weiss. In 1893, *Studien und Kritiken*, Weiss had already to some extent given in his adhesion to Spitta's theory, and had treated Clemen's redactors R.J. and R.A., one of whom always follows the other to undo the effects of his working, with little ceremony; but in opposition to Spitta he sees in i.-v. only source B, a strong Jewish-Christian document, and in this respect he ap- proaches more nearly to B. Weiss and Feine, although he does not attach equal weight to the historical value of the document in question. Unlike Spitta, he refers the speech of Stephen (upon the unity of which Spitta so strongly insists) not to A, but to B. In 1897 J. Weiss admits only A as the source for the second half of Acts, except in some passages in which he cannot refrain from introducing a redactor, *Über die Absicht und den literarischen Charakter der A. G.*, 1897, p. 38. The view taken by J. Weiss certainly has the merit of appearing less complicated than that of Jüngst and Clemen.

Heitmüller, *u. s.*, pp. 94, 139, highly commends the service rendered by J. Weiss in insisting upon the fact that, even if it is derived from sources, the book of Acts forms a whole, written with a definite purpose and aim, and it is no doubt true that the more we recognise this, the more readily shall we recognise parts or sources which are inconsistent with a unity of aim, whether we derive them from oral or written traditions. But what kind of man must the final reviser have been in that he was entirely unaware of the discrepancies and difficulties which the sharp eyes of modern critics have discovered, and allowed them to remain instead of dismissing or explaining them with a few strokes of his pen? Or if he was so skilful as to be able to combine together sources often so unlike, how is it that he was notwithstanding so unskilful as to leave such patent and glaring discrepancies? And if the final revision took place in the second century, how is it that we have no colouring, not even in the speeches, of second-century ideas? (See especially Ramsay, *St. Paul*, p. 10.) In other respects it will be noticed that these theories, far from possessing even the recommendation of novelty, are nothing but a rehabilitation of the exploded "tendency" theories of Baur and Zeller, or of the discredited "parallelism" between Peter and Paul (see above); in numberless cases one critic flatly contradicts another in the details of his confident partition of sources into verses, or even portions of verses. At the same time hardly any of the writers in question seem able to separate themselves entirely from the traditional view that Luke, the companion of Paul, was more or less concerned in the composition of the book, which, as we believe, is so justly ascribed to him.

Before we pass from this question of sources, a few words must be said as to the alleged dependence of St. Luke upon Josephus. A century and a half ago points of contact between the two historians were collected by Ott and Krebs (see Wendt, *u. s.*, p. 36, and Krenkel, *Josephus und Lucas*, p. 1). But only in comparatively recent times has the question been seriously discussed as to whether the author of the third Gospel and of Acts was dependent in a literary sense upon Josephus. At the outset it is well to bear in mind that both men were historians, writing at the same period, and often of necessity referring to the same events. A certain amount, therefore, of parallel description and even of similarity of diction might fairly be expected.[1] But that the author of Acts often showed a know-

---

[1] Amongst recent critics who have rejected the idea of St. Luke's dependence on Josephus may be mentioned Reuss, Schürer, Gloël, Harnack, Belser, Bousset, and in England, Salmon, Sanday, Plummer (in his review of the latter's *St. Luke* J. Weiss, however, now inclines to the opposite view).

ledge of independent tradition is admitted even by those who maintain the dependence in question ; see, *e.g.*, Krenkel, *u. s.*, p. 207,
Clemen, *Die Chronologie der Paulinischen Briefe*, p. 68 (see further
in commentary, v. 36, xii. 19, xxi. 38, and Zahn's instances of this
independent knowledge of events and persons, *Einleitung*, ii., p. 416).

But more extraordinary than the variations of certainty and
uncertainty in these critics is the position taken up by Wendt in his
latest edition (1899) of Meyer's Commentary. In his former edition
(1888) he maintained that the points of contact between Josephus
and Luke were too general in their character to justify the notion
of literary dependence, and that the author of Acts would naturally
possess independent knowledge of contemporary events and person-
alities, and he still admits this general similarity and the want of
proof in many of the dependencies alleged by Krenkel in his lengthy
examination of the question : *e.g.*, the fact that both writers speak of
Porcius Festus as the διάδοχος of Felix is no proof of literary
dependence (Acts xxiv. 27, Jos., *Ant.*, xx., 8, 9). But Wendt
fastens on the one passage, v. 36, *cf.* Jos., *Ant.*, xx., 5, 1, as proving
a real dependence (see notes in commentary), and argues that if this
is so, the same dependence may be naturally expected in other
places. Thus, in what appears to be quite an arbitrary manner, he
asserts that some notices in Acts are dependent upon Josephus,
whilst some may be taken by the author of the book out of his own
chief source, *e.g.*, the account of the Egyptian, xxi. 38, and of the
high priest Ananias, xxiii. 2, xxiv. 1, etc. But having said all this,
Wendt proceeds to point out that we must not measure too highly
the influence of Josephus on Acts ; even the passage v. 36, in
which that influence is most marked, proves to us at the same time
the nature of the influence in question : it did not consist in an
exact familiarity with the words of Josephus, and in a careful
employment of his material, but in a superficial reminiscence of an
earlier reading of the Jewish historian ; thus the deviations side by
side with the likenesses are explained. But the most conservative
critic might allow as much as this.

Wendt further admits that this dependence cannot extend to the
later works of Josephus, *c. Apion.* and his *Vita*. This last work,
which must have been written after the year 100 A.D. (see " Josephus "
(Edersheim), *Dict. of Chr. Biog.*, iii., p. 448), contains the expression,
c. 29, θανεῖν μὲν, εἰ δίκαιόν ἐστιν, οὐ παραιτοῦμαι, and Krenkel maintains
that there is a clear trace of dependence upon this in the words
used in Acts xxiv. 11 (pp. 255, 256, so Holtzmann and Steck). But
in the first place the supposed dependency is not admitted by Wendt,

and not only may parallels be found to a similar use of the verb
παραιτοῦμαι in other Greek writers (Wetstein), but it is also noticeable that in the same speech of St. Paul Krenkel discovers, xxv. ver.
9, what he calls "the most striking reference" to the language of
Josephus in the phrase χάριτα, χάριν κατατίθεσθαί τινι (cf. also xxiv.
27, Jos., *B.J.*, vi., 3, and commentary, *in loco*).   But the phrase
is distinctly classical, cf. Thuc., i., 33, 138, and if Josephus was
acquainted with Thucydides (see Kennedy, *Sources of N.T. Greek*,
p. 56) why not St. Luke?   (*Cf.* Belser, *Theol. Quartalschrift*, p. 653,
1895.)

But what can we think of these supposed dependencies upon
a book of Josephus written in the early years of the second
century, when we read further that St. Paul's account of his
dream, xxiii. 11, is modelled upon the dream in Josephus,
Vita, 42?   In the former passage we read σε δεῖ καὶ εἰς Ῥώμην
μαρτυρῆσαι, and in the latter ὅτι καὶ Ῥωμαίοις δεῖ σε πολεμῆσαι, in
each case the dream takes place in the night, and in each case
some one stood over the dreamer (ἐπιστάς) (see Bousset's review of
Krenkel, *Theol. Literaturzeitung*, p. 392, 1895, No. 15).   The alleged
similarity between the introduction to the third Gospel and the
Acts, and the introduction to the *Ant.* of Josephus and to his
book, *c. Apionem*, is of the slightest when compared with the
likeness between the language of St. Luke in his preface to his
Gospel and the introduction of Dioscorides of Anazarbus to his
Materia Medica, cf. Bousset, *u. s.*, Vogel, *Zur Charakteristik des
Lukas*, p. 17, and J. Weiss, Meyer's Commentary, *Evangelium des
Lukas*, p. 286; indeed much more might be said for an imitation by
St. Luke in his preface of the introduction to the history of Thucydides (cf. Belser, *u. s.*, pp. 642, 658, 659, etc.).   It would have been
very advantageous if Krenkel in his long list of words common to
Josephus and Luke, p. 304 ff., had not only given us references in
classical writers to the use of the words which he adduces (*e.g.*,
the phrase πυρετῷ συνέχεσθαι, Luke iv. 38, *Ant.*, xiii., 15, 5, finds
frequent parallels in Plato and Thucydides), but also to the authors
whose books form the Apocrypha, and especially to 1 Macc. and 2
Macc.   It is also noteworthy that no mention whatever is made of
Polybius (Zahn, *u. s.*, p. 414).   The whole list requires revision, and
it is preposterous to class amongst literary dependencies technical
terms like ἀνθύπατος, κολωνία, νεωκόρος, ναύκληρος, σικάριος, στρατοπεδάρχης, τετραρχέω, or ordinary words which since Homer had been
common to all Greek literature, *e.g.*, ἐκεῖσε, μόγις, πλοῦς, παροίχομαι,
παραπλέω.   So far as language is concerned, what is more improbable,

as Zahn points out, than that the man who wrote Luke i. 1-4 should go to school and learn from Josephus? (*Cf. C. Apion.*, i., 9 ; *Ant.*, xx., 12.) But again what can we expect from an author who can find a parallel between Luke ii. 42 and Jos., *Vita*, 2 ? (See Gloël, *Die jüngste Kritik des Galaterbriefes*, p. 65.) The " We " sections equally with the other parts of the book contain many points of contact with Josephus, and Krenkel is somewhat puzzled to explain this, p. 281 ; but when we consider that Josephus has given us a long description of his own voyage to Rome, and of his shipwreck on the way, *Vita*, 3, it was only to be expected that similar nautical terms would be found in the two narratives, and some similarity of description, and the two accounts help to show us how easily and naturally two writers narrating the same experiences would express themselves in the same style and language.

But this question of the author's relation to Josephus is also important in its bearing upon the date of Acts.

The *Antiquities* of Josephus are placed at 93, 94 A.D., and if it could be proved that traces of dependence on the Jewish historian may be found in the third Gospel, those who maintain that a considerable period of time elapsed between the writing of that book and of Acts would be obliged to place the latter work some few years later still. But here again we may see the uncertainty which prevails when conclusions are built upon such *data*. Wendt (p. 40) can find no sure traces of any acquaintance with Josephus in the third Gospel, and so he inclines to date Acts in the interval between 95 and 100 A.D. (although he admits the possibility of a later date still). But 95, 96 A.D. would place the book under Domitian, and the question arises as to whether it can be said with any certainty that Acts was composed at a time when the Christians had gone through such a period of persecution as marked the close of that emperor's reign. Harnack decides without hesitation in the negative, *Chron.*, i., pp. 248-250, and whilst he gives 93 as the *terminus ad quem*, it is satisfactory to find that he holds that the book may have been composed between 80 and 93 A.D. The limit which he thus fixes Harnack regards as in approximate agreement with his other argument (see above) against the later date of Acts, *viz.*, its non-use of St. Paul's Epistles, a fact which alone would prevent us from dating the book in the second century (p. 249). So far as date is concerned, Ramsay would seem to occupy to some extent the same position, at least approximately, for he maintains that the book could not possibly have been written as late as the reign of Trajan, when the Church had long suffered persecution from the State, or even by a writer who had passed through the reign of Domitian, *St. Paul*, p. 387, and he dates its publication in the year immediately following 81 A.D., *i.e.*, in the early years of Domitian. But whilst Harnack's language might be employed by one who even dated the book *before* the persecution of Nero, Ramsay maintains that there runs through the entire work a purpose which could hardly have been conceived before the State had begun to persecute on political grounds (p. 388). But *when* did this kind of persecution begin? The evidence for the origin of a definite State policy against the Christians points presumably to Nero, and not to Vespasian, *cf.* Hardy, *Christianity and the Roman Government*, p. 80 (1890), Mommsen's letter, *Expositor*, July, 1893, Hort, *First Epistle of St. Peter*, p. 3, Pullan, *Early Christianity*, p. 106 ff., 1898. Professor Ramsay speaks of the Flavian policy as declaring Christianity illegal and proscribing the Name, but the first of the three Flavian emperors was Vespasian, and there is no positive evidence to refer the adoption of a definite State policy against the new religion to him (*cf.* Ramsay, *Church in the Roman Empire*, p. 256).

But if, from this point of view, there is nothing in the book itself to militate against an earlier date even than that mentioned by Ramsay and Harnack, are we justified in placing it, with Blass, before the fall of Jerusalem? Blass indeed would place it as early as 57-59 A.D., following St. Jerome, and the Gospel in 56, *Evangelium secundum Lucam*, p. lxxix., *Philology of the Gospels*, p. 33 ff. But however this may be, Blass has done invaluable service by pointing out that there is nothing in St. Luke's words, Luke xxi. 20 ff., which can give colour to the theory which regards them as a mere *vaticinium post eventum*, by showing that Daniel ix. 36 ff. already contained much which Luke is alleged to have added from his own knowledge of events already fulfilled, and by adding from modern history at least one remarkable prophecy and its fulfilment. Savonarola foretold as early as 1496 the capture of Rome, which happened in 1527, and he did this not merely in general terms but in detail; his words were realised to the letter when the sacred Churches of St. Peter and St. Paul became, as the prophet had foretold, stables for the conquerors' horses. The difficulties of foreseeing this capture of the Holy City at all by an army which would not have refrained from such an act of sacrilege is vividly depicted by Blass, *Philology of the Gospels*, p. 42 ff.[1]

---

[1] *Cf. Evangelium secundum Lucam*, p. viii., where he adds: "Major utique Christus propheta quam Savonarola; hujus autem vaticinium longe difficilius fuit quam illius; nam hostis Romanus prævideri poterat, exercitus Lutheranus non poterat".

But if on other grounds, *e.g.*, on account of the prologue to St. Luke's Gospel (Harnack, *u. s.*, p. 248, Sanday, *B.L.*, p. 278, Page, *Acts*, p. xviii.), we are asked to place that book after the destruction of Jerusalem, it is further maintained by Harnack that some considerable interval must have elapsed after that event before Acts was written; for if it had been composed immediately after the destruction, the writer would have mentioned it as useful for his aim; and so the book must have been composed at a time, *c.* 80, when the overthrow of the Holy City no longer stood, as it were, in the foreground of events. But it may be doubted if this is a very convincing argument, for the Epistle of Barnabas, written, as Harnack holds, between the wide limits of 80 and 132 A.D., does refer to the destruction, and for the writer of this Epistle equally as for the writer of Acts the event would have been a *fait accompli*. It is doubtful whether, in fact, anything can be gained as to the fixture of date from this omission of any reference to the fate of the Holy City; if anything, the omission would point to the years *before* the destruction for the composition of the book, as Harnack himself allows, if we were not obliged, according to the same writer, by the date of the Gospel to place Acts also after the overthrow. Both in England and in Germany representative writers can be named in support of the earlier and of the later date, Dr. Salmon maintaining that Acts was written a little more than two years after St. Luke's arrival in Rome (*cf.* also Rackham, *Journal of Theol. Studies*, i., p. 77), whilst Dr. Sanday would apparently place Acts about 80 A.D., and the Gospel 75-80, *B. L.*, p. 279, so too Dr. Plummer, *St. Luke*, p. xxxi., both being influenced to a great extent by the presumption that the Gospel followed the fall of Jerusalem. In this the English critics are in interesting agreement with Zahn in his recent volume, *Einleitung*, ii., pp. 433, 434, so far as date is concerned, in that he too regards 80 A.D. as the *terminus ad quem* for both Gospel and Acts, assigning them probably to 75 A.D., but unable to find a place for them before the fall of Jerusalem.[1]

---

[1] Sir J. Hawkins in his valuable *Horæ Synopticæ*, p. 143, has recently drawn attention to the *difference* of vocabulary between the third Gospel and Acts, and whilst maintaining that it is quite insufficient to destroy the argument for the identity of authorship, he thinks that it points to a considerable lapse of time between the two works. But we are dealing with a versatile author acquainted apparently with many writers, Vogel, *Zur Charakteristik des Lucas nach Sprache und Stil*, pp. 15, 17, 38, and the differences in question cannot have weighed with Blass, inasmuch as he places the completion of Acts three years after the Gospel, and still less with Zahn, who still maintains that the two books were published

It would appear then that the date of Acts must be determined to a great extent by the date assigned to the third Gospel; and this apparently was the view of Bishop Lightfoot (*cf.* Plummer, *St. Luke*, p. xxix., and Zöckler, *Apostelgeschichte*, p. 163, 2nd edit.), inasmuch as he leaves the question of the date of Acts undetermined, and refers for its solution to the date assigned to St. Luke's Gospel; although it should be noted that he does not attach any weight to the argument which finds in Luke xxi. 20-24 a proof that the Gospel was written after Jerusalem had fallen (*cf.* also Headlam, "Acts," Hastings' B.D., p. 30, and Wendt, *Apostelgeschichte*, p. 40, for various dates).

As in the case of the Gospel, so in that of the Acts, it is impossible to say at what *place* it was written. The traditional view since the days of St. Jerome, *De Vir. Illust.*, 7, has favoured Rome (although elsewhere Jerome refers the writing of the Gospel to parts of Achaia and Bœotia, *Præf.* to *Comm. in Matt.*), *cf.* Schneckenburger, Lekebusch, Godet, Felten, Blass, amongst others (Wendt, 1899, although rejecting the traditional account of St. Jerome, adds that he knows of no decisive grounds *against* Rome, p. 40). Lekebusch, *Apostelgeschichte*, pp. 393, 429, in supporting the claims of Rome argues for the probability that St. Luke, like many medical men at the time, would be likely to find in Rome a good field for his professional work. Achaia, Macedonia, Asia Minor, Alexandria have all been mentioned, and Lightfoot also mentions Philippi. Pfleiderer has supported Ephesus on the ground that the writer manifests a special interest in that city, whilst Zöckler thinks that something may be said for Antioch in Syria, owing to St. Luke's traditional connection with the place, Eus., *H. E.*, iii., 4; Jerome, *De Vir. Illust.*, 7, *cf.* Acts xi. 28, D., if there was the slightest ground for supposing that Luke at the period when the book was written had any residence in the Syrian town. On the whole it seems best with Nösgen, *Apostelgeschichte*, p. 42; Lightfoot, *u. s.*, p. 40; Zahn, *Einleitung*, ii., pp. 337, 439, to leave the locality undetermined; see especially the latter as to the bearing on the question of the mention of insignificant places such as Tres Tabernæ, Appii Forum, in the

---

in the same year, 75. It is remarkable no doubt that τε is used so often in Acts in all parts of the book: nevertheless it occurs also in the third Gospel nine or ten times, but in St. Mark not at all, and in St. Matthew and St. John only three times in each; μὲν οὖν, although no doubt frequent in Acts, does not occur at all in St. Matthew and St. Mark, although it is found once in St. Luke, iii. 18 (twice in St. John); and καὶ αὐτός, although occurring very frequently in the third Gospel, is not dropped in Acts, although proportionately it is rarely found (eight times).

neighbourhood of Rome, and on the evident ignorance of Theophilus as to the localities of Palestine, and apparently also in some respects, and in comparison with the author, of Macedonia and Greece (*cf.* xvi. 12; xvii. 19, 21).

If we turn to external testimony in favour of the book we find it full and satisfactory (*cf.* Zöckler, *Apostelgeschichte*, 2nd edit., p. 160, Headlam, "Acts," Hastings' B.D., i., p. 26, and Gore on the points of contact between the earlier chapters and the *Didache*; see *Church and the Ministry*, p. 416). To Wendt in his latest edition, p. 41 (1899), we again owe much that is of value, both in what he allows, and in what he declines to recognise. One very important point calls for determination at the outset. The likeness between the language of Acts xiii. 22 and Clem. Rom., *Cor.*, xviii., 1, in relation to Ps. lxxxviii. 20 (LXX) cannot, as both Clemen and Wendt admit, be accidental. Indeed Wendt is of opinion that it is no more probable that Clement depends upon Acts than Acts upon Clement, while at the same time he holds that a third alternative is possible, *viz.*, that both writings may be dependent on some common third source. But there is no evidence forthcoming as to the existence of this common source, and Lightfoot rightly presses the significance of the threefold coincidence between the language of Acts and Clement, which cannot easily be explained away (*u. s.*, p. 120). In Acts we have three features introduced which are not found in the original of the Psalm, *viz.*, the mention of the "witness," and the addition (*a*) of "a man after my heart," *cf.* 1 Sam. xiii. 14, and (*b*) of "the son of Jesse," but all these are also found in the passage in St. Clement. So again Wendt with many other critics would explain the words ἥδιον διδόντες ἢ λαμβάνοντες, Clem. Rom., *Cor.*, ii., 1, *cf.* Acts xx. 35, not by dependence upon Acts, but by a common tradition of the words of the Lord. But Wendt admits, although very guardedly, the use of Acts in Polycarp, *Phil.*, i., 2, *cf.* Acts ii. 34, Ignat., *Ad Smyrn.*, 3, Acts x. 41, and he does not deny the connection between Ignat., *Ad Magn.*, 5, and Acts i. 25, whilst he admits that in Justin Martyr the references become more clear and frequent (see, for a full and good estimate of the references to Ignatius and Polycarp, Headlam, "Acts," Hastings' B.D., i., p. 26).

But it is most important to observe that Wendt fully recognises the influence of the Canonical Acts upon the Apocryphal Acts of the second century, although he points out that of this literature we only possess a small portion, and he expects great things from the recently discovered fragments of the *Acta Pauli* of the middle of the second century; *cf. Acta Pauli et Theclæ* (apparently a part of the *Acta Pauli*), which are frequently dependent upon our Acts for their notices of persons and places, and also *Acta Petri* dependent again upon our Acts, as in the notice of the meeting of Peter and Simon Magus, *cf.* Zöckler, *Apostelgeschichte*, p, 159, and Harnack, *Chron.*, i., pp. 498 and 554 (although Harnack places the *Acta Petri* as late as the middle of the third century, whilst Zahn takes 170 as the *terminus ad quem*).   From other writings and documents of the second century the testimony to our book is clear, *cf. Epist. ad Diognetum*, 3, *cf.* Acts xvii. 24; the *Epistle of Vienne and Lyons*, *cf.* Acts vii. 59 ff. (Euseb., *H.E.*, v., 2; *Didache*, iv. 8, Acts iv. 32), and two other references to St. Paul's address at Athens, in Tatian, *Orat. ad Græc.*, 4, and Athenagoras, *Legat.*, 13 (Wendt) (*cf.* possibly Dionysius of Corinth, Euseb., *H.E.*, iv., 23); so too in Justin Martyr, references to the book are found in *Apol.*, i. and ii., and *Dial. cum Tryph.*, *cf.*, *e.g.*, Acts i. 8, 9, ii. 2, *Apol.*, i., 50; Acts xvii. 23, *Apol.*, ii., 10; Acts xxvi. 22 f., *Dial.*, 36 (Wendt, Zöckler, Headlam); and not only so, but it is definitely assigned to St. Luke and treated as Scripture in the Muratorian Fragment, *l.* 34; *cf.* Iren., *Adv. Hær.*, iii., 14, 15, Tertull., *C. Marcion.*, v., 2; *De Jejun.*, 10; Clem. Alex., *Strom.*, v., 12.   Moreover, we must not lose sight of the fact that "all the evidence which testifies to the authorship of the third Gospel is available also for Acts, and conversely, and that the early testimony in favour of St. Luke as the author of the third Gospel is absolutely unbroken and undisputed for nearly eighteen centuries," Lightfoot, *u. s.*, p. 30; Plummer, *St. Luke*, pp. xiv., xvi.

Space forbids us to enter into the many vexed questions which surround the *chronology* of Acts, but an attempt is made to discuss some of them in the pages of the commentary.   A glance at the various tables given us in Meyer-Wendt (1888), p. 31, or in Farrar's *St. Paul*, ii., p. 624, is enough in itself to show us the number and complexity of the problems raised.   But fresh interest has been aroused not only by Professor Ramsay, but by the recent return of Harnack and O. Holtzmann (*cf.* also McGiffert, *Apostolic Age*, p. 359; Blass, *Proleg.*, p. 22) to the earlier chronology of Eusebius (although O. Holtzmann does not mention him, *Neutestamentliche Zeitgeschichte*, pp. 128, 132), formerly advocated by Bengel.   According to Eusebius the recall of Felix must be dated between October 55 and 56.   Harnack places the entry of Festus upon office in the summer of 56, since Paul embarks for Rome some few months after the arrival of Festus in the autumn, *Chron.*, i., p. 237.   The

Apostle would thus arrive in Rome in the spring of 57, and his release follows in 59. (O. Holtzmann from other *data* places the arrival of Festus in Palestine in the summer of 55, and both he and McGiffert place Paul's arrival in Rome in 56, and his imprisonment 56-58.)

This chronology has been severely criticised by Wendt, *Apostelgeschichte*, p. 57 (1899), and it fails to commend itself to Ramsay, *Expositor*, March, 1897, as also more recently to Zahn, *Einleitung*, ii., p. 626. It has been objected to it, *inter alia*, that its supporters, or at all events Harnack and O. Holtzmann, place the conversion of Paul so soon after the death of our Lord that it is doubtful whether sufficient time is allowed for the events recorded in Acts i.-vi. (*cf.* xxvi. 10), although Holtzmann, p. 133, sees no difficulty in placing the conversion in 29, the date of the death of Jesus, as the events in Acts i.-viii. in his view follow quickly upon one another. (Ramsay thinks that the interval before Stephen's murder was short, but he allows two and a half or three years for the event after the great Pentecost ; see notes in commentary for the difficulties connected with the martyrdom.) Harnack places the date of the conversion in 30, *i.e.*, according to him, either in the year following, or in the year of, the death of Jesus. On the other hand the chronology in question allows some considerable time for Paul's release from his first captivity (a release admitted by Harnack and Spitta, as earlier by Renan), and for his subsequent journeys east and west, if Mr. Turner, "Chronology," Hastings' B.D., i., 420, is right in placing the death of both Peter and Paul in 64-65 (Harnack placing the death of St. Paul in 64 and of St. Peter in 67, Eusebius, however (so Blass), from whom Harnack here departs, placing the former event in 67 (68)). The received chronology, making 60, 61, the date for the arrival of Festus in Judæa, allows but little interval between the close of St. Paul's first imprisonment and his death, if his martyrdom was in 64. The difficulty is met by Mr. Turner, *u. s.*, p. 421, by assigning 58 (Ramsay 59) as the precise year for the accession of Festus to office, placing the close of the Acts, after the two years' captivity in Rome, early in 61, and so allowing an interval of three years between St. Paul's first and second imprisonment. Unfortunately it must be admitted that we cannot positively fix 58 as the year for the event in question, and this uncertainty sadly interferes with the adoption of any precise chronology for Acts, although on all sides the importance of the date of Festus' arrival is recognised—" the crucial date," Mr. Turner calls it ; all depends upon ascertaining it, says Harnack (*cf.* also Wendt, *u. s.*, p. 56 ;

Page, *Acts*, xxxviii.; Zahn, *Einleitung*, ii., p. 639; Lightfoot, B.D.[2], i., 42).

If we adopt Mr. Turner's date for Festus—a date intermediate between the earlier and later dates assigned above—and work back, we get 56 as the date for St. Paul's arrest in Jerusalem and imprisonment in Cæsarea, 55 for his leaving Ephesus, 52 for the commencement of his third missionary journey (for he stayed at Ephesus considerably over two years; Lewin, *Fasti Sacri*, p. 310, says three), 50 for his reaching Corinth (late in the year), where he sojourned eighteen months, 49 for Council at Jerusalem and second missionary journey. But if we identify the Council at Jerusalem, Acts xv., with the second visit to Jerusalem according to Gal. ii. 1, but the third visit according to Acts, the question arises as to whether the notices in Gal. i. 18 and ii. 1 involve seventeen years as an interval between the Conversion and the Council (with Lightfoot, Harnack, Zahn), or whether the fourteen years, Gal. ii. 1, should be reckoned from the Conversion, *i.e.*, eleven years from the first visit of St. Paul to Jerusalem, including the three in the fourteen (with Ramsay, Turner, McGiffert).[1]

Against the former view Mr. Turner urges the objection that in this case the first visit to Jerusalem would be carried back to 35-36, whereas in all probability Aretas was not ethnarch of Damascus until 37 (2 Cor. xi. 32, Acts ix. 25, 26; see commentary), and he therefore includes the three years in the fourteen, and thus gets 35-36 for the conversion, and 38 (under Aretas) for the first visit. As Mr. Turner places the Crucifixion 29 A.D., his scheme is thus free from the objection referred to above as against Harnack and O. Holtzmann, since it allows some six or seven years for the events in the early chapters of Acts (see further on the whole question of chronology Mr. Turner's full and valuable article already mentioned; Zahn, *u. s.*, ii.; *Excursus*, ii.; Professor Ramsay, "Pauline Chronology," *Expositor*, March, 1897; Professor Bacon (Yale), "Criticism of the New Chron. of Paul," *Expositor*, February, 1898; Wendt, *u. s.* (1899), p. 53 ff.; *Biblical World*, November, 1897; Mr. Vernon Bartlet's article on "Pauline Hist.

---

[1] But Professor Ramsay, it must be remembered, identifies Gal. ii. with Acts xi. 30, xii. 25 (see notes in commentary), and an interval of fourteen years between St. Paul's conversion and the famine would be more probable than an interval of seventeen, which would throw the conversion back too early, and Dr. McGiffert identifies the accounts of both visits in Acts xi. and xv.—the former for famine relief and the latter for the settlement of the controversy with the Judaisers—with the visit mentioned in Gal. ii. 1, *Apostolic Age*, p. 208.

and Chron.," *Expositor*, October, 1899, written too late for more than a brief mention here, as also Professor Bacon's more recent contribution, *Expositor*, November, 1899).

But although there are so many points of contact between secular history and the Acts, it seems that we must still be content with what Harnack describes as a relative rather than an absolute Chronology. We cannot say, *e.g.*, that we can fix precisely the date of the famine, or the edict of Claudius, or the proconsulship of Gallio, or the reign of Aretas, to take the four events mentioned by Lightfoot, "Acts," B.D.², i., p. 4, as also by Harnack, *Chron.*, i., p. 236, *cf.* Zahn, *u. s.*, ii.; *Excursus* ii. But in this respect no blame attaches to St. Luke as an historian. His object was to connect the history of the rise and progress of the Christian Faith with the course of general imperial history around him, and if his chronological sense seems deficient to modern judgment, it was a deficiency in which he was by no means peculiar, but which he shared with his contemporaries and his age, *cf.* Ramsay, *St. Paul*, pp. 18, 23, and *Was Christ born at Bethlehem?* pp. 204, 256.

STATE OF THE TEXT. It is not too much to say that during the last fifteen years chief interest has centred around the Western text and its relative importance (*cf.* Blass, *Studien und Kritiken*, p. 86 ff., 1894; *Acta Apostolorum*, 1895, and *Acta Apostolorum*, 1896, also *Evangelium secundum Lucam*, 1897, both edited *secundum formam quæ videtur Romanam*; see also Dräseke, *Zeitschrift für wissenschaft. Theol.*, p. 192 ff., 1894).[1]

Codex D, its most important representative, contains an unusually large number of variations from the received text in Acts (see for the number Zöckler, *Apostelgeschichte*, 2nd edit., p. 165; he reckons, *e.g.*, some 410 additions or interpolations), and it is no wonder that attempts should have been made to account for this diversity. Bornemann's endeavour some half-century ago (1848) to represent D as the original text, and the omissions in the common text as due to the negligence or ignorance of copyists, found no acceptance, and whilst in one sense Blass may be said to have returned to the position of Bornemann, he has nevertheless found his predecessor's solution totally inadequate, *Philology of the Gospels*, p. 105. Joannes Clericus, Jean Leclerc, the Dutch philologist (born 1657), had already suggested that St. Luke had made two

---

[1] The main division of MSS. of Acts into three groups, with references to W. H. and Blass, is well given in *Old Latin Biblical Texts*, iv., pp. xvii., xviii. (H. J. White, Oxon., 1897).

editions of Acts, and is said by Semler to have published his opinion, although under an assumed name (Zahn, *Einleitung*, ii., p. 348; see also on the same page Zahn's interesting acknowledgment that he was himself in 1885-6 working on much the same lines as Blass). Meanwhile Tisch., W. H., B. Weiss have sought to establish the text of Acts essentially on the basis of ℵABC, and it was left for Blass to startle the world of textual criticism by boldly claiming a fresh originality for Codex D. But this originality was not exclusive; St. Luke has given us two originals, first a rough copy β, R(omana), in Blass, and then a fair copy α, and A(ntiochena), for the use of Theophilus; the rough copy remained in Rome and became the foundation of the Western text, copies of it having reached Syria and Egypt in the second century, while the latter abridged by Luke reached Theophilus in Antioch (so Blass), and was thence propagated in the East.[1]

But Codex D is by no means the sole witness, although a very weighty one, upon which Blass depends for his β text. He derives help from Codex E (Laudianus), from the minuscule 137 (M) in Milan, especially for the last chapters in which D is deficient, and in some passages also from Codex Ephraem, C; from the Philoxenian Syriac version with the marginal annotations of Thomas Harkel (unfortunately we have no Old Syriac text as for the Gospels), the Sahidic version, the Latin text in D, d, and E, e, the Fleury palimpsest (Samuel Berger, 1889), Flor. in Blass; the so-called "Gigas" Latin version in Stockholm (Belsheim, 1879), Gig. in Blass; the Codex Parisinus, 321 (S. Berger, 1895), Par. in Blass; a Latin version of the N.T., fifteenth century, in Wernigerode, Wernig., *w.*, in Blass, and a Latin version of the thirteenth century, "in linguam provinciæ Gallicæ Romanæ facta," Prov. in Blass.[2]

In addition to these MSS. and versions Blass also appeals to the

---

[1] On the difference between the circulation of the two copies in the case of the third Gospel see *Philology of the Gospels*, p. 103. In England Bishop Lightfoot had previously conjectured that the Evangelist might himself have issued two separate editions of both Gospel and Acts, *On a Fresh Revision of the N.T.*, p. 29. For similar instances of the issue of a double edition in classical and other literature see Dräseke, *u. s.*, p. 194; Zöckler, *Greifswalder Studien*, p. 132, and Blass, *Proleg.*, p. 32.

[2] To these may be added fragments of an old Latin translation of Acts in the *Anonymi de prophetis et prophetiis* containing six passages, notably Acts xi. 27, 28, in agreement with Codex D, *cf. Miscellanea Cassinese*, 1897, and Harnack, *Theol. Literaturzeitung*, p. 171, No. 6, 1898; the Greek Codex Athous, derived according to Blass, *Philology of the Gospels*, p. 250, from an old and very valuable original, and taken into some account by Hilgenfeld, *Acta Apostolorum*, p. ix. (1899), and *cf.*

text employed by Irenæus, which contains many resemblances to D; to the text of St. Cyprian, which shows the same peculiarity; to the text of St. Augustine, especially in his treatises against the Manicheans, containing Acts i.-ii. 13, x. 13, 15, parts which are not found in the Fleury palimpsest: *cf.* also Tertullian, whose text, although it contains few quotations from Acts, resembles that of Irenæus (add to these the work *De promissionibus et prædicationibus Dei*, referred, but wrongly, to Prosper, Prom. in Blass; and the *Contra Varimadum* of Vigilius, Vigil. in Blass: works not valued so highly by Hilgenfeld in his list of authorities for the Western text, *Acta Apostolorum*, p. xiii., 1899). By these aids Blass constructs his β text, even for those portions where D is wanting, *viz.*, from viii. 29, πρόσελθε to x. 14, ἔφαγον; from xxi. 2, ἐπιβάντες to ver. 10, ἀπὸ τῆς; xxii. 10, ὧν τέτακται to ver. 20, συνευδοκῶν, and from xxii. 29, οἱ μέλλοντες to the end of the book, and his aim is to restore the Western text as it existed about the time of Cyprian, *cf. Evangelium secundum Lucam*, p. xxxi. The merit of his work in showing how widespread and interesting was the Western form of text is acknowledged even by those who do not accept his conclusions, see, *e.g.*, Wendt, *Apostelgeschichte* (1899), p. 46, and Bousset, *Theol. Rundschau*, p. 413, 1898, although both object that Blass does not rightly estimate his different witnesses.

But Blass is able to refer in support of his use of some of the authorities mentioned to the important investigation of Dr. P. Corssen in his *Der Cyprianische Text der Acta Apostolorum*, 26 pp., 1892. This Latin text carries us back at least to the middle of the third century (and earlier still according to Harris, *Four Lectures*, etc., p. 53 ff., who thinks that the text might be called Tertullianic equally as well as Cyprianic; but see on the other hand Blass, *Acta Apost.*, edit. m., p. xxxi.), as Corssen shows by comparing the readings of the Fleury palimpsest (sixth century) (1) with St. Cyprian's quotations from Acts, (2) with similar quotations in the works of St. Augustine referred to above, *De Actis cum Felice Manichæo* and *Contra epistolam Manichæi*, (3) with the quotations in the work mentioned above as that of Prosper (Harris, *u. s.*, p. 53). Behind these various texts Corssen concludes that there was a common Latin primitive, *i.e.*, the Cyprian text, as he calls it. Moreover, this Cyprian text is a Western witness superior in value

Acts xv. 20, 29. Hilgenfeld also adds to the Latin versions, Codex Vindobonensis *s.* (probably sixth century), *cf.* xxviii. 20, and see *Old Latin Biblical Texts*, iv. (H. J. White, Oxon., 1897).

even to the Greek of Codex Bezæ, since it has in Corssen's opinion an internal unity and sequence wanting in the latter, although it agrees in many peculiarities with the Greek of that Codex (Harris, *u. s.*, p. 53; Salmon, *Introd.*, p. 594). Corssen thus helps materially to prove the antiquity of the Western Latin.

But Dr. Blass further acknowledges that Corssen has done most valuable service in proving the composite nature of Codex D, and that in it we have not β in its purity, but in a state of frequent mixture and conflation with α. Whilst, however, Blass regards the β text as the older, Corssen regards α in that light, and β as revealing the character of a later revision (*Göttingische gelehrte Anzeigen*, pp. 433, 436, 446 : 1896); in β he somewhat strangely maintains that we have the hand of a Montanist reviser at work (*cf.* Blass's strictures, *Evang. secundum Lucam*, p. xxiv. ff.), a theory formerly adopted by Professor Harris, but afterwards abandoned by him.

But how far do the variations between the two forms of text justify the hypothesis of Blass that both may be referred to one author, β as the primary, α as the secondary text ?[1]

In the *apparatus criticus* of the following pages, in which the variations for the most part in the two texts are stated and examined, it cannot be claimed for a moment that any definite conclusion is reached, simply because the matter is one which may be said to call for suspension of judgment. Certainly there are many difficulties in the way of accepting the theory of Blass in its entirety. There are passages, *e.g.*, of which it may be said that the more detailed form is the original, which was afterwards shortened, while it may be maintained often with equal force that the shortened form may well have been the original ; there are passages where a local knowledge or an exact knowledge of circumstances is shown, *e.g.*, xii. 10, xix. 9, xx. 15, xxi. 1, but such passages do not prove the priority of the β text, for if both α and β are referred to the same author, the same hand which omitted in a revision could also have added, although such instances may be cited for the originality of the β text in comparison with α (see notes *in loco* for each passage). To these may be added the famous addition in xi. 28 (see *in loco*), which Blass makes the starting-point for his inquiry, and to which Hilgenfeld, Zahn, Zöckler, Salmon, as against Harnack and B. Weiss, attach so much importance. There are again other passages in which it may be

---

[1] Blass still maintains, as against Corssen, that the language of the additions, and generally in the variants of β, is Lucan, *Philology of the Gospels*, p. 113 ff., and *Evangelium secundum Lucam*, p. xxvii. ff.

maintained that if α is original we can understand the smoothness of β, but not *vice versâ*, and it must always be remembered that this love of paraphrase and simplification has been urged on high authority as a marked characteristic of the Western readings in general, *cf.* W. H., p. 122 ff., and B. Weiss, *Der Codex D in der Apostelge-schichte*, pp. 52, 105 : 1897. There are, moreover, other passages in which Blass seems to assimilate α and β, although the witnesses would differentiate them, *cf.* v. 28, 34, xv. 33, or in which there is a manifest blunder, not only in D but in other Western witnesses, which Blass corrects by α, although such blunders really belong to the β text, *cf.* v. 31, xiii. 48, xv. 15. There are cases in which D affords weighty support to readings otherwise testified to only by B, *e.g.*, xix. 8, xxi. 25, or only by ℵ, *cf.* ii. 20 (Wendt).

But a careful consideration of the whole of the instances justi-fies the attachment of far greater importance to the Western text than formerly (*cf.*, *e.g.*, Holtzmann's review of Blass's edit. min. of Acts, *Theol. Literaturzeitung*, p. 350, 1897, No. 13), and goes some way to break down the former prejudice against Codex Bezæ : not only is it allowed that one revising hand of the second century may be the main source of the most important readings, but that these readings may contain original elements, since they must be based upon a text which carries us back very near to the date of the composition of the book of Acts (Wendt, *u. s.*, p. 52 ; Bousset, *Theol. Rundschau*, p. 414, 1898). The same tendency to attach more importance to the Western text is observable in Professor Ramsay, for although he regards the most vivid additions of the Western text in Acts as for the most part nothing but a second-century commentary, and while he refuses to introduce xi. 27, 28, D, into his own text, yet he speaks of the high value of D in that it preserves with corruptions a second-century witness to the text, and he places the home of the revision on the line of intercourse between the Syrian Antioch and Ephesus, arguing from xi. 28 that the reviser was acquainted with Antioch (*Church in the Roman Empire*, p. 151 ; *St. Paul*, p. 27, and review of Professor Blass, *Expositor*, 1895, and *cf.* Zöckler, *Greifswalder Studien*, pp. 131, 140).

On the other hand the most thorough advocates of Dr. Blass's theory support his view of the priority and originality of β by reference to three classes of passages : (1) those in which the later α has abbreviated the reading of β, *cf.* iii. 1, iv. 1, 3, 24, 32, vii. 29, ix. 5-8, x. 23, xi. 2, xiv. 1-20, xvi. 19, xvii. 12, 15, xxi. 39, xxii. 26 ; (2) those in which β contains exact and specific notices of time which are wanting in α, *cf.* xv. 30, xvi. 11, xvii. 19, xviii. 19, xix. 9,

xx. 18, xxvii. 1, etc.; (3) those in which exact information appears to characterise the references of β to places, circumstances, persons, *cf.*, in addition to passages of this character already noticed under (1), xi. 28, xii. 1, 10, xvi. 35, xviii. 18, 27, xix. 14, xx. 15, xxi. 16, xxiv. 27, xxviii. 16, 19 (see for these passages Zöckler, *Greifswalder Studien*, p. 134 ff., and notes in *apparatus criticus*, and in opposition to the view of Zöckler Mr. Page's detailed list of passages in D, all of which he regards as bearing traces of being subsequent corrections of the text by a second-rate hand, *Classical Review*, p. 319, July, 1897, and Blass's reply, *Philology of the Gospels*, p. 123).[1]

If an examination of these passages, which vary considerably in value and importance, and the proofs of the existence of a second-century Latin text convince us that the readings in β are not to be hastily rejected as the glosses of a careless or blundering scribe, it cannot be said that we are in a position to account for the origin of the Western readings, or that a solution of the problem is yet attained. The hypothesis of Blass, tempting as it is, and simple as it is, wants verification, and the very simplicity which commends it to its supporters is often a sore stumbling-block to its acceptance, inasmuch as it does not seem to account for all the facts of the case. But at the present stage of the controversy it is of interest to note that the honoured name of Theodor Zahn, *Einleitung*, ii., 340, 1899, may be added to those who accept in the main Blass's position, amongst whom may be mentioned Nestle, Belser, Zöckler, Salmon.[2] Zahn makes some reservations, *e.g.*, with regard to xv. 29 (see *in*

---

[1] In 1891 Professor Harris regarded the readings of Codex D (see Blass, edit. min., p. xx.) as the result of their adaptation to the Latin version of a bilingual MS. which carries us back to the middle of the second century, a view which he has somewhat modified in 1894, *Four Lectures*, etc., p. viii., although still maintaining a certain amount of Latinisation. Schmiedel, *Enc. Bibl.*, i., 52, 1899, recently supports Harris, and maintains that the Greek of D rests partly on retranslation from the Latin. In his later book Dr. Harris examines the theory of Dr. Chase, that the peculiarities of Codex D are due to retranslation from an old Syriac version, pp. 14, 68, and maintains that whilst Dr. Chase's position is justified in so far that we possess evidence of an old Syriac text of Acts, yet his explanation of the Western variants as due to a Syriac glossator cannot be sustained, see also Zöckler, *u. s.*, p. 131, and Headlam, "Acts," Hastings' B.D.

[2] Amongst the keenest attacks upon the theory may be noted that of B. Weiss in *Codex D in der Apostelgeschichte*, 1897; Page, *Classical Review*, July, 1897, and more recently, Harnack, see notes on xi. 28 and xv. 29; Schmiedel in *Enc. Bibl.*, 50-56, 1899. Wendt's examination of the question, *Apostelgeschichte* (1899), pp. 43-53, should also be carefully considered, whilst Blass has replied to the strictures of Harnack and Zahn in *Studien und Kritiken*, i., 1900.

loco, and Harnack, *Sitzungsberichte d. königl. Preuss. Akad. d. Wissenschaften zu Berlin,* xi., 1899), whilst he lays stress upon xi. 28, and maintains the genuine Lucan character of the words used, *e.g.,* ἀγαλλίασις, συστρέφειν.

Still more recently Hilgenfeld, *Acta Apostolorum,* 1899, has again, and more fully, expressed his conviction of the priority of the β text (although he differs from Blass and Zahn in not referring α and β to the same original author[1]), and he has reconstructed it much on the same lines as Blass, and somewhat more boldly. References to the text adopted by Hilgenfeld will be frequently found in the *apparatus criticus* (as also to his annotations which deal largely with the criticisms of B. Weiss in his *Codex D*). In his *Proleg.* Hilgenfeld divides the authorities for the Western text as against אABC into various groups: (1) Græco-Latin MSS.: Codex D and E; (2) Latin versions: Flor., Gig., Par., Wernig., Prov., as Blass calls them, see above on p. 42; (3) Oriental versions: especially the marginal readings of Thomas Harkel in the Philoxenian Syriac; also the Sahidic version; (4) the Fathers: especially Irenæus, Cyprian, Tertullian (with reference to Corssen's pamphlet, see above); (5) some readings even in the four great MSS. אABC. Hilgenfeld evidently attaches some weight (as Blass) to 137 (M), and to Codex Athous Lauræ, p. ix. (see Blass, *Philology of the Gospels,* p. 250; and further, *Studien und Kritiken,* i., 1900).

For *Literature* bearing on Acts see the valuable lists in Headlam, "Acts," Hastings' B.D., pp. 34, 35, and Wendt, *Apostelgeschichte,* pp. 1-4, 1899. The present writer would venture to add to the former: (1) *Commentaries:* Felten, *Apostelgeschichte,* 1892; Knabenbauer, *Actus Apostolorum* (Paris, 1899), two learned and reverent works by Romanists, the latter dealing with the most recent phase of modern problems of text, chronology and sources; Wendt, *Apostelgeschichte* (Meyer-Wendt), 1899, with a full Introduction, pp. 1-60, discussing all recent problems, with constant reference in the text to Professor Ramsay's writings, and altogether indispensable for the study of Acts; Matthias, *Auslegung der Apostelgeschichte,* 1897, a compendium useful in some respects, based chiefly upon Wendt's earlier edition; Zöckler, *Apostelgeschichte,* 2nd edit., 1894; to these constant reference is made. (2) *Introductions:* Zahn, *Einleitung,* ii.,

---

[1] " Blassio debemus alterum Actorum app. textum non ortum ex jam fere recepto, sed hinc ab ipso Actorum app. auctore postea breviante et emendante in chartam puram scriptum esse minime demonstravit, lima ita potitus est, ut etiam genuina et necessaria non pauca sublata sint," p. xiv.

1899 ; B. Weiss, *Einleitung*, 3rd edit., 1897 ; Jülicher, *Einleitung*, 1894 ; (3) *Special Treatises :* Hilgenfeld, *Acta Apostolorum*, Græce et Latine, 1899 ; J. Weiss, *Über die Absicht und den literarischen Charakter der Apostelgeschichte*, 1897 ; Bethge, *Die Paulinischen Reden der Apostelgeschichte*, 1887, a reverent and in many respects valuable treatment of the text and sources of St. Paul's addresses ; Bishop Williams of Connecticut, *Studies in Acts*, 1888 ; Gilbert, *Student's Life of St. Paul*, 1899 : with appendix on Churches of Galatia ; Luckock, *Footprints of the Apostles as traced by St. Luke in the Acts*, 1897 ; (4) *Early Church History :* McGiffert, *Apostolic Age ;* Hort, *Ecclesia ;* Nösgen, *Geschichte d. Neut. Offenbarung*, ii., 1892 ; (5) *Monographs on Special Points :* E. H. Askwith, *Epistle to the Galatians*, 1899 (an enlargement of the Norrisian Prize Essay on *The Locality of the Churches of Galatia*) ; Vogel, *Zur Charakteristik des Lukas nach Sprache und Stil*, 1897, and his *Einführung in das Griechische N.T.*, 2nd edit., 1899 ; Nestle, *Philologica Sacra* (*Bemerkungen über die Urgestalt der Evangelien und A.G.*), 1896, frequently referred to by Zahn and Dalman ; Blass, *Philology of the Gospels*, and *Præf.* to *Evangelium secundum Lucam*, 1897 ; Klostermann, *Probleme im Aposteltexte*, 1883, and *Vindiciæ Lucanæ*, 1866 ; Hawkins, *Horæ Synopticæ*, pp. 140-158, *on the Linguistic Relations between St. Luke's Gospel and Acts ;* Bousset, *Der Text des N.T.*, 1898 (*Theol. Rundschau*, p. 405 ff.) ; B. Weiss, *Der Codex D*, 1897, dealing with the hypothesis of Dr. Blass ; Harnack, *Sitzungsberichte der königlich Preussischen Akad. der Wissenschaften zu Berlin*, xi. and xvii., 1899 ; Curtius, " Paulus in Athen " (*Gesammelte Abhandlungen*, ii., pp. 528-543, 1894) ; see also Ramsay, various articles of great value in Hastings' B.D., i., ii., "Ephesus," "Galatia," "Corinth," etc., and Schmiedel, "Acts," in *Enc. Bibl.*, 1899, which appeared too late for more than a few references here. For literature connected with special points, and the text and sources of Acts, see above, pp. 8, 22, 41, and for grammatical questions and syntax see references in commentary to Simcox, *Language of the N.T. ;* Blass, *Grammatik des Neutestamentlichen Griechisch*, 1896 ; Viteau, *Le Grec du N.T.*, 1893 and 1896 ; and to the numbers of Winer-Schmiedel, *Grammatik des Neutestamentlichen Sprachidioms*, now in course of publication.[1]

---

[1] In the preparation of the textual criticism my best thanks are due to the kind and valuable help of the Rev. Harold Smith, M.A., St. John's College, Cambridge, sometime Lecturer in King's College, London.

ΠΡΑΞΕΙΣ[1] ΑΠΟΣΤΟΛΩΝ.

I. 1. ΤΟΝ μὲν πρῶτον λόγον ἐποιησάμην περὶ πάντων, ὦ Θεόφιλε,
ὧν ἤρξατο ὁ[2] Ἰησοῦς ποιεῖν τε καὶ διδάσκειν, 2. ἄχρι ἧς ἡμέρας

[1] B and also the subscription of ℵ; so Lach., W.H., Wendt. D has πραξις
αποστολων. ℵ merely πραξεις, so Tisch. πραξεις των αποστολων 31, 61; so
Griesb., Meyer, whilst των αγιων before αποστολων is found in subscription of
EGH. Clem. Alex., *Strom.*, v., 12, has πραξεις των αποστ. Tertullian, *Adv. Marc.*,
v., 1, 2, has *Acta Apostolorum*. *Cf.* Iren., *Adv. Hær.*, iii., 13, 3, and also lat. title as
in Clem. Alex., *Adumbr.*, 1 Pet., v., 13, *Actus Apostolorum*; sometimes simply *Acta*
or *Actus*; see further Zahn, *Einleitung in das N. T.*, ii., 334, 388 (1899).

[2] ὁ ℵAE, Orig. and Blass in β, so also Weiss. Omit. BD, W.H. (see Blass,
Grammatik, p. 148).

CHAPTER I.—Ver. 1. τὸν μὲν πρῶτον
λόγον, a reference beyond all reasonable
doubt to St. Luke's Gospel. Not merely
the dedication of both writings to Theophilus, but their unity of language and
style is regarded by critics of all schools
as convincing proof of the identity of
authorship of Acts and the third Gospel;
see *Introd.* and Zöckler, *Greifswalder
Studien*, p. 128 (1895). In the expression πρῶτος λόγος Ramsay finds an
intimation from St. Luke's own hand
that he contemplated a third book at
least, otherwise we should have had
πρότερος λόγος, *St. Paul the Traveller*,
pp. 23, 27, 28; see to the same effect
Zahn, *Einleitung in das N. T.*, ii., 371
(1899), Rendall, *Acts of the Apostles,
in loco*, and *cf.* comment. on Acts xxviii.
31. So, too, *primus* is used in Latin not
simply as former but as first in a series,
Cicero, *De Invent.*, ii., 3. On the other
hand, Blass, *Grammatik des N. G.*, p. 34,
Acta Apost., p. 16, and more recently
Philology of the Gospels, p. 38, maintains
that πρῶτος simply = πρότερος (so also
Holtzmann and Felten). But Ramsay,
whilst pointing out instances in which St.
Luke apparently uses πρῶτος differently
from this, p. 28 (*cf.* also Zahn, *u. s.*, p.
389), admits that we cannot attain to any
absolute certainty in the passage before
us, since no instance occurs of the use of
πρότερος by St. Luke.—λόγος: frequently
used by classical writers in the sense of
a narrative or history contained in a
book; see instances in Wetstein. The
passage in Plato, *Phædo*, p. 61, B., is
valuable not only for the marked contrast
between λόγος and μῦθος, ποιεῖν μύθους
ἀλλ᾽ οὐ λόγους, but also for the use of
ποιεῖν (Wendt). Amongst other instances
of the phrase ποιεῖν λόγον *cf.* Galen, *De
Usu Part.*, ii., περὶ πρώτων τῶν δακτύλων
ἐποιησάμην τὸν λόγον. St. Chrysostom
sees in the phrase a proof of the unassuming character of the author: St. Luke
does not say "The former Gospel which
I preached". For the anomalous μέν,
"solitarium," without the following δέ,
frequent in Luke, see Blass, *Grammatik
des N. G.*, p. 261, *cf.* Luke viii. 5, Acts
iii. 21, xxviii. 22, etc., and several times
in St. Paul. μέν occurs thus six times
in the Acts without οὖν—on μὲν οὖν see
ver. 6.—ὦ Θεόφιλε: the interjection used
here simply in address, as common in
Attic Greek, *cf.* xviii. 14, xxvii. 21, 1 Tim.
vi. 11; without the epithet κράτιστε, as
in Luke i. 3, and without ὦ, Θεόφ. alone
would have seemed too bold, Winer-
Schmiedel, p. 258. It has been suggested
that the omission of the epithet κράτιστε,
Luke i. 3, denotes that St. Luke's friendship had become less ceremonious, just
as a similar change has been noted

ἐντειλάμενος τοῖς ἀποστόλοις διὰ Πνεύματος Ἁγίου, οὓς ἐξελέξατο,
ἀνελήφθη.[1] 3. οἷς καὶ παρέστησεν ἑαυτὸν ζῶντα μετὰ τὸ παθεῖν

[1] ανελήφθη B[3] and probably all cursives, but -λημφθη אAB*CDE, so Tisch.,W.H.,
Weiss (see Blass, *Gram.*, pp. 24, 55). αχρι ης . . . ανελήφ. Aug., Vig. read "in
die quo Apostolos elegit per Spiritum Sanctum," omitting ανελήφ. altogether,
and continuing with D, Lux., Syr. Harcl. mg., Sah. και εκελευσεν κηρυσσειν
το ευαγγελιον (*et præcepit prædicare evangelium*). This reading of Aug. Blass
adopts (so Corssen, *Der Cyprianische Text der Acta Apost.*, p. 18, and Graefe,
Stud. und Krit., p. 136 (1898)) and therefore refers the day mentioned to Luke vi. 12,
the day of the choice of the Apostles. But Belser well points out that St. Luke's
Gospel (quite apart from chaps. i. and ii.) does not begin with the choice of the
Twelve, but with the public appearance of the Baptist and that of Jesus Himself, and
with His public teaching. Nor is there anything said, as Blass himself admits, in
St. Luke's account of the choice of the Twelve, vi. 12, as to any commission given
to them at that time to preach the Gospel (although in his edition of St. Luke's
Gospel Blass compares Mark iii. 14, but even then the expression used, κηρυσσειν
το ευαγγελιον, cannot be called Lucan, see Weiss on Codex D, p. 53). Further, D
contains ανελήφθη, after ημερας, apparently to simplify the structure ; there is no
Greek authority for its omission, and it is contained in Codex Parisinus (which in
many respects approaches so closely to D), where we find it at the end of the verse:
assumptus est. Blass, *Philology of the Gospels*, p. 132 ff., contends for the reading
which he had previously adopted in β, and sees in it the original draft of Luke who
in α "has encumbered the clause in order to bring in the Ascension without leaving
out the choice of the Apostles " (p. 136).

in the dedication of Shakespeare's two
poems to the Earl of Southampton;
cf. also Zahn, *Einleitung*, ii. 360. The
way in which the epithet κράτιστε is
employed elsewhere in the book in addressing Roman officials, xxiii. 26, xxiv.
3, xxvi. 25, has been thought to indicate
that Theophilus held some high official
post, or that he was at least of equestrian
rank (Ramsay, *St. Paul the Traveller*, pp.
388, 389, and his inferences as to the date
of Acts). Ramsay is of opinion that the
name was given at baptism, and that it
was used or known only among Christians,
and he infers that this baptismal name is
used in Acts because the book was probably written at a time when it was
dangerous for a Roman of rank to be
recognised as a Christian. But Theophilus was by no means uncommon as a
Jewish name; *cf.* B. D.[2], i., p. 25, and also
article " Theophilus," B. D.[1] (see also
Deissmann, *Bibelstudien*, p. 19). The
epithet κράτιστος was peculiarly appropriated to Romans holding high office,
and actually became during the second
century a technical title to denote equestrian rank ; and from its use here Zahn
maintains not only that Theophilus was
a man of some social position, but that
he was, when Luke wrote his gospel,
not a member of the Christian Church,
since there is no instance in the first two
centuries of a Christian addressing his
fellow-Christians in a title corresponding

as it were to " your Excellency " (*Einleitung in das N. T.*, ii., 360, 383). The
instance of the address of the *Epist. ad
Diognetum*, κράτιστε Διόγνητε, is alleged
by Blass as an instance that the epithet
is not always used in the technical sense
mentioned ; but to this Ramsay replies
that if Diognetus was the friend and
teacher of Marcus Aurelius, the emperor
might well raise his teacher to equestrian
rank ; Septimius Severus raised his sons'
tutor to the high dignity of the consul-
ship. Ramsay discusses κράτιστος at
length in *Was Christ born at Bethlehem?*
(1898), pp. 65, 71, 72, as against Blass,
Philology of the Gospels, p. 19. Blass
fully recognises that Theophilus held
a high position, and that the title in
question would naturally occur in a book
dedicated to a patron ; but it must be
borne in mind that Blass regards Theophilus as of Greek extraction, possibly
a fellow-citizen with Luke of Antioch,
whilst Ramsay sees in him a citizen of
Rome and a resident in the imperial city.
Theophylact asks why Luke should have
cared to write to one man only and to
value him so highly, and makes answer
that it was because the Evangelist was a
guardian of the words spoken by the Lord:
" It is not the will of my Father that one
of these little ones should perish ". There
seems no great reason to doubt that
Theophilus was a real personage, and
the epithet κράτιστε, at all events in its

αὐτόν, ἐν πολλοῖς τεκμηρίοις, δι᾽ ἡμερῶν τεσσαράκοντα [1] ὀπτανόμενος
αὐτοῖς, καὶ λέγων τὰ περὶ τῆς βασιλείας τοῦ Θεοῦ.   4. Καὶ συναλιζό-

---

[1] τεσσαρακοντα, so B³E 1, 13, Meyer; but τεσσερακοντα אAB*CD 61, so Tisch.,
W.H., Weiss. D omits δια, so Blass in β.

technical significance, is hardly consistent
with any other supposition (see Sanday,
Inspiration, p. 319, note). The recent
attempt to identify Theophilus with
Seneca, referred to by Zöckler, *Apostelgeschichte*, p. 163, must be dismissed
as equally groundless and fanciful as
the former conjecture that he was no
other than Philo.—περὶ πάντων ὧν: the
use of πᾶς (mostly after a prep., as here)
followed by an attracted relative may
be classed amongst the mannerisms of
St. Luke (Simcox, *Writers of the N. T.*,
p. 24, where other instances are given);
see also Friedrich, *Das Lucasevangelium*,
pp. 1, 2.—ὧν: in St. Luke's Gospel and
in the Acts the frequency of the attraction
of the relative again specially characterises
him amongst the N.T. writers, Friedrich,
u. s., pp. 36 and 100.—ἤρξατο: often regarded as simply pleonastic, but sometimes
as emphatic, to intimate that the work
which Jesus began on earth He continued
in heaven, or that He began the work of
the Gospel and committed its continuance
to His followers; Zahn, *u. s.*, p. 366 ff.
In Winer's view to regard ἄρχεσθαι as
pleonastic is a mere subterfuge to avoid
a difficulty, and he renders the passage
"what Jesus began both to do and to teach,
and *continued to do* until," etc. (see also
Grimm-Thayer, *sub v.*), treating it as
an example of breviloquence (Winer-
Moulton, lxvi., 1). On the whole it is
perhaps best to consider the phrase ἤρξ.
ποιεῖν with Bengel (*in loco*) as equivalent
to *fecit ab initio*, although no doubt there
is a sense in which, with every Christian
for nineteen centuries, St. Luke would
regard the *whole* earthly life of Jesus as
a *beginning*, a prelude to the glory and
mighty working to be revealed and perfected in the ascended Lord. The verb
is of frequent use in St. Luke's writings
(Friedrich, Zeller, Lekebusch), although
in St. Mark's Gospel it is also constantly
found. In the LXX it is often found like
לָלֵחַ hi., and also in Apocr. ποιεῖν
τε καὶ διδάσκειν, "Scilicet prius fecit,
deinde docuit; prius docuit exemplo,
deinde verbo. Unde prius non docuit,
quod prius ipse non fecit" (Corn. à Lap.).
Ver. 2. ἄχρι ἧς ἡμέρας. In Matt.
ἄχρι occurs once or twice, in Mark and

and John not at all, in Luke four times,
and in Acts sixteen; whilst the commoner
μέχρι is found only once in the Gospels
and twice in the Acts (Winer-Schmiedel,
p. 227, and on the use of the form ἄχρι
or ἄχρις see Grimm-Thayer, *sub v.*). It
is seldom used in the LXX, but in 2
Macc. xiv. it occurs twice, vv. 10 and
15; *cf.* also Symm., 2 Kings xxi. 16;
Theod., Job xxxii. 11.—διὰ πνεύματος
ἁγίου. The older commentators, and
Wendt, Holtzmann, Zöckler, Hilgenfeld,
amongst moderns, connect the words with
ἐξελέξατο, the reference to the choice
of the Apostles through the Holy Ghost
standing significantly at the opening of a
book in which their endowment with the
same divine power is so prominent. On
the other hand, it is urged that there is
no need to emphasise further the divine
choice of the Apostles (*cf.* Luke vi. 13,
and see below on ver. 25), but that it was
important to show that the instructions
to continue the work and teaching of
Jesus were a divine commission (Weiss),
and to emphasise from the commencement
of the Acts that Jesus had given this commission to His Apostles through the same
divine Spirit Whom they received shortly
after His Ascension (Felten). Spitta (who
refers i. 1-14 to his inferior source B),
whilst he connects διὰ πνεύμ. ἁγ. with
ἐντειλάμενος, curiously limits the latter to
the command to the Apostles to assemble
themselves on the Mount of Olives (so too
Jüngst). For other connections of the
words see Alford *in loco*.—ἐξελέξατο,
always in N.T. ἐκλέγομαι, middle (except,
perhaps, in Luke ix. 35, but see R.V.
and W.H.). Another verb very frequent
in LXX, used constantly of a divine
choice: of God's choice of Israel, of
Jacob, Aaron, David, the tribe of Judah,
Zion, and Jerusalem. The verb is also
found in the same sense in the middle
voice in classical Greek.—ἀνελήμφθη:
the verb is used of Elijah's translation to
heaven in the LXX, 2 Kings ii. 9-11, also
in Ecclesiasticus xlviii. 9 and 1 Macc. ii.
58, and perhaps of Enoch in Ecclesiasticus
xlix. 14 (A, μετετέθη). In addition to the
present passage (*cf.* vv. 11, 12) it is also
used in Mark xvi. 9 and 1 Tim. iii. 16
(where it probably forms part of an early
Christian Hymn or confession of faith)

μενος[1] παρήγγειλεν αὐτοῖς ἀπὸ Ἱεροσολύμων μὴ χωρίζεσθαι, ἀλλὰ
περιμένειν τὴν ἐπαγγελίαν τοῦ πατρός, ἣν ἠκούσατέ μου[2]· 5. ὅτι

[1] συναλιζομενος, some good cursives συναυλιζομενος. Aug. prefixes ὡς to συναλ.;
so β (see also Belser). D reads συναλισκομενος (-σγομ. D²). D, Gig., Par.¹, Sah.
add μετ' αυτων, perhaps explanatory addition, Syriac (Chase), or Latin, to bring
out force of συν. retained by Blass in β. R.V. omits μετ' αυτων; so W.H., Wendt,
and Weiss.

[2] ην ηκουσατε μου; in place of this, D, Par.², Vulg. (Clem.), Hil., Aug. read ην
ηκουσατε φησιν δια του στοματος μου, so Blass in β and Hilgenfeld (see also Belser),
may be mere amplification of μου in T.R., possibly assimilated to xv. 7 (Chase).
Harris ascribes it to a Montanist. ηκουσα in D¹.

of our Lord's Ascension; cf. also Gospel of
Peter, 19, in a doubtfully orthodox sense.
It is to be noted that the word is here
used absolutely, as of an event with which
the Apostolic Church was already familiar.
On the cognate noun ἀνάληψις, used only
by St. Luke in N.T., and absolutely, with
reference to the same event, in his Gospel,
ix. 51, see Psalms of Solomon, iv., 20,
ed. Ryle and James, p. 49. In the latter
passage the word is apparently used for
the first time in extant Greek literature,
but its meaning is very different from its
later technical use with reference to the
Assumption of the Blessed; see instances,
p. 49, ubi supra. St. Irenæus, i., 10, 1,
whilst using the noun of our Lord's
Ascension, is careful to say τὴν ἔνσαρ-
κον εἰς τοὺς οὐρανοὺς ἀνάληψιν; see
especially Swete, The Apostles' Creed,
pp. 70-72, and below on verse 11.
Ver. 3. οἷς καὶ παρέστησεν, "he
also showed himself," R.V., but margin
"presented himself" (cf. ix. 41), praebuit
se, Vulg. In ix. 41 monstravit, h. l.
magis demonstravit (Blass). The verb
is used thirteen times in Acts (once
in a quotation, iv. 26), both transitively
and intransitively. St. Luke in his
Gospel uses it three times, and as in
Acts both transitively and intransitively.
In this he is alone amongst the Evangelists. In the Epistles it is found only
in St. Paul, and for the most part in a
transitive sense.—μετὰ τὸ παθεῖν, "after
his passion," so in A. and R.V.; post
passionem suam, Vulg.; "too sacred a
word to be expunged from this the only
place where it occurs in the Bible,"
Humphry, Commentary on R.V.; cf.
iii. 18, xvii. 3, xxvi. 23.—ἐν πολλοῖς
τεκμηρίοις — τεκμήριον only here in
N.T. — twice in Wisdom v. 11, xix.
13, and 3 Macc. iii. 24. The A.V.
followed the Genevan Version by inserting the word "infallible" (although the
latter still retained "tokens" instead of
"proofs"). But R.V. simply "proofs"

expresses the technical use of the word
τεκμήριον, convincing, certain evidence.
Although in a familiar passage, Wisdom
v. 11, τεκμήριον and σημεῖον are used as
practically synonymous, yet there is no
doubt that they were technically distinguished, e.g., Arist., Rhet., i., 2, τῶν
σημείων τὸ μὲν ἀναγκαῖον τεκμ. This
technical distinction, it may be observed,
was strictly maintained by medical men,
although St. Luke may no doubt have
met the word elsewhere. Thus it is used
by Josephus several times, as Krenkel
mentions, but he does not mention that
it is also used by Thucydides, ii., 39, to
say nothing of other classical writers.
Galen writes τὸ μὲν ἐκ τηρήσεως σημεῖον
τὸ δὲ ἐξ ἐνδείξεως τεκμήριον, and the
context states that rhetoricians as well as
physicians had examined the distinction;
Hobart, Medical Language of St. Luke,
p. 184. The word also occurs in the
Proem of Dioscorides to his De Materia
Medica, p. 3, which Vogel and Meyer-
Weiss hold that Luke imitated in the
Prologue to his Gospel (but see Zahn,
Einleitung, ii., 384).—δι' ἡμερῶν τεσσαράκοντα. St. Chrysostom comments
οὐ γὰρ εἶπε τεσσαράκοντα ἡμέρας, ἀλλὰ
δι' ἡμερῶν τεσσαράκοντα· ἐφίστατο γὰρ
καὶ ἀφίστατο πάλιν. To this interpretation of the genitive with διά Blass refers,
and endorses it, Grammatik des Neutestamentlichen Griechisch, p. 129, following
the Scholiast. The meaning, if this
interpretation is adopted, would therefore be that our Lord did not remain with
His disciples continuously (οὐ διηνεκῶς,
Schol.) as before, but that He appeared
to them from time to time; non perpetuo,
sed per intervalla, Bengel. But cf. also
Simcox, Language of the N.T., p.
140. Men have seen in this period of
forty days, mentioned only by St. Luke
in N.T., what we may reverently call
a symbolical fitness. But in a certain
sense the remark of Blass seems justified:
Parum ad rem est quod idem (numerus)

Ἰωάννης [1] μὲν ἐβάπτισεν ὕδατι, ὑμεῖς δὲ βαπτισθήσεσθε ἐν Πνεύματι
Ἁγίῳ, οὐ μετὰ πολλὰς ταύτας ἡμέρας.[2] 6. Οἱ μὲν οὖν συνελθόντες

[1] Ἰωάννης; in D almost throughout Ἰωάνης, see W.H., *Notes on Orthography*, p. 166, on authority of B and D. Nestle (*Expository Times*, Nov., 1897, p. 93) points out that in D νν prevails in Matt., Mk., John (νν 66, ν 7), while in Luke and Acts the reverse is the case (νν 3, ν 48); but see also Winer-Schmiedel, p. 57.

[2] After ἡμέρας D, Sah. insert ἕως τῆς πεντηκοστῆς. Blass sees in the addition an intimate knowledge of the facts (see also Belser); *cf.* ii. 1, but *cf.* on the other hand Weiss on Codex D, p. 54.

alias quoque occurrit. The parallels in the histories of Moses and Elijah to which Holtzmann and Spitta refer are really no parallels at all, and if it be true to say that there was nothing in contemporary Jewish ideas to suggest our Lord's Resurrection *as it is represented as taking place*, it is equally true to maintain that there was nothing to suggest the after sojourn of the forty days on earth as it is represented as taking place; see Edersheim, *Jesus the Messiah*, ii., 624.—ὀπτανόμενος: if we could call this a frequentative verb with some scholars, it would in itself give the meaning "appearing from time to time," but it is rather a late Hellenistic present, formed from some parts of ὁρᾶν; Blass, *Grammatik des N. G.*, pp. 57, 181. But it certainly does not mean that our Lord's appearances were merely visionary. The verb is found only here in N.T., but also in LXX 1 Kings viii. 8 and in Tobit xii. 19 (not in S.). In these two passages the word cannot fairly be pressed into the service of visionary appearances. In 1 Kings the reference is to the staves of the ark which were so long that the ends were seen from the holy place before the oracle, but they were not seen from without, *i.e.*, from the porch or vestibule. In Tobit it is not the appearance of the angel which is represented as visionary, quite the contrary; but his eating and drinking are represented as being only in appearance. But even if the word could be pressed into the meaning suggested, St. Luke's view of our Lord's appearances must be judged not by one expression but by his whole conception, *cf.* Luke xxiv. 39-43 and Acts x. 41. That he could distinguish between visions and realities we cannot doubt; see note below on xii. 12.—τὰ περὶ τῆς βασιλείας τοῦ θ.: "speaking the things concerning," R.V., not "speaking of the things," A.V., but speaking the very things, whether truths to be believed, or commands to be obeyed (Humphry, *Commentary on R.V.*). On St. Luke's fondness for τὰ περί τινος in his writings

see Friedrich, *Das Lucasevangelium*, pp. 10 and 89 (so also Zeller and Lekebusch). The exact phrase is only found in *Acts*, where it occurs twice (in T.R. three times); *cf.* xix. 8 (viii. 12), and see also xx. 25 and xxviii. (23), 31. The expression ἡ βασ. τοῦ θ., instead of τῶν οὐρανῶν of the Hebrew Evangelist St. Matthew, is characteristic of St. Luke's writings, although it is found frequently in St. Mark and once in St. John. In St. Luke's Gospel it occurs more than thirty times, and six times in Acts (only four times in St. Matt.). Possibly the phrase was used by St. Luke as one more easily understood by Gentile readers, but the two terms ἡ βασ. τοῦ θ. and τῶν οὐρ. were practically synonymous in the Gospels and in Judaism in the time of our Lord (Schürer, *Jewish People*, div. ii., vol. ii., p. 171; E. T. and Taylor, *Sayings of the Jewish Fathers* (second edit.), p. 67; Edersheim, *Jesus the Messiah*, i., 267; and Dalman, *Die Worte Jesu*, p. 76 ff.). Dr. Stanton, *Jewish and Christian Messiah*, p. 226, draws attention to the important fact that the preaching of the original Apostles after the Ascension is not described as that of the preaching of the kingdom of God, but that the phrase is only used of the preaching of St. Paul, and of St. Philip the associate of St. Stephen. But in view of the fact that the original Apostles heard during the Forty Days from their Master's lips τὰ περὶ τῆς βασιλ. τοῦ θεοῦ, we cannot doubt that in deed and in word they would proclaim that kingdom. On the question as to whether they conceived of the kingdom as present, or future, or both, see Wendt, *Teaching of Jesus*, i., 409, E. T., and *Witness of the Epistles* (Longmans), p. 309 ff., and on the conception of the kingdom of God in the Theology of A. Ritschl and his school see Orr, *Ritschlian Theology*, p. 258 ff. For the relation of the Church and the Kingdom see also Moberly, *Ministerial Priesthood*, pp. 28, 36 ff., "Church," Hastings, B.D., p. 425; Hort, *Ecclesia*, p. 5 ff.

ἐπηρώτων αὐτὸν λέγοντες, Κύριε, εἰ ἐν τῷ χρόνῳ τούτῳ ἀποκαθιστάνεις τὴν βασιλείαν τῷ Ἰσραήλ; 7. εἶπε δὲ πρὸς αὐτούς, Οὐχ ὑμῶν

Ver. 4. συναλίζομενος: a strong array of modern commentators renders "eating with them," following the Vulgate *convescens illis* (so both A. and R.V. in margin, and Wycl. and Rhem.). It is thus rendered by Overbeck (as against De Wette), Wendt, Holtzmann, Felten, Weiss, Matthias, Knabenbauer, and Blass, who adopts the reading ὡς συναλ., and regards the particle as showing that the recapitulation is continued of the events already mentioned in Luke xxiv. 42 ff. It is evidently taken in the same sense by Spitta, Feine, Jüngst. If we so translate it, we must derive it from ἅλς (salt), so Schol. κοινωνῶν ἁλῶν, τραπέζης, in the sense given to the expression by Chrys., Theophyl., Œcum. In Ps. cxl. 4 LXX, to which Wendt refers, μὴ συνδυάσω (although the reading is somewhat doubtful—the word is used by Symmachus, I Sam. xxvi. 19) is also rendered συναλισθῶ (Alius) as an equivalent of the Hebrew אַל־תַּלְחֵם, μὴ συμφάγοιμι, Symmachus. Blass gives no classical references, but points out that the word undoubtedly exists in the sense referred to in *Clem. Hom.*, xiii., 4 (but see Grimm-Thayer, *sub v.*). Hilgenfeld (*Zeitschrift für wissenschaft. Theol.*, p. 74 (1894)) contends that the use of the word in the psalm quoted and in the passage from the Clementines refers not to the use of salt at an ordinary meal, but rather to the sacrificial and symbolical use of salt in the Old and New Testaments. Thus in the passage *Clem. Hom.*, xiii., 4, τότε αὐτοῖς συναλιζόμεθα, τότε means "after the Baptism"; *cf.* also Ignatius, *ad Magnes.*, x., ἁλίσθητε ἐν αὐτῷ, "be ye salted in him". Wendt takes the word quite generally as meaning that the sharing in a common meal with His disciples, as on the evening of the Resurrection, was the habitual practice of the Lord during the Forty Days; *cf.* Acts x. 41 and Luke xxiv. 36 ff. Feine similarly holds that the word presupposes some such incidents as those mentioned in Luke xxiv., and that Luke had derived his information from a source which described the final instructions to the disciples as given at a common meal. On the other hand it must be borne in mind that in classical Greek, as in Herodotus and Xenophon (Wetstein) (as also in Josephus, *B. J.*, iii., 9, 4), συναλίζω = to assemble, *cf.* Hesy-

chius, συναλιζ. = συναλισθείς, συναχθείς, συναθροισθείς, and it is possible that the preceding present participles in the immediate context may help to account for the use of the same participle instead of the aorist συναλισθείς. The verb is then derived from σύν and ἁλής (ᾱ), meaning lit., close, crowded together. Mr. Rendall (*Acts of the Apostles*, p. 32) would derive it from Ἀλίη (-α), a common term for a popular assembly amongst Ionian and Dorian Greeks, and he supposes that the verb here implies a general gathering of believers not limited to the Twelve; but the context apparently points back to Luke xxiv. 49 to a command which was certainly given only to the Twelve.— παρήγγειλεν, "he charged them," R.V., which not only distinguishes it from other verbs rendered "to command," but also gives the emphatic meaning which St. Luke often attaches to the word. It is characteristic of his writings, occurring four times in his Gospel and ten or eleven times in Acts, and it is very frequent in St. Paul's Epistles (Friedrich, Lekebusch).— Ἱεροσολύμων: a neuter plural (but *cf.* Matt. ii. 3 and Grimm *sub v.*). St. Luke most frequently uses the Jewish form Ἱερουσαλήμ—twenty-seven times in his Gospel, about forty in Acts—as against the use of Ἱεροσόλυμα four times in his Gospel and over twenty in Acts (Friedrich, Lekebusch). Blass retains the aspirate for the Greek form but not for the Jewish, *cf. in loco* and *Grammatik des N. G.*, pp. 17, 31, but it is very doubtful whether either should have the aspirate; W.H., ii., 313; Plummer's *St. Luke*, p. 64; Winer-Schmiedel, p. 93. Grimm points out that the Hebrew form is used in the N.T.: "ubi in ipso nomine tanquam sancta vis quædam reponitur ut, Gal. iv. 25; ita in compellationibus, Matt. xxiii. 37, Luke xiii. 34;" see further *sub v.* Ἱεροσόλυμα.—μὴ χωρίζ.: it was fitting that they should not depart from Jerusalem, not only that the new law as the old should go forth from Zion and the word of the Lord from Jerusalem, Isa. ii. 3 (Felten), but that the Apostles' testimony should be delivered not to men unacquainted with the facts, but to the inhabitants of the city where Jesus had been crucified and buried. Εἰ δὲ εὐθὺς ἐχωρίσθησαν Ἱεροσολύμων, καὶ τούτων οὐδὲν ἐπηκολούθησεν, ὕποπτος ἂν ἡ ἀνάστασις ὑπῆρξεν, Œcumenius, *in loco*; see also Theophyl. —περιμένειν: not else-

ἐστι γνῶναι χρόνους ἢ καιροὺς οὓς ὁ Πατὴρ ἔθετο ἐν τῇ ἰδίᾳ ἐξουσίᾳ·
8. ἀλλὰ λήψεσθε δύναμιν, ἐπελθόντος τοῦ Ἁγίου Πνεύματος ἐφ᾽ ὑμᾶς,

where in N.T. (but see x. 24, D), but used in classical Greek of awaiting a thing's happening (Dem.). The passage in LXX in which it occurs is suggestive: τὴν σωτηρίαν περιμένων κυρίου, Gen. xlix. 18 (cf. Wisd. viii. 12). On the tradition that the Apostles remained in Jerusalem for twelve years in obedience to a command of the Lord, and the evidence for it, see Harnack, *Chronologie*, i., p. 243 ff. Harnack speaks of the tradition as very old and well attested, and maintains that it is quite in accordance with Acts, as the earlier journeys of the Apostles are there described as missionary excursions from which they always returned to Jerusalem.—τὴν ἐπαγγελίαν: Bengel notes the distinction between ὑπισχνέομαι and ἐπαγγέλλομαι, the former being used of promises in response to petitions, the latter of voluntary offers (Ammonius): "quæ verbi Græci proprietas, ubi de divinis promissionibus agitur, exquisite observanda est". It is therefore remarkable that in the Gospels the word ἐπαγγελία is never used in this technical sense of the divine promise made by God until Luke xxiv. 49, where it is used of the promise of the Holy Spirit, as here. But in Acts and in St. Paul's Epistles and in the Hebrews the word is frequent, and always of the promises made by God (except Acts xxiii. 21). See Sanday and Headlam on *Romans* i. 2, and Lightfoot on *Gal.* iii. 14, and *Psalms of Solomon*, xii., 8 (cf. vii., 9, and xvii., 6), ed. Ryle and James, p. 106. "The promise of the Father," cf. Luke xxiv. 49, is fulfilled in the baptism with the Holy Ghost, and although no doubt earlier promises of the gift of the Spirit may be included, cf. Luke xii. 11, as also the promise of the Spirit's outpouring in Messianic times (cf. Joel ii. 28, Isaiah xliv. 3, Ezek. xxxvi. 26), yet the phraseology may be fairly said to present an undesigned coincidence with the more recent language of the Lord to the Twelve, John xiv. 16, xv. 26, xvi. 14. On the many points of connection between the opening verses of Acts and the closing verses of St. Luke's Gospel see below.

Ver. 5. ἐν πνεύματι: the omission of ἐν before ὕδατι and its insertion before πνεύμ. may be meant to draw a distinction between the baptism with water and the baptism *in* the Spirit (R.V. margin "in"). But in Matt. iii. 11 we have the preposition ἐν in both parts of the verse; cf.

John i. 31. On ἐν with the instrumental dative see Blass, *Grammatik des N. G.*, p. 114, and Grotius, *in loco*; cf. the Hebrew ְּ.—οὐ μετὰ πολλὰς ταύτας ἡμέρας: not after many, *i.e.*, after few. This use of οὐ with an adjective or adverb is characteristic of St. Luke, cf. Luke xv. 13, Acts xxvii. 14, in which places οὐ πολύς = ὀλίγος as here; cf. οὐ μετρίως, Acts xx. 12; οὐ μακράν, Luke vii. 6, Acts xvii. 27; οὐκ ἄσημος, Acts xxi. 39; οὐχ ὁ τυχών, Acts xix. 11, xxviii. 2, cf. Hawkins, *Horæ Syn.*, p. 153. No doubt μετ᾽ οὐ would be more correct, but the negative is found both before and after the preposition, so in Luke xv. 13; cf. Josephus, *Ant.*, i., 12, and xiii., 7, 1, for similar changes of allocation in the same words. ταύτας closely connects the days referred to with the current day; cf. also Winer-Schmiedel, p. 221. οὐ μετὰ πολλάς, φησὶν ἵνα μὴ εἰς ἀθυμίαν ἐμπέσωσιν· ὡρισμένως δὲ πότε, οὐκ εἶπεν, ἵνα ἀεὶ ἐκγρηγορῶσιν ἐκδεχόμενοι, Theophylact, *in loco*.

Ver. 6. οἱ μὲν οὖν: the combination μὲν οὖν is very frequent in Acts in all parts, occurring no less than twenty-seven times; cf. Luke iii. 18. Like the simple μέν it is sometimes used without δέ in the apodosis. Here, if δέ is omitted in ver. 7 after εἶπεν, there is still a contrast between the question of the Apostles and the answer of Jesus. See especially Rendall, *Acts of the Apostles*, Appendix on μὲν οὖν, p. 160 ff.; cf. Weiss *in loco*.—συνελθόντες: the question has often been raised as to whether this word and μὲν οὖν refer back to ver. 4, or whether a later meeting of the disciples is here introduced. For the former Hilgenfeld contends (as against Weiss) and sees no reference to any fresh meeting: the disciples referred to in the αὐτοῖς of ver. 4 and the ὑμεῖς of ver. 5 had already come together. According to Holtzmann there is a reference in the words to a common meal of the Lord with His disciples already mentioned in ver. 4, and after this final meal the question of ver. 6 is asked on the way to Bethany (Luke xxiv. 50). The words οἱ μὲν οὖν συνελθ. are referred by Felten to the final meeting which formed the conclusion of the constant intercourse of ver. 3, a meeting thus specially emphasised, although in reality only one out of many, and the question which follows in ver. 6 was asked, as Felten also supposes

καὶ ἔσεσθέ μοι μάρτυρες ἔν τε Ἱερουσαλὴμ καὶ ἐν πάσῃ τῇ Ἰουδαίᾳ
καὶ Σαμαρείᾳ¹ καὶ ἕως ἐσχάτου τῆς γῆς.   9. Καὶ ταῦτα εἰπών,

¹ Σαμαρείᾳ, but אADE Σαμαριᾳ (but Blass in β, -ειᾳ) ; so Tisch., W.H. although
-εια is given as alternative ; see also Winer-Schmiedel, p. 45.

(see too Rendall on vv. 7 and 8), on the way to Bethany. But there is no need to suppose that this was the case (as Jüngst so far correctly objects against Holtzmann), and whilst we may take συνελθ. as referring to the final meeting before the Ascension, we may place that meeting not in Jerusalem but on the Mount of Olives. Blass sees in the word συνελθ. an assembly of all the Apostles, cf. ver. 13 and 1 Cor. xv. 7, and adds: "Aliunde supplendus locus ubi hoc factum, ver. 12, Luke xxiv. 50".—ἐπηρώτων: imperfect, denoting that the act of questioning is always imperfect until an answer is given (Blass, cf. iii. 3), and here perhaps indicating that the same question was put by one inquirer after another (see on the force of the tense, as noted here and elsewhere by Blass, Hermathena, xxi., pp. 228, 229).—εἰ: this use of εἰ in direct questions is frequent in Luke, Blass, Grammatik des N. G., p. 254; cf. vii. 1, xix. 2 (in Vulgate si) ; it is adopted in the LXX, and a parallel may also be found in the interrogative הֲ in Hebrew (so Blass and Viteau).—ἐν τῷ χρόνῳ τούτῳ: such a promise as that made in ver. 5, the fulfilment of which, according to Joel ii. 28, would mark the salvation of Messianic times, might lead the disciples to ask about the restoration of the kingdom to Israel which the same prophet had foretold, to be realised by the annihilation of the enemies of God and victory and happiness for the good. As in the days of old the yoke of Pharaoh had been broken and Israel redeemed from captivity, so would the Messiah accomplish the final redemption, cf. Luke xxiv. 21, and set up again, after the destruction of the world-powers, the kingdom in Jerusalem; Weber, Jüdische Theologie, pp. 360, 361 (1897). No doubt the thoughts of the disciples still moved within the narrow circle of Jewish national hopes: "totidem in hac interrogatione sunt errores quot verba," writes Calvin. But still we must remember that with these thoughts of the redemption of Israel there mingled higher thoughts of the need of repentance and righteousness for the Messianic kingdom (Psalms of Solomon, xvii., xviii.; ed. Ryle and James, p. lvii.), and that the disciples may well have shared, even if imperfectly, in the hopes of a Zacharias or a Simeon. Dr. Edersheim notes "with what wonderful sobriety" the disciples put this question to our Lord (ubi supra, i., p. 79); at the same time the question before us is plainly too primitive in character to have been invented by a later generation (McGiffert, Apostolic Age, p. 41).—ἀποκαθιστάνεις: ἀποκαθιστάνω, a form of ἀποκαθίστημι which is found in classical Greek and is used of the restoration of dominion as here in 1 Macc. xv. 3; see also below on iii. 21 and Malachi LXX iv. 5. On the form of the verb see W.H., ii., 162, and on its force see further Dalman, u. s., p. 109. "Dost thou at this time restore . . . ?" R.V.; the present tense marking their expectation that the kingdom, as they conceived it, would immediately appear—an expectation enhanced by the promise of the previous verse, in which they saw the foretaste of the Messianic kingdom. Ver. 7. χρόνους ἢ καιρούς: Blass regards the two as synonymous, and no doubt it is difficult always to maintain a distinction. But here χρόνους may well be taken to mean space of time as such, the duration of the Church's history, and καιρούς the critical periods in that history: ὁ μὲν καιρὸς δηλοῖ ποιότητα χρόνου, χρόνος δὲ ποσότητα (Ammonius). A good instance of the distinction may be found in LXX Neh. x. 34: εἰς καιροὺς ἀπὸ χρόνων, "at times appointed"; cf. 1 Thes. v. 1. So here Weiss renders: „zu kennen Zeiten und geeignete Zeitpunkte". In modern Greek, whilst καιρός means weather, χρόνος means year, so that " in both words the kernel of meaning has remained unaltered; this in the case of καιρούς is changeableness, of χρόνων duration " (Curtius, Etym., p. 110 sq.) ; cf. also Trench, N. T. Synonyms, ii., p. 27 ff.; Kennedy, Sources of N. T. Greek, p. 153 ; and Grimm-Thayer, sub v. καιρός. —ἐξουσία, authority, R.V.—either as delegated or unrestrained, the liberty of doing as one pleases (ἔξεστι) ; δύναμις, power, natural ability, inherent power, residing in a thing by virtue of its nature, or, which a person or thing exerts or puts forth—so δύναμις is ascribed to Christ, now in one sense, now in another, so also

βλεπόντων αὐτῶν ἐπήρθη, καὶ νεφέλη ὑπέλαβεν αὐτὸν ἀπὸ τῶν ὀφθαλμῶν αὐτῶν.[1] 10. καὶ ὡς ἀτενίζοντες ἦσαν εἰς τὸν οὐρανόν,

[1] For T.R. καὶ ταυτα . . . οφθ. αυτων D, Sah., Aug., with var. καὶ ταυτα ειποντος αυτου νεφ. υπελ. αυτον και απηρθη απ' αυτων. Chase explains from Syriac, but καὶ απηρ. κ.τ.λ. may be an assimilation to Matt. ix. 15. Omission of βλεπ. αυτων and απο των οφθαλ. in Western texts curious ; may to some extent support Blass's view or may have been intentional omissions. Vulg. and Flor. retain both omissions. Weiss regards the whole in D as secondary ; Hilgenfeld follows D.

to the Holy Spirit as in ver. 8; *cf.* x. 38, Luke iv. 14, Rom. xv. 13 ; Bengel, Luke iv. 36, and Grimm-Thayer, *Synonyms.* *Sub v.* δύναμις.

Ver. 8. ἔσεσθέ μου μάρτυρες, "my witnesses," R.V., reading μου instead of μοι, not only witnesses to the facts of their Lord's life, *cf.* i. 22, x. 39, but also *His* witnesses, His by a direct personal relationship ; Luke xxiv. 48 simply speaks of a testimony to the facts.—ἔν τε Ἱερουσαλὴμ κ.τ.λ.: St. Luke on other occasions, as here, distinguishes Jerusalem as a district separate from all the rest of Judæa (*cf.* Luke v. 17, Acts x. 39), a proof of intimate acquaintance with the Rabbinical phraseology of the time, according to Edersheim, *Sketches of Jewish Social Life*, pp. 17, 73. In this verse, see *Introduction*, the keynote is struck of the contents of the whole book, and the great divisions of the Acts are marked, see, *e.g.*, Blass, p. 12 in *Prologue* to Acts—Jerusalem, i.-vii. ; Judæa, ix., 32 ; xii., 19 ; Samaria, viii. ; and if it appears somewhat strained to see in St. Paul's preaching in Rome a witness to "the utmost parts of the earth," it is noteworthy that in *Psalms of Solomon*, viii., 16, we read of Pompey that he came ἀπ' ἐσχάτου τῆς γῆς, *i.e.*, Rome—the same phrase as in Acts i. 8. This verse affords a good illustration of the subjective element which characterises the partition theories of Spitta, Jüngst, Clemen and others. Spitta would omit the whole verse from his sources A and B, and considers it as an interpolation by the author of Acts ; but, as Hilgenfeld points out, the verse is entirely in its place, and it forms the best answer to the "particularism" of the disciples, from which their question in ver. 6 shows that they were not yet free. Feine would omit the words ἕως ἐσχάτου τῆς γῆς because nothing in the conduct of the early Church, as it is described to us in the Jewish-Christian source, Acts i.-xii., points to any knowledge of such a commission from the Risen Christ. Jüngst disagrees with both Spitta and Feine, and thinks that the hand of the redactor is visible in prominence given to the little Samaria.

Ver. 9. ἐπήρθη: the word in ver. 2 is different, and ἐπήρθη seems not merely to denote our Lord's first leaving the ground (as Weiss, Overbeck), but also to be more in accordance with the calm and grandeur of the event than ἀπήρθη ; this latter word would rather denote a taking away by violence.—καὶ νεφέλη ὑπέλαβε: the cloud is here, as elsewhere, the symbol of the divine glory, and it was also as St. Chrysostom called it : τὸ ὄχημα τὸ βασιλίκον ; *cf.* Ps. civ. 3. In 1 Tim. iii. 16 we read that our Lord was received up ἐν δόξῃ, "in glory," R.V.

Ver. 10. ἀτενίζοντες ἦσαν : this periphrasis of ἦν or ἦσαν with a present or perfect participle is very frequently found in St. Luke's writings (Friedrich, pp. 12 and 89, and compare the list in Simcox, *u. s.*, pp. 130-134). The verb is peculiar to St. Luke and St. Paul, and is found ten times in Acts, twice in St. Luke's Gospel, and twice in 2 Cor. ; it denotes a fixed, steadfast, protracted gaze : "and while they were looking steadfastly into heaven as he went," R.V., thus expressing more clearly the longing gaze of the disciples watching the Lord as He was going (πορευομένου αὐτοῦ, the present participle denoting that the cloud was still visible for a considerable time), as if carrying their eyes and hearts with Him to heaven : "Ipse enim est amor noster ; ubi autem amor, ibi est oculus et cor " (Corn. à Lapide). The word is also found in LXX 1 Esdr. vi. 28 and 3 Macc. ii. 26 (*cf.* Aquila, Job vii. 8), and also in Josephus, *B. J.*, v., 12, 3, and Polybius. Ramsay, *St. Paul*, 38, 39, gives a most valuable account of the use of the word in St. Luke, and concludes that the action implied by it is quite inconsistent with weakness of vision, and that the theory which makes Paul a permanent sufferer in the eyes, as if he could not distinctly see the persons near him, is hopelessly at variance with St. Luke ; *cf.* too the meaning of the word as used by St. Paul himself in 2 Cor. iii. 7, 13, where not weak but strong sight is implied in the word. The verb thus common in St. Luke is frequently employed by medical writers

πορευομένου αὐτοῦ, καὶ ἰδοὺ ἄνδρες δύο παρειστήκεισαν [1] αὐτοῖς ἐν
ἐσθῆτι λευκῇ,[2] 11. οἳ καὶ εἶπον, Ἄνδρες Γαλιλαῖοι, τί ἑστήκατε
ἐμβλέποντες εἰς τὸν οὐρανόν; οὗτος ὁ Ἰησοῦς ὁ ἀναληφθεὶς ἀφ'
ὑμῶν εἰς τὸν οὐρανόν, οὕτως ἐλεύσεται, ὃν τρόπον ἐθεάσασθε αὐτὸν
πορευόμενον εἰς τὸν οὐρανόν. 12. τότε ὑπέστρεψαν εἰς Ἰερουσαλὴμ

---

[1] παρειστηκεισαν; W.H. read παρισ., but see also Winer-Schmiedel, p. 100.

[2] εσθητι λευκη C³DE Syr. Harcl., Aeth., Orig.-int., Chrys., so Hilgenfeld; but in
R.V. εσθησεσι λευκαις ℵABC and good cursives, Vulg., Syr. Pesh., Arm., Sah.
Boh., Tisch., W.H., Weiss; so also Blass in β.

---

to denote a peculiar fixed look (Zahn); so
in Luke xxii. 56, where it is used for the
servant-maid's earnest gaze at St. Peter,
a gaze not mentioned at all by St.
Matthew, and expressed by a different
word in St. Mark xiv. 67; Hobart,
Medical Language of St. Luke, p. 76.
In LXX, as above, it is employed in a
secondary sense, but by Aquila, *u. s.*, in
its primary meaning of gazing, beholding.
—καὶ ἰδού: καί at the commencement of
the apodosis is explained as Hebraistic,
but instances are not wanting in classical
Greek; *cf.* Blass, *Grammatik des N. G.*,
p. 257, and see also Simcox, *ubi supra*,
p. 160 ff. For the formula καὶ ἰδού *cf.*
the Hebrew וְהִנֵּה, and on St. Luke's
employment of it in sudden interpositions,
see Hort, *Ecclesia*, p. 179. The use of
καί (which in the most Hebraic books of
the N.T. is employed much more extensively than in classical Greek) is most
frequent in Luke, who also uses more
frequently than other writers the formula
καὶ ἰδού to introduce an apodosis; *cf.*
Friedrich, *ubi supra*, p. 33.—παρειστήκεισαν αὐτοῖς: in the appearance of
angels which St. Luke often narrates
there is a striking similarity between the
phraseology of his Gospel and the Acts;
cf. with the present passage Acts x. 30,
xii. 7, and Luke xxiv. 4, ii. 9. The description of the angels' disappearances is
not so similar, *cf.* Acts x. 7 and Luke ii.
15, but it must be remembered that there
is only one other passage in which the
departure of the angels is mentioned,
Rev. xvi. 2; Friedrich, *ubi supra*, pp. 45,
52, and Zeller, Acts ii., p. 224 (E. T.).
For the verb *cf.* Luke i. 19, xix. 24, Acts
xxiii. 2, 4, and especially xxvii. 23.—ἐν
ἐσθῆτι λευκῇ: in R.V. in the plural, see
critical notes and also Deissmann, *Neue
Bibelstudien*, p. 90.
Ver. 11. ἄνδρες Γαλ.: the ἄνδρες in
similar expressions is often indicative of
respect as in classical Greek, but as ad-

dressed by angels to men it may denote the
earnestness of the address (Nösgen). St.
Chrysostom saw in the salutation a wish
to gain the confidence of the disciples:
"Else, why needed they to be told of
their country who knew it well enough?"
Calvin also rejects the notion that the
angels meant to blame the slowness and
dulness of apprehension of Galilæans.
At the same time the word Γαλ. seems
to remind us that things which are despised (John vii. 52) hath God chosen.
*Ex Galilæa nunquam vel certe raro fuerat
propheta; at omnes Apostoli* (Bengel); see
also below.—οὗτος ὁ Ἰησοῦς: if the
mention of their northern home had reminded the disciples of their early choice
by Christ and of all that He had been to
them, the personal name Jesus would
assure them that their master would still
be a human Friend and divine Saviour;
*Hic Jesus: qui vobis fuit eritque semper
Jesus, id est, Salvator* (Corn. à Lap.).
—πορευόμενον: on the frequency of the
verb in St. Luke as compared with other
N.T. writers, often used to give effect
and vividness to the scene, both Friedrich and Zeller remark; St. Peter uses
the same word of our Lord's Ascension,
1 Peter iii. 22. As at the Birth of Christ,
so too at His Ascension the angels' message was received obediently and joyfully,
for only thus can we explain Luke xxiv. 52.
Ver. 12. τότε: frequent in Acts and
in St. Luke's Gospel, but most frequent
in St. Matthew; on its use see Grimm-
Thayer, and Blass, *Gramm. des N. G.*,
p. 270.—ὑπέστρεψαν: a word characteristic of Luke both in his Gospel and
in Acts, occurring in the former over
twenty times, in the latter ten or eleven
times. Only in three places elsewhere,
not at all in the Gospels, but see Mark
xiv. 40 (Moulton and Geden, *sub v.*);
Friedrich, *ubi supra*, p. 8. On the
Ascension see additional note at end of
chapter.—τοῦ καλ. Ἐλαιῶνος: *ubi captus
et vinctus fuerat.* Wetstein. Although

ἀπὸ ὄρους τοῦ καλουμένου Ἐλαιῶνος, ὅ ἐστιν ἐγγὺς Ἰερουσαλήμ, σαββάτου ἔχον ὁδόν.

13. Καὶ ὅτε εἰσῆλθον, ἀνέβησαν εἰς τὸ ὑπερῷον οὗ ἦσαν καταμέ-νοντες, ὅ τε Πέτρος καὶ Ἰάκωβος καὶ Ἰωάννης [1] καὶ Ἀνδρέας, Φίλιππος

[1] Ιακωβος και Ιωαννης, so E, Syr. Harcl., Arm. Zoh., Chrys., Theodrt. ; but in inverse order in ℵABCD 61, Vulg. and good versions, so Tisch., W.H., R.V., Wendt, Weiss.

St. Matthew and St. Mark both speak of the Mount of Olives they do not say τοῦ καλ. (neither is the formula found in John viii. 1). It is therefore probable that St. Luke speaks as he does as one who was a stranger to Jerusalem, or, as writing to one who was so. Blass, *ubi supra*, pp. 32, 84, contends that Ἐλαιῶνος ought to give place to ἐλαιῶν, which he also reads in Luke xix. 29, xxi. 37 (W.H. Ἐλαιὼν, and in Luke xix. 37, xxii. 39, τῶν Ἐλαιῶν, in each case as genitive of ἐλαία), the former word being found only here and in Josephus, *Ant.*, vii., 9, 2. But it is found in all the MSS. in this passage, although *falso D. cum cæt.*, says Blass. Blass would thus get rid of the difficulty of regarding Ἐλαιῶν as if used in Luke xix. 29, xxi. 37 as an indeclinable noun, whilst here he would exchange its genitive for ἐλαιῶν. Deissmann, however, is not inclined to set aside the consensus of authoritities for Ἐλαιῶνος, and he regards ἐλαιών in the two passages above as a lax use of the nominative case. As the genitive of ἐλαιῶν it would correspond to the Latin *Olivetum* (so Vulgate), an olive-orchard ; *cf.* ἄμπελος and ἀμπελῶν in N.T., the termination ών in derivative nouns indicating a place set with trees of the kind designated by the primitive. For instances *cf.* Grimm-Thayer, *sub* Ἐλαιῶν, but see on the other hand Deissmann, *Neue Bibelstudien*, p. 36 ff. With regard to the parallel between our verse and Josephus, *Ant.*, vii., 9, 2, it is evident that even if St. Luke had read Josephus he was not dependent upon him, for he says here τοῦ καλ. just as in his Gospel he had written τὸ καλ., probably giving one or more popular names by which the place was known ; Gloël, *Galaterbrief*, p. 65 (see also on the word W.H., ii., Appendix, p. 165 ; Plummer, *St. Luke*, p. 445 ; and Winer-Schmiedel, p. 93).—σαββάτου ἔχον ὁδόν, not ἀπέχον : the distance is represented as something which the mountain has, Meyer-Wendt ; *cf.* Luke xxiv. 13. There is no real discrepancy between this and the statement of St. Luke's Gospel

that our Lord led His disciples ἕως πρὸς Βηθανίαν, xxiv. 50, a village which was more than double a sabbath day's journey, fifteen furlongs from Jerusalem. But if the words in St. Luke, *l. c.*, mean "over against Bethany," ἕως πρός (so Feine, *Eine vorkanonische Uberlieferung des Lucas*, p. 79, and Nösgen, *Apostelgeschichte*, p. 80; see also Rendall, *Acts*, p. 171—Blass omits ἕως and reads only πρός and remarks *neque vero πρός est εἰς*; *cf.* also Belser, *Theologische Quartalschrift*, i., 79 (1895)), the difficulty is surmounted, for St. Luke does not fix the exact spot of the Ascension, and he elsewhere uses the Mount of Olives, Luke xxi. 37, as the equivalent of the Bethany of Matthew (xxi. 17) and Mark (xi. 1). Nor is it likely that our Lord would lead His disciples into a village for the event of His Ascension. It should be remembered that Lightfoot, *Hor. Heb.*, says that "the Ascension was from the place where that tract of the Mount of Olives ceased to be called Bethphage and began to be called Bethany". The recent attempt of Rud. Hoffmann to refer the Ascension to a "Galilee" in the Mount of Olives rests upon a tradition which cannot be regarded as reliable (see *Galilæa auf dem Oelberg*, Leipzig, 1896), although he can quote Resch as in agreement with him, p. 14. On Hoffmann's pamphlet see also *Expositor* (5th series), p. 119 (1897), and *Theologisches Literaturblatt*, No. 27 (1897). This mention of the distance is quite characteristic of St. Luke ; it may also have been introduced here for the benefit of his Gentile readers ; Page, *Acts*, *in loco*, and *cf.* Ramsay's remarks, *Was Christ born at Bethlehem?* pp. 55, 56.

Ver. 13. τὸ ὑπερῷον : "the upper chamber," R.V., as of some well-known place, but there is no positive evidence to identify it with the room of the Last Supper, although here and in Mark xiv. 15, as also in Luke xxii. 12, the Vulgate has *cœnaculum*. Amongst recent writers Hilgenfeld and Feine see in this definite mention of a room well known to the readers a reference to

καὶ Θωμᾶς, Βαρθολομαῖος καὶ Ματθαῖος,[1] Ἰάκωβος Ἀλφαίου [2] καὶ
Σίμων ὁ Ζηλωτής, καὶ Ἰούδας Ἰακώβου. 14. οὗτοι πάντες ἦσαν

[1] **Ματθαιος** AB[3]CE, Boh. **Μαθθαιος** אB*D, Sah.; so Tisch., W.H., Weiss; see
Winer-Schmiedel, pp. 60, 61. For **Ιακ. Αλφαιου** D, Sah. read **Ιακ. ο του Αλφ.**, may
be assimilation to Matt. x. 3 and Mc. iii. 18 (not Lc.); Chase explains by Syriac
idiom; retained by Blass in **β**.

[2] **και τη δεησει** C[3], Chrys. Omitted by אABC*DE 61, and others, Vulg., Sah.,
Boh., Arm., Aeth., Chrys.; so Tisch., W.H., R.V., Wendt, Weiss, Hilgenfeld. **συν
γυναιξιν**, D adds **και τεκνοις**, so Hilgenfeld, but rejected by Blass ("male D"), for
which see criticism of Weiss, Codex D, p. 54; probably occasioned by mention of
the women, cf. xxi. 5. **ουτοι παντες** omit. Aug., Cypr. **Μαρια** אACD, Boh., Chrys.

the author's first book, Luke xxii. 11, 12.
But the word used in St. Mark and in St.
Luke's Gospel is different from that in
the passage before us—ἀνάγαιον, but
here ὑπερῷον. If we identify the former
with the κατάλυμα, Luke xxii. 11, it
would denote rather the guest-chamber
used for meals than the upper room or
loft set apart for retirement or prayer,
although sometimes used for supper or
for assemblies (ὑπερῷον). Both words
are found in classical Greek, but only the
latter in the LXX, where it is frequent.
In the N.T. it is used by St. Luke alone,
and only in Acts. Holtzmann, following Lightfoot and Schöttgen, considers
that an upper room in the Temple is
meant, but this would be scarcely probable under the circumstances, and a
meeting in a private house, ii. 46, iv. 23,
v. 42, is far more likely.—ὅ τε Π.: in a
series of nouns embraced under one category only the first may have the article,
Winer-Schmiedel, pp. 154-157. In comparing this list of the Apostles with that
given by the Synoptists we notice that
whilst St. Peter stands at the head in
the four lists, those three are placed in
the first group who out of the whole
band are prominent in the Acts as also
in the Gospels, viz., Peter, John, and
James; all the Synoptists, however, place
St. James as the elder brother before St.
John. In St. Luke's first list, as in St.
Matthew's list, the brothers Peter and
Andrew stand first, followed by another
pair of brothers James and John; but in
Acts Andrew gives place, as we might
expect, to the three Apostles who had
been admitted to the closest intimacy
with Jesus during His earthly life, and
St. John as St. Peter's constant companion in the Gospel narrative makes a
pair with him. The list in Acts agrees
with that given by St. Luke in his
Gospel in two particulars (see Friedrich,
ubi supra, p. 50, and so too Zeller): (1)
Simon the Zealot is called not ὁ Καναν-

αῖος, as in Matthew and Mark, but ὁ
Ζηλωτής, cf. Luke vi. 15; (2) instead of
Thaddæus (or Lebbæus) we have "Judas
of James," cf. Luke vi. 16.—Ἰούδας
Ἰακώβου, "the son of James," R.V. (so
too above Ἰάκωβος Ἀλφαίου, "James
the son of Alphæus"), placing the words
"or, brother, see Jude i.," in the margin,
so too in Luke vi. 16. The rendering of
the words as Jude the brother of James
was probably caused by Jude i., and it is
difficult to believe, as Nösgen argues (see
also Winer-Schmiedel, p. 262), that in
the same list and in such close proximity these two meanings "the son of"
and "the brother of" should occur for
the genitive, although no doubt it is
possible grammatically; see Nösgen and
Wendt, in loco. On the other hand, see
Felten, note, p. 66. But Winer, to whom
the latter refers, is by no means positive,
and only expresses the opinion that
ἀδελφός is perhaps to be supplied here
and in Luke vi. 16 if the same Apostle is
referred to in Jude i. (Winer-Moulton,
p. 238). But the identification with the
latter is very improbable, as he was most
likely the brother of James, known as
"the Lord's brother" (see Plummer on
Luke, vi., 16, and Salmon, Introduction to
N.T., pp. 473, 474, fifth edit.). It is also
noteworthy that St. Luke uses ἀδελφός
where he means "brother," cf. Luke iii.
1, vi. 14; Acts xii. 2. Blass, Grammatik
des N.G., gives the same reference to
Alciphr., ii., 2, as Winer, Τιμοκράτης ὁ
Μητροδώρου, sc. ἀδελφός, but at the
same time he declines to commit himself
as to the passage in Acts and Luke vi.
The list, it has been thought, is given
here again by St. Luke to show the recovery of the Apostolic band from their
denial and flight—so St. Chrysostom
remarks that Luke did well to mention
the disciples, for since one had betrayed
Christ and another had been unbelieving,
he hereby shows that, except the first, all
were preserved (so to the same effect

προσκαρτεροῦντες ὁμοθυμαδὸν τῇ προσευχῇ καὶ τῇ δεήσει, σὺν γυναιξὶ καὶ Μαρίᾳ [1] τῇ μητρὶ τοῦ Ἰησοῦ, καὶ σὺν τοῖς ἀδελφοῖς αὐτοῦ.

[1] **Μαριαμ** BE (some very good cursives), Sah., Aeth., Chrys.; so Tisch., W.H., Weiss—the latter is said to be put always for the Virgin, but here evidence seems equally divided (see Winer-Schmiedel, pp. 90, 91).

Œcumenius, *in loco*). There may also have been the desire of the author to intimate that although only the works of a few on the list would be chronicled, yet all alike were witnesses to Christ and workers for Him (Lumby).

Ver. 14. **καὶ ἦσαν προσκαρτεροῦντες**: on the construction see ver. 10. In N.T. found only in St. Luke and St. Paul (except once in St. Mark iii. 9); most frequently with the dative of the thing, of continuing steadfast in prayer; *cf.* vi. 4, Rom. xii. 12, Col. iv. 2, and *cf.* also ii. 42 or ii. 46 of continuing all the time *in* (ἐν) a place; in Acts viii. 13, x. 7, it is used with the dative of the person, and in Rom. xiii. 6 with **εἴς τι**. It is found in Josephus with the dative of the thing, *Ant.*, v., 2, 6, and in Polybius, who also uses it with the dative of the person. In LXX it is found in Numbers xiii. 21 and in Susannah ver. 6, Theod., also in Tobit v. 8, S.—**ὁμοθυμαδὸν**, a favourite word of St. Luke: *Lucæ in Actis in deliciis est* (Blass) —used ten or eleven times in Acts, only once elsewhere in N.T., Rom. xv. 6, where it has the same meaning, Vulgate *unanimiter*. In the LXX it is oftener found as the equivalent of Hebrew words meaning simply "together," and Hatch, *Essays in B. G.*, p. 63, would limit it to this meaning in the N.T., but the word cannot be confined to mere outward assembling together; *cf.* Dem., *Phil.*, iv., 147, **ὁμοθυμαδὸν ἐκ μιᾶς γνώμης** (Meyer-Wendt); so Luther *einmüthig*. It was very natural that St. Luke should lay stress upon the absolute unanimity of the early believers, and the word is used with reference to the Twelve, to the hundred-and-twenty, to the whole number of believers; truly the Holy Ghost was "amator concordiæ" (Corn. à Lapide). —**τῇ προσευχῇ καὶ τῇ δεήσει**: the latter noun cannot be supported by MS. authority; the two words mark the difference between general and specific prayer; *cf.* Bengel on 1 Tim. ii. 1, and *cf. Luke*, v., 33. It is very doubtful whether we can confine **προσευχή** here to the Temple prayers; rather the article, *cf.* vi. 4 and ii. 42, seems to point to a definite custom of common prayer as a bond of Christian fellowship (Hort, *Ecclesia*, p. 43, so *Speaker's Commentary, in loco*). As in his Gospel, so here and elsewhere in Acts, St. Luke lays stress upon frequency in prayer, and that too in all parts of the book (Friedrich, pp. 55-60).—**σὺν γυναιξὶ**: it is natural to include the women already mentioned in St. Luke's Gospel, *cf.*, *e.g.*, viii. 2, 3, xxiii. 55, "with the women," R.V., or the expression may be quite indefinite as in margin R.V. In this mention of the presence of women, as in the stress laid upon prayer, there is another point of unity between the book and the third Gospel, "The Gospel of Womanhood" (see also Ramsay, *Was Christ born at Bethlehem?* p. 50). (The mention of women would certainly indicate a private house rather than the Temple.) Erasmus and Calvin both interpret the words *cum uxoribus*, probably not without desire to make a point against celibacy. J. Lightfoot allows that this meaning may be correct, since the Apostles and disciples who had wives took them with them, "but," he adds, "it is too strait ".—**Μαριάμ** (for **Μαρία**), so always according to W.H. of the Blessed Virgin, nominative, vocative, accusative, dative, except twice in a few of the best MSS. (Matt. i. 20, and Luke ii. 19). *Cf.* Appendix, p. 163. See also Simcox, *Language of the N. T.*, p. 28, and Winer-Schmiedel, p. 91, note. The **καί** may be taken either to comprehend her under the other women, or as distinguishing her from them. This is the last mention of her in the N.T., and the Scripture leaves her "in prayer".—**σὺν τοῖς ἀδελφοῖς αὐτοῦ**: they are previously mentioned as unbelieving (John vii. 5, and compare Mark vi. 4), but not only the Resurrection of the Lord but also that of Lazarus may well have overcome their unbelief. St. Chrysostom (so too Œcumenius) conjectures that Joseph was dead, for it is not to be supposed, he says, that when the brethren had become believers Joseph believed not. As the brethren are here distinguished from the Eleven, it would seem that they could not have been included in the latter (see, however, "Brethren," B.D.[2] pp. 13, 14). But whatever meaning we give to the word "brethren" here or in the Gospels, nothing could be more significant than the fact that they had now left their

15. ΚΑΙ ἐν ταῖς ἡμέραις ταύταις ἀναστὰς Πέτρος ἐν μέσῳ τῶν μαθητῶν[1] εἶπεν (ἦν τε ὄχλος ὀνομάτων ἐπὶ τὸ αὐτὸ ὡς ἑκατὸν εἴκοσιν·),

[1] μαθητων; but אABC*, Vulg., Tisch., W.H., R.V., so Weiss, Wendt αδελφων.

settled homes in Galilee to take part in the lot of the disciples of Jesus, and to await with them the promise of the Father (Felten). It may have been that James, "the Lord's brother," was converted by the Resurrection, 1 Cor. xv. 5, and that his example constrained the other "brethren" to follow him.

Ver. 15. καὶ ἐν ταῖς ἡμέραις ταύταις: St. Luke often employs such notes of time, used indefinitely like similar expressions in Hebrew—e.g., 1 Sam. xxviii. 1, both in his Gospel and in Acts. Friedrich, p. 9, Lekebusch, p. 53.—ἀναστὰς: it is very characteristic of St. Luke to add a participle to a finite verb indicating the posture or position of the speaker. This word is found in St. Luke's Gospel seventeen times, and in Acts nineteen times, only twice in Matthew, six or seven times in Mark; cf. also his use of σταθείς, three times in Gospel, six times in Acts, but not at all in the other Evangelists. — Πέτρος: that St. Peter should be the spokesman is only what we should naturally expect from his previous position among the Twelve, but, as St. Chrysostom observes, he does everything with the common consent, nothing imperiously. The best fruits of his repentance are here seen in the fulfilment of his commission to strengthen his brethren. ἐν μέσῳ: another favourite expression of St. Luke both in his Gospel and in the Acts, in the former eight times, in the latter five times (four times in St. Matthew, twice in St. Mark).

Blass compares the Hebrew בְּתוֹךְ, Grammatik des N. G., p. 126, and in loco. —μαθητῶν: Blass retains and contends that ἀδελφ. has arisen from either ver. 14 or ver. 16; but there is strong critical authority for the latter word; cf. vi. 1. In LXX it is used in three senses; a brother and a neighbour, Lev. xix. 17; a member of the same nation, Exod. ii. 14, Deut. xv. 3. In the N.T. it is used in these three senses, and also in the sense of fellow-Christians, who are looked upon as forming one family. The transition is easily seen: (1) member of the same family; (2) of the same community (national), of the same community (spiritual). Kennedy, Sources of N.T. Greek, pp. 95, 96. On its use in religious as-

sociations in Egypt see Deissmann, Bibelstudien, i., 82, 140, 209. — τε: here for the first time solitarium. On the frequent recurrence of this word in Acts in all parts, as compared with other books of the N.T., see Blass, Grammatik des N. G., pp. 257, 258.— ὀνομάτων: R.V., "persons". Lightfoot compares the use of the word in Rev. iii. 4, xi. 13 (so too Wendt), where the word is used to signify any persons without distinction of sex, so that the word may have been used here to include the women also. But he considers that it rather means men as distinct from women, and so, as he says, the Syriac and Arabic understand it here. Its use in the sense of persons reckoned up by name is Hebraistic שֵׁמוֹת LXX, Numb. i. 2, 18, 20; iii. 40, 43; xxii. 53 (Grimm-Thayer, sub v.), but see also for a similar use on the Egyptian papyri, Deissmann, Neue Bibelstudien, p. 24 (1897).—ἐπὶ τὸ αὐτὸ, "gathered together," R.V.; cf. Matt. xxii. 34, Luke xvii. 35, Acts ii. 1, 44, 47 (so W.H., R.V., see in loco, Wendt, Weiss), 1 Cor. xi. 20, xiv. 23. Holtzmann, in loco, describes it as always local, and it is no doubt so used in most of the above passages, as also in LXX Psalm ii. 2 (cf. Acts iv. 26), 2 Sam. ii. 13, 3 Macc. iii. 1, Sus. v. 14, and in classical Greek. But when we remember the stress laid by St. Luke in the opening chapters of the Acts upon the unanimity of the believers, it is not unlikely that he should use the phrase, at all events in ii. 44, 47, with this deeper thought of unity of purpose and devotion underlying the words, even if we cannot render the phrase in each passage in Acts with Rendall (Acts, p. 34), "with one mind," "of one mind".— ὡς ἑκατὸν εἴκοσιν. Both Wendt and Feine reject the view that the number is merely mythical (Baur, Zeller, Overbeck, Weizsäcker), and would rather see in it a definite piece of information which St. Luke had gained. It is quite beside the mark to suppose that St. Luke only used this particular number because it represented the Apostles multiplied by 10, or 40 multiplied by 3. If he had wished to emphasise the number as a number, why introduce the ὡς?

16. Ἄνδρες ἀδελφοί, ἔδει ¹ πληρωθῆναι τὴν γραφὴν ταύτην, ἣν προεῖπε τὸ Πνεῦμα τὸ Ἅγιον διὰ στόματος Δαβίδ, περὶ Ἰούδα τοῦ γενομένου ὁδηγοῦ τοῖς συλλαβοῦσι τὸν Ἰησοῦν · 17. ὅτι κατηριθμημένος ἦν σὺν

¹ εδει ℵABCD²E, Origen, Eus., Ath., W.H., Weiss.　δει D*, Vulg., Boh.; so Gig., Par., Aug. (Iren., Vig.), Hilgenfeld.　Blass, p. xvii., in his Preface to β, argues that as Irenæus omits 17ᵃ-20 and elsewhere seems to be ignorant of the death of Judas, so his text also omitted from κατηρ. εν ημιν to γενηθητω.　In his revised edition Luke added 17ᵃ-20 and also substituted εδει for the original δει : "ut significaretur ex parte jam esse ratum factum vetus vaticinium, exitu nempe Judæ".　But the omission of Irenæus may be accidental, or it has been suggested that he too may have regarded 17ᵃ-20 as a parenthesis and not actually part of Peter's speech. Δαβιδ ; but in ℵBD, so W.H., Weiss Δανειδ.　ACE read ΔΑΔ ; see Winer-Schmiedel, p. 65, Blass, Proleg. (Acta Apost.), p. 34.

Ver. 16. Ἄνδρες ἀδελφοί : a mode of address indicating not only respect but also the solemnity of the occasion and the importance of the subject.　There is nothing unclassical in this use of the vocative without ὦ at the beginning of speeches.　Demosthenes, at least on some occasions, used the phrase Ἄνδρες Ἀθηναῖοι without ὦ.　Simcox, ubi supra, p. 76, note, and see also Winer-Schmiedel, p. 258, note.—ἔδει : very frequent in St. Luke's Gospel and the Acts ; in the former nineteen, in the latter twenty-five times, and in all parts of the book, Friedrich, ubi supra, p. 22 (Lekebusch). It expresses a divine necessity, and is used by all the Evangelists, as by St. Peter here, and by St. Paul (1 Cor. xv. 25), of the events connected with and following upon the Passion.—δεῖ, oportet, expresses logical necessity rather than personal moral obligation ὤφειλεν, debuit, or the sense of fitness, ἔπρεπεν, decebat.　The three words are all found in Heb. ii. 1, 17, 10, on which see West-cott, Hebrews, p. 36, and Plummer's St. Luke, p. 247.　St. Peter's speech falls into two parts, one introduced by ἔδει, and the other introduced by δεῖ, ver. 21. —τὴν γραφὴν : the reference is undoubtedly to the particular passages in the O.T. which follow, cf. Luke iv. 20, Acts viii. 35 ; see Lightfoot on Galatians iii. 22. There is no reference to Psalm xli. 9, or this passage would have been quoted, but to the passages in ver. 20.—πληρωθῆναι, cf. Luke xxiv. 44, 45.　πληρόω (which is very frequently used by St. Luke, Friedrich, ubi supra, p. 40) means more than "fulfil" in the popular acceptation of the word ; it implies "to fill up to the full" ; "Not only is our Lord the subject of direct predictions in the Old Testament, but His claims go to the full extent of affirming that all the truths which are imperfectly, and frequently very darkly shadowed forth in the pages, are realised in Him as the ideal to which they pointed" (Row, Bampton Lectures, pp. 202, 203).—τὸ πνεῦμα τὸ ἅγιον.　St. Luke uses this, or a similar expression, πνεῦμα ἅγιον or τὸ ἅγιον πνεῦμα, about forty times in Acts alone, whilst in St. Luke's Gospel alone it is used about as many times as in the three other Evangelists together (Lekebusch, Apostelgeschichte, p. 65, and Plummer, St. Luke, p. 14).—ὁδηγοῦ τοῖς συλλ. τὸν Ἰησοῦν.　St. Peter simply states a fact, but does not heap scorn or abuse upon Judas (Chrysostom, Hom., iii., cf. Theophylact).　St. Matthew, St. Mark, St. John simply say of Judas ὁ παραδιδούς, "he who delivered Him up," or employ some similar expression ; he is never called "the traitor" (St. Luke vi. 16, ἐγένετο προδότης, "became a traitor," see Plummer, in loco).　This self-restraint is remarkable on the part of men who must have regarded their Master's Death as the most atrocious of murders (see Row, Bampton Lectures, pp. 179, 180, note).　At the same time the word ὁδηγός seems to bring before us the scene in Gethsemane, how Judas went before the multitude, and drew near to Jesus to kiss Him (Luke xxii. 47), and to show us how vividly the memories of the Passion were present to St. Peter ; cf. 1 Peter ii. 21 ff.).

Ver. 17. ὅτι κατηριθμημένος ἦν κ.τ.λ. For the construction see ver. 10. ὅτι introduces the ground upon which the Scripture to be cited, which speaks of the vacancy in the Apostolic office, found its fulfilment in Judas ; "he was numbered," "triste est numerari non manere," Bengel.—καὶ ἔλαχεν τὸν κλῆρον : lit., "and obtained by lot the lot" : κλῆρος, a lot, that which is assigned by lot, the portion or share so assigned ; so amongst the Greeks, and somewhat similarly in English, cf. in LXX Wisdom ii. 9, v. 5, Ecclesiasticus

ἡμῖν, καὶ ἔλαχε τὸν κλῆρον τῆς διακονίας ταύτης. 18. οὗτος μὲν
οὖν ἐκτήσατο χωρίον ἐκ τοῦ[1] μισθοῦ τῆς ἀδικίας, καὶ πρηνὴς γενό-

[1] τοῦ om. ℵABCDE, Tisch., W.H., R.V., Weiss, Wendt, Hilgenfeld. After
ἀδικιας D inserts αυτου; so Syr. Harcl., Sah., Aug., so Blass in β, and Hilgenfeld.
Blass added at first, but see Hilg., note, p. 4, καὶ κατεδησεν αυτου τον τραχηλον.

xxv. 19. The word is used elsewhere in Acts three times, i. 26, viii. 21, xxvi. 18; cf. with the last passage its use by St. Paul elsewhere, Col. i. 12. Here the word no doubt may be used by St. Peter with reference to the actual selection by lot which was about to follow. The same word is used elsewhere by the same Apostle, 1 Peter v. 3, "neither as lording it over *the charge allotted* to you," τῶν κλήρων. Tyndale and Cranmer render the word here "parishes," which really gives a good interpretation of it = the "lots" assigned to the elders as their portions in God's heritage; and so we have by an easy transition *clerici* = clergy, those to whom such "lots" are assigned: Humphry, *Commentary on R. V.*, p. 446, Lightfoot, *Philippians*, p. 246 ff.—ἔλαχεν: here and in 2 Peter i. 1 with an accusative, as in classical Greek, "received his portion" R.V. On the construction of the verb with the genitive, cf. Blass, *Grammatik des N. G.*, pp. 100, 230, and Plummer's *St. Luke*, p. 11; with Luke i. 9, cf. 1 Sam. xiv., 47. In classical Greek it is used as the opposite of χειροτονηθῆναι, *to be elected*, more commonly with the infinitive.—διακονίας: "Apostleship the highest form of ministration is repeatedly designated thus," Hort, *Ecclesia*, p. 204, *e.g.*, ver. 25, xx. 24, xxi. 19, 2 Cor. iv. 1, v. 18, vi. 3, Rom. xi. 13, and see further on the word, chap. vi. below. It would be difficult to find in such a general term, or in any part of the speech, any reference to a hierarchical constitution of the Church (Zeller, Overbeck). Jüngst cannot derive any such view from this verse, although he sees in the description of διακονία as ἀποστολή, ver. 25, the mark of a later period than that of the delivery of the speech (so too Wendt).

Ver. 18. οὗτος μὲν οὖν κ.τ.λ. This verse and the next are regarded in R.V. as a parenthesis (compare also W.H.), μὲν οὖν making the transition from St. Peter's own words to the explanatory statement of St. Luke; see Rendall's Appendix on μὲν οὖν, although he would place ver. 20 also in a parenthesis, *Acts*, p. 160 ff. For this frequent use of μὲν οὖν in Acts, see also Blass, who regards μέν as used here, as in other

places, without any following antithesis expressed by δέ, *Grammatik des N. G.*, pp. 261, 267, see also Hackett's note *in loco*. Spitta, Feine, Weiss, see in these two verses an editorial interpolation.— ἐκτήσατο χωρίον. To harmonise this with Matt. xxvii. 5, an explanation has been often used to this effect, that although Judas did not purchase the field, it was purchased by his money, and that thus he might be called its possessor. This was the explanation adopted by the older commentators, and by many modern. Theophylact, *e.g.*, describes Judas as rightly called the κύριος of the field for the price of it was his. It is no doubt quite possible that St. Peter (if the words are his and not St. Luke's) should thus express himself rhetorically (and some of his other expressions are certainly rhetorical, *e.g.*, ἐλάκησε μέσος), or that Judas should be spoken of as the possessor of the field, just as Joseph of Arimathæa is said to have hewn his own tomb, or Pilate to have scourged Jesus, but possibly Dr. Edersheim's view that the blood-money by a fiction of law was still considered to belong to Judas may help to explain the difficulty, *Jesus the Messiah*, ii., 575. Lightfoot comments, "Not that he himself bought the field, for Matthew resolves the contrary—nor was there any such thing in his intention when he bargained for the money," and then he adds, "But Peter by a bitter irrision showeth the fruit and profit of his wretched covetise:" *Hor. Heb.* (see also Hackett's note). Without fully endorsing this, it is quite possible that St. Peter, or St. Luke, would contrast the portion in the ministry which Judas had received with the little which was the result of the price of his iniquity. —ἐκ τοῦ μισθοῦ τῆς ἀδικίας pro τοῦ ἀδίκου μισθοῦ, a Hebraism, Blass, *in loco*, see also Winer-Schmiedel, p. 268. The phrase only occurs again in 2 Peter ii. 13, 15; on this use of ἐκ see Simcox, *Language of the N. T.*, p. 146. Combinations of words with ἀδικία are characteristic of St. Luke (Friedrich). In the other Evangelists the word is only found once, John vii. 18. — καὶ πρηνὴς γενόμ. Wendt (following Zeller and Overbeck) and others maintain

μενος ἐλάκησε μέσος, καὶ ἐξεχύθη πάντα τὰ σπλάγχνα αὐτοῦ · 19.
καὶ γνωστὸν ἐγένετο πᾶσι τοῖς κατοικοῦσιν Ἱερουσαλήμ, ὥστε
κληθῆναι τὸ χωρίον ἐκεῖνο τῇ ἰδίᾳ διαλέκτῳ αὐτῶν Ἀκελδαμὰ,[1]

---

[1] Ἀκελδαμα, so C, Syr. Harcl., Chrys., Vulg.; Ἀχελδαμαχ ℵA 40, 61, Tisch.;
Ἀκελδαμαχ B, so W.H., Weiss; Ἀκελδαιμαχ D (Blass in β -δεμαχ), so Hilg., and other
variants; in Gig., Par. -emac(h). Final χ (-ακ) seems certain—see comment below.

that St. Luke here follows a different
tradition from St. Matthew, xxvii. 6 ff.,
and that it is only arbitrary to attempt
to reconcile them. But Felten and
Zöckler (so too Lumby and Jacobson)
see in St. Luke's description a later stage
in the terrible end of the traitor. St.
Matthew says καὶ ἀπελθὼν ἀπήγξατο : if
the rope broke, or a branch gave way
under the weight of Judas, St. Luke's
narrative might easily be supplementary
to that of St. Matthew. Blass, in loco,
adopts the former alternative, and holds
that thus the narrative may be harmon-
ised with that of St. Matthew, rupto
fune Iudam in terram procidisse. It is
difficult to see (as against Overbeck) why
πρηνὴς γεν. is inconsistent with this.
The words no doubt mean strictly "falling flat on his face" opposed to ὕπτιος,
not "falling headlong," and so they do
not necessarily imply that Judas fell over
a precipice, but Hackett's view that Judas
may have hung himself from a tree on
the edge of a precipice near the valley of
Hinnom, and that he fell on to the rocky
pavement below is suggested from his
own observation of the locality, p. 36,
Acts of the Apostles (first English edition),
see also Edersheim, ubi supra, pp. 575,
576. At all events there is nothing disconcerting in the supposition that we
may have here "some unknown series
of facts, of which we have but two fragmentary narratives": "Judas," B.D.[2],
and see further Plummer sub v. in Hastings' B.D. ἐλάκησε : here only in the
N.T. λάσκω : a strong expression, signifying bursting asunder with a loud noise,
Hom., Iliad, xiii., 616 ; cf. also Acta
Thomæ, 33 (p. 219, ed. Tdf.): ὁ δράκων
φυσηθεὶς ἐλάκησε καὶ ἀπέθανε καὶ
ἐξεχύθη ὁ ἰὸς αὐτοῦ καὶ ἡ χολή, for the
construction cf. Luke xxiii. 45.
Ver. 19. καὶ γνωστὸν . . . πᾶσιν τοῖς
κατοικοῦσιν Ἱερουσ.: the words have
been taken to support the view that we
have here a parenthesis containing the
notice of St. Luke, but if St. Peter was
speaking rhetorically he might easily express himself so. But many critics, who
refuse to see in the whole of the two
verses any parenthetical remarks of the

historian, adopt the view that τῇ διαλέκτῳ
αὐτῶν and τοῦτ' ἔστιν χωρίον αἵματος
are explanations introduced by St. Luke,
who could trust to his Gentile readers to
distinguish between his words and those
of St. Peter (Wendt, Holtzmann, Zöckler,
Nösgen, Jüngst. Matthias).—τῇ διαλέκτῳ:
only in Acts in the N.T., where it is used
six times in all parts; it may mean dialect or language, but here it is used in
the latter sense (R.V.) to distinguish
Aramaic from Greek (cf. its use in Polybius).—αὐτῶν, i.e., the dwellers of Jerusalem, who spoke Aramaic—unless the
whole expression is used rhetorically, it
would seem that it contains the words,
not of St. Peter, who himself spoke
Aramaic, but of the author (see Blass, in
loco).—Ἀκελδαμά: the Aramaic of the

Field of Blood would be חֲקֵל דְּמָא,

and it is possible that the χ may be added
to represent in some way the guttural א,
just as Σιράχ = סִירָא, cf. Blass, in loco,
and Grammatik des N. G., p. 13. W.H. (so
Blass) read Ἀκελδαμάχ (and Ἀχελδαμάχ,
Tisch. and Treg.); see also on the word
Winer-Schmiedel, pp. 60 and 63. A
new derivation has been proposed by
Klostermann, Probleme in Aposteltexte,
p. 6 ff., which has gained considerable
attention (cf. Holtzmann, Wendt, Felten,

Zöckler, in loco), viz.: דְּמַק = κοιμᾶσθαι,

so that the word = κοιμητήριον, cf. Matt.
xxvii. 8. This is the derivation preferred
by Wendt, and it is very tempting, but
see also Enc. Bibl., I., 32, 1899, sub v.
It is true that the two accounts in St.
Matthew and St. Luke give two reasons
for the name Field of Blood. But why
should there not be two reasons ? if the
traitor in the agony of his remorse rushed
from the Temple into the valley of Hinnom, and across the valley to "the potter's field" of Jeremiah, the old name of
the potter's field might easily become
changed in the popular language into
that of "field of blood," whilst the reason given by St. Matthew for the name
might still hold good, since the blood-
money, which by a fiction of law was

τουτέστι χωρίον αἵματος. 20. γέγραπται γὰρ ἐν βίβλῳ Ψαλμῶν,
" Γενηθήτω ἡ ἔπαυλις αὐτοῦ ἔρημος, καὶ μὴ ἔστω ὁ κατοικῶν ἐν
αὐτῇ·" καί, " Τὴν ἐπισκοπὴν αὐτοῦ λάβοι ἕτερος." 21. Δεῖ οὖν
τῶν συνελθόντων ἡμῖν ἀνδρῶν ἐν παντὶ χρόνῳ ἐν ᾧ εἰσῆλθε καὶ

still considered to belong to Judas, was employed for the purchase of the accursed spot as a burial ground for strangers. See Edersheim, *Jesus the Messiah*, ii., 574, 575. Whatever may be alleged as to the growth of popular fancy and tradition in the later account in Acts of the death of Judas, it cannot be said to contrast unfavourably with the details given by Papias, *Fragment*, 18, which Blass describes as "insulsissima et foedissima".

Ver. 20. The quotation is twofold, the first part from Psalm lxix. 26 (LXX, lxviii.); in the LXX we have αὐτῶν, changed here into αὐτοῦ with reference to Judas, whilst ἐν τοῖς σκηνώμασιν is omitted and the words ἐν αὐτῇ, referring to ἔπαυλις, are added. The omission would make the application of the words more general than in the original, which related to the desolation of the encampment and tents of a nomadic tribe. The other part of the quotation is *verbatim* from Psalm cviii. 8 (cix.), called by the ancients the Iscariot Psalm. With the exception of Psalm xxii., no Psalm is more frequently quoted in the N.T. than lxix. ; *cf.* ver. 9 with John ii. 17 ; ver. 21 with Matt. xxvii. 34, and with John xix. 28; ver. 22 and 23 with Rom. xi. 9, 10 ; and ver. 9 with Rom. xv. 3. In these Psalms, as in the twenty-second Psalm, we see how the history of prophets and holy men of old, of a David or a Jeremiah, was typical of the history of the Son of man made perfect through suffering, and we know how our Lord Himself saw the fulfilment of the words of the suffering Psalmist (xli. 9) in the tragic events of His own life (John xiii. 18). So too St. Peter in the recent miserable end of the traitor sees another evidence, not only of the general truth, which the Psalmists learnt through suffering, that God rewarded His servants and that confusion awaited the unrighteous, but also another fulfilment in the case of Judas of the doom which the Psalmists of old had invoked upon the persecutors of the faithful servants of God. But we are not called upon to regard Psalm cix. as the Iscariot Psalm in all its details (see Perowne, *Psalms*, p. 538 (smaller edition)), or to forget, as Delitzsch reminds us, that the spirit of Elias is not that of the N.T.

St. Peter, although he must have regarded the crime of Judas as a crime without a parallel, does not dwell upon his punishment, but passes at once to the duty incumbent upon the infant Church in view of the vacant Apostleship.— ἔπαυλις: by many commentators, both ancient and modern (Chrys., Oecum., so too Nösgen, Overbeck, Wendt, Blass, Holtzmann, Zöckler, Jüngst), this is referred to the χωρίον, which was rendered desolate by the death of Judas in it, on the ground that γάρ thus maintains its evident relation to what precedes. But if the two preceding verses are inserted by St. Luke, and form no part of St. Peter's words, it would seem that ἔπαυλις must be regarded as parallel to ἐπισκοπή in the second quotation.—ἐπισκοπήν: "his office," R.V. ("overseership," margin), so for the same word in LXX, Ps. cix. 8, from which the quotation is made. In the LXX the word is used, Num. iv. 16, for the charge of the tabernacle. St. Peter uses the word ἐπίσκοπος in 1 Peter ii. 25, and it is significant that there the translators of 1611 maintain the use of the word "bishop," as here "bishoprick" (so R.V., "overseer," margin), whilst they use "overseer" and "oversight" (ἐπισκοπή), Acts xx. 28 and 1 Peter v. 2, where the reference is to the function of the elders or presbyters. The word ἐπισκοπή, of course, could not have its later ecclesiastical force, but the Apostolic office of Judas might well be described as one of oversight, and care of others; and it is significant that it is so described, and not only as a διακονία (see below on ver. 25, and on ἐπίσκοπος, xx. 28, note): "St. Peter would not have quoted the Psalm containing the expression ἐπισκοπή unless he had instinctively felt the word to be applicable to Judas' position" (Canon Gore in *Guardian*, 16th March, 1898).

Ver. 21. δεῖ οὖν, see ver. 16. As the one prophecy had thus already been fulfilled, so for the fulfilment of the other it was imperative upon the Church to elect a successor to Judas.—εἰσῆλθε καὶ ἐξῆλθεν: a Hebraistic formula expressing the whole course of a man's daily life ; ix. 28 ; *cf.* LXX Deut. xxviii. 6, 1 Sam. xxix. 6, Psalm cxx. 8, and for other instances, Wetstein, *in loco*. There is no occasion

ἐξῆλθεν ἐφ᾽ ἡμᾶς ὁ κύριος Ἰησοῦς, 22. ἀρξάμενος ἀπὸ τοῦ βαπτίσματος Ἰωάννου ἕως¹ τῆς ἡμέρας ἧς ἀνελήφθη ἀφ᾽ ἡμῶν, μάρτυρα τῆς
ἀναστάσεως αὐτοῦ γενέσθαι σὺν ἡμῖν ἕνα τούτων.   23. Καὶ ἔστησαν
δύο, Ἰωσὴφ τὸν καλούμενον Βαρσαββᾶν,² ὃς ἐπεκλήθη Ἰοῦστος, καὶ

¹ εως BCDE, so W.H., Wendt doubtful, Weiss ; αχρι ℵA 61—both εως and αχρι,
as Wendt points out, are frequent in Luke.

² Βαρσαβαν C, Vulg. clem., Syrr. ; Βαρσαββαν, so ℵABE, Tisch., W.H., R.V.,
Weiss, Wendt ; Βαρναβαν D, Gig., Par. tol., Aeth.—but Blass reads = W.H. in
his β text—Wendt thinks that D may have been a confusion with iv. 36—see also
Winer-Schmiedel, p. 56, on the spelling.

to render ἐφ᾽ ἡμᾶς, " over us," R.V., margin, for in full the phrase would run :
εἰσῆλθεν ἐφ᾽ ἡμᾶς καὶ ἐξῆλθεν ἀφ᾽ ἡμῶν.
The formula shows that St. Peter did not
shrink from dwelling upon the perfect
humanity of the Ascended Christ, whilst
in the same sentence he speaks of Him
as ὁ Κύριος.

Ver. 22. ἀρξάμενος, cf. note on verse
1. The word need not be restricted to
our Lord's own baptism, but would include the time of the baptism preached
by John, as his baptism and preaching
were the announcement of, and a preparation for, the Christ. If St. Mark's
Gospel, as there is every reason to believe,
was closely connected with St. Peter, its
opening verses give us a similar date for
the commencement of the Apostolic testimony ; cf. Schmid, Biblische Theologie
des N. T., p. 436.—ἕως τῆς ἡμέρας ἧς :
according to Wendt and Weiss, the
relative is not attracted for ῇ, but is to
be regarded as a genitive of time, but cf.
Lev. xxiii. 15, Haggai ii. 18, Bar. i. 15 ;
Winer-Schmiedel, p. 226; Blass, ubi supra,
p. 170.—μάρτυρα τῆς ἀναστάσεως. It
has been noted as remarkable that St.
Peter here lays down experience of matters of fact, not eminence in any subjective grace or quality, as one of the conditions of Apostleship, but it is evident
that from the first the testimony of the
Apostles was not merely to the facts, but
to their spiritual bearing, cf. chap. v. 32 :
"On the one side there is the historical witness to the facts, on the other, the internal
testimony of personal experience " (Westcott's St. John, xv., 27), and the appeal to
Him "Who knew the hearts," showed
that something more was needed than
intellectual competency. Spitta and
Jüngst (so Weiss) regard the whole clause
ἐν παντὶ χρόνῳ . . . ἀφ᾽ ἡμῶν as introduced by a reviser, but on the other hand
Hilgenfeld considers the words to be in
their right place. He also rebukes Weiss
for maintaining that the whole passage,

vv. 15-26, could not have been composed
by the author of the book, who gives no
intimation of the number of the Apostles,
with whom the Twelve as such play no
part, and who finds his hero outside their
number. But Hilgenfeld points out that
the Twelve have for his "author to
Theophilus" a very important place ;
cf. ii. 14, 22, iv. 33, v. 12, 40, viii. 1,
14, ix. 27.

Ver. 23. ἔστησαν, not ἔστησεν : the
latter reading, "nimium Petro dat, nihil
concilio relinquit" (Blass). "They put
forward," R.V., not "appointed," A.V.,
for the appointment had not yet been
made.—Ἰωσὴφ τὸν καλ. Βαρσαββᾶν,
"Joseph called Barsabbas". We cannot identify him with Joseph Barnabas (iv. 36), or with Judas Barsabbas
(xv. 22). Barsabbas may have been a
patronymic "son of Sabba," but cf. Enc.
Bibl., I., 487, 1899. It is only a conjecture
that he was the brother of Judas Barsabbas just mentioned. The name Justus is
probably a Roman surname, as Ἰοῦστος
indicates, adopted after the custom of the
time, just as the second Evangelist took
the Roman name Marcus in addition to
the Hebrew John. Nothing more is said
of him in the N.T. Eusebius ranks him
with Matthias as one of the Seventy,
H.E., i., 12, and Papias is said to have
related concerning him that he drank
deadly poison but escaped all harm,
Euseb., H.E., iii., 39. On the connection
of this tradition with Aristion see Nestle,
Einführung in das G. N. T., p. 240, and
Zahn, Einleitung, ii., p. 231. If the
reading of Blass in β, supported by the
Latin, τὸν καὶ Ἰοῦστον (qui et Justus)
may claim acceptance, it affords, as Belser
notes, an interesting parallel with the
Σαῦλος ὁ καὶ Παῦλος of xiii. 8. On the
spelling of the word, see W.H. Appendix
p. 166, and also Winer-Schmiedel, pp. 56,
57.—Ματθίαν. Nothing more is known
of him with certainty than that he must
have fulfilled the qualifications required

Ματθίαν.[1]   24. καὶ προσευξάμενοι εἶπον, Σὺ Κύριε, καρδιογνῶστα πάντων, ἀνάδειξον ἐκ τούτων τῶν δύο ἕνα ὃν ἐξελέξω, 25. λαβεῖν τὸν

[1] Ματθιαν; but Μαθ. in B*D, Sah., so T., W.H., Hilg. (see Winer-Schmiedel, p. 60; W.H., App., pp. 162, 166).

by St. Peter. Both Eusebius and Epiphanius rank him in the Seventy, and he is said to have suffered martyrdom in Ethiopia. An apocryphal Gospel was ascribed to him, Euseb., *H.E.*, iii., 25, and from Clem. Alex., *Strom.*, iv., 6, 35, we find that the words of Zacchæus, Luke xix. 8, were supposed to be his; so too Hilgenfeld, *Actus Apost.*, p. 202, 1899.

Ver. 24. Κύριε καρδιογνῶστα . . . ὃν ἐξελέξω. The words may well have been addressed to Christ: St. Peter had just spoken of Him as the Lord, his own experience and that of his fellow-disciples must have taught him that Jesus was One Who knew the hearts of all men (John ii. 25, xxi. 17), and he had heard his Master's claim to have chosen the Apostles (*cf.* Luke vi. 13, and v. 2 above, where the same verb is used). On the other hand Wendt regards as decisive against this view that St. Peter himself in xv. 7 says ἐξελέξατο ὁ θεός and then in ver. 8 calls God καρδιογνώστης (*cf.* Jeremiah xvii. 10, where Jehovah is said to search the heart). But the passage in Acts xv. is much too general in its reference to consider it decisive against any special prerogative ascribed to Jesus here (*viz.*, the choice of His own Apostles), and the references to 2 Cor. i. 1, Ephes. ii. 1, where St. Paul refers his Apostleship to God, may be fairly met by Acts ix. 17 and xxvi. 16. It is quite true that in iv. 29 Κύριε is used in prayer plainly addressed to the Lord Jehovah, but it is equally certain that prayer was directed to Christ in the earliest days of the Church (Zahn, *Skizzen aus dem Leben der alten Kirche*, pp. 1-38 and notes), see also below on ii. 21 (and *cf.* 1 Thess. iii. 11, 12, and 2 Thess. ii. 16; Archbishop of Armagh in *Speaker's Commentary*, iii., 690). — ἀνάδειξον: in Luke x. 1 the only other passage in the N.T. where the word is used, it is applied to our Lord's appointment of the Seventy, and is rendered "appointed," A. and R.V. But here R.V. renders "show" as A.V. (Rendall, "appoint"). The verb however may be used in the sense of showing forth or clearly, and hence to proclaim, especially a person's appointment to an office (*cf.* the noun ἀνάδειξις also used by St. Luke only in his Gospel, i. 80); *cf.* for the former meaning, 2 Macc. ii. 8, *cf.*

v. 6, and for the latter, 2 Macc. ix. 14, 23, 35; x. 11; xiv. 12, 26; 1 Esdras i. 35, viii. 23; so too the use of the word in Polybius and Plutarch (see Grimm-Thayer, *sub v.*, and Weiss, *in loco*).

Ver. 25. τὸν κλῆρον: R.V. τόπον marking the antithesis between the place in the Apostleship and "his own place" to which Judas had gone, Vulg. *locum.* —τῆς διακονίας ταύτης καὶ ἀποστολῆς: as above we have not only the word διακονία used but also ἐπισκοπή, v. 17 and 20, so here too we have not only διακονία but also ἀποστολή, although no doubt there is a sense in which we may truly say with Dr. Hort (*Ecclesia*, p. 204) that Apostleship is the highest form of ministration. On the word ἀπόστολος see xiii. 2, 3; the term was undoubtedly used in N.T. to include others besides the Twelve, although there is no reason to suppose that the qualification of having "seen the Lord" was in any case invalidated (*cf.* Gwatkin, "Apostle," Hastings' B.D., p. 126). The whole narrative before us which relates the solemn appeal of the Church to her Ascended Lord, and the choice determined upon in immediate sequence to that appeal, is clearly at variance with any conception of Apostleship as other than a divine commission received directly from Christ Himself (Moberly, *Ministerial Priesthood*, p. 130).—παρέβη, "fell away," R.V. *cf.* LXX Exod. xxxii. 8, ἐκ τῆς ὁδοῦ, so Deut. ix. 12, xvii. 20, ἀπὸ τῶν ἐντολῶν

(*cf.* xxviii. 14, A.), so the Heb. סוּר

followed by מִן. A.V. following Tyndall renders "by transgression fell," which lays too much stress upon "fell," which is not the prominent notion of the Greek verb, elsewhere "transgressed" (Humphry on *Revised Version*, p. 188). —εἰς τὸν τόπον τὸν ἴδιον: on τόπος in the sense of social position, dignity, see *Ecclesiasticus*, xii., 12, and also Deissmann, *Neue Bibelstudien*, p. 95, of succeeding to the vacant place caused by death in a religious community. Here the phrase is usually explained as the place of punishment, Gehenna, *cf. Baal-Turim* on Numb. xxiv. 25 (and Gen. xxxi. 55) "Balaam ivit in locum suum," *i.e.*, Gehenna, Lightfoot, *Hor. Heb.*, while

κλῆρον [1] τῆς διακονίας ταύτης καὶ ἀποστολῆς, ἐξ [2] ἧς παρέβη Ἰούδας,
πορευθῆναι εἰς τὸν τόπον τὸν ἴδιον.   26. καὶ ἔδωκαν κλήρους αὐτῶν, [3]

[1] κλῆρον ℵC³E, Syrr., Arm., Eus., Bas., Chrys. τοπον ABC*D, Vulg., Sah.,
Boh.; so Tisch., W.H., R.V., Weiss, Wendt, Hilg. (κλῆρον probably gloss ver. 17).

[2] εξ; but αφ' in ℵABCD 61, Bas., Aug., so Tisch., W.H., R.V., Weiss, Wendt,
Hilg.

[3] αυτων D*E, Syr. Harcl., Arm.; so Blass in β with Gig. and Par.¹, so Hilg. αυτοις
ℵABCD², Vulg., and good versions; so Tisch., W.H., R.V., Weiss, Wendt (probably the dative was misunderstood, see comment.).

on the other hand Schöttgen sees no
need to explain the expression in this
way. In each of the passages in the
O.T. the word ἴδιος does not occur in
the LXX, although in the still more fanciful comment of the Rabbis on Job ii. 11,
we have ἐκ τῆς ἰδίας χώρας. That the
phrase ἴδιος τόπος may be used in a
good or bad sense is plain from Ignat.,
Magn., v., in a passage which is naturally
referred to the verse before us, where a
man's "own place" denotes the place
of reward, or that of punishment, *cf.*, *e.g.*,
εἰς τὸν ὀφειλόμενον τόπον, Polycarp,
Phil., ix., where the words refer to the
martyrs who were with the Lord, and
εἰς τὸν ὀφειλ. τόπον τῆς δόξης said of
St. Peter, Clem. Rom., *Cor.* v. Nösgen
argues, *Apostelgeschichte*, pp. 88, 89, that
we are not justified in concluding from
a few Rabbinical passages which contain
such fanciful interpretations of simple
words (*cf.* the comment on Job ii. 11,
quoted by Wetstein) that St. Peter must
have meant "Gehenna". In his wilful
fall from the place chosen for him by God,
Judas had chosen in self-will ἴδιος τόπος,
and this wilful and deliberate choice St.
Peter would emphasise in contrast to the
τόπος ἀποστολῆς about to be bestowed,
ver. 25 (see also Rendall, *Acts*, p. 174).
But however this may be, the words
may well indicate a reserve on the part
of St. Peter in speaking of the fate and
destiny of Judas, characteristic of his
reference to him *cf.* note on ver. 16.
None of the other explanations offered
can be deemed satisfactory, as, *e.g.*, that
the word πορευθῆναι κ.τ.λ. refers to the
successor of Judas; that Matthias should
undertake the Apostolic circuit assigned
to Judas (so Oecumenius, and amongst
English commentators, Hammond); or,
that the words refer to the house or
home of Judas, or to his association with
the Pharisees, or to his suicide and dishonoured burial, or to the χωρίον mentioned above. Spitta, amongst recent
commentators, stands almost alone in
referring the words back to ver. 16, and

holds that they refer to the position of
Judas as the guide to those who took
Jesus. The sense of the passage is expressed in the reading of A δίκαιον
instead of ἴδιον.
Ver. 26. καὶ ἔδωκαν κλήρους αὐτῶν,
"they gave forth their lots," A.V. But
R.V. reads αὐτοῖς, "they gave lots for
them". R.V. margin, "unto them". It
is difficult to decide whether the expression means that they gave lots unto
the candidates themselves or whether
they cast lots for them—*i.e.*, on their
behalf, or to see which of the two would
be selected. How the lot was decided
we cannot positively say. According
to Hamburger (*Real-Encyclopädie des
Judentums*, i., 5, p. 723) the Bible does
not tell us, as the expressions used point
sometimes to a casting, sometimes to a
drawing out, of the lots; *cf.* Proverbs
xvi. 33: "Quo modo et ratione uti sunt
Apostoli incertum est. Certum est Deum
per eam declarasse Mathiam tum diri-
gendo sortem ut caderet in Mathiam
juxta illud Prov. xvi. 33" (Corn. à
Lapide). For the expression *cf.* Lev.
xvi. 8. *Hebraismus* (Wetstein), so
Blass. καὶ ἔπεσεν, *i.e.*, through shaking the vessel, Jonah i. 7; *cf.* Livy,
xxiii., 3; so in Homer and Sophocles
πάλλειν, *cf.* Josephus, *Ant.*, vi., 5.—
συγκατεψηφίσθη: only here in N.T.
"he was numbered with the eleven
Apostles," *i.e.*, as the twelfth. The verb
is used in the middle voice for condemning with others, Plut., *Them.*, 21, but
as it occurs nowhere else we have no
parallels to its use here. Grimm explains it "deponendo (κατά) in urnam
calculo, *i.e.*, suffragando assigno (alicui)
locum inter (σύν)". But here it is used
rather as an equivalent of συγκαταριθ-
μεῖσθαι; *cf.* ver. 17 (and also xix. 19),
(Blass and Wendt, *in loco*) = ἐναρίθμιος,
συμψηφισθείς, καταριθμηθείς, Hesychius. Wendt as against Meyer maintains
that it is not proved that recourse was
never again had to lots, because no other
instance of such an appeal is recorded in

καὶ ἔπεσεν ὁ κλῆρος ἐπὶ Ματθίαν, καὶ συγκατεψηφίσθη [1] μετὰ τῶν ἔνδεκα ἀποστόλων.

[1] συγκατεψηφισθη; but συν—ABCE 61, so W.H., Weiss; ℵ* has κατεψηφ. (cf. Const. Apost., vi., 12, 1); D has συ(νε)ψηφ.; probably variants caused by the unusual word. των ενδεκα, D reads ιβ′ = δωδεκα, δωδεκατος Aug., so Blass in β (see p. xx., Pref.); both readings are probably due to taking μετα των ενδεκα in an inclusive sense.

Acts. But it is most significant that this one instance should be recorded between the departure of the Lord and the out-pouring of the Spirit on the Day of Pentecost, and that after Pentecost no further reference is made to such a mode of decision. Cf., e.g., x. 19, xvi. 6. With regard to the historical character of the election of Matthias, Wendt sees no ground to doubt it in the main, although he is not prepared to vouch for all the details, but he finds no reason to place such an event at a later date of the Church's history, as Zeller proposed. To question the validity of the appointment is quite unreasonable, as not only is it presupposed in ii. 14, vi. 2, but even the way in which both St. Paul (1 Cor. xv. 5) and the Apocalypse (xxi. 14) employ the number twelve in a technical sense of the Twelve Apostles, makes the after choice of Matthias as here described very probable (so Overbeck, in loco). No mention is made of the laying on of hands, but "non dicuntur manus novo Apostolo impositæ; erat enim prorsus immediate constitutus," Bengel. See also on ver. 25, and xiii. 3.

Ascension of our Lord.—Friedrich in his Das Lucasevangelium, p. 47 ff., discusses not only similarity of words and phrases, but similarity of contents in St. Luke's writings. With reference to the latter, he examines the two accounts of the Ascension as given in St. Luke's Gospel and in the Acts. There are, he notes, four points of difference (the same four in fact as are mentioned by Zeller, Acts of the Apostles, i., 166, E. T.): (1) Bethany as the place of the Ascension, Luke xxiv. 30; Acts i. 12, the Mount of Olives; (2) the time of the Ascension; according to Acts the event falls on the fortieth day after the Resurrection, i. 3; according to the Gospel on the Resurrection day itself; (3) the words of Jesus before the Ascension are not quite the same in the two narratives; (4) in the Gospel the words appear to be spoken in Jerusalem, in the Acts at the place of the Ascension. Friedrich points out what Zeller fully admitted, that (1) has no importance, for Bethany lay on the Mount of Olives, and the neighbourhood of Bethany might be described quite correctly as ὄρος ἐλαιῶνος; (3) is not of any great importance (as Zeller also admitted), since Luke xxiv. 47-49 and Acts i. 4-8 agree in the main. With regard to (4), Friedrich is again in agreement with Zeller in holding that the difficulty might easily be solved by supposing some slight inaccuracy, or that the words in question were uttered on the way from Jerusalem to the Mount of Olives; but he agrees also with Zeller in maintaining that the time of the Ascension as given in Luke's Gospel and in Acts constitutes the only definite contradiction between the two writings. But even this difficulty presents itself to Friedrich as by no means insuperable, since the author has not attempted to avoid apparent contradictions in other places in the Acts, and therefore he need not have felt himself called upon to do so in the passage before us, where the book seems at variance with his Gospel (see pp. 48, 49).

But Friedrich proceeds to emphasise the many points in which the history of the Ascension in Acts reminds us of the close of the Gospel (see also Zeller, u. s., ii., pp. 226, 227, E.T., and also Feine). Only St. Luke knows of the command of Jesus, that the Apostles should not leave Jerusalem, and of the promise of the Holy Spirit associated with it, Luke xxiv. 49, and Acts i. 4-8. So also Luke xxiv. 47 reminds us unmistakably of Acts i. 8; also Luke xxiv. 52 and Acts i. 12, Luke xxiv. 53 and Acts i. 14 (ii. 14) (cf. also Acts i. 5 and Luke iii. 16). But there is no need to adopt Friedrich's defence of the supposed contradiction with regard to the time of the Ascension. Certainly in the Gospel of St. Luke nothing is said of any interval between the Resurrection and the Ascension, but it is incredible that "the author can mean that late at night, vv. 29, 33, Jesus led the disciples out to Bethany and ascended in the dark!" Plummer, St. Luke, p. 569, see also Felten, Apostelgeschichte, p. 59, and Blass, Acta Apostolorum, p. 44. It is of course possible that St. Luke may have gained his information as to the interval of the forty days between the writing of his two works, but

II. 1. ΚΑΙ ἐν τῷ συμπληροῦσθαι [1] τὴν ἡμέραν τῆς Πεντηκοστῆς, ἦσαν ἅπαντες [2] ὁμοθυμαδὸν ἐπὶ τὸ αὐτό.   2. καὶ [3] ἐγένετο ἄφνω ἐκ τοῦ

[1] συμπληρουσθαι ℵB³; συνπλ. AB*CDE, so Tisch., W.H., Weiss.

[2] απαντες cursives; παντες ℵcABC 61, so Tisch., W.H., R.V. (omit in ℵE). ομοθυμαδον C³E, Chrys.; ομου ℵABC* 61, e, Vulg., Ath., so Tisch., W.H., R.V., Weiss, Wendt; ομοθ. very common in Acts, ομου only elsewhere in John (3 times). D instead of και εν τω συμπλ. reads και εγενετο εν ταις ημεραις εκειναις του συμπλ., very likely as Blass says in notes on β text, "ut in principio lectionis". d, e, Gig., Par., Vulg., Aug. read τας ημερας (e.g., Par., "et dum complerentur dies"—εν τω συμπληρουσθαι την ημεραν is now read by Blass in β, see comment.). (See Page, *Classical Review*, July, 1897, p. 319, and *cf.* also Weiss, Codex D, p. 55, note.) D also reads before επι το αυτο the words οντων αυτων παντων. Hilg. follows D.

[3] After και D inserts ιδου (*cf.* Syriac characteristic, Chase).

however this may be (*cf.* Plummer, but against this view Zöckler, *Apostelgeschichte*, p. 173), it becomes very improbable that even if a tradition existed that the Ascension took place on the evening of the Resurrection, and that Luke afterwards in Acts followed a new and more trustworthy account (so Wendt), that the Evangelist, the disciple of St. Paul, who must have been acquainted with the continuous series of the appearances of the Risen Christ in 1 Cor. xv., should have favoured such a tradition for a moment (see Zöckler, *u. s.*). On the undue stress laid by Harnack upon the famous passage in Barnabas, *Epist.*, xv., see Dr. Swete, *The Apostle's Creed*, p. 68, Plummer, *u. s.*, p. 564, and on this point and also the later tradition of a lengthy interval, Zöckler, *u. s.* For the early testimony to the fact of the Ascension in the Apostolic writings, and for the impossibility of accounting for the belief in the fact either from O.T. precedents or from pagan myths, see Zahn, *Das Apostolische Symbolum*, pp. 76-78, and *Witness of the Epistles* (Longmans), p. 400 ff. The view of Steinneyer that St. Luke gives us a full account of the Ascension in the Acts rather than in his Gospel, because he felt that the true position of such an event was to emphasise it more as the beginning of a new period than as a conclusion of the Gospel history, *Die Auferstehungsgeschichte des Herrn*, pp. 226, 227, deserves attention, and may be fitly compared with W.H., *Notes on Select Readings*, p. 73.

CHAPTER II.—Ver. 1. ἐν τῷ συμπληροῦσθαι, lit., "when the day of Pentecost was being fulfilled" (filled up). R.V. renders "was now come," and a question arises as to whether the words mean this, or that the day was only being filled up, and not fully come. Blass interprets the expression to mean

a short time before the day of Pentecost, not the day itself. Weiss and others suppose that the expression refers to the completing of the interval of time between the Paschal Feast and Pentecost. Vulgate (*cf.* Syriac) reads "cum complerentur dies Pentecostes," and so all English versions have "days" except A. and R.V. The verb is only used by St. Luke in the N.T., twice in his Gospel, viii. 23, and in the same sense as here, ix. 51, and once more in the passage before us. We have the noun συμπλήρωσις in the same sense in LXX 2 Chron. xxxvi. 21, Dan. (Theod.) ix. 2, 1 Esdras i. 58; see Friedrich, *ubi supra*, p. 44. The mode of expression is Hebraistic, as we see also from Exod. vii. 25, Jeremiah xxxvi. 10 (LXX). St. Luke may be using the expression of a day which had begun, according to Jewish reckoning, at the previous sunset, and which thus in the early morning could not be said to be either fulfilled or past, but which was in the process of being fulfilled (Hilgenfeld, *Zeitschrift für wissenschaft. Theol.*, p. 90, 1895; Knabenbauer, *in loco*). The parallel passage in Luke ix. 51 cannot be quoted to support the view that the reference here is to a period *preceding* the day of Pentecost, since in that passage we have ἡμέρας, not ἡμέραν as here, and, although the interpretation of the word as referring to the approach of the Feast is possible, yet the circumstances and the view evidently taken by the narrator point decisively to the very day of the Feast (see Schmid, *Biblische Theol.*, p. 283). On the construction ἐν τῷ with the infinitive, see Blass, *Grammatik des N. G.*, pp. 232, 234, and Dalman, *Die Worte Jesu*, p. 27. It is quite in the style of St. Luke, who frequently employs it; *cf.* the Hebrew use of בְ, Fried-

οὐρανοῦ ἦχος ὥσπερ φερομένης πνοῆς βιαίας, καὶ ἐπλήρωσεν ὅλον
τὸν οἶκον οὗ ἦσαν καθήμενοι · [1] 3. καὶ ὤφθησαν αὐτοῖς διαμεριζόμεναι

[1] καθήμενοι; CD read καθεζομενοι, so Lach., Meyer, Hilg.; but reading in text
ℵABE, minusc., Ath., Cyr.-Jer., Cyr.-Al., Theodrt., Wendt (as against Meyer),
W.H., Weiss.

rich, p. 13, *ubi supra*, Lekebusch, *Apos-telgeschichte*, p. 75). On Spitta's forced interpretation of the word, see p. 100. —τῆς Πεντηκοστῆς: no occasion to add ἡμέρα, as the word was used as a proper name (although as an adjective ἡμέρα would of course be understood with it); *cf.* 2 Macc. xii. 32 (Tob. ii. 1), μετὰ δὲ τὴν λεγομ. Πεντηκοστήν.— ἅπαντες, *i.e.*, the hundred-and-twenty as well as the Apostles (Chrysostom, Jerome), and the expression may also have included other disciples who were present in Jerusalem at the Feast (so Hilgenfeld, Wendt, Holtzmann). This interpretation appears to be more in accordance with the wide range of the prophecy, ii. 16-21.—ὁμοθυμαδὸν, see above on ver. 14. ἐπὶ τὸ αὐτό may simply = "together," so that of the two expressions ὁμοῦ, R.V., and this phrase "alterum abundat" (Blass, Weiss); but the reference may be to the room in which they were previously assembled; *cf.* i. 15.

Ver. 2. ἄφνω: only in Acts, here, and in xvi. 26, xxviii. 6; Klostermann's *Vin-diciæ Lucanæ*, p. 55; several times in LXX, but also in classical Greek in Thuc., Dem., Eur.—ἦχος ὥσπερ φερομ. πν. βιαίας, lit., "a sound as if a violent gust were being borne along". St. Chrysostom rightly emphasises the ὡς, so that the sound is not that of wind, but as of the rushing of a mighty wind (so too the tongues are not of fire, but *as of fire*). The words describe not a natural but a supernatural phenomenon, as Wendt pointedly admits. Wind was often used as a symbol of the divine Presence, 2 Sam. v. 24, Psalm civ. 3, 1 Kings xix. 11, Ezekiel xliii. 2, etc.; *cf.* Josephus, *Ant.*, iii., 5, 2; vii., 4; here it is used of the mighty power of the Spirit which nothing could resist. St. Luke alone of the N.T. writers uses ἦχος— Heb. xii. 19 being a quotation, and it is perhaps worth noting that the word is employed in medical writers, and by one of them, Aretæus, of the noise of the sea (*cf.* ἤχους θαλάσσης, Luke xxi. 25).— ὅλον τὸν οἶκον. If the Temple were meant, as Holtzmann and Zöckler think, it would have been specified, iii. 2, 11, v. 21.

Ver. 3. διαμεριζόμ. γλῶσσαι: the audible σημεῖον is followed by a visible: γλῶσσαι the organs of speech by which the wonderful works of God were to be proclaimed, so that the expression cannot be explained from Isaiah v. 24, where the tongue of fire is represented as an organ of destruction (Wendt, note, *in loco*). ὡσεὶ πυρός in their appearance and brightness. The words themselves therefore forbid reference to a natural phenomenon, to say nothing of the fact of the spiritual transformation of the Apostles which followed. Fire like wind was symbolic of the divine Presence, Exod. iii. 2, and of the Spirit who purifies and sanctifies, Ezekiel i. 13, Malachi, iii. 2, 3 (see Wetstein for classical instances of fire symbolical of the presence of the deity; *cf.*, *e.g.*, Homer, *Iliad*, xviii., 214; Virgil, *Æn.*, ii., 683). διαμεριζ., lit., dividing or parting themselves off. R.V. "tongues parting asunder," so that originally they were one, as one mighty flame of fire. This rendering is strictly in accordance with the meaning of the verb. Vulgate *dispertitæ* (the word used by Blass). διαμερίζω is used once again in Acts ii. 45 in the active voice, and once only by St. Matthew and St. Mark (once by St. John as a quotation) in the middle voice, but six times by St. Luke in his Gospel; frequently in the LXX.—ἐκάθισε (not -αν), *sc.*, γλῶσσα (not πῦρ or πνεῦμα ἅγιον), although the latter is advocated by Chrysostom, Theophylact, Bengel: "it sat," R.V. The singular best expresses the result of the tongues parting asunder, and of the distribution to each and all. So too ἐφ᾽ ἕνα ἕκαστον αὐτῶν, "upon each one of them," R.V., *cf.* ver. 6 εἰς ἕκαστος (and ver. 8). The resting of a flame of fire upon the head as a token of the favour of Heaven may be illustrated from classical sources (see above and instances in Wetstein), but the thought here is not so much of fire as the token of divine favour, as of the tongue (as of fire) conferring a divine power to utter in speech divine things.

Ver. 4. ἀποφθέγγεσθαι—a word peculiar to Acts, *cf.* v. 14 and xxvi. 25; in the LXX used not of ordinary conversation, but of the utterances of prophets; *cf.* Ezek. xiii. 9, Micah v. 12, 1 Chron. xxv.

γλῶσσαι ὡσεὶ πυρὸς, ἐκάθισέ[1] τε ἐφ᾽ ἕνα ἕκαστον αὐτῶν, 4. καὶ
ἐπλήσθησαν ἅπαντες Πνεύματος Ἁγίου, καὶ ἤρξαντο λαλεῖν ἑτέραις
γλώσσαις, καθὼς τὸ Πνεῦμα ἐδίδου αὐτοῖς ἀποφθέγγεσθαι. 5. Ἦσαν
δὲ ἐν Ἱερουσαλὴμ κατοικοῦντες Ἰουδαῖοι ἄνδρες εὐλαβεῖς ἀπὸ παντὸς
ἔθνους τῶν ὑπὸ τὸν οὐρανόν. 6. γενομένης δὲ τῆς φωνῆς ταύτης,
συνῆλθε τὸ πλῆθος καὶ συνεχύθη · ὅτι ἤκουον εἰς ἕκαστος τῇ ἰδίᾳ

---

[1] εκαθισαν ℵ*D, probably emendation from γλωσσαι, but overwhelming evidence
for -σεν.

1, so fitly here: (cf. ἀποφθέγματα, used by the Greeks of the sayings of the wise and philosophers, and see also references in Wendt).—ἑτέραις γλώσσαις, see additional note.

Ver. 5. κατοικοῦντες, probably used not merely of temporary dwellers for the Feast, but of the devout Jews of the Diaspora, who for the purpose of being near the Temple had taken up their residence in Jerusalem, perhaps for the study of the Law, perhaps to live and to die within the city walls (see St. Chrysostom's comment on the word). They were not proselytes as is indicated by Ἰουδαῖοι, but probably devout men like Symeon, Luke ii. 25, who is described by the same word εὐλαβής, waiting for the consolation of Israel. The expression, as Zöckler points out, is not quite synonymous with that in ver. 14 (or with Luke xiii. 4), and he explains it as above. There is certainly no need to consider the word, with Spitta and Hilgenfeld, as an epithet added by a later editor, or to omit Ἰουδαῖοι, as Blass strongly urges (while Hilgenfeld desires to retain this word). The word may fairly be regarded as contrasted with Γαλιλαῖοι (ver. 7). The same view of it as applied here to foreign Jews who had their stated residence in Jerusalem is maintained by Schürer, Jewish People, div. ii., vol. ii., p. 291 (note) E.T.—κατοικεῖν is used generally of taking up a permanent abode as in contrast to παροικεῖν used of temporary sojourn, and on the frequent use of the word in St. Luke, Friedrich, ubi supra, p. 39. But here it is followed most probably by εἰς not ἐν, constructio prægnans, cf. Wendt and Weiss as against W.H. (T.R. ἐν and so Blass in β). Weiss, Apostelgeschichte, p. 36, regards this frequent use of εἰς as characteristic of the style of Acts, cf. ix. 21, xiv. 25, and considers it quite inconceivable that ἐν would be changed into εἰς, although the reverse is likely enough to have happened (Wendt).—εὐλαβεῖς, see viii. 2.—ἀπὸ

παντὸς ἔθνους: "from every nation," so R.V.; "out of," A.V., but this would represent ἐκ rather than ἀπό, and would imply that they belonged to these different nations, not that they were born Jews residing among them and coming from them (Humphry, Commentary on R.V.).—τῶν ὑπὸ τὸν οὐρανόν, sc. ἐθνῶν. The phrase is used frequently in LXX, cf. Deut. ii. 25, and in classical literature by Plato and Dem. If κατοικοῦντες includes the Jews who had come up to the Feast as well as those who had settled in Jerusalem from other countries, this expression is strikingly illustrated by the words of Philo, De Monarchia, ii., i, p. 223. The Pentecost would be more largely attended even than the Passover, as it was a more favourable season for travelling than the early spring (see Wetstein, in loco), and cf. Schürer, Jewish People, div. ii., vol. ii., pp. 291, 307, E.T.

Ver. 6. φωνῆς ταύτης: "when this sound was heard," R.V. "Hic idem quod ἦχος comm. 2," so Wetstein, who compares for φωνή in this sense Matt. xxiv. 31, 1 Cor. xiv. 7, 8 (2 Chron. v. 13), and so most recent commentators (cf. John iii. 8); if human voices were meant, the plural might have been expected. But the word in singular might refer to the divine voice, the voice of the Spirit, cf. Matt. iii. 17, xvii. 5. The A.V., so too Grotius, following Erasmus, Calvin, render the word as if φήμη, but the two passages quoted from LXX to justify this rendering are no real examples, cf., e.g., Gen. xlv. 16, Jer. xxvii. 46.—τὸ πλῆθος: a characteristic word of St. Luke, occurring eight times in his Gospel, seventeen in Acts, and only seven times in rest of the N.T.; on the frequency with which St. Luke uses expressions indicative of fulness, see Friedrich, Das Lucasevangelium, pp. 40, 102. In inscriptions the word seems to have been used not only of political but of religious communities, see Deissmann, Neue Bibel-

διαλέκτῳ λαλούντων αὐτῶν.[1] 7. ἐξίσταντο δὲ πάντες καὶ ἐθαύμαζον,
λέγοντες πρὸς ἀλλήλους, Οὐκ[2] ἰδοὺ πάντες οὗτοί εἰσιν οἱ λαλοῦντες
Γαλιλαῖοι; 8. καὶ πῶς ἡμεῖς ἀκούομεν ἕκαστος τῇ ἰδίᾳ διαλέκτῳ
ἡμῶν ἐν ᾗ ἐγεννήθημεν, 9. Πάρθοι καὶ Μῆδοι καὶ Ἐλαμῖται,[3] καὶ οἱ

[1] τῇ ἰδίᾳ διαλ. λαλουντων; in D λαλουντας ταις γλωσσαις αυτων, Syr. Harcl.,
(Aug. conflate), but not received by Blass in β although retained by Hilg.; may
be retranslation from Syriac (Chase), but see Weiss, Codex D, p. 56.

[2] ουκ AC; ουχ ℵDE 61, so Tisch., W.H. marg.; ουχι B, so W.H. text, Weiss
(Wendt doubtful); see further Winer-Schmiedel, p. 39.

[3] Ελαμιται ℵ[3]EIP, but Ελαμειται A(B)(C)D (ℵ omits), so Tisch., W.H., Weiss;
Blass in β reads Αιλαμιται, cf. B.

studien, pp. 59, 60 (1897), and see below on xv. 30.—συνεχύθη—from συνχύνω (συνχέω), only found in Acts, where it occurs five times (cf. also σύγχυσις, Acts xix. 29), see Moulton and Geden, sub v. For its meaning here cf. Gen. xi. 7, 9, 1 Macc. iv. 27, 2 Macc. xiii. 23, xiv. 28; Vulg., mente confusa est.— διαλέκτῳ: only in the Acts in N.T. The question has been raised as to whether it meant a dialect or a language. Meyer argued in favour of the former, but the latter rendering more probably expresses the author's meaning, cf. i. 19, and also xxi. 40, xxii. 2, xxvi. 14. The word is apparently used as the equivalent of γλῶσσα, ver. 11, A. and R.V. "language". As the historian in his list, vv. 9, 10, apparently is following distinctions of language (see Rendall, Acts, p. 177, and Appendix, p. 359), this would help to fix the meaning of the word διάλεκτος here. Wendt in revising Meyer's rendering contends that the word is purposely introduced because γλῶσσα, vv. 3, 4, had just been employed not in the sense of language but tongue, and so might have been misunderstood if repeated here with λαλεῖν. On the other hand it may be urged that some of the distinctions in the list are those of dialect, and that St. Luke intentionally used a word meaning both language and dialect. Ver. 7. ἐξίσταντο: frequent in St. Luke, three times in his Gospel, eight in the Acts, elsewhere once in St. Paul, once in St. Matthew, four times in St. Mark. The word is often found in the LXX in various senses; cf. for its meaning here Gen. xliii. 33, Judith xiii. 17, xv. 1, 1 Macc. xv. 32, xvi. 22. πάντες—Γαλιλαῖοι: there is no need to suppose with Schöttgen (so Grotius, Olshausen) that the term implies any reference to the want of culture among the Galileans, as if in this way to emphasise the surprise of the questioners,

or to explain the introduction of the term because the Galileans were "magis ad arma quam ad litteras et linguas idonei" (Corn. à Lapide). But if there is a reference to the peculiar dialect of the Galileans this might help to explain the introduction of Ἰουδαίαν in ver. 9 (Wetstein followed by Weiss, but see below). Weiss sees here, it is true, the hand of a reviser who thinks only of the Apostles and not of the hundred-and-twenty who could not be supposed to come under the term Γαλιλαῖοι. But whilst no doubt Γαλ. might be considered a fitting description of the Apostolic band (except Judas), Hilgenfeld well asks why the hundred-and-twenty should not have been also Galileans, if they had followed Jesus from Galilee to Jerusalem. Ver. 8. τῇ ἰδίᾳ διαλ. . . . ἐν ᾗ ἐγεννήθημεν—used distributively as ver. 11 ταῖς ἡμετ. γλώσσαις shows—and hence cannot be taken to mean that only one language common to all, viz., Aramaic, was spoken on the outpouring of the Spirit. Vv. 9-11. The list which follows has been described as showing the trained hand of the historian, whilst it has also been regarded as a distinctly popular utterance in Greek style (Ramsay, Church in the Roman Empire, p. 149; but see also Rendall, Acts, Introd., p. 13). But, as Dean Plumptre well remarks, the omission of many countries which one might have expected shows that the list was not a made up list after the event, but that St. Luke had accurately mentioned the nations present at the Feast. The reference throughout is of course to Jews of the Dispersion, and Schürer (see too Schöttgen) well parallels the description given here of the extent of the Diaspora with the description in Agrippa's letter to the Emperor Caligula given by Philo (Legat. ad Gaium, 36,

κατοικοῦντες τὴν Μεσοποταμίαν, Ἰουδαίαν τε καὶ Καππαδοκίαν,
Πόντον καὶ τὴν Ἀσίαν, 10. Φρυγίαν τε καὶ Παμφυλίαν, Αἴγυπτον
καὶ τὰ μέρη τῆς Λιβύης τῆς κατὰ Κυρήνην, καὶ οἱ ἐπιδημοῦντες

Mang., ii., 587). All commentators seem to be agreed in regarding the list as framed to some extent on geographical lines, beginning from Parthia the furthest east. Mr. Page holds that the countries named may be regarded as grouped not only geographically but historically. Of the Jews of the Dispersion there were four classes : (1) *Eastern* or *Babylonian* Jews, corresponding in the list to Parthians, Medes, Elamites ; (2) *Syrian* Jews, corresponding to Judæa, Cappadocia, Pontus and Asia, Phrygia and Pamphylia ; (3) *Egyptian* Jews, corresponding to Egypt and the parts of Libya over against Cyrene ; (4) *Roman* Jews. (1) Parthia, mentioned here only in the N.T., is placed first, not only because of the vast extent of its empire from India to the Tigris, but because it then was the only power which had tried issues with Rome and had not been defeated, " Parthia " B.D. (Rawlinson). In Mesopotamia, Elam, and Babylonia were to be found the descendants of the kingdom of the Ten Tribes and of the kingdom of Judah, transported thither by the Assyrians and Chaldeans, now and until the reign of Trajan the subjects of the Parthians, but always of political importance to Rome from their position on the eastern borders of the Empire (Schürer, *ubi supra*, div. ii., vol. ii., pp. 223, 224 E.T.). At the head of (2), Ἰουδαίαν is placed by Mr. Page, *i.e.*, at the head of the group with which in his view it is geographically connected. Of Asia, as of Syria, it could be said that Jews dwelt in large numbers in every city, and the statement that Jews had settled in the most distant parts of Pontus is abundantly confirmed by the Jewish inscriptions in the Greek language found in the Crimea. Seleucus Nicator granted to the Jews in Syria and Asia the same privileges as those bestowed upon his Greek and Macedonian subjects (Jos., *Ant.*, xii., 31) ; and to Antiochus the Great was due the removal of two thousand Jewish families from Mesopotamia and Babylonia to Lydia and Phrygia (Schürer, *l. c.*, and "Antiochus III.," B.D.[2]; Jos., *Ant.*, xii., 3, 4). Mr. Page uses the word Ἰουδαία as equivalent to the land of the Jews, *i.e.*, Palestine and perhaps also to some part of Syria. In the former sense the word could undoubtedly be employed (Hamburger, "Judäa," *Real-Encyclopädie des Judentums*, i., 5 ; so too by classical writers and by Strabo, "Judæa," B.D.). But it is very doubtful how far the term can be extended to include any part of Syria, although Josephus (*B.J.*, iii., 3, 5) speaks of the maritime places of Judæa extending as far as Ptolemais. It may well be that Syria was regarded as a kind of outer Palestine, intermediate between it and heathendom (Edersheim, *Sketches of Jewish Social Life*, pp. 16-19, 71, 73). St. Jerome reads Syria instead of Judæa, a reading to which Blass apparently inclines. Tertullian conjectured Armenia, *c. Jud.*, vii., and Idumæa (so again Spitta), Bithynia and India have been proposed. It is often very difficult to say exactly what is meant by Asia, whether the term refers to the entire Roman province, which had been greatly increased in the first century B.C. since its formation in 133 B.C., or whether the word is used in its popular sense, as denoting the Ægean coast lands and excluding Phrygia. Here the term is used with the latter signification (Ramsay, *Church in the Roman Empire*, p. 150, and also "Asia" in Hastings, B.D.). At the head of (3) stands Egypt, where the Jewish Dispersion, especially in Alexandria, played so important a part in the history of civilisation. The greatest prosperity of the Jews in Egypt began with Alexander the Great, but long before his time, in the seventh century B.C., Jewish immigrants were in the country (Schürer, *ubi supra*, pp. 226, 227, and "Alexandria," B.D.[2]). From Egypt the Dispersion penetrated further westward (Schürer, *u. s.*, pp. 230, 231, and note), and in Libya Cyrenaica or Pentapolitana, the modern *Tripoli*, the Jews were very numerous ; *cf.* for their history in Cyrene 1 Macc. xv. 23 ; 2 Macc. ii. 23 ; Jos., *Ant.*, xvi., 6, 1, 5, and Acts vi. 9, xi. 30, xiii. 1 ; Schürer, *u. s.*, p. 232, and Merivale, *Romans under the Empire*, pp. 364, 365. The expression used here, τὰ μέρη τῆς Λ. τῆς κατὰ Κ., affords a striking parallel to that used by Dio Cassius, ἡ πρὸς Κυρήνην Λιβύη, liii., 12 ; *cf.* also Jos., *Ant.*, xvi., 16 ; "Cyrene," B.D.[2], and Hastings' B.D. In (4) we have οἱ ἐπιδ. Ῥωμαῖοι. There is no ground for supposing that any Jews dwelt permanently in Rome before the

Ῥωμαῖοι, Ἰουδαῖοί τε καὶ προσήλυτοι, 11. Κρῆτες καὶ Ἄραβες,
ἀκούομεν λαλούντων αὐτῶν ταῖς ἡμετέραις γλώσσαις τὰ μεγαλεῖα

time of Pompey, although their first appearance there dates from the days of
the Maccabees (1 Macc. viii. 17, xiv. 24,
xv. 15 ff.). Of the numerous Jewish
families brought to Rome by Pompey
many regained their freedom, and settled
beyond the Tiber as a regular Jewish
community with the rights of Roman
citizenship. In 19 A.D., however, the
whole Jewish population was banished
from the imperial city, Jos., *Ant.*, xviii.,
3, 5; but after the overthrow of Sejanus
it may be safely assumed that Tiberius
allowed their return to Rome (Schürer, *u.s.*,
p. 232 ff.).—οἱ ἐπιδημοῦντες Ῥωμαῖοι,
" Sojourners from Rome," R.V., *i.e.*, the
Jews who live at Rome as sojourners—
Roman Jews. Others take ἐπιδ. as referring to the Roman Jews who were
making a temporary sojourn in Jerusalem for the Feast, or for some other purpose, the word being thus in a certain
degree opposed to the κατοικοῦντες (of
permanent dwelling) in ver. 5. Others
again apparently take the expression as
describing Roman Jews who, born in
Rome, had taken up their dwelling in Jerusalem, and who are thus distinguished from
those Jews who, born in Jerusalem, were
Romans by right of Roman citizenship.
The only other passage in which ἐπιδημοῦντες occurs is Acts xvii. 21 (but *cf.*
xviii. 27, D and β (Blass), and it is there
used of the ξένοι sojourning in Athens,
and so probably thus making a temporary
sojourn, or who were not Athenians by
birth or citizenship, as distinct from the
regular inhabitants of Athens. *Cf.* Athenæus, viii., p. 361 F.—οἱ Ῥώμην κατοικοῦντες, καὶ οἱ ἐνεπιδημοῦντες τῇ πόλει,
which passage shows that ἐπιδ. " minus
significat quam κατοικεῖν " (Blass), and
other instances in Wetstein. Hilgenfeld,
whose pages contain a long discussion of
recent views of the words in question,
argues that according to what precedes we
should expect καὶ οἱ κατοικοῦντες Ῥώμην,
and according to what follows we should
expect simply Ῥωμαῖοι, and he solves
the difficulty by the arbitrary method of
omitting καὶ οἱ ἐπιδ. before Ῥωμαῖοι,
and Ἰουδ. τε καὶ προσήλυτοι after it,
Zeitschrift für wissenschaft. Theol., p.
93 ff. (1895); see further *Actus Apost.*,
p. 260, 1899.—Ἰουδαῖοί τε καὶ προσήλυτοι. Not only would St. Luke in
writing to a Roman convert of social
rank like Theophilus be likely to mention

the presence of *Roman* Jews at the first
Christian Pentecost, but he would also
emphasise the fact that they were not
only Jews, or of Jewish origin, but that
proselytes from heathendom were also
included (Felten, Belser). In thus explaining the words Felten refers them,
with Erasmus and Grotius, to οἱ ἐπιδ.
Ῥωμαῖοι only, whilst Overbeck, Weiss,
Holtzmann, Wendt, Belser, so Page,
Hackett, refer them to the whole of the
preceding catalogue. It is evident that
Schürer takes the same view, for in speaking of the large offerings contributed by
proselytes to the Temple at Jerusalem
he mentions that in stating the number of
Jews of every nationality living in Jerusalem the *Acts* does not forget to mention the proselytes along with the Jews,
ii. 10 (*u. s.*, p. 307).

Ver. 11. Κρῆτες καὶ Ἄραβες : both
names seem to have been added to the
list as an after-thought. Even if we cannot accept Nösgen's idea that St. Luke
is repeating *verbatim* the account which
he had received orally from an eyewitness who had forgotten the Arabians
and Cretans in going through the list
geographically, yet the introduction of
the two names in no apparent connection with the rest ought to show
us that we are not dealing with an artificial list, but with a genuine record
of the different nations represented
at the Feast. Belser, who endorses
this view, supposes that St. Luke
obtained his information from an eye-
witness who added the Cretans and
Arabians supplementarily, just as a person might easily forget one or two names
in going through a long list of representative nations at a festival. It is possible,
as Belser suggests, that the Cretans and
Arabians were thinly represented at the
Pentecost, although the notices in Josephus and Philo's letter mentioned
above point to a large Jewish population
in Crete. The special mention of the
Cretans is strikingly in accordance with
the statement of the Jewish envoys to
Caligula, *viz.*, that all the more noted
islands of the Mediterranean, including
Crete, were full of Jews, " Crete," B.D.,[2]
and Schürer, *u. s.*, p. 232. In R.V.
" Cretans "; which marks the fact that
the Greek Κρῆτες is a dissyllable; in A.V.
" Cretes " this is easily forgotten (*cf.*
Titus i. 12).—μεγαλεῖα only found here

τοῦ Θεοῦ; 12. ἐξίσταντο δὲ πάντες καὶ διηπόρουν,[1] ἄλλος πρὸς ἄλλον λέγοντες, Τί ἂν θέλοι τοῦτο εἶναι; 13. ἕτεροι δὲ χλευάζοντες[2] ἔλεγον, Ὅτι γλεύκους μεμεστωμένοι εἰσί.

[1] διηπόρουν CDEI, Bas., Chrys., so Lach.; διηπορουντο ℵAB, so Tisch., Weiss, W.H., R.V. After προς αλλον D adds επι τω γεγονοτι, so Blass in β, and Hilg. (Syr. Harcl., Aug.); cf. iii. 10, iv. 21, and Weiss, Codex D, p. 56.

[2] χλευάζοντες, but διαχλευαζ. R.V., W.H., Weiss, Wendt, beyond doubt to be read.

in N.T.; the reading of T.R., Luke i. 49, cannot be supported; cf. Psalm lxx. (lxxi.) 19, where the word occurs in LXX. (Hebrew, גְּדֹלוֹת) Ecclesiasticus xvii. 9, xviii. 4, xxxiii. (xxxvi.) 8, xlii. 21, 3 Macc. vii. 22, R. The word is found in Josephus, and also in classical Greek: used here not only of the Resurrection of the Lord (Grotius), but of all that the prophets had foretold, of all that Christ had done and the Holy Ghost had conferred.

Ver. 12. διηπόρουν: not found in LXX (only in Psalm lxxvi. 5, and Dan. ii. 3, Symmachus), and peculiar to St. Luke in the N.T., once in his Gospel, ix. 7 (xxiv. 4 ἀπορεῖσθαι, W.H. and R.V.), and three times in Acts, cf. v. 24, x. 17. διηποροῦντο in R.V. "were perplexed"; A.V. "were in doubt," although in Luke xxiv. 4 this or a similar word is rendered as in R.V., "were (much) perplexed". The Greek conveys the thought of utter uncertainty what to think, rather than doubt as to which opinion of several is right (Humphry). The word no doubt is frequently found in classical writers, and is found also in Philo (not in Josephus), but it may be worth noting that ἀπορία, εὐπορία, διαπορεῖν, εὐπορεῖν are all peculiar to St. Luke, and were terms constantly employed by medical writers (Hobart, Medical Language, etc., p. 163). τί ἂν θέλοι τοῦτο εἶναι—θέλω was constantly used in this sense in classical writers, see instances in Wetstein. On the popular use of θέλω instead of βούλομαι in later Greek, cf. Blass, Acta Apostolorum, p. 15. Blass points out that St. Luke's employment of βούλομαι is characteristic of his culture, although it must be remembered that the Evangelist uses θέλω (as here) very frequently.

Ver. 13. ἕτεροι δὲ: although the word is ἕτεροι, not ἄλλοι, it is doubtful how far it indicates a distinct class from those mentioned as speaking in vv. 7-12. At the same time not only πάντες, ver. 12, but also the behaviour of the ἕτεροι, seems to separate them from the εὐλαβεῖς in

ver. 5.—χλευάζοντες: but stronger with the intensifying διά than the simple verb in xvii. 32; used in classical Greek, Dem., Plato, and in Polybius—here only in N.T., not found in LXX, although the simple verb is used (see below).— γλεύκους: if the rendering R.V. "new wine" is adopted, the ridicule was indeed ill-timed, as at the Pentecost there was no new wine strictly speaking, the earliest vintage being in August (cf. Chrysostom and Oecumenius, who see in such a charge the excessive folly and the excessive malignity of the scoffers). Neither the context nor the use of the word elsewhere obliges us to suppose that it is used here of unfermented wine. Its use in Lucian, Ep., Sat., xxii. (to which reference is made by Wendt and Page), and also in LXX, Job xxxii. 19, ὥσπερ ἀσκὸς γλεύκους ζέων δεδεμένος, points to a wine still fermenting, intoxicating, while the definition of Hesychius, τὸ ἀπόσταγμα τῆς σταφυλῆς πρὶν πατηθῇ, refers its lusciousness to the quality of its make (from the purest juice of the grape), and not of necessity to the brevity of its age, see B.D. "Wine". It would therefore be best to render "sweet wine," made perhaps of a specially sweet small grape, cf. Gen. xlix. 11. "The extraordinary candour of Christ's biographers must not be forgotten. Notice also such sentences as 'but some doubted,' and in the account of Pentecost, 'these men are full of new wine'. Such observations are wonderfully true to human nature, but no less wonderfully opposed to any 'accretion' theory": Romanes, Thoughts on Religion, p. 156.

Ver. 14. σταθεὶς δὲ Πέτρος: St. Chrysostom rightly remarks on the change which had passed over St. Peter. In the place where a few weeks before he had denied with an oath that he knew "the man," he now stands forth to proclaim him as the Christ and the Saviour. It is quite characteristic of St. Luke thus to introduce participles indicating the position or gesture of the speaker (cf. Friedrich, Zöckler, Overbeck); cf. St.

14. Σταθεὶς δὲ Πέτρος σὺν τοῖς ἕνδεκα,[1] ἐπῆρε τὴν φωνὴν αὐτοῦ, καὶ ἀπεφθέγξατο αὐτοῖς, Ἄνδρες Ἰουδαῖοι καὶ οἱ κατοικοῦντες Ἰερουσαλὴμ ἅπαντες, τοῦτο ὑμῖν γνωστὸν ἔστω, καὶ ἐνωτίσασθε τὰ ῥήματά μου. 15. οὐ γὰρ, ὡς ὑμεῖς ὑπολαμβάνετε, οὗτοι μεθύουσιν· ἔστι γὰρ ὥρα τρίτη τῆς ἡμέρας· 16. ἀλλὰ τοῦτό ἐστι τὸ εἰρημένον διὰ τοῦ προφήτου Ἰωὴλ,[2] 17. "Καὶ[3] ἔσται ἐν ταῖς ἐσχάταις ἡμέραις,

[1] ἐνδεκα D, Gig., Par., Syr., Pesh., Aug. add αποστολοις; cf. i. 20. D reads δεκα for ενδεκα, perhaps through carelessness (Weiss). After επηρεν D, Par.[2] insert πρωτος; E has προτερον after την φωνην αυτου; πρωτος retained by Blass in β, and by Hilg.; it seems a needless addition as it is implied in the verse (see also Harris, *Four Lectures*, p. 58).

[2] Ιωηλ אABCEIP, Vulg., Bas., Chrys., Cyr.-Jer.; so W.H., R.V., Weiss. Om. D, Iren., Aug., Hil. "Rebapt.," so Hilg. Blass regards it as an interpolation even in α text.

[3] και om. by D, Gig., Par., Ir., Aug., Sah., Boh.; but in LXX.

Luke xviii. 11, 40, xix. 8, Acts v. 40, xi. 13, xvii. 2, xxv. 18, xxvii. 21.—**σὺν τοῖς ἕνδεκα,** and so with Matthias; cf. v. 32, and i. 22.—**ἐπῆρε τὴν φωνὴν αὐτοῦ:** this phrase is only found in St. Luke's Gospel (xi. 29) and the Acts (xiv. 11, xxii. 22), but it is quite classical, so in Demosthenes, and in LXX it occurs several times.— **ἀπεφθέγξατο:** "spake forth," R.V., cf. xxvi. 25, expressive of the solemnity of the utterance, see above in ver. 4, and showing that St. Peter's words were inspired no less than the speaking with tongues (Weiss).—**ἄνδρες Ἰουδαῖοι:** no word of reproach, but an address of respect; the words may be taken quite generally to indicate not only those previously present, but also those who were attracted by the noise. There is no need to suppose that St. Peter addressed the inhabitants of Jerusalem and the Jews as if they had been the only scoffers as distinct from the pilgrims from other lands. It is no doubt possible that the first part of the speech was addressed to the native home-bred residents, and that in ver. 22 St. Peter in the word **Ἰσραηλῖται** includes all the Jews whether resident in Jerusalem or not.—**ἐνωτίσασθε:** only here in N.T., but frequent in LXX, especially in the Psalms. It usually translates Hebrew

הַאֲזִין from Hebrew אֹזֶן = ear; cf. *inaurire;* Kennedy, *Sources of N. T. Greek,* p. 130. "Give ear unto my words," R.V. *Auribus percipite,* Vulg.

Ver. 15. **ὥρα τρίτη τῆς ἡμέρας:** if the words refer to the hour of early prayer, 9 A.M., the Jews previously did not partake of food, and on festal days

they abstained from food and drink until the sixth hour (twelve o'clock). But if Schürer (see on iii. 1, and Blass, *in loco*) is right in specifying other hours for prayer, the expression may mean that St. Peter appeals to the early period of the day as a proof that the charge of drunkenness was contrary to all reasonable probability.

Ver. 17. **ἐν ταῖς ἐσχ. ἡμέρ.,** *i.e.,* the time immediately preceding the Parousia of the Messiah (Weber, *Jüdische Theologie,* p. 372). The expression is introduced here instead of **μετὰ ταῦτα,** LXX, to show that St. Peter saw in the outpouring of the Spirit the fulfilment of Joel's prophecy, ii. 28-31 (LXX), and the dawn of the period preceding the return of Christ in glory, Isaiah ii. 2, Micah iv. 1 (2 Tim. iii. 1, James v. 3, Heb. i. 1).— **λέγει ὁ Θεός:** introduced possibly from Joel ii. 12, although wanting in LXX and Hebrew.—**ἐκχεῶ:** Hellenistic future, Blass, *Grammatik des N.G.,* pp. 41, 42, 58, cf. x. 45, Titus iii. 6. In LXX the word is used as here, not only in Joel, but in Zach. xii. 10, Ecclus. xviii. 11, xxiv. 33, but very often of pouring forth anger.— **ἀπὸ τοῦ πνεύμ. μου,** "I will pour forth of my Spirit," R.V., so in LXX, but in Heb., "I will pour out my Spirit". The partitive **ἀπό** may be accounted for by the thought that the Spirit of God considered in its entirety remains with God, and that men acquire only a certain portion of its energies (so Wendt, Holtzmann). Or the partitive force of the word may be taken as signifying the great diversity of the Spirit's gifts and operations. See also Viteau, *Le Grec du N. T.,* p. 151 (1893).— **πᾶσαν σάρκα,** *i.e.,* all men; but this ex-

λέγει ὁ Θεὸς, ἐκχεῶ ἀπὸ τοῦ πνεύματός μου ἐπὶ πᾶσαν σάρκα, καὶ
προφητεύσουσιν οἱ υἱοὶ ὑμῶν [1] καὶ αἱ θυγατέρες ὑμῶν· καὶ οἱ νεανίσκοι ὑμῶν ὁράσεις ὄψονται, καὶ οἱ πρεσβύτεροι ὑμῶν ἐνύπνια [2]
ἐνυπνιασθήσονται, 18. καί γε ἐπὶ τοὺς δούλους μου καὶ ἐπὶ τὰς
δούλας μου ἐν ταῖς ἡμέραις ἐκείναις [3] ἐκχεῶ ἀπὸ τοῦ πνεύματός μου,

[1] For υμων . . . υμων D, Gig., Tert., "Rebapt." Hil. read αυτων (referred by
Harris to a Montanistic application).

[2] ενυπνια EP, Tert., Chrys. (cf. LXX, but AS³ has -ιοις) ; but ενυπνιοις אABCD²
13, 27, 61, Epiph., so Tisch., W.H., R.V., Wendt, Weiss, Hilg.

[3] εν ταις ημεραις εκειναις om. D, Gig. (Cypr.), Acta Perpetuæ. και προφητευ-
σουσιν om. D, Par.¹, Tert. (Cypr.), Acta Perpetuæ (not in LXX). The two clauses
come together in Syriac and may have been omitted together (Chase).

pression in itself suggests a contrast
beween the weakness and imperfection
of humanity and the all-powerful working
of the divine Spirit. The expression is
Hebraistic, cf. Luke iii. 6, John xvii. 2,
and Ecclus. xlv. 4, and often in LXX.
In Joel's prophecy the expression only
included the people of Israel, although
the divine Spirit should be no longer
limited to particular prophets or favoured
individuals, but should be given to the
whole nation. If we compare ii. 39, the
expression would include at least the
members of the Diaspora, wherever they
might be, but it is doubtful whether we
can take it as including the heathen as
such in St. Peter's thoughts, although
Hilgenfeld is so convinced that the verse
ii. 39 can only refer to the heathen that
he refers all the words from καὶ πᾶσι to
the end of the verse to his "author to
Theophilus". Spitta on the other hand
regards the expression as referring only
to the Jews of the Diaspora; if the
Gentiles had been intended, he thinks
that we should have had τοῖς εἰς μακρὰν
ἔθνεσιν as in xxii. 21. Undoubtedly we
have an analogous expression to ii. 39 in
Eph. ii. 13, οἱ ποτε ὄντες μακράν, where
the words evidently refer to the heathen,
but we must not expect the universalism
of St. Paul in the first public address of
St. Peter: for him it is still ὁ θεὸς ἡμῶν,
"our God," ver. 39, and even the expression, πρῶτον, iii. 26, in which Holtzmann
sees a reference to the extension of the
Messianic blessings to the Jew first and
then to the Gentile, need only mean that
in St. Peter's view these blessings could
only be secured by the Gentile through
becoming a proselyte to the faith of
Israel. It is thus only that St. Peter's
subsequent conduct becomes intelligible.
The reading αὐτῶν instead of ὑμῶν in
the next clause before both υἱοὶ and

θυγατέρες if it is adopted (Blass β)
would seem to extend the scope of the
prophecy beyond the limits of Israel
proper.—θυγατέρες: as Anna is called
προφῆτις, Luke ii. 36, so too in the
Christian Church the daughters of Philip
are spoken of as προφητεύουσαι, xxi. 9.
—νεανίσκοι: in LXX and Hebrew the
order is reversed. It may be that Bengel
is right in drawing the distinction thus :
"Apud juvenes maximi vigent sensus
externi, visionibus opportuni : apud senes
sensus interni, somniis accommodati".
But he adds "Non tamen adolescentes
a somniis, neque sensus a visionibus
excluduntur" (see also Keil, in loco),
and so Overbeck, Winer, Wendt see
in the words simply an instance of the
Hebrew love of parallelism.—καί γε
(in LXX) = Hebrew וְגַם—only here in
N.T. and in xvii. 27 W.H. (and possibly
in Luke xix. 42) = "and even," Blass,
Grammatik des N. G., p. 255. The only
good Attic instance of καί γε with an
intervening word is to be found in Lysias,
in Theomn., ii., 7, although not a strict
parallel to the passage before us, Simcox,
Language of the N. T., p. 168.
Ver. 18. As there was to be no limit of
sex or age, so too there was no limit of condition. The word μου is not in the Hebrew,
only in the LXX, but as it is found in the
latter and in Acts it is argued that the
words δούλους and δούλας do not mean
those of servile rank, but are applied in
a general sense to those who are worshippers, and so servants of God. But
in retaining the word μου we are not
obliged to reject the literal meaning
"bond-servants," just as St. Peter himself, in addressing household servants
and slaves, commands them to act ὡς
δοῦλοι θεοῦ (1 Peter ii. 16): "Intelliguntur
servi secundum carnem, diversi a liberis,

καὶ προφητεύσουσι. 19. καὶ δώσω τέρατα ἐν τῷ οὐρανῷ ἄνω, καὶ
σημεῖα ἐπὶ τῆς γῆς κάτω,[1] αἷμα καὶ πῦρ καὶ ἀτμίδα καπνοῦ. 20. ὁ
ἥλιος μεταστραφήσεται εἰς σκότος, καὶ ἡ σελήνη εἰς αἷμα,[2] πρὶν ἢ

[1] αιμα και πυρ και ατμιδα καπνου om. D, Gig., Par.[1], Hilg.

[2] πριν η BP, Chrys., so W.H., marg.; retained by Weiss (Wendt doubtful). η
omitted in אABCDE 13, 61; so Tisch., W.H., Hilg. text, R.V. (omitted also in LXX).
την ημεραν, article omitted by א*BD; so Tisch., W.H., Weiss, Wendt, Hilg.

ver. 17, sed iidem servi Dei," Bengel. According to Maimonides, no slave could be a prophet, but as in Christ there was neither Jew nor Gentile, neither male nor female, so in Him there was neither bond nor free (see also Keil, *in loco*). — **καὶ προφητεύσουσι**: an explanatory addition of the speaker, or an interpolation from ver. 17, not found either in Hebrew or LXX.

Ver. 19. The word **σημεῖα** is wanting in the Hebrew and the LXX, but the co-ordination of the two words **τέρας** and **σημεῖον** is frequent in the N.T. (John iv. 48, Acts iv. 30, Rom. xv. 19, 2 Cor. xii. 12), and even more so in the LXX (Exod. vii. 3, 9, Deut. iv. 34, Neh. ix. 10, Dan. vi. 27), so also in Josephus, Philo, Plutarch, Polybius. For the distinction between the words in the N.T., see below on ver. 22. **τέρας** is often used of some startling portent, or of some strange appearance in the heavens, so here fitly used of the sun being turned into darkness, etc. But God's **τέρατα** are always to those who have eyes to see, and significantly in the N.T. the former word is never found without the latter. It is no doubt true to say that St. Peter had already received a sign from heaven above in the **ἦχος ἐκ τοῦ οὐρανοῦ**, and a sign upon the earth below in the **λαλεῖν ἑτέραις γλώσσαις** (Nösgen), but the whole context, vv. 19-21, shows that St. Peter's thoughts had passed from the day of Pentecost to a period of grace and warning which should precede the Parousia. No explanation, therefore, of the words which limits their fulfilment to the Pentecostal Feast (see Keil, *in loco*, and also his reference to the interpretation of the Rabbis) is satisfactory.—**σημεῖα** is probably introduced into the text to emphasise the antithesis, as also are **ἄνω** and **κάτω**.— **αἷμα καὶ πῦρ**: if we see in these words **σημεῖα ἐπὶ τῆς γῆς κάτω**, there is no need to refer them to such startling phenomena as rain of blood, or fiery meteors, or pillars of smoke rising from the earth (so De Wette, Overbeck), but rather

to the bloodshed and devastation of war (so Holtzmann, Wendt, Felten); *cf.* our Lord's words, Matt. xxiv. 6, 29. Dean Plumptre thinks of the imagery as drawn from one of the great thunderstorms of Palestine, and *cf.* Weber, *Jüdische Theologie*, pp. 350, 351 (1897).

Ver. 20. For similar prophetic imagery taken from the startling phenomena of an eclipse in Palestine, *cf.* Isaiah xiii. 10, Ezek. xxxii. 7, Amos viii. 9.—**πρὶν ἢ ἐλθεῖν**. The LXX omit **ἤ**, and Weiss contends that this is the reason of its omission here in so many MSS. Weiss retains it as in vii. 2, xxv. 16; *cf.* also Luke ii. 26 (but doubtful). Blass omits it here, but retains it in the other two passages cited from Acts: "Ionicum est non Atticum"; *cf.* Viteau, *Le Grec du N. T.*, p. 130 (1893).—**τὴν ἡμέραν Κυρίου**. It is most significant that in the Epistles of the N.T. this O.T. phrase used of Jehovah is constantly applied to the Coming of Jesus Christ to judgment; *cf.* 1 Thess. v. 2, 1 Cor. i. 8, 2 Cor. i. 14, Phil. i. 10; Sabatier, *L'Apôtre Paul*, p. 104.—**καὶ ἐπιφανῆ**: if the word is to be retained, it means a day manifest to all as being what it claims to be, Vulgate *manifestus*, "clearly visible"; Luke xvii. 24; also 1 Tim. vi. 14, 2 Thess. ii. 8, where the word **ἐπιφάνεια** is used of the Parousia (*cf.* Prayer-Book, "the Epiphany *or* Manifestation of Christ to the Gentiles").

But in the Hebrew the word הַנּוֹרָא

= "terrible," not "clearly visible," and the LXX here, as elsewhere, Hab. i. 7, Mal. i. 14 (Judges xiii. 6, A.), etc., has failed to give a right derivation of the word which it connects with רָאָה,

to see, instead of with יָרֵא, to fear

(Niph. נוֹרָא and Part., as here, "terrible"). Zöckler holds that the LXX read not הַנּוֹרָא, but הַנּוֹדָא.

see
Addenda.
p. 290.

Vol. I.

ἐλθεῖν τὴν ἡμέραν Κυρίου τὴν μεγάλην καὶ ἐπιφανῆ.[1] 21. καὶ ἔσται,
πᾶς ὃς ἂν ἐπικαλέσηται τὸ ὄνομα Κυρίου σωθήσεται." 22. Ἄνδρες
Ἰσραηλῖται,[2] ἀκούσατε τοὺς λόγους τούτους · Ἰησοῦν τὸν Ναζωραῖον,
ἄνδρα ἀπὸ τοῦ Θεοῦ ἀποδεδειγμένον εἰς ὑμᾶς δυνάμεσι καὶ τέρασι

[1] ἐπιφανη ABCEP, Vulg., Chrys., W.H., Weiss, R.V. ; but om. אD, Gig., so
Tisch., Wendt, Hilg., Blass, who adds " del. igitur et in α, et fort. omnino per locum
4-14 (i.e., vv. 17-20) forma α male interpolata ".

[2] Ισραηλιται P ; Ισραηλειται אABCDE, so Tisch., W.H., Weiss.

Ver. 21. ἐπικαλέσηται τὸ ὄνομα, the
usual LXX rendering of a common Hebrew phrase. The expression is derived
from the way in which prayers addressed
to God begin with the invocation of the
divine name, Psalm iii. 2, vi. 2, etc., and
a similar phrase is found in classical
writers, ἐπικαλεῖσθαι τοὺς θεούς, Xen.,
Cyr., vii., 1., 35 ; Plat., Tim., p. 27, c. ;
Polyb., xv., 1, 13. From this it was an
easy step to use the phrase as meaning
the worshippers of the one God, Gen.
iv. 26, xii. 8, 2 Kings v. 4. It is therefore significant that the Christian converts at Corinth are described by the
same phrase, 1 Cor. i. 2. But just as in
Rom. x. 12 this same prophecy of Joel
is beyond all doubt referred by St. Paul
to the Lord Jesus, so here the whole
drift of St. Peter's speech, that the same
Jesus who was crucified was made both
Lord and Christ, points to the same conclusion, ii. 36. In Joel Κύριος is undoubtedly used of the Lord Jehovah, and
the word is here transferred to Christ.
In its bearing on our Lord's Divinity
this fact is of primary importance, for it
is not merely that the early Christians
addressed their Ascended Lord so many
times by the same name which is used
of Jehovah in the LXX—although it is
certainly remarkable that in 1 Thess.
the name is applied to Christ more than
twenty times—but that they did not
hesitate to refer to Him the attributes
and the prophecies which the great prophets of the Jewish nation had associated
with the name of Jehovah, Zahn, Skizzen
aus dem Leben der alten Kirche, pp. 8,
10, 16 (1894), and for the force of the expression, ἐπικ. τὸ ὄνομα, in 1 Cor. i. 2,
see Harnack, History of Dogma, i., p.
29, E.T.—ὃς ἂν ἐπικ., "whosoever": it
would seem that in St. Peter's address
the expression does not extend beyond
the chosen people ; cf. v. 36.—σωθήσεται : to the Jew salvation would
mean safety in the Messianic kingdom,
and from the penalties of the Messianic
judgment ; for the Christian there would

be a partial fulfilment in the flight of the
believers to Pella for safety when the
Son of Man came in the destruction of
Jerusalem ; but the word carries our
thoughts far beyond any such subordinate
fulfilment to the fulness of blessing for
body and soul which the verb expresses
on the lips of Christ ; cf. Luke vii. 50.
And so St. Luke places in the forefront
of Acts as of his Gospel the thought of
Jesus not only as the Messiah, but also
as the Σωτήρ, Luke ii. 14 ; cf. Psalms of
Sol., iv., 2 (Ryle and James).
Ver. 22. Ἰσραηλῖται : the tone of St.
Peter throughout is that of a man who
would win and not repulse his hearers, cf.
v. 29, and so he commences the second
part of his speech, in proof that Jesus was
both Lord and Christ, with a title full
of honour, reminding his hearers of their
covenant relation with God, and preparing them for the declaration that the
covenant was not broken but confirmed
in the person of Jesus.—Ἰ. τὸν Ναζ.,
"the Nazarene," the same word (not
Ναζαρηνός) formed part of the inscription
on the Cross, and it is difficult to believe
with Wendt that there is no reference to
this in St. Peter's words (cf. προσπήξαντες, vv. 23 and 36), although no
doubt the title was often used as a
description of Jesus in popular speech,
iv. 10, xxvi. 9. No contrast could be
greater than between Ἰησοῦς the despised Nazarene (ὁ Ν. οὗτος, vi. 14)
dying a felon's death, and Ἰησοῦς
Χριστός, v. 38, ὑψωθείς, v. 33, no longer
upon the Cross, but at a seat on the
right hand of the Father (cf. John xii.
12) ; again the marvellous change which
had passed over St. Peter is apparent :
"If Christ had not risen," argues St.
Chrysostom, "how account for the fact
that those who fled whilst He was alive,
now dared a thousand perils for Him
when dead ? St. Peter, who is struck
with fear by a servant-maid, comes
boldly forward" (so too Theophylact).—
ἄνδρα ἀποδεδειγ. ἀπὸ τοῦ Θεοῦ εἰς ὑμᾶς,
"a man approved of God unto you,"

καὶ σημείοις, οἷς ἐποίησε δι᾽ αὐτοῦ ὁ Θεὸς ἐν μέσῳ ὑμῶν, καθὼς καὶ [1]
αὐτοὶ οἴδατε, 23. τοῦτον τῇ ὡρισμένῃ βουλῇ καὶ προγνώσει τοῦ

[1] και αυτοι; but και om. in אABC*DE, Vulg. versions (Syr. Pesh.), Ir[int.], so Tisch., W.H., R.V., Weiss, Wendt.

R.V. The word, only used by St. Luke and St. Paul in the N.T. (cf. xxv. 7, 1 Cor. iv. 9, 2 Thess. ii. 4) = demonstrated, and "approved" in its old meaning would be a good equivalent; so in classical Greek, in Plato and Aristotle, shown by argument, proved, cf. xxv. 7. The sense of the word is given by the gloss in D δεδοκιμασμένον. It occurs in Esther ii. 9, AB, and iii. 13 (LXX), and several times in the Books of the Maccabees (see Hatch and Redpath, sub v.).—ἄνδρα: Erasmus commends the wisdom of Peter, "qui apud rudem multitudinem Christum magnifice laudat, sed virum tantum nominat, ut ex factis paullatim agnoscant Divinitatem".—ἀπό: probably here not simply for ὑπό (as Blass, and Felten, and others). The phrase means "a man demonstrated to have come unto you from God by mighty works," etc. If the words may not be pressed to mean our Lord's divine origin, they at least declare His divine mission (John iii. 2), divinitus (Wendt in loco).—δυνάμεσι καὶ τέρασι καὶ σημείοις: cf. 2 Cor. xii. 12, Heb. ii. 4, and 2 Thess. ii. 9; cf. Rom. xv. 19.—σημεῖα καὶ τέρατα: no less than eight times in Acts.—δυνάμεις is often rendered in a way which rather obscures its true form and meaning. Lit. = "powers," and so here in R.V. margin, where in the text we have "mighty works," so in Heb. ii. 4. St. Luke is fond of using δύναμις of the power inherent in Christ, and so the plural might well be used of the outward manifestations of this power in Christ, or through Him in His disciples. The word therefore seems in itself to point to the new forces at work in the world (Trench, N. T. Synonyms, ii., p. 177 ff.).—τέρατα: the word is never used in the N. T. alone as applied to our Lord's works or those of His disciples, and this observation made by Origen is very importaut, since the one word which might seem to suggest the prodigies and portents of the heathen world is never used unless in combination with some other word, which at once raises the N.T. miracles to a higher level. And so whilst the ethical purpose of these miracles is least apparent in the word τέρατα, it is brought

distinctly into view by the word with which τέρατα is so often joined—σημεῖα, a term which points in its very meaning to something beyond itself. Blass therefore is not justified in speaking of σημεῖα and τέρατα as synonymous terms. The true distinction between them lies in remembering that in the N.T. all three words mentioned in this passage have the same denotation but a different connotation—they are all used for miracles, but miracles regarded from different points of view (see Sanday and Headlam, Romans, p. 406).—οἷς ἐποίησεν . . . ὁ Θεός. The words, as Alford points out against De Wette, do not express a low view of our Lord's miracles. The favourite word used by St. John for the miracles of Christ, ἔργα, exactly corresponds to the phrase of St. Peter, since these ἔργα were the works of the Father Whom the Son revealed in them (cf. St. John v. 19, xiv. 10).—καθὼς καὶ αὐτοὶ οἴδατε: Weiss rightly draws attention to the emphatic pronoun. The fact of the miracles was not denied, although their source was so terribly misrepresented; cf. "Jesus Christ in the Talmud," Laible, E.T. (Streane), pp. 45-50 (1893).

Ver. 23. τοῦτον, emphatic, ἔκδοτον delivered up, by Judas, not by God; only here in the N.T., but see instances from Josephus, also from classical Greek, in Wetstein. In Dan., Theod., Bel and the Dragon ver. 22.—ὡρισμένῃ βουλῇ: both favourite words of St. Luke: ὡρισ. used by him five times in the Acts, x. 42, xi. 29, xvii. 26, 31; once by St. Paul, Rom. i. 4; once in Hebrews, iv. 7, and only in St. Luke amongst the Evangelists, xxii. 22, where our Lord Himself speaks of the events of His betrayal by the same word, κατὰ τὸ ὡρισμένον (cf. xxiv. 26).—βουλῇ: Wendt compares the Homeric Διὸς δ᾽ ἐτελείετο βουλή. The phrase βουλή τοῦ Θ. is used only by St. Luke; once in his Gospel, vii. 30, and three times in Acts, xiii. 36, xx. 27 (whilst βουλή is used twice in the Gospel, eight times in the Acts, and only three times elsewhere in the N.T., 1 Cor. iv. 5, Ephes. i. 11, Heb. vi. 17), but cf. Wisdom vi. 4, ix. 13, and often ἡ βουλή Κυρίου in LXX.—προγνώσει: the word is only found again in 1 Peter i. 2, and its

Θεοῦ ἔκδοτον λαβόντες,[1] διὰ χειρῶν ἀνόμων προσπήξαντες ἀνείλετε · 24. ὃν ὁ Θεὸς ἀνέστησε, λύσας τὰς ὠδῖνας τοῦ θανάτου,[2] καθότι οὐκ

[1] λαβοντες om. ℵ*ABC 61, Vulg., Sah., Boh., Syr. Pesh., Arm., Aeth., Ath., Irint., Victorin.; so Tisch., W.H., R.V., Weiss— but omitted by Blass in β although found in Dℵ³EC³P, Syr. Harcl., Eus., Chrys.; Hilg. retains. χειρων; but χειρος in ℵABC*D 13, 15, 61, Syr. Harcl., Aeth., Eus., Ath., Cyr., so Tisch., W.H., R.V., Weiss, Wendt, Hilg. (plural probably out of the following ανομων). ανειλετε minusc., but ανειλατε ℵABCDEP, so Tisch., W.H., Weiss—see W.H., Appendix, p. 172, and Winer-Schmiedel, p. 112.

[2] θανατου ℵABCEP, Syr. Harcl., Sah., Arm., Aeth., Eus., Ath., Cyr., Theodrt.; so Tisch., W.H., Wendt, Weiss. ᾳδου D, Vulg., Syr. Pesh., Boh., Gig., Par., Polyc., Epiph., Irenint.—similar var. l. in 1 Cor. xv., 55, cf. Ps. xvii. (xviii.) 5, 6; ᾳδου out of ver. 27, 31 (Wendt).

occurrence in that place, and the thoughts which it expresses, may be classed amongst the points of contact between Acts and 1 Peter (see at end of chap. iii.). In the Passion and Resurrection of Christ, which at one time seemed to Peter impossible, cf. Matt. xvi. 22, he now sees the full accomplishment of God's counsel, cf. iii. 20, and 1 Peter i. 20 (Nösgen, Apostelgeschichte, p. 53, and also 48-52). In this spiritual insight now imparted to the Apostle we see a further proof of the illuminating power of the Holy Ghost, the gift of Pentecost, which he himself so emphatically acknowledges in his first epistle (i. 1-12).—διὰ χειρῶν, best explained as a Hebraism. Cf. for the frequent use of this Hebraistic expression, Blass, Grammatik des N. G., pp. 126, 127; and Simcox, Language of the N. T., p. 141. In the LXX, cf. 2 Kings xiv. 27, 1 Chron. xi. 3, xxix. 5. St. Luke is very fond of these paraphrases with πρόσωπον and χείρ, see Friedrich, Das Lukasevangelium, pp. 8, 9, and Lekebusch, Apostelgeschichte, p. 77; cf. v. 12, vii. 25, xi. 30, xiv. 3, xv. 23, xix. 11, so ἐν χειρί, εἰς χεῖρας.—ἀνόμων: "lawless," R.V., generally taken to refer to the Roman soldiers who crucified our Lord, i.e., Gentiles without law, as in 1 Cor. ix. 21, Rom. ii. 14. In Wisdom xvii. 2 the same word is used of the Egyptians who thought to oppress the holy nation—they are described as ἄνομοι. —προσπήξαντες, sc., τῷ σταυρῷ: a graphic word used only here, with which we may compare the vivid description also by St. Peter in v. 29-32, x. 39, cf. 1 Peter ii. 24—the language of one who could justly claim to be a witness of the sufferings of Christ, 1 Peter v. 1. The word is not found in LXX, cf. Dio Cassius.—ἀνείλατε: an Alexandrian form, see for similar instances, Kennedy,

Sources of N. T. Greek, pp. 159, 160. The verb is a favourite with St. Luke, nineteen times in Acts, twice in the Gospel, and only once elsewhere in the Evangelists, viz., Matt. ii. 16, and the noun ἀναίρεσις is only found in Acts viii. 10 (xxii. 20), cf. its similar use in classical Greek and in the LXX. The fact that St. Peter thus describes the Jewish people as the actual murderers of Jesus is not a proof that in such language we have an instance of anti-Judaism quite inconsistent with the historical truth of the speech (Baur, Renan, Overbeck), but the Apostle sees vividly before his eyes essentially the same crowd at the Feast as had demanded the Cross of Jesus before the judgment-seat of Pilate, Nösgen, Apostelgeschichte, p. 103.—ὃν ὁ Θεὸς ἀνέστησε, "est hoc summum orationis," Blass, cf. v. 32, and i. 22.

Ver 24. λύσας τὰς ὠδῖνας τοῦ θαν.: R.V. "pangs" instead of "pains" (all previous versions) approaches nearer to the literal form of the word—"birth-pangs," the resurrection of Christ being conceived of as a birth out of death, as the Fathers interpreted the passage. The phrase is found in the Psalms, LXX xvii. 4, cxiv. 3, but it is most probable that the LXX has here mistaken the force of the Hebrew חבל which might mean "birth-pangs," or the cords of a hunter catching his prey. In the Hebrew version the parallelism, such a favourite figure in Hebrew poetry, decides in favour of the latter meaning, as in R.V. Ps. xviii. 4, 5 (LXX xvii.), Sheol and Death are personified as hunters lying in wait for their prey with nooses and nets (Kirkpatrick, Psalms, in loco, the word מוֹקֵשׁ meaning snares by which birds or beasts are taken (Amos iii. 5)). In

ἦν δυνατὸν κρατεῖσθαι αὐτὸν ὑπ' αὐτοῦ. 25. Δαβὶδ γὰρ λέγει εἰς αὐτὸν, "Προωρώμην[1] τὸν Κύριον ἐνώπιόν μου διὰ παντός· ὅτι ἐκ δεξιῶν μού ἐστιν, ἵνα μὴ σαλευθῶ· 26. διὰ τοῦτο εὐφράνθη ἡ καρδία

---

[1] προωρωμην B³P; προορ. אAB*CDE, so Tisch., W.H., Weiss, Wendt, Hilg. (see Winer-Schmiedel, p. 101).

---

the previous verse the parallelism is also maintained if we read "the waves of death" (cf. 2 Sam. xxii. 5) "compassed me, the *floods* of ungodliness made me afraid". It is tempting to account for the reading ὠδῖνας by supposing that St. Luke had before him a source for St. Peter's speech, and that he had given a mistaken rendering of the word חֶבְלִ. But it would certainly seem that λύσας and κρατεῖσθαι are far more applicable to the idea of the hunter's cords, in which the Christ could not be bound, since He was Himself the Life. A similar mistake in connection with the same Hebrew word חֶבְל may possibly occur in 1 Thess. v. 3 and Luke xxi. 34. There is no occasion to find in the word any reference to the death-pains of Christ (so Grotius, Bengel), or to render ὠδῖνες *pains* and *snares* (Olshausen, Nösgen), and it is somewhat fanciful to explain with St. Chrysostom (so Theophylact and Oecumenius) ὁ θάνατος ὤδινε κατέχων αὐτὸν καὶ τὰ δεινὰ ἔπασχε.—καθότι: only found in St. Luke, in Gospel twice, and in Acts four times (Friedrich); generally in classical Greek καθ' ὅ τι (cf. Tobit i. 12, xiii. 4).—οὐκ ἦν δυνατὸν ... γὰρ: the words primarily refer to the proof which St. Peter was about to adduce from prophecy, and the Scripture could not be broken. But whilst Baur sees in such an expression, as also in iii. 15, a transition to Johannine conceptions of the Person of Jesus, every Christian gladly recognises in the words the moral impossibility that the Life could be holden by Death. On the impersonal construction, see Viteau, *Le Grec du N. T.*, p. 151 (1893). — κρατεῖσθαι ... ὑπ', *cf.* Luke xxiv. 16 (John xx. 23), only in these passages in passive voice in N.T., but *cf.* for similar use of the passive voice, 4 Macc. ii. 9, and so in Dem. Schmid compares this verse where the internal necessity of Christ's resurrection is thus stated with 1 Peter iii. 18, showing that the πνεῦμα in Him possessed this power of life (*Biblische Theologie des N. T.*, p. 402).

Ver. 25. Δανεὶδ γὰρ λέγει: the words which follow are quoted by St. Peter from Psalm xvi.; and it has been said that the Apostle's argument would be the same if the Psalm were the work of some other author than David. But if the following Psalm and the Psalm in question may with considerable reason be attributed to the same author, and if the former Psalm, the seventeenth, may be referred to the period of David's persecution by Saul, then David's authorship of Psalm sixteen becomes increasingly probable (Kirkpatrick). In Delitzsch's view whatever can mark a Psalm as Davidic we actually find combined here, *e.g.*, coincidences of many kinds which he regards as undoubtedly Davidic (cf. v. 5 with xi. 6, v. 10 with iv. 4, v. 11 with xvii. 15), and he sees no reason for giving up the testimony afforded by the title. But it is plain that David's experience did not exhaust the meaning of the Psalm, and St. Peter in the fulness of the gift of Pentecost interprets the words εἰς αὐτὸν, "with reference to Him," *i.e.*, the Messiah (*cf.* St. Paul's interpretation of the same Psalm in xiii. 35). On the application of the Psalm as Messianic, *cf.* Edersheim, *Jesus the Messiah*, ii., p. 717.—Προωρώμην: not "I foresaw," but "I beheld the Lord always before my face," LXX; Heb., "I have set the Lord always before me".—Κύριον = Jehovah.—ἐκ δεξιῶν μου: as a defence and helper. *Cf.* παραστάτης, Xen., *Cyr.*, iii., 3, 21. The imagery may be taken from that of the trials in which advocates stood at the right hand of their clients (Psalm cix. 31), or there may be a reference to a champion who, in defending another, would stand on his right hand; *cf.* Psalm cx. 5, cxxi. 5 (Kirkpatrick, and Robertson Smith, *Expositor*, 1876, p. 351).—ἵνα μὴ σαλευθῶ: although the verses which follow contain the chief Messianic references in St. Peter's interpretation, yet in the fullest sense of the words the Christ could say προωρ. κ.τ.λ. (see Felten, *in loco*). But because the Father was with Him, He could add διὰ τοῦτο εὐφράνθη ἡ καρδία μου: "the heart" in O.T. is not only the heart of the affections, but the centre of the man's whole moral and intellectual nature (Oehler, *Theol. des A.T.*, p. 71).—εὐφράνθη

μου, καὶ ἠγαλλιάσατο ἡ γλῶσσά μου · ἔτι δὲ καὶ ἡ σάρξ μου κατα-
σκηνώσει ἐπ' ἐλπίδι · 27. ὅτι οὐκ ἐγκαταλείψεις τὴν ψυχήν μου εἰς

refers rather to a joyous state of mind, "was glad," R.V., ἠγαλλιάσατο used of outward and active expression of joy is rendered "rejoiced," R.V. (in A.V. the meaning of the two verbs is transposed). At the same time εὐφράνθη is sometimes used in LXX and N.T., as in modern Greek of *festive* enjoyment, Kennedy, *Sources of N. T. Greek*, p. 155.—ἡ γλῶσσά μου : in Hebrew כְּבוֹדִי "my glory," *i.e.*, my soul, my spirit (*cf.* Gen. xlix. 6, Schöttgen). The Arabs use a similar expression for the eye, the hand, or any member of the body held in special honour (*cf.* Lumby on Psalm cviii. 1).— ἔτι δὲ καὶ ἡ σάρξ : *flesh* does not here mean the dead corpse but the living body (Perowne, Kirkpatrick).—κατασ-κηνώσει, "shall dwell in safety," R.V., "confidently," margin (O.T.); the expression is used frequently of dwelling safely in the Promised Land. In N.T. the R.V. translates "shall dwell," "tabernacle" margin, shall dwell as in a tent, a temporary abode. In its *literal* meaning, therefore, there is no reference to the rest of the body in the grave, or to the hope of resurrection from the grave, but the words must be understood of *this life* (Perowne); *cf.* Deut. xxxiii. 12, 28, Psalm iv. 8, xxv. 13, Jer. xxiii. 6, xxxiii. 16. For the hope of the Psalmist, expressed in the following words, is primarily for preservation from death : "Thou wilt not give up my soul to Sheol [*i.e.*, to the underworld, so that one becomes its prey], neither wilt thou suffer thy beloved one [singular] to see the pit" (so Delitzsch and Perowne, as also R. Smith and Kirkpatrick). Ver. 27. In LXX and N.T. rightly εἰς ᾅδην. W.H.; *cf.* also Briggs, *Messianic Prophecies*, p. 24; although in T.R. as usually in Attic, εἰς ᾅδου, *sc.*, δόμον. Blass regards εἰς as simply usurping in the common dialect the place of ἐν, but we can scarcely explain the force of the preposition here in this way. ἐγκαταλείψεις used of utter abandonment, *cf.* Psalm xxii. 1 (*cf.* 2 Tim. iv. 10, 16).—εἰς ᾅδην or whilst it is true that the Psalmist "says nothing about what shall happen to him *after* death" (Perowne), he expresses his conviction that his soul would not be given up to the land of gloom and forgetfulness, the abode of the dead, dark and cheerless,

with which the Psalmist cannot associate the thought of life and light (see also on ver. 31).—οὐδὲ δώσεις : in R.V. (O.T.) the word "suffer" is retained, but in R.V. (N.T.) we find "thou wilt not give," the Hebrew נָתַן being used in this sense to permit, to suffer, to let, like δίδωμι and *dare*, Viteau, *Le Grec du N. T.*, p. 156 (1893).—τὸν ὅσιόν σου : the Hebrew *Chāsīd* which is thus sometimes translated in the LXX (Vulgate, *Sanctus*) is often rendered "thy beloved one," and the word denotes not only one who is godly and pious, but also one who is the object of Jehovah's loving-kindness. The word might well be used of Him, Who was not only the Holy One of God, but ὁ ἀγαπητὸς υἱός, "the beloved Son". On the word *Chāsīd* see Kirkpatrick, *Psalms*, Appendix, p. 221.—ἰδεῖν διαφθοράν : "corruption" or "the pit," margin R.V. (O.T.), but in the N.T. simply "corruption" (A. and R.V.), Vulgate, *corruptio*. In the LXX the Hebrew שַׁחַת is often rendered διαφθορά, "corruption," as if derived from שַׁחַת διαφθείρειν, "to corrupt"; not, however, in the sense of corruption, putridity, but of destruction. The derivation however is probably from שׁוּחַ, to sink down, hence it means a pit, and sometimes a sepulchre, a grave, Psalm xxx. 10, lv. 24, so here "to see the grave," *i.e.*, to die and be buried, *cf.* Psalm xlix. 10 (see Robinson's *Gesenius*, p. 1053, note, twenty-sixth edition). Dr. Robertson Smith maintains that there are two Hebrew words the same in form but different in origin, one masculine = *putrefaction* or *corruption*, the other feminine = the *deep* or the *pit*. So far he agrees with the note in *Gesenius*, *u.s.*, that the word διαφθορά should here be rendered by the latter, the *pit*, but he takes the rendering, the *deep* or the *pit*, as an epithet not of the grave but of Sheol or Hades (see *Expositor*, p. 354, 1876, the whole paper on "The Sixteenth Psalm," by Dr. R. Smith, should be consulted, and p. 354 compared with the note in *Gesenius*), and this view certainly seems to fit in better with the parallelism.

ᾅδου,[1] οὐδὲ δώσεις τὸν ὅσιόν σου ἰδεῖν διαφθοράν. 28. ἐγνώρισάς μοι ὁδοὺς ζωῆς· πληρώσεις με εὐφροσύνης μετὰ τοῦ προσώπου σου." 29. Ἄνδρες ἀδελφοί, ἐξὸν εἰπεῖν μετὰ παρρησίας πρὸς ὑμᾶς περὶ τοῦ πατριάρχου Δαβίδ, ὅτι καὶ ἐτελεύτησε καὶ ἐτάφη, καὶ τὸ μνῆμα

---

[1] ᾅδου EP, Chrys. (in LXX A) ; ᾅδην ℵABCD, Clem., Epiph., so Tisch., W.H., Weiss, Wendt (so in LXX B—τον αδην S[1]).

Ver. 28. ἐγνώρισάς μοι ὁδοὺς ζωῆς : St. Peter quotes from the LXX, which has the plural ὁδούς—so in Proverbs v. 6, where Hebrew has the same word as here in the singular, the LXX translates ὁδοὺς ζωῆς.—μετὰ τοῦ προσώπου σου, " with thy countenance " = " in thy presence," margin ; = Hebrew, " in thy presence ". The LXX πρόσωπον is a literal translation of the Hebrew פָּנִים, face or countenance, in the O.T. The expression is a common one in the O.T., " in God's presence " ; cf. Psalm iv. 6, xvii. 15, xxi. 6, cxl. 13. Grimm-Thayer explains (με) ὄντα μετά, etc., " being in thy presence " (see sub μετά, i. 2 b). The force of the expression is strikingly seen in its repeated use in Numbers vi. 25 ; cf. Exodus xxxiii. 14 ; Oehler, Theologie des A. T., pp. 46, 56, 62, and Westcott, Hebrews, p. 272. And so the Psalm ends as it had begun with God ; cf. ver. 2, and ver. 11. The Psalmist's thoughts carried him beyond mere temporal deliverance, beyond the changes and chances of this mortal life, to the assurance of a union with God, which death could not dissolve ; while as Christians we read with St. Peter a deeper and a fuller meaning still in the words, as we recall the Life, Death, Resurrection, and Ascension of Him, of Whom it was written : ὁ λόγος σὰρξ ἐγένετο καὶ ἐσκήνωσεν ἐν ἡμῖν. Ver. 29. ἄνδρες ἀδελφοί : an affectionate form of address as compared with vv. 14 and 22 (cf. vii. 2, xxii. 1), but still much more formal than iii. 17, where we have ἀδελφοί alone in St. Peter's pity for those who crucifying the Saviour knew not what they did.—ἐξὸν, sc., ἐστι (with infinitive), cf. 2 Cor. xii. 4, only in N.T. Viteau, Le Grec du N. T., p. 200 (1893), cf. LXX Esther iv. 2 ; 4 Macc. v. 18 ; not " may I speak unto you," but " I may say unto you," R.V., not ἔστω, but ἐστί (ἔξεστι), Wendt, in loco.—μετὰ παρρησίας : on the phrase, see below, iv. 13, and its repeated use by St. Luke ; cf. Heb. iv. 16 ; Lat., cum fiducia, Westcott, Hebrews, p. 108. In the LXX

the phrase is found, Lev. xxvi. 13, Esther viii. 12, 1 Macc. iv. 18, 3 Macc. iv. 1, vii. 12. St. Peter will first of all state facts which cannot be denied, before he proceeds to show how the words used of David are fulfilled in " great David's greater Son ". He speaks of David in terms which indicate his respect for his name and memory, and as Bengel well says, " est igitur hoc loco προθεραπεία, praevia sermonis mitigatio " (" est haec προθερ. ut aiunt rhetores," Blass, in loco). —τοῦ πατριάρχου, the name is emphatically used in the N.T. of Abraham ; cf. Heb. vii. 4 (properly the ἄρχων (auctor), πατριᾶς), and of the sons of Jacob, Acts vii. 8, 9, and cf. 4 Macc. vii. 19, used of Abraham, Isaac and Jacob. In the LXX it is used of the " heads of the fathers' houses," 1 Chron. ix. 9, xxiv. 31, in a comparatively lower sense. Here used, as a term of high honour, of David, regarded as the ancestor of the kingly race. See on the word and its formation, Kennedy, Sources of New Testament Greek, p. 114.—ὅτι καὶ ἐτελεύτησε καὶ ἐτάφη : " that he both died and was buried," R.V. St. Peter states notorious facts, and refers to them in a way which could not wound the susceptibilities of his hearers, whilst he shows them that David's words were not exhausted in his own case. The argument is practically the same as that of St. Paul in xiii. 36 from the same Psalm.—καὶ τὸ μνῆμα αὐτοῦ ἐστιν ἐν ἡμῖν, i.e., in Jerusalem, the mention of the tomb emphasises the fact and certainty of the death of David, and implies that his body had seen corruption. That David's tomb was shown in the time of Nehemiah we know from Neh. iii. 16. From Jos., Ant., vii., 15, 3 ; xiii., 8, 4 ; B. J., i., 2, 5, we learn that Solomon had buried a large treasure in the tomb, and that on that account one of its chambers had been broken open by Hyrcanus, and another by Herod the Great. According to Jos., Ant., xvi., 7, 1, Herod, not content with rifling the tomb, desired to penetrate further, even as far as the bodies of David and Solomon, but a flame burst

αὐτοῦ ἐστιν ἐν ἡμῖν ἄχρι τῆς ἡμέρας ταύτης. 30. προφήτης οὖν
ὑπάρχων, καὶ εἰδὼς ὅτι ὅρκῳ ὤμοσεν αὐτῷ ὁ Θεός, ἐκ καρποῦ τῆς
ὀσφύος αὐτοῦ τὸ κατὰ σάρκα ἀναστήσειν τὸν Χριστόν,[1] καθίσαι ἐπὶ
τοῦ θρόνου αὐτοῦ, 31. προϊδὼν ἐλάλησε περὶ τῆς ἀναστάσεως τοῦ
Χριστοῦ, ὅτι οὐ κατελείφθη[2] ἡ ψυχὴ αὐτοῦ εἰς ᾅδου, οὐδὲ ἡ σὰρξ

[1] το κατα σ. . . . τον Χ. om. ℵABCD² 61, Vulg., good versions, Eus., Cypr.,
Irenint., so Tisch., W.H., R.V., Weiss, Wendt (rejects as a marginal gloss, so Alford);
but although a *similar* reading is found in DE Blass does not receive it in his β text
(see Weiss on Codex D, p. 57). οσφυος, D reads καρδιας; Gig., Par., Syr. Pesh.,
so Hilg., Iren. κοιλιας (*ventris*); so in β (LXX Ps. cxxxi. 11, S²R).

[2] εγκατελειφθη ℵBCDE, Eus., Chrys., Theodrt., so Tisch., W.H., Weiss, Wendt,
εν. A (alt. in W.H.), too well testified to suppose that it is simply derived from ver. 27
(Wendt). ᾳδου ACDEP, Chrys., Lach. ; αδην ℵB, Eus., Thaum., so Tisch., W.H.,
Wendt, Weiss. η ψυχη αυτου om. ℵABC*D 61, 81, Syr. Pesh., Boh., Sah., Aeth.,
Eus., Irenint., Didint., Victorin. so Tisch., W.H., R.V., Weiss, Wendt (from ver. 27,
so also ου . . . ουδε, instead of ουτε . . . ουτε. ουδε; but ουτε ℵACD, Eus.,
Chrys., Cyr., so Tisch., W.H., Wendt; but Weiss ουτε . . . ουδε, following B).

forth and slew two of his guards, and the
king fled. To this attempt the Jewish
historian attributed the growing troubles
in Herod's family. In the time of
Hadrian the tomb is said to have fallen
into ruins. Whatever its exact site, it
must have been within the walls, and
therefore could not correspond with the
so-called "tombs of the kings" which
De Saulcy identified with it. Those
tombs are outside the walls, and are of the
Roman period (Schürer, *Jewish People*,
div. i., vol. i., p. 276, E.T., "David,"
B.D.²). Wetstein, *in loco*, quotes the testimony of Maundrell as to the sepulchres of
David and his family being the only
sepulchres within the walls. St. Jerome,
Epist., xlvi., writing to Marcella, expresses a hope that they might pray together in the mausoleum of David; so
that at the end of the fourth century
tradition must still have claimed to mark
the spot.
Ver. 30. προφήτης: as David could
not have spoken this Psalm of himself,
he spoke it of some other, who was none
other than the Messiah—here the word
is used in the double sense of one
declaring God's will, and also of one
foretelling how that will would be fulfilled.—ὑπάρχων: another favourite word
of St. Luke, in his Gospel, and especially
in Acts; in the former it is found seven
times, and in the latter no less than
twenty-four times, and in all parts (excluding τὰ ὑπάρχοντα), Friedrich, *Das
Lucasevangelium*, p. 7. It is not used
by the other Evangelists. In the N.T.,
as in later Greek, it is often weakened
into an equivalent of εἶναι; Blass, *Gram-*

matik des N. G., p. 239. Here it may
indicate that David was a prophet, not
only in this one instance, but constantly
with reference to the Messiah.—ὅρκῳ
ὤμοσεν, Hebraistic; *cf.* ver. 17. Viteau,
Le Grec du N. T., p. 141 (1896); for the
oath *cf.* Ps. cxxxii. 11, 2 Sam. vii. 16.—
ἐκ καρποῦ τῆς ὀσφύος αὐτοῦ, *i.e.*, of
his offspring. It is a common Hebraistic
form of expression—ὀσφύς read here,
but κοιλία in Ps. cxxxi. 11 (LXX); *cf.*
Gen. xxxv. 11 and 2 Chron. vi. 9 (Heb.
vii. 5). With regard to the human element in the Person of Jesus, Peter speaks
of him as a descendant of David according to prophecy, as in the Synoptists and
Rom. i. 3 (Schmid). The exact expression, καρπὸς τῆς ὀσφύος, is not found in
the LXX, but καρ. τῆς κοιλίας is found,
not only in the Psalm quoted but in
Mic. vi. 7 (Lam. ii. 20), where the same
Hebrew words are used as in the Psalm:
ὀσφύς in the LXX is several times a translation of another Hebrew word חֲלָצִים
(dual). This partitive construction
(supply τινα) is also a Hebraistic mode
of expression, and frequent in the LXX;
cf. ii. 18, v. 2. See Viteau, *Le Grec
du N. T.*, p. 151 (1896).
Ver. 31. προϊδών, *cf.* Gal. iii. 8.
The word ascribes prophetic consciousness to David in the composition of the
Psalm, but, as we learn from St. Peter
himself, that prophetic consciousness did
not involve a distinct knowledge of the
events foretold (1 Pet. i. 10-12); that
which the Holy Ghost presignified was
only in part clear to the prophets, both
as to the date of fulfilment and also as

αὐτοῦ εἶδε διαφθοράν. 32. τοῦτον τὸν Ἰησοῦν ἀνέστησεν ὁ Θεός,
οὗ πάντες ἡμεῖς ἐσμεν μάρτυρες. 33. τῇ δεξιᾷ οὖν τοῦ Θεοῦ
ὑψωθεὶς, τήν τε ἐπαγγελίαν τοῦ Ἁγίου Πνεύματος[1] λαβὼν παρὰ τοῦ

[1] τοῦ Ἁγ. Πν.; but τὸν πν. τὸν αγ. ℵABCE 13, 61, 130, Vulg., Chrys., so W.H.;
Weiss; but TR. in DP, Ir int., and accepted by Blass in β and by Hilg.

to historical shaping (Schmid, *Biblische Theol. des N. T.*, p. 395, and Alford, *in loco*).—ὅτι: introducing the words which follow as a fuller explanation, or simply as expressing a well-known fact.—ἐγκατελείφθη ... εἶδεν: aorists, not futures, because from St. Peter's standpoint the prophecy had been already fulfilled (Felten, Wendt). With this verse we naturally compare the mention of Christ's descent into Hades and His agency in the realms of the dead in St. Peter's First Epistle, iii. 19 (*cf.* Phil. ii. 10, Ephes. iv. 9, Rom. x. 7; Zahn, *Das Apost. Symbolum*, pp. 71-74; but see also Schmid, *ubi supra*, p. 414). Thus while the words bore, as we have seen, a primary and lower reference to David himself, St. Peter was led by the Holy Ghost to see their higher and grander fulfilment in Christ.—εἰς ᾅδου: on the construction see above on ver. 27, and on the Jewish view of Sheol or Hades in the time of our Lord as an intermediate state, see Charles, *Book of Enoch*, p. 168 and p. 94, and compare also the interesting although indirect parallel to 1 Pet. iii. 19, which he finds in *The Book of the Secrets of Enoch*, p. xlv. ff.; Weber, *Jüdische Theologie*, pp. 163, 341.

Ver. 32. οὗ: may be masculine = Christ, *cf.* xiii. 31, but is taken as neuter by Blass (so too Overbeck, Holtzmann, Weiss, Wendt, Felten). Bengel remarks "nempe Dei qui id fecit," and compares v. 32, x. 41, and 1 Cor. xv. 15.

Ver. 33. οὖν: the Ascension is a necessary sequel to the Resurrection, *cf.* Weiss, *Leben Jesu*, iii., 409 ff. and *in loco*. Or the word may mark the result of the assured and manifold testimony to the Resurrection, to which the Apostle had just appealed: "Confirmata resurrectione Christi, ascensio non potest in dubium vocari," Bengel.—τῇ δεξιᾷ τοῦ Θεοῦ: best to take the words as an instrumental dative, so in v. 31, with the majority of recent commentators. On grammatical grounds it would be difficult to justify the rendering "*to the right hand*" (although taken in connection with v. 34 it would give very good sense), since such a combination of the dative alone is found only in the poets,

and never in prose in classical Greek. The only other instances adduced, Acts xxi. 16 and Rev. ii. 16, can be otherwise explained, *cf.* Winer-Moulton, xxxi., p. 268. On Judg. xi. 18 (LXX) quoted in support of the local rendering by Fritzsch, see Wendt's full note *in loco*. The instrumental meaning follows naturally upon ver. 32 — the Ascension, as the Resurrection, was the mighty deed of God, Phil. ii. 9. There is therefore no occasion to regard the expression with De Wette as a Hebraism, see Wetstein, *in loco*.— ὑψωθείς, *cf.* especially John xii. 32, and Westcott's note on John iii. 14. The word is frequently found in LXX. As Lightfoot points out, in our Lord Himself the divine law which He Himself had enunciated was fulfilled, ὁ ταπεινῶν ἑαυτὸν ὑψωθήσεται (Luke xiv. 11, xviii. 14).—τήν τε ἐπαγγελίαν τοῦ ἁγίου πνεύματος κ.τ.λ., see above on i. 4 (Gal. iii. 14). The language of St. Peter is in agreement with, but yet independent of, that in St. John, whilst it calmly certifies the fulfilment of our Lord's promise. — ἐξέχεε: "hath poured forth," R.V. All previous English versions except Rhem. = A.V. The verb is used in the LXX in the prophecy cited above, Joel ii. 28, 29 (*cf.* also Zech. xii. 10), although it is not used in the Gospels of the outpouring of the Spirit.— τοῦτο: either the Holy Ghost, as the Vulgate takes it, or an independent neuter "this which ye see and hear," *i.e.*, in the bearing and speech of the assembled Apostles. St. Peter thus leads his hearers to infer that that which is poured out is by its effects nothing else than the Holy Ghost. It is noteworthy that just as Joel speaks of God, the Lord Jehovah, pouring out of His Spirit, so the same divine energy is here attributed by St. Peter to Jesus. See above on ver. 17.

Ver. 34. St. Peter does not demand belief upon his own assertion, but he again appeals to the Scriptures, and to words which could not have received a fulfilment in the case of David. In this appeal he reproduces the very words in which, some seven weeks before, our Lord Himself had convicted the scribes of error in their interpretation of this

πατρὸς, ἐξέχεε[1] τοῦτο ὃ νῦν ὑμεῖς βλέπετε καὶ ἀκούετε. 34. οὐ γὰρ Δαβὶδ ἀνέβη εἰς τοὺς οὐρανούς, λέγει δὲ αὐτός, "Εἶπεν ὁ Κύριος τῷ κυρίῳ μου, Κάθου ἐκ δεξιῶν μου, 35. ἕως ἂν θῶ τοὺς ἐχθρούς σου ὑποπόδιον τῶν ποδῶν σου." 36. Ἀσφαλῶς οὖν γινωσκέτω πᾶς οἶκος Ἰσραὴλ ὅτι καὶ[2] Κύριον καὶ Χριστὸν αὐτὸν ὁ Θεὸς ἐποίησε, τοῦτον τὸν Ἰησοῦν ὃν ἡμεῖς ἐσταυρώσατε.

---

[1] After εξεχεε and before τουτο D (Par.) insert υμιν, and E, Syrr. (Pesh. and Harc), Sah. tol. demid., Ir., Did., Ambr., Par. *hoc donum*. Harris ascribes this second addition, though dubiously, to a Montanist; but *cf.* ver. 38, x. 45, xi. 17, although in these passages δωρεα, not δωρον, is used.

[2] και K.; και in all uncials, also Vulg., Syr. H., W.H., R.V., Weiss; *om.* by many cursives, also Syr. Pesh. και Χ. αυτον EP 61, Ath., Epiph.; αυτον και Χ. ℵABCD² 15, 18, 61, 130, Vulg., Arm., Bas., Ir^{int.}, so Tisch., W.H., R.V., Weiss.

same Psalm (Matt. xxii. 44, Mark xii. 35, Luke xx. 41), and, "unlearned" in the eyes of the scribes, had answered the question which they could not answer, how David's Son was also David's Lord. No passage of Scripture is so constantly referred to in the N.T. as this 110th Psalm, *cf.* references above, and also 1 Cor. xv. 25, Heb. i. 13, v. 6, vii. 17, 21, x. 13. The Psalm was always regarded as Messianic by the Jews (Weber, *Jüdische Theologie*, p. 357 (1897); Edersheim, *Jesus the Messiah*, ii., 720 (Appendix); Cheyne, *Origin of the Psalter*, p. 35; Driver, *Introduction to O. T.*, pp. 362, 363; and if it had not been so in the time of our Lord, it is obvious that His argument would have missed its point if those to whom He addressed His question "What think ye of the Christ?" could have answered that David was not speaking of the coming Messiah. For earlier interpretations of the Psalm, and the patristic testimony to its Messianic character, see *Speaker's Commentary*, iv., 427, and on the authorship see Gifford, *Authorship of the 110th Psalm*, with Appendix, 1895 (SPCK), and Delitzsch, *Psalms*, iii., pp. 163-176, E.T.—κάθου ἐκ δεξιῶν μου: κάθου contracted for κάθησο (*cf.* also Mark xii. 36, Heb. i. 13); this "popular" form, which is also found in the Fragments of the comic writers, is the present imperative of κάθημαι in modern Greek, Kennedy, *Sources of N. T. Greek*, p. 162. In the LXX it is frequently used (see Hatch and Redpath, *sub. v.*).—ἕως: the word does not imply that Christ shall cease to reign subsequently: the word here, as elsewhere, does not imply that what is expressed will *only* have place up to a certain time (*cf.* Gen. xxxiii. 15, Deut. vii. 4, 2 Chron. vi. 23; *cf.* 1 Tim. iv. 13), rather is it

true to say that Christ will only then rightly rule, when He has subjugated all His enemies.—ἂν with ἕως as here, where it is left doubtful *when* that will take place to which it is said a thing will continue (Grimm-Thayer, and instances *sub* ἕως, i., 1 *b*).—ὑποπόδιον, *cf.* Josh. x. 24, referring to the custom of conquering kings placing their feet upon the necks of their conquered enemies (so Blass, *in loco*, amongst recent commentators).

Ver. 36. ἀσφαλῶς: used here emphatically; the Apostle would emphasise the conclusion which he is about to draw from his three texts; *cf.* xxi. 34, xxii. 30, and Wisdom xviii. 6 (so in classical Greek).—πᾶς οἶκος Ἰσρ., without the article, for οἶκος Ἰ. is regarded as a proper name, *cf.* LXX, 1 Sam. vii. 2, 1 Kings xii. 23, Neh. iv. 16, Ezek. xlv. 6, or it may be reckoned as Hebraistic, Blass, *Grammatik des N. G.*, pp. 147, 158.—καὶ Κύριον καὶ Χριστόν: the Κύριος plainly refers to the prophetic utterance just cited. Although in the first verse of Ps. cx. the words τῷ Κυρίῳ μου are not to be taken as a name of God, for the expression is Adoni not Adonai (" the LORD saith unto my Lord," R.V.), and is simply a title of honour and respect, which was used of earthly superiors, *e.g.*, of Abraham, Moses, Elijah, Sisera, Naaman, yet St. Peter had called David a Prophet, and only in the Person of the Risen and Ascended Christ Who had sat down with His Father on His Throne could the Apostle see an adequate fulfilment of David's prophecy, or an adequate realisation of the anticipations of the Christ. So in the early Church, Justin Martyr, *Apol.*, i., 60, appeals to the words of "the prophet David" in this same Psalm as foretelling the Ascension of Christ and His reign

37. Ἀκούσαντες¹ δὲ κατενύγησαν τῇ καρδίᾳ, εἰπόν τε πρὸς τὸν
Πέτρον καὶ τοὺς λοιποὺς² ἀποστόλους, Τί ποιήσομεν, ἄνδρες ἀδελφοί;

¹ ακουσαντες; before this word D (so Syr. Harcl. mg.) reads τοτε παντες οι
συνελθοντες και, and after κατενυγ. την καρδ. D adds και τινες εξ αυτων (ειπαν), so
Hilg. According to Blass's theory this would show more account and detailed information, . . . all were pricked, etc., but only some inquired—but on the other hand it may
have been inserted to explain an apparent difficulty. According to Weiss, Codex D,
p. 57, this and the following addition in D, υποδειξατε ημιν, are emendations of a
kind similar to those which we find in ii. 45. In τοτε κ.τ.λ. in D, Harris sees either
a lectionary preface or reader's expansion. Others find a case of assimilation, e.g.,
to Luke xxiii. 48 (Chase points out that similar words occur in the Syriac of the two
passages). In τοτε Weiss can only see one of the frequent ways in which the
characteristic alterations of D are introduced.

² λοιπους om. by D, Gig., Aug.—Hilg., and Blass, who omits it in β also, say "recte
fort. et in α"; cf. v. 29. ποιησωμεν ℵABCEP, Epiph., Chrys.; so Tisch., W.H.,
R.V., Weiss, Wendt (as against Meyer), so also Blass in β; but Hilg. follows T.R.
αδελφοι; after this word D adds υποδειξατε ημιν, so E, Gig., Par., Wer. tol., Syr.
Harcl. mg., Aug., Prom.; so Hilg. The word could be well connected with the και
τινες as indicating their earnestness and willingness; cf. Luke iii. 7, Matt. iii. 7 (to
which Chase sees an assimilation), Acts ix. 16, xx. 35.

over His spiritual enemies. On the
remarkable expression Χριστὸς Κύριος
in connection with Ps. cx. 1, see Ryle
and James, *Psalms of Solomon*, pp.
141-143, cf. with the passage here x.
36, 42. In 1 Peter iii. 15 we have the
phrase Κύριον δὲ Χριστὸν ἁγιάσατε κ.τ.λ.
(R.V. and W.H.), "sanctify in your
hearts Christ as Lord" (R.V.), where St.
Peter does not hesitate to command that
Christ be sanctified in our hearts as
Lord, in words which are used in the
O.T. of the Lord of hosts, Isa. viii. 13,
and His sanctification by Israel. If it is
said that it has been already shown that
in Ps. cx. 1 Christ is referred to not as
the Lord but as "my lord," it must not
be forgotten that an exact parallel to 1
Peter iii. 15 and its high Christology
may be found in this first sermon of St.
Peter, cf. note on vv. 18-21 and 33.—
τοῦτον τὸν Ἰ. ὃν ὑμεῖς ἐσταυρώσατε,
"hath made Him both Lord and Christ,
this Jesus whom ye crucified," R.V., so
Vulgate. The A.V., following Tyndale
and Cranmer, inverts the clauses, but
fails to mark what Bengel so well calls
aculeus in fine, the stinging effect with
which St. Peter's words would fall on
the ears of his audience, many of whom
may have joined in the cry, Crucify Him!
(Chrysostom). Holtzmann describes this
last clause of the speech as "ein schwerer
Schlusstein zur Krönung des Gebäudes".

Ver. 37. κατενύγησαν τὴν καρδίαν:
no word could better make known that
the sting of the last word had begun to
work (see Theophylact, *in loco*) = *com-
pungo*, so in Vulg. The word is not

used in classical Greek in the same sense
as here, but the simple verb νύσσειν is
so used. In LXX the best parallels
are Gen. xxxiv. 7, Ps. cviii. 16 (cix.):
cf. Cicero, *De Orat.*, iii., 34. "Hoc
pœnitentiæ initium est, hic ad pietatem
ingressus, tristitiam ex peccatis nostris
concipere ac malorum nostrorum sensu
vulnerari . . . sed compunctioni accedere
debet promptitudo ad parendum," Calvin,
in loco.—τί ποιήσωμεν; conj., delib., cf.
Luke iii. 10, 12, 14, Mark xii. 14, xiv. 12,
John xii. 27, Matt. xxvi. 54, Burton,
Moods and Tenses of N. T. Greek, pp. 76,
126, and Viteau, *Le Grec du N. T.*,
p. 28 ff. (1893).—ἄνδρες ἀδελφοί: indicating respect and regard—St. Peter's
address had not been in vain—"*non ita
dixerant prius*" Bengel; but now the
words come as a response to St. Peter's
own appeal, v. 29, cf. also Oecumenius,
(so too Theophylact), καὶ οἰκειωτικῶς
αὐτοὺς ἀδελφοὺς καλοῦσιν, οὓς πρώην
ἐχλεύαζον.—μετανοήσατε, Luke xxiv. 47.
The Apostles began, as the Baptist began,
Matt. iii. 2, as the Christ Himself began,
Matt. iv. 17, Mark i. 15, with the exhortation to repentance, to a change of heart
and life, not to mere regret for the past.
On the distinction between μετανοεῖν and
μεταμέλομαι, see Trench, *N. T. Synonyms*, i., 208. Dr. Thayer remarks that
the distinction drawn by Trench is hardly
sustained by usage, but at the same
time he allows that μετανοεῖν is undoubtedly the fuller and nobler term, expressive
of moral action and issues, as is indicated
by the fact that it is often employed in
the imperative (μεταμέλομαι never), and

38. Πέτρος δὲ ἔφη πρὸς αὐτούς, Μετανοήσατε, καὶ βαπτισθήτω
ἕκαστος ὑμῶν [1] ἐπὶ τῷ ὀνόματι Ἰησοῦ Χριστοῦ εἰς ἄφεσιν ἁμαρτιῶν·
καὶ λήψεσθε τὴν δωρεὰν τοῦ Ἁγίου Πνεύματος. 39. ὑμῖν γάρ ἐστιν
ἡ ἐπαγγελία καὶ τοῖς τέκνοις ὑμῶν, καὶ πᾶσι τοῖς εἰς μακράν, ὅσους

[1] ἐπι ℵAEP, Bas., Chrys., so Tisch. and Weiss; but ἐν in BCD, Cyr.-Jer., Epiph.,
Cyr., Theodrt., so W.H., R.V.; both expressions seem to be equally common in
Luke and Acts.

by its construction with ἀπό, ἐκ, cf. also
Acts xx. 31, ἡ εἰς θεὸν μετάνοια (Synonyms in Grimm-Thayer, sub μεταμέλομαι). Christian Baptism was not
admission to some new club or society
of virtue, it was not primarily a token of
mutual love and brotherhood, although
it purified and strengthened both, cf. ver.
44 ff.

Ver. 38. βαπτισθήτω: "Non satis est
Christo credere, sed oportet et Christianum
profiteri, Rom. x. 10, quod Christus per
baptismum fieri voluit," Grotius. John's
baptism had been a baptism of repentance
for the remission of sins, but the work
of St. Peter and of his fellow-Apostles
was no mere continuation of that of the
Baptist, cf. xix. 4, 5. Their baptism was
to be ἐπὶ (ἐν) τῷ ὀνόματι Ἰ. Χ. St. Peter's
address had been directed to the proof
that Jesus was the Christ, and it was
only natural that the acknowledgment
of the cogency of that proof should form
the ground of admission to the Christian
Church: the ground of the admission to
baptism was the recognition of Jesus
as the Christ. The reading ἐπί (see
especially Weiss, Apostelgeschichte, pp.
35, 36) brings this out more clearly than ἐν.
It is much better to explain thus than
to say that baptism in the name of one of
the Persons of the Trinity involves the
names of the other Persons also, or to
suppose with Bengel (so Plumptre) that
the formula in Matt. xxviii. 19 was used
for Gentiles, whilst for Jews or Proselytes
who already acknowledged a Father and
a Holy Spirit baptism in the name of
the Lord Jesus sufficed; or to conjecture
with Neander that Matt. xxviii. 19 was
not at first considered as a formula to be
adhered to rigidly in baptism, but that
the rite was performed with reference to
Christ's name alone. This difficulty, of
which so much has been made, does not
appear to have pressed upon the early
Church, for it is remarkable that the
passage in the Didache, vii., 3, which is
rightly cited to prove the early existence
of the Invocation of the Holy Trinity in
baptism, is closely followed by another

in which we read (ix. 5) μηδεὶς δὲ φαγέτω
μηδὲ πιέτω ἀπὸ τῆς εὐχαριστίας ὑμῶν,
ἀλλ' οἱ βαπτισθέντες εἰς ὄνομα Κυρίου,
i.e., Christ, as the immediate context
shows.—εἰς ἄφεσιν τῶν ἁμαρτιῶν ὑμῶν:
εἰς, "unto" R.V., signifying the aim.
It has been objected that St. Peter lays
no stress upon the death of Christ in
this connection, but rather upon His
Resurrection. But we cannot doubt that
St. Peter who had emphasised the fact
of the crucifixion would have remembered
his Master's solemn declaration a few
hours before His death, Matt. xxvi. 28.
Even if the words in this Gospel εἰς ἄφεσιν
ἁμαρτιῶν are rejected, the fact remains
that St. Peter would have connected the
thought of the forgiveness of sins, a
prerogative which, as every Jew was
eager to maintain, belonged to God and
to God alone, with the (new) covenant
which Christ had ratified by His death.
Harnack admits that however difficult it
may be to explain precisely the words of
Jesus to the disciples at the Last Supper,
yet one thing is certain, that He connected
the forgiveness of sins with His death,
Dogmengeschichte, i., pp. 55 and 59, see
also "Covenant," Hastings, B.D., p.
512.—ὑμῶν: the R.V. has this addition,
so too the Vulgate (Wycl. and Rheims).
As each individual ἕκαστος was to be
baptised, so each, if truly penitent, would
receive the forgiveness of his sins.—τὴν
δωρεάν, not χάρισμα as in 1 Cor. xii. 4,
9, 28, for the Holy Ghost, the gift, was a
personal and abiding possession, but the
χαρίσματα were for a time answering to
special needs, and enjoyed by those to
whom God distributed them. The word
is used specially of the gift of the Holy
Ghost by St. Luke four times in Acts,
viii. 20, x. 45, xi. 17, but by no other
Evangelist (cf., however, Luke xi. 13), cf.
Heb. vi. 4 (John iv. 10).

Ver. 39. ὑμῖν γάρ: the promise was
made to the very men who had invoked
upon themselves and upon their children,
St. Matt. xxvii. 25, the blood of the
Crucified. See Psalms of Solomon, viii.,
39 (Ryle and James' edition, p. 88).—

ἂν προσκαλέσηται Κύριος ὁ Θεὸς ἡμῶν. 40. ἑτέροις τε λόγοις πλείοσι διεμαρτύρετο καὶ παρεκάλει λέγων, Σώθητε ἀπὸ τῆς γενεᾶς τῆς σκολιᾶς ταύτης. 41. Οἱ μὲν οὖν ἀσμένως [1] ἀποδεξάμενοι τὸν

[1] ασμενως EP, Syrr. (Pesh. and Harcl.), Arm., Chrys.; but om. by ℵABCD 61, Vulg., Sah., Boh., Aeth., Clem., so Tisch., W.H., R.V., Weiss, Wendt. For αποδεξαμενοι D substitutes πιστευσαντες, and Syr. Harcl. mg., Aug. add και πιστευσαντες. (Harris sees a Montanist addition, necessity of faith for baptism.)

πᾶσι τοῖς εἰς μακράν: no occasion with Wendt and others to limit the words to the Jews of the Diaspora. It must not be forgotten that the Apostles were not surprised that the Gentiles should be admitted to the Christian Church, but only that they should be admitted without conforming to the rite of circumcision. If we compare iii. 26, and Ephes. ii. 13, 17 (cf. Rom. x. 13), it would seem that no restriction of race was placed upon the declaration of the Gospel message, provided that it was made to the Jew first (as was always Paul's custom). Hilgenfeld interprets the words as referring beyond all doubt to the Gentiles, since ὑμῖν . . . ὑμῶν had already expressed the Diaspora Jews. But he contends that as ver. 26 plainly intimates that the address was delivered only to Israelites, the words in question are added by "the author to Theophilus". He therefore places them in brackets. Jüngst in the same way thinks it well to refer them to the Redactor, and Feine refers them to Luke himself as Reviser. Weiss sees in the words an allusion to an O.T. passage which could only have been applied at first to the calling of the Gentiles, but which (in the connection in which it is here placed by the narrator) must be referred to the Jews of the Diaspora. It may well have been that (as in Holtzmann's view) St. Peter's audience only thought of the Jews of the Diaspora, but we can see in his words a wider and a deeper meaning, cf. Isaiah v. 26, and cf. also Isaiah ii. 2, Zech. vi. 15. Among the older commentators Oecumenius and Theophylact referred the words to the Gentiles.—ὅσους ἂν προσκαλέσηται Κύριος ὁ Θεὸς ἡμῶν. Wendt presses the ἡμῶν to favour his view that St. Peter thinks only of the Jews and not of the Gentiles, since he speaks of "our God," but Blass catches the meaning much better in his comment: "ἡμῶν Israelitarum, qui idem gentes ad se vocat". This gives the true force of προσκαλ., "shall call unto him" (so R.V.). Oecumenius also comments on the words as revealing the true peni-

tence and charity of Peter, ψυχὴ γὰρ ὅταν ἑαυτὴν καταδικάσῃ, οὐκ ἔτι φθονεῖν δύναται.

Ver. 40. ἑτέροις τε λόγοις πλείοσιν: τε (not δὲ), as so frequent in Acts; "inducit quæ similia cognataque sunt, δέ diversa," Blass, in loco, and Grammatik des N. G., p. 258.—διεμαρτύρατο: the translation "testified," both in A. and R.V., hardly gives the full form of the word. Its frequent use in the LXX in the sense of protesting solemnly, cf. Deut. iv. 26, viii. 19, 1 Sam. viii. 9, Zech. iii. 7 (6), seems more in accordance with St. Peter's words, who here as elsewhere (x. 42, xliii. 5, xx. 21) was not simply acting as a witness μαρτυρεῖν, but was also protesting against the false views of those he was addressing. It must not, however, be forgotten that in other passages in the LXX the verb may mean to bear witness (see Hatch and Redpath, sub v.). In the N.T., as Wendt notes, it is used by St. Paul in the former sense of protesting solemnly in 1 Tim. v. 21, 2 Tim. ii. 14, iv. 1. With this Mr. Page rightly compares its use in Acts xx. 23 (cf. also v. 20, μαρτύρομαι), and Luke xvi. 28. So too in classical writers.—παρεκάλει: the imperfect suggests the continuous exhortation which followed upon the Apostles' solemn protest (Weiss, in loco).—τῆς γενεᾶς τῆς σκολιᾶς ταύτης: the adjective is used to describe the rebellious Israelites in the wilderness, LXX, Deut. xxxii. 5 (and Ps. lxxvii. 8), a description used in part by our Lord Himself, Matt. xvii. 17, Luke ix. 41, and wholly by St. Paul, Phil. ii. 15. The correct translation "crooked," R.V. (which A.V. has in Luke iii. 5, Phil. ii. 15), signifies perversity in turning off from the truth, whilst the A.V. "untoward" (so Tyndale) signifies rather backwardness in coming to the truth (Humphry, Commentary on R. V.), Hort, Judaistic Christianity, pp. 41, 42.

Ver. 41. Οἱ μὲν οὖν: a truly Lucan formula, see i. 6. There is no anacoluthon, but for the answering δέ see v. 43. The words therefore refer to those mentioned in v. 37; in contrast to the three

λόγον αὐτοῦ ἐβαπτίσθησαν· καὶ προσετέθησαν[1] τῇ ἡμέρᾳ ἐκείνῃ ψυχαὶ ὡσεὶ τρισχίλιαι.

42. Ἦσαν δὲ προσκαρτεροῦντες τῇ διδαχῇ τῶν ἀποστόλων καὶ τῇ

---

[1] προσετέθησαν; after the verb ἐν inserted by ℵABCD 15, 18, 61, Vulg., so Tisch., W.H., R.V., Weiss, Wendt, Hilg.

---

thousand fear came upon every person, ψυχή, so Mr. Page, on μὲν οὖν, *in loco*. Mr. Rendall finds the answering δέ in v. 42; two phases of events are contrasted; three thousand converts are added in one day—they clave stedfastly to the Christian communion. See also his Appendix on μὲν οὖν, p. 162.—ἀποδεξάμενοι τὸν λόγον αὐτοῦ: used in classical Greek, especially in Plato, of receiving a teacher or his arguments with acceptance, and in the N.T. of receiving with approval; *cf.* xxiv. 3. The verb is only found in St. Luke in the N.T. with varying shades of meaning, twice in his Gospel, and five times in Acts in all parts. Only found in LXX in Apocryphal books, Tob. vii. 17, Judith xiii. 13 (but see Hatch and Redpath, *sub v.*), and in the Books of the Maccabees; *cf.* xviii. 27, xxi. 17, xxiv. 3, xxxviii. 30, see below. —ἐβαπτίσθησαν. There is nothing in the text which intimates that the Baptism of the three thousand was performed, not on the day of Pentecost, but during the days which followed. At the same time it is not said that the Baptism of such a multitude took place at one time or in one place on the day of the Feast, or that the rite was performed by St. Peter alone. Felten allows that others besides the Twelve may have baptised. See his note, *in loco*, and also Zöckler, *Apostelgeschichte*, p. 183.—προσετέθησαν, *cf.* ver. 47, and v. 14, xi. 24. In the LXX the same verb is used, Isa. xiv. 1, for a proselyte who is joined to Israel, so too Esth. ix. 27.—ψυχαὶ, "souls," *i.e.*, persons. See on ver. 43.—ὡσεὶ τρισχίλιαι: the adverb is another favourite word of St. Luke (Friedrich)—it is not found in St. John, and in St. Mark only once, in St. Matthew three times, but in St. Luke's Gospel eight or nine times, and in Acts six or seven times. As in i. 15 the introduction of the adverb is against the supposition that the number was a fictitious one. We cannot suppose that the influence and the recollection of Jesus had vanished within a few short weeks without leaving a trace behind, and where the proclamation of Him as the Christ followed upon the wonderful gift of tongues, in which many of the people

would see the inspiration of God and a confirmation given by Him to the claims made by the disciples, hearts and consciences might well be stirred and quickened—and the movement once begun was sure to spread (see the remarks of Spitta, *Apostelgeschichte*, p. 60, on the birthday of the Church, in spite of the suspicion with which he regards the number three thousand).

Ver. 42. The growth of the Church not merely in numbers but in the increase of faith and charity. In R.V. by the omission of καὶ before τῇ κλάσει two pairs of particulars are apparently enumerated—the first referring to the close adherence of believers to the Apostles in teaching and fellowship, the second expressing their outward acts of worship; or the first pair may be taken as expressing rather their relation to man, the second their relation to God (Nösgen). Dr. Hort, while pointing out that the first term τῇ διδαχῇ τῶν ἀποστόλων ("the teaching," R.V., following Wycliffe; *cf.* Matt. vii. 28, "doctrine," A.V., which would refer rather to a definite system, unless taken in the sense of the Latin *doctrina, teaching*) was obviously Christian, so that the disciples might well be called scribes to the kingdom, bringing out of their treasures things new and old, the facts of the life of Jesus and the glory which followed, facts interpreted in the light of the Law and the Prophets, takes the next words τῇ κοινωνίᾳ as separated altogether from τῶν ἀποστόλων, "and with the communion": κοινωνία, in Dr. Hort's view by parallelism with the other terms, expresses something more external and concrete than a spirit of communion; it refers to the help given to the destitute of the community, not apparently in money, but in public meals, such as from another point of view are called "the daily ministration" (*cf.* Acts vi. 2, τραπέζαις). There are undoubtedly instances of the employment of the word κοινωνία in this concrete sense, Rom. xv. 26, 2 Cor. viii. 4, ix. 13, Heb. xiii. 26, but in each of these cases its meaning is determined by the context (and Zöckler, amongst recent commentators, would so

κοινωνίᾳ [1] καὶ τῇ κλάσει τοῦ ἄρτου καὶ ταῖς προσευχαῖς. 43. ἐγένετο
δὲ πάσῃ ψυχῇ φόβος, πολλά τε τέρατα καὶ σημεῖα διὰ τῶν ἀποσ-

[1] καὶ τῇ κλασει; om. καὶ ℵ*ABCD* 61, so Tisch., W.H., R.V., Weiss, Wendt,
Hilg., so Alford. κοινωνια τῆς κλασεως του αρτου, so d, Vulg., Sah. (so in Gig.,
Par. του αρ. τῆς κλ.), of which Blass says "recte, nisi delenda τ. κλ.". But the
Western readings look like attempts to remove a difficulty.

restrict its meaning here). But, on the other hand, there are equally undoubted instances of κοινωνία referring to spiritual fellowship and concord, a fellowship in the spirit; cf. 2 Cor. vi. 4, xiii. 14, Phil. ii. 1, Gal. ii. 9, 1 John i. 3, 6, 7; cf. also in classical writers, Arist., *Ethic.*, viii., 9, 12, ἐν κοινωνίᾳ ἡ φιλία ἐστί. Here, if the word can be separated from ἀποσ., it may be taken to include the inward fellowship and its outward manifestation, ver. 44. May not a good parallel to this signification of the word be found in Phil. i. 5, where κοινωνία, whilst it signifies co-operation in the widest sense, including fellowship in sympathy, suffering and toil, also indicates the special and tangible manifestation of this fellowship in the ready alms-giving and contributions of the Philippian Church; see Lightfoot, *Philippians, in loco.* The word naturally suggests the community of goods, as Weizsäcker points out, but as it stands here without any precise definition we cannot so limit it, and in his view Gal. ii. 9 gives the key to its meaning in the passage before us—the bond which united the μαθηταί was the consciousness of their belief in Christ, and in the name ἀδελφοί the relationship thus constituted gained its complete expression.— τῇ κλάσει τοῦ ἄρτου: no interpretation is satisfactory which forgets (as both Weizsäcker and Holtzmann point out) that the author of Acts had behind him Pauline language and doctrine, and that we are justified in adducing the language of St. Paul in order to explain the words before us, cf. 1 Cor. x. 16, xi. 24, Acts xx. 7 (and xxvii. 35, Weizsäcker). But if we admit this, we cannot consistently explain the expression of a mere common meal. It may be true that every such meal in the early days of the Church's first love had a religious significance, that it became a type and evidence of the kingdom of God amongst the believers, but St. Paul's habitual reference of the words before us to the Lord's Supper leads us to see in them here a reference to the commemoration of the Lord's death, although we may admit that it is altogether indisputable that this commemoration at first followed a common meal. That St. Paul's teaching as to the deep religious significance of the breaking of the bread carries us back to a very early date is evident from the fact that he speaks to the Corinthians of a custom long established; cf. "Abendmahl I." in Hauck's *Real-Encyklopädie*, heft i. (1896), p. 23 ff., on the evidential value of this testimony as against Jülicher's and Spitta's attempt to show that the celebration of the Lord's Supper in the early Church rested upon no positive command of Jesus. Weizsäcker's words are most emphatic: "Every assumption of its having originated in the Church from the recollection of intercourse with Him at table, and the necessity felt for re-calling His death is precluded—the celebration must rather have been generally observed from the beginning" *Apostolic Age*, ii., p. 279, E.T., and cf. *Das apostol. Zeitalter*, p. 594, second edition (1892), Beyschlag, *Neutestamentliche Theol.*, i., p. 155. Against any attempt to interpret the words under discussion of mere benevolence towards the poor (Isaiah lviii. 7) Wendt regards xx. 6, 7 (and also xxvii. 35) as decisive. Weiss refers to Luke xxiv. 30 for an illustration of the words, but the act, probably the habitual act of Jesus, which they express there, does not exhaust their meaning here. Spitta takes vi. 2, διακονεῖν τραπέζαις as = κλάσις ἄρτου, an arbitrary interpretation, see also below. The Vulgate connects τῇ κλάσει τοῦ ἄρτου with the preceding κοινωνία, and renders in *communicatione fractionis panis*, a rendering justified in so far as the κοινωνία has otherwise no definite meaning, and by the fact that the brotherly intercourse of Christians specially revealed itself in the *fractio panis*, cf. 1 Cor. x. 16, and Blass, *in loco*, and also β where he reads καὶ τῇ κοινωνίᾳ τῆς κλάσεως τοῦ ἄρτου. But whilst Felten refers to the evidence of the Vulgate, and also to that of the Peshitto, which renders the words before us "in the breaking of the Eucharist" (so too in xx. 7), it is worthy of note that he refuses to follow the usual Roman

τόλων ἐγίνετο.¹   44. πάντες δὲ οἱ πιστεύοντες ἦσαν ἐπὶ τὸ αὐτό, καὶ
εἶχον ² ἅπαντα κοινά, 45.³ καὶ τὰ κτήματα καὶ τὰς ὑπάρξεις ἐπίπρασ-

---

¹ In ver. 43 ℵACE 13, many cursives, Vulg., Syr. Pesh., Boh. add εν ιερουσαλημ (which is added by D to των αποστ. in ver. 42); so Tisch., R.V. marg. But the addition is not found in BD 1, 31, 61, Sah., Syr. Harcl., Arm., Aeth., Chrys.; so W.H., R.V. text, Weiss, Wendt. ℵAC 40, Vulg., Boh. add also φοβος τε ην μεγας επι παντας, so Tisch.; but omitted by BDE, Sah., Syrr. (P. and H.), Arm., Aeth., Chrys.—perhaps assimilation to iv. 33, v. 5; it has been already expressed in the first clause of the verse, and as the authorities for its retention are mainly the same as for εν ιερ., it would seem that the former addition may also be rejected.

² ησαν επι το αυτο και ειχον, so Tisch., Hilg.; but B 57, Orig., so W.H., Weiss, Wendt have only επι το αυτο ειχον—ησαν and και might easily be added, but their falling out is difficult to imagine.

³ D (cf. Pesch.) reads και οσοι κτηματα ειχον η υπαρξεις επιπρασκον; so Hilg. Before πασι D, Gig., Par. insert καθ᾽ ημεραν. For καθοτι . . . ειχε D reads τοις αν τις χρειαν ειχεν (τοις χρειαν εχουσιν in β); cf. iv. 35. The remarks of Belser and Weiss on the passage should be compared—the former sees in β a more precise account and, at the same time, a more moderate account of the "community of goods" at Jerusalem than is sometimes derived from this passage (see comments), whilst here Weiss sees in D nothing but fruitless and even senseless emendations.

---

interpretation, viz., that the words point to a communion in one kind only, Apostelgeschichte, p. 94. It is possible that the introduction of the article before at least one of the words τῇ κλάσει (cf. R.V.) emphasises here the Lord's Supper as distinct from the social meal with which it was connected, whilst ver. 46 may point to the social as well as to the devotional bearing of the expression (cf. Zöckler, note in loco), and this possibility is increased if we regard the words τῶν ἀποστόλων as characterising the whole sentence in ver. 42. But unless in both verses some deeper meaning was attached to the phrases τῇ κλάσει τοῦ ἄρτου—κλῶντες ἄρτον, it seems superfluous, as Schöttgen remarked, to introduce the mention of common food at the time of a community of goods. No doubt St. Chrysostom (so Oecum., Theophyl.) and Bengel interpret the words as simply = victus frugalis, but elsewhere St. Chrysostom speaks of them, or at least when joined with κοινωνία, as referring to the Holy Communion (see Alford's note in loco), and Bengel's comment on ver. 42 must be compared with what he says on ver. 46. —καὶ ταῖς προσευχαῖς, "and [in] the prayers" R.V. Dr. Hort suggests that the prayers may well have been Christian prayers at stated hours, answering to Jewish prayers, and perhaps replacing the synagogue prayers (not recognised in the Law), as the Apostles' "teaching" had replaced that of the scribes (Judaistic Christianity, p. 44, and Ecclesia, p. 45). But the words may also be taken to include prayers both new and old, cf. iv. 24, James v. 13 (Eph. ii. 19, Col. iii. 16), and also Acts iii. 1, where Peter and John go up to the Temple "at the hour of prayer," cf. Wendt, Die Lehre Jesu, ii., p. 159.

Ver. 43. πάσῃ ψυχῇ, i.e., every person, and so iii. 23, Hebraistic, cf. כָּל־נֶפֶשׁ, Lev. vii. 17, xvii. 12, etc., and cf. 1 Macc. ii. 38. In ver. 41 the plural is used rather like the Latin capita in enumerations, cf. Acts vii. 14, xxvii. 37, and LXX, Gen. xlvi. 15, Exod. i. 5, Num. xix. 18, etc. But Winer-Moulton (p. 194, xxii. 7) would press the meaning of ψυχή here, and contends that the fear was produced in the heart, the seat of the feelings and desires, so that its use is no mere Hebraism, although he admits that in Rom. xiii. 1 (1 Peter iii. 20) the single πᾶσα ψυχή = every person, but see l.c. —φόβος, cf. iii. 10, i.e., upon the non-believers, for "perfect love casteth out fear". Friedrich notes amongst the characteristics of St. Luke that in his two books one of the results of miraculous powers is fear. Here the φόβος means rather the fear of reverential awe or the fear which acted quasi freno (Calvin), so that the early growth of the Church was not destroyed prematurely by assaults from without. There is surely nothing inconsistent here with ver. 47, but Hilgenfeld ascribes the whole of ver. 43 to his "author to Theophilus," partly on the ground of this supposed inconsistency, partly be-

κον, καὶ διεμέριζον αὐτὰ πᾶσι, καθότι ἄν τις χρείαν εἶχε · 46.[1] καθ᾽
ἡμέραν τε προσκαρτεροῦντες ὁμοθυμαδὸν ἐν τῷ ἱερῷ, κλῶντές τε κατ᾽

[1] D omits καθ᾽ ημεραν (see previous note) and reads παντες τε προσκαρτερουν,
perhaps for additional clearness, or perhaps some confusion (see also Weiss's
comments). D reads also και κατοικουσαν επι το αυτο—D² del. αν, and so Blass
corrects και κατ οικους ησαν; so too Hilg. Belser sees in κατ᾽ οικους an answer
to the objection that κατ᾽ οικον in α text refers to the house of assembly of the
Christians, and that as the number 3000 could not assemble in a single dwelling it
must be an exaggeration—no doubt if Luke had meant one house of assembly he
would have written κατα τον οικον, but the reading κατ᾽ οικους puts the matter beyond
a doubt, and shows how κατ᾽ οικον must be taken as = vicissim per domos.

cause the mention of miracles is out of place. But it is nowhere stated, as Hilgenfeld and Weiss presuppose, that the healing of the lame man in iii. 1 ff. was the *first* miracle performed (see note there, and Wendt and Blass).

Ver. 44. πάντες δε κ.τ.λ., *cf.* iii. 24, all, *i.e.*, not only those who had recently joined, ver. 41.—ἐπὶ τὸ αὐτὸ, see note on i. 15; here of place. Theophylact takes it of the unanimity in the Church, but this does not seem to be in accordance with the general use of the phrase in the N.T. = ὁμοῦ, ἐπὶ τὸν αὐτὸν τόπον (Hesychius). Blass points out that ἐπὶ τὸ αὐτὸ demands ἦσαν, and if we omit this word (W.H.) we must supply ὄντες with ἐπὶ τὸ αὐτὸ, as ἐπὶ τὸ αὐτὸ εἶχον could not stand (W.H.). The difficulty raised by Hilgenfeld, Wendt, Holtzmann, Overbeck, in this connection as to the number is exaggerated, whether we meet it or not by supposing that some of this large number were pilgrims who had come up to the Feast, but who had now returned to their homes. For in the first place, ἐπὶ τὸ αὐτὸ cannot be taken to mean that all the believers were always assembled in one and the same place. The reading in β, ver. 46, may throw light upon the expression in this verse καὶ κατ᾽ οἴκους ἦσαν ἐπὶ τὸ αὐτό, or the phrase may be referred to their assembling together in the Temple, ver. 46, and v. 12 may be quoted in support of this, where all the believers apparently assemble in Solomon's Porch. It is therefore quite arbitrary to dismiss the number here or in iv. 4 as merely due to the idealising tendency of the Apostles, or to the growth of the Christian legend. —εἶχον ἅπαντα κοινά, "held all things common," R.V. Blass and Weiss refer these words with ἐπὶ τὸ αὐτὸ to the assembling of the Christians together for common meals and find in the statement the exact antithesis to the selfish conduct in 1 Cor. xi. 20, 21. But the words also demand a much wider reference. On the "Community of Goods," see additional note at end of chapter.

Ver. 45. τὰ κτήματα . . . τὰς ὑπάρξεις: according to their derivation, the former word would mean that which is acquired, and the latter that which belongs to a man for the time being. But in ordinary usage κτήματα was always used of real property, fields, lands, *cf.* v. 1, whilst ὑπάρξεις was used of personal property (=τὰ ὑπάρχοντα in Heb. x. 34). This latter word, τὰ ὑπάρχοντα, was a favourite with St. Luke, who uses it eight times in his Gospel and in Acts iv. 32. No doubt κτῆμα is used in LXX for field and vineyard, Prov. xxiii. 10, xxxi. 16, but the above distinction was not strictly observed, for τὰ ὑπάρχοντα, ὕπαρξις, are used both of movable and immovable property (see Hatch and Redpath, *sub v.*).—ἐπίπρασκον: all three verbs are in the imperfect, and if we remember that this tense may express an action which is done often and continuously without being done universally or extending to a complete accomplishment (*cf.* iv. 34, xviii. 8, Mark xii. 41), considerable light may be thrown upon the picture here drawn (see Blass, *Grammatik des N. G.*, p. 186, on the tense and this passage): "And kept getting . . . and distributing to all, as any man [τις] [not 'every man,' A.V.] had need". See Rendall, *Acts, in loco*, and on iv. 32, and *Expositor*, vii., p. 358, 3rd series.— καθότι: peculiar to St. Luke; in Gospel twice, and in Acts four times. ἄν makes the clause more indefinite: it is found in relative clauses after ὅς, ὅστις, etc., with the indicative—here it is best explained as signifying "accidisse aliquid non certo quodam tempore, sed quotiescumque occasio ita ferret," quoted by Wendt from Herm., *ad Vig.*, p. 820; *cf.* Mark vi. 56, Blass, *in loco*, and Viteau, *Le Grec du N. T.*, p. 142 (1893). Grimm renders καθότι ἄν here "in so far," *or* "so often as," "according as". Spitta refers vv. 45-47 to the Apostles only, but to justify this he is obliged to refer ver. 44 to his reviser. Hilgenfeld brackets the whole verse, referring it to his "author to Theophilus," retaining ver. 44, whilst Weiss also refers the whole verse to a reviser, who introduced it in imitation of St. Luke's love of poverty as indicated in his Gospel. But by such expedients the picture of the whole body of the believers sharing in the Apostles' life and liberality is completely marred.

Ver. 46. ὁμοθυμαδόν, see note on i. 14.—προσκαρτεροῦντες, cf. i. 14.—ἐν τῷ ἱερῷ: we are not told how far this participation in the Temple extended, and mention is only made in one place, in xxi. 26, of any kind of connection between the Apostles or any other Christians and any kind of sacrificial act. But that one peculiar incident may imply that similar acts were not uncommon, and their omission by the Christians at Jerusalem might well have led to an open breach between them and their Jewish countrymen (Hort, *Judaistic Christianity*, pp. 44, 45). No doubt the Apostles would recommend their teaching to the people by devout attendance at the Temple, cf. iii. 1, v. 20, 42, like other Jews.—κατ' οἶκον, R.V. "at home" (so in A.V. margin). But all other English versions except Genevan render the words "from house to house" (Vulgate, *circa domos*), and this latter rendering is quite possible, cf. Luke viii. 1, Acts xv. 21, xx. 20. If we interpret the words of the meeting of the believers in a private house (*privatim* in contrast to the ἐν τῷ ἱερῷ, *palam*), cf. Rom. xvi. 3, 5, 1 Cor. xvi. 19, Col. iv. 15, Philemon 2, it does not follow that only one house is here meant, as Wendt and Weiss suppose by referring to i. 13 (see on the other hand Blass, Holtzmann, Zöckler, Spitta, Hort) —there may well have been private houses open to the disciples, *e.g.*, the house of John Mark, cf. Dr. Edersheim, *Sketches of Jewish Social Life*, pp. 259, 260. Hilgenfeld, with Overbeck, rejects the explanation given on the ground that for this κατ' οἴκους, or κατὰ τοὺς οἴκους, would be required—an argument which does not however get over the fact that κατά may be used distributively with the singular—according to him all is in order if ii. 42 follows immediately upon 41ᵃ, *i.e.*, he drops 41ᵇ altogether, and proceeds to omit also the whole of vv. 43 and 45.—κλῶντες ἄρτον: the question has been raised as to whether this expression has the same meaning here as

in ver. 42, or whether it is used here of merely ordinary meals. The additional words μετελάμβανον τροφῆς have been taken to support this latter view, but on the other hand if the two expressions are almost synonymous, it is difficult to see why the former κλῶντες ἄρτον should have been introduced here at all, cf. Knabenbauer *in loco*. It is not satisfactory to lay all the stress upon the omission of the article before ἄρτον, and to explain the expression of ordinary daily meals, an interpretation adopted even by the Romanist Beelen and others. In the *Didache* the expression κλάσατε ἄρτον, chap. xiv. 1, certainly refers to the Eucharist, and in the earlier chap. ix., where the word κλάσμα occurs twice in the sense of broken bread, it can scarcely refer to anything less than the *Agape* (Salmon, *Introd.*, p. 565, and Gore, *The Church and the Ministry*, p. 414, on the value of the Eucharistic teaching in the *Didache*).—μετελ.: the imperf. denotes a customary act, the meaning of the verb with the gen. as here is frequently found in classical Greek; cf. LXX, Wisdom xviii. 9, 4 Macc. viii. 8, AR., and xvi. 18.—ἐν ἀγαλλιάσει: exulting, bounding joy; Vulgate, *exultatione*, "extreme joy," Grimm, used by St. Luke twice in his Gospel, i. 14, 44—only twice elsewhere in the N.T., Heb. i. 9, quotation, and in Jude, ver. 24. The word, though not occurring in classical Greek, was a favourite in the LXX, where it occurs no less than eighteen times in the Psalms alone. This "gladness" is full of significance —it is connected with the birth of the forerunner by the angel's message to Zacharias, Luke i. 14; the cognate verb ἀγαλλιάω, -άομαι, common to St. Luke's Gospel and the Acts, denotes the spiritual and exultant joy with which the Church age after age has rejoiced in the Song of the Incarnation, Luke i. 47.—ἀφελότητι καρδίας: rightly derived from a priv. and φελλεύς, *stony ground* = a smooth soil, free from stones (but see Zöckler, *in loco*, who derives ἀφέλεια, the noun in use in Greek writers, from φέλα, πέλλα, Macedon. *a stone*). The word itself does not occur elsewhere, but ἀφέλεια, ἀφελής, ἀφελῶς are all found (Wetstein), and just as the adj. ἀφελής signified a man ἁπλοῦς ἐν τῷ βίῳ, so the noun here used might well be taken as equivalent to ἁπλότης (Overbeck) "in simplicity of heart," *simplicitate*, Bengel. Wendt compares the words of Demosthenes, ἀφελὴς καὶ παρρησίας μεστός.

Ver. 47. αἰνοῦντες τὸν Θεὸν: a favourite expression with St. Luke, cf. Gospel

οἶκον ἄρτον, μετελάμβανον τροφῆς ἐν ἀγαλλιάσει καὶ ἀφελότητι
καρδίας, 47. αἰνοῦντες τὸν Θεὸν καὶ ἔχοντες χάριν πρὸς ὅλον τὸν

ii. 13, 20, xix. 37, Acts iii. 8, 9, else-where only in Rom. xv. 11 (a quotation), and Rev. xix. 5, with dative of person, W.H. The praise refers not merely to their thanksgivings at meals, but is characteristic of their whole devotional life both in public and private; and their life of worship and praise, combined with their liberality and their simplicity of life, helped to secure for them the result given in the following words, and an un-molested hearing in the Temple: "Hunc inveniunt (favorem) qui Deum laudant" Bengel. αἰνέω is very frequent in the LXX, and nearly always of the praise of God, but cf. Gen. xlix. 8, Prov. xxxi. 28, 30, 31, Ecclus. xliv. 1, etc.— ἔχοντες χάριν: if the life of the Church at this stage has been compared with that of her divine Master, inasmuch as it increased in wisdom and stature, another point of likeness may be found in the fact that the Church, like Christ, was in favour with God and man.—χάριν: very frequent in St. Luke's Gospel and the Acts (Friedrich), only three times in the Gospel of St. John, and not at all in St. Matthew or St. Mark. In the O.T. it is often used of finding favour in the sight of God, and in the N.T. in a similar sense, cf. Luke i. 30, Acts vii. 46. It is also used in the O.T. of favour, kind-ness, goodwill, especially from a superior to an inferior (Gen. xviii. 3, xxxii. 5, etc.), so too in the N.T., here, and in Acts vii. 10. See further note on Acts xiv. 3. In Luke's Gospel eight times, in Acts seventeen times. See also Plum-mer's full note on Luke iv. 22, Sanday and Headlam's *Romans*, p. 10, and Grimm-Thayer, *sub v.* Rendall would render "giving Him thanks before all the people," and he refers to the fact that the phrase is always so rendered elsewhere (though once wrongly trans-lated, Heb xii. 28). But the phrase is also found in LXX, Exodus xxxiii. 12, 1 Esdras vi. 5 (see also Wetstein, *in loco*) in the sense first mentioned.—ὁ δὲ κύριος προσετίθει, *i.e.*, the Lord Christ, *cf.* ver. 36 (as Holtzmann, Wendt, Weiss, amongst others). The pure and simple life of the disciples doubtless commended them to the people, and made it easier for them to gain con-fidence, and so converts, but the growth of the Church, St. Luke reminds us, was not the work of any human agency or attractiveness.—τοὺς σωζομένους: natur-

ally connected with the prophecy in ver. 21 (*cf. v.* 40), so that the work of salva-tion there attributed to Jehovah by the Old Testament Prophet is here the work of Christ: the inference is again plain with regard to our Lord's divinity. The expression is rightly translated in R.V. (so too in 1 Cor. i. 18, 2 Cor. ii. 15. See Burton, *Moods and Tenses in N. T. Greek*, pp. 57, 58). It has nothing to do, as Wetstein well remarks, with the secret counsels of God, but relates to those who were obeying St. Peter's com-mand in ver. 40. An apt parallel is given by Mr. Page from Thuc., vii., 44.

Gift of Tongues, ii. 4. λαλεῖν ἑτέραις γλώσσαις.—There can be no doubt that St. Luke's phrase (*cf.* γλώσσαις καιναῖς, Mark xvi. 17, W.H., margin, not text), taken with the context, distinctly asserts that the Apostles, if not the whole Christian assembly (St. Chrysostom, St. Jerome, St. Augustine, including the hundred-and-twenty), received the power of speaking in foreign languages, and that some of their hearers at all events understood them, vv. 8, 11 (ἡμετέραις). (On the phrase as distinguished from those used elsewhere in Acts and in 1 Cor., see Grimm-Thayer, *sub v.*, γλῶττα 2, and Blass, *Acta Apost.*, p. 50, "γλῶττα etiam ap. att. per se est lingua peregrina vel potius vocabulum pere-grinum".) Wendt and Matthias, who have recently given us a lengthy account of the events of the first Christian Pente-cost, both hold that this speaking with tongues is introduced by St. Luke him-self, and that it is a legendary embel-lishment from his hand of what actually took place; the speaking with tongues at Pentecost was simply identical with the same phenomenon described else-where in x. 46, xix. 6, and in 1 Cor. xii.-xiv. This is plain from St. Peter's own words in xi. 15, 17; so in xix. 6, the speaking with tongues is the immediate result of the outpouring of the Spirit. So too Wendt lays stress upon the fact that St. Paul says λαλεῖν γλώσσαις or γλώσσῃ, but not λαλ. ἑτέρ. γλ. The former was evidently the original mode of describing the phenomenon, to which Luke recurs in his own description in x. 46 and xix. 6, whereas in the passage before us his language represents the miraculous enhancement of the events of Pentecost. M'Giffert, in the same way, thinks that the writer of Acts, far removed from the events, could hardly avoid investing even the common phenomena of the *Glossolalia* with marvel and mystery. Wendt however admits that this embellishment was already accomplished by Christian tradition before Luke. But if St. Luke must have had every means of knowing from St. Paul the character of the speaking with tongues at Corinth, it does not seem unfair to maintain that he also had means of knowing from the old Palestinian Christians, who had been in union with the Church at Jerusalem from the beginning, *e.g.*, from a John Mark, or a Mnason (ἀρχαῖος μαθητής, xxi. 16), the exact facts connected with the great outpouring of the Spirit on the day of Pentecost (Schmid, *Biblische Theologie*, pp. 278, 279). But it is further to be noted that Wendt by no means denies that there was a miraculous element, as shown in the outpouring of the Spirit, in the events of the Pentecostal Feast, but that he also considers it quite unlikely that Luke's introduction of a still further miraculous element was prompted by a symbolising tendency, a desire to draw a parallel between the Christian Pentecost and the miraculous delivery of the Law, according to the Jewish tradition that the one voice which proceeded from Sinai divided into seventy tongues, and was heard by the seventy nations of the world, each in their mother tongue (so Zeller, Pfleiderer, Hilgenfeld, Spitta, Jüngst and Matthias, and so apparently Clemen in his " Speaking with Tongues," *Expository Times*, p. 345, 1899). But in the first place there is no convincing evidence at the early date of the Christian Pentecost of any connection in Jewish tradition between the Feast of Pentecost and the giving of the Law on Sinai (*cf.* Schmid, *Biblische Theologie*, p. 286; Hamburger, *Real-Encyclopädie des Judentums*, i., 7, 1057, and Holtzmann, *Apostelgeschichte*, p. 330), and it is significant that neither Philo nor Josephus make any reference to any such connection ; and in the next place it is strange, as Wendt himself points out, that if Luke had started with the idea of the importance of any such symbolism, no reference should be made to it in the subsequent address of Peter, whereas even in the catalogue of the nations there is no reference of any kind to the number seventy ; the number actually given, vv. 9, 11, might rather justify the far-fetched notice of Holtzmann (*u. s.*, p. 331), that a reference is meant to the sixteen grandsons of Noah, Gen. x. 1, 2,

6, 21. Certainly Heb. ii. 2-4 cannot, as Schmid well points out against Holtzmann, lead to any such connection of ideas as the μερισμοὶ πνεύμ. ἀγ. are evidently the distribution of the gifts of the Spirit. We may readily admit that the miracle on the birthday of the Christian Church was meant to foreshadow the universal progress of the new faith, and its message for all mankind without distinction of nation, position, or age. But even if the Jewish tradition referred to above was in existence at this early date, we have still to consider whether the narrative in Acts could possibly be a copy of it, or dependent upon it. According to the tradition, a voice was to be expected from Heaven which would be understood by different men in their mother tongues, but in our narrative the Apostles themselves speak after the manner of men in these tongues. For to suppose that the Apostles all spoke one and the same language, but that the hearers were enabled to understand these utterances, each in his own language, is not only to do violence to the narrative, but simply to substitute one miraculous incident for another. Nor again, as Wendt further admits, is there any real ground for seeing in the miraculous event under consideration a cancelling of the confusion of tongues at Babel which resulted from rebellion against God, for the narrative does not contain any trace of the conception of a unity of language to which the Jewish idea appears to have tended as a contrast to the confusion of Babel (Test. xii., Patr., *Jud.*, xxv.). The unity is not one of uniformity of speech but of oneness of Spirit and in the Spirit. At the same time there was a peculiar fitness in the fact that the first and most abundant bestowal of this divine gift should be given at a Feast which was marked above all others by the presence of strangers from distant lands, that a sign should thus be given to them that believed not, and that the firstfruits of a Gentile harvest should be offered by the Spirit to the Father (Iren., *Adv. Haer*, iii., 17), an assurance to the Apostles of the greatness and universality of the message which they were commissioned to deliver. But there is no reason to suppose that this power of speaking in foreign languages was a permanent gift. In the first place the Greek language was known throughout the Roman Empire, and in the next place Acts xiv. 11 (see *in loco*) seems to forbid any such view. The speaking

λαόν.[1] ὁ δὲ Κύριος προσετίθει τοὺς σωζομένους καθ᾽ ἡμέραν τῇ ἐκκλησίᾳ.[2]

[1] τον λαον; D has τον κοσμον. Nestle and Chase point out Syriac as probable source; the former, with Blass, thinking that St. Luke first of all translated the word wrongly, κοσμον, and corrected it in later edition to λαον, whilst Chase gives the variation a much later origin. Harris supposes that the translator first introduced "mundum" (cf. "tout le monde") and thence it crept into the Greek. Belser finds no need for Syriac influence, as St. Luke in revising might easily substitute "people" for the more general term "world". Some Syriac influence may have been at work, or possibly a corruption of the Greek may be suggested. Hilg. also has κοσμον. See further Dalman, *Die Worte Jesu*, p. 54.

[2] τη εκκλησια. επι το αυτο (iii.) EP, Syrr. (P. and H.); but for omitting τη εκκλ. and concluding ii. with επι το αυτο ℵABCG 61, Vulg., Sah., Boh., Arm., Aeth., so Bengel, Tisch., W.H., R.V., Weiss, Wendt. The T.R. was followed by Meyer, De Wette, Nösgen, on account of the extreme difficulty of the proposed correction, but the latter is too well attested. Hilg. has επι το αυτο εν τη εκκλησια, so D.

with tongues in Acts ii. and in other passages of the N.T. may be classed as identical in so far as each was the effect of the divine Πνεῦμα, each a miraculous spiritual gift, marking a new epoch of spiritual life. But in Acts we have what we have not elsewhere—the speaking in foreign tongues—this was not the case in Corinth; there the speaking with tongues was absolutely unintelligible, it could not be understood without an interpreter, *i.e.*, without another gift of the divine Spirit, *viz.*, interpretation, 1 Cor. xii. 10, 30 (the word *unknown* inserted in A.V. in 1 Cor. xiv. is unfortunate), and the fact that the Apostle compares the speaking with tongues to a speaking in foreign languages shows that the former was itself no speaking in foreign tongues, since two identical things do not admit of comparison (Schmid, *u. s.*, pp. 288, 289).

Peter might well express his belief that Cornelius and those who spoke with tongues had also received the Holy Ghost, *cf.* x. 44, xi. 17, 24, *in loco ;* but it does not follow that the gift bestowed upon them was identical with that bestowed at Pentecost—there were diversities of gifts from the bounty of the One Spirit. Felten, *Apostelgeschichte*, p. 78; Evans in *Speaker's Commentary* on 1 *Cor.*, p. 334; Plumptre, B.D.[1] "Tongues, Gift of"; Weizsäcker, *Apostolic Age*, ii., pp. 272, 273, E.T., and Feine, *Eine Vorkanonische Ueberlieferung des Lukas*, n., p. 167; Zöckler, *Apostelgeschichte*, p. 177; Page, *Acts of the Apostles*, note on chap. ii., 4; and A. Wright, *Some N. T. Problems*, p. 277 ff.

The objection urged at length by Wendt and Spitta that foreign languages could not have been spoken, since in that case there was no occasion to accuse the Apostles of drunkenness, but that ecstatic incoherent utterances of devotion and praise might well have seemed to the hearers sounds produced by revelry or madness (*cf.* 1 Cor. xiv. 23), is easily met by noting that the utterances were not received with mockery by all but only by some, the word ἕτεροι apparently denoting quite a different class of hearers, who may have been unacquainted with the language spoken, and hence regarded the words as an unintelligible jargon.

Spitta attempts to break up Acts ii. 1-13 into two sources, i.ᵃ, 4, 12, 13, belonging to A, and simply referring to a *Glossolalia* like that at Corinth, whilst the other verses are assigned to B and the Redactor, and contain a narrative which could only have been derived from the Jewish tradition mentioned above, and introducing the notion of foreign tongues at a date when the *Glossolalia* had ceased to exist, and so to be understood. Spitta refers συμπληροῦσθαι ii. 1 to the filling up of the number of the Apostles in chap. i., so that his source A begins καὶ ἐν τῷ συμπλ. . . . ἐπλήσθησαν πάντες π. ἁγ., *Apostelgeschichte*, p. 52. It is not surprising that Hilgenfeld should speak of the narrative as one which cannot be thus divided, upon which as he says Spitta has in vain essayed his artificial analysis.

Community of Goods.—The key to the two passages, ii. 42 ff. and iv. 32 ff., is to be found in the expression in which they both agree, occurring in ii. 45 and iv. 35, καθότι ἄν τις χρείαν εἶχεν. Such expressions indicate, as we have seen, not reckless but judicious charity (see also Ramsay, *St. Paul*, etc., p. 373, and reading in D, ii., 45); they show wise management, as in early days St. Chrysostom noted in commenting on the words, so that the Christians did not act recklessly like many philosophers among the Greeks, of whom some gave up their lands, others cast great quantities of money into the sea, which was no contempt of riches, but only folly and madness (*Hom.*, vii.). Not that St. Luke's glowing and repeated description (on St. Luke's way of sometimes repeating himself as here, see Harris, *Four Lectures on the Western Text*, p. 85) is to be confined to the exercise of mere almsgiving on the part of the Church. Both those who had, and those who had not, were alike the inheritors of a kingdom which could only be entered by the poor in spirit, alike members of a family and a household in which there was one Master, even Christ, in Whose Name all who believed were brethren. In this poverty of spirit, in this sense of brotherhood, "the poor man knew no shame, the rich no haughtiness" (Chrys.).

But whilst men were called upon to give ungrudgingly, they were not called upon to give of necessity : what each one had was still his own, τὰ ὑπάρχοντα αὐτῷ, iv. 32, although not even one (οὐδὲ εἷς) of them reckoned it so; the daily ministration in vi. 1 seems to show that no equal division of property amongst all was intended ; the act of Barnabas was apparently one of charity rather than of communism, for nothing is said of an absolute surrender of all that he had ; the act of Ananias and Sapphira was entirely voluntary, although it presented itself almost as a duty (Ramsay, *u. s.*); Mark's mother still retains her home at Jerusalem, xii. 12, and it would seem that Mnason too had a dwelling there (see on xxi. 16). At Joppa, ix. 36, 39, and at Antioch, xi. 29, there was evidently no absolute equality of earthly possessions —Tabitha helps the poor out of her own resources, and every man as he prospered sent his contributions to the Church at Jerusalem.

It is sometimes urged that this enthusiasm of charity and of the spirit (ἐνθουσιασμός, as Blass calls it), which filled at all events the Church at Jerusalem, was due to the expectation of Christ's immediate return, and that in the light of that event men regarded lands and possessions as of no account, even if ordinary daily work was not neglected (O. Holtzmann, *Neutest. Zeitgeschichte*, p. 233). But it is strange that if this is the true account of the action of the Church at Jerusalem, a similar mode of life and charity should not have found place in other Churches, *e.g.*, in the Church at Thessalonica, where the belief in Christ's speedy return was so overwhelmingly felt (Felten). No picture could be more extraordinary than that drawn by O. Holtzmann of the Christian Church at Jerusalem, driven by the voice of Christian prophets to enjoin an absolutely compulsory community of goods in expectation of the nearness of the Parousia, and of Ananias and Sapphira as the victims of this tyrannical product of fanaticism and overwrought excitement. It is a relief to turn from such a strange perversion of the narrative to the enthusiastic language in which, whilst insisting on its idealising tendency, Renan and Pfleiderer alike have recognised the beauty of St. Luke's picture, and of the social transformation which was destined to renew the face of the earth, which found its pattern of serving and patient love in Jesus the Friend of the poor, whose brotherhood opened a place of refuge for the oppressed, the destitute, the weak, who enjoyed in the mutual love of their fellows a foretaste of the future kingdom in which God Himself will wipe all tears from their eyes. Whatever qualifications must be made in accepting the whole description given us by Renan and Pfleiderer, they were at least right in recognising the important factor of the Person of Jesus, and the probability that during His lifetime He had Himself laid the foundations of the social movement which so soon ennobled and blessed His Church. It is far more credible that the disciples should have continued the common life in which they had lived with their Master than that they should have derived a social system from the institutions of the Essenes. There is no proof of any historical connection between this sect and the Apostolic Church, nor can we say that the high moral standard and mode of common life adopted by the Essenes, although in some respects analogous to their own, had any direct influence on the followers of Christ. Moreover, with points of comparison, there were also points of contrast. St. Luke's notice, ii. 46, that the believers continued steadfastly in the Temple, stands out in contrast to the perpetual absence of the Essenes from the Temple, to which they sent their gifts (Jos., *Ant.*, xviii. 2, 5); the common meals of the Essene brotherhood naturally present a likeness to St. Luke's description of the

III. 1.[1] ἘΠΙ τὸ αὐτὸ δὲ Πέτρος καὶ Ἰωάννης ἀνέβαινον εἰς τὸ
ἱερὸν ἐπὶ τὴν ὥραν τῆς προσευχῆς τὴν ἐνάτην.　2. καί[2] τις ἀνὴρ

[1] D begins εν δε ταις ημεραις ταυταις, so Par. Blass (so Harris) regards the
phrase as addition " in principio novæ lectionis," but the addition is characteristic of
Luke; Hilg. retains.　After ιερον D also inserts το δειλινον (the acc. of time, like τὸ
πρώι, v. 21—defended by Belser (and by Zöckler), who argues that it is more likely
to have been struck out on revision than added by a later hand); Hilg. retains.

[2] After και D, Par.[2], Syr. Pesh. insert ιδου.　υπαρχων om. D, Gig., Par.

early Christian Church, but whilst the
Essenes dined together, owing to their
scrupulosity in avoiding all food except
what was ceremonially pure, the Christians saw in every poor man who partook
of their common meal the real Presence
of their Lord.　Of all contemporary sects
it may no doubt be said that the Christian society resembled most nearly the
Essenes, but with this admission Weizsäcker well adds : " The Essenes, through
their binding rules and their suppression
of individualism, were, from their very
nature, an order of limited extent.　In
the new Society the moral obligation of
liberty reigned, and disclosed an unlimited future," *Apostolic Age*, i., 58 (E.T.).
It is often supposed that the after-poverty
of the Church in Jerusalem, Rom. xv. 26,
Gal. ii. 10, etc., was the result of this
first enthusiasm of love and charity, and
that the failure of a community of goods
in the mother city prevented its introduction elsewhere.　But not only is the
above view of the " communism " of the
early Christians adverse to this supposition, but there were doubtless many causes
at work which may account for the poverty
of the Saints in Jerusalem, *cf*. Rendall,
Expositor, Nov., 1893, p. 322.　The collection for the Saints, which occupies such a
prominent place in St. Paul's life and
words, may not have been undertaken for
any exceptional distress as in the earlier
case of the famine in Judæa, Acts xi. 26,
but we cannot say how severely the
effects of the famine may have affected
the fortunes of the Jerusalem Christians.
We must too take into account the persecution of the Christians by their rich
neighbours ; the wealthy Sadducees were
their avowed opponents.　From the first
it was likely that the large majority of the
Christians in Jerusalem would possess
little of this world's goods, and the constant increase in the number of the disciples would have added to the difficulty
of maintaining the disproportionate number of poor.　But we cannot shut our eyes
to the fact that there was another and a
fatal cause at work—love itself had grown

cold—the picture drawn by St. James
in his Epistle is painfully at variance
with the golden days which he had himself
seen, when bitter jealousy and faction
were unknown, for all were of one heart
and one soul, Zahn, *Skizzen aus dem
Leben der alten Kirche*, p. 39 ff.; Zöckler,
u.s., pp. 191, 192; Wendt, *in loco*;
M'Giffert, *Apostolic Age*, p. 67 ; Conybeare, "Essenes," Hastings' B.D. ;
Kaufmann, *Socialism and Communism*,
p. 5 ff.

CHAPTER III.—Ver. 1.　St. Luke
selects out of the number of τέρατα καὶ
σημεῖα the one which was the immediate
antecedent of the first persecution.　" Non
dicitur primum hoc miraculum fuisse, sed
fuit, quanquam unum e multis, ipso loco
maxime conspicuum," Blass, as against
Weiss, Hilgenfeld, Feine.—ἀνέβαινον, *cf*.
Luke xviii. 10.　"Two men went up into
the Temple to pray," *i.e.*, from the lower
city to Mount Moriah, the hill of the
Temple, "the hill of the house," on its
site see "Jerusalem," B.D.[2].　The verb
is in the imperfect, because the Apostles
do not enter the Temple until ver. 8.
St. Chrysostom comments: Πέτρος καὶ
Ἰωάννης ἦσαν καὶ τὸν Ἰησοῦν εἶχον
μέσον, Matt. xviii. 20.—ἐπὶ τὴν ὥραν
τῆς προσευχῆς, not *during* or *about*, but
marking a definite time, *for the hour*,
i.e., to be there during the hour—sometimes the words are taken to mean
"towards the hour": see Plummer on
Luke x. 35 (so apparently Weiss).　Page
renders "for, *i.e.*, to be there at the
hour" (so Felten, Lumby).　In going
thus to the Temple they imitated their
Master, Matt. xxvi. 55.—τὴν ἐνάτην, *i.e.*,
3 P.M., when the evening sacrifice was
offered, Jos., *Ant.*, xiv., 4, 3.　Edersheim
points out that although the evening
sacrifice was fixed by the Jews as "between the evenings," *i.e.*, between the
darkness of the gloaming and that of
the night, and although the words of
Psalm cxxxiv., and the appointment of
Levite singers for night service, 1 Chron.
ix. 33, xxiii. 30, seem to imply an evening service, yet in the time of our Lord

χωλὸς ἐκ κοιλίας μητρὸς αὐτοῦ ὑπάρχων ἐβαστάζετο· ὃν ἐτίθουν
καθ' ἡμέραν πρὸς τὴν θύραν τοῦ ἱεροῦ τὴν λεγομένην Ὡραίαν, τοῦ

the evening sacrifice commenced much earlier, *The Temple; its Ministry and Services*, pp. 115, 116. According to Schürer, followed by Blass who appeals to the authority of Hamburger, there is no ground for supposing that the third, sixth, and ninth hours of the day were regular stated times for prayer. The actual times were rather (1) early in the morning at the time of the morning sacrifice (see also Edersheim, *u. s.*, p. 115); (2) in the afternoon about the ninth hour (three o'clock), at the time of the evening sacrifice; (3) in the evening at sunset (*Jewish People*, div. ii., vol. i., 290, E.T.). The third, sixth, and ninth hours were no doubt appropriated to private prayer, and some such rule might well have been derived from Psalm lv. 7; *cf.* Dan. vi. 11. This custom of prayer three times a day passed very early into the Christian Church, *Didache*, viii. 3. To Abraham, Isaac and Jacob the three daily times of prayer are traced back in the *Berachoth*, 26 *b;* Charles, *Apocalypse of Baruch*, p. 99.

Ver. 2. τις, by its position as in Luke xi. 27 directs attention to this man, "the man was conspicuous both from the place and from his malady" Chrys., *Hom.*, viii.—χωλὸς ... ὑπάρχων: "a certain man that was lame" R.V., otherwise ὑπάρχων is not noticed, fittingly used here in its classical sense expressing the connection between the man's present state and his previous state, see on ii. 30.—ἐβαστάζετο: imperf., expressing a customary act, the man was being carried at the hour of worship when the Temple would be filled with worshippers (Chrysostom); or the verb may mean that he was being carried in the sense that the bearers had not yet placed him in the accustomed spot for begging, *cf.* 2 Kings xviii. 14, Ecclesiasticus vi. 25, Bel and the Dragon, ver. 36; Theod.—ὃν ἐτίθουν: the imperfect used of customary or repeated action in past time, Burton, *Syntax of Moods and Tenses*, etc., p. 12, on the form see Winer-Schmiedel, p. 121; Blass, *Grammatik des N. G.*, p. 48: in Acts there are several undoubted instances of the way in which the imperfect 3rd plural of verbs in μι was often formed as if from a contract verb, *cf.* iv. 33, 35, xxvii. 1.—πρὸς τὴν θύραν: R.V. "door," although in ver. 10 we have not θύρα but πύλη. —τὴν λεγ. Ὡραίαν: it may have been the

gate of Nicanor (so called because Judas Maccabæus had nailed to the gate the hand of his conquered foe, 1 Macc. vii. 47). The description given of it by Josephus, *B. J.*, v., 5, 3, marks it as specially magnificent, *cf.* also Hamburger, *Real-Encycl.*, ii., 8, p. 1198. This view was held by Wetstein, see, *in loco*, Nicanor's gate. Another interpretation refers the term to the gate Shushan, which was not only close to the Porch of Solomon, but also to the market for the sale of doves and other offerings, and so a fitting spot for a beggar to choose (Zöckler). The gate may have been so called because a picture of the Persian capital Susa was placed over it (Hamburger, *u. s.*), *i.e.*, Town of Lilies. *Cf.* Hebrew Shushan, a lily, the lily being regarded as the type of beauty. Wendt suggests that the title may be explained from the decoration on the pillars of lily work מַעֲשֵׂה שׁוּשָׁן.

Mr. Wright, *Some N.T. Problems*, 1898, has recently argued that the eastern gate of the Court of the Women is meant, p. 304 ff. (so too Schürer, *Jewish People*, div. ii., vol. i., p. 180, E.T.). This court was the place of assembly for the services, and a beggar might naturally choose a position near it. The decision as to which of these gates reference is made to is rendered more difficult by the fact that, so far as we know, no gate bore the name "Beautiful". But the decision apparently lies between these alternatives, although others have been proposed, *cf.* John Lightfoot, *Hor. Heb.*, *in loco*, and Wright, *u. s.* In such notices as the mention of the Beautiful Gate, Solomon's Porch, Feine sees indications of a true and reliable tradition.—τοῦ αἰτεῖν: genitive of the purpose, very frequent in this form, genitive of the article with the infinitive both in the N.T. and in the LXX, *cf.* Gen. iv. 15, 1 Kings i. 35, Ezekiel xxi. 11; Luke xxiv. 16, see especially Burton, *Syntax of Moods and Tenses*, p. 159. It is very characteristic of St. Luke, and next to him of St. Paul —probably indicates the influence of the LXX, although the construction is found in classical Greek, *cf.* Xen., *Anab.*, iii., 5, see Viteau, *Le Grec du N. T.*, p. 172 (1893). It was a common thing for beggars amongst the Jews as amongst the Christians (just as amongst the Romans, Martial, i., 112) to frequent the Temple

αἰτεῖν ἐλεημοσύνην [1] παρὰ τῶν εἰσπορευομένων εἰς τὸ ἱερόν. 3. ὃς
ἰδὼν [2] Πέτρον καὶ Ἰωάννην μέλλοντας εἰσιέναι εἰς τὸ ἱερὸν ἠρώτα [3]
ἐλεημοσύνην λαβεῖν. 4.[4] ἀτενίσας δὲ Πέτρος εἰς αὐτὸν σὺν τῷ
Ἰωάννῃ, εἶπε,[5] Βλέψον εἰς ἡμᾶς. 5.[6] ὁ δὲ ἐπεῖχεν αὐτοῖς, προσδοκῶν

[1] For παρα των εισπ. εις το ιερον D has παρ' αυτων εισπορ. αυτων εις το ιερ., but
not received by Blass in β (Chase sees in first part exact reproduction of Syriac
αυτων being carelessly repeated).

[2] For ος ιδων D, Flor. read ουτος (so Gig., Par.) ατενισας τοις οφθαλμοις αυτου
και ιδων (Chase: interpolation arose in Syriac). Belser again sees the longer form
which Luke abbreviated in α.

[3] After ηρωτα D, Flor., Par.[1] insert αυτους. λαβειν (𝕹ABCE, b, 13, 61, Vulg.,
Boh., Arm., Chrys.) om. by DP, h, Fl., Gig., Par.[1], Syr. Harcl., Lucif.—Blass
"recte ut vid.".—added by T.R., W.H., Weiss.

[4] For ατενισας D, Flor., Par.[2] read εμβλεψας (εμβλεπειν not uncommon in the
Gospels); (συν Ιωανην in D is attributed by Chase to Syriac influence, cf. Aquila,
συν τον ουρανον και συν την γην); Hilg. follows D.

[5] For ειπε Flor. has "(ad)stans dixit ei"; so in β επιστας ειπεν αυτω, in which
Belser sees the simpler form of Luke's own revision. For βλεψ. εις ημας D, Flor.
ατενισεν εις εμε (ημας D); εμε is curious, but may be earlier edition, or introduced
later because John here says nothing. Throughout the passage D, as compared
with T.R. or with W.H., introduces different synonyms for "see". Thus T.R.
ιδων . . . ατενισας . . . βλεψον, D ατενισας (τους οφθ. και ιδων) . . . εμβλεψας
. . . ατενισον, or from Belser's point of view, we must see in the T.R. three words
for "see" which may be introduced by Luke in revising his rough draft. But it is
difficult to account even in a rough draft for ατενισας in ver. 5 instead of ητενισεν,
and for the και introduced before ειπεν without any construction in ver. 4.

[6] επειχεν αυτοις; D reads ατενισας; Flor. represents ητενισεν εις αυτον (so β),
see above. But in the fact that D reads αυτοις instead of εις αυτους (ον), as we
might expect after ατεν., Weiss sees a further proof of the secondary character of
the reading.

and Churches for alms. St. Chrysostom
notes the custom as common as it is to-
day in continental cathedrals or modern
mosques. — ἐλεημοσύνην: common in
the LXX but not classical, sometimes used for the feeling of mercy
(ἔλεος), Prov. iii. 3, xix. 22, and constantly through the book; and then for
mercy showing itself in acts of pity,
almsgiving, Tobit i. 3, xii. 8, cf. Acts
ix. 36, x. 2, where it is used in the plural,
as often in the LXX. Our word alms
is derived from it and the German
Almosen, both being corruptions of the
Greek word.
    Ver. 3. ἠρώτα λαβεῖν: "asked to
receive," R.V., as other English versions
except A.V. The expression is quite
classical, αἰτῶν λαβεῖν, Aristoph., Plut.,
240, cf. Mark i. 17, and LXX, Exodus
xxiii. 15, for similar instances of a re-
dundant infinitive. The verb is in the
imperfect, because the action of asking
is imperfect until what is asked for is
granted by another, Blass, in loco, and
Grammatik des N. G., pp. 187, 236, and
Salmon, Hermathena, xxi. p. 228.

Ver. 4. ἀτενίσας, cf. i. 10. βλέψον
εἰς ἡμᾶς: it has sometimes been thought
that the command was given to see
whether the man was a worthless beggar
or not (Nösgen), or whether he was
spiritually disposed for the reception of
the benefit, and would show his faith (as
in our Lord's miracles of healing), or it
might mean that the man's whole attention was to be directed towards the
Apostles, as he evidently only expects
an alms, ver. 5. At the same time, as
Feine remarks, the fact that the narrative does not mention that faith was
demanded of the man, forms an essential
contrast to the narrative often compared
with it in xiv. 9.
    Ver. 5. ὁ δὲ ἐπεῖχεν, sc., νοῦν (not
τοὺς ὀφθαλμούς); cf. Luke xiv. 7, 1
Tim. iv. 16, Ecclesiasticus xxxi. (xxxiv.)
2, 2 Macc. ix. 25 (Job xxx. 26, A.S.[2]
al.) with dative rei; so in Polybius.
    Ver 6. ἀργύριον καὶ χρυσίον: the words
do not suggest the idea of a complete communism amongst the believers, although
Oecumenius derives from them a proof
of the absolute poverty of the Apostles.

τι παρ᾽ αὐτῶν λαβεῖν. 6. εἶπε δὲ Πέτρος, Ἀργύριον καὶ χρυσίον
οὐχ ὑπάρχει μοι· ὃ δὲ ἔχω, τοῦτό σοι δίδωμι. ἐν τῷ ὀνόματι Ἰησοῦ
Χριστοῦ τοῦ Ναζωραίου, ¹ ἔγειραι καὶ περιπάτει. 7. καὶ πιάσας

¹ ἔγειραι καὶ περιπατει ; AEGP 61 read ἔγειρε, found in ACEGP 61, Vulg., Boh.,
Syrr. (P. and H.), Arm., Aeth., Ir^{int.}; but omitted by אBD, Sah., so Tisch., W.H.,
R.V., Weiss, Hilg., Wendt (who sees in the preceding words assimilation to passages
in the Gospels). αναστα Epiph.

They may perhaps be explained by remembering that if the Apostles had no
silver or gold with them, they were
literally obeying their Lord's command,
Matt. x. 9, or that whatever money
they had was held by them in trust for
the public good, not as available for
private charity. Spitta, who interprets
ii. 45 of the Apostles alone (pp. 72-74),
sees in St. Peter's words a confirmation
of his view, and a further fulfilment of
our Lord's words in Luke xii. 33, but if
our interpretation of ii. 44 ff. is correct,
our Lord's words were fully obeyed, but
as a principle of charity, and not as a
rule binding to the letter. St. Chrysostom (*Hom.*, viii.) justly notes the unassuming language of St. Peter here, so
free from boasting and personal display.
Compare 1 Peter i. 18 (iii. 3), where the
Apostle sharply contrasts the corruptible gold and silver with higher and
spiritual gifts (Scharfe).—ὃ δὲ ἔχω: the
difference between this verb and ὑπάρχει
may be maintained by regarding the
latter as used of worldly belongings,
ἔχω of that which was lasting and
surely held.—ἐν τῷ ὀνόματι: no occasion
to prefix such words as λέγω σοι for the
expression means "in the power of this
name" (*cf.* Matt. vii. 22, Luke x. 17,
Acts iv. 10, xvi. 18, James v. 14, Mark
xvi. 17). So too the Hebrew בְּשֵׁם
in the name of any one, *i.e.*, by his authority, Exodus v. 23, and thus "in the
name of Jehovah," *i.e.*, by divine authority, Deut. xviii. 22, 1 Chron. xxii. 19,
Jer. xi. 21, and frequently in the Psalms,
cf. also *Book of Enoch*, xlviii. 7 (Charles,
p. 48). On the use, or possible use, of
the phrase in extra-biblical literature, see
Deissmann, *Bibelstudien*, p. 145, and
also *Neue Bibelstudien*, p. 25 (1897).
When Celsus alleged that the Christians
cast out demons by the aid of evil spirits,
Origen claims this power for the name of
Jesus: τοσοῦτον γὰρ δύναται τὸ ὄνομα
τοῦ Ἰησοῦ, *cf.* also Justin Martyr, *Dial.
c. Tryph.*, 85.—Ἰ. Χ. τοῦ Ναζωραίου: the
words must in themselves have tested

the faith of the lame man. His part has
sometimes been represented as merely
passive, and as if no appeal of any kind
were made to his faith contrasted with
xiv. 9 (ver. 16 in this chapter being
interpreted only of the faith of the
Apostles), but a test of faith was implied
in the command which bade the man
rise and walk in the power of a name
which a short time before had been
placed as an inscription on a malefactor's
cross, but with which St. Peter now bids
him to associate the dignity and power
of the Messiah (see Plumptre, *in loco*).
It is necessary from another point of
view to emphasise this implied appeal
to the man's faith, since Zeller and
Overbeck regard the omission of faith
in the recipient as designed to magnify
the magic of the miracle. Zeller remarks: "Our book makes but one observation on his state of mind, which
certainly indicates a receptivity, but unfortunately not a receptivity for spiritual
gifts". But nothing was more natural
than that the man should at first expect
to receive money, and his faith in St.
Peter's words is rather enhanced by the
fact that the Apostle had already declared his utter inability to satisfy his
expectations. St. Luke much more frequently than the other Evangelists names
our Lord from His early home Nazareth,
in which frequency Friedrich sees another point of likeness between St.
Luke's Gospel and the Acts, *Das Lucasevangelium*, p. 85. Holtzmann attempts
to refer the whole story to an imitation
of Luke v. 18-26, but see as against such
attempts Feine, *Eine vorkanonische
Überlieferung des Lukas*, pp. 175, 199, 200 .
Ver. 7. πιάσας, *cf.* xii. 4: so in LXX,
Cant. ii. 15, Ecclesiasticus xxiii. 21, A. *al.*
χειρὸς very similar to, if not exactly, a
partitive genitive, found after verbs of
touching, etc., inasmuch as the touching
affects only a part of the object (Mark v.
30), and so too often after verbs of *taking
hold of*, the part or the limit grasped is
put in the genitive, Mark v. 41 (accusative being used when the whole person is

αὐτὸν τῆς δεξιᾶς χειρὸς [1] ἤγειρε · παραχρῆμα δὲ ἐστερεώθησαν αὐτοῦ
αἱ βάσεις καὶ τὰ σφυρά,[2] 8. καὶ [3] ἐξαλλόμενος ἔστη καὶ περιεπάτει,
καὶ εἰσῆλθε σὺν αὐτοῖς εἰς τὸ ἱερὸν περιπατῶν καὶ ἁλλόμενος καὶ

[1] ηγειρε ℵABCG 15, 18, 61, Syr. (P. and H.), Arm., Sah., Boh., Aeth., Bas., Cypr.,
Lucif. insert αυτον; so Tisch., W.H., R.V., Weiss, Wendt (but omitted by Meyer)
—omitted in DEP.

[2] αυτου αι βασεις DEGP, Chrys.; but αι β. αυτου ℵABC 61, Vulg., Bas., Tert.,
Lucif., so Tisch., W.H., Weiss. σφυρα ℵ³B³C²DEGP, so Hilg.; but σφυδρα
ℵ*B*C*, so Tisch., W.H., Weiss, Blass (Winer-Schmiedel, p. 64).

[3] και εξαλλομενος εστη omit Flor. περιεπατει, after this word D inserts χαιρομενος
(χαιρων E), Flor. *gaudens et exultans* = χαιρων και εξαλλομενος in β, so Hilg. περι-
πατων και αλλ. και omitted by D, Flor. It is difficult to determine the precise order of
events—possibly "leaping" is not mentioned at all in Western text, and in it the
healed man does not at all events "leap" in the Temple. It is again difficult to
believe that in this passage the common text comes from a revision of the author,
and not rather through corruption and confusion.

seized, Matt. xiv. 3), Blass, *Grammatik
des N. G.*, p. 100, *cf.* classical use in
Eurip., *Hec.*, 523. The meaning of
πιάζω in N.T. and in the LXX has
passed into modern Greek = πιάνω =
seize, apprehend (Kennedy). For a
similar use see also 2 Cor. xi. 32, Rev.
xix. 20, and John vii. 30, 32, 33, 44,
viii. 20, x. 39, xi. 57, xxi. 3, 10.—παραχρῆμα, *i.e.*, παρὰ τὸ χρῆμα, forthwith,
immediately, *auf der Stelle*, on the spot,
specially characteristic of St. Luke, both
in Gospel and Acts (*cf.* εὐθύς of St. Mark).
It is found no less than ten times in the
Gospel, and six to seven times in Acts,
elsewhere in N.T. only twice, Matt. xxi.
19, 20; several times in LXX, Wisdom
xviii. 17, Tobit viii. 3, S., 2 Macc. iv. 34,
38, etc., 4 Macc. xiv. 9, Bel and the
Dragon, ver. 39, 42, Theod., and in
Num. vi. 9, xii. 4, AB²R., Isaiah xxix.
5, for Hebrew, פִּתְאֹם; frequent in
Attic prose; see also Dalman, *Die Worte
Jesu*, pp. 22, 29. But as the word is so
manifestly characteristic of St. Luke it
is noteworthy that in the large majority
of instances it is employed by him in
connection with miracles of healing or
the infliction of disease and death, and
this frequency of use and application
may be paralleled by the constant employment of the word in an analogous
way in medical writers; see, *e.g.*, Hobart,
Medical Language of St. Luke, and instances in Hippocrates, Galen, Dioscorides. — ἐστερεώθησαν: στερεόω =
to make firm or solid; it cannot by
any means be regarded only as a technical medical term, but as a matter of fact
it was often employed in medical language (so also the adjective στερεός),

and this use of the word makes it a
natural one for a medical man to employ
here, especially in connection with βάσεις
and σφυρά. It is used only by St.
Luke in the N.T. (ver. 16 and xvi. 5), but
very frequently in the LXX. The nearest approach to a medical use of the
word is given perhaps by Wetstein, *in
loco*, Xen., *Pæd.*, viii.—αἱ βάσεις, "the
feet" (βαίνω). The word is constantly
used in LXX, but for the most part in
the sense of something upon which a
thing may rest, but it is found in the
same sense as here in Wisdom xiii. 18;
cf. also Jos., *Ant.*, vii., 3, 5, so in Plato,
Timæus, 92, A. It was in frequent use
amongst medical men, and its employment here, and here only in the N.T.,
with the mention of the other details,
e.g., the more precise σφυρά, "ankle-
bones," also only found in this one passage in N.T., has been justly held to
point to the technical description of a
medical man; see not only Hobart, p.
34 ff., *u. s.*, and Belcher's *Miracles of
Healing*, p. 41, but Bengel, Zöckler,
Rendall, Zahn.
Ver. 8. ἐξαλλόμενος: not leaping out
of his couch (as has sometimes been supposed), of which there is no mention,
but leaping up for joy (*cf.* Isaiah lv. 12,
Joel ii. 5) (on the spelling with one λ see
Blass, p. 51); *cf.* also Isaiah xxxv. 6.
This seems more natural than to suppose
that he leaped because he was incredulous, or because he did not know how to
walk, (or to avoid the suspicion of hypocrisy (Chrys., *Hom.*, viii., so too Oecumenius). St. Chrysostom remarks that
it was no less than if they saw Christ
risen from the dead to hear Peter saying:
"In the name," etc., and if Christ is not

αἰνῶν τὸν Θεόν. 9. καὶ εἶδεν αὐτὸν πᾶς ὁ λαὸς περιπατοῦντα καὶ αἰνοῦντα τὸν Θεόν· 10. ἐπεγίνωσκόν τε αὐτὸν ὅτι οὗτος ἦν ὁ πρὸς τὴν ἐλεημοσύνην καθήμενος ἐπὶ τῇ Ὡραίᾳ πύλῃ τοῦ ἱεροῦ· καὶ ἐπλήσθησαν θάμβους καὶ ¹ ἐκστάσεως ἐπὶ τῷ συμβεβηκότι αὐτῷ.

¹ εκστασεως, before this word Flor., Par.¹ insert παντες. For θαμβ. και εκστασ. Flor., Par.¹ read εκστασ. και εθαμβουντο εφ' ῳ αυτῳ συμβεβηκεν ιαοις; but D with α accepts γεγενημενω instead of συμβεβ., cf. iv. 22; so Hilg.

raised, how account for it, he asks, that those who fled whilst He was alive, now dared a thousand perils for Him when dead?—ἔστη καὶ περιεπάτει: "he stood and began to walk" R.V., thus marking the difference between the aorist and the imperfect. Such vivid details may have been derived from St. Peter himself, and they are given here with a vividness characteristic of St. Mark's Gospel, of which St. Peter may reasonably be regarded as the main source. If St. Luke did not derive the narrative directly from St. Peter, he may easily have done so from the same Evangelist, John Mark, see on chap. xii., and Scharfe, *Die petrinische Strömung der N. T. Literatur*, pp. 59, 60 (1893).—αἰνῶν τὸν θεόν: commentators from the days of St. Chrysostom have noted that by no act or in no place could the man have shown his gratitude more appropriately; characteristic of St. Luke, to note not only fear, but the ascription of praise to God as the result of miraculous deeds; cf., e.g., Luke xix. 37, xxiv. 53, Acts iii. 9, iv. 21, xi. 18, and other instances in Friedrich (*Das Lucasevangelium*, pp. 77, 78). On the word see further, p. 97. Spitta regards ver. 8 as modelled after xiv. 10, a passage attributed by him to his inferior source B. But on the other hand both Feine and Jüngst regard the first part of ver. 8 as belonging to the original source. Ver. 10. ἐπεγίνωσκόν τε: "took knowledge of him" or perhaps better still "recognised". The word is so used of recognising any one by sight, hearing, or certain signs, to perceive who a person is (Grimm), cf., e.g., Luke xxiv. 16, 31, Matt. xiv. 35, Mark vi. 54.—ὁ . . . καθήμενος: imperfect, may refer to the customary action of the man: or may be equivalent here to an imperfect, a force of the imperfect usual in similar cases when reference is made to a time before the actual time of recognition, Blass, *Grammatik des N. G.*, p. 188.—ἐπὶ: for the local dative cf. v. 9, Matt. xxiv. 33, Mark xiii. 29, John v. 2, Rev. ix. 14.—θάμβους, cf. Luke iv. 36 and v. 9. A

word peculiar to St. Luke in the N.T. (so St. Luke alone uses ἔκθαμβος, ver. 11); used from Homer downwards, of amazement allied to terror or awe, cf. LXX, Ezek. vii. 18, Cant. iii. 8, vi. 3 (4), 9 (10).—ἐκστάσεως: for the word in a similar sense, Mark v. 42, xvi. 8, Luke v. 26. Its use in ordinary Greek expresses rather distraction or disturbance of mind caused by a shock. The word is very common both in Hippocrates and Aretaeus. In the LXX it is employed in various senses, cf. Deut. xxviii. 28, ἐκστάσει διανοίας; elsewhere it is used of agitation, trouble, 2 Chron. xxix. 8, and most frequently of terror, fear, 1 Sam. xi. 7, Ezek. xxvi. 16. See further on. Here the word expresses more than simple astonishment as its collocation with θάμβος shows (Wendt, *in loco*), rather "bewilderment," cf. Mark v. 42. See on ii. 43 for this characteristic of St. Luke. But there is no occasion to conclude with Weiss that these strong expressions as to the effect of the miracle show that it must have been the first which the disciples performed. It was the unique nature of the miracle which affected the beholders so powerfully. Ver. 11. κρατοῦντος: in his joy and gratitude, "holding them" in a physical sense, although it is possible that it signifies that the healed man joined himself to the Apostles more closely as a follower (iv. 14), fearing like the demoniac healed by Christ (Luke viii. 38) lest he should be separated from his benefactors, cf. Cant. iii. 4.—ἐπὶ τῇ στοᾷ τῇ καλ. Σ.: better "portico," R.V. margin; colonnade, or cloister (John x. 23). It derived its name from Solomon, and was the only remnant of his temple. A comparison of the notices in Josephus, *B. J.*, v., 5, 1; *Ant.*, xv., 11, 5 and xx., 9, 7, make it doubtful whether the foundations only, or the whole colonnade, should be referred back to Solomon. Ewald's idea that the colonnade was so called because it was a place of concourse for the wise in their teaching has not found any support: Stanley's *Jewish Church*, ii.,

11. Κρατοῦντος δὲ [1] τοῦ ἰαθέντος χωλοῦ τὸν Πέτρον καὶ Ἰωάννην, συνέδραμε πρὸς αὐτοὺς πᾶς ὁ λαὸς ἐπὶ τῇ στοᾷ τῇ καλουμένῃ Σολομῶντος, ἔκθαμβοι. 12. ἰδὼν δὲ Πέτρος ἀπεκρίνατο πρὸς τὸν λαόν, Ἄνδρες Ἰσραηλῖται, τί θαυμάζετε ἐπὶ τούτῳ, ἢ ἡμῖν τί ἀτενί-ζετε,[2] ὡς ἰδίᾳ δυνάμει ἢ εὐσεβείᾳ πεποιηκόσι τοῦ περιπατεῖν αὐτόν;

[1] του ιαθεντος; but αυτου in אABCDE 61, Vulg., Syrr. P. H., Sah., Boh., Arm., so Tisch., W.H., R.V., Weiss; Rec.=prob. beginning of a church lectionary. But in ver. 11 Western text quite different. D, Flor. εκπορευομενου (Fl. -νων) δε του Π. και Ιω. συνεξεπορευετο κρατων αυτους, and D continues (not Flor. = α) οι δε θαμβηθεντες εστησαν εν τη στοα τη καλ. Σ. εκθαμβοι (but in β Blass brackets the last word); Hilg. follows D. There is a distinction evidently drawn between the area of the Temple and Solomon's Porch, "nam porticus illa extra aream sacram fuit," Blass; and ιερον might perhaps be so used as distinct from the outer court or cloisters. If so, the Western text may contain the more precise account of a writer who wishes to bring the Apostles and the lame man from the one into the other, in accordance with the topography with which he was familiar. But if, as Weiss admits, εκπορ. . . . συνεξεπορευετο is implied in the κρατων and change of locality, cf. vv. 8 and 11, we may have another case in which the theory of Blass may hold good, and Luke him-self may have revised for shortness (see Belser's retention of the β reading, and Blass, Acta Apost., in loco). Σολομωντος א(A)BCP 1, 13, 31, 61; so Tisch., W.H., Weiss (but see Winer-Schmiedel, p. 93).

[2] D, Flor., Par. begin αποκριθεις δε ο Π. ειπεν προς αυτους—ο λαος and πας ο λαος both omitted. ως ιδια . . . περιπ. αυτον, for this D, Flor., Gig., Severian. read ως ημων τη ιδια δυν. η ευσεβ. πεποιηκοτων του περιπ. αυτον, so Hilg.—gen. abs. characteristic of the Western text (see Weiss, Codex D, p. 60); cf. ii. 1, 15; may be careless transcription or through translation. D has τουτο both before and after πεποιηκοτων (Harris, Latinising; Chase, due to Syriac); but see iv. 7—the second τουτο perhaps confusion with του or το.

184; Edersheim, *Temple and its Services*, pp. 20, 22, and Keim, *Geschichte Jesu*, iii., 161. It was situated on the eastern side of the Temple, and so was some-times called the Eastern Cloister, and from its position it was a favourite re-sort.—τῇ καλ.: the present participle is used just as the present tense is found in the notice in St. John's Gospel, chap. v. 2 (see Blass, *Philology of the Gospels*, pp. 241, 242), and if we cannot conclude from this that the book was composed before the destruction of the Temple, the vividness of the whole scene and the way in which Solomon's Porch is spoken of as still standing, points to the testi-mony of an eye-witness. Nösgen argues that this narrative and others in the early chapters may have been derived directly from St. John, and he instances some verbal coincidences between them and the writings of St. John (*Apostelgeschichte*, p. 28). But if we cannot adopt his conclu-sions there are good reasons for referring some of these Jerusalem incidents to St. Peter, or to John Mark, see introduction and chap. xii. Feine rightly insists upon this notice and that in ver. 2 as bearing the stamp of a true and trustworthy tradition.

Ver. 12. This address of St. Peter divides itself into two parts, 12-16, 17-26, and although it covers much of the same ground as in chap. ii., there is no need to regard it with Overbeck and Holtz-mann as unhistorical: see Blass, *in loco*, and Feine; the latter points out that St. Peter would naturally, as in chap. iii., take the incident before him as his text, place it in its right light, and draw from it an appeal to repentance and conver-sion. But whilst we may grant the common and identical aim of the two discourses, to proclaim the Messiahship of Jesus before the Jews, none can fail to see that in chap. iii. the Messianic idea becomes richer and fuller. Jesus is the prophet greater than Moses: Jesus is the fulfilment of the Abrahamic covenant, through which the blessing of Abraham is to extend to all the earth, Matt. viii. 11. And more than this: St. Peter has learnt to see in the despised Nazarene not only the suffering servant of Jehovah (παῖς), but in the servant the King, and in the seed of David the Prince of Life. And in the light of that revela-tion the future opens out more clearly before him, and he becomes the first prophet in the Messianic age—the spirit-

13.[1] ὁ Θεὸς ᾿Αβραὰμ καὶ ᾿Ισαὰκ καὶ ᾿Ιακώβ, ὁ Θεὸς τῶν πατέρων ἡμῶν, ἐδόξασε τὸν παῖδα αὐτοῦ ᾿Ιησοῦν· ὃν ὑμεῖς[2] παρεδώκατε, καὶ

[1] ὁ Θ. Αβρ. και Ισ. και Ιακ. BEP 61, Sah., Syr. (Pesh. Harcl.); so W.H., Weiss, R.V., T.R.; Wendt, who explains the reading in Tisch., Hilg. introducing (ο) Θεος (אACD) before Ισ. and before Ιακ. as out of LXX, Exod. iii. 6 (cf. Matt. xxii. 32).

[2] παρεδώκατε; D adds εις κρισιν, so Hilg.; E εις κριτηριον (cf. also Flor., Par.[1], Syr. Harcl. mg., Iren., cf. Luke xxiv. 30; see also Chase, in loco).

ual presence which the believers now enjoyed, and by which those mighty deeds are wrought, is only a foretaste of a more visible and glorious Presence, when the Messiah should return in His glory; and for that return repentance and remission of sins must prepare the way (see Briggs, *Messiah of the Apostles*, pp. 31, 32). On St. Peter's discourses see additional note at end of chapter.— ἀπεκρίνατο: *cf.* Luke xiii. 14, xiv. 3, answered, *i.e.*, to their looks of astonishment and inquiry. The middle voice as here, which would be the classical usage, is seldom found in the N.T., but generally the passive aorist, ἀπεκρίθη, and so in the LXX. "In Biblical Greek the middle voice is dying, in modern Greek it is dead," Plummer. Thus in modern Greek, ὑποκρίνομαι in the passive = to answer, Kennedy, *Sources of N.T. Greek*, p. 155, and Blass, *Grammatik des N.G.*, p. 44.— ὡς πεποιηκόσιν τοῦ περιπατεῖν: this use of the infinitive with the genitive of the article, instead of the simple infinitive with or without ὥστε, to express a purpose, or result as here: "non de consilio sed de eventu" (Blass), may be illustrated from the LXX, Gen. xxxvii. 18, 1 Chron. xliv. 6, Isaiah v. 6.— εὐσεβείᾳ: "godliness," R.V., as always elsewhere in A.V., *i.e.*, by our piety towards God, as always in the Bible, although εὐσέβεια may be used like the Latin *pietas* of piety towards parents or others, as well as of piety towards God. It is frequently used in the LXX of reverence towards God, εἰς, so too in Josephus, πρὸς τὸν Θεόν, *cf.* Prov. i. 7, xiii. 11, Isaiah xi. 2, Wisdom x. 12, and often in 4 Macc. In Trench, *N.T. Synonyms*, ii., p. 196, and Grimm-Thayer, *sub v.* In the N.T. the word is used, in addition to its use here, by St. Paul ten times in the Pastoral Epistles, and it is found no less than four times in 2 Peter, but nowhere else. St. Chrysostom, *Hom.* ix., comments: "Do you see how clear of all ambition he is, and how he repels the honour paid to him?" so too Joseph: Do not interpretations belong to God?

Ver. 13. ὁ Θεὸς ᾿Αβραὰμ κ.τ.λ.: the words were wisely chosen, not only to gain attention and to show that the speaker identified himself with the nation and hope of Israel, but also because in Jesus St. Peter saw the fulfilment of the promise made to Abraham.— ἐδόξασε, John viii. 54, xi. 4. Again we mark the same sharp contrast as in St. Peter's former address—God hath *glorified* . . . but *you* put to an open shame. The objections of Weiss, who traces a reviser's hand in the double mention of the glorification of Jesus in ver. 13 and in 15, fail to secure the approval of Spitta, Feine, Jüngst, who all hold that ἐδόξασε refers to the power of the Risen Jesus, shown in the healing of the lame man, which Peter thus expressly emphasises. But the glorification was not, of course, confined to this miracle: "auxit gloria hoc quoque miraculo" (Blass).— τὸν παῖδα: "his Servant," R.V. (margin, "Child"). Vulgate has *filium*, which all other English versions (except A.V., "Child") seem to have followed. But the rendering "Servant" is undoubtedly most appropriate, *cf.* ver. 26, and iv. 27, 30 (employed in the Messianic sense of Isa. xlii. 1, lii. 13, liii. 11), where the LXX has παῖς, Hebrew עֶבֶד. In Matt. xii. 18 the Evangelist sees the fulfilment of the first passage in Jesus as the Christ, the Servant of Jehovah. Wendt rightly emphasises the fact that no Apostle ever bears the name παῖς Θεοῦ, but δοῦλος; *cf.* iv. 29. In the LXX Moses is called both παῖς and δοῦλος. The rendering of R.V. is generally adopted, and by critics of very varying schools, *e.g.*, Overbeck, Nösgen, Holtzmann, Felten, Hilgenfeld, whilst he adopts the rendering "Servant," still maintains that Luther's translation, *Kind Gottes*, cannot be regarded as incorrect (*cf.* the double meaning of the word in classical literature). Certainly he seems justified in maintaining that in the numerous parallels in the sub-apostolic writings the conception of the Servant by no means always excludes that of the Son, *e.g.*, *Epist. ad Diogn.*, viii., 11 and 9, where of

ἠρνήσασθε αὐτὸν κατὰ πρόσωπον [1] Πιλάτου, κρίναντος ἐκείνου ἀπολύειν.　14. ὑμεῖς δὲ τὸν ἅγιον καὶ δίκαιον [2] ἠρνήσασθε, καὶ ᾐτήσασθε

---

[1] **Πιλατου**; B*D read **Πειλ.**, so Tisch., W.H., Weiss, Hilg.—see Winer-Schmiedel, p. 43. **κριναντος εκεινου απολ.**; D adds **αυτου θελοντος** and prefixes **του** (om. in D²); conflate **θελοντος** assim. to Luke xxiii. 20.

[2] **ηρνησασθε**, but D, Iren., Aug. have **εβαρυνατε** (*aggravastis*), so Hilg.; Nestle (so Blass, Chase, and see also Belser) believes confusion arose in Syriac between כברתם‎כפרתם; see Nestle, *Philologia Sacra*, 1896, p. 40, and *Einführung in das G. N. T.*, p. 240 (and also Harris, who explains through **ητησατε**, ver. 6, for **ητησασθε**, displaced **ηρνησασθε**, and became corrupted into **ηττησατε**, transl. *aggravastis*); see also Blass, *Philology of the Gospels*, p. 194, and also Dalman, *Die Worte Jesu*, p. 54, and *Enc. Bibl.*, i., 56. **φονεα**; after this word D inserts **ζην και**, so E, Flor., Aug. Gloss.; but Belser sees in it a marked contrast to **φονεα**, "that a murderer should live," original. **αυτον** om. א ABC, Tisch., W.H., R.V.

God's great scheme it is said **ἀνεκοινώσατο μόνῳ τῷ παιδί** (to His Son alone), called in 11 **τοῦ ἀγαπητοῦ παιδός**; *cf. Martyr. Polyc.*, xiv., 3, where the same phrase occurs, reminding us of Matt. iii. 17 (Col. i. 13, Eph. i. 6) and xiv. 1, where God is spoken of as **ὁ πατήρ** of the well-beloved Son **παιδός**. In Clem. Rom., *Cor.* lix. 2-4, the word is used three times of Jesus Christ, and twice with **τοῦ ἠγαπημένου** (**παιδός**), and if there is nothing in the context to determine the exact sense of the word, in the previous chapter St. Clement had written **ζῇ γὰρ ὁ Θεὸς καὶ ζῇ ὁ Κύριος Ἰησοῦς Χριστὸς καὶ τὸ πνεῦμα τὸ ἅγιον κ.τ.λ.**; *cf.* also Barnabas, *Epist.* (iii., 6), vi., 1; *Apost. Const.*, viii., 5, 14, 39, 40, 41; and *Didache*, ix., 2, 3; x., 2, 3, where, however, at the first introduction of the word, David and Jesus are both called by it in the same sentence. In the *Didache* the title is found altogether five times, once as above, and four times as applied to Jesus alone. But these passages all occur in the Eucharistic Prayers of the *Didache* (placed by Resch as early as 80-90 A.D.), and in them we find not only the title "Lord" used absolutely of Jesus, ix., 5, but He is associated with the Father in glory and power, ix., 4. Knowledge, faith, and immortality are made known by Him, spiritual food and drink, and eternal life are imparted by Him, x., 2, 3. Zöckler, *Apostelgeschichte*, *in loco*; Lock, *Expositor*, p. 183 ff. (1891), "Christology of the Earlier Chapters of the Acts"; Schmid, *Biblische Theologie*, p. 405. But further: if we bear in mind all that the "Servant of the Lord" must have meant for a Jew, and for a Jew so well versed in the O.T. Prophets as St. Peter, it becomes a marvellous fact that he should have seen in Jesus of Nazareth the realisation of a character and of a work so unique (*cf.* Isaiah xlii. 1 ff., xlix. 1-3, 5, 8, l. 4-9, lii. 13-liii. 12). For if we admit that the word "Servant" may be used, and is sometimes used, of the nation of Israel (*cf.* Isaiah xli. 8, xlv. 4), and if we admit that some of the traits in the portrait of Jehovah's "Servant" may have been suggested by the sufferings of individuals, and were applicable to individual sufferers, yet the portrait as a whole was one which transcended all experience, and the figure of the ideal Servant anticipated a work and a mission more enduring and comprehensive than that of Israel, and a holiness and innocency of life which the best of her sons had never attained (Driver, *Isaiah*, pp. 175-180). But not only in His miraculous working, but in His Resurrection and Ascension St. Peter recognised how God had glorified His Servant Jesus; and whilst it was natural that the word "Servant" should rise to his lips, as he recalls the submission to betrayal and death, whilst he never forgets the example of lowliness and obedience which Christ had given, and commends to poor Christian slaves the patience and humility of Him Who was "the first Servant in the world" (1 Peter ii. 18-25), he sees what prophets and wise men had failed to see, how the suffering "Servant" is also "the Prince of Life," *cf.* chap. v. 15, and v. 31.—**ὑμεῖς μὲν**: there is no regular answering **δὲ** in the text (*cf.* i. 1), but the words in ver. 15 **ὁ Θεὸς ἤγειρεν** express the antithesis (Blass, Wendt, Holtzmann). In dwelling upon the action of Pilate and the guilt of the Jews, the Apostle loses the direct grammatical construction; he emphasises the denial (**ἠρνήσασθε** twice) and its baseness; but nothing in reality was more natural, more like St. Peter's impetuosity. —**κατὰ πρόσωπον**, *coram*, *cf.* Luke ii. 31,

ἄνδρα φονέα χαρισθῆναι ὑμῖν, 15. τὸν δὲ ἀρχηγὸν τῆς ζωῆς ἀπεκτείνατε· ὃν ὁ Θεὸς ἤγειρεν ἐκ νεκρῶν, οὗ ἡμεῖς μάρτυρές ἐσμεν.

2 Cor. x. 1—the expression need not be explained as a Hebraism, it is found several times in Polybius; see Dalman, *Die Worte Jesu*, p. 23. In the LXX it is frequent in various senses, and sometimes simply in the sense of before, in the presence of, a person, 1 Sam. xvii. 8, 1 Kings i. 23, 1 Chron. xvii. 25, Ecclesiasticus xlv. 3, Jer. lii. 12, 33, Judith x. 23, xi. 5, etc. Rendall takes the words as usually denoting open encounter with an opposite party face to face, *cf.* xxv. 16, Gal. ii. 11, and so here; the Jews met Pilate's proposal to free the prisoner with a point-blank denial. 13[b] is referred by Hilgenfeld to the revising hand of "the author to Theophilus," and he sees in its introduction a proof of the anti-Judaism of the reviser, whilst Jüngst prefers to regard the first part of ver. 14 as an insertion, but this Hilgenfeld will not accept, as thus the antithesis in ver. 15 is not marked.—κρίναντος: "when he had determined," R.V., not a purpose only, but a decision, Luke xxiii. 16.—ἐκείνου, not αὐτοῦ, emphasising the antithesis between what *Pilate* had determined and what *they* had done: ὑμεῖς ἐκείνου θελήσαντος οὐκ ἠθελήσατε (Chrys.).
Ver. 14. τὸν ἅγιον καὶ δίκαιον: both epithets are used of John the Baptist, Mark vi. 20, ἄνδρα δίκαιον καὶ ἅγιον, but Jesus is emphatically "the Holy and Righteous One" R.V. Not only is the sinlessness of His human character emphasised, but also associated with the language of prophecy. St. Peter had already spoken of Jesus as God's Holy One, ii. 27, and if the word used here means rather one consecrated to God's service, it is the thought involved in the παῖς Θεοῦ (ἅγιος, *e.g.*, ἐκλεκτὸς Θεοῦ, see Grimm, *sub v.*, and *cf.* Isaiah xlii. 1 LXX). The word was used by the demoniacs as they felt the power of the unique holiness of Christ, Mark i. 34, Luke iv. 34, and in St. John's Gospel vi. 69, it is the title given to Jesus by St. Peter in his great confession.—τὸν δικ.: the reference to the language of prophecy is unmistakable. The suffering Servant of Jehovah was also the righteous Servant, Isaiah liii. 11 (*cf.* xi. 5, and Jer. xxiii. 5), see Acts vii. 52, xxii. 14. Later, in the *Book of Enoch*, the title is applied to the Messiah as the *Righteous One*, xxxviii. 2, liii. 6, xlvi. 3 (Charles' edition, pp. 48, 112, 144). In Acts vii. 52, 56, the

title is found on the lips of St. Stephen, and in xxii. 14, Ananias, a Jewish Christian, announces to Paul that God had chosen him to see the *Righteous One*. When we remember too that this title is used again in the writings of each of the Apostles, who now appealed to it, 1 Peter iii. 18, 1 John ii. 1, *cf.* ver. 20 (Rev. iii. 7), it would seem that it was not only a favourite one amongst these early believers, but that it affords in itself a marvellous proof of the impression made by the human life of Jesus upon those who knew Him best, or who at all events, like St. Stephen, had ample opportunities of learning the details of that life of holiness and righteousness, *cf.* also Matt. xxvii. 19, 24, Luke xviii. 47.—ἄνδρα φονέα: nearly all commentators dwell upon the marked contrast between this description of Barabbas and that just given of Jesus. Both St. Mark, xv. 7, and St. Luke, xxiii. 19, notice that Barabbas was not only a robber but a murderer. The addition, ἄνδρα, common in Luke, makes the expression stronger than the simple φονέα; *cf.* Soph., *O. C.*, 948, ἄνδρα πατροκτόνον, *O. R.*, 842, ἄνδρας λῃστάς. No crime was more abhorrent to the Christian life, as St. Peter himself indicates, 1 Peter iv. 15.—χαρισθῆναι: to be granted to you as a χάρις or favour, as if St. Peter would recall the fact that Pilate had given them a gratification! The verb is used several times in Luke, three times in his Gospel, vii. 21, 42, 43, and four times in Acts, *cf.* xxv. 11, 16, xxvii. 24, elsewhere only in St. Paul's Epistles, where it is found fifteen times. In the LXX, *cf.* Esther viii. 7, Ecclus. xii. 3, and several times in the Books of the Maccabees, *cf.* 2 Macc. iii. 31, 33, and other instances in Hatch and Redpath, *sub v.* St. Chrys. writes: "Peter shows the great aggravation of the act. As he has them under his hand, he strikes hard; while they were hardened he refrained from such language, but when their minds are most moved then he strikes home, now that they are in a condition to feel it" (*Hom.*, ix.).
Ver. 15. τὸν δὲ ἀρχηγὸν τῆς ζωῆς: again the words stand in marked contrast not only to φονέα but also to ἀπεκτείνατε; magnificum antitheton, Bengel. The word is rendered "Author" in the margin of R.V. (Vulgate, *auctorem*) but "Prince" in the text and so in v. 31 (Vulg., *principem*). In the two other passages in

16. καὶ [1] ἐπὶ τῇ πίστει τοῦ ὀνόματος αὐτοῦ, τοῦτον, ὃν θεωρεῖτε καὶ
οἴδατε, ἐστερέωσε τὸ ὄνομα αὐτοῦ · καὶ ἡ πίστις ἡ δι' αὐτοῦ ἔδωκεν

[1] επι ℵ³ACDEP, Vulg., Sah., Boh., Ir^{int}., so Tisch., and so Weiss ; but om. ℵ*B
61, Arm., so W.H. (Lachmann and Blass punctuate εστερεωσεν · το ονομ.)

which the word occurs in the N.T., *viz.*,
Heb. ii. 10, xii. 2, R.V. renders "Author,"
"the author of their salvation," "the
author and perfecter of our faith," margin "captain" (Vulgate, *auctorem*) ; see
Westcott, *Hebrews*, pp. 49, 395. Christ
is both the Prince of life and the Source
(*auctor*) of life : "Vitam aliis dat
Christus, opp. φονεύς qui admit"
(Blass). Grimm and others draw a distinction between the meaning attaching to
the word here and in v. 31. The use of
the word in the LXX may help to justify
such a distinction, for whilst it is found
in the sense of a leader or a captain
(Num. xiv. 4, Judith xiv. 2), or the chief
of a family or tribe (R.V. renders it
"every one a prince" in Num. xiii. 2, but
in the next verse "heads of the children
of Israel"), it is also used to signify the
author, or beginner, the source, *cf.* 1
Macc. ix. 61, x. 47, Micah i. 13 (although
it was never used for a prince or to describe kingly attributes) ; but in many
respects the rendering "Prince" may be
compared with the Latin *princeps*, which
signifies the first person in order, a chief,
a leader, an originator, the founder of a
family (in the time of the emperors it was
used of the heir to the throne). So in
classical Greek the word was used for a
leader, a founder, Latin *auctor*, for the
first cause, author, so God τῶν πάντων,
Plat., and also for a prince, a chief, and,
especially in later Greek, of the person
from whom anything good or bad first
proceeds in which others have a share,
e.g., ἀρχηγὸς καὶ αἴτιος combined (*ante-
signanus et auctor*), Polyb., i., 66, 10 ;
Hdian., ii., 6, 22, and as Alford points
out in Heb. ii. 10, this later usage
throws a light upon its meaning in
Acts iii. 15, *cf.* Chrys. on Heb. ii. 10,
ἀρχηγὸν τῆς σωτηρίας τούτεστι τὸν
αἴτιον τῆς σωτηρίας. Christ is the source
of life, a life in which others share
through Him ; in this very place where
St. Peter was speaking our Lord had
spoken of Himself as the giver of eternal
life, John x. 28, although doubtless the
expression may include the thought that
in Him was life in its fullest and widest
sense — physical, intellectual, moral,
spiritual. St. Chrysostom comments on
the words "Prince of Life," *Hom.*, ix. :

"It follows that the life He had was not
from another, the Prince or Author of
Life must be He who has life from Himself". Theophylact and Oecumenius see
in the words a contrast to the φονέα, in
that Christ gives life, while the murderer
takes it away—a contrast deepened by the
words of St. Peter's fellow-disciple whom
he here associates with himself in his
appeal to the people, *cf.* 1 John iii. 15.
In ver. 31 ἀρχ. in its rendering "Prince"
of kingly dignity may be compared with
the use of the word in Thuc., i., 132,
Æsch., *Agam.*, 259. Rendall sees in the
expression both here and Acts v. 31 a
reference to Jesus (the name used by St.
Peter) as the second Joshua. As Joshua
was the captain of Israel and led them
across the Jordan into the land of promise, so Jesus was the Captain of the
living army of the Resurrection ; and for
Saviour, v. 31, he compares Matt. i. 21.
Such associations may be included in St.
Peter's words, but they seem much more
applicable to v. 31. In modern Greek the
word ἀρχηγός = leader, in the ordinary
sense, Kennedy, *Sources of N. T. Greek*,
p. 153 ; see Grimm, *sub v*. — οὗ may
refer to ὄν, *cf.* i. 8, xiii. 31, or to the
fact of the Resurrection, *cf.* ii. 32, v. 32,
x. 39. R.V. reads "of whom" in the
margin.

Ver. 16. ἐπὶ : so T.R., and so Weiss
and Wendt : "on the ground of faith
in His name," R.V. margin ; *cf.* Luke v.
5 (not expressing the aim as if it meant
with a view to faith in His name). But
the name is no mere formula of incantation, see xix. 13, nor is it used as, in
Jewish tradition, the name of God, inscribed on the rod of Moses, was said to
have given him power to work his
miracles in Egypt and the wilderness,
see above on ver. 5. On the use of
ὄνομα in formulæ of incantation, see
Deissmann, *Bibelstudien*, pp. 25-54.—ἡ
πίστις ἡ δι' αὐτοῦ : "the faith which is
through Him," not by it, *i.e.*, the name
—not only the healing power is through
Christ, but also the faith of the Apostles
as of the man who was healed, *cf.*,
especially, 1 Pet. i. 21. τοὺς δι' αὐτὸν
πιστοὺς εἰς Θεόν, *i.e.*, his converts who
through Christ are believers in God : He
is the object and the author of our faith.

αὐτῷ τὴν ὁλοκληρίαν ταύτην ἀπέναντι πάντων ὑμῶν.   17. καὶ νῦν,
ἀδελφοί,[1] οἶδα ὅτι κατὰ ἄγνοιαν ἐπράξατε, ὥσπερ καὶ οἱ ἄρχοντες
ὑμῶν·   18. ὁ δὲ Θεὸς ἃ προκατήγγειλε διὰ στόματος πάντων τῶν

[1] Before αδελφοι DE, Flor., Par.[1] insert ανδρες.   For οιδα οτι D, Flor. read
επισταμεθα οτι υμεις μεν, perhaps for emphasising contrast (cf. vv. 13, 14) with
ver. 18, o δε Θεος (Chase, Syriac). επραξατε, D, Fl., Gig., Par., Syr. H. mg., Irint.,
Aug., Ambrst. add το πονηρον, so Hilg., a gloss to explain επραξ. since it is not in
accordance with the exculpating tone of the context (Weiss).

Cf. also Nestle, *Expository Times*, Feb.,
1899, p. 238, and the connection of this
phrase with Codex D, xviii. 8, and xx.
21 (see Blass, *l. c.*).—ὁλοκληρίαν: only
here in N.T., *integram sanitatem*, Vulgate, but the adjective ὁλόκληρος in an
ethical sense, 1 Thess. v. 23, James i. 4.
The noun is only used once in the LXX,
and there in a physical sense, Isaiah i.
6. The adjective is used by Josephus
of a sacrifice complete in all its parts
(*integer*), *Ant.*, iii., 12, 2, *cf.* its use in
Philo., but in LXX, Zach. xi. 16, its use
in a physical sense is a very doubtful
rendering of the Hebrew, see further
Trench, *N. T. Synonyms*, i., 85, and
Mayor's *St. James*, p. 34. *Cf.* Plato,
Tim., 44.—ὁλόκληρος ὑγιὴς τε παντελῶς.
In Plutarch the noun is joined with
ὑγίεια, and also with τοῦ σώματος
(Grimm), but whilst the noun does not
seem to be used by the strictly medical
writers, ὁλόκληρος is frequently used of
complete soundness of body (Hobart,
Zahn).
Ver. 17. καὶ νῦν: favourite formula
of transition, *cf.* vii. 35, x. 5, xx. 25,
xxii. 16, 1 John ii. 28, 2 John 5.   See
Wendt and Page, *in loco*. Bengel describes it as "formula transeuntis a præ-
terito ad præsens". Blass, "i.e., quod at-
tinet ad ea quæ nunc facienda sunt, ver.
19".—ἀδελφοί: affectionate and conciliatory, *cf.* ver. 12, where he speaks
more formally because more by way of
reproof: "One of the marks of truth
would be wanting without this accordance between the style and the changing
mental moods of the speaker" (Hackett).
—κατὰ ἄγνοιαν: the same phrase occurs
in LXX, Lev. xxii. 14 (*cf.* also Lev. v.
18, Eccles. v. 5).   On κατά in this
usage, see Simcox, *Language of the
N. T.*, p. 149, who doubts whether it is
quite good Greek. It is used in Polybius, and Blass compares κατ' ἀνάγκην
(Philem., ver. 14), which is found in Xen.,
Cyr., iv., 3. Their guilt was less than
if they had slain the Messiah κατὰ
πρόθεσιν, κατὰ προαίρεσιν, or ἐν χειρὶ
ὑπερηφανίας, Num. xv. 30, and therefore their hope of pardon was assured
on their repentance (*cf.* 1 Pet. i. 14, ἐν
ἀγνοίᾳ, and *Psalms of Solomon*, xviii., 5,
for the same phrase).   St. Peter speaks
in the spirit of his Master, Luke xxiii.
34. See instances in Wetstein of the
antithesis of the two phrases κατ'
ἄγνοιαν and κατὰ πρόθεσιν (προαίρεσιν)
in Polybius.—οἱ ἄρχοντες ὑμῶν, *cf.* 1
Cor. ii. 8. The guilt of the rulers was
greater than that of the people, but even
for their crime St. Peter finds a palliation
in the fact that they did not recognise
the Messiah, although he does not hold
them guiltless for shutting their eyes to
His holiness and innocence.
Ver. 18.   δὲ: a further mitigation ;
whilst they were acting in their ignorance, God was working out His unerring
counsel and will.—πάντων τῶν προφητῶν:
not to be explained by simply calling it
hyperbolic. The prophets are spoken of
collectively, because the Messianic redemption to which they all looked forward was to be accomplished through
the death of Christ, *cf.* x. 43. The view
here taken by St. Peter is in striking
harmony with his first Epistle, i. 11, and
ii. 22-25.—παθεῖν τὸν Χ. αὐτοῦ, R.V.,
"his Christ," *cf.* Luke xvii. 25, xxiv. 26.
The phrase, which (W.H.) is undoubtedly
correct, is found in Psalm ii. 2, from
which St. Peter quotes in iv. 26, and the
same expression is used twice in the
Apocalypse, but nowhere else in the
N.T.; xi. 15, xii. 10 (*cf.* also Luke ii.
26, ix. 20). See also the striking passage in *Psalms of Solomon*, xviii., 6
(and ver. 8), ἐν ἀνάξει Χριστοῦ αὐτοῦ,
and Ryle and James on *Psalm* xvii.
36. The paradox that the suffering
Messiah was also the Messiah of Jehovah,
His Anointed, which the Jews could not
understand (hence their ἄγνοια), was
solved for St. Peter in the Passion,
Death, and Resurrection of Jesus. On
the suffering Messiah, see note xxvi.
23.—ἐπλήρωσεν οὕτω: "He thus fulfilled," *i.e.*, in the way described, vv. 14,
15. On πληρόω, see i. 16. "In the
gardens of the Carthusian Convent . . .

προφητῶν αὐτοῦ, παθεῖν τὸν Χριστὸν, ἐπλήρωσεν οὕτω.   19. μετανοήσατε οὖν καὶ ἐπιστρέψατε, εἰς τὸ ἐξαλειφθῆναι ὑμῶν τὰς ἁμαρτίας,

near Dijon . . . is a beautiful monument. . . . It consists of a group of
Prophets and Kings from the O.T., each
holding in his hand a scroll of mourning
from his writings—each with his own
individual costume and gesture and
look, each distinguished from each by the
most marked peculiarities of age and
character, absorbed in the thoughts of
his own time and country. But above
these figures is a circle of angels, as like
each to each as the human figures are
unlike. They, too, as each overhangs
and overlooks the Prophet below him,
are saddened with grief. But their expression of sorrow is far deeper and
more intense than that of the Prophets,
whose words they read. They see something in the Prophetic sorrow which the
Prophets themselves see not : they are
lost in the contemplation of the Divine
Passion, of which the ancient saints
below them are but the unconscious and
indirect exponents : " Stanley's *Jewish
Church*, pref. to vol. ii.
Ver. 19. ἐπιστρέψατε : "turn again,"
R.V. ; *cf.* also Matt. xiii. 15, Mark iv. 12,
and Acts xxviii. 27 (Luke xxii. 32), in
each of these passages, as in the text,
A.V., " should be converted," following
the Vulgate, *convertantur.* But the verb
is in the active voice in each of the passages mentioned ; *cf.* LXX, 1 Kings viii.
33, 2 Chron. vi. 24, 37, Isaiah vi. 10
(" turn again," R.V.), Tobit xiii. 6—ἐπιστρέψατε ἁμαρτωλοί : this passive rendering in the Vulgate and A.V. testifies
to the unwillingness in the Western
Church to recognise the " conversion "
to God as in any degree the spontaneous
act of the sinner himself—men have enlarged upon Lam. v. 21, but have
forgotten James iv. 8 (Humphry, *Commentary on the R. V.*, pp. 31, 32).—πρὸς
τὸ ἐξαλειφθῆναι : in the LXX the verb
is found in the sense of obliterating
ἀνομίας, Ps. l. (li.) 1, 9 ; Isaiah xliii. 25,
Ecclesiasticus xlvi. 20, Jer. xviii. 23,
with ἁμαρτίας, 2 Macc. xii. 42, with
ἁμάρτημα (*cf.* 3 Macc. ii. 19, ἀπαλείφειν
with ἁμαρτίας), and in N.T. ; *cf.* Col. ii.
14. For other instances of its use in the
N.T., *cf.* Rev. iii. 5, with Deut. ix. 14,
Ps. ix. 5, etc., and see also Rev. vii. 17,
xxi. 4. In *Psalms of Solomon* it is used
twice—once of blotting out the memories
of sinners from off the earth, Psalm ii.
19 ; *cf.* Exod. xvii. 14, etc., and once of
blotting out the transgressions of Saints

by the Lord, Psalm xiii. 9. Blass speaks
of the word as used " de scriptis proprie ;
itaque etiam de debita pecunia " ; *cf.*
Dem., 791, 12 (Wendt), and see also
Wetstein, *in loco.* The word can
scarcely be applied here to the Baptism
(as Meyer), for which a word expressing
washing would rather be required, *cf.*
xxii. 16, although no doubt, as in ii. 38,
Baptism joined with Repentance was required for the remission of sins.—ὅπως
ἄν : not "when" (as if ὅπως = ὅτε), but
"that so there may come," R.V., ἄν with
ὅπως indicates that the accomplishment
of the purpose is dependent upon certain conditions ; here dependent upon the
repentance. In the N.T. there are only
four instances of this use of ὅπως ἄν, all
in pure final clauses, *viz.*, in the text,
Luke ii. 35, and in two quotations from
the LXX, Acts xv. 17 (where ἄν is wanting in LXX, Amos ix. 12), and Rom. iii. 4
= LXX, Ps. l. (li.) 4, so that this usage
is practically peculiar to St. Luke in the
N.T. Viteau, *Le Grec du N. T.*, p. 80
(1893) ; Blass, *Grammatik des N. G.*, p.
207, and Burton, *N.T. Moods and Tenses*,
p. 85.—καιροὶ ἀναψύξεως : the word
ἀνάψυξις, used only by St. Luke, means
refreshing or refreshment. In the LXX
it occurs in Exod. viii. 15 (but *cf.* Aq.
on Isaiah xxviii. 12, and Sym. on
Isaiah xxxii. 15), where it is translated
" respite," although the same Hebrew
word רְוָחָה, in the only other place
in which it occurs, Lam. iii. 56, may
have the sense of "relief" (see Dr.
Payne Smith, *in loco, Speaker's Commentary*, vol. v.). In Strabo ἀνάψυξις is
found in the sense of recreation, refreshment, x., p. 459 ; see also Philo, *De Abr.*,
29, and *cf.* the verb ἀναψύχω in 2 Tim.
i. 16 (*cf.* Rom. xv. 32, ἀναψύξω μεθ' ὑμῶν,
DE, *refrigerer vobiscum*, Vulgate, and
Nösgen on Acts iii. 19). Rendall would
render it here " respite," as if St. Peter
urged the need of repentance that the
people might obtain a respite from the
terrible visitation of the Lord. But the
καιροὶ ἀναψ. are identified by most commentators with the ἀποκατα. πάντων, and
ἀναψ. need by no means be rendered
"respite". Nösgen, connecting the words
with the thought of ἀνάπαυσις (*cf.* the
various renderings in Rom. xv. 32), would
see here a fulfilment of Christ's promise,
κἀγὼ ἀναπαύσω ὑμᾶς, Matt. xi. 28, to
those who turned to Him in true re-

ὅπως ἂν ἔλθωσι καιροὶ ἀναψύξεως ἀπὸ προσώπου τοῦ Κυρίου, 20. καὶ
ἀποστείλῃ τὸν προκεκηρυγμένον ὑμῖν Ἰησοῦν Χριστόν, 21. ὃν δεῖ

pentance, and so in his view the expression applies to the seasons of spiritual refreshment which may be enjoyed by the truly penitent here and now, which may occur again and again as men repent (Isaiah lvii. 16); so J. Lightfoot, *Hor. Heb.*, interprets the word of the present refreshing of the Gospel, and God's present sending of Christ in His ministry and power, and in the same manner ἀποστείλῃ, *i.e.*, not at the end of the world, when Christ shall come as Judge, but in the Gospel, which is His voice. But the context certainly conceives of Christ as enthroned in Heaven, where He must remain until His Second Advent, although we may readily admit that there is a spiritual presence of the enthroned Jesus which believers enjoy as a foretaste of the visible and glorious Presence at the Parousia, Briggs, *Messiah of the Apostles*, p. 31 ff.—ἀπὸ προσώπου τοῦ Κ. πρόσωπ., lit., face, often used as here for "the presence"; *cf.* Hebrew, מִפְּנֵי, frequently in LXX, and see above on ii. 28, here of the refreshment which comes from the bright and smiling presence of God to one seeking comfort (so Grimm). The phrase occurs three times in Acts v. 41, vii. 45, elsewhere in 2 Thess. i. 9, and three times in Apoc. On St. Luke's fondness for phrases with πρόσωπον (ἀπό, πρό, κατά), see Friedrich (*Das Lucasevangelium*, pp. 8, 9, 89). The Lord is evidently God the Father, the καιροί are represented as present before God, already decreed and determined, and as coming down from His presence to earth (Weiss, Wendt). Christ speaks, i. 6, of the seasons which the Father hath set in His own power, and so St. Chrysostom speaks of God as αἴτιος of the seasons of refreshment.

Ver. 20. καὶ ἀποστείλῃ, *i.e.*, at His Parousia. The construction is still ὅπως ἂν with the verb. ἀποστ. is here used as in Luke iv. 18, 43, expressing that the person sent is the envoy or representative of the sender (πέμπω is also used of the mission of our Lord).—τὸν προκεκηρυγμένον, T.R., see on ver. 18; but W.H., Blass, Weiss, τὸν προκεχειρισμένον ὑμῖν Χριστόν, Ἰησοῦν: "the Christ who hath been appointed for you, *even* Jesus". So R.V. This verb is found with accusative of the person in the sense of choosing, appointing, in Acts xxii. 14, xxvi. 16, and nowhere else in the N.T.; *cf.* Josh.

iii. 12, 2 Macc. iii. 7, viii. 9, Exod. vi. 13 (*cf.* its use also in Dem., Polyb., Plut., and instances in Wetstein); Latin *eligere, destinare*. The expression here refers not only to the fact that Jesus was the appointed Christ, inasmuch as the covenant with Abraham was fulfilled in Him, ver. 25, but also to the return of Jesus as the Christ, the Messianic King, at His Parousia, in accordance with the voices of the Prophets. This is more natural than to suppose that the expression means foreordained, *i.e.*, from eternity, although St. Peter's words elsewhere may well be considered in connection with the present passage, 1 Pet. i. 20.

Ver 21. μέν: no answering δέ expressed, but the antithesis is found in the ἄχρι χρόνων ἀποκ., " quasi dicat : ubi illud tempus venerit, ex coelo in terras redibit," Grotius (so Weiss, Blass).—ὃν δεῖ οὐρανὸν δέξασθαι: the words have been rendered in three ways: (1) "whom the heaven must receive," *i.e.*, as the place assigned to Him by God until the Parousia, Phil. iii. 20, Col. iii. 4. In this case δεῖ is not used for ἔδει, as if St. Luke were referring to the past historical fact of the Ascension only, but Christ's exaltation to heaven is represented as a fact continually present until His coming again ; or (2) the words have been taken as if ὅν were the subject, "who must possess the heaven". But the former seems the more natural rendering, so in A.V. and R.V., as more in accordance with the use of δέχεσθαι, and κατέχειν would be rather the word in the second rendering (see Wendt's note). Zöckler takes the words to mean "who must receive heaven," *i.e.*, from the Father. Here St. Peter corrects the popular view that the Messiah should remain on earth, John xii. 34, and if we compare the words with the question asked in i. 6, they show how his views had changed of his Master's kingdom (see Hackett's note).—ἄχρι χρόνων ἀποκαταστάσεως : the latter noun is not found either in LXX or elsewhere in N.T., but it is used by Polybius, Diodorus, Plutarch. In Josephus, *Ant.*, xi., 3, 8, 9, it is used of the restoration of the Jews to their own land from the captivity, and also in Philo., *Decal.*, 30, of the restoration of inheritances at the Jubilee. The key to its meaning here is found not in the question of the disciples in i. 6, but in our Lord's own saying, Matt. xvii. 11, Mark ix. 12, "Elias truly

οὐρανὸν μὲν δέξασθαι ἄχρι χρόνων ἀποκαταστάσεως πάντων, ὧν
ἐλάλησεν ὁ Θεὸς διὰ στόματος [1] πάντων ἁγίων αὐτοῦ προφητῶν ἀπ'

[1] αγιων, prefix των instead of παντων ℵABCD 27, 61, Vulg. verss., Irint., Chrys.,
Orig.; so Tisch., W.H., R.V., Weiss, Wendt. αυτου προφ. απ' αιωνος; but
ℵ*AB*C 61, 69 read απ' αιωνος αυτου προφητων, so Tisch., W.H., R.V., Weiss,
Wendt. In D, Flor., Gig., Par., Iren., Tert., so Arm. απ' αιωνος omitted; so in Hilg.

first cometh, and shall restore all things,"
καὶ ἀποκαταστήσει πάντα, and cf. LXX,
Mal. iv. 6, where the same verb is found
(ἀποκαταστήσει). It was the teaching
of the Scriptures that Elias should be
the forerunner of the Messiah, Mal. iv. 5,
and Matt. xvii. 11, and xi. 14. But his
activity embraced both an external and an
internal, i.e., a moral restoration, Ecclesiasticus xlviii. 10. He is said καταστῆσαι
φυλὰς 'Ιακώβ, to enable those who had
been illegally excluded from the congregation to attain their inheritance.
But he is eager also for the moral
and religious renewal of his people. All
disputes would be settled by him at his
coming, and chiefly and above all he
conducts the people to a great repentance, which will not be accomplished
before he comes, Luke i. 16, 17 (Mal. iv.
6, LXX). This is the inward and moral
side of the ἀποκατάστασις, Matt. xvii. 11,
Mark ix. 12. But as in Acts i. 6 our
Lord had corrected the ideas of the disciples as to an external restoration of the
kingdom to Israel, so in the Gospels He
had corrected their ideas as to the coming
of Elias, and had bidden them see its
realisation in the preaching of John the
Baptist in turning the hearts of the
fathers to the children, and the disobedient to the wisdom of the just. And so
the ἀποκατάστασις πάντων had already
begun, in so far as men's hearts were
restored to obedience to God, the beginning of wisdom, to the purity of family
affection, to a love of righteousness and
a hatred of iniquity. Even when the
thoughts of the N.T. writers embrace the
renewal of the visible creation, the moral
and spiritual elements of restoration were
present and prominent; cf. 2 Pet. iii. 13,
Rom. viii. 19-21, Rev. xxi. 5. So too
the παλινγενεσία, in Matt. xix. 28, is
joined with the rule which the disciples
would share with their Lord, and involved great moral issues. A renewal
of all things had no doubt been foretold by the prophets, Is. xxxiv. 4, li. 6,
lxv. 17; it was dwelt upon in later Jewish writings, and often referred to by
the Rabbis (cf., e.g., Book of Enoch, xlv.,
2; lxii., 1; xci., 16, 17; Apocalypse of

Baruch, xxxii., and instances in Edersheim, Jesus the Messiah, ii., p. 343);
but even amongst pious Israelites there
was always a danger lest their hopes for
the future should be mainly associated
with material prosperity and national
glorification. It is perhaps significant
thas Josephus uses the two terms ἀποκατάστασις and παλινγενεσία in close
conjunction of the restoration of the
Jews to their own land after the exile.
How this restoration of all things was
to be effected, and what was involved
in it, St. Peter does not say, but his
whole trend of thought shows that it
was made dependent upon man's repentance, upon his heart being right
with God, see Weber, Jüdische Theologie, p. 352 ff. (1897); Edersheim,
Jesus the Messiah, ii., pp. 343, 706;
Hauck's Real-Encyclopädie, "Apokatas-
tasis," p. 616 ff. (1896).—ὧν refers to
χρόνων, so R.V. "whereof," i.e., of
which times. Holtzmann and Wendt
on the other hand refer ὧν to πάντων.
But the words of our Lord in Matt. xvii.
11 certainly point to the former reference,
and the words are so taken by Weiss,
Page, Hackett. In the article from
Hauck quoted above, the writer speaks
of the reference to χρόνων as the more
correct, and points out that if ὧν is the
relative to πάντων, the restoration spoken
of would no longer be a restoration of
all things, but only of those things of
which the prophets had spoken. On
the prophecies referred to see above.
All the words from πάντων to προφητῶν
are ascribed by Hilgenfeld to his "author
to Theophilus"; the thought of the
prophets existing ἀπ' αἰῶνος (Luke i. 70)
belongs in his opinion to the Paulinism
of this reviser, just as in Luke's Gospel
he carries back the genealogy of Jesus not
to Abraham but to Adam. To a similar Pauline tendency on the part of the
same reviser, Hilgenfeld refers the introduction in vv. 25, 26 of the promise made
to Abraham embracing all the nations of
the earth (Gal. iii. 16), and also the
introduction of the word πρῶτον (Rom.
i. 16, ii. 9), to show that not only upon
the Jews, but also upon the Gentiles had

αἰῶνος. 22.[1] Μωσῆς μὲν γὰρ πρὸς τοὺς πατέρας εἶπεν, "Ὅτι προφήτην ὑμῖν ἀναστήσει Κύριος ὁ Θεὸς ὑμῶν ἐκ τῶν ἀδελφῶν ὑμῶν,
ὡς ἐμέ· αὐτοῦ ἀκούσεσθε κατὰ πάντα ὅσα ἂν λαλήσῃ πρὸς ὑμᾶς.
23. ἔσται δέ, πᾶσα ψυχή, ἥτις ἂν μὴ ἀκούσῃ τοῦ προφήτου ἐκείνου,

[1] Μωσης, so אEP; but Μωυσης in ABCD, so Tisch., W.H., Weiss, Hilg., so
Winer-Schmiedel, p. 51. μεν γαρ; but only μεν in אABCDE, vers., Iren., Chrys.,
so Tisch., W.H., R.V., Weiss, Wendt. προς τους πατερας om. אABC 15, 18, 61,
Vulg., Syr. Pesh., Boh.; so Tisch., W.H., R.V., Weiss, Wendt.

God conferred the blessings of the Christ; *cf.* ii. 39, where the same revising hand is at work. But St. Peter's "universalism" here is in no way inconsistent with that of a pious Jew who would believe that all nations should be blessed *through Israel*, so far, *i.e.*, as they conformed to the covenant and the law of Israel. Spitta sees no difficulty in referring both the passage before us and ii. 39 to the Jewish Diaspora (so too Jüngst).—διὰ στόματος τῶν ἁγ. προφ.: *cf.* Luke i. 70, a periphrasis of which St. Luke is fond (Plummer), *cf.* i. 16, iii. 18, iv. 25, 30, xv. 7, not found in the other Evangelists except once in St. Matthew in a quotation, iv. 4.—ἀπ' αἰῶνος: in the singular the phrase is only used by St. Luke in the N.T., Luke i. 70, Acts iii. 21, and xv. 18, but the plural ἀπ' αἰώνων is used twice, Col. i. 26, Ephes. iii. 9 (Friedrich), *cf.* in LXX, Gen. vi. 4, Isaiah xlvi. 9, Jer. xxxv. (xxviii.) 8. The phrase here may be taken simply = "of old time," *cf.* Tobit iv. 12.

Ver. 22. μὲν: answered by, or rather connected with, καὶ πάντες δὲ (ver. 24), "Moses indeed, yea and all the Prophets from Samuel"—not "truly" as in A.V., as if μὲν were an adverb. The quotation is freely made from Deut. xviii. 15. On the Messianic bearing of the passage see Weber, *Jüdische Theologie*, p. 364 (1897), and Lumby, *Acts*, *in loco*. Wetstein sees no necessity to refer the word προφήτην, ver. 22, to Jesus, but rather to the succession of prophets who in turn prophesied of the Coming One. But "similitudo non officit excellentiæ" (Bengel, so Wendt), and the words in Deuteronomy were *fulfilled* in Christ alone, the new Law-giver; the Revealer of God's will, of grace and truth, "Whom the Lord knew face to face," Who was from all eternity "with God". But the N.T. gives us ample reason for referring the verse, if not to the Messiah, yet at least to the Messianic conceptions of the age. To say nothing of St. Stephen's significant reference to the same pro-phecy, vii. 37, it would certainly seem that in the conversation of our Lord with the Samaritan woman, John iv. 19 ff., the conception of the Messianic prophet is in her mind, and it was upon this prediction of a prophet greater than Moses that the Samaritans built their Messianic hopes (Briggs, *Messiah of the Gospels*, p. 272, and see also for Deut. xviii. 15, and its Messianic fulfilment, *Messianic Prophecy*, p. 110 ff.). On other allusions in St. John's Gospel to the anticipation in Deut. xviii. 15 see Bishop Lightfoot, *Expositor*, i. (fourth series), pp. 84, 85; there are, he thinks, four passages, John i. 21, 25, vi. 14, vii. 40, in all of which "*the* prophet" is mentioned (so R.V. in each place). But whilst in St. John the conception is still Jewish (that is to say, St. John exhibits the Messianic conceptions of his countrymen, who regard *the* Christ and *the* prophet as two different persons), in Acts it is Christian. St. Peter identified *the* prophet with the Christ (and so inferentially St. Stephen). (But see also Alford's note on St. John vi. 14, and also Weber, *ubi supra*, p. 354, for the view that Jeremiah was ὁ προφ., in John i. 21, 25, vii. 40 (*cf.* 2 Macc. xv. 14), whilst Wendt's *Teaching of Jesus*, i., pp. 67-69, E.T., should also be consulted.)—ὡς ἐμέ: rendered by A.V. and R.V. "like me" (the meaning of the Hebrew, *in loco*), but in margin R.V. has "as he raised up me," a rendering adopted as the only admissible one of the Greek by Page and Rendall; as no doubt it is, if we read ὥσπερ, as in LXX, Deut. xviii. 18. But ὡς is found in the LXX in v. 15. Certainly the rendering in A.V. and R.V. could not be applied to any one prophet so truly as to Christ, and the ὡς ἐμέ is a rendering of the familiar Hebrew כ (Lumby), which is so frequent in the LXX; see also Grimm-Thayer, *sub v.*, and Delitzsch, *Messianische Weissagungen*, p. 46 ff., second edition (1899).

Ver. 23. ἔσται δὲ, *cf.* ii. 17. The expression, which is not in the Hebrew,

ἐξολοθρευθήσεται ἐκ τοῦ λαοῦ." 24. καὶ πάντες δὲ οἱ προφῆται
ἀπὸ Σαμουὴλ καὶ τῶν καθεξῆς,[1] ὅσοι ἐλάλησαν, καὶ προκατήγγειλαν

[1] ὅσοι, D has ὃ ελαλησεν—Harris accounts for as *quodquod* of *d*, read as *quod*,
and so ὃ. T.R. has the support of ℵBC³EP; so W.H., Weiss. οι in ℵC²D², Vulg.,
Gig., Par.².

seems to call attention to what follows.—
ἐξολεθρευθήσεται ἐκ τοῦ λαοῦ : " shall be
utterly destroyed " (ἐξ), R.V. In the
LXX, Deut. xviii. 19, following the
Hebrew, the words are ἐγὼ ἐκδικήσω
ἐξ αὐτοῦ, " I will require it of him ".
But the phrase which St. Peter uses
was a very common one, from Gen.
xvii. 14, for the sentence of death,
cf. also Exod. xii. 15, 19, Lev. xvii. 4,
9, Num. xv. 30. Here again the quotation is evidently made freely or from
memory. The strong verb, although
frequent in the LXX, is found only here
in the N.T. It is used by Josephus and
by Philo, but not in classical Greek.
The warning is evidently directed against
wilful disobedience, and is expressed in
terms signifying the utterness of the destruction from the people. But in their
original meaning in the O.T. they need
not refer to anything more than the
penalty of the death of the body, and it
is not necessary to see in them here any
threat of eternal punishment in Gehenna
(so Wendt, Holtzmann, Felten). If the
word has any eschatological bearing it
would support the theory of annihilation
more easily. Grotius explains ἐξολεθ.,
" morte violenta aut immatura," and he
adds " mystice etiam Rabbini hoc ad
poenas post hanc vitam referunt," but
this is quite apart from the primary meaning of the word.
Ver. 24. Σαμουὴλ : On Samuel as the
founder of the prophetic schools and the
pattern of all later prophets, see Hamburger, *Real-Encyclopädie des Judentums*, i., 6, p. 854 ; " Prophet," *cf. Midrash
Shemuel*, c. 24, where Samuel is called
the Rabban, the chief and teacher of the
prophets (Wetstein, *in loco*, and Lumby),
cf. also Heb. xi. 32, Δαυείδ τε καὶ Σ. καὶ
τῶν προφητῶν.—καὶ τῶν καθεξῆς : an
unmistakable tautology. Wendt considers the expression as inaccurate, see
his note, and for a full discussion *cf.*
Winer-Moulton, lxvii. 2, who compares
Luke xxiv. 27, = " all the series of
prophets beginning from Samuel "
(Page) ; " longa tamen successione, uno
tamen consensu " (Calvin). καθεξ. used
by St. Luke alone, Luke i. 3, viii. 1,
Acts xi. 4, xviii. 23. In Greek writers =

ἐφεξῆς, not found in LXX.—καὶ κατήγγ.
τὰς ἡμέρας ταύτας : " have also told of
these days," *i.e.*, the present days, *cf.*
v. 36, Luke xxiv. 18. This interpretation does not prevent the identification
of " these days " with the χρόνοι τῆς
ἀποκαταστάσεως, since in one sense
the restoration had already begun with
the coming of the forerunner and
of the Christ, and in the acceptance
of the repentance which they had
preached. Rendall renders " yea, so
said all the prophets from Samuel
. . . as many as have spoken and told
of these days," as if the fact which St.
Peter wished to emphasise was that all
the prophets had spoken threats of utter
destruction like Moses. But the Greek
does not by any means of necessity bear
this construction (Viteau, *Le Grec du N.
T.*, p. 55 (1896), and such an interpretation seems too harsh. As Wendt admits,
the reference is not merely to the prophetical sayings relating to the last judgment, but also to the promises of salvation and to all which is connected with
the χρόνοι ἀποκατ. Moreover the reference to Samuel is made because of
Nathan's prediction, " the fundamental
prophecy respecting the seed of David,"
2 Sam. vii. 12 ff., in which it is foretold
that mercy shall not be taken away even
in the midst of punishment. Blass explains the expression τὰς ἡμερ. ταύτ.
" regni felicis Messianici " ; but we must
remember that it does not follow that the
popular views of the Messianic kingdom
and judgment were still held by St. Peter.
Ver. 25. ὑμεῖς, as in ver. 26, emphatic,
" obligat auditores " Bengel, *cf.* ii. 39,
Rom. ix. 4, xv. 8 ; their preference and
destiny ought to make them more sensible
of their duty in the reception of the
Messiah ; υἱοί, " sons " as in Matt. viii.
12, R.V. The rendering " disciples "
(Matt. xii. 2), even if υἱοί could be so
rendered with προφητῶν (J. Lightfoot,
Kuinoel), could not be applied to τῆς
διαθήκης. The expression is Hebraistic,
see Grimm-Thayer, *sub* υἱός, 2, and on
many similar expressions Deissmann,
Bibelstudien, p. 163 ff.—διαθ. διέθετο, *cf.*
Heb. viii. 10, x. 16, Gen. xv. 18, 1 Macc.
i. 11, for a similar construction in LXX

τὰς ἡμέρας ταύτας. 25. ὑμεῖς ἐστε[1] υἱοὶ τῶν προφητῶν, καὶ τῆς
διαθήκης ἧς διέθετο ὁ Θεὸς πρὸς τοὺς πατέρας[2] ἡμῶν, λέγων πρὸς

[1] υἱοι, prefix οι ℵABCE 61, Boh., Sah.; so Tisch., W.H., R.V., Weiss.

[2] ημων ℵ*CDP 1, 13, 31, Vulg., Boh., Sah., Syrr. (P. and H.), Arm., Aeth., so
Tisch., W.H. margin, Hilg.; υμων ℵ³ABE, Sahwoi., Armcodd., Chrys., so W.H.
text, Weiss, Wendt.

in more than seventy places, so also frequently in classical writers.—**διαθήκης**:
on the word, see below, vii. 8.—**ἐν τῷ
σπέρματί σου**, cf. Gen. xxii. 18, xii. 3.
For the application of the prophecy to
the Messiah as the seed of Abraham by
the Rabbinical writers, see Wetstein on
Gal. iii. 16 (and Edersheim, *Jesus the
Messiah*, ii., p. 712); so by St. Luke, although the words of the prophecy were
first uttered in a collective sense.—
πατριαί: "families," R.V., Luke ii. 4,
Eph. iii. 15; "kindreds," A.V., is the
rendering of other words, iv. 5, vii. 3.
πατριά is found in LXX (and in Herodotus); in Gen. xii. 3 **φυλαί** is used, and
in xviii. 18 **ἔθνη**, but in Ps. xxii. 27 and
in 1 Chron. xvi. 28 we have the phrase
αἱ πατριαὶ τῶν ἐθνῶν (but see Nösgen,
in loco). In this quotation, cf. Gal. iii.
8, 16, and in the **πρῶτον** of the next
verse we may see a striking illustration
of the unity of Apostolic preaching,
and the recognition of God's purpose
by St. Peter and St. Paul alike (Rom.
i. 16, ii. 9, 10).—**ἐνευλογηθήσονται**:
ἐν of the instrument as often: the verb
is not used in classical writers, but Blass
gives several instances of verbs similarly
compounded with **ἐν**, cf. **ἐνευδαιμονεῖν,
ἐνευδοκιμεῖν**. The compound verb is
found several times in LXX.
Ver. 26. **ὑμῖν πρῶτον—ὑμῖν**: again
emphatic. In the words of St. Peter
we may again note his agreement with
St. Paul, xiii. 46, Rom. i. 16 (x. 11), although no doubt St. Peter shared the
views of his nation in so far that Gentiles
could only participate in the blessings of
the Messianic kingdom through acceptance of Judaism.—**ἀναστήσας**, cf. ver.
22, **τὸν παῖδα**, "his servant," R.V., see
above on ver. 13. **ἀπέστειλεν** also shows
that **ἀναστ.** here refers not to the Resurrection but to the Incarnation.—**εὐλογοῦντα**: as in the act of blessing, present
participle; the present participle expressing that the Christ is still continuing
His work of blessing on repentance, but
see also Burton, *N. T. Moods and Tenses*,
p. 171.—**ἐν τῷ**: this use of **ἐν** governing
the dative with the infinitive is most
commonly temporal, but it is used to

express other relations, such as manner,
means, as here (cf. iv. 30, where the
attempt to give a temporal sense is very
far-fetched, Hackett, *in loco*); see Burton,
u. s., p. 162, and Blass, *Grammatik des
N. G.*, p. 232. This formula of **ἐν** with
the dative of the article and the infinitive
is very common in St. Luke, both in his
Gospel and in the Acts, and is characteristic of him as compared with
the number of times the same formula
is used by other writers in the N.T.,
Friedrich, *Das Lucasevangelium*, p.
37, and also Zeller, *Acts of the
Apostles*, ii., p. 196, E.T.; so also in
the LXX the same construction is found,
cf. Gen. xix. 16, xxxiv. 15, etc.—**ἀποστρέφειν**: probably intransitive (Blass,
Grimm, and so often in LXX, although
the English A. and R.V. may be understood in either sense). Vulgate renders
"ut convertat se unusquisque," but the
use of the verb elsewhere in Luke xxiii.
14 (cf. also Rom. xi. 26, Isa. lix. 20)
makes for the transitive sense (so Weiss,
in loco). The argument from ver. 19 (as
Alford points out) does not decide the
matter either way (see also Holtzmann).
—**πονηριῶν**, cf. Luke xi. 39, and adjective
πονηρός frequent both in the Gospel and
in the Acts; in LXX both words are very
common. The word may denote miseries
as well as iniquities, as Bengel notes,
but the latter sense is demanded by the
context. **πρῶτον** according to Jüngst
does not mark the fact that the Jews
were to be converted first and the Gentiles afterwards, but as belonging to the
whole clause, and as referring to the first
and past sending of Jesus in contrast to
the second (ver. 20) and future sending
in glory. But to support this view
Jüngst has no hesitation in regarding
25b as an interpolation, and so nothing
is left but a reference to the **διαθήκη** of
God with the fathers, *i.e.*, circumcision,
which is quite in place before a Jewish
audience.

St. Peter's Discourses.—More recent
German criticism has departed far from
the standpoint of the early Tübrigen
school, who could only see in these discourses the free composition of a later

 Ἀβραάμ, " Καὶ τῷ σπέρματί σου ἐνευλογηθήσονται πᾶσαι αἱ πατριαὶ
τῆς γῆς." 26. ὑμῖν πρῶτον ὁ Θεὸς ἀναστήσας τὸν παῖδα αὐτοῦ

age, whilst Dr. McGiffert, in spite of his denial of the Lucan authorship of Acts, inclines to the belief that the discourses in question represent an early type of Christian teaching, derived from primitive documents, and that they breathe the spirit of St. Peter and of primitive Jewish Christianity. Feine sees in the contents of the addresses a proof that we have in them a truthful record of the primitive Apostolic teaching. Just the very points which were of central interest in this early period of the Church's life are those emphasised here, e.g., the proof that Jesus of Nazareth, the Crucified One, is the Messiah, a proof attested by His Resurrection, the appeal to Israel, the chosen people, to repent for the remission of sins in His name. Nor is there anything against the speeches in the fact of their similarity; in their first and early preaching, as Feine urges, the Apostles' thoughts would naturally move in the same circle, they would recur again and again to the same facts, and their addresses could scarcely be otherwise than similar. Moreover we have an appeal to the facts of the life of Jesus as to things well known in the immediate past: " Jesus of Nazareth " had been working in the midst of them, and Peter's hearers were witnesses with him of His signs and wonders, " as ye yourselves know," ii. 23 ; we become conscious in such words and in their context of all the moral indignation and the deep pain of the Apostles at the crucifixion of their Master, just as in iii. 13 we seem to listen to another personal reminiscence of the Passion history (see Beyschlag, *Neutest. Theol.*, i., pp. 304, 305; Scharfe, *Die Petrinische Strömung*, 2 c., pp. 184, 185).

The fact that no reference is made to, or at all events that no stress is laid upon, the doctrinal significance of the death of Christ, as by St. Paul, is again an intimation that we are dealing with the earliest days of Apostolic teaching—the death of the Cross was in itself the fact of all others which was the insuperable offence to the Jew, and it could not help him to proclaim that Christ died for his sins if he had no belief in Jesus as the Christ. The first and necessary step was to prove to the Jew that the suffering of the Messiah was in accordance with the counsels of God and with the voices of the prophets (Lechler, *Das Apostolische Zeitalter*, pp.

230, 231). But the historical fact accepted, its inner and spiritual significance would be imparted, and there was nothing strange in the fact that disciples who had themselves found it so difficult to overcome their repugnance to the mention of their Master's sufferings, should first direct their main efforts to remove the like prejudice from the minds of their countrymen. But we cannot adduce from this method that the Apostles had never heard such words as those of Christ (Matt. xx. 28, Mark x. 45, *cf.* 1 Peter i. 18) (*cf.* the striking passage in Beyschlag, *u. s.*, pp. 306, 307), or that they were entirely ignorant of the atoning significance of His Death. St. Paul, 1 Cor. xv. 1-3, speaks of the tradition which he had received, a tradition in which he was at one with the Twelve, ver. 11, *viz.*, that Christ died for our sins according to the Scriptures (Feine, *Die vorkanonische Ueberlieferung des Lukas;* see p. 230).

When we pass to the consideration of St. Peter's Christology, we again see how he starts from the actual experience of his hearers before him : " Jesus of Nazareth, a man," etc.—plainly and fearlessly St. Peter emphasises the manhood of his Lord—the title which is never found in any of the Epistles leads us back to the Passion and the Cross, to the early records of the Saviour's life on earth, Acts xxiv. 9, xxii. 8. And yet the Crucified Nazarene was by a startling paradox the Prince or Author of Life (see note on ἀρχηγός) ; by a divine law which the Jews could not discern He could not save Himself—and yet— another paradox—there was no other Name given amongst men whereby they must be saved.

St. Paul could write of Him, Who took upon Him the form of a servant, Who humbled Himself, and became obedient to the death of the Cross, Phil. ii. 6 ; and St. Peter, in one familiar word, which so far as we know St. Paul never used, brings before his hearers the same sublime picture of obedience, humility, death and glory ; Jesus is the ideal, the glorified " Servant " of God (see note on iii. 13). But almost in the same breath St. Peter speaks of the Servant as the Holy and Righteous One, iii. 14 ; holy, in that He was consecrated to the service of Jehovah (ἅγιος, iv. 27, 30, see note, and ii. 27) ; righteous, in that He was

Ἰησοῦν,[1] ἀπέστειλεν αὐτὸν εὐλογοῦντα ὑμᾶς, ἐν τῷ ἀποστρέφειν ἕκαστον ἀπὸ τῶν πονηριῶν ὑμῶν.

[1] Ἰησουν om. ℵBCDE 61, Vulg.; so Tisch., W.H., R.V., Weiss, Hilg. υμων ℵAC³DEP 1, 31, 61, Syrr. (P. and H.), Arm., Aeth., so Tisch. [W.H.]., Weiss; in B, Chrys., Theophyl. omitted; C³ 13, Vulg., Sah., Boh., Irint. read αυτων.

also the impersonation of righteousness, a righteousness which the Law had proclaimed, and which Prophets and Kings had desired to see, but had not seen (Isaiah liii. 11). But whilst we note these titles, steeped each and all of them in O.T. imagery, whilst we may see in them the germs of the later and the deeper theology of St. Paul and St. John (see Dr. Lock, " Christology of the Earlier Chapters of the Acts," *Expositor*, iv. (fourth series), p. 178 ff.), they carry us far beyond the conception of a mere humanitarian Christ. It is not only that Jesus of Nazareth is set before us as " the very soul and end of Jewish Prophecy," as Himself the Prophet to whom the true Israel would hearken, but that He is associated by St. Peter even in his earliest utterances, as none other is associated, with Jehovah in His Majesty in the work of salvation, ii. 34; the salvation which was for all who called upon Jehovah's Name, ii. 21, was also for all in the Name, in the power of Jesus Christ, iv. 12 (see notes, *l. c*, and *cf.* the force of the expression ἐπικαλεῖσθαι τὸ ὄνομα in 1 Cor. i. 2, Schmid, *Biblische Theologie*, p. 407); the Spirit which Joel had foretold would be poured forth by Jehovah had been poured forth by Jesus raised to the right hand of God, ii. 18, 33 (see further notes in chap. x. 36, 42, 43).

One other matter must be briefly noticed—the correspondence in thought and word between the St. Peter of the early chapters of the Acts and the St. Peter of the First Epistle which bears his name. A few points may be selected. St. Peter had spoken of Christ as the Prince of Life; quite in harmony with this is the thought expressed in 1 Pet. i. 3, of Christians as " begotten again " by the resurrection of Jesus Christ from the dead. St. Peter had spoken of Christ as the Holy and Righteous One, so in the First Epistle he sets forth this aspect of Christ's peculiar dignity, His sinlessness. As in Acts, so also in 1 Pet. the thought of the sufferings of Christ is prominent, but also that of the glory which should follow, chap. i., ver. 11. As in Acts, so also in 1 Pet. these

sufferings are described as undeserved, but also as foreordained by God and in accordance with the voices of the Prophets, 1 Pet. i. 11 and ii. 22-25. As in Acts, so in 1 Pet. it is the special task of the Apostles to be witnesses of the sufferings and also of the resurrection of Christ, chap. v. 1. As in Acts, so in 1 Pet. we have the clearest testimony to the δόξα of Christ, 1 Pet. i. 21 and iv. 11. As in Acts stress is laid not only upon the facts of the life of Christ, but also upon His teaching, x. 34 ff., so also in 1 Pet., while allusions are made to the scenes of our Lord's Passion with all the force of an eye-witness, we have stress laid upon the word of Christ, the Gospel or teaching, i. 12, 23, 25, ii. 2, 8, iii. 19, iv. 6. As in Acts, so in 1 Pet. we have a reference to the agency of Christ in the realm of the dead, 1 Pet. iii. 19, iv. 6. As in Acts, x. 42, so in 1 Pet. Christ is Himself the judge of quick and dead, iv. 6, or in His unity with the Father shares with Him that divine prerogative, *cf.* i. 17. As in Acts, so in 1 Pet. the communication of the Holy Spirit is specially attributed to the exalted Christ, *cf.* Acts ii. 33, 1 Pet. i. 11, 12. As in Acts, so in 1 Pet. Christ is the living corner-stone on which God's spiritual house is built, Acts iv. 12 and 1 Pet. ii. 4-10. As in Acts, so in 1 Pet. not only the details but the whole scope of salvation is regarded in the light and as a fulfilment of O.T. prophecy, *cf.* Acts iii. 18-25, 1 Pet. ii. 22, 23, and i. 10-12. But this correspondence extends to words, amongst which we may note πρόγνωσις, Acts ii. 23, 1 Pet. i. 2, a word found nowhere else in the N.T., and used in each passage in the same sense; ἀπροσωπολήμπτως, 1 Pet. i. 17, and only here in N.T., but *cf.* Acts x. 34, οὐκ ἔστιν προσωπολήμπτης. ξύλον twice used by St. Peter in Acts v. 30, x. 39 (once by St. Paul), and again in 1 Pet. ii. 24; ἀθέμιτος only in the Cornelius history, Acts x. 28, by St. Peter, and in 1 Pet. iv. 3; μάρτυς with the genitive of that to which testimony is rendered, most frequently in N.T. used by St. Peter, *cf.* Acts i. 22, vi. 32, x. 39, and 1 Pet. v. 1; and further, in

IV. 1. ΛΑΛΟΥΝΤΩΝ δὲ αὐτῶν πρὸς τὸν λαόν, ἐπέστησαν αὐτοῖς οἱ ἱερεῖς [1] καὶ ὁ στρατηγὸς τοῦ ἱεροῦ καὶ οἱ Σαδδουκαῖοι, 2. διαπονού-

---

[1] ιερεις ℵADEP 1, 31, 61, Vulg., Sah., Boh., Syrr. (P. and H.), Lucif., Chrys., so Tisch., W.H. margin, R.V. text, Weiss, Hilg.; αρχιερεις BC 4, Arm., Aeth., so W.H. text, R.V. margin, Wendt; ο στρατ. του ιερου om. by D, but accepted by Blass in β.

Acts iv. 11 = 1 Pet. ii. 7, Acts x. 42 = 1 Pet. iv. 5, the verbal correspondence is very close.

See on the whole subject Nösgen, *Apostelgeschichte*, p. 48; Lechler, *Das Apost. Zeitalter*, p. 428 ff.; Scharfe, *Die Petrinische Strömung*, 2 c., p. 122 ff.; Lumby, *Expositor*, iv. (first series), pp. 118, 123; and also Schmid, *Biblische Theologie*, p. 389 ff. On the striking connection between the *Didache*, and the language of St. Peter's sermons, and the phraseology of the early chapters of Acts, see Gore, *Church and the Ministry*, p. 416.

CHAPTER IV.—Ver. 1. λαλούντων δὲ αὐτῶν: the speech was interrupted, as the present participle indicates, and we cannot treat it as if we had received it in full. It is no doubt possible to infer from αὐτῶν that St. John also addressed the people.—ἐπέστησαν αὐτοῖς: commonly used with the notion of coming upon one suddenly, so of the coming of an angel, xii. 7, xxiii. 11, Luke ii. 9, xxiv. 4, sometimes too as implying a hostile purpose, cf. vi. 12, xvii. 5, and St. Luke (x. 40), xx. 1. For its use in the LXX cf. Wisdom vi. 5, 8, xix. 1.—οἱ ἱερεῖς: "the priests," so A. and R.V., but the latter, margin, "the chief priests," see critical note. ἀρχιερεῖς would comprise probably the members of the privileged high-priestly families in which the high-priesthood was vested (Schürer, *Jewish People*, div. ii., vol. i., pp. 203-206, E.T.), Jos., *B. J.*, vi., 2, 2. That the members of these families occupied a distinguished position we know (cf. iv. 6), and there is nothing improbable in the supposition that the description ἀρχιερεῖς would include them as well as the ex-high-priests, and the one actually in office; this seems justified from the words of Josephus in the passage referred to above (Derenbourg, *Histoire de la Palestine*, p. 231). —ὁ στρατηγὸς τοῦ ἱεροῦ: the captain of the Temple (known chiefly in Jewish writings as "the man of the Temple Mount "). He had the chief superintendence of the Levites and priests who were on guard in and around the Temple, and under him were στρατηγοί, who were also captains of the Temple police,

although subordinate to the στρατηγός as their head. The στρατ. τοῦ ἱεροῦ was not only a priest, but second in dignity to the high-priest himself (Schürer, *u. s.*, pp. 258, 259, 267, and Edersheim, *u. s.*, and *History of the Jewish Nation*, p. 139), Acts v. 24, 26, Jos., *Ant.*, xx., 6, 2, *B. J.*, vi., 5, 3. For the use of the term in the LXX, see Schürer, *u. s.*, p. 258. In 2 Macc. iii. 4 the "governor of the Temple " is identified by some with the officer here and in v. 24, but see Rawlinson's note *in loco* in *Speaker's Commentary*. —καὶ οἱ Σαδδουκαῖοι: at this time, as Josephus informs us, however strange it may appear, the high-priestly families belonged to the Sadducean party. Not that the Sadducees are to be identified entirely with the party of the priests, since the Pharisees were by no means hostile to the priests as such, nor the priests to the Pharisees. But the Sadducees were the aristocrats, and to the *aristocratic* priests, who occupied influential civil positions, the Pharisees were bitterly opposed. Jos., *Ant.*, xvii., 10, 6, xviii., 1, 4, xx., 9, 1. Schürer, *u. s.*, div. ii., vol. ii., pp. 29-43, and div. ii., vol. i., p. 178 ff. The words οἱ Σαδδ. and ἡ οὖσα αἵρεσις τῶν Σ., ver. 17, are referred by Hilgenfeld to his "author to Theophilus," as also the reference to the preaching of the Resurrection as the cause of the sore trouble to the Sadducees; but the mention of the Sadducees at least shows (as Weizsäcker and Holtzmann admit) that the author of *Acts* had correct information of the state of parties in Jerusalem: "The Sadducees were at the helm, and the office of the high-priest was in Sadducean hands, and the Sadducees predominated in the high-priestly families " (Weizsäcker, *Apostolic Age*, i., 61, E.T.).

Ver. 2. διαπονούμενοι, cf. xvi. 18, only in *Acts* in the N.T., not, as often in classical Greek, referring to the exertions made by them, but to the vexation which they felt, "being sore troubled," R.V. (πόνος, *dolor*, Blass), cf. LXX, Eccles. x. 9, used of pain caused to the body, and 2 Macc. ii. 28, R. (A. *al.* ἀτονοῦντες), but cf. Aquila, Gen. vi. 6, xxxiv. 7, 1 Sam. xx. 3, 34, of mental grief.—ἐν τῷ Ἰησοῦ:

μενοι διὰ τὸ διδάσκειν αὐτοὺς τὸν λαόν, καὶ¹ καταγγέλλειν ἐν τῷ
Ἰησοῦ τὴν ἀνάστασιν τὴν ἐκ νεκρῶν· 3. καὶ ἐπέβαλον αὐτοῖς τὰς
χεῖρας,² καὶ ἔθεντο εἰς τήρησιν εἰς τὴν αὔριον· ἦν γὰρ ἑσπέρα ἤδη.
4. πολλοὶ δὲ τῶν ἀκουσάντων τὸν λόγον ἐπίστευσαν· καὶ ἐγενήθη ὁ

¹ D reads αναγγελλειν τον Ι. εν τη αναστασει των νεκρων, but Blass rejects (Chase
contends for Syriac); την εκ νεκρων ΝABCE, Vulg., Boh., Syrr. (P. and H.); των
νεκρων DP, h, 31, Flor., Gig., Par., Sah., Arm., Aeth., Lucif., Ir., Chrys.

² χειρας; after this word Flor. inserts εκρατησαν αυτους (which Zöckler and
Belser regard as original); for επεβαλον D reads επιβαλοντες.

not "through," but as in R.V., "in
Jesus," i.e., "in persona Jesu quem resur-
rexisse dicebant" (Blass). Others render
it "in the instance of Jesus" (so Holtzmann, Wendt, Felten, Zöckler).—τὴν
ἀνάστασιν τὴν ἐκ νεκρῶν: on the form
of the expression see Plummer on St.
Luke, xx. 35, and Lumby's note, in loco.
It must be distinguished from (ἡ) ἀνάστασις τῶν νεκρῶν. It is the more limited
term implying that some from among the
dead are raised, while others as yet are
not; used of the Resurrection of Christ
and of the righteous, cf. with this passage 1 Peter i. 3 (Col. i. 18), but see also
Grimm-Thayer, sub ἀνάστασις. It was
not merely a dogmatic question of the
denial of the Resurrection which concerned the Sadducees, but the danger to
their power, and to their wealth from
the Temple sacrifices and dues, if the Resurrection of Jesus was proclaimed and
accepted (see Wendt and Holtzmann, in
loco, and Plummer on Luke xxiii. 1-7,
note). Spitta agrees with Weiss, Feine,
Jüngst, in regarding the mention of the
distress of the Sadducees at the preaching
of the Apostles as not belonging to the
original source. But it is worthy of
notice that in estimating the positive
value of his source, A., he decides to
retain the mention of the Sadducees in
iv. 1—it would have been more easy, he
thinks, for a forger to have represented
the enmity to the Church as proceeding
not from the Sadducees but from the
Pharisees, as in the Gospels. But the
Sadducees, as Spitta reminds us, according to Josephus, included the high-priestly
families in their number, and it was by
this sect that at a later date the death of
James the Just was caused. Only once
in the Gospels, John xii. 10, the chief
priests, rather than the Pharisees, take
the initiative against our Lord, but this
was in the case of what was essentially a
question for the Sadducees (as here in
Acts iv. 2), the advisability of getting rid
of Lazarus, a living witness to the truth

which the Sadducees denied. It is no
unfair inference that the chief priests in
St. John occupy the place of the Sadducees in the Synoptists, as the latter are
never mentioned by name in the fourth
Gospel; and if so, this is exactly in accordance with what we should expect
from the notices here and in Acts v. 17,
and in Josephus; see on the point Lightfoot in Expositor, 1890, pp. 86, 87.
Ver. 3. ἐπέβαλον αὐτοῖς τὰς χεῖρας:
the verb is always as here joined with
the same noun in Acts, and twice in the
Gospel; the phrase is found once in
Matthew and Mark, and twice in John;
see Luke xx. 19, xxi. 12, Acts iv. 3, v. 18,
xii. 1, xxi. 27, cf. in LXX, Gen. xxii. 12,
2 Sam. xviii. 12; Esther vi. 2, so also in
Polybius.—τήρησιν, cf. v. 18, only used
elsewhere in N.T. by St. Paul, 1 Cor.
vii. 19; in Thuc., vii., 86 (Wendt),
it denotes not only the act of guarding,
but also a place of custody. Five
times in LXX, but in the former sense.
For another instance of its meaning
as a place of custody (see Deissmann,
Neue Bibelstudien, p. 55), on papyrus in
Egypt, second or third century after
Christ.—ἦν γὰρ ἑσπέρα ἤδη, cf. iii. 1,
the judicial examination must therefore
be postponed until the next day, see Jer.
xxi. 12, on which it appears that the
Rabbis founded this prohibition against
giving judgment in the night (Lumby
and Felten, in loco).—ἑσπέρα: only in
St. Luke in the N.T., Luke xxiv. 29,
Acts iv. 3 (xx. 15, W.H. margin) and
xxviii. 23.
Ver. 4. ἐγενήθη: "came to be" R.V.,
only here in St. Luke, except in the quotation in i. 20 (see also vii. 13, D., and
Blass in β—hellenistic, frequently in LXX;
in N.T. cf. 1 Thess. ii. 14, Col. iv. 11; also
Jos., Ant., x., 10, 2, Winer-Schmiedel, p.
108, note).—ἀνδρῶν. This word here appears to be used of men only (so Wetstein, Blass), cf. Matt. xiv. 21, Mark vi.
40, for although we cannot argue with
Weiss from v. 14, that women in great

ἀριθμὸς [1] τῶν ἀνδρῶν ὡσεὶ χιλιάδες πέντε. 5. Ἐγένετο δὲ ἐπὶ τὴν
αὔριον [2] συναχθῆναι αὐτῶν τοὺς ἄρχοντας καὶ πρεσβυτέρους καὶ γραμματεῖς εἰς Ἰερουσαλήμ, 6. καὶ Ἄνναν [3] τὸν ἀρχιερέα καὶ Καϊάφαν καὶ
Ἰωάννην καὶ Ἀλέξανδρον, καὶ ὅσοι ἦσαν ἐκ γένους ἀρχιερατικοῦ.

[1] ὁ αριθμος, so AEP 31, 61, Chrys.; but article om. אBD, so Tisch., W.H., R.V.,
Weiss. ωσει EP, Chrys.; ως BD, so W.H., Weiss, Hilg.; om. אA 61, Vulg. verss.,
so Tisch., Wendt (who compares ii. 41 and regards ως or ωσει as added accordingly).

[2] After αυριον D, Flor. add ημεραν, so Hilg.; Chase by assim. to Syriac, Harris by
assim. to Bezan Latin—*crastinum diem*. But *cf*. σημερον ημερα in N.T., Acts xx. 26,
Rom. xi. 8, 2 Cor. iii. 14. εις ιερ. אP 1, 31, Syr. Harcl., so Tisch., Wendt; εν
ABDE 61, Chrys., so W.H., R.V., Weiss, Hilg.; Flor., Syr. Pesh. omit. συναχθηναι,
D, Flor. change constr. συνηχθησαν οι αρχ.

[3] Ανναν, acc., EP 1, 31, 61, Chrys.; Αννας, nom. (and so all the proper names),
אBD 15, 18, 36, 61, so Tisch., W.H., R.V., Weiss, Wendt (who holds, as against
Meyer, that the noms. are not derived from συνηχθησαν in D, but that the latter
was occasioned by the noms.). Ιωαννην, D, Gig., Par.[1] read Ιωναθας. Blass contends
for the correctness of D, so Hilg., Ιωναθας = Jonathan, son of Annas, who succeeded
Caiaphas, Josephus, *Ant.*, xviii., 4, 3 (see Blass, *Acta Apost.*, 72 and 35), Ιωαννης
being a common name and an unknown man. But we cannot conceive that Luke
would himself have altered Ιωναθας into Ιωαννης, so Blass regards the former as the
reading in α and β—Ιωαννης a later blunder.

numbers did not join the Church until a
later period (*cf*. also ii. 41, where women
may well have been included), yet it
seems that St. Luke, by his use of one
word, ἀνδρῶν, here refers to the additional
number of *men*. St. Luke does not say
that five thousand of St. Peter's hearers
were converted, in addition to those already converted at Pentecost (although
Dr. Hort, following Chrys., Aug., Jer.,
takes this view, *Judaistic Christianity*,
p. 47), or that five thousand were added,
but his words certainly mark the growing
expansion of the Church in spite of threatening danger, as this is also evident on
the view that five thousand represent the
total number of believers. The instances
above from the Gospels are generally
quoted to confirm the view here taken,
but Wendt, *in loco*, curiously quotes the
same passages in proof that ἀνδρῶν here
includes women. The numbers are regarded by him as by Weizsäcker as artificial, but see above on i. 15.

Ver. 5. ἐγένετο δὲ: the formula is
another characteristic of St. Luke's style,
Friedrich, *Das Lucasevangelium*, p. 13,
also Dalman, *Die Worte Jesu*, pp. 26, 29.
Compare for the type of construction,
according to which what takes place is
put in the infinitive mood, depending
upon ἐγένετο, ix. 32, 37, 43, xi. 26,
xiv. 1, and other instances in Dr.
Plummer's exhaustive note, *St. Luke*,
p. xlv.—ἐπὶ τὴν αὔριον: here only and
in Luke x. 35, in N.T. For the tem-

poral use of ἐπί iii. 1.—συναχθῆναι,
i.e., the Sanhedrim. ἄρχοντας here =
ἀρχιερεῖς, who are mentioned first as
a rule, where the N.T. enumerates the
different orders of the Sanhedrim,
whilst οἱ ἄρχοντες is an interchangeable expression, both in the N.T. and
in Josephus (see, for instance, Schürer,
Jewish People, div. ii., vol. i., pp. 177,
205, E.T.), although there are two
instances in which both words occur
together, Luke xxiii. 13 and xxiv. 20.
Whatever may have been the precise
significance of the term ἀρχιερεῖς,
Schürer, *u. s.*, pp. 203-206, E.T., it included, beyond all doubt, the most prominent representatives of the priesthood,
belonging chiefly, if not entirely, to the
Sadducean party.—πρεσβυτέρους: those
members were known simply by this title
who did not belong to either of the two
special classes mentioned.—γραμματεῖς:
the professional lawyers who adhered to
the Pharisees, Jos., *Ant.*, xvii., 6, 2. Even
under the Roman government the Sanhedrim possessed considerable independence
of jurisdiction, both civil and criminal.
Not only could it order arrests to be
made by its own officers, but it could
dispose, on its own authority, of cases
where the death penalty was not involved, Schürer, *u. s.*, p. 187, E.T., and
Edersheim, *History of the Jewish
Nation*, p. 103 ff.—εἰς Ἰερουσαλήμ:
Weiss would restrict ἐν Ἰερ. to the
scribes of Jerusalem to distinguish them

7. καὶ στήσαντες αὐτοὺς ἐν τῷ μέσῳ, ἐπυνθάνοντο, Ἐν ποίᾳ δυνάμει
ἢ ἐν ποίῳ ὀνόματι ἐποιήσατε τοῦτο ὑμεῖς; 8. Τότε Πέτρος, πλησθεὶς
Πνεύματος Ἁγίου, εἶπε πρὸς αὐτούς, Ἄρχοντες τοῦ λαοῦ καὶ πρεσ-

from the scribes of Galilee, but it is doubtful whether the words can bear this (see also Rendall, who favours the same view as Weiss). Holtzmann and Wendt, on the other hand, defend εἰς, and suppose that the members of the Sanhedrim were obliged to hurry into the city from their country estates. Zöckler applies ἐν ᾽Ιερ. not only to γραμματεῖς, but also to the other members of the Sanhedrim, and sees in the words an intimation that the sitting was hurriedly composed of the members actually present in Jerusalem.

Ver. 6. Ἄννας: Caiaphas, the son-in-law of Annas, was the high priest actually in office, but like other retired high priests, the latter retained not only the title, but also many of the rights and obligations of the office. Josephus certainly appears to extend the title to ex-high priests, and so in the N.T. where ἀρχιερεῖς appear at the head of the Sanhedrim as in this passage (ἄρχοντες), the ex-high priests are to be understood, first and foremost, as well as the high-priest actually in office. The difficulty here is that the title is given to Annas alone, and this seems to involve that he was also regarded as president of the Sadducees, whereas it is always the actual ἀρχιερεύς who presides, cf. Acts v. 17, vii. 1, ix. 1, xxii. 5, xxiii. 2, 4, xxiv. 1. But not only is the laxity of the term to be considered, but also the fact that Annas on account of his influence as the head of the γένος ἀρχιερατικόν may have remained the presiding ἀρχιερεύς in spite of all the rapid changes in the tenure of the high-priestly office under the Romans. These changes the Jews would not recognise as valid, and if the early chapters of Acts came to St. Luke as seems probable from Jewish Christian sources, Annas might easily be spoken of as high-priest. His relationship to Caiaphas helps to explain the influence and power of Annas. On Hamburger's view (Real-Encyclopädie des Judentums, ii., 8, p. 1151, "Synhedrion"), that a Rabbi and not the high-priest presided over the Sadducees, see Edersheim, History of the Jewish Nation, p. 522, and Schürer, u. s., p. 180. For Annas, see Jos., Ant., xviii., 2, 12, xx., 9, 1, and see further "Annas" in B.D.[2] and Hastings' B.D.—᾽Ιωάννης: identified by J. Lightfoot (cf. also Wetstein) with

the famous Johanan ben Zacchai, president of the Great Synagogue after its removal to Jamnia, who obtained leave from Vespasian for many of the Jews to settle in the place. But the identification is very uncertain, and does not appear to commend itself to Schürer; see critical note above.—Ἀλέξανδρος: of him too nothing is known, as there is no confirmatory evidence to identify him with the brother of Philo, alabarch of Alexandria, and the first man of his time amongst the Jews of that city, Jos., Ant., xviii., 8, 1, xix., 5, 1, xx., 5, B.D.[2] and Hastings' B.D., "Alexander".

Ver. 7. ἐν τῷ μέσῳ: according to the Mishnah the members of the court sat in a semicircle, see Hamburger, u. s., to be able to see each other. But it is unnecessary to press the expression, it may be quite general, cf. Matt. xiv. 6, Mark iii. 3, John viii. 3. On the usual submissive attitude of prisoners, see Jos., Ant., xiv., 9, 4. In this verse R.V. supplies "was there" as a verb, Annas being its subject. Various attempts to amend the broken construction—all the proper names are in the nominative (not in accusative as T.R.), so W.H., R.V., Wendt, Weiss; D. reads συνήχθησαν, so Blass in β.—ἐν ποίᾳ: by what kind of power; or may = τίνι, xxiii. 34.—ἐν ποίῳ ὀνόματι: in virtue of what name? "nomen hic vis ac potestas" Grotius and Wetstein, in loco. They ask as if they would accuse them of referring to some magical name or formula for the performance of the miracles, xix. 13 (on ὄνομα see iii. 16), cf. LXX, Exodus v. 23. Probably they would like to bring the Apostles under the condemnation pronounced in Deut. xiii. 1. "So did they very foolishly conceit that the very naming of some name might do wonders—and the Talmud forgeth that Ben Sadha wrought miracles by putting the unutterable name within the skin of his foot and then sewing it up," J. Lightfoot. —ὑμεῖς: as if in scorn, with depreciatory emphasis at the close of the question, so Wendt, and Blass, Grammatik des N. G., p. 160.—τοῦτο: not this teaching (Olshausen), but the miracle on the lame man.

Ver. 8. πλησθεὶς πνεύ. ἁγ.: the whole phrase is characteristic of St. Luke, who employs it in the Gospel

βύτεροι τοῦ Ἰσραήλ,[1] 9. εἰ ἡμεῖς σήμερον ἀνακρινόμεθα ἐπὶ εὐεργεσίᾳ
ἀνθρώπου ἀσθενοῦς, ἐν τίνι οὗτος σέσωσται · 10. γνωστὸν ἔστω
πᾶσιν ὑμῖν καὶ παντὶ τῷ λαῷ Ἰσραήλ, ὅτι ἐν τῷ ὀνόματι Ἰησοῦ
Χριστοῦ τοῦ Ναζωραίου, ὃν ὑμεῖς ἐσταυρώσατε, ὃν ὁ Θεὸς ἤγειρεν ἐκ

---

[1] του Ισραηλ om. ℵAB, Vulg., Sah., Boh., Aeth., Cyr., so Tisch., W.H., R.V.,
Weiss; but retained in DEP, Flor., Par., Syrr. (P. and H.), Irint., Chrys., Cypr.,
so Meyer, Blass, Hilg. D adds εν αλλω δε ουδενι to this verse, so E, Flor., Syr.
Harcl. mg., Cypr.; but see Weiss, Codex D, p. 64, and, on the other hand, Belser.

---

three times and in Acts five (Friedrich,
Lekebusch, Zeller). Acts has sometimes
been called the Gospel of the Holy Spirit,
and the number of times St. Luke uses
the title "Holy Spirit" justifies the
name, see above also p. 63. All three
expressions, πνεῦμα ἅγιον, τὸ ἅγιον
πνεῦμα, and τὸ πνεῦμα τὸ ἅγιον are
found in the Gospel and Acts, though
much more frequently in the latter, the
first expression (in the text) occurring
quite double the number of times in
Acts as compared with the Gospel, cf. in
the LXX, Ps. l. (li.) 11, Isa. lxiii. 10, 11,
Wisdom i. 5, ix. 17; and with 1 Cor. ii.
10, 12, cf. Wisdom ix. 17, and Isa. lxiii.
10, 11. On the omission of the article
see Simcox, Language of N. T. Greek,
p. 49. πλησθεὶς—the verb πίμπλημι
common both in Gospel and in Acts,
only found twice elsewhere in N.T., as
against thirteen times in Gospel and nine
times in Acts (Friedrich, Lekebusch).
The word was also very frequent in LXX,
cf. Ecclesiasticus xlviii. 12, A. The
phrase πλησθῆναι πνεύμ. ἁγ. is peculiar
to St. Luke, in Gospel three times, i. 15,
41, 67, and Acts ii. 4, iv. 31, ix. 17, xiii.
9, cf. Luke xii. 12, and xxi. 14; see
also Matt. x. 20, Mark xiii. 11. St.
Peter's courage in thus openly proclaiming the Crucified for the first time before
the rulers of his people might well be
significantly emphasised, as in ver. 13.
St. Chrysostom comments (Hom., x.) on
the Christian wisdom of St. Peter on
this occasion, how full of confidence he
is, and yet how he utters not a word of
insult, but speaks with all respect.
Ver. 9. εἰ: chosen not without oratorical nicety, if, as is the case = ἐπεὶ
ἡμεῖς, expressing at the same time the
righteous indignation of the Apostles in
contrast to the contemptuous ὑμεῖς of
ver. 7, and their surprise at the object of
the present inquiry; so too in ἐπ' εὐεργεσίᾳ St. Peter again indicates the un-
fairness of such inquisitorial treatment
("cum alias dijudicari debeant, qui malum
fecerunt," Bengel).—ἀνακρινόμεθα: used

here of a judicial examination, see xii.
19 and Luke xxiii. 14, and cf. Acts xxiv.
8, xxviii. 18, and 1 Cor. ix. 3, although
the strictly technical sense of ἀνάκρισις
as a preliminary investigation cannot be
pressed here.—ἐπ' εὐεργ. ἀ. ἀσθενοῦς:
"concerning a good deal done to an
impotent man"—the omission of the
articles in both nouns adds to St. Peter's
irony; "he hits them hard in that they
are always making a crime of such acts,
finding fault with works of beneficence,"
Chrys., Hom., x.; ἀνθρώπου on the objective genitive, Winer-Schmiedel, pp.
260 and 267.—ἐν τίνι: "by what means,"
R.V.; "in whom," margin. The neuter
instrumental dative, cf. Matt. v. 13, is
supported by Blass, Weiss, Holtzmann,
and others, as if the expression embraced
the two questions of ver. 7. Rendall,
following the older commentators, regards the expression as masculine.—
οὗτος: the healed man is thought of as
present, although nothing is said of his
summons; "this man," R.V.—σέσωσται:
the word familiar to us in the Gospels,
Luke vii. 50, Mark x. 52, with the pregnant meaning of health for body and soul
alike.
Ver. 10. St. Peter does not hesitate to
refer his judges to the same passage of
Scripture which a few short weeks before
Jesus of Nazareth had quoted to a deputation of the Sanhedrim. In that case
too the question put to Jesus had been
as to the authority by which He acted,
Matt. xxi. 42, Mark xii. 10, Luke xxi. 17.
It is possible that the words from Ps.
cxviii. 22 were already regarded as Messianic, from the fact that the people had
welcomed Jesus at His public entry into
Jerusalem with part of a verse of the
same Psalm, ver. 26, Edersheim, Jesus
the Messiah, ii., 368. Moreover, the passage, Isa. xxviii. 16, which forms the
connecting link between the Psalm and
St. Peter's words, both here and in his
First Epistle (1 Pet. ii. 7, cf. Rom. ix.
33, x. 11), was interpreted as Messianic,
apparently by the Targums, and un-

νεκρῶν, ἐν τούτῳ οὗτος παρέστηκεν ἐνώπιον ὑμῶν ὑγιής.　11. οὗτός
ἐστιν ὁ λίθος ὁ ἐξουθενηθεὶς ὑφ᾽ ὑμῶν τῶν οἰκοδομούντων, ὁ γενόμενος
εἰς κεφαλὴν γωνίας.　12.[1] καὶ οὐκ ἔστιν ἐν ἄλλῳ οὐδενὶ ἡ σωτηρία·
οὔτε γὰρ ὄνομά ἐστιν ἕτερον ὑπὸ τὸν οὐρανὸν τὸ δεδομένον ἐν ἀνθρώποις, ἐν ᾧ δεῖ σωθῆναι ἡμᾶς.

---

[1] και ουκ . . . η σωτηρια omit Flor., Ir., Cypr., Aug.; D and Par.[1] omit also
η σωτηρια.

---

doubtedly by Rashi in his Commentary, cf. also Wetstein on Matt. xxi. 42; Edersheim, u. s., ii., 725. In the original meaning of the Psalm Israel is the stone rejected by the builders, i.e., by the heathen, the builders of this world's empires, or the expression may refer to those in Israel who despised the small beginnings of a dawning new era (Delitzsch); but however this may be, in the N.T. the builders are the heads and representatives of Israel, as is evident from our Lord's use of the verse, and also by St. Peter's words here, "you the builders," R.V. But that which the Psalmist had spoken of the second Temple, that which was a parable of the history of Israel, had its complete and ideal fulfilment in Him Who, despised and rejected of men, had become the chief corner-stone of a spiritual Temple, in whom both Jew and Gentile were made one (1 Cor. iii. 11, Eph. ii. 20).—ἐσταυρώσατε: mentioned not merely to remind them of their fault, cf. ii. 36, but perhaps also that they might understand how vain it was to fight against God (Calvin).—ἐν τούτῳ: "in him," or "in this name" R.V. margin. For the former Wendt decides, although in the previous verse he takes ἐν τίνι as neuter; so too Page and Holtzmann. On the other hand Rendall (so De Wette, Weiss) adopts the latter rendering, while admitting that the reference to Jesus Himself is quite possible, as in ver. 12.—ἐνώπ. ὑμῶν: Hebraism, characteristic of St. Luke in his Gospel and in the Acts. The expression is never used in Matthew and Mark, and only once in John, xx. 30, but thirty-one times in the Hebraistic Apocalypse—frequent in LXX, but not found in classical or Hellenistic Greek, although τὰ ἐνώπια in Homer, Blass, in loco, and Grammatik des N. G., p. 125. The word is also found on papyri twice, so Deissmann, Neue Bibelstudien, p. 40.

Ver. 11. οὗτος: "He," as in R.V. All E.V. previously translated it "this," referring it to ὁ λίθος, but in the next verse a person is directly spoken of, not under the metaphor of a stone, and the pronoun finds its subject better in the ἐν τούτῳ, masculine of ver. 10. See Winer-Schmiedel, p. 216.—ὁ ἐξουθενηθεὶς: in the LXX and in the Gospels the word used is ἀπεδοκίμασαν. St. Peter, quoting apparently from memory, used a word expressing still greater contempt. It is used, e.g., very significantly by St. Luke in his Gospel, xxiii. 11, and again in xviii. 9. The word is found in none of the other Gospels, and is characteristic of St. Luke and of St. Paul (cf. Rom. xiv. 3, 10, 1 Cor. i. 28, 1 Cor. vi. 4, etc.). It occurs several times in the LXX; cf. Wisdom, iii. 11, iv. 18, Ecclesiasticus xix. 1, 2 Macc. i. 27, and Psalms of Solomon, ii., 5. In classical writers it is not found at all.—ὁ γενόμ. εἰς, "which was made," R.V. Blass compares the Hebrew phrase הָיָה לְ and finds parallels in v. 36, Luke xiii. 19, but γίγνεσθαι εἰς, while common in the LXX, is a correct expression in classical Greek, although the places in the N.T. in which the formula is found in O.T. quotations are undoubtedly Hebraisms (see below on v. 36), Winer-Schmiedel, p. 257, and with this may be connected the frequency of its occurrence in the Apocalypse (see Simcox on the phrase, Language of the N. T., p. 143).—κεφαλὴν γωνίας: not "the topmost pinnacle-stone," but a corner-stone uniting two walls, on which they rested and were made firm, cf. the meaning of ἀκρογωνιαῖος (Isa. xxviii. 16), 1 Pet. ii. 6-8, Eph. ii. 20, which is used here by Symmachus instead of κεφ. γων. The Hebrew פִּנָּה elsewhere always refers not to the upper part of the building, but to the lower (Isa. xxviii. 16, Jer. li. 26, Job xxxviii. 6, ὁ βαλὼν λίθον γωνιαῖον, Delitzsch). Probably therefore the expression here refers to a foundation-stone at the base of the corner. On the occurrence of the phrase from Ps. cxviii. 22 in St. Peter's First Epistle, and in his speech here, see p. 119, and also Scharfe, Die Petrinische Strömung, 2 c., p. 126.

13. Θεωροῦντες δὲ τὴν τοῦ Πέτρου παρρησίαν καὶ Ἰωάννου, καὶ καταλαβόμενοι ὅτι ἄνθρωποι ἀγράμματοί εἰσι καὶ ἰδιῶται, ἐθαύ-

Ver. 12. ἡ σωτηρία, *cf.* v. 31, xvii. 11, *i.e.*, κατ᾽ ἐξοχήν, the Messianic salvation. The interpretation which would limit ἡ σωτ. to bodily healing is less satisfactory; infinitely higher than the healing of one man, ver. 9, stands the Messianic salvation, for which even the Sanhedrists were hoping and longing, but see also Rendall's note, *in loco.* A parallel to the expression is found in Jos., *Ant.*, iii., 1, 5, but there are many passages in the O.T. which might have suggested the words to St. Peter, *cf.* Isa. xii. 2, xlix. 6-8, lii. 10.—οὔτε γὰρ ὄνομα, see on i. 15, ii. 21. οὐδέ is the best reading, Winer-Moulton, liii. 10, "for not even is there a second name"—the claim develops more precisely and consequently from the statement ἐν ἄλλῳ οὐδενί· ἕτερος μὲν, ἐπὶ δυοῖν· ἄλλος δὲ, ἐπὶ πλειόνων (*cf.* 1 Cor. xii. 8, 2 Cor. xi. 1, Gal. i. 6, 7), Ammonius, quoted by Bengel.—τὸ δεδομένον: on the force of the article with the participle, see Viteau, *Le Grec du N. T.*, pp. 183, 184 (1893) = τοῦτο γὰρ τὸ ὄνομα, τὸ δεδομ. ἐν ἀνθρώποις, μόνον ἐστὶν ἐν ᾧ δεῖ . . . and Blass, *Grammatik des N. G.*, p. 238; *cf.* Luke xviii. 9, Gal. i. 7, Col. ii. 8.—ᾧ δεῖ σωθῆναι: "Jesus when He spoke of the rejection as future, predicted that the stone would be a judgment-stone to destroy the wicked builders. But Peter takes up the other side, and presents the stone as the stone of Messianic salvation; this name is the only name under heaven that is a saving name. Here Peter apprehends the spiritual significance of the reign of the Messiah," Briggs, *Messiah of the Apostles*, p. 34, and the whole passage.

Ver. 13. θεωροῦντες δὲ, *cf.* iii. 16, not merely βλέπ., as in ver. 14, but "inest notio contemplandi cum attentione aut admiratione," Tittm., *Synon. N. T.*, p. 121. The present participle marks this continuous observation of the fearless bearing of the Apostles during the trial (Rendall).—παρρησίαν: either boldness of speech, or of bearing; it was the feature which had characterised the teaching of our Lord; *cf.* Mark viii. 32, and nine times in St. John in connection with Christ's teaching or bearing; and the disciples in this respect also were as their Master, *c.* iv. 29, 31 (ii. 29); so too of St. Paul, xxviii. 31, and frequently used by St. Paul himself in his Epistles; also by St. John four times in his First Epistle

of confidence in approaching God: "urbem et orbem hac parrhesia vicerunt," Bengel. *Cf.* παρρησιάζεσθαι used of Paul's preaching, ix. 27, 28, and again of him and Barnabas, xiii. 46, xiv. 3, of Apollos, xviii. 26, and twice again of Paul, xix. 8, xxvi. 26; only found in Acts, and twice in St. Paul's Epistles, Eph. vi. 20, 1 Thess. ii. 2, of speaking the Gospel boldly. For παρρησία, see LXX, Prov. xiii. 5, 1 Macc. iv. 18, Wisdom v. 1 (of speech), *cf.* also Jos., *Ant.*, ix., 10, 4, xv., 2, 7.—Ἰωάννου: even if St. John had not spoken, that "confidence towards God," which experience of life deepened, 1 John iv. 17, v. 14, but which was doubtless his now, would arrest attention; but it is evidently assumed that St. John had spoken, and it is quite characteristic of St. Luke's style thus to quote the most telling utterance, and to assume that the reader conceives the general situation, and procedure in the trial, Ramsay's *St. Paul*, pp. 371, 372.—καὶ καταλαβόμενοι: "and had perceived" R.V., rightly marking the tense of the participle; either by their dress or demeanour, or by their speech (*cf.* x. 34, xxv. 25, Eph. iii. 18, Blass, *Grammatik des N. G.*, p. 181).—ὅτι . . . εἰσι . . . ὅτι σὺν τῷ Ἰ. ἦσαν in dependent clauses where English usage would employ a past tense and a pluperfect, N.T. usage employs a present and an imperfect "perceived that they *were* . . . that they *had been* . . .," Blass, and see Salmon on Blass's Commentary, *Hermathena*, xxi., p. 229.—ἄνθρωποι: Wendt sees in the addition something depreciatory.—ἀγράμματοι: lit., unlettered, *i.e.*, without acquaintance with the Rabbinic learning in τὰ ἱερὰ γράμματα (2 Tim. iii. 15), the Jewish Scriptures (lit., letters), hence γραμματεύς, *cf.* John vii. 15, Acts xxvi. 24, where the word is used without ἱερά, so that it cannot be confined to the sacred Scriptures of the O.T., and includes the Rabbinic training in their meaning and exposition. In classical Greek the word = "illiterati," joined by Plato with ὄρειος, ἄμουσος, see also Xen., *Mem.*, iv., 2, 20; by Plutarch it is set over against the μεμουσωμένος, and elsewhere joined with ἄγροικος, Trench, *N. T. Synonyms*, ii., p. 134, and Wetstein, *in loco*, *cf.* Athenæus, x., p. 454 B., βοτὴρ δ᾽ ἐστὶν ἀγράμματος.—ἰδιῶται: the word properly signifies a private person (a man occupied with τὰ ἴδια), as opposed to any one who

μαζον, ἐπεγίνωσκόν τε αὐτοὺς ὅτι σὺν τῷ Ἰησοῦ ἦσαν· 14. τὸν δὲ
ἄνθρωπον βλέποντες σὺν αὐτοῖς ἑστῶτα τὸν τεθεραπευμένον, οὐδὲν

holds office in the State, but as the Greeks held that without political life there was no true education of a man, it was not unnatural that ἰδιώτης should acquire a somewhat contemptuous meaning, and so Plato joins it with ἀπράγμων, and Plutarch with ἄπρακτος and ἀπαίδευτος (and instances in Wetstein). But further: in Trench, *u. s.*, p. 136, and Grimm, *sub v.*, the ἰδιώτης is "a layman," as compared with the ἰατρός, "the skilled physician," Thuc. ii. 48, and the word is applied by Philo to the whole congregation of Israel as contrasted with the priests, and to subjects as contrasted with their prince, *cf.* its only use in the LXX, Prov. vi. 8 (*cf.* Herod., ii., 81, vii., 199, and instances in Wetstein on 1 Cor. xiv. 16). Bearing this in mind, it would seem that the word is used by St. Paul (1 Cor. xiv. 16, 23, 24) of believers devoid of special spiritual gifts, of prophecy or of speaking with tongues, and in the passage before us it is applied to those who, like the ἀγράμματοι, had been without professional training in the Rabbinical schools. The translation "ignorant" is somewhat unfortunate. ἰδιώτης certainly need not mean ignorant, *cf.* Plato, *Legg.*, 830, A., ἀνδρῶν σοφῶν ἰδιωτῶν τε καὶ συνετῶν. St. Paul uses the word of himself, ἰδιώτης ἐν λόγῳ, 2 Cor. xi. 6, in a way which helps us to understand its meaning here, for it may well have been used contemptuously of him (as here by the Sadducees of Peter and John) by the Judaisers, who despised him as "unlearned" and a "layman": he would not affect the Rabbinic subtleties and interpretations in which they boasted. Others take the word here as referring to the social rank of the Apostles, "plebeians" "common men" (Kuinoel, Olshausen, De Wette, Bengel, Hackett), but the word is not so used until Herodian, iv., 10, 4. See also Dean Plumptre's note on the transition of the word through the Vulgate *idiota* to our word "idiot": Tyndale and Cranmer both render "laymen".—ἐπεγίνωσκόν τε: if we take those words to imply that the Sanhedrim only recognised during the trial that Peter and John had been amongst the disciples of Jesus, there is something unnatural and forced about such an interpretation, especially when we remember that all Jerusalem was speaking of them, vv. 16, 21, and that one of them was personally known to the high priest (John xviii. 15).

In Codex D (so β) an attempt is apparently made to meet this difficulty by reading τινες δὲ ἐξ αὐτῶν ἐπεγίνωσκον αὐτούς. Others have pointed out that the same word is used in iii. 10 of the beggar who sat for alms, and that here, as there, ἐπεγίν. implies something more than mere recognition (see especially Lumby's note on the force of ἐπί); thus the revisers in both passages render "took knowledge of". But here as elsewhere Professor Ramsay throws fresh light upon the narrative, *St. Paul*, p. 371. And however we interpret the words, St. Chrysostom's comment does not lose its beauty: ἐπεγίν. τε ... ἦσαν, *i.e.*, in His Passion, for only those were with Him at the time, and there indeed they had seen them humble, dejected—and this it was that most surprised them, the greatness of the change; *Hom.*, x.—The τε after ἐπεγίν., and its repetition at the commencement of ver. 14 (so R.V., W.H., Weiss), is very Lucan (see Ramsay's paraphrase above); for this closely connecting force of τε *cf.* Weiss's commentary, *passim*. With σύν κ.τ.λ. Weiss compares Luke viii. 38, xxii. 56.

Ver. 14. ἑστῶτα: standing, no longer a cripple, *firmo talo* (Bengel), and by his presence and attitude affording a testimony not to be gainsaid. — σὺν αὐτοῖς, *i.e.*, with the disciples. We are not told whether the man was a prisoner with the disciples, but just as the healed demoniac had sought to be with Jesus, so we may easily imagine that the restored cripple, in his gratitude and faith, would desire to be with his benefactors: "great was the boldness of the man that even in the judgment-hall he had not left them: for had they (*i.e.*, their opponents) said that the fact was not so, there was he to refute them," St. Chrysostom, *Hom.*, x. On St. Luke's fondness for the shorter form, ἑστώς not ἑστηκώς, both in Gospel and Acts, see Friedrich, *Das Lucasevangelium*, p. 8.—οὐδὲν εἶχον ἀντ.: this meaning of ἔχω with the infinitive is quite classical; *cf.* the Latin *habeo dicere;* on St. Luke's fondness for phrases with εὑρίσκειν and ἔχειν see Friedrich, *u. s.*, pp. 11, 12.— ἀντειπεῖν: only used by St. Luke in the N.T., Luke xxi. 15. The miracle, as St. Chrysostom says, spoke no less forcibly than the Apostles themselves, but the word may be taken, as in the Gospel, of contradicting personal adversaries, *i.e.*,

εἶχον ἀντειπεῖν.[1] 15. κελεύσαντες δὲ αὐτοὺς ἔξω τοῦ συνεδρίου
ἀπελθεῖν, συνέβαλον πρὸς ἀλλήλους, 16. λέγοντες, Τί ποιήσομεν[2]
τοῖς ἀνθρώποις τούτοις; ὅτι μὲν γὰρ γνωστὸν σημεῖον γέγονε δι’
αὐτῶν, πᾶσι τοῖς κατοικοῦσιν Ἱερουσαλὴμ φανερόν,[3] καὶ οὐ δυνάμεθα
ἀρνήσασθαι · 17. ἀλλ’ ἵνα μὴ ἐπὶ πλεῖον διανεμηθῇ εἰς τὸν λαόν,
ἀπειλῇ[4] ἀπειλησώμεθα αὐτοῖς μηκέτι λαλεῖν ἐπὶ τῷ ὀνόματι τούτῳ

[1] αντειπειν; D, Flor. insert before, ποιησαι η. D also omits last clause of ver.
13, and puts in altered form at end of ver. 14 τινες δε εξ αυτων κ.τ.λ. The τινες δε
would follow naturally enough if we read with Flor. ακουσαντες δε παντες at the
beginning of ver. 13 ; but see connection of passage in comment.

[2] ποιησομεν DP, Flor., Gig., Par., Vulg., Bas., Chrys., so Meyer and Hilg. ; ποιησωμεν ℵABE, so Tisch., W.H., R.V., Weiss, Wendt, and so Blass in β.

[3] φανερον, D reads φανερωτερον, according to Blass (in β retained), for superl.
defended by Belser and Hilg.

[4] απειλη om. ℵABD vers., Lucif., Bas., so Tisch., W.H., R.V., Hilg. ; but retained
by EP, Syr. Harcl., Chrys., so by Meyer and Weiss (Wendt doubtful but on the whole
against retention) ; cf. v. 28, Blass retains : “optime”.

here, the Apostles, so Weiss, and cf.
Rendall, in loco.

Ver. 15. συνέβαλον πρὸς ἀλλήλους,
sc., λόγους : only in St. Luke's writings,
in different significations ; cf. for the
construction here, Eurip., Iphig. Aul.,
830, and Plutarch, Mor., p. 222, C.—see
on xvii. 18.

Ver. 16. τί ποιήσομεν : for the
deliberative subjunctive, which should
be read here, cf. ii. 37 ; it may express
the utter perplexity of the Sanhedrists
(so Rendall) ; in questions expressing
doubt or deliberation, the subjunctive
would be more usual in classical Greek
than the future indicative, Blass, u. s., p.
205.—ὅτι μέν : μέν answered by ἀλλά in
ver. 17 (omitted by D.), cf. Mark ix. 12,
see Simcox, Language of the N. T., p.
168, and for other instances of μέν similarly used, see also Lekebusch, Apostelgeschichte, pp. 74, 75.—γνωστὸν, that
which is a matter of knowledge as opposed to δοξαστόν, that which is matter
of opinion (so Plato). The word is
characteristic of St. Luke, being used by
him twice in the Gospel, ten times in
Acts, and elsewhere in N.T. only three
times (Friedrich).

Ver. 17. ἐπὶ πλεῖον may be taken as
= latius (2 Tim. ii. 16, iii. 9) or =
diutius (Acts xx. 9, xxiv. 4), but the context favours the former. The phrase is
quite classical, and it occurs several
times in LXX, cf. Wisdom viii. 12 ; 3
Macc. v. 18.—διανεμηθῇ : only here in
N.T. but frequently used in classical
writers in active and middle—to divide
into portions, to distribute, to divide

among themselves — here = lest it
should spread abroad (or better perhaps in D (β)). It has been taken by
some as if it had a parallel in ὡς γάγ-
γραινα νομὴν ἕξει, 2 Tim. ii. 17, and expressed that the report of the Apostles’
teaching and power might spread and
feed like a cancer (see Bengel, Blass,
Zöckler, Rendall), but although νέμω in
the middle voice (and possibly ἐπινέμω)
could be so used, it is very doubtful how
far διανέμω could be so applied. At the
same time we may note that διανέμω
is a word frequently used in medical
writers, Hobart, Medical Language of
St. Luke, pp. 196, 197, and that it, with
the two other great medical words of
similar import, διασπείρειν and ἀναδιδόναι, is peculiar to St. Luke. In the
LXX διανέμω is only found once,
Deut. xxix. 26 (25), in its classical sense
as a translation of the Hebrew חלק.
—ἀπειλῇ ἀπειλησώμεθα : if we retain
the reading in T.R., the phrase is a
common Hebraism, cf. v. 28, xxiii. 14,
ii. 17, 30, Luke xxii. 15, cf. John vi. 29,
James v. 7, and from the LXX, Matt.
xiii. 14, xv. 4. The form of the Hebrew
formula giving the notion of intenseness
is rendered in A.V. by “straitly,” as by
the revisers (who omit ἀπειλῇ here) in v.
28. Similar expressions are common in
the LXX, and also in the Apocrypha, cf.
Ecclus. xlviii. 11, Judith vi. 4, and occasionally a similar formula is found in
Greek authors, see especially Simcox,
Language of the N. T., p. 83, and Blass,
Grammatik des N. G., pp. 116, 117.—

μηδενὶ ἀνθρώπων. 18.[1] καὶ καλέσαντες αὐτούς, παρήγγειλαν αὐτοῖς τὸ καθόλου μὴ φθέγγεσθαι μηδὲ διδάσκειν ἐπὶ τῷ ὀνόματι τοῦ Ἰησοῦ. 19. ὁ δὲ Πέτρος καὶ Ἰωάννης ἀποκριθέντες πρὸς αὐτοὺς εἶπον, Εἰ δίκαιόν ἐστιν ἐνώπιον τοῦ Θεοῦ, ὑμῶν ἀκούειν μᾶλλον ἢ τοῦ Θεοῦ, κρίνατε. 20. οὐ δυνάμεθα γὰρ ἡμεῖς ἃ[2] εἴδομεν καὶ ἠκούσαμεν μὴ

---

[1] At begin. of ver. D, Flor., Syr. Harcl. mg., Lucif., Hilg. add συγκατατιθεμενων δε αυτων τη γνωμη. Belser sees here the hand of Luke who omitted the clause in revision, as he thinks no one could have added it (so τα ρηματα αυτων after λαον in ver. 17, see β); but, on the other hand, Weiss, Codex D, p. 61. καλεσαντες, D has φωνησαντες. αυτοις om. ℵABDE 13, Vulg., Syr. Harcl., Arm., Chrys., so Tisch., W.H., R.V., Wendt, Weiss; so το before καθολου ℵ*B, Tisch., W.H., Weiss, Wendt.

[2] ειδομεν B³EP, Chrys., Cyr.; ειδαμεν ℵAB*D 4, Chrys., so Tisch., W.H., Weiss, Hilg.; see W.H., App., p. 171 (so for ειπαν above), Winer-Schmiedel, p. 112.

ἐπὶ τῷ ὀνόματι: on the name, i.e., resting on, or with reference to, this name, as the basis of their teaching, Winer-Moulton, xlviii. c., cf. v. 28, and Luke xxiv. 47, ix. 48, xxi. 8. The phrase has thus a force of its own, although it is apparently interchangeable with ἐν, ver. 10 (Simcox, see also Blass, in loco); Rendall takes it = "about the name of Jesus," ἐπί being used as often with verbs of speech.—τούτῳ: "quem nominare nolunt, v. 28, vid. tamen 18," Blass; (on the hatred of the Jews against the name of Jesus and their periphrastic titles for him, e.g., otho ha'ish, "that man," "so and so," see "Jesus Christ in the Talmud," H. Laible, pp. 32, 33 (Streane)). Ver. 18. καθόλου: only here in N.T. The word which had been very common since Aristotle (previously καθ' ὅλου) is quite classical in the sense in which it is used here, and it is also found a few times in the LXX (see Hatch and Redpath for instances of its use without and with the art., as here in T.R.). It is frequently used by medical writers, Hobart, Medical Language of St. Luke, p. 197.—μὴ φθέγγεσθαι: "not to utter a word," so Rendall, ne muttire quidem (Blass). The word seems to indicate more than that the disciples should not speak, "ne hiscerent aut ullam vocem ederent," Erasmus. In contrast to διδάσκειν we might well refer it to the utterance of the name of Jesus in their miracles, as in iii. 6; only found twice elsewhere in N.T., and both times in 2 Peter, ii. 16, 18, but its use is quite classical, and it is also found several times in LXX. Ver. 19. Parallel sayings may be quoted from Greeks and Romans, and from Jewish sources, see instances in Wetstein, cf. Plato, Apol., 29, D., the famous words of Socrates: πεισόμεθα τῷ θεῷ μᾶλλον ἢ ὑμῖν, and Livy, xxxix., 37; Jos., Ant., xvii., 6, 3; xviii. 8, 2; on ἐνώπιον see ver. 10; ἀκούειν = πειθαρχεῖν, v. 29, and cf. iii. 22, Luke x. 16, xvi. 31; μᾶλλον = potius, cf. Rom. xiv. 13, 1 Cor. vii. 21.—κρίνατε: this appeal to the Sadducees could only be justified on the ground that the Apostles were sure of the validity of their own appeal to a higher tribunal. No man could lay down the principle of obedience to every ordinance of man for the Lord's sake, whether to the king or to governors, more plainly than St. Peter (1 Pet. ii. 13, cf. Rom. xiii. 1), and he and his fellow-disciples might have exposed themselves to the charge of fanaticism or obstinacy, if they could only say οὐ δυν. . . . μὴ λαλεῖν; but they could add ἃ εἴδομεν καὶ ἠκούσ., cf. Acts i. 8. The same appeal is made by St. John, both in his Gospel (i. 14) and in his First Epistle (i. 1, 2), in vindication of his teaching; and here the final answer is that of St. John and St. Peter jointly. Ver. 20. οὐ . . . μὴ: on the two negatives forming an affirmative cf. 1 Cor. xii. 15; Viteau, Le Grec du N. T., p. 220 (1893). Winer-Moulton, lv., 9, compares Aristoph., Ran., 42; see also Burton, N. T. Moods and Tenses, p. 184. Ver. 21. προσαπειλησάμενοι: "when they had further threatened them" R.V., or the word may mean "added threats to their warning" ver. 18 ("prius enim tantum praeceperunt," Erasmus). So Wendt as against Meyer; cf. in LXX, Ecclus. xiii. 3, S., and Dem., p. 544, 26.—ἀπέλυσαν: "dimiserunt [iii. 13] non absolverunt," Blass; see St. Chrysostom's striking contrast between the boldness of the Apostles and the fear of their judges (Hom., xi.).—

λαλεῖν. 21. οἱ δὲ προσαπειλησάμενοι ἀπέλυσαν αὐτούς,[1] μηδὲν εὑρίσκοντες τὸ πῶς κολάσωνται αὐτούς, διὰ τὸν λαόν, ὅτι πάντες ἐδόξαζον τὸν Θεὸν ἐπὶ τῷ γεγονότι. 22. ἐτῶν γὰρ ἦν πλειόνων τεσσαράκοντα[2] ὁ ἄνθρωπος ἐφ᾽ ὃν ἐγεγόνει τὸ σημεῖον τοῦτο τῆς ἰάσεως.

23. Ἀπολυθέντες δὲ ἦλθον πρὸς τοὺς ἰδίους, καὶ ἀπήγγειλαν ὅσα πρὸς αὐτοὺς οἱ ἀρχιερεῖς καὶ οἱ πρεσβύτεροι εἶπον. 24. οἱ δὲ ἀκούσαντες,[3] ὁμοθυμαδὸν ἦραν φωνὴν πρὸς τὸν Θεόν, καὶ εἶπον,

[1] D seems to read μη ευρισκοντες αιτιαν, so Hilg., see Harris (p. 90).

[2] τεσσαρ., see on i. 3.

[3] After ακουσαντες D adds και επιγνοντες την του θεου ενεργειαν, so Hilg.—Belser and Zöckler hold that the clause cannot be a later addition, but Weiss objects that no reference is found to the words in ver. 29 which follows. επιγινωσκω is used more frequently by St. Luke than by the other Evangelists, but ενεργεια is entirely confined to St. Paul in the N.T.

τὸ πῶς: finding nothing, namely (τὸ), how they might, etc.; this use of the article is quite classical, drawing attention to the proposition introduced by it and making of it a compound substantive expressing one idea, most commonly with an interrogation; it is used by St. Luke and St. Paul, and both in St. Luke's Gospel and in the Acts, cf. Luke i. 62, ix. 46, xix. 48, xxii. 2, 4, 23, 24, Acts xxii. 30, Rom. viii. 26, 1 Thess. iv. 1, cf. Mark ix. 23. So here the Sanhedrists are represented as asking themselves τὸ πῶς κολ. (Friedrich and Lekebusch both draw attention to this characteristic of St. Luke's writings). See Viteau, Le Grec du N. T., pp. 67, 68 (1893). κολ. only here and in 2 Pet. ii. 9 in N.T.; cf. 3 Macc. vii. 3, where it is also used in middle, expressing to cause to be punished, cf. 1 Macc. vii. 7, AS.—διὰ τὸν λαόν belongs not to ἀπέλυσαν, but rather to μὴ εὑρίσκ. κ.τ.λ.—ἐδόξαζον: see on ii. 46; cf. Luke ii. 20, 2 Cor. ix. 13, for the construction; the verb never has in Biblical Gr. mere classical meaning of to think, suppose, entertain an opinion (but cf. Polyb., vi., 53, 10; δεδοξασμένοι ἐπ᾽ ἀρετῇ); in the LXX very frequently of glory ascribed to God, see Plummer's note on Luke ii. 20.

Ver. 22. Characteristic of St. Luke to note the age, as in the case of Æneas, ix. 33, and of the cripple at Lystra, xiv. 8, cf. also Luke viii. 42 (although Mark also here notes the same fact), xiii. 11. The genitive with εἶναι or γίγνεσθαι, instead of the accusative, in reference to the question of age, is noted by Friedrich as characteristic of St. Luke; cf.

Luke ii. 42 (iii. 23), viii. 42, and here; but cf. Mark v. 42.—ἐγεγόνει: in this episode "with its lights and shades" Overbeck (so Baur) can only see the idealising work of myth and legend, but it is difficult to understand how a narrative which purports to describe the first conflict between the Church and the Sanhedrim could be free from such contrasts, and that some collision with the authorities took place is admitted to be quite conceivable (Weizsäcker, Apostolic Age, i., 46, E.T.); we should rather say that St. Luke's power as an historian is nowhere more visible than in the dramatic form of this narrative (Ramsay, St. Paul, u. s.).

Ver. 23. τοὺς ἰδίους: not necessarily limited to their fellow-Apostles (so Meyer, Blass, Weiss), but as including the members of the Christian community (so Overbeck, Wendt, Hilgenfeld, Zöckler), cf. xxiv. 23, John xiii. 1, 1 Tim. v. 8, and also of one's fellow-countrymen, associates, John i. 11, 2 Macc. xii. 22.

Ver. 24. ὁμοθυμαδὸν, see above on i. 14. The word must not be pressed to mean that they all simultaneously gave utterance to the same words, or that they were able to do so, because they were repeating a familiar Hymn; it may mean that the Hymn was uttered by one of the leaders, by St. Peter, or St. James (Zöckler), and answered by the responsive Amen of the rest, or that the words were caught up by the multitude of believers as they were uttered by an inspired Apostle (so Felten, Rendall).— ἦραν φωνήν: the same phrase is used in Luke xvii. 13, so in Acts ii. 14, xiv. 11,

Δέσποτα, σὺ [1] ὁ Θεὸς ὁ ποιήσας τὸν οὐρανὸν καὶ τὴν γῆν καὶ τὴν
θάλασσαν καὶ πάντα τὰ ἐν αὐτοῖς, 25.[2] ὁ διὰ στόματος Δαβὶδ τοῦ
παιδός σου εἰπὼν, "Ἵνα τί ἐφρύαξαν ἔθνη, καὶ λαοὶ ἐμελέτησαν

[1] ο Θεος DEP, Gig., Par., verss., Irint., Luc., so Meyer, so Hilg.; but om. אBA, best
MS. of Vulg., Boh., so Tisch., W.H., R.V., Weiss, Wendt (who refers the construction
of the words to Isaiah xxxvii. 16).

[2] ο δια στοματος Δαβιδ του παιδος σου ειπων P 1, 31, Chrys., so Meyer; but του
omitted by אABDEP. ο του πατρος ημων δια πνευματος αγιου στοματος Δανειδ
παιδος σου ειπων, so אABE 13, 15, 27, 29, 36, 38; so Lach., Treg., Tisch., W.H.,
R.V., Alford. ο δια πν. αγ. δια στομ., του πατρος ημων Δ., so Vulg., Iren.,
apparently for improvement in order. D reads δια πν. αγ. δια του στοματος
λαλησας Δ., omit. του πατρος ημων; so apparently Syr. Pesch., Boh. P, Hil.,
and Aug. omit πνευματος αγιου—Syr. Harcl., Arm. place δια πν. αγ. after παιδος
σου; so Par. Blass in β omits του πατρος ημων and brackets πν. αγ., practically agreeing with T.R. (see also *Acta Apost.*, p. 77). W.H. mention the
extreme difficulty of the text and hold that it contains a primitive error (so also
Holtzmann), and each makes an attempt at solution, App., *Select Readings*, p. 92.
Felten follows the solution offered by Westcott. Weiss, *Apostelgeschichte*, pp. 39,
40 (1893), speaks of πνευματος αγιου as perfectly senseless (so too Zöckler, who
follows T.R.) and regards the expression as an old gloss for στομα Δ., but which
afterwards came into the text with the latter words; or some scribe, as he thinks,
may have introduced δια πν. αγ. expected by him from i. 2, 16 (see also Blass, *in
loco*), and then continued the text lying before him. Weiss therefore follows P
although it omits του πατρος ημων, which Weiss retains and reads ο του πατρος
ημων δια στομ. Δ. παιδος σου ειπων. Wendt and Alford maintain that the more
complicated readings could scarcely have arisen through additions to the simpler
text of T.R. and that the contrary is more probable.

xxii. 22, ἐπαίρειν, and also in Luke xi.
27. Both phrases are peculiar to St.
Luke, but both are found in the LXX,
and both are classical (Friedrich, *Das
Lucasevangelium*, p. 29, and Plummer
on Luke xi. 27).—Δέσποτα κ.τ.λ.: the
words form the earliest known Psalm of
Thanksgiving in the Christian Church.
In its tenor the Hymn may be compared
with Hezekiah's Prayer against the
threats of Assyria, Isa. xxxvii. 16, 20.
It begins like many of the Psalms (xviii.,
xix., liii.) with praising God as the
Creator, a thought which finds fitting
expression here as marking the utter
impotence of worldly power to with-
stand Him. The word Δέσποτα, thus
used in the vocative in addressing God
here and in Luke ii. 29 only (found
nowhere else in Gospels, although several
times in the Epistles), expresses the
absolute control of a Master over a
slave, *cf.* also Luke ii. 29, where τὸν
δοῦλόν σου answers to it, as here τοῖς
δούλοις in ver. 29. It also expresses
here as often in the LXX the sovereignty
of God over creation, *cf.* Job v. 8, Wisdom vi. 7, Judith ix. 12. So Jos., *Ant.*,
iv., 3, 2, puts it into the mouth of Moses.
It is very rarely used in the N.T. as a
name of God or of Christ, but *cf.* Rev.

vi. 10 of God, and 2 Pet. ii. 1 of Christ
(where the metaphor of the master and
slave is retained), and see Jude ver. 4,
R.V. (although the name may refer
to God); and so in writings ascribed to
men who may well have been present, and
have taken part in the Hymn. The word
is also used of the gods in classical
Greek; but the Maker of heaven and
earth was no "despot," although His
rule was absolute, for His power was
never dissociated from wisdom and love,
cf. Wisdom xi. 26, Δέσποτα φιλόψυχε.
On the use of the word in *Didache*, x.,
3, in prayer to God, see Biggs' note.
Ver. 25. The words form an exact
quotation from the LXX (Psalm ii.
1). ἵνα τί, again in quotation, vii.,
26; *cf.* Luke xiii. 7, 1 Cor. x. 29; twice
in Matt. ix. 4, xxvii. 46, quotation;
W.H., Blass (Weiss, ἱνατί, *sc.*, γένηται,
Blass, *Grammatik des N.G.*, p. 14, and
Winer-Schmiedel, p. 36.—ἐφρύαξαν: in
the active form the verb occurs once in
LXX, *viz.*, in this passage, as a translation of רָגַשׁ, φρυάσσομαι, primarily of
the snorting and neighing of a high-
spirited horse, then of the haughtiness
and insolence of men; twice it is used as
a dep. in LXX, 2 Macc. vii. 34, R.; iii. 2,

κενά; 26. παρέστησαν οἱ βασιλεῖς τῆς γῆς, καὶ οἱ ἄρχοντες συνήχθησαν ἐπὶ τὸ αὐτὸ κατὰ τοῦ Κυρίου, καὶ κατὰ τοῦ Χριστοῦ αὐτοῦ."
27. συνήχθησαν γὰρ [1] ἐπ' ἀληθείας ἐπὶ τὸν ἅγιον παῖδά σου, Ἰησοῦν,
ὃν ἔχρισας, Ἡρώδης τε καὶ Πόντιος [2] Πιλάτος, σὺν ἔθνεσι καὶ λαοῖς

[1] ἐπ' αληθειας; אABDE, Vulg., Syr. P. H., verss., Eus., Ir., Tert.; so Tisch.,
W.H., R.V., Weiss, Wendt, Hilg. add εν τη πολει ταυτη (wanting in the Psalm).

[2] Πιλατος; but B* Πειλατος, so Tisch., W.H.; see on iii. 13.

2, and so in profane writers.—ἔθνη, i.e.,
the Gentiles, see on ver. 27. λαός might
be used, and is used of any people, but
it is used in Biblical Greek specially of
the chosen people of God, cf. Luke ii.
32, Acts xxvi. 17, 23, Rom. xv. 10, and
it is significant that the word is transferred to the Christian community, which
was thus regarded as taking the place of
the Jewish theocracy, Acts xv. 14, xviii.
10, Rom. ix. 25, 1 Peter ii. 10; Hort,
Ecclesia, pp. 11, 12, Grimm, sub v., λαός;
so too in the LXX, ἔθνος in the plural
is used in an overwhelming number of
instances of other nations besides Israel,
cf. Psalm lvi. (lvii.) 9, Zech. i. 15; in
N.T., ἔθνη = pagans, Rom. iii. 29, and
Roman Christians, Rom. xv. 27, cf. populus, the Roman people, as opposed to
gentes, Lucan, Phars., i., 82, 83 (Page);
Kennedy, Sources of N. T. Greek, p. 98.
Ver. 26. παρέστησαν: not necessarily
of hostile intent, although here the context indicates it; R.V., "set themselves
in array," lit. "presented themselves,"
an exact rendering of the Hebrew יָצַב,
which sometimes implies rising up against
as here, Psalm ii. 2, and cf. 2 Sam.
xviii. 13 (R.V. margin). Of the generally
accepted Messianic interpretation of the
Psalm, and of the verses here quoted,
there can be no doubt, cf. Edersheim,
Jesus the Messiah, ii., 716 (appendix on
Messianic passages), and Wetstein, in
loco. The Psalm is regarded as full of
Messianic references (Briggs, Messianic
Prophecy, pp. 132-140, and 492, 493),
cf., e.g., the comment on this verse of
the Psalm in the Mechilta (quoted in
the Yalkut Shimeoni, ii., f. 90, 1 Sch.
p. 227), Perowne, Psalms (small edition),
p. 16; and Edersheim, u. s. The Psalm
carries us back to the great Davidic promise in 2 Sam. vii. 11-16, and it reflects
the Messianic hopes of the Davidic period.
That hope the N.T. writers who quote
this Psalm very frequently or refer to
it, cf. xiii. 33, Heb. i. 5, v. 5, see fulfilled in Christ, the antitype of David and

of Solomon. Thus the gathering together
of the nations and their fruitless decrees
find their counterpart in the alliance of
Herod and Pilate, and the hostile combination of Jew and Gentile against the
holy Servant Jesus, the anointed of God,
and against His followers; although the
words of the Psalm and the issues of the
conflict carry on our thoughts to a still
wider and deeper fulfilment in the final
triumph of Christ's kingdom, cf. the
frequent recurrence of the language of
the Psalm in Rev. xii. 5, xix. 15, and cf.
i. 5, ii. 26, 27.
Ver. 27. γάρ: confirms the truth of
the preceding prophecy, by pointing to its
historical fulfilment, and does not simply
give a reason for addressing God as ὁ
εἰπών—to emphasise this fulfilment
συνήχ. is again quoted, and placed first
in the sentence.—ἐπ' ἀληθείας, of a
truth, i.e., assuredly, Luke iv. 25, xx. 21,
xxii. 59, Acts x. 34; so too in LXX,
Job ix. 2, and also in classical Greek.
The phrase is characteristic of St. Luke,
and is only used elsewhere in N.T. in
Mark xii. 14, 32, the usual expression
being ἐν ἀληθείᾳ, never used by St.
Luke (Friedrich).—παῖδα, see on iii. 13.
—ὃν ἔχρισας: showing that Jesus =
τοῦ Χριστοῦ named in the quotation
just made, cf. Luke iv. 18, and Isa. lxi. 1
and Acts x. 38. Nösgen compares also
John x. 36, and refuses to limit the reference to iii. 21. The words may no
doubt be referred to the Baptism, but
they need not be confined to that.—
Ἡρώδης = βασιλεῖς of the Psalm, Π.
Πειλᾶτος = ἄρχοντες, but Nösgen, referring to iii. 17, regards the ἄρχ. as included in the λαοί. Ἡρ. instead of
Ἡρωίδης, Blass, in loco, and Grammatik
des N. G., pp. 7, 8, the iota subscript
W.H. thus accounted for; Winer-Schmiedel, p. 41.—ἔθνεσιν καὶ λαοῖς Ἰ.: the
first word = the centurion and soldiers,
those who carried out the orders of Pilate;
λαοί the plural (quoted from the Psalm)
does not refer with Calvin to the different nationalities out of which the Jews

Ἰσραήλ, 28. ποιῆσαι ὅσα ἡ χείρ σου καὶ ἡ βουλή σου[1] προώρισε
γενέσθαι. 29. καὶ τὰ νῦν, Κύριε, ἔπιδε ἐπὶ τὰς ἀπειλὰς αὐτῶν, καὶ
δὸς τοῖς δούλοις σου μετὰ παρρησίας πάσης λαλεῖν τὸν λόγον σου,
30. ἐν τῷ τὴν χεῖρά σου ἐκτείνειν σε εἰς ἴασιν, καὶ σημεῖα καὶ
τέρατα γίνεσθαι διὰ τοῦ ὀνόματος τοῦ ἁγίου παιδός σου Ἰησοῦ.

---

[1] σου omit A*B, Arm., Lucif. (Cod. Am. of Vulg.), so W.H., Weiss, Wendt; retained by ℵAªDEP, Vulg., vers., Irint., so Tisch. Here, as commonly, Tisch. follows ℵ, W.H., B—and difficult, as often, to decide; insertion appears more obvious than omission.

---

who came up to the Feast were gathered, but possibly to the tribes of Israel, Grimm-Thayer, sub, λαός, like עַמִּים, Gen. xlix. 10, Deut. xxxii. 8, Isa. iii. 13, etc., R.V., "the peoples of Israel". St. Luke's Gospel alone gives us the narrative of Herod's share in the proceedings connected with the Passion, xxiii. 8-12; see Plumptre, in loco, and Friedrich, Das Lucasevangelium, pp. 54, 55.—Ver. 28. ποιῆσαι, infinitive of purpose, see on iii. 2; but even this purpose was overruled by God to the accomplishment of His will, cf. Luke xxii. 22, xxiv. 26, συνῆλθον μὲν γὰρ ἐκεῖνοι ὡς ἐχθροὶ . . . ἐποίουν δὲ ἃ σὺ ἐβούλου, Oecum. —ἡ χείρ σου, a common expression to signify the controlling power of God, cf. in the N.T. (peculiar to St. Luke's Gospel and the Acts) the phrases χεὶρ Κυρίου, Luke i. 66, Acts xi. 21, xiii. 11. —ἡ βουλή: only used by St. Luke, cf. Luke vii. 30, Acts ii. 23, xiii. 36, xx. 27. —προώρισε: only in St. Luke and St. Paul, but never in LXX or Apocrypha, Rom. viii. 29, 30, 1 Cor. ii. 7, Ephes. i. 5, 11, but the thought which it contains is in striking harmony with St. Peter's words elsewhere; cf. ii. 23, x. 42, and 1 Pet. i. 2, 20, ii. 4-6—see above on Peter's speeches—cf. Ignat., Ephes., tit.—ἡ χείρ connected with β. by Zeugma, since only βουλή directly suits the verb; cf. 1 Cor. iii. 2, and Luke i. 64. (The two verses (27, 28) are referred by Hilgenfeld to the "author to Theophilus". In his view there is a want of fitness in introducing into the Church's prayer the words of the Psalm, and their reference to the closing scenes of the life of Jesus; he thinks with Weiss that in the αὐτῶν of ver. 29 there is quite sufficient reference to the words of the Psalm.) Ver. 29. τὰ νῦν (cf. iii. 17) only used in the Acts v. 38, xvii. 30, xx. 32, xxvii. 22, but frequently found in classical writers (Wetstein), cf. also 1 Macc. vii.

35, ix. 9; 2 Macc. xv. 8, Klostermann, Vindiciæ Lucanæ, p. 53. As elsewhere St. Peter's words have a practical bearing and issue, ii. 16, iii. 12 (Felten).—ἔπιδε: only used here and in Luke i. 25, and both times of God; so in Homer, of the gods regarding the affairs of men (and so too in Dem. and Herod.), cf. the use of the simple verb ἰδεῖν in Gen. xxii. 14, and also of ἐπιδεῖν in Gen. xvi. 13, 1 Chron. xvii. 17, Ps. xxx. (xxxi. 7), 2 Macc. i. 27, and viii. 2.—τὸν λόγον σου: a characteristic phrase in St. Luke; his use of ὁ λόγ. τοῦ Θεοῦ, ver. 31, four times in his Gospel, and twelve times in Acts, as against the use of it once in St. Mark, St. John and St. Matthew, xv. 6 (W.H.). The phrase is of frequent occurrence in St. Paul's Epistles, and it is found several times in the Apocalypse.— μετὰ παρρησίας, see above on iv. 13. There is an antithesis in the Greek words, for boldness of speech was usually the privilege, not of slaves, but of freemen —but it is the duty of those who are in the service of Christ (Humphry, Acts, in loco). Ver. 30. ἐν τῷ κ.τ.λ., iii. 26: a Hebraistic formula; for similar expressions used of God cf. Exodus vii. 5, Jeremiah xv. 6, Ezek. vi. 14, etc., most frequently in the act of punishment; but here the context shows that it is for healing, Luke v. 13, vi. 10; "while thou stretchest forth thine hand"—the construction is very frequent in Luke and the Acts, see Burton, N. T. Moods and Tenses, p. 162, and Friedrich, p. 37. Commenting on the prayer, St. Chrysostom writes: "Observe they do not say 'crush them, cast them down,' . . . let us also learn thus to pray. And yet how full of wrath one would be when fallen upon by men intent upon killing him, and making threats to that effect! how full of animosity! but not so these saints." —γίγνεσθαι: A. and R.V. make γιγ. to depend upon δός, but better to regard it

31. Καὶ δεηθέντων αὐτῶν ἐσαλεύθη ὁ τόπος ἐν ᾧ ἦσαν συνηγμένοι, καὶ ἐπλήσθησαν ἅπαντες Πνεύματος Ἁγίου, καὶ ἐλάλουν τὸν λόγον τοῦ Θεοῦ μετὰ παρρησίας.[1]

[1] At end of ver. D (E, Ir., Aug.) adds παντι τω θελοντι πιστευειν (last word omitted by Aug.); so Hilg. Chase points out that Syriac often inserts "will" when nothing corresponding in Greek, but see Harris on a primitive Latin redaction, *Four Lectures*, etc., pp. 89, 90.

as infinitive of purpose, subordinate to ἐν τῷ κ.τ.λ. (see Wendt and Page). Weiss regards from καὶ σημ. to γιγ. as the reviser's insertion.—εἰς ἴασιν : St. Luke alone employs the good medical word ἴασις, see ver. 22, and Luke xiii. 32, so whilst ἰᾶσθαι is used only three or four times by St. Matthew, two or three times by St. John, and once by St. Mark, it is used by St. Luke eleven times in his Gospel, and three or four times in the Acts. The significant use of this strictly medical term, and of the verb ἰᾶσθαι in St. Luke's writings, comes out by comparing Matt. xiv. 36, Mark vi. 56, and Luke vi. 19, see Hobart. ἴασιν —'Ἰησοῦ, paronomasia ; Wordsworth. In this ver., 30, Spitta, agreeing with Weiss as against Feine, traced another addition in the reviser's hand through the influence of source B, in which the Apostles appear, not as preachers of the Gospel, but as performers of miraculous deeds.

Ver. 31. δεηθέντων, *cf.* xvi. 26, where a similar answer is given to the prayer of Paul and Silas : the verb is characteristic of St. Luke and St. Paul, and is only used by these two writers with the exception of one passage, Matt ix. 38 ; in St. Luke's Gospel it is found eight times, and in Acts seven times, and often of requests addressed to God as here, *cf.* x. 2, viii. 24, Luke x. 2, xxi. 36, xxii. 32, 1 Thess. iii. 10. See on αἰτέω, Grimm-Thayer (Synonyms). This frequent reference to prayer is characteristic of St. Luke both in his Gospel and the Acts, *cf.* Acts i. 14, ii. 42, iv. 31, vi. 4, x. 2, xiii. 3, xiv. 23, xvi. 13, 25, xxviii. 8 ; Friedrich, *Das Lucasevangelium*, pp. 59, 60.—ἐσαλεύθη, xvi. 26 ; Luke (vi. 38, 48, vii. 24) xxi. 26 ; Heb. xii. 26, 27 ; in the O.T. we have similar manifestations of the divine Presence, *cf.* Ps. cxiv. 7, Amos ix. 5, where the same word is used ; *cf.* also Isa. vi. 4, Hag. ii. 6, Joel iii. 16, Ezek. xxxviii. 19. For instance of an earthquake regarded as a token of the presence of a deity, see Wetstein, *in loco ;* Virgil, *Æneid*, iii., 90 ; Ovid, *Met.*, xv., 672, and so amongst the Rabbis,

Schöttgen, *Hor. Heb., in loco.* In the Acts it is plainly regarded as no chance occurrence, and with regard to the rationalistic hypothesis that it was merely a natural event, accidentally coinciding with the conclusion of the prayer, Zeller admits that there is every probability against the truth of any such hypothesis ; rather may we see in it with St. Chrysostom a direct answer to the appeal to the God in whose hands were the heaven and the earth (*cf.* Iren., *Adv. Haer.*, iii., 12, 5). " The place was shaken, and that made them all the more unshaken " (Chrysostom, Theophylact, Oecumenius). —συνηγμένοι, "were gathered," so in ver. 27 ; the aorist in the former verse referring to an act, but here the perfect to a state, but impossible to distinguish in translation, Burton, *N. T. Moods and Tenses*, p. 45. That the shaking is regarded as miraculous is admitted by Weiss, who sees in it the reviser's hand introducing a miraculous result of the prayer of the Church, in place of the natural result of strengthened faith and popular favour.—καὶ ἐπλήσθησαν, ver. 8. So here the Holy Ghost inspired them all with courage: He came *comfortari*, to strengthen ; they had prayed that they might speak the word μετὰ παρρ. and their prayer was heard and fulfilled to the letter (ver. 31) as Luke describes " with simple skill ".—ἐλάλουν : mark the force of the imperfect. ἐπλησθ. (aorist), the prayer was immediately answered by their being filled with the Holy Ghost, and they proceeded to speak, the imperfect also implying that they continued to speak (Rendall) ; there is no need to see any reference to the speaking with tongues. Feine sees in the narrative a divine answer to the Apostles' prayer, so that filled with the Holy Ghost they spoke with boldness. And he adds, that such divine power must have been actually working in the Apostles, otherwise the growth of the Church in spite of its opposition is inexplicable—a remark which might well be considered by the deniers of a miraculous Christianity. It is in reality the same

32. ΤΟΥ δὲ πλήθους τῶν πιστευσάντων ἦν ἡ καρδία καὶ ἡ ψυχὴ μία¹· καὶ οὐδὲ εἷς τι τῶν ὑπαρχόντων αὐτῷ ἔλεγεν ἴδιον εἶναι, ἀλλ᾽ ἦν αὐτοῖς ἅπαντα κοινά. 33. καὶ μεγάλη δυνάμει ἀπεδίδουν τὸ μαρτύριον οἱ ἀπόστολοι τῆς ἀναστάσεως τοῦ Κυρίου Ἰησοῦ, χάρις

¹ After μια DE, Cypr., Amb., Zeno. insert και ουκ ην διακρισις (χωρισμος, E) εν αυτοις ουδεμια (τις, E) ; so Hilg. Belser (so too Zöckler) again sees an original reading which, beautiful as it is, was sacrificed to brevity ; but Weiss objects that the words are no explanation of the preceding words, which point, as the context shows, to a fulness of love rather than to the mere absence of division. But it is possible that the words may at first have been written in close connection with what follows as a fuller picture of the ψυχη μια and afterwards abbreviated. Chase suggests Syriac— assim. to John ix. 16, where Greek has σχισμα—see further on this and other points in connection with parallel passage in ii. 44 ff., Harris, Four Lectures, etc., pp. 57, 85.

argument so forcibly put by St. Chrysostom : "If you deny miracles, you make it all the more marvellous that they should obtain such moral victories— these illiterate men !" Jüngst refers the whole verse to a redactor, recording that there was no one present with reference to whom the παρρησία could be employed. But the distinction between the aorist ἐπλήσ. and the imperfect ἐλάλουν shows that not only the immediate but the continuous action of the disciples is denoted.

Ver. 32. δέ marks no contrast between the multitude and the Apostles ; it introduces a general statement of the life of the whole Christian community, cf. xv. 12, 30. On St. Luke's frequent use of words expressing fulness, see iv. 32. Deissmann, Neue Bibelstudien, p. 59 (1897), points out that in the inscriptions πλῆθος with a genitive has a technical significance, not only in official political life, but also in that of religious communities, cf. Luke i. 10, xix. 37, Acts ii. 6, but especially xv. 30 ; so too iv. 32, vi. 2, 5, xv. 12, xix. 9, xxi. 22, where the word=not Menge or Masse, but Gemeinde. —καρδία καὶ ψυχὴ μία : it is difficult to distinguish precisely between the two words, but they undoubtedly imply entire harmony in affection and thought according to a common Hebrew mode of expression ; cf. passages in the LXX in which both ψυχή and καρδία occur as here with μία, 1 Chron. xii. 38, 2 Chron. xxx. 12 (Wetstein) ; but in each passage the Hebrew word is the same, לֵב, and it would include not only affection and emotion, but also understanding, intelligence, thought ; cf. Phil i. 27, ii. 2, 20. " Behold heart and soul are what make the together !" Chrys. δύο φίλοι, ψυχὴ μία, Plutarch, cf. instances in Blass, in loco, from Aristotle and Cicero. Grotius

comments "erant ut Hebræi loquuntur בְּאִישׁ אֶחָד".—καὶ οὐδὲ εἷς, "and not one of them said," R.V., i.e., not one among so many ; cf. John i. 3. οὐδὲ ἕν, "not even one thing " ; cf. Rom. iii. 10 ; see above on ii. 45 and J. Lightfoot, Hor. Heb., in loco. On the difference between the classical and N.T. use of the infinitive after verbs of declaring, see Viteau, Le Grec du N. T., pp. 51, 52, 153, 155 (1896) ; except in Luke and Paul the infinitive tends to disappear, whilst these two writers retain the more literary usage.

Ver. 33. ἀπεδίδουν τὸ μαρτύριον, "gave the Apostles their witness," R.V. See ver. 12. τὸ μαρτ., prop., "res quæ testimonio est," but sometimes in N.T. pro μαρτυρία (Blass). ἀπεδ., however, implies paying or rendering what is due ; it suggests that there is a claim in response to which something is given (Westcott on Heb. xiii. 11) ; cf. Matt. xii. 36, Luke xii. 59, xvi. 2, xx. 25, Rom. xiii. 7, 1 Cor. vii. 3, etc. This was its first and strict significance in classical Greek, cf. also its use in LXX, frequently. The Apostles therefore bear their witness as a duty to which they were pledged, cf. i. 8, 22, iv. 20 ; καὶ ὡς περὶ ὀφλήματος λέγει αὐτό, Oecum.—δυνάμει μεγάλη : the words may include miraculous powers, as well as stedfast witness. But the τε must not, as Weiss maintains, be so taken as to indicate that χάρις μεγάλη was the result, as in ii. 47. For if we regard χάρις as referring to the favour of the people (as in the former narrative in ii.), the γάρ in ver. 34 seems to point to the love and liberality of the Christians as its cause. But many commentators prefer to take χάρις as in vi. 8 (and as in Luke ii. 40, Hilgenfeld), of the grace of God, since here as there it is used absolutely, and ver. 34 would thus be a proof of the efficacy of this grace, cf. 2 Cor. ix. 14.

τε μεγάλη ἦν ἐπὶ πάντας αὐτούς.　34. οὐδὲ γὰρ ἐνδεής τις ὑπῆρχεν [1]
ἐν αὐτοῖς · ὅσοι γὰρ κτήτορες χωρίων ἢ οἰκιῶν ὑπῆρχον, πωλοῦντες
ἔφερον τὰς τιμὰς τῶν πιπρασκομένων, 35. καὶ ἐτίθουν παρὰ τοὺς
πόδας τῶν ἀποστόλων · διεδίδοτο [2] δὲ ἑκάστῳ καθότι ἄν τις χρείαν
εἶχεν.

[1] τις υπηρχεν DEP, Chrys.; τις ην ℵAF² 15, 69, so Tisch., W.H., R.V., Weiss;
ην τις B.　D reads οσοι κτητορες ησαν οικ. η χωρ. υπηρχον πωλουντες και φεροντες
combination, so Hilg.; Harris thinks *erant* Lat. brought in ησαν out of place, while
Chase refers to fusion of true Greek text with Syr. trans.　Whatever theory we adopt
it seems that both ησαν and υπηρχον got into the text, and that alteration was made
so as to include them both.　Blass's theory seems difficult to accept although St.
Luke, with whom υπαρχειν is such a favourite word, might conceivably have written
υπηρχον πωλοντες και φεροντες in a rough draft.

[2] διεδιδοτο B³P; διεδιδετο ℵAB¹DE, so Tisch., W.H., Weiss, Winer-Schmiedel,
p. 121; Blass, *Grammatik*, p. 48; Kennedy, *Sources of N. T. Greek*, p. 159.

χάρις, as Bengel maintains, may include
grace, favour with God and man, as in
our Lord Himself, *Gratia Dei et favor
populi*.

Ver. 34.　οὐδὲ γὰρ ἐνδεής: cf. Deut.
xv. 4, where the same adjective occurs;
cf. xv. 7, 11, xxiv. 14, Isa. xli. 17.　No
contradiction with vi. 1, as Holtzmann
supposes; here there is no ideal immunity
from poverty and want, but distribution
was made as each fitting case presented
itself: "their feeling was just as if they
were under the paternal roof, all for a
while sharing alike," Chrys., *Hom.*, xi.—
ὅσοι γὰρ . . . ὑπῆρχον, "non dicitur:
omnes hoc fecerunt [aorist] ut jam nemo
vel fundum vel domum propriam haberet,
sed: vulgo [saepe] hoc fiebat [imperfect]
ad supplendum fiscum communem pau-
peribus destinatum; itaque nunquam
deerat quod daretur," Blass, *in loco*, cf.
remarks on ii. 47.—τὰς τιμὰς τῶν πιπρασκομένων, "the prices of the things which
were being sold".　The language shows
that we are not meant to infer that the
men sold all that they had (cf. Wetstein,
especially Appian, *B. Civ.*, v., p. 1088,
τιμὰς τῶν ἔτι πιπρασκ.).　πωλοῦντες et
πιπρασκ. both imperfect (Blass), and see
also Burton, *N. T. Moods and Tenses*, p.
58.—κτήτορες in N.T. only here, rarely
elsewhere, see instances in Wetstein;
not in LXX, but cf. Symmachus, Joel
i. 11.

Ver. 35.　The statement marks, it is
true, an advance upon the former narrative, ii. 44, but one which was perfectly
natural and intelligible.　Here for the
first time we read that the money is
brought and laid at the Apostles' feet.
As the community grew, the responsibilities of distribution increased, and to
whom could the administration of the
common fund be more fittingly committed
than to the Apostles?　The narrative
indicates that this commital of trust was
voluntary on the part of the Ecclesia,
although it was marked by an act of
reverence for the Apostles' authority.
The fact that Barnabas is expressly
mentioned as laying the value of his field
at the Apostles' feet, may be an indication that the other members of the community were acting upon his suggestion;
if so, it would be in accordance with what
we know of his character and forethought,
cf. ix. 27, xi. 22-24, Hort, *Ecclesia*, pp.
47, 48.　There is no reason to reject this
narrative as a mere repetition of ii. 44,
45.　The same spirit prevails in both
accounts, but in the one case we have
the immediate result of the Pentecostal
gift, in the case before us we have the
permanence and not only the vitality of
the gift marked—the Christian community is now organised under Apostolic
direction, and stress is laid upon the
continuance of the "first love," whilst
the contrast is marked between the self-
sacrifice of Barnabas and the greed of
Ananias and Sapphira, see Rendall, *Acts*,
p. 196, and also Zöckler, *Apostelgeschichte*,
p. 198, in answer to recent criticisms.—
παρὰ τοὺς πόδας: the Apostles are represented as sitting, perhaps as teachers,
xxii. 3, cf. Luke ii. 46, and also as an
indication of their authority: the expression in the Greek conveys the thought
of committal to the care and authority of any one, cf. v. 2, vii. 58,
xxii. 20, so Matt. xv. 30, or that of reverence and thankfulness. Oecumenius
sees in the words an indication of the
great honour of the Apostles, and the

36. Ἰωσῆς¹ δὲ ὁ ἐπικληθεὶς Βαρνάβας ὑπὸ τῶν ἀποστόλων (ὅ ἐστι μεθερμηνευόμενον, Υἱὸς παρακλήσεως), Λευΐτης, Κύπριος τῷ γένει,

¹ Ἰωσης P 1, 13, 31, Sah., Syr. Harcl., Chrys., Theophy., Meyer, Alford; Ἰωσηφ ℵABDE, Vulg., Boh., Syr. Pesh., Arm., Aeth., Epiph., so Tisch., W.H., R.V., Weiss, Wendt, Hilg.—see Blass, *Grammatik*, p. 30.

reverence of those who brought the money. Friedrich notes the expression as characteristic of St. Luke's style, since it is used by him five times in the Gospel, six times in Acts, and is found in the N.T. only once elsewhere, see above, *cf.* Cicero, *Pro Flacco*, 28, and instances in Wetstein.—διεδίδετο: impersonal, or τὸ ἀργύριον may be supplied, Viteau, *Le Grec du N. T.*, p. 57 (1896), and in St. Luke's Gospel twice, xi. 22, xviii. 22; only once elsewhere in N.T., John vi. 11; on the abnormal termination ετο for οτο, *cf.* LXX, Kennedy, *Sources of N. T. Greek*, p. 159, *cf.* Exodus v. 13, ἐδίδοτο, but A -ετο; Jer. lii. 34, ἐδίδοτο, but AB¹S -ετο; 1 Cor. xi. 23, Winer-Schmiedel, p. 121.—καθότι: only found in St. Luke in N. T., twice in Gospel, four times in Acts; Luke i. 7, xix. 9, Acts ii. 24, 45, iv. 35, xxii. 31; on the imperfect with ἄν in a conditional relative clause, Burton, *N. T. Moods and Tenses*, pp. 13, 125, and Viteau, *Le Grec du N. T.*, p. 142 (1893), *cf.* ii. 45.   33ᵇ-35 are ascribed by Hilgenfeld to his "author to Theophilus," but this reviser must have been very clumsy to introduce a notice involving a general surrender of all landed property, as Hilgenfeld interprets the verse, which could not be reconciled with St. Peter's express words in v. 4—words which, on Hilgenfeld's own showing, the reviser must have had before him.

Ver. 36. Ἰωσῆς δὲ: δέ introduces the special case of Barnabas after the general statement in ver. 34.—ὁ ἐπικ., *cf.* i. 23.   On what occasion this surname was conferred by the Apostles nothing certain is known (ἀπό as often for ὑπό, ii. 22), although the fact that it was conferred by them may indicate that he owed his conversion to them. Possibly it may not have been bestowed until later, and reference may here be made to identify him (Nösgen).—βαρνάβας: most commonly derived from בַּר נְבוּאָה ("quod neque ad sensum neque ad litteras prorsus convenit," Blass) = properly υἱὸς προφητείας. But St. Luke, it is argued, renders this υἱὸς παρακλήσεως, because under the threefold uses of prophecy,

1 Cor. xiv. 3, the special gift of παράκλησις distinguished Barnabas, *cf.* Acts xi. 23. So Harnack (whose full article "Barnabas" should be consulted, *Real-Encyclopädie für prot. Theol. und Kirche*," xv., 410) explains it as indicating a *prophet* in the sense in which the word was used in the early Church, Acts xv. 32 (xi. 23), παράκλησις = edifying exhortation.   But not only is בַּר an Aramaic word, whilst נְבוּאָה is Hebrew, but the above solution of St. Luke's translation is by no means satisfactory (see Zöckler, *in loco*). In 1 Cor. xiv. 3 παράκ. might equally mean consolation, *cf.* 2 Cor. i. 3-7, and it is translated "comfort" (not "exhortation") in the R.V.   In St. Luke's Gospel the word is used twice, ii. 25, vi. 24, and in both passages it means comfort, consolation, *cf.* the cognate verb in xvi. 25.   Another derivation has been suggested by Klostermann, *Probleme im Aposteltexte*, pp. 8-14. He maintains that both parts of the word are Aramaic, בַּר and נְוָחָא, *solatium*, and that therefore St. Luke's translation is quite justified.   Blass however points out that as in the former derivation so here there is a difficulty in the connection between βαρνάβας and the somewhat obscure Aramaic word.   In the conversion of Barnabas, the first man whose heart was so touched as to join him, in spite of his Levitical status and culture, to ignorant and unlettered men, the Apostles might well see a source of hope and comfort (*cf.* Gen. v. 29), Klostermann, p. 13.   It is also worthy of note that the LXX frequently uses παράκλησις as a translation of the common Hebrew words for comfort or consolation; *cf.* Job xxi. 2, Ps. xciii. 19, Isa. lvii. 8, Jer. xvi. 17, etc., and *cf. Psalms of Solomon* xiii., title, παράκλησις τῶν δικαίων.   On the whole question, Deissmann, *Bibelstudien*, p. 175 ff., should be consulted. Deissmann, referring to an inscription recently discovered in Northern Syria, in the old Nicopolis, probably of the third or fourth century A.D., explains the word as follows: The inscription contains the

37. ὑπάρχοντος αὐτῷ ἀγροῦ,[1] πωλήσας ἤνεγκε τὸ χρῆμα, καὶ ἔθηκε παρὰ[2] τοὺς πόδας τῶν ἀποστόλων.

[1] αγρου; D has χωριον, but αγρος only here in Acts. For χωριον cf. iv. 34, v. 3, 8.

[2] παρα BP, Chrys., so W.H. (so Lach.); προς אE 15, 18, 37, so Tisch., Weiss, Wendt; cf. ver. 35 and v. 2.

name βαρνεβοῦν, which D. considers rightly = Son of Nebo; cf., e.g., Symmachus, Isa. xlvi. 1, who renders נבו‍, Nebo (transcribed by the LXX, Aquila and Theodotion, Ναβώ), by Νεβοῦς. The view of the connection or identity of βαρνάβας with βαρνεβοῦς is facilitated by the fact that in other words the ε sound in Nebo is replaced by α; cf. Nebuchadnezar = LXX Ν α βουχοδονοσορ, so Nebuzaradan = LXX Ν α βουζαραδαν. Very probably therefore βαρναβοῦς will occur instead of βαρνεβοῦς—and the Jews themselves might easily have converted βαρναβοῦς into βαρναβᾶς—ας being the constant termination of Greek names. In his Neue Bibelstudien, p. 16, Deissmann is able to refer to an Aramaic inscription from Palmyra, dating 114 A.D., with the word Barnebo, and cf. also Enc. Bibl., i., 484.—Λευείτης: although the Levites were not allowed to hold possessions in land, since God Himself was their portion (Num. xviii. 20, Deut. x. 9), yet they could do so by purchase or inheritance, cf. Jer. xxxii. 7-12, or it is possible that the field of Barnabas may not have been in Palestine at all (see Bengel, but, on the other hand, Wendt, in loco), and that the same Messianic regulations may not have applied to the Levites in other countries (Wetstein). It would also seem that after the Captivity the distribution of land, according to the Mosaic Law, was no longer strictly observed (Overbeck, Hackett (Hastings' B.D.), "Barnabas," e.g., Josephus, a Levite and Priest, has lands in the vicinity of Jerusalem, and gains others in exchange for them from Vespasian, Vita, 76.— Κύπριος τῷ γένει: soon after the time of Alexander, and possibly before it, Jews had settled in Cyprus, and 1 Macc. xv. 23 indicates that they were there in good numbers. This is the first mention of it in the N.T.; see also xi. 19, 20, xiii. 4-13, xv. 39, xx. 16, and the geographical notices in xxi. 3, xxvii. 4. From the neighbouring island, Cyprus, Barnabas might well have been sent to the famous University of Tarsus, and so have made the acquaintance of Saul. In this way the previous acquaintance between the two men goes far to explain succeeding events, ix. 27: see "Cyprus," B.D. (Hastings), Hamburger, Real-Encyclopädie des Judentums, i. 2, 216.—γένει, "a man of Cyprus by race," R.V., not "of the country of Cyprus": γένει refers to his parentage and descent, cf. xviii. 2, 24.

Ver. 37. ἀγροῦ, better "a field" R.V.; the possession was not great, but if the field lay in the rich and productive island of Cyprus, its value may have been considerable. — τὸ χρῆμα: rarely in this sense in the singular, only here in the N.T., and never in Attic Greek, but cf. Herod., iii., 38, and instances in Wetstein, and see Blass, in loco. The money, i.e., the proceeds, the money got (German Erlös). Lumby suggests that the word may be used here to indicate the entirety, the sum without deduction, in contrast to the action of Ananias and Sapphira, v. 2. The same unselfish spirit manifested itself in Barnabas at a later date, when he was content to live from the produce of his hands, 1 Cor. ix. 6. Possibly at Tarsus, so near his own home, he may have learnt with Saul in earlier days the craft of tent-making, for which the city was famous (Plumptre). In connection with this passage, and ix. 26, see Renan's eulogy on the character of Barnabas. In him Renan sees the patron of all good and liberal ideas, and considers that Christianity has done him an injustice in not placing him in the first rank of her founders, Apostles, p. 191, E.T.

Chapter V.—Ver. 1. Ἀνὴρ δέ τις: in striking contrast to the unreserved self-sacrifice of Barnabas, St. Luke places the selfishness and hypocrisy of Ananias and Sapphira. It is in itself no small proof of the truth of the narrative, that the writer should not hesitate to introduce this episode side by side with his picture of the still unbroken love and fellowship of the Church. He makes no apology for the facts, but narrates them simply and without comment. — Ἀνανίας — written in W.H. (so Blass) Ἀ., prob. Hebrew חֲנַנְיָה = Hananiah = to whom Jehovah

V. 1. Ἀνὴρ δέ τις Ἀνανίας [1] ὀνόματι, σὺν Σαπφείρῃ τῇ γυναικὶ αὐτοῦ, ἐπώλησε κτῆμα, 2. καὶ ἐνοσφίσατο ἀπὸ τῆς τιμῆς, συνειδυίας καὶ τῆς γυναικὸς αὐτοῦ, καὶ ἐνέγκας μέρος τι παρὰ τοὺς πόδας τῶν ἀποστόλων ἔθηκεν. 3. εἶπε δὲ [2] Πέτρος, Ἀνανία, διατί ἐπλήρωσεν ὁ Σατανᾶς τὴν καρδίαν σου, ψεύσασθαί σε τὸ Πνεῦμα τὸ Ἅγιον, καὶ νοσφίσασθαι ἀπὸ τῆς τιμῆς τοῦ χωρίου; 4. οὐχὶ μένον σοὶ ἔμενε, καὶ πραθὲν ἐν τῇ σῇ ἐξουσίᾳ ὑπῆρχε; τί ὅτι ἔθου ἐν τῇ καρδίᾳ σου

---

[1] Αν. ονοματι ℵBEP, so Tisch., W.H., Weiss, Winer-Schmiedel, p. 256; ον. Αν. AD, Vulg., Chrys. Σαπφειρῃ AP, so Tisch., W.H., so Blass in β; Σαπφειρα B, so Weiss. Many variations: ℵ Σαμφιρῃ, D σαφφυρα, corr. Σαφφιρᾳ (so Hilg.); E has Σαφφιρῃ; see comment.

[2] Πετρος DP; but ὁ Π. ℵABE, Chrys., so Tisch., W.H., Wendt, Weiss.

---

has been gracious (the Hebrew name of Shadrach, Dan. i. 6, LXX, Jer. xxviii. 1, Tob. v. 12,(Song of the Three Children, ver. 66) (Lumby, but see also Wendt, note, *in loco*).—Σαπφείρῃ, so also W.H., either from σάπφειρος (σάμφ., so here Σαμφ., ℵ*, Blass), a sapphire, or from the Aramaic שַׁפִּירָא, beautiful. The latter derivation is adopted by Blass (*Grammatik des N. G.*, p. 8), and Winer-Schmiedel, p. 76. It is declined like σπεῖρα, μάχαιρα, Acts x. 1, xii. 2, etc., in N.T., and so makes dative ῃ, Winer-Schmiedel, pp. 80, 93, and Blass, *u. s.* —κτῆμα = χωρίον, ver. 3: but may mean property of any kind. It is used in the singular several times in the LXX, as a possession, heritage, etc., Job xx. 29, Prov. xii. 27, xxxi. 16, Wisdom viii. 5, Ecclus. xxxvi. 30, li. 21, etc.

Ver. 2. ἐνοσφίσατο: may merely mean from its derivation, to set apart νόσφι. But both in LXX and N.T. it is used in a bad sense of appropriating for one's own benefit, purloining, Josh. vii. 1, of Achan, 2 Macc. iv. 32, so here and in ver. 3, and Tit. ii. 10, *cf.* also a similar use of the word in Jos., *Ant.*, iv., 8, 29 (so in Greek authors, Xen., Polyb., Plut.). —ἀπό: the same combination in Josh. vii. 1 (*cf.* ii. 17 above, ἐκχεῶ ἀπό, *cf.* Hebrew מִן. See Bengel's note, *in loco*, on the sin of Achan and Ananias).— συνειδυίης: it was thus a deliberate and aggravated offence. On the irregular form, instead of -υιας, *cf.* the LXX, Exod. viii. 21, 24, 1 Sam. xxv. 20; and see also Winer-Schmiedel, p. 81, note, and Blass on instances from the papyri, *in loco.*— παρὰ τοὺς πόδας: a further aggravation (iv. 35), since the money was brought ostentatiously to gain a reputation for the

donors. Blass well comments: "in conventu ecclesiæ hoc liberalitatis documentum editum"; *cf.* Calvin, who in marking the ambition of Ananias to gain a reputation for liberality adds: "ita fit ut pedes Apostolorum magis honoret quam Dei oculos".

Ver. 3. διὰ τί: not simply "why?" but "how is it that?" R.V., *cf.* Luke ii. 49; the force of the Greek seems to emphasise the fact that Ananias had it in his power to have prevented such a result, *cf.* James iv. 7, 1 Peter v. 9.—ἐπλήρωσεν, *occupavit* (*cf.* John xvi. 6), so that there is room for no other influence, Eccles. ix. 3. On the Vulgate, *tentavit*, which does not express the meaning here, see Felten's note. — ψεύσασθαι, *sc.*, ὥστε, often omitted; *cf.* Luke i. 54, the infinitive of conceived result, see Burton, *N. T. Moods and Tenses*, pp. 148, 154. The verb with the accusative of the person only here in N.T., but in LXX, Deut. xxxiii. 29, Psalm lxv. 3, Isa. lvii. 11, Hos. ix. 2, 4 Macc. v. 34, etc., and frequently in classical writers.

Ver. 4. οὐχὶ, "id quaerit quod sic esse nemo negat," Grimm, "while it remained, did it not remain thine own?" R.V. Very frequent in Luke as compared with the other Evangelists, see also vii. 50. This rendering better retains the kind of play upon the word μένω, to which Weiss draws attention, and compares 1 Macc. xv. 7 for the force of ἔμενεν. —πραθὲν, *i.e.*, the price of it when sold (*rectius* πραθέντος τὸ ἀργύριον, *cf.* Viteau, *Le Grec du N. T.*, p. 57 (1896)); so αὐτά in ii. 45 is used for the prices of the possessions and goods sold. The whole question, while it deprived Ananias of every excuse, also proves beyond doubt that the community of goods in the Church of Jerusalem was not compulsory

τὸ πρᾶγμα τοῦτο [1]; οὐκ ἐψεύσω ἀνθρώποις, ἀλλὰ τῷ Θεῷ. 5. ἀκούων
δὲ ᾿Ανανίας τοὺς λόγους τούτους, πεσὼν ἐξέψυξε · καὶ ἐγένετο φόβος

[1] το πραγμα τουτο ; but D, Par., Sah. read ποιησαι (το) πονηρον τουτο—πραγμα
once elsewhere in Luke's Gospel i. 1, once in St. Matt., four times in St. Paul.
Αν. ΝΑΒΕΡ, Chrys. prefix article, so Tisch., W.H., Weiss, Wendt. πεσων ; D, Par.,
so Hilg., prefix παραχρημα—and Par. also adds after πεσ. επι την γην, cf. ix. 4,
read by Blass in β. ταντα om. Ν*ABD, verss., Orig., Lucif., so Tisch., W.H., R.V.,
Wendt, Weiss ; cf. ver. 11 end.

but voluntary.—ἐξουσίᾳ, power or right (ἔξεστι): "The Ecclesia was a society in which neither the community was lost in the individual, nor the individual in the community," Hort, *Ecclesia*, p. 48.—τί ὅτι, *sc.*, τί ἔστιν ὅτι, *cf.* Luke ii. 49, and Viteau, *Le Grec du N. T.*, p. 101 (1893), Blass, *Grammatik des N. G.*, p. 173.— ἔθου ἐν τῇ καρδίᾳ σου, xix. 21, and Luke xxi. 14. The phrase is rightly described as having a Hebraistic colouring, *cf.* LXX, 1 Sam. xxi. 12, Dan. i. 8, Hag. ii. 16, 19, Mal. i. 1, and the Homeric θέσθαι ἐν φρεσί, ἐν θυμῷ βάλλεσθαι. —τὸ πρᾶγμα τοῦτο: so frequently in LXX, Gen. xliv. 15, Exod. i. 18, Josh. ix. 24, 1 Chron. xxi. 8; Viteau, *Le Grec du N. T.*, p. 149 (1896).—οὐκ ἐψεύσω: the words do not here of course mean that Ananias had not lied unto men, but an absolute negative is employed in the first conception, not to annul it, but rhetorically to direct undivided attention to the second, *cf.* Matt. x. 20, Mark ix. 37, 1 Thess. iv. 8, Winer-Moulton, lv. 8, 6. The dative of the person is found after ψεύδεσθαι in the LXX, but not in classical Greek. The sin of Ananias was much more than mere hypocrisy, much more than fraud, pride or greed—hateful as these sins are—the power and presence of the Holy Spirit had been manifested in the Church, and Ananias had sinned not only against human brotherhood, but against the divine light and leading which had made that brotherhood possible. In the words there lies an undeniable proof of the personality and divinity of the Holy Ghost, and a refutation of Macedonius long before he was born (see Bede's note *in loco*, and on patristic authorities, Felten). We cannot satisfactorily explain the words by supposing that offence against the public spirit of that Church is meant, and that the sin against the Holy Ghost may be identified with this. Ver. 5. ἀκούων, "as he heard these words" = μεταξὺ ἀκούων, so Weiss, Blass, Rendall.—ἐξέψυξεν : only found here, in ver. 10 of Sapphira, and xii. 23 of the

death of Herod, in the N.T.; not found in classical writers, and only twice in the LXX, Judg. iv. 21 where A reads it to describe the death of Sisera, but = a Hebrew word which may only mean to faint, to faint away ; Ezek. xxi. 7 (12) where it translates a Hebrew word כָּהֲתָה meaning to be faint-hearted, to despond, to be dim. But as Blass points out it is used by Hippocrates ; indeed it would seem that its use is almost altogether confined to medical writers (Hobart, Zahn). It is therefore a word which may probably be referred to St. Luke's employment of medical terms ; Hobart, *Medical Language of St. Luke*, p. 37, for instances of its use not only in Hippocrates but in Galen and Aretaeus (Lumby refers to *Acta Andr. et Matth. Apocr.*, 19, where the word is also used of men suddenly falling down dead). In classical Greek ἀποψύχειν (βίον), or ἀποψ. absolutely is the term employed. There can be no doubt that the narrative implies the closest connection between the guilt of Ananias and his sudden death. It therefore cannot be regarded as a narrative of a chance occurrence or of the effect of a sudden shock caused by the discovery of guilt in St. Peter's words. No one has shown more clearly than Baur (*Paulus*, i., 27-33, especially against Neander) that all such explanations are unsatisfactory (see also Zeller and De Wette). In the early history of the Church, Origen, *Tract. ix. in Matt.*, had espoused the view that Ananias had died overcome by shame and grief at the sudden detection of his sin. But no such explanation could account for the death of Sapphira which Peter foretells as about to follow without delay. That the narrative is not without historical foundation is frankly admitted by Wendt, and also by Baur, Zeller, Overbeck, and most recently by Weizsäcker, Holtzmann, Spitta. But this stern condemnation of any attempt to lie unto God is a stumbling-block even to those who with Wendt recognise not only some historical fact underlying the

μέγας ἐπὶ πάντας τοὺς ἀκούοντας ταῦτα. 6. ἀναστάντες δὲ οἱ
νεώτεροι συνέστειλαν αὐτόν, καὶ ἐξενέγκαντες ἔθαψαν. 7. Ἐγένετο

narrative, but also the danger and culpability of the action of Ananias and his
wife. It may however be justly observed that our Lord Himself had condemned no sin so severely as that of
hypocrisy, and that the action of Ananias
and Sapphira was hypocrisy of the worst
kind, in that they sought by false pre-
tences to gain a reputation like the
Pharisees for special sanctity and charity;
the hypocrisy of the leaven of the Pharisees had entered the Church (Baumgarten), and if such a spirit had once
gained ground in the Christian community, it must have destroyed all
mutual affection and all brotherly kindness, for how could men speak the truth,
every one with his neighbour, unless their
love was without hypocrisy? Rom. xii. 9 ;
how could they claim to be citizens of a
city, into which none could enter who
"made a lie"? Rev. xxi. 27, xxii. 15. The
sin before us was not one sin but many
(Chrys., *Hom.*, xii., on ver. 9), and in its
deliberateness it came perilously near
that sin against the Holy Ghost which,
whatever else it may mean, certainly
means a wilful hardening against divine
guidance. For further considerations on
the necessity of this unhesitating condemnation of such a sin at the outset of
the life of the Church, see St. Chrysostom's remarks. We must guard against
supposing that St. Peter had imprecated
the death-penalty upon Ananias (as
Porphyry asserted, see against such a
view, Jerome, *Epist.*, 130). St. Jerome
speaks of Ananias and Sapphira as not
only deceitful, but also as timid stewards,
keeping back a part of the price "through
fear of famine which true faith never
fears". On his judgment that the avenging stroke was inflicted, not in cruelty to
them, but as a warning to others, see
below.—καὶ ἐγένετο φόβος μέγας κ.τ.λ.,
i.e., upon all who were present, as distinct
from ver. 11—but see Page's note. Overbeck, with De Wette, regards the remark as proleptical, as if the writer
hurried to describe the impression made
—but why should the words not include
the judgment uttered by St. Peter? for
the construction see Luke i. 65, iv. 36.
On the characteristic reference to φόβος
as following upon the exhibition of divine
miraculous power both in St. Luke's
Gospel and the Acts, see Friedrich,
Das Lucasevangelium, p. 77, and above
on ii. 43.

Ver. 6. ἀναστάντες, see on ii. 14.—
οἱ νεώτεροι: the fact that they are called
simply νεανίσκοι in ver. 10 seems decisive against the view that reference is
made to any definite order in the Church.
Nor is it certain that we can see in the
fulfilment of such duties by the νεώτεροι
the beginnings of the diaconate, although
on the natural distinction between πρεσβύτεροι and νεώτεροι it may well have
been that official duties in the Church
were afterwards based, *cf.* 1 Tim. v. 1,
Tit. ii. 1-6, 1 Pet. v. 5, Clem. Rom., i., 3 ;
iii., 3 ; xxi., 6 ; Polycarp, *Epist.*, v., 3 (*cf.*
Luke xxii. 26). In comparatively early
days it belonged to the duties of the
deacons to provide for the burial of the
strangers and the poor, but it seems
hardly probable that οἱ νεώτεροι were
appointed as a separate body to bury the
dead, before any attempt had been made
to relieve the Apostles of the more
pressing duty of distributing the public
funds, vi. 1. On the other hand it is
possible that the company of public
"buriers" whom the prophet saw in
vision, Ezek. xxxix. 12-16, may have
become quite customary in N.T. days.
R.V. margin renders simply "the younger
men". — συνέστειλαν, "wrapped him
round," R.V., probably in their own
mantles (for no formal laying-out in robes
can be supposed by the context), for which
περιστέλλω would be the usual word,
cf. Eur., *Troad.*, 378 (see Grimm, Blass,
Weiss). But Meyer on the other hand
is against the parallel, and argues, following Grotius, that the word should be
rendered "placed him together," *i.e.*,
laid out or composed his limbs, so that
he might be carried out more con-
veniently (so too Overbeck, Holtzmann,
Zöckler). Vulgate, *amoverunt*, followed
by Luther, Erasmus, Beza, cannot be
said to be supported by any parallel use
of the word (Par.² also same verb as Vulg.).
The word is frequently used by medical
writers in various senses, one of which,
to bandage, to compress by bandaging,
is that which seems to afford a possible
parallel to its use here, Hobart, *Medical
Language*, etc., pp. 37, 38. The use of
the word by Josephus, *Ant.*, xviii., 3 ; xix.,
4, is not sufficient to justify us in taking it here to express all the preparations for burial.—ἐξενέγκαντες : outside
the walls of the city, the usual place for
graves—only prophets and kings had
their graves in the city—Hamburger,

δὲ ὡς ὡρῶν τριῶν διάστημα, καὶ ἡ γυνὴ αὐτοῦ μὴ εἰδυῖα τὸ γεγονὸς εἰσῆλθεν. 8. ἀπεκρίθη δὲ αὐτῇ ὁ Πέτρος,[1] Εἰπέ μοι, εἰ τοσούτου τὸ χωρίον ἀπέδοσθε; ἡ δὲ εἶπε, Ναί, τοσούτου. 9. ὁ δὲ Πέτρος εἶπε πρὸς αὐτήν, Τί ὅτι συνεφωνήθη[2] ὑμῖν πειράσαι τὸ πνεῦμα Κυρίου; ἰδοὺ οἱ πόδες τῶν θαψάντων τὸν ἄνδρα σου ἐπὶ τῇ θύρᾳ, καὶ ἐξοίσουσί σε. 10. ἔπεσε δὲ παραχρῆμα παρὰ τοὺς πόδας αὐτοῦ, καὶ ἐξέψυξεν· εἰσελθόντες δὲ οἱ νεανίσκοι εὗρον αὐτὴν νεκράν, καὶ ἐξενέγκαντες

---

[1] For ειπε μοι ει . . . απεδ. D reads επερωτησω σε ει αρα το χ. τοσ. απεδ., so Hilg.; cf. Sah.

[2] συνεφωνηθη, D has συνεφωνησεν, so Hilg.; but in β Blass has T.R. (see Chase on retrans. from Syriac—possibly active may be a retranslation of Latin *convenit*, Harris).

Real-Encyclopädie des Judentums, i., 4, 475, "Grab"; Edersheim, *Jewish Social Life*, p. 169, cf. the use of ἐκφέρω and ἐκκομίζω in classical Greek, Latin, *efferre*. —ἔθαψαν: partly for sanitary reasons, partly to avoid defilement; the interval between death and burial was very brief, especially in Jerusalem (Numb. xix. 11, Deut. xxi. 23; Hamburger, *u. s.*, i., 2, 161, "Beerdigung," with reference to this passage, Edersheim, *u. s.*, p. 168; for the existing custom in Jerusalem of speedy burial, see Hackett, *in loco*, and Schneller, *Kennst du das Land?* (eighth edition), p. 188). Ver. 7. ἐγένετο δὲ . . . καὶ, cf. for construction Luke v. 1, 17, viii. 1, 22, ix. 51, xiv. 1, etc. Hebraistic, if not strictly a Hebraism; on καί thus uniting two co-ordinate statements with ἐγένετο see Plummer's valuable note, p. 45; *St. Luke*, first edition; and on the use of καί see Simcox, *Language of the N. T.*, pp. 161, 162; Blass, *Grammatik des N. G.*, pp. 256, 257.—διάστημα: as if a nominative absolute, here parenthetical from ὡς, cf. Luke ix. 28. Cf. Viteau, *Le Grec du N. T.*, p. 83 (1896). St. Luke alone uses διάστημα (only here in N.T.), cf. Polyb., ix., 1, 1; διάστημα τετραετές, and the verb διΐστημι, cf. Luke xxii. 59, xxiv. 51, Acts xxvii. 28. In *Apocryph. Act. Andreæ*, 14, we have ἡμιωρίου διάστημα (Lumby), and in LXX, cf. Ecclesiast., *prol.*, 24, 3 Macc. iv. 17.—ὡς = ὡσεί, *fere*, cf. i. 15, ii. 4, etc.—ὡρῶν τριῶν: Nösgen supposes the approach of the next hour of prayer in this mention of the time, μὴ *pro* οὐ (Blass), see also Lumby's note. Ver. 8. τοσούτου, *monstrat pecuniam*, Blass, so Zöckler, Holtzmann, Felten, Weiss, and others: genitive of the price. The position of the word in the question is emphatic, cf. Luke xv. 29. Blass

would render *non pluris* (Bornemann, *tantilli*), but this is implied rather than expressed by the word here (see Wendt's note for classical instances). The question of St. Peter and the emphatic reply of Sapphira show that opportunity was given her by the inquiry to retract, and that she wilfully persisted in her sin (Chrys.; so Calvin, "tempus illi ad resipiscendum datur"). Ver. 9. τί ὅτι, ver. 4. συνεφωνήθη: only here in the N.T. in the passive, for its use in the active, xv. 15. Blass maintains that this passive usage συμφωνεῖταί τισι is Latin rather than Greek (*convenit inter aliquos*), and that it may have arisen from the intercourse between Greeks and Romans, see *in loco*, and *Grammatik des N. G.*, pp. 112, 235; in LXX only in the active. Cf. also Viteau, *Le Grec du N. T.*, p. 155 (1893). "The aggravation was that they committed the deed as with one soul, just as upon a settled compact between them," Chrys., *Hom.*, xii.; cf. the plural ἀπέδοσθε.— πειράσαι: the rendering "to tempt," does not seem to express the idea so well as "to try," to make trial whether the Holy Ghost would discover their deception, whether He knew all things: cf. xv. 10, and in LXX, Exod. xvii. 2, 7, Ps. lxxvii. (lxxviii.) 41, 56, etc. (in Rev. ii. 2 the same verb as here = "try," A. and R.V.).—ἰδού, see on i. 10. οἱ πόδες, cf. Luke i. 79, Rom. iii. 15, x. 15. A Hebraistic expression—the whole description is full of dramatic intensity— the returning steps of the νεώτεροι are heard ἐπὶ τῇ θύρᾳ. But Alford thinks that they were probably bare-footed, and that the words mean that the time was just at hand for their return, cf. James v. 9.— ἐξοίσουσίν σε, see on ver. 6. Ver. 10. παραχρῆμα, see on iii. 7. The introduction of the word shows that

ἔθαψαν[1] πρὸς τὸν ἄνδρα αὐτῆς. 11. καὶ ἐγένετο φόβος μέγας ἐφ᾽ ὅλην τὴν ἐκκλησίαν, καὶ ἐπὶ πάντας τοὺς ἀκούοντας ταῦτα.

12. Διὰ δὲ τῶν χειρῶν τῶν ἀποστόλων ἐγίνετο σημεῖα καὶ τέρατα ἐν τῷ λαῷ πολλά· (καὶ ἦσαν ὁμοθυμαδὸν ἅπαντες[2] ἐν τῇ στοᾷ Σολομῶντος· 13. τῶν δὲ λοιπῶν οὐδεὶς ἐτόλμα κολλᾶσθαι αὐτοῖς,

---

[1] εξενεγκαντες, D reads συστειλαντες εξηνεγκαν; so Hilg.

[2] ἅπαντες, D, Sah., Aeth. add εν τω ιερω—E εν τω ναω συνηγμενοι. But the words εν τω ιερω are not received by Blass in β; *Acta Apost. in loco*, he says: "*cf.* ii. 43, videtur interpolatio esse; nam sec. iii. 10, haec porticus extra τὸ ἱερόν erat, *cf.* ver. 21". Σολομῶντος, see above, iii. 11.

---

the writer regarded the death as supernatural, see above on ver. 5. πρός, by, beside her husband = παρά with dative, Blass, *Grammatik des N. G.*, p. 135, note; Winer-Moulton, xlix. h. Although the whole narrative shows that in each case the death was caused by the judgment of God, yet nothing whatever is said as to the world beyond the grave: "As it is, both the man himself is benefited, in that he is not left to advance further in wickedness, and the rest, in that they are made more earnest," Chrys., *Hom.*, xii. Wendt points out that the punishment inflicted by St. Paul, 1 Cor. v. 5, was of a wholly different kind, because it had the avowed aim of saving the spirit of the sinner in the day of the Lord by delivering him over to Satan for the destruction of the flesh; but it should not be forgotten that St. Peter himself speaks of a judgment according to men in the flesh, which has its issue in a life according to God in the spirit (1 Pet. iv. 6). St. Augustine's words may fairly be quoted not against him but in favour of applying to the cases before us the principle of judgment employed by St. Paul: "Credendum est autem quod post hanc vitam eis pepercerit Deus. . . . Correpti sunt mortis flagello, ne supplicio puniantur æterno," Serm., *de Verbis Act.* v., 4, *cf.* Origen, *Tract.* viii., *in Matth.*, and Jerome, *Epist.*, cxxx. See *Speaker's Commentary, in loco*, and Bengel, Felten, Zöckler, Plumptre. Felten's reverent thoughts, p. 124, may well be compared with the remarks of Dr. Pusey on the case of Ananias, *What is of Faith? etc.*, p. 14.

Ver. 11. φόβος μέγας: evidently one purpose in the infliction of this stern penalty was at once obtained, see above on ver. 5.—ἐφ᾽ ὅλην τὴν ἐκκλησίαν: St. Luke, as it seems, uses the word ἐκκλησία here for the first time. Dr. Hort thinks that he may employ it by anti-

cipation, and that we cannot be sure that it was actually in use at this early date (*Ecclesia*, p. 49), but, as the same writer reminds us, our Lord's saying to St. Peter, Matt. xvi. 18, must have had its influence upon the minds and teaching of the Apostles. Moreover, we can see a special fitness in the employment here, after the preceding description, not only of the growth, but of the organisation of the Christian community, iv. 32 ff., and of the judgment which followed upon the attempt to challenge its powers and to violate its harmony, *cf.* Bengel's note, *in loco*. The context too probably marks a distinction between the members of the ἐκκλησία and those without (Weiss, Hort, Blass).

Ver. 12. δέ: merely transitional; ἐγίνετο marking the continuance of the miracles; διὰ τῶν χειρῶν characteristic of St. Luke in Acts, *cf.* ii. 23, vii. 25, xi. 30, xiv. 3, xv. 23, xix. 11. On Luke's fondness for this and similar phrases with χείρ, see Friedrich, *Das Lucasevangelium*, p. 8; Lekebusch, *Apostelgeschichte*, p. 77. Such phrases, *cf.* διὰ στόματός τινος, are thoroughly Hebraistic; so also in iii. 13, Luke iii. 21, κατὰ πρόσωπον, and for other instances, Blass, *Grammatik des N. G.*, pp. 126, 147.—Στοᾷ Σολ., iii. 11.—ἅπαντες, *cf.* ii. 1, including other believers as well as the Apostles, see below. ὁμοθυμαδὸν, see i. 14.

Ver. 13. τῶν δὲ λοιπῶν: variously interpreted (1) of the rest of the believers in contrast to the Apostles, but this is unnatural, as the Apostles are not elsewhere regarded as objects of fear to their fellow-believers, and ἅπαντες above certainly need not = ἀπόστολοι as Hilgenfeld interprets it. See, however, Alford, *in loco*, and Gore, *Church and the Ministry*, p. 256, note. J. Lightfoot applies ἅπαντες to the hundred-and-eight (the Apostles making up the hundred-and-twenty), who durst not join themselves

ἀλλ' ἐμεγάλυνεν αὐτοὺς ὁ λαός · 14. μᾶλλον δὲ προσετίθεντο
πιστεύοντες τῷ Κυρίῳ, πλήθη ἀνδρῶν τε καὶ γυναικῶν ·) 15. ὥστε
κατὰ ¹ τὰς πλατείας ἐκφέρειν τοὺς ἀσθενεῖς καὶ τιθέναι ἐπὶ κλινῶν
καὶ κραββάτων, ἵνα ἐρχομένου Πέτρου κἂν ἡ σκιὰ ἐπισκιάσῃ τινὶ

---

¹ κατα (τας) D*P 1, Chrys., Theoph., so Meyer ; και εις τας ℵABD²(E), Tisch.,
W.H., R.V., Weiss, Wendt. κλινων EP, Chrys., Theodrt. ; κλιναριων ℵABD,
Cyr.-Jer., so Tisch., W.H., R.V., Weiss, Wendt, Hilg. κραββατων B³EP ; κραβαττων
ℵAB*D, so W.H., Weiss, Hilg. ; but see Blass, *Grammatik*, p. 12, who reads in β,
κραβατος (*grabatus*), and Winer-Schmiedel, p. 56. επισκιαση ℵADEP, so Tisch.
(W.H. alt.), Weiss, Hilg. ; επισκιασει B 13, 31, W.H. following B, Wendt (probable).
At end of verse D, Par. (Gig.¹, Wern.) add απηλλασσοντο γαρ απο πασης ασθενειας
ην ειχε εκαστος αυτων, whilst E (Vulg., Lucif.) adds και ρυσθωσιν απο πασης ασθενειας ης ειχον. Variations between D and E may be due to retranslation from
Latin, see Harris ; Chase from assim. of Acts xix. 12, through Syriac ; an explanatory
addition of the result of Peter's shadow falling upon them according to Weiss, Codex
D, p. 64 ; but Belser sees in vv. 15 and 16 in β original, revised in α.

in the dignity and office of Apostleship,
properly so called, having seen the judgment that one of the Twelve had brought
upon Ananias, one of their own number
(as Lightfoot ranks Ananias amongst the
hundred-and-twenty) ; (2) of non-believers as contrasted with ἅπαντες ; this is
adopted by Blass, but it obliges him to
translate κολλᾶσθαι, *se eis immiscere =
interpellare, vexare*, whereas the word is
more often used, as he admits, both in the
Acts and in the LXX of friendly intercourse דבק, Deut. x. 20, 2 Sam. xx.
2, 2 Kings xviii. 6, Ps. cxviii. (cxix.) 31, *cf.*
Acts viii. 29, ix. 26, x. 28, xvii. 34 ; (3) of
the rest including ὁ λαός, who stood
aloof from joining their lot, but at the
same time regarded them with respect ;
(4) of the rest, *i.e.*, rulers, scribes, priests,
men of position, as contrasted, ἀλλά, with
the λαός, the populace, *cf.* iv. 21, where
the same contrast is marked (so Hort,
Page, Rendall), see also Luke xxi. 38.
For κολλᾶσθαι see further on ver. 36.

Ver. 14. μᾶλλον δὲ προσετίθεντο : the
favour of the people which still protected
the Church (*cf.* ver. 17) resulted in further
increase of believers, "were the more
added," *um so mehr ;* imperfect, signifying
the continuous growth of the Church ; on
the verb see ii. 41. πλήθη, plural (only
here in N.T.), because not only men as
in iv. 4, but women also (Weiss), but
Bengel "pluralis grandis : jam non initur
numerus, uti 4, 4," to the same effect
Blass, "saepe fiebat ut magnus numerus
accederet, inde plur. hic tantum N.T.".
On St. Luke's characteristic fondness
for this and similar words see iv. 32.
γυναικῶν : this mention of women forms
as it were an introduction to the further

mention in vi. 1 ff., *cf.* viii. 3, where
women are again mentioned amongst the
victims in the general persecution of the
Church (see Plumptre's note, *in loco*).
This constant reference to the share of
women in the ministry of the Gospel and
the life of the Church is characteristic of
St. Luke in both his writings.

Ver. 15. ὥστε καὶ εἰς, "insomuch
that they even," R.V.—κατά, T.R., so
Alford, Meyer, "all down the streets,"
as if the streets were entirely beset with
sick folk (see Holtzmann, *in loco*).—
πλατείας, feminine of the adjective
πλατύς, *sc.*, ὁδός, a broad way, so here,
the open streets, in classical Greek, and
frequently in LXX, chiefly for Hebrew,
רחב, Tobit xiii. 17, Judith i. 14, vii.
14, 22, 1 Macc. i. 55, ii. 9, 3 Macc. i. 18,
used by St. Luke three times in his
Gospel, x. 10, xiii. 26, xiv. 21, but only
here in Acts, see below on ix. 11.
For κλινῶν read κλιναρίων, which is found
only here in N.T., not at all in LXX,
and very rarely in other Greek authors,
Aristoph., *Frag.*, 33, d, and Arrian,
Epict. Diss., iii., 5, 13, where it is used
for the couch of a sick person ; Artem.,
Oneir., ii., 57. As Dr. Hobart points
out, St. Luke employs no less than four
different words for the beds of the sick,
two in common with the other Evangelists, *viz.*, κλίνη (not in John), and κρά-
βαττος (not in Matthew). But two are
peculiar to him, *viz.*, κλινίδιον (Luke v.
19, 24), and κλινάριον only here.
Neither word is found in the LXX, but
κλινίδιον, although rare elsewhere, is
used in Artem., also in Plutarch, and
Dion. Hal. (*Antiq. Rom.*, vii., 68), for a
litter for carrying the sick, Hobart, *Medical*

αὐτῶν. 16. συνήρχετο δὲ καὶ τὸ πλῆθος τῶν πέριξ πόλεων εἰς
Ἰερουσαλήμ, φέροντες ἀσθενεῖς καὶ ὀχλουμένους ὑπὸ πνευμάτων
ἀκαθάρτων, οἵτινες ἐθεραπεύοντο ἅπαντες.[1]

[1] εἰς DEP demid., Arm., Chrys., so Meyer; om. ℵAB vers., so Tisch., W.H.,
R.V., Weiss, Wendt. οιτινες εθεραπευοντο απαντες, D, Par. (Gig., Lucif.) read και
ιωντο παντες; both verbs almost equally common. At end of verse "duo codices
Bergeri" add *et magnificabant Dominum J. C.*, added by Blass in β (Greek); *cf.*
Acts xix. 17.

Language, etc., pp. 116, 117. Dr. Kennedy
sees in κλινίδιον an instance of rare
words used by the comic poets, especially Aristophanes, found also in the
N.T., and almost nowhere else, and
hence a proof of the "colloquial" language of the N.T. writers (*Sources of
N. T. Greek*, pp. 76-79). But the fact remains that the word in question is found
only in St. Luke, and that both it and
κλινάριον were employed for the couch
of a sick person.—ἐρχομένου Πέτρου,
genitive absolute, "as Peter came by,"
R.V. (very frequent in Luke), it does
not mean, as Felten admits, that none
of the other Apostles possessed such
powers.—κἄν = καὶ ἐάν—even if it
were only his shadow, "at the least his
shadow," R.V., *cf.* Mark v. 28, vi. 56, 2
Cor. xi. 16; the usage is not unclassical,
Soph., *Elect.*, 1483; Simcox, *Language
of the N. T.*, p. 170; Viteau, *Le Grec du
N. T.*, p. 118 (1893).—ἐπισκιάσῃ with
dative, Luke i. 35, Mark ix. 7; B so W.H.,
future indicative σει, a construction common with ὅπως in classical Greek (Page);
for other examples of the future indicative
with ἵνα see Viteau, *Le Grec du N. T.*, p.
81 (1893), of which several are found
in the N.T., although not in classical
Greek; *cf.* Luke xiv. 10, xx. 10, 1 Cor.
ix. 18, 1 Pet. iii. 1, Acts xxi. 24, W.H.;
John vii. 3, Gal. ii. 4, etc.; Burton,
u. s., p. 86. Undoubtedly this action of
the people showed the lively power of
their faith (Chrys., Theod., Aug.), but
the further question arises in spite of the
severe strictures of Zeller, Overbeck,
Holtzmann, as to how far the narrative
indicates that the shadow of Peter actually produced the healing effects. Ver.
16 shows that the sick folk were all
healed, but Zöckler maintains that there
is nothing to show that St. Luke endorses
the enthusiastic superstition of the people
(so J. Lightfoot, Nösgen, Lechler, Rendall). On the other hand we may compare Matt. ix. 20, Mark vi. 56, John ix. 5,
Acts xix. 12; and Baumgarten's comment
should be considered that, although it is
not actually said that a miraculous

power went forth from Peter's shadow,
it is a question why, if no such power is
implied, the words should be introduced
at all into a narrative which evidently
purports to note the extraordinary
powers of the Apostles. The parallels
just instanced from the Gospels could, of
course, have no weight with critics who
can only see in such comparisons a
proof that the Acts cannot rise above the
superstitious level of the Gospels, or who
start like Renan with "an absolute rule
of criticism," *viz.*, the denial of a place in
history to all miraculous narratives. β
adds ἀπηλλάσσοντο γὰρ κ.τ.λ.: but
even here, as Blass says, Luke does not
distinctly assert that cures were wrought
by the shadow of Peter, although there
is no reason to deny that the Evangelist
had this in mind, since he does not hesitate to refer the same miraculous powers
to St. Paul. Hilgenfeld refers vv. 14-16
to his "author to Theophilus," and sees
in the expressions used in ver. 16 a reminiscence of Luke vi. 17.

Ver. 16. δὲ καὶ: very common in
St. Luke, Luke ii. 4, iii. 9, v. 10, ix. 61,
xiv. 12, etc., and also nine times in Acts.
St. John uses it frequently, but seldom
in Matt. and Mark; used for the sake
of giving emphasis.—πέριξ only here,
strengthened for περί, not in LXX, but
see Hatch and Redpath, found in *Acta
Andr. et Matth. Apocr.*, 26 (see Lumby's
note), in classics from Æschylus.—
τῶν π. πόλεων, "the cities round about
Jerusalem," omitting εἰς before Ἰερουσ.
—ὀχλουμένους: only here in N.T., *cf.*
Luke vi. 18, οἱ ἐνοχλούμενοι (W.H.,
R.V.) ὑπὸ πν. ἀκαθ. Both verbs are
peculiar to St. Luke in the N.T. in connection with disease (ἐνοχλεῖν is used in
Heb. xii. 15 in a different sense), and
both were often used by medical writers.
In Tobit vi. 8, ὀχλῇ the simple verb is
used of the vexing and disturbing of an
evil spirit, and ἐνοχλεῖν is used several
times in the LXX, of being troubled with
sicknesses, Gen. xlviii. 1, 1 Sam. xix. 14,
xxx. 13, Mal. i. 13. So J. Weiss, who is
by no means inclined to overrate Dr.

17. Ἀναστὰς[1] δὲ ὁ ἀρχιερεὺς καὶ πάντες οἱ σὺν αὐτῷ, ἡ οὖσα αἵρεσις τῶν Σαδδουκαίων, ἐπλήσθησαν ζήλου, 18. καὶ ἐπέβαλον τὰς χεῖρας αὐτῶν ἐπὶ τοὺς ἀποστόλους, καὶ ἔθεντο αὐτοὺς ἐν τηρήσει

[1] αναστας, Par. reads Αννας, "cod. Dubl. ap. Berger" (Blass); so also Prov. after αναστ. δε—Blass follows Par. in β. αναστας is no doubt a very common word, but it is quite characteristic of St. Luke. Western reading may have possessed the true text, cf. iii. 6, but if Αννας is original then αναστας is a corruption, not a revision.

Hobart's work, regards the use of the two verbs just mentioned as the employment in St. Luke of technical medical terms, *Evangelium des Lukas*, pp. 273, 274 (1892); found in Hipp., Galen, Dioscorides, cf. in the latter, *Mat. Med.*, iii., 116, τοὺς ὑπὸ ξηρᾶς βηχὸς καὶ ὀρθοπνοίας ὀχλουμένους θεραπεύει, see also Luke vi. 19, viii. 46, for a like effect following on the manifestation of the miraculous powers of Christ.

Ver. 17. ἀναστὰς, see on i. 15, cf. vi. 9: it may denote a hostile intention (but need not force this), Mark iii. 26, Luke x. 35, Matt. xii. 41, in LXX, Job xvi. 8; see Overbeck, Blass, Weiss; ὁ ἀρχ., i.e., Annas not Caiaphas, iv. 6.— πάντες οἱ σὺν αὐτῷ: the context seems to imply that more are included than referred to in iv. 6.—ἡ οὖσα αἵρεσις(= οἱ εἰσιν αἵρεσις), a rare employment of the relative in the N.T., but found in Luke and Paul, most of all in the latter; cf. Acts xvi. 12, 1 Cor. iii. 17, Gal. iii. 16, Ephes. iii. 13, vi. 2, Phil. i. 28, etc. (cf. Rev. iv. 5, v. 9); Viteau, *Le Grec du N. T.*, p. 192 (1896).—αἵρεσις: (1) a choosing, choice, so in classical writers, cf. also LXX, Lev. xxii. 18, 21, 1 Macc. viii. 30; (2) that which is chosen, a chosen method of thought and action; (3) later, a philosophic principle; those who have chosen certain principles, a school, a sect, so six times in Acts. It is used thrice elsewhere in N.T., 1 Cor. xi. 29, Gal. v. 20, 2 Pet. ii. 1 in the plural, of factions or parties *within* the Church; in its later ecclesiastical use, applied to doctrines, "heresies," which tended to cause separation from the Church. The word need not therefore be used in a bad sense, although it is so used of the Nazarenes, cf. xxiv. 5, 14, xxviii. 22, whilst on the other hand St. Paul uses it of the Pharisees xxvi. 5 (cf. xv. 5), in no depreciatory sense (cf. its use by Josephus of the Sadducees, *Ant.*, xx., 9, 1). Lumby gives a disparaging use of the word in *Apocr. Act. Phil. in Hellad.*, 10, see his note. It is not expressly said by St. Luke that Annas was a Sadducee, although he seems to imply it. But this

is not in itself inconceivable (see iv. 1) in spite of the strictures of Zeller and Overbeck; Josephus distinctly says, *u. s.*, that the son of Annas who bore his father's name was of the sect of the Sadducees, and if he mentions this as something peculiar, and as showing why the younger Annas was so bold and insolent (Zeller, cf. Nösgen's note, *in loco*), yet there is no difficulty in supposing that the elder Annas was at least associated with the Sadducees if only for political reasons.—ζήλου: jealousy, R.V., so rightly A.V. in xiii. 45; Wycliffe "envy," cf. Rom. xiii. 13, 1 Cor. iii. 3, 2 Cor. xi. 2, Gal. v. 20, James iii. 14, 16, Clem. Rom., *Cor.*, iii., 4 and iv.-vi. (cf. Numb. xxv. 10, 11, 1 Macc. viii. 16, οὐκ ἐστι φθόνος οὐδὲ ζῆλος ἐν αὐτοῖς, and ii. 54, 58, *Psalms of Solomon*, ii., 27), and in some places of the jealousy which God has, as in 2 Cor. xi. 2, Numb. xxv. 10, 11, and cf. *Psalms of Solomon*, i., 27, iv., 2, 1 Macc. ii. 54. But φθόνος is capable only of an evil signification. By Aristotle ζῆλος is used in its nobler sense (*Rhet.*, ii., 11), as opposed to τὸ φθονεῖν, but it seems to be used by other writers as = φθόνος or coupled with it. The meaning is defined by the context. Trench, *N. T. Synonyms*, i., 99. Here the envy and jealousy of the Sanhedrim was provoked by the popular favour shown to the disciples, and hence to their doctrine of the resurrection.

Ver. 18. ἐπέβαλον τὰς χεῖρας: a phrase used twice in St. Luke's Gospel, and three times in the Acts, cf. Gen. xxii. 12. Cf. Hebrew שָׁלַח יָד אֶל. —ἐν τηρήσει δημοσίᾳ, "in public ward," R.V. δημ. used here as an adjective, only found in N.T. in Acts, in the three other passages used as an adverb, xvi. 37, xviii. 28, xx. 20 (2 Macc. vi. 10, 3 Macc. ii. 2), cf. Thuc., v., 18, where τὸ δημόσιον = the public prison. See note above on iv. 3. Hilgenfeld is so far right in pointing out that the two imprisonments, iv. 3 and v. 18, are occasioned by two different causes, in the first case by the preaching of the Apostles

δημοσίᾳ.[1] 19. ἄγγελος δὲ Κυρίου διὰ τῆς νυκτὸς ἤνοιξε τὰς θύρας τῆς φυλακῆς, ἐξαγαγών τε αὐτοὺς εἶπε, 20. Πορεύεσθε, καὶ σταθέντες

[1] αυτων om. אABD 15, Vulg., Syr. Pesh., Arm., Lucif., so Tisch., W.H., R.V., Weiss, Wendt; but retained by EP, verss., Bas., Chrys., Meyer. At end of verse D adds και επορευθη εις εκαστος εις τα ιδια, so Hilg.; cf. John vii. 55; see Harris and Chase, who both think that the gloss comes from John, l. c., but the resemblance is not verbal. εις τα ιδια is characteristic of St. John, but it is also found in Acts xxi. 6.

to the people, and in the second by the reverence which their miracles gained from the people.

Ver. 19. ἄγγελος δὲ K.: the narrative must be accepted or rejected as it stands. As Wendt, following Zeller in earlier days, candidly admits, every attempt to explain the narrative by referring the release of the prisoners to some natural event, such as an earthquake or lightning, or to some friendly disposed person, who with the assistance of the gaoler opened the prison doors, and who was mistaken by the Apostles for an angel in the darkness and excitement of the night, is shattered at once against the plain meaning of the text. Nor can it be deemed satisfactory to believe that St. Luke has unconsciously given us two narratives of the liberation of St. Peter, here and in xii., and that the former is merely an echo of the later deliverance transferred to an earlier date (Weiss, Sorof, Holtzmann). But St. Luke had the best means of knowing accurately the events narrated in xii. from John Mark (see below on chap. xii., and Ramsay, St. Paul, etc., p. 385), Introd., p. 17, and there is no ground whatever for supposing that xii. is simply an embellished version of this former incident. Attempts have been made to show that St. Luke introduces the same doubling of narratives in his Gospel (Wendt, Holtzmann), e.g., the sending forth of the disciples in ix. 3 and x. 1, but the former chapter is concerned with the mission of the Twelve, and the latter with that of the Seventy. Further objections have been made as to the uselessness of the miracle—the disciples are found, to be imprisoned again! But not only was the miracle a source of fresh strength and faith to the disciples, but—as Hilgenfeld notes—their release can scarcely be described as purposeless, since it called forth a public transgression of the command of silence imposed upon the two chief Apostles, iv. 17-21. Moreover, the deliverance was another indication to the Sadducees, if they would have accepted it, that it was useless for them to attempt to stay the movement. "Quis ergo usus

angeli?" asks Blass; and he answers: "Sed est aliquis: augetur enim apostolorum audacia (21), tum ira adversariorum magis accenditur; nihilominus Deus suos perire non patitur". That the Sadducees should ignore the miracle (ver. 28) is surely not strange, although it may well have influenced their subsequent deliberations; that the action of the Sadducees should now be more coercive than on the former occasion was only natural on the part of men who feared that vengeance would be taken on them for the death of Jesus by an uprising of the people (vv. 28 and 26).—διὰ νυκτὸς = νυκτός, νύκτωρ (cf. Luke ii. 8) in classical Greek. The phrase is used four times by St. Luke in Acts, cf. xvi. 19, xvii. 10, xxiii. 31, and cf. Luke v. 5 (and ix. 37, D, διὰ τῆς ἡμέρας): nowhere else in N.T. In all the passages Meyer thinks that the expression means throughout the night, but such a meaning would be inconsistent with the context at all events here and in xvi. 19; and xvii. 10 is doubtful.—See Blass, Grammatik des N. G., p. 129, "by night" (nachts). Simcox speaks of this expression in Acts as an "almost adverbial phrase," Language of N. T., p. 140.

Ver. 20. Πορεύεσθε: characteristic of St. Luke both in Gospel and Acts. The word appears here in Acts for the first time, and it is found in St. Luke's Gospel about fifty times, and in this book nearly forty (Friedrich, Lekebusch).—σταθέντες, ii. 14, on this pictorial use of the word, see Page's note, and Friedrich, Das Lucasevangelium, p. 42; so also ἀναστάς, ἐπιστάς, ἐγερθείς, καθίσας, στραφείς—here it intimates the boldness with which the Apostles were to proclaim their message.—ἐν τῷ ἱερῷ: they were to speak not only boldly but publicly.—τῆς ζωῆς ταύτης (cf. xiii. 26, τῆς σωτηρίας ταύτης, and Rom. vii. 24), i.e., the life to which the whole Apostolic preaching referred, the life which the Sadducees denied, bestowed by Him who was Himself the Resurrection and the Life, cf. iii. 15, iv. 12. This or a similar explanation is accepted by Holtzmann,

λαλεῖτε ἐν τῷ ἱερῷ τῷ λαῷ πάντα τὰ ῥήματα τῆς ζωῆς ταύτης. 21.
ἀκούσαντες δὲ εἰσῆλθον ὑπὸ τὸν ὄρθρον εἰς τὸ ἱερόν, καὶ ἐδίδασκον.[1]
παραγενόμενος δὲ ὁ ἀρχιερεὺς καὶ οἱ σὺν αὐτῷ, συνεκάλεσαν[2] τὸ
συνέδριον καὶ πᾶσαν τὴν γερουσίαν τῶν υἱῶν Ἰσραήλ, καὶ ἀπέστειλαν

---

[1] ακουσαντες δε, E, Pesh. read εξελθοντες δε εκ της φυλακης, received by Blass in
β; but cf. xvi. 40; may have been omitted on revision, or added for exactness. After
εδιδασκον Prov., Wern. add εν τω ονοματι Κ. Ι.; cf. iv. 18, ix. 27.

[2] For συνεκαλεσαν D has εγερθεντες το πρωι και συγκαλεσαμενοι (so also Hilg.);
may be addition for sake of clearness, or omitted in revision; assim. to our Lord's trial
and the Jewish authorities seems unnecessary.

Wendt, Weiss, Zöckler, Blass. On the
attempt to explain the words as simply
= these words of life, see Winer-Moulton,
xxxiv. 3, b., and see also Grimm, sub v.
ῥῆμα.
Ver. 21. ὑπὸ τὸν ὄρθρον, "about daybreak," R.V., i.e., without delay they
obeyed the angel's command (Weiss).
The words may also indicate the customary usage of Palestine where the heat
was great in the daytime. The people
rose early and came to our Lord to hear
Him, Luke xxi. 38 (John viii. 2). ὑπὸ
= sub, circa (of time), so in classical
Greek, Blass, Grammatik des N. G., p.
132. The first sacrifice took place in
the Temple very early, Edersheim,
Temple and its Services, p. 132, and it
may be that the Apostles went to catch
the people at the hour of their early
devotions (Plumptre).—ὑπό is used nowhere else in the N.T. with an accusative
in this sense, cf. Tobit vii. 11, S, al; ὑπὸ
τὴν νύκτα, 3 Macc. v. 2.—παραγενόμενος:
having come, i.e., to the place where the
Sadducees met, not merely pleonastic; the
verb may fairly be regarded as character-
istic of St. Luke—it occurs eight times in his Gospel and thirty
in the Acts, and frequently absolutely
as here—elsewhere in N.T. only eight or
nine times, frequent in LXX.—τὸ συνέδριον καὶ πᾶσαν τὴν γερουσίαν: does
γερουσία represent an assembly or body
in addition to the συνέδριον, or do the
two words represent the same Court?
The word γερ. appears nowhere else in
the N.T., but in the LXX it is used in
several places of the Jewish Sanhedrim,
1 Macc. xii. 6, 2 Macc. i. 10, iv. 44, xi.
27, Jud. iv. 8, xiv. 4, xv. 8. In the N.T.
the Sanhedrim is also called πρεσβυ-
τέριον, Luke xxii. 66, Acts xxii. 5. If
the two words denote the same body καί
must be regarded as merely explicative
(so Wendt as against Meyer) to emphasise the solemn importance and representative nature of the assembly (so

Grimm-Thayer to signify the full Sanhedrim sub v. γερ. and so apparently
Blass). If we adopt Rendall's view καί
may still be explicative, but in another
way, specifying the comprehensive character of this meeting as compared with
the hasty and informal gathering in iv.
5, 6 (cf. Kuinoel's view, in loco). The
difficulty has caused others to suggest
that γερ. refers to men of age and experience who were asked to join the
Council as assessors, or to some other
assembly larger than the Sanhedrim and
only summoned on special occasions.
For the former view, Lumby and
Plumptre (see also Page's note) refer
to Mishna, Joma, i., 1, where mention is made of "the chamber of the
assessors," parhedrin = πάρεδροι. Further we may note, Schürer, Jewish People,
div. ii., vol. i., p. 172, E.T., in a note on
this passage points out that as there can
be no doubt as to the identity of the two
conceptions συνέδριον and γερουσία (so
too Zöckler and Weiss, in loco), καί
must be taken as explanatory, or St.
Luke makes a mistake in assuming
that the συνέδριον was of a less comprehensive character than the γερουσία,
"the Sanhedrin and all the elders of the
people together". Schürer prefers the
latter alternative, but the former may
reasonably be maintained not only from
the Greek text but also because St.
Luke's information admittedly derived
from a Jewish-Christian source is not
likely to have been inaccurate. Hilgenfeld agrees with Weiss that in the source
the O.T. expression γερουσία, Exod. iii.
16, iv. 29, xii. 21, stood alone, but that
the reviser prefixed the usual expression
συνέδριον which in v. 27 and 34 is found
without any addition. On "Synhedrion,"
see Hamburger, Real-Encyclopädie des
Judentums, ii., 8, 1149, and "Aelteste,"
i., 1, pp. 59, 60, and O. Holtzmann,
Neutestamentliche Zeitgeschichte, pp. 175,
176 (1895).—δεσμωτήριον, xvi. 26; Thuc.

εἰς τὸ δεσμωτήριον, ἀχθῆναι αὐτούς. 22. οἱ δὲ ὑπηρέται παραγενόμενοι [1] οὐχ εὗρον αὐτοὺς ἐν τῇ φυλακῇ· ἀναστρέψαντες δὲ
ἀπήγγειλαν, λέγοντες, 23. Ὅτι τὸ μὲν δεσμωτήριον εὕρομεν κεκλεισ-
μένον ἐν πάσῃ ἀσφαλείᾳ, καὶ τοὺς φύλακας ἔξω [2] ἑστῶτας πρὸ τῶν
θυρῶν· ἀνοίξαντες δέ, ἔσω οὐδένα εὕρομεν. 24. ὡς δὲ ἤκουσαν
τοὺς λόγους τούτους ὅ τε ἱερεὺς καὶ ὁ στρατηγὸς [3] τοῦ ἱεροῦ καὶ οἱ
ἀρχιερεῖς, διηπόρουν περὶ αὐτῶν, τί ἂν γένοιτο τοῦτο. 25. παραγενόμενος δέ τις ἀπήγγειλεν αὐτοῖς λέγων, Ὅτι ἰδού, οἱ ἄνδρες οὓς
ἔθεσθε ἐν τῇ φυλακῇ, εἰσὶν ἐν τῷ ἱερῷ ἑστῶτες καὶ διδάσκοντες τὸν

[1] After **παραγενόμενοι** D adds **και ανοιξαντες την φυλακην**, so Par., Vulg., Syr.
H. mg.; cf. ver. 23, assimilation or revision?

[2] **εξω** om. ℵABDEP, Vulg., verss., Chrys., Lucif., so Tisch., W.H., R.V., Weiss,
Wendt, Hilg. **προ** EP, Vulg.-Clem., Boh., Syr. Harcl., Chrys.; **επι** ℵABD, so
"ad" d, e, am. fu. demid., Sah., Syr. Pesh., so Tisch., W.H., R.V., Weiss, Wendt.

[3] **ο τε ιερευς και ο στρατηγος** P 13, 31 (E), so Meyer; **ο τε στρατηγος**, om. **ιερευς
και ο** ℵABD, Vulg., Sah., Boh., Arm., Syr. Pesh., Aeth., so Tisch., W.H., R.V.,
Weiss, Wendt, Alford, Hilg. (other variations in Wendt and Alford).

vi. 60 and LXX, Gen. xxxix. 20-23, xl.
3-5. On the jurisdiction of the Sanhedrim and its right to order arrests by its
own officers, and to dispose of cases not
involving capital punishment, Schürer,
Jewish People, div. ii., vol. i., 187, 188,
E.T., O. Holtzmann, *u. s.*, p. 173.
Ver. 22. ὑπηρέται: apparently some
of the Temple guard, ver. 26; see above
on ὁ στρατηγός, iv. 1, and Edersheim,
Temple and its Services, pp. 119, 120. In
the N.T. the word is not used of the
military.—ἀναστρέψαντες: used only
here in this sense (xv. 16 is not strictly
a parallel), cf. LXX, Gen. viii. 9, 1
Kings xxi. (xx.) 5, and frequently.
Ver. 23. ἐν πάσῃ ἀσφαλείᾳ, "in all
safety," R.V. (not *cum omni diligentia*,
Vulgate); "in omni firmitate," Flor.;
in LXX generally μετά with genitive;
cf. 2 Macc. iii. 22, xv. 1, μετὰ πάσης
ἀσφ. The Vulgate is misleading; the
words mean not that the prison had been
carefully shut, but that it was found in a
state of perfect security.
Ver. 24. ὅ τε ἱερεὺς καὶ ὁ στρατηγὸς
τοῦ ἱεροῦ καὶ οἱ ἀρχ.: if we retain ὁ
ἱερεύς it must mean the high priest, ver.
27, cf. 1 Macc. xv. 1; Jos., *Ant.*, vi.,
12, 1. But Weiss and Wendt both follow W.H. and R.V., and omit ἱερεὺς καὶ
ὁ (so Blass β). ὁ στρατ. and οἱ ἀρχ. are
thus closely united by the τε καὶ, inasmuch
as the former in the flight of the prisoners
had the greatest responsibility, and the
ἀρχ. had occasioned the imprisonment,
ver. 17. The στρατ. τοῦ ἱερ. was pre-

sent at the meetings of the Sanhedrim,
and assisted in their deliberations.—
ἀρχιερεῖς: see on iv. 1. The word is
probably used as including the heads of
the twenty-four courses, those who had
been high priests and still retained the
title, and also those referred to in iv. 6.
Schürer, *Jewish People*, div. ii., vol. i.,
203-206; O. Holtzmann, *Neutestamentliche Zeitgeschichte*, p. 142.—διηπόρουν,
ii. 12, "were much perplexed," R.V.—See
on περὶ αὐτῶν, sc., λόγοι: not the Apostles,
as Alford and Meyer.—τί ἂν γένοιτο
τοῦτο, "whereunto this might grow," so
A. and R.V. Blass interprets *quomodo
hoc factum esse posset*, cf. x. 17; *Grammatik des N. G.*, p. 173. St. Luke alone
uses the optative with ἄν in the N.T.,
cf. Luke i. 62, vi. 11, ix. 46, Acts v. 24,
viii. 31, x. 17, xvii. 18 (Luke xv. 26, xviii.
36, Acts xxvi. 29, doubtful text); Burton,
N. T. Moods and Tenses, pp. 80 and 133;
see also Viteau, *Le Grec du N. T.*, p. 66
(1893).
Ver. 25. ἰδοὺ . . . εἰσὶν: on the
characteristic use of the verb εἶναι after
ἰδοὺ or ἴδε in St. Luke's writings as
compared with other N.T. writers and
the LXX, see Viteau, *Le Grec du N. T.*,
pp. 200, 205 (1896); cf. ii. 7, xvi. 1, and
Luke ii. 25, vii. 25, xi. 41, etc.—παραγεν.,
see on ver. 22.—ἑστῶτες, cf. ver. 20.
antitheton: *posuistis* (Bengel).
Ver. 26. ἤγαγεν: but imperfect with
W.H. and Weiss, so Blass "quia modus
quo res gesta est describitur; perfecta
res indicatur, ver. 27, ἀγαγόντες".—οὐ

λαόν. 26. Τότε ἀπελθὼν ὁ στρατηγὸς σὺν τοῖς ὑπηρέταις, ἤγαγεν αὐτούς, οὐ μετὰ βίας, ἐφοβοῦντο γὰρ τὸν λαόν, ἵνα μὴ λιθασθῶσιν.[1] 27. ἀγαγόντες δὲ αὐτοὺς ἔστησαν ἐν τῷ συνεδρίῳ· καὶ ἐπηρώτησεν αὐτοὺς ὁ ἀρχιερεύς,[2] λέγων, 28. Οὐ[3] παραγγελίᾳ παρηγγείλαμεν ὑμῖν μὴ διδάσκειν ἐπὶ τῷ ὀνόματι τούτῳ; καὶ ἰδού, πεπληρώκατε[4] τὴν Ἱερουσαλὴμ τῆς διδαχῆς ὑμῶν, καὶ βούλεσθε ἐπαγαγεῖν ἐφ' ἡμᾶς τὸ

---

[1] ηγαγεν AEP, Vulg., Chrys., Lucif.; D* ηγαγον; ηγεν ℵBD², so Tisch., W.H., Weiss. εφοβουντο . . . λιθασθωσιν, Flor. om., represents φοβουμενος μηποτε λιθασθη υπο του λαου; D φοβουμενος γαρ. ινα om. ℵBDE 5, 13, 40, 96, so Tisch., W.H., R.V., Wendt, Weiss, Hilg.; but ins. AP, Chr., Theophyl., T.R., Meyer.

[2] αρχιερευς; D, Gig., Par., Lucif. have ιερευς, Flor. praetor = στρατηγος, instead; other additions in Flor., but no difference in sense.

[3] ου ℵ³DEP, Flor., Par., Sah., Syrr. P. and H., Arm., Aeth., Ath., Bas.; but om. ℵ*B 13, Gig., Vulg., Boh., Ath., Cyr., Lucif., so Tisch., W.H., R.V., Weiss, Wendt (who thinks with Alford that it was suggested by επηρωτησεν); Blass retains the negative, so Hilg.

[4] πεπληρωκατε BDEP, Bas., Tisch., Weiss, W.H., Hilg.; επληρωσατε ℵA 15, Chrys., Cyr. In Western text Flor., Pesh. insert υμεις δε instead of και before ιδου, and D*, Flor., Gig., Sah. read εκεινου for τουτου, emphasis.

μετὰ βίας, "but without violence," R.V. Weiss compares with the whole phrase ἤγεν . . . βίας (Exod. xiv. 25); βία three or four times in Acts only, xxi. 35, xxiv. 7 (omit W.H., R.V.), xxvii. 41; used in the LXX in the same sense as here and with the genitive, cf. Exod. xiv. 25 (cf. i. 14), 3 Macc. iv. 7; classical usage more frequently has βίᾳ, ἐκ βίας, etc.—ἐφοβοῦντο γὰρ: the favour of the people which the Apostles so fully enjoyed at this time might well have caused an outbreak of fanaticism as later in the case of Stephen. The subjects to ἐφοβ. and to ἔστησαν (27) are ὁ στρατ. and οἱ ὑπηρέται. St. Chrysostom well comments on those who would thus fear — not God, but the people. On the Greek of the verse, see Viteau, Le Grec du N.T., p. 116 (1896).—ἵνα μὴ λιθασθῶσιν: the reading μὴ undoubtedly correct, so W.H., Wendt, Weiss, Blass.—τὸν λαόν: denoting the persons feared, and μὴ λιθασ., the thing feared, so that the meaning is as in R.V., "for they were afraid that they should be stoned by the people," or ἐφοβοῦντο γὰρ τὸν λαὸν may be taken as parenthetical (so Weiss), and μὴ λιθασ. as limiting ἤγεν . . . βίας. In the N.T. after verbs of fearing the subjunctive only is used where after secondary tenses we should have expected the optative, or sometimes the subjunctive is explained as implying more certainty of a result. Burton, N.T. Moods and Tenses, pp. 95, 96.—λιθασ.: very seldom in Attic Greek,

where we should expect καταλεύειν; only twice in LXX, 2 Sam. xvi. 6, 13, where usually λιθοβολέω (not used in classical writers, but six or seven times in N.T.); but λιθάζειν is found eight or nine times in N.T.

Ver. 27. ἔστησαν, cf. iv. 7, during the investigation the judges would sit, vi. 15, xxiii. 3, the accused, the witnesses, and those speaking, stood, Mark xiv. 57, 60, Acts iv. 7, v. 27, 34, vi. 13, xxiii. 9, O. Holtzmann, Neutestamentliche Zeitgeschichte, p. 177.

Ver. 28. παραγγελίᾳ παρηγγείλαμεν: for the Hebraism cf. iv. 17, "we straitly," etc., R.V. (and A.V.), expressing intensity — "commanding, we commanded you," Wycliffe. The T.R. makes the clause a question, commencing with οὐ, but the evidence is too strong against it, evidently it was occasioned by the ἐπηρώτησεν, but St. Chrysostom adopts it, see Hom., xiii., 1. Bengel remarks on παραγγελίᾳ, "pudet dicere minando, iv. 17, nam non poterant punire". But St. Chrysostom rightly notes that they ought to have asked πῶς ἐξήλθετε, i.e., from the prison, but they ask as if nothing had happened. —ἐπὶ τῷ ὀνόματι τούτῳ, iv. 17, here as there the Council do not mention the name of Jesus, perhaps because they disdained it; in sharp contrast stands not only St. Peter's mention of the name, but his glorying in it, ver. 30, 31.—τὴν Ἱερουσαλήμ: fem. here and elsewhere, cf. Gal. iv. 25, Rev. iii. 12, so in Matt.

αἷμα τοῦ ἀνθρώπου τούτου. 29.[1] ἀποκριθεὶς δὲ ὁ Πέτρος καὶ οἱ ἀπόστολοι εἶπον, Πειθαρχεῖν δεῖ Θεῷ μᾶλλον ἢ ἀνθρώποις. 30. ὁ Θεὸς τῶν πατέρων ἡμῶν ἤγειρεν Ἰησοῦν, ὃν ὑμεῖς διεχειρίσασθε

[1] ο Π., article om. אABEHP, Bas., Chrys., so W.H., Weiss; ειπον, but -αν אABE, so Tisch., W.H., Weiss. At the commencement of the verse αποκ. . . . προς αυτον is omitted in D, and the words πειθαρχειν δει (δε in D) follow as part of the high priest's remarks; but Blass in β, following Flor., Gig., Lucif., adds to αποκ. δε Πετρος the words ειπεν προς αυτον, and proceeds "τινι πειθαρχειν δει Θεω η ανθρωποις;" making these words a question asked by Peter of the high priest, who replies, according to a further addition of Flor., Gig., ο δε ειπεν "Θεω". Weiss, Codex D, p. 64, thinks that the emendator took offence at the repetition of iv. 19, and thereupon places the words πειθαρχειν δε (not δει) κ.τ.λ. on the lips of the high priest as if he thus took up their own words contemptuously in addressing the Apostles, and the whole from βουλεσθε might thus originally have formed a question: "You wish to bring this man's blood upon us—but thus, indeed, to obey God rather than man? Such blood revenge cannot surely be the command of God;" but see further Blass, in loco, and Weiss, u. s. D, Flor., Gig. all add at the end of ver. 29, as introductory to ver. 30, ο δε Πετρος ειπεν προς αυτους.

ii. 3, Blass, *Grammatik des N. G.*, p. 32; Winer-Schmiedel, p. 153.—διδαχῆς, "teaching," R.V., *cf.* Matt. vii. 28.— βούλεσθε: the charge was untrue—the wish was their own, not that of the Apostles, *cf.* Matt. xxvii. 25. St. Peter's earnest desire was that they should be saved.—ἐπαγαγεῖν, xviii. 6, xxii. 20, and 2 Sam. i. 16, *cf.* 2 Peter ii. 1, 5; nowhere else in N.T.—ἐφ' ἡμᾶς: to bring His blood upon us, *i.e.*, the vengeance of the people for His murder. αἷμα pro φόνον, Hebraistic—no thought of divine punishment from their point of view; *cf.* LXX. Gen. xx. 9, Exod. xxxii. 34, Judges ix. 24, and *cf.* Josh. xxiii. 15 (in N.T., Matt. xxiii. 35, Rev. xviii. 24). Ver. 29. St. Peter as the spokesman, *primus inter pares;* the Apostles as a body are associated with him in his answer: "but Peter and the Apostles," R.V. A.V. renders "Peter and the other Apostles," and we may understand an ellipse of ἄλλοι or λοιποί before οἱ ἀπόστολοι, Blass, *Grammatik des N. G.*, p. 286.—ἀποκ., *cf.* Viteau, *Le Grec du N. T.*, p. 112 (1896).—πειθαρχεῖν: only used by St. Luke and St. Paul; *cf.* ver. 32, xxvii. 21, Titus iii. 1; in this chapter and in St. Paul, in its classical use, obeying one in authority, or τοῖς νόμοις, etc. The word is used in Polybius, and Josephus, and frequently in Philo, but only three times in the LXX; *cf.* 1 Esd. viii. 94, of obeying the law of the Lord. The reply of St. Peter, who speaks for all the Apostles, is practically the same as in iv. 19, but still more decisive in its tone as was natural after the recent command, ver. 20.

Ver. 30. ὁ Θεὸς τῶν πατέρων ἡμῶν, *cf.* iii. 13. St. Peter, as before, will not dissociate himself from the commonwealth of Israel, or his hearers from the message and works of the Christ.— ἤγειρεν: does this word refer to the Resurrection, or to the sending of Jesus into this world, and His raising up by God as the Messiah? The former is the view taken by St. Chrysostom, Oecumenius, Erasmus, and amongst moderns by Meyer-Wendt, Nösgen, Alford, Overbeck, Felten, Blass, Holtzmann, Weiss, Hilgenfeld; but in iii. 15, iv. 10, the phrase is ἤγειρεν ἐκ νεκρῶν (*cf.* Ecclesiast. xlviii. 5: ὁ ἐγείρας νεκρὸν ἐκ θανάτου), although in x. 40, xiii. 37, the word evidently refers to the Resurrection. Others interpret the word as ἀνίστημι in iii. 22, and as in xiii. 22, ἤγειρεν αὐτοῖς τὸν Δαυείδ (*cf.* Luke i. 69, vii. 16), so Calvin, Bengel, De Wette, Lechler, Hackett, Page. One of the chief arguments for the former interpretation is the contrast marked in the next clause between the death of the Cross and the Resurrection, but this contrast would still be marked by the following verb. Is it not possible that, as in the days of old God had raised up a Saviour, or Saviours, for Israel, *cf.* Jud. ii. 18, ἤγειρε Κ. αὐτοῖς κριτάς, Jud. iii. 9, 15, ἤγειρε Κ. σωτῆρα τῷ Ἰ., St. Peter may now speak of Him as raising up Ἰησοῦς, *i.e.*, a Saviour? see further, ver. 31.—διεχειρίσασθε, *cf.* xxvi. 21, "whom ye slew, hanging Him on a tree," R.V., not as in A.V., "whom ye slew and hanged on a tree," which would make the words refer to a Jewish mode of punishment, for, according to Jewish

κρεμάσαντες ἐπὶ ξύλου· 31. τοῦτον ὁ Θεὸς ἀρχηγὸν καὶ σωτῆρα
ὕψωσε τῇ δεξιᾷ αὐτοῦ, δοῦναι μετάνοιαν τῷ Ἰσραὴλ καὶ ἄφεσιν
ἁμαρτιῶν. 32. καὶ ἡμεῖς ἐσμεν αὐτοῦ μάρτυρες[1] τῶν ῥημάτων
τούτων, καὶ τὸ Πνεῦμα δὲ τὸ Ἅγιον, ὃ ἔδωκεν ὁ Θεὸς τοῖς πειθαρχοῦσιν αὐτῷ.

[1] εσμεν αυτου μαρτυρες D²EHP, Syr. Harcl., Aeth., Chrys; εσμεν μαρτ., om. αυτου
ℵD*, Vulg., Sah., Boh., Arm., Did., Chrys., so Tisch., W.H. text, R.V. text, Hilg.;
εν αυτω μαρτ., so B, W.H. marg., Wendt (crit. note, p. 141) om. εσμεν αυτου; εσμεν
εν αυτω μαρτ. R.V. marg.; εσμεν αυτω μαρτυρες Weiss, see comment. δε D²EHP,
Syr. Harcl., Chrys.; om. ℵABD* 31, Did. Chrys., so Vulg., d, Syr. Pesh., Arm.,
Aeth., Irint., so Tisch., W.H., R.V., Weiss, Wendt. After μαρτυρες D, Flor., Par.
add παντων; Par. omits των ρηματων, Blass brackets in β. ο ℵAD²HP, so Weiss;
om. B 17, Ægypt., so W.H. marg., R.V. marg.; ον DE—Harris refers to Latin *quem*,
but if article originally omitted possibly the ον of αγιον may have been repeated, and
= an after-correction.

law, only those were hanged who were
already dead (Deut. xxi. 22, Josh. x. 26).
The word which means in middle to lay
hands upon, and so to slay, to kill, is only
used by St. Luke (not in LXX), and forcibly represents the guilt of the Jews in
the murder of Jesus, as if they had perpetrated it with their own hands (*cf.*
xxvi. 24), "made away with violently,"
Page; *cf.* instances in Wetstein (*truci-
dastis*).—κρεμάσαντες ἐπὶ ξύλου, LXX,
Gen. xl. 19, Deut. xxi. 22, 23, Josh. x.
26, Esth. v. 14, vi. 4 (Gal. iii. 13). Although St. Luke uses κρεμασθείς of
crucifixion, Luke xxiii. 39, St. Peter
alone uses the exact phrase of the text
given in x. 39, and so he too has ξύλον,
1 Pet. ii. 24, for the Cross (although St.
Paul uses the same word, Acts xiii. 29).
The word may therefore have a place
amongst the many coincidences between
St. Peter's addresses and the language
of his Epistles, see above on pp. 121 ff.
The fact that their victim was thus accursed in the eyes of the law aggravated
their guilt, and at the same sharply contrasted their act and that of God; for a
similar contrast see iii. 14, 15.

Ver. 31. ἀρχηγὸν καὶ σωτῆρα: the
former word as it is used here without
any qualification, *cf.* iii. 15, may imply,
like σωτῆρα, a reference to the earlier
days of Israel's history, when God raised
up for them from time to time judges of
whom the title ἀρχηγός, Jud. xi. 6, 11,
might be used no less than σωτήρ. In
Jesus of Nazareth, the Christ, St. Peter
saw the true Leader and Saviour. For
St. Peter no less than for St. Paul the
ascended Jesus had led captivity captive
and received gifts for men, *cf.* Luke
xxiv. 47-49.—ὕψωσεν τῇ δεξιᾷ αὐτοῦ, *cf.*
ii. 33: "exalt with his right hand," R.V.,

"at" margin. Here as elsewhere Briggs
interprets τῇ δεξιᾷ as local not instrumental, and prefers R.V. margin, *Messiah
of the Apostles*, p. 37, note; but see note
on ii. 33 above. The verb is used also
by St. John, iii. 14, viii. 28, xii. 32, and
also by St. Paul, Phil. ii. 9 (see Westcott on St. John iii. 14). But in the passive (as twice in St. John) it is employed
in the LXX of the high exaltation of the
Servant of God, in the picture which
had evidently passed before the eyes
of St. Peter, Isaiah lii. 13; and he sees in
the ascension of his Lord, and His spiritual sovereignty, a fulfilment of the prophecy of the suffering Servant, who is
also a Prince and a Saviour.

Ver. 32. "And we are witnesses of
these things," R.V. (W.H.), but in margin, "witnesses in Him," ἐν αὐτῷ (*cf.*
Luke xxiv. 47); "nos in eo testes sumus,"
Iren., see also above critical notes.
For an explanation of the reading in
T.R. and the two genitives, see Simcox,
Language of the N. T., p. 84, note, and
compare 2 Cor. v. 1, Phil. ii. 30, 1 Thess.
i. 3.—ῥημάτων: here = Hebrew דָּבָר, *cf.*
x. 37 (Grotius, Blass), the words standing
for their contents, *i.e.*, the things, the
facts. Meyer understood the facts to be
the Resurrection and Ascension of Jesus,
but Wendt understands them to be the
gifts of the Messianic salvation mentioned
in ver. 31, and compares ver. 20. But the
use of the word in ver. 20 need not limit
its use here: the Apostles were called
above all things to witness to the facts of
Christ's life, x. 37, and the ζωή in ver. 20
depended upon the Resurrection. In Luke
i. 37 R.V. has "no word," ῥῆμα, where
A.V. has "no thing," *cf.* Luke i. 65,
where A.V. has "things" in the margin

33. Οἱ δὲ ἀκούσαντες διεπρίοντο, καὶ ἐβουλεύοντο ἀνελεῖν αὐτούς.

34. ἀναστὰς δέ τις ἐν τῷ συνεδρίῳ [1] Φαρισαῖος, ὀνόματι Γαμαλιήλ,

[1] ἐν τῷ συνεδρίῳ; DE, Flor., Par. read (τις) εκ του συνεδριου, E adds αυτων.

(ῥήματα), and R.V. reads "sayings" in text: Luke ii. 15, where R.V. has "this thing" (ῥῆμα) in the text, and "saying" in margin; in ii. 19, 51, R.V. has "sayings" in the text, "things" in the margin —so in LXX, the same uncertainty, cf. Gen. xv. 1, xviii. 14, Exod. ii. 14, 15. ῥῆμα is used frequently by St. Luke in his writings, and much more so than by the other Evangelists; although it is found in all parts of the Acts, it is noticeable that it is employed more frequently in the earlier chapters, as in the first two chapters of the Gospel.—καὶ τὸ πνεῦμα τὸ ἅγιον δὲ: on the expression see iv. 8. The Holy Ghost συμμαρτυρεῖ with the Apostles, Rom. viii. 16 (cf. Acts xv. 28). We may well compare with these words of St. Luke our Lord's parting words in John xv. 26, 27. Here we have also the twofold witness—the historical witness borne to the facts—and the internal witness of the Holy Ghost in bringing home to men's hearts the meaning of the facts (see Westcott on St. John, in loco).— τοῖς πειθαρχοῦσιν αὐτῷ: not to be limited to the Apostles, although by repeating this verb used at the opening of the speech St. Peter intimates that the ὑπακοὴ τῆς πίστεως (Rom. i. 5) was the first requisite for the reception of the divine gift. In their own case the witness of the Spirit had been clearly shown, not only in the miracles which the Apostles had done, but also in the results of their preaching, in the enthusiasm of their charity, and we need not limit with Nösgen the thought of the gift of the Holy Spirit to the events of Pentecost. If this short speech of St. Peter, 29-32, reads like a summary of much which he is represented as saying on former occasions, we have no warrant for dismissing it as unhistorical, or even for supposing that St. Luke has only given us a summary of the address. It is rather "a perfect model of concise and ready eloquence," and a striking fulfilment of the Lord's promise, Matt. xi. 19. Nothing was more natural than that St. Peter and his fellow-Apostles, like men whose minds were finally made up, should thus content themselves with an emphatic reassertion of the main issues involved in teaching which was already widely known, and with a justification of their

disobedience to man by an appeal to the results which accompanied their obedience to God.

Ver. 33. διεπρίοντο: lit., were sawn asunder (in heart), dissecabantur, Vulgate (cf. use of findo in Persius and Plautus), cf. vii. 54 (Luke ii. 35), Euseb., H. E., v., i., 6 (see Grimm, sub v.). The word is used in its literal sense in Aristoph., Equites, 768, Plato, Conv., p. 193 a, and once in the LXX, 1 Chron. xx. 3. The rendering "sawed their teeth" would certainly require τοὺς ὀδόντας as in other cases where the verb (and the simple verb also) has any such meaning. Dr. Kennedy, Sources of N. T. Greek, pp. 72, 73, also refers to its use in the comic poet Eubulus (Meineke), 3, 255, and classes it among the words (colloquial) common to the comic poets (including Aristophanes) and the N.T. Here we have not the pricking of the heart, ii. 37, which led to contrition and repentance, but the painful indignation and envy which found vent in seeking to rid themselves of the disciples as they had done of their Master.—ἀνελεῖν: the verb is found no less than nineteen times in Acts, twice in St. Luke's Gospel, and only two or three times in the rest of the N.T., once in Matt. ii. 16, Heb. x. 9 (2 Thess. ii. 8); often used as here in LXX and classical Greek; it is therefore not one of those words which can be regarded as distinctly medical terms, characteristic of St. Luke (so Hobart and Zahn), although it is much used in medical writers. The noun ἀναίρεσις, viii. 1, is only found in St. Luke, and is also frequent in medical writers, Hobart, Medical Language of St. Luke, pp. 209, 210; but this word is also used in LXX of a violent death or destruction, cf. Numb. xi. 15, Judith xv. 4, 2 Macc. v. 13. At the same time it is interesting to note that ἐπιχειρεῖν, another medical word characteristic of St. Luke, and used by him in the sense of attempting, trying, is found with ἀνελεῖν in Acts ix. 29, cf. Zahn, Einleitung, ii., p. 384, with which Hobart compares ὁ μὲν γὰρ ἰατρὸς ἀνελεῖν ἐπιχειρεῖ τὸ νόσημα (Galen), see in loco.

Ver. 34. ἀναστὰς, see ver. 17.— συνεδρίῳ: the word is used here and in ver. 27 above, without γερουσία, and

νομοδιδάσκαλος τίμιος παντὶ τῷ λαῷ, ἐκέλευσεν ἔξω βραχύ τι τοὺς
ἀποστόλους [1] ποιῆσαι, 35. εἶπέ τε πρὸς αὐτούς,[2] Ἄνδρες Ἰσραηλῖται,
προσέχετε ἑαυτοῖς ἐπὶ τοῖς ἀνθρώποις τούτοις τί μέλλετε πράσσειν.

[1] τι HP (put by many before ποιησαι); om. ℵABDE, vers., Chrys., so Tisch.,
W.H., R.V., Weiss, Wendt, Hilg. τους αποστολους DEHP, Par., Flor., Gig.
(Vulg. am.corr. tol.), Sah., Syrr. P. and H., Aeth., Chrys.; τους ανθρωπους
ℵAB (Vulg.), Boh., Arm., Chrys., so Tisch., W.H., R.V., Wendt, Weiss, so also
Blass in β; cf. vv. 35, 38, but here in narrative ανθρωπ. seemed undignified word.

[2] αυτους; D (Flor.), Sah. has τους αρχοντας και τους συνεδρους (-ιους), d has
"concilium," Flor. "ad totum concilium". Ισραηλιται, see above.

this seems to indicate that in ver. 21 the
Sanhedrim is meant, and no additional
council.—Γαμαλιήλ: it has sometimes
been urged that Saul, the persecutor,
could not have been the pupil of such a
man as is here described—a man who
was so liberal in his religious opinions,
and so adverse to political agitation.
But whatever may have been the extent
of his liberality, Gamaliel remained firmly
attached to the traditions of the fathers,
and whilst we see in his recorded
principle his abhorrence of wrangling and
over-scrupulosity, we may also see in it
a proof of his adherence to traditionalism:
"Procure thyself a teacher, avoid being
in doubt; and do not accustom thyself
to give tithes by guess" (Edersheim,
History of the Jewish Nation, p. 128).
But in itself there is nothing strange in
the fact that Saul should surpass the
zeal of Gamaliel, for not only does history often show us how one side of the
teaching of a master may be exaggerated
to excess by a pupil, but also the specific
charge against Stephen of destroying the
Temple and of changing the customs of
Moses had not been formulated against
St. Peter and his brother-Apostles, who
still attended the Temple worship, and
whose piety gained them the regard of
the people. That charge against the
first martyr was nothing less than the
charge brought against Jesus of Nazareth: the burning words and scathing
denunciations of Stephen could only be
answered, as those of Jesus had been
answered, by the counter charge of blasphemy, and the punishment of death
(see Sabatier's L'Apôtre Paul, 21 ff.).
Gamaliel appears as an ordinary member, and there can be no reasonable doubt
that the high priest was always the President during the Roman-Herodian period.
Not until after the destruction of Jerusalem, when the priesthood had lost its
importance, was a Rabbi chosen as
President of a reconstituted Sanhedrim.

For a summary of the views for and
against the Rabbinic tradition that this
Gamaliel was the President of the Sanhedrim, see Appendix iii., "The President
of the Sanhedrim," by the late Rev. H.
A. White, in Dr. Edersheim's History
of the Jewish Nation, p. 522 ff. The
influence of Gamaliel may easily be
understood (1) when we remember that
whilst the ἀρχιερεῖς belonged chiefly if
not exclusively to the Sadducees, the
Pharisees who also had seats in the
Sanhedrim (cf. Acts xxiii. 6, and Jos.,
B. J., ii., 17, 3, Vita, 38, 39, C. Apion, ii.,
22) possessed practically a predominating
influence in the Council. The remark
of Jos., Ant., xviii., 1, 4, gives us, as
Schürer says, "a deep insight into the
actual position of matters," Schürer,
Jewish People, div. ii., vol. i., p. 178 ff.,
E.T., and O. Holtzmann Neutest. Zeitgeschichte, p. 175. (2) But we have also
to take into account the personal influence of the man, which was no doubt
at its height about the time described in
Acts v.—he died A.D. 57-58. Not only
was he the first teacher of the seven
to whom the title Rabban was given
(higher than that of Rab or Rabbi), but
Jewish tradition respecting him shows the
dignity and influence which attached to
his name, Hamburger, Real-Encyclopädie
des Judentums, ii., 2, 236, and see on
the titles given to Gamaliel, Derenbourg,
Histoire de la Palestine, pp. 239-246, and
Schürer, u. s., p. 364. We may see a
further proof of his influence in the fact
that a certain proviso with regard to the
determining leap year, which was passed
in the Sanhedrim in his absence, was only
to come into force if it received the
confirmation of Gamaliel (Edajoth, vii.,7).
So far then St. Luke's account of the
weight which would be carried by Gamaliel in the assembly is amply justified,
and Schürer's description of the constitution of the Sanhedrim, u. s., p. 174 ff., is
sufficient reply to the strictures of Jüngst

36. πρὸ γὰρ τούτων τῶν ἡμερῶν ἀνέστη Θευδᾶς, λέγων εἶναί τινα ἑαυτόν,[1] ᾧ προσεκολλήθη[2] ἀριθμὸς ἀνδρῶν ὡσεὶ τετρακοσίων· ὃς ἀνῃρέθη,[3] καὶ πάντες ὅσοι ἐπείθοντο αὐτῷ διελύθησαν καὶ ἐγένοντο

[1] εαυτον ℵA*BCHP, Vulg., Sah., Boh., Syr. Harcl., Arm., Eus., Chrys., so Tisch., W.H., R.V.; εαυτον μεγαν (or μεγαν εαυτον) A²DE tol., Flor., Gig., Syr. Pesh., Cyr., Or., Hier.

[2] προσεκολληθη 13, Chrys., Cyr.; προσεκλιθη ℵABC² 17, 31, Cyr., so Tisch., W.H., R.V., Weiss, Wendt (Blass in β), Hilg.; προσεκληθη C*D*EHP—προσεκλιθη orig. only here in N.T., others = interpretations of it. ωσει ℵHP, Cyr.; but ως ℵcABCDE, Chrys., so Tisch., W.H., R.V., Weiss, Hilg.

[3] ανηρεθη, instead D has διελυθη αυτος δι᾽ αυτου (διελυθησαν omitted below). Eus. and Par. read κατελυθη (the latter dissolutus est = διελ. or κατελ.); see Blass, who maintains with Belser that this word rather than ανηρεθη is required by Gamaliel's argument, but why? αυτω, after this word διελ. omitted by D, και om. in d, and και εγεν. in Par.[1] but διελ. (dissoluti sunt) retained. (Weiss holds that the corrector refers ος the subject of κατελυθη not to Θευδας but to αριθμος.)

against Gamaliel's appearance as a member of the Council, cf. Derenbourg, u. s., pp. 201, 213. On the words attributed to Gamaliel see below.—νομοδιδάσκαλος: only in St. Luke and St. Paul, cf. Luke v. 17, 1 Tim. i. 7, almost = γραμματεύς, νομικός, not found in LXX.—βραχύ (τι): = "a little while," R.V., Luke xxii. 58, "a little space," A.V.; ambiguous, in classical Greek the word might be used as either βραχύ, a short distance, Xen., Anab., iii., 3, 7, or ἐν βραχεῖ, "in a short time," Herod., v., 24, cf. Thuc., vi., 12. In Acts xxvii. 28 the word may be taken either of space or time (see Blass). In the LXX it is used of space in 2 Sam. xvi. 1, and 2 Sam. xix. 36, and most likely of degree in Psalm viii. 6 (although the expression may be taken of time, cf. Heb. ii. 7, 9, R.V.), and of time in Psalm xciii. 17, and in Isa. lvii. 17 (Weiss, Westcott; but see Hatch and Redpath, doubtful). But whether we take the word of space or time in this passage, it is noteworthy that St. Luke alone of the N.T. writers can be said to use βραχύ temporally (in Hebrews it is a quotation), Friedrich, and so Klostermann, Vindiciæ Lucanæ, p. 54.—ἔξω ποιεῖν (hinausthun): only here in this sense, cf. Blass, in loco, for classical instances, and cf. Psalm cxli. 8 (Symmachus)—Weiss, Wendt. Ver. 35. ἄνδρες Ἰσραηλεῖται, see on ii. 22. προσέχετε ἑαυτοῖς: phrase only found in St. Luke, cf. Luke xii. 1, xvii. 3, xxi. 34, and Acts xx. 28. προσέχειν without the pronoun is found six times in Matthew alone of the Evangelists, but in LXX frequently used in the phrase πρόσεχε σεαυτῷ. The phrase may be connected with ἐπὶ τοῖς ἀνθρώποις τού-

τοις, "as touching these men, what you are about to do," R.V., hence the reading ἀπὸ τῶν, etc., E. Or we may take it with μέλλετε πράσσειν, "what you are about to do to these men". In favour of the latter it may be said that the construction πράσσειν τι ἐπί τινι is very common, whereas προσέχειν ἑαυτοῖς is never found in construction with ἐπί, and that this rendering rightly marks the evidently emphatic position of τοῖς ἀνθρώποις (so Weiss, Wendt, Holtzmann, Hackett).—τί μέλλετε πράσσειν, quid acturi sitis, Vulgate. Burton, N. T. Moods and Tenses, p. 36, μέλλειν never found with future infinitive except in the phrase μέλλειν ἔσεσθαι used in Acts, almost always has a present infinitive, although its force is akin to that of the future (Grimm-Thayer); also Simcox, Language of the N. T., p. 120. μέλλειν is used over thirty times in Acts in all its parts, and is found very often in St. Luke's Gospel. Ver. 36. πρὸ γὰρ τούτων τῶν ἡμερῶν: Gamaliel appeals to the experience of the past—the phrase is placed first with emphasis, cf. xxi. 38; on St. Luke's fondness for phrases with ἡμέρα see above, and Friedrich, pp. 9, 89. But whilst Gamaliel appeals to the past, his appeal is not to a remote but to a near past which was still fresh in the memories of his generation, perhaps because, as St. Chrysostom urges, such recent examples μάλιστα πρὸς πίστιν ἦσαν ἰσχυρά.—ἀνέστη, cf. vii. 18, like the Hebrew קוּם, and so constantly in LXX, Exod. i. 8, Deut. xiii. 1, xxxiv. 10, Judg. ii. 10, iv. 9, v. 7, etc.—Θευδᾶς: St. Luke evidently places Theudas before Judas. But

εἰς οὐδέν. 37. μετὰ τοῦτον ἀνέστη Ἰούδας ὁ Γαλιλαῖος, ἐν ταῖς ἡμέραις τῆς ἀπογραφῆς, καὶ ἀπέστησε λαὸν ἱκανὸν[1] ὀπίσω αὐτοῦ·

[1] ικανον om. ℵA*B 81, d, Vulg., Eus., Cyr.; so Tisch., W.H., R.V., Weiss, Wendt. πολυν in CD, so Hilg., but not retained by Blass in β. απωλετο, Par. reads κατελυθη; "recte," says Blass, who receives κατελ. in β. This will be only consistent with the former rejection of ανηρεθη.

a difficulty arises from the fact that the only Theudas of this period known to us is placed by Josephus in the reign of Claudius, about the year 44, 45. He gave himself out as a false prophet, gathered round him " a great part of the people," and persuaded them to follow him to the Jordan with a promise that its waters should miraculously divide before him as in the days of Moses. But the Roman procurator, Cuspius Fadus, sent a troop of horse to meet him, some of his followers were slain, others taken captive, whilst he himself was made prisoner and beheaded, and his head sent to Jerusalem, Jos., Ant., xx., 5, 1. But a serious chronological discrepancy must be faced if the Theudas of Josephus is the Theudas of St. Luke. Gamaliel speaks of a Theudas who arose before the days of the enrolment, R.V., which marked the attempt of Judas, i.e., about 6-7 A.D. But are they the same ? As early as the days of Origen their identity was denied (c. Cels., i., 57), see " Acts," B.D.[2], Bishop Lightfoot, p. 40, and in comparing the two accounts in Josephus and Acts there is no close resemblance beyond the name, see Nösgen, in loco, and Belser, Theol. Quartalschrift, i., p. 70 (1896). St. Luke speaks definitely of 400 followers ; Josephus evidently considers that the pretender was much more successful, so far as numbers were concerned, for he writes : πείθει τὸν πλεῖστον ὄχλον. These and similar discrepancies are also well insisted upon by Zahn in his recent Introduction, ii., 416, 417 (1899), and his own conclusion is that only such ordinary words are common to the two accounts as Luke, ἀνηρέθη ; Jos., ἀνεῖλε ; Luke, ἐπείθοντο ; Jos., ἔπειθε ; and that we cannot get beyond the bounds of possibility that the two authors refer to the same fact (on Zahn's criticism of Krenkel's view of the dependence of Luke on Josephus in the narrative, see u. s.). In referring to the appearance of the many false Messiahs, such as the Theudas of Josephus, Ant., xx., 5, 1, Dr. Edersheim, Sketches of Jewish Social Life, p. 66, remarks : " Of course this could not have been the Theudas of Acts v. 36, 37, but both the name and the movement were not solitary in Israel at the time " ; see also Ramsay, Was Christ born in Bethlehem ? p. 259. And no testimony could be stronger than that of Josephus himself to the fact that at the time of the Advent Judæa was full of tumults and seditions and pretenders of all kinds, Ant., xvii., 10, 4, 8 ; B. J., ii., 4, 1. The view has been maintained by many commentators that the Theudas of Josephus may reasonably be supposed to be one of the many false teachers and leaders mentioned by the Jewish historian and not always by name, who pandered to the feverish hopes of the people and gave themselves out as of kingly rank—(so recently Belser, Felten, Page, Plumptre, Knabenbauer). The name Theudas contracted from Theodorus may not have been so common as that of Simon or Judas (although on the other hand, see Nösgen, Apostelgeschichte, p. 147)—" Josephus describes four men bearing the name of Simon within forty years, and three that of Judas within ten years, all of whom were instigators of rebellion "—but it was the Greek equivalent to several familiar Hebrew names, e.g., Jonathan, Matthias ; and Bishop Lightfoot allows that there is something to be said for Wieseler's suggestion that on the ground of the name the Theudas here may be identified with Matthias, the son of Margalothus, an insurgent in the time of Herod, prominent in the pages of Josephus, Ant., xvii., 6, 2 (see also Zöckler on the whole question, Apostelgeschichte, p. 197, 2nd edit.). We must admit the objection of Wendt that this and other identifications of names and persons cannot be proved (and some of them certainly are very precarious, as Alford pointed out), but we cannot suppose that St. Luke could have made the gross blunder attributed to him in the face of his usual accuracy (see Blass, Acta Apostolorum, p. 90), or endorse with Schürer what he calls " the slight authority of the Acts in such matters " (Jewish People, div. i., vol. ii., p. 169). If it is hardly possible that Josephus can have been mistaken, although some writers

κἀκεῖνος ἀπώλετο, καὶ πάντες ὅσοι ἐπείθοντο αὐτῷ διεσκορπίσθησαν.
38. καὶ τὰ νῦν λέγω ὑμῖν, ἀπόστητε ἀπὸ τῶν ἀνθρώπων τούτων, καὶ

have held that it is by no means impossible that even here he may have been (cf. Alford, Rendall, Belser, and compare the remarks of Zahn, ubi supra), we may at least claim the same probability of freedom from error for St. Luke, "temporum bene memorem se scriptor monstrat: quo minus est probabile eum de Theuda tam graviter errasse quam plerique putant" (Blass), and see the recent remarks of Ramsay, Was Christ born at Bethlehem? p. 252 ff. It cannot be said that some recent attempts at a solution of the difficulty are very promising; for whilst H. Holtzmann severely blames Blass for maintaining that some Christian had interpolated the name Theudas in the text of Josephus (see Blass, in loco, and p. xvi., edit. min.), he himself is prepared to endorse the view recently maintained amongst others by Clemen that the writer of Acts in his mention of Theudas gives us a vague but yet recognisable recollection of Jos., Ant., xx., 5, 1; see in loco and Theol. Literaturzeitung, 3, 1896, and 13, 1897. B. Weiss thinks that the notorious difficulty may easily be got rid of by supposing that the reviser inserted the example of Theudas in the wrong place, Einleitung in das N. T., p. 574.—λέγων εἶναί τινα ἑαυτόν: of consequence, really "somebody," cf. viii. 9 (and R.V.); "ein grosser Mann," Blass, Grammatik des N. G., p. 76; so we have its opposite, οὐδείς, cf. instances in Wetstein in classical Greek; so in Latin quidam, aliquis, Juvenal, i., 74; Cicero, ad Atticum, iii., 15; and cf. also 1 Cor. iii. 7, Gal. ii. 6, vi. 3; Viteau, Le Grec du N. T., p. 148 (1893). And yet the jealous eye of the Pharisees was blind to the difference between such a man as Theudas, whom Gamaliel so contemptuously described, and the Apostles who sought not their own honour (Nösgen); cf. Vulgate, "dicens se esse aliquem," so Rhem. and Wycl., "saying that he was somebody".—προσεκολλήθη: better reading προσεκλίθη, a word not found elsewhere in N.T., cf. 2 Macc. xiv. 24; and so also in LXX, cf. Ps. xxxix. (xl.) 2, Symmachus; cf. Polyb., iv., 51, 5; so also πρόσκλισις; for its further use see Clem. Rom., Cor., xlvii., 4.—ὡσεὶ (ὡς) τετρακοσίων, see above on "Theudas".—ἀνῃρέθη, see also on ἀναιρέω, ver. 33, often of violent death in Acts. The two clauses stand in sharp contrast—the one emphasises the large number which joined Theudas, the other the fact that notwithstanding he was slain; cf. iv. 10.—διελύθησαν κ.τ.λ.: nowhere else in N.T., but its use is quite classical, cf. Thuc., ii., 12; Xen., Cyr., v., 5, 43; Polyb., iv., 2. Blass remarks that the whole phrase "apte de secta quæ paullatim dilabitur, minus apte de multitudine per vim disjecta".—ἐγένοντο εἰς οὐδέν: phrase only here in N.T. (cf. xix. 27), but see in LXX, Job xxiv. 25, Isa. xl. 17, Wisd. iii. 17, xx. 16. γίνομαι εἰς in LXX and also in classics; in N.T. cf. Luke xiii. 19, xx. 17, Acts iv. 11, and cf. 1 Thess. iii. 5. In the first passage it is Hebraistic; in the passage before us and in 1 Thess. the phrases are quite possibly Greek, cf. especially Simcox, Language of the N. T., p. 143. The phrase is more frequent in St. Luke's writings than in any other books of the N.T., except the Apocalypse.

Ver. 37. Ἰούδας ὁ Γαλ.: here too an inaccuracy might have been charged against St. Luke, but it is to be noted that while Josephus speaks of Judas as a Gaulonite in one passage, Jos., Ant., xviii., 1, 1, he frequently, as both Belser and Wendt point out, speaks of him as a Galilean, cf. Ant., xviii., 1, 6; xx., 5, 2; B. J., ii., 8, 1, and 17, 8. But the name Galilean might easily be given to him because Galilee was the scene of his exploits, or because Gamala, his home, belonged to Lower Gaulonitis, which was reckoned as part of Galilee. The accuracy of St. Luke in the account of Judas is remarkable, for Gamaliel speaks of his insurrection as coming to nothing. He could so speak, say in 34 or 35 A.D., but not some ten years later, when the followers of Judas had again gathered together, and formed a kind of school or party, to say nothing of the rebellion of his three sons, James, Simon, and later, Menahem; see Belser, u. s., p. 61, so Lightfoot, u. s., Nösgen, and Alford's note.

As we consider the characteristics of such men as Theudas and Judas, it is difficult to suppose that the age which produced them could have produced the Messiah of the Gospels. He is, in truth, the Anti-Christ of Judaism. Instead of giving Himself out to be somebody, Jesus is meek and lowly of heart; instead of stirring revolt in Galilee, a burning furnace of sedition, His blessing is upon

ἐάσατε αὐτούς[1] · ὅτι ἐὰν ᾖ ἐξ ἀνθρώπων ἡ βουλὴ αὕτη ἢ τὸ ἔργον τοῦτο, καταλυθήσεται · 39. εἰ δὲ ἐκ Θεοῦ ἐστιν, οὐ δύνασθε καταλῦσαι

---

[1] After **αφετ. αυτους** (W.H., R.V.) DE, Flor. insert **μη μιαναντες τας χειρας** (E has **μολυνοντες**), d *non coinquinatas manus*, e *non coinquinantes manus*, Flor. *non maculetis manus vestras*. Blass and Hilg. follow D. Chase thinks that the gloss arose in Syriac by assim. of O.T. passages, *cf.* Isa. lix. 3 ; but see Harris, *Four Lectures*, etc., p. 79 ff., as against this, and for the possible deriv. from Syriac through the trans. of **δυνησεσθε** (W.H., R.V.), and for theories that the gloss has moved away (as in other instances according to H.) from its right place. Belser sees in each word of the **β** recension in vv. 38 and 39 "the stamp of originality". Mr. Harold Smith suggests that there was a gloss on **εασατε (αφετε) αυτους** from ver. 33 : **μη αναιρουντες**—**MHANAIPOYNTEC**—then **μη** became repeated—**MHMHANAIPOYNTEC**—the second **μη** became **MI** (by itacism), while **AIP** dropped out after **AN**. This produces **MHMIANOYNTE**C which would easily be read **μη μιαναντες—τας χειρας** being added for sense. **ἀναιρεῖν** is very common in *Acts*.

the peace-makers ; instead of seeking a kingly crown, like Judas the Gaulonite, He withdraws from those who would take Him by force, and make Him a king ; instead of preaching revolt and licence in the name of liberty for merely selfish ends, He bade men render unto Caesar the things that are Caesar's ; instead of defiantly bidding His followers to be in subjection to no man, and inaugurating a policy of bloodshed and murder, He bade them remember that whilst One was their Master and Teacher, they all were brethren. Schürer, *Jewish People*, div. ii., vol. iii., p. 80, E.T., well points out that we have a literary memorial of the views and hopes of the Zealots in the *Assumption of Moses*, which goes so far as to prophesy that Israel will tread on the neck of the eagle, *i.e.*, the Romans, x. 8; but see also edition of *Assumption of Moses* by Prof. Charles, p. 42.

Ver. 37. **ἐν ταῖς ἡμέραις τῆς ἀπογ.**, see Blass, *in loco*, on St. Luke's accuracy. We must be careful to distinguish this from Luke ii. 1. The tribal method of numbering which forms an essential part of St. Luke's story in the Gospel may explain why no such serious disturbance followed as resulted from the Roman numbering and valuation which marked Quirinius' second Roman administration, "the great census," **ἡ ἀπογ.** (in 6-8 A.D.), taken when Judæa had just become a part of the Roman province of Syria. This "great census," taken after the Roman method, involved the imposition of a tax, Jos., *Ant.*, xviii., 1, 1, and it was this import which roused the indignation of Judas. To pay tribute to a foreign power was to violate an Israelite's allegiance to Jehovah : "We have no Lord and Master

but God," was the watchword of Judas and his followers. For the whole subject see Ramsay, *Expositor*, April and June, 1897, and *Was Christ born at Bethlehem ?* (1898), *e.g.*, pp. 107, 108, 127, 139.—**καὶ ἀπέστησε λαὸν** : used here transitively, and here only in the N.T., *cf.* Deut. vii. 4, and in classical writers, Herod., i., 76. The verb **ἀφίστημι** is not found in any of the Gospels except St. Luke's, where it occurs four times, and in the Acts six times. It is not only one of the words characteristic of the two books, but also of St. Luke and St. Paul (so also **μεθίστημι**, see on xix. 26), as it is only found once outside St. Paul's Epistles (in which it is employed four times), *viz.*, Heb. iii. 12 ; "drew away *some of the people*," R.V. There is no word which actually expresses this as in T.R., where we have **ἱκανόν** = "much," A.V.—**ὀπίσω αὐτοῦ** : this prepositional use of **ὀπ.** is not found in classical writers, where the word is always an adverb. In the N.T. and LXX the prepositional use is derived from Hebrew אַחֲרֵי, *cf.* xx. 30, Luke ix. 23, xxi. 8. Blass, *Grammatik des N. G.*, p. 126.—**διεσκορπίσθησαν** : it is true that the sect revived under the name of Zealots, and played an active part in the Jewish wars, but there is no reason for charging St. Luke's account with inaccuracy (so Overbeck following De Wette). The fate of the leader and the dispersion of his followers was quite sufficient to point the moral which Gamaliel wished to draw.

Ver. 38. **καὶ τὰ νῦν**, *cf.* also in iv. 29, xvii. 30, xx. 32, xxvii. 22. **τὰ** neuter accusative absolute — as respects the present, now, *cf.* 2 Macc. xv. 8 ; thus in all parts of Acts, *Vindiciæ Lucanæ*, Klostermann, p. 53, so Zeller, Leke-

αὐτό,[1] μήποτε καὶ θεομάχοι εὑρεθῆτε.　40. Ἐπείσθησαν δὲ αὐτῷ, καὶ
προσκαλεσάμενοι τοὺς ἀποστόλους, δείραντες παρήγγειλαν μὴ λαλεῖν

[1] αυτο C*HP, Vulg. (clem. and demid.), Sah., Boh., Syr. Pesh., Chrys.; αυτους
אABC²DE, Vulg. (am. fu.), Syr. Harcl., Arm., Aeth., Bede, so Tisch., W.H., R.V.,
Weiss, Wendt, Hilg.—αυτο may have come in from το εργον τουτο. Flor. apparently
paraphrases latter part of verse, see Blass β. After αυτους E, Gig., Wern. add ουτε
υμεις ουτε οι αρχοντες υμων; D, Flor., Syr. Harcl. mg. demid. add ουτε υμεις ουτε
βασιλεις ουτε τυραννοι, so Hilg.　Belser lays special stress on these words, whilst
Weiss only sees here and in the following words of D unfortunate attempts at emend-
ing; cf. Wisd. xii. 14, ουτε βασιλευς η τυραννος, and see also below on vi. 10.　D,
Syr. Harcl. mg., Flor. demid., 33 mg., 180 add απεχεσθε ουν απο των ανθρωπων τουτων.　Weiss sees an empty repetition of ver. 38, but Belser finds in απεχ. that which
enables the construction of the following μηποτε και κ.τ.λ. to run quite smoothly.

busch, Friedrich.　The expression is
quite classical. — ἐάσατε: ἐάω characteristic of Luke, and is only used once
elsewhere in the Gospels, Matt. xxiv. 43
(also in 1 Cor. x. 13), but twice in Acts.
Luke's Gospel, and seven times in Acts
—ἀφίημι occurs only thrice in Acts;
viii. 22, xiv. 17.—καταλυθήσεται, "will
be overthrown," R.V. evertere, Blass,
so Rendall.　This rendering gives the
proper force of the word; it is not διαλύομαι
as in ver. 36, which might be rendered
"will be dissolved," but κατά indicates
subversion, cf. Rom. xiv. 20, Acts vi. 14,
Gal. ii. 18; cf. 2 Macc. ii. 22, 4 Macc. iv.
16, and frequently ibid., Vulgate, "dis-
solvetur".

Ver. 39. ἐάν . . . εἰ δὲ: it has sometimes been thought that the change of
mood from subjunctive to indicative, "but
if it is of God," as if indicating that the
second supposition were the more probable (cf. Gal. i. 8, 9), indicates sympathy
on the part of Gamaliel.　It is of course
possible that he may have been rendered
favourably disposed towards the Christians by their strict observance of the
Law, and by their appeal to a doctrine
which widely divided Pharisees and
Sadducees.　Others have attributed the
change in mood, not to Gamaliel at all,
but to the author (so Overbeck, Holtzmann), and have maintained (so Blass,
Weiss, cf. Winer-Moulton, xli. 2) that the
indicative may be used because the second
is the case with which the Council had
actually to deal, the assertion, i.e., of
the Apostles.　There may also be an
underlying contrast between the transi-
toriness of all mere human schemes, all
of which would be overthrown, and the
certainty of that which is "of God," and
which has Him for its Author.　There
cannot be the least ground for supposing
that Gamaliel's counsel was in its tenor
a mere invention, as it bears the impress

of a thorough Rabbinical wise saying,
cf. Sayings of the Jewish Fathers, v.,
24 (Taylor, p. 93, second edition).　See
too Herod., ix., 16; Eur., Hippol., vi.,
76; for the construction, cf. Burton,
N. T. Moods and Tenses, p. 96, and
Viteau, Le Grec du N. T., pp. 103, 113
(1893), who compares LXX, Gen. xliv.
23, 26.—οὐ δύνασθε: R.V. and W.H.,
δυνήσεσθε.　καταλῦσαι with accusative
of person in Xen., Cyr., viii., 5, 24; Plato,
Legg., iv., p. 714, C., cf. 4 Macc. iv. 16.
But without this addition it is usual to
refer back to προσέχετε in ver. 35 (cf.
Luke xxi. 34) for the construction of
μήποτε; but μήποτε . . . εὑρεθῆτε may
be explained on the principle that a verb
of fearing is sometimes unexpressed, the
idea of fear being supplied by the context
(in clauses where μή with the subjunctive
is found), Burton, u. s., p. 96.—μήποτε,
"lest haply," its use in later Greek,
Blass, Grammatik des N. G., p. 208.
καί sometimes interpreted (so Alford,
Wendt, Holtzmann), as if it meant not
only against man but also against God.
θεομάχοι: not found elsewhere, but cf.
LXX, Job xxvi. 5, Symm., and in Prov.
ix. 18, xxi. 16, applying the word to the
Rephaim (see B.D.² "Giants"); in 2
Macc. vii. 19 we have θεομαχεῖν ἐπε-
χείρησας.　In classical Greek the same
verb is found, see Grimm and Wendt
for instances; θεομαχία, Plato, Rep., 378,
D. (as certain books of the Iliad were
called, especially the xix.).　The tolerance of the sentiments here attributed
to Gamaliel is undoubtedly in perfect accordance with what we know of his
character and opinions; the decisions
attributed to him, e.g., that relating to
the law of the Sabbath (Hamburger,
Real-Encyclopädie des Judentums, ii., 2,
237; see also Derenbourg, Histoire de la
Palestine, pp. 239-246, and cf. also Renan,
Apostles, p. 153, E.T.), are marked by a

ἐπὶ τῷ ὀνόματι τοῦ Ἰησοῦ, καὶ ἀπέλυσαν αὐτούς.　41. Οἱ μὲν οὖν [1]
ἐπορεύοντο χαίροντες ἀπὸ προσώπου τοῦ συνεδρίου, ὅτι ὑπὲρ τοῦ

[1] μεν ουν (Flor. δε), D, Par. add αποστολοι, so Hilg.; Flor. adds απολυθεντες,
cf. iv. 23; Blass in β combines both.

tendency to mildness and liberality; and perhaps a still more remarkable illustration of the same tendency is afforded by the enactment so often referred to him (Hamburger, u. s.) to allow to the poor of the heathen, as well as of Israel, the gleaning and a participation in the corn left standing in the corner of the fields, to inquire after the welfare of the Gentile poor, to maintain them, to visit their sick, to bury their dead (the prayer against heretics belonged not to this Gamaliel, but to Gamaliel II.).　But the decision of Gamaliel was not prompted by any sympathy with the Christians; it was the judgment of toleration and prudence, but certainly nothing more, although it scarcely falls under the head of "cynical"; it was rather, as Ewald called it, that of an ordinary politician.　No credence whatever can be attributed to the tradition that Gamaliel became a Christian, or that he was secretly a Christian, although we may sympathise with St. Chrysostom's words, "it cannot be that he should have continued in unbelief to the end".　The Talmud distinctly affirms that he died a Jew, and, if he had betrayed his faith, we cannot understand the honour which Jewish tradition attaches to his name, "Gamaliel," B.D.[2]; Schürer, _Jewish People_, div. ii., vol. i., p. 364. Wendt, while he refuses to admit the historical character of the speech of Gamaliel, is evidently puzzled to discover any definite grounds for St. Luke's wilful introduction of the famous Rabban into the scene (so too Feine).　He therefore supposes that the decision in ver. 38, in which he sees a wise saying similar to those attributed to other Rabbis, was assigned by tradition to Gamaliel, and that St. Luke, who was in possession of the further tradition that Gamaliel had given a decisive judgment in the trial of the Apostles, introduces this saying into the speech which he attributes to Gamaliel as fitting to the occasion.　But there is no indication in our authorities that the sentiment thus attributed to Gamaliel was in any way different from what might have been expected of him (see Schürer, _Jewish People_, u. s.).　The chief objection to the speech, viz., the alleged anachronism involved in the mention of Theudas, really begs the question as to its authenticity, and even on the supposition of an inaccuracy in the point mentioned, we cannot get rid of the fact that the attitude of Gamaliel in itself betrays no inconsistency.　It was this alleged anachronism which caused Spitta to refer the incident of Gamaliel in this chapter to his inferior source B., and to refuse to adopt the solution of Weiss and Feine, who solved the difficulty involved in the mention of Theudas by introducing the hand of a reviser.

Ver. 40.　ἐπείσθησαν δὲ αὐτῷ: whatever scruples Gamaliel may have had in pressing matters against the Apostles, or even if the teaching of Christ, as some have conjectured, with much of which he might have sympathised as a follower of Hillel, had influenced his mind, or if, like Joseph of Arimathea, he too had not consented to the counsel and will of his fellow-Sanhedrists, there is no reason to suppose (see above) that he ever advanced beyond the compromise here suggested.　It may be that Neander was right in his judgment that Gamaliel was too wise a man to render a fanatical movement more violent still by opposing it.　Others however see in his words a mere _laisser-aller_ view of matters, or a timid caution which betokened a mere waiter upon Providence.　But at the same time there are occasions when Gamaliel's advice may not be out of place, see Bengel on ver. 38, and Farrar, _St. Paul_, i., 110 ff.—δείραντες, Deut. xxv. 3, 2 Cor. xi. 24: the punishment was for minor offences, and it was now inflicted upon the Apostles because they had trangressed the command enjoined upon them previously, iv. 18.　The Pharisees, probably by their superior number in the Sanhedrim (Jos., _Ant._, xiii., 10, 6), were able to secure the following of Gamaliel's advice, and to prevent extreme measures against the Apostles, but they were not prepared to disregard the previous injunction of the Council which bade the Apostles refrain from uttering a word in the name of Jesus.　But the Apostles themselves must have seen in the punishment a striking fulfilment of their Lord's words, as in the closing hours of His earthly life He foretold their future sufferings for His Name.　The

ὀνόματος αὐτοῦ [1] κατηξιώθησαν ἀτιμασθῆναι · 42. πᾶσάν τε ἡμέραν ἐν τῷ ἱερῷ καὶ κατ' οἶκον οὐκ ἐπαύοντο διδάσκοντες καὶ εὐαγγελιζόμενοι Ἰησοῦν τὸν Χριστόν.[2]

[1] After ονοματος a few cursives read αυτου; but om. ℵABCDHP, Tisch., W.H., R.V., Weiss, Wendt.

[2] Flor., Gig. add *Jesu*, Par. adds *Christi* (see for variations Alford and Wendt). R.V., W.H., Weiss have τον Χριστον Ιησουν; D, Flor., Par. τον κυρον Ι. Χ., so Hilg.

penalty which must have been a very painful one, although the command not to exceed forty stripes often led to its mitigation, was often inflicted by the synagogues, and not only by the great Sanhedrim, for all kinds of offences as against heretics and others. These verses 40-42, with the exception of the words ἐπείσθησαν δὲ αὐτῷ, were referred by Jüngst to the redactor on the ground that they do not fit in well after Gamaliel's speech, and that the Apostles would have been at once released, but the Apostles were punished for a transgression of the command previously laid upon them in iv. 18. According to Jüngst, who here follows Spitta, the original conclusion of the narrative is to be found in inserting after ver. 39, chap. vi. 7 ! Here we are told is a notice, which is quite out of place where it now stands, that a great number of the priests were obedient to the faith : this was the result of the speech of Gamaliel, and his warning not to be found " fighting against God "; a speech delivered in the Sanhedrim in the midst of the priests !

Ver. 41. οἱ μὲν οὖν : no answering δέ as after i. 6, ii. 41, but explained because immediately upon ἐπορεύοντο (which answers to ἀπέλυσαν) follows χαίροντες, marking the attitude of the Apostles, and showing how little they proposed to obey the injunction from fear of further punishment. But see also Mr. Rendall's note, and also his Appendix on μὲν οὖν, *Acts*, p. 163, in which he examines this view at length; according to him there is an answering δέ, but it is found in the antithesis to this sentence in chap. vi. 1, the connection being that the Apostles now became more absorbed in their spiritual work, and a murmuring arose in consequence of their neglect of the distribution of the common funds. But this antithesis does not seem natural, and a censure on the Apostles is not necessarily contained in vi. i. ff.—ἐπορεύοντο χαίροντες: "imperf. quia describitur modus" (Blass, *Grammatik des N. G.*, p. 186 ; if one prophecy of their Lord had

been already fulfilled, another was fulfilled in the sequel, Matt. v. 11, 12, Phil. i. 29.—κατηξιώθησαν . . . ἀτιμασθῆναι: oxymoron, *cf.* 2 Cor. vi. 8-10 ; *cf.* Bengel's note—he calls it " eximium oxy.". The verb καταξ. is used by St. Luke in his Gospel, xx. 35 (xxi. 36, T.R., but not W.H. or R.V.), and here ; only found once elsewhere, 2 Thess. i. 5, in a passage where the thought of Christian suffering and inheritance is combined ; 2 Macc. xiii. 12, 3 Macc. iii. 21, iv. 11, 4 Macc. xviii. 3. ἀτιμασθῆναι only used once elsewhere by St. Luke, *cf.* Luke xx. 11, where it is also found in connection with δέρω.—ὑπὲρ τοῦ ὀνόμ., "the Name"—*i.e.*, the Name κατ' ἐξοχήν, *cf.* 3 John 7, and James v. 14 (ii. 7) (τοῦ Κ. doubtful), *cf.* also Clem. Rom., 2 *Cor.* (so called), xiii., 4, Ignat., *Ephes.*, iii., 1, used here as the absolute use of שֵׁם in Lev. xxiv. 11, 16, by which the Jews understood Jehovah. See Grimm, Mayor's *St. James* above, and Taylor, *Pirke Aboth*, p. 67, second edition ; *cf.* τῆς ὁδοῦ, "the Way," ix. 2, etc.— πᾶσάν τε ἡμέραν: the τε joins the imperfect ἐπαύοντο closely to the preceding, indicating the continuance of the work of the Apostles in spite of threats and blows, and of their resolve to welcome suffering for Christ as an honour = κατὰ πᾶσαν ἡμέραν. This use of παύεσθαι with the participle almost entirely in Luke and Paul may be regarded as a remains of literary usage, Luke v. 4, Col. i. 9, Ephes. i. 16 (Heb. x. 2) ; Viteau, *Le Grec du N. T.*, p. 193 (1893).—ἐν τῷ ἱερ. καὶ κατ' οἶκον : the words may mark a contrast between the public preaching which was not discontinued, *cf.* ver. 21, and the teaching continued at home in a household assembly, or κατά may be taken distributively, and refer to the Christian assemblies met together in various houses in the city, as in ii. 46. See Zöckler's note, and Edersheim, *Jewish Social Life*, pp. 259, 260.—τὸν Χρ. Ἰ. : "Jesus *as* the Christ," R.V. The contents of the first Apostolic preaching, the sum and substance of the Apostles'

VI. 1. ἘΝ δὲ ταῖς ἡμέραις ταύταις πληθυνόντων τῶν μαθητῶν,
ἐγένετο γογγυσμὸς τῶν Ἑλληνιστῶν πρὸς τοὺς Ἑβραίους, ὅτι παρε-

message to their fellow-countrymen. This is allowed and insisted upon by Schwegler, Renan, and others, but in the statement what an intimate knowledge of the life of Jesus is presupposed, and how great must have been the impression made by Him upon His daily companions!

CHAPTER VI.—Ver. 1. δὲ; cf. i. 15, and see above in v. 41. There seems no occasion to regard δὲ as marking a contrast between v. 41 and the opening of this chapter, or as contrasting the outward victory of the Church with its inward dissensions (as Meyer, Holtzmann, Zechler, see Nösgen's criticism in loco); simply introduces a new recital as in iii. 1. It may refer back to the notice in v. 14 of the increase of the disciples, and this would be in harmony with the context. On the expression ἐν ταῖς ἡμέρ. ταύτ., as characteristic of Luke, see above, and Friedrich, Das Lucasevangelium, p. 9; in both his Gospel and the Acts expressions with ἡμέρα abound. Harnack admits that in passing to this sixth chapter "we at once enter on historical ground," Expositor, v., p. 324 (3rd series). For views of the partition critics see Wendt's summary in new edition (1899), p. 140, Hilgenfeld, Zeitschrift für wissenschaft. Theol., p. 390 ff. (1895), and also in commentary below. Wendt sees in vi. 1-7 the hand of the redactor, the author of Acts ii. 5; others suppose that we have in vi. the commencement of a new Hellenistic source; so Feine, J. Weiss, Hilgenfeld. Clemen refers vi. 7, 8 to his Historia Petri, whilst ver. 9 commences his Historia Hellenistarum (vv. 1-6 belong to a special source); others again see in chap. vi. the continuance of an earlier source or sources.—πληθυνόντων, when the number of the disciples was multiplying (present part.); verb frequent in LXX, sometimes intrans. as here, Exod. i. 20, etc., and see Psalms of Solomon, x., 1, and note in Ryle and James' edition; cf. also its classical use in its more correct form, πληθύω, in the Acts: vi. 7, vii. 17, ix. 31, xii. 24. On St. Luke's fondness for this and similar words (Friedrich) see p. 73. Weiss calls it here a very modest word, introduced by one who knew nothing of the conversions in many of the preceding chapters. But the word, and especially its use in the present participle, rather denotes that the numbers went on increasing, and so

rapidly that the Apostles found the work of relief too great for them.—μαθητῶν, the word occurs here for the first time in the Acts (surely an insufficient ground for maintaining with Hilgenfeld that we are dealing with a new source). The same word is found frequently in each of the Gospels, twenty-eight times in Acts (μαθήτρια once, ix. 36), but never in the Epistles. It evidently passed into the ancient language of the early Church from the earthly days of the ministry of Jesus, and may fairly be regarded as the earliest designation of the Christians; but as the associations connected with it (the thought that Jesus was the διδάσκαλος and His followers His μαθηταί) passed into the background it quickly dropped out of use, although in the Acts the name is still the rule for the more ancient times and for the Jewish-Christian Churches; cf. xxi. 16. In the Acts we have the transition marked from μαθηταί to the brethren and saints of the Epistles. The reason for the change is obvious. During the lifetime of Jesus the disciples were called after their relationship to Him; after His departure the names given indicated their relation to each other and to the society (Dr. Sanday, Inspiration, p. 289). And as an evidential test of the date of the various N.T. writings this is just what we might expect: the Gospels have their own characteristic vocabulary, the Epistles have theirs, whilst Acts forms a kind of link between the two groups, Gospels and Epistles. It is, of course, to be remembered that both terms ἀδελφοί and ἅγιοι are also found in Acts, not to the exclusion of, but alongside with, μαθηταί (cf., e.g., ix. 26, 30, xxi. 4, 7, 16, 17): the former in all parts of the book, and indeed more frequently than μαθηταί, as applied to Christians; the latter four times, ix. 13, 32, 41, xxvi. 10. But if our Lord gave the charge to His disciples recorded in St. Matt. xxviii. 19, bidding them make disciples of all the nations, μαθητεύσατε (cf. also Acts xiv. 21 for the same word), then we can understand that the term would still be retained, as it was so closely associated with the last charge of the Master, whilst a mutual discipleship involved a mutual brotherhood (Matt. xxiii. 8). St. Paul in his Epistles would be addressing those who enjoyed through Christ a common share with himself in a holy fellowship and calling, and whom he would therefore address not as μαθηταί but as ἀδελφοί and ἅγιοι. They were still μαθηταί, yet not of man but of the Lord (only in one passage in Acts, and that a doubtful one, ix. 43, is the word μαθηταί or μαθητής used of any human teacher), and the word was still true of them with that significance, and is still used up to a period subsequent (we may well believe) to the writing of several of Paul's Epistles, Acts xxi. 16. How the word left its impress upon the thought of the Church, in the claim of the disciple to be as his Master, is touchingly evidenced by the expressions of St. Ign., *Ephes.* i. 2; *Magn.*, ix., 2; *Rom.* iv. 2; *Tral.*, v., 2 (St. Polyc., *Martyr*, xvii., 3, where the word is applied to the martyrs as disciples of the Lord, and the prayer is offered : ὧν γένοιτο καὶ ἡμᾶς συγκοινωνούς τε καὶ συμμαθητὰς γενέσθαι). — γογγυσ-μὸς and γογγύζειν are both used by St. Luke (*cf.* Luke v. 30), by St. John, and also by St. Paul, Phil. ii. 14, and I Cor. x. 10, the noun also by St. Peter, i. 4, 9. The noun is found seven times in the LXX of Israel in the wilderness (*cf.* I Cor. x. 10); so in Phil. ii. 14 it is probable that the same passage, Exod. xvi. 7, was in the Apostle's mind, as in the next verse he quotes from the Song of Moses, Deut. xxxii. 5, LXX; so γόγγυσις is also found in LXX with the same meaning, Numb. xiv. 27. γογγυσμός is also found in Wisd. i. 10, Ecclus. xlvi. 7, with reference to Numb. xiv. 26, 27, and twice in Psalms of Solomon v. 15, xvi. 11. In Attic Greek τονθυρισμός would be used (so τονθρίζω and τονθυρίζω). Phrynichus brands the other forms as Ionian, but Dr. Kennedy maintains that γογγυσμός and γογγύζειν from their frequent use in the LXX are rather to be classed amongst "vernacular terms" long continued in the speech of the people, from which the LXX drew. Both words are probably onomatopoetic.—Kennedy, *Sources of N. T. Greek*, pp. 38-40, 72, 73, 76; see also Rutherford, *New Phrynichus*, p. 463; Deissmann, *Bibelstudien*, p. 106. Here the word refers rather to *indignatio clandestina*, not to an open murmuring. —Ἑλληνιστῶν. The meaning of the term, which was a matter of conjecture in St. Chrysostom's day, cannot be said to be decided now (Hort, *Judaistic Christianity*, p. 48). The verb Ἑλλη-νίζειν, to speak Greek (Xen., *Anab.*, vii., 3, 25), helps us reasonably to define it as a Greek-speaking Jew (so also Holtzmann and Wendt). The term occurs again in ix. 29 (and xi. 20 ? see

in loco), and includes those Jews who had settled in Greek-speaking countries, who spoke the common Greek dialect in place of the vernacular Aramaic current in Palestine, and who would be more or less acquainted with Greek habits of life and education. They were there-fore a class distinguished not by descent but by language. This word "Grecians" (A.V.) was introduced to distinguish them from the Greeks by race, but the rendering "Grecian Jews" (R.V.) makes the dis-tinction much plainer. Thus in the Dispersion "the cultured Jew was not only a Jew but a Greek as well"; he would be obliged from force of circum-stances to adapt himself to his surround-ings more or less, but, even in the more educated, the original Jewish element still predominated in his character; and if this was true of the higher it was still more true of the lower classes amongst the Hellenists—no adoption of the Greek language as their mode of speech,no sepa-ration of distance from the Holy City, no defections in their observances of the law, or the surrender as unessential of points which the Pharisees deemed vital, could make them forget that they were members of the Commonwealth of Israel, that Palestine was their home, and the Temple their pride, see B.D.[2], "Hellen-ist," Schürer, *Jewish People*, div. ii., vol. ii., p. 282, E.T.; Hamburger, *Real-Encyclopädie des Judentums*, ii., 3, "Griechenthum". But bearing this de-scription in mind, we can the more easily understand the conflict with Stephen, and his treatment by those who were probably his fellow-Hellenists. If as a cultured Hellenist St. Stephen's sym-pathies were wider and his outlook less narrow than that of the orthodox Jew, or of the less educated type of Hellenist, such a man, who died as St. Stephen died with the prayer of Jesus on his lips (see Feine's remarks), must have so lived in the spirit of his Master's teaching as to realise that in His Kingdom the old order would change and give place to new. But the same considerations help us to understand the fury aroused by St. Stephen's attitude, and it is not difficult to imagine the fanatical rage of a people who had nearly risen in insur-rection because Pilate had placed in his palace at Jerusalem some gilt shields in-scribed with the names of heathen gods, against one who without the power of Pilate appeared to advocate a change of the customs which Moses had delivered (see Nösgen, *Apostelgeschichte*, p. 69).— Ἑβραῖοι—in W.H. with smooth breath-

θεωροῦντο ἐν τῇ διακονίᾳ τῇ καθημερινῇ αἱ χῆραι αὐτῶν.[1] 2. προσκαλεσάμενοι δὲ[2] οἱ δώδεκα τὸ πλῆθος τῶν μαθητῶν, εἶπον, Οὐκ

[1] At end D adds εν τη διακονια των Εβραιων, according to Flor. οτι εν τ. καθ.
διακ. αι χ. των Ελλ. υπο των διακονων των Εβρ. παρεθεωρ. Blass in β reads simply
after αι χ. αυτων the words υπο των διακ. των Εβραιων.

[2] ουν CEHP, Vulg.; δε אB, so Tisch., W.H. text, R.V. marg., Weiss, Wendt;
δη A, so Lach., W.H. marg. D reads τι ουν εστιν αδελφοι; επισκεψ., so Flor.,
Par.; cf. xxi. 22 (Weiss).

ing, see W.H., Introduction, p. 313, and
Winer-Schmiedel, p. 40; here those Jews
in Palestine who spoke Aramaic; in the
Church at Jerusalem they would probably
form a considerable majority, cf. Phil.
iii. 5, and Lightfoot's note. In the N.T.
ʼΙουδαῖος is opposed to Ἕλλην (Rom. i.
16), and Ἑβραῖος to Ἑλληνιστής, Acts vi.
1. In the former case the contrast lies in
the difference of race and religion; in the
latter in the difference of customs and
language. A man might be called ʼΙουδαῖος, but he would not be Ἑβραῖος in the
N.T. sense unless he retained in speech
the Aramaic tongue; the distinction
was therefore drawn on the side of language, a distinction which still survives
in our way of speaking of the *Jewish*
nation, but of the *Hebrew* tongue. See
Trench, *Synonyms*, i., p. 156 ff. In the
two other passages in which Ἑβρ. is
used, Phil. iii. 5 and 2 Cor. xi. 22, whatever difficulties surround them, it is probable that the distinctive force of the
word as explained above is implied. But
as *within* the nation, the distinction is
not recognised by later Christian writers,
and that it finds no place at all in Jewish
writers like Philo and Josephus, or in
Greek authors like Plutarch and Pausanias (Trench, *u. s.*).—πρὸς, cf. St. Luke
v. 30, ἐγόγγυζον πρὸς τ. μαθητὰς αὐτοῦ.
—παρεθεωροῦντο: not found elsewhere
in N.T. and not in LXX, but used in this
sense in Dem. (also by Diodorus and Dion.
Hal.) = παρορᾶν, Attic: imperfect, denoting that the neglect had been going on for
some time; how the neglect had arisen
we are not told—there is no reason to
suppose that there had been previously
Palestinian deacons (so Blass in β, critical notes), for the introduction of such a
class of deacons, as Hilgenfeld notes, is
something quite new, and does not arise
out of anything previously said, although
it would seem that in the rapidly growing
numbers of the Church the Hebrew Christians regarded their Hellenist fellow-
Christians as having only a secondary
claim on their care. Possibly the supply
for the Hellenists fell short, simply be-

cause the Hebrews were already in possession. The Church had been composed
first of Galileans and native Jews resident
in Jerusalem, and then there was added
a wider circle—Jews of the Dispersion.
It is possible to interpret the incident as
an indication of what would happen as
the feeling between Jew and Hellenist
became more bitter, but it is difficult to
believe that the Apostles, who shared
with St. James of Jerusalem the belief
that θρησκεία consisted in visiting the
fatherless and widows in their affliction,
could have acted in a spirit of partiality,
so that the neglect, if it was due to them,
could be attributed to anything else than
to their ignorance of the greatness of the
need.—διακονίᾳ, see below on ver. 2.—
καθημερινῇ: not found elsewhere in N.T.
or in LXX, only in Judith xii. 15. It is
a word only used in Hellenistic Greek,
cf. Josephus, *Ant.*, iii., 10, 1; but it may
be noted that it is also a word frequently
employed by medical writers of a class
of fevers, etc. See instances in Hobart,
pp. 134, 135, and also in Wetstein, *in loco*.
—αἱ χῆραι αὐτῶν: not merely a generic
term for the poor and needy—under the
Mosaic dispensation no legal provision
was made for widows, but they would
not only receive the privileges belonging
to other distressed classes, but also specific regulations protected them — they
were commended to the care of the community, and their oppression and neglect
were strongly condemned—it is quite
possible that the Hellenistic widows had
previously been helped from the Temple
Treasury, but that now, on their joining
the Christian community, this help had
ceased. On the care of the widow in the
early Church, see James i. 27 (Mayor's
note); Polycarp, *Phil.*, vi., 1, where
the presbyters are exhorted to be εὔσ-
πλαγχνοι μὴ ἀμελοῦντες χήρας ἢ ὀρ-
φανοῦ ἢ πένητος, and *cf.* iv. 3. The
word χήρα occurs no less than nine times
in St. Luke's Gospel, three times in the
Acts, but elsewhere in the Evangelists
only three times in St. Mark (Matt. xxiii.
14, omitted by W.H. and R.V.), and two

of these three in an incident which he and St. Luke alone record, Mark xii. 42, 43, and the other time in a passage also peculiar to him and St. Luke (if we are justified in omitting Matt. xxiii. 14), *viz.*, Mark xii. 40.

Ver. 2. προσκαλεσάμενοι δὲ οἱ δώδεκα: whatever may have been the irritation caused by the pride or neglect of the Hebrews, the Apostles recognised that there was ground for complaint, and thus showed not only their practical capacities, but also their freedom from any partiality. οἱ δώδ.: only here in Acts, but *cf.* 1 Cor. xv. 5, where St. Paul uses the title as if it were well and widely known, and required no explanation from him. It is found six times in St. Luke's Gospel, and no less than ten in St. Mark's. See also above i. 26, ii. 14. — τὸ πλῆθος = the whole Church, not the hundred-and-twenty, as J. Lightfoot. The expression is a general one, and need not imply that every single member of the Church obeyed the summons. For the word πλῆθος and the illustration of its use in religious communities on the papyri by Deissmann, see p. 73. The passage has been quoted in support of the democratic constitution of the Apostolic Church, but the whole context shows that the government really lay with the Apostles. The Church as a whole is under their direction and counsel, and the Apostles alone determine what qualification those chosen should possess, the Apostles alone lay hands upon them after prayer: "The hand of man is laid upon the person, but the whole work is of God, and it is His hand which toucheth the head of the one ordained, if he be duly ordained" (Chrys., *Hom.*, xiv.). The dignity of the Apostles, and their authority as leaders of the Church and ordainers of the Seven, is fully recognised by Feine, but he considers that their position is so altered, and the organisation of the Church so much more developed, that another source and not the Jerusalem *Quellenschrift* must be supposed; but if, as Feine allows, such passages as iv. 34, v. 2, belong to the Jerusalem source, it would appear that the authority of the Apostles in the passage before us was a very plain and natural development.— καταλείψαντας: on the formation of the first aorist see Blass, *Grammatik*, p. 43, and also Deissmann, *Neue Bibelstudien*, p. 18; Winer-Schmiedel, p. 109.— διακονεῖν τραπέζαις: there seems to be an intentional antithesis between these words and τῇ διακονίᾳ τοῦ λόγου in ver.

3. The Twelve do not object to the work of ministering, but only to the neglect of ministering to the higher sustenance for the sake of the lower (Hort, *Ecclesia*, p. 206); thus Bengel speaks of the expression as used with indignation, "Antitheton, *ministerium verbi*". διακονία and διακονεῖν are used for ministrations to man, although more usually of man to God; *cf.* Acts xix. 22, of service to St. Paul, διακονία, Acts xi. 29, xii. 25, of service to the brethren of Judæa in the famine, Rom. xv. 25, 31, 2 Cor. viii. 4, ix. 1, 12, 13, of the Gentile collections for the same purpose, so too probably in Rom. xvi. 1 of the service rendered by Stephanas to travelling Christians, *cf.* Heb. vi. 10, and its use of the verb in the Gospels of ministering to our Lord's earthly wants, Luke viii. 3, x. 40 (both noun and verb), John xii. 2; *cf.* also Luke xii. 37, xxii. 27, Matt. iv. 11, Luke iv. 39; see further on the use of the word in classical Greek, Hort, *Ecclesia*, p. 203. The word had a high dignity conferred upon it when, in contrast to the contemptuous associations which surrounded it for the most part in Greek society, Epictetus remarks that it is man's true honour to be a διάκονος of God (*Diss.*, iii., 22, 69; 24, 65; iv. 7, 20; *cf.* iii. 26, 28), and a dignity immeasurably higher still, when the Son of Man could speak of Himself as in Matt. xx. 28, Mark x. 45; *cf.* Luke xxii. 27. "Every clergyman begins as a deacon. This is right. But he never ceases to be a deacon. The priest is a deacon still. The bishop is a deacon still. Christ came as a deacon, lived as a deacon, died as a deacon: μὴ διακονηθῆναι, ἀλλὰ διακονῆσαι" (Lightfoot, *Ordination Sermons*, p. 115). In the LXX the verb does not occur at all, but διάκονος is used four times in Esther i. 10, ii. 2, vi. 3, 5, of the king's chamberlains and of the servants that ministered to him, and once in 4 Macc. ix. 17; διακονία is also found in two of the passages in Esther just quoted, vi. 3 and 5, where in A we read οἱ ἐκ τῆς διακονίας (BS διάκονοι), and once in 1 Macc. xi. 58, of the service of gold sent by Jonathan to Antiochus. What is meant by the expression here? does it refer to distribution of money or in kind? The word in itself might include either, but if we were to limit διακονία to alms, yet the use of the word remarked upon above renders the service higher than that of ordinary relief: "*ministration*," says St. Chrysostom (although he takes it of alms, *Hom.*, xiv.), "extolling by this at once the doers, and

ἀρεστόν ἐστιν ἡμᾶς, καταλείψαντας τὸν λόγον τοῦ Θεοῦ, διακονεῖν
τραπέζαις. 3. ἐπισκέψασθε οὖν, ἀδελφοί, ἄνδρας ἐξ ὑμῶν μαρτυρου-

those to whom it was done ". But τραπέζαις presents a further difficulty; does it refer to the tables of exchange for money, a rendering which claims support from Matt. xxi. 12, xxv. 27, Luke xix. 23, John ii. 15, or to tables for food, Luke xvi. 21, xxii. 21, 30 ? Possibly the use of the word in some passages in the N.T., and also the fact that the διακονία was καθημερινή, may indicate the latter, and the phrase may refer to the actual serving and superintending at the tables at which the poor sat, or at all events to the supplying in a general way those things which were necessary for their bodily sustenance. Zöckler, *Apostelgeschichte* (second edition), refers the word to the ministration of the gifts of love offered at the Eucharist in the various Christian houses (so Scaliger understood the expression of the Agapæ). Mr. Humphry reminds us that the words were quoted by Latimer (1548) in a sermon against some bishops of his time who were comptrollers of the mint.

Ver. 3. ἐπισκέψασθε οὖν : the verb, though frequently used by St. Luke in both his writings, is not elsewhere used in the sense of this verse, "look ye out," *cf.* σκέπτεσθαι in Gen. xli. 33.— μαρτυρουμένους, *cf.* Heb. xi. 2, 39, and *cf.* 4, 5, and 1 Tim. v. 10, Acts x. 22, xxii. 12, also xvi. 2 ; *cf.* its use also in Clem. Rom., *Cor.*, xvii., 1 ; xviii. 1, etc. ; Ignat., *Phil.*, xi., 1 ; *Ephes.*, xii. 2. See also the interesting parallels in Deissmann, *Neue Bibelstudien*, p. 93. In Jos., *Ant.*, iii., 2, 5, and xv., 10, 5, it is used as here, but of hostile testimony in Matt. xxiii. 31, John xviii. 23.— ἑπτά : why was the number chosen? Various answers have been given to the question : (1) that the number was fixed upon because of the seven gifts of the Spirit, Isa. xi. 2, Rev. i. 4 ; (2) that the number was appointed with regard to the different elements of the Church : three Hellenists, three Hebrews, one Proselyte ; (3) that the number was regulated by the fact that the Jerusalem of that day may have been divided into seven districts ; (4) that the number was suggested by the Hebrew sacred number— seven ; (5) Zöckler thinks that there is no hypothesis so probable as that the small Jerusalem ἐκκλησίαι κατ' οἶκον were seven in number, each with its special worship, and its special business connected with alms-giving and distribu-

tion—alms-giving closely related to the Eucharist or to the Love-Feasts ; (6) the derivation of the number from Roman usage on the analogy of the *septemviri epulones* advocated by Dean Plumptre, officials no doubt well known to the *Libertini* (see also B.D.[2] "Deacon," and the remarks of Ramsay, *St. Paul*, p. 375, on Roman organisation and its value). This is far more probable than that there should be any connection between the appointment of the Seven and the two heathen inscriptions quoted by Dr. Hatch (*Bampton Lectures*, p. 50, note 56), in which the word διάκονος is used of the assistants in the ritual of sacrificial and temple feasts at Anactorium in Acarnania and Metropolis in Lydia (on the other hand, Hort, *Ecclesia*, p. 210), for in the incident before us the word διάκονος is not used at all, and later in the history, xxi. 8, Philip is described not by that title but as one of the Seven. Nor is there any real likeness to be found between the office assigned to the Seven and that of the Chazzan or officer of the Jewish synagogue (ὑπηρέτης, Luke iv. 20), who corresponded rather to our parish-clerk or verger, and whose duties were confined to the synagogue ; a nearer Jewish parallel is to be found in the צְדָקָה גַּבָּאֵי, collectors of alms, but these officers would rather present a parallel to the tax-gatherers than to those who ministered to the poor (see "Deacon" in Hastings, B.D.). Whilst, however, these analogies in Jewish offices fail us, we stand on much higher ground if we may suppose that as our Lord's choice of the Twelve was practically the choice of a number sacred in its associations for every Israelite, so the number Seven may have been adopted from its sacredness in Jewish eyes, and thus side by side with the sacred Apostolic College there existed at this period another College, that of the Seven. What was the nature of the office? Was it the Diaconate in the modern sense of the term ? But, as we have noted above, the Seven are never called Deacons, and therefore it has been thought that we have here a special office to meet a special need, and that the Seven were rather the prototypes of the later archdeacons, or corresponded to the elders who are mentioned in xi. 30 and xiv. 23. On the other hand St. Luke,

μένους ἑπτά, πλήρεις Πνεύματος [1] Ἁγίου καὶ σοφίας, οὓς καταστήσω-
μεν [2] ἐπὶ τῆς χρείας ταύτης · 4. ἡμεῖς δὲ τῇ προσευχῇ καὶ τῇ διακονίᾳ

[1] **αγιου** om. 𝕏BC²D 137, 180 (Vulg. am. fu. lux), Syr. Harcl., Chrys.; so Tisch.,
W.H., R.V., Weiss, Wendt.

[2] **καταστησομεν** 𝕏ABCDE, Bas., Chrys., Wendt, Weiss, W.H; **καταστησωμεν**
HP (d, e, Vulg.).

from the prominence given to the narrative, may fairly be regarded as viewing the institution of the office as establishing a new departure, and not as an
isolated incident, and the emphasis is
characteristic of an historian who was fond
of recording " beginnings " of movements.
The earliest Church tradition speaks of
Stephen and Nicolas as ordained to the
diaconate, Iren., *Adv. Haer.*, i., 26;
iv., 15, and the same writer speaks of
Stephen as "the first deacon," iii., 12;
cf. also the testimony of St. Cyprian,
Epist., 3, 3, and the fact that for centuries the Roman Church continued to
restrict the number of deacons to seven
(Cornelius, ap. *Euseb. H. E.*, vi., 43). It
is quite true that the first mention of
διάκονοι in the N.T. (although both
διακονία and **διακονεῖν** are used in the
passage before us) is not found until
Phil. i. 1, but already a deaconess had
been mentioned in writing to the Church
at Rome (xvi. 1, where Phœbe is called
διάκονος), in the Church at Philippi the
office had evidently become established
and familiar, and it is reasonable to assume
that the institution of the Seven at Jerusalem would have been well known to
St. Paul and to others outside Palestine,
" and that analogous wants might well
lead to analogous institutions " (Hort,
and to the same effect, Gore, *The Church
and its Ministry*, p. 403). But if the
Seven were thus the prototypes of the
deacons, we must remember that as the
former office though primarily ordained
for helping the Apostles in distribution
of alms and in works of mercy was by
no means confined to such duties, but
that from the very first the Seven were
occupied in essentially spiritual work,
so the later diaconate was engaged in
something far different from mere charity
organisation ; there were doubtless qualifications demanded such as might be
found in good business men of tact and
discretion, but there were also moral and
spiritual qualities which to a great extent
were required of the **διάκονοι** no less than
of the **πρεσβύτεροι** and **ἐπίσκοποι** : there
was the holding the mystery of the faith
in a pure conscience, there was the

moral and spiritual courage which would
enable the **διάκονοι** to gain even in the
pursuit of their **διακονία** " great boldness
in the faith which is in Christ Jesus," 1
Tim. iii. 13 (Moberly, *Ministerial Priesthood*, p. 138 ff.) ; see also on the whole
subject, Felten, *Apostelgeschichte*, p. 139
ff. ; Zöckler, *Apostelgeschichte*, p. 206 ff. ;
Lightfoot, *Philippians*, " Dissertation on
the Christian Ministry," and *Real-Encyclopädie für protest. Theol. und Kirche*
(Hauck), " Diakonen " (Heft 38, 1898).
—**σοφίας**: practical wisdom, *prudentia,
cf.* 1 Cor. vi. 5 (Blass, so Grimm) ; in
ver. 10 the use of the word is different,
but in both places **σοφία** is referred to
the Spirit, " it is not simply spiritual
men, but full of the Spirit and of wisdom
. . . for what profits it that the dispenser of alms speak not, if nevertheless
he wastes all, or be harsh and easily provoked ?" Chrys., *Hom.*, xiv.—**οὓς κατα-
στήσομεν** (on the reading *whom ye*,
which was exhibited in some few editions
of A.V., see *Speaker's Commentary, in
loco*) : the appointment, the consecration, and the qualifications for it, depend
upon the Apostles—the verb implies at
all events an exercise of authority if it
has no technical force, *cf.* Titus i. 5.
The same shade of meaning is found in
classical writers and in the LXX in the
use of the verb with the genitive, with
ἐπί, sometimes with a dative, sometimes
with an accusative : Gen. xxxix. 4, xli.
41, Exod. ii. 14, xviii. 21, Num. iii. 10,
Neh. xii. 44, Dan. ii. 48, 49, 1 Macc. vi.
14; *cf.* its use in Luke xii. 14, 42, 44.
The opposite is expressed by **μεταστή-
σασθαι ἀπὸ τῆς χρ.**, Polyb., iv., 87, 9 ; 1
Macc. xi. 63 (Wendt).—**χρείας**: the word
might mean need in the sense of necessity, Latin *opus*, want, 2 Chron. ii. 16,
Wisdom xiii. 16, 1 Macc. iii. 28, or it
might mean business, Latin *negotium,
officium*. In the LXX it seems to be
employed in both senses, as also in
classical writers, but here both A. and
R.V. render " business " (so in Polybius),
cf. Judith xii. 10 AB., 1 Macc. x. 37, xi.
63, xii. 45 (**χρεία** is found no less than
eight times in 1 Macc., seven times in 2
Macc., once in 3 Macc.) ; see Wetstein

τοῦ λόγου προσκαρτερήσομεν.[1] 5. καὶ ἤρεσεν ὁ λόγος [2] ἐνώπιον παντὸς
τοῦ πλήθους · καὶ ἐξελέξαντο Στέφανον, ἄνδρα πλήρη [3] πίστεως καὶ
Πνεύματος Ἁγίου, καὶ Φίλιππον, καὶ Πρόχορον καὶ Νικάνορα, καὶ

[1] προσκαρτερησομεν ; D, Flor., Gig., Par., Vulg. read εσομεθα . . . προσκαρ-
τερουντες. This participial construction with the substantive verb is characteristic
of St. Luke, and occurs with the same verb as here in i. 14, ii. 42, viii. 13.

[2] ο λογος ; D, Flor. (Gig.) add ουτος ; Harris refers to retrans. from Latin,
παντος του πληθους ; D adds των μαθητων, so Hilg. ; Flor. substitutes παντων των
μαθητων, so Blass in β.

[3] πληρη BC corr., T.R. ; so Weiss, Wendt, W.H., R.V. ; πληρης אBC*DEHP,
so Lach. See further below.

for uses of the word in Philo and
Josephus.

Ver. 4. ἡμεῖς δὲ : in marked contrast
to the service of tables, etc., but still every
work in the Church, whether high or
low, was a διακονία.—τῇ διακ. τοῦ λ.,
see above.—προσκαρτερήσομεν, "will
continue steadfastly," R.V., see above
on i. 14.—τῇ προσ., "the prayer"
(Hort) ; the article seems to imply not
only private prayer and intercession, but
the public prayer of the Church.

Ver. 5. ἤρεσεν ἐνώπιον : phrase not
usual in classical Greek ; but ἐνώ. in this
sense, so κατενώπιον ἔναντι κατέναντι,
derived from the LXX (ἐναντίον
frequent in LXX, is also classical) ; cf.,
e.g., Deut. i. 23 A, 2 Sam. iii. 36, 1
Kings iii. 10, xx. (xxi.) 2, Jer. xviii. 4,
Ju. vii. 16, xiii. 20, 1 Macc. vi. 60,
viii. 21 (ἐναντίον, S), where the whole
phrase occurs. Blass, Grammatik, p.
125, and see on iv. 10.—πλήθους, cf.
Deissmann, Neue Bibelstudien, p. 60,
and above on p. 73.—ἐξελέξαντο, see
above, cf. xv. 22, 25, always in the
middle in N.T. (Luke ix. 35 doubtful), so
in LXX. Blass, Grammatik, p. 181,
nearly always = בָּחַר. On the importance of the step thus taken as marking
a distinct stage in the organisation of
the Church, and in the distribution of
work amongst the members of what was
now a true body politic, see Ramsay, St.
Paul, p. 372 ; Hort., Ecclesia, p. 52, and
on its further importance in the emancipation of the Church, see Lightfoot's " Paul
and the Three". The choice of the
names has often been held to indicate
the liberal spirit in which the complaint
of the Hellenists was met, since the Seven
bear purely Greek names, and we infer
that the bearers were Hellenists, "ele-
gerunt ergo Graecos non Hebræos, ut
magis satisfacerent murmuri Graecorum"
Cornelius à Lapide. But the inference
is not altogether certain, however pro-

bable (see Wendt, Felten), for Greek
names, e.g., Philip, Didymus, Andrew,
were also found amongst the Palestinian
Jews. Bengel holds that part were
Hebrew, part Hellenist, whilst Gieseler
hazarded the opinion that three were
Hebrews, three Hellenists, and one a
proselyte. But we cannot conclude
from the fact that they were probably
Hellenists, that the Seven were only
charged with the care of distribution
amongst the Hellenist section of the
Church, as there is nothing in the narrative to warrant this. We cannot say
that we know anything of the Seven
except Stephen and Philip—Stephen
the preacher and martyr of liberty,
Philip the practical worker (Lightfoot,
" Paul and the Three "). Baronius
hazarded the fanciful conjecture that
Stephen as well as Saul was a pupil of
Gamaliel. Both Stephen and Philip were
said to have been amongst the Seventy,
Epiphanius, Haer., xx., 4 (but see Hooker,
v., lxxviii., 5). If so, it is possible that
they may have been sent to labour in
Samaria as our Lord had laboured there,
Luke ix. 52, xvii. 11 ; and possibly the
after work of Philip in that region, and
possibly some of the remarks in St.
Stephen's speech, may be connected
with a mission which had been committed to Hellenistic Jews. See further
on his name and work, Dean Plumptre,
in loco, and also below, notes on chap.
vii. He may well be called not only the
proto-martyr, but also the first great
Christian Ecclesiastic (B.D.[1] "Stephen").
—The description given of Stephen (as
of Barnabas, so closely similar, xi. 24,
cf. Numb. xxvii. 18 of Joshua) shows that
the essential qualifications for office were
moral and spiritual ; see also below on
Φίλιππον.—πλήρη : in some MSS. the
word appears as indeclinable, W.H.
margin, so in ver. 3, xix. 28, Mark viii. 19,
2 John 8. Blass, Grammatik, p. 81.
St. Luke uses the adjective twice in his

Τίμωνα καὶ Παρμενᾶν, καὶ Νικόλαον προσήλυτον Ἀντιοχέα, 6. οὓς
ἔστησαν ἐνώπιον τῶν ἀποστόλων· καὶ προσευξάμενοι ἐπέθηκαν αὐτοῖς

Gospel, and eight times in the Acts; on his fondness for such words, see p. 73.— πίστεως: not in the lower sense of honesty or truthfulness, but in the higher sense of religious faith, *cf.* xi. 24, "non modo fidelitate sed fide spirituali," Bengel.— Φίλιππον, *cf.* viii. 5, xxi. 8: we may probably trace his work also along the coasts of Palestine and Phœnicia, *cf.* viii. 40, xv. 3, xxi. 3, 7 (Plumptre's notes on these passages), and no doubt St. Luke would have learnt from him, when he met him at Cæsarea, xxi. 8, much that relates to the early history of the Church, *Introd.*, 17. It would appear both in his case and in that of St. Stephen that the duties of the Seven could not have been confined to service of the tables. In the deacons M. Renan saw a proclamation of the truth that social questions should be the first to occupy the attention of man, and the deacons were, for him, the best preachers of Christianity; but we must not forget that they did not preach merely by their method and works of charity, but by a proclamation of a Saviour and by the power of the Holy Ghost. In the reference to Philip in xxi. 8 as simply "one of the Seven" we may fairly see one of the many proofs of the unity of the authorship of *Acts*, see Salmon, *Introd.*, chapter xviii., and Lightfoot, "Acts," B.D.[2], and see further, Salmon in the same chapter, on the proof which is afforded in the account of Philip of the antiquity of the *Acts;* see below also on xxi. 8.—Πρόχορον: tradition says that he was consecrated by St. Peter Bishop of Nicomedia, and a fabulous biography of John the Evangelist had his name attached to it, as a companion of the Apostle in Asia, and his biographer—but we cannot attach any credence to any such professed information; see Blass, *in loco*, Hilgenfeld, *Zeitschrift für wissenschaft. Theol.*, 1895, p. 426; B.D.[1] iii. *sub v.* Of Simon, Parmenas, Nicanor, it cannot be said that anything is known, as is frankly admitted by the Romanist commentator Felten.—Νικόλαον προσήλυτον Ἀ.: that the name proselyte is given to him has been held by many to mark him out as the only proselyte among the Seven; otherwise it is difficult to see why he alone is so designated (so Ramsay, *St. Paul*, p. 375, Lightfoot, Hort, Weiss, Felten, and amongst earlier writers, De Wette and Ewald). No doubt he was a proselyte of the higher and more com-

plete type (a "proselyte of the gate," the lower type—as distinct from a "proselyte of righteousness"—is always in Acts φοβούμενος or σεβόμενος τὸν θεόν), but Ramsay sees in his election to office another distinct step in advance : "the Church is wider than the pure Jewish race, and the non-Jewish element is raised to official rank," although, as Ramsay himself points out, there was nothing in this step out of harmony with the principle of the extreme Judaistic party (*St. Paul*, p. 375, *cf.* 157). The case of Cornelius was of a different kind, see below on chap. x. But the notice is all the more interesting because it contains the first mention of the Church afterwards so important, the Mother Church of the Gentiles, Antioch in Syria, and this may point to the reason of the description of Nicolaus as a proselyte of Antioch. It was a notice of special interest to St. Luke if his own home was at Antioch, but we cannot say positively that the notice means that Nicolaus was the *only* proselyte among the Seven. That the Jews were numerous at Antioch and had made many proselytes we learn from Jos., *B. J.*, vii., 3, 3 : of the supposed connection between this Nicolaus and the sect of the Nicolaitans, Rev. ii. 6, 14, we may hesitate to say with Blass that it is worthy of no more credit than the notice which attaches to Prochorus, although we may also well hesitate to accept it, but it has been advocated by Lightfoot, *Galatians*, p. 297, and recently by Zöckler, *Apostelgeschichte*, p. 199. Zöckler goes so far as to see in the list of the Seven a copy of the list of the Apostles, inasmuch as the most distinguished is placed first, the traitor last. But Nicolaus would be fitly placed last if he were the only proselyte. The Patristic evidence in support of the connection in question is by no means conclusive, see Ritschl, *Altkatholische Kirche*, p. 135 and note (second edition), Felten, *Apostelgeschichte*, p. 140, and Wendt, *in loco*, Hilgenfeld, *Zeitschrift für wissenschaft. Theol.*, p. 425 (1895). Holtzmann on Rev. ii. 6 holds that the Nicolaitans, who are not to be connected with Nicolaus the deacon, may = symbolically, the Bileamites, ver. 14; so Grimm, *sub. v.* Νικολαΐτης, if we take the latter as coinciding with the Hebrew

בִּלְעָם = *destruction of the people.*

τὰς χεῖρας.　7. καὶ ὁ λόγος τοῦ Θεοῦ [1] ηὔξανε, καὶ ἐπληθύνετο ὁ
ἀριθμὸς τῶν μαθητῶν ἐν Ἱερουσαλὴμ σφόδρα, πολύς τε ὄχλος τῶν
ἱερέων [2] ὑπήκουον τῇ πίστει.

[1] θεου ‭ℵ‬ABCHP; but DE 180, Vulg., Par., Syr. Harcl., Chrys., Orint. read Κυριου.

[2] ιερεων; but ‭ℵ‬* Syr. Pesh., Theophyl. read ιουδαιων.　(See below.)

Ver. 6. ἔστησαν, cf. i. 23 ; for ἐνώπιον,
see above.—καὶ προσευξάμενοι ἐπέθηκαν
αὐτοῖς τὰς χεῖρας: change of subject.
This is the first mention of the laying on
of hands in the Apostolic Church. No
doubt the practice was customary in the
Jewish Church, Num. xxvii. 18, Deut.
xxxiv. 9; see also Edersheim, *Jewish
Social Life*, p. 281, and *Jesus the Messiah*, ii., 382, and Hamburger, *Real-
Encyclopädie*, ii., 6, pp. 882-886, "Ordini-
rung, Ordination"; Hort, *Ecclesia*, p.
216; Gore, *Church and the Ministry*, pp.
187, 382; but the constant practice of it
by our Lord Himself was sufficient to
recommend it to His Apostles. It soon
became the outward and visible sign of
the bestowal of spiritual gifts in the
Apostolic Church, *cf.* Acts viii. 15, xiii.
3, 1 Tim. iv. 14, v. 22, 2 Tim. i. 6, and
every convert was instructed in its meaning as one of the elementary teachings
of the faith, Heb. vi. 2. That the act
was a means of grace is evident from St.
Paul's words, for he reminds Timothy of
the grace thus bestowed upon him, 1
Tim. iv. 14, 2 Tim. i. 6, and from the
narrative of St. Luke in viii. 15, 17, and
passages below. But that it was not
a mere outward act dissociated from
prayer is evident from St. Luke's words
in the passage before us, in viii. 17, xiii.
3, and xix. 6. See especially Hooker, v.,
lxvi., 1, 2; see below in viii. and xiii.,
and Gore, *Church and the Ministry*,
especially note G. Holtzmann would
draw a distinction between the laying on
of hands here and in viii. 17, xix. 6.
Here, he contends, it only corresponds
to the customary usage at the ordination
of a Rabbi, as the Seven had already
received the Holy Ghost, ver. 3, 5, *cf.*
xiii. 1. But ver. 8 undoubtedly justifies
us in believing that an accession of power
was granted after the laying on of hands,
and now for the first time mention is
made of St. Stephen's τέρατα καὶ σημεῖα
μεγάλα (see St. Chrysostom's comment).
Ver. 7. τῶν ἱερέων: the reading
Ἰουδαίων is advocated by Klostermann,
Probleme in Aposteltexte, pp. 13, 14, but
not only is the weight of critical evidence
overwhelmingly against it, but we can

scarcely doubt that St. Luke would have
laid more stress upon the first penetration
of the Christian faith into districts outside
Jerusalem—this is represented as the result of the persecution about Stephen,
viii. 4; *cf.* John xii. 42 (see also Wendt,
1899, p. 145, note). The whole verse
shows that the γογγυσμός had not interfered with the growth of the Church.
The conjecture that in the word ὄχλος
reference is made to the priests of the
plebs in contrast to the learned priests is
in no way satisfactory; if this had been
the meaning, the words would have been
πολλοί τε ἱερεῖς τοῦ ὄχλου, and no such
distinction of priests is anywhere noticed
in the N.T., see further below.—ἐν Ἱερουσαλήμ: Hilgenfeld (so Weiss) considers
that, as this notice implies that there
were disciples outside Jerusalem, such a
remark is inconsistent with the statements of the after-spread of the Church
in this chapter and in viii., and that
therefore the words ἐν Ἱ. are to be referred to the "author to Theophilus".
But so far from the words bearing the
interpretation of Hilgenfeld, the historian
may have introduced them to mark the
fact that the growth of the Church continued in Jerusalem, in the capital where
the hierarchical power was felt, and that
the growth included the accession of
priests no less than of laymen.—ὑπήκουον
τῇ πίστει: the imperfect may denote repetition—the priests kept joining the new
community, Blass, *in loco ; cf.* Rom. i. 5,
vi. 16, 17, x. 16, 2 Thess. i. 8—the verb
(very frequent in LXX) is only used in
Acts in this place in the sense given, but
often in St. Paul's Epistles. No doubt
when the number of Jewish priests was
so large (according to Josephus, twenty
thousand) both poor and wealthy would
have been included in the statement, and
we cannot limit it to the Sadducees. It
must be borne in mind that the obedience
of these priests to the Christian faith
need not of necessity have interfered
with the continuance of their duties in
the Temple (so Felten), especially when
we remember the attitude of Peter and
John; but the words certainly seem to
mark their complete obedience to the

8. ΣΤΕΦΑΝΟΣ δὲ πλήρης πίστεως [1] καὶ δυνάμεως ἐποίει τέρατα καὶ σημεῖα μεγάλα ἐν τῷ λαῷ.　9. ἀνέστησαν δέ τινες τῶν ἐκ τῆς συνα-

[1] πιστεως HP, Syr. Harcl., Chrys.; cf. ver. 5.　χαριτος ℵABD, Vulg., Sah., Boh., Syr. Pesh., Arm., Bas., Did.; so Tisch., W.H., R.V., Weiss, Hilg. After λαω D (Syr. H. mg.), Par. (E, Flor., Gig.), so Hilg., add δια του ονοματος κυριου I. X.; cf. iv. 30 (and in *Classical Review*, July, 1897, p. 319).

faith (see Grimm-Thayer, *sub v.* πίστις, i. *b*, *a*), and in face of the opposition of the Sadducees and the more wealthy priestly families, an open adherence to the disciples of Jesus may well have involved a break with their former profession (Hort, *Judaistic Christianity*, p. 49, and *Ecclesia*, p. 52).　May there not have been many among the priests waiting for the consolation of Israel, men righteous and devout like the Pharisee priest or priests, to whom perhaps we owe that expression of the hopes of the pious Jew in the *Psalms of Solomon*, which approach so nearly in style and character to the Hymns of the priest Zacharias and the devout Symeon in the early chapters of St. Luke's Gospel ? see Ryle and James's edition, *Psalms of Solomon*, Introd., lix., lx.　Spitta refers the whole verse to his source B, as a break in the narrative, without any connection with what follows or precedes. Clemen assigns vi. 1-6 to his special source, H(*istoria*) H(*ellenistarum*) ; vi. 7 to his H(*istoria*) Pe(*tri*).　Jüngst assigns vi. 1-6. 7b, c, to his source B, 7a to his R(edactor).　The comment of Hilgenfeld on ver. 7 is suggestive (although he himself agrees with Spitta, and regards the verse as an interpretation), "Clemen und Jüngst nicht einmal dieses Verstein ungeteilt".

Ver. 8.　πλήρης πίστεως, but χάριτος, R.V. Vulgate, *gratia* = divine grace, xviii. 27, not merely favour with the people—the word might well include, as in the case of our Lord, the λόγοι χάριτος which fell from his lips (Luke iv. 22).　On the word as characteristic of St. Luke and St. Paul, see Friedrich, *Das Lucasevangelium*, pp. 28, 96 ; in the other Gospels it only occurs three times; *cf.* John i. 14, 16, 17.　See Plummer's note on the word in *St. Luke*, *l. c.*—δυνάμεις : not merely power in the sense of courage, heroism, but power to work miracles, supernatural power, *cf.* viii. 13 and Luke v. 17.　That the word also means spiritual power is evident from ver. 10.—ἐποίει, "was doing," imperfect, during Stephen's career of grace and power the attack was made ; notice

imperfect combined with aorist, ἀνέστησαν, see Rendall's note.　In ver. 8 Spitta sees one of the popular legendary notices of his source B.　St. Stephen is introduced as the great miracle-worker, who is brought before the Sanhedrim, because in v. 17, a parallel incident in B, the Apostles were also represented as miracle-doers and brought before the same assembly ; it would therefore seem that the criticism which can only see in the latter part of the Acts, in the miracles ascribed to St. Paul, a repetition in each case of the miracles assigned in the former part to St. Peter, must now be further utilised to account for any points of likeness between the career of St. Stephen and the other leaders of the Church.　But nowhere is it said that Stephen was brought before the Sanhedrim on account of his miracles, and even if so, it was quite likely that the ζῆλος of the Sanhedrim would be stirred by such manifestations as on the former occasion in chap. v.

Ver. 9.　ἀνέστησαν : in a hostile sense, *cf.* Luke x. 25, Mark xiv. 57, and see above on v. 17.—τῆς συναγωγῆς : in Jerusalem, Alexandria, Rome and the larger towns there was no doubt a considerable number of synagogues, but the tradition that assigned no less than four hundred and eighty to Jerusalem alone is characterised by Schürer as a Talmudic myth (*Jewish Temple*, div. ii., vol. ii., p. 73, E.T., so too Edersheim, *Jewish Social Life*, pp. 83, 252, but see also Renan, *Apostles*, p. 113, E.T.).　The number four hundred and eighty was apparently fixed upon as the numerical equivalent of the Hebrew word for "full," in Isa. i. 21, a city "full of judgment". The names which follow have been variously classified, but they have always proved and still prove a difficulty.　Ramsay considers that the bad form of the list is due to the fact that St. Luke is here dependent on an authority whose expressions he either translated *verbatim* or did not understand, *Expositor* (1895), p. 35.　One thing seems certain, *viz.*, that Λιβερτίνων does not refer to any town Libertum in the neighbourhood of

γωγῆς τῆς λεγομένης [1] Λιβερτίνων, καὶ Κυρηναίων καὶ Ἀλεξανδρέων,
καὶ τῶν ἀπὸ Κιλικίας καὶ Ἀσίας,[2] συζητοῦντες τῷ Στεφάνῳ· 10. καὶ

[1] τῆς λεγομένης BCDEHP, Vulg. Syrr. P.H., Arm., Aeth. (Chrys.), so Lach.,
W.H., Weiss, Wendt; τῶν λεγομενων ℵA 13, 47, Gig., Sah., Boh., Chrys., so Tisch.

[2] Ασιας om. AD² d, so Lach., Hilg. brackets; may easily have dropped out after
Κιλικιας. συζητουντες, B³HP.

Carthage, which has been urged as an explanation of the close juxtaposition of Cyrene, also in Africa. The existence of a town or region bearing any such name is merely conjectural, and even if its existence could be demonstrated, it is improbable that many Jews from such an obscure place should have been resident in Jerusalem. There is therefore much probability that St. Chrysostom was correct in referring the word to the Libertini, Ῥωμαῖοι ἀπελεύθεροι. The Libertini here were probably Roman "freedmen" who were formerly captive Jews brought to Rome by Pompey, B.C. 63 (Suet., *Tib.*, 36; Tac., *Ann.*, ii., 85; Philo, *Legat. ad Gaium*, 23), and afterwards liberated by their Roman masters. These men and their descendants would enjoy the rights of Roman citizenship, and some of them appear to have returned to Jerusalem, where they had their own community and a synagogue called συναγ. Λιβερτίνων (according to Grimm-Thayer, *sub v.* Λιβερτ., some evidence seems to have been discovered of a "synagogue of the Libertines" at Pompeii), see Schürer, *Jewish Temple*, div. ii., vol. ii., pp. 57, 276, 277; O. Holtzmann, *Neutest. Zeitgeschichte*, p. 89; and Zöckler, *Apostelgeschichte*, p. 201 (second edition). But a further question arises as to the number of synagogues intended. Thus it has been maintained that they were five in number. This is Schürer's decided view, Weiss, Meyer (in earlier editions), so Hackett, so Matthias, *Handbuch zum N. T.*, V. *Apostelgeschichte*, 1897. By other writers it is thought that reference is made to two synagogues. This is the view advocated by Wendt as against Meyer. Wendt admits that as in the places named there were undoubtedly large numbers of Jewish inhabitants, so it is possible that in Jerusalem itself they may have been sufficiently numerous to make up the five synagogues, but his own view is based upon the ground that τῶν before ἀπὸ Κ. καὶ Ἀ. is parallel with the τῶν after τινες (so Holtzmann, Felten). So too Zöckler, who depends upon the simple καί before Κυρηναίων and Ἀλεξ. as pointing to one group with the Libertines; τῶν ἀπὸ Κ. καὶ Ἀσίας forming a second group. Dr. Sanday, *Expositor*, viii., p. 327 (third series), takes the same view of two synagogues only, as he considers that it is favoured by the Greeks (so too Dean Plumptre and Winer-Moulton, xix., 5a, note, but see also Winer-Schmiedel, p. 158; *cf.* critical note above). Mr. Page is inclined to think that three synagogues are intended: (1) *i.e.*, of the Libertini, (2) another of the men of Alexandria and Cyrene, (3) another of the men of Cilicia and Asia; whilst many writers from Calvin, Bengel and others to O. Holtzmann and Rendall hold that only one synagogue is intended; so Dr. Hort maintains that the Greek suggests only the one synagogue of the Libertines, and that the other names are simply descriptive of origin—from the south, Cyrene, and Alexandria; from the north, Cilicia, and Proconsular Asia. On the whole the Greek seems to favour the view of Wendt as above; καὶ Κυρην. καὶ Ἀλεξ. seem to form, as Blass says, a part of the same appellation with Λιβερτίνων. Blass himself has recently, *Philology of the Gospels*, p. 49 ff., declared in favour of another reading, Λιβυστίνων, which he regards as the correct text, Λιβερτίνων being corrupt although differing only in two letters from the original. In the proposed reading he is following Oecumenius and Beza amongst others; the same reading is apparently favoured also by Wetstein, who gives both the passages to which Blass refers, one from Catullus, lx., 1, "Leæna montibus Libystinis," and the other from the geographical Lexicon of Stephanus Byzantinus. Λιβυστίνων would mean Jews inhabitants of Libya, not Libyans, and the synagogue in question bore the name of Λιβυσ. καὶ Κυρηναίων καὶ Ἀλεξ., thus specifying the African Jews in the geographical order of their original dwelling-places.— Κυρηναίων, see on ii. 9, and below, xi. 20, xiii. 1.—Ἀλεξ.: probably there was no city, next to Jerusalem and Rome, in which the Jewish population was so numerous and influential as in Alexan-

οὐκ ἴσχυον ἀντιστῆναι τῇ σοφίᾳ¹ καὶ τῷ πνεύματι ᾧ ἐλάλει.² 11. τότε³
ὑπέβαλον ἄνδρας λέγοντας, Ὅτι ἀκηκόαμεν αὐτοῦ λαλοῦντος ῥήματα

¹ After σοφίᾳ DE, Flor. add τη ουση εν αυτω, so Hilg., and after πνευματι DE,
Flor., Gig., Par. add τω αγιω. (Harris regards as Montanist additions.)

² At end of verse 10 D (E), Syr. Harcl. mg., Flor., Wern. add δια το ελεγχεσθαι
υπ' αυτου μετα πασης παρρησιας; (11) μη δυναμενοι ουν αντοφθαλμειν τη αληθειᾳ,
so Hilg., Blass. E, διοτι ηλεγχοντο . . . επειδη ουκ ηδυναντο αντιλεγειν τη
αληθειᾳ, possible influence of Luke xxi. 15, 2 Tim. iii. 8 (see Chase); Harris refers
to Latin and regards as Montanistic. μετα π. παρρησιας characteristic of Luke
and Paul, iv. 29, etc.; αντοφθαλμειν Acts xxvii. 15. Blass refers to Wisdom xii. 14
(also in Polyb.); cf. also v. 39 with Wisdom l.c.

³ Both ουν and τοτε are retained by Blass in β, but see Weiss, Codex D, p. 66,
Flor. reads τοτε ουν μη δυν.

dria. In his new city Alexander the
Great had assigned the Jews a place:
their numbers rapidly grew, and, according to Philo, two of the five districts of
the town, named after the first five letters
of the alphabet, were called "the Jewish,"
from the number of Jews dwelling in
them, one quarter, Delta, being entirely
populated by them. Julius Caesar and
Augustus confirmed their former privileges, and they retained them for the
most part, with the important exception
described by Philo, during subsequent
reigns. For some time, until the reign
of Claudius, they had their own officer
to represent them as ethnarch (alabarch),
and Augustus appointed a council who
should superintend their affairs according
to their own laws, and the Romans
evidently recognised the importance of a
mercenary race like the Jews for the
trade and commerce of the city. Here
dwelt the famous teacher Philo, B.C.
20-A.D. 50; here Apollos was trained,
possibly under the guidance of the famous
philosopher, and here too St. Stephen
may have belonged by birth and education (Edersheim, *Jewish Social Life*, p.
253). St. Paul never visited Alexandria,
and it is possible that the Apostle may
have felt after his experience at Corinth,
and the teaching of Apollos (1 Cor. i.
12), that the simplicity of his own message of Christ Crucified would not have
been acceptable to hearers of the word of
wisdom and the lovers of allegory. On the
causes which tended to produce a distinct
form of the Jewish character and faith in
the city, see B.D.² "Alexandria," and
Hastings, B.D., *sub v.*; Stanley's *Jewish
Church*, iii., xlvii.; Hamburger, *Real-
Encyclopädie des Judentums*, ii., 1, 47.
We know that Alexandria had, as was
only likely, a synagogue at Jerusalem,
specially gorgeous (Edersheim, *Jewish
Social Life*, p. 253); on the history

of the place see, in addition to literature already mentioned, Schürer, *Jewish
People*, div. ii., vol. ii., pp. 73, 228,
229, 244, E.T.; Jos., *Ant.*, xiv., 7, 2;
x., 1; xix., 5, 2.—Κιλικίας: of special interest because Saul of Tarsus would probably be prominent amongst "those of
Cilicia," and there is no difficulty in
supposing with Weiss and even Spitta
(*Apostelgeschichte*, p. 115) that he belonged to the members of the Cilician
synagogue who disputed with Stephen.
To the considerable Jewish community
settled in Tarsus, from the time of the
Seleucidæ, Saul belonged. But whatever
influence early associations may have had
upon Stephen, Saul by his own confession
was not merely the son of a Pharisee, but
himself a Pharisee of the Pharisees in
orthodoxy and zeal, Gal. i. 14, Phil. iii.
5. It would seem that there was a synagogue of the Tarsians at Jerusalem,
Megilla, 26a (Hamburger, *u. s.*, ii., 1,
148); see also B.D.² "Cilicia," Schürer,
u. s., p. 222; O. Holtzmann, *Neutest.
Zeitgeschichte*, p. 100. The "Jews from
Asia" are those who at a later date,
xxi. 27, are again prominent in their zeal
for the sacredness of the Holy Place, and
who hurl against Paul the same fatal
charge which he now directs against
Stephen (Plumptre, *in loco*; Sabatier,
L'Apôtre Paul, p. 20).—συνζητοῦντες: not
found in LXX or other Greek versions of
the O.T., or Apocrypha, although it may
occur, Neh. ii. 4, in the sense of request,
but the reading is doubtful (see Hatch
and Redpath). In the N.T. it is used
six times by St. Mark and four times by
St. Luke (twice in his Gospel), and
always in the sense of questioning, generally in the sense of disputatious questioning. The words of Josephus in his
preface (sect. 5), *B. J.*, may help us to
understand the characteristics of the
Hellenists. The same verb is used by

βλάσφημα[1] εἰς Μωσῆν[2] καὶ τὸν Θεόν.   12. συνεκίνησάν τε τὸν λαὸν καὶ
τοὺς πρεσβυτέρους καὶ τοὺς γραμματεῖς, καὶ ἐπιστάντες συνήρπασαν

[1] βλασφημα ℵABCEHP, so Tisch., W.H., Weiss; βλασφημιας ℵ*D, Vulg.,
Flor., Gig., so Blass in β, and Hilg.

[2] Μωσην; but Μωυσην ℵABCDH, so Tisch., W.H., Weiss, Hilg. (See esp.
Winer-Schmiedel, pp. 51, 52, and note 43.)

St. Paul himself, as in this same Jerusalem he disputed, possibly in their synagogue, with the Hellenists on behalf of
the faith which he was now seeking to
destroy, Acts ix. 29. In modern Greek
the verb has always the meaning to discuss, to dispute (Kennedy).

Ver. 10. καὶ οὐκ ἴσχυον ἀντιστῆναι:
the whole phrase is an exact fulfilment
of Luke xxi. 15, cf. 1 Cor. i. 17, ii. 6.
πνεῦμα, as Wendt points out, was the
Holy Spirit with which Stephen was
filled, cf. 3, 5. Vulgate renders " Spiritui
Sancto qui loquebatur," as if it read ὅ;
see critical notes.

Ver. 11. ὑπέβαλον: only found here
in N.T., not in LXX in this sense; sub-
ornaverunt; Vulgate, submiserunt (Suet.,
Ner., 28), cf. Appian, B. C., i., 74,
ὑπεβλήθησαν κατήγοροι, and Jos., B. J.,
v., 10, 41, μηνυτής τις ὑπόβλητος.—
ῥήματα βλασφημίας = βλάσφημα, Hebraism, cf. Rev. xiii. 1, xvii. 3, Winer-
Schmiedel, p. 266.—εἰς Μωυσῆν καὶ τὸν
Θεόν: Rendall draws a distinction between λαλοῦντος . . . εἰς and λαλῶν
ῥήματα κατά in ver. 13, the former denoting charges of blasphemy about Moses,
and the latter against, etc., cf. ii. 25,
Heb. vii. 14, but it is doubtful whether
this distinction can be maintained, cf.
Luke xii. 10 and xxii. 65. The R.V.
renders both prepositions against: cf.
Dan., LXX, vii., 25, and iii. 29 (96;
LXX and Theod.).

Ver. 12. συνεκίνησαν: not found in
LXX or other Greek versions of O.T., or
in the Apocrypha, cf. Polyb., xv., 17, 1,
so too in Plutarch. As this word and
συνήρπασαν are found only in St. Luke
it is perhaps worth noting that they are
both frequent in medical writers, see
below.—τὸν λαὸν: a crafty design to
gain the people first, not only because
they had hitherto favoured the Nazarenes,
but because the Sanhedrim would be
more inclined to take action if they felt
that the people were with them, cf. iv.
26.—ἐπιστάντες, see on iv. 1.—συνήρπασαν, "seized him," R.V.; "caught,"
A.V., signifies rather capture after pursuit than a sudden seizure (Humphry);

only in St. Luke in the N.T., once in his
Gospel, viii. 29, and Acts xix. 29, xxvii.
15. In the first passage it is used of the
demoniac of the country of the Gerasenes;
many times the evil spirit συνηρπάκει
αὐτόν; see 2 Macc. vii. 27, Prov. vi. 25,
2 Macc. iv. 41, 4 Macc. v. 4. The word
is also quite classical, see Hobart, Medical Language, pp. 204, 243; on the
hostility against Stephen and its causes,
see above. At this word συνήρπ. Hilgenfeld would stop, and the rest of the
verse, ἤγαγον to vii. 2, is referred by
him to his "author to Theophilus". The
leading Stephen before the Sanhedrim
is thus excluded by Hilgenfeld, because
nothing is said of the previous summoning of the Council as in iv. 5, 6! and the
introduction of false witnesses and their
accusation is something quite different
from the charge of blasphemous words
against Moses and God! In somewhat
the same manner Spitta refers vi. 1-6,
9-12ᵃ, to his source A, and sees so far
a most trustworthy narrative, no single
point in which can fairly be assailed by
criticism, Apostelgeschichte, p. 115, whilst
vi. 7 f., 12ᵇ-15 constitute B, a worthless
document on account of its legendary
and fictitious character — instituting a
parallel between the death of Stephen
and that of Christ, and leaving nothing
historical except the fact that Stephen
was a conspicuous member of the early
Church who died as a martyr by stoning.
But whilst Hilgenfeld and Spitta thus
treat the passage beginning with καὶ
ἤγαγον, Jüngst refers these verses and
the rest of the chapter as far as ver. 14
to his source A, whilst the previous part
of ver. 12, συνεκίνησαν—αὐτόν, is in
his view an insertion of the Redactor.
Clemen regards the whole incident of the
bringing before the Sanhedrim as a later
addition, and as forming part of his
Historia Petri, the revolutionary nature
of Stephen's teaching being placed in the
mouth of false witnesses, and the fanaticism of the Jews being lessened by their
susceptibility at any rate to the outward
impression made by their opponents (ver.
15).

αὐτόν, καὶ ἤγαγον εἰς τὸ συνέδριον, 13. ἔστησάν τε μάρτυρας ψευδεῖς[1]
λέγοντας, Ὁ ἄνθρωπος οὗτος οὐ παύεται ῥήματα βλάσφημα[2] λαλῶν
κατὰ τοῦ τόπου τοῦ ἁγίου τούτου καὶ τοῦ νόμου · 14. ἀκηκόαμεν γὰρ
αὐτοῦ λέγοντος, Ὅτι Ἰησοῦς ὁ Ναζωραῖος οὗτος καταλύσει τὸν τόπον

[1] ψευδεις; D, Flor. add κατα αυτου, so Hilg.; ℵABCD om.

[2] βλασφημα, om. Tisch., W.H., R.V., Weiss, Wendt, Hilg.

Ver. 13. οὗτος: here and in ver. 14 used contemptuously, iste, so Vulgate; cf. vii. 40, xviii. 18, xix. 26, ὁ Παῦλος οὗτος.—οὐ παύεται λαλῶν: the words in themselves are sufficient to indicate the exaggerated and biassed character of the testimony brought against Stephen —" invidiam facere conantur," Bengel, βλάσφημα omitted, see above. — μάρτυρας ψευδεῖς, "false," inasmuch as they perverted the meaning of Stephen's words, which were no blasphemy against Moses or against God, although no doubt he had taught the transitory nature of the Mosaic law, and that the true worship of God was not confined to the Temple (see Weizsäcker, Apostolic Age, i., 64, 83, E.T., and Wendt, p. 148 (1899)). So also in the very same manner Christ's words had been perverted (John ii. 21, cf. Mark xiv. 56, Matt. xxvii. 63), and it is likely enough that the spirit of His teaching as to the Sabbath, the laws of purifying, the fulfilling of the law, breathed again in the words of His disciples. But such utterances were blasphemous in the eyes of the Jewish legalists, and Stephen's own words, vii. 48, 49, might well seem to them an affirmation rather than a denial of the charges brought against him.—κατὰ τοῦ τόπου τοῦ ἁγίου τούτου: if τούτου is retained (W.H.), phrase could refer not only to the Temple as the holy place, but also to the place of assembly of the Sanhedrim, where according to ver. 15 the charge was brought, which was probably situated on the Temple Mount on the western side of the enclosing wall, Schürer, Jewish People, div. ii., vol. i., p. 190, E.T., so Hilgenfeld and Wendt, and also Blass, who adds " itaque etiam τούτου (B, cf. 14) recte se habet," although he omits the word in his own text. Weiss thinks that the word dropped out because it could have no reference to a scene in the Sanhedrim.

Ver. 14. ὁ Ναζ. οὗτος: not part of the words of Stephen, but of the witnesses—see however Blass, in loco.— καὶ καταλύσει: the closest similarity to the words in Mark xiv. 58 (cf. Matt. xxvi. 61), and in both passages the same verb καταλύειν is used. It is also found in all three Synoptists in our Lord's prophecy of the destruction of the Temple, Matt. xxiv. 2, Mark xiii. 2, Luke xxi. 6, and we find it again in the bitter scorn of the revilers who passed beneath the cross (Mark xv. 29, Matt. xxvii. 40). The prophecy, we cannot doubt, had made its impression not only upon the disciples, but also upon the enemies of Jesus, and if St. Stephen did not employ the actual words, we can easily understand how easily and plausibly they might be attributed to him.— ἀλλάξει τὰ ἔθη, cf. Ezra vi. 11, Isaiah xxiv. 5. ἔθος is used by St. Luke seven times in Acts, three times in his Gospel, and it is only found twice elsewhere in the N.T., John xix. 40, Heb. x. 25; in the Books of the Maccabees it occurs three or four times, in Wisdom iv. 16 (but see Hatch and Redpath), in Bel and the Dragon v. 15, in the sense of custom, usage, as so often in the classics. Here it would doubtless include the whole system of the Mosaic law, which touched Jewish life at every turn, cf. xv. 1, xxi. 21, xxvi. 3, xxviii. 17. For the dignity which attached to every word of the Pentateuch, and to Moses to whom the complete book of the law was declared to have been handed by God, see Schürer, Jewish People, div. ii., vol. i., p. 307, E.T., and Weber, Jüdische Theologie, p. 378 (1897). We have moreover the testimony of Jewish literature contemporary with the N.T. books, cf., e.g., Book of Jubilees, placed by Edersheim about 50 A.D., with its ultra-legal spirit, and its glorification of Moses and the Thorah, see too Apocalypse of Baruch, e.g., xv., 5; xlviii., 22, 24; li., 3; lxxxiv., 2, 5.

Ver. 15. ἀτενίσαντες, see above on i. 10.—ὡσεὶ πρόσωπον ἀγγέλου, cf. LXX, Esth. v. 2, where Esther says to the king in reverence εἶδόν σε κύριε, ὡς ἄγγελον Θεοῦ; in 2 Sam. xiv. 17, 20, the reference is not to outward appearance, but to inward discernment (see Wetstein,

τοῦτον, καὶ ἀλλάξει τὰ ἔθη ἃ παρέδωκεν ἡμῖν Μωϋσῆς. 15. καὶ
ἀτενίσαντες εἰς αὐτὸν ¹ ἅπαντες οἱ καθεζόμενοι ἐν τῷ συνεδρίῳ, εἶδον
τὸ πρόσωπον αὐτοῦ ὡσεὶ πρόσωπον ἀγγέλου.²

¹ ἀτενίσαντες εις αυτον, but in D ητενιζον δε αυτῳ; and at the end of verse
D, Flor. add εστωτος εν μεσῳ αυτων; cf. iv. 7, etc. (and see below).

² On the words in Flor., "stantis inter illos," see esp. Harris, *Four Lectures*, etc.,
p. 70 ff. Blass regards the words as favourable to his theory and as part of Luke's
own text. Hilg. retains them. Harris sees in them an instance (amongst many
in D) of a wrongly inserted gloss from vii. 1; cf. Mark xiv. 60.

who refers also to Gen. xxxiii. 10, and
quotes other instances from the Rabbis,
e.g., Dixit R. Nathanael: parentes Mosis
viderunt pulchritudinem ejus tanquam
angeli Domini: and we have the same
expression used by St. Paul in *Acta
Pauli et Theklæ*, 2; ἀγγέλου πρόσωπον
εἶχεν. See too Schöttgen, *in loco*. R.
Gedalja speaks of Moses and Aaron
when they came to Pharaoh as angels
ministering before God). At such a
moment when Stephen was called upon
to plead for the truth at the risk of his
life, and when not only the calmness
and strength of his convictions, but also
the grace, the beauty of his Master, and
the power of His spirit rested upon him,
such a description was no exaggeration,
cf. a striking passage in Dr. Liddon's
Some Elements of Religion, p. 180. It
was said of the aged Polycarp, as he
faced a martyr's death: τὸ πρόσωπον
αὐτοῦ χάριτος ἐπληροῦτο, and "to have
lived in spirit on Mount Tabor during
the years of a long life, is to have caught
in its closing hours some rays of the
glory of the Transfiguration". But if
the brightness on the face of St. Stephen
is represented by St. Luke as supernatural (as Wendt admits), we are not
called upon to conclude that such a
description is due to the glorification of
the Saint in Christian legend: "the
occasion was worthy of the miracle,"
the ministration of the Spirit, ἡ διακονία
τοῦ πνεύματος, in which St. Stephen
had shared, might well exceed in glory;
and a brightness like that on the face of
Moses, above the brightness of the sun,
might well have shone upon one who
like the angels beheld the face of the
Father in heaven, and to whom the glory
of the Lord had been revealed: "As if
in refutation of the charge made against
him, Stephen receives the same mark of
divine favour which had been granted
to Moses" (Humphry). St. Chrysostom
speaks of the face of Stephen as being
terrible to the Jews, but lovable and

wonderful to the Christians (cf. Theophylact, *in loco*). But although St. Stephen's
words must afterwards have proved
terrible to his opponents, we scarcely
associate the thought of terror with the
verse before us; we may speak of such
faces as that of the proto-martyr as
αἰδέσιμα but scarcely as φοβερά. It is
possible that the representation of St.
Stephen in sacred art as a young man
may be due to this comparison of his face
to that of an angel, angels being always
represented as in the bloom of youth
(Dr. Moore, *Studies in Dante*, first series,
p. 84).

CHAPTER VII.—Ver. 1. The question
of the high priest breaks in upon the
silence (Holtzmann). St. Chrysostom,
Hom., xv., thought that the mildness of
the inquiry showed that the assembly
was overawed by St. Stephen's presence,
but the question was probably a usual
interrogation on such occasions (Felten,
Farrar).—On εἰ see i. 6, and Blass,
Grammatik, p. 254.

Ver. 2. Ἄνδρες ἀδελφοὶ καὶ πατέρες,
cf. St. Paul's address, xxii. 1, and also
note on xxiii. 1. On St. Stephen's
speech see additional note at the end of
chapter.—ὁ Θεὸς τῆς δόξης: lit., "the
God of the glory," i.e., the glory peculiar
to Him, not simply ἔνδοξος, a reference
to the Shechinah, Exod. xxiv. 16, 17,
Ps. xxix. 3, Isa. vi. 3, and in the N.T.
cf. 1 Cor. ii. 8, and James ii. 1 (John i.
14). The appearances to Abraham and
Moses were similar to those later ones
to which the term Shechinah was applied. Such words were in themselves
an answer to the charge of blasphemy;
but Stephen proceeds to show that this
same God who dwelt in the Tabernacle
was not confined to it, but that He
appeared to Abraham in a distant heathen
land. ὤφθη: there was therefore no
need of a Temple that God might appear
to His own (Chrys., *Hom.*, xv.; see Blass,
in loco).—τῷ πατρὶ ἡμῶν: emphatic,
cf. vv. 19, 38, 39, 44, 45; St. Stephen

VII. 1. Εἶπε δὲ ὁ ἀρχιερεύς, Εἰ ἄρα ταῦτα οὕτως ἔχει; 2. ὁ δὲ ἔφη, Ἄνδρες ἀδελφοὶ καὶ πατέρες, ἀκούσατε. ὁ Θεὸς τῆς δόξης ὤφθη τῷ πατρὶ ἡμῶν Ἀβραὰμ [1] ὄντι ἐν τῇ Μεσοποταμίᾳ, πρὶν ἢ κατοικῆσαι

[1] vii. 2-4. For T.R. Blass reads (2) (οντι εν τη Μεσοποταμια εν Χαρραν μετα το αποθανειν τον πατερα αυτου); (3) και ειπεν προς αυτον "Εξελθε απο . . . δειξω"; (4) και μετωκισεν αυτον. In Par. we read "cum esset in Mesopotamia in Charran postquam mortuus est pater ipsius, et dixit . . . monstravero, et inde transtulit eum," etc. This reading agrees almost entirely with that adopted by Blass, but it contains the word bracketed by him in ver. 2, and also apparently κακειθεν (*et inde*) (see below). The difficulties in these verses are attributed by Blass and Belser to Alexandrian copyists. An explanatory note was added very early to ver. 2. οτε Α. εξελθεν εκ γης Χαλδαιων και κατωκησεν εν Χαρραν κακει ην μετα το αποθανειν τον πατερα αυτου. These words (which may easily have been derived from the narrative in Genesis) were thought by the Alexandrian copyists to be the additional words of Luke himself, and they inserted them (*inferserunt in ver.* 4, Blass) in ver. 4 as they could not add them at the end of ver. 2, οτε being changed into τοτε, Αβρααμ being omitted, and κακειθεν being substituted for κακει, whilst the words μετα το αποθ. τον πατερα αυτου, originally belonging to ver. 2 (so Par. above), were then omitted altogether and added in the text after κακειθεν; then between the words Μεσοπ. and εν Χαρραν, which are joined together in Par., these copyists (*audacissimum*, Blass) inserted πριν η κατοικησαι αυτον, no doubt with the view of showing that Stephen referred not only to the later injunction from Haran to Canaan but to the earlier one from Ur to Haran. But there is no need to suppose that the text was thus tampered with (see Wendt's note, p. 154, edit. 1899), and whatever difficulties this part of the speech contains, they may be easily explained on the supposition that Stephen in these verses, as elsewhere, was expressing himself in accordance with well-known traditions. In support of his view Blass (so Belser) appeals to Irenæus, iii. 12, who quotes the whole passage from vii. 2, ὁ θεὸς τῆς δ., to ver. 8, τὸν Ἰσαάκ, omitting what Par. omits, and thus being in agreement with it on the whole in Belser's judgment. But Blass admits that Irenæus (who apparently leaves out all not in LXX) also omits words which occur in ver. 2, partly in all authorites and partly in Par. (Gig.): οντι εν τη Μ. εν Χαρραν μετα το αποθ. τον πατερα αυτου: "delenda igitur haec quoque" (see above) "neque ea quidquam desiderabit," Blass, *Praef.* xv. (*Acta Apost. secundum formam quae videtur Romanam*). Belser is not prepared to go so far as this, but he sees in the original text of Luke a much simpler version of Stephen's speech; no reference is made to the original dwelling-place of Abraham in Ur, and only the call given to him in Mesopotamia (in Haran) is specified. According to Belser the original text reads thus: (Ver. 2) ὁ θεος της δοξης ωφθη τω πατρι ημων Α. οντι εν τη Μ. μετα το αποθανειν τον πατερα αυτου, (Ver. 3) και ειπεν προς αυτον· εξελθε εκ της γης σου και της συγγενειας σου, και δευρο εις την γην, ην αν σοι δειξω. (Ver. 4) και μετωκισεν αυτον εις την γην ταυτην, etc. (*Beiträge zur Erklärung der Apostelgeschichte*, p. 48). See further on Gen. xii. 1-3 and the quotation here, in the passages in Philo, and in Clem. Rom., *Cor.*, x., 2, Hatch, *Essays in Biblical Greek*, p. 154.

thus closely associates himself with his hearers. Wetstein comments: "Stephanus ergo non fuit proselytus, sed Judæus natus," but it would seem from Wetstein himself that a proselyte might call Abraham father; *cf.* his comment on Luke i. 73, and *cf. Ecclus.*, xliv. 21; *Speaker's Commentary*, "Apocrypha," vol. ii.; see also Lumby's note, *in loco*, and *cf.* Schürer, *Jewish People*, div. ii., vol. ii., p. 326, note, E.T.— Μεσοποταμίᾳ: a difficulty at once arises in comparing this statement with the Book of Genesis. Here the call of Abraham is said to have come to him *before* he dwelt in Haran, but in Gen. xii. 1, *after* he removed thither. But, at the same time Gen. xv. 7, *cf.* Josh. xxiv. 3, Neh. ix. 7, distinctly intimates that Abraham left "Ur of the Chaldees" (see "Abraham," Hastings' B.D., p. 14, and Sayce, *Patriarchal Palestine*, pp. 166-169, as to its site) in accordance with the choice and guidance of God. St. Stephen applies the language of what we may describe as the second to the first call, and in so doing he was really following on the lines of Jewish literature, *e.g.*, Philo, *De Abrah.*, ii., 11, 16, Mang., paraphrases the divine counsel,

αὐτὸν ἐν Χαρράν, 3. καὶ εἶπε πρὸς αὐτόν, "Ἔξελθε ἐκ τῆς γῆς σου
καὶ ἐκ τῆς συγγενείας σου, καὶ δεῦρο εἰς γῆν ἣν ἄν σοι δείξω." 4.
τότε ἐξελθὼν ἐκ γῆς Χαλδαίων, κατῴκησεν ἐν Χαρράν· κἀκεῖθεν,
μετὰ τὸ ἀποθανεῖν τὸν πατέρα αὐτοῦ, μετῴκισεν αὐτὸν εἰς τὴν γῆν

and then adds διὰ τοῦτο τὴν πρώτην ἀποικίαν ἀπὸ τῆς Χαλδαίων γῆς εἰς τὴν Χαρραίων λέγεται ποιεῖσθαι. Moreover the manner of St. Stephen's quotation seems to mark the difference between the call in Ur and the call in Haran (R.V., not Charran, Greek form, as in A.V.). In Gen. xii. 1 we have the call to Abraham in Haran given as follows: ἔξελθε ἐκ τῆς γῆς σου καὶ ἐκ τῆς συγγενείας σου καὶ ἐκ τοῦ οἴκου τοῦ πατρός σου. But the call in Ur, according to St. Stephen's wording, is one which did not involve the sacrifice of his family, for Abraham was accompanied by them to Haran, and so the clause ἐκ τοῦ οἴκου κ.τ.λ. is omitted because inappropriate. Of course if we omit ἐκ before τῆς συγγενείας (see critical notes), St. Stephen's words become more suitable still to the position of Abraham in Ur, for we should then translate the words, "from thy land and the land of thy kindred" (Rendall, cf. Lightfoot, Hor. Heb.). St. Stephen may naturally have referred back to Abraham's first migration from Ur to Haran, as desiring to emphasise more plainly the fact that since the call of God came to him before he had taken even the first step towards the Holy Land by settling in Haran, that divine revelation was evidently not bound up with any one spot, however holy.—Χαρράν, Gen. xi. 31, xii. 5, xxvii. 43, LXX, in the old language of Chaldea = road (see Sayce, u. s., pp. 166, 167, and "Haran" Hastings' B.D., and B.D.², i. (Pinches)), in Mesopotamia; little doubt that it should be identified with the *Carræ* of the Greeks and Romans, near the scene of the defeat of Crassus by the Parthians, B.C. 53, and of his death, Lucan, i., 104; Pliny, N.H., v., 24; Strabo, xvi., p. 747. In the fourth century *Carræ* was the seat of a Christian bishopric, with a magnificent cathedral. It is remarkable that the people of the place retained until a late date the Chaldean language and the worship of the Chaldean deities, B.D.², "Haran," and see Hamburger, *Real-Encyclopädie des Judentums*, i., 4, p. 499, and references cited by him for identification with *Carræ* (*cf.* Winer-Schmiedel, p. 57).

Ver. 4. μετὰ τὸ ἀποθανεῖν: St. Stephen apparently falls into the same chronologi-cal mistake as is made in the Pentateuch and by Philo (*De Migr. Abrah.*, i., 463, Mang.). According to Gen. xi. 26 Terah lived seventy years and begat Abraham, Nahor, Haran; in xi. 32 it is said that Terah's age was 205 years when he died in Haran; in xii. 4 it is said that Abraham was seventy-five years old when he left Haran. But since 70 + 75 = 145, it would seem that Terah must have lived some sixty years *after* Abraham's departure. Perhaps the circumstance that Terah's death was *mentioned*, in Gen. xi. 32, *before* the command to Abraham to leave Haran, xii. 1, may be the cause of the mistake, as it was not observed that the *mention* of Terah's death was anticipatory (so Alford). Blass seems to adopt a somewhat similar view, as he commends the reading in Gigas: "priusquam mortuus est pater ejus," for the obedience of the patriarch, who did not hesitate to leave even his father, is opposed to the obstinacy of the Jewish people (see Blass, *in loco*). Other attempts at explanation are that reference is made to *spiritual* death of Terah, who is supposed to have relapsed into idolatry at Haran, a view which appears to have originated with the Rabbis, probably to get rid of the chronological difficulty (Lightfoot, *Hor. Heb.*; Meyer-Wendt, *in loco*), but for which there is absolutely no justification in the context; or that Abraham need not have been the eldest son of Terah, but that he was mentioned first because he was the most famous, a view adopted with more or less variation by Wordsworth, Hackett, and recently by Felten (see too B.D.², p. 16, note), but apparently in opposition to the authority of Hamburger, who states that Terah was seventy years old when Abraham was born, that he was alive when Abraham departed at the age of seventy-five, being released from the duty of caring for his father by the more imperative command to obey the call of God. Lumby quotes from *Midrash Rabbah*, on Genesis, cap. 39, that God absolved Abraham from the care of his father, and yet, lest Abraham's departure from Terah should lead others to claim the same relaxation of a commandment for themselves, Terah's death is mentioned in Holy Scripture before Abra-

ταύτην εἰς ἣν ὑμεῖς νῦν κατοικεῖτε[1] · 5. καὶ οὐκ ἔδωκεν αὐτῷ κληρονομίαν ἐν αὐτῇ, οὐδὲ βῆμα ποδός · καὶ[2] ἐπηγγείλατο αὐτῷ δοῦναι εἰς
κατάσχεσιν αὐτήν, καὶ τῷ σπέρματι αὐτοῦ μετ᾽ αὐτόν, οὐκ ὄντος
αὐτῷ τέκνου. 6. ἐλάλησε δὲ οὕτως ὁ Θεός, "Ὅτι ἔσται τὸ σπέρμα
αὐτοῦ πάροικον ἐν γῇ ἀλλοτρίᾳ, καὶ δουλώσουσιν αὐτὸ[3] καὶ κακώσουσιν,

[1] After κατοικειτε DE, Syr. Harcl. mg., Aug. add και οι πατερες υμων (ημων)
προ υμων (ημων); Weiss (Codex D, p. 67) points out that the addition demands
κατωκησαν; the words might have been easily added, cf. O.T. phraseology.

[2] For και επηγ. D, Gig., Vulg. read αλλ᾽ επηγ., so Hilg.

[3] αυτο; D, Gig., Vulg. read αυτους, so Hilg.; cf. LXX, Gen. xv. 13.

ham's departure, cf. Gen. xi. 32, and xii.
1. One other solution has been attempted
by maintaining that μετῴκισεν does not
refer to the removal, but only to the quiet
and abiding settlement which Abraham
gained *after* his father's death, but this
view, although supported by Augustine
and Bengel, amongst others, is justly
condemned by Alford and Wendt. The
Samaritan Pentateuch reads in Gen. xi. 32,
145 instead of 205, probably an alteration
to meet the apparent contradiction. But
it is quite possible that here, as elsewhere
in the speech, Stephen followed some
special tradition (so Zöckler).—μετά with
infinitive as a temporal proposition frequent in Luke (analogous construction in
Hebrew), cf. Luke xii. 5, xxii. 20, etc.,
cf. LXX, Baruch i. 9; Viteau, *Le Grec
du N. T.*, p. 165 (1893).—μετῴκισεν,
subject ὁ Θεός: cf. for a similar
quick change of subject vi. 6. Weiss
sees in this the hand of a reviser, but the
fact that Stephen was speaking under
such circumstances would easily account
for a rapid change of subject, which would
easily be supplied by his hearers; verb
only in ver. 43 elsewhere, in a quotation
—found several times in LXX, and also
in use in classical Greek.

Ver. 5. κληρονομίαν: the field which
Abraham bought, Gen. xxiii. 9-17, could
not come under this title—the field was
Abraham's purchase, not God's gift as
κληρονομία (see Meyer - Wendt, and
Westcott, Heb. vi. 12, additional note,
also Bengel, *in loco*); ver. 16 sufficiently
shows that Stephen was fully acquainted
with Abraham's purchase of the field.—
οὐδὲ βῆμα ποδός, cf. Deut. ii. 5, xi. 24,
same Hebrew (cf. Heb. xi. 9), "spatium
quod planta pedis calcatur" (Grimm);
cf. also its use in Xen. It may have been
a kind of proverbial expression, cf. Gen.
viii. 9 (Schöttgen).—καὶ ἐπηγγείλατο,
cf. Gen. xii. 7 (xvii. 8, xlviii. 4), so that
here again God appeared unto Abraham

in what was a strange and heathen land.
See also for verb, James i. 12, ii. 5. On
the force of the word see p. 54.—εἰς
κατάσχεσιν: "in possession," R.V., the
A.V. renders the word in its secondary
or derivative sense, which is found in
ver. 45.—οὐκ ὄντος αὐτῷ τέκνου: the
faith of Abraham "tecte significatur"
(Blass), first because nothing was given
—there was only a promise—and secondly
because the promise was made while yet
he had no child.

Ver. 6. δέ: not in contrast to the
fact just mentioned that Abraham had
no child, but introducing a fuller account
of God's promise. The quotation is
from LXX, Gen. xv. 13, with a few
alterations; in LXX and Heb., the second
person, not the third, is used; instead of
οὐκ ἰδίᾳ in LXX, ἀλλοτρίᾳ, cf. Heb. xi.
9; and instead of αὐτούς, αὐτό corresponding to σπέρμα. Wendt takes ὅτι
as "recitantis," and not with Meyer as
a constituent part of the quotation itself,
LXX: Γιγνώσκων γνώσῃ ὅτι κ.τ.λ.—
πάροικον in LXX as a stranger or so-
journer in a country not one's own,
several times in combination with ἐν γῇ
ἀλλοτρίᾳ, cf. Gen. xxi. 23, 34, xxvi. 3,
and in N.T. cf. this passage and ver. 29.
In Eph. ii. 19, 1 Pet. ii. 11, the word is
also used, but metaphorically, although
the usage may be said to be based on
that of the LXX; cf. *Epist. ad Diognet.*
v., 5, and Polycarp, *Phil.*, inscript. See
Kennedy, *Sources of N. T. Greek*, p. 102.
—ἔτη τετρακόσια: so too Gen. xv. 13.
The period named belongs not only to
κακώσουσιν but also to ἔσται, as Meyer
rightly observes. But in Exod. xii. 40
four hundred and thirty years are mentioned as the sojourning which Israel
sojourned in Egypt, and in both passages
the whole space of time is so occupied;
or, at all events it may be fairly said
that this is implied in the Hebrew text
in both Gen. xv. 13 and Exod. xii. 40:

ἔτη τετρακόσια. 7. καὶ τὸ ἔθνος, ᾧ ἐὰν [1] δουλεύσωσι, κρινῶ ἐγώ,"
εἶπεν ὁ Θεός· "καὶ μετὰ ταῦτα ἐξελεύσονται, καὶ λατρεύσουσί μοι
ἐν τῷ τόπῳ τούτῳ." 8. καὶ ἔδωκεν αὐτῷ διαθήκην περιτομῆς· καὶ
οὕτως ἐγέννησε τὸν Ἰσαάκ, καὶ περιέτεμεν αὐτὸν τῇ ἡμέρᾳ τῇ ὀγδόῃ·

---

[1] εαν ﹏ΑϹΕΗΡ, so Tisch., W.H. alt., Weiss; αν BD, so W.H. δουλευσωσι
﹏ΒΕΗΡ, d, Vulg., Chrys., Lach., Weiss, Wendt, so in LXX, Gen. xv. 14;
δουλευσουσι ΑCD 26, 96, Sah., Ir., so Tisch., Alford, W.H., R.V., so Blass in β
(see his Proleg. to *Acta Apost.*, p. 35, and *Grammatik*, p. 212). In vii. 3 on the
contrary the LXX has ην αν σοι δειξω; only ﹏ reads εαν, perhaps anticipating the
reading in vv. before us (Weiss). Winer-Schmiedel, p. 52, points out that δουλευ-
σουσιν, though well attested, is open to suspicion.

cf. also for the same mode of reckoning
Philo, *Quis rer. div. her.*, 54, p. 511,
Mang. But neither here nor in Gal.
iii. 17 is the argument in the least degree
affected by the precise period, or by the
adoption of one of the two chronological
systems in preference to the other, and
in a speech round numbers would be
quite sufficient to mark the progressive
stages in the history of the nation and of
God's dealings with them. For an explanation of the point see Lightfoot,
Gal. iii. 17, who regards the number in
Genesis as given in round numbers, but
in Exodus with historical exactness (to
the same effect Wendt, Felten, Zöckler).
But in the LXX version, Exod. xii. 40,
the four hundred and thirty years cover
the sojourn both in Egypt and in Canaan,
thus including the sojourn of the Patriarchs in Canaan before the migration,
and reducing the actual residence in
Egypt to about half this period, the
Vatican MS. reading four hundred and
thirty-five years after adding καὶ ἐν
γῇ Χαναὰν (the word *five*, however, πέντε,
being erased), and the Alexandrian MS.
reading after ἐν Χαναὰν the words αὐτοὶ
καὶ οἱ πατέρες αὐτῶν, making the revision in the chronology more decisive.
This is the chronology adopted in Gal.
iii. 17, and by Josephus, *Ant.*, ii., 15, 2;
but the latter writer in other passages,
Ant., ii., 9, 1, and *B.J.*, v., 9, 4, adopts
the same reckoning as we find here in
Acts. But see also Charles, *Assumption
of Moses*, pp. 3, 4 (1897).

Ver. 7. The *oratio recta* is introduced
by the words εἶπεν ὁ Θεός . . . κρινῶ
ἐγώ emphatic, *cf.* Rom. xii. 19. In this
verse the quotation is a free rendering of
Gen. xv. 14, the words ὧδε μετὰ ἀποσ-
κευῆς πολλῆς being omitted after ἐξελ.,
and the latter part of the verse being
apparently introduced from Exod. iii. 12.
And so at length, after so long a time,
God appointed for Himself a "holy

place," *cf.* vi. 13 (Blass).—ᾧ ἐὰν δουλεύσωσι, *cf.* LXX, Gen. xv. 14, and see
critical note above, *cf.* also Burton, *N. T.
Moods and Tenses*, p. 123.

Ver. 8. διαθήκην, *fœdus* (Grimm,
Blass), the same word is used in LXX,
Gen. xvii. 10, and with two or three
exceptions uniformly in LXX for "covenant," so too in the Apocrypha with
apparently two exceptions. The ordinary
word for "covenant," συνθήκη, is very
rare in LXX (though used by the later
translators, Aquila, Sym., Theod., for
בְּרִית, but see also Ramsay, *Expositor*,
ii., pp. 322, 323 (1898)). But the word διαθ.
would be suitably employed to express a
divine covenant, because it could not be
said that in such a case the contractors
are in any degree of equal standing
(συνθήκη). In the N.T. the sense of
"covenant" is correct (except in Gal.
iii. 15 and Heb. ix. 16). But in *classical*
writers from the time of Plato διαθήκη
generally has the meaning of a will, a
testament, a disposition of property, and
in the Latin renderings of the word in
the N.T. we find uniformly *testamentum*
in cases where the sense of "covenant"
is beyond dispute (Luke i. 72, Acts iii.
25 d. *dispositionis;* and here d. has *dis-
positionem*, also in Rom. xi. 27), *cf.*, *e.g.*,
in this verse, Vulgate and Par. No
doubt the early translators would render
διαθήκη by its ordinary equivalent, although in the common language it is
quite possible that *testamentum* had a
wider meaning than the classical sense
of *will*, see Westcott, *Hebrews*, additional
note on ix. 16; Lightfoot on Gal. iii. 15;
A. B. Davidson, *Hebrews*, p. 161; and
"Covenant" in Hastings' B.D. and
Grimm-Thayer, *sub v.;* Hatch, *Essays
in Biblical Greek*, pp. 47, 48; and more
recently Ramsay, *Expositor*, ii., pp. 300
and 321 ff. (1898).

Ver. 9. ζηλώσαντες, *cf.* Gen. xxxvii.

καὶ ὁ Ἰσαὰκ τὸν Ἰακώβ, καὶ ὁ Ἰακὼβ τοὺς δώδεκα πατριάρχας.   9.
καὶ οἱ πατριάρχαι ζηλώσαντες τὸν Ἰωσὴφ ἀπέδοντο εἰς Αἴγυπτον·
10. καὶ ἦν ὁ Θεὸς μετ' αὐτοῦ, καὶ ἐξείλετο αὐτὸν ἐκ πασῶν τῶν
θλίψεων αὐτοῦ, καὶ ἔδωκεν αὐτῷ χάριν καὶ σοφίαν ἐναντίον Φαραὼ
βασιλέως Αἰγύπτου, καὶ κατέστησεν αὐτὸν ἡγούμενον ἐπ' Αἴγυπτον
καὶ ὅλον τὸν οἶκον αὐτοῦ.   11. ἦλθε δὲ λιμὸς ἐφ' ὅλην τὴν γῆν
Αἰγύπτου καὶ Χαναάν, καὶ θλίψις μεγάλη· καὶ οὐχ εὕρισκον χορτάσματα οἱ πατέρες ἡμῶν.   12. ἀκούσας δὲ Ἰακὼβ ὄντα σῖτα [1] ἐν Αἰγύπτῳ,
ἐξαπέστειλε τοὺς πατέρας ἡμῶν πρῶτον·   13. καὶ ἐν τῷ δευτέρῳ
ἀνεγνωρίσθη Ἰωσὴφ τοῖς ἀδελφοῖς αὐτοῦ, καὶ φανερὸν ἐγένετο τῷ

---

[1] σιτα HP, Chrys.; σιτια אABCDE 5, 8, so Tisch., W.H., R.V., Weiss, Wendt,
Hilg. (see Wendt, crit. note, p. 168, and Field, *Otium Norvic.*, iii., 76).

11, and so in Gen. xxvi. 14, xxx. 1, Isa.
xi. 13, Ecclus. xxxvii. 10; used also in a
bad sense in Acts xvii. 5, 1 Cor. xiii. 4,
James iv. 2, and so in classical writers.
It may be used here absolutely, as in
A.V. (see Grimm, Nösgen), or governing
Ἰωσήφ, as in R.V.—ἀπέδ. εἰς, *cf.* for
construction Gen. xlv. 4.

Ver. 10. ἦν ὁ Θεὸς μετ' αὐτοῦ, *cf.*
Gen. xxxix. 2, 21, 23 (*cf.* Luke i.
28, 66).—ἐξείλετο . . . ἐκ: the same
construction in Gen. xxxii. 11, Exod. iii.
8, and in N.T., Acts xii. 11, xxvi. 17,
Gal. i. 4; so in classical Greek. The
middle force of the verb in the sense of
causing to be saved is lost.—χάρις, *cf.*
ii. 41. The word means primarily, as the
context shows, favour with man, *cf.* Gen.
xxxix. 21; but this χάρις was also a divine
gift: ἔδωκεν. It is significant also that
Pharaoh speaks of Joseph, Gen. xli. 38,
as a man in whom the spirit of God is,
although no doubt the expression refers
primarily to Joseph's skill in foretelling
and providing against the famine.—
σοφίαν: in interpreting the king's decree, Gen. xli. 25 ff.—ἐναντίον, so in
Gen. xxxix. 21.—βασ. Αἰγ.: without the
article as in Hebrew (Blass), *cf.* Gen.
xli. 46; see also Winer-Schmiedel, p.
185.—καὶ κατέστησεν, *sc.*, Pharaoh, *cf.*
change of subject as in ver. 4, in which
Weiss also sees the hand of a reviser,
but see above. The same word is used
in Gen. xli. 43, and *cf.* for ἡγούμενον the
same chap., ver. 41, where the sense of
the title is shown—the exact word is used
of Joseph in Ecclus. xlix. 15 (ἡγούμενος
ἀδελφῶν); in N.T. four times in Luke,
see Luke xxii. 26, Acts vii. 10, xiv. 12,
xv. 22; elsewhere only in Hebrews, *cf.*
xiii. 7, 17, 24.

Ver. 11. λιμὸς, *cf.* Luke iv. 25, where

ἐπί follows.—χορτάσματα: sustenance,
R.V., fodder, provender for their cattle,
cf. Gen. xxiv. 25, 32, xlii. 27, Judg. xix.
19; only here in N.T., *cf.* Polyb., ix., 43.
The want of it would be a most pressing
need for large owners of flocks. Blass
takes it as meaning *frumentum*, corn,
food for man as well as for beasts, since
χορτάζειν, both in LXX and N.T. (Mark
viii. 4, *cf.* vii. 27, 28), is used of the food
of man, *cf.* Kennedy, *Sources of N. T.
Greek*, pp. 82, 156.

Ver. 12. σῖτα, but σιτία in R.V.
(Blass follows T.R.), *cf.* LXX, Prov. xxx.
22 = properly food made of corn opposed
to χόρτος (σῖτα not elsewhere in N.T.,
but in LXX τὰ σῖτα, corn, *frumenta*).
In Gen. xlii. 2 we have σῖτος. But as
Wendt points out, in the words which
follow: πρίασθε ἡμῖν μικρὰ βρώματα we
have what may well correspond to σιτία.
—ὄντα: on the participle after verbs of
sense, *e.g.*, ὁρῶ, ἀκούω, οἶδα, in classical
Greek, construction same as here—
especially in Luke and Paul in N.T., *cf.*
Viteau, *Le Grec du N. T.*, p. 196 (1893).
—πρῶτον = "the first time," R.V. = τὸ
πρότερον opposed to ἐν τῷ δευτέρῳ, ver.
13, which is only found here in N.T.:
generally δεύτερον (*cf.* ἐκ δευτέρου, 1
Macc. ix. 1 and Dan. ii. 7 (LXX)).

Ver. 13. ἀνεγνωρίσθη: the compound
verb apparently from LXX, Gen. xlv. 1.
—φανερὸν ἐγέν., *cf.* Luke viii. 17, iv. 36,
i. 65, vi. 49, etc.; on Luke's fondness
for periphrasis with γίνομαι, see Plummer
on Luke iv. 36.—τὸ γένος τοῦ Ἰ.: R.V.
"race," so ver. 19, *cf.* iv. 36, because
wider than συγγένειαν, "kindred," in
ver. 14. R.V. "became manifest"
strictly; the captain of the guard, Gen.
xli. 12, had previously mentioned that
Joseph was a Hebrew, but the fact which

Φαραὼ τὸ γένος τοῦ Ἰωσήφ.[1]　14. ἀποστείλας δὲ Ἰωσὴφ μετεκαλέσατο
τὸν πατέρα αὐτοῦ Ἰακώβ, καὶ πᾶσαν τὴν συγγένειαν αὐτοῦ, ἐν ψυχαῖς
ἑβδομηκονταπέντε.[2]　15. κατέβη δὲ Ἰακὼβ εἰς Αἴγυπτον,[3] καὶ ἐτε-

[1] το γενος του Ιωσηφ DHP, Chrys., so Hilg.; om. Ιωσηφ BC 47, so Lach., W.H.,
Wendt, Weiss.　το γενος αυτου ℵAE 40, Vulg., Arm., so Tisch., Blass; την συγγ.
αυτου—αυτου om. ℵABCHP, Vulg. (am. fu. demid.), Syr. Harcl., Arm., Chrys., so
Tisch., W.H., R.V., Weiss, Wendt.

[2] DH, Gig. read εν εβδ. και πεντε ψυχαις (*cf.* Deut. x. 22), so Blass and Hilg.

[3] εις Αιγυπτον om. B (W.H. in brackets)—Wendt regards as an addition from
LXX—but retained in ℵACDEHP, Vulg., Syrr. (P.H.), etc.; so Weiss and Hilg.

had been only mentioned incidentally
"became manifest" when Joseph's
brethren came, and he revealed himself
to them, so that Pharaoh and his household were aware of it, ver. 16. It was
not until later that five of Joseph's
brethren were actually presented to
Pharaoh, xlvii. 1 ff. (Hackett).

Ver. 14. μετεκαλέσατο: four times in
Acts, and nowhere else in N.T., *cf.* x.
32, xx. 17, xxiv. 25, only once in LXX,
H. and R., *cf.* Hosea xi. 2, A; so εἰσκα-
λέομαι, only once in N.T., *cf.* Acts x. 23;
not in LXX or Apocrypha. Both compounds are peculiar to St. Luke in N.T.,
and are frequent in medical writers, to
"send for" or to "call in" (although Polyb.
in middle voice, xxii. 5, 2, in same sense)
a physician, Hobart, *Medical Language*,
etc., p. 219. In Attic Greek we should
have μεταπέμπεσθαι.—ἐν ψυχαῖς ἑβδομήκοντα πέντε: ἐν = Hebrew ‏ב‎, *cf.* Deut.
x. 22, in (consisting in) so many souls,
cf. Luke xvi. 31. Here in Deut., LXX,
as also in Hebrew, we have the number
given as seventy (although in A, seventy-
five, which seems to have been introduced to make the passage similar to
the two others quoted below) who went
down into Egypt. But in Gen. xlvi. 27,
and in Exod. i. 5, LXX, the number is
given as seventy-five (the Hebrew in
both passages however giving seventy as
the number, although in Gen. xlvi. 26
giving sixty-six, making up the seventy by
adding Jacob, Joseph, and his two sons).
For the curious Rabbinical traditions
current on the subject, see Lumby, *Acts*,
p. 163. In Gen. xlvi. 27 the LXX make
up the number to seventy-five by adding
nine sons as born to Joseph while in
Egypt, so that from this interpolation it
seems that they did not obtain their
number by simply adding the sons and
grandsons, five in all, of Ephraim and
Manasseh from Gen. xlvi. 20 (LXX) to
the seventy mentioned in the Hebrew

text, as Wetstein and others have maintained. But there is nothing strange
in the fact that Stephen, as a Hellenist,
should follow the tradition which he
found in the LXX. Josephus in *Ant.*,
ii., 7, 4; vi., 5, 6, follows the Hebrew
seventy, and Philo gives the two numbers, and allegorises about them. See
Meyer-Wendt, p. 174, note, Hackett,
Lumby, *in loco*, and Wetstein. Nothing
in the argument is touched by these variations in the numbers.

Ver. 15. The frequent mention of
Egypt may perhaps indicate that Stephen
meant to emphasise the fact that there,
far away from the land of promise, God's
Presence was with the chosen race (who
were now all in a strange land) and His
worship was observed.— μετετέθησαν:
only here in this sense in N.T. Some
have supposed that only οἱ πατέρες and
not αὐτός is the subject; this would no
doubt avoid the first difficulty of the
verse, *viz.*, that Jacob was buried in
Shechem, whereas according to Gen. l.
13 he was laid to rest in the cave of
Machpelah. But a further difficulty
must be met. Joseph is the only son of
the Patriarch who is expressly stated to
have been buried in Shechem, Josh. xxiv.
32, and of the removal of the bodies from
Egypt nothing is said. But the silence
as to the latter fact need not trouble us,
as whether we accept the tradition mentioned by Josephus or by St. Jerome,
they both presuppose the removal of the
bodies of the Patriarchs to the promised
land, *cf.* the discussion on Exod. xiii. 19,
Mechilta (Lumby, p. 164), Wetstein, *in
loco*, and see also the tradition in the
Book of Jubilees, chap. xlvi., that the
children carried up the bones of the sons
of Jacob, and buried them in Machpelah,
except those of Joseph. But another
tradition is implied in *Sot.* 7 *b*. According to Josephus, who probably repeats a
local tradition, *Ant.*, ii., 8, 2, they were
buried at Hebron. But according to

λεύτησεν αὐτὸς καὶ οἱ πατέρες ἡμῶν · 16. καὶ μετετέθησαν¹ εἰς Συχέμ,
καὶ ἐτέθησαν ἐν τῷ μνήματι ὃ ὠνήσατο² Ἀβραὰμ τιμῆς ἀργυρίου παρὰ
τῶν υἱῶν Ἐμμὸρ³ τοῦ Συχέμ. 17. Καθὼς δὲ ἤγγιζεν ὁ χρόνος τῆς
ἐπαγγελίας ἣν ὤμοσεν⁴ ὁ Θεὸς τῷ Ἀβραάμ, ηὔξησεν ὁ λαὸς καὶ
ἐπληθύνθη ἐν Αἰγύπτῳ, 18. ἄχρις⁵ οὗ ἀνέστη βασιλεὺς ἕτερος, ὃς οὐκ

¹ μετετεθησαν; but in D μετηχθησαν, so Hilg. and Blass, who thinks μετετεθ.
suggested by ετεθ. below—but D stands alone.

² ο ωνησ. HP, Chrys.; ῳ ℵABCDE, so Tisch., W.H., Weiss, Wendt, Hilg.

³ εν for του is read by ℵ¹BC, and so Tisch., Blass (α and β), Weiss.

⁴ ωμοσεν HP 31, 61, Syrr. Pesh. Harcl. text, Boh., Chrys.; ωμολογησεν ℵABC 15,
36, Vulg., Sah., Arm. (Syr. Harcl. mg.), Aeth., so Tisch., W.H., R.V., Weiss, Wendt
(gloss, after LXX), rare in sense of "promised," and so επηγγειλατο DE tol. (Syr.
Harcl. marg.), also Hilg., gloss for ωμολ. corrupted into ωμοσε.

⁵ αχρις ℵAB³EHP; αχρι B*CD, so Tisch., W.H., Weiss, Hilg. (see Grimm-
Thayer, sub v., on the two forms and Winer-Schmiedel, p. 63).   After ετερ. ℵABC,
so W.H., R.V., Weiss, add επ' Αιγυπτον.

St. Jerome their tombs were shown at
Shechem, and the Rabbinical tradition
mentioned by Wetstein and Lightfoot
places their burial there, a statement
supported by a Samaritan tradition existing to this day (*Palestine Exploration
Fund*, December, 1877, see Felten and
Plumptre, *in loco*). When we consider
the prominent position of Shechem as
compared with Hebron in the time of
Joshua, there is nothing strange in the
fact that the former place rather than
Machpelah should have been chosen
as the resting-place not only of Joseph
but also of his brethren. Plumptre has
ingeniously contended that St. Stephen
might have followed the Samaritan
tradition, *cf.* Acts vi. 5, and see *Expositor*, vol. vii., first series : " The
Samaritan element in the Gospels and
Acts," p. 21 ff., although we need not
suppose that in this reference to the
hated Samaritans Stephen proposed to
show that not even they had been rejected by God. There is certainly no
difficulty in supposing that here and elsewhere Stephen might easily have adopted some popular tradition, and at all
events the fact that the mistake, if it is
one, is left unnoticed by the historian is
a plain proof of the truthfulness of the
record. But a further difficulty. Abraham purchases the cave of Machpelah,
but from Ephron the Hittite, Gen. xxiii.
16. The sons of Hamor sell a field, but
to Jacob—a field at Shechem, Gen. xxxiii.
19, Josh. xxiv. 32. How can we explain
this with reference to the statement in the
text? Shechem was the earliest settlement of Abraham when he entered
Canaan, and there he built an altar, Gen.

xii. 6, 7. But no devout Hebrew worshipper, with all his reverence for holy
places, would be content to see the altar
so consecrated belonging to others, and
so exposed to desecration ; the purchase
of the ground on which an altar stood
would therefore seem to follow as a kind
of corollary from the erection of an altar
on that ground. This is at all events
a more satisfactory solution than omitting
the word Ἀβραάμ or exchanging it for
Ἰακώβ (see Hackett). Of course the reading of R.V., W.H. (as above), prevents
a further difficulty as to the rendering
of τοῦ Συχέμ if the reading τοῦ Συχέμ is
retained, *cf.* Wendt, critical note, p. 157
(edition 1899), who follows A.V. in supporting "the father of Sichem," so
Hackett, but see on the other hand
Plumptre, *Acts, in loco*, and Felten, *in
loco*. For the way in which the two
purchases and the two burials may have
been confused in popular tradition, see
Zöckler, *Apostelgeschichte*, p. 302, 2nd
edit. (*cf.* Bengel, Stier, Nösgen).

Ver. 17. καθὼς: not "when" as in
A.V., but "as" R.V., *prout, quemadmodum, cf.* Mark iv. 33: "in the degree
that": Felten thinks that it is temporal,
as in 2 Macc. i. 31.—τῆς ἐπαγγελίας,
cf. ii. 33.—ἧς: Attic attraction.—
ὤμοσεν: but if we read with R.V.,
etc., ὡμολόγησεν "vouchsafed," so in
classical Greek, *cf.* Jer. li. 25 (LXX),
Matt. xiv. 7 (ὤμοσεν, a gloss from the
LXX according to Wendt).—ηὔξησεν ὁ λ.
καὶ ἐπληθύνθη, *cf.* Exod. i. 7, so in a
strange land the blessing was continued
(Weiss).

Ver. 18. *Cf.* Exod. i. 8, and Jos., *Ant.*,
ii., 9, 1. After ἕτερος add ἐπ' Αἰγ., see

ᾔδει τὸν Ἰωσήφ. 19. οὗτος[1] κατασοφισάμενος τὸ γένος ἡμῶν, ἐκάκωσε τοὺς πατέρας ἡμῶν, τοῦ ποιεῖν ἔκθετα τὰ βρέφη αὐτῶν, εἰς τὸ μὴ ζωογονεῖσθαι. 20. Ἐν ᾧ καιρῷ ἐγεννήθη Μωσῆς,[2] καὶ ἦν ἀστεῖος τῷ

---

[1] ουτος, D reads και, so Hilg.

[2] Μωσης AEP; Μωυσης ℵBCDH, W.H., Weiss.

---

above. ἕτερος not ἄλλος, probably meaning the native sovereign after the expulsion of the Shepherd Kings, "Joseph," B.D.[2]; "Egypt," B.D.[2], pp. 886, 887; Hamburger, *Real-Encyclopädie des Judentums*, i., 5, pp. 759, 760; Sayce, *Higher Criticism and the Monuments*, p. 237.—ἄχρις οὗ: only in Luke amongst the Evangelists, Luke xxi. 24, Acts vii. 18, xxvii. 33. Sayce, following Dr. Naville, argues in favour of Ramses II. as the Pharaoh of the Oppression, see *u. s.* and *Expository Times*, January and April, 1899, but see on the other hand the number of February, p. 210 (Prof. Hamond), and *Expositor*, March, 1897, Prof. Orr on the Exodus. Joseph settled under the Hyksos or Shepherd Kings, but the words "who knew not Joseph" should apparently refer, according to Dr. Sayce, not to the immediately succeeding dynasty, *i.e.*, the eighteenth, in which a Canaanite might still have occupied a place of honour, but rather to the nineteenth, which led to the overthrow of the stranger, and to a day of reckoning against the Hebrews. But it becomes difficult to speak with absolute confidence in the present state of Egyptological research, see *Expositor, u. s.*, p. 177. οὐκ ᾔδει: in Robinson's *Gesenius*, p. 380, the word is taken literally, or it may mean "who does not know Joseph's history or services"; others take it "who had no regard for his memory or services". Hamburger understands by it that Joseph was quite forgotten under the new national dynasty, whilst Nösgen refers to the use of οἶδα in Matt. xxv. 12.

Ver. 19. κατασοφισάμενος: in Exod. i. 10 we have the same verb "let us deal wisely with them" here translated "deal subtilly"; Vulgate, "circumveniens," *cf.* Rhemish version: "circumventing our stock" (γένος, as in iv. 36); *cf.* Judith v. 11, x. 19, in both passages the same verb is used, translated (R.V.), v. 11, "dealt subtilly"—the Syriac, probably nearest to the Hebrew, "*dealt* wisely with them," *i.e.*, the Egyptians dealt so with the Hebrews. In the second passage, R.V., word is rendered "might deceive"; same verb in Syriac as in Exod. i. 10, Heb.;

Speaker's Commentary, "Apocrypha," i., p. 290. Josephus and Philo use verb in same sense as in text; see for the force and meaning of κατά here, Page and Rendall. —ἐκάκωσε, *cf.* Exod. i. 11, where the same word is used of task-masters afflicting the people with burdens. For other ways in which Pharaoh is said to have afflicted the people, see Jos., *Ant.*, ii., 9, 1.—τοῦ ποιεῖν κ.τ.λ., "that they [*or he, margin*] should cast out their babes," R.V. But a comparison with Exod. i. 22 (LXX) justifies us in taking these words, as in R.V. margin, as describing the tyranny of Pharaoh, not as declaring that the parents themselves exposed their children. For the construction see Blass, *Grammatik*, p. 231; *cf.* 1 Kings xvii. 20, etc., genitive of result, see Page on iii. 12, and *in loco*, and Burton, *N. T. Moods and Tenses*, p. 157.—ἔκθετα: only here in N.T. and not in LXX, but used with γόνος in Eur., *Andr.*, 70.—εἰς τὸ: expressing the purpose, *cf.* Luke v. 17.—ζωογονεῖσθαι: in the active the verb is used three times, in Exod. i., of the midwives saving the Hebrew children alive, ver. 17, 18, 22 (*cf.* Judg. viii. 19, etc.), *vivum conservare*. In the N.T. the word is only used by St. Luke here and in his Gospel, chap. xvii. 33, and once by St. Paul, 1 Tim. vi. 13 (see R.V. margin). St. Chrysostom comments on the thought that where man's help was despaired of, and the child was cast forth, then God's benefit did shine forth conspicuous, *Hom.*, xvi.

Ver. 20. ἐν ᾧ καιρῷ, *cf.* i. 7, iii. 19, characterising the time, comp. Bengel, *tristi, opportuno*: on the name Μωυσῆς see Blass, *Grammatik*, p. 10, and Hamburger, *Real-Encyclopädie des Judentums*, i., 5, p. 768, and critical notes.—ἀστεῖος τῷ Θεῷ: if we render the expression as in A. and R.V., "exceeding fair," the dative τῷ Θεῷ is used as an equivalent of the Hebrew expression employed almost in a superlative sense, לֵאלֹהִים, Jonah iii. 3, πόλις μεγ. τῷ Θεῷ. Or the expression may be rendered "fair to God," *i.e.*, in the judgment of God; *cf.* δυνατὰ τῷ Θεῷ, 2 Cor. x. 4 and James ii. 5, τοὺς πτωχοὺς τῷ κόσμῳ. Page and Wendt

Θεῷ· ὃς ἀνετράφη μῆνας τρεῖς ἐν τῷ οἴκῳ τοῦ πατρὸς αὐτοῦ. 21.
ἐκτεθέντα δὲ αὐτόν,[1] ἀνείλετο αὐτὸν ἡ θυγάτηρ Φαραώ, καὶ ἀνεθρέψατο
αὐτὸν ἑαυτῇ εἰς υἱόν. 22. καὶ ἐπαιδεύθη Μωσῆς πάσῃ σοφίᾳ

[1] DE, Syr. Harcl. mg. add παρα (E εις) τον ποταμον after εκτ. . . . αυτον, Blass
in β, so Hilg. ανειλετο; but -ατο in אABCDE (H) 61, so Tisch., W.H., Weiss,
Hilg., Winer-Schmiedel, p. 112.

compare Æsch., *Agam.*, 352, and see also
Simcox, *Language of the N. T.*, p. 81.
ἀστεῖος, lit., belonging to the city (opposite to ἄγροικος), witty, clever; then,
elegant, pretty; Vulgate, *elegans*, used
as a general word of praise: applied to
Moses here, in Exod. ii. 2, and Heb. xi.
23, and also by Philo, *cf.* also Jos., *Ant.*,
ii., 97, and see Hamburger, *u. s.*, i., 5, p.
773; *Jalkut Rubeni*, f. 75, 4. For other
instances of the use of the word see LXX,
Num. xxii. 32, Judges iii. 17, and Judith
xi. 23, Susannah, ver. 7; in the last two
passages used of physical fairness, pretti-
ness (*cf.* Arist., *Eth. Nic.*, iv., 3, 5, and
instances in Wetstein). In 2 Macc. vi.
23 it is also used, and ἀστείως in 2 Macc.
xii. 43 in the general sense of right and
good, honestly.—ἀνετράφη μῆνας τρεῖς,
cf. Exod. ii. 2, verb used only by St.
Luke, twice in this chapter, and in xx. 3,
once in Luke iv. 16, but *cf.* margin, W.H.
—not used in LXX, but in Wisdom vii.
4 (where A has ἀνεστρ.), and see also 4
Macc. x. 2 and xi. 15 (but A.R., τραφ.).
The word is used in classical Greek, as
in Wisdom vii. 4 and here, of a child
nourished to promote its growth (although
sometimes with the idea of improving the
mind, *cf.* Acts xx. 3). In the N.T. it is
peculiar to St. Luke, and it is just the
word which a medical man would use,
frequently found in medical writings, opposed to ἰσχναίνω; see L. and S., *sub
v.*, and Hobart, *Medical Language*, p.
207.
   Ver. 21. ἐκτεθ.: the regular word for
exposure of children in classical Greek;
see also Wisdom xviii. 5, peculiar to
Luke in N.T., and only here in this
sense; *cf.* Exod. ii. 3, and β critical note
above.—ἀνείλετο—same word in Exod. ii.
5. The verb, though very frequent in Luke
in the sense of *to kill*, is only used here
in the sense of A. and R.V., Vulgate,
sustulit—but *cf.* Aristoph., *Nub.*, 531;
Epict., *Diss.*, i. 23, 7. ἑαυτῇ: as in contrast to the child's own mother. According to tradition, Pharaoh's daughter
designed him for the throne, as the
king had no son, Jos., *Ant.*, ii., 9, 7.—
εἰς υἱόν, Exod. ii. 10; *cf.* xiii. 22, 47;
Simcox, *Language of N. T.*, p. 80.

Ver. 22. ἐπαιδεύθη, *cf.* xxii. 3 here
with instrumental dative, or, better, dative
of respect or manner; not mentioned in
Exodus, but see Philo, *Vita Moys.*, ii.,
83, Mang., and also Schürer, *Jewish
People*, div. ii., vol. i., p. 343, E.T.; *cf.* the
knowledge of magic ascribed to Pharaoh's
wise men in Exod. vii. 11, and "Jannes
and Jambres," B.D.[2], and also 1 Kings
iv. 30, and Isa. xix. 2, 11, 12; Hamburger, *Real-Encyclopädie des Judentums* "Zauberei," i., 7, 1068, and references in Wetstein, *in loco*. παιδεύω,
both in LXX and N.T., used in the
sense of *training*; *cf.* Prov. v. 13 (Jos.,
C. Apion, i., 4), 1 Tim. i. 20, Titus ii.
12, and also in the sense of *chastising*,
so often in LXX and in N.T., and also
similarly used in classical Greek. The
passage is also important because it
helped to fix the attention of cultivated
early Christian writers upon the wisdom
of Greek poets and philosophers, and to
give a kind of precedent for the right
pursuit of such studies; *cf.* Clem. Alex.,
Strom., i., 5, 28; vi., 5, 42; Justin
Martyr, *Dial. c. Tryph.*, c., 1-4; see
Dean Plumptre's note, *in loco*.—ἦν δὲ
δυνατὸς, *cf.* xviii. 24, and especially
Luke xxiv. 19; see also Ecclus. xxi.
7, Judith xi. 8. If αὐτοῦ is retained, the
mode of expression is Hebraistic (Blass).
There is no contradiction with Exod. iv.
10, and no need to explain the expression
of Moses' writings, for Stephen has in
his thoughts not so much, as we may
believe, the oratorical form as the powerful contents of Moses' words (*e.g.*, his prophetical teaching, Hamburger, "Moses,"
Real-Encyclopädie des Judentums, i., 5,
772). Josephus speaks of him as πλήθει
ὁμιλεῖν πιθανώτατος, *Ant.*, iii., 1, 4 (see
also Jos., *Ant.*, ii., 10, 1, for the traditional exploits of Moses, and Hamburger,
u. s., p. 771).
   Ver. 23. ὡς, *cf.* i. 10, Lucan. The
exact age is not mentioned in O.T., but
it was traditional (Weiss refers its mention to the reviser, perhaps introduced
as a parallel to ver. 30). According to
the tradition, which Stephen apparently
followed, Moses lived forty years in
Pharaoh's palace, but some accounts

Αἰγυπτίων· ἦν δὲ δυνατὸς ἐν λόγοις καὶ ἐν ἔργοις. 23. Ὡς δὲ
ἐπληροῦτο αὐτῷ τεσσαρακονταετὴς¹ χρόνος, ἀνέβη ἐπὶ τὴν καρδίαν
αὐτοῦ ἐπισκέψασθαι τοὺς ἀδελφοὺς αὐτοῦ τοὺς υἱοὺς Ἰσραήλ. 24.
καὶ ἰδών τινα ἀδικούμενον² ἠμύνατο καὶ ἐποίησεν ἐκδίκησιν τῷ

¹ τεσσαρακονταετης B³EHP, so Hilg.; but τεσσερακον. ℵAB*C, so Tisch., W.H.,
Weiss (Winer-Schmiedel, pp. 45, 54).

² After αδικουμενον, DE, Gig., Syr. Harcl. mg. read εκ του γενους αυτου, so Hilg.

give twenty years; his dwelling in Midian
occupied forty years, and he governed
Israel for the same period, xiii. 18. See
Midrash Tanchuma on Exod. ii. 6 (Wetstein, with other references, so too Lumby).—**ἐπληροῦτο**, "but when he was
well-nigh," etc., R.V., lit. "when the age
of forty years was being fulfilled to him"
(imperf. tense), *cf.* Luke xxi. 24, Acts
ii. 1, ix. 23, xxiv. 27, and ver. 30 below;
so repeatedly in LXX.—**ἀνέβη ἐπὶ τὴν
καρδίαν αὐτοῦ**, *cf.* 1 Cor. ii. 9 for the
expression, probably taken from LXX,
Isa. lxv. 17, *cf.* Jer. iii. 16, xxxii. 35,
Ezek. xxxviii. 10, and 2 Kings xii. 4.
The phrase is an imitation of the Hebrew.
Gesenius compares the phrase before us
with Heb., Ezek. xiv. 3, 4; see also
Viteau, *Le Grec du N. T.*, p. 66 (1896).—
ἐπισκέψασθαι, *cf.* Luke i. 68, 78, and vii.
16, *cf.* Exod. iv. 31, of God visiting
His people by Moses and Aaron (Acts
xv. 14). In each of these passages the
verb is used of a divine visitation, and
it is so used by St. Luke only amongst
N.T. writers, except Heb. ii. 6 = Ps. viii.
5, LXX. It is used elsewhere in Matt.
xxv. 36, 43, James i. 27, Acts vi. 3, xv. 36
(*cf.* Judg. xv. 1). The word is used of
visits paid to the sick, *cf.* Ecclus. vii. 35,
and so in classical Greek (see Mayor on
James i. 27), often in medical writings
and in Plutarch (Grimm, *sub v.*, and
Kennedy, *Sources of N. T. Greek*, p. 105);
mostly in the LXX, as always in the
N.T., in good sense (Gen. xxi. 1, Ps.
viii. 4, lxxix. 14, Ecclus. xlvi. 14, Judith
viii. 33, but also with reference to divine
punishment, Ps. lxxxviii. 31, 32, Jer. ix.
9, 25, xi. 22, xxxiv. (xxvii.) 8, etc.), *cf.* its
use in *Psalms of Solomon*, where it is
generally employed with reference to
divine visitation, either for purposes of
punishment or deliverance. In modern
Greek = *to visit*, same sense as in LXX
and N.T.; Kennedy, *u. s.*, p. 155. For
its old English sense of *visit*, as looking
upon with kindness, Lumby compares
Shaks., *Rich. II.*, i., 3, 275: "All places
that the eye of heaven *visits*".—**τοὺς**

ἀδελφοὺς αὐτοῦ: though in a king's
palace, and far removed in one sense
from his people, Moses remembers that
he is an Israelite, and that he has brethren; while others forgot their brotherhood he reminded them of it: "motivum
amoris quod Moses etiam aliis adhibuit
ver. 26," Bengel, *cf.* Exod. ii. 10, and
Heb. xi. 24, 25.

Ver. 24. **ἀδικούμενον**, "wronged," *i.e.*,
by blows, Exod. ii. 11.—**ἠμύνατο**: only
here in N.T. (*sc.*, **τὸν ἀδικοῦντα**); in
active the verb means to defend, "debebat scribere **ἤμυνε**," says Blass, but in
the middle it means defence of oneself,
or of a friend, with the collateral notion
of requital or retaliation on an enemy
(see Rendall). In the middle it has also
the meaning of avenging, and therefore
might mean here "he took vengeance
on" or "he repulsed" (*cf.* Josh. x. 13,
2 Macc. x. 17, Wisdom xi. 3, and Jos.,
Ant., ix., 1, 2), although this is expressed
in the next words.—**ἐποίησεν ἐκδίκησιν**,
cf. Luke xviii. 7, 8, xxi. 22; lit., "wrought
an avenging," Rom. xii. 19 (*cf.* Heb. x.
30), 2 Cor. vii. 11, 2 Thess. i. 8, 1 Pet.
ii. 14. This and similar expressions are
common in LXX, Judg. xi. 36, Ps. cxlix. 7,
Ezek. xxv. 17, 1 Macc. iii. 15, vii. 9, 24,
38; **ἐκδ**. in Polybius with **ποιεῖσθαι**, iii.,
8, 10.—**καταπονουμένῳ**: only here and in
2 Pet. ii. 7; *cf.* 2 Macc. viii. 2 (R has **κατα-
π α τ ούμ.**, of the Jews oppressed, trodden
down, in the days of Judas Maccabæus),
3 Macc. ii. 2, 13; used in Polyb. and
Josephus, etc. The exact word is found
in *Didache*, v., 2.—**πατάξας**: lit., to strike,
hence to kill, in Biblical language only,
cf. Exod. ii. 12 and 14, and ver. 28 below:
so also in Matt. xxvi. 31, Mark xiv. 27
(Zech. xiii. 7, LXX). The verb is very
frequent in LXX. "Smiting the Egyptian," R.V.—**τὸν Αἰγ.**: not previously
mentioned, but implied in **ἀδικ.**, which
involves an oppressor; as in ver. 26 the
facts are regarded by St. Stephen as
known to his audience.

Ver. 25. **ἐνόμιζε δὲ**: a comment by
St. Stephen, but we are not told upon

καταπονουμένῳ, πατάξας τὸν Αἰγύπτιον.[1] 25. ἐνόμιζε δὲ συνιέναι
τοὺς ἀδελφοὺς αὐτοῦ, ὅτι ὁ Θεὸς διὰ χειρὸς αὐτοῦ δίδωσιν αὐτοῖς
σωτηρίαν · οἱ δὲ οὐ συνῆκαν. 26. τῇ τε ἐπιούσῃ ἡμέρᾳ ὤφθη αὐτοῖς
μαχομένοις, καὶ συνήλασεν[2] αὐτοὺς εἰς εἰρήνην, εἰπών, "Ἄνδρες,
ἀδελφοί ἐστε ὑμεῖς[3] · ἱνατί ἀδικεῖτε ἀλλήλους ;" 27. ὁ δὲ ἀδικῶν τὸν
πλησίον ἀπώσατο αὐτόν, εἰπών, "Τίς σε κατέστησεν ἄρχοντα καὶ

---

[1] After Αιγυπτιον, D (Wer.) add και εκρυψεν αυτον εν τη αμμω ; cf. Exodus ii. 12
(Blass rejects, Hilg. retains).

[2] συνηλασεν AEP, Chrys., some verss., so Meyer, Alford ; συνηλλασσεν ℵBCD e,
Vulg., Syrr. (P. and H.), Sah., so Tisch., W.H., R.V., Weiss, Wendt, Hilg. After
μαχομενοις D adds ειδεν αυτους αδικουντας (not retained by Blass but by Hilg.).

[3] υμεις HP, Boh., Syr. Harcl., Aeth. ; om. ℵABCDE 27, 61, Vulg., Sah., Arm.,
Chrys., so Tisch., W.H., R.V., Weiss, Wendt. For ανδρες αδελφοι εστε, D, Prom.
read τι ποιειτε, ανδρες αδελφοι ;

---

what grounds Moses based his expectation (see however Lumby's note, *in
loco*). The verb is found in Luke ii. 44,
iii. 23, and seven times in Acts, but elsewhere in the Gospels only three times
in St. Matthew ; it is used three times
by St. Paul. It is frequently found
in ii. and iv. Macc., twice in Wisdom and once in Ecclesiasticus.—διὰ
χειρὸς αὐτοῦ, ii. 23. δίδωσι, "was
giving them," R.V. (not "would give,"
A.V.), as if the first step in their deliverance was already taken by this act, so
συνιέναι, "understood," R.V. (not "would
understand," A.V.). In Jos., *Ant.*, ii., 9,
2, 3, reference is made to the intimation
which was said to have been vouchsafed
by God to Amram the father of Moses
that his son should be the divine agent
who was expected to arise for the deliverance of the Hebrews, and whose
glory should be remembered through
all ages. It has been sometimes
thought that St. Stephen had this
tradition in mind.—οἱ δὲ οὐ συνῆκαν :
Mr. Page notes the rhetorical power in
these words, cf. ver. 53 καὶ οὐκ ἐφυλάξατε.
Ver. 26. ὤφθη : Wendt commends
Bengel, who sees in the word the thought
that he appeared *ultro, ex improviso*, cf.
ii. 3, vii. 2, Heb. ix. 28.—συνήλασεν :
but if we read συνήλασσεν, see critical
note = imperfect, *de conatu*, cf. Matt.
iii. 14, Luke i. 59, xv. 14, Acts xxvi.
11, see Burton, *N. T. Moods and Tenses*,
p. 12, from συναλλάσσω, only found
here in N.T., not in LXX or Apocrypha,
but in classical Greek, cf. Thuc., i., 24.
—ἱνατί = ἵνα τί γένηται ; cf. iv. 25,
and Luke xiii. 7 (Matt. ix. 4, xxvii.
46, 1 Cor. x. 29), and with the words

ἱνατί ἀδικεῖτε ἀλλήλους ; Exod. ii.
13 (Moulton and Geden) ; used several
times in LXX, also by Aristoph. and
Plato. Like the Latin *ut quid?* see
Grimm, *sub v.*, and for spelling ; and comp.
also Blass, *Gram.*, p. 14, and Winer-
Schmiedel, p. 36.—ἄνδρες, ἀδελφοί ἐστε :
the fact of their brotherhood aggravated
their offence ; it was no longer a matter
between an Egyptian and a Hebrew as
on the previous day, but between brother
and brother—community of suffering
should have cemented and not destroyed
their sense of brotherhood. Hackett and
Alford take ἄνδρες as belonging to
ἀδελφοί (not as = κύριοι, 'Sirs' in A. and
R.V.), *men* related as *brethren are ye*, cf.
Gen. xiii. 8.
Ver. 27. ἀπώσατο for Attic ἀπεώσατο
(see also ver. 45), not found in the O.T.
parallel, but added by Stephen, cf. ver.
38, compare LXX, Jer. iv. 30. The
word may be introduced to empha-
size the contumaciousness of the people,
which in Stephen's narrative is the
motive of the flight of Moses ; in Exodus,
Moses flees from fear of Pharaoh, and
the answer of the Hebrew demonstrates
to him that his deed of yesterday was
known—but there is no contradiction in
the two narratives. The matter would
become known to Pharaoh, as the words
of the Hebrew intimated ; it could not
be hidden ; and in spite of the attempt
at concealment on the part of Moses by
hiding the body in the sand, his life was
no longer safe, and so he fled because he
had nothing to hope for from his people.
Stephen's words would be quite consistent with the narrative in Exodus (Nösgen, *Apostelgeschichte*, p. 163, as against
Overbeck).

δικαστὴν ἐφ' ἡμᾶς[1]; 28. μὴ ἀνελεῖν με σὺ θέλεις, ὃν τρόπον ἀνεῖλες
χθὲς[2] τὸν Αἰγύπτιον;" 29.[3] ἔφυγε δὲ Μωσῆς ἐν τῷ λόγῳ τούτῳ, καὶ
ἐγένετο πάροικος ἐν τῇ Μαδιάμ, οὗ ἐγέννησεν υἱούς δύο.   30. Καὶ
πληρωθέντων ἐτῶν τεσσαράκοντα, ὤφθη αὐτῷ ἐν τῇ ἐρήμῳ τοῦ ὄρους

[1] ημας DE, Chrys., so Meyer, Hilg.; ημων ℵABCHP 13, 61, so Tisch., W.H.,
R.V., Weiss, Wendt.

[2] χθες AEHP, Chrys; εχθες ℵB*CD 34, so Tisch., W.H., Weiss (Winer-
Schmiedel, p. 54).

[3] D reads ουτως και εφυγαδευσεν Μωυσης (και ουτως d), so Hilg.; E reads εφυγαδευσεν δε Μωυσην; Gig. has *fugatus est autem M.;* and Par. *effugavit autem se M.*
Weiss (Codex D, p. 67) inclines to consider φυγαδ. as the original reading (so Zöckler),
and to take it trans., understanding ο αδικων as the nom. φυγαδευω nowhere else
in N.T.; in LXX found both trans. and intrans. but gen. the latter; commoner εφυγεν
may be corruption of it here; φυγαδεύω frequent in Letters of Pseudo-Heraclitus.

Ver. 28. *Cf.* Exod. ii. 14.

Ver. 29. ἐν τῷ λόγῳ τούτῳ: Weiss
points out that Moses fled on account
of this word, because he saw that his
people would not protect him against
the vengeance of Pharaoh. Jos., *Ant.*,
ii., 11, 1, makes the cause of the flight
of Moses not the words which told him
that his deed was known, but the jealousy
of the Egyptians, who represented to
the king that he would prove a seditious
person. — Μαδιάμ: generally taken to
mean or to include the peninsula of
Sinai (Exod. ii. 15, and iii. 1), and thus
agrees with the natural supposition that
his flight did not carry Moses far
beyond the territory of Egypt (*cf.* Exod.
xviii. 1-27). The name Midianites would
be applied to the descendants of Abraham's fourth son by Keturah, who in
various clans, some nomadic, some mercantile (*e.g.*, those to whom Joseph was
sold), may be described as Northern
Arabs. (Dr. Sayce, *u. s.*, p. 270, maintains that Moses to get beyond Egyptian
territory must have travelled further than
to the S. peninsula of our modern maps,
and places Sinai in the region of Seir,
with Midian in its close neighbourhood.) Amongst one of these tribes
Moses found a home in his flight,
Hamburger, "Midian," *Real-Encyclopädie des Judentums*, i., 5, 755. Hackett, *Acts*, p. 104, "Midian," B.D.[1].
—οὗ ἐγένν., *cf.* Exod. ii. 22, iv. 20,
xviii. 3. Weiss thinks the notice due
to a reviser, who wished to show
that Moses had given up his people,
and made himself a home in a strange
land.

Ver. 30. πληρωθέντων, see ver. 23,
cf. Exod. vii. 7, "fulfilled," R.V. ὤφθη,
ver. 2, so the second fundamental re-

velation of God to Israel took place in
the wilderness far away from the Promised Land (Weiss), see also ver. 33.—
τεσσαράκοντα, *cf.* i. 3.—Σινᾶ: there is
no contradiction between this and Exod.
iii. 1, where the appearance is said to
take place in Horeb, for whilst in the
N.T. and Josephus Sinai only is named
for the place of the law-giving, in the
O.T. the two names are interchanged,
cf. also Ecclus. xlviii. 7. According to
Hamburger the two names are identical,
signifying in a narrower sense only one
mountain, the historical mountain of the
giving of the law, but in a wider sense
given to a whole group of mountains.
Thus Hamburger declines to accept the
view that Horeb was the name of the
whole ridge of mountain-cluster, whilst
Sinai specially denotes the mountain of
the law-giving, since Horeb is also used
for the same event (*cf.* Exod. iii. 1, xvii.
6, xxxiii. 6), *Real-Encyclopädie des Judentums*, i., 7, 940. See also B.D.[1], "Sinai,"
Wendt, edition (1899), *in loco;* Schaff-
Herzog, *Encyclopædia*, iv., "Sinai" (also
for literature); and Grimm-Thayer, *sub v.*
According to Sayce, *Higher Criticism and
the Monuments*, p. 263 ff., Sinai is a mountain of Seir, rather than of the Sinaitic peninsula so called. The same writer lays
stress upon the fact that Sinai is associated with Seir and Edom, Deut. xxxiii.
2, Judg. v. 4, 5, and maintains that it is
nowhere in the O.T. transported to the
Sinaitic peninsula of our modern maps.
The word Σινᾶ is an indeclinable noun
τό (*sc.*, ὄρος); Josephus τὸ Σιναῖον and
τὸ Σιναῖον ὄρος; Grimm-Thayer, Winer-
Schmiedel, p. 91, Blass, *Gram.*, 8, 32;
and see also Sayce, *u. s.*, p. 268, 269,
and *Patriarchal Palestine*, p. 259, who
renders as adjective "(the mountain)

Σινᾶ ἄγγελος Κυρίου [1] ἐν φλογὶ πυρὸς [2] βάτου. 31. ὁ δὲ Μωσῆς ἰδὼν
ἐθαύμασε [3] τὸ ὅραμα· προσερχομένου δὲ αὐτοῦ κατανοῆσαι, ἐγένετο
φωνὴ Κυρίου πρὸς αὐτόν, 32. "Ἐγὼ ὁ Θεὸς τῶν πατέρων σου, ὁ
Θεὸς Ἀβραὰμ καὶ ὁ Θεὸς Ἰσαὰκ καὶ ὁ Θεὸς Ἰακώβ." ἔντρομος δὲ
γενόμενος Μωσῆς οὐκ ἐτόλμα κατανοῆσαι. 33. εἶπε δὲ αὐτῷ ὁ
Κύριος, "Λῦσον τὸ ὑπόδημα τῶν ποδῶν σου· ὁ γὰρ τόπος ἐν ᾧ

[1] **Κυριου** om. ℵABC 61, 81, Vulg., Sah., Boh.; so Tisch., W.H., R.V., Blass (a
and β, although found in D), Weiss, Wendt (prob. added from Exod. iii. 2); Hilg.
retains.

[2] **εν φλογι πυρος** ℵBDHP, Sah., Boh., Syr. Harcl., Arm., Aeth., Chrys., so
W.H., R.V., Weiss, Wendt, and Hilg.; **εν πυρι φλογος** ACE, Vulg., Syr. Pesh.
(so LXX, Exod. iii. 2, varies: **εν πυρι φλογος** in B; **εν φλογι πυρος** AF).

[3] **εθαυμασε** ABC 13, Vulg., Chrys., so Lach., Meyer, W.H., R.V.; **εθαυμαζεν**
ℵDEHP 1, 31, 61, Aug., so Tisch., Weiss (Wendt doubtful), Hilg. Blass and Hilg.
both read **ακηκοα** (D) for **ηκουσα**; cf. Exod. iii. 7.

which belongs to Sin," i.e., like desert
which it overlooked, to the worship of
the Babylonian Moon-God Sin in that
region.—**ἄγγελος**: in Exod. iii. 2 "the
angel of the Lord," but in ver. 7 "the
Lord said," so here in ver. 31 "the voice
of the Lord said," cf. ver. 33. For the
same mode of expression cf. Acts xxvii.
23 with xxiii. 11. In this Angel, the
Angel of the Lord, cf. Exod. iii. 2 with
vv. 6, 14, and Gen. xxii. 11 with ver. 12;
the Angel of the Presence, Exod. xxxiii.
11, cf. Isa. lxiii. 9 (ver. 38 below),
although Jewish interpreters varied,
the Fathers saw the Logos, the Eternal
Word of the Father. See references in
Felten, in loco, and Liddon, Bampton
Lectures, Lect. ii., and "Angel," B.D.².
Otherwise we can only say that Jehovah
Himself speaks through the Angel
(Weiss, Blass, in loco).—**ἐν φλογὶ πυρὸς
βάτου**: words interchanged as in LXX
A, Exod. iii. 2; according to Hebrew
πυρὸς ἐκ τοῦ βάτου—**πυρός** here = an
adjective, rubus incensus (Blass, Weiss);
cf. 2 Thess. i. 8, **ἐν πυρὶ φλογός**. For
gender of **βάτος** see ver. 35.
Ver. 31. **κατανοῆσαι**: this careful observation is implied in the narrative of
Exodus though the word is not employed.
It is a favourite word with St. Luke, and
is used by him four times in his Gospel
and four times in Acts, elsewhere in
Gospels only in Matt. vii. 3 (five times in
Epistles). On its force see Westcott on
Heb. iii. 1: "oculos vel mentem de-
figere in aliquo" Grimm; properly =
to take notice of, so in classical Greek;
it is used also in the sense of observing, looking at, cf. James i. 27; and
in a general sense, to see, cf. LXX, Ps.

xciii. 9, cf. xc. 8; and also, to consider,
Heb. x. 24 (Mayor, note on James
i. 27). In the LXX, where it is frequent, it is used with both shades of
meaning.
Ver. 32. **ἔντρομος γεν.** (cf. x. 4, **ἔμφοβος γεν.**), xvi. 29, cf. Exod. iii. 6, expression used only in Acts in these two
passages (Heb. xii. 21, quotation from
LXX). **ἔμφοβος** is found five times in
Luke, in Gospel xxiv. 5, 37, in Acts x.
4, xxiv. 25 (only once elsewhere, in Rev.
xi. 33, with **ἐγένοντο**), and in each passage with **γενόμενος**. **ἔντρομος**, Dan.
(Theod.) x. 11, Wisdom xvii. 10, 1 Macc.
xiii. 2, and in Ps. xvii. (xviii.) 7, lxxvi.
(-vii.) 18, **ἔντρομος ἐγενήθη ἡ γῆ**—the
word is also used by Plutarch.
Ver. 33. **λῦσον**, cf. Josh. v. 15, **λῦσον**
A., cf. Exod. iii. 5; in classical Greek
λῦσαι, omitting **σου**. On the custom of
worshipping bare-footed, as the priests
when actually engaged in the Temple,
or as the Arabs enter their mosques with
bare feet, or the Samaritan the holiest
place on Gerizim, see instances, both
classical, Juvenal, Sat., vi., 158, and from
Josephus and others, Wetstein and
Wendt, in loco. The latter refers to an
Egyptian custom of the order of Pythagoras **ἀνυπόδητος θῦε καὶ προσκύνει,**
Jamblich., Vit. Pyth., 23, and cf. 18 in
Wetstein.—**τὸ ὑπόδημα**, cf. xiii. 25, and
John i. 27, where in each passage the
singular is used. Both Weiss and Wendt
note the significance of the verse—a
strange land is consecrated (cf. vi. 13,
τόπος ἅγιος) by the presence of God—
the Jews thought that the Temple was
the only holy place, cf. add. note for
significance in connection with the aim

ἔστηκας γῆ ἁγία ἐστίν. 34. ἰδὼν εἶδον τὴν κάκωσιν τοῦ λαοῦ μου τοῦ ἐν Αἰγύπτῳ, καὶ τοῦ στεναγμοῦ αὐτῶν ἤκουσα· καὶ κατέβην ἐξελέσθαι αὐτούς· καὶ νῦν δεῦρο, ἀποστελῶ [1] σε εἰς Αἴγυπτον." 35. τοῦτον τὸν Μωϋσῆν ὃν ἠρνήσαντο εἰπόντες, "Τίς σε κατέστησεν ἄρχοντα καὶ δικαστήν [2];" τοῦτον ὁ Θεὸς ἄρχοντα [3] καὶ λυτρωτὴν ἀπέστειλεν [4] ἐν χειρὶ ἀγγέλου τοῦ ὀφθέντος αὐτῷ ἐν τῇ βάτῳ. 36. οὗτος ἐξήγαγεν αὐτούς, ποιήσας τέρατα καὶ σημεῖα ἐν γῇ Αἰγύπτου καὶ ἐν Ἐρυθρᾷ θαλάσσῃ, καὶ ἐν τῇ ἐρήμῳ ἔτη τεσσαράκοντα.

[1] αποστελω HP.; αποστειλω ℵABCDE 61, Chrys., so Tisch., Alford, W.H., R.V., Wendt, Weiss, Hilg.

[2] δικαστην, ℵCD 61, Gig., Par., Syr. Harcl. mg. add εφ' ημων (εφ' ημας in E and Chrys.), so Hilg., but text in ABHP, Vulg., Syr. Harcl. text, so Tisch., W.H., R.V., Blass, Weiss.

[3] αρχοντα, before this word και inserted by ℵABDE 15, 18, 61, Syr. Harcl.; so Tisch., W.H., R.V., Blass, Wendt, Weiss, Hilg.

[4] απεστειλεν CHP, Chrys., so Blass; απεσταλκεν ℵABDE, so Tisch., W.H., R.V., Weiss, Wendt, Hilg.; εν ℵHP d, Syr. Pesh., Boh., Arm., Aeth., Meyer; συν ABCDE, Vulg., Sah., Syr. Harcl., Chrys., so Tisch., Alford, W.H., R.V., Weiss, Wendt, Hilg.; εν probably from confusion with last syll. in απεσταλκεν. συν χειρι only here in N.T.; εν χειρι not uncommon.

of St. Stephen's speech, and St. Chrysostom's comment *in loco*.

Ver. 34. ἰδὼν εἶδον: Hebraism, so LXX, Exod. iii. 7, and so frequently, *e.g.*, Ps. xl. 1, *cf.* Matt. xiii. 14, Heb. vi. 14 (Gen. xxii. 17), the participle with the verb emphasising the assurance. But similar collocations are not wanting in classical Greek, see Page, *in loco*, and Wendt, who compares 1 Cor. ii. 1. The phrase ἰδὼν εἶδον occurs in Lucian, *Dial. Mar.*, iv., 3 (Wetstein). "I have surely seen," R.V., so in A. and R.V., Exod. iii. 7, see Simcox, *Language of N. T.*, p. 130, and Viteau, *Le Grec du N. T.*, p. 217 (1896).—καὶ νῦν δεῦρο ἀποστελῶ, but *cf.* Exod. iii. 10; ἀποστείλω; see critical notes. On the hortatory subj. in first person singular with δεῦρο or ἄφες prefixed, see Burton, *N. T. Moods and Tenses*, p. 74, *cf.* Matt. vii. 4, Luke vi. 42, but translated by the revisers, "I will send," with an imperative force as of a divine command (see Rendall's note, *in loco*). For classical instances *cf.* Wendt, *in loco*.

Ver. 35. τοῦτον: followed by the triple οὗτος, a significant and oratorical repetition—*anaphora* or repetition of the pronoun, *cf.* ii. 23, v. 31 (so Bengel, Blass, Viteau, see also Simcox, *Language of the N. T.*, pp. 65, 66). It plainly appears to be one of the purposes, although we cannot positively say the chief purpose, of the speech to place Moses in typical comparison to Jesus and the be-

haviour of the Jews towards Him, ver. 25.—(καὶ) ἄρχοντα καὶ λυτρωτήν: Moses was made by God a ruler and even more than a judge—not δικαστής but λυτρωτής. But just as the denial of the Christ is compared with the denial of Moses, *cf.* ἠρνήσαντο and ἠρνήσασθε in Acts iii. 13, so in the same way the λύτρωσις wrought by Christ is compared with that wrought by Moses, *cf.* Luke i. 68, ii. 38, Heb. ix. 12, Tit. ii. 14 (so Wendt, *in loco*) "omnia quæ negaverant Judæi Deus attribuit Moysi" (Blass). λυτρωτής in LXX and in Philo, but not in classical Greek. In the Sept. the word is used of God Himself, Ps. xix. 14, lxxviii. 35 (*cf.* Deut. xiii. 5, and *Psalms of Solomon*, ix. 1).—ἐν χειρί, *cf.* xi. 21, but σύν is closer to the classical σὺν θεοῖς with the helping and protecting hand, ἐν χειρὶ = בְּיַד, *cf.* Gal. iii. 19.—τῇ βάτῳ: ὁ Attic, ἡ Hellenistic, but in N.T. it varies, in Luke xx. 37 feminine, in Mark xii. 26 (and in LXX) masculine (W.H.); Blass, *Gram.*, p. 26; Grimm-Thayer, *sub v.*

Ver. 36. On οὗτος see ver. 35.— ἐξήγαγεν, Exod. iii. 10, καὶ ἐξάξεις τὸν λαόν μου.—Ἐρυθρᾷ θαλάσσῃ in LXX frequent, יַם סוּף sometimes with, sometimes without the article, here as in the Heb. without: *cf.* the parallel in *Assumption of Moses*, iii., 11 (ed. Charles), and see below on ver. 38.

37. Οὗτός ἐστιν ὁ Μωϋσῆς ὁ εἰπὼν τοῖς υἱοῖς Ἰσραήλ, " Προφήτην
ὑμῖν ἀναστήσει Κύριος ὁ Θεὸς ὑμῶν [1] ἐκ τῶν ἀδελφῶν ὑμῶν, ὡς ἐμέ·
αὐτοῦ ἀκούσεσθε." [2] 38. οὗτός ἐστιν ὁ γενόμενος ἐν τῇ ἐκκλησίᾳ ἐν
τῇ ἐρήμῳ μετὰ τοῦ ἀγγέλου τοῦ [3] λαλοῦντος αὐτῷ ἐν τῷ ὄρει Σινᾶ καὶ

[1] Κυριος CEHP, Boh., Syr. Harcl., Aeth., Chrys., so LXX, Deut. xviii. 15; om.
ℵABD 61, Vulg., Sah., Aeth., so Tisch., W.H., R.V., Weiss, Wendt, Hilg. υμων
(1) om. ℵABCD 61, Vulg. verss., Chrys.; so Tisch., W.H., R.V., Weiss.

[2] αυτου ακουσεσθε CDE, Gig., Par., Wern., Vulg., Syrr. (P. and H.), Boh., Arm.,
Aeth.; om. ℵABHP 61, Sah., Chrys., so Tisch., W.H., R.V., Blass, Weiss, Wendt
(cf. Deut. xviii. 15, and Acts iii. 22).

[3] αγγελου του om. Gig., "recte ut videtur," according to Blass, cf. ver. 44—
Blass brackets in β.

Ver. 37. οὗτός, cf. ver. 35, cf. Deut. xviii. 15, and iii. 22, above. The introduction of the prophecy may mean that St. Stephen wished in this as in the preceding and following verse to emphasise the position and the work of Moses, and to mark more strongly the disobedience of the people. Blass regards οὗτός ἐστιν ὁ Μ. κ.τ.λ. as intended to show that Moses, whom the Jews accused Stephen of injuring, was himself by his own words a supporter of the claims of Christ: " hic est ille M. qui dixit ".
Ver. 38. οὗτός : again emphatic use. —ἐκκλησίᾳ : " in the congregation," R.V. margin: held in the wilderness for the giving of the law, although the word does not occur in Exod. xix., but cf. Deut. xxxi. 30, Josh. viii. 35 (ix. 2). By Wycliffe the word was translated " Church " here, but afterwards " congregation," so in Tynd., Cranm., Gen., until A.V. again rendered " Church," cf. Heb. ii. 12, and on the word see above on v. 11, Hort, Ecclesia, p. 3 ff., and B.D.[2] " Church ". In Heb. ii. 12, R.V. reads " congregation " in text (but " Church " in margin), following Tynd. and Cranm., and Ps. xxii. 22 from which the quotation is made (where both A. and R.V. have " congregation "). Schmiedel would dismiss the word as a later gloss, which has been inserted here in a wrong place, see Wendt (edit. 1899), p. 160, note.—γενόμ. . . . μετὰ, cf. ix. 19, xx. 18 (Mark xvi. 10); no Hebraism, cf. σύν in Luke ii. 13.—τοῦ ἀγγέλου τοῦ λαλ., but in Exodus Moses is said to speak with God, cf. ver. 30 above, and see also ver. 53, " who was with the angel . . . and with our fathers," i.e., who acted as the mediator between the two parties, who had relations with them both, cf. Gal. iii. 19, and Philo, Vit. Moys., iii., 19, where Moses is called μεσίτης καὶ διαλλακ-

τής, cf. also Heb. ii. 2, and Jos., Ant., xv., 5, 3 ; the latter passage represents Herod as saying that the Jews learned all that was most holy in their law δι' ἀγγέλων παρὰ τοῦ Θεοῦ (see Westcott Hebrews, and Wetstein on Gal. iii. 19). On the title μεσίτης as given to Moses, see further Assumption of Moses, i., 14, and Charles' note and introd. lxiii., but it does not follow that the inference is justified that the Apocryphal Book in question was known to the writer of St. Stephen's speech. Dr. Charles maintains this on the ground of three passages, but of (1) it may be said that the term μεσίτης evidently could have been known from other sources than Acts, (2) the parallel between ver. 36 and Assumption of Moses, iii., 11, is, as Dr. Charles admits, an agreement verbally " for the most part," but the words " Egypt, the Red Sea, and the wilderness for forty years " might often be used as a summary of the history of Israel at a particular period, whilst the context with which the words are here associated is quite different from that in Assumption of Moses, l.c., and (3) there is no close resemblance between the prophecy from Amos quoted in ver. 43 below and the prophecy in Assumption of Moses, ii., 13 ; in both the phraseology is quite general. Perhaps the omission of the word μετά before τῶν πατέρων gives emphasis to the privilege of " our fathers," when one can speak of being with the angel and with them, Simcox, Language of the N. T., p. 159. Thus Moses prefigures the Mediator of the new covenant, cf. Heb. viii. 15, ix. 15, xii. 24, and the mention of this honour bestowed upon Moses emphasises still more fully the indignity which he received from his countrymen, cf. St. Chrysostom on the force of οὗτος in this verse.—λόγια, cf. Rom. iii. 2, as in LXX

τῶν πατέρων ἡμῶν, ὃς ἐδέξατο λόγια ζῶντα δοῦναι ἡμῖν.[1] 39. ᾧ οὐκ
ἠθέλησαν ὑπήκοοι γενέσθαι οἱ πατέρες ἡμῶν, ἀλλ᾽[2] ἀπώσαντο, καὶ
ἐστράφησαν[3] ταῖς καρδίαις αὐτῶν εἰς Αἴγυπτον, 40. εἰπόντες τῷ
Ἀαρών, "Ποίησον ἡμῖν θεοὺς οἳ προπορεύσονται ἡμῶν· ὁ γὰρ
Μωσῆς οὗτος, ὃς ἐξήγαγεν ἡμᾶς ἐκ γῆς Αἰγύπτου, οὐκ οἴδαμεν τί
γέγονεν[4] αὐτῷ." 41. καὶ ἐμοσχοποίησαν ἐν ταῖς ἡμέραις ἐκείναις,
καὶ ἀνήγαγον θυσίαν τῷ εἰδώλῳ, καὶ εὐφραίνοντο ἐν τοῖς ἔργοις τῶν
χειρῶν αὐτῶν. 42. Ἔστρεψε δὲ ὁ Θεός, καὶ παρέδωκεν αὐτοὺς
λατρεύειν τῇ στρατιᾷ τοῦ οὐρανοῦ· καθὼς γέγραπται ἐν βίβλῳ τῶν
προφητῶν, "Μὴ σφάγια καὶ θυσίας προσηνέγκατέ μοι ἔτη τεσσαρά-

---

[1] ημιν; but אB read υμιν, so W.H. text, Weiss.

[2] αλλ'; but αλλα in אABCDEH, so Tisch., W.H., Weiss, Hilg.

[3] εστραφησαν, D reads απεστραφησαν, so Hilg. ταις καρδιαις DE, Vulg., Arm.,
Syr. Pesh., Chrys., Iren[int].; so Meyer; εν pref. in אABC, so W.H., R.V., Weiss.

[4] εγενετο אABC, so W.H., R.V., Blass (cf. Exod. xxxii. 1, pr. R.V.).

---

of the words of God, cf. Numb. xxiv. 4,
16, and chiefly for any utterance of God
whether precept or promise, only once of
human words (Ps. xviii. (xix.) 14); so
Philo speaks of the decalogue as τὰ δέκα
λόγια, and Jos., B. J., vi., 5, 4, of the
prophecies of God in the O.T., and Philo
writes τὸ λόγιον τοῦ προφήτου (i.e.,
Moses), Vit. Moys., iii., 35, see Grimm-
Thayer, sub v., λόγιον, lit., a little word,
from the brevity of oracular responses.—
ζῶντα: "vim vitalem habentia," Blass,
cf. Heb. iv. 12, 1 Pet. i. 23, cf. Deut.
xxxii. 47. The words again show how
far St. Stephen was from despising the
Law of Moses, cf. Heb. iv. 12, "living,"
R.V. ("quick," A.V.); 1 Pet. i. 3, and
ii. 5, where R.V. has "living" instead
of "lively"; in Ps. xxxviii. 19 "lively"
is retained in R.V. (see also in Exod. i.
19, in contrast to feeble, languid), cf.
Spenser, Faërie Queene, iii., 8, 5. Here
the word has the sense of living, i.e.,
enduring, abiding, cf. "thy true and
lively [living] word" in prayer for the
Church Militant, cf. 1 Pet. i. 23, R.V.

Ver. 39. ἐστράφησαν, i.e., in their
desires after the Egyptian gods, cf. ver.
40, not "turned back again," but
simply "turned" (Rendall, in loco), the
words cannot be taken literally (as Corn.
à Lap. and others), or we should have
to render "who may go before us in our
return to Egypt," which not only is unsupported by the Greek, but cf. Exod.
xxxii. 4, 1 Kings xii. 28; see also on this
verse, Exod. xvi. 3, Num. xi. 4, 5, but
the desires there expressed marked a later
date.

Ver. 40. προπορεύσονται (Exod. xvi.
3, Num. xi. 4, 5), only elsewhere in N.T.,
in Luke i. 76, with which cf. Deut. xxxi.
3. The words in Acts are taken from
Exod. xxxii. 1, 23; frequent in LXX, 1
Macc. ix. 11 (but see H. and R.), and
also in Xen. and Polyb.—οὗτος, iste, cf.
vi. 14, the same anacoluthon as in LXX,
Exod. xxxii. 23, so in the Heb., "who
brought us up": no mention of God—
they ascribed all to Moses (Chrysostom);
see Viteau, Le Grec du N. T., p. 135
(1896).

Ver. 41. ἐμοσχοποίησαν: not in LXX
or in classical Greek; in Exod. xxxii. 2,
ἐποίησαν μόσχον.—ἀνήγαγον θυσίαν,
cf. 1 Kings iii. 15 (and 2 Sam. vi. 17, A.),
for similar use of the word, "quia victima
in aram tollitur," Grimm.—εὐφραίνοντο,
cf. Exod. xxxii. 6 and 18; the word is
very frequent in LXX, and several
times with ἐν, cf., e.g., 2 Chron. vi. 41,
Ecclesiast. xiv. 5, 1 Macc. iii. 7; χαίρειν
ἐν, Luke x. 20; used only by St. Luke
amongst the Evangelists, six times in his
Gospel, twice in Acts (but ii. 26 is a
quotation). Bengel points out that God
rejoices in the works of His own hands,
and men in the work of God's hands,
but not as here—half irony in the words.

Ver. 42. ἔστρεψε: properly intransitive. Weiss takes it transitively: God
turned them from one idol worship to
another; but here probably means that
God turned away from them, in the sense
that He cared no longer for them as before; so Grimm, sub v.; or that He
actually changed so as to be opposed to
them; cf. Josh. xxiv. 20, Heb., so Wet-

κοντα ἐν τῇ ἐρήμῳ, οἶκος Ἰσραήλ; 43. καὶ ἀνελάβετε τὴν σκηνὴν
τοῦ Μολόχ, καὶ τὸ ἄστρον τοῦ θεοῦ ὑμῶν Ῥεμφάν,[1] τοὺς τύπους
οὓς ἐποιήσατε προσκυνεῖν αὐτοῖς· καὶ μετοικιῶ ὑμᾶς ἐπέκεινα[2]

[1] υμων ℵACEHP, Vulg., Boh., Syr. Harcl., Aeth., Chrys. (so LXX, Amos v. 26),
so Blass; om. BD 15, 18, Syr. Pesh., Sah., Arm., Ir., Or., Philast., so Tisch., W.H.,
R.V., Weiss, Wendt, Hilg. Ρεμφαν 1, 31, Or., Chrys.; Ρεμφαμ D, Flor., Gig.,
Par., Wern., Vulg., Iren., so Blass in β, and Hilg.; Ρεφαν ℵ³ACE, Syrr. (P. and
H.), Boh., Sah., so R.V.; Ρομφαν ℵ* 3, so Tisch.; Ρομφα B, so W.H., Weiss.
In LXX Ραιφαν or Ρεφαν. Wendt prefers Ρομφαν or Ρομφα.

[2] επεκεινα; D¹, Gig., Par. read επι τα μερη, so Blass in α and β, so Hilg., cf.
LXX; originality of Western reading not imposs., or επι τα μερη may have been
substituted for a phrase unique in N.T. (see also Wendt, p. 163, edit. 1899).

stein "Deus se ab iis avertit," and cf.
LXX, Isa. lxiii. 10.—παρέδωκεν, cf. Rom.
i. 24, and εἴασε in xiv. 16; Ephes. iv. 19,
"gave themselves up".—ἑαυτοὺς παρέδω-
καν, from the side of man.—λατρεύειν τῇ
στρατιᾷ τοῦ οὐρ., cf. Deut. xvii. 3, 2
Kings xvii. 16, xxi. 3, 2 Chron. xxxiii. 3, 5,
Jer. viii. 2, xix. 13, a still grosser idolatry:
"antiquissima idolatria, ceteris speci-
osior" Bengel. The created host was
worshipped in place of Jehovah Sabaoth,
"the Lord of Hosts". The word,
though used always in the N.T. of religious service, is sometimes applied to the
worship of idols, as well as of the One
God; cf. Rom. i. 25 (LXX, Exod. xx. 5,
xxiii. 24, Ezek. xx. 32), so λατρεία is
used of the worship of idols in 1 Macc. i.
43; see Trench, Synonyms, i., p. 142 ff.—
ἐν βίβλῳ τῶν προφ.: here part of the
Hebrew Scriptures which the Jews
summed up under the title of "the Prophets," as a separate part, the other two
parts being the Law and the Hagio-
grapha (the Psalms, Luke xxiv. 44);
or Twelve Minor Prophets which probably formed one book.—Μὴ σφάγια
κ.τ.λ.: a quotation from Amos v. 25-27,
with little variation—the quotation in
ver. 42 is really answered by the
following verse. The question does
not mean literally that no sacrifices were
ever offered in the wilderness, which
would be directly contrary to such passages as Exod. xxiv. 4, Num. vii. 9. The
sacrifices no doubt were offered, but
how could they have been real and
effectual and acceptable to God while in
their hearts the people's affections were
far from Him, and were given to idol
deities? μή, expecting a negative answer = num (see Zöckler's note, in
loco).—οἶκος: nominative for vocative,
as often, as if in apposition to the
ὑμεῖς contained in προσηνέγκατε (Blass).
Some emphasise μοι = mihi soli, or

suppose with Nösgen that the question
is ironical.

Ver. 43. The answer of God to His
own question: καί should be explained
"ye actually took up" ("yea," R.V., in
Amos v. 26); ἀνελάβετε, "ye took up,"
i.e., to carry in procession from one halting place to another. τὴν σκηνὴν, properly
σκηνή = סֻכָּה, which has sometimes
been explained as the tent or tabernacle
made by the idolatrous Israelites in
honour of an idol, like the tabernacle of
the covenant in honour of Jehovah, but
R.V. renders "Siccuth your king" (margin, "the tabernacle of your king"),
Amos v. 26, see below.—τοῦ Μολόχ: s
in LXX, but in Hebrew, מַלְכְּכֶם, i.e.,
your king (as A.V. in margin, Amos v.
26). The LXX, either as explanatory, or
perhaps through another reading מִלְכֹּם,
2 Kings xxiii. 13, here render by the name
of the idol. Sayce also (Patriarchal
Palestine, p. 258) renders "Sikkuth your
Malik," i.e., the Babylonian god Sikkuth also represents "Malik," the king,
another Babylonian deity (=Moloch of
the O.T.). Most commentators maintain
that ver. 26 (Amos v.) is not in the
original connected with ver. 25 as the
LXX render, referring the latter verse
back to Mosaic times. The LXX may
have followed some tradition, but not only
does the fact that the worship of Moloch
was forbidden in the wilderness seem to
indicate that its practice was a possibility,
but there is also evidence that long before the Exodus Babylonian influence
had made itself felt in the West, and the
statement of Amos may therefore mean
that the Babylonian god was actually
worshipped by the Israelites in the wilderness (Sayce, u. s., p. 259). In margin
of R.V. we have "shall take up," i.e.,

Βαβυλῶνος." 44. Ἡ σκηνὴ τοῦ μαρτυρίου ἦν ἐν τοῖς πατράσιν ἡμῶν ἐν τῇ ἐρήμῳ, καθὼς διετάξατο ὁ λαλῶν τῷ Μωσῇ, ποιῆσαι

carry away with you into exile (as a threat), while others take the verb not in a future but in a perfect sense, as referring to the practice of the contemporaries of the prophet: "de suo tempore hæc dicit Amos" (Blass). *Siccuth* or rather *Saccuth* is probably a proper name (a name given to Nin-ip, the warlike sun-god of Babylonia (Sayce)), and both it and *Kewan* (*Kaivan*), כִּיּוּן, represent Babylono-Assyrian deities (or a deity), see Schrader, *Cun. Inscript. and the O. T.*, ii., 141, 142, E.T.; Sayce, *u. s.*, Art. "Chiun" in Hastings' B.D., and Felten and Wendt, *in loco*. For the thought expressed here there is that their gods should go into captivity with the people, *cf.* Isa. xlvi. 2.—**καὶ τὸ ἄστρον . . . Ῥεμφάν,** T.R.—but R.V. Ῥεφάν, on the reading see critical notes, and Wendt, p. 177.

For the Hebrew (Amos v. 26) כִּיּוּן *Chiun*, the LXX has Ῥαιφάν. How can we account for this? Probably LXX read the word not *Chiun* but *Kewan* כֵּיוָן (so in Syr. Pesh., *Kewan* = Saturn your idol), of which Ῥαιφάν is a corruption through Καιφάν (*cf.* similar change of כ into ר in Nah. i. 6, כְּאֵשׁ in LXX **ἀρχάς** as if רְאֵשׁ, Robinson's *Gesenius*, p. 463). *Kewan* = Ka-ai-va-nu, an Assyrian name for the planet Saturn, called by the same name in Arabic and Persian (Hamburger, *Real-Encyclopädie des Judentums*, i., 2, 216, and Art. "Chiun," *u. s.*); and this falls in perfectly with the Hebrew, "the star of your god" (your star-god) — אֱלֹהֵיכֶם כּוֹכַב, the previous word, צַלְמֵיכֶם, "your images," being placed after the two Hebrew words just quoted, *cf.* LXX (but see also Sayce, *u. s.*, who renders "Chiun, your Zelem," Zelem denoting another Babylonian deity = the image or disc of the sun). It seems plain at all events that both in the Hebrew and in the LXX reference is made to the divine honours paid to the god Saturn. In the words "ye took up the star," etc., the meaning is that they took up the star or image which represented the god Saturn—*your* god with some authorities

(so in LXX, see Blass, *in loco*). ὑμῶν, *i.e.*, the deity whom these Israelites thus placed on a level with Jehovah. If we take כִּיּוּן *Chiun* = the litter, or pedestal, of your gods, *i.e.*, on which they were carried in procession, as if from כּוּן (a meaning advocated by Dr. Robertson Smith), and not as a proper name at all: "the shrines of your images, the star of your God," R.V. margin, Amos v. 26, we may still infer from the mention of a star that the reference is to the debasement of planet worship (so Jerome conjectured Venus or Lucifer). It is to be noted that the vocalisation of *Siccuth* and *Chiun* is the same, and it has been recently suggested that for the form of these two names in our present text we are indebted zeal of the misplaced zeal of the Massoretes, by the familiar trick of fitting the pointing of one word to the consonant skeleton of another—here the pointing is taken from the word שִׁקּוּץ, "abomination," see Art. "Chiun," *u. s.*—**τοὺς τύπους**, *simulacra:* in LXX, in opposition to σκηνή and ἄστρον. If the σκηνή is to be taken as meaning the tent or tabernacle containing the image of the god, it might be so described. τύποι is used, Jos., *Ant.*, i., 19, 11; xv. 9, 5, of the images of Laban stolen by Rachel.—**προσκυνεῖν αὐτοῖς**: not in LXX, where we read τοὺς τύπους αὐτῶν οὓς ἐποιήσατε ἑαυτοῖς.—**ἐπέκεινα Βαβυλῶνος**: in LXX and Hebrew "Damascus". ἐπέκ. only here in N.T., but in classical authors, and in LXX, Gen. xxxv. 16 (21), Jer. xxii. 19 (and Aquila on passage in Genesis). "Babylon" may have been due to a slip, but more probably spoken designedly: "interpretatur vaticinium Stephanus ex eventu" (as the Rabbis often interpreted passages), see Wendt, *in loco*, and Lightfoot. It may be that St. Stephen thus closes one part of his speech, that which shows how Israel, all through their history, had been rebellious, and how punishment had followed. If this conjecture is correct, we pass now to the way in which Stephen deals with the charge of blasphemy against the temple.

Ver. 44. Here again we notice that the first sanctuary of the fathers was not the temple, nor was it erected on holy ground, but ἐν τῇ ἐρήμῳ according to

αὐτὴν κατὰ τὸν τύπον ὃν ἑωράκει · 45. ἦν καὶ εἰσήγαγον διαδεξάμενοι
οἱ πατέρες ἡμῶν μετὰ Ἰησοῦ, ἐν τῇ κατασχέσει τῶν ἐθνῶν ὧν ἐξῶσεν [1]
ὁ Θεὸς ἀπὸ προσώπου τῶν πατέρων ἡμῶν, ἕως τῶν ἡμερῶν Δαβίδ ·
46. ὃς εὗρε χάριν ἐνώπιον τοῦ Θεοῦ, καὶ ᾐτήσατο εὑρεῖν σκήνωμα

---

[1] εξωσεν ℵ³ABCDHP, Chrys., so W.H., Weiss, Hilg. ; εξεωσεν ℵ*E 5, Tisch.,
so Blass, *Grammatik*, p. 37.

God's direct command.—ἡ σκηνὴ τοῦ
μαρτ. : it is possible that there was in the
speaker's mind a contrast to the σκηνή
in ver. 43, but the connection is not
clearly drawn out, ἀσυνδέτως, "ut in
oratione concitatiore" (Blass).—ἡ σ. τοῦ
μαρτυρίου, "the tabernacle of the testimony". The same phrase in LXX is
used (incorrectly as Meyer noted) to
translate the Hebrew tabernacle of the
congregation *or* tabernacle of meeting,
i.e., of God with His people, *cf.* Exod.
xxvii. 21. But the tabernacle was justly
called μαρτυρίου, because it contained
"the ark of the testimony," LXX, Exod.
xxv. 9 (10), κιβωτὸς μαρτυρίου, and so
frequently in the rest of the book, and
xxxi. 18, τὰς δύο πλάκας τοῦ μαρτυρίου.
The tabernacle might properly be so
called as a witness of God's presence,
and a testimony to the covenant between
God and His people. See also Westcott
on Heb. viii. 5, additional note.—διετάξατο, *cf.* xx. 13, xxiv. 23 ; only in St.
Luke and St. Paul in N.T., except once
in Matt. xi. 1 ; in Gospel four times, in
Acts four or five times, and frequent in
LXX. Grimm compares *disponere* (ver-
ordnen).—καθὼς δ. ὁ λαλῶν : "even as
he appointed who spake," R.V. ; "per
reverentiam appellatio siletur" Blass ;
cf. Exod. xxv. 40, Heb. viii. 5.—κατὰ
τὸν τύπον, *cf.* Wisdom ix. 8, where the
command is given to Solomon.—μίμημα
σκηνῆς ἁγίας ἣν προητοίμασας : "according to the figure," R.V., *i.e.*, pattern,
likeness, *cf.* ver. 43 and Rom. v. 14.
Again we see how far Stephen was from
denying the divine sanction given to
Moses for the tabernacle. In the thought
thus implied lies the germ of Hooker's
great argument, *Eccles. Pol.*, iii., 11
(Plumptre).
Ver. 45. διαδεξάμενοι : having received
in their turn, *i.e.*, from Moses, only here
in N.T., *cf.* 4 Macc. iv. 15 ; so also in
classical Greek, in Dem. and in Polyb.,
cf. διαδοχῆς, "in their turn," Herod.,
viii., 142 : (on the technical meaning of
διάδοχος, to which in the LXX διαδεχό-
μενος is akin to the term of a deputy, or
of one next to the king, see Deissmann,

Bibelstudien, pp. 111, 112).—μετὰ Ἰησοῦ,
cf. Heb. iv. 8, where Syr. Pesh. has
"Jesus the son of Nun" (but not here).
—ἐν τῇ κατασχέσει τῶν ἐθνῶν : "when
they entered on the possession of the
nations," R.V., lit., in the taking possession of the nations, *i.e.*, of the land in-
habited by the nations (Wendt). A.V.
follows Vulgate ; frequent in LXX, *cf.*
Jos., *Ant.*, ix., 1, 2, and *Test. xii. Patr.*, x.,
used by Philo in the sense of a portion
given to keep (Grimm-Thayer).—ὧν :
Attic attraction, *cf.* i. 1.—ἀπὸ προσώπου : for a similar phrase *cf.* Deut. xi. 23,
xii, 29, 30, etc., and frequently in LXX,
Hebrew מִפְּנֵי.—ἕως τῶν ἡμ. Δ. : to be
connected with the first part of the verse,
"which also our fathers brought in . . .
unto the days of David" (inclusively),
see Wendt, *in loco*, *i.e.*, "et mansit
tabernaculum usque ad tempora Davidis"
(Blass). Rendall takes the words as
closely joined to ὧν ἐξῶσεν, but the
clause ὧν ἐξῶσεν . . . ἡμῶν is rather
subordinate.
Ver. 46. ὃς εὗρε χάριν, *cf.* Luke i. 30,
Hebraistic, *cf.* Gen. vi. 8 ; it may be
tacitly implied that had the temple been
so important as the Jew maintained,
God would have allowed the man who
found favour before him to build it ; on
the phrase ἐνώπ. Κ. or Θεοῦ see above
on iv. 10.—ᾐτήσατο εὑρεῖν, *i.e.*, σκήνωμα,
cf. iii. 3 ; ἠρώτα λαβεῖν, and instances in
Wetstein, "asked to find," not only
"desired," LXX, 2 Sam. vii. 2 ff., 1
Chron. xxii. 7, Ps. lxxxi. 5.—σκήνωμα :
perhaps used by David (as in the
Psalm quoted) in his humility (Meyer) ;
used of the temple in 1 Esdras i. 50.
David of course desired to build not a
σκηνή, which already existed.—τῷ Θεῷ
Ἰακώβ, see critical notes.
Ver. 47. Σολομῶν, see above on iii. 11.
—δὲ : "But" or "And"—δὲ, adversative
as in A. and R.V., *cf.* 2 Chron. vi. 7-9,
where Solomon is represented as claiming God's promise that he should build the
house—a favour denied to his father David.
Ver. 48. ἀλλ᾽ οὐχ : But the presence
of the Most High (in contrast to the

τῷ Θεῷ [1] Ἰακώβ · 47. Σολομῶν [2] δὲ ᾠκοδόμησεν [3] αὐτῷ οἶκον. 48. Ἀλλ᾽ οὐχ ὁ ὕψιστος ἐν χειροποιήτοις ναοῖς [4] κατοικεῖ, καθὼς ὁ προφήτης λέγει, 49. "Ὁ οὐρανός μοι θρόνος, ἡ δὲ γῆ ὑποπόδιον τῶν ποδῶν μου · ποῖον οἶκον οἰκοδομήσετέ μοι; λέγει Κύριος · ἢ τίς [5] τόπος τῆς

[1] θεω ℵ3ACEP, Vulg., Syrr. (P. and H.), Sah., Boh., Arm., Aeth., Chrys.; οικω ℵ1BDH, so Weiss (*Apostelgeschichte*, p. 7), so also Hilg. W.H. (Appendix, 92) think that although θεω is a very ancient correction of οικω the latter can hardly be genuine and that there is apparently a primitive error, and with this judgment Wendt agrees. Hort suggests κυριω, and concludes that τωοικω may have come from τωκω (so too Wendt), and refers to LXX, Ps. cxxxi. 5; but we have still to ask if the expression "Lord of Jacob" ever occurred, whilst no doubt "God of Jacob," "House of Jacob" are familiar expressions. In LXX, Ps. cxxxi. 3, we have σκηνωμα οικου, and a similar expression *may* have been the orig. reading here; again, in Ps. xxiv. 6, Heb., we have "Jacob" = "the God of Jacob" (see LXX), and it has been suggested that some such abbreviation or mode of speech lies at the bottom of the difficulty here. Blass holds that οικω comes from the next verse "corrupte" (orig. a gloss on σκηνωμα).

[2] Σολομών BDEHP, so Blass in β, Weiss; Σολομῶν W.H., Hilg.; Σαλωμων AC, so Tisch.; Σαλομων ℵ. (See Winer-Schmiedel, p. 93; Blass, *Gram.*, p. 29.)

[3] ᾠκοδομησεν ℵAB3CEHP, so Tisch.; οικοδομησεν BD, so W.H., Weiss, Blass in β, Hilg., but see W.H., App., 170. (Winer-Schmiedel, p. 100; Blass, *Gram.*, p. 37.)

[4] ναοις om. ℵABCDE; so Tisch., W.H., R.V., Blass, Weiss, Wendt, Hilg. (*cf.* xvii. 24).

[5] τις; D, Flor. read ποιος, so Blass in β, and Hilg.—assim. either to preceding ποιον or to LXX.

smallness of any building made by hands) was not so confined—the previous words must not be misunderstood by Stephen's hearers. Solomon's οἶκος might have given the idea of greater permanency, but still Isaiah had taught, lxvi. 1, 2, and even the builder of the temple, Solomon himself, had acknowledged that God was not confined to any single place of worship, 1 King viii. 27, 2 Chron. vi. 18 (Hackett), *cf.* also David's prayer, 1 Chron. xxix. 10-19.—ἐν χειροποιήτοις ναοῖς κατοικεῖ—omit ναοῖς, probably an exegetical addition, *cf.* xvii. 24, where the word is found. The omission makes the contrast with οἶκος still more emphatic. "But Solomon . . . a *house*, howbeit the Most High dwelleth not in *houses* made with hands" (R.V.). For χειροποίητος and ἀχειρ. see Westcott on Heb. ix. 11, 24. Both words occur in Mark xiv. 58, in the charge of the false witness against our Lord. In the LXX χειροποίητος is used several times of idols made with hands, and occasionally found in classical Greek. Weiss compares as a parallel with its use here Isa. xvi. 12 (see R.V.), but the meaning is doubtful. — ὁ ὕψιστος, emphatic—Solomon's building a house must not be

misunderstood — see too ver. 49. ὁ ὕψ., xvi. 17, used here absolutely (*cf.* Luke i. 32, 35, 76, vi. 35, without the article), so often in LXX, 2 Sam. xxii. 14, Ps. xvii. 13, and often in Psalms, Isa. xiv. 14, Ecclus. xii. 6, etc. R.V. writes "Most High," instead of A.V. "most High," thus making the proper name of God more emphatic, *cf.* Winer-Schmiedel, p. 172—so in classical Greek Ζεὺς ὕψιστος; ὁ ὕψιστος θεός in Greek inscriptions of Asia Minor; for the Hebrew equivalents, see Grimm-Thayer, *sub v.* St. Stephen's words apparently impressed at least one of his hearers, for the same thought is reproduced in the words of St. Paul at Athens, where he asserts the same truth, and makes St. Stephen's words as it were his text to emphasise the real power and worship of God: "atque similiter hic Judæi atque illic Græci castigantur" (Blass), *cf.* the teaching of our Lord in John iv. 21 (and see Plumptre's note on this passage in Acts). —καθὼς ὁ προφ., Isa. lxvi. 1, 2 (LXX). The quotation is almost identical with few slight changes, as *e.g.*, Ver. 49. τίς τόπος for ποῖος, and οὐχὶ introducing the conclusion instead of γάρ. Although Solomon had expressed the

καταπαύσεώς μου; 50. οὐχὶ ἡ χείρ μου ἐποίησε ταῦτα πάντα[1];"
51. Σκληροτράχηλοι καὶ ἀπερίτμητοι τῇ καρδίᾳ[2] καὶ τοῖς ὠσίν, ὑμεῖς
ἀεὶ τῷ Πνεύματι τῷ Ἁγίῳ ἀντιπίπτετε, ὡς οἱ πατέρες ὑμῶν καὶ
ὑμεῖς.[3] 52. τίνα τῶν προφητῶν οὐκ ἐδίωξαν οἱ πατέρες ὑμῶν[4]; καὶ
ἀπέκτειναν τοὺς προκαταγγείλαντας περὶ τῆς ἐλεύσεως τοῦ δικαίου,

[1] Flor. omits whole verse, but Blass and Hilg. retain it. Variation from LXX decisive for retention.

[2] (τῇ) καρδίᾳ EHP 61, Flor., Gig., Syr. Pesh., Sah., Boh., Eus., Lucif., so Blass, Meyer, Alford; καρδίαις (א)ACD 7, 14 (Chrys.), Cyr. (Vulg., Syr. Harcl., Arm., Aeth.), so Tisch., W.H., R.V., Weiss, Wendt, Hilg.; καρδίας B, W.H. marg. Meyer and Alford retain καρδίᾳ because (they think) καρδίαις was introduced to suit plural subject, but cf. Ezek. xliv. 7. καρδίας in LXX, Jer. ix. 26, but the reading can scarcely be original here on account of the following dat. τοῖς ωσιν (Wendt). But on the whole W.H.'s decision is best.

[3] καὶ υμεις om. D², Flor., Gig., but Blass retains; Hilg. omits.

[4] οι πατερες υμων; D, Flor. read εκεινοι.

same truth in the dedicatory prayer of his temple, St. Stephen appeals to the great Messianic prophet. It is not, as some have thought, the worthlessness of the temple, but rather its relative value upon which Stephen insists. Those who take the former view of the words must suppose that St. Stephen had forgotten that Solomon had given utterance to the same thought at the moment when he was consecrating the temple (so Wendt, Felten, McGiffert, in loco). Weiss sees in the question another proof of the thought running through the whole address, that God's presence, with the blessings which He confers and the revelations which He imparts, is not confined to the temple : cf. the use of the same quotation as here against the Jews, Epist. Barn., xvi., 2, after the destruction of the temple. Ver. 51. σκληροτράχηλοι καὶ ἀπερίτμητοι τῇ καρδίᾳ, cf. Exod. xxxiii. 3, 5, xxxiv. 9, Deut. ix. 6, Baruch ii. 30, etc., Ecclus. xvi. 11 (cf. Cicero, Verr., iii., 95, "tantis cervicibus est"). Both adjectives had been used to describe the sins of Israel in former days. On this reading see above and Wendt, critical note, p. 190, cf. Kennedy, Sources of N. T. Greek, p. 116. For the expression ἀπερ., cf. Deut. x. 16, Jer. iv. 4, and ἀπερ. τὰ ὦτα, Jer. vi. 10. In the N.T. cf. Rom. ii. 25, 29 (which sounds like another echo of St. Stephen's teaching), cf. also Epist. Baru., ix. (Jer. iv. 4). Similar expressions occur in Philo and the Rabbis, and also 1 Macc. i. 48, ii. 46, and see further Deissmann, Bibelstudien, pp. 150, 151. Many writers have maintained that St. Stephen's sharp and abrupt declaration

marks the increasing impatience of his hearers at this point, as if the speaker felt that the murmurs of his audience would not allow him much more speech. But on the other hand St. Stephen's whole speech led up to this point, and his words were not so much an interruption, but a continuance and a summary of what had gone before. No doubt the speech was left unfinished : " cujus cursus ad Iesum tendebat" (Blass); since in His rejection the obstinacy of the people which had marked and marred their history had reached its climax ; and the indignant words of St. Stephen bring to mind the indignation of a greater than he against the hyprocrisy and wilfulness of the nation—"the wrath of the Lamb" against the Pharisees and the oppressors (Briggs, Messiah of the Apostles, p. 68). — ἀεὶ : "summa tractationis — semper quotiescumque vocamini" Bengel.—ἀντιπίπτετε, cf. Num. xxvii. 14, of Israel striving against God, and also in Polyb. and Plut. Ver. 52. τίνα τῶν προφ.—ἀσυνδέτως, to mark the vehemence of the speech, as above, verse 51: cf. 2 Chron. xxxvi. 16 for the general statement, and for individual cases, Jeremiah, Amos, and probably Isaiah, the prophet just quoted. We may compare the words of our Lord, Matt. v. 12, Luke xiii. 34, and also Luke xi. 49, Matt. xxiii. 29-37 where the same words ἐδίωξαν and ἀπέκτειναν are used of the treatment of the prophets.—καὶ ἀπέκ. : "they even slew"—perhaps the force of καὶ (Wendt), "they slew them also" (Rendall).—ἐλεύσεως : only here in the N.T., not in LXX or Apocrypha, or

οὖ νῦν ὑμεῖς προδόται καὶ φονεῖς γεγένησθε [1] · 53. οἵτινες ἐλάβετε
τὸν νόμον εἰς διαταγὰς ἀγγέλων, καὶ οὐκ ἐφυλάξατε. 54. Ἀκούοντες
δὲ ταῦτα, διεπρίοντο ταῖς καρδίαις αὐτῶν, καὶ ἔβρυχον τοὺς ὀδόντας

[1] γεγενησθε HP, Chrys.; εγενεσθε ℵABCDE, Orig., so Tisch., W.H., R.V.,
Blass, Weiss, Wendt, Hilg.

in classical writers, but found in *Acta
Thomæ* 28, and in Iren., i., 10, in plural,
of the first and second advent of Christ
(see also Dion. Hal., iii., 59).—τοῦ δικαίου,
see Acts iii. 14 and note. It has been
suggested that it is used here and elsewhere of our Lord from His own employment of the same word in Matt. xxiii.
29, where He speaks of the tombs τῶν
δικαίων whom the fathers had slain
whilst the children adorned their sepulchres. But it is more probable that the
word was applied to our Lord from the
LXX use of it, *cf.* Isa. liii. 11. Even
those Jews who rejected the idea of an
atoning Messiah acknowledged that His
personal righteousness was His real
claim to the Messianic dignity, Weber,
Jüdische Theologie, p. 362; Taylor, *Sayings of the Jewish Fathers,* p. 185, second
edition. We cannot forget that one of
those present who heard St. Stephen's
burning words was himself to see the
Just One and to carry on the martyr's
work, *cf.* xxii. 14, ἰδεῖν τὸν δίκαιον κ.τ.λ.
—νῦν ἐγένεσθε: "of whom ye have now
become," R.V., the spirit of their fathers
was still alive, and they had acted as
their fathers had done; ὑμεῖς again emphatic.

Ver. 53. οἵτινες, *quippe qui* (" ye who,"
R.V.), as often in Acts and Epistles not
simply for identification, but when as
here the conduct of the persons already
mentioned is further enlarged upon (Alford), *cf.* viii. 15, ix. 35, x. 41, 47, and
Winer-Schmiedel, p. 235, but see also
Blass, *Grammatik,* p. 169.—εἰς διαταγὰς
ἀγγέλων: " as it was ordained by angels,"
R.V. εἰς: at the appointment of, *cf.* its
use in Matt. xii. 41, or better εἰς as in
ver. 21 = received the law as ordinances
of angels (νόμον being regarded as an
aggregate of single acts and so with
plural " ordinances "), so Rendall, who
takes εἰς = ὡς, and Page, *cf.* Heb. xi. 8,
i.e., it was no human ordinance. But
see on the other hand Wendt's note, p.
192, where he points out that the law was
not received as commands given by angels
but by God. This was undoubtedly the
case, but St. Stephen was here probably
referring to the current tradition in Philo

and Josephus, and LXX, Deut. xxxiii. 2.
ἐκ δεξιῶν αὐτοῦ ἄγγελοι μετ' αὐτοῦ, *cf.*
Ps. lxvii. 17; Philo, *De Somn.*, p. 642
Mang., so Jos., *Ant.*, xv., 5, 3, and also
Book of Jubilees, chap. i. (see Wetstein
and Lightfoot (J. B.) on Gal. iii. 19).
Others again take εἰς = ἐν, "accepistis
legem ab angelis promulgatam" = διατασ-
σόντων ἀγγέλων, so Blass. Certainly it
does not seem possible to take διαταγή
= διάταξις = *agmen dispositum* (*cf.* Judith i. 4, viii. 36), and to render "præ-
sentibus angelorum ordinibus," so that
here also εἰς = ἐν (Meyer and others).
Lightfoot (J.) takes the "angels" as =
Moses and the Prophets; Surenhusius as
= the elders of the people, whilst St.
Chrysostom sees a reference to the angel
of the burning bush. It must not be
thought that St. Stephen is here de-
preciating the Law. From a Christian
standpoint it might of course be urged
that as Christ was superior to the angels,
so the introduction of angels showed the
inferiority of the Law to the Gospel (*cf.*
Heb. ii. 2, Gal. iii. 19), but St. Stephen's
point is that although the Law had
been given with such notable sanctions,
yet his hearers had not kept it, and that
therefore they, not he, were the real
law-breakers. — οὐκ ἐφύλαξατε: "cum
omnibus *phylacteriis* vestris," Bengel.
Note the rhetorical power of the words
cf. ver. 25 (Page).

Ver. 54. No charge could have been
more hateful to such an audience, *cf.* our
Lord's words, John vii. 19; see Schürer,
Jewish People, vol ii., div. ii., p. 90 ff.,
E.T. Schürer twice quotes St. Paul's
words, pp. 96, 124, ζῆλον Θεοῦ ἔχουσιν
ἀλλ' οὐ κατ' ἐπίγνωσιν; no words could
better characterise the entire tendency
of the Judaism of the period.—διεπρίοντο,
cf. v. 33.—ἔβρυχον: not elsewhere in
N.T., in LXX, Job xvi. 10 (9), Ps. xxxiv.
(v.) 16, xxxvi. (vii.) 12, *cf.* cxi. (xii.) 10;
Lam. ii. 16, *cf.* Plutarch, *Pericles,* 33
(without ὀδόντας, intransitive). The
noun βρύχη is found in the same sense,
Ap. Rh., ii., 83, of brute passion, not the
despair so often associated with the
cognate noun; *cf.* Matt. viii. 12, xiii. 42,
etc.

ἐπ' αὐτόν.　55.¹ Ὑπάρχων δὲ πλήρης Πνεύματος Ἁγίου, ἀτενίσας εἰς
τὸν οὐρανόν, εἶδε δόξαν Θεοῦ, καὶ Ἰησοῦν ² ἑστῶτα ἐκ δεξιῶν τοῦ Θεοῦ,³
56. καὶ εἶπεν, Ἰδού, θεωρῶ τοὺς οὐρανοὺς ἀνεῳγμένους, καὶ τὸν υἱὸν
τοῦ ἀνθρώπου ἐκ δεξιῶν ἑστῶτα τοῦ Θεοῦ.　57. κράξαντες δὲ φωνῇ
μεγάλῃ, συνέσχον τὰ ὦτα αὐτῶν, καὶ ὥρμησαν ὁμοθυμαδὸν ἐπ' αὐτόν ·

¹ υπαρχων δε πληρης Π. Α., Flor. represents ὁ δε υπαρχων (or ων) ἐν πνευματι
αγιω; possibly assim. to Apoc. i. 10, iv. 2, as it has been thoughtfully suggested
that to be "in the spirit" would account for his vision, whereas the expression in
T.R. would not seem to account for it.

² Ιησουν; D, Flor., Gig. add τον Κυριον, so Hilg.

³ For του θεου Par., Wern. read *virtutis Dei*; Const. Apost. της δυναμεως, "recte
ut videtur" Blass, so in β ; *cf.* Matt. xxvi. 64, Luke xxii. 69.

Ver. 55. ἀτενίσας, *cf.* i. 10, εἰς τὸν
οὐρανόν, *cf.* John xvii. 1, "ubi enim est
oculus, ibi est cor et amor". In the
power of the Holy Ghost, with which
Stephen is represented as being full, as
in life so in death, he saw δόξαν Θεοῦ, in
which He had appeared to Abraham,
cf. ver. 2, πλήρης, "crescente furore hos-
tium, in Stephano crescit robur spiritus,
omnisque fructus Spiritus," Bengel.—
Ἰησοῦν ἑστῶτα: elsewhere He is represented as sitting, ii. 34. If St. Luke had
placed this saying in the mouth of St.
Stephen in imitation of the words of
Jesus, Matt. xxi. 64, Mark xvi. 19, Luke
xxii. 69, he would, without doubt, have
described Him as sitting, *cf.* also the
expression "Son of Man," only here
outside the Gospels, and never in the
Epistles (Rev. i. 13, a doubtful instance),
a noteworthy indication of the primitive
date and truthfulness of the expression
and the report. See especially Wendt's
note on p. 194 (1888). Standing, as if
to succour and to receive His servant,
ἵνα δείξῃ τὴν ἀντίληψιν τὴν εἰς αὐτόν
(Oecum., and so Chrys.); "quasi obvium
Stephano," Bengel, so Zöckler, and see
Alford's note and Collect for St. Stephen's
day. St. Augustine represents Christ as
standing: "ut Stephano stanti, patienti,
et reo, ipse quoque stans, quasi patiens
et reus compatiatur". Alford supposes
reference in the vision to that of Zech.
iii. 1.—ἐκ δεξιῶν: as the place of honour,
cf. 1 Kings ii. 19, Matt. xx. 21. The
Sanhedrin would recall the words "the
Son of Man," as they had been spoken
by One Who was Himself the Son of
Man, and in Whom, as in His follower,
they had seen only a blasphemer. On
the expression "Son of Man" *cf.* Charles,
Book of Enoch, Appendix B, p. 312 ff.,
and *Witness of the Epistles*, p. 286
(1892).

Ver. 57. κράξαντες: so as to silence
him.—συνέσχον τὰ ὦτα αὐτῶν: in order
that the words which they regarded as
so impious should not be heard, *cf.* Matt.
xxvi. 65. Blass compares the phrase
LXX, Isa. liii. 15, καὶ συνέξουσι βασιλεῖς
τὸ στόμα αὐτῶν. — ὥρμησαν . . . ἐπ'
αὐτόν, *cf.* 2 Macc. x. 16, and in several
places in 2 Macc. the verb is found with
the same construction (although not
quite in the same sense).

Ver. 58. ἔξω τῆς πόλεως: according
to the law, Lev. xxiv. 14, so in Luke iv.
29, our Lord is cast out of Nazareth to
be stoned.—ἐλιθοβόλουν: as guilty of
blasphemy. St. Stephen's closing remarks were in the eyes of his judges a
justification of the charge; imperf. as
in ver. 59, see note below. The judicial
forms were evidently observed, at least
to some extent (Weiss attributes the
introduction of the witnesses to a reviser), and whilst the scene was a
tumultuous one, it was quite possible that
it was not wholly bereft of judicial appearances.—μάρτυρες: whose part it was to
throw the first stone, *cf.* Deut. xvii. 7
(John viii. 7).—ἀπέθεντο τὰ ἱμάτια
αὐτῶν: to perform their cruel task with
greater ease and freedom, *cf.* xxii. 20.—
νεανίου: only used in Acts, where it
occurs three or four times, xx. 9, xxiii.
17 (18), several times in LXX. It has
been thought (Wendt) that the term
could not have been used of Saul if he
had been married, or if he was at this
time a widower, but if νεανίας might be
used to denote any man of an age between
twenty-four and forty, like Latin *adule-
scens* and the Hebrew נַעַר, Gen. xli.
12 (Grimm-Thayer), Saul might be so
described. Josephus applies the term to
Agrippa I. when he was at least forty.
Jos., *Ant.*, xviii., 6, 7. See further on

58. καὶ ἐκβαλόντες ἔξω τῆς πόλεως, ἐλιθοβόλουν. καὶ οἱ μάρτυρες[1] ἀπέθεντο τὰ ἱμάτια αὐτῶν[2] παρὰ τοὺς πόδας νεανίου καλουμένου

[1] μάρτυρες, Gig., Par. *falsi testes;* cf. vi. 12. Blass rejects in β.

[2] αυτων; B has εαυτων, so Weiss, but W.H. as in T.R.

xxvi. 10.—Σαύλου: "If the Acts are the composition of a second-century writer to whom Paul was only a name, then the introduction of this silent figure in such a scene is a masterpiece of dramatic invention" (Page, *Acts*, Introd., xxxi.); for the name see below on xiii. 9, and also on its genuineness, Zahn, *Einleitung in das N. T.*, ii., 49, as against Krenkel. Of Saul's earlier life we gather something from his own personal notices, see notes on xxii. 3, xxiii. 6, xxiv. 14, xxvi. 4, and cf. ix. 13. He was a Hebrew sprung from Hebrews, Phil. iii. 5; he was a Roman citizen, and not only so, but a Tarsian, a citizen of no mean city; cf. for the two citizenships, xxi. 39 (ix. 11) and xxii. 27, "Citizenship," Hastings' B.D.; Zahn, *u. s.*, p. 48; Ramsay, *St. Paul*, p. 30. Zahn, *u. s.*, pp. 35, 49, maintains that Saul's family had only recently settled in Tarsus (but see Ramsay, *u. s.*), and defends the tradition that his parents had come there from Gischala, their son being born to them in Tarsus. On Saul's family and means see notes on xxiii. 16 and xxiv. 26. But whatever his Roman and Tarsian citizenship may have contributed to his mental development, St. Paul's own words clearly lead us to attach the highest and most significant influence to the Jewish side of his nature and character. Paul's Pharisaism was the result not only of his training under Gamaliel, but also of the inheritance which he claimed from his father and his ancestors (xxiii. 6, Φαρισαίων not Φαρισαίου, cf. Gal. i. 14). His early years were passed away from Jerusalem, xxvi. 4 (the force of τε (R.V.) and the expression ἐν τῷ ἔθνει μου, Zahn, *u. s.*, p. 48), but his home-training could not have been neglected (cf. 2 Tim. i. 3), and when he went up to the Holy City at an early stage to study under Gamaliel (xxii. 3, ἀνατεθραμμένος, on its force see Sabatier *L'Apôtre Paul*, p. 30) he "lived a Pharisee," and nothing else than his well-known zeal is needed to account for his selection to his dreadful and solemn office at St. Stephen's martyrdom. As a Pharisee he had been "a separated one," and had borne the name with pride, not suspecting that a day was at hand when he would speak of himself as ἀφωρισμένος in a far higher and fuller sense, Rom. i. 1, Gal. i. 15 (Zahn, *u. s.*, p. 48); as a Pharisee he was "separated from all filthiness of heathenism" around (Nivdal), but he was to learn that the Christian life was that of the true "Chasid," and that in contrast to all Pharisaic legalism and externalism there was a cleansing ourselves from all filthiness of the flesh and spirit, a perfecting holiness in the fear of God—God Who chooseth before all temples the upright heart and pure (Edersheim, *Jewish Social Life*, p. 231). On the question whether St. Paul ever saw our Lord in the flesh, see Keim, *Geschichte Jesu*, i., 35, 36, and references, and for the views of more recent writers, *Witness of the Epistles* (Longmans), chaps. i. and ii.

Ver. 59. καὶ ἐλιθ. τὸν Σ. ἐπικ.: imperf., as in ver. 58, "quia res morte demum [60] perficitur," Blass. ἐπικ., present participle, denoting, it would seem, the continuous appeal of the martyr to his Lord. Zeller, Overbeck and Baur throw doubt upon the historical truth of the narrative on account of the manner in which the Sanhedrists' action is divided between an utter absence of formal proceedings and a punctilious observance of correct formalities; but on the other hand Wendt, note, p. 195 (1888), points out with much force that an excited and tumultuous crowd, even in the midst of a high-handed and illegal act, might observe some legal forms, and the description given by St. Luke, so far from proceeding from one who through ignorance was unable to distinguish between a legal execution and a massacre, impresses us rather with a sense of truthfulness from the very fact that no attempt is made to draw such a distinction of nicely balanced justice, less or more. The real difficulty lies in the relations which the scene presupposes between the Roman Government and the Sanhedrim. No doubt at this period the latter did not possess the power to inflict capital punishment (Schürer, *Jewish People*, div. ii., vol. i., p. 187, E.T.), as is evident from the trial of our Lord. But it may well be that at the time of Stephen's murder Roman authority was somewhat relaxed in Judæa. Pilate had just been suspended from his functions, or was on the point of being so, and he may well have been tired of refusing the madness and violence of the Jews, as Renan supposes, or at all events he may well have refrained, owing to his bad odour with them, from calling them to account for their illegal action in the case before us (see McGiffert, *Apostolic Age*, p. 91). It is of course possible that the stoning took place with the connivance of the Jewish authorities, as Weizsäcker allows, or that there was an interval longer than Acts supposes between the trial of Stephen and his actual execution, during which the sanction of the Romans was obtained. In the absence of exact dates it is difficult to see why the events before us should not have been transacted during the interregnum between the departure of Pontius Pilate, to answer before Tiberius for his misgovernment, and the arrival of Marcellus, the next Procurator. If this was so, we have an exact historical parallel in the illegal murder of James the Just, who was tried before the high priest, and stoned to death, since Ananias thought that he had a good opportunity for his violence when Festus was dead, and Albinus was still upon his road (Jos., *Ant.*, xx., 9, 1). But if this suggestion of an interregnum is not free from difficulties, we may further take into consideration the fact that the same Roman officer, Vitellius, prefect of Syria, who had caused Pilate to be sent to Rome in disgrace, was anxious at the same time to receive Jewish support, and determined to effect his object by every means in his power. Josephus, *Ant.*, xviii., 4, 2-5, tells us that Vitellius sent a friend of his own, Marcellus, to manage the affairs of Judæa, and that, not content with this, he went up to Jerusalem himself to conciliate the Jews by open regard for their religion, as well as by the remission of taxation. It is therefore not difficult to conceive that both the murder of Stephen and the persecution which followed were connived at by the Roman government; see, in addition to the above references, Rendall's *Acts*, Introd., p. 19 ff.; Farrar, *St. Paul*, i., p. 648 ff., and note, p. 649. But this solution of the difficulty places the date of Saul's conversion somewhat late—A.D. 37—and is entirely at variance with the earlier chronology adopted not only by Harnack (so too by McGiffert), but here by Ramsay, *St. Paul*, 376, 377, who places St. Stephen's martyrdom in A.D. 33 at

the latest. In the account of the death of Stephen, Wendt, following Weiss, Sorof, Clemen, Hilgenfeld, regards vii. 58b, viii. 1a, 3, as evidently additions of the redactor, although he declines to follow Weiss and Hilgenfeld in passing the same judgment on ver. 55 (and 56, according to H.), and on the last words of Stephen in ver. 59b. The second ἐλιθοβόλουν in 59b, which Hilgenfeld assigns to his redactor, and Wendt now refers to the action of the witnesses, as distinct from that of the whole crowd, is repeated with dramatic effect, heightened by the present participle, ἐπικ., "ruthless violence on the one side, answered by continuous appeals to heaven on the other"; see Rendall's note, *in loco*.—ἐπικ.: "calling upon *the Lord*," R.V. ("calling upon *God*," A.V.), the former seems undoubtedly to be rightly suggested by the words of the prayer which follow—on the force of the word see above, ii. 21.—Κύριε Ἰησοῦ, δέξαι τὸ πνεῦμά μου: a direct prayer to our Lord, *cf.* for its significance and reality, Zahn, "Die Anbetung Jesu" (*Skizzen aus dem Leben der alten Kirche*, pp. 9, 288), Liddon, *Our Lord's Divinity*, lect. vii.; *cf.* Luke xxiii. 46. (Weiss can only see an imitation of Luke, and an interpolation here, because the kneeling, and also another word follow before the surrender of the spirit; but see on the other hand the remarks of Wendt, note, p. 196.)

Ver. 60. θεὶς δὲ τὰ γόνατα: a phrase not used in classical writers, but Blass compares Ovid, *Fasti*, ii., 438; five times in St. Luke's writings, Luke xxii. 41, Acts ix. 40, xx. 36, xxi. 5; only once elsewhere in N.T., Mark xv. 19. The attitude of kneeling in prayer would no doubt commend itself to the early believers from the example of their Lord. Standing would seem to have been the more common attitude among the Jews, but *cf.* instances in the O.T. of kneeling in prayer, LXX, 1 Kings viii. 54, Ezra ix. 5, Dan. vi. 10, and also the expression used twice by St. Paul, κάμπτειν τὰ γόνατα, 1 Chron. xxix. 20, 1 Esdras viii. 73, Isa. xlv. 23, etc., Ephes. iii. 14, and Phil. ii. 10 (Rom. xi. 4, xiv. 11). See Friedrich, *Das Lucasevangelium*, p. 42.— φωνῇ μεγάλῃ, *cf.* Luke xxiii. 46. The last final effort of the strong love which showed itself also in the martyr's bended knees (see Wendt, *in loco*). Eusebius, *H. E.*, v., 2, tells us how the martyrs of Vienne and Lyons took up St. Stephen's words in their own prayer for their persecutors (*cf.* the famous instance of the last words of Sir Thomas More before

Σαύλου, 59. καὶ ἐλιθοβόλουν τὸν Στέφανον, ἐπικαλούμενον καὶ λέγοντα, Κύριε Ἰησοῦ, δέξαι τὸ πνεῦμά μου. 60. θεὶς δὲ τὰ γόνατα,

his judges, and Dante, *Purgatorio*, xv., 106 ff., on the dying Stephen): μὴ στήσῃς αὐτοῖς τὴν ἁμαρτίαν ταύτην: the negative expression best corresponds to the positive ἀφιέναι τὴν ἁμαρτίαν (Wendt), *cf*. 1 Macc. xiii. 38, 39, xv. 5, 8, where the contrast marked between ἱστάναι and ἀφιέναι seems to favour this explanation. Blass takes it as marking a contrast like that between ἱστάναι and ἀναιρεῖν, *cf*. Heb. x. 9. Weiss lays stress upon ταύτην, and regards the prayer as asking that their present sin might not be weighed out to them in an equivalent punishment, *cf*. Grotius on the Hebrew שָׁקַל, 1 Kings xx. 39, whilst De Wette (so Felten) takes it as simply "reckon it not," *i.e.*, "weigh it not," *cf*. Zech. xi. 12. Schöttgen sees a reference to the Rabbinical notion " si quis bonum aut malum opus facit, hoc sequitur eum, et stat juxta eum in mundo futuro," Rev. xiv. 13, and *cf*. a similar view quoted by Farrar, *St. Paul*, i., 167. Rendall regards it as a judicial term, as if Stephen appealed to Christ as *Judge* not to impute their sin to the murderers in condemnation (Rom. x. 3). The words of St. Stephen again recall the words of his Master, Luke xxiii. 34, words which (Eusebius, *H. E.*, *cf*. ii., 20) also formed the dying prayer of James, "the Lord's brother". In James as in Stephen we may see how the true Christian character, whilst expressing itself in righteous indignation against hypocrisy and wrong, never failed to exhibit as its counterpart the meekness and gentleness of Christ.—ἐκοιμήθη (*cf*. 1 Cor. xv. 18), a picture-word of rest and calmness which stands in dramatic contrast to the rage and violence of the scene. The word is used of death both in LXX and in classical Greek, *cf*., *e.g*., Isa. xiv. 8, 18, xliii. 17, 1 Kings xi. 43, 2 Macc. xii. 45, etc.; Homer, *Il*., xi., 241; Soph., *Elect*., 509. Blass well says of this word, " sed nullo loco æque mirandum," and describes the reference in Homer, κοιμήσατο χάλκεον ὕπνον, as " et simile et dissimile ": Christians sleep in death, but no " brazen sleep "; they sleep ἐν Χριστῷ; simple words which formed the epitaph on many a Christian grave—in Him, Who is Himself " the Resurrection and the Life ". Page notes the cadence of the word expressing rest and repose, *cf*. Farrar, *St. Paul*, i., 167, note, and ἀκωλύτως, xxviii. 31.

St. Stephen's Speech.— Many and varied explanations have been given of the drift and purpose of St. Stephen's address. But the various explanations need not be mutually exclusive, and St. Stephen, like a wise scribe instructed unto the kingdom, might well bring out of his treasury things new and old. It is often said, *e.g*., that the address is no reply to the charges alleged, that it would be more intelligible how the charges were framed from a perversion of the speech, than how the speech could be framed out of the charges; whilst, on the other hand, it is possible to see from the opening to the closing words an implicit repudiation of the charges of blasphemy against God and contempt of the law. The speech opens with a declaration of the divine majesty of Jehovah; it closes with a reference to the divine sanction of the law, and with the condemnation of those who had not kept it. This implicit repudiation by Stephen of the charges brought against him is also contained in St. Chrysostom's view of the purpose of the martyr, *viz*., that he designed to show that the covenant and promises were before the law, and sacrifice and the law before the temple. This view, which was adopted by Grotius and Calvin, is in some degree retained by Wendt (so also Felten), who sums up the chief aim of the speech as a demonstration that the presence of God is not confined to the holy place, the temple, but that long before the temple was built, and before the people had settled in the promised land, God had given to the fathers a share in the proofs of this revelation, and that too in strange countries (although there is no reason to suppose that Stephen went so far as to contend that Jew and Gentile were on a precisely equal footing). But Wendt is conscious that this view does not account for the whole of the speech, and that it does not explain the prominence given in it to the obstinacy of Israel against the revelation of God vouchsafed to Moses, with which the counter accusation against Stephen is so closely connected (see Spitta's severe criticism, *Apostelgeschichte*, pp. 111, 112, and Weizsäcker's evident failure to maintain the position that the climax of the whole address is to be found in the declaration about Solomon's temple, which he is obliged to explain as a later thought belonging to a later time, *Apostolic Age*, i., pp. 68-71, E.T.). Thus in his last edition, p. 151 (1899), he points out that in section vv. 35-43, as also in vv. 25 and 27, the obstinacy of the people against Moses, sent to be their deliverer, is evidently compared with their obstinacy in rejecting Jesus as the Messiah, and in vv. 51-53 the murder of Jesus is condemned as a fresh proof of the opposition of the people to God's revelation to them : here is a point of view which in Wendt's judgment evidently had a share in the composition of the address. Wendt urges his view against the older one of Meyer and to some extent at all events that of Baur, Zeller and Overbeck, that the central point of the speech is to be found in ver. 51, to which the whole preceding sketch of the history of the people led up : however great had been the benefits bestowed by God upon His people, on their part there had been from the beginning nothing in return but a corresponding thanklessness and resistance to this purpose. McGiffert, *Apostolic Age*, pp. 87, 88, also recognises that the theme of the address is to be found in vv. 51-53, but he also admits the double purpose of St. Stephen, *viz.*, not only to show (as Meyer and others) that at all stages of their history Israel had been stiffnecked and disobedient, but also (as Wendt) to draw a parallel between their conduct and the treatment of Jesus by those whom he is addressing.

This leads us to a consideration of the view of Spitta as to the main purpose of St. Stephen's speech. Whatever may be thought of its merits, it gives a unity to the speech which is wanting in many earlier and more recent expositions of it, as Hilgenfeld recognises, although he himself holds a different view, and one essentially similar to that of Baur. According to Spitta, in vv. 2-16 we have an introduction to the chief section of the address which begins with ver. 17, καθὼς δὲ ἤγγιζεν ὁ χρόνος τῆς ἐπαγ. Moses, ver. 20, was the person through whom God would save His people, and lead them to His true service in the promised land, vv. 7, 35, 38, 44. If we ask why Moses occupies this important place in the speech, the answer is found in ver. 37, which forms the central point of the description of Moses, and divides it into two parts (a verse in which Clemen and Hilgenfeld can only see an interpolation of a redactor, and in which Weiss finds something suspicious, see Zöckler's note, *in loco*). In the first part, 17-36, we are told how Moses by divine and miraculous guidance grows up

to be the deliverer of Israel. But when he would commence his work of deliverance his brethren will not understand his aim and reject him, 23-28. In the wilderness he receives a fresh commission from God to undertake the delivery of the people, 29-34. But *this* Moses (οὗτος) who was thus repulsed God had sent to be a ruler and deliverer—*this* man was he who led these people forth— and it was *this* Moses who said to the children : "A prophet" etc., v. 37. Why is this prophecy introduced except to support the inference that as Moses, a type of the Messiah, was thus repulsed, and afterwards raised to be a ruler and deliverer, so must, according to Moses' own words, the Messiah of Israel be first rejected by His people ? In the next division, vv. 38-50, the same parallel is again instituted between Moses and the Messiah. The former had delivered a law which consisted of "living oracles," but instead of receiving it, Israel had given themselves up to the worship of idols, 35-43 ; instead of establishing a worship well-pleasing to God, those who came after Moses, not content with the tabernacle, which was not confined to one place, and which represented the heavenly archetype, had built a temple which called forth the cutting words of the prophet, 47-50. In his explanation of these last verses there lies at least one weakness of Spitta's explanation, for he does not seem in his disapproval of the temple to allow that it had even a relative value, and that Solomon was well aware that God did not dwell only in temples made with hands. But Spitta's main point is to trace again a connection with the verse which forms his centre, ver. 37 (Deut. xviii. 15). As Moses in vain communicated a spiritual law and a corresponding worship to a people whose heart turned after idols and the service of a temple, so the Messiah must also experience that the carnal mind of the people would oppose His revelation of the divine will in relation to a rightful service. Thus the whole speech becomes a proof of the Messiahship of Jesus as against those who appealed to the authority of Moses, and saw in Jesus a twofold cause of offence : (1) that He was rejected by His people and crucified ; (2) that He had treated with impiety that which they held most sacred—the law and the temple.

In all this Spitta sees no direct answer to the false witnesses ; but the speech, he maintains, is much rather an answer to the two causes of offence which must

ἔκραξε φωνῇ μεγάλῃ,[1] Κύριε, μὴ στήσῃς αὐτοῖς τὴν ἁμαρτίαν ταύτην.
καὶ τοῦτο εἰπὼν ἐκοιμήθη.[2] Σαῦλος δὲ ἦν συνευδοκῶν τῇ ἀναιρέσει
αὐτοῦ.

[1] D, Vulg., Gig. (not Flor.) add λεγων, so Blass in β, and Hilg. ; prob. assim. to
more usual λεγων after κραζειν where the words are given.

[2] εκοιμηθη, Par., Wern., Vulg. add *in Domino*, but not Blass.

have been discussed in every synagogue,
and which the infant Church must have
been obliged to face from the first, especially as it took its stand upon the proof
that Jesus was the Christ. Stephen in
his disputations, vi. 9, must have often
faced opponents who thus sought to
invalidate the Messianic claims of Jesus ;
what more natural than that he should
now repeat before the whole assembly
the proofs which he had before given in
the synagogue, where no one could resist the spirit and the wisdom with which
he spake ? In this way Spitta maintains
that the charges in vv. 52, 53 occupy
their proper place ; the Jews had rejected
the prophets—Moses and his successors
—finally they rejected the Messiah,
whom the prophets had foretold (*Apostelgeschichte*, p. 105 ff.). Whatever strictures we may be inclined to pass upon
Spitta (see, *e.g.*, Wendt in new edition,
1899, pp. 150, 151), it is not unlikely
that he has at all events grasped what
others have failed to see, *viz.*, that in the
nature of the case, Stephen in his ἀπολογία, or counter-accusation—whichever
it was—could not have been unmindful
of the Prophet like unto Moses, whom
Moses had foretold : his dying prayer
revealed the Name, not uttered in the
speech, which was enshrined in his inmost heart ; Jesus was the Christ—He
came οὐ καταλῦσαι ἀλλὰ πληρῶσαι,
whether that fulfilment was made by a
spiritual temple or a spiritual law. In
thus keeping the thought of Jesus of
Nazareth prominent throughout the
speech, whilst not actually uttering His
Name, in thus comparing Moses and
Christ, Stephen *was answering* the
charges made against him. "This
Nazarene" (so it was said in the charge
made against Stephen) "would destroy
this place and change the customs," etc.
—the prophet Moses had given the
people living oracles, not a law which
should stifle the spirit in the letter ; the
prophet Isaiah had spoken of a presence
of God far transcending that which filled
any earthly temple ; and if these prophets
had pointed on to the Messiah, and if

the Nazarene were indeed the Christ thus
foretold, what wonder that He should
reveal a commandment unto life, and a
worship of the Father in spirit and in
truth ? Nor must it be forgotten that
if Stephen was interrupted before his
speech was concluded, he may well have
intended to drive home more closely
the manifest fulfilment in Christ of the
deliverance dimly foreshadowed in the
work of Moses and in the freedom
from Egyptian bondage. This was the
true parallel between Moses and the
Messiah on which the Rabbis were wont
to dwell. Thus the Messiah, in comparison with Moses, was the second, but
in comparison with all others the great,
deliverer ; as Moses led Israel out of
Egypt, so would the Messiah accomplish
the final deliverance, and restore Israel to
their own land (Weber, *Jüdische Theologie*, pp. 359, 364 (1897)). It is to be
observed that Spitta warmly supports the
historical character of the speech, which
he ascribes without interpolations to his
source A, although in vv. 55-60 he refers
some "insertions" to B. His criticism
as against the *tendency* critics, especially
Overbeck, is well worth consulting (pp.
110-123), and he quotes with approval the
judgment of Gfrörer—"I consider this
speech unreservedly as the oldest monument of Gospel history". So too
Clemen, pp. 97, 288, allows that the
speech is essentially derived, with the
exception of ver. 37, as also the whole
chapter with the exception of ver. 60, from
an old written source, H.H., *Historia
Hellenistarum ;* and amongst more recent
writers, McGiffert holds that whilst
many maintain that the author of the
Acts composed the speech and put it
into the mouth of Stephen, its contents
are against such a supposition, and that
Luke undoubtedly got the substance of
the discourse from an early source, and
reproduced it with approximate accuracy
(p. 89 and note). So Weiss refers the
speech to his Jewish-Christian source,
and refuses to admit that with its profound knowledge of the O.T. it could
have been composed by the author of

VIII. 1. Ἐγένετο δὲ ἐν ἐκείνῃ τῇ ἡμέρᾳ διωγμὸς μέγας ἐπὶ τὴν ἐκκλησίαν τὴν ἐν Ἱεροσολύμοις· πάντες τε διεσπάρησαν κατὰ τὰς

the book. The attempt of Feine (so also Holtzmann and Jüngst) to split up the speech into two distinct parts is based upon the idea that in one part an answer is made to the charge that Stephen had spoken against God, and that the other part contains an answer to the charge that he had spoken against the temple. The first part is contained in vii. 2-21, 29-34, 44-50, and the second part in vii. 22-28, 35-43, 51-53. The latter sections are taken from Feine's Jerusalem source; they are then added to those which belong to a new source, and finally combined by the canonical Luke. Hilgenfeld may well ask how it is possible to break up in this manner the narrative part of the speech relating to Moses, so as to regard vv. 22-28 as a section alien from what precedes and what follows! (see especially Hilgenfeld's criticism on Feine, *Zeitschrift für wissenschaft. Theol.*, p. 396 (1895) and Knabenbauer, p. 120); on the truthful record of the speech see Lightfoot's striking remarks "Acts," B.D.², i., p. 33. Whatever may be said as to the various difficulties which the speech contains, two things are apparent: (1) that these difficulties do not touch the main drift of the argument; (2) that the fact of their presence, where their removal was easy, bears witness to the accuracy of the report.

Chapter VIII.—Ver. 1. Σαῦλος δὲ κ.τ.λ., R.V. joins these words to the conclusion of the previous chapter, and thus brings them into a close and fitting connection with vii. 58. So too Wendt, Blass, Nösgen, Zöckler.—ἦν συνευδοκῶν: for this characteristic Lucan use of the imperfect of the substantive verb with a participle, see chap. i. 10. The formula here indicates the lasting and enduring nature of Saul's "consent". The verb συνευδοκέω is peculiar to St. Luke and St. Paul, and is used by the former in his Gospel as well as in Acts, *cf.* Luke xi. 48, Acts xxii. 20 (by St. Paul himself with reference to his share in the murder of St. Stephen), Rom. i. 32, 1 Cor. vii. 12, 13. The word is also found in 1 Macc. i. 57 (iv. 28), 2 Macc. xi. 24, 35, signifying entire approval; it is also twice used by St. Clement, *Cor.*, xxxv., 6; xliv., 3: "consent" does not express the force of the word—"was approving of his death" (Rendall).—ἀναιρέσει: used only here in N.T. (on St. Luke's favourite

word ἀναιρέω, see Friedrich, *Das Lucasevangelium*, p. 22); both verb and noun were frequent in medical language (Hobart, Zahn), see below on ix. 29, but the noun in LXX, Num. xi. 15, Judith xv. 4, 2 Macc. v. 13, and in classical Greek, *e.g.*, Xen., *Hell.*, vi., 3, 5.— ἐγένετο δὲ: another characteristic formula in St. Luke, Friedrich, *u. s.*, p. 13; here introduces a new section of the history.—ἐν ἐκείνῃ τῇ ἡμέρᾳ: R.V. "on that day" (A.V. "at that time"), *cf.* ii. 41; the persecution broke out at once, "on that very day" (so Wendt, Rendall, Hort, Hackett, Felten, Zöckler, Holtzmann), the signal for it being given by the tumultuous stoning of the first martyr (but see on the other hand Alford, *in loco*). Weiss draws attention to the emphatic position of ἐκείνῃ before τῇ ἡμέρᾳ.—ἐπὶ τὴν ἐκκλησίαν τὴν ἐν Ἱ.: hitherto as, *e.g.*, v. 11, the Church has been thought of as one, because limited in fact to the one city Jerusalem, but here we have a hint that soon there would be new Ecclesiæ in the one Ecclesia, as it spread throughout the Holy Land (Hort, *Ecclesia*, pp. 53-56, 227, and Ramsay, *St. Paul*, etc., pp. 41, 127, 377).—πάντες τε: "ridiculum est hoc mathematica ratione accipere" (Blass)—it is evident from ver. 3 that there were some left for Saul to persecute. In ix. 26 we have mention of a company of disciples in Jerusalem, but there is no reason to suppose (Schneckenburger, Zeller, Overbeck) that Luke has made a mistake in the passage before us, for there is nothing in the text against the supposition that some at least of those who had fled returned again later. —διεσπάρησαν: only in St. Luke in N.T., here and in ver. 4, and in xi. 19. This use of the word is quite classical, and frequent in LXX, *e.g.*, Gen. ix. 19, Lev. xxvi. 33, 1 Macc. xi. 47. Feine remarks that even Holtzmann allows that the spread of Christianity throughout Judæa and Samaria may be regarded as historical. — χώρας: here rendered "regions": Blass takes the word as almost = κώμας, and see also Plummer on Luke xxi. 21, ἐν ταῖς χώραις "in the country," R.V. The word is characteristic of St. Luke, being used in his Gospel nine times, and in Acts eight; it is used thrice by St. Matthew and by St. John, four times by St. Mark, but elsewhere in N.T. only once, James v. 4.

χώρας τῆς Ἰουδαίας καὶ Σαμαρείας, πλὴν τῶν ἀποστόλων.[1] 2.
συνεκόμισαν δὲ τὸν Στέφανον ἄνδρες εὐλαβεῖς, καὶ ἐποιήσαντο

[1] **Σαμαρειας** ABCHP, so W.H. alt. App., p. 160, Blass, Weiss, Hilg.; **Σαμαριας**
אDE, so Tisch., W.H., see Winer-Schmiedel, p. 45. After **διωγμος** D, Flor., Sah.
και θλιψις, assim. to Matt. xiii. 21, 2 Thess. i. 4, so Hilg. The same addition
occurs in Western text in xiii. 50. After **αποστολων** D[1], Flor., Gig., Prov., Sah., Aug.
add **οι εμειναν εν Ιερ.**, retained by Blass in β, so Belser, *Beiträge*, p. 49, and Hilg.

It is found frequently in LXX and in
1, 2, 3 Macc.—τῆς Ἰουδαίας καὶ Σαμαρείας: thus the historian makes another
step in the fulfilment of the Lord's command, i. 8, and see also Ramsay, *St. Paul*,
etc., p. 41. St. Chrysostom remarks ὅτι
οἰκονομίας ὁ διωγμὸς ἦν, since the persecution became the means of spreading
the Gospel, and thus early the blood of
the martyrs became the seed of the
Church.—πλὴν τῶν ἀποστόλων—πλήν:
characteristic of St. Luke, sometimes as
an adverb, sometimes as a preposition
with genitive as here and in xv. 28,
xxvii. 22; elsewhere it is only found once
as a preposition with genitive, in Mark
xii. 32, although very frequent in LXX.
The word occurs at least thirteen times
in the Gospel, four times in Acts, in St.
Matthew five times, in St. Mark once,
and in John viii. 10; see Friedrich, *Das
Lucasevangelium*, pp. 16, 91. This mention of the Apostles seems unlikely to
Schneckenburger, Schleiermacher, and
others, but, as Wendt points out, it is
quite consistent with the greater steadfastness of men who felt themselves to
be πρωταγωνισταί, as Œcumenius calls
them, in that which concerned their
Lord. Their position too may well have
been more secure than that of the Hellenists, who were identified with Stephen,
as they were held in favour by the people,
v. 13, and as regular attendants at the
temple services would not have been
exposed to the same charges as those
directed against the proto-martyr. There
was, too, a tradition (very old and well
attested according to Harnack, *Chronologie*, i., 243) to the effect that the
Apostles were commanded by Christ not
to depart from Jerusalem for twelve
years, so that none should say that he
had not heard the message, Euseb.,
H. E., v., 18, 14; nor is there anything
inconsistent with this tradition in the
visit of St. Peter and St. John to Samaria,
since this and other journeys are simply
missionary excursions, from which the
Apostles always returned to Jerusalem
(Harnack). The passage in Clem. Alex.,
Strom., vi., 5, 43, limited the Apostles'

preaching for the time specified not to
Jerusalem, but to Israel.—Σαμαρείας: our
Lord had recognised the barrier between
the Samaritan and the Jew, Matt. x. 5;
but now in obedience to His command
(i. 8) both Samaritan and Jew were admitted to the Church, for although the
Apostles had not originated this preaching they very plainly endorsed it, ver.
14 ff. (*cf.* Hort, *Judaistic Christianity*,
p. 54). Possibly the very fact that Philip
and others were flying from the persecution of the Jewish hierarchy would have
secured their welcome in the Samaritan
towns.
    Ver. 2. Spitta connects ver. 2 with
xi. 19-21, and all the intermediate section, viii. 5-xi. 19; forms part of his source
B (so also Sorof, Clemen, who joins his
H.H., viii. 1 to xi. 19; but on the other
hand see Hilgenfeld, *Zeitschrift für
wissenschaft. Theol.*, p. 501 (1895), and
Jüngst, *Apostelgeschichte*, p. 79). According to Spitta the whole narrative of
Philip's ministry in viii. ought not to be
connected so closely with the death of
Stephen, but should fall after ix. 31.
The only reason for its earlier insertion
is the desire to connect the second deacon
with the first (but Hilgenfeld, *u. s.*, pp.
413, 414 (1895), as against both Spitta
and Clemen, regards the account of
Philip and that of Stephen as inseparable). Spitta strongly maintains that
Philip the Apostle, and not the deacon,
is meant; and if this be so, he would
no doubt help us to answer the objection
that in viii. 14-17, and indeed in the
whole section 9-24 we have an addition
of the sub-Apostolic age inserted to show
that the Apostles alone could bestow
the Holy Spirit. But it cannot be said
that Spitta's attempt at the identification
of Philip in viii. with the Apostle is in any
way convincing, see, *e.g.*, Zöckler, *Apostelgeschichte*, p. 212; Hilgenfeld, *u. s.*, p. 416
(note), and Jüngst, *u. s.*, p. 81. Feine's
objection to viii. 14-17 leads him, whilst
he admits that the meeting with Simon
Magus is historical, to regard the conversion of the sorcerer as doubtful, because the whole passage presupposes

κοπετὸν μέγαν ἐπ' αὐτῷ. 3. Σαῦλος δὲ ἐλυμαίνετο τὴν ἐκκλησίαν,
κατὰ τοὺς οἴκους εἰσπορευόμενος, σύρων τε ἄνδρας καὶ γυναῖκας

(vv. 18-24) that the laying on of the
Apostles' hands bestowed the Spirit;
so Clemen refers the whole representation
in its present form of the communication
of the Spirit, not through Baptism, but
through the laying on of the Apostles'
hands, to his Redactor Antijudaicus (cf.
xix. 6), and to the same hand he attributes the πλὴν τῶν ἀποστόλων, ver. 1,
and cf. ver. 25, introduced for the purpose of showing that the Apostles Peter
and John sanctioned the Samaritan
mission from the central home of the
Christian Church.—συνεκόμισαν: in its
primary sense the verb means to carry
or bring together, of harvest; to gather
in, to house it; so also in LXX, Job v.
26; in a secondary sense, to help in
burying; so Soph., *Ajax*, 1048; Plut.,
Sull., 38. The meaning is not "carried
to his burial," as in A.V., but rather as
R.V., "buried," for, although the Greek is
properly "joined in carrying," the word
includes the whole ceremony of burial—
it is used only here in the N.T., and in
LXX only in *l. c.*—εὐλαβεῖς: only found
in St. Luke in N.T., and used by him
four times, once in Luke ii. 25, and in
Acts ii. 5, xxii. 12 (εὐσεβής, T.R.). The
primary thought underlying the word is
that of one who handles carefully and
cautiously, and so it bears the meaning of
cautious, circumspect. Although εὐλάβεια and εὐλαβεῖσθαι are both used in
the sense of caution and reverence towards the gods in classical Greek, the
adjective is never expressly so used.
But Plato connects it closely with δίκαιος
(cf. Luke ii. 25), *Polit.* 311 A and 311 B
(so εὐσεβῶς and εὐλαβῶς are used together by Demosthenes). In the LXX
all three words are found to express reverent fear of, or piety towards, God;
εὐλαβεῖσθαι, frequently, εὐλάβεια in
Prov. xxviii. 14, where σκληρὸς τὴν
καρδίαν in the second part of the verse
seems to point to the religious character
of the εὐλαβ., whilst εὐλαβής is found in
Micah vii. 2 as a rendering of חָסִיד (cf.
Psalms of Solomon, p. 36, Ryle and
James' edition); cf. also Ecclus. xi.
17 (but see for both passages, Hatch
and Redpath); in Lev. xv. 31 we find
the word εὐλαβεῖς ποιήσετε τοὺς υἱοὺς
'Ι. ἀπὸ τῶν ἀκαθαρσιῶν αὐτῶν, נָזַר,
hi. The adverb εὐλαβῶς is found once,
2 Macc. vi. 11. St. Luke uses the word

chiefly at all events of O.T. piety. In
Luke ii. 45 it is used of Simeon, in Acts
ii. 5 of the Jews who came up to worship
at the feasts in Jerusalem, and in xxii.
12, although Ananias was a Christian,
yet the qualifying words εὐλ. κατὰ
τὸν νόμον point again to a devout observance of the Jewish law. Trench, *N. T.
Synonyms*, i., pp. 38, 198 ff.; Westcott,
Hebrews, on v. 7; Grimm-Thayer, *sub
v.*, and *sub v.* δειλία.—ἄνδρες εὐλ.:
much discussion has arisen as to whether
they were Jews or Christians. They
may have been Christians who like
the Apostles themselves were still Jews,
attending the temple services and
hours of prayer, some of whom were
doubtless left in the city. But these
would have been described more probably as ἀδελφοί or μαθηταί (so Felten,
Page, Hackett). Or they may have been
devout Jews like Nicodemus, or Joseph
of Arimathea, who would show their
respect for Stephen, as Nicodemus and
Joseph for Jesus (so Holtzmann, Zöckler).
Wetstein (so too Renan and Blass)
explains of Gentile proselytes, men like
Cornelius, who rendered the last offices
to Stephen out of natural respect for the
dead, and who stood outside the jurisdiction of the Sanhedrim, so that the
funeral rites need not have been performed in secret. But St. Luke as a
rule uses other words to denote Gentile
proselytes, and the Sanhedrim would
probably not have interfered with the
burial, not only on account of the known
Jewish care for the dead, but also because
devout Jews would not have been obnoxious in their eyes to the charges brought
against Stephen, vi. 14 (so Nösgen).
The word might therefore include both
devout Jews and Jewish Christians who
joined together in burying Stephen.—
κοπετὸν μέγαν, from κόπτω, κόπτομαι,
cf. *planctus* from *plango*, to beat the
breast or head in lamentation. Not used
elsewhere in N.T., but frequent in LXX;
cf., *e.g.*, Gen. l. 10, 1 Macc. ii. 70, iv.
39, ix. 20, xiii. 26, for the same allocation
as here, and for ποιῆσαι κοπετόν, Jer.
vi. 26, Mic. i. 8, and cf. also Zech. xii.
10. In classical Greek κομμός is found,
but see Plut., *Fab.*, 17, and Kennedy,
Sources of N. T. Greek, p. 74, for reference to the comic poet Eupolis (cf. also
Blass), and Grimm-Thayer, *sub v.* For
the Jewish customs of mourning cf.
Matt. ix. 23, Hamburger, *Real-Encyclo-*

παρεδίδου εἰς φυλακήν. 4. οἱ μὲν οὖν διασπαρέντες διῆλθον, εὐαγγελιζόμενοι τὸν λόγον.[1]

[1] διῆλθον; for this word Gig., Par., Wern. seem to have read επορευοντο, *ibant*. After λογον Par., Wern. and other Latin authorities add "circa (per) civitates et castella Judææ," κατα τας πολεις και κωμας της Ι., Blass in β, evidently for the sake of clearness, as also in previous επορ., *cf.* Wendt. After λογον E, Vulg., Par[2], Wern. add του θεου, again addition apparently for clearness (if not omission). Blass rejects in β; where ὁ λόγος is used in Acts in this sense we almost always have this addition or του Κυριου.

pädie des *Judentums*, i., 7, 996, "Trauer"; Edersheim, *Jesus the Messiah*, i., p. 616, and *Sketches of Jewish Social Life*, p. 172 ff. If the mourners included Jews as well as Jewish Christians, it may well have been that the lamentation was not only a token of sorrow and respect, but also in the nature of a protest on the part of the more moderate section of the Pharisees (see also Trench's remarks, *u. s.*, p. 198). According to the tradition accepted by St. Augustine, it is said that both Gamaliel and Nicodemus took part in the burial of Stephen, and were afterwards laid in the same grave (Felten, *Apostelgeschichte*, p. 167, and Plumptre *in loco*).

Ver. 3. ἐλυμαίνετο: deponent verb, used in classical Greek of personal outrage (λύμη), of scourging and torturing, of outraging the dead, of the ruin and devastation caused by an army (Wetstein). In the LXX it is found several times, *cf.* especially Ps. lxxix. (lxxx.) 13, of a wild boar ravaging a vineyard, and *cf.* also Ecclus. xxviii. 23. As the word is used only by St. Luke it is *possible* that it may have been suggested by its frequent employment in medical language, where it is employed not only of injury by wrong treatment, but also of the ravages of disease, Hobart, *Medical Language*, pp. 211, 212. R.V. renders "laid waste," A.V. (so Tyndale) "made havoc of," but the revisers have rendered πορθέω by the latter, *cf.* Acts ix. 21, Gal. i. 3. St. Paul's description of himself as ὑβριστής, 1 Tim. i. 13, may well refer to the infliction of personal insults and injuries, as expressed here by λυμαίνομαι (*cf.* Paley, *Horæ Paulinæ*, xi., 5).—τὴν ἐκκλησίαν, *i.e.*, the Church just mentioned at Jerusalem—Saul's further persecution, even to Damascus, probably came later (Hort, *Ecclesia*, p. 53).—κατὰ τοὺς οἴκους εἰσπορ.: the expression may denote "entering into every house," R. and A.V., or perhaps, more specifically, the houses known as places of Christian assembly, the ἐκκλησίαι κατ᾽ οἶκον, see on ii. 46.

In any case the words, as also those which follow, show the thoroughness and relentlessness of Saul's persecuting zeal. —σύρων: haling, *i.e.*, hauling, dragging (*schlappend*), *cf.* James ii. 6. The word is used by St. Luke three times in Acts (only twice elsewhere in N.T.), and he alone uses κατασύρω, Luke xii. 58, in the same sense as the single verb (where St. Matthew has παραδῷ). For its employment in the Comic Poets see Kennedy, *Sources of N. T. Greek*, p. 76, and also Arrian, *Epict.*, i. 29, 22, and other instances in Wetstein; *cf.* LXX, 2 Sam. xvii. 13, 4 Macc. vi. 1, ἔσυραν ἐπὶ τὰ βασανιστήρια τὸν Ἐλ.—γυναῖκας: repeated also in ix. 2, and xxii. 4, as indicating the relentless nature of the persecution. Some of the devout and ministering women may well have been included, Luke viii. 2, 3, Acts i. 14.

Ver. 4. οἱ μὲν οὖν: marking a general statement, δὲ in following verse, introducing a particular instance (so Rendall, Appendix on μὲν οὖν, Acts, p. 162, and see also p. 64).—διῆλθον: the word is constantly used of missionary journeys in *Acts*, *cf.* v. 40, xi. 19, ix. 32 (Luke ix. 6), *cf.* xiii. 6, note.—εὐαγγελιζόμενοι: it is a suggestive fact that this word is only used once in the other Gospels (Matt. xi. 5 by our Lord), but no less than ten times in St. Luke's Gospel, fifteen in Acts, and chiefly elsewhere by St. Paul; truly "a missionary word," see ver. 12. Simcox, *Language of the N. T.*, p. 79, speaks of its introduction into the N.T. with "such a novel force as to be felt like a new word". It is used several times in LXX, and is also found in *Psalms of Solomon*, xi., 2 (*cf.* Isa. xl. 9, lii. 7, and Nah. i. 15). On its construction see Simcox, *u. s.*, p. 79, and Vogel, p. 24.

Ver. 5. Φίλιππος δὲ: the Evangelist, *cf.* xxi. 8, and note on vi. 5.—εἰς πόλιν: if we insert the article (see above on critical notes), the expression means "the city of Samaria," *i.e.*, the capital of the district (so Weiss, Wendt,

5. ΦΙΛΙΠΠΟΣ δὲ κατελθὼν εἰς πόλιν τῆς Σαμαρείας,[1] ἐκήρυσσεν αὐτοῖς τὸν Χριστόν. 6. προσεῖχόν τε[2] οἱ ὄχλοι τοῖς λεγομένοις ὑπὸ τοῦ Φιλίππου ὁμοθυμαδόν, ἐν τῷ ἀκούειν αὐτοὺς καὶ βλέπειν τὰ σημεῖα ἃ ἐποίει. 7.[3] πολλῶν γὰρ τῶν ἐχόντων πνεύματα ἀκάθαρτα βοῶντα μεγάλῃ φωνῇ ἐξήρχετο· πολλοὶ δὲ παραλελυμένοι καὶ χωλοὶ

[1] εἰς Σ. τὴν πολιν Par. (" Samaria in civitate," again for clearness (Wendt)), so Blass in β; Σαμαρειας ABHP, so Blass; -ιας ℵ³DE, so Tisch., W.H., see on ver. 1. (See on the reading Winer-Schmiedel, p. 266.)

[2] προσειχον τε EHP, Chrys.; but δε ℵABCD² 61, e, Vulg., Sah., Boh., Syr. Harcl., so Tisch., W.H., R.V., Blass, Wendt, Weiss. In D this verse begins ως δε ηκουον παν(τες) οι οχλοι προσειχον τοις λεγ. παν (omnis turba, d), but Blass rejects; Hilg. retains. Weiss, Codex D, p. 68, expresses surprise at this rejection by Blass, as the reading is not more superfluous than countless additions in D; the words already lay in the following εν τω ακουειν αυτους. Chase refers to Syriac with considerable probability.

[3] πολλων HP, Boh., Arm., Chrys. (D¹ παρα πολλοις, D² απο πολλοι, a multis, d); πολλοι ℵABCD²E 18, 36, 40, 61, Vulg., Sah. Syr., Aeth., so Tisch., W.H., R.V., Blass, Wendt, Weiss, Hilg. Blass inserts ἃ after ακαθαρτα, so Hilg., " bene " Blass (see below and Wendt, note, p. 172, eighth edition).

Zöckler, see Blass, in loco), or Sebaste, so called by Herod the Great in honour of Augustus, Σεβαστή (Jos., Ant., xv., 7, 3; 8, 5; Strabo, xvi., p. 860), see Schürer, Jewish People, div. ii., vol. 1, p. 123 ff., E.T., and O. Holtzmann, Neutest. Zeitgeschichte, p. 93.—ἐκήρυσσεν: the revisers distinguish between this verb and εὐαγγελ. in ver. 4, the latter being rendered "preaching," or more fully, preaching the glad tidings, and the former "proclaimed" (see also Page's note on the word, p. 131), but it is doubtful if we can retain this full force of the word always, e.g., Luke iv. 44, where R.V. translates κηρύσσων, "preaching".—αὐτοῖς, i.e., the people in the city mentioned, see Blass, Grammatik, p. 162, and cf. xvi. 10, xx. 2.
Ver. 6. προσεῖχον . . . τοῖς λεγ. cf. xvi. 14, 1 Tim. i. 4, Tit. i. 14, 2 Pet. i. 9, see note on v. 35, used in classical Greek sometimes with νοῦν, and sometimes without as here; frequent in LXX, cf. with this passage, Wisdom viii. 12, 1 Macc. vii. 12.—ὁμοθυμαδόν, see above on i. 14.
Ver. 7. πολλῶν γὰρ κ.τ.λ.: if we accept reading in R.V. (see critical notes above), we must suppose that St. Luke passes in thought from the possessed to the unclean spirits by which they were possessed, and so introduces the verb ἐξήρχοντο (as if the unclean spirits were themselves the subject), whereas we should have expected that ἐθεραπεύθησαν would have followed after the first πολλοί, as after the second, in the second

clause of the verse. Blass conjectures that ἃ should be read before βοῶντα, which thus enables him, while retaining ἐξήρχοντο, to make πολλοί in each clause of the verse the subject of ἐθεραπ. One of the most striking phenomena in the demonised was that they lost at least temporarily their own self-consciousness, and became identified with the demon or demons, and this may account for St. Luke's way of writing, as if he also identified the two in thought, Edersheim, Jesus the Messiah, i., 479, 647, ff. As a physician St. Luke must have often come into contact with those who had unclean spirits, and he would naturally have studied closely the nature of their disease. It is also to be noted that πολλοί with the genitive, τῶν ἐχόντων (not πολλοὶ ἔχοντες), shows that not all the possessed were healed, and if so, it is an indication of the truthfulness of the narrative. Moreover, St. Luke not only shows himself acquainted with the characteristics of demoniacal possession, cf. his description in Luke viii. 27, ix. 38, 39, but he constantly, as in the passage before us, distinguishes it from disease itself, and that more frequently than the other Evangelists. Hobart draws special attention to Luke vi. 17, viii. 4, xiii. 32, which have no parallels in the other Gospels, and Acts xix. 12. To which we may add Luke iv. 40, Acts v. 16 (Wendt); see further on xix. 12.—βοῶντα, cf. Mark i. 26, Luke iv. 33.—παραλελυμένοι: St. Luke alone of the Evangelists uses the participle of παρα-

ἐθεραπεύθησαν.[1] 8. καὶ ἐγένετο χαρὰ μεγάλη [2] ἐν τῇ πόλει ἐκείνῃ.
9. Ἀνὴρ δέ τις ὀνόματι Σίμων προϋπῆρχεν [3] ἐν τῇ πόλει μαγεύων καὶ

[1] εθεραπευθησαν; D reads εθεραπευοντο, so Hilg., perhaps assim. to εξηρχοντο, Blass in β rejects.

[2] χαρα μεγαλη DEHP, Vulgclem., Syr. Harcl., Arm., Chrys.; πολλη χαρα ℵABC 47, 61, so Tisch., W.H., R.V., Weiss, Wendt; χαρα τε μεγαλη εγενετο, so Gig., Par., Syr. Pesh., Blass in β, and Hilg. χαρα often joined with μεγ. elsewhere in N.T.; cf. Luke ii. 10, xxiv. 52, Acts xv. 3.

[3] προϋπῆρχεν . . . εξιστων, D reads προϋπαρχων . . . εξιστανεν; Par., Vulg., Iren. also read προυπαρχων, so Hilg. Σαμαρειας, see on ver. 1. μεγαν, "delevi," so Blass on the authority of some codices of Iren. see comment. below.

λύειν, instead of παραλυτικός, the more popular word; and here again his usage is exactly what we should expect from a medical man acquainted with technical terms (Hobart, Zahn, Salmon), cf. ix. 33 and Luke v. 18, 24 (παραλυτικῷ, W.H. margin). Dr. Plummer, St. Luke, Introd., lxv., points out that Aristotle, a physician's son, has also this use of παραλελυμένος (Eth. Nic., i., 13, 15), but he adds that its use in St. Luke may have come from the LXX, as in Heb. xii. 12, where we have the word in a quotation from Isa. xxxv. 3 (cf. also Ecclesiast. xxv. 23). It may be added that the participle is also found in 3 Macc. ii. 22, καὶ τοῖς μέλεσι παραλελυμένον, and cf. 1 Macc. ix. 15, where it is said of Alcimus, καὶ παρελύθη. But the most remarkable feature in St. Luke's employment of the word is surely this, that in parallel passages in which St. Matthew and St. Mark have παραλυτικός he has παραλελυμένος, cf. Luke v. 18, Matt. ix. 2, Mark ii. 3; in Luke v. 24 this same distinction is also found in the Revisers' text (but see W.H. above), when this verse is compared with Matt. ix. 6 and Mark ii. 10.

Ver. 8. This detail, and indeed the whole narrative, may have been derived by St. Luke from the information of St. Philip himself, cf. xxi. 8, xxiv. 27, or from St. Paul as he travelled through Samaria, xv. 3.

Ver. 9. Σίμων: very few of the most advanced critics now dismiss Simon as an unhistorical character, or deny that the account before us contains at least some historical data; see McGiffert's note, Apostolic Age, p. 100. Hilgenfeld and Lipsius may be reckoned amongst those who once refused to admit that Simon Magus was an historical personage, but who afterwards retracted their opinion. But it still remains almost unaccountable that so many critics should have more or less endorsed, or developed, the theory first advocated by Baur that the Simon Magus of the Clementine Homilies is none other than the Apostle Paul. It is sufficient to refer for an exposition of the absurdity of this identification to Dr. Salmon "Clementine Literature" (Dict. of Christ. Biog., iii., pp. 575, 576; see also Ritschl's note, Die Entstehung der altkatholischen Kirche, p. 228 (second edition)). This ingenuity outdid itself in asking us to see in Simon's request to buy the power of conferring the Holy Ghost a travesty of the rejection of Paul's apostolic claims by the older Apostles, in spite of the gift of money which he had collected for the poor Saints in Jerusalem (Overbeck). No wonder that Spitta should describe such an explanation as "a perfect absurdity" (Apostelgeschichte, p. 149). Before we can believe that the author of the Acts would make any use of the pseudo-Clementine literature in his account of Simon, we must account for the extraordinary fact that an author who so prominently represents his hero as triumphing over the powers of magic, xiii. 6-12, xix. 11-19, should have recourse to a tradition in which this same hero is identified with a magician (see Spitta, u. s., p. 151; Salmon, "The Simon of Modern Criticism," Dict. of Christian Biog., iv., p. 687; Zöckler, Apostelgeschichte, p. 212, and Wendt's note, p. 201). In Acts xxi. 8 we read that St. Luke spent several days in the house of Philip the Evangelist, and if we bear in mind that this same Philip is so prominent in chap. viii., there is nothing impossible in the belief that St. Luke should have received his narrative from St. Philip's lips, and included it in his history as an early and remarkable instance of the triumph of the Gospel—we need not search for any more occult reason on the part of the historian (see Salmon, u. s., p. 688). Simon then is an historical personage, and it is not too much to say that to all the stories which have gathered round his name the narrative of

ἐξιστῶν τὸ ἔθνος τῆς Σαμαρείας, λέγων εἶναί τινα ἑαυτὸν μέγαν·
10. ᾧ προσεῖχον πάντες [1] ἀπὸ μικροῦ ἕως μεγάλου, λέγοντες, Οὗτός

[1] πάντες ℵABCDE 61, Vulg., many other verss., Chrys., so all edd.; om. HP, Aethᵖᵖ., Iren.; Blass brackets: "nec opus".

Acts always stands in a relation of priority—the two facts mentioned in Acts, that Simon was a magician, and that he came into personal antagonism with St. Peter, always recur elsewhere—but Acts tells us nothing of the details of Simon's heretical preaching, and it draws the veil entirely over his subsequent history. But "the hero of the romance of heresy" comes into prominence under the name of Simon in Justin Martyr, *Apol.*, i., 26, Irenæus, i., 23 (who speaks of Simon the Samaritan, from whom all heresies had their being), and in the Clementine literature. But there is good reason for thinking that St. Irenæus, whilst he gives us a fuller account, is still giving us an account dependent on Justin, and there is every reason to believe that the Clementine writers also followed the same authority; see further, Salmon, "Simon Magus," *u. s.*, iv., p. 681 ff., and for a summary of the legends which gathered round the name of the Samaritan magician Plumptre's note, *in loco*, may be consulted. To the vexed question as to the identification of the Simon of Justin with the Simon of the Acts Dr. Salmon returns a decided negative answer, *u. s.*, p. 683, and certainly the Simon described by Justin seems to note rather the inheritor and teacher of a Gnostic system already developed than to have been in his own person the father of Gnosticism. Simon, however, was no uncommon name, *e.g.*, Josephus, *Ant.*, xx., 7, 2, speaks of a Simon of Cyprus, whom there is no valid reason to identify with the Simon of the Acts (although famous critical authorities may be quoted in favour of such an identification). On the mistake made by Justin with reference to the statue on the Tiberine island with the words *Semoni Sanco Deo Fidio* inscribed (*cf.* the account of the marble fragment, apparently the base of a statue, dug up in 1574, marked with a similar inscription, in Lanciani's *Pagan and Christian Rome*) in referring it to Simon Magus, *Apol.*, i., 26, 56, Tertullian, *Apol.*, c. xiii., and Irenæus, i., 23, whilst in reality it referred to a Sabine god, Semo Sancus, the Sabine Hercules, see further, Salmon, *u. s.*, p. 682, Rendall,

Acts, p. 220. (Van Manen, followed by Feine, claims to discover two representations of Simon in Acts—one as an ordinary magician, viii. 9, 11, the other as a supposed incarnation of the deity, ver. 10—so too Jüngst, who refers the words from μαγεύων to Σαμαρίας to his Redactor; but on the other hand Hilgenfeld and Spitta see no contradiction, and regard the narrative as a complete whole.) —μαγεύων: only here in N.T., not found in LXX (but *cf.* μάγος in Dan. i. 20, ii. 2), though used in classical Greek. The word μάγος was used frequently by Herodotus of the priests and wise men in Persia who interpreted dreams, and hence the word came to denote any enchanter or wizard, and in a bad sense, a juggler, a quack like γόης (see instances in Wetstein). Here (*cf.* xiii. 6) it is used of the evil exercise of magic and sorcery by Simon, who practised the charms and incantations so extensively employed at the time in the East by quacks claiming supernatural powers (Baur, *Paulus*, i., p. 107; Neander, *Geschichte der Pflanzung*, *cf.* i., 84, 85 (fifth edit.); Wendt, *Apostelgeschichte*, p. 202; Blass, *in loco*; Deissmann, *Bibelstudien*, p. 19, and see below on xiii. 6.—ἐξιστῶν, from ἐξιστάω (ἐξίστημι); so ἐξιστάνων, W. H. from ἐξιστάνω (hellenistic), see Blass, *Grammatik*, pp. 48, 49, transitive in present, future, first aorist active, *cf.* Luke xxiv. 22 —so ἐξεστακέναι, ver. 11, perfect active, hellenistic form, also transitive; see Blass, *u. s.* (also Winer-Schmiedel, p. 118, and Grimm-Thayer, *sub v.*) (in 3 Macc. i. 25 ἐξιστάνειν also occurs).— ἵσταμαι, intransitive, ver. 13, Blass, *u. s.*, p. 49—the revisers have consistently rendered the verb by the same English word in the three verses 9, 11, 13, thus giving point and force to the narrative, see on ver. 13.—λέγων κ.τ.λ., *cf.* v. 36. Blass, *Grammatik*, p. 174, regards μέγαν as an interpolation, and it is not found in the similar phrase in v. 36 (so too Winer-Schmiedel, p. 243), *cf.* Gal. ii. 6, and vi. 3, and the use of the Latin *aliquis*, Cicero, *Att.*, iii., 15, so too vii. 3, etc. It may be that Simon set himself up for a Messiah (see Ritschl's note, p. 228, *Die Entstehung der altkatholischen Kirche*, second edition), or a Prophet, Jos.,

ἐστιν ἡ δύναμις τοῦ Θεοῦ ἡ μεγάλη.[1]　11. προσεῖχον δὲ αὐτῷ, διὰ
τὸ ἱκανῷ χρόνῳ ταῖς μαγείαις[2] ἐξεστακέναι αὐτούς.　12. Ὅτε δὲ

[1] ἡ μεγαλη HLP, Sah., Syr. Pesh., Aethpp., Chrys.; ἡ καλουμενη μεγαλη ℵABCDE,
Vulg., Boh., Syr. Harcl., Arm., Aethr., Irint., Orig., so Tisch., W.H., R.V., Blass,
Weiss, Hilg.

[2] μαγειαις BLP, so Blass, Weiss, Hilg.; μαγιαις ℵACDEH, so Tisch., W.H.
(see Winer-Schmiedel, p. 44).

Ant., xviii., 4, 1, but ver. 14 points to a
definite title, and it is likely enough that
the people would repeat what Simon had
told them of himself. His later followers
went further and made him say, "Ego
sum sermo Dei, ego sum speciosus, ego
paraclitus, ego omnipotens, ego omnia
Dei" Jerome, Commentar. in Matt., c.
xx., 24 (Neander, Geschichte der Pflanzung, cf. i., 85, note).—ἑαυτὸν: contrast
Philip's attitude; he preached Christ, not
himself (cf. Rev. ii. 20).
Ver. 10. ἡ δύναμις τοῦ Θεοῦ ἡ μεγάλη:
in R.V. the power of God which is called
(καλουμένη) Great, see above, critical
notes. T.R. may have omitted the word
because it appeared unsuitable to the
context; but it could not have been used
in a depreciatory sense by the Samaritans,
as if to intimate that the person claimed
was the so-called "Great," since they
also gave heed to Simon. On the other
hand it has been argued that the title
"Great" is meaningless in this relation,
for every divine power might be described
by the same epithet (so Wendt, in loco,
and Blass: "mirum maxime ἡ καλ. quasi
δύναμις Θ. μικρά quoque esse possit".
This difficulty leads Blass in his notes to
introduce the solution proposed by Klostermann, Probleme im Aposteltexte, pp.
15-20 (1883), and approved by Wendt,
Zöckler, Spitta, and recently by Zahn,
Einleitung in das N. T., ii. 420; see also
Salmon's remarks in Hermathena, xxi.,
p. 232), viz., that μεγάλη is not a translation of the attribute "great" רב, but
rather a transcription of the Samaritan
word מגלי or מגלא meaning qui
revelat (cf. Hebrew גָּלָה, Chaldean
גְּלָא גְּלָה, to reveal). The explanation would then be that in contrast to
the hidden essence of the Godhead,
Simon was known as its revealing power.
Nestle however (see Knabenbauer in loco)
objects on the ground that καλουμένη is
not read at all in many MSS. But
apart from Klostermann's explanation

the revised text might fairly mean that
amongst the "powers" of God (cf. the
N.T. use of the word δυνάμεις in Rom.
viii. 38, 1 Peter iii. 22, and cf. Book of
Enoch lxi. 10) Simon was emphatically
the one which is called great, i.e., the
one prominently great or divine. The
same title was assigned to him in later
accounts, cf. Irenæus, i., 23 (Clem. Hom.,
ii., 22; Clem. Recog., i., 72; ii., 7; Tertullian, De Præscr., xlvi.; Origen, c. Celsum,
v.). But whatever the claims made by
Simon himself, or attributed to him by his
followers, we need not read them into
the words before us. The expression
might mean nothing more than that
Simon called himself a great (or revealing) angel of God, since by the Samaritans
the angels were regarded as δυνάμεις,
powers of God (cf. Edersheim, Jesus the
Messiah, i., 402, note 4, and De Wette,
Apostelgeschichte, p. 122, fourth edition).
Such an explanation is far more probable
than the attribution to the Samaritans of
later Gnostic and philosophical beliefs,
while it is a complete answer to Overbeck,
who argues that as the patristic literature
about Simon presupposes the emanation
theories of the Gnostics so the expression
in the verse before us must be explained
in the same way, and that thus we have
a direct proof that the narrative is influenced by the Simon legend. We may
however readily admit that Simon's
teaching may have been a starting-point
for the later Gnostic developments, and
so far from ver. 10 demanding a Gnostic
system as a background, we may rather
see in it a glimpse of the genesis of the
beliefs which afterwards figure so prominently in the Gnostic schools (Nösgen,
Apostelgeschichte, in loco, and p. 186, and
see McGiffert, Apostolic Age, p. 99, and
"Gnosticism," Dict. of Christ. Biog., ii.,
680). On the close connection between
the Samaritans and Egypt and the widespread study of sorcery amongst the
Egyptian Samaritans see Deissmann,
Bibelstudien, pp. 18, 19. In Hadrian's
letter to Servianus we find the Samaritans
in Egypt described, like the Jews and
Christians there, as all astrologers, sooth-

ἐπίστευσαν τῷ Φιλίππῳ εὐαγγελιζομένῳ τὰ[1] περὶ τῆς βασιλείας τοῦ
Θεοῦ καὶ τοῦ ὀνόματος τοῦ Ἰησοῦ Χριστοῦ, ἐβαπτίζοντο ἄνδρες τε
καὶ γυναῖκες.   13. ὁ δὲ Σίμων καὶ αὐτὸς ἐπίστευσε, καὶ βαπτισθεὶς
ἦν προσκαρτερῶν τῷ Φιλίππῳ· θεωρῶν τε σημεῖα καὶ δυνάμεις
μεγάλας γινομένας, ἐξίστατο.   14. Ἀκούσαντες δὲ οἱ ἐν Ἱεροσολύμοις
ἀπόστολοι, ὅτι δέδεκται ἡ Σαμάρεια τὸν λόγον τοῦ Θεοῦ, ἀπέστειλαν

---

[1] τα omit W.H., R.V., Blass, Weiss.

---

sayers and quacks (Schürer, *Jewish
People*, div. ii., vol. ii., p. 230 E.T.).: no
doubt an exaggeration, as Deissmann
says, but still a proof that amongst these
Egyptian Samaritans magic and its
kindred arts were widely known. In a
note on p. 19 Deissmann gives an interesting parallel to Acts viii. 10, ἐπι-
καλοῦμαί σε τὴν μεγίστην δύναμιν τὴν
ἐν τῷ οὐρανῷ (ἄλλοι· τὴν ἐν τῇ ἄρκτῳ)
ὑπὸ Κυρίου Θεοῦ τεταγμένην (*Pap. Par.
Bibl. nat.*, 1275 ff.; Wessely, i., 76) (and
he also compares *Gospel of Peter*, ver.
19, ἡ δύναμίς μου (2)). The expression
according to him will thus have passed
from its use amongst the Samaritans
into the *Zauber-litteratur* of Egypt.
Ver. 11. ἱκανῷ χρόνῳ: dative for
accusative, *cf.* xiii. 20, and perhaps Luke
viii. 29, Rom. xvi. 25—the usage is not
classical, Blass, *Grammatik*, p. 118, but
see also Winer-Moulton, xxxi. 9 *a*. St.
Luke alone uses ἱκανός with χρόνος,
both in his Gospel and in Acts (Vogel,
Klostermann).—μαγείαις: only here in
N.T., not found in LXX or Apocryphal
books, but used in Theophrastus and
Plutarch, also in Josephus. It is found
in a striking passage in St. Ignatius
(*Ephes.*, xix., 3) in reference to the shining forth of the star at the Incarnation,
ὅθεν ἐλύετο πᾶσα μαγεία καὶ πᾶς δεσμός,
and it is also mentioned, *Didache*, v., 1,
amongst the things comprised under
"the way of death," and so in ii. 1 we
read οὐ μαγεύσεις οὐ φαρμακεύσεις.—ἐξεστακέναι, see above on ver. 9.
Ver. 12. εὐαγγελ. περὶ: only here
with περί, *cf.* Rom. i. 3 (Jos., *Ant.*, xv.,
7, 2). Amongst the Samaritans Philip
would have found a soil already prepared
for his teaching, *cf.* John iv. 25, and a
doctrine of the Messiah, in whom the
Samaritans saw not only a political but
a religious renewer, and one in whom
the promise of Deut. xviii. 15 would be
fulfilled (Edersheim, *Jesus the Messiah*,
i., 402, 403; Westcott, *Introduction to the
Study of the Gospels*, pp. 162, 163).—
ἄνδρες τε καὶ γυναῖκες, *cf.* v. 14:

"etiam mulieres quae a superstitionibus
difficilius abstrahuntur," Wetstein, *cf.*
John iv. 35 ff.
Ver. 13. καὶ αὐτὸς: characteristic of
St. Luke, see Friedrich, *Das Lucasevangelium*, p. 37.—βαπτισθεὶς—ἐβαπτίσθη ἀλλ' οὐκ ἐφωτίσθη (St. Cyril).—ἦν
προσκαρτερῶν: on ἦν with a participle as
characteristic of St. Luke see on i. 10,
and Friedrich, *u. s.*, p. 12; on προσκαρτ.
see on i. 14. Here with dative of the
person (*cf.* x. 7); the whole expression
shows how assiduously Simon attached
himself to Philip.—θεωρῶν: the faith of
Simon rested on the outward miracles
and signs, a faith which ended in
amazement, ἐξίστατο—but it was no permanent abiding faith, just as the amazement which he had himself inspired in
others gave way before a higher and
more convincing belief. The expression
δυνάμεις μεγάλας may have been purposely chosen; hitherto men had seen
in Simon, and he himself had claimed to
be, ἡ δύν. ἡ μεγάλη (Weiss).—ἐξίστατο:
"Simon qui alios obstupefaciebat, jam
ipse obstupescit," Wetstein. ἐξίσταμαι,
intransitive, Blass, *Grammatik*, p. 49.
Irenæus speaks of him as one who pretended faith, i. 23 (so too St. Cyril, St.
Chrysostom, St. Jerome, St. Ambrose):
he may have believed in the Messianic
dignity of Christ, and in His Death and
Resurrection, constrained by the miracles
which Philip wrought in attestation of
his preaching, but it was a belief about
the facts, and not a belief in Him whom
the facts made known, a belief in the
power of the new faith, but not an
acceptance of its *holiness*, ver. 18 (see
further, Rendall's note *in loco*, and on
the Baptism of Simon, "Baptism," in
Hastings' B.D.).
Ver. 14. ἡ Σαμ.: here the district;
Weiss traces the revising hand of St.
Luke (but see on the other hand Wendt,
in loco). There is nothing surprising in
the fact that the preaching of the Gospel
in the town should be regarded by the
Apostles at Jerusalem as a proof that the

πρὸς αὐτοὺς τὸν Πέτρον καὶ Ἰωάννην· 15. οἵτινες καταβάντες προσηύξαντο περὶ αὐτῶν, ὅπως λάβωσι Πνεῦμα Ἅγιον. (16. οὔπω γὰρ ἦν ἐπ᾽ οὐδενὶ αὐτῶν ἐπιπεπτωκός, μόνον δὲ βεβαπτισμένοι

good news had penetrated throughout the district, or that the people of the town should themselves have spread the Gospel amongst their countrymen (*cf.* John iv. 28).—**δέδεκται τὸν λόγον τοῦ Θ.**: the phrase is characteristic of St. Luke, as it is used by him, Luke viii. 13, Acts xi. 1, xvii. 11, but not by the other Evangelists—it is found once in St. Paul, 1 Thess. i. 6 (*cf.* ii. 13 and James i. 21). In the mention of John here, as in iii. 4, Weiss can only see the hand of a reviser, since the beloved disciple is mentioned with Peter in a way for which, as Weiss alleges, no reason can be assigned, iii. 4, 11, iv. 13; but nothing was more likely than that Peter and John should be associated together here as previously in the Gospels, see Plumptre's note on Acts iii. 1.

Ver. 15. **οἵτινες**: on this form of the relative see Rendall, *in loco;* Blass however regards it as simply = **οἵ**, *Grammatik,* p. 169, *cf.* xii. 10.—**καταβάντες**, *cf.* xxiv. 1 (Luke ii. 42), xi. 2, xxi. 12, 15. Wendt defends the historical character of this journey to Samaria as against Zeller and Overbeck.—**προσηύξαντο περὶ**: here only with **περὶ**; the verb is characteristic of St. Luke, and he alone has the construction used in this verse, *cf.* Luke vi. 28, W.H. The exact phrase is found in St. Paul's Epistles four or five times (and once in Hebrews), but often in LXX, and *cf.* Baruch i., 11, 13; 2 Macc. i. 6, xv. 14. The laying on of hands, as in vi. 7 and xiii. 3, is here preceded by prayer, see Hooker, *Eccles. Pol.,* v., chap. lxvi., 1-4.—**ὅπως λάβωσι Πν. Ἅγιον**: the words express the chief and highest object of the Apostles' visit: it was not only to ascertain the genuineness of the conversions, or to form a connecting link between the Church of Samaria and that of Jerusalem, although such objects might not have been excluded in dealing with an entirely new and strange state of things —the recognition of the Samaritans in a common faith. It has been argued with great force that the expression Holy Spirit is not meant here in its dogmatic Pauline sense; Luke only means to include in it the ecstatic gifts of speaking with tongues and prophecy. This view is held to be supported by **ἰδών** in ver. 18, intimating that outward manifestations which meet the eye must have shown

themselves, and by the fact that the same verb, **ἐπέπεσε**, is used in cases where the results which follow plainly show that the reception of the Holy Ghost meant a manifestation of the outward marvellous signs such as marked the day of Pentecost, x. 44, 46, xi. 15 (*cf.* xix. 6). In the case of these Samaritans no such signs from heaven had followed their baptism, and the Apostles prayed for a conspicuous divine sanction on the reception of the new converts (Wendt, Zöckler, Holtzmann, and see also Hort, *Ecclesia,* pp. 54, 55). But even supposing that the reception of the Holy Ghost could be thus limited, the gift of tongues was no mere magical power, but the direct result of a supernatural Presence and of a special grace— of that Presence speaking with tongues, prophesyings, and various gifts, 1 Cor. xiv. 1, 14, 37, were no doubt the outward manifestations, but they could not have been manifested apart from that Presence, and they were outward visible signs of an inward spiritual grace. In a book so marked by the working of the Holy Spirit that it has received the name of the "Gospel of the Spirit" it is difficult to believe that St. Luke can mean to limit the expression **λαμβάνειν** here and in the following verse to anything less than a bestowal of that divine indwelling of the spirit which makes the Christian the temple of God, and which St. Paul speaks of in the very same terms as a permanent possession, Gal. iii. 2, Rom. viii. 15 (Gore, *Church and the Ministry,* p. 258). St. Paul's language, 1 Cor. xii. 30, makes it plain that the advent of the Holy Spirit was not of necessity attested by any peculiar manifestations, nor were these manifestations essential accompaniments of it: "Do all speak with tongues?" he asks, "Are all prophets?" See further on ver. 17.

Ver. 16. **ἐπιπεπτωκός**: the verb is characteristic of St. Luke, and used by him both in his Gospel and in Acts of the occurrence of extraordinary conditions, *e.g.,* the sudden influence of the Spirit, *cf.* Luke i. 12, Acts x. 44, xi. 15, xix. 17, *cf.* Rev. xi. 11 (Acts x. 10 cannot be supported, and in xiii. 11 read **ἔπεσεν**). Similar usage in LXX, Exod. xv. 16, 1 Sam. xxvi. 12, Ps. liv. 4, Judith ii. 28, xi. 11, etc., Friedrich, *Das Lucasevangelium,* p. 41.

ὑπῆρχον εἰς τὸ ὄνομα τοῦ Κυρίου Ἰησοῦ.) 17. τότε ἐπετίθουν [1] τὰς χεῖρας ἐπ᾽ αὐτούς, καὶ ἐλάμβανον Πνεῦμα Ἅγιον. 18. Θεασάμενος [2] δὲ ὁ Σίμων, ὅτι διὰ τῆς ἐπιθέσεως τῶν χειρῶν τῶν ἀποστόλων δίδοται

[1] επετιθουν, see Winer-Schmiedel, p. 121; Blass, *Gram.*, p. 48.

[2] θεασαμενος HLP, Chrys.; ιδων ℵABCDE, so Tisch., W.H., R.V., Blass, Weiss, Wendt, Hilg.

For the word as used by St. Luke in another sense also characteristic of him, see below on xx. 37, and Plummer on xv. 20. On the formula of baptism see above p. 91, and "Baptism," B.D.[2], p. 352, and Hastings' B.D.—ὑπῆρχον here perhaps = "made a beginning," took the first step (Lumby).

Ver. 17. There cannot be any reason to doubt the validity of St. Philip's baptism, and it is therefore evident that the laying on of hands (*cf.* xix. 6) is here distinct from baptism, and also from the appointment to any Church office (as in vi. 6, xiii. 3), or the bestowal of any special power of healing as in the person of Ananias, ix. 12, 17, although gifts of healing might no doubt accompany it. But both here and in xix. 6 (*cf.* Heb. vi. 2) it follows closely upon baptism, and is performed by Apostles, to whom alone the function belongs, although it is reasonable to suppose that the prophets and teachers who were associated with them in their Apostolic office, and who could lay on hands in Acts xiii. 1-3, could do so in other cases also for the reception of the Holy Ghost (Gore, *Church and the Ministry*, p. 258). The question why St. Philip did not himself "lay hands" upon his converts has been variously discussed, but the narrative of Acts supplies the answer, inasmuch as in the only two parallel cases, *viz.*, the verse before us and xix. 6, the higher officers alone exercise this power, and also justifies the usual custom of the Church in so limiting its exercise ("Confirmation," *Dict. of Christian Antiq.* (Smith & Cheetham), i., p. 425; B.D.[1], iii., *App.*; and Hooker, *Eccles. Pol.*, v., ch. lxvi. 5, and passage cited; Jerome, *Advers. Lucif.*, c. 4, and St. Cyprian, *Epis.* 73, *ad Jubaianum* (reference to the passage before us)). Undoubtedly there are cases of baptism, Acts iii. 41, xvi. 15, 33, where no reference is made to the subsequent performance of this rite, but in these cases it must be remembered that the baptiser was an Apostle, and that when this was the case its observance might fairly be assumed. For the special

case of Cornelius see below on x. 44, see further "Confirmation," B.D.[2], i., 640. Weizsäcker contrasts this account in viii., v. 16, which he describes as this crude conception of the communication of the Spirit solely by the imposition of the Apostles' hands (*Apostolic Age*, ii., 254 and 299, E.T.), and which represents baptism as being thus completed, with the account of baptism given us by St. Paul in 1 Cor. i. 14-17. But in the first place we should remember that Acts does not describe *baptism* as being completed by the laying on of hands; the baptism was not invalid, the Samaritan converts became by its administration members of the Church; and the laying on of hands was not so much a completion of baptism as an addition to it. And, in the next place, Heb. vi. 2 certainly indicates that this addition must have been known at a very early period (see Westcott, *in loco*). It may also be borne in mind that 2 Cor. i. 21 is interpreted of confirmation by many of the Fathers (*cf.* too Westcott's interpretation of 1 John ii. 20, 27), and that St. Paul is writing a letter and not describing a ritual. — ἐλάμβανον: Dr. Hort, who holds that the reception of the Holy Spirit is here explained as in x. 44 by reference to the manifestation of the gift of tongues, etc., points out that the verb is not ἔλαβον, but imperfect ἐλάμβανον, and he therefore renders it "showed a succession of signs of the Spirit" (see also above). But this interpretation need not conflict with the belief in the gift of the Spirit as a permanent possession, and it is well to remember that ἐπετίθεσαν (ἐπετίθουν) is also imperfect. Both verbs may therefore simply indicate the continuous administration of the laying on of hands by the Apostles, and the continuous supernatural result (not necessarily external manifestation) which followed upon this action; *cf.* ἐβαπτίζοντο in ver. 12, imperfect, and so in xviii. 8.

Ver. 18. θεασάμενος: the word would seem to point on (so ἰδών, see critical notes) to some outward manifestation of

τὸ Πνεῦμα τὸ Ἅγιον, προσήνεγκεν αὐτοῖς χρήματα,[1] λέγων, 19. Δότε κἀμοὶ τὴν ἐξουσίαν ταύτην, ἵνα ᾧ ἐὰν ἐπιθῶ τὰς χεῖρας, λαμβάνῃ Πνεῦμα Ἅγιον. 20. Πέτρος δὲ εἶπε πρὸς αὐτόν, Τὸ ἀργύριόν σου σὺν σοὶ εἴη εἰς ἀπώλειαν, ὅτι τὴν δωρεὰν τοῦ Θεοῦ ἐνόμισας διὰ

[1] D, Gig. Par. read παρακαλων και λεγων (cf. ver. 24 where παρακαλω is also found in D), so Hilg.; combination not infrequent, Matt. viii. 5, Acts ii. 40, xvi. 9, to strengthen the request. After ινα D, Par. Const. apost. insert καγω. εαν ℵABCELP, so Tisch., W.H., Weiss; αν DH 36, Const. apost., Bas., Chrys., Cyr.-Jer. (so Blass in β, and Hilg.).

the inward grace of the Spirit, so Weiss, Wendt, Zöckler; so Felten, although he does not of course limit the reception of the Holy Spirit to such outward evidences of His Presence. The word may further give us an insight into Simon's character and belief—the gift of the Spirit was valuable to him in its external manifestation, in so far, that is, as it presented itself to ocular demonstration as a higher power than his own magic.—διὰ τῆς ἐπιθ. τῶν χ. τῶν ἀποστ., see above on ver. 17, cf. διά, "the laying on of hands" was the instrument by which the Holy Ghost was given in this instance: "Church," Hastings' B.D., i., 426.—προσήνεγκεν αὐτοῖς χρήματα: Simon was right in so far as he regarded the gift of the Spirit as an ἐξουσία to be bestowed, but entirely wrong in supposing that such a power could be obtained without an inward disposition of the heart, as anything might be bought for gold in external commerce. So De Wette, Apostelgeschichte, p. 124 (fourth edition), and he adds: "This is the fundamental error in 'Simony,' which is closely connected with unbelief in the power and meaning of the Spirit, and with materialism" (see also Alford in loco). (See further on "Simony," Luckock, Footprints of the Apostles as traced by St. Luke, i., 208.) Probably Simon, after the manner of the time, cf. xix. 19, may already have purchased secrets from other masters of the magical arts, and thought that a similar purchase could now be effected.

Ver. 19. ἵνα ᾧ ἐὰν ἐπιθῶ: "that on whomsoever I lay my hands," i.e., quite apart from any profession of faith or test of character; no words could more plainly show how completely Simon mistook the essential source and meaning of the power which he coveted.

Ver. 20. τὸ ἀργύριόν σου κ.τ.λ.: the words are no curse or imprecation, as is evident from ver. 22, but rather a vehement expression of horror on the part of St. Peter, an expression which would warn Simon that he was on the way to destruction. Rendall considers that the real form of the prayer is not that Simon may perish, but that as he is already on the way to destruction, so the silver may perish which is dragging him down, to the intent that Simon himself may repent and be forgiven: so Page, "thy money perish, even as thou art now perishing," cf. Œcumenius, in loco (and to the same effect St. Chrys.): οὐκ ἔστι ταῦτα ἀρωμένου ἀλλὰ παιδεύοντος, ὡς ἄν τις εἴποι · τὸ ἀργύριόν σου συναπόλοιτό σοι μετὰ τῆς προαιρέσεως. But see also on the optative of wishing, Burton, N. T. Moods and Tenses, p. 79, where he speaks of Mark xi. 14 and Acts viii. 20 as peculiar, being imprecations of evil, and cf. also Blass, Grammatik, p. 215.—εἴη εἰς ἀπώλειαν: a frequent construction, "go to destruction and remain there," see Felten, Wendt, Page, and cf. ver. 23, εἰς χολὴν . . . ὄντα. The noun occurs no less than five times in St. Peter's Second Epistle, cf. also 1 Peter i. 7. εἰς ἀπώλ. occurs five times elsewhere, Rom. ix. 22, 1 Tim. vi. 9, Heb. x. 39, Rev. xvii. 8, 11, and it is frequent in LXX; cf. 1 Chron. xxi. 17, Isa. xiv. 23, liv. 16, Dan. iii. 29, and ii. 5, Theod., etc.; 1 Macc. iii. 42, Bel and the Dragon, ver. 29, and several times in Ecclus.—τὴν δωρεὰν: and so, not to be bought, cf. Matt. x. 8, and our Lord's own words in Samaria, John iv. 10, εἰ ἤδεις τὴν δωρεὰν τοῦ Θεοῦ κ.τ.λ.—ὅτι . . . ἐνόμισας διὰ χ. κτᾶσθαι: "because thou hast thought to obtain," to acquire, gain possession of, κτᾶσθαι, deponent verb, so in classical Greek, not passive as in A.V., see Matt. x. 9, and elsewhere twice in St. Luke's Gospel, xviii. 12, xxi. 19, and three times in Acts, i. 18, viii. 20, xxii. 28, and once in St. Paul, 1 Thess. iv. 4, frequent in LXX, and in same sense as here of acquiring by money.—ἐνόμ.: it was not a mere error of judgment, but a sinful intention, which

χρημάτων κτᾶσθαι. 21. οὐκ ἔστι σοι μερὶς οὐδὲ κλῆρος ἐν τῷ λόγῳ
τούτῳ · ἡ γὰρ καρδία σου οὐκ ἔστιν εὐθεῖα ἐνώπιον[1] τοῦ Θεοῦ. 22.
μετανόησον οὖν ἀπὸ τῆς κακίας σου ταύτης, καὶ δεήθητι τοῦ Θεοῦ,[2] εἰ
ἄρα ἀφεθήσεταί σοι ἡ ἐπίνοια τῆς καρδίας σου · 23. εἰς[3] γὰρ χολὴν

[1] ενωπιον EHLP; εναντι אABD 15, 36, so Tisch., W.H., R.V., Blass, Hilg. (cf.
Luke i. 8, a rarer word).

[2] Θεου HLP, Vulg., Syr. Pesh., Irint., Blass in β (prob. after ver. 21); Κυριου
אABCDE, Sah., Boh., Syr. Harcl., Arm., Const. apost., Bas., so Tisch., W.H., R.V.,
Weiss, Wendt, so Hilg.

[3] D[1] has ην (=εν (?)) γαρ πικριας χολη και συνδεσμω αδικ., so Blass and Hilg.,
prob. caused by the difficult εις. ορω—DE read θεωρω, so Const. apost., Chrys.;
"recte" Blass, so in α and β, and Hilg.; but there seems no real reason why ορω
should not occur here.

had come from a heart not right before
God, ver. 21; cf. Matt. xv. 19.
Ver. 21. μερὶς οὐδὲ κλῆρος, cf. Deut.
xii. 2, xiv. 27, 29, xviii. 1, Isa. lviii. 6, and
instances in Wetstein, see on i. 17.—
λόγῳ τούτῳ: both A. and R.V. "in this
matter," i.e., in the power of communicating the Holy Spirit, but Grotius,
Neander, Hackett, Blass, Rendall and
others refer it to the Gospel, i.e., the
word of God which the Apostles preached,
and in the blessings of which the Apostles
had a share. λόγος is frequently used
in classical Greek of that de quo agitur
(see instances in Wendt). Grimm, sub
v., compares the use of the noun in
classical Greek, like ῥῆμα, the thing
spoken of, the subject or matter of the
λόγος, Herod., i., 21, etc.—ἡ γὰρ καρδία
. . . εὐθεῖα, cf. LXX, Ps. vii. 10, x. 3,
xxxv. 10, lxxii. 1, lxxvii. 37, etc., where
the adjective is used, as often in classical
Greek, of moral uprightness (cf. εὐθύτης
in LXX, and Psalms of Solomon, ii., 15,
ἐν εὐθύτητι καρδίας), so also in Acts
xiii. 10, where the word is used by St.
Paul on a similar occasion in rebuking
Elymas; only found once in the Epistles,
where it is again used by St. Peter, 2
Pet. ii. 15.
Ver. 22. κακίας: not used elsewhere
by St. Luke, but it significantly meets us
twice in St. Peter, cf. 1 Pet. ii. 1, 16.—
ἀφεθ.: if we read above, Κυρίου, the
meaning will be the Lord Jesus, in
whose name the Apostles had been
baptising, ver. 16, and ἀφεθ. may also
point to the word of the Lord Jesus in
Matt. xii. 31 (so Alford, Plumptre).—
εἰ ἄρα, Mark xi. 13 (Acts xvii. 27). R.
and A.V. both render "if perhaps," but
R.V. "if perhaps . . . shall be forgiven
thee"; A.V. "if perhaps . . . may be
forgiven thee". St. Peter does not throw

doubt on forgiveness after sincere repentance, but the doubt is expressed, because
Simon so long as he was what he was
(see the probable reading of the next
verse and the connecting γάρ) could not
repent, and therefore could not be forgiven, cf. Gen. xviii. 3. "If now I have
found favour in thine eyes," εἰ ἄρα
(אִם־נָא), which I hope rather than
venture to assume; see also Simcox,
Language of N. T. Greek, pp. 180, 181,
and compare Winer-Moulton, xli., 4 c.,
and liii., 8 a; and Viteau, Le Grec du
N. T., p. 62 (1893).—ἐπίνοια: only here
in N.T.; cf. Jer. xx. 10, Wisdom vi. 16,
etc., 2 Macc. xii. 45, 4 Macc. xvii. 2, and
often in classical Greek.
Ver. 23. εἰς γὰρ χολὴν: The passages in LXX generally referred to as
containing somewhat similar phraseology
are Deut. xxix. 18, xxxii. 32, Lam. iii.
15. But the word χολή is found in
LXX several times, and not always as
the equivalent of the same Hebrew. In
Deut. xxix. 18, xxxii. 32, Ps. lxix. 21,
Jer. viii. 14, ix. 15, Lam. iii. 19, it is used
to translate רֹאשׁ (רוֹשׁ, Deut. xxxii.
32), a poisonous plant of intense bitterness and of quick growth (coupled with
wormwood, cf. Deut. xxix. 18, Lam. iii.
19, Jer. ix. 15). In Job xvi. 14 (where,
however, AS[2] read ζωήν for χολήν) it is
used to translate מְרֵרָה, bile, gall;
in xx. 14 of the same book it is the
equivalent of מְרֹרָה in the sense of
the gall of vipers, i.e., the poison of
vipers, which the ancients supposed to
lie in the gall. In Prov. v. 4 and Lam.
iii. 15 it is the rendering of לַעֲנָה,

πικρίας καὶ σύνδεσμον ἀδικίας ὁρῶ σε ὄντα. 24. ἀποκριθεὶς δὲ ὁ
Σίμων εἶπε, Δεήθητε ὑμεῖς ὑπὲρ ἐμοῦ πρὸς τὸν Κύριον, ὅπως μηδὲν
ἐπέλθῃ ἐπ᾽ ἐμὲ ὧν εἰρήκατε.[1] 25. Οἱ μὲν οὖν διαμαρτυράμενοι καὶ
λαλήσαντες τὸν λόγον τοῦ Κυρίου, ὑπέστρεψαν[2] εἰς Ἱερουσαλήμ,
πολλάς τε κώμας τῶν Σαμαρειτῶν εὐηγγελίσαντο.

[1] Before δεηθητε D, Gig., Syr. Harcl. mg., Const. apost. prefix παρακαλω; cf.
ver. 19, so Hilg. For ων D has τουτων των κακων, and adds μοι after ειρηκατε, so
Hilg. At end of verse D adds ος πολλα κλαιων ου διελιμπανεν, so Syr. H. mg.
without ος—so Blass in β, but και for ος; Hilg. follows D; see Belser, *Beiträge*,
p. 4, who refers to xx. 27, xvii. 13, for διαλιμπανειν, διαλειπειν, constr. with participle as here, instances which he regards as beyond doubt Lucan; cf. Luke vii. 45,
where διαλειπω, *used only by Luke*, is found with a similar constr., διαλιμπανω only
found elsewhere in Tobit x. 7 (but S *al.*), but also in Galen, cf. Grimm, *sub v.*, and L.
and S. But in spite of the Lucan phraseology it seems difficult to suppose that Luke
would himself have struck out the words, unless, indeed, he had gained further information about Simon which led him to conclude that the repentance was not
sincere. Such an omission could scarcely be made for the sake of brevity. Weiss,
Codex D, p. 68, evidently regards the words as added by a later hand, not as omitted
by Luke himself; see also Wendt, edit. 1899, p. 177, note.

[2] υπεστρεψαν CEHLP, several verss., Chrys.; υπεστρεφον ℵABD 15, 61, Vulg.,
so Tisch., W.H., R.V., Blass, Weiss, Wendt, Hilg. Σαμαρειτων ABCDHLP, so
W.H. (and see App., p. 161), Hilg.; Σαμαριτων ℵE, so Tisch., Blass. ευηγγελι-
σαντο HLP, Boh., Syr. Pesh., Aeth., Chrys.; ευηγγελιζοντο ℵABCD, Vulg., Sah.,
Syr. Harcl., Arm., Aug., so Tisch., W.H., R.V., Blass, Weiss, Wendt, Hilg.

wormwood; and in the former passage
we have **πικρότερον χολῆς.** If we take
the most usual signification of **χολή** in
the LXX, *viz.*, that of the *gall plant* (see
R.V., margin, *in loco*, *gall*, or *a gall
root*), the thought of bitterness would
naturally be associated with it (in the
passage which presents the closest parallel to the verse before us, Deut xxix. 18,
ἐν χολῇ καὶ πικρίᾳ, πικρία is a translation of the Hebrew word for *wormwood*);
ἐν χολῇ πικρίας might therefore denote
the intense malignity which filled the
heart of Simon. (On the word **χολή** in
its sense here, and in Matt. xxvii. 34, see
Meyer-Weiss, *Matth.*, p. 546.) The preposition **εἰς** is generally taken as = **ἐν**
in this passage; but Rendall suggests
that here, as is sometimes elsewhere, it
= **ὡς,** and he therefore renders: "I see
that thou art as gall of bitterness," denoting the evil function which Simon
would fulfil in the Church if he continued
what he was. Westcott's note on Heb.
xii. 15 should also be consulted.—**σύνδεσμον ἀδικίας:** R.V. translates "thou
art . . . in the bond of iniquity". But
if the passage means that Simon "will
become . . . a bond of iniquity," R.V.,
margin, or that he is now *as a* bond of
iniquity (Rendall), the expression denotes,
not that Simon is bound, but that he
binds others in iniquity. Blass refers to

Isa. lviii. 6, where a similar phrase occurs,
σύνδ. ἀδικ., and explains: "improbitate
quasi vinctus es"; so Grimm, while
pointing out that the phrase in Isa. lviii.
6 is used in a different sense from here,
explains "vinculum improbitatis, *i.e.*,
quod ab improbitate nectitur ad con-
stringendos animos". Others again
take the expression to denote a *bundle,*
fasciculus (Wetstein) (cf. Hdian., iv., 12,
11), Simon being regarded "quasi ex
improbitate concretum," cf. especially
Cicero, *in Pison.*, ix., 21; but such a rendering is rejected by Grimm, as no examples can be adduced of this tropical
use of the noun, and by Wendt, on the
ground that **ἀδικία** is not in the plural,
but in the singular. Combinations with
ἀδικία are characteristic of St. Luke;
cf. Luke xiii. 27, xvi. 8, 9, xviii. 6; cf.
Act i. 18; the word only occurs once
elsewhere in the Gospels, John vii. 18;
Friedrich, *Das Lucasevangelium*, p. 23.
Ver. 24. **Δεήθητε:** the verse is often
taken (as by Meyer and others) as a
further proof of the hollowness of Simon's
belief, and his ignorance of the way of
true repentance—he will not pray for
himself, and he only asks for deliverance
from fear of the penalty and not from
hatred of the sin (so Bengel). But on
the other hand Wendt, in criticising
Meyer, objects to this further condemna-

26. Ἄγγελος δὲ Κυρίου ἐλάλησε πρὸς Φίλιππον, λέγων, Ἀνάστηθι
καὶ πορεύου κατὰ μεσημβρίαν, ἐπὶ τὴν ὁδὸν τὴν καταβαίνουσαν ἀπὸ

tion of Simon as not expressed in the text. So far as the petition for the Apostles' prayers is concerned, it is of course possible that it may have been prompted by the belief that such prayers would be more efficacious than his own (so Blass, Wendt, see also conclusion of the story in D); he does not ask them to pray instead of himself but ὑπέρ, on his behalf.—ἐπέλθῃ: not used by the other Evangelists, but three times in St. Luke's Gospel and four times in Acts, with ἐπί and accusative both in Gospel (i. 35, cf. xxi. 35) and Acts.

Ver. 25. οἱ μὲν οὖν: the μὲν οὖν and δέ in ver. 26 may connect the return of the party to Jerusalem and the following instructions to Philip for his journey, and so enable us to gather for a certainty that Philip returned to Jerusalem with the Apostles, and received there his further directions from the Lord; see Rendall's Appendix on μὲν οὖν, Acts, p. 164, but cf. on the other hand, Belser, Beiträge, pp. 51, 52. On the frequent and characteristic use of μὲν οὖν in Luke, see above on i. 6, etc.—ὑπέστρεψαν: if we read the imperfect, we have the two verbs in the verse in the same tense, and the sense would be that the Apostles did not return at once to Jerusalem, but started on their return (imperfect), and preached to the Samaritan villages on the way (as Belser also allows)—the τε closely unites the two verbs (Weiss). The verb is characteristic of St. Luke: in his Gospel twenty-one or twenty-two times; in Acts, eleven or twelve times; in the other Evangelists, only once, Mark xv. 40, and this doubtful; only three times in rest of N.T. (Lekebusch, Friedrich).

Ver. 26. ἄγγελος: on the frequency of angelic appearances, another characteristic of St. Luke, see Friedrich, Das Lucasevangelium, pp. 45 and 52 (so Zeller, Acts, ii., 224, E.T.), cf. Luke ii. 9 and Acts xii. 7, Luke i. 38 and Acts x. 7, Luke xxiv. 4 and Acts i. 10, x. 30. There can be no doubt, as Wendt points out, that St. Luke means that the communication was made to Philip by an angel, and that therefore all attempts to explain his words as meaning that Philip felt a sudden inward impulse, or that he had a vision in a dream, are unsatisfactory.— ἀνάστηθι, as Wendt remarks, does not support the latter supposition, cf. v. 17, and its frequent use in Acts and in O.T. see below.—δέ may be taken as above,

see ver. 25, or as simply marking the return of the narrative from the chief Apostles to the history of Philip. As in vv. 29, 39, πνεῦμα and not ἄγγελος occurs; the alteration has been attributed to a reviser, but even Spitta, Apostelgeschichte, p. 153, can find no reason for this, and sees in the use of πνεῦμα and ἄγγελος here nothing more strange than their close collocation Matt. iv. 1, 11.— ἀνάστηθι καὶ πορεύου, words often similarly joined together in LXX.—κατὰ μεσημβρίαν: towards the south, i.e., he was to proceed "with his face to the south," cf. xxvii. 12 (Page).—ἐπὶ τὴν ὁδὸν (not πρός), on, i.e., along the road (not "unto," A.V.). R.V. margin renders κατὰ μεσ. "at noon"; so Rendall, cf. xxii. 6, as we have κατά not πρός; so Nestle, Studien und Kritiken, p. 335 (1892) (see Felten's note, Apostelgeschichte, p. 177; but as he points out, the heat of the day at twelve o'clock would not be a likely time for travelling, see also Belser, Beiträge, p. 52, as against Nestle). Wendt, edition 1899, p. 177, gives in his adhesion to Nestle's view on the ground that in LXX, cf. Gen. xviii. 1, etc., the word μεσημβρ. is always so used, and because the time of the day for the meeting was an important factor, whilst there would be no need to mention the direction, when the town was definitely named (see also O. Holtzmann, Neutest. Zeitgeschichte, p. 88).—αὕτη ἐστὶν ἔρημος: opinion is still divided as to whether the adjective is to be referred to the town or the road. Amongst recent writers, Wendt, edition 1899, p. 178; Zahn, Einleitung in das N. T., ii., 438 (1899); Belser, Rendall, O. Holtzmann, u. s., p. 88, Knabenbauer (so too Edersheim, Jewish Social Life, p. 79; Conder in B.D.² "Gaza," and Grimm-Thayer) may be added to the large number who see a reference to the route (in Schürer, Jewish People, div. ii., vol. i., p. 71, E.T., it is stated that this view is the more probable). But, on the other hand, some of the older commentators (Calvin, Grotius, etc.) take the former view, and they have recently received a strong supporter in Prof. G. A. Smith, Historical Geog. of the Holy Land, pp. 186-188. O. Holtzmann, although referring αὕτη to ὁδός, points out that both Strabo, xvi., 2, 30, and the Anonymous Geographical Fragment (Geogr. Græc. Minores, Hudson, iv., p. 39) designate Gaza as ἔρημος. Dr.

Ἱερουσαλὴμ εἰς Γάζαν· αὕτη ἐστὶν ἔρημος. 27. καὶ ἀναστὰς
ἐπορεύθη· καὶ ἰδοὺ ἀνὴρ Αἰθίοψ εὐνοῦχος δυνάστης Κανδάκης τῆς [1]
βασιλίσσης Αἰθιόπων, ὃς ἦν ἐπὶ πάσης τῆς γάζης αὐτῆς, ὃς ἐληλύθει

[1] τῆς HLP, Chrys.; om. NABC(D)E 61, so Tisch., W.H., R.V., Blass, Weiss,
Wendt, Hilg.; D adds τινος, but Blass rejects in β, Hilg. retains.   ος (2)
N³BC²D²EHLP, Syr. Harcl., Arm., Chrys., so Weiss (see comment. below),
[W.H.]; om. N¹AC¹D¹, Vulg., Sah., so Tisch., Blass, Hilg. Blass suggests orig.
reading was ουτος, which might easily fall out after αυτης—ουτος in Gig., Boh.
For αυτης D reads αυτου, but Blass rejects, so Hilg.—suggested as due from retrans.
of Latin, or unpointed Syriac. εις om. in D¹, εν in D².

Smith strengthens these references, not
only by Jos., *Ant.*, xiv., 4, 4, and
Diodorus Siculus, xix., 80, but by maintaining that the New Gaza mentioned
in the Anonymous Fragment was on
the coast, and that if so, it lay off the
road to Egypt, which still passed by the
desert Gaza; the latter place need not
have been absolutely deserted in Philip's
time; its site and the vicinity of the great
road would soon attract people back, but
it was not unlikely that the name Ἔρημος
might still stick to it (see also ver. 36
below). If we take the adjective as referring to the road, its exact force is still
doubtful ; does it refer to one route,
specially lonely, as distinguished from
others, or to the ordinary aspect of a
route leading through waste places, or to
the fact that at the hour mentioned,
noon-day (see above), it would be deserted? Wendt confesses himself unable to decide, and perhaps he goes as
far as one can expect to go in adding
that at least this characterisation of the
route so far prepares us for the sequel, in
that it explains the fact that the eunuch
would read aloud, and that Philip could
converse with him uninterruptedly.
Hackett and others regard the words
before us as a parenthetical remark by
St. Luke himself to acquaint the reader
with the region of this memorable occurrence, and αὕτη is used in a somewhat
similar explanatory way in 2 Chron. v. 2,
LXX, but this does not enable us to
decide as to whether the explanation is
St. Luke's or the angel's. Hilgenfeld
and Schmiedel dismiss the words as an
explanatory gloss. The argument sometimes drawn for the late date of Acts by
referring ἔρημος to the supposed demoli-
tion of Gaza in A.D. 66 cannot be maintained, since this destruction so called
was evidently very partial, see G. A.
Smith, *u. s.*, and so Schürer, *u. s.*
Ver. 27. καὶ ἀναστὰς ἐπορεύθη: immediate and implicit obedience. — καὶ
ἰδού, see on i. 11; *cf.* Hort, *Ecclesia*,

p. 179, on the force of the phrase ; used
characteristically by St. Luke of sudden
and as it were providential interpositions, i. 10, x. 17, xii. 7, and see note
on xvi. 1.—εὐνοῦχος: the word can be
taken literally, for there is no contradiction involved in Deut. xxiii. 1, as he
would be simply "a proselyte of the
gate" (Hort, *Judaistic Christianity*, p.
54). The instances sometimes referred
to as showing that the exclusion of
eunuchs from the congregation of the
Lord was relaxed in the later period of
Jewish history can scarcely hold good,
since Isa. lvi. 3 refers to the Messianic
future in which even the heathen and
the eunuchs should share, and in Jer.
xxxviii. 7, xxxix. 15 nothing is said which
could lead us to describe Ebed Melech,
another Ethiopian eunuch, as a Jew in
the full sense. On the position and influence of eunuchs in the East, both in
ancient and modern times, see "Eunuch,"
B.D.², and Hastings' B.D. St. Luke's
mention that he was a eunuch is quite
in accordance with the "universalism"
of the Acts; gradually the barriers of a
narrow Judaism were broken down, first
in the case of the Samaritans, and now
in the case of the eunuch. Eusebius,
H. E., ii., 1, speaks of him as πρῶτος ἐξ
ἐθνῶν, who was converted to Christ, and
even as a "proselyte of the gate" he
might be so described, for the gulf which
lay between a born Gentile and a genuine
descendant of Abraham could never be
bridged over (Schürer, *Jewish People*,
div. ii., vol. ii., p. 326, E.T.). Moreover,
in the case of the Ethiopian eunuch, descended from the accursed race of Ham,
this separation from Israel must have
been intensified to the utmost (*cf.* Amos
ix. 7). No doubt St. Luke may also
have desired to instance the way in
which thus early the Gospel spread to
a land far distant from the place of its
birth (McGiffert, *Apostolic Age*, p. 100).
—δυνάστης: noun in apposition to ἀνὴρ
Αἰθ., only used by St. Luke here and in

προσκυνήσων εἰς Ἰερουσαλήμ, 28. ἦν τε ὑποστρέφων καὶ καθήμενος
ἐπὶ τοῦ ἅρματος αὐτοῦ, καὶ ἀνεγίνωσκε τὸν προφήτην Ἠσαΐαν.[1] 29.
εἶπε δὲ τὸ Πνεῦμα τῷ Φιλίππῳ, Πρόσελθε καὶ κολλήθητι τῷ ἅρματι

[1] τον προφ. Ησ. EHLP 61, Boh., Syr. Harcl.; Ησ. τον προφ. אABC 13, 69,
Vulg., Syr. Pesh., Sah., Arm., Aeth., so Tisch., W.H., R.V. See for this note v. 30.

his Gospel, i. 52, and once again by St. Paul, 1 Tim. vi. 15. In LXX frequent (used of God, Ecclus. xlvi. 5, 2 Macc. xv. 3, 23, etc. ; so too of Zeus by Soph.), for its meaning here *cf.* Gen. I. 4, Latin, *aulicus.*—**Κανδάκης**: not a personal name, but said to be a name often given to queens of Ethiopia (*cf.* Pharaoh, and later Ptolemy, in Egypt), Pliny, *N. H.*, vi., 35, 7. In the time of Eusebius, *H. E.*, ii., 1, Ethiopia is said to be still ruled by queens, Strabo, xvii., I., 54; Bion of Soli, *Ethiopica* (Müller, *Fragm. Hist. Græc.*, iv., p. 351). According to Brugsch the spelling would be Kanta-ki: *cf.* "Candace," B.D.[2], and "Ethiopia," Hastings' B.D.—**γάζης**: a Persian word found both in Greek and Latin (*cf.* Cicero, *De Off.*, ii., 22 ; Virg., *Æn.*, i., 119; and see Wetstein, *in loco*). In LXX, Ezra vi. 1 (Esth. iv. 7), *treasures;* v. 17, vii. 20, *treasury ;* vii. 21, *treasurers ; cf.* also Isa. xxxix. 2, and γαζοφυλάκιον in LXX, and in N.T., Luke xxi. 1, Mark xii. 41 (2), 43, John viii. 20. "Observat Lucas, et locum, ubi præfectus Gazæ Philippo factus est obviam, Gazam fuisse vocatum" Wetstein; see also on the *nomen et omen* Felten and Plumptre, and compare on the word Jerome, *Epist.*, cviii., 11. If the second ὅς is retained (R.V.) it emphasises the fact that the eunuch was already a proselyte (Weiss).—**προσκυνήσων**: proves not that he was a Jew, but that he was not a heathen (Hackett). The proselytes, as well as foreign Jews, came to Jerusalem to worship. We cannot say whether he had gone up to one of the feasts; St. Chrysostom places it to his credit that he had gone up at an unusual time.

Ver. 28. **ἅρματος**: the chariot was regarded as a mark of high rank: very frequent word in LXX, but in N.T. only here, and in Rev. ix. 9, *cf.* xviii. 13. "Chariot," Hastings' B.D., properly in classics a war-chariot, but here for ἁρμάμαξα, a covered chariot (Blass), Herod., vii., 41.—**ἀνεγίνωσκεν**: evidently aloud, according to Eastern usage; there is no need to suppose that some slave was reading to him (Olshausen, Nösgen, Blass). As the following citation proves, he was

reading from the LXX, and the widespread knowledge of this translation in Egypt would make it probable *a priori* (Wendt), *cf.* Professor Margoliouth, "Ethiopian Eunuch," Hastings' B.D. It may be that the eunuch had bought the roll in Jerusalem "a pearl of great price," and that he was reading it for the first time ; ver. 34 is not quite consistent with the supposition that he had heard in Jerusalem rumours of the Apostles' preaching, and of their reference of the prophecies to Jesus of Nazareth : Philip is represented as preaching to him Jesus, and that too as good news. "The eunuch came to worship—great was also his studiousness—observe again his piety, but though he did not understand he read, and after reading, examines," Chrys., *Hom.*, xix., and Jerome, *Epist.*, liii., 5. See also Corn. à Lapide, *in loco*, on the diligence and devotion of the eunuch.

Ver. 29. **τὸ πνεῦμα εἶπεν**: nothing inconsistent with the previous statement that an angel had spoken to him, as Weiss supposes by referring the angel visit to a reviser. There was no reason why the angel should accompany Philip, or reappear to him, whilst the inward guidance of the Spirit would be always present, as our Lord had promised.—**κολλήθητι**, *cf.* v. 13, in Acts five times, and in each case of joining or attaching oneself closely to a person, of social or religious communion with a person, twice in Luke's Gospel, *cf.* xv. 15 for its sense here, and elsewhere only once in the Evangelists, Matt. xix. 5, and that in a quotation, Gen. ii. 24, *cf.* its use three times in St. Paul, Rom. xii. 9, 1 Cor. vi. 16, 17. In classical Greek similar usage, and *cf.* LXX, Ruth ii. 8, Ecclus. ii. 3, xix. 2, 1 Macc. iii. 2, vi. 21, etc. Hebrew

דָבֵק, see Wetstein on x. 28.

Ver. 30. **προσδραμὼν δὲ**: rightly taken to indicate the eagerness with which Philip obeyed.—Ἄρά γε—the γε strengthens the ἄρα, dost thou really understand ? *num igitur ?* ἄρα without γε is only found elsewhere in Luke xviii. 8, and in Gal. ii. 17 (W.H., and also Lightfoot, *Galatians, l.c.*), see Blass, *in*

τούτῳ. 30. προσδραμὼν δὲ ὁ Φίλιππος ἤκουσεν αὐτοῦ ἀναγινώσκοντος
τὸν προφήτην Ἡσαΐαν, καὶ εἶπεν, Ἆρά γε γινώσκεις ἃ ἀναγινώσκεις ;
31. ὁ δὲ εἶπε, Πῶς γὰρ ἂν δυναίμην, ἐὰν μή τις ὁδηγήσῃ [1] με ;
παρεκάλεσέ τε τὸν Φίλιππον ἀναβάντα καθίσαι σὺν αὐτῷ. 32. ἡ δὲ
περιοχὴ τῆς γραφῆς ἣν ἀνεγίνωσκεν, ἦν αὕτη, "Ὡς πρόβατον ἐπὶ
σφαγὴν ἤχθη, καὶ ὡς ἀμνὸς ἐναντίον τοῦ κείροντος [2] αὐτὸν ἄφωνος,
οὕτως οὐκ ἀνοίγει τὸ στόμα αὐτοῦ. 33. ἐν τῇ ταπεινώσει αὐτοῦ ἡ
κρίσις αὐτοῦ ἤρθη,[3] τὴν δὲ γενεὰν αὐτοῦ τίς διηγήσεται ; ὅτι αἴρεται

---

[1] ὁδηγήσῃ AB³HLP, Chrys., so Blass, Weiss; ὁδηγήσει ℵB¹CE 13, so Tisch.,
W.H., R.V., Wendt, Hilg.

[2] κείροντος BP, Orig., so Lach., W.H. text, Blass, Weiss; κείραντος ℵACEHL,
Chrys., so Tisch., W.H. marg., Hilg.   But as Wendt points out, readings vary as
in LXX.

[3] εν τῃ ταπει. . . . ηρθη D, Par., Iren. omit.   Blass brackets in β; may have
been a "Western non-interpolation," or the omission may have been for shortness.
αυτου CEHLP, Syrr. (P. and H.), several verss., Chrys.; om. ℵAB, Vulg., Irint., so
Tisch., W.H., R.V., Blass, so LXX.

loco, and *Grammatik*, p. 254. In LXX
very rare, see Hatch and Redpath, *sub
v.*, and Viteau, *Le Grec du N. T.*, p. 22
(1893).—γιν. ἃ ἀναγ.: for *paronomasia*,
see Blass, *Gram.*, p. 292, where other
instances in N.T. are given, and also
Wetstein, *in loco*.   Julian's well-known
saying with reference to the Christian
writings, and the famous retort, are
quoted by Alford, Plumptre, Page, Meyer-
Wendt, *in loco*.

Ver. 31. γάρ; "elegans particula hoc
sensu *quid quaeris?*" implies, Why do
you ask? for how should I be able? (*cf.*
Matt. xxvii. 23, Mark xv. 14, Luke xxiii.
22); see Simcox, *Language of N. T.
Greek*, p. 172; Grimm-Thayer, *sub v.*, I.
—ἂν δυναίμην: optative with ἄν; occurs
only in Luke, both in his Gospel and
Acts, expressing what would happen on
the fulfilment of some supposed condition: see, for a full list of passages, Burton, *N. T. Moods and Tenses*, p. 80;
Simcox, *u. s.*, p. 112: twice in direct
questions, here and in xvii. 18, but only
in this passage is the condition expressed,
cf. also Viteau, *Le Grec du N. T.*, pp. 33
and 66 (1893).—ὁδηγήσῃ, see critical
notes, and Blass, *Grammatik*, p. 210; if
we read future indicative it will be an
instance of a future supposition thus expressed with more probability, Burton,
u. s., pp. 104, 105, 109, and see also
Simcox, note on the passage, *u. s.*, p.
112.   Burton compares Luke xix. 40
(W.H.), see also Viteau, *u. s.*, pp. 4, 111,
226, whilst Blass maintains that there is
no one certain example of this usage of

ἐάν with future indicative.   The word
used here ("insignis modestia eunuchi,"
Calvin) is used also by our Lord Himself
for the Holy Spirit's leading and guidance, John xvi. 13, and also in the LXX,
as in the Psalms, of divine guidance.
—παρεκάλεσέν: "he besought," R.V.
("desired" A.V.), the word is rightly
taken to denote both the humility and
the earnestness of the eunuch (Bengel):
a verb frequent both in St. Luke and
St. Paul, six or seven times in Gospel,
twenty-two or twenty-three times in Acts.
—τε: note the closing connecting particle, showing the necessary result of the
question (Weiss).

Ver. 32. περιοχὴ τῆς γραφῆς "the
contents of the passage of Scripture" *i.e.*,
the one particular passage, Isa. liii. 7, 8
(so Meyer-Wendt, Holtzmann, Hackett),
cf. i. 16, and 1 Pet. ii. 6: περιέχει ἐν
τῇ γραφῇ and ταύτης in ver. 35 below;
περιοχή has been taken to mean a
section, as in Cicero, *Epist. ad Att.*, xiii.,
25 (so in Codex A, before the Gospel
of St. Mark, its περιοχαί, *i.e.*, *sectiones*,
are prefixed), but in Cicero also Meyer-
Wendt take the word to mean the *contents*
of a passage, *cf.* notes, edit. 1888 and 1899;
see also Felten and Plumptre, *in loco*.
St. Chrysostom apparently takes γραφή
here as = αἱ γραφαί, "totum corpus
scripturae sacræ," see Blass, *in loco*,
but if so, the plural would be used as
always; see above references and Lightfoot on *Gal.*, iii., 22.   The fact that the
eunuch was reading Isaiah is mentioned
by St. Chrysostom as another indication

ἀπὸ τῆς γῆς ἡ ζωὴ αὐτοῦ." 34. ἀποκριθεὶς δὲ ὁ εὐνοῦχος τῷ
Φιλίππῳ εἶπε, Δέομαί σου, περὶ τίνος ὁ προφήτης λέγει τοῦτο ; περὶ
ἑαυτοῦ, ἢ περὶ ἑτέρου τινός ; 35. ἀνοίξας δὲ ὁ Φίλιππος τὸ στόμα
αὐτοῦ, καὶ ἀρξάμενος ἀπὸ τῆς γραφῆς ταύτης, εὐηγγελίσατο αὐτῷ

of character, since he had in hand the prophet who is more sublime than all others, *Hom.*, xix.

Ver. 33. ἐν τῇ ταπεινώσει κ.τ.λ., *cf.* Isa. liii. 7, 8, "in his humiliation his judgment was taken away" (LXX), so A. and R.V., generally taken to mean by his humbling himself his judgment was cancelled, *cf.* Phil. ii. 6, 7, so Wendt in seventh and eighth editions: *cf.* Grimm-Thayer, *sub v.*, κρίσις, the punishment appointed for him was taken away, *i.e.*, ended, and so *sub v.*, αἴρω = to cause to cease, Col. ii. 14. But the words "in his humiliation" etc., may also fairly mean that in the violence and injustice done to him his judgment, *i.e.*, the fair trial due to him, was withheld, and thus they conform more closely to the Hebrew "by oppression and by (unjust) judgment he was taken away," so Hitzig, Ewald, Cheyne and R.V. So to the same effect Delitzsch takes the words to mean that hostile oppression and judicial persecution befel him, and out of them he was removed by death (*cf.* R.V. margin). (The words have been taken to mean that by oppression and judgment he was hurried off and punished, *raptus est ad supplicium*.)—τὴν (δὲ) γενεὰν αὐτοῦ τίς διηγήσεται; (LXX), "his generation who shall declare?" R.V., the words may mean "who shall declare the wickedness of the generation in which he lived?" (see Grimm-Thayer, *sub v.*, γενεά)—their wickedness, *i.e.*, in their treatment of him; so De Wette (and Meyer in early editions), and to the same effect, Lumby, Rendall, *cf.* our Lord's own words, Matt. xii. 39-42, etc. In Meyer-Wendt (seventh and eighth edition) the words are taken to mean "who can fitly declare the number of those who share his life?" *i.e.*, his posterity, his disciples, so Felten (but see on the other hand, Delitzsch, *in loco*). The Hebrew seems to mean, as in R.V. text, "and as for his generation who *among them* considered that he was cut off out of the land of the living? for the transgression of my people" etc., see Cheyne, *in loco* ; Briggs, *Messianic Prophecy*, p. 358, and Delitzsch, *Jesaia*, pp. 523, 524, fourth edition (see also Page's note, and Wendt, edition 1899). The references by the

Fathers (*cf.* Bede and Wordsworth) to the eternal generation of the Son, and the mystery of His Incarnation, do not seem to find support in the Hebrew or in the Greek rendering. On the *oldest* Jewish interpretations of Isaiah liii., see Dalman's *Der leidende und der sterbende Messias*, pp. 21-23, 27-35, 89, 91 ; and see also in connection with the passage before us, Athanasius, *Four Discourses against the Arians*, i., 13, 54, and Dr. Robertson's note ; see also above on St. Peter's Discourses in chap. iii., and below on xxvi. 23.—αἴρεται ἀπὸ τῆς γῆς : "is taken," *i.e.*, with violence (here = Hebrew גזר), *cf.* use of αἴρω, LXX, Acts xxii. 22, xxi. 36, Matt. xxiv. 39, Luke xxiii. 18, John xix. 15.

Ver. 34. ἀποκ., see above iii. 12, v. 8. It has been sometimes supposed that the eunuch was acquainted with the tradition that Isaiah had been sawn asunder by Manasseh — Felten, see Wetstein on Heb. xi. 37.

Ver. 35. ἀνοίξας τὸ στ. αὐτοῦ : the phrase is used to introduce some weighty and important utterance, *cf.* x. 34, xviii. 14, and Luke i. 64, so too Matt. v. 2, 2 Cor. vi. 11, also frequent in LXX ; "aperire os in Scriptura est ordiri longum sermonem de re gravi et seria. Significat ergo Lucas coepisse Philippum pleno ore disserere de Christo," Calvin, *cf.* Hebrew phrase פתח את־פיו, in various senses.—ἀρξάμενος, see on i. 22, *cf.* Luke xxiv. 27.—ταύτης, see above on ver. 32.—εὐηγγελίσατο : used with an accusative both of the person addressed, as in vv. 25, 40, and of the message delivered, *cf.* Luke viii. 1, Acts v. 42, viii. 4, 12, etc., but when the two are combined the person is always expressed by the dative, *cf.* Luke i. 19, ii. 10 (Acts xvii. 18), Simcox, *Language of the N. T.*, p. 79. From the sequel it is evident that Philip not only preached the glad tidings of the fulfilment of the prophecies in Jesus as the ideal and divine Sufferer, but that he also pointed out to the eunuch the door of admission into the Church of Jesus ; *cf.* Jerome, *Epist.*, liii., 5.

Ver. 36. ἰδοὺ ὕδωρ : "intus *fides*, foris *aqua* praesto erat" Bengel. According

τὸν Ἰησοῦν. 36. ὡς δὲ ἐπορεύοντο κατὰ τὴν ὁδόν, ἦλθον ἐπί τι ὕδωρ· καί φησιν ὁ εὐνοῦχος, Ἰδοὺ ὕδωρ· τί κωλύει με βαπτισθῆναι; 37.[1] εἶπε δὲ ὁ Φίλιππος, Εἰ πιστεύεις ἐξ ὅλης τῆς καρδίας, ἔξεστιν. ἀποκριθεὶς δὲ εἶπε, Πιστεύω τὸν υἱὸν τοῦ Θεοῦ εἶναι τὸν Ἰησοῦν Χριστόν. 38. καὶ ἐκέλευσε στῆναι τὸ ἅρμα· καὶ κατέβησαν ἀμφότεροι εἰς τὸ ὕδωρ, ὅ τε Φίλιππος καὶ ὁ εὐνοῦχος· καὶ ἐβάπτισεν

---

[1] The whole verse as it stands in T.R. is read in one form or another, with varying variations, also in Patristic quotations, by E (D is wanting from viii. 29ᵇ–x. 14), 15, and other good cursives, Gig., Par., Wern., Vulg. (clem. + am.ˣˣ demid. tol.), Arm., Syr. Harcl. mg., Iren., Cypr., R.V. marg., and by Hilg.; *om.* by ℵABCHLP 13, 61, Vulg. (am.ˣ fu.), Syr. Pesh. Harcl. text, Sah., Boh., Aeth., Chrys., so Tisch., W.H., Weiss, Wendt, R.V. text. The verse is strongly defended by Belser, *Beiträge*, p. 50, as originally Lucan, but omitted by Luke for brevity as in many other cases—but on the other hand Wendt, edit. 1899, p. 180, note, justly points out that it is difficult to see any reason for its omission, whilst it is easily conceivable that the words would have been inserted perhaps originally as a marginal note, since otherwise the belief of the eunuch is nowhere expressly stated in the text; *cf.* Rom. x. 9 (but *cf.* ii. 41, xvi. 33). But they were evidently known as early as Irenæus, *Adv. Hær.*, iii., 12, as also to Oecumenius and Theophylact, and they may well have expressed what actually happened, as the question in ver. 36 evidently required an answer. Augustine did not question its genuineness, although he refused to shorten the profession at Baptism on account of it, *De Fide et Operibus*, ix. (see W.H., *App.*, p. 93; Felten, crit. notes, p. 177; *Speaker's Comm.*, *in loco*).

---

to Jerome (*Epist.*, ciii.) and Eusebius (περὶ τόπων), the site of the baptism was placed at Bethsura (Bethzur, Josh. xv. 28, 2 Chron. xi. 17, Neh. iii. 16, etc.), about twenty miles from Jerusalem, and two from Hebron. Robinson (*Biblical Researches*, ii., 749) thinks that the place is more probably to be found on the road between Eleutheropolis (Beit-Jibrin) and Gaza, whilst Professor G. A. Smith (see above on ver. 26) considers that the fact that Philip was found immediately after at Azotus suggests that the meeting and baptism took place, not where tradition has placed them, among the hills of Judæa, but on the Philistine plain (*Hist. Geog. of the Holy Land*, pp. 186, 240). But as he finds it impossible to apply the epithet "desert" to any route from Jerusalem to Gaza, whether that by Beit-Jibrin, or the longer one by Hebron, he does not hesitate to apply the epithet to Gaza itself, and as the meeting (according to his view) took place in its neighbourhood, the town would naturally be mentioned. Gaza and Azotus, ver. 40, are the only two Philistine towns named in the N. T.—τί κωλύει με βαπτισθῆναι; "mark the eager desire, mark the exact knowledge . . . see again his modesty; he does not say Baptise me, neither does he hold his peace, but he utters somewhat betwixt strong desire and reverent fear" Chrys., *Hom.*, xix.

Ver. 38. εἰς τὸ ὕδωρ: even if the words are rendered "unto the water" (Plumptre), the context ἀνέβησαν ἐκ indicates that the baptism was by immersion, and there can be no doubt that this was the custom in the early Church. St. Paul's symbolic language in Rom. vi. 4, Col. ii. 12, certainly seems to presuppose that such was the case, as also such types as the Flood, the passage of the Red Sea, the dipping of Naaman in Jordan. But the *Didaché* is fairly quoted to show that at an early period immersion could not have been regarded as essential, *cf.* vii. 3. See also "Teaching of the Apostles," iv., 807, in *Dict. of Christ. Biog.* (Smith & Wace), "Apostellehre" in *Real-Encyclopädie für protestant. Theol. und Kirche* (Hauck), p. 712; "Baptism" in B.D.². "Mutavit Æthiops pellem suam" is the comment of Bede, "id est sorde peccatorum abluta, de lavacro Jesu dealbatus ascendit."

Ver. 39. Πνεῦμα Κ. ἥρπασε: although the expression is simply Πνεῦμα Κ. the reference is evidently to the same divine power as in ver. 29, and cannot be explained as meaning an inward impulse of the Evangelist, or as denoting a hurricane or storm of wind (as even Nösgen and Stier supposed). The article is omitted before Πνεῦμα Κ. in Luke iv. 18, so also in LXX, Isa. lxi. 1, and we

αὐτόν. 39. ὅτε δὲ ἀνέβησαν ἐκ τοῦ ὕδατος, Πνεῦμα Κυρίου ἥρπασε
τὸν Φίλιππον¹· καὶ οὐκ εἶδεν αὐτὸν οὐκέτι εὐνοῦχος, ἐπορεύετο γὰρ

¹ Πνευμα Κ. ηρπασε τον Φ.; instead of this A², Par., Wern., Syr. H. mg., Jer., Aug.
read πνευμα αγιον επεπεσεν επι τον ευνουχον, αγγελος δε Κ. ηρπασεν τον Φ. Wendt
regards as interpolation partly according to ver. 26 and partly according to ver. 44.
Hilg. retains and Belser, p. 51, defends as Lucan. It is fitting that in Scripture the
Holy Ghost is not represented as given after Philip's Baptism, because his work was
to be completed by the advent of Peter and John; but in the case before us no Apostle
was present, and so the Holy Spirit came down miraculously after Philip had baptised
the eunuch. So, too, Hilgenfeld leans towards the reading *l. c.*, and regards it as
just possible that the ordinary text is a set-off against the contradiction involved with
viii. 15-18, in accordance with which the Holy Spirit was only bestowed through the
laying on of the hands of the Apostles. Blass rejects, and follows T.R. (see below).
After Φίλιππον Par., Syr. H. mg. (no other authorities) add "ab eo"; so Hilg., and
so Blass in β, απ' αυτου, which seems somewhat strange in the case of the latter
writer.

cannot therefore conclude anything from
its omission here. ἥρπασε, *abripuit*, the
disappearance, as the context shows, was
regarded as supernatural, *cf.* LXX, 1
Kings xviii. 12, 2 Kings ii. 16 (Ezek. iii.

14, Hebrew only רוח). Thus Hilgenfeld recognises not only a likeness here
to the O.T. passages quoted, but that
a miraculous transference of Philip to
another place is implied. No doubt, as
Hilgenfeld points out, πνεῦμα may mean
wind, John iii. 8, but this by no means
justifies exclusion of all reference here to
the Holy Spirit. No doubt we may see
with Blass a likeness in the language of the
narrative to the O.T. passages just cited,
and St. Luke's informants may have been
the daughters of Philip, who were themselves προφήτιδες (see Blass, *in loco*);
but there is no reason why he should not
have heard the narrative from St. Philip
himself, and the rendering πνεῦμα by
ventus is not satisfactory, although Blass
fully recognises that Philip departed by
the same *divine* impulse as that by which
he had come. Holtzmann endorses the
reference to the O.T. passages above, but
specially draws attention to the parallel
which he supposes in Bel and the
Dragon, ver. 34 ff. But this passage
should be contrasted rather than compared with the simple narrative of the
text, so free from any fantastic embellishment, while plainly implying a supernatural element: *cf.* for the verb ἁρπάζω,
1 Thess. iv. 17, 2 Cor. xii. 2, 4 (a reference
to which as explaining Philip's withdrawal is not to the point, since the narrative cannot imply that Philip was ἐκτὸς
τοῦ σώματος), Rev. xii. 5, used of a
snatching or taking up due to divine
agency, *cf.* Wisdom iv. 11, where it is

said of Enoch ἡρπάγη. Both in classical
Greek and in the LXX the word implies
forcible or sudden seizure (John vi. 15).
—καὶ οὐκ εἶδεν . . . ἐπορεύετο γὰρ κ.τ.λ.
If these two clauses are closely connected
as by R.V., they do not simply state
that the eunuch went on *his own* way
(Rendall), (in contrast with Philip who
went *his* way), rejoicing in the good
news which he had heard, and in the
baptism which he had received; and
R.V. punctuation surely need not prevent
the disappearance of Philip from being
viewed as mysterious, even if the words
καὶ οὐκ εἶδον αὐτὸν οὐκέτι do not
imply this. Moreover αὐτοῦ may rather
emphasise the fact that the eunuch went
his way, which he would not have done
had he seen Philip, but would perhaps
have followed him who had thus enlightened his path (so Weiss, *in loco*,
reading αὐτοῦ τὴν ὁδόν—αὐτοῦ emphatic:
see also St. Chrysostom's comment *in
loco*).—χαίρων: "the fruit of the Spirit
is . . . joy," Gal. v. 22 (the word at the
end of a clause is characteristic of Luke;
Luke xv. 5, xix. 6, see Vogel, p. 45).
Eusebius describes the eunuch, to whom
he gives the name of Indich, as the first
preacher to his countrymen of the tidings
of great joy, and on the possible reception
in the earliest Christian times of the
Gospel message in the island of Meroë at
least, see "Ethiopian Church," *Dict. of
Christ. Biog.*, ii., 234 (Smith & Wace).
In the conversion of the Ethiopian eunuch
men have seen the first fulfilment of the
ancient prophecy, Ps. lxviii. 31 (Luckock,
*Footprints of the Apostles as traced
by St Luke*, i., 219, and C. and H.,
p. 66).
Ver. 40. εὑρέθη εἰς "Α.: *constructio
prægnans* = was borne to and found at,

τὴν ὁδὸν αὐτοῦ χαίρων. 40. Φίλιππος δὲ εὑρέθη εἰς Ἄζωτον· καὶ
διερχόμενος εὐηγγελίζετο τὰς πόλεις πάσας, ἕως τοῦ ἐλθεῖν αὐτὸν
εἰς Καισάρειαν.[1]

[1] Καισαρειαν BCHLP, so Blass, Weiss, Hilg.; Καισαριαν ‭א‬AE 61, so Tisch.,
W.H. (see W.H., *App.*, p. 160, and Winer-Schmiedel, p. 45).

cf. xxi. 13; or, as εἰς means more than
ἐν, implying that he had come *into* the
city and was staying there, *cf.* Esth. i. 5;
marg. Hebrew "found," A.V., εὑρίσκω,
‭מצא‬, is very often found in the LXX
in similar phrases, *e.g.*, 1 Chron. xxix.
17, 2 Chron. xxxi. 1, 1 Sam. xiii. 15, etc.
The word may imply, however, much
more than the fact that Philip *was present*
at Azotus, and Alford sees in it a probable reference to 2 Kings ii. 17 (*cf.*
passages in O.T. above), where the same
word is used, εὑρέθη. Blass takes it to
mean "vento quasi ibi dejectus," but see
above on ver. 39.—Ἄζωτον, ‭אשׁדוד‬:
only mentioned here in N.T., but in
LXX Ashdod, Josh. xi. 22, xiii. 3, xv. 46,
1 Sam. v. 5, 2 Chron. xxvi. 6, Neh. iv. 7,
xiii. 20, Jer. xx. 20, xlvii. 5, Amos i. 8,
Zeph. ii. 4, Zech. ix. 6; Azotus in 1 Macc.
v. 18, x. 84; Herod., ii., 157: Herod. speaks
of the siege of the twenty-nine years under
Psammetichus as the longest in history
(ζ = σδ, as in Ὡρομάζης, *Ahuramazda*,
Blass, *in loco*). An old Philistine town,
and one of the five chief cities—it might
be regarded as the half-way station on the
great road between Gaza and Joppa.
Schürer holds that the population was
Jewish to a considerable extent, as we
find that Vespasian was obliged to place
a garrison there (Jos., *B. J.*, iv., 3, 2);
it is now a mere village of no importance, and still bearing the name *Esdûd*.
Schürer, *Jewish People*, div. ii., vol. i.,
pp. 62, 67 ff., E.T.; G. A. Smith, *Hist.
Geog. of the Holy Land*, pp. 192, 193; Hamburger, *Real-Encyclopädie des Judentums*,
i., 1, 124, "Ashdod," B.D.[2], "Azotus,"
and also Col. Conder *sub v.*, Hastings'
B.D.—διερχόμενος εὐηγγελ., see above
on ver. 4 and also xiii. 6, and *cf.*
Luke ix. 6 for a similar combination
of the two verbs.—τὰς πόλεις πάσας:
from their position between Azotus and
Cæsarea, Lydda and Joppa may well
have been included, *cf.* ix. 32, 36, in
which we may see something of the
effects of St. Philip's preaching, "hic
quoque, uti in urbe Samariæ, Apostolis
auditores præparavit," Bengel. — Και-
σαρείαν (mentioned no less than fifteen

times in Acts): its full name was Και-
σαρεία Σεβαστή, so named by Herod
the Great in honour of Augustus (Jos.,
Ant., xvi., 5, 1); sometimes also παρά-
λιος or ἡ ἐπὶ θαλάττη (Jos., *B. J.*, iii.,
9, 1; vii., 1, 3); it was also called
"Straton's Tower" (*cf.* Κ. ἡ Στράτωνος,
Apost. Const., vi., 12), although it was
virtually a fresh site. Schürer derives this
latter name from Straton, the name of
one or more of the last kings of Sidon,
who towards the end of the Persian
period were probably in possession of
the strip of coast upon which the tower
was built (Schürer, *u. s.*, div. ii., vol. i.,
p. 84 ff.). Herod's lavish expenditure
and enlargement gave it such importance that it came to be called *Caput
Judaeæ*, Tacitus, *Hist.*, ii., 79, *i.e.*,
of the Roman Province, for it never
could be called truly Judæan. For its
magnificence, see Jos., *Ant.*, xv., 9;
B. J., i., 21, *cf. Ant.*, xvi., 5. It
was a seaport suited to his taste,
which Herod wanted, and in Cæsarea
he found it—"Joppa, Jerusalem's port,
was Jewish, national, patriotic; Cæsarea,
Herodian, Roman in obedience, Greek
in culture". The buildings were
magnificent — a temple with its two
statues of Augustus and of Rome, a
theatre, an amphitheatre; but above all,
the haven was the chief work of art,
Sebastos Limen, so large and important
that the name of the city was even
dwarfed beside it (see especially Dr. G.
A. Smith, *u. s.*, p. 140). Here the Roman
procurators had their abode, both before
and after Agrippa's reign; here, too, was
the chief garrison of the troops of the
province. The population was chiefly
heathen, but with a considerable mixture
of Jews, and so both Gentile and Jew
had equal rights, while each claimed exclusive powers. In the time of Felix
things came to such a pass that bloodshed ensued, and Felix exasperated the
Jews by leaving the sole direction of the
town in the hands of the heathen party.
It was this which in the first place provoked the great rising of the Jews, A.D.
66 (Jos., *Ant.*, xx., 8, 7, 9; *B. J.*, ii., 13,
7; 14, 4, 5). The war broke out, and,
according to Josephus, all the Jewish in-

IX. 1. Ὁ ΔΕ Σαῦλος ἔτι ἐμπνέων ἀπειλῆς καὶ φόνου εἰς τοὺς μαθητὰς τοῦ Κυρίου, προσελθὼν τῷ ἀρχιερεῖ, 2. ᾐτήσατο παρ᾽ αὐτοῦ ἐπιστολὰς εἰς Δαμασκὸν πρὸς τὰς συναγωγάς, ὅπως ἐάν τινας εὕρῃ τῆς ὁδοῦ ὄντας ἄνδρας τε καὶ γυναῖκας, δεδεμένους ἀγάγῃ εἰς

habitants, twenty thousand in number, were massacred in an hour. Here the famous Rabbi Akiba met a martyr's death, here Eusebius of Cæsarea and Procopius were born, and hither Origen fled. See Schürer, *u. s.;* Hamburger, *Real-Encyclopädie des Judentums,* ii., 1, 123; G. A. Smith, *u. s.,* pp. 138, 143 ff., B.D.[2]; Edersheim, *History of the Jewish Nation,* pp. 21, 23, 156, 199, 251, 265, etc. Among the Jews Cæsarea was called by the same name by which we know it, but sometimes from its fortifications, Migdal Shur, or after its harbour, Migdal Shina, or after both, and once by its ancient name, "Straton's Tower" (*cf.* also *Strabo,* xvi., p. 758), but as the seat of the Roman power, and for its preponderating heathen population, it was specially hated; and so it was designated "the daughter of Edom," although the district, so rich and fertile, was still called "the land of life". Edersheim, *Jewish Social Life,* pp. 24, 72, 202, and Hamburger, *u.s.* Cæsarea is mentioned in the verse before us not because of its political and commercial importance, but because it became the after home of Philip, xxi. 8. But it also might be named here as marking a further and interesting stage in the progress of the Gospel (see also below on chap. x.). We cannot say whether at the time of the narrative in chap. x. Philip had already settled and worked in Cæsarea.

CHAPTER IX.—Ver. 1. Ὁ δὲ Σαῦλος: takes up and continues the narrative from viii. 3; the resumptive use of δέ.—ἔτι: "Sic in summo fervore peccandi ereptus et conversus est" Bengel.—ἐμπνέων: only here in N.T., not "breathing out," A.V., but rather "breathing of," lit., "in" (R.V. simply "breathing"), *cf.* LXX, Josh. x. 40; πᾶν ἐμπνέον ζωῆς (*cf.* Ps. xvii. 15)—threatening and murdering were as it were the atmosphere which he breathed, and in and by which he lived, *cf.* Stobæus, *Flor.,* 85, 19, ὀδμῆς ἐμπνέοντα, L. and S. and Blass, *in loco* (*cf.* also Aristoph., *Eq.,* 437, οὗτος ἤδη κακίας καὶ συκοφαντίας πνεῖ, and Winer-Moulton, xxx., 9).—τῷ ἀρχιερεῖ: probably Joseph Caiaphas, who continues thus to persecute the Church, see on iv. 6 (v. 17); he held office until 36 A.D., see Zöckler's note, *in loco,* and

"Caiaphas," B.D.[2], and Hastings' B.D. "Saul as a Pharisee makes request of a Sadducee!" says Felten.

Ver. 2. ᾐτήσατο, see on iii. 2, with παρά, in iii. 3, we have the imperfect, but "inest in aoristo quod etiam accepit," Blass; on the use of the verb in N.T., see also Blass, *Gram.,* p. 182, and Grimm-Thayer, *sub v.*—ἐπιστολάς, *cf.* xxii. 5, xxvi. 12; on the jurisdiction of the Sanhedrim, see above on iv. 5; Weber, *Jüdische Theol.,* p. 141 (1897); O. Holtzmann, *Neutest. Zeitgeschichte,* pp. 174, 175; and Schürer, *Jewish People,* div. ii., vol. i., p. 185, E.T.: only within the limits of Judæa had the Sanhedrim any direct authority, although its orders were regarded as binding over *every* Jewish community. But the extent to which this obligation prevailed depended on the disposition of the Jewish communities towards the Sanhedrim.—Δαμασκόν: "In the history of religion," writes Dr. G. A. Smith, "Damascus was the stage of two great crises. She was the scene of the conversion of the first Apostle of Christianity to the Gentiles; she was the first Christian city to be taken by Islam. It was fit that Paul's conversion, with his first sense of a mission to the Gentiles, should not take place till his journey had brought him to Jewish soil." If Damascus was not the oldest, it may at all events be called the most enduring city in the world. According to Josephus, *Ant.,* i., 6, 4, it was founded by Uz, the grandson of Shem, whilst a Moslem tradition makes Eliezer its founder, and Abraham its king (see also Jos., *Ant.,* i., 7, 2). Here, too, was the traditional scene of the murder of Abel (Shakespeare, 1 *King Henry VI.,* i., 3). Damascus was situated some seventy miles from the seaboard (about six or eight days' journey from Jerusalem), to the east of Anti-Lebanon in a great plain, watered by the river Abana with her seven streams, to which the city owes her beauty and her charm. Travellers of every age and of every nationality have celebrated the gardens and orchards, the running waters and the fountains of Damascus, and as the Arab passes from the burning desert to its cooling streams and rich verdure, it is not surprising that he hails it as an earthly paradise. From

Ἰερουσαλήμ. 3. ἐν δὲ τῷ πορεύεσθαι, ἐγένετο αὐτὸν ἐγγίζειν τῇ
Δαμασκῷ, καὶ ἐξαίφνης¹ περιήστραψεν αὐτὸν φῶς ἀπὸ τοῦ οὐρανοῦ ·

¹ ἐξαιφνης—in אB¹CE 13 ἐξεφνης, so W.H., but see xxii. 6. ; see Winer-
Schmiedel, p. 47.

a commercial point of view Damascus
has been called the meeting-place and
mart of the nations, and whilst the
armies of the ancient world passed
through her streets, she was also the
great avenue of communication for the
wealth of north and south, east and
west (cf. the significant passage, Ezek.
xxvii. 16, 18, and Amos iii. 12, R.V.,
from which it seems that the city was
known at an early date for her own
manufactures, although the passing trade
of the caravans would be its chief source
of income). For its political position at
the period of Acts, see below on ver.
24, and for its history in the O.T., its
after struggles, and its present position as
still the chief city of Syria, see G. A.
Smith, *Hist. Geog.*, p. 641 ff.; Hamburger, *Real-Encyclopädie des Judentums*,
i., 2, p. 220, B.D.² ; and Hastings'
B.D., Conybeare and Howson (smaller
edition, p. 67 ff.) ; Schürer, *Jewish
People*, div. ii., vol. i., p. 96, E.T.—
πρὸς τὰς συναγωγάς, cf. vi. 9, as at
Jerusalem—the number of Jews dwelling
in Damascus was so numerous that in a
tumult under Nero ten thousand were
put to death, Jos., *B. J.*, vii., 8, 7 ; ii., 20,
2 ; as at Jerusalem, the Christians of
Damascus may not as yet have formally
separated from their Jewish brethren ;
cf. the description of Ananias in xxii.
12 ; but as communication between
Damascus and the capital was very frequent, refugees from Jerusalem would
no doubt have fled to Damascus, and it
is difficult to believe that the views advocated by Stephen had in him their sole
representative. There is no reason to
question with Overbeck the existence in
Damascus of a community of believers in
the claims of Jesus at this early date ;
but whilst those Christians who de-
voutly observed the law would not have
aroused hostility hitherto, Saul came
armed with a commission against all
who called on the name of Christ, and
so probably his object was not only to
bring back the refugees to Jerusalem,
but also to stir up the synagogue at
Damascus against their own fellow-
worshippers who acknowledged that
Jesus was the Christ.—ἐάν τινας εὕρῃ :
the phrase does not mean that the exist-

ence of Christians was doubtful, but
whether Saul would succeed in finding
them out (Weiss).—ὄντες τῆς ὁδοῦ : the
genitive with εἶναι or γίγνεσθαι, very common in N.T. (as in classical Greek) ; may
be explained as the genitive of the *class* to
which a man belongs, or as the genitive
of the property in which any one partici-
pates, expressed by the genitive singular
of an abstract noun, and also, as here, of
a concrete noun, Winer-Moulton, xxx.,
5, *c.* (and Winer-Schmiedel, pp. 269,
270). "The Way," R.V., all E.V.,
"this way," except Wycliff, who has " of
this life," apparently reading *vitæ* instead
of *viæ* in the Vulgate ; see Humphry on
the R.V., *in loco*. (In xviii. 25 we have
τὴν ὁδὸν τοῦ K. of the instruction given
to Apollos, cf. the common metaphorical
use of the word in LXX.) In the text
(as in xix. 9, xxii. 4, xxiv. 14, 22) the
noun is used absolutely, and this use is
peculiar to St. Luke (cf. ὁ λόγος, sc., τοῦ
θ., x. 44, xiv. 25, etc., and τὸ ὄνομα, v.
41). The term may have originated
amongst the Jews who saw in the
Christians those who adopted a special
way or mode of life, or a special form of
their own national belief, but if so, the
Christians would see in it *nomen et
omen*—in Christ *they* had found the
Way, the Truth, the Life, John xiv. 6
(so Holtzmann points out the parallel in
St. John, and thus accounts for the
article τῆς ὁδοῦ—there is only one way
of salvation, *viz.*, Christ). Chrysostom
(so Theophylact) thinks that the believers were probably so called because
of their taking the direct way that leads
to heaven (*Hom.*, xix.) : see also Dean
Plumptre's interesting note. The expression seems to point to the early date
of Acts. As it is used thus, absolutely,
and with no explanation in the context, Hilgenfeld sees in chap. ix. the
commencement of a third source C
(see *Introd.*, p. 29). — γυναῖκας, see
above on viii. 3. Although no doubt
the women referred to were Jewesses,
yet it is of interest to note the remark of
Josephus, *B. J.*, ii., 20, 2, *viz.*, that the
women of Damascus were addicted to
the Jewish religion. Their mention
also indicates the violence of Saul :
" quod nullum sexus respectum habuit,

4. καὶ πεσὼν ἐπὶ τὴν γῆν,[1] ἤκουσε φωνὴν λέγουσαν αὐτῷ, Σαούλ,
Σαούλ, τί με διώκεις; 5. εἶπε δέ, Τίς εἶ, Κύριε[2]; ὁ δὲ Κύριος εἶπεν,

[1] After γην Par. (Flor.) add "cum magna mentis alienatione"; μετα μεγαλης
εκστασεως, so Blass; cf. rendering of εκστασις in x. 10. Hilg. adds the words
αληθως και after γην. After διωκεις E. Syr. Harcl. mg. add σκληρον σοι κ.τ.λ.,
but cf. xxvi. 14—Blass rejects.

[2] Κυριος ειπεν HLP, Syrr. (P. and H.), Sah.; om. ABC, Vulg., so Tisch., W.H.,
R.V., Blass, Weiss; om. K., reading ο δε ειπεν, א,‎ Boh., Arm.

cui etiam armati hostes in medio belli
ardore parcere solent" Calvin.

Ver. 3. ἐν δὲ τῷ πορεύεσθαι, ἐγένετο:
on the frequency of the infinitive as here,
and of ἐγένετο in St. Luke, see Friedrich,
Das Lucasevangelium, p. 13, but whilst
St. Luke, even more than the other
Evangelists, connects his narratives by
more or less Hebraistic formulæ, so he
often tones down the Hebraism by
changes of order or other modifications,
cf. Luke i. 8, 9, v. 17, vi. 1, Acts iv. 5,
and ix. 3, etc., see especially Simcox,
Writers of the N. T., p. 19, cf. also
Blass, Gram., pp. 232, 234.—ἐγγίζειν τῇ
Δ.: for a recent description of the three
roads which lead from Jerusalem to
Damascus, see Luckock, Footprints of
the Apostles as traced by St. Luke, i., pp.
223, 224. We may well believe that
Saul in his haste and passion would
choose the quickest and best frequented
route which ran straight to Shechem,
and after inclining to the east, by the
shores of the lake of Galilee, leads straight
to Damascus, with an entrance on the
south; possibly he may have been stirred
to "exceeding madness" by seeing in
the Samaritan villages indications of
the spread of the faith which it was his
purpose to destroy (Plumptre, Expositor,
p. 28 (1878)). Ramsay, Expositor, p. 199,
note (1898), follows the old tradition as
to the locality (following Sir C. Wilson).
But, as he points out, this locality fixed
at Kaukab (so Luckock, also u. s.), some
ten or twelve miles from Damascus, was
changed in modern times for a site
nearer the city (so the Romanist commentator Felten, p. 185, laying stress
on ἐγγίζειν); but the spot so chosen
seems an impossible one from the fact
that it is on the east side of the city,
not on the south; see also "Damascus"
Hastings' B.D., i., 548. Moreover the
tradition for this site (one out of four
selected at different times) does not
appear to have existed for more than some
two hundred years, and although we
can well understand the action of the
Christians in Damascus, who, on St.

Paul's Day, walk in procession to this
traditional site, and read the narrative of
the Apostle's wonderful conversion, it
seems that there is no adequate evidence
in support of the spot selected. "It
was a true instinct that led the Church
to take the Conversion as the day of
St. Paul. For other saints and martyrs
their day of celebration was their dies
natalis, the day on which they entered
their real life, their day of martyrdom.
But the dies natalis of St. Paul, the day
on which his true life began, was the
day of his Conversion," Ramsay, Expositor, p. 28 (1898).—ἐξαίφνης: the word
is used by St. Luke twice in his Gospel
and twice in the Acts—only once elsewhere, Mark xiii. 36. Hobart and Zahn
claim it as a medical term, and it was no
doubt frequent amongst medical writers,
as in Hippocrates and Galen (Hobart,
Medical Language of St. Luke, pp. 19, 20),
but the word is also used in LXX several
times in same sense as here.—περιήστραψεν: only twice in N.T.—not found
at all in classical Greek, but see 4 Macc.
iv. 10. The simple verb occurs in Luke
xvii. 24, xxiv. 4. The word is used in St.
Paul's own account of the event (xxii. 6),
(and περιλάμψαν in his second account
xxvi. 13); noun in classical Greek of
flashing like lightning. In xxii. 6 the time
is fixed "about noon," and in xxvi. 13 it
is said that the light was "above the
brightness of the sun," and shone round
about those who journeyed with Paul.
But St. Luke states the general fact, and
St. Paul, as was natural, is more explicit
in his own account. But St. Paul's
mention of the time of day, when an
Eastern sun was at its brightest, and
of the exceeding glory of the light,
evidently indicates that no natural
phenomenon was implied.

Ver. 4. καὶ πεσὼν ἐπὶ τὴν γῆν, cf.
xxii. 7, both expressions show the overwhelming impression made by the sudden
bright light. In xxvi. 14 all fall to the
ground, but there is no contradiction with
ix. 7, see below on verse 7. Lewin, Farrar
(so Hackett, and some early interpreters)

Ἐγώ εἰμι Ἰησοῦς[1] ὃν σὺ διώκεις[2]· σκληρόν σοι πρὸς κέντρα λακτίζειν.
6. τρέμων τε καὶ θαμβῶν εἶπε, Κύριε, τί με θέλεις ποιῆσαι; καὶ ὁ

[1] Ἰησους ℵABLP, Vulg., Sah., Boh., Syr. Harcl. text, Arm., Orig., so Tisch.,
W.H., Blass, Weiss; Ι. ο Ναζ. ACE 25, Par., Flor. (Vulg. demid.), Syr. (Pesh. and
Harcl.), Aeth., Hil., but cf. xx. 8—Blass rejects; Hilg. retains.

[2] After διωκεις Flor., Gig., Par., Wern., Vulg. (fu. demid.), Syr. Harcl. mg. read
σκληρον σοι Ι. κ.τ.λ. So, too, the same authorities (– Gig., Wer. + Hil.) read also
ο δε τρεμων τε και θαμβων ειπε, Κυριε . . . αυτον—Blass receives, so too Hilg.
For all this between διωκ. and αναστηθι the true reading appears to be αλλα (all
else omitted), ℵABCEHLP, Vulg. (am.), Syr. P. and H. text, Sah., Boh., Arm.,
Tisch., Chrys.; evidence for insertions purely Western—inserted under influence of
xxii. and xxvi. After θαμβων all these Western authorities except Vulg. add επι τω
γεγονοτι αυτω; this is a clear case of assimilation to iii. 10. There seems no Greek
authority for the whole insertion; apparently a retranslation by Erasmus from
the Latin.

have held that Saul and some at least
of his companions were mounted, since
Saul was the emissary of the high priest,
and the journey would occupy some days.
On the other hand Felten (following
Corn. à Lapide) holds that the text makes
no suggestion of this, and that the expression " they led him by the hand " and
the command "rise and enter into the
city" are against it; but the near neighbourhood of Damascus might easily
account for the fact that his companions
led Saul by the hand for the remaining
distance, which could not have been
long, although the immediate proximity
of the traditional site cannot be maintained (see above on ver. 3). As the
strict Jews, like the Pharisees, seldom
used horses, Felten may be right in con-
jecturing that Saul rode upon an ass or
a mule (p. 186, note).—ἤκουσε φωνὴν
λέγουσαν: in St. Paul's own account we
have ἤκουσα φωνῆς λεγούσης, xxii. 7,
and ἤκουσα φωνὴν λέγ., as here, in xxvi.
14. It would seem therefore that the
distinction between ἀκούειν with (1)
accusative, and (2) genitive; (1) to hear
and understand, (2) to hear, merely,
cannot be pressed (so Alford, in loco, and
Simcox, Language of N. T., p. 90, and
Weiss on xxii. 7; but see on the other
hand Rendall on ix., ver. 7). Thus in
the passage before us it has been usual
to explain ἀκούειν with φωνήν, ver. 4,
as indicating that Saul not only heard
but understood the voice, cf. xxii. 14,
whilst ἀκούειν with φωνῆς, ver. 7, has
been taken to show that his comrades
heard, but did not understand (so Weiss,
in loco, and also on xxii. 9). But there
is (1) no contradiction with xxii. 9, for
there it is said of Paul's companions : τὴν
δὲ φωνὴν οὐκ ἤκουσαν τοῦ λαλοῦντός
μοι—they heard the utterance, ix. 7, xxii.

7, but did not hear definitely, or understand who it was that spoke, μηδένα δὲ
θεωροῦντες. But (2) on comparing the
passages together, it appears that in ix.
4 and 7 a distinction is drawn between the
contents of the utterance and the mere
sound of the voice, a distinction drawn
by the accusative and genitive; in xxii. 7
the same distinction is really maintained,
and by the same cases, since in xxii. 7
Paul, in speaking of himself, says that he
heard a voice, i.e., was conscious of a
voice speaking to him (genitive, φωνῆς),
(Simcox, u. s., p. 85), whilst in ver. 9
(accusative φωνήν) the contents of the
utterance are referred to, cf. ver. 14 in the
same chapter; in xxvi. 14 the accusative
is rightly used for the contents of the
utterance which are given there more
fully than elsewhere.—Σαούλ, Σαούλ:
in each of the three narratives of the
Conversion it is significant that the
Hebrew form is thus given, and it is
also found in the address of Ananias,
probably himself a Hebrew, ver. 17, to
the new convert. On the emphatic and
solemn repetition of the name cf. Gen.
xxii. 11, and in the N.T., Luke x. 41,
xxii. 31, Matt. xxiii. 37, and on the frequency of this repetition of a name as
characteristic of Luke in Gospel and Acts
see Friedrich, pp. 75, 76, cf. Luke viii.
24, x. 41, xxii. 31, cf. xxiii. 21 (see also
Deissmann's note Bibelstudien, p. 184,
on the introduction of the Hebrew name).
—τί με διώκεις; cf. vii. 52, and 1 Cor.
xv. 9, Gal. i. 13. " Saul's first lesson
was the mystical union between Christ
and His Church " cf. Matt. x. 40, xxv.
40, 45, John x. 16, etc. No wonder that
Felten sees " an ineffable pathos " in the
words; Wendt quotes St. Augustine:
" caput pro membris clamabat," cf. also
Corn. à Lapide: " corpus enim mysti-

Κύριος πρὸς αὐτόν, Ἀνάστηθι καὶ εἴσελθε εἰς τὴν πόλιν, καὶ λαληθήσεταί σοι τί σε δεῖ ποιεῖν. 7. οἱ δὲ ἄνδρες οἱ συνοδεύοντες αὐτῷ
εἱστήκεισαν ἐννεοί,[1] ἀκούοντες μὲν τῆς φωνῆς, μηδένα δὲ θεωροῦντες.
8. ἠγέρθη δὲ ὁ Σαῦλος ἀπὸ τῆς γῆς· ἀνεῳγμένων δὲ τῶν ὀφθαλμῶν
αὐτοῦ, οὐδένα ἔβλεπε, χειραγωγοῦντες δὲ αὐτὸν εἰσήγαγον εἰς

---

[1] εννεοι L; but ενεοι ℵABCEHP 61, Syr. Harcl. mg., so Tisch., W.H., Blass,
Hilg.; see Winer-Schmiedel, p. 55. Blass reconstructs the conclusion of ver. 7 and
the first half of ver. 8; Flor. (and partly Gig., Par., Wern.) μηδενα δε θεωρ. μεθ᾽ ου
ελαλει· εφη δε προς αυτους· εγειρατε με απο της γης και εγειραντων δε αυτον ουδεν
εβλ. ανεωγμ. τ. οφθ. χειραγωγ. τε—probably these additions arose partly from the
wish to explain the μηδενα standing absolutely in ver. 7 (cf. xxii. 9), partly to represent the blindness as coming on Saul at once (and not after he had risen), and thus
making him need immediate help.

---

cum Christi est ecclesia, membra sunt
fideles".

Ver. 5. **Τίς εἶ, Κύριε;** the title is here
used in reverent and awestruck response
to the question of a speaker, in whose
voice, accompanied as it was by the
supernatural light, Saul recognised a
divine utterance—it is therefore more
than a mere word of respect, as in xvi.
30, xxv. 26; it indicates, as St. Chrysostom noted, a purpose to follow the
voice, whether it was that of an angel
or of God Himself (Felten), "Jam parat
se ad obediendum, qui prius insaniebat ad
persequendum," Augustine.—**Ἐγὼ . . .
σὺ**: both pronouns are emphatic, and
contrasted: **Ἰησοῦς**, cf. xx. 8, and note.
For rest of verse see critical notes.

Ver. 6. For this verse see critical
notes and also xxii. 10. **Ἀνάστηθι**: verb
characteristic of St. Luke, see on v. 7.
Here, if we compare xxvi. 16 (xiv. 10), it
is evidently used in a literal sense.—**καὶ
λαληθήσεταί σοι,** see note on xxvi. 15.

Ver. 7. **οἱ συνοδεύοντες**: probably
riding in company with him; not found
in classical Greek, but used in the same
sense as here in Plutarch—not elsewhere
in N. T; but see Wisdom vi. 23, and Tobit
v. 16 S (AB al.), so according to S[1] in
Zech. viii. 21 (ABS[3] al.), cf. also Symm.
in Gen. xxxiii. 12.—**εἱστήκεισαν ἐννεοί.**
The form **ἐννεός** is incorrect, see critical
notes: in LXX, cf. Prov. xvii. 28, Isa. lvi.
10, Epist. of Jer. 41 (Symm. in Hos. ix. 7);
see critical notes. It is frivolous to find
a contradiction here with xxvi. 14. No
stress is laid upon **εἱστήκ.**, which may be
used like **εἶναι**, and even if there is, it
does not preclude a previous falling. We
have merely to suppose that the sight
and sound had affected Saul's companions in a less degree than Saul, and
that they rose from the ground before

him, to make the narratives quite consistent (see Felten, p. 193, Hackett, in
loco; B.D.[1], iv., "Paul" p. 733). Or it
is quite possible, as Weiss points out on
xxvi. 14, that here the narrative emphasises the impression made by the
hearing of the voice, and in xxvi. 14 the
immediate result produced by the light,
and that the narrator is quite unconscious
of any contradiction in his recital (see
notes below on xxii., xxvi.).—**μηδένα δὲ
θεωροῦντες**: there is no contradiction between this statement and xxii. 9, where
it is said that they saw the light—here it
is not denied that they saw a light, but
only that they saw no person. Holtzmann apparently forgets this, and says
that whilst in xxix. 9 they see the light,
in ix. 7 they see nothing; but the pronoun is not neuter, but masculine; **μηδένα**
(see critical notes and reading in β). The
inference is that Saul saw Jesus, but although this is not stated in so many
words here, it is also to be inferred from
the words of Ananias in ver. 17, and xxii.
14, and from St. Paul's own statement in
1 Cor. xv. 8, and ix. 1. St. Chrysostom
refers **ἀκούοντες μὲν τῆς φ.** to the words
of Saul, but this is certainly not natural,
for **τῆς φ.** evidently refers back to **ἤκουσα
φωνήν** in ver. 4.

Ver. 8. **ἀνεῳγμένων**; see critical notes.
—**οὐδένα ἔβλεπε**: his eyes, which he
had closed mechanically, as he fell overwhelmed with the dazzling brightness
of the light, and of the appearance of
Jesus, he now opens, but only to find
that he saw nothing (**οὐδέν**) (see critical
note)—he had become blind (so Weiss
and Wendt, cf. xxii. 11). This blindness was the clearest proof that the
appearances vouchsafed to him had been
a reality (Felten), see also ver. 18.—
χειραγωγοῦντες: the necessary result of

Δαμασκόν. 9. καὶ ἦν ἡμέρας τρεῖς μὴ βλέπων, καὶ οὐκ ἔφαγεν
οὐδὲ ἔπιεν. 10. Ἦν δέ τις μαθητὴς ἐν Δαμασκῷ ὀνόματι Ἀνανίας,
καὶ εἶπε πρὸς αὐτὸν ὁ Κύριος ἐν ὁράματι, Ἀνανία. ὁ δὲ εἶπεν, Ἰδοὺ

his blindness, cf. Judg. xvi. 26 and Tob. xi. 16, but in each case the reading is varied (see H. and R.); in N.T. only in Acts, cf. xxii. 11 (and see xiii. 11); it is also found in the Apocryphal *Gospel of Peter*, x. (ver. 40 in Harnack's edition). "He who would strike others was himself struck, and the proud Pharisee became a deeply humbled penitent—a guide of the blind" he was himself to be guided by others (Felten).

Ver. 9. ἦν . . . μὴ βλέπων: on ἦν with participle, characteristic, see above on chap. i. 10. Wendt (in seventh edition, not in eighth), and so Felten, Alford, Hackett, distinguish between μή and οὐ with ἔφαγεν and ἔπιεν, and see especially Winer-Moulton, lv., 5. οὐ β. would have simply meant *blind; μὴ β.* is *not seeing (not able to see)*—said of one who had been, and might appear to be again, possessed of sight; the not eating and not drinking are related simply as matters of fact; see the whole section. Blass regards μή with participle as simply = οὐ, so in ver. 7 μηδένα with participle = οὐδένα, *ut alias* (see also Lumby's note).—οὐκ ἔφαγ. κ.τ.λ.: there is no reason why the words should not be taken literally, in spite of Wendt's objection as against Meyer *in loco*, as an expression of penitential sorrow and contrition for his perversity (so Weiss and Holtzmann, no less than Felten): "with what fervour must he then have prayed for 'more light'" (Felten). On Saul's blindness and its possibly lasting effects, see Plumptre, *in loco*, Felten, p. 196, and on the other hand Lightfoot on Gal. vi. 11, and Ramsay, *St. Paul the Traveller*, etc., pp. 38, 39.

Ver. 10. Ἀνανίας: *nomen et omen*, "Jehovah is gracious" (*cf.* xxii. 12). No doubt a Jewish Christian (he is supposed by some, as by St. Augustine, to have been the presbyter to whose care the Church at Damascus was committed). For more details and traditions concerning him, see Dr. James, "Ananias," Hastings' B.D., and Felten, *in loco*. The objections raised against the historical character of the meeting between Ananias and Saul, by Baur, Zeller, Overbeck, are considered by Wendt as quite insufficient. Weizsäcker regards the narrative of the blindness and its cure by Ananias as transparently symbolical,

and adds that in any case it is suggestive that Paul, Gal. iv. 15, seems, at least in later days, to have had a severe ailment in his eyes (see however on this point ver. 9 above). But the weakness, if it existed, might have been caused by the previous blindness at Damascus, and this suggestion, if it is needed, has at all events more probability than the supposition that the narrative in the text was due to the fact that in after years Saul's eyes were affected! (so Weizsäcker, *Apostolic Age*, i., 72). Zeller indeed admits, *Acts*, i., 289, E.T., that the connection of Saul with Ananias, "irrespective of the visions and miracles," may have been historical, and he falls back upon Schneckenburger's theory that the author of Acts had a special aim in view in introducing a man so avowedly pious in the law (xxii. 12) to introduce Paul to Christianity. But Schneckenburger does not seem to deny the main fact of the meeting between the two men (*Ueber den Zweck der Apostelgeschichte*, pp. 168, 169), and St. Paul would scarcely have spoken as he did later (xxii. 12) before a Jewish crowd, in a speech delivered when the capital was full of pilgrims from all parts, and at a time when the constant communication between Damascus and Jerusalem would have exposed him to instant refutation, had his statements with regard to Ananias been incorrect. It is evident that the supernatural element in the narrative is what really lay at the root of Zeller's objections. —ὁ Κύριος, *i.e.*, Jesus, as is evident from a comparison of vv. 13, 14, 17.—ἐν ὁράματι: critical objections have been raised by Baur and others against the double vision narrated here of Saul and Ananias, as against the double vision of Cornelius and St. Peter in x. 3 and xi., but see Lumby's note, *in loco*, and reference to Conybeare and Howson, quoted also by Felten. The idea of the older rationalists that Saul and Ananias had previously been friends, and that thus the coincidence of their visions may be accounted for, is justly regarded by Wendt as entirely arbitrary. The vision, as narrated by Luke, is evidently regarded as something objective, *cf.* vv. 10, 13.

Ver. 11. ἀναστὰς: the word as has been previously remarked is characteristic of Luke (*cf.* its use in O.T.), and does

ἐγώ, Κύριε.   11. ὁ δὲ Κύριος πρὸς αὐτόν, Ἀναστὰς [1] πορεύθητι ἐπὶ
τὴν ῥύμην τὴν καλουμένην Εὐθεῖαν, καὶ ζήτησον ἐν οἰκίᾳ Ἰούδα
Σαῦλον ὀνόματι,[2] Ταρσέα.   ἰδοὺ γὰρ προσεύχεται, 12.[3] καὶ εἶδεν ἐν
ὁράματι ἄνδρα ὀνόματι Ἀνανίαν εἰσελθόντα καὶ ἐπιθέντα αὐτῷ χεῖρα,

[1] Αναστας ℵACEHLP, Vulg. (am. demid. tol.), so Tisch., W.H. marg., Weiss,
Hilg. (cf. x. 13, 20); but αναστα in B and most verss., so Lach., W.H. text, Wendt.

[2] Before Ταρσεα Flor. and Par. have γενει, not an unusual word with adjectives
of nationality.

[3] Blass in β, following Flor., omits the whole verse, Hilg. brackets; but there seems
no reason for its insertion if not genuine, as it is not influenced by any parallel passage
(cf. long discussion in Corssen, *Der Cyprianische Text*, p. 21 ff.).   Wendt (edit. 1899)
decides for its retention, but another and a further question arises as to the original
reading if the verse is retained.   εν οραματι om. ℵA 61, Vulg., Sah., Boh., Aeth.,
so Tisch. R.V., Wendt.   The words may be an explanatory gloss.   In BC 163, so
Blass [W.H.] Weiss εν οραμ. follow ανδρα.   Instead of χειρα the plural χειρας is
found in ℵABCE, Vulg., Boh., Arm., so W.H., R.V., Weiss, Wendt, but the art.
τας is doubtful, probably to be omitted (Wendt) with ℵ*AC 61, so Tisch., Weiss;
but retained by ℵcBE, R.V. [W.H.].

not in the least support the idea that the
vision was a dream of the night, cf. viii.
26.—ἐπὶ τὴν ῥύμην τ. κ. Εὐθεῖαν: ῥύμη,
cf. xii. 10, Matt. vi. 2.   In Luke xiv. 21
it seems to be used in contrast to πλα-
τεῖα, but in LXX at least in one passage
it is used as its equivalent, Isa. xv. 3, cf.
R.V., " broad places," רְחֹב. It is found
also in Ecclus. ix. 7 (perhaps twice) and
in Tobit xiii. 18, where in the previous
ver., 17, we have πλατεῖαι, although it is
very doubtful whether we can press a
contrast here, and ῥύμη, ver. 18, might
perhaps be taken as meaning a city-
quarter, Latin vicus, see Speaker's Commentary, in loco.   On the stages in the
history of the word, and its occurrence
in Attic Greek, e.g., in the comic writers
Antiphanes (380 B.C.) and Philippides
(323 B.C.), see Kennedy, Sources of N. T.
Greek, pp. 15, 16; Rutherford, New
Phrynichus, p. 488. — Εὐθεῖαν: " the
street called Straight " may be traced
from the eastern to the western gate,
and it still bears the name, Derb el-Mus-
takîm, Schneller, Apostelfahrten, pp. 254,
255, " Damascus," Hastings' B.D.   The
"house of Judas," also that of Ananias,
are still pointed out, but considerable
uncertainty attaches to the attempts at
identification, see " Damascus," u. s., also
Felten, in loco.—Ταρσέα: Tarsus was
the capital of the Roman Province of
Cilicia.   Curtius has called it the Athens
of Asia Minor, and Strabo emphasises
its celebrity for the production of men
famous in all branches of science and

art.   As a celebrated university town it
may have ranked amongst its students
not only St. Paul but his companion St.
Luke, attracted it may be by the renown
of its medical school; and if this be so,
the acquaintance of the two men may
date from their student days.   To Tarsus, moreover, and to a country where
Stoicism was cradled, St. Paul may
have been indebted for his evident
familiarity with the ideas and tenets of
the Stoic philosophy.   From Cyprus
came Zeno and Persæus, from Soli,
Chrysippus and Aratus, whilst Anazarba
in Cilicia was the birthplace of the
physician Dioscorides, contemporary of
St. Luke as of St. Paul.   It is indeed
possible to enumerate at least six Stoic
teachers whose home was Tarsus.   See
notes on St. Paul at Athens and at
Ephesus, and see J. Lightfoot, Hor. Heb.,
on Acts vi. 9; Curtius, Gesammelte
Abhandlungen, ii., p. 538 ff.; Zahn,
Einleitung i., pp. 37, 50; Lightfoot,
Philippians, p. 303 ff.; Salmon, Introd.,
p. 317.—ἰδοὺ γὰρ προσεύχεται: " oran-
tes videt Jesus " Bengel; present tense,
continuous prayer, 1 Thess. v. 17.
   Ver. 12.   ἐν ὁράματι, see critical notes.
—ἄνδρα Ἀ. ὀνόμ.: the words would
certainly indicate, as Wendt points out
(seventh edition, not eighth), that Saul
was previously unacquainted with Ananias.   Jesus communicates the contents
of the vision, and speaks as it were
from the standpoint of Saul (see Felten's
note, p. 190).—ἐπιθέντα κ.τ.λ., see above
on viii. 17.

ὅπως ἀναβλέψῃ. 13. ἀπεκρίθη δὲ ὁ Ἀνανίας, Κύριε, ἀκήκοα[1] ἀπὸ πολλῶν περὶ τοῦ ἀνδρὸς τούτου, ὅσα κακὰ ἐποίησε τοῖς ἁγίοις σου ἐν Ἰερουσαλήμ· 14. καὶ ὧδε ἔχει ἐξουσίαν παρὰ τῶν ἀρχιερέων, δῆσαι πάντας τοὺς ἐπικαλουμένους τὸ ὄνομά σου. 15. Εἶπε δὲ πρὸς αὐτὸν ὁ Κύριος, Πορεύου, ὅτι σκεῦος ἐκλογῆς μοι ἐστιν οὗτος, τοῦ βαστάσαι τὸ ὄνομά μου ἐνώπιον[2] ἐθνῶν καὶ βασιλέων, υἱῶν τε Ἰσραήλ.

[1] ακηκοα HLP, Chrys.; ηκουσα ℵABCE, so Tisch., W.H., R.V., Blass, Weiss, Wendt, Hilg.

[2] εθνων, but art. των prefixed in BC*, so Lach., R.V. (W.H.), Weiss, Wendt (probably); but των apparently does not suit the context.

Ver. 13. Ananias naturally hesitates to go to a man who had undoubtedly inflicted harm upon the Christians, and had come to Damascus with the same intent. But there is nothing inconsistent in the fact that Ananias should not be acquainted with Saul personally, whilst he knew of his persecuting zeal.—τοῖς ἁγίοις σου: used here for the first time as a name for the Christians; cf. vv. 32, 41, xxvi. 10. Every Israelite was ἅγιος by the mere fact of his membership in the holy Ecclesia of Israel, and Ananias, himself a Jew, does not hesitate to employ the same term of the members of the Christian Ecclesia (see Hort, Ecclesia, pp. 56, 57, and Grimm, sub v., 2). Its use has therefore a deep significance: "Christus habet sanctos, ut suos: ergo est Deus," says Bengel. The force of the words can be more fully appreciated in connection with the significance of the phrase in ver. 14, τοῖς ἐπικ. τὸ ὄνομά σου. In xxvi. 10 it is noticeable that the word occurs on St. Paul's own lips as he stood before Agrippa "in the bitterness of his self-accusation for his acts of persecution, probably in intentional repetition of Ananias's language respecting those same acts of his. It was a phrase that was likely to burn itself into his memory on that occasion." And so we find St. Paul addressing at least six of his Epistles to those who were "called to be Saints," indicating that every Christian as such had this high calling. If Christians individually had realised it, the prophetic vision of the Psalms of Solomon (xvii. 36) would have been fulfilled in the early Church of Christ: ὅτι πάντες ἅγιοι, καὶ βασιλεὺς αὐτῶν Χριστὸς Κύριος (see Ryle and James' edition, p. 141).—ἐν Ἰερ. belongs to ἐποίησε, and so points back to viii. 3, and to Saul as the soul of the persecution which broke out in Jerusalem, cf.

Paul's own language before Agrippa, xxvi. 10.

Ver. 14. ὧδε hic et huc (Blass), ver. 21.—τοὺς ἐπικ. τὸ ὄνομά σου—note the repeated pronoun and compare 1 Cor. i. 2, where ἐπικ. is closely joined with ἅγιοι, and on the whole phrase see above ii. 21.

Ver. 15. σκεῦος ἐκλογῆς, cf. St. Paul's own language in Gal. i. 15, genitive of quality; common Hebraistic mode of expression (cf. viii. 23) = ἐκλεκτόν, see Blass, Gram., p. 96; cf. Luke xvi. 8, xviii. 6, etc. For σκεῦος similarly used see Jer. xxii. 28, Hosea viii. 8, and Schöttgen, Horæ Hebraicæ, in loco; and in N.T. Rom. ix. 22, 23, 1 Thess. iv. 4. Grimm and Blass both compare σκ. de homine in Polyb., xiii., 5, 7; xv., 25, 1. Vas electionis: the words are written over what is said to be St. Paul's tomb in the church dedicated to him near the city of Rome.—τοῦ βαστάσαι, genitive of purpose; verb as used here continues the metaphor of σκεῦος; may mean simply to bear, to carry, or it may denote to bear as a burden; cf. 2 Kings xviii. 14, Ecclus. vi. 25; cf. Luke xiv. 27, Acts xv. 10, Rom. xv. 1, etc.—ἐθνῶν καὶ βασιλέων — ἐθν., placed first because Saul's special mission is thus indicated. —βασιλ., cf. xxvi. 12, 2 Tim. i. 16; also before the governors of Cyprus, Achaia, Judæa.—υἱῶν τε Ἰ., see critical notes above, again the closely connecting τε, all three nouns being comprehended under the one article τῶν—the Apostle's work was to include, not to exclude, his brethren according to the flesh, whilst mission to the Gentiles is always emphasised; cf. xxii. 15 and 21, xxvi. 17; cf. Rom. i. 13, 14.

Ver. 16. ἐγὼ γὰρ: he is a chosen vessel unto me, and therefore ὑποδ. Wendt disagrees with Meyer, who finds the showing in the experiences of the sufferings (so Hackett and Felten), and

16. ἐγὼ γὰρ ὑποδείξω αὐτῷ, ὅσα δεῖ αὐτὸν ὑπὲρ τοῦ ὀνόματός μου παθεῖν.

17.[1] Ἀπῆλθε δὲ Ἀνανίας καὶ εἰσῆλθεν εἰς τὴν οἰκίαν, καὶ ἐπιθεὶς ἐπ᾽ αὐτὸν τὰς χεῖρας εἶπε, Σαοὺλ ἀδελφέ, ὁ Κύριος ἀπέσταλκέ με, Ἰησοῦς ὁ ὀφθείς σοι ἐν τῇ ὁδῷ ᾗ ἤρχου, ὅπως ἀναβλέψῃς καὶ πλησθῇς Πνεύματος Ἁγίου. 18. καὶ εὐθέως ἀπέπεσον ἀπὸ τῶν ὀφθαλμῶν αὐτοῦ ὡσεὶ λεπίδες, ἀνέβλεψέ τε παραχρῆμα,[2] καὶ ἀναστὰς ἐβαπτίσθη, καὶ λαβὼν τροφὴν ἐνίσχυσεν.[3] 19. Ἐγένετο δὲ ὁ Σαῦλος μετὰ τῶν ἐν

---

[1] Blass, following Flor., reconstructs (so very simil. Hilg.) τοτε εγερθεις (as if the vision came in sleep; cf. Corssen, G. G. A., p. 437 (1896), who thinks that the expression is an interpolation and compares β text in xvi. 9 ff., p. 436, u. s.) Αν. απηλθεν και εισ. εις την οικ.; so again Flor. has επεθηκε αυτω την χειρα εν τω ονομ. Ι. Χ. λεγων.

[2] παραχρημα om. ℵABCHP, Vulg., Boh., Syr. Pesh., Arm., so Tisch., W.H., R.V., Weiss, Wendt. ℵC² 40, Boh. read δε instead of τε.

[3] ενισχυσεν, so Tisch., Blass, Weiss, Hilg.; ενισχυθη BC*, so W.H., Wendt (probably). ὁ Σαυλος om. ℵABCE 13, 61, Vulg., many vers., so Tisch., W.H., R.V.; beginning, perhaps, of a Church lectionary. Flor. reads " dies autem plurimos et in civitate. D cum discentibus transegit," perhaps some influence of xvi. 12, xiv. 28, xxv. 14. Blass suspects Δαμασκῳ and brackets in β. Blass places St. Paul's visit to Arabia before this period, a visit which St. Luke omits.

---

refers the word with De Wette, Overbeck, to a revelation or to some directing counsel of Christ, cf. xiii. 2, xvi. 6, 9, xx. 20, so too Blass—cf. 2 Cor. xi. 25-28. Either interpretation seems better than that of Weiss, who refers the γάρ back to πορεύου, as if Christ were assuring Ananias that Saul would not inflict suffering upon others, but *I* will show him how much *he* (αὐτόν, with emphasis) must suffer, etc., cf. also Bengel's comment.

Ver. 17. ἐπιθεὶς ἐπ᾽ ἀ. τὰς χ.: not as bestowing the Holy Ghost (for see context), but as recovering from his blindness, cf. Mark xvi. 18. Σαούλ, see on ver. 4, perhaps too the word used by Jesus would reassure Saul. — ἀδελφέ: as a Christian brother, and not merely as a brother in nationality, ii. 29, xxii. 1, xxviii. 17—for the word see further, Kennedy, p. 95, and see on i. 15.— ὁ Κ. . . . Ἰησοῦς: the words must have further reassured Saul—the title by which he had himself addressed Jesus is more than justified.

Ver. 18. καὶ εὐθέως: as the immediate result of the laying on of hands the recovery of sight is given, but the baptism follows for the reception of the Holy Ghost, cf. xxii. 13 ff.—ἀπέπεσον . . . ὡσεὶ λ.: the words cannot be taken as merely figurative with Weiss or Zöckler, or with Blass as merely indicating the speediness of the cure—some scaly

substance had formed over the eyes, probably as the result of the dazzling brightness which had struck upon them, cf. Tobit iii. 17, xi. 13, and ii. 10 (cf. vi. 8), λευκώματα = white films (see H. and R., sub v., λεύκωμα). St. Chrysostom's comment is also to be noted: καὶ ἵνα μὴ νομίσῃ φαντασίαν τις εἶναι τὴν πήρωσιν, διὰ τοῦτο αἱ λεπίδες. Here, as elsewhere, we may see traces of St. Luke's accuracy as a physician. Both ἀποπίπτειν and λεπίς are used only by St. Luke in N.T. (λεπίς, although found six times in LXX, does not occur in the sense before us), and both words are found conjoined in medical writers, the former for the falling off of scales from the cuticle and particles from the diseased parts of the body or bones, etc., and λεπίς as the regular medical term for the particles or scaly substances thrown off from the body (see instances in Hobart, p. 39, and Felten, in loco), and cf. also Zahn, Einleitung in das N. T., ii., p. 436 (1899).— ἀναστάς, see above on viii. 26; the word may here be taken literally (although not necessarily so), as of Saul rising from a sitting or reclining position (so Weiss). —ἐβαπτίσθη: no doubt by Ananias— there was no reception into the Church without this.—λαβὼν τροφήν, see on ver. 9.—ἐνίσχυσεν: here used intransitively (1 Macc. vii. 25, 3 Macc. ii. 32), if we adopt reading of T.R. which is

Δαμασκῷ μαθητῶν ἡμέρας τινάς· 20.[1] καὶ εὐθέως ἐν ταῖς συναγωγαῖς
ἐκήρυσσε τὸν Χριστόν,[2] ὅτι οὗτός ἐστιν ὁ υἱὸς τοῦ Θεοῦ. 21. ἐξίσταντο
δὲ πάντες οἱ ἀκούοντες καὶ ἔλεγον, Οὐχ οὗτός ἐστιν ὁ πορθήσας ἐν
Ἰερουσαλὴμ τοὺς ἐπικαλουμένους τὸ ὄνομα τοῦτο, καὶ ὧδε εἰς τοῦτο
ἐληλύθει ἵνα δεδεμένους αὐτοὺς ἀγάγῃ ἐπὶ τοὺς ἀρχιερεῖς; 22.
Σαῦλος δὲ μᾶλλον ἐνεδυναμοῦτο, καὶ συνέχυνε[3] τοὺς Ἰουδαίους τοὺς
κατοικοῦντας ἐν Δαμασκῷ, συμβιβάζων ὅτι οὗτός ἐστιν ὁ Χριστός.

[1] Flor., Par., Wern. read καὶ εἰσελθὼν εἰς τὰς συναγωγας των Ι., cf. xiii. 5, xiv. 1,
xix. 8, so Hilg. The phrase "synagogue of the Jews" usually implies contrast between Jews and Gentiles, which is hardly the case here, but the writer might wish
to emphasise the boldness of Saul: Flor., Iren. read μετα πασης παρρησιας, so
Hilg. ο Χριστος after εστι 68, Flor., Iren[lat]. (Iren[gk.] after Θεου), retained by Blass
and by Hilg., perhaps from ver. 22 (cf. John xx. 31).

[2] Χριστον HLP, Chrys.; Ιησουν אABCE 61, Iren., Vulg., so Tisch., W.H.,
R.V., Blass, Weiss, Wendt; Hilg. has τον κυριον Ιησουν with Flor.; ουτος in ver.
22 seems to demand a preceding Ιησουν.

[3] συνεχυνε AB³HLP, so Blass; συνεχυννε אB*C, Tisch., W.H., App., p. 172, and
see also Winer-Schmiedel, p. 111; Hilg. has συνεχεεν. τους Ιουδ., but τους om.
by א*B, so W.H., R.V., Weiss, Wendt, Blass. At end of verse Flor., Gig., Par.
add εις ον ευδοκησεν ο Θεος—retained by Blass and Hilg.

retained by Weiss. We have the verb,
in the N.T. peculiar to St. Luke, used in
the transitive sense (cf. Luke xxii. 43
and 44, W. H., App., 67, and Plummer,
in loco), and in this sense its use outside
the LXX is confined to Hippocrates and
St. Luke, Hobart, p. 80 (cf. 2 Sam. xxii.
40, Ecclus. l. 4); but cf. Psalms of
Solomon, xvi. 12. The reading here to
which Wendt apparently inclines is
ἐνισχύθη (see critical notes), as this
would be in accordance with the transitive use of the verb in Luke xxii. 43,
and other instances.

Ver. 19. ἡμέρας τινάς: used here apparently, as in x. 48, xvi. 12, xxiv. 24,
etc., of a short period; see note on ver.
23, and cf. critical notes, Blass in β, and
see ver. 23.

Ver. 20. ἐν ταῖς συναγωγαῖς—publicly
in the Jewish Assemblies: οὐκ ἠσχύνετο
(Chrys.).—ὁ υἱὸς τοῦ Θεοῦ: only here in
Acts. As the preaching was in the synagogue the term would be used in its
Messianic sense (cf. John i. 49), according to the early Messianic interpretation
of Psalm ii. 7; cf. xiii. 33 and St. Paul's
reference to the Psalm in another address
to Jews, in the Pisidian Antioch. For
the use of the term as applied to the
Messiah by the Jews see further Book of
Enoch, cv., 2, and Dr. Charles' note.

Ver. 21. πορθήσας: same word used
by St. Paul of himself in Gal. i. 13, 23;
nowhere else in N.T., but see 4 Macc.
iv. 23, xi. 4; used often in classical Greek.

Blass draws attention to the coincidence
between this passage and the use of the
word in Gal., and adds: "ut a Paulo
hoc ipsum verbum scriptorem accepisse
dicas". Wendt (1899) dismisses the
point of connection in the use of the
word by the two authors Luke and Paul
as accidental. He bases his objection,
p. 35, upon the view that St. Paul's
Epistles and Acts are independent of
each other; but this would not prevent St.
Luke from receiving the narrative of the
events at Damascus from the lips of Paul
himself.—τοὺς ἐπικ., see above on ver.
14.—ἐληλύθει, pluperfect: "inest indicatio
voluntatis mulctæ," Blass, cf. also Burton, N. T. Moods and Tenses, p. 44, and
Blass, Gramm., p. 197. On the jurisdiction of the Sanhedrim and their com-
missions to their officers see iv. 5, and
Lewin, St. Paul, i., 52 (smaller edition).
For ἵνα followed by the conjunctive after
a past tense in preference to the optative
cf. v. 26, xxv. 26, in Winer-Moulton, xli.
b. 1 a.

Ver. 22. ἐνεδυναμοῦτο: only used
here by St. Luke, and elsewhere only by
St. Paul (five or six times), and always
of religious and spiritual strength; used
also three times in the LXX; twice with
reference to the power of the Spirit, Judg.
vi. 34, 1 Chron. xii. 18; in Psalm li. 7,
perhaps the simple verb δυναμόω.—συνέχυνε: "confounded," so A. and R.V., or
rather, "continued to confound," imperfect active, cf. ii. 6, "were con-

23. ὡς δὲ ἐπληροῦντο ἡμέραι ἱκαναί, συνεβουλεύσαντο οἱ Ἰουδαῖοι ἀνελεῖν αὐτόν· 24. ἐγνώσθη δὲ τῷ Σαύλῳ ἡ ἐπιβουλὴ αὐτῶν. παρε-

founded," passive, see also xix. 32, xxi. 31 (critical notes above): from συνχύννω (συνχύνω), nowhere used except in Acts, as above (see Moulton and Geden). συνχύννω: not found in classical Greek nor in LXX, a later form of συγχέω, συνχέω T. W. H. (cf. ἐκχύννομαι from ἐκχέω, three times in Acts, also two or three times in Luke's Gospel; in Matthew twice, in Mark once, also Rom. v. 5, Jude ver. 11; not found in LXX, but see Theod., 2 Sam. xiv. 14); in Acts, xxi. 27. συνέχεον from συνχέω (but see *in loco*), Moulton and Geden. According to the best MS., Tisch., W.H., read the double ν, but elsewhere we have only one ν, Winer-Schmiedel, p. 132, Blass, *Gram.*, p. 41.— συμβιβάζων: only used by St. Luke and St. Paul, cf. xvi. 10, xix. 33, see especially for this last passage, Grimm-Thayer, *sub v.*, cf. 1 Cor. ii. 16. In the LXX the word is used in the sense of teaching, instructing, Exod. iv. 12, 15, xviii. 16, Isa. xl. 13, etc., this usage is purely Biblical (in Attic Greek rather προσβ. in this sense): lit., (1) to bring together; (2) then like συμβάλλω, to put together, to compare, to examine closely; (3) so to deduce, to prove; thus here the word may well imply that Saul compared Messianic passages of the O.T. with the events of the life of Jesus of Nazareth, and hence deduced the proof that He was the Christ, cf. παρατιθέμενος in xvii. 3. So Theophylact explains διδάσκων καὶ ἑρμηνεύων out of the Scriptures which the Jews themselves knew.

Ver. 23. ἡμέρας ἱκανάς: whether the period thus described was meant to cover the definite period in Gal. i. 16, *i.e.*, as including St. Paul's visit to Arabia, it is difficult to decide. Lightfoot holds that ἱκανός in St. Luke's language is connected rather with largeness than with smallness, Luke vii. 12, Acts xx. 37, and that the Hebrew phrase יָמִים which St. Luke is copying admits of almost any extension of time (*Galatians*, p. 89, note). Paley, *Horæ Paulinæ*, v., 2, pointed out in the Hebrew of 1 Kings ii. 38, 39, an instance of the use of the phrase "many days" = a period of three years (so Lewin, Felten). It is therefore possible that St. Luke might employ an indefinite, vague expression, an expression which at all events is characteristic of him. On the other hand, Wendt (1899), whilst seeing here a longer period than in ver.

19, compares ver. 43, xviii. 18, xxvii. 7, and decides that the phrase cannot denote time measured by years (so Blass). A reason for St. Luke's indefiniteness may perhaps be that St. Paul's visit to Arabia was not within the scope and purpose of his narrative; or Belser, *Beiträge* (p. 55), and others may be right in maintaining that the visit may lie between vv. 22 and 23, and that, as such intervals are not wanting in Luke's Gospel, it is not strange that they should occur in Acts, but that it does not at all follow that the historian was unacquainted with St. Luke's Arabian journey, as Wendt maintains: "sed aliquid omittere non est idem atque illud negare" Knabenbauer, *in loco*. But if we take the expression, ver. 19, *certain* days to indicate the first visit to Damascus, and the expression, ver. 23, *many* days to indicate a second visit, the visit to Arabia, Gal. i. 19, may lie between these two (Knabenbauer), and if we accept the reading Ἰησοῦν in ver. 20, it may be that Saul first preached that Jesus was the Son of God, and then after his first retirement in Arabia he was prepared to *prove* on his return to Damascus that He was also *the Christ*, ver. 22 (see Mr. Barnard's article, *Expositor*, April, 1899).

Ver. 24. ἐπιβουλή: "plot"; N.T. only used in Acts; in three other passages, xx. 3, 19, xxiii. 30. It is used in the same sense in LXX, Esth. ii. 22 (for other instances of the word see H. and R.), and frequently in classical Greek.— παρετήρουν: if we follow R.V., see critical notes, we have the middle for the active, cf. Luke xiv. 1, vi. 7, Gal. iv. 10. There is no contradiction involved with 2 Cor. xi. 32. The ethnarch acted as the instrument of the Jews, at their instigation, or they acted by his permission, or possibly as the Jews were the actual originators of the persecution of Saul, St. Luke for brevity speaks of them as carrying it out, cf. ii. 23, xxviii. 27. See to this effect, Blass, Zöckler, Felten, Wendt.—τε: if we add καὶ R.V., see critical notes, the two words τε καὶ signify that they not only laid wait for him, but also watched the city gates day and night, to secure the success of their design; "and they watched the gates also," R.V. In 2 Cor. xi. 32, according to Paul's own statement, the ethnarch under Aretas the king guarded the walls to prevent his escape. But this seems

τήρουν[1] τε τὰς πύλας ἡμέρας τε καὶ νυκτός, ὅπως αὐτὸν ἀνέλωσι·
25. λαβόντες δὲ αὐτὸν οἱ μαθηταὶ[2] νυκτός, καθῆκαν διὰ τοῦ τείχους,

[1] παρετηρουν HLP, Chrys.; παρετηρουντο ℵABCEFa 61, Vulg., Or., so Tisch., W.H., R.V., Blass, Weiss, Wendt, Hilg. Instead of τε, ℵABCEFa 61, Vulg., Or., Tisch., W.H., R.V., Blass, Weiss, Hilg. read δε και—Alford supposes that το in παρετηρουντο became mistaken for τε, and then δε και was struck out, no other copula being wanted.

[2] οι μαθηται, after these words ℵABCFa 61, Vulg. (am. fu. demid. tol.), Or. read αυτου, so Tisch., W.H., R.V., Weiss, Wendt, Zöckler, Holtzmann; perhaps omitted because in vv. 19 and 26 μαθηται is used absolutely. σπυριδι—but in ℵC σφυρ., so W.H. (but not Weiss, who follows AB, etc.), although with σπ. as alternative, App., pp. 155, 156, and Winer-Schmiedel, pp. 59, 60; see also Deissmann, Bibelstudien, p. 157, and Neue Bibelstudien, p. 13.

strange, as Damascus was part of the Roman province of Syria. The difficulty is met by a large number of modern writers by the assumption that Caligula, whose reign began in 37 A.D., gave Damascus to Aretas, to whose predecessors it had belonged (Jos., Ant., xiii., 5, 2). On the accession of Caligula a great change of policy occurred—Antipas, the old foe of Aretas, who was indignant with him for the divorce of his daughter, was shortly after deposed, and his kingdom was added to that of Herod Agrippa, who had already received from the emperor the tetrarchy of Philip and Lysanias (Jos., Ant., xviii., 6, 10). But this latter grant was one of the first acts of Caligula's reign, and there is nothing improbable in the supposition that the new ruler should also bestow some gift of territory on the great foe of the Herodian house, who apparently reigned until 40 A.D. Added to this there is the fact that we have no coins of Damascus with the imperial superscription from 34-62 A.D. In 62-63 the image of Nero begins, but there are no coins marked with that of Caligula or Claudius. The latter emperor died in 54 A.D., and in a few years Damascus must have passed again into Roman hands, if the above theory is correct. Certainly this theory is more feasible than that which supposes that Aretas had actually seized Damascus himself in 37 A.D., when upon the death of Tiberius (who had supported Antipas), Vitellius, the governor of Syria, had withdrawn his troops and the expedition which the emperor had despatched against Aretas. But whether this forcible taking possession of the city is placed before, during, or after the expedition of Vitellius, we should expect that it would have met with energetic punishment at the hands of the governor of Syria, but of this there is no mention or trace (P. Ewald). McGiffert,

who favours an earlier chronology, and dates Paul's conversion in 31 or 32 A.D., contends that the flight from Damascus may have occurred as well in the year 35, i.e., in the reign of Tiberius, as in 38, when no change had taken place in the status of Damascus; the city was subject to Rome, but Aretas may have had control over it, just as Herod had control over Jerusalem. There is at all events no ground for supposing that the term ethnarch denotes that Aretas was only head of the Arabian colony in Damascus (so O. Holtzmann, following Keim, Nösgen, etc.), or that he was only a chance visitor who exercised his authority to the detriment of Paul (Anger); any such suggestion utterly fails to account for the fact that he is represented as guarding Damascus. It has been suggested that the wife of Aretas may well have been a proselyte, but the fact that the Jews of Damascus were both numerous and powerful is quite sufficient to explain the attitude of the governor, Jos., B. J., ii., 20, 2; vii., 8, 7. See "Aretas" in Hastings' B.D., and B.D.². McGiffert, Apostolic Age, pp. 164, 165; G. A. Smith, Hist. Geog., pp. 619, 620; O. Holtzmann, Neutest. Zeitgeschichte, p. 97; Schürer, Jewish People, div. i., vol. ii., p. 356, and div. ii., vol. i., p. 98, E.T.; Real-Encyclopädie für protestant. Theol. (Hauck), i., pp. 795-797, by P. Ewald. See further on the title ἐθνάρχης Schürer, Studien und Kritiken, 1899 (1), which he explains by the conditions of the Nabatean kingdom, in which tribes not cities were concerned—the head of such a tribe being actually so called in more than one inscription.

Ver. 25. οἱ μαθηταί—if we add αὐτοῦ, see critical notes, the words would apparently refer to Jews converted by Saul, so Chrysostom: "but his disciples" R.V. Alford, who reads αὐτοῦ, supposes that we have here an unusual government of

χαλάσαντες ἐν σπυρίδι. 26. Παραγενόμενος δὲ ὁ Σαῦλος εἰς Ἱερουσαλήμ, ἐπειρᾶτο ¹ κολλᾶσθαι τοῖς μαθηταῖς· καὶ πάντες ἐφοβοῦντο
αὐτόν, μὴ πιστεύοντες ὅτι ἐστὶ μαθητής· 27. Βαρνάβας δὲ
ἐπιλαβόμενος αὐτόν, ἤγαγε πρὸς τοὺς ἀποστόλους, καὶ διηγήσατο
αὐτοῖς πῶς ἐν τῇ ὁδῷ εἶδε τὸν Κύριον, καὶ ὅτι ἐλάλησεν αὐτῷ, καὶ

---

¹ επειρατο—but אABC 61, 81 read επειραζεν, so Tisch., W.H., R.V., Weiss,
Wendt (against Meyer) ; latter verb much more common in N.T., but elsewhere is
used in a different sense from this passage, and so επειρατο introduced. Hilg. has
this latter verb here.

---

the genitive by λαβόντες, and compares
Luke viii. 54 and classical instances, see
in loco.—διὰ τοῦ τείχους : "through the
wall," R.V., cf. 2 Cor. xi. 33, where we
read διὰ θυρίδος . . . διὰ τοῦ τείχους,
perhaps a window in the external face
of the wall opening into the house on
the inside, rather than simply a window
of a house overhanging the wall ; cf.
Josh. ii. 16, 1 Sam. xix. 12. Blass takes
it of a window made " in ipso muro scil.
ad tormenta mittenda," but there is no
need for this explantion ; see Hackett's
note on his own observations at Damascus of two or three windows built in
the wall as above.—χαλάσαντες ἐν
σπυρίδι : "lowering him," R.V., not
expressed in A.V. ; on spelling of
σπυρ. see critical note. In 2 Cor.
xi. 33 Paul uses the word σαργάνη,
a basket of wickerwork, σπυρ. a basket
larger than the κόφινος, the small hand-
basket of the Jew, Juv., iii., 14 ; vi., 541,
probably a provision basket of considerable size, used as by the Paeonians for
fishing, Herod., v., 16. σαργάνη too is
used of a fish basket by Timokles, Ληθ.,
i., see further, " Basket," Hastings'
B.D., and Plummer on Luke ix. 17.
Neither word is met with in the LXX or
Apocrypha. For the naturalness of the
incident according to the present customs of the country see Hackett, in loco.
The traditional spot of its occurrence is
still shown, but we can only say of it as
of the " house of Judas," see above on
ver. ii. Wendt, p. 35 (1899), thinks that
here we have a coincidence with the
account in 2 Cor., which cannot be
accounted for except by the acquaintance
of the author of Acts with the Epistle.
Ver. 26. παραγενόμενος : on its
frequency in St. Luke's Gospel and
Acts see v. 21 ; apparently presupposes
that Saul betook himself immediately
to Jerusalem, so that the stay in Arabia
cannot be inserted here (Weiss, in loco),

a stay which Weiss holds was unknown
to the author of Acts, see his note on
ver. 19. παραγ. is found four times in
Acts with εἰς, c. acc. loci, elsewhere only
in Matt. ii. 1 (cf. John viii. 2).—ἐπειρᾶτο :
the verb πειράομαι only found once in
N.T., viz., xxvi. 21, and the true reading
here is ἐπείραζε, which is used in a
similar sense in xvi. 7, xxiv. 6, only in
the active in this sense = Attic πειρῶμαι,
according to Blass, in loco, and Gram.,
56, 221 ; " he assayed," R.V. = to essay,
attempt, try, Deut. iv. 34, 2 Macc. ii. 23.
—κολλᾶσθαι, cf. v. 13, x. 28, and also
Matt. xix. 5, Luke xv. 5, 1 Cor. vi. 16—
evidently means that he sought to join
himself to them intimately.—καὶ πάντες
ἐφοβ. αὐτόν—καὶ " and," R.V., not
" but," A.V. ; it is not adversative, but
simply introduces the unfavourable result of Saul's endeavour. This does not
necessarily require that the conversion
should have been recent, as Weiss maintains. If three years had elapsed, Gal.
i. 16, during a portion of which at all
events Saul had been in retirement, the
Christians in Jerusalem might very
naturally still feel apprehensive when
their former persecutor was thus for the
first time since his conversion actually
present amongst them, and the memory
of his former fierce hatred could not have
been effaced. If it seems unlikely that
this should have been their attitude had
they known of Saul's profession of faith
at Damascus, there are critics who would
have expressed great surprise if the
Apostle had been received with open
arms, and without any credentials : " cre-
do si contrarium exstaret, hoc rursus
mirarentur " (Blass).
Ver. 27. Βαρνάβας, cf. iv. 36. Saul
and Barnabas may have been previously
acquainted, see J. Lightfoot, Hor. Heb.,
and note on iv. 36. St. Chrysostom,
Hom., xxi. (so Theophylact and Oecumenius), sees here a proof of the kindly

πῶς ἐν Δαμασκῷ ἐπαρρησιάσατο ἐν τῷ ὀνόματι τοῦ Ἰησοῦ. 28. καὶ
ἦν μετ᾽ αὐτῶν εἰσπορευόμενος καὶ ἐκπορευόμενος ἐν Ἱερουσαλήμ·
καὶ παρρησιαζόμενος[1] ἐν τῷ ὀνόματι τοῦ Κυρίου Ἰησοῦ, 29. ἐλάλει τε

---

[1] ἐν Ἰ. καὶ π.—but εἰς Ἰ. παρρησ. ΝΑΒCΕLΡ 61, so Tisch., W.H., R.V., Blass,
Weiss, Wendt; εἰς perhaps not understood.　Blass takes εἰς = ἐν *ut alias*.

---

nature of Barnabas, so truly called
"Son of Consolation". For an appreciative notice of the goodness and
generosity of Barnabas, from a very
different standpoint, see Renan, *Apostles*,
p. 191 E.T.—ἐπιλ., *cf.* xxiii. 19; so as
to disarm fear: on the force of this characteristic word of St. Luke see Ramsay,
St. Paul, p. 245, Friedrich, p. 27, and
below xvii. 19; generally constructed
with genitive, but here αὐτὸν is probably
governed by ἤγαγε; *cf.* xvi. 19, and xviii.
17, where also the accusative is found in
cases of a finite transitive verb following the participle, ἐπιλ. Blass, *Gram.*,
p. 100, note 2, refers αὐτόν to ἤγαγε,
and understands αὐτοῦ with ἐπιλ.—
πρὸς τοὺς ἀποστόλους, *cf.* Gal. i. 19;
there is no contradiction, although St.
Paul's own narrative confines Saul's introduction to Peter and James: "though
most of the Apostles were absent, yet
the two real leaders were present" (Ramsay), and this was the point which St.
Luke would emphasise. Wendt (1899)
rejects the narrative of Acts as indistinct when compared with Gal. i., but see
Lightfoot, *Galatians*, p. 91, and Drummond, *Galatians*, p. 67; see below on ver.
30 also.—διηγήσατο, *exposuit, i.e.*, Barnabas (but Beza and Meyer make Saul
the subject, although unlikely from construction and context); verb twice in
Luke's Gospel, viii. 39, ix. 10, and three
times in Acts, viii. 33 (quotation), xii.
17; *cf.* Heb. xi. 32, and Mark v. 16,
ix. 9; and nowhere else in N.T.; frequent in LXX to recount, narrate, declare, *cf.* 1 Macc. v. 25, viii. 2, x. 15,
xi. 5, and several times in Ecclesiasticus.
Similarly used in classical Greek; Grimm
compares figurative use of German *durch-
führen*.—πῶς εἶδε Κ.: while it is not said
in any part of the three accounts of the
Conversion that Saul *saw* Jesus, it is distinctly asserted here in a statement which
Barnabas may well have received from
Saul himself, and also in the two expressions of Ananias, *cf.* ver. 17, xxii. 14;
cf. also the Apostle's own words, 1 Cor.
ix. 1, xv. 8.—ἐπαρρησιάσατο, *cf.* the
verb with the expression μετὰ παρρησίας
λαλεῖν, see above on iv. 13, and of

the preaching of the other Apostles and
of the Church, *cf.* xxviii. 31 (of Paul).
Verb only used by Luke and Paul, and
always of speaking boldly the truths of
the Gospel; so seven times in Acts, and
also in 1 Thess. ii. 2, Ephes. vi. 20.
Ver. 28. ἦν . . . εἰσπ.: for characteristic construction see i. 10, etc.
εἰς καὶ ἐκπ., *cf.* i. 21. Hebraistic formula to express the daily confidential
intercourse with the Apostles; *cf.* 1 Sam.
xviii. 13, 2 Chron. xxiii. 7 (1 Macc.
xiii. 49, xv. 14, 25, for somewhat
similar expressions, but see H. and R.).
—ἐν: if we read εἰς, see critical note.
Weiss connects closely with ἐκπ. and
takes it to signify that Saul was not only
associated with the Apostles privately,
but openly in the town, so Wendt and
Holtzmann, *privatim* and *publice*. Page
connects ἦν εἰς together, and thinks εἰς
probably due to the intervention of the
verbs expressing motion. Zöckler compares xxvi. 20, and takes εἰς as referring
to Jerusalem and its neighbourhood (but
see critical notes).
Ver. 29. συνεζήτει, *cf.* vi. 9.—πρὸς
τοὺς Ἑλλην., of whom Saul himself
was one; see critical notes. Saul's
visit was a short one (Gal. i. 18), and
although we must not limit his opportunities of disputation to the two Sabbaths
with Blass (note the two imperfects), yet
it is evident that the Hellenists were at
once enraged against the deserter from
their ranks. There is no contradiction
with xxii. 17, as Zeller and Overbeck
maintained—it is rather a mark of truth
that Luke gives the outward impulse,
and Paul the inner ground (Hackett,
Lightfoot, Lumby); but see on the other
hand Ramsay, *St. Paul*, p. 62, against
the identification of xxii. 17 with Paul's
first visit; according to Ramsay, xxii. 17,
18 refer to the close of the Apostle's
second visit. Wendt (1899) still identifies xxii. 18 with the passage before
us, ix. 29; in seventh edition he speaks
more fully of the fulfilment of the
negative prophecy in xxii. 18, by the
positive fact here narrated.—ἐπεχείρουν:
only used by St. Luke; St. Luke i. 1,
Acts xix. 13; it is used in same sense in

καὶ συνεζήτει πρὸς τοὺς Ἑλληνιστάς[1]· οἱ δὲ ἐπεχείρουν αὐτὸν ἀνελεῖν.
30. ἐπιγνόντες δὲ οἱ ἀδελφοὶ κατήγαγον αὐτὸν εἰς Καισάρειαν, καὶ

[1] Ἑλληνιστας אABCEHLP ; but A has Ἑλληνας, and Vulg. (not am. demid.) has "loquebatur quoque gentibus et disputabat cum Græcis," see Felten's note, *in loco.*

classical Greek ; and it also occurs in Esther ix. 25, 1 Esd. i. 28, 2 Macc. ii. 29, vii. 19, ix. 2, etc., and 3 Macc. vii. 5, where it occurs as here with ἀνελεῖν (see also below), and for other instances *cf.* Hatch and Redpath. The word was frequently employed in medical language, sometimes in its literal sense "to apply the hand to," but generally as in N.T. Both Hippocrates and Galen use the verb as St. Luke does, with γράφειν— ἐπεχείρησαν γράφειν. Hobart, pp. 87 and 210, points out that Galen also employs the verb with ἀνελεῖν, as here. It is true that the word is also used in the same sense by Josephus, *c. Apion,* ii., with συγγράφειν, but the medical use of the term is so striking in Hippocrates that its use here is noted by J. Weiss, *Evangelium des Lukas,* p. i., as a probable reminiscence by the writer, and still more positively so by Zahn, *Einleitung in das N. T.,* ii., p. 384 (1899).

Ver. 30. ἐπιγνόντες : the preposition may signify here as elsewhere accurate and certain knowledge or information—a favourite word with St. Luke, in the Gospel seven times, in Acts thirteen times ; it was also a favourite word with St. Paul, *cf., e.g.,* 1 Cor. xiii. 12, 2 Cor. vi. 9 ; frequent in LXX, or it may simply mean to find out, to ascertain (Grimm) ; see Blass *in loco* on its force in LXX. 5.—οἱ ἀδελφοὶ : the expression seems expressly used to imply that the disciples at Jerusalem recognised Saul as a brother. Wendt (1899) rejects all the narrative in Acts as unhistorical, and compares with the statement here Gal. i. 22 ; but there mention is only made of the "Churches of Judæa," whilst the inference that Paul could scarcely fail to have been known to the members of the Church in Jerusalem seems quite justifiable, Lightfoot, *Galatians,* p. 86.—κατήγαγον, *i.e.,* brought him down to the sea coast, *ad mare deduxerunt,* word used only by Luke and Paul ; but by St. Luke only as a nautical expression, *cf.* xxvii. 3, xxviii. 12 (xxi. 3), and Luke v. 11 ; so in classical writers.— εἰς Κ. as in viii. 40 (not Cæsarea Philippi which is always so called) ; if he found Philip there (xxi. 8), the friend and the accuser of the proto-martyr would meet

face to face as brethren (Plumptre).— ἐξαπέστειλαν : the word might mean by sea or by land, but the former is supported amongst recent commentators by Blass, so too Page (*cf.* Lightfoot on Gal. i. 21, p. 85), Knabenbauer, p. 174. But if so, there is no contradiction with Gal. i. 21, where Paul speaks of coming into the regions of Syria and Cilicia, as if he went to the latter through the former. The expressions in *Galatians* have sometimes been explained on the supposition that the two countries, Syria and Cilicia, are named there as elsewhere in that order, Acts xv. 23, 41, as a kind of general geographical expression (Felten), the most important country being mentioned first, so Lightfoot, Nösgen, Conybeare and Howson ; or that as Paul would remain at Syrian ports on the way to Cilicia, he might fairly speak as he does, or that he went first to Tarsus, and thence made missionary excursions into Syria. If neither of these or similar explanations are satisfactory, we can scarcely conclude with Blass that Gal. i. 21 is accounted for "inverso per incuriam ordine". Ramsay has lately argued with much force that here as elsewhere Paul thinks and speaks of the Roman divisions of the empire (*cf.* Zahn, *Einleitung in das N. T.,* i., p. 124 (1897)), and that here the two great divisions, Syria and Cilicia, of the Roman province are spoken of ; and he accordingly reads, with the original text of א, τὰ κλίματα τῆς Σ. καὶ Κ., the article used once, and thus embracing the two parts of the one province (sometimes three parts are enumerated, Phœnicia being distinguished from Syria). There is apparently no example of the expression *Prov. Syria et Cilicia,* but Ramsay points to the analogy of Bithynia-Pontus ; see *Expositor,* p. 29 ff., 1898, and "Cilicia" and "Bithynia" (Ramsay) in Hastings' B.D. Ramsay therefore concludes that Gal. i. 21 simply implies that Paul spent the following period of his life in various parts of the province Syria-Cilicia.—Ταρσόν, see above, ver. 11 ; on the years of quiet work at Tarsus and in its neighbourhood, see Ramsay, *St. Paul,* pp. 46, 47, and below on xi. 25.

ἐξαπέστειλαν αὐτὸν εἰς Ταρσόν.   31. Αἱ μὲν οὖν ἐκκλησίαι [1] καθ᾽ ὅλης τῆς Ἰουδαίας καὶ Γαλιλαίας [2] καὶ Σαμαρείας εἶχον εἰρήνην, οἰκοδομούμεναι καὶ πορευόμεναι τῷ φόβῳ τοῦ Κυρίου, καὶ τῇ παρακλήσει τοῦ Ἁγίου Πνεύματος ἐπληθύνοντο.

[1] αι εκκλησιαι; but sing. η εκκλη. ℵABC, Vulg., Syr. Pesh., Sah., Boh., Arm., Aeth., so Tisch., W.H., R.V., Blass, Wendt, Weiss, Hilg.; see Ramsay, *St. Paul*, p. 128.

[2] καὶ Γαλιλαίας, Blass brackets in β because om. by Chrys., Cassiod., perhaps because nothing has been said of the Church in Galilee, but it obviously must have existed there, though never actually mentioned in Acts (see Plumptre's note, *in loco*), see also below.

Ver. 31.   αἱ ἐκκλησίαι—if we read the singular ἡ ἐκκλ. with the great MS. the word shows us that the Church, though manifestly assuming a wider range, is still one: Hort, *Ecclesia*, p. 55, thinks that here the term in the singular corresponds by the three modern representative districts named, *viz.*, Judæa, Galilee, Samaria, to the ancient Ecclesia, which had its home in the whole land of Israel; but however this may be, the term is used here markedly of the unified Church, and in accordance with St. Paul's own later usage of the word; see especially Ramsay, *St. Paul*, pp. 126, 127, and also p. 124.—καθ᾽ ὅλης: the genitive in this sense is peculiar to St. Luke, and always with the adjective ὅλος; Luke iv. 14, xxiii. 5, Acts ix. 42, x. 37, the phrase, although not the best classically, seeming to "sound right," because καθόλου, only in Acts iv. 18 in N.T., had come into common use since Aristotle (Simcox, *Language of the N. T.*, p. 148; Vogel, p. 45).—οὖν connects with the preceding narrative; so Bengel, Weiss, Wendt, Blass, Zöckler; the Church had rest because the persecutors had become converted; but see also Rendall, Appendix, on μὲν οὖν, p. 164, and Hackett, Felten. —οἰκοδομούμεναι: "being edified," R.V. (see critical notes) (not "and were edified," A.V.)—as an accompaniment of the peace from persecutors. The term may refer primarily to the organisation of the Church as a visible institution, but would also indicate the spiritual edification which is so often expressed by the word in St. Paul's Epistles, where both the verb and its cognate noun are so frequent; *cf.* xx. 32, and note. The fact that the verb is employed only once in the Gospels, Matt. xvi. 18, of the Church, as here in a non-literal sense, as compared with its constant use by St. Paul as above, is a striking indication of the early date of the Synoptic Gospels or

their source (see Page, *in loco*). For the metaphorical use of the word in the O.T. of good fortune and prosperity, *cf.* LXX, Ps. xxvii. (xxviii.) 5, Jer. xii. 16, xl. (xxxiii.) 7, xxxviii. (xxxi.) 4, xlix. (xlii.) 10. (Hilgenfeld refers the whole section ix. 32-42 to the same source A from which his "author to Theophilus" derived the founding, and the first incidents in the history, of the early Church, i. 15-iv. 42, although the "author to Theophilus" may have added the words καὶ τῇ παρακ. ... ἐπληθύνοντο. But if we desire a good illustration of the labyrinth (as Hilgenfeld calls it) through which we have to tread, if we would see our way to any coherent meaning in ix. 31-xii. 25, it is sufficient to note the analysis of the sources of the modern critics given us by Hilgenfeld himself, *Zeitschrift für wissenschaft. Theol.*, pp. 481, 482; 1895.)— οἰκοδ.: may refer to the inward spiritual growth, ἐπληθ. to the outward growth in numbers; a growth attributed not to human agency but to the power of the Holy Ghost. παράκλησις only here in Acts of the Holy Ghost. Hort renders "and walking by the fear of the Lord and by the invocation [παρακ.] of the Holy Spirit [probably invoking His guidance as Paraclete to the Ecclesia] was multiplied" (*Ecclesia*, p. 55), and it is not strange that the working of the Παράκλητος should be so described; while others connect the word with the divine counsel or exhortation of the prophets in opening hearts and minds; others again attach παρακ. to ἐπληθ. as expressing increase of spiritual strength and comfort (see Blass, Rendall, Felten, and *cf.* Col. i. 11, 1 Pet. i. 2). On the verb and its frequency in Acts see p. 73.

Vv. 32-35. *Healing of Aeneas.*—Ver. 32. ἐγένετο δὲ Π. διερχ.: on the formula and its frequency in Luke see Friedrich, p. 13, and above on p. 124. We have here a note of what may fairly be

32. ΈΓΕΝΕΤΟ δὲ Πέτρον διερχόμενον διὰ πάντων,[1] κατελθεῖν καὶ πρὸς τοὺς ἁγίους τοὺς κατοικοῦντας Λύδδαν. 33. εὖρε δὲ ἐκεῖ ἄνθρωπόν τινα Αἰνέαν ὀνόματι, ἐξ ἐτῶν ὀκτὼ κατακείμενον ἐπὶ

[1] διὰ πάντων, instead of this Par. and Wern. read " per omnes civitates et regiones," accepted by Blass ; no doubt to explain διὰ πάντων, which is difficult, see below.

taken as a specimen of many similar missionary journeys, or rather journeys of progress and inspection, mentioned here perhaps more in detail because of the development which followed upon it, cf. with chap. x. New congregations had been formed, and just as Peter and John had gone down to Samaria to the Christians converted by Philip, so it became necessary that the congregations which had grown up in many towns (viii. 14, 25, 40) should be visited and kept in touch with the centre at Jerusalem (see Ramsay, St. Paul, pp. 41, 42 ; Felten and Plumptre, in loco).—διερχ. διὰ πάντων, see note on xiii. 6, and for the construction Luke ix. 6, xi. 24.—κατελθεῖν, i.e., probably from Jerusalem, cf. viii. 5, Luke iv. 31 devenire, cf. Plummer's note on Luke iv. 31. On the frequent use of διέρχομαι and κατέρχομαι in Luke, see Friedrich, p. 7.—διὰ πάντων, sc., ἁγίων, so Meyer-Wendt, Weiss, Bengel, Alford, Hackett, De Wette, Holtzmann ; cf. for similar construction 2 Cor. i. 16, and cf. Acts xx. 25, Rom. xv. 28, or it may mean "through all parts," R.V., so Belser, Beiträge, p. 58 (see critical notes). Hort seems to take it of the whole land (Ecclesia, p. 56).—ἁγίους, see on ver. 13.—Λύδδαν, Hebrew לֹד, Lod, perpetuated in the modern Ludd ; on the word see critical notes, cf. 1 Chron. viii. 2, Ezra ii. 23, Neh. vii. 37, xi. 35, 1 Macc. xi. 34 ; "a village not less than a city" Jos., Ant., xx., 6, 2 ; three hours from Joppa in the plain of Sharon : its frontier position often involved it in battle, and rendered it a subject of treaty between Jews and Syrians, and Jews and Romans. At this period not only Jerusalem but Joppa and Lydda were centres of Jewish national feeling, and were singled out by Cestius Gallus as the centres of the national revolt. On its importance as a place of refuge and a seat of learning after the destruction of Jerusalem, see Hamburger, Real-Encyclopädie des Judentums, i., 5, p. 721 ; Edersheim, History of the Jewish People, pp. 155, 215, 479, 512, and also Jewish Social Life, pp. 75-78 ; G. A. Smith, Hist. Geog. of the Holy Land, pp. 141, 160 (and his interesting remarks on

the connection of St. George of England with Lydda) ; Schürer, Jewish People, div. ii., vol. i., p. 159, E.T. As the place lay on the route from Azotus to Cæsarea the planting or at any rate the strengthening of its Christianity may be referred to Philip the Evangelist, viii. 40. But on the other hand the close proximity to Jerusalem, within an easy day's journey, may induce us to believe that Lydda had its congregation of "saints" almost from the first, Edersheim, Jewish Social Life, p. 75. On the curious Talmudical notices with reference to our Lord and the Virgin Mother, e.g., that He was condemned at Lydda, see Edersheim, u. s., p. 76. Such passages perhaps indicate a close connection between Lydda and the founding of Christianity. Ver. 33. Αἰνέαν : the name in this form is found in Thuc., Xen., Pindar, and is not to be identified with that of the Trojan Αἰνείας, although in a fragment of Sophocles we have for the sake of the verse Αἰνέας instead of Αἰνείας ; see Wendt, seventh edition, and Wetstein, in loco. The name is also used of a Jew, Jos., Ant., xiv., 10, 22. Probably a Hellenistic Jew ; but although he is not expressly named a disciple (as in the case of Tabitha), yet as Peter visited him, and he knew the name of Jesus Christ, he may have become a Christian (so Blass) ; the fact that Peter went to the "saints" may imply this ; but see Alford's note, and so too Hilgenfeld.—ἐξ ἐτῶν ὀκτώ : characteristic of Luke as a medical man ; in the cases of disease which he alone mentions, St. Luke frequently gives their duration, e.g., xiii. 11, Acts iii. 2, iv. 22, xiv. 8, see Hobart, p. 40, Zahn, Einleitung in das N. T., ii., p. 427.—κραββάτῳ, see above on v. 15, and spelling.—παραλελυμένος, see above on viii. 7, and cf. also Zahn, Einleitung in das N. T., ii., p. 436 (1899). Ver. 34. ἰᾶται σε ᾽Ι.: perhaps a paronomasia, iv. 30 (see Page, in loco) ; present tense, indicating that the healing was immediately effected, Burton, N. T. Moods and Tenses, p. 9 ; Blass, Gram., p. 183 ; verb much more frequent in St. Luke than in the other N.T. writers ; in Gospel eleven times, in Acts three times,

κραββάτῳ, ὃς ἦν παραλελυμένος. 34. καὶ εἶπεν αὐτῷ ὁ Πέτρος,
Αἰνέα, ἰαταί σε Ἰησοῦς ὁ Χριστός· ἀνάστηθι καὶ στρῶσον σεαυτῷ.
καὶ εὐθέως ἀνέστη· 35. καὶ εἶδον αὐτὸν πάντες οἱ κατοικοῦντες
Λύδδαν καὶ τὸν Σάρωνα,[1] οἵτινες ἐπέστρεψαν ἐπὶ τὸν Κύριον.

36. Ἐν Ἰόππῃ δέ τις ἦν μαθήτρια ὀνόματι Ταβιθά,[2] ἢ διερμηνευο-
μένη λέγεται Δορκάς· αὕτη ἦν πλήρης ἀγαθῶν ἔργων καὶ ἐλεημοσυνῶν

---

[1] Λυδδαν: but in אAB, so Tisch., W.H., Blass, Weiss, Λυδδα; see Winer-
Schmiedel, p. 93, Blass, Gram., pp. 25, 31 (so for ver. 25). Σαρωνα אABCE, so
Tisch., W.H., Weiss, Blass, Hilg., but with varying accent; Blass, Gram., p. 31.
א has Σαρρωνα.

[2] Ταβιθα; but BC Ταβειθα, so W.H., Weiss, but in W.H., alt., see App., p.
162.

and one quotation; in St. Matthew three
times, and same quotation; in St. John
twice, and same quotation; in St. Mark
only once; in Epistles three times, but
perhaps only figuratively; so in Deut.
xxx. 3, of the diseases of the soul. The
term is used by St. Luke in a passage
where a similar statement is made by
St. Matthew and St. Mark, in which they
employ another verb, less precise, σώζειν,
διασώζειν, and not so strictly medical, cf.
Matt. xiv. 36, Mark vi. 56, Luke vi. 19,
Hobart, p. 9. ἴασις: the cognate noun,
only in St. Luke, Luke xiii. 32, Acts iv.
32, and see further also Hobart, pp. 23,
24. Both noun and verb are also frequent in LXX, and cf. Plummer on
Luke v. 19, who points out that ἰᾶσθαι
in its active significance is peculiar to
St. Luke, except in the quotations from
LXX (Matt. xiii. 15, John xii. 40, both
figurative), and in John iv. 47.—στρῶσον
σεαυτῷ, cf. xxii. 12, where, as here, the
context must be supplied. The aorist
denotes performance without delay—
now and at once make thy bed for
thyself—an act which hitherto others
have done for thee.—καὶ εὐθ. ἀνέστη
corresponds to ἀνάστηθι and indicates
the completeness of the healing.

Ver. 35. τὸν Σάρωνα, on accentuation
see critical notes: "at Lydda and in
Sharon," R.V. In Sharon, because it
was not a town as Lydda, but rather a
level tract, the maritime plain between
Carmel and Joppa, so called in Hebrew
(with article), meaning "the Level"; in
Greek, the Forest, δρυμός, LXX, because
it was once covered by a great oak
forest; full of quiet but rich beauty;
cf. 1 Chron. xxvii. 29, Isa. xxxiii. 9,
xxxv. 2, xxxvii. 24, lxv. 10, celebrated
for its pasturage, Cant. ii. 1. "The
masculine article doth show that it is
not named of a city, and so doth the

LXX article in Isa. 33, 9," J. Lightfoot,
Hor. Heb. There is no ground for supposing that it meant a village in the
neighbourhood, as no place bearing the
name Saron can be satisfactorily cited,
but cf. Nösgen, in loco; see G. A. Smith,
Hist. Geog. of the Holy Land, pp. 52,
147, 148; Edersheim, Jewish Social
Life, p. 74; Hamburger, Real-Encyclopädie des Judentums, i., 6, p. 897.—
πάντες: the expression may be taken to
mean that a general conversion of the
inhabitants followed. Rendall renders
" and all that dwelt, etc., who had turned
to the Lord, saw Him," i.e., attested the
reality of the miracle, Acts, pp. 72 and
232. But it might fairly be urged that
many would see the man besides those
who had become Christians. It helps us
to understand the passage if we remember
with Nösgen (so Bengel) that the expression ἐπὶ τὸν K. applies not to God the
Father, but to Jesus Christ, so that we
learn that a conversion of the Jewish
population at Lydda to the claims of
Jesus as the Messiah was the result of
the miracle (see also Hackett's useful
note). On the use of οἵτινες see Alford's
note on vii. 53, quoted by Page (Winer-
Schmiedel, p. 235). For the phrase ἐπισ.
ἐπὶ τὸν K. cf. xiv. 15.

Vv. 36-43. Tabitha raised from the
dead.—Ver. 36. Ἰόππῃ, on the spelling,
Winer-Schmiedel, p. 56; and below on
ver. 43.—μαθήτρια: only here in N.T.:
the word occurs in the Apocryphal Gospel
of Peter: Mary Magdalene is described as
μ. τοῦ Κυρίου: it is also used by Diod.,
ii., 52; Diog. Laert., iv., 2; viii., 2. The
form μαθητρίς is found in Philo.—Ταβιθά,
see critical notes. מְבִיתָא, Aramaic,

= צְבִי, Hebrew: (1) splendour, beauty;
(2) Greek Δορκάς, specially prized by

ὧν ἐποίει · 37. ἐγένετο δὲ ἐν ταῖς ἡμέραις ἐκείναις ἀσθενήσασαν
αὐτὴν ἀποθανεῖν · λούσαντες δὲ αὐτὴν ἔθηκαν ἐν ὑπερῴῳ. 38. ἐγγὺς
δὲ οὔσης Λύδδης [1] τῇ Ἰόππῃ, οἱ μαθηταὶ ἀκούσαντες ὅτι Πέτρος ἐστὶν
ἐν αὐτῇ, ἀπέστειλαν δύο ἄνδρας πρὸς αὐτόν, παρακαλοῦντες μὴ
ὀκνῆσαι [2] διελθεῖν ἕως αὐτῶν. 39. ἀναστὰς δὲ Πέτρος συνῆλθεν
αὐτοῖς · ὃν παραγενόμενον ἀνήγαγον εἰς τὸ ὑπερῷον, καὶ παρέστησαν
αὐτῷ πᾶσαι αἱ χῆραι κλαίουσαι καὶ ἐπιδεικνύμεναι χιτῶνας καὶ

---

[1] Λύδδης; but Tisch., Blass, W.H. -ας, see on ver. 35, and W.H., App., p. 163.

[2] δυο ανδρας ℵABCE; om. HLP, Chrys. οκνησαι; but οκνησης ℵABC¹E 40, 61, 81, Vulg., Sah., Boh., so Tisch., W.H., R.V., Blass, Weiss, Wendt, Hilg.

---

the Orientals for its elegance, Cant. ii. 9,—so called from the large bright eyes of the animal (δέρκομαι). The name was found as a feminine name amongst both Greek and Jews, see instances in Wetstein (e.g., Jos., B. J., iv., 3, 5), Plumptre, Wendt, seventh edition, sub v., and more recently Deissmann, Neue Bibelstudien, p. 17. This Greek equivalent (found several times in LXX) may not have been actually borne by Tabitha as a name, for St. Luke may only mean to interpret the Aramaic word for his Gentile readers ; but she may have been known by both names. Like Æneas, she may have been an Hellenist. There is nothing to indicate that she should be called a deaconess, nor can we tell from the narrative what was the state of this true Sister of Charity, whether she was a widow, whether married or unmarried (Weiss) ; see further, "Dorcas," Hastings' B.D., and Edersheim, Jewish Social Life, p. 78. On the phrase here see Winer-Schmiedel, p. 232.—ἐλεημοσυνῶν in singular, iii. 2 ; in plural x. 2, as here ; "species post genus ut, 41," Blass, but by the former term also ἀγαθ. ἔργων works of charity may be more especially intended ; see Weber, Jüdische Theol., p. 284 (1897) ; cf. Ecclus. xx. 16, τὰ ἀγαθά μου (and xviii. 15 ; Tobit xii. 13) ; "Dorcas" and "Almsgiving," Hastings' B.D.—ὧν, see on i. 1.

Ver. 37. ἐγέν. δὲ: on the frequency of the formula in Luke see above p. 124, and Plummer, St. Luke, p. 45, on the use of ἐγένετο. — ἀσθενήσασαν : aorist, marking the time when she fell sick (Weiss).—λούσαντες : after the manner of the Jews as well as of the Greeks, cf. instances in Wetstein and Hamburger, Real-Encyclopädie des Judentums, i., 2, 162, "Beerdigung".

Outside Jerusalem three days might elapse between the death and burial, but in Jerusalem no corpse lay over night, see Hamburger, u. s., p. 161 ; in the case of Ananias and Sapphira we may note the accuracy of this distinction.—ἔθηκαν : burial did not take place until the danger of an apparent death was considered past ; in uncertain cases a delay as above might be allowed, or for other special reasons, and children were forbidden to hasten the burial of their parents, Hamburger, u. s., p. 161 ; and further for burial and mourning customs, Edersheim, Jewish Social Life, p. 168, and History of the Jewish Nation, p. 311.—ἐν ὑπερῴῳ : the body was usually laid in an upper chamber when burial was delayed ; see Hackett's note and also on ver. 39, and Alford on the article.

Ver. 38. Λύδδης, on the form see above on ver. 35 ; nine miles from Joppa. —παρακαλοῦντες ; the only passage in which the oratio recta follows if we read μὴ ὀκνήσῃς, see critical notes ; this also best represents the urgency of the message (cf. John xi. 3), as in R.V.—μὴ ὀκν.: "fides non tollit civilitatem verborum," Bengel. Verb only here in N.T., cf. LXX, Num. xxii. 16, of Balak to Balaam, a phrase almost identically similar.—διελθεῖν, cf. Luke ii. 15, and ver. 32 above, and below xi. 19. Like other compounds of ἔρχομαι very frequent in Luke, as compared with other writers (Friedrich, p. 7).—ἕως αὐτῶν : use of ἕως locally, common in St. Luke (Friedrich, p. 20) ; ἕως with genitive of the person as here, cf. Luke iv. 42, 1 Macc. iii. 26 ; not so used in classical writers (Plummer).

Ver. 39. It is not said that they sent for St. Peter to work a miracle, but his near presence at Lydda would naturally make them turn to him in a time of sorrow.

ἱμάτια [1] ὅσα ἐποίει μετ᾽ αὐτῶν οὖσα ἡ Δορκάς.   40. ἐκβαλὼν δὲ ἔξω
πάντας ὁ Πέτρος, θεὶς τὰ γόνατα προσηύξατο · καὶ ἐπιστρέψας πρὸς
τὸ σῶμα, εἶπε, Ταβιθά,[2] ἀνάστηθι.   ἡ δὲ ἤνοιξε τοὺς ὀφθαλμοὺς

[1] After **ιματια** Par., Ps.-Aug. add **διηγουντο αυτῳ**, accepted by Blass. Belser
supports, pp. 58, 59, as being clearer, and showing that the widows not only pointed
to the garments with them in proof of the charity of Dorcas, but also showed how
much good work she had down besides.

[2] After **αναστηθι** Syr. Harcl., Sah., Gig., Par., Cypr., Ps.-Aug., Cassiod. add " in
nomine domini nostri Jesu Christi ".   Cypr. and Cassiod. omit " domini nostri ".
Blass accepts this latter form, Hilg. the former.   Belser, *u. s.*, thinks that the words
might easily be omitted on revision by an author who was not afraid of any obscurity arising after ver. 34

—**παραγενόμενον** : a characteristic Lucan
expression (Weiss), see above v. 21.—
τὸ ὑπερ. : here the article would naturally be used on referring to the chamber,
cf. ver. 37, in which the body lay.—**αἱ
χῆραι** : they may have been the poor of
the Church, vi. 1, whom Dorcas had
befriended, or those who had been associated with her in good works (see also
Plumptre's suggestive note). In connection with St. Luke's marked sympathy
with women, we may note that the word
χήρα is used by him no less than nine
times in his Gospel, three in Acts.—
κλαίουσαι, *cf.* Luke vii. 13, viii. 52, Hamburger, *u. s.* (ver. 37).—**ἐπιδεικ.** : only
here in middle voice, perhaps as pointing
to the garments which they were themselves wearing (so Blass, Wendt, Felten,
Grimm-Thayer), which Dorcas had given
them.—**χιτῶνας** : "coats," close-fitting
undergarments ; the word was used in
classical Greek of men and women, more
perhaps like a dressing-gown or cassock ;
"Coat," "Dress," Hastings' B.D.—**ἱμάτια,** the long flowing outer robes.—**ὅσα** :
"all which," *i.e.*, so many (Blass, Page,
Hackett, Knabenbauer) ; see reading in
β (Blass), critical notes.—**ἐποίει** : imperfect as denoting her customary mode
of action.
Ver. 40. **ἐκβαλὼν δὲ ἔξω πάντας** :
nothing could be more natural than this
action of St. Peter as a reminiscence of
his Master's action, when He was about
to perform a similar miracle, *cf.* Matt.
ix. 25, Mark v. 40 (*cf.* 2 Kings iv. 33,
and vv. 4, 5 in same chapter), but· in
Luke viii. 54 it is noteworthy that the
similar words are omitted by W.H. and
the revisers, see above. In St. Matthew
the multitude ὁ ὄχλος is put out, but in
St. Mark (and St. Luke), whilst all are
described as put out (the same verb),
Peter, James and John, with the parents,

are allowed to be present at the miracle.
Weiss points out the reminiscence of
Mark v. 40, but this we might expect
if St. Mark's Gospel comes to us through
St. Peter. St. Chrysostom marks the
action of St. Peter as showing how
entirely free he was from any attempt
at display.—**θεὶς τὰ γόνατα**, see note
on vii. 60, "hoc Dominus ipse non
fecerat" Blass.   St. Peter had been
present on each of the three occasions
recorded in the Gospels when his Master
had raised the dead, but he does not
venture at once to speak the word of
power, but like Elijah or Elisha kneels
down in prayer (see Rendall's note).—
Τ. ἀνάστηθι, *cf.* Mark v. 41. Here
again we note the close agreement with
St. Mark's narrative—the words to the
damsel are not given at all by St.
Matthew ix. 25, and by St. Luke in
Greek, viii. 54, not in Aramaic as by
Mark. On the absurdity of identifying
the **Ταβιθά** here with the **Ταλιθά** of
Mark v. 41 see Nösgen and Zöckler, *in
loco.* It may suffice to note with Lumby
that in each case an interpretation of
the word used is given.—**ἀνεκάθισε** :
not found in LXX, and used only by St.
Luke in this passage and in his Gospel,
vii. 15 (but B has **ἐκάθισεν**, which W.H.
reads only in margin), in both cases of a
person restored to life and sitting up.
In this *intransitive* sense it is almost
entirely confined to medical writers, to
describe patients sitting up in bed. It
occurs in Plato, *Phædo*, 60 B, but in the
middle voice, and with the words ἐπὶ τὴν
κλίνην expressed : in Xen., *Cyr.*, v., 7, it is
also·used, but in a different sense (to sit
down again),*cf.* Hobart, pp. 11,40,41, who
also notices that the circumstantial details
of the gradual recovery of Tabitha are
quite in the style of medical description.
τὸ σῶμα, Luke xvii. 37, the word is quite

αὐτῆς · καὶ ἰδοῦσα τὸν Πέτρον, ἀνεκάθισε.   41. δοὺς δὲ αὐτῇ χεῖρα,
ἀνέστησεν αὐτήν · φωνήσας δὲ τοὺς ἁγίους καὶ τὰς χήρας, παρέστησεν
αὐτὴν ζῶσαν.   42. γνωστὸν δὲ ἐγένετο καθ᾽ ὅλης τῆς Ἰόππης,[1]
43. καὶ πολλοὶ ἐπίστευσαν ἐπὶ τὸν Κύριον · ἐγένετο δὲ ἡμέρας
ἱκανὰς μεῖναι αὐτὸν[2] ἐν Ἰόππῃ παρά τινι Σίμωνι βυρσεῖ.

---

[1] **της Ιοππης**, on spelling see Winer-Schmiedel, p. 56.   Art. om. by W.H. after
BC¹, but retained here by Weiss.

[2] **αυτον** om. א¹B, so Tisch., W.H. (Weiss) ; and there are various other readings
but none possessing such strong support.

classical for a dead body, so too in LXX,
cf. Deut. xxi. 23, 1 Kings xiii. 24, 1 Macc.
xi. 4, 2 Macc. ix. 29. Everything, as
Wendt admits (1888), points to the fact
that no apparent death, or a raising by
natural means, is thought of by the
narrator. Holtzmann and Pfleiderer can
only find a parallel here with xx. 9-12,
but none can read the two narratives
without seeing their independence, except in the main fact that both narrate
a similar miracle.—**ἤνοιξε τοὺς ὀφθ.** : to
this there is nothing corresponding in the
details given by the Gospel narratives, as
Blass points out.

Ver. 41. **δοὺς δὲ αὐτῇ χ.** : here for help
to her to rise, after she had been restored
to life, but in the Gospels Christ takes
the damsel by the hand *before* she is restored, Mark v. 41, Luke viii. 54. Thus,
while retaining a close resemblance, as
we might surely expect, to our Lord's
action in St. Mark's narrative, there is yet
sufficient independence of detail to show
that one description is not a slavish imitation of the other.—**τὰς χήρας** : Rendall
sees in the words reference to an organised body, 1 Tim. v. 11-16, engaged in
the service of the Church, but the context only points to the widows who had
been previously mentioned, *species post
genus*, as in ver. 36 (Blass).

Ver. 42. **καθ᾽ ὅλης,** see above on ver. 31.
Ver. 43. **ἐγένετο δὲ,** see on ver. 37,
Plummer, *St. Luke*, p. 45, on the use of
ἐγένετο. The phrase also marks (as often
in Luke) a transition to the following
narrative (Nösgen).—**ἡμέρας ἱκανὰς,** see
on viii. 11, and xxvii. 7. Kennedy speaks
of the adjective as used in the vernacular
sense of "long," "many," Aristoph.,
Pax., 354.—**βυρσεῖ,** in classics **βυρσοδέ-
ψης** : it is difficult to suppose that the
common estimate of the work of a tanner
amongst the Jews as unclean, on account
of their constant contact with dead animals, has here no significance. At least
the mention of the trade seems to show

that St. Peter was already in a state of mind
which would fit him for the further revelation of the next chapter, and for the instructions to go and baptise the Gentile Cornelius. On the detestation in which this
trade was held by the Jews, see Wetstein,
in loco ; Edersheim, *Jewish Social Life*,
p. 158; *cf.* Mishna, *Khethuboth*, vii., 10.
It does not in any way militate against
the historical character of the narrative,
as Overbeck maintains, to admit that the
description is meant to introduce the
" universalism " of the following incident. Both Chrysostom and Theophylact
(so too Erasmus) dwell upon this incident in St. Peter's life as illustrating
his unassuming conduct.—**Ἰόππη,** see
on ver. 36. Heb. יָפוֹ, "beauty," *Jaffa ;*
see for references Josh. xix. 46, 2 Chron.
ii. 16, Jonah i. 3, Ezra iii. 7; the port of
Jerusalem from the days of Solomon
(from which it was distant some thirty-
five miles), situated on a hill so high that
people affirmed, as Strabo mentions, that
the capital was visible from its summit.
It was *comparatively* (Schürer) the best
harbour on the coast of Palestine (although Josephus, *B. J.*, iii., 9, correctly
describes it as dangerous), and in this lay
its chief importance. The Maccabees
were well aware of this, and it is of
Simon that the historian writes : " With
all his glory he took Joppa for an haven,
and made an entrance to the isles of the
sea " 1 Macc. xiv. 5 (about 144 B.C.).
The Judaising of the city was the natural
result of the Maccabean occupation, although the Syrians twice retook Joppa,
and twice Hyrcanus regained it for the
Jews. Taken by Pompey B.C. 63, restored to the Jews by Cæsar 47, Jos.,
Ant., xiv., 4, 4; *B. J.*, i., 7, 7, and
Ant., xiv., 10, 6, and at length added to
the kingdom of Herod the Great, *Ant.*,
xv., 7, 3 ; *B. J.*, i., 20, 3, Joppa remained
Jewish, imbued with all the fanatic
patriotism of the mother-city, and in

X. 1. ᾿ΑΝΗΡ δέ τις ἦν ἐν Καισαρείᾳ ὀνόματι Κορνήλιος,
2. ἑκατοντάρχης ἐκ σπείρης[1] τῆς καλουμένης ᾿Ιταλικῆς, εὐσεβὴς καὶ
φοβούμενος τὸν Θεὸν σὺν παντὶ τῷ οἴκῳ αὐτοῦ, ποιῶν τε ἐλεημοσύνας

---

[1] σπειρης ℵACEL, so Tisch., W.H., Blass, Weiss, Hilg.; but σπειρας in BP, Chrys., W.H., alt., App., p. 164.

---

the fierce revolt of 66 A.D. Joppa still remained alone in her undivided allegiance to Judaism, and against Joppa the first assault of Cestius Gallus was directed. On the Joppa which St. Peter entered, Acts x., and its contrast to the neighbouring Cæsarea, see viii. 40 and G. A. Smith, *Hist. Geog.*, p. 136 ff.; see also Schürer, *Jewish People*, div. ii., vol. i., p. 79 ff. E.T.; Hamburger, *Real-Encyclopädie des Judentums*, i., 4, 601; B.D.[2], "Joppa".

CHAPTER X. *Baptism of Cornelius and his friends.*—Ver. 1. ἀνήρ τις: on the expression see Ramsay, *St. Paul*, p. 202.—ἐν Κ., see viii. 40.

Ver. 2. ἑκατοντάρχης: form general in N.T., and so in later Greek, although χιλίαρχος is always retained in N.T., and ἑκατόνταρχος is also found, Matt. viii. 5, 8 (W.H.), Luke vii. 2, Acts xxii. 25 (W.H.); so πατριάρχης, πολιτάρχης, ἐθνάρχης, see Winer-Schmiedel, p. 82, and note on forms employed in Josephus and LXX; W.H., Appendix, p. 163; Blass, *Gram.*, pp. 28, 68; and Grimm-Thayer, *sub v.*, for various authorities.—ἐκ σπείρης τῆς ᾿Ι.: the word σπεῖρα here = *cohors*, although used in the N.T. in a more general way as of the band which arrested Jesus, and so also of Jewish troops in Judith xiv. 11, 2 Macc. viii. 23, xii. 20, 22. Each legion was subdivided into ten cohorts, but besides the legionary cohorts there were auxiliary cohorts, and Josephus mentions that five of these cohorts were stationed at Cæsarea at the time of the death of Herod Agrippa, composed to a great extent at all events of the inhabitants of Cæsarea and Sebaste, *Ant.*, xix., 9, 2; xx., 8, 7. There were in the provinces Italic cohorts composed of volunteer Roman citizens born in Italy, and in answer to the strictures of Schürer, who contends that there was no Italic cohort in Cæsarea at this time, Blass, *in loco*, asks why one of the five cohorts mentioned by Josephus may not have been composed of Roman citizens who had made their home at Cæsarea or Sebaste, a cohort known by the name mentioned. But Ramsay has given great

interest to the subject by his account of a recently discovered inscription at Carnuntum—the epitaph of a young Roman soldier, a subordinate officer in the second Italic cohort, who died at Carnuntum while engaged on detached service from the Syrian army. He sees reason to infer that there was an Italic cohort stationed in Syria in A.D. 69, and although the new discovery does not prove anything with certainty for the period in Acts x., say 40-44 A.D., yet it becomes in every way probable that at that date, when Cornelius is described as in x. 1, an Italic cohort recruited from the east was stationed in the province Syria. But even if it could be shown that no Italic cohort was stationed at Cæsarea from A.D. 6-41, or again from 41-44 in the reign of Herod, it by no means follows that a centurion belonging to the cohort may not have been on duty there. He may have been so, even if his cohort was on duty elsewhere, and it would be a bold thing to deny such a possibility when the whole subject of detached service is so obscure; Ramsay, *Expositor*, September, 1896, also *Expositor*, December, 1896 (Schürer's reply), and January, 1897 (Ramsay); Schürer, *Jewish People*, div. i., vol. ii., p. 53 ff. E.T.; Ramsay, *Was Christ born at Bethlehem?* pp. 260-269; O. Holtzmann, *Neutest. Zeitgeschichte*, p. 108; and Wendt, *in loco*, (1899).—εὐσεβὴς καὶ φ. τὸν Θεόν: the adjective is only used here and in ver. 7 (xxii. 12), and once again in 2 Peter ii. 9 in the N.T. In the LXX it is found four times in Isaiah, thrice as an equivalent of צַדִּיק, xxiv. 16, xxvi. 7 (2), righteous, upright, *cf.* also Prov. xii. 12, once as an equivalent of נָדִיב, liberal, generous, see on viii. 2 above; frequent in Ecclus. and Macc., see also Trench, *N.T. Synonyms*, i., p. 196. Taken by itself the word might denote goodness such as might characterise a Gentile, *cf.* xvii. 23, and its classical use (like the Latin *pietas*); but construed with φ. τὸν Θεόν it certainly seems to indicate that Cornelius was "a God-fearing proselyte" (not to

πολλὰς τῷ λαῷ, καὶ δεόμενος τοῦ Θεοῦ διὰ παντός · 3. εἶδεν ἐν
ὁράματι φανερῶς,[1] ὡσεὶ ὥραν ἐννάτην τῆς ἡμέρας, ἄγγελον τοῦ Θεοῦ

[1] ἐν οραματι φαν. om. by Iren. ; Blass brackets, and see Pref. to β text, p. xviii.
ωσει add περι, so ℵABCE, many min., Syr. (P. and H.), Boh., Irint., Dam., so
Tisch., W.H., R.V., Weiss, Wendt, Hilg. ; Blass omits in β ; evidence for the addition seems conclusive, and περι may have dropped out as superfluous after ωσει.
εννατην ; ℵABCEP have ενατην, and Tisch., W.H., Blass, Hilg., see Winer-
Schmiedel, p. 55.

be identified it would seem with "proselytes of the gate," although the confusion is common (Schürer, *Jewish
People*, div. ii., vol. ii., p. 316 E.T.)). In
Acts this class of proselyte is always so
described (or σεβόμενοι τὸν Θ.) "they
that fear God," *i.e.*, the God of the Jews,
cf. x. 22, 35, xiii. 16, 26, etc. All the
incidents of the story seem to point to
the fact that Cornelius had come into
relations with the synagogue, and had
learned the name and the fear of the God
of Israel, *cf.* x. 2, 22, 25, without accepting circumcision, see especially Ramsay,
Expositor, p. 200 (1896), where he corrects
his former remarks in *St. Paul*, p. 43 ;
Hamburger, *Real-Encyclopädie des Judentums*, " Fremder," i., 3, p. 382 ; Hort,
Ecclesia, p. 58 ; O. Holtzmann, *Neutest.
Zeitgeschichte*, pp. 184, 185 ; Weizsäcker,
Apostolic Age, i., 103 E.T. ; McGiffert,
Apostolic Age, p. 101, note, and for a
further explanation of the distinction between the σεβόμενοι and the " proselytes
of the gate " *cf.* Muirhead *Times of Christ*
(T. & T. Clark), pp. 105, 106.—σὺν παντὶ
τῷ οἴκῳ αὐτοῦ : the centurions of the N.T.
are always favourably represented, *cf.*
Matt. viii. 5, Luke vii. 9, xxiii. 47, Acts
xxvii. 3. οἶκος here includes not only
the family but the whole household, *cf.*
vii. 10, xi. 14, xvi. 31, xviii. 8, etc. ; Luke
i. 27, x. 5, xix. 9, thus the soldier "who
waited on him continually " is also called
εὐσεβής. οἶκος (*cf.* πᾶς ὁ οἶκ. ὅλος ὁ οἶκ.),
favourite word with St. Luke in the sense
of "family" (Lekebusch, Friedrich) as
compared with the other Evangelists, but
often found in St. Paul (*cf.* Hebrews), so
also LXX, Gen. vii. 1, xlvii. 12. St.
Peter uses the word so in xi, 14, and in
1 Peter ii. 18 we have οἰκέτης. St.
Chrysostom well says: " Let us take
heed as many of us as neglect those of
our own house " (*Hom.*, xxii.). *Cf.* too
Calvin, *in loco*.—ποιῶν ἐλεημ. τῷ λαῷ,
see note on ix. 36; the word occurs
frequently in Ecclus. and Tobit, and its
occurrence here and elsewhere in Acts
illustrates the Jewish use of the term ;
but although it is true to say that it

does not occur in Acts in any Christian
precept, St. Paul applies the word to
the collection made from the Christian
Churches for his nation at Jerusalem,
xxiv. 17, a collection to which he attached so much importance as the true
outcome of Christian love and brotherhood, see *l.c.* How highly almsgiving
was estimated amongst the Jews we may
see from the passages referred to in
Hastings' B.D. and B.D.[2]; Uhlhorn's
Christian Charity in the Ancient Church,
p. 52 ff. E.T. ; but it should be remembered that both in Ecclus. and
Tobit there are passages in which both
almsgiving and fasting are also closely
connected with prayer, Ecclus. vii. 10,
Tob. xii. 8.—τῷ λ., *i.e.*, Israel, as always
in Luke, see above on iv. 25. Both
this and his continuous prayer to God,
ver. 30, characterise him as half a Jew
(Weiss).—διὰ παντός : Luke xxiv. 53, and
three times in Acts (once in a quotation, ii. 25), but only used once in Matthew and Mark, and not at all by St.
John ; on St. Luke's predilection for πᾶς
and its compounds see Friedrich, pp. 5, 6.
The description of the centurion no
doubt reminds us of the description of
another centurion in Luke vii. 5 (so
Weiss), but we are not obliged to conclude that the centurion here is merely
pictured after the prototype there ; but the
likeness may possibly point to the same
source for both narratives, as in some
respects the language in the two cases
is verbally alike, see Feine.—δεόμενος :
"*preces* et *liberalitas* commendantur hic ;
accedit *jejunium*, ver. 30"; so Bengel,
and he adds, "Benefici faciunt, quod
Deus vult : precantes iidem quod volunt,
Deus facit ".
   Ver. 3. εἶδεν : there is no ground for
explaining away the force of the words
by assuming that Cornelius had formerly
a longing to see Peter. — φανερῶς :
"openly," R.V. ; *manifeste*, Vulgate.
The words plainly are meant to exclude
any illusion of the senses, not in a trance
as in ver. 10, *cf.* xxii. 17 ; only here in
Luke's writings, *cf.* 2 Macc. iii. 28.—ὡσεὶ

εἰσελθόντα πρὸς αὐτόν, 4. καὶ εἰπόντα αὐτῷ, Κορνήλιε. ὁ δὲ ἀτενίσας
αὐτῷ καὶ ἔμφοβος γενόμενος εἶπε, Τί ἐστι, Κύριε; εἶπε δὲ αὐτῷ, Αἱ
προσευχαί σου καὶ αἱ ἐλεημοσύναι σου ἀνέβησαν εἰς μνημόσυνον
ἐνώπιον τοῦ Θεοῦ. 5. καὶ νῦν πέμψον εἰς Ἰόππην ἄνδρας, καὶ
μετάπεμψαι Σίμωνα¹ ὅς ἐπικαλεῖται Πέτρος· 6. οὗτος ξενίζεται παρά
τινι Σίμωνι βυρσεῖ, ᾧ ἐστιν οἰκία παρὰ θάλασσαν· οὗτος λαλήσει
σοι τί σε δεῖ ποιεῖν.² 7. ὡς δὲ ἀπῆλθεν ὁ ἄγγελος ὁ λαλῶν τῷ
Κορνηλίῳ, φωνήσας δύο τῶν οἰκετῶν αὐτοῦ, καὶ στρατιώτην εὐσεβῆ

¹ After **Σίμωνα** add **τινα** W.H., R.V., Blass, Weiss.

² **ουτος λαλησει . . . δει ποιειν**, whole clause om. אABCELP 13, 61, Vulg.
(am. fu. tol.), Syr., P. and H., etc., so W.H., R.V., Hilg., retained by Blass in β on
the authority of Vulg^cl., Par.², and a few min., evidently case of insertion, cf. ix. 6,
xi. 14.

(**περί**) : the **ὡσεί**, as Blass points out, intimates the same as **περί**—the dative which is read here by Chrysostom (omit **περί**) is sometimes confused with the accusative in the sense of duration of time, see Blass on ver. 30, and viii. 11 (for the accusative see John iv. 52, Rev. iii. 3), and *Gram.*, p. 93. Cornelius observed without doubt the Jewish hours of prayer, and the vision is represented as following upon, or whilst he was engaged in, prayer, and in answer to it.
Ver. 4. **Κορνήλιε**, *cf.* ix. 10 (1 Sam. iii.). Of Cornelius the words of the Evangelical Prophet were true, xliii. 1, "Fear not, for I have redeemed thee, I have called thee by thy name; thou art mine".—**ἀτενίσας**, see above on i. 10.—**ἔμφοβος** : four times in St. Luke, twice in Gospel, twice in Acts, and always with second aorist participle of **γίγνομαι** as here, only once elsewhere in N.T., Rev. xi. 13 (with **ἐγένοντο**); *cf.* Ecclus. xix. 24 (21), of the fear of God; and in 1 Macc. xiii. 2 both **ἔντρομος** and **ἔμφοβος** are apparently found together, *cf.* Acts vii. 32 and xvi. 29, but in classical Greek the word is used properly actively, *formidolosus*.—**τί ἐστι, Κύριε**; the words, similar to those used by Paul at his conversion, reveal the humility and the attentive attitude and readiness of Cornelius.—**αἱ προσ.**, *cf.* ii. 22, with article : of regular prayers. —**ἀνέβησαν**: *tanquam sacrificia*, *cf.* Ps. cxli. 2, Phil. iv. 18, Heb. xiii. 15, and for the word, 2 Kings iii. 20, Job xx. 6, Ezek. viii. 11, 1 Macc. v. 31.—**εἰς μνημόσυνον**: in Lev. ii. 2, 9, 16, v. 12, vi. 15, Num. v. 26 (*cf.* Ecclus. xxxviii. 11, xlv. 16), the word is used as a translation of the Hebrew אַזְכָּרָה, "a name given to that portion of the vegetable oblation which was

burnt with frankincense upon the altar, the sweet savour of which ascending to heaven was supposed to commend the person sacrificing to the remembrance and favour of God," *a remembrance offering*. The words at all events express the thought that the prayers and alms of Cornelius had gained the favourable regard of God, and that they would be remembered, and are remembered accordingly (see notes by Wendt, Felten and Holtzmann), the alms being regarded by zeugma as ascending like the prayers. With this passage *cf.* Tob. xii. 12, 15, and Mr. Ball's note in *Speaker's Commentary*, i., p. 231. "O quam multa in terram cadunt, non ascendunt" Bengel, and *cf. Hamlet*, Act iii., Sc. 3 : "My words fly up," etc.: see *Book of Enoch*, xlix., 3, for a striking parallel to the thought of raising prayers as a memorial to God, Charles' edition, pp. 70, 284.
Ver. 5. **μετάπεμψαι**: middle, his messengers were to perform his wishes; only in Acts in N.T., where it occurs nine times, but found twice in LXX and in Maccabees; so too mostly in the middle in classical writers, although the active is also found in same sense.—**Σίμωνά** (**τινα**), see critical notes; as unknown to Cornelius, marked out by his surname as the one of the many who were called Simon.
Ver. 6. **ξενίζεται**, see ver. 33.—**παρὰ θάλασσαν**: perhaps to secure water for the purpose of his trade, perhaps because it seems that a tanner was not allowed to carry on his business unless outside the walls of a town, see on ix. 43, at a distance of fifty cubits, see Wendt, *in loco;* Hackett, p. 135.
Ver. 7. **οἰκετῶν**: one related to the **οἶκος**, a milder and a narrower term than **δοῦλος**, which would simply de-

17. Ὡς δὲ ἐν ἑαυτῷ [1] διηπόρει ὁ Πέτρος, τί ἂν εἴη τὸ ὅραμα ὃ εἶδε,
καὶ ἰδού, οἱ ἄνδρες οἱ ἀπεσταλμένοι ἀπὸ τοῦ Κορνηλίου, διερωτήσαντες
τὴν οἰκίαν Σίμωνος, ἐπέστησαν ἐπὶ τὸν πυλῶνα · 18. καὶ φωνήσαντες
ἐπυνθάνοντο, εἰ Σίμων ὁ ἐπικαλούμενος Πέτρος ἐνθάδε ξενίζεται. 19.
Τοῦ δὲ Πέτρου ἐνθυμουμένου [2] περὶ τοῦ ὁράματος, εἶπεν αὐτῷ τὸ
Πνεῦμα, Ἰδού, ἄνδρες τρεῖς [3] ζητοῦσί σε · 20. ἀλλὰ ἀναστὰς κατάβηθι,
καὶ πορεύου σὺν αὐτοῖς, μηδὲν διακρινόμενος · διότι ἐγὼ ἀπέσταλκα
αὐτούς. 21. καταβὰς δὲ Πέτρος πρὸς τοὺς ἄνδρας τοὺς ἀπεσταλ-
μένους ἀπὸ τοῦ Κορνηλίου πρὸς αὐτόν, εἶπεν, Ἰδού, ἐγώ εἰμι ὃν

[1] After εαυτω D, Par., Aug., add εγενετο, " when P. came to himself, he doubted
. . .," so Hilg., cf. xii. 11.

[2] ενθυμουμενου, but אABCDELP have διενθ., so all edd. αυτω το Πν. om. B,
Boh., so W.H. text, Weiss, Wendt (probably). Par. prefixes ετι before διεν., and
Par., Syr. Harcl. και διαπορουντος before περι.

[3] τρεις אACE 13, 61, many verss.; Lach. [W.H. marg.], R.V., Hilg.; δυο B, W.H.
text, Weiss; om. DHLP, Syr. H., Apost. Const., Cyr.-Jer., Chrys., Aug., Amb.; so
Tisch., Blass, Wendt. Those who favour omission contend that τρεις comes from
xi. 11, δυο from ver. 7. But Weiss maintains that δυο is quite correct, as in ver. 7,
the soldier is regarded as a guard for the two servants who convey the message : this
was overlooked, and δυο was either allowed to drop out, or was changed into τρεις, cf.
xi. 11. It is possible that if τρεις was original it fell out after ανδρες (-ΔΡΕΣΤΡΕΙΣ).

ness where God had already bestowed His
cleansing mercy in Christ " (Rendall).
We cannot limit the words, as has been
attempted, to the single case of Cornelius,
or refer them only to the removal of the
distinction between clean and unclean
meats.

Ver. 16. πάλιν : if we read εὐθύς,
see critical notes, we have St. Mark's
characteristic word (used by St. Luke
only here in Acts, and once in Luke vi.
49), a suggestive fact in a section of the
book in which the pen or the language
of St. Peter may fairly be traced.

Ver. 17. διηπόρει : "was much perplexed," R.V., cf. ii. 12, v. 24 ; see Page's
note, Acts, p. 145.—τί ἂν εἴη : on the
optative in indirect questions used by
St. Luke only, with or without ἂν, see
Simcox, Language of the N. T., p. 112 ;
Burton, N. T. Moods and Tenses, pp. 80,
133.—διερωτήσαντες : only here in N.T.,
not in LXX, but in classical Greek for
asking constantly or continually ; preposition intensifies. Here it may imply
that they had asked through the town
for the house of Cornelius (Weiss).—
πυλῶνα, cf. xii. 13 (and Blass, in loco).
R.V. renders not "porch," as in Matt.
xxvi. 71, but " gate," as if it were θύρα.
The πυλών was properly the passage
which led from the street through the
front part of the house to the inner
court. This was closed next the street

by a heavy folding gate with a small
wicket kept by a porter (see Alford on
Matt., u. s., and Grimm-Thayer, sub v.).
Ver. 18. φωνήσαντες : "having called out
some one of the servants" (Blass, Alford,
Kuinoel), but = "called " simply, R.V.;
" vocantes portæ curatorem," Wetstein.
Ver. 19. ἐνθυμουμένου : compound
verb best, see critical notes : "pondered
on the vision," Rendall ; διενθ. verb =
to weigh in the mind, only here, not
found in LXX or elsewhere, except in
ecclesiastical writers.—ἄνδρες τρεῖς, so
A. and R.V., see critical notes.

Ver. 20. μηδὲν διακ. : "nothing doubting," i.e., without hesitation as to its
lawfulness, cf. Matt. xxi. 21, Rom. xiv.
23, Mark xi. 23, James i. 6 ; the verb is
not so used in classical Greek. See
Mayor's note on James i. 6, apparently
confined in this sense to N.T. and later
Christian writings. For the active voice
see xi. 12, xv. 9. If we read a stop
after διακ. and διότι or ὅτι immediately
following, we may translate, "nothing
doubting ; for I have sent them," R.V.;
but if no punctuation (so Rendall, Weiss)
translate, "nothing doubting that I have
sent them," i.e., the fact that I have
sent them. In either case ἐγώ emphatic.
Nothing had been spoken to him of his
journey, but in the path of unhesitating
obedience he was led to the meaning of
the revelation (cf. John xiii. 7).

ζητεῖτε [1] · τίς ἡ αἰτία δι' ἣν πάρεστε; 22. οἱ δὲ εἶπον, Κορνήλιος
ἑκατοντάρχης, ἀνὴρ δίκαιος καὶ φοβούμενος τὸν Θεόν, μαρτυρούμενός
τε ὑπὸ ὅλου τοῦ ἔθνους τῶν Ἰουδαίων, ἐχρηματίσθη ὑπὸ ἀγγέλου
ἁγίου, μεταπέμψασθαί σε εἰς τὸν οἶκον αὐτοῦ, καὶ ἀκοῦσαι ῥήματα
παρὰ σοῦ. 23. εἰσκαλεσάμενος [2] οὖν αὐτοὺς ἐξένισε. Τῇ δὲ ἐπαύριον
ὁ Πέτρος ἐξῆλθε σὺν αὐτοῖς, καί τινες τῶν ἀδελφῶν τῶν ἀπὸ τῆς [3]
Ἰόππης συνῆλθον αὐτῷ. 24. καὶ τῇ ἐπαύριον εἰσῆλθον [4] εἰς τὴν
Καισάρειαν · ὁ δὲ Κορνήλιος ἦν προσδοκῶν αὐτούς, συγκαλεσάμενος

[1] After ζητειτε D, Syr. Harcl. add τι θελετε; (ἤ) κ.τ.λ. looks like an anticipatory
gloss of τις ἡ αιτια.

[2] For εισκαλεσαμενος D, Par. read εισαγαγων, a fairly common word (six times in
Acts), but εισκ. "απ. λεγ." in N.T.

[3] The art. before Ι. should be omitted, on the evidence of אABCDEHLP ; Tisch.,
W.H., Weiss, Wendt, Hilg.

[4] εισηλθον—but BD 47, 61, Vulg., Syr. Harcl. text, Aeth. εισηλθεν, so W.H.,
R.V., marg., Weiss, Hilg.—but plural AEHLP (εισηλθαν in אC), and several vers.,
Chrys., Tisch., Blass. Alford thinks sing. a corrn. to suit εξηλθεν above ; but, on
the other hand, as the sing. lies between several plurals, transcriptural prob. seems
to favour it. Καισαρειαν, see on viii. 40. D, Syr. Harcl. Par.[1] add περιεμενεν at
the end of verse retained by Blass and Hilg., see Weiss, Codex D, p. 68, on its
possible force here.

Ver. 22. δίκαιος: "sensu Judaico"
(Blass), cf. Luke i. 6, ii. 25, xxiii. 50.—
μαρτ., see on vi. 3. τε closely joins it,
as confirming the judgment. On construction with ὑπό in inscriptions, Deissmann, *Neue Bibelstudien*, p. 95.—ἔθνους
τῶν Ἰ.: ἔθνος in the mouth of Gentiles,
cf. Luke vii. 5 and see above on iv.
25.—ἐχρηματίσθη: "was warned of God,"
R.V., Matt. ii. 12, 22, Luke ii. 26,
cf. Heb. viii. 5, xi. 7, and Jos., *Ant.*,
iii., 8, 8 ; see Westcott, *Hebrews*, p.
217. For use of the active in LXX,
see Jer. xxxiii. (xxvi.) 2, cf. also xi. 26.—
ἁγίου: only here with ἀγγέλου, expressing the reverence of these pious men
(Weiss).
Ver. 23. εἰσκ.: only used here in
N.T., so μετακ. in ver. 32 ; both verbs
are also frequent in medical writers, as
Hobart urges, but both are found in
classical Greek, and the latter three
times in LXX, although the former not
at all.—ἐξένισε, *recepit hospitio*, Vulgate,
cf. Heb. xiii. 2, and Westcott, *l.c.*; verb
used six times in Acts in this sense, but
nowhere else in N.T.; cf. Ecclus. xxix.
25. In this Christian hospitality to Gentile strangers Peter had taken another
step towards understanding what the will
of the Lord was.—τινες τῶν ἀδελφῶν =
xi. 12.
Ver. 24. On the route see Edersheim,
Jewish Social Life, p. 27 ; and on this and
the following verse in β text as specially
supporting his theory, see Blass, *Philology of the Gospels*, pp. 116 ff. and 127.—
ἦν προσδοκῶν: characteristic Lucan construction, see above i. 10; cf. Luke i. 21.
προσδ., favourite with St. Luke ; six times
in Gospel, five in Acts, elsewhere in
Gospels only twice in Matthew.—συγκ.,
i.e., on the day on which he expected the
advent of Peter and the returning messengers as to a feast ; they were probably also
fearers of the true God, and of a like mind
with Cornelius.—ἀναγκαίους, *necessarios*,
cf. Jos., *Ant.*, vii., 14, 4 ; xi., 6, 4 ; xiii.,
7, 2, etc., and instances in Wetstein.
Ver. 25. ὡς δὲ ἐγέν. (τοῦ) εἰσ.: for
τοῦ see critical notes ; "and when it
came to pass that Peter entered," R.V.,
i.e., into the house, see Burton, *N. T.
Moods and Tenses*, p. 139. It may be
regarded as an extension of τοῦ beyond
its usual sphere, see Viteau, *Le Grec du
N. T.*, for instances in LXX, pp. 166, 170
(1893). Simcox regards the sense as
much the same as in the common (and
specially Lucan), ἐγένετο τὸν Π. εἰσελθεῖν.—προσεκύνησεν (cf. xiv. 15): expressive of lowliest humiliation, but not
of necessity involving divine worship, cf
LXX, Gen. xxiii. 7, 12, etc. Weiss
thinks that as the verb is used here
absolutely, as in viii. 27, the act was

τοὺς συγγενεῖς αὐτοῦ καὶ τοὺς ἀναγκαίους φίλους. 25.[1] Ὡς δὲ
ἐγένετο εἰσελθεῖν τὸν Πέτρον, συναντήσας αὐτῷ ὁ Κορνήλιος, πεσὼν
ἐπὶ τοὺς πόδας προσεκύνησεν. 26. ὁ δὲ Πέτρος αὐτὸν ἤγειρε λέγων,
Ἀνάστηθι[2]· κἀγὼ αὐτὸς ἄνθρωπός εἰμι. 27. καὶ συνομιλῶν αὐτῷ,
εἰσῆλθε, καὶ εὑρίσκει συνεληλυθότας πολλούς, ἔφη τε πρὸς αὐτούς,
28. Ὑμεῖς[3] ἐπίστασθε ὡς ἀθέμιτόν ἐστιν ἀνδρὶ Ἰουδαίῳ κολλᾶσθαι ἢ
προσέρχεσθαι ἀλλοφύλῳ· καὶ ἐμοὶ ὁ Θεὸς ἔδειξε μηδένα κοινὸν ἢ
ἀκάθαρτον λέγειν ἄνθρωπον· 29. διὸ καὶ ἀναντιρρήτως[4] ἦλθον μετα-

---

[1] For the whole verse D, Syr. Harcl., Gig. read προσεγγιζοντος δε του Π. (εις
την Κ.) προδραμων εις των δουλων διεσαφησεν παραγεγονεναι αυτον. D, Syr.
Harcl. read also ο δε Κ. εκπηδησας και συναντησας αυτω. Hilg. reads as above and
Belser strongly supports β text, p. 60 ; so Harris, *Four Lectures*, etc., p. 63, who calls
these details " as lifelike as anything we could wish," but see also Corssen, *G. G. A.*,
p. 437, Weiss, Codex D, p. 68, and Wendt, *in loco*, edit. 1899, where he refers the
expansion in Western text to a misunderstanding of εισελθειν in a text. After εγεν.
ℵABCELP, Tisch, Weiss., W.H. read του.

[2] D, Syr. Harcl., Par., Wern. read τι ποιεις; (*cf.* Acts xiv. 15) ; whilst D omits
αναστηθι, the others read it after ποιεις. Par.[2], Wern. add τον Θεον προσκυνει,
cf. Apoc. xix. 10, xxii. 9, so after ειμι DE, Gig., Par., Wern. add ως και συ.

[3] After υμεις D, Aug. insert βελτιον, so Hilg. (*cf.* compar. in iv. 16, β).

[4] αναντιρρητως, so Tisch., Blass, Weiss ; but αναντιρητως BD, 61, W.H., Hilg.

---

one of worship towards one regarded
after the vision as a divine being ; but
on the other hand the language of the
vision by no means involved such a belief on the part of Cornelius (see ver. 5),
and as a worshipper of the one true God
he would not be likely to pay such divine
worship.

Ver. 26. The conduct of Christ may
be contrasted with that of His Apostles,
so Blass : " illi (Petro) autem is honor
recusandus erat, *cf.* Apoc., 19, 10 ; 22, 8 ;
quem nunquam recusavit Jesus, Luc., 4,
8 ; 8, 41 " (see Hackett's note and Knabenbauer *in loco*).

Ver. 27. καὶ συνομιλῶν αὐτῷ : "and
as he talked with him," R.V. ; only here
in N.T., not in LXX (but συνόμιλος,
Symm. Job xix. 19), *cf.* xx. 11 for
similar use of the simple verb ὁμιλέω,
which is also used in a similar sense in
LXX and in Josephus (so too in Xen.),
and also in modern Greek (Kennedy).—
εἰσῆλθε, *i.e.*, into the room, in distinction to ver. 25 of entrance into the
house, or it may signify the *completion*
of his entering in (so De Wette, Weiss).

Ver. 28. ἀθέμιτον : only once again in
N.T., and significantly in 1 Pet. iv. 3, but
cf. for a similar sense to its use here 2
Macc. vi. 5, vii. 1. On the extent to which
this feeling was carried see Edersheim,
Jewish Social Life, pp. 26-28 ; Taylor's
Sayings of the Jewish Fathers, pp. 15, 26,
137 (second edition) ; Weber, *Jüdische*

Theologie, p. 68 ; so too Jos., *c. Apion*,
ii., 28, 29, 36 ; Juvenal, xiv., 103 ; Tacitus,
Hist., v., 5.—κολλᾶσθαι, see on v. 13 and
Lightfoot, *Hor. Heb.*, *in loco*.—προσέρχεσθαι : objected to by Zeller and Overbeck, because we know of instances
where Jews went without scruple into
the houses of Gentiles (*cf.* Jos., *Ant.*,
xx., 2, 3) ; but here the whole context
plainly shows what kind of intercourse
was intended (see also Wetstein). Hilgenfeld too regards the notice as unhistorical, but an answer may be found
to his objections in the references above
and in Feine, pp. 202, 204, although his
language seems inconsistent with that
on p. 205.—ἀλλοφύλῳ : in the LXX and
Apocrypha, so in Philo and Josephus as
here ; nowhere else in N.T. but here
with a certain delicate touch, avoiding
the use of the word "heathen" ; in xi. 3
no such delicacy of feeling.—καὶ : not
"but," A.V., but as in R.V., "and yet,"
i.e., in spite of all these prohibitions
and usages.—ὁ Θ. : emphatic, preceding ἔδειξε (Weiss). How fully Peter
afterwards lived and preached this
truth his First Epistle shows, *cf.* 1 Pet.
ii. 17.

Ver. 29. ἀναντιρρήτως : only here in
N.T., but see xix. 36 ; on spelling see
critical notes ; used also by Polyb. ;
" sanctum fidei silentium " (Calvin).—
μεταπεμφθείς : only here in passive in
N.T., see ver. 22.

πεμφθείς. πυνθάνομαι οὖν, τίνι λόγῳ μετεπέμψασθέ με; 30. Καὶ ὁ
Κορνήλιος ἔφη, Ἀπὸ τετάρτης ἡμέρας[1] μέχρι ταύτης τῆς ὥρας ἤμην
νηστεύων, καὶ τὴν ἐννάτην ὥραν προσευχόμενος ἐν τῷ οἴκῳ μου· καὶ
ἰδού, ἀνὴρ ἔστη ἐνώπιόν μου ἐν ἐσθῆτι λαμπρᾷ, 31. καί φησι,
Κορνήλιε, εἰσηκούσθη σου ἡ προσευχή, καὶ αἱ ἐλεημοσύναι σου
ἐμνήσθησαν ἐνώπιον τοῦ Θεοῦ· 32. πέμψον οὖν εἰς Ἰόππην, καὶ
μετακάλεσαι Σίμωνα ὃς ἐπικαλεῖται Πέτρος· οὗτος ξενίζεται ἐν οἰκίᾳ
Σίμωνος βυρσέως παρὰ θάλασσαν· ὃς[2] παραγενόμενος λαλήσει σοι.
33. ἐξαυτῆς οὖν ἔπεμψα πρὸς σέ· σύ τε καλῶς ἐποίησας παραγενόμενος.[3] νῦν οὖν πάντες ἡμεῖς ἐνώπιον τοῦ Θεοῦ πάρεσμεν ἀκοῦσαι
πάντα τὰ προστεταγμένα σοι ὑπὸ τοῦ Θεοῦ.[4]

[1] απο τ. ημερας; Blass emends: τεταρτην ημεραν ταυτην, a more usual construction, but β emendation has no support. τεταρτης—D reads της τριτης, due,
perhaps, to diff. modes of calculation, so Hilg. For ταυτης της ωρας D reads της
αρτι ωρας (cf. 1 Cor. iv. 11), so Hilg. νηστευων και om. ℵABC 61, Vulg., Boh.,
Arm., Aeth., so Tisch., W.H., R.V., Blass, Weiss, Wendt(against Meyer). εννατην,
on spelling see above. ωραν om. ℵABCD 40, 61, so Tisch., W.H., Blass, Hilg.

[2] ος παραγεν. . . . σοι om. ℵAB 3, 15, 18, 61, Vulg., Boh., Aethro·, so Tisch.,
W.H., R.V., Weiss, Wendt; retained by Blass in β and by Hilg., following CDEHLP,
Syr. P. and H., Sah., Gig. and Par.

[3] παραγενομενος, D inserts εν ταχει before (ix. 38), and so Hilg. Instead of
ενωπιον του Θ. Blass (so Hilg.) reads σου ("verum puto"), so D, d, Vulg., Syr.
Pesh., Sah., Aeth., Par.—here Western reading may be correct, as ενωπ. του Θ. is
so common in N.T., and might easily creep in, but see also Weiss, Codex D, p. 69.

[4] Θεου DHLP, Par., Syr. Pesh., Sah., Chrys., so Hilg.; but Κυριου ℵABCE, Vulg.,
Boh., Syr. Harcl., Arm., so Tisch., W.H., R.V., Weiss, Wendt, and so too Blass.

Ver. 30. For readings see critical
notes. "Four days ago, until this hour,
I was keeping the ninth hour of prayer,"
R.V., this hour, i.e., the present hour, the
hour of Peter's visit; four days ago
reckoned from this present hour, lit.,
"from the fourth day," "quarto abhinc
die". The four days according to the
Jewish mode of reckoning would include
the day of the vision and departure of
the messengers, the day they reached
Joppa, the day of their return with Peter,
and the day of their reaching Cæsarea.
Cornelius wishes to signify two things: (1)
that the vision occurred, even to the hour,
four days before Peter's arrival; (2) that
this period of time when it occurred was
the ninth hour.—ἐν ἐσθῆτι λαμπρᾷ, see on
i. 11, "cur illum contemneremus et fuge-
remus cui angeli ministrant?" Wetstein.
Ver. 31. εἰσηκούσθη: perhaps "was
heard" or "has been heard" is best
(see Rendall and Hackett). ἡ προσ. may
refer to his present prayer, as it is in the
singular, but the burden of all his past
prayers had doubtless been the same, cf.
ver. 33 for God's guidance into truth.—

ἐμνήσθησαν, cf. LXX, Ps. xix. 3, Ezek.
xviii. 22, 24; Rev. xvi. 19.
Ver. 33. ἐξαυτῆς, sc., ὥρας: four times
in Acts, otherwise only once in Mark vi.
25 and once in Phil. ii. 23, not in LXX;
for instances in Polyb., Jos., see Wetstein,
sub Mark l.c.—καλῶς ἐποίησας, cf. Phil.
iv. 14, 2 Pet. i. 19, 3 John ver. 6, 1 Macc.
xii. 18, 22. In some instances it may be
described as a formula of expressing
thanks, see Page's note.—ἀκοῦσαι: as in
iv. 20, i.e., to obey.—ἐνώπ. τοῦ Θ.: this
is the way we ought to attend to God's
servants, Chrys., Hom., xxii.
Ver. 34. ἀνοίξας κ.τ.λ.: a solemn
formula, cf. viii. 35, xviii. 14, Matt. v. 2,
xiii. 35; Hort, Judaistic Christ., p. 57.—
ἐπ' ἀληθ.: used in Luke's Gospel three
times, iv. 25, xx. 21, xxii. 59, and in Acts
twice, iv. 27, x. 34, elsewhere only twice
in N.T., Mark xii. 14, 32; the customary
ἐν ἀληθείᾳ is altogether wanting in
Luke.—καταλαμβ.: three times in Acts,
not found in Luke's Gospel; here=mente
comprehendo, cf. Eph. iii. 15, similar
sense; so in Plato, Polybius, and Philo.
—προσωπολήπτης, see Mayor on James

34. Ἀνοίξας δὲ Πέτρος τὸ στόμα εἶπεν, Ἐπ᾿ ἀληθείας καταλαμβάνομαι, ὅτι οὐκ ἔστι προσωπολήπτης ὁ Θεός, 35. ἀλλ᾿ ἐν παντὶ ἔθνει ὁ φοβούμενος αὐτὸν καὶ ἐργαζόμενος δικαιοσύνην δεκτὸς αὐτῷ ἐστι. 36. τὸν λόγον ὃν [1] ἀπέστειλε τοῖς υἱοῖς Ἰσραήλ, εὐαγγελιζόμενος εἰρήνην διὰ Ἰησοῦ Χριστοῦ, (οὗτός ἐστι πάντων Κύριος,) 37. ὑμεῖς οἴδατε τὸ γενόμενον ῥῆμα καθ᾿ ὅλης τῆς Ἰουδαίας, ἀρξάμενον [2] ἀπὸ

[1] ον 𝔑*CDEHLP, Syr. Chrys., Weiss; but wanting in 𝔑ᵃAB 61, W.H., R.V. marg. Blass rejects Κυριος: the word which God sent, this (word) applies to, appertains to, all men. But it has been not unfairly said that almost as good result follows by omitting ον on good authority, as by omitting K. on no authority. Blass parallels for his explanation xxvii. 23, Luke iv. 7, but it may be questioned whether these are quite exact. See also below. Clemen (p. 108) regards the whole verse as marg. note of his R. Antijud., which crept into the text by mistake with 37ᵃ.

[2] αρξαμενον LP 31, 61, and so Weiss, Wendt; αρξαμενος 𝔑ABCDEH 40, so Lach., Tisch., W.H., R.V., see below. Blass regards αρξ. . . . Γαλ. as interpolated after Luke xxiii. 5, and brackets in β. See also Wendt, note edit. 1899. Clemen, p. 108, refers the whole of 37ᵇ to his R. Antijud.; cf. i. 22. After αρξ. DA, Par., Vulg., Iren. add γαρ, so Hilg.; Blass rejects.

ii. 1, πρόσωπον-λαμβάνειν. The actual word is not found in LXX (or in classical Greek), but for the thought of God as no respecter of persons see Deut. x. 17, Lev. xix. 15, Mal. ii. 9, etc., etc., and Luke xx. 21, Gal. ii. 16 (so too προσωποληψία in N.T. three times). The expression πρόσ. λαμβ. is Hebraistic, not necessarily in a bad sense, and in the O.T. more often in a good one, but in the N.T. always in a bad sense, since πρόσωπον acquired the meaning of what was simply external (through its secondary signification a mask) in contrast to a man's real intrinsic character, but the noun and adj. always imply favouritism: see Lightfoot on Gal. ii. 6 and Plummer on Luke xx. 21. Even the enemies acknowledged our Lord's God-likeness at least in this respect, Matt. xxii. 16, Mark xii. 14, Luke xx. 21. Ver. 35. ἀλλ᾿ ἐν παντὶ ἔθνει κ.τ.λ. The words are taken by Ramsay to mean that Cornelius was regarded as a proselyte by Peter, and that only on that condition could he be admitted to the Christian Church, i.e., through Judaism; so apparently St. Paul, pp. 42, 43. On the other hand the general expression ἐργαζ. δικαι. inclines Weiss to refer all the words to the piety attainable by a heathen, who need not be a proselyte. Bengel's words should always be borne in mind: "non indifferentissimus religionum sed indifferentia nationum hic asseritur," see also below, and Knabenbauer, p. 193.—δεκτὸς: "acceptable to him," R.V., and this is best, because it better expresses the thought that fearing God and working righteousness place a

man in a state preparatory for the salvation received through Christ, a reception no longer conditioned by nationality, but by the disposition of the heart. St. Peter does not speak of each and every religion, but of each and every nation, and ver. 43 plainly shows that he by no means loses sight of the higher blessedness of the man whose sin is forgiven through conscious belief in Christ; cf. the language of St. Paul, Rom. x. 9-14. δεκτὸς only in Luke and Paul in N.T., in LXX frequently, and once in the recently discovered Sayings of Jesus, No. 6, which agrees remarkably with St. Luke iv. 24.

Ver. 36. For readings see critical notes; translate: "the word he sent unto" R.V., cf. Ps. cvii. 20.—λόγον, ι, for use of the word as a divine message iv. 31, viii. 14, 25, xiii. 26, xiv. 3, xvi. 32; here it may mean the Gospel message sent to Israel as distinct from the τὸ ῥῆμα, i.e., the previous teaching of John the Baptist (see Rendall); but R.V. like A.V. regards ῥῆμα and Ἰ. τὸν ἀπὸ Ν. as in apposition to λόγον, but Rendall and Weiss place a full stop after Κύριος, and begin a new sentence with ὑμεῖς.—εὐαγγελ. εἰρήνην with the accusative as signifying the contents of the glad tidings, cf. v. 42. —οὗτός ἐστι πάντων Κ.: the parenthetical turn given to the words seem to express the way in which the speaker would guard against the thought that Jesus of Nazareth was simply on a level with those who were spoken of as ἀπόστολοι, as the ἀπέστειλε might perhaps suggest to his hearers (see Nösgen). The words are simply the natural ex-

τῆς Γαλιλαίας, μετὰ τὸ βάπτισμα ὃ ἐκήρυξεν Ἰωάννης · 38. Ἰησοῦν
τὸν ἀπὸ Ναζαρέτ, ὡς ἔχρισεν αὐτὸν ὁ Θεὸς Πνεύματι Ἁγίῳ καὶ
δυνάμει, ὃς διῆλθεν εὐεργετῶν καὶ ἰώμενος πάντας τοὺς καταδυνα-
στευομένους ὑπὸ τοῦ διαβόλου, ὅτι ὁ Θεὸς ἦν μετ᾽ αὐτοῦ · 39. καὶ
ἡμεῖς ἐσμεν μάρτυρες πάντων ὧν ἐποίησεν ἔν τε τῇ χώρᾳ τῶν
Ἰουδαίων καὶ ἐν Ἰερουσαλήμ. ὃν ἀνεῖλον[1] κρεμάσαντες ἐπὶ ξύλου.
40. τοῦτον ὁ Θεὸς ἤγειρε τῇ τρίτῃ ἡμέρᾳ,[2] καὶ ἔδωκεν αὐτὸν ἐμφανῆ

---

[1] ανειλον; in אABCDE και ανειλαν, so Tisch., W.H., Blass, R.V., Weiss, Hilg.,
see Kennedy, p. 160, and Winer-Schmiedel, p. 112. After ον Blass inserts απεδοκιμασαν οι Ιουδαιοι, but no Greek MS., quite insuff.

[2] τη τριτη ημερα א℠ABD²EHLP, so W.H., Blass; with prep. εν prefixed א*C 31,
so Tisch., Weiss (Wendt doubtful). Hilg. follows D and reads the phrase in the acc.

---

pression of the divine power and authority
already assigned by St. Peter to our Lord,
cf. ii. 33, 36 (cf. Rom. x. 12); on their explanation by St. Athanasius and their
place in the Arian controversy, see *Four
Discourses against the Arians*, iv., 30,
E.T. (Schaff and Wace edition). On
Blass's "brilliant suggestion" to omit
κ., see Blass, *in loco* (he seems to think
that κοινός is possible), and Page, *Classical Review*, p. 317, July, 1897.

Ver. 37. τὸ ῥῆμα: so far Peter has
referred to a message which would be
unknown to Cornelius, the message of
peace through Christ, but he now turns
to what Cornelius probably did know by
report at all events; τὸ ῥ. not the λόγος
of ver. 36, but only the "report".—καθ᾽
ὅλης τῆς Ἰ., *i.e.*, all Palestine including
Galilee, cf. ii. 9, xi. 1, 29, St. Luke i. 5
(iv. 44), vii. 17, xxiii. 5, see on ix. 31, 42
above.—ἀρξάμενον, see critical notes;
cf. i. 22 and Luke xxiii. 5. If we read
the accusative it agrees with ῥῆμα (see
above); if the nominative, *cf.* for a
similar construction Luke xxiv. 47, and
see Blass, *Gram.*, p. 81. The abruptness of the construction is quite in
accordance with that elsewhere marked in
St. Peter's speeches, cf. ii. 22-24, iii. 14 ff.
Ver. 38. Ἰησοῦν τὸν ἀπὸ Ν.: in apposition to ῥῆμα, the person in Whom
all else was centred, and in Whom
Peter had found and now preached "the
Christ"; or may be treated as accusative
after ἔχρισεν.—ὡς ἔχρ.: taken by St.
Ambrose, St. Cyril of Jerusalem (so by
Bede) to refer to the Incarnation, by St.
Athanasius to the Baptism only. But
the expression may also be connected
with the entrance of our Lord upon His
ministry at Nazareth, cf. Luke iv. 14;
cf. in this passage the mention of Nazareth and Galilee.—εὐεργετῶν: our Lord

was really εὐεργέτης, *cf.* Luke xxii. 25
(only in St. Luke); "far more truly used
of Christ than of Ptolemy the king of
Egypt," Cornelius à Lapide.—καταδυνα-
στευομένους: only elsewhere in James
ii. 6 in N.T., but *cf.* Wisdom ii. 10,
xv. 14, Ecclus. xlviii. 12, Jos., *Ant.*,
xii., 2, 3. No doubt other diseases besides those of demoniacal possession
are included, *cf.* especially Luke xiii. 11,
16; but a special emphasis on the former
exactly corresponds to the prominence
of a similar class of disease in Mark i.
23.—ὁ Θεὸς ἦν μετ᾽ αὐτοῦ, *cf.* vii. 9,
John iii. 2, so also Luke i. 28, 66, and in
LXX, Judg. vi. 16. We cannot see in the
expression a "low" Christology; St. Peter
had first to declare that Jesus was the
Christ, and it is not likely that he would
have entered upon a further exposition of
His Person in his introductory discourse
with a Gentile convert; but vv. 42 and
43 below, to say nothing of St. Peter's
public addresses, certainly do not point
to a humanitarian Christ.

Ver. 39. ἀνεῖλον, see above, p. 155.
—κρεμάσαντες, p. 154.

Ver. 40. ἐν τῇ τ. ἡμ.: only alluded to
here in Acts, but a positive testimony from
St. Peter to the resurrection appearances
on the third day, 1 Cor. xv. 4; the
expression is specially emphasised by St.
Luke in his Gospel, where it occurs some
six times.—ἐμφανῆ γεν.: a phrase only
found here and in Rom. x. 20, in a
quotation from Isa. lxv. 1, "to be made
manifest," R.V., *viz.*, that He was the
same Person as before His Passion, not
"openly showed," A.V., which gives an
idea not in accordance with the present
context.

Ver. 41. οὐ παντὶ τῷ λαῷ, and therefore
Cornelius could not have known the details fully. Theophylact well remarks,

γενέσθαι, 41. οὐ παντὶ τῷ λαῷ, ἀλλὰ μάρτυσι τοῖς προκεχειροτονημένοις ὑπὸ τοῦ Θεοῦ ἡμῖν, οἵτινες συνεφάγομεν καὶ συνεπίομεν [1] αὐτῷ,
μετὰ τὸ ἀναστῆναι αὐτὸν ἐκ νεκρῶν· 42. καὶ παρήγγειλεν [2] ἡμῖν
κηρύξαι τῷ λαῷ, καὶ διαμαρτύρασθαι, ὅτι αὐτός ἐστιν ὁ ὡρισμένος
ὑπὸ τοῦ Θεοῦ κριτὴς ζώντων καὶ νεκρῶν. 43. τούτῳ πάντες οἱ
προφῆται μαρτυροῦσιν, ἄφεσιν ἁμαρτιῶν λαβεῖν διὰ τοῦ ὀνόματος
αὐτοῦ πάντα τὸν πιστεύοντα εἰς αὐτόν. 44. Ἔτι λαλοῦντος τοῦ
Πέτρου τὰ ῥήματα ταῦτα, ἐπέπεσε [3] τὸ Πνεῦμα τὸ Ἅγιον ἐπὶ πάντας

---

[1] After συνεπ. αυτω D, Par., Syr. H. (cf. Wern.) add και συνανεστραφημεν ; D[1]
has συστραφημεν, cf. Matt. xvii. 22 ; συστρεφομενων, W.H. ; αναστρεφομενων in
CD, etc. St. Luke himself never uses συστρεφω in this sense, nor αναστρεφω at
all ; but Hilg. συνεστραφημεν, and compares D xi. 28, and xvi. 39 ; see, however,
note on xi. 28. After νεκρων D, Sah. (Wern.), Apost. Const. (Syr. H. mg.) (cf. E
also) add ημερας τεσσαρακοντα, so Hilg., see Harris, *Four Lectures*, etc., p. 44 ;
Ephrem's commentary implies such a reading of the old Syriac. Par. also adds και
ανεβη εις τον ουρανον, see Harris, *u. s.*, for addition in Ephrem.

[2] παρηγγειλε, D has ενετειλατο ; but παραγγελλω is also a favourite word with
Luke ; an instance where D seems to be a reminiscence of i. 2. τω λαω om. Par.,
Blass brackets, see below. αυτος but ουτος BCDE, Syrr. P. and H., Sah., Boh.,
Lach., W.H., Hilg., Wendt, Weiss, R.V. ; Tisch. and Meyer follow אAHP 61,
Vulg., Aeth., Iren., Chrys., and read αυτος, see Wendt's note in 1899, and also
former edit. in favour of ουτος.

[3] επεπεσε אBEHLP ; all edd. επεσε AD.

" If even the disciples were incredulous,
and needed touch and talk, what would
have happened in the case of the many?"
—προκεχειροτονημένοις, *i.e.*, by God;
only here, not used in LXX or Apocrypha ; in classical Greek in same sense
as here, see xiv. 23 for the simple verb.
The preposition points back to the choice
of the disciples with a view to bearing
their testimony, i. 18, so that their
witness was no chance, haphazard assertion.—συνεφάγ., *cf.* Luke xxiv. 41, 43
(John xxi. 13), see also Ignat., *ad Smyrn.*,
iii., 3 (*Apost. Const.*, vi., 30, 5).—
συνεπίομεν : it is surely a false method
of criticism which cavils at this statement, because in St. Luke's Gospel
nothing is said of drinking, only of eating (see Plummer, *in loco*). Bede comments : " here Peter mentions what is not
in the Gospel, unless intimated when He
says ' until I drink it new ' " etc.
Ver. 42. παρήγγειλεν : charged us,
see on i. 4.—διαμαρτύρ., see above on
ii. 40, viii. 25.—ὁ ὡρισμένος, see ii. 23,
cf. xvii. 31, in a strikingly similar statement by St. Paul at Athens. St. Peter
and St. Paul are both at one in their
witness to the Resurrection of the Christ
on the third day, and also in their witness
to His appointment as the future Judge
of mankind. This startling claim made

by St. Peter with reference to Jesus of
Nazareth, with Whom he had lived on
terms of closest human intimacy, and in
Whose death he might well have seen
the destruction of all his hopes, is a
further evidence of the change which
had passed over the Apostle, a change
which could only be accounted for by
the belief that this same Jesus was risen
and declared to be the Son of God with
power ; *cf.* Enoch xli. 9, edition Charles ;
Witness of the Epistles, p. 403.—κριτὴς
ζ. καὶ ν., *cf.* 1 Pet. iv. 5 ; the words
point back to the universal lordship
of Christ over Jew and Gentile alike, ver.
36, *cf.* Rom. xiv. 9.
Ver. 43. πάντα τὸν πιστεύοντα, *cf.*
Rom. x. 11, whether Jew or Gentile ;
the phrase emphatic at the close of the
verse, *cf.* Rom. iii. 22. There is no
occasion to refer the words to a reviser
in their Pauline meaning (Weiss) ; St.
Peter in reality says nothing more than
he had already said and implied, ii. 38,
iii. 16, 26.
Ver. 44. ἔτι λ. : the Apostle is apparently interrupted (*cf.* xi. 15) ; but in this
instance we can agree with Overbeck
that the concluding phrase, in its relation to ver. 34 and its proof that God
was no respecter of persons, gives to the
whole speech a perfect completeness (so

τοὺς ἀκούοντας τὸν λόγον. 45. καὶ ἐξέστησαν οἱ ἐκ περιτομῆς πιστοὶ ὅσοι [1] συνῆλθον τῷ Πέτρῳ, ὅτι καὶ ἐπὶ τὰ ἔθνη ἡ δωρεὰ τοῦ Ἁγίου Πνεύματος ἐκκέχυται· 46. ἤκουον γὰρ αὐτῶν λαλούντων γλώσσαις,[2] καὶ μεγαλυνόντων τὸν Θεόν. 47. τότε ἀπεκρίθη ὁ Πέτρος, Μήτι τὸ ὕδωρ κωλῦσαι δύναταί τις τοῦ μὴ βαπτισθῆναι τούτους, οἵτινες τὸ Πνεῦμα τὸ Ἅγιον ἔλαβον καθὼς [3] καὶ ἡμεῖς ; 48. προσέταξε τε αὐτοὺς [4] βαπτισθῆναι ἐν τῷ ὀνόματι τοῦ Κυρίου.[5] τότε ἠρώτησαν αὐτὸν ἐπιμεῖναι ἡμέρας τινάς.

[1] οσοι retained by Tisch., W.H. marg., Blass, Hilg., and even Weiss with ℵADEHLP; but Lach., W.H. text, Wendt follow B, d, Vulg.

[2] γλωσσαις, D¹ prefixes καιναις, d *prævaricatis* (= ποικιλαις, so Hilg.), Sah., *aliis*, see below.

[3] καθως EHLP ; ως ℵAB, Iren., Chrys., Epiph., so Tisch., W.H., R.V., Blass, Weiss. Hilg. has ωσπερ with D.

[4] αυτους BDEHLP, Cyr.-Jer., Chrys., so W.H., Blass, Weiss, Wendt, Hilg. ; αυτοις, Tisch. following ℵA 33.

[5] του Κ. ℵABE verss. have instead Ιησου Χριστου, so all edd., so also Blass in β ; but D has του κ. Ι. Χ., so Hilg. ; Meyer retains T.R.

Zöckler).—ἐπέπεσε, *cf.* x. 44, xi. 15, and for the frequency of the word in Acts and its use in Luke's Gospel, see Friedrich, p. 41. By this wonderful proof St. Peter and his Jewish brethren with him saw that, uncircumcised though they were, Cornelius and his household were no longer "common or unclean": "The Holy Ghost," said the Jews, "never fell upon a Gentile". Bengel comments, "Alias baptismus susceptus est ante adventum Spiritus Sancti . . . Liberum gratia habet ordinem ".—ἀκούοντας, as in ver. 33.

Ver. 45. οἱ ἐκ π., see ver. 23, *cf.* Rom. iv. 12, and for the phrase as describing St. Paul's most bitter and narrow opponents, see Gal. ii. 12, Col. iv. 11, Tit. i. 10. The fact was thus fully testified, even by those who were not in sympathy with it.—καὶ ἐπὶ τὰ ἔθνη: "nam uno admisso jam nulli clausa est janua " Bengel. *Cf.* ii. 38, a gift which they thought did not appertain to the Gentiles ; see on ver. 44, and Schöttgen, *Hor. Heb.*, *in loco*.

Ver. 46. λαλούντων γλώσσαις, see on ii. 13 ; here no speaking in different languages is meant, but none the less the gift which manifested itself in jubilant ecstatic praise was a gift of the Spirit, and the event may well be called "the Gentile Pentecost"; see on xi. 15 and Plumptre, *in loco ;* Wendt, edition 1899. The words of ver. 47 need not mean that this gift of tongues

was manifested precisely as the Pentecostal gift.

Ver. 47. μήτι τὸ ὕ. . . . τοῦ μὴ βαπτισθῆναι, *cf.* xiv. 18 : on construction, Burton, p. 159 ; so also in LXX and classical Greek, Blass, *Gram.*, p. 230 ; Viteau, *Le Grec du N. T.*, p. 172 (1893). —οἵτινες, *quippe qui*, so Blass in this passage.—τὸ ὕδωρ: "the water" R.V., not simply "water" as A.V., as Bengel admirably says, "Non dicit : jam habent Spiritum, ergo aqua carere possunt ". In baptism both the water and the Spirit were required, xi. 16. The greater had been bestowed ; could the lesser be withheld ? See the striking passage in Moberly, *Ministerial Priesthood*, p. 108, on the fact that Cornelius and his companions, even after they had first received the presence of the Holy Ghost, were nevertheless ordered to be baptised.

Ver. 48. προσέταξε, *cf.* St. Paul's rule, 1 Cor. i. 17. If Philip the Evangelist was at Cæsarea at the time, the baptism may have been intrusted to him. —ἐπιμεῖναι : *diutius commorari*, Blass, so *manere amplius*, Bengel, *cf.* xxi. 4, 10, xxviii. 12, 14, and xv. 34 β (Blass) ; only in Luke and Paul, frequent in Acts, not found in Luke's Gospel, *cf.* John viii. 7 ; only once in LXX, Exod. xii. 39, in classics as in text.—ἡμέρας τινάς, no doubt spent in further instruction in the faith : *aurei dies*, Bengel.

CHAPTER XI.—Ver. 1. For Western readings see critical notices.—κατὰ τὴν

XI. 1. Ἤ́ΚΟΥΣΑΝ δὲ οἱ ἀπόστολοι καὶ οἱ ἀδελφοὶ οἱ ὄντες κατὰ τὴν Ἰουδαίαν, ὅτι καὶ τὰ ἔθνη ἐδέξαντο τὸν λόγον τοῦ Θεοῦ. 2.[1] καὶ ὅτε ἀνέβη Πέτρος εἰς Ἱεροσόλυμα, διεκρίνοντο πρὸς αὐτὸν οἱ ἐκ περιτομῆς, λέγοντες, 3. Ὅτι πρὸς ἄνδρας ἀκροβυστίαν ἔχοντας εἰσῆλθες,[2] καὶ συνέφαγες αὐτοῖς. 4. Ἀρξάμενος δὲ ὁ Πέτρος ἐξετίθετο

---

[1] The Western text is here considerably expanded. Blass, following D, Syr. Harcl., Par., Wern. (with differences in particulars), reads in **β** : o μεν ουν Π. δια ικανου χρονου ηθελησεν πορευθηναι εις Ι. και προσφωνησας τους αδελφους και επιστηριξας (αυτους) εξηλθεν, πολυν τε χρονον ποιουμενος (επορευετο) δια των χωρων διδασκων αυτους. οτε δε κατηντησεν εις Ι. και απηγγειλεν αυτοις την χαριν του Θεου οι εκ περιτομης αδελφοι διεκρινοντο προς αυτον, λεγοντες· This, according to Belser, is an irrefutable proof that **β** gives us the original text of Luke, p. 63, and see also Blass, *Phil. of the Gospels*, p. 129, and *cf.* xxi. 16. It is true that in the first part of the addition all the words and clauses are Lucan (although if we read with D ος και κατηντησεν αυτοις instead of οτε δε κατην. εις Ι. we have no instance in Luke of **καταντάω** in construction with a dative). But Weiss, Codex D, takes a very opposite view from Belser (see also Wendt (1899)), p. 206, and it is, of course, quite possible that the additions were made on account of the apparent abrupt ending of the passage about Cornelius, and to show that Peter, too, did not break off his missionary work hurriedly, etc.

[2] εισηλθες και συνεφαγες ; W.H., following BL, Syrr., Arm., has the 3rd person sing., but Weiss has the 2nd person sing., as in TR (so Tisch.).

Ἰ.: not simply *in* but *throughout* Judæa, "all about Judæa," Hort, *Ecclesia*, p. 57, *cf.* viii. 1.

Ver. 2. **διεκρίνοντο**, *cf.* Jude, ver. 9, with dative of the person (Polyb., ii., 22, 11). For similar construction as here see LXX, Ezek. xx. 35, 36, see Grimm-Thayer, *sub v.* Otherwise in x. 20.—**οἱ ἐκ περιτομῆς**, *cf.* Gal. ii. 12 ; we can scarcely confine the term here to those mentioned in x. 45 (although Dr. Hort takes this view as most probable), but how far there was a section of the Church at Jerusalem who could thus be described at this time it is difficult to say, see Ramsay, *St. Paul*, p. 44.

Ver. 3. **ἀκροβυστίαν ἔχοντας**: the expression intimates the bitterness of the opposition. Bengel curiously comments "benigne loquuntur". On **ἀκροβ.** see especially Kennedy, *Sources of N. T. Greek*, p. 111.—**καὶ συνέφαγες αὐτοῖς**: this was the real charge, the violation of the ceremonial law, *cf.* x. 28 ; see on the intolerant division between Pharisaical Jews and Gentiles, Weber, *Jüdische Theol.*, pp. 59, 60 ; Edersheim, *Jewish Social Life*, pp. 26-28. There is therefore nothing in the statement to justify the objection raised by Zeller and others against the whole narrative of the baptism of Cornelius (so Wendt, edition 1888 and 1899). But if the complaint against Peter was based not upon the fact that he had baptised Cornelius but

had eaten with him, then we can see a great difference between the narrative here and that of the Ethiopian eunuch in chap. viii. In the latter case there was no question of the obligations of the ceremonial law ; the baptism was administered and Philip and the eunuch separated, but here the whole stress of the narrative lies in the fact referred to in ver. 3, so that if the eunuch and Cornelius both belonged to the class of "half-proselytes" their cases are not parallel. But even if they were, in other respects there would still remain a distinction between them. It was one thing for the Ethiopian to be received into the Church of Christ by the Hellenist Philip, but it was another thing—and a marked advance—when the principle asserted by Philip was ratified by the Apostles of the circumcision in the case of Cornelius. Wendt, edition 1899, pp. 181, 198, and Lightfoot, *Galatians*, p. 300.

Ver. 4. **ἀρξ. δὲ ὁ Π.** "But Peter began, and expounded the matter ": **ἀρξ.** may be pleonastic, i. 4, *cf.* **καθεξῆς**, or may be used graphically, or because the reproaches of **οἱ ἐκ περιτ.** gave the *first* incentive to St. Peter's recital.—**καθ.** only in Luke, Gospel and Acts, see iii. 24.—**ἐξετίθετο**, xviii. 26, xxviii. 23, Jos., *Ant.*, i., 12, 2, so also in Polyb., x., 9, 3. Perhaps used here by St. Luke from its use by Dioscorides ; familiar word to him also as a physician, see Vogel, p. 17.

αὐτοῖς καθεξῆς λέγων, 5. Ἐγὼ ἤμην ἐν πόλει Ἰόππῃ προσευχόμενος,
καὶ εἶδον ἐν ἐκστάσει ὅραμα, καταβαῖνον σκεῦός τι ὡς ὀθόνην μεγάλην[1]
τέσσαρσιν ἀρχαῖς καθιεμένην ἐκ τοῦ οὐρανοῦ, καὶ ἦλθεν ἄχρις ἐμοῦ ·
6. εἰς ἣν ἀτενίσας κατενόουν, καὶ εἶδον τὰ τετράποδα τῆς γῆς καὶ τὰ
θηρία καὶ τὰ ἑρπετὰ καὶ τὰ πετεινὰ τοῦ οὐρανοῦ. 7. ἤκουσα δὲ
φωνῆς λεγούσης μοι, Ἀναστάς, Πέτρε, θῦσον καὶ φάγε. 8. εἶπον
δέ, Μηδαμῶς, Κύριε[2] · ὅτι πᾶν κοινὸν ἢ ἀκάθαρτον οὐδέποτε εἰσῆλθεν
εἰς τὸ στόμα μου. 9. ἀπεκρίθη δέ μοι φωνὴ ἐκ δευτέρου[3] ἐκ τοῦ
οὐρανοῦ, Ἃ ὁ Θεὸς ἐκαθάρισε, σὺ μὴ κοίνου. 10. τοῦτο δὲ ἐγένετο
ἐπὶ τρίς, καὶ πάλιν ἀνεσπάσθη ἅπαντα εἰς τὸν οὐρανόν. 11. καὶ
ἰδού, ἐξαυτῆς τρεῖς ἄνδρες ἐπέστησαν ἐπὶ τὴν οἰκίαν ἐν ᾗ ἤμην,[4]
ἀπεσταλμένοι ἀπὸ Καισαρείας πρός με. 12. εἶπε δέ μοι τὸ Πνεῦμα
συνελθεῖν αὐτοῖς, μηδὲν διακρινόμενον[5] · ἦλθον δὲ σὺν ἐμοὶ καὶ οἱ ἓξ

---

[1] μεγαλην, but λαμπραν in Syr. Harcl., Par.[1] has μεγαλην λαμπραν. Blass rejects (cf. x. 11).

[2] Orig. has κυριε συ οισθα οτι, Blass rejects.

[3] εκ δευτερου D omits, as also some Western authorities in x. 15, and Blass in β.

[4] ημην EHLP, Vulg., Syrr. (P. and H.), Boh., Sah., Aeth., Chrys., so Blass, W.H. marg.—assim. apparently to ver. 5. ημεν ℵABD 40, Tisch., W.H. text, R.V., Wendt, Weiss, Hilg.

[5] διακρινομενον HLP, Chrys. (cf. x. 20, Meyer, who suspects it here). διακριναντα ℵcAB 13, 40, 61, so Tisch., W.H., Weiss, Wendt, R.V. ; διακρινοντα ℵ*E 15, 18*, 36. Blass rejects altogether, so Hilg., with D, Syr. H. (text and margin), Par.[1]. But cf. Acts xv. 9, where act. occurs in similar context.

Evidently St. Luke by the two accounts attaches great significance to this first reception, exceptional case as it was, of a Gentile proselyte like Cornelius into the Christian Church, but it was an isolated case, and moreover a case within Palestine, not beyond its borders, so that the great questions of a mission to the Gentiles of the heathen world, and of the conditions for their reception as Christians, were not matter for consideration as afterwards in chap. xv., see Wendt, edition 1899, p. 211 ; Hort, *Ecclesia*, pp. 58, 59 ; and see below on ver. 12.—Ver. 6. κατενόουν, cf. vii. 31, 32, Matt. vii. 3, Luke vi. 41, R.V., etc., the seeing is the result of the considering—" *contemplabar singula, effectus comprehenditur aoristo*" εἶδον.—θηρία: not specially mentioned in x. 12 (see critical notes), but there πάντα precedes τετράποδα.—Ver. 8. εἰσῆλθεν, cf. Matt. xv. 11, 17. Blass sees in the phrase " locutio hebraismum redolens," cf. viii. 35 ; on the other hand the Hebraistic πᾶν of x. 14 is omitted (Weiss).—Ver. 10. ἀνεσπάσθη : only found in

Luke xiv. 5 in N.T., another touch of vividness as in vv. 5, 6. In LXX three times, and possibly once in Bel and the Dragon, ver. 42, of drawing up Daniel from the den (but reading may be the simple verb, see H. and R.).—Ver. 12. μηδὲν διακρινόμενον, cf. x. 20, but if we read (see critical notes) μ. διακρίναντα, " making no distinction," R.V.—οἱ ἓξ ἀδελφοὶ οὗτοι : who had been with Peter at Cæsarea, and had returned with him to Jerusalem, see x. 45. Hilgenfeld would regard them as constant companions of St. Peter on his Apostolic journeys. Differences such as these between the narrative here and that in x. 23 where the brethren are mentioned without their number constrain Feine to regard xi. 1-18 as derived like the earlier narrative in x. from one and the same source, not as added by a reviser (although he excludes vv. 1 and 18 in xi. from the original narrative). Spitta agrees with Feine in this view of xi. 2-17 ; a forger writing with a " tendency " would have smoothed away any apparent discrepancies, as Zöckler well points out. With regard to the whole Cornelius

ἀδελφοὶ οὗτοι, καὶ εἰσήλθομεν εἰς τὸν οἶκον τοῦ ἀνδρός, 13. ἀπήγγειλέ τε ἡμῖν πῶς εἶδε τὸν ἄγγελον ἐν τῷ οἴκῳ αὐτοῦ σταθέντα καὶ εἰπόντα αὐτῷ Ἀπόστειλον εἰς Ἰόππην ἄνδρας, καὶ μετάπεμψαι Σίμωνα τὸν ἐπικαλούμενον Πέτρον, 14. ὃς λαλήσει ῥήματα πρὸς σέ, ἐν οἷς σωθήσῃ σὺ καὶ πᾶς ὁ οἶκός σου · 15. ἐν δὲ τῷ ἄρξασθαί με λαλεῖν, ἐπέπεσε [1] τὸ Πνεῦμα τὸ Ἅγιον ἐπ᾽ αὐτούς, ὥσπερ καὶ ἐφ᾽ ἡμᾶς ἐν ἀρχῇ. 16. ἐμνήσθην δὲ τοῦ ῥήματος Κυρίου, ὡς ἔλεγεν, "Ἰωάννης μὲν ἐβάπτισεν ὕδατι, ὑμεῖς δὲ βαπτισθήσεσθε ἐν Πνεύματι Ἁγίῳ." 17. εἰ οὖν τὴν ἴσην δωρεὰν ἔδωκεν αὐτοῖς ὁ Θεὸς ὡς καὶ ἡμῖν, πιστεύσασιν ἐπὶ τὸν Κύριον Ἰησοῦν Χριστόν, ἐγὼ δὲ τίς ἤμην δυνατὸς κωλῦσαι τὸν Θεόν [2]; 18. Ἀκούσαντες δὲ ταῦτα ἡσύχασαν, καὶ ἐδόξαζον [3] τὸν Θεόν, λέγοντες, Ἄραγε [4] καὶ τοῖς ἔθνεσιν ὁ Θεὸς τὴν μετάνοιαν ἔδωκεν εἰς ζωήν.

[1] επεπεσε, but D reads simple verb, which Blass rejects here, although he accepts it in x. 44 (AD). Hilg. has simple verb.

[2] ο Θεος om. D, Aug., so Hilg., but Blass retains. D, Syr. Harcl. mg., Par. Aug. (Hilg. follows D) add του μη δουναι αυτοις π. αγ., and D further adds τοις πιστευσασιν επ᾽ αυτω and Syr. Harcl. πιστ. εις τον Κ. Ι. Χ. Blass omits these last two additions (with Aug.), but places πιστευσασιν επ᾽ αυτω in brackets; additions apparently to explain of what the κωλ. τον Θ. consisted, described by Weiss as quite superfluous, see Codex D, p. 71, and note.

[3] εδοξαζον AEHLP, Arm., so Meyer; Blass (see force of imperf. in his comment.), Wendt, Weiss. εδοξασαν ℵBD[b], Vulg., Sah., Boh., Syr. P. and H., Aeth., so Gig., Par.; Tisch., W.H., Hilg. But aor. manifestly conformed to aor. ησυχασαν (so Weiss, Wendt).

[4] αραγε, but αρα only in ℵABD 40, 61, 65, 133; so Tisch., W.H., R.V., Weiss, Blass, Wendt (against Meyer). D omits την before μετανοιαν.

episode, Spitta and Feine (so Weiss and Wendt), inasmuch as they regard St. Luke's narrative as containing at least a genuine historical kernel, and as marking a special exceptional case, and not a general rule as existing at such an early time, are much less radical than Weizsäcker, Holtzmann, and Clemen. For a good review of the relation of modern criticism to the narrative see Wendt (1899) on x. 1 and Zöckler, *Apostelgeschichte*, pp. 226, 227 (second edition).

Ver. 13. σταθέντα—σταθείς: used only by St. Luke, in Gospel and Acts: Luke xviii. 11, 40, xix. 8, Acts ii. 14, v. 20, xi. 13, xvii. 22, xxv. 18, xxvii. 21, found therefore in *all* parts of Acts (Friedrich, Vogel).

Ver. 14. ἐν οἷς σωθ. σὺ καὶ πᾶς ὁ οἶκ. σου: words not found in x., but may be fairly taken as implied; the prayers of Cornelius we can scarcely doubt had been that he might see the salvation of God, and his household were devout like himself, *cf.* x. 2-6.

Ver. 15. ἄρξασθαι: somewhat more precisely stated than in x. 44. The speech has there no abruptness, but St. Peter may well have intended to say much more; if this was so, the notice here is quite natural, Winer-Moulton, lxv., 7 *d*.—ἐν ἀρχῇ, *i.e.*, at the great Pentecost.

Ver. 16. Words not found in the Gospels, but in Acts i. 5, quoted here with the omission of οὐ μετὰ πολλὰς ταύτας ἡμέρας, showing that St. Peter regarded the baptism of the Holy Ghost received by Cornelius as equally decisive of the Spirit's presence as the bestowal upon himself and others at Pentecost.—ὡς ἔλεγεν: not merely pleonastic, *cf.* Luke xxii. 61; Winer-Moulton, lxv., 1 *a*, Wendt, Felten.

Ver. 17. πιστεύσασιν, see R.V., best to take participle as referring both to αὐτοῖς and to ἡμῖν; in each case the Holy Spirit was bestowed, and in each case as a result of the preceding belief, not as a result of circumcision, or of

19. Οἱ μὲν οὖν διασπαρέντες ἀπὸ τῆς θλίψεως τῆς γενομένης ἐπὶ
Στεφάνῳ,¹ διῆλθον ἕως Φοινίκης καὶ Κύπρου καὶ Ἀντιοχείας, μηδενὶ
λαλοῦντες τὸν λόγον εἰ μὴ μόνον Ἰουδαίοις.   20. ἦσαν δέ τινες
ἐξ αὐτῶν ἄνδρες Κύπριοι καὶ Κυρηναῖοι, οἵτινες εἰσελθόντες εἰς
Ἀντιόχειαν ἐλάλουν πρὸς τοὺς Ἑλληνιστάς,² εὐαγγελιζόμενοι τὸν

---

¹ επι Στεφανω ℵBHLP 61, Bas., Chrys., Theophl., best supported; επι Στεφανου
perhaps a gloss since επι was taken temporally; απο του Στεφανου D, so Hilg. (but
not Blass in β). Κυπρου, Par. reads Τυρου; Blass rejects.

² Ελληνιστας BD²EHLP 61, W.H., R.V. marg., so Sanday (cf. Shirley, Apostolic
Age, pp. 27, 28; Wordsworth, and Hastings' B.D., art. "Christian," p. 384); Ελληνας
ℵ³A (discounted by reading Ελληνας wrongly in ix. 27), D¹, Arm., Eus., Chrys.,
Tisch., Weiss, Blass, R.V. text. ℵ¹ ευαγγελιστας claimed as supporting Ελληνιστας, but see Sanday, u. infra. Lightfoot and a large number of recent writers
(Page, Ramsay, Zöckler, Holtzmann, Felten, Rendall, G. A. Smith, McGiffert)
accept Ελληνας (although, in some cases, admitting that MS. authority is adverse),
because demanded as antithetical to the preceding Ιουδαιοι. It is urged that
Ελληνιστ. are included under Ιουδ., but whilst in one sense this is so, it is also
possible to draw a distinction between the two, Ιουδ. may be used as = Εβραιοι
in vi. 1, or as in xiv. 1, xviii. 4 where evidently Jews and proselytes (not heathen)
are distinguished, so that whilst as far as Antioch Jews only had been addressed,
now the Cyprians and Cyrenians addressed Hellenists, God-fearers (like Cornelius),
"Greeks who came into relations with the Jews," whilst not addressing as yet
those who were entirely heathen. In view of the great importance and future
position of the Church of Antioch, it is not unlikely that Luke should carefully note
the elements of which it was originally composed. The real turning-point in the
sphere of Peter and Paul is not yet, but in xiii. 46. See W.H., Select Readings, p.
94; Hort, Judaistic Christianity, pp. 59, 60; Ecclesia, p. 61; Sanday, Expositor,
pp. 60-62, and Ramsay, p. 47 (1896).

---

uncircumcision; sometimes referred to
ἡμῖν, so Bengel, Nösgen, Wendt, sometimes to αὐτοῖς, so Weiss, Blass.—τίς
ἤμην δ., cf. Exod. iii. 11, 2 Kings viii. 13,
Blass, Gram., p. 173; in reality two questions: Who was I? Was I able to with-
stand God? Winer-Moulton, lxvi., 5.—
ἐγὼ,emphatic,"merum organon," Bengel.
Ver. 18. ἡσύχασαν, cf. xxi. 14 and
Luke xiv. 3, so in LXX, Neh. v. 8 (Job
xxxii. 6, Hebrew different); also in a
different sense in Luke xxiii. 56, 1 Thess.
iv. 11, only in Luke and Paul in N.T.—
ἐδόξαζον, see critical notes, imperfect of
continuous action—the writer about to
pass to other things thus depicts the
state of things which he leaves, cf. viii.
3 (Blass).—Ἄραγε, see critical notes.
Vv. 19-26. Further spread of the Gos-
ael to Antioch.
Ver. 19. οἱ μὲν οὖν, cf. viii. 4. μὲν οὖν
introduces a general statement, whilst
δέ (ver. 20) marks a particular instance.
—ἐπὶ Σ.: "about Stephen" A. and R.
V. (best); some render "against Stephen,"
and others "post Stephanum". See
also critical note.
Ver. 20. ἄνδρες Κύπ. καὶ Κυρ., cf.
iv. 36, xxi. 16; ii. 10, vi. 9.—Ἑλληνιστάς,

see critical notes.—εὐαγγελιζόμενοι τὸν
Κ. Ἰ.: on construction with accusative
of the message, Simcox, Language of the
N. T., p. 79. We can scarcely take the
phrase given here, instead of "preaching
that Jesus was the Christ," as a proof
that the word was preached not to Jews
but to Gentiles.—Ἀντιόχειαν: on the
Orontes, distinguished as Ἀ. ἡ πρός, or
ἐπὶ Δάφνῃ, and bearing the title μητρόπολις. There appear to have been at
least five places in Syria so called under
the Seleucids. For the Arabs Damascus
was the capital, but the Greeks wanted
to be nearer the Mediterranean and Asia
Minor. The city built in 500 B.C. by
Seleucus Nicator I. became more and
more beautiful, whilst all the trade of the
Mediterranean was connected with it
through its harbour Seleucia. All the
varied elements of the life of the ancient
world found a home there. From the
first there were Jews amongst its inhabitants. But in such a mixed population, whilst art and literature could gain
the praise of Cicero, vice as well as
luxury made the city infamous as well as
famous. Josephus calls it the third city
of the empire, next to Rome and Alex-

Κύριον Ἰησοῦν. 21. καὶ ἦν χεὶρ Κυρίου μετ᾽ αὐτῶν· πολύς τε
ἀριθμὸς πιστεύσας ἐπέστρεψεν ἐπὶ τὸν Κύριον. 22. Ἠκούσθη δὲ ὁ
λόγος εἰς τὰ ὦτα τῆς ἐκκλησίας τῆς ἐν Ἰεροσολύμοις περὶ αὐτῶν·
καὶ ἐξαπέστειλαν Βαρνάβαν διελθεῖν [1] ἕως Ἀντιοχείας. 23. ὃς παραγενόμενος καὶ ἰδὼν τὴν χάριν [2] τοῦ Θεοῦ ἐχάρη, καὶ παρεκάλει πάντας
τῇ προθέσει τῆς καρδίας προσμένειν τῷ Κυρίῳ· 24. ὅτι ἦν ἀνὴρ
ἀγαθὸς καὶ πλήρης Πνεύματος Ἁγίου καὶ πίστεως. καὶ προσετέθη
ὄχλος ἱκανὸς τῷ Κυρίῳ. 25.[3] Ἐξῆλθε δὲ εἰς Ταρσὸν ὁ Βαρνάβας
ἀναζητῆσαι Σαῦλον, καὶ εὑρὼν αὐτὸν ἤγαγεν αὐτὸν εἰς Ἀντιόχειαν.

[1] διελθεῖν om. אAB 61, Vulg., Syr. Pesh., Boh., Arm., Aeth., so Tisch., W.H.,
R.V., Weiss, Wendt (against Meyer); but retained by Blass and Hilg., so in D,
Syr. Harcl., Chrys.—perhaps added from xi. 19.

[2] χαριν την του Θ., so אAB, so Tisch., W.H., R.V., Blass, Weiss, Wendt om.
την in T.R., so DEHLP, Chrys., Hilg.

[3] Blass (cf. Hilg.) reconstructs according to D, Gig., Par., Syr. Harcl. mg. : ακουσας
δε οτι Σαυλος εστιν εις Ταρσον εξηλθεν αναζητων αυτον και συντυχων παρεκαλεσεν
ελθειν εις Α. οιτινες παραγενομενοι ενιαυτον ολον συνηχθησαν τη εκκ. κ. εδιδαξαν
οχλον ικανον (D has ενι. ολ. συνεχυθησαν οχλ. ικ., omits και εδιδ.). It is difficult to
see why this should have been shortened if original; perhaps added to definitely show
why Barnabas went to Tarsus, and to mark that Saul was not brought to Tarsus
but "besought to come". συνεχυθησαν, D (Par.¹), evident mistake, Blass emends;
see Weiss, Codex D, pp. 71, 72. Hilg. has συνεχυσαν.

andria, but Ausonius hesitates between
Antioch and Alexandria, as to the rank
they occupied in eminence and vice. The
famous words of Juvenal : "in Tiberim
defluxit Orontes," Sat., iii., 62, describe
the influences which Antioch, with its
worthless rabble of Greeks and para-
sites, with its quacks and impostors,
its rivalries and debaucheries, exercised
upon Rome. Gibbon speaks of the city
in the days of Julian as a place where
the lively licentiousness of the Greek was
blended with the hereditary softness of
the Syrian. Yet here was the μητρόπολις, not merely of Syria, but of the
Gentile Christian Churches, and next to
Jerusalem no city is more closely associated with the early history and spread
of the Christian faith. See "Antioch"
(G. A. Smith) in Hastings' B.D.; Gibbon,
Decline and Fall of the Roman Empire,
chaps. xxiii., xxiv.; Renan, Les Apôtres,
chaps. xii., xiii. — ἐλάλουν: "used to
speak," so Ramsay.
Ver. 21. χεὶρ Κ., cf. iv. 28, 30, xiii.
11, Luke i. 66; frequent in O.T. τε
closely connects the two clauses, showing
that the result of "the hand of the Lord"
was that a great number, etc. (Weiss).
Ver. 22. τῆς ἐκκ. τῆς ἐν Ἰ.: in contrast here to Antioch, in which the existence of an Ecclesia was not yet formally
recognised; but cf. ver. 26, Hort, Ecclesia,

pp. 59-61.—περὶ αὐτῶν: "concerning
them" R.V., i.e., the persons who had
believed and turned to the Lord. Meyer
takes it of the preachers, Felten of both
preachers and converts.
Ver. 23. τὴν χάριν: if we add τὴν, see
critical notes, "the grace that was of
God" Hort, Ecclesia, p. 60, so Alford.—
παρεκάλει: a true son of encouragement, exhortation—see on iv. 36, imperfect because Barnabas remained at
Antioch, and the result is indicated in
ver. 24, προσετέθη. This mention of
Barnabas and the part played by the
primitive Church is referred by Clemen to
his Redactor Antijudaicus, p. 109. If we
read ἐν τῷ Κ. with R.V. margin we could
render "to abide by the purpose of their
heart in the Lord," so Hort, u. s., p. 60;
Rendall; cf. 2 Tim. iii. 10; and Symmachus, Ps. x. 17 (Weiss). τῷ Κ., i.e.,
Christ; with this verse cf. xv. 32, where
St. Luke similarly insists upon the due
qualification of divine gifts; Ramsay, St.
Paul, p. 45.
Ver. 25. Luke gives no reason why
Barnabas goes to seek Saul, but Barnabas
who had already vouched for Saul's sincerity before the Church of Jerusalem, ix.
27, could scarcely be ignorant that the
sphere of his friend's future work was to
be the Gentile world. In ix. 30 Saul
was sent away to Tarsus, and now Bar-

26. ἐγένετο δὲ αὐτοὺς ἐνιαυτὸν [1] ὅλον συναχθῆναι ἐν τῇ ἐκκλησίᾳ, καὶ διδάξαι ὄχλον ἱκανόν, χρηματίσαι τε πρῶτον [2] ἐν Ἀντιοχείᾳ τοὺς

[1] αυτους, but αυτοις אABE 13, 61, so Tisch., W.H., R.V., Wendt. ενιαυτον אAB 13, Syr. Harcl., Did., Ath.; Tisch., W.H., R.V., Weiss, Wendt prefix και, but see Blass's comment on β, *in loco*, p. 136.

[2] πρωτον אBD² 36, 163, so Tisch., W.H., Blass, Weiss, Wendt; πρωτως, see also Alford's note on its force; D, Gig., Par. read και τοτε πρωτον, so Hilg. Harnack regards the τοτε as secondary, and introduced by the Western reviser to mark that the disciples were *then* called Christians, which in Harnack's opinion was very improbable, see *Sitzungsberichte d. Königl. preuss. Akad. d. Wissenschaften zu Berlin*, xvii., p. 4, 1899. Χριστιαν. א[1] has Χρηστιανοι, "recte," Blass (so 61), but there is no reason to suppose that this was the original, although it may well have been a corrupted form, *cf.* the testimony of Tert., Just. Mar., Lactant.; D has Χρειστ.

nabas goes to Tarsus to seek him; each statement is the complement of the other, and a long period intervenes not marked by any critical event in Saul's history. So also Paul's own statement, Gal. i. 21, 22, marks the same period, and the two writers complete each other. Ramsay, *St. Paul*, pp. 45, 46, on Luke's style and reading in D above.—ἀναζητῆσαι, *cf.* Luke ii. 44, 45, nowhere else in N.T., a word therefore not only common to, but peculiar to Luke's writings.—ἀνά: giving idea of thoroughness; it was not known at what precise spot Saul was prosecuting his work, so the word implies effort or thoroughness in the search; εὑρὼν implies the same uncertainty. In LXX, *cf.* Job iii. 4, x. 6, 2 Macc. xiii. 21. Calvin comments on the fresh proof of the " simplicitas " of Barnabas ; he might have retained the chief place at Antioch, but he goes for Paul : " videmus ergo ut sui oblitus nihil aliud spectat, nisi ut emineat unus Christus ".

Ver. 26. ἐγένετο δὲ αὐτοὺς, see critical notes, if dative αὐτοῖς = *accidit eis*, see Plummer, *St. Luke*, p. 45, on the use of ἐγένετο.—ἐνιαυτὸν ὅλον : " even a whole year " R.V.—συναχθῆναι ἐν τῇ ἐκκλ. : " they were gathered together *in* the Church," so R.V. margin. Rendall holds that ἐν is fatal to the A.V. and R.V. text, and renders " they [*i.e.*, Barnabas and Saul] were brought together in the Church," an intimate association of inestimable value. Hort adopts as " the least difficult explanation of this curious word " " were hospitably received in the Church," so Wendt, Weiss, Nösgen, *cf.* Matt. xxv. 35 ; Deut. xxii. 18, Josh. ii. 18, Judg. xix. 18, 2 Sam. xi. 27.—διδάξαι . . . χρηματίσαι: *both* infinitives depend upon ἐγένετο, " and that the disciples," etc., suggesting that the name " Christian " followed as result upon the widespread teaching of the Apostles amongst the Gentiles. If St. Luke, as Eusebius states, was himself a native of Antioch, it has been well noted that he might well record such a distinction for his city as the origin of the name " Christian ".—χρηματίσαι : prim. to transact business (χρῆμα), passes into the meaning of taking a name from one's public business, so to receive a name, to be called, *cf.* Rom. vii. 3, so in Josephus and Philo, and instances in Grimm-Thayer. See also x. 22 for another shade of meaning, and so elsewhere in N.T.; and for its use to express a reply or information by a king or those in authority to inquiry, see Deissmann, *Bibelstudien*, p. 118.—πρῶτον, see critical notes.—Χριστιανούς : in the N.T. the Christians always named themselves μαθηταί, ἀδελφοί, ἅγιοι, πιστοί, etc., but on no occasion " Christians," whilst the Jews not only refused to recognise that Jesus had any claim to be the Christ, but also called His followers Ναζωραῖοι (xxiv. 5), or spake of them as ἡ αἵρεσις αὕτη (xxviii. 22, *cf.* xxiv. 14). On the probably contemptuous use of the word in 1 Peter iv. 16 and Acts xxvi. 28 as not inconsistent with the above statements, see Wendt, edition 1899, *in loco*, and " Christian " in Hastings' B.D. But whilst it is difficult to find an origin for the title amongst Christians or amongst Jews, there is no difficulty in attributing it to the keen-witted populace of Antioch, already famous for their bestowal of nick-names, although perhaps the possibility that the name may have originated amongst the Latin - speaking official retinue of the *legatus* at Antioch should not be excluded (though there is no evidence whatever that it became at this early date an official name). But there is no need to suppose that the name

μαθητὰς Χριστιανούς. 27. Ἐν ταύταις δὲ ταῖς ἡμέραις κατῆλθον ἀπὸ Ἱεροσολύμων προφῆται εἰς Ἀντιόχειαν.¹ 28. ἀναστὰς δὲ εἷς ἐξ

¹ At end of verse and commencement of ver. 28 we have the remarkable reading in β: ην δε πολλη αγαλλιασις. συνεστραμμενων δε ημων εφη εις εξ αυτων, so D, Aug., Par., Wern., and also, a new witness, Fragment of the Old Latin translation of Acts in the *Miscellanea Cassinese*, 1897 (see Harnack's note in *Theol. Literatur-zeitung*, p. 172, 1898). αγαλλιασις is quite Lucan, *cf.* ii. 46, and the solutions of Weiss and Corssen are not sufficient to weaken the view that here, at least, we may have an original draft. If it is said that the words are introduced to show the impression made by the visit of the prophets (so Weiss), we must remember that they stand in strange contrast to the announcement of the coming famine, and that it would have been a bold thing for an emendator to introduce them here. The circumstances in viii. 8 are quite different. Blass sees in the following words, p. 137, "luculen-tissimum testimonium, quo auctor sese Antiochenum fuisse monstrat," see also *Philology of the Gospels*, p. 131; we get by these three words, συνεσ. δε ημων, a fresh *we-section*; to the same effect Zöckler, *Greifswalder Studien*, p. 137; Salmon, *Introd.*, pp. 597, 602; Belser, p. 64; see also Harnack, *u. s.*, and Zahn, *Einleitung in das N. T.*, ii., pp. 341, 350. Wendt (1898), p. 216, note, inclines to accept the reading as original, and even Weiss, Codex D, p. 111, thinks it not impossible; so too Hilgenfeld, *Zeitschrift für wissenschaft. Theol.*, p. 505 (1895); and *cf.* Jülicher, *Einleitung in das N. T.*, p. 271. Harnack, *u. s.*, admits, p. 6, that the language is not un-Lucan, but he regards the other passages in which συστρεφ. occurs as Western interpolations, and ην δε πολλη αγαλλ. as a mere amplification, as in viii. 24, xiii. 8.

was of Roman origin, although we may readily concede that the Latin termina-tion -*ianus* was common enough at this period. There is ample proof of the use of the same termination not only in Latin but in Greek, even if we do not regard -ιανός with Wendt as a termination of a native "Asiatic type". The notice in Tacitus, *Ann.*, xv., 44 (*cf.* Suetonius, *Nero*, 16), who was probably in Rome during Nero's persecution, A.D. 64, is very signi-ficant, for he not only intimates that the word was commonly and popularly known, but also that the title had been in vogue for some time: "quos vulgus Christianos appellabat," note the imper-fect tense. Against the recent strictures of Weizsäcker and Schmiedel we may place the opinion of Spitta, and also of Zahn, *Einleitung*, ii., 158. How soon the title given in mockery became a name of honour we may gather from the Ignatian Epistles, *cf. Rom.*, iii., 3; *Magn.*, iv.; *Ephes.*, xi., 2, and *cf. Mart. Polyc.*, x. and xii., 1, 2. See further Lightfoot, *Phil.*, p. 16; Lechler, *Das Apostolische Zeitalter*, p. 129 ff.; Smith, B.D.² "Christian," Conybeare and Howson, p. 100 (smaller edition), and *Expositor*, June, 1898. Ver. 27. Antioch sends relief to Jerusalem.—ἐν ταύταις δὲ ταῖς ἡ., *cf.* i. 15, vi. 1. ταύταις emphatic, by its position and also by its significance, days full of importance for Barnabas and Saul, who were still at Antioch (Weiss). —προφῆται: the coming of the prophets gave an additional sanction to the work

at Antioch. There is no reason in the uncertainty of the dates to suppose that they had been driven from Jerusalem by persecution. For the position of the Christian prophets in the N.T. *cf.* Acts xiii. 1, where Barnabas and Saul are spoken of as prophets and teachers; afterwards as Apostles, xiv. 4; xv. 32, where Judas and Silas are described as prophets, having been previously spoken of, ver. 22, as ἡγούμενοι amongst the brethren at Jerusalem (while Silas later bears the name of Apostle); *cf.*, further, 1 Cor. xii. 28, xiv. 29-33, 39, Ephes. iv. 11, where in each case the Prophet is placed next to Apostles (al-though in 1 Cor. he may have been merely a member of a local com-munity), perhaps because "he belonged to the same family as the great prophets of the Old Testament," for whilst foreknowledge of events was not necessarily implied by the word either in the O.T. or in the N.T., the case of Agabus, both here and in xxi. 10, 11, shows that predictiveness was by no means excluded. The Christian pro-phets, moreover, as we see them in Acts, combine the duty of "ministering to the Lord" with that of preaching the word; they are not only foretellers, but forth-tellers of God's will, as in the case of a Samuel or an Elijah, Gore, *Church and the Ministry*, pp. 240, 261, 393, etc.; Mo-berly, *Ministerial Priesthood*, p. 160 ff.; and for *Sub-Apostolic Age*, p. 179 ff.; Bigg, *Doctrine of the Twelve Apostles*, p.

αὐτῶν, ὀνόματι Ἄγαβος, ἐσήμανε¹ διὰ τοῦ Πνεύματος, λιμὸν μέγαν²
μέλλειν ἔσεσθαι ἐφ' ὅλην τὴν οἰκουμένην· ὅστις καὶ ἐγένετο ἐπὶ
Κλαυδίου³ Καίσαρος.   29. τῶν δὲ μαθητῶν⁴ καθὼς ηὐπορεῖτό τις,

¹ εσημανε ‫א‬AEHLP, most verss., so Tisch., W.H. marg.; but B, d, Vulg., Chron.,
Aug., so Lach., W.H., Weiss read imperf. εσημαινε—Wendt undecided.

² μεγαν D¹EHLP, Chrys., Chron.; but ‫א‬ABD² 61, so Tisch., W.H., Blass,
Weiss, Wendt, Hilg. have μεγαλην (ητις).

³ Καισαρος om. ‫א‬ABD 13, 61, Vulg., several verss., so Tisch., W.H., R.V., Blass,
Weiss, Wendt, so Hilg.

⁴ των δε μαθητων, D, Par., Vulg. (Gig.) read οι δε μαθηται, and so D καθως
ευπορουντο instead of ευπ. τις.

28 (1898); Harnack, "Apostellehre" in *Real-Encyclopädie für Protestant. Theol.* (Hauck), p. 716, and see, further, on xiii. 1.

Ver. 28. Ἄγαβος: on derivation see W.H., ii., 313, from עֲגַב "to love"; or from חָגָב "a locust," Ezra ii. 45, Neh. vii. 48, with rough breathing Ἄγ. W.H. follow Syriac and read the former as in T.R., so Weiss; Blass doubtful; Klostermann would connect it with Ἀγανός, *Probleme im Aposteltexte*, p. 10. As a Jewish prophet he would naturally use the symbolic methods of a Jeremiah or an Ezekiel, see on xxi. 10, 11. On insertion in D see critical notes. —μέλλειν ἔσεσθαι: future infinitive only used in N.T. with μέλλειν in this one phrase, and only so in Acts, *cf.* xxiv. 15, xxvii. 10. In xxiii. 30 μέλλειν omitted (although in T.R.), and in xxiv. 25 ἔσεσθαι omitted (although in T.R.). Klostermann, *Vindiciæ Lucanæ*, p. 51, Simcox, *Language of the N. T.*, p. 120, and Viteau, *Le Grec du N. T.*, p. 158 (1893).—λιμὸν: masculine in Luke iv. 25, and so in common usage, but in Doric usage, as it is called, feminine, and so also in later Greek; feminine in Luke xv. 14 and here; see critical notes; Blass, *Gram.*, p. 26.—ἐφ' ὅλην τὴν οἰκ. —the civilised world, *i.e.*, the Roman Empire. *Cf.* xxiv. 5, and Luke ii. 1, see Plummer's note on Luke iv. 5 (and Hackett's attempt, *in loco*, to limit the expression), and Ramsay, *Was Christ born at Bethlehem?* p. 118. We have ample evidence as to a widespread dearth over various parts of the Roman Empire, to which Suetonius, Dion Cassius, Tacitus, and Eusebius all bear witness, in the reign of Claudius; and in no other reign do we find such varied allusions to periodical famines, "assiduae sterilitates,"

Suetonius, *Claudius*, xviii., *cf.* Dion Cassius, lx., 11; Tac., *Ann.*, xii., 43, etc. These and other references are given by Schürer, *Jewish People*, div. i., vol. ii., p. 170, E.T. (so also by O. Holtzmann, *Neutest. Zeitgeschichte*, p. 124), but instead of drawing from these varied references the inference that the author of Acts had ample justification for his statement as to the prevalence of famine over the Roman Empire, he takes him to task for speaking of a famine "over the whole world". See Ramsay, *St. Paul*, pp. 48, 49, and also *Was Christ Born at Bethlehem?* pp. 251, 252, *cf.* vv. 29 and 30. At least there is no ground to suppose, with Clemen and others, that the writer of Acts was here dependent on Josephus for the mention of the famine which that historian confined to Judæa, but which the writer of Acts, or rather Clemen's Redactor Antijudaicus, magnified according to his usual custom.

Ver. 29. καθὼς ηὐπορεῖτό τις: only here in N.T., and the cognate noun in xix. 25, but in same sense in classical Greek; *cf.* Lev. xxv. 26, 28, 49, and Wisdom x. 10 (but see Hatch and Redpath on passages in Lev.). "According to his ability," so A. and R.V., *i.e.*, as each man prospered, in proportion to his means. The expression intimates that the community of goods, at least in a communistic sense, could not have been the rule, *cf.* 1 Cor. xvi. 2, but a right view of "the community of goods" at Jerusalem invokes no contradiction with this statement, as Hilgenfeld apparently maintains, *Zeitschrift für wissenschaft. Theol.*, p. 506, 1895. On the good effect of this work of brotherly charity and fellowship, this practical exhibition of Christian union between Church and Church, between the Christians of the mother-city and those of the Jewish dispersion, see Hort, *Ecclesia*, p. 62; Ram-

ὥρισαν ἕκαστος αὐτῶν εἰς διακονίαν πέμψαι τοῖς κατοικοῦσιν ἐν τῇ
Ἰουδαίᾳ ἀδελφοῖς· 30. ὃ καὶ ἐποίησαν, ἀποστείλαντες πρὸς τοὺς
πρεσβυτέρους διὰ χειρὸς Βαρνάβα καὶ Σαύλου.

say, u. s., p. 52; Baumgarten (Alford, in loco).—εἰς διακονίαν: "for a ministry," R.V. margin, cf. Rom. xv. 31, 2 Cor. ix. 1, etc., Acta Thomæ, 56; "contributions for relief" Ramsay, see further below; on the construction and complexity of the sentence see especially Page's note, and Wendt.—ἀδελφοῖς: not merely as fellow-disciples, but as brethren in the One Lord.

Ver. 30. ὃ καὶ ἐποίησαν κ.τ.λ.: a question arises as to whether this took place during, or at a later date than, Herod's persecution in 44 A.D.—the year of his death. Bishop Lightfoot (with whom Dr. Sanday and Dr. Hort substantially agree) maintains that Barnabas and Saul went up to Jerusalem in the early months of 44, during Herod's persecution, deposited their διακονία with the elders, and returned without delay. If we ask why "elders" are mentioned, and not Apostles, the probability is suggested that the Apostles had fled from Jerusalem and were in hiding. Against this view Ramsay strongly protests, not only on account of the part assigned to the leading Apostles, but also because of the meaning which he attaches to the διακονία of Barnabas and Saul (see on xii. 25). The elders, not Apostles, are mentioned because the embassy was of a purely business kind, and it was not fit that the Apostles should serve tables. Moreover, Ramsay places the visit of Barnabas and Saul to Jerusalem in 45, or preferably in 46, at the commencement of the great famine in Judæa—not in 44, but in 45. Still, as Dr. Sanday urges, the entire omission of any reference to the Apostles is strange (cf. Blass on xi. 30, xii. 17, who holds that the Apostles had fled), especially as elsewhere Apostles and elders are constantly bracketed together as a single body (xv. 2, 4, 6, 22, 23, xvi. 4, cf. xxi. 18). Nor does it follow that because James, presumably "the brother of the Lord," is mentioned as remaining in Jerusalem during the persecution (but see Lightfoot, Gal., p. 127, note), which his reputation for sanctity amongst his countrymen might have enabled him to do, that the other Apostles could have done so with equal safety. But Ramsay at all events relieves us from the difficulty involved in the entrance of Paul into Jerusalem at a time of persecution, and the more so in view of the previous plots against his life, a difficulty which is quite unsatisfactorily met by supposing that Paul did not enter the city at all for some unknown reasons, or more unsatisfactorily still by attributing to the author of Acts a mistake in asserting that any visit of Paul to Jerusalem was made at this time. On the chronological order involved in accordance with the two views mentioned, see Ramsay, St. Paul, pp. 48 ff., 68, 69; Lightfoot, Gal., p. 124, note; and, as space forbids more, for the whole question Expositor for February and March, 1896; Lightfoot, Gal., p. 123 ff.; Hort, Judaistic Christianity, p. 61, and Ecclesia, p. 62; Wendt, p. 265 (1888) and p. 218 (1899).— τοὺς πρεσβυτέρους, see previous verse. It is also noticeable that St. Luke gives no account of the appointment of the elders; he takes it for granted. These Christian elders are therefore in all probability no new kind of officers, but a continuation in the Christian Church of the office of the זְקֵנִים, πρεσβύτεροι, to whom probably the government of the Synagogue was assigned—hence we may account for St. Luke's silence (Moberly, Ministerial Priesthood, p. 141; Hort, Ecclesia, p. 62; Lightfoot, Phil., pp. 191-193; "Bishop" (Gwatkin), Hastings' B.D.). In the Christian συναγωγή (James ii. 2) there would naturally be elders occupying a position of trust and authority. There is certainly no reason to regard them as (so Zeller, Ritschl), although it is quite conceivable that if the Seven represented the Hellenists, the elders may have been already in existence as representing the Hebrew part of the Church. But there is need to guard against the exaggeration of the Jewish nature of the office in question. In the N.T. we find mention of elders, not merely so on account of age, not merely as administrative and disciplinary officers (Hatch, Bampton Lectures, pp. 58, 61), as in a Jewish synagogue, but as officers of the Christian Church with spiritual functions, cf. James v. 14, 1 Pet. v. 2, Acts xx. 17, Tit. i. 5, and also 1 Thess. v. 12-14, Heb. xiii.7 (see Mayor, St. James, p. cxxviii; Gore, Church and the Ministry, pp. 253, 263, and note

XII. 1. ΚΑΤ᾽ ἐκεῖνον δὲ τὸν καιρὸν ἐπέβαλεν Ἡρώδης ὁ βασιλεὺς τὰς χεῖρας κακῶσαί τινας τῶν ἀπὸ τῆς ἐκκλησίας.[1] 2. ἀνεῖλε δὲ Ἰάκωβον τὸν ἀδελφὸν Ἰωάννου μαχαίρᾳ. 3. καὶ ἰδὼν ὅτι ἀρεστόν ἐστι τοῖς Ἰουδαίοις,[2] προσέθετο συλλαβεῖν καὶ Πέτρον· (ἦσαν δὲ

[1] After εκκλησιας D, Syr. Harcl. mg., Par., Wern. add της εν τη Ιουδαια—if the words were original it seems difficult to account for their omission ; but see Belser's defence, p. 64, of this and β in vv. 3 and 5.

[2] After Ιουδαιοις D, Syr. H. mg., Par., so Hilg., add η επιχειρησις αυτου επι τους πιστους—this again may be an explanatory gloss, defining what pleased the Jews— but επιχ. and πιστ. are used by Luke in his writings.

K). At the same time there is nothing to surprise us in the fact that the administration of alms should be connected *in loco* with the office of elders. If they were representing the Apostles at the time in Jerusalem, it is what we should expect, since the organisation of almsgiving remained part of the Apostolic office, Gal. ii. 10, 2 Cor. viii., etc. ; and if in a passage from Polycarp (quoted by Dr. Hatch) we find the two connected— the presbyterate and what looks like the administration of alms, Polycarp, *Phil.,* vi., xi.—this again need not surprise us, since not only in the N.T., but from the passage referred to in Polycarp, it is evident that the elders, whilst they exercised judicial and administrative functions, exercised also spiritual gifts, and discharged the office of teachers, functions to which there was nothing analogous in the Jewish presbyters (see Gore, *u. s.,* note K, and Gwatkin, *u. s.,* p. 302). *To turn back the sheep that are gone astray* (ἐπιστρέφοντες τὰ ἀποπεπλανημένα) is one of the first commands laid by Polycarp in his Epistle upon the Christian Presbyters (vi., quoted by Hatch), and from this alone it would appear that a familiar title in the Jewish Church passed into the Church of Christ, gaining therein a new and spiritual power. See further on xx. 17, and for the use of the word in inscriptions, Deissmann, *Bibelstudien,* p. 153, and *Neue Bibelstudien,* p. 160.

CHAPTER XII. *Persecution by Herod ; St. Peter's deliverance.*—Ver. 1. κατ᾽ ἐκεῖνον τὸν καιρόν : "about that time," or more precisely "at that time," Rendall, *cf.* Rom. ix. 9, so in Gen. xviii. 10, 2 Macc. iii. 5 : in the early part of 44 A.D.—Ἡρώδης ὁ β., Herod Agrippa I. : only in this chapter in the N.T. : on his character and death, see below xii. 3, 23. Born in B.C. 10 and educated in his early life in Rome, he rose from a rash adventurer to good fortune and high position first through

the friendship of Caligula and afterwards of Claudius. He united under his own sway the entire empire of his grandfather, Herod the Great, while his Pharisaic piety and also his attachment to the Roman supremacy found expression in the titles which he bore, βασιλεὺς μέγας φιλόκαισαρ εὐσεβὴς καὶ φιλορώμαιος. On the pathetic story told of him in connection with the Feast of Tabernacles (A.D. 41) see Hamburger, *Real-Encyclopädie des Judentums,* ii., 1, p. 28, and the whole article ; Schürer, *Jewish People,* div. i., vol. ii., p. 150 ff., E.T. ; Farrar, *The Herods,* p. 179 ff. (1898).—ἐπέβαλεν τὰς χεῖρας, Luke xx. 19, xxi. 12, and *cf.* Acts iv. 3, v. 18, xxi. 27, once in Matthew and Mark, in John twice ; Friedrich, p. 39, *cf.* LXX, Gen. xxii. 12, 2 Sam. xviii. 12 (so in Polyb.), *cf.* for similar construction of the infinitive of the purpose xviii. 10, not in the sense of ἐπεχείρησε, *conatus est,* but to be rendered quite literally ; *cf.* also the context, ver. 3.—κακῶσαι : five times in Acts, only once elsewhere in N.T., 1 Peter iii. 13, "to afflict," R.V., A.V. "vex," so Tyndale.—τῶν ἀπὸ τῆς ἐκ., for the phrase *cf.* vi. 9, xv. 5, Grimm-Thayer, *sub v.,* ἀπό, ii., but see also Blass, *Gram.,* p. 122 and *in loco.*

Ver. 2. ἀνεῖλε, characteristic word, see on v. 33.—Ἰάκωβον τὸν ἀ. Ἰ. : St. Chrysostom reminds us of our Lord's prophecy in Mark x. 38 ff. (Matt. xx. 23), distinguished thus from the James of i. 13. Possibly his prominent position, and his characteristic nature as a son of Thunder marked him out as an early victim.—μαχαίρᾳ : so in the case of John the Baptist. This mode of death was regarded as very disgraceful among the Jews (J. Lightfoot, Wetstein), and as in the Baptist's case so here, the mode of execution shows that the punishment was not for blasphemy, but that James was apprehended and killed by the political power. For the touching account of his

ἡμέραι τῶν ἀζύμων ·) 4. ὃν καὶ πιάσας ἔθετο εἰς φυλακήν, παραδοὺς
τέσσαρσι τετραδίοις στρατιωτῶν φυλάσσειν αὐτόν, βουλόμενος μετὰ
τὸ πάσχα ἀναγαγεῖν αὐτὸν τῷ λαῷ. 5. ὁ μὲν οὖν Πέτρος ἐτηρεῖτο
ἐν τῇ φυλακῇ[1] · προσευχὴ δὲ ἦν ἐκτενὴς[2] γινομένη ὑπὸ τῆς ἐκκλησίας
πρὸς τὸν Θεὸν ὑπὲρ αὐτοῦ.

[1] After φυλακῇ Syr. H. mg., Par. add υπο της σπειρης του βασιλεως—here, again,
the words may be a gloss to explain ετηρειτο, unnecessary after ver. 4.

[2] εκτενης A²EHLP 61, Bas., Chrys., so Meyer; εκτενως ℵA¹B 13, 40, 81, Vulg.,
Lucif., so Tisch., W. H., Weiss, Wendt, R. V. ; D has εν εκτενεια (cf. xxvi. 7), so Hig.

martyrdom narrated by Clement of Alexandria, see Eus., H. E., ii., 9. Whatever
St. Luke's reason for the brevity of the
account, whether he knew no more, or
whether he intended to write a third book
giving an account of the other Apostles
besides Peter and Paul, and so only mentioned here what concerned the following
history (so Meyer, but see Wendt, p. 267
(1888)), his brief notice is at least in
striking contrast (ἁπλῶς καὶ ὡς ἔτυχεν,
Chrys.) with the details of later martyr-
ologies.
　Ver. 3. ἀρεστόν . . . τοῖς Ἰ.: exactly
what we should expect from the character
and policy of Herod in his zeal for the
law, and from the success with which
during his short reign he retained the
favour of Jews and Romans alike. Holtzmann, p. 370, seems inclined to doubt
the truth of this description of Herod,
and lays stress upon the mention of the
king's mild disposition in Josephus, Ant.,
xix., 7, 3. But Josephus also makes it
quite plain how zealous Agrippa was, or
pretended to be, for the laws and ordinances of Judaism, u. s. and xx., 7, 1, and
see Schürer, u. s., and Feine, p. 226.
Nor is it at all certain that Agrippa's
reputed mildness and gentleness would
have kept him from rejoicing in the persecution of the Christians, cf. the description of his delight in the bloody gladia-
torial games, Jos., Ant., xix., 9, 5.—
προσέθετο συλλ.: a Hebraism, cf. Luke
xix. 11, xx. 11 : LXX, Gen. iv. 2, viii. 12,
xxv. 1, Exod. xiv. 13, etc., peculiar to St.
Luke in N.T., Viteau, Le Grec du N. T.,
p. 209 (1893).—αἱ ἡ. τῶν ἀζύμων, and
therefore a large number of Jews would
be in Jerusalem, and Herod would thus
have a good opportunity of gaining wide
popularity by his zeal for the law.
　Ver. 4. ὃν καὶ πιάσας, iii. 7, really
Doric form of πιέζω (cf. Luke vi. 38, nowhere else in N.T.), used in this sense
also in LXX, and elsewhere in N.T., cf.
Cant. ii. 15, Ecclus. xxiii. 21 (not A).

Modern Greek πιάνω = seize, apprehend.
—καὶ : "when he had taken him, indeed,"
so Rendall, as if a delay had taken place,
before the arrest was actually made.—
τέσσαρσι τετραδ. : the night was divided
by the Romans—a practice here imitated
by Herod—into four watches, and each
watch of three hours was kept by four
soldiers, quaternio, two probably guarding
the prisoner within the cell, chained to
him, and two outside. τετραδ., cf. Philo,
in Flaccum, 13 ; Polyb., xv., 33, 7, and
see for other instances, Wetstein.—μετὰ
τὸ πάσχα, "after the Passover," R.V.,
i.e., after the whole festival was over :
Herod either did not wish, or affected
not to wish, to profane the Feast : "non
judicant die festo" (Moed Katon., v., 2).—
ἀναγαγεῖν : only here in this sense (in
Luke xxii. 66, ἀπήγαγον, W. H.), probably
means to lead the prisoner up, i.e., before
the judgment tribunal (John xix. 13), to
sentence him openly to death before the
people.
　Ver. 5. ὁ μὲν οὖν . . . προσευχὴ δὲ :
both A. and R.V. regard προσ. δὲ in the
same verse as the antithesis, but see
Page's note, where the antithesis is found
in ver. 6, ὅτε δέ. If we retain the former
interpretation, ver. 5 may be regarded as
a kind of parenthesis, the ὅτε δέ in ver. 6
forming a kind of antithesis to ver. 4.—
ἐκτενής, see critical notes; if we read
ἐκτενῶς = "earnestly," R.V. (Latin, intente), adverb is Hellenistic, used (by St.
Luke xxii. 44, and) once elsewhere in 1
Peter i. 22 (cf. the adjective in 1 Peter
iv. 8), so of prayer in Clem. Rom., Cor.,
xxxiv., 7. In LXX cf. the use of the word
in Joel i. 14 (but see H. and R.), Jonah iii.
8, Judith iv. 12 (see H. and R.), 3 Macc.
v. 9. The adjective is also found in 3
Macc. iii. 10 and v. 29. Their praying
shows "non fuisse animis fractos,"
Calvin. The word passed into the
services of the Church, and was often
repeated by the deacon : δεηθῶμεν ἐκ. or
ἐκτενέστερον.

6. Ὅτε δὲ ἔμελλεν αὐτὸν προάγειν [1] ὁ Ἡρώδης, τῇ νυκτὶ ἐκείνῃ ἦν ὁ Πέτρος κοιμώμενος μεταξὺ δύο στρατιωτῶν, δεδεμένος ἁλύσεσι δυσί, φύλακές τε πρὸ τῆς θύρας ἐτήρουν τὴν φυλακήν. 7. καὶ ἰδού, ἄγγελος Κυρίου ἐπέστη,[2] καὶ φῶς ἔλαμψεν ἐν τῷ οἰκήματι· πατάξας δὲ τὴν πλευρὰν τοῦ Πέτρου, ἤγειρεν αὐτὸν λέγων, Ἀνάστα ἐν τάχει. καὶ ἐξέπεσον[3] αὐτοῦ αἱ ἁλύσεις ἐκ τῶν χειρῶν. 8. εἶπέ τε ὁ ἄγγελος πρὸς αὐτόν, Περίζωσαι, καὶ ὑπόδησαι τὰ σανδάλιά σου. ἐποίησε δὲ οὕτω. καὶ λέγει αὐτῷ, Περιβαλοῦ τὸ ἱμάτιόν σου, καὶ ἀκολούθει

[1] προαγειν DEHLP, Chrys., so Meyer, Blass, and Hilg.; προαγαγειν A 8, 15, 61, so Tisch., W.H., marg., Weiss; προσαγειν ℵ 5, 29; προσαγαγειν B 13, 57, so W.H. text, Wendt. Compounds in προ and προς often interchanged (see Weiss, p. 20).

[2] Western text, β, adds τω Πετρω after επεστη, for ελαμψεν reads επελαμψεν, adds απ' αυτου (the angel), and instead of τω οικ. reads τω τοπω εκεινω. παταξ., instead D, Gig. read νυξας, so Hilg., cf. John xix. 34.

[3] εξεπεσον, but -εσαν ℵABDE 61, Tisch., W.H., Blass, Hilg., Weiss, W.H., App., p. 171, and Kennedy, p. 169.

Ver. 6. τῇ νυκτὶ ἐκείνῃ: "that very night," i.e., the night before the trial.—κοιμώμενος, cf. 1 Peter v. 7 and Ps. cxxxvii. 2: "for so He giveth His beloved sleep": "and there too it is beautiful that Paul sings hymns, whilst there Peter sleeps," Chrys., Hom., xxvi: cf. xvi. 25. τὸ πᾶν ῥίψας ἐπὶ τὸν Κύριον, Oecumenius (cf. Blass, in loco).—ἁλύσεσι δυσί, cf. xxi. 33; on the usual Roman custom see Jos., Ant., xviii., 6, 7, in the account of Herod's own imprisonment by Tiberius; cf. Pliny, Epist., x., 65; Seneca, Epist., i., 5, "eadem catena et custodiam (vinctum) et militem copulabat," perhaps most natural to suppose that Peter was bound on either hand to each of the soldiers, the two chains being used perhaps for greater security on account of the former escape. —φύλακες, i.e., the other two of the quaternion to make escape impossible. Ver. 7. ἐπέστη: often as here with the notion of coming suddenly, in classical Greek it is often used of dreams, as in Homer; or of the coming of heavenly visitors, very frequent in Luke, and with the same force as here, Friedrich, pp. 7 and 87, and almost always in second aorist, see also Plummer on Luke ii. 9.— οἰκήματι: only here in N.T., used in Wisdom xiii. 15 (and perhaps in Tobit ii. 4), but not in same sense. Dem. and Thuc. use it for a prison: R.V. "the cell," lit., the chamber.—πατάξας δὲ τὴν πλευρὰν: to rouse him, an indication of the sound and quiet sleep which the prisoner slept in spite of the fateful morrow (so Weiss); cf. vii. 24, and ver. 23).

Ver. 8. περίζωσαι, but simple verb in R.V., W.H., Weiss, Wendt; bind thy tunic with a girdle: during the night the long flowing undergarment was loosened, but fastened up by day, so as not to impede the movements. Wettstein, Weiss, Page, and others contrast Hor., Sat., i., 2, 132. "Colligit sarcinulas nec festinat" (Wetstein), simple verb only twice elsewhere in N.T., and there also of St. Peter, cf. John xxi. 18.—σανδάλιά: Mark vi. 9, elsewhere ὑποδήματα. St. Peter still observed his Master's rule to be shod with sandals (Mark, u. s.), i.e., the shoes of the poor as distinguished from those of the more wealthy: dim. of σάνδαλον, a wooden sole. In LXX cf. Josh. ix. 5, Isa. xx. 2; in Judith x. 4, xvi. 9, of the sandals of the richer class.—περιβαλοῦ, only here in Acts; Luke xii. 27, xxiii. 11, often elsewhere in N.T., and in LXX.—τὸ ἱμάτιον: the outer garment worn over the χιτών, and laid aside at night with the sandals. Lumby compares Didache, i., 4. Mark the distinction between the aorist and present tense, περίζωσαι . . . ὑπόδ.; περιβ., but ἀκολούθει (cf. John ii. 16). "Præsens propter finem non indicatum" Blass; Simcox, Language of N. T., p. 114. Ver. 9. ἐδόκει δὲ ὅραμα βλέπειν: even those who regard the narrative as unhistorical can scarcely say that the writer cannot understand how to distinguish between an actual fact and a vision; moreover, this same writer describes visions such as that of Peter, x. 10, and of Paul, xxii. 17, as ecstacies; once in xxvi. 19 Paul speaks of the appearance of Christ vouchsafed to him before Damascus as a

μοι. 9. καὶ ἐξελθὼν ἠκολούθει αὐτῷ· καὶ οὐκ ᾔδει ὅτι ἀληθές ἐστι
τὸ γινόμενον διὰ τοῦ ἀγγέλου, ἐδόκει δὲ ὅραμα βλέπειν. 10. διελθόντες δὲ πρώτην φυλακὴν καὶ δευτέραν, ἦλθον ἐπὶ τὴν πύλην τὴν
σιδηρᾶν, τὴν φέρουσαν εἰς τὴν πόλιν, ἥτις αὐτομάτη ἠνοίχθη[1] αὐτοῖς·
καὶ ἐξελθόντες[2] προῆλθον ῥύμην μίαν, καὶ εὐθέως ἀπέστη ὁ ἄγγελος
ἀπ᾽ αὐτοῦ. 11. καὶ ὁ Πέτρος γενόμενος ἐν ἑαυτῷ εἶπε, Νῦν οἶδα
ἀληθῶς ὅτι ἐξαπέστειλε Κύριος τὸν ἄγγελον αὐτοῦ, καὶ ἐξείλετό με
ἐκ χειρὸς Ἡρώδου καὶ πάσης τῆς προσδοκίας τοῦ λαοῦ τῶν Ἰουδαίων·

[1] ηνοιχθη EHLP, Chrys.; ηνοιγη A, so Tisch., W.H., Blass, Weiss, Hilg.; see
Winer-Schmiedel, p. 103; Deissmann, *Neue Bibelstudien*, p. 17.

[2] After εξελθοντες D, Par. add κατεβησαν τους επτα βαθμους και. Both Weiss
(p. 110) and Corrsen (p. 441) (see too Harris, p. 63, *Four Lectures*, etc.) regard
this as possibly original, so Wendt (p. 221, edit. 1899), whilst Belser (p. 65),
Zahn (ii., 350), Salmon (pp. 600, 601), Zöckler incline still more strongly to its
acceptance, and Blass and Hilg. retain. The addition has been referred to the
mention of the seven steps in Ezek. xl. 22 (*cf.* 26, 31) as its source (so Chase),
but, on the other hand, Zahn can see no explanation of the present passage in the
seven or the eight (ver. 31) steps of Ezekiel. It is quite possible, he thinks, that the
writer might introduce a detail of the kind into his first draft, but omit it afterwarde
as unnecessary for distant readers. In xxi. 35, 40, the steps lead not into the street,
but from Antonia into the Temple, and there is no connection between them and the
definite seven steps here, which are evidently presupposed (note the article) to be
well known to the reader.

vision, ὀπτασία, but this word is not confined to appearances which the narrators
regard as visions, *cf.* Luke i. 22, xxiv. 23,
cf. Beyschlag, *Studien und Kritiken*, p.
203, 1864; *Witness of the Epistles* (Longmans, 1892).

Ver. 10. φυλακὴν: "ward," perhaps
the best translation here with διελθόντες
so often used of traversing a place. The
first ward might be the place outside
the cell where the other soldiers of the
quaternion were on guard, and the second
ward might refer to some other part of
the prison or fortress Antonia (see Blass
in loco) where sentinels were stationed.
Weiss apparently takes the expression
to refer to the two φύλακες, ver. 6, *cf.*
1 Chron. xxvi. 16.—σιδηρᾶν: specially
noted since such a gate, when shut,
would effectually bar their way; but it
opened αὐτομάτη, only here in N.T. and
in Mark iv. 28, *cf.* Lev. xxv. 5, 11, 2
Kings xix. 29, Wisdom xvii. 6, and in
classical writers the striking parallel,
Hom., *Iliad*, v., 749 (Wendt, Blass);
Virgil, *Æneid*, vi., 81 (Wetstein).—φέρουσαν εἰς: only here in N.T., but
quite usual in classical Greek. If the
narrative means that immediately they
were out of the prison they were in the
street (so Weiss), evidently the prison
was in the city, and εἰς τὴν π. would
simply mean the open town, in contrast

to the confined prison-house (so Weiss
and Wendt, 1899). Blass decides for the
tower of Antonia on account of D.—
ἠνοίχθη, see critical notes.—ἐξελθόντες:
for remarkable addition in D see critical
notes.—εὐθέως: used several times in
Acts, but εὐθύς only once, see x. 16.—
ἀπέστη: when there were no further
hindrances to the Apostle's flight, then
the angel departed (Chrys.).

Ver. 11. γενόμενος ἐν ἑαυτῷ, *cf.* Luke
xv. 17, and compare instances of similar
phrases in Greek and Latin classical
writers in Wetstein and Blass.—Κύριος,
see critical notes, if without the article
Nösgen (so Weiss) takes it of God,
Jehovah.—ἐξαπέστειλε: a compound
only found in Luke and Paul; four times
in Luke's Gospel, six or seven times in
Acts, and Gal. iv. 4, 6; very frequent in
LXX, and used also in active voice by
Polybius.—ἐξείλετο ἐκ χ.: close parallels
in LXX, *cf.* Exod. iii. 8, 2 Sam. xxii. 1,
Isa. xliii. 13, Baruch iv. 18, 21, etc.—
ἐκ χειρὸς: Hebraism, *cf.* Luke i. 74.
The expression is also classical, Blass,
Gram., p. 127, for close parallel.—προσδοκία: only in Luke here and in Luke
xxi. 26, *cf.* Gen. xlix. 10, but more allied
to its sense here Ps. cxix. 116, Wisdom xvii.
13, Ecclus. xl. 2, and in 2 and 3 Macc.
(see H. and R.), and *Psalms of Solomon*,
Tit. xi.; frequently in classics. Ho-

12. συνιδών τε ἦλθεν ἐπὶ τὴν οἰκίαν[1] Μαρίας τῆς μητρὸς Ἰωάννου τοῦ ἐπικαλουμένου Μάρκου, οὗ ἦσαν ἱκανοὶ συνηθροισμένοι καὶ προσευχό- μενοι. 13. Κρούσαντος δὲ τοῦ Πέτρου[2] τὴν θύραν τοῦ πυλῶνος, προσῆλθε παιδίσκη ὑπακοῦσαι, ὀνόματι Ῥόδη · 14. καὶ ἐπιγνοῦσα τὴν φωνὴν τοῦ Πέτρου, ἀπὸ τῆς χαρᾶς οὐκ ἤνοιξε τὸν πυλῶνα, εἰσδραμοῦσα δὲ ἀπήγγειλεν ἑστάναι τὸν Πέτρον πρὸ τοῦ πυλῶνος.

---

[1] **Μαρ.**, but with art. τῆς preceding ℵABD 33, 61, Tisch., W.H., Weiss, Wendt —Blass omits.

[2] Instead of **του Π.**, great preponderance of authorities for **αυτου** ℵABDLP 61, maj. of vers., W.H., R.V., etc.

---

bart claims as a medical word, especially as the verb **προσδοκᾶν** is also so frequent in Luke; so too Zahn, *Einleitung in das N. T.*, p. 436; but see Plummer on Luke xxi. 36. Both verb and noun are also frequent in classical use.

Ver. 12. **συνιδών,** *cf.* xiv. 6; so several times in Apocrypha, so in classical writers, and also in Josephus. It may also include a consideration of the future (Bengel and Wetstein), but the aorist refers rather to a single act and not to a permanent state (so Alford).—**Μαρίας**: as no mention is made of Mark's father, she may well have been a widow, possessed of some wealth like Barnabas; see below.—**Ἰωάννου τοῦ ἐπικ.,** i. 23; iv. 36; x. 5, 18, 32; xi. 13; and below, xiii. 9. As in the case of Paul, his Roman name is used most frequently, *cf.* xv. 39, 2 Tim. iv. 11, Philem. 24, although in xiii. 5, 13 he is spoken of as John. No reason to doubt the identity of this John Mark with the second Evangelist: the notice of Papias that Mark was the **ἑρμηνευτής** of Peter, Eusebius, *H. E.*, iii., 39, is quite in accordance with the notice here of the Apostle's intimacy with the family of Mark, and with his mention in 1 Pet. v. 13. Blass comments on **Μάρκου,** "quasi digito monstratur auctor narrationis," and similarly Proleg., p. 11; *Philology of the Gospels*, pp. 192, 193. In Col. iv. 10 the A.V. calls him "sister's son to Barnabas," **ὁ ἀνεψιός,** but **ἀνεψ.** properly means "first cousin"; so R.V. the cousin of Barnabas (*cf.* LXX, Num. xxxvi. 11, Tob. vii. 2), Lightfoot on Col. iv. 10; see on xv. 39.— **προσευχόμενοι,** *cf.* James v. 16; "media nocte," Bengel; they betook them to prayer, "to that alliance which is indeed invincible," Chrys., *Hom.*, 26. On **ἦσαν** with participle as characteristic of St. Luke, see i. 10. As in the former miraculous deliverance, v. 16, all at-

tempts to get rid of the supernatural in St. Luke's narrative are unsuccessful. This is frankly admitted by Wendt, although he also maintains that we cannot discern the actual historical conditions owing to the mingling of legend and history. But he does not deny that St. Peter was liberated, and the same fact is admitted by Weizsäcker, see Wendt (1899), p. 219; and Zöckler, *Apostelgeschichte*, p. 230, and Wendt (1888), pp. 269, 270, for an account of the different attempts to explain the Apostle's liberation. In contrast to all such attempts the minute circumstantiality and the naturalness of the narrative speak for themselves, and we can hardly doubt (as Wendt is inclined to admit in some details) that John Mark has given us an account derived partly from St. Peter himself, *cf.* vv. 9, 11, and partly from his own knowledge, *cf.* the peculiarly artless and graphic touches in vv. 13, 14, which could scarcely have come from any one but an inmate of the house, as also the mention of the name of the servant; *cf.* Ramsay, *St. Paul*, p. 385; Blass, *Acta Apostolorum*, p. 142; Belser, *Theol. Quartalschrift*, Heft ii. (1895), p. 257; Zahn, *Einleitung*, ii., 244.

Ver. 13. **τὴν θ. τοῦ πυλῶνος**: the door of the gateway, *cf.* x. 17. **πυλών** as in Matt. xxvi. 71, of the passage leading from the inner court to the street, so that strictly the door in the gateway opening upon this passage would be meant, *cf.* **εἰσδ.,** ver. 14 (and **προσῆλθε,** ver. 13).— **κρούσαντος**: to knock at a door on the outside, *cf.* Luke xiii. 25, but elsewhere in Luke without **τὴν θύραν,** Luke xi. 9, 10, xii. 36 (Matt. vii. 7, Rev. iii. 20); so too in classical Greek, Xen., *Symp.*, i., 11, see Rutherford, *New Phrynichus*, p. 266; in LXX, Judg. xix. 22, Cant. v. 2, Judith xiv. 14.—**παιδίσκη,** *i.e.*, the portress, *cf.* John xviii. 17, see Rutherford, *u. s.*, p. 312; Kennedy, *Sources of N. T. Greek*,

15. οἱ δὲ πρὸς αὐτὴν εἶπον, Μαίνῃ. ἡ δὲ διϊσχυρίζετο οὕτως ἔχειν. οἱ δ᾽ ἔλεγον,[1] Ὁ ἄγγελος αὐτοῦ ἐστιν. 16. ὁ δὲ Πέτρος[2] ἐπέμενε κρούων· [3]ἀνοίξαντες δὲ εἶδον αὐτόν, καὶ ἐξέστησαν. 17. κατασείσας δὲ αὐτοῖς τῇ χειρὶ σιγᾶν,[4] διηγήσατο αὐτοῖς πῶς ὁ Κύριος αὐτὸν ἐξήγαγεν ἐκ τῆς φυλακῆς. εἶπε δέ, Ἀπαγγείλατε Ἰακώβῳ καὶ τοῖς

---

[1] Before ο αγγ. D (Pesh.) prefix τυχον, so Blass, Hilg. (as if only a possible solution, see Weiss, p. 72). (τυχον only occurs in N.T. in 1 Cor. xvi. 6, but in classical Greek adv.)

[2] D omits Π. with Par., but all edit. retain except Blass in β and Hilg.

[3] D reads εξανοιξαντες δε και ιδοντες αυτον εξεστ., a graphic touch perhaps orig., but if so, hardly corrected for brevity.

[4] For σιγαν D (Vulg., Gig., Par.) ινα σιγησωσιν, and D, Syr. H. mg., Par. εισηλθεν και—may be explanatory by reviser; Belser defends as orig., p. 65.

---

p. 40.—ὑπακοῦσαι, R.V., "to answer," cf. above, Xen., Symp., i., 11 (so in Plato, Phædo, 59 e, etc.).—Ῥόδη: a rose, cf. Dorcas and other names of the same class. The name occurs in myths and plays, see Blass's note.

Ver. 14. τῆς χαρᾶς: with article, the joy which she felt at the voice of Peter, cf. Luke xxiv. 41 for the same emphatic expression.—εἰσδ.: see above on ver. 10, only here in N.T., cf. 2 Macc. v. 26.

Ver. 15. Μαίνῃ: used as in a colloquial expression, not meaning literal insanity, see Page's note on xxvi. 24, so in 2 Kings ix. 11, ἐπίληπτος seems to be used.—διϊσχυρίζετο: only here and in Luke xxii. 59 (cf. xv. 2 β). In Luke, A.V. renders "confidently affirmed" as it should be here, and as it is in R.V.; found in classical Greek, and so also in Jos., Ant., ii., 6, 4, but not in LXX; cf. also its use in Acta Petri et Pauli Apocryph., 34, 39 (Lumby). Both ἰσχυρίζεσθαι and its compound here are used in medical language, and both in the same way as in this passage. If we compare the parallel passages, Matt. xxvi. 73, Mark xiv. 70, Luke xxii. 59, in Matthew we have εἶπον, in Mark ἔλεγον, but in Luke the strong word in the passage before us; Hobart, p. 77, and see also a similar change in parallel passages on p. 76.—Ὁ ἄγγελος αὐτοῦ ἐστιν, cf. Matt. xviii. 10, Heb. i. 14. According to Jewish ideas they would believe that Peter's guardian angel had assumed his form and voice, and stood before the door, see Edersheim, Jesus the Messiah, ii., 748-755, especially 752; "Apocrypha" ("Speaker's Commentary") "Angelology," i., 171 ff.; Weber, Jüdische Theol., pp. 170, 171 (1897); "Angels," B.D., 1², Blass, Nösgen, J.

Lightfoot, in loco. We may contrast the reserve of the canonical books of the Jews with the details of their later theology, "Engel," Hamburger, Real-Encyclopädie des Judentums, i., 2 and 3.

Ver. 16. ἐπέμενε, cf. John viii. 7, with a participle as here; only found elsewhere in N.T. in Luke and Paul; see on x. 48.—ἀνοίξ., another natural touch; those assembled went to the door themselves.

Ver. 17. κατασείσας ... σιγᾶν: only in Acts xiii. 16, xix. 33, xxi. 40, prop. to shake down (as fruit from trees), thus to shake up and down (the hand), to beckon with the hand for silence, used with accusative, and later with dat. instrument. χειρί: so in classical Greek and Josephus, cf. Ovid, Met., i., 206; Æneid, xii., 692, and instances in Wetstein; not in LXX as parallel to this; on the phrase, and also on σιγᾶν, as characteristic of Luke, see further Friedrich, pp. 26, 79.—διηγήσατο, ix. 27, only in Luke and Mark (except Heb. xi. 32). — Ἀπαγγείλατε: "tell," R.V., characteristic of Luke, eleven times in his Gospel, thirteen or fourteen in Acts.—Ἰακώβῳ: "the Lord's brother," Gal. i. 19, ii. 9, 1 Cor. xv. 7 (from Mark vi. 3 it has been inferred that he was the eldest of those so called). This James may have become more prominent still since the murder of James the son of Zebedee. On his position in the Church at Jerusalem see below on xv. 13, and also on xi. 30. For arguments in favour of the identification of this James with James the son of Alphæus, see B.D., 1², p. 1512; Felten, Apostelgeschichte, p. 239; and, on the other hand, Mayor, Introd. to Epistle of

ἀδελφοῖς ταῦτα. καὶ ἐξελθὼν ἐπορεύθη εἰς ἕτερον τόπον. 18.
Γενομένης δὲ ἡμέρας, ἦν τάραχος οὐκ ὀλίγος [1] ἐν τοῖς στρατιώταις, τί
ἄρα ὁ Πέτρος ἐγένετο. 19. Ἡρώδης δὲ ἐπιζητήσας αὐτὸν καὶ μὴ
εὑρών, ἀνακρίνας τοὺς φύλακας, ἐκέλευσεν [2] ἀπαχθῆναι· καὶ κατελθὼν
ἀπὸ τῆς Ἰουδαίας εἰς τὴν Καισάρειαν διέτριβεν.

[1] ουκ ολιγος om. D, Gig., Par., so Blass in β, and Hilg., may be " Western
non-interpolation," and for ordinary reading cf. xx. 23. At end of verse β adds
η πως εξηλθεν, cf. Par.[2] " aut quomodo exisset"; cf. Blass, p. ix., for defence, so
Belser, p. 65.

[2] απαχθ., D[1] reads αποκτανθηναι, so Hilg., but Blass rejects—certainly looks like
a gloss.

St. James; Zahn, Einleitung in das
N. T., i., 72; Lightfoot, Galatians, pp. 252
ff. and 364; Hort, Ecclesia, pp. 76, 77. In
this mention of James, Feine points out
that a knowledge as to who he was is
evidently presupposed, and that therefore
we have another indication that the
" Jerusalem tradition " is the source of
St. Luke's information here.—εἰς ἕτερον
τόπον: all conjectures as to the place,
whether it was Antioch, Rome, Cæsarea,
are rendered more arbitrary by the fact
that it is not even said that the place was
outside Jerusalem (however probable this
may have been); ἐξελθών need not mean
that he went out of the city, but out of
the house in which he had taken refuge,
cf. ver. 9. For all that can be said in
support of the view that he went to
Rome, see Felten, u. s., pp. 240-244,
Knabenbauer, p. 214. Harnack, Chronol.,
i., p. 243, apparently is prepared to
regard the visit to Rome in the reign of
Claudius, A.D. 42, as not impossible,
although unprovable. But see the whole
question treated from the opposite side
by Zöckler, Apostelgeschichte, pp. 233,
234 (second edition). The notice is so
indefinite that we cannot build anything
upon it, and we can scarcely go beyond
Wendt's view that if Peter left Jerusalem
at all, he may have undertaken some
missionary journey, cf. 1 Cor. ix. 5.
Ver. 18. τάραχος (generally ταραχή):
only in Acts xix. 23, although several
times in LXX.—οὐκ ὀλίγος: only found
in Acts, where it occurs eight times
(litotes), cf. xix. 11, xx. 12, xxvii. 14,
and for similar expressions Luke xv. 13
(Acts i. 5), vii. 6: see Klostermann,
Vindiciæ Lucanæ, p. 52, and Page, in
loco. The guards would answer for
the escape of the prisoner by suffering
a like penalty, cf. Cod. Just., ix., 4, 4.
—τί ἄρα (cf. Luke i. 66), Peter has
disappeared, what, then, has become of

him? (Grimm, sub v. ἄρα (i.), and Winer-
Moulton, liii. 8); it thus marks the perplexity of the soldier as to what had
become of Peter.—ἐγέν.: Blass, quid
Petro (ablat.) factum sit.
Ver. 19. μὴ for οὐ, as often with a
participle. Simcox, Language of the
N. T., p. 188.—ἀνακρίνας, Acts iv. 9, xxiv.
8, xxviii. 18, Luke xxiii. 14, of a judicial
investigation, cf. also 1 Cor. ix. 3 for this
judicial use by St. Paul, see Grimm sub
v.—ἀπαχθῆναι, "to be put to death,"
R.V., only here in this sense in N.T.
absolutely; so Latin duci in Pliny, ad
Traj., 96 (Page); Nestle, Philologia
Sacra (1896), p. 53, cf. Gen. xxxix. 22,
xl. 3, xlii. 16, LXX, use of the same verb
of carrying off to prison.—κατελθών:
Herod was wont to make his residence
for the most part at Jerusalem, Jos., Ant.,
xix., 7, 3, and we are not told why he
went down to Cæsarea on this occasion.
Josephus, xix., 8, 2, tells us that the festival during which the king met his death
was appointed in honour of the emperor's
safety, and the conjecture has been made
that the thanksgiving was for the return
of Claudius from Britain (see Farrar, St.
Paul, i., 315), but this must remain uncertain; he may have gone down to
Cæsarea "propter Tyros," Blass, see
also B.D., i[2], p. 135.
Ver. 20. θυμομαχῶν: lit., "to fight
desperately" Polyb., ix., 40, 4; xxvii., 8, 4,
and it might be used not only of open
warfare, but of any violent quarrel; here
almost = ὀργίζεσθαι. There could be no
question of actual warfare, as Phœnicia
was part of the province of Syria, and
Herod had no power to wage war against
it. Probably the cause of this θυμομαχία
lay in commercial interests. The word
is not found in LXX, or elsewhere in
N.T.—ὁμοθυμαδόν, i. 14.—πείσαντες, cf.
Matt. xxviii. 14, possibly with bribes, as
Blass and Wendt suggest.—τὸν ἐπὶ τοῦ

20. Ἦν δὲ ὁ Ἡρώδης θυμομαχῶν Τυρίοις καὶ Σιδωνίοις [1]· ὁμοθυμαδὸν δὲ παρῆσαν πρὸς αὐτόν, καὶ πείσαντες Βλάστον τὸν ἐπὶ τοῦ κοιτῶνος τοῦ βασιλέως, ᾐτοῦντο εἰρήνην, διὰ τὸ τρέφεσθαι αὐτῶν τὴν χώραν ἀπὸ τῆς βασιλικῆς. 21. Τακτῇ δὲ ἡμέρᾳ ὁ Ἡρώδης ἐνδυσάμενος ἐσθῆτα βασιλικήν, καὶ καθίσας ἐπὶ τοῦ βήματος, ἐδημηγόρει πρὸς αὐτούς· 22. ὁ δὲ δῆμος ἐπεφώνει, Θεοῦ φωνὴ καὶ οὐκ ἀνθρώπου. 23. παραχρῆμα δὲ ἐπάταξεν αὐτὸν ἄγγελος Κυρίου, ἀνθ᾽ ὧν οὐκ ἔδωκε τὴν δόξαν τῷ Θεῷ [2]· καὶ γενόμενος σκωληκόβρωτος, ἐξέψυξεν.

[1] ομοθ., D, Syr. H. mg. (Par. Vulg.), so Blass and Hilg. read οι δε ομοθ. εξ αμφοτερων των πολεων παρησαν., may be a gloss on ομοθ. meaning that the two cities made common cause, cf. τας χωρας for την χωραν in same verse (Western). D, Par.[2] (Wern.) add at end of ver. 21 καταλλαγεντος δε αυτου τοις Τ. και τοις Σ. D omits και τοις Σ. Syr. H. mg. has κατηλλαγη δε αυτοις. But this appears to introduce a fresh connection into the narrative, and to divert attention from the main point, viz., the speech. So Weiss, p. 73, thinks φωναι (β), for φωνη, ver. 22, is introduced to indicate the contents of the speech.

[2] D reads καταβας απο του βηματος after Θεω και. After σκωλ. D adds ετι ζων και ουτως, so Blass and Hilg. Blass in β reads εγεν. for γενομ.; insertions avoid possible misunderstandings, see comment.

κοιτῶνος, "chamberlain," perhaps best. κοιτών will imply that he was over the king's bed-chamber. Exod. viii. 3, cf. 2 Sam. iv. 7, 2 Kings, vi. 12, 1 Esd. iii. 3 = Latin cubicularius. κοιτών, in Dio Cassius, lxi., 5, is used of the king's treasury, but the ordinary usage is as above. In Attic Greek δωμάτιον, not κοιτών.—τρέφεσθαι, i.e., with corn (cf. 1 Kings v. 9, Ezra iii. 7, Ezek. xxvii. 17; Jos., Ant., xiv., 10, 6), and see Blass, note in loco. Ver. 21. τακτῇ: only here in N.T.; cf. Jos., Ant., xix., 8, 2 (cf. xviii., 6, 7), δευτέρᾳ δὲ τῶν θεωριῶν ἡμέρᾳ. It is quite true that Josephus says nothing directly of the Tyrians and Sidonians, but the audience was evidently granted to them on the second day of the public spectacle ; cf. for the expression, Polyb., iii., 34, 9. The description of Josephus evidently implies some special occasion, and not the return of the ordinary Quinquennalia ; see on ver. 19 and also below. Josephus does not menion Blastus, or those of Tyre and Sidon, but this is no reason against the narrative, as Krenkel maintains. Belser, much more reasonably, contends that Luke's narrative supplements and completes the statement of Josephus.—ἐνδ. ἐσθῆτα βασιλικήν, cf. Jos., Ant., xix., 8, 2, στολὴν ἐνδυσάμενος ἐξ ἀργυρίου πεποιημένην πᾶσαν.; on ἐσθ. see i. 10.—βήματος : Josephus speaks of the event happening in the theatre, and the βῆμα here = rather "the throne," R.V. (margin, "judgment-seat"), the

royal seat in the theatre from which the king saw the games and made his harangues to the people (so of an orator's pulpit, Neh. viii. 4, 2 Macc. xiii. 26), see Blass and Grimm-Thayer, sub v.—ἐδημηγόρει: only here in N.T. In 4 Macc. v. 15 = contionari, frequent in classical Greek.—πρὸς αὐτούς, i.e., to the Tyrian and Sidonian representatives, but the word ἐδημ. might well be used of what was in any case an address, ad populum, cf. ver. 22. Ver. 22. δῆμος : only in Acts, xvii. 5, xix. 30, 33, but in the same signification in classical Greek.—ἐπεφώνει: later Greek in this sense (cf. the flatterers in the description of Josephus, u. s., ἀνεβόων, that Herod was θεός, and so in the words εὐμενὴς εἴης). In N.T. only in Luke, cf. Luke xxiii. 21, Acts xxi. 34, xxii. 24; cf. 2 Macc. i. 23, 3 Macc. vii. 13, 1 Esd. ix. 47. The imperfect quite corresponds to the description of Josephus: ἄλλος ἄλλοθεν φωνῆς ἀνεβ. θ. φωνή; for instances of similar flattery see Wetstein, and cf. Josephus, u. s. Ver. 23. παραχρῆμα, see above, p. 106. —ἐπάταξεν, cf. Exod. xi. 23, 2 Sam. xxiv. 17, 2 Kings xix. 35, 1 Chron. xxi. 15, Isa. xxxvii. 36, 1 Macc. vii. 41. See p. 188. On the confusion in the reading of Eusebius, H.E., ii., 10, where for the owl whom Josephus describes as appearing to Herod as ἄγγελος κακῶν we have the reading "the angel" of the Acts, the unseen minister of the divine will, see B.D. 1², p. 1345, and Eusebius, Schaff and Wace's

24. Ὁ δὲ λόγος τοῦ Θεοῦ ηὔξανε καὶ ἐπληθύνετο.　25. Βαρνάβας δὲ καὶ Σαῦλος¹ ὑπέστρεψαν ἐξ Ἰερουσαλήμ, πληρώσαντες τὴν διακονίαν, συμπαραλαβόντες καὶ Ἰωάννην τὸν ἐπικληθέντα Μάρκον.

¹ After **Σαῦλος** Syr. H. mg., Par. add ὁ επικαλουμενος Παυλος. Par. also reads **Παυλος** in xiii. 1, 2. This seems a mere anticipation of xiii. 9. Blass in β follows Par. (p. ix.), and regards **Παυλος** as original. So Belser, pp. 65, 66, warmly defends, as showing that there is no need to see in xiii. 9 a sudden introd. of the name Paul, but that Luke, at least in the first draft of his work, had already spoken of him here as bearing a double name, like John Mark. **υπεστρεψαν εξ Ι.** A 13, 27, Syr. P. and H., Sah., Boh., Arm., Aeth., Chrys., so Tisch., Weiss, W.H. marg., R.V.; but ℵBHLP 61, Syr. H. mg., Aeth^ro.; W.H., Wendt, R.V. marg. read **εις Ι.**, and DE 15, 180, Vulg., Chrys. read **απο**, so Blass in β, and so Hilg. Tisch. maintains that scribe began to write **απο** but turned it into **εις**. The latter prep. would not be understood if taken with **υπεστρεψαν**, as it would have no meaning, and so **εξ** and **απο** substituted. E, Syr. Pesh., Sah., and so Par. and Blass in β, added **εις Αντιοχειαν** (but see Weiss, Introd. to *Apostelgeschichte*, p. 37). But the reading **εις Ι.** can be fairly explained if the words are connected with **πληρ. την διακ.**, so Wendt and W.H. (*App.*, p. 94), and Zöckler, *Apostelgeschichte*, p. 232. Ramsay, *St. Paul*, p. 64, holds that **εις** was a deliberate alteration of an editor who thus brought the text into conformity with xxii. 17 because the two passages referred to the same visit.

edition, *in loco;* see also Bengel's impressive note on this verse on the difference between human history and divine. —ἀνθ᾽ ὧν = ἀντὶ τούτων ὅτι, *cf.* Luke i. 20, xix. 44, see also xii. 3; only once outside St. Luke's writings in N.T., 2 Thess. ii. 10; see Simcox, *Language of N. T.*, p. 137; Plummer on Luke i. 20 and xii. 3; quite classical and several times in LXX.—ἔδωκε τὴν δ.: *debitum honorem, cf.* Isa. xlviii. 11, Rev. xix. 7; article elsewhere omitted (*cf.* Luke xvii. 18); a Hebrew phrase. How different the behaviour of St. Peter and of St. Paul, x. 26, xiv. 14. Josephus expressly says that the king did not rebuke the flatterers or reject their flattery.—καὶ γενόμ. σκ.: see below. St. Luke does not say that Herod died on the spot, but simply marks the commencement of the disease, παραχρῆμα; Josephus describes the death as occurring after five days. Wendt (1899 edition) admits that the kind of death described may well have been gradual, although in 1888 edition he held that the ἐξέψυξεν meant that he expired immediately; see also Zöckler and Hackett, as against Weiss. ἐξέψ., see on v. 5, 10.—σκωλ.: only here in N.T.; no contradiction with Josephus, but a more precise description of the fatal disease, *cf.* 2 Macc. ix. 5, 9, with which detailed and strange account the simple statement of the fact here stands in marked contrast. The word cannot be taken metaphorically, *cf.* Herod., iv., 205: and Jos., *Ant.*, xvii., 6, 5, of the death of Herod the Great. Such a death was regarded as a punishment for pride; so in 2 Macc. and Herod., Farrar, *St. Paul,*

i., 318. The term itself was one which we might expect from a medical man, and St. Luke may easily have learnt the exact nature of the disease during his two years residence in Cæsarea (Belser). See Hobart, pp. 42, 43, Knabenbauer *in loco.* The word was used of a disease of plants, but Luke, no less than his contemporary Dioscorides, may well have been acquainted with botanical terms (Vogel). To think with Baur and Holtzmann of the gnawing worm of the damned is quite opposed to the whole context. If we place the two narratives, the account given by Josephus and that given by St. Luke side by side, it is impossible not to see their general agreement, and none has admitted this more unreservedly than Schürer. On reasons for the silence of Josephus as to the death as a punishment of the king's impiety in contrast with the clear statement of St. Luke; and also on the whole narrative as against the strictures of Spitta, see Belser, *Theologische Quartalschrift*, p. 252 ff., 2ᵉ Heft, 1895; for a full examination; *cf.* also Nösgen to the same effect, *Apostelgeschichte*, p. 242, Zahn, *Einleitung*, ii., 417. Belser should also be consulted as against Krenkel, *Josephus und Lucas*, p. 203 ff. It should be noted that Krenkel does not affirm that Luke derived his material from Josephus in xii. 1-23, but only that he was influenced by the Jewish historian, and that with regard to the hapax-legomenon, σκωληκόβρωτος, he can only affirm that Josephus affords us an analogous expression, *B. J.*, vii., 8, 7.

Ver. 24. δὲ, marking the contrast, not

XIII. 1. ᾽ΗΣΑΝ δέ τινες [1] ἐν ᾽Αντιοχείᾳ κατὰ τὴν οὖσαν ἐκκλησίαν προφῆται καὶ διδάσκαλοι, ὅ τε [2] Βαρνάβας καὶ Συμεὼν ὁ καλούμενος Νίγερ, καὶ Λούκιος ὁ Κυρηναῖος, Μαναήν τε ᾽Ηρώδου τοῦ τετράρχου

[1] τινες om. $\aleph$ABD 61, Vulg., Syr. Pesh., Sah., Boh., Aeth., so Tisch., W.H., R.V., Weiss, Wendt.

[2] For ο τε D, Vulg. read εν οις, and before Κυρ. D omits ο—Blass, "recte," but there may have been some other Lucius from whom this one was distinguished. Σαυλος, Par. reads Παυλος, so in ver. 2, and Blass in β ; see on xii. 25.

only between the death of the persecutor and the growth of the Word, but also between the persecution and the vitality of the Church.—ηὔξανε καὶ ἐπληθ. imperfects, marking the continuous growth in spite of all obstacles ; cf. Luke viii. 11, Matt. xiii. 32, 2 Cor. ix. 10.

Ver. 25. ὑπέστρεψαν ἐξ ῾Ι., see critical notes, and Ramsay, St. Paul, pp. 63, 64, and note on xxii. 17, below.—πληρ. τὴν διακ. ; if the visit extended over as long a period as Ramsay believes, viz., from the time when the failure of harvest in 46 turned scarcity into famine until the beginning of 47 (u. s., pp. 51, 63), no doubt the delegates could not have simply delivered a sum of money to the elders, but would have administered the relief (not money), and carried a personal message of cheer to the distressed (Ramsay, p. 49 ff., u. s.), and so have "fulfilled" their ministry. But the word διακονία does not of necessity involve this personal and continuous ministration, e.g., cf. Rom. xv. 31, where St. Paul uses the word of the money collection brought by him to Jerusalem for the poor, a passage in which the Western gloss is δωροφορία, cf. Rom. xv. 25, 2 Cor. viii. 4, ix. 1, 12, 13. Grimm writes that the word is used of those who succour need by either collecting or bestowing benefactions ; see further, Expositor, March and July, 1896 (Ramsay), April, 1896 (Sanday), also Hort, Ecclesia, p. 206, and above on xi. 29. —Σαῦλος, see critical notes for Western addition. — συμπαραλαβόντες, cf. xv. 37, 38, of bringing as a companion in N.T., only once elsewhere in same sense, Gal. ii. i. (cf. 3 Macc. i. 1). This incidental notice of John Mark may well emphasise the fact that he was taken with Paul and Barnabas as a supernumerary, and to mark his secondary character as compared with them. In view of subsequent events, it would be important to make this clear by introducing him in a way which showed that he was not essential to the expedition, Ramsay, St. Paul, pp. 71, 170, 177 ; cf. xv. 37, 40. CHAPTERS XIII.-XIV. First Missionary

Journey of St. Paul.—On the unity of xiii. and xiv. with the rest of the book see additional note at end of chap. xiv.—Ver. 1. κατὰ τὴν οὖσαν ἐκκ.: the word οὖσαν may well be used here, as the participle of εἰμί is often used in Acts to introduce some technical phrase, or some term marked out as having a technical force, cf. v. 17, xiv. 13, xxviii. 17, so that a new stage in the history of the Christians at Antioch is marked—no longer a mere congregation, but " the Church that was there " (Ramsay, Church in the R. E., p. 52). So also Weiss, in loco ; οὖσαν stands in contrast to xi. 21-26 : there was no longer a mere company of believers at Antioch, but a Church.—ἐν ᾽A.: Blass maintains that the order of words as compared with the mention of the Church in Jerusalem, xi. 22, emphasises the fact that Antioch is the starting-point of the succeeding missionary enterprise, and is named first, and so distinctively set before men's eyes.—προφῆται καὶ διδάσκαλοι, see above on xi. 27. From 1 Cor. xii. 28 it would seem that in Corinth at all events not all teachers were prophets, although in a sense all prophets were teachers, in so far as they edified the Church. The two gifts might be united in the same person as in Paul himself, Gal. ii. 2, 2 Cor. xii. 1 (Zöckler). In Ephes. iv. 11, as in 1 Cor. xii. 28, Apostles stand first in the Church, Prophets next, and after them Teachers. But whilst it is quite possible to regard the account of the gift of προφητεία in 1 Cor. xii.-xiv. as expressing " inspiration " rather than " official character," this does not detract from the pre-eminent honour and importance assigned to the prophets and teachers at Antioch. Their position is such and their powers are such in the description before us that they might fairly be described as " presbyters," whose official position was enhanced by the possession of a special gift, " the prophecy " of the New Testament, " presbyters " who like those in 1 Tim. v. 17 might also be described as κοπιῶντες ἐν διδασκαλίᾳ, Moberly, Ministerial Priest-

σύντροφος, καὶ Σαῦλος. 2. λειτουργούντων δὲ αὐτῶν τῷ Κυρίῳ καὶ
νηστευόντων, εἶπε τὸ Πνεῦμα τὸ Ἅγιον, Ἀφορίσατε δή μοι τόν τε
Βαρνάβαν καὶ τὸν Σαῦλον εἰς τὸ ἔργον ὃ προσκέκλημαι αὐτούς.

hood, pp. 159, 160, 166, 208. See further on the relation of the prophets and teachers in the *Didaché* "Church," Hastings' B.D., i. 436, Bigg, *Doctrine of the Twelve Apostles*, p. 27 ; and on the relation of prophecy and teaching in the N.T., McGiffert, *Apostolic Age*, p. 528, Zöckler, *in loco*.—τε ... καὶ : a difficulty arises as to the force of these particles. It is urged that two groups are thus represented, the first three names forming one group (prophets), and the last two another group (teachers), so Ramsay (p. 65), Weiss, Holtzmann, Zöckler, Harnack, Knabenbauer, and amongst older commentators Meyer and Alford ; but on the other hand Wendt, so Nösgen, Felten, Hilgenfeld think that there is no such separation intended, as Paul himself later claims the prophetic gift (1 Cor. xiv. 6), to which Zöckler would reply that at this time Paul might well be described as a teacher, his prophetic gift being more developed at a later date. Amongst recent English writers both Hort and Gore regard the term "prophets and teachers" as applying to all the five (so Page).—Συμεών : nothing is known of him. Spitta would identify him with Simon of Cyrene, Matt. xxvii. 32, but the epithet Niger may have been given to distinguish him from others of the same name, and possibly from the Simon to whom Spitta refers. — Λούκιος ὁ Κ. : Zöckler describes as "quite absurd" the attempt to identify him with Luke of the Acts. The names are quite different, and the identification has been supported on the ground that Cyrene was a famous school of medicine. This Lucius may have been one of the men of Cyrene, xi. 20, who first preached the Gospel at Antioch. Others have proposed to identify him with the Lucius of Rom. xvi. 21. —Μαναήν : of the three names, as distinct from Barnabas and Paul, Blass says *ignoti reliqui*, and we cannot say more than this. For although Mark is described as σύντροφος of Herod the Tetrarch (Antipas), the description is still very indefinite. A.V. "brought up with," R.V. " foster - brother," *collactaneus*, Vulgate. For an ingenious study on the name and the man see Plumptre, *in loco*, *cf.* also Wetstein and Zöckler. The name occurs in 1 Macc. i. 6, but the reading must apparently give place to

συνέκτροφοι. It is also found in 2 Macc. ix. 29, and once in the N.T. in the present passage. Deissmann, from the evidence of the inscriptions, regards it as a court title, and quotes amongst other places an inscription in Delos of the first half of the second century B.C., where Heliodorus is described as σύντροφος τοῦ βασιλέως Σελεύκου Φιλοπάτορος. So Manaen also might be described as a confidential friend of Herod Antipas, *Bibelstudien*, pp. 173, 178-181.—Σαῦλος, placed last probably because the others were older members of the Church. The position certainly does not mark the list as unhistorical ; if the account came from the Apostle himself, the lowest place was eminently characteristic of him.

Ver. 2. λειτουργούντων : "as they ministered to the Lord," A. and R. V., *ministrantibus Domino*, Vulgate. It would be difficult to find a more appropriate rendering. On the one hand the word is habitually used in the LXX of the service of the priests and Levites (*cf.* Heb. viii. 2, x. 11), although it has a wider meaning as, *e.g.*, when used to describe the service of Samuel to God, 1 Sam. ii. 18, iii. 1, or of service to man, 1 Kings i. 4, 15, 2 Chron. xvii. 19, Ecclus. x. 25. So too in the N.T. it is used in the widest sense of those who aid others in their poverty, Rom. xv. 27 (*cf.* 2 Cor. ix. 12), Phil. ii. 25, 27, and also λειτουργία τῆς πίστεως ὑμῶν, Phil. ii. 17, of the whole life of the Christian Society. But here the context, see on ver. 3 (*cf.* xiv. 23), seems to point to some special public religious service (Hort, *Ecclesia*, p. 63, but see also Ramsay's rendering of the words, and Zöckler, *in loco*). In this early period λειτουργία could of course not be applied to the Eucharist alone, and the Romanist commentator Felten only goes so far as to say that a reference to it cannot be excluded in the passage before us, and in this we may agree with him. At all events it seems somewhat arbitrary to explain *Didaché*, xv. 1, where we have a parallel phrase, of the service of public worship, whilst in the passage before us the words are explained of serving Christ whether by prayer or by instructing others concerning the way of salvation ; so Grimm-Thayer. In each passage the verb should certainly be taken as referring to the

3. τότε νηστεύσαντες καὶ προσευξάμενοι, καὶ ἐπιθέντες τὰς χεῖρας αὐτοῖς, ἀπέλυσαν.[1]   4. Οὗτοι μὲν οὖν ἐκπεμφθέντες ὑπὸ τοῦ Πνεύματος

[1] ἀπελυσαν D omits, Blass retains, so Hilg.; its omission ruins the construction. (τον Β. και) τον Σ., om. τον אaABCDE, Tisch., W.H., Blass, Weiss, Hilg.; cf. Ramsay, "Forms of Classif. in Acts," Expositor, July, 1895.

ministry of public worship. In the N.T. the whole group of words, λειτουργέω, λειτουργία, λειτουργός, λειτουργικός, is found only in St. Luke, St. Paul, and Hebrews. See further on the classical and Biblical usage Westcott, Hebrews, additional note on viii. 2. Deissmann, Bibelstudien, p. 137, from pre-Christian papyri points out that λειτουργία and λειτουργέω were used by the Egyptians of the sacred service of the priests, and sometimes of a wider religious service. —αὐτῶν: not the whole Ecclesia, but the prophets and teachers: "prophetarum doctorumque qui quasi arctius sunt concilium," Blass.—νηστευόντων, cf. x. 30, xiv. 23, xxvii. 9, and in O.T. 1 Sam. vii. 5, 6, Dan. ix. 3, on the union of fasting and prayer. In Didaché, viii., 1, while the fasts of the "hypocrites" are condemned, fasting is enjoined on the fourth day of the week, and on Friday, i.e., the day of the Betrayal and the Crucifixion. But Didaché, vii., 4, lays it down that before baptism the baptiser and the candidate should fast. The conduct therefore of the prophets and teachers at Antioch before the solemn mission of Barnabas and Saul to their work is exactly what might have been expected, cf. Edersheim, Temple and its Services, p. 66.—εἶπε τὸ Π.: we may reasonably infer by one of the prophets; it may have been at a solemn meeting of the whole Ecclesia held expressly with reference to a project for carrying the Gospel to the heathen (Hort, Felten, Hackett). Felten sees in δή an indication of an answer to a special prayer. But it does not follow that the "liturgical" functions should be assigned to the whole Ecclesia. —Ἀφορίσατε, cf. the same word used by St. Paul of himself, Rom. i. 1, Gal. i. 15, LXX, Lev. xx. 26, Numb. viii. 11. μοι. Such words and acts indicate the personality of the Holy Ghost, cf. δή emphatic, signifying the urgency of the command (cf. use of the word in classical Greek). A. and R.V. omit altogether in translation. In Luke ii. 15 both render it "now," in Matt. xiii. 23, R.V. "verily," Act xv. 36, "now," 1 Cor. vi. 20, A. and R.V. "therefore," to emphasise a demand as here. With this force the word is

thus peculiar to Luke and Paul (in other passages, reading contested). The translation of the word may have been omitted here, since the rendering "now" would have been taken in a temporal sense which δή need not suggest.—δ for εἰς δ, cf. i. 21, Luke i. 25, xii. 46. Grimm-Thayer, Winer-Moulton, l., 7 b, so in Greek writers generally.—προσκέκλημαι, cf. ii. 39, xvi. 10. Grimm-Thayer, sub v. b. Winer-Moulton, xxxix. 3.
Ver. 3. τότε probably indicating a new and special act of fasting and prayer. But is the subject of the sentence the whole Ecclesia, or only the prophets and teachers mentioned before? Ramsay maintains that it cannot be the officials just mentioned, because they cannot be said to lay hands on two of themselves, so that he considers some awkward change of subject takes place, and that the simplest interpretation is that the Church as a whole held a meeting for this solemn purpose (cf. πάντες in D). But if the whole Church was present, it does not follow that they took part in every detail of the service, just as they may have been present in the public service of worship in ver. 2 (see above) without λειτουργ. τῷ Κ. equally with the prophets and teachers (cf. Felten and also Wendt). There is therefore no reason to assume that the laying on of hands was performed by the whole Church, or that St. Luke could have been ignorant that this function was one which belonged specifically to the officers of the Church. The change of subject is not more awkward than in vi. 6. Dr. Hort is evidently conscious of the difficulty, see especially Ecclesia, p. 64. No doubt, on the return of the two missionaries, they report their doings to the whole Church, xiv. 27, but this is no proof that the laying on of hands for their consecration to their mission was the act of the whole Church. That prophets and teachers should thus perform what is represented in Acts as an Apostolic function need not surprise us, see Gore, u. s., pp. 241, 260, 261. A further question arises as to whether this passage conflicts with the fact that St. Paul

τοῦ ʿΑγίου,[1] κατῆλθον εἰς τὴν Σελεύκειαν, ἐκεῖθέν τε ἀπέπλευσαν εἰς
τὴν Κύπρον. 5. καὶ γενόμενοι ἐν Σαλαμῖνι, κατήγγελλον τὸν λόγον

[1] εκπεμφ. υπο του Π., Par. has *egressi e sanctis* = οι μεν ουν εξελθοντες απο των
αγιων, Blass in β, and for απηλθον D has καταβαντες (so Blass and Hilg.).

was already an Apostle, and that his
Apostleship was based not upon his
appointment by man, or upon human
teaching, but upon a revelation from God,
and upon the fact that he had seen the
Lord. It is certainly remarkable that
both Barnabas and Saul are called
Apostles by St. Luke in connection with
this first missionary journey, and that
under no other circumstance does he
apply the term to either, xiv. 4, 14, and
it is possible that the title may have been
given here in a limited sense with reference to their special mission; see Hort,
Ecclesia, pp. 28, 64, 65. But at the
same time we must remember that in
the N.T. the term ἀπόστολος is never
applied to any one who may not very well
have satisfied the primary qualification
of Apostleship, *viz.*, to have seen the
Lord, and to bear witness to His Resurrection, see Lightfoot, *Galatians*, p. 95 ff.
(as against the recent statements of
McGiffert, *Apostolic Age*, p. 653): "We
have no reason to suppose that this condition was ever realised, unless we throw
forward the *Teaching* into the second
century," Gwatkin, "Apostle," Hastings'
B.D.: see further, Lightfoot, *Philippians*, p. 350, additional note on the
Didaché. This we may accept, except
in so far as it bears upon the *Didaché*, in
which the Apostles (only mentioned in
one passage, xi. 3-6) may be contrasted
rather than compared with the Apostles
of the N.T., inasmuch as they are represented as wandering missionaries, itiner-
ating from place to place, in days of
corruption and gross imposture, and inasmuch as the picture which the *Didaché*
reveals is apparently characteristic of a
corner of Church life rather than of the
whole of it; Moberly, *Ministerial Priesthood*, p. 176; Bright, *Some Aspects of
Primitive Church Life*, p. 34, and the
strictures of Bigg, *Doctrine of the Twelve
Apostles*, pp. 27, 40 ff. It may of course
be urged that we know nothing of Barnabas and of the others, to whom Lightfoot and Gwatkin refer as to their special
call from Christ, whilst in the case of St.
Paul we have his·own positive assertion.
But even in his case the laying on of
hands recognised, if it did not bestow,
his Apostolic commission, and "the

ceremony of Ordination when it was not
the channel of the grace was its recognition," Gore, *u. s.*, pp. 257-267, 383, 395,
etc., and see especially the striking passage in Moberly, *Ministerial Priesthood*,
pp. 107, 108.
Ver. 4. μὲν οὖν answered by δέ in
ver. 5, so Weiss and Rendall, Appendix
on μὲν οὖν, p. 161. Page takes διελ.
δέ in ver. 6 as the antithesis, see his note
on ii. 41.—ἐκπεμφ., *cf.* ver. 2; only in
N.T. in xvii. 10, *cf.* 2 Sam. xix. 31, where
it denotes personal conduct. Mr. Rendall's note takes the verb here also of the
personal presence of the Holy Spirit
conducting the Apostles on their way.—
κατῆλθον: "went down," R.V., of a
journey from the interior to the coast, *cf.*
xv. 30; Vulgate, *abierunt*, and so A.V.
"departed," which fails to give the full
force of the word.—Σελεύκειαν: the port of
Antioch, built by the first Seleucus, about
sixteen miles from the city on the Orontes;
Seleucia ad mare and ἡ ἐν Πιερίᾳ to distinguish it from other places bearing the
same name, see Wetstein for references
to it. On its mention here and St. Luke's
custom see Ramsay, *St. Paul*, p. 70.—
Κύπρον, *cf.* iv. 36. Although not expressly
stated, we may well believe that the place
was divinely intimated. But it was
natural for more reasons than one that
the missionaries should make for Cyprus.
Barnabas was a Cypriote, and the nearness of Cyprus to Syria and its productive
copper mines had attracted a large settlement of Jews, *cf.* also xi. 19, 20, and the
Church at Antioch moreover owed its
birth in part to the Cypriotes, xi. 20
(xxi. 16).
Ver. 5. Σαλαμῖνι: the nearest place to
Seleucia on the eastern coast of Cyprus.
A few hours' sail in favourable weather
would bring the traveller to a harbour convenient and capacious. The Jewish
colony must have been considerable since
mention is made of synagogues.—κατήγγελλον: "they began to proclaim" . . .
ἐν ταῖς συν., it was St. Paul's habitual
custom to go to the synagogues first, *cf.*
ix. 20, xiv. 1, etc.—Ἰωάννην: the marked
silence about him previously seems to
emphasise the fact that he was not
selected by the Holy Ghost in the same
solemn way as Barnabas and Saul.—

τοῦ Θεοῦ ἐν ταῖς συναγωγαῖς τῶν Ἰουδαίων· εἶχον δὲ καὶ Ἰωάννην ὑπηρέτην.[1] 6. διελθόντες[2] δὲ τὴν νῆσον ἄχρι Πάφου, εὑρόν τινα μάγον

[1] ὑπηρετην, D, Par., Syr. Harcl. mg. read ὑπηρετουντα αυτοις (E reads εις διακονιαν). Weiss considers that this is in order to avoid describing Mark as ὑπηρετης.

[2] διελθοντες δε, D[1] reads και περιελθοντων αυτων, and so Blass and Hilg., and D[2] διελθοντων δε αυτων. περι may have been changed into δια, as the latter prep. may have been thought to mean that they went straight through, instead of going about the island; see also Weiss, Codex D, p. 73. ολην την νησον, so ℵABCDE 61, Vulg., several vers., so Tisch., W.H., R.V., Blass, Weiss, Wendt, Hilg.—perhaps fell out, as in T.R., because the situation of Paphos was not known, and ολην seemed to contradict αχρι Π. (Wendt). D reads ονοματι καλουμενον; ῳ ονομα is common in Gospels but not elsewhere in Acts, ονοματι and καλου. are both common; cf. also Luke xix. 1. Βαρϊησοῦς BCE 13, Sah., Chrys., so W.H., Weiss; Βαριησοῦν AD²HLP, Syr. H. mg.; Βαριησοῦ ℵ 40, Vulg., Boh., Syr. H. text, Arm., Tisch.; Βαριησουα D, so Blass, Hilg. with ν or μ added (D²)—other variations. E, Gig., Wer., Lucif. add ο μεθερμηνευεται Ετοιμας (see on ver. 8) according to Blass in β (E reading Ελυμας, Gig., Wer., Lucif. reading paratus = Ετοιμος). In ver. 8 almost all authorities read Ελυμας, but D, Lucif. have Ετοιμας (not Gig., Par.). This reading is defended by Klostermann, Prob. im Aposteltexte, p. 21, and adopted by Blass (although he is not satisfied with Klostermann's derivation) and also by Ramsay. Blass holds that this name Ετοιμας, whatever it is, must be interpretation of Βαριησους—not μαγος of it. It is possible that some desire may have been at work to avoid any connection between the name of the Magian and the name of Jesus, and thus the words ουτος γαρ μεθ. . . . αυτου in ver. 8, which are omitted by Blass without any authority, simply because of the reading in ver. 6 in E, etc., may have crept into ver. 6 as more appropriate. See also "Barjesus," Hastings' B.D. Weiss, Codex D, p. 74, points out that Ετοιμας may be an old corruption for Ελυμας, and this seems very probable. See further, Schmiedel, Enc. Bibl., i., 478 ff.

ὑπηρέτην, cf. Luke iv. 20, and many writers give it here a kind of official sense (although the word may be used of any kind of service), "velut ad baptizandum," cf. x. 48 (1 Cor. i. 14), Blass; so Alford, Felten, Overbeck, Weiss. But the word may express the fact that John Mark was able to set the Apostles more free for their work of evangelising.

Ver. 6. διελθόντες δὲ (ὅλην) τὴν ν.: "and they made a missionary progress through the whole island," Ramsay, St. Paul, pp. 72 and 384, and "Words denoting Missionary Travel in Acts," Expositor, May, 1896; on ὅλην, see critical notes. Ramsay gives nine examples in Acts of this use of διέρχεσθαι or διελθεῖν with the accusative of the region traversed, the only other instance in the N.T. being 1 Cor. xvi. 5. In each of these ten cases the verb implies the process of going over a country as a missionary, and it is remarkable that in i.-xii. this construction of διέρχομαι never occurs, though there are cases in which the idea of a missionary tour requires expression. Ramsay therefore sees in the use of the word in the second part of the book a quasi technical term which the writer had caught from St. Paul himself, by whom alone it is also employed.—

Πάφου: Nea Paphos—the chief town and the place of residence of the Roman governor—some little distance from the old Paphos (Παλαίπαφος, Strabo) celebrated for its Venus temple. The place still bears the name of Baffa, Renan, St. Paul, p. 14; O. Holtzmann, Neutest. Zeitgeschichte, p. 101; C. and H., smaller edition, p. 125.—μάγον, cf. viii. 9; "sorcerer," A. and R.V. margin, cf. Matt. ii. 1, but word used here as among the Greeks and Romans in a bad sense. Wycl. has "witch," and this in its masculine form "wizard" has been suggested as an appropriate rendering here. On the absurd attempt to show that the whole narrative is merely introduced as a parallel to St. Peter's encounter with Simon, chap. viii., see Nösgen, p. 427; Zöckler, in loco, and Salmon, Introduction, p. 310. The parallel really amounts to [this, that both Peter and Paul encountered a person described under the same title, a magician—an encounter surely not improbable in the social circumstances of the time (see below)! For other views see Holtzmann, who still holds that the narrative is influenced by viii. 14 ff. The word is entirely omitted by Jüngst, p. 120, without any authority whatever. Elymas, according

ψευδοπροφήτην Ἰουδαῖον ᾧ ὄνομα Βαριῆσοῦς, 7. ὃς ἦν σὺν τῷ
ἀνθυπάτῳ Σεργίῳ Παύλῳ, ἀνδρὶ συνετῷ. οὗτος προσκαλεσάμενος
Βαρνάβαν καὶ Σαῦλον,[1] ἐπεζήτησεν ἀκοῦσαι τὸν λόγον τοῦ Θεοῦ.

[1] **Σαυλον,** so in all auth. Blass says "even by Par."—to distinguish him from
Sergius Paulus—see above on ver. 1; Blass, p. ix., and Wendt (1899), p. 230, note.

to the narrative, says Jüngst, was either
a magician *or* a false prophet. But the
proconsul is styled **ἀνὴρ συνετός,** and this
could not have been consistent with his
relation with a magician: Elymas was
therefore a kind of Jewish confessor.
But neither supposition does much to
establish the wisdom of Sergius Paulus.
—**ψευδοπροφήτην** like **ψευδόμαντις** in
classical writers, here only in Acts; and
Luke vi. 26, by St. Luke. But frequently
used elsewhere in N.T., and in the LXX,
and several times in *Didaché*, xi. On the
"Triple beat," Magian, false prophet,
Jew, see Ramsay, *St. Paul*, p. 415.—
Βαριῆσοῦς, on the name see critical
notes.
Ver. 7. **ὃς ἦν σὺν τῷ ἀ.,** *cf.* iv. 13.
Nothing was more in accordance with
what we know of the *personnel* of the
strange groups which often followed the
Roman governors as *comites*, and it is
quite possible that Sergius Paulus may
have been keenly interested in the powers
or assumed powers of the Magian, and
in gaining a knowledge of the strange
religions which dominated the East. If
the Roman had been completely under
the influence of the false prophet, it is
difficult to believe that St. Luke would
have described him as **συνετός** (a title in
which Zöckler sees a distinction between
Sergius Paulus and another Roman,
Felix, over whom a Jewish Magian
gained such influence, Jos., *Ant.*, xx.,
7, 2), although magicians of all kinds
found a welcome in unexpected quarters
in Roman society, even at the hands of
otherwise discerning and clear-sighted
personages, as the pages of Roman
writers from Horace to Lucian testify.
It was not the first time in the world's
history that credulity and scepticism had
gone hand in hand: Wetstein, *in loco;*
Farrar, *St. Paul*, i., pp. 351, 352; Ramsay,
St. Paul, p. 74 ff.—**ἐπεζήτησεν**; perhaps
means, as in classical Greek, "put questions to them". The typical Roman is
again marked by the fact that he was
thus desirous to hear what the travellers
would say, and it is also indicated that
he was not inclined to submit himself
entirely to the Magian.—**τῷ ἀνθυπάτῳ:**
"the proconsul," R.V., "deputy," A.V.

In the reign of James I. the Lord Lieu-
tenant of Ireland was called "the deputy" (*cf.* Shakespeare, *Measure for
Measure*, i., 2, 161). Under Augustus,
B.C. 27, the Roman provinces had been
divided into two classes: (1) imperial and
(2) senatorial, the former being governed
by proprætors or generals, and the latter
by proconsuls. But as the first kind
of government would often be required
when a province was unruly, it frequently
happened that the same province might
be at one time classed under (1) and at
another time under (2). Cyprus had
been originally an imperial province,
Strabo, xiv., but in 22 B.C. it had been
transferred by Augustus to the Senate,
and was accordingly, as Luke describes
it, under a proconsul, Dio Cassius, liii.,
12, liv., 4. Under Hadrian it appears
to have been under a proprætor; under
Severus it was again under a proconsul.
At Soloi, a town on the north coast of
Cyprus, an inscription was discovered by
General Cesnola, *Cyprus*, 1877, p. 425
(*cf.* Hogarth, *Devia Cypria*, 1889, p. 114),
dated **ἐπὶ Παύλου (ἀνθ)υπάτου,** and
the probable identification with Sergius
Paulus is accepted by Lightfoot, Zöckler,
Ramsay, Knabenbauer, etc.; see especially amongst recent writers Zahn, *Einleitung*, ii., Excurs. ii., p. 632, for a
similar view, and also for information
as to date, and as to another and more
recent inscription (1887), bearing upon
the connnection of the Gens Sergia
with Cyprus; see also McGiffert, *Apostolic Age*, p. 175, note, and Wendt,
edition 1899.—**συνετῷ**: R.V., "a man
of understanding," *cf.* Matt. xi. 25. A.V.
and other E.V. translate "prudent,"
Vulgate, *prudens*, but see Genevan Version on Matt., *u. s.;* frequent in LXX in
various significations: **σύνεσις,** practical
discernment, intelligence, so **συνετός,** one
who can "put things together" (**συνιέναι**): **σοφία,** the wisdom of culture
(Grimm-Thayer); on "prudent," see
Humphry, Commentary on R.V., p. 28.
Ver. 8. **ἀνθίστατο**: because he saw
that his hope of gain was gone, *cf.* xvi.
19, xix. 27, and the hope of retaining
influence with the proconsul; see reading
in D, *cf.* 2 Tim. iii. 8, where St. Paul

8. ἀνθίστατο δὲ αὐτοῖς Ἐλύμας, ὁ μάγος, (οὕτω γὰρ μεθερμηνεύεται
τὸ ὄνομα αὐτοῦ,) ζητῶν διαστρέψαι τὸν ἀνθύπατον ἀπὸ τῆς πίστεως.[1]
9. Σαῦλος δέ, ὁ καὶ Παῦλος, πλησθεὶς Πνεύματος Ἁγίου, καὶ ἀτενίσας
εἰς αὐτόν, εἶπεν, 10. Ὦ πλήρης παντὸς δόλου καὶ πάσης ῥᾳδιουργίας,
υἱὲ διαβόλου, ἐχθρὲ πάσης δικαιοσύνης, οὐ παύσῃ διαστρέφων τὰς

---

[1] After πιστεως D, Syr. Harcl. mg. add επειδη ηδιστα ηκουεν αυτων (cf. E). We
may compare Mark vi. 20 ; see also Ramsay, St. Paul, p. 81.

uses the same verb of the magicians withstanding Moses.—Ἐλύμας, see critical
notes in answer to Klostermann, who
finds in Ἐ. a translation of Bar-Jesus;
Wendt points out (1899) that in this
case οὕτω γὰρ μεθ. would follow im
mediately after Ἐ., but as οὕτω κ.τ.λ.
follows immediately upon ὁ μάγος, Ἐ.
can only be a translation of that word;
see also MS. authority, so Blass in β,
where he adds to βαρïησοῦς the words
ὁ μεθ. Ἑτοιμᾶς. In Ἐλύμας we have
the Greek form either of Aramaic Alīmā,
strong, or more probably of an Arab
word ʿalim, wise; we cannot arrive at any
derivation closer than this, cf. " Bar-
Jesus," Hastings' B.D., and for a similar
explanation Zöckler, in loco; and Wendt
(1899), Grimm-Thayer, sub v., Ramsay,
St. Paul, p. 74, and so Blass, in loco,
read Ἑτοιμᾶς, and render " Son of
the Ready ".—διαστρέψαι, Exod. v. 4,
same construction with ἀπό; 1 Kings
xviii. 17, 18, Matt. xvii. 17, Luke ix. 41,
Phil. ii. 15 ; see also critical notes.
Ver. 9. Σαῦλος δέ, ὁ καὶ Παῦλος :
since the days of St. Jerome (De Vir.
Ill., chap. vi., cf. Aug., Confess., viii., 4,
etc., cf. amongst moderns Bengel, Olshausen, Ewald, Meyer) it has been
thought that there is some connection
here emphasised by the writer between
the name Sergius Paulus and the assumption of the name Paul by the Apostle
at this juncture. (Wendt (1899) inclines
to the view that the name Paul was first
used in ver. 1. See in loco and critical
notes.) So too Baur, Zeller, Hausrath,
Overbeck, Hilgenfeld are of opinion that
Luke intended some reference to the
name of the proconsul, although they
regard the narrative of his conversion as
unhistorical. But Wendt rightly maintains (1899) that the simple ὁ καὶ without
the addition of ἀπὸ τότε would not
denote the accomplishment of a change
of name at this juncture, and that if the
change or rather addition of name had
been now effected, the mention of it
would naturally have followed after the
mention of the conversion of the pro-

consul in ver. 13. The connection
seemed so strained and artificial to many
that they abandoned it, and regarded the
collocation of the two names as a mere
chance incident, whilst Zöckler (whose
note should be consulted, Apostelgeschichte, in loco, second edition), who
cannot thus get rid of the striking similarity in the names of the two men,
thinks that the narrative of St. Luke is
too condensed to enable us fully to solve
the connection. But since it was customary for many Jews to bear two names,
a Hebrew and a Gentile name, cf. Acts
i. 23, xii. 25, xiii. 1, Col. iv. 11, Jos.,
Ant., xii., 9, 7, and frequent instances in
Deissmann, Bibelstudien, pp. 182, 183,
cf. Winer-Schmiedel, p. 149 note, it may
well be that Luke wished to intimate
that if not at this moment, yet during
his first missionary journey, when the
Apostle definitely entered upon his Gentile missionary labours, he employed not
his Jewish but his Gentile name to mark
his Apostleship to the Gentile world
(„ Seit 13. 1. ist der jüdische Jünger
Σαῦλος Weltapostel," Deissmann); by a
marvellous stroke of historic brevity the
author sets before us the past and the
present in the formula ὁ καὶ Π.—a simple
change in the order of a recurring pair
of names : see Ramsay's striking remarks,
St. Paul, p. 83 ff., with which however,
mutatis mutandis, his more recent remarks, Was Christ born at Bethlehem ?
p. 54, should be carefully compared. See
also Deissmann, u. s., Nösgen, Wendt,
Hackett, Felten, and Zöckler, in loco,
and McGiffert, Apostolic Age, p. 176.
This preference by St. Luke of the Gentile for the Hebrew name has its analogy
in St. Paul's own use in his Epistles
(and in his preference for Roman provincial names in his geographical references, cf. 1 Cor. xvi. 1, 2 Cor. viii. 1, ix.
2, Rom. xv. 26, Phil. iv. 15).
Ver. 10. πλήρης : for an interesting parallel in Plato cf. Wetstein, in loco, Plato,
Legg., 908 D.—ῥᾳδιουργίας : only here
in N.T., cf. xviii. 14, hellenistic, R.V.
" villainy," A.V. " mischief " (so Genevan),

ὁδοὺς Κυρίου[1] τὰς εὐθείας; 11. καὶ νῦν ἰδοὺ χεὶρ τοῦ Κυρίου ἐπὶ σέ, καὶ ἔσῃ τυφλὸς μὴ βλέπων τὸν ἥλιον ἄχρι καιροῦ. παραχρῆμα δὲ ἐπέπεσεν[2] ἐπ᾽ αὐτὸν ἀχλὺς καὶ σκότος, καὶ περιάγων ἐζήτει χειραγωγούς. 12. τότε ἰδὼν ὁ ἀνθύπατος τὸ γεγονὸς ἐπίστευσεν,[3] ἐκπλησσόμενος ἐπὶ τῇ διδαχῇ τοῦ Κυρίου.

[1] Κυριου, but ℵ*B του Κ., so W.H. text, cf. Hos. xiv. 9 (10) (but see var. lec.), so Weiss, Wendt.

[2] επεπεσεν, but επεσεν ℵABD 61, Tisch., W.H., R.V., Blass, Wendt, Hilg.; see, on the other hand, Weiss, Apostelgeschichte, Introd., pp. 19, 20.

[3] επιστευσεν—DE prefix εθαυμασεν και; after επισ. D adds τῳ Θεῳ, so Blass and Hilg.

but other E.V. "deceit"; the idea of deceit, however, is more properly contained in δόλου R.V., "guile". ῥᾳδ., lit., ease in doing, so easiness, laziness, and hence fraud, wickedness, cf. πανουργία, frequently used, although not necessarily so, in a bad sense.—υἱὲ διαβόλου, John viii. 44, the expression may be used in marked and indignant contrast to the name "Son of Jesus," cf. iii. 25, iv. 36. But without any reference to ver. 6 the expression would describe him as the natural enemy of the messengers of God. On the phrase and its use here see Deissmann, Bibelstudien, p. 163. Note the thrice παντὸς — πάσης — πάσης, "ter repetitur emphatice" Wetstein. — διαστρέφων, cf. LXX, Prov. x. 9, and Isa. lix. 8, Micah iii. 9.—τὰς ὁδοὺς . . . τὰς εὐθείας: similar expressions frequent in LXX, so of the ways of the Lord in contrast to the ways of men, Ezek. xxxiii. 17, Ecclesiast. xxxix. 24, Song of the Three Children, ver. 3.

Ver. 11. καὶ νῦν ἰδοὺ, cf. Hort, Ecclesia, p. 179.—μὴ βλέπων τὸν ἥλιον: emphasising the punishment, as it would imply that he should be stone-blind (Weiss).—ἄχρι καιροῦ: "until a season," R.V. margin, "until the time" (Rendall), i.e., the duly appointed time when it should please God to restore his sight, cf. Luke iv. 13, xxi. 24 (Acts xxiv. 25). The exact expression is only found here and in Luke iv. 13. Wendt (1899) asks if the ceasing of the punishment is conceived of as ceasing with the opposition in ver. 8. See his earlier edition, 1888, and the comment of Chrys., so Oecumenius: οὐκ ἄρα τιμωρία ἦν ἀλλ᾽ ἴασις: so too Theophylact.—παραχρῆμα, see above on p. 106. - ἐπέπεσεν, see critical notes. If we retain T.R. with Weiss, the word may be called characteristic of St. Luke, see above on p. 216 its use as denoting an attack of disease

is quite medical, Hobart, p. 44.—ἀχλὺς: only here in N.T., not in LXX. Galen in describing diseases of the eye mentions ἀχλύς amongst them. So Dioscorides uses the word of a cataract, and Hippocrates also employs it, Hobart, p. 44. The word is no doubt frequent in Homer, sometimes of one deprived of sight by divine power, and it also occurs in Polyb. and Josephus. But here it is used in conjunction with other words which may also be classed as medical, παραχ., σκότος, to say nothing of (ἐπ)έπεσεν.—σκότος: marks the final stage of blindness—the word is no doubt a common one, but it is used, as also some of its derivatives, by medical writers in a technical sense, and Dioscorides in one place connects σκοτώματα and ἀχλύς together.—περιάγων: only absolutely here in N.T., so sometimes in classical Greek, and sometimes with acc. loci, as also in N.T. (cf. Matt. iv. 23, ix. 35, etc.).—ἐζήτει, imperf., he sought but did not find.—χειραγωγούς: only here in N.T., not in LXX, cf. the verb in ix. 8, xxii. 11, and in LXX, Judg. xvi. 26 A, Tobit xi. 16 (but not A, B); used by Plutarch, etc.

Ver. 12. ἐπίστευσεν: "the blindness of Elymas opened the eyes of the proconsul" (Felten). If the verb is understood in its full sense, viz., that Sergius Paulus became a convert to the faith, ver. 48, ii. 44, iv. 4, xi. 21, baptism would be implied, viii. 12.—ἐκπλησσ., Matt. vii. 28, Mark i. 22, xi. 18, Luke iv. 32, ix. 43, etc., so in classical Greek with ἐπί. The verb is also found in Eccl. vii. 17 (16), Wisdom xiii. 4, 2 Macc. vii. 12, 4 Macc. viii. 4, xvii. 16. Bengel's comment is suggestive, "miraculo acuebatur attentio ad doctrinam": the conversion is not represented as the result of the miracle alone. The conversion of a Roman proconsul is regarded as absolutely incredible by Renan (so more recent critics). But if

13. Ἀναχθέντες δὲ ἀπὸ τῆς Πάφου οἱ περὶ τὸν Παῦλον ἦλθον εἰς Πέργην τῆς Παμφυλίας. Ἰωάννης δὲ ἀποχωρήσας ἀπ᾽ αὐτῶν ὑπέστρεψεν εἰς Ἱεροσόλυμα. 14. αὐτοὶ δέ, διελθόντες ἀπὸ τῆς Πέργης, παρεγένοντο εἰς Ἀντιόχειαν τῆς Πισιδίας,[1] καὶ εἰσελθόντες

---

[1] τῆς Πισιδιας, DEHLP but acc. in ℵABC, so Tisch., W.H., Weiss, Wendt. Blass (so Hilg.) retains gen. on the ground that the adj. Πισίδιος "non exstat," but see Ramsay, and Wendt (1899), p. 231 ; also Grimm-Thayer, sub v. and sub Ἀντιόχεια, 2.

---

the narrative had been a mere fiction to magnify Paul's powers in converting such an important personage in his first encounter with the powers of heathenism, the forger would not have contented himself with the brief Σαῦλος ὁ καὶ Π. of ver. 9 ; see Zöckler's *Apostelgeschichte*, p. 245, second edition, on this and other objections against the narrative. See *Introd.* for the favourable light in which St. Luke describes the relations between the Roman government and Christianity.

Ver. 13. Ἀναχθέντες, "set sail," R.V. So in classical use, here in its technical nautical sense—so too, in opposite sense, κατάγεσθαι. In this sense thirteen times in Acts, and once in Luke's Gospel, viii. 22, but not in the other Gospels at all ; it is only used once, in another sense, by St. Matthew among the Evangelists, *cf.* iv. 1. ἄγειν and its compounds with ἀνά, κατά, εἰς, are characteristic of Luke's writings, Friedrich, p. 7.—οἱ περὶ τὸν Π.: Paul now taking the first place as the leader of the company, see Ramsay, *St. Paul*, p. 84, the order henceforth is Paul and Barnabas, with two significant exceptions, xv. 12, 25, and xiv. 12, see *in loco*. —Ἰ. δὲ . . . ὑπέστρεψεν : Ramsay refers St. Mark's withdrawal to the above circumstances, inasmuch as he disapproved of St. Paul's change of place, which he regarded as an abandonment of the work. But the withdrawal on the part of Mark is still more difficult to understand, if we are to suppose that he withdrew because Paul and Barnabas made, as it were, a trip to Antioch for the recovery of the former ; and xv. 38 seems to imply something different from this. Various reasons may have contributed to the desertion of Mark, perhaps the fact that his cousin Barnabas was no longer the leader, or Paul's preaching to the Gentiles may have been too liberal for him, or lack of courage to face the dangers of the mountain passes and missionary work inland, or affection for his home at Jerusalem and anxiety for the coming famine (he withdrew, says Holtzmann,

"zu seinem Mutter "). See Deissmann's striking note, *Bibelstudien*, p. 185, on the fact that here, where John Mark leaves Paul for Jerusalem, he is simply " John," his Jewish name ; in xv. 39 he goes with Barnabas to Cyprus, and on that occasion only he is described by his Gentile name " Mark " alone. On the " perils of rivers, and perils of robbers," see Ramsay, *Church in the Roman Empire*, p. 23, and in connection with the above, pp. 62, 65, also C. and H. (smaller edition), p. 129, Hausrath, *Neutest. Zeitgeschichte*, iii., 133.

Ver. 14. διελθόντες : in this journey northwards to Antioch the Apostles would probably follow the one definite route of commerce between Perga and that city ; the natural and easy course would lead them to Adada, now *Kara Bavlo*, and the dedication there of a church to St. Paul may point to the belief that he had visited the place on his way to Antioch (Ramsay, *Church in the Roman Empire*, p. 21, and Zöckler, *in loco*, who agrees here with Ramsay's view). Although disagreeing with C. and H. in bringing the Apostles to Adada, Ramsay fully agrees with them in emphasising the dangers of the journey across the Pisidian highlands, and in referring to his travels from Perga across Taurus to Antioch and back his perils of rivers, and perils of robbers, 2 Cor. xi. 26 (see too Wendt, *in loco* (1899), in agreement with Ramsay, whose instances of the dangers of the way, from the notices of the inscriptions, should be consulted, *u. s.*).—Ἀντιόχειαν τῆς Πισιδίας, see critical notes. If we adopt with R.V., etc., Ἀ. τὴν Πισιδίαν=an adjective, τὴν Πισιδικήν, "Pisidian Antioch," or, as it was also called, Antioch towards Pisidia, or on the side of Pisidia, to distinguish it from Antioch on the Maeander, or Carian Antioch. At this period Antioch did not belong to Pisidia at all (Strabo, pp. 557, 569, 577), but later the term Pisidia was widened, and so the expression " Antioch of Pisidia " came into vogue. Ptolemy, v., 4, 11, employs it,

εἰς τὴν συναγωγὴν τῇ ἡμέρᾳ τῶν σαββάτων, ἐκάθισαν. 15. Μετὰ
δὲ τὴν ἀνάγνωσιν τοῦ νόμου καὶ τῶν προφητῶν, ἀπέστειλαν οἱ
ἀρχισυνάγωγοι πρὸς αὐτούς, λέγοντες, Ἄνδρες ἀδελφοί, εἰ ἔστι λόγος

and so some MSS. in the passage before us; see critical notes, and Ramsay,
" Antioch in Pisidia," in Hastings' B.D.,
Church in the Roman Empire, p. 25, and
Wendt (1899), in loco; see further on
xvi. 6. On the death of Amyntas, B.C.
25, Antioch became part of the Roman
province Galatia, and a little later,
some time before 6 B.C., it was made
a colonia by Augustus, with Latin
rights, and as such it became an
administrative and military centre in
the protection of the province against
the Pisidian robbers in their mountain
fortresses, Ramsay, u. s. There can be
no doubt that Paul would also find there
a considerable Jewish population, as the
Jews were trusty supporters of the
Seleucid kings, and found a home in
many of the cities which they founded.—
ἀπὸ τῆς Πέργης : Ramsay supposes that
the travellers hurried on from Perga (chief
town of Pamphylia on the Cestrus,
and an important place of commerce) to
Antioch, without any evangelisation on
their way, because in Perga the Apostle
had been smitten with an attack of
malarial fever, which obliged him to
seek the higher ground of Antioch. In
Gal. iv. 13 Ramsay finds a corroboration
of this view, a passage in which Paul himself states that an illness occasioned his
first preaching to the Churches of Galatia,
i.e., of the Roman province Galatia. The
suggestion has much to recommend it,
see St. Paul, p. 92. McGiffert's remarks,
however, should be consulted in support
of the view that the illness overtook
the Apostle at Antioch rather than at
Perga, Apostolic Age, p. 177, and Weizsäcker, Apostolic Age, i., 275, E.T.—
εἰς τὴν συναγωγὴν, "to the Jew first,"
was Paul's primary rule, and here
amongst those φοβ. τὸν Θεόν he would
find, perhaps, the best soil for his labours,
cf. xvi. 14, and also xiii. 5, xiv. 1, xvi. 13,
xvii. 2, 10, 17, xviii. 4, xix. 8. Against
the doubts raised by the Tübingen School
as to the historical character of the notice,
see especially Wendt, 1888 and 1899 editions. It is inconceivable, as he says,
that Paul, who could express himself as
in Rom. i. 16, ix. 32, x. 16, xi. 30, should
entirely disregard the Jews in his missionary efforts. The notice in xvi. 13,
from a "We-source," of St. Paul's first
Sabbath at Philippi enables us to form

a correct judgment as to his probable
course in other places.—τῇ ἡμέρᾳ τῶν
σαβ. ; not necessarily the first Sabbath
after their arrival ; some time may have
been spent previously in mission work
before a critical event took place, Ramsay, St. Paul, pp. 99, 100.—ἐκάθισαν :
the word may mean that they sat down
in the seat of the Rabbis, so J. Lightfoot,
in loco, as intimating that they expected
to be called upon to preach, or we may
infer, ver. 15, that they were called upon
on the present occasion because they
were well known in the city as men who
claimed to have a message to deliver, and
the rulers of the synagogue could invite
whom they would, Edersheim, Jewish
Social Life, p. 281 ; Lumby, p. 252, "on
the Jewish Manner of reading the Scriptures ".
Ver. 15. τὴν ἀνάγ. τοῦ ν. καὶ τῶν π. :
the first and second lesson, Edersheim,
u. s., p. 278, History of the Jewish Nation, p. 443 ; Schürer, Jewish People,
div. ii., vol. ii., p. 79 ff., E.T., the first
from the Pentateuch, and the second a
paragraph from the Prophets, including
the older historical books. As there is
no evidence that the lectionary of the
Prophets existed in the time of our Lord,
it is precarious to attempt to fix the particular Sabbath for St. Paul's address.
It is however significant that he uses
two remarkable words from the LXX,
Deut. i. 31 : ἐτροφ. (see critical notes), in
ver. 18, and from Isa. i. 2 : ὕψωσεν
in ver. 17, and that in the present table
of Jewish lessons that from the Law
for the forty-fourth Sabbath in the year
is Deut. i.-iii. 22, while the corresponding
lesson from the Prophets is Isa. i. 1-22 ;
see Bengel on ver. 18, and Farrar, St.
Paul, i., pp. 368, 369 ; Plumptre, in loco.
But we cannot safely go beyond the
view of Ramsay, St. Paul, p. 100, who
points out that the present list of Jewish
lessons is of decidedly later origin, but adds
that "probably it was often determined
by older custom and traditional ideas of
suitable accompaniment ".—ἀπέστειλαν :
the words seem hardly consistent with
Lumby's view that St. Paul was himself the Haphtarist.—οἱ ἀρχισυνάγωγοι ;
generally only one, Luke xiii. 14, but cf.
Mark v. 22 (Weiss, in loco), and the passage before us ; the office was specially
concerned with the care of public worship,

ἐν ὑμῖν παρακλήσεως [1] πρὸς τὸν λαὸν λέγετε. 16. ἀναστὰς δὲ Παῦλος, καὶ κατασείσας τῇ χειρὶ, εἶπεν, Ἄνδρες Ἰσραηλῖται, καὶ οἱ φοβούμενοι τὸν Θεόν, ἀκούσατε. 17. ὁ Θεὸς τοῦ λαοῦ τούτου Ἰσραὴλ ἐξελέξατο τοὺς πατέρας ἡμῶν· καὶ τὸν λαὸν ὕψωσεν ἐν τῇ παροικίᾳ ἐν γῇ Αἰγύπτῳ, καὶ μετὰ βραχίονος ὑψηλοῦ ἐξήγαγεν αὐτοὺς ἐξ αὐτῆς·

[1] D reads λογος σοφιας εν υμιν παρακλησεως. Blass inserts η before παρακ.; cf. 1 Cor. xii. 8.

and the name was given to those who conducted the assemblies for that purpose. They had to guard against anything unfitting taking place in the synagogue (Luke xiii. 14), and to appoint readers and preachers, Schürer, *Jewish People*, div. ii., vol. ii., p. 65, E.T.; Edersheim, *Jewish Social Life*, p. 281, and on the present passage, *Jesus the Messiah*, i., 434, and for the title in inscriptions, Grimm-Thayer, *sub v.*; see also below on xiv. 2. —ἄνδρες ἀδελφοί: courteous address, ii. 37, " Gentlemen, brethren " (Ramsay). Ver. 16. κατασείσας, see above on xii. 17, and *cf.* xix. 33, xxi. 40 (xxvi. 1), " made a gesture with his hand," a gesture common to orators, " nam hoc gestu olim verba facturi pro contione silentium exigebant," and here a graphic touch quite characteristic of Acts. The speech which follows may well have remained in the memory, or possibly may have found a place in the manuscript diary of one of Paul's hearers (Ramsay, *St. Paul*, p. 100), or St. Paul may himself have furnished St. Luke with an outline of it, for the main sections, as Ewald suggested, may have formed part of the Apostle's regular mode of addressing similar audiences; and if not St. Paul himself, yet one of those who are described as οἱ περὶ Παῦλον, ver. 13 (Zöckler), may have supplied the information. On the other hand it is maintained that the speech in its present form is a free composition of the author of Acts, since it is so similar to the early addresses of St. Peter, or to the defence made by St. Stephen, and that St. Luke wished to illustrate St. Paul's method of proclaiming the Messianic salvation to Jews. But considering the audience and the occasion, it is difficult to see how St. Paul could have avoided touching upon points similar to those which had claimed the attention of a St. Peter or a St. Stephen: " non poterat multum differre vel a Petri orationibus, vel a defensione Stephani . . . hæc igitur non magis in Paulum cadunt quam in quemvis novae salutis praeconem " (Blass), while at the same time it is quite possible to press this similarity too far and to ignore the points which are confessedly characteristic of St. Paul, *cf.*, *e.g.*, vv. 38, 39 (Bethge, *Die Paulinischen Reden der Apostelgeschichte*, pp. 19-22; Zöckler, *Apostelgeschichte*, pp. 244, 245; Lechler, *Das Apostolische Zeitalter*, p. 272; Hilgenfeld, *Zeitschrift für wissenschaft. Theol.*, i., p. 46 (1896)); see further, Farrar, *St. Paul*, i., p. 369, note, and Alford references for the several Pauline expressions, and the remarkable list of parallels drawn out recently by Ramsay between the speech at Pisidian Antioch and the thoughts and phrases of the Epistle to the Galatians, *Expositor*, December, 1898 (see below on pp. 295, 297); also Nösgen's list of Pauline expressions, *Apostelgeschichte*, p. 53, in this and in other speeches in Acts.— ἄνδρες Ἰ., *cf.* ii. 22, iii. 12, v. 35, a mode of address fitly chosen as in harmony with the references to the history of Israel which were to follow.—οἱ φ. Θεόν, *cf.* x. 2, xiii. 43, 50, xvi. 14, etc. Ver. 17. τούτου: this points back to Ἰσρ.: an appeal to the national pride of the people in their theocratic privileges and names, *cf.* 2 Cor. xi. 22, Rom. ix. 6. —ἐξελ. so often in LXX of God's choice of Israel.—ὕψωσεν: "exalted," A. and R.V. Weiss and Wendt, with Bethge and Blass, restrict its meaning to increase in numbers, Gen. xlviii. 19, Acts vii. 17, so also Overbeck; whilst others refer it to the miraculous events connected with their sojourn as well as to their increase in numbers (so St. Chrysostom), others take it of the exaltation of the people under Joseph. But the word may certainly mean something more than numerical increase, and include increase in strength and power (so Hackett, Page). It is used once by St. Paul elsewhere, 2 Cor. xi. 7, in contrast with ταπεινόω, *cf.* its similar use in Luke i. 52. Rendall refers its use here to 2 Kings xxv. 27, "lifted up," *i.e.*, at the end of a miserable state of bondage, a passage where the verb is closely joined with ἐξήγαγεν. In Isaiah i. 2 and xxiii.

18. καὶ ὡς τεσσαρακονταετῆ χρόνον ἐτροποφόρησεν [1] αὐτοὺς ἐν τῇ
ἐρήμῳ· 19.[2] καὶ καθελὼν ἔθνη ἑπτὰ ἐν γῇ Χαναάν, κατεκληροδότησεν
αὐτοῖς [3] τὴν γῆν αὐτῶν. 20.[4] καὶ μετὰ ταῦτα, ὡς ἔτεσι τετρακοσίοις

---

[1] ετροπ. אBC²DHLP 36, 61, Vulg., Syr. Harcl. mg., so W.H., Blass, R.V. text,
Rendall, Weiss; ετροφ. AC*E 13, d, Gig., Sah., Boh., Syrr. Pesh. Harcl. text, so Tisch.,
R.V. marg., and Hilg. Wendt cannot decide, although he considers ετροφ. as more
fitting here, while he regards ετροπ. as the more original reading in LXX Deut. i. 31
(B*, Orig.). Tischendorf, however, regards ετροφ. as best attested in Deut. i. 31
and as best suited to the context both there and here. W.H., App., p. 94, maintain
that τροπ. is the more obvious rendering of נָשָׂא, but that when the orig. meaning
was forgotten, the context in Deut. i. 31 led to the change to τροφοφ. This corruption in LXX was doubtless widely current in the Apostolic age, and might have
been followed here. W.H. conclude that there can be no reason to question a reading
supported by אB 61, Vulg., and many good cursives, a reading which they regard
as best authenticated in the LXX and as agreeing with the Heb., especially when it
was liable to be changed by the influence of the common and corrupt text of the LXX.
They add that both here and in Deut. either reading gives excellent sense.

[2] και om. B 61, Sah., W.H. text, Wendt—but Blass, Hilg. and Weiss retain.
W.H. take ως in ver. 18 as "when," not "about".

[3] κατεκληροδοτησεν, but κατεκληρονομησεν אABCDEHLP 13, 61, Chrys., Tisch.,
W.H., Blass, Weiss, Wendt, Hilg. -δοτ- arose from missing active use of κληρονομ.
Similar instances of confusion between the two verbs in LXX; cf. H. and R. αυτοις
om. אBD* 13, 40, 61, Sah., Boh., so Tisch., W.H., R.V., Weiss, Wendt. For αυτων
D, Syr. Harcl. read των αλλοφυλων, so Blass and Hilg.

[4] The words ως ετεσιν τετρ. κ. πεντ. are to be placed before και μετα ταυτα—so
אABC, Vulg., Sah., Boh., Arm., Tisch., W.H., R.V., Weiss. Wendt thinks with
Meyer and Holtzmann that the transposition may have been made to meet a difficulty;
see also Farrar, St. Paul, i., 370. D, Sah., Syr. Harcl. mg. omit μετα ταυτα
altogether, so Blass and Hilg.

---

4 it is used of bringing up children.—
παροικία, cf. vii. 6, and for the noun as
here, LXX, 2 Esdras viii. 35, Wisdom
xix. 10. Prologue of Ecclus., ver. 26,
Ps. cxx. 5.—μετὰ βραχίονος ὑψ., cf.
Exod. vi. 1, 6, Deut. v. 15, etc., Ps.
cxxxvi. 12, Baruch ii. 11, etc. Hebraistic, cf. Luke i. 51, where we have ἐν
as in Hebrew, but in LXX μετά as of the
accompanying the arm of God, and not
merely of his power as bringing the
people out.
Ver. 18. ἐτροποφόρησεν, see critical
notes. ἐτροπ., "suffered he their
manners," so A. and R.V. ἐτροφ.,
"bare he them as a nursing father,"
R.V. margin. This latter rendering is
supported by Bengel, Alford, Bethge,
Nösgen, Hackett, Page, Farrar, Plumptre,
etc., as more agreeable to the conciliatory
drift of the Apostle's words, but see
above, cf. 2 Macc. vii. 27.
Ver. 19. καθελὼν, cf. Deut. vii. 1. In
LXX the stronger verb ἐξαίρειν is used,
but καθαιρεῖν in LXX often means to
destroy, Jer. xxiv. 6, Ps. xxvii. 5, and so

in classical Greek. Weiss prefers the
force of the verb as in Luke i. 52, to cast
down, i.e., from their sovereignty.—
κατεκληροδότησεν, see critical notes. If
we adopt reading of R.V. W.H.: "he
gave them their land for an inheritance".
Ver. 20. If we follow the best attested
reading, see critical notes, we may connect the dative of time ἔτεσι, cf. viii.
11, closely with the preceding words as
signifying the period within which an
event is accomplished. The κληρονομία
was already assured to the fathers as
God's chosen, vii. 5, and the four hundred years of the people's sojourn in a
strange land, Acts vii. 6, Gen. xv. 13,
forty years in the wilderness, and some
ten years for the actual conquest of the
land made up the four hundred and fifty
years (so Weiss, Felten, see Wendt, in
loco). If reading in T.R. is accepted
(strongly defended by Farrar, St. Paul,
i., p. 370), although it is at variance
with 1 Kings vi. 1, according to which
Solomon began his Temple in the 480th
(LXX 440th) year after the Exodus, we

καὶ πεντήκοντα, ἔδωκε κριτὰς ἕως Σαμουὴλ τοῦ προφήτου · 21.
κἀκεῖθεν ᾐτήσαντο βασιλέα, καὶ ἔδωκεν αὐτοῖς ὁ Θεὸς τὸν Σαοὺλ
υἱὸν Κίς, ἄνδρα ἐκ φυλῆς Βενιαμίν, ἔτη τεσσαράκοντα · 22. καὶ
μεταστήσας αὐτόν, ἤγειρεν αὐτοῖς τὸν Δαβὶδ εἰς βασιλέα, ᾧ καὶ εἶπε
μαρτυρήσας, "Εὗρον Δαβὶδ τὸν τοῦ Ἰεσσαί, ἄνδρα κατὰ τὴν καρδίαν
μου, ὃς ποιήσει πάντα τὰ θελήματά μου." 23. Τούτου ὁ Θεὸς ἀπὸ
τοῦ σπέρματος κατ᾽ ἐπαγγελίαν ἤγειρε [1] τῷ Ἰσραὴλ σωτῆρα Ἰησοῦν,
24. προκηρύξαντος Ἰωάννου πρὸ προσώπου τῆς εἰσόδου αὐτοῦ βάπτισμα μετανοίας παντὶ τῷ λαῷ Ἰσραήλ. 25. ὡς δὲ ἐπλήρου ὁ
Ἰωάννης τὸν δρόμον, ἔλεγε, "Τίνα με [2] ὑπονοεῖτε εἶναι ; οὐκ εἰμὶ ἐγώ,
ἀλλ᾽ ἰδού, ἔρχεται μετ᾽ ἐμέ, οὗ οὐκ εἰμὶ ἄξιος τὸ ὑπόδημα τῶν ποδῶν

---

[1] ἠγειρε, cf. ver. 22 ; but ηγαγε ℵABEHLP 61, Vulg., Boh., Aeth., Ath., Chrys.,
Tisch., W.H., R.V., Blass, Weiss, Wendt.

[2] τινα με, but τι εμε ℵAB 61, Sah., Aeth., so Tisch., W.H., R.V., Weiss, Wendt ;
Blass follows T.R. with CDEHLP, Vulg., Boh., Syrr. P. and H., so Hilg., but in
Blass punctuation differs from T.R.

---

have merely to suppose that the Apostle
followed the popular chronology adopted
by Josephus, *Ant.*, viii., 3, 1 ; x., 8, 5,
especially when we remember that speaking in round numbers (ὡς) that chronology
tallies very fairly with that of the Book
of Judges. See Meyer-Wendt, Alford,
and *cf.* also the almost similar reckoning
in Wetstein, and Bethge, *Die Paulinischen Reden*, pp. 30, 31. Another explanation is given by Rendall, *in loco*,
where ἔτεσι is taken as marking not
duration of time (which would require
the accusative), but the limit of time
within which, etc.
Ver. 21. κἀκεῖθεν : only here of time
in N.T. as in later Greek. Weiss even
here interprets the expression to mean
that they asked for a king from him, *i.e.*,
Samuel, in his character as prophet.—ἔτη
τεσσαράκοντα : not mentioned in O.T.,
but *cf.* Jos., *Ant.*, vi., 14, 9. The period
does not seem much too long for Saul's
reign when we remember that Ishbosheth
was forty years old at his father's death,
when he was placed on the throne by
Abner, 2 Sam. ii. 10.—Σαοὺλ κ.τ.λ., *cf.*
Paul's description of himself in Phil.
iii. 5.
Ver. 22. μεταστήσας, Luke xvi. 4 :
refers here to Saul's deposition from the
throne, 1 Sam. xv. 16, *cf.* Dan. ii. 21, 1
Macc. viii. 13, not as Bethge thinks to
his removal from the presence of God,
cf. 2 Kings xvii. 23, nor to his death, 3
Macc. iii. 1, vi. 12. Saul therefore could
not have been the bringer of the promised
salvation.—εὗρον κ.τ.λ. : a combination

of two passages, Ps. lxxxix. 20 and 1
Sam. xiii. 14, and freely referred to as a
saying pronounced by God Himself, but
the latter part was pronounced by Samuel
in God's name.—τὸν τοῦ Ἰεσσαί, but in
LXX τὸν δοῦλόν μου. ἄνδρα to mark the
dignity (Bethge).—κατὰ τὴν καρδίαν, *cf.*
Jer. iii. 15.—ὃς ποιήσει, *cf.* Isa. xliv. 28,
Ps. xl. 8. The fact that these quotations
are thus left in their present shape with
no attempt to correct them justifies the
belief that we have here St. Paul's own
words. With the first part of the quotation *cf.* Clem. Rom., *Cor.*, xviii., 1, a
striking agreement ; see on the one hand
as against its dependence on Acts, Wendt,
p. 41 (1899), and on the other hand,
Bethge, *in loco*, and *Introd.*, p. 37.
Ver. 23. κατ᾽ ἐπαγγελίαν : phrase only
found in Gal. iii. 29, 2 Tim. i. 1 : the
Messianic promises generally, or more
specifically 2 Sam. vii. 12, Ps. cxxxii. 11,
Isa. xi. 1, 10, Jer. xxiii. 5, 6, Zech. iii. 8.
In the last prophecy the LXX read the
verb ἄγω which is found in the verse
before us, see critical notes.—Ἰησοῦν :
emphatic at the end of the clause, as
τούτου at the beginning of the verse.
Ver. 24. προκηρύξ. not in LXX or
Apocrypha, but in classical Greek, *cf.*
also Josephus, *Ant.*, x., 5, 1, and also
in Plut., Polyb.—πρὸ προσώπου τῆς
εἰσόδου : "before the face of his entering
in," R.V. margin, *cf.* Luke i. 76 ; here
used temporally, really a Hebraistic
pleonasm, *cf.* Mal. iii. 1, an expression used as still under the influence
of that passage, Simcox, *Language of the*

λῦσαι." 26. Ἄνδρες ἀδελφοί, υἱοὶ γένους Ἀβραάμ, καὶ οἱ ἐν ὑμῖν φοβούμενοι τὸν Θεόν, ὑμῖν ὁ λόγος τῆς σωτηρίας ταύτης ἀπεστάλη.[1] 27. οἱ γὰρ κατοικοῦντες ἐν Ἱερουσαλὴμ καὶ οἱ ἄρχοντες αὐτῶν,[2] τοῦτον ἀγνοήσαντες, καὶ τὰς φωνὰς τῶν προφητῶν τὰς κατὰ πᾶν σάββατον ἀναγινωσκομένας, κρίναντες ἐπλήρωσαν· 28. καὶ μηδεμίαν αἰτίαν

---

[1] υμιν CEHLP, Vulg., Syrr. P. and H. (text), Boh., Arm., Aeth., Chrys., so Blass; ημιν ℵABD 13, 61, Sah., Syr. Harcl. mg.; so Tisch., W.H., R.V., Weiss, Wendt, so Hilg. απεσταλη EHLP; εξαπεσ. ℵABCD 13, 61, Tisch., W.H., Blass, R.V., Weiss, Wendt, Hilg.

[2] For τουτον αγν. . . . των προφ. τας D has μη συνιεντες τας γραφας των π. τας . . ., cf. Luke xxiv. 45. D also reads και κριναντες επληρ., so Hilg. Par. reads reprobaverunt for επληρωσαν, so Blass τουτον απεδοκιμασαν (omitting κριναντες επληρ.), reading κριναντες in the next verse; see on ver. 29.

N. T., p. 154, and also Dalman, *Die Worte Jesu*, p. 23.—εἰσόδου: the entry of Jesus upon His public Messianic ministry, a word which may also have been suggested by Mal. iii. 2, LXX.

Ver. 25. ἐπλήρου: "*i.e.*, non multo ante finem vitæ," Blass, *cf.* vii. 23.—δρόμον: "Paulum sapit," *cf.* xx. 24, 2 Tim. iv. 7, Gal. ii. 2.—ὑπονοεῖτε: three times in Acts, *cf.* xxv. 18, xxvii. 27; nowhere else in N.T., but see Judith xiv. 14, Tob. viii. 16, Ecclus. xxiii. 21. Note this free reproduction of the words of the Evangelists—essentially the same but verbally different.—οὐκ εἰμὶ ἐγώ, I am not he, *i.e.*, the Messiah; best to punctuate as in A. and R.V., so Wendt; but see on the other hand Bethge and Weiss, and the reading they adopt: τί ἐμὲ ὑπον. εἶναι, οὐκ εἰμὶ ἐγώ; the gloss ὁ XC. after ἐγώ, old enough to have crept into the text, shows that the punctuation in A.V. was a natural one, Simcox, *u. s.*, p. 70.

Ver. 26. ἄνδρες ἀδελφοί: the address of ver. 16 is here renewed in more affectionate tones, and here as in ver. 16 both Jews and proselytes are two classes, here both regarded by Paul as ἀδελφοί.—ὑμῖν, see critical notes. Some take it as marking a sharp antithesis between the Jews of Antioch and those of Jerusalem (an antithesis not removed by ἡμῖν), as if the Jews at Antioch and of the Dispersion were contrasted with the Jews of the capital. But γὰρ need not mark a contrast, it may rather confirm the implication in σωτ. ταύτης that Jesus was the Saviour, for He had suffered and died, and so had fulfilled the predictions relating to the Messiah. Nor indeed was it true that those who crucified the Saviour had excluded themselves from the offer of the Gospel: ὁ λόγος τῆς σ., *cf.* Ephes. i. 13, Phil. ii. 16, 1 Thess. ii. 13, etc.—

ἀπεστάλη: if we read the compound ἐξαπ., critical notes, R.V. "is sent forth," *i.e.*, from God, *cf.* x. 36. Weiss takes the verb as simply referring to the sending forth of the word from the place where it was first announced. But *cf.* on the other hand Gal. iv. 4, 6, and ver. 23 above, where God is spoken of as the agent in the Messianic salvation, and on the possible force of ὁ λόγος τῆς σωτ. and ἐξαπεστάλη here see Ramsay, *Expositor*, December, 1898.

Ver. 27. Both A. and R.V. take ἀγνοήσαντες as governing τοῦτον and τὰς φωνάς. But καί may be not copulative but intensive—not only did they not recognise the Christ, but even condemned Him to death; so Rendall. Meyer rendered καί = "also," and makes τὰς φωνάς the direct object of ἐπλήρ. Wendt renders as A. and R.V., see critical notes.—ἀγνοήσαντες, *cf.* iii. 14, it is very doubtful how far we can see in the expression an excuse in the former passage, and guiltiness here. Paul speaks of himself as acting ἀγνοῶν and yet obtaining mercy, 1 Tim. i. 13, *cf.* also for the use of the word by Paul xvii. 23, and frequently in his Epistles.

Ver. 29. ὡς δὲ ἐτέλεσαν ἅπαντα: St. Paul was evidently acquainted with the details of the Passion as well as with the main facts of the death and burial, *cf.* 1 Cor. xi. 23; and for the verb used here Luke xviii. 31, xxii. 37, John xix. 28, 30; only here in Acts. Weiss regards the subject of ἐτέλ., καθέλ., ἔθηκαν as presupposed as known in accordance with the Gospel history, but St. Paul may have been speaking in general terms of the action of the Jews, although not the enemies of Christ but His friends actually took Him down and buried Him. Taken literally, St. Paul's statement agrees with

θανάτου εὑρόντες, ᾐτήσαντο ¹ Πιλάτον ἀναιρεθῆναι αὐτόν. 29. ὡς δὲ
ἐτέλεσαν ² ἅπαντα τὰ περὶ αὐτοῦ γεγραμμένα,³ καθελόντες ἀπὸ τοῦ
ξύλου ἔθηκαν εἰς μνημεῖον. 30. ὁ δὲ Θεὸς ἤγειρεν αὐτὸν ἐκ νεκρῶν,
31. ὃς ὤφθη ἐπὶ ἡμέρας πλείους τοῖς συναναβᾶσιν αὐτῷ ἀπὸ τῆς
Γαλιλαίας εἰς Ἰερουσαλήμ, οἵτινες ⁴ εἰσὶ μάρτυρες αὐτοῦ πρὸς τὸν
λαόν. 32. καὶ ἡμεῖς ὑμᾶς εὐαγγελιζόμεθα τὴν πρὸς τοὺς πατέρας
ἐπαγγελίαν γενομένην, 33. ὅτι ταύτην ὁ Θεὸς ἐκπεπλήρωκε τοῖς
τέκνοις αὐτῶν ἡμῖν,⁵ ἀναστήσας Ἰησοῦν· ὡς καὶ ἐν τῷ ψαλμῷ τῷ

¹ ητησαντο—ℵ reads ητησαν, so W.H. marg., but mid. better, "asked for themselves". D reads κριναντες αυτον παρεδωκαν Πιλατω ινα εις αναιρεσιν; Blass and
Hilg. omit ινα; see ver. 29.

² ετελεσαν, in D ετελουν.

³ D reads after γεγρ.: ητουντο τον Π. τουτον μεν σταυρωσαι και επιτυχοντες
παλιν . . . The reason of these insertions, as has been suggested, seems the same
as in the previous verses—to gain a complete, although summary, account according
to the Gospels. Syr. Harcl. mg. after γεγρ. *postquam crucifixus esset, petierunt a
Pilato ut de ligno detraherent eum. Impetraverunt* . . . Blass combines the two
in β (*cf.* also Hilg.). But one seems rather a corruption of the other, although
the same motive mentioned above might lead to the insertion of either.

⁴ After οιτινες ℵAC 13, 15, 18, 61, Sah., Boh., Syrr. P. (H.), Arm., Aeth. read νυν,
so Tisch., R.V., [W.H.]; but om. BEHLP, Chrys., so Blass, Weiss, [W.H.]. Perhaps
it fell out because the Apostles not only now first, but for a long time past, were
witnesses. D, Vulg., Syr. Harcl. read αχρι νυν, so Blass in β, and Hilg.

⁵ αυτων ημιν C³EHLP 61, Syr. P. and H., Arm., Chrys., Weiss, Hilg.; ημων (om.
αυτων) ℵABC*D, Vulg., Aeth., Hil., Tisch., W.H., R.V., Wendt; αυτων (om. ημων)
Sah., Gig., Amb., Blass. Wendt (1899) attaches great prob. to W.H. explanation,
see *App.*, p. 95; ημιν alone being the orig. reading. DE, Gig., Vulg., so Blass
and Hilg., add ημων after πατερας, which shows how easily additions would follow
τεκνοις.

the *Gospel of Peter*, 21-24, as Hilgenfeld
noted. But Joseph of Arimathæa and
Nicodemus were both Jews and members
of the Council.—τοῦ ξύλου, *cf.* v. 30, x. 39.
Jüngst, without any ground, as Hilgenfeld
remarks, refers ver. 29 partly on account
of this expression to a reviser, and so
34-37. On ξύλον, significant here and
in Gal. iii. 13, see Ramsay, *Expositor*,
December, 1898.—εἰς μν., *cf.* 1 Cor. xv.
4, the death followed by the burial, and
so the reality of the death, "ἐκ νεκρῶν,"
was vouched for.

Ver. 31. ὤφθη, see Milligan's note
on the word, *Resurrection of our Lord*,
p. 265; *Witness of the Epistles* (1892),
pp. 369, 377, 386; and Beyschlag, *Leben
Jesu*, i., p. 434 (second edition), *cf.* Luke
xxiv. 34, 1 Cor. xv. 5 ff.—ἐπί: with
accusative of duration of time, *cf.* xvi. 18,
xviii. 20, xix. 8, 10, 34, xxvii. 20, *cf.* Luke
iv. 25, xviii. 4; in classical writers, but
only in St. Luke in N.T., except Heb. xi.
30, *Vindiciæ Lucanæ*, p. 53.—οἵτινες: if
we add νῦν, see critical notes, the word

intimates that this announcement of Jesus
as the Messiah was not first made by Paul,
as some new thing, but that His Apostles
were still bearing the same witness to
the Jews (λαόν) as a living message in
the same city in which Jesus had been
crucified.

Ver. 32. καὶ ἡμεῖς, *cf.* 1 Cor. xv. 11,
"whether it were I or they," etc., "ut
illi illis, sic nos vobis".—εὐαγγελ., see
above on p. 210, and Simcox, *u. s.*,
pp. 78, 79.—τὴν πρὸς τοὺς π. ἐπαγγελίαν
γεν., *cf.* Rom. xv. 8, Acts xxvi. 6.

Ver. 33. ἐκπεπλήρωκε: "hath fulfilled to the utmost," *cf.* 3 Macc. i. 2, 22,
Polyb., i., 67, 1, τὰς ἐπαγγελίας ἐκπ.—
τοῖς τέκνοις αὐτῶν ἡμῖν, see critical
notes.—ἀναστήσας: "in that he raised
up Jesus," R.V.; "in that he hath raised
up Jesus again," A.V. The former
rendering is quite compatible with the
view that the reference of the word here
is not to the resurrection of Jesus, but to
the raising up of Jesus as the Messiah,
cf. iii. 22, vii. 37, Deut. xviii. 15. The

δευτέρῳ[1] γέγραπται, "Υἱός μου εἶ σύ· ἐγὼ σήμερον γεγέννηκά σε."
34. ὅτι δὲ ἀνέστησεν αὐτὸν ἐκ νεκρῶν, μηκέτι μέλλοντα ὑποστρέφειν
εἰς διαφθοράν, οὕτως εἴρηκεν, "Ὅτι δώσω ὑμῖν τὰ ὅσια Δαβὶδ τὰ
πιστά." 35. διὸ[2] καὶ ἐν ἑτέρῳ λέγει, "Οὐ δώσεις τὸν ὅσιόν σου ἰδεῖν
διαφθοράν." 36. Δαβὶδ μὲν γὰρ ἰδίᾳ γενεᾷ ὑπηρετήσας τῇ τοῦ Θεοῦ
βουλῇ ἐκοιμήθη, καὶ προσετέθη πρὸς τοὺς πατέρας αὐτοῦ, καὶ εἶδε

---

[1] τῳ ψαλμῳ τῳ δευτερῳ γεγ. ELP, Vulg., Syr. H., R.V. (T.R.); τῳ ψ. γεγ. τῳ δευτ. ℵABC 13, 61, Arm., W.H. But in D (τῳ) πρωτῳ ψ. γεγ., cf. Or., Hil., Gig., Latin MS. known to Bede, Tisch., Meyer, Blass. The δευτ. and πρωτ. is the only important var., and the authority for the latter is almost entirely Western. According to Origen the Jews frequently combined Ps. i. and ii. (cf. also Justin, Apol., i., 40; Tert., adv. Marc., iv., 22; Cypr., Testim., i., 13), "so that a 'Western' scribe, being probably accustomed to read the two Psalms combined, would be under a temptation to alter δευτ. to πρωτ. and not vice versâ," W.H., App., p. 95. In D, Syr. Harcl. marg. the quotation also comprises Ps. ii. 5 (cf. Blass in β, and Hilg.); see Wendt (1899), note, p. 241; Belser, p. 69. Wern. omits εν τ. πρ. ψ. altogether; "fort. recte," Blass.

[2] εν ετερῳ, D, Gig., Vulg., Hilg. read ετερως—may have been changed into εν ετερ. διοτι, so ℵAB, R.V., W.H., under influence of Heb. v. 6, but more probably corruption.

---

first prophecy, ver. 33, would be fulfilled in this way, whilst in vv. 34 and 35 the prophecy would be fulfilled by the resurrection from the dead, ἀνασ. ἐκ νεκρῶν (see Knabenbauer in loco, p. 233 ff.). Wendt argues that Heb. i. 5, where the same prophecy is quoted as in ver. 33, also refers to the raising up as the Messiah, but see on the other hand Westcott, Hebrews, in loco.

Ver. 34. μηκέτι μ. ὑποσ. εἰς διαφθ., cf. Rom. vi. 9, "no more to return to corruption," does not of course mean that Christ had already seen corruption, so that there is no need to understand διαφθ. of the place of corruption, sepulchrum, with Beza, Kuinoel. Hilgenfeld refuses to follow Jüngst, Sorof, Clemen in referring vv. 34-37 to a reviser, for he justly remarks that the speech which was intended to move the Israelites to a recognition of Jesus as the promised Saviour of the seed of David, would have been imperfect, unless it had set forth His sufferings and after-resurrection.— Δώσω κ.τ.λ.: "I will give you the holy and sure blessings of David". This rendering makes the connection with the next verse more evident, cf. Isa. lv. 3, καὶ διαθήσομαι ὑμῖν διαθήκην αἰώνιον τὰ ὅσια Δαυὶδ τὰ πιστά. "By David was understood the Messiah, which yet the Rabbis themselves have well observed:" J. Lightfoot, Hor. Heb. (so Schöttgen), in loco. "The everlasting covenant," what was it but the holy and sure blessings promised to David? But these blessings, ὅσια, sancta promissa Davidi data, are connected with the resurrection of Christ because (" διότι not διό, T.R., see critical notes, stating the cause, not the consequence ") only in the triumph of God's Holy One (τὸν ὅσιον) are these blessings ratified and assured. Just as Peter (ii. 47), so here Paul applies the passage in Ps. xvi. directly to Christ, Briggs, Messianic Prophecy, p. 151.

Ver. 36. γὰρ: David is contrasted with Christ by St. Paul as by St. Peter, ii. 29.—ἰδίᾳ γενεᾷ ὑπηρ.: "after he had in his own generation served the counsel of God, fell on sleep," R.V., but in margin the rendering of A.V. is practically retained. It seems best to take ἰδίᾳ γενεᾷ as a dative of time, cf. ver. 20, Ephes. iii. 5 (so Blass, Wendt, Zöckler, Felten), and not as dat. commodi. St. Paul's point seems to be (1) the contrast between the service of David which extended only for a generation, and the service of Christ which lasted through all ages permanently. But this contrast would be also marked if we adopt R.V. margin rendering and govern ἰδίᾳ γεν. by ὑπηρ. (see Weiss). (2) The second point of contrast is between the corruption which David saw, and the incorruption of the Holy One of God. Weiss still connects τῇ Θεοῦ βουλῇ with ἐκοιμήθη; see margin (2) in R.V.; but this does not seem so significant as the contrast drawn between David serving the counsel or purpose of God for one, or during one generation, whilst in Christ the eternal purpose of God was realised.—προσετέθη πρὸς τοὺς π. αὐτοῦ: Hebraistic expression, lit., "was added," i.e., in Sheol, cf. Gen. xxvi. 8, Judg. ii. 10, 1 Macc. ii. 69.

διαφθοράν. 37. ὃν δὲ ὁ Θεὸς ἤγειρεν, οὐκ εἶδε διαφθοράν. 38.
Γνωστὸν οὖν ἔστω ὑμῖν, ἄνδρες ἀδελφοί, ὅτι διὰ τούτου ¹ ὑμῖν ἄφεσις
ἁμαρτιῶν καταγγέλλεται · 39. καὶ ² ἀπὸ πάντων ὧν οὐκ ἠδυνήθητε ἐν
τῷ νόμῳ Μωσέως δικαιωθῆναι, ἐν τούτῳ πᾶς ὁ πιστεύων δικαιοῦται.

¹ δια τουτου ℵAB³CDLP, so all edd. ; δια τουτο B* 15, 18, 180—Weiss here follows
above authorities.

² και BC³(D)ELP, Sah., Boh., Syrr. P. and H., Arm., Aethro., Chrys., W.H.,
Weiss, R.V. (T.R.) ; om. ℵAC, Vulg. (am. fu. demid.), Aethᵖᵖ., Tisch., Blass ; και
might easily drop out after ΤΑΙ (Weiss). D 137, Syr. H. mg. add παρα θεω after δικαι.

Ver. 37. ἤγειρεν: more than resurrection from the dead, "hic non notatur
resuscitatio ex mortuis ; quippe quæ ipsa
in conclusione evincitur : sed *quem Deus
suscitavit* est *Sanctus Dei*, ver. 35, ut
hæc Subjecti descriptio contineat ætio-
logiam," Bengel.

Ver. 38. γνωστὸν οὖν: "incipit ad-
hortatio quæ orationem claudit," Blass.—
ἄφεσις ἁμαρ.: the keynote of St. Paul's
preaching, *cf*. xxvi. 18, as it had been of
St. Peter's, ii. 38, v. 31, x. 43 ; and as it
had been of the preaching of the Baptist,
and of our Lord Himself.—διὰ τούτου,
i.e., Christ—through Him Who died,
and was risen again—the phrase is
characteristically Pauline, *cf*. x. 43.

Ver. 39. So far the words represent
the entire harmony between the preaching of St. Peter and St. Paul, and
there is no reason to attribute this verse,
as also x. 43, with Jüngst, to any reviser ;
δικαιοῦσθαι ἀπό *only* elsewhere in Rom.
vi. 7. But *if* St. Paul's next words seem
to imply that within certain limits, *i.e*.,
so far as it was obeyed, the law of Moses
brought justification, they affirm at the
same time the utter inefficacy of all legal
obedience, since one thing was certain,
that the law exacted much more than
Israel could obey ; complete justification
must be found, if anywhere, elsewhere.
Can we doubt that St. Paul is here giving
us what was really his own experience ?
(See Briggs, *Messiah of the Apostles*, p.
76.) In spite of all his efforts to fulfil
the law, there was still the feeling that
these efforts were hopelessly deficient ;
there was an area of transgression in
which the law, so far from justifying,
condemned. But in the Messiah, the
Holy One of God, he saw a realisation
of that perfect holiness to which in the
weakness of the flesh he could not attain,
and in Him, Who died, and rose again,
for us—that Righteous One, Whom he
saw, not only on the road to Damascus,
but ever on his right hand by the eye of
faith—he found complete and full justi-

fication. That this forgiveness of sins is
not connected specially with the Death
of Christ, but with His Resurrection, or
rather with His whole Messianic character, to which the Resurrection put the
final seal, is certainly not to be regarded
as an indication of a non-Pauline view,
cf. Romans iv. 25, viii. 34, 2 Cor. v. 15.
Moreover, if we consider the connection
of the whole address, the Resurrection
is not regarded apart from the Death of
Christ : vv. 26-29 show us that the
Message of Salvation starts from the
Death of Christ, and is based upon that,
cf. Bethge, *Die Paulinischen Reden*, p.
54. It is unreasonable to complain that
St. Paul's conception of justification in
this address falls below his characteristic
and controlling idea of it (McGiffert, p.
186). We could not justly expect that
the Apostle's utterances, thus summarised
by St. Luke, would contain as full and
complete a doctrinal exposition as his
Galatian and Roman Epistles. To the
former Epistle McGiffert points as giving
us what Paul actually taught in Galatia ;
but there is no contradiction between the
teaching given us in St. Luke's account
of the address in Pisidian Antioch and
St. Paul's account of his teaching to his
converts in his letter : "the coincidences
between the two are so striking as to
make each the best commentary on the
other . . . and there is no such close resemblance between the Epistle and any
other of Paul's addresses reported in
Acts," Ramsay, *Expositor*, December,
1898. "Historical Commentary on Gal."
see below, and also Lightfoot, on Gal. iii.
11. St. Paul's teaching is essentially the
same in the synagogue at Antioch as
when he is writing to his Galatian converts : only in Christ is justification, and
in the law as such there is no forgiveness
of sins. He does not say in so many
words that there was no sin from which
men could be freed under the law of
Moses, but it is evident that the most
solemn warning with which the Apostle

40. βλέπετε οὖν μὴ ἐπέλθῃ ἐφ᾽ ὑμᾶς τὸ εἰρημένον ἐν τοῖς προφήταις,
41. "Ἴδετε, οἱ καταφρονηταί, καὶ θαυμάσατε καὶ ἀφανίσθητε· ὅτι
ἔργον ἐγὼ ἐργάζομαι ἐν ταῖς ἡμέραις ὑμῶν, ἔργον ᾧ οὐ μὴ πιστεύσητε,
ἐάν τις ἐκδιηγῆται ὑμῖν.[1]"

42. Ἐξιόντων δὲ ἐκ τῆς συναγωγῆς τῶν Ἰουδαίων,[2] παρεκάλουν τὰ
ἔθνη εἰς τὸ μεταξὺ σάββατον λαληθῆναι αὐτοῖς τὰ ῥήματα ταῦτα.

---

[1] At end D adds και εσιγησαν, Syr. Harcl. mg. και εσιγησεν. In the former case
points to the impression the speech made; in the latter, merely to the fact that he
finished it; cf. xv. 12, 13. Blass reads εσιγησεν (β), so Hilg.; see Weiss, Codex D,
p. 76.

[2] εκ της σ. των Ι., but αυτων only in אABCDEI 13, 61,Vulg., Sah., Boh., Syr. (Pesh.)
and Harcl., Arm., Chrys., so Tisch., W.H., R.V., Blass, Weiss, Wendt, Hilg. τα
εθνη, but om. אA(B)CD(E), Syr. P. and H., Sah., Boh., Arm., Aeth., Chrys., so
Tisch., W.H., Blass, R.V., Weiss, Wendt, Hilg. Evidence overwhelming for R.V.;
the subject of the verbs not being clear the sentence was interpreted wrongly. BE
(81) omit παρεκαλουν—B inserting ηξιουν after σαβ., while Chrys. substitutes ηξιουν
for παρεκ. W.H., App., p. 95, suspect primitive corruption, probably in opening
words, and see Hort's suggestion. μεταξυ—D reads εξης, Hilg. retains; Blass
rejects, although he thinks it good as an explanation.

---

follows up his declaration could only be
justified on the ground that some essential principle was involved in the acceptance or rejection of the work of Christ.
On δικαιόω in classical literature, in LXX,
and in N.T., see Kennedy, Sources of N.
T. Greek, pp. 104, 105, and Sanday and
Headlam, Romans, pp. 30, 31.

Ver. 40. ἐν τοῖς προφ., cf. Luke xxiv.
44, and Acts xxiv. 14; John vi. 45.—
ἐπέλθῃ: quite Lucan in this sense, cf.
viii. 24, Luke xi. 22, xxi. 26 (James v. 1).
Ver. 41. Hab. i. 5, but here slightly
different from the Hebrew "behold, ye
among the nations," in LXX through the
possible mistake of reading the Hebrew
noun as if = deceitful ones (with the idea
perhaps of impudence, shamelessness). On
βλέπ. μὴ ἐπέλ. see Burton, pp. 85, 89;
Viteau, p. 83 (1893).—ἀφανίσθητε: added
by LXX to the "wonder marvellously"
of Heb. and LXX: "perish," "vanish
away," R.V. margin, an idea involved in
Heb. though not expressed: verb frequent
in LXX, in N.T. three times, in Matt. vi.,
and nowhere else except James iv. 14; see
Mayor's note, in loco. The Apostle here
transfers the prophecies of the temporal
judgments following on the Chaldean
invasion to the judgment of the nation
by the Romans, or to the punishment
which would fall upon the Jews by the
election of the Gentiles into their place.
Perhaps the latter is more probable before
his present audience. The πᾶς ὁ πιστ.
naturally leads him to the warning for
those who disbelieved (ἔργον ᾧ οὐ μὴ

πιστεύσητε). It is tempting to regard
the words with Ramsay (Expositor, December, 1898), as insisting upon the
marvellous and mysterious nature of
God's action in the sending forth of His
Son, but the context (cf. ἐπέλθῃ) here,
and the O.T. prophecy, both point to
the imminence of judgment and penalty.
—ἐργάζομαι: the present (so in LXX),
because the result was so certain that
it was regarded as actually in process.
With true rhetorical force St. Paul concludes his speech, as at Athens, by an
appeal to awaken all consciences, cf.
St. Peter's closing words, ii. 36, iii. 26—
possibly, as at the close perhaps of St.
Stephen's speech, signs of impatience
had begun to manifest themselves in his
audience (Plumptre).

Ver. 42. ἐξιόντων: "and as they
went out," i.e., the Apostles, before the
synagogue broke up the congregation of
Jews and proselytes besought them—
not "when they had gone out," which
would introduce a confusion of time; see
critical notes. Wendt refers to ver. 15,
and takes ἀρχισυ. as the subject of
παρεκάλουν.—εἰς τὸ μ. Σ.: "the next
Sabbath," A. and R.V., cf. for εἰς iv. 3.
μετ. here an adverb, later Greek, cf. Barn.,
Epist., xiii., 5; Clem. Rom., Cor., i. 44,
and so in Josephus; ver. 44 apparently
decides for the rendering above. Others
take it of the days during the intervening
week, between the Sabbaths, cf. J. Lightfoot, in loco, and Schöttgen.

Ver. 43. λυθ. δὲ: Paul and Barnabas

43. λυθείσης δὲ τῆς συναγωγῆς, ἠκολούθησαν πολλοὶ τῶν Ἰουδαίων καὶ τῶν σεβομένων προσηλύτων τῷ Παύλῳ καὶ τῷ Βαρνάβᾳ[1] · οἵτινες προσλαλοῦντες αὐτοῖς, ἔπειθον αὐτοὺς ἐπιμένειν τῇ χάριτι τοῦ Θεοῦ.

44. Τῷ δὲ ἐρχομένῳ[2] σαββάτῳ σχεδὸν πᾶσα ἡ πόλις συνήχθη ἀκοῦσαι τὸν λόγον τοῦ Θεοῦ. 45.[3] ἰδόντες δὲ οἱ Ἰουδαῖοι τοὺς ὄχλους ἐπλήσθησαν ζήλου, καὶ ἀντέλεγον τοῖς ὑπὸ τοῦ Παύλου λεγομένοις, ἀντιλέγοντες καὶ βλασφημοῦντες. 46. παρρησιασάμενοι δὲ ὁ Παῦλος καὶ ὁ Βαρνάβας εἶπον, Ὑμῖν ἦν ἀναγκαῖον πρῶτον λαληθῆναι τὸν λόγον τοῦ Θεοῦ · ἐπειδὴ δὲ[4] ἀπωθεῖσθε αὐτόν, καὶ οὐκ ἀξίους κρίνετε

[1] Βαρναβᾳ, 137, Syr. Harcl. mg. add αξιουντες βαπτισθηναι, so Blass in β. Belser supports, p. 69, and thinks that it explains context, but if thus important it seems curious that it should have been omitted. At end of verse D, Syr. H. mg., Prov. add εγεν. καθ᾽ οληs της πολεωs διελθειν τον λογον (cf. E, Wern.), so Blass in β., and Hilg. επιμενειν, but προσμ. ℵABCDE 61, Chrys., Tisch., W.H., Blass, R.V., Weiss, Wendt, Hilg.

[2] ερχομενῳ ℵBC*DE²LP 61, Chrys., Tisch., W.H., Wendt, Weiss, Hilg; εχομενῳ AC²E* 13, 40, W.H. marg., Blass (ἡ ἐχομένη several times in Luke). For τον λογον του Θ. (K.) D reads only Παυλου ; so Blass and Hilg. Belser defends (with addition in previous verse) as marking exactly what the people would be likely to say, p. 69. But as D reads τον λογον του Θ. in previous verse, probably the change may have been made here merely to avoid repetition, Weiss, Codex D, p. 76.

[3] D commences πολυν τε λογον ποιησαμενου περι του κυριου (all this following upon Παυλου at close of previous verse): may be meant to mark that the opposition showed itself after Paul had spoken at length. αντιλ. και DIP 40, Syr. Harcl., Chrys., Theophyl., Par.¹, Tisch., Wendt, Hilg. ; om. ℵABCL 13, 61, Vulg., Syr. Pesh., Sah., Boh., Arm., Aeth., W.H., Blass, R.V., Weiss. εναντιομενοι (sic) και E, Gig. ; Blass in β αντιτασσομενοι (cf. xviii. 6).

[4] επειδη δε, but δε om. ℵ*BD* 180, Syr. H., Sah., Boh., Tisch., W.H., R.V., Wendt (Weiss retains, so Blass and Hilg.). απωθ. . . . κρινετε . . ., Gig., Par., Wern., Cypr., Prom., so Blass in β, read απωσασθε . . . εκρινατε, marking that the opportunity was past and gone.

had gone out before the synagogue was formally broken up; δέ marks the contrast in the case of those who followed them to hear more.—τῶν σεβ. προσ.: only here. σεβ. τὸν Θεόν or φοβ. τὸν Θεόν: used elsewhere of the uncircumcised Gentiles who joined the Jewish synagogue, whilst προσήλυτοι means those who became circumcised and were full proselytes: "devout," R.V., referring rather to the outward worship, "religious," A.V., rather to inward feelings (but in ver. 50, "devout," A.V.).—οἵτινες (ix. 35, xi. 28) refers to the Apostles, but see on the other hand Rendall's note, pp. 92, 165, referring it to the people (so apparently Calvin). The Apostles thought by the eager following of the people that the grace of God had found an entrance into their souls, see critical notes for D. —προσλαλοῦντες: in N.T. only elsewhere in xxviii. 20, cf. Wisdom xiii. 17 (Exod. iv. 16, A B²).

Ver. 44. ἐρχ., see critical notes.— σχεδὸν: cf. xix. 26, Heb. ix. 22, each time before πᾶς, and in 2 Macc. v. 2, 3 Macc. v. 14, 45. In classical use as in text, often with πᾶς.—συνήχθη, i.e., in the synagogue, not, as some have thought, before the lodging of the Apostles. Ver. 45. οἱ Ἰ.: not the proselytes with them (Ramsay, St. Paul, p. 101). —τοὺς ὄχλους, cf. ver. 48, τὰ ἔθνη.— ἀντιλ. καὶ, see critical notes ; if retained, participle emphasises finite verb: "not only contradicting but blaspheming"; see Simcox, Language of the N. T., p. 130.—βλασ.: nomen Christi, xviii. 6, xxvi. 11. Ver. 46. παρρησιασάμενοι, see on ix. 27.—ἦν ἀναγκαῖον, cf. on ver. 14.— ἐπειδὴ δὲ, see critical notes. δέ marks the contrast, but its omission emphasises it even more vividly and sternly.—ἀπω-θεῖσθε: "ye thrust it from you," R.V.; repellitis, Vulgate; only in Luke and

ἑαυτοὺς τῆς αἰωνίου ζωῆς, ἰδοὺ στρεφόμεθα εἰς τὰ ἔθνη· 47. οὕτω
γὰρ ἐντέταλται ἡμῖν ὁ Κύριος, "Τέθεικά[1] σε εἰς φῶς ἐθνῶν, τοῦ εἶναί
σε εἰς σωτηρίαν ἕως ἐσχάτου τῆς γῆς." 48. ἀκούοντα δὲ τὰ ἔθνη
ἔχαιρον, καὶ ἐδόξαζον[2] τὸν λόγον τοῦ Κυρίου, καὶ ἐπίστευσαν ὅσοι
ἦσαν τεταγμένοι εἰς ζωὴν αἰώνιον. 49. διεφέρετο δὲ ὁ λόγος τοῦ
Κυρίου δι' ὅλης τῆς χώρας. 50. οἱ δὲ Ἰουδαῖοι παρώτρυναν τὰς
σεβομένας γυναῖκας[3] καὶ τὰς εὐσχήμονας καὶ τοὺς πρώτους τῆς
πόλεως, καὶ ἐπήγειραν διωγμὸν ἐπὶ τὸν Παῦλον καὶ τὸν Βαρνάβαν,

---

[1] DE, Cypr. prefix ιδου to quot., so LXX. D, Cypr., Gig. read φως τεθ. σε τοις
εθν., so Blass and Hilg., but here variance from LXX.

[2] εδοξαζον, D, Gig., Aug. read εδεξαντο, so Hilg.—rejected by Blass in β, but
see also his Commentary, *in loco*; for the phrase *cf.* 2 Thess. iii. 1. του Κυριου,
but του Θ. BD*E 180, Boh., Arm., Aug., W.H. text, R.V. text, Blass, Hilg.—
Weiss retains του Κ., so Tisch., W.H. mg. following ℵACLP 61, Vulg., Sah., Chrys.

[3] και (1) om. ℵcABCD 61, 180, Sah., Boh., Syrr. P. and H., Arm., Tisch., W.H.,
R.V., Weiss, Hilg. Gig. τινας των σεβ. (τον θεον) γυναικας ευσχημονας. DE
(Ephraem, Harris, *Four Lectures*, p. 23) read θλιψιν μεγ. και διωγμον, *cf.* viii. 11,
Western text, and Phil. i. 16; see also Ramsay, *St. Paul*, p. 106.

Paul, *cf.* 1 Tim. i. 19, Rom. xi. 1, Acts
vii. 27, 39; frequent in LXX, *cf.*, *e.g.*,
Ps. xciii. 14, Ezek. xliii. 9, and 3 Macc.
iii. 22, vi. 32, 4 Macc. ii. 16.—οὐκ ἀξίους,
cf. Matt. xxii. 8.

Ver. 47. γὰρ: this action of the
Apostles in turning to the Gentiles was
not arbitrary.—Τέθεικα, *cf.* Isa. xlix. 6
(Luke ii. 32). In LXX B reads δέδωκα
instead of Τέθ., and inserts after it εἰς
διαθήκην γένους; not in Hebrew.—σε
really refers to the Servant of the Lord,
the Messiah; *cf.* Delitzsch, *Das Buch
Jesaia*, p. 486, fourth edition; but the
Apostles speak of an ἐντολή given to
them, because through them the Messiah
is proclaimed to the Gentiles; see note
on i. 8.

Ver. 48. ἐδόξ. τὸν λ. τοῦ Κ.: δοξ. τὸν
Θ.; frequent in Luke and Paul, *cf.* 2
Thess. iii. 1 for the nearest approach to
the exact phrase here. — ὅσοι ἦσαν
τεταγ.: there is no countenance here for
the *absolutum decretum* of the Calvinists,
since ver. 46 had already shown that the
Jews had acted through their own choice.
The words are really nothing more than
a corollary of St. Paul's ἀναγκαῖον: the
Jews as a nation had been ordained to
eternal life—they had rejected this election—but those who believed amongst
the Gentiles were equally ordained by
God to eternal life, and it was in accordance with His divine appointment that
the Apostles had turned to them. Some
take the word as if middle, not passive:
"as many as had set themselves unto

eternal life," and in support of this
Rendall refers to 1 Cor. xvi. 15, ἔταξαν
ἑαυτοὺς (see also Blass, *in loco*). The
rendering here given by Rendall may be
adopted without pressing the military
metaphor in the verb, as has sometimes been done; see Wendt's note,
p. 308 (1888). St. Chrysostom takes
the expression (rightly as Wendt
thinks): ἀφωρισμένοι τῷ Θεῷ. Mr.
Page's note, *in loco*, should be consulted.

Ver. 49. διεφέρετο; *divulgabatur*,
"was spread abroad," R.V.; not only by
the preaching of the Apostles themselves,
but by small knots of Christians in other
towns, see Ramsay, *St. Paul*, p. 105,
and so Blass, *in loco*; only here in N.T.
in this sense, so in (Wisdom xviii. 10)
Plut.; Lucian; imperfect, a certain lapse
of time is implied, see Ramsay, *St.
Paul*, p. 105.—ὅλης τῆς χώρας: the
phrase, "the whole *Region*," indicates
that Antioch was the centre of a
Region, a notice which introduces us
to an important fact of Roman imperial
administration. Antioch, as a Roman
colony, would be the natural military
and administrative centre of a certain
Regio, and there is evidence that in
Southern Galatia there were also other
distinct *Regiones*, χῶραι, Ramsay, *St.
Paul*, pp. 102-104, 109, 110-112.

Ver. 50. παρώτρυναν: "urged on,"
R.V.; only here in N.T., not in LXX
or Apocrypha; so in Pind., Lucian,
and so too in Josephus, *Ant.*, vii., 6, 1,

καὶ ἐξέβαλον αὐτοὺς ἀπὸ τῶν ὁρίων αὐτῶν. 51. οἱ δὲ ἐκτιναξάμενοι
τὸν κονιορτὸν τῶν ποδῶν αὐτῶν ἐπ' αὐτούς, ἦλθον [1] εἰς Ἰκόνιον. 52. οἱ
δὲ μαθηταὶ ἐπληροῦντο χαρᾶς καὶ Πνεύματος Ἁγίου.

XIV. 1. ἘΓΕΝΕΤΟ δὲ ἐν Ἰκονίῳ, κατὰ τὸ αὐτὸ εἰσελθεῖν αὐτοὺς
εἰς τὴν συναγωγὴν τῶν Ἰουδαίων, καὶ λαλῆσαι οὕτως ὥστε πιστεῦσαι

[1] ἦλθον, D reads κατηντησαν, so Blass and Hilg., a common word in Acts but not
necessary here.

and also in Hippocrates and Aretaeus.—
ἐπήγειραν, cf. xiv. 2; nowhere else in
N.T., several times in LXX, and also
frequently in Hippocrates and Galen,
Hobart, pp. 225, 226. On the addition in
Codex D see critical notes, and Ramsay,
St. Paul, pp. 105, 106.—τὰς εὐσχ.: "of
honourable estate," R.V.; not of character, but of position, cf. Mark xv. 43.
This influence assigned to women at
Antioch, and exerted by them, is quite
in accordance with the manners of the
country, and we find evidence of it in all
periods and under most varying conditions. Thus women were appointed
under the empire as magistrates, as
presidents of the games, and even the
Jews elected a woman as an Archisyna-
gogos, at least in one instance, at Smyrna,
Ramsay, St. Paul, p. 102; Church in the
Roman Empire, p. 67; C. and H., p. 144;
"Antioch," Hastings' B.D.; Loening,
Die Gemeindeverfassung des Urchristenthums, p. 15.—τοὺς πρώτους: perhaps
approaching them through their wives.
On the addiction of women to the Jewish
religion cf. Jos., B. J., ii., 20, 2; Strabo,
vii., 2; Juvenal, vi., 542; see Blass,
Felten, Plumptre, in loco, and instances in
Wetstein.—ἐξέβαλον αὐτούς, see xiv. 21.
Ver. 51. ἐκτιναξάμενοι, cf. Matt. x.
14, Luke x. 11, Mark vi. 11. The
symbolic act would be understood by
the Jews as an intimation that all further
intercourse was at an end. There is no
reason to see in the words a late addition
by the author of Acts to the source; the
disciples mentioned in ver. 52 need not
have been Jews at all, but Gentiles, and
in xiv. 21 nothing is said of any intercourse except with those who were
already disciples.—Ἰκόνιον, see on xiv. 1.
Ver. 52. χαρᾶς, cf. 1 Thess. i. 6,
Rom. xiv. 17, 2 Tim. i. 4.
CHAPTER XIV.—Ver. 1. ἐν Ἰκονίῳ
(Konia), sometimes regarded as a Roman
colony towards the end of the reign of
Claudius, thus dignified on account of the
title conferred upon the frontier town,
Claudio-Derbe. But Hadrian, not Claudius, constituted it a colony. In ver. 6
the Apostles flee from Iconium to the

cities of Lycaonia, Lystra and Derbe,
and the inference from this statement
is that Iconium was not itself Lycaonian. But this inference justifies the
local accuracy of the historian, as it
would appear that the people of
Iconium regarded themselves as Phrygian even after Iconium had been
united with Lycaonia in one district
of Roman administration: cf. Ramsay,
Church in the Roman Empire, p. 37 ff.,
and the testimony of the Christian
Hierax, 163 A.D., before his Roman
judge: "I have come hither (i.e., as
a slave), torn away from Iconium of
Phrygia": on the road travelled by the
Apostles see also Ramsay, u. s., p. 27
ff. Strictly speaking, Lystra and Derbe
were cities of Lycaonia-Galatica, while
Iconium reckoned itself as a city of
Phrygia-Galatica, all three being comprised within the Roman province of
Galatia. See also Rendall, Acts, p. 262.
On the place and its importance, situated
with a busy trade on the principal lines
of communication through Asia Minor,
see C. and H., smaller edition, p. 145,
B.D.[2]. Iconium is the scene of the famous
Acts of Paul and Thekla, forming a part
of the Acts of Paul, C. Schmidt's translation of which we must await with interest.
See Harnack, Chronol., i., p. 493, Wendt
(1899), p. 42, Ramsay, Church in the Roman Empire, p. 375, and "Iconium,"
Hastings' B.D. — κατὰ τὸ αὐτὸ, "together," so R. and A.V., cf. LXX, 1 Sam.
xi. 11, or it may mean "at the same
time". Blass however (so Ramsay, Weiss,
Rendall) renders "after the same fashion,"
i.e., as at Antioch. But for this meaning
cf. xvii. 2, where a different phrase is
used.—Ἑλλήνων: on the whole best
taken as referring to the σεβ. or φοβ.
τὸν Θεόν, because in ver. 2 we have
ἔθνη, which would signify the Gentiles
generally, as opposed to those devout
persons who as proselytes had joined
the Jewish synagogue.
Ver. 2. ἀπειθοῦντες, see critical notes.
If we read ἀπειθήσαντες, "that were disobedient," R.V., but cf. John iii. 36, and
Page's note in loco. Lumby quotes

Ἰουδαίων τε καὶ Ἑλλήνων πολὺ πλῆθος. 2. οἱ δὲ ἀπειθοῦντες[1]
Ἰουδαῖοι ἐπήγειραν καὶ ἐκάκωσαν τὰς ψυχὰς τῶν ἐθνῶν κατὰ τῶν
ἀδελφῶν. 3. ἱκανὸν μὲν οὖν χρόνον διέτριψαν παρρησιαζόμενοι ἐπὶ

[1] απειθουντες, but aor. απειθησαντες אABC 13, 61, Tisch., W.H., R.V., Weiss,
Wendt. D, Syr. Harcl. mg., cf. Blass in β, and Hilg., read οι δε αρχισυναγωγοι
των Ιουδαιων και οι αρχοντες της συναγωγης (τ. σ. om. by Syr. H.), and for
επηγειραν DE, Gig., Wern., Syr. H. read επηγαγον (αυτοις om. by Syr. H.)
διωγμον κατα των δικαιων. These readings may have arisen from the seeming
inconsequence of vv. 1-3 as they stand in the ordinary text. We read of the
opposition of the Jews, and yet the Apostles abode a long time, etc. Ramsay
therefore maintains that there is some corruption, and is prepared to follow
Spitta in omitting ver. 3 (although for a different reason). But as the text
stands it is quite possible to suppose that the effect of the preaching in the
synagogue would be twofold, ver. 2 thus answering to the last clause of ver. 1,
and that the disciples continued to speak boldly, encouraged by success on the one
hand and undeterred by opposition on the other, the consequence being that the
division in the city was still further intensified. Ramsay sees in the reading at the
commencement of the verse which marks the distinction between αρχοντες and
αρχισυναγωγοι a proof that the Bezan reading here cannot be an original first
century one, although in its carefulness to enumerate the different classes of Jews
it may embody an actual popular tradition (see his article on "The Rulers of the
Synagogue," *Expositor*, April, 1895, and compare *C. R. E.*, p. 46). On κατα των
δικαιων see also Ramsay, *C. R. E.*, p. 46; δικαιοι is not used by Luke of *Christians*,
rather αγιοι or αδελφοι. At the end of the verse D(E), Gig., Par., Wern., Syr. H.
mg. add ὁ δε κυριος εδωκεν ταχυ ειρηνην, which seem introduced to make an easy
transition from ver. 2 to ver. 3, a second tumult being referred to in ver. 5; see
crit. notes. Cf. εκ δευτερου, Blass in β. See further Weiss, Codex D, p. 77;
Wendt (1899), pp. 247, 248; Harris, *Four Lectures*, etc., pp. 23, 69; and for decided
support of β, Belser, p. 70 ff.; Hilgenfeld, *Zeitschrift für wissenschaft. Theol.*, i.,
pp. 52, 53, 1896, and *Acta Apost.*, p. 245, 1899; and especially Blass, *Philology of
the Gospels*, pp. 121, 127; Zöckler, *Greifswalder Studien*, p. 135; see also Salmon,
Introd., p. 598; but on the other hand Schmiedel, *Encycl. Bibl.*, i., p. 53.

Baruch i. 19, and regards the expression
here as stronger than "unbelieving,"
rather unbelief breaking forth into rebellion, as in the case of these Jews at
Iconium and elsewhere. Ramsay renders
"the disaffected".—ἐκάκωσαν: "exasperated," Ramsay; only here in N.T. in
this sense, five times in Acts, once in
quotation; only once elsewhere in N.T.,
1 Pet. iii. 13, cf. for its use here Jos.,
Ant., xvi., 1, 2; vii., 3; viii., 6. It is used
several times in LXX, but not in this
sense, the nearest approach to it is Ps.
cv. (LXX) 32. The same phrase occurs
twice, Num. xxix. 7, xxx. 14, but with a
different meaning or reading in D. See
critical notes.

Ver. 3. ἱκανὸν μὲν οὖν χ. οὖν: as a
result from the two previous verses, the
accession to their numbers and the dis-
affection. Blass sees in the aorists
ἐπήγ. and ἐκάκ. a proof that the disaffected Jews succeeded in their attempts,
and he asks if this was so, how were the
Apostles able to remain? The answer
is to be found, he thinks, in D, see

above, so Hilgenfeld, who holds that
this reading makes it conceivable how
Paul and Barnabas could continue their
work. On ἱκανός with χρόνος, peculiar
to St. Luke, see p. 215. Ramsay sees
the same force in the aorists, and therefore ver. 3 seems so disconnected that
he can only regard it as an early gloss
similar to many which have crept into
the Bezan text. He thus inclines to adopt
here Spitta's hypothesis, and to regard
vv. 1, 2, 4, 5, 6, 7 as a primitive document. The Bezan text is to him simply
an attempt to remedy the discrepancy
which was felt to exist between vv. 2 and
3, and it presupposes two tumults: one
in ver. 2, and the other in vv. 4 and 5.
But there seems nothing unnatural in
taking οὖν as marking a result from the
events of the two previous verses, not
from the second alone, or in the extended
stay of the Apostles in the divided city.
(Wendt (1899) supposes that in the
original source ver. 3 preceded ver. 2,
which makes the sequence quite easy.
Clemen is much more drastic in his

τῷ Κυρίῳ τῷ μαρτυροῦντι τῷ λόγῳ[1] τῆς χάριτος αὐτοῦ, καὶ διδόντι
σημεῖα καὶ τέρατα γίνεσθαι διὰ τῶν χειρῶν αὐτῶν. 4. ἐσχίσθη[2] δὲ
τὸ πλῆθος τῆς πόλεως · καὶ οἱ μὲν ἦσαν σὺν τοῖς Ἰουδαίοις, οἱ δὲ
σὺν τοῖς ἀποστόλοις. 5.[3] Ὡς δὲ ἐγένετο ὁρμὴ τῶν ἐθνῶν τε καὶ
Ἰουδαίων σὺν τοῖς ἄρχουσιν αὐτῶν, ὑβρίσαι καὶ λιθοβολῆσαι αὐτούς,

[1] Wendt (1899), p. 248, maintains that ver. 3 preceded ver. 2 in the source, thus
simplifying, as he thinks, the order of thought. τῳ λογῳ, in אA, Syr. Pesh. επι
precedes, so Tisch., Wendt, and Weiss; cf. Heb. xi. 4, but prep. om. by אcBCDELP,
Chrys., so W.H., Blass, Hilg. και διδ., om. και ABDEP, Chrys., so W.H., Blass,
R.V., Wendt, Weiss, Hilg.; διδοντος so א 4, 21, 133, Tisch.

[2] εσχισθη, D, Syr. Pesh. ην εσχισμενον, and for οι δε D reads αλλοι δε, so Hilg.;
Harris regards these as cases of Latinisation, so Corssen, p. 43. At end of verse, D,
Syr. Harcl. mg. add κολλωμενοι δια τον λογον του Θεου (so Blass in β and so Hilg.),
the verb is Lucan, but we cannot say that it is original.

[3] Syr. Harcl. mg. has " et iterum excitaverunt persecutionem secundo Judæi cum
Gentibus et lapidantes eos eduxerunt eos ex civitate," so Blass in β; cf. also Ephrem;
Harris, Four Lectures, etc., p. 23. Hilg. follows T.R. Harris also quotes "et
iniuriaverunt et lapidaverunt eos," d, which he suspects to be more archaic than
its Greek. It is difficult to see how this can agree with συνιδοντες in the next verse,
which could not be used of an assault actually committed, but Syr. Harcl. omits
συνιδ.

methods, and refers ver. 2 and vv. 4-6a to
his Redactor Antijudaicus.)—παῤῥης.:
speaking boldly in spite of the opposition
of the Jews, see above on the verb, p. 242.
—ἐπὶ, cf. iv. 17, 18 (elsewhere with ἐν),
the Lord being the ground and support of
their preaching; Calvin notes that the
words may mean that they spoke boldly
in the cause of the Lord, or that relying
on His grace they took courage, but that
both meanings really run into each other.
—τῷ Κυρίῳ: difficult to decide whether
the reference is to Jesus; Nösgen takes it
so, not only on account of St. Luke's
usual way of giving Him this title, but
also because the Acts speak expressly
of the miracles of the Apostles as works
of Christ, iii. 16, cf. iv. 30. On the other
hand Meyer-Wendt appeals to iv. 29, xx.
24, 32 (but for last passage see var. lect.),
Heb. ii. 4.

Ver. 4. ἐσχίσθη δὲ, better "and the
multitude" (see Page's note on ver. 3),
cf. xxiii. 7, John vii. 43. There is no
such marked success in ver. 3 as in
Ramsay's view. In Thessalonica, xvii.
4, 5, a similar division, cf. Luke xii. 51.—
ἀποστόλοις: the note of Weiss here
takes the word, not in its technical sense
at all, but only as missionaries; but see
above on xiii. 1.

Ver. 5. The real contrast is marked
in this verse, ὡς δὲ ἐγέν. Hitherto the
evil results indicated in ver. 2 had not
resulted in an open combination of Jews
and Gentiles to injure Paul and Barnabas,
but now the Jews and their rulers were
prepared to act in concert with the Gentiles, so that the opposition assumed a
public shape, and a definite accusation of
blasphemy could be formulated against
the Apostles.—ὁρμή, "onset," R.V.; "assault," A.V., but neither word seems appropriate, since neither onset nor assault
actually occurred. It seems therefore
better to take the word as expressing
the inclination, or hostile intention, or
instigation, and to connect it with the
infinitives. In classical Greek the word
is used of eagerness (joined with ἐπιθυμία), of impulse, of eager desire of,
or for, a thing, cf. Thuc. iv. 4, Plat.,
Phil., 35 D, although it is also used of
an assault or attack. The only other
place in the N.T. in which it occurs
is James iii. 4 (R.V. renders "impulse").
Hesychius regards it as equivalent to
βουλή, ἐπιθυμία, but see also for its use as
expressing attack, violence, 3 Macc. i. 16,
23; iv. 5.—σὺν τοῖς ἄρχουσιν αὐτῶν,
i.e., of the Jewish synagogues, as αὐτῶν
shows. Hackett and Lumby take it of
the heathen magistrates. On the distinction between these and the ἀρχισυνάγωγος, see Schürer, div. ii., vol. ii., pp.
64, 250, E.T. The magistrates of the
city could not have participated in an
act of mob-violence, and the plot to stone
the Apostles seems to point to Jewish
instigation for enforcing the punishment
of blasphemy.—ὑβρίσαι, "to entreat them
shamefully," so A. and R.V., indicating

6.¹ συνιδόντες κατέφυγον εἰς τὰς πόλεις τῆς Λυκαονίας, Λύστραν
καὶ Δέρβην, καὶ τὴν περίχωρον, 7. κἀκεῖ ἦσαν εὐαγγελιζόμενοι.²

¹ Syr. Harcl. mg. (cf. Flor.) reads "et fugientes pervenerunt in Lycaoniam, in
civitatem quandam, quæ vocatur Lystra, et Derben," so Blass in β; in civit. quandam
does not sound Lucan. After περιχωρον DE (Flor., Vulg.) add ολην, so Blass and
Hilg., but see Ramsay, St. Paul, p. 113.

² At end of verse D(E), Flor., Wern., Prov. add εκινηθη ολον το πληθος επι τη
διδαχη, and also apparently by way of transition to the following narrative ὁ δε Π.
και Β. διετριβον εν Λυστροις, so Blass and Hilg., but see Ramsay, u. s., and Weiss,
Codex D, p. 78. E has εξεπλησσετο πασα ἡ πολυπληθεια επι τη διδαχη αυτων, and
Harris thinks that the gloss arose in Latin and points out the closeness of d and e
here (see also Blass, Proleg., p. 28). But it has been pointed out that the Latin
of d and Flor. also differ.

outrage, insolence in act, cf. Matt. xxii.
6, Luke xviii. 32, 2 Macc. xiv. 42, 3 Macc.
vi. 9; in Luke xi. 45 of insulting words.
St. Paul uses the same word of treatment
at Philippi, 1 Thess. ii. 2, and he describes
his own conduct towards the Christians
by the cognate noun ὑβριστής, 1 Tim.
i. 13.
  Ver. 6. συνιδόντες, cf. xii. 12, v. 2, only
in Luke and Paul, 1 Cor. iv. 4; 1 Macc.
iv. 21; 2 Macc. iv. 41, xiv. 26, 30; 3 Macc.
v. 50.—κατέφυγον, cf. Matt. x. 23: "We
ought not to run into danger, but to flee
from it if needful, like these leaders of the
Church wishing to extend their preaching, and to multiply by persecution"
Oecumenius; only elsewhere in N.T.,
Heb. vi. 18; see Westcott, l.c., cf. Deut.
iv. 42, Numb. xxxv. 26; 1 Macc. v. 11,
etc. So in classical Greek with εἰς, ἐπί,
πρός.—εἰς τὰς πόλεις τῆς Λ. Λύστραν
καὶ Δέρβην, καὶ τὴν περίχωρον: in these
words Ramsay sees a notable indication
of St. Luke's habit of defining each new
sphere of work according to the existing
political divisions of the Roman Empire:
"Lystra and Derbe and the surrounding
Region"; in going from Antioch to
Iconium the travellers entered no new
Region (χώρα), but in ver. 6 another
Region is referred to, comprising part of
Lycaonia, consisting of two cities and a
stretch of cityless territory; and if this is
so, we see also in the words an indication
of St. Paul's constant aim in his missionary efforts, viz., the Roman world and
its centres of life and commerce; when
he reached the limit of Roman territory
(Derbe) he retraced his steps. The position of Lystra, about six hours south-
south-west from Iconium, near the
village Khatyn Serai, is now considered
as established by Professor Sterrett's
evidence based on an inscription; and
from similar evidence of inscriptions it
appears that Lystra had been a Roman

colonia since Augustus, Ramsay, Church
in the Roman Empire, p. 47 ff., and Wendt
(1899), p. 248; O. Holtzmann, Neutestamentliche Zeitgeschichte, p. 102. The
site of Derbe cannot be quite so satisfactorily determined, but probably near the
village Losta or Zosta; about three miles
north-west of this place, a large mound, by
name Gudelissin, is marked by evident
traces of the remains of a city, "Derbe,"
Hastings' B.D.; Ramsay, Church in the
Roman Empire, p. 54 ff., and Wendt
(1899), p. 249. From 41-72 A.D. Derbe
was the frontier city of the Roman
province on the south-east. But if St.
Paul thus found in Lystra and Derbe
centres of Roman commercial life, we
must modify our view of the wild and
uncivilised nature of the region into
which the Apostles penetrated after
leaving Antioch and Iconium, cf. C.
and H., p. 147, with Ramsay, Church
in the Roman Empire, pp. 56, 57. If
Paul had gone to the ruder parts of
Lycaonia, it is very doubtful whether
the inhabitants could have understood
him, or any one addressing them in
Greek (see also Rendall, Acts, p. 263).
  Ver. 7. See critical notes for reading
in D.—κἀκεῖ; found in four other places
in Acts, but not at all in Luke's Gospel.
—εὐαγγελ. ἦσαν: "they were engaged
in preaching the Gospel," Ramsay; on
participle with ἦν or ἦσαν see i. 10.
  Ver. 8. ἐν Λύστροις: here neuter
plural, and not as in vv. 6 and 21, feminine. Clemen, p. 115, and Jüngst, p. 131,
see a proof in this that 8-18, or 21ª, was
interpolated by a redactor. But Hilgenfeld points out that the same interchange
of feminine singular and neuter plural
recurs in xvi. 1, 2; cf. also 2 Tim. iii. 11.
The miracle which follows has often been
compared with those narrated in iii. 1 ff.,
and it has been alleged that this second
miracle is a mere imitation of the first, to

8. Καί τις ἀνὴρ ἐν Λύστροις¹ ἀδύνατος τοῖς ποσὶν ἐκάθητο, χωλὸς ἐκ κοιλίας μητρὸς αυτοῦ ὑπάρχων,² ὃς οὐδέποτε περιεπεπατήκει.³ 9. οὗτος ἤκουε⁴ τοῦ Παύλου λαλοῦντος · ὃς ἀτενίσας αὐτῷ, καὶ ἰδὼν ὅτι πίστιν ἔχει τοῦ σωθῆναι, 10. εἶπε μεγάλῃ τῇ φωνῇ, Ἀνάστηθι

¹ εν Λυστροις, D omits (so Hilg. and Blass in β, where he reads και (εκει))—attractive, although probably due to the previous interpolation, because it would do away with the perplexity of the two readings εν Λ. αδυν. (so Weiss) and αδυν. εν Λ. (W.H.).

² εκ κ. μητρος Blass thinks out of iii. 2, so apparently Wendt—χωλος om. D, Gig., but see Ramsay, St. Paul, p. 114.

³ περιεπεπατηκει, but περιεπατησεν ℵABC 61, so Tisch., W.H., Weiss, Wendt, R.V., Blass. At end of verse Flor. reads υπαρχων εν φοβω του θεου, so Blass in β; D omits του θεου and puts the clause after λαλουντος in ver. 9; so Hilg. υπαρχ. omitted above, where it seems clearly an interpolation in T.R. out of iii. 2. According to Flor. the man would be a proselyte, see Ramsay, St. Paul, p. 116, Hilgenfeld, Blass; but Weiss, Codex D, p. 78, regards the reading in Flor. as quite secondary, and it is to be noticed that D omits entirely the words του θεου after φοβω.

⁴ ηκουε BCP, Sah., Syr. Harcl., so W.H., R.V., Blass, Wendt, Weiss; ηκουσεν ℵADEHL 13, 61, Syr. Pesh., Boh., Arm., Æth., Chrys., so Tisch. Flor. adds "libenter," and Gig. adds επιστευσεν, so Blass in β.

keep up the parallel between Peter and Paul. But whilst there are, no doubt, features in common in the two narratives—no great matter for surprise in similar healings, where a similarity of expressions would fitly recur, especially in the literary usage of a medical writer (see Zöckler, p. 240)—the differences are also marked: e.g., in the Petrine miracle the man is a beggar, and asks only for alms; in the Pauline nothing is said of all this, even if the first fact is implied—in the Petrine miracle nothing is said of the man's faith, although it is implied (see notes, in loco); here it is distinctly stated—in the earlier miracle Peter is represented as taking the man and raising him up; here nothing of the kind is mentioned (see further on the two miracles, and the different motive in their performance, Nösgen, Apostelgeschichte, p. 267). On St. Paul's own claim to work miracles see 2 Cor. xii. 12, Rom. xv. 19, Gal. iii. 5. If the latter passage occurs in an Epistle addressed amongst other Churches to Christians in Lystra, in accordance with the South Galatian theory, the assertion of miraculous powers is the more notable; see also McGiffert, Apostolic Age, p. 189.—ἀδύν. τοῖς π.: adjective only here in N.T. in this sense, cf. LXX, S. Tobit ii. 10, v. 9, ἀδύν. τοῖς ὀφθαλμοῖς. It is used frequently in a similar sense by medical writers, Hobart, p. 46.—ἐκάθητο; not "dwelt" Hebraistic; but simply "used to sit," cf. Luke xviii. 35, John ix. 8; probably in the forum, cf. ver. 11 (Blass).—ἐκ κοιλ. μητρὸς α.; "no mendicant pretender, but one whose history from infancy was well known". See Ramsay on the "triple beat," St. Paul, p. 115.

Ver. 9. οὗτος; a genuine Lucan mark of connection, Friedrich, p. 10.—ἤκουε "used to hear," or "was listening to," i.e., was an habitual hearer of Paul's preaching, see critical notes on D. Ramsay, St. Paul, pp. 114, 116, regards the man as a proselyte, cf. additions in Bezan text, but for another view of the additions here and in ver. 10, Page, Classical Review, July, 1899.—ἀτεν., see above, i. 10.—τοῦ σ., Burton, Moods and Tenses, p. 158.

Ver. 10. ἀνάσ. . . . ὀρθός: verb, as elsewhere, ix. 34, 40, but only here with ἐπὶ τοὺς π., hitherto they had been too weak to support him, ὀρθός signifying that he was entirely whole, cf. reading in D. On ὀρθός see Hobart, p. 46: it was frequently used by medical writers, so by Hippocrates and Galen, with ἵστημι; only elsewhere in N.T. in a figurative sense and in a quotation, Heb. xi. 13. The collocation is also found in classical Greek, and cf. 1 Esdras ix. 46 (see also Hatch and Redpath), but cf. also ἀνορθόω, Luke xiii. 13, and the combination in Galen of ὀρθόω and τὸ ἀδύνατον κῶλον.—ἥλλετο καὶ περιεπ., see also reading in D. If we read ἥλατο, note aorist and imperfect, he sprang up with a single bound, whilst the walking is a continuous action, or inceptive: "he began to walk".

ἐπὶ τοὺς πόδας σου ὀρθός. καὶ ἥλλετο [1] καὶ περιεπάτει. 11. Οἱ δὲ
ὄχλοι ἰδόντες ὃ ἐποίησεν ὁ Παῦλος, ἐπῆραν τὴν φωνὴν αὐτῶν
Λυκαονιστὶ λέγοντες, Οἱ θεοὶ ὁμοιωθέντες ἀνθρώποις κατέβησαν πρὸς
ἡμᾶς· 12. ἐκάλουν τε τὸν μὲν Βαρνάβαν, Δία [2]· τὸν δὲ Παῦλον,

[1] ηλλετο, but ηλατο ℵABC 61, Vulg., Sah., Boh., Chrys., so Tisch., W.H., R.V.,
Wendt, Weiss. D, Syr. H. mg. (Flor.), Hilg. have και ευθεως παραχρημα ανηλατο,
so Vulg., Gig. ανηλ. for ηλ. (εξηλ. E).

[2] Δια ℵABCP, Syr. H. mg., so Weiss, W.H., Blass in β; Διαν DEHLP² 15, 40,
61, so Hilg.; cf. Grimm-Thayer and Winer-Schmiedel, p. 89.

Ver. 11. ἐπῆραν τὴν φ. αὐτῶν: aorist;
lifted up their voices with a sudden outburst, and then went on to devise names
for the two: ἐκάλουν, "were for calling,"
imperfect; cf. Luke i. 54 (Rendall). The
phrase here only found in ii. 14,
xxii. 22 and Luke xi. 27; Friedrich, p.
29, cf. LXX, Judg. ix. 7; phrase also
found in classical Greek.—οἱ ὄχλοι: the
common city mob; the crowd, who
would speak in their own native tongue.
The Apostles had evidently spoken in
Greek, which the native Lycaonians
would understand and speak, Church
in the Roman Empire, p. 57. But in
moments of excitement their native
tongue would rise more naturally to
their lips, and they would give expression
to their old superstitious beliefs, see
Church in the Roman Empire, p. 58,
and Wendt (1888), p. 313.—Λυκαονιστὶ:
specially mentioned not only on account
of its naturalness here (see above) but
also because, as St. Chrysostom noted,
this mention of the fact would explain
why Paul and Barnabas made no protest.
Bethge's objection that ὁμοιοπαθεῖς (ver.
15) shows that St. Paul understood the
words of ver. 11 is no answer, because
the preparations for the sacrifice, rather
than the words of the people, enabled
the Apostles to understand the bearings
of the scene. On the speech of L. see
Conder, Palestine Explor. Fund, October,
1888.—Οἱ θεοὶ κ.τ.λ.: the knowledge of
the story of Baucis and Philemon, according to which Jupiter and Mercury visited
in human form the neighbouring district,
Ovid, Met., viii., 611 ff., would render such
words quite natural (cf. Fasti, v., 495, and
Dio Chrys., Orat., xxxiii., p. 408). Baur,
Zeller, and Overbeck, followed by Wendt,
object that the people would not have
thought of such high gods, but rather of
magicians or demons, and the latter
evidently thinks that St. Luke has
coloured the narrative by introducing
into it the form which in his opinion the

adoration of the Apostles would assume;
but the same narrative emphasises the
fact that the miracle was a notable one,
and we can scarcely limit the bounds of
excitement on the part of a superstitious
people who were wont to make their
pilgrimages to the spot where Jupiter
and Mercury conversed with men. At
Malta a similar result follows from the
miracle of Paul, and heathen mythology
was full of narratives of the appearances
of high gods, which were by no means
strange to N.T. times (see Holtzmann's
note, Hand-Commentar, p. 378). Moreover, the people, rude as they were, might
easily have seen that Paul and Barnabas
were not altogether like the common
magicians of the day. The main incident,
McGiffert admits, was entirely natural
under the circumstances, and is too striking and unique to have been invented,
Apostolic Age, pp. 188, 189.
Ver. 12. ἐκάλουν, see above on ver.
11.—τὸν μὲν Β. Δία· τὸν δὲ Π. Ἑρμῆν.
The relative estimate of the Lycaonians
was strikingly in accordance with Oriental notions—Barnabas, the more silent
and passive, is identified with Jupiter;
and Paul, the more active, with Mercury.
Ramsay, Church in the Roman Empire,
p. 57; St. Paul, pp. 84, 85; McGiffert,
Apostolic Age, p. 189. With the reason
given for the identification of Paul
with Mercury, cf. Iamblichus, De Myst.
Ægypt., i., where Mercury is designated
as Θεὸς ὁ τῶν λόγων ἡγεμών (see also
Wetstein). The comparison could not
have been because of the Apostle's insignificant appearance (although the
fact that he was the younger of the two
men may be taken into account), since
Hermes is always represented as of
a graceful well-formed figure. On the
traditional accounts of Paul's personal
appearances see Wendt (1888), in loco,
Blass, Renan, and Plumptre, Acts (Excursus, pp. 191, 192). It is of interest to
note that in Gal. iv. 14 Paul writes to

Ἑρμῆν, ἐπειδὴ αὐτὸς ἦν ὁ ἡγούμενος τοῦ λόγου.¹ 13. ὁ δὲ ἱερεὺς
τοῦ Διὸς τοῦ ὄντος πρὸ τῆς πόλεως² αὐτῶν, ταύρους καὶ στέμματα

¹ Flor. om. ἐπειδη αυτος . . . του λ., and Blass brackets, comparing xvii. 18, xviii. 3, where some Western authorities omit explanatory clause. Ramsay also rejects clause, St. Paul, p. 117, but Hilg. retains. It is quite possible that in these cases the Western reading may be original, and the explanation may have been added later.

² D reads του οντος Διος προ πολεως (Blass accepts, so Hilg., adding της before πολ.), and D, Gig. read οι ιερεις, so Hilg. (Blass rejects), so D reads επιθυειν, so Hilg. (not Blass). Ramsay, C. R. E., p. 51, and St. Paul, p. 118, defends all these readings as indications of local accuracy; see notes. Perhaps he forces too much his rendering of ἐπιθύειν.

the Galatians: "Ye received me as a messenger of God," Ramsay, St. Paul, p. 117.
Ver. 13. ὁ δὲ ἱερεύς. Plural in D; strongly rejected by Blass, with other details. Ramsay defends D (p. 118), and points out that at each of the great temples in Asia Minor a college of priests would be in regular service: see also Church in the Roman Empire, pp. 52, 53.—τοῦ Διὸς τοῦ ὄντος πρὸ τῆς π. αὐτῶν, see critical notes. R.V., omitting αὐτῶν, renders "whose temple was before the city," i.e., enshrined in the temple outside the gate as the protecting deity. Zöckler, with Ramsay, compares "Ζεὺς Προάστιος" on an inscription at Claudiopolis, cf. also παρὰ Διΐ (=ad fanum Jovis), παρ' Ἥρῃ, and modern, the name of a church in Rome, "S. Paolo fuori le mura" (see also Holtzmann and Wendt). Here again the reading of D seems to bring out the technical force of the phrase more accurately, τοῦ ὄντος Δ. πρὸ πόλεως (so Blass in β)—possibly = Προπόλεως (cf. an unpublished inscription of Smyrna with the phrase ἱέρεια πρὸ πόλεως or Προπόλεως). In this phrase, as read in D, the force of the participle is retained in a way characteristic of Acts, as almost = τοῦ ὀνομαζομένου: see on xiii. 1, a characteristic lost by the transposition of ὄντος; see on the whole question Ramsay, Church in the Roman Empire, p. 51 ff., and also on the possible site of the temple. The words cannot refer to the statue of Jupiter (so lately Rendall), to which no priests would be attached. See Blass in Studien u. Kritiken, 1900, p. 27, n. 1.—ταύρους καὶ στέμματα: brought by the ministri who would be included in the generic term priests. On the sacrifice of a bull to Jupiter, Ovid, Met., iv., 755, as also to Mercury, Persius, Sat., ii., 44. On the garlands to wreathe and adorn the victims, Æneid, v., 366; Eur., Heracl., 529, perhaps also for the priests and the

altars, the doors, and the attendants; see instances in Wetstein, and cf. Tertullian, De Corona, x. The words do not refer to the Apostles; the aim seems to be indicated in ἤθελε θύειν.—ἐπὶ τοὺς πυλῶνας: some see a reference to the gates of the city, mainly because of the collocation τοῦ ὄντος πρὸ τῆς Π. Blass supposes that the priest came from the temple outside to the city gates, but in that case Ramsay urges that Lucan usage would = πύλη rather than πυλών, cf. ix. 24, xvi. 13. Others take it of the gates of the temple in front of which the altar stood, cf. οἱ μὲν ἱεροὶ τοῦ νεὼ πυλῶνες, Plut., Tim., xii. Ramsay suggests that the priests probably prepared their sacrifices at the outer gateway of the temple grounds, as something beyond the usual ritual, and so not to be performed at one of the usual places, cf. ἐπιθύειν D; St. Paul, p. 119. Others again refer the words to the gates leading into the atrium or courtyard of the house in which the Apostles were lodging, partly on the ground that the word ἐξεπήδησαν is best referred to the house (cf. Judith xiv. 17, and Susannah, ver. 39). But the verb may mean that they ran hastily out of the city to the temple, and there mingled with the crowd: in 2 Macc. iii. 18 the same verb is used of a general rush of the people to the temple for supplication to heaven.—ἤθελε θύειν: What was his motive? Was he acting in good faith, or out of complaisant regard to the wishes of the multitude (Ewald), or for the sake of gain? On the attitude of the native priests see Ramsay, Church in the Roman Empire, p. 144. In the present instance it would appear that they had known of the Apostles' preaching for some time at all events, and also, it may be, of its success, cf. D., xiv. 7, critical notes, and apparently they were willing to honour the Apostles with divine honours, and to turn the religious revival to their own ends.

ἐπὶ τοὺς πυλῶνας ἐνέγκας, σὺν τοῖς ὄχλοις ἤθελε θύειν. 14. Ἀκούσαντες δὲ οἱ ἀπόστολοι [1] Βαρνάβας καὶ Παῦλος, διαρρήξαντες τὰ
ἱμάτια αὐτῶν εἰσεπήδησαν [2] εἰς τὸν ὄχλον, κράζοντες καὶ λέγοντες,
15. Ἄνδρες, τί ταῦτα ποιεῖτε; καὶ ἡμεῖς ὁμοιοπαθεῖς ἐσμεν ὑμῖν
ἄνθρωποι, εὐαγγελιζόμενοι ὑμᾶς ἀπὸ τούτων τῶν ματαίων ἐπιστρέφειν
ἐπὶ τὸν Θεὸν τὸν ζῶντα,[3] ὃς ἐποίησε τὸν οὐρανὸν καὶ τὴν γῆν καὶ τὴν

---

[1] οι αποστολοι om. D, Flor., Gig., Syr. Pesh., Blass "recte". Weiss thinks om.
caused because offence was taken at the extension of the title to Barnabas. In ver. 4
Barnabas is not expressly mentioned, while here he is not only mentioned by name
but placed first.

[2] εισεπηδησαν, but εξεπ. ℵABCDE 13, 61, Chrys., so Tisch., W.H., R.V., Blass,
Weiss, Wendt, Hilg.

[3] επι τον Θεον τον ζωντα ℵcABCD2E 13, 40, 61, Ath., so Tisch., W.H., R.V.,
Weiss, Wendt; cf. Blass, Gram., p. 144. D has ευαγγ. υμιν τον Θεον (so Iren.),
and again επι τον Θεον ζωντα τον ποιησαντα, thus reading τον Θεον in both places
(whilst Blass in β and Hilg. follow Flor. in omitting τον Θεον the second time).
Ramsay however also retains the words in both places, as "the God" was the title
under which the supreme God was worshipped in Asia Minor, St. Paul, p. 118.

Ver. 14. ἀκούσ.: how, we are not told;
whether, as Blass supposes, they had
returned to their lodgings, and hurried
forth to the city gates when they heard
what was going on, or whether, later in
the day, they hurried from the city to the
temple when they heard of the approaching sacrifice, we do not know, and a
better knowledge of the localities would
no doubt make many points clearer.
The crowd who had seen the miracle,
ver. 11, would naturally be eager to
follow the priest to the sacrifice, σὺν
τοῖς ὄχλοις, ver. 13.—διαρρήξαντες: in
token of distress and horror, cf. Gen.
xxxvii. 29, 34; Josh. vii. 6; Matt. xxvi.
65; frequently in LXX, and several
times in 1 Macc.—εἰσεπήδησαν: xvi.
29, see critical notes.
Ver. 15. ἄνδρες: brief address in accordance with the hurry of the moment.
—ὁμοιοπαθεῖς, James v. 17, "of like
passions," so R.V. in both passages, but
'nature' in margin, so Ramsay. But to
others the latter word seems too general,
and they explain it as meaning equally
capable of passion or feeling, as opposed
to the ἀπάθεια of the idols; or, equally
prone to human weakness, and not all-
powerful as the people seemed to infer
from the miracle (Bethge); whilst others
again take it as meaning ὁμοίως θνητός
(so Blass). On its meaning in Wisdom
vii. 3 see Grimm, sub v., and Speaker's
Commentary. In 4 Macc. xii. 13 it is
also used to mark the atrocious nature
of persecution inflicted by one who, a
man himself, was not ashamed τοὺς

ὁμοιοπαθεῖς γλωττοτομῆσαι: cf. its use
in medical writers and in classical Greek
(Wetstein); by the Fathers it was used
of our Lord Himself, Euseb., H. E.,
i., 2, cf. Heb. iv. 15 (see Mayor on James
v. 17).—εὐαγγελιζ.: we preach not ourselves—Paul was a "messenger of God"
in a higher sense than the people
conceived; on the construction see
above p. 210 and Simcox, Language of
the N. T., p. 79. For reading in D see
critical note = bringing you glad tidings
of "the God"—in Asia Minor a familiar
term for the great God, so that just as
St. Paul introduces the Christian God at
Athens as "the Unknown God," whom
the Athenians had been worshipping, so
here he may have used a familiar term
known to the crowd around him at Lystra,
Ramsay, St. Paul, p. 118.—ἐπιστρέφειν
ἐπὶ, cf. especially 1 Thess. i. 9, in Acts
ix. 35, xi. 21, xv. 19, xxvi. 20; on the
construction see Wendt, and Weiss, in
loco, cf. iv. 18, v. 28, 40, infinitive after
παραγγέλλειν.—τὸν ζῶντα, see critical
note.—τούτων: may be used contemptuously, as if St. Paul pointed to the preparations for the sacrifice.—ματαίων,
cf. Jer. ii. 5, x. 3, of the gods of the nations
and their worship, cf. also 2 Kings xvii.
15 B, Jer. viii. 19; cf. Rom. i. 21, Ephes.
iv. 17. R.V. and A.V. take it as neuter,
others as masculine, sc., Θεῶν.—ὃς ἐποίησε
κ.τ.λ., cf. especially Jer. x. 11, 12-15, 16,
for the contrast between the gods who
are no gods, and the God Who made the
heavens, and cf. also Acts xvii. 24 for a
similar appeal from the same Apostle.

θάλασσαν καὶ πάντα τὰ ἐν αὐτοῖς· 16. ὃς ἐν ταῖς παρῳχημέναις
γενεαῖς εἴασε πάντα τὰ ἔθνη πορεύεσθαι ταῖς ὁδοῖς αὐτῶν· 17.
καίτοιγε¹ οὐκ ἀμάρτυρον ἑαυτὸν ἀφῆκεν, ἀγαθοποιῶν,² οὐρανόθεν ἡμῖν
ὑετοὺς διδοὺς καὶ καιροὺς καρποφόρους, ἐμπιπλῶν τροφῆς καὶ

¹ καιτοιγε ℵ*C³HLP 61**, Chrys., Theodt.; καιτοι ℵcABC* 13, 61*, so Tisch.,
W.H., Blass, R.V., Weiss, Wendt; καιγε DE, so Hilg. (see Wendt's note (1888),
p. 312); cf. xvii. 27.

² αγαθοποιων, but ℵABC 13, 61, 180 αγαθουργων, and so Tisch., W.H., Blass,
R.V., Weiss, Wendt.

The "living" God manifests His life in creation—a manifestation to which St. Paul would naturally appeal before such an audience; even in writing to Christian converts of the deepest mysteries of the faith he does not forget that the God of Nature and the God of Redemption are one, cf. Ephes. iii. 9, R.V.; so too St. Peter prefaces the first Christian hymn with the same words used here by the Apostle of the Gentiles, iv. 24. On the tact of St. Paul at Lystra and at Athens, laying the foundation of his teaching as a wise master-builder in the truths of natural religion, and leading his audience from them as stepping-stones to higher things, see notes on xvii. That he did not even at Lystra confine his teaching or his appeal simply to Nature's witness, see notes on vv. 22 and 23.

Vv. 16-17. ὃς: God working not only in creation, but in history, not only the source of life but the personal living Guide and Ruler of man, even in His tolerance far removed from the easy indifference of the gods of Olympus. The three present participles ἀγαθ. . . . διδ. . . . ἐμπ. . . . mark the continuous activity and goodness of God, and are all three epexegetical of ἀμάρτυρον; whilst the second participle is generally regarded as specifying a mode of the first, and the third as expressing a consequence of the second.—οὐρανόθεν: only again in xxvi. 13 in N.T., see 4 Macc. iv. 10; so n Hom. and Hes., old genitive of οὐρανός. —ὑετοὺς διδοὺς καὶ καιροὺς καρπ.: the Apostle's appeal becomes more significant when we remember that Zeus was spoken of as ὑέτιος, ἐπικάρπιος (Bethge); the rain was regarded in the East as a special sign of divine favour, and here, as in the O.T., God's goodness and power in this gift are asserted as against the impotence of the gods of the heathen, see especially Jer. xiv. 22, and cf. 1 Kings xviii. 1 and 1 Sam. xii. 17 where this same phrase ὑετ. διδόναι is used of God.—καρπ. :

here only in N.T., cf. LXX, Jer. ii. 21, Ps. cvi. 34, and also classical; cf. for the whole passage Cicero, De Nat. Deorum, ii., 53.—ἐμπιπλῶν (ἐμπιπλάω), cf. Luke i. 53, vi. 25, Rom. xv. 24, John vi. 12, frequent in LXX, e.g., Ps. cvi. 9, Isa. xxix. 19, Jer. xxxviii. 14, Ecclus. iv. 12; see also below on εὐφροσ.—καρδίας: Blass compares Luke xxi. 34, where the heart is spoken of as overcharged with surfeiting, as here it is spoken of as filled with food. But the word may be used not merely as = ὑμᾶς, or in a merely material sense, but as including the idea of enjoyment, cf. LXX, Ps. ciii. 15 ; Winer-Moulton, xxiii. 1, and Alford on James v. 5.— εὐφροσύνης: in its ordinary Greek use might simply mean "good cheer," although we need not limit it here with Grotius to wine as in Ecclus. xxxi. 28 ; very frequently used in LXX (only here and in ii. 28 in N.T.), sometimes of mere festive joy, Gen. xxxi. 27, sometimes of religious gladness, Deut. xxviii. 47. Although St. Paul could not have used it here as it is employed in ii. 28, yet he might perhaps have used it as a kind of transition word to lead his hearers on to a deeper gladness of heart, a richer gift of God than corn and wine, cf. Ps. iv. 7, and for the phrase ἐμπ. εὐφροσ. Isa. xxix. 19, Ecclus. iv. 12. It may well be that whilst we have in this address the germ of the thoughts afterwards developed in Rom. i. 18, 23, etc., St. Paul did not press his argument on this occasion as in his Epistle, but took the first step to arrest the attention of his hearers by an appeal to the goodness, not to the severity, of God—the goodness which leadeth to repentance. It has been thought that the words οὐρ. ἡμῖν διδούς κ.τ.λ. are rhythmical, and may have been some familiar fragment of a song, or a citation from a Greek poet, in which the Apostle expressed his thoughts; others have maintained that they may have formed part

εὐφροσύνης τὰς καρδίας ἡμῶν.[1] 18. καὶ ταῦτα λέγοντες, μόλις[2] κατέπαυσαν τοὺς ὄχλους τοῦ μὴ θύειν αὐτοῖς.

19.[3] Ἐπῆλθον δὲ ἀπὸ Ἀντιοχείας καὶ Ἰκονίου Ἰουδαῖοι, καὶ πείσαντες τοὺς ὄχλους, καὶ λιθάσαντες τὸν Παῦλον, ἔσυρον ἔξω τῆς

---

[1] ημιν . . . ημων, but υμιν . . . υμων ℵ*BCDE, Syr. Harcl., Arm., Ir., Ath., so Tisch., W.H., Blass, R.V., Weiss, Wendt, Hilg. ; υμιν however is om. by ℵcA 13, 61, Vulg.

[2] μόλις, D reads μογις, and for κατεπαυσαν . . . αυτοις Flor. has "vix persuaserunt ne immolarent sibi illi homines" (so Blass in β, cf. Hilg.). C, many min., and Syr. H. mg. add αλλα πορευεσθαι εκαστον εις τα ιδια, cf. v. 18 D, John vii. 53 ; Flor. adds "et discedere eos ab se" (so Blass in β preceding previous addition ; Hilg. omits).

[3] At the begin. of verse CDE (Flor. Cassiod.), Syr. H. mg., Arm., Bed. read διατριβοντων δε αυτων και διδασκοντων evidently to show that the outbreak did not ensue immediately upon the intended worship. D, Flor., Syr. H. mg. (E, Vulg.) insert τινες before Ιουδ. and change order. C, Syr. H. mg., Flor. proceed και διαλεγομενων αυτων παρρησια επεισαν τους οχλους αποστηναι απ' αυτων ("ne crederent illis docentibus," Flor.), λεγοντες οτι ουδεν αληθες λεγουσιν αλλα παντα ψευδονται— so Blass throughout in β, and Hilg., see Belser, p. 71, in support, on the ground that β thus explains fully the change in the attitude of the people ; but the whole might proceed from a reviser, and need not be original.

---

of the hymn sung in the procession for the sacrifice, and that St. Paul made the words his text ; see Humphry, in loco ; Farrar, St. Paul, i., p. 384 ; Felten, in loco ; but it may be fairly said that the O.T. language was in itself quite sufficient to suggest the Apostle's words. On the remarkable parallels between this speech and the sayings of Pseudo-Heracleitus in his letters see Gore, Ephesians, p. 253 ff., but see also Bernays, Die Heraklitischen Briefe, p. 29.—πάντα τὰ ἔθνη: "all the Gentiles," R.V., the words divided mankind into two classes, but there was the same Lord over all, Rom. iii. 29.— ἐν ταῖς παρῳχ. γενεαῖς: "in the generations gone by," R.V. παρῳχ.: not in LXX or Apocrypha, but classical, and used also by Josephus.—εἴασε (cf. xvii. 30, Rom. iii. 25, 26) . . . πορεύ. ταῖς ὁδοῖς αὐτῶν, i.e., without summoning them as now to repent, cf. for the combination ix. 31, and for the expression 2 Cor. xii. 18, Jude v. 11, James v. 20 (in classical Greek cf. Thuc., iii., 64, ἄδικον ὁδὸν ἰέναι), cf. also the contrast between God's ways and the wilfulness of Israel in the past, Ps. lxxxi. 13 and previous verses, expressed in the same phraseology.

Ver. 17. καίτοιγε, see critical notes. If we read καίτοι the word is only found in the N.T. here and in Heb. iv. 3 ; used here as an adversative conjunction ; see Simcox, Language of the N. T., p. 168, and further Blass, Gramm., pp. 242, 264 ; Viteau, Le Grec du N. T., p. 118 (1893) ;

see 4 Macc. ii. 6.—ἀμάρτυρον: not in LXX or Apocrypha ; only here in N.T., but in classical Greek, and also in Josephus, see instances in Wetstein. This witness is not as at Athens, xvii. 27, Rom. ii. 15, to man's consciousness and conscience, but rather to God's presence in nature, cf. for the expression LXX, Ps. lxxxviii. 37, ὁ μάρτυς ἐν οὐρανῷ πιστός, and Pseudo-Heracleitus, letter iv., where the moon is spoken of as God's οὐράνιος μαρτυρία ; see below on ver. 17.—οὐκ ἀφῆκεν: non reliquit sed sivit (Blass), see critical notes. Neither ἀγαθοποιῶν, ἀγαθουργέω nor ἀγαθοεργέω, 1 Tim. vi. 18, occur in classical Greek or LXX. T.R. uses the more familiar word ; found three times in Luke's Gospel and elsewhere in N.T., and also a few times in LXX (in different senses), but not in classical Greek ; see Plummer on Luke vi. 33, and Hatch, Essays in B. G., p. 7.

Ver. 18. μόλις: used only by Luke and Paul (with one exception of a quotation, 1 Pet. iv. 18), Luke ix. 39, W.H. ; four times in Acts, and Rom. v. 7.— κατέπαυσαν τοῦ μὴ, x. 47, Burton, N. T. Moods and Tenses, pp. 159, 184.

Ver. 19. ἐπῆλθον δὲ: on readings to account for the interval see critical notes. Nothing in the narrative forbids some kind of interval, whilst nothing is said as to its duration.—Ἰουδαῖοι: a proof of their enmity in that they undertook a long journey of some one hundred and

πόλεως, νομίσαντες¹ αὐτὸν τεθνάναι. 20.² κυκλωσάντων δὲ αὐτὸν τῶν μαθητῶν, ἀναστὰς εἰσῆλθεν εἰς τὴν πόλιν· καὶ τῇ ἐπαύριον ἐξῆλθε σὺν τῷ Βαρνάβᾳ εἰς Δέρβην. 21. εὐαγγελισάμενοι³ τε τὴν πόλιν ἐκείνην, καὶ μαθητεύσαντες ἱκανούς, ὑπέστρεψαν εἰς τὴν Λύστραν

¹ νομίζοντες ℵABD 13, 40, 61, so Tisch., W.H., Blass, R.V., Weiss, Wendt, Hilg.

² Flor. reads "tunc circumdederunt eum discentes et cum surressisset (x) populus vespere . . ." Par.² adds μογις before ανασ., so Blass in β; cf. Belser, p. 71.

³ εὐαγγελισαμενοι ℵcBCL 61, Bas., Chrys., so W.H., Blass, R.V.; ευαγγελιζομενοι ADEHP, Lach., Tisch., Weiss, Wendt, Hilg., the aor. part. probably a mechanical conformity to the following part.

thirty miles.—πείσαντες τοὺς ὄ.: *mobile vulgus*. The change in their attitude need not surprise us, *cf.* the fickleness of the inhabitants of Malta, xxviii. 6, and, more notably still, the change of feeling in the multitudes who could cry Hosannah! and Crucify! The Scholiast, Homer, *Il.*, iv., 89-92, has ἄπιστοι γὰρ Λυκάονες, ὡς καὶ ᾿Αριστοτέλης μαρτυρεῖ. These Jews may have received help from their fellow-countrymen, some few of whom were resident in Lystra, xvi. 1, or possibly, as McGiffert suggests, it may have been easy to incite the populace against Paul and Barnabas, because of the Apostles' rejection of the divine honours offered to them. But probably the persuasion implies that they influenced the multitudes to regard the miracle, the reality of which they could not dispute, as the work not of beneficent gods but of evil demons. The form of punishment, λιθάσαντες, would seem at all events to point to Jewish instigation, although the stoning took place not outside but inside the city, *cf.* 2 Cor. xi. 25, 2 Tim. iii. 11, and Wendt (1888), p. 318, as against Zeller. In Gal. vi. 17 the Apostle may allude to the scars marked on him by these same people (Ramsay, Zahn), *cf.* also Clem. Rom., *Cor.*, v. 6. λιθασθείς: "Uti Paulus prius lapidationi Stephani consenserat: ita nunc veterem culpam expiat, 2 Cor. xi. 25" (Wetstein). On the undesigned coincidence between this narrative and the notice in 2 Tim. *cf.* Paley, *Horæ Paulinæ*, xii., 5. Hilgenfeld refers this verse to his "author to Theophilus," but the change in the multitude and the hatred of the Jews are not surprising, but perfectly natural. —ἔσυρον: perhaps as a last indignity, *cf.* viii. 3, xvii. 6.—νομίσαντες: St. Luke's words do not require us to infer that St. Paul was rendered lifeless, and we need not suppose that he was more than stunned. But at the same time the

narrative undoubtedly leads us to recognise in St. Paul's speedy recovery from such an outrage, and his ability to resume his journey, the good hand of God upon him. We may again notice St. Luke's reserve in dwelling on the Apostle's sufferings, and his carefulness in refraining from magnifying the incident. Ver. 20. κυκλ.: Bengel says "tanquam sepeliendum," and others have held the same view, but the word need not imply more than that the disciples surrounded him, to help if human aid could profit, and to lament for him in his sufferings. Amongst the mourners the youthful Timothy may well have found a place. On Timothy's means of knowing of the Apostle's sufferings here narrated see Paley, *Horæ Paulinæ, u. s.*—μαθητῶν: the Apostles' work had not therefore been unsuccessful: there were converts willing to brave persecution, and to avow themselves as disciples.—τῇ ἐπαύριον: the journey to Derbe was one of some hours, not free from risk, and the mention of Paul's undertaking and finishing it on the morrow indicates how wonderfully he had been strengthened in his recovery. The word is found ten times in Acts, and not at all in Luke's Gospel, but *cf.* αὔριον Luke x. 35, Acts iv. 5 only; Hawkins' *Horæ Syn.*, p. 144. It occurs three times in chap. x., no less than in the second half of the book.—σὺν τῷ Β.: apparently he had been free from attack, since Paul was the chief speaker, and consequently provoked hostility.

Ver. 21. εὐαγγελ.: continuous preaching, present participle, and the result, many disciples; not "having taught many," A.V., but "had made many disciples," R.V., *cf.* Matt. xxviii. 19. No doubt they pursued the same course as at Lystra, and again we have direct proof that the teaching of the Gospel was not in vain: it is therefore quite unwarrantable to suppose that Paul's

καὶ Ἰκόνιον καὶ Ἀντιόχειαν, 22. ἐπιστηρίζοντες τὰς ψυχὰς τῶν
μαθητῶν, παρακαλοῦντες ἐμμένειν τῇ πίστει, καὶ ὅτι διὰ πολλῶν
θλίψεων δεῖ ἡμᾶς εἰσελθεῖν εἰς τὴν βασιλείαν τοῦ Θεοῦ. 23.
χειροτονήσαντες δὲ αὐτοῖς πρεσβυτέρους κατ᾽ ἐκκλησίαν, προσευξάμενοι μετὰ νηστειῶν, παρέθεντο αὐτοὺς τῷ Κυρίῳ εἰς ὃν

speech at Lystra indicates the powerlessness of the message of the Gospel in
contact with deep-rooted heathenism
(Bethge) ; in vv. 22, 23 we have abundant proof that Paul had not limited his
first preaching in Lystra to truths of
natural religion, for now on his return
the disciples are bidden ἐμμένειν τῇ
πίστει, and they are commended to the
Lord, εἰς ὃν πεπιστεύκεισαν, "on whom
they had believed". No persecution is
mentioned at Lystra, with which cf. 2
Tim. iii. 11.—ὑπέστρεψαν: how they
were able to do this after they had been
recently expelled, cf. Ramsay, Church in
the Roman Empire, p. 70 ff., and McGiffert,
Apostolic Age, pp. 190, 191—no permanent
disability could be inflicted on them by
the magistrates, and the person expelled
might return after a little, especially if new
magistrates had been appointed in the
interim. Moreover, on their return journey the Apostles may have refrained
from open and public preaching, and
devoted themselves rather to the organisation of the Christian communities. (There
is therefore no ground for Hilgenfeld's and
Wendt's reference of ver. 19 to a different
source from the verse before us.) At the
same time the courage of the Apostle is
also noteworthy: "neque enim securum
petit, ubi instar emeriti militis otio fruatur,
sed etiam repetit loca, in quibus paullo
ante male tractatus fuerat," Calvin.

Ver. 22. ἐπιστηρίζοντες: only in Acts,
cf. xv. 32, 41 ; for the simple verb see
xviii. 23 (W.H., R.V.), and Luke xxii. 32,
and six times in St. Paul's Epistles, frequent in LXX, but not in any similar
sense, although for the simple verb cf.
Ps. li. (l.) 12.—ἐμμένειν, Gal. iii. 10, Heb.
viii. 9, two quotations : in the former,
with the simple dative ; in the latter,
with ἐν ; several times in LXX, and with
both constructions, cf. Xen., Mem., iv., 4.
—τῇ πίστει: subjective or objective, as
a feeling of trust, or a belief, a creed ?
That it was used in the latter sense by St.
Paul we cannot doubt, in such passages as
Col. i. 23, 1 Tim. v. 8 (cf. 1 Pet. v. 9, Jude
vv. 3, 20), and St. Luke may have used the
word in this latter sense in recording the
incident. But cf. also vi. 7, xiii. 8, where
the word may be used, as perhaps here,

in a kind of intermediate stage.—ὅτι, cf.
xi. 3, xv. 1, we have the language of the
preachers themselves, but it is precarious
to conclude that ἡμᾶς includes the presence of the author of the book, St. Luke
himself. The ἡμᾶς may simply mean that
the speakers thus associated themselves
with their hearers, and drew a general
lesson similar to that drawn by St. Paul
in 2 Tim. iii. 12, as he looked back upon
these same sufferings at the close of his
life. The teaching thus expressed may
have struck deep root in the heart of one
of St. Paul's hearers—why not Timothy ?
—and have been repeated by him to St.
Luke as the Apostle had uttered it ; see
further in its bearing on the date, Ramsay, St. Paul, p. 123. Alford's note
strongly maintains that Luke himself
was present, see in loco and also Proleg.,
pp. 6, 7. On the possibility that the
words contain an Agraphon of the Lord
see Resch, Agrapha, pp. 148, 278, and
cf. Epist. Barn., vii., 11.—θλίψεων, cf.
xx. 23, quite a Pauline word, not used by
Luke at all in his Gospel (five times
in Acts), cf. 1 Thess. iii. 3 and ii. 12, and
Epist. Barn., u. s. On St. Paul's reference
to "the kingdom of God," sometimes as
future, sometimes as actually present,
see Witness of the Epistles, p. 311, note
(1892).

Ver. 23. χειροτονήσαντες δὲ αὐτοῖς
πρεσβ., see above, x. 41, where the compound verb is used, "chosen of God,"
ὑπὸ Θ. The simple verb is only used
here and in 2 Cor. viii. 19 : lit., to elect by
popular vote, by show of hands, but it is
by no means a word of certain meaning,
and came to be used, as Ramsay admits,
in the sense of appointing or designating.
Here evidently the word is not used in
the literal sense given above, as Paul and
Barnabas appoint, and that the idea of
popular election did not necessarily belong
to the word, at least in later Greek, is
evident from Josephus, Ant., vi., 13, 9,
τὸν ὑπὸ τοῦ Θεοῦ κεχειροτονημένον
βασιλέα : cf. xiii. 2, 2, of the appointment of Jonathan as high priest by Alexander. On the later use of the word, of
which there is no early trace, as referring
to the stretching out of the bishop's
hands in the laying on of hands, cf.

πεπιστεύκεισαν. 24. καὶ διελθόντες τὴν Πισιδίαν, ἦλθον εἰς Παμ-
φυλίαν· 25. καὶ λαλήσαντες ἐν Πέργῃ [1] τὸν λόγον, κατέβησαν εἰς

---

[1] ἐν Πέργῃ ℵcBCDEHLP, so Lach., W.H. text, Rendall, Hilg.; εἰς τὴν Π. ℵ*A (without art.) 61, so Tisch., W.H. marg., Weiss, Wendt, Blass—the change of εν into εις is quite inconceivable, so Weiss, who compares other frequent uses of εις as characteristic of Acts ii. 5, ix. 21 (*Apostelgeschichte*, p. 36).

"Ordination" (Hatch, *Dict. of Chr. Ant.*, ii., p. 1501 ff.). Blass takes the word here as = καθιστάναι, and compares Titus i. 5, although he thinks that nothing is said here about the mode of election, and that the Church may have had some share in it. So too Ramsay compares the same passage, Titus i. 5, and concludes that St. Paul doubtless followed there the same method which he followed here, a method in which the votes and voices of each congregation were considered, cf. 2 Cor. viii. 19. But the office to which Luke was appointed in 2 Cor., *l. c.*, was not an office which involved ordination, and we could not argue from it alone to the method of the appointment of elders in the passage before us. At the same time it may be fully admitted that the Church was not without some share in the election of the elders, and it must not be forgotten that, in the case of the Seven, the Church had elected, and the Apostles had ordained, Acts vi. 3. In Clem. Rom., *Cor.*, xliv., whilst the Apostles took care to secure that after their death distinguished men should appoint presbyters and deacons, yet the latter were elected *with the consent of the whole Church*, and they were exposed, as it were, to the judgment of the Church (see on this voice of the Church, Moberly, *Ministerial Priesthood*, p. 89, and Gore, *Church and the Ministry*, p. 100 ff.). If we compare the language of Acts vi. 3, Tit. i. 5, Clem. Rom., *Cor.*, xliii., 4, xliv., 2, 3, and the use of the verb καθίστημι in each, it would seem that the κατάστασις was throughout reserved to the Apostles or their representatives, whilst the Church, if not always selecting, may at least be regarded as consenting, συνευδοκησάσης τῆς ἐκκλησίας πάσης, Clem. Rom., *u. s.*, xliv., 3; see "Bishop" (Haddan), *Dict. of Chr. Ant.*, i., p. 213. But, further, in the passage before us it is not impossible that the choice as well as the ordination of the presbyters may be referred to Paul and Barnabas, cf. the pronoun αὐτοῖς: "having appointed for them," and in newly founded communities it was not unnatural that the Apostles should

exercise such choice and authority. On the use of the verb in the *Didaché*, xv., 1, and its compatibility with ordination in accordance with Apostolic practice and injunction, see Gore, *Church and the Ministry*, p. 281; and further, *Church Quarterly Review*, 42, p. 265 ff., on the strictures passed by Loening, *Die Gemeindeverfassung*, 61, 62.—κατ' ἐκκλησίαν, "in every Church," distributive, ii. 46, v. 42, cf. Titus i. 5, Clem. Rom., *Cor.*, xlii., 4. On the spread of Christianity in Asia Minor see additional note at end of chapter.—προσευξ. μετὰ νησ.: Ramsay, *St. Paul*, p. 122, speaks of the solemn prayer and fasting which accompanied the appointment of the elders, and of this meeting and rite of fasting, as the form permanently observed, cf. xiii. 1-3. The two participles χειροτ. and προσευξ. evidently refer to the appointment, and not to the subsequent commendation. See also Harnack, Proleg. to *Didaché*, p. 148; and on the other hand, Overbeck, Wendt, Weiss, Zöckler.—παρέθεντο, xx. 32, cf. Luke xii. 48, xxiii. 46, 1 Pet. iv. 19, cf. 1 Tim. i. 18, 2 Tim. ii. 2 (in no parallel sense in the other Evangelists). In the first three passages above used as here of solemn committal to God; also of giving into another's charge or keeping, cf. παραθήκη, 1 Tim. vi. 20, 2 Tim. i. 12, 14. In classical Greek of money or property entrusted to one's care. In Tobit x. 12 (cf. i. 14, iv. 1, 20) both verb and noun are found together, παρατίθεμαί σοι τὴν θυγατέρα μου ἐν παραθήκη S (see Hatch and Redpath).—αὐτοὺς may refer to the believers in general, cf. Hort, *Ecclesia*, p. 66.—τῷ Κ., *i.e.*, Christ, as the πιστεύω indicates: the phrase πιστ. εἰς, or ἐπί τινα, is peculiarly Christian, cf. Lightfoot on Gal. ii. 16.

Ver. 24. διελ. τὴν Π. "having made a missionary journey through Pisidia," see above on xiii. 6. Here it seems clearly implied that Pisidian Antioch was not in Pisidia, see above on xiii. 14, and Ramsay, *St. Paul*, p. 124.

Ver. 25. καὶ λ. ἐν Πέργῃ τὸν λόγον: in the beginning of their journey they probably made a slight stay at Perga, but without preaching there—possibly

'Ατταλειαν· 26. κἀκεῖθεν ἀπέπλευσαν εἰς 'Αντιόχειαν, ὅθεν ἦσαν παραδεδομένοι τῇ χάριτι τοῦ Θεοῦ εἰς τὸ ἔργον ὃ ἐπλήρωσαν.

for the reason mentioned above which prompted them to hurry on to Antioch, and possibly because, as C. and H. (so Felten) think, the inhabitants at the time of the Apostles' first visit were all leaving Perga for the cool mountain districts, their summer retreats, whereas on the return journey of the missionaries Perga would again be full (C. and H., pp. 131, 158, smaller edition).—ἐν Π., see critical notes. — κατέβησαν, went down, i.e., to the sea coast where Attalia lay, cf. xvi. 8 (xiii. 4), Jonah i. 3, so in classical Greek ἀναβαίνω, to go up from the coast.—'Ατταλειαν: mentioned because it was the harbour of embarkation, and so called from Attalus II. Philadelphus, king of Pergamus, its builder, B.C. 159-138; is a port for the trade of Egypt and Syria, Strabo, xiv., 4. It bears the modern name of Adalia, and until quite recent days it was the chief harbour of the south coast of Asia Minor. See B.D.[2], and Hastings' B.D., "Attalia" (Ramsay). The distance from Perga was about sixteen miles, and the travellers would reach it across the plain: formerly they had gone up the Cestrus to Perga, and probably they now go to Attalia to find a ship for Antioch. See Hackett, in loco, and C. and H.

Ver. 26. κἀκεῖθεν, cf. vii. 3, and Luke xi. 53, in six other places in Acts in a local sense as here, only once elsewhere in N.T., in Mark ix. 30, in same sense; see also xiii. 21.—ἦσαν παραδεδομ.: "they had been committed," R.V., in xv. 40 "commended"; in both passages A.V. "recommended," a rendering which has changed its meaning; only in these two passages in this sense, but cf. 1 Pet. ii. 23 (John xix. 30).—ὃ ἐπλήρωσαν, cf. xii. 25, xiii. 25, still, as hitherto, St. Paul found the χάρις of God "sufficient".

Ver. 27. συν. τὴν ἐκκλ., cf. xv. 30, as was natural, for they had been sent out by them.—ἀνήγγειλαν: xv. 4 (xx. 20, 27), lit., to carry back tidings (so in classical Greek, as from a less to a greater), cf. 2 Cor. vii. 7; used here as in Æschylus, Xen., Polyb., of messengers reporting what they had seen or heard (Grimm). Blass takes it as simply = ἀπαγγέλλω as in LXX and later Greek. —ὅσα: "how many (or 'how great') things". — μετ' αὐτῶν, i.e., on their behalf; cf. xv. 4, Luke i. 58, 72, x. 37, cf. 1 Sam. xii. 24, Ps. cxxvi. 2,

3, Hebrew עָשָׂה עִם, Ps. cxix. 65, and cannot = per ipsos, which would require διά—the phrase may therefore be described as a Hebraism; it occurs only in Luke; Friedrich, p. 33.—ὅτι ἤνοιξε . . . θύραν: a striking coincidence with St. Paul's use of the same metaphor elsewhere, cf. 1 Cor. xvi. 9, 2 Cor. ii. 12, Col. iv. 3, and cf. Rev. iii. 8. St. Paul's Galatian Epistle clearly shows that his missionary work in Galatia had met with much success, and that the Churches now founded held a large place in his affections, cf. Gal. iv. 14, 15. Enough had been accomplished, even if all his desires were still unfulfilled, to make him eager for a continuation of the work to which he had been called as an Apostle of the Gentiles, see McGiffert, Apostolic Age, pp. 191, 192; Hort, Ecclesia, p. 66: "perhaps the greatest epoch in the history of the Ecclesia at large": Spitta refers the whole verse to his Redactor, p. 171.

Ver. 28. χρόνον οὐκ ὀλίγον: only in Acts, where it occurs eight times, cf. xii. 18, etc.; on the length of time thus spent see "Chronology of the N.T.," Hastings' B.D., and also Ramsay, Church in the Roman Empire, p. 74, with which cf. Lewin, Fasti Sacri, p. 288.

Additional Note.—In chapters xiii. and xiv. many critics find the commencement of a new source, a belief based to a great extent upon the view that Barnabas and Saul are here introduced as if they had not been previously mentioned. But whilst some description is given of each of the remaining persons in the list (xiii. 1), nothing is added to the name of Barnabas or of Saul, so that it seems quite permissible to argue that these two are thus simply mentioned by name because they were already known. It is therefore not surprising to find that some writers, e.g., Hilgenfeld, regard these chapters as part of a previous source, so too Wendt, Spitta, Jüngst. Others see in these chapters a separate document, possibly not used again by the author of Acts; a document composed by a different hand from that to which we owe the "We" sections, and incorporated by the author of the whole book into his work (McGiffert). Others again see in these same chapters the commencement of a Travel-Document, containing not only these two chapters, but also the later journeys of St. Paul, coming to us from

27. παραγενόμενοι δὲ καὶ συναγαγόντες τὴν ἐκκλησίαν, ἀνήγγειλαν[1]
ὅσα ἐποίησεν ὁ Θεὸς μετ᾽ αὐτῶν, καὶ ὅτι ἤνοιξε τοῖς ἔθνεσι θύραν
πίστεως.　28. διέτριβον δὲ ἐκεῖ χρόνον οὐκ ὀλίγον σὺν τοῖς μαθηταῖς.

---

[1] ανηγγειλαν, but imperf. אABC 18, 40, 61, Syr. Pesh., Boh., Tisch., W.H., R.V.,
Weiss, Wendt—Blass and Hilg. follow T.R.　For μετ᾽ αυτων D, Gig., so Hilg.,
read μετα των ψυχων αυτων, perhaps Syriac influence (Harris).　Blass brackets
και οτι . . . θ. πιστεως without any authority, and adds the same words to xv. 4,
see below l. c.

the same hand as the "We" sections,
and from the same hand as the rest of
the book (Ramsay).　It is disappointing
to find how Clemen, while referring xiii.,
xiv. to his good source, *Historia Pauli*,
goes even further than Spitta in breaking
up the different parts of the narrative:
e.g., xiv. 8-11, we owe to the Redactor
Judaicus, and vv. 19, 20, 22*b*, 23 in
the same chapter to the Redactor Anti-
Judaicus.　(See on the whole question
Hilgenfeld, *Zeitschrift für wissenschaft.*
Theol., 1e Heft, 1896; Wendt (1899),
p. 225, note; Zöckler, *Apostelgeschichte*,
pp. 243, 244 (second edition).)　It is no
wonder in face of the unsatisfactory
attempts to break up these chapters, or
to separate their authorship from that
of the rest of the book, that Zahn should
maintain that a man like Luke needed for
the composition of chapters xiii.-xxviii.
no other source than his recollections of
the narratives recited by St. Paul himself, or of the events in which he, as
St. Paul's companion, had participated,
Einleitung in das N. T., ii., 412 (1899),
cf. Nösgen, *Apostelgeschichte*, pp. 25, 26.
Certainly the unity of authorship between
the two chapters under consideration and
the rest of the book seems most clearly
marked in language and style: *e.g.*,
κατασείειν, xiii. 6, only found elsewhere
in N.T., Acts xii. 17, xix. 33, xxi. 40;
ἐπαίρειν τὴν φωνήν, xiv. 11, only elsewhere in N.T., Luke xi. 27, Acts ii. 14,
xxii. 22; παραχρῆμα, xiii. 11, elsewhere
in N.T., ten times in Luke's Gospel (only
twice in St. Matthew, and not at all in
the other Evangelists), Acts iii. 7, v. 10,
xii. 23, xvi. (26), 33; ἦν, with participle,
xiii. 48, xiv. 7, 12, 26; δή, xiii. 2; ἄχρι,
xiii. 6, 11; ἱκανός with χρόνος, xiv. 3,
elsewhere in N.T. in Luke only, and
eight times in Acts in all parts; ἀτενίζειν
in xiii. 9 and xiv. 9 and the frequent recurrence of τέ in both chapters.　It is
also perhaps worthy of observation that
out of some twenty-one words and phrases
found only in the "We" sections, and in
the rest of Acts (Hawkins, *Horæ Synop-*
ticæ, p. 151), six occur in these two

chapters, and two of them twice : ἀπο-
πλέω, xiii. 4, xiv. 26; διατρίβω with
accusative of time, xiv. 3; ἔξειμι, xiii.
42; ἡμέραι πλείους, xiii. 31; προσκέκλημαι with accusative, xiii. 2, 7; ὑπονοέω,
xiii. 25.　On the position of these two
chapters relatively to chap. xv. see below.
Additional note on xiv. 23.—On the
rapid spread of Christianity in Asia
Minor see Ramsay, *Cities and Bishop-*
rics of Phrygia, i., pp. 87, 94, 95, 135-
137, and *Church in the Roman Em-*
pire, pp. 161, 397.　The old nature
religion with its negation of moral distinctions and family ties was doomed, a
religion which on the one hand made
woman the head of the family, and on
the other hand compelled her to a so-
called sacred service which involved the
surrender of all which in a civilised
community womanhood held most dear.
The strength of the old ritual, however,
was so great that it seems to have been
maintained in Phrygia even after a higher
type of society became known in the
Roman period.　But with the growth of
Roman organisation and educational influences the minds of men were at least
prepared for new ideas, and at this
juncture St. Paul came preaching a
gospel of home life, of Christian purity;
and wherever higher social ideas had
already penetrated he found converts
disposed to follow his teaching as "a more
excellent way".　In connection with the
wide spread of Christianity in Asia Minor
see also Orr, *Some Neglected Factors in*
the Study of the Early Progress of
Christianity, p. 48 ff. (1899).

CHAPTER XV.—Ver. 1. τινες κατελ.
ἀπὸ τῆς Ἰ.: on the vagueness of the
expression see Ramsay, *St. Paul*, pp.
158, 159.—κατελ., *i.e.*, to Antioch; see
critical notes for β reading, and additional
note at end of chapter on the identification of Gal. ii. 1-10 with Acts xv.: in
the early Church in favour of the identification, *cf.* Iren., *Hær.*, iii., 13, 3;
Tertullian, *Adv. Marc.*, v., 2.—ἐδίδασκον:
imperfect, representing perhaps their continuous efforts to force their teaching on

XV. 1. ΚΑΙ τινες κατελθόντες ἀπὸ τῆς Ἰουδαίας ἐδίδασκον τοὺς
ἀδελφούς, Ὅτι ἐὰν μὴ περιτέμνησθε¹ τῷ ἔθει Μωϋσέως, οὐ δύνασθε

¹ περιτεμνησθε, but περιτμηθητε ℵABCD 13, 40, 180, Const. Apost., Epiph., so
Tisch., W.H., Blass, R.V., Weiss, Wendt, Hilg. After ιουδαιας Syr. Harcl. mg.,
8, 137 add των πεπιστευκοτων απο της αιρεσεως των Φαρισαιων, obviously anticipating ver. 5. After Μωυσεως Const. App. add και τοις αλλοις απασιν (εθεσιν)
οις διεταξατο περιπατητε: in D, Syr. Harcl. mg. (Sah.) after περιτ. και τω εθει Μ.
περιπατητε, cf. xxi. 21. Blass in β follows Const. App. The Western reading
may be original, but it may also be due to assimilation to ver. 5 and xxi. 21.

the brethren.—περιτέμνησθε, see critical
note.—τῷ ἔθει Μ.: R.V. as in vi. 15,
"custom of Moses"; in A.V. "manner,"
which might be used of a temporary
fashion or habit; ἔθος marks a national
custom, but see also Deissmann, *Neue
Bibelstudien*, p. 79. On its national
significance, see art. "Circumcision,"
B.D.², and Hastings' B.D., "Beschnei-
dung"; Hamburger, *Real-Encyclopädie
des Judentums*, i., 2, 174; Weber,
Jüdische Theol., p. 266 (1897); Renan,
Saint Paul, p. 66; and cf. *Book of
Jubilees*, xv., cf. i.; *Assumption of Moses*,
viii.; Jos., *Ant.*, xx., 2, 4; *c. Apion.*, ii.,
14; *Vita*, xxiii.—σωθῆναι, i.e., in the
Messianic salvation, cf. ii. 40, iv. 12, xi.
14. On the tradition that Cerinthus was
amongst these Judaisers, as he and his
had already rebuked Peter, Acts xi. 2,
see "Cerinthus," *Dict. of Christ. Biog.*,
i., 447. It is very probable that the
successful mission of Paul and Barnabas
was really the immediate cause of this
protest on the part of the narrow Judaic
party. This party, as the Church in
Jerusalem grew, may well have grown
also; the case of Cornelius had been
acquiesced in, but it was exceptional, and
it was a very different thing to be asked
to embrace all Gentiles in the new covenant, and to place them on a level with
the Jewish Christians, whether they did
homage or not to the Mosaic law, Hort,
Ecclesia, p. 67; McGiffert, *Apostolic Age*,
p. 192.
Ver. 2. στάσεως: the word, with the
exception of Mark xv. 7, and Heb. ix. 8
(in a totally different sense), is peculiar
to St. Luke: twice in his Gospel, and
five times in Acts; used in classical
Greek of sedition, discord, faction, and
so of the factious opposition of parties in
the state; frequent in LXX, but only
once in any similar sense, Prov. xvii. 14.
—συζητήσεως, but ζητ.: "questioning,"
R.V., cf. John iii. 25; three times in St.
Paul, 1 Tim. vi. 4, 2 Tim. ii. 23, Tit.
iii. 9, in a depreciatory sense in each
case; not in LXX or Apocrypha.—οὐκ

ὀλίγης, see on xii. 18 and xiv. 28; eight
times in Acts.—ἔταξαν, sc., οἱ ἀδελφοὶ,
ver. 1; no discrepancy with Gal. ii. 2,
see additional note.—τινας ἄλλους: Titus
amongst them, Gal. ii. 1, 3; expression
found only here in N.T.; men like the
prophets and teachers in xiii. 1 may have
been included. On the attempt to identify
Titus with Silas see Zöckler, *in loco*,
and further Ramsay, *St. Paul*, p. 390, for
the entire omission of Titus from Acts and
its probable reason; Lightfoot, *Biblical
Essays*, p. 281; Farrar, *St. Paul*, ii., 532;
Alford, iii., 106, Proleg. A Gentile convert, and so keenly concerned in the
settlement of the question, and in himself
a proof of the "repentance unto life"
granted to the Gentiles.—πρεσβ.: first
mentioned in xi. 30, cf. note, in all official
communications henceforth prominent,
xv. 2, 4, 6, 22, 23, xvi. 4, xxi. 18, Lightfoot, *Phil.*, p. 193.—ζητήματος: five
times in Acts, nowhere else in N.T.;
once in LXX, Ezek. xxxvi. 37 A (see
Hatch and Redpath), and in classical
Greek; "question," A. and R.V.
Ver. 3. οἱ μὲν οὖν: Phœnicia and
Samaria on the one hand welcome them
with joy, but on the other hand the
Church in Jerusalem is divided, ver. 5,
see Rendall, Appendix on μὲν οὖν, p.
161. Blass however thinks that the
words are used "without opposition" as
often.—διήρχοντο τὴν Φ. καὶ Σ., see note
on xiii. 6. In both cases the presence of
brethren is presupposed, cf. viii. 25, xi.
19, imperfect, "peragrabant donec pervenerunt," ver. 4 (Blass).—προπεμφ.:
escorted on their way, not as Tit. iii. 13,
of being provided with necessaries for
the journey (Wisdom xix. 2); cf. xx. 38,
xxi. 5, and so in classical Greek, only in
Luke and Paul in N.T. (except once,
3 John 6), cf. Rom. xv. 24; but in 1
Cor. xvi. 6, 11, 2 Cor. i. 16, R.V. renders
as in Titus, *l. c.*, and John, *l. c.*; cf. 1
Esd. iv. 47, Judith x. 15, 1 Macc. xii. 4,
see Grimm-Thayer, *sub v.*; Polycarp,
Phil., i., 1, of the conduct of St. Ignatius
through Macedonia, amongst the early

σωθῆναι. 2. γενομένης οὖν στάσεως καὶ συζητήσεως [1] οὐκ ὀλίγης τῷ
Παύλῳ καὶ τῷ Βαρνάβᾳ πρὸς αὐτούς, ἔταξαν ἀναβαίνειν Παῦλον καὶ
Βαρνάβαν καί τινας ἄλλους ἐξ αὐτῶν πρὸς τοὺς ἀποστόλους καὶ
πρεσβυτέρους εἰς Ἰερουσαλήμ, περὶ τοῦ ζητήματος τούτου. 3. οἱ
μὲν οὖν προπεμφθέντες ὑπὸ τῆς ἐκκλησίας, διήρχοντο τὴν Φοινίκην
καὶ Σαμάρειαν, ἐκδιηγούμενοι τὴν ἐπιστροφὴν τῶν ἐθνῶν · καὶ ἐποίουν
χαρὰν μεγάλην πᾶσι τοῖς ἀδελφοῖς. 4. παραγενόμενοι δὲ εἰς Ἰερουσαλήμ, ἀπεδέχθησαν [2] ὑπὸ τῆς ἐκκλησίας καὶ τῶν ἀποστόλων καὶ τῶν

[1] συζητησεως, but ζητησεως ℵABCDHLP, Const., Apost., Chrys., so Tisch.,W.H.,
Blass, R.V., Weiss, Wendt. Blass in β reads without authority εγενετο δε στασις
και ζητησις ουκ ολιγη, to give good construction, and on the supposition that all
authorities have been influenced by α. After αυτους D, Syr. Harcl. mg., Gig., Wer.,
Prov. add ελεγεν γαρ ο Π. μενειν (εκαστον) ουτως καθως επιστευσεν διισχυριζομενος ;
cf. ι Cor. vii. 17, 20, 24. Hilg. brackets all this. διισχυριζ. only in Luke in N.T.,
Luke xxii. 59, Acts xii. 15 (Zahn). In place of εταξαν D, Syr. Harcl. mg. read οι
δε εληλυθοτες απο Ιερ. παρηγγειλαν αυτοις. The subject of εταξαν is probably
the Antiochian Christians, the brethren, vv. 1 and 3, but "those from Jerusalem"
was assumed to be the subject, and so to remove all doubt the gap was supplied as
above, and παρηγγειλαν appeared more fitting than εταξαν, which seemed too dic-
tatorial when applied to men in the high position of Paul and Barnabas (Weiss,
Codex D, p. 80). Blass reading αυτοις omits Π. και Β. . . . εξ αυτων. But D,
which alone has αυτοις, has the rest as well, and it is uncertain whether αυτοις
ever stood alone. After εις Ι. D 137, Syr. Harcl. mg. insert οπως κριθωσιν επ'
αυτοις (137, αυτων) περι τ. ζητηματος τουτου, cf. xxv. 9 ; so Blass and Hilg.

[2] απεδεχθησαν, but παρεδεχ. ℵABD² 61, so Tisch., W.H., R.V., Wendt, Weiss,
Hilg. ; Blass retains T.R. ; D¹ has παρεδοθησαν. υπο ℵADEHLP 31, 61, Chrys.,
so Tisch., Blass, Hilg. ; απο BC 18, 180, W.H., Weiss, Wendt (as the more probable). After παρεδ. CD 137, Syr. Harcl. mg., Sah., Cassiod. insert μεγαλως, so
Blass and Hilg., but ασμενως, xxi. 17, would seem to be a fitter word ; D¹ has μεγως.
At end of verse C³HL add και οτι ηνοιξεν τοις εθνεσιν θυραν πιστεως, cf. xiv. 27,
where all authorities read it ; Blass however inserts it here (so also Hilg.) on the
ground of its suitability and rejects it in the former passage ; see also Blass, p. xv.

Christians, as amongst the Jews (Gen.
xviii. 16), a mark of affection and
respect. The meaning of the word,
as Wendt points out, depends on the context.—ἐκδιηγ. : only here and in quotation, xiii. 41 in N.T., "telling the tale of
the conversion of the Gentiles"; so διη-
γεῖσθαι and ἐξηγεῖσθαι more frequently
in Luke than in other N.T. writers.
Hobart describes all three as medical
terms but all three also occur frequently
in LXX. ἐκδ. : cf. Hab. i. 5 ; several
times in Ecclus., also in Josephus and
Arist. (Grimm-Thayer, sub v.).—χ. μεγάλην : on Luke's fondness for the predicate
μέγας, Friedrich, p. 41, with χαρά as
here, cf. Luke ii. 10, xxiv. 52, Acts viii.
8 (Matt. ii. 10, xxviii. 8), cf. LXX, Jon.
iv. 6, Isa. xxxix. 2, A. S.—ἐποίουν, imperfect, continuous joy, as they went
from place to place, perhaps visiting
Cornelius or Philip the Evangelist, viii.
40, in their progress. — ἐπιστροφὴν :
only here in N.T. (cf. 1 Thess. i. 9),
Ecclus. xviii. 21 (20), xlix. 2.

Ver. 4. Council at Jerusalem.—
παραγεν., Lucan, see above on v. 21.
—ἀπεδέχθησαν—if we read παρεδέχ.,
cf. 2 Macc. iv. 22 (but see Hatch and
Redpath) ; with the idea of receiving
with welcome, cf. Mark iv. 20, Heb. xii. 6
(quotation); see Syn. δέχ. and λαμβ.,
Grimm-Thayer ; in classical Greek = ὑπο-
δέχομαι. — ὑπὸ τῆς ἐκκ. : the whole
Church is regarded as concerned in the
matter ; as present at the public discussion in ver. 12 and as concurring in the
decision, ver. 22 (30) ; the decree is issued
by the Apostles and Elders, see on ver.
23.—μετ' αὐτῶν, see above on xiv. 27.
Ver. 5. For D see critical note.—
ἐξανέστησαν : compound verb in this
sense here only in N.T. (only elsewhere
in quotation, Mark xii. 19, Luke xx. 28),
but in classical Greek and in LXX,
cf. Obad. i. 1, Ecclus. viii. 11, xvii. 23, 1
Macc. ix. 40. The double compound
apparently gives at least some measure of
emphasis, Simcox, Language of the N. T.,
p. 43.—τινες τῶν ἀπὸ τῆς αἱρ. τῶν Φ. :

πρεσβυτέρων, ἀνήγγειλάν τε ὅσα ὁ Θεὸς ἐποίησε μετ᾽ αὐτῶν.   5.
ἐξανέστησαν ¹ δέ τινες τῶν ἀπὸ τῆς αἱρέσεως τῶν Φαρισαίων πεπισ-
τευκότες, λέγοντες, Ὅτι δεῖ περιτέμνειν αὐτούς, παραγγέλλειν τε
τηρεῖν τὸν νόμον Μωϋσέως.   6. Συνήχθησαν δὲ οἱ ἀπόστολοι καὶ οἱ
πρεσβύτεροι ² ἰδεῖν περὶ τοῦ λόγου τούτου.

¹ D, Syr. Harcl. mg. begin verse οι δε παραγγειλαντες αυτοις αναβαινειν προς
τους πρεσ. εξανεστησαν λεγοντες, so Blass in β, so Hilg., but with αποστολους
instead of πρεσβ., Blass "male," omitting τινες . . . πεπιστευκοτες. According
to this reading the Jerusalem Christians who stirred up the disputed question in
Antioch are now identified with those who rise up against Paul and Barnabas in
Jerusalem.   A.V. margin, following Beza and some of the older commentators,
make this sentence part of the narrative of Paul and Barnabas, "there rose up, said
they (ελεγον)," etc.   Weiss, Völter, Spitta, see here a proof of a combination of two
sources.   But there does not seem to be any reason why, as in T.R., the Pharisees
at Jerusalem should not represent the same point of view as had been presented by
the Jews who had come down to Antioch; that they did so with accentuated bitterness in Jerusalem is quite in accordance with the notice in Gal. ii. 4, but this fact
need not exclude the previous raising of the question against the Apostles in
Antioch, especially as the Jews who had come thither from Jerusalem were plainly
not merely Jews but Judaisers.   See Wendt (1899), following Meyer, and for a
favourable judgment of the Bezan text Salmon, Introd., p. 598; see also Hilgenfeld,
Zeitschrift für wissenschaft. Theol., i., 1896, and Acta Apost., p. 246, 1899; on the
other hand Weiss, Codex D, p. 80, and Wendt (1899), Introd., p. 49, and on this
occasion Zahn, Einleitung, ii., p. 344.

² After πρεσβ. 137, Syr. Harcl. mg. add συν τω πληθει so Blass in β, and Hilg.
The πληθος here, although not mentioned except in authorities just named, is plainly
presupposed in vv. 12 and 22, and Wendt (1899) opposes the view that we have
before us in its omission elsewhere a trace of distinct sources.

probably in some smaller and more
private assembly in answer to the ἀνήγγ.
of ver. 4, which seems to mean that the
delegates at first announced informally
in Jerusalem what had happened, just as
they had done in Phœnicia and Samaria,
cf. παρείσακτοι ἀδελφοί, Gal. ii. 4.   The
Pharisees took up their remarks, objected
—probably basing their teaching on the
necessity of circumcision on such passages as Isa. lvi. 6, cf. lii. 1 (Lumby);
and then followed as a consequence the
official assembly in ver. 6 (see Zöckler's
note, ver. 4, and in loco, p. 246, second
edition).   Or if we consider that a representative meeting of the whole Church
is implied in ver. 4, and that the Apostles
spoke before it, then the private conference of Gal. ii. 2 may be regarded as
taking place between the first public
assembly, ver. 4, and the second in ver.
6 (Hort, Ecclesia, p. 69, cf. Lightfoot,
Galatians, p. 126).—αἱρέσεως, see above
p. 148.—τῶν Φ.: the Pharisaic spirit had
already shown itself in xi. 2, but this is
the first definite mention in the book of
the conversion of any of the Pharisees;
not strange after the conversion of the
priests, see note on vi. 7, or after the

attitude of men like Nicodemus or Joseph
of Arimathæa towards our Lord, and the
moderate counsels of Gamaliel.—πεπισ-
τευκότες: believed, i.e., that Jesus was
the Messiah, and the fulfiller of the law
—but still only as the Head of a glorified
Judaism, from which Gentiles were to be
rigidly excluded unless they conformed to
the enactments relating to circumcision.
How difficult it was for a Pharisee Quietist
probably of the earlier part of the first
century to acknowledge that the law of
circumcision and of Moses could possibly
be regarded as unessential we may learn
from Assumption of Moses, ix., 4-6, and
viii., on circumcision, and see references
on ver. 1.—αὐτούς, i.e., the Gentiles,
speaking generally, not the τινας ἄλλους
of ver. 2 (Lekebusch), the uncircumcised
companions of Paul and Barnabas, although in accordance with Gal. ii. 3-5
such persons would no doubt have been
included.—τηρεῖν: only used here by St.
Luke of keeping the law, and only elsewhere in James ii. 10 in a similar phrase,
cf. Mark vii. 9, John ix. 16, of keeping the
law of the Sabbath; Matt. xix. 17, of
keeping the commandments; Tobit xiv.
9 (S, al.), Jos., Ant., xiii., 10, 6.

7. Πολλῆς δὲ συζητήσεως [1] γενομένης, ἀναστὰς Πέτρος εἶπε πρὸς αὐτούς, Ἄνδρες ἀδελφοί, ὑμεῖς ἐπίστασθε ὅτι ἀφ᾽ ἡμερῶν ἀρχαίων ὁ Θεὸς ἐν ἡμῖν ἐξελέξατο [2] διὰ τοῦ στόματός μου ἀκοῦσαι τὰ ἔθνη τὸν λόγον τοῦ εὐαγγελίου, καὶ πιστεῦσαι. 8. καὶ ὁ καρδιογνώστης Θεὸς ἐμαρτύρησεν αὐτοῖς, δοὺς αὐτοῖς τὸ Πνεῦμα τὸ Ἅγιον, καθὼς καὶ ἡμῖν· 9. καὶ οὐδὲν διέκρινε μεταξὺ ἡμῶν τε καὶ αὐτῶν, τῇ πίστει καθαρίσας τὰς καρδίας αὐτῶν. 10. νῦν οὖν τί πειράζετε τὸν Θεόν,[3] ἐπιθεῖναι ζυγὸν ἐπὶ τὸν τράχηλον τῶν μαθητῶν, ὃν οὔτε οἱ πατέρες

---

[1] συζητησεως, but ζητησεως as in ver. 1 אAB, so Tisch., W.H., Blass, R.V., Weiss, Wendt. Meyer retains T.R. with Lach. (so Hilg. and Blass) on the ground of alteration to ζητ. after ver. 1.

[2] εν ημιν εξελ., but εν υμιν אABC 13, 40, 61, Arm., Const., so Tisch., W.H., R.V., Weiss, Wendt (as against Meyer, Blass, Hilg.).

[3] After πειραζετε one Latin MS. and several Latin Fathers omit τον Θεον. Blass says "recte fort.," but does not follow in β. But no need to omit the words or to regard πειραζειν = πειρασθαι (Wendt in loco).

Ver. 6. λόγου: "de causâ quæ in disceptationem venit" (Blass), cf. viii. 21, xix. 38. The Ecclesia at large was in some manner also present at this final assembly, cf. vv. 12, 22, although the chief responsibility would rest with the Apostles and Elders, cf. Iren., Hær., iii., chap. xii. 14, " cum universa ecclesia convenisset in unum," Zöckler, in loco, p. 246, and cf. p. 254 ; Hort, Ecclesia, pp. 66, 70, and see critical notes above.

Ver. 7. ἀναστὰς, Lucan, see v. 17 ; the position of Peter is one of authority, not of pre-eminence—the latter belongs to James. The part which Peter had formerly taken in the conversion of Cornelius would naturally make him the most fitting person to introduce the discussion. From Gal. ii. 3 we learn that the general principle was debated with reference to the individual case of Titus.—ἀφ᾽ ἡμερῶν ἀρχαίων : " a good while ago," meaning probably from the beginnings of the Christian Church, cf. xi. 15, xxi. 16 ; cf. Phil. iv. 15 (see Lightfoot's note, l. c.), and cf. Clem. Rom., Cor., xlvii., 2, and Polycarp, Phil., i., 2 ; or, if the words are referred to the one definite incident of the conversion of the Gentile Cornelius, some ten or twelve years (Blass, " fortasse ") may have passed since that event, possibly longer, see Zöckler, Page, Knabenbauer, in loco. Others take the words as referring to our Lord's declaration to St. Peter as long ago as at Cæsarea Philippi, Matt. xvi. 13-20; see Speaker's Commentary, so Bishop Williams of Connecticut, Studies in the Book of Acts, p.

139 (1888). Rendall connects ἐν ἡμῖν with ἀρχ. on the ground that thus the whole phrase would point to early Christian days, whereas, without qualification, confusion as to its meaning would arise, cf. ver. 21. But a reference to the case of Cornelius need not exhaust the meaning of the phrase, and St. Peter would naturally think of his own choice by God as going back earlier still, dating from the foundation of the Church, and receiving its confirmation and significance in the acceptance of the Gospel by Cornelius.—ἐξελέξατο, see on i. 2.—τοῦ εὐαγγ. : not used by St. Luke in his Gospel, but here and in xx. 24 ; used once by St. Peter, 1 Pet. iv. 17 ; so also εὐαγγελίζομαι, three times in the same Epistle.

Ver. 8. ὁ καρδιογνώστης, i. 24, where the same word is used by St. Peter ; cf. Jer. xvii. 10. ἐτάζων καρδίας, and cf. St. Peter's words in x. 34.—καθὼς καὶ ἡμῖν, x. 44, xi. 15.

Ver. 9. τῇ πίστει καθαρίσας τ. κ. : the thought is described by Zöckler as equally Petrine, Pauline, and Johannine; cf. iii. 16, 19, 1 Pet. i. 18-21, xiii. 38, Rom. iii. 24, 1 John i. 8, ii. 2, Rev. vii. 14; here it stands in contrast to the outward purification of circumcision upon which the Judaisers insisted, cf. also x. 15, and for the phrase καθαρ. τὴν κ., Ecclus. xxxviii. 10. Rendall renders τῇ πίστει, the faith, i.e., the Christian faith, and he is no doubt right in this, in so far as the faith is faith in Jesus Christ (Schmid, Bibl. Theol. des N. T., pp. 424, 425), cf. St. Peter's language in 1 Pet. i. 18-22.

ἡμῶν οὔτε ἡμεῖς ἰσχύσαμεν βαστάσαι; 11. ἀλλὰ διὰ τῆς χάριτος Κυρίου Ἰησοῦ Χριστοῦ πιστεύομεν σωθῆναι, καθ᾿ ὃν τρόπον κἀκεῖνοι. 12.[1] Ἐσίγησε δὲ πᾶν τὸ πλῆθος, καὶ ἤκουον Βαρνάβα καὶ Παύλου ἐξηγουμένων ὅσα ἐποίησεν ὁ Θεὸς σημεῖα καὶ τέρατα ἐν τοῖς ἔθνεσι

[1] D, Syr. Harcl. mg. prefix συγκατατιθεμενων δε των πρεσβυτερων τοις υπο του Πετρου ειρημενοις, so Blass and Hilg., an addition which shows why the multitude kept silence, and connects Peter's speech with Paul and Barnabas. Weiss, p. 84, sees here the characteristic love of D for the gen. abs., cf. ii. 1, iv. 18, etc., and notes that the same stress is here laid as in ver. 5 upon the πρεσβυτεροι rather than upon the Apostles.

Ver. 10. νῦν οὖν: in Acts four times, nowhere else in N.T.; cf. x. 35, nunc igitur: LXX, Gen. xxvii. 8, etc.; 1 Macc. x. 71.—τί πειράζετε τὸν Θ., cf. v. 9, they put God to the proof, as to whether He had not admitted unworthy persons into the Church.—ἐπιθ. ζυγὸν: on the infinitive see Burton, N. T. Moods and Tenses, p. 151; Blass, Gram., p. 221: metaphor common among the Rabbis, and also in classical literature, cf. Jer. v. 5, Lam. iii. 27, Ecclus. li. 26 (Zeph. iii. 9), and Matt. xi. 29 (Luke xi. 46), Gal. v. 1. Possibly in Jer. v. 5 reference is made to the yoke of the law, but Psalms of Solomon, vii., 8, cf. xvii., 32, present undoubted instances of the metaphorical use of the term "the yoke" for the service of Jehovah. In Sayings of the Jewish Fathers, iii., 8 (Taylor, second edition, p. 46), we have a definite and twice repeated reference to the yoke of Thorah, cf. Apocalypse of Baruch, xli., 3 (Charles' edition, p. 66 and note), and also Psalms of Solomon, Ryle and James, p. 72, note. It would seem therefore that St. Peter uses an almost technical word in his warning to the first Christians.—τῶν μαθητῶν, i.e., of those who had learnt of Christ and knew the meaning of His yoke, Matt. xi. 29.— ἰσχ. βαστάσαι: cf. xiii. 39. St. Peter no less than St. Paul endorses the charge made by St. Stephen, vii. 53.—οὔτε ἡμεῖς: a remarkable confession on St. Peter's lips: the conversations with Paul and Barnabas, Gal. ii. 7, may well have confirmed the attitude which he had taken after the baptism of Cornelius (Zöckler). Ver. 11. διὰ τῆς χ.: twice in his First Epistle St. Peter speaks of the grace of God, of the God of all grace; so also of the grace prophesied beforehand, of the grace brought to them, cf. also iii. 7 and 2 Pet. iii. 18. The exact phrase here is not found elsewhere in St. Peter, although common in St. Paul, but see Plumptre (Cambridge Bible) on 1

Pet. v. 12. In R.V. σωθῆναι is joined more clearly with διά than in A.V.— κἀκεῖνοι, i.e., the Gentile Christians, not οἱ πατέρες (as St. Aug. and Calvin). For points of likeness between these, the last words of St. Peter in Acts, and his previous utterances, with characteristic idioms and expressions, see Alford on Acts xv. 7 ff., cf. Schmid, Bibl. Theol. des N. T., p. 427. Ver. 12. ἐσίγησε: may mean "became silent," "itaque antea non tacuerant" (Blass), cf. Burton, N.T. Moods and Tenses, 21, A. and R.V., "kept silence". —πᾶν τὸ πλῆθος: implying a general assembly of the Church; on the word see ii. 6, iv. 32, etc.—ἤκουον: imperfect, marking a continuous hearing; the silence and the audience both testified to the effect produced by St. Peter's words. Βαρ. καὶ Π., on the order here and in ver. 25 cf. Ramsay, St. Paul, p. 84.— ἐξηγουμένων: setting forth in detail; see above on ver. 3, and x. 8.—ὅσα ἐποί., cf. xiv. 27 and ver. 4. In each case the appeal is made to what God had done, and to the further answer to the prayer of iv. 30 by the miracles wrought among the Gentiles: it was an answer which a Jewish audience would understand, John iii. 2. The historical truthfulness of Paul and Barnabas thus recounting the facts, and leaving the actual proof of the rightfulness of their method of working to Peter and James, is to Zeller inconceivable—an objection sufficiently answered by the consideration that Luke wished to represent not so much the attitude of Paul and Barnabas, but that of the original Apostles to the Gentile-question; and in Jerusalem it was only natural that Peter and James should be the spokesmen. Ver. 13. μετὰ δὲ τὸ σ., i.e., after Barnabas and Paul had ceased speaking. —ἀπεκ. Ἰ. λ.: his speech may be divided into two parts: (1) reference to the prophecy foretelling the reception of the

δι' αὐτῶν. 13. Μετὰ δὲ τὸ σιγῆσαι αὐτούς, ἀπεκρίθη Ἰάκωβος λέγων, Ἄνδρες ἀδελφοί, ἀκούσατέ μου· 14. Συμεὼν ἐξηγήσατο, καθὼς πρῶτον ὁ Θεὸς ἐπεσκέψατο λαβεῖν ἐξ ἐθνῶν λαὸν ἐπὶ[1] τῷ ὀνόματι αὐτοῦ· 15. καὶ τούτῳ συμφωνοῦσιν οἱ λόγοι τῶν προφητῶν, καθὼς γέγραπται, 16. "Μετὰ ταῦτα ἀναστρέψω καὶ ἀνοικοδομήσω τὴν σκηνὴν Δαβὶδ τὴν πεπτωκυῖαν· καὶ τὰ κατεσκαμμένα[2] αὐτῆς

---

[1] επι, but om. ℵABCDE 61, Vulg., Sah., Syr. P. and H., Arm., Iren., Const., Rebapt., so Tisch., W.H., R.V., Blass, Weiss, Wendt, Hilg.

[2] κατεσκαμμενα ACDEHLP, Const., Chrys., so Lach., Blass in β, and Hilg.; κατεστραμμενα ℵ(B) 13, 33, 34, so Tisch., W.H., R.V., Wendt, Weiss. Similar variation in the passage in LXX.

Gentiles; (2) his opinion on the conditions of that reception. ἀ. ἀκούσατέ μου: only here and in James ii. 5.—Ver. 14. Συμεὼν: Peter so named only here and in 2 Pet. ii. 1. The use of the word here in its old Hebrew form by James is exactly what we should expect, cf. Luke ii. 25, 34, W.H.; probably therefore the form current in Jerusalem, a form which reappears in the list of the successors of St. James in the bishopric of the Holy City, Eusebius, H. E., iv., 5, cf. Luke xxiv. 34, from which also it would appear that the Hebrew name of Peter, in the contracted or uncontracted form, was current in Jerusalem.—πρῶτον like ἀπ' ἀρ. ἡμ. in ver. 7.—ἐπεσκέψατο, cf. James i. 27, and above on vii. 23, Kennedy, Sources of N. T. Greek, p. 105.—λαβεῖν: infinitive of purpose, ἐξ ἐθνῶν λαὸν, ex gentibus populum, "egregium paradoxon" Bengel; the converts from among the Gentiles were no less than Israel the people of God. On ἔθνος and λαός see iii. 25. — τῷ ὀνόματι, i.e., who should bear His Name as a people of God, or may mean simply "for Himself," God's name being often so used. On the "pregnant use" of the word cf. James ii. 7, v. 10, 14. St. James thus in his address agrees with St. Peter.—Ver. 15. καὶ τούτῳ, "and to this agree," A. and R.V., i.e., to the fact just stated (so Wendt, Weiss, Blass, Ramsay); if the pronoun referred to St. Peter, as some take it, we should have had οἱ προφῆται, not as in text, οἱ λ. τῶν π. The quotation Amos. ix. 11, 12, is freely cited from the LXX, and indeed the chief point made by St. James depends upon that version.—τῶν προφ., plural, as including those prophets whose words of prophecy had been of similar import.

Ver. 16. Μετὰ ταῦτα: both Hebrew and LXX, ἐν τῇ ἐκει. τῇ ἡμέρᾳ, i.e., in the Messianic times, after the predicted chastisement of Israel: the house of David is in ruins, but it is to be re-erected, and from the restoration of its prosperity the Messianic blessings will flow: "the person of the Messiah does not appear in this prophecy, but there is the generic reference to the house of David, and the people of Israel," Briggs, Messianic Prophecy, p. 163, Delitzsch, Messianische Weissagungen, second edition, p. 94. St. James sees the spiritual fulfilment of the prophecy in the kingdom of Christ erected on the Day of Pentecost, and in the ingathering of the Gentile nations to it. On the Messianic interpretations of the passage amongst the Jews see Edersheim, Jesus the Messiah, ii., 734.—ἀναστρέψω καὶ ἀνοι.: like Hebrew אָשׁוּב=I will return and do, i.e., I will do again—but not in LXX or Hebrew. In the latter we have simply אָקִים, and in LXX ἀναστήσω, where St. James has ἀνοικοδομήσω: the idea of restoration is fully contained in the twice repeated ἀνοι. and in ἀνορθώσω.—τὴν σκ. Δ. πεπτ.: the noun is used to show how low the house of David (2 Sam. vii. 12) had fallen—it is no longer a palace but a hut, and that in ruins: the Hebrew word might be used for a temporary structure of the boughs of trees as at the Feast of Tabernacles. We may compare the way in which this hope of restoration asserted itself in Psalms of Solomon, xvii., 23, where Ryle and James, p. 137, compare the words with Amos ix. 11, Jer. xxx. 9, etc. From the passage before us the Messiah received the name of Bar Naphli, "Son of the fallen".—κατεσκαμμένα, see critical note. In LXX B has κατεσκαμ., A κατεστρ.

ἀνοικοδομήσω, καὶ ἀνορθώσω αὐτήν· 17. ὅπως ἂν ἐκζητήσωσιν οἱ
κατάλοιποι τῶν ἀνθρώπων τὸν Κύριον, καὶ πάντα τὰ ἔθνη, ἐφ᾽ οὓς
ἐπικέκληται τὸ ὄνομά μου ἐπ᾽ αὐτούς· λέγει Κύριος ὁ[1] ποιῶν ταῦτα
πάντα." 18.[2] γνωστὰ ἀπ᾽ αἰῶνός ἐστι τῷ Θεῷ πάντα τὰ ἔργα αὐτοῦ.
19. διὸ ἐγὼ[3] κρίνω μὴ παρενοχλεῖν τοῖς ἀπὸ τῶν ἐθνῶν ἐπιστρέφουσιν

[1] ο ποιων, art. om. א*B, Vulg., Irint., Tisch., W.H., Blass, Weiss, Wendt. ταυτα,
om. παντα אABCD 61, Vulg., Boh., Aeth., Irint., Rebapt., Const., so Lach., Tisch.,
W.H., Blass, R.V., Weiss, Wendt, and Hilg. (παντα ταυτα ELP, Syr. H.).
Amos ix. 12 ο ποιων ταυτα.

[2] γνωστα απ᾽ αιωνος, om. rest, so אBC 61, 180, Sah., Boh., Arm., so also Tisch.,
Alford, W.H., R.V., Weiss, Wendt; see W.H., App., p. 96, and for the same explanation Wendt, 1888 and 1899, in loco. The quot. in Amos ix. does not contain
γνωστα απ᾽ αιωνος, so that the words were separated from the clause and formed
into an independent sentence. T.R. is supported by EHLP, Syr. H., Const., Chrys.;
whilst AD, Vulg., Syr. H. mg., Irint., Blass in both texts, and Hilg. read γνωστον
απ᾽ αιωνος εστι τω κυριω το εργον αυτον.

[3] After εγω Iren. adds το κατ᾽ εμε "secundum me," cf. Rom. i. 15; may be translator's paraphrase; retained by Blass in β.

Ver. 17. ὅπως ἂν ἐκζητ. οἱ κ. τῶν
ἀνθρώπων τὸν K.: LXX and Hebrew
are here considerably at variance. Hebrew: "that they may possess the remnant of Edom". In LXX: "that the
rest of men may seek after (the
Lord)" (so also Arabic Version, whilst
Vulgate, Peshitto, and Targum support the Massoretic text, see Briggs,
u. s., p. 162). In LXX A τὸν K. is found,
but not in B. In LXX rendering אָדָם,
men, takes the place of אֱדוֹם, Edom,
and יִדְרְשׁוּ instead of יִירְשׁוּ, i.e.,
דָּרַשׁ, to seek, instead of יָרַשׁ, to possess.—καὶ πάντα τὰ ἔθνη : explicative,
"the rest of men," i.e., the heathen :
" sine respectu personarum et operum ".
—ὅπως ἂν, Winer-Moulton, xlii., 6;
Burton, N. T. Moods and Tenses, p. 85;
cf. Luke ii. 35, Acts iii. 19, Rom. iii. 4,
and in no other instances, three of these
quotations from LXX.—ἐφ᾽ οὓς ἐπικέκ.
. . . ἐπ᾽ α.: "upon whom my name is
called [pronounced]": Hebraistic formula, cf. LXX, Jer. xli. 15; and Deut.
xxviii. 10, Isa. lxiii. 19, 2 Macc. viii. 15.
In James ii. 7, and only there in the
N.T. does the same formula recur (see
Mayor, Introd., and Nösgen, Geschichte
der Neutest. Offb., ii., 51).
Ver. 18. In R.V. the phrase ἀπ᾽
αἰῶνος is connected closely with the
preceding clause, see critical notes:
" who maketh these things known from
the beginning of the world " (" of

time," Ramsay), or margin, " who doeth
these things which were known " etc. St.
James may perhaps have added the
words freely to the LXX to emphasise
his argument that the call of the Gentiles was a carrying out of God's eternal
purpose, but there is nothing corresponding to the words in the Hebrew, although at the end of ver. 11 we have
כִּימֵי עוֹלָם: LXX, καθὼς αἱ ἡμέραι
ἀπ᾽ αἰῶνος, and somewhat similar phrase
in Isa. xlv. 21, see Zöckler, in loco, for
different authorities, and for further discussion of the words, Klostermann, Probleme im Aposteltexte, p. 128. ἀπ᾽ αἰῶνος
is peculiar to Luke in N.T., cf. Luke i.
70, Acts iii. 21; it may simply = " of
old time," see Plummer, St. Luke, l. c.,
but here it may intimate that St. James
refers to that purpose of God revealed by
all the prophets, as in iii. 21. In Psalms of
Solomon, viii., 7, ἀπ᾽ αἰῶνος seems to be
equivalent to " from the creation of the
heaven and earth," cf. Ps. cxviii. 52. If
the conference was held in Greek, as we
may reasonably conclude from the fact
that Gentile interests were at stake, and
that many of the Gentiles, as of the Hellenistic Jews, would probably be present,
it is very significant that St. James, a Hebrew of the Hebrews, quotes the rendering of the LXX so apposite for his
purpose, and that he should see the
spiritual restoration of the house of David
in the kingdom of Jesus, and the fulfilment of prophecy in the reception of the
Gentiles into the kingdom of the Messiah,
so exclusively guarded by the Jews.

ἐπὶ τὸν Θεόν· 20. ἀλλὰ ἐπιστεῖλαι αὐτοῖς τοῦ ἀπέχεσθαι [1] ἀπὸ τῶν
ἀλισγημάτων τῶν εἰδώλων καὶ τῆς πορνείας καὶ τοῦ πνικτοῦ καὶ τοῦ

[1] απο om. אBD 61, 180, so Tisch., W.H., Blass, Weiss, Wendt, Hilg. και του
πνικτου om. art. AB 13, 61, so W.H., Weiss. D, Gig., Iren. omit και του πνικτου (see
also ver. 29). Wendt (1888) accounts for the omission partly by the fact that no such
command was precisely given in Lev. xvii. 13 (so Meyer, Alford), and partly from
the laxer views of the Western Church; but (1899, Introd., p. 50) he now gives in
his adherence to Corssen's view (G. G. A., p. 442; 1896), with which compare for
similarity Zahn's explanation, Einleitung, ii., pp. 344, 345 (1899), Weiss, Codex D,
p. 198, that the omission, as also the addition following (see below), were intended
to do away with the Judaic and ceremonial character of the decree, and to substitute
the comprehensive moral prescription of the Sermon on the Mount; so too recently
Harnack. του πνικ. being eliminated αιμα can be referred to homicidium, Tert.,
De Pud., xii., so that the decree means that they should abstain from pollutions, viz.,
idolatry, fornication, bloodshed (cf. the punctuation in β), and that they should love
their neighbours (the negative injunction of the Golden Rule); see below. See
further in favour of the omission Blass, Præf., Evang. sec. Lucam, p. xxv. (1897);
Philology of the Gospels, p. 250; but for a very different reason; as against the interpretation given above by Harnack and others to αιμα, see also Blass, Studien und
Kritiken, i., 1900; Hilgenfeld, also Corssen, C. G. G., p. 445 ff., remark on the probability of Montanistic influences in the Bezan text of the passage before us, and in
reply to their strictures see Blass, Evang. sec. Lucam, Præf., p. xxiv. ff. At the end
of the clause we have και οσα μη θελουσιν εαυτοις γινεσθαι ετεροις μη ποιειν, so
D, 11 minuscules, Sah., Aeth., Iren. (cf. also ver. 29). Harris, Four Lectures, etc.,
pp. 31, 32, points out that the addition was known to Aristides (Seeberg, Die Apologie
des A., p. 213), and that therefore the Acts was known and used and interpolated by
the middle of the second century. But he refrains from speaking positively as to
the source of this variant in Acts, as "the negative precept turns up everywhere in the
early Church, having been absorbed in the first instance from Jewish ethics"; cf. also
Weiss, Codex D, p. 109. So Theophilus, Didache, Const. Apost. and Ephrem on
Rom. iii. 21 and viii. 7; see Harris, u. s.; Resch, Agrapha, p. 95; W.H., App., 96.
Zahn unhesitatingly refers the addition to the Didache, but it is very doubtful how
far the Didache enjoyed the high and wide credit which Zahn attaches to it: about
110-140 the words were interpolated in the text in the East, and soon after, but by
no means with universal acceptance, they found their way into the Western text.
Blass in Studien und Kritiken, u. s., replies further to Harnack. Harnack asks why
the "golden rule," if genuine, is not found in xxi. 25. Blass replies that Luke kept
a rough draft for himself in which were both πνικτα and the rule, and thus omitted
πνικτα in β, and in α the rule "brevitati consulens".

Ver. 19. διὸ ἐγὼ κρίνω: "wherefore
my judgment is". St. James apparently
speaks as the president of the meeting,
Chrysostom, Hom., xxxiii., and his words
with the emphatic ἐγώ (Weiss) may express more than the opinion of a private
member—he sums up the debate and
proposes "the draught of a practical
resolution" (see however Hort, Ecclesia,
79; Hackett, in loco; and on the other
hand Moberly, Ministerial Priesthood,
p. 147). If a position of authority is thus
given to St. James at the conference, it
is very significant that this should be so
in Jerusalem itself, where the Twelve
would naturally carry special weight.
But this presidency and Apostolic authority of St. James in Jerusalem is exactly
in accordance with the remarkable order
of the three names referred to by St. Paul

in Gal. ii. 9 (cf. Acts xii. 17, xxi. 18). At
the same time ver. 22 shows us that
neither the authority of St. James nor
that of the other Apostles is conceived
of as overriding the general consent of
the whole Church. — μὴ παρενοχλεῖν:
only here in N.T.; "not to trouble," A.
and R.V.; it may be possible to press
the παρά, "not to trouble further," i.e.,
by anything more than he is about to
mention, or in their conversion to God.
The verb is found with dative and
accusative in LXX; for the former cf.
Judg. xiv. 17, 1 Macc. x. 63 SR, xii. 14;
and for the latter Jer. xxvi. (xlvi.) 27,
1 Macc. x. 35. Bengel takes παρά as =
præter, but whilst it is very doubtful how
far the preposition can be so rendered
here, he adds fides quieta non obturbanda.
— τοῖς ἐπισ. cf. xi. 21, "who are turn-

αἵματος· 21.[1] Μωσῆς γὰρ ἐκ γενεῶν ἀρχαίων κατὰ πόλιν τοὺς κηρύσσοντας αὐτὸν ἔχει ἐν ταῖς συναγωγαῖς κατὰ πᾶν σάββατον ἀναγινωσκόμενος.

[1] Blass in β brackets whole verse on the ground of its omission by Irenæus, but the latter may easily have omitted it as superfluous or irrelevant to his argument, whilst the obscurity of the verse has been well noted as a reason for its retention.

ing to God"; present participle, as in acknowledgment of a work actually in progress.

Ver. 20. ἐπιστεῖλαι (xxi. 25), Heb. xiii. 22; the verb is used of a *written* injunction, Westcott, *l. c.* (so Wendt here and in xxi. 25, and so Klostermann), and so often in ecclesiastical writers; here it may mean to write or enjoin, or may well include both, *cf.* Hort, *Ecclesia*, p. 70, Westcott, *u. s.*, Weiss, *in loco*; in classical Greek it is used in both senses. In LXX it is not used, except in a few passages in which the reading is doubtful, ἀπ. for ἐπ., see Hatch and Redpath, *sub v.*—τοῦ ἀπέχεσθαι: Burton, *N. T. Moods and Tenses*, p. 159, *cf.* Jer. vii. 10, 1 Pet. ii. 11, 1 Tim. iv. 3; generally without ἀπό.—τῶν ἀλισγημάτων: from Hellenistic verb, ἀλισγεῖν, LXX, Dan. i. 8, Mal. i. 7, 12, Ecclus. xl. 29 (S, *al*); may mean the pollution from the flesh used in heathen offerings = εἰδωλοθύτων in ver. 29 (xxi. 25), *cf.* 1 Cor. viii. 1, x. 14 ff., but see further Klostermann, *Probleme im Aposteltexte*, p. 144 ff., and Wendt, 1888 and 1899, *in loco*. The phrase stands by itself, and the three following genitives are not dependent upon it. If St. James's words are interpreted more widely than as = εἰδωλοθύτων, ver. 29, they would involve the prohibition for a Christian not only not to eat anything offered to idols, or to share in the idolatrous feasts, but even to accept an invitation to a domestic feast of the Gentiles or at least to a participation in the food on such an occasion. That it was easy for Christians to run these risks is evident from 1 Cor. viii. 10 when St. Paul refers to the case of those who had not only eaten of the flesh offered to idols, but had also sat down to a feast in the idol's temple.—τῆς πορνείας: the moral explanation of this close allocation of idolatry and uncleanness is that the former so often involved the latter. But Dr. Hort whilst pointing out that such an association is not fanciful or accidental, reminds us that we ought not to lay too much stress on the connection, since many forms of idolatry might fairly be regarded as free from that particular stain. The language, however, of St. James in his Epistle shows us how imperative it was in the moral atmosphere of the Syria of the first century to guard the Christian life from sexual defilement, and the burning language of St. Paul in 1 Cor. vi. 15 and 1 Thess. iv. 3, etc., shows us the terrible risks to which Christian morality was exposed, risks enhanced by the fact that the heathen view of impurity was so lax throughout the Roman empire, *cf.* Horace, *Sat.*, i., 2, 31; Terence, *Adelphi*, i., 2, 21; Cicero, *Pro Cælio*, xx.; and on the intimate and almost universal connection between the heathen religious guilds and societies and the observance of nameless breaches of the Christian law of purity, see Loening, *Die Gemeindeverfassung des Urchristenthums*, and his references to Foucart, p. 12 ff. Without some special prohibition it was conceivable that a man might pass from some scene of licentious indulgence to the participation in the Supper of the Lord (Plumptre, Felten). An attempt has been made to refer the word here to the sin of incest, or to marriage within the forbidden degrees, rather than to the sin of fornication, so Holtzmann, Ritschl, Zöckler, Wendt, Ramsay; but on the other hand Meyer, Ewald, Godet, Weiss, and others take the word in its general sense as it is employed elsewhere in the N.T. From what has been said above, and from the way in which women might be called upon to serve impurely in a heathen temple (to which religious obligation, as Zöckler reminds us, some have seen a reference in the word here, *cf.* also Wendt, p. 332 (1888)), we see the need and the likelihood of such a specific enjoinder against the sin of fornication. Bentley conjectured χοιρείας or πορκείας.—τοῦ πνικτοῦ: "from that which has been strangled," lit., such beasts as had been killed through strangling, and whose blood had not been let out when they were killed. For this prohibition reference is usually made to Lev. xvii. 13, Deut. xii. 16, 23, so Weiss, Wendt, Zöckler, Plumptre, Felten, Hackett. But on the other hand Dr. Hort

22. Τότε ἔδοξε τοῖς ἀποστόλοις καὶ τοῖς πρεσβυτέροις σὺν ὅλῃ τῇ ἐκκλησίᾳ, ἐκλεξαμένους ἄνδρας ἐξ αὐτῶν πέμψαι εἰς Ἀντιόχειαν σὺν τῷ Παύλῳ καὶ Βαρνάβᾳ, Ἰούδαν τὸν ¹ ἐπικαλούμενον Βαρσαβᾶν, καὶ

¹ επικ., but καλ. ℵABCDEL, Tisch., W.H., Blass, Weiss, Wendt. Βαρσαβαν Vulg., Arm., Chrys.; βαρσαββαν ℵABCEHLP 61, Sah., Boh., Const., Tisch., W.H., Blass, R.V., Weiss, Wendt; see on the word Winer-Schmiedel, pp. 56, 57; βαραββαν D, so Hilg.

contends that all attempts to find the prohibition in the Pentateuch quite fail, although he considers it perfectly conceivable that the flesh of animals strangled in such a way as not to allow of the letting out of blood would be counted as unlawful food by the Jews, cf. Origen, c. Cels., viii., 30; Judaistic Christianity, p. 73, and Appendix, p. 209. But his further remark, that if such a prohibition had been actually prescribed (as in his view it is not) we should have a separate fourth precept referring only to a particular case of the third precept, viz., abstinence from blood, is probably the reason why in D, cf. Irenæus, Hær., iii., 12, 14; Cyprian, Testim., iii., 119; Tertullian, De Pudicitia, xii., the words καὶ τοῦ πνικτοῦ are omitted here and in the decree, ver. 29, although it is also possible that the laxer views on the subject in the West may have contributed to the omission (see Zöckler and Wendt). Dr. Hort leaves the difficulty unsolved, merely referring to the "Western" text without adopting it. But in xxi. 25 the words are again found in a reference to, and in a summary of, the decree, although here too D consistently omits them (see critical notes).—τοῦ αἵματος: specially forbidden by the Jewish law, Lev. xvii. 10, cf. iii. 17, vii. 26, xix. 26, Deut. xii. 16, 23, xv. 23, and we may refer the prohibition, with Dr. Hort, to the feeling of mystery entertained by various nations of antiquity with regard to blood, so that the feeling is not exclusively Jewish, although the Jewish law had given it such express and divine sanction. "The blood is the life," and abstinence from it was a manifestation of reverence for the life given by and dedicated to God. This was the ground upon which the Jews based, and still base, the prohibition. Nothing could override the command first given to Noah, Gen. ix. 4, together with the permission to eat animal food, and renewed in the law. αἷμ. cannot refer (so Cyprian and Tertullian) to homicide, as the collocation with πνικτοῦ (if retained) is against any such interpretation. See additional note (2) at end of chapter.

Ver. 21. ἐκ γενεῶν ἀρχαίων: pointing back to the first days when the Diaspora had first spread to any considerable extent in heathen lands: see on ver. 7. The exact phrase (ἀπὸ) γενεῶν ἀρχ. occurs in Psalms of Solomon, xviii., 14—from the generations of old the lights of heaven have not departed from their path. For the custom referred to here, see Schürer, Jewish People, div. ii., vol. ii., p. 55, E.T. The words seem closely connected in sense with the preceding in this way, viz., that the Gentile proselytes could long ago in the synagogues have been acquainted week by week with the spirit and enactments of the Mosaic law, and they would thus be the more easily inclined to take upon themselves the few elementary precepts laid down in the decree of the Jerusalem Church, so as to avoid any serious cause of offence to their Jewish-Christian brethren. Others however take the meaning to be that, as the Jewish Christians in their continual association with the synagogue would still hear the law read every Sabbath, there would be no intercourse between them and the Gentile Christians, unless the latter observed the necessary restrictions enjoined by the decree for brotherly intercommunion. There is no occasion to interpret the meaning to be that it is superfluous to write the decree to the Jewish Christians, since they knew its contents already from the law (so St. Chrysostom, and Blass), for a decree for the Jewish Christians is not in question, see ver. 23. Others again interpret: there is no fear that the Mosaic law should be neglected or despised "for Moses, etc.". See further, Wendt, Weiss, McGiffert, Knabenbauer.

Ver. 22. ἔδοξε: the word is often found in public resolutions and official decrees, Herod., i., 3; Thuc., iv., 118 (L and S.).—τοῖς ἀποσ. . . . ἐκλεξ. . . . γράψ.: on the irregular construction see Page and Rendall, and instances in Alford and Lumby; and further, Burton, N. T. Moods and Tenses, p. 173.—σὺν ὅλῃ τῇ ἐκκλ., cf. ver. 12, πᾶν τὸ πλῆθος, cf. Iren., Hær., iii., 12.—

Σίλαν, ἄνδρας ἡγουμένους ἐν τοῖς ἀδελφοῖς, 23. γράψαντες διὰ χειρὸς
αὐτῶν τάδε · Οἱ ἀπόστολοι καὶ οἱ πρεσβύτεροι¹ καὶ οἱ ἀδελφοί, τοῖς
κατὰ τὴν Ἀντιόχειαν καὶ Συρίαν καὶ Κιλικίαν ἀδελφοῖς τοῖς ἐξ ἐθνῶν,

¹ καὶ οἱ αδελφοι אᶜEHLP, Syrr. P. and H., Arm^Zoh., Aeth^ut., Chrys., so Weiss,
Apostelgeschichte, p. 57; om. καὶ οἱ א*ABCD, 13, 61, Arm^usc., Irint., Ath., Tisch.,
W.H., R.V., Wendt. Blass, following Sah., Orig., reads αδελφοις here and brackets
the same word after Κιλ., so Ramsay, *St. Paul*, p. 171, rejecting the word as an
accidental corruption ; "The Apostles and the Elders unto the brethren," etc., R.V.
renders "The Apostles and the elder brethren," a title which the Jerusalem Church
might use in addressing younger Churches (Rendall), but see commentary.

ἐκλεξ. ἄνδρας πέμψαι: "to choose men
out of their company, and send," R.V.
In A.V. we lose sight of the fact that the
choice was thus made in the rendering
"chosen men," a rendering which takes
ἐκλεξ. middle as if passive (see Wendt's
just criticism, and *cf.* ver. 40 ἐπιλεξ.).—
Ἰούδαν τὸν ἐπικ. B., see critical note,
sometimes regarded as a brother of
Joseph Barsabbas in i. 23. Ewald thinks
that he was actually identical with him.
Nothing further is known of him, but if
he was a brother of Joseph Barsabbas,
he too may have been amongst the personal followers of the Lord; hence his
leading position, see also B.D.² "Judas,"
p. 1830.—Σίλαν, *cf.* ver. 40, xvi. 19, 25,
29, xvii. 4, 10, 14, xviii. 5, 2 Cor. i. 19, 1
Thess. i. 1, 2 Thess. i. 1, 1 Pet. v. 12.
The name may have been contracted
for Silvanus, but it may also have been
a Greek equivalent for a Hebrew name
שְׁלֵשׁ = Tertius, or שְׁלֹחַ, Gen. x. 24,
see especially Winer-Schmiedel, p. 143,
note, and Zahn, *Einleitung*, i., p. 23,
who prefers שָׁאַל, „bitten, erfragen".
Paul always used the form Σιλουανός
(so 1 Pet. v. 12), Blass, *Gram.*, pp. 70,
71, Winer-Schmiedel, *u. s.*, and also pp.
74, 75. On the supposed identity of
Silas with Titus, who is never mentioned
in Acts, see above; and Wendt, *in loco*.
If the two passages, 2 Cor. i. 19 and
viii. 23, on which the advocates of this
view rely make the identity possible, the
description of Titus, Gal. ii. 3, is completely at variance with the description
of Silas in this chapter ("perversa, ne
quid durius dicam, conjectura" Blass,
in commenting on the supposed identity).
—ἡγουμένους, *cf.* ver. 32, προφῆται
ὄντες: the word is also used in Heb.
xiii. three times, once of those who had
passed away, ver. 7, and in vv. 17 and
24 of actual authorities to be obeyed.
The word is applied in the LXX to

various forms of authority and leadership
(see also references to the word in
classical Greek, Grimm-Thayer), and *cf.*
Clem. Rom., *Cor.*, i., 3 (xxi., 6), with v. 7,
xxxvii. 2, lv. 1, lx. 4. It is quite possible
that it may have essentially = διδάσκαλοι, xiii. 1 (*cf.* xiv. 12, ἡγούμ. τοῦ
λόγου), *cf.* Heb. *u. s.*, with *Didaché*, iv.,
1, and see Zöckler, *Apostelgeschichte*, p.
249; Harnack, *Proleg.* to *Didaché*, p.
95; or the mere fact that Judas and
Silas may both have been personal
followers of Jesus would have conferred
upon them a high degree of authority
(Plumptre); or the term ἡγου. may be
used as a general one, and we cannot
say to what particular office or qualification it may have extended besides that
involved in ver. 32. For use of the
word in sub-apostolic times see Gore,
Church and the Ministry, p. 322, etc.,
Moberly, *Ministerial Priesthood*, pp. 166,
186. The word may be called characteristic of St. Luke (Friedrich, p. 22, *cf.*
Luke xxii. 26, Acts vii. 10 (of civil rule),
xiv. 12).

Ver. 23.—οἱ ἀπόστ. καὶ οἱ πρεσβ. καὶ
οἱ ἀδελ., but in R.V. "the Apostles and
the elder brethren," see critical notes.
The phrase as it stands in R.V. has been
called meaningless (Page), but Hort,
Ecclesia, p. 71, while admitting that the
phrase is unusual, defends it as indicating that they who held the office of elder
were to be regarded as bearing the characteristic from which the title itself had
arisen, and that they were but elder
brethren at the head of a great family of
brethren (*cf.* Knabenbauer *in loco*). It
is of course quite possible that ἀδελ. is
merely to be taken as in apposition to
ἀπόστ. and πρεσβ., meaning that as
brethren they sent a message to brethren
(Wendt, Felten, Page).—τοῖς κατὰ τὴν
Ἀ. κ.τ.λ., see below.—χαίρειν: amongst
the Epistles of the N.T. only that of St.
James thus commences, as has been often
pointed out by Bengel and others. The

χαίρειν. 24. ἐπειδὴ ἠκούσαμεν ὅτι τινὲς ἐξ ἡμῶν [1] ἐξελθόντες ἐτάραξαν ὑμᾶς λόγοις, ἀνασκευάζοντες τὰς ψυχὰς ὑμῶν,[2] λέγοντες περιτέμνεσθαι καὶ τηρεῖν τὸν νόμον, οἷς οὐ διεστειλάμεθα · 25. ἔδοξεν ἡμῖν γενομένοις ὁμοθυμαδόν,[3] ἐκλεξαμένους ἄνδρας πέμψαι πρὸς ὑμᾶς, σὺν τοῖς

[1] εξελθοντες om. א*B, Arm., Aethro., Const., Ath., Chrys., so W.H., R.V. marg., Weiss, Wendt; but retained אcACDEP, Vulg., Syrr. P. and H., Sah., Boh., Aethpp., Iren., so Tisch., Blass, Hilg. It might have been introduced (cf. ver. 1, κατελ.) to guard against the appearances that τινες εξ ημων belonged to the senders of the letter (see Wendt's note, 1888).

[2] λεγ. . . . τον νομον om. אABD 13, 61, Vulg., Sah., Boh., Aethro., Or., Const., Ath., so Tisch., W.H., Blass., R.V., Weiss, Wendt; but Blass retains in β, following CEHLP, Gig., Iren. (Chrys.), so Hilg.

[3] εκλεξαμενους אCDEHP, Const., Iren., Chrys., so Tisch., W.H. marg., Blass, Weiss and Hilg.; -οις ABL 61, Lach., W.H. text. Wendt unable to decide whether acc. after ver. 22 or dat. for gram. was the later reading.

coincidence may be a chance one, but it is the more remarkable, since the letter may well have been written and dictated by St. James in his authoritative position. On the phrase in letters see Mayor's interesting note on James i. 1. It occurs again in Acts xxiii. 26, but nowhere else in N.T.

Ver. 24. On the similarity of this verse in phraseology to St. Luke's preface, Luke i. 1, Schwegler, Zeller, Weiss, Friedrich, Hilgenfeld, and others have commented. But, after all, in what does the likeness consist? Simply in the fact that here as there we have ἐπειδή introducing the antecedent clause, and ἔδοξεν the subsequent clause. Friedrich (p. 46) considers this as too striking to be a matter of chance, but strangely he writes each of the two passages as if they commenced with the same word, see below on ver. 28 —ἐπειδήπερ. This word is a curious one, and is only found in Luke i. 1 (not in LXX), but there is no authority for reading it in the passage before us in Acts. Nösgen, Apostelgeschichte, p. 45, refers to instances of a similar formula and phraseology as in use in Jewish writings, cf. Jost, Jüd. Gesch., i., 284.—τινὲς ἐξ ἡμῶν, cf. for the expression Gal. ii. 12.— ἐξελ., see critical notes.—ἐτάραξαν ἡμᾶς, cf. Gal. i. 7, v. 10. λόγοις may mean with words only, words without true doctrine.—ἀνασκευάζοντες, "subverting," A. and R.V.; not in LXX, and only here in N.T., in classical Greek, primarily colligere vasa, to pack up, and so to carry away; or to dismantle a place; to destroy, overthrow, and so trop. as in text—of breaking treaties (Polyb.), of destroying an opponent's arguments (Arist.). Nösgen and Felten note it amongst the non-

Lucan words in the decree, so βάρος, τὸ ἐπάναγκες, διὰ λόγον, ἀπαγγέλλειν, εὖ πράττειν, ἔρρωσθε, ἀγαπητός.—οἷς οὐ διεστειλάμεθα: "to whom we gave no commandment," R.V., omitting "such," not in text, and weakens; in Tyndale, Cramner, and Genevan Version; cf. Gal. ii. 12, and Acts xxi. 20; only used once in passive in N.T., Heb. xii. 20, often in LXX in middle voice, meaning to warn, cf. also its meaning in Judith xi. 12 with Mark v. 43, etc.

Ver. 25. γενομ. ὁμοθυμαδόν: "having come to one accord," "einmutig geworden," Weiss: ὁμοθ., though frequent in Acts, see i. 14, only here with γεν. For the form of the phrase as indicating mutual deliberation on the part of the Church collectively see "Council," Dict. of Chr. Ant., i., 474.—ἐκλεξ. ἄνδρας: "to choose out men and send them unto you," R.V., whether we read accusative or dative see critical note, and cf. ver. 22.—ἀγαπητοῖς: very frequent in St. Paul's Epistles; used three times by St. James in his Epistle, twice by St. Peter in his First Epistle, four times in the Second, cf. iii. 15, where the word is used by St. Peter of St. Paul, ten times by St. John: it was therefore a very natural word to occur in the letter, and we may compare it with the right hand of fellowship given by the three Apostles just named to Barnabas and Paul, Gal. ii. 9.—Β. καὶ Π.: this order because in Jerusalem Church; see above on ver. 12. Meyer, Bleek, Nösgen, Wendt, all note its truthful significance.

Ver. 26. παραδεδωκόσι τὰς ψ. α.: "hazarded their lives," A. and R.V.; so in classical Greek, and in LXX, Dan. iii. 28 (95). The sufferings of the mission-

ἀγαπητοῖς ἡμῶν Βαρνάβᾳ καὶ Παύλῳ, 26. ἀνθρώποις παραδεδωκόσι τὰς ψυχὰς αὐτῶν ὑπὲρ τοῦ ὀνόματος τοῦ Κυρίου ἡμῶν Ἰησοῦ Χριστοῦ.[1] 27. ἀπεστάλκαμεν οὖν Ἰούδαν καὶ Σίλαν, καὶ αὐτοὺς διὰ λόγου ἀπαγγέλλοντας τὰ αὐτά. 28. ἔδοξε γὰρ τῷ Ἁγίῳ Πνεύματι καὶ ἡμῖν, μηδὲν πλέον ἐπιτίθεσθαι ὑμῖν βάρος πλὴν τῶν ἐπάναγκες

---

[1] At end of verse, DE 137, Syr. Harcl. mg. add εις παντα πειρασμον, so Blass in β, Hilg. Harris, *Four Lectures*, etc., pp. 85, 86, describes this as the best example extant of a Syriac assimilation in the text of Acts ; παραδεδωκασιν in D, ambiguous, but in *Sirach*, ii., 1, Syriac had rendered "thou hast surrendered thy soul to all temptations" (ετοιμασον την ψυχην σου εις πειρασμον, LXX) ; gloss added here for clearness. Weiss, Codex D, p. 82, refers the words to a reminiscence of Acts xx. 19.

---

aries in their first journey were evidently well known, and appeal was fittingly made to them in recognition of their self-sacrifice, and in proof of their sincerity. Ver. 27. Ἰ. καὶ Σ. καὶ αὐτοὺς: "who themselves also shall tell you the same things by word of mouth," R.V. Judas and Silas were sent to confirm personally the contents of the letter, as they could speak with authority as representing the Church at Jerusalem, while Barnabas and Saul alone would be regarded as already committed to the conciliatory side (Alford). The present participle, as the writer thinks of Judas and Silas as actually present with the letter at its reception, cf. ἀπεστάλκαμεν, "we have sent" by a common idiom, and also xxi. 16; Blass compares Thuc., vii., 26, ἔπεμψαν ἀγγέλλοντας, *Gram.*, p. 194.— τὰ αὐτὰ: not the same things as Barnabas and Paul had preached, but, as διὰ λ. intimates, the same things as the letter contained, see critical notes. Ver. 28. ἔδοξε γὰρ τῷ Ἁ. Π. καὶ ἡμῖν: "causa principalis" and "causa ministerialis" of the decree. The words of Hooker exactly describe the meaning and purpose of the words, *E. P.*, iii., 10, 2, cf. viii., 6, 7, and cf. St. Chrysostom's words, *Hom.*, xxxiii., "not making themselves equal to Him [i.e., the Holy Ghost]—they are not so mad—the one to the Holy Ghost, that they may not deem it to be of man ; the other to us, that they may be taught that they also themselves admit the Gentiles, although themselves being in circumcision". On other suggested but improbable meanings see Alford's and Wendt's notes. The words became a kind of general formula in the decrees of Councils and Synods, cf. the phrase commonly prefixed to Councils : *Sancto Spiritu suggerente* (*Dict. Chr. Ant.*, i., 483). On this classical construction of ἔδοξε τῷ with the infinitive see Nestle's note, *Expository Times*, December, 1898. Moreover it would seem that this ἔδοξε is quite in accordance with the manner in which Jewish Rabbis would formulate their decisions.— μηδὲν πλέον . . . βάρος: the words indicate authority on the part of the speakers, although in ver. 20 we read only of "enjoining". St. Peter had used the cognate verb in ver. 10, cf. Rev. ii. 24, where the same noun occurs with a *possible* reference to the decree, see Lightfoot, *Galatians*, p. 309, and Plumptre, *in loco*. —ἐπάναγκες, *i.e.*, for mutual intercourse, that Jewish and Gentile Christians might live as brethren in the One Lord. There is nothing said to imply that these four abstinences were to be imposed as necessary to salvation; the receivers of the letter are only told that it should be well with them if they observed the decree, and we cannot interpret εὖ πράξετε as = σωθήσεσθε. At the same time the word was a very emphatic one, and might be easily interpreted, as it speedily was, in a narrower sense, Ramsay, *St. Paul*, p. 172; Lightfoot, *Galatians*, p. 310. Rendall compares the use of ἀναγκαῖος in Thuc., i., 90. Ver. 29. ἀπέχ.: preposition omitted as in ver. 20, W.H. ; so usually in classical Greek, but in N.T. ἀπέχ. ἀπό, 1 Thess. iv. 3, v. 22; so in LXX, Job i. 1, 8, ii. 3, etc. On the difference in meaning in the two constructions, see Alford and Wendt, *in loco*.—εἰδωλοθύτων, see ver. 20.— πνικτοῦ: omitted in Western text ; see critical notes. — διατηροῦντες ἑαυτοὺς: verb, only in Luke, cf. Luke ii. 51 (in LXX with ἐκ or ἀπό, Ps. xi. 7, Prov. xxi. 23). In Jas. i. 27 we have a somewhat striking similarity of expression (cf. also John xvii. 15).—εὖ πράξετε : "it shall be well with you," R.V. ; *viz.*, through the peace and concord established in the Christian community, cf. 2 Macc. ix. 19, so in classical Greek. The reading in A.V. is somewhat ambiguous, but the Greek signifies

τούτων, 29. ἀπέχεσθαι εἰδωλοθύτων καὶ αἵματος καὶ ¹ πνικτοῦ καὶ
πορνείας. ἐξ ὧν διατηροῦντες ἑαυτοὺς εὖ ² πράξετε. ἔρρωσθε.

30. Οἱ μὲν οὖν ἀπολυθέντες ³ ἦλθον εἰς Ἀντιόχειαν · καὶ συναγαγόντες τὸ πλῆθος, ἐπέδωκαν τὴν ἐπιστολήν. 31. ἀναγνόντες δὲ
ἐχάρησαν ἐπὶ τῇ παρακλήσει. 32. Ἰούδας δὲ καὶ Σίλας, καὶ αὐτοὶ
προφῆται ὄντες,⁴ διὰ λόγου πολλοῦ παρεκάλεσαν τοὺς ἀδελφούς, καὶ

¹ **καὶ πνικτοῦ** *om*. D, Iren., Tert., Cypr., Amb., Pac., Aug., so Blass in **β** ; see
above on ver. 20, and Zahn, *Einleitung*, ii., p. 353 ; **πνικτου** אcA²EHLP, Vulg.,
Syrr. P. and H., Arm., Aeth., Const., Chrys., etc. ; **πνικτων** א*A*BC 61, 137, Sah.,
Boh., Clem., Or., so Tisch., W.H., R.V., Weiss, Wendt (**πνικτου** introduced after ver.
20). After **πορνειας** D, Par., Wer.², Syr. Harcl. mg., Sah., Aeth., Irint., Cypr. (with
many variations) read **και οσα μη θελετε εαυτοις γινεσθαι, ετερω μη ποιειν**, so Blass
in **β**, and Hilg.

² **πραξετε** אAB, Vulg., all edd. ; **πραξατε** CDHL ; **πραξητε** E ; see Zahn, *u. s.*,
p. 354. After **πραξ.** D, Iren., Tert. (Ephrem) add **φερομενοι εν τω αγιω πνευματι**,
so Blass in **β**. Harris, *Four Lectures*, etc., p. 77, thinks that the gloss has been
misplaced, and declining all references to Montanus or Marcion or to N.T. parallels,
regards it as simply an expansion or explanation of **απολυθεντες**, ver. 30 ; *cf*. xiii. 4.
Weiss also declines all Montanist influence, but takes the words after **εν πραξ.** as
meaning that they would fare well being guided by the Holy Spirit, by Whom the
decree, ver. 28, had been inspired. **ερρωσθε**, Blass brackets in **β**, *om*. by Irenæus ;
see also Zahn, *u. s.*, p. 354.

³ **ηλθον**, but **κατηλθον** אABCD 61, Vulg., Arm., Aeth., Theophyl., so Tisch.,
W.H., Blass, R.V., Weiss, Wendt. After **απολυθεντες** D* adds **εν ημεραις ολιγαις**,
so Blass in **β**, and Hilg. Belser, *Beiträge*, p. 72, speaks of the addition as more
valuable than much gold, as showing their eagerness to bring the good news to
Antioch, and the speed of their travelling, contrasted with ver. 3. Weiss however
would connect it (p. 82), not with the time consumed in the journey, but with the
time of their departure, *i.e.*, they set off a few days after the Council to put an end
to the disquietude at Antioch.

⁴ After **οντες** D adds **πληρεις πνευματος αγιου**, so Blass and Hilg., no Montanistic
source ; either explanation of **προφ.** (unnecessary), or may be connected with **δια
λογου** implying that their oral words no less than the written letter were spoken in
the Holy Ghost (Weiss, p. 82). Mr. Page, *Classical Review*, p. 320 (1897), refers
this addition, with similar ones in vv. 7 and 29 of this chap., to the characteristic of
D " to emphasise words and actions as inspired ".

prosperity. For D, see critical notes.—
ἔρρωσθε, see critical notes, 2 Macc. xi.
21 and 33, 3 Macc. vii. 9, etc., and often
in classics ; a natural conclusion of a
letter addressed to Gentile Christians,
see additional note (2) at end of chapter.
Ver. 30. **οἱ μὲν οὖν . . . ἀναγνόντες
δέ**: two parties are presented as acting
in concert as here (or in opposition), see
Rendall, *Acts*, Appendix on **μὲν οὖν**, p.
161.—**ἦλθον**, but **κατῆλθον** R.V.: Jerusalem is still the centre from which Barnabas and Paul go down. See reading in
D, critical note.—**τὸ πλῆθος** = **ἡ ἐκκλησία**,
cf. xiv. 27 ; Deissmann, *Neue Bibelstudien*, p. 59, especially refers to this passage : **τὸ πλ.** = *Christengemeinde* at Antioch, *cf. plebs, populus* in Lat. Chr. authors.
—**ἐπέδωκαν τὴν ἐπισ.**, see instances in
Wetstein of same phrase in same sense.

Ver. 31. **παρακλήσει**: A. and R.V.
" consolation " (" exhortation " margin,
R.V.). The former rendering seems suitable here, because the letter causes rejoicing, not as an exhortation, but as a
message of relief and concord. Ramsay
and Hort render " encouragement ".
Barnabas was a fitting bearer of such a
message, *cf*. iv. 36.
Ver. 32. **καὶ αὐτοὶ προφ. ὄντες**:
Wendt, so Meyer, takes **καὶ αὐτοί** not
with **προφ. ὄντες** (these words in com-
mas), but with the words which follow,
indicating that Judas and Silas gave
encouragement to the brethren personally (*cf*. ver. 27), as the letter had verbally ; but punctuation of T.R. in R.V.,
W.H., Weiss, etc. On **καὶ αὐτοί** and
its frequency in St. Luke, Friedrich, p.
37 ; Hawkins, *Horæ Synopticæ* (1899), p.

ἐπεστήριξαν.   33. Ποιήσαντες δὲ χρόνον, ἀπελύθησαν μετ᾿ εἰρήνης ἀπὸ τῶν ἀδελφῶν πρὸς τοὺς ἀποστόλους.¹   34.² ἔδοξε δὲ τῷ Σίλα

¹ αποστολους EHLP, Syrr. P. and H., Bohwi., Arm., Chrys.; but αποστειλαντας αυτους ℵABCD, Vulg., Sah., Bohboett., Aethro., so Tisch., W.H., Blass, R.V., Weiss, Wendt, Blass and Hilg.

² Om. ℵABEHLP 61, Vulg. (am. fu. demid.), Syr. Pesh., Syr. H. text, Bohboett., Chrys., so Tisch., W.H., R.V. text, Weiss, Wendt.   In CD 13, Vulgclem. + tol., Sah., Bohwi., Syr. Harcl. mg., Arm., Aethut., so Blass and Hilg.   Also D, Gig., Wern., Prov., Vulg.clem., Cassiod. add μονος δε Ιουδας επορευθη (Wern. adding "reversus est Hierosolyma," cf. also Vulg.cl.).   It is difficult to see why if 34ᵃ was genuine it should have been omitted, but the sentence may have been introduced to account for the presence of Silas at Antioch in ver. 40; so Weiss and Corssen.   (In C and D αυτους instead of αυτου, and in a few mins. αυτοθι.)   Ver. 34ᵃ is defended as genuine by Ramsay, St. Paul, pp. 174, 175; Zahn, Einleitung, i., p. 148 (whilst both regard 34ᵇ as a gloss); cf. Belser, Beiträge, p. 73, on the same ground, viz., that ver. 33 does not declare that Judas and Silas actually departed, but only that they were free to depart.   The Bezan reviser found the first part of the verse in his text and added the second.   Blass retains both parts of the verse in β.   If the first clause was introduced to explain a supposed difficulty about Silas, it must be remembered that the difficulty was more fanciful than real, since Barnabas takes Mark from Jerusalem, xiii. 13 (see Ramsay, u. s.).   W.H., App., p. 96, considers the first clause as probably Alexandrian, as well as Western, while Corssen regards them both as Western.

33.—παρεκάλεσαν: A. and R.V., "exhorted"; R.V. margin, "comforted," Ramsay, "encouraged" (so Hort; or "exhorted").   Possibly the word may include something of all these meanings (see also Alford's note).—ἐπεστήριξαν, cf. xiv. 22.

Ver. 33. ποιήσαντες δὲ χρόνον, cf. xviii. 23, and xx. 3, only in Acts in N.T., cf. 2 Cor. xi. 25, James iv. 13.   For the phrase both in LXX and classical Greek (so in Latin), see Wetstein, Blass, Grimm. In LXX cf. Prov. xiii. 23, Eccl. vi. 12 (Tob. x. 7), so Hebrew עָשָׂה יָמִים.—μετ᾿ εἰρήνης: exact phrase only Heb. xi. 31 in N.T.; in LXX several times; in Apocryha, in 1 and 3 Macc.—πρὸς τοὺς ἀποσ.: but if as in R.V., "unto those that had sent them" (see critical notes and Hort, Ecclesia, p. 73), i.e., the whole synod at Jerusalem, not only the Apostles.

Ver. 34. Omitted in R.V. text, but not in margin.   See critical notes.

Ver. 35. διέτριβον, cf. xii. 19, and see also on xvi. 12.   In LXX cf. Lev. xiv. 8, Jer. xlii. (xxxv.) 7, Judith x. 2, 2 Macc. xiv. 23.   So also in classics with or without χρόνον.—διδάσ. καὶ εὐαγγ.: possibly the first may refer to work inside the Church, and the second to work outside, but the distinction can scarcely be pressed.   Within this time, according to Wendt, falls the incident between Paul and Peter, Gal. ii. 11.   On the other hand, see Weiss, Apostelgeschichte, p. 194, who thinks that the τινας ἡμέρας

excludes, Gal. ii., etc., but the phrase is very indefinite, and may have included months as well as days, cf. xvi. 12, and ix. 23.   On the incident referred to see additional note at end of chapter.

Ver. 36. μετὰ δέ: second missionary journey commences, ending xviii. 22. — ἐπιστρέψαντες, reversi, cf. Luke ii. 39, W.H., xvii. 31.   The word is so used in LXX, and in modern Greek (Kennedy, p. 155).—δή, see on xiii. 2.— ἐπισκεψ., see above on vi. 3.   The word was characteristic of a man like St. Paul, whose heart was the heart of the world, and who daily sustained the care of all the churches.—πῶς ἔχουσι: "in fide, amore, spe . . . nervus visitationis ecclesiasticæ" Bengel.

Ver. 37. ἐβουλεύσατο, but ἐβούλετο see critical note, "wished," volebat; R.V., "was minded" almost too strong.   Possibly owing to his kinship, Barnabas may have taken a more lenient view than Paul.

Ver. 38. ἠξίου, cf. xxviii. 22 (Luke vii. 7), and cf. 1 Macc. xi. 28, 2 Macc. ii. 8, etc.—ἐβούλ. is a mild word compared with this.—συμπαραλαβεῖν, cf. xii. 25, used also by Paul in Gal. ii. 1 of taking Titus with him to Jerusalem, and nowhere else in N.T. except in this passage, cf. Job i. 4, 3 Macc. i. 1, so in classical Greek.—τὸν ἀποστάντα ἀπ᾿ αὐτῶν: the neutral word ἀποχωρεῖν ἀπ᾿ αὐτῶν, xiii. 13, is not used here, but a word which may denote not disloyalty in the sense of apostasy from Christ, but to the mission,

ἐπιμεῖναι αὐτοῦ. 35. Παῦλος δὲ καὶ Βαρνάβας διέτριβον ἐν
Ἀντιοχείᾳ, διδάσκοντες καὶ εὐαγγελιζόμενοι, μετὰ καὶ ἑτέρων πολλῶν, τὸν λόγον τοῦ Κυρίου.

I Tim. iv. I (Rendall); it is doubtful, however, whether we can press this (see Weiss, *in loco*).—τοῦτον: significant at the end of the verse, and note also decisive contradiction between συμπαραλ., ver. 37, and μὴ συμπαραλ. here.

Ver. 39. παροξυσμός, Heb. x. 24, in different sense, nowhere else in N.T. The verb is found twice, Acts xvii. 16, I Cor. xiii. 5; in the former passage of Paul's righteous provocation in Athens, and in the latter of irritation of mind as here; the noun twice in LXX of God's righteous anger, Deut. xxix. 28, Jer. xxxix. (xxxii.) 37 (*cf.* also the verb, Deut. ix. 7, 8, etc.), so too in Dem. Both noun and verb are common in medical language (Hobart); παροξυσμός, φησίν, ἐγένετο οὐχ ἔχθρα οὐδὲ φιλονεικία; in the result good, for Mark was stirred up to greater diligence by Paul, and the kindness of Barnabas made him cling to him all the more devotedly, *cf.* Oecumenius, *in loco.*—ἀποχωρισθῆναι: "they parted asunder," R.V., *cf.* διαχωρίζεσθαι ἀπό, Gen. xiii. 11, 14, *cf.* Luke ix. 33.—παραλαβόντα: not the compound verb, because Barnabas alone takes Mark.—ἐκπλεῦσαι: with εἰς also in xviii. 18, with ἀπό in xx. 6; on πλέω and the number of its compounds in St. Luke, *cf.* xxvii. 4, etc. —εἰς K.: where he could be sure of influence, since by family he belonged to the Jews settled there, iv. 36. Barnabas is not mentioned again in Acts, and it is to be noted that St. Paul's friendship was not permanently impaired either with him or with Mark (see Chrysostom, *in loco*, and *cf.* I Cor. ix. 6). In Gal. ii. 13 St. Paul in speaking of Barnabas marks by implication his high estimate of his character and the expectations he had formed of him; καὶ B. "even Barnabas" (Lightfoot, *Gal.*, *in loco*, and Hackett). According to tradition Barnabas remained in Cyprus until his death, and the appearance of Mark at a later stage may point to this; but although possibly Mark's rejoining Paul may have been occasioned by the death of Barnabas, the sources for the life of Barnabas outside the N.T. are quite untrustworthy, "Barnabas," B.D.²; Hackett, *Acts*, p. 192. Whatever his fortunes may have been, St. Luke did not estimate his work in the same category as that of Paul as a main factor in the development

of the Church, although we must never forget that "twice over did Barnabas save Saul for the work of Christianity". —Μάρκον: In his two imprisonments St. Paul mentions Mark in terms of high approval, Col. iv. 10, 11, Philem. 24, 2 Tim. iv. 11. In the first imprisonment St. Paul significantly recommends him to the Colossians as being the cousin of Barnabas, one of his own fellow-labourers unto the kingdom of God, one amongst the few who had been a παρηγορία, a comfort unto him. In such words as these St. Paul breaks the silence of the years during which we hear nothing of the relations between him and Mark, although the same notice in *Colossians* seems to indicate an earlier reconciliation than the date of the letter, since the Churches of the Lycus valley had already been instructed to receive Mark if he passed that way, *Expositor*, August, 1897, "St. Mark in the N.T." (Dr. Swete), p. 85.

Ver. 40. Π. δὲ ἐπιλεξ. Σ.: not in the place of Mark, but in the place of Barnabas, Ramsay, *St. Paul*, p. 171; having chosen, *i.e.*, for himself: *sibi eligere;* only in N.T. in this sense, but in classical Greek and in LXX, I Sam. ii. 28 A, 2 Sam. x. 9 R, Ecclus. vi. 18, I Esdras ix. 16, I Macc. i. 63 R, v. 17, etc.; "elegit ut socium, non ut ministrum" (Blass). If Silas had not returned to Jerusalem, but had remained in Antioch (see above on ver. 35), he had doubtless recommended himself to Paul by some special proof of fitness for dealing sympathetically with the relations of the Jewish Christians and the Gentile converts. This sympathy on the part of Silas would be the more marked and significant as he was himself almost certainly a Hebrew; otherwise we cannot account for his high position in the Jerusalem Church, ver. 22, although his Roman citizenship is implied in xvi. 37; perhaps this latter fact may account for his freedom from narrow Jewish prejudices. If we may identify, as we reasonably may, the Silas of Acts with the Silas (Silvanus) of the Epistles, 2 Cor. i. 19, I Thess. i. 1, 2 Thess. i. 1, I Pet. v. 12, the last mention of him by St. Peter becomes very suggestive. For St. Peter's First Epistle contains the names of the two men, Mark and Sil-

36. ΜΕΤΑ δέ τινας ἡμέρας εἶπε Παῦλος πρὸς Βαρνάβαν, Ἐπιστρέψαντες δὴ ἐπισκεψώμεθα τοὺς ἀδελφοὺς ἡμῶν [1] κατὰ πᾶσαν πόλιν, ἐν

[1] ημων om. with ℵABCDE, Vulg., Sah., Boh., Syrr. P. and H., Arm., Chrys.,
Tisch., W.H., Blass, R.V., Weiss, Wendt, and Hilg.

vanus, who had originally been members
of the Jerusalem Church, Acts xii. 12,
xv. 22, and moreover the two oldest of
St. Paul's associates, whose brotherly
Christian concord had been broken for
the time (when Paul chose the latter in
the place of Barnabas, and rejected
Mark's services altogether), but who are
now both found at St. Peter's side in
Rome (assuming that Babylon is Rome),
evidently at one with him and with each
other; the one the bearer of a letter, the
other the sender of greetings, to *Pauline*
Churches. If St. Paul had passed to his
rest, and the leader had thus changed,
the teaching was the same, as the names
of Silvanus and Mark assure us, and St.
Peter takes up and carries on the work of
the Apostle of the Gentiles, see Dr. Swete,
u. s., pp. 87, 88.—ἐξῆλθε, *cf.* Luke ix. 6,
3 John, ver. 7, where the word is used of
going forth for missionary work.—παραδοθεὶς, *cf.* xiv. 26. Possibly we may
infer that the Church took Paul's view
of the point at issue between himself and
Barnabas, but on the other hand we
cannot prove this, because the writer's
thoughts are so specially fixed upon
Paul as the great and chief worker in
the organisation and unification of the
Church.

Ver. 41. διήρχετο, see above on xiii.
6.—Συρίαν καὶ Κιλικίαν: as Barnabas
had turned to Cyprus, the scene of his
early labours in the Gospel, and perhaps
also his own home, so Paul turned to
Syria and Cilicia, not only because his
home was in Cilicia, but also because he
had worked there in his early Christian
life and labours, *Gal.*, i., 21, 23. It is a
coincidence with the notice in *Gal.* that
St. Luke here and in ver. 23 presupposes
the existence of Churches in Syria and
Cilicia, although nothing had been previously said of their foundation, whilst
the presence of Saul at Tarsus is twice
intimated, ix. 30, xi. 25. Moreover the
commencement of the letter, vv. 22, 23,
indicates that these regions had been the
centre of the teaching of the Judaisers,
and St. Paul's presence, together with
the fact that Silas, a prominent and leading member of the Jerusalem Church,
was his colleague, would doubtless help
to prevent further disquiet. On the ad-

dition to the verse in the Bezan text see
critical note.

Additional note (1).

Amongst recent writers on the *Acts*,
Mr. Rendall has stated that the evidence
for the identification of Acts xv. with
Gal. ii. 1-10 is overwhelming, *Appendix*
to Acts, pp. 357, 359. If we cannot fully
endorse this, it is at all events noticeable
that critics of widely different schools
of thought have refused to regard the
alleged differences between the two as
irreconcilable; in this conservative writers
like Lechler, Godet, Belser, Knabenbauer and Zahn, *Einleitung*, ii., 627, 628;
scientific critics, as we may call them,
like Reuss, B. Weiss; and still more
advanced critics like Lipsius and H.
Holtzmann are agreed. This general
agreement is recognised and endorsed
by Wendt, p. 255 (1899), see also K.
Schmidt, "Apostelkonvent," in *Real-
Encyclopädie für protest. Theol.* (Hauck),
p. 704 ff. Amongst English writers
Lightfoot, Hort, Sanday, Salmon, Drummond, Turner may be quoted on the
same side (so too McGiffert, *Apostolic
Age*, p. 208), (see for the points of agreement, Lightfoot, *Galatians*, p. 123;
Drummond, *Galatians*, p. 73 ff.; Salmon,
"Galatians," B.D.[2]; Reuss, *Geschichte
des h. S. des N. T.*, p. 60, sixth edition,
and very fully in Belser, *Die Selbstvertheidigung der h. Paulus im Galaterbriefe*, p. 83 ff., 1896; for the difficulty in
identifying Gal. ii. with any other visit
of St. Paul to Jerusalem, *cf.* Salmon,
Lightfoot, *u. s.*, and Zahn, *u. s.*, Felten,
Introd. to *Apostelgeschichte*, p. 46). But
the recent forcible attempt of Professor
Ramsay to identify Gal. ii. 1-10 with St.
Paul's second visit to Jerusalem, Acts
xi. 30, xii. 25, and not with the third
visit, Acts xv., has opened up the whole
question again (see on the same identification recently proposed from a very different point of view by Völter, *Witness
of the Epistles*, p. 231, and also by
Spitta, *Apostelgeschichte*, p. 184). At
first sight it is no doubt in favour of this
conclusion that according to Acts the
journey, xi. 30, is the second made by
St. Paul to Jerusalem, and the journey
in xv. the third, whilst Gal. ii. 1 also
describes a journey which the Apostle

αἷς κατηγγείλαμεν τὸν λόγον τοῦ Κυρίου, πῶς ἔχουσι · 37.[1] Βαρνάβας
δὲ ἐβουλεύσατο συμπαραλαβεῖν τὸν Ἰωάννην τὸν καλούμενον Μάρκον ·

[1] After πως εχουσι and at commencement of verse Syr. Harcl. mg. prefixes "placuit
autem cogitatio Barnabæ," so Blass in β. εβουλευσατο, but with ℵABCE 13, 61,
Vulg. verss., so Tisch., W.H., Blass, R.V., Weiss, Wendt, εβουλετο; D, Gig.
εβουλευετο, so Hilg.

himself represents as his second to the
mother-city. We cannot fairly solve
this difficulty by cutting the knot with
McGiffert, who regards Acts xi. 30 and xv.
as = Gal. ii. 1-10, and thinks that Luke
found two independent accounts of the
same journey, and supposed them to
refer to separate events (*Apostolic Age*,
p. 171); or by concluding with Drummond, *Galatians*, p. 78, that the writer
of Acts made a mistake in bringing St.
Paul to Jerusalem at the time of the
famine, so that Gal. ii. and Acts xv.
both refer to his second visit (*cf.* to the
same effect, Wendt, p. 218 (1899), who
looks upon the visit described in xi. 25
as a mistake of the author, at all events
as regards Paul). But McGiffert and
Drummond are both right in emphasising
one most important and, as it seems to
us, crucial difficulty in the way of the
view advocated by Ramsay; if he is
correct, it is difficult to see any object
in the visit described in Acts xv. After
the decision already arrived at in Gal. ii.
1-10: Acts xi. 30, xii. 25, the question
then *ex hypothesi* at issue could scarcely
have been raised again in the manner
described in Acts xv. Moreover, whilst
Ramsay admits that another purpose was
achieved by the journey to Jerusalem
described in Gal. ii. 1-10, although only
as a mere private piece of business, *St.
Paul*, p. 57, he maintains that the special
and primary object of the visit was to
relieve the poor. But if the pillars of
the Church were already aware, as *ex
hypothesi* they must have been aware,
that St. Paul came to Jerusalem bringing
food and money for the poor (Acts xi.
29, 30), we may be pardoned for finding
it difficult to believe that the "one charge
alone" (Gal. ii. 10) which they gave him
was to do the very thing which he
actually came for the purpose of doing.
If, too, Barnabas and Saul had just been
associated in helping the poor, and if
the expression ὃ καὶ ἐσπούδασα, Gal. ii.
10, refers, as Professor Ramsay holds, to
this service, we should hardly have expected Paul to use the first person singular, but rather to have associated
Barnabas with himself in his reference

to their work of love and danger. Professor Ramsay emphasises the fact (*Expositor*, p. 183, March, 1896) that Luke
pointedly records that the distribution
was carried out to its completion by
Barnabas and Saul in person (Acts xii.
25). Why then does Paul only refer to
his own zeal in remembering the poor
in Acts xi. 29, and xii. 25 = Gal. ii. 1-10?
(On the force of the aorist as against
Professor Ramsay's view, see *Expositor*,
March, 1899, p. 221, Mr. Vernon Bartlet's
note.) Gal. ii. 10 should rather be read
in the light of 1 Cor. xvi. 1-3; if the first-
named Epistle was also the first in point
of time, then we can understand how,
whilst it contains no specific and definite
mention of a collection for the Church
at Jerusalem, which is so emphasised in
1 Cor. xvi. 1, 2 Cor. viii. 9, etc., yet the
eager desire of the pillars of the Church
that the poor in Judæa should be remembered, and the thought of a fund for
supplying their needs, may well have
been working in St. Paul's mind from
the earlier time of the expression of that
desire and need, Gal. ii. 10, *Expositor*,
November, 1893, " Pauline Collection
for the Saints," and April, 1894,
"The Galatians of St. Paul," Rendall;
Hort, *Judaistic Christianity*, p. 67.

For reasons why St. Paul did not refer
to his second visit to Jerusalem when
writing to the Galatians see on xi. 30,
and Salmon, "Galatians," B.D.[2], p. 1111;
Sanday, *Expositor*, February, 1896, p.
92; Hort, *Judaistic Christianity*, p. 61;
"Acts of the Apostles," p. 30, Hastings'
B.D. and "Chron. of the N.T.," *ibid.*, p.
423; Zahn, *Einleitung*, ii., 629. Further:
Dr. Sanday has emphasised the fact that
at the time of St. Paul's second visit to
Jerusalem the state of things which we
find in Acts xv. (the third visit) did not
exist; that a stage in the controversy as
to the terms of admission of Gentile converts had been reached by the date of
Acts xv. which had not been reached at
the date of xi. 30; that at this latter
date, *e.g.*, there was no such clear de-
marcation of spheres between St. Peter
and St. Paul, and that it is not until Acts
xiii. 46 that the turning-point is actually

38. Παῦλος δὲ ἠξίου,[1] τὸν ἀποστάντα ἀπ᾿ αὐτῶν ἀπὸ Παμφυλίας, καὶ μὴ συνελθόντα αὐτοῖς εἰς τὸ ἔργον,[2] μὴ συμπαραλαβεῖν τοῦτον.

[1] For ηξιου D reads ουκ εβουλετο λεγων.

[2] For μη συμπ. τουτον D reads τουτον μη ειναι συν αυτοις; see on the passage Weiss, Codex D, p. 83; but if Weiss is correct, it has been well asked, how came Paul to take Silas? Hilg. reads ιεναι for ειναι. συμπαραλαβειν, cf. ver. 37, but pres. infin. ℵABC 61, 180, Tisch., W.H., Blass, R.V., Wendt, Weiss.

reached: henceforth St. Paul assumes his true "Apostleship of the Gentiles," and preaches a real "Gospel of the uncircumcision"; see especially *Expositor*, July, 1896, p. 62. Of course Professor Ramsay's theory obliges us to place Gal. ii. 1-10 *before* the Apostolic Conference, and to suppose that when the events narrated in Gal. ii. took place, the journey of Acts xiii., xiv. was still in the future. But is not the whole tone and attitude of St. Paul in Gal. ii. 1-10, placing himself, *e.g.*, before Barnabas in ver. 9 and evidently regarding himself as the foremost representative of one sphere of missionary work, as St. Peter was of the other, ver. 8, more easily explained if his first missionary journey was already an accomplished fact and not still in the future?

In the two short references to Paul's second visit to Jerusalem, Acts xi. 30, xii. 25, it is still "Barnabas and Saul," so too in xiii. 1, 2, 7; not till xiii. 9 does the change come: henceforth Paul takes the lead, vv. 13, 16, 43, 45, 50, etc., with two exceptions as Professor Ramsay pointedly describes them (see above on xiii. 9), and in the account of the Conference and all connected with it St. Luke and the Church at Antioch evidently regard Paul as the leader, xv. 2 (2), 22 (although the Church at Jerusalem places Barnabas first, vv. 12, 25). But in xi. 30, xii. 25 the historian speaks of "Barnabas and Saul". The whole position of St. Paul assigned to him by St. Luke in Acts xv. is in harmony with the Apostle's own claims and prominence in Gal. ii. 1-10; it is not in harmony with the subordinate place which the same St. Luke assigns to him in the second visit to Jerusalem. In other words, if Gal. ii. 1-10 = Acts xv., then St. Paul's claim to be an Apostle of the Gentiles is ratified by the Gentile Luke; but if Gal. ii. 1-10 = Acts xi. 30, xii. 25, then there is no hint in Acts that Luke as yet regarded Paul in any other light than a subordinate to the Hebrew Barnabas; he is still Saul, not Paul. For the points of discrepancy between Gal. ii. 1-10 and Acts xv. see

same authorities as above; one point upon which Ramsay strongly insists, *viz.*, that a visit which is said to be "by revelation," Gal. ii. 2, cannot be identified with a visit which takes place by the appointment of the Church, Acts xv. 2, is surely hypercritical; it would not be the first occasion on which the Spirit and the Church had spoken in harmony; in Acts xiii. 3, 4 the Church ἀπέλυσαν sent away Paul and Barnabas, and yet in the next verse we read οἱ ἐκπεμφθέντες ὑπὸ τοῦ ἁγίου πνεύματος, see Lightfoot, *Galatians*, p. 125; Drummond, *Galatians*, p. 75; Turner, "Chronology of the N.T.," Hastings' B.D., p. 424; *cf.* also Wendt, p. 258 (1899), and Zahn, *Einleitung*, ii., 632, who both point out that the statements referred to are by no means mutually exclusive. On the whole question see Wendt's 1899 edition, p. 255 ff., and *Expositor*, 1896 (February, March, April, July) for its full discussion by Dr. Sanday and Professor Ramsay.

A further question arises as to the position to be assigned to the incident in Gal. ii. 11-14. Professor Ramsay, *St. Paul*, p. 157 ff., supposes that it took place *before* the Apostolic Conference, and finds a description of the occasion of the incident in Acts xv. 1, Acts xv. 24, Gal. ii. 12, *i.e.*, in the words of three authorities, St. Luke, the Apostles at Jerusalem, and St. Paul himself; the actual conflict between St. Peter and St. Paul took place after the latter's second visit to Jerusalem, but before his third visit. The issue of the conflict is not described by Paul, but it is implied in the events of the Jerusalem Conference, Acts xv. 2, 7. Barnabas had wavered, but had afterwards joined Paul; Peter had been rebuked, but had received the rebuke in such a way as to become a champion of freedom in the ensuing Conference, employing to others the argument which had convinced himself, *cf.* Acts xv. 10, Gal. ii. 14. Mr. Turner, "Chronology of the N.T.," Hastings' B.D., i., 424, is inclined to adopt this view, which identifies the two Judaising missions from Jerusalem to Antioch, Gal.

39. ἐγένετο οὖν παροξυσμός, ὥστε ἀποχωρισθῆναι αὐτοὺς ἀπ' ἀλλήλων,
τόν[1] τε Βαρνάβαν παραλαβόντα τὸν Μάρκον ἐκπλεῦσαι εἰς Κύπρον·

[1] D amplifies after αλληλων τοτε Β. παραλαβ. τον Μ. επλευσεν εις Κ., so Blass
and Hilg.   Weiss sees in τοτε a characteristic of D; cf. ii. 37.

ii. 12 and Acts xv. 1, while he still maintains the ordinary view that Gal. ii. 1-10
= Acts xv. This, as he points out, we
may easily do, whilst Gal. ii. 11-14 may
be allowed to precede Gal. ii. 1-10 in
order of time, and in the absence of the
ἔπειτα in Gal. i. 18, 21, ii. 1 there is
nothing to suggest that the chronological
series is continued.   It may be noted
that Paley, *Horæ Paulinæ*, v., 9, had remarked that there is nothing to hinder
us from supposing that the dispute at
Antioch was prior to the Conference at
Jerusalem.   Moreover it may be fairly
urged that this view puts a more favourable construction on the conduct of St.
James and St. Peter in relation to the
compact which they had made with Paul
at the Jerusalem Conference. But on
the attitude of St. James and the expression ἐλθεῖν τινὰς ἀπὸ 'Ιακώβου, see Hort,
Judaistic Christianity, p. 79; Lightfoot
on Gal. ii. 12; Drummond, *Galatians*, p.
85; and with regard to the conduct of
St. Peter, see Hort, *u. s.*, p. 76; Lightfoot on the collision at Antioch, *Galatians*, p. 125 ff.; and Salmon, "Galatians," B.D.[2], p. 1114; Drummond, *u. s.*,
p. 78.
On Zahn's position that the dispute
between Peter and Paul took place before the Apostolic Conference, when the
former betook himself to Antioch after
his liberation, Acts xii. 5 ff., a view put
forward also by Schneckenburger, *Zweck
der Apostelgeschichte*, p. 109 ff., see
Neue Kirchl. Zeitschr., p. 435 ff., 1894,
and Belser's criticism, *Die Selbstvertheidigung des h. Paulus im Galaterbriefe*,
p. 127 ff., 1896 (*Biblische Studien*).
Wendt, pp. 211, 212 (1899), while
declining to attempt any explanation
either · psychological or moral of St.
Peter's action in Gal. ii. 11-14, points out
with justice how perverse it is to argue
that Peter could not have previously
conducted himself with reference to Cornelius as Acts describes when we remember that in the incident before us
Barnabas, who had been the constant
companion of St. Paul in the Gentile
mission, shared nevertheless in St. Peter's
weakness.
Additional note (2), *cf.* ver. 29.
A further question arises as to why the
particular prohibitions of the Decree are
mentioned.   According to a very common
view they represented the Seven Precepts
of Noah, six of which were said to have
been given by God to Adam, while the
seventh was given as an addition to
Noah.   The Seven Precepts were as
follows: (1) against profanation of God's
name; (2) against idolatry; (3) against
fornication; (4) against murder; (5)
against theft; (6) to obey those in authority; (7) against eating living flesh, *i.e.*,
flesh with the blood in it, see Schürer
Jewish People, div. ii., vol. ii., p. 318,
E.T.; Hort, *Judaistic Christianity*, p.
69.   No doubt there are points of contact between these Precepts and the four
Prohibitions of the Decree, but at the
same time it would seem that there are
certainly four of the Precepts to which
there is nothing corresponding in the
Decree.   The Precepts were binding on
every *Gêr Toshav*, a stranger sojourning
in the land of Israel, but it has been
erroneously supposed that the *Gêr
Toshav* = σεβόμενος, and thus the conclusion is drawn that the idea of the
four prohibitions was to place Gentiles on
the footing of σεβόμενοι in the Christian
community.   Against this identification
of the *Gêr Toshav* and the σεβόμενος
Schürer's words are decisive, *u. s.*, pp.
318, 319.   But if this view was valid
historically, the position of the Gentile
Christians under such conditions would
have been far from satisfactory, and we
cannot suppose that Paul would have
regarded any such result as a success;
still circumcision and the keeping of the
law would have been necessary to entitle
a man to the full privilege of the Christian
Church and name. Ritschl, who takes
practically the same view as Wendt
below, admits that in a certain degree
the Gentile Christians would be regarded
as in an inferior position to the Jewish
Christians, *Altkatholische Kirche*, pp. 131,
133, second edition.
It seems even more difficult to trace
the prohibitions of the Decree to the
Levitical prohibitions, Lev. xvii., xviii.,
which were binding on strangers or
sojourners in Israel (LXX προσήλυτοι),
since, if the written law was to be the
source of the Jerusalem prohibitions, it
is inexplicable that the variations from
it both in matter and number should be

40. Παῦλος δὲ ἐπιλεξάμενος Σίλαν ἐξῆλθε, παραδοθεὶς τῇ χάριτι τοῦ Θεοῦ [1] ὑπὸ τῶν ἀδελφῶν.   41. διήρχετο δὲ τὴν Συρίαν καὶ Κιλικίαν,

[1] τοῦ Θεου, cf. xiv. 26, but best τοῦ K. with אAB(D), Vulg. (am. fu. demid. tol.), Sah., so Tisch., W.H., Blass, R.V., Wendt, Weiss, Hilg.

so observable (Hort, u. s., p. 70); and although Wendt (so Ritschl, Overbeck, Lipsius, Zöckler, Holtzmann, and others; see on the other hand, Weiss, *Biblische Theol.*, p. 145; Felten, *Apostelgeschichte*, p. 297; Lightfoot, *Galatians*, p. 306; Hilgenfeld, *Zeitschrift für wissenschaft. Theol.*, i., 72, 73, 1896) adopts the view that in the four prohibitions of the Jerusalem Decree we have the form in which prohibitions binding upon proselytes in the wider sense, *i.e.*, upon the uncircumcised φοβούμ. or σεβ. τὸν Θεόν, existed in the Apostolic days, he can only say that this is "very probable": of direct historical evidence, as Zöckler admits, there is none. The difficulty is so great in supposing that Paul and Barnabas could have submitted to the distinction drawn between the Jewish Christians and Gentile Christians that it has led to doubts as to the historical character of the decree. Weizsäcker and McGiffert maintain that the decree was formulated after Paul's departure, when James had reconsidered the matter, and had determined that some restriction should be put upon the complete Gentile liberty which had been previously granted. But this view can only be maintained by the sacrifice of xvi. 4, where Paul is distinctly said to have given the decrees to the Churches to keep.

Ramsay, agreeing with Lightfoot, calls the Decree a compromise, and although, as he points out, it seems impossible to suppose that St. Paul would have endorsed a decree which thus made mere points of ritual compulsory, it is probable, he thinks, that after the exordium in which the Jewish party had been so emphatically condemned, the concluding part of the Decree would be regarded as a strong recommendation that the four points should be observed in the interests of peace and amity (*St. Paul*, p. 172). In a previous passage, p. 167, he seems to take a very similar view to Wendt, who answers the question as to how the Precepts of the Decree were to be observed by the Gentile converts by maintaining that they were an attempt to make intercourse more feasible between the Jewish Christians and their Gentile brethren, p. 265 (1899).

We naturally ask why the Decree apparently fell so quickly into abeyance, and why it did not hold good over a wider area, since in writing to Corinth and Rome St. Paul never refers to it. But, to say nothing of the principle laid down in the reading of Codex D (see above on p. 323), St. Paul's language in 1 Cor. viii. 1-13, x. 14-22, Rom. xiv., may be fairly said to possess the spirit of the Decree, and to mark the discriminating wisdom of one eager to lead his disciples behind the rule to the principle; and there is no more reason to doubt the historical truth of the compact made in the Jerusalem Decree, because St. Paul never expressly refers to it, than there is to throw doubt upon his statement in Gal. ii. 10, because he does not expressly refer to it as an additional motive for urging the Corinthians to join in the collection for the poor saints, 2 Cor. viii. 9. But further, there is a sufficient answer to the above question in the fact that the Decree was ordained for the Churches which are specifically mentioned, *viz.*, those of Antioch (placed first as the centre of importance, not only as the local capital of Syria, but as the mother of the Gentile Churches, the Church from which the deputation had come), Syria and Cilicia. In these Churches Jewish prejudice had made itself felt, and in these Churches with their constant communication with Jerusalem the Decree would be maintained. The language of St. James in xxi. 25 proves that some years later reference was naturally made to the Decree as a standard still regulating the intercourse between Jewish and Gentile Christians, at least in Jerusalem, and we may presume in the Churches neighbouring. St. Paul's attitude towards the Decree is marked by loyal acceptance on the one hand, and on the other by a deepening recognition of his own special sphere among the Gentiles as the Apostle of the Gentiles, Gal. ii. 9. Thus we find him delivering the Decrees to the Churches of his first missionary journey, xvi. 4, although those Churches were not mentioned in the address of the Decree (no mention is made of the same action on his part towards the Churches in Syria and Cilicia, xv. 41, doubtless because they were already aware of the enactments prescribed). It may well be that St. Paul regarded himself as the missionary-Apostle of the Church at Antioch, sent forth from that Church for a special work, and that he would recognise that if the Antiochian Christians were to be loyal to the compact of Jerusalem, he as their representative and emissary must enforce the requirements of that compact in revisiting those regions in which the converts had been so instrumental in causing the Decree to be enacted.

But the work upon which he had been specially sent forth from Antioch had been fulfilled, xiv. 27 ; the Conference at Jerusalem had assigned a wider and a separate sphere to his labours ; henceforth his Apostleship to the Gentiles εἰς τὰ ἔθνη was more definitely recognised, and more abundantly fulfilled ; and in what may be called strictly Gentile Churches, in Churches not only further removed from Palestine, but in which his own Apostleship was adequate authority, he may well have felt that he was relieved from enforcing the Decree. In these Churches the stress laid upon such secondary matters as "things strangled and blood" would simply have been a cause of perplexity, a burden too heavy to bear, the source of a Christianity maimed by Jewish particularism, see Lightfoot, *Galatians*, pp. 127, 305 ; Hort, *Ecclesia*, pp. 88, 89 ; *Judaistic Christianity*, p. 74 ; *Speaker's Commentary*, Acts, p. 325 ; Zöckler, *Apostelgeschichte*, p. 254 ; "Apostelkonvent," K. Schmidt in *Real-Encyclopädie für protest. Theol.* (Hauck), pp. 710, 711 (1896) ; Wendt, p. 269 (1899) ; and for the after-history of the Decree, K. Schmidt, *u. s.*, Lightfoot, *u .s.*, Plumptre, Felten, and *cf.* also Hooker's remarks, *Eccles. Pol.*, iv., 11, 5 ff.

On the attempt to place the Apostolic Conference at Jerusalem *before* chaps. xiii. and xiv., see *Apostelgeschichte*, Wendt (1899), pp. 254, 255, and McGiffert, *Apostolic Age*, p. 181. Weizsäcker adopts this view because no mention is made in Gal. i. 21 of the missionary journey in Acts xiii., xiv., and he therefore maintains that it could only have taken place after the Conference, but the Epistle does not require that Paul should give a complete account of all his missionary experiences outside Judæa ; he is only concerned to show how far he was or was not likely to have received his Gospel from the older Apostles.

Moreover, it is very difficult to find a place for the close companionship of Paul and Barnabas, and their mutual labours in xiii., xiv. subsequent to the incident described in Gal. ii. 13, whether that incident took place just before or just after the Jerusalem Conference ; in either case a previous mutual association between Paul and Barnabas in mission work amongst the Gentiles, such as that described in Acts xiii., xiv., accounts for the expectations Paul had evidently formed of Barnabas, Gal. ii. 13, and also for the position which the latter holds in Gal. ii. 1-10.

Space forbids us to make more than a very brief reference to the attempts to break up chap. xv. into various sources. Spitta, who places the whole section xv. 1-33 before chap. xiii., refers vv. 1-4, 13-33 to his inferior source B, which the reviser has wrongly inserted here instead of in its proper place after xii. 24, and has added vv. 5-12. Clemen in the same section, which he regards as an interpolation, assigns vv. 1-4, 13-18, 20-22, to his Redactor Judaicus, and vv. 5-12, 19, 23-33 to Redactor Antijudaicus. Clemen, like Spitta, holds that ver. 34 simply takes up again xiv. 28 ; further, he regards xxi. 17-20ª as the source of xv. 1-4, but Jüngst cautiously remarks that there is nothing strange in the fact that an author should use similar expressions to describe similar situations (p. 146)—a piece of advice which he might himself have remembered with advantage on other occasions. Hilgenfeld's "author to Theophilus" plays a large part in the representation of the negotiations at Jerusalem in respect to the Conference and the Decree, and this representation is based, according to Hilgenfeld, upon the narrative of the conversion of Cornelius whom the same author had formerly embellished, although not without some connection with tradition (*Zeitschrift für wissenschaft. Theol.*, p. 59 ff., 1896). Still more recently Wendt (1899) credits the author of Acts with a tolerably free revision of the tradition he had received, with a view of representing the harmony between Paul and the original Apostles in the clearest light : thus the speeches of Peter and James in xv. are essentially his composition ; but Wendt concludes by asserting that it seems in his judgment impossible to separate exactly the additions made by the author of Acts from the tradition, another note of caution against hasty subjective conclusions.

CHAPTER XVI.—Ver. 1. κατήντησε : only in Luke and Paul, nine times in Acts, four times in Paul, xviii. 19, 24, xx.

ἐπιστηρίζων τὰς ἐκκλησίας.¹ XVI. 1.² Κατήντησε δὲ εἰς Δέρβην
καὶ Λύστραν· καὶ ἰδού, μαθητής τις ἦν ἐκεῖ ὀνόματι Τιμόθεος, υἱὸς
γυναικός τινος Ἰουδαίας πιστῆς, πατρὸς δὲ Ἕλληνος· 2. ὃς ἐμαρ-

¹ At end of verse D, Gig., Vulg., Syr. H. mg. add παραδιδους τε και εντολας των
αποστολων και (αποστ. και *om.* D, Cassiod) πρεσβυτερων, so Blass in β and Hilg.
(*cf.* vv. 5, 12 for omission of αποστολοι in β). The words look like an obvious addition,
cf. xvi. 4, but Belser, *Beiträge*, p. 73, defends as "very interesting," as showing that
whilst the mission of Judas and Silas was limited to Antioch, Paul was afterwards
in person the bearer of the decree to the Churches in Syria and Cilicia; see however
Ramsay, *St. Paul*, pp. 173, 174; *C. R. E.*, p. 87.

² Before εἰς Δ. και with AB, Boh., Syr. Harcl. text, so W.H., R.V., Weiss,
Wendt, R.V. ℵAB 61 insert εἰς before Λ., so Tisch., W.H., Blass, R.V., Weiss,
Wendt. τινος *om.* with ℵABCDE 61, Vulg., many verss., so Tisch., W.H., Blass,
R.V., Weiss, Wendt, Hilg. After γυν. 25 (Gig., Prov., Wern.) has χηρας—Blass
rejects. At beginning of verse D, Syr. Harcl. mg. (Gig., Cassiod.) prefix διελθων δε
τα εθνη ταυτα, to show that Lystra and Derbe were not included in Syria and Cilicia,
so also the και in AB may point to the same reason; see Ramsay, *C. R. E.*, p. 87.

15, xxi. 7, xxv. 13, xxvi. 7, xxvii. 12,
xxviii. 13, 1 Cor. x. 11, xiv. 36, Ephes. iv.
13, Phil. iii. 11. But whilst in St. Paul it
is used in a figurative sense, it is used eight
times by St. Luke of arriving at a place
and making some stay there, *cf.* 2 Macc.
iv. 21, 44. The fact that the verb is thus
used frequently in the second part of
Acts and not in i.-xii. is surely easily
accounted for by the subjects of the narrative (Hawkins, *Horæ Synopticæ*, p.
147).—εἰς Δέρβην καὶ Λ.: if we read εἰς
before Λ., also (see critical note): "he
came also to Derbe and to Lystra". The
purpose was implied in xv. 36, but here
places mentioned in the inverse order
of xiv. 6 since coming from Cilicia
through the "Cilician Gates" St. Paul
would visit Derbe first, see Hastings'
B.D., "Derbe" (Ramsay). The two
places are grouped together as a *region*
according to the Roman classification
(Ramsay, *St. Paul*, pp. 110, 179). The
second εἰς before Λ. marks that while
Derbe is mentioned as a place visited,
Lystra is the scene of the events in the
sequel.—καὶ ἰδού: indicating the surprising fact that a successor to Mark was
found at once (so Weiss); whilst Hort
still more significantly marks the form of
the phrase by pointing out that St. Luke
reserves it for sudden and as it were providential interpretations, *Ecclesia*, p. 179,
cf. i. 10, viii. 17, x. 17, xi. 7: however
disheartening had been the rupture
with Barnabas, in Timothy Paul was to
find another "son of consolation," *cf.*
Hort's comment on 1 Tim. i. 18 in this
connection, *u. s.*, pp. 179-185. It must
not however be forgotten that there are
good reasons for seeing in Timothy not

the successor of Barnabas (this was Silas),
but of Mark. It could hardly be said of
one in the position of Silas that he was
like Mark a ὑπηρέτης, on a mere subordinate footing, whereas on the other hand
the difference of age between Barnabas
and Timothy, and their relative positions
to St. Paul would have naturally placed
Timothy in a subordinate position from
the first.—ἐκεῖ, *i.e.*, at Lystra, most probably. The view that reference is made
not to Lystra but to Derbe arises from
supposing that in xx. 4 the word Δερβαῖος refers to Timothy and not to
Gaius, the truth being that Timothy is
not described because already well known.
Certainly the fact that his character was
testified of by those of Lystra, as well as
St. Paul's reference to Lystra in 2 Tim.
iii. 11, seems to favour Lystra as being
at all events the home of Timothy, if not
his birthplace. There is no reason why
the Gaius mentioned as of Macedonia,
xix. 29, should be identified with the
Gaius of xx. 4. Gaius was a very common name, and in the N.T. we have
apparently references to four persons
bearing the name. Blass however refers Δερβαῖος in xx. 4 to Timothy.—
υἱὸς γυναικός τ. Ἰουδ. πιστῆς π. δὲ
Ἕ.: such marriages although forbidden
by the law, Ezra x. 2, were sanctioned under certain conditions, *cf.*
xxiv. 24 in the case of Drusilla, wife of
Aziz, king of Emesa (see also C. and H.,
p. 203), who became a proselyte and
actually accepted circumcision. In the
Diaspora such marriages would probably
be more or less frequent, especially
if the husband became a proselyte. In
this case even if he were ranked as one,

τυρεῖτο ὑπὸ τῶν ἐν Λύστροις καὶ Ἰκονίῳ ἀδελφῶν. 3. τοῦτον
ἠθέλησεν ὁ Παῦλος σὺν αὐτῷ ἐξελθεῖν, καὶ λαβὼν περιέτεμεν αὐτὸν
διὰ τοὺς Ἰουδαίους τοὺς ὄντας ἐν τοῖς τόποις ἐκείνοις · ᾔδεισαν

it could only have been as a "proselyte
of the gate," otherwise Timothy would
surely have been circumcised. We cannot argue from the fact that the boy had
been trained in the Jewish Scriptures
that his father was a proselyte, for the
early training of the child was evidently
the work of the mother, 2 Tim. iii. 15.
But such a duty according to Jewish law
rested primarily upon the father, and the
fact that the father here is described as a
Greek, without any qualifying adjective
as in the case of the wife, indicates that
he was a heathen, see Weiss, *in loco ;*
Edersheim, *Jewish Social Life*, p. 115.
The mother, Eunice (on spelling see
Hastings' B.D.), may conceivably have
been a proselyte, as the name is Greek,
as also that of Lois, but Ἰουδ. seems to
indicate that she was a Jewess by birth.
Whether she was a widow or not we
cannot say, although there is some evidence, see critical note, which points to
the influence of some such tradition.
On the picture of a Jewish home, and
the influence of a Jewish mother, see
Edersheim, *u. s.*—πιστῆς : Lydia was
the same term of herself in ver. 15. Both
mother and son were probably converted
in St. Paul's former visit, and there is no
reason to suppose with Nösgen that the
conversion of the latter was a proof of
the growth of the Church in the Apostle's
absence.

Ver. 2. ἐμαρτυρεῖτο, *cf.* vi. 3, x. 22,
xxii. 12. The good report which may
well have been formed to some extent by
the aptitude and fitness which Timothy
had shown in the Church during St.
Paul's absence may also have helped the
Apostle in the selection of his future
companion. The union of Lystra and
Iconium is quite natural for common intercourse, Ramsay, *St. Paul*, p. 178. There
is no reason to suppose with Rendall that
Iconium would be the home of Eunice,
as the synagogue and principal Jewish
colony were there, see Edersheim, *u. s.*

Ver. 3. περιέτεμεν αὐτὸν : the act might
be performed by *any Israelite ; cf.* Gen.
xvii. 23 for a similar phrase which may indicate that St. Paul performed the act himself. See also Ramsay, *Cities and Bishoprics of Phrygia*, ii., 674 ; the marriage and
the exemption of Timothy from the Mosaic
law may be regarded as typical of a relaxation of the exclusive Jewish standard in

Lycaonia and Phrygia, and an approximation of the Jew to the pagan population
around him, confirmed as it is by the evidence of inscriptions.—διὰ τοὺς Ἰ. : the
true answer to the objection raised against
Paul's conduct may be found in his own
words, 1 Cor. ix. 20 (*cf.* 1 Cor. vii. 19).
As a missionary he would have to make
his way amongst the unbelieving Jews in
the parts which were most hostile to him,
viz., Antioch and Iconium, on his road
into Asia. All along this frequented route
of trade he would find colonies of Jews
in close communication, and the story of
Timothy's parentage would be known
(Ramsay, *St. Paul*, p. 180). But if so,
his own usefulness and that of Timothy
would be impaired, since his Jewish
countrymen would take offence at seeing
him in close intercourse with an uncircumcised person (a reason which
McGiffert admits to be conceivable,
Apostolic Age, p. 232), and Timothy
would have been unacceptable to them,
since with a Jewish mother and with a
Jewish education he would be regarded
as one who refused to adhere to the
Jewish rule : " partus sequitur ventrem "
(see Wetstein and Nösgen), and to
remedy the one fatal flaw which separated him from them : see, however, B.
Weiss, *Die Briefe Pauli an T.*, Introd.,
p. 2, who disagrees with this reason,
whilst he lays stress on the other reason
mentioned above. On the other hand,
both among unbelieving and Christian
Jews alike the circumcision of Timothy
would not fail to produce a favourable
impression. Amongst the former the
fact that the convert thus submitted even
in manhood to this painful rite would
have afforded the clearest evidence that
neither he nor his spiritual father despised
the seal of the covenant for those who
were Jews according to the flesh, whilst
the Christian Jews would see in the act
a loyal adherence to the Jerusalem decree.
It was no question of enforcing circumcision upon Timothy as if it were necessary to salvation ; it was simply a question
of what was necessary under the special
circumstances in which both he and Paul
were to seek to gain a hearing for the
Gospel on the lines of the Apostolic
policy : " to the Jew first, and also to the
Greek"; "neque salutis æternæ causa
Timotheus circumciditur, sed utilitatis,"

γὰρ ἅπαντες¹ τὸν πατέρα αὐτοῦ, ὅτι ῞Ελλην ὑπῆρχεν. 4.² ὡς δὲ
διεπορεύοντο τὰς πόλεις, παρεδίδουν αὐτοῖς φυλάσσειν τὰ δόγματα
τὰ κεκριμένα ὑπὸ τῶν ἀποστόλων καὶ τῶν πρεσβυτέρων τῶν ἐν
῾Ιερουσαλήμ. 5. αἱ μὲν οὖν ἐκκλησίαι ἐστερεοῦντο τῇ πίστει, καὶ
ἐπερίσσευον τῷ ἀριθμῷ καθ᾽ ἡμέραν.

¹ ℵABC 13, 31, 180, Vulg., Sah., Boh., Aethwi.; W.H., R.V., Weiss, Wendt
read οτι Ελλην ο πατηρ αυτου υπηρχεν; Blass, Hilg., Tisch. follow T.R. (DEHLP).

² D, Gig. read διερχομενοι δε τας πολεις; D, Syr. Harcl. mg. continue εκηρυσσον
αυτοις μετα πασης παρρησιας τον κυριον Ιησουν Χριστον, and D adds αμα παραδι-
δοντες και τας εντολας των αποστ. . . ., see Weiss, Codex D, p. 85, who regards the
addition as made to account for the growth of the Church described in ver. 5, but
also cf. Blass, Philology of the Gospels, p. 158.

Blass, cf. Godet, Epître aux Romains, i.,
pp. 43, 44; Hort, Judaistic Christianity,
pp. 85-87; Knabenbauer, in loco. "There
is no time in Paul's life when we should
suppose him less likely to circumcise one
of his converts," says McGiffert, u. s., p.
233, but there were converts and converts,
and none has pointed out more plainly
than McGiffert that the case of Titus and
that of Timothy stood on totally different
grounds, and none has insisted on this
more emphatically than St. Paul himself:
ἀλλ᾽ οὐδὲ Τίτος, Gal. ii. 3. The case of
Titus was a case of principle: Titus was a
Greek, and if St. Paul had yielded, there
would have been no need for the Apostle's
further attendance at the conference as
the advocate of freedom for the Gentile
Churches. In the words ῞Ελλην ὤν, Gal.
ii. 3, there may have been a tacit allusion
to the different position of Timothy,
whose parentage was different, and not
wholly Gentile as in the case of Titus.
For a defence of the historical nature of
the incident as against the strictures of
Baur, Zeller, Overbeck, Weizsäcker, see
Wendt, 1898 and 1899, who regards St.
Paul's action as falling under the Apostle's
own principle, 1 Cor. ix. 19.—ὑπῆρχεν:
Blass translates fuerat, and sees in the
word an intimation that the father was no
longer living, otherwise we should have
ὑπάρχει, cf. Salmon, Hermathena, xxi.,
p. 229.

Ver. 4. A proof of St. Paul's loyalty
to the Jerusalem compact. The decree
had not been delivered in Syria and
Cilicia (where the letter had been already
received), but in Galatia St. Paul delivers
it. Wendt regards vv. 4 and 5 as interpolated by the author, who desires
to give a universal importance to the
decree which had previously been read to
a few specified Churches (so too Spitta,
Jüngst, Hilgenfeld, Clemen, who refers

the verses to his Redactor Antijudaicus).
But St. Paul might well feel himself bound
to deliver the decree to the Churches
evangelised by him before the conference
in Jerusalem. Weiss, therefore, is probably right in pointing out that as no
mention is again made of any similar
proceeding, the action was confined to
the Pauline Churches which had been
previously founded, Churches which were,
as it were, daughter Churches of Antioch.
—δόγματα: in the N.T. only in Luke
and Paul (cannot be supported in Heb.
xi. 23), and only here of the decrees of the
Christian Church relative to right living,
cf. Ignat., Magnes., xiii., 1; Didaché, xi.,
3. In 3 Macc. i. 3 it is used of the rules
and requirements of the Mosaic Law, cf.
its use by Philo, see further Plummer on
Luke ii. 1, and Grimm, sub v. Dr. Hort
refers the word back to xv. 22, ἔδοξεν,
and so κεκρ. to κρίνω, xv. 19 (cf. xxi. 25),
used by St. James. In these expressions
he sees "more than advice," but "less
than a command," and so here he regards
"resolutions" as more nearly expressing
the force of this passage, Ecclesia, pp. 81,
82; see however above on xv. 19.

Ver. 5. αἱ μὲν οὖν ἐκκ.: the last
time ἐκκλησία is used by St. Luke,
except of the Jerusalem Church, and in
the peculiar case of the elders at Ephesus,
Hort, Ecclesia, p. 95. Rendall, Appendix,
μὲν οὖν, p. 165, connects this verse with
the following paragraph, cf. ix. 31, so
apparently Blass in β.—ἐστερεοῦντο:
only used in N.T. in Acts, cf. iii. 7, 16,
and only here in this figurative sense,
and it is very possible that St. Luke as
a medical man might thus employ the
verb which he had twice used in its
literal sense, cf. similar instances in
Hobart's Introd., p. xxxii.; here as in
vi. 7, ix. 31, we have the outward growth
of numbers and the inward in the stead-

6.¹ Διελθόντες δὲ τὴν Φρυγίαν καὶ τὴν Γαλατικὴν χώραν, κωλυθέντες ὑπὸ τοῦ Ἁγίου Πνεύματος λαλῆσαι τὸν λόγον ἐν τῇ Ἀσίᾳ, 7.² ἐλθόντες κατὰ τὴν Μυσίαν ἐπείραζον κατὰ τὴν Βιθυνίαν πορεύεσθαι· καὶ οὐκ

¹ διελθόντες HLP, . . . Chrys.; διῆλθον אABCDE 61, Syrr. Pesh.-Harcl., Sah., Boh., Arm., Aeth., so Tisch., W.H., Blass, R.V., Weiss, Wendt, Hilg. This latter has therefore overwhelming evidence in its favour, however the passage may be interpreted. τὴν Γαλ., om. τὴν אABCD 13, 61, so Tisch., W.H., R.V., Weiss, Wendt. Par. reads "Phrygiam et Galatie regiones," and so Blass in β: τὴν Φρυγιαν και τας Γαλατικας χωρας (i.e., "vicos Galatiæ"). Belser, following Blass, sees in the expression sufficient to destroy the South Galatian theory. cf. Beiträge, p. 74. But it can scarcely be said that this reading in Par. is of any special value.

² ελθοντες κατα, but δε after ελθ. in אABC(D)E 13, 61, Vulg., so Tisch., W.H., R.V., Weiss. Blass and Hilg. read γενομενοι for ελθοντες. κατα την B., but εις in אABCD, Epiph., Did., Cyr., Chrys., so Tisch., W.H., R.V., Blass, Weiss, Wendt, Hilg. πορευεσθαι CDHLP, so Hilg., but -θηναι אABE 31, 61, so Tisch., W.H., R.V., Blass, Wendt, Weiss. πνευμα, add Ιησου אABC²DE, Vulg., Syrr. Pesh.-Harcl., Boh., Armcodd. 3, Aethut., Did., Cyr., so Tisch., W.H., Blass, R.V., Weiss, Wendt, Hilg.; for a gloss one would have added το αγιον, cf. ver. 6, but the expression πνευμα Ι. is not found elsewhere in N.T. For επειραζον D reads ηθελαν, so Blass in β, and Hilg.; see Ramsay, C. R. E., p. 88.

fast holding of the faith, extensive and intensive.

Ver. 6. διελθόντες δὲ τὴν Φ. καὶ τὴν Γ. χώραν, see critical notes, and also additional note at the end of chap. xviii. If we follow R.V. text and omit the second τὴν, and regard both Φ. and Γ. as adjectives with Ramsay and Lightfoot (so Weiss and Wendt, cf. adjective Πισιδίαν, xiii. 14; but see also xviii. 23), under the vinculum of the one article we have one district, "the Phrygo-Galatic country," i.e., ethnically Phrygian, politically Galatian; see also Turner, "Chronology of the N.T.," Hastings' B.D., i., 422, and "The Churches of Galatia," Dr. Gifford, Expositor, July, 1894. But Zahn, Einleitung, i., 134, objects that if Ramsay sees in ver. 6 a recapitulation of the journey, and action in vv. 4 and 5, and includes under the term Phrygo-Galatia the places visited in the first missionary journey, we must include under the term not only Iconium and Antioch, but also Derbe and Lystra. But the two latter, according to xiv. 6, are not Phrygian at all, but Lycaonian. Ramsay, however, sufficiently answers this objection by the distinction which he draws between the phrase before us in xvi. 6 and the phrase used in xviii. 23: τὴν Γαλατικὴν χώραν καὶ Φρυγίαν. In the verse before us reference is made to the country traversed by Paul after he left Lystra, and so we have quite correctly the territory about Iconium and Antioch described as Phrygo-Galatic; but in xviii. 23 Lystra and Derbe are also included, and therefore we might expect "Lycaono-Galatic and Phrygo-Galatic," but to avoid this complicated phraseology the writer uses the simple phrase: "the Galatic country," while Phrygia denotes either Phrygia Galatica or Phrygia Magna, or both, and see Ramsay, Church in the Roman Empire, pp. 77 and 91-93, and Expositor, August, 1898. Dr. Gifford, in his valuable contribution to the controversy between Prof. Ramsay and Dr. Chase, Expositor, July 1894, while rejecting the North-Galatian theory, would not limit the phrase "the Phrygian and Galatian region" to the country about Iconium and Antioch with Ramsay, but advocates an extension of its meaning to the borderlands of Phrygia and Galatia northward of Antioch.— κωλυθέντες: a favourite word in St. Luke, both in Gospel and Acts, six times in each, cf. viii. 36, x. 47. How the hindrance was effected we are not told, whether by inward monitions, or by prophetic intimations, or by some circumstances which were regarded as providential warnings: "wherefore they were forbidden he does not say, but that they were forbidden he does say—teaching us to obey and not ask questions," Chrys., Hom., xxxiv. On the construction of κωλυθ. with διῆλθον (see critical notes) cf. Ramsay, Church in the Roman Empire, p. 89; St. Paul, p. 211; Expositor (Epilogue), April, 1894, and Gifford, u. s., pp. 11 and 19. Both writers point out that the South Galatian theory need not depend upon this construction, whether we render it according to A.V. or R.V.,

εἴασεν αὐτοὺς τὸ Πνεῦμα. 8.[1] παρελθόντες δὲ τὴν Μυσίαν, κατέβησαν εἰς Τρωάδα. 9. καὶ ὅραμα διὰ τῆς νυκτὸς ὤφθη τῷ Παύλῳ[2] · ἀνήρ τις ἦν Μακεδὼν ἑστώς, παρακαλῶν αὐτὸν καὶ λέγων, Διαβὰς εἰς

[1] For παρελθόντες D, Gig., Vulg. read διελθόντες, so Blass ("recte") in α and β. But the meaning of παρελ. is disputed. In its ordinary sense of "passing along-side" it can hardly stand, or even "passing along Mysia," *i.e.*, on border of Mysia and Bithynia (Weiss, Codex D, p. 26), as the travellers to reach Troas would pass through Mysia, see below in comment. It seems unlikely that διελθ., a common word, should be changed to παρελθ.—the converse is far more probable; see also Harris, *Four Lectures, etc.*, p. 83, note. For κατεβησαν D has κατηντησαν : "nos venimus," Iren., iii., 14, 1 ; see especially Harris, *u. s.*, pp. 64, 65.

[2] In R.V. (ανηρ) Μακεδων τις ην, so ℵABCD² 13, 31, 61, Vulg., so Tisch., W.H., Blass, Weiss, Wendt ; Μακ. τις, *om.* ην DE ; so D reads also εν οραματι, and before ανηρ D, Syr.-Pesh., Sah. insert ωσει. After εστως D, Syr. Harcl. mg., Sah. add κατα προσωπον αυτου. Belser points out that the phrase occurs only in Luke, Luke ii. 31, Acts iii. 13, xxv. 16, and regards it as original ; but see also Corssen, *u. s.*, pp. 436, 437, who compares α and β, and holds that in the latter the reviser has purposely added words for clearness in the description. Blass in β and Hilg. both read these additions.

see further Askwith, *Epistle to the Galatians*, p. 46, 1899.
Ver. 7. κατὰ τὴν Μ. : "over against Mysia," R.V., *i.e.*, opposite Mysia, or perhaps, on the outskirts of Mysia, *cf.* xxvii. 7, and Herod., i., 76, κατὰ Σινώπην, Ramsay, *St. Paul*, p. 194, Wendt, p. 354 (1888), and Gifford, *u. s.*, p. 13. If we read εἰς for κατά (2), it means that they endeavoured to go out of Asia into the Roman province Bithynia on the north, Ramsay, *St. Paul*, p. 195.—ἐπεί-ραζον : for a similar use of the verb *cf.* ix. 26, xxiv. 6.—τὸ Πνεῦμα, add Ἰησοῦ, see critical note. Doctrinally, the expression shows that the Spirit may be called the Spirit of Christ, *Rom.* viii. 9, or of Jesus, no less than the Spirit of God, *Rom., l. c.*, Matt. x. 20 ; see West-cott, *Historic Faith*, p. 106.
Ver. 8. παρελθόντες : "passing by Mysia". Ramsay renders "neglecting Mysia," *cf. St. Paul*, pp. 194, 196, 197, *i.e.*, passing through it without preaching. McGiffert, p. 235, so Wendt (1899), following Ramsay. Rendall, p. 278, explains "passing along or alongside of Mysia," *i.e.*, skirting it, the southern portion of it. The words cannot mean passing by without entering. Mysia was part of Asia, but there was no dis-obedience to the divine command, which, while it forbade them to preach in Mysia, did not forbid them to enter it. Troas could not be reached without crossing Mysia ; Blass sees this clearly enough (but note his reading) : "non prætereunda sed transeunda erat Mysia, ut ad Ægæum mare venirent," Blass, *in loco, cf.* also

Ramsay, *Church in the Roman Empire*, p. 76 ; Wendt (1899), *in loco.*—Τρωάδα : a town on the sea coast (Alexandria Troas, in honour of Alexander the Great), a Roman colony and an important port for communication between Europe and the north-west of Asia Minor, opposite Tenedos, but not to be identified with *New Ilium*, which was built on the site of ancient Troy, considerably further north. It was not reckoned as belong-ing to either of the provinces Asia or Bithynia, *cf.* also xx. 5, 2 Cor. ii. 13, 2 Tim. iv. 13 : C. and H., pp. 215 and 544, Renan, *St. Paul*, p. 128, Zöckler, *in loco.*
Ver. 9. καὶ ὅραμα : used by St. Luke eleven times in Acts elsewhere (in N.T. only once, Matt. xvii. 19), three times in i.-xii., and eight times in xii.-xxviii. (see Hawkins, *Horæ Synopticæ*, p. 144). But St. Luke never uses ὄναρ ; sometimes ὅρ. διὰ νυκτός as here, sometimes ὅρ. alone. It is quite arbitrary on the part of Baur, Zeller, Overbeck to interpret this as a mere symbolical representation by the author of the Acts of the eagerness of the Macedonians for the message of sal-vation ; see as against this view not only Wendt and Zöckler but Spitta, p. 331. Hilgenfeld, *Zeitschrift für wissenschaft. Theol.*, ii., p. 189, 1896, thinks that the "author to Theophilus" here used and partly transcribed an account of one of the oldest members of the Church of Antioch who had written the journey of St. Paul partly as an eye-witness, and see for the question of the "We" sections Introduction.—ἀνήρ τις ἦν Μ. : Ramsay,

Μακεδονίαν βοήθησον ὑμῖν.   10.¹ ὡς δὲ τὸ ὅραμα εἶδεν, εὐθέως
ἐζητήσαμεν ἐξελθεῖν εἰς τὴν Μακεδονίαν, συμβιβάζοντες ὅτι προσ-
κέκληται ἡμᾶς ὁ Κύριος εὐαγγελίσασθαι αὐτούς.   11. Ἀναχθέντες
οὖν ἀπὸ τῆς Τρωάδος, εὐθυδρομήσαμεν εἰς Σαμοθράκην, τῇ τε

---

¹ D, Sah. read διεγερθεὶς οὐν διηγησατο το οραμα ημιν, and D continues και
ενοησαμεν οτι προσκεκληται ημας ο κ. ευαγγελισασθαι τους εν τη Μακεδονια, so
Blass in β, and Hilg. Wendt (1899) refers to Corssen, *u. s.*, and regards addition
as simply elaboration of the vision.

---

here in agreement with Renan, identifies this man with St. Luke, *St. Paul*, pp. 202, 203. But it can scarcely be said that anything in the narrative justifies this identification. Ramsay asks: Was Luke already a Christian, or had he come under the influence of Christianity through meeting Paul at Troas? and he himself evidently sympathises entirely with the former view. The probability, however, of previous intercourse between Luke and Paul has given rise to some interesting conjectures—possibly they may have met in student days when Luke studied as a medical student in the university (as we may call it) of Tarsus; in the passage before us the succeeding words in ver. 10 lead to the natural inference that Luke too was a preacher of the Gospel, and had already done the work of an Evangelist. Ramsay admits that the meeting with Luke at Troas may have been sought by Paul on the ground of the former's professional skill, p. 205. He further maintains that Paul could not have known that the man was a Macedonian unless he had been personally known to him, but surely the man's own words sufficiently implied it (Knabenbauer), even if we do not agree with Blass, *in loco*, that Paul must have recognised a Macedonian by his dress. At all events it is quite unnecessary with Grotius (so Bede) to suppose that reference is made to the angel of Macedonia, "angelus Macedoniam curans," Dan. x. 12. On the importance of this verse in the "We" sections see Introduction: Ramsay, p. 200, Blass, *Proleg.*, p. x.

Ver. 10. **εἰς Μ.** : It is easy to understand St. Paul's eagerness to follow the vision after he had been twice hindered in his purpose, although it may well be that neither he nor St. Luke regarded the journey from Troas to Philippi as a passage from one continent to another continent—Macedonia and Asia were two provinces of the Roman empire, Ramsay, p. 199. But in the good Providence of Him Who sees with larger other eyes

than ours St. Paul's first European Church was now founded, although perhaps it is venturesome to say that the Gospel was now first preached on the continent of Europe, as the good tidings may have reached Rome through the Jews and proselytes who heard St. Peter on the day of Pentecost, *cf.* Acts ii. 9 ; see McGiffert's remarks, pp. 235, 236, on the providential guidance of St. Paul at this juncture, and Lightfoot, *Biblical Essays* "The Churches of Macedonia".—συμβιβάζοντες, see on ix. 22.

Ver. 11. ἀναχθέντες, see on xiii. 13. —εὐθυδρομήσαμεν : only in Acts here and in xxi. 1, nowhere else in N.T., not in LXX or Apocrypha but used by Philo, *cf.* St. Luke's true Greek feeling for the sea, Ramsay, p. 205. Strabo used εὐθύδρομος, p. 45, and elsewhere St. Luke's language may point to the influence of the great geographer; see Plumptre's *Introduction* to St. Luke's Gospel.—Σαμοθράκην : an island of the Ægean sea on the Thracian coast about half-way between Troas and Neapolis, but with adverse winds or calms the voyage from Philippi to Troas takes five days, xx. 6. Samothracia, with the exception of Mount Athos, was the highest point in this part of the Ægean, and would have been a familiar landmark for every Greek sailor, see C. and H., pp. 220, 221.—Νεάπολιν : modern *Cavallo*, the harbour of Philippi, lying some miles further north : Thracian, but after Vespasian reckoned as Macedonian ; opposite Thasos, C. and H., p. 221 ; Renan, *Saint Paul*, p. 139.—τῇ τε ἐπιούσῃ, *sc.*, ἡμέρᾳ, *cf.* xx. 15, xxi. 18, with ἡμέρᾳ added, vii. 26, xxiii. 11, so too in classical Greek, Polyb., Jos. ; in N.T., phrase only found in Acts : mark the exact note of time.

Ver. 12. ἐκεῖθέν τε εἰς Φ. : on or near the site of Krenides (*Wells* or *Fountains*), so called from its founder Philip, the father of Alexander the Great. Near Philippi, Octavius and Anthony had decisively defeated Brutus and Cassius,

ἐπιούσῃ εἰς [1] Νεάπολιν, 12. ἐκεῖθέν τε εἰς Φιλίππους, ἥτις ἐστὶ πρώτη [2] τῆς μερίδος τῆς Μακεδονίας πόλις κολωνία.

Ἦμεν δὲ ἐν ταύτῃ τῇ πόλει διατρίβοντες ἡμέρας τινάς, 13. τῇ τε ἡμέρᾳ τῶν σαββάτων ἐξήλθομεν ἔξω τῆς [3] πόλεως παρὰ ποταμόν, οὗ ἐνομίζετο προσευχὴ εἶναι, καὶ καθίσαντες ἐλαλοῦμεν ταῖς συνελθούσαις

---

[1] **Νεαπολιν,** but **Νεαν Πολιν** ℵABD[2], so Tisch., W.H., Blass, R.V., Weiss; see Winer-Schmiedel, p. 37; D 137, Syr. Harcl. mg. prefix **τη δε επαυριον,** so Blass and Hilg. If this is a revision, it is a further proof of the oft-recurring fact that the Western reviser takes nothing for granted.

[2] **πρωτη της μεριδος της M. πολις κολωνια;** *om.* **της** before M. ℵACE 31, 40, 61, 180, Tisch., W.H., R.V., but retained in BDHLP, so by Weiss; B has the article before M. instead of before **μεριδος.** ℵAC read **πρωτης της μεριδος Μακεδονιας π. κ.;** B has **πρωτη μεριδος της Μακ.;** D has **κεφαλη της Μακ.** (so Hilg.). Blass in β (so Prov.) (see p. xx.) inserts **πρωτης μεριδος της Μακ.** and rejects **κεφαλη,** which is read in D and Syr.-Pesh., Lat. *caput,* while **μεριδος** is omitted by D 137, Syr. Pesh. and Harcl.; see W.H., App., for Hort's conjecture, **Πιεριδος;** Lightfoot, *Phil.,* p. 50; Wendt, 1888 and 1899; and Ramsay, *St. Paul,* p. 100, and *C. R. E.,* p. 156; see additional note at end of chapter.

[3] **πολεως,** but **πυλης** ℵABCD 13, 40, 61, Vulg., Sah., Boh., W.H., R.V., Weiss, so Blass and Hilg.; **πολ.** may have been a marginal expl. of **πυλης** (see Alford and Wendt). **ενομιζετο προσευχη ειναι,** so EHLP, Amm., Chrys., Theophyl., but Ramsay and Wendt both follow T.R.—Tisch., W.H., Weiss, R.V. prefer **ενομιζομεν προσευχην,** following ℵC 13, 40, 61, Boh., Aethro. (ℵ **ενομιζεν**)—AB have **ενομιζομεν προσευχη,** but this may testify to the originality of the nom., so D **εδοκει προσευχη** (Blass in β, so Hilg.); *cf.* Vulg., "videbatur oratio". In a text Blass conjectures **ου ενομιζον εν προσευχη ειναι.** Weiss maintains that in AB the **ν** in **προσευχην** has dropped out, and regards ℵC as unquestionably correct.

---

and to that event it owed the honour of being made a Roman colony with the *jus Italicum* (R.V., " a *Roman* colony "), or in other words, " a miniature likeness of the great Roman people," *cf.* Lightfoot, *Philippians,* p. 51. Hence both in St. Luke's account of the place, and in St. Paul's Epistle we are constantly face to face with the political life of Rome, with the power and pride of Roman citizenship. But its geographical position really invested Philippi with its chief importance, thoroughfare as it was on the great Egnatian Way for the two continents of Europe and Asia. At Philippi we are standing at the confluence of the stream of Europe and Asiatic life; we see reflected in the evangelisation of Philippi as in a mirror the history of the passage of Christianity from the East to the West, Lightfoot, *Phil.,* p. 49; Renan, *St. Paul,* p. 140; McGiffert, *Apostolic Christianity,* p. 239; *Speaker's Commentary,* vol. iii., 580; C. and H., p. 202 ff.—**πρώτη τῆς μερίδος,** see Additional note. — **κολωνία :** " a *Roman* colony," R.V., there were many Greek colonies, **ἀποικία** or **ἐποικία,** but **κολ.** denoted a Roman colony, *i.e.,* a colony enjoying

the *jus Italicum* like Philippi at this time, governed by Roman law, and on the model of Rome; see " Colony " in B.D.[2] and Hastings' B.D.—**ἦμεν . . . διατρ.,** see above on i. 10; characteristic Lucan construction.

Ver. 13. **πόλεως,** see critical notes, and C. and H., p. 226, note.—**παρὰ ποταμόν :** " by a river side," A. and R.V., see critical notes; here Ramsay sees in the omission of the article a touch of local familiarity and renders " by the river side ". On the other hand Weiss holds that the absence of the article merely denotes that they supposed they should find a place of prayer, since a river provided the means for the necessary purifications.—**οὗ ἐνομ. προσευχὴ εἶναι,** see critical notes: " where there was wont to be held a meeting for prayer " (Ramsay); on the nominative see above. A further difficulty lies in the word **ἐνομίζετο.** Can it bear the above rendering? Rendall, p. 103, thinks that it hardly admits of it; on the other hand Wendt and Grimm compare 2 Macc. xiv. 4, and see instances of the use of the passive voice in L. and S., Herod., vi., 138, Thuc., iv., 32. Wendt renders

γυναιξί. 14. Καί τις γυνὴ ὀνόματι Λυδία, πορφυρόπωλις πόλεως
Θυατείρων, σεβομένη τὸν Θεόν,[1] ἤκουεν · ἧς ὁ Κύριος διήνοιξε τὴν

[1] ηκουεν, D*E, Vulg., Chrys. read ηκουσεν; Blass rejects.

"where there was according to custom a place for prayer". The R.V. reads οὗ ἐνομίζομεν προσευχὴν εἶναι, "where we supposed there was a place of prayer". There is very good authority for rendering προσευχή, "a place of prayer," cf. 3 Macc. vii. 20; Philo, In Flacc., 6; Jos., Vita, 54, cf. also Juvenal, iii., 295, and Tertullian, Adv. Nat., i., 13, etc. To these instances we may add a striking use of the word in an Egyptian inscription, possibly of the third century B.C., Deissmann, Neue Bibelstudien, pp. 49, 50, see also Curtius, Gesammelte Abhandlungen, ii. 542. No doubt the word occurs also in heathen worship for a place of prayer, Schürer, Jewish People, div. ii., vol. ii., p. 69, E.T., cf. also Kennedy, Sources of N. T. Greek, p. 214. Where there were no synagogues, owing perhaps to the smallness of the Jewish believers or proselytes, there may well have been a προσευχή, and St. Luke may have wished to mark this by the expression he chooses (in xvii. 1 he speaks of a συναγωγή at Thessalonica), although on the other hand it must not be forgotten that προσευχή might be used of a large building capable of holding a considerable crowd (Jos., u. s.), and we cannot with certainty distinguish between the two buildings, Schürer, u. s., pp. 72, 73. That the river side (not the Strymon, but a stream, the Gangas or Gangites, which flows into the larger river) should be chosen as the place of resort was very natural for the purpose of the Levitical washings, cf. also Juvenal, Sat., iii., 11, and long before Tertullian's day the Decree of Halicarnassus, Jos., Ant., xiv., 10, 23, cf. Ps. cxxxvii. 1, Ezra viii. 15, 21, cf. Plumptre's note on Luke vi. 12.—ταῖς συνελθούσαις γυν.: "which were come together," R.V., i.e., on this particular occasion; A.V. "resorted". It is noticeable that in the three Macedonian towns, Philippi, Thessalonica, Beroea, women are specially mentioned as influenced by the Apostle's labours, and, as in the case of Lydia, it is evident that the women of Philippi occupied a position of considerable freedom and social influence. See this picture fully borne out by extant Macedonian inscriptions, which assign to women a higher social position in Macedonia than was the case for instance in Athens, Lightfoot, Philippians, pp. 55, 56; Ramsay, St. Paul, pp. 224, 227, 252. In this lies an answer to the strictures of Hilgenfeld, who regards the whole of ver. 13 as an interpolation of the "author to Theophilus," and so also the expression πορ. ἡμῶν εἰς τὴν προσευχήν, whereas it was quite natural that Paul should go frequently to the Jewish house of prayer.

Ver. 14. Λυδία: she may have taken her name "a solo natali," as Grotius and others have thought, like many of the libertinae, Afra, Graeca, Syra; but the name was a popular one for women, cf. its frequent use in Horace. Renan takes it as meaning "the Lydian," and compares Κορινθία in inscriptions, St. Paul, p. 116, cf. also Zahn, Einleitung, i., 375, but on the other hand, Nösgen, in loco.—πορφυρόπωλις: a seller of purple at Philippi of the purple dyed garments from Thyatira, which formed the finest class of her wares. It is evident that she must have possessed a considerable amount of capital to carry on this trade, and we may note that she was thus in a position to help Paul in the expenses connected with his trial, without endorsing Renan's view that she was his wife, St. Paul, p. 148; see below on xxiv. 26. The expression σεβ. τὸν Θεόν shows that she was "a proselyte of the gate"; she could easily have gained her knowledge of the Jewish religion as she was πόλεως Θυατείρων where a Jewish colony had been planted, and there is reason to believe that the Jews were specially devoted to the dyeing industry for which Thyatira and the Lydian land in general were noted. Thus the inscriptions make it certain that there was a guild of dyers οἱ βαφεῖς at Thyatira, cf. Spohn, Miscell. erud. ant., p. 113; Blass in loco; Ramsay, Cities and Bishoprics of Phrygia, i., p. 145; Renan, St. Paul, p. 146, note; Zahn, Einleitung, i., p. 376. According to Strabo, Thyatira was a Mysian town, but Ptolemy, v. 2, describes it as belonging to Lydia.—ἤκουεν: imperfect, denoting continuous hearing; the baptism would naturally follow after a period of hearing and instruction, "quod evenit aor. διήνοιξεν declaratur" Blass, see also Bengel.—διήνοιξε τὴν καρδίαν, cf. xvii. 3, Eph. i. 18; in LXX, cf. Hos. ii.

καρδίαν, προσέχειν τοῖς λαλουμένοις ὑπὸ τοῦ Παύλου. 15. ὡς δὲ ἐβαπτίσθη, καὶ ὁ οἶκος αὐτῆς, παρεκάλεσε λέγουσα, Εἰ κεκρίκατέ με πιστὴν τῷ Κυρίῳ εἶναι, εἰσελθόντες εἰς τὸν οἶκόν μου[1] μείνατε· καὶ παρεβιάσατο ἡμᾶς. 16. Ἐγένετο δὲ πορευομένων ἡμῶν εἰς προσευχήν,[2] παιδίσκην τινὰ ἔχουσαν[3] πνεῦμα Πύθωνος ἀπαντῆσαι ἡμῖν, ἥτις ἐργασίαν πολλὴν παρεῖχε τοῖς κυρίοις αὐτῆς μαντευομένη.

[1] μείνατε—μενετε ℵABDE 13, 61, Tisch., W.H., Weiss, Wendt, Blass, Hilg.

[2] εἰς π., but ℵABCE 13, 18, 40, 61, 180, Or. insert art. before π., so Tisch., W.H., R.V., Blass, Weiss, Wendt (not Hilg.).

[3] πνευμα Πυθωνος, but acc. ℵABC*D* 13, 33, 61, Vulg., Or., so Tisch., W.H., R.V., Blass, Weiss, Wendt, Hilg.; T.R. has in its favour C³D²EHLP, tol., Syr. H. mg. gr., Chrys., Eustath., Lucif., Gig.

15 (17), 2 Macc. i. 4. The verb is frequent in St. Luke, Luke xxiv. 31, 32, 45, and in ii. 23 quotation, Acts vi. 56, xvii. 3; only once elsewhere in N.T., Mark vii. 34. "To open is the part of God, to pay attention that of the woman," Chrysostom: ὥστε καὶ θεῖον καὶ ἀνθρώπινον ἦν.—τοῖς λ. ὑπὸ τοῦ Π.: C. and H. see an indication of St. Luke's own modesty: "we spake" in ver. 13, but now only Paul is mentioned. Ver. 15. ὁ οἶκος: as in the case of Cornelius, so here, the household is received as one into the fold of Christ, cf. ver. 33 and xviii. 8. We cannot say whether children or not were included, although we may well ask with Bengel: "quis credat in tot familiis nullum fuisse infantem?" but nothing against infant baptism, which rests on a much more definite foundation, can be inferred from such cases, "Baptism," Hastings' B.D., p. 242. Possibly Euodia and Syntyche and the other women, Phil. iv. 2, 3, may have been included in the familia of Lydia, who may have employed many slaves and freed women in her trade.—εἰ κεκρίκατε: almost=since you have judged me, viz., by my baptism; or εἰ if instead of ἐπεὶ chosen with delicate modesty.—μείνατε: this has been called the first instance of the hospitality which was afterwards so characteristic of the early Church, and enforced by the words of St. Peter, St. Paul, and St. John alike; 1 Pet. iv. 9, Rom. xii. 13, 1 Tim. v. 10, etc., 3 John 5, cf. Clement, Cor., i., 17, and see Westcott on Heb. xiii. 2, Uhlhorn, Charity in the Early Church, pp. 91, 325, E.T.; "Hospitality" in B.D.², and Smith and Cheetham, Dict. of Christ. Antiq. Another trait is thus marked in the character of Lydia, the same generosity which afterwards no doubt made her one of the contributors to the Apostle's necessities, as a member of a Church which so frequently helped him. —παρεβιάσατο: only used by St. Luke, once in Luke xxiv. 29, in the same sense as here, cf. LXX, 1 Sam. xxviii. 23, Gen. xix. 9, 2 Kings ii. 17, v. 16 (A omits). The word expresses urgency, but not compulsion (in classical Greek it is used of violent compulsion). The word may imply that Paul and his companions at first declined, cf. 2 Cor. xi. 9 (so Chrys., Bengel), although on occasion he accepted the aid of Christian friends, Phil. iv. 15, and the hospitality of a Christian host, Rom. xvi. 23; or it may refer to the urgent entreaty of Lydia in expression of her thankfulness. Ver. 16. If we add the article τὴν, see critical note: "to the place of prayer," R.V.—πνεῦμα Πύθωνος: in R.V., accusative, see critical note, "a spirit, a Python," margin, i.e., a ventriloquist (Ramsay). The passage most frequently quoted in illustration is Plutarch, De defectu Orac., ix., from which it appears that ventriloquists who formerly took their name from Εὐρυκλῆς a famous ventriloquist (cf. Arist., Vesp., 1019) were called Πύθωνες. The word ἐγγαστρίμυθος, ventriloquist (Hebrew אוֹב), of which Πύθων is thus used as an equivalent, is the term employed in the LXX, Lev. xix. 31, xx. 6, 27, 1 Sam. xxviii. 7, etc., for those that have a familiar spirit (cf. also the use of the two words ἐγγαστρ. and Πύθων amongst the Rabbis, R. Salomo on Deut. xviii. 11, and instances in Wetstein), i.e., a man or a woman in whom is the spirit of divination; Gesenius uses אוֹב for the divining spirit, the python, supposed to be present in the body of a sorcerer or conjurer,

17. αὕτη¹ κατακολουθήσασα τῷ Παύλῳ καὶ ἡμῖν, ἔκραζε λέγουσα,
Οὗτοι οἱ ἄνθρωποι δοῦλοι τοῦ Θεοῦ τοῦ ὑψίστου εἰσίν, οἵτινες

¹ κατακολουθοῦσα is read by ℵBD 180, Tisch., W.H., R.V., Weiss, Hilg.; but
Blass in β follows T.R.   ἡμῖν (2)—ὑμῖν is best supported, ℵBDE, Vulg., Syrr.
P. and H., Arm., Aethₚₚ., Theodt., so Tisch., W.H., R.V., Blass, Weiss, Wendt,
Hilg.; Meyer and Lach. follow T.R. (AC²HLP, Sah., Boh., Aethro., Or., Chrys.,
Eusth.).   ἡμιν would have been easily changed, as it seemed unfitting for the
demons.

and illustrates from this passage in Acts, and adds that the LXX usually render אוֹב correctly by ἐγγαστρίμυθοι, *ventriloquists*, since amongst the ancients this power of ventriloquism was often misused for the purposes of magic. But in addition to ventriloquism, it would certainly seem from the narrative in Acts that some prophetic power was claimed for the maiden, μαντευομένη, so Blass in describing the ἐγγαστρ. "credebatur dæmon e ventre illorum loqui et vaticinari," *cf.* τὴν Εὐρυκλέους μαντείαν, Arist., *u. s.*); so too Suidas explains Πύθων as δαιμόνιον μαντικόν, connecting the word directly with the Pythian serpent or dragon, the reputed guardian of the oracle at Delphi, slain by Apollo, the successor to the serpent's oracular power. If therefore the girl was regarded as inspired by the Pythian Apollo, the expression in T.R. simply expresses the current pagan estimate of her state; this is the more probable as the physicians of the time, *e.g.*, Hippocrates, spoke of the way in which some symptoms of epilepsy were *popularly* attributed to Apollo, Neptune, etc.; article "Divination," B.D.², i., 490; C. and H., p. 231, smaller edition; Lightfoot, *Phil.*, p. 54; Plumptre and Wendt, *in loco*, and Page on the derivation of the word.—ἐργασίαν: only in Luke and Paul; A. and R.V. "gain," although primarily the word denotes work done, so Rendall, "business"; Wisdom xiii. 19 well illustrates its use here. The word is used of gain (*quæstus*), Xen., *Mem.*, iii., 10, 1.—τοῖς κυρίοις αὐτῆς, ver. 19, seems to imply not successive but joint owners (on the plural in Luke see Friedrich, p. 21).—μαντευ.: if Luke had believed in her power he would more probably have used προφητεύειν. μαντευ. used only here in N.T., but it is significant that in LXX it is always employed of lying prophets or of divination contrary to the law, *e.g.*, Deut. xviii. 10, 1 Sam. xxviii. 8 (9), Ezek. xiii. 6, xxi. 29 (34), Micah iii. 11, etc. The Greeks themselves distinguished between the two verbs and recognised the superior dignity of προφητεύειν; *e.g.*, Plato contrasts the μάντις who more or less *rages* (*cf.* derivation μανία, μαίνομαι, thus fitly used of Pythonesses, Sibyls, and the like) with the προφήτης, *Timæus*, 71 E, 72 A, B, Trench, *Synonyms*, i., 26.

Ver. 17. κατακολουθήσασα, but if we follow R.V. the present participle denotes that she continuously followed after (κατά), and kept crying (ἔκραζε). The verb is only used by St. Luke in N.T., *cf.* Luke xxiii. 35; in LXX, Jer. xvii. 16, Dan., LXX, ix. 10, 1 Esd. vii. 1, Jud. xi. 6, 1 Macc. vi. 23, but not in same literal sense as here; used by Polyb., Plut., Jos. —οὗτοι: placed emphatically first (see also Friedrich, pp. 10, 89). If we turn to the Gospel narratives of those possessed with evil spirits, as affording an analogy to the narrative here, we recall how Jesus had found recognition, *cf.* Mark i. 24, iii. 11, Luke iv. 41 (where the same verb, κράζω, is used of the ἀκάθαρτα πνεύματα καὶ δαιμόνια).—τοῦ Θ. τοῦ ὑψ.: similar title used by the demoniacs in Mark v. 7, Luke viii. 28; see Plumptre's note on former passage. Both Zeller and Friedrich note that Luke alone employs ὁ ὑψ. of God without any word in apposition, Luke i. 32, 35, 76, vi. 35, Acts vii. 48, and that we have the title with τοῦ Θεοῦ, both in his Gospel and Acts. (Heb. vii. 1, probably from Gen. xiv. 18.) — ἡμῖν — ὑμῖν very strongly supported, see critical note. But ἡμῖν might easily have been altered into ὑμῖν, as the former would appear to be an unfitting expression for the evil spirit: but ἡμῖν may point to that disturbed and divided consciousness which seems to have been so characteristic of the possessed (Edersheim); at one time the girl was overmastered by the evil spirit who was her real Κύριος, at another she felt a longing for deliverance from her bondage, and in ἡμῖν she associates herself with those around her who felt a similar longing for some way of salvation, for we must by no means regard her as a mere impostor (Ramsay).

καταγγέλλουσιν ὑμῖν ὁδὸν σωτηρίας. 18. τοῦτο δὲ ἐποίει ἐπὶ πολλὰς ἡμέρας. διαπονηθεὶς δὲ ὁ Παῦλος, καὶ ἐπιστρέψας, τῷ πνεύματι εἶπε, Παραγγέλλω σοι ἐν τῷ ὀνόματι Ἰησοῦ Χριστοῦ ἐξελθεῖν¹ ἀπ' αὐτῆς. καὶ ἐξῆλθεν αὐτῇ τῇ ὥρᾳ. 19. Ἰδόντες δὲ οἱ κύριοι αὐτῆς,² ὅτι ἐξῆλθεν ἡ ἐλπὶς τῆς ἐργασίας αὐτῶν, ἐπιλαβόμενοι τὸν Παῦλον καὶ τὸν Σίλαν εἵλκυσαν εἰς τὴν ἀγορὰν ἐπὶ τοὺς ἄρχοντας³ ·

¹ Instead of εξελ. D has ινα εξελθης; instead of εξ. αυτη τη ωρα D has ευθεως; so Blass in β, and Hilg. Belser strongly supports D, see his remarks, *Beiträge*, p. 77; Blass retains changes in β.

² Instead of οτι εξηλθεν η ελπις Blass and Hilg. read οτι απεστερηνται της εργ. αυτων, and adds with D ης ειχον δι' αυτης; but this spoils the play on the εξηλθεν, see below.

³ αρχοντας, but Gig., Lucif. (not D), Blass ("recte"), read στρατηγους, omitting στρατηγοις in ver. 20.

Ver. 18. διαπονηθεὶς, only here and in iv. 2 in N.T.; its use in LXX in two passages only does not help us much, see iv. 2, and in classics it is not used in the sense required here. Aquila uses it four times of the Hebrew עָצַב in passages which show that the word may combine the ideas of grief, pain, and anger, Gen. vi. 6, xxxiv. 7, 1 Sam. xx. 3, 34. It may be noticed that the word and other compounds of πονεῖν are frequent in medical writers.—Παραγγέλλω, see on i. 4. The same strong word is used of our Lord, Luke viii. 29, where He charged another unclean spirit to come out.—ὀνόματι, see above on iii. 6, "Demonology," Hastings' B.D., where reference is made to Sayce, *Hibbert Lect.*, pp. 302-347, as to the belief in the powerful efficacy of the *name*, the *name* meaning to an ancient Semite personal power and existence.—ἐξελθεῖν ἀπ' αὐτῆς: the phrase occurs in Luke much more frequently than in any other N.T. writer; nine times in his Gospel of the coming out of evil spirits, as here. Rendall sees in the phrase the medical accuracy of the writer in describing the process of the cure; the evil spirit must not only come out, but depart, pp. 104, 280; it must however be remembered that St. Matthew uses the same phrase twice of the departure of evil spirits from men, xii. 43, xvii. 18. Paul charges the evil spirit to depart; it departed, and with it *departed* the master's hope of gain (see also Weiss, *in loco*). —αὐτῇ τῇ ὥρᾳ: "that very hour," R.V., *cf.* xxii. 13, *eo ipso tempore*; peculiar to Luke, *cf.* Luke ii. 38, x. 21, xii. 12, xx. 19, xxiv. 33 (so too Friedrich, p. 37). We are not told anything further of the history of the girl, but we may well believe that she too would partake of the generous help of Lydia, and of the other Christian women at Philippi, who would see in her no longer a bondservant to the many lords who had had dominion over her, but a sister beloved in the One Lord.

Ver. 19. ὅτι ἐξ. ἡ ἐλπὶς κ.τ.λ.: "The most sensitive part of 'civilised' man is his pocket," Ramsay, *St. Paul*, p. 237, and we can see how bitter was the hostility excited both here and at Ephesus when the new faith threatened existing pecuniary profits.—ἐπιλαβ.: here with hostile intent, see above on ix. 27 and further on xvii. 19.—εἵλκυσαν: with violence, so ἕλκω in James ii. 4 (Acts xxi. 30), *cf.* Saul before his conversion, viii. 3, σύρων. "Everywhere money the cause of evils: O that heathen cruelty! they wished the girl to be still a demoniac, that they might make money by her!" Chrys., *Hom.*, xxx., 5.—εἰς τὴν ἀγ.: where the magistrates would sit, as in the Roman *forum*.—ἄρχοντας ... στρατηγοῖς: it is of course possible that the two clauses mean the same thing, and that the expressions halt, as Lightfoot and Ramsay maintain, between the Greek form and the Latin, between the ordinary Greek term for the supreme board of magistrates in any city ἄρχοντες, and the popular Latin designation στρατηγοί, *prætores* ("non licet distinguere inter ἄρχ. et στρατ.," Blass, so O. Holtzmann, Weiss, Wendt). But the former may mean the magistrates who happened to be presiding at the time in the *forum*, whereas the milder verb προσαγαγόντες may imply that there was another stage in the case, and that it was referred to the στρατηγοί, the prætors (as they

20.¹ καὶ προσαγαγόντες αὐτοὺς τοῖς στρατηγοῖς, εἶπον, Οὗτοι οἱ
ἄνθρωποι ἐκταράσσουσιν ἡμῶν τὴν πόλιν, Ἰουδαῖοι ὑπάρχοντες ·
21. καὶ καταγγελλουσιν ² ἔθη ἃ οὐκ ἔξεστιν ἡμῖν παραδέχεσθαι οὐδὲ
ποιεῖν, Ῥωμαίοις οὖσι.   22. καὶ συνεπέστη ὁ ὄχλος κατ᾽ αὐτῶν ·
καὶ οἱ στρατηγοί, περιρρήξαντες αὐτῶν τὰ ἱμάτια, ἐκέλευον ῥαβδίζ-

---

¹ Gig., Lucif. read at beginning of verse και προσηνεγκαν αυτους λεγοντες; see
Ramsay, *St. Paul*, p. 217.

² εθη, D reads τα εθνη, but Blass and Hilg. reject.

---

called themselves), because they were the
chief magisterial authorities, and the accusation assumed a political form. Meyer
and Zöckler, H. Holtzmann distinguish
between the two, as if ἄρχ. were the
local magistrates of the town, *cf.* πολιτάρχης, xvii. 6. In the *municipia* and
coloniæ the chief governing power was in
the hands of *duoviri* who apparently
in many places assumed the title of
prætors, *cf.* Cicero, *De Leg. Agr.*, ii.,
34, where he speaks with amusement of
the *duoviri* at Capua who showed their
ambition in this way, *cf.* Horace, *Sat.*, i.,
5, 34. A *duumvir* of Philippi is a title
borne out by inscriptions, Lightfoot,
Phil., p. 51, note; Felten, p. 315.

Ver. 20. οὗτοι, contemptuously Ἰουδ.
ὄντες: If the decree of Claudius expelling
the Jews from Rome had been enacted,
it would have easily inflamed the minds
of the people and the magistrates at
Philippi against the Jews (*cf.* xviii. 2,
so Holtzmann). Of the bad odour in
which the Jews were held we have also
other evidences, *cf.* Cicero, *Pro Flacco*,
xxviii.; Juvenal, xiv., 96-106. On the
attitude of the Romans towards the Jews
see Sanday and Headlam, *Romans*, p.
xix. ff. It was of this intense feeling of
hatred and contempt felt by Romans and
Greeks alike that the masters of the
maiden availed themselves: "causa
autem alia atque prætextus caussæ,"
Blass; the real cause was not a religious
but a social and mercenary one, see
above on ver. 19, and Ramsay, *Church
in the Roman Empire*, p. 131; where
the accusation was brought on purely
religious grounds, as, *e.g.*, at Corinth,
xviii. 13, the Roman governor declined
to be judge of such matters.—ἐκταράσσουσιν: "exceedingly trouble" (ἐκ), *cf.*
LXX, Ps. xvii. 4, lxxxvii. 16, Wisd. xvii.
3, 4, see Hatch and Redpath, xviii., 7;
Plut., *Cor.*, xix., more often in classical
Greek, συνταράσσω.

Ver. 21. ἔθη: religious customs here;
the charge ostensibly put forward was
really that of introducing a *religio illicita*,
licita as it was for the Jews themselves.
No doubt the fact that they were Jews
presented in itself no ground of accusation, but their Jewish nationality would
suggest the kind of customs with the
introduction of which it would be easy
to charge them, *e.g.*, circumcision. The
introduction of Jewish habits and mode
of life included under ἔθη, *cf.* vi. 14, xxi.
21, would upset the whole social system,
so that here, as on other occasions, the
missionaries suffered from being identified
with their Jewish countrymen.—οὐκ ἔξ.
παραδέχεσθαι: Wetstein, *in loco*; Mar-
quardt, *Röm. Staatsrecht*, iii., 70, and
see preceding verse, *cf.* xv. 5, xxi. 21.
In LXX, *cf.* Exod. xxiii.—Ῥωμαίοις οὖσι:
in natural contrast (at the end of the
sentence) to the despised Jews: as inhabitants of a Roman *colonia* they could
lay claim to the proud title. On the force
of ὑπάρχοντες and οὖσι see Alford's note
in loco.

Ver. 22. συνεπέστη: only here in
N.T., *cf.* xviii. 12, not in LXX, but *cf.*
Num. xvi. 3, used in classical Greek, but
not in same sense. No reason is given,
but the ὄχλος would have been easily
swayed by hatred of the Jews, and further
incensed perhaps at finding an end put
to their love of the revelations of fortune-
telling.—περιρρήξ. αὐτῶν τὰ ἱμάτια, *i.e.*,
they rent off the garments of Paul and
Silas; just as there is no change of subject
before ἐπιθ., so here probably what was
done by the lictors is said to have been
done by the magistrates. There is no
need to suppose with Bengel that the
prætors tore off the prisoners' clothes
with their own hands. Grotius (but see
on the other hand Calvin's note *in loco*)
takes the words as meaning that the
prætors rent off their own clothes (reading αὐτῶν); so Ramsay speaks of the
prætors rending their garments in horror
at the ἀσέβεια, the impiety. But not
only would such an act be strange on
the part of Roman magistrates, but also

εἰν· 23. πολλάς τε ἐπιθέντες αὐτοῖς πληγάς, ἔβαλον εἰς φυλακήν, παραγγείλαντες τῷ δεσμοφύλακι ἀσφαλῶς τηρεῖν αὐτούς· 24. ὃς παραγγελίαν τοιαύτην εἰληφώς, ἔβαλεν αὐτοὺς εἰς τὴν ἐσωτέραν φυλακήν, καὶ τοὺς πόδας αὐτῶν ἠσφαλίσατο εἰς τὸ ξύλον. 25. Κατὰ δὲ τὸ μεσονύκτιον Παῦλος καὶ Σίλας προσευχόμενοι ὕμνουν τὸν Θεόν·

the verb seems to make against the interpretation; it means in classical and in later Greek to rend all round, tear off, cf. the numerous instances in Wetstein, and so it expresses the rough way in which the lictors tore off the garments of the prisoners. In 2 Macc. iv. 38 the word is used of tearing off the garments of another, see Wendt's (1888) note *in loco*.—ῥαβδίζειν: to beat with rods: thrice St. Paul suffered this punishment, 2 Cor. xi. 25, grievous and degrading, of a Roman scourging, cf. his own words in 1 Thess. ii. 2, ὑβρισθέντες ὡς οἴδατε ἐν Φιλίπποις. Nothing can be alleged against the truthfulness of the narrative on the ground that Paul as a Roman citizen could not have been thus maltreated. The whole proceeding was evidently tumultuary and hasty, and the magistrates acted with the high-handedness characteristic of the fussy provincial authorities; in such a scene St. Paul's protest may well have been made, but would very easily be disregarded. The incident in xxii. 25, which shows us how the Apostle barely escaped a similar punishment amidst the tumult and shouts of the mob in Jerusalem, and the instances quoted by Cicero, *In Verr.*, v., 62, of a prisoner remorselessly scourged, while he cried "inter dolorem crepitumque plagarum" *Civis Romanus sum*, enables us to see how easily Paul and Silas (who probably enjoyed the Roman citizenship, cf. ver. 37) might have protested and yet have suffered.

Ver. 23. δεσμοφύλακι, Lucian, *Tox.*, 30; Jos., *Ant.*, ii., 5, 1, LXX ἀρχιδεσμοφύλαξ, Gen. xxxix. 21-23, xl. 3 A, xli. 10 A (cf. the word ἀρχισωματοφύλαξ, Deissmann, *Neue Bibelstudien*, p. 93). Chrysostom and Oecumenius identify him with Stephanus, but he was the first-fruits of Achaia, 1 Cor. xvi. 15.

Ver. 24. ἐσωτέραν: comparative for superlative, as often in N.T. (Blass). Not necessarily underground, but a part of the prison which would have been further from such light and air as could be had.—τὸ ξύλον, Hebrew סַד, Job xxxiii. 11 (A κυκλώματι), cf. Arist., *Eq.*, 367, 393, 705; Herod., vi., 75; ix., 37; and

instances in Wetstein, Liv., viii., 28, Plaut., *Capt.*, iii., 70, Latin *nervus*. So Eusebius uses the word of the martyrs in Gaul (see Alford). In Jeremiah's case another and equivalent word is used in the Heb. xxix. 26 = LXX ἀπόκλεισμα. The same Hebrew is used in 2 Chron. xvi. 10, where LXX has simply φυλακή.—ἠσφαλίσατο: only elsewhere in N.T. in Matt. xxvii. 64, 65, 66; in LXX and Polyb., cf. critical note, ver. 30 in β.

Ver. 25. κατὰ δὲ τὸ μεσονύκτιον: neuter of the adjective μεσονύκτιος, cf. xx. 7, Luke xi. 5, elsewhere only in Mark xiii. 35, often in medical writers, also in Arist., Strabo, Plutarch; in LXX, Judg. xvi. 3 A, Ruth iii. 8, Ps. cxviii. 62 (Isaiah lix. 10).—προσευχόμενοι, see on chap. xii. 12.—ὕμνουν with accusative Heb. ii. 12 only, cf. Ephes. v. 19, Col. iii. 16, Trench, *Syn.*, ii., 129. "Hoc erat *gaudium in Spiritu sancto*: in carcere ubi nec genua flectere, nec manus tollere poterant" Wetstein, cf. too the often-quoted words of Tertullian *Ad Martyres*, ii.: "Nihil crus sentit in nervo quum animus in cœlo est," and Chrys., *Hom.*, xxxvi., "This let us also do, and we shall open for ourselves—not a prison, but heaven. If we pray, we shall be able even to open heaven. Elias both shut and opened heaven by prayer."—ἐπηκροῶντο: used by Plato (Comicus), and referred to by Kennedy, *Sources of N. T. Greek*, p. 73, as one of the rare words mainly colloquial common to N.T. and the comic poets; it occurs also in Lucian, and in *Test.*, xii., *Patr.* Not found in LXX (but the cognate noun of hearing so as to obey in 1 Sam. xv. 22). But it is peculiar to St. Luke in N.T., and it was the technical word in medical language for auscultation; the word might therefore naturally be employed by him to denote attentive hearing as God "gave songs in the night". Both verbs ὕμν. and ἐπηκ. are in the imperfect; they were singing, and the prisoners were listening, when the earthquake happened.

Ver. 26. ἄφνω, see on ii. 2.—σεισμὸς, cf. iv. 31, where the divine nearness and presence were manifested in a similar manner; the neighbourhood and the period were conspicuous for such con-

ἐπηκροῶντο δὲ αὐτῶν οἱ δέσμιοι. 26. ἄφνω δὲ σεισμὸς ἐγένετο
μέγας, ὥστε σαλευθῆναι τὰ θεμέλια τοῦ δεσμωτηρίου[1] · ἀνεῴχθησάν
τε παραχρῆμα αἱ θύραι πᾶσαι, καὶ πάντων τὰ δεσμὰ[2] ἀνέθη. 27.
ἔξυπνος δὲ γενόμενος ὁ δεσμοφύλαξ, καὶ ἰδὼν ἀνεῳγμένας τὰς θύρας
τῆς φυλακῆς, σπασάμενος[3] μάχαιραν ἔμελλεν ἑαυτὸν ἀναιρεῖν, νομίζων
ἐκπεφευγέναι τοὺς δεσμίους. 28. ἐφώνησε δὲ φωνῇ μεγάλῃ ὁ Παῦλος
λέγων, Μηδὲν πράξῃς σεαυτῷ κακόν · ἅπαντες γάρ ἐσμεν ἐνθάδε.

---

[1] ανεωχθησαν, but BCD 31, 33, 40, 180; so Lach., Alford, W.H., Blass, Weiss,
Hilg. have ηνεωχθησαν, whilst אAE 13, 54, 61, Or., Tisch have ηνοιχθησαν;
Wendt cannot decide. παραχρημα om. B, Lucif., Gig., so Blass; Hilg. retains.

[2] ανεθη, א¹D¹ ανελυθη, so Hilg.

[3] μαχαιραν, BCD 61* prefix την, so Lach., W.H., R.V., Weiss, Blass, Hilg.

---

vulsions of nature, cf. Plumptre on Matt.
xxiv. 7, and Ramsay, St. Paul, p. 221.—
παραχρῆμα, see critical notes.—ἀνεῴχθησάν τε . . . αἱ θύραι πᾶσαι: any one
who has seen a Turkish prison, says
Prof. Ramsay, will not wonder at this;
"each door was merely closed by a bar,
and the earthquake, as it passed along
the ground, forced the door-posts apart
from each other, so that the bar slipped
from its hold, and the door swung open,"
and see further description on same page.
—ἀνέθη, cf. xxvii. 40, nowhere else in N.T.
in same sense; in LXX we have the same
collocation of words in Mal. iv. 2. See
also for the phrase, Plut., Alex., 73; see
Winer-Schmiedel, p. 101. If we ask, Why
did not the prisoners escape? the answer
is that a semi-Oriental mob would be
panic-stricken by the earthquake, and
there is nothing strange in the fact that
they made no dash for safety; moreover,
the opportunity must have been very
quickly lost, for the jailor was not only
roused himself, but evidently called at
once to the guard for lights; see Ramsay's description, u. s., and the comments
of Blass, in loco, and Felten, note, p.
318, to the same effect as Ramsay, that
the prisoners were panic-stricken, and
had no time to collect their thoughts for
flight.
Ver. 27. ἔξυπνος: only here in N.T.,
once in LXX, 1 Esd. iii. 3, of Darius
waking from sleep.—μάχαιραν: article
omitted in T.R., see critical note. Weiss
thinks that the omission occurs since in
xii. 2, and five times in Luke, no article
is found with μάχαιρα. τὴν = his sword,
cf. Mark xiv. 47.—ἤμελλεν, cf. iii. 3, v.
35, xii. 6, etc., characteristic Lucan word,
see Friedrich, p. 12. The act was quite
natural, the act of a man who had lost
in his terror his self-control (Weiss).—

ἑαυτὸν ἀναιρεῖν: to avoid the disgraceful
fate which would be allotted to him by
Roman law, according to which the jailor
was subjected to the same death as the
escaped prisoners would have suffered
(Wetstein, in loco), cf. xii. 19, xxvii. 42.—
νομίζων, see on vii. 25. It seems hypercritical to ask, How could Paul have seen
that the jailor was about to kill himself?
That there must have been some kind of
light in the outer prison is evident, otherwise the jailor could not have even seen
that the doors were open, nor is there
any difficulty in supposing that Paul out
of the darkness of the inner prison would
see through the opened doors any one in
the outer doorway, whilst to the jailor
the inner prison would be lost in darkness. Moreover, as Blass notes, Paul
may have heard from the jailor's utterances what he meant to do: "neque
enim tacuisse putandus est" (see also
Ramsay, Felten, Hackett, Lumby, in
loco).
Ver. 28. μηδὲν πράξ. σεαυτῷ κακόν:
Blass remarks that the distinction between πράσσειν and ποιεῖν is not always
precisely observed in N.T., and takes it
as = Attic, μ. ποιησῇς. πράσσειν is
not found in St. Matthew or St. Mark,
and only twice in St. John, whilst by St.
Luke it is used six times in his Gospel,
thirteen times in Acts, elsewhere in N.T.
only by Paul. Philippi was famous in
the annals of suicide (C. and H.); see
also Plumptre's note in loco.—ἅπαντες
γάρ ἐ.: "Multa erant graviora, cur non
deberet se interficere; sed Paulus id
arripit, quod maxime opportunum erat"
Bengel.
Ver. 29. φῶτα: "lights," R.V., plural,
and only in plural in later Greek, cf. 1
Macc. xii. 29, of fires in a military encampment; "the prisoners' chains were

29.[1] αἰτήσας δὲ φῶτα εἰσεπήδησε, καὶ ἔντρομος γενόμενος προσέπεσε
τῷ Παύλῳ καὶ τῷ Σίλᾳ · 30. καὶ προαγαγὼν αὐτοὺς ἔξω,[2] ἔφη, Κύριοι,
τί με δεῖ ποιεῖν ἵνα σωθῶ; 31. οἱ δὲ εἶπον, Πίστευσον ἐπὶ τὸν Κύριον
Ἰησοῦν Χριστόν, καὶ σωθήσῃ σὺ καὶ ὁ οἶκός σου. 32. καὶ ἐλάλησαν
αὐτῷ τὸν λόγον[3] τοῦ Κυρίου, καὶ πᾶσι τοῖς ἐν τῇ οἰκίᾳ αὐτοῦ. 33.
καὶ παραλαβὼν αὐτοὺς ἐν ἐκείνῃ τῇ ὥρᾳ τῆς νυκτὸς ἔλουσεν ἀπὸ
τῶν πληγῶν, καὶ ἐβαπτίσθη αὐτὸς καὶ οἱ αὐτοῦ πάντες παραχρῆμα ·
34. ἀναγαγών τε αὐτοὺς εἰς τὸν οἶκον αὐτοῦ, παρέθηκε τράπεζαν,
καὶ ἠγαλλιάσατο πανοικὶ πεπιστευκὼς τῷ Θεῷ.

[1] At beginning of verse Blass in β prefixes ακουσας δε ο δεσμοφυλαξ (*quo audito
cust. carc.* Gig., Wer.).

[2] D, Syr. H. mg. add (και) τους λοιπους ασφαλισαμενος after εξω, see on this
touch Ramsay, *St. Paul*, p. 222, who accepts it as most prob. genuine, retained by
Blass and Hilg. ; Syr. H. mg. adds "appropinquavit et" (προσηλθεν in β).

[3] του Κ., W.H. text, R.V. marg., Blass, Wendt, Weiss, following ℵ*B, read Θεου ;
see Weiss, *Apostelgeschichte*, p. 5.

loosed, and worse chains were loosed
from himself; he called for a light, but
the true heat was lighted in his own
heart" Chrys., *Hom.*, xxxvi.—εἰσεπήδησε, *cf.* xiv. 14, ἐκπ., both verbs only in
Luke in N.T. In LXX, *cf.* Amos v. 19,
Sus., ver. 26, especially the latter, found
also in classical Greek.—ἔντρομος γεν.,
see above.—προσέπεσε : he may have
known of the words of the maiden, ver.
17, and recognised their truth in the
earthquake, and in the calmness and demeanour of Paul ; hence too his question.
Ver. 30. Κύριοι, in respect, *cf.* John
xx. 15.—ἵνα σωθῶ; the word of the
maiden σωτηρία and the occurrence of
the night may well have prompted the
question. The context, ver. 31, seems
to indicate the higher meaning here, and
the question can scarcely be limited to
mere desire of escape from personal
danger or punishment. On the addition
in D see critical note.
Ver. 31. ἐπὶ τὸν Κ. : "non agnoscunt
se *dominos*" Bengel—they point him to
the One Lord.—οἶκος . . . οἰκίᾳ: the
first word is most frequently used in Attic
Greek, and in the N.T. for household,
cf. ver. 15, but both words are used in
Attic, and in the N.T., for *familia*.
σὺ καὶ ὁ οἶκός σου : "and thou shalt be
saved, thou and thy house," R.V., not as
if *his* faith could save his household, as
A.V. might imply, but that the same
way was open to him and to them
(Alford, see also Meyer-Wendt, and
Page).
Ver. 32. καὶ ἐλάλησαν : before baptism instruction.

Ver. 33. ἐν ἐκείνῃ τῇ ὥρᾳ τῆς νυκτὸς,
cf. ver. 18, "at that hour of the night";
the jailor will not delay for a moment his
first Christian duty, Matt. xxv. 36.—
ἔλουσεν ἀπὸ τῶν πληγῶν : "and washed
them of their stripes," Ramsay ; *i.e.*, the
stains of the wounds caused by the lictors
(for similar construction of λούειν ἀπὸ see
Deissmann, *Neue Bibelstudien*, p. 54).
Hobart, p. 112, compares Galen's words,
τὸ αἷμα τοῦ τετρωμένου μέρους ἀπο-
πλῦναι.—καὶ οἱ αὐτοῦ πάντες : for the
bearing of the words on Infant Baptism,
see on ver. 15. It may of course be said
that the expression evidently implies the
same persons who are instructed in ver.
32, but it cannot be said that the phrase
may not include any other members of
the household. The two washings are
put in striking juxtaposition : the waters
of baptism washed the jailor from deeper
stains and more grievous wounds than
those of the lictors' rods, Chrys., *Hom.*,
xxxvi.—παραχρῆμα, emphatic, see above
on p. 106.
Ver. 34. ἀναγαγών τε αὐτοὺς : τε
closely connects this second proof of his
thankfulness with the first ἀναγ. : "he
brought them up into," R.V. ; Blass
thinks that the ἀνά means that he brought
them up from underground, but it may
simply mean that the house was built
over the prison ; see also Knabenbauer
in loco.—παρέθηκε τράπ. : the phrase
is a classical one, so in Homer, also in
Polyb. ; so in Homer a separate table is
assigned to each guest, *Odys.*, xvii., 333;
xxii., 74. But the word is also used as
implying the meal on the table, see L.

35. Ἡμέρας δὲ γενομένης [1] ἀπέστειλαν οἱ στρατηγοὶ τοὺς ῥαβδούχους λέγοντες, Ἀπόλυσον τοὺς ἀνθρώπους ἐκείνους. 36. ἀπήγγειλε
δὲ ὁ δεσμοφύλαξ τοὺς λόγους τούτους πρὸς τὸν Παῦλον, Ὅτι ἀπεστάλ-
κασιν οἱ στρατηγοί, ἵνα ἀπολυθῆτε · νῦν οὖν ἐξελθόντες πορεύεσθε [2] ἐν
εἰρήνῃ. 37. ὁ δὲ Παῦλος ἔφη πρὸς αὐτούς,[3] Δείραντες ἡμᾶς δημοσίᾳ,
ἀκατακρίτους, ἀνθρώπους Ῥωμαίους ὑπάρχοντας, ἔβαλον εἰς φυλακήν,
καὶ νῦν λάθρα ἡμᾶς ἐκβάλλουσιν; οὐ γάρ · ἀλλὰ ἐλθόντες αὐτοὶ

[1] D, Syr. H. mg., after γεν., add συνηλθον οι στρατηγοι επι το αυτο εις την
αγοραν και αναμνησθεντες τον σεισμον τον γεγονοτα εφοβηθησαν, so Blass in
β, and Hilg. Belser and Zöckler both defend this and subsequent additions in D
as valuable in explanation of the sudden change of resolve on the part of the
magistrates; but see also Weiss, Códex D, p. 86, and Ramsay, St. Paul, p. 223.
After εκεινους D 137, Syr. Harcl. add ους εχθες παρελαβες.

[2] After πορευεσθε Blass and Hilg. omit εν ειρηνη, following D and Gig.

[3] At beginning of verse Blass, following D, prefixes αναιτιους (so Hilg.), but
brackets ακατακριτους.

and S., cf. Tobit ii. 2, παρετέθη μου ἡ
τράπεζα, S. Ps. lxxvii. 20. Paul makes
no question about sitting at meat with the
uncircumcised (Weiss).—ἠγαλλιάσατο:
it is suggestive that St. Luke uses the
cognate noun of this same verb to describe the intense exulting gladness of
the early Church at Jerusalem in their
social life, ii. 46—here was indeed an
Agape, a Feast of Love, cf. 1 Pet. i. 6, 8,
iv. 13 (Matt. v. 12, Rev. xix. 7) ; in St.
Luke the word occurs twice in his
Gospel, i. 47, x. 21, and in Acts ii. 26,
quotation (see above); not found in
classical Greek, but formed probably
from ἀγάλλομαι, Hellenistic, often in
LXX. At the same time the word
πεπιστευκώς, perfect participle, shows
that this fulness of joy was caused by
his full profession of belief; it was the
joy of the Holy Ghost which followed
on his baptism : "rejoiced greatly with
all his house, having believed on the
Lord," gaudebat quod crediderat, Blass
(reading imperfect ἠγαλλιᾶτο, see critical
note). See also Viteau, Le Grec du
N. T., p. 194 (1893).—πανοικὶ (-εὶ, W.H.,
App., p. 154), cf. παραπληθεί, Luke
xxiii. 18. In LXX the word is found,
Exod. i. 1, but A has -κία 3 Macc. iii. 27,
where A has also -κίᾳ. On St. Luke's
fondness for πᾶς and its related forms
see Friedrich, p. 6. The form preferred
in Attic is πανοικησία. The word in
text is found in Jos., Philo, and in Plato,
Eryx., p. 392 C., cf. Blass, in loco, and
Proleg., p. 19.
Ver. 35. ἀπέσ. οἱ στρατηγοὶ : we are
not told the reason of this sudden change
in the action of the prætors, and no

doubt the omission may fairly account
for the reading in D, see critical notes.
At the same time it is quite characteristic
of St. Luke to give the plain facts without entering upon explanations. Meyer
thinks that they were influenced by the
earthquake, while Wendt rather inclines
to the view that they were incited to this
action, so inconsistent with their former
conduct, by fresh intelligence as to their
own hasty treatment of the missionaries ;
Ramsay combines both views, and see also
St. Paul, p. 224, on the contrast brought
out by St. Luke, and also on the Bezan
text; see to the same effect Zöckler, in
loco. Blass accounts for the change of
front on the part of the prætors by supposing that they saw in the earthquake
a sign that they had insulted a foreign
deity, and that they had therefore better
dismiss his servants at once, lest further
mischief should result.—τοὺς ῥαβ. : "the
lictors" R.V. margin, apparently as the
duoviri aped the prætors, so the lictors
carried the fasces and not the baculi, cf.
Cicero, De Leg. Agr., ii., 34; Farrar,
St. Paul, i., 493; Grimm-Thayer, sub v.,
and references in Wetstein : διὰ τί λικτώ-
ρεις τοὺς ῥαβδούχους ὀνομάζουσι; Plut.,
Quæst. Rom. 67.
Ver. 36. νῦν οὖν, Lucan, cf. x. 33, xv.
10, xxiii. 15.—ἐν εἰρήνῃ (omitted by D) :
the jailor may well have used the words
in a deeper sense after the instruction of
Paul, and his own admission to citizenship in a kingdom which was "righteousness, peace, joy in the Holy Ghost".
Ver. 37. Δείραντες ἡμᾶς δ. : in flagrant
violation of the Lex Valeria, B.C. 509, and
the Lex Porcia, B.C. 248; see also Cicero,

ἡμᾶς ἐξαγαγέτωσαν. 38. ἀνήγγειλαν δὲ τοῖς στρατηγοῖς οἱ ῥαβδοῦ-
χοι τὰ ῥήματα ταῦτα · ¹ καὶ ἐφοβήθησαν ἀκούσαντες ὅτι Ῥωμαῖοί
εἰσι, 39. καὶ ἐλθόντες παρεκάλεσαν αὐτούς, καὶ ἐξαγαγόντες ἠρώτων

¹ D reads at beginning of verse καὶ παραγενομενοι μετα φιλων πολλων εις την
φυλακην (εις τ. φ. 137, Syr. H. mg.). After εξελθειν the same authorities continue
ειποντες Ηγνοησαμεν τα καθ' υμας οτι εστε ανδρες δικαιοι. D then continues
(137, Syr. H. mg., Ephr.) και εξαγαγοντες παρεκαλεσαν αυτους λεγοντες · Εκ
της πολεως ταυτης εξελθατε, μηποτε παλιν συστραφωσιν ημιν επικραζοντες καθ'
υμων (so practically the other authorities above, followed here by Blass in β, and
Hilg.). Ramsay, St. Paul, p. 224, points out that the Bezan text hits off the situation
with obvious truth, and the way in which in the Ægean cities the weak municipal
government was always a danger to order, "one would gladly think this Lucan".
Belser draws attention to the fact that συστραφ. has a parallel in Acts xxiii. 12 ;
see Harris, Four Lectures, etc., pp. 26, 27, for Ephraem's commentary on vv. 35-37, 39,
and likenesses to the Bezan text. Schmiedel, Encycl. Bibl., p. 52, regards this
passage as plainly derived from a fusion of two texts, and as militating strongly
against Blass.

In Verrem, v., 57, 66, it was the weightiest
charge brought by Cicero against Verres.
To claim Roman citizenship falsely was
punishable with death, Suet., Claud.,
xxv. — ἀκατακρίτους: "uncondemned"
gives a wrong idea, cf. also xxii. 25,
although it is difficult to translate the
word otherwise. The meaning is "without investigating our cause," res incognita, "causa cognita multi possunt
absolvi ; incognita quidem condemnari
nemo potest," Cicero, In Verrem, i., 9, see
also Wetstein, in loco. The word is only
found in N.T., but Blass takes it as=
Attic, ἄκριτος, which might be sometimes
used of a cause not yet tried. The rendering "uncondemned" implies that the
flogging would have been legal after a
fair trial, but it was illegal under any
circumstances, Ramsay, St. Paul, p. 224.
—δημοσίᾳ contrasted with λάθρα, so a
marked contrast between ἔβαλον εἰς φυλ.
and ἐκβάλλουσιν.—Ῥωμαίους ὑπάρχοντας: "Roman citizens as we are," the
boast made by the masters of the girl,
ver. 21. St. Paul, too, had his rights as
a Roman citizen, see below on xxii. 28.
The antithesis is again marked in the
Apostles' assertion of their claim to
courtesy as against the insolence of the
prætors — they wish ἐκβάλλειν λάθρα ;
nay, but let them come in person (αὐτοί),
and conduct us forth (ἐξαγαγέτωσαν).—
οὐ γὰρ : non profecto ; Blass, Grammatik,
pp. 268, 269, "ut sæpe in responsis," see
also Page, in loco.—ἐξαγ.: not only his
sense of justice, but the fact that the
public disgrace to which they had been
subjected would seriously impede the
acceptance of the Gospel message, and
perhaps raise a prejudice to the injury of

his Philippian converts, would prompt
Paul to demand at least this amount of
reparation. Wetstein's comments are
well worth consulting.
    Ver. 38. ἀνήγγειλαν, see critical notes.
—ἐφοβήθησαν, so the chief captain, xxii.
29 ; and no wonder, for the illegal punishment of Roman citizens was a serious
offence. If convicted, the magistrates
would have been degraded, and incapable
in future of holding office ; cf. Cicero, In
Verrem, v., 66 ; Rep., ii., 31 ; and see Blass,
note on xxii. 29, Grotius, in loco, and O.
Holtzmann, Neutest. Zeitgeschichte, p.
99. In A.D. 44 the Rhodians had been
deprived by Claudius of their privileges
for putting some Roman citizens to death
(Speaker's Commentary, in loco).
    Ver. 39. See addition in D, critical
note. The fear of a further riot expressed
by the magistrates is exactly what we
should expect in the cities of the Ægean
lands, which were always weak in their
municipal government. D also expresses
the naïve way in which the magistrates
not only try to throw the blame upon the
people, but wanted to get out of a difficulty by procuring the withdrawal from
the city of the injured parties, Ramsay,
u. s., p. 224. The Greek pointedly and
dramatically expresses the change in the
whole situation : ἐλθόντες—παρεκάλεσαν
—ἐξαγαγόντες ἠρώτων ! (Wendt).
    Ver. 40. εἰς, see critical notes ; they
would not leave the city without once
more visiting the household out of which
grew the Church dearest to St. Paul ; see
Lightfoot's remarks on the growth of the
Church from "the Church in the house,"
Philippians, pp. 57, 58.—ἐξῆλθον : the third
person indicates that the narrator of the

ἐξελθεῖν τῆς πόλεως. 40. ἐξελθόντες δὲ ἐκ τῆς φυλακῆς εἰσῆλθον
εἰς τὴν Λυδίαν· καὶ ἰδόντες τοὺς ἀδελφούς,[1] παρεκάλεσαν αὐτούς,
καὶ ἐξῆλθον.

[1] After **ἀδελφούς** D adds **διηγησαντο οσα εποιησεν Κυριος αυτοις**, so Blass in β, and Hilg.

"We" section, xvi. 9, 10, remained at Philippi, Timothy probably accompanying Paul and Silas. In xx. 5 we again have **ἡμᾶς** introduced, and the inference is that St. Luke remained at Philippi during the interval, or at least for a part of it; and it is reasonable to infer that he laboured there in the Gospel, although he modestly refrains (as elsewhere) from any notice of his own work. The Apostle's first visit to Philippi represented in epitome the universality of the Gospel, so characteristic of St. Luke's record of our Lord's teaching, and so characteristic of the mind of St. Paul. Both from a religious and social point of view the conversions at Philippi are full of significance. The Jew could express his thankfulness in his morning prayer that God had not made him a Gentile—a woman—a slave. But at Philippi St. Paul taught in action the principle which he enforced in his Galatian Epistle, iii. 28, and again in writing to the Colossians, iii. 11 : "Christ was all and in all"; in Him the soothsaying slave-girl, the proselyte of Thyatira, the Roman jailor, were each and all the children of God, and fellow-citizens with the saints, Lightfoot, Introduction to *Philippians;* Taylor, *Sayings of the Jewish Fathers*, pp. 15, 26, 137 (second edition).

The narrative of St. Paul's visit to Philippi has been made the object of attack from various quarters. Most of the objections have been stated and met by Professor Ramsay, and a summary of them with their refutation is aptly given in a recent article by Dr. Giesekke (*Studien und Kritiken*, 1898) described at length in the *Expository Times*, March, 1898, see also Knabenbauer, pp. 292, 293. The view that the narrative is simply a fiction modelled upon the escape of St. Peter in iv. 31 and xii. is untenable in face of the many differences in the narratives (see the points of contrast in Nösgen, *Apostelgeschichte*, pp. 315, 316). (Schneckenburger in his list of parallels between Peter and Paul in Acts apparently makes no mention of the supposed parallel here.) Zeller's attempt to connect the narrative with the story in Lucian's *Toxaris*, c. 27, is still more absurd, cf. Zöckler, *Apos-

telgeschichte*, p. 262 (second edition), and Farrar, *St. Paul*, i., 501, whilst more recently Schmiedel (1898) attempts to find a parallel in Euripides, *Bacchæ*, 436-441, 502, 602-628, see Wendt's note, p. 282 (1899). Weizsäcker boldly refuses to admit even the imprisonment as a fact, and regards only the meeting of Paul with the soothsayer as historical. But it should be noted that he allows the Apostle's intercourse with Lydia and his instruction of the women to be genuine historical incidents, and he makes the important remark that the name of Lydia is the more credible, since the Philippian Epistle seems to support the idea that women received Paul and contributed to the planting of the Church (*Apostolic Age*, i., 284, E.T.). Holtzmann represents in a general manner the standpoint of modern advanced criticism, when he divides the narrative of the events at Philippi into two parts, the one concerned with events transacted under the open heaven, belonging not only to the "We" source but bearing also the stamp of reality, whilst the other part is not guaranteed by the "We" source, and is full of legendary matter. Thus vv. 25-34 are dismissed as a later addition, and Ramsay's fresh and careful explanations are dismissed by Holtzmann as "humbug"! *Theologische Literaturzeitung*, No. 7, 1899.

Additional Note. — Chap. xvi. 12, "which is a city of Macedonia, the first of the district," R.V. This *might* mean, so far as **πρώτη** is concerned, that Philippi was the city nearest in the district, and the city which they first reached. Neapolis, which actually came first on the route, was not generally regarded as Macedonian but Thracian; so Lightfoot, Rendall, O. Holtzmann. Or it might also mean that it was "the chief" (A.V.), the leading city of its division of Macedonia (Ramsay). Here again Ramsay sees a proof of St. Luke's intimate acquaintance with the rivalries of the Greek cities, and of his special interest in Philippi. In B.C. 167 the province Macedonia had been divided by the Romans into four districts, **μερίς**, and even if this division were obsolete at the time, another would be

XVII. 1. ΔΙΟΔΕΥΣΑΝΤΕΣ δὲ τὴν Ἀμφίπολιν καὶ [1] Ἀπολλωνίαν, ἦλθον εἰς Θεσσαλονίκην, ὅπου ἦν ἡ συναγωγὴ τῶν Ἰουδαίων.

[1] τὴν before Ἀπολ. ℵABE 13, 40, 61, 180, so Tisch., W.H., Weiss.   η before συν. om. ℵABD 13, 40, 61, 180, Sah., Boh., Arm., W.H., R.V., Weiss, Wendt, Zöckler, Blass, Hilg.

likely to succeed to it (so Ramsay, *Church in the Roman Empire*, p. 158, as against Lightfoot, *Phil.*, p. 50, who takes πρώτη as denoting not the political but the geographical position of Philippi.) At this time Amphipolis was the chief (πρώτη) city of the district to which both it and Philippi belonged, but though Amphipolis held the rank, Philippi claimed the same title, a case of rivalry between two or even three cities which often occurred. This single passage Ramsay regards as conclusive of the claims of Philippi, see *St. Paul*, p. 207, and *Cities and Bishoprics of Phrygia*, ii., 429. As to whether μερίς can be used in the sense of a division of a province, *cf.* Ramsay, *Church in the Roman Empire*, p. 158, and the instances quoted from Egypt, and also *Expositor*, October, 1897, p. 320, as against Hort's limitation of the term. Hort, W.H., App. 96 (to whose view Rendall inclines, *cf.* also Zahn, *Einleitung*, i., p. 375), thinks that μερίδος must be a corruption, and proposes Πιερίδος, Pieria being an ancient name of that part of Macedonia; but he declines to draw any positive conclusion in its favour. Wendt, following Meyer, regards πρώτη as signifying rank, and so far he is in agreement with Ramsay. But as Amphipolis was really the chief town of the district, he contends that πόλις κολωνία might be taken as one phrase (see also Hackett, Overbeck, Weiss, Holtzmann), and so he regards the whole expression as signifying that Philippi is spoken of as the most considerable colony-town in that district of Macedonia, whilst he agrees with Hort and Lightfoot in maintaining that πρώτη is only classical as an absolute title of towns in Asia Minor. This Ramsay allows, but the title was frequent in Asia and Cilicia, and might easily have been used elsewhere. *Church in the Roman Empire*, p. 156; Holtzmann quite admits that the term may have been applied as in Asian towns to signify the enjoyment of certain privileges. For Ramsay's criticism of Codex D, which substitutes κεφαλὴ τῆς M. and omits μερίδος altogether, see *Church in the Roman Empire*, pp. 156, 157, and *Expositor*, *u. s.*, κεφαλή being evidently

substituted because the term πρώτη is ambiguous, and so liable to be misunderstood. Blass himself finds fault with D, and also considers πρώτη wrong, not only because Amphipolis was superior in rank, but because Thessalonica was called πρώτη Μακεδόνων, *C. T. Gr.*, 1967. But this would not prevent the rivalry amongst other towns in the various subdivisions of the province. Blass reads in β πρώτης μερίδος (a reading which Lightfoot thinks might deserve some consideration, though unsupported, if the original Roman fourfold division of the provinces were still maintained, see above, p. 355), and takes it as referring to Philippi as a city of the first of the four *regiones*.

Chapter XVII.—Ver. 1. διοδεύσαντες δὲ: "and they went along the *Roman road*" (Ramsay): verb only found in Luke, Luke viii. 1, and here, but frequent in LXX, and used also by Polyb. and Plut., *cf.* Gen. xiii. 17, etc., so in 1 Macc. three times. The famous road, the *Via Egnatia*, Horace, *Sat.*, i., 5, 97, extended for a distance of over five hundred miles from the Hellespont to Dyrrhachium; it was really the continuation through Macedonia of the *Via Appia*, and it might be truly said that when St. Paul was on the Roman road at Troas or Philippi, he was on a road which led to the gates of Rome; see some interesting details in C. and H., p. 244. The article "certam atque notam viam designat," Blass, *in loco*, and *Gram.*, p. 149, but see also Weiss, *in loco*.—Ἀμφ., thirty-two or thirty-three miles from Philippi. The *Via Egnatia* passed through it (*cf.* C. and H., and Hackett, *in loco*). The import of its name may be contained in the term applied to it, Thuc., iv., 102, περιφανής, conspicuous towards sea and land, "the all around [visible] city"; or the name may simply refer to the fact that the Strymon flowed almost round the town, Thuc., *u. s.* Its earlier name, "Nine Ways," Ἐννέα ὁδοί, Thuc., i., 100; Herod vii., 114, indicated its important position, and no doubt this occasioned its colonisation by the Athenians in B.C. 437. In the Peloponnesian War it was famous as the scene of the battle in which both Brasidas

2. κατὰ δὲ τὸ εἰωθὸς τῷ Παύλῳ εἰσῆλθε πρὸς αὐτούς, καὶ ἐπὶ σάββατα τρία ¹ διελέγετο αὐτοῖς ἀπὸ τῶν γραφῶν, 3. διανοίγων καὶ παρατιθέμενος, ὅτι τὸν Χριστὸν ἔδει παθεῖν καὶ ἀναστῆναι ἐκ νεκρῶν, καὶ ὅτι

¹ διελέξατο (*pro* -λεγετο, which Meyer retains) ℵAB 13, 61, 103, Syrr. P. and H., Boh., so Tisch., W.H., R.V., Weiss, Wendt ; διελέχθη, Hilg. with D.

and Cleon fell, Thuc., v., 6-11, whilst for his previous failure to succour the place Thucydides had himself been exiled (Thuc., i., 26). From the Macedonians it passed eventually into the hands of the Romans, and in B.C. 167 Æmilius Paulus proclaimed the Macedonians free and Amphipolis the capital of the *first* of the four districts into which the Romans divided the province (Liv., xlv., 18, 29). In the Middle Ages *Popolia*, now *Neochori*: B.D.² and Hastings' B.D., C. and H. The route may well have been one of the most beautiful of any day's journey in St. Paul's many travels, Renan, *St. Paul*, pp. 154, 155.—'Απολλωνίαν : to be carefully distinguished from the more celebrated Apollonia in Illyria — apparently there were three places in Macedonia bearing this name. The *Antonine Itinerary* gives it as thirty miles from Amphipolis, and thirty-seven from Thessalonica, but the other authorities, for example, the *Jerusalem Itinerary*, differ a little. The *Via Egnatia* passed through it, and the name is probably retained in the modern *Pollina*. It is quite possible that the two places are mentioned as having formed St. Paul's resting-place for a night, see references above. — Θεσσαλονίκην : *Saloniki* ; formerly Therme ; the name had been most probably changed by Cassander in honour of his wife Thessalonica, the sister of Alexander the Great, Polyb., xxiii., 4, 4. Under the Romans it became the capital of the *second* of the four districts of Macedonia Provincia (Liv., xlv., 29), and later it was made the metropolis of the whole when the four districts were united into one. It was the largest as well as the most populous city in Macedonia, and like Ephesus and Corinth it had its share in the commerce of the Ægean. From its geographical position it could not cease to be important ; through the Middle Ages it may fairly be described as the bulwark of Christendom in the East, and it still remains the second city in European Turkey. St. Paul, with his usual wisdom, selected it as marking a centre of civilisation and government in the district : " posita in gremio imperii

Romani," as Cicero says. C. and H., p. 247 ff. ; Zahn, *Einleitung*, i., p. 151; Lightfoot, *Biblical Essays*, p. 253 ff. ; Schaff-Herzog, *Encycl.*, iv.—ὅπου ἦν ἡ συν. : implying that there was no synagogue at Amphipolis or Apollonia, the former being a purely Hellenic town, and the latter a small place. ὅπου may = οὗ simply, but if distinguished from it implies *oppidum tale in quo esset* (as in distinction to the other places named) ; see Wendt and Blass. In Agrippa's letter to Caligula we have plain evidence of the existence of Jews in Macedonia, O. Holtzmann, *Neutest. Zeitgeschichte*, p. 180 ; Schürer, *Jewish People*, div. ii., vol. ii., E.T., pp. 222, 232. As the name remains in the modern *Saloniki*, *manent Judaei quoque* (Blass), C. and H., 250, see also in this connection, Ramsay, *St. Paul*, p. 236. Ver. 2. κατὰ τὸ εἰωθὸς : phrase peculiar to St. Luke, only here and in Luke iv. 16. St. Paul follows his usual principle : " to the Jew first ".—ἐπὶ σάββατα τρία : " for three Sabbath days " or " weeks," R.V., margin, the latter strongly supported by Zahn, *Einleitung*, i., 152. This may be the exact period of work *within* the synagogue. For ἐπὶ *cf.* iii. 1, iv. 15, xiii. 31, xvi. 18, etc. ; Hawkins, *Horæ Synopticæ*, p. 152, used in the " We " sections, and also predominantly, though not exclusively, in the rest of Acts or Luke or either of them ; see on Acts xxvii. 20, xxviii. 6 ; Klostermann, *Vindiciæ Lucanæ*, p. 53 ; see also Blass, *Gram.*, p. 133.—διελέγετο αὐτοῖς : he reasoned, rather than disputed, as the word is sometimes rendered—ten times in Acts, seven times rendered by R.V., " reasoned," *cf.* also Heb. xii. 5, and twice " discoursed," xx. 7, 9, once only " disputed," xxiv. 12, *cf.* Jude 9. Here the word may point to a conversational intercourse between St. Paul and his fellow-countryman (*cf.* ver. 17 and Mark ix. 34) ; so Overbeck, Holtzmann, Wendt, on the force of the verb with the dative or πρός. That such interchange of speech could take place in the synagogue we learn from John vi. 25, 29, Matt. xii. 9. In classical Greek with the dative or πρός the word means to converse with,

οὗτός ἐστιν [1] ὁ Χριστός, Ἰησοῦς, ὃν ἐγὼ καταγγέλλω ὑμῖν. 4. καί τινες ἐξ αὐτῶν ἐπείσθησαν, καὶ προσεκληρώθησαν τῷ Παύλῳ καὶ τῷ Σίλᾳ, τῶν τε [2] σεβομένων Ἑλλήνων πολὺ πλῆθος, γυναικῶν τε τῶν

[1] ο Χρ. I., so HLP and most mins., Theophyl., but B has ο Χρ. ο I., so W.H. text, Weiss, Wendt, R.V., Blass in α; א, so Vulg clem., Syr. Pesh., Boh., Arm codd. have I. Χρ.; AD Χρ. I., so Tisch., W.H. marg., so Hilg. with comma after X.; Χρ. ο I., so E 32, 177, 180. Probably the many changes arose from the unusual description in B with the double article.

[2] σεβ. Ελλ., AD 13, 40, 61, Vulg., Boh., Gig. have σεβ. και Ελλ., so Lach. This reading is defended by Ramsay, St. Paul, p. 235, and Hilgenfeld, Zw. Th., 1896, p. 198, so in 1899, Acta Apost. (but not by Blass in β text); see notes in comment. Wendt (1899) finds a solution of the reading in the wish to express that Paul won converts amongst other Gentiles than the proselytes. γυναικων τε, but D, Gig. και γυναικες των πρ. ουκ ολιγ. Probably the reviser took πρωτων as referring only to the men, and thought that the expression meant "wives of the chief men" (so too Weiss explains the words), and then altered above to bring out this sense more clearly. πρωτων of course could be taken as masc., but better to refer it to γυν. = ενοχ., xiii. 50, xvii. 12 (Wendt, 1899). Belser, however, pp. 81, 82, strongly supports the originality of D; he points out that in Acts we never have the expression των πρ. used of women, and that the reading in D harmonises with the thought that the influence of these women as wives of the leading citizens may account for the mild treatment of the Apostles.

to argue, and thus in Xen., Mem., i., 6, 1, ii., 10, 1, we have the construction διαλ. π. τινι or πρὸς τινα to discuss a question with another, so that the word might easily have the meaning of arguing or reasoning about a question, but not of necessity with any hostile intent; even in Heb. xii. 5 it is the fatherly παράκλησις which reasoneth with sons. Blass supports the imperfect as in T.R., Gram., p. 186.—ἀπὸ γραφῶν, i.e., drawing his proofs from them, or if a discussion is meant, starting from them; Winer-Moulton, xlvii., Grotius, so Overbeck, Kuinoel, Weiss, Wendt take the word with διανοίγων.

Ver. 3. διανοίγων, sc., αὐτάς, a favourite word with St. Luke, cf. xvi. 14; here, as in Luke xxiv. 32, 45, he alone uses it of making plain to the understanding the meaning of the Scriptures, "opening their meaning".—καὶ παρατιθ. "and quoting to prove" (Ramsay), i.e., bringing forward in proof passages of Scripture; so often amongst profane writers in a similar way, instances in Wetstein; lit., the word means "to set forth," and this was the older English meaning of allege; in middle voice, to set forth from oneself, to explain; to quote in one's own favour, as evidence, or as authority, "Non other auctour allegge I," Chaucer, Hours of Fame, 314.—τὸν X. ἔδει παθεῖν: "that it behoved the Christ to suffer," R.V., cf. Luke xxiv. 25, 46; now as ever "to

the Jews a stumbling-block," see above on p. 113, and cf. xxvi. 23; so also in writing to the Thessalonian Church the Apostle insists on the same fundamental facts of Christian belief, 1 Thess. iv. 14.— καὶ ὅτι οὗτος κ.τ.λ.: "and that this Jesus whom, said he, I proclaim unto you is the Christ," R.V. adds ὁ before Ἰ. The words said he are inserted because of the change of construction, cf. i. 4, xxiii. 22, Luke v. 14, specially frequent in Luke. On St. Paul's preaching that "Jesus was the Christ," and what it involved, see Witness of the Epistles, p. 307 ff.

Ver. 4. προσεκληρώθησαν: "there were in addition gathered to them" (Ramsay), giving the verb a passive meaning answering to its form; or " these were allotted to them, associated with them, as disciples [by God]," cf. Ephes. i., 11. The verb is often used in Philo, also found in Plutarch, Lucian, but only here in N.T. Mr. Rendall, while pointing out that the A.V. and R.V. "consorted" gives the impression of outward association only, regards the passive aorist as a middle in meaning, and renders "threw in their lot with Paul and Silas". According to A.V. and R.V., W. H., Weiss, and Hort, Judaistic Christianity, p. 89, two classes seem to be mentioned besides the Jews, viz., devout Greeks, and some of the chief women. According, however, to Ramsay, comparing A and D (see p. 235, St. Paul),

πρώτων οὐκ ὀλίγαι. 5. ζηλώσαντες δὲ οἱ ¹ ἀπειθοῦντες Ἰουδαῖοι, καὶ
προσλαβόμενοι τῶν ἀγοραίων τινὰς ἄνδρας πονηρούς, καὶ ὀχλοποιή-
σαντες, ἐθορύβουν τὴν πόλιν· ἐπιστάντες τε τῇ οἰκίᾳ Ἰάσονος,

¹ απειθουντες *om.* ℵABE, Vulg., Syr. P. H., Sah., Boh., Arm., Aethpp., so Tisch.,
R.V., Weiss, Wendt, W.H.; προσλ. δε οι Ι. οι απειθ. HLP; reading in T.R. very
ill supported; and there are other variations. Probably απειθ. is an addition after
xiv. 2. D reads οι δε απειθ. Ι. συνστρεψαντες (συστροφη occurs twice in Acts, not
elsewhere in N.T., but not συστρεφω in sense demanded here), so Blass in β,
and Hilg. αγαγειν, but προ- ℵAB, Vulg., Tisch., Weiss, Wendt, W.H., R.V.,
Blass in β; Meyer follows T.R. with HP; προσαγ. in E; αναγαγ. in L; εξαγαγ.
in D, so Hilg.

we have three classes besides the Jews,
viz., proselytes, Greeks, chief women
(added as a climax), see critical note,
but also McGiffert, *Apostolic Age*, p. 247.
The difficulty in T.R. and authorities
first mentioned is that their rendering
restricts St. Paul's work not only to three
Sabbaths or weeks, but to the synagogue
and its worshippers, whereas from 1
Thess. i. 9, ii. 14, it would appear that
the Church contained a large number of
converted heathens. McGiffert thinks it
possible that St. Luke may have only
recorded the least important of Paul's
labours, just as he only mentions his
work in three Macedonian towns,
whereas he may easily have laboured over
a wider area, 1 Thess. i. 7; but see Paley,
Horæ Paulinæ, ix., 6, and on the reading,
Zahn, *Einleitung*, i., p. 152. In any
case it would seem that a small minority
of Jews is contrasted with a large number of born Gentiles, so that the Thessalonian Church may have been spoken of
by St. Paul as one of Gentile Christians,
who had been opposed not only to
Christianity, but earlier still to Judaism,
1 Thess. i. 9, 10.—γυν. τε τῶν πρώτων
οὐκ ὀλίγαι: here, as at Philippi and
Berœa, the three Macedonian towns,
the prominence assigned to women quite
in accordance with what we know from
other sources; see above. The mention
both here and in ver. 12 that the women
were the leading high-born women
intimates that the poorer women would
follow the men of the lower orders, ver.
5. Dr. Hort regards the women here
as the Jewish wives of heathen men
of distinction, as in xiii. 50, *Judaistic
Christianity*, p. 89, but in xiii. 50 the
opposition to the Apostles proceeds from
these women of the higher classes, and it
seems much more likely that those mentioned here were Macedonian women.
    Ver. 5. ἀπειθ., see critical note.—
ζηλώσαντες: the jealousy is apparent,
whether the word is read or not (*cf.* β),
a jealousy aroused not only by the
preaching of a Messiah, but also by the
success of such preaching.—προσλαβ.,
cf. xviii. 26 for similar sense of the verb,
cf. 2 Macc. viii. 1, x. 15.—τῶν ἀγοραίων
. . . πον.: "certain vile fellows of the
rabble," R.V.; πον. translated in A.V.
"lewd" (A.-S. loewede) means simply
"people," hence (1) the common people
and (2) the ignorant and rude among
the people, *cf.* Spenser, *Shep. Kal. Feb.*,
245: "But little ease of thy *lewd* tale I
tasted" (Skeat); and in the sense of
vicious, Ezek. xvi. 27, A. and R.V. (see
Lumby's note *in loco* — the German
Leute is the word nearest akin to it.)—
ἀγορ.: hangers-on in the market-place;
Blass renders "tabernarii aliique in foro
versantes," see instances in Wetstein
(Aristophanes, Xen., Plut.), who compares "canalicolæ" hodie *canaille*. In
Latin, subrostrani, subbasilicani; Germ.
Pflastertreter, our *Loafer*, Grimm-Thayer,
Farrar, *St. Paul*, i., 513, and Nösgen, *in
loco*. On the distinction sometimes but
probably fancifully maintained between
ἀγοραῖος and ἀγόραιος, see Alford on
xix. 38; Wendt (1888), *in loco;* Winer-
Schmiedel, p. 69; Grimm-Thayer, *sub v.*
For the accent of πονηρός see also Winer-
Schmiedel, *u. s.*—τῇ οἰκίᾳ Ἰ.: in which
the Apostles were lodging, or in which
the Christian assemblies were held. We
know nothing further for certain of this
Jason, *cf.* Rom. xvi. 21 where a Jason is
mentioned as a companion of Paul, and
amongst his συγγενεῖς. If he was a Jew,
as is most probable, we may infer that
his Jewish name was Joshua or Jesus, but
that he used the name Jason, the nearest
Greek equivalent, in his intercourse with
Greeks and Hellenists; *cf.* for a similar
change of the two names 2 Macc. i. 7,
iv. 7, and *cf.* Jos., *Ant.*, xii., 5, 1, where
we read that Jason's real name was
Joshua, but that he changed it into the

ἐζήτουν αὐτοὺς ἀγαγεῖν εἰς τὸν δῆμον· 6. μὴ εὑρόντες δὲ αὐτούς,
ἔσυρον τὸν Ἰάσονα καί τινας ἀδελφοὺς ἐπὶ τοὺς πολιτάρχας, βοῶντες,
Ὅτι οἱ τὴν οἰκουμένην ἀναστατώσαντες, οὗτοι καὶ ἐνθάδε πάρεισιν,
7. οὓς ὑποδέδεκται Ἰάσων· καὶ οὗτοι πάντες ἀπέναντι τῶν δογμάτων

former, owing no doubt to his Hellenising ; see Deissmann, *Bibelstudien*, p. 184,
note ; Wendt and Zöckler express themselves doubtfully, and hold that the name
may be here a Greek name, and its
bearer not a Jew at all.—ἐπιστάντες, *cf.*
iv. 1, vi. 12, Friedrich, p. 87.—δῆμον : to
a public meeting, or to the crowd who
shall inflict vengeance on them, there and
then (so Weiss, Lumby) ; C. and H.
take it of the free assembly of the people,
so Ramsay. A true cause does not need
such methods or supporters, "non tali
auxilio nec defensoribus istis".
Ver. 6. ἔσυρον : the word indicates
the violence of the mob.—πολιτάρχας :
the word is an excellent instance of the
accuracy of St. Luke ; it is not used by
any classical author of the magistrates of
any city (in classical Greek we have only
the form πολίαρχος and πολίταρχος),
but an inscription on an arch spanning a
street of the modern city has been preserved containing the title (and also
containing the names which occur
among the names of St. Paul's converts,
Sosipater, Gaius, Secundus), see Bœckh,
C. I. Gr., 1967. The arch is assigned
to the time of Vespasian, and the
entablature preserved by the British consul at the instance of Dean Stanley in
1876 is in the British Museum, see Blass,
in loco, Speaker's Commentary, C.
and H. (small edition), p. 258, Knabenbauer *in loco*, and for other inscription
evidence, Zahn, *Einleitung*, i., 151. But
more recently Burton (*Amer. Jour. of
Theol.*, July, 1898, pp. 598-632) has collected no less than seventeen inscriptions
on which the word πολιτάρχαι or πολι-
ταρχοῦντες (πολειταρχ-), the latter more
frequently, occurs : of these thirteen are
referred to Macedonia, and of these
again five to Thessalonica, extending
from the beginning of the first to the
middle of the second century, A.D. The
number of the politarchs in Thessalonica
varies from five to six (see *Theol. Literaturzeitung*, 1899, 2, for notice of
Burton's article by Schürer), and on
spelling, Winer-Schmiedel, p. 82 note.—
τὴν οἰκουμένην : no doubt in the political
sense "the Roman Empire" since the
charge was a political one, and was
naturally exaggerated through jealousy

and excitement. There is therefore no
need for the hypercritical remarks of
Baur, Zeller, Overbeck, against the truthfulness or accuracy of the expression.—
ἀναστατώσαντες : only in Luke and Paul,
xxi. 38, Gal. v. 12, see LXX, Dan. vii.
23 (in a different sense), Deut. xxix. 27,
Græc. Venet. (Grimm-Thayer, *sub v.*),
and several times in the O.T., fragments
of Aquila, Symmachus, and in Eustathius,
see also Hatch and Redpath, *sub v.*).
οὗτοι, contemptuous.
Ver. 7. ὑποδέδεκται : no notion of
secrecy as Erasmus and Bengel, but as
in Luke x. 38, xix. 6 ; only found in these
three passages in Luke, and in James ii.
25, *cf.* LXX, Tob. vii. 8, Jud. xiii. 13 (see
Hatch and Redpath for both instances),
1 Macc. xvi. 15, and 4 Macc. xiii. 17, often
in classical Greek without any notion of
secrecy.—οὗτοι πάντες : the words may
be taken as referring not only to Jason
and the accused, but with Alford, "all
these people," *i.e.*, Christians wherever
found.—ἀπέναντι : only here in N.T.
in this sense (common in LXX and
Apocrypha, so also Polyb., i., 86, 3),
cf. Ecclus. xxxvi. (xxxiii.) 14.—δογμάτων, see on xvi. 4. The word may here
refer to the successive decrees of the
emperors against treason, and there is
no need to refer it in this passage to the
decree of Claudius, see on xviii. 2, but
rather to the Julian *Leges Majestatis*.—
β. λέγοντες ἕτερον εἶναι : this was the
charge, the political charge of high
treason, brought against our Lord Himself by the Jews, Luke xxiii. 2, John xix.
12, 15. The nature of this charge may
fairly point to a Jewish source, for the
Jews thought of the Messiah as a king,
and in their hostility to Paul they could
easily accuse him of proclaiming Jesus or
another king, another emperor (Ramsay),
instead of Caesar ; so McGiffert on this
passage, "whose trustworthiness can
hardly be doubted" (*Apostolic Age*, p.
246). The Epistles to the Thessalonians
contain passages which might be as easily
perverted in the same direction, 1 Thess.
ii. 12, iv. 14, v. 2, 23 ; 2 Thess. i. 5-8, or
the fact that Jesus was so often spoken
of as Κύριος, "that deathless King Who
lived and died for men," might have
given colour to the charge, *cf.* on the

Καίσαρος πράττουσι, βασιλέα λέγοντες ἕτερον εἶναι,[1] Ἰησοῦν. 8. ἐτάραξαν δὲ τὸν ὄχλον καὶ τοὺς πολιτάρχας ἀκούοντας ταῦτα · 9. καὶ λαβόντες τὸ ἱκανὸν παρὰ τοῦ Ἰάσονος καὶ τῶν λοιπῶν, ἀπέλυσαν αὐτούς. 10. Οἱ δὲ ἀδελφοὶ εὐθέως διὰ τῆς νυκτὸς ἐξέπεμψαν τόν τε Παῦλον καὶ τὸν Σίλαν εἰς Βέροιαν · οἵτινες παραγενόμενοι, εἰς

---

[1] Before Ιησουν Blass reads τινα ποτε (*nescio quem*) with Gig., and cod. Lat. Sangermanensis ap. Berger. *Cf.* xxv. 19.

---

coincidence and accuracy of the Acts and 1 Thess. ii. 14-16, Paley, *Horæ Paulinæ*, ix., 5, and McGiffert, *u. s.*

Ver. 8. ἐτάραξαν: the people would be disturbed at intelligence which might point to a revolution, and the politarchs, lest they should themselves be liable to the same charge of treason for not defending the honour of the emperor. No charge would be more subtle in its conception, or more dangerous in the liabilities which it involved, *cf.* Tacitus, *Ann.*, iii., 38.

Ver. 9. λαβόντες τὸ ἱκανὸν = *satis accipere* (*cf.* Mark xv. 15, and Wetstein, *in loco*). Blass regards the phrase as a commercial one, due to the frequency of commercial intercourse, and *cf.* v. 31, xviii. 15, xix. 38 (xxiv. 24, β); properly a pecuniary surety, or sureties, here security for good behaviour from Jason and the others, that nothing illegal should be done by them, and certainly nothing against the majesty of the emperor. The words have been explained as meaning that securities were given for the production of the Apostles, and that thus Jason and his friend, by sending them off at night, ran a risk of their lives (Chrys., Grotius), or that the Apostles should not be sheltered any longer, or that they should be obliged to depart at once. Evidently the magistrates did not consider the evidence very weighty = ἀπέλυσαν αὐτούς.

Ver. 10. εὐθέως . . . ἐξέπεμ.: there was need of immediate action, either in obedience to the direct charge of the magistrates that Paul should not come again to Thessalonica, or from danger of a revival of the tumult. That St. Paul left Thessalonica with grief and pain is evident from 1 Thess. ii. 17-20, but he felt that the separation was necessary at least for a time. But still he looked back upon Thessalonica and his work with an ungrudging affection, and his converts were his glory and joy. In the opening words of his First Epistle, i. 7 (*cf.* 2 Thess. i. 4, 2 Cor. viii. 1), he speaks

in a way which not only implies that his own work extended further in and from Thessalonica than the Acts alone enables us to learn, but that the furtherance of the Gospel was due to the Thessalonians themselves. See McGiffert, p. 255, on St. Paul's quiet hand-to-hand work at Thessalonica. For it was not only in the synagogue that St. Paul laboured, as if the message of the Gospel was formal and official, but amongst them who were working like himself for their daily bread, 1 Thess. ii. 9, 2 Thess. iii. 8, see Ramsay's note, *Church in the Roman Empire*, p. 85, on St. Paul's work at Thessalonica. The phrase "night and day," 1 Thess. ii. 9, need not imply, as the *Speaker's Commentary*, that Paul had only the Sundays for preaching, because his other days were so fully occupied; but the phrase means that he started work before dawn, and thus was able to devote some of the later part of the day to preaching. On the striking parallel between the characteristics of the Thessalonians of St. Paul's Epistles and the Acts and the characteristics which were marked by St. Jerome in his day, see *Speaker's Commentary*, iii., 701.—Βέροιαν (or Βέρροια): in the district of Macedonia called Emathia, Ptol., iii., 12, originally perhaps Pheræa, from Pheres, its founder (see Wetstein): about fifty miles southwest of Thessalonica. It was smaller and less important than the latter, but still possessing a considerable population and commerce, owing to its natural advantages, now *Verria* or *Kara Feria*, see B.D.[2] and Hastings' B.D., Renan, *St. Paul*, p. 162, and C. and H., small edition, p. 261. According to the Itineraries, two roads led from Thessalonica to Beroea. Wetstein quotes a curious passage from Cicero, *In Pisonem*, xxvi.; which may possibly indicate that Paul and Silas went to Beroea on account of its comparative seclusion (so Alford, Farrar, Felten): Cicero calls it "oppidum devium".—εἰς τὴν συν. The Jewish population was at least considerable

τὴν συναγωγὴν τῶν Ἰουδαίων ἀπῄεσαν. 11. οὗτοι δὲ ἦσαν [1] εὐγενέστεροι τῶν ἐν Θεσσαλονίκῃ, οἵτινες ἐδέξαντο τὸν λόγον μετὰ πάσης
προθυμίας, τὸ καθ᾽ ἡμέραν ἀνακρίνοντες τὰς γραφάς, εἰ ἔχοι ταῦτα
οὕτως. 12. πολλοὶ μὲν οὖν ἐξ αὐτῶν ἐπίστευσαν,[2] καὶ τῶν Ἑλληνίδων

[1] For ευγενεστεροι D, Par.[1] read ευγενεις, but not Blass or Hilg. Whether το
is to be retained (W.H., Weiss, Blass) before καθ᾽ ημεραν or omitted is difficult
to decide (Wendt); it may easily have fallen out, or may have been added, cf. Luke
xi. 3, and at end of verse καθως Π. απαγγελλει is added by β, after 137, Gig., Syr.
H. mg., so Hilg.

[2] After επιστ. D adds τινες δε ηπιστησαν, cf. xxviii. 24; see Ramsay, C. R. E.,
p. 160 (also Corssen, u. s., p. 444, who thinks that the addition proceeded from anti-
Jewish feeling). In the same verse D reads και των Ελληνων και των ευσχημονων
α. και γ. ικανοι επιστευσαν. Here Ramsay holds that D misses a characteristic of
Macedonia, viz., the prominent part played by the women, C. R. E., pp. 160, 161.
Blass omits και after Ελλην. Hilg. follows D here and above.

enough to have a synagogue, and thither
Paul, according to his custom, went first.
—ἀπῄεσαν: only here in N.T., cf. 2
Macc. xii. 1, 4 Macc. iv. 8; here it may
imply that on their arrival Paul and Silas
left their escort, and went into the synagogue. Ver. 11. εὐγενέστεροι: only in Luke
and Paul in the N.T., so in classics the
word is used of noble birth, Luke xix. 12,
1 Cor. i. 26 (Job i. 3), or of nobility of
character as here, cf. also its use in
4 Macc. iii. 5, ix. 23, 27 (and εὐγενῶς in
2 Macc. xiv. 42, and several times in
4 Macc.). We may compare the wide
and varying use of the Latin ingenuus
in accordance with the context, its meaning here is that the Berœans were far
from the strife and envy of the Thessalonian Jews; see Ramsay, Church in the
Roman Empire, pp. 154, 160, 163, on the
less favourable attitude of Codex Bezæ
to the Berœans than the T.R., and critical
note; see also above on xiii. 50.—
προθ.: another word only in Luke and
Paul, cf. 2 Cor. viii. 11, 12, 19, ix. 2;
not in LXX, but once in Ecclus. xlv. 23,
frequent in classical Greek.—τὸ καθ᾽
ἡμέραν: indicates that St. Paul made a
lengthy stay at Berœa also, cf. Luke xi.
3, xix. 47, but elsewhere without the
article, with the article peculiar to Luke
(see Plummer's note on Luke xi. 3).
On the frequency of καθ᾽ ἡμέραν in
Luke's writings see Friedrich, p. 9, and
above on Hawkins, Horæ Synopticæ, p.
33. If τό is read, see critical note, it
particularises the repetition or constancy
of the act.—ἀνακρ.: "examining," R.V.
(the word in St. John v. 39, which A.V.
also renders "search," is ἐρευνάω), cf.
1 Cor. x. 25, 27, used elsewhere by

St. Luke of a judicial inquiry or investigation, Luke xxiii. 14, Acts iv. 9, xii. 19,
xxiv. 8, xxviii. 18. The word is only found
in Luke and Paul, once in LXX, 1 Sam.
xx. 12, in a general sense, and in Susannah, vv. 48, 51, where it is connected
with a judicial inquiry, as elsewhere in
Luke. In classical Greek used also in
the general sense of examining closely,
questioning, sifting.—τὰς γραφάς: Blass
explains "locos a Paulo allatos," but
although these were ipso facto included,
the term can hardly be so limited, cf.
xviii. 24, 28, and Lightfoot on Gal. iii. 22.
"Character veræ religionis, quod se dijudicari patitur," Bengel.—εἰ ἔχοι, Burton, p. 52, cf. Luke i. 29, iii. 15. Wendt
rightly points out that the positive praise
bestowed on the Jews of Berœa tends in
itself to contradict the theory that Acts
was written to emphasise the unbelief of
the Jews, and to contrast their unbelief
with Gentile belief. Ver. 12. See critical note and Ramsay, Church in the Roman Empire, u. s.
As at Thessalonica, so here the Apostles'
work extended beyond the limits of the
synagogue. Ἑλληνίδων: the term relates
to the men as well as to the women—the
Jewish men had already been included
in the first word πολλοί, see Alford,
Weiss, Wendt, Zöckler.—εὐσχημόνων,
see above on xiii. 50. Blass refers the
term to ἀνδρῶν also, and points out that
Sopater of Berœa alone in Acts is named
πατρόθεν according to Greek custom,
cf. xx. 4 (R.V., W.H., Weiss, Wendt).
See also Orr, Neglected Factors in the
Early Progress of Christianity, p. 107. Ver. 13. οἱ ἀπὸ τῆς Θ. Ἰ.: as before
in the first journey, the bitter and en-
during malice of the Jews followed Paul

γυναικῶν τῶν εὐσχημόνων καὶ ἀνδρῶν οὐκ ὀλίγοι. 13. ὡς δὲ ἔγνωσαν
οἱ ἀπὸ τῆς Θεσσαλονίκης Ἰουδαῖοι, ὅτι καὶ ἐν τῇ Βεροίᾳ κατηγγέλη
ὑπὸ τοῦ Παύλου ὁ λόγος τοῦ Θεοῦ, ἦλθον κἀκεῖ σαλεύοντες [1] τοὺς
ὄχλους. 14. εὐθέως δὲ τότε τὸν Παῦλον ἐξαπέστειλαν οἱ ἀδελφοὶ
πορεύεσθαι ὡς [2] ἐπὶ τὴν θάλασσαν · ὑπέμενον δὲ ὅ τε Σίλας καὶ ὁ
Τιμόθεος ἐκεῖ. 15. Οἱ δὲ καθιστῶντες τὸν Παῦλον ἤγαγον αὐτὸν

[1] After **σαλ.** ℵABD 13, 40, 61, verss., except Aeth., so Tisch., W.H., R.V., Weiss,
Wendt, Blass, Hilg., add **και ταρασσοντες.** Meyer thinks the words a gloss and *cf.*
ver. 8. D also reads **οτι (ο) λογος του Θεου κατηγγελη εις Βεροιαν και επιστευσαν,**
so Hilg. and Blass in β. The **και επιστ.**, the reception of the Gospel, was the
reason of this turbulent action. At end of verse D, Syr. Pesh. add **ου διελιμπανον**
(*cf.* Acts viii. 24 β), so Blass and Hilg. In Luke vii. 45 we have **διαλειπω,** and only
in that place in N.T. But **διαλιμπανω** occurs also, Tob. x. 7, **ου διελιμπανε**
θρηνουσα Τωβιαν (but S *al.*). This *may* have suggested viii. 24. It may perhaps
be noted that **διαλιμπανω** is a medical word = **διαλειπω** (Galen).

[2] Before **επι** read according to ℵABE 13, 40, 61, Vulg., Syr. Pesh., Boh., so Tisch.,
W.H., R.V., Weiss, Wendt, **εως** instead of **ως ;** Meyer retains **ως.** In D, Sah., Aeth.,
word omitted. **υπεμενον,** but **υπεμειναν** ℵB 61, Tisch., W.H., R.V., Weiss, Wendt;
υπεμεινεν AD 27, 137, Sah., Syr. Pesh., so Lach, Hilg., and Blass in β. **τε** (for **δε**)
ℵABE, Syr. P. and H., Aeth., so Tisch., W.H., R.V., Weiss, Wendt.

from one place to another, and the use
of his name alone shows that he was
their chief aim.—**κἀκεῖ:** the word is
often taken with **σαλεύοντες,** for it was
not their advent which had happened
previously, but their incitement to risk
against Paul, so Page, Weiss, Wendt,
Rendall, etc.; on the word see above on
xiv. 7.—**σαλεύοντες,** *cf.* also for its figurative use 2 Thess. ii. 2, very frequent in
LXX, and sometimes in figurative sense,
as often in the Psalms, *cf.* 1 Macc. vi. 8,
see above on ii. 25, and critical note
on D.
Ver. 14. **εὐθέως δὲ τότε:** evidently the
same riot and danger followed as at
Thessalonica; St. Luke often passes over
the difficulties and dangers which drove
Paul from place to place (Ramsay).—**ὡς:**
if we read **ἕως,** R.V., see critical note,
"as far as to the sea," but **ὡς ἐπί** might
well mean *ad mare versus, ad mare,* so
Alford, Blass, and instances in Wetstein.
There is no need to suppose that the
words express a feigned movement to
elude pursuit, "as if towards the sea"
(see this meaning supported by Rendall,
p. 108).—**ἐπὶ τὴν θ.:** probably he would
embark at Dium near the foot of Olympus, which was connected by a direct
road with Berœa (Lewin, C. and H., but
see, however, Renan, *Saint Paul,* p. 166,
note).—**ὑπέμ. . . . ἐκεῖ,** *i.e.,* remained
behind at Berœa, probably to gain the
first intelligence from Thessalonica as
to the possibility of St. Paul's return,

and to bring the news to the Apostle,
whose next stage may not have been
decided upon until he reached the coast.
Ver. 15. **καθιστῶντες,** see critical note,
i.e., the Berœan brethren. In N.T. only
here in this sense, *cf.* Josh. vi. 23, 2
Chron. xxviii. 15, so also in classical
Greek and in later Greek (instances in
Wetstein); they accompanied Paul probably for protection as well as guidance
(it has sometimes been supposed that
disease of the eyes rendered the guidance
necessary, but the word is used quite
generally); see further additional note at
end of chapter and critical note above,
Ramsay, *Church in the Roman Empire,*
pp. 159, 160. If we compare xviii. 5 it
looks as if Timothy and Silas only overtook Paul at Corinth, and that he had
left Athens before they reached that city.
But from 1 Thess. iii. 1 it appears that
Timothy was with Paul at Athens, and
was sent from thence by him to Thessalonica, and this is quite in accordance
with Paul's earnest wish that Timothy
and Silas should come to him as quickly
as possible (if we suppose that they only
rejoined him in xviii. 5, they must have
taken a much longer time than was
necessary for the journey). But if Paul
remained alone, as he states, 1 Thess. iii.
1, at Athens, Silas must also have been
sent away; and we may well suppose
that as Timothy was sent to comfort the
Thessalonians for St. Paul's delay in
returning to them, so Silas may have

ἕως Ἀθηνῶν¹· καὶ λαβόντες ἐντολὴν πρὸς τὸν Σίλαν καὶ Τιμόθεον,
ἵνα ὡς τάχιστα ἔλθωσι πρὸς αὐτόν, ἐξῄεσαν.

16. Ἐν δὲ ταῖς Ἀθήναις ἐκδεχομένου αὐτοὺς τοῦ Παύλου, παρωξύνετο τὸ πνεῦμα αὐτοῦ ἐν αὐτῷ θεωροῦντι² κατείδωλον οὖσαν τὴν
πόλιν. 17. διελέγετο μὲν οὖν ἐν τῇ συναγωγῇ τοῖς Ἰουδαίοις καὶ
τοῖς σεβομένοις, καὶ ἐν τῇ ἀγορᾷ κατὰ πᾶσαν ἡμέραν πρὸς τοὺς

---

¹ καθιστανοντες in AB 25, Tisch., W.H., R.V., Weiss, Wendt; D καταστανοντες,
so Hilg. Blass in β follows reading in T.R. After Ἀθηνων D adds παρηλθεν δε
την Θεσσαλιαν· εκωλυθη γαρ εις αυτους κηρυξαι τον λογον, so Blass in β, and
Hilg.; cf. also Ephraem (Harris, Four Lectures, etc., pp. 28, 47, 83). Ramsay,
C. R. E., p. 160, thinks that the reviser did not observe that Paul probably
sailed direct from the coast of Macedonia to Athens; in other words, he mistook a sea voyage for a journey by land. But Harris, u. s., p. 83, holds that
Ramsay may be incorrect in this, and that the reviser meant to imply that St. Paul
went to Athens by sea, but that he did not go through Thessaly, but coasted by it.
It is also possible that παρηλθεν may mean "neglected" Thessaly in the sense that
he did not preach to them, and in this sense Harris, p. 84, believes that Blass would
find it possible to defend the Lucanity of the gloss; see also Wendt (1899), p. 288, note.

² θεωρουντος, instead of dat. as in T.R., אABE 40, 61, 180, Tisch., W.H., R.V.,
Weiss, Wendt; D has the dat., so Blass in β, and Hilg., which seems conformity
to αυτω.

---

been sent to Philippi, with which St.
Paul was frequently in communication
at this time, Phil. iv. 15. But after their
return to Corinth from their mission,
they found that St. Paul had already
gone on to Corinth, and there they rejoined him. See on the whole subject,
Ramsay, St. Paul, pp. 233, 240, as against
McGiffert; Wendt (1899) and Felten, in
loco; Paley, Horæ Paulinæ, ix., 4.
Ver. 16. ἐκδεχομένου, cf. 1 Cor. xi.
33, xvi. 11, rare in classical Greek in this
sense.—παρωξύνετο: "was provoked,"
R.V., only found elsewhere in N.T. in
St. Paul's own description of ἀγάπη, 1
Cor. xiii. 5, and cf. xv. 39 (see note) and
Heb. x. 24 for the cognate noun, see on
the latter, Westcott, in loco. In LXX
both verb and noun are used for burning
with anger, or for violent anger, passion,
Hos. viii. 5, Zech. x. 3, Deut. xxix. 28,
Jer. xxxix. (xxxii.) 37; cf. Dem., 514, 10;
ὠργίσθη καὶ παρωξύνθη (Meyer-Wendt).
—τὸ πνεῦμα: expression principally used
in Paul, cf. 1 Cor. ii. 11, Rom. i. 9,
viii. 16, etc. Blass calls it periphrasis
hebraica, and cf. Luke i. 47.—θεωροῦντες: "beheld," R.V., as of contemplation in thought, Latin, contemplari.—
κατείδωλον: "full of idols," R.V.—the
rendering "wholly given to idolatry"
was not true, i.e., idolatry in the sense
of worshipping the innumerable idols. If
the city had been sincerely devoted to
idol worship St. Paul might have had
more to appeal to, "verum monumenta

pietatis reperiebat Paulus, non ipsam,
quæ dudum evanuerat," Blass. A.V.
follows Vulgate, "idololatriæ deditum".
The adjective is found only here, but it
is formed after the analogy of κατάδεν-
δρος, κατάμπελος, so Hermann, ad Vig.,
p. 638 (1824), "κατείδωλος πόλις non est,
uti quidam opinantur, simulacris dedita
urbs, sed simulacris referta". No word
could have been more fitly chosen to
describe the aspect of Athens to St. Paul
as he wandered through it, a city which
had been described as ὅλη βωμός, ὅλη
θῦμα θεοῖς καὶ ἀνάθημα, see below on
ver. 17. Before he actually entered the
city, as he walked along the Hamaxitos
road, St. Paul would have seen altars
raised at intervals to the unknown gods,
as both Pausanias and Philostratus testify,
see "Athens," F. C. Conybeare, in Hastings' B.D. "He took these incomparable
figures for idols," writes Renan (Saint
Paul, p. 172) as he describes the beautiful sculptured forms upon which the eyes
of the Apostle would be fixed, but the
man who could write Rom. i. must have
been keenly alive to the dangers which
followed upon "the healthy sensualism
of the Greeks".
Ver. 17. μὲν οὖν . . . τινὲς δὲ, see
Rendall, p. 162, Appendix on μὲν οὖν,
for the antithesis; a simple instance of
two parties acting in opposition. Page
however finds the antithesis to μὲν οὖν
in ver. 19. ἐπιλαβ. δὲ (so W. H.), and
regards τινὲς δὲ . . . συνέβαλλον αὐτῷ

παρατυγχάνοντας. 18. τινὲς δὲ τῶν Ἐπικουρείων καὶ τῶν Στωϊκῶν [1] φιλοσόφων συνέβαλλον αὐτῷ· καί τινες ἔλεγον, Τί ἂν θέλοι ὁ

[1] After δὲ ℵBDHLP, Syr. Pesh., Chrys., Tisch., W.H., R.V., Weiss, Wendt, Blass, Hilg. add καὶ; instead of Ἐπικουρείων W.H. read Ἐπικουριων, and Weiss, W.H. alt., Hilg. Στοϊκων for Στωικων; see W.H., pp. 159, 161, *App.*

as almost parenthetical, see below on ver. 19. — διελέγετο: "he reasoned," R.V. (so Ramsay), see above on ver. 2. —ἐν τῇ συν.: on the synagogue see "Athens," F. C. Conybeare, in Hastings' B.D., but St. Paul did not confine himself to the synagogue, although undeterred by their hatred he went first to his own countrymen, and to the proselytes. But probably they were not numerous (see Farrar, *St. Paul*, i., 533), and the Apostle carried the same method of reasoning into the market-place—as was natural in the city of Socrates, he entered into conversation with those whom he met, as the same philosopher had done four hundred years before. Thus he became an Athenian to the Athenians: see the striking parallel in the description of Socrates, "he was to be seen in the market-place at the hour when it was most crowded," etc., and the words used by Socrates of himself, Plato, *Apol.*, 31 A, quoted by Grote, viii., 211, 212, small edit., p. 212. F. C. Conybeare, *u. s.*, compares the experiences in Athens of the Apostle's contemporary Apollonius with those of St. Paul; he too reasoned διελέξατο with them on religious matters, Philostr., *Vit. Apollonii Tyanæ*, iv., 19. The words ἐν τῇ συν. are placed in brackets by Hilgenfeld, and referred by Clemen to his Redactor Antijudaicus, whilst Jüngst retains the words but omits 16b, and with Van Manen and Clemen regards the whole of Paul's subsequent speech to the philosophers as the interpolation of a Redactor, p. 161 ff.— ἐν τῇ ἀγορᾷ: not the market-place like that which fills a bare space in a modern town, but rather to be compared with its varied beauty and its busy crowd to the square of some Italian city, *e.g.*, the *Piazza di Marco* of Venice. There the Apostle's eye would fall on portico after portico, adorned by famous artists, rich in noble statues, see F. C. Conybeare, *u. s.*, and Renan, *Saint Paul*, p. 180. On the west lay the *Stoa Pœcile*, whence the Stoics received their name, and where Zeno met his pupils, whilst the quiet gardens of Epicurus were probably not far distant (see on the site of the Agora to which St. Luke refers, "Athens," B.D.[2], i., 292, 293, and also C. and H.,

smaller edition, p. 273, Hackett, *in loco*, for different views as to its site).—κατὰ πᾶσαν ἡμέραν: every day, for he could take advantage by this method not only of the Sabbaths and days of meeting in the synagogues, but of every day, *cf.* the words of Socrates, Plato, *u. s.*, in describing his own daily work of conversation with every one τὴν ἡμέραν ὅλην πανταχοῦ προσκαθίζων. The phrase seems to denote some time spent at Athens. — παρατυγχάνοντας: "chance comers" (like another Socrates), used only here in N.T., but *cf.* Thuc., i., 22, not in LXX or Apocrypha. Athens was full not only of philosophers, but we can imagine from the one phrase applied to it, Tac., *Ann.*, ii., 55, what a motley group might surround the Apostle, *illa colluvies nationum.*

Ver. 18. συνέβαλλον αὐτῷ: a word peculiar to St. Luke; three times in his Gospel, four times in Acts; it need not have necessarily a hostile sense as in Luke xiv. 31, but simply means that amongst the chance comers in the Agora there were some who "engaged in discussions" with him (so Blass like Latin, *consilia conferre, sc.* λόγους), a meaning perhaps suggested by the imperfect. Grotius and others take it as "translatio de prœliis sumpta, ut apparet, Luc. xiv. 31. Utitur ita sæpe Polybius, quem sequi amat Lucas."—Ἐπικουρείων: so called from Epicurus, 342-270 B.C.; his disciples were known also as the School of the Garden, from the garden in Athens where the master instructed them, in distinction from the disciples of the Porch or the Academy. We must be careful to remember that as in numberless other cases, so the system of the founder suffered at the hands of his successors, and that the life of Epicurus himself was far removed from that of a mere sensualist, or "Epicure" in its later sense. But it was evident that a life which made pleasure and happiness the be-all and end-all of existence, however safeguarded by the conditions imposed at the outset by Epicurus, was liable to degenerate into a mere series of prudential calculations, or a mere indulgence of the senses and appetites. In his determination to rid men of the

σπερμολόγος οὗτος λέγειν; οἱ δέ, Ξένων δαιμονίων δοκεῖ καταγγελεὺς εἶναι¹· ὅτι τὸν Ἰησοῦν καὶ τὴν ἀνάστασιν αὐτοῖς εὐηγγελίζετο.

¹ οτι τον Ι. . . . . ευηγγελιζετο *om.* by D, Gig., one of these places where explanatory clauses are omitted in D, and also by Blass in β, and Hilg. Blass, p. x., *cf.* xiv. 12, xvii. 18, "a scriptore potius in α adjecta puto, qui videret ea lectoribus vel omnibus vel quibusdam vel necessaria esse vel utilia". It is possible that the writer scrupled to appear to class Ιησους among the δαιμονια. Ramsay, *St. Paul*, p. 242, thinks the clause foreign to Luke's fashion; apparently a gloss, suggested by ver. 32.

superstitious fears which were the chief cause of the miseries of humanity, Epicurus opposed the popular Polytheism, and regarded the gods as living a life of passionless calm far removed from mundane strifes and sorrows, "careless of mankind". The Stoics branded Epicurus as an Atheist, but the materialistic creed of Epicurus and his followers had at all events this merit, that its bold criticism of existing beliefs was serviceable in undermining the prevailing acceptance of a gross and crude mythology, whilst it helped to assert in contradistinction to a paralysing fatalism the doctrine of the freedom of man's will (see F. C. Conybeare, "Epicureans," Hastings' B.D.; Westcott, "Epicureans," B.D.²; Wallace, *Epicureanism*).—Στωϊκῶν: The Stoics, so called from the *Stoa Pœcile* at Athens where Zeno of Citium, the founder of the school, 340-260 B.C., met his pupils, and where his successors debated (Capes, *Stoics*, p. 30), spoke in their theology of a providence ruling the world, of a first cause and a governing mind. But their creed was essentially Pantheistic, although the verses of Cleanthes' Hymn ("the most important document of the Stoic theology," Ueberweg) seemed to breathe the accents of a higher and nobler belief. But no devotional phrases could disguise a Pantheism which regarded the world as the body of God, and God as the soul of the world, which held that apart from external nature the Supreme God had no existence which identified Him with fate and necessity, while the history of the universe was an unfolding of the providence of God, but a providence which was but another name for the chain of causation and consequences, inviolable, eternal. The leading maxims of the ethical system of the Stoics was the injunction to live according to nature, although the expression of the rule varied in the earlier and later schools. But as this life was best realised in conformity to the law of the universe, in conformity with reason as the highest element in man, the Stoic ideal, in spite of its recognition of virtue, became not merely stern and intellectual, but impassive and austere; in aiming at *apathy* the Stoic lost *sympathy* with the most ennobling and energetic emotions, and thus wrapped up in the cloak of his own virtue he justified, at least from an ethical point of view, the description which classed him as the Pharisee of Greek philosophy. In addressing an audience composed at all events in part of the representatives of these two great philosophic schools it may be said that St. Paul was not unmindful of his own former training in the early home of Stoicism (see on p. 235). And so in speaking of creation and providence, of the unity of nations in the recognition of all that was true even in Pantheism, St. Paul has been described as taking the Stoic side against the Epicureans, or at least we may say that he in his speech asserts against some of the cardinal errors of the Epicureans the creative and superintending power of God. But to the Stoic and Epicurean alike the Christian Creed would proclaim that *All's Love, yet all's Law;* to the Stoic and Epicurean alike, the Pharisee and Sadducee of the world of philosophy, the bidding came to repent and obey the Gospel, no less than to the crowd whom sages and philosophers despised: "Paulus summa arte orationem suam ita temperat, ut modo cum vulgo contra Philosophos, modo cum Philosophis contra plebem, modo contra utrosque pugnet," Wetstein; see Capes, *Stoicism;* Lightfoot, *Philippians,* "St. Paul and Seneca"; Zahn, *Der Stoiker Epiktet und sein Verhältniss zum Christenthum;* Ueberweg, *Hist. of Phil.,* i., p. 185 ff.; Rendall, *Marcus Antoninus,* Introd. (1898); Gore, *Ephesians,* p. 253 ff.—καὶ τινες ἔλεγον: these are generally taken to include the philosophers, and the remarks following are referred to them; sometimes the first question to the Epicureans, and the second criticism to the Stoics. But it has recently been maintained that we need not refer to the two sects of philosophers this unfavourable criticism on St. Paul; "Epicureans," Conybeare in Hastings' B.D. Certainly the οἱ δέ has no οἱ μέν as if two opposing schools were meant. The punctuation in R.V., which simply states the fact that amongst those in the Agora certain also τινὲς δὲ καὶ of the philosophers, etc., admits of this view that the criticisms were uttered not by the philosophers, but by the curious crowd which thronged the Agora. Ramsay however takes the verse as marking the opinions of the philosophers, and the use of the word σπερμολόγος by Zeno of one of his followers may help to confirm this.—τί ἂν θέλοι: "what would this babbler say?" R.V., not future as in A.V.; the ἂν with optative being used to express what would happen as the fulfilment of some supposed condition, Burton, p. 79, so Viteau, Le Grec du N. T., p. 33 (1893), the condition being if we would listen to him, or if his words have any meaning; optative with ἂν only in Luke, see Burton, u. s.— σπερμολόγος: primarily an adjective, -ον; as a substantive ὁ σπερ. of a rook or crow, or some small bird, picking up seeds, cf. Arist., Av., 233, 580. σπέρμα-λέγω: so far as derivation is concerned it is not connected with σπείρω-λόγους, Latin, seminiverbius (so Augustine, Wycliffe, "sower of words"). The accent shows that this latter derivation is incorrect. Hence a man hanging about the shops and the markets, picking up scraps which fell from the loads and thus gaining a livelihood, so a parasite, one who lives at the expense of others, a hanger-on, Eustathius on Hom., Odys., v., 490; see in Grimm, sub v.; so Dem. speaks of Aeschines, 269, 19, as σπερ. περίτριμμα ἀγορᾶς. The word thus came to be used of a man who picked up scraps of information, and retailed them at second hand. So Eustathius speaks of rhetoricians who were mere collectors of words and consistent plagiarists δι' ὅλου σπερμολογοῦντες; so again he remarks that the word is applied to those who make a show in unscientific style of knowledge which they have got from misunderstanding of lectures (see for these quotations Ramsay, Expositor, September, 1899, p. 222, and the whole article "St. Paul in Athens"). Ramsay maintains therefore that there is no instance of the classical use of the word as a babbler or mere talker, and he sees in the word a piece of Athenian slang, caught up as the Athenians had themselves used it ("sine dubio hoc ex ipso ore Atheniensium auctor excepit" Blass), and applied to one who was quite outside any literary circle, an ignorant, vulgar plagiarist. At the same time it is perhaps difficult to find any single word more to the point than "babbler," A. and R.V. (Tyndall), for, as Alford urges, it both signifies one who talks fluently to no purpose, and hints also that his talk is not his own. We may, however, well owe this rendering to the fact that σπερμολόγος was wrongly derived, as if it meant seminator verborum, whereas its true derivation is given above. De Wette, Overbeck, Nösgen, Weiss, Holtzmann, Zöckler, Wendt, all so render it. An ingenious attempt has been made to connect the word with the Aretalogi (Juvenal, Sat., xv., 16; Suet, Aug., 74) or praters about virtue, who hired themselves as entertainers for the wealthy Roman nobles at their dinners: "mendax aretalogus," Juv., u. s.; Zöckler, in loco. For instances of the use of the word see Wetstein, Ramsay, Nösgen, Bethge, Die Paulinischen Reden, p. 77; Rendall (who agrees with Ramsay), and "Babbler," Hastings' B.D.—ξένων δαιμ. δοκεῖ καταγ.: The same kind of accusation had been already made against Socrates, Xen., Mem., i., 1, as also against Anaxagoras and Protagoras, see Josephus, C. Apion., ii., 38, who also tells us how a certain priestess had been condemned in Athens ὅτι ξένους ἐμύει θεούς. In Athens the introduction of strange gods was a capital offence, if by such an introduction the home deities were rejected and the state religion disturbed, but there is nothing to show that the Athenians regarded Paul's teaching in this light, and there is no evidence that the Areopagus had cognisance of serious charges of impiety or of the introduction of foreign religion (Ramsay, St. Paul, p. 247).—ξένων: "strange," i.e., foreign.— δαιμονίων used here like the Greek δαιμόνιον in a neutral sense which might refer to deities good or bad. In classical Greek we have καινὰ δαιμόνια, cf. the charge against Socrates, Xen., Mem., i., 1; Plato, Apol., 24 B. καταγγελεύς: only here in N.T., not found in LXX or classical Greek, the verb καταγγέλλειν occurs twice in 2 Macc. viii. 36, ix. 17, of declaring abroad the power of the God of the Jews. In Plutarch we have κατάγγελος.—δοκεῖ, see Burton, p. 153; on the personal construction with δοκεῖ cf. Gal. ii. 9, Jas. i. 26, etc.—τὸν Ἰ. καὶ τὴν ἀνάστασιν, see critical note. It is possible that the Athenians thought that Paul was preaching two strange

19. ἐπιλαβόμενοί τε αὐτοῦ, ἐπὶ τὸν Ἄρειον [1] πάγον ἤγαγον λέγοντες,
Δυνάμεθα γνῶναι, τίς ἡ καινὴ αὕτη ἡ ὑπὸ σοῦ λαλουμένη διδαχή;

[1] In אADE, Sah., Boh. we have Αριον, but Αρειον in BHP, Weiss, W.H., Blass,
Hilg. η after αυτη omitted in BD, Lach. [W.H.], Blass, Hilg., but retained in
R.V. and by Weiss.

deities, Jesus and Resurrection (the latter as a female deity Ἀνάστασις), just as they had their own altars erected to Pity, Piety, Modesty, a view which gains support not only from the collocation of the words, but from the use of the article with both, and from the supposition that Paul was held to be a preacher of more than one strange God; so Chrys., Oecum., Selden, and list given by Wendt (1888), *in loco*. Wendt also (1899) inclines to this view, which is adopted by Renan, Overbeck, Holtzmann, Felten, McGiffert, Knabenbauer, *cf.* also the punctuation in R.V., which may imply this view (see Humphry on R.V., *in loco*). As against this view see Hackett's note, p. 213, who thinks it hardly conceivable that the Apostle could express himself so obscurely on the subject as to afford any occasion for this gross mistake (so also Farrar). The article before ἀνάσ. is taken by Nösgen as referring simply to the general resurrection, a view which he regards as agreeing with the prominence given to the doctrine in ver. 31. It is argued that if ἀνάσ. referred to the resurrection of Jesus we should have αὐτοῦ which has crept into some copies, but the address itself shows that the Apostle spoke of the resurrection of Jesus as affording a pledge of a general resurrection.

Ver. 19. ἐπιλαβ.: as to whether we regard this as done with hostile intent, or not, will depend upon the view taken of the meaning of the Areopagus. If the latter means "the Hill of Mars," to which the Apostle was taken for a quiet hearing and for unimportant discussion, then the former is clearly inadmissible; if, however, the Areopagus meant the *Council of* Areopagus, then that action would seem to have been indicative at least of malice and dislike. The verb in the N.T. is used only in the middle, with accusative or genitive, and most frequently by St. Luke, five times in his Gospel, seven times in Acts, twice by St. Paul, only once by St. Matthew and by St. Mark. In each case it can be determined by the context whether it is used in a favourable or unfavourable sense. So too in LXX (always with genitive), where it is frequently used, the context

alone decides. Certainly ix. 27 presents a close verbal parallel in language, as the participle ἐπιλ. is followed as here by ἤγαγον (Weiss), but the context there expresses beyond all doubt a friendly action. Grotius (so Weiss, Wendt, Felten, Zöckler, Bethge) attributes friendliness to the action here, and renders "manu leniter prehensum," so too F. C. Conybeare, "Areopagus," Hastings' B.D., renders it "took Paul by the hand," but in three of the four parallels to which he refers χείρ is expressed, and for the fourth see above. But the view taken of the following words will help us to decide, Ramsay, *St. Paul*, p. 245, and *Expositor*, September, 1895, pp. 216, 217.—ἐπὶ τὸν Ἄ. πάγον, Curtius, *Gesammelte Abhandlungen*, ii., p. 528, note, and Ramsay, *Expositor, u. s.*, p. 217, point out that ἐπί with accusative would be the correct expression for taking any one before an official court, *cf.* ix. 21, xvi. 19, xvii. 6, xviii. 12—a regular Lucan preposition in this sense—*cf.* also Herod., iii., 46, 156; viii., 79. But it does not therefore follow that a regular trial was instituted, as Chrys., Theophylact and others have held, since there is nothing in the context to indicate this. But the form of expression certainly does seem to indicate that Paul was taken not *to* the Hill of Mars, as is generally held, but *before* a court or council. And there is substantial evidence for believing that the term Areopagus (as Blass admits) was not merely local, but that it was sometimes used as = the Council or Court of Areopagus, *cf.* Cicero, *Ad Atticum*, i., 14, 5; *De Nat. Deorum*, ii., 29; *Rep.*, i., 27. Moreover, there is good reason to believe that the council, although deriving its name from the hill, did not always meet on the hill, and also that it had the power of taking official action in questions bearing upon public teaching in the city (*cf.* Renan, *Saint Paul*, pp. 193, 194, and authorities cited). It is therefore not an improbable inference that Paul would be brought before such a court for inquiry into his teaching; beyond this inference perhaps we cannot go; even to call the inquiry a **προδικασία** (so Curtius) may be to apply a technical term unwarranted by the con-

20. ξενίζοντα γάρ τινα εἰσφέρεις εἰς τὰς ἀκοὰς ἡμῶν· βουλόμεθα οὖν γνῶναι, τί ἂν θέλοι ¹ ταῦτα εἶναι. 21. Ἀθηναῖοι δὲ πάντες καὶ οἱ ἐπιδημοῦντες ξένοι εἰς οὐδὲν ἕτερον εὐκαίρουν,² ἢ λέγειν τι καὶ ἀκούειν καινότερον.

¹ τι αν θελοι DEHLP, Chrys., so Meyer; τινα θελει ℵAB 18, 36, 40, 61, 180, Tisch., R.V., W.H., Weiss, Wendt.

² ευκαιρουν, but ηυκ. ℵABDE 13, 40, 61, Tisch., W.H., Blass, Weiss. Instead of και ακου ℵABD 25, 44, Vulg., Sah., Syr. H., Arm., Tisch., W.H., Weiss, Wendt, Blass read η ακου.

text, which bears no trace of a criminal procedure, cf. Curtius, u. s., pp. 528, 529 ; Ramsay, u. s. ; Plumptre and Rendall, in loco. But where did the council meet for the discharge of such duties as inquiries into the qualification of teachers, as a public court for the maintenance of public order ? Probably in the Stoa Basileios ; here Demosthenes informs us that some of its duties were transacted (see Expositor, October, 1895, p. 272, and Curtius, u. s., p. 528), and the scene before us is full of the life of the Agora with the corona of people thronging to listen, rather than of the sacred or solemn associations of the Hill of Mars, or of the quietude of a spot far removed from the busy life of the market-place. So too the name "Areopagus" might have been easily transferred to the council sitting in a place other than the hill, so that ἡ βουλὴ ἡ ἐξ Ἀ. π. might easily become Ἄρειος Πάγος informally and colloquially, and the word as used here by St. Luke may really be another proof that, as in σπερμολόγος, the author catches the very word which the Athenians would use, Ramsay, Expositor, September, 1895, p. 216, and Renan, u. s., p. 194, note. But it has further been urged both by Curtius and Ramsay (so also Renan, u. s.) that the Hill of Mars would be a most inconvenient place for public assemblies and speakers, see Ramsay, u. s., p. 213, and Curtius, u. s., p. 529, and even if the spot had been suitable for such purposes, there would have been a want of fitness in the Athenians taking this σπερμολόγος to harangue them on a spot so inseparably associated with the dignity and glory of their city ; see also below on vv. 22 and 33.—Δυνάμεθα γνῶναι: like the Latin, Possum scire ? the question may have been asked in courtesy, or in sarcasm, or ironically ; in the repetition of the article the irony may be accentuated.—ἡ ὑπὸ σοῦ λαλ.: "which is spoken by thee," R.V., the Apostle

was not speaking about the doctrine, A.V., his words were the doctrine (Lumby). Felten regards the question as courteously put, and sees in it a decisive proof that Paul was not put upon his trial, since a man could not be tried on a charge of which his accusers had no knowledge. But this would not prevent a preliminary inquiry of some kind before the court, prompted by dislike or suspicion.

Ver. 20. ξενίζοντα: rather perhaps startling or bewildering than strange— so too in Polyb., cf. 1 Peter iv. 12, but see Grimm-Thayer, sub v. Ramsay renders "some things of foreign fashion" as if the words were connected with the opinion that the Apostle was an announcer of foreign gods, cf. also 2 Macc. ix. 6, Diod. Sic., xii., 53.—τινα: the rhetorical use of the indefinite τις here strengthening the participle, cf. viii. 9, v. 6, Heb. x. 27.—εἰσφ. . . . ἀκοάς: Blass suggests a Hebraism, but on the life of Greeks we must look no further than the parallel which the same writer adduces, Soph., Ajax, 147, cf. also Wetstein. The verb is only used here in this sense in N.T.—τί ἂν θέλοι, see critical note and Simcox, Language of the N. T., p. 112 : "de rebus in aliquem exitum tendentibus," Grimm ; cf. ii. 12 ; so Bethge.

Ver. 21. Ἀθην. δὲ πάντες: "now all Athenians," without any article, a characteristic of the whole people, cf. xxvii. 4, but see Ramsay, Expositor, October, 1895, p. 274, and Blass, Gram., p. 157.—ἐπιδημοῦντες: "sojourning there," R.V., A.V. takes no notice of the word = resident strangers : "unde iidem mores," Bengel ; on the population of Athens see F. C. Conybeare, "Athens," Hastings' B.D. ; Renan, Saint Paul, pp. 183, 185, 187.—εὐκαίρουν: "had leisure for nothing else," R.V. margin, cf. Mark vi. 21 (only elsewhere in N.T. in 1 Cor. xvi. 12), used by Polyb., Rutherford, New Phrynichus, p. 205. How fatally the more important

22 Σταθεὶς δὲ ὁ Παῦλος ἐν μέσῳ τοῦ Ἀρείου πάγου, ἔφη,
Ἄνδρες Ἀθηναῖοι, κατὰ πάντα ὡς δεισιδαιμονεστέρους ὑμᾶς θεωρῶ.

interests of life were sacrificed to this characteristic (note imperfect tense), restless inquisitiveness, their great orator, Demosthenes, knew when he contrasted this idle curiosity with the vigour and ability of Philip of Macedon, *Philippic I.*, p. 43. The words go to support the interpretation that there was no formal indictment, but they do not destroy the view that there may have been an examinaton into the Apostle's teaching, Curtius, *u. s.*, p. 529.—καινότερον: certainly there is, as Blass says, "mirus consensus" as to this characteristic of the Athenians; see instances in Wetstein: Dem., *Philippic I.*, 43, and *Philipp. Epist.*, 156, 157; Thuc., iii., 38; Theophr., *Char.*, iii., περὶ λογοποίας μὴ λέγεταί τι καινότερον; *cf.* Seneca, *Epist.*, 74. Lit., "some newer thing," something newer than that which had just preceded it as *new* up to the time of asking. The comparative may therefore indicate more vividly the voracious appetite of the Athenians for news, although it may be also said that the comparative was the usual degree used by the Greeks in the question *What news?* (usually νεώτερον); indeed their fondness for using the comparative of both νέος and καινός is quite singular (Page, see also Winer-Moulton, xxxv., 4; Blass, *Gram.*, p. 138). The words of Bengel are often quoted, "nova statim sordebant, *noviora* quærebantur," but it should be noted that he adds "*Noviora* autem quærebant, non modo in iis quæ gentilia accidunt; sed, quod nobilius videtur, in philosophicis," see for a practical and forcible lesson on the words, F. D. Maurice, *Friendship of Books*, pp. 84, 85. Ver. 22. σταθεὶς, Lucan, see i. 15.—ἐν μέσῳ τοῦ Ἀ. π., *i.e.*, in the midst of the Council or Court of Areopagus, see above on ver. 19, *cf.* iv. 7, Peter stood in the midst of the Sanhedrim. Ramsay pertinently remarks that the words "in the middle of Mars' hill" are far from natural or clear, and those who adopt them usually omit the word "midst," and say that Paul stood on Mars' hill, justifying the expression by supposing that ἐν μέσῳ is a Hebraism for ἐν, i. 15, ii. 22. But whilst a Hebraism would be natural in the earlier chapters referred to, it would be quite out of place here in this Attic scene, *cf.* also ver. 33, Ramsay, *Expositor*, September, 1895, so too Curtius, *u. s.*, p. 529, in support of the rendering adopted by Ramsay.—Ἄνδρες Ἀθην.:

usual way of beginning a speech; strange to allege it as a proof that the speech is not genuine: "according to the best MS. evidence, Demosthenes habitually, at least in some speeches, said ἄνδρες Ἀθηναῖοι without ὦ. It is therefore a mistake to note as unclassical the use of the vocative here without ὦ, *cf.* i. 14, xix. 35," Simcox, *Language of the New Testament*, p. 76, note.—κατὰ πάντα: "in all things I perceive that ye are," R.V., meaning that wherever he looked he had evidence of this characteristic—the A.V. would imply that in all their conduct the Athenians were, etc. The phrase which is common in classics is only found here, in iii. 22, Col. iii. 20, 22, Heb. ii. 5, iv. 15, in N.T.—ὡς, see Grimm-Thayer, *sub v.*, i., d., Winer-Moulton, xxxv., 4.—δεισιδαιμ.: "somewhat superstitious," R.V., but in margin, "somewhat religious," so in xxv. 19 the noun is rendered "religion," R.V. (in margin, "superstition"), where Festus, in speaking to Agrippa, a Jew, would not have been likely to call the Jewish religion a superstition. R.V. gives a better turn to the word than A.V. with Tyndale, "too superstitious," *cf.* Vulgate, *superstitiosiores*, as it is incredible that St. Paul should have commenced his remarks with a phrase calculated to offend his hearers. The R.V. has modified the A.V. by introducing "somewhat" instead of "too," according to the classical idiom by which the comparative of an adjective may be used to express the deficiency or excess (slight in either case) of the quality contained in the positive. But the quality in this case may be good or bad, since the adjective δεισιδαίμων and the cognate noun may be used of reverence or of superstition, *cf.* for the former Xen., *Cyr.*, iii., 3, 58; Arist., *Pol.*, v., 11; *cf. C. I. Gr.*, 2737b; Jos., *Ant.*, x., 32; Polyb., vi., 56, 7, and for the latter, Theoph., *Char.*, xvi.; Plut., *De Superstit.*, 10; Jos., *Ant.*, xv., 8, 2; M. Aurelius, vi., 30, and instances in Philo, *cf.* also Justin Martyr, *Apol.*, i., 2 (see Hatch, *Biblical Essays*, p. 43). Ramsay renders: "more than others respectful of what is divine"; so Renan, "le plus religieux"; Holtzmann, "Gottesfürchtige," so Weiss, so Zöckler, "religiosiores ceteris Græcis" (Horace, *Sat.*, i., 9, 70), *cf.* Winer-Moulton, xxxv., 4. In thus emphasising the religious spirit of the Athenians, St. Paul was speaking in

23. διερχόμενος γὰρ καὶ ἀναθεωρῶν [1] τὰ σεβάσματα ὑμῶν, εὗρον καὶ
βωμὸν ἐν ᾧ ἐπεγέγραπτο,[2] Ἀγνώστῳ Θεῷ. ὃν οὖν ἀγνοοῦντες

[1] For ἀναθεωρῶν D (Clem.) has διιστορων (nowhere found in N.T., not used in LXX or classical Greek).

[2] For επεγεγραπτο D (Gig.) has ην γεγραμμενον, so Hilg., and reads Αγνωστων Θεων, see Blass, *in loco*, for authorities who think this reading original, although in β text he follows T.R. ον ... τουτον אcA²EHLP, Arm., Clem., Ath., Chrys., Cosm., Aug.; ο ... τουτο א*A*BD¹, Vulg., Or., Hier., Tisch., W.H., R.V., Weiss, Wendt, Blass; ο ... τουτον 61.

strict accordance with similar testimonies from various quarters, *cf.* Thuc., ii., 40; Soph., *O. C.*, 260; Jos., *C. Apion.*, ii., 11; Pausanias, *In Attic.*, 24; Petronius, *Sat.*, c. 17. The context, ver. 24, where εὐσεβεῖτε, *religiose colitis* (Wetstein), is one result of this δεισιδαιμονία, strengthens the view that the adjective is used here in a good sense; *cf.* the comment on its good use here by St. Chrys., *Hom.*, xxxviii., and Theophylact. There is therefore no reason to suppose that Paul's words were an accommodation to the usual practice of Athenian orators to commence with a mere compliment. At the same time it is possible that with delicate tact the Apostle made use of a word of doubtful meaning, *verbum per se μέσον*, which could not possibly provoke hostility at the outset, while it left unexpressed his own judgment as to the nature of this reverence for the divine " with kindly ambiguity," Grimm-Thayer.

Ver. 23. διερχόμενος γὰρ: "for as I passed along," R.V., through the streets, or perhaps "was wandering through" —Renan has *passant dans vos rues*, see also on ver. 16 above, and also on viii. 40. A.V., "as I passed by" does not give the force of the word, and apparently means "passed by the objects of your devotion".—ἀναθεωρῶν: *accurate contemplari*, "observed," R.V., only in later Greek, and in N.T. only in Heb. xiii. 7, "*considering* with attentive survey again and again," see Westcott, *in loco*: Weiss renders it here ,, immer wieder betrachtend," *cf.* critical notes, *cf.* Diod. Sic., xiv. 109, and references in Grimm.—τὰ σεβάσματα: "the objects of your worship," R.V., Vulgate, *simulacra*, the thing worshipped, not the act or manner of worshipping. The A.V. margin gives "gods that ye worship," *cf.* 2 Thess. ii. 4, where A. and R.V. both render "that is worshipped," σέβασμα in text, and R.V. in margin, " an object of worship"; Bel and the Dragon,

ver. 27, Wisdom xiv. 20, xv. 17.—καὶ βωμὸν: "I found also an altar," R.V., *i.e.*, in addition to those with definite dedications; only here in N.T., often in LXX, sometimes of heathen altars, Exod. xxxiv. 13, Numb. xxiii. 1, Deut. vii. 5.— ἐπεγέγραπτο, *cf.* Luke xvi. 20; on the pluperfect with augment, Blass, *Gram.*, p. 37, see critical note: Farrar, *St. Paul*, i., 542, takes the word as implying permanence, and perhaps antiquity, so in *Speaker's Commentary* as of an ancient decayed altar, whose inscription had been forgotten; Mark xv. 26, Rev. xxi. 12 (Heb. viii. 10, x. 16).—Ἀγνώστῳ Θεῷ: "to an unknown God," R.V.: all previous versions like A.V., but there is no definite article, although in inscriptions it was often omitted. For the existence of altars of this kind the testimony of Pausanias and Philostratus may be fairly quoted; Pausan., i., 1, 4 (*cf.* v. 14, 6), βωμοὶ θεῶν τε ὀνομαζομένων ἀγνώστων καὶ ἡρώων, and Philost., *Vit. Apollon.*, vi., 2, σωφρονέστερον περὶ πάντων θεῶν εὖ λέγειν, καὶ ταῦτα Ἀθήνησιν, οὗ καὶ ἀγνώστων θεῶν βωμοὶ ἵδρυνται, see references in Wetstein, and *cf.* F. C. Conybeare, *u. s.*; Renan, *Saint Paul*, p. 173; Neander, *Geschichte der Pflanzung*, ii., 32 ff.; Wendt, etc. Baur, Zeller, Overbeck have maintained that there could have been no such inscription in the singular number as the plural is so much more in harmony with polytheism, although the last named admits that the authorities cited above admit at least the possibility of an inscription as in the text. To say nothing of the improbability that Paul would refer before such an audience to an inscription which had no existence, we may reasonably infer that there were at Athens several altars with the inscription which the Apostle quotes. A passage in Diog. Laert., *Epim.*, 3, informs us how Epimenides, in the time of a plague, brought to the Areopagus and let loose white and black sheep, and wherever the sheep lay down, he bade the Athenians

εὐσεβεῖτε, τοῦτον ἐγὼ καταγγέλλω ὑμῖν. 24. ὁ Θεὸς ὁ ποιήσας τὸν κόσμον καὶ πάντα τὰ ἐν αὐτῷ, οὗτος οὐρανοῦ καὶ γῆς κύριος ὑπάρχων,

to sacrifice τῷ προσήκοντι θεῷ, and so the plague ceased, with the result that we find in Athens many βωμοὺς ἀνωνύμους, see the passage quoted in full in Wetstein; from this it is not an unfair inference that in case of misfortune or disaster, when it was uncertain what god should be honoured or propitiated, an altar might be erected ἀγνώστῳ Θεῷ. (It is curious that Blass although he writes ἀγνώστῳ Θεῷ in β thinks that the true reading must have been the plural.) To draw such an inference is much more reasonable than to suppose with Jerome, *Tit.*, i., 12, that the inscription was not as Paul asserted, but that he used the singular number because it was more in accordance with his purpose, the inscription really being " Diis Asiæ et Europæ et Africæ, Diis ignotis et peregrinis," *cf.* the inscription according to Oecumenius θεοῖς ᾿Ασίας καὶ Εὐρώπης καὶ Λιβύης Θεῷ ἀγνώστῳ καὶ ξένῳ. But at the very commencement of his speech the Apostle would scarcely have made a quotation so far removed from the actual words of the inscription, otherwise he would have strengthened the suspicion that he was a mere σπερμολόγος. St. Chrysostom, *Hom.*, xxxviii., sees in the inscription an indication of the anxiety of the Athenians lest they should have neglected some deity honoured elsewhere, but if we connect it with the story mentioned above of Epimenides, it would be quite in accordance with the religious character of the Athenians, or perhaps one might rather say with the superstitious feeling which prompted the formula so often employed in the prayer of Greeks and Romans alike *Si deo si deæ*, or the words of Horace (*Epod.*, v., 1), "At deorum quidquid in coelo regit". There is no reason for the view held amongst others by Mr. Lewin that the inscription refers to the God of the Jews. But in such an inscription St. Paul wisely recognised that there was in the heart of Athens a witness to the deep unsatisfied yearning of humanity for a clearer and closer knowledge of the unseen power which men worshipped dimly and imperfectly, a yearning expressed in the sacred Vedic hymns of an old world, or in the crude religions of a new, *cf.* Max Müller, *Selected Essays*, i., p. 23 ff.; Zöckler, *in loco*, "Altar," B.D.[2]; Plumptre, *Movements of Religious Thought*, p. 78 ff.—ὃν οὖν ἀγνοοῦντες, see critical

notes. If we read ὅ for ὅν, we may render with R.V., "what therefore ye worship in ignorance": Vulgate, *quod colitis*. The mere fact of the erection of such an inscription showed that the Athenians did reverence to some divine existence, although they worshipped what they knew not, St. John iv. 22; not "ignorantly worship," as in A.V., this would have been alien to the refinement and tact of St. Paul.— εὐσεβεῖτε: used here as elsewhere of genuine piety, which St. Paul recognised and claimed as existing in the existence of the altar—the word throws light on the meaning which the Apostle attached to the δεισιδαιμονία of ver. 22; in N.T. only in Luke and Paul, *cf.* 1 Tim. v. 4, of filial piety (*cf. pietas*), *cf.* Susannah, ver. 64 (LXX), and 4 Macc. xi. 5, 8, 23, xviii. 2. "That *divine nature* which you worship, not knowing *what it is*" (Ramsay).—τοῦτον ἐγὼ καταγγέλλω ὑμῖν: in these words lay the answer to the charge that he was a σπερμ. or a καταγγελεύς of strange gods. ἐγὼ, emphatic; I whom you regard as a mere babbler proclaim to you, or set forth, the object which you recognise however dimly, and worship however imperfectly. Since the days of St. Chrysostom the verse has been taken as a proof that the words of St. Paul were addressed not to a select group of philosophers, but to the *corona* of the people.

Ver. 24. ὁ Θεὸς ὁ ποιήσας: "the God Who made all," R.V., the definiteness of the words and the revelation of God as Creator stand in marked contrast to the imperfect conception of the divine nature grasped by the Athenian populace, or even by the philosophers: ἐφθέγξατο φωνὴν μίαν, δι᾽ ἧς πάντα κατέστρεψε τὰ τῶν φιλοσόφων. οἱ μὲν γὰρ ᾿Επικούρειοι αὐτόματά φασιν εἶναι τὰ πάντα, καὶ ἀπὸ ἀτόμων συνεστάναι· οἱ δὲ Στωϊκοὶ σῶμα καὶ ἐκπύρωσιν· ὁ δὲ ἔργον Θεοῦ λέγει κόσμον καὶ πάντα τὰ ἐν αὐτῷ. Ὁρᾷς συντομίαν, καὶ ἐν συντομίᾳ σαφήνειαν. St. Paul's language is that of a Jew, a Monotheist, and is based upon Gen. i. 1, Exod. xx. 11, Isa. xlv. 7, Neh. ix. 6, etc., but his use of the word κόσμος (only here in Acts, only three times in St. Luke's Gospel) is observable. The word is evidently not used in the moral sense, or in the sense of moral separation from God, which is so common in St. John, and which is sometimes employed by the Synoptists, and it may well have been

οὐκ ἐν χειροποιήτοις ναοῖς κατοικεῖ, 25. οὐδὲ ὑπὸ χειρῶν ἀνθρώπων
θεραπεύεται προσδεόμενός τινος, αὐτὸς διδοὺς πᾶσι ζωὴν καὶ πνοὴν

chosen by Paul as a word familiar to his hearers. Both by Aristotle and Plato it had been used as including the orderly disposition of the heaven and the earth (according to some, Pythagoras had first used the word of the orderly system of the universe), and in this passage οὐρανοῦ καὶ γῆς may perhaps both be taken or included in the κόσμος, cf. iv. 24, xiv. 15. In the LXX κόσμος is never used as a synonym of the world, i.e., the universe (but cf. Prov. xvii. 6, Grimm, sub v.), except in the Apocryphal books, where it is frequently used of the created universe, Wisdom vii. 17, ix. 3; 2 Macc. vii. 23, viii. 18; 4 Macc. v. 25 (24), etc., Grimm, sub v., and Cremer, Wörterbuch.— οὗτος: "He being Lord of heaven and earth," R.V., more emphatic and less ambiguous than A.V., "seeing that".— ὑπάρχων "being the natural Lord" (Farrar), "He, Lord as He is, of heaven and earth" (Ramsay); see Plummer's note on Luke viii. 41; the word is Lucan, see above on οὐρ. καὶ γῆς κ., cf. Isa. xlv. 7, Jer. x. 16, and 1 Cor. x. 26.—οὐκ ἐν χειροποιήτοις ναοῖς κ.: as the Maker of all things, and Lord of heaven and earth, He is contrasted with the gods whose dwelling was in temples made with hands, and limited to a small portion of space, cf. 1 Kings viii. 27; Jos., Ant., viii., 4, 2, and St. Stephen's words, vii. 48, of which St. Paul here as elsewhere may be expressing his reminiscence, cf. for the thought Cicero, Leg., ii., 10, and in early Christian writers Arnobius and Minucius Felix (Wetstein), see also Mr. Page's note.

Ver. 25. οὐδὲ . . . θεραπεύεται: used in LXX and in classical Greek of the service of the Gods, significantly twice in Epist. Jer., vv. 27, 39, of the worshippers and priests of the idols overlaid with silver and gold, which are contrasted with the true God in that they can save no man from death, or show mercy to the widow and the fatherless, before which the worshippers set offerings and meat as before dead men. "Non quærit ministros Deus. Quidni? ipse humano generi ministrat," Seneca, Epist., 95, and instances in Wetstein; but St. Chrysostom's comment must also be noted, λέγων δέ, μὴ ὑπὸ χ. ἀνθ. θεραπεύεσθαι τὸν θεόν, αἰνίττεται ὅτι διανοίᾳ καὶ νῷ θεραπεύεται.—προσδεόμενός τινος: only here in N.T., to need in addition, as if necessary to perfection, "qui habet

quidem aliquid, sed non satis, qui insuper eget," Wetstein, so "cum . . . nullius boni desideret accessionem," Erasmus; a close parallel is found in 2 Macc. xiv. 35 (3 Macc. ii. 9); in both passages the word ἀπροσδεής is used of God, and in the former reference is made to the fact that God was pleased that the temple of His habitation should be amongst the Jews, cf. also Ecclus. lii. 21. Blass and Wetstein both quote a striking Pythagorean saying from Hierocles, see in loco, and to this αὐτάρκεια of the divine nature both the Jewish philosopher Philo and the Roman Epicurean Lucretius from their varying standpoints bore witness, see the instances in Wetstein (cf. Psalm li. 9).—Luther takes τινος as masculine, which as Wendt admits corresponds well to the preceding and also to the following πᾶσι, but it seems best to take it as neuter, of the service which men render, cf. Clem., Cor., lii., 1, ἀπροσδεής, ἀδελφοί, ὁ δεσπότης ὑπάρχει τῶν ἁπάντων, οὐδὲν οὐδενὸς χρήζει εἰ μὴ τὸ ἐξομολογεῖσθαι αὐτῷ, and Epist. ad Diognetum, iii., 5.—αὐτὸς διδοὺς: "seeing he himself giveth," R.V., so Vulgate ipse, but although αὐτός is so emphatic it was unfortunately ignored in Wycl., Genevan and A.V. The best commentary on the words is in David's words, 1 Chron. xxix. 14, cf. the striking passage in Epist. ad Diognetum, iii., 4.— πᾶσι: taken as neuter or masculine, but perhaps with Bengel "omnibus viventibus et spirantibus, summe προσδεομένοις indigentibus. De homine speciatim, v. seq."—ζωὴν καὶ πνοήν, cf. Gen. ii. 7, not a mere hendiadys, vitam animalem, or spiritum vitalem, but the first word = life in itself, existence; and the second the continuance of life, "per spiritum (halitum) continuatur vita," Bengel: on the paronomasia, see Winer-Moulton, lxviii., 1. For πνοή LXX, Ps. cl. 6, Job xxvii. 3, Isa. xlii. 5, Ecclus. xxx. 29 (xxxiii. 20), 2 Macc. iii. 31, and vii. 9, etc.—τὰ πάντα: omnia quæcumque, Rom. viii. 32, the expression need not be limited with Bethge to all things necessary for the preservation of life and breath.

Ver. 26. "And he hath made of one every nation of men for to dwell," R.V., so also A.V. takes ἐποίησε separately from κατοικεῖν, not "caused to dwell"; ἐποίησε, cf. ver. 24, he made, i.e., created of one; see Hackett's note.— κατοικεῖν: infinitive of purpose.—ἐξ ἑνὸς

καὶ τὰ πάντα · 26. ἐποίησέ τε ἐξ ἑνὸς αἵματος [1] πᾶν ἔθνος ἀνθρώπων, κατοικεῖν ἐπὶ πᾶν τὸ πρόσωπον τῆς γῆς, ὁρίσας προτεταγμένους [2]

[1] αιματος om. ℵAB 13, 40, 61, Vulg., Sah., Boh., Aethᵖᵖ·, Clem., so Tisch., W.H., R.V. [Blass], Wendt; Meyer retains with DEHLP, Syrr. P. and H., Arm., Irint., Theodt., Chrys., Cosm., Hilg. Alford brackets like Blass, see his note. For παν το προσ. ℵABD, R.V., W.H., Weiss, Wendt read παντος προσωπου; Meyer follows T.R.

[2] προστεταγμενους, overwhelming support ℵABD²EHLP, Clem., Chrys., Theodt., Tisch., W.H., R.V., Weiss, Wendt; D* 13 has προτεταγ., so Blass in β. Lach. wrote προς τεταγμ.

(αἵματος), see critical note. Rendall renders "from one father" as the substantive really understood, the idea of offspring being implied by ἐξ, cf. Heb. ii. 11, xi. 12 : Ramsay, "of one *nature*, every race of men," etc. Such teaching has often been supposed to be specially directed against the boast of the Athenians that they were themselves αὐτόχθονες (so recently Zöckler, and see instances in Wetstein, cf., e.g., Arist., *Vesp.*, 1076; Cicero, *Pro Flacco*, xxvi.); but whilst the Apostle's words were raised above any such special polemic, yet he may well have had in mind the characteristic pride of his hearers, whilst asserting a truth which cut at the root of all national pride engendered by polytheism on the one hand, by a belief in a god of this nation or of that, or of a philosophic pride engendered by a hard Stoicism on the other. When Renan and others speak of Christianity extending its hand to the philosophy of Greece in the beautiful theory which it proclaimed of the moral unity of the human race (*Saint Paul*, p. 197) it must not be forgotten that Rome and not Greece manifested the perfection of Pagan ethics, and that, even so, the sayings of a Seneca or an Epictetus wanted equally with those of a Zeno "a lifting power in human life". The cosmopolitanism of a Seneca no less than that of a Zeno failed; the higher thoughts of good men of a citizenship, not of Ephesus or elsewhere, but of the world, which were stirring in the towns where St. Paul preached, all these failed, *Die Heraklitischen Briefe*, p. 91 (Bernays); it was not given to the Greek or to the Roman, but to the Jew, separated though he was from every other nation, to safeguard the truth of the unity of mankind, and to proclaim the realisation of that truth through the blood of a Crucified Jew (Alford). On the Stoic cosmopolitanism see amongst recent writers G. H. Rendall, *Marcus Antoninus*, Introd., pp. 88, 118, 137 (1898).—ἐπὶ πᾶν τὸ πρόσωπον τῆς γῆς,

cf. Gen. ii. 6, xi. 8, etc.; Winer-Moulton, xviii., 4, cf. in Latin, *maris facies*, Æn. v., 768, *naturæ vultus*, Ovid, *Met.*, i., 6. —ὁρίσας προτεταγ. καιροὺς : if we read προστεταγ. see critical note, "having determined *their* appointed seasons," R.V. καιρ. not simply seasons in the sense used in addressing the people of Lystra, xiv. 17, as if St. Paul had in mind only the course of nature as divinely ordered, and not also a divine philosophy of history. If the word was to be taken with κατοικίας it would have the article and χρόνος would be more probably used, cf. also πρόσταγμα, Jer. v. 24, Ecclus. xxxix. 16. It is natural to think of the expression of our Lord Himself, Luke xxi. 24, καιροὶ ἐθνῶν, words which may well have suggested to St. Paul his argument in Rom. ix.-xi., but the thought is a more general one. In speaking thus, before such an audience, of a Providence in the history of mankind, assigning to them their seasons and their dwellings, the thought of the Stoic πρόνοια may well have been present to his mind; but if so it was by way of contrast (" sed non a Stoicis Paulo erat discenda πρόνοια," Blass, *in loco*). St. Paul owed his doctrine of Providence to no school of philosophy, but to the sacred Scriptures of his nation, which had proclaimed by the mouth of lawgiver, patriarch, psalmist, and prophet alike, that the Most High had given to the nations their inheritance, that it was He Who had spread them abroad and brought them in, that it was His to change the times and the seasons, Deut. xxxii. 8, Job xii. 23, Ps. cxv. 16, Dan. ii. 21, see further the note on πρόνοια, Wisdom of Solomon xiv. 3 (xvii. 2), *Speaker's Commentary* (Farrar). — τὰς ὁροθεσίας τῆς κατοικίας : the first noun is not found elsewhere either in classical or biblical Greek, but cf. Blass, *Gram.*, p. 69. κατοικία : only here in N.T., but frequent in LXX; found also in Polyb., of a dwelling; so in

καιροὺς καὶ τὰς ὁροθεσίας τῆς κατοικίας αὐτῶν· 27. ζητεῖν τὸν
Κύριον,¹ εἰ ἄρα γε ψηλαφήσειαν ² αὐτὸν καὶ εὕροιεν, καίτοιγε ³ οὐ

¹ Θεον for Κυριον ℵABHL 61, Vulg., Syrr. P. H., Boh., Sah., Arm., Chrys., so
Tisch., W.H., R.V., Wendt, Weiss; D, Gig., Iren., Clem. read το Θειον; and Syr.
H. mg. adds τι; and D, Syr. H. mg. add εστιν (Iren.). Blass omits; Weiss thinks
arbitrarily.

² ψηλαφησειαν, -σειεν (cf. Luke vi. 11) Winer-Schmiedel, p. 114, -σαισαν Hilg.;
W.H., App., 174.

³ καιτοιγε ℵP², Chrys., Cosm., so Meyer; but και γε BD² (D* και τε), HLP*
13, 61, 137, 180, Tisch., W.H., R.V., Weiss, Wendt, Blass; AE, Clem. have
καιτοι. Instead of ημων A*L 31, 180 read υμων.

Strabo, of a settlement, a colony.
Here, as in the former part of the
verse, we need not *limit* the words to
the assertion of the fact that God has
given to various nations their different
geographical bounds of mountain, river
or sea; as we recognise the influence
exerted upon the *morale* of the inhabitants of a country by their physical
surroundings, St. Paul's words teach us
to see also in these conditions "the
works of the Lord"—the words of the
most scientific observer perhaps of Palestine, Karl Ritter, are these: "Nature and
the course of history show that here,
from the beginning onwards there cannot be talk of any chance": G. A. Smith,
Historical Geography of the Holy Land,
pp. 112, 113, and 302, 303 ff.; Curtius,
"Paulus in Athen.," *Gesammelte Abhandlungen*, ii., 531, 536.
Ver. 27. ζητεῖν = ὅπως ζητῶσι, telic
infinitive, Winer - Moulton, xliv. 1.—
Κύριον, see critical note. Θεόν : the
more fitting word before this audience—
Ramsay renders "the God".—εἰ ἄρα γε :
"if haply," A. and R.V., ἄρα strengthened by γε ; in classical Greek we have
ἄρα followed by γε, but not ἄρα. This
ἄρα and ἄρα γε are generally regarded as
= Latin *si forte* (Blass, *Grammatik*, p.
211), although Simcox, *Language of the
New Testament*, pp. 180, 181, in admitting this, is careful to point out that
it is misleading to regard ἄρα as = *forte*.
Alford (so Page) maintains that the expression here, as in viii. 22, indicates a
contingency which is apparently not
very likely to happen. On the other
hand Rendall holds that the particle here,
as in viii. 22, should be rendered not
perhaps or *haply*, but *indeed* : "if they
might *indeed* feel after him," etc., expressing a very real intention of God's
providence, the optative pointing to the
fact that this intention had not yet been
realised (pp. 66, 110), cf. also Mark xi.

13, and in 1 Cor. xv. 15, εἴπερ ἄρα (see
further Blass, *Gram.*, pp. 254, 267; Burton, pp. 106, 111). With the whole passage, Wisdom xiii. 6 should be compared.
On St. Paul's study of the Book of
Wisdom at some time in his life see
Sanday and Headlam, *Romans*, p. 52.
—ψηλαφήσειαν, Æolic aorist, the verb
is used several times in LXX for the act
of groping in the dark, Deut. xxviii. 29,
Job v. 14, xii. 25 ; Isa. lix. 10 ; cf. its use
also in classical Greek, *Odys.*, ix., 416 ;
so Plato, *Phædo*, 99 B, where it is used
of vague guesses at truth (Wendt, Page).
The word would therefore fitly express
the thought of men stretching lame
hands of faith and groping, and calling
to what they feel is Lord of all. Weiss
finds the idea of the word as used here,
not in the LXX as above, but in 1 John
i. 1, of some palpable assurance, which
was everywhere possible in a world made
by God, ver. 24, Rom. i. 20, and where
men's dwellings had been apportioned by
Him. But the word might still be used
in the above sense, since the recognition
of God in His Creation is after all only a
partial recognition, and not the highest
knowledge of Him ; and the inscription
"To an Unknown God" testified in itself
how imperfect that recognition had been.
For the meaning of the verb in modern
Greek see Kennedy, p. 156.— καίτοιγε,
see critical note. καὶ γε, cf. ii. 18, *quin
etiam* (*quamvis* καίτοιγε "vix aptum,"
Blass). The word ψηλαφ. had intimated "et proximum esse Deum et oculis
occultum" (Blass, Knabenbauer), and
the Apostle now proclaims the nearness
of God, not only in creation, in its maintenance and preservation, but in the
spiritual being of man : "Closer is he than
breathing, and nearer than hands and
feet".—οὐ μακρὰν : the word implies not
mere local nearness, but spiritual, cf.
Jer. xxiii. 23, and Ephes. ii. 13. With
this we may compare Seneca, *Ep. Mor.*,

μακρὰν ἀπὸ ἑνὸς ἑκάστου ἡμῶν ὑπάρχοντα.   28. ἐν αὐτῷ γὰρ ζῶμεν
καὶ κινούμεθα καί ἐσμεν · ὡς καί τινες τῶν καθ᾿ ὑμᾶς ποιητῶν

xli., I. "God is near thee; He is with thee; He is within" (quoted by Lightfoot, *Philippians*, p. 290). The relation of man to God is a personal relationship: God is not "careless of the single life": ἀπὸ ἑνὸς ἑκάστου ἡμῶν, "from each one of us," R.V. The words may well have struck a responsive chord in the hearts, not only of some in the crowd, but of some of the Stoics who were listening, contradictory and incongruous as their system was, with its strange union of a gross material pantheism, and the expression of belief in the fatherly love and goodness of God (see further Lightfoot, *u. s.*, p. 298, and Curtius, *Gesammelte Abhandlungen*, ii., 530, 531).

Ver. 28. St. Chrysostom comments (*Hom.*, xxxviii.): Τί λέγω μακράν; οὕτως ἐγγύς ἐστιν, ὡς χωρὶς αὐτοῦ μὴ ζῆν. ἐν αὐτῷ γὰρ ζῶμεν κ.τ.λ. . . . καὶ οὐκ εἶπε, δι᾿ αὐτοῦ, ἀλλ᾿ ὃ ἐγγύτερον ἦν, ἐν αὐτῷ. In the three verbs it has been sometimes maintained there is an ascending scale; in God we possess the gift of life, in Him we move, in Him we *are* (not "have our being" simply), *i.e.*, we are what we are, personal beings. Bethge and Plumptre may be named as two chief supporters of some such view as this, whilst others regard the words (Bengel, Weiss) as merely expressing what had been already expressed in ver. 25, or as referring simply (so Overbeck, Wendt, Felten) to our physical life and being.—τῶν καθ᾿ ὑμᾶς π.: "of your own poets," see Grimm., *sub v.* κατά, with the accusative as a periphrasis for the possessive pronoun; see also Winer-Moulton, xxii., 7, xlix. d. Blass takes it as = ὑμέτεροι., on the reading see W. H. marg. καθ᾿ ἡμᾶς, though the limited range of attestation prevents them from reading this in the text: "there would be a striking fitness in a claim by St. Paul to take his stand as a Greek among Greeks, as he elsewhere vindicates his position as a Roman (xvi. 37; xxii. 25, 28), and as a Pharisee (xxiii. 6)": W. H., ii., p. 310.—τοῦ γὰρ καὶ γένος ἐσμέν: half of an hexameter, the γὰρ καί has nothing to do with the meaning of the quotation in the N.T., but see Winer-Moulton, liii. 10. The words are found in Aratus, B.C. 270, *Phænom.*, 5, and Cleanthes, B.C. 300, *Hymn to Jove*, 5; for other parallels see Blass, *in loco*, and Wetstein, so that Zöckler may go too far in saying that St. Paul quoted from

the former as his fellow-countryman, Aratus being of Soli in Cilicia. Both poets named were Stoics, and the words may have been well known as a familiar quotation, see on Tarsus, chapter ix. II. In Cleanthes the actual words are rather different, ἐκ σοῦ γὰρ γένος ἐσμέν, where origin rather than kinship may be meant. No doubt it is possible to exaggerate, with Bentley, St. Paul's knowledge of classical literature, but on the other hand it is not perhaps an unfair inference that a man who could quote so aptly from the poets as here in I Cor. xv. 35, and in Tit. i. 12, could have done so at other times if occasion had required, *cf.* Curtius, *ubi supra*, Blass, *in loco*, and Farrar, "Classical Quotations of St. Paul," *St. Paul*, ii., *Exc.*, iii. As the words of the hymn were addressed to Zeus, a difficulty has been raised as to the Apostle's application of them here, and it has been questioned whether he was acquainted with the context of the words, or whether he was aware of their application. But he must at least have known that they were not originally written of the God Whom he revealed. If so, however, there seems no more difficulty in supposing that he would apply such a hemistich to a higher purpose, than that he should make the inscription on a heathen altar a text for his discourse.

Ver. 29. γένος οὖν ὑπάρχοντες: for ὑπάρχειν, see above on ver. 24; is the inference simply that because we are dependent upon God for all things, it is absurd to suppose that the divine nature can be like to the work of men's hands? This is correct so far as it goes, but is not the further thought implied that as men are the offspring of God, they ought not to think that man is the measure of God, or that the divine nature, which no man hath seen at any time, can be represented by the art of man, but rather as conscious of a sonship with a Father of spirits they ought to worship a Father in spirit and in truth? see quotations from Seneca in Lightfoot, *Philippians*, p. 290: "The whole world is the temple of the immortal gods. Temples are not to be built to God of stones piled on high . . . ." *Fragm.* 123 in Lactant. *Div. Inst.*, vi., 25: "God is near thee; He is with thee; He is within," *Ep. Mor.*, xcv., 47: "Thou shalt not form Him of silver and gold, a true likeness of

εἰρήκασι, "Τοῦ γὰρ καὶ γένος ἐσμέν". [1] 29. γένος οὖν ὑπάρχοντες
τοῦ Θεοῦ, οὐκ ὀφείλομεν νομίζειν χρυσῷ ἢ ἀργύρῳ [2] ἢ λίθῳ, χαράγματι

[1] καθ υμας, see note in comment., B 33, W.H. mg. read ημας. After εσμεν D adds
το καθ ημεραν, so Blass in β, and Hilg. ποιητων om. D, Gig.. Aethro., Irint., Ambr.,
Blass in β.

[2] Blass reads (β) χρυσιω η αργυριω; χρ. ℵAE, Theodt.; αργ. AE 13, 15, 18,
χρυσος et αργυρος materiem denotant; χρυσια et αργυρια sunt ex auro argentove
facta (Blass, in loco).

God cannot be moulded of this material,"
Ep. Mor., xxxi., 11. See also the striking
parallels from *Letters of Pseudo-Heracleitus*, Gore, *Ephesians*, p. 254. For a
recent view of the possible acquaintance
of Seneca with the Christian teaching of
St. Paul see Orr, *Some Neglected Factors
in Early Christianity*, pp. 178 ff.—
τὸ θεῖον: not "godhead," but "that
which is divine," R.V. margin, "the
divine nature"; probably the word
which the Athenians themselves used,
Xen., *Mem.*, i., 4, 18, see instances in
Grimm, *sub v.*, of its use in Philo and
Josephus, who employ it in the neuter of
the one God, Grimm thinks, out of regard
for Greek usage.—χρυσῷ ἢ ἀργ. ἢ λίθῳ:
(on the form of the word see Blass and
critical notes) including, we may suppose, the chryselephantine statues of
Phidias in the Parthenon, and a reference
to the silver mines of Laurium, and the
marble hewn from Pentelicus, *cf. Epist.
ad Diognetum*, ii., 2.—χαράγματι: in
apposition to χρύσῳ. χαράσσω, Latin,
sculpo, insculpo, only here in N.T. in
this sense. Polyb. uses the words of
coins stamped (so in Anth. P., v., 30) τὸ
χαραχθὲν νόμισμα.—τέχνης καὶ ἐνθ.:
"artis externæ, cogitationis internæ".
ἐνθ.: a rare word (in the plural, *thoughts*,
cf. Matt. ix. 4, etc.), but used by Thuc.,
Eur., and also by Hippocrates. See the
remarks of Curtius (*Gesammelte Abhandlungen*, ii., 535) on the words, as indicating that Paul was acquainted with the
phrases of Greek authors. The passage
in Wisdom xiii. 6 should be carefully
noted (see ver. 27 above), and also ver.
10, in which the writer speaks of gods
which are the work of men's hands, gold
and silver to show art in, *i.e.*, lit., an
elaboration of art, ἐμμελέτημα τέχνης.
In the words Bethge further sees an intimation that the Apostle had an eye for
the forms of beauty represented in the
carved statues and idols which met his
gaze in Athens; but for a very different
view of St. Paul's estimate of art see
Renan, *Saint Paul*, p. 172, Farrar, *St.
Paul*, i., 525, McGiffert, *Apostolic Age*,

p. 260.—ἀνθρώπου: stands contrasted
with τὸ θεῖον; it is the device of man
which forms the material into the idol
god, and thus human thought becomes
the measure of the divine form; Xeno-
phanes (570 B.C.) had ridiculed the way
in which the Thracians represented *their*
gods, with blue eyes and fair complexions,
whilst the Æthiopians had represented
their gods as flat-nosed and swarthy.
Zeno had renewed the protest, but some
of the best of the heathen philosophers
had spoken in inconsistent language on
the subject; St. Paul's plain and direct
words were the utterances of a man who
had in mind the severe and indignant
protests of the Hebrew prophets, *cf.* Isa.
xliv. 12.—οὐκ ὀφείλομεν: at the same time
the use of the 1st person plural again
points to the conciliatory tone of the
speech, "clemens locutio" (so Bengel,
Wendt); or possibly the words may
mean that he is referring in a general
way to the beliefs of the people, to the
crowd and not to the philosophers:
πρὸς τοὺς πολλοὺς ὁ λόγος ἦν αὐτῷ,
Chrys. But Nestle has lately called
attention to the question as to whether
we should not translate: "we are not
obliged, not bound to think, we are at
liberty not to think so," and thus, instead
of a reproof, the words become a plea
for freedom of religious thought. The
first shade of meaning, he adds, *i.e.*,
"clemens locutio," as above, comes
nearer to ὀφειλ. μὴ νομίζειν, the second
agrees with the other passage in the
N.T., 2 Cor. xii. 14, where the negative
particle is connected with ὀφείλειν; see
Nestle's note in *Expository Times*,
March, 1898, p. 381.
Ver. 30. τοὺς μὲν οὖν χρ.: a contrast
drawn between the past times of ignorance, and the present times with God's
summons to repentance, but instead of
a finite verb we have the participle
ὑπεριδών, and so δέ is omitted in the
apodosis; see Rendall, *in loco*, and Appendix on μὲν οὖν, p. 163, and to the
same effect, Blass, *in loco*.—τῆς ἀγνοίας:
simply "the times of ignorance," R.V.,

τέχνης καὶ ἐνθυμήσεως ἀνθρώπου, τὸ θεῖον εἶναι ὅμοιον. 30. Τοὺς μὲν οὖν χρόνους τῆς ἀγνοίας ὑπεριδὼν ὁ Θεός, τανῦν παραγγέλλει [1]

---

[1] παραγγέλλει ℵcADEHLP, so Blass in β, and Hilg.; απαγγελλει ℵ*AB, Tisch., W.H., R.V. marg., Weiss, Wendt. πασι, but παντας ℵABD²E, Ath., Cyr., Tisch., W.H., R.V., Blass, Weiss, Wendt. For ὑπεριδων D has παριδων, "recte," Blass (β); neither word occurs elsewhere in N.T.

not "this," as in Vulgate and all E.V. "*Ignorantia* objicitur Atheniensibus? Hanc ipsi sunt fassi. ἀγνώστῳ, *ignoto*; ἀγνοοῦντες, *ignorantes*, v. 23."—ὑπεριδὼν: "overlooked," R.V., "winked at," A.V. The latter rendering occurs three times in LXX, Wisdom xiii. 23, Ecclus. xxviii. 7, and xxx. 11 R.; for the verb παρορᾶν Skeat quotes Lever, *Serm.*, p. 81: "For if ye *winke at* such matters, God wyl scoull upon you," when the word evidently means to connive at, but not the sense required here, *cf.* also Chapman, *Il.*, iv., 66. The verb ὑπερορᾶν is frequent in the LXX, but rather in the sense of despising, neglecting, Gen. xlii. 21, Deut. xxii. 3, 4, Ps. liv. (lv.) 1, Job xxxi. 19, and Ecclus. ii. 10, etc. But here it is used rather as the opposite of ἐφορᾶν, a verb used in classical Greek of overseeing, observing, as of the divine providence of the gods (*cf.* in N.T. Luke i. 25, Acts iv. 29); so ὑπερορᾶν = (1) to look over, (2) to overlook, *i.e.*, not attend to, to let pass (*cf.* the use of ὑπεριδεῖν in LXX, Lev. xxvi. 44 and 3 Macc. vi. 15). Tyndale rendered "regarded not," with which we may compare: "et cum videas perinde te gerere quasi non videas," Erasmus. Both Chrys. and Oecum. comment on the words, pointing out that it is not παρεῖδεν or εἴασεν, but ὑπερεῖδεν, τουτέστιν, οὐκ ἀπαιτεῖ κόλασιν ὡς ἀξίους ὄντας κολάσεως. With the statement of St. Paul here *cf.* Acts xiv. 16, Rom. iii. 25. But it must be remembered that πάρεσις, Rom. iii. 25, is by no means the same as ἄφεσις ("idem paene est παριέναι quod ὑπεριδεῖν, Acts xvii. 30," Bengel); in considering the strictures of Overbeck against the use of the passage in Romans as a parallel to our present passage, it is not alleged, let it be noted, either here or there that God inflicted no punishment upon the sins of the heathen. Rom. i. 19 is a decided proof of the contrary in the case of the very sin of idolatry which St. Paul condemns in Athens; see the words of Chrys. and Oecum. above, and *cf.* the comments of Weiss, Wendt, Felten, Plumptre, and McGiffert's note, pp. 260, 261.—τὰ νῦν, see above p. 135; "hic dies, haec hora, inquit Paulus," Bengel, in contrast to the "overlooking" on account of ignorance, and so relatively of excuse (*cf.* ἐν τῷ νῦν καιρῷ, Rom. iii. 26, *i.e.*, from the N.T. times of salvation to the final judgment).—παραγγέλλει: "commandeth," but in margin, R.V., ἀπαγ., "he declareth": *cf.* Friedrich, p. 29, on the constant use of the latter in St. Luke's writings, but used twice by St. Paul elsewhere, 1 Cor. xiv. 25, 1 Thess. i. 9.—πᾶσι πανταχοῦ: on this and other collocations with πᾶς as frequent in Luke see Friedrich, p. 5. πανταχοῦ is used in the N.T. four times by St. Luke, *cf.* Luke ix. 6, Acts xxiv. 3, xxviii. 22 (elsewhere in the Gospels, Mark i. 28, xvi. 20), but it is also used, although only once, by St. Paul, 1 Cor. iv. 17. Wetstein quotes instances of the same collocation in Dem., Philo, and adds: "ex toto terrarum orbe plurimi Athenas advenerant, adeoque hac ipsa Pauli oratione omnibus prædicatur doctrina Evangelii".—μετανοεῖν: for all had sinned, and all would be judged; infinitive after verbs *dicendi*, expressing what they must do, *cf.* xiv. 15, iv. 18, v. 28, 40. The context requires something more than a reference of the words to the turning from idol worship to the true God (Holtzmann), it points to the change of mind which was demanded of those whose consciences by sin were accused. To both Stoic and Epicurean the counsel would appear not merely needless, but objectionable. To the latter because it would conflict not only with his denial of immortality, but with his whole idea of the gods, and to the Stoic because the wise man was himself a king, self-sufficing, who stood in no need of atonement, who feared no judgment to come; the famous picture of Josephus was so far realised, and the Epicurean might be called the Sadducee, and the Stoic the Pharisee of ancient philosophy; but in one respect both Stoic and Epicurean were at one—whether they were just persons or not, they "needed no repentance," Bethge, *Die Paulinischen Reden*, p. 115; Lightfoot, "Paul and Seneca" (*Philippians*, pp. 280, 296, 305); Plumptre, *in loco*; Zahn, *Der Stoiker Epiktet, und sein Verhältniss zum Christenthum*, pp. 26, 33, etc.

τοῖς ἀνθρώποις πᾶσι πανταχοῦ μετανοεῖν· 31. διότι¹ ἔστησεν ἡμέραν,
ἐν ᾗ μέλλει κρίνειν² τὴν οἰκουμένην ἐν δικαιοσύνῃ, ἐν ἀνδρὶ ᾧ ὥρισε,
πίστιν παρασχὼν πᾶσιν, ἀναστήσας αὐτὸν ἐκ νεκρῶν. 32. Ἀκού-

---

¹ καθοτι for διοτι is supported by ℵABDE, Ath., Bas., Cyr., Theodt., Tisch.,
W.H., R.V., Weiss, Wendt, Blass. For εν η μελλει κρινειν D, Gig., Iren. simply
κριναι, so Blass in β, and Hilg.

² Tisch., R.V., W.H., Weiss read περι τουτου και παλιν, so ℵAB.

Ver. 31. διότι—καθότι, R.V., see
critical note, only found in St. Luke =
quia (Blass) in Luke i. 7, xix. 9, Acts ii.
24, ii. 45, iv. 35 = according as : see
Plummer on Luke i. 7, and Blass, Gram.,
p. 268.—ἔστησεν ἡμέραν : hence the command to repent, cf. 1 Macc. iv. 59 and
Blass, in loco.—μέλλει κρίνειν, LXX, Ps.
ix. 8, xcv. (xcvi.) 13, xcvii. (xcviii.) 9 ; its
form here may = xii. 6, "on the point of
judging" (Weiss).—τὴν οἰκ., so often in
LXX, as in instances above.—ἐν δικαιοσύνῃ = δικαίως (as of the moral element
in which the judgment will take place),
cf. 1 Peter ii. 24 and Rev. xix. 11, cf.
Psalms as above, and Ecclus. xlv. 26.
—ἐν ἀνδρὶ : in the person of the man (so
Ramsay, Meyer, Alford), not ἄνθρωπος
but ἀνήρ, in viro (cf. 1 Cor. vi. 12, ἐν
ὑμῖν κρίνεται) ; above we have ἀνθρώποις, but here the nobler appellation.
We may compare with the Christian
doctrine Book of Enoch, xli. 9, although
according to other Jewish statements
it would seem that God, and not the
Messiah, was to judge the dead.—ᾧ
ὥρισε : ᾧ attraction, cf. ii. 22, see
Winer-Schmiedel, p. 225, cf. x. 42, Rom.
i. 4. The whole statement, as indeed the
general tenor of the address, is entirely in
line with the preaching to the Thessalonians in the Epistles written some few
months later, cf. 1 Thess. i. 9, 10, iii. 13,
iv. 6, v. 2, 2 Thess. i. 7, ii. 12 ; McGiffert,
Apostolic Age, p. 259, and Plumptre, in
loco. "Pour un juif, dire que Jésus
présidera au jugement, c'était à peu près
dire qu'il est créateur. Aussi je ne sais
pas de preuve plus éclatante de l'immense
impression produite par le Galiléen que
ce simple fait . . . après qu'il eut été
crucifié, un pharisien, comme l'avait été
Paul, a pu voir en lui le juge des vivants et
des morts," Colani, J. C. et les Croyances
Messianiques de son temps.—πίστιν παρασχὼν : in classical Greek to afford assurance, a guarantee, see instances in
Wetstein. But it is difficult to say how
much St. Paul included in the words—
to a Jewish audience he would no doubt,
like St. Peter, have insisted upon the resur-

rection of Christ as a final proof given
by God that the claims of Christ were
true ; but to an audience like that at
Athens he might well insist upon the fact
of the resurrection of the Man ordained
by God as a guarantee that all men would
be raised ; R.V., "whereof he hath given
assurance," "whereof" implied in the
Greek : marginal rendering in A.V.
"offered faith" is omitted in R.V. ; "and
He hath given all a guarantee in that He
hath raised Him from the dead" : so Ramsay. Others have taken the words to
mean that God thus affords assurance
that He will judge the world righteously
in that He hath shown His righteousness
by raising Christ, others again connect
πίστιν closely with ἐν ἀνδρί (so Bethge).
If at this point the Apostle was interrupted
he may have intended to pursue the theme
further, if not then, on some other occasion. But the fact that the speech contains so little that is distinctively Christian
is a strong proof of its genuineness ; none
would have invented such a speech for
Paul, any more than they could have invented his discourse at Lystra, see below
on p. 381, and Ramsay, St. Paul, pp.
150 and 250, 251. Yet in this short address at Athens the Apostle had preached
both Jesus and the Resurrection.
Ver. 32. οἱ μὲν ἐχλ. . . . οἱ δὲ : verb
only here in N.T., implies outward gesture as well as words of scorn (χλεύη,
χεῖλος, cf. μυκτηρίζω, μυκτήρ). We
usually think of the οἱ μέν as the Stoics,
and the οἱ δέ as the Epicureans ; e.g.,
Wetstein after describing the Epicureans
adds οἱ δέ = Stoici : cf. Cicero, De Natura
Deorum, ii., 17, and Plutarch, De Or. Def.,
32. But if the Epicureans ridiculed a
resurrection and judgment to come, the
Stoics also were separated by a wide
gulf from the teaching of St. Paul. Even
if it may be said that in general they
approximated towards the doctrine of
personal existence after death, some of
their most famous representatives departed from it ; Capes, Stoicism, p. 173 ;
Wallace, Epicureanism, p. 121 ; Ueberweg, Hist. of Phil., i., p. 196 ; E.T.

σαντες δὲ ἀνάστασιν νεκρῶν, οἱ μὲν ἐχλεύαζον· οἱ δὲ εἶπον, Ἀκουσόμεθά σου πάλιν περὶ τούτου.　33. καὶ οὕτως ὁ Παῦλος ἐξῆλθεν ἐκ

Rendall, *Marcus Antoninus*, Introd., pp. 107, 108. "On one point alone were the professors of this school [Stoic] agreed; an *external* existence of the human soul was out of the question," Lightfoot, *Philippians*, p. 323. The idea of retribution beyond the grave would have been equally alien to the Stoic as to the Epicurean, and both Stoic and Epicurean alike would have ridiculed the idea of a resurrection of the body. Zöckler, *in loco*, while referring the οἱ μέν without hesitation to the Epicureans, thinks that possibly Platonists rather than Stoics may be represented by the οἱ δέ. If St. Paul was addressing not only a philosophical but a popular audience, as we have seen reason to believe, it is quite possible that while the majority would laugh at his closing words, Juvenal, *Sat.*, ii., 149, there may have been others who clung to the popular mythology and its crude conceptions, and the Apostle's prediction of a judgment to come may have sufficiently interested them to prompt a desire for further disclosures. — ἀκουσόμεθά σου πάλιν (περὶ τούτου, R.V., neuter, we can hardly refer it to the αὐτόν of ver. 31). The words are often taken to imply a polite rejection of the Apostle's appeal, a courteous refusal to hear anything further; or at all events to express a very cold interest in his announcement. But if we adopt the reading καὶ πάλιν (see critical note) "yet again," R.V., the words rather indicate that a real interest had been excited in some of the hearers (so Calvin, Grotius, Weiss, Alford) and that the marked and defined division of opinion was not merely a dramatic device of the author.

Ver. 33. οὕτως: may mean, with this scanty result, or simply, after these events, in this state of the popular mind, with an expectation of being heard again (Alford); "ancipiti auditorum obsequio; nullo edito miraculo": Bengel. — ἐκ μέσου αὐτῶν: at the opening Paul stood ἐν μέσῳ, ver. 22, τοῦ Ἀ. π.: "the two expressions correspond to and explain each other, . . . he that 'went forth from the midst of them' must have been standing 'in the midst of them'"; *cf.* Ramsay, *Expositor*, September, 1895, and for the bearing of the words see above on ver. 22. For similar phrase with μέσου as frequent in St. Luke's writings, Friedrich, p. 22. Ramsay thinks that some

danger is indicated, but nothing is said of this; the words apparently refer to no trial, although, perhaps, to some kind of preliminary inquiry, see above, ver. 22.

Ver. 34. τινὲς δὲ: may contrast the favourable with the unfavourable, or perhaps merely continuous.—κολληθέντες, see above on v. 13, implies close companionship upon which their conversion followed, see additional note.—Διονύσιος ὁ Ἀ.: "quam doctrinam scurræ rejecerunt, Areopagita vir gravis accipit". Dionysius was a member of the Council, the words can mean nothing less—it is evident, therefore, that this convert must have been a man of some distinction, as an Areopagite would previously have filled the office of Archon. On the honour attached to the term *cf.* Cicero, *Pro Balbo*, xii., and instances cited by Renan, *Saint Paul*, p. 209, note. It is not improbable that St. Luke may have received from him the draft of St. Paul's address. On the other hand the conversion of a man occupying such a position has excited suspicion, and Baur, *Paulus*, i., 195, considers that the whole scene on the Areopagus is unhistorical, and owes its origin to the tradition that an Areopagite named Dionysius was converted. So Holtzmann holds that the whole scene was placed on the Areopagus, because, according to report, a member of the Areopagus was converted, *Apostelgeschichte*, p. 393, similarly Weizsäcker. See further, "Dionysius," B.D.[2], Hastings' B.D., Smith and Wace, *Dictionary of Christian Biography*, i., p. 846; Felten, *Apostelgeschichte*, p. 337 and notes below. — Δάμαρις: perhaps Δάμαλις, a heifer, a name popular amongst the Greeks, so Grotius, Wetstein, and Renan, *Saint Paul*, p. 209, note; see critical note above. We know nothing certain about her, but Ramsay makes the interesting conjecture that as the woman is not described as εὐσχήμων (*cf.* the description of the women at Thessalonica, Berœa, and Pisidian Antioch, xiii. 50, xvii. 4, 12), she may have been a foreign woman (perhaps one of the educated *Hetairai*), as at Athens no woman of respectable position would have been present amongst St. Paul's audience. St. Chrysostom (so St. Ambrose and Asterius) thought that she was the wife of Dionysius, but St. Luke calls her γυνή, not ἡ γυνὴ αὐτοῦ. No mention is made of her in D (but see above

μέσου αὐτῶν. 34. τινὲς δὲ ἄνδρες κολληθέντες αὐτῷ ἐπίστευσαν·
ἐν οἷς καὶ Διονύσιος ὁ Ἀρεοπαγίτης, καὶ γυνὴ ὀνόματι Δάμαρις,[1] καὶ
ἕτεροι σὺν αὐτοῖς.

[1] Before και ετερ. D (Flor.) add ευσχημων. The words και γυνη ονομ. Δ. are
omitted in D (retained by Blass in β), see comment., and also by Hilg., who adds
ευσχημων after Αρεοπ.

critical note), and Ramsay accounts for
this by the view that the reviser of Codex
Bezæ was a Catholic, who objected to
the prominence given to women in Acts,
and that under the influence of this feeling the changes occurred in xvii. 12 (see
above) and 34 : this prominence assigned
to women was, in Ramsay's view, firstly,
pagan rather than Christian, and, secondly,
heretical rather than Catholic ; *Church in
the Roman Empire*, pp. 160, 161 ; see
" Damaris," Hastings' B.D., and Felten,
Apostelgeschichte, p. 337.—**καὶ ἕτεροι** : a
significant contrast to the precise results
of the Apostle's preaching elsewhere,
and yet a contrast which carries with it
an evidence of truth. Spitta, p. 242,
justly remarks that he knows not how the
author of the " We " sections, who was
not present at Athens, could have represented the activity of St. Paul in that
city better than he has done ; the idle
curiosity of the Athenians, ver. 21, and
after a speech received with ridicule and
indifference, a scanty result, graphically
represented by two names, of which it is
a mere assertion to say that they refer to
the sub-apostolic age. Spitta thus refuses to allow any justification for
Weizsäcker's rejection of the historical
worth of the narrative. Thus in the
simple notice of the results of St. Paul's
preaching we gain an indication of the
historical truthfulness of the narrative.
If anywhere, surely at Athens a forger
would have been tempted to magnify
the influence of St. Paul's intellectual power, and to attribute an overwhelming victory to the message of the
Gospel in its first encounter with the
philosophic wisdom of the world in a
city which possessed a university, the
greatest of any of that time, which was
known as " the eye of Greece, mother of
arts," whose inhabitants a Jewish philosopher (Philo) had described as the
keenest mentally of all the Greeks.
In answer to the earlier criticism of
Zeller and Overbeck, we may place the
conclusion of Weiss that the result of
St. Paul's labours is plainly not described
after a set pattern, but rests upon definite information, whilst Wendt, who

refers the composition of the speech, as
we have it, to St. Luke, and regards it
as derived from information of a speech
actually delivered at Athens, insists
equally strongly upon the difficulty of
supposing that such slender results would
be represented as following, if the speech
had been composed with a view of ex-
alting Jewish and Christian monotheism
against polytheism. Moreover the narrative bears the stamp of truthfulness in
its picture of the local condition of Athens,
and also in its representation of St. Paul's
attitude to the philosophical surroundings
of the place and its schools. " One must
be at home in Athens," writes Curtius,
" to understand the narrative rightly,"
and no one has enabled us to realise
more fully the historical character and
vividness of the scene than Curtius himself in the essay to which reference is
made above, of which the concluding words
are these, that " he who refuses to accept
the historical value of the narrative of
Paul in Athens, tears one of the weightiest
pages out of the history of humanity "
(*Gesammelte Abhandlungen*, ii., p. 543,
" Paulus in Athens " : see further, Knabenbauer, pp. 308, 309). The character of
the people, the moving life of the Agora,
the breadth of view which could comprehend in one short speech the crude errors
of the populace and the fallacious theology
of the schools, " the heart of the world "
too generous to ignore all that was best
in men's thoughts of God's providence
and of human brotherhood, and yet too
loving to forget that all men had sinned,
and that after death was the judgment—
we recognise them all. If we turn to
the speech itself we find abundant evidence of characteristic Pauline thoughts
and teaching (*cf.*, *e.g.*, ver. 27 and Rom.
i. 19, ii. 14 ; ver. 26 and Rom. v. 12,
1 Cor. xv. 45 ; ver. 30 and Rom. iii. 25,
etc., Zöckler, p. 268, and instances in
notes above, McGiffert, *Apostolic Age*,
p. 259), and it is worthy of note that
Weizsäcker, while rejecting with Baur,
Zeller, Schwegler, and Overbeck the account of St. Paul's visit to Athens as
unhistorical, fully recognises, after an
examination of the Apostle's method of

XVIII. 1. ΜΕΤΑ δὲ ταῦτα χωρισθεὶς ὁ Παῦλος [1] ἐκ τῶν Ἀθηνῶν
ἦλθεν εἰς Κόρινθον · 2. καὶ εὑρών τινα Ἰουδαῖον ὀνόματι Ἀκύλαν,

[1] ℵAB 13, 69, Vulg., Boh., Arm., so Tisch., W.H., R.V., Weiss, Wendt, omit δε.
ℵBD, Vulg., Sah., Boh., Tisch., W.H., R.V., Weiss, Wendt omit ο Παυλος.

dealing with idolatry and polytheism in Rom. i. 20, that if we compare with the Apostle's own indications the fine survey of the world, and especially of history from a monotheistic standpoint, ascribed to him by the Acts at Lystra, xiv. 15, and afterwards at Athens, xvii. 24, the latter, whatever its source, also gives us a true idea of Paul's method and teaching, *Apostolic Age*, i., p. 117, E.T. On the whole tone of the speech as incredible as a later composition, see Ramsay, *St. Paul*, p. 147 ff., whilst no one perhaps has drawn up more clearly than Wetstein, see on Acts xvii. 25, the consummate skill of the speech addressed to an audience comprising so many varieties of culture and belief. (To the strange attempt of Holtzmann to reproduce at some length the argument of Zeller, who maintains that the scene at Athens was a mere counterpart of the scene of Stephen's encounter with his foes at Jerusalem, a sufficient answer may be found in Spitta, *Apostelgeschichte*, p. 240.)

If we ask from whom the report of the speech was received, since Luke, Silas, Timothy all were absent, it is possible that a Christian convert like Dionysius the Areopagite may have preserved it (Zöckler); but a speech so full of Pauline thoughts, and so expressive of Athenian life and culture, may well have been received at least in substance from St. Paul himself, although it is quite conceivable that the precise form of it in Acts is due to St. Luke's own editing and arrangement (see for an analysis of the language of the speech Bethge, *Die Paulinischen Reden der Apostelgeschichte*, p. 82). The results of St. Paul's work at Athens were small if measured by the number of converts, although even amongst them it must not be forgotten that it was something to gain the allegiance to the faith of a man holding the position of Dionysius the Areopagite (see further an interesting account of the matter in *Expository Times*, April, 1898). But in addition to this, it is also important to remember that St. Paul has given us "an invaluable method of missionary preaching" (Lechler, *Das Apost. Zeitalter*, p. 275), that to the Church at Athens Origen could appeal

against Celsus as a proof of the fruits of Christianity (Bethge, p. 116), that its failing faith was revived in time of persecution by its bishop Quadratus, the successor of the martyr-bishop Publius; that in the Christian schools of Athens St. Basil and St. Gregory were trained; and that to an Athenian philosopher, Aristides, a convert to Christ, we owe the earliest *Apology* which we possess (Athenagoras too was an Athenian philosopher), see Farrar, *St. Paul*, i., p. 551; Humphry, *Commentary on the Acts*. It is significant that St. Paul never visited Athens again, and never addressed a letter to the Saints at Athens, although he may well have included them in his salutation to "the Saints which are in the whole of Achaia," 2 Cor. i. 1.

CHAPTER XVIII.—Ver. 1. μετὰ δὲ ταῦτα: in continuation of the narrative, *cf.* Luke x. 1.—χωρισθεὶς: in i. 4 with ἀπό, and so usually—only here with ἐκ, departure from Athens emphasised, because events had compelled the Apostle to alter his intended plan (Ramsay, *St. Paul*, p. 240, and Blass, *in loco*), *cf.* 1 Chron. xii. 8 (A *al.*); 2 Macc. v. 21, xii. 12, with an accusative of place.—Κόρινθον: Corinth from its position as the capital of the Roman province Achaia was the centre of government and commerce, while Athens was still the great educational centre of Greece. St. Paul, with his keen eye for the most important and prominent stations of Roman government and the meeting points of East and West, might be expected to choose a place from whence the influence of the Gospel could spread over the whole province. Like Ephesus, Corinth lay on the great highway between East and West; like Ephesus it was, as Professor Ramsay terms it, one of the knots on the line of communication, the point of convergence for many subordinate roads. But Corinth, with all its external beauty, its wealth and fame, had become a byword for vice and infamy, *cf.* Κορινθιάζεσθαι, Κορινθιάζειν, Wetstein, 1 Cor. i. 2, and references in Farrar, *St. Paul*, i., 557 ff., and it has not been unfairly termed the Vanity Fair of the Roman empire: at once the London and the Paris of the first century after Christ

Ποντικὸν τῷ γένει, προσφάτως ἐληλυθότα ἀπὸ τῆς Ἰταλίας, καὶ
Πρίσκιλλαν γυναῖκα αὐτοῦ,[1] διὰ τὸ διατεταχέναι Κλαύδιον χωρίζεσθαι

[1] Instead of Π. γυναικα αυτου Syr. Harcl. mg., Flor., Gig., Blass in β read συν
Π. γυναικι αυτου, and Flor. adds ησπασατο αυτους, so Blass in β. After αυτους
Syr. Harcl. mg., Flor., so Blass in β, add ουτοι δε εξηλθον απο της Ρωμης (urbe
Flor.), (Blass brackets απο της P. after Ιουδαιους). D, Syr. Harcl. mg., Flor.
insert after Ρωμης οι και κατωκησαν εις την Αχαιαν (Blass in β brackets οι). δια-
τεταχεναι ℵcABH, Chrys., so Lach., W.H., Weiss, Wendt, following T.R.;
τεταχεναι ℵ*DELP, so Tisch. απο instead of εκ in ℵABDEL, Vulg., Tisch.,
W.H., R.V., Weiss, Wendt, Blass.

(Farrar, u. s., p. 556). To this infamous
notoriety not only the cosmopolitanism
of the city contributed, but the open consecration of shameless impurity in its
temple service of Venus, see Ramsay,
"Corinth," Hastings' B.D.; C. and H.,
small edition, p. 324 ff.; McGiffert,
Apostolic Age, p. 262, and notes below.
Ver. 2. Ἀκύλαν, cf. ver. 18, Rom.
xvi. 3, 1 Cor. xvi. 19, 2 Tim. iv. 19: the
Latin Aquila in its Greek form; the
name may have been assumed, as often
the case, in place of the Jewish name.
It is altogether unreasonable to suppose
that Luke made a mistake and that this
Aquila's name was Pontius Aquila, which
he bore as a freedman of the Gens Pontia,
a distinguished member of which was
called by the same two names, Pontius
Aquila, Cic., Ad Fam., x., 33; Suet., Jul.
Cæs., 78. The fact that another Aquila,
who is famous as giving us the earliest
version A.D. of the O.T. in Greek, is also
described as from Pontus goes far to
show that there is nothing improbable in
St. Luke's statement (Schürer, Jewish
People, div. ii., vol. ii., p. 226, E.T.).
The name, moreover, was also a slave
name (Ramsay, p. 269), as a freedman of
Mæcenas was called (C. Cilnius) Aquila.
But it is probable that as the greater
part of the Jews in Rome were freedmen, Aquila may also have belonged
to this class, see Schürer, u. s., p. 234,
and also further, Sanday and Headlam,
Romans, p. xxvii., 418; Lightfoot, Philippians, p. 173.—τῷ γένει: "by race," R.V.,
cf. iv. 36, of Barnabas, and xviii. 24, of
Apollos; the word need not mean more
than this.—Ἰουδαῖον: The word has been
pressed sometimes to indicate that Aquila
was still unconverted to Christianity.
But the fact that he is called a Jew may
simply refer to the notice which follows
"that all Jews," etc. Whether Aquila
was a Christian before he met St. Paul
is very difficult to determine. He is not
spoken of as a disciple, and similarity of
employment rather than of Christian be-

lief may account for the Apostle's intercourse with him and Priscilla, Zahn,
Einleitung, i., 189. But the suspicion
with which most of his countrymen regarded St. Paul rather indicates that
Aquila and Priscilla must at least have
had some leanings towards the new faith,
or they would scarcely have received him
into their lodgings. It is quite possible that, as at the great Pentecost Jews
from Rome had been present, cf. ii. 10,
Christianity may have been carried by this
means to the imperial city, and that such
tidings may have predisposed Aquila and
Priscilla to listen to St. Paul's teaching,
even if they were not Christians when they
first met him. If they were converted,
as has been supposed, by St. Paul at
Corinth, it is strange that no mention is
made of their conversion. That they
were Christians when St. Paul left them
at Ephesus seems to be beyond a doubt.
Renan describes them as already Christians when they met the Apostle, so too
Hilgenfeld, on the ground that their
conversion by St. Paul could scarcely
have been passed over, see further
"Aquila," B.D.², and Hastings' B.D.;
Wendt, in loco; Lightfoot, Phil., pp. 16
and 17, Hort, Rom. and Ephes., p. 9.—
προσφάτως: here only, lit., lately
slaughtered or killed; hence recent,
fresh; Latin, recens (Grimm). In LXX,
Deut. xxiv. 5, Ezek. xi. 3, Jud. iv. 3, 5,
2 Macc. xiv. 36, so too in Polybius,
Westcott on Heb. x. 20 πρόσφατος regards all derivations from σφάω (σφάζω)
φάω (φένω) φάω (φημί) as unsatisfactory.
—Πρίσκιλλαν: in Epistles, Rom. xvi. 3,
1 Cor. xvi. 19, 2 Tim. iv. 9, Prisca, R.V.,
W.H., Priscilla, perhaps the diminutive,
cf. Lucilla, Domitilla. Probably St. Luke
used the language of conversation, in
which the diminutive forms were usually
employed, St. Paul, p. 268. On Bezan
text see critical note, Ramsay, u. s., and
Church in the Roman Empire, p. 158.
In vv. 18 and 26 we have Priscilla mentioned before her husband, and so by

πάντας τοὺς Ἰουδαίους ἐκ τῆς Ῥώμης, προσῆλθεν αὐτοῖς· 3.¹ καὶ
διὰ τὸ ὁμότεχνον εἶναι, ἔμενε παρ᾽ αὐτοῖς καὶ εἰργάζετο· ἦσαν γὰρ

¹ At the commencement of the verse Syr. Harcl. mg., Flor. (Aug.) add ο δε Π.
εγνωσθη τω Ακυλα, and before ομοτεχνον Syr. Harcl. mg., Aug. add ομοφυλον και,
so Blass in β (cf. Flor. in ver. 2, salutavit eos) ; see Belser, Beiträge, p. 84, on the
bearing of this reading on the conversion of Aquila and Priscilla. For ειργαζετο
ℵ*B, Boh. Orig., Tisch,, W.H., R.V., Weiss, Wendt read ηργαζοντο. τη τεχνη
(for acc.), so ℵABELP, Chrys., Lach., Tisch., W.H., R.V., Weiss, Wendt. D. Gig.
(not Flor.) omit the clause ησαν γαρ σκη. τη τεχνη, and so Blass in β, and see
Blass, p. x., and note above on xvii. 18. Ramsay follows Western text in supporting
omission, see St. Paul, p. 253, and, on the other hand, Weiss, Codex D, p. 43.

St. Paul, except in 1 Cor. xvi. 19. The
reason may be that she was of higher
social status, and indeed not a Jewess at
all, as this seems the best way of accounting for the curious arrangement of the sentence here, the point being to emphasise
the fact that Aquila was a Jew. Her
name may indicate some connection
with the Priscan Gens ; whilst Sanday
and Headlam, Romans, p. 420, in an
interesting discussion find reasons to
connect both her (and possibly her
husband) with the Acilian Gens. That
she was a woman of education is evident
from ver. 26, and it is possible that her
marriage with Aquila may afford us another proof amongst many of the influence
of the Jewish religion over educated
women in Rome, Jos., Ant., xviii., 3, 5.
But many commentators from St. Chrysostom have referred the precedence of
Priscilla not to social rank, but to her
greater fervency of spirit or ability of
character ; or it may be simply due to
the fact that she was converted first.—
διὰ τὸ διατετοχέναι: St. Luke's statement is fully corroborated by Suet.,
Claudius, 25 : " Judæos impulsore Christo
assidue tumultuantes Roma expulit ".
But Dio Cassius, lx. 6, in referring to
what is most probably the same edict,
states that the Jews were not expelled,
because of the difficulty in carrying such
an order into effect on account of their
great numbers. Another passage in
Suet., Tiberius, 36, gives us the probable
explanation : " expulit et mathematicos
sed deprecantibus veniam dedit " : an instance of a contemplated expulsion, afterwards abandoned. If we thus interpret
the meaning of Suetonius with reference
to the edict of Claudius by giving the same
force to " expulit," it explains the silence
of Tacitus and Josephus, who do not
mention the edict, while the words of Dio
Cassius emphasise the fact that although
no expulsion took place the assemblies
of the Jews were prohibited, and on that

account, we may fairly suppose, that many
Jews would leave the city, Schürer, u. s.,
p. 237. On any view the edict could not
have remained in force very long, cf.
xxviii. 15, and also the return of Aquila
and Priscilla to Rome, Rom. xvi. 3.
Ramsay dates the edict at the end of
50 A.D. on the ground that although
Orosius, Hist., vii., 6, 15, states that it
occurred in the ninth year of Claudius,
49 A.D., the historian here, as elsewhere
(e.g., cf. the famine) in connection with the
events of this reign, is a year too early.
Wendt (1899), p. 59, gives 49-50 as the
year of the edict. But it must be remembered that the authority of Orosius is not
altogether reliable in this case, as there
is no proof that he had any direct reference to Josephus, to whom he appeals
for his date ; see O. Holtzmann, Neutest.
Zeitgeschichte, p. 129 ; Blass, Proleg.,
23, and Turner, " Chronology of the New
Testament " Hastings' B.D. McGiffert,
p. 362, maintains that as the date of
the edict is thus unknown, we cannot
base any chronological conclusions
upon it, cf. Zahn, Einleitung, ii., 634.
Meyer maintained that by Chrestus Suetonius meant a Jewish agitator so called,
but it is more probable that the historian
confused Christus with Chrestus—an
unfamiliar name with one in use among
both Greeks and Romans. This Chrestus
Suetonius speaks of as actually living, as
the historian might have heard enough
to lead him to regard the commotions
between Jews and Jewish Christians in
Rome as instigated by a leader bearing
this name, commotions like those excited
in the Pisidian Antioch, in Thessalonica,
and elsewhere ; or it may be that he
thus indicates the feverish hopes of the
Messiah amongst the Jews resident in
Rome, hopes so often raised by some
pretentious deliverer. But Lightfoot
makes the important remark that even
in this case we may fairly suppose that
the true Christ held a prominent place in

σκηνοποιοὶ τὴν τέχνην.   4. διελέγετο¹ δὲ ἐν τῇ συναγωγῇ κατὰ πᾶν
σάββατον, ἔπειθέ τε Ἰουδαίους καὶ Ἕλληνας.   5. Ὡς δὲ κατῆλθον

¹ After διελέγετο (δε) D, Flor. Gig., Vulgcl., Syr. Harcl. mg., Blass in β, so Hilg.
add εντιθεις το ονομα του κυριου I. If in contrast to ver. 5 it is difficult to see why
omitted, nor does the introduction of the name of Jesus seem likely in itself (*inter-
ponens*, Flor.) to have persuaded both Jews and Greeks, unless we take επειθε as
conative only. εντιθημι is not found elsewhere in the N.T. Belser thinks that here
εντιθεις means "insinuating" (p. 85), and that the passage in β reminds us of Paul's
own description of his preaching in 1 Cor. ii. 3 (so Blass). ου μονον I. αλλα και
Ελλ., so D and Flor., Blass in β, supported by Belser, *u. s.*

these reports, for He must have been not
less known at this time than any of the
false Christs (*Philippians*, p. 16, note).
Such indifference on the part of a Roman
of the period is surely not surprising,
and the probability is more generally
maintained that this Chrestus was really
Christ, the leader of the Christians, see
Weiss, *Einleitung in das N. T.*, p. 227;
Wendt (1899), *in loco;* Ramsay, *St.
Paul*, pp. 47, 254; McGiffert, *Apostolic
Age*, p. 362, note, but, on the other
hand, Zahn, *Einleitung*, i., p. 306.
Ver. 3. διὰ τὸ ὁμότεχνον: the word
is peculiar to St. Luke, and although it
is found in classical Greek and in Josephus, it is not used in the LXX, and it
may be regarded as a technical word
used by physicians of one another; the
medical profession was called ἡ ἰατρικὴ
τέχνη, physicians were ὁμότεχνοι; thus
Dioscorides in dedicating his work to
Areus speaks of his friendly disposition
towards fellow-physicians (ὁμοτέχνους),
Hobart, p. 239, Weiss in Meyer's *Kommentar*, Luke i. 6, and also Vogel, *Zur
Charakteristik des Lukas*, p. 17 (1897).
On the dignity of labour as fully recognised by Judaism at the time of the
Advent, see Edersheim, *Jewish Social
Life*, chapter xi.; *Sayings of the Jewish
Fathers*, pp. 18, 19, 141 (Taylor, 2nd
edit.).—ἔμενε παρ' αὐτοῖς: "In Alexandria the different trades sat in the
synagogue arranged into guilds; and
St. Paul could have no difficulty in
meeting in the bazaar of his trade
with the like-minded Aquila and Priscilla
(Acts xviii. 2, 3), with whom to find a
lodging," Edersheim, *u. s.*, p. 89, and
see passage from T. B. *Sukkah*, 51 b,
quoted by Lumby, *in loco*, and on vi.
9.—ἠργάζετο: "at Corinth St. Paul's
first search seems to have been for
work," *cf.* Acts xx. 34, 35, 1 Thess. ii.
9, 2 Thess. iii. 8, 1 Cor. iv. 11, 12,
2 Cor. xi. 9, Phil. iv. 12. In close
connection with this passage *cf.* "St.
Paul a Working Man and in Want,"

An Expositor's Note-Book, pp. 419-438
(the late Dr. Samuel Cox), see also
Ramsay, *St. Paul*, pp. 34-36.—σκηνοποιοὶ: only here in N.T. (σκηνοποιεῖν,
Symm., Isa. xiii. 20, xxii. 15); much has
been said about the word, but there
seems no reason to depart from the
translation "tent-makers," *i.e.*, σκηνορράφος, Aelian, *V.H.*, ii., 1, and so St. Paul
is called by Chrysostom and Theodoret,
although Chrysostom also calls him
σκυτοτόμος, 2 Tim. ii., *Hom.*, iv., 5, 3.
It is no doubt true that tents were often
made of a rough material woven from
the hair of the goats in which Cilicia
abounded, and that the name κιλίκιον
(Lat. *cilicium*, Fr. *cilice*, hair-cloth) was
given to this material; but the word in
the text does not mean "makers of materials for tents". There is no ground for
rendering the word with Renan *tapissier*,
or with Michaelis "Kunst-Instrumenten-
macher". On the curious notion that
St. Paul was a landscape painter, which
appears to have arisen from a confusion
between σκηνορράφος and σκηνογράφος,
and the fact that he is described as
ἡνιοποιός, probably a confusion with
σκηνοποιός, see *Expository Times*, and
notes by Ramsay, Nestle, Dec., 1896,
Jan. and March, 1897. As it was often
enjoined upon a son not to forsake the
trade of his father, perhaps from respect,
perhaps because a similar trade might be
more easily learnt at home, it is likely
that Saul followed his father's trade,
which both father and son might easily
have learnt at Tarsus. Schürer, *Jewish
People*, div. ii., vol. i., p. 44, E.T. In a
commercial city like Corinth the material
would be easily obtainable, see critical
note.
Ver. 4. διελέγετο δὲ . . . ἔπειθέ τε:
"and he used to discourse . . . and
tried to persuade," so Ramsay, marking
the imperfects, see also Hackett's note.—
Ἕλληνας: proselytes, since they are
represented as in the synagogue, *cf.* xiv.
1. The heathen are not addressed until

ἀπὸ τῆς Μακεδονίας ὅ τε Σίλας καὶ ὁ Τιμόθεος, συνείχετο τῷ πνεύματι [1]
ὁ Παῦλος, διαμαρτυρόμενος τοῖς Ἰουδαίοις τὸν Χριστὸν Ἰησοῦν. 6.[2]
ἀντιτασσομένων δὲ αὐτῶν καὶ βλασφημούντων, ἐκτιναξάμενος τὰ
ἱμάτια, εἶπε πρὸς αὐτούς, Τὸ αἷμα ὑμῶν ἐπὶ τὴν κεφαλὴν ὑμῶν·

[1] Instead of πνευματι ℵABDE 13, 40, verss., Bas., Theodt., Tisch., W.H., Weiss,
Blass, Wendt, R.V. read λογῳ. Blass reads συνειχε in β. After Ιουδ. ℵABD 13,
36, Vulg., verss., Bas. insert ειναι, so Tisch., W.H., R.V., Blass, Weiss, Wendt.

[2] D, Syr. Harcl. mg., Flor. prefix πολλου δε λογου γενομενου και γραφων διερ-
μηνευομενων. Flor. continues (so Blass in β) αντετασσοντο Ιουδαιοι τινες και
εβλασφημουν, see especially Corssen, G. G. A., p. 431. For πορευσομαι D[1]H[1]L,
Flor. πορευομαι. For απο του νυν D[1], not D[2], reads αφ᾽ υμων νυν, "nunc vado ad
(gentes) ab vobis," Flor.; Blass rejects in β.; Hilg. retains.

ver. 6. McGiffert considers that this
notice of work in the synagogue is untrustworthy (p. 268) and at variance with
the fact that in St. Paul's own Epistles
there is no hint of it, but cf. 1 Cor. ix. 20,
words which we may reasonably suppose
had a special application to Corinth, or
the Apostle would scarcely have so expressed himself. It would have been
strange if in such a commercial centre
there had been no Jewish synagogue.

Ver. 5. See note on xvii. 15; McGiffert,
Apostolic Age, p. 269, recognises this
among the striking points of contact
between Acts and the Epistles to the
Corinthians. Here Silas and Timothy
are said to have been with St. Paul in
Corinth, cf. St. Paul's own statement
in 2 Cor. i. 19, to the fact that the same
two names occur in the salutations of
1 and 2 Thess., both of which were
written from Corinth, see also Paley,
Horæ Paulinæ, iv., 6, 7, and viii. 4.—
συνείχετο τῷ πνεύματι: "he was wholly
absorbed in preaching," λόγῳ, so Ramsay; "in teaching the word," Grimm-
Thayer, cf. Wisdom xvii. 11 (cf. 2 Cor.
v. 14). The verb occurs frequently in
Luke, six times in his Gospel, three times
in Acts, twice in St. Paul, only once elsewhere in N.T., but nowhere as in the
particular phrase here. It looks as if St.
Paul's preaching in Corinth was specially
characterised by "greater concentration
of purpose and simplicity of method," cf.
1 Cor. ii. 2. The philosophic style in
which he had addressed the Athenians is
now abandoned, and so too, at least
primarily, the proclamation of the living
and true God, and of the coming of
His Son to save His people in the day
of wrath, with which apparently he had
commenced at Thessalonica, 1 Thess. i.
9, 10. Such methods and truths had
their place, but in Corinth "Jesus Christ
and Him crucified" was to be preached

as the power of God and the wisdom of
God, and in both his Epistles all that
the Apostle says about the duties of
the Christian life is brought into relation
with this fundamental truth (see McGiffert,
u. s., p. 266). Silas and Timothy found
him wholly possessed by and engrossed
in the word (so the imperfect, Page, Alford, Wendt). On the other hand it has
been maintained that the arrival of Silas
and Timothy brought St. Paul help from
Macedonia, and that on the account,
Phil. iv. 15, 2 Cor. xi. 9, he was able to
give himself up to preaching, as he was
thus relieved from the strain of working
for his bread (so Wordsworth, Lewin,
Rendall). But 1 Cor. ix. 1 seems to
imply that St. Paul still continued to
work for his livelihood at Corinth. Blass
seems to find in the uniqueness of the
phrase a reason for its alteration; see
critical note for his view. Plumptre
refers the words to the Apostle's desire to
see Rome, which the Apostle cherished
for many years, and which had been further
kindled by finding himself in company
with those who came from Rome; and
the announcement of a journey to Rome,
xix. 21, after the Apostle had been some
time in the company of Aquila and Priscilla both at Corinth and Ephesus, is
emphasised by Ramsay, St. Paul, p. 255.
But on the whole, Ramsay's interpretation is very striking, p. 252, cf. the
remarks of McGiffert much to the
same effect, Apostolic Age, pp. 263-
266.—διαμαρτ., see above on p. 92.—
τὸν Χ. Ἰ.: "that the Anointed One is
Jesus," cf. xvii. 3, so Ramsay, St. Paul,
p. 226. So far the message was evidently
for Jews. See critical note for reading
in D.

Ver. 6. ἀντιτασσ.: classical use, of
an army ranged in hostile array, or of
those opposed to each other in opinion,
Thuc., iii., 83. So in later Greek, in Polyb.,

καθαρὸς ἐγὼ ἀπὸ τοῦ νῦν εἰς τὰ ἔθνη πορεύσομαι.   7. καὶ μεταβὰς
ἐκεῖθεν ἦλθεν εἰς οἰκίαν τινὸς ὀνόματι Ἰούστου,[1] σεβομένου τὸν Θεόν,
οὗ ἡ οἰκία ἦν συνομοροῦσα τῇ συναγωγῇ.   8.[2] Κρίσπος δὲ ὁ ἀρχισυνάγωγος ἐπίστευσε τῷ Κυρίῳ σὺν ὅλῳ τῷ οἴκῳ αὐτοῦ· καὶ πολλοὶ

[1] B*D², Syr. H.; Tisch., W.H., Weiss, Wendt have Τιτιου Ι. אE, Vulg., Boh.,
Arm. have Τιτου Ι., so R.V. Instead of εκειθεν D* 137, Flor. read απο του Ακυλα,
not Blass in β, but Hilg.; see Corssen, u. s., p. 428.

[2] For doublets in D in this verse, so in Flor., Blass in β, see Harris, Four Lectures, etc., p. 60.

generally to oppose, to resist. Ramsay renders "and when they began to
form a faction against him," but cf.
Rom. xiii. 2, James iv. 6, v. 6, 1 Pet.
v. 5, Prov. iii. 34.—βλασφ., cf. xiii. 45,
or it may be used generally as in xix.
9, and 2 Peter ii. 2.—ἐκτιναξ., cf. xiii.
51, note; cf. Matt. x. 14, and LXX,
Neh. v. 13, "undoubtedly a very ex-
asperating gesture," Ramsay, St. Paul,
p. 256; but we must remember that the
opposition at Corinth seems to have been
unusually great, as Ramsay himself points
out, u. s., pp. 143, 256.—τὸ αἷμα ὑμῶν,
cf. xx. 26, Hebraistic, cf., e.g., Matt.
xxvii. 25, and in LXX, Lev. xx. 16, 2
Sam. i. 16, 1 Kings ii. 37, Ezek. iii. 18,
etc., i.e., ἐλθέτω, Matt. xxiii. 35. Both
here and in xx. 26 we can scarcely doubt
that St. Paul had in mind the words of
the prophet, Ezek. xxxiii. 6.—ἐπὶ τὴν
κεφ., i.e., upon yourselves, the head
being used for the person—for other ideas
of the word see Wendt (1888), in loco.
De Wette interprets of moral ruin, and
others of the eternal ἀπωλεία, but we
cannot refine so much upon a figurative
phrase. In vv. 5b and 6 Spitta and
Jüngst see the hand of a Reviser, the
former holding that the whole passage
runs smoothly with these omissions,
whilst Jüngst ascribes also the word
ἐκεῖθεν, ver. 7, to the Reviser. According
to Clemen, 4 and 5b, the preaching in
the synagogue belongs to Redactor
Judaicus, the Jewish persecution in ver.
6 to the Redactor Antijudaicus. Hilgenfeld agrees with Spitta in so far that he
ascribes 5b and 6b to "the author to
Theophilus".—καθαρὸς ἐγὼ: scarcely
enough to say "I am pure," have discharged my duty with a clear conscience,
cf. xx. 26, the same idea here, better to
punctuate at ἐγώ, but see Blass, in loco.
—ἀπὸ τοῦ νῦν: from henceforth, i.e., so
far as he is concerned. It is evident that
the words did not apply to other places,
for in xix. 8 St. Paul goes to the synagogue according to his wont. The phrase

is found five times in St. Luke's Gospel,
but only here in Acts. It is used once
elsewhere in N.T, and there by St. Paul,
2 Cor. v. 16 (cf. John viii. 11). See
Friedrich, p. 16, and Hawkins, Horæ
Synopticæ, p. 29.

Ver. 7. μεταβὰς ἐκεῖθεν, i.e., from
the synagogue, cf. Luke x. 7, "he removed," Rendall; "he changed his place
from the synagogue," Ramsay: the verb
is found three times with ἐκεῖθεν in St.
Matthew, and in each place "departed"
R.V., this gives perfectly good sense:
cf. Ramsay, Church in the Roman Empire,
p. 158, and critical note.—Ἰούστου: if
the addition Τίτου or Τιτίου is correct,
there is no need to discuss the possible
identification with the companion of St.
Paul in Gal. ii. 1, etc.; see Alford and
Page, in loco, and critical note. The
identification was adopted by Chrysostom and Grotius, and for a statement of
the evidence on either side see Plumptre,
in loco. It should be remembered that
we have Barsabbas Justus, i. 23, and
Jesus Justus, Col. iv. 11, see also Lightfoot "Acts of the Apostles," B.D.², i.,
32. The house of a proselyte may have
been chosen because it offered easy
access to those who wished to come,
whether Greeks or Hebrews (see Chrysostom's comment), but in Paul's thus
going into the house of a proselyte hard
by the synagogue we may see how his
spirit had been stirred. But further: this
Titus Justus was evidently a Roman
citizen, one of the coloni in Corinth, and
thus St. Paul would gain access through
him to the more educated class in the
city, Ramsay, St. Paul, p. 256, and
"Corinth," Hastings' B.D., i. 480.—
συνομοροῦσα: there is no need to suppose that he left his lodgings with Aquila
—this house became Paul's place of
meeting (so in Ephesus, cf. xix. 9, 10);
he had his own synagogue there (Blass);
in classics simple verb ὁμορέω, ὁμουρέω;
compound only found here; συνόμορος,
Eccl. writers.

τῶν Κορινθίων ἀκούοντες ἐπίστευον καὶ ἐβαπτίζοντο. 9. Εἶπε δὲ ὁ Κύριος δι᾽ ὁράματος ἐν νυκτὶ τῷ Παύλῳ, Μὴ φοβοῦ, ἀλλὰ λάλει καὶ μὴ σιωπήσῃς· 10. διότι ἐγώ εἰμι μετὰ σοῦ, καὶ οὐδεὶς ἐπιθήσεταί σοι τοῦ κακῶσαί σε· διότι λαός ἐστί μοι πολὺς ἐν τῇ πόλει ταύτῃ.

Ver. 8. **Κρίσπος**, *cf.* 1 Cor. i. 14, coincidence with, admitted by McGiffert, p. 269 (so too by Holtzmann), "no reason to doubt that he is the man whose conversion Luke reports," according to tradition he became Bishop of Ægina, *Const. Apost.*, vii., 46. Though a Jew he bore a Latin name, *cf.* for a parallel case J. Lightfoot, *Hor. Heb.*, *in loco.*—ὁ ἀρχισ., if we *cf.* ver. 17 it looks as if in the Corinthian synagogue there was only one person bearing this title, and that Sosthenes succeeded Crispus when the latter became a Christian, see "Corinth" (Ramsay), Hastings' B.D., i., p. 482, and see also Ramsay, *Expositor*, April, 1895, and above on xiii. 15: on the reason of St. Paul's baptism of Crispus, Gaius, Stephanas, see B.D.², and Hastings' B.D., *u. s.* There is certainly no ground for supposing that St. Paul depreciated baptism although he baptised so few in Corinth with his own hands, *Speaker's Commentary* on 1 Cor. i. 17. It is evident from this notice that St. Paul's preaching had not been without its effect on the Jewish residents, and probably one reason why the feeling against the Apostle was so strong, xx. 3, was because this influence extended to persons of importance in Corinth; the next words show good results among the Gentile population of the city.—σὺν ὅλῳ τῷ οἴκῳ, *cf.* xvi. 15, 1 Cor. i. 16.—τῶν Κ., not Ἰουδαῖοι, who are always so called, but Ἕλληνες, ver. 4, including for the most part "proselytes of the gate".—ἀκού. ἐπίστευον καὶ ἐβαπτ.: "used to hear, and believe, and receive baptism," imperfects; the spread of the new faith was gradual but continuous. ἀκού. is taken by some to refer to the hearing of the fact that Paul had separated himself from the synagogue (so Wendt, Weiss); see critical note.

Ver. 9. So at other crises in the Apostle's life, *cf.* xxii. 17, xxvii. 23. —ὁ Κ., *i.e.*, Jesus.—μὴ φοβοῦ, *cf.* Isa. xlii. 6, xliii. 2, and for the phrase Luke i. 13, ii. 10, v. 10, viii. 50, xii. 7, 32, Acts, *in loco*, and xxvii. 24, characteristic of the Evangelist; Friedrich, p. 35, and Plummer on Luke i. 13. *Cf.* xx. 3 for the continued malignity of these Corinthian Jews; the Apostle's apprehension as expressed here is confirmed by the statements in 1 Thess. ii. 15, iii. 7, which describe the Jewish opposition as existing at the time he wrote (see this fully acknowledged by McGiffert, *Apostolic Age*, p. 270). Hilgenfeld sees no reason to refer vv. 9 and 10 to the Reviser (with Jüngst). He finds them in his source C of which they are characteristic, *cf.* xvi. 9, 10; the vision refers not to what had preceded, but to what follows, and explains the stay of Paul at Corinth mentioned in ver. 11.—ἀλλὰ λάλει καὶ μὴ σιωπ., *i.e.*, "continue to speak," "speak on," *cf.* Isa. lviii. 1, affirmation and negation; solemnity in the double form; see too Jer. i. 6-8, xv. 15-21; on the form of the tenses see Weiss, *in loco*. In 1 Cor. ii. 3, 4 we have a proof of the effect of this assurance, and of the confidence with which the Apostle was inspired.

Ver. 10. **διότι ἐγώ**: *fundamentum fiduciæ*, Bengel.—ἐπιθ.: only here in this sense, but so in LXX, *aggrediri*, *cf.* Gen. xliii. 18, Exod. xxi. 14, 2 Chron. xxiii. 13, Jud. xvi. 7.—τοῦ κακῶσαι: infinitive with τοῦ, probably to express conceived or intended result, Burton, p. 157 and also p. 148, *i.e.*, an event indicated by the context not to have actually taken place.—λαός: "qui mei sunt et mei fient": Bengel—even in Corinth, proverbial for its vice, Christ has His "chosen people," and in Cenchreae, where all the vices of a seafaring population found a home, "Christianity wrought its miracle," so Renan, *Saint Paul*, p. 219, *cf.* the Apostle's own description, 1 Cor. vi. 9-11: "in Corinth the Gospel had been put to a supreme test, and nowhere had it triumphed more gloriously". No wonder that in facing this stronghold of the powers of darkness St. Paul needed an assurance similar to that which cheered the heart of an Elijah, 1 Kings xix. 18. But whilst the new faith thus gained adherents chiefly from the lowest social grade, *cf.* also 1 Cor. i. 26, which indicates that there were some in the higher social ranks and some versed in the learning of the schools who welcomed the Gospel; to a Crispus, a Gaius, a Stephanas, we may add Erastus, the public treasurer of the city, Rom. xvi. 23, an office which in a place like Corinth carried with it considerable influence and position (as even

11. ἐκάθισέ τε ἐνιαυτὸν καὶ μῆνας ἕξ, διδάσκων ἐν αὐτοῖς τὸν λόγον τοῦ Θεοῦ.

12. Γαλλίωνος δὲ ἀνθυπατεύοντος[1] τῆς Ἀχαΐας, κατεπέστησαν ὁμοθυμαδὸν οἱ Ἰουδαῖοι τῷ Παύλῳ, καὶ ἤγαγον αὐτὸν ἐπὶ τὸ βῆμα,

[1] אABD 15, 18, 36, 40, Tisch., Alford, W.H., Weiss, Wendt, Hilg. read ανθυπατου οντος. Meyer follows T.R., so Blass. D and Flor. expand as follows in 12 and 13, so Blass in β, κατεπ. οι Ι. συλλαλησαντες μεθ᾽ εαυτων επι τον Π. και επιθεντες τας χειρας ηγαγον αυτον επι το βημα καταβοωντες και λεγ.

Renan admits, although he regards him as the only adherent won from the upper classes), and the readiness with which the Corinthian Church responded to St. Paul's appeal for the poor saints indicates that many of its members had some means at their disposal (cf. the striking account of Paul's work at Corinth by McGiffert, p. 267, and Orr, *Some Neglected Factors in Early Christianity*, p. 108).

Ver. 11. ἐκάθισε, see critical note, "he dwelt," R.V., cf. Luke xxiv. 49, but not elsewhere in N.T. in this sense, but constantly in LXX, 1 Macc. ii. 1, 29. Rendall renders "he took his seat," i.e., as a teacher, a Rabbi, and see also the remarks of Ramsay on the way in which St. Paul was evidently regarded at Corinth as one of the travelling lecturers on philosophy and morals so common in the Greek world, "Corinth," Hastings' B.D.[1], p. 482. The word may be purposely used here instead of the ordinary μένειν to indicate the quiet and settled work to which the Apostle was directed by the vision which had calmed his troubled spirit, and had taught him that his cherished plan of revisiting Macedonia must be postponed to preaching the Word in Corinth. During this period 1 and 2 Thess. were probably written. The year and a half is taken to include the whole subsequent residence in Corinth, ver. 18, in which vv. 12-17 form an episode. Men attacked him with a view of injuring him, but without success, and his continuous abode in Corinth was a fulfilment of the promise in ver 10 (indicated perhaps more clearly by τε than by δέ in ver. 11). On ἡμέρας ἱκανὰς, ver. 18, see below—the words are taken to mark simply a note of the time spent between the incident of vv. 12-17 and the departure of Paul from the city. In this period the Apostle would have founded the Church at Cenchreae, and his labours seem to have extended still further, for in 2 Cor i. 1 we read of the saints in the whole of Achaia (cf. 2 Cor. xi. 10) and the household of Stephanas is spoken of as the firstfruits not of Corinth but of Achaia.

Ver. 12. ἀνθ., cf. xiii. 7, another proof of St. Luke's accuracy, Achaia from B.C. 27 (when it had been separated from Macedonia, to which it had been united since B.C. 146, and made into a separate province) had been governed by a proconsul. In A.D. 15 Tiberius had reunited it with Macedonia and Mysia, and it was therefore under an imperial legatus as an imperial province, Tac., *Ann.*, i., 76. But a further change occurred when Claudius, A.D. 44, made it again a senatorial province under a proconsul, Suet., *Claudius*, 25. On subsequent changes in its government see Ramsay, "Achaia," Hastings' B.D. Corinth was the chief city of the province Achaia, and so probably chosen for the residence of the governors.—Γαλλίωνος: we have no direct statement save that of St. Luke that Gallio governed Achaia. Gallio's brother Seneca tells us that Gallio caught fever in Achaia, *Ep. Mor.*, 104, and took a voyage for change of air (Ramsay, *St. Paul*, p. 258) (see also the same reference in Zahn, *Einleitung*, ii., p. 634, and as against Clemen, Ramsay, *St. Paul*, p. 260), a remark which Ramsay justly regards as a corroboration of St. Luke; on the date see Ramsay, *St. Paul*, p. 258, and *Expositor*, March, 1897, p. 206; "Corinth," Hastings' B.D.[1], p. 481; Turner, "Chronology of the New Testament," *ibid*. Gallio could not have entered on the proconsulship of Achaia *before* 44 A.D., and probably not before 49 or 50: Ramsay thinks during the summer of A.D. 52 (Renan and Lightfoot, A.D. 53), whilst recently Schürer (so Wendt, 1899) places the proconsulship of Gallio between 51-55 A.D., *Zw. Th.*, 1898, p. 41 f. (as against O. Holtzmann, *Neutest. Zeitgeschichte*, who places it before 49 A.D.). The description of Gallio in Acts is quite consistent with what we know of his personal character, and with his attitude as a Roman official.

13. λέγοντες, Ὅτι παρὰ τὸν νόμον οὗτος ἀναπείθει τοὺς ἀνθρώπους σέβεσθαι τὸν Θεόν. 14. μέλλοντος δὲ τοῦ Παύλου ἀνοίγειν τὸ στόμα, εἶπεν ὁ Γαλλίων πρὸς τοὺς Ἰουδαίους, Εἰ μὲν οὖν [1] ἦν ἀδίκημά τι ἢ ῥᾳδιούργημα πονηρόν, ὦ Ἰουδαῖοι, κατὰ λόγον ἂν ἠνεσχόμην ὑμῶν ·

[1] ουν om. ‭א‬ABDE, Chrys., verss., Tisch., W.H., R.V., Weiss, Wendt, Blass. D, Flor., Vulg. read ω ανδρες Ιουδ.

Statius, *Silv.*, ii., 7, 32, speaks of him as "dulcis Gallio," and his brother Seneca writes of him : " Nemo mortalium uni tam dulcis est quam hic omnibus," *Quæst. Nat.*, iv., Præf., and see other references and testimonies, Renan, *Saint Paul*, p. 221, and "Gallio," B.D.[2]. It is quite possible that the Jews took advantage of his easy-going nature and affability, or, if he had recently arrived in the province, of his inexperience. Gallio's Hellenic culture may have led to his selection for the post (Renan, *u. s.*, p. 222). The notion that as a Stoic he was friendly disposed towards the Christians, and on that account rejected the accusations of the Jews, is quite without foundation, see Zöckler, *in loco*. The name of Junius Gallio was an assumed one ; its bearer, whose real name was Marcus Annæus Novatus, had been adopted by the rhetorician, L. Junius Gallio, a friend of his father.—κατεπέστησαν, *cf.* xvi. 22, verb, only found here. Rendall, *in loco*, renders " made a set assault upon Paul," expressing the culmination of the Jewish hostility in a set assault (not *against*, as in A. and R.V.).—ὁμοθ., as in xv. 25.—τὸ βῆμα : of the proconsul, probably erected in some public place, a movable seat of judgment.

Ver. 13. λέγοντες : in the set accusation which follows there is probably an indication that the Jews could not stir up the crowd against Paul as at Philippi and Thessalonica, for already he had gained too good an influence over the common people (Weiss).—ἀναπείθει : only here in N.T., " persuadendo excitare, sollicitare," it is used of evil persuasion in LXX, Jer. xxxvi. (xxix.) 8 and in 1 Macc. i. 11.—παρὰ τὸν νόμον : " contrary to the law " : what law ? Roman or Jewish ? in a certain sense the expression might include both, for as a *religio licita* the Jewish law was under the protection of the Roman law, and Josephus tells us how leave had been granted to the Jews to worship according to their own law, *Ant.*, xiv., 10, 2 ff. But Paul's teaching was to these Jews the introduction of something illegal, contrary to the religion

which they were allowed to practise, and so they sought to bring his teaching under the cognisance of the proconsul (see Zahn, *Einleitung*, i., p. 190). They may therefore have designedly used a phrase which had a double meaning. But whatever their design, Gallio saw through it, and drew a hard and fast distinction between a charge of illegality against the state and of illegality against Jewish, νόμου τοῦ καθ' ὑμᾶς, not Roman law. In this reply Gallio showed that he knew more about the matter than the Jews supposed, and he may have had some intelligence of the Jewish disturbances at Rome about " Chrestus ". Both ἀνθρώπους and σέβ. τὸν Θεόν point to the general nature of the charge, as including Paul's efforts to convert not only Jews but proselytes. At least the Jews would try to give their accusation a colour of illegality against the Roman law, for they would themselves have dealt with it if it had been simply connected with their own religious observances, see " Corinth," Hastings' B.D., i., 481.

Ver. 14. μέλλοντος : Lucan ; see Burton, p. 71, on οὖν, see critical note and Alford, *in loco*, for its retention.—ἀδίκημα, *cf.* xxiv. 20, only once elsewhere in N.T., Rev. xviii. 5, here it may perhaps mark a legal wrong, a wrong against the state — the word is used in classical Greek of a breach of law ἀδίκ. τῶν νόμων, Dem., 586, 11, while ῥᾳδιούργημα marks rather the moral wrong. ῥᾳδ., *cf.* xiii. 10, not elsewhere either in classical Greek or LXX, but *cf.* Plut., *Pyrrh.*, 6, " if a misdemeanour or a crime " : so Ramsay.—κατὰ λόγον : *ut par est, merito* ; *cf.* use of the phrase in Polyb. and 3 Macc. iii. 14 (παρὰ λ., 2 Macc. iv. 46, 3 Macc. vii. 8).—Ἰουδαῖοι without ἄνδρες perhaps in contempt (so Knabenbauer), but see critical note.—ἠνεσχόμην, *cf.* Luke ix. 41, and so several times in St. Paul's Epistles, 2 Cor. xi. 1, 4 ; on the augment and construction see Blass, *Gram.*, pp. 39, 102, Simcox, *Language of the New Testament*, p. 34, note, and Burton, p. 103.

15. εἰ δὲ ζήτημά¹ ἐστι περὶ λόγου καὶ ὀνομάτων καὶ νόμου τοῦ καθ᾽ ὑμᾶς, ὄψεσθε αὐτοί· κριτὴς γὰρ² ἐγὼ τούτων οὐ βούλομαι εἶναι. 16. καὶ³ ἀπήλασεν αὐτοὺς ἀπὸ τοῦ βήματος. 17. ἐπιλαβόμενοι δὲ πάντες⁴ οἱ Ἕλληνες Σωσθένην τὸν ἀρχισυνάγωγον ἔτυπτον ἔμπροσθεν τοῦ βήματος· καὶ οὐδὲν τούτων τῷ Γαλλίωνι ἔμελεν.

¹ The plur. ζητήματα read by אABD²E, verss., Tisch., W.H., R.V., Weiss, Wendt, Blass.

² γαρ after κριτης *om.* אABD 13, Vulg., Boh., Tisch., W.H., R.V., Weiss, Wendt, Blass.

³ For απηλασεν, D¹, Flor., Hilg. απελυσεν, but not Blass.

⁴ אAB Vulg., Boh., Arm. *om.* οι Ελληνες, so R.V., W.H., Wendt, Weiss; Blass retains (Flor. *om.* παντες), so Belser and Hilg. Blass in β reads και ο Γαλλιων προσεποιειτο αυτον μη βλεπειν. Flor. "simulat se non videre" (d); Belser holds that this is original, p. 87. Some later MSS. read Ιουδαιοι.

Ver. 15. If we read the plural ζητήματα we may regard it as expressing contempt: "a parcel of questions," Alford; but if they are questions of word (teaching) not deed (opposite ἔργον, *factum*) and of names not things, *verba*, opposite πράγματα (Blass); *i.e.*, the arguments as to whether Jesus could rightly or not claim the title of Messiah, see also Page's note.—νόμου τοῦ καθ᾽ ὑμᾶς: of your law—not Roman law; with the phrase *cf.* xvii. 28 (xvi. 39 β), xxiv. 22. It is used only once elsewhere in N.T., by St. Paul, Eph. i. 15 (*cf.* Acts xxvi. 3).—ὄψεσθε αὐτοί, *cf.* Matt. xxvii. 4, 24; pronoun emphatic, xiii. 18, 19; so in LXX, Num. xiii. 19, Judg. vii. 17, xxi. 21, etc. Blass quotes two passages from Epictetus, ii., 5, 30, and iv., 6, 41.—κριτὴς γὰρ ἐγὼ: omit γάρ; pronoun more emphatic; they could determine their matters according to their own law; so Lysias, xxiii., 29, Festus, xxv., 19.—οὐ βούλομαι: "I am not minded," R.V.; the decision while it testifies to the strength of Gallio's character, since unlike Pilate he would not allow himself to be influenced against his better judgment, expresses at the same time his sovereign contempt for the Jews and their religion; to him as to his brother Seneca the Jews were only *sceleratissima gens* (Aug., *De Civ. Dei*, vi., 10). The decision shows no favourable inclination to Christianity itself, but this does not take away from its importance as proving that so far as the Roman authorities were concerned the freedom of speech thus granted would enable the religion of the Christ to make its way through the civilised, *i.e.*, the Roman world; *cf.* Ramsay, *St. Paul*, p. 260, who sees in his residence at Corinth an epoch in Paul's life not only as regards

his doctrine and his presentation of it, but also as regards his aim that Christianity should be spread throughout the empire, an aim made more clear by the imperial policy of which Gallio was the exponent.

Ver. 16. ἀπήλασεν: probably by his lictors who would be commanded to clear the court. This interpretation of the word is in accordance with the next verse, which describes the crowd of Greeks as prepared to follow up the decision of Gallio by similar treatment of a leading Jew on their own account. See critical note.

Ver. 17. ἐπιλαβ. δὲ: of hostile action, xvii. 19, xvi. 19.—οἱ Ἕλληνες, see critical note. If πάντες alone is read it seems clear from the context that only the Jews could be meant, and Weiss supposes that when they had failed so ignominiously they vented their rage on their own leader, Sosthenes, who as head of the synagogue would naturally have been prominent in presenting the complaint to Gallio. Some of the later MSS. insert οἱ Ἰουδαῖοι after πάντες to make the meaning clearer. Probably confusion arose in the MSS. from identifying Sosthenes either rightly or wrongly with the Sosthenes in 1 Cor. i. 1, and therefore οἱ Ἕλληνες was omitted on the supposition that the Jews were allowed to console themselves by beating a Christian. But not only is it difficult to conceive that Gallio would have allowed them to do this, but there is no occasion to suppose that the Sosthenes here is the same as in 1 Cor. i. 1 (for the name was common), and even if so, he may have become a Christian at a later date. It is much more conceivable that the Corinthians in their hatred of the Jews proceeded to

18. Ὁ δὲ Παῦλος ἔτι προσμείνας ἡμέρας ἱκανάς, τοῖς ἀδελφοῖς
ἀποταξάμενος ἐξέπλει εἰς τὴν Συρίαν, καὶ σὺν αὐτῷ Πρίσκιλλα καὶ

second as it were the supercilious treatment dealt out to them by Gallio, and
they would naturally fix upon Sosthenes
as the leading spirit in the Jewish community. So far as he cared at all, Gallio
may have been pleased rather than otherwise at the rough and ready approval of
his decision by the populace, see Ramsay,
St. Paul, p. 250, and "Corinth," Hastings' B.D.[1], p. 482 ; Plumptre, *in loco*,
and Wendt (1899). The whole of the
section, vv. 12-17, is regarded by Clemen,
p. 126, Jüngst, p. 165, as an interpolation,
but Hilgenfeld puts aside their varying
grounds of rejection as unconvincing,
and finds it very conceivable that the
Jews attempted to hinder the preaching
of Paul as is here described (1 Thess. ii.
16). With regard to the whole narrative
of Paul at Corinth, vv. 1-17, Spitta, p.
244, concludes, as against Weizsäcker's
attack on its historical character, that
we may regard it as scanty or even one-
sided, but that there is no valid reason
to regard it as unhistorical.—ἔτυπτον :
Hackett interprets the imperfect as
showing how thorough a beating Sosthenes received ; but "exitus rei quæ
depingitur (imperf.) non indicatur, quia
nihil gravius secutum est," Blass ; the
imperfect may simply mean "began to
strike".—οὐδὲν . . . ἔμελεν, *cf.* Luke x.
40, a Gallio has become a proverbial
name for one indifferent to religion, but
there is nothing in St. Luke's statement
to support such a view. All the words
show is that Gallio was so little influenced
by the accusations of the Jews against
Paul that he took no notice of the
conduct of the Greeks (?) in beating
Sosthenes. And if the beating was
administered by the Jews, Gallio might
well overlook it, as he would regard it as
the outcome of some question which only
concerned *their* religion (Weiss).

Ver. 18. ἔτι προσμείνας : this may be
an addition to the year and a half, or
may be included in it ; on ἔτι see critical
note.—ἱκανάς, Lucan, see on viii. 11, etc.
the expression shows how little the
attack upon the Apostle had injured his
prospects of evangelising the city and
neighbourhood.—ἀποταξ., Vulgate, *vale-
facio*, used by Luke and Paul only, except
Mark vi. 46, Luke ix. 61, xiv. 33, Acts,
in loco, and ver. 21, 2 Cor. iii. 13 ; in this
sense only in middle voice in N.T., in
classical Greek not used in this sense,
but ἀσπάζεσθαί τινα (Grimm, *sub v.*) ;

cf. also its use in Jos., *Ant.*, xi., 6, 8
(so too in Philo), like Latin, *renuntio*,
to forsake (*cf.* Luke xiv. 33), and in Eccl.
writers, Ignatius, *Ad Philadelph.*, xi., 1 ;
Euseb., *H.E.*, ii., 17, 5 (2 Clem., vi., 4, 5).
—ἐξέπλει : "he set about the voyage,"
in xx. 6, aorist, not imperfect as here ;
"recte impf., nam de perfecta navigatione,
ver. 22, demum agitur," Blass.—κειρ. . . .
εὐχήν : in the interpretation of this
passage it is undoubtedly best to refer
the vow to Paul ; grammatically it would
refer to Aquila, but it is difficult to see
what point there would then be in the
statement. If it is urged that Aquila's
name placed after Priscilla's indicates
that he is the subject of the following
verb, we have clearly seen that this is
not the only occasion on which Priscilla's
name preceded her husband's, see above,
and ver. 26, and Rom. xvi. 3. The
argument that the notice is intended by
St. Luke to show that Paul counselled
observance of the law, and did not tempt
him to break it, as he was afterwards
accused of doing, xxi. 21, is still more
irrelevant, for so far nothing has been
definitely said as to Aquila's conversion.
And if the vow involved any obligation
to appear at Jerusalem, it is quite evident
that Paul and not Aquila went up to the
Holy City. A list of the names on either
side is given by Alford, Felten, Wendt.
Amongst recent writers we may add
Wendt, Zöckler, Blass, Jüngst, Matthias
as favouring the view that Aquila is
the subject, whilst Weiss, Felton, Ramsay, Hort, Rendall, Page, Knabenbauer,
Luckock take the opposite view. What
then was the nature and occasion of the
vow ? Those who connect this vow with
the journey to Jerusalem, as if the latter
was obligatory in the fulfilment of the
former, are justified in regarding the vow
as a modified form of the Nazirite vow,
Num. vi. 1-21. The man under the
Nazirite vow was to drink no wine or
strong drink, and to let no razor pass
over his head or face. At the end of
the time during which the vow lasted,
his hair was shaven at the door of the
Tabernacle (the Temple), and burnt in
the fire of the altar as an offering. But
it is to be observed that in this passage
the word is κειράμενος, whilst of thus
completing the Nazirite vow, xxi. 24,
the word ξυρήσωνται is used (*cf.* 1 Cor.
xi. 6), and there is evidence (Wordsworth,
in loco) that a man who had taken a

Ἀκύλας,[1] κειράμενος τὴν κεφαλὴν ἐν Κεγχρεαῖς · εἶχε γὰρ εὐχήν.
19. κατήντησε[2] δὲ εἰς Ἔφεσον, κἀκείνους κατέλιπεν αὐτοῦ · αὐτὸς δὲ

[1] After Ἀκύλας Blass in β reads ος ευχην εχων εν Κεγχρεαις την κεφαλην εκειρατο, following Flor.; see Belser, pp. 89-92, who strongly opposes Blass, and *cf.* Ramsay, *St. Paul*, p. 263, and comment.

[2] κατηντησαν, plur. in אABE 13, 40, d, tol., Sah., Boh., Syrr., Arm., Tisch., W.H., R.V., Weiss, Wendt. Blass omits κακεινους κατελιπεν αυτον, so Flor., which ends " cum venisset Ephesum in se ". Blass, with D, Flor., reads καταντησας δε εις Σ., and continues with D 137, Syr. H. mg., Sah., τῳ επιοντι σαββατῳ εισελθων. διελεχθη EHLP; διελεξατο אAB 13, 68, 69, 105, Tisch., Weiss, Wendt, W.H.; διελεγετο D, Gig., Vulg., so Blass in β.

Nazirite vow in a foreign land was allowed to poll or cut his hair shorter (κείρω), provided that the hair so polled was taken to the Temple and burnt there as an offering together with the hair shorn off at the completion of the vow. That the Jews took upon themselves a modified form of the Nazirite vow is proved from Josephus, *B. J.*, ii., 15, 1, when they were afflicted by disease or any other distress. Possibly therefore the vow followed upon St. Paul's deliverance from an attack of sickness, and the warm praise bestowed upon Phœbe, the deaconess of the Church at Cenchreae (Rom. xvi. 1), for her personal aid to himself may be taken as some confirmation of this. But if we thus place St. Paul's vow here under the category of the vows mentioned by Josephus, the journey to Jerusalem must be immediately connected with it, as the description given by the Jewish historian plainly shows that the vows in question were modified forms of the regular Nazirite vow. It is a very reasonable conjecture that the vow may be connected with St. Paul's danger at Corinth, and with his safe deliverance from it. As one consecrated to the service of the Lord, he would allow his hair to grow until the promise of his safety had been fulfilled and his embarkation from Corinth was assured. The vow was thus analogous to the Nazirite vow, inasmuch as the same idea of consecration lay at the root of each; but it was rather a private vow (Hort, *Judaistic Christianity*, p. 91, and Weiss, *in loco*), and in this case the journey of the Apostle to Jerusalem would not be conditioned by the vow, but by his desire to be present at some great festival, beyond doubt that of the Passover. On the custom amongst other nations to cut off the hair, and to let it grow in votive offering to the gods, see Holtzmann, *Apostelgeschichte*, p. 395, and Page, *in loco*. Hilgenfeld ascribes the narrative of the

incident to his " author to Theophilus," whether the vow refers to Paul or Aquila, and considers that the story is intended to connect St. Paul as much as possible with Judaism. One of the most curious instances of perverse interpretation is that of Krenkel, who thinks that the κειρ. may be referred to Paul, who shaved his head to counteract the epileptic fits with which he was afflicted, 2 Cor. xiii. 7, see Zöckler's note.—Κεγχρεαῖς, see notices of the place in Renan, *Saint Paul*, p. 218, and Hastings' B.D., modern *Kalaniki* (in Thuc. Κεγχρειαί): the eastern harbour of Corinth, about nine miles distant, connecting the trade with Asia; Lechæum, the other port ("bimaris Corinthi," Horace, *Odes*, i., 7, 2), connecting it with Italy and the West. Τούτῳ μὲν οὖν χρῶνται πρὸς τοὺς ἐκ τῆς Ἀσίας, πρὸς δὲ τοὺς ἐκ τῆς Ἰταλίας τῷ Λεχαίῳ, Strabo, viii., 6, p. 380.

Ver. 19. κατήντησε, see critical note. —εἰς Ἔφεσον: a voyage of two or three days with unfavourable wind. Cicero mentions two occasions when the voyage from Ephesus to Athens took two weeks, *Ad Attic.*, vi., 8, 9; iii., 9, but in both instances extraordinary delays were the cause of the lengthy voyage; on Ephesus see xix. 1. — κἀκείνους κατέλ. αὐτοῦ: Ephesus, famous for its commerce, where they might carry on their trade, although it is perhaps somewhat hazardous to regard the city as the centre of the particular trade in which they were engaged. Lewin quotes two passages in support of this, but they both refer to one event, the presentation of a tent by the Ephesians to Alcibiades, " Ephesus " B.D.[2].—αὐτὸς δὲ: this does not mean that Paul for his part (in contradiction to Aquila and Priscilla) went into the synagogue; such an interpretation seems unnatural. Others explain that Aquila and Priscilla were left in the town, and that the synagogue was *outside* the town (so Alford), but this does not seem satisfactory as a full explanation,

εἰσελθὼν εἰς τὴν συναγωγὴν διελέχθη τοῖς Ἰουδαίοις. 20. ἐρωτώντων
δὲ αὐτῶν ἐπὶ πλείονα χρόνον μεῖναι παρ' αὐτοῖς,[1] οὐκ ἐπένευσεν·
21. ἀλλ' ἀπετάξατο αὐτοῖς, εἰπών,[2] Δεῖ με πάντως τὴν ἑορτὴν τὴν
ἐρχομένην ποιῆσαι εἰς Ἱεροσόλυμα· πάλιν δὲ ἀνακάμψω πρὸς ὑμᾶς,

[1] παρ' αυτοις *om.* ℵAB 36, 40, Vulg., Syr. H. text, Aeth., so Tisch., W.H., R.V.,
Weiss, Wendt, Blass.

[2] After ειπων ℵABE 13, 15, 105, 180, Vulg. (*exc.* demid.), Sah., Boh., Arm., Aethro.
om. δει . . . Ιεροσ., so Tisch., W.H., R.V., Weiss, Wendt; retained by T.R., so
Meyer, after (D)HLP 36, 40, Syrr., demid., Chrys., Oec., Thl., Gig., Wer.; D has
την εορτην ημεραν, omitting the second την. Blass, p. xx., thinks D here affected
by the corresponding Latin, "sollemnem diem advenientem ". The reading may have
arisen from a desire to give a reason for St. Paul's urgency in making a brief journey
to Jerusalem, a journey to which the αναβας of ver. 22 was regarded as referring (*cf.*
xx. 16). But whether we follow the Bezan text or not, Ramsay holds that the shorter
reading of the great MSS. still implies a hurried visit to Jerusalem, which could only
be for some great occasion—the Feast of the Passover close at hand (so Ramsay,
St. Paul, p. 263). Possibly the performance of his vow may have occasioned this
urgent desire (Belser). But in xix. 1 D has a further expansion of the text, and speaks
of a purposed but unaccomplished journey of St. Paul to Jerusalem, so that we cannot
find in xviii. 22 an intimation of the accomplishment of this journey (*cf.* Corssen,
G. G. A., p. 440, 1896 ; Hilgenfeld, *Zw. Th.*, 1896, p. 82), and αναβας, xviii. 22, does
not refer to a journey to Jerusalem at all on this view. But the reference of β in xix.
1 to the proposed journey in xviii. 21 has been doubted : Paul may have visited Jerusalem, xviii. 22, then travelled through Galatia and Phrygia, ver. 23, and have formed
anew an intention to pay another visit to Jerusalem (so Belser, strongly against Blass,
Beiträge, p. 97, and also *Die Selbstvertheidigung des heiligen Paulus*, p. 140 ff.,
App. I.; the visit in xviii. 22 having been already accomplished for the performance
of his vow). But if xix. 1 does refer back to the journey of xviii. 21, Wendt maintains
that the original occasion for the addition in that verse may still have been the fact
that αναβας was understood of a journey to Jerusalem. For the two additions may
proceed from different hands ; that in xviii. 21 has much better attestation than that
in xix. 1, and may owe its origin to the correct reference of αναβας in ver. 22 to a
journey to Jerusalem ; whilst the later addition in xix. 1 may have been occasioned
by that of xviii. 21, because the reference in ver. 22 to a journey to Jerusalem was no
longer recognised (Wendt, 1899, note, p. 306) ; see further on xix. 1.

especially after xvi. 13. It seems most
probable that St. Luke uses the words in
an anticipatory way, and passes on to
the doings of the chief figure, Paul. In
spite of all that he had suffered at the
hands of his countrymen, St. Paul is still
an Israelite, yearning for the hope of
Israel, and desirous that others should
participate in his hope, see critical note
on β and Wendt (1899), note, p. 305.—
διελέχθη: aorist, not imperfect as in ver.
4 ; "delivered a discourse to the Jews,"
so Ramsay, in contrast to the continued
stay at Corinth marked by the imperfect ;
so Alford.

Ver. 20. ἐπένευσεν : only here in N.T.,
but *cf.* 2 Macc. xi. 10, xi. 15, xiv. 20,
frequent in classical Greek. St. Paul
must have had some very pressing reason
for refusing such an invitation from his
own countrymen.

Ver. 21. See critical note. The Feast,
as Ramsay maintains, *St. Paul*, p. 264

(so Ewald, Renan, Zöckler, Rendall,
Blass and others), was the Passover, the
one which seems most reconcilable with
the chronology ; others maintain Pentecost, so Anger, Alford, Wieseler, Plumptre
—see Alford, *in loco*, and Turner, *Chron.
of the N. T.*, p. 422 ; Lewin favours
Tabernacles.—ἀνακάμψω, *cf.* xix. 1 : used
by St. Luke, Luke x. 6, Matt. ii. 12,
Heb. xi. 15 ; used also several times in
LXX, Jud. xi. 39 A, 2 Sam. viii. 13, 1
Kings xii. 20, Job xxxix. 4, Sus. 14,
and other instances, so in classical
Greek, to return to a place, Herod., ii.,
8.—τοῦ Θ. θέλ., *cf.* 1 Cor. iv. 19, xvi. 17,
James iv. 15. Not only amongst Jews
and Arabs but amongst Greeks and
Romans similar phrases were in vogue,
see Meyer's note on James iv. 15 ; see
critical note on β.—ἀνήχθη, see above on
xiii. 13.

Ver. 22. κατελθὼν εἰς Κ., *i.e.*, Cæsarea
Stratonis, *i.e.*, came down from the

τοῦ Θεοῦ θέλοντος. καὶ ἀνήχθη ἀπὸ τῆς Ἐφέσου · 22.[1] καὶ κατελθὼν
εἰς Καισάρειαν, ἀναβὰς καὶ ἀσπασάμενος τὴν ἐκκλησίαν, κατέβη εἰς
Ἀντιόχειαν.   23. καὶ ποιήσας χρόνον τινὰ ἐξῆλθε, διερχόμενος
καθεξῆς τὴν Γαλατικὴν χώραν καὶ Φρυγίαν, ἐπιστηρίζων πάντας
τοὺς μαθητάς.

---

[1] 137, Syr. Harcl. mg., Pesh. read τον δε Ακυλαν ειασεν εν Εφεσω· αυτος δε
αναχθεις ηλθεν εις Καισ., so as to bring in the words omitted above, κατελιπεν
αυτους εκει—no mention of Priscilla; this would be characteristic of the Bezan
reviser, cf. ver. 26, etc.

high sea to the coast, the shore, cf. xxvii.
5 (xxi. 3), so in Homer, and also of
coming down from the high land to the
coast, see Grimm-Thayer, sub v.—ἀναβὰς, i.e., to Jerusalem, the usual expression for a journey to the capital, cf. xi. 2,
xv. 2 (b), xxv. 1, 9, Matt. xx. 18, Mark
x. 32, see Luke ii. 42, xviii. 31, xix. 28,
John ii. 13, vii. 8, Gal. ii. 1; cf. xxiv. 1,
22, xxv. 6, where "to go down" is used
of the journey from Jerusalem to Cæsarea.
To suppose that the word is used to indicate simply that they landed in the
harbour, or because the town lay high up
from the shore, or because the place of
assembly for the Church was on high
ground, is quite arbitrary, and cannot be
set against the usage of the term "going
up" and "going down" in relation to
Jerusalem; see Hort, Ecclesia, p. 96;
Ramsay, St. Paul, p. 264; so Bengel,
Neander, Meyer, Hackett, Zöckler, Rendall, Page, Weiss, Weizsäcker, Spitta,
Jüngst, Hilgenfeld, Wendt, Knabenbauer,
and Belser, Beiträge, p. 89, who opposes
here the position of Blass (and if the T.R.
in ver. 21 is retained in β certainly "the
going up" to Jerusalem seems naturally
to follow). Blass maintains that Cæsarea
is meant, but he is evidently led to adopt
this view by his desire to retain the reading in D, xix. 1, see Zöckler, in loco, and
Ramsay, p. 264, and Belser, u. s., for a
criticism of Blass's view. Amongst the
more recent critics, Zahn, Einleitung, ii.,
343, 350, combats the reasons alleged by
Belser, and takes the going up and the
Church mentioned to refer to Cæsarea
and the Church there, not to Jerusalem.
This visit of St. Paul to Jerusalem is
disputed by McGiffert, although he does
not deny with Weizsäcker the whole
journey, but admits that the Apostle
went as far as Antioch. So too Wendt
is not prepared to follow Weizsäcker
entirely, although he holds that as the
Apostle went to Syria, Luke concluded
that he must have gone up to Jerusalem
(so McGiffert). On the other hand, the
historical truthfulness of the journey to
Jerusalem is stoutly defended by Spitta
(pp. 246-248). The silence of the Galatian Epistle is admitted by Wendt to be
in itself no proof against its occurrence,
and still less objection can be based on
the supposed variance at this time between St. Paul and the Jewish Christians
of the capital. See Zöckler's note, p.
272, and also Alford, in loco.—τὴν ἐκκ. :
the Church at Jerusalem may be fairly
regarded as indicated, the ἐκκ. κατ'
ἐξοχὴν : "primariam, ex qua propagatæ
sunt reliquæ," Bengel. If St. Luke had
meant the Christians in Cæsarea, he
would probably have said that Paul
saluted the brethren or the disciples, cf.
xxiv. 7 (see Belser, u. s., p. 90). This
visit of St. Paul to Jerusalem would probably be his fourth, ix. 26, xi. 30 (xii. 25),
xv. 4, and if he went on this fourth occasion to complete a vow, this fact alone
would prove that the visit was not wanting in an object: see however note on
ver. 18.—ἀσπασ. : the word indicates a
short stay. Blass interprets that the
Apostle went up from the harbour to the
city of Cæsarea, and then "went down
to Antioch". But Ramsay, p. 264, urges
that it is impossible to use the term
κατέβη of a journey from the coast town
Cæsarea to the inland city Antioch; on
the contrary, one regularly "goes down"
to a coast town, xiii. 4, xiv. 25, xvi. 8, etc.
At the Syrian Antioch, the mother of the
Gentile churches, St. Paul would find a
welcome after his second journey, as after
his first—this so far as we know was his
last visit to a place which was now no
longer an effective centre for the Apostle's
work, or for the supervision of his new
churches.

Ver. 23. ποιήσας χρόνον τινὰ : St.
Paul would naturally have spent some
time in a place so associated with the
origin of Gentile Christianity, and with
his own labours, the starting place of
each of his missionary journeys; on the
phrase in St. Luke see Friedrich, cf.

24. Ἰουδαῖος δέ τις Ἀπολλῶς[1] ὀνόματι, Ἀλεξανδρεὺς τῷ γένει, ἀνὴρ λόγιος, κατήντησεν εἰς Ἔφεσον, δυνατὸς ὢν ἐν ταῖς γραφαῖς. 25. οὗτος ἦν κατηχημένος τὴν ὁδὸν τοῦ Κυρίου, καί, ζέων τῷ πνεύματι, ἐλάλει καὶ ἐδίδασκεν ἀκριβῶς τὰ περὶ τοῦ Κυρίου,[2] ἐπιστάμενος

[1] D reads Ἀπολλωνιος, possibly correct, so Blass in β, and Hilg., but cf. Ramsay, St. Paul, p. 268, C. R. E., p. 151, and see below; see also Wendt (1899), p. 308, note, who thinks with Blass that orig. in Acts Ἀπελλης as in ℵ*.

[2] For Κυριου ℵABDEL 13, 36, 40, verss., Tisch., W.H., R.V., Weiss, Wendt, Blass, Hilg. read Ιησου. After κατηχ. D (Gig.) reads εν τη πατριδι. For την οδον D has τον λογον, but not Blass. For ελαλει D[1] has απελαλει (d, eloquebatur), so Blass in β, and Hilg.; see also below.

xv. 33, xx. 3, James iv. 13, Rev. xiii. 5, St. Matt. xx. 12, 2 Cor. xi. 25.—The stay was probably not lengthy, especially if advantage was to be taken of the travelling season for the highlands of Asia Minor, Turner, *Chronology of N. T.*, p. 422, Hastings' B.D. On the connection of the Galatian Epistle with this stay in Antioch see Ramsay, especially *St. Paul*, pp. 190, 265.—ἐξῆλθε, on his third missionary journey.—καθεξῆς, see above on p. 118.—διερχόμενος, see above on xiii. 6.

Ver. 24. Ἀλεξ., cf. vi. 9, Schürer, *Jewish People*, div. ii., vol. ii., p. 226, E.T. At Alexandria the LXX was written and Philo lived; here too was the magnificent mosque of which it was said that he who had not worshipped in it had not witnessed the glory of Israel, Edersheim, *History of the Jewish People*, pp. 67, 186, 405, 409; on the contact of Jewish and Greek thought in Alexandria, "Alexandria," B.D.[2] (Westcott). What was the exact influence of his Alexandrian training upon Apollos we are not told, but as a cultured Jew of such a centre of Hellenistic influence, it is quite possible that Aquila and Priscilla chose him for the work at Corinth because they thought that his training and learning would attract the attention of a Corinthian audience. Possibly his preaching may have included some Philonian speculations, but the difference between him and St. Paul in their teaching at Corinth may have consisted in outward form and delivery rather than in substance; see Canon Evans, *Speaker's Commentary*, iii., p. 240. No doubt the subtle Corinthian would admire the eloquence of Apollos and pervert his words, but there is no reason to suppose that Apollos encouraged any such party spirit. On his work at Corinth and the last notice of him, Titus iii. 13, see "Apollos," B. D.[2], and Has-

tings' B.D., cf. 1 Cor. xvi. 12, for his unambitious and peaceful character, and Plumptre, *in loco*. The Book of Wisdom was attributed to Apollos by Dean Plumptre, but see on the other hand "Wisdom of Solomon," B.D.[2] (Westcott), and *Speaker's Commentary*, "Apocrypha," vol. i., p. 413.—λόγιος; "learned," R.V., "eloquent," margin; A.V., "eloquent"; the word may include both learning and eloquence. In classical Greek of a man learned, as, *e.g.*, in history (Herod.), but in Plutarch λογιότης, eloquence, and so λόγιος, eloquent. Meyer rendered the word "eloquent," so Weiss, Zöckler, Page, Alford, Hackett, Felten, Blass (*doctus ap. antiquos*), δυνατός referring rather to his learning and acquaintance with the Scriptures: "a good speaker and well read in the Scriptures" (Ramsay). Rendall however takes δυνατός as conveying the idea of eloquence, but in vii. 22 the word cannot mean eloquent as applied to Moses, but rather denotes the wise and weighty nature of his utterances, see Lobeck, *Phryn.*, p. 198.

Ver. 25. See critical note on the proposed omission of the verse and reading also in D.—κατηχ., cf. Luke i. 4, "taught by word of mouth," R.V., margin; D. adds ἐν τῇ πατρίδι, and Blass holds that we may learn from this that some form of Gospel teaching had already been known in Egypt. But how far had Apollos been instructed? It is commonly held that he only knew the Baptism of John and nothing further, and that he was imperfectly acquainted with the facts of our Lord's life. But he is said to have taught accurately (ἀκριβῶς) "the things concerning Jesus" (see critical note), and not only so, but, as Blass also points out, the mention of the twelve disciples at Ephesus has previously been taken to mean literally that these men were disciples of the Baptist, and had never

μόνον τὸ βάπτισμα Ἰωάννου· 26. οὗτός τε ἤρξατο παρρησιάζεσθαι
ἐν τῇ συναγωγῇ. ἀκούσαντες δὲ αὐτοῦ [1] Ἀκύλας καὶ Πρίσκιλλα,

[1] Ἀκύλας καὶ Πρισκίλλα, so DHLP, Syrr. P. and H., Sah., Arm., Chrys., Gig. ;
but Πρ. καὶ Ἀκ. ABE 13, Vulg., Boh., Aeth., Tisch., W.H., R.V., Weiss, Wendt, so
Blass, although in β we might have expected the other order, as characteristic of the
Bezan text; see Ramsay, St. Paul, p. 268, and see below on verse 2.

heard of Jesus, whereas the words used
to describe them, μαθηταί and πιστεύσαντες, are never used except of Christians. What is the conclusion? That
whilst Apollos, like these twelve men, was
acquainted with no other Baptism than
John's, he may have known quite as
much of our Lord's words and deeds as
was contained in the Gospel of St.
Mark in its mutilated form, xvi. 8, which
tells us nothing of Christian Baptism.
And if we further ask from what source
did Apollos gain this accurate information, Blass answers: "videlicet non sine
scripto aliquo Evangelio". If, he urges,
it had been otherwise, and Apollos had
been instructed by some disciple of the
Apostles and not through a written Gospel, the position of things in the text
would be reversed, and Apollos would
have been imperfectly acquainted with
our Lord's life and teaching, whilst he
could not have failed to know of Christian
Baptism as the admission to Christian
churches. Blass therefore believes that
before the year 50 (he places the Conference in 45 or 46) written Gospels were
in existence, and he evidently leans to
the belief that St. Mark's Gospel, or
some first edition of it, was the Gospel
from which Apollos was instructed (see
in loco, and cf. also Philology of the
Gospels, p. 30). But the word κατηχ. on
this view must be taken not to include
but to exclude, at all events mainly, a
reference to catechetical teaching, and
this from the use of the word in the
N.T. is most unlikely. In the majority
of the cases, as Blass admits, the word
denotes oral teaching, although he maintains that this meaning is not always
strictly kept. In the N.T. the word is
used only by Luke and Paul, altogether
eight times, in six of which it is used
with reference to oral instruction, according to Mr. Wright: "Apollos: a study
in Pre-Pauline Christianity," Expository
Times, October, 1897 (but see also in
answer, Blass, Philology of the Gospels,
p. 31). Mr. Wright suggests that
Apollos may have derived his knowledge
of "the facts concerning Jesus" from
one of the many Catechists who were
sent out from Jerusalem, and visited

in large numbers the capital of Egypt,
and by him Apollos like Theophilus
was instructed in the way of the
Lord. This view certainly gives an
adequate meaning to κατηχ., but still it
seems strange that a Catechist, even if
his chief business was to catechise or
instruct in the facts of the Gospel history,
should say nothing about Christian Baptism; surely a Catechist would himself
be a baptised member of Christ. It
is possible that Apollos may have deliberately decided to abide as he was;
he may have said that as the Master
Himself had fulfilled all righteousness in
John's Baptism, so that Baptism was
sufficient for the servant. But on this
view one has to suppose that no news of
the events of Pentecost had reached Alexandria, although Egyptian Jews had been
present at the feast. But the news which
Apollos may have received had been imperfect, cf. xix. 2, 3, and he had not
therefore abandoned his position as a
follower of the Baptist, who accepted the
teaching that Jesus was the Messiah
without knowing fully how that claim
had been fulfilled, who had been baptised
with the Baptism of the Baptist unto
repentance without knowing the higher
blessings conferred by membership in the
Body of the Risen and Ascended Lord:
see further Expository Times, vol. vii.,
pp. 564, 565; Hermathena, xxi. (1895);
Weiss and Zöckler, in loco.—ἐλάλει καὶ
ἐδίδασκεν: Blass prefers D ἀπελάλει,
which Wright, u. s., p. 11, renders "repeated by rote".—ζέων τῷ πνεύματι, cf.
Rom. xii. 11, this fervency was shown
not only in speaking what he knew, but
in teaching it to others; cf. ver. 11, where
the same word is used of Paul's instructions. We can scarcely take ἐλάλει as
privatim, ἐδίδασκεν publice (Bengel).—
ἀκριβῶς: "accurately," so often in
classics, and as agreeing best here with
this verse and the comparative in ver.
26; on the use of the word in medical
writers see Hobart, p. 251; Weiss,
Meyer's Kommentar, Luke i. 3, also compares the similarity between St. Luke's
phrase and Galen's dedication of his work
to a friend (he also finds a parallel in
Jos., C. Apion, i., 10); see also below on

προσελάβοντο αὐτόν, καὶ ἀκριβέστερον αὐτῷ ἐξέθεντο τὴν τοῦ Θεοῦ ὁδόν. 27.[1] βουλομένου δὲ αὐτοῦ διελθεῖν εἰς τὴν Ἀχαΐαν, προτρεψά-

---

[1] In D, Syr. Harcl. mg. εν δε Εφεσω επιδημουντες τινες Κορινθιοι και ακουσαντες αυτου παρεκαλουν διελθειν συν αυτοις εις την πατριδα αυτων. συγκατανευσαντος δε αυτου οι Εφεσιοι εγραψαν τοις εν Κορινθω μαθηταις, οπως αποδεξωνται τον ανδρα, ος επιδημησας εις την Αχαιαν πολυ συνεβαλλετο εν ταις εκκλησιαις. If the work of a reviser, object seems to be to show more clearly why Apollos came to Corinth. επιδημειν is Lucan; συγκατανευειν occurs nowhere in N.T. Belser, pp. 87, 88, argues for the value of the β text here, esp. in the addition εν ταις εκκλησιαις, which shows St. Paul had not confined his attention to Corinth. But if original, why omitted? See Ramsay, *St. Paul*, p. 267; W.H. marg.; Holtzmann, *Apostelgeschichte*, p. 396. δια της χαριτος *om*. D 137, Gig., Par., Vulg., Syr. Harcl., so Blass in β.

ἀκριβέστερον and its employment by Dioscorides. The word occurs in Luke twice, Luke i. 3, Acts xviii. 25, and elsewhere in Matt. ii. 8, and twice in St. Paul, 1 Thess. v. 2, Eph. v. 15, whilst ἀκριβέστερον occurs four times in N.T., and each time in Acts, *cf*. ver. 26, xxiii. 15, 20, xxiv. 22.

Ver. 26. παρρησιάζεσθαι, see above on p. 242; whatever was the exact form of the belief of Apollos, he had at all events the courage of his convictions. — ἀκούσαντες showing that Priscilla and Aquila had not separated themselves from their fellow-countrymen.—προσελάβοντο, *cf*. xvii. 5, *i.e.*, for instruction in private.—ἀκριβέστερον: on its use by St. Luke see above on ver. 25. The word is used by Dioscorides in his preface to his *De Materia Medica*: see Weiss-Meyer's *Kommentar* on Luke i. 1, and Vogel, p. 17, as an instance of medical language. — ἐξέθεντο: we are not told whether he was baptised, but xix. 5 makes it probable that he was; see Zöckler's note. "Qui Jesum Christum novit, potentes in Scriptura docere potest," Bengel, and Vogel *u. s.*

Ver. 27. διελθεῖν εἰς, *cf*. Luke viii. 22, Mark iv. 35, Latin, *trajicere.*—προτρεψ. . . . ἔγραψαν: "encouraged him and wrote," R.V., so Chrysostom, Erasmus, Grotius, Bengel, Felten, Lumby, Rendall, Knabenbauer: "currentem incitantes," Bengel. But others refer it to the disciples, "wrote exhorting the disciples," *i.e.*, wrote letters of commendation, 2 Cor. iii., so Luther, De Wette, Ewald, Zöckler, Alford, Wendt, Weiss, Nösgen, Hackett. Blass thinks that the word can be referred to neither in the sense of *cohortari*, and prefers the rendering in accordance with the Syriac *anteverterunt*, but *cf*. Wisdom xiv. 18, 2 Macc. xi. 7 for the former sense, so in classical Greek; only here in N.T., classed not only by

Hobart, but also by Vogel, as amongst the medical words in St. Luke, *u. s.*, p. 17.—συνεβάλετο: only here in N.T. in middle, with dative of the person, *profuit*, so often in Greek authors, especially Polybius; Wisdom v. 8, Xen., *Cyr.*, i., 2, 8; *cf*. 1 Cor. iii. 6, "rigavit A. non plantavit" Bengel.—διὰ τῆς χ.: "helped much through grace them which had believed" R.V., margin. This connection of the words seems preferable, as stress is laid upon the fact that the gifts and eloquence of Apollos were only available when God gave the increase—the position of the words is not against this, as they may have been so placed for emphasis. Blass, who joins the phrase with πεπιστ., adds "quamvis ibi abundat". It does not seem natural to explain the word χάρις here as the Gospel, or to refer it to the grace of the eloquence of Apollos.

Ver. 28. εὐτόνως: "powerfully," only in Luke, *cf*. Luke xxiii. 10, "vehemently," like Latin, *intente, acriter*, Josh. vi. (7), 8 (-νος, 2 Macc. xii. 23, 4 Macc. vii. 10, A R); found also in classical Greek, and may be one of the "colloquial" words common to the N.T. and Aristophanes, *cf*. *Plutus*, 1096 (Kennedy, p. 78). But as the word is used only by St. Luke, it may be noted that it is very frequently employed by medical writers, opposed to ἄτονος.—διακατηλέγχετο: "powerfully confuted," R.V. The word does not prove that Apollos convinced them (A.V. "mightily convinced"), lit., he argued them down; but to confute is not of necessity to convince. The double compound, a very strong word, is not found elsewhere, but in classical Greek διελέγχω, to refute utterly (in LXX, middle, to dispute), κατελέγχω, to convict of falsehood, to belie. — ἐπιδεικνὺς: only once elsewhere in N.T., Heb. vi. 17, and in classical Greek as in Plato, to prove, to demonstrate.

μενοι οἱ ἀδελφοὶ ἔγραψαν τοῖς μαθηταῖς ἀποδέξασθαι αὐτόν· ὃς
παραγενόμενος συνεβάλετο πολὺ τοῖς πεπιστευκόσι διὰ τῆς χάριτος·

Additional note on Acts xviii. 23 (see on xvi. 6).

In a brief attempt to refer to a few difficulties connected with this verse, it is well to bear in mind at the outset that St. Luke never uses the noun Γαλατία (which is twice used by St. Paul, 1 Cor. xvi. 1, Gal. i. 2), but the adjective Γαλατικός, xviii. 23 and xvi. 6, in both cases with the noun χώρα; St. Paul in each case is speaking of the "Churches of Galatia"; St. Luke in each case is speaking of the Apostle's journeys. How may we account for this different phraseology? If St. Luke had meant Galatia proper, we may believe that he would have used the word Γαλατία, but as he says Γαλατικὴ χώρα he speaks as a Greek and indicates the Roman province Galatia, or the Galatic province; a name by which the Greek-speaking natives called it, whilst sometimes they enumerated its parts, e.g., Pontus Galaticus, Phrygia Galatica, Expositor, pp. 126, 127, August, 1898 (Ramsay), and Hastings' B.D., "Galatia" (Ramsay), pp. 87-89, 1899; cf. the form of the derived adjective in -ικός in the pair Λακωνικὴ γῆ and Λακωνία. St. Paul on the other hand, speaking as a Roman citizen, used the word Γαλατία as = the Roman province, for not only is there evidence that Γαλ. could be so employed in current official usage (the contrary hypothesis is now abandoned by Schürer, one of its former staunch supporters, see Expositor, u. s., p. 128, and Hastings' B.D., ii., 86), but it seems beyond all dispute that St. Paul in other cases classified his Churches in accordance with the Roman provinces, Asia, Macedonia, Achaia, Expositor, u. s., p. 125; Zahn, Einleitung, i., 124; Renan, Saint Paul, p. 51; Hausrath, Neutest. Zeitgeschichte, iii., p. 135; Clemen, Chron. der Paulinischen Briefe, p. 121. Why then should the Churches of Galatia be interpreted otherwise? Ramsay ("Questions," Expositor, January, 1899) may well appeal to Dr. Hort's decisive acceptance of the view that in 1 Peter i. 1 (First Epistle of St. Peter, pp. 17, 158) the Churches are named according to the provinces of the Roman empire (a point emphasised by Hausrath, u. s., in advocating the South-Galatian theory), and that in provincial Galatia St. Peter included at least the Churches founded by St. Paul in Galatia proper, i.e., in Phrygia and Lycaonia, although it must be re-

membered that Dr. Hort still followed Lightfoot in maintaining that the Galatians of St. Paul's Epistle were true Galatians, and not the inhabitants of the Roman province. "But if St. Peter, as Hort declares, classed Antioch, Iconium, Derbe and Lystra among the Churches of Galatia, must not Paul have done the same thing? Is it likely that 1 Peter, a letter so penetrated with the Pauline spirit, so much influenced by at least two Pauline Epistles, composed in such close relations with two of Paul's coadjutors, Silas and Mark, should class the Pauline Churches after a method that Paul would not employ?" (Ramsay, Expositor, January, 1899.) The Churches which in this view are thus included in the province Galatia, viz., Pisidian Antioch, Iconium, Lystra, Derbe, would be fitly addressed as Galatians by a Roman citizen writing to provincials proud of Roman names and titles (although Wendt (1899) urges this mode of address, Gal. iii. 1, as one of two decisive points against the South Galatian theory). For we must not forget that two of the four Churches in South Galatia were Roman coloniæ, Antioch and Lystra, whilst the two others mentioned in Acts xiv. bore an emperor's name, Claudio-Iconium, Claudio-Derbe. That the title "Galatians" might be so applied to the people of Roman "Galatia" has been sufficiently illustrated by Zahn, Einleitung, i., p. 130, and Ramsay, Expositor, August, 1898, cf. Tac., Ann., xiii., 35, xv., 6; Hist., ii., 9; and it is very noteworthy that in Phil. iv. 15 St. Paul in addressing the inhabitants of a Roman colonia addresses them by a Latin and not a Greek form of their name, Φιλιππήσιοι = Latin, Philippenses, so that in addressing the four Churches of South Galatia, so closely connected with Rome as we have seen, St. Paul would naturally address them by the one title common to them all as belonging to a Roman province, Γαλάται, Galatians; Ramsay, Expositor, August, 1898; McGiffert, Apostolic Age, pp. 177-179.

St. Paul then uses the term Galatia as a Roman citizen would use it, while St. Luke employs the phraseology common in the Ægean land amongst his contemporaries; he does not speak of Galatia, by which term he would as a Greek mean North Galatia, but of the "Galatic territory" or of the region or regions with which he was concerned; see on

28. εὐτόνως γὰρ τοῖς Ἰουδαίοις διακατηλέγχετο [1] δημοσίᾳ, ἐπιδεικνὺς διὰ τῶν γραφῶν εἶναι τὸν Χριστὸν Ἰησοῦν.

[1] δημοσια επιδεικνυς, D 137 has δημ. διαλεγομενος και, so Blass in β, and Hilg., but apparently superfluous after διακατηλεγχετο (Weiss).

this Expositor, August, 1898, pp. 126, 127, and Hastings' B.D., "Galatia". In xvi. 6 he writes of a missionary tour (see on διῆλθον, note, l. c.) through the Phrygo-Galatic region; in xviii. 23 he speaks of a missionary tour through the Galatic region (Derbe and Lystra) and the Phrygian (Iconium and Antioch). It is, moreover, important to note that whether we take Φρυγία, xviii. 23, as an adjective, χώρα being understood, or as a noun, the same sense prevails, for we have evidence from inscriptions of Antioch that Galatic Phrygia was often designated by the noun, "and St. Luke may be allowed to speak as the people of Antioch wrote," Ramsay, Hastings' B.D., ii., p. 90, 1899. See further the same writer's reference to the testimony of Asterius, Bishop of Amasia in Pontus Galaticus, A.D. 400, in favour of the above view, who paraphrases xviii. 23, τὴν Λυκαονίαν καὶ τὰς τῆς Φρυγίας πόλεις, and places the journey through Lycaonia and Phrygia immediately before the visit to Asia, xix. 1; see especially Ramsay, Studia Biblica, iv., p. 16 ff. and p. 90; Hastings' B.D., u. s., as against Zahn, Einleitung, i., p. 136.

But further: if the Phrygo-Galatic district thus lay on the road to Ephesus, it is difficult to see how St. Paul could be conceived of as going to a distance of some 300 miles out of his route to Galatia in the narrower ethnical sense of the word; and this is one of the many points which influences Mr. Turner to regard the South Galatia view as almost demonstrably true, Chron. of the N.T.; Hastings' B.D., i., 422 (see also to the same effect, Renan, Saint Paul, p. 52; and Rendall, Acts, p. 275; Salmon, Introd., p. 377). McGiffert (so too Renan, Hausrath) maintains that if the North Galatian theory is correct, and St. Paul is not addressing the Churches founded on his first missionary journey, but only those founded, as we must suppose, during a period of missionary labour in North Galatia, a period inserted without a hint from St. Luke in xvi. 6, it seems incomprehensible why Barnabas should be mentioned in the Galatian Epistle. The Churches in North Galatia could scarcely have known anything about

him, especially as ex hypothesi they had been evangelised after the rupture between Paul and Barnabas, Acts xv. 36 ff. If, however, the Churches of the Epistle = the Churches founded in Acts xiii., xiv., then we can at once understand the mention of Barnabas. But Mr. Askwith has lately pointed out with much force (Epistle to the Galatians, p. 77, 1899) that this argument must not be pressed too far. The introduction of Barnabas in the Galatian Epistle does not prove that he was known personally to the Galatians (although it may reasonably warrant the inference that he was known by name) any more than the allusion to him, 1 Cor. ix. 6, proves that he was personally known to the Corinthians, cf. also Lightfoot, Colossians, p. 28.

One more significant and weighty fact deserves mention. In St. Paul's collection for the poor Saints (on the importance of which see xxiv. 17) there is every reason to believe that all the Pauline Churches shared; in 1 Cor. xvi. 1 appeal is made to the Churches of Galatia and Achaia, and the Churches of Macedonia and Asia subsequently contributed to the fund. If by Galatia we understand Galatia proper, and not the Roman province, then the four South Galatian Churches are not included in the list of subscribers, and they are not even asked to contribute. This appears inconceivable; whereas, if we look at the list of delegates, Acts xx. 4, whilst Macedonia and Asia are represented, and Gaius and Timothy represent the Churches of South Galatia, no delegate is mentioned from any North Galatian community (see Rendall: "Pauline collection for the Saints," Expositor, Nov., 1898, and "The Galatians of St. Paul," Expositor, April, 1894; also Weizsäcker, Apostolic Age, i., 272, E.T., and McGiffert, Apostolic Age, p. 180, Askwith, Epistle to the Galatians, p. 88 ff. (1899)). For the literature of the question see Ramsay, "Galatia," Hastings' B.D., ii., p. 89, 1899; Zahn, Einleitung, i., pp. 129, 130; Wendt (1899), p. 276, and "Galatians, Epistle to the," Marcus Dods, Hastings' B.D., ii., 94. To the list given in the last reference may be added the names of Wendt, O. Holtzmann, Clemen, V. Weber (Würsburg), Page, Rendall, McGiffert,

XIX. 1.[1] ᾿ΕΓΕΝΕΤΟ δὲ ἐν τῷ τὸν ᾿Απολλὼ εἶναι ἐν Κορίνθῳ, Παῦλον, διελθόντα τὰ ἀνωτερικὰ μέρη, ἐλθεῖν εἰς ῎Εφεσον· 2. καὶ

[1] D, Syr. Harcl. mg. read at commencement of verse Θελοντος δε του Παυλου κατα την ιδιαν βουλην πορευεσθαι εις Ιεροσολυμα, ειπεν αυτω το πνευμα υποστρεφειν εις την Ασιαν. διελθων δε τα ανωτερικα μερη. See above on xviii. 21, and Ramsay, St. Paul, p. 266—the supposed failure to pay the visit to Jerusalem is explained by the interpolation of the above statement; cf. Harris, Four Lectures, etc., p. 48, who quotes Ephrem, in loco. The omission of the notice about Apollos is explained by Weiss, Codex D, p. 93, on the ground that it had no meaning for the reviser, but it may have been accidental because of the other changes. Απολλω ℵc, so W.H., Weiss, Wendt; Απολλων A²L 40; Απελλην ℵ¹ 180. ευρειν instead of ευρων, so ℵAB, Vulg., Boh., Arm.; Tisch., Weiss, Wendt, W.H., R.V. adding τε after ειπεν.

in favour of the South Galatian view, and most recently Askwith, *Epistle to the Galatians* (1899); whilst to the other side may be added Volkmar, Schürer, Holsten, who has examined the whole subject closely in his *Das Evangelium des Paulus*, p. 35 ff. (chiefly in reply to Hausrath's strong support of the opposing view), Zöckler, Jülicher, Hilgenfeld, *Zeitschrift für wissenschaft. Theol.*, p. 186 ff. and p. 353, 1896, Schmiedel, and amongst English writers, Findlay, *Epistles of St. Paul*, p. 288 ff., and very fully Dr. Chase, *Expositor*, 1893, 1894.

We can only make a passing allusion to the date or possible date of the Galatian Epistle. Ramsay, *St. Paul*, p. 189 ff., places it at the close of the Apostle's second missionary journey during his stay at Antioch, xviii. 22 (A.D. 55), whilst McGiffert also places it at Antioch, but *before* the Apostle started on this same journey, not at its close, *Apostolic Age*, p. 226. Rendall, *Expositor*, April, 1894, has assigned it an earlier date, 51, 52, and places it amongst the earliest of St. Paul's Epistles, and more recently Zahn has dated it almost equally early in the beginning of 53, and upon somewhat similar grounds, *Einleitung*, i., p. 139 (the three oldest Epistles of St. Paul according to him being the group of Galatians, 1 Thessalonians, 2 Thessalonians, all written in the same year). But on the other hand, Lightfoot, *Galatians*, p. 43 ff., and Salmon, *Introd.*, p. 376, not only place the Epistle later than any of the dates suggested above, but assign it a place between 2 Corinthians and Romans, arguing from the similarity of subject and style between the three Epistles. Most of the continental critics would place it in the same group, but as the earliest of the four great Epistles written

in the earlier period of the Apostle's long residence at Ephesus, Acts xix. 1.

Lightfoot places it apparently on the journey between Macedonia and Achaia, Acts xx. 2, 2 Corinthians having been previously written during the Apostle's residence in Macedonia (so Zahn), Romans being dated a little later whilst St. Paul stayed in Corinth, Acts xx. 2, 3 (*Galatians*, pp. 39, 55). Dr. Clemen has since defended at great length his view, first put forward in *Chronol. der Paul. Briefe*, p. 199 ff., that Romans preceded Galatians, in *Studien und Kritiken*, 1897, 2, pp. 219-270; but see as against Clemen, Zahn, *Einleitung*, i., p. 142; Zöckler, *Die Briefe an die Thess. und Galater*, p. 71; Sanday and Headlam, *Romans*, p. xxxviii. Mr. Askwith has recently discussed the points at issue between Ramsay and Lightfoot as to the date of Galatians, and in accepting the latter's position as his own, he has shown that this is not incompatible with a firm recognition of the South Galatian theory, *Epistle to the Galatians*, p. 98 ff. Harnack, *Chronol.*, p. 239, declines to commit himself to any definite date for Galatians, and perhaps this conclusion is not surprising in relation to an Epistle of which it may be truly said that it has been placed by different critics in the beginning, in the close, and in every intermediate stage of St. Paul's epistolary activity, *cf.* Dr. Marcus Dods, "Galatians," Hastings' B.D.

CHAPTER XIX.—Ver. 1. See critical note for Bezan reading.—᾿Απολλὼ, *cf.* xxi. 1; see Blass, *Gram.*, p. 31, and Winer-Schmiedel, p. 95.—τὰ ἀνωτερικὰ μέρη: The main road to Ephesus which passed through Colosse and Laodicea was not apparently taken by Paul, but a shorter though less frequented route running through the Cayster valley. This route leads over higher ground than the

εὑρών τινας μαθητάς, εἶπε πρὸς αὐτούς, Εἰ Πνεῦμα Ἅγιον ἐλάβετε
πιστεύσαντες ; οἱ δὲ εἶπον πρὸς αὐτόν, Ἀλλ' οὐδὲ εἰ Πνεῦμα Ἅγιον

other, and St. Paul in taking it would be passing through the higher-lying districts of Asia on his way from Pisidian Antioch to Ephesus. According to Col. ii. 1 the Apostle never visited Colosse and Laodicea, which seems to confirm the view taken above (but see Ramsay, *Church in the Roman Empire*, p. 94, on Mr. Lewin's view of Col. ii. 1). The expression τὰ ἀνωτ. μέρη is really a description in brief of the same district, " the region of Galatia and Phrygia," mentioned in xviii. 23. If the journey passed through North Galatia, Ramsay contends with great force that the expressions in xviii. 23 καθεξῆς and πάντας τοὺς μαθητάς would be meaningless, as καθ. would apply not to Churches already known to us, but to Churches never mentioned in the book, and if St. Paul did not visit the South Galatian Churches, how could St. Luke mention " all the disciples"? Zöckler, *Apostelgeschichte* (second edition), *in loco*, as a supporter of the North Galatian theory, takes the term as the equivalent of the places referred to in xviii. 23, but he does not include in these places as far north as Tavium or Ancyra, and a route through Cappadocia is not thought of; so here Pessinus, Amorion, Synnada, Apameia, Philadelphia, and Sardis would be visited by the Apostle, and from Sardis he would go down to Ephesus ; the expression τὰ ἀνωτ. μέρη would thus in Zöckler's view include churches founded on the second missionary journey, but the most northerly are excluded as lying too far away, p. 273 ; see Ramsay, *Church in the Roman Empire*, p. 93 ; "Ephesus," Hastings' B.D., and *Cities and Bishoprics of Phrygia*, ii., 715 ; McGiffert, *Apostolic Age*, p. 275. Blass takes the words to mean districts more remote from the sea ; Rendall (so Hackett) explains them as referring to the land route through the interior of Asia Minor by way of distinction to the sea route which Paul had before pursued on his way from Ephesus to Jerusalem. Grimm explains as the parts of Asia Minor more remote from the Mediterranean, farther east, and refers only to Hippocrates and Galen for the use of the adjective, which was evidently a very rare one (see Hobart, p. 148) ; see also Zöckler on xix. 1 and illustrations of Latin expressions similarly used. R.V. renders " the upper country," lit., the upper parts, *i.e.*, inland ; A.V., " coasts," *i.e.*, borders, as in Matt. ii. 16,

etc., Humphry, *Commentary on R. V.*— εἰς Ἔφεσον : Ephesus and Athens have aptly been described as two typical cities of heathendom, the latter most Hellenic, the heart and citadel of Greece, the former the home of every Oriental quackery and superstition in combination with its Hellenism ; the latter inquisitive, philosophical, courteous, refined, the former fanatical, |superstitious, impulsive. And yet *Acts* portrays to the life the religious and moral atmosphere of the two cities, no less than their local colouring (Lightfoot, " Acts of the Apostles," B.D.[2], p. 36). Under the empire it was a regulation that the Roman governor should land at Ephesus, and from all quarters of the province the system of Roman roads made Ephesus easily accessible. St. Paul with his wonted judgment fixed upon it as a fitting centre for the message and for the spread of the Gospel. Like Corinth, with which close intercourse was maintained, Ephesus is described as one of the great knots in the line of communication between Rome and the East ; see further notes in commentary, Ramsay, " Ephesus," Hastings' B.D. ; " Ephesus," B.D.[2] ; E. Curtius, *Gesammelte Abhandlungen*, i., 233 ff.

Ver. 2. μαθ. . . . πιστεύσαντες : Blass points out that both these words are used only of Christians. From St. Chrysostom's days the men have often been regarded merely as disciples of the Baptist (so McGiffert, p. 286), and Apollos has been named as the person to whom they owed their conversion, whilst amongst recent writers Mr. Wright, *u. s.*, argues that they had been baptised by the Baptist himself. But if we realise the force of the remark made by Blass on the two words, they were men simply in the same position as Apollos, *i.e.*, " ignorabant illi ea quæ post resurrectionem facta erant" (Blass)—their knowledge was imperfect like that of Apollos. There may have been many who would be called μαθηταί in the same immature stage of knowledge. Much difficulty has arisen in insisting upon a personal connection of these men with Apollos, but St. Luke's words quite admit of the supposition that the twelve men may not have come to Ephesus until after Apollos had left for Corinth, a consideration which might answer the question of Ramsay, p. 270, as to how the Twelve had escaped the

ἐστιν [1] ἠκούσαμεν. 3. εἶπέ τε πρὸς αὐτούς, Εἰς τί οὖν ἐβαπτίσθητε ; οἱ δὲ εἶπον, Εἰς τὸ Ἰωάννου βάπτισμα. 4. εἶπε δὲ Παῦλος, Ἰωάννης μὲν [2] ἐβάπτισε βάπτισμα μετανοίας, τῷ λαῷ λέγων, εἰς τὸν ἐρχόμενον μετ᾽ αὐτὸν ἵνα πιστεύσωσι, τουτέστιν εἰς τὸν Χριστὸν Ἰησοῦν. 5. ἀκούσαντες δὲ ἐβαπτίσθησαν εἰς τὸ ὄνομα τοῦ Κυρίου Ἰησοῦ. 6. καὶ ἐπιθέντος αὐτοῖς τοῦ Παύλου τὰς χεῖρας, ἦλθε [3] τὸ Πνεῦμα τὸ Ἅγιον

[1] Instead of εστιν D[1], Syr. Harcl. mg., Sah. read λαμβανουσιν τινες, so Blass and Hilg. εστιν very likely misunderstood; it seems impossible that λαμβ. τινες should be replaced by the difficult εστιν.

[2] μεν om. אABD, Vulg., Sah., Arm., so Tisch., W.H., R.V., Weiss, Wendt. Χριστον om. אABE 13, 25, 40, Vulg., Boh., Syr. H., Aethro., so Tisch., W.H., R.V., Weiss, Wendt, Blass ; although Sah., Gig., Pesh. read εις τον I. X., and D (so Hilg.) has εις X.

[3] D, Jer., instead of ηλθεν, have ευθεως επεπεσεν. After γλωσσαις, Sah., Syr. H. mg. add ετεραις, and Syr. H. mg. (Par.) continue και επεγινωσκον εν εαυτοις, ωστε και ερμηνευειν αυτας εαυτοις, τινες δε και επροφητευον. Both Wendt (1899) and Weiss regard as interpolations after 1 Cor. xiv. Blass, on the other hand, accepts in β, cf. also p. xxviii., and speaks of this as "locus gravissimus".

notice of Apollos (see Felten, p. 351, note).—εἰ, cf. i. 6.—πιστεύσ.: "when ye became believers," or "when ye believed," R.V., in contrast with A.V.—the question was whether they had received the Holy Ghost at their Baptism, and there is no allusion to any subsequent time. The two aorists, as in R.V., point to one definite occasion.—εἰ Π.Ἅ. ἐστιν: "whether the Holy Ghost was *given*," R.V. (cf. John vii. 39): (the spirit was not yet *given*), A.V., but in margin, R.V. follows A.V. in the passage before us: ἐστιν, *accipitur*, Bengel. There could not be any question as to the *existence* of the Holy Ghost, for the Baptist had pointed to the future Baptism of the Spirit to be conferred by the Messiah, and the O.T. would have taught the existence of a Holy Spirit—the meaning is that they had not heard whether their promised Baptism of the Spirit by the Messiah had been already fulfilled or not. So δοθέν, ἐκχυνόμενον may be understood. Alford holds that the stress should be laid on ἠκούσαμεν—when we received Baptism we did not even *hear* of a Holy Ghost.

Ver. 3. οὖν: presupposes that if they had been baptised into the name of Jesus, they would have received the Spirit at Baptism.—εἰς: "to baptise into" (R.V.) may have been suggested by the original practice to baptise by dipping or plunging, see Humphry, *Comment. on R.V., in loco.*—εἰς τὸ Ἰ. βάπτισμα, i.e., into or unto repentance. For the strange notion that they were baptised into John as the Messiah see Hackett's note.

Ver. 4. εἰς τὸν ἐρχ.: placed first before ἵνα, perhaps for emphasis. The phrase had been a favourite one with the Baptist (cf. Matt. iii. 1). John's own words showed that his Baptism was insufficient. ἵνα may express both the purport and the purpose (so Alford).

Ver. 5. ἀκούσαντες δὲ: neither grammatical nor in accordance with fact can these words be regarded (as by Beza and others) as part of St. Paul's words, as if they meant, "and the people when they heard him," *i.e.*, John.

Ver. 6. καὶ ἐπιθ. αὐτοῖς τοῦ Π. τὰς χ., see above on viii. 16.—ἐλάλουν τε γλ. καὶ προεφ.: the imperfects may mean that they began to speak, or that the exercise of the gifts mentioned continued. The two gifts are discussed in 1 Cor. xii. 10, xiv., in an Epistle which was written probably during this stay at Ephesus—no doubt the gifts are specially mentioned because the bestowal of such gifts distinguished Christian Baptism from that of John. McGiffert, p. 286, while admitting the accuracy of the account as a whole, thinks that its representation is moulded, as in viii., in accordance with the work of Peter and John in Samaria ; so too Hilgenfeld refers the account to his "author to Theophilus," who also, in viii. 16, narrates that the baptised Samaritans received the Holy Ghost by the laying on of Peter's hands. This is in some respects not unlike the older view of Baur, who held that the narrative was introduced to parallel Paul's dignity and work with that of Peter in x. 44—the first speaking with tongues in

ἐπ᾽ αὐτούς, ἐλάλουν τε γλώσσαις καὶ προεφήτευον. 7. ἦσαν δὲ οἱ
πάντες ἄνδρες ὡσεὶ¹ δεκαδύο. 8. Εἰσελθὼν δὲ εἰς τὴν συναγωγὴν
ἐπαρρησιάζετο,² ἐπὶ μῆνας τρεῖς διαλεγόμενος καὶ πείθων τὰ περὶ
τῆς βασιλείας τοῦ Θεοῦ. 9. Ὡς δέ τινες ἐσκληρύνοντο καὶ ἠπείθουν,
κακολογοῦντες τὴν ὁδὸν ἐνώπιον τοῦ πλήθους, ἀποστὰς ἀπ᾽ αὐτῶν
ἀφώρισε τοὺς μαθητάς, καθ᾽ ἡμέραν διαλεγόμενος ἐν τῇ σχολῇ

¹ For δεκαδυο(T .R., so Meyer, HLP, Chrys.), ℵABDE, Tisch., W.H., Blass,
Weiss, Wendt read δωδεκα.

² Before επαρρησιαζετο D, Syr. H. mg. read εν δυναμει μεγαλη ; see Harris, *Four
Lectures*, etc., pp. 60, 61. τα before περι ℵAEHLP 13, 36, Chrys., retained by T.R.,
Tisch., but om. by Lach., W.H., Weiss, Wendt, Blass (*cf.* viii. 12), in accordance
with BD.

ii. is narrated in relation to Jews, the
second in relation to Gentiles, x., and the
third in relation to a kind of middle
class, half-believers like the Samaritans !
(so Zeller and Schneckenburger). But
not only does this require us to identify
ii. with x. and xix., the speaking of
tongues at Pentecost with subsequent
bestowal of the gift, but it seems strange
that a narrative should not have been
constructed more free from liability to
misconception and misinterpretation if
the leading purpose of its introduction
had been as supposed above.

Ver. 7. ὡσεὶ, as Weiss admits, excludes any special significance attaching
to the number twelve on account of
which the narrative would be constructed.
See also Knabenbauer, *in loco*. We
know so little about these men that
it seems hazardous to attempt to define
them more clearly (see Plumptre, *in
loco*).

Ver. 8. The Apostle follows his usual
method—to the Jew first, and also to the
Greek. διαλεγ., see above ; *cf.* xvii. 2,
"reasoning," R.V. ("discoursing," Rendall).

Ver. 9. ἐσκληρύνοντο: only here and
in Rom. ix. 18, but four times in Hebrews,
three times as a quotation from Ps. xcv.
8, and once in direct reference to that
passage, iii. 13, *cf.* Exodus vii. 3, Deut.
ii. 30, etc. In Ecclus. xxx. 12 it is
found as here with ἀπειθέω, *cf.* also
Clem. Rom., li., 3, 5.—ἠπείθ.: "were disobedient," R.V., unbelief is manifested in
disobedience, Westcott, *Hebrews*, pp. 87,
97, *cf.* Ign., *Magn.*, viii., 2 ; Polyc., *Phil.*,
ii., 1.—τὴν ὁδὸν: "the Way," see on ix.
2.—κακολ., Mark ix. 39, used by our
Lord of speaking evil of Him, Matt. xv.
4, and Mark vii. 10, as a quotation from
Exod. xxi. 17 ; in LXX five times, and
once in same sense in 2 Macc. iv. 1.

—ἀποστὰς: as in xviii. 7, at Corinth ;
verb only in Luke and Paul, except Heb.
iii. 12, see Friedrich, p. 7, and above
on xv. 38, seven times in N.T. with ἀπό
and a genitive as here.—ἀφώρισε: except
Matt. xiii. 49, xxv. 32 (2), only in Luke
and Paul, *cf.* Luke vi. 22, Acts xiii. 2,
Rom. i. 1, 2 Cor. vi. 17, quotation, Gal.
i. 15, ii. 12 ; *cf.* Grimm-Thayer for different shades of meaning, both in a good
and bad sense, in classical Greek and
also in LXX frequently. It is evidently
presupposed that as in xviii. 26 there
were still disciples who held fast to the
common worship of a Jewish community
in the synagogue.—καθ᾽ ἡμέραν: on the
days when synagogue worship was held,
and so the separation was complete.—
ἐν σχολῇ Τυράννου τινός, see critical
note. We cannot tell whether reference
is made to the lecture-hall of some heathen
sophist hired by Paul or to the *Beth
Hammidrash* kept by a Jew. Others
have thought that Tyrannus, like Titius
Justus, xviii. 7, may have been "a proselyte of the gate," but if so, one might
expect it to be signified as in the case of
Justus. The name was common enough,
Jos., *Ant.*, xvi., 10, 3 ; *B. J.*, i., 26, 3 ;
2 Macc. iv. 40, and see Plumptre's note,
in loco. Overbeck's view is quite possible,
that the expression referred to the standing
name of the place, so called from its
original owner, *cf.* Hort, *Judaistic Christianity*, p. 93. Probably, if we take the
first-mentioned view, in teaching in such
a school or lecture-hall the Apostle himself would appear to the people at large
as one of the rhetors or travelling sophists
of the time, Ramsay, *St. Paul*, pp. 246,
271 (so McGiffert, p. 285, who regards
the notice as taken from a trustworthy
source). For instances of the use of
σχολή as a school of the philosophers
for teaching and lecturing see Wetstein,

Τυράννου[1] τινός. 10. τοῦτο δὲ ἐγένετο ἐπὶ ἔτη δύο, ὥστε πάντας
τοὺς κατοικοῦντας τὴν Ἀσίαν ἀκοῦσαι τὸν λόγον τοῦ Κυρίου[2] Ἰησοῦ,
Ἰουδαίους τε καὶ Ἕλληνας. 11. Δυνάμεις τε οὐ τὰς τυχούσας
ἐποίει ὁ Θεὸς διὰ τῶν χειρῶν Παύλου, 12. ὥστε καὶ ἐπὶ τοὺς
ἀσθενοῦντας[3] ἐπιφέρεσθαι ἀπὸ τοῦ χρωτὸς αὐτοῦ σουδάρια ἢ σιμικίνθια, καὶ ἀπαλλάσσεσθαι ἀπ' αὐτῶν τὰς νόσους, τά τε πνεύματα

---

[1] τινος om. ℵAB 13, 27, 29, 81, Sah., Boh., Syr. Pesh., Vulg. fu.-tol., Tisch., W.H.,
R.V., Weiss, Wendt. After T. D, Gig., Wer., Syr. H. mg. add απο ωρας πεμπτης
εως δεκατης. The addition is accepted by Blass, Belser, Nestle, Zöckler as original,
whilst even Wendt sees in it a passage in which D has retained some elements of
the original text otherwise lost, p. 313 (1899), and Weiss, Codex D, p. 110, thinks
that it may have been added according to an old oral tradition, cf. xii. 10. Ramsay, C. R. E., p. 152, and St. Paul, p. 271, maintains that the tradition is probably
true, and he gives proofs from Martial, ix., 68, xii., 57, and Juv., vii., 222-6, that
the schools opened at daybreak; so that by eleven o'clock the scholars would be
dismissed, and Paul could use the school.

[2] Ιησου after K. om. ℵABDE, Vulg., Syrr : P.H., Boh., Sah., Arm., Aeth., Tisch.,
W.H., R.V., Blass, Weiss, Wendt.

[3] επιφ., but αποφ. ℵABE 13, 36, 40, Vulg., Arm., Tisch., W.H., R.V., Weiss,
Wendt. Blass in β has επιφ.

---

in loco, cf. Latin, auditorium, Zöckler
compares St. Augustine's lecture-hall in
Rome before his conversion.

Ver. 10. ἐπὶ ἔτη δύο: exclusive of
the quarter of a year in ver. 8 and in xx.
31 the Apostle speaks of three years'
residence in Ephesus, "in the usual
ancient style of reckoning an intermediate
period by the superior round number,"
Turner, "Chron. of N. T.," Hastings'
B. D., see also Page and Wendt, in loco.
—πάντας: not only the position of
Ephesus, but the fact that it was just the
place which would be frequented for
its famous temple and festivals by crowds
of strangers, both Jew and Greek, from
all parts of proconsular Asia, "Ephesus,"
Hastings' B. D., i., 720. Nor must we
suppose that St. Paul and his fellow-
workers confined themselves literally to
Ephesus. The seven Churches of Asia
may reasonably be referred for their foundation to this period—all of which were
centres of trade, and all within reach of
Ephesus. Timothy, moreover, may well
have been working at Colosse, since in
the Epistle to the Colossians he is mentioned with Paul in the inscription of the
letter, although the latter had not been
personally known to the Churches of
Colosse and Laodicea, Ramsay, "Co-
lossæ," Hastings' B.D., and St. Paul,
p. 274.—Ἕλληνας: comprising no doubt
Hellenists and Greeks, cf. xi. 20.
Ver. 11. οὐ τὰς τυχ., cf. xxviii. 2, the
phrase is peculiar to St. Luke, "not the
ordinary," i.e., extra-ordinary, with which
the deeds of the Jewish exorcists could
not be compared, see Klostermann, Vindiciæ Lucanæ, p. 52, for the same phrase
cf. 3 Macc. iii. 7, and also Deissmann,
Neue Bibelstudien, p. 83; so too in
classical Greek.—ἐποίει: "continued to
work," or ex more, Blass.
Ver. 12. ὥστε καὶ: so that even to
the sick, i.e., to those who could not be
reached by the hands of the Apostle.—
χρωτὸς: the σουδ. and σιμικ. had been
in contact with the body of the Apostle,
and thence derived their healing power;
so in LXX used for both בָּשָׂר, and עוֹר
(twice), see Hatch and Redpath; Zahn,
Einleitung, ii., 435, sees in its use here the
use of a medical term, so Hobart, p. 242.—
σουδάρια: Latin, sudaria, used for wiping
off sweat, as the noun indicates, cf. Luke
xix. 20, John xix. 44, xx. 7.—σιμικίνθια:
Latin, semicinctium, only here in N.T.,
aprons worn by artisans at their work,
cf. Martial, xiv., 153. Oecumenius and
Theophylact apparently regarded the
word as simply = handkerchiefs, but the
meaning given is far more likely both
from the etymology of the word and its
use in Martial. For other Latinisms see
Blass, in loco, and Wetstein.—ἀπαλ. ἀπ'
αὐτῶν, cf. Luke xii. 58, Heb. ii. 15, here
in connection with sickness, and this use
is very frequent in medical writers, Hobart, p. 47; the word is found with ἀπὸ
both in classical writers and in the LXX.

τὰ πονηρὰ [1] ἐξέρχεσθαι ἀπ' αὐτῶν.   13. Ἐπεχείρησαν δέ τινες [2] ἀπὸ
τῶν περιερχομένων Ἰουδαίων ἐξορκιστῶν ὀνομάζειν ἐπὶ τοὺς ἔχοντας
τὰ πνεύματα τὰ πονηρὰ τὸ ὄνομα τοῦ Κυρίου Ἰησοῦ, λέγοντες,

[1] Instead of εξερ. απ' αυτων, (HLP (Sah.), Chrys.), ℵABDE, Tisch., Weiss,
Wendt, R.V., W.H., Blass in α and β have one word εκπορευεσθαι.

[2] After τινες ℵABE add και and omit απο, so Tisch., Weiss, Wendt, W.H.,
R.V., Blass in β. HP have και απο, D 43 εκ, so Hilg. ορκιζω ℵABDE, Vulg.,
Boh., Arm., Tisch., W.H., Weiss, Wendt, R.V., Blass, Hilg.

It should also be noted that here as elsewhere St. Luke distinguishes between
natural diseases and the diseases of the
demonised, and that he does so more
frequently than the other Evangelists,
Hobart, pp. 12, 13, so " Demon," Hastings' B.D., i., p. 593, cf. especially Luke
vi. 17, viii. 2, xiii. 32, which have no
parallels in the other Gospels.—πονηρὰ:
is applied to evil spirits by St. Luke three
times in his Gospel and four times in this
passage, and only once elsewhere, St.
Matt. xii. 45, although the word is very
frequent in St. Matthew's Gospel and in
the Epistles; the word was constantly
used by medical writers in connection
with disease, Hobart, u. s. Blass quotes
as a parallel to the present passage εἰ αἱ
νόσοι ἀπαλλαγείησαν ἐκ τῶν σωμάτων
(Plat.) Eryx, 401 c.—τά τε πνεύματα
. . . Were the aprons brought for the
healing of the diseases and the banishing
of the demons equally? The τε seems
to indicate that this was the case (Weiss,
Wendt); Blass on the other hand holds
that it is not said that the demons were
driven out by the sudaria. According
to some interpretations of the verse the
carrying of the aprons to the sick is only
to be regarded as a result of the wonderful impression made by St. Paul's miraculous power; the writer says nothing of
the effect of these aprons, although he
places both the healing of the diseases
and the expulsion of the demons
amongst the δυνάμεις of St. Paul. From
this point of view the carrying of the
σουδάρια would only illustrate the
superstitious practices which showed how
often, in the homes of culture, quackery
was also found, and the Evangelist gives
them no word of commendation, see also
note on v. 15. On the other hand we
must remember that the miracles are
distinctly spoken of as οὐ τὰς τυχ., and
even in the means employed we may
perhaps see a possible appeal to the
populace, who would recognise that these
charms and amulets in which they put
such confidence had not the same potency
as the handkerchiefs and aprons of the

Apostle. But in this accommodation to
special forms of ignorance we are never
allowed to forget that God is the source
of all power and might.
Ver. 13. If we read καὶ after ἀπὸ (see
critical note), it contrasts the Jewish
exorcists who endeavoured to gain this
power with those like St. Paul who really
possessed it.—περιερχ.: "vagabond,"
A.V., the word as it is now used colloquially does not express the Greek; R.V.
" strolling," Vulgate, circumeuntibus;
Blass renders circumvagantes. The word
" vagabond " is used only here in N.T.:
in the O.T. we have it in Gen. iv. 12, 14,
R.V. " wanderer," and in Ps. cix. 10,
R.V. " vagabonds," cf. Milton, Paradise
Lost, xi., 16.—ἐξορκιστῶν: the word
points to a class of Jews who practised
exorcisms as a profession, cf. Jos., Ant.,
viii., 2, 5. The usual method of exorcism
was the recitation of some special name
or spell, and these Jewish exorcists having seen the power which Paul wielded
by his appeal to the name of Jesus endeavoured to avail themselves of the
same efficacy. It would be difficult to
say how far these Jewish exorcists
would employ the incantations so
widely in vogue in a place like Ephesus,
but there is a notable passage in Justin
Martyr in which, whilst admitting that
a Jew might exorcise an evil spirit by the
God of Abraham, he complains that as a
class the Jewish exorcists had adopted
the same superstitions and magical
aids as the heathen, " Exorcist," B.D.[2],
i., 1028. In the Didaché, iii., 4, the use
of charms and sorceries is expressly forbidden since they led to idolatry.—
ὁρκίζομεν: with double accusative = of the
one adjured and of the one by whom he
is adjured, cf. Mark v. 7 (1 Thess. v. 27),
see Grimm-Thayer, sub v., cf. Deissmann,
Bibelstudien, p. 25 ff., for the constant
use of the verb in inscriptions in formulæ
of adjuration as here, see further " Demon " and " Exorcist " for examples of
such formulæ, Hastings' B.D., i., pp.
593, 812, and for the absurdities involved
in them.

Ὁρκίζομεν ὑμᾶς τὸν Ἰησοῦν ὃν ὁ Παῦλος κηρύσσει. 14. ἦσαν
δέ τινες[1] υἱοὶ Σκευᾶ Ἰουδαίου ἀρχιερέως ἑπτὰ οἱ τοῦτο ποιοῦντες.

[1] τινες ℵAHLP, Vulg., Syr. H., so Alford, but Lach., W.H., Weiss,
Blass, Hilg., R.V. after B (D), E 36, 180, Syr. Pesh., Boh., Arm. read τινος (τινες in
connection with the following επτα υιοι is very difficult), υιοι om. after τινες, but
placed by ℵABE 13, 15, 18, 40, Vulg., Arm., after επτα; Meyer follows T.R.
In D, Syr. H. mg. εν οις και υιοι (Syr. H. mg. has υιοι επτα) Σκευα τινος ιερεως
ηθελησαν το αυτο ποιησαι, (οι) εθος ειχαν τους τοιουτους εξορκιζειν. Και
εισελθοντες προς τον δαιμονιζομενον ηρξαντο επικαλεισθαι το ονομα λεγοντες·
παραγγελλομεν σοι εν Ιησου ον Π. κηρυσσει εξελθειν, so Hilg. and so Blass in
β, but with αρχοντος, Gig.[2], instead of ιερεως. Blass considers that this was
orig. both in α and β, then ιερεως was written over αρχοντος, hence ιερεως D,
Syr. H. mg., Gig., and in most αρχιερεως; but why should ιερεως be inserted at
all? No doubt the omission of επτα removes much difficulty. Belser thinks that
the omis. is orig., and argues strongly in favour of β text, pp. 103, 104, so also
Zöckler, and Ramsay, *C. R. E.*, p. 153, speaks of D as giving a reading here which
is intelligent, consistent, and possible. Overbeck conjectured δυο (Gig. has δυο)
instead of επτα with reference to ver. 16, on the ground that the numerical
signs B and Z might be confused, but as Wendt (1888) points out, it is difficult to
explain how a mistake so troublesome for the understanding of the passage could
be perpetuated. The greatest difficulty is to explain how επτα came in if not
original, and it is easy to understand that it might be omitted because of αμφοτερων, ver. 16, see Weiss, Codex D, p. 95.

Ver. 14. See critical note. Σκευᾶ:
probably a Latin name adapted to Greek,
see Blass, *in loco*, who gives instances of
its occurrence, see also *Gram.*, p. 13, and
Winer-Schmeidel, p. 75. Ewald refers
it to the Hebrew שְׁכַבְיָה.—ἀρχ.: the
description is difficult, as it seems incredible if we take it in its strictest sense;
it may have denoted one who had been
at the head of one of the twenty-four
courses of priests in Jerusalem, or perhaps used loosely to denote one who
belonged to the high-priestly families
(*cf.* iv. 6). We cannot connect him with
any special sacred office of the Jews in
Asia Minor, as Nösgen proposes, for the
Jews in the Diaspora had no temple,
but synagogues; see reading in D, critical note. Nothing further is known
of Sceva, but there is no reason to suppose that he was an impostor in the
sense that he pretended to be a high
priest.—ἦσαν . . . ποιοῦντες, Lucan,
see above on i. 10.
Ver. 15. γινώσκω . . . ἐπίσταμαι:
"I know," R.V. for both verbs, but for
the former "I recognise," margin, as a
distinction is drawn between Paul and
Jesus in the formula of adjuration, it is
natural to expect a distinction in the
reply; γιν. probably denotes a more
personal knowledge, ἐπίστ., I know as
of a fact. "Jesus I know and about Paul
I know," Rendall; Lightfoot would render "Jesus I acknowledge and Paul I

know": *On a Fresh Revision of N. T.*
p. 60. Wordsworth also, *in loco*, holds
that ἐπίστ. denotes knowledge of a
lower degree such as acquaintance with
a *fact*, and compares the distinction between the two verbs in Jude ver. 10.
ἐπίστ. is only once used in the Gospels,
Mark xiv. 68. But see also Page, *in
loco*, as to the difficulty in making any
precise distinction.—ὑμεῖς placed first
here in a depreciatory sense, τίνες indicating contempt.
Ver. 16. ἐφαλλόμενος; only here in
N.T.; in LXX, 1 Sam. x. 6, xi. 6, xvi.
13.—κατακυρ.; only here in Luke;
Matt. xx. 25, Mark x. 42, 1 Pet. v. 3;
frequent in LXX.—αὐτῶν, see critical
note. There is no real difficulty if we
read ἀμφοτέρων after ἑπτά, ver. 14; St.
Luke had mentioned that seven of the
sons of Sceva made the attempt to imitate Paul, but the incident which he
describes introduces two of them only.
ἀμφ. cannot be taken distributively, or
with Ewald, neuter, as if = ἀμφοτέρωθεν.
—γυμνοὺς: may mean with torn garments, not literally naked, so Grimm-
Thayer, *sub v.*, and Alford.—ἐκείνου:
the pronoun seems to imply that the
writer had a definite place before his eyes,
although it is not fully described. But it is
surely a mark of truthfulness that the narrative ends where it does; a forger, we
may well believe, would have crowned
the story by a picture of the man, after
baffling the impostors, healed by the word

15. ἀποκριθὲν δὲ τὸ πνεῦμα τὸ πονηρὸν εἶπε, Τὸν [1] Ἰησοῦν γινώσκω, καὶ τὸν Παῦλον ἐπίσταμαι· ὑμεῖς δὲ τίνες ἐστέ; 16. καὶ [2] ἐφαλλόμενος ἐπ' αὐτοὺς ὁ ἄνθρωπος ἐν ᾧ ἦν τὸ πνεῦμα τὸ πονηρόν, καὶ κατακυριεύσας [3] αὐτῶν, ἴσχυσε κατ' αὐτῶν, ὥστε γυμνοὺς καὶ τετραυματισμένους ἐκφυγεῖν ἐκ τοῦ οἴκου ἐκείνου. 17. τοῦτο δὲ ἐγένετο γνωστὸν πᾶσιν Ἰουδαίοις τε καὶ Ἕλλησι τοῖς κατοικοῦσι τὴν Ἔφεσον, καὶ [4] ἐπέπεσε φόβος ἐπὶ πάντας αὐτούς, καὶ ἐμεγαλύνετο τὸ ὄνομα τοῦ Κυρίου Ἰησοῦ. 18. Πολλοί τε τῶν πεπιστευκότων ἤρχοντο ἐξομολογούμενοι

[1] After τον (1), אᶜBE 40, 73, 137, Syr. H. Cass. read μεν [W.H.], so Weiss.

[2] εφαλλ., but εφαλ. א*AB 104, Tisch., W.H., Weiss, Wendt, R.V., Blass in β, but D εναλλομενος.

[3] αμφοτερων (not αυτων), אABD 13, 36, 40, Vulg., Boh., Arm., Tisch., W.H., R.V., Weiss, Wendt, Blass, Hilg.

[4] επεσεν AD, so Hilg., but not Gig. or Blass in β.

or touch of Paul (see Plumptre's remarks, *in loco*). The marked contrast between the New Testament in its description of the demonised and their healing, and the notions and practices which meet us in the Jewish Rabbi, may be seen in Edersheim's valuable appendix, *Jesus the Messiah*, ii., 770 ff., and the same decisive contrast is also seen between the N.T. and the prevailing ideas of the first century in the cures of the demonised attributed to Apollonius of Tyana in this same city Ephesus and in Athens; Smith and Wace, *Dictionary of the Christian Biography*, i., 136. Ramsay is very severe on the whole narrative, *St. Paul*, p. 273, and regards it as a mere piece of current gossip; so, too, very similarly, Wendt (1899), note, p. 313, who refers, as so many have done, to the analogy between the narrative in ver. 11 and that in v. 12, 15; in other words, to the parallel between Peter and Paul (which the writer of Acts is supposed to draw on every possible occasion; see introd.). So too Hilgenfeld ascribes the whole section vv. 11-20 to his "author to Theophilus," and sees in it a story to magnify St. Paul's triumph over sorcery and magic, as St. Peter's over Simon Magus in viii. 13. Clemen with Spitta, Van Manen, and others regard the whole section as interrupting the connection between vv. 10 and 21—but even here, in ver. 14, Clemen sees in addition the hand of his Redactor Antijudaicus, as distinct from the Redactor to whom the whole narrative is otherwise attributed.

Ver. 17. φόβος ἐπέπ.: characteristic phrase in St. Luke; see above on Luke i. 12, and Friedrich, pp. 77, 78.—καὶ

ἐμεγαλύνετο: "continued to be magnified," imperfect, as in Luke vii. 16, praise follows upon fear, Luke xxiii. 47; *cf.* with Matt. xxvii. 54, Friedrich, p. 78.—τὸ ὄνομα 'I. : "jam cuncta illa nomina inania irritaque pro Iesu nomine putabantur" (Blass), see on ver. 19.

Ver. 18. πολλοί τε: the τε shows another immediate result in the fact that those who were already believers were now fully convinced of the pre-eminence of the name of Jesus, and were all the more filled with a reverential fear of His holy name: "many also of those who had believed," R.V. So Wendt in latest edition. — ἤρχοντο *ultro*, Bengel. — ἐξομολ.: Rendall renders "giving thanks" to God for this manifestation of His power. But it is usually taken, not absolutely, but as governing πράξεις, *cf.* Matt. iii. 6, Mark i. 5, James v. 16; Jos., *Ant.*, viii., 4, 6; *B. J.*, v., 10, 5, so in Plutarch several times, "confessing," *cf.* also Clem. Rom., *Cor.*, li., 3; Barn., *Epist.*, xix., 12; Kennedy, *Sources of N. T. Greek*, p. 118, and Mayor on James v. 16; Felten, *Apostelgeschichte*, p. 361.—πράξεις, *cf.* Luke xxiii. 51; also in a bad sense. So too in Rom. viii. 13, Col. iii. 9, so often in Polyb. (3 Macc. i. 27). Deissmann, *Bibelstudien*, p. 5, maintains that the passage before us shows acquaintance with the technical terminology of magic, and instances πράξεις as a *terminus technicus* for a magic prescription; see also Knabenbauer's note *in loco*. — ἀναγγέλλοντες: instead of continuing secretly practising or approving of the deeds of magic, they declared their wrongdoings. Rendall takes it as meaning that they reported the deeds of those men, *i.e.*,

καὶ ἀναγγέλλοντες τὰς πράξεις αὐτῶν.   19. ἱκανοὶ δὲ τῶν τὰ περίεργα
πραξάντων, συνενέγκαντες τὰς βίβλους κατέκαιον ἐνώπιον πάντων·
καὶ συνεψήφισαν τὰς τιμὰς αὐτῶν, καὶ εὗρον ἀργυρίου μυριάδας
πέντε.   20. οὕτω κατὰ κράτος[1] ὁ λόγος τοῦ Κυρίου ηὔξανε καὶ ἴσχυεν.

21. Ὡς δὲ ἐπληρώθη ταῦτα, ἔθετο ὁ Παῦλος ἐν τῷ πνεύματι,
διελθὼν τὴν Μακεδονίαν καὶ Ἀχαΐαν πορεύεσθαι εἰς Ἱερουσαλήμ,
εἰπών, Ὅτι μετὰ τὸ γενέσθαι με ἐκεῖ, δεῖ με καὶ Ῥώμην ἰδεῖν.

---

[1] D has after κρατος, ενισχυσεν και η πιστις του Θεου ηυξανε και επληθυνετο.
Syr. Pesh. has ενισχυεν et crescebat fides Dei (only).   Blass reads ενισχυεν η
πιστις του Θεου και (ηυξανεν και) επληθυνετο.   Weiss, Codex D, p. 96, objects that
Blass omits the και necessary before η πιστ. του Θ., and adds an impossible και
after Θεου.   Belser defends and points out that ενισχυεν is Lucan, only found in
Luke's writings ; but on the other hand, whilst no doubt η πιστις is used objectively
in Acts, we never have η πιστις του Θεου in Luke's writings.

the magicians ; but can the Greek bear this?

Ver. 19. ἱκανοὶ δὲ: to be referred probably to the magicians, as the previous verse refers to their dupes : a Lucan word, see above on viii. 11.—τὰ περίεργα: "curious," Wyclif and A. and R.V. ("magical," R.V., margin), cf. Vulgate, curiosa (Latin, curiosus, inquisitive, prying), of a person who concerns himself with things unnecessary and profitless to the neglect of the duty which lies nearest, cf. 1 Tim. v. 13, 2 Thess. iii. 11, so in classical Greek, Xen., Mem., i., 3, 1. The word is also used of things over and above what is necessary, and so of magical, arts in which a man concerns himself with what has not been given him to know, cf. Aristaenetus, Epist., ii., 18, and the striking passage in Plat., Apol., 19 B, where περιεργά-ζεσθαι is used of Socrates in an accusatory sense (Wendt, Page) ; the verb is found in Ecclesiast. iii. 23, and περιεργασία, Ecclesiast. xli. 22 S[2], but the adjective does not occur either in LXX or Apocrypha.   But see especially Deissmann, Bibelstudien, u. s., who finds here another instance of acquaintance with the terminology of magic, and illustrates from the papyri.   The R.V. margin gives best sense, as "curious" in the passive sense as here need not have a bad or depreciatory meaning, cf. for a good parallel for "curious" = "magical," Bacon, Essays, 35; and see "Curious," Hastings' B.D.; Skeat, Glossary of Bible Words. — συνενέγκαντες: only here in N.T. in this sense, elsewhere frequently, as συμφέρει it is expedient, profitable.— τὰς βίβλους: parchments containing the magical formulæ.   For these Ephesus, with its Ἐφέσια γράμματα worn as amulets and cherished as charms, was famous; "Ephesus" (Ramsay), Hastings' B.D., i., p. 723 ; Wetstein, in loco ; amongst other references, Plut., Sympos., vii., 5 ; Clement of Alex., Strom., v., 8, 46, and also in Renan, Saint Paul, p. 344 ; Blass, in loco ; C. and H., small edition, p. 371 ; and see also Deissmann, Bibelstudien, u. s.—κατέκαιον: imperfect, "describes them as throwing book after book into the burning fire," Hackett, see also Blass, in loco.   Plumptre recalls a parallel scene when the artists and musicians of Florence brought their ornaments, pictures, dresses, and burnt them in the Piazza of St. Mark at the bidding of Savonarola.—συνεψή-φισαν: only here in this sense, not in LXX (cf. i. 26).—ἀργ. μυρ. πέντε, sc., δραχμῶν ἀργ.: the sum is very large, nearly £2000, but probably such books would be expensive, and we must take into account in estimating it the immense trade and rich commerce of Ephesus, and the fact that we need not suppose that all the Christian converts were to be found only amongst the slaves and poorer classes (Nösgen).   Such books would certainly fetch a fancy price.   It may no doubt be maintained that their measuring all things by money value indicates the Oriental popular tale (Ramsay), but may we not see in the statement the knowledge of a writer who thus hits off the Oriental standard of worth, especially in a chapter otherwise so rich and exact in its description of Ephesian localities and life ?

Ver. 20. κατὰ κράτος: adverbial, so only here in N.T., cf. Judg. iv. 3, and Jos., Ant., viii., 11, 3, in classical Greek, Xen., Cyr., i., 4, 23, etc.—ηὔξ. καὶ ἴσ.: in contrast to the empty superstitions and vanities the continuous growth (imperfect) of the Church.

Ver. 21. διελθὼν, see on the force of

22. ἀποστείλας δὲ εἰς τὴν Μακεδονίαν δύο τῶν διακονούντων αὐτῷ, Τιμόθεον καὶ Ἔραστον, αὐτὸς ἐπέσχε χρόνον εἰς τὴν Ἀσίαν. 23. Ἐγένετο δὲ κατὰ τὸν καιρὸν ἐκεῖνον τάραχος οὐκ ὀλίγος περὶ τῆς ὁδοῦ. 24. Δημήτριος γάρ τις [1] ὀνόματι, ἀργυροκόπος, ποιῶν ναοὺς ἀργυροῦς [2] Ἀρτέμιδος, παρείχετο τοῖς τεχνίταις ἐργασίαν οὐκ ὀλίγην ·

[1] ην *pro* ονοματι, so D, Syr. P., Blass, Hilg.

[2] αργυρους *om.* B, Gig. [W.H.], but retained by Blass in β ; παρειχετο ℵBHLP, so W.H., R.V., Weiss, Wendt ; παρειχεν A*DE 65, 67, 133, so Blass in β, who inserts o before παρειχε for ος in D, και in Pesh.

the word Ramsay, *Expositor*, May, 1895, and above on xiii. 6. Ramsay regards this as perhaps the most conclusive of the ten cases he cites of the use of the verb as denoting missionary travel. There is no reason to suppose that Paul paid a visit to Corinth during his stay at Ephesus ; vv. 9, 10 intimate that he resided at Ephesus through the whole period. Wendt thinks that the notice of this second visit to Corinth was omitted by Luke because it did not fit in with his representation of the ideal development of the Church. But is there any real argument to be found for it in the Epistles ? The passages usually quoted are 2 Cor. ii. 1, xii. 14, xiii. 1. But τρίτον τοῦτο ἔρχομαι may well express "I am meaning to come," so that Paul would mean that this was the third time he had purposed to come to them, not that he had come for the third time ; and this rendering is borne out by the Apostle's own words, 2 Cor. xii. 14, Paley, *Horæ Paulinæ*, iv., 11, whilst with regard to 2 Cor. ii. 1 the words may simply mean that he resolves that his new, *i.e.*, his second visit, πάλιν ἐλθεῖν, should not be ἐν λύπῃ, for we are not shut up to the conclusion that πάλιν must be connected with ἐν λύπῃ as if he had already paid one visit in grief ; and this interpretation is at all events in harmony with 2 Cor. xiii. 2, R.V. margin, and with i. 23, R.V., see especially "II. Cor." (Dr. A. Robertson), Hastings' B.D., p. 494, and compare "Corinth" (Ramsay), *ibid.*, p. 483 ; see also Farrar, *Messages of the Books*, pp. 211, 216 ; *St. Paul*, ii. 101, 118 ; Felten, note, p. 364 ; Renan, *Saint Paul*, p. 450, note ; and in favour of the second visit to Corinth, McGiffert, p. 310, following Alford, Neander, Weizsäcker (so too in early days St. Chrysostom). In 1 Cor. xvi. 5-9 Paul speaks of his intention to go through Macedonia to Corinth, but previously, 2 Cor. i. 16, he had intended to sail from Ephesus to Corinth, then to go to Macedonia,

and afterwards to return to Corinth. Why had he changed his plans ? Owing to the bad news from Corinth, 2 Cor. i. 23. But although he did not go to Corinth in person, he determined to write to reprove the Corinthians, and this he did in 1 Cor. It is possible that the Apostle's determination to see Rome— the first notice of the desire so long cherished, Rom. i. 13, xv. 23—may be closely connected with his friendship with Aquila and Priscilla (Ramsay, *St. Paul*, p. 255, and Plumptre, *in loco*, Hort, *Rom. and Ephes.*, p. 11). Ver. 22. ἀποστείλας . . . Τιμ. καὶ Ἐρ., *cf.* 1 Cor. iv. 17, xvi. 10, 11, Paley, *Horæ Paulinæ*, iii., 3, 4 ; McGiffert, *Apostolic Age*, p. 297, note.—διακ. αὐτῷ : for a few instances of διακονεῖν and cognate words used of ministrations rendered to Paul himself, see Hort, *Ecclesia*, p. 205, *cf.* Philem., ver. 13.—Ἔραστον : here, as in 2 Tim. iv. 20, the person bearing this name appears as an itinerant companion of St. Paul, and it therefore seems difficult to identify him with the Erastus of Rom. xvi. 23, who is described as "treasurer" of the city, *i.e.*, Corinth, since the tenure of such an office seems to presuppose a fixed residence. That the identification was not impossible is maintained by Wendt as against Meyer, but see "Erastus," Hastings' B.D. The name, as Meyer remarks, Rom. xvi. 23, was very common.—ἐπέσχε χρόνον : verb, only used by Luke and Paul, and only here in this sense. ἑαυτόν : supplied after the verb ; LXX, Gen. viii. 10, 12 ; in classical Greek, Xen., *Cyr.*, v., 4, 38.— εἰς pro ἐν, Blass ; but see on the other hand, Alford, *in loco*. As Asia, not Ephesus, is mentioned, the word may well include work outside Ephesus itself. Ver. 23. ἐγένετο δὲ : on the frequency of the formula in Luke's writings see Friedrich, p. 13, and above on iv. 5. —τάραχος οὐκ ὀλίγος : the same phrase as in xii. 18, nowhere else in N.T., for οὐκ ὀλίγος as Lucan see above, xii. 18.

25.[1] οὓς συναθροίσας, καὶ τοὺς περὶ τὰ τοιαῦτα ἐργάτας, εἶπεν,
Ἄνδρες, ἐπίστασθε ὅτι ἐκ ταύτης τῆς ἐργασίας ἡ εὐπορία ἡμῶν

[1] Blass (so Hilg.) reconstructs in β text, according to Syr. Pesh., ουτος συνα-
θροισας παντας τους τεχνιτας και τους συνεργατας αυτων εφη προς αυτους; this
was shortened in α, τεχν. and συνεργ. being combined under one word εργαται,
ουτος being still read instead of ους and και omitted; see further Blass, p. vii.,
and in loco. After ανδρες D, Sah., Syr. H. mg. add συντεχνιται, but if original,
it is not easy to see why omitted. For ημων אABDE, Vulg., Sah., Boh., Arm.,
Tisch., W.H., R.V., Weiss, Wendt, Blass, Hilg. read ημιν.

—τῆς ὁδοῦ: as in ix. 2, xix. 9, xxiv. 22;
much better than to refer it with Weiss
merely to the method adopted by Paul in
ver. 26.

Ver. 24. Δημ.: a sufficiently common
name, as St. Luke's words show (Blass).
There is no ground for identifying him
with the Demetrius in 3 John, ver. 12,
except the fact that both came from the
neighbourhood of Ephesus; see, however,
"Demetrius," Hastings' B.D.—ἀργυροκόπος, LXX, Judg. xvii. 4 (A al.), Jer. vi.
29; on the trade-guilds in Asia Minor cf.
Ramsay, Cities and Bishoprics of Phrygia,
i., p. 105, and "Ephesus," Hastings'
B.D.; Church in the Roman Empire, p.
128; Demetrius may have been master of
the guild for the year.—ναοὺς ἀργ. Ἀρτέμιδος: "silver shrines of Diana," R.V.,
i.e., representing the shrine of Diana
(Artemis) with the statue of the goddess within (ὡς κιβώρια μικρά, Chrys.).
These miniature temples were bought up
by Ephesians and strangers alike, since
the worship of the goddess was so widely
spread, and since the "shrines" were
made sufficiently small to be worn as
amulets on journeys, as well as to be
placed as ornaments in houses. There
is no need to suppose that they were
coins with a representation of the temple
stamped upon them, and there is no evidence of the existence of such coins;
Amm. Marc., xxii., 13, Dio Cass., xxxix.,
20, cf. Blass and Wendt, in loco. They
were first explained correctly by Curtius,
Athenische Mittheilungen, ii., 49. Examples of these ναοί in terra-cotta or
marble with dedicatory inscriptions
abound in the neighbourhood of Ephesus.
No examples in silver have been found,
but they were naturally melted down
owing to their intrinsic value, "Diana"
(Ramsay), Hastings' B.D., and Church in
the Roman Empire, u. s. On the interesting but apparently groundless hypothesis
(as Zöckler calls it, Apostelgeschichte, p.
277, second edition) that Demetrius should
be identified with Demetrius, the νεοποιός
of an inscription at Ephesus which pro-

bably dated from a considerably later
time, the very close of the first century,
νεοποιός being really a temple warden, the words νεοποιὸς Ἀρτέμιδος
being mistaken by the author of Acts
and rendered "making silver shrines of
Diana," see Zöckler, u. s.; and Ramsay,
Church in the Roman Empire, p. 112 ff.;
and Wendt (1899), p. 317. As Ramsay
puts it, there is no extant use of such a
phrase as νεοπ. Ἀρτ. in any authority
about A.D. 57, νεοποιοί simply being the
term used in inscriptions found at Ephesus—as Hicks himself allows (Church in
the Roman Empire, pp. 122, 123).—παρείχετο, see critical note or reading in Blass.
Rendall distinguishes between active
voice, xvi. 16, where the slave girl finds
work for her masters, whilst here, middle
voice, Demetrius finds work for himself and
his fellow-craftsmen in their joint employment.—ἐργασίαν "business," R.V., in
xvi. 16, 19, "gain"; here the two meanings run into each other, in ver. 25
"business," R.V., is perhaps more in
accordance with the context οὐκ ὀλίγην,
Lucan, see on ver. 23.—τεχνίταις . . .
ἐργάταις: "alii erant τεχνῖται, artifices
nobiliores; alii ἐργάται, operarii," so
Zöckler and Grimm-Thayer following
Bengel. But Blass regards them as the
same, cf. reading in D, and Ramsay,
Church in the Roman Empire, p. 128,
note. There were no doubt shrines of
widely differing value, for the rich of
silver made by the richer tradesmen, for
the poorer classes of marble and terra-
cotta, so that several trades were no
doubt seriously affected, Ramsay, St.
Paul, p. 278, and "Ephesus," u. s.,
Church in the Roman Empire, p. 128,
and to the same effect Wendt (1899), p.
317. The word ἐργάται occurs in one
of the inscriptions at Ephesus, ἐργ. προ-
πυλεῖται πρὸς τῷ Ποσειδῶνι, "Ephesus,"
u. s., p. 723, note.

Ver. 25. περὶ τὰ τοιαῦτα, cf. Luke
x. 40, 41, for a similar use of περί with
accusative, but see W. H., l. c., and
2 Macc. xii. 1.—εὐπορία: wealth, or gain,

ἐστι· 26. καὶ θεωρεῖτε καὶ ἀκούετε ὅτι οὐ μόνον[1] Ἐφέσου, ἀλλὰ σχεδὸν πάσης τῆς Ἀσίας ὁ Παῦλος οὗτος πείσας μετέστησεν ἱκανὸν ὄχλον, λέγων ὅτι οὐκ εἰσὶ θεοὶ οἱ διὰ χειρῶν γινόμενοι. 27. οὐ μόνον δὲ τοῦτο κινδυνεύει ἡμῖν τὸ μέρος εἰς ἀπελεγμὸν ἐλθεῖν, ἀλλὰ καὶ τὸ τῆς μεγάλης θεᾶς Ἀρτέμιδος ἱερὸν εἰς οὐδὲν[2] λογισθῆναι, μέλλειν τε καὶ καθαιρεῖσθαι τὴν μεγαλειότητα αὐτῆς, ἣν ὅλη ἡ Ἀσία

[1] Before Ἐφέσου D prefixes εως, so Blass in β (comparing xxiii. 23), and Hilg. After ουτος D¹ adds τις ποτε, Gig., "nescio quem," so Blass in β, comparing xvii. 7, where we have the same addition in Gig. and β text.

[2] λογισθηναι ℵBHLP, Chrys., so not only T.R., but Alford, R.V., Weiss, Wendt ; μελλειν ℵA²BD²EHLP, Chrys. ; τε ℵABEP, Sah., Boh., Syrr., P.H., Arm., in both cases R.V., W.H., Weiss, Wendt, as in T.R. Blass following ADE, Vulg. reads in β, λογισθησεται, and μελλει with A*D*, Vulg. But in D the whole passage is confused. την μεγαλειοτητα, but the gen. in ℵABE 13, 15, 18, 40, R.V., W.H., Weiss, Wendt. In β text Blass reads μελλει τε και καθαιρεισθαι η μεγαλειοτης αυτης ην ολη η A. following Gig., Par., Vulg., " sed et destrui incipiet majestas ejus quam," etc. ; D reading " lacunose et corrupte," in the first part : αλλα καθερισθαι μελλει (-ειν Db) η ολη A.

only here in N.T., in classical Greek " in different senses in different authorities," Grimm-Thayer ; in LXX, 2 Kings xxv. 10, but in a different sense (see Hatch and Redpath's references to its use by Aquila, Symm., and others). Rendall takes it of comfort and well-being, in the old English sense *weal*.

Ver. 26. οὐ μόνον . . . ἀλλά: *non modo . . . sed.*—σχεδόν, xiii. 44, we cannot take the genitive with ὄχλον, as Hackett suggests.—Ἀσίας : the Roman province, so Ramsay, *St. Paul*, p. 278, where he corrects his former interpretation of the word in this passage in *Church in the Roman Empire*, p. 166 ; see above on Paul's work outside Ephesus.—οὗτος : contemptuous. — μετέστησεν, *cf.* Josh. xiv. 8. The testimony thus borne to the wide and effective influence of the Apostles even by their enemies is well commented on by St. Chrys., *Hom.*, xlii., and see also below.

Ver. 27. τοῦτο . . . τὸ μέρος, *sc.*, τῆς ἐργασίας ἡμῶν, ver. 25, Grimm-Thayer—this branch of their trade, which was concerned with the making of the shrines. Others take μέρος = *trade*, the part assigned to one.—κινδυνεύει : "the most sensitive part of ' civilised ' man is his pocket," Ramsay, *St. Paul*, p. 277, and the opposition thus naturally came not from the priests as instigators of the riot against Paul, but from the fact that trade connected with the Artemis-worship was endangered ; so at Philippi, " when the masters saw that the hope of this was gone," xvi. 19 ; see Ramsay, *Church in the Roman Empire*, p. 129 ff.,

as against Hicks. " See how wherever there is idolatry, in every case we find money at the bottom of it, both in the former instance it was for money, and in the case of this man for money ; it was not for their religion, because they thought that in danger ; no, it was for their lucrative craft, that it would have nothing to work upon," Chrys., *Hom.*, xlii.—εἰς ἀπελεγμὸν ἐλθεῖν : noun, not found either in classical Greek or in the LXX ; the verb ἀπελέγχειν is found in 4 Macc. ii. 11 (*cf.* Symm., Ps. cxix. 118), and ἐλεγμός is not uncommon in LXX, *confutatio, repudiatio* (for the phrase *cf.* Mark v. 26), *in contemptum venire*, Wetstein ; but *in redargutionem venire*, Vulgate.—ἀλλὰ καί : the utilitarian aspect of the appeal stands first, but speciously seconded by an appeal to religious feelings (" non tam pro aris ipsos quam pro focis pugnare," Calvin).—τῆς μεγ. θεᾶς Ἀ. : St. Luke appears to have retained the precise title of the goddess, according to the witness of the inscription ; " Diana " (Ramsay), Hastings' B.D., p. 605, so Blass, *in loco.*—τὸ . . . ἱερὸν : the Temple of Artemis was burnt to the ground by the fanatic Herostratus in B.C. 356 on the night of the birth of Alexander the Great, but its restoration was effected with great magnificence, and it was regarded as one of the seven wonders of the world. Its dimensions are given by Pliny, xxxvi., 95. For references, and a description of its worship, see C. and H., p. 422, small edition ; Renan, *Saint Paul*, p. 427 ; Ramsay, " Diana," *u. s. ;* Wood's *Ephesus*, pp. 4-

καὶ ἡ οἰκουμένη σέβεται. 28. Ἀκούσαντες δὲ καὶ γενόμενοι πλήρεις
θυμοῦ,[1] ἔκραζον, λέγοντες. Μεγάλη ἡ Ἄρτεμις Ἐφεσίων. 29. καὶ[2]
ἐπλήσθη ἡ πόλις ὅλη συγχύσεως· ὥρμησάν τε ὁμοθυμαδὸν εἰς τὸ
θέατρον, συναρπάσαντες Γάϊον καὶ Ἀρίσταρχον Μακεδόνας, συνεκδή-

[1] After θυμου D 137, Syr. H. mg. add δραμοντες εις την αμφοδον, so Blass,
Hilg. ; see Ramsay, C. R. E., p. 153. Μεγ. η Αρ. om. η D[1], Ramsay emphasises, St.
Paul, p. 274 ; C. R. E., u. s., see note in comment.

[2] After και, β reads after D[1], Gig., Syr. Pesh. συνεχυθη ολη η πολις (αισχυνης) ;
D reads αισχ., which Blass rejects ; apparently for Lat. "confusione," see Blass,
p. xx. ; "confusio," common rendering of αισχυνη, Harris, Study in Codex Bezæ, p.
106 ; D prob. conflate ; see also Corssen, G. G. A., p. 430, 1896. αισχ. = confusio, Phil. iii. 19, Heb. xii. 12.

45 ; Greek Inscrip. at British Museum,
iii., 1890, and for a complete account of
the temple, its structure, and literature
relating to its history and site, B.D.[2],
"Ephesus". So sumptuous was the
magnificence of this sanctuary that it
could be said ὁ τῆς Ἀρτέμιδος ναὸς ἐν
Ἐφέσῳ μόνος ἐστὶ θεῶν οἶκος, Philo Byz.,
Spect. Mund., 7, and the sun, so the saying ran, saw nothing in his course more
magnificent than Diana's temple.—εἰς
οὐδὲν λογ., cf. for a similar phrase LXX,
Isa. xl. 17, Wisdom iii. 17 and ix. 6 (εἰς
om. S[1]), and Dan. Theod., iv., 32. The
verb λογίζομαι is also frequent in St. Paul
with εἰς and the accusative.—τε καὶ, cf.
xxi. 28, not correlative, but : "and that
she should even," etc., Simcox, Language
of the New Testament, p. 163.—τὴν μεγαλειότητα, see critical note, if we read
the genitive, "and that she should even
be deposed from her magnificence," R.V.,
cf. Winer-Schmiedel, xxx., 6. Grimm-
Thayer regards the genitive as partitive,
aliquid de majestate ejus, as if it was inconceivable that all her magnificence
should be lost : so Meyer, Zöckler,
Weiss, cf. Xen., Hellen., iv., 4, 13 ; Diod.
Sic., iv., 8. But Wendt (as against
Meyer) regards τὸ ἱερόν as the subject ;
cf. 1 Tim. vi. 5. The word is used,
Luke ix. 43, of the majesty of God, cf.
2 Pet. i. 16 (Friedrich, p. 30) ; in LXX,
Jer. xl. (xxxiii.) 9 ; 1 Esd. i. 5, iv. 40,
Dan. vii. 27.—ὅλη ἡ Ἀσία : "multitudo
errantium non efficit veritatem": Bengel.
The temple was built by contributions
from the whole of Asia, tota Asia exstru-
ente, Pliny, Nat. Hist., xvi., 40, so that
the goddess was evidently held in venera-
tion by the whole province, cf. ibid.,
xxxvi., 21 ; Liv., i., 45. According to the
testimony of Pausanias, iv., 31, 8 ; cf.
Xen., Anab., v., 3, 4, no deity was more
widely worshipped by private persons
(Wetstein, Ramsay, Blass), see also

Apuleius, 2, quoted by Mr. Page from
Wordsworth. For the way in which the
imperial government allied itself with the
Artemis worship and the revival of
paganism in the second century, and the
universal honour paid to Artemis by
Greek and barbarian alike, cf. Greek
Inscriptions of the British Museum
(Hicks), iii., pp. 135, 145.—οἰκουμένη,
see above on xi. 28. Plumptre points
out that the language is almost identical
with that of Apuleius (perhaps from this
passage) : "Diana Ephesia cujus nomen
unicum . . . totus veneratur orbis".
Ver. 28. ἔκραζον : "they cried continuously," imperfect, see addition in D.
—Μεγάλη ἡ Ἄ. : omitting ἡ we have apparently the popular cry, or rather
invocation : Great Artemis ! as it was
actually used in the cultus—the cry was
not an argument against Paul's doctrine,
but rather a prayer to the goddess and
queen of Ephesus, and so regarded it
gives a vividness and naturalness to the
scene, Ramsay, Church in the Roman
Empire, p. 135 ff., and "Diana," u. s.,
p. 105 ; see D, critical note.
Ver. 29. συγχύσεως : the noun only
here in N.T. (συγχέω : only in Luke,
see above p. 238), in LXX, Gen. xi. 9,
1 Sam. v. 11, 1 Sam. xiv. 20, used in
classical Greek in the sense of confusion,
disturbance ; τε, the immediate result
was that they rushed (Weiss), ὁμοθυμαδὸν,
see above i. 14, "with one accord,"
uno animo, Vulgate (not simul).—τὸ
θέατρον : no doubt the great theatre
explored by Mr. Wood, Ephesus, pp. 73,
74, App. vi. ; Lightfoot, Contemp. Rev.,
xxxii., p. 293 ; the theatre was the usual
place for public assemblies in most towns,
cf. Jos., B. J., vii. 3, 3 ; Tac., Hist., ii., 80 ;
Blass, in loco, and Wetstein, and also
Pseudo-Heraclitus, Letter vii., 47, condemning the Ephesians for submitting
grave and weighty matters to the decision

μους τοῦ Παύλου.   30. τοῦ δὲ Παύλου βουλομένου εἰσελθεῖν εἰς τὸν
δῆμον, οὐκ εἴων αὐτὸν οἱ μαθηταί.   31. τινὲς δὲ καὶ τῶν Ἀσιαρχῶν
ὄντες αὐτῷ φίλοι, πέμψαντες πρὸς αὐτόν, παρεκάλουν μὴ δοῦναι

of the mobs in the theatre, *Die Heraklitischen Briefe*, p. 65; Gore, *Ephesians*, p.
255. The theatre was capable of holding,
it is calculated, 24,500 people, its dia-
meter was 495 feet, and it was probably
the largest in the world (Renan). Wetstein remarks that the position of the
places tended in no small degree to increase and foment the tumult, since the
temple was in full view of the theatre.—
συναρπάσαντες, *cf.* vi. 12, *i.e.*, being
carried off with them in their rush; we
are not told whether they met Gaius and
Aristarchus by chance, and seized them
as well-known companions of Paul,
συνεκδήμους, or whether they searched
for them in their lodgings, and seized
them when they could not find the
Apostle. — Ἀρίσταρχον: a native of
Thessalonica, *cf.* xx. 4; he accompanied
Paul on his last journey to Jerusalem,
and hence to Rome, xxvii. 2. It is
possible, as Lightfoot thinks, that the
words "Aristarchus, a Macedonian of
Thessalonica, being with us" in the
latter passage intimate that Aristarchus
accompanied Luke and Paul on the
former part of this route because he was
on his way home, and that leaving Paul
at Myra he may have returned to Thessalonica, Lightfoot, *Philippians*, p. 35.
But however this may be, it is evident
from Col. iv. 10, Philem., ver. 24, that he
was with the Apostle at Rome, probably
sharing his captivity. ὁ συναιχμάλωτός
μου, Col., *u. s.*, can hardly refer to this
incident at Ephesus, Lightfoot, *Philippians*, p. 11, "Aristarchus," B.D.², or
to a captivity in a spiritual sense, as
bound and captive to Christ together
with Paul; see also Salmon, *Introd.*,
p. 383.—Μακεδόνας: nothing was more
natural than that devoted Christians
from Thessalonica should be among St.
Paul's companions in travel when we
consider his special affection for the
Thessalonian Church. With this reading
the Gaius here is of course to be distinguished from the Gaius of xx. 4, of
Derbe, and from the Gaius of Rom. xvi.
23, 1 Cor. i. 14, a Corinthian. But if we
could read Μακεδόνα, Ramsay, *St. Paul*,
p. 280, the Gaius here may be identified
with the Gaius of xx. 4. In xx. 4 Blass
connects Δερβαῖος with Timothy, making
Gaius a Thessalonian with Aristarchus,
Secundus, see *in loco*; but against this

we must place the positive statement of
xvi. 1, that Timothy was a Lystran.—
συνεκδήμους: used only by Luke and
Paul, 2 Cor. viii. 19, not in LXX, but
in Plut. and Josephus. The word may
look forward to xx. 4 (so Ramsay, *u. s.*),
or we may take it with Blass as referring
to the part which the two men played as
representatives of the Thessalonians, who
were carrying with St. Paul the contribution to the Church at Jerusalem (2 Cor.
ix. 4). These two men, as Weiss points
out, may be our informants for some of
the details which follow.
Ver. 30. τοῦ δὲ Π. βουλ.: St. Paul
was not the man to leave his comrades
in the lurch, and he would have followed
them with his life in his hands to face
the mob of Ephesus; if we may depend
upon the picture of Ephesian life given
us in Pseudo-Heraclitus, Letter vii., we
can understand the imminent danger in
which St. Paul was placed at the mercy
of men who were no longer men but
beasts, ἐξ ἀνθρώπων θηρία γεγονότες
(*Die Heraklitischen Briefe*, p. 65 (Bernays), and Ramsay, *u. s.*, p. 280).—δῆμον,
ver. 33, xii. 22, xvii. 5, so sometimes in
classical Greek of the *plebs*, *vulgus*—in
N.T. only in Acts. Both before and
after the riot the passions of the vulgar
mob were no doubt a real and serious
danger to St. Paul, *cf.* 1 Cor. xv. 32, xvi.
9, 2 Cor. i. 8-10. In the former passage
the word ἐθηριομάχησα is generally referred to this danger in Ephesus, the
multitude in its ferocious rage being
compared to wild beasts, see Ramsay,
St. Paul, p. 230, "Ephesus," Hastings'
B.D., and Plumptre's note, *in loco*. With
the expression used in 1 Cor. xv. 32 we
may compare Ignat., *Rom.*, v., 1, and
cf. Ephes., vii., 1; *Smyrn.*, iv., 1; so too
Pseudo-Heraclitus, *u. s.*, and Renan,
Saint Paul, p. 351, note; Grimm-Thayer,
sub v. McGiffert, p. 280 ff., maintains
that the word ἐθηριομάχησα refers to an
actual conflict with wild beasts in the
arena (so Weizsäcker), and that 2 Cor. i.
9 more probably refers to the danger
from the riot of Demetrius; but if the
literal interpretation of the verb in 1 Cor.
is correct, it is strange that St. Paul
should have omitted such a terrible encounter from his catalogue of dangers in
2 Cor. xi. 23; see also below at end of
chapter.

ἑαυτὸν εἰς τὸ θέατρον.   32. ἄλλοι μὲν οὖν ἄλλο τι ἔκραζον· ἦν γὰρ
ἡ ἐκκλησία συγκεχυμένη, καὶ οἱ πλείους οὐκ ᾔδεισαν τίνος ἔνεκεν
συνεληλύθεισαν.   33. ἐκ δὲ τοῦ ὄχλου [1] προεβίβασαν Ἀλέξανδρον,
προβαλόντων αὐτὸν τῶν Ἰουδαίων· ὁ δὲ Ἀλέξανδρος, κατασείσας

[1] Instead of **προεβίβασαν** ℵABE, Tisch., W.H., Weiss, Wendt, R.V. read
συνεβίβασαν, whilst D²HLP, Chrys. have **προεβ**. (so T.R.).   **προεβ**. adds nothing
to **προβαλλόντων** and the difficulty of **συνεβ**. might easily lead to change. D* reads
κατεβίβασαν, so Blass in both texts, cf. Hilgenfeld, Zw. Th., pp. 364, 366, 1896,
and note in comment.   Gig., Vulg., "detraxerunt".

Ver. 31. **Ἀσιαρχῶν**: "the chief officers
of Asia," R.V., cf. **Γαλατάρχης, Βιθυ-
νιάρχης, Συριάρχης,** etc.; Mommsen,
Röm. Gesch., v., 318 (Knabenbauer),
officers, i.e., of the province of Asia, and so
provincial, not merely municipal officers.
Each province united in an association for
the worship of Rome and the Empire,
hence **Κοινὸν Ἀσίας**, of which the Asiarchs
would probably be the high priests. But
in addition to their religious office the
Asiarchs were called upon to provide
games, partly if not solely at their own
expense, and to preside over them. These
festivals were called **Κοινὰ Ἀσίας ἐν
Σμύρνῃ, Λαοδικείᾳ, κ.τ.λ.** It is doubtful
whether the office was annual, or whether
it was held for four years; but as an
Asiarch still retained his title after his
term of office had expired, there may
evidently have been in Ephesus several
Asiarchs, although only one was actually
performing his duties (cf. the title **ἀρχιερεῖς** amongst the Jews, iv. 6, 23). If
there were a sort of Council of Asiarchs,
this Council may well have assembled
when the **Κοινὰ Ἀσίας** were being held,
and this might have been the case at
Ephesus in the narrative before us; such
a festival would have brought together a
vast crowd of pilgrims and worshippers
actuated with zeal for the goddess, and
ready to side with Demetrius and his
followers. The title was one of great
dignity and repute, as is evident from
inscriptions which commemorate in
various cities the names of those who
had held the office. Whether the Asiarchs
were in any sense high priests has been
disputed, but see Polycarp, Mart., cf.
xii. 2 and xxi.; on the whole subject
"Asiarch" (Ramsay), Hastings' B.D.
and B.D.²; St. Ignatius and St. Polycarp,
ii., p. 987, Lightfoot; Renan, Saint Paul,
p. 353; Wendt, p. 318; O. Holtzmann,
Neutest. Zeitgeschichte, p. 102.—**φίλοι**:
not only does the notice show that St.
Paul had gained at least the toleration of
some of the leading men of the province,

but that the attitude of the imperial
authorities was not unfriendly. We
cannot of course suppose with Zimmer-
mann that the Asiarchs were friendly
because the Apostle had been less opposed to the imperial cultus than to
that of Diana, and that so far the Asiarchs
stood with him on common ground.
See Ramsay, Church in the Roman Empire, on the probable attitude of the
priests, and cf. chap. xiv.—**δοῦναι ἑαυτὸν**:
only here in N.T., cf. Polyb., v., 14, 9,
the expression involves the thought of
danger, so in A. and R.V.
   Ver. 32. **ἄλλοι μὲν οὖν**: **μὲν οὖν** probably as often in Acts without any opposition expressed, but see Rendall, App.,
p. 162; the antithesis may be in **δὲ** of
ver. 33.—**ἔκραζον**: "kept on crying,"
imperfect.—**ἐκκλησία**, see below on ver.
39; here of an unlawful tumultuous assembly.—**συγκεχ.**, see above ver. 29.—
οἱ πλείους: "sensu vere comparativo"
Blass = major pars.
   Ver. 33. **ἐκ δὲ τοῦ ὅ.**, sc., **τινές**, cf.
xxi. 16. If we read **συνεβίβασαν** (see
critical note), and render "instructed
Alexander," R.V., margin; cf. 1 Cor. ii.
16, and often in LXX, it seems to mean
that the Jews instructed Alexander, a
fellow-Jew, to come forward and dissociate himself and them from any coali-
tion with Paul and his companions
against the Diana worship (**ἀπολογεῖσθαι**). Erasmus takes the word to mean
that the Jews had instructed him beforehand as their advocate. **συμβιβάζω** in
Col. ii. 19, Ephes. iv. 16 = to join together, to knit together, in Acts xvi. 10,
to consider, to conclude, so Weiss thinks
here that it = concluded that Alexander
was the reason why they had come together; but the sentence and the context
does not seem to bear out this rendering.
Meyer retains T.R., and holds that Alexander was a Jewish Christian who was
put forward by the Jews maliciously,
hoping that he might be sacrificed to the
popular tumult — hence **ἀπολογεῖσθαι**.

τὴν χεῖρα, ἤθελεν ἀπολογεῖσθαι τῷ δήμῳ. 34. ἐπιγνόντων [1] δὲ ὅτι
Ἰουδαῖός ἐστι, φωνὴ ἐγένετο μία ἐκ πάντων, ὡς ἐπὶ ὥρας δύο κραζόν-
των, Μεγάλη ἡ Ἄρτεμις Ἐφεσίων. 35. Καταστείλας δὲ ὁ γραμματεὺς
τὸν ὄχλον, φησίν, Ἄνδρες Ἐφέσιοι, τίς γάρ ἐστιν ἄνθρωπος ὃς οὐ
γινώσκει τὴν Ἐφεσίων πόλιν νεωκόρον οὖσαν τῆς μεγάλης [2] θεᾶς

[1] Instead of επιγνοντων, אABDEHLP, Tisch., W.H., R.V., Weiss, Wendt, Blass,
Hilg. read επιγνοντες, and instead of κραζοντων (Hilg.), BDEHLP, which Lach.,
W.H., Blass retain in, Tisch., Weiss, Wendt read κραζοντες, following אA.

[2] θεας om. אABDE, so Tisch., W.H., R.V., Weiss, Wendt, Blass, Hilg.

This latter view seems to be adopted practically by Blass (so by Knabenbauer), although he reads κατεβίβασαν (Luke x. 15), descendere coegerunt, i.e., into the theatre, as he cannot see that συνεβίβ. is intelligible; in which Grimm-Thayer agrees with him, and renders with R.V., margin, as above (see sub v.).—ὁ δὲ Ἀ.: if ὁ χαλκεύς in 2 Tim. iv. 14 is taken in a wider sense to mean a worker in any metal, it is, of course, possible that Alexander might be so described as one of the craftsmen of Demetrius. But the name was very common, although the omission of τις may be taken to imply that Alexander in ver. 33 was well known in Ephesus (cf. ver. 9 above). We cannot pass beyond conjecture, especially as the notice in Acts, when compared with 2 Tim., contains no further mark of identification than the similarity of name, although the Alexander in the latter passage was no doubt in some way connected with Ephesus, or the warning to Timothy against him would be without force. Against the identification see Meyer-Weiss, Die Briefe Pauli an Timotheus und Titus, p. 347, and so also Holtzmann, Pastoralbriefe, in loco (who identifies the Alexander in 2 Tim. iv. 14 with the Alexander in 1 Tim. i. 20). Holtzmann's view is that the author of the Pastoral Epistles, whoever he may have been, mistook the notice in Acts, and concluded that the Alexander there mentioned was a Christian, and a treacherous one, who allowed himself to be utilised by the Jews against Paul. The pseudonymous author of 2 Tim. therefore names Alexander χαλκεύς, and refers also to him the βλασφημεῖν of 1 Tim. i. 20.—κατασείσας τὴν χεῖρα, see on xii. 17.—ἀπολ.: peculiar to Luke and Paul, twice in St. Luke's Gospel, and six times in Acts, so in Rom. ii. 15, 2 Cor. xii. 19. In the last-named passage with same construction as here (see for various constructions Grimm-Thayer, sub v.).

Ver. 34. ἐπιγνόντων: "when they recognised" by his dress and his features, "when they perceived," R.V. If we read ἐπιγνόντες, see critical note, φωνὴ ἐγέν. = "anacoluthon luculentissimum" cf. Mark ix. 20 (Blass).—μία ἐκ πάντων: callida junctura, arresting the reader's attention (Hackett). Alexander was thus unable to obtain a hearing because he was a Jew, a fact which sufficiently justifies the apprehension for Paul entertained by his friends.—Μεγάλη κ.τ.λ., see on ver. 28, the cry in B, and β text is doubled, which marks its continuance and its emphatic utterance (Weiss).—ὡς ἐπὶ ὥρας δύο κραζ.: probably they regarded this as in itself an act of worship, cf. 1 Kings xviii. 26, and Ramsay, Church in the Roman Empire, p. 142, "Diana," Hastings' B.D., p. 605. "A childish understanding indeed! as if they were afraid lest their worship should be extinguished, they shouted without intermission:" Chrys., Hom., xlii.

Ver. 35. καταστείλας: only here in N.T. and in ver. 36, "had quieted," R.V., cf. 2 Macc. iv. 31, 3 Macc. vi. 1, Aquila, Ps. lxiv. (lxv.) 8, also in Josephus and Plutarch.—ὁ γραμματεύς: "the secretary of the city" Ramsay; Lightfoot was the first to point out the importance of the officer so named—called also ὁ Ἐφεσίων γραμ. or γραμ. τοῦ δήμου; he was the most influential person in Ephesus, for not only were the decrees to be proposed drafted by him and the Strategoi, and money left to the city was committed to his charge, but as the power of the Ecclesia, the public assembly, declined under imperial rule, the importance of the secretary's office was enhanced, because he was in closer touch with the court of the proconsul than the other city magistrates, and acted as a medium of communication between the imperial and municipal government, "Ephesus" (Ramsay), Hastings' B.D., p. 723, Cities and

Ἀρτέμιδος καὶ τοῦ Διοπετοῦς; 36. ἀναντιρρήτων [1] οὖν ὄντων τούτων,
δέον ἐστὶν ὑμᾶς κατεσταλμένους ὑπάρχειν, καὶ μηδὲν προπετὲς
πράττειν. 37. ἠγάγετε γὰρ τοὺς ἄνδρας τούτους, οὔτε ἱεροσύλους

[1] αναντιρητων B*L, so W.H. (not Weiss).

Bishoprics of Phrygia, i., 66; St. Paul, pp. 281, 304; Hicks, Greek Inscriptions in the British Museum, iii., p. 154, and Wood's Ephesus, App., p. 49, often with Asiarchs and proconsul; Lightfoot, Contemp. Review, p. 294, 1878. St. Luke's picture therefore of the secretary as a man of influence and keenly alive to his responsibility is strikingly in accordance with what we might have expected. — τίς γάρ ἐστιν ἄνθρωπος: "what man is there then?" etc. Rendall: the γάρ looks back to the action of the speaker in quieting the crowd, as if he would say that there is no need for this excitement, for all that you have said about your goddess is universally acknowledged. — νεωκόρον: "temple-keeper," R.V., "a worshipper," A.V., cultricem, Vulgate, lit., "a temple-sweeper" (on derivation see Grimm-Thayer, sub v.), and so found in classical Greek, a sacristan, a verger, Lat., ædituus, cf. Jos., B. J., v., 9, 4, where= worshippers, οὓς ὁ θεὸς ἑαυτῷ νεωκόρους ἦγεν. The title "Warden of the Temple of Ephesus" was a boast of the city, just as other cities boasted of the same title in relation to other deities. It would seem that the title at Ephesus was generally used in connection with the imperial cultus; in the period of this narrative, Ephesus could claim the title as Warden of one Temple of this cultus, and later on she enjoyed the title of δὶς, τρὶς νεωκόρος, as the number of the temples of the imperial cultus increased. But there is ample justification from inscriptions for the mention of the title in the verse before us in connection with the Artemis worship. For references, Ramsay, "Ephesus," Hastings' B.D., p. 722; Cities and Bishoprics of Phrygia, i., 58; Wendt, Blass, in loco; Lightfoot, Cont. Rev., p. 294, 1878; Wood, Ephesus, App., p. 50.—τοῦ Δ., sc., ἄγαλμα: or some such word; the image was believed to have fallen from the sky (heaven, R.V. margin), like that of the Tauric Artemis, cf. Eur., Iph. T., 977, 1384, where we find οὐρανοῦ πέσημα given as the equivalent and explanation of διοπετὲς ἄγαλμα (Herod., i., 11). The worship of Diana of the Ephesians was entirely Asian and not Greek, although the Greek colonists attempted to establish an identification with their own Artemis on account of certain analogies between them. According to Jerome, Præfat. ad Ephesios, the Ephesian Artemis was represented as a figure with many breasts, multimammia ("quam Græci πολύμαστον vocant"), symbolising the reproductive and nutritive powers of Nature which she personified. This description is fully borne out by the common representations of the goddess on coins and statues. No one could say for certain of what the ἄγαλμα was made: according to Petronius it was made of cedar wood, according to Pliny of the wood of the vine, according to Xen. of gold, and according to others of ebony. For a fuller description of the image, and for some account of the wide prevalence of worship of the goddess and its peculiar character, Ramsay, Cities and Bishoprics of Phrygia, "Diana of the Ephesians," Hastings' B.D., B.D.[2]; Wendt, 1888, in loco; Farrar, St. Paul, ii., p. 13, and references in Wetstein.

Ver. 36. ἀναντιρρήτων: only here in N.T., but the adverb in x. 29, not in LXX but Symm., Job xi. 2, xxxiii. 13; Polyb., xxiii., 8, 11; on spelling see critical note.—δέον ἐστὶν, 1 Peter i. 6 (1 Tim. v. 13), cf. Ecclus., Prol., vv. 3, 4, 1 Macc. xii. 11, 2 Macc. xi. 18, also in classical Greek.—προπετὲς: only in Luke and Paul in N.T., 2 Tim. iii. 4, of thoughtless haste (Meyer-Weiss); in LXX of rash talk, cf. Prov. x. 14, xiii. 3, Ecclus. ix. 18, Symm., Eccles. v. 1, Clem. Rom., Cor., i., 1, of persons.—κατεσταλμένους, see also on ver. 35; only in these two verses in N.T.

Ver. 37. γὰρ: "for," i.e., they had done something rash.—τοὺς ἄνδρ. τούτους: Gaius and Aristarchus, ἱεροσύλους, "robbers of temples," R.V., in A.V. "of churches," the word "church" being applied as often in the Elizabethan age to pagan temples. Ramsay however renders "guilty neither in act nor in language of disrespect to our goddess," i.e., to the established religion of our city, ἱεροσυλία = Latin, sacrilegium, and here for emphasis the speaker uses the double term οὔτε ἱεροσ. οὔτε βλασφ., "Churches, Robbers of," Hastings' B.D., Ramsay, and St. Paul, pp. 260, 282, 401.

οὔτε βλασφημοῦντας τὴν[1] θεὰν ὑμῶν. 38. εἰ μὲν οὖν Δημήτριος[2]
καὶ οἱ σὺν αὐτῷ τεχνῖται πρός τινα λόγον ἔχουσιν, ἀγοραῖοι ἄγονται,
καὶ ἀνθύπατοί εἰσιν· ἐγκαλείτωσαν ἀλλήλοις. 39. εἰ δέ τι περὶ

[1] For την θεαν אABD²E*HL, Chrys., so Tisch., W.H., R.V., Weiss, Wendt,
Blass read την θεον, and for υμων אABD, Syr. P., Sah., Arm., Aeth., Tisch., W.H.,
R.V., Blass, Weiss, Wendt read ημων.

[2] After Δημ. D, Syr. Pesh., Ephr., Blass, Hilg. add ουτος.

In 2 Macc. iv. 42 we have the same word
ἱερόσυλος, R.V., "Author of the sacrilege," "Church-robber," A.V., used of
Lysimachus, brother of Menelaus the
high priest, who perished in a riot which
arose from the theft of the sacred vessels
by his brother and himself (quoted by
Ramsay, u. s.). Canon Gore, *Ephesians*,
p. 41, note, however, points out that the
word is used in the former sense of
"robbers of temples," in special connection with Ephesus by Strabo, xiv. 1, 22,
and Pseudo-Heraclitus, Letter vii., p.
64 (Bernays); *cf.* Rom. ii. 22. The cognate noun is found in inscriptions at
Ephesus, describing a crime involving
the heaviest penalties, Wood, *Ephesus*,
vi., 1, p. 14; Lightfoot, *Cont. Rev.*, p.
294, 1878.

Ver. 38. λόγον ἔχουσιν: no exact
equivalent elsewhere in N.T., but Grimm
(so Kypke) compares Matt. v. 32 (see
also Col. iii. 13).—ἀγοραῖοι ἄγονται:
"the courts are open," R.V., perhaps
best to understand σύνοδοι, "court-
meetings are now going on," *i.e.*, for
holding trials (in the forum or agora);
Vulgate, *conventus forenses aguntur*, the
verb being in the present indicative.
Or ἡμέραι may alone be supplied = court
days are kept, *i.e.*, at certain intervals,
not implying at that particular time, but
rather a general statement as in the
words that follow: "there are proconsuls,"
see Page, *in loco*. For ἄγειν, *cf.* Luke
xxiv. 21, Matt. xiv. 6, 2 Macc. ii. 16, *cf.*
Strabo, xiii., p. 932, Latin, *conventus
agere*. Alford, so Wendt (1888), speaks of
the distinction drawn by the old grammarians between ἀγοραῖος and ἀγόραιος
as groundless, but see also Winer-
Schmiedel, p. 69.—ἀνθύπατοί εἰσιν: the
plural is used: "de eo quod nunquam
non esse soleat," Bengel (quoted by Blass
and Wendt), although strictly there would
be only one proconsul at a time. There
is no need to understand any assistants
of the proconsul, as if the description was
meant for them, or, with Lewin, as if there
were several persons with proconsular
power. It is quite possible that in both

clauses the secretary is speaking in a
mere colloquial way, as we might say,
"There are assizes and there are judges".
Lightfoot calls it "a rhetorical plural"
Cont. Rev., p. 295, 1878, and quotes Eur.,
I. T., 1359, κλέπτοντες ἐκ γῆς ξόανα καὶ
θυηπόλους, though there was only one
image and one priestess.—ἐγκαλείτωσαν
ἀλλήλοις: "accuse," R.V. The verb
need not have a technical legal sense as
is implied by "implead" in A.V. So in
LXX it may be used quite generally, or
of a criminal charge, and so in classical
Greek, *cf.* Wisd. xii. 12 and Ecclus.
xlvi. 19. In the N.T. it is used six
times in Acts with reference to judicial
process, and only once elsewhere by St.
Paul in Rom. viii. 33 in a general sense.
The verb only occurs in the second part
of Acts in accordance no doubt with the
subject-matter; see Hawkins, *Horæ Synopticæ*, p. 147, note, and Weiss, *Einleitung
in das N. T.*, p. 570, note.

Ver. 39. εἰ δέ τι περὶ ἑτέρων: if we
read περαιτέρω, *cf.* Plato, *Phædo*, p. 107
B, the meaning is anything further than
an accusation against an individual, a
public and not a personal matter: if
they desired to get any resolution passed
with regard to the future conduct of citizens and of resident non-citizens in this
matter, see Ramsay, *Expositor*, February,
1896, reading περαιτ.—ἐπιλυθήσεται (*cf.*
Mark iv. 34), nowhere else in N.T. the
verb is found in LXX, Aquila, Gen. xl. 8,
xli. 8, 12; Th., Hos., iii. 4; Philo., Jos.).
—τῇ ἐννόμῳ ἐκκλησίᾳ: "the regular
assembly," R.V. Mr. Wood, *Ephesus,
App.*, p. 38, quotes an inscription in
which it was enjoined that a statue of
Minerva should be placed in a certain
spot, κατὰ πᾶσαν ἔννομον ἐκκλησίαν.
But A.V. has "the lawful assembly":
which is the better rendering? "regular"
seems to restrict us to νόμιμοι ἐκκλησίαι held on stated customary days,
and to exclude from the secretary's
statement any reference to extraordinary
meetings, meetings summoned for special
business, whereas he would be likely to
use a term which would cover all legal

ἐτέρων[1] ἐπιζητεῖτε, ἐν τῇ ἐννόμῳ ἐκκλησίᾳ ἐπιλυθήσεται. 40. καὶ
γὰρ κινδυνεύομεν[2] ἐγκαλεῖσθαι στάσεως περὶ τῆς σήμερον, μηδενὸς
αἰτίου ὑπάρχοντος περὶ οὗ δυνησόμεθα ἀποδοῦναι λόγον τῆς συστροφῆς ταύτης. 41. Καὶ ταῦτα εἰπὼν ἀπέλυσε τὴν ἐκκλησίαν.

[1] περι ετερων, so ℵADHLP, so Tisch., R.V., Hilg., but B (d Gig., Vulg.), so
Lach., W.H., Blass, Weiss, Wendt have περαιτερω, see further Harris, *Four Lectures*, p. 29, on Ephrem's text. The περι ετερων is the correction of a word not
found elsewhere in N.T. (so Wendt, p. 320 (1899)). E has περ ετερον.

[2] D has σημερον εγκαλεισθαι στασεως, *argui seditionis hodiernæ*, Vulg., *accusari
quasi seditiosi hodie*, Gig., but these look like paraphrases. περι ου ου in W.H.
and R.V. is supported by ℵBHLP, Syrr., P.H., Arm., Chrys.; and after λογον
the addition of περι is supported by ℵBE, Arm., so Tisch., W.H., R.V., Weiss,
Wendt. DE omit negative ου, and περι after λογον is omitted by D*HLP d,
so T.R. (Meyer and Lach.), Hilg. and Blass in both texts; see Wendt (1899), note
p. 321. W.H., see *App.*, p. 97, thinks some primitive error probable, perhaps
αιτιοι υπαρχοντες instead of αιτιου υπαρχοντος. D has οντος instead of υπαρ.,
so Blass in β.

meetings. But on the other hand
Blass quotes the phrase given above
from the inscriptions, and explains
ἔννομοι ἐκκλησίαι *sunt, quæ ex lege certis
diebus fiebant* (so too Wendt, Lightfoot); and if this is correct, " regular "
would be the more appropriate rendering,
ἔννομος = νόμιμος. But in Ephesus we
have to consider how far the old Greek
assembly ἐκκλησία was or was not under
the control of the imperial government.
In considering this with reference to the
special incident before us, Ramsay, with
whom Wendt agrees, p. 321 (1899),
gives good reason for regarding the
" regular " as equivalent to the " lawful " assemblies : *i.e.*, extraordinary assemblies which in the Greek period had
been legal, but were now so no longer
through the jealous desire of Rome to
control popular assemblies, abroad as at
home. The ἐκκλησία could not be
summoned without the leave of the
Roman officials, and it was not at all
likely that that sanction would be extended beyond a certain fixed and regular
number, Ramsay, *Expositor*, February,
1896: " The Lawful Assembly," and
" Ephesus," Hastings' B.D., p. 723.

Ver. 40. ἐγκαλεῖσθαι στάσεως περὶ
τῆς σήμερον, A.V., " to be called in question for this day's uproar," but R.V., " to
be accused concerning this day's riot,"
rendering ἐγκαλ., as in ver. 38, and
στάσεως, as in Mark xv. 7. θόρυβος
being rather the word for uproar or
tumult, *cf.* Vulgate: " argui seditionis
hodiernæ ". But a further question
arises from the marginal rendering of
R.V., " to be accused of riot concerning
this day ": so Page, Meyer-Wendt, Zöck-

ler. But Blass, Weiss, Rendall, so Ramsay: " to be accused of riot concerning
this day's assembly," *sc.*, ἐκκλησία, although Blass thinks it still better to omit
περὶ τῆς altogether, and to connect
σήμερον with ἐγκαλ., *cf.* iv. 9.—μηδενὸς
αἰτίου ὑπάρχοντος : with this punctuation
R.V. renders " there being no cause *for
it*," taking αἰτίου as neuter, and closely
connecting the phrase with the foregoing,
so W.H. Overbeck (so Felten, Rendall)
takes αἰτίου as masculine : " there being
no man guilty by reason of whom," etc.,
and Wendt considers that the rendering
cannot be altogether excluded. Vulgate
has " cum nullus obnoxius sit ". But
αἰτίου may be strictly a noun neuter
from αἴτιον = αἰτία, and not an adjective as the last-mentioned rendering
demands, *cf.* Plummer on Luke xxiii. 4,
14, 22, and nowhere else in N.T., so
Moulton and Geden, who give the adjective αἴτιος only in Heb. v. 9.—περὶ
οὗ δυνησόμεθα : Ramsay (so Meyer and
Zöckler) follows T.R. and Bezan text in
omitting the negative οὐ before δυν., but
see on the other hand Wendt (1899), p.
322; and critical note. R.V. (introducing
negative οὐ, so Weiss and Wendt) renders " and as touching it we shall not be
able to give account of this concourse ".
—συστροφῆς, Polyb., iv., 34, 6, of a
seditious meeting or mob. In xxiii. 12
used of a conspiracy; *cf.* LXX, Ps. lxiii.
2, Amos vii. 10.

Ver. 41. τὴν ἐκκλησίαν : the word
may imply, as Ramsay thinks, that the
secretary thus recognised the meeting as
an ἐκκλησία to shield it, as far as he
could, from Roman censure. The attitude of the secretary is that of a man

XX. I. ΜΕΤΑ δὲ τὸ παύσασθαι τὸν θόρυβον,[1] προσκαλεσάμενος ὁ
Παῦλος τοὺς μαθητὰς καὶ ἀσπασάμενος ἐξῆλθε πορευθῆναι εἰς τὴν
Μακεδονίαν.　2. διελθὼν δὲ τὰ μέρη ἐκεῖνα, καὶ [2] παρακαλέσας αὐτοὺς

---

[1] For προσκαλ. אBE, Sah., Boh., Aethro., so Tisch., W.H., R.V., Wendt, Weiss,
Blass read μετακαλ.; Lach. follows T.R. according to ADHLP, Chrys. After και
AB 13, 33, Boh. add παρακαλεσας (και παρακ. και ασπασ. אE), Tisch., W.H.,
R.V., Wendt, Weiss; T.R., so Meyer, om. παρακαλ. D, Gig. read εξηλθεν εις
Μακεδ., so Blass in β.

[2] παρακαλ. χρησαμενος λ. π., so D (and Blass in β) om. αυτους.

altogether superior to, and almost contemptuous of, the vulgar mob (cf. οὗτος
in D, ver. 38), and there is no apparent
desire on his part to deny Paul's right to
preach, provided that the Apostle respected the laws and institutions of the
city.

On the historical character of the incidents narrated at Ephesus, the graphic
description and the intimate knowledge
of the life of the city, see Ramsay,
Church in the Roman Empire, p. 143,
and the same writer "Ephesus," Hastings' B.D. Every detail tends to confirm
the faithfulness of the picture drawn of
Ephesian society A.D. 57 (cf. Knabenbauer, p. 340). Wendt also is so impressed with the vividness of the scene
as it is narrated, that he considers that we
are justified in referring the narrative to
a source which we owe to an actual
companion of St. Paul, and in regarding
it as an historical episode, and he refers
in justification to Lightfoot, *Cont. Rev.*,
p. 292 ff., 1878; see Wendt's edition,
1888, pp. 429, 430, and also edition
1899, p. 316, note. Whilst Baur and
Overbeck give an unfavourable verdict
as to the historical truthfulness of the
Ephesian tumult, a verdict which Wendt
condemns, Zeller is constrained to acknowledge the very minute details
which tell in favour of the narrative, and
for the invention of which there is no
apparent reason. Amongst more recent
critics, Weizsäcker can only see in the
story the historian's defence of Paul and
the same tendency to make events issue
in the success of his missionary propa-
ganda: I Cor. xv. 32 he takes literally,
and the tumult recorded in Acts gives us
only a faint and shadowy outline of
actual reminiscences: nothing is left of
the wild beasts except a tumult in the
theatre, and the Apostle against whom
the violence is mainly directed is himself
absent. But as Wendt rightly maintains,
I Cor. xv. 32 is much rather to be taken
as referring figuratively to a struggle
with men raging against the Apostle's

life; nor are we shut up of necessity to
the conclusion that I Cor. xv. 32 and
Acts xix. 23 ff. refer to one and the same
event (so Hilgenfeld, Zöckler), see note
on p. 414. McGiffert, whilst taking I
Cor. xv. 32 literally (although he inclines
to identify Acts xix. with 2 Cor. i. 8, so too
Hilgenfeld), admits as against Weizsäcker
the general trustworthiness of St. Luke's
account, since it is too true to life, and is
related too vividly to admit any doubt as
to its historic reality (p. 282). Hilgenfeld
too, *Zw. Th.*, p. 363, 1896, agrees that
the whole narrative is related in a way
true to life, and refers it with the possible
exception of ὡς ἐπὶ ὥρας δύο in ver. 34
to his good source C: it could not possibly have been invented by the "author
to Theophilus". Even here Clemen and
Jüngst can only see an interpolation,
referred by the former to Redactor, i.e.,
vv. 15-41 with the possible exception of
ver. 33 to Redactor Antijudaicus; and by
the latter also to his Redactor, i.e., vv.
23-41.

CHAPTER XX.—Ver. I. μετὰ δὲ τὸ
παύσ.: the words may indicate not only
the fact of the cessation of the tumult,
but that Paul felt that the time for departure had come.—θόρ., cf. Matt. xxvi.
5, xxvii. 24, Mark xiv. 2; three times
in Acts, xxi. 34, xxiv. 18, and several
times in LXX. In xxi. 34 it is used more
as in classics of the confused noise of an
assembly (cf. Mark v. 38), but in the
text it seems to cover the whole riot, and
may be translated "riot". — ἀσπασάμενος: " non solum salutabant osculo
advenientes verum etiam discessuri,"
Wetstein, and references; so in classical
Greek, cf. also xxi. 6, 7, 19.

Ver. 2. διελθὼν δὲ, see above on xiii.
6, " and when he had gone through," in a
missionary progress τὰ μέρη ἐκεῖνα, i.e.,
of Macedonia, the places where he had
founded Churches, Thessalonica, Berœa,
Philippi. From Rom. xv. 19 it would
appear that his work continued some
time, and that round about even unto
Illyricum he fully preached the Gospel.

λόγῳ πολλῷ, ἦλθεν εἰς τὴν Ἑλλάδα · 3. ποιήσας τε μῆνας τρεῖς,
γενομένης αὐτῷ ἐπιβουλῆς ὑπὸ τῶν Ἰουδαίων¹ μέλλοντι ἀνάγεσθαι εἰς

¹ D, Syr. H. mg., Ephr. read after Ιουδαιων ηθελησεν αναχθηναι εις Σ., which
gives rather a different idea, viz., that a plot of the Jews induced Paul to leave
Corinth (so Belser, p. 108; Hilgenfeld also adopts, Zw. Th., 1896, p. 368); but Blass
transposes the clauses and reads in β: ποιη. τε μ. τ. ηθελ. αναχθηναι εις Σ. και
γεννθεισης αυτω επιβουλης υπο των Ι.; see as against this transposition by Blass,
Wendt (1899), p. 50. For εγενετο γνωμης του υπο. D, Syr. H. mg., Gig. read ειπεν
δε το πνευμα. Blass omits δε in β, and so the antithesis is not maintained. Weiss,
p. 98 (note), condemns Blass for making ειπεν το πν. the equivalent of εγεν. γνωμης,
whilst in xix. 1 a distinction is decisively drawn between the ιδια βουλη (= γνωμη)
of the Apostle and the guidance of the Spirit. γνωμη, but gen. γνωμης is read by
ℵAB*E 13, 15, 18, Tisch., W.H., R.V., Weiss, Wendt.

On the connection of 2 Cor. with this
part of Acts, see " II. Corinthians "
(Robertson), Hastings' B.D., i., pp. 493,
495; Ramsay, St. Paul, p. 286; and on the
coincidence between Acts and Romans,
l. c., see Paley, Horæ Paulinæ, ii., 4.—τὴν
Ἑλλάδα, i.e., Achaia in its Roman sense
(approximately at all events); the stay
might have included a visit to Athens,
but at all events Corinth was visited. A
wider sense of the epithet "Greek"
would comprise Macedonia also, and
Macedonia and Achaia are thus spoken
of in close connection as forming the
Greek lands in Europe, cf. xix. 21, and
Rom. xv. 26, 2 Cor. ix. 2, 1 Thess. i. 8,
"Achaia" (Ramsay), Hastings' B.D.
Ver. 3. ποιήσας τε μῆνας τρεῖς, cf.
xv. 33, xviii. 23.—ἐπιβουλῆς: only here
in Acts in N.T., see above on ix. 24; the
plot may have been formed in the anticipation that it would be easy to carry it
through on a pilgrim ship crowded with
Jews of Corinth and Asia, hostile to the
Apostle; or it may have been the purpose of the conspirators to kill Paul in a
crowded harbour like Cenchreæ before
the ship actually started.—μέλλ. ἀνάγ.,
see on xiii. 13. If we read ἐγέν. γνώμης
(genitive) (cf. 2 Peter i. 20), nowhere else
in N.T., cf. Thuc., i., 113, ὅσοι τῆς αὐτῆς
γνώμης ἦσαν, see also Winer-Schmiedel,
p. 269.—τοῦ ὑποσ., i.e., the return journey to Jerusalem (Ramsay), but see also
Wendt (1899), p. 323.
Ver. 4. συνείπετο δὲ αὐτῷ: only here
in N.T., cf. 2 Macc. xv. 2, 3 Macc. v. 48,
vi. 21, but frequent in classics.—ἄχρι
τῆς Ἀ.: among more recent writers
Rendall has argued strongly for the retention of the words, whilst he maintains,
nevertheless, that all the companions of
the Apostle named here accompanied
him to Jerusalem. In his view the
words are an antithesis to Ἀσιανοὶ δέ,
so that whilst on the one hand one party,
viz., six of the deputies, travel with Paul

to Philippi, on the other hand the
other party consisting of two, viz., the
Asian representatives, waited for them at
Troas. At Philippi the six deputies and
Paul were joined by St. Luke, who henceforth speaks of the deputation in the first
person plural, and identifies himself with
its members as a colleague. Then from
Troas the whole party proceed to Jerusalem (Acts, pp. 119, 303). In this way
οὗτοι in ver. 5 is restricted to Tychicus
and Trophimus (see also Ramsay, as
below), whereas A. and R.V. refer the
pronoun to all the deputies, so too Weiss
and Wendt. If this is so, the ἡμᾶς, ver.
5, might refer (but see further below)
only to Paul and Luke, as the latter
would naturally rejoin Paul at Philippi
where we left him, cf. xvi. 17. Ramsay
explains (St. Paul, p. 287) that the
discovery of the Jewish plot altered
St. Paul's plan, and that too at the
last moment, when delegates from the
Churches had already assembled. The
European delegates were to sail from
Corinth, and the Asian from Ephesus,
but the latter having received word of
the change of plan went as far as Troas
to meet the others, οὗτοι thus referring
to Tychicus and Trophimus alone (but
see also Askwith, Epistle to the Galatians (1899), pp. 94, 95).
Wendt also favours retention of ἄχρι
τῆς Ἀ. and prefers the reading προσελθόντες, but he takes ἡμᾶς in ver. 5 to
exclude St. Paul, and refers it to other
friends of the Apostle (as distinct from
those who accompanied him through
Macedonia "as far as Asia"), viz., the
author of the " We " sections and others
who only now meet the Apostle and his
company at Troas. But this obliges us to
make a somewhat artificial distinction between ἡμᾶς in ver. 5 with ἡμεῖς in ver. 6,
and ἐξεπ. and ἤλθομεν on the one hand,
and διετρίψαμεν, ver. 6, on the other, as
the latter must be taken to include St.

τὴν Συρίαν, ἐγένετο γνώμη τοῦ ὑποστρέφειν διὰ Μακεδονίας. 4.
συνείπετο δὲ αὐτῷ¹ ἄχρι τῆς Ἀσίας² Σώπατρος³ Βεροιαῖος . Θεσσα-

¹ συνειπετο δε αυτω, Blass follows D and also inserts προηρχοντο, whilst D omits verb altogether, Syr. H. mg. reads συνειποντο. Apparently D takes μεχρι της Α. with εξιεναι, and the names may have been taken with προηρχοντο if Blass is right in regarding this as original; see his *Proleg.*, p. 27.

² αχρι της Ασιας *om.* ℵB 13, Vulg., Sah., Boh., Aethpp., so Tisch., W.H. text, R.V. marg., Weiss; but retained ADEHLP, Syr. P. and H., Arm., Chrys.; (Gig., Wer.) Blass in β (μεχρι); see also W.H., *App.*, p. 97. Wendt also considers that it is probably to be retained, see note in comment.; *cf.* προελθ., *u. s.*

³ After Σωπατρος ℵABDE, Vulg., Boh., Syr. H. mg., Arm., Origint., so Tisch., Alford, W.H., R.V., Weiss, Wendt, Blass add Πυρρου.

Paul, St. Luke, and the whole company, although Wendt justifies the distinction by pointing out that in ver. 13 ἡμεῖς is used exclusive of Paul (*cf.* xxi. 12).

Mr. Askwith, *u. s.*, p. 93 ff., has recently argued that ἡμεῖς in ver. 6 includes not only St. Luke and St. Paul, but with them the representatives of Achaia (who are not mentioned by name with the other deputies) who would naturally be with St. Paul on his return from Corinth, vv. 2, 3, and he would not travel through Macedonia unaccompanied. In 2 Cor. viii. St. Luke, "the brother," according to tradition, whose praise in the Gospel was spread through all the Churches, had been sent to Corinth with Titus and another "brother," and so naturally any representatives from Achaia would come along with them, pp. 93, 94. No names are given because St. Luke himself was amongst them, and he never mentions his own name, p. 96. The fact that Timothy and Sopater who had been with the Apostle at Corinth when he wrote to the Romans (chap. xvi. 21, if we may identify Σωσίπατρος with the Σώπατρος Πύρρου Βεροιαῖος, Acts xx. 4) are amongst those who waited at Troas is accounted for on the supposition that Timothy and others might naturally go across to inform the Asiatic delegates of Paul's change of plan, and would then proceed with these Asian representatives to Troas to meet the Apostle (p. 94). The presence of Aristarchus and Secundus at Troas is accounted for on the ground that St. Paul, on his way to Achaia, did not expect to return through Macedonia, and so would naturally arrange for the Macedonian delegates, who were not accompanying him into Greece, to meet him somewhere. And the delegates from Thessalonica would naturally cross to Troas with the intention of proceeding to Ephesus (or Miletus), where St. Paul would have touched even if he had sailed

for Palestine from Cenchreæ (*cf.* Acts xviii. 18, 19), p. 95. But against this it may be fairly urged that there is no reason to assume that the Macedonian delegates did *not* accompany Paul into Greece; Timothy and Sosipater had evidently done so, and all the delegates mentioned seem to have been together in St. Paul's company, συνείπετο αὐτῷ, ver. 4. In the uncertain state of the text it is difficult to come to any decision on the passage. The words ἄχρι τῆς Ἀσίας may easily have been omitted on account of the supposed difficulty connected with the fact that two at least of St. Paul's companions who are named, Trophimus and Aristarchus, went further than Asia, *cf.* xxi. 29, xxvii. 2, while on the other hand it is somewhat hard to believe that the words could be inserted by a later hand.

On "The Pauline Collection for the Saints and its importance," and the representatives of the Churches in the different provinces, see Rendall, *Expositor*, November, 1893; Ramsay, *St. Paul*, p. 287, and "Corinth," Hastings' B.D.; Wendt, p. 325 (1899); Hort, *Rom.* and *Ephes.*, pp. 39 ff. and 173. Nothing could more clearly show the immense importance which St. Paul attached to this contribution for the poor saints than the fact that he was ready to present in person at Jerusalem the members of the deputation and their joint offerings, and that too at a time when his presence in the capital was full of danger, and after he had been expressly warned of the peril, *cf.* Acts. xxiv. 17, Rom. xv. 25. On the suggestion for the fund and its consummation see 1 Cor. xvi. 1-8, Acts xx. 16, 2 Cor. viii. 10, ix. 2; A.D. 57-58, Rendall, Lightfoot; 56-57, Ramsay. Such a scheme would not only unite all the Gentile Churches in one holy bond of faith and charity, but it would mark their solidarity with the Mother Church

λονικέων δὲ Ἀρίσταρχος καὶ Σέκουνδος,[1] καὶ Γάϊος Δερβαῖος καὶ
Τιμόθεος[2]· Ἀσιανοὶ δέ, Τυχικὸς καὶ Τρόφιμος. 5.[3] οὗτοι προελθόντες
ἔμενον ἡμᾶς ἐν Τρωάδι· 6. ἡμεῖς δὲ ἐξεπλεύσαμεν μετὰ τὰς ἡμέρας
τῶν ἀζύμων ἀπὸ Φιλίππων, καὶ ἤλθομεν πρὸς αὐτοὺς εἰς τὴν Τρωάδα

[1] καὶ Γαιος Δ., Blass reads Δερβαιος δε Τιμοθεος, but against this we have the
"insurmountable" statement in xvi. 1, so Ramsay, p. 280, so too Wendt (1899),
p. 323.

[2] Ασιανοι, D, Syr. H. mg. read Εφεσιοι, so Blass; Wendt approves; see Ramsay, C. R. E., p. 154.

[3] ουτοι, add δε ℵABE, Boh., Syr. H., Tisch., W.H., R.V., Weiss, Wendt; omit
Blass, with DHLP, Vulg., Gig. προελθοντες, this reading of T.R. is retained by
Lach., Tisch., Weiss, R.V., W.H. mg.; Blass in text following B³D; and it corresponds
with the omission of αχρι της A. in ver. 4 and the view that Paul was included in
the ημας of ver. 5. If, however, the words αχρι της A. are retained, Wendt argues
that προσελθοντες is quite intelligible, and that this verb, which he regards as best supported, ℵAB*EHLP [so W.H.], becomes thus an indirect confirmation of the former
disputed words in ver. 4. According to Wendt's view Paul is not included in the
ημας of ver. 5, but the ημας refers to the writer of the "We" sections with one or
two companions who had not journeyed with Paul through Macedonia to Asia, but
only met him in Troas. But a difficulty connected with Wendt's solution would
seem to lie in the fact that he is obliged to refer the ημεις in ver. 6 only to the writer
of the "We" sections and those with him, whilst the first person in διετριψαμεν
includes Paul and his party who have been hitherto excluded from the ημεις and
ημας. After εμενον D reads αυτον, so Blass in β, thus plainly separating Paul from
the ουτοι.

at Jerusalem; it would be a splendid
fulfilment by their own generous and
loyal effort of the truth that if one member of the body suffered all the members
suffered with it. We know how this
vision which St. Paul had before his
eyes of a universal brotherhood throughout the Christian world seemed to tarry;
and we may understand something of
the joy which filled his heart, even amidst
his farewell to the elders at Miletus, as
he anticipated without misgiving the
accomplishment of this διακονία to the
saints, a "ministry" which he had received from the Lord Jesus, Acts xx. 24.
On the coincidence between the narrative
of the Acts cf. xx. 2, 3, xxiv. 17-19, and
the notices in St. Paul's Epistles given
above, see especially Paley, Horæ
Paulinæ, chap. ii., 1.—Σώπατρος Πύρρου
Β., see critical note; whether he is the
same as the Sopater of Rom. xvi. 21 who
was with St. Paul at Corinth we cannot
say—possibly the name of his father may
be introduced to distinguish him, but
perhaps, as Blass says, added in this one
case "quod domi nobilis erat".—Γάϊος
Δ. καὶ Τ., see above on p. 414, and
Knabenbauer's note as against Blass.—
Τυχικὸς: Ephes. vi. 21, Col. iv. 7 show
that Timothy was in Rome at the time
of St. Paul's first imprisonment. He is
spoken of as a beloved and faithful

minister, and it would appear that as St.
Paul was about to send him to Ephesus,
he was presumably the bearer of the
Epistle which at all events included the
Ephesian Church. In Tit. iii. 12 we
have another reference which shows the
high place Timothy occupied amongst
St. Paul's trusted confidential friends,
and from 2 Tim. iv. 12 we learn that he
had been a sharer in the Apostle's second
and heavier captivity, and had only left
him to fulfil another mission to Ephesus.
—Τρόφιμος: probably like Tychicus an
Ephesian. In xxi. 29 he was with St.
Paul at Jerusalem, and from 2 Tim. iv.
20 we learn that he was at a later stage
the companion of the Apostle after his
release from his first imprisonment, and
that he had been left by him at Miletus
sick. On the absurd attempt to connect
this notice of Miletus in the Pastoral
Epistles with Acts xx. 4 see Weiss, Die
Briefe Pauli an Timotheus und Titus,
p. 354; Salmon, Introd., fifth edition, p.
401.
Ver. 5. προελθόντες, see critical note.
If we read προσελ. render as in R.V.
(margin), "these came, and were waiting
for us at Troas," cf. Ramsay, St. Paul,
p. 287, and Rendall, in loco.—ἡμᾶς: the
introduction of the word is fatal to the
idea that Timothy could have been the
author of this "We" section.

ἄχρις [1] ἡμερῶν πέντε, οὖ διετρίψαμεν ἡμέρας ἑπτά. 7. Ἐν δὲ τῇ μιᾷ τῶν σαββάτων, συνηγμένων [2] τῶν μαθητῶν τοῦ κλάσαι ἄρτον, ὁ Παῦλος διελέγετο αὐτοῖς, μέλλων ἐξιέναι τῇ ἐπαύριον, παρέτεινέ τε τὸν λόγον μέχρι μεσονυκτίου · 8. ἦσαν δὲ [3] λαμπάδες ἱκαναὶ ἐν τῷ ὑπερῴῳ οὖ

[1] D has πεμπταιοι instead of αχ. η. π., so Blass in β. It may be simply explanatory of the difficult αχ. η. π. (Weiss).

[2] τῶν μαθητῶν, according to ℵABDE, Tisch., W.H., R.V., Weiss, Wendt, Blass ημων.

[3] λαμπαδες, D (not Blass in β) reads υπολαμπαδες. According to *Phylarch. ap. Ath.* υπολ. seems to be a sort of window or look-out (L. and S., edit. 7). This reading is suggestive, but Blass is of opinion that υπολ. "nusquam exstat".

Ver. 6. μετὰ τὰς ἡμ. τῶν ἀ., *cf.* xii. 3, *i.e.*, the Passover. 1 Cor. v. 7 shows us how they would "keep the Feast". Ramsay's "fixed date in the life of St. Paul," *Expositor*, May, 1896, depends partly on the assumption that Paul left Philippi the very first day after the close of the Paschal week, but we cannot be sure of this, see Wendt's criticism on Ramsay's view, p. 326, edition 1899, and also Dr. Robertson "I. Corinthians" Hastings' B.D., p. 485.— ἄχρις ἡμ. πέντε : "in five days," *i.e.*, the journey lasted until the fifth day, so D πεμπταῖοι, *cf.* δευτεραῖοι, xxviii. 13. In xvi. 11 the journey only lasted two (three?) days, but here probably adverse winds must be taken into account; or the five days may include a delay at Neapolis, the port of Philippi, or the land journey to the port; on ἄχρις see above i. 2. —ἡμέρας ἑπτά, so as to include a whole week, and so the first day of the week, *cf.* 2 Cor. ii. 12, 13, which shows how reluctantly Paul left Troas on his former visit, but see on the other hand, Ramsay, *St. Paul*, p. 295, who thinks that St. Paul would not have voluntarily stayed seven days at Troas. Ver. 7. τῇ μιᾷ τῶν σ., "on the first day of the week," μιᾷ being used, the cardinal for the ordinal πρῶτος, like Hebrew אֶחָד, in enumerating the days of the month, see Plummer's note on Luke xxiv. 1 and *cf.* xviii. 12 (so Blass). We must remember that 1 Cor. had been previously written, and that the reference in 1 Cor. xvi. 2 to "the first day of the week" for the collection of alms naturally connects itself with the statement here in proof that this day had been marked out by the Christian Church as a special day for public worship, and for "the breaking of the bread". On the significance of this selection of the "first day," see Milligan, *Resurrection*,

pp. 67-69; Maclear, *Evidential Value of the Lord's Day*, "Present Day Tracts" 54; and for other references, *Witness of the Epistles*, pp. 368, 369; Wendt (1899), p. 326.—μέλλων: Burton, *Moods and Tenses*, p. 71. — παρέτεινε, see μῦθον, Arist., *Poet.*, xvii., 5, λόγους, and ix. 4, μῦθον.—μεσονυκτίου, *cf.* xvi. 25. Ver. 8. λαμπάδες ἱκαναί, see critical note and reading in D. The words have been taken to indicate clearly that the accident was not due to darkness coming on through Paul's lengthy discourse (so Weiss and Wendt), whilst Meyer regards them as introduced to show that the fall of the young man was not perceived at once. Others (so Felten) hold that the words mark the joy at the Sacramental Presence of the Lord and Bridegroom of the Church (Matt. xxv. 1), and Nösgen sees in them a note of joy in the celebration of the Christian Sunday (see also Kuinoel). But it is also allowable to see in this notice the graphic and minute touch of one who was an eye-witness of the scene, and who described it, as he remembered it, in all its vividness (Hackett, Blass). We can scarcely see in the words with Ewald an intention on the part of the narrative to guard against any suspicion attaching to the night meetings of the Christians (so Calvin, Bengel, Lechler); the date, as Nösgen says, is too early (so too Overbeck). Lewin also takes Ewald's view, but with the alternative that the lights may have been mentioned to exclude any suspicion in the reader's mind of any deception with regard to the miracle. Ver. 9. Εὔτυχος : we are not told what position he occupied, but there is no hint that he was a servant.—ἐπὶ τῆς θυρ. : on the window sill—there were no windows of glass, and the lattice or door was open probably on account of the heat from the lamps, and from the number present—the fact that Eutychus thus sat

ἦσαν συνηγμένοι. 9. καθήμενος δέ τις νεανίας ὀνόματι Εὔτυχος ἐπὶ τῆς θυρίδος, καταφερόμενος ὕπνῳ[1] βαθεῖ, διαλεγομένου τοῦ Παύλου ἐπὶ πλεῖον, κατενεχθεὶς ἀπὸ τοῦ ὕπνου, ἔπεσεν ἀπὸ τοῦ τριστέγου κάτω, καὶ ἤρθη νεκρός. 10. καταβὰς δὲ ὁ Παῦλος ἐπέπεσεν αὐτῷ, καὶ συμπεριλαβὼν εἶπε, Μὴ θορυβεῖσθε· ἡ γὰρ ψυχὴ αὐτοῦ ἐν αὐτῷ ἐστιν. 11. ἀναβὰς δὲ καὶ κλάσας[2] ἄρτον καὶ γευσάμενος, ἐφ᾽ ἱκανὸν

[1] D, Gig., so Blass in β, βαρει pro βαθει.

[2] Before αρτον ℵ*ABCD* 13, so Tisch., W.H., R.V., Weiss, Wendt add τον.

at the window points to the crowded nature of the assembly, cf. 2 Kings i. 2, where a different word is used in LXX, although θυρίς is also frequently found. —καταφερ. ὕ. β.: the two participles are to be carefully distinguished (but R.V. does not); "who was gradually oppressed," or "becoming oppressed with sleep," present participle; "being borne down by his sleep," i.e., overcome by it, aorist. Rendall takes ἐπὶ πλεῖον with κατενεχθεὶς (so W.H. margin), "and being still more overcome with the sleep," but the words are usually taken with διαλεγ. See Bengel, Nösgen, Alford, Holtzmann, Weiss, Ramsay, Page on the force of the participles: "sedentem somnus occupavit . . . somno oppressus cecidit," Bengel. καταφέρεσθαι: used only in Luke in N.T., and in no corresponding sense in LXX; a medical term, and so much so that it was used more frequently absolutely than with ὕπνος in medical writings, and the two participles thus expressing the different stages of sleep would be quite natural in a medical writer.—βαθεῖ: one of the epithets joined with ὕπνος by the medical writers, see Hobart, pp. 48, 49, and his remarks on Luke xxii. 45, p. 84. The verb is also used in the same sense by other writers as by Aristotle, Josephus, see instances in Wetstein, but Zahn reckons the whole phrase as medical, Einleitung, ii., p. 436.—καὶ ἤρθη νεκρός: the words positively assert that Eutychus was dead—they are not ὡσεὶ νεκρός, cf. Mark ix. 26, and the attempt to show that the words in ver. 10, "his life is in him," indicate apparent death, or that life is still thought of as not having left him (so apparently even Zöckler, whilst he strongly maintains the force of the preceding words), cannot be called satisfactory; see on the other hand Ramsay, St. Paul, pp. 290, 291, and Wendt, in loco. Ver. 10. καταβὰς: by the outside staircase common in Eastern houses.—

ἐπέπεσεν αὐτῷ καὶ συμ., cf. 1 Kings xvii. 21, 22; 2 Kings iv. 34; there as here the purport of the act was a restoration to life.—Μὴ θορ.: "make ye no ado," R.V., cf. Mark v. 39 (Mark ix. 23), where the word is used of the loud weeping and wailing of the mourners in the East; see above on ix. 39.—ἡ γὰρ ψ., see above. Ver. 11. κλάσας ἄρτον: if we read τὸν ἄρ., see critical note, "the bread," so R.V., i.e., of the Eucharist; so Syriac. The words evidently refer back to ver. 7, see Blass, Gram., p. 148.—γευσ.: often taken to refer not to the Eucharist, but to the partaking of the Agape or common meal which followed. If so, it certainly appears as if St. Paul had soon taken steps to prevent the scandals which occurred in Corinth from the Holy Communion being celebrated during or after a common meal, 1 Cor. ix. 23, since here the Eucharist precedes, Luckock, Footprints of the Apostles as traced by St. Luke, ii., 199. Wendt, who still identifies the breaking of the bread with the Agape (so Holtzmann, Weiss), protests against the view of Kuinoel and others that reference is here made to a breakfast which St. Paul took for his coming journey. Dean Plumptre refers to the use of γεύομαι in Heb. vi. 4 as suggesting that here too reference is made to the participation of the Eucharist; but, on the other hand, in Acts x. 10 (see Blass, in loco) the word is used of eating an ordinary meal, and Wendt refers it to the enjoyment of the Agape (cf. also Knabenbauer, in loco). Weiss urges that the meaning of simply "tasting" is to be adopted here, and that τε shows that Paul only "tasted" the meal, i.e., the Agape, and hurried on with his interrupted discourse, whilst Lewin would take γευσ. absolutely here, and refer it to a separate ordinary meal; although he maintains that the previous formula κλάσ. τὸν ἄρτον must refer to the Eucharist. In LXX the verb is

τε ὁμιλήσας ἄχρις αὐγῆς, οὕτως ἐξῆλθεν. 12.[1] ἤγαγον δὲ τὸν παῖδα
ζῶντα, καὶ παρεκλήθησαν οὐ μετρίως. 13. Ἡμεῖς δὲ[2] προελθόντες
ἐπὶ τὸ πλοῖον, ἀνήχθημεν εἰς τὴν Ἄσσον, ἐκεῖθεν μέλλοντες ἀναλαμβάνειν τὸν Παῦλον· οὕτω γὰρ ἦν διατεταγμένος, μέλλων αὐτὸς

---

[1] Instead of ηγαγον D has ασπαζομενων δε αυτων ηγαγεν τον νεανισκον ζωντα.
Blass and Hilgenfeld, however, read ηγαγον in the β text. But Wendt thinks that
ηγαγεν may not be a mere error, and that Paul is conceived of in D as himself
bringing the boy alive at the scene of departure, and thus conferring comfort,
Wendt (1899), p. 327.

[2] προελθοντες ℵB²CL, Tisch., W.H. text, Weiss, Wendt; but προσ- AB*EHP,
W.H. marg. D has κατελθοντες. επι for εις ℵABCE, so Tisch., W.H., R.V.,
Blass, Weiss, Wendt.

---

frequent, but there is no case in which it means definitely more than to taste, although in some cases it might imply eating a meal, e.g., Gen. xxv. 30; for its former sense see, e.g., Jonah iii. 7. In modern Greek γευματίζω = to dine, so γεῦμα = dinner.—ἐφ᾽ ἱκανόν τε ὁμιλ.: on St. Luke's use of ἱκανός with temporal significance see above on p. 215, cf. with this expression 2 Macc. viii. 25. ὁμιλ.: only in Luke in N.T., cf. Luke xxiv. 14, 15, Acts xxiv. 26; here, "talked with them," R.V., as of a familiar meeting, elsewhere "communed," R.V.; so in classical Greek, and in Josephus, and also in modern Greek (Kennedy); in LXX, Dan. i. 19: ὡμίλησεν αὐτοῖς ὁ β., "the king communed with them". In the passage before us the alternative rendering "when he had stayed in their company" is given by Grimm-Thayer, sub v.—ἄχρις αὐγῆς, cf. Polyaen., iv., 18, κατὰ τὴν πρώτην αὐγὴν τῆς ἡμέρας (Wetstein); only here in N.T., found in Isa. lix. 9, 2 Macc. xii. 9, but not in same sense as here.—οὕτως, cf. xx. 7, after a participle, as often in classical Greek, Simcox, Language of the N. T., p. 175, see also xxvii. 17, and Viteau, Le Grec du N. T., p. 190 (1893).

Ver. 12. ἤγαγον: the subject must be supplied; probably those who had attended to the boy, and who, now that he was sufficiently recovered, brought him back to the room. Rendall thinks that the expression means that they took the lad home after the assembly was over. The comfort is derived from the recovery of the boy, as is indicated by ζῶντα, and it is forced to refer it to the consolation which they received from the boy's presence, as a proof which the Apostle had left behind him of divine and miraculous help (so Wendt, Weiss); see also D, critical note, and Ramsay, St. Paul, p. 291.—ζῶντα: the word is

pointless unless on the supposition that the accident had been fatal. It is in fact impossible to deny that a miracle is intended to be narrated; otherwise the introduction of the whole story is meaningless, as Overbeck insists against Baur and Renan. The word νεκρός, the action of Paul, the word ζῶντα all point to an actual death, whilst the vivid details in the narrative also indicate the presence of an eye-witness as an informant. Schneckenburger has shown exhaustively, as Zeller admits, that an actual raising of the dead is intended; but we are asked to see in the narrative only an attempt to set off the raising of Eutychus against the raising of Tabitha at Joppa, a parallel between Paul and Peter; so Baur, and recently Overbeck and Weizsäcker. But the conclusion of Overbeck is disappointing in face of the fact that he dwells (p. 333) most pointedly upon the difference between the narrative here and in ix. 36—how in this latter case we have the expectation of the miracle emphasised, whilst here it is entirely wanting; how too the laudatory description of Tabitha may be contrasted with the simple mention of the name, Eutychus here.—οὐ μετρίως: often in Plutarch, cf. 2 Macc. xv. 38. On Luke's use of οὐ with an adjective, to express the opposite, see Lekebusch, Apostelgeschichte, p. 62; Klostermann, Vindiciæ Lucanæ, p. 52; and four times in "We" sections (twelve times in rest of Acts, rare in rest of N.T.), xx. 12, xxvii. 14, 20, xxviii. 2; Hawkins, Horæ Synopticæ, p. 153.

Ver. 13. ἡμεῖς, i.e., without Paul.— Ἄσσον: south of Troas in the Roman province of Asia, and some miles east of Cape Lectum. The opposite coast of Lesbos was about seven miles distant. Its harbour gave it a considerable importance in the coasting trade of former days. A Roman road connected it with

πεζεύειν.　14. ὡς δὲ¹ συνέβαλεν ἡμῖν εἰς τὴν Ἄσσον, ἀναλαβόντες αὐτὸν ἤλθομεν εἰς Μιτυλήνην· 15. κἀκεῖθεν ἀποπλεύσαντες, τῇ ἐπιούσῃ κατηντήσαμεν ἀντικρὺ Χίου² · τῇ δὲ ἑτέρᾳ παρεβάλομεν εἰς Σάμον·

¹ συνέβαλεν CDH², Blass, Hilg.; this is more fitting to the sense than the imperfect (Wendt), but the latter tense, συνέβαλλεν, is read in אABEP 40, 100, Tisch., W.H., R.V., Weiss.

² Instead of ετερα B 15, 19, 73, has the remarkable reading εσπερα, which Weiss accepts, W.H. marg. But Wendt (1899), p. 428, discusses and rejects, on the ground that the charge was introduced by a scribe who did not take κατην. αντικρυ Χιου as meaning a station for the night at Chios, and therefore represented the next station as the stopping place for the night of the same day.

Troas and the Troad coast. The sculptures from the Temple of Athena erected on the hill on which Assos itself was built form some of the most important remains of archaic Greek art: most of them are now in Paris. "Assos" (Ramsay), Hastings' B.D., B.D.². Steph. Byz. describes Assos as situated ἐφ᾽ ὑψηλοῦ καὶ ὀξέος καὶ δυσανόδου τόπου. —ἀναλαμβάνειν: assumere in navem; cf. Polyb., xxx., 9, 8. The only other instance at all parallel in N.T. is 2 Tim. iv. 11, where we might render "to pick him up on the way," Lightfoot, Biblical Essays, p. 437.—διατεταγ.: with middle significance, cf. vii. 44, xxiv. 23; Winer-Moulton, xxxix., 3.—πεζεύειν: "to go by land," R.V. (margin, "on foot"): "de terrestri (non necessario pedestri) itinere," Blass; a much shorter route than the sea voyage round Cape Lectum. The land journey was about twenty miles, Itin. Anton., B.D.². Probably Paul took the journey in this way for ministerial purposes; others suggest that he did so for the sake of his health, others to avoid the snare of the Jews, or from a desire for solitude. But it may be questioned whether this somewhat lengthy foot journey would be accomplished without any attendant at all. It does not follow, as has been supposed, that the ship was hired by Paul himself, but that he used its putting in at Assos for his own purpose. Ver. 14. συνέβαλεν, cf. xvii. 18. The verb is peculiar to St. Luke; its meaning here is classical, cf. also Jos., Ant., ii., 7, 5. Rendall thinks that the imperfect (see critical note) may mean that Paul fell in with the ship while still on his way to Assos, and was taken on board at once; he therefore renders "as he came to meet us at Assos".—Μιτυλήνην: the capital of Lesbos, about thirty miles from Assos, and so an easy day's journey; Lewin, St. Paul, ii., 84, cf. Hor., Od., i., 7, 1; Ep., i., 11, 17. Its northern harbour

into which the ship would sail is called by Strabo, xiii., 2, μέγας καὶ βαθύς, χώματι σκεπαζόμενος (Wetstein). Ver. 15. κἀκεῖθεν, see on xvi. 12, xiv. 26.—κατηντήσαμεν, cf. xvi. 1, xviii. 19, 24, "we reached a point on the mainland," Ramsay, ἀντικρὺ X. over against, i.e., opposite Chios; often in Greek writers, only here in N.T., but W.H., Weiss, ἄντικρυς, 3 Macc. v. 16 (Neh. xii. 8, see Hatch and Redpath). On καταντᾶν εἰς, and καταντᾶν ἀντ. as here, see on xvi. 1, xviii. 19; Klostermann, Vindiciæ Lucanæ, p. 49.—Χίου: The island Chios (Scio) in the Ægean was separated from the Asian coast by a channel which at its narrowest was only five miles across. The ship carrying St. Paul would pass through this picturesque channel on its way south from Mitylene. An interesting comparison with the voyage of St. Paul may be found in Herod's voyage by Rhodes, Cos, Chios and Mitylene, towards the Black Sea (Jos., Ant., xvi., 2, 2). Amongst the seven rivals for the honour of being the birthplace of Homer, the claims of Chios are most strongly supported by tradition. On the legendary and historic connections of the places named in this voyage see Plumptre, in loco, and "Chios" (Ramsay), Hastings' B.D.—τῇ δὲ ἑτέρᾳ: (see critical note). Wetstein calls attention to the variety of phrases, τῇ ἑτ., τῇ ἐπιούσῃ, τῇ ἐχομ. The phrase before us is found in xxvii. 3, so that it only occurs in the "We" sections and nowhere else in Acts, but the expression "the next day" occurs so much more frequently in the "We" sections than in any other passages of the same length that we might expect a larger variety of phrases to express it, Hawkins, Horæ Synop., pp. 153, 154; and Klostermann, Vindiciæ Lucanæ, p. 50.—παρεβάλομεν εἰς Σ.: "we struck across to Samos," Ramsay, cf. Thuc., iii., 32, where the verb means "to cross over to Ionia" (see Mr. Page's note, and

καὶ [1] μείναντες ἐν Τρωγυλλίῳ, τῇ ἐχομένῃ ἤλθομεν εἰς Μίλητον. 16.
ἔκρινε [2] γὰρ ὁ Παῦλος παραπλεῦσαι τὴν Ἔφεσον, ὅπως μὴ γένηται
αὐτῷ χρονοτριβῆσαι ἐν τῇ Ἀσίᾳ · ἔσπευδε γάρ, εἰ δυνατὸν [3] ἦν αὐτῷ,
τὴν ἡμέραν τῆς Πεντηκοστῆς γενέσθαι εἰς Ἱεροσόλυμα.

[1] καὶ μείναντες εν T., so DHLP, Syr. P. H., Sah., Chrys., so Meyer, Alford, Blass
in β, and even by Weiss (not by Wendt), Introd., p. 57, and Codex D, p. 109; *cf.*
xxi. 1.   Corssen, too, regards favourably, *G. G. A.*, p. 441, 1896, supported by
Ramsay, *St. Paul*, p. 294, Belser and Zöckler.   Weiss cannot see any reason for
its omission, and therefore retains it.   The words may, however, have been omitted
because in the text Trogyllium seems to be placed in Samos, but see also Wendt,
note, p. 328 (1899).   For the omission, אABCE, Vulg., Boh., Arm., Aethpp., Tisch.,
R.V. only in marg., W.H. describe as Western and Syrian; these authorities read
in text τῇ δε εχομ.   Ramsay's interesting note, *C. R. E.*, p. 155, should also be consulted in favour of the retention of the words.   Τρωγιλια, so Blass in β, see note *in
loco*; Τρωγυλιῳ W.H. and Winer-Schmiedel, p. 47.

[2] κεκρικει is read for εκρινε in אAB*DE, Tisch., W.H., R.V., Wendt, Weiss, Blass.
Instead of οπως μη γενηται α. χρονοτριβ. D (Gig.) has μηποτε γενηθη αυτω κατασχεσις τις—Weiss considers this as a mere explanation of the rare χρονοτριβ.
κατασχεσις is used twice in N.T., Acts vii. 5, 45, but not in the sense required here;
"mora" in Gig.   Blass accepts in β text, and there is much better authority for
χρονοτριβ. in classical Greek than for κατασχεσις in the sense of this passage.

[3] ην, but ειη is supported by אABCE 13, 15, 18, 36, 180, Tisch., W.H., R.V.,
Weiss, Wendt.   Meyer and Alford regard as gram. corr., but too well supported
(Wendt).

the passage quoted also in Wetstein, and
L. and S.).   On the frequency of this and
other nautical terms in Acts *cf.* Klostermann, *u. s.*, p. 49.—καὶ μείν. ἐν Τρω.,
see critical note.—Μίλητον : practically
the port of Ephesus.   The latter city
had long gained the pre-eminence once
enjoyed by Miletus, the former capital of
Ionia, Pliny, *N. H.*, v., 31; *cf.* Herod.,
v., 28-36, for the revolt of Miletus against
Persia and its disastrous consequences.
Miletus had been the mother of some
eighty colonies.   Here Thales and Anaxi-
mander were born.   The silting up of
the Menander had altered its position
even in St. Paul's day, and now it is
several miles from the sea; Lewin, *St.
Paul*, ii., 90; Renan, *Saint Paul*, p. 501;
Ramsay, *Church in the Roman Empire*,
p. 480.
    Ver. 16.   ἔκρινε (see critical note) . . .
παραπλεῦσαι τὴν Ἔ. : " to sail past
Ephesus," R.V., *i.e.*, without stopping
there.   The words have sometimes been
interpreted as if St. Paul had control
over a ship which he had hired himself,
and could stop where he pleased, so
Alford, Hackett, Rendall.   But if so,
there seems no definite reason for his
going to Miletus at all, as it would have
been shorter for him to have stopped at
Ephesus, or to have made his farewell
address there.   According to Ramsay
the probabilities are that Paul experienced

at Troas some delay in continuing his
journey.   In starting from Troas he had
therefore to choose a vessel making no
break in its voyage except at Miletus, or
a vessel intending to stop at Ephesus,
perhaps as its destination, perhaps with
a previous delay elsewhere.   He determined for the former by the shortness of
the time, and his desire to reach Jerusalem.   He may no doubt have been also
influenced to some extent by the thought
that it would be difficult to tear himself
away from a Church which had so many
claims upon him, and by the reflection
that hostilities might be aroused against
him and his progress further impeded
(*cf.* McGiffert, p. 339, who thinks that the
author's reason for St. Paul's desire not
to visit Ephesus "is entirely satisfactory").   — χρονοτριβ. : nowhere else in
N.T. or in LXX, but in Arist., Plut.—
γένηται αὐτῷ, *cf.* xi. 26 for construction.
—ἔσπευδε γάρ : if the verb expresses as
the imperfect intimates the whole character of the journey (Blass, *Gram.*, p.
216), the repeated long delays at first
sight seem inexplicable, but we know
nothing definitely of the special circumstances which may have occasioned each
delay, and we must not lose sight of the
fact that the Apostle would have to guard
against the constant uncertainty which
would be always involved in a coasting
voyage.   Whether St. Paul reached

17. Ἀπὸ δὲ τῆς Μιλήτου πέμψας εἰς Ἔφεσον, μετεκαλέσατο τοὺς πρεσβυτέρους τῆς ἐκκλησίας. 18. ὡς δὲ παρεγένοντο πρὸς αὐτόν,[1] εἶπεν αὐτοῖς, Ὑμεῖς ἐπίστασθε, ἀπὸ πρώτης ἡμέρας ἀφ᾽ ἧς ἐπέβην εἰς τὴν Ἀσίαν,[2] πῶς μεθ᾽ ὑμῶν τὸν πάντα χρόνον ἐγενόμην, 19. δουλεύων τῷ Κυρίῳ μετὰ πάσης ταπεινοφροσύνης καὶ πολλῶν δακρύων καὶ πειρασμῶν, τῶν συμβάντων μοι ἐν ταῖς ἐπιβουλαῖς τῶν Ἰουδαίων ·

[1] After αυτον (A)D (E, Gig., Vulg.) add ομοσε οντων αυτων, so Blass in β text. Harris, *Four Lectures*, etc., p. 61, thinks conflation here of α and β, so Gig. is double and reads "cum convenissent ad eum simulque essent".

[2] After Ασιαν D adds ως τριετιαν η και πλειον, the form of the phrase does not look original; τριετια occurs in xx. 31 and nowhere else in N.T. Vogel, it may be noted, classes it as one of the medical words in Luke's writings; see on ver. 31. For πως D has ποταπως, nowhere else in N.T.; but ποταπος six times in N.T., twice in Luke, only once in LXX.

Jerusalem in time we are not told. St. Chrysostom maintained that he did, see also Ramsay, *St. Paul*, pp. 296, 297; McGiffert, p. 340 (on the other hand, Weiss, Renan, Felten). Mr. Turner, *Chron. of N. T.*, p. 422, holds that the Apostle probably reached Jerusalem just in time, while Farrar sees in xxiv. 11 an intimation that he arrived on the very eve of the Feast. The Pentecostal Feast was the most crowded, most attended by foreigners, *cf.* ii. 1.

Ver. 17. Ἀπὸ δὲ τῆς Μ. π.: Apparently the Apostle could reckon on a stay of some days at Miletus. If we take into account the landing, the despatching a messenger to Ephesus, and the summoning and journeying of the elders to Miletus, probably, as Ramsay thinks, the third day of the stay at Miletus would be devoted to the presbyters.— μετεκαλέσατο: "called to him," R.V., *cf.* ii. 39 (and see on vii. 14, only in Acts), indicating authority or earnestness in the invitation.—τοὺς πρεσβ., see on xii. 25, and also below on ver. 28. For Pauline words and phraseology characterising the addresses, see following notes.

When Spitta remarks (*Apostelgeschichte*, p. 252 ff.) that the speech at Miletus is inferior to no part of Acts, not even to the description of the voyage in chap. xxvii., in vividness of expression and intensity of feeling, he expresses the opinion of every unbiassed reader. He justly too lays stress upon the fact that while criticism admits the forcible and direct impression derived from the speech, it fails to account for it in the most natural way, *viz.*, by the fact that whilst for the addresses delivered in the Pisidian Antioch and in Athens we are dependent upon a report

derived from hearsay, we are here in possession of the testimony of an eyewitness, and of a hearer of the speech (p. 252). Spitta (p. 254) defends the speech against the usual objections. It is disappointing to find that Hilgenfeld is content to regard the whole speech as interpolated by his "author to Theophilus". Clemen refers the whole speech to his R. or to R.A.; thus whilst ver. 19a is referred to R., 19b with its reference to the plots of the Jews is ascribed to R.A. (Redactor Antijudaicus); Jüngst ascribes ver. 19b from the words καὶ δακρύων . . . Ἰουδ. to the Redactor, but the previous part of the chap. xxi. to ταπεινοφροσύνης, ver. 19, to his source A. So ver. 38 with its reference to ver. 25 is referred to the Redactor; whilst Clemen refers ver. 38a to his R.A., 38b to R.

Ver. 18. ὑμεῖς : " ye yourselves," R.V., *ipsi*, emphatic, *cf.* x. 37, xv. 7.— ἀπὸ π. ἡ. : to be connected with what follows, although it is quite possible that the word may hold a middle place (Alford), connected partly with ἐπίσ. and partly with ἐγεν.—ἐπέβην : " set foot in Asia," R.V., only in Acts, except Matt. xxi. 5, also with the dative of place, Acts xxv. 1, but the local meaning is doubtful (LXX, Josh. xiv. 9). Rendall renders " I took ship for Asia," but although the expression elsewhere refers to a voyage, *cf.* xxi. 2, 4, 6, xxvii. 2, it is not always so used, *e.g.*, xxv. 1.—πῶς μεθ᾽ ὑ. . . . ἐγεν., *cf.* vii. 38 (*versor cum*), ix. 19, Mark xvi. 10. Bethge points out that the phrase is always used of intimate association and contrasts the less intimate significance of σύν. See also critical note and reading in D.

Ver. 19. δουλεύων : the word occurs

20. ὡς οὐδὲν ὑπεστειλάμην τῶν συμφερόντων, τοῦ μὴ ἀναγγεῖλαι ὑμῖν
καὶ διδάξαι ὑμᾶς δημοσίᾳ καὶ κατ᾽ οἴκους, 21. διαμαρτυρόμενος

six times in St. Paul's Epistles of serving God, the Lord, Christ, 1 Thess.
i. 9, Rom. xii. 11 (R., margin, τῷ
καιρῷ), xiv. 18, xvi. 18, Ephes. vi. 7,
Col. iii. 24 (once in Matthew and Luke,
of serving God, Matt. vi. 24, Luke xvi.
13), and *cf.* St. Paul's expression δοῦλος
of himself, Rom. i. 1, Gal. i. 10, Phil. i.
1, Tit. i. 1.—μετὰ πάσης ταπεινοφ. :
this use of πᾶς may be called eminently
Pauline, *cf.* Ephes. i. 3, 8, iv. 2, vi. 18,
2 Cor. viii. 7, xii. 12, 1 Tim. iii. 4; 2
Tim. iv. 2, Tit. ii. 15, iii. 2 (see Hackett's
note). ταπειν., a word which may justly
be called Pauline, as out of seven places
in the N.T. it is used five times by St.
Paul in his Epistles, and once in his
address in the passage before us ; Ephes.
iv. 2, Phil. ii. 3, Col. ii. 18, 23, iii. 12
(elsewhere, only in 1 Peter v. 5). It will
be noted that it finds a place in three
Epistles of the First Captivity, although
used once disparagingly, Col. iii. 18. In
pagan ethics ταπεινός was for the most
part a depreciatory characteristic, although some few notable exceptions
may be quoted, Trench, *Synonyms*, i.,
171 ff. In the LXX and Apocrypha it
has a high moral significance and is
opposed to ὕβρις in all its forms. The
noun is not found either in LXX or
Apocrypha, and the adjective ταπεινό-
φρων (1 Peter iii. 8) and the verb ταπεινο-
φρονεῖν (not in N.T.), although each
found in LXX once, the former in Prov.
xxix. 23 and the latter in Ps. cxxx.
2 (*cf.* instances in Aquila and Symmachus, Hatch and Redpath), cannot be
traced in classical Greek before the
Christian era, and then not in a laudatory sense. The noun occurs in Jos.,
B. J., iv., 9, 2, but in the sense of pusil-
lanimity, and also in Epictet., *Diss.*, iii.,
24, 56, but in a bad sense (Grimm-
Thayer). But for St. Paul as for St.
Peter the life of Christ had conferred a
divine honour upon all forms of lowliness
and service, and every Christian was
bidden to an imitation of One Who had
said : πραΰς εἰμι καὶ ταπεινὸς τῇ καρδίᾳ,
Lightfoot on Phil. ii. 3 ; "Ethics" (T.
B. Strong), Hastings' B.D., i., 786;
Cremer, *Wörterbuch*, *sub v.* ταπεινός.—
δακρύων, *cf.* ver. 31, 2 Cor. ii. 4, Phil.
iii. 18. "Lachrymæ sanctæ . . . cum
his tamen consistit *gaudium*": Bengel.
St. Paul was no Stoic, for whom ἀπάθεια
was a virtue, the accompaniment of
wisdom and the passport to perfection ;

see Rom. xii. 15 : "in every age the
Christian temper has shivered at the
touch of Stoic apathy". Here the word
refers not to the Apostle's *outward* trials
which were rather a source of joy, but to
his sorrow of heart for his brethren and
for the world, ἔπασχε γὰρ ὑπὲρ τῶν
ἀπολλυμένων, Chrysostom.—πειρασμῶν,
cf. St. Paul's own words, 1 Thess. iii. 3,
Phil. i. 27, 2 Cor. i. 6, vi. 4-10, 2 Cor. xi.
26, κινδύνοις ἐκ γένους (Gal. iv. 14). In
our Lord's own life and ministry there
had been "temptations," Luke iv. 13,
xxii. 28 ; and a beatitude rested upon the
man who endured temptation, James i.
12 and 2. The noun is found no less
than six times in St. Luke's Gospel, but
only here in Acts. It occurs four times
in St. Paul's Epistles, and may be fairly
classed as Lucan-Pauline (Bethge). On
its use in N.T. and LXX see Hatch,
Essays in Biblical Greek, p. 71 ff., and
compare Mayor, *Epistle of St. James*,
i., 2.—ἐπιβ. τῶν Ἰ.: evidently classed
amongst the πειρασμῶν, Hatch, *u. s.*,
although we must not suppose that St.
Luke tells us of all the Apostle's dangers,
trials and temptations here any more
than elsewhere. Nothing of the kind is
mentioned in connection definitely with
the Ephesian Jews, "sed res minime
dubia, xxi. 27," Blass. The noun has
not been found in any classical author,
but it occurs in Dioscorides, *Præf.*, i.,
see Grimm, *sub v.*, and several times
in LXX, six times in Ecclus. and in 1
Macc. ii. 52.

Ver. 20. ὑπεστειλάμην : "how that I
shrank not from declaring unto you anything that was profitable," R.V., *cf.* ver.
27, where βουλήν follows the same verb
ἀναγγέλλειν, here followed by οὐδέν ; on
the construction see Page's note, *in
loco*. The verb means to draw or shrink
back from, out of fear or regard for
another. In the same sense in classical
Greek with οὐδέν or μηδέν : "locutio
Demosthenica." Blass and Wendt, *cf.*
also Jos., *B. J.*, i., 20, 21 ; *Vita*, 54 ; in
LXX, Deut. i. 17, Exod. xxiii. 21, Job
xiii. 8, Wisd. vi. 7, Hab. ii. 4 ; see Westcott on Heb. x. 38. It is used once in
Gal. ii. 12 by Paul himself. It is possible
that the verb may have been used metaphorically by St. Paul from its use in the
active voice as a nautical term to reef or
lower sail, and there would be perhaps a
special appropriateness in the metaphor,
as St. Paul had just landed, and the sails

Ἰουδαίοις τε καὶ Ἕλλησι τὴν εἰς¹ τὸν Θεὸν μετάνοιαν, καὶ πίστιν
τὴν εἰς τὸν Κύριον ἡμῶν Ἰησοῦν Χριστόν. 22. καὶ νῦν ἰδοὺ ἐγὼ
δεδεμένος τῷ πνεύματι πορεύομαι εἰς Ἱερουσαλήμ, τὰ ἐν αὐτῇ
συναντήσοντά μοι μὴ εἰδώς, 23. πλὴν ὅτι τὸ Πνεῦμα τὸ Ἅγιον κατὰ
πόλιν διαμαρτύρεται λέγον, ὅτι δεσμά με καὶ θλίψεις μένουσιν.

¹ τον Θεον, *om.* art. ℵBCE, Tisch., W.H., Weiss, Wendt, Blass; after πιστιν
ℵBCD 18, 36, Arm. *om.* την, so Tisch., W.H., R.V., Weiss, Wendt, Blass. At end
of verse BHLP, Sah., Syr. H., Aethᵣₒ·, Lucif., so W.H., Weiss, Wendt (probably),
read simply Ιησουν; but Tisch., R.V. text, W.H. marg. (Blass) Ι. Χριστον with
ℵAC(D)E, Vulg., Syr. Pesh., Boh., Arm., Aethᵖᵖ. Blass reads gen. with D, δια
του Κυριου; *cf.* iii. 16.

of the ship may have been before his
eyes in speaking, to say nothing of the
fact that the word would become familiar
to him day by day on the voyage (see
Humphry, Plumptre, Farrar); but it is
not well to press this special metaphorical
usage too far here, especially as the word
is frequently used elsewhere of military
rather than nautical ways (see Lightfoot's note on Gal. ii. 12, and the use of
the verb in Polybius).—τῶν συμφ., *cf.* I
Cor. vii. 35, x. 33; Pauline: "the things
profitable for their salvation," a message
not always agreeable, but which nevertheless the Apostle spoke with the same
παρρησία (ὑποστέλλεσθαι is the opposite of παρρησιάζεσθαι, Page) which
characterised him. Blass compares also
the whole phrase ὑποστείλασθαι περὶ ὧν
ὑμῖν συμφέρειν ἡγοῦμαι, Dem., i., 16.—
δημ. καὶ κατ᾽ οἴκους: *publice et privatim*,
another and a further glimpse of the
Apostle's work at Ephesus: publicly in
the synagogue and in the school of
Tyrannus, privately as in the Church in
the house of Aquila and Priscilla, I Cor.
xvi. 19.

Ver. 21. διαμαρτ., see above on p. 92;
Lucan - Pauline.— μετάν. καὶ πίστιν,
cf. the earliest notes in the preaching of
Jesus, Mark i. 15, and these were equally
the notes of the preaching of St. Peter
and St. Paul alike. Whether Paul was
preaching to Jews or Gentiles, to philosophers at Athens or to peasants at
Lystra, the substance of his teaching
was the same under all varieties of
forms, *cf.* xiv. 15, xvii. 30, xxvi. 20. It
is quite arbitrary to refer μετάνοια to the
Gentile and πίστις to the Jew.—Ἰουδ. τε
καὶ Ἕλλησι, Pauline, *cf.* Rom. i. 16, ii.
9, 10, iii. 9, 12, I Cor. i. 24.

Ver. 22. καὶ νῦν ἰδού: the exact
phrase occurs again in ver. 25, and only
once elsewhere in words ascribed to
Paul, xiii. 11 (ἰδού νῦν, twice in Paul
only, 2 Cor. vi. 2).—δεδεμένος τῷ πνεύ-

ματι: "bound in the spirit," *compulsus
animo*, Blass; so δέω in classical Greek,
Xen., *Cyr.*, viii., 1, 12; Plato, *Rep.*, viii.,
p. 567 *e*, *cf.* xix. 21, xviii. 25, I Cor. v. 3.
The fact that the Holy Spirit is specifically so called in ver. 23 seems to decide
for the above rendering in this verse; but
see Weiss on ver. 23; Ramsay also renders "constrained by the Spirit". Possibly πνεῦμα is named as that part of the
man in closest union with the Spirit of
God, *cf.* Rom. viii. 16, so that the sense
is not affected. If we compare with xix.
21 the expression presents an advance in
the Apostle's thought—his purpose becomes plainer, and the obligation more
definite, as the Spirit witnesses with his
spirit. The expression may mean that
the Apostle regarded himself as already
bound in the spirit, *i.e.*, although not
outwardly bound, he yet knows and feels
himself as one bound. For St. Paul's
frequent use of πνεῦμα *cf.* Rom. i. 9,
viii. 16, xii. 11, I Cor. ii. 11, v. 3, 4, xiv.
14, etc. Oecumenius and Theophylact
take πνεύματι with πορεύομαι, *i.e.*, bound,
as good as bound, I go by the leading of
the Spirit to Jerusalem; but this seems
forced. Paley, *Horæ Paulinæ*, ii., 5, remarks on the undesigned coincidence
with Rom. xv. 30.—συναντήσοντά μοι:
the verb is found only in Luke in N.T.
(except Heb. vii. 10 as a quotation, Gen.
xiv. 17), and only here in this sense, *cf.*
Eccles. ii. 14, ix. 11, also Plut., *Sulla*, 2;
Polyb., xx., 7, 14; middle, τὰ συναντώ-
μενα. On the rarity of the future
participle in Greek, and its use in this
passage "an exception which proves the
rule," see Simcox, *Language of the N. T.*,
p. 126.

Ver. 23. πλὴν ὅτι: The collocation is
found nowhere else in N.T. except in
Phil. i. 18, *only that* (so Alford, Lightfoot, W.H., see Lightfoot, *l. c.*, for parallels), *i.e.*, knowing one thing only, etc.,
"I do not ask to see the distant scene;

24.[1] ἀλλ᾽ οὐδενὸς λόγον ποιοῦμαι, οὐδὲ ἔχω τὴν ψυχήν μου τιμίαν
ἐμαυτῷ, ὡς τελειῶσαι τὸν δρόμον μου μετὰ χαρᾶς, καὶ τὴν διακονίαν
ἣν ἔλαβον παρὰ τοῦ Κυρίου Ἰησοῦ, διαμαρτύρασθαι τὸ εὐαγγέλιον
τῆς χάριτος τοῦ Θεοῦ.   25. καὶ νῦν ἰδοὺ ἐγὼ οἶδα, ὅτι οὐκέτι ὄψεσθε
τὸ πρόσωπόν μου ὑμεῖς πάντες, ἐν οἷς διῆλθον κηρύσσων τὴν [2] βασιλ-

---

[1] T.R. is supported by EHLP; Lachmann's reading, which is the same as Blass
in β text, **αλλ᾽ ουδενος λογον εχω ουδε ποιουμαι την ψυχην τιμιαν εμ.** (= D, with
add. of **μοι** after **εχω** and **μου** after **ψυχην**), is found in ℵcA 13, 40, 43, 68, Vulg. But
R.V. is supported by Tisch., W.H., Weiss, following ℵ*BCD², so Sah., Boh., Syr.
P., Arm., Gig., Lucif., Or.   See also Field., *Ot. Norv.*, iii., p. 85 ; Weiss, Codex D,
p. 100.   **ως τελειωσαι,** but W.H. (Weiss, Rendall) **ως τελειωσω** (-**σαι** W.H. mg.) ;
see comment.   Blass in α conjectures **ωστε τελειωσαι;** **τε** could easily drop out
before the **τελ.**   In β Blass reads **του τελειωσαι** with D ; **ωστε** E ; **ως το** C.   **μετα
χαρας** *om.* ℵABD 13, 40, 81, Vulg., several verss., Tisch., Blass, W.H., R.V., Weiss,
Wendt.   After **διαμαρτ.** D, Sah., Gig., Lucif., Ephr. insert **Ιουδαιοις τε και Ελλησι,**
see ver. 21.

[2] After **βασ.** ℵABC 13 omit **του Θ.,** so Tisch., W.H., R.V., Weiss, Wendt.   D,
Sah., Hilg. read **του Ιησου** (Gig., Lucif. *domini I.*) ; Blass rejects—contrary to
usage of Acts (Weiss).

---

one step enough for me," so from step
to step **κατὰ πόλιν,** on his journey, St.
Paul was warned and guided, *cf.* xxi. 4,
11.—**κατὰ πόλιν,** Lucan-Pauline ; **κατά**
used several times by Luke, alone
amongst the synoptists, in his Gospel
and in the Acts with this distributive force
in connection with **πόλις ;** Luke viii. 1,
4, xiii. 22, *cf.* xv. 21 ; in the text, as also
in Titus i. 5 ; the only other passage in
which the collocation occurs in N.T.,
the phrase is adopted by St. Paul.—
δεσμὰ καὶ θλίψεις : δεσμά in St. Luke ;
Luke viii. 29, Acts xvi. 26, but it is
noticeable that the two nouns are found
together in Phil. i. 17, and in 2 Cor. i. 8.
θλίψις is used of the affliction which
befel the Apostle in Asia, including that
of public danger, as well as illness and
mental distress.   On the variation between masculine and neuter in **δεσμός**
and in other nouns see Blass, *Gram.*, p.
28.—**μένουσιν :** only twice in N.T., with
accusative of the person, here and in
ver. 5.
Ver. 24.   See critical note.   "But I
hold not my life of any account, as dear
unto myself," R.V., reading **λόγου** for
λόγον, omitting **οὐδὲ ἔχω** and **μου.**   Both
verbs **ἔχω** and **ποιοῦμαι** are found in
similar phrases in LXX, Tobit vi. 16,
Job xxii. 4, so also in classical Greek
(Wetstein).   The former verb is used in
N.T. as = *habere, æstimare, cf.* Luke
xiv. 18 and by St. Paul, Phil. ii. 29.—
ὡς τελειῶσαι, see critical note.   "So
that I may accomplish my course," R.V.,
"in comparison of accomplishing my
course," margin.   Difficulty has arisen

because this is the only case in the N.T.
in which **ὡς** appears in a final clause,
Burton, p. 85 (but see W.H., Luke ix.
52, and Viteau, *Le Grec du N. T.*, p. 74
(1893)).   The whole phrase is strikingly
Pauline, *cf.* Phil. iii. 12, where the
same verb immediately seems to suggest the
δρόμος (Alford), Gal. ii. 2, 1 Cor. ix. 24,
2 Tim. iv. 7.—**μετὰ χαρᾶς,** see critical
note, *cf.* Phil. i. 4, Col. i. 11, Heb. x. 34.
The words are strongly defended by
Ewald.—**τὴν διακονίαν,** see above on p.
422 "saepe apud Paulum," *cf.* Rom.
xi. 13.   Apostleship is often so designated,
Acts i. 17, 25, xxi. 19, 2 Cor. iv. 1, and
other instances in Hort, *Ecclesia*, p. 204.
—**διαμαρτ.,** *cf.* vi. 4, where the **διακ. τοῦ
λόγου** is the highest function of the
Apostles.
Ver. 25.   **καὶ νῦν,** see on ver. 22.—
οἶδα : no infallible presentiment or prophetic inspiration, but a personal conviction based on human probabilities,
which was overruled by subsequent
events.   The word cannot fairly be taken
to mean more than this, for in the same
context the Apostle himself had distinctly
disclaimed a full knowledge of the future,
ver. 23.   And if **οἶδα** is to be pressed here
into a claim of infallible knowledge, it is
difficult to see why it should not be also
so pressed in Phil. i. 25, where the Apostle
expresses his sure conviction **πεποιθὼς
οἶδα** of a release from his Roman imprisonment, *cf.* xxvi. 27 where Paul uses
the same verb in expressing his firm
persuasion of Agrippa's belief, but surely
not any infallible knowledge of Agrippa's
heart.   For a full discussion of the word

εἴαν τοῦ Θεοῦ. 26.[1] διὸ μαρτύρομαι ὑμῖν ἐν τῇ σήμερον ἡμέρᾳ, ὅτι
καθαρὸς ἐγὼ ἀπὸ τοῦ αἵματος πάντων · 27.[2] οὐ γὰρ ὑπεστειλάμην τοῦ

[1] For διο ﬡABEP read διοτι, so Tisch., W.H., R.V., Weiss, Wendt; but Blass
as T.R. But in β text Blass reads (instead of διο . . . οτι) αχρι ουν της σημερον
ημερας with D[1] (possibly point not grasped—Weiss). After καθαρος ﬡBCDE, Vulg.,
Syr. H., Sah., Ir[int]., Lucif. read ειμι, so Tisch., R.V., W.H., Weiss, Wendt; T.R.
= xviii. 6 (Wendt).

[2] Instead of ου γαρ υπεστ. του μη αναγ. υμιν Gig., Lucif., so Blass in β, read και
ου διελιπον κηρυσσων. Gig., Lucif. also omit υμιν, but Blass retains with emphasis
as last word in verse, so Tisch., W.H., Weiss, Alford, following ﬡ*BC(D) 13, 81, Vulg.

see amongst recent writers Steinmetz,
*Die zweite römische Gefangenschaft des
Apostels Paulus*, p. 14 ff. (1897); Zahn,
Einleitung, i., p. 436.—οὐκέτι ὄψεσθε:
" shall no longer see," see Rendall,
whereas A. and R.V. rendering " no
more," οὐκέτι, give the impression that
St. Paul definitely affirms that he would
never return. Rendall compares Rom. xv.
23, but on the other hand Acts viii. 39
seems to justify the usual rendering.
The Apostle's increasing anxiety is quite
natural when we remember how even in
Corinth he had thought of his journey to
Jerusalem with apprehension, Rom xv.
30, Paley, *Horæ Paulinæ*, ii., 5. On the
inference drawn by Blass from this passage as to the early date of Acts, see his
remarks *in loco*, and *Proleg.*, p. 3, and to
the same effect, Salmon, *Introd.*, p. 407,
fifth edition.—διῆλθον: the word taken
in the sense of a missionary tour, see
xiii. 6, indicates that representatives not
only of Ephesus but of other Churches
were present, hence ὑμεῖς πάντες, διῆλθον
κηρύσσων, coalescing into a single idea;
the Apostle could not say διῆλθον ὑμᾶς,
and so we have ἐν ὑμῖν substituted. If
the word is Lucan it is also Pauline, and
that too in this particular sense, *cf.* 1
Cor. xvi. 5.—κηρ. τὴν βασ.: if Lucan,
also Pauline—*cf.* Col. iv. 11. As our
Lord had sent His first disciples to
preach (κηρύσσειν) the kingdom of God,
and as He Himself had done the same,
Luke viii. 1, ix. 2, we cannot doubt that
St. Paul would lay claim to the same
duty and privilege; in his first Epistle, 1
Thess. ii. 12, as in his latest, 2 Tim. iv.
18, the kingdom of God, its present and
its future realisation, is present to his
thoughts; in his first journey, xiv. 22, no
less than in his third it finds a place in
his teaching and exhortation; in his first
Epistle, 1 Thess. ii. 9, as in his latest, 2
Tim. i. 11, iv. 17, he does the work of a
herald, κῆρυξ. No less than five times in
1 Corinthians, one of the Epistles written
during his stay at Ephesus, the phrase

βασιλεία Θεοῦ occurs (it is not found
at all in 2 Corinthians).
Ver. 26. If we read διότι, critical
note, we have a word which is not used
by the other Evangelists, but three times
in Luke's Gospel and five times in Acts;
in each passage in Acts it is referred to
Paul, xiii. 35, xviii. 10 (2), xx. 26, xxii.
18, and it occurs nine or ten times in
Paul's Epistles. On account of the
Apostle's approaching departure, such a
reckoning is demanded.—μαρτύρομαι:
only in Luke and Paul, and in both
cases in Acts referred to Paul, here and
in xxvi. 22, Gal. v. 3, Ephes. iv. 17, 1
Thess. ii. 12, "I protest," properly "I
call to witness," but never = μαρτυρῶ in
classical Greek; in Judith vii. 28 we
have the fuller construction, of which
this use of the dative here is a remnant,
Lightfoot, *Gal.*, v., 3. The verb occurs
once more in 1 Macc. ii. 56 S (but
AR, *al.*).—ἐν τῇ σήμερον ἡμέρᾳ: Attic,
τήμερον, *i.e.*, ἡμ. with pronom. prefix
(*cf.* Matt. xxviii. 15 but ἡμέρας [W. H.]),
the very day of my departure; the exact
phrase occurs twice elsewhere, but both
times in Paul's writings, 2 Cor. iii.
14, W. H., Rom. xi. 8 (quotation);
" Hoc magnam declarandi vim habet,"
Bengel. Several times in LXX, *cf.*
Jos., *Ant.*, xiii., 2, 3, found frequently
in classical Greek.—καθαρὸς ἀπὸ, *cf.*
xvii. 6, where a similar phrase is used
by St. Paul; the adjective is found
seven times in St. Paul's Epistles, but
only here and in xvii. 6 in Luke's writings. In LXX, *cf.* Job xiv. 4, Prov.
xx. 9, Tobit iii. 14, Susannah, ver. 46; in
Psalms of Solomon, xvii. 41, and, for the
thought, Ezek. iii. 18-20. In classics
for the most part with genitive, but in
later Greek with ἀπό, see however Blass,
Gram., p. 104, and instances from Demosthenes; and Deissmann for instances
from papyri, *Neue Bibelstudien*, pp. 24,
48; Ramsay, " Greek of the Early
Church," etc.; *Expository Times*, December, 1898, p. 108. Only a Paul

μὴ ἀναγγεῖλαι ὑμῖν πᾶσαν τὴν βουλὴν τοῦ Θεοῦ. 28. προσέχετε οὖν
ἑαυτοῖς, καὶ παντὶ τῷ ποιμνίῳ ἐν ᾧ ὑμᾶς τὸ Πνεῦμα τὸ Ἅγιον ἔθετο
ἐπισκόπους, ποιμαίνειν τὴν ἐκκλησίαν [1] τοῦ Θεοῦ, ἣν περιεποιήσατο

---

[1] τοῦ Θεου, so אB 68, Vulg., Syr. H. (Syr. Pesh. MSS.), Epiph., Bas., Ps.-Ath.,
Theod.-Mops., Cyr.-Al.: τοῦ κυριου AC*DE, 13, 15, 36, 40, 69, 110, 118 (eight
others), Gig., Sah., Boh., Syr. H. mg., Arm., Irint., Const., Ath., Did., Chrys., Jer.,
Lucif. Here W.H., Weiss have Θεου, so Bengel, Alford in later editions; Tisch.,
R.V. marg., Blass, Wendt, Hilg. κυριου; του κυριου και Θεου C³HLP, most mins.,
Slavonic, Theophl.; and there are other variations. Against Θεου it is objected
that St. Paul would not apply the word to Christ, although we have in Clem.
Rom., *Cor.*, ii., 1; Ignat., *Ephes.*, i., 1; *Rom.*, vi., 3; Tert., *Ad Uxor.*, ii., 3;
Clem. Alex., *Quis dives salv.*, xxxiv., similar language; but there are also passages
in the N.T., *e.g.*, Rom. ix. 5, Tit. ii. 13, in which there is at least a very considerable amount of evidence for referring Θεος to Jesus, "and when it is objected that
these are disputed passages, it is just to remind the objector that this will exclude
his original statement as well as the rebuttal of it" (Warfield). The evidence in
its favour comes to us afforded by a strong combination (*cf.* too the intrinsic
evidence in its favour from Ps. lxxiv. 2, W.H., *App.*, 99); so far from the unusual
nature of the phrase being regarded as fatal to its genuineness, it might be fairly
maintained that Θεου as it is the more difficult reading is also on that very
ground recommended to our confidence. We should also give weight to the
fact that the words εκκλησια του θ., which find a place in this address full of
Pauline expressions, are found no less than eleven times in St. Paul's Epistles,
but that εκκ. του κυριου is not found at all in the N.T. (we have αιμα του
K. once in 1 Cor. xi. 27). Weiss endeavours to solve the difficulty by taking
ιδιου, masc., the blood of his own; *cf.* Rom. viii. 32. But while disagreeing with
this solution, Hort, in W.H., *App.*, 99, thinks it by no means impossible that υιου
dropped out after του ιδιου (its insertion solves every difficulty (so too Rendall)).
Hort, reading δια του αιματος του ιδιου, renders "through the blood that was His
own," *i.e.*, His Son's, following אABCDE 13, 36, 40, Vulg., so too Weiss, R.V.;
cf. the language which finds repeated expression in the *Apost. Const.*, and em-
bodies a conception familiar to us in one of our Ember Collects (1662). See
further W.H., *u. s.*; Dr. Ezra Abbot, *Bibliotheca Sacra*, p. 313 ff. (1876); Page,
in loco; Wendt (1899), p. 335; Warfield, *Textual Criticism*, pp. 184-189, 5th edit.
Mr. Page, *Classical Review*, p. 317, 1897, warmly approves of the note of Dr. Blass
on Acts xx. 28, and of his support of the reading Κυριον, on the ground that Θεος
would be easily substituted for it in days when "moris factum erat ut Θεος Jesus
diceretur"; but is this explanation so certain? Dr. Hort indicates that the prevalent instinct would be to change του Θεου into του κ., and not *vice versâ*, as the
fear of sanctioning "Monarchian," or (in later times) "Monophysite" language
would outweigh any other doctrinal impulse.

---

could say this with fitness; we could
not dare to say it, Chrys., *Hom.*, xliv.
Ver. 27. ὑπεστ., see above on ver.
20.—τὴν β. τοῦ Θεοῦ, see on ii. 23, and
cf. especially Ephes. i. 11 for the phrase,
and iii. 4 for the thought. No Epistle
excels that to the Ephesians in the richness of its thoughts, and in its conception of a divine purpose running through
the ages; no Epistle dwells more fully
upon the conception of the Church as
the Body of Christ, or exhorts more
touchingly to diligence in keeping the
unity of the Spirit, or insists more practically upon the sanctifying power of the
One Spirit, and the sense of a divine
membership in every sphere of human
life. The rich and full teaching of the

Epistle is addressed to men who are able
to understand the Apostle's knowledge
of the mystery of Christ; in other words,
to those to whom he had announced
more fully than to others the counsel of
God. The Ephesian Epistle may have
been an encyclical letter, but it was
addressed principally to the Ephesians
as the representatives of the leading
Church of the province of Asia. See
amongst recent writers Gore, *Ephesians*,
pp. 42, 43; and Lock, "Ephesians,"
Hastings' B.D., p. 718.—ὑμῖν: emphatically at the end, W.H.; this revelation
had been made to the presbyters before
him, and the responsibility would rest
with them of communicating it to others
when their spiritual father had left them.

διὰ τοῦ ἰδίου αἵματος.   29. ἐγὼ γὰρ οἶδα τοῦτο, ὅτι εἰσελεύσονται
μετὰ τὴν ἄφιξίν μου λύκοι βαρεῖς εἰς ὑμᾶς, μὴ φειδόμενοι τοῦ

Ver. 28. προσέχετε . . . ἑαυτοῖς (cf.
1 Tim. iv. 16), Luke xvii. 3, xxi. 34, Acts
v. 35, viii. 6. In LXX with ἐμαυτῷ,
Gen. xxiv. 6, Exod. x. 28, Deut. iv. 9.
"Non tantum jubet eos gregi attendere,
sed primum sibi ipsis ; neque enim aliorum
salutem sedulo unquam curabit, qui suam
negliget . . . cum sit ipse pars gregis,"
Calvin, in loco, and also Chrys. (Bethge,
p. 144).—ποιμνίῳ: the figure was common in the O.T. and it is found in St.
Luke, xii. 32, in St. John, in St. Peter,
but it is said that St. Paul does not use
it, cf. however Ephes. iv. 11, where, and
nowhere else, he writes καὶ αὐτὸς ἔδωκε
. . . τοὺς δὲ ποιμένας.—ἐν ᾧ: "in the
which," R.V., not "over which".—ὑμᾶς
is again emphatic, but the presbyters
were still part of the flock, see Calvin,
u. s.—ἔθετο, cf. 1 Cor. xii. 28, 1 Tim. i.
12, ii. 7, 2 Tim. i. 11. There is no ground
whatever for supposing that the ἐπισκό-
ποι here mentioned were not ordained,
as the words τὸ Π. τὸ Ἅγ. ἔθετο may be
used without any reference whatever to
the actual mode of appointment. Dr.
Hort allows that here the precedent of
vi. 3-6 may have been followed, and the
appointment of the elders may have been
sealed, so to speak, by the Apostle's
prayers and laying-on-of-hands, Ecclesia,
pp. 99, 100. The thought of appointment by the Holy Spirit, although not
excluding the ordination of Apostles,
may well be emphasised here for the
sake of solemnly reminding the Presbyters of their responsibility to a divine
Person, and that they stand in danger of
losing the divine gifts imparted to them
in so far as they are unfaithful to their
office.—ποιμαίνειν: "to tend" as distinct from βόσκειν "to feed," although the
act of feeding as well as of governing is
associated also with the former word ;
see on John xxi. 16. The figurative
pastoral language in this passage was
probably not unknown as applied to
Jewish elders, Edersheim, Jewish Social
Life, p. 282 ; Hort, Ecclesia, p. 101.—
ἐπισκόπους: the word, which occurs five
times in the N.T., is applied four times
to officers of the Christian Church : in
this passage, again at Ephesus in 1 Tim.
iii. 2, at Philippi in Phil. i. 1, at Crete in
Titus i. 7 ; and once to our Lord Himself, 1 Peter ii. 25 (cf. the significant
passage, Wisdom i. 6, where it is applied
to God). In the LXX it is used in
various senses, e.g., of the overseers of

Josiah, 2 Chron. xxxiv. 12, 17 ; of task-
masters or exactors, Isa. lx. 17 ; of minor
officers, Neh. xi. 9, 14 ; of officers over
the house of the Lord, 2 Kings xi. 18 ;
and in 1 Macc. i. 51 of overseers or local
commissioners of Antiochus Epiphanes
to enforce idolatry, cf. Jos., Ant., xii., 5,
4. In classical Greek the word is also
used with varied associations. Thus in
Attic Greek it was used of a commis-
sioner sent to regulate a new colony or
subject city like a Spartan "harmost,"
cf. Arist., Av., 1032, and Boeckh, Inscr.,
73 (in the Roman period ἐπιμεληταί); but
it was by no means confined to Attic
usage. In another inscription found at
Thera in the Macedonian period mention is made of two ἐπίσκοποι receiving
money and putting it out at interest,
and again at Rhodes, in the second century B.C., ἐπίσ. are mentioned in inscriptions, but we do not know their functions,
although Deissmann claims that in one
inscription, I. M. A. e., 731, the title is
used of a sacred office in the Temple of
Apollo, but he declines to commit himself to any statement as to the duties of
the office: cf. also Loening, Die Gemeindeverfassung des Urchristenthums, pp. 21,
22 ; Gibson, "Bishop," B.D.²; Gwatkin,
"Bishop," Hastings' B.D. ; Deissmann,
Neue Bibelstudien, p. 57 ; Lightfoot,
Philippians, p. 95. M. Waddington
has collected several instances of the
title in inscriptions found in the Haurân,
i.e., the south-eastern district of the
ancient Bashan (see the references to
Le Bas-Waddington in Loening, u. s.,
p. 22, note, and Gore, Church and the
Ministry, p. 402), but none of these give
us precise and definite information as to
the functions of the ἐπίσκοποι. But it
is important to note that M. Waddington
is of opinion that the comparative frequency of the title in the Haurân points
to the derivation of the Christian use of
the word from Syria or Palestine rather
than from the organisation of the Greek
municipality (Expositor, p. 99, 1887).
It has been urged that the officers of
administration and finance in the contemporary non-Christian associations,
the clubs and guilds so common in the
Roman empire, were chiefly known by
one or other of two names, ἐπιμελητής
or ἐπίσκοπος, Hatch, B.L., p. 36, and
hence the inference has been drawn that
the primary function of the primitive
ἐπίσκοποι in the Christian Church was

ποιμνίου · 30. καὶ ἐξ ὑμῶν αὐτῶν ἀναστήσονται ἄνδρες λαλοῦντες
διεστραμμένα, τοῦ ἀποσπᾶν τοὺς μαθητὰς ὀπίσω αὐτῶν. 31. διὸ

the administration of finance; but Dr.
Hatch himself has denied that he laid
any special stress upon the financial
character of the ἐπίσκοποι, although he
still apparently retained the description
of them as " officers of *administration
and* finance," see *Expositor, u. s.*, p. 99,
note, thus adopting a position like that
of Professor Harnack, who would extend
the administration duties beyond finance
to all the functions of the community.
But however this may be (see below),
there is certainly no ground for believing
that the title ἐπίσκοπος in the Christian
Church was ever limited to the care of
finance (see the judgment of Loening on
this view, *u. s.*, p. 22), or that such a limitation was justified by the secular use of
the term. If indeed we can point to any
definite influence which connects itself
with the introduction of the title into the
Christian Church, it is at least as likely,
one might say more likely when we
consider that the Apostles were above
all things Jews, that the influence lies in
the previous use in the LXX of ἐπίσκοπος and ἐπισκοπή, and the direct appeal
of St. Clement of Rome, *Cor.*, xlii., 5,
to Isaiah (LXX) lx. 17 in support of
the Christian offices of ἐπίσκοποι and
διάκονοι may be fairly quoted as pointing
to such an influence. But whatever
influences were at work in the adoption
of the term by the early believers, it
became, as it were, baptised into the
Christian Church, and received a Christian and a higher spiritual meaning.
This one passage in Acts xx. 28 is sufficient to show that those who bore the
name were responsible for the spiritual
care of the Church of Christ, and that
they were to feed His flock with the
bread of life (see the striking and impressive remarks of Dr. Moberly, *Ministerial
Priesthood*, p. 266). This one passage
is also sufficient to show that the
" presbyter " and " bishop " were at first
practically identical, *cf.* vv. 17 and 28,
Steinmetz, *Die zweite römische Gefangenschaft des Apostels Paulus*, p. 173,
1897, and that there is no room for the
separation made by Harnack between
the two, see his *Analecta zu Hatch*,
p. 231, or for his division between the
" patriarchal " office of the πρεσβύτεροι
and the " administrative " office of the
ἐπίσκοποι (Loening, *u. s.*, pp. 23-27;
Sanday, *Expositor, u. s.*, pp. 12, 104;
Gwatkin, *u. s.*, p. 302). In the Pastoral
Epistles the identity between the two is
even more clearly marked, although
Harnack cannot accept Tit. i. 5-7 as a
valid proof, because he believes that
vv. 7-9 were interpolated into the received
text by a redactor; *cf.* also for proof of the
same I Tim. iii. 1-7, 8-13, v. 17-19;
I Pet. v. 1, 2, although in this last
passage Harnack rejects the reading
ἐπισκοποῦντες (and it must be admitted
that it is not found in אB, and that it is
omitted by Tisch. and W. H.), whilst he
still relegates the passages in the Pastoral
Epistles relating to bishops, deacons
and Church organisation to the second
quarter of the second century, *Chron.*, i.,
p. 483, note. In St. Clement of Rome,
Cor., xlii., 4, xliv., 1, 4, 5, the terms are
still synonymous, and by implication in
Didaché, xv., 1 (Gwatkin, *u. s.*, p. 302,
and Gore, *u. s.*, p. 409, note). But if
we may say with Bishop Lightfoot
that a new phraseology began with
the opening of a new century, and
that in St. Ignatius the two terms are
used in their more modern sense, it
should be borne in mind that the transition period between Acts and St. Ignatius is exactly marked by the Pastoral
Epistles, and that this fact is in itself no
small proof of their genuineness. In
these Epistles Timothy and Titus exercise not only the functions of the ordinary presbyteral office, but also functions
which are pre-eminent over those of the
ordinary presbyter, although there is no
trace of any special title for these Apostolic delegates, as they may be fairly
called. The circumstances may have
been temporary or tentative, but it is
sufficiently plain that Timothy and Titus
were to exercise not only a general
discipline, but also a jurisdiction over
the other ministers of the Church, and
that to them was committed not only
the selection, but also the ordination of
presbyters (Moberly, *Ministerial Priesthood*, p. 151 ff.; Bright, *Some Aspects of
Primitive Church Life*, p. 28 ff., 1898;
Church Quarterly Review, xlii., pp. 265-
302).—τὴν ἐκκ. τοῦ Θεοῦ, see critical
note.—περιεποιήσατο, *cf.* Psalm lxxiv. 2.
It has been thought that St. Paul
adopts and adapts the language of this
Psalm; in comparing his language with
that of the LXX we can see how by the
use of the word ἐκκλησία instead of
συναγωγή in the Psalm he connects the
new Christian Society with the ancient

γρηγορεῖτε, μνημονεύοντες ὅτι τριετίαν νύκτα καὶ ἡμέραν οὐκ ἐπαυσά-
μην μετὰ δακρύων νουθετῶν ἕνα ἕκαστον. 32. καὶ τανῦν παρατίθεμαι
ὑμᾶς, ἀδελφοί,[1] τῷ Θεῷ καὶ τῷ λόγῳ τῆς χάριτος αὐτοῦ, τῷ δυναμένῳ
ἐποικοδομῆσαι καὶ δοῦναι ἡμῖν κληρονομίαν ἐν τοῖς ἡγιασμένοις

---

[1] τῷ Θεῳ, but B 33, 68, Sah., Boh., so Gig., W.H. text, R.V. marg., and Weiss
read τῷ Κυριῳ (Wendt doubtful), Alford, Tisch., Blass, R.V. text follow T.R., so
W.H. marg. For εποικοδ. ℵABCDE 18 read οικοδ., so Tisch., W.H., R.V.,
Weiss, Wendt, so Blass in β; DE, Gig. οικοδ. υμας.

ἐκκλησία of Israel, whilst in employing
περιεποιήσατο instead of ἐκτήσω (LXX),
and retaining the force of ἐλυτρώσω,
LXX, by reference to the λύτρον of the
new Covenant, a deeper significance is
given to the Psalmist's language : a
greater redemption than that of Israel
from the old Egyptian bondage had been
wrought for the Christian Ecclesia (Hort,
Ecclesia, pp. 14 and 102). The verb
περιποιεῖσθαι only in St. Luke and St.
Paul in N.T., but in a different sense in
the former, Luke xvii. 33. In 1 Tim.
iii. 13 (1 Macc. vi. 44) it is found in the
sense of "gaining for oneself," so in
classical Greek. But it is to be noted
that the cognate noun περιποίησις is
associated by St. Paul in his Ephesian
letter with the thought of redemption,
εἰς ἀπολύτρωσιν τῆς περιποιήσεως
"unto the redemption of *God's* own possession," R.V.—τοῦ ἰδ. τοῦ αἷμ., see
critical note.

Ver. 29. ἐγὼ γὰρ οἶδα, see critical
note. Baur and Zeller could only see in
this assertion a *vaticinium post eventum*
—the heresiarchs are portrayed in the
general expressions in vogue in the
second century; so too Renan thinks that
the writer gives us the ideas of a later
date, although he does not carry us further
than 75-80 A.D. But if we accept the
early date of the *Didaché*, that document
is quite sufficient to show us that similar
phraseology to that in the address before
us was current in the Church at an
earlier date than Baur and Zeller supposed. If St. Paul had been engaged all
his life in struggling with false teachers,
it would have been inconceivably short-
sighted if he had thought that such dangers
would cease after his departure, and still
more inconceivable if with such presenti-
ments he had neglected to warn the
Church. The vagueness of the description of the heretical teachers is in itself
a proof of genuineness, and a writer of
a later date would have made it far less
general, and more easily to be identified
with some current error. It has been

further objected by Zeller and Overbeck,
and even by Wendt, that it is strange
that with present opponents before him,
1 Cor. xvi. 8, 9, St. Paul should speak
only of the future; but whilst he had
himself been present among them
he had been their protector against
their enemies, but now that he was
about to withdraw from them nothing
was more natural than that he should
warn them against the subtle attacks
which might be more easily made when
his own careful superintendence was no
more.—εἰσελεύσονται: so men outside
the fold—the *when* of their entrance is
not specified precisely, but the words
were amply fulfilled in the presence of the
emissaries of the Judaisers, creeping in
from the Jewish communities into the
Churches of Asia, as they had slunk into
the Churches of Galatia, *cf.* Hort, *Judaistic
Christianity*, pp. 130-146, on the teaching
of the Judaisers and its evil influence in
the Pastoral Epistles. There is at all
events no need to refer the words with
Grotius to outward persecution, such as
that of Nero.—ἄφιξιν, *i.e.*, his departure
from amongst them (not necessarily
including his death), not arrival, although
the latter meaning attaches to the word
in classical Greek, so too 3 Macc. vii.
18; Jos., *Ant.*, iv., 8, 47 (but see both
Alford and Blass, *in loco*).—λύκοι: continuing the imagery of ver. 28, *cf.* Matt.
vii. 15, Luke x. 3, John x. 12; so in the
O.T. λύκοι of presumptuous and cruel
rulers and judges, Ezek. xxii. 27, Zeph.
iii. 3. The similar kind of language used
by Ignat., *Philadelph.*, ii., 1, 2; Justin
Martyr, *Apol.*, i., 58; Iren., *Adv. Hær.*,
i., Præf. 2, may well have been borrowed
from this, not *vice versâ* as Zeller maintained; but such imagery would no doubt
be widely known from its employment in
O. and N.T. alike.—βαρεῖς, *cf.* for the
sense of the adjective, Hom., *Il.*, i., 89;
Xen., *Ages.*, xi., 12; so too Diog. Laert.,
i., 72.—μὴ φειδ.: *litotes*, *cf.* John x.
12. The verb occurs six times in St.
Paul's Epistles, twice in Romans and four

πᾶσιν. 33. ἀργυρίου ἢ χρυσίου ἢ ἱματισμοῦ οὐδενὸς ἐπεθύμησα ·
34. αὐτοὶ[1] δὲ γινώσκετε ὅτι ταῖς χρείαις μου καὶ τοῖς οὖσι μετ᾽ ἐμοῦ

[1] δε omit. after αυτοι, W.H., R.V. on overwhelming evidence. After χρειαις μου
Blass adds πασαις in β ; D has πασιν.

times in the Corinthian Epistles (only
twice elsewhere in N.T. in 2 Pet.).
Ver. 30. καὶ ἐξ ὑμῶν αὐτῶν: αὐτῶν
adds emphasis, "from your own
selves". The Pastoral Epistles afford
abundant evidence of the fulfilment
of the words, cf. 1 Tim. i. 20, 2
Tim. i. 15, ii. 17, iii. 8, 13. To some
extent the Apostolic warning was effectual at all events in Ephesus itself, cf.
Rev. ii. 2; Ignat., Ephes., vi., 2.—ἀναστήσονται: common word in Acts, see
on v. 17, used here perhaps as in v. 36.
—διεστραμμένα, cf. LXX, Deut. xxxii.
5. The verb is found twice in Luke ix.
41 (Matt. xvii. 17), xxiii. 2, three times
in Acts xiii. 8, 10, and once again by St.
Paul, Phil. ii. 15, in a similar sense, cf.
Arist., Pol., iii., 16, 5, viii., 7, 7; Arrian,
Epict., iii., 6, 8.—ἀποσπᾶν τοὺς μαθητάς: "the disciples," R.V. with art. meaning that they would try and draw away
those that were already Christians, μαθ.
always so used in Acts. ἀποσ. to tear
away from that to which one is already
attached; used by St. Matt. xxvi. 51, and
elsewhere only by St. Luke xxii. 41, Acts
xxi. 1; compare with the genitive of
purpose after ἀνίστημι, 2 Chron. xx. 23.
—ὀπίσω αὐτῶν, "after themselves," cf.
v. 37, not after Christ, Matt. iv. 19.
Ver. 31. γρηγ.: the pastoral metaphor
continued; verb used four times by St.
Paul, and it may well have passed into
familiar use in the early Church by the
solemn injunction of our Lord on the
Mount of Olives to watch, cf. also Luke
xii. 37, 1 Pet. v. 8, Rev. iii. 2, 3, xvi. 15,
and the names Gregory, Vigilantius,
amongst the early converts.—τριετίαν:
the three years may be used summarily
i.e., as speaking in round numbers, or
literally. It would have seemed out of
place in such an appeal to say "two
years and three months," or whatever
the exact time may have been. The
intention was to give a practical turn to
this watchfulness: triennium celeste, Bengel. The word is regarded by Vogel as
a decided employment of a medical term
by Luke from Dioscorides, see also to
the same effect Meyer-Weiss, Evangelium
des Lukas, note on i., 1. The word is
found only here in N.T., not at all in
LXX, but used by Theophr., Plut.,
Artem.—νύκτα: perhaps placed first

because it corresponded more closely to
the idea of watching against attacks, or
perhaps because it emphasised the cease-
lessness of the Apostle's labours, cf. xxvi.
7, 1 Thess. ii. 9, iii. 10, 1 Tim. v. 5,
2 Tim. i. 3.—μετὰ δακρύων, cf. 2 Cor.
ii. 4, Chrys., Hom., xliv. "Quod cor
tamen saxatum, ut hisce lacrimis non
emolliatur ? qui non fleat flente Paulo ? "
Corn. à Lapide; see also Farrar, St. Paul,
ii., 283.—νουθετῶν: only here in Acts,
but seven times in St. Paul's Epistles,
but nowhere else in N.T., "admonish,"
R.V. In classical Greek it is joined both
with παρακαλεῖν and κολάζειν ; St. Paul
too used it in gentleness, or "with a
rod ". In LXX, Job iv. 3 ; Wisd. xi. 10,
xii. 2.—ἕνα ἕκαστον, 2 Cor. xi. 29 and
John x. 3 ; εἰς ἕκαστος twice in St.
Luke's Gospel, iv. 40, xvi. 5, six times in
Acts, five times in St. Paul's Epistles
(only once elsewhere in N.T., Matt. xxvi.
22, but not in T.R.).
Ver. 32. καὶ τὰ νῦν, see above on iv. 29.
—παρατίθ., cf. xiv. 23.—τῷ λόγῳ τῆς χ.
αὐτοῦ: as in the fourth Gospel, John i.
14-17, so here and in the Epistle to the
Ephesians, we find great stress laid on
χάρις, but we cannot conclude with Stier
and others that in the word λόγος we
have any reference here to the Word of
St. John's Gospel, although the similarity
between St. John's doctrine of the Word
and St. Paul's conception of our Lord's
Person is very close elsewhere ; the
thought here is however closely akin to
that of St. James i. 21 (Heb. iv. 12). In
his earliest Epistle the Apostle had
spoken of the Word, 1 Thess. ii. 13,
ὃς καὶ ἐνεργεῖται ἐν ὑμῖν. The Word
here is able to build up and to give, etc.,
which certainly seems to ascribe to it a
quasi-personal character, even more so
than in 2 Tim. iii. 15, where the Apostle
uses a somewhat similar phrase of the
O.T. Scriptures, τὰ δυνάμενά (the same
verb as here) σε σοφίσαι εἰς σωτηρίαν
κ.τ.λ. The same phrase as here occurs
in Acts xiv. 3, which points to its derivation from one imbued with Paul's words
and habits of thought, if not from the
Apostle himself (Alford). Weiss and
others refer τῷ δυν. to τῷ Θεῷ (Κυρίῳ, see
critical note), cf. Rom. xvi. 25, Ephes.
iii. 20, Gal. iii. 21, on the ground that
although ἐποικοδομῆσαι (οἰκοδ.) may re-

ὑπηρέτησαν αἱ χεῖρες αὗται. 35.[1] πάντα ὑπέδειξα ὑμῖν, ὅτι οὕτω
κοπιῶντας δεῖ ἀντιλαμβάνεσθαι τῶν ἀσθενούντων, μνημονεύειν τε τῶν
λόγων τοῦ Κυρίου Ἰησοῦ, ὅτι αὐτὸς εἶπε, "Μακάριόν ἐστι διδόναι

[1] Lach. and Blass add παντα to the previous verse, so Overbeck, Nösgen, Bethge
(Wendt doubtful). For των λογων LP read τον λογον; Bengel του λογου; no
doubt changes made because only one saying is quoted. D[1], Gig. read μακαριος
εστι μαλλον διδ. η λαμβ.; Blass in β reads μακαριον μαλλον τον διδοντα υπερ τον
λαμβανοντα; cf. Const. Apost., iv., 3, μακαριον ειπεν ειναι τον διδοντα ηπερ
(υπερ Anastas. Sin.) τον λαμβανοντα.

fer to λόγος, yet the λόγος cannot be said
δοῦναι κληρ. To the latter phrase Bethge,
p. 158, strives to find some Scriptural
analogies in the work attributed to ὁ
λόγος, cf. 1 Cor. i. 18, John xii. 48. But
it is best and simplest on the whole to
regard the entire phrase τῷ Θ. καὶ τῷ λ.
as one, "quasi una notio sunt; agit enim
Deus per verbum suum," Blass; so Page.
—ἐποικοδ., Ephes. ii. 20, in the passive,
see critical note. Whether we read the
compound or the simple verb, the metaphor of building is prominent in the
Ephesian Epistle ii. 21, iv. 12, 16, 29, as
also in 1 Cor., cf. iii. 10 (2), 12, 14; iii.
9, xiv. 3, 5, 12, 26, and cf. 2 Cor. v. 1, x.
8, xii. 19, xiii. 10. See note above on
ix. 31. τὴν κληρ., vii. 5, see note; nowhere else in Acts, cf. for the thought
Ephes. iii. 18, i. 11; and words elsewhere
spoken by St. Paul, Acts xxvi. 18; the
word itself occurs three times in Ephesians, i. 14, 18, v. 5. In Ephes. iii. 18
we have closely conjoined with κληρ. the
ἡ βασιλ. τοῦ χ., cf. St. Paul's words
ver. 25 above. The word is frequent in
Psalms of Solomon, cf. xiv. 6, 7, where
the inheritance of the saints is contrasted
with the inheritance of sinners in the
Messianic consummation, and also xv.
11, 12, xvii. 26; see further on the word,
Kennedy, p. 100.
Ver. 33. Cf. 1 Sam. xii. 3, ἱματ., frequent in LXX, in N.T. only in Luke and
Paul (except John xix. 24, quotation)|;
Luke vii. 25, ix. 29, 1 Tim. ii. 9. In
1 Macc. xi. 24 we have silver, gold and
raiment, joined together as in this verse,
describing Eastern riches, cf. James v.
2, 3.—ἐπεθ., "he takes away that which
is the root of all evil, the love of money";
he says not "I have not taken," but
"not even coveted," Chrys., Hom., xlv.
Ver. 34. αὐτοί: placed first for emphasis, so too emphasised in ii. 22, xvi.
37, xviii. 15. In 1 Cor. iv. 12 we may
see an undesigned coincidence, and cf.
the word κοπιῶντας in ver. 35, Paley,
H.P., iii., 6.—ταῖς χρείαις μου καὶ τοῖς
οὖσι μετ᾽ ἐμοῦ: so the work of the

Christian convert ἐργαζ. τὸ ἀγ. ταῖς
χερσίν is to be done ἵνα ἔχῃ μεταδιδόναι
τῷ χρείαν ἔχοντι, Ephes. iv. 28, and for
the word χρεία as used by St. Paul elsewhere in same sense, cf. Rom. xii. 13,
Phil. ii. 25, iv. 16, Tit. iii. 14.—ὑπηρέτησαν: only in Acts xiii. 36, used by
Paul, xxiv. 23, used of Paul (cf. 1 Cor.
iv. 1); Wisd. xvi. 24.—αὗται: "callosæ,
ut videtis," Bengel, so Blass; quite in
Paul's manner, cf. xxvi. 29, xxviii. 20;
so also πάντα, 1 Cor. ix. 25, x. 33, xi. 2,
Ephes. iv. 15. Paul pursued his trade
at Ephesus probably with Aquila and
Priscilla, possibly with Philemon, Philem.
ver. 17.
Ver. 35. πάντα ὑπέδ.: "in all things
I gave you an example," R.V., see also
critical note. The verb and the cognate
noun are both used in Greek in accordance with this sense, Xen., Oec., xii.,
18, Isocr., v., 27, see Plummer on Luke
iii. 7, etc., so ὑπόδειγμα, Xen., De re
eq., ii., 2, and for other instances of the
similar use of the word see Westcott on
Heb. viii. 5, Ecclus. xliv. 16, 2 Macc.
vi. 28, 31, 4 Macc. xvii. 23, cf. also Clem.
Rom., Cor., v., 1, xlvi., 1. οὕτως, i.e.,
as I have done, cf. Phil. iii. 17.—κοπιῶντας: not of spiritual labours, but of
manual, as the context requires. No
doubt the verb is used in the former
sense, 1 Cor. xvi. 16, Rom. xvi. 12,
1 Thess. v. 12, but also in the latter,
1 Cor. iv. 12, Ephes. iv. 28, 2 Tim. ii. 6
(so also κόπος by Paul). In St. Paul's
writings it occurs no less than fourteen
times, in St. Luke only twice, Luke v. 5
(xii. 27). In classical Greek, so in Josephus, it has the meaning of growing
weary or tired, but in LXX and N.T.
alone, laboro viribus intentis (Grimm).
—δεῖ, see above on p. 63.—ἀντιλαμβ.:
only in Luke and Paul, Luke i. 54, 1
Tim. vi. 2, cf. 1 Cor. xii. 28. The verb
= to take another's part, to succour (so
too cognate noun), in LXX, Isa. xli. 9,
Ecclus. ii. 6, iii. 12, xxix. 9, 20, of
helping the poor, cf. also Psalms of
Solomon, xvi. 3, 5, vii. 9, see further Psalms

μᾶλλον ἢ λαμβάνειν". 36. καὶ ταῦτα εἰπών, θεὶς τὰ γόνατα αὐτοῦ,
σὺν πᾶσιν αὐτοῖς προσηύξατο. 37. Ἱκανὸς δὲ ἐγένετο κλαυθμὸς
πάντων· καὶ ἐπιπεσόντες ἐπὶ τὸν τράχηλον τοῦ Παύλου κατεφίλουν
αὐτόν· 38. ὀδυνώμενοι μάλιστα ἐπὶ τῷ λόγῳ ᾧ εἰρήκει, ὅτι οὐκέτι
μέλλουσι τὸ πρόσωπον αὐτοῦ θεωρεῖν. προέπεμπον δὲ αὐτὸν εἰς τὸ
πλοῖον.

of Solomon, Ryle and James edit., p. 73 ; on ἀντίληψις, H. and R., *sub. v.* In classical Greek used in middle voice with genitive as here.—τῶν ἀσθενούν., *cf.* 1 Thess. v. 14, for a similar precept. The adjective need not be limited to those who sought relief owing to physical weakness or poverty, but may include all those who could claim the presbyters' support and care, bodily or spiritual, *cf.* Rom. xii. 13. The usage of the gospels points to those who are weak through disease and therefore needing help, *cf., e.g.,* Matt. x. 8, **Mark** vi. 56, Luke ix. 2, John v. 3, so also by St. Paul, Phil. ii. 26, 27, 2 Tim. iv. 20, although there are instances in LXX where the word is used of moral rather than of physical weakness. When the word is used of moral or spiritual weakness in the N.T., such a meaning is for the most part either determined by the context, or by some addition, *e.g.,* τῇ πίστει, Rom. xiv. 1.—μνημονεύειν τε : the verb is used seven times by St. Paul in his Epistles, once by St. Luke in his Gospel, Luke xvii. 32, and twice in Acts in the words of St. Paul, *cf.* ver. 31. Twice in the Epistle of St. Clement of Rome we find a similar exhortation in similar words, chap. xiii. 1 and xlvi. 7, and in each case the word may refer to a free combination of our Lord's words (*cf.* Luke vi. 30, xiv. 14), so too in St. Polycarp, *Epist.,* ii., 3. From what source St. Paul obtained this, the only saying of our Lord, definitely so described, outside the four Gospels which the N.T. contains, we cannot tell, but the command to "remember" shows that the words must have been familiar words, like those from St. Clement and St. Polycarp, which are very similar to the utterances of the Sermon on the Mount. From whatever source they were derived the references given by Resch, *Agrapha,* pp. 100, 150, show how deep an impression they made upon the mind of the Church, Clem. Rom., *Cor.,* ii., 1, *Did.,* i., 5, *Const. Ap.,* iv., 3, 1 ; *cf.* also Ropes, *Die Sprüche Jesus,* p. 136. In thus appealing to the words of the Lord Jesus, St. Paul's manner in his address is very similar to that employed in his Epistles, where he is apparently able to quote the words of the Lord in support of his judgment on some religious and moral question, *cf.* 1 Cor. vii. 10, 11, 12, 25, and the distinction between his own opinion, γνώμη, and the command of Christ, ἐπιταγή (*Witness of the Epistles,* p. 319). τε : Weiss (so Bethge) holds that the word closely connects the two clauses, and that the meaning is that only thus could the weak be rightly maintained, *viz.,* by remembering, etc., ὅτι being causal. But however this may be, in this reference, ὅτι αὐτὸς εἶπεν, "how he *himself* said," R.V. (thus implying that the fact was beyond all doubt), we may note one distinctive feature in Christian philanthropy, that it is based upon allegiance to a divine Person, and upon a reference to His commands. The emphatic personal pronoun seems to forbid the view that the Apostle is simply giving the sense of some of our Lord's sayings (see above). Similar sayings may be quoted from pagan and Jewish sources, but in Aristotle, *Eth. Nicom.,* iv., 1, it is the part τοῦ ἐλευθερίου to give when and where and as much as he pleases, but only because it is beautiful to give ; even in friendship, generosity and benevolence spring from the reflection that such conduct is decorous and worthy of a noble man, *Eth. Nicom.,* ix., 8. In Plato's *Republic* there would have been no place for the ἀσθενεῖς. Even in Seneca who sometimes approaches very nearly to the Christian precept, when he declares, *e.g.,* that even if we lose we must still give, we cannot forget that pity is regarded as something unworthy of a wise man ; the wise man will help him in tears, but he will not weep with him ; he helps the poor not with compassion, but with an impassive calm. —μακάριον : emphatic in position, see critical note. Bengel quotes from an old poet, *cf.* Athenæus, viii., 5, μακάριος, εἴπερ μεταδίδωσι μηδενί . . . ἀνόητος ὁ διδούς, εὐτυχὴς δ' ὁ λαμβάνων. The lines are by no means to be regarded as the best expression of pagan ethics, but the μακάρ., which occurs more than thirty

XXI. 1. ΄ΩΣ δὲ ἐγένετο ἀναχθῆναι ἡμᾶς¹ ἀποσπασθέντας ἀπ'
αὐτῶν, εὐθυδρομήσαντες ἤλθομεν εἰς τὴν Κῶν, τῇ δὲ ἑξῆς εἰς τὴν

¹ W.H. in marg., following BE²L, read **αποσπασθεντες**, placing a comma after
ημας; Weiss here is uninfluenced by B, and reads as in text. **Κων**, but **Κω ℵABCDE**,
Tisch., W.H., R.V., Blass, Weiss. At beginning of sentence β text **αποσπασθεντων**
δε ημων απ' αυτων επιβαντες ανηχθημεν; D¹ has **και επιβαντες ανηχθημεν αποσ-**
πασθεντων δε ημων απ' αυτων. Either from next verse, or from the usual desire of
reviser to take nothing for granted (Weiss).

times on the lips of our Lord, bids us
aim at something altogether higher and
deeper and fuller than happiness—blessedness. In Judaism, whilst compassion for
the poor and distressed is characteristic of
a righteous Israelite, we must still bear in
mind that such compassion was limited by
legality and nationality; the universality
of the Christian precept is wanting,
Uhlhorn, *Christian Charity*, pp. 1-56,
E.T., instances in Wetstein, and Bethge
and Page, *in loco*.

Ver. 36. θεὶς τὰ γόν., see above on p. 203.

Ver. 37. ἱκανὸς, *cf*. viii. 13.—ἐπιπεσόντες: an exact parallel only in
Luke xv. 22 (*cf*. also κατεφίλησεν in
same verse), *cf*. above on ἐπιπίπτειν
and in LXX, Gen. xxxiii. 4, xlv. 14, xlvi.
29, Tobit xi. 8, 3 Macc. v. 49.—κατεφίλουν, imperfect, *i.e.*, repeatedly and
tenderly. The verb occurs three times
in St. Luke's Gospel, vii. 38, 45, xv. 20,
and once in Matthew and Mark of the
kiss of Judas, *cf*. Xen., *Mem*., ii., 6, 33.

Ver. 38. ὀδυνώμενοι: common in Luke
and Acts, only three times elsewhere in
N.T., Luke ii. 48, xvi. 24, 25.—θεωρεῖν,
Lucan, *cf*. xvii. 16, 22, "to behold," R.V.,
to gaze with reverence upon his face.—
μέλλουσι, see above p. 157.—προέπεμπον
δὲ αὐτὸν: "and they brought him on
his way," R.V., *cf*. xv. 3 (see note), xxi.
5; the harbour was some little distance
from the town.

CHAPTER XXI.—Ver. 1. ἀναχθῆναι,
see above on xiii. 13.—ἀποσ., *cf*. xx. 30,
"were parted from them," R.V. The
word expresses a separation difficult and
painful; it adds to the pathos of the
scene, and marks the close affection
which could not bear the thought of
a parting, "divulsi ab eorum complexu,"
Blass (see Chrys., comment. *in loco*).
—εὐθυδ., see on xvi. 11.—Κῶν, *Stanchio*
or *Stanko*, an island of great trading
importance off the coast of Caria, south of
Miletus and Samos, and north of Rhodes.
Historically it had several points of connection with the Jews, *cf*. 1 Macc. xv. 23,
Jos., *Ant*., xiv., 7, 2, and 10, 15, *B. J.*, i.,
21, 11, and owing to its commerce it

became one of the centres of Jewish life
in the Ægean. It lay about forty nautical miles from Miletus, and it was famous
as the birthplace not only of Hippocrates, but of Apelles, and as being one
of the great medical schools of the ancient
world. See further "Cos" (Ramsay),
Hastings' B.D., and B.D.²; Farrar, *Saint
Paul*, ii., 284; Lewin, *St. Paul*, ii., 96;
cf. Strabo, xiv., 2, Hor., *Od*., iv., 13,
13, Tac., *Ann*., xii., 61. C. and H. think
that the chief town of the same name at
the east of the island is referred to in the
narrative before us. The place must have
had, as C. and H. note, a special interest
for St. Luke. — ΄Ρόδον: off the south
coast of Caria. According to the proverb the sun shone every day on Rhodes,
and it might well be called the sunny
island of roses. Her coins, stamped on
one side with Apollo's head radiated,
and on the other with the rose-flower,
bear their witness to the brightness and
fertility of the island. Moreover, it was
a seat not only of commerce but of
learning. St. Paul does not appear to
have landed, but only to have touched at
the island. The great Colossus representing the sun, counted as one of the
wonders of the world, lay prostrate,
having been broken down by an earthquake, Pliny, *N. H.*, xxxiv., 18; Strabo,
xiv., 2. In the time of the Peloponnesian
War Rhodes had been famous for its
strong navy, as its timber was abundant.
A notice of Jewish residents in Rhodes
meets us in 1 Macc. xv. 23. On subsequent history see the excellent account
in C. and H., small edit., p. 357; Farrar,
Saint Paul, ii., p. 285.—Πάταρα: a seaport on the Lycian coast, now in ruins,
but probably a place of some importance
and splendour. C. and H. say that
Patara was to the city Xanthus what the
Piræus was to Athens. On the modern
discoveries in Patara see C. and H.,
small edit., note p. 560, *cf*. Herod., i.,
182, Hor., *Od*., iii., 4, 64, Lewin, *St.
Paul*, ii., 99, O. Holtzmann, *Neutest. Zeitgeschichte*, p. 101. "The voyage may be
taken as typical of the course which hun-

Ῥόδον, κἀκεῖθεν εἰς Πάταρα.[1] 2. καὶ εὑρόντες πλοῖον διαπερῶν εἰς
Φοινίκην ἐπιβάντες ἀνήχθημεν. 3.[2] ἀναφανέντες δὲ τὴν Κύπρον, καὶ
καταλιπόντες αὐτὴν εὐώνυμον, ἐπλέομεν εἰς Συρίαν, καὶ κατήχθημεν
εἰς Τύρον· ἐκεῖσε γὰρ ἦν τὸ πλοῖον ἀποφορτιζόμενον τὸν γόμον.
4. καὶ ἀνευρόντες τοὺς μαθητάς, ἐπεμείναμεν αὐτοῦ ἡμέρας ἑπτά·
οἵτινες τῷ Παύλῳ ἔλεγον διὰ τοῦ Πνεύματος, μὴ [3] ἀναβαίνειν εἰς

---

[1] After **Πάταρα** D (Gig., Wer., Sah.) add **καὶ Μύρα**, so Blass in β, and Hilg.,
another accurate geographical touch; *cf*. xx. 15 and Ramsay, *C. R. E.*, p. 153, and
St. Paul, p. 297; but after a long discussion of the passage in *Expositor*, March,
1895, Ramsay decides against the originality of the reading, but see also Zöckler,
Greifswalder Studien, p. 138, who declines to be persuaded by these recent arguments urged by R. Wendt thinks that it may be original, p. 338 (1899), so Corssen,
G. G. A., p. 441. Weiss, Codex D, p. 109, while accepting D in xx. 15, finds here
assimilation to xxvii. 5. On the other hand the words may have been omitted in
view of Paul's haste in xx. 16 (Wendt). See also Schmiedel, *Enc. Bibl.*, i., 54.

[2] **ἀναφανέντες** אB* 66, Tisch., W.H., Weiss, Blass, but **-φανέντες** AB³CEHLP,
Lach., Treg., Alford. **κατηλθομεν** for **κατηχ.** אABE, Vulg., Sah., Boh., Syr. H.,
Aeth., Tisch., W.H., R.V., Blass, Weiss.

[3] For **ἀναβ.** אABC, mins., Tisch., W.H., R.V., Blass, Weiss, read **ἐπιβ.**

---

dreds of ships took every year," Ramsay,
St. Paul, p. 297, and *cf*. the illustrations
from Roman history in C. and H., p. 560
note.

Ver. 2. They went at Patara on board
a ship about to start on the direct Syrian
course, ἐπιβ., *cf*. xx. 18.

Ver. 3. ἀναφ.: "when we had come
in sight of," R.V., Doric form of 1st
aorist active, Winer-Schmiedel, p. 112,
here a technical word (only in Luke, *cf*.
Luke xix. 11, but in a different sense),
i.e., after we had rendered Cyprus visible
(to us) = *facere ut appareat* (Blass);
Virgil, *Æneid*, iii., 275, 291, see also
Rendall's note *in loco* (for the opposite
idiom, ἀποκρύπτειν, *cf*. Thuc., v., 65).—
καταλιπόντες αὐτὴν εὐώ.: sailing south-
east they would have passed close to
Paphos in Cyprus.—ἐπλέομεν: "imperf.
cursum, aorist. κατήλθομεν finem denotat" (Blass).—εἰς Τύρον: now a free
town of the R. province of Syria,
Strabo, xvi., 2, in honour of its ancient
greatness; it is still a place of considerable commerce and consequence, still
famous for its fabrics and its architecture.
At present it numbers amongst its five
thousand inhabitants a few Jews, the
rest being Mohammedans and Christians.
Besides O.T. references, see 1 Macc. xi.
59, 2 Macc. iv. 18, 44, and further for its
history, C. H., small edit., p. 563, Hamburger, *Real-Encyclopädie des Judentums*,
i., 7, 998, Schaff-Herzog, *Encyclopædia*,
iv., "Tyre".—ἐκεῖσε: the adverb may be
used here with something of its proper
force, but in xxii. 5, the only other

place in which it occurs in N.T., simply
= ἐκεῖ, Simcox, *Language of the New
Testament*, p. 179. Page (*in loco*) renders
"for there the ship was unlading her
cargo," ἐκεῖσε being used because of the
idea of movement and carrying into the
town contained in the "unloading".—
ἦν ἀποφ.: taken sometimes as the
present for the future, Burton, p. 59, but
see also Winer-Moulton, xlv., 5, and
Wendt (1888) *in loco* (Philo, *De Præm.
et Pœn.*, 5; and Athenæus, ii., 5, of
lightening a ship in a storm).—γόμον
(γέμω): so in classical Greek, Herod.,
Dem., etc., in LXX of the load of a beast
of burden, Exod. xxiii. 5, 2 Kings v. 17;
in N.T. only elsewhere in Rev. xviii. 11,
of any merchandise.

Ver. 4. ἀνευρόντες τοὺς μ.: more
than simply to find, *quærendo reperire*,
Blass; "having found out," as colloquially "having looked up"; only in
Luke, *cf*. Luke ii. 16, but in middle,
4 Macc. iii. 14.—τοὺς μαθ.: W. H. The
article indicates that the existence of the
disciples was known, but it was difficult
to find out their whereabouts in a great
town, *cf*. xv. 3, 41.—ἐπεμείναμεν, see on
x. 48.— ἡμέρας ἑπτά: the period
would at all events enable Paul to enjoy
a first day of the week with the Church.
Apparently he and his went on in the
same ship, ver. 6, evidently it was a
trading vessel of the larger size, as it
took this time to unload; on the genuineness of the narration here see Salmon,
Introd., p. 300. — διὰ τοῦ Π.: there
is no contradiction between this state-

Ἰερουσαλήμ.　5. ὅτε δὲ ἐγένετο[1] ἡμᾶς ἐξαρτίσαι τὰς ἡμέρας, ἐξελθόντες ἐπορευόμεθα, προπεμπόντων ἡμᾶς πάντων σὺν γυναιξὶ καὶ
τέκνοις ἕως ἔξω τῆς πόλεως, καὶ θέντες τὰ γόνατα ἐπὶ τὸν αἰγιαλὸν
προσηυξάμεθα.　6. καὶ[2] ἀσπασάμενοι ἀλλήλους, ἐπέβημεν εἰς τὸ

---

[1] ημας εξαρτισαι ℵ(*or)², CHLP, so Tisch., W.H. marg. ; but εξαρ. ημας AB*E
68, W.H. text, Weiss.　At beginning of verse, instead of οτε . . . τας ημερας d, so
Blass in β, has *sequenti die*—τη δε εξης ημερᾳ.

[2] προσευξαμενοι απησπασαμεθα in R.V., Tisch., W.H., Blass.　Instead of T.R.,
ℵ*AC, Tisch. have ανεβημεν, so Wendt (probably) ; but ℵcBE 68, 73, Chrys., so
Lach., W.H., R.V., Weiss ενεβημεν.

ment and St. Paul's assertion that he was
proceeding to Jerusalem under the same
divine guidance.　That the prophets
at Tyre should foresee the Apostle's
danger was only in accordance with his
own words in xx. 23, and their affectionate regard for him might well prompt
them to dissuade him from such perilous
risks.　There is therefore no occasion to
suppose that the clause has been interpolated into the "We" source.　Hilgenfeld refers οἵτινες . . . Ἰερ. (ver. 4), as
also the whole of ver. 9, τούτῳ δὲ . . .
προφ. to his "author to Theophilus," on
the ground that this writer had already
spoken of Paul's tribulations as awaiting
him in city by city, xx. 23, and that the
notices in vv. 4 and 9 here are added by
him in confirmation.　But Hilgenfeld
(with Clemen and Jüngst) retains vv.
10-14, the episode of Agabus, as belonging to the "We" source, and sees a
fitness in the prophecy of Agabus foretelling, after the manner of the O.T.
prophets, in the last station before Jerusalem, the imprisonment of the Apostle,
whilst Paul in spite of all entreaties is
unmoved in his determination.　But (1)
it is quite arbitrary to refer the whole
speech at Miletus (see above, chap. xx.)
to the "author to Theophilus," and (2)
although it was quite fitting that the
warning of danger should be more vivid
on its approach, yet one fails to see why
the more definite symbolical act of Agabus should exclude previous intimations
of danger on the part of affectionate
friends speaking of the Holy Ghost.
In ver. 9 nothing is said as to the
prophecies of the daughter of Philip and
Paul's imprisonment, but see below.
　　Ver. 5. ἐξαρτίσαι: here in the sense
of accomplishing the days, *i.e.*, finishing
the time, the seven days during which
we had to remain for the cargo to be
unloaded or for other business = ἀπαρ-
τίζειν (and *cf.* Luke xiv. 28), Vulgate,
"expletis diebus," Chrys., πληρῶσαι,

so Oecum., Theoph.　The verb is only
used once elsewhere in N.T., and there
by St. Paul, 2 Tim. iii. 17 = furnishing,
completing, so Jos., *Ant.*, iii., 2, 2, where
the verb is used as in 2 Tim., *l. c.*, and
some have thought that here the verb
means that the ship was completely prepared for the continuance of her voyage.
So Rendall who takes ἡμᾶς (reading ἐξαρ.
ἡμᾶς) as the object, and renders "and
when it proved that the days furnished
us"; on St. Paul's stay and its reason
see Ramsay, *St. Paul*, p. 300, and for
other explanations, Nösgen and Weiss,
in loco.　There is no reason to interpret
the words as meaning that the Apostle
found that his desire, xx. 16, could not
be fulfilled, and that so he was content
to remain the seven days.—προπεμ., see
above: πάντων.　The clause has been
taken (Wendt) to intimate that the number of disciples at Tyre was small; this
was probably the case, but it is not clear
from the words here.　σὺν γυν. καὶ τέκ.,
a descriptive touch of an eyewitness
(Zöckler) ; on this local use of ἕως as
characteristic of Luke, *cf.* Friedrich, p.
20.—θέντες . . . αἰγ., see xx. 36.　αἰγ.,
a smooth shore in distinction to one
precipitous and rocky, xxvii. 39, also
found in Matt. xiii. 2, 48, John xxi. 4.
In LXX, Judg. v. 17, Ecclus. xxiv.
14 (S² *al.*, and *cf.* note in *Speaker's
Commentary, in loco*).　See Hackett's
note on this accurate description of the
beach on both sides of the site of the
ancient Tyre, and also a parallel to the
scene described in this passage from
modern missionary life.
　　Ver. 6. R.V. ἀπησπασάμεθα ἀλλ.
"bade each other farewell," see critical
note. ἀπασπάζομαι: only here in N.T.,
in Tobit x. 13 S (AR *al.*); Himerius,
p. 194; here of salutations at departure,
as simple verb in ver. 7, of salutations on
arrival (1 Macc. xii. 17).—τὸ πλοῖον:
article indicates that it was the same
ship (ver. 2 without the article) which

πλοῖον, ἐκεῖνοι δὲ ὑπέστρεψαν εἰς τὰ ἴδια. 7. Ἡμεῖς δὲ τὸν πλοῦν διανύσαντες ἀπὸ Τύρου κατηντήσαμεν εἰς Πτολεμαΐδα, καὶ ἀσπασά-μενοι τοὺς ἀδελφοὺς ἐμείναμεν ἡμέραν μίαν παρ᾽ αὐτοῖς. 8. τῇ δὲ ἐπαύριον ἐξελθόντες[1] οἱ περὶ τὸν Παῦλον ἤλθομεν εἰς Καισάρειαν · καὶ εἰσελθόντες εἰς τὸν οἶκον Φιλίππου τοῦ εὐαγγελιστοῦ, τοῦ ὄντος ἐκ

---

[1] οι περι τον Π. om. ﹡ABCE, Vulg., and other verss. ; Tisch., W.H., R.V., Weiss, Wendt, Blass.

was going on to Ptolemais.—**εἰς τὰ ἴδια**, cf. John xvi. 32, xix. 27, cf. β text v. 18, xiv. 18 (**τὰ ἴδια** not in Synoptists, but cf. Luke xviii. 28), in LXX, Esther v. 10, vi. 12, 3 Macc. vi. 27, 37, vii. 8.

Ver. 7. **διανύσαντες**: "and when we had finished the voyage from Tyre we arrived at Ptolemais," R.V. (so in effect A.V.), but Page (so Wendt) renders "but we having (thereby) completed our voyage (i.e., from Macedonia, xx. 6), came from Tyre to Ptolemais," on the ground that **διανύω** would not be used of the short journey to Ptolemais from Tyre.—**Πτολε-μαΐδα**: the ancient Accho and the modern *Acre*, Arab. *Akka*: *St. Jean d'Acre*, mentioned here for the last time in Scrip-ture. About thirty miles south of Tyre. In Judg. i. 31 it was assigned to Asher, but it was never taken by Israel, and was always reckoned as belonging to the Philistine towns, and later by the Greeks as belonging to Phœnicia. In its stormy history it was held in succession by Babylonians and Persians (Strabo, xvi., 2, 25), and on the first division of Alexan-der's kingdom it was assigned to Ptolemy Soter (Ptolemy I.), from whom it may have derived its name (so Hamburger). Schürer however refers the name to Ptolemy II. (Philadelphus), and others to Ptolemy Lathurus. In the Syro-Egyptian wars its importance as a mili-tary station was manifested, since the power which held it could close the road down the Syrian coast to Egypt. To the Jews it was always hostile, 1 Macc. v. 15, Jos., *Ant.*, xii., 8, 2, 1 Macc. xii. 45, Jos., *Ant.*, xiii., 6, 2, and later in history when the Jewish War broke out against Rome, the Jews, two thousand in number, were slaughtered in Ptolemais, Jos., *B.J.*, ii., 18, 5. After falling to the Parthians, it finally passed under the dominion of Rome, but although it was called *colonia Ptolemais* under the Em-peror Claudius, Pliny, v., 19, it does not seem to have possessed the actual privi-leges of a colony (Schürer). See on its earlier and modern history, Hamburger, *Real-Encyclopädie des Judentums*, i., 1,

p. 41 ; "Acco," Hastings' B.D., "Accho," B.D.[2]; Schürer, *Jewish People*, div. ii., vol. i., p. 90, E.T. It was only separated from Tyre by a short day's voyage, if the wind was favourable. Here Herod landed on his return from Italy to Syria, Jos., *Ant.*, xiv., 15, 1.—**τοὺς ἀδελφοὺς**: a Chris-tian Church at Ptolemais ; founded perhaps by Philip the Evangelist. It is also very possible that a Church may have existed there ever since the dispersion after the death of St. Stephen, Acts xi. 19. On the times which St. Paul probably visited it see "Ptolemais" B.D.[1].

Ver. 8. **Φ. τοῦ εὐαγγ.**: the title, as Wendt and Hilgenfeld think, may have been given to Philip on account of his evangelising work, cf. viii., 12, 40; "*the* Evangelist": the honourable title gained by some signal service to the Gospel ; and the two incidents noted in his career, his preaching to the Samaritans, and to the Ethiopian eunuch, each mark an advance in the free development of the Church (Lightfoot, *Galatians*, p. 299). He had originally been set apart for other work, vi. 2, but both he and St. Stephen had been called to higher duties, and it is not sufficient to say that he was called an "evangelist" to distinguish him from Philip the Apostle, for that would have been done sufficiently by calling him "one of the Seven". The word only occurs twice elsewhere in the N.T., Ephes. iv. 11, 2 Tim. iv. 5. In the for-mer passage the Evangelists are placed between the Apostles and Prophets on the one hand, and the Pastors and Teachers on the other. The latter two offices suggested those who were attached to a settled community, whilst the Apostles and Prophets were non-local. Between the two pairs stood the Evangelists, whose work like that of Philip was to preach the Word. But it is to be care-fully noted that as the title is used of the work of Philip, "one of the Seven," and of that of Timothy, an Apostolic dele-gate, 2 Tim. iv. 5, it may have denoted an employment rather than an office, "a work rather than an order," and it

τῶν ἑπτά, ἐμείναμεν παρ' αὐτῷ.   9. τούτῳ δὲ ἦσαν θυγατέρες
παρθένοι τέσσαρες προφητεύουσαι.   10. ἐπιμενόντων δὲ ἡμῶν
ἡμέρας πλείους, κατῆλθέ τις ἀπὸ τῆς Ἰουδαίας προφήτης ὀνόματι

might be truly said that every Apostle was an Evangelist, but that not every Evangelist was an Apostle. At the same time their work may well have been more restricted locally than that of the Apostles, cf. Theodoret on Ephes. iv. 11, and also Eusebius, *H.E.*, ii., 3, iii. 37, itinerant work of an Evangelist, "Evangelist," B.D.[2]. The title is not found in the Apostolic Fathers or in the *Didaché*, and the latter omission Harnack would explain on the ground that the "Apostles" in the *Didaché* were just Evangelists; but it would seem, if we admit the reference to 2 Tim. iv. 5, that the title was already in general use, and that it was not limited to Apostles. Meyer sees in the Evangelists those who transmitted orally the facts of our Lord's life and teaching, before the existence of written Gospels; but however tempting this view may be, we can scarcely define the Evangelists' work so precisely, and still less thus distinguish it from that of the Apostles; but see, however, as favouring Meyer's view, "Evangelist," Hastings' B.D. Ewald's remarks on Philip as an Evangelist are still of interest, *Die drei ersten Evangelien*, i., 48 ff.; on the mistake which confused this Philip with Philip the Apostle, see Salmon, *Introd.*, 313.— εἰς Κ.: on two occasions St. Paul had already visited Cæsarea, ix. 30, xviii. 22, and he would probably have met Philip previously; but we have no knowledge of any previous meeting between St. Luke and Philip. We can conceive something of the importance of such a meeting when we remember the advantage which the latter's knowledge of the events in the early history of the Church would possess for the future historian. Philip's presence in Cæsarea at once connects itself with the notice in viii. 40, and thus indicates a unity of authorship in the whole book.—ὄντος ἐκ τῶν ἑπτά: the notice shows us how the early part of the book is taken for granted by the writer of the latter part (so Lightfoot and Salmon). This is surely more intelligible and satisfactory than to refer the words to the "author to Theophilus," or to regard it with Clemen as a later addition perhaps by his R., who already betrayed, xiv. 8, a knowledge of the sources of the first part of the book, or perhaps by R.J., who then connected *Historia Petri*

and *Historia Pauli*. Jüngst refers the notice in viii. 40 to a Reviser who thus seeks to connect the Philip of chap. viii. with Cæsarea, and so to identify him with the Philip here.

Ver. 9. παρθένοι: an unwedded life might enable them to wait on the Lord without distraction, and thus to be more free for the exercise of their gift of prophecy, but nothing is said of any separate order, or anything to lead us to suppose that they did not share the home life of their father, or that they had devoted themselves to God by any special vow (see however in support of this latter view Felten, Knabenbauer, Plumptre, C. and H.). St. Jerome, *Epist.*, v., 8, cviii., 8, in relating the story of Paula mentions how she saw at Cæsarea the house of Cornelius now turned into a Christian church, and the humble abode of Philip, and the chambers of his daughters, the four virgins "which did prophesy".—προφητεύουσαι, cf. Joel ii. 28, 29, Acts ii. 17, xix. 6, 1 Cor. xi. 5, xiv. 24, although nothing is said of their possessing the power of *prediction*, or foretelling anything concerning Paul. Since women were forbidden to teach it would seem that the prophet as such was not a teacher; Bigg, *Doctrine of the Twelve Apostles*, p. 29. But whilst there is no reason to suppose that they prophesied in the church, although even Felten supposes that in Churches not founded by Paul different rules might have prevailed, they would be able to speak and to teach in private or at home especially amongst the women both Jews and Gentiles, to whom in the East men would have had no access (Luckock, *Footprints of the Apostles as traced by St. Luke*, ii., p. 214). This verse is regarded by Hilgenfeld as an addition made by the "author to Theophilus" (so Renan). Spitta however thinks that something ought to have been said as to the nature of the prophecies uttered by the four daughters, but that instead of this we have the notice of Agabus in ver. 10. He therefore believes that the "We" section was interrupted at ver. 10, and that the verses following are interpolated from his inferior source B. The reference to weeping in ver. 13 is much more natural if we presuppose the presence of women, so he therefore reads

Ἄγαβος· 11. καὶ ἐλθὼν πρὸς ἡμᾶς, καὶ ἄρας τὴν ζώνην τοῦ Παύλου, δήσας¹ τε αὐτοῦ τὰς χεῖρας καὶ τοὺς πόδας, εἶπε, Τάδε λέγει τὸ Πνεῦμα τὸ Ἅγιον· Τὸν ἄνδρα οὗ ἐστιν ἡ ζώνη αὕτη, οὕτω δήσουσιν ἐν Ἰερουσαλὴμ οἱ Ἰουδαῖοι, καὶ παραδώσουσιν εἰς χεῖρας ἐθνῶν. 12. ὡς δὲ ἠκούσαμεν ταῦτα, παρεκαλοῦμεν ἡμεῖς τε καὶ οἱ ἐντόπιοι, τοῦ μὴ ἀναβαίνειν αὐτὸν εἰς Ἰερουσαλήμ. 13.² ἀπεκρίθη δὲ ὁ Παῦλος, Τί ποιεῖτε κλαίοντες καὶ συνθρύπτοντές μου τὴν καρδίαν; ἐγὼ γὰρ οὐ μόνον δεθῆναι, ἀλλὰ καὶ ἀποθανεῖν εἰς Ἰερουσαλὴμ

¹ Instead of τε αυτου 𝕹ABCDE, Tisch., W.H., R.V., Blass, Wendt read εαυτου (HLP αὐτοῦ, others αὐτοῦ), see W.H., *App.*, p. 151.

² 𝕹ABC*E, Tisch., W.H. (omit o). 𝕹AE add και ειπεν, so Tisch. (Wendt perhaps); but *om.*, W.H., R.V., Weiss, after BCHLP, Bas., Chrys., D has ειπεν δε προς ημας ο Π., so Blass and Hilg. Instead of συνθ. D has θορυβουντες; D also reads δεθηναι βουλομαι, but not Blass.

"they prophesied with tears over the fate of Paul" (p. 339); so somewhat similarly Jüngst (p. 177).

Ver. 10. ἡμέρας πλείους: "many days," R.V., "some" margin; literally "more days," the phrase is used vaguely with what Ramsay calls Luke's usual defective sense of time, *cf.* xiii. 31, xxv. 14. The phrase is also found in xxvii. 20, so that it occurs twice in the "We" sections and twice in the rest of Acts, but nowhere else in N.T., see Hawkins, *Horæ Synopticæ*, p. 151, Klostermann, *Vindiciæ Lucanæ*, p. 53. Often in LXX. Weiss thinks that the phrase here, *cf.* ver. 4, shows that Paul had given up all idea of reaching Jerusalem for Pentecost; but see on the other hand Ramsay, *St. Paul*, p. 297, and Salmon, *Introd.*, p. 300: probably the Apostle had several days to spare when he reached Cæsarea, and he would naturally calculate his time differently when he had made a prosperous voyage, so that there is no contradiction with xx. 16.—προφ. ὀνόμ. Ἄ.: probably the same who is mentioned in xi. 25, since he too came from Jerusalem. It has seemed strange to Blass and to others that St. Luke mentions Agabus here so indefinitely, but in this "We" section it would seem that St. Luke refers to Agabus in this vague way because this was the first time that he had seen the prophet (unless we accept D in xi. 28). It is therefore quite unnecessary to regard the mention of his name in xi. 28 as an interpolation. Agabus is evidently enabled not only to declare the will of God, but also to predict the future.

Ver. 11. ἄρας τὴν ζώνην: the symbolic action by Agabus reminds us of the O.T. prophets, *cf.* 1 Kings xxii. 11, Isa. xx. 2, Jer. xiii. 1, Ezek. iv. and v. Agabus as a dweller in Jerusalem would know something of that bitter feeling against Paul, and would wish to warn him.—παραδώσ. εἰς χ., *cf.* the words of our Lord, Luke ix. 44, xxiv. 7; phrase frequent in LXX both in Psalms and Prophets, *cf.* Ecclus. iv. 19, xi. 6; 1 Macc. iv. 30.

Ver. 12. παρεκ. ἡμεῖς: St. Luke joins in the entreaty.—ἐντόπ., *i.e.*, the Christians of Cæsarea, including of course the inmates of Philip's house; not in LXX or Apocr., but in classical Greek.—τοῦ μὴ ἀναβ., Burton, p. 159.

Ver. 13. τί ποιεῖτε κλαί.: what do ye, weeping? (as we might say "what are you about?" etc.), *cf.* Mark xi. 5 (Acts xiv. 15).—συνθ.: in Attic Greek, to break in pieces, and so ἀποθρύπτω is used of (1) breaking in pieces, (2) breaking in spirit, enervating τὰς ψυχάς, *cf.* Plat., *Rep.*, 495 E.; here συνθ. means to weaken the Apostle's purpose rather than to break his heart in sorrow. —ἐγὼ, emphatic, I for my part.—οὐ μόνον in N.T., rather than μὴ μόνον with the infinitive, Burton, p. 183.—ἑτοίμως ἔχω: the exact phrase only once elsewhere in N.T., and there used by St. Paul, 2 Cor. xii. 14 (*cf.* 1 Pet. iv. 5): "qui paratus est, ei leve onus est," Bengel. Ewald compares this firm determination and courage of St. Paul with our Lord's last journey to Jerusalem, *cf.* Luke ix. 51.

Ver. 14. ἡσυχάσαμεν: only in Luke and Paul, *cf.* Luke xiv. 3, Acts xi. 18. In LXX, Job xxxii. 6, Neh. v. 8.—τὸ θέλ. τοῦ Κ., *cf.* Matt. vi. 10, Luke xxii. 42, and also St. Paul's own expression in

ἑτοίμως ἔχω ὑπὲρ τοῦ ὀνόματος τοῦ Κυρίου Ἰησοῦ. 14. μὴ πειθο-
μένου δὲ αὐτοῦ, ἡσυχάσαμεν εἰπόντες, Τὸ θέλημα τοῦ Κυρίου γενέσθω.

15. Μετὰ δὲ τὰς ἡμέρας ταύτας [1] ἀποσκευασάμενοι ἀνεβαίνομεν εἰς
Ἱερουσαλήμ. 16. συνῆλθον δὲ καὶ τῶν μαθητῶν ἀπὸ Καισαρείας
σὺν ἡμῖν,[2] ἄγοντες παρ' ᾧ ξενισθῶμεν, Μνάσωνί τινι Κυπρίῳ, ἀρχαίῳ
μαθητῇ.

[1] Instead of **αποσ.** ℵABELP, Tisch., Wendt, Weiss, R.V., W.H. read **επισ.** D
has **αποταξαμενοι**, so Blass in **β**, and Hilg. Blass proposed **απασπασαμενοι**;
but did not put in text; see Ramsay's criticism of Blass on this passage, *Exposi-*
tor, March, 1895.

[2] Instead of **αγοντες κ.τ.λ.** Blass in **β** text (following D, Syr. H. mg.) **ουτοι δε**
ηγον ημας προς ους ξενισθωμεν, και παραγενομενοι εις τινα κωμην εγενομεθα παρα
Μνασονι Κ. μαθητη αρχ. κακειθεν εξιοντες ηλθομεν εις Ι. From the trans. given in
comment. it would appear that the Cæsarean disciples accompanied Paul on a
journey of no less than sixty-four miles to Jerusalem to introduce him to Mnason, who
lived in the Holy City. But the improbability of this has been justly urged by Blass,
Philology of the Gospels, p. 128 (so too Salmon, *Hermathena*, xxi., p. 239; Zahn,
Einleitung, ii., p. 343), not only on account of the long distance, too long for one
day, but also because Paul might presumably have relied upon the hospitality of
private friends, already known in Jerusalem, to say nothing of the brethren referred
to in ver. 17. But the **β** text makes Paul rest at the house of Mnason, not at Jerusalem, but at some village on the way, and the Cæsarean disciples might naturally
accompany Paul to a village known to them, but not to Paul, where their fellow-
disciple (Mnason) dwelt. The originality of the **β** text is supported not only by
Belser and Zöckler, but by Holtzmann, *Th. Zs.*, p. 81, 1896, and Hilgenfeld; but,
on the other hand, see Corssen, *G. G. A.*, p. 438, 1896, and Weiss, Codex D, p. 101;
Page, *Classical Review*, pp. 318, 319 (1897), Wendt (1899), p. 342, and Schmiedel,
u. s. Wendt cannot see why, if **β** text was original, it could have been altered into
T.R., whereas if we note that the arrival of Paul at Jerusalem is only notified in
ver. 17, the lodging with Mnason might well have been placed previously at some
village on the route. But if we give the proper force to **ανεβαινομεν**, ver. 15, the
α text properly understood (as Zahn admits) implies the same fact as is brought
out in **β**, *viz.*, that Mnason entertained the company, not at Jerusalem, but on the
evening of the first day of their journey thither; ver. 15, they set about the
journey; ver. 16, they lodged with Mnason on the introduction of the Cæsarean
disciples; ver. 17, they came to Jerusalem, see especially Ramsay, *Expositor*, March,
1895, and his preference for the "Eastern" as against the "Western" reading
(although Zöckler is still unpersuaded by Ramsay's arguments, *Greifswalder*
Studien, p. 138).

xviii. 21, 1 Cor. iv. 19, xvi. 7 (Heb.
vi. 3), *cf.* Mayor's note on James iv.
15 for similar phrases amongst Greeks
and Romans, as also amongst Jews and
Arabians, Taylor's *Sayings of the Jewish*
Fathers, pp. 29, 95, 128, 2nd edit.
Ver. 15. **αποσ.**: A.V., "took up our
carriages," but the latter word is not
used now in a passive sense for luggage
or *impedimenta*, as in O.T., Judg. xviii.
21, 1 Sam. xvii. 22, Isa. x. 18, *cf.* Shakes.,
Tempest, v. 1, 3: "Time goes upright
with his carriage" (burden); see also
Plumptre's interesting note on the word.
R.V., reading **επισ.**, renders "we took up
our baggage," margin "made ready our
baggage," **τὰ πρὸς τὴν ὁδοιπορίαν λα-**
βόντες, Chrys., Ramsay renders "having

equipped *horses*," Xen., *Hell.*, v., 3, 1,
and see *St. Paul*, p. 302: the journey on
foot, some sixty-four miles, was scarcely
probable for Paul, especially if, as it would
seem from D, it was accomplished in two
days. Grotius took it as = "sarcinas
jumentis imponere," as if **ὑποζύγια**, Xen.,
Hell., vii., 2, 18. Hackett and Rendall
refer the word to the packing up of the
valuable alms which St. Paul was carrying to Jerusalem, but this interpretation
seems fanciful, although Hackett supposes that the contribution might have
consisted in part of raiment or provisions.
Belser still more curiously refers it to
getting change in the current money of
Palestine for the alms collected in the
coin of various lands.—**ἀνεβ.**: imperfect,

17. ΓΕΝΟΜΕΝΩΝ δὲ ἡμῶν εἰς Ἱεροσόλυμα, ἀσμένως [1] ἐδέξαντο
ἡμᾶς οἱ ἀδελφοί. 18. τῇ δὲ ἐπιούσῃ εἰσῄει ὁ Παῦλος σὺν ἡμῖν
πρὸς Ἰάκωβον, πάντες τε παρεγένοντο οἱ πρεσβύτεροι. 19. καὶ
ἀσπασάμενος αὐτούς, ἐξηγεῖτο καθ᾽ ἓν ἕκαστον ὧν ἐποίησεν ὁ Θεὸς
ἐν τοῖς ἔθνεσι διὰ τῆς διακονίας αὐτοῦ. 20. οἱ δὲ ἀκούσαντες
ἐδόξαζον τὸν [2] Κύριον· εἶπόν τε αὐτῷ, Θεωρεῖς, ἀδελφέ, πόσαι μυριάδες
εἰσὶν [3] Ἰουδαίων τῶν πεπιστευκότων· καὶ πάντες ζηλωταὶ τοῦ νόμου

[1] εδεξαντο, but ℵABCE, Tisch., W.H., R.V., Wendt απεδ.

[2] Κυριον, but Θεον ℵABCEL, Syr. Pesh., Boh., Aeth., so Tisch., W.H., R.V.,
Wendt, Weiss.

[3] After μυριαδες εισιν ABCE, Vulg., Boh., Aeth. 13, 36, 40, W.H., R.V., Weiss,
Wendt εν τοις Ιουδαιοις; om. in Tisch. with ℵ* 34*, 95*, 97. D, Syr. Pesh.,
Par., Sah., Aug. read εν τη Ιουδαια, so Blass in β text.

to denote the start on the journey (cf.
viii. 25: ὑπέστρεφον, R.V.). Both A.
and R.V. here render "went up," but it
should be rendered "we set about the
journey to Jerusalem," end of third m. j.
Ver. 16. ἄγοντες παρ᾽ ᾧ ξενισ.: A.
and R.V. render "bringing with them
Mnason with whom we should lodge,"
but Meyer-Wendt, so Page and Rendall,
render "bringing us to the house of
Mnason," etc., cf. also Spitta, Apostelgeschichte, p. 234. This is more in accordance with Codex D, on which see
critical note = ἄγ. πρὸς Μνάσ. ἵνα ξενισθῶμεν παρ᾽ αὐτῷ κ.τ.λ., see Blass, Gram.,
pp. 171, 213, and Winer-Schmiedel, p.
229. Vulgate (so Erasmus, Calvin)
renders "adducentes secum apud quem
hospitaremur Mnasonem," but harsh,
and presupposes that Mnason was at
Cæsarea.—Μνάσωνι, Att. Μνήσων, in
late MS., Νάσων and Ἰάσων, a name
common among the Greeks, and Mnason
was probably a Hellenist.—ἀρχαίῳ, cf.
xv. 7, may mean that he was an early
disciple, R.V., or even from the beginning, the great Pentecost, xi. 15 (Hum-
phrey), see also Ramsay, St. Paul,
p. 303; he may have been converted
by his fellow-countryman Barnabas. If
Blass is right in β, Acts xi. 2, he may
have been a convert instructed by St.
Peter (and in this sense ἀρχαῖος).
Ver. 17. There is no good reason to
doubt that they were in time for the
Feast; it is a legitimate inference from
their tarrying at Cæsarea that they were
easily able to reach Jerusalem: possibly
the presence of Jews from Asia may be
taken, as Rendall points out, to indicate
that the time of the Feast was near at
hand.—ἀσμένως: only here, significantly;
omitted in ii. 41 (R.V., W.H.); 2 Macc.

iv. 12, x. 33 A, 3 Macc. iii. 15, v. 21, so
in classical Greek. Even if the welcome
only came, as Wendt supposes, from
those who were comparatively few
amongst many in Jerusalem, St. Paul
found himself a brother amongst brethren.
—ἐδέξ., see on xviii. 27, ἀποδέχομαι.
Ver. 18. τῇ ἐπιούσῃ, three times in
"We" sections, twice in rest of Acts;
nowhere else in N.T. (in vii. 26 with
ἡμέρᾳ), Hawkins, u. s.—σὺν ἡμῖν: the
writer thus again claims to be an eye-
witness of what passed; it may well
have been the occasion for the reception of the alms collected from
the Churches.—Ἰάκωβον: on the authoritative position of St. James as
further shown here see Hort, Ecclesia,
p. 105, and Moberly, Ministerial Priesthood, p. 147. Nothing is said of the
Apostles, and they may have been absent
from Jerusalem on missionary work, or
at least the chief of them. They would
scarcely have been included under the
term πρεσβ. as Wendt supposes.
Ver. 19. ἀσπαζ.: used of farewell
greetings, xx. 1, xxi. 6, and of greetings
on arrival, xviii. 22, xxi. 7, for its use
here cf. 1 Macc. xi. 6.—ἐξηγ., see on x. 8,
etc.—καθ᾽ ἓν ἕκαστον: "one by one,"
R.V., cf. Ephes. v. 33.—διακονίας, see
note on vi. 1, 2.
Ver. 20. ἐδόξ.: "recte imperf. quia
finis verbo εἶπαν indicatur," Blass.—
θεωρεῖς: the word seems to imply that
Paul had already become cognisant of
the fact by his own observations in his
ministerial work.—ἀδελφέ: St. Paul is
recognised as an ἀδελφός not only by
St. James but by the assembled elders
(see also Weiss, in loco).—Ἰουδ., see
critical note.—μυριάδες, cf. Luke xii. 1,
of a large but indefinite number (cf. 1

ὑπάρχουσι. 21.[1] κατηχήθησαν δὲ περὶ σοῦ, ὅτι ἀποστασίαν διδάσκεις ἀπὸ Μωσέως τοὺς κατὰ τὰ ἔθνη πάντας Ἰουδαίους, λέγων μὴ περιτέμνειν αὐτοὺς τὰ τέκνα, μηδὲ τοῖς ἔθεσι περιπατεῖν. 22. τί οὖν ἐστι; πάντως[2] δεῖ πλῆθος συνελθεῖν· ἀκούσονται γὰρ ὅτι ἐλήλυθας. 23. τοῦτο οὖν ποίησον ὅ σοι λέγομεν· εἰσὶν ἡμῖν ἄνδρες τέσσαρες εὐχὴν ἔχοντες[3] ἐφ᾽ ἑαυτῶν· 24. τούτους παραλαβὼν ἁγνίσθητι σὺν αὐτοῖς, καὶ δαπάνησον[4] ἐπ᾽ αὐτοῖς, ἵνα[5] ξυρήσωνται τὴν κεφαλήν, καὶ γνῶσι πάντες ὅτι ὧν κατήχηνται περὶ σοῦ οὐδέν ἐστιν, ἀλλὰ στοιχεῖς καὶ

---

[1] D[1], Gig. κατηκησαν, *diffamaverunt*, instead of κατηχηθησαν, not Blass.

[2] δει πληθος συνελθειν *om.* BC* 15, 36, 137, 180, several verss., W.H., R.V., Weiss, but retained by Tisch., Blass, with אAC²DEHLP, Vulg., Chrys. γαρ. *om.* R.V., W.H., Weiss.

[3] εφ᾽ εαυτων W.H. marg., in text αφ᾽, following אB, but Weiss reads εφ᾽.

[4] επ᾽ αυτοις אAcorr.BCEHLP, επ᾽ αυτους, A* 13, 27, Theodrt.; Blass in β reads εις αυτους with D.

[5] ξυρησωνται AB³CHL, so Lach., Weiss, Blass; ξυρησονται אB*D², EP, Tisch., W.H., R.V. γνωσι HLP, Chrys.; γνωσονται אABCDE, W.H., Blass, Weiss, Wendt, R.V.

Cor. iv. 15), referring to the number of believers not only in Jerusalem but in Judæa present in large numbers for the Feast. The word cannot refer to Jewish Christians in a wider sense, as Overbeck took it, because they would not need to be informed of Paul's teaching relative to the Mosaic law.—ζηλωταὶ τοῦ ν., *cf.* Gal. i. 14, Tit. ii. 14, 1 Pet. iii. 13 (2 Macc. iv. 2, we have the same phrase, *cf.* 4 Macc. xviii. 12). The extreme party of the Pharisees prided themselves on the title "zealots of the law, zealots of God"; it was a title which St. Paul himself had claimed, Lightfoot, Gal. i. 14.

Ver. 21. κατηχήθησαν: the word seems to imply definite instruction, not merely *audierunt*, Vulgate. Hort refers to the term as implying here assiduous talking and lecturing, *Judaistic Christianity*, p. 107.—ἀποστασίαν, *cf.* 1 Macc. ii. 15 (S ἀπόστασιν) when the officers of Antiochus Epiphanes, in the time of Mattathias, tried to compel the people of Modin to forsake the law and to sacrifice upon the idol altar.—μὴ περιτέμνειν: these words and those which follow were an entire perversion of St. Paul's teaching, just as his enemies gave a perverted view of the Apostle's supposed intrusion with Trophimus into the temple, ver. 29. The exemption from the Mosaic law was confined to Jewish converts, xvi. 3, 1 Cor. vii. 18.—τοῖς ἔθεσι, *cf.* vi. 14, xv. 1. —περιπατεῖν: only here in Luke, but often in the Epistles in this sense, *cf.* Mark vii. 5.

Ver. 22. τί οὖν ἐστι; *cf.* 1 Cor. xiv. 15, 26, *cf.* vi. 3 in β text.—δεῖ πλῆθος συνελθεῖν, see critical note.—ἀκούσονται, *i.e.*, the Judaising Christians referred to in κατηχήθησαν, ver. 26. The words refer, not to an assembly of the whole Church, or to a tumultuary assembly, ver. 27, but to an assembly of the Judaising Christians as above.

Ver. 23. εἰσὶν ἡμῖν, *cf.* xviii. 10. The four men certainly seem to have been members of the Church at Jerusalem, *i.e.*, Jewish Christians.—εὐχὴν ἔχοντες: a temporary Nazirite vow, Num. vi. 1 ff. The length of time was optional, but thirty days seems to have been the shortest time, Jos., *B.J.*, ii., 15, 1.— ἐφ᾽ ἑαυτῶν, see critical note, the Nazirite vow lies upon them as an unfulfilled obligation. If we read ἀφ᾽ it would mean him to affirm that the vow had been taken by them of their own will, on their own initiation, *cf.* Luke xii. 57, 2 Cor. iii. 5, John v. 19, 30, etc., see further Grimm-Thayer, *sub v.* ἀπό, ii., 2 d, aa; and Rendall, *in loco*. Blass however renders ἐφ᾽ "quia votum *in se* receperunt," so that it is difficult to distinguish very definitely.

Ver. 24. παραλαβών, *cf.* ver. 26, xv. 39 (xvi. 33): take in a friendly way, associate thyself with them as a companion.— ἁγνίσθητι σὺν αὐτοῖς: the advice is characteristic of the Apostle who had lived as St. James had lived, Eusebius, *H.E.*, ii., 23, and it certainly seems to demand that St. Paul should place him-

αὐτὸς τὸν νόμον φυλάσσων. 25. περὶ δὲ τῶν πεπιστευκότων ἐθνῶν ἡμεῖς [1] ἐπεστείλαμεν, κρίναντες μηδὲν τοιοῦτον τηρεῖν αὐτούς, εἰ μὴ φυλάσσεσθαι αὐτοὺς τό τε εἰδωλόθυτον καὶ τὸ αἶμα καὶ πνικτὸν καὶ πορνείαν. 26. Τότε ὁ Παῦλος παραλαβὼν τοὺς ἄνδρας, τῇ [2] ἐχομένῃ ἡμέρᾳ σὺν αὐτοῖς ἀγνισθεὶς εἰσῄει εἰς τὸ ἱερόν, διαγγέλλων τὴν ἐκπλήρωσιν τῶν ἡμερῶν τοῦ ἁγνισμοῦ, ἕως οὗ προσηνέχθη ὑπὲρ ἑνὸς

---

[1] επεστειλαμεν ℵACEHLP, Vulg., Syr. Pesh., Sah., Chrys., Tisch., W.H. marg., R.V. text, Weiss (cf. xv. 20); απεστειλαμεν BD 40, Syr. H., Arm., W.H. text, R.V. marg., Wendt, Blass; see Wendt, p. 346 (1899). After εθνων D, Gig., Sah. add ουδεν εχουσι λεγειν προσ σε· ημεις γαρ, so Blass in β, Hilgenfeld, *Zw. Th.*, p. 382 (1896). The words in T.R. (after κριναντες) μηδεν . . . ει μη are supported by DCEHLP, Gig., Syr. H., Chrys., so Meyer, Alford, Blass, but om. ℵAB 13, 81, Vulg., Syr. Pesh., Sah., Boh., Tisch., W.H., R.V., Wendt, Weiss (Codex D, p. 103), και πνικτον om. D, Gig., Sah., Jer., Aug.

[2] εχομενη, D has επιουση; for εως ου D has οπως, but not Blass.

---

self on a level with the four men and take upon himself the Nazirite vow, *cf.* Num. vi. 3. The σὺν αὐτοῖς can hardly be explained otherwise. But how far the obligation of the vow extended in such a case is not clear (Edersheim, *Temple and its Services*, p. 326), and the time specified does not seem to allow for the commencement and completion of a vow on the part of the Apostle, although we cannot satisfactorily explain such expressions as the one before us, *cf.* ἡγνισμένον, xxiv. 18, on the supposition that St. Paul only associated himself with the company of the four votaries and incurred the expenses of their sacrifices. Dr. Hort suggests that the Apostle may have been himself about to offer sacrifices in the Temple in connection with some previous vow, or that in connection with the Gentile offerings which he had brought to Jerusalem and safely delivered (as it would seem) he may have proposed to offer a solemn peace-offering in the Temple, *cf.* καὶ προσφοράς, xxiv. 17, and Rom. xv. 16, *Judaistic Christianity*, pp. 109, 110; on the verb ἁγνίζω see also Hort's *First Epistle of St. Peter*, p. 87.—δαπάνησον ἐπ᾿ αὐτοῖς: "be at charges for them," R.V., spend money upon them. It was considered a meritorious act thus to defray the expenses of their sacrifices for poor Nazirites; Josephus, *Ant.*, xix., 6, 1, how King Agrippa on his arrival at Jerusalem acted thus with a view to conciliate popular favour, Edersheim, *u. s.*, p. 326, Renan, *Saint Paul*, p. 519, Kypke, *Observ.*, ii., 113; *cf.* Mishna, *Nazir*, ii., 6. J. Weiss supposed that the money would have been furnished out of the contributions brought by Paul, and that such em-

ployed for the poor members of the Jerusalem Church would have been quite in accordance with the objects for which the contributions were made; but on the other hand, Ramsay, *St. Paul*, p. 310.—ἵνα ξυρήσ., see critical note; at the conclusion of their vow, Num. vi. 18, when the sacrifice was offered by the Nazirites, Num. vi. 14.—On the future indicative with ἵνα in N.T. in pure final clauses see Burton, p. 86, if we adopt R.V. If we read γνώσονται, see critical note, the future is not dependent on ἵνα, "and all shall know," R.V., *viz.*, by this act of thine. On this independent future see Viteau, *Le Grec du N.T.*, p. 81 (1893).—καὶ αὐτὸς, *i.e.*, as well as other Jewish Christians.—στοιχεῖς: a neutral word, as the walk might be right or wrong, but here to be taken with φυλάσσων, "so walkest as to keep the law," Grimm-Thayer, *sub v.*, no need for "orderly".

Ver. 25. ἡμεῖς, *cf.* reading in β text, but in any case ἡμεῖς is emphatic, intimating that St. James and the Church at Jerusalem could not condemn St. Paul's attitude towards Gentile Christians, since they had themselves consented to place these Gentile Christians on a different footing from that of the born Jews who became Christians.—ἐπεστείλαμεν, see critical note, *cf.* xv. 20 (Zöckler).—μηδὲν τοιοῦτον τηρ., see critical note.—Wendt with Schürer objects to the whole reference to the Apostolic Conference, and sees in the verse the hand of a Redactor, as in xvi. 4 (see note, p. 346, edit. 1899). But the reference may well imply that St. James on his part was quite prepared to adhere to the compact entered into at the Conference with regard to

ἑκάστου αὐτῶν ἡ προσφορά. 27. ὡς δὲ ἔμελλον [1] αἱ ἑπτὰ ἡμέραι
συντελεῖσθαι, οἱ ἀπὸ τῆς Ἀσίας Ἰουδαῖοι, θεασάμενοι αὐτὸν ἐν τῷ
ἱερῷ, [2] συνέχεον πάντα τὸν ὄχλον, καὶ ἐπέβαλον τὰς χεῖρας ἐπ᾽ αὐτόν,

[1] αι επτα ημ., art. om. in E (in α text Blass brackets), D has συντελουμενης δε
της εβδομης ημερας (so Blass in β text, Hilg.).

[2] συνεχεαν is preferred by Blass with C and some mins., who thinks that the 1st
aor. is to be read here, because usually χυνω is pres. in N.T., but see, on the other
hand, Wendt (1899), p. 350 (Winer-Schmiedel, p. 111). επεβαλαν ℵ¹A, so W.H.,
Weiss (Winer-Schmiedel, p. 112). Blass in β reads επιβαλλουσιν with D, so Hilg.

Gentile Christians, and that he expects
St. Paul on his side to show that he has
no desire to disparage the law in the
eyes of Jewish Christians.

Ver. 26. τότε ὁ Παῦλος: St. Paul's
conduct was another illustration of the
rule laid down for himself when writing
to Corinth, cf. 1 Cor. ix. 20. This is in
itself an answer to the captious criticism
which doubts the truth of his action on
this occasion, so amongst recent writers
Hilgenfeld (1896). The vow of Acts
xviii. 18 is sufficient to show us that
there is no reason to suppose that the
Apostle was merely acting a part in
following the advice of St. James.
McGiffert discusses the question at length,
p. 340 ff., and concludes that the Apostle
may well have done just what he is
reported to have done; and further, that
as a simpler explanation of Paul's arrest
would have answered every purpose, the
explanation given may fairly be assumed
to be the true one. Renan, *Saint Paul*,
p. 517, also accepts the narrative as an
illustration of St. Paul's own principle
referred to above in 1 Cor. ix. 20, so too
Wendt, J. Weiss, Pfleiderer. It seems
strange that Wesley should have gone
so far in the opposite direction as to
believe that the Apostle actually suffered
for his compliance with the wishes of
James, ver. 33, *cf. Speaker's Commentary*,
in loco.—τῇ ἐχομ. ἡμέρᾳ, taken either
with παραλ. or with σὺν αὐτοῖς ἀγν.,
so R.V.; only in Luke, *cf.* Luke xiii.
33, Acts xx. 15, without ἡμέρᾳ (so in Polybius); *cf.* xiii. 44, W. H. margin. In LXX
1 Chron. x. 8; 2 Macc. xii. 39 (1 Macc.
iv. 28).—εἰσῄει: according to our interpretation of the passage, the word means
that Paul entered into the Temple, and
stayed there for seven days with the four
poor men until the period of their vow
was fulfilled, Renan, *Saint Paul*, p. 520;
but the expression need not mean more
than that he entered into the Temple to
give notice, or rather, giving notice, for
the convenience of the priests of the day
when the vow would be ended, and the
necessary offerings brought.—διαγγέλλων: "declaring," R.V., *i.e.*, to the
priests, not *omnibus edicens* (Grotius, so
Grimm), "to signify" as in A.V., makes
the participle future; verb only used by
St. Luke in N.T. (Rom. xi. 17, quotation
from LXX), 2 Macc. i. 33 (*cf.* its use in
the sense of publication, Ps. ii. 7, lviii.
13, *cf.* 2 Macc. i. 33, iii. 34, Ecclesiast.
xliii. 2).—τὴν ἐκπ. τῶν ἡ. τοῦ ἁγ., *i.e.*,
the seven days, ver. 27, which remained
until the period of the vow was fulfilled,
when the sacrifice was offered. Others
however take ἕως οὗ with εἰσῄει, "he
entered in . . . (and remained) until the
offering," etc.—ὑπὲρ ἑνὸς ἑκάστου αὐτῶν:
there is no need to suppose with Nösgen
that these words mean that the period
of the full accomplishment of the vow
was different in each of the four cases—
at all events the whole period of "purification" did not extend over more than
seven days.

Ver. 27. αἱ ἑπτὰ ἡμέραι: it does not
appear that the seven days were enjoined
by the law—not even in Num. vi. 9;
indeed it would appear from Jos., *B.J.*,
ii., 15, that a period of thirty days was
customary before the sacrifice could be
offered. The seven days cannot therefore include the whole period of the
vow, although they might well include
the period of the Apostle's partnership
with the four men. Wendt and Weiss
suppose that a reference is here made to
a rule that the interval between the
announcement to the priest and the
conclusion of the Nazirite vow should
include a period of seven days, but as
there is admittedly no reference to any
such ordinance elsewhere, it is precarious to depend too much upon it. It
seems impossible to refer the expression
to the seven days observed as the Feast
of Pentecost; the article before ἑπτὰ ἡμ.
refers to the "days of purification" just
mentioned, see further critical note and
Knabenbauer for summary of different
views.—οἱ ἀπὸ τῆς Ἀ. Ἰ.: "the Jews
from Asia," R.V., *cf.* vi. 9, where we

28. κράζοντες, Ἄνδρες Ἰσραηλῖται, βοηθεῖτε· οὗτός ἐστιν ὁ ἄνθρωπος ὁ κατὰ τοῦ λαοῦ καὶ τοῦ νόμου καὶ τοῦ τόπου τούτου πάντας[1] πανταχοῦ διδάσκων· ἔτι τε καὶ Ἕλληνας εἰσήγαγεν εἰς τὸ ἱερόν, καὶ[2] κεκοίνωκε τὸν ἅγιον τόπον τοῦτον. 29. (ἦσαν γὰρ προεωρακότες Τρόφιμον τὸν Ἐφέσιον ἐν τῇ πόλει σὺν αὐτῷ, ὃν[3] ἐνόμιζον ὅτι εἰς τὸ ἱερὸν εἰσήγαγεν ὁ Παῦλος.) 30. ἐκινήθη τε ἡ πόλις ὅλη, καὶ ἐγένετο συνδρομὴ τοῦ λαοῦ· καὶ ἐπιλαβόμενοι τοῦ Παύλου, εἷλκον αὐτὸν ἔξω τοῦ ἱεροῦ·

[1] πανταχη אABCDE (W.H. and Blass in β -χη), so Weiss; var. often in classical Greek.

[2] For κεκοινωκε D[1] has εκοινωνησεν, D[2] εκοινωσεν, but Blass follows T.R.

[3] ενομιζον, D has ενομισαμεν, not Blass.

read of the Jews of Cilicia, etc., who disputed with Stephen. — θεασάμ., cf. xxiv. 18, where St. Paul tells us how these Jews had found him in the Temple purified, i.e., with the Nazirite vow upon him, and in the act of presenting offerings—not of creating a disturbance, as his enemies alleged. These Jews, who were of course not believers, may have come from Ephesus, and were full of enmity against the Apostle for escaping them there, cf. xx. 3—they had come up to worship at Pentecost.—συνέχεον, see on ix. 22.—ἐπέβ. τὰς χ., cf. xii. 1.

Ver. 28. Ἄνδρες Ἰσ.: the title which would remind them of the special dignity and glory of their nation, of its hopes and obligations. — βοηθεῖτε: as if against some outrage, or perhaps as if to apprehend Paul, or to attack him — in doing anything to admit the Gentiles, ἔθνη, to God's fold, St. Paul was exposing himself to the hatred of these unbelievers amongst his countrymen, 1 Thess. ii. 16, Hort, Judaistic Christianity, p. 107.—οὗτός: contemptuous.—κατὰ τοῦ λαοῦ: the name for Israel, see on iv. 25, the same charge in almost the same words had been brought against St. Stephen, vi. 13; "before the Jewish authorities blasphemy was alleged, before the Roman, sedition".—πάντας πανταχοῦ, πανταχῇ or -ῇ, W.H., cf. xvii. 30, 1 Cor. iv. 17.—πανταχῇ: only here. The three words show the exaggerated nature of the charge; on St. Luke's characteristic use of πᾶς and kindred words see p. 51.—ἔτι τε καί, connecting thus closely the alleged act of introducing Gentiles into the Temple with the foregoing, as an illustration that Paul did not confine himself to preaching against the Holy Place, but had proceeded to defile it by his action; but cf. Simcox, Language of the N.T., p. 163, "and further hath brought

Greeks also," cf. xix. 27.—Ἕλληνας: only one man, Trophimus, had been actually seen with Paul, so that we again note the exaggerated charge, and even with regard to Trophimus, ἐνόμιζον, they only conjectured—they had no positive proof.—κεκοίνωκε: perfect, "sed manet pollutio," Blass, in loco, see also Gram., p. 194.

Ver. 29. τὸν Ἐφέσ.: if some of these Jews, as is very probable, came from Ephesus, they would have recognised Trophimus. The latter had not only come "as far as Asia," xx. 4, but had evidently accompanied Paul to Jerusalem; on the statement and its bearing upon 2 Tim. iv. 20, see Salmon, Introd., p. 401, and Weiss, Die Briefe Pauli an Timotheus und Titus, p. 354.—προεωρακότες: antea videre; in classical Greek nowhere as here, but referring to future, or space, not to past time; Blass, in loco, compares 1 Thess. ii. 2, Rom. iii. 9, for πρό.—εἰς τὸ ἱερόν, i.e., from the Court of the Gentiles (into which the uncircumcised Greeks like Trophimus and others might enter) into the inner Court, open to Jews only. The punishment for such transgression by a Gentile was death, even if he was a Roman citizen, Jos., B.J., vi., 2, 4. At the foot of the stair by which "the Court" in the strict sense of the word was approached there was a railing bearing notice in Greek and Latin with the prohibition and the punishment due to its violation. For one of these inscriptions discovered and published in 1871 by Clermont-Ganneau see Revue archéologique, xxiii., 1872, Schürer, Jewish People, div. i., vol. ii., p. 74, and div. ii., vol. i., p. 266. E.T. (where other references are given), Edersheim, Temple and its Services, p. 24, Plumptre, Acts, in loco, Blass, in loco, cf. Jos., Ant., xv., 11, 5, B.J., v., 5, 2.

καὶ εὐθέως ἐκλείσθησαν αἱ θύραι. 31. ζητούντων δὲ αὐτὸν ἀποκτεῖναι, ἀνέβη φάσις τῷ χιλιάρχῳ τῆς σπείρης, ὅτι ὅλη [1] συγκέχυται Ἰερουσαλήμ· 32. ὃς ἐξαυτῆς [2] παραλαβὼν στρατιώτας καὶ ἑκατοντάρχους, κατέδραμεν ἐπ᾽ αὐτούς. οἱ δὲ ἰδόντες τὸν χιλίαρχον καὶ τοὺς στρατιώτας, ἐπαύσαντο τύπτοντες τὸν Παῦλον. 33. τότε ἐγγίσας ὁ χιλίαρχος ἐπελάβετο αὐτοῦ, καὶ ἐκέλευσε δεθῆναι ἁλύσεσι δυσί·

---

[1] συγκέχυται אcEHLP; συνχυννεται א*AB* (συγχ.), D 13 (συγχυνεται), Vulg., Tisch., W.H., Weiss; συγχυννεται Wendt; συγχυνεται R.V., Blass (cf. Winer-Schmiedel, p. 111, W.H., *App.*, p. 172). Blass in β, so Hilg., adds after ιερου. **ορα ουν μη ποιωνται επαναστασιν** with Syr. H. mg.; noun not in N.T., but **επανιστημι**, although not in Luke.

[2] παραλ. אADEHLP, Tisch., W.H. text, R.V., Blass, Weiss, but λαβων B, W.H. marg.

Ver. 30. ἐκινήθη, as in vi. 12, cf. xxiv. 5.—συνδρομὴ τοῦ λ., Jud. iii. 18, 3 Macc. iii. 8, used of a tumultuous concourse of people, Arist., *Rhet.*, iii., 10, 7, Polyb., i., 67, 2.—ἐπιλ. τοῦ Π.: see p. 368, here of violent seizing; they wanted to get Paul outside the Temple precincts, so that the latter might not be polluted with his blood, ver. 31.—ἐκλείσθησαν αἱ θ.: no doubt by the Levitical guard, perhaps lest Paul should return, and so gain a place of safety in the Temple, or more probably to save the sacred precincts from any further pollution and uproar.

Ver. 31. ἀνέβη φάσις: "tidings came up," R.V., vividly, of the report which would reach the Roman officer in the tower of Antonia, overlooking and connected with the Temple at two points by stairs. The ἀνέβη seems to indicate that the writer was well acquainted with the locality. Stier supposes that a report was brought to the Roman authorities by the Christians, or the word may refer to an official report. The troops would be in readiness as always during the Festivals in case of riot, Jos., *Ant.*, xx., 5, 3, *B.J.*, v., 5, 8, etc. φάσις: only here in N.T. Blass and Grimm derive it from φαίνω (in classical Greek, especially of information against smugglers, and also quite generally), but in Susannah ver. 55 (Theod.) φάσις is derived by some from φημί, see *Speaker's Commentary, in loco*, while Grimm classes it there also under the same derivation as here.—τῷ χιλ.: "military tribune," R.V. margin; his thousand men consisted of 760 infantry and 240 cavalry, cf. xxiii. 23, Blass, *in loco*. This officer who was evidently in command at Fort Antonia is called by Josephus φρούραρχος, *Ant.*, xv., 11, 4, xviii., 4, 3; Schürer, *Jewish People*, div. ii., vol. ii., p. 55, E.T.—τῆς

σπείρης, cf. x. 1, "cohort," R.V. margin. —συγκέχυται, see p. 238, and also critical note, "was in confusion," R.V., lit. (so Rhem.).

Ver. 32. ἐξαυτῆς, cf. x. 33.—παραλ. στρ. καὶ ἑκατοντ., indicating that he thought the tumult considerable.—κατέδραμεν ἐπ᾽ αὐτούς, "ran down upon them" from Antonia, so R.V. vividly; verb found only here in N.T. In Job xvi. 10 (11) A we have the verb with accusative and ἐπί.—ἐπαύσαντο τύπτοντες after παύομαι: the act or state desisted from, indicated by the addition of a present participle, frequent in Luke, cf. Luke v. 4, Acts v. 42, vi. 13, xiii. 10, xx. 31; cf. also Ephes. i. 16, Col. i. 9, so in LXX, Grimm, *sub v.*, Winer-Moulton, xlv. 4.

Ver. 33. ἐπελ. αὐτοῦ: with a hostile intention, see xvii. 19.—δεθ. ἁλύσεσι δυσὶ: as a malefactor and seditious person, ver. 38, to be guarded securely as the cause of the tumult, cf. xii. 6.—τίς ἂν εἴη, καὶ τί ἐστι πεποιηκώς: the difference in the moods in dependent sentences after τις may be noted: the centurion had no clear idea as to who Paul was, but he feels sure that he had committed some crime, Winer-Moulton, xli., 4c, Weiss, Wendt, *in loco*, on the other hand Page. On Luke's thus mingling the optative obliqua with direct narrative alone among the N.T. writers, Viteau, *Le Grec du N.T.*, p. 225 (1893).

Ver. 34. ἐβόων: if we read ἐπεφώνουν, see critical note, a verb peculiar to St. Luke, Luke xxiii. 21, Acts xii. 22, xxii. 24 = "shouted," R.V., cf. xix. 31. —μὴ δυνάμ., see critical note. — τὸ ἀσφαλὲς: adjective, three times in St. Luke with this same shade of meaning, xxii. 30, xxv. 26 (cf. ii. 36, and Wisd. xviii. 6, ἀσφαλῶς).—παρεμ.: the word may mean an army, Heb. xi. 34, or

καὶ ἐπυνθάνετο τίς [1] ἂν εἴη, καὶ τί ἐστι πεποιηκώς.　34. ἄλλοι δὲ
ἄλλο τι [2] ἐβόων ἐν τῷ ὄχλῳ · μὴ δυνάμενος δὲ γνῶναι τὸ ἀσφαλὲς διὰ
τὸν θόρυβον, ἐκέλευσεν ἄγεσθαι αὐτὸν εἰς τὴν παρεμβολήν.　35. ὅτε
δὲ ἐγένετο [3] ἐπὶ τοὺς ἀναβαθμούς, συνέβη βαστάζεσθαι αὐτὸν ὑπὸ τῶν
στρατιωτῶν διὰ τὴν βίαν τοῦ ὄχλου.　36. ἠκολούθει γὰρ τὸ πλῆθος
τοῦ λαοῦ [4] κράζον,[5] Αἶρε αὐτόν.

37. Μέλλων τε εἰσάγεσθαι εἰς τὴν παρεμβολὴν ὁ Παῦλος λέγει
τῷ χιλιάρχῳ, Εἰ ἔξεστί μοι εἰπεῖν τι πρὸς σέ ; ὁ δὲ ἔφη, Ἑλληνιστὶ

---

[1] τις αν ειη *om.* αν ℵABD 18, 36, 105, 180, Tisch., W.H., R.V., Blass, Weiss,
Wendt.

[2] εβοων HLP, Chrys. ; επεφωνουν ℵABDE, Tisch., W.H., etc., as above. δυνα-
μενου δε αυτου (instead of δυναμενος δε HLP), ℵAB(D)E 13, 31, 40, 68, same auth.

[3] επι τους αναβ., D has εις (*adhuc esset in gradus* d).

[4] Instead of κραζον (DHLP, Syr. H., Chrys.), which seems to be a gram.
emend., ℵABE, Syr. Pesh., Theophl., same auth. as in ver. 34 have κραζοντες.

[5] D *pro* αιρε has αναιρεισθαι (Gig., Sah. add τον εχθρον ημων, *cf.* xxiv. 18,
xxviii. 19).

---

the camp which it occupies (so in LXX
= Heb. מַחֲנֶה Judg. iv. 16, viii. 10,
1 Macc. v. 28). In this passage may =
the castle itself, as A. and R.V., or
perhaps the barracks in the castle. A
Macedonian word according to Phryn.,
but see Kennedy, *Sources of N.T. Greek*,
pp. 15, 16, and also for its meaning Ant.,
Schürer, *Jewish People*, div. i., vol. ii.,
p. 55, E.T.

Ver. 35. ἐγέν. ἐπὶ, *cf.* ver. 17, and
Luke xxiv. 22, Grimm, *sub* γίν., 5,
g. ἀναβ. : the steps which led up to the
fortress from the Temple area. *B.J.*, v.,
5, 8, describes the surroundings of the
scene vividly, and the καταβάσεις which
led down from Antonia to the Temple ;
see above on ver. 31, and O. Holtzmann,
Neutest. Zeitgeschichte, p. 138.—συνέβη
βαστάξ. : the σύν is not superfluous
(see Meyer-Wendt and Hackett), it indicates the peril of the situation ; the
pressure of the people became increasingly violent as they saw that St. Paul
would escape them, and compelled the
soldiers to carry him, that he might not
be torn from them altogether, so that the
carrying was not merely "propter an-
gustias loci". βαστάξ., *cf.* iii. 2, see
Schürer, *u. s.*

Ver. 36. ἠκολούθει, imperfect, "kept
following".—Αἶρε αὐτόν : the cry was
continuous ; it was the same cry which
had been raised against another and a
greater prisoner Who had been delivered to the Romans as a malefactor,

cf. Luke xxiii. 18, John xix. 15, and also
Polycarp, *Martyr*, iii., 19.

Ver. 37. παρεμβ., see on ver. 34.—
εἰ, *cf.* i. 6.—Ἑλλη. γινώσκεις ; no need
to supply λαλεῖν, *cf.* Xen., *Cyr.*, vii., 5, 31 ;
so in Latin, *Græcè nescire*, Cic., *Pro
Flacco*, iv., Vulgate, literally, *Græcè
nosti ?*

Ver. 38. οὐκ ἄρα σὺ εἶ : *mirantis est*,
cf. Arist., *Av.*, 280 (Blass). Vulgate,
Eras. render *Nonne tu es . . . ?* but
emphasis on οὐκ "Thou art not then "
(as I supposed). No doubt the false prophet to whom reference is made by
Josephus. Whilst Felix was governor
he gathered the people around him on
the Mount of Olives to the number of
30,000, and foretold that at his word the
walls of the city would fall. But Felix
attacked him and the impostor fled
although the majority (πλεῖστοι) of his
followers were captured or slain, Jos.,
B.J., ii., 13, 5. In another account,
Ant., xx., 8, 6, Josephus states that 400
were killed and 200 wounded, so that he
evidently contradicts himself and his
numbers are untrustworthy. For the
various attempts to reconcile these different notices, *cf.* Krenkel, *Josephus und
Lukas*, p. 243. But apart from this,
there is no positive discrepancy with St.
Luke. It is possible that the chiliarch as
a soldier only reckoned those who were
armed, whilst Josephus spoke of the
whole crowd of followers. Evidently the
Roman officer thought that the Egyptian
had returned after his flight, and that he

γινώσκεις ; 38. οὐκ ἄρα σὺ εἶ ὁ Αἰγύπτιος ὁ πρὸ τούτων τῶν ἡμερῶν
ἀναστατώσας καὶ ἐξαγαγὼν εἰς τὴν ἔρημον τοὺς τετρακισχιλίους
ἄνδρας τῶν σικαρίων ; 39. εἶπε δὲ ὁ Παῦλος, Ἐγὼ ἄνθρωπος μέν
εἰμι Ἰουδαῖος¹ Ταρσεύς, τῆς Κιλικίας οὐκ ἀσήμου πόλεως πολίτης·
δέομαι δέ σου, ἐπίτρεψόν μοι λαλῆσαι πρὸς τὸν λαόν.

¹ Instead of Τ. τῆς Κ. ουκ ασημ. πολεως πολ. D has εν Ταρσῳ δε της Κ. γεγεν-
νημενος, so Blass in β text, and Hilg. ; instead of επιτρεψον D has συγχωρησαι
(cf. Gig.), so Blass in β text, and Hilg.

was now set upon by the people as an
impostor (so also Schürer, *Jewish People*,
div. i., vol. ii., p. 180, note, E.T.). There
is no sign whatever that St. Luke was
dependent upon Josephus, as Krenkel
maintains, but it is of course quite possible that both writers followed a different
tradition of the same event. But St.
Luke differs from Josephus in his numbers, there is no connection in the Jewish
historian, as in St. Luke, between the
Egyptian and the Sicarii, and whilst
Josephus mentions the Mount of Olives,
St. Luke speaks of the wilderness; Belser,
Theol. Quartalschrift, pp. 68, 69, Heft i.,
1896, "Egyptian, The" (A. C. Headlam),
Hastings' B.D.—ὁ . . . ἀναστ. καὶ ἐξαγ.:
"stirred up to sedition and led out,"
R.V., this rendering makes the first verb
(used only in Luke and Paul) also active,
as in other cases in N.T. where it occurs,
Acts xviii. 6, Gal. v. 12. The verb is
not known in classical writers, but *cf.*
LXX, Dan. vii. 23, and also in the O.T.
fragments, Aquila and Symm., Ps. x. 1,
lviii. 11, Isa. xxii. 3 (Grimm-Thayer).—
τοὺς: "the 4000," R.V., as of some
well-known number.—τῶν σικαρίων : " of
the Assassins," R.V. The word *sicarius*
is the common designation of a number,
A.V., *cf.*, *e.g.*, the law passed under Sulla
against murderers, " *Lex Cornelia de Si-
cariis et Veneficis* "; so in the Mishna in
this general sense, but here it is used of
the Sicarii or fanatical Jewish faction
(and we note that the writer is evidently
aware of their existence as a political
party) which arose in Judæa after Felix
had rid the country of the robbers of
whom Josephus speaks, *Ant.*, xx., 8, 5,
B.J., ii., 13, 2, so called from the short
daggers, *sicæ*, which they wore under
their clothes. They mingled with the
crowds at the Festivals, stabbed their
political opponents unobserved, and drew
suspicion from themselves by apparent
indignation at such crimes, "Assassin"
(A. C. Headlam), Hastings' B.D., Schürer, *Jewish People*, div. i., vol. ii., p. 178,
E.T.

Ver. 39. Ἐγὼ ἄνθρωπος μέν εἰμι Ἰ.
. . . δέομαι δέ . . .: there is no strict
antithesis, "I am indeed a Jew of
Tarsus" (and therefore free from your
suspicion); but without speaking further
of this, and proceeding perhaps to demand
a legal process, the Apostle adds "but I
pray you," etc. Mr. Page explains, from
the position of μέν : " I (ἐγώ) as regards
your question to me, am a man (ἄνθρωπος μέν), etc., but, as regards my
question to you, I ask (δέομαι δέ . . .),"
see reading in β. On St. Paul's citizenship see note below on xxii. 28. St. Paul
uses ἄνθρωπος here, but ἀνήρ, the more
dignified term, xxii. 3, in addressing his
fellow-countrymen ; but according to
Blass, " vix recte distinguitur quasi
illud (ἄνθρωπος) ut ap. att. sit humilius,"
cf. Matt. xviii. 23, and xxii. 2.—λαλῆσαι:
Blass has a striking note on Paul's hope-
fulness for his people, and the proof
apparent here of a man " qui populi sui
summo amore imbutus nunquam de eo
desperare potuit," Rom. ix.-xi.—Ἰουδ.
not only Ταρ., which would have distinguished him from Ἀιγ., but Ἰουδ.,
otherwise the chiliarch from his speaking
Greek might have regarded him as no
Jew, and so guilty of death for profaning
the Temple. — οὐκ ἀσήμου πόλεως :
litotes, xx. 29, on Tarsus see ix. 11.
The city had on its coins the titles
μητρόπολις αὐτόνομος. For ἄσημος, *cf.*
3 Macc. iii. 1, and in classical Greek,
Eurip., *Ion.*, 8. οὐκ ἀσ. Ἑλλήνων πόλις,
i.e., Athens (Wetstein), see further xxii.
27. Hobart (so too Zahn) mentions
ἄσημος as one of the words which show
that Luke, when dealing with unpro-
fessional subjects, shows a leaning to the
use of professional language ; ἄσημος is
the technical term for "a disease without
distinctive symptoms," and Hippocrates,
just as Luke, says, μία πόλεων οὐκ
ἄσημος, *Epis.*, 1273. So again in xxiii.
13, ἀναδιδόναι, a word applied to the
distribution of nourishment throughout
the body, or of blood throughout the
veins, is used by Hippocrates, as by

40. Ἐπιτρέψαντος δὲ αὐτοῦ, ὁ Παῦλος ἑστὼς ἐπὶ τῶν ἀναβαθμῶν
κατέσεισε¹ τῇ χειρὶ τῷ λαῷ· πολλῆς δὲ σιγῆς γενομένης, προσεφώνησε

¹ D has καὶ σείσας instead of κατέσεισε, not Blass ; so D has ἡσυχίας instead of
σιγῆς, see note in comment.

Luke, *l.c.*, of a messenger delivering a letter, *Epis.*, 1275 (see Hobart and Zahn) ; but it must be admitted that the same phrase is found in Polybius and Plutarch. Still the fact remains that the phraseology of St. Luke is here illustrated by a use of two similar expressions in Hippocrates, and it should be also remembered that the verb with which St. Luke opens his Gospel, ἐπιχειρεῖν, was frequently used by medical men, and that too in its secondary sense, just as by St. Luke, *e.g.*, Hippocrates begins his treatise *De Prisca Med.*, ὁκόσοι ἐπεχείρησαν περὶ ἰατρικῆς λέγειν ἢ γράφειν (see J. Weiss on Luke i. 1) ; so too Galen uses the word similarly, although it must be admitted that the same use is found in classical Greek and in Josephus, c. *Apion.*, 2.

Ver. 40. ἐπιτρέψ.: because he no doubt saw that Paul's purpose was to inform and pacify the people, so that there is nothing strange in such permission to speak.—κατέσεισε, see on xii. 17. "What nobler spectacle than that of Paul at this moment! There he stands bound with two chains, ready to make his defence to the people. The Roman commander sits by to enforce order by his presence. An enraged populace look up to him from below. Yet in the midst of so many dangers, how self-possessed is he, how tranquil!" Chrys., *Hom*, xlvii. —πολλῆς δὲ σιγῆς γεν., *cf.* Virg., *Aen.*, i., 148-152, ii., 1 ; but probably the phrase means not "a great silence," but rather "aliquantum silentii" (Blass), xxii. 2, *cf.* Xen., *Cyr.*, vii., 1, 25.—Ἑβραΐδι: in W.H. Ἑβ., see *Introd.*, 408 ; so as to gain the attention, and if possible the hearts, of the people, by using the language of the people, the Aramaic dialect of Palestine (Grimm-Thayer however points out that this is not rightly described as Syro-Chaldaic, it was rather Chaldee): see also Schürer, *Jewish People*, div. ii., vol. i., E.T., pp. 47, 48.

CHAPTER XXII.—Ver. 1. ἄνδρες ἀ. καὶ π., *cf.* vii. 2. So St. Stephen had addressed a similar assembly, in which had been Saul of Tarsus, who was now charged with a like offence as had been laid to the charge of the first Martyr.

Those whom he addressed were his brethren according to the flesh, and his fathers, as the representatives of his nation, whether as Sanhedrists, or priests, or Rabbis. The mode of address was quite natural, since St. Paul's object was conciliatory: τοῦτο τιμῆς, ἐκεῖνο γνησιότητος, Chrys., *Hom.*, xlvii.—ἀκούσατε: "hear from me," *cf.* John xii. 47, a double genitive of the person and thing, as in classical Greek, or "hear my defence," *cf.* 2 Tim. iv. 16.—ἀπολογίας: five times in St. Paul's Epistles, once elsewhere in Acts xxv. 16, in a strictly legal sense (*cf.* 1 Peter iii. 15). Used with the verb ἀπολογέομαι of defending oneself against a charge, Wisd. vi. 10, Xen., *Mem.*, iv., 8, 5. In 2 Macc. xiii. 26 the verb is also used of Lysias ascending the *rostrum* and addressing the people in defence.

Ver. 2. προσεφώνει: only in Luke and Paul, except Matt. xi. 16, *cf.* Luke vi. 13, vii. 32, xiii. 12, xxiii. 20, xxi. 40, see Friedrich, p. 29, for the frequency of other compounds of φωνεῖν in Luke.— μᾶλλον παρ. ἡσυχ: the phrase is used similarly in Plut., *Coriol.*, 18, Dion Hal., ii., 32, and LXX, Job xxxiv. 29 ; on the fondness of St. Luke for σιγή, σιγᾶν, ἡσυχάζειν, and the characteristic way in which silence results from his words and speeches, or before or during the speech, see Friedrich, p. 26, *cf.* Luke xiv. 4, xv. 26, Acts xi. 18, xv. 12, Acts xii. 17, xxi. 40, and for ἡσυχάζειν, 1 Thess. iv. 11, Luke xiv. 4, Acts xi. 18, xxi. 14, so too παρέχειν with accusative of the thing offered by any one, xix. 24, xxviii. 2 (xvi. 16). The verb is used only in Matt. xxvi. 10, and parallel, Mark xiv. 6, except in Luke and Paul, Luke vi. 29, vii. 4, xi. 7, xviii. 5, Acts xvi. 16, xvii. 31, and as above, and five times in St. Paul's Epistles.

Ver. 3. γεγενν. ἐν Τ., see above p. 202.—ἀνατεθ. δὲ: although by birth a foreign Jew, yet brought up in Jerusalem, and so belonging to his hearers. It was important for the Apostle to emphasise this, as his close association with Jerusalem had a significant bearing on his future life. The comma best after Γαμ., so that each clause begins with a participle, but Weiss places comma after

τῇ Ἑβραΐδι διαλέκτῳ λέγων, XXII. 1. Ἄνδρες ἀδελφοὶ καὶ πατέρες, ἀκούσατέ μου τῆς πρὸς ὑμᾶς νῦν [1] ἀπολογίας. 2. Ἀκούσαντες δὲ ὅτι τῇ Ἑβραΐδι διαλέκτῳ προσεφώνει [2] αὐτοῖς, μᾶλλον παρέσχον ἡσυχίαν. 3. καί φησιν, Ἐγὼ μέν [3] εἰμι ἀνὴρ Ἰουδαῖος, γεγεννημένος ἐν Ταρσῷ τῆς Κιλικίας, ἀνατεθραμμένος δὲ ἐν τῇ πόλει ταύτῃ παρὰ τοὺς πόδας Γαμαλιήλ, πεπαιδευμένος κατὰ ἀκρίβειαν τοῦ πατρῴου νόμου, ζηλωτὴς ὑπάρχων τοῦ Θεοῦ, καθὼς πάντες ὑμεῖς ἐστε σήμερον. 4. ὃς ταύτην τὴν ὁδὸν ἐδίωξα ἄχρι θανάτου, δεσμεύων καὶ παραδιδοὺς εἰς φυλακὰς

[1] νυν, but all good authorities νυνι.

[2] προσεφώνει ℵABP, most verss., Tisch., R.V., W.H., Wendt, Weiss; L, Syr. Harcl. have προσεφωνησεν; whilst DEH προσφωνει, so Blass in β, and Hilg.

[3] μεν om. ℵABDE, Vulg., Sah., Arm., Tisch., Weiss, Wendt, W.H., Blass, R.V.; Meyer retains with HLP, Boh., Syr. H., Aeth^utr., but it may have been added after xxi. 39. The punctuation of the verse varies considerably; W.H. have ανατεθ. . . . Γαμ., πεπαιδ. . . . νομου, ζηλ. . . . σημερον·; Blass has ανατεθ. . . . ταυτη, παρα . . . ακριβειαν, του πατ. νομον ζηλ. (του Θεου); and Tisch. has ανατεθ. . . . ταυτη, παρα . . . νομου, ζηλωτης . . . σημερον·. T.R. = W.H., except comma after Θεου.

ταύτῃ (so De Wette, Hackett). Probably Paul went to Jerusalem not later than thirteen, possibly at eleven, for his training as a teacher of the law. ἀνατεθ.: only in Luke, cf. Acts vii. 20, 21, Luke iv. 16 (W.H. margin), "educated," so in classical Greek, 4 Macc. x. 2, xi. 15, but in latter passage AR τραφ. In Wisd. vii. 4 we have ἐν σπαργάνοις ἀνετράφην (A ἀνεστρ.).—παρὰ τοὺς πόδας: the more usual attitude for teacher and taught according to the N.T. and the Talmud; according to later Talmudic tradition the sitting on the ground was not customary until after the death of Gamaliel I., J. Lightfoot, Hor. Heb., on Luke ii. 46; cf. also Schürer, Jewish People, div. ii., vol. 1, p. 326, E.T., and Taylor, Sayings of the Jewish Fathers, pp. 14, 15, 2nd edit.; even if the later tradition was true, the scholar standing would still be at the feet of his teacher on his raised seat.—κατὰ ἀκρίβειαν: noun only here in N.T., but cf. xxvi. 5, "according to the strict manner of the law of our fathers," R.V., and so practically A.V. For a comment on the words cf. Jos., Ant., xvii., 2, 4, Vita, 38, and B.J., ii., 8, 18. Φαρισαῖοι οἱ δοκοῦντες μετὰ ἀκριβείας ἐξηγεῖσθαι τὰ νόμιμα: Edersheim, Jesus the Messiah, ii., 314, note on ἀκρίβεια as used by Josephus and St. Paul, Schürer, Jewish People, div. ii., vol. ii., p. 54, E.T. Whether therefore τοῦ πατ. νόμου (3 Macc. i. 23) included anything besides the Mosaic law or not, the words before us at least refer to the strictness upon which the Pharisees prided themselves in the observance of the law. In Gal. i. 14 St. Paul speaks of being a zealot of the traditions handed down from his fathers, πατρικῶν, where the traditions are apparently distinguished from the written law, Jos., Ant., xiii., 16, 2, and 10, 6; but the "oral law" which the scribes developed was apparently equally binding with the written Thorah in the eyes of the Pharisees, Schürer, Jewish People, div. ii., vol. ii., pp. 10, 11, E.T., but cf. also Lightfoot, u. s. The word πατρῴου would appeal to the hearts of the people, who loved the Thorah as the chief good, but St. Chrysostom's words are also to be remembered: "all this seems indeed to be spoken on their side, but in fact it told against them, since he, knowing the law, forsook it" Hom., xlvii.—ζηλωτὴς ὑπάρ. τοῦ Θεοῦ: St. Paul might have called himself a zealot of the law, or a zealot of God (Lightfoot, u. s.), cf. 2 Macc. iv. 2, ζηλ. τῶν νόμων, sued of Phinehas, 4 Macc. xviii. 12.— καθὼς πάντες . . . σήμερον: he recognises that their present zeal was a zeal for God, as his own had been, ἀλλ' οὐ κατ' ἐπίγνωσιν, Rom. x. 2: argumentum concilians, Bengel.

Ver. 4. ταύτην τὴν ὁδὸν, see above ix. 2.—ἄχρι θανάτου: sometimes taken to mean not that he prosecuted the Christians "unto death" (for if this was the meaning the following participles would sound feeble), but that this was his aim; ver. 20 and xxvi. 10, however, seem fully to justify the former meaning.—φυλακὰς:

ἄνδρας τε καὶ γυναῖκας, 5. ὡς καὶ ὁ ἀρχιερεὺς[1] μαρτυρεῖ μοι, καὶ πᾶν τὸ πρεσβυτέριον· παρ᾽ ὧν καὶ ἐπιστολὰς δεξάμενος πρὸς τοὺς ἀδελφοὺς εἰς Δαμασκὸν ἐπορευόμην, ἄξων καὶ τοὺς ἐκεῖσε ὄντας δεδεμένους εἰς Ἰερουσαλήμ, ἵνα τιμωρηθῶσιν. 6. ἐγένετο δέ μοι πορευομένῳ καὶ ἐγγίζοντι τῇ Δαμασκῷ περὶ μεσημβρίαν ἐξαίφνης ἐκ τοῦ οὐρανοῦ περιαστράψαι φῶς ἱκανὸν περὶ ἐμέ· 7.[2] ἔπεσόν τε εἰς τὸ ἔδαφος, καὶ ἤκουσα φωνῆς λεγούσης μοι, Σαούλ, Σαούλ, τί με διώκεις; 8. ἐγὼ δὲ ἀπεκρίθην, Τίς εἶ, Κύριε; εἶπέ τε πρός με, Ἐγώ εἰμι Ἰησοῦς ὁ Ναζωραῖος ὃν σὺ διώκεις. 9. οἱ δὲ σὺν ἐμοὶ ὄντες τὸ μὲν φῶς ἐθεάσαντο,[3] καὶ ἔμφοβοι ἐγένοντο· τὴν δὲ φωνὴν οὐκ ἤκουσαν τοῦ λαλοῦντός μοι. 10. εἶπον δέ, Τί ποιήσω, Κύριε; ὁ δὲ Κύριος εἶπε πρός με, Ἀναστὰς πορεύου εἰς Δαμασκόν· κἀκεῖ σοι λαληθήσεται περὶ πάντων ὧν τέτακταί σοι ποιῆσαι. 11. ὡς δὲ[4] οὐκ ἐνέβλεπον ἀπὸ τῆς δόξης τοῦ φωτὸς ἐκείνου, χειραγωγούμενος ὑπὸ

---

[1] D has μαρτυρησει, so Blass in β, and Hilg.; B has εμαρτυρει (but Weiss and W.H. reject).

[2] For επεσον אABEHP have επεσα, so Tisch., W.H., Weiss, but Blass in β has επεσον with DL, so Hilg.

[3] אABH, Syr. P., Boh., Arm. om. και εμφ. εγενοντο, so Tisch., W.H., R.V., Weiss, Wendt, but the reading is retained by DELP, Sah., Syr. H., Gig., so Blass in β, and Hilg.; on εμφ. εγεν. see x. 40. See Alford's note (he brackets the words).

[4] Blass reads ως δε ανεστην ουκ εβλ. with d, Syr. H. mg., Gig. ουκ ενεβλεπον, but B has ουδεν εβλεπον, so W.H. marg., Blass in β; εμβλεπειν not used absolutely elsewhere, B may therefore be original (Wendt).

---

plural, perhaps in relation to xxvi. 11, where Paul's persecuting fury extends to strange cities; usually singular.

Ver. 5. ὡς καὶ ὁ ἀρχ.: not the high priest at the time he was speaking, for that was Ananias, xxiii. 2, but rather to the high priest Caiaphas who gave him his commission to Damascus, and who may have been still alive, hence μαρτυρεῖ, present.—τοὺς ἀδελ.: the word was used by the Jews of each other, Exod. ii. 14, Deut. xv. 3, and St. Paul uses it here to show that he regarded the Jews as still his brethren, cf. Rom. ix. 3.—τοὺς ἐκεῖσε ὄντας, cf. xxi. 3, the adverb may imply those who had come thither only, so that refugees, not residents in Damascus, are meant, but the word may simply = ἐκεῖ, see on xxi. 3, and Winer-Moulton, liv. 7. In Hipp., Vict. San., ii., 2, p. 35, we have οἱ ἐκεῖσε οἰκέοντες.— τιμωρηθῶσιν: only here and in xxvi. 11 in N.T.: used as here in classical Greek, but in this sense more frequent in middle.

Ver. 6. περὶ μεσημ., cf. xxvi. 12, not mentioned in ix., note of a personal recollection.—ἐξαίφνης: only here in Acts

and in ix. 3, see note; twice in Luke's Gospel, only once elsewhere in N.T.; see further on xxvi. 12 note, on the three accounts of St. Paul's Conversion.— περιαστράψαι: so also in ix. 3, nowhere else in N.T., see note above, cf. xxvi. 13, περιλάμπειν (note); the supernatural brightness of the light is implied here in δόξης, ver. 11.

Ver. 7. ἔπεσον: on the form ἔπεσα W.H. see Kennedy, Sources of N.T. Greek, p. 159, Winer - Schmiedel, p. 111.—ἔδαφος: only here in N.T. (in LXX, 1 Kings vi. 15, Wisd. xi. 5, etc., and in 4 Macc. vi. 7, πίπτων εἰς τὸ ἔδ.), but the verb ἐδαφίζειν is found in Luke xix. 44, and there only in N.T.—ἤκουσα φωνῆς, see on ix. 4 and 7, cf. Dan. x. 6-9.—Σαοὺλ, Σαοὺλ, as in ix. 4, see note on xxvi. 14 (and cf. reading in β text).

Vv. 8 and 9. See on ix. 5 and ix. 4, 7, 9.—ἔμφ. ἐγέν., see critical note.

Ver. 11. οὐκ ἐνέβλεπον, cf. Xen., Mem., iii., 11, 10, here absolute, Grimm-Thayer, sub v.: chap. ix., 8, gives the fact of the blindness, here we have its cause as from St. Paul's personal remini-

τῶν συνόντων μοι ἦλθον εἰς Δαμασκόν. 12. Ἀνανίας δέ τις, ἀνὴρ εὐσεβὴς[1] κατὰ τὸν νόμον, μαρτυρούμενος ὑπὸ πάντων τῶν κατοικούντων Ἰουδαίων, 13. ἐλθὼν πρός με καὶ ἐπιστὰς εἶπέ μοι, Σαοὺλ ἀδελφέ, ἀνάβλεψον. κἀγὼ αὐτῇ τῇ ὥρᾳ[2] ἀνέβλεψα εἰς αὐτόν. 14. ὁ δὲ εἶπεν, Ὁ Θεὸς τῶν πατέρων ἡμῶν προεχειρίσατό σε γνῶναι τὸ θέλημα αὐτοῦ, καὶ ἰδεῖν τὸν δίκαιον, καὶ ἀκοῦσαι φωνὴν ἐκ τοῦ στόματος αὐτοῦ· 15. ὅτι ἔσῃ μάρτυς αὐτῷ πρὸς πάντας ἀνθρώπους, ὧν ἑώρακας καὶ ἤκουσας. 16. καὶ νῦν τί μέλλεις; ἀναστὰς βάπτισαι καὶ ἀπό-

---

[1] εὐλαβης for ευσ. אBHLP, Chrys., Theophl., Tisch., W.H., Wendt, Weiss, Blass.

[2] After ανεβλεψα Blass in β omits εις αυτον, so d, Sah., Hilg. (Schmiedel also omits), but see Wendt, note, p. 355 (1899).

scence.—**δόξης**: Heb. כָּבוֹד cf. 1 Cor. xv. 40, 2 Cor. iii. 7, and Luke ix. 31.

Ver. 12. **Ἀναν.**, ix. 10. The description is added, ἀνὴρ εὐ. Ἰ., manifestly fitting before a Jewish audience, and a proof that the brother who came to Saul was no law-breaker, Lewin, *St. Paul*, ii., 146. On the reading εὐλαβής, cf. ii. 5.—**τῶν κατοικ.**: seems to imply that Ananias had dwelt for some time in Damascus, ix.

Ver. 13. **ἐπιστὰς**: "standing over one," used frequently in Acts of the appearance of an angel, or of the intervention of a friend (or of an enemy), see Luke ii. 9, iv. 39, x. 40, xii. 7, xxiv. 4, only found in Luke and Paul, Friedrich, p. 42, see above xii. 7. **μαρτ.**, vi. 3. **ἀδελφέ**, ix. 17.—**ἀνάβλεψον . . . ἀνέβλ. εἰς αὐτόν**: "receive thy sight, and in that very hour I recovered my sight *and looked* upon him," R.V. margin. **ἀναβλέπειν** may mean (1) to recover sight, ix. 17, 18, or (2) to look up, Luke xix. 5, but used frequently as if combining both meanings, Humphry on R.V., and Page, *in loco*. Meyer and Zöckler render "to look up" in both clauses.—**αὐτῇ τῇ ὥρᾳ**, see note on xvi. 18.

Ver. 14. **ὁ Θεὸς τῶν πατ. ἡμῶν**: again a conciliatory phrase, cf. vii. 32, so St. Peter in iii. 13, v. 30.—**προεχειρ.**: "hath appointed," only in Acts in N.T., iii. 20, and in xxvi. 16, again used by Paul in narrating his conversion and call. In LXX, cf. Exod. iv. 13, Josh. iii. 12, 2 Macc. iii. 7, viii. 9, always with the notion of some one selected for an important duty (Lumby): to which may be added Dan., LXX, iii. 22 (see H. and R.), cf. note on iii. 20.—**τὸν δίκαιον**, see on iii. 14, and vii. 52.—**φ. ἐκ τοῦ στ.**: "a voice from his mouth," R.V., so Rhem., as the Apostle heard it at his conversion. στ. is often used in phrases of a Hebra-

istic character, so here fitly by Ananias, cf. xv. 7.

Ver. 15. **μάρτυς αὐτῷ**: "a witness for him," R.V., cf. i. 8.—**πάντας ἀνθ.**: we may see another evidence of the Apostle's tact in that he does not yet employ the word ἔθνη.—**ὧν ἑώρακας καὶ ἤκουσας**, Blass well compares for the former verb the Apostle's own words, 1 Cor. ix. 1; perfect tense, marks what was essential in giving him enduring consecration as an Apostle, cf. Blass, *Gram.*, p. 237.

Ver. 16. **καὶ νῦν**: so by St. Paul in xx. 22, 25, xxvi. 6, xvi. 37, xiii. 11; also found in iii. 17, x. 5, but no instances in Luke's Gospel of καὶ νῦν beginning a sentence, Hawkins, *Horæ Synopticæ*, p. 145.—**τί μέλλεις**: only here in this sense in N.T., cf. 4 Macc. vi. 23, ix. 1, and so often in classical Greek, Aesch., *Prom.*, 36, etc.— **ἀναστὰς**, see v. 17.—**βάπτισαι**: middle voice (so perhaps in 1 Cor. x. 2, W.H. text, but passive in margin, as Blass), as a rule naturally in the passive, "to be baptised," cf. ix. 18, but the convert in "getting baptised" was conceived as doing something for himself, not merely as receiving something (Simcox, *Language of the N.T.*, pp. 97, 98), so apparently Blass, *Gram.*, p. 182, or the middle may mean that he submitted himself to Christian Baptism, Bethge, p. 197, and Alford.—**ἀπόλουσαι**: also middle, cf. ii. 38, and 1 Cor. vi. 11, the result of the submission to Baptism, Tit. iii. 5, Ephes. v. 26.—**ἐπικαλ.**, cf. p. 81, on the significance of the phrase. This calling upon the name of Christ, thus closely connected with Baptism and preceding it, necessarily involved belief in Him, Rom. x. 14. There is no contradiction in the fact that the commission to the Apostleship here and in ix. comes from Ananias, whilst in xxvi. he is not men-

λοῦσαι τὰς ἁμαρτίας σου, ἐπικαλεσάμενος τὸ ὄνομα[1] τοῦ Κυρίου. 17.
ἐγένετο δέ μοι ὑποστρέψαντι εἰς Ἱερουσαλήμ, καὶ προσευχομένου μου
ἐν τῷ ἱερῷ, γενέσθαι με ἐν ἐκστάσει, 18. καὶ[2] ἰδεῖν αὐτὸν λέγοντά
μοι, Σπεῦσον καὶ ἔξελθε ἐν τάχει ἐξ Ἱερουσαλήμ· διότι οὐ παρα-
δέξονταί σου τὴν μαρτυρίαν περὶ ἐμοῦ. 19. κἀγὼ εἶπον, Κύριε,
αὐτοὶ ἐπίστανται, ὅτι ἐγὼ ἤμην φυλακίζων καὶ δέρων κατὰ τὰς
συναγωγὰς τοὺς πιστεύοντας ἐπὶ σέ· 20. καὶ ὅτε[3] ἐξεχεῖτο τὸ αἷμα
Στεφάνου τοῦ μάρτυρός σου, καὶ αὐτὸς ἤμην ἐφεστὼς καὶ συνευδοκῶν
τῇ[4] ἀναιρέσει αὐτοῦ, καὶ φυλάσσων τὰ ἱμάτια τῶν ἀναιρούντων

---

[1] Instead of **K.** ℵABE, verss., Tisch., W.H., R.V., Weiss, Wendt, Blass, Hilg.
have αυτου.

[2] ιδειν ABEHLP, Vulg., Chrys., Lach., W.H., Weiss; Tisch. after ℵ 18, 36, 180, d
has ιδον (ειδον, so Blass in β, and Hilg.).

[3] Instead of εξεχειτο ℵAB*. W.H., Weiss, Wendt have εξεχυννετο; Blass -υνετο
with B³E. Στεφ. om. A 68, but no other authorities.

[4] τη αναιρεσει αυτου om. ℵABE 40, Vulg., Sah., Boh., Aethutr.; Tisch., W.H.,
R.V., Blass, Weiss, Wendt, Hilg.; cf. viii. 1.

tioned at all, and the commission comes
directly from the mouth of the Lord. It
might be sufficient simply to say "quod
quis per alium facit id ipse fecisse puta-
tur," but before the Roman governor it
was likely enough that the Apostle should
omit the name of Ananias and combine
with the revelation at his conversion and
with that made by Ananias other and
subsequent revelations, cf. xxvi. 16-18.
Festus might have treated the vision to
Ananias with ridicule, Agrippa would
not have been influenced by the name of
a Jew living in obscurity at Damascus
(Speaker's Commentary).
Ver. 17. ἐγέν. δέ μοι ὑποσ.: refers
to the first visit of St. Paul to Jerusalem
after his Conversion, Lightfoot, Galatians, pp. 84, 93, 125. Ramsay, St.
Paul, p. 60, refers it to the second visit,
(1) because the reason for Paul's departure from Jerusalem is given differently
here and in ix. 29. But may not St.
Luke be describing the occurrence in
relation to the Jews and the Church,
and St. Paul in relation to his own
private personal history, St. Luke giving
us the outward impulse, St. Paul the
inner motive (Hackett), so that two
causes, the one natural, the other supernatural, are mentioned side by side? cf.
Acts xiii. 2-4 (so Lightfoot, Felten,
Lumby). (2) Ramsay's second reason is
that Paul does not go at once to the
Gentiles, but spends many years of quiet
work in Cilicia and Antioch, and so the
command of the vision in vv. 20, 21, is

not suitable to the first visit. But the
command to go to the Gentiles dates
from the Apostle's Conversion, quite
apart from the vision in the Temple, cf.
ix. 15, xxvi. 17, and the same commission is plainly implied in xxii. 15; the
words of the command may well express
the ultimate and not the immediate issue
of the Apostle's labours. On ἐγέν. δέ, Luke
seventeen times, Acts twenty-one, and
ἐγέν. followed by infinitive, see Hawkins,
Horæ Synopticæ, p. 30, and Plummer's
St. Luke, p. 45. For the reading in xii.
25, ὑπέστ. εἰς Ἱ., and its bearing on the
present passage see Ramsay, St. Paul,
pp. 63, 64, and also above, xi. 29, xii. 25.
—προσευχ. . . . τῷ ἱερῷ: there was a
special reason for the mention of the fact
before St. Paul's present audience; it
showed that the Temple was still for
him the place of prayer and worship, and
it should have shown the Jews that he
who thus prayed in the Temple could not
so have profaned it, Lewin, St. Paul, ii.,
p. 146.—ἐν ἐκστάσει, x. 10. For the
construction see Burton, p. 175, Simcox,
Language of the N.T., p. 58, Blass,
Gram., p. 247.
Ver. 18. σπεῦσον καὶ ἔξ.: implying
danger, cf. ix. 29.—σου μαρτ.: grounded
upon the occurrence before Damascus,
and so a striking testimony.
Ver. 19. Κύριε, ix. 5.—αὐτοὶ ἐπίσ.:
Paul seems as it were to plead with his
Lord that men cannot but receive testimony from one who had previously been
an enemy of Jesus of Nazareth; the words

αὐτόν.　21. καὶ εἶπε πρός με, Πορεύου, ὅτι ἐγὼ εἰς ἔθνη μακρὰν
ἐξαποστελῶ[1] σε.

22. Ἤκουον δὲ αὐτοῦ ἄχρι τούτου τοῦ λόγου, καὶ ἐπῆραν τὴν
φωνὴν αὐτῶν λέγοντες, Αἶρε ἀπὸ τῆς γῆς τὸν τοιοῦτον· οὐ γὰρ
καθῆκον[2] αὐτὸν ζῆν.　23. κραυγαζόντων δὲ[3] αὐτῶν, καὶ ῥιπτούντων

[1] εξαποστειλω, but W.H. marg. αποστελω, so B; D has εξαποστελλω, but Blass
in β = T.R.

[2] καθηκον, D², but καθηκεν ℵABCDEHLP (Blass).　Other var. καθηκει, καθηκαν
in minsc. show imperf. not understood.

[3] After κραυγαζ. τε is read by Lach., W.H., Weiss, Wendt with ABC, Syr. P.,
Aeth., but Tisch. with T.R. keeps δε, so ℵDEHLP, Vulg., Boh., Syr. H., Arm.,
Chrys.

too are directed to his hearers, so that
they may impress them with the strength
of the testimony thus given by one who
had imprisoned the Christians.—δέρων:
on the power of the Sanhedrim outside
Jerusalem see on p. 151.—κατὰ τὰς συν.,
cf. viii. 3, xx. 20, and for such punishments in the synagogues cf. Matt. x. 17,
xxiii. 34, Mark xiii. 9, Luke xxi. 12, 17,
Luke xii. 11, Edersheim, History of the
Jewish Nation, p. 374.
Ver. 20. τοῦ μ. σου: he identifies
himself with Stephen, his testimony like
that of the martyr is borne to Christ; on
the word see p. 67; the term is
here in a transition stage from "witness"
to "martyr," cf. also Rev. xvii. 6: Hackett
quotes the Christians of Lyons, towards
the close of the second century, refusing
to be called "martyrs" because such an
honourable name only belonged to the
true and faithful Witness, or to those
who had sealed their testimony by constancy to the end, and they feared lest
they should waver: Euseb., Hist., v.,
2.—καὶ αὐτὸς, cf. viii. 13, xv. 32,
xxi. 24, xxiv. 15, 16, xxv. 22, xxvii. 36,
here it is placed in sharp contrast to the
preceding words about Stephen (with
whose witness he was now identified).
On καὶ αὐτὸς as characteristic of Luke in
his Gospel and Acts see Hawkins, Horæ
Synopticæ, p. 33, as compared with its
employment by the other Synoptists,
sometimes it is inserted with emphasis,
Plummer on Luke i. 16.—συνευδ., see
note on viii. 1.
Ver. 21. εἰς ἔθνη: the mere mention
of the Gentiles roused their fury, and
they saw in it a justification of the charge
in xxi. 28; the scene closely resembled
the tumultuous outburst which led to the
murder of St. Stephen.
Ver. 22. ἐπῆραν τὴν φ., see on ii. 14.
—αἶρε, cf. xxi. 36, emphasised here by

ἀπὸ τῆς γῆς; present tense, a continu-
ous cry.—καθῆκον: only used by St.
Paul elsewhere in N.T., cf. Rom. i. 28.
The imperfect, καθῆκεν, see critical note,
implies that long ago he ought to have
been put to death "for it was not fit,"
etc., non debebat (or debuerat) vivere,
Winer-Moulton, xli. 2.—καθ = προσῆκον
Att. In LXX, Deut. xxi. 17, Ezek. xxi.
27 (32), and other passages, also several
times in Books of Macc. (see H. and R.).
For construction cf. Burton, p. 15.
Ver. 23. κραυγαζόντων δὲ (τε, Weiss,
Wendt, W.H.), only here in Acts (cf.
Luke iv. 41, but doubtful: W.H. read
κράζοντα), six times in St. John, and
four times in his narrative of the Passion
of the cries of the Jewish multitude, cf.
especially xix. 15, so too in 2 Esdras iii.
13, in classical Greek rare (Dem.), used
by Epict., Diss., iii., 4, 4, of the shouts
in the theatres.—ῥιπτ. τὰ ἱμάτια: not
throwing off their garments as if preparing to stone Paul (for which Zöckler
compares vii. 58, and see Plato, Rep.,
474 A), for the fact that the Apostle was
in the custody of the Romans would
have prevented any such purpose. The
verb may be used as a frequentative,
ῥιπτεῖν, jactare, ῥίπτειν, jacere, while
some of the old grammarians associate
with it a suggestion of earnestness or
effort, others of contempt, Grimm-Thayer,
sub v. (for the form in LXX cf. Dan.,
Theod., ix., 18, 20). The word here rather
means "tossing about their garments,"
a manifestation of excitement and un-
controllable rage, cf. Ovid, Am., iii., 2, 74,
and also instances in Wetstein, cf. Chrys.,
who explains ῥιπτάζοντες, ἐκτινάσσον-
τες. Dean Farrar refers to Pal. Expln.
Fund, 1879, p, 77, for instances of the
sudden excitability of Oriental crowds,
and for similar illustrations see Hackett,
in loco.—κονιορτὸν βαλλ.: best taken as

τὰ ἱμάτια, καὶ κονιορτὸν βαλλόντων εἰς τὸν[1] ἀέρα, 24. ἐκέλευσεν
αὐτὸν ὁ χιλίαρχος ἄγεσθαι εἰς τὴν παρεμβολήν, εἰπὼν μάστιξιν
ἀνετάζεσθαι αὐτάν, ἵνα ἐπιγνῷ δι᾽ ἣν αἰτίαν οὕτως ἐπεφώνουν αὐτῷ.
25. ὡς δὲ[2] προέτεινεν αὐτὸν τοῖς ἱμᾶσιν, εἶπε πρὸς τὸν ἑστῶτα
ἑκατόνταρχον ὁ Παῦλος, Εἰ ἄνθρωπον Ῥωμαῖον καὶ ἀκατάκριτον
ἔξεστιν ὑμῖν μαστίζειν; 26. ἀκούσας δὲ ὁ ἑκατόνταρχος, προσελθὼν
ἀπήγγειλε τῷ χιλιάρχῳ λέγων,[3] Ὅρα τί μέλλεις ποιεῖν· ὁ γὰρ
ἄνθρωπος οὗτος Ῥωμαῖός ἐστι. 27. προσελθὼν δὲ ὁ χιλίαρχος

[1] Instead of αερα D, Gig., Syr. P., Cassiod. have ουρανον, so Blass in β.
ριπτοντων in DEHL, Blass, Hilg., but text ℵABC, all edd.

[2] προετειναν ℵBL, so Tisch., W.H., Weiss, Wendt, Blass in β, Hilg.; AE 68
have προετεινον; CD 40, 137, προσετειναν; P 31, προετεινεν, plural changed into
sing. ο χ. λ. regarded as still the subject.

[3] ορα before τι om. ℵABCE, Vulg., Syrr. P.H., Boh., Arm., Tisch., W.H., Weiss,
Wendt, but retained by Blass with DHLP. After εκατον. Blass in β, and Hilg. add
οτι Ρωμαιον εαυτον λεγει with D, Gig., Wern.

another sign of the same rage and fury,
a similar demonstration; this is preferable
to the supposition that they threw dust
into the air to signify that they would
throw stones if they could. εἰς τὸν ἀέρα
seems to imply the interpretation adopted; the dust could scarcely have been
aimed at Paul, for he was out of reach;
but see 2 Sam. xvi. 13.

Ver. 24. ὁ χιλ., see xxi. 31.—παρεμ.,
xxi. 34.—εἰπὼν: whether the chiliarch
understood Paul's words or not, he evidently saw from the outcries of the mob
that the Apostle was regarded as a dangerous person, and he probably thought
to obtain some definite information from
the prisoner himself by torture.—μάστιξιν, cf. 2 Macc. vii. 1, 4 Macc. vi. 3, ix.
12, etc., and 1 Kings xii. 11, Prov. xxvi.
3, and in N.T., Heb. xi. 36; the Roman
scourging was a terrible punishment; for
its description cf., e.g., Keim, Geschichte
Jesu, iii., p. 390 (for Jewish scougings
see Farrar, St. Paul, ii., Excurs., xi.).—
ἀνετάζεσθαι: not found in classical Greek,
but ἐξετάζεσθαι used specially of examination by torture. It is found in the active
voice in Judg. vi. 29 A, and Susannah,
ver. 14.—ἐπεφ.: "shouted against him,"
R.V., see on xxi. 34, and 3 Macc. vii. 13
—only here with dative.

Ver. 25. προέτειναν: "and when
they had tied him up with the thongs,"
R.V., i.e., with the ligatures which kept
the body extended and fixed while under
flogging; Vulgate, "cum astrinxissent
eum loris"; but προέ. is rather "stretched
him forward with the thongs," i.e., bound
him to a pillar or post in a tense posture
for receiving the blows, see critical note.

Blass takes προέτειναν as an imperfect.
cf. xxviii. 2.—τοῖς ἱμᾶσιν: referring to
the thongs usually employed for so binding, and this seems borne out by ver. 29
δεδεκώς: not "for the thongs," as in
R.V. margin, so Lewin, Blass, Weiss and
others, as if = μάστιξ. Grimm admits
that the word may be used either of the
leathern thongs with which a person was
bound or was beaten, but here he prefers
the latter.—τὸν ἑστῶτα ἑκατόν.: the
centurion who presided over the scourging, just as a centurion was appointed to
be in charge over the execution of our
Lord; on the form ἑκατόν., only here in
Acts, see Simcox, Lauguage of the N.T.,
p. 30, and see Moulton and Geden, sub v.
-άρχης, and above on x. 1.—εἰ: "in-
terrogatio subironica est, confidentiæ
plena," Blass (so Wendt).—καὶ: "and
that too," δύο τὰ ἐγκλήματα· καὶ τὸ
ἄνευ λόγου καὶ τὸ Ῥωμαῖον ὄντα, Chrys.,
cf. xvi. 37. The torture was illegal in
the case of a Roman citizen, although it
might be employed in the case of slaves
and foreigners: Digest. Leg. 48, tit. 18,
c. 1. "Et non esse a tormentis incipi-
endum Div. Augustus constituit." At
Philippi St. Paul had probably not been
heard in his protests on account of the
din and tumult: "nunc quia illi negotium
est cum Romanis militibus, qui modestius
et gravius se gerebant, occasione utitur"
Calvin.

Ver. 26. ὅρα, see critical note.—τί
μέλλεις ποιεῖν, cf. 2 Macc. vii. 2 R, τί
μέλλεις ἐρωτᾶν;—ὁ γὰρ ἄν. οὗτος, on St.
Luke's fondness for οὗτος in similar
phrases, Friedrich, pp. 10, 89.

Ver. 28. πολλοῦ κεφ., cf. LXX, Lev.

καταγαγὼν τὸν Παῦλον ἔστησεν εἰς αὐτούς. XXIII. 1. Ἀτενίσας
δὲ ὁ Παῦλος τῷ συνεδρίῳ εἶπεν, Ἄνδρες ἀδελφοί, ἐγὼ πάσῃ συνειδήσει
ἀγαθῇ πεπολίτευμαι τῷ Θεῷ ἄχρι ταύτης τῆς ἡμέρας.　2. ὁ δὲ
ἀρχιερεὺς Ἀνανίας ἐπέταξε τοῖς παρεστῶσιν αὐτῷ τύπτειν αὐτοῦ τὸ

addressed the assembly not as judges but as fellow-countrymen. On ἀδελ. see on i. 15. It is of course possible, as Chrysostom observes, that he did not wish to appear εὐκαταφρόνητος before the chiliarch.—συνειδήσει: the word occurs no less than thirty times in N.T., R.V., so also in John viii. 9, but 1 Cor. viii. 7, συνηθείᾳ, R.V., and of these no less than twenty times in St. Paul's Epistles, twice in Acts, on both occasions by St. Paul, three times in 1 Peter, and five times in Hebrews. It may therefore be almost reckoned as a Pauline word. It does not occur at all in the Gospels (but cf. John viii. 9), but it need hardly be said that our Lord distinctly appeals to its sanction, although the word is never uttered by Him. The N.T. writers found the word ready to their use. In Wisd. xvii. 10 (11) we have the nearest anticipation of the Christian use of the word, whilst it must not be forgotten that it first appears at least in philosophical importance amongst the Stoics. (In Eccles. x. 20 it is used but in a different sense, and in Ecclus. xlii. 18, but in the latter case the reading is doubtful, and if the word is retained, it is only used in the same sense as in Eccles. x. 20.) It is used by Chrysippus of Soli, or Tarsus, in Cilicia, Diog. Laert., vii., 8, but not perhaps with any higher meaning than self-consciousness. For the *alleged* earlier use of the word by Bias and Periander, and the remarkable parallel expression ἀγαθὴ συνείδησις attributed to the latter, see W. Schmidt, *Das Gewissen*, p. 6 (1889), and for two quotations of its use by Menander, Grimm-Thayer, *sub v.*; *cf.* also Davison, *The Christian Conscience* (Fernley Lectures), 1888, sec. ii. and vi.; Cremer, *Wörterbuch, sub v.*; Sanday and Headlam, Rom. ii. 15, and for literature "Conscience," Hastings' B.D. For the scriptural idea of the word *cf.* also Westcott, additional note, on Heb. ix. 9.—πεπολ.: however loosely the word may have been used at a later date, it seems that when St. Paul spoke, and when he wrote to the Philippians, it embraced the public duties incumbent on men as *members of a body*, Hort, *Ecclesia*, p. 137, Lightfoot on Phil. i. 27 (iii. 20), *cf.*

Jos., *Vita*, ii. St. Paul was a covenant member of a divine πολιτεία, the commonwealth of God, the laws of which he claims to have respected and observed. The word is also found in LXX, Es. viii. 13 (H. and R.), 2 Macc. vi. 1, xi. 25, and four times in 4 Macc. Lightfoot, *u. s.*, parallels the use of the verb in Phil. by St. Paul from Clem. Rom., *Cor.*, xxi., 1, and Polycarp, *Phil.*, v., 5. But Clem. Rom., *u. s.*, vi., 1, has the phrase τοῖς ἀνδράσιν ὁσίως πολιτευσαμένοις, referring to the O.T. Saints, and so St. Peter and St. Paul. To this latter expression Deissmann, *Bibelstudien*, i., p. 211, finds a parallel in the fragment of a letter dating about 164 B.C. (Pap., *Par.*, 63, *coll.* 8 and 9), τοῖς θεοῖς πρὸς οὓς ὁσίως καὶ . . . δικαίως (πολι)τευσάμενος.—τῷ Θεῷ: in another moment of danger at the close of his career, 2 Tim. i. 3, the Apostle again appeals to a higher tribunal than that of the Sanhedrim or of Caesar. For the dative of the object *cf.* Rom. xiv. 18, Gal. ii. 19.—ἄχρι ταύτης τῆς ἡμ., emphatic, because the Apostle wished to affirm that he was still in his present work for Christ a true member of the theocracy, *cf.* Rom. ix. 1 ff.

Ver. 2. Ἀναν.: not the Ananias of iv. 7, Luke iii. 2, John xviii. 13, but the son of Nebedæus, appointed to his office by Herod of Chalcis, high priest from *c.* 47-59. He was sent to Rome on account of the complaints of the Samaritans against the Jews, but the Jewish cause prevailed, and there is no reason to suppose that Ananias lost his office. The probabilities are that he retained it until he was deposed shortly before the departure of Felix. Josephus gives us a terrible picture of his violent and unscrupulous conduct, *Ant.*, xx., 9, 2. But his Roman sympathisers made him an object of hatred to the nationalists, and in A.D. 66, in the days of the last great revolt against the Romans, he was dragged from a sewer in which he had hidden, and was murdered by the weapons of the assassins whom in his own period of power he had not scrupled to employ, Jos., *B.J.*, ii., 17, 9, "Ananias," B.D.², and Hastings' B.D., O. Holtzmann, *Neutest. Zeitgeschichte*, pp. 130,

στόμα. 3. τότε ὁ Παῦλος πρὸς αὐτὸν εἶπε, Τύπτειν σε μέλλει ὁ
Θεός, τοῖχε κεκονιαμένε· καὶ σὺ κάθη κρίνων με κατὰ τὸν νόμον,
καὶ παρανομῶν κελεύεις με τύπτεσθαι; 4. οἱ δὲ παρεστῶτες εἶπον,
Τὸν [1] ἀρχιερέα τοῦ Θεοῦ λοιδορεῖς; 5. ἔφη τε ὁ Παῦλος, Οὐκ ᾔδειν,
ἀδελφοί, ὅτι ἐστὶν ἀρχιερεύς· γέγραπται γάρ, "Ἄρχοντα τοῦ λαοῦ

---

[1] Blass reads in β text (with approval of Belser) ουτως εμπαιζεις τῳ αρχιερει
του Θεου λοιδορων; *sic insilis in sacerdotem Dei male dicendo,* Cypr.

146.—**τύπτειν**: because Paul had forgotten that he was before his judges,
and ought not to have spoken before
being asked, *cf.* Luke vi. 29, John xviii.
22, 2 Cor. xi. 20, 1 Tim. iii. 3, Titus i. 7.
The act was illegal and peculiarly offensive to a Jew at the hands of a Jew,
Farrar, *St. Paul,* ii., p. 323.

Ver. 3. Wetstein sees in the words the
customary formula of malediction among
the Jews. But we need not regard
Paul's words as an imprecation of evil
on the high priest, but only an expression
of the firm belief that such conduct would
meet with punishment, *cf.* Knabenbauer,
in loco. The terrible death of Ananias
was a fulfilment of the words. On the
paronomasia and other instances of the
same figure see Blass, *Gram.,* p. 292.—
τοῖχε κεκον., *cf.* Matt. xxiii. 27, Luke xi.
44, the expression may have been proverbial, in LXX, *cf.* Prov. xxi. 9. A
contrast has been drawn between St.
Paul's conduct and that of our Lord
under provocation, as, *e.g.,* by St. Jerome,
Adv. Pelag., iii., 1, but there were occasions when Christ spoke with righteous
indignation, and never more severely
than when He was condemning the same
sin which St. Paul censured—hypocrisy.
—**καὶ σύ,** emphatic, *cf.* Mark iv. 13, Luke
x. 29. **καὶ** at the commencement of a
question expressing indignation or astonishment (Page).—**κάθη κρίνων,** later
form for **κάθησαι,** *cf.* for the phrase
Luke xxii. 30.—**παρανομῶν**: only here
in N.T., but *cf.* LXX, Ps. lxxv. 4, cxviii.
51; the verb also occurs several times
in 4 Macc.

Ver. 4. **τὸν ἀρχ. τοῦ Θεοῦ**: of God,
emphatic, *i.e.,* sitting on the judgment-
seat as God's representative, *cf.* Deut.
xvii. 8 ff., and also the name Elohim, by
which the priestly and other judges
were sometimes known, Exod. xxi. 6,
xxii. 8, 9, Psalm lxxxi. 1.

Ver. 5. **οὐκ ᾔδειν**: the subject of **ἐστιν**
is not expressed as in A. and R.V., in
the Greek it is simply "I wist not that it
was the high priest (who spoke)". If it
be said that St. Paul could scarcely have

been ignorant that Ananias was high
priest, we must bear in mind that not
even the high priest wore a distinctive
dress when not engaged in actual service
(Edersheim, *Temple and its Services,* p.
67, with reference to this same passage),
if we are not prepared to accept the view
of Chrysostom and Oecumenius amongst
others, that the Apostle, owing to his
long absence from Jerusalem, did not
know the high priest by sight, or to
suppose that his weakness of eyesight
might have prevented him from seeing
clearly (so Lewin, Plumptre). The interpretation that St. Paul spoke ironically, or by way of protest, as if such
behaviour as that of Ananias on his
nomination to office by Herod of Chalcis
was in itself sufficient to prevent his
recognition as high priest, is somewhat
out of harmony with the Apostle's quotation of Scripture in his reply, nor are the
attempts to translate **οὐκ ᾔδειν** as =
non agnosco or *non reputabam* successful. See further Zöckler's summary of
the different views, *Apostelgeschichte,* 2nd
edition, *in loco.*—**ἀδελφοί**: the word indicates St. Paul's quick recovery from
his moment of just anger to a conciliatory tone.—**γέγ. γάρ**: in this appeal
to the law, St. Paul showed not only his
acquaintance with it, but his reverence for
it—another proof of his wisdom and tact.
—**ἄρχοντα τοῦ λαοῦ σου κ.τ.λ.**: LXX,
Exod. xxii. 28, the Apostle apparently
only quotes the latter part of the verse;
in the Hebrew we have "thou shalt not
revile God (*margin,* the judges), nor
curse a ruler of thy people". *Cf.* the
ruling principle of the Apostle's conduct,
Rom. xiii. 1-7 (1 Pet. ii. 13-17).

Ver. 6. **γνοὺς . . . τὸ ἓν . . . τὸ δὲ
ἕτερον.** On **ἕν . . . ἕτερον**: see Simcox,
Language of the N.T., pp. 71, 72. That
Pharisees and Sadducees alike had seats
in the Sanhedrim during this period is
borne out not only by the N. T., but by
Jos., *Ant.,* xx., 9, 1, *B.J.,* ii., 17, 3, *Vita,*
38, 39. It is possible that the Pharisees
might have attracted the attention of the
Apostle by their protest against the be-

σου οὐκ ἐρεῖς κακῶς". 6. Γνοὺς δὲ ὁ Παῦλος ὅτι τὸ ἓν μέρος ἐστὶ
Σαδδουκαίων, τὸ δὲ ἕτερον Φαρισαίων,[1] ἔκραξεν ἐν τῷ συνεδρίῳ,
Ἄνδρες ἀδελφοί, ἐγὼ Φαρισαῖός εἰμι, υἱὸς Φαρισαίου · περὶ ἐλπίδος

[1] εκραξεν, but imperf. εκραζεν ℵBC 36, Syr. Pesh.; so Tisch., W.H., R.V.,
Weiss, Wendt (see note ed. 1899). Blass has εκραξεν, so Hilg. Φαρισαιου, but
plural Φαρισαιων in ℵABC, Vulg., Syr. Pesh., Tert., and other authorities as
above, with Blass also, perhaps altered into sing., because one only thought of the
relation of father and son (Wendt). B, Sah. Boh., Tert. omit εγω before κρινομαι;
Lach. and Tisch. retain, but other authorities above with Blass omit (but W.H. in
marg.); it may have been added in accordance with xxiv. 21.

haviour of Ananias and their acceptance
of the words of apology (so Felten,
Zöckler), but it is equally probable that
in St. Luke's apparently condensed account the appeal to the Pharisees was
not made on a sudden impulse (see
below), but was based upon some manifestation of sympathy with his utterances.
In ver. 9 it is evidently implied that the
story of Paul's conversion on the road to
Damascus had been narrated, and his
acceptance of the Messiahship of the
Risen Jesus carried with it his belief in
a resurrection.—ἔκραξεν: the word may
here as sometimes elsewhere, cf. John
vii. 37, xii. 44, indicate no isolated cry,
but a reference to something previously
said, and it is probable that St. Luke
may have passed over here as elsewhere
some portions of the Apostle's speech,
which were less intimately connected
with the development and issue of events.
It must however be noted that the verb
may mean that the Apostle cried aloud
so that all might hear him amidst the
rising confusion.—ἐγὼ Φαρι. εἰμι κ.τ.λ.:
the words have been severely criticised,
but in a very real sense they truthfully
expressed the Apostle's convictions. Before Felix St. Paul made practically the
same assertion, although he did not use
the word Φαρ. (cf. also xxvi. 5), Hort,
Judaistic Christianity, p. 111. Moreover it is difficult to see why the Apostle
should not describe himself as a Pharisee
in face of the statement, xv. 5, that
many members of the sect were also
members of the Christian Church.
They, like St. Paul, must have acknowledged that Jesus was the Messiah.
But that Messiahship was attested
by the avowal of the resurrection of
Jesus, and the resurrection was a prominent article of the Pharisees' creed.
In the acceptance of this latter doctrine
St. Paul was at one not only with the
" Pharisees who believed," but with the
whole sect, and that he used the title
in this limited way, viz., with rela-

tion to the hope of the resurrection, is
plain from the context, which fixes the
limitation by the Apostle's own words.
But because the declaration shows the
tact of St. Paul, because it is an instance
of his acting upon the maxim Divide et
impera, has it no higher side in relation
to his character and purpose? May we
not even say that to the Pharisees he
became as a Pharisee in order to save
some, to lead them to see the crown and
fulfilment of the hope in which he and
they were at one, in the Person of Jesus,
the Resurrection and the Life? That
the Apostle's action met with Divine
approval seems evident, ver. 11. See
"Paul" (Dr. Llewellyn Davies), B.D.[1],
iii., 754, 755, and amongst recent
writers, Luckock, but on the other hand
Gilbert, Student's Life of Paul, p. 187 ff.
Bethge attributes to the Apostle an
apologetic aim, viz., to show the chiliarch that Christianity should be protected by the State, since it was no new
religion, but really proceeded from
Judaism; and in support he refers to the
words of Lysias, xxiii. 29; but although
the Apostle's appeal may have helped
Lysias to form his judgment, it seems
somewhat strained to attribute to the
Apostle the motive assigned by Bethge.
—υἱὸς Φαρ.: "a son of Pharisees," R.V.
plural, which is the best reading, i.e.,
his ancestors, 2 Tim. i. 3, Phil. iii. 5,
possibly including his teachers by a
familiar Hebraism.—περὶ ἐλπίδος καὶ
ἀνασ.: generally taken as a hendiadys
(so Page), "hope of a resurrection of the
dead" (see, however, Winer-Moulton,
lxvi. 7). In xxvi. 6 ἐλπίς is used of the
hope of a future Messianic salvation—
the hope of Israel—but in xxiv. 15 St.
Paul distinctly makes mention of the
hope of a resurrection of the dead, and
his own words again in xxiv. 21 seem
to exclude anything beyond that question
as under discussion on the present occasion.

Ver. 7. στάσις: There is no difficulty

καὶ ἀναστάσεως νεκρῶν ἐγὼ κρίνομαι. 7. Τοῦτο δὲ αὐτοῦ [1] λαλήσαντος, ἐγένετο στάσις τῶν Φαρισαίων καὶ τῶν Σαδδουκαίων, καὶ ἐσχίσθη τὸ πλῆθος. 8. Σαδδουκαῖοι [2] μὲν γὰρ λέγουσι μὴ εἶναι ἀνάστασιν, μήτε ἄγγελον μήτε πνεῦμα· Φαρισαῖοι δὲ ὁμολογοῦσι τὰ ἀμφότερα. 9. ἐγένετο δὲ κραυγὴ μεγάλη· καὶ ἀναστάντες [3] οἱ γραμματεῖς τοῦ μέρους τῶν Φαρισαίων διεμάχοντο λέγοντες, Οὐδὲν κακὸν εὑρίσκομεν ἐν τῷ ἀνθρώπῳ τούτῳ· εἰ δὲ πνεῦμα ἐλάλησεν αὐτῷ ἢ ἄγγελος,

[1] Instead of λαλησαντος W.H., Weiss, Wendt, following B, read λαλουντος; Tisch., Meyer, Blass have λαλησαντος with T.R., following CHLP, Syr. H.; R.V. (W.H. marg.), with Lach. and Hilgenfeld, has ειποντος, so אcAE, Vulg., Syr. Pesh.; א* reads ειπαντος. For εγενετο B* (Syr. H.) has επεπεσεν, so W.H. marg. Blass brackets και εσχισθη το πληθος, see below on ver. 9.

[2] After Σαδδ. B, Vulg., Sah. omit μεν, so W.H. (text), Weiss, Blass; but retained by Tisch., R.V., W.H. marg., Hilg. Instead of μηδε as in T.R. (so Meyer, Wendt, Blass), μητε in אABCE, so Tisch., W.H., Weiss, Hilgenfeld. In edit. 1899 Wendt decides to follow T.R., and to read μηδε, although he admits that MS. authority is against him. μηδε is supported by HLP, Chrys., Theophyl. But μητε may have been altered to μηδε to suit τα αμφοτερα. Instead of τα αμφ. Blass in β (Sah., Flor.) reads ειναι αναστασιν και αγγελον και πνευμα.

[3] Instead of οι γραμματεις אBC, Sah., Arm. read τινες των γραμματεων, Tisch., W.H., R.V., Weiss, Wendt, Blass, Hilg.; AE 13, Vulg., Boh. read simply τινες, so Lach., T.R. very little support; HLP, Aeth. read γραμματεις (om. οι). του μερους om. AE 13, Vulg., Boh., but retained in אBCHLP, Syr. P. and H., Arm., Chrys., Tisch., W.H., R.V., Weiss, Wendt, Blass. In β at commencement of verse Blass reads και κραυγης γενομενης εν εαυτοις (inter eos, Flor.) εσχισθησαν with Flor.; ανασταντες omit. in β text with Flor. μη θεομαχωμεν om. אABCE 13, 40, 66, verss. Instead of ουδεν κακον κ.τ.λ. Blass in β text (Flor.) reads τι δε κακον εν τω ανθρωπω τουτω ευρισκομεν;

in supposing that this dissention took place in the Assembly; it may have been no sudden result, because the Apostle had evidently said much more than is mentioned in the preceding verse (see above), and there is good evidence that one of the fundamental differences between the two sects was concerned with the question which St. Paul had raised, Edersheim, *Jesus the Messiah*, i., 315; Jos., *Ant.*, xviii., 1, 4; *B.J.*, ii., 8, 14.—ἐσχίσθη τὸ πλ., *Æn.*, ii., 39, and instances in Wetstein.

Ver. 8. ἄγγελον . . . πνεῦμα: are joined together by the speaker as one principal conception, so that the following ἀμφότερα presents no difficulty, see Winer-Moulton, lv., 6, Page, *in loco.* πνεῦμα would include the spirits of the dead, to one of which Paul would appear to have appealed, xxii. 7, 18 (Weiss). On the denial see Schürer, *Jewish People*, div. ii., vol. ii., p. 13, E.T., *cf.* also the remarks of Dr. A. B. Davidson, "Angel," Hastings' B.D., as to the possible sense of this denial and its possible limitation, with which we may compare Hamburger, *Real-Encyclopädie des Judentums*, ii., 7,

1046.—ὁμολ., *i.e.*, as part of their religious creed, their confession and open profession of faith : "but the faith of the Sadducees is well described by negations".

Ver. 9. κραυγὴ μεγ.: "there arose a great clamour," R.V., so A.V. in Ephes. iv. 31; the noun also denotes not only the loud cry of partisan applause as here, but of joyful surprise, Luke i. 42, of grief, Rev. xxi. 4, of anger, Ephes. u. s., Westcott on Heb. v. 7, *cf.* LXX, Exod. xii. 30, Judith xiv. 19, 2 Macc. xv. 29.—ἀναστάντες, characteristic, see on v. 17.—γραμματεῖς, the professional lawyers exercised considerable influence in the Sanhedrim, belonging chiefly to the Pharisees, but also numbering in their ranks some Sadducean scribes, Schürer, *Jewish People*, div. ii., vol. i., pp. 178, 319, E.T. The notice may therefore be placed to the writer's accuracy. —διεμάχοντο: only here in N.T., *cf.* LXX, Dan. x. 20, Ecclesiast. viii. 1, 3, li. 19 R., frequent in classics. Overbeck and Holtzmann can only see in this scene a repetition of chap. v. 33.—εἰ δὲ πνεῦμα: "And what if a spirit hath

μὴ θεομαχῶμεν. 10. πολλῆς δὲ [1] γενομένης στάσεως, εὐλαβηθεὶς ὁ
χιλίαρχος μὴ διασπασθῇ ὁ Παῦλος ὑπ᾽ αὐτῶν, ἐκέλευσε τὸ στράτευμα
καταβὰν ἁρπάσαι αὐτὸν ἐκ μέσου αὐτῶν, ἄγειν τε [2] εἰς τὴν παρεμβολήν.

11. ΤΗι δὲ ἐπιούσῃ νυκτὶ ἐπιστὰς αὐτῷ ὁ Κύριος εἶπε, Θάρσει,
Παῦλε [3] · ὡς γὰρ διεμαρτύρω τὰ περὶ ἐμοῦ εἰς Ἰερουσαλήμ, οὕτω σε
δεῖ καὶ εἰς Ῥώμην μαρτυρῆσαι. 12. γενομένης δὲ ἡμέρας,[4] ποιή-
σαντές τινες τῶν Ἰουδαίων συστροφὴν ἀνεθεμάτισαν ἑαυτούς, λέγοντες

[1] Instead of γεν. אB 98*, read γιν.; Lach., Alford, Hilg. follow T.R., but Tisch.,
Weiss, Wendt, W.H., R.V., Blass read γιν. εὐλαβηθεις retained by Meyer
as the rarer word in N.T., but φοβηθεις אABCE, Chrys., and authorities above,
so Hilgenfeld.

[2] After αγειν, W.H., following B, Boh., 31, omit τε in text (not in marg.), but
Weiss retains in spite of B. If omitted, αρπασαι would depend upon καταβαν, and
αγειν upon εκελευσε.

[3] Παυλε om. אABC*E, verss., so Tisch., W.H., R.V., Weiss, Wendt, Blass
(although retained in Flor. and by Hilg.).

[4] Instead of T.R., אABCE 13, 61, Boh., Arm., Aeth. read -τες συστροφην οι
Ιουδαιοι; so authorities in ver. 11 except Blass. The latter reads with T.R.
συστροφην τινες των Ιουδ., so L(HP), Vulg., Syr. Pesh., Gig., Flor., Lucif. (see also
Hilg.).

spoken to him, or an angel?" R.V.
reading after ἄγγελος a mark of interrogation. Often explained as *aposiopesis*
(so Weiss), *cf.* W.H. reading—John vi.
62, Rom. ix. 22, but see Blass, *Gram.*,
p. 288, Burton, pp. 109-110. The words
may have been followed by a significant
gesture or look towards the Sadducees,
or by some such words as St. Chrysostom
suggests: ποῖον ἔγκλημα! or, without any
real *aposiopesis*, the words may have
been interrupted by the tumult, Winer-
Moulton, lxiv., ii. πνεῦμα: the word
evidently refers back to St. Paul's own
statements, xxii. 6, 7, while at the same
time it indicates that the Pharisees were
far from accepting Paul's account of the
scene before Damascus as an appearance
of Jesus of Nazareth.

Ver. 10. εὐλ., see critical note.—μὴ:
after verbs of *fear* and *danger* in classical
Greek, with subjunctive after primary
tenses, with optative (more usually) after
secondary tenses, but in N.T. only the
subjunctive, Burton, p. 95, and Viteau,
Le Grec du N.T., p. 83 (1893), Acts
xxvii. 17, 2 Cor. xi. 3, xii. 20, Heb. iv. 1.
—διασπασθῇ, *cf.* LXX, Hos. xiii. 8, for
use in same sense as here, to tear like a
wild beast tears its prey in pieces (elsewhere in N.T., Mark v. 4, *cf.* LXX, Jer.
ii. 20), *cf.* in classical Greek, Herod., iii.,
13, Dem., 58, 8.—καταβὰν from Antonia.
—ἁρπάσαι ἄγειν τε = ἁρπάσαν ἄγειν
(Blass), see critical note.

Ver. 11. τῇ ἐπι. νυκτί, see Knabenbauer's note, p. 385, on Hilgenfeld's
strictures; and below on the need and
fitness of the appearance of the Lord on
this night.—ἐπιστὰς, *cf.* xii. 7, and xviii.
9.—ὁ κ., evidently Jesus, as the context
implies.—θάρσει: only in the imperative
in N.T. (seven times); the word on the
lips of Christ had brought cheer to the
sick and diseased, Matt. ix. 2, 22, Mark
x. 49; to the disciples sailing on the sea,
Matt. xiv. 27, Mark v. 50; to the same
disciples in an hour of deeper need, John
xvi. 33, *cf.* its use in LXX as a message
of encouragement (elsewhere we have
the verb θαρρεῖν, so in Paul and Heb.,
but *cf. Apoc. of Peter*, v., Blass, *Gram.*,
p. 24). The Apostle might well stand in
need of an assurance after the events of
the day that his labours would not be
cut short before his great desire was
fulfilled. The words of the Lord as
given to us by St. Luke intimate that
the Evangelist regarded Paul's visit to
Rome as *apex Evangelii*, so far as
his present work was concerned.—
διεμαρτύρω: the word seems to imply
the thoroughness of the Apostle's testimony, and to show that his method
of bearing it was approved by his Lord,
see on ii. 40.

Ver. 12. συστροφήν, xix. 40.—ἀνεθεμάτισαν ἑαυτούς: literally "they placed
themselves under an anathema," *i.e.*,
declared themselves liable to the direst
punishments of God unless, etc. In N.T.
the verb is only used in this passage, *cf.*

μήτε φαγεῖν μήτε πιεῖν ἕως οὗ ἀποκτείνωσι τὸν Παῦλον · 13. ἦσαν
δὲ πλείους τεσσαράκοντα οἱ ταύτην τὴν συνωμοσίαν[1] πεποιηκότες ·
14. οἵτινες προσελθόντες τοῖς ἀρχιερεῦσι[2] καὶ τοῖς πρεσβυτέροις
εἶπον, Ἀναθέματι ἀνεθεματίσαμεν ἑαυτούς, μηδενὸς γεύσασθαι[3] ἕως
οὗ ἀποκτείνωμεν τὸν Παῦλον. 15. νῦν οὖν ὑμεῖς ἐμφανίσατε τῷ
χιλιάρχῳ σὺν τῷ συνεδρίῳ, ὅπως[4] αὔριον αὐτὸν καταγάγῃ πρὸς ὑμᾶς,
ὡς μέλλοντας διαγινώσκειν ἀκριβέστερον τὰ περὶ αὐτοῦ · ἡμεῖς δέ,

---

[1] Instead of πεποι. ℵABCE have ποιησαμενοι, so R.V. and authorities above,
except Blass in β text, εαυτους αναθεματισαντες, following Flor.

[2] Blass in β brackets και τοις πρεσβ. Lucif. "recte ut videtur" (Blass).

[3] After γευσ. Blass in β (Flor., Gig.) adds καθολου.

[4] αυριον om. ℵABCE 18, 36, 61, verss., and authorities above, so Hilg. ℵABE
61 have εις, so R.V. and as above.

14, 21, and once by St. Mark, xiv. 71,
cf. the use of the verb in LXX, Josh. vi.
21, 1 Macc. v. 5. In N.T. the noun
ἀνάθεμα is only found in Luke and Paul,
see Lightfoot on Gal. i. 8, Sanday and
Headlam on Rom. ix. 3. For instances
of similar bindings by oath, Jos., Vita,
liii., and a similar combination of ten
men to murder Herod, Ant., xv., 8, 3, 4.
Of whom the band consisted we are not
told, although probably Ananias would
not have scrupled to employ the Sicarii,
Jos., Ant., ix. 2. The conspirators seem
to have affected to be Sadducees, ver.
14, but Edersheim evidently holds that
they were Pharisees, and he points out
that the latter as a fraternity or "guild,"
or some of their kindred guilds, would
have furnished material at hand for such
a band of conspirators, Jewish Social
Life, p. 227 ff.—πεποι. see critical note,
ἕως οὗ, cf. Matt. v. 25, xiii. 33, John ix.
18 ; Burton, p. 128.

Ver. 14. τοῖς ἀρχ., cf. iv. 23, see
critical note on reading in β (Blass).—
ἀναθέματι ἀνεθεμ.: "we have bound ourselves under a great curse," thus representing the emphatic Hebrew idiom, cf.
v. 28, and for the same phrase cf. Deut.
xiii. 15, xx. 17. The conspirators may
have been instigated by the knowledge
that the Sanhedrim could no longer inflict
capital punishment, and from despair of
obtaining the sanction of the Roman
authorities for violence against Paul. It
is quite certain that sentence of death
must at all events be ratified by the procurator. Another serious restriction of
the Jewish powers lay in the fact that
the Roman authorities could step in at
any moment and take the initiative, as in
the case of Paul. Moreover the incidents

before us illustrate the strange fact that
even the chiliarch of the Roman force
stationed in Jerusalem seems to be able
to summon the Sanhedrim for the purpose
of submitting to it any question upon
which the Jewish law had to be learnt,
cf. xxii. 30, Schürer, Jewish People, div.
ii., vol. i., p. 188 ff., with which, however,
should be compared O. Holtzmann,
Neutest. Zeitgeschichte, pp. 175, 176.—
γεύσασθαι: "to taste nothing," R.V.
"Hoc certe tam praeposterum concilium
nunquam probassent sacerdotes, si qua
in illis fuisset gutta pii rectique affectus,
imo sensus humani," Calvin. Edersheim
quotes a curious illustration of the rash
vow before us, which shows how easily
absolution from its consequences could
be obtained, Jewish Social Life, p. 229,
J. Lightfoot, Hor. Heb.

Ver. 15. νῦν οὖν: only in Acts in
N.T., where it occurs four times, frequent
in LXX.—ἐμφανίσατε: "signify" in A.
and R.V.; this rendering apparently
conveys a wrong idea, for it implies that
the Council had the authority, whereas
this lay with the Roman officer, cf. xxiv.
1, xxv. 2, 15. In LXX, Esther ii. 22,
2 Macc. iii. 7, xi. 29.—σὺν τῷ συν.: with
the whole Council, including both those
who had previously inclined to favour
Paul as well as his opponents ; the former could not object to the pretext that
further inquiries were to be made into
Paul's position, especially when the
Sadducees urged such an inquiry.—
ὅπως, Burton, p. 87.—ὡς μέλλοντας: this
use of ὡς with the participle expressing
the pretext alleged by another, often in
Luke, cf. Luke xvi. 1, xxiii. 14, Acts
xxiii. 20, xxvii. 30, Viteau, Le Grec du
N.T., p. 189 (1893), but we may also

πρὸ τοῦ ἐγγίσαι αὐτόν, ἕτοιμοί[1] ἐσμεν τοῦ ἀνελεῖν αὐτόν. 16. ἀκούσας
δὲ ὁ υἱὸς τῆς ἀδελφῆς Παύλου τὴν ἐνέδραν, παραγενόμενος καὶ
εἰσελθὼν εἰς τὴν παρεμβολὴν ἀπήγγειλε τῷ Παύλῳ. 17. προσκαλεσάμενος δὲ ὁ Παῦλος ἕνα τῶν ἑκατοντάρχων, ἔφη, Τὸν νεανίαν
τοῦτον ἀπάγαγε πρὸς τὸν χιλίαρχον· ἔχει γάρ τι ἀπαγγεῖλαι αὐτῷ.
18. ὁ μὲν οὖν παραλαβὼν αὐτὸν ἤγαγε πρὸς τὸν χιλίαρχον, καί
φησιν, Ὁ δέσμιος Παῦλος προσκαλεσάμενός με ἠρώτησε τοῦτον τὸν
νεανίαν ἀγαγεῖν πρὸς σέ, ἔχοντά τι λαλῆσαί σοι. 19. ἐπιλαβόμενος
δὲ τῆς χειρὸς αὐτοῦ ὁ χιλίαρχος, καὶ ἀναχωρήσας κατ᾽ ἰδίαν, ἐπυν-

---

[1] Blass in β reads **εσομεθα** instead of **εσμεν** with Flor., and at end of verse **εαν
δεη και αποθανειν** with 137, Syr. H. mg., Flor.

---

compare 1 Cor. iv. 18 (Burton).—**διαγ.**:
" as though ye would judge of his case
more exactly," R.V., *accurate cognoscere ;*
the word need not be used here in the
forensic sense as in xxiv. 22 (xxv. 21),
Grimm, Blass; the "inquiry" is expressed by the usual word in ver. 20.
The verb is used in 2 Macc. ix. 15.—
πρὸ τοῦ ἐγγίσαι: so that the crime
could not be imputed to the priests.—
ἕτοιμοί ἐσμεν τοῦ: for genitive of the
infinitive after a noun or an adjective, in
Luke and Paul (1 Pet. iv. 17), (Viteau, *u. s.*,
p. 169, Burton, p. 158. In LXX, *cf.*
Mich. vi. 8, Ezek. xxi. 10, 11 (15, 16),
1 Macc. iii. 58, v. 39, xiii. 37.—**ἀνελεῖν
αὐτὸν,** *cf.* Hackett's note, which gives a
formal justification from Philo for the
assassination of apostates.
Ver. 16. **ὁ υἱὸς τῆς ἀδελφῆς**: whether
he and his mother lived in Jerusalem, as
Ewald conjectured, we are not told.
Probably not, as the mother is not otherwise mentioned. Paul's nephew may
have been a student in Jerusalem, as
the Apostle had been in his earlier days.
Edersheim, *Jewish Social Life*, p. 227,
gives an interesting account of the way
in which the young man as a member of
the Pharisaic "Chabura," or guild,
might have gained his knowledge of the
conspiracy. At the same time nothing
is told us in the text, and we cannot
wonder at the comment "quis is fuerit,
unde rescierit, ignoratur" (Blass).—
παραγεν.: "having come in upon *them*,"
R.V. margin, "and he entered into the
castle," etc. **παραγεν.** is thoroughly
Lucan, and often gives a graphic touch
to the narrative, but it is doubtful whether
we can press it as above, although the
rendering is tempting.—**ἀπήγγειλε τῷ
Π.**: evidently Paul's friends were allowed
access to him, and amongst them we
may well suppose that St. Luke himself

would have been included. On the
different kinds of Roman custody see
below, xxiv. 23, note.
Ver. 17. **τὸν νεανίαν τοῦτον,** see on
vii. 58 and previous note above. The
narrative gives the impression that he
was quite a young man, if we look at his
reception by the chiliarch and the charge
given to him.
Ver. 18. **ὁ δέσμιος Π.**: used by Paul
five times of himself in his Epistles, here
for the first time in Acts with reference
to him.
Ver. 19. **ἐπιλαβ.**: "ut fiduciam
adolescentis confirmaret," Bengel, so
Knabenbauer; on **ἐπιλ.** see note, xvii.
19.—**τῆς χειρὸς αὐτοῦ,** *cf.* Luke viii. 54,
Winer-Moulton, xxx. 8 d; see Calvin's
note on the *humanitas* (as he calls it) of
the centurion in thus receiving the young
man.—**ἀναχ.**: used also in xxvi. 31, but
not by Luke in his Gospel, although
found in the other Evangelists.—**κατ᾽
ἰδίαν ἐπυν.**: "asked him privately,"
R.V., as suggested by the order of the
Greek.
Ver. 20. **συνέθεντο,** Luke xxii. 5,
John ix. 22, so in classical Greek in
middle, *cf.* 1 Sam. xxii. 13, Dan. (Th.) ii.
9.—**τοῦ ἐρωτῆσαι**: the word certainly
points to a certain equality with the
person asked (not **αἰτέω**), see above on
ver. 15—but still a request, not a demand.—**μέλλοντες,** see critical note; if
plural, the clause intimates the pretext
put forward by the conspirators; if
singular, it is perhaps more in accordance with the deference of the youth,
who would refer the control of the proceedings to the chiliarch.
Ver. 21. **ἐνεδρ.**: only in Luke in
N.T., Luke xi. 54, with the accusative
also in classical Greek, and several times
in LXX, 1 Macc. v. 4, Jos., *Ant.*, v., 2,
12.—**καὶ νῦν,** see on xx. 22.—**προσδεχ.**:

θάνετο, Τί ἐστιν ὃ ἔχεις ἀπαγγεῖλαί μοι; 20. εἶπε δέ, Ὅτι οἱ
Ἰουδαῖοι συνέθεντο τοῦ ἐρωτῆσαί σε, [3] ὅπως αὔριον εἰς τὸ συνέδριον
καταγάγῃς τὸν Παῦλον, ὡς μέλλοντές[1] τι ἀκριβέστερον πυνθάνεσθαι
περὶ αὐτοῦ. 21. σὺ οὖν μὴ πεισθῇς αὐτοῖς· ἐνεδρεύουσι γὰρ αὐτὸν
ἐξ αὐτῶν ἄνδρες πλείους τεσσαράκοντα, οἵτινες ἀνεθεμάτισαν ἑαυτοὺς
μήτε φαγεῖν μήτε πιεῖν ἕως οὗ ἀνέλωσιν αὐτόν· καὶ νῦν ἕτοιμοί εἰσι
προσδεχόμενοι τὴν ἀπὸ σοῦ ἐπαγγελίαν. 22. ὁ μὲν οὖν χιλίαρχος
ἀπέλυσε τὸν νεανίαν, παραγγείλας μηδενὶ ἐκλαλῆσαι ὅτι ταῦτα
ἐνεφάνισας πρός με. 23. καὶ προσκαλεσάμενος[2] δύο τινὰς τῶν
ἑκατοντάρχων εἶπεν, Ἑτοιμάσατε στρατιώτας διακοσίους, ὅπως πορ-
ευθῶσιν ἕως Καισαρείας, καὶ ἱππεῖς ἑβδομήκοντα, καὶ δεξιολάβους

---

[1] μέλλοντες minscl. verss., so Blass, Hilg., with Gig., Flor. (as in ver. 15);
μελλων ABE, Boh., Aeth., Tisch., W.H., Weiss; μελλον, so Wendt, with א* 13,
sc. το συνεδρ.

[2] אB 13, 61, Tisch., W.H., Blass, Weiss, Wendt read τινας before δυο. Blass
(so Flor.) brackets διακ. and και before ιππεις, and instead of εβδομηκοντα he reads
εκατον with 137, Flor., Syr. H. mg., Sah., so Hilg.

---

only once elsewhere in Acts, xxiv. 15,
probably in same sense as here, so R.V.
text. In the Gospels, the word is found
once in Mark xv. 43 (= Luke xxiii. 51),
and five times in Luke, four times translated in R.V. as here; Luke ii. 25, 38,
xii. 36, xxiii. 51, cf. also Tit. ii. 13, Jude
ver. 21, and Wisd. xviii. 7, 2 Macc. viii. 11.
In classical Greek two meanings as in
N.T.: (1) to accept, receive favourably,
(2) to wish for or expect a thing.—ἐπαγγελίαν: only here in N.T. of a human
promise, see above on i. 4, cf. 1 Esd. i. 7,
Esther iv. 7, 1 Macc. x. 15.

Ver. 22. ἐκλαλῆσαι, Judith xi. 9
(but S al.), "to divulge," here only in
N.T., but in classical Greek, and in
Philo. As in i. 4, transition to oratio
recta, cf. Luke v. 14, Mark vi. 9, etc.,
very common in Greek prose, Winer-
Moulton, lxiii., ii., 2, Blass, Gram., p.
280.

Ver. 23. See critical note; if we place
τινάς before δύο, Blass, Weiss, Knabenbauer take it of two centurions whom
he could specially trust, see their notes
in loco, and Blass, Gram., p. 174. In
Luke vii. 19 the order is different, Blass
compares Herman, Vis., i., 4, 3, δύο
τινὲς ἄνδρες (but see on the other hand
Page's note, and Wendt, edit. 1899).—
ἑτοιμάσατε: here only in Acts, but
frequent in Luke's Gospel, more so than
in Matthew or Mark, in John only
twice. On the aorist imperfect see
Winer-Moulton, xliii., 3, "have immediately . . . in readiness to march".—

στρατ. διακ.: milites gravis armaturæ.
Blass brackets the first διακ., and καὶ
before ἱππεῖς, so that στρατ. includes
under it both ἱππεῖς and δεξιολάβους,
see critical note.—δεξιολ.: apparently a
special class of light-armed soldiers
(javelin-throwers, Livy, xxii., 21, or
slingers), Schürer, Jewish People, div. i.,
vol. ii., p. 56, E.T., who says that this
much only is certain. The word only
occurs elsewhere twice, and that in
later Greek literature of the seventh and
tenth century (see references in Grimm-
Thayer, sub v., and Meyer-Wendt, in
loco), where they are distinguished from
the τοξοφόροι and πελτασταί. Probably
from δεξιός and λαμβάνω, grasping their
weapons by the right hand, so here of
those who carried their light weapon,
a lance, in their right hand, Vulgate,
lancearios. This is more probable than
the derivation from λαβή, a sword-hilt,
as if the word referred to spiculatores
cum lanceis, who wore their swords fastened not on the left but on the right (so
Ewald). Still more fanciful is the derivation of Egli who accented thus δεξιο-
λάβοι, and took the word to refer to
those who were unable to use the right
hand, Judg. iii. 15, xx. 16, so "left-
handed" slingers. Others interpret as if
the word meant military lictors who
guarded captives bound by the right
hand, but their large number here seems
to conflict with such an interpretation
(Grimm-Thayer), see the full notes of
Meyer-Wendt, 1888, 1899, and cf. Renan,

διακοσίους, ἀπὸ τρίτης ὥρας τῆς νυκτός · 24.[1] κτήνη τε παραστῆσαι,
ἵνα ἐπιβιβάσαντες τὸν Παῦλον διασώσωσι πρὸς Φήλικα, τὸν ἡγεμόνα ·
25. γράψας ἐπιστολὴν [2] περιέχουσαν τὸν τύπον τοῦτον · 26. Κλαύδιος
Λυσίας τῷ κρατίστῳ ἡγεμόνι Φήλικι, χαίρειν. 27. τὸν ἄνδρα τοῦτον
συλληφθέντα ὑπὸ τῶν Ἰουδαίων, καὶ μέλλοντα ἀναιρεῖσθαι ὑπ' αὐτῶν,
ἐπιστὰς σὺν τῷ στρατεύματι [3] ἐξειλόμην αὐτόν, μαθὼν ὅτι Ῥωμαῖός

---

[1] In β text Blass reads κτηνος, Par.[2], Syrr. P. and H., Prov., and before διασωσωσι
the words δια νυκτος, so Flor., Syr. H. mg. Belser approves as precise notes of exact
information. Blass adds (so Hilg.) after τον ηγεμονα the words εις Καισ. with 137,
and continues εφοβηθη γαρ, μηποτε αρπασαντες αυτον οι ιουδαιοι αποκτεινωσιν,
και αυτος μεταξυ εγκλημα εχη ως χρηματα ειληφως, 137, Gig., Wer., Par.[2], Vulgcl.,
Syr. H. mg.

[2] περιεχουσαν, so Meyer, Blass, Hilgenfeld, with AHLP; but εχουσαν ℵBE 61,
137, so R.V., and other authorities as above.

[3] εξειλαμην ℵABE, Tisch., W.H., Blass, Weiss. Instead of μαθων Blass in β
reads (Gig.) βοωντα και λεγοντα εαυτον ειναι Ρωμαιον.

Saint Paul, p. 532, Overbeck for various
interpretations, and Winer - Schmiedel,
p. 69. A reads δεξιοβόλους (Syr. Pesh.
jaculantes dextra, Ar͏e *jaculatores*), which
would be a correct interpretation if we
understood the word of javelin-throwers
or slingers.—ἀπὸ τρίτης ὥρας: about
nine in the evening; the journey was to
commence *from* that time, so that by
daybreak Paul would be in safety, *cf.*
x. 30. The number of the escort was
meant to guard against surprise.
Ver. 24. παραστῆσαι: depending on
εἶπεν, ver. 23; a change to indirect
speech, *cf.* references in ver. 22.—κτήνη
(κτάομαι): *jumenta*, Vulgate, almost
always in plural, property in general,
herds or flocks, cattle; in LXX, where
it is very frequent, and in N.T. it is used
of beasts of burden or for riding, *cf.*
Luke x. 34, Rev. xviii. 13, sometimes
quite generally in LXX, as in 1 Cor. xv.
39.—ἐπιβ.: only in Luke and Acts in
N.T., Luke x. 34, xix. 35, in each case
in same sense; so in classical Greek and
LXX. The reason why the plural κτήνη
is used *vix satis perspicitur* (Blass); the
word has sometimes been taken to apply
to the soldiers, as if they were all mounted,
but taking the word in relation to Paul,
one or more beasts might be required for
relays or for baggage, so Weiss, Wendt,
Hackett, or, as the prisoner was chained
to a soldier, another κτῆνος would be
required (Kuinoel, Felten).—διασώσωσι:
five times in Acts, once in Luke's Gospel, only twice elsewhere in N.T., "ut
P. salvum perducerent," Vulgate, frequent in LXX, *cf.* its use in Polyb. and
Jos., see further on xxvii. 44.—Φήλικα,
see on xxiv. 3.—τὸν ἡγεμόνα: used of a

leader of any kind, or of an emperor or
king; in N.T. of the procurator, of
Pilate, Felix, Festus, so by Josephus of
Pilate, *Ant.*, xviii., 3, 1, of governors
more generally, Luke xxi. 12, 1 Pet. ii.
14, etc.
Ver. 25. περιέχουσαν, see critical
note above.—τύπον: "form," R.V., a
précis or summary of the contents of a
letter, 3 Macc. iii. 30. Such a letter
would be called *elogium*, Alford, *in loco*,
Renan, *Saint Paul*, p. 532. It is quite
true that τύπος does not demand that
the letter should have been given verbally,
and in an oft-quoted passage, Plato,
Polit., 3, p. 414, ἐν τύπῳ is contrasted
with δι' ἀκριβείας, but the letter bears
the marks of genuineness, *e.g.*, the part
which Lysias claims to have played, and
the expression "questions of their law"
(see below). Moreover St. Luke might
have easily learnt its contents, as there
is reason for supposing that the letter
would have been read in open court
before Felix, as containing the preliminary inquiry, and that a copy may have
been given to Paul after his appeal, see
Bethge, *Die Paulinischen Reden Apostelgeschichte*, p. 226.
Ver. 26. κρατίστῳ, see note on i. 1.—
χαίρειν (λέγει or κελεύει), *cf.* xv. 23.
Ver. 27. ἄνδρα, not ἄνθρωπον: Bengel and Wendt take the word to indicate
a certain degree of respect.—συλλ.: used
in various senses, but in all four Gospels
of the capture of Jesus, and in Luke,
where the word is frequent, often of the
capture of prisoners, Acts i. 16, xii. 3,
xxvi. 21, Luke xxii. 54 (Plummer) so in
LXX.—μέλλοντα ἀναι.: "was about to be
killed," R.V.—ἐπιστὰς: the word seems

ἐστι. 28. βουλόμενος δὲ[1] γνῶναι τὴν αἰτίαν δι᾽ ἣν ἐνεκάλουν αὐτῷ, κατήγαγον αὐτὸν εἰς τὸ συνέδριον αὐτῶν · 29. ὃν εὗρον ἐγκαλούμενον περὶ[2] ζητημάτων τοῦ νόμου αὐτῶν, μηδὲν δὲ ἄξιον θανάτου ἢ δεσμῶν ἔγκλημα ἔχοντα. 30. μηνυθείσης δέ μοι ἐπιβουλῆς εἰς τὸν ἄνδρα μέλλειν[3] ἔσεσθαι ὑπὸ τῶν Ἰουδαίων, ἐξαυτῆς ἔπεμψα πρὸς σέ, παραγγείλας καὶ τοῖς κατηγόροις λέγειν[4] τὰ πρὸς αὐτὸν ἐπὶ σοῦ.[5] Ἔρρωσο.

[1] ἐπιγνωναι ℵAB 13, other authorities as in ver. 27, so also in R.V. and Wendt. κατηγαγον . . . αυτων B* 61 om. [W.H.], R.V. marg. om.

[2] ζητηματων, Blass in β om. (Gig.); περι του νομου Μωυσεως και Ιησου τινος, so Blass in β, with 137, Gig., Syr. H. mg.; β text continues: μηδεν δε αξιον θανατου πρασσοντα (Gig.), εξηγαγον αυτον μολις τη βια, 137, Syr. H. mg. (Gig.), so Hilgenfeld.

[3] μελλειν om. ℵABE, so R.V., W.H., Weiss, Wendt, Blass. υπο των I. om. ℵABE, and other authorities as above. εξαυτης BHLP, Syr. Pesh., Sah., Boh., so W.H., Blass, Weiss, Wendt; but Lach., Tisch. read εξ αυτων with ℵAE, Syr. H., Arm.

[4] τα προς αυτον, om. τα B, Syr. Pesh., Arm., so W.H., R.V., Weiss. For the three words Lach., Tisch., with ℵA 13, 40, Vulg., read αυτους, whilst EHP insert τα before προς αυτον (not seeing that the phrase was taken as in xix. 38); see Weiss, Apostelgeschichte, p. 37. Blass in β text (Gig.) reads (instead of λεγειν . . . σου) εκει ερχεσθαι προς την σην διαγνωσιν.

[5] ερρωσο om. AB 13, Sah., Boh., Aethro·, Gig., Tisch., W.H., Weiss, R.V. in text; Blass brackets in β; ℵEL d, Syrr. P. H., Arm., Aethpp· retain, so Hilg.; HP read ερρωσθε, xv. 29.

to intimate that he was ready at the right moment to rescue the prisoner.— τῷ στρατ.: "with the soldiers," R.V., those under his command.—ἐξειλόμην, vii. 10.—μαθὼν ὅτι ʿΡ.: "qua ratione id compererit, tacere satius erat," Blass. The chiliarch wishes to put the best interpretation on his own conduct after his hastiness in xxi. 33, xxii. 24, see reading in β text. Overbeck and Wendt (and even Zöckler) defend the chiliarch from a crafty misrepresentation, and compare the condensed explanation of the letter and the facts given in the narrative to the different accounts of Saul's conversion, but the chiliarch had a motive for dissembling his real part in the transaction, viz., fear of punishment.

Ver. 28. δέ: if we read τε Weiss regards it as closely connecting the wish of the chiliarch with the previous rescue affected by him, and as hoping to veil his conduct in the interim which was so open to censure.—ἐνεκάλουν αὐτῷ, xix. 38, with dative of the person as here, and in classical Greek, cf. Ecclus. xlvi. 19. In N.T. only in Luke and Paul, cf. Simcox, Language of the N.T., p. 148.—In the letter of Lysias Hilgenfeld omits vv. 28, 29, as an addition of the "author to Theophilus". Vv. 26, 30, are quite sufficient, he thinks,

for "military brevity," whilst ver. 28 could not have been written by Lysias since he would have written an untruth. But it is quite conceivable that the Roman would not only try to conceal his previous hastiness, but to commend himself to the governor as the protector of a fellow-citizen. Spitta omits ver. 28 in the letter, and Jüngst also ver. 29. But Jüngst equally with Hilgenfeld declines to omit the whole letter as Clemen proposes.

Ver. 29. ζητημάτων, cf. xviii. 14, 15, "a contemptuous plural" (Page).—ἔγκλημα ἔχοντα: phrase only here in N.T., criminis reum esse, accusari, as in classical Greek, cf. Thuc., i., 26; the noun occurs again in xxv. 16, but not elsewhere in N.T., not found in LXX.

Ver. 30. A mingling of two constructions, Blass, Gram., p. 247, Winer-Moulton, lxiii., 1, 1. ἔσεσθαι: on the future infinitive denoting time relatively to the time of the principal verb see Burton, pp. 48, 52.—ἔπεμψα: epistolary aorist, cf. 1 Cor. v. 11, Phil. ii. 28, Ephes. vi. 22, Col. iv. 8, Philem., ver. 11; Burton, p. 21. ἐξαυτῆς, see critical note.—λέγειν τὰ πρὸς αὐτὸν, cf. xix. 38, omitting τὰ, see critical note.—ἐπὶ σοῦ: coram, cf. xxiv. 20, 21, xxv. 9, 26, xxvi. 2, 1 Cor. vi. 1 (1 Tim. vi. 13), Winer-Moulton, xlvii.

31. Οἱ μὲν οὖν στρατιῶται, κατὰ τὸ διατεταγμένον αὐτοῖς, ἀναλαβόντες τὸν Παῦλον ἤγαγον διὰ[1] τῆς νυκτὸς εἰς τὴν Ἀντιπατρίδα. 32.[2] τῇ δὲ ἐπαύριον ἐάσαντες τοὺς ἱππεῖς πορεύεσθαι σὺν αὐτῷ, ὑπέστρεψαν εἰς τὴν παρεμβολήν· 33. οἵτινες εἰσελθόντες εἰς τὴν Καισάρειαν, καὶ ἀναδόντες τὴν ἐπιστολὴν τῷ ἡγεμόνι, παρέστησαν καὶ τὸν Παῦλον αὐτῷ. 34. ἀναγνοὺς δὲ[3] ὁ ἡγεμών, καὶ ἐπερωτήσας ἐκ ποίας[4] ἐπαρχίας ἐστί, καὶ πυθόμενος ὅτι ἀπὸ Κιλικίας, 35.[5] Διακούσομαί σου, ἔφη, ὅταν καὶ οἱ κατήγοροί σου παραγένωνται. ἐκέλευσέ τε αὐτὸν ἐν τῷ πραιτωρίῳ τοῦ Ἡρώδου φυλάσσεσθαι.

[1] אABE *om.* art. before νυκτος, so Tisch., W.H., Weiss, Wendt, Blass, R.V.

[2] At the beginning of the verse Blass in β reads (Gig.) τη δε επαυριον εασαντες τους στρατιωτας (υποστρεφειν) εις την παρεμβολην μετα μονων των ιππεων ηλθον εις την Κ. Instead of πορευεσθαι אABE, Tisch., W.H., R.V., Weiss, Wendt, Hilg. read απερχεσθαι.

[3] ο ηγεμων *om.* אABE ; other authorities above.

[4] επαρχειας אAB*, so W.H., Weiss, Wendt ; Blass has -ιας, so Hilg.

[5] ακουσ., so Blass in β for διακ. with other, but slight variations, after 137, Syr. H. mg. For T.R., R.V. reads παραγενωνται· κελευσας, so אcABE 40, 61 (א* κελευσαντος), so Tisch., W.H., R.V., Weiss, Wendt, Blass, Hilg. After φυλασσ. אABE add αυτον, so R.V., and other authorities above.

Ver. 31. **οἱ μὲν οὖν . . . τῇ δὲ ἐπαύριον**: Rendall, appendix on **μὲν οὖν**, p. 162. Page finds the antithesis in **μετὰ δέ**, xxiv. 1, referring the five days there not to Paul's arrival in Cæsarea, but to his despatch from Jerusalem by Lysias, "so then the soldiers, etc. . . . but after five days . . ." (see also note below).—**ἀναλαβόντες**, *cf.* xx. 13.—**διὰ (τῆς) νυκτός**: "by night," this use of διά with genitive of time passed through (*cf.* i. 3) is comparatively rare, Luke v. 5, Heb. ii. 15, except in almost adverbial phrases as here, *cf.* v. 19, xvi. 9, xvii. 10, Simcox, *Language of the N.T.*, p. 140.—**εἰς τὴν Ἀντιπατρίδα**: founded by Herod the Great, on the road from Jerusalem to Cæsarea, not apparently as a fortress but as a pleasant residence, giving it its name in honour of his father, most probably on the site now called *Râs el ʿAin*, "the spring-head," and not where Robinson placed it, on the site of the present *Kefr Saba*. The more modern site, the discovery of which is due to Conder, is more in accordance with the abundant supply of water referred to by Josephus. It is to be noted that while Josephus in one passage identifies Antipatris with Kefr Saba, in another his description is more general, and he places it in the Plain of Kefr Saba (for notices *cf. Ant.*, xiii., 15, 1, xvi. 5, 2, *B.J.*, i., 21, 9). They were now more than half way to

Cæsarea, and the road traversed the open plain so that they were no longer in danger of surprise, G. A. Smith, *Historical Geography*, p. 165, B.D.[2], Hastings' B.D. (Conder). On the Greek article in notices of stations on journeys, peculiar to Acts, see Blass, *Gram.*, p. 149, *cf.* xvii. 1, xx. 13, xxi. 1, 3 (but xx. 14 no article).

Ver. 32. **τῇ δὲ ἐπ.**: not necessarily the morrow after they left Jerusalem, but the morrow after they arrived at Antipatris. In this interpretation **διὰ νυκτὸς** might be taken to mean *by night* in distinction to *by day*, so that they may have occupied two nights on the road, see Hackett's note, *in loco.*—**ἐάσαντες**, Lucan, see xxvii. 32, 40; xxviii. 4.—**εἰς τὴν παρεμβολήν**, here "to the castle" A. and R.V., the barracks in Antonia.—**ὑπέστρεψαν**, Lucan (Friedrich, p. 8), *cf.* i. 12.

Ver. 33. **οἵτινες**: "and they when they . . ." R.V., *sc.* **ἱππεῖς.**—**ἀναδόντες**: not elsewhere in N.T., or in LXX in this sense, of delivering a letter. Zahn, following Hobart, sees in the phrase **ἀναδ. τὴν ἐπιστολήν** a phrase characteristic of a medical man, since Hippocrates, *Epis.*, 1275, uses the verb instead of **διδόναι** or **ἀποδιδόναι** of a messenger delivering a letter, and thus shows a leaning common to the Greek medical writers of employing a verb already

XXIV. 1. ΜΕΤΑ δὲ πέντε ἡμέρας κατέβη ὁ ἀρχιερεὺς Ἀνανίας μετὰ[1] τῶν πρεσβυτέρων καὶ ῥήτορος Τερτύλλου τινός, οἵτινες ἐνεφάνι-

[1] Instead of των πρεσβ. ℵABE, Vulg., Sah., Syr. H. read πρεσβ. τινων, so Tisch., W.H., R.V., Weiss, Wendt, Blass, Hilg.; Meyer follows T.R.

familiar to them in a professional way; but it must be remembered that both Polybius and Plutarch use the verb in a similar sense.

Ver. 34. ἀναγνοὺς, see reading in β text. ποίας: of what kind of province, imperial or senatorial, as the governor desired to complete the report, cf. ver. 27. Blass takes it as simply = τίνος, as in iv. 7.—It appears that during the first century, although perhaps with variations from time to time, Cilicia formed part of the great Roman province Syria-Cilicia-Phœnice, cf. "Cilicia" (Ramsay), Hastings' B.D. A procurator of Judæa like Felix was only subordinate to the governor of Syria inasmuch as the latter could bring his supreme power to bear in cases of necessity. The military command and the independent jurisdiction of the procurator gave him practically sole power in all ordinary transactions, but the governor could take the superior command if he had reason to fear revolutionary or other serious difficulties. Schürer, Jewish People, div. i., vol. ii., p. 44 ff., E.T.—ἐπαρχίας: the word is used to describe either a larger province, or an appendage to a larger province, as Judæa was to that of Syria, see Schürer, u.s., and Grimm-Thayer, sub v.

Ver. 35. διακούσομαί σου: "I will hear thy cause," R.V., the word implies a judicial hearing (cf. LXX, Deut. i. 16 (Job ix. 33)), and so in classical Greek of hearing thoroughly. The word is used of a judicial hearing, Dio Cassius, xxxvi., 53 (36), and Deissmann, Neue Bibelstudien, p. 57, gives examples of similar usages on Egyptian papyri, 2nd to 3rd century A.D.—πραιτωρίῳ: "palace," R.V., Herod's palace at Cæsarea, where the procurator resided; it was not only a palace but also a fortress, and would contain a guard-room in which Paul would be confined. The word "palace" might well express its meaning in all the passages in which it occurs in the Gospels and Acts (but on Phil. i. 13 see Lightfoot, in loco). The Romans thus appropriated palaces already existing, and formerly dwelt in by kings or princes, cf. Cicero, Verr., ii., 5, 12, 30, Grimm-Thayer, sub v., and Lightfoot, On a Fresh Revision of N.T., p. 49. It

seems from the context that the place could not have been far from the quarters occupied by Felix, since Paul could be easily sent for.—φυλάσσεσθαι: the kind of custodia depended on the procurator, and no doubt the elogium had its effect; custodia satis levis (Blass).

CHAPTER XXIV.—Ver. 1. πέντε ἡμέρας: most probably to be reckoned from the arrival of St. Paul at Cæsarea, not from his apprehension in Jerusalem, or from his start from Jerusalem on the way to Cæsarea. This latter view is that of Mr. Page, who takes οἱ μὲν οὖν, xxiii. 31, as answered by the δέ in this verse. But δέ, xxiii. 32, seems quite sufficiently to answer to μέν in the previous verse. Wendt reckons the days from the arrival of Paul at Cæsarea, and regards the day of the arrival of the high priest as the fifth day, cf. Mark viii. 31. μετὰ τρεῖς ἡμέρας = Matt. xvi. 21, Luke ix. 22, τῇ τρίτῃ ἡμ., see below, ver. 11. On the truthfulness of the narrative see also on same verse.—κατέβη: "came down," R.V., i.e., from the capital.—Ἀνανίας, see on xxiii. 2. If we read πρεσ. τινῶν, see critical note, "with certain elders," R.V., i.e., a deputation of the Sanhedrim.—ῥήτορος Τ. τινὸς: "an orator, one Tertullus," R.V., ῥη. here = causidicus, a barrister; here the prosecuting counsel συνήγορος (as opposed to σύνδικος the defendant's advocate), see note, Blass, in loco. Tert.: a common name, diminutive of Tertius; but it does not follow from the name that he was a Roman, as both Greeks and Jews often bore Roman names. Blass speaks of him as a Jew "erat Judæus et ipse" (so Ewald, Bethge), whilst Wendt (1899) inclines against this view, although if the words in ver. 6, κατὰ τὸν ἡμέτερον νόμον, are retained, he admits that it would be correct; in addition to this the expression ἔθνος τοῦτο, ver. 3, seems in Wendt's view to indicate that the speaker was not a Jew (so too Wetstein). Tertullus was apparently one of the class of hired pleaders, often employed in the provinces by those who were themselves ignorant of Roman law. The trial may have been conducted in Greek, Lewin, St. Paul, ii., 684, Felten, in loco. —ἐνεφάνισαν, cf. xxv. 2, 15, the verb appears to be used in these passages as

σαν τῷ ἡγεμόνι κατὰ τοῦ Παύλου. 2. κληθέντος δὲ[1] αὐτοῦ, ἤρξατο
κατηγορεῖν ὁ Τέρτυλλος, λέγων, 3. Πολλῆς εἰρήνης τυγχάνοντες διὰ
σοῦ, καὶ[2] κατορθωμάτων γινομένων τῷ ἔθνει τούτῳ διὰ τῆς σῆς
προνοίας πάντη τε καὶ πανταχοῦ, ἀποδεχόμεθα, κράτιστε Φῆλιξ,
μετὰ πάσης εὐχαριστίας. 4. ἵνα δὲ μὴ ἐπὶ πλεῖόν σε[3] ἐγκόπτω,

[1] αυτου om. B, so Weiss [W.H.], Wendt perhaps.

[2] κατορθ. HLP; διορθ. ℵABE 13, 61, 137, 180; Tisch., W.H., R.V., Blass,
Weiss, Wendt, Hilg.

[3] For εγκοπτω ℵAB[1]E have ενκοπτω, so Tisch., W.H., Weiss, Wendt, Hilgenfeld (see Winer-Schmiedel, p. 54), Blass reads κοπτω (fatigans, Syr[utr].; molestus
sim, Sah., Boh.), A* 13, 19, 31.

a kind of technical term to indicate laying formal information before a judge,
cf. Jos., Ant., xiv., 10, 8, in LXX, Esther,
ii., 22. Blass takes it here = χάρτην
ἔδωκαν, see also Wetstein.

Ver. 2. ἤρξατο: he began with a
captatio benevolentiæ after the usual oratorical style, cf. Cicero, De Oratore, ii.,
78, 79, on the exordium and its rules.—
If obtaining such artificial support was
not as Calvin calls it "signum malæ
conscientiæ," it may well indicate the
weakness of the Jews' cause, and their
determination to leave nothing untried
against Paul.

Ver. 3. πολλῆς εἰρ. τυγχ.: the governors specially prided themselves on
keeping peace in their provinces (Wetstein). On the phrase see 2 Macc. iv.
6, xiv. 10.—κατορθωμάτων: "very worthy
deeds," A.V., the word might mean
"successes," cf. Polyb., i., 19, 12, or it
might mean recte facta, cf. Cic., De
Fin., iii., 14 (see also in Wetstein;
the word is found in 3 Macc. iii.
23, R); but διορθώματα, see critical
note, in Arist., Plut. = corrections, reforms (cf. R.V.), so διόρθωσις in Polyb.,
Vulgate, multa corrigantur. In LXX
διορθοῦν is used of amending, Jer. vii. 3,
5.—προνοίας: foresight, cf. Rom. xiii.
14, nowhere else in N.T.; cf. for a close
parallel to its use here 2 Macc. iv. 6,
referred to above (Lumby). It is possible
that the word may be a further proof of
the sycophancy of the orator; twice the
Latin providentia, A. and R.V. "providence," was used of the emperors on
coins, and also of the gods (Humphry on
R.V.), "hoc vocabulum sæpe diis tribu-
erunt," Bengel, in loco.—πάντη τε καὶ
πανταχοῦ ἀποδεχ., so A. and R.V.,
"non in os solum laudamus" (Wetstein);
but Meyer joins πάν. τε κ. παντ. with
what precedes (Lach.), and in this he is
followed by Weiss, Wendt, Page and

Blass. For similar phrases in Plato,
Aristotle, Philo, Josephus, see Wetstein.
πάντη: only here in N.T., but cf. Ecclus. l. 22, 3 Macc. iv. 1, cf. Friedrich,
p. 5, on Luke's fondness for πᾶς and
kindred words.—τῷ ἔθνει τούτῳ, see
above on ver. 1 and also ver. 10. If he
had been a Jew Wetstein thinks that he
would have said τῷ ἔθνει τῷ ἡμετέρῳ,
but see Blass, in loco, on ἔθνος "in sermone elegantiore et coram alienigenis".
—ἀποδ.: only in Luke and Acts; for its
meaning here cf. ii. 41, 1 Macc. ix. 71
(S al.), so in classical Greek.—εὐχ.:
except Rev. iv. 9, vii. 12, elsewhere in
N.T. only in St. Paul's Epistles (frequent);
the word is also found in Esth. (LXX)
viii. 13, Ecclus. xxxvii. 11, Wisd.
xvi. 28, 2 Macc. ii. 27, and for other
references see Kennedy, Sources of N.T.
Greek, p. 73, and Grimm-Thayer, sub v.
—There was very little, if anything, to
praise in the administration of Felix, but
Tertullus fastened on the fact of his
suppression of the bands of robbers who
had infested the country, Jos., B.J., ii.,
13, 2, Ant., xx., 8, 5, "ipse tamen his
omnibus erat nocentior" (Wetstein).
His severity and cruelty was so great
that he only added fuel to the flame of
outrage and sedition, Jos., Ant., xx., 8,
6, B.J., ii., 13, 6, whilst he did not
hesitate to employ the Sicarii to get rid
of Jonathan the high priest who urged
him to be more worthy of his office. In
the rule of Felix Schürer sees the turning-
point in the drama which opened with
the death of Herod and terminated with
the bloody conflict of A.D. 70. The
uprisings of the people under his predecessors had been isolated and occasional; under him rebellion became
permanent. And no wonder when we
consider the picture of the public and
private life of the man drawn by the hand
of the Roman historian, and the fact that

παρακαλῶ ἀκοῦσαί σε ἡμῶν συντόμως τῇ σῇ ἐπιεικείᾳ. 5. εὑρόντες
γὰρ τὸν ἄνδρα τοῦτον λοιμόν, καὶ κινοῦντα στάσιν[1] πᾶσι τοῖς Ἰουδαίοις
τοῖς κατὰ τὴν οἰκουμένην, πρωτοστάτην τε τῆς τῶν Ναζωραίων αἱρέσεως, 6. ὃς καὶ τὸ ἱερὸν ἐπείρασε βεβηλῶσαι· ὃν καὶ ἐκρατήσαμεν

---

[1] The plural στασεις for στασιν is supported by אABE 13, 40, 61, 68, Vulg.,
Boh., Chrys., so Tisch., W.H., R.V., Blass, Weiss, Wendt, Hilg. Blass in β text
with Gig. adds ου μονον τω γενει ημων αλλα σχεδον παση τη οικουμενη.

trading upon the influence of his infamous
brother Pallas he allowed himself a free
hand to indulge in every licence and
excess, Tac., *Hist.*, v., 9, and *Ann.*, xii.,
54, Schürer, *Jewish People*, div. i., vol.
ii., p. 177-181, E.T.

Ver. 4. **δέ**: *autem,* "innuit plura dici
potuisse in laudem Felicis," Bengel.—
ἐγκόπτω, *impedire*, as if Felix was so
busy in his reforms that Tertullus would
not interrupt him, but see critical note,
cf. Rom. xv. 22, Gal. v. 7.—**ἐπὶ πλεῖον**,
cf. iv. 17, xx. 9; in 2 Tim. ii. 16, iii. 9,
with the opposite verb **προκόπτω**.—
συντόμως: so in classical Greek, with
λέγειν, εἰπεῖν; in Jos., *c. Apion.*, i., 1,
6, with **γράψαι** and **διδάσκειν**, see Wetstein on Rom. ix. 28, *cf*. 2 Macc. ii. 31,
for the adjective and for the adverb, Prov.
xiii. 23, 3 Macc. v. 25; "est hæc communis
oratorum promissio" (Blass).—**ἐπιεικείᾳ**:
only in Luke and Paul, see 2 Cor. x. 1,
"pro tua clementia," Vulgate, derived
from **εἴκω**, *cedo*, it properly might be
rendered *yieldingness;* equity as opposed
to strict law; so Aristotle sets the **ἐπιεικής**
against the **ἀκριβοδίκαιος**, *Eth. Nic.*, v.,
10, 6. It is often joined with **φιλανθρω-
πία, πραότης**. Its architype and pattern
is to be found in God, *cf*. Wisd. xii. 18,
2 Macc. ii. 22, x. 4 R., Ps. lxxxv. 5, and
so also in *Psalms of Solomon*, v., 14. The
word also occurs, Baruch ii. 27, Song of
the Three Children, ver. 19 (Dan., LXX
and Theod. iii. 42), where it is used of
God, also in Wisd. ii. 19, 3 Macc. iii. 15,
vii. 6. For a valuable account of the
word see Trench, *Synonyms*, i., p. 176 ff.

Ver. 5. **εὑρόντες γὰρ τὸν ἄνδρα** . . .
ὃς καὶ . . . **ὃν καὶ ἐκρατ.**: on the anacolouthon, Blass, *Gram. des N.G.*, p. 277,
Winer-Moulton, xlv., 6 *b*. Blass remarks
that Luke gives no address so carelessly
as that of Tertullus, but may not the
anacolouthon here be the exact expression
of the orator's invective? see critical
note.—**λοιμόν**: 1 Sam. ii. 12, x. 27, xxv.
17, 25, Ps. i. 1 (plural), 1 Macc. xv. 21;
1 Macc. x. 61, xv. 3 R, **ἄνδρες λοιμοί** (*cf*.
Prov. xxiv. 9, xxix. 8 A). So in classical
Greek, Dem., and in Latin *pestis*, Ter.,

Cic., Sallust. In 1 Macc. x. 6 A, **ἄνδρες
παράνομοι** is a further description of "the
pestilent fellows" (so 1 Sam. ii. 12, **υἱοὶ
λοιμοί = ἀνὴρ ὁ παράνομος**, 2 Sam.
xvi. 7).—**κινοῦντα στάσιν**, *cf*. Jos., *B.J.*,
ii., 9, 4. **κιν. ταραχήν**: not against the
Romans but amongst the Jews themselves—such a charge would be specially
obnoxious to Felix, who prided himself
on keeping order.—**τὴν οἰκ.**: the Roman
empire, see on p. 270, *cf*. xvii. 6, and
xxi. 28; see addition in β text.—**πρωτοστάτην**: the **τε** closely connecting the
thought that the prisoner does all this as
the leader, etc., literally one who stands
in the front rank, so often in classical
Greek, in LXX, Job xv. 24, AB.—**τῶν
Ναζ.**: "the disciple is not above his
Master," and the term is applied as a
term of contempt to the followers of
Jesus, as it had been to Jesus Himself,
Who was stamped in the eyes of the
Jews as a false Messiah by His reputed
origin from Nazareth, John i. 46, vii. 41,
42 ; see for the modern employment of
the name amongst Jews and Mohammedans Plumptre, *in loco*, and further,
Harnack, *History of Dogma*, i., 301,
E.T. Blass compares the contemptuous
term used by the Greeks, **Χρηστιανοί**,
xi. 26.—**αἱρέσεως**, see above on v. 17, all
references to the question of law, xxiii.
6, 29, were purposely kept in the background, and stress laid upon all which
threatened to destroy the boasted "peace"
(Weiss).

Ver. 6. **ἐπείρασε**: the charge could
not be proved, *cf*. xxi. 28, but the verb
here used is an aggravation not a modi-
fication of the surmise (**ἐνόμιζον**, ver. 29)
of the Jews.—**βεβ.**, *cf*. Matt. xii. 5 (**βαίνω,
βηλός**, threshold), Judith ix. 8, 1 Macc.
ii. 12, iv. 38, 44, 54, 2 Macc. x. 5, etc.,
and frequent in LXX, *cf*. *Psalms of
Solomon* i. 8, and **βέβηλος** four, **βεβή-
λωσις** three times.—Probably Tertullus
wanted to insinuate that the prisoner was
punishable even according to Roman
law, see above on xxi. 29; but Trophimus as a Greek and not Paul would
have been exposed to the death penalty,

καὶ¹ κατὰ τὸν ἡμέτερον νόμον ἠθελήσαμεν κρίνειν, 7. παρελθὼν δὲ
Λυσίας ὁ χιλίαρχος μετὰ πολλῆς βίας ἐκ τῶν χειρῶν ἡμῶν ἀπήγαγε,
8. κελεύσας τοὺς κατηγόρους αὐτοῦ ἔρχεσθαι ἐπὶ σέ · παρ' οὗ δυνήσῃ
αὐτὸς ἀνακρίνας περὶ πάντων τούτων ἐπιγνῶναι ὧν ἡμεῖς κατηγοροῦμεν
αὐτοῦ. 9.² συνέθεντο δὲ καὶ οἱ Ἰουδαῖοι, φάσκοντες ταῦτα οὕτως
ἔχειν.

¹ T.R. καὶ . . . ἐπὶ σε (ver. 8) is supported by E, Vulg., Gig., Syr. P. and H.;
Blass retains, R.V. marg. But the whole is omit. by ℵABHLP 61 (many others),
Sah., Boh., so Lach., Tisch., W.H., Weiss, Wendt; Alford places in dark brackets.
The words, however, have been recently defended by Zöckler, H. Holtzmann, Hilgenfeld, and Belser, following Blass in his two texts. It is possible that the abruptness
of ἐκρατησαμεν may have prompted a desire for additions and completeness, and it
is difficult to understand the omission of the disputed words if they were original.
If we retain them, παρ' οὑ refers to Lysias, but not only is it somewhat strange that
a professional orator should throw blame upon the Roman chiliarch, but it is also
difficult to see how Lysias could in any way bear testimony against Paul in relation
to accusations with regard to which he had professed himself ignorant, and after the
hearing of which he had concluded that the prisoner had done nothing worthy of
death or bonds. Moreover, the omission of any reference on Paul's part to Lysias
in ver. 20 raises another difficulty, if Tertullus had appealed to the evidence which
the Roman could give (Wendt, 1899). On the other hand the decision of Felix in
ver. 22, and the postponement for the arrival of Lysias, have been held to prove the
genuineness of the doubtful words. It is possible that there may be some antecedent corruption or abridgment in the text. For further variations see W.H., *App.*,
p. 100.

² συνεπεθεντο R.V., W.H., Weiss, Wendt, Blass (instead of συνεθεντο), with
ℵABEHLP.

to say nothing of the fact that the charge
was only one of suspicion. Schürer,
Jewish People, div. i., vol. ii., p. 74, note,
and references in chap. xxi., ver. 29.—
ἐκρατήσαμεν: the word could be used
"de conatu vel mero vel efficaci," and so
Bengel adds "aptum igitur ad calum-
niam". The orator identifies himself
with his clients, and ascribes to the
hierarchy the seizing of Paul, as if it was
a legal act, whereas it was primarily the
action of the mob violence of the people,
xxi. 30; frequently used *in same sense* as
here by Matthew and Mark, but not at
all by St. John, and only in this passage
by Luke, *cf.* Rev. xx. 2, LXX, Ps. lv.,
tit., Judg. viii. 12, xvi. 21 (A *al.*).—καὶ
κατὰ . . . ἐπὶ σέ, ver. 8, see critical
note, omitted by R.V. in text, retained
by Blass and Knabenbauer, so in Vulgate.
Zöckler amongst others has recently
supported Blass, and for the same reason,
viz., because if the words are retained
the judge is asked to inquire of Paul, and
thus the Apostle becomes a witness as
well as a prisoner. But, on the other
hand, Paul though still a prisoner is
allowed to speak for himself before both
Felix and Festus. If the words are
retained, παρ' οὑ would refer to Lysias,
and this would be in agreement with the
remarks of Felix in ver. 22. Certainly
ἐκρατήσαμεν seems very bald without
any sequel, and this may have caused
the insertion of the words; but the insertion was a bold one, although we can
understand that the Jews would have
been incensed against Lysias, who had
twice protected Paul from their violence.
The omission of the words if they formed
part of the original text is no doubt difficult to explain.—ἠθελ. κρίνειν, *cf.* xxi.
31, 36, xxii. 22, xxiii. 12, passages which
give us a very different idea of the
wishes of the Jews.

Ver. 7. μετὰ π. βίας: another statement
directly at variance with the facts, xxi. 32.

Ver. 8. ἀνακ.: not an examination
by torture, which could not be legally
applied either to Paul or to Lysias as
Roman citizens, but in the sense of a
judicial investigation—in this sense peculiar to Luke, *cf.* iv. 9, and Plummer on
Luke xxiii. 14, *cf.* xxv. 26 below. A.V.,
"by examining of whom thyself," etc.,
which is quite misleading whether we
retain the words omitted above in R.V.
or not, because this rendering reads as if
Felix was to examine the accusers,
whereas the relative pronoun is in the
singular, παρ' οὑ.

Ver. 9. συνέθεντο: in R.V. συνεπεθ.,

10. Ἀπεκρίθη δὲ ὁ Παῦλος, νεύσαντος αὐτῷ τοῦ ἡγεμόνος λέγειν,
Ἐκ πολλῶν ἐτῶν ὄντα σε κριτὴν τῷ ἔθνει τούτῳ ἐπιστάμενος,[1] εὐθυμό-

---

[1] ευθυμοτερον HLP, Chrys. (Meyer); ευθυμως ℵABE, Vulg., Ath., Tisch., W.H.,
R.V., Weiss, Wendt, Blass, Hilg.

"joined in the charge," cf. xviii. 10, so in classical Greek; in LXX (Deut. xxxii. 27), Ps. iii. 6 AS, Zach. i. 15, here only in N.T.—φάσκοντες, cf. xxv. 19, Rom. i. 22, dictitantes, but sometimes with the notion of alleging what is untrue, to pretend, cf. LXX, Bel and the Dragon, ver. 8. The verb is found elsewhere, Gen. xxvi. 20, 2 Macc. xiv. 27, 32, 3 Macc. iii. 7. Ver. 10. On the language of the speech see Bethge, p. 229.—This short apology before Felix is not without its traces of Paul's phraseology, e.g., ἐλπίδα ἔχων, ver. 15, with which we may compare Rom. xv. 4, 2 Cor. iii. 12, x. 15, Ephes. ii. 12, 1 Thess. iv. 13, in all of which we have the phrase ἐλπ. ἔχειν (only once elsewhere in N.T., 1 John iii. 3); προσδέχονται in ver. 15, with which we may compare Tit. ii. 13; προσφοράς, ver. 17, cf. Rom. xv. 16; δι' ἐτῶν, ver. 17, with Gal. ii. 1 (διά with genitive of time, only once elsewhere in N.T., Mark ii. 1), and more especially ἀπρόσκοπον συνειδ., cf. 1 Cor. x. 32, Phil. i. 10, and for συνείδησις, see xxiii. 1 (cf. Nösgen, Apostelgeschichte, p. 54, and Alford, Acts, Introd., p. 14). Wendt regards the whole speech as a free composition of the author of Acts, and even this view contrasts favourably with what Wendt himself calls the wilful attempts to refer different words and phrases in the speech to various Redactors, see for illustrations of this arbitrariness his note on p. 369 (1899). —νεύσαντος: in N.T., elsewhere only John xiii. 24. Friedrich draws attention to the frequent mention of beckoning, or making signs, as characteristic of Luke's writings, p. 29, cf. Luke i. 22 and 62 (διανεύω, ἐννεύω), v. 7 (κατανεύω); Acts xiii. 16, xxvi. 1, xxiv. 10, etc.—Ἐκ πολλῶν ἐτῶν: in view of the constant change of procurators a period of five to seven years would quite justify St. Paul's words. Ewald argued for ten years from the statement, Tac., Ann., xii., 54, that Felix had been joint procurator with Cumanus before he had been appointed sole procurator of Judæa, Samaria, Galilee, Peræa. But no mention is made of this by Jos., Ant., xx., 7, 1. If, however, so it is argued, Felix had occupied a position of importance in Samaria in the time of the rule of Cumanus without being himself actually joint procurator, this would perhaps account for Jonathan the high priest asking that he might be appointed procurator after the departure of Cumanus (Jos., Ant., xx., 8, 5, B.J., ii., 12, 6); such a request is difficult to understand unless Jonathan had some ground for supposing that Felix would be acceptable to the Jews. But the description of Tacitus, l.c., is also difficult to understand, since we naturally ask what was the relative rank of Felix and Cumanus? or were there two procuratorial districts? and the statement of Josephus seems clearly to intimate that Felix was first appointed to the province after the deposition of Cumanus, and that he went to Palestine as his successor, B.J., ii., 12, 6, cf. Ant., xx., 8, 5, Schürer, Jewish People, div. i., vol. ii., p. 173 ff., and "Felix," Hastings' B.D.—Both Tacitus and Josephus are taken to imply that Felix succeeded Cumanus in 52 A.D. as procurator, Ann., xii., 54, Jos., Ant., xx., 7, 1. But if O. Holtzmann and McGiffert are right in placing St. Paul's imprisonment in Cæsarea in 53-55 A.D., it seems scarcely intelligible that St. Paul should speak of the "many years" of the rule of Felix, unless on the supposition that Tacitus is right and that Felix had ruled in Samaria and Judæa whilst Cumanus had ruled in Galilee. Harnack, Chron., i., 236, following Eusebius, assigns the eleventh year of Claudius, 51 A.D., as the year in which Felix entered upon office, and thinks that a procuratorship lasting from 51-54 might be described in St. Paul's words, but, as Wendt justly points out (1899), the expression πολλὰ ἔτη is much more fitting if spoken some years later. Schürer follows Josephus, Jewish People, div. i., vol. ii., p. 173 ff., and so more recently Dr. A. Robertson, "Felix," Hastings' B.D., and Dr. Zahn, Einleitung, ii., p. 635 (so also article, Biblical World, Nov., 1897), whilst Wendt, p. 58 (1899), would appear to incline to the same view.—But it is to be noted that St. Paul speaks of Felix as κριτής, and in this expres-

τερον τὰ περὶ ἐμαυτοῦ ἀπολογοῦμαι · 11. δυναμένου σου [1] γνῶναι ὅτι
οὐ πλείους εἰσί μοι ἡμέραι ἢ δεκαδύο, ἀφ' ἧς ἀνέβην προσκυνήσων

[1] For γνῶναι ℵABE, Tisch., W.H., and other authorities in ver. 10 read ἐπιγνῶναι. η om. with all better authorities, cf. iv. 22. δωδεκα (instead of δεκαδυο)
ℵABE, and other authorities above. εις for εν ℵABEH, and other authorities, as
above.

sion it may be possible to find a
point of reconciliation between the
divergencies resulting from a com-
parision of Josephus and Tacitus. Felix
may have held an office during the
procuratorship of Cumanus which may
have given him some judicial authority,
although of course subordinate to the
procurator, whilst on the other hand his
tenure of such an office may well have
prompted Jonathan's request to the
emperor that Felix should be sent as
procurator (a request upon which both
Schürer and Zahn lay such stress).
The phrase πόλλα ἔτη may thus be
further extended to include the tenure
of this judicial office which Felix held
earlier than 52 A.D., see also Turner,
"Chronology," Hastings' B.D., i., 418,
419, McGiffert, Apostolic Age, p. 358,
O. Holtzmann, Neutest. Zeitgeschichte,
p. 128, Ramsay, St. Paul, p. 313, Gilbert, Student's Life of Paul, p. 249
ff., 1899.—κριτὴν, see above, p. 480;
on the addition δίκαιον, defended by
St. Chrysostom (so E, Syr. H.), Blass
remarks "continet adulationem quæ
Paulum parum deceat, quidquid dicit
Chrysostomus".—τῷ ἔθνει τούτῳ: St.
Paul is speaking of the Jews as a
nation in their political relationship, in
addressing a Roman governor, not as
God's people, λαός.—εὐθυμότερον: adverb only here in N.T., not in LXX, but
in classical Greek, for the adjective see
xxvii. 36 (2 Macc. xi. 26), and the verb
εὐθυμεῖν, ver. 22.—St. Paul also begins
with a captatio benevolentiæ, but one
which contains nothing but the strict
truth; he might fairly appeal to the
judicial experience of Felix for the due
understanding of his case. — τὰ περὶ
ἐμαυτοῦ: for the phrase τὰ περί τινος
as characteristic of St. Luke, three times
in Gospel, eight times in Acts (six times
in St. Paul's Epistles and not in other
Gospels, except Mark v. 27, R.V.), cf.
Hawkins, Horæ Synopticæ, p. 38, Friedrich, p. 10 (so Lekebusch and Zeller).—
ἀπολογοῦμαι: only in Luke and Paul,
Luke xii. 11, xxi. 14, Acts xix. 33, xxv.
8, xxvi. 1, 2, 24; Rom. ii. 15, 2 Cor. xii.
19, each time in Acts, except xix. 38, with

reference to Paul: R.V. "I make my
defence"; see Grimm-Thayer, sub v., for
the construction of the verb, in classical Greek as here, Thuc., iii., 62, Plat.,
Phædo, 69 D. In LXX, cf. Jer. xii. 1,
2 Macc. xiii. 26.
Ver. 11. δυν. σοῦ γνῶναι: "seeing
that thou canst take knowledge" (ἐπιγ.),
R.V., the shortness of the time would
enable Felix to gain accurate knowledge
of the events which had transpired, and
the Apostle may also imply that the time
was too short for exciting a multitude to
sedition.—οὐ πλείους εἰσί μοι ἡμ. ἢ δεκαδύο: on οὐ πλείους see ver. 1 and critical
note.—The number is evidently not a
mere round number, as Overbeck thinks,
but indicates that Paul laid stress upon
the shortness of the period, and would
not have included incomplete days in his
reckoning. It is not necessary therefore
to include the day of the arrival in Jerusalem (ἀφ' ἧς points to the day as something past, Bethge), or the day of
the present trial; probably the arrival
in Jerusalem was in the evening, as
it is not until the next day that Paul
seeks out James (Wendt). The first
day of the twelve would therefore be the
entry in to James, the second the commencement of the Nazirite vow, the
sixth that of the apprehension of Paul
towards the close of the seven days, xxi.
27; the seventh the day before the
Sanhedrim, the eighth the information
of the plot and (in the evening) Paul's
start for Cæsarea, the ninth the arrival
in Cæsarea; and, reckoning from the
ninth five days inclusively, the day of
the speech of Tertullus before Felix
would be the thirteenth, i.e., twelve
full days; cf. xx. 6, where in the seven
days are reckoned the day of arrival and
the day of departure (Wendt, in loco).
Meyer on the other hand reckons the
day of St. Paul's arrival in Jerusalem as
the first day, and the five days of xxiv.
1 from his departure from Jerusalem for
Cæsarea. For other modes of reckoning
see Wendt's note, Farrar, St. Paul, ii.,
338, Alford, Rendall, and Lumby, in
loco. Weiss points out that it is simplest
to add the seven days of xxi. 27 and the

ἐν Ἱερουσαλήμ· 12. καὶ οὔτε ἐν τῷ ἱερῷ εὗρόν με πρός τινα διαλεγό-
μενον ἢ[1] ἐπισύστασιν ποιοῦντα ὄχλου, οὔτε ἐν ταῖς συναγωγαῖς, οὔτε
κατὰ τὴν πόλιν· 13.[2] οὔτε παραστῆσαί με δύνανται περὶ ὧν νῦν
κατηγοροῦσί μου. 14. ὁμολογῶ δὲ τοῦτό σοι, ὅτι κατὰ τὴν ὁδὸν
ἣν λέγουσιν αἵρεσιν, οὕτω λατρεύω τῷ πατρῴῳ Θεῷ, πιστεύων πᾶσι

[1] For ἐπισυστασιν HLP, Chrys. (Meyer), ℵABE 13, 40, and other authorities as
above read ἐπιστασιν.

[2] For ουτε ℵB 61 read ουδε; R.V. with other authorities as above, but not Hilgenfeld. For νυν ℵAB read νυνι, so Tisch., W.H., Weiss, Blass, Hilgenfeld.

five days of xxiv. 1, but we cannot by
any means be sure that xxi. 27 implies a
space of full seven days: "varie nume-
rum computant; sed simplicissimum est
sine dubio, e septem diebus, xxi. 27, et
quinque, xxiv. 1, eum colligere," so
Blass, but see his note on the passage.—
προσκυνήσων, cf. xx. 16, the purpose
was in itself an answer to each accusation—reverence not insurrection, conformity not heresy, worship not profanity.
"To worship I came, so far was I from
raising sedition," Chrys. There were
other reasons no doubt for St. Paul's
journey, as he himself states, ver. 17, cf.
Rom. xv. 25, but he naturally places
first the reason which would be a defence in the procurator's eyes. Overbeck
and Wendt contend that the statement
is not genuine, and that it is placed by
the author of Acts in St. Paul's mouth,
but see on the other hand Weiss, in loco.
It seems quite captious to demand that
Paul should explain to the procurator all
the reasons for his journey, or that the
fact that he came to worship should
exclude the fact that he also came to
offer alms.
Ver. 12. οὔτε ἐν τῷ ἱερῷ . . . οὔτε
. . . οὔτε: step by step he refutes
the charge.—οὔτε εὗρον, cf. ver. 5, εὑρόντες, a flat denial to the allegation of Tertullus; R.V. reads more plainly: both acts,
the disputing and the exciting a tumult,
are denied with reference to the Temple,
the synagogue, the city. In διαλ. there
would have been nothing censurable, but
even from this the Apostle had refrained.
—ἢ ἐπισύστασιν ποι. ὄχ.: R.V. reads
ἐπίστασιν; the Apostle had been accused as κινοῦντα στάσεις, ver. 5; here
is his answer to the charge, they had not
found him "stirring up a crowd," R.V.
This rendering however seems to make
ἐπίστασις almost = ἐπισύστασις, a
stronger word, cf. Numb. xxvi. 9, 1 Esdras v. 73, conjuratio. In 2 Macc. vi. 3
we have ἐπίστασις τῆς κακίας, incursio

malorum, Vulgate, but its meaning here
would seem to be rather concursus, in the
sense of a concourse, an assembly, not
an onset or attack; and the phrase expresses that the Apostle had not been
guilty of even the least disturbance, not
even of causing the assembling of a
crowd (see Wendt and Weiss, in loco),
"aut concursum facientem turbæ," Vulgate.—In 2 Cor. xi. 28 it is possible that
ἐπισύστασις may be used of the presence of a multitude, almost like ἐπίστασις, see Grimm-Thayer.—συναγωγαῖς: plural, because so many in Jerusalem, cf. vi. 9.—κατὰ τὴν πόλιν: Alford
renders "up and down the streets,"
cf. Luke viii. 39, xv. 14.
Ver. 13. οὔτε: οὐδὲ, R.V. (so Blass,
Gram., p. 260, Simcox, Z.N.T., p. 165);
the Apostle after denying the specific
charges made against him in Jerusalem, now proceeds further to a general
denial of the charge that he had been an
agitator amongst the Jews throughout
the empire.—παραστῆσαι: argumentis
probare, only here in N.T. in this sense,
but in classical Greek, Philo, Jos.,
Epictet.—νῦν, see critical note.
Ver. 14. ὁμολ.: "verbum forense
idemque sacrum," Bengel. "Unum
crimen confitetur," viz., that of belonging
to the sect of the Nazarenes, "sed
crimen non esse docet".—κατὰ τὴν ὁδὸν
ἣν λέγ. αἵρεσιν: "according to the
way which they call a sect," R.V. For
ὁδὸν see ix. 2, and for the reading in
β text critical note. αἵρεσιν: a word of
neutral significance, which Tertullus had
used in a bad sense. For St. Paul
Christianity was not αἵρεσις, a separation
from the Jewish religion, but was rather
πλήρωσις, cf. xiii. 32.—τῷ πατρ. Θεῷ,
cf. xxii. 3. The Apostle may have used
the expression here as a classical one
which the Roman might appreciate, cf.
θεοὶ πατρῷοι, Thuc., ii., 71; Æn., ix.,
247, and instances in Wetstein. (On the
distinctions between πατρῷος and πατρι-

τοῖς κατὰ τὸν νόμον καὶ[1] ἐν τοῖς προφήταις γεγραμμένοις, 15. ἐλπίδα
ἔχων εἰς τὸν Θεόν, ἣν καὶ αὐτοὶ οὗτοι προσδέχονται, ἀνάστασιν
μέλλειν ἔσεσθαι[2] νεκρῶν, δικαίων τε καὶ ἀδίκων· 16. ἐν τούτῳ[3] δὲ
αὐτὸς ἀσκῶ, ἀπρόσκοπον συνείδησιν ἔχειν πρὸς τὸν Θεὸν καὶ τοὺς

[1] After καὶ ℵ*BE read τοις εν, so Tisch., W.H., R.V., Weiss, Wendt, Hilg.; Blass
in β text follows T.R. (Steph.) and omits ἐν. (On the force of κατα and εν see
Wendt (1899), in loco.)

[2] After εσεσθαι, νεκρων is om. by ℵABC 13, 40, 61, 68, Vulg., Sah. Boh., Arm.,
Chrys., Tisch., W.H., R.V., Weiss, Wendt, Blass (but retained by Hilg.).

[3] και (for δε) ℵABCEL, Vulg., Syr. P. and H., Sah., Aeth., R.V., and other
authorities as in ver. 15.

κός, Gal. i. 14, see Syn., Grimm-Thayer.)
Moreover St. Paul could appeal to the
fact that liberty had been given to the
Jews by the Romans themselves to
worship the God of their fathers (see
Alford's note, in loco).—λατρεύω: "so
serve I," R.V., see on vii. 42; if it is
true that the word always describes
a divine service like λατρεία, and
that this idea appears to spring from
the conception of complete devotion of
powers to a master which lies in the
root of the word (Westcott), no verb
could more appropriately describe the
service of one who called himself δοῦλος
of God and of Christ.—πᾶσι τοῖς κατὰ
τὸν ν. κ.τ.λ.: "all things which are
according to the law," R.V., "iterum
refutat Tertullum, ver. 6," Bengel; "and
which are written in the prophets," R.V.
The mention of the prophets as well as
of the law shows that a reference to the
Messianic hopes is intended.

Ver. 15. ἐλπίδα ἔχων, cf. xxiii. 6:
St. Paul speaks of the hope as a frequent
possession, "habens id plus quam προσδ.
expectant," Bengel; in LXX very frequent
with ἐπί, but for εἰς cf. Isa. li. 5, Ps.
cxviii. 114 S¹, so here, a hope supporting itself upon God.—καὶ αὐτοὶ οὗτοι:
the Apostle makes no distinction between Sadducees and Pharisees, but
regards the Jews who were present as
representing the nation.—προσδ., xxiii.
21, cf. St. Paul's words in Tit. ii. 13,
Gal. v. 5.—μέλλειν ἔσεσθαι, see above on
xi. 28, and cf. xxvii. 10, future infinitive
with μέλλειν only in this one phrase
in N.T.—ἀνάστασιν . . . δικ. τε καὶ
ἀδίκων: the belief was firmly held in all
circles where the teaching of the Pharisees prevailed. But was this belief a belief
in the resurrection of Israelites only?
Was it a belief in the resurrection of
the righteous only? The book of Daniel
plainly implies a resurrection of the
just and the unjust, xii. 2, but we cannot say that this became the prevailing

belief, e.g., in Psalms of Solomon, although
iii. 16 may probably be based upon the
passage in Daniel, yet in ver. 13 there is
no thought of the resurrection of the
sinner (cf. 2 Macc. vii. 14, σοὶ μὲν γὰρ
ἀνάστασις εἰς ζωὴν οὐκ ἔσται, addressed to Antiochus Epiphanes). So
Josephus, in giving an account of the
ordinary Pharisaic doctrine, speaks only
of the virtuous reviving and living again,
Ant., xviii., 1, 3. So too in the Talmudic
literature the resurrection of the dead is
a privilege of Israel, and of righteous
Israelites only—there is no resurrection
of the heathen. On the other hand
there are passages in the Book of Enoch
where a resurrection of all Israelites is
spoken of, cf. xxii., with the exception
of one class of sinners, i.-xxxvi., xxxvii.-
lxx., lxxxiii.-xc., Apocalypse of Baruch
l.-li. 6, but in Enoch xli.-liv. we have a
resurrection of the righteous Israelites
only, cf. Apoc. of Baruch xxx. 1 (cf.
with this verse in Acts). See further
Charles, Book of Enoch, pp. 139, 262,
and Apocalypse of Baruch, l.c., Psalms
of Solomon, Ryle and James, Introd.,
li., pp. 37, 38, Schürer, Jewish People,
div. ii., vol. ii., p. 179, Weber, Jüdische
Theol., p. 390 ff. (1897). Enoch xci.-civ.
is placed by Charles at 104-95 B.C., and
Baruch xxx. is ascribed to B², written
after the destruction of Jerusalem.

Ver. 16. ἐν τούτῳ: "herein" is rather
ambiguous, A. and R.V.; the expression
may be used as = propterea, as the result of the confession of faith in vv. 14,
15, cf. John xvi. 30 (Xen., Cyr., i., 3, 14).
Rendall takes it = meanwhile (so apparently Wetstein), sc. χρόνῳ, i.e., in this
earthly life; "hanc spem dum habeo,"
Bengel. If we read καί, not δέ, perhaps
best explained "non minus quam illi,"
Blass, "I also exercise myself," R.V.,
ἀσκῶ, cf. 2 Macc. xv. 4; ἄσκησις, 4 Macc.
xiii. 22; ἀσκητής, 4 Macc. xii. 11; so in
classical Greek, laborare, studere, Soph.,
Elect., 1024.—ἀπρόσκοπον: only by Paul

ἀνθρώπους διαπαντός. 17. δι᾿ ἐτῶν δὲ πλειόνων [1] παρεγενόμην
ἐλεημοσύνας ποιήσων εἰς τὸ ἔθνος μου καὶ προσφοράς· 18.[2] ἐν
οἷς εὑρόν με ἡγνισμένον ἐν τῷ ἱερῷ, οὐ μετὰ ὄχλου οὐδὲ μετὰ

[1] R.V. transposes παρεγ., placing it after μου, with ℵ*BC, Tisch., W.H., Weiss,
Blass (but not Hilg.), who places it after προσφορας; A omits.

[2] εν οις HLP, so Blass, but εν αις ℵABCE, Blass in β text, Tisch., W.H., R.V.'
Weiss, Wendt, Hilg. οις may have been changed into αις on account of the
immediately preceding προσφοραις; but the fem. may also have been changed into
οις, because no definite reference is made to offerings in xxi. 27, where the tumult
took place, and the expression εν οις would express a more general reference to ver.
17. See note below, and also Winer-Schmiedel, pp. 193, 228; Wendt (1899), note,
in loco.

in N. T., cf. 1 Cor. x. 32, where used
actively, and cf. Ecclus. xxxii. (xxxv.)
21, 3 Macc. iii. 8. In Phil. i. 10 Lightfoot points out that the word may be
taken either transitively or intransitively,
although he prefers the latter. Mr. Page
in his note on the word in this passage
commends A.V. "void of offence" as
including the two images, not offending,
upright, ἀπροσ. πρὸς τὸν Θεόν; not
causing offence, ἀπροσ. πρὸς τοὺς ἀνθρώπους. "Ad Deum et homines congruit
quod sequitur eleemosynas et oblationes,"
Bengel.—διὰ παντός, see Plummer on
Luke xxiv. 53, cf. Acts ii. 25, x. 2, Matt.
xviii. 10, Mark v. 5, Heb. ii. 15, emphatic here at the end of sentence, implying that the Apostle's whole aim in
life should free him from the suspicion
of such charges as had been brought
against him.
Ver. 17. πλειόνων: "many," R.V.,
but margin, "some," so Rendall: if
xviii. 22 refers to a visit to Jerusalem
(see note) at the close of the Apostle's
second missionary journey, the number
expressed by πλειόνων would not exceed
four or five.—ἐλεημοσύνας ποιήσων, see
above on collection for the Saints at
Jerusalem. ἐλεη.: not elsewhere used
by Paul, who speaks of κοινωνία, διακονία εἰς τοὺς ἁγίους, see on x. 2.—
παρεγενόμην, Lucan, but cf. also 1 Cor.
xvi. 3, for the word again used by St.
Paul.—εἰς τὸ ἔθνος μου: quite natural
for St. Paul to speak thus of the Jewish
nation, for the Jewish-Christian Church
naturally consisted of Jews, cf. Rom. ix.
3. For this allusion in Acts to the great
work of the collection, and its evidential
value, as corroborating the notices in
the Epistles, see above on p. 422, and
Paley, H.P., chap. ii., 1. On this use of
εἰς cf. 1 Cor. xvi. 1, 2 Cor. viii. 4, ix. 1,
13, Rom. xv. 26, and see Deissmann,
Bibelstudien, p. 113.—καὶ προσφοράς:

no mention is made of offerings as part
of the purpose of St. Paul's visit to
Jerusalem, but we know that he came
up to Jerusalem to worship, ver. 11, and
to be present at the Feast of Pentecost,
xx. 16, and even if he did not present
some offering in connection with that
Feast (a thank-offering as Bethge supposes), Dr. Hort's view may well commend itself that the Apostle wished to
make some offering on his own account,
or it may be a solemn peace-offering in
connection with the Gentile contribution
for the Jewish Christians, and its acceptance, see on xxi. 26, and also Weiss,
in loco. The position of προσφ. seems
against the supposition that we can take
it simply with ἐλεη., and in combination
with it, as if both words referred to the
collection for the Saints. Jüngst would
omit the words καὶ προσφ. . . . ἱερῷ
altogether, whilst even Hilgenfeld regards vv. 17-21 as an addition of his
"Author to Theophilus".
Ver. 18. ἐν οἷς, see critical note.
If we read ἐν αἷς = "amidst which,"
R.V., "in presenting which," margin,
with reference to προσφοράς, including
not only the offerings in connection with
the Apostle's association of himself with
the poor men in the Nazirite vow, but
also offerings such as those referred to
in ver. 17. ἐν οἷς = inter quæ (Winer-
Schmiedel, pp. 193, 228), i.e., in reference
to these matters generally, cf. xxvi. 12.—
εὑρον, cf. ver. 5: "they found me," indeed, as they have said, but οὐ μετὰ
ὄχλου κ.τ.λ.; a direct answer to the
charge of profaning the Temple: he had
gone there for worship and sacrifice, "then
how did I profane it?" Chrys., Hom., L.
—ἡγνισμένον: the expression is generally
taken to refer to the offerings involved
in the association with the vow, xxi. 26,
but it may also include other acts of
worship and purification in the Temple.

θορύβου, τινὲς[1] ἀπὸ τῆς Ἀσίας Ἰουδαῖοι, 19. οὓς ἔδει ἐπὶ σοῦ
παρεῖναι καὶ κατηγορεῖν εἴ τι ἔχοιεν πρός με. 20. ἢ αὐτοὶ οὗτοι
εἰπάτωσαν,[2] εἴ τι εὗρον ἐν ἐμοὶ ἀδίκημα, στάντος μου ἐπὶ τοῦ συνεδρίου · 21. ἢ περὶ μιᾶς ταύτης φωνῆς, ἧς[3] ἔκραξα ἑστὼς ἐν αὐτοῖς,
Ὅτι περὶ ἀναστάσεως νεκρῶν ἐγὼ κρίνομαι σήμερον[4] ὑφ᾽ ὑμῶν.

[1] After τινες אABCE 13, 40, 61, Sah., Boh., Syr. H.; Tisch., W.H., Weiss,
R.V., Wendt [Blass] add δε; omitted by HLP.

[2] Instead of τι ευρ. W.H., R.V., Blass, Weiss, Wendt, T.R. has ει τι ευρ. with
very slight attestation; cf. ver. 19. εν εμοι om. אAB 13, 40, 61, Tisch., W.H.,
R.V., Weiss, Wendt, Blass, but not Hilg.

[3] For εκραξα (Lach., Hilgenfeld) the form εκεκραξα is found in אABC 13, 40, 61,
Chrys., Tisch., W.H., Blass, Weiss; redupl. form only here in N.T., but often in
LXX; see Winer-Schmiedel, p. 104.

[4] Instead of υφ᾽ ABC 13, 40, 61, Syr. Pesh., Aeth^utr. read εφ᾽, so Tisch., W.H.,
R.V., Weiss, Wendt, Blass in β; υφ᾽ is supported by אEHLP, Chrys. (so Vulg.,
Gig., Boh., Syr. H., a vobis, and Hilg.).

—τινὲς: in A.V. the word is simply referred to εὗρον and there is no difficulty;
but if we insert δέ after it (see critical
note). R.V. renders "but *there were*
certain Jews from Asia," etc. The
sentence breaks off, and the speaker
makes no direct reference to xxi. 27, but
implies that these Asiatic Jews should
have been present to accuse him if they
had any accusation to make—their absence was in the prisoner's favour; "the
passage as it stands (*i.e.*, with this break)
is instinct with life, and seems to exhibit the abruptness so characteristic of
the Pauline Epistles," *cf.* xxvi. 9, see
Page's note *in loco*. Others take δέ
though less forcibly as more strictly in
opposition to the preceding words,
meaning that his accusers had not
found him as they alleged, and as Tertullus alleged, ver. 5, but that certain
Jews of Asia had found him. Hackett
retains δέ, and sees in the words a retort of the charge of riot upon the true
authors of it: "but certain Jews from
Asia"—it is they who excited a tumult,
not I; the verb could be omitted, a true
picture of the Apostle's earnestness, because so readily suggested from θορύβου, but this interpretation seems hardly
borne out by the context.
Ver. 19. ἔδει without ἄν, *cf.* Luke xi.
42, xv. 32; on the force of this imperfect,
see Burton, p. 14, Winer-Moulton, xli.
2.—εἴ τι ἔχοιεν πρός με: the optative of
subjective possibility, representing the
subjective view of the agent — if they
had anything against me (in their own
belief), Winer-Moulton, xli. *b* 2, Viteau,
Le Grec du N. T., p. 111 (1893), Burton,

p. 106.—κατηγορεῖν: "to make accusation," R.V., *cf.* ver. 2.
Ver. 20. ἢ αὐτοὶ οὗτοι: "quandoquidem absunt illi, hi dicant," Blass;
as the Jews from Asia are not present as
accusers, he appeals to those Jews who
are—he cannot demand speech from the
absent, but he claims it from the present
(Weiss): "or else let these men themselves say," R.V., since they are the
only accusers present. Kuinoel refers
the words to the Sadducees, and thinks
this proved from the next verse, but the
context does not require this reference,
nor can the words be referred with
Ewald to the Asiatic Jews, since στάντος μου ἐπὶ τοῦ συν. is against such an
interpretation.—τι, see critical note.
Ver. 21. ἤ = ἄλλο ἤ after ἀδίκημα
(Rendall); St. Paul, of course, uses the
word (ἀδίκημα) of his accusers. St. Paul
is taken by some to speak ironically . . .
strange ἀδίκημα, a question of belief
with regard to which the Jews themselves were at variance, and which the
procurator would regard as an idle contention! Weiss renders "or let them
say, if in other respects they have found
nothing wrong, concerning this one
utterance," etc.—"in what respect they
regard it as an ἀδίκημα," supplying εἰπάτωσαν from the previous verse. On the
whole verse see further Blass, *Gram.*, p.
168, Winer-Schmiedel, p. 187; and also
p. 225 on ἧς ἔκραξα—ἧς probably not
for ᾗ (*cf.* Matt. xxvii. 50), but here
φωνή is used in the sense of a loud cry,
so that the construction resolves itself
into φωνὴν κράζειν, *cf.* Rev. vi. 10,
v. l. (and for the expression in LXX.

22.[1] Ἀκούσας δὲ ταῦτα ὁ Φῆλιξ ἀνεβάλετο αὐτούς, ἀκριβέστερον εἰδὼς τὰ περὶ τῆς ὁδοῦ, εἰπών, Ὅταν Λυσίας ὁ χιλίαρχος καταβῇ, διαγνώσομαι τὰ καθ᾽ ὑμᾶς· 23. διαταξάμενός τε τῷ ἑκατοντάρχῃ τηρεῖσθαι τὸν Παῦλον, ἔχειν τε ἄνεσιν, καὶ μηδένα κωλύειν τῶν ἰδίων αὐτοῦ ὑπηρετεῖν [2] ἢ προσέρχεσθαι αὐτῷ.

24. Μετὰ δὲ ἡμέρας τινὰς παραγενόμενος ὁ Φῆλιξ σὺν Δρουσίλλῃ τῇ[3] γυναικὶ αὐτοῦ οὔσῃ Ἰουδαίᾳ, μετεπέμψατο τὸν Παῦλον, καὶ

[1] The words ακουσας δε ταυτα *om.*; ανεβαλ. δε αυτ. ο Φ. with ℵABCE, Tisch., W.H., R.V., Blass, Weiss, Wendt, Hilg.

[2] η προσερχ. *om.* ℵABCE 13, 61, Vulg., Syr. P. and H., Boh., Arm., Tisch., R.V., and other authorities in ver. 22.

[3] Instead of T.R. BC² 36, Syr. H. mg., Tisch., W.H., R.V., Weiss [Blass] have τη ιδια γυν. (*om.* αυτου). T.R. as ℵ*E, τη γυναικι in C*HLP (Meyer, Hilgenfeld); ℵ^aA, 13, 18, 6, have τη ιδ. γυν. αυτου. At the beginning of verse Blass in β text after ημ. τινας reads Δρουσιλλα η γυνη του Φηλικος ουσα Ιουδαια ηρωτα ιδειν τον Παυλον και ακουσαι τον λογον. βουλομενος ουν το ικανον ποιησαι αυτη (Cassiod. Compl., p. 205 (1402, Mign.) and Syr. H. mg.).

Isa. vi. 4). Farrar, *St. Paul*, ii., 328, thinks that he sees in this utterance some compunction on St. Paul's part for his action in dividing the Sanhedrim, and for the tumult he had caused, but see above, p. 467.

Ver. 22. ἀνεβάλετο: *ampliavit eos*, a technical expression, only here in N. T., the judges were wont to say *Amplius* in cases where it was not possible to pass at once a judgment of condemnation or acquittal before further inquiry, Cic., *In Verr.*, i., 29.—ἀκριβ.: "having more exact knowledge concerning the Way" than to be deceived by the misrepresentation of the Jews; he may have learnt some details of the Christian sect during his years of office from his wife Drusilla, or possibly during his residence in Cæsarea, where there was a Christian community and the home of Philip the Evangelist, and where Cornelius had been converted. This knowledge, the writer indicates, was the real reason: the reason which Felix alleged was that he required the evidence of Lysias in person. Wendt, Zöckler, Bethge, Nösgen take the words to mean that the address of Paul had offended Felix's more accurate knowledge, and on this account he put off any decision. On the comparative see Blass, *Gram.*, p. 139.—τὰ περὶ: characteristic of Luke and Paul, see p. 481.—διαγ. τὰ καθ᾽ ὑμᾶς: "I will determine your matter," R.V., *cf.* xxv. 21, and see above on xxiii. 15. τὰ καθ᾽ ὑμᾶς: probably refers to both accusers and accused. On τὰ before κατά characteristic of

Luke see instance in Moulton and Geden, and Hawkins, *Horæ Synopticæ*, p. 38.

Ver. 23. τηρεῖσθαι: that he should he kept in charge as a prisoner; not middle as in A.V.—ἔχειν τε ἄνεσιν: "and should have indulgence," R.V., not "liberty," A.V., word only elsewhere in Paul in N.T., 2 Cor. ii. 13, vii. 5, viii. 13, 2 Thess. i. 7, *cf.* also Ecclus. xxvi. 10, 1 Esd. iv. 62. From ver. 27 it appears that the prisoner was still bound, but the indulgence involved a *custodia liberior*, and extended to food, and the visits of friends, and remission from the severer form of custody, *cf.* Jos., *Ant.*, xviii., 6, 7, 10, where Agrippa has similar indulgence in his imprisonment at Rome, but is still chained.—μηδένα κωλύειν τῶν ἰδίων, *cf.* iv. 23, Luke, Aristarchus, perhaps Trophimus, *cf.* Jos., *Ant.*, xviii., *u. s.*, for the same indulgence; change of subject to centurion in κωλύειν.—ὑπηρετεῖν, xiii. 36, xx. 34.

Ver. 24. Δρουσίλλη: of the three daughters of Agrippa I. Drusilla was the youngest, her sisters being Bernice (see below) and Mariamne. Married, when about fourteen, to Azizus king of Emeza, she had been seduced from her husband by Felix, who had employed for his evil purpose a certain impostor and magician, Simon by name, Jos., *Ant.*, xx., 7, 2. The account in Josephus implies that she was unhappy in her marriage with Azizus, and asserts that she was exposed on account of her beauty to the envious ill-treatment of her sister Bernice. She married Felix ("trium reginarum mari-

ἤκουσεν αὐτοῦ περὶ τῆς εἰς¹ Χριστὸν πίστεως. 25. διαλεγομένου
δὲ αὐτοῦ περὶ δικαιοσύνης καὶ ἐγκρατείας καὶ τοῦ κρίματος² τοῦ
μέλλοντος ἔσεσθαι, ἔμφοβος γενόμενος ὁ Φῆλιξ ἀπεκρίθη, Τὸ νῦν
ἔχον πορεύου· καιρὸν δὲ μεταλαβὼν μετακαλέσομαί σε· 26. ἅμα
δὲ καὶ ἐλπίζων, ὅτι χρήματα δοθήσεται αὐτῷ ὑπὸ τοῦ Παύλου,³ ὅπως

¹ After Χριστον Ⅸ*BEL 61, Vulg., Gig., Boh., Syr. H., Chrys. add Ιησουν, so
Tisch., W.H., R.V., Weiss, Wendt, but *om.* by Blass in β text, so by Meyer.

² C 15, 31, 40, 180, Arm., Chrys. read του μελλ. κριματος, but text retained as in
T.R. by all edd. εσεσθαι *om.* ⅨABCE, W.H., R.V., Blass. Instead of text Blass
in β, so Hilg. with E. Gig., Vulg. (Cassiod.) read καιρω δε επιτηδειω μετα-
καλεσομαι σε.

³ οπως λυση αυτον *om.* ⅨABCE, Vulg., Syr. P. and H., Arm., Aethʳᵒ·, Tisch.,
W.H., R.V., Blass, Weiss, Wendt, Hilgenfeld. After μεταπεμπ. Gig. adds
" secrete," but not Blass in β. Instead of χαριτας Ⅸ*ABC 13, 61, Vulg., Syr. P.
and H., Boh. read χαριτα, so Tisch., and authorities as above (see note below).
χαριν ⅨᶜEL.

tus," as Suetonius calls him, *Claud.*, 28),
and her son by him, Agrippa by name,
perished under Titus in an eruption of
Vesuvius, Jos., *u. s.* It has been sometimes thought that his mother perished
with him, but probably the words σὺν τῇ
γυναικί in Josephus refer not to Drusilla,
but to the wife of Agrippa (so Schürer);
"Herod" (Headlam), Hastings' B.D.,
The Herods (Farrar), p. 192 ff.—τῇ γυν.
αὐτοῦ, see critical note, the addition of
ἰδίᾳ before γυν. (omit. αὐτοῦ) perhaps to
emphasise that Drusilla, though a Jewess,
was the wife of Felix, or it may point to
the private and informal character of the
interview, due to the request of Drusilla.
Possibly both ἰδίᾳ and αὐτοῦ were
additions to intimate that Drusilla was
really the wife of Felix, but the article
before γυναικί would have been sufficient
to indicate this.—οὔσῃ Ἰουδαίᾳ, *cf.* β
text, which states how Felix acted thus
to gratify Drusilla, who as a Jewess
wished to hear Paul, as her brother
Agrippa afterwards, *cf.* xxv. 22, see
Knabenbauer, *in loco.*—μετεπέμψατο,
see on x. 5.—Χριστὸν, see critical
note.

Ver. 25. περὶ δικαι.: Paul does not
gratify the curiosity of Felix and Drusilla,
but goes straight to the enforcement of
those great moral conditions without
which, both for Jew and Greek, what
he had to say of the Messiahship of
Jesus was unintelligible; how grievously
Felix had failed in righteousness the
events of his period of government proved,
cf. Tac., *Ann.*, xii., 54, "cuncta male-
facta sibi impune ratus," through the
evil influence of Pallas, Tac., *Hist.*, v., 9.
—ἐγκρατ.: R.V. margin "self-control,"

Latin, *temperantia,* Vulgate, *castitate.*
The presence of Drusilla by his side was
in itself a proof how Felix had failed in
this virtue also, ἐγκρ. being specially
applicable to continence from sensual
pleasures (Wetstein); opposed to it is
ἀκρασία, 1 Cor. vii. 5 (= ἀκράτεια),
"incontinence," Arist., *Eth.*, vii., 4, 2.
In N.T., Gal. v. 23, 2 Pet. i. 6 (*bis*), *cf.*
Tit. i. 8. The word is found in Ecclesiast. xviii. 15 S, 30, 4 Macc. v. 34.
St. Paul gives a double proof of his
courage in reasoning thus not only before
Felix but before his wife, for like another
Herodias her resentment was to be feared.
—τοῦ κρίματος τοῦ μέλλ.: "the judgment to come," R.V., preserving the force
of the article omitted in all E.V. except
Rhem.: "ubi etiam illi, qui nunc judices
sedent, judicandi erunt" (Wetstein).—
ἐμφ. γεν., see on x. 4, *cf.* the attitude of
Antipas with regard to the Baptist, Mark
vi. 30.—Τὸ νῦν ἔχον, *cf.* Tob. vii. 11 (B¹
ἔχων), and for instances in Greek writers
see Wetstein.—καιρὸν δὲ μεταλ., *cf.*
Polyb., ii., 16, 15. μεταλαβόντες καιρ.
ἁρμόττοντα (Alford, Blass). So far as
we know, no more convenient season
ever came, see reading in β text.

Ver. 26. ἅμα δὲ καὶ ἐλπ.: connected
by some with ἀπεκ. (*cf.* xxiii. 25), so
Weiss, Wendt, Hackett; others punctuate as W.H., R.V., and render it as a
finite verb.—ὅτι: on the construction
with ἐλπίζειν see Simcox, *Language of
the N.T.*, p. 121, and Blass, *in loco;*
Luke xxiv. 31, 2 Cor. i. 13, xiii. 6,
Philem. ver. 22 (not in Attic Greek).—
On ἅμα *cf.* Blass, *Gram.*, p. 247, Col.
iv. 3, Philem. ver. 22, 1 Tim. v. 13. ἅμα
καί: only in Luke and Paul; on its use

λύσῃ αὐτόν· διὸ καὶ πυκνότερον αὐτὸν μεταπεμπόμενος ὡμίλει αὐτῷ.
27. Διετίας δὲ πληρωθείσης ἔλαβε διάδοχον ὁ Φῆλιξ Πόρκιον

by them see further Viteau, *Le Grec du N.T.*, p. 187 (1893). — χρήματα: the mention of "alms," ver. 17, had perhaps suggested the thought that Paul was in a position to purchase his freedom with money, and it was also evident to Felix that the prisoner was not without personal friends, ver. 23. Spitta, *Apostelgeschichte*, p. 280, points to ver. 17, and to the fact that Felix could not be unaware that Paul was a man of wide influence and supported by many friends, as a sufficient answer to the supposed improbability urged by Pfleiderer that Felix could hope for money from a poor tent-maker and missionary. Spitta thinks that *Philippians* may have been written from Cæsarea, and that therefore (Phil. iv. 10) Felix had double cause to suppose that the poor missionary had command of money; but without endorsing this view as to the place of writing of *Philippians*, it may be suggested that St. Paul's friends at Philippi might have helped to provide financial help for the expenses of his trial: Lydia, *e.g.*, was not only ready with large-hearted hospitality, but her trade in itself required a considerable capital: see on the other hand the view of Ramsay, *St. Paul*, p. 312. It is urged, moreover, that a poor man would never have received such attention or aroused such interest. But St. Luke himself has told us how Herod desired to see the Son of Man, Who had not where to lay His head, and the same feeling which prompted Herod, the feeling of curiosity, the hope perhaps of seeing some new thing, may have prompted the desire of an Agrippa or a Drusilla to see and to hear Paul.—ἐλπίζ. . . . δοθ.: "sic thesaurum evangelii omisit infelix Felix," Bengel. When Overbeck expresses surprise that Felix did not deliver Paul to the Jews for money, he forgets that Paul's Roman citizenship would make such an action much more dangerous than his detention. —διὸ καὶ: characteristic of Luke and Paul, and common to Luke's Gospel and Acts, *cf.* Luke i. 35, Acts x. 29, Rom. iv. 22, xv. 22, 2 Cor. i. 20, iv. 13, v. 9, Phil. ii. 9, only twice elsewhere in N.T., Heb. xi. 12, xiii. 12; "ut illiceret eum ad se pecunia temptandum," Blass, Knabenbauer.—πυκνότερον, *cf.* Luke v. 33, 1 Tim. v. 23; and LXX, Esther viii. 13, 2 Macc. viii. 8, 3 Macc. iv. 12. The comparative here is "verus comparativus": *quo sæpius*, Blass. Nothing

could more plainly show the corruption of the Roman government than the conduct of Felix in face of the law: "Lex Julia de repetundis præcepit, ne quis ob hominem in vincula publice conjiciendum, vinciendum, vincirive jubendum, exve vinculis dimittendum; neve quis ob hominem condemnandum, absolvenduum . . . aliquid acceperit," *Digest.*, xl., 11, 3 (Wetstein); see further on ver. 3.—ὡμίλει: only in Luke, see above xx. 11; imperfect denoting frequent occurrence.

Ver. 27. διετίας δὲ πληρ.: on the question of chronology see below, *cf.* xx. 30, and for τριετία, xx. 31; on διετία in inscriptions see two instances in Deissmann, *Neue Bibelstudien*, p. 86. πληρ.: perhaps indicating that two full years are meant. Weizsäcker throws doubt upon the historical character of this imprisonment, and thinks that the episode is merely introduced by the writer of Acts, who in his ignorance of the name of the procurator doubles the incident before Felix and Festus; but Wendt declines to value so lightly the definite notices and accounts in Acts, and adds that the delay of the trial under a procurator devoid of a sense of duty was no improbable event. The recall of Felix has been assigned to very varying dates, Lightfoot naming 60, Wendt (1899) 61, Schürer, at the earliest 58, at the latest 61, probably 60, Ramsay 59, whilst McGiffert, following the Chronology recently advocated by O. Holtzmann (with a few earlier writers), places it as early as 55 (Harnack 55-56, following Eusebius, whilst Blass has also defended the Eusebian date). Both McGiffert and Holtzmann fix upon 55 because before the end of this year Pallas, the brother of Felix, was in disgrace; and yet, according to Josephus, Felix escaped the accusations brought against him by shielding himself behind his brother Pallas, whom Nero was then holding in special honour, Jos., *Ant.*, xx., 8, 9, Tac., *Ann.*, xiii., 14. "Either Josephus is in error," says O. Holtzmann, *Neutest. Zeitgeschichte*, p. 128, "or Festus went to Palestine in 55". But there is good reason for thinking that Josephus was in error in stating that Felix escaped by his brother's influence, then at its height, Jos., *u. s.* It is no doubt true that the influence of Pallas may have been very substantial

Φῆστον[1] · θέλων τε χάριτας καταθέσθαι τοῖς Ἰουδαίοις ὁ Φῆλιξ, κατέλιπε τὸν Παῦλον δεδεμένον.

[1] Instead of θελων τε χαρ. Blass in β text with 137, Syr. H. mg. reads τον δε Παυλον ειασεν εν τηρησει δια Δρουσιλλαν, so Zöckler, Belser, Hilg., and J. Weiss, who thinks that T.R. is simply conformed to xxv. 9 ; but see on the other hand Schmiedel, *Enc. Bibl.*, i., 53.

long after his fall from court favour; but if the intervention of Pallas was subsequent to his fall, what becomes of the synchronism between his disgrace and the recall of Felix? But further, Pallas, according to the statement of Tacitus, *Ann.*, xiii., 14, was disgraced before the fourteenth birthday of Britannicus, in Feb. 55, but, if so, how could Felix have reached Rome at such an early period of that year? Nero came to the throne on 13th Oct., 54, and we have to suppose that the order for recall was sent and the return journey of Felix to the capital accomplished in spite of the winter season which made a sea voyage impossible (Ramsay, Zahn, Bacon); "one can therefore no longer base the chronology of an Apostle's life upon the dismissal of a court favourite". But are there no chronological data available? Albinus, the successor of Festus, was already procurator in 62. How long he had been in office we cannot say, but he was certainly procurator in the summer of that year (Schürer, *Jewish People*, div. i., vol. ii., p. 188, E.T.; *Biblical World*, p. 357, 1897). From Jos., *Ant.*, xx., 9, 1, we learn that there was an interval of some few months full of disturbance and anarchy between the death of Festus and the arrival of Albinus in Jerusalem, so that we seem justified in inferring that Festus died probably in the winter of 61-62; and whilst the events of his procuratorship can scarcely have extended over five years (as would be demanded by the earlier chronology)—for in this case Josephus would surely have given us more information about them—it seems equally difficult to suppose that the events which Josephus does record could have been crowded into less than a year, or portions of two (Schürer). The entrance of Festus upon his office might thus be carried back to 59-60, and St. Paul's departure for Rome would fall probably in 60. But a further contribution to the subject has been made by Mr. Turner, "Chronology of the N.T.," Hastings' B.D., pp. 418, 419, and he argues for the exclusion of a date as late as 60 for the accession of Festus, and for placing the recall of Felix in 57-59, *i.e.*, between the earlier and later dates mentioned above; or, more definitely still, in 58, *cf.* p. 420. With this date Dr. Gilbert agrees, *Student's Life of Paul*, p. 252, 1899. See further Zahn, *Einleitung*, ii., 634; Wendt (1899), p. 56; *Expositor*, March, 1897, Feb., 1898; "Festus" (A. Robertson), Hastings' B.D. and B.D².—ἔλαβε διάδοχον, Ecclus. xlvi. 1, xlviii. 8. In 2 Macc. iv. 29, xiv. 26, the meaning of successor is doubtful, and it would seem that the title rather denoted a high office about the court of the Ptolemies, *cf.* Deissmann, *Bibelstudien*, p. 111. In classical Greek it is used as here for successor, *cf.* Jos., *Ant.*, xx., 8, 9, so *successorem accepit*, Plin., *Epist.*, ix., 13.—Φῆστον: we know nothing of him except from the N.T. and Josephus. The latter, however, contrasts him favourably with his successor Albinus: "et Albinum cum ei dissimillimum fuisse tradit, scelestum hominem, simul illum laudat" (Blass). So far as our information goes, Festus also contrasts favourably with his predecessor; he acted with promptness to rid the country of robbers and *sicarii*, and amongst them of one impostor whose promises were specially seductive, *Ant.*, xx., 8, 9, 10, and *B.J.*, ii., 14, 1. But although, as Schürer says, he was disposed to act righteously, he found himself unable to undo the mischief wrought by his predecessor, and after a short administration death prevented him from coping further with the evils which infested the province. For his attitude towards St. Paul as his prisoner see notes below. Two other events marked his procuratorship: (1) the quarrel between the priests and Agrippa, because the latter built on to his palace so as to overlook the Temple, and the priests retaliated by building so as to shut off his view. Festus sided with Agrippa, but allowed the priests to appeal to Rome. (2) The decision of the emperor in favour of the Syrian against the Jewish inhabitants of Cæsarea, which caused a bitterness provoking in A.D. 66 the disturbances in which Josephus marked the beginnings of the great War, *Ant.*, xx., 8, 9.—θέλων τε χάριτας καταθέσθαι τοῖς Ἰ.: "desiring to gain favour with

XXV. 1. ΦΗΣΤΟΣ οὖν, ἐπιβὰς [1] τῇ ἐπαρχίᾳ, μετὰ τρεῖς ἡμέρας ἀνέβη εἰς Ἱεροσόλυμα ἀπὸ Καισαρείας. 2. ἐνεφάνισαν δὲ [2] αὐτῷ ὁ ἀρχιερεὺς καὶ οἱ πρῶτοι τῶν Ἰουδαίων κατὰ τοῦ Παύλου, καὶ παρεκάλουν αὐτόν, 3. αἰτούμενοι χάριν κατ' αὐτοῦ, ὅπως μεταπέμψηται αὐτὸν εἰς Ἱερουσαλήμ, ἐνέδραν ποιοῦντες ἀνελεῖν αὐτὸν κατὰ τὴν

[1] επαρχιᾳ, so also Lach., Hilgenfeld, Blass, W.H. text. επαρχεια, so B; but Tisch., Weiss, and W.H. marg. (so Wendt probably) following ℵ*A have επαρχειω. Weiss regards επαρχιᾳ (-εια) as a thoughtless emendation in accordance with xxiii. 34. See also Winer-Schmiedel, p. 44, and note below.

[2] For δε ℵABC, Vulg., Syr. Pesh., Aeth. read τε, so Tisch., W.H., Weiss, R.V., Wendt, Blass. ο αρχ., but instead of the sing. ℵABCEL read the plural, so Tisch. and authorities above. For T.R. cf. xxiv. 1.

the Jews," R.V., literally to lay down or deposit a favour with the Jews as a deposit for which a due return might be expected, cf. 1 Macc. x. 23 R.; Jos., Ant., xi., 6, 5, so too in classical Greek, Thuc., i., 33, 128; Herod., vi., 41, etc. The policy of Felix was to gain popularity with the Jews in view of the accusations which followed him on his return to Rome, Jos., Ant., xx., 8, 9. That the pursuit of such a policy was not alien to the character of Roman officials see Jos., Ant., xx., 9, 5, where we learn that Albinus, desiring to gain the gratitude of the Jews, took money of all those in prison for some trifling fault, by which means the prisons indeed were emptied, but the country was full of robbers. In B.J., ii., 14, 1, we learn that the same system was pursued by Albinus, the successor of Festus, until no one was left in the prisons but those who gave him nothing. According to β text Felix leaves Paul in prison to please his wife, but, as Blass points out, both reasons may be true.— χάριτα (W.H., R.V.) only (in N.T.) in Jude, ver. 4, cf. xxv. 9 A; found in classics, though rarer than χάριν, Winer-Schmiedel, p. 88; in LXX, Zech. vi. 14. —δεδεμ.: this does not at all imply that Paul had been quite free, and was now rebound, cf. ver. 23. ἄνεσις did not mean perfect freedom, and the custodia militaris might still continue. Nösgen thinks that the word in its position at the end of the verse indicates a severer form of custody, but this is by no means necessary, although as the last word of the episode, and as the result of all the intercourse with Felix, it has a dramatic force and pathos. Zeller, Acts, ii., p. 83, E.T., although he thinks it remarkable that Felix and Festus are represented as acting from the same motive, as Pilate for a similar reason had consented to the

execution of Jesus, is constrained to admit that conduct such as that of the two procurators is too natural for its repetition to be surprising; unscrupulous officials are always ready by complaisance at the expense of others to appease those to whom they have given just cause for complaint.

CHAPTER XXV.—Ver. 1. ἐπιβὰς: "having come into the province," A. and R.V., or, "having entered upon his province," R.V. margin. If we read τῇ ἐπαρχείῳ with Weiss and W.H. margin, the word is an adjective of two terminations, sc. ἐξουσίᾳ, i.e., having entered on his duties as governor of the province (see Weiss, Apostelgeschichte, p. 8), and cf. xxiii. 34. For the adjective in inscriptions see Blass, in loco.—μετὰ τρεῖς ἡμ.: "sat cito," Bengel.—ἀνέβη: went up to Jerusalem officially as the capital; the visit had nothing necessarily to do with St. Paul, but the close-connecting τε may indicate that the action of the priests in again bringing up their case was to be expected.

Ver. 2. ἐνεφάνισαν, cf. xxiii. 15, xxiv. 1: here the context evidently implies that legal and formal information was laid against Paul.—If we read οἱ ἀρχ., cf. iv. 5. οἱ πρῶτοι: sometimes taken as = πρεσβ. in ver. 15, cf. xxiii. 14, xxiv. 1, but in Luke xix. 47 we have οἱ ἀρχ. καὶ οἱ γράμμ. καὶ οἱ πρῶτοι τοῦ λαοῦ. The difference of designation seems to indicate that they were not identical with the πρεσβ., although perhaps including them, or possibly as their chief representatives: see also Plummer on Luke, l. c. Blass seems to identify πρῶτοι with ἀρχιερεῖς, cf. iv. 5, ἄρχοντες.— παρεκάλουν: the word and the tense mark their importunity.

Ver. 3. αἰτουμ., cf. ver. 15. "Postulantes gratiam non justitiam," Corn.

ὁδόν.[1] 4. ὁ μὲν οὖν Φῆστος ἀπεκρίθη, τηρεῖσθαι τὸν Παῦλον[2] ἐν Καισαρείᾳ, ἑαυτὸν δὲ μέλλειν ἐν τάχει ἐκπορεύεσθαι· 5. Οἱ οὖν δυνατοὶ ἐν ὑμῖν, φησί, συγκαταβάντες, εἴ τί ἐστιν[3] ἐν τῷ ἀνδρὶ τούτῳ, κατηγορείτωσαν αὐτοῦ. 6. Διατρίψας δὲ ἐν αὐτοῖς ἡμέρας[4] πλείους ἢ δέκα, καταβὰς εἰς Καισάρειαν, τῇ ἐπαύριον καθίσας ἐπὶ τοῦ

[1] After οδον Syr. H. mg. adds *illi qui votum fecerant se pro virili (facturos esse) ut in manibus suis esset ;* but not β text.

[2] For εν Καισ. 𝕹ABCE 13, 40, 61, read εις, so Tisch., W.H., and authorities above. R.V., Weiss, Blass, Hilg. have **Καισαρειαν** with BC 13, 40 ; whilst W.H. read **Καισαριαν**.

[3] Instead of T.R. (so Meyer) 𝕹ABCE, Vulg., Boh., Arm., Lucif. read εν τῳ ανδρι ατοπον, so Tisch., W.H., R.V., Weiss, Wendt, Blass, Hilg.

[4] R.V., following 𝕹ABC, Vulg., Arm., reads ου πλειους οκτω η δεκα instead of T.R., so too W.H., Weiss, Wendt, Blass, Hilgenfeld. Other variations, *e.g.*, 137, Syr. P.H., Sah. omit ου πλειους. See Alford's note and Meyer-Wendt on probable confusion between **οκτω** of the more ancient MSS. and **η** of later ones, the former **η** representing the numeral being absorbed in the second **η**.

à Lapide. — **ἐνέδραν ποιοῦντες**, not **ποιήσοντες**, they were making and contriving the ambush *already* (Alford) : priests and elders were willing as before to avail themselves of the assassin. — **κατὰ τὴν ὁδόν**, *cf.* Luke x. 4, and three times in Acts, viii. 36, xxvi. 13, nowhere else in N. T. Syr. H. mg. adds a distinct reference to the forty conspirators previously mentioned, xxiii. 12, but Blass omits in β text—doubtless, as he says, there were many others ready for the deed at the service of the Sanhedrim.

Ver. 4. **μὲν οὖν** : no antithesis expressed ; but Rendall, Appendix on **μὲν οὖν**, *Acts*, p. 162, holds that two phases of events are here contrasted : Festus refused to bring Paul away from Cæsarea, but he undertook to hear the charges of the Jews there. — **ἐν Και.**, see critical note, perhaps here **εἰς** simply = **ἐν**, so Blass, and Simcox, *cf.* Mark xiii. 9, Acts xix. 22. On the other hand *cf.* Weiss on the frequent force of **εἰς** peculiar to Acts, viii. 40, ix. 21 (where he reads **εἰς**), intimating that Paul had been brought to Cæsarea with the purpose that he should be kept there. The Jews had asked Festus **ὅπως μεταπέμψ. α. εἰς Ἱ.**, but Festus intimates that the prisoner was in custody at Cæsarea, and that as he was himself going there, the prisoner's accusers should go there also ; in other words, he returns a refusal to their request, *cf.* ver. 16.—**ἐν τάχει**, Luke xviii. 8, and three times in Acts, xii. 7, xxii. 18, not in the other Evangelists ; Rom. xvi. 20, 1 Tim. iii. 14, Rev. i. 1, xxii. 6.—

ἐκπορ. : for the verb used absolutely as here *cf.* Luke iii. 7.

Ver. 5. **φησί** : change to the *oratio recta*, *cf.* i. 4. For other instances of the insertion of the single words **ἔφη** or **φησίν**, rare in N. T., see Simcox, *Language of the New Testament*, p. 200 ; *cf.* xxiii. 35, xxvi. 25, 1 Cor. vi. 16, 2 Cor. x. 10, Heb. viii. 5.—**οἱ . . . δυνατοί** : " Let them therefore, saith he, which are of power among you," R.V. ; not simply " which are able," A.V., " qui in vobis potentes sunt," Vulgate. The word may be used by Festus, because he was not acquainted with the Jewish official terms, or it may be used in a general way as in 1 Cor. i. 26. In Jos., *B.J.*, i., i2, 5, we have the expression, **ἦκον Ἰουδαίων οἱ δυνατοί**, *cf.* Thuc. i. 89, Polyb., ix., 23, 4 ; but in addition to this general use of the word Jos. frequently conjoins the **ἀρχιερεῖς** with the **δυνατοί** as members of the Sanhedrim, Schürer, *Jewish People*, div. ii., vol. i., p. 178, E.T. This interpretation of the word is more natural than that adopted by Bengel : " *qui valent ad iter faciendum* : **ἦθος** urbanum Festi respondentis Judæis molestiam viae causantibus ; " for other explanations see Wendt-Meyer, *in loco*.—**συγκαταβάντες** : " go down with me," R.V., *mecum ;* only here in N. T., in LXX, Ps. xlviii. 17, Wisd. x. 13, Dan. iii. 49 (Theod. iii. 49) = Song of the Three Children, ver. 26.— **ἄτοπον**, see critical note, and further on xxviii. 6.

Ver. 6. **ἡμέρας πλ.**, see critical note, " not more than eight or ten days," R.V., *i.e.*, the whole period of Festus'

βήματος ἐκέλευσε τὸν Παῦλον ἀχθῆναι. 7. παραγενομένου δὲ
αὐτοῦ, περιέστησαν¹ οἱ ἀπὸ Ἱεροσολύμων καταβεβηκότες Ἰουδαῖοι,
πολλὰ καὶ βαρέα² αἰτιάματα φέροντες κατὰ τοῦ Παύλου, ἃ οὐκ
ἴσχυον ἀποδεῖξαι· 8. ἀπολογουμένου αὐτοῦ, Ὅτι οὔτε εἰς τὸν νόμον
τῶν Ἰουδαίων, οὔτε εἰς τὸ ἱερόν, οὔτε εἰς Καίσαρά τι ἥμαρτον. 9.
ὁ Φῆστος δέ, τοῖς Ἰουδαίοις θέλων χάριν καταθέσθαι, ἀποκριθεὶς τῷ
Παύλῳ εἶπε, Θέλεις, εἰς Ἱεροσόλυμα ἀναβάς, ἐκεῖ περὶ τούτων

¹ ΝΑΒCL, so Tisch., W.H., R.V., Weiss, Blass, Hilg. read αυτον after περι-
εστησαν; E has αυτω; Meyer follows T.R.

² For αιτιαματα ΝΑΒCEHLP, so Tisch. and authorities above read αιτιωματα,
a word which does not occur elsewhere, although Eustath. has αιτιωσις for
αιτιασις. ΝΑΒC 13, 40, 61, so Tisch. and authorities above read καταφεροντες
instead of φεροντες κατα τον Π.

stay ἐν αὐτοῖς. Blass sees in the words
an indication of the vigour of action
characterising Festus. The expression
may, however, be used from the standpoint of Paul and his friends at Cæsarea,
who did not know how much of his
absence Festus had spent in Jerusalem,
or how much on the journey (so Weiss
and Wendt).—τῇ ἐπαύριον: ten times
in Acts, but nowhere in Luke's Gospel,
cf., however, ἐπὶ τὴν αὔριον, Luke x. 35
and Acts iv. 5 only (Hawkins). This evidently implies that the accusers had come
down with Festus, and it may again indicate his promptness, cf. ver. 17. There
does not seem any indication that this
immediate action shows that he had been
prejudiced against Paul in Jerusalem
(Chrys.).—ἐπὶ τοῦ βήματος, xii. 21, xviii.
12, and ver. 10 below: seven times in
Acts in this sense (Matt. xxvii. 19, John
xix. 13), but nowhere in Luke's Gospel;
twice by St. Paul, Rom. xiv. 10, 2 Cor. v.
10.—καθ. ἐπὶ τοῦ β.: a necessary formality, otherwise no legal effect would
be given to the decision, cf. Schürer, Jewish People, div. i., vol. ii., p. 15, E.T.,
for this and other instances.—ἀχθῆναι, cf.
προσάγεσθαι, Polyc., Mart., ix., 1 and 2.
Ver. 7. περιέστησαν: if we add
αὐτόν, see critical note, "stood round
about him," i.e., Paul, R.V., "peri-
culum intentantes," Bengel. (Cf. John
xi. 42, Judith v. 22, omit S¹.)—πολλὰ
καὶ βαρέα: "many and (indeed) heavy,"
etc., Winer-Moulton, lix., 3, perhaps as
in Matt. xxiii. 23, weighty, of great
moment.—αἰτιάματα φέρ., see critical
note. αἰτίαμ. in Æschylus and Thucydides. For καταφέροντες, xxvi. 10, cf.
Deut. xxii. 14.
Ver. 8. Evidently the charges classed
as before under three heads, (1) the Law,

(2) the Temple, (3) the Empire. In
this verse Hilgenfeld ascribes ὅτι . . .
ἥμαρτον to his "author to Theophilus"
(Jüngst, too, omits the words). But, not
content with this, he concludes that the
whole narrative which follows about
Agrippa is to ratify the innocence of
Paul before a crowned head of Judaism,
cf. ix. 15, where υἱῶν τε Ἰσ. is also
ascribed to the "author to Theophilus,"
and perhaps also τε καὶ βασιλέων; we
are therefore to refer to this unknown
writer the whole section xxv. 13-xxvi.
32.—ἥμαρτον with εἰς only here in Acts,
three times in Luke's Gospel, three
times in 1 Cor., only once elsewhere in
N.T., Matt. xviii. 21.
Ver. 9. χάριν καταθέσθαι, xxiv. 27.—
τοῖς Ἰ., best placed emphatically before
χάριν κατ. (W.H.), so as to show that
it was the compliance of Festus to the
Jews which caused the turn which things
took (Weiss).—θέλεις εἰς Ἰ.: "injustum
videbatur condemnare, incommodum
absolvere," Blass.—ἐκεῖ: he makes himself the same proposal to the prisoner
which had previously been suggested by
the accusers, ver. 3.—ἐπ' ἐμοῦ: "me
præsente," for the Sanhedrists would be
the judges; otherwise, where would be
the favour to the Jews? Felix may have
added the words speciose, so as to reassure Paul and to obtain his acqui-
escence to the proposal; in ver. 20
omitted, but evidently from their close
connection with περὶ τούτ. κρίν. they
indicate that Festus would play some
judicial part in the matter; cf. xxiv. 21
and 1 Cor. vi. 1. But Paul's answer
plainly shows that he thought from the
words of Felix that a Jewish and not a
Roman tribunal awaited him: ἐπ' ἐμοῦ
would therefore seem to mean that the

κρίνεσθαι [1] ἐπ᾽ ἐμοῦ; 10. εἶπε δὲ ὁ Παῦλος, Ἐπὶ τοῦ βήματος Καίσαρος [2] ἑστώς εἰμι, οὗ με δεῖ κρίνεσθαι. Ἰουδαίους οὐδὲν [3] ἠδίκησα, ὡς καὶ σὺ κάλλιον ἐπιγινώσκεις· 11. εἰ μὲν [4] γὰρ ἀδικῶ καὶ ἄξιον θανάτου πέπραχά τι, οὐ παραιτοῦμαι τὸ ἀποθανεῖν· εἰ δὲ οὐδέν ἐστιν ὧν οὗτοι κατηγοροῦσί μου, οὐδείς με δύναται αὐτοῖς

[1] For κρινεσθαι 𝕭ABCE, so Tisch., W.H., Weiss, Wendt, Blass, Hilg. read κριθηναι.

[2] 𝕭* has εστως at commencement of verse, B has it in both places, Tisch., W.H., Weiss, Blass, Wendt place it at commencement.

[3] For ηδικησα (T.R. Lach.) 𝕭B have ηδικηκα, so Tisch., W.H., Weiss, Wendt, Blass.

[4] For γαρ 𝕭ABCEgr. 61 read ουν, so Tisch., W.H., Weiss, Wendt, Hilg. but [Blass].

Sanhedrim would judge, whilst Festus would ratify their judgment or not as seemed good to him, as Pilate had acted in the case of Christ. On the other hand it is possible that Festus may have been quite sincere in his proposal: his words at least showed that in his judgment there was no case against Paul of a political nature, and he may have thought that religious questions could be best decided before the Sanhedrim in Jerusalem, whilst he could guarantee a safe-conduct for Paul as a Roman citizen.
Ver. 10. ἑστώς εἰμι: "I am standing," used rhetorically, Blass, *Gram.*, p. 198; on the position of ἑστ. see critical note.—Καίσαρος: because the procurator was the representative of Cæsar: "quæ acta gestaque sunt a procuratore Cæsaris sic ab eo comprobantur, atque si a Cæsare ipso gesta sint," Ulpian, *Digest.*, i., 19, 1.—δεῖ: because a Roman citizen, no need to suppose that the word has reference here to any divine intimation.—Ἰουδ. . . . : "to Jews have I done no wrong," the omission of the article in translation makes Paul's denial more forcible and comprehensive; for ἀδικεῖν with οὐδέν and the double accusative *cf.* Luke x. 19.—ὡς καὶ σὺ κάλλιον ἐπιγ.: "as thou also art getting to know better," Rendall (see also Page and Weiss): this rendering, it is said, saves us from the ungracious and unjust retort which A. and R.V. ascribe to Paul. But ver. 18 seems to show us by the confession of Festus himself that the Apostle might fairly have imputed to him a keeping back of his better and fairer judgment, whilst in the expression χαρίσασθαι, ver. 11, there seems to be an intimation that the Apostle felt that Festus might make him a victim. Zöckler sees in the comparative "a gentle reproach," as if

St. Paul would intimate to Festus that he really knew better than his question (ver. 9) would imply.
Ver. 11. εἰ μὲν γὰρ, see critical note, "if then (οὖν) I am a wrongdoer," referring to his standing before Cæsar's judgment-seat, and not to the ἠδίκησα in ver. 10.—ἀδικεῖν: only here absolutely in N.T.; the verb occurs five times in Acts, once in Luke's Gospel, and once in St. Matthew, but not elsewhere in the Gospels (Friedrich, p. 23).—ἄξιον θαν., *i.e.*, according to Roman law.—οὐ παραιτοῦμαι τὸ ἀποθανεῖν: *non recuso*, Vulgate, so Blass; the verb is only used here in Acts, but it occurs three times in St. Luke's Gospel, three times in Hebrews, once in Mark xv. 6, W.H. —In the present passage, and in 1 Tim. iv. 7, v. 11, 2 Tim. ii. 23, Tit. iii. 10, Heb. xii. 25 (twice), the word is rendered "refuse," R.V. text; but in Luke xiv. 18, 19, the word is rendered "to make excuse"; "excused": Jos., *Ant.*, vii., 8, 2; but in each case the Greek verb literally means "to beg off from," and the Latin *deprecor* might well express the verb both here and in Luke xiv., *l.c.*, *cf.* Esth. iv. 8 in the sense of supplicating, and for the sense as above 2 Macc. ii. 31, 3 Macc. vi. 27; see also Grimm *sub v.* for different shades of meaning. In Jos., *Vita*, 29, we have the phrase θανεῖν οὐ παραιτοῦμαι: upon which Krenkel insists as an instance of dependence upon Josephus, but not only is the phrase here somewhat different verbally, οὐ παραι. τὸ ἀποθ., the article expressing more emphatically, as Bengel says, *id ipsum agi;* but *cf.* the instances quoted by Wetstein of the use of similar phrases in Greek, and of the Latin *deprecor*, *e.g.*, Dion. Hal., *A.V.*, 29. τὸν μὲν οὖν θάνατον . . . οὐ παραιτοῦμαι. See

χαρίσασθαι· Καίσαρα ἐπικαλοῦμαι. 12. τότε ὁ Φῆστος, συλλαλή-
σας μετὰ τοῦ συμβουλίου, ἀπεκρίθη, Καίσαρα ἐπικέκλησαι, ἐπὶ
Καίσαρα πορεύσῃ.

further *Introd.*, p. 31.— **χαρίσασθαι**: "to
grant me by favour," R.V. margin, *cf.*
iii. 14, xxv. 16, xxvii. 24 (Philem. ver. 22),
only in Luke and Paul in N.T.; see on
its importance as marking the "We"
section, xxvii. 24, and other parts of
Acts, Zeller, *Acts*, ii., 318, E.T. Paul
must have known what this "giving up"
to the Jews would involve.—**Καίσαρα
ἐπικ.**: *Appello: provoco ad Cæsarem:*
"Si apud acta quis appellaverit, *satis*
erit si dicat|: Appello." *Digest.*, xlix., 1, 2,
except in the case of notorious robbers
and agitators whose guilt was clear, *ibid.*,
16. But we must distinguish between
an appeal against a sentence already
pronounced, and a claim at the commencement of a process that the whole
matter should be referred to the emperor.
It would appear from this passage, *cf.*
vv. 21, 26, 32, that Roman citizens
charged with capital offences could make
this kind of appeal, for the whole narrative is based upon the fact that Paul
had not yet been tried, and that he was
to be kept for a thorough inquiry by the
emperor, and to be brought to Rome for
this purpose, *cf.* Pliny, *Epist.*, x., 97,
quoted by Schürer, Alford, and others,
and similar instances in Renan, *Saint
Paul*, p. 543, Schürer, *Jewish People*,
div. i., vol. ii., p. 59, and div. ii., vol. ii.,
p. 278, E.T., and also "Appeal," Hastings' B.D., and below, p. 514.—
This step of St. Paul's was very natural.
During his imprisonment under Felix
he had hoped against hope that he
might have been released, but although
the character of Festus might have given
him a more reasonable anticipation of
justice, he had seen enough of the
procurator to detect the vacillation which
led him also to curry favour with the
Jews. From some points of view his
position under Festus was more dangerous than under Felix: if he accepted the
suggestion that he should go up to
Jerusalem and be tried before the Sanhedrim, he could not doubt that his judges
would find him guilty; if he declined,
and Festus became the judge, there was
still the manifest danger that the better
judgment of the magistrate would be
warped by the selfishness of the politician.
Moreover, he may well have thought
that at a distant court, where there might
be difficulty in collecting evidence against

him, he would fare better in spite of the
danger and expense of the appeal.
But whilst we may thus base St. Paul's
action upon probable human motives,
his own keen and long desire to see
Rome, xix. 21, and his Lord's promise of
the fulfilment of that desire, xxiii. 11,
could not have been without influence
upon his decision, although other motives
need not be altogether excluded, as St.
Chrysostom, Ewald, Neander and Meyer
(see Nösgen, 435). It has been maintained that there was every reason to
suppose that St. Paul would have obtained his acquittal at the hands of the
Roman authorities, especially after
Agrippa's declaration of his innocence,
xxvi. 32. But St. Paul's appeal had
been already made before Agrippa had
heard him, and he may well have come
to the conclusion that the best he
could hope for from Festus was a further
period of imprisonment, whilst his release
would only expose him to the bitter and
relentless animosity of the Jews. Two
years of enforced imprisonment had been
patiently borne, and the Apostle would
be eager (can we doubt it?) to bear
further witness before Gentiles and
kings of his belief in Jesus as the Christ,
and of repentance and faith towards
God.

Ver. 12. **μετὰ τοῦ συμβ.**, *i.e.*, his
assessors, *assessores consiliarii*, with
whom the procurators were wont to
consult in the administration of the law.
They were probably composed, in part
at all events, of the higher officials of
the court, *cf.* Suet., *Tiber.*, 33, Lamprid.,
Vita Alex. Sev., 46, Jos., *Ant.*, xiv., 10,
2, Schürer, *Jewish People*, div. i., vol.
ii., p. 60, E.T.; and see further on the
word Deissmann, *Neue Bibelstudien*, p.
65, and references in Grimm-Thayer, *sub
v.* It would seem that the procurator
could only reject such an appeal at his
peril, unless in cases where delay might
be followed by danger, or when there
was manifestly no room for an appeal,
Dig., xlix., 5, and see Bethge, *Die
Paulinischen Reden*, p. 252, and Blass,
in loco.—**K. ἐπικ.**: no question, W.H.,
R.V., Weiss (as in A.V.); "asynd. rhetori-
cum cum anaphora," Blass, *cf.* 1 Cor.
vii. 18, 21, 27. The decision of the
procurator that the appeal must be allowed, and the words in which it was

13. Ἡμερῶν δὲ διαγενομένων τινῶν, Ἀγρίππας ὁ βασιλεὺς καὶ
Βερνίκη κατήντησαν εἰς Καισάρειαν,[1] ἀσπασόμενοι τὸν Φῆστον. 14.
ὡς δὲ πλείους ἡμέρας διέτριβον ἐκεῖ, ὁ Φῆστος τῷ βασιλεῖ ἀνέθετο
τὰ κατὰ τὸν Παῦλον, λέγων, Ἀνήρ τίς ἐστι[2] καταλελειμμένος ὑπὸ

[1] For ασπασαμενοι (instead of -ομενοι) ℵABEgr·HLP 13, 31, 68, 105, Boh., Aeth.,
so Tisch., Weiss, Wendt, R.V. Hort (not Westcott) says the authority for -αμενοι
is absolutely overwhelming, and as a matter of transmission -ομενοι can be only a
correction. But he adds that it is difficult to remain satisfied that there is no prior
corruption of some kind. Blass, *Gram.*, p. 193, rejects -αμενοι as impossible, and
reads, -ομενοι, so Hilg. Wendt (1899), p. 386, strongly supports -αμενοι, and
explains the aor. part. after the anal. of i. 24, x. 13, xiii. 27.

[2] καταλελειμμ., W.H. have -λιμμ. ; *cf.* Winer-Schmiedel, p. 45.

announced were not meant to frighten
Paul, as Bengel supposed, but at the
same time they may have been uttered,
if not with a sneer, yet with the implication "thou little knowest what an appeal
to Cæsar means". Moreover, Festus
must have seen that the appeal was
based upon the prisoner's mistrust of
his character, for only if the accused
could not trust the impartiality of the
governor had he any interest in claiming
the transference of his trial to Rome.

Ver. 13. Ἀγρ. ὁ βασιλεὺς: this was
Herod Agrippa II., son of Agrippa I.,
whose tragic end is recorded in chap. xii.
At the time of his father's death he was
only seventeen, and for a time he lived
in retirement, as Claudius was persuaded
not to entrust him with the kingdom of
Judæa. But on the death of Herod,
king of Chalcis, A.D. 48, Claudius not
only gave the young Agrippa the vacant
throne, A.D. 50, but transferred to him
the government of the Temple, and the
right of appointing the high priest. His
opinion on religious questions would
therefore be much desired by Festus.
Subsequently he obtained the old te-
trarchies of Philip and Lysanias, and the
title of king was bestowed upon him.
We have thus a proof of St. Luke's
accuracy in that he calls him βασιλεύς,
cf. xxvi. 27, but not king of Judæa, although he was the last Jewish king in
Palestine. Bernice and Drusilla were his
sisters. He offended the Jews not only
by building his palace so as to overlook the
Temple, but also by his constant changes
in the priesthood. In the Jewish war he
took part with the Romans, by whom at
its close he was confirmed in the government of his kingdom, and received considerable additions to it. When Titus,
after the fall of Jerusalem, celebrated his
visit to Cæsarea Philippi—Herod's capital, called by him *Neronias* in honour

of Nero—by magnificent games and
shows, it would seem that Agrippa must
have been present; and if so, he doubtless joined as a Roman in the rejoicings
over the fate of his people, Hamburger,
Real-Encyclopädie des Judentums, ii., 1,
30, "Agrippa II."; Schürer, *Jewish
People*, div. i., vol. ii., p. 191 ff., "Herod"
(6), Hastings' B.D., Farrar, *The Herods*,
p. 193 ff. (1898).—Βερνίκη (Βερεν. = Macedonian form of Φερενίκη, see Blass, *in
loco*, and *C.I.G.*, 361; *C.I. Att.*, iii.,
i., 556, Headlam in Hastings' B.D.): the
eldest of the three daughters of Agrippa
I. She was betrothed, but apparently
never married, to Marcus, son of Alexander, the Alabarch of Alexandria (see
Schürer for correct reading of Jos., *Ant.*,
xix., 5, 1, *Jewish People*, div. i., vol. ii.,
p. 342, note). On his death at the age of
thirteen she was married to her uncle,
Herod of Chalcis, Jos., *u. s.*, but after a few
years she was left a widow, and lived in
the house of her brother Agrippa II. In
order to allay the worst suspicions
which were current as to this intimacy,
she married Polemon, king of Cilicia,
Ant., xx., 7, 3 (Juv., *Sat.*, vi., 156 ff.), but
she soon left him and resumed the
intimacy with her brother. Like
Agrippa she showed openly at least a
certain deference for the Jewish religion,
and on one occasion, says Schürer, *u.s.*,
p. 197, we find even her, a bigot as well
as a wanton, a Nazirite in Jerusalem,
B.J., ii., 15, 1. This was in A.D. 66, and
she endeavoured while in the capital to
stay the terrible massacre of Florus—"the
one redeeming feature of her career,"
B.D.[2]. But later on, exasperated by the
Jewish populace who burnt her palace,
she became, like her brother, a partisan
of the Romans, and in turn the mistress
of Vespasian and of Titus, Tac., *Hist.*, ii.,
81; Suet., *Tit.*, 7; Jos., *B.J.*, ii., 17, 6. O.
Holtzmann, *Neutest. Zeitgeschichte*, p. 83,

Φῆλικος δέσμιος, 15. περὶ οὗ, γενομένου μου εἰς Ἱεροσόλυμα, ἐνεφάνισαν οἱ ἀρχιερεῖς καὶ οἱ πρεσβύτεροι τῶν Ἰουδαίων, αἰτούμενοι κατ᾽ αὐτοῦ[1] δίκην· 16. πρὸς οὓς ἀπεκρίθην, ὅτι οὐκ εστιν ἔθος Ῥωμαίοις χαρίζεσθαί τινα ἄνθρωπον[2] εἰς ἀπώλειαν, πρὶν ἢ ὁ κατηγορούμενος κατὰ πρόσωπον ἔχοι τοὺς κατηγόρους, τόπον τε ἀπολογίας λάβοι περὶ τοῦ ἐγκλήματος. 17. συνελθόντων οὖν[3] αὐτῶν ἐνθάδε, ἀναβολὴν μηδεμίαν ποιησάμενος, τῇ ἑξῆς καθίσας ἐπὶ τοῦ βήματος ἐκέλευσα ἀχθῆναι τὸν ἄνδρα· 18. περὶ οὗ σταθέντες οἱ κατήγοροι οὐδεμίαν αἰτίαν[4] ἐπέφερον ὧν ὑπενόουν ἐγώ· 19. ζητήματα δέ τινα περὶ τῆς ἰδίας δεισιδαιμονίας εἶχον πρὸς αὐτόν, καὶ περί τινος

---

[1] For δικην ℵABC read καταδικην, so Tisch., W.H., R.V., Weiss, Wendt, Blass. Meyer explains καταδ. as an interpretation of δικην, but more probably καταδ. was altered into δικην on account of ver. 3 (Wendt).

[2] εις απωλ. *om.* ℵABCE, so Tisch., W.H., R.V., Weiss, Wendt, but retained by Blass, Hilg., with HLP, Syr. P. and H., Chrys., Gig.

[3] αυτων *om.* B 40, so Weiss, W.H., Blass in β text; retained by Lach., Tisch., R.V., Hilg.; Wendt doubtful.

[4] For επεφερον ℵABCEL 13, 40, 61, Tisch., W.H., Weiss, Wendt, Blass, Hilgenfeld, R.V. read εφερον. At end of verse ℵcBE 61, 100, add πονηρων, so R.V., Weiss, W.H. text, Blass; AC read πονηραν, so Lach., Tisch., Hilgenfeld, W.H. margin; ℵ*C² read πονηρα.

---

speaks of Drusilla as a worthy sister of Bernice: he might have said the same of the other sister, Mariamne, since she too left her husband for the wealth ot Demetrius, the Jewish Alabarch of Alexandria, Jos., *Ant.*, xx.,7,3.—ἀσπασόμενοι, see critical note. No doubt an official visit of congratulation paid by Agrippa as a Roman vassal upon the procurator's entry on his office. The future participle makes the sense quite easy, but if we read the aorist it looks as if Agrippa and Bernice had previously saluted Felix, and afterwards came to his official residence, Cæsarea. Rendall includes in κατήντησαν not only the notion of arrival but also of settling down for a stay short or long: "came to stay at Cæsarea and saluted Felix" (aorist), but see Simcox, *Language of the N. T.*, p. 125.

Ver. 14. ἀνέθετο: only in Luke and Paul, *cf.* Gal. ii. 2. "Laid Paul's case before the king," R.V., *cf.* 2 Macc. iii. 9, and instances in Wetstein, Gal. ii. 2. In the middle voice the idea is that of relating with a view to consulting, so here (*cf.* vv. 20, 26, Lightfoot on Gal. ii. 2); it was natural for Festus thus to consult Agrippa, see above on ver. 13.

Ver. 15. ἀρχ. καὶ οἱ πρεσβ., see on ver. 2.—ἐνεφάνισαν, see ver. 21.—δίκην, see critical note. If we read καταδίκην ="sentence," R.V., *i.e.*, of condemnation; LXX, Symm., Ps. lxxxix. 3, Wisd. xii. 27; so in Polyb., xxvi., 5, 1.

Ver. 16. ἔθος, see vi. 14.—χαρίζ., p. 489.—πρὶν ἤ . . . ἔχοι, *cf.* Luke ii. 26, the only two passages where a finite verb occurs after πρὶν in N. T., see further Burton, pp. 52, 129, 133, and Plummer, Luke, *l. c.*—κατὰ πρόσωπον, see on iii. 13.—τόπον: "opportunity," Rom. xv. 23, Ephes. iv. 27, Heb. xii. 17, Ecclus. iv. 5, *cf.* Jos., *Ant.*, xvi., 8, 5 (Polyb., i., 88, 2).

Ver. 17. ἀναβ. μηδ. ποιησάμενος, xxiv. 22, for the phrase see Thuc., ii., 42; Plut., *Camill.*, 35, and Wetstein, *in loco*.

Ver. 18. οὐδ. αἰτίαν ἐπέφ.: classical, *cf.* Thuc., v., 76; Herod., i., 26, so in Polyb. and Jos., but see critical note.—αἰτίαν: *criminis delatio, accusatio*, and so in ver. 27; see for various meanings Grimm, *sub v*.—ὑπενόουν: possibly he supposed that there were to be some charges of political disturbance or sedition like that which had recently given rise to such bloody scenes and a conflict between Greeks and Jews in the streets of Cæsarea. St. Chrys., *Hom.*, well emphasises the way in which the charges against Paul had repeatedly broken down.

Ver. 19. ζητήματα . . . τινα: plural contemptuously (Weiss). — δεισιδαιμονίας, see on xvii. 22, "religion," R.V.: in ad-

Ἰησοῦ τεθνηκότος, ὃν ἔφασκεν ὁ Παῦλος ζῆν. 20. ἀπορούμενος δὲ
ἐγὼ¹ εἰς τὴν περὶ τούτου ζήτησιν, ἔλεγον, εἰ βούλοιτο πορεύεσθαι
εἰς Ἱερουσαλήμ, κἀκεῖ κρίνεσθαι περὶ τούτων. 21. τοῦ δὲ Παύλου
ἐπικαλεσαμένου τηρηθῆναι αὐτὸν εἰς τὴν τοῦ Σεβαστοῦ διάγνωσιν,
ἐκέλευσα τηρεῖσθαι αὐτόν, ἕως οὗ² πέμψω αὐτὸν πρὸς Καίσαρα.

¹ εἰς om. ℵABHP, Tisch., W.H., R.V., Weiss, Wendt, but retained by Blass,
Hilgenfeld. Although απορ. not elsewhere in N.T. with simple acc., but as this is
good Greek no need to read the prep. For τουτου ℵABCEL read τουτων, so
Tisch. and authorities above, so Blass, but brackets περι τουτων at end of verse.

² For πεμψω ℵABCE 13, 31, 40, 61, 137, read αναπεμψω, so Tisch., W.H.,
Weiss, Wendt, Blass, Hilg., R.V. After διαγνωσιν Blass in β with Gig. adds
επειδη τε αυτον ουκ εδυναμην κριναι.

dressing a Jewish king Felix would not
have used the term offensively, especially
when we consider the official relation
of Agrippa to the Jewish religion (see
above, ver. 13), but he may well have
chosen the word because it was a neutral
word (verbum μέσον, Bengel) and did
not commit him to anything definite.—
περί τινος Ἰ.: we note again the almost
contemptuous, or at least indifferent,
tone of Festus. At the same time this
and the similar passage xviii. 15 are
proofs of the candour of St. Luke in
quoting testimonies of this kind from
men of rank: in this "aristocratic ignorance of the Roman" Zeller sees a
trait taken from life, so in Agrippa's
answer to Paul's urgency, xxvi. 28.
Festus does not even deign to mention
the kind of death (but he accepts the fact
of the death as certain); "crucem aut
nescivit, aut non curavit," Bengel; see
further Luckock, Footsteps of the Apostles
as traced by St. Luke, ii., p. 269.—ἔφασκεν: with the notion of groundless
affirmation, "alleging"; see Page, in
loco, and Meyer on Rom. i. 22 (Rev. ii.
2). Blass and Knabenbauer take it as =
dictitabat.
    Ver. 20. ἀπορούμενος δὲ: "being
perplexed how to inquire concerning,"
R.V., omitting εἰς, the verb ἀπορ. talking a direct accusative. See above on
ii. 12. Festus might have truly said that
he was perplexed, as he still was, concerning Paul, and it is possible that the
positive motive assigned for his action in
ver. 9 was an honest attempt on his part
to get more definite information at Jerusalem than he would obtain in Cæsarea—
but we know how St. Paul viewed his
question. On the other hand he may
have wished to conceal his real motive
(Weiss).
    Ver. 21. ἐπικ. τηρηθῆναι αὐτόν: on
the construction after words of request

or command of the infinitive passive see
Simcox, Language of the N. T., p. 121,
and also Blass, Gram., p. 222.—εἰς τὴν
τοῦ Σεβαστοῦ διάγνωσιν: "for the decision of the Emperor," R.V., "the Augustus," margin; cf. xxiv. 22, and for the
noun Wisd. iii. 18.—Σεβ.: here and in
ver. 25 rendered "Emperor," R.V.—the
title Augustus, A.V., might lead to confusion. The Cæsar Augustus in Luke ii.
1 was Octavian, upon whom the title of
Augustus was first conferred, Suet., Aug.,
7, B.C. 27. The title was inherited by
his successors, and thus it is ascribed
to Nero here and in ver. 25. The
divine sacredness which the title seemed
to confer (cf. its Greek form, and the
remark of Dio Cassius, liii., 16, 18, that
Augustus took the title as being himself
something more than human) excited
the scruples of Tiberius, but succeeding
emperors appear to have adopted it
without hesitation.—πέμψω, see critical
notes; the reading ἀναπέμψω would
mean, literally, "till I should send him
up," i.e., to a higher authority, cf.
Luke xxiii. 7, where it is used of "referring" to another jurisdiction, and in
vv. 11, 15, of "sending back" (Philem.
ver. 12); see Plummer's note. For
the use of this word in its technical
sense of sending to a higher authority
(as it is used in Plut., Phil., Jos.,
Polyb.) see further instances from inscriptions, Deissmann, Neue Bibelstudien, ii., 56. The verb is only used
by Luke and Paul.—Καίσαρα: in N.T.
the name is always official, never personal. It was first assumed as an official
title by Octavius, the nephew of Julius
Cæsar (see above), who doubtless took
it on account of the fame of his
uncle, and as a name not likely to be
hated and despised by the Romans like
that of "king". After the death of
Gaius Cæsar, the last of the Julian stock,

22. Ἀγρίππας δὲ πρὸς τὸν Φῆστον [1] ἔφη, Ἐβουλόμην καὶ αὐτὸς τοῦ ἀνθρώπου ἀκοῦσαι. ὁ δέ, Αὔριον, φησίν, ἀκούσῃ αὐτοῦ.

23. Τῇ οὖν ἐπαύριον ἐλθόντος τοῦ Ἀγρίππα καὶ τῆς Βερνίκης μετὰ πολλῆς φαντασίας, καὶ εἰσελθόντων εἰς τὸ ἀκροατήριον, σύν τε τοῖς χιλιάρχοις καὶ ἀνδράσι [2] τοῖς κατ' ἐξοχὴν οὖσι τῆς πόλεως,

[1] εφη om. אAB 13, so Tisch. and other authorities as in ver. 21, except Hilg. ο δε om. אAB, Vulg., Boh., so Tisch. and other authorities as above.

[2] For τοις . . . πολεως Syr. H. mg. reads *qui descendissent de provincia;* in β text Blass *adds* the words after πολεως (και). τοις om. before χιλ., so אABCE, so Tisch. and other authorities as above.

it was adopted by Claudius and by succeeding emperors, Tac., *Hist.*, ii., 80, until the third century, when the title Augustus was reserved for the supreme ruler, and that of Cæsar was adopted for those who shared his government as his possible heirs, as earlier still it had been conferred upon the heir presumptive: "Cæsar," Hastings' B.D. and B.D.².

Ver. 22. ἐβουλόμην καὶ αὐτὸς: "I also was wishing to hear the man myself," R.V., margin, imperfect, as of a wish entertained for some time; it was probable from Agrippa's position, and his official relationship to Judaism, that he would have been already interested in Paul. Bethge takes it as if it meant that a strong desire had been already awakened by the governor's statement to hear Paul, see also Winer-Moulton, xli. *a*, 2; but it is most usual to explain the imperfect here (without ἄν) rather than the direct present as used out of politeness, softening the request, "I should like," Burton, p. 16, Page, *in loco;* Lightfoot, *On a Fresh Revision, etc.*, p. 16. Calvin strangely takes the imperfect to mean that Agrippa had long cherished the wish to hear Paul, but had checked it hitherto, lest he should seem to have come with any other motive than to see Festus.— αὔριον: emphatic (and emphasised by φησίν), indicating the immediate compliance with Agrippa's wish.

Ver. 23. φαντασίας, Polyb., xv., 25, 15, etc.; Diod. Sic., xii., 83, and instances in Wetstein, *cf.* Herod., vii., 10. φαντάζεσθαι (Page); "in eadem urbe, in qua pater ipsorum a vermibus corrosus ob superbiam perierat" (Wetstein). The word here in the description may point to the presence of an eyewitness (Plumptre).—τὸ ἀκροατήριον: *auditorium*, but the article need not be pressed, as here the word may simply imply the chamber used on this occasion; it would scarcely

have been the place of formal trial, as this was not in question.—χιλιάρχοις: there were five cohorts stationed at Cæsarea, Jos., *B.J.*, iii., 4, 2, but see the remarks of Belser, *Beiträge*, pp. 138-140.—ἀνδράσι τοῖς κατ' ἐξοχὴν: evidently from the context to be regarded as heathen. Both Jew and heathen in Cæsarea had equal civil rights, and had to conduct the public affairs in common; the expression here used does not mean that Jews were excluded from the government, although it is quite in accordance with the fact of the preponderating Gentile element mentioned by Josephus, *B.J.*, iii., 9, 1; Schürer, *Jewish People*, div. ii., vol. i., p. 86, note, E.T.—κατ' ἐξοχήν: here only in N.T., not in classical Greek in this sense; primarily of any prominence, *cf.* LXX, Job xxxix. 28, ἐξόχως, 3 Macc. v. 31; *cf.* for its meaning here Cic., *Ad Att.*, iv., 15, 7, in classical Greek ἔξοχος; for the phrase, Winer-Moulton, li., 2, *g*.

Ver. 24. βασιλεῦ, see above on p. 495. —συμπαρόντες: only here in N.T., *cf.* Wisd. ix. 10, Tobit xii. 12 AB.—πᾶν τὸ πλ.: the statement is not in the least inconsistent with vv. 2, 7, 15. In Jerusalem at all events it is easily intelligible that a noisy crowd would second the actual accusers, *cf.* xvii. 5, 6, while in connection with Cæsarea we know from the latter years of the government of Felix how bitter the Jews were against the Gentiles, and how natural it would be for them to oppose the Apostle of the Gentiles, Jos., *B. J.*, ii., 13, 7; *Ant.*, xx., 8, 7.—ἐνέτυχόν μοι: "made suit to me," R.V., Wisd. viii. 20, 3 Macc. vi. 37, so in Plut., *Pomp.*, 55, *cf.* Polyc., *Martyr.*, xvii., 2, with dative only; it is used also of those making complaint before some authority, 1 Macc. viii. 32, x. 61, xi. 35, 2 Macc. iv. 36, see Westcott on Heb. vii. 25. The verb with the exception of Heb. vii. 25 and text is only found in

καὶ κελεύσαντος τοῦ Φήστου, ἤχθη ὁ Παῦλος.   24. καί φησιν ὁ
Φῆστος, Ἀγρίππα βασιλεῦ, καὶ πάντες οἱ συμπαρόντες ἡμῖν ἄνδρες,
θεωρεῖτε τοῦτον, περὶ οὗ πᾶν τὸ πλῆθος τῶν Ἰουδαίων [1] ἐνέτυχόν μοι
ἔν τε Ἱεροσολύμοις καὶ ἐνθάδε, ἐπιβοῶντες μὴ δεῖν ζῆν αὐτὸν μηκέτι.
25. ἐγὼ δὲ [2] καταλαβόμενος μηδὲν ἄξιον θανάτου αὐτὸν πεπραχέναι,
καὶ [3] αὐτοῦ δὲ τούτου ἐπικαλεσαμένου τὸν Σεβαστόν, ἔκρινα πέμπειν
αὐτόν.   26. περὶ οὗ ἀσφαλές [4] τι γράψαι τῷ κυρίῳ οὐκ ἔχω· διὰ
προήγαγον αὐτὸν ἐφ᾽ ὑμῶν, καὶ μάλιστα ἐπὶ σοῦ, βασιλεῦ Ἀγρίππα,
ὅπως τῆς ἀνακρίσεως γενομένης σχῶ τι γράψαι.   27. ἄλογον γάρ
μοι δοκεῖ, πέμποντα δέσμιον, μὴ καὶ τὰς κατ᾽ αὐτοῦ αἰτίας σημᾶναι.

[1] ενετυχον ℵCAEHLP, Tisch., W.H. marg., Weiss, but in text W.H. read ενετυχεν
(so Blass in β text), with B.H. 40, 105. For επιβοωντες ℵAB 61, Tisch., W.H.,
R.V., Weiss, Wendt read βοωντες. After ενετυχον μοι Blass in β text omits τε and
και ενθαδε (retained by Hilgenfeld) with Cod. Dublin, Berger, and proceeds with
the same Codex, and Vers. Bohem. (Tisch.), and especially with Syr. H. mg. to
reconstruct the text in β (see also Hilgenfeld's reconstruction).   οπως παραδω αυτον
εις θανατον.   (εν) ακατηγορητον δε ουκ ηδυναμην παραδουναι αυτον δια τας εντολας
ας εχομεν παρα του Σεβαστου.   εαν δε τις αυτου κατηγορειν θελη, ελεγον ακολουθειν
μοι εις Καισαρειαν, ου φυλασσεται.   ελθοντες δε εβοησαν αιρεισθαι αυτον.   ακουσας
δε αμφοτερων κατελαβομην εν μηδενι αυτον ενοχον θανατου ειναι.   λεγοντος δε μου·
θελεις κρινεσθαι μετ᾽ αυτων εν Ιεροσολυμοις; Καισαρα επεκαλεσατο.   Belser sees
in this, as compared with the shortened form in α, a weighty confirmation of Blass's
theory, p. 140, and cf. Blass, *Philology of the Gospels*, p. 150.

[2] For καταλαβ. ℵcABCE 40, 61, 68, Vulg., Boh., Syr. P., read κατελαβομην; so
Tisch., W.H., Weiss, Wendt, R.V., Hilg.

[3] και before αυτου om. ℵABCE 13, 40, 68, Vulg., Boh., and other authorities as
above.

[4] For τι γραψαι ℵABC 5, Syr. H., Tisch., and other authorities above; so Blass,
τι γραψω, but Hilg., γραψαι.

Rom. viii. 27, 34, xi. 2, in each place of
making supplication to God.   For its
use cf. ἔντευξις and ἐντυχία, of making
request to one in authority, cf. Deissmann, *Bibelstudien*, i., pp. 117, 118, 143,
144, e.g., the frequent formula on the
papyri, ἔντευξις εἰς τὸ τοῦ βασιλέως
ὄνομα.   Clemen regards the whole speech
of Festus to Agrippa, vv. 24-27, as an
interpolation on account of the repetition
of ver. 21 in ver. 25, and of the contradiction supposed to exist between vv.
27 and 19.   But Jüngst differs from
him with regard to the latter point,
and although admitting the hand of a
reviser freely in the first speech, and also
in vv. 14-21, he hesitates to define the
revision too exactly in the latter speech.
Ver. 25. καταλαβόμενος, cf. iv. 13
and x. 34; Ephes. iii. 18.—τὸν Σ.:
"sanctius hoc nomen erat quam *Cæsar*,"
Blass.—αὐτοῦ δὲ τούτου, cf. xxiv. 15,
Thuc., vi., 33 (Wetstein).
Ver. 26. ἀσφαλές τι γράψαι, *Dig.*,
xlix., 6.   "Post appellationem interpo-

sitam litteræ dandæ sunt ab eo, a quo
appellatum est, ad eum qui de appellatione cogniturus est, sive principem, sive
quem alium, quas litt. dimissorias sive
Apostolos appellant" (Wetstein and
Blass).—τῷ κυρίῳ: title refused by
Augustus and Tiberius because it
savoured too much of the relationship
between a master and a slave, and perhaps because it seemed a title more
fitting to God (as Wetstein explains it),
cf. Suet., *Aug.*, 53, *Tiber.*, 27, and Tacitus,
Ann., ii., 87.   It was accepted by Caligula and succeeding emperors (cf.
Pliny's Letter to Trajan with the
frequent *Dominus*), although Alexander
Severus forbade it to be applied to
him; for other instances, and instances on inscriptions, see Wetstein, *in
loco*, Deissmann, *Neue Bibelstudien*, 44,
and *Bibelstudien*, 77, 78, and Tert.,
Apol., 34, Polyc., *Martyr.*, viii., 2, ix. 2,
who refused to utter it with reference to
Cæsar.   For the due significance of the
word in St. Luke, who uses it more fre-

XXVI. 1. ᾽ΑΓΡΙΠΠΑΣ δὲ πρὸς τὸν Παῦλον ἔφη, ᾽Επιτρέπεταί σοι
ὑπὲρ[1] σεαυτοῦ λέγειν. τότε ὁ Παῦλος[2] ἀπελογεῖτο, ἐκτείνας τὴν
χεῖρα, 2. Περὶ πάντων ὧν ἐγκαλοῦμαι ὑπὸ ᾽Ιουδαίων, βασιλεῦ
᾽Αγρίππα, ἥγημαι ἐμαυτὸν μακάριον[3] μέλλων ἀπολογεῖσθαι ἐπὶ σοῦ
σήμερον, 3. μάλιστα γνώστην ὄντα σε πάντων τῶν κατὰ ᾽Ιουδαίους
ἐθῶν τε καὶ ζητημάτων[4] · διὸ δέομαί σου μακροθύμως ἀκοῦσαί μου.

[1] υπερ, so BLP, W.H., Weiss, but W.H. marg. have περι, so Tisch., Wendt
undecided, but apparently preferring περι.

[2] After Παυλος Blass in β adds θαρρων και εν τω αγιω πνευματι παρακλησιν
λαβων with Syr., Harcl., mg.

[3] R.V. reads επι σου μελλων σημερον απολογεισθαι, with ℵABC, Tisch., W.H.,
R.V., Weiss, Blass.

[4] After ζητηματων ℵcAC add επισταμενος, so Blass and Hilgenfeld to avoid the
anacoluthon; for the same purpose after οντα σε, 6, 29, 31, insert ειδως, but
neither part. is retained by W.H., R.V., Wendt, Weiss.

quently of Christ than the other Evangelists, see especially Wetstein, *in loco.*
—ἀνακρίσεως: here not in its strictly
legal and judicial sense of a preliminary
inquiry, but an inquiry into the case, *cf.*
ver. 22 (iv. 9), with a view to sending
a report to the emperor as judge, Renan,
Saint Paul, p. 544, and Zöckler, *in loco.*
Festus knew what the charges were, but
not their significance, and he hoped to
obtain some definite information from
Agrippa or Paul—he wanted something
ἀσφαλές; Paul had contradicted the
charge of treason, and what was left,
ver. 19, seemed full of obscurity and
absurdity.

Ver. 27. ἄλογον, *cf.* Thuc., vi., 85,
Xen., *Ages.*, xi., 1 (elsewhere in N.T.,
2 Pet. ii. 12, Jude ver. 10, *cf.* Wisd. xi. 15,
16, 3 Macc. v. 40 (A *om.*), 4 Macc. xiv.
14, 18). It would seem from the verse
that the procurator was not bound to
send the *litteræ dimissoriæ* (O. Holtzmann).—πέμποντα: for construction *cf.*
Heb. ii. 10, or the expression may be
quite general "that any one sending,"
etc.—σημᾶναι: here *per litteras signi-
ficare*, as in classical Greek (Wetstein).
This decisive turn given to events by
Paul's appeal is regarded by Weizsäcker
(*Apostolic Age*, ii., 124, E.T.) as the
most certain event in the whole history
of the case; Paul as a prisoner could
only be taken to Rome if he was to be
brought before the emperor's court, and
this had to be done if he invoked such
intervention. On Zeller's and Weizsäcker's attempt to see in the appearance
of Paul before Agrippa a mere repetition
of the episode of our Lord before Annas
cf. Spitta's reply, *Apostelgeschichte*, p.
281.

CHAPTER XXVI.—Ver. 1. ἐπιτρέ-
πεται, Burton, p. 9, on "the aoristic
present". Agrippa as a king and as a
guest presides; and Paul addresses himself specially to him, *cf.* vv. 2, 7, 13,
19, 27; *cf.* xxviii. 16, 1 Cor. xiv. 34, for
the passive with infinitive, and for other
instances of the word in the same sense
as here xxi. 39, 40, xxvii. 3; the verb is
similarly used in all of the Gospels (three
times in Luke), and in 1 Cor. xvi. 7, 1
Tim. ii. 12, Heb. vi. 3.—ἐκτείνας: not
the same as in xii. 17, xiii. 16; here not to
ensure silence, but *gestus est oratorius*,
cf. ver. 29. — ἀπελογεῖτο, see above,
xxiv. 10, although not formally on trial,
the word shows that the Apostle was
defending himself.

Ver. 2. ἐπὶ σοῦ, *cf.* xxiv. 19.—ἐγκαλοῦμαι, see on xix. 38.—ὑπὸ ᾽Ιουδ.: "by
Jews" simply (*cf.* xxv. 10), and therefore
he is glad to address one acquainted with
Jewish customs, but see on ver. 4.—
ἥγημαι ἐμαυτὸν μακ.: only here by Luke
in this sense, but frequently so used by
St. Paul in his Epistles eleven times, *cf.*,
e.g., Phil. iii. 7, 1 Tim. vi. 1. St. Paul
too commences with a "captatio benevolentiæ," "sed absque adulatione,"
Blass: "and yet had he been conscious
of guilt, he should have feared being
tried in the presence of one who knew
all the facts; but this is a mark of a clear
conscience, not to shrink from a judge
who has an accurate knowledge of the
circumstances, but even to rejoice and to
call himself happy," Chrys., *Hom.*, liii.

Ver. 3. μάλιστα: (1) "especially because thou art expert," R.V. (so Blass,
Felten, Weiss), or (2) "because thou
art specially expert," margin, R.V. (so
Wendt, Rendall, Bethge, Zöckler). See

4. τὴν μὲν οὖν βίωσίν μου [1] τὴν ἐκ νεότητος, τὴν ἀπ᾽ ἀρχῆς γενομένην ἐν τῷ ἔθνει μου ἐν Ἱεροσολύμοις, ἴσασι πάντες οἱ Ἰουδαῖοι, 5. προγινώσκοντές με ἄνωθεν, (ἐὰν θέλωσι μαρτυρεῖν,) ὅτι κατὰ τὴν ἀκριβεστάτην αἵρεσιν τῆς ἡμετέρας [2] θρησκείας ἔζησα Φαρισαῖος·

[1] τὴν before εκ νεοτ., retained by Tisch., Blass and Hilg., is omitted by Weiss, W.H., Wendt, with BC*H. την απ᾽ αρχης om. by Blass in β, with Gig. After εν ℵABEgr 40, Syr. P., Tisch., W.H., R.V., Wendt, Weiss, Hilg. add τε, Blass omits in β text.

[2] θρησκειας, so W.H., Weiss, Blass, Hilg., with ABHLP; Tisch. with ℵCE read θρησκιας, Winer-Schmiedel, p. 44.

critical notes, and for construction Winer-Moulton, lxiii., 2, *a*, and xxxii. 7, Wendt (1899), p. 389.—γνώστην ὄντα: an anacoluthon, as if an accusative had been previously used, πρός σε . . . ἀπολ., *cf.* xxii. 1. Zöckler takes it as an accusative absolute, following A. Buttmann (see Winer-Moulton., *u. s.*), but no clear example (*cf.* Ephes. i. 18, and Hackett's note, *in loco*).—γνώστην, *cf.* Susannah, ver. 42 (Theod., not LXX), with genitive as here.—ἐθῶν τε καὶ ζητ.: "*consuetudinum* in practicis, *quæstionum* in theoreticis," Bengel, on ver. 32 see above, xxv. 19.—μακροθύμως, only here in N.T., but μακροθυμία frequent in St. Paul's Epistles (*cf.* Ecclus. v. 11).

Ver. 4. μὲν οὖν: with no formal antithesis, but as marking the opposition between his present and former mode of life, a contrast dropped for the moment, and resumed again in ver. 9; see Rendall, Appendix on μὲν οὖν, but also Page, *in loco*, and notes below on ver. 9.—βίωσιν: *vivendi et agendi ratio*, Grimm; *cf.* the same word used in the description of a life very similar to that of Paul before he became a Christian, Ecclus., *Prol.*, 12, διὰ τῆς ἐννόμου βιώσεως (Symm., Ps. xxxviii. (xxxix.) 6).—νεότητος, 1 Tim. iv. 12, only elsewhere in N.T. in Luke xviii. 21, and in parallel passage, Mark x. 20, in LXX Gen. xliii. 33, Job xxxi. 18, etc. From its use with reference to Timothy it is evident that the word did not imply the earliest years of life, and although Paul may probably have removed to Jerusalem at an early age, the context does not require a reference to the years he had lived before his removal.—τὴν ἀπ᾽ ἀρχῆς γεν.: explanatory of preceding,— the commencement of his training, which was not only amongst his own nation, but also specially τε, at Jerusalem, *cf.* xxii. 3. The Apostle presses the point to show that he was most unlikely to act in violation of Jewish feeling—he is still a Jew.—ἴσασι: only here in N.T., per-

haps a conscious classicism, Simcox, *Language of the N.T.*, p. 33; on the classical forms in this speech see Blass, *Proleg.*, p. 14, and *Gram.*, p. 49, and especially p. 5, *Philology of the Gospels*, p. 9. These literary forms are what we should have expected the Apostle to employ before an audience so distinguished. —Ἰουδαῖοι: Blass gives a further reason for the omission of article, "abest ut 2, 3, 7, 21, sec. usum Atticorum, *cf.* xvii. 21".

Ver. 5. προγιν. με: knowing me beforehand, *i.e.*, ἄνωθεν, from the beginning of my public education in Jerusalem. προγ.: twice elsewhere by Paul, Rom. viii. 29, xi. 2, also in 1 Pet. i. 20, 2 Pet. iii. 17. For ἀπ᾽ ἀρχῆς and ἄνωθεν *cf.* Luke i. 2, 3, and for the former also 2 Thess. ii. 13.—ἀκριβ.: "the straitest sect," R.V. on the double accusative in A.V. see Humphry, *Commentary on R.V.* For this classical form, the only instance of a superlative in -τατος in N.T., see especially Blass, *u. s.*, *cf.* ver. 4; on the term in its close connection with Pharisaism *cf.* Jos., *B.J.*, i., 5, 2; *Ant.*, xvii., 2, 4, and references above on xxii. 3. Their "straitness" included not only observance and interpretation of the Mosaic law, but also of the whole παράδοσις τῶν πρεσβυτέρων.—αἵρεσιν, see on v. 17, the word in the sense of "a sect" was rightly applied to the exclusiveness of Pharisaism as in the N.T., *cf.* xv. 5, and in Jos., *cf. Vita*, 38. —θρησκείας: "*cultus religionis*, potissimum *externus*," Grimm, so here and in the other places where it occurs in N.T., Col. ii. 18, James i. 26, 27; twice in Wisdom, xiv. 18, 27, of the worship of idols; in Ecclus. xxii. 5 the reading is doubtful; in 4 Macc. v. 6, 13, of the religion of the Jews. The instances of its use both in Philo and Josephus show that it was plainly distinguished from εὐσεβεία and ὁσιότης. Thus it is contrasted with the latter by Philo, *Quod det. potiori insid.*, c. 7: θρησκείαν ἀντὶ

6 καὶ νῦν ἐπ' ἐλπίδι τῆς [1] πρὸς τοὺς πατέρας ἐπαγγελίας γενομένης ὑπὸ τοῦ Θεοῦ ἕστηκα κρινόμενος, 7. εἰς ἣν τὸ δωδεκάφυλον ἡμῶν ἐν ἐκτενείᾳ νύκτα καὶ ἡμέραν λατρεῦον ἐλπίζει [2] καταντῆσαι· περὶ ἧς ἐλπίδος ἐγκαλοῦμαι, βασιλεῦ Ἀγρίππα, ὑπὸ τῶν Ἰουδαίων. 8. τί;

[1] For πρὸς ℵABE have εἰς; so Tisch., W.H., Blass, R.V., Weiss, Wendt, Hilgenfeld; for T.R., cf. xiii. 32. After πατέρας ℵABCE 61, Vulg., Syr. P.H., Boh. add ημων, so Tisch., W.H., R.V., Weiss, Wendt, Hilg., but Blass brackets.

[2] For καταντησαι B has καταντησειν, so W.H. marg., Weiss, βασ. at end of verse ℵBCEI, Tisch., W.H., R.V., Blass, Weiss, Wendt, Hilg. After υπο, των is omitted by ℵABCEHLP, so by Tisch and other authorities above.

ὁσιότητος ἡγούμενος; and in Josephus it is frequently used of the public worship of God, worship in its external aspect, cf. Ant., ix., 13, 3; xii., 5, 4; v., 10, 1; xii., 6, 2. It was therefore a very natural word for St. Paul to use, and it is not necessary to suppose that he did so merely for the sake of Festus and the Romans (Blass), although the word was used of one mode of worship when contrasted with another; see further Hatch, Essays in B.G., p. 55; Trench, Synonyms, i., p. 200, and Mayor on James i. 26.—Φαρισαῖος: emphatic at the end, expressing the "straitest sect" by name, cf. Gal. i. 14, Phil. iii. 5, 6.

Ver. 6. καὶ νῦν: the expression does not indicate any contrast with ver. 4: this hope for which he stands to be judged is in full accord with his whole past life.—ἐπ' ἐλπίδι: phrase only found elsewhere in St. Paul's Epistles, where it is frequent; Rom. viii. 20, 1 Cor. ix. 10, Tit. i. 2. A hope not merely of the resurrection of the dead, but of the Messiah's kingdom with which the resurrection was connected, as the context points to the national hope of Israel; cf. Schürer, Jewish People, div. ii., vol. ii., p. 175, E.T., see also pp. 137, 148, 149, and Edersheim, Jesus the Messiah, i., pp. 75, 79, on the strong bond of the common hope of Israel.—πρὸς τοὺς πατέρας, see critical note. With either preposition we have a Pauline expression; on the force of εἰς see Alford and Weiss, in loco. If we read ἡμῶν after πατ. perhaps including Agrippa with himself as a Jew.

Ver. 7. εἰς ἣν: unto which promise, not spem (Grotius, Bengel), καταντῆσαι εἰς, cf. the same construction with the same verb, Phil. iii. 11, Ephes. iv. 13, only in Luke and Paul, but never by the former elsewhere in metaphorical sense; in classical Greek after verbs of hoping we should have had a future, but in N.T. generally aorist infinitive, Viteau, Le

Grec du N.T., p. 154 (1893).—τὸ δωδεκάφυλον: here only in biblical Greek; perhaps used after the mention of the fathers, as the heads of the tribes; for the word cf. Prot. Jac., i., 3, Clem. Rom., Cor., lv., 6 (cf. xxxi. 4), and Orac. Syb., λαὸς ὁ δωδεκάφυλος; the expression was full of hope, and pointed to a national reunion under the Messiah; for the intensity of this hope, and of the restoration of the tribes of Israel, see on iii. 21 (p. 115), and references in ver. 6, Edersheim, Jewish Social Life, p. 67, and especially Psalms of Solomon, xviii., 28, 30, 50.—ἐν ἐκτενείᾳ, cf. xii. 5, 2 Macc. xiv. 38, 3 Macc. vi. 41, Jud. iv. 9 (twice?); Cic., Ad Att., x., 17, 1. See Hatch, u. s., p. 12.—νύκτα καὶ ἡμέραν, cf. xx. 31, also used by Paul; elsewhere in his Epistles five times, and once in Mark v. in genitive, 1 Thess. ii. 9, iii. 10; 2 Thess. iii. 8; 1 Tim. v. 5; 2 Tim. i. 3; Mark v. 5. The precise phrase in the accusative also occurs in Luke ii. 37, Mark iv. 25.—λατρεῦον, cf. Luke ii. 37, joined with νύκτα καὶ ἡμ. as here, and in both places of the earnest prayer for the Messiah's coming; same phrase elsewhere in N.T. only in Rev. vii. 15. For the force of the expression here and its relation to the Temple worship see Blass, in loco, and Schürer, Jewish People, div. ii., vol. ii., p. 174, E.T.—ὑπὸ Ἰουδ.: by Jews, O King! Agrippa knew that this hope, nowever misdirected, was the hope of every Israelite, and the Apostle lays stress upon the strange fact that Jews should thus persecute one who identified himself with their deepest and most enduring hopes.

Ver. 8. R.V. gives more clearly the significance of the original, "Why is it judged incredible with you, if God (as He does) raises the dead?" εἰ with indicative assumes that the hypothesis is true, Vulgate "si Deus mortuos suscitat?" cf. Luke xvi. 31. It has sometimes been thought that St. Paul

ἄπιστον κρίνεται παρ' ὑμῖν, εἰ ὁ Θεὸς νεκροὺς ἐγείρει; 9. ἐγὼ μὲν
οὖν ἔδοξα ἐμαυτῷ πρὸς τὸ ὄνομα Ἰησοῦ τοῦ Ναζωραίου δεῖν πολλὰ
ἐναντία πρᾶξαι· 10. ὃ καὶ ἐποίησα ἐν Ἱεροσολύμοις, καὶ πολλοὺς
τῶν ἁγίων ἐγὼ φυλακαῖς κατέκλεισα, τὴν παρὰ τῶν ἀρχιερέων

here makes a special appeal to the Sadducean part of his audience—**παρ' ὑμῖν**—including among them Agrippa, with his indifference and practical Sadduceism (Alford), with his policy favouring the Sadducees in the appointment of the high priests (Felten): others have seen in the words a reference to the general resurrection with which the Apostle's Messianic belief was connected, or to cases of resurrection in the history of Israel, as, *e.g.*, 1 Kings xvii., 2 Kings iv., as if the speaker would ask: Why is it judged a thing incredible in your judgment when you have instances before you in the sacred books accepted by Agrippa and the Jews? But it is far better to consider the words in connection with the great truth to which the whole speech was meant to lead up, ver. 23, *viz.*, that Jesus, although crucified, had risen again, that He was at this moment a living Person, and by His resurrection had been proved to be the Messiah, the fulfiller of the hope of Israel. Zöckler regards the question as forming a kind of transition from the general hope of the Jews in a Messiah to the specific Christian hope in Jesus.—**ἄπιστον**: only here in Acts, twice in Luke's Gospel, but frequent in St. Paul's Epistles of those who believed not. See further Nestle, *Philologica Sacra*, p. 54, 1896, and Wendt, p. 391 and note (1899). Nestle proposes to place the verse as out of connection here between vv. 22 and 23, with a full stop at the end of the former; and Wendt commends this view.

Ver. 9. **ἐγὼ μὲν οὖν**: the words may be taken as simply resuming the narrative of the Apostle's life which he had commenced in vv. 4 and 5, the three succeeding verses forming a parenthesis, or as an answer to the question of ver. 8, the real antithesis to **μὲν οὖν**, ver. 9, and the narrative, vv. 9-11, being found in ver. 12 and what follows. On **μὲν οὖν** see Rendall, *Acts*, Appendix, p. 163, and also Page on ii. 41, *Acts*, pp. 94, 95; see also critical note above.—**ἔδοξα ἐμαυτῷ**: *mihi ipsi videbar;* so in classical Greek. If with Weiss, Wendt, Bethge we lay stress on **ἐμαυ.**, the Apostle explains the fact that this obligation was his own wilful self-delusion. In classical Greek

instead of the impersonal construction we have frequently the personal construction with the infinitive as here, *cf.* 2 Cor. x. 9—only in Luke and Paul, indication of literary style, Viteau, *Le Grec du N.T.*, p. 152 (1893).—**τὸ ὄνομα Ἰ. τοῦ Ν.**, see on iv. 10, 12.—**ἐναντία πρᾶξαι**, *cf.* xxviii. 17, and also 1 Thess. ii. 15, Tit. ii. 8.

Ver. 10. **ὃ καὶ ἐποίησα**, *cf.* Gal. ii. 10 (Bethge, p. 272), on the distinction between **πράσσειν** and **ποιεῖν** Westcott on St. John iii. 22.—**ἐγὼ**: emphatic.—**τῶν ἁγίων**, see above ix. 13, *cf.* its use in ix. 32; the word aggravates St. Paul's own guilt. Agrippa too would know of pious Jews by the same designation.—**ἀναιρ. τε αὐτῶν**: probably pointing to more deaths, not as expressing the death of Stephen alone, *cf.* viii. 1, ix. 1, xxii. 4. The state of affairs which rendered the murder of St. Stephen possible in the capital would easily account for similar acts of outrage in other places, so that there is no need to suppose with Weiss that the notice here is unhistorical.—**κατήνεγκα ψῆφον**: "I gave my vote," R.V., the **ψῆφος**, literally the pebble used in voting, *calculum defero* sc. *in urnam* (Grimm), *i.e.*, *addo calculum, approbo*, *cf.* **ψῆφον φέρειν**, **ἐπιφ.** or **ἐκφ.** If the phrase is taken quite literally, it is said to denote the vote of a judge, so that Paul must have been a member of the Sanhedrim, and gave his vote for the death of St. Stephen and other Christians. On the other hand the phrase is sometimes taken as simply = **συνευδοκεῖν τῇ ἀναιρέσει** (so amongst recent writers, Knabenbauer), xxii. 20. (C. and H. think that if not a member of the Sanhedrim at the time of Stephen's death, he was elected soon after, whilst Weiss holds that if the expression does not imply that the writer represents Paul by mistake as a member of the Sanhedrim, it can only be understood as meaning that by his testimony Paul gave a decisive weight to the verdict in condemnation of the Christians.) Certainly it seems, as Bethge urges, difficult to suppose that Paul was a member of such an august body as the Sanhedrim, not only on account of his probable age at the time of his conversion, but also because of his comparatively obscure circumstances. The Sanhedrim was an

ἐξουσίαν λαβών. ἀναιρουμένων τε αὐτῶν κατήνεγκα ψῆφον. 11.
καὶ κατὰ πάσας τὰς συναγωγὰς πολλάκις τιμωρῶν αὐτούς, ἠνάγκαζον
βλασφημεῖν· περισσῶς τε ἐμμαινόμενος αὐτοῖς, ἐδίωκον ἕως καὶ
εἰς τὰς ἔξω πόλεις. 12. ἐν οἷς [1] καὶ πορευόμενος εἰς τὴν Δαμασκὸν
μετ᾽ ἐξουσίας καὶ ἐπιτροπῆς τῆς παρὰ τῶν ἀρχιερέων, 13. ἡμέρας
μέσης κατὰ τὴν ὁδὸν εἶδον, βασιλεῦ, οὐρανόθεν ὑπὲρ τὴν λαμπρότητα

---

[1] καὶ *om.* ℵABCEI, 13, 40, 61, so Tisch. and other authorities in ver. 7. For
T.R. read της των αρχ. ℵ*B, Tisch., Weiss, Wendt, R.V., Blass; της παρα *om.*
AEI 40, 68, Lach.

---

assembly of aristocrats, composed too of
men of mature years and marked influence, and the question may be asked
how Saul of Tarsus, who may not even
have had a stated residence in the Holy
City, could have found a place in the ranks
of an assembly numbering the members
of the high priestly families and the
principal men of Judæa: see *Expositor*,
June, 1897, and also for the bearing of
the statement on the question of Paul's
marriage, with Hackett's note, *in loco*.
For the voting in the Sanhedrim see
Schürer, div. ii., vol. i., p. 194. E.T.
Rendall, p. 336, meets the difficulty above
by referring the expression under discussion to a kind of popular vote confirming
the sentence of the court against Stephen,
for which he finds support in the language
of the law and in the narrative of the
proto-martyr's condemnation.

Ver. 11. τιμωρῶν (*cf.* xxii. 5), more
usually in the middle voice in this sense,
although the active is so used sometimes
in classical Greek, Soph., *O. T.*, 107, 140,
Polyb., ii., 56, 15. For ecclesiastial
censures and punishments see Edersheim,
History of the Jewish Nation, p. 374, *cf.*
Matt. x. 17, xxiii. 34.—ἠνάγκαζον: "I
strove to make them blaspheme," R.V.,
all other E.V. render "I compelled them
to blaspheme," but the imperfect leaves
it quite doubtful as to whether the persecutor succeeded in his attempts or not.
The imperfect may thus be regarded as
conative, Burton, p. 12, *cf.* Luke i. 59,
Matt. iii. 14. Blass points out that it
may have the force of repeated action (*cf.*
ἐδίωκον), but even if so, it does not say
that the compulsion was effectual, *Gram.*,
p. 186. See further Page, *in loco*, for
the rendering of R.V., which he regards as correct. A striking parallel
may be adduced from Pliny's Letter to
Trajan, x., 97, where the Christians are
urged to call upon the gods, to worship the emperor, and to blaspheme
Christ, "quorum nihil cogi posse dicuntur

qui sunt revera Christiani," *cf.* Polycarp, *Martyr.*, ix., 2, 3.—βλασφημεῖν, *i.e.*,
Jesus, "maledicere Christo," Pliny, *u. s.*,
James ii. 7; *cf.* 1 Tim. i. 13 with this
passage, and Paul's later reflections on
his conduct.—ἕως καὶ εἰς τὰς ἔξω π.:
"even unto foreign cities," R.V., so that
other cities besides Damascus had been
included in the persecution, or would
have been included if Saul's attempt
had been successful.—ἐδίωκον: "I set
about persecuting them". The imperfect
ἐδίωκ. may however denote repeated
action, and may indicate that Saul had
already visited other foreign cities. Weiss
regards the τε as connecting the two
imperfects *de conatu* together—the latter
imperfect being regarded as a continuation of the former, in case the victims
sought to save themselves by flight.
—ἐμμαιν.: only in Josephus once, *Ant.*,
xvii., 6, 5, but ἐμμανής in Wisd. xiv. 23,
and in classical Greek, so also ἐκμαίνεσ-
θαι.

Ver. 12. ἐν οἷς, *i.e.*, as I was thus
engaged, *inter quæ*, "on which errand,"
R.V. margin, see xxiv. 18.—ἐπιτροπῆς,
2 Macc. xiii. 14, Polyb., iii., 15, 7, "commission," A. and R.V. "Paulus erat
commissarius," Bengel, the two nouns
show the fulness of the authority committed to Paul.

Ver. 13. ἡμέρας μέσης: temporal
genitive, Blass, *Gram.*, p. 107 (in classical
Greek ἡμ. μεσούσα). The expression is
perhaps stronger than in xxii. 6, in the
bright full light of day.—κατὰ τὴν ὁδὸν:
"on the way," and so foreboding nothing
(Weiss).—βασιλεῦ: "advertitur rex ad
miraculum rei," Blass, *cf.* ver. 7, so
Weiss.—ὑπὲρ τὴν λαμπ.: here only
expressly, but implied in ix. 3, xxii. 6,
indicating the supernatural nature of the
light; noun only here in N.T., *cf.* Dan.
xii. 3.—περιλάμψαν: only in Luke, *cf.*
Luke ii. 9, where the word is also used
for a light from heaven; nowhere else in
N.T., but the verb is found in Plutarch,

τοῦ ἡλίου περιλάμψαν με φῶς καὶ τοὺς σὺν ἐμοὶ πορευομένους. 14.
πάντων δὲ [1] καταπεσόντων ἡμῶν εἰς τὴν γῆν, ἤκουσα φωνὴν λαλοῦσαν
πρός με, καὶ λέγουσαν τῇ Ἑβραΐδι διαλέκτῳ, Σαούλ, Σαούλ, τί με
διώκεις; σκληρόν σοι πρὸς κέντρα λακτίζειν. 15. ἐγὼ δὲ εἶπον,

[1] For δε ℵABEI, Syrr. H.P., Vulg. read τε, Tisch., W.H., R.V., Blass, Weiss,
Wendt, Hilgenfeld. For T.R. φωνην λ. . . . και λεγ. ℵBCI, Vulg., Syrr. P.H.,
Boh., read φ. λεγουσαν προς με, so Tisch., W.H., Weiss, Wendt, R.V. After γην
Blass in β adds δια τον φοβον εγω μονος, 137 Syr. H. mg. (Gig.), so Hilg.

Josephus. The fact that the light shone round about Paul and his companions is at any rate not excluded by ix. 7 or xxii. 9, as Weiss notes. It is quite in accordance with the truth of the facts that the more vivid expression should occur in Paul's own recital.

Ver. 14. See notes on ix. 7 and xxii. 7, and reading above in β.—τῇ Ἑβραΐδι διαλ.: this is intimated in ix. 4 and xxii. 7 by the form Σαούλ, but here the words are inserted because Paul was speaking in Greek, or perhaps he spoke the solemn words, indelible in his memory, as they were uttered, in Hebrew, for Agrippa (Alford). — σκληρόν σοι κ.τ.λ.: a proverb which finds expression both in Greek and in Latin literature (see instances in Wetstein): cf. Scholiast on Pind., Pyth., ii., 173 : ἡ δὲ τροπὴ ἀπὸ τῶν βοῶν· τῶν γὰρ οἱ ἄτακτοι κατὰ τὴν γεωργίαν κεντριζόμενοι ὑπὸ τοῦ ἀροῦντος, λακτίζουσι τὸ κέντρον καὶ μᾶλλον πλήττονται. Cf. also Aesch., Agam., 1633 (cf. Prom., 323), Eur., Bacch., 791, and in Latin, Terence, Phorm., i., 2, 27; Plautus, Truc., iv., 2, 59; and there may have been a similar proverb current among the Hebrews. Blass, Gram., pp. 5, 6, thinks that the introduction of the proverb on this occasion before Festus and Agrippa points to the culture which Paul possessed, and which he called into requisition in addressing an educated assembly. It is not wise to press too closely a proverbial saying with regard to Saul's state of mind before his conversion; the words may simply mean to intimate to him that it was a foolish and inefficacious effort to try to persecute Jesus in His followers, an effort which would only inflict deeper wounds upon himself, an effort as idle as that described by the Psalmist, Ps. ii. 3, 4. At all events Paul's statement here must be compared with his statements elsewhere, 1 Tim. i. 13; see Witness of the Epistles, p. 389 ff., and Bethge, Die Paulinischen Reden, p. 275.

Ver. 15. Evidently the following verses contain a summary of what in the other two accounts of the Conversion is spoken to Paul by Ananias, and revealed by the Lord in a vision, cf. ix. 15, xxii. 14 (so Alford, Felten, Zöckler). This is far more satisfactory than to suppose that the two narratives in ix. and xxii. are really dependent upon xxvi., the author having employed in them an oral tradition relating to Ananias, without being at all aware that by introducing such an account he was really contradicting a point upon which Paul lays special stress, viz., the fact that he had received his apostleship neither from man nor through man, Gal. i. 1 (so Wendt (1899), p. 189, and McGiffert, pp. 120 and 355). But in the first place nothing is said as to the Apostle receiving his Apostleship from Ananias; he receives recovery of sight from him, but his call to his Apostleship commences with his call before Damascus: "epocha apostolatus Paulini cum hoc ipso conversionis articulo incipit," Bengel; and see specially Beyschlag, Studien und Kritiken, p. 220, 1864, on Gal. i. 15 (Witness of the Epistles, p. 379, 1892); and, further, the introduction and omission of Ananias are in themselves strong corroborations of the naturalness of the three accounts of the Conversion. Thus in chap. xxii., ver. 12, cf. ix. 10, "non conveniebat in hunc locum uberior de An. narratio, ix. 10 ff., sed conveniebat præconium ejus, quod non est illic" (Blass); so too it was natural and important to emphasise before a Jewish audience the description of Ananias (in ix. 10 he is simply τις μαθητής) as εὐλαβὴς κατὰ τὸν νόμον, well reported of by all the Jews, whereas in xxvi. "tota persona Ananiæ sublata est, quippe quæ non esset apta apud hos auditores" (Blass). The three narratives agree in the main facts (see notes in comment., and Zöckler, Apostelgeschichte, 2nd edit., p. 216), and "the slight variations in the three accounts do not seem to be of any consequence," Ramsay, Saint Paul, p. 379, cf. also

Τίς εἶ, Κύριε; ὁ δὲ[1] εἶπεν, Ἐγώ εἰμι Ἰησοῦς ὃν σὺ διώκεις. 16. ἀλλὰ ἀνάστηθι, καὶ στῆθι ἐπὶ τοὺς πόδας σου· εἰς τοῦτο γὰρ ὤφθην σοι, προχειρίσασθαί σε ὑπηρέτην καὶ μάρτυρα ὧν τε εἶδες[2] ὧν τε ὀφθήσομαί σοι, 17. ἐξαιρούμενός σε ἐκ τοῦ λαοῦ καὶ[3] τῶν ἐθνῶν, εἰς οὓς

[1] ὁ δε, *add* Κυριος ℵABCEIL, so Tisch., W.H., R.V., Blass, Weiss, Wendt, Hilg.

[2] After ειδες BC* 105, 137, Syrr. P.H., Arm., Ambr., Aug. add με, so W.H., Weiss, Hilg., R.V. text, but R.V. marg. Blass and Wendt omit; see the latter's note, p. 394 (1899), as against Weiss.

[3] Before των εθνων ℵABEgr.I 13, 40, 61, repeat εκ, so Tisch., W.H., R.V., Blass, Hilg., Weiss, Wendt. For νυν ℵABCEHILP read εγω, so other authorities above.

Renan, *Apostles*, p. 13, E.T., Salmon, *Introd.*, p. 121. Clemen, who agrees in the main with Wendt in regarding xxvi. as the original narrative, refers chap. ix. to his Redactor Antijudaicus, and chap. xxii. to his Redactor Judaicus; he sees evidences of the hand of the former in ix., 10, 15, 17, and of the latter in xxii. 12, 14. If xxii. 17 f., and the words in ver. 15, πρὸς πάντας ἀνθρώπους, do not fit in with this theory, they are ascribed by Clemen to the later Redactor Antijudaicus; but the latter expression πρὸς π. ἀνθ. is already contained in the meaning of the original source, xxvi. 17, 20 a and c (20b belonging, according to Clemen, to the Redactor Judaicus). Space forbids any further examination of passages in the three narratives with regard to which the partition critics, Clemen and Jüngst, are again hopelessly at variance with each other, but *cf.* Jüngst, *Apostelgeschichte*, pp. 84, 87, 89, 94, and the strictures of Knabenbauer, *Actus Apostolorum*, p. 11 (1899). But it is strange to find that Clemen should be prepared to fall back upon the view of Baur, *Paulus*, ii., 13, that the narrative of Paul's blindness was derived from the spiritual blindness referred to in xxvi. 17, and that *therefore* this narrative is evidently older than the other accounts in ix. and xxii., which introduce a tragical blindness. As Wendt points out, there is no hint in the text that Paul's blindness was symbolical, and there is nothing to suggest the circumstantial narratives relating to Ananias in the phrase xxvi. 17, which relates not to the Apostle's own conversion, but to his power of converting others.

Ver. 16. ἀλλὰ ἀνάστηθι: "Prostravit Christus Paulum ut eum humiliaret; nunc eum erigit ac jubet bono esse animo," Calvin; for the expression *cf.* Ezek. ii. 1, 2.—προχειρ., *cf.* iii. 14, xxii.

14, ix. 15, σκεῦος ἐκλογῆς.—ὑπηρέτην καὶ μάρτυρα ὧν τε εἶδες, so like the Twelve, and *cf.* also αὐτόπται καὶ ὑπηρέται τοῦ λόγου, Luke i. 1; in Cor. iv. 1 St. Paul speaks of himself as ὑπηρέτης. —ὧν τε εἶδές με, see critical note, "wherein thou hast seen me," R.V., *cf.* 1 Cor. ix. 1, quite in harmony with the stress which the Apostle there lays upon "seeing the Lord".—ὧν τε ὀφθ. = τούτων ἅ: "and of the things wherein I will appear to thee," so A. and R.V. *Cf.* Acts xviii. 9, xxii. 18, 21, xxiii. 11, 2 Cor. xii. 2. ὀφθ., future passive (Grimm-Thayer), cannot be rendered "I will make thee to see," or "I will communicate to thee by vision," as if = ἐγὼ ὑποδείξω, ix. 16. For construction see Page, and Blass, *in loco*.

Ver. 17. ἐξαιρούμενός σε: "delivering," A. and R.V. Vulgate, *eripiens*, and so the word is elsewhere rendered in N.T., *cf.* vii. 10, 34, xii. 11, xxiii. 27, Gal. i. 4, and below, ver. 22; so very frequently in LXX (although twice in the sense below, Job xxxvi. 21, Isa. xlviii. 10). It may be called a Lucan-Pauline word (only twice elsewhere in N.T.; in St. Matt. v. 29, xviii. 9, but in an entirely different signification). Blass renders it as above, and points out that there is no reason for rendering it "choosing" in this one passage, a sense which is not at all fitted to the context; for the language *cf.* 1 Chron. xvi. 35, Jer. i. 8, so Wendt (1899, but in the sense below previously), Weiss, Felten, Hackett, Bethge, Knabenbauer. It is no objection to say that Paul was not delivered, but was persecuted all his life long, for he was delivered in the sense of deliverance to proclaim the message for which he was sent as an Apostle. On the other hand Overbeck, Rendall, Page, so C. and H. take it in the sense of "choosing," *cf.* ix. 15, σκεῦος ἐκλογῆς. Grimm-Thayer is

νῦν σε ἀποστέλλω, 18. ἀνοῖξαι ὀφθαλμοὺς αὐτῶν, τοῦ ἐπιστρέψαι ἀπὸ
σκότους εἰς φῶς καὶ τῆς ἐξουσίας τοῦ Σατανᾶ ἐπὶ τὸν Θεόν, τοῦ
λαβεῖν αὐτοὺς ἄφεσιν ἁμαρτιῶν, καὶ κλῆρον ἐν τοῖς ἡγιασμένοις,

doubtful. Rendall urges that the word cannot mean "delivering" without some phrase such as ἐκ χειρός, as common in the LXX, but *cf.* on the other hand LXX, Judg. x. 15, xviii. 28 A, Ps. xxx. 2, xlix. 15, Hosea v. 14, etc. But how could Paul be said to be chosen ἐξ ἐθνῶν? The phrase would certainly sound strange to him as a description of his own position. Rendall also objects that in 1 Chron. xvi. 35 the word means to gather the scattered exiles from among the heathen as the context shows, but the Hebrew verb נָצַל means to deliver, and is so rendered, *l. c.*, in A. and R. V. It is also urged that λαός is always the name of honour, and that elsewhere the enemies of the Apostle were named Ἰουδαῖοι; but not only is the collocation "the people and the Gentiles" a common one, *cf.* ver. 23, Rom. xv. 10, but λαός is used of the unbelieving Jews in describing hostility to the Gospel, *cf.* iv. 27, xii. 4. Agrippa would understand the distinction between λαός and ἔθνη. ἐγὼ "denotat auctoritatem mittentis," Bengel.—ἀποστέλλω: Paul receives his Apostolic commission direct from Christ as much as the Twelve; Gal. i. 1, 16, 17, Rom. i. 5 (Matt. x. 16, John xx. 21-23); *cf.* Acts i. 25.
Ver. 18. ἀνοῖξαι ὀφθ. αὐτῶν, *cf.* Acts ix. 8, 40, and also Matt. ix. 30; so too Isai. xxxv. 5, xlii. 7. Both Jews and Gentiles were blinded (οὓς above, referring to both), the former because seeing they saw not, Matt. xiii. 13, Rom. xi. 8; the latter in that knowing God in His creation they glorified Him not as God, and their senseless heart was darkened, Rom. i. 21; and to both St. Paul proclaimed the light of the knowledge of the glory of God in the face of Jesus Christ, 2 Cor. iv. 6, Ephes. i. 18. The infinitive of purpose depending on ἀποστέλλω, Burton, p. 157; Viteau, *Le Grec du N.T.*, p. 169 (1893).—ἐπιστρέψαι: "that they may turn," R.V. ("to turn them," margin, so A.V.); in St. Luke, who uses the verb more frequently than any other N.T. writer, it is nearly always intransitive, except in Luke i. 16, 17, Moulton and Geden, while Grimm adds ver. 20 below; so here all E.V. before the authorised, *cf.* Vulgate, "ut convertan-

tur" (Humphry). If we thus take ἐπισ. as intransitive, it is subordinate to the previous infinitive of purpose, ἀνοῖξαι, and τοῦ λαβεῖν again subordinate to ἐπιστ., expressing the final result aimed at (Page, and see also Wendt's note, *in loco* (1899)).—ἀπὸ σκότους εἰς φῶς: throughout St. Paul's Epistles the imagery was frequent with reference not only to Gentiles but also to Jews, *cf.* Rom. ii. 19, xiii. 12, 1 Thess. v. 5, Ephes. v. 18, Col. i. 12. The words gain in interest here if we think of them as corresponding with the Apostle's own recovering from blindness, spiritual and physical (Plumptre).—τοῦ Σατανᾶ, Blass, *Gram.*, pp. 32, 144; no less than ten times by St. Paul in his Epistles; *cf.* 2 Cor. iv. 4, Ephes. ii. 2, vi. 12 (Col. i. 13. ἐξουσία σκότους, Luke xxii. 53). There is no reason to suppose with Bengel that St. Paul is here referring to Gentiles rather than to Jews, for whilst the Jews no doubt would regard the Gentiles as loving σκότος and in the power of Satan, *cf.* also Luke xiii. 16, xxii. 31, Acts v. 3. For current ideas with regard to Satan and the teaching of the N.T. *cf.* Edersheim, *Jesus the Messiah*, ii., p. 775; Charles, *Book of Enoch*, Introd., p. 52, and *Assumption of Moses*, x., 1, where Satan is apparently represented as the head of the kingdom of evil; *cf.* in the N.T. Ephes. i. 21, vi. 12, Col. ii. 15, for the whole hierarchy of evil spirits at the disposal of Satan, and 2 Thess. ii. 9; *cf.* 2 Cor. xi. 14 for his supernatural powers of deceiving or preventing men; see especially Sanday and Headlam, *Romans*, p. 145.—τοῦ λαβεῖν: expressing the ultimate object of ἀνοῖξαι (see above, and Weiss, *in loco*).—ἄφεσιν ἁμαρ., iii. 16, the language here is quite Pauline, *cf.* Col. i. 12-14, where also deliverance out of the power of darkness and forgiveness of sins in the Son of God's love are connected as here.— τῇ πίστει εἰς ἐμέ: may be connected with λαβεῖν, faith in Christ as the condition of forgiveness placed emphatically at the end; *cf.* x. 43, A. and R.V. connect the words with ἡγιασμένοις, so Vulgate.— κλῆρον ἐν τοῖς ἡγιασ., *cf.* xx. 32, Col. i. 12.
Ver. 19. ὅθεν: "wherefore," R.V., so in Heb. ii. 17, iii. 1, vii. 25, viii. 3, ix. 18 (locally in Luke xi. 24, Acts xiv. 26, xxviii. 13); probably best taken here as

πίστει τῇ εἰς ἐμέ.   19. Ὅθεν, βασιλεῦ Ἀγρίππα, οὐκ ἐγενόμην ἀπειθὴς τῇ οὐρανίῳ ὀπτασίᾳ, 20. ἀλλὰ τοῖς ἐν Δαμασκῷ πρῶτον [1] καὶ Ἱεροσολύμοις, εἰς πᾶσάν τε τὴν χώραν τῆς Ἰουδαίας, καὶ τοῖς ἔθνεσιν, ἀπήγγελλον μετανοεῖν καὶ ἐπιστρέφειν ἐπὶ τὸν Θεόν, ἄξια

---

[1] After πρωτον ℵAB 25, 61, add τε, so Tisch. and other authorities in ver. 17, except Hilg. Before Ιερ. AE read εν. Hilg. has και τοις εν Ιερ. εις om. ℵAB, so Tisch., R.V., W.H., but retained by Weiss, Hilg. and Wendt, may easily have dropped out after the preceding -οις. Blass reads in α and β εις πασαν τε (την) χωραν Ιουδαιοις και τοις εθνεσιν, with support by Par.² "Judæis," see note below, and Wendt (1899), p. 396. Clemen, p. 144, regards τε και Ιερ. . . . Ιουδαιας as a gloss of R. Judaicus (ver. 21 being added by R. Antijudaicus), and both Wendt and McGiffert view the whole reference as added to the original source.

---

referring to the whole revelation from ver. 12, marking the natural result of what had gone before; not used in St. Paul's Epistles.—βασ. Ἀ.: "cum ad sua facta redeat, apte regem denuo compellat," Blass, marking the commencement of his real defence.—ἀπειθὴς: only in Luke and Paul in N.T., cf. Luke i. 17 ; Rom. i. 30, 2 Tim. iii. 2, Tit. i. 16, iii. 3 ; in LXX and in classical Greek.—ὀπτασίᾳ: here and here only Paul himself apparently speaks of the appearance of Christ vouchsafed to him before Damascus by this word, but ὀπτασία, as Beyschlag shows, is not confined to appearances which the narrators regard as visions, cf. Luke i. 22, xxiv. 23, and its meaning must be explained from the entire "objectivity" with which St. Paul invests the whole narrative of his Conversion, cf. Witness of the Epistles, p. 383 (1892), and p. 380 for further reference to Beyschlag in Studien und Kritiken, 1864, 1890, and his Leben Jesu, i., p. 435. In modern Greek ὀπτασία = a vision (Kennedy).

Ver. 20. ἀλλὰ τοῖς ἐν Δ.: "both to them of Damascus first, and at Jerusalem," reading τε (see critical note) after πρῶτον, thus closely connecting Damascus and Jerusalem as the scenes of Paul's first activity, cf. ix. 20, 28.—εἰς πᾶσάν τε τὴν χώραν τῆς Ἰ., see critical note. If we read accusative simply without εἰς = accusative of space marking the extension of the preaching. Blass solves the difficulty by regarding εἰς = ἐν, ut sæpe. The statement seems to contradict Gal. i. 22, and there is no mention of such a widely extended preaching at this time in Acts. It has therefore been held by some that reference is made to the preaching at the time of Saul's carrying relief with Barnabas from Antioch to Jerusalem, xi. 30, xii. 25 (Zöckler and Rendall), while others refer the passage to Rome xv. 10 (Weiss), and

others combine xi. 29, 30, xv. 3 = Rom. xv. 10. Ramsay, St. Paul, p. 382, regards the statement as so directly contradictory to all other authorities that he practically follows Blass in β text, and reads εἰς πᾶσαν χώραν Ἰουδαίοις τε καὶ τοῖς ἔθνεσι, "in every land to both Jews and Gentiles". The text he regards as not Lucan and hardly Greek; see also Blass, in loco; ἡ χώρα τῆς Ἰουδαίας ought to be τῶν Ἰουδ., as in x. 39, etc. But see in defence of reading in T.R. as against Blass, and the reference of the words to the journeys in xi. 30, xv. 3, Wendt, in loco (1899). The general meaning given to the words by Blass is at all events in accordance with the view of the speech as a summary, and not as an account in detail, of the Apostle's work (C. and H., p. 620). Dr. Farrar, St. Paul, i., 228, ingeniously supposes that Paul may have preached on his way from Damascus to Jerusalem in the guest chambers of the Jewish synagogues, so that he may not have come into contact with any Christian communities, and he would thus explain Gal. i. 22.—ἀπήγγελλον: imperfect, denoting continuous preaching; here only of preaching the Gospel, but cf. xvii. 30 W.H., where God announces to men everywhere to repent, μετανοεῖν, a striking similarity in language with Paul's words here (cf. 1 John i. 2, 3).—ἐπιστρέφειν, cf. for the expression xiv. 15, and see above on ver. 18.—ἄξια τῆς μετανοίας ἔργα: "worthy of their repentance," R.V. margin, i.e., of the repentance which they profess. In the Gospels καρπούς, καρπόν, here ἔργα, but cf. Ephes. ii. 10, v. 11, Col. i. 10, Tit. iii. 8, and ἀξίους with genitive rei, more frequent in St. Luke and St. Paul than in any other N.T. writers.—πράσσοντας: used in N.T. sometimes of good, sometimes of evil, actions; in

τῆς μετανοίας ἔργα πράσσοντας. 21. ἕνεκα τούτων με[1] οἱ Ἰουδαῖοι συλλαβόμενοι ἐν τῷ ἱερῷ ἐπειρῶντο διαχειρίσασθαι. 22. ἐπικουρίας οὖν τυχὼν τῆς[2] παρὰ τοῦ Θεοῦ, ἄχρι τῆς ἡμέρας ταύτης ἕστηκα, μαρτυρούμενος μικρῷ τε καὶ μεγάλῳ, οὐδὲν ἐκτὸς λέγων ὧν τε οἱ

[1] The art. before ιουδ. om. ℵ*BL 13, 61, 105, so Tisch., R.V., Hilgenfeld, W.H., Blass, Weiss, Wendt, but Lach. and Meyer follow T.R. After συλλ. Tisch., Hilgenfeld, with ℵcE, Vulg. Chron. reads οντα, but the word may easily have been added to express more clearly that the temple, xxi. 30, was the place where they found Paul, not where they sought to kill him (Wendt).

[2] For παρα ℵABE, Chron. read απο, so Tisch., R.V., W.H., Hilgenfeld, Blass, Weiss, Wendt. ℵABHLP, Chrys., so Tisch. and authorities in ver. 21, read μαρτυρομενος.

classical Greek ποιεῖν is more frequent de inhonestis, cf. Xen., Mem., iii., 9, 4, see Grimm, sub v.

Ver. 21.—ἕνεκα τούτων: because I preached to Jews and Gentiles alike, proclaiming one Gospel to both, and placing both on an equality before God (not for profaning the Temple), cf. xxi. 28. On ἕνεκα see Blass, Gram., p. 21. This Attic form of the word is read here by all authorities, and Blass notes it as characteristic of the literary style of this address before Agrippa, see above on ver. 4.—συλλαβόμενοι, i. 16, xii. 3. So also in each of the Gospels in the active voice, of a violent arrest; in passive see above, xxiii. 27, and frequent in same sense in LXX, and 1 and 2 Macc.—ἐπειρῶντο: here only in N.T. in middle, but see critical note on ix. 26. Cf. 1 Macc. xii. 10, 2 Macc. x. 12, 3 Macc. i. 25, ii. 32, 4 Macc. xii. 3. Imperfect because the attempt was not actually made.—διαχειρ., see on v. 30. The whole description ranks as a summary without giving all the details of the events which led up to the Apostle's imprisonment.

Ver. 22. ἐπικουρίας . . . τῆς παρὰ (ἀπὸ) Θεοῦ: "the help that is from God," R.V., i.e., the help which cometh from God only; only here in N.T., cf. Wisdom xiii. 18 (ἐμπειρίας, S²), for the use of the same phrase cf. instances in Wetstein from Polybius; the word is found in Josephus, but also frequently in classical Greek, of succour against foes.—τυχὼν: no idea of chance, cf. 2 Tim. ii. 10; the aid was divine, not human.—οὖν, see Wendt, and references, Blass, Gram., p. 267, Winer-Moulton, liii., 10, 4.—ἕστηκα: sto salvus, Bengel, after these repeated dangers. The A.V. hardly gives the force of the word; it is a Pauline expression, cf. Ephes. vi. 13, 14, Col. iv. 12, so Knabenbauer, subsisto incolumis.—μαρ-

τυρούμενος: "testifying," A.V., yet μαρτυρόμενος, see critical note, would rather signify "testifying," so R.V., see on vi. 3. Grimm-Thayer, if the reading in T.R. is retained, evidently considers that it should be rendered as passive, "testified to both by small and great". But μαρτυρόμενος marks most appropriately the office of bearing testimony to which Paul was appointed.—μικρῷ τε καὶ μεγάλῳ: if taken to mean "both small and great," the words would have a special force in thus being spoken before Festus and Agrippa, but if = young and old, i.e., before all men, cf. viii. 10, Heb. viii. 11; cf. Gen. xix. 4, 11, etc., but in Rev. xi. 18, xiii. 16, xix. 5, reference is made rather to rank than to age, and the latter meaning may well be included here; cf. Deut. i. 17, Job iii. 19, Wisd. vi. 7.—οὐδὲν ἐκτὸς λ. ὧν τε οἱ πρ. . . . μελλόντων = οὐδὲν ἐκτὸς τούτων ἅ . . . ἐλάλησαν μέλλοντα, cf. Rev. xvii. 8, Simcox, Language of the N.T., p. 135. μελλ. γίγ., cf. Luke xxi. 36; ἐκτὸς, cf. 1 Cor. xv. 27; the word is only used by St. Paul elsewhere in N.T. (except Matt. xxiii. 26), cf. 1 Kings x. 13, 2 Chron. ix. 12, xvii. 19.—οἱ προφ. . . . καὶ Μ.: more naturally Moses and the prophets, Luke xvi. 29, 31, and cf. xxviii. 23, but Moses may have been mentioned to influence the Sadducean element in the audience: the historical Christ was always the subject of St. Paul's preaching "Jesus is the Christ," and the historical Christ was also the ideal Christ; cf. iii. 13, 1 Cor. xv. 3. See on this verse critical note, and Wendt (1899), p. 397, note.

Ver. 23. εἰ = Heb. vii. 15, i.e., as is most certain from the authority of Scripture, "how that the Christ," R.V.—παθητὸς: "must suffer," R.V. ("although is subject to suffering," margin), cf. Vulgate, passibilis (not patibilis); no question here of the abstract possibility of, or

προφῆται ἐλάλησαν μελλόντων γενέσθαι ¹ καὶ Μωσῆς, 23.² εἰ παθητὸς ὁ Χριστός, εἰ πρῶτος ἐξ ἀναστάσεως νεκρῶν φῶς μέλλει καταγγέλλειν τῷ λαῷ καὶ τοῖς ἔθνεσι.   24. Ταῦτα δὲ αὐτοῦ ἀπολογουμένου, ὁ Φῆστος μεγάλῃ τῇ φωνῇ ἔφη,³ Μαίνῃ, Παῦλε· τὰ πολλά σε γράμματα

¹ For καὶ Μωσῆς Flor. and Gig. have "scriptum est in Moysen". Blass regards this as the remaining fragment of the original β text, which ran somewhat as follows : γεγραπται γαρ εν Μωυσει και τοις προφ. πολλα περι τουτων, τοις ερευνησασιν (1 Pet. i. 11).

² ει παθητος κ.τ.λ., Corssen, *G. C. A.*, 1896, p. 429, points out that Tert., *De resurr. carn.*, 39, presupposes the reading of Flor. and Gig., and regards the passage, Gen. ix. 5, in support of bodily resurrection, as quoted by Paul.   According to Corssen's view, this passage was noted in the margin of the Western text.   Flor. and Gig. make Paul refer to some particular passage of the Pentateuch, instead of generally to Moses and the prophets, but in Corssen's view Blass has not helped the recovered reading, but rather destroyed its force by his conjectural additions (see further Wendt (1899), p. 397).   But Blass in his β text leaves a lacuna : γεγραπται γαρ εν Μωυσει (και τοις προφηταις) . . .

³ Blass reads in β text Εμανης Παυλε εμανης with Flor., so περιετρεψεν with Flor. (ut videtur), so ηγεμων for Φηστε on the same authority.

capacity for, suffering, although primarily the Greek word implies this, but of the divine destination to suffering, *cf.* Luke xxiv. 26, 44, 1 Cor. xv. 2, 3, see Grimm-Thayer, *sub v.;* Justin Martyr, *c. Tryph.*, c. 89, παθητὸν τὸν Χριστόν, ὅτι αἱ γραφαὶ κηρύσσουσι, φανερόν ἐστι.   But the same dialogue, c. 90, enables us to realise that even where the idea of a suffering Messiah was entertained, nothing was more abhorrent than the idea of the cross as the outward expression of such sufferings : "If the Messiah can suffer," cries the Jew Trypho, "yet he cannot be crucified ; he cannot die such a shameful, dishonourable death".   See also cc. 36, 76. For the incompatibility of the idea of a suffering Messiah with the ideas current in the time of Jesus see Dalman, *Der Leidende und der Sterbende Messias*, p. 30, and references may be made to *Witness of the Epistles*, pp. 360, 361, for other authorities to the same effect ; *cf.* Matt. xvi. 22, Luke xviii. 34, xxiv. 21, John xii. 34, 1 Cor. i. 23, Gal. v. 11 ; see above on iii. 18 (p. 113).   If we render εἰ *if* or *whether* it does not indicate that there was any doubt in Paul's mind ; but he simply states in the hypothetical form the question at issue between himself and the Jews.—εἰ πρῶτος : "that he first by the resurrection of the dead," R.V., closely connected with the preceding ; the Messiah was to suffer, but "out of his resurrection from the dead" assurance was given not only that the Suffering Messiah and the Triumphant Messiah were one, but that in Him, the true Messiah, all the O.T. prophecies of the blessings of light and life, to Jew and Gentile alike, were to be fulfilled, *cf.* Isai. xlix. 6, Acts xiii. 47 (Isai. ix. 1, 2, lx. 1).   This on the whole seems better than to limit the words to the fact that life and immortality had been brought to light by the resurrection of the Christ : φῶς means more than the blessing of immortality in the future, it means the present realisation of the light of life, *cf.* ver. 18, and Luke ii. 32, of a life in the light of the Lord. πρῶτος closely connected with ἐξ ἀναστ., as if = πρωτότοκος ἐκ νέκρων, Col. i. 18, 1 Cor. xv. 20, 23, or as if the Apostle would emphasise the fact that Christ first rose in the sense of rising to die no more, Rom. vi. 9, and so proclaimed light, etc.—καταγγέλλειν : " to proclaim," R.V., *cf.* xvi. 17, xvii. 3, 23.—λαῷ καὶ τοῖς ἔθνεσι, see above ver. 17.; even in the Pharisaic hope expressed in *Psalms of Solomon*, xvii., *cf.* ver. 32, we see how far the Gentiles would necessarily be from sharing on an equality with the Jews in the Messianic kingdom, see Ryle and James, Introd., liii., and also for later literature, *Apocalypse of Baruch*, lxxii., Edersheim on Isaiah lx., *Jesus the Messiah*, ii., pp. 728, 729.

Ver. 24.   ἀπολ. : the present participle, indicating that Festus broke in upon the speech, *cf.* iv. 1.—μεγ. τῇ φ. : raising his voice, because interrupting in surprise and astonishment, and no doubt with something of impatience if not of anger (Chrysostom). — Μαίνῃ : a hyperbolic, but not a jesting expression ; the mention

εἰς μανίαν περιτρέπει. 25. ὁ δέ, Οὐ μαίνομαι, φησί, κράτιστε Φῆστε,
ἀλλ᾽ ἀληθείας καὶ σωφροσύνης ῥήματα ἀποφθέγγομαι. 26. ἐπίσταται γὰρ περὶ τούτων ὁ βασιλεύς, πρὸς ὃν καὶ[1] παρρησιαζόμενος
λαλῶ[2]· λανθάνειν γὰρ αὐτόν τι τούτων οὐ πείθομαι οὐδέν· οὐ γάρ

[1] και after προς ον is omitted by W.H., following B, Boh., Arm., but retained by
W.H. marg., Weiss, Hilg.

[2] λανθ. γαρ αυτον κ.τ.λ., Wendt decides in favour of T.R. here, with ℵHLP.
In B 36, 69, 137, 180, τι is omitted, so by W.H. text, Weiss, Blass; in ℵcAE 13,
ουδεν is omitted, so by Lach. ℵB read ουθεν, see Winer-Schmiedel, p. 61.
Blass in β text, following Flor., reads ουδεν γαρ τουτων αυτον λανθανει, and omits
ου γαρ . . . τουτο.

not only of a resurrection, but the expressed belief that this Christ Whom
Festus could only describe as "one who
was dead," xxv. 19, should bring light
not only to Jews but even to Gentiles,
to Romans like himself, was too much—
such a belief could only result from a
disturbed brain, cf. xvii. 32 for the effect of
the announcement of a resurrection and a
judgment on the polished Athenians, cf.
St. John x. 20, where our Lord's words
provoked a similar pronouncement by
the Jews, the learned Jews of the
capital. μαίνεσθαι: "qui ita loquitur ut
videatur mentis non compos esse,"
Grimm, cf. xii. 15, 1 Cor. xiv. 23, opposite to σωφροσύνης ῥήματα ἀποφθ. (see
also Page's note); cf. the passage in
Wisd. v. 3, 4, and Luckock, Footsteps of
the Apostles, etc., ii., p. 263.—τὰ πολλά
σε γράμματα: "thy much learning,"
R.V., giving the force of the article perhaps even more correctly, "that great
learning of thine". It is possible that
the words may refer simply to the learning which Paul had just shown in his
speech, of which we may have only a
summary, and γράμμ. may be used of
the sacred writings from which he had
been quoting, and to which in his utterances he may have applied the actual
word, and so Festus refers to them
by the same term, cf. 2 Tim. iii. 15.
Others refer the word to the many rolls
which St. Paul had with him, and which he
was so intent in studying. It is possible
that the word may be used here as in
John vii. 15, of sacred learning in general,
of learning in the Rabbinical schools,
and perhaps, as it is employed by a
Roman, of learning in a more general
sense still, although here including sacred
learning = μαθήματα, cf. Plat., Apol.,
26 D. If books alone had been meant
βιβλία or βίβλοι would have been the
word used. — περιτρέπει εἰς μανίαν:
"doth turn thee to madness," R.V.,

cf. our English phrase "his head is
turned," literally "turn thee round"
(Humphry), cf. Jos., Ant., ix., 4, 4, ii.,
4, 1. It is possible that Festus used the
expression with a certain delicacy, since
in using it he recognises how much
wisdom Paul had previously shown
(Weiss, Bethge). After such an expression of opinion by Festus, and owing to
the deference of Agrippa to the Romans,
Knabenbauer thinks that the king could
not have expressed himself seriously in
the words which follow in ver. 28.
Ver. 25. Οὐ μαίνομαι κ. Φ.: whatever
may have been the sense in which Festus addressed Paul, there is no doubt as
to the courtesy of the Apostle's answer,
μετὰ ἐπιεικείας ἀποκρινόμενος, Chrys.
κράτιστε: "most excellent," R.V., see
above, i. 1.—ἀληθ. καὶ σωφροσ.: veritas
not veracitas, objective truth; no suspicion had been raised against St. Paul's
truthfulness of character (cf. John xviii.
37); as our Lord stood before Pilate
as a witness for the truth, so His Apostle
stands face to face with a Roman sceptic
as a witness to the existence of a world
of real existences and not of mere shadows and unrealities (Bethge, p. 294).
σωφρ.: the opposite of madness, cf.
Plato, Protag., 323 B (Xen., Mem., i.,
1, 16), ὁ ἐκεῖ σωφροσύνην ἡγοῦντο εἶναι
τἀληθῆ λέγειν, ἐνταῦθα μανίαν. The
two nouns are only found here in St.
Luke's writings, but cf. σωφρονεῖν, Luke
viii. 35, Rom. xii. 3, 2 Cor. v. 13; cf.
ῥήματα ζωῆς, chap. v. 20.—ἀποφθ., cf.
ii. 4 and 14, of the Pentecostal utterances,
and of the solemn utterances of St. Peter;
"aptum verbum," Bengel. St. Paul was
speaking with boldness like St. Peter,
and under the same divine inspiration; in
LXX of the utterances of the prophets,
cf. 1 Chron. xxv. 1, of philosophers, and of
oracular responses; like the Latin profari
and pronuntiare, see above on ii. 4, and
Grimm-Thayer, sub v.

ἐστιν ἐν γωνίᾳ πεπραγμένον τοῦτο. 27. πιστεύεις, βασιλεῦ Ἀγρίππα, τοῖς προφήταις; οἶδα ὅτι πιστεύεις. 28. ὁ δὲ Ἀγρίππας πρὸς τὸν Παῦλον ἔφη,[1] Ἐν ὀλίγῳ με πείθεις Χριστιανὸν γενέσθαι.

[1] εν ολιγω με πειθεις Χριστ. ποιησαι אB 13, 17, 40, 61, Syr. H., mg., Boh., Tisch., Weiss. Instead of πειθεις A, so Lach., Blass (Nösgen, Belser, Alford) πειθη, but prob. this was an attempt to solve the difficulty of the reading given above, and with the same purpose EHLP, Vulg., Syr. P. Harcl. text, Cyr.-Jer., Chrys. have γενεσθαι for ποιησαι, so Meyer and Hilg. Both Alford and Blass, while adopting πειθη, read ποιησαι. W.H. (and to this view apparently Wendt inclines, 1899) think that there must be some corruption in text, see *App.*, p. 100. Hort adds that possibly πεποιθας should be read for με πειθεις, for the personal με loses no force by being left to implication, and the changes of letters are inconsiderable, but at the same time he thinks it equally possible that the error may lie elsewhere.

Ver. 26. ἐπίσταται γὰρ: here only with περί: in proof that his words were words of soberness, and that he was basing his statements on facts, St. Paul appeals to the knowledge of Agrippa, a knowledge which he would have gained from his close connection with the Jewish religion, but also to some extent perhaps from the events of his father's reign, for Herod Agrippa had beheaded James with a sword, and had cast Peter into prison: "patet hoc," says Bengel, "nam etiam *Christianum* nomen sciebat".—If καὶ is retained, "to whom also," *i.e.*, because of his knowledge just mentioned.—παρρησιαζ.: "freely," R.V., everywhere else R.V. renders "boldly"; verb only in Luke and Paul, see on ix. 27; the Apostle spoke freely because of the king's full knowledge, but his boldness is also shown in his question to the king, and to the reply which he makes to it in the king's name, ver. 27.—λανθάνειν γὰρ αὐτόν κ.τ.λ.: if οὐδέν and τι are both retained, see critical note, τι may be taken adverbially, "in any degree," but see Winer-Moulton, lv., 9, b., and Wendt's note, *in loco*, p. 399 (1899).—ἐν γωνίᾳ πεπραγ., *cf.* Luke vii. 17, xxiii. 8. Blass notes this expression, *Gram.*, p. 4, as a proof that Paul used more literary expressions than usual in addressing his audience, and no doubt the expression was used by classical writers, *cf.* Plato, *Gorg.*, 485 D; Epict., *Diss.*, ii., 12, 17, and other instances in Wetstein, *cf. angulus*, Ter., *Adelph.*, v., 2, 10.

Ver. 27. πιστεύεις; the question and answer were quite natural as addressed to a Jewish king; it was a belief which St. Paul could justly presuppose in every Jew, even in one like Agrippa, educated amongst the Romans. The question may well have been asked as a proof that the words which had preceded were

words of truth and soberness, and that the king could so regard them, even if Festus could not; if Agrippa believed the prophets—as Paul affirmed—he could not regard the fulfilment of their prophecies as irrational. Or we may view the question as taking up, after the interruption of Festus, the statement of vv. 22, 23, and as a forcible appeal to Agrippa, as to one who could judge whether in the death and resurrection of Jesus of Nazareth there was anything really contrary to the picture of the Messiah drawn by the Hebrew prophets. It is possible that the Apostle meant to add a second ground for the knowledge of the king; not only were these events not done in a corner, but they had been prophesied by the prophets, in whom Agrippa believed; but instead of thus stating a fact, he addresses the king with increasing urgency and emotion, as one specially interested in religious questions, ver. 3 (Zöckler, Meyer).

Ver. 28. ἐν ὀλίγῳ με πείθεις Χ. γένεσθαι, see critical note, "with but little persuasion thou wouldest fain make me a Christian," R.V. reading ποιῆσαι, and πείθεις being used *de conatu* (so Zöckler in his 2nd edition); *cf.* προσήλυτον ποιεῖν, Matt. xxiii. 15. Schmiedel, *Encycl. Bibl.*, i., 754, inclines to explain the phrase Χ. ποιῆσαι as a Latinism: *Christianum agere*, to play the part of a Christian. Weiss sees in the words a gentle irony, as if Agrippa would answer St. Paul's appeal to his belief in the prophets by intimating that it was not so simple a matter to become a Christian, even if one, as a Jew, believed in the prophets. Or we may regard Agrippa as rejecting, not so much in banter as in cold disdain, the enthusiasm of the orator, and adopting the tone of a certain Jewish orthodoxy (Zöckler), not, *i.e.*, the indifference of

29. ὁ δὲ Παῦλος [1] εἶπεν,[2] Εὐξαίμην ἂν τῷ Θεῷ, καὶ ἐν ὀλίγῳ καὶ ἐν πολλῷ οὐ μόνον σέ, ἀλλὰ καὶ πάντας τοὺς ἀκούοντάς μου σήμερον, γενέσθαι τοιούτους ὁποῖος κἀγώ εἰμι, παρεκτὸς τῶν δεσμῶν τούτων.

[1] After ο δε Π. אAB, Vulg., Syr. Harcl. *om.* ειπεν, so Tisch., W.H., R.V., Weiss, Wendt, Hilg.

[2] ευξαιμην אcAB, so Lach., W.H., Weiss, Wendt, Blass, Hilg.; but א*HLP 61, so Tisch. ευξαμην. For πολλω (HLP, Chrys.) אAB 13, 40, 61, Vulg., Syrr. P. H., Boh., so Tisch., W.H., R.V., Blass, Weiss, Wendt, Hilg. have μεγαλω.

the Roman, but that of the Sadducees to the prophets. The A.V. "almost" must be abandoned, even if we retain γενέσθαι, for ἐν ὀλίγῳ cannot be so rendered, either here or elsewhere in the N.T.; παρ' ὀλίγον, or ὀλίγου or ὀλίγῳ δεῖ would be required as the classical expression for "almost". The best parallel is Ephes. iii. 3, ἐν ὀλίγῳ: "in a few words": so A. and R.V. (*cf.* 1 Pet. v. 12). But if in the next verse we read μεγάλῳ instead of πολλῷ, so R.V. (see critical note), it seems best to understand πόνῳ with ὀλίγῳ, as this noun could fitly stand with both μεγάλῳ and ὀλίγῳ = with little trouble, with little cost. The R.V. rendering of the two verses reads as if πολλῷ was retained in ver. 29, whereas μεγάλῳ is the reading adopted in R.V. text. So far as N.T. usage is concerned, ἐν ὀλίγῳ might be rendered "in a short time" (*cf.* James iv. 14, 1 Pet. i. 6, Rev. xvii. 10, so in classical Greek), but this rendering also is excluded by ἐν ὀλίγῳ καὶ ἐν μεγάλῳ in the next verse. Wendt maintains that ἐν ὀλίγῳ may still be rendered "almost"; the phrase is instrumental, as if expressing the thought contained in ὀλίγου δεῖ, and meaning that a little was wanted to attain the aim = almost; so St. Chrysostom, St. Cyril of Jerusalem; Luther, Beza, Grotius = *propemodum*. The answer of Agrippa, therefore, need not be taken ironically, as by most moderns, but in earnest (*cf.* ver. 32, where his favourable opinion supports this view), although Wendt acknowledges that his confession was only half-hearted, as is seen by his desire to conclude the interview (Wendt, 1888, note, p. 530, and 1899, p. 400, to the same effect, so too Schürer, *Jewish People*, div. i., vol. ii., p. 198, note). If we read πείθῃ, see critical note, we render "with but little thou art persuading thyself that thou canst make me a Christian," taking up πείθομαι of ver. 26. This reading is adopted by Blass and Belser, but the former takes ἐν ὀλίγῳ as meaning *brevi tempore* in this verse (so in Plato, *Apol.*, 22 B), but in ver. 29 he takes it as =

facile, whilst ἐν μεγάλῳ (which he reads) = *difficile*. Belser, however, takes the phrase ἐν ὀλίγῳ in the same sense in both verses, "with little trouble or pains". St. Chrysostom thought that the phrase ἐν ὀλίγῳ was used by Agrippa in one sense and by St. Paul in another (so too Lewin, *cf.* Grimm-Thayer and Plumptre); Blass apparently obliges us to adopt the same view, but there is nothing in the context to support it (Wendt, Belser).—Χριστ.: there is nothing strange in this use of the word by Agrippa; he may have become acquainted with it in his knowledge of the Christian movement (see above), and the term could easily have spread from Antioch over the district which he ruled. It is difficult to say in what sense he used the term; and no doubt the shade of meaning which we attach to his employment of it will depend upon the meaning which we give to the rest of his answer—a meaning earnest or contemptuous. Thus on the former supposition it is possible that he may have used the word instead of the despised "Nazarene," to indicate his half-friendly attitude towards Christianity, and his relative recognition of it by connecting it with the name which was cherished by every Jew, although the context shows that he had no intention whatever of allowing Paul's persuasive powers further scope; see Wendt (1899), who points out as against Lipsius that there is nothing unhistorical in the introduction of the name here, as if the writer presupposed that it would be familiar to every Jew. On the other hand, although a Jew, Agrippa, before such an audience, might well have used a term with which the Romans also would probably have been familiar, and if he spoke contemptuously (so Blass, Rendall) he would naturally employ a title which had been given in scorn, and which apparently at this period even the Christians themselves had not accepted; see below, and note on xi. 26.

Ver. 29. εὐξαίμην ἄν: on the optative with ἄν, Burton, p. 80, Blass, *Gram.*, p. 202, Viteau, *Le Grec du N.T.*, p. 40

30.[1] Καὶ ταῦτα εἰπόντος αὐτοῦ, ἀνέστη ὁ βασιλεὺς καὶ ὁ ἡγεμών, ἥ τε Βερνίκη, καὶ οἱ συγκαθήμενοι αὐτοῖς, 31. καὶ ἀναχωρήσαντες ἐλάλουν πρὸς ἀλλήλους λέγοντες, Ὅτι οὐδὲν θανάτου ἄξιον[2] ἢ δεσμῶν πράσσει ὁ ἄνθρωπος οὗτος. 32. Ἀγρίππας δὲ τῷ Φήστῳ ἔφη, Ἀπολελύσθαι ἐδύνατο ὁ ἄνθρωπος οὗτος, εἰ μὴ[3] ἐπεκέκλητο Καίσαρα.

[1] και ταυτα ειπ. αυτου HLP (137), Syr. H., Flor., so Blass in β text, and Hilg.; but otherwise unsupported, R.V. omit.

[2] After αξιον Wendt is inclined to retain with Tisch. and W.H. marg. τι, so ℵA 13, 31, 40, 61, 68, Vulg., Boh.; BHLP om., so T.R., Lach., W.H., Weiss, Blass, Hilg.

[3] επεκ., but AL; Blass επικ., but in β text Blass has επεκ., so ℵBHP, etc.

(1893); with dative only here in N.T.—καὶ ἐν ὀλ. καὶ ἐν μεγ.: "whether with little or with much," R.V. See critical note and ver. 28, i.e., with little or much trouble, and cost.—σήμερον: to be joined not with γενέσθαι (as Chrysostom, Bengel), but with τοὺς ἀκούοντάς μου.—οὐ μόνον, Burton, pp. 183, 184, μὴ μόνον with infinitive only in Gal. iv. 18.—τοιούτους ὁποῖος κἀγώ εἰμι, he does not repeat the word "Christian," which perhaps he would not recognise (Blass): "tales qualis ego sum, sive Chr. appellare vis, sive alio vel contemptiore nomine". γενέσθαι . . . εἰμι: "might become such as I am," R.V., thus giving the difference between γέν. and εἰμι; by whatever name he might be called, the Apostle knew what he actually was (1 Cor. ix. 9).—παρεκτὸς τῶν δεσμῶν τούτων; not figurative but literal; although the plural may be used rhetorically (Weiss), cf. Tac., Ann., iv., 28. παρεκτὸς: Matt. v. 32, xix. 9 (see W.H.) (2 Cor. xi. 28, adv.), Didaché, vi., 1, Test., xii., Patr., Zab., 1; "suavissima ἐπιθεραπεία et exceptio," Bengel. Faith and Hope—of these the Apostle had spoken, and his closing words reveal a Love which sought not its own, was not easily provoked, and took no account of evil: "totum responsum et urbanissimum et Christiano nomine dignissimum," Blass.

Ver. 30. καὶ ταῦτα εἰπόντος αὐτοῦ: if these words are not retained, see critical note, their omission seems to make the rising up more abrupt (subito consurgit, Blass), and probably this is the meaning of the passage, although the order of rank is maintained in leaving the chamber. For the vividness of the whole narrative see Zöckler and Wendt, and cf. McGiffert, Apostolic Age, p. 355.—ἀνέστη, Lucan, see on ἀναχωρ. Suet., Nero, 15; cf. xxiii. 19, and note on xxv. 12.

Ver. 31. πράσσει, present tense: "agit de vitæ instituto" (Grotius, Blass).

Ver. 32. ἐδύνατο: a true affirmative imperfect of verbs denoting obligation or possibility, when used to affirm that a certain thing could or should have been done under the circumstances narrated; therefore not correct to speak of an omitted ἄν, since the past necessity was not hypothetical or contrary to fact, but actual, Burton, p. 14, but cf. Simcox, Language of the N.T., cf. xxiv. 19, xxvii. 21.—εἰ μὴ ἐπεκ. Καίσαρα: the appeal had been made and accepted and Paul must be sent to Rome, but doubtless the decision of Agrippa would have great weight with Festus, and would greatly modify the letter which he would send to Rome with the prisoner (see above, p. 499), and we may thus account for the treatment of Paul on his arrival in the capital, xxviii. 16. The circumstance that the innocence of Paul is thus established at the mouth of various personages, and now by Agrippa, himself a Jew, as well as by Festus, a Roman, has been made the ground of objection to the narrative by Baur, Zeller, Overbeck, Weizsäcker, Schmiedel. But whilst we may frankly admit that St. Luke no doubt purposely introduced these varied testimonies to Paul's innocence, this is no proof of the incorrectness of his statements (Wendt, Matthias). If we grant, as St. Luke affirms, that the primary cause of the Apostle's imprisonment was the fanatical rage of the Jews against him as a despiser and enemy of the national religion, it is quite conceivable that those who were called to inquire into the matter without such enmity and prejudice should receive a strong impression of his innocence, and should give expression to their impressions. On the other hand, the description in Acts enables us to see how Paul, in spite of

XXVII. 1.[1] 'ΩΣ δὲ ἐκρίθη τοῦ ἀποπλεῖν ἡμᾶς εἰς τὴν Ἰταλίαν,
παρεδίδουν τόν τε Παῦλον καί τινας ἑτέρους δεσμώτας ἑκατοντάρχῃ,

[1] With Flor., Gig., Syr. H. mg., Blass reconstructs the β text: ουτως ουν ο
ηγεμων πεμπεσθαι αυτον Καισαρι εκρινεν, και τη επαυριον προσκαλεσαμενος
εκατονταρχην τινα σπειρης Σεβαστης ονοματι Ιουλιον, παρεδωκεν αυτω τον Παυλον
συν τοις λοιποις δεσμωταις, so Hilgenfeld, 1899.

such declarations in his favour, might find himself compelled to appeal to Cæsar. Had he acted otherwise, and if release had followed upon the verdict of his innocence, he was sure that sooner or later the implacable Jews would make him their victim. McGiffert, *u. s.*, p. 356, observes that even if both Agrippa and Festus were convinced of the Apostle's innocence, this would not prevent Festus from seeing in him a dangerous person, who would stir up trouble and cause a riot wherever he went; such a man could not have been set at liberty by Festus as a faithful Roman official; but see above on xxv. 12. On the whole narrative see Zöckler, p. 311; Bethge, p. 260 (for phraseology). Zöckler supposes as a foundation for the narrative a written account by Luke himself, perhaps an eyewitness, at an early period after the events. Wendt (1899) also takes the view that the writer of the narrative had probably been in the personal company of St. Paul at Cæsarea before the start on the journey for Rome, xxvii. 1, and that the reason that he does not employ the first person in the narrative of xxv., xxvi., is because the facts narrated in these two chapters did not immediately concern him, although he was in Cæsarea during their process. In referring to the account of St. Paul's conversion as given in ch. xxvi. it is noteworthy that McGiffert, p. 120, speaks of it as occurring "in a setting whose vividness and verisimilitude are unsurpassed".

CHAPTER XXVII.—Ver. 1. Blass at the outset speaks of this and the next chapter as "clarissimam descriptionem" of St. Paul's voyage, and he adds that this description has been estimated by a man skilled in nautical matters as "monumentum omnium pretiosissimum, quæ rei navalis ex tota antiquitate nobis relicta sint". He refers to *Die Nautik der Alten* by Breusing, formerly Director of the School of Navigation in Bremen, 1886; a book which should be read side by side with J. Smith's well-known *Voyage and Shipwreck of St. Paul*, 4th edit., 1880 (*cf.* also J. Vars, *L'Art Nautique*, 1887, and see also Introd., p. 8).—

ὡς: *particula temporalis*, often so used by St. Luke in Gospel and Acts, and more frequently than by the other Evangelists; in St. Matthew not at all, in St. Mark once; often in O.T., Apoc., and especially in 1 Macc.—ἐκρίθη τοῦ ἀποπ.: common construction in LXX with kindred words, *e.g.*, βουλεύομαι, but no other instances of the genitive with infinitive after κρίνω (except 1 Cor. ii. 2, T.R.) in N.T., Lumby; see also Burton, p. 159. ἀποπ.: St. Luke stands alone amongst N.T. writers in the number of compounds of πλεῖν which he employs, no less than nine, J. Smith, *u.s.*, p. 28, 61.—ἡμᾶς: "with this section we tread the firm ground of history, for here at Acts xxvii. 1 the personal record of the book again enters, and that in its longest and fullest part" (Weizsäcker): see also on ἡμᾶς, as intimating by its recurrence the narrative of an eyewitness, Hilgenfeld, *Zw. Th.*, iv., p. 549 (1896), Wendt (1899), p. 402, note. The ἡμᾶς included Paul, Luke, Aristarchus; Ramsay, *St. Paul*, p. 315, maintains that both Luke and Aristarchus must have accompanied Paul as his slaves, and that they would not have been permitted to go as his friends, but see Gilbert, *Student's Life of Paul*, p. 201; and Wendt (1899) in reply to Ramsay points out that as the ship was not sailing as a transport vessel with the prisoners direct to Rome, but that a vessel engaged in private enterprise and commerce was employed, it is quite possible that Paul's friends may have travelled on the same ship with him as independent passengers. But see further Ramsay, p. 323. So far as Luke is concerned, it is possible that he may have travelled in his professional capacity as a medical man, Lekebusch, *Apostelgeschichte*, p. 393.—παρεδίδουν: assimilated to form of contracted verbs, so most certainly in Acts, *cf.* iii. 2, iv. 33, 35, Simcox, *Language of the N.T.*, p. 37. Winer-Schmiedel, p. 121.—δεσμώτας, see below, p. 516.—That Paul commanded respect is implied by the whole narrative: some of the other prisoners may also have been sent to Rome on the ground of an appeal, *cf.* Josephus, *Vita*, 3, but others may have been already condemned, Ramsay, p.

ὀνόματι Ἰουλίῳ, σπείρης Σεβαστῆς. 2. ἐπιβάντες δὲ πλοίῳ Ἀδρα-
μυττηνῷ, μέλλοντες πλεῖν[1] τοὺς κατὰ τὴν Ἀσίαν τόπους, ἀνήχθημεν,

[1] After πλειν אAB add εις, so Tisch., W.H., R.V., Weiss, Wendt. Instead of μελ-λοντες אAB, Tisch., W.H., R.V., Weiss, Wendt read μελλοντι; perhaps changed into plural after επιβαντες. Blass reconstructs with Flor., Gig., Syr. P. μελλοντες δε πλειν επεβημεν πλοιω Αδραμυττηνω, omitting μελλοντι πλειν . . . τοπους with Flor., retained, however, by Hilgenfeld, 1899, with Gig. and Syr. P. Blass continues in β text, so Hilgenfeld, επεβη δε συν ημιν Αρισταρχος Μακεδων Θεσσαλον-ικευς with the same authority, except that Flor. omits Θεσσ. AB*, so Weiss, W.H. read Αδραμυντηνω; see further Winer-Schmiedel, p. 58, and W.H., p. 313 (for aspirate Ἀδρα.), and App., p. 167.

314.—ἑτέρους: Meyer and Zöckler take the word to indicate prisoners of a character different from Paul, i.e., heathen, not Christians; but Wendt (so Hackett) points out that Luke in Acts uses ἕτερος in singular and plural as simply = another, or other, additional; vii. 18, viii. 34, xv. 35, xvii. 34. As against this Zöckler quotes Luke xxiii. 32, Gal. i. 7. —Ἰουλίῳ: name far too common for any identification; Tacitus speaks of a Julius Priscus, Hist., ii., 92, iv., 11, a centurion of the prætorians, but see below on xxviii. 16.—σπείρης Σ.: "of the Augustan band," R.V. It is suggested that the term is here used is a popular colloquial way by St. Luke, and that it is not a translation of a correct Roman name, but rather "the troops of the emperor," denoting a body of legionary centurions who were employed by the emperor on confidential business between the provinces and the imperial city, the title Augustan being conferred on them as a mark of favour and distinction. If this is so we gather from this notice in Acts a fact which is quite in accordance with what is known from other sources, although nowhere precisely attested. But can any connection be established between such a body and any branch of the imperial service which is actually known to us? There were certain legionary centurions who went by the name of frumentarii, who were employed not only, as their name implied, on duties connected with the commissariat, but also with the custody of prisoners and for purposes of police. In xxviii. 16, A.V. and R.V. margin, we have the remarkable reading: "and the centurion delivered the prisoners to the captain of the [prætorian] guard" (see on l.c.). But it is urged that we cannot understand by this expression the Prefect of the Prætorian Guard, who would not be concerned with the comparatively humble duty of receiving and guarding prisoners. But in the Old L.V. called

Gigas (unfortunately the only representative of the Old Latin for this passage) we have for a translation of the Greek στρατοπεδάρχης, in itself a very rare word, princeps peregrinorum. Now the legionary centurions who formed the frumentarii were regarded in Rome as being on detached duty, and were known as peregrini; on the Cælian Hill they occupied the camp known as the castra peregrinorum, and their commander bore the name of princeps peregrinorum. If therefore we may identify the Strato-pedarch in Acts xxviii. 16 with this commanding officer, we may also infer that Julius was one of the Peregrini, and that he hands over his prisoners to his superior officer, Ramsay, St. Paul, pp. 315, 347, Mommsen, Sitzungsberichte d. Berl. Akad., 1895, p. 495 ff., Rendall, Acts, p. 340. But see on the other hand Zahn, Einleitung, i., p. 389 (1897), Knabenbauer, Actus Apostolorum, p. 448, Belser, Beiträge, p. 147 ff., who point out amongst other reasons (1) that there is no clear evidence of the title princeps peregrinorum before the reorganisation of Sept. Severus, (2) that we have evidence that prisoners were sent from the provinces and committed to the care of the præfectus prætorio, cf. Traj., Ad Plin., 57, with reference to one who had appealed: "vinctus mitti ad præfectos prætorii mei debet," and other instances in Zahn, u. s., and Knabenbauer. See further for the value of the Old Latin reading in Gigas "Julius" (Headlam), Hastings' B.D., and below on xxviii. 16. But whether we adopt the explanation suggested by Prof. Ramsay or not, it is still open to us to maintain that the title "Augustan" was a title of honour and not a local title; not connected with Sebaste the chief town of Samaria, or with Cæsarea Sebaste. Schürer in answer to Mr. Headlam's criticism ("Julius," Hastings' B.D.) is still of opinion, Theol. Literaturzeitung,

ὄντος σὺν ἡμῖν Ἀριστάρχου Μακεδόνος Θεσσαλονικέως. 3. τῇ τε
ἑτέρᾳ κατήχθημεν εἰς Σιδῶνα · φιλανθρώπως τε ὁ Ἰούλιος τῷ Παύλῳ
χρησάμενος, ἐπέτρεψε πρὸς φίλους ¹ πορευθέντα ἐπιμελείας τυχεῖν.

¹ Tisch., W.H., Weiss, Wendt read πορευθεντι with ℵAB 13, 36, 68. Blass in
β text follows Flor. according to which Paul's friends come to him, "permisit
amicis qui veniebant (ad eum) uti curam ejus agerent".

20, 1899, that reference is here made to
one of the five cohorts of Cæsareans and
Sebasteni mentioned by Josephus (for
references see *Jewish People*, div. i., vol.
ii., p. 53, E.T., and Schmiedel, *Encyclop.
Biblica*, i., 909, 1899), and therefore
a σπεῖρα Σεβαστηνῶν ; but he maintains
that this same cohort was distinguished
by the title Augusta from the other four
cohorts, and that the writer of Acts is
rendering this title in the word Σεβαστή
(see also below). It is *possible* (as Wendt
admits, although he prefers Schürer's
view, 1899) that Julius might have belonged to the *cohors Augusta, cf. C.I.L.*,
iii., 66, 83, Augustiani, Suet., *Nero*, 25,
Augustani, Tac., *Ann.*, xiv., 15, etc. (Belser, *Beiträge*, p. 154, Knabenbauer, p.
425), a select number of Roman knights
who formed a kind of body-guard for the
emperor, instituted about 59 A.D., and
that he may have been in Cæsarea on
some temporary special duty ; but on the
other hand see Page's note, *in loco* (*cf.*
note on x. 1). Grimm-Thayer, *sub v.*
Σεβαστός (2), describes it as (an adj.) a
title of honour given to certain legions,
or cohorts, or battalions, for "valour":
"Ala Augusta ob virtutem appellata," *C.
I. L.*, vii., 340, 341, 344, but there is no
inscriptional *proof* that this title was
given to any Cæsarean cohort; see
"Augustan Band" (Barnes), Hastings'
B.D., and Wendt can only refer to the
bestowal of the title as "probable".

Ver. 2. πλοίῳ Ἀδραμ.: a boat which
belonged to Adramyttium in Mysia, in
the Roman province Asia, situated at the
top of the gulf *Sinus Adramyttenus*, to
which it gives its name (Ramsay, Hastings'
B.D., *sub v.*). It was of considerable
importance as a seaport and commercial
centre, and under Roman rule it was the
metropolis of the north-west district of
Asia. Not to be confounded as by
Grotius and others with Adrumetum on
the north coast of Africa. For the
spelling see critical note.—μέλλοντες:
the usual route to Rome would have
been by way of Alexandria, *cf.* the route
taken by Titus from Judæa to the capital, Suet., *Tit.*, 5. But apparently there
was no ship sufficiently large at hand.

From some of the great harbours of the
Asian coast the centurion might have
passed to Italy, or probably from Adramyttium (if the ship was going home) he
intended to go to Neapolis, and take the
great high road to Rome, if no ship
could be found in the Asian harbours so
late in the season.—τοὺς κατὰ τὴν Ἀ.
τόπους: "to sail by the coasts of Asia,"
A.V.; but with εἰς after πλεῖν see critical note, "to sail unto the places on
the coast of Asia," R.V., *cf.* for the
phrase, xi. 1, Polyb., i., 3, 6. In xvi. 3
τόποι is similarly used. See J. Smith's
note, *u.s.*, p. 63.—ἀνήχ., see above on
xiii. 13 ; in the preceding verse we have
the corresponding nautical term κατάγεσθαι, to come to land.—Ἀριστ., *cf.*
xix. 39, xxi. 4. Perhaps the expression
σὺν ἡμῖν may mean that he was with
them, but only for a time, not being
actually one of them, *i.e.*, of Paul's
company; he may have gone in the
Adramyttian ship on his way to his
native home, and left Paul at Myra. On
the other hand, Col. iv. 10, he is named
as one of Paul's companions in Rome, and
as his "fellow-prisoner," see Salmon,
Introd., p. 383. Whether he made the
journey as an actual fellow-prisoner with
Paul cannot be proved, although Col.,
u. s. (Philem. ver. 24), may point to it,
see Lightfoot, *Philippians*, 35, 36, Lewin,
St. Paul, ii. 183; "one Aristarchus,"
A.V., as if otherwise unknown; R.V.
gives simply his name. Jüngst refers
Μακεδ. Θεσσ. to his Redactor.

Ver. 3. τῇ δὲ ἑτέρᾳ: an easy journey
to Sidon—distance 69 sea miles (Breusing).—κατήχ.: technical nautical term,
opposite of ἀνάγειν in ver. 2, see above.
—φιλανθ. τε ὁ Ἰούλιος . . . χρησ.: "and
Julius treated Paul kindly," R.V., *cf.*
xxviii. 2. Bengel says "videtur audisse
Paulum," xxv. 32. Hobart, so also Zahn,
sees in φιλανθ., which is peculiar to Luke
in N.T., the word a medical man might
be likely to use. See also on φιλαν-
θρωπία, xxviii. 2, below, but in Dem.,
411, 10, we have the phrase φιλανθ. τινὶ
χρῆσθαι, so in Plutarch, and the adverb
occurs in 2 Macc. ix. 27, 3 Macc. iii. 20.
χρησ. only in Luke and Paul, *cf.* 2 Cor.

4. κἀκεῖθεν ἀναχθέντες ὑπεπλεύσαμεν τὴν Κύπρον, διὰ τὸ τοὺς ἀνέμους εἶναι ἐναντίους. 5.[1] τό τε πέλαγος τὸ κατὰ τὴν Κιλικίαν καὶ Παμφυλίαν διαπλεύσαντες, κατήλθομεν εἰς Μύρα τῆς Λυκίας. 6. Κἀκεῖ εὑρὼν ὁ ἑκατόνταρχος πλοῖον[2] Ἀλεξανδρινὸν πλέον εἰς τὴν Ἰταλίαν, ἐνεβίβασεν ἡμᾶς εἰς αὐτό· 7. ἐν ἱκαναῖς δὲ ἡμέραις βραδυπλοοῦντες, καὶ μόλις γενόμενοι κατὰ τὴν Κνίδον, μὴ[3] προσεῶντος

[1] At the beginning of verse Blass in β text, with Flor., reads καὶ μετα ταυτα διαπλευσαντες τον Κιλικιον κολπον και το Παμφυλιον πελαγος, and with 137, Syr. H. c*, Flor. adds δι᾽ ημερων δεκαπεντε, which Wendt (1899) seems inclined to retain, and which is read by Hilg. (1899), W.H. marg. Μυρα, neut. plur.; in B Μυρρα, so Tisch., W.H., Weiss, but the reading in T.R. is supported by inscriptions, Winer-Schmiedel, p. 58, so Hilg., Blass, Wendt; אA have Λυστραν, and see further W.H., App., p. 167.

[2] Blass accentuates Ἀλεξανδρῖνον.

[3] Blass corrects, on his own authority, προεωντος for προσ.

xiii. 10, in LXX Gen. xxvi. 29.—πρὸς τοὺς φίλους πορευθέντα: probably with the soldier to whom he was chained, but see also β text, critical note.—ἐπιμελείας τυχεῖν: "to receive attention," R.V. margin, cf. Isocr., 113 D. The noun is found in Prov. iii. 8, 1 Macc. xvi. 14, 2 Macc. xi. 23, 3 Macc. v. 1, and also in classical Greek; it was also frequently employed in medical language for the care bestowed upon the sick, and it may be so here; so Hobart, Zahn, Felten, Vogel, Luckock. St. Luke alone uses the word in the N.T., and he alone uses the verb ἐπιμελεῖσθαι in the sense of caring for the needs of the body, Luke x. 24, 35, another word frequently employed with this meaning by medical writers (Zahn). A delay would be made at Sidon, no doubt, for merchandise to be shipped or unladen. There is no occasion to regard the verse, with Overbeck, as an interpolation; see Wendt's note in favour of its retention, p. 543 (1888)).

Ver. 4. ὑπεπλεύσαμεν τὴν Κ.: "we sailed under the lee of Cyprus," R.V. So Wetstein with whom James Smith is in agreement, i.e., to the east of the island, as was usual for ships westward bound, to avoid the prevalent west winds. Otherwise the direct course would have been to make for Patara in Lycia across the open sea to the south-west of Cyprus (cf. xxi. 1-3, where Paul makes a direct run from Patara to the Syrian coast (Ramsay, Goerne)).

Ver. 5. τό τε πέλαγος τὸ κατὰ τὴν Κ. καὶ Π. διαπλ.: the ship in its northerly course would reach the coast of Cilicia, and then creep slowly along from point to point along the Cilician and Pamphylian coast, using the local land breezes when possible, and the current constantly running to the westward along the southern coast (Ramsay, J. Smith, Breusing). Blass takes πέλαγος as "mare vaste patens" and thinks that the ship did not coast along the shore, but J. Smith gives several instances of ships following St. Paul's route. On the additional reading in β text see critical note.—Μύρα τῆς Λυκίας: two and a half miles from the coast of Lycia; on the spelling see critical notes. On its importance as one of the great harbours in the corn trade between Egypt and Rome see Ramsay, St. Paul, p. 298, 318, Lewin, Saint Paul, ii., 186, and for later notices Zöckler, in loco. As a good illustration of the voyage of the Adramyttian and Alexandrian ship see Lucian's dialogue, Πλοῖον ἢ Εὐχαί, 7-9; Ramsay, p. 319; Breusing, 152.

Ver. 6. πλοῖον: St. Luke does no mention what kind of ship, but the fact that it was on its way from Egypt to Italy, and that in ver. 38 the cargo was evidently grain, makes it a reasonable inference that the ship was carrying corn for conveyance to Rome. On this trade to Rome, Seneca, Epist., 77, and for the large size of the ships (cf. ver. 37) so employed cf. references in Wetstein to Lucian and Plutarch, and Breusing, p. 157, Goerne, and also for the reputation of the Alexandrian ships and sailors.— εὑρὼν: there was nothing unlikely in this, if Myra was situated as above described. The ship, therefore, Ramsay holds, had not been blown out of her

ἡμᾶς τοῦ ἀνέμου, ὑπεπλεύσαμεν τὴν Κρήτην κατὰ Σαλμώνην · 8.
μόλις τε παραλεγόμενοι αὐτήν, ἤλθομεν εἰς τόπον τινὰ καλούμενον
Καλοὺς Λιμένας, ᾧ ἐγγὺς ἦν πόλις[1] Λασαία. 9. Ἱκανοῦ δὲ χρόνου
διαγενομένου, καὶ ὄντος[2] ἤδη ἐπισφαλοῦς τοῦ πλοός, διὰ τὸ καὶ
τὴν νηστείαν ἤδη παρεληλυθέναι, παρῄνει ὁ Παῦλος, λέγων αὐτοῖς,

---

[1] Λασαια, so HLP, Chrys., Arm., Blass in β text, Weiss, Hilgenfeld, but ℵ*
Λασσαια ; B, so W.H., Λασεα ; Λαῖσσα ℵc ; A 40, 96, Αλασσα (Lach.), Syr. H.
mg., Alasa ; Vulg., Thalassa ; see further W.H., *App.*, p. 167, and Winer-Schmiedel,
pp. 47, 58.

[2] ηδη omit. in β text by Blass with Flor., Gig.

---

course, and the westerly winds, preju-
dicial to the run of the Adramyttian ship
from Sidon to Myra, were favourable for
the direct run of a ship from Alexandria,
cf. ver. 9, and the course taken by the
Alexandrian ship was probably a customary one during a certain season of the
year for the voyage from Alexandria to
Italy. Blass, on the other hand, quoting
from Lucian, maintains that the ship
was obliged to quit the usual course
owing to the winds, but Ramsay has
here the entire support of J. Smith, *u. s.*,
p. 73.—ἐνεβίβασεν : *vox nautica*, Holtzmann, *cf.* Thuc., i., 53.
Ver. 7. ἐν ἱκαναῖς ἡμέραις or ἱκανός :
in temporal sense only in Luke in N.T.,
see Hawkins, p. 151, and *cf. Vindiciæ
Lucanæ* (Klostermann), p. 51.—βραδυπλοοῦντες : Artemid., *Oneir.*, iv., 30 ;
ταχυπλοεῖν, Polyb. (Blass), evidently on
account of the strong westerly winds ;
the distance was about a hundred and
thirty geographical miles to Cnidus.—καὶ
μόλις γεν. κατὰ τὴν Κ. : "and were come
with difficulty off Cnidus," R.V., to this
point the course of the two ships would be
the same from Myra ; here they would no
longer enjoy the protection of the shore,
or the help of the local breezes and cur-
rents ; "so far the ship would be sheltered from the north-westerly winds, at
Cnidus that advantage ceased" (J.
Smith).—Κνίδον : the south-west point
of Asia Minor, the dividing line between
the western and southern coast ; a Dorian
colony in Caria having the rank of a free
city like Chios ; see 1 Macc. xv. 23.—
μὴ προσεῶντος : "as the wind did not
permit our straight course onwards,"
Ramsay, so Blass, J. Smith, p. 79 : the
northerly wind in the Ægean effectually prevented them from running straight
across to the island of Cythera, north
of Crete ; *cf.* Wendt's note (1899), *in
loco*, inclining to agree with Ramsay, see
critical note ; others take the words to
mean "the wind not permitting us

unto it," *i.e.*, to approach Cnidus (Hackett), so too R.V., margin. But there
does not seem to have been any reason
why they should not have entered the
southern harbour of Cnidus. They might
have done so, and waited for a fair wind,
had they not adopted the alternative of
running for the east and south coast of
Crete. The verb προσεῶντος does not
occur elsewhere, and the same must be
said of the conjecture of Blass, προ-
εῶντος. — ὑπεπλεύ. : "we sailed under
the lee of Crete off Cape Salmone "
(Ramsay), *i.e.*, a promontory on the east
of the island, and protected by it from a
north-westerly wind (Ramsay). Strabo
has Σαλμώνιον and Σαμώνιον (Pliny,
Sammonium) ; Σαλμώνις is also found ;
Σαλμώνιον (or Σαμμ.) may be explained,
sc. ὄρος, Winer-Schmiedel, p. 65.
Ver. 8. μόλις τε παραλεγ. αὐτήν :
"and with difficulty coasting along it,"
i.e., Crete on the southern side—with
difficulty because under the same conditions as in their journey along the coast
of Asia Minor (Breusing) (this is better
than to refer αὐτήν to Σαλμώνην, and
render to work past, to weather, *cf.*
Grimm - Thayer) ; παραλέγομαι, *oram
legere*, Diodorus Siculus, Strabo.—Καλοὺς
Λιμένας : a small bay two miles east of
Cape Matala, in modern Greek, Λιμε-
ῶνας Καλούς, J. Smith, p. 82, and
Appendix, p. 251 ff., 4th edition ; not mentioned, however, elsewhere. This harbour
would afford them shelter for a time, for
west of Cape Matala the land trends
suddenly to the north, and they would
have been again exposed to the north-
westerly winds ; see further for a description of the place Findlay's *Mediterranean Directory*, p. 66, quoted by Breusing and Goerne, who also have no doubt
that the place is identical with that mentioned by St. Luke (see also Wendt,
1898 and 1899).—Λασαία, see critical
note ; like the Fair Havens not mentioned by name in any ancient writer,

10. Ἄνδρες, θεωρῶ ὅτι μετὰ ὕβρεως καὶ πολλῆς ζημίας οὐ μόνον
τοῦ[1] φόρτου καὶ τοῦ πλοίου, ἀλλὰ καὶ τῶν ψυχῶν ἡμῶν, μέλλειν

[1] ℵABHLP, Chrys., and Tisch., W.H., R.V., Blass, Weiss, Wendt read φορτιον.

but since 1856 it may be fairly said that
its identification has been established
with a place some four miles to the east
of Fair Havens, or rather the ruins of a
place to which the name Lasea was still
given, see J. Smith, 4th edition, p. 82,
and p. 268 (Appendix); Alford, *Proleg.*
to Acts, p. 27. If Lasea was one of
"the (ninety or) hundred towns of
Crete," and one of the smaller amongst
them, it ceases to be strange that no
precise mention of it should occur in
ancient writers (Grimm).

Ver. 9. ἱκανοῦ δὲ χρ. γεν.: not since
the commencement of the voyage (as
Meyer), but since they lay weather-
bound. Wendt (1899) agrees with Meyer
as against Weiss and Ramsay, on the
ground that there is no ἐκεῖ, so Hackett.
—ἐπισ. τοῦ πλοός: "terminus proprie
nauticus," Klostermann, *Vindiciæ Lucanæ*, J. Smith, p. 84, who refers to Jul.
Pollux, i., 105, although the adjective
was not distinctively so. It is only used
by St. Luke, and although it is frequently
employed by medical writers, it is found
also in Plato, Polybius, Plutarch (*cf.*
also Wisd. ix. 14, and for the adverb iv.
4). τοῦ πλοός: "the voyage," R.V.,
but perhaps "sailing," A.V., is best, so
Ramsay—the dangerous season for *sailing*
had commenced; in the next verse =
"voyage," *i.e.*, to Rome (Alford); only in
Luke, *cf.* xxi. 7, on the form of the genitive
see Winer-Schmiedel, p. 84, *cf.* 1 Cor.
xiv. 15, 19, 2 Thess. ii. 2. The dangerous
season was reckoned from 14th September
to 11th November, and from 11th November to 5th March all navigation was
discontinued; see Blass, *in loco*, and
Ramsay, *Saint Paul*, p. 322; according
to Hesiod, *Works and Days*, 619, navigation ceased after the setting of the
Pleiades about 20th October. The
Jewish period for navigation ended 28th
September.— διὰ τὸ καὶ τὴν νηστείαν
ἤδη παρεληλυθέναι: the mention of the
fact that the Fast, *i.e.*, the Great Day of
Atonement, Lev. xvi. 29, Jos., *Ant.*, xiv.,
16, 4, was over, Tisri the 10th, made the
danger more apparent. According to
Mr. Turner, "Chronology," Hastings'
B.D., the great Fast on Tisri 10 in 58
A.D. fell *circa* 15th September, so that
the dangerous sailing season would
have just commenced. In A.D. 59, the

date preferred by Ramsay, the Fast
would be on 5th October. Starting from
the view that a considerably later point
of time than Tisri 10 is implied, *cf.*
xxviii. 11, various attempts have been
made to interpret νηστεία differently, and
it has been referred to the Athenian festival of the Thesmophoria, the third day of
which was so called; or to some nautical
mode of expression not elsewhere employed equivalent to *extremum autumni*,
but all such attempts are based upon no
authority (Zöckler, *in loco*), and there
can be no doubt that the expression "the
Fast" κατ᾽ ἐξοχήν refers to the Jewish
Fast as above. St. Paul usually reckoned
after the Jewish calendar, 1 Cor. xvi. 8,
and as Wendt observes there is nothing
strange in the fact that his travel-com-
panion should also so reckon, *cf.* xx.
6 above, even if he was a Gentile
Christian, an observation to be noted in
face of Schmiedel's recent arguments
against the Lucan authorship, *Encycl.
Biblica*, p. 44, 1899. The indication that
St. Paul kept the Jewish Fast Day is
significant. — παρῄνει: "admonished,"
R. and A.V., in N.T. only here, and in
ver. 22, see note. The Apostle had
sufficient experience to justify him, 2
Cor xi. 25 (Weiss), his interposition is
all an indication of the respect which he
had secured: "the event justified St.
Paul's advice," J. Smith.

Ver. 10. θεωρῶ: here used of the
result of experience and observation,
not of a revelation, *cf.* xvii. 22, xix.
26, xxi. 20. — θεωρῶ ὅτι . . . μέλλειν
ἔσεσθαι: anacoluthon. ὅτι: forgotten by the number of words intervening in the flow of speech—a vivid
dramatic touch; *cf.* Xen., *Hell.*, ii., 2, 2,
see Blass, *Gram.*, p. 279, Winer-Moulton,
xliv., 8, A 2. μέλλειν ἔσεσθαι, *cf.* xi.
28, xxiv. 15, 25, only in Luke, Simcox,
Language of the N.T., p. 120. μετὰ
ὕβρεως καὶ πολλῆς ζημίας, *cf.* ver. 21:
"with injury and much loss," A. and
R.V. ὕβρις: used of the injury inflicted
by the elements, *injuria tempestatis*, *cf.*
Jos., *Ant.*, iii., 6, 4. τὴν ἀπὸ τῶν ὄμβρων
ὕβριν: *Anthol.*, vii., 291,'3. δείσασα
θαλάττης ὕβριν: Grimm-Thayer renders
"injury inflicted by the violence of a
tempest," and this well combines the
active and passive shades of meaning;

ἔσεσθαι τὸν πλοῦν. 11.[1] ὁ δὲ ἑκατόνταρχος τῷ κυβερνήτῃ καὶ τῷ ναυκλήρῳ ἐπείθετο μᾶλλον ἢ τοῖς ὑπὸ τοῦ Παύλου λεγομένοις. 12. ἀνευθέτου δὲ τοῦ λιμένος ὑπάρχοντος πρὸς παραχειμασίαν, οἱ πλείους ἔθεντο βουλὴν ἀναχθῆναι κἀκεῖθεν, εἴ πως δύναιντο καταντήσαντες εἰς Φοίνικα παραχειμάσαι, λιμένα τῆς Κρήτης βλέποντα κατὰ

---

[1] Blass in β text reconstructs with Flor.: ο δε κυβ. και ο ναυκ. εβουλευοντο πλειν ει πως δυναιντο καταντ. εις Φ. λιμενα της Κ. (και) επειθετο εκεινοις μαλλον ο εκατονταρχης η τοις υπο Π. λεγ.; all the rest of ver. 12 omitted by Flor., see especially Blass, *Præf.* to β text, pp. x., xi.

---

for the passive signification of ὕβρις *cf.* 2 Cor. xii. 10. ζημίαν: only elsewhere in Paul, *cf.* Phil. iii. 7, 8. οὐ μόνον: occurs regularly with the infinitive in the N.T. instead of μὴ μόνον, Burton, p. 183. φόρτου, see critical note, if we read φορτίου the word which is dim. in form not in significance is often found of the freight of a ship; but see also Blass and Wetstein, *in loco*, for distinction between φορτίον and φόρτος.

Ver. 11. ὁ δὲ ἑκατόν.: the centurion evidently presides at the Council as the superior officer, see Ramsay, *St. Paul*, pp. 324, 325, but, as Wendt notes (and so Blass), the majority decide, not the centurion alone. — τῷ κυβερ. καὶ τῷ ναυκλ.: "to the master and to the owner of the ship," A. and R.V., better "to the pilot and the captain"; ναύκληρος was not the owner, although the word might denote ownership as well as command of the ship, for the ship if it was a corn ship would belong to the imperial service, and would form a vessel of the Alexandrian fleet. In Breusing's view, p. 160, ναύκληρος is owner of the ship, but κυβερνήτης is better rendered, he thinks, "captain" than "pilot," *cf.* Plut., *Mor.*, 807 B (Wetstein and Blass). — ἐπείθετο μᾶλλον τοῖς λεγ.: "locutio Lucana," *cf.* xxviii. 24, the centurion's conduct was natural enough; what would be said of him in Rome, where provision ships for the winter were so eagerly expected, if out of timidity he, though a soldier, had hindered the captain from continuing his voyage? Breusing, pp. 161, 162, and quotations from Suet., *Claudius*, 18, as to the compensation offered by the emperor to merchants for losses in winter and storm. Goerne points out that it may have been also to their interest to proceed on the voyage, rather than to incur the responsibility of providing for the keep of the large crew during a long stay at Fair Havens.

Ver. 12. ἀνευθέτου: here only, but in later Greek we have δύσθετος, so in Jos.

St. Luke, however, uses εὔθετος in his Gospel, ix. 62, xiv. 35 (found only once elsewhere in N.T., Heb. vi. 7). We may compare J. Smith's 1st and 4th edition, p. 85. In the latter he points out that recent surveys show that Fair Havens may have been a very fair winter harbour, and that even on nautical grounds St. Paul's action may have been justified, but Blass, *in loco*, adheres to the view that the harbour was only fit for use during the summer. — πρὸς παραχειμασίαν: noun only here in N.T., not found in LXX, but in Polyb. and Diod. Sic. παραχειμάσαι: only in Luke and Paul in N.T., 1 Cor. xvi. 6, *cf.* Acts xxviii. 11, Tit. iii. 12, not in LXX, but used by Dem., Polyb., Plut., Diod. Sic. — οἱ πλείονες: πλείονες (πλείους) with the article only by Luke and Paul in N.T., *cf.* xix. 32; by St. Paul seven times in his Epistles. Bengel well says, "plura suffragia non semper meliora". — ἔθεντο βουλὴν: on the noun and its use by St. Luke see above, ii. 23, and for the phrase *cf.* Luke xxiii. 51, in LXX, Ps. xii. 2 (Judg. xix. 30, A *al.*); so also in classical Greek. — ἀναχθῆναι: "to put to sea," R.V., see on xiii. 13. — εἴ πως δύναιντο: on the optative see Simcox, *Language of the N.T.*, p. 172; and Burton, p. 111; *cf.* Mark xi. 13, Acts viii. 22, xviii. 27, Rom. i. 10, xi. 14, Phil. iii.

11. — καταντήσαντες: Lucan and Pauline, see above, xvi. 1. — εἰς Φοίνικα, Strabo, x., 4; Ptolemy, iii., 17. Generally taken as = modern *Lutro*, so Ramsay, Alford, Renan, Rendall, Blass, J. Smith (pp. 87, 88), Lewin, Rendall, Plumptre, and Muir in Hastings' B.D., "Fair Havens"; so amongst recent German writers on this voyage, *cf.* Breusing, p. 162, and Goerne, *u. s.*, p. 360, both of whom quote Findlay, *Mediterranean Directory*, p. 67, "Port Lutro, the ancient Phœnix, or Phœnice, is the only bay on the south coast where a vessel could be quite secure in winter"; but on the other hand Hackett, *in loco*, Wordsworth,

λίβα καὶ κατὰ χῶρον. 13. ὑποπνεύσαντος δὲ νότου,[1] δόξαντες τῆς προθέσεως κεκρατηκέναι, ἄραντες[2] ἆσσον παρελέγοντο τὴν Κρήτην.

[1] Flor. om. δοξ. . . . κεκρατ., so Blass in β.

[2] For ασσον Blass in β with Flor. reads θασσον, so Hilg. (1899); Vulg., so Erasmus, "cum sustulissent de Asson," taking Assos as Ασος (Asus, Pliny) as the name of one of the Cretan towns; Luther takes it as acc., "cum sustulissent Assum". Wycl. and Rhem. follow the Vulg., and Tynd. and Cranm. follow Luther, but there is no clear trace of the existence of a town so called in Crete, and Assos lay far to the north, xx. 13 (Plumptre).

Humphry and Page (whose full note should be consulted) suppose the modern Phineka to be meant; so also C. H. Prichard in Hastings' B.D., "Crete"; see below. Alford, *Acts*, Proleg., p. 28, quotes from J. Smith's Appendix (2nd edition) the words from Mr. G. Brown's Journal (1855, 1856) stating that Lutro is the only secure harbour *in all winds* on the south coast of Crete, words quoted by Ramsay, *St. Paul*, p. 326, and Muir, Hastings' B.D., "Fair Havens".—λιμένα τῆς Κ. κ.τ.λ.: "a harbour of Crete which faces south-west and north-west," so Ramsay, and so A.V. and Vulgate. But R.V. so Rendall, "looking north-east and south-east," which is a correct description of the entrance of the harbour of Lutro, so J. Smith, Alford, Lumby and Plumptre, who interpret "looking down the south-west and north-west winds," literally translated as = in the direction of these winds, *i.e.*, the direction *to* which they blew, and so north-east and south-east, κατά indicating the line of motion, *cf.* R.V. margin, and so Rendall and Knabenbauer, *in loco*. C. and H., so Ramsay and Farrar, find an explanation of the rendering in A.V. in the subjectivity of the sailors, who describe a harbour from the direction in which they sail into it; and thus by transmission from mouth to mouth the wrong impression arose that the harbour itself looked south-west and north-west. As against Rendall's interpretation and that of R.V., see Page and Hackett's learned notes *in loco*. Both lay stress upon the phrase, βλέπειν κατά τι, as used only of that which is *opposite*, and which you *face*. *Cf.* Luke's own use of κατά, iii. 13, viii. 26, xvi. 7, xxvii. 7. Page, and so C. H. Prichard, Hastings' B.D., "Crete," would adopt A.V. reading, but would apply it to the harbour Phineka, opposite Lutro, which does look south-west and north-west. λίψ, (prob. λείβω) Herod., ii., 25, Polyb., x.,

103, etc., south-west wind *Africus*, χῶρος, north-west wind *Corus* or *Caurus*. Ver. 13. ὑποπνεύσαντος: *leniter afflante, aspirante, cf.* ὑποκινέω, ὑπομειδιάω, a moderate breeze from the south arose which would favour their westerly course. *Cf.* Luke xii. 55, not in LXX or Apocrypha, but see Heliod., iii., 3 (Wetstein). — δόξαντες, xii. 9, τῆς προθ. κεκρατηκέναι: their purpose, *i.e.*, of starting from Fair Havens for the more desirable anchorage of Lutro some forty miles distant. προθέσεως, *cf.* xi. 23; in N.T. only in Luke and Paul in this sense; *cf.* 2 Macc. iii. 8. κεκρατ.: only here in this sense in N.T., *cf.* Diod. Sic., xvi. 20, κεκρατηκότες ἤδη τῆς προθέσεως (Grimm-Thayer, Page), and for instances of the same collocation of words in Galen, and in Polyb. (κατακρατεῖν), see Wettstein and Blass, *in loco*. Breusing, p. 164, takes the phrase to refer here to their purpose of continuing their voyage to the end (so too Goerne).— ἄραντες: "they weighed anchor," R.V. So Ramsay, J. Smith, pp. 65, 97; only here in N.T. in this sense, *sc.* τὰς ἀγκύρας, *cf.* Thuc., i., 52, and ii., 23, but the word may imply simply *profecti*, of movement, whether by sea or by land, of armies or ships; so Breusing takes it intransitively, no need of any noun, Thuc., iv., 129; vii., 26 (p. 164): see also ver. 17. For aorist participle of an action antecedent in time to that of the principal verb *cf.* xiv. 19: Burton, pp. 63, 64.—ἆσσον παρελ. τὴν Κ.: "sailed along Crete, close in-shore," R.V., *i.e.*, as they rounded Cape Matala, about six miles west of Fair Havens; the statement so emphatically introduced by St. Luke seems to imply that their ability to weather the point was for some time doubtful, Ramsay, *St. Paul*, p. 326. ἆσσον: "if the wind went round a point towards the west they would fail; and the anxious hour has left its record in the single word of ver. 13, 'ἆσσον,'" Ramsay, *u. s.* See critical note, and

14. μετ᾽ οὐ πολὺ δὲ ἔβαλε κατ᾽ αὐτῆς ἄνεμος τυφωνικός, ὁ καλούμενος ¹ Εὐροκλύδων.   15. συναρπασθέντος δὲ τοῦ πλοίου, καὶ μὴ

¹ Εὐρακυλων א AB*, Tisch., W.H., R.V., Weiss, Wendt, Blass, HLP, Chrys.
have Εὐροκλυδων, so Hilg. (1899) ; B³ 40, 133 ; Εὐρυκλυδων (Griesbach, Meyer,
Nosgen) ; i.e., a wind causing broad waves, the Wide-washer (Grimm-Thayer, sub v.,
" der Breitspülende " supported "by respectable authorities "). Vulg., Cassiod.
have " Euro-aquilo," see Hastings' B.D., sub v., and comment. below.

above on ver. 8. ἆσσον, an adverb comparative of ἄγχι ; the comparative degree
makes it more emphatic (see above), as
they had been coasting for weeks, and
they now went "closer" in shore (see
R.V.) ; Wendt (1899) takes it, however,
not as a comparative with reference to
ver. 8 (so Meyer, Weiss), but as a superlative, cf. xxiv. 22, xxv. 10.
Ver. 14. μετ᾽ οὐ πολὺ δὲ, cf. xx. 12.
οὐ μετρίως, Luke xv. 15, Acts i. 5, "observe the 'Litotes' of οὐ with an adjective or adverb, four times in 'We'
sections, twelve in rest of Acts, twice in
Luke vii. 6, xv. 13, rare in rest of N.T.,"
Hawkins, p. 153.—ἔβαλε κατ᾽ αὐτῆς :
intransitive, as often in classical Greek
since Homer : " there beat down from
it," R.V., i.e., from Crete and its mountains over 7,000 feet in height ; so also
Blass, Holtzmann, Ramsay, Zöckler,
Page, Rendall, Wendt, Weiss, Knabenbauer, and J. Smith, in later editions, see
p. 100, 4th edition ; a graphic description
of a common experience in the Cretan
waters ; as the ship crossed the open bay
between Cape Matala and Phœnice, the
wind suddenly shifting to the north, a
violent hurricane (strictly from east-north-
east) burst upon them from Mount Ida,
cf. St. Luke's κατέβη, Luke viii. 23, of a
squall descending from the hills on the
Lake of Gennesaret, and κατὰ τοῦ κρημ-
νοῦ, Luke viii. 33, cf. Matt. viii. 32 (J.
Smith, Weiss, Zöckler). Breusing, p.
164 (so Hackett, Lewin, Farrar), takes
κατ᾽ αὐτῆς as = against the ship, but
the word πλοῖον is used for ship, and not
ναῦς until ver. 41. Luther regarded αὐτῆς
as agreeing with προθέσεως (so Tyndale
and Cranmer).—τυφωνικός : formed from
τυφώς, turbo, denoting not the direction,
but the vehemence of the wind (Breusing,
Page), a heavy, eddying squall (J. Smith,
Ramsay), vorticosus (Bentley).—Εὐροκλύδων, see critical note. If we read
with א AB* Εὐρακύλων, render "which
is called Euraquilo," R.V. Perhaps the
irregularly formed Euraquilo occasioned
the corrections. V. Euroaquilo. Blass
calls it vox hybrida from εὖρος and
Aquilo (qui Latin = κϋ, ut Ἀκύλας,

xviii. 2), strictly the " East-north-east "
wind (Breusing thinks " North-east "
sufficient ; so Wycliffe and Tyndale in
their translations). Such a wind would
drive the ship into the African Syrtis as
the pilot feared, ver. 17, and the word is
apposite to the context, to all the circumstances, and is so well attested as to
fairly claim admission as the word of St.
Luke. The Latin had no name for the
Greek Καικίας blowing between Aquilo
and Eurus, and it is quite possible that
the Roman seamen, for want of a specific
word, might express this wind by the
compound Euro-Aquilo ; cf. ὁ καλούμενος,
which seems to point to some popular
name given to the wind ; for similar compounds cf. Εὐρόνοτος and Euro-Auster,
and Gregalia, the name given to the
same wind by the Levantines, as Euripus
has become Egripou (Renan, Saint Paul,
p. 551) ; see Bentley, Remarks on a late
Discourse on Freethinking, p. 97, quoted
at length by Breusing, " Euraquilo,"
Hastings' B.D. and B.D.², i.
Ver. 15. συναρπασθέντος δὲ τοῦ
πλοίου : " and when the ship was caught
by it " (Ramsay), a graphic word as if
the ship was seized in the grasp of the
wind ; only in Luke, cf. Luke viii. 29,
Acts vi. 12, xix. 29 ; in LXX cf. Prov.
vi. 25, 2 Macc. iii. 27, iv. 41, 4 Macc. v.
4 ; so in classical Greek, e.g., Soph.,
Electr., 1150.—ἀντοφθαλμεῖν : "and could
not face the wind," R.V., "look at the
wind eye to eye " : eyes were painted on
the prows of vessels, but Alford thinks
that the word was not originally a nautical
term derived from this practice, but that
more probably the expression was transferred to a ship from its usage in common life ; it is used in Polybius of facing
an enemy, Polyb., i., 17, 3, of resisting
temptation, xxviii. 17, 18, with δύνασθαι
as here, and also with δύνασθαι in Wisd.
xii. 14, cf. Acts vi. 11, β text. For the
fit application of the word to a ship
see Breusing, p. 168.—ἐπιδόντες ἐφερόμεθα : " we gave way to it (to the wind),
and were driven," or τὸ πλοῖον may be
regarded as the object, " we gave up the
ship to the winds," " data nave fluctibus

δυναμένου ἀντοφθαλμεῖν τῷ ἀνέμῳ, ἐπιδόντες[1] ἐφερόμεθα. 16. νησίον
δέ τι ὑποδραμόντες καλούμενον[2] Κλαύδην, μόλις ἰσχύσαμεν περι-
κρατεῖς γενέσθαι τῆς σκάφης· 17. ἦν ἄραντες, βοηθείαις ἐχρῶντο,

[1] After ἐπιδ. Blass in β text, so Hilg. (1899) add τῷ πνεοντι και συστειλαντες
τα ιστια with 137, Syr. H. (cf. Cassiod., Bede), and before εφερ. Blass has κατα
το συμβαινον (Hilg. τυχον) with Syr. H.

[2] Κλαυδην HLP d; ℵ* Κλαυδα Syr. H., Arm., Boh., so Tisch., Weiss; A has
first three letters Κλα; but ℵcB, Vulg. have Καυδα, W.H., Blass, so R.V. text
(Κλαυδα marg.), Hilg. (1899), and the form Κλαυδα is supported by Κλαυδος in
Ptolem., iii., 15, 8, and other authorities in Hastings' B.D., "Cauda" (Ramsay).
See note in comment., and Wendt, p. 408 (1899). The variation cannot be ac-
counted for by the mere dropping out of Λ before Α as Weiss maintains, for the
difference of spelling occurs in other than MS. authorities. But see further
Winer-Schmiedel, p. 65, note.

ferebamur," Vulgate, so Holtzmann,
Zöckler, Hackett, Wordsworth, and J.
Smith, p. 106. The instances in Wetstein
justify either rendering, see also references in Blass, *in loco*. ἐφερόμεθα: "and
let the ship drive," Ramsay and A.V.,
others render as passive, so Grimm-
Thayer, *sub v.*; in classical Greek it is
often used passively for being borne
along by wind, or storm, or wave, *cf.*
Hom., *Odys.*, v., 343 (Page); Diod.
Sic., xx., 16.

Ver. 16. ὑποδραμόντες: "and running
under the lee of a small island," R.V.
J. Smith calls attention to the nautical
accuracy of St. Luke's terms; they ran
before the wind to leeward of Cauda;
ὑποδραμ., they sailed with a side wind
to leeward of Cyprus and Crete, ὑπεπλεύσαμεν, ver. 4, see also Ramsay,
Saint Paul, p. 328, to the same effect;
here was calmer water, and the island
(see below) would afford them a refuge
for a time from the gale. Breusing, pp.
167, 168, 181, thinks that the great sail
had been struck at once, and that the
artemon or small foresail was kept up as
a storm sail; otherwise the ship would
have been simply the plaything of the
waves. But Ramsay and others (see Farrar) think, on the contrary, that the one
huge sail, in comparison with which all
others were of little importance, was kept
up, but that the strain of this great sail
on the single mast was more than the
hull could sustain; the timbers would
have started, and the ship foundered, had
she not gained the smooth water to the
lee of Cauda.—μόλις ἰσχύσ.: "we were
able with difficulty to secure the boat,"
R.V., the boat had not been hauled in, as
the storm was so sudden; and now as it
was nearly filled with water, and battered
by the waves and storm, it was hard work
to haul it in at all (J. Smith), as Luke

himself experienced (pressed into this
service of hauling in the boat; note first
person, Hackett, Ramsay, p. 327); clearly
they could not afford to lose such a means
of safety; even as it was, the boat was
dragging along as a heavy weight retarding the ship (Breusing, p. 169).—
περικ., *cf.* Susannah, ver. 39, A, for
ἐγκρατεῖς in B.—σκάφης: a small boat
towed behind, only in this passage in
N.T., *cf.* vv. 30, 32, Latin, *scapha*; Cic.,
De Invent., ii., 51 (Humphry).—Κλαύδην, see critical note, an island twenty-
three miles from Crete, nearly due
south of Phœnice. Ramsay (but see on
the other hand Wendt, p. 408, 1899)
maintains that preference be given to the
forms of the name in which the letter
L is omitted, *cf.* the modern *Gavdho* in
Greek, and *Gozzo* in Italian; not to be confounded with *Gozzo* near Malta (Renan,
Saint Paul, p. 551), and see further on
its present name, J. Smith, pp. 95, 259,
4th edition.

Ver. 17. ἦν ἄραντες: "and when they
had hoisted it up" into the ship, see on
ver. 13.—βοηθ. ἐχρῶντο: they used helps
ὑποζ. τὸ πλοῖον undergirding the ship,
A. and R.V., on ἐχρῶντο see ver. 3, *cf.*
1 Cor. ix. 12, 15; often compared to the
custom called in modern language *frap-
ping*, or undergirding the ship with
cables to prevent the timbers from being
strained, or to hold them together during
a storm, Plato, *Rep.*, 616, C, Polyb.,
xxvii., 3, 3, Horace, *Od.*, i., 14, 6. The difficult point to decide is whether the girders
were put longitudinally round the ship,
i.e., passed from stem to stern, or under
the ship transversely. Breusing, p. 670
(so Goerne and Vars), defends the former
at great length, following Böckh. The
passage from Plato, *u. s.*, he admits may
possibly make for the latter view, but it
is evident that the description is not

ὑποζωννύντες τὸ πλοῖον· φοβούμενοί τε μὴ εἰς τὴν σύρτιν ἐκπέσωσι, χαλάσαντες ¹ τὸ σκεῦος, οὕτως ἐφέροντο. 18. Σφοδρῶς δὲ χειμαζο-

¹ For χαλασ. το σκενος Blass has in β text εχαλασαν τι σκενος φερεσθαι following Gig. "vas quoddam dimiserunt, quod traheret," so Hilg. (1899), χαλασ. τι σκ. εφελκυστικον; see note below.

very definite or precise, and the passage in Isidore of Seville, Orig., xix., 4, 4, "tormentum (ὑπόζωμα) funis in navibus longus, qui a prora ad puppim extenditur, quo magis constringantur," which Böckh quotes (so also Vars, L'Art Nautique, p. 219) is much clearer. Moreover, the girding was often performed when the ships were on land, on the stocks, and it is not likely that the operation in the circumstances under discussion could have meant passing a cable under the keel. Further, by girding the ship transversely, i.e., underneath the ship (p. 175), only the timbers in the middle of the ship would be held together, whilst a girding longitudinally was needed to secure the whole plankage of the ship. But see on the other hand Ramsay, p. 329, who agreeing with Smith holds that the cables were passed underneath round the ship transversely. Either operation, one would suppose, would have been difficult during a storm. For instances of this practice in modern times, see Smith, and C. and H., small edit., p. 645. Wendt (1899) refers to Naber's conjecture of βοείαις for βοηθ. as very plausible.—μὴ εἰς τὴν Σ.: "on the great quicksands," Ramsay; "the Syrtis," R.V., not merely "the quicksands," as A.V., but the Syrtis Major, "the Goodwin Sands of the Mediterranean" (Farrar), lying at a distance to the south-west of Clauda; upon them the sailors knew that they would be cast, unless they could manage by some means to alter their course.—ἐκπέσωσι: a regular nautical term, to fall off, ἐκ, i.e., from a straight course, εἰς—Eur., Hel., 409, Herod., viii., 13, others supply "from deep water" and render ἐκπ. to be cast away, Grimm-Thayer, sub v., cf. vv. 26, 29.—χαλάσ. τὸ σκεῦος: "lowered the gear," R.V., "they reduced sail," Ramsay; here and in ver. 30 used as a nautical term; the tempting reference to Isa. xxxiii. 23, LXX, cannot be sustained, for the meaning of the words is very doubtful. The article with the singular (in ver. 19, the plural) seems to indicate "the gear," the mainyard carrying the mainsail (so Page, Wordsworth, Humphry). Of the A.V., J. Smith says that no more erroneous translation could be imagined, as "they struck sail" would imply that the ship

had no means of escaping danger, but was left to flounder hopelessly in the storm, although Meyer-Wendt take the words to mean that they preferred to let the ship drift without any mast or sail than to be driven on upon the Syrtis, as was inevitable with the ship kept in full sail. Chrysostom explains τὸ σκ. as = τὰ ἱστία, but some sail was necessary, and they had still the artemon or storm sail, so J. Smith, who thinks that they lowered the great sail and mainyard some way, but not apparently entirely. The aim of the sailors was not merely to delay their course (which would only bring them upon the Syrtis), but to alter it, and it is therefore quite possible that χαλάσ. τὸ σκεῦος may denote a series of operations, slackening sail, lowering as much of the gear as they could, but leaving enough sail spread to keep the ship's head to the wind, i.e., to the north instead of drifting to south-west upon the quicksand (Ramsay). Breusing, p. 177 ff., who thinks that the mainsail had been lowered at the commencement of the storm, adopts quite a different meaning for the words, and interprets them as implying that weights and great stones were let down by ropes into the sea for the purpose of retarding the progress of the vessel, and with this view Blass and Knabenbauer are in agreement (Wendt, 1899, evidently inclines to it, and Goerne adopts it); this curious view, which Ramsay finds it difficult to regard seriously, Breusing supports by a passage in Plut., Moral., p. 507, A (so Hesychius' explanation, ἄγκυρα τὸ ναυτικὸν σκεῦος), which intimates that σπεῖραι and ἄγκυραι were frequently employed to check the course of a ship in a storm; but even if the Greek words admit of this explanation, the object of the sailors was nothing less than to alter the course of the vessel, and Breusing's supposition would not conduce to this.—οὕτως ἐφέροντο: "so were driven," R.V., i.e., in this state, "and drove on so," Rendall; meaning that we let the ship drift in that position, viz., undergirded, with storm sail set and on the starboard tack; J. Smith, so Ramsay, not simply "were driven hopelessly". For οὕτως, xvii. 33, xx. 11.

Ver. 18. σφοδρῶς δὴ χειμαζ. ἡμῶν:

μένων ἡμῶν, τῇ ἑξῆς ἐκβολὴν ἐποιοῦντο· 19. καὶ τῇ τρίτῃ αὐτόχειρες
τὴν σκευὴν τοῦ πλοίου[1] ἐρρίψαμεν· 20.[2] μήτε δὲ ἡλίου μήτε ἄστρων
ἐπιφαινόντων ἐπὶ πλείονας ἡμέρας, χειμῶνός τε οὐκ ὀλίγου ἐπικει-

[1] Instead of 1st pers. pl. ℵAB*C, Vulg., Arm., so Tisch., W.H., R.V., Blass in β,
Weiss, Wendt have 3rd pers. (W.H., so Tisch., with one ρ with ℵB*, while AB³C
have double ρ); HLP, Syr. H. and P., Boh. have 1st pers. pl., and so Hilg.
(1899) with one ρ. 137 Syr. H., Wern. add εἰς τὴν θαλασσαν, so Blass in β text,
and Hilg.; Winer-Schmiedel, p. 56.

[2] At beginning of verse Blass in β and Hilg. (1899) add επιμενοντος δε του
χειμωνος και with Gig., Syr. P. (the latter with επι πλ. ημ. after χειμωνος), whilst
χειμ. . . . to λοιπον is omitted.

"and as we laboured exceedingly with the storm," R.V., Ramsay, Rendall, a regular nautical and classical term; cf. Thuc., ii., 25; iii., 69; viii., 99; Plato, Ion, 540 B. In Attic Greek usually σφόδρα, but cf. LXX, Josh. iii. 16, Ecclus. xiii. 13, 4 Macc. vi. 11; only here in N.T. Weiss thinks that it is used to express how severely they were distressed by the storm.—τῇ ἑξῆς . . . καὶ τῇ τρίτῃ, cf. Luke xiii. 32, connected with the words which follow in R.V. and by Ramsay. For τῇ ἑξ. cf. Luke vii. 11 (but see W.H.), ix. 37, and above on xxi. 1, xxv. 17; nowhere else in N.T. — ἐκβολὴν ἐποιοῦντο: "they began to throw the freight overboard," R.V., Ramsay, Felten, a technical term, so in classical Greek, for throwing out cargo to lighten a ship; Latin jactura, LXX, Jonah i. 5, with τῶν σκευῶν, and Julius Pollux, i., 99, who also has the phrase κουφίσαι τὴν ναῦν, cf. ver. 38 below. The imperfect marks that they began by throwing away the cargo, probably what was on deck, so that the vessel would ship less water; and in ver. 19 they cast out (ἔρριψαν, aorist) the furniture of the ship, its fittings and equipment, anything movable lying on the deck upon which the passengers could lay their hands (αὐτόχειρες only here in N.T. representing the haste, Weiss). Others include under the word the actual baggage of the passengers, but we should have expected ἡμῶν instead of τοῦ πλοίου, whilst others explain of beds and crockery, tables, etc., furniture in this sense (Zöckler and Felten, exclusive of beds which were not in use). Breusing rejects this interpretation as "too silly," and he thinks that the expression really means that by thus throwing overboard the poles and tackling, room was found for the crowd of passengers on the deck, as the hatchways could not be kept open, since the heavy sea would have swamped the ship, p. 186. J. Smith takes σκευή to mean the mainyard, but the word is here apparently used in a more general sense, as above, R.V., margin, "furniture of the ship".

Ver. 19. ἐρρίψαμεν, see critical note. Ramsay prefers the first person, although not well supported, because it increases the effect; but in any case the scene is graphically described, ἔρριψαν may be due to ἐποιοῦντο, but, as Wendt notes, ἐρρίψαμεν may have been equally due to αὐτόχειρες. Breusing rejects the first person, p. 187, from a seaman's point of view; the sailors would have kept the passengers in their places, and not have allowed them to engage in a work in which they might perchance have done more harm than good.

Ver. 20. μήτε δὲ ἡλίου μήτε ἄστρων: the omission of the article here intensifies the meaning, Blass, Gram., p. 143, "weder etwas von Sonne".—ἐπιφαινόντων, cf. Luke i. 79; only in Luke and Paul, Tit. ii. 11, iii. 4; "shone upon us," R.V., thus their only guidance, humanly speaking (for, of course, they had no compass), was taken from them, cf. Æneid, i., 88; iii., 195; Horace, Epod., x., 9, and for the phrase, Polyb., v., 6, 6.—ἐπὶ πλείονας: often in Luke ἐπί with acc. of time, cf. xxviii. 6, and for instances in Luke and other parts of Acts of the same usage as predominant (though not exclusive) in Luke see Hawkins, Horæ Synopticæ, p. 152; Klostermann, Vindiciæ Lucanæ, p. 53; Luke x. 35, xviii. 4, Acts iii. 1, iv. 5, xiii. 31, xvi. 18, xvii. 2, xviii. 20, xix. 8, 10, 34.—οὐκ ὀλίγου: only in Luke, eight times in Acts; see above on ver. 14.— ἐπίκειμ., cf. 1 Cor. ix. 16, Heb. ix. 10, Luke v. 1, xxiii. 23 (John xi. 38, xxi. 9, literal sense), and for its use here, Plut., Timol., 28, τέλος δὲ τοῦ χειμῶνος ἐπικειμένου. In LXX, Job xix. 3, Wisd. xvii. 21 S, 1 Macc. vi. 57, 3 Macc. i. 22, etc.—

μένου, λοιπὸν περιῃρεῖτο πᾶσα ἐλπὶς τοῦ σώζεσθαι ἡμᾶς.   21.
πολλῆς δὲ[1] ἀσιτίας ὑπαρχούσης, τότε σταθεὶς ὁ Παῦλος ἐν μέσῳ
αὐτῶν εἶπεν, Ἔδει μέν, ὦ ἄνδρες, πειθαρχήσαντάς μοι μὴ ἀνάγεσθαι
ἀπὸ τῆς Κρήτης, κερδῆσαί τε τὴν ὕβριν ταύτην καὶ τὴν ζημίαν.

[1] For δε 𝕬ABC have τε, so Tisch., W.H., Blass, R.V., Hilg., Weiss, Wendt.

λοιπὸν (cf. Matt. xxvi. 45), "now,"
R.V., jam, Blass; often = ἤδη, L. and S.;
others render it: for the future (2 Tim.
iv. 8), finally, at last.—περιῃρεῖτο:
"was gradually taken away," Ramsay,
"imperf. quod in dies magis," Blass;
Page renders "was being gradually
stripped from us," a very vivid word, cf.
2 Cor. iii. 16, Heb. x. 11 (ver. 40, see
below), and its use in LXX and Psalms
of Solomon, ii. 22; cf. Westcott's note
on Heb., l.c., but on the other hand
Blass, in loco, regards the force of περί
as lost in the word in N.T. J. Smith (so
Breusing) sees in the expression more
than the hopelessness arising from the
force of the storm—we have also to
consider the fact that they could not see
their course, and the increasing leakage
of the vessel.

Ver. 21. δέ: if we read τε, see critical
note, the word closely connects what
follows as the result of the hopelessness.
—πολλῆς δὲ (τε) ἀσιτίας ὑπαρχ.: "and
when they had been long without food,"
R.V.; "abstinence," A.V. and Tyndale,
"fasting" in Wycl., Rhem., imply rather
a voluntary refraining which is not in the
Greek; disinclination for food may have
resulted from their anxiety (Humphry),
and to the same effect Breusing, Goerne,
"and little heart being left for food,"
Rendall. But the storm may also have
prevented the preparation of food (so
Smith, Ramsay, Page, Farrar); the former gives instances to show that ἀσιτία
was one of the most frequent concomit-
ants of heavy gales, owing to the impossibility of cooking food, and to the
destruction of provisions by leakage.
ἀσιτίας, see below, ver. 33, for the adjective: both noun and adjective peculiar to
St. Luke, and much employed in medical
language, both so noted by Hobart and
Zahn, the noun often meaning "want
of appetite," see instances in Hobart, p.
276, Hipp., Galen, Aret. The word was
no doubt similarly used in classical Greek,
so in Jos., but cf. the striking parallel in
ver. 33 in medical phraseology. For the
genitive absolute cf. locutiones Lucanæ
(Klostermann, p. 53), xv. 7, xix. 40, xxi.
40, xxiii. 10. Felten, Zöckler, Bethge

(and so Wendt, 1888, but cf. p. 410
(1899)), rightly refuse to regard vv. 21-
26 or ver. 10 as interpolations in the
"We" section, or a "vaticinium post
eventum," and no one has contended
more forcibly than Weizsäcker that the
narrative is to be taken as an indivisible
whole, and that it is impossible to disentangle the mere history of travel
from it, or to strip away the miraculous
additions, see especially Apostolic Age,
ii., pp. 126, 127, E.T.—τότε: in this
state of things, at this juncture,—
hungry, and thirsty, and their soul faint-
ing in them; cf. xxviii. 1, so also in
classical Greek.—σταθεὶς ὁ Π. ἐν μέσῳ
αὐτῶν, cf. i. 15, ii. 14, xvii. 22; vividness
and solemnity of the scene (αὐτῶν, not
ἡμῶν), characteristically marked by Luke;
Mr. Page well says that it is impossible
not to recall Horace, Od., iii., 3, 1, "vir
justus et propositi tenax," unmoved
amidst the storms "inquieti Adriæ".—
ἔδει μέν: antithesis, not strictly expressed.
. . . καὶ τὰ νῦν, ver. 22, "modestiam
habet," Bengel. For μέν answered not
by δέ, but occasionally by other particles,
as here by καί, cf. Luke xxii. 22, Acts
iv. 16; see Simcox, Language of the
N.T., p. 168, and for τὰ νῦν, see ver. 29,
v. 38, xvii. 30, xx. 32, and note on p. 135.
On the imperfect ἔδει cf. Burton, p. 14;
Winer-Moulton, xli., 2.—ὦ ἄνδρες:
"gentlemen," "viri quos decet virtus,"
Bengel, the word may thus mark St.
Paul's courtesy, and also his firmness;
in counsel, ver. 10, he had been prudent
and confident; in danger he was equally
so; cf. especially Weizsäcker, u. s.—
πειθαρχ.: only in Acts in N.T., v. 29,
32, except once again as used by St.
Paul, Tit. iii. 1.—ἀνάγ., see above, xiii.
13, and Blass, in loco, on the tense.—
κερδῆσαι: "and have gotten this injury
and loss," R.V., carrying on μή; Page on
the other hand prefers the combination
ἔδει τε κερδῆσαι ("hoc non pendet a μή,"
Bengel), i.e., you ought not to have put
to sea, and (you ought by so not putting
to sea) to have gained this loss, i.e., not
suffered it; with nouns signifying loss,
injury, the verb κερδαίνειν is used of
the gain arising from shunning or escap-

22. καὶ τανῦν παραινῶ ὑμᾶς εὐθυμεῖν· ἀποβολὴ γὰρ ψυχῆς οὐδεμία
ἔσται ἐξ ὑμῶν, πλὴν τοῦ πλοίου. 23. παρέστη γάρ μοι τῇ νυκτὶ
ταύτῃ ἄγγελος τοῦ Θεοῦ, οὗ εἰμι,[1] ᾧ καὶ λατρεύω, 24. λέγων, Μὴ
φοβοῦ, Παῦλε· Καίσαρί σε δεῖ παραστῆναι· καὶ ἰδού, κεχάρισταί σοι
ὁ Θεὸς πάντας τοὺς πλέοντας μετὰ σοῦ. 25. διὸ εὐθυμεῖτε, ἄνδρες·
πιστεύω γὰρ τῷ Θεῷ ὅτι οὕτως ἔσται καθ' ὃν τρόπον λελάληταί μοι.
26. εἰς νῆσον δέ τινα δεῖ ἡμᾶς ἐκπεσεῖν. 27. Ὡς δὲ τεσσαρεσκαιδεκάτη νὺξ ἐγένετο, διαφερομένων ἡμῶν ἐν τῷ Ἀδρίᾳ, κατὰ μέσον

[1] After ειμι Tisch. reads εγω, but om. W.H., Weiss, Wendt, etc., with B*CHLP.
αγγελος best after λατρ. with אABC, so W.H., Weiss, Blass, Wendt, R.V., Hilgenfeld instead of before του Θεου.

ing from the evil, Grimm-Thayer, sub v.,
see Eur., Cycl., 312, with ζημίαν, to
escape a loss, and cf. Jos., Ant., ii., 3, 2,
and the Latin lucrifacere, Pliny, N.H.,
vii., 40, "lucri fecit injuriam". The
Genevan Version adds an explanatory
note, "that is, ye should have saved the
losse by avoyding the danger"; see
also ver. 10. κερδῆσαι = κερδᾶναι,
-δῆναι; almost always in N.T., cf.
Winer-Schmiedel, p. 110.

Ver. 22. καὶ τὰ νῦν, see on ver 21,
Paul would spare their reproaches, and
rather awaken hope in their hearts
(Bethge).—παραινῶ: only in Luke, here
and in ver. 9. Hobart speaks of it as
the verb employed for a physician giving
his advice, and although the word is common in classical Greek, cf. also 2 Macc.
vii. 25, 26 R, 3 Macc. v. 17, vii. 12 A, its
frequency in medical usage may account
for its occurrence in this "We" section
only; see also Hawkins, Horæ Synopticæ,
p. 153.—εὐθυμεῖν, cf. vv. 25, 36, and xxiv.
10, elsewhere in N.T. only in James v. 10,
but in classical Greek, and εὔθυμος in 2
Macc. xi. 26. The verb, adjective, and
adverb εὐθύμως are used in medical language of the sick keeping up spirit, opposed to ἀθυμία and δυσθυμία; εὐθυμεῖν
παραινῶ might therefore well be a medical expression, Hobart, p. 280, although
the verb εὐθ. is used intransitively, as
here, in classical Greek, and in Plutarch.
—ἀποβολὴ: only here in N.T., "there
shall be no loss of life among you, but
only of the ship," R.V., Winer-Moulton,
lxvii. I.e., πλὴν with the genitive, Acts
viii. 1, xv. 28 (once elsewhere in N.T.,
Mark xii. 32).

Ver. 23. παρέστη . . . ἄγγελος: on
this Lucan phrase and description of
angelic appearances cf. Luke ii. 9, xxiv.
4, Acts xii. 7 (xxiii. 11), and see above, i. 10.
—τοῦ Θεοῦ: "of the God whose I am,

whom also I serve," R.V., Ramsay,
Rendall, not "an angel of God," as A.V.;
the R.V. rendering gives the force of
the Greek more naturally in addressing
a heathen; see also critical note.—λατρεύω, see on xxiv. 14; cf. Rom. i. 9,
and LXX, Jonah i. 9.

Ver. 24. μὴ φοβοῦ, see above, xviii. 9.
—παραστῆναι, cf. Rom. xiv. 10, the words
emphatically bear out the prominence
already laid upon the Apostle's witness in
Rome.—καὶ ἰδού, see on i. 10.—κεχάρισταί σοι: "hath granted them as a
favour"; see on iii. 14, no doubt Paul had
prayed for this, cf. especially Philemon
ver. 22. The statement in ver. 24 looks
back to xxiii. 11, which, as Wendt allowed (1888), is only to be rejected if one
presupposes that Paul could not have
confidently looked forward to a visit to
Rome, or at least if we suppose that the
confidence could not have been created
and sustained by a heavenly vision.
Wendt, however, in 1899 edition, speaks
much more doubtfully as to the existence
of vv. 21-26 as part of the original source;
see also on ver. 21.

Ver. 25. πιστεύω γὰρ τῷ Θ. ὅτι οὕτως
ε. καθ' ὃν τρόπον, cf. xv. 11, and also
i. 11, Klostermann, Vindiciæ Lucanæ,
p. 53.

Ver. 26. εἰς νῆσον δέ κ.τ.λ.: the
words do not form part of the message
of the angel as they stand, but they may
be considered as forming part of the
contents of that message, and the Apostle
may himself be regarded as speaking
μαντικῶς. With Jüngst's question "How
could Paul know anything of an island?"
and his dismissal of the statement here
as a vaticinium ex eventu, cf. Weizsäcker,
u. s., see ver. 21; in the section, vv. 33-36,
which Jüngst defends and refers to his
source A, the element of prophecy is
equally present, ver. 34, as in the verse

τῆς νυκτὸς ὑπενόουν οἱ ναῦται¹ προσάγειν τινὰ αὐτοῖς χώραν· 28. καὶ
βολίσαντες, εὗρον ὀργυιὰς εἴκοσι· βραχὺ δὲ διαστήσαντες, καὶ πάλιν

¹ προσαγειν אcACHLP Chrys., Tisch., W.H. text, Weiss, Blass in β text;
προσαγαγειν א*; προσαχειν B*, cf. resonare, Gig., which suggests an earlier Greek
reading προσηχειν (Ramsay, Harris, Rendall): Hilgenfeld (1899) reads προσεγγιζειν,
so 137 cscr., Syr. P.; B³ has προσανεχειν, Vulg. apparere; Winer-Schmiedel, p. 52.

before us.—ἐκπεσεῖν, cf. ver. 17, and
further instances in Wetstein, see also
vv. 29, 32, below.

Ver. 27. τεσσαρεσκαιδεκάτη νύξ, i.e.,
since their departure from Fair Havens,
cf. vv. 18, 19, see also the reckonings of
mileage in Breusing, p. 189, and Goerne,
who reckons from the departure from
Cauda.—διαφερομένων ἡμῶν: "as we
were driven to and fro," R.V., so Ramsay; "huc illuc ferri," Blass, cf. for a
similar meaning of the verb Philo, De
Migr. Abr., 27, Strabo, 3, p. 144, and
other instances as in Plutarch, see
Wetstein, Grimm-Thayer, sub v. But
J. Smith (so Breusing, Goerne, Rendall) takes the word as signifying that
they were driven through the waters of
the Adria uniformly in the same direction, i.e., right across from Cauda to
Malta, and not as moving up and down,
or to and fro. Ramsay (so Farrar) holds
that St. Luke writes as a landsman who
supposes that they drifted to and fro,
whilst a sailor would have known that
they drifted in a uniform direction (an
explanation which Page describes as easy
but unsatisfactory, but he thinks that the
Greek word cannot be used as J. Smith
believes); Rendall however maintains
that throughout the Acts the habitual
force of διά in composition, e.g., διέρχεσθαι, διαπλεῖν, διαφεύγειν, διαπερᾶν,
διοδεύειν, whether governing an accusative or used absolutely is to express
continuous movement onwards over an
intervening space.—ἐν τῷ Ἀδρίᾳ: "in the
sea of Adria," R.V. (on the form of the
word see Hastings' B.D., more properly
"Adrias"); not in the narrower sense of
the Adriatic, the Gulf of Venice, or as we
now speak of "the Adriatic," but as
including the whole sea which lay between Malta, Italy, Greece and Crete;
St. Luke probably used the term as it
was colloquially used by the sailors in this
wider sense. For Mommsen's objection
to the term here see above, Introd., p. 8.
The passage in Strabo, ii., 123 (cf. vii.,
187), where the Ionian sea is spoken of
as a part of what is now called Adria
plainly justifies a wider use of the term
in St. Paul's day than had been originally attached to it, cf. Ptolemy, Geogr.,

iii., 4, 14, 15, 16, who applies it to the sea
extending from Sicily to Crete, and thus
represents, although living some sixty
or seventy years after him, what was
no doubt the current usage in St. Luke's
day; so J. Smith, Breusing, Goerne,
Vars, Ramsay, Renan, Blass, etc. Josephus, Vita, 3, speaks of being taken up
in the middle of Adria, κατὰ μέσον τὸν
Ἀδρίαν, when his ship foundered, by a
vessel sailing from Cyrene to Puteoli.
See further "Adria," Hastings' B.D.,
where a full criticism of the attempt
made by W. Falconer (and others), Dissertation on St. Paul's Voyage, 1817, republished with additions in 1870, to limit
the term to the branch of the sea between Italy and Illyria, and to identify
Melita with an island off its Illyrian
shore, will be found; see further on
xxviii. 1, and C. and H., small edition,
p. 660 ff., for other references to the
meaning of the term "Adria," and Renan,
Saint Paul, p. 552, J. Smith, p. 280 ff.,
4th edit. (editor's note), and Encycl. Bibl.,
i., 72, 1899.—κατὰ μέσον τῆς ν., cf. xvi.
25 for a similar expression, only in Luke.
—ὑπενόουν: only in Luke; "surmised,"
R.V., less decided than "deemed," A.V.,
see on xiii. 25 (cf. 1 Tim. vi. 4).—προσάγειν τινὰ αὐτοῖς χ.: "that some land
was approaching them," R.V., so Breusing and Ramsay; intransitive in LXX,
Josh. iii. 9, 1 Sam. ix. 18, Jer. xxvi. (xlvi.)
3, etc., "Lucas optice loquitur, nautarum
more," Kypke; the opposite verb would
be ἀναχωρεῖν, recedere, see Wetstein and
Blass for illustrations. J. Smith thinks
that probably they heard the breakers on
the shore, but Breusing and Goerne (so
Blass) think that the anchor or whatever weight was dragged behind the ship
appeared to strike the ground, see above
on ver. 17, cf. critical note for προσαχεῖν,
Doric for προσηχεῖν.—χώραν: the
point of Koura, east of St. Paul's Bay,
J. Smith; the ship would pass within a
quarter of a mile of it, and while the
land is too low to be seen when the night
is stormy, the breakers can be heard for
a considerable distance; cf. the description of the wreck of the Lively in 1810,
Smith, p. 123, 4th edition.
Ver. 28. βολίσαντες: having let down

βολίσαντες, εὖρον ὀργυιὰς δεκαπέντε· 29. φοβούμενοί τε[1] μήπως εἰς
τραχεῖς τόπους ἐκπέσωσιν, ἐκ πρύμνης ῥίψαντες ἀγκύρας τέσσαρας,
ηὔχοντο ἡμέραν γενέσθαι. 30. τῶν δὲ ναυτῶν ζητούντων φυγεῖν ἐκ
τοῦ πλοίου, καὶ χαλασάντων τὴν σκάφην εἰς τὴν θάλασσαν,[2] προφάσει

[1] For μηπως, Tisch., W.H., R.V., Blass, Weiss read μηπου with ℵBC 13, 40, 61.
Hilgenfeld (1899) retains μηπως with HLP (A μηπω). Instead of εις ℵABC have
κατα, so Tisch., W.H., R.V., Weiss, Wendt, Blass, but Hilgenfeld has εις (Vulg.,
Gig., *in*). εκπεσωμεν ℵABCHLP Vulg., Syr. P. and H., Boh., Tisch., W.H., R.V.,
Blass, Weiss, Wendt, Hilg. After γενεσθαι Blass in β text (so Hilg.) adds του
ειδεναι ει σωθηναι δυναμεθα with Gig.

[2] After θαλ. Blass in β text adds ευκαιριαν ζητουντων, so Hilgenfeld (1899) with
Gig., and after εκτ. both add on the same authority του ασφαλεστερον το πλοιον
εσταναι.

the sounding-lead (**βολίς**), elsewhere only
in Eustath., in active voice, but see also
Grimm-Thayer, *sub v.*—**ὀργυιὰς**: five
or six feet, a fathom, Grimm; Breusing
compares Herod., iv., 41, and gives
six feet; on the accent see Winer-
Schmiedel, p. 72. "The ancient fathom
so nearly agrees with the English that
the difference may be neglected," J.
Smith, p. 131.—**βραχὺ δὲ διαστήσαντες**:
"and after a little space," so Ramsay,
Rendall; the phrase may refer to space
or time; if we understand τὸ πλοῖον or
ἑαυτούς we should take it of the
former (Grimm); but if we explain
= βραχὺ διάστημα ποιήσαντες (Blass),
it may be taken of either. διΐστημι is
only found in Luke for signifying any
space of time, Luke xxii. 59, *cf.* Acts
v. 7; but Luke xxiv. 51, **διέστη ἀπ'
αὐτῶν**. J. Smith shows how exactly the
geographical details in the traditional
St. Paul's Bay correspond with the
description here. Before a ship drifting
from Cauda could enter the bay it would
not only pass within a quarter of a mile
of Point Kaura, north-east of Malta, but
the measurements of 20 and 15 fathoms
exactly correspond to ascertained soundings according to the vessel's average of
speed.
Ver. 29. **φοβούμενοι**: the diminution
of the depth of water increased the
danger of running aground, perhaps on
some hidden reef of rocks.—**τραχεῖς
τόπους**, *cf.* Luke iii. 5, in quotation Isa.
xl. 4; nowhere else in N.T., *cf.* Bar. iv.
26 (3 Macc. i. 23), so in Diod. Sic., xii.,
72, of rocks, Polyb., i., 54. It was evidently a hydrographic term, and classed
with δύσορμος, ἀλίμενος, etc., Jul. Pollux,
i., 101; J. Smith, p. 132.—**ἐκπέσωμεν**, see
ver. 17, "to cast ashore," R.V., or simply
"cast on rocky ground," which is more
indefinite than the former rendering, and

perhaps correctly so, as there were possible dangers from sunken reefs as well
as from a rocky coast. On the subjunctive after verbs of fear and danger *cf.*
Burton, p. 15.—**ἐκ πρύμνης**: this was
unusual, but to anchor was their only
chance of safety, and four anchors would
make the vessel more secure: ancient
vessels carried as a rule several anchors.
Athenæus speaks of a ship which had
eight iron anchors, *cf.* for the number
here, and the security which they gave,
Cæsar, *Bell. Civ.*, i., 25, "naves quaternis
anchoris destinabat, ne fluctibus move-
rentur"; anchorage from the prow would
have caused the ship to swing round
from the wind, whereas anchorage from
the stern would enable the sailors to
manage the ship far more easily, and to
bring her under control of the helm
when they wished to run her aground
(see the description in Ramsay, Rendall,
Farrar, and J. Smith). On the interesting parallels of anchoring ships from
the stern in our own naval engagements see C. and H., small edition, p.
653, and J. Smith, p. 133, 4th edition.—
ηὔχοντο: "prayed," R.V. margin, the
Greek sailors might pray at such a crisis
(Rendall).—**ἡμέραν γενέσθαι**, *cf.* vv. 33,
39, characteristic of Luke, *cf.* Luke iv.
42, vi. 13, xxii. 26, Acts xii. 18, xvi. 35,
xxiii. 12.
Ver. 30. **ζητούντων**: "and as the
sailors were seeking," R.V., "about to
flee," A.V. is incorrect, for they were
planning possible means of escape, and
could scarcely be said to be about to
escape, *cf.* β text—if they succeeded the
passengers and the soldiers would thus be
left to their fate.—**προφ. ὡς**: under colour,
under pretence, *specie*, *cf.* Mark xii. 40,
Luke xx. 47, John xv. 22, Phil. i. 18, 1
Thess. ii. 5. *Cf.* for its use here Thuc.,
v., 53, vi., 76. For ὡς *cf.* xvii. 14, xxviii.

ὡς ἐκ πρῴρας μελλόντων ἀγκύρας ἐκτείνειν, 31. εἶπεν ὁ Παῦλος τῷ
ἑκατοντάρχῃ καὶ τοῖς στρατιώταις, Ἐὰν μὴ οὗτοι μείνωσιν ἐν τῷ
πλοίῳ, ὑμεῖς σωθῆναι οὐ δύνασθε.   32. τότε οἱ στρατιῶται ἀπέκοψαν
τὰ σχοινία τῆς σκάφης, καὶ εἴασαν αὐτὴν ἐκπεσεῖν.   33. ἄχρι δὲ οὗ
ἔμελλεν ἡμέρα γίνεσθαι, παρεκάλει ὁ Παῦλος ἅπαντας μεταλαβεῖν
τροφῆς, λέγων, Τεσσαρεσκαιδεκάτην σήμερον ἡμέραν προσδοκῶντες,

19, Luke xxiii. 14, and ὡς μέλλων with present infinitive active as here, Acts xxiii. 15, 20, Klostermann, *Vindiciæ Lucanæ*, p. 54.—ἐκτείνειν: "lay out anchors," R.V., Ramsay, *i.e.*, at the full length of the cable. The sailors pretended that more anchors from the prow would help to steady the ship, and that they must go off in a boat to carry them out to cable's length, rather than drop them out as in ver. 29.—ἐκτ.: a technical expression (*cf. élonger*, Vars, p. 248, and so ῥίπτειν in ver. 29, *mouiller*), Breusing, p. 195. It seems impossible to suppose with Breusing, p. 194, and Vars, p. 248 (so also Goerne), that the sailors may have been actuated by an honourable motive, and that they wished to put off in the boat to see if the soundings and the nature of the ground allowed the ship to get nearer shore, for although St. Paul's words do not expressly accuse them of treachery, yet the narrative of his companion does so, *cf.* προφάσει, etc. But, as Breusing himself points out, St. Paul's words issued in the best result, for the centurion's counsel prevented a terrible scene of *sauve qui peut* (as in the stranding of the *Cimbria*, Goerne).

Ver. 31. ὑμεῖς not ἡμεῖς: St. Paul appeals to the law of self-preservation, and the centurion acts promptly on his advice; although safety had been divinely promised, human means were not excluded, and it is altogether hypercritical to find any contradiction here with vv. 24-26, as Holtzmann supposes.

Ver. 32. τότε οἱ στρ. ἀπέκ.: Lewin, *Saint Paul*, ii., 202, sees in this the absolute ascendency which St. Paul had gained; he had said that their lives should be spared, and although, humanly speaking, the boat offered the best prospect of reaching land, yet at a word from St. Paul the soldiers deprived themselves even of this last resource.—σχοινία: only elsewhere in N.T. in John ii. 15; in classical Greek, and also frequently in LXX. For the terrible scene which would doubtless have ensued if the soldiers had not thus acted, Breusing and Vars (so Wetstein, *in loco*) strikingly compare the description of a

shipwreck in Achilles Tatius, iii., 3; the whole passage is cited by Breusing, p. 194.

Ver. 33. ἄχρι δὲ οὗ: only used by Luke in the historical books of the N.T., *cf.* Luke xxi. 24, Acts vii. 18; in St. Paul's Epistles three or four times, Heb. iii. 13, Rev. ii. 25. Ramsay renders "and while the day was coming on," so A. and R.V.; *dum* with imperfect, Heb. iii. 13 (Blass). But Rendall takes it as = *until*, as if Paul had continued his entreaties until close on dawn (imperfect).—μεταλαβεῖν τροφῆς, *cf.* ii. 46 for the same phrase, only in Luke in N.T.—τεσσαρεσκ. . . . προσδοκῶντες κ.τ.λ.: "this is the fourteenth day that ye wait (A.V. 'tarry,' Ramsay, 'watch') and continue fasting". Rendall renders "this is the fourteenth day that ye have continued fasting on the watch for the dawn"—προσδ. *sc.* ἡμέραν, as if St. Paul did not mean a fourteenth day of continuous fasting, but fourteen successive nights of anxious watching for the dawn, all alike spent in restless hungry expectation of what the day might reveal (*Acts*, p. 347), but προσδοκᾶν is here without an object as in Luke iii. 15 (Weiss). For the word see further xxviii. 6, and *cf.* προσδοκία only in Acts xii. 11 and Luke xxi. 26. On the accusative of time, as expressed here, *cf.* Blass, *Gram.*, p. 93.—ἄσιτοι διατελεῖτε: precisely the same collocation of words occur in Galen, εἴ ποτε ἄσιτος διετέλεσεν, so also καὶ ἄδιψοι διατελοῦσιν, and Hippocrates speaks of a man who continued suffering πάσχων διατελέει for fourteen days (see Hobart and Zahn). It must however be admitted that the same collocation as in this verse ἄσιτοι and διατελεῖν is found in Dion. Hal. (Wetstein, *in loco*). For the construction see Winer-Moulton, xlv., 4; *cf.* Thuc., i., 34.—μηδὲν προσλ., *i.e.*, taking no regular meal, so Weiss, Blass, Zöckler, Alford, Plumptre, Felten, Bethge, Wendt. Breusing, p. 196, and Vars, p. 250, both explain the word as meaning that in their perilous and hopeless condition those on board had not gone to fetch their regular food and rations, but had subsisted on any bits of

ἄσιτοι διατελεῖτε, μηδὲν¹ προσλαβόμενοι. 34. διὸ παρακαλῶ ὑμᾶς
προσλαβεῖν² τροφῆς· τοῦτο γὰρ πρὸς τῆς ὑμετέρας σωτηρίας ὑπάρχει·
οὐδενὸς γὰρ ὑμῶν θρὶξ³ ἐκ τῆς κεφαλῆς πεσεῖται. 35. εἰπὼν δὲ
ταῦτα, καὶ λαβὼν ἄρτον, εὐχαρίστησε τῷ Θεῷ ἐνώπιον πάντων, καὶ
κλάσας ἤρξατο ἐσθίειν.⁴ 36. εὔθυμοι δὲ γενόμενοι πάντες, καὶ αὐτοὶ

¹ Instead of προσλαβ. Lach. with A 40 reads προσλαμβανομενοι, prob. change
to suit προσδοκωντες.

² Instead of προσλ. ℵABC, Chrys., so Tisch., W.H., R.V., Blass, Weiss, Wendt
read μεταλ. For υμετ. ALP have ημετ., so Hilg.

³ For εκ ABC minusc., Tisch., W.H. and other authorities above read απο,
but Hilg. has εκ with ℵHLP. For πεσειται ℵABC Vulg., Syr. P., Boh., Arm.,
Aethpp. have απολειται, so Tisch., W.H. and other authorities above; but πεσ. is
supported by HLP, Sah., Syr. H., so Hilg. and Meyer who suppose that απολ.
is from Luke xxi. 18; but see on the other hand Alford's note. After υπαρχει
Blass in β text and Belser, so Hilg., add ελπιζω γαρ εν τω Θεω μου οτι with Gig.

⁴ After εσθιειν Blass and Hilgenfeld add επιδιδους και ημιν with 137 Sah., Syr.
H., c*.

food they might have by them; in ancient ships there were no tables spread,
or waiters to bring food to the passengers,
and each one who wanted refreshment
must fetch it for himself. Plumptre
takes πρός as meaning no extra food,
only what would keep body and soul
together, but it is doubtful whether the
Greek will bear this or Breusing's interpretation. Ver. 34. διό: so that they might be
ready for the work which would be necessary.—προσλαβεῖν, see critical note.
—πρὸς: here only with genitive in N.T.,
cf. Blass, Gram., p. 136; i.e., stands, so
to speak, on the side of our deliverance,
Latin a parte, cf. Thuc., ii., 86; iii., 59;
Plat., p. 459 C; Winer-Moulton, xlviii. f.
—ὑμετ.: emphatic. — σωτ.: "safety,"
R.V., only used here and in Heb. xi. 7
of the preservation of physical life, safety,
so in classical Greek and in Greek
medical writers, see on xvi. 17; "health,"
A.V., not limited formerly as now to the
condition of body and mind, cf. Luke
i. 77, "science of health" Wycliffe =
"knowledge of salvation," and cf. also
Ps. lxvii. 2, "thy saving health," literally
"thy salvation" (Humphry). Effort on
their part was necessary, and yet no hair
of their heads should perish; what a significant union of faith in God and self-
help! (Bethge.)—οὐδενὸς γὰρ . . . πεσεῖται, see ver. 22, cf. Luke xxi. 18,
nowhere else in N.T., but the proverbial
phrase, as it apparently was, is found in
1 Sam. xiv. 45, 2 Sam. xiv. 11, 1 Kings
i. 52 (cf. Matt. x. 29), see critical note,
and cf. Shakespeare, Tempest, Act i.,
Scene 2.

Ver. 35. λαβὼν ἄρτον εὐχαρίστησε
τῷ Θ., cf. Luke xxii. 19, xxiv. 30, with intentional solemnity (Weiss, Weizsäcker).
The words are sometimes taken to mean
that Paul simply encourages them by
his own example to eat. But Blass, see
critical note, who comments "et oratione
confirmat et exemplo," adds in β text
ἐπιδιδοὺς καὶ ἡμῖν, i.e., to Luke and
Aristarchus, in which he sees a distinct
reference to the cœna sacra (so Belser).
But quite apart from this reading in β the
peculiar language of St. Luke seems to
intimate such a reference. Olshausen
and Ewald (so Plumptre) take the words
to refer to the Agape, whilst Meyer (so
Hackett) sees a reference to the act
of the Jewish house-father amidst his
household; but Wendt simply refers it
to the act of a pious Jew or Christian
giving thanks before eating a meal and
sharing it, so Zöckler. Bethge, more
specifically, sees in the act a thanksgiving
of a Christian to God the Father, an instance of what St. Paul himself recommends, Ephes. v. 20, Col. iii. 17, and both
Felten and Knabenbauer apparently
prefer to interpret the words as marking
Paul's reverence towards God before
the Gentiles around him. Breusing
shows, p. 196, that ἄρτος might = panis
nauticus, but in the passage which he
quotes from Lucian we have ἄρτους
ναυτικούς.

Ver. 36. τροφῆς: with a partitive
meaning; cf. γεύσασθαι, xxiii. 14, μεταλαβεῖν, ver. 33, κορέννυσθαι, ver. 38. Cf.
Herod., viii., 90. Luckock points out
that St. Luke distinguishes between the
bread of which the Apostle partook and

προσελάβοντο τροφῆς · 37. ἦμεν δὲ ἐν τῷ πλοίῳ αἱ πᾶσαι ψυχαὶ διακόσιαι¹ ἑβδομηκονταέξ. 38. κορεσθέντες δὲ τροφῆς, ἐκούφιζον τὸ

¹ For **διακόσιαι** W.H. read in text **ὡς** (so R.V. marg.) (in marg. **διακ.**) with B, Sah. Epiph., so Hilgenfeld; Weiss however declines here to follow B, and speaks of "the impossible" **ὡς** before 76 which is no round number, *Apostelgeschichte*, p. 34 (so Blass); the mistake seems best explained by supposing that the last letter of **πλοιω** was read as if **Σ** = 200, and thus = **ΩΣ**. Or, to explain it more fully, by supposing that the sign for 200, **Σ**, was misunderstood, and with the double reading of the **ω** in **πλοιω** easily became **ὡς**; this is of course if we read with W.H. **αι πασαι ψ. εν τω πλοιω**, a different order from T.R. (see also Hilgenfeld's note, where explanation of the reading **διακ.** from **ὡς** is certainly not so obvious). For **εξ** A has **πεντε**.

the food, **τροφῆς**, taken by the rest, and certainly the expression **κλάσας** is remarkable, *cf.* Luke xxii. 19, 1 Cor. xi. 23, 24; but it is perhaps noteworthy that the Romanist Felten (see above) sees no reference to the Eucharist, although he fully admits that this act of Paul in thus giving thanks must have made a great impression at such a moment.—**εὔθυμοι**, ver. 22, *cf.* 2 Macc. xi. 26.—**καὶ αὐτοί**: "also themselves," following his example. For the second time Paul had restored their courage by his faith and prudence; the event had already shown that he deserved confidence, and it is evident that he inspired it; see the testimony of Breusing, pp. 198, 199.

Wendt, so too Jüngst, and Clemen see no reason to regard vv. 33-36 as an interpolation in the "We" source, as vv. 21-26 above. Overbeck regards both sections as standing or falling together, and treats them both as interpolations, but Ramsay, whilst regarding the two sections as inseparably connected, treats them both as belonging to the original "We" source, and he rightly expresses surprise at those who accept ver. 33 ff., and refuse to accept vv. 21-26 (*Saint Paul*, p. 337); much more intelligible is the judgment of Weizsäcker than that of the other German critics in question when he describes the narrative as an indivisible whole, and considers it impossible to disentangle the mere history of travel from it, or to strip away the miraculous additions.

Ver. 37. The number was large, but nothing is told us of the size and manning of the Alexandrian ship, and Josephus, *Vita*, 3, mentions that there were about 600 in the ship which took him to Italy. On the large size of the ships engaged in a traffic similar to that of the corn ship in this chapter see Breusing, p. 157; Vars, p. 191; Hackett and Blass, *in loco*, and ver. 6; Lucian, **Πλοῖον ἢ Εὐχαί.**, 5. The

number may be mentioned at this point that they might know afterwards that all had been saved. But Breusing thinks that it would have come perhaps more naturally at the end of the narrative, and that it is given here because the rations were distributed to each on board at this juncture. For the phrase *cf.* xix. 7.

Ver. 38. **κορεσθ.**, 1 Cor. iv. 8, nowhere else in N.T., with genitive of the thing with which one is filled, as in classical Greek. Alford refers to LXX, Deut. xxxi. 20, but see Hatch and Redpath, *sub v.*—**ἐκούφιζον**: *de nave*, Polyb., i., 60, 8; LXX, Jonah i. 5.—**τὸν σῖτον**: "the wheat," A. and R.V., Vulgate, *triticum;* so Ramsay, Breusing, Vars, J. Smith, Page, and so too Erasmus, Bengel, etc., *i.e.*, the cargo, *cf.* ver. 6. Blass thinks that the word used is decisive in favour of this interpretation; otherwise we should have had **σιτία** or **ἄρτοι** if merely food had been meant; not only was the cargo of sufficient weight really to lighten the ship, but there was need for the ship being as clear as possible for the operations in ver. 40. Wendt 1899 appears also to favour this view, *cf.* his comments with those in 1888 edition, where he adopts the view of Meyer and Weiss, that the word means provisions of food, as at first sight the context seems to indicate. But the latter would not have made much appreciable difference in weight, nor would those on board have been likely to throw them away, since they could not tell on what shore they might be cast, whether hospitable or not, or how long they would be dependent on the food which they had in the ship. In ver. 18 the reference may be to the cargo on deck, or at all events only to a part of the cargo (Holtzmann). Naber conjectured **ἱστόν**, but no such emendation is required (Wendt).

πλοῖον, ἐκβαλλόμενοι τὸν σῖτον εἰς τὴν θάλασσαν.　39. Ὅτε δὲ
ἡμέρα ἐγένετο,[1] τὴν γῆν οὐκ ἐπεγίνωσκον· κόλπον δέ τινα κατενόουν
ἔχοντα αἰγιαλόν, εἰς ὃν[2] ἐβουλεύσαντο, εἰ δύναιντο,[3] ἐξῶσαι τὸ πλοῖον.
40. καὶ τὰς ἀγκύρας περιελόντες εἴων εἰς τὴν θάλασσαν, ἅμα ἀνέντες
τὰς ζευκτηρίας τῶν πηδαλίων· καὶ ἐπάραντες τὸν[4] ἀρτέμονα τῇ

[1] Before τὴν γῆν Gig., Syr. P. add οἱ ναῦται, so Blass in β and Hilg.

[2] For εβουλευσαντο ℵBC, Vulg., Syrr. P. and H., Boh., Tisch., W.H., R.V.,
Blass, Weiss, Wendt, Hilgenfeld read εβουλευοντο ; A 40, 61 have εβουλοντο.

[3] For εξωσαι B*C, Boh., Aeth., Arm. have εκσωσαι, so W.H. text, R.V. marg.,
but Tisch., W.H. mg., R.V. text, Blass, Weiss, Hilgenfeld read εξωσαι (Wendt
doubtful).

[4] αρτεμονα LP, Chrys., but -ωνα W.H., Weiss, Blass with ℵABCH, B¹ has
αρτομωνα, see Winer-Schmiedel, p. 86.

Ver. 39. τὴν γῆν οὐκ ἐπεγ.: "they
did not recognise the land," Ramsay ;
the sailors probably knew Malta, since,
xxviii. 11, there was evidently nothing
unusual in eastern ships touching at the
island on their way to Rome. But they
did not know St. Paul's Bay, which is
remote from the great harbour, and was
not distinguished by any marked features
to secure recognition, Ramsay, J. Smith ;
see also note on xxviii. 1. C. and H. lay
stress on the imperfect, "they tried to
recognise . . ., but could not"; but in
xxviii. 1 we have the aorist indicating that
the land was recognised immediately on
landing.—κατενόουν: "perceived," R.V.,
cf. Matt. vii. 3, Luke vi. 41, xx. 23.—
κόλπον τινα: a sort of bay or creek, "a
bay," R.V., the word means a bay either
small or large, and St. Paul's Bay may be
described as a small bay or creek (Rendall) ; ἔχοντα αἰγιαλόν "with a sandy
beach," Ramsay, with a beach, R.V., i.e.,
smooth and fit for a vessel's landing-
place, cf. xxi. 5, Matt. xiii. 2, 48, John
xxi. 4; cf. Xen., Anab., vi., 4, 4 (see
Page's note) ; in LXX, Judg. v. 17 A,
Ecclus. xxiv. 14 S², al. J. Smith
adds that St. Luke here again employs
the correct hydrographical term, frequently used by Arrian in this sense.
The traditional St. Paul's Bay may certainly well have been the place meant (so
Wendt, 1899, and Blass). On the
smooth, sandy beach see Hackett, note,
p. 334, who has also visited the spot, and
confirmed Smith's view, although both
admit that the former sandy beach has
been worn away by the action of the
sea ; Smith, p. 247, 4th edition, and see
also Ramsay, St. Paul, p. 341.—ἐξῶσαι
τὸ πλοῖον: "to drive the ship upon it,"
R.V., i.e., the beach, so Ramsay, Rendall, Breusing, Vars, Goerne, J. Smith

(4th edit., p. 142) ; the object was not to
save the ship from being destroyed, but
the crew from perishing ; under like circumstances the same would be done to-
day (so Breusing, Vars), cf. Arrian,
Peripl. Pont. Eux., 6. ἐξῶσαι: so in
Thuc., ii., 90; viii., 104 (and see Wetstein) ; see also critical note on ἐκσῶσαι
εἰ δύναιντο, and Burton, p. 106, and
Grimm-Thayer, sub εἰ, i., 7, c., with
optative, where the condition represents
the mind and judgment of others . . . , as
if the sailors had said amongst themselves
ἐξώσομεν εἰ δυνάμεθα, cf. xxiv. 19.

Ver. 40. καὶ τὰς ἀγκ. περιελόντες:
"and casting off the anchors," R.V., cf.
ver. 20 for the same verb, so that the
meaning cannot be as A.V., following
Vulgate, "having taken up"; in fact it is
the very reverse. The sailors loosed the
cables of the anchors which were fastened
within the ship, that they might fall off into
the sea (Blass) ; Breusing and Vars compare Xen., Hell., xvi., 21, τὰς ἀγκύρας
ἀποκόπτοντες = τὰ σχοινία τῶν ἀγκυρῶν.
—εἴων εἰς τὴν θάλασσαν: "they left them
(the anchors) in the sea," R.V., relinque-
bant, Blass ; so Breusing, Vars, Goerne,
as against A.V., and Vulgate, committe-
bant se, or Luther's rendering (Beza
and Grotius), εἴων τὸ πλοῖον ἰέναι εἰς
τὴν θάλασσαν. Grimm-Thayer renders
"they let down into the sea," i.e., abandoned, which gives better the force of
εἰς than regarding it simply as = ἐν.—
ἅμα: "at the same time," R.V., "simul
laxantes," Vulgate, "loosing withal,"
Rhem., but in no other E.V. (Speaker's
Commentary).—τὰς ζευκτ. τῶν πηδαλίων:
the bands of the rudders, the fastenings
of the rudders, i.e., the two paddle-rud-
ders with which Greek and Roman ships
were supplied, one on each quarter, C.
and H. and J. Smith, p. 183, 4th edition,

πνεούσῃ κατεῖχον εἰς τὸν αἰγιαλόν.   41. περιπεσόντες δὲ εἰς τόπον
διθάλασσον,[1] ἐπώκειλαν τὴν ναῦν· καὶ ἡ μὲν πρῷρα ἐρείσασα ἔμεινεν

[1] For ἐπωκειλαν (B³LP, Chrys., Meyer, Hilgenfeld), ℵAB*C 13, 40, 61, 73 have
επεκειλαν, so Tisch., W.H., R.V., Blass, Weiss, Wendt, see note below (and
Wendt's note in both edit., 1888 and 1899), and Blass, *in loco*.   After τὴν ναυν Blass
in β and Hilgenfeld adds εις συρτιν with Syr. H. c* (so Hilg.).

these rudders had been lifted from the
water and lashed up while the ship was
anchored by the stern (see Breusing's
description, p. 98, *cf.* Eur., *Hel.*, 1536:
πηδάλια ζεύγλαισι παρακαθίετο), but
the rudders were wanted when the
ship again got under weigh.—τῇ πνεούσῃ, *sc.* αὔρᾳ. — ἐπάραντες : technical
word for spreading out the sail, opposite
to ὑφίεσθαι. — κατεῖχον εἰς τὸν αἰγ.:
"they made for the beach," R.V., in
order to land, *cf.* Xen., *Hell.*, ii., 1, 29 ;
others take it as meaning to check the
ship's headway, but better, to *hold* or *head*
the ship, Herod., vii., 59, 188, so Grimm-
Thayer, *sub v.*, *sc.* τὴν ναῦν, whilst
others take the verb intransitively as above
in R.V.—τὸν ἀρτέμονα : "the foresail,"
R.V., Ramsay, J. Smith.   The word has
been interpreted by various writers as
meaning nearly every sail which a vessel
carries.   If the interpretation of ver. 17 is
correct, it could not mean the mainsail as
A.V.   Others apply it to the stern-sail,
which bears the name to-day (Italian,
artimone; French, *voile d'artimon*), but to
set this sail would have been the most
foolish thing they could have done, so
Vars, Breusing.   The word is found only
here for the foresail, and its meaning is
fixed by the fact that no other sail could
be so well used by sailors under the circumstances, see Breusing, p. 79, J. Smith,
pp. 141 and 193 ff., 4th edit. In his edition,
1899, Wendt thinks it probable that the
sail here meant is otherwise called δόλων,
but see J. Smith, p. 200, 4th edit. In
his former edition he preferred to interpret it of the topsail (Meyer, Weiss,
Zöckler, Baumgarten), but Breusing, p.
xii., points out that only in the sixteenth
century were topsails introduced; see
also Vars, p. 93.
   Ver. 41.   περιπ. δὲ εἰς τ. διθ.: Luke
x. 30, James i. 2, with the dative, as
generally, but Arrian, περιπίπτειν εἰς
τόπους πετρώδεις (Wetstein), 2 Macc.
vi. 13, x. 4, Polyb., i., 37, 1.   εἰς τόπον
διθ.: a bank or a ridge between two
seas, which has sea on both sides; *cf.*
Dio Chrys., 5, p. 83, where reference is
made to the dangers of the sea: βραχέα
καὶ διθάλαττα καὶ ταινίαι μακραὶ . . .

ἄπορον . . . παρέχουσι τὸ πέλαγος
(Wetstein and Blass).   Breusing, Vars
and Goerne (so Blass) take the words
εἰς τ. δ. to refer to a hidden ridge beneath
the water, and the aorist περιπ. in contrast to the imperfect κατεῖχον seems
to favour this, as expressing that they
came upon a τόπ. διθ. unexpectedly, *cf.*
Page's note and Ramsay's translation,
"chancing on a bank between two seas".
But the latter writer adds that the περιπ.
does not imply want of purpose, as
ἐπώκειλαν shows, and the meaning is
that while at anchor they could not see
the exact character of the spot (see also
C. and H.), but as they approached they
found that they had lighted on the channel
not more than a hundred yards in breadth
between the island of Salmonetta and
the mainland ; this might very properly
be called "a place where two seas meet,"
A. and R.V., as it formed a communication between the sea within the bay and
the sea outside.   The adjective διθ. is as
applicable to *water* uniting two seas,
e.g., the Bosphorus, *cf.* Strabo, ii., 5,
12 (quoted by Smith), as to *land* like the
Isthmus of Corinth; see J. Smith, pp.
142, 178, 4th edit., Hackett, C. and H.,
Lumby, Rendall, and note in *Speaker's
Commentary*.   Breusing, p. 204, Goerne,
Wendt (1899) take it of St. Paul's Bank
which lies just in front of St. Paul's Bay,
so too Vars, p. 258, for the same view
and its support.—ἐπώκειλαν τὴν ναῦν:
"they ran the vessel aground" (*cf.* J.
Smith, p. 143, 4th edit.), see critical note.
ἐποκέλλω and ἐπικέλλω are both used in
classical Greek, but the latter is "altogether poetical " (Blass), and more usually
intransitive.   In Homer, *Odys.*, ix., 148,
however, we have νῆας . . . ἐπικέλσαι,
and 546, νῆα ἐκέλσαμεν (*cf. adpellere
navem*).   Blass, *Philology of the Gospels*,
p. 186, sees in this sudden introduction of
the phrase ἐπώκειλαν τὴν ναῦν an indication that St. Luke had read his Homer,
since in no other passage in the N.T. do
we find the obsolete word ἡ ναῦς, the
commoner expression τὸ πλοῖον occurring
in this chapter no less than thirteen
times.   R.V. renders τὴν ναῦν "the
vessel," all other E.V. "the ship," and

ἀσάλευτος, ἡ δὲ πρύμνα ἐλύετο ὑπὸ τῆς βίας τῶν κυμάτων.[1]   42.
τῶν δὲ στρατιωτῶν βουλὴ ἐγένετο ἵνα [2] τοὺς δεσμώτας ἀποκτείνωσι,
μήτις ἐκκολυμβήσας [3] διαφύγοι.   43. ὁ δὲ [4] ἑκατόνταρχος, βουλόμενος
διασῶσαι τὸν Παῦλον, ἐκώλυσεν αὐτοὺς τοῦ βουλήματος, ἐκέλευσέ τε
τοὺς δυναμένους κολυμβᾷν,[5] ἀπορρίψαντας πρώτους ἐπὶ τὴν γῆν ἐξιέναι,
44. καὶ τοὺς λοιποὺς, οὓς μὲν ἐπὶ σανίσιν, οὓς δὲ ἐπί τινων τῶν ἀπὸ
τοῦ πλοίου.   καὶ οὕτως [6] ἐγένετο πάντας διασωθῆναι ἐπὶ τὴν γῆν.

[1] των κυμ., but אּ*AB, so Tisch., W.H., R.V. have only υπο τ. βιας.   The
words των κυμ. are, however, retained here by Weiss, Blass, Hilg.; Vulg., Gig.
have maris.

[2] Before τους δεσμ. Blass (not Hilg.) with Gig. in β text adds παντας.

[3] διαφυγοι, but very slight authority.   Tisch., W.H., Blass, Hilg., Weiss, Wendt
διαφυγη אּABCHLP 61, Chrys.

[4] After εκατον. Blass adds with Gig. εκωλυσεν τουτο γενεσθαι, μαλιστα δια τον
Π. ινα διασωση αυτον.

[5] απορρ. for the one ρ W.H., see ver. 19, and Winer-Schmiedel, p. 56.

[6] Afte τουτως Blass with Gig. reads πασαι αι ψυχαι διεσωθησαν (επι την γην).

it has been thought that the word is so
changed here because that which had
hitherto been a πλοῖον capable of sailing
was now reduced to a mere hulk (Wordsworth, Humphry).—καὶ ἡ μὲν πρῶρα ἐρείσασα: "and the prow struck," R.V.,
Ramsay, this is accounted for by the
peculiar nature of the bottom in St.
Paul's Bay, see J. Smith, Ramsay, Hackett, Alford, "a bottom of mud graduat-
ing into tenacious clay, into which the
fore part would fix itself, and be held fast
while the stern was exposed to the force
of the waves".   For the verb in intransitive sense as here cf. Prov. iv. 4,
cf. Æneid, v., 206 (Wetstein).—ἀσάλ.:
only in Heb. xii. 8 in N.T., but σαλεύειν
several times in Luke, in Gospel and
Acts; in classical Greek and LXX;
adverb -τως, Polyb., ix., 9, 8, cf. also
Ecclus. xxix. 18.—ἡ δὲ πρύμνα ἐλύετο
ὑπὸ τῆς βίας: "but the stern began to
break up," R.V., marking the imperfect
as distinguished from aorist ἔμεινεν,
Blass, Gram., p. 186; Æn., x., 303, Cic.,
Att., xv., 11 (Wetstein).—βίας τῶν κυμ.,
see critical note. βία: four times in
Acts, see on v. 26, nowhere else in N.T.,
but frequent in LXX, Vulgate, "a vi
maris," which Breusing, p. 203, strongly
endorses.
Ver. 42. τῶν δὲ στρατ.: only the
soldiers, since they and not the sailors
were responsible for the safety of the
prisoners, cf. xii. 7, xvi. 27; C. and H.,
small edit., p. 236.—ἐκκολ.: "swim
away" (Ramsay), literally "out," Eur.,
Hel., 1609, Dion H., v., 24.—διαφ.:

only here in N.T., LXX, Josh. viii. 22,
Judg. vii. 19, Prov. xix. 5, 1 Macc. xv.
21, 2 Macc. xii. 35, etc., so absolutely in
Herod., i., 10.
Ver. 43. βουλόμενος: "desiring,"
R.V.; the centurion had from the first,
ver. 3, treated Paul with respect, and the
respect had no doubt been deepened by
the prisoner's bearing in the hour of
danger, and he would naturally wish to
save the man to whom he owed his own
safety, and that of the whole crew.
διασῶσαι, even if he cared little for the
rest he was determined "to save Paul to
the end," literally, so C. and H.   There
is no reason whatever to regard the
words βουλ. . . . τὸν Π. as an interpolation.—ἐκώλυσεν αὐτοὺς τοῦ β.: only
here with this construction, accusative
of person and genitive of thing, but
similar usage in Xenophon, Polybius.
For the resultative aorist, i.e., the aorist
of a verb whose present implies effort or
intention, commonly denoting the success of the effort, cf. also Matt. xxvii. 20,
Acts vii. 36, Burton, p. 21.—τοὺς δυν.
κολυμβᾷν: probably Paul was amongst the
number; he had thrice been shipwrecked,
and had passed a day and a night in the
open sea, 2 Cor. xi. 25 (Felten, Plumptre).
—ἐξιέναι: four times in Acts, nowhere
else in N.T., xiii. 42, xvii. 15, xx. 7.—
ἀπορρίψαντας: "should cast themselves
overboard and get first to the land,"
R.V., where they could help the others to
safety, so Breusing, Goerne, Renan; A.V.
not so expressive. ἀπορρίπτειν: here
used reflexively, see instance in Wetstein.

XXVIII. 1. ΚΑΙ διασωθέντες, τότε[1] ἐπέγνωσαν ὅτι Μελίτη ἡ νῆσος
καλεῖται. 2. Οἱ δὲ βάρβαροι παρεῖχον οὐ τὴν τυχοῦσαν φιλανθρωπίαν
ἡμῖν· ἀνάψαντες γὰρ πυράν,[2] προσελάβοντο πάντας ἡμᾶς, διὰ τὸν

[1] Instead of επεγνωσαν ℵABC* 13, 61, 68, 137, Syrr. P. and H., Boh. read
επεγνωμεν, so Tisch., W.H., R.V., Weiss, Wendt, Blass, Hilg. διασ. om. by
Blass with Gig., Syr. Pesh., but retained by Hilg. Instead of Μελιτη (Tisch.,
R.V. text, Weiss, Blass, Hilg.), W.H., R.V. marg. read Μελιτηνη with B*, Syr. H.
mg. Gk., Arm., Boh., Gig.

[2] ℵ* has προσανελαμβανον, so Blass and Hilg.; 137 has προσελαμβανον; Vulg.,
Par. reficiebant; Gig. refecerunt, and Blass takes the word in his text as = reficie-
bant. Wendt thinks that this may have been the original reading. For αναψ.
(Meyer) ℵABC 61, 68, Tisch., W.H., Blass, Hilg., Weiss read αψαντες.

Ver. 44. τοὺς λ., sc. ἐξιέναι ἐπὶ τὴν
γῆν.—οὓς μὲν . . . οὓς δὲ, Luke xxiii.
33, and in classical Greek.—ἐπὶ σανίσιν:
"some on planks and some on pieces
from the ship," Ramsay; the planks
which were in use in the ship as distinguished from actual parts or fragments
of the ship in the next clause; in LXX,
Ezek. xxvii. 5, the word is used of planks
for the deck of a ship (Cant. viii. 9,
2 Kings xii. 9 (?)). Breusing, pp. 45,
203 (so Blass), takes it of the boards or
planks which were used for keeping the
cargo firmly in its place. The furniture
of the vessel had already been thrown
overboard, so that we can only think
of the pieces broken away as the ship
stranded, or perhaps broken off by the
escaping crew. ἐπί: here used pro-
miscuously with dative and genitive in
the same sense.—ἐγένετο: with infinitive
following, characteristic of St. Luke,
Friedrich, p. 13.—διασωθῆναι: on its
use by St. Luke here and in xxviii. 1, 4
(Luke vii. 3), see Hobart, pp. 9, 10, 284.
For the remarkable correspondence between the details of the scene of the
shipwreck and the topography of St.
Paul's Bay see not only J. Smith and
Ramsay, but Goerne, p. 374, Breusing,
p. 204, and Vars, p. 257. Breusing and
Vars both admit that it is not safe to
trust too much to tradition, but in this
case, as they both point out, it was only
likely that St. Paul would have won
loyal adherents in the island who would
have handed down every detail of his
visit to their children, and the local tradition is in striking accordance with the
description of the sacred narrative; see
further Introd., p. 8.

CHAPTER XXVIII.— Ver. 1. διασωθέντες, see on xxvii. 43. Used by
Josephus of his own shipwreck and
escape, Vita, 3, and in Xen. and Thuc.
of coming safely to a place.—τότε ἐπέγ.:

not imperfect as in xxvii. 39; here denoting the immediate recognition of the
place after they had once gained safety
(Weiss, Rendall, C.H.). St. Paul's Bay
is several miles distant from Valetta, the
harbour which the sailors doubtless knew
previously, see also Breusing, p. 190,
Vars, p. 243, and J. Smith, pp. 140 and
148, 4th edition.—Μελίτη, see critical
note; Malta, cf. Diod. Sic., v., 12,
Strabo, vi., 2, Ovid, Fasti, iii., 567,
Sicula Melita as distinct from Melita
Illyrica (Meleda). There is no need here
to refute the view that the latter, in the
Adriatic Sea on the coast of Dalmatia,
is meant. This view depends chiefly
upon the narrow view of the meaning of
the Adria xxvii. 27, see also below on vv.
2, 3. It was first put forward in the
tenth century by Constantine the Por-
phyrogenite, and was advocated in the
last century by a Dalmatian monk, Padre
Georgi, himself a native of Meleda, no
doubt jealous for the honour of his birthplace and his monastery. Its chief champion may be said to be W. Falconer, in
his Dissertation on St. Paul's Voyage,
1817, republished in 1870 by his nephew,
Judge Falconer. This last was an unsuccessful attempt to controvert the arguments of J. Smith in favour of Malta,
who may be said to have established his
case to demonstration (see for a candid
description of Falconer's view "Adria"
(Dickson), Hastings' B.D.). More recent
nautical authorities have most decisively
confirmed the view of J. Smith, cf. Breusing, p. 190, and Vars, p. 242. Quite
apart from the strong local tradition in
favour of Malta, and the testimony of the
Apocryphal Acta Petri et Pauli in favour
of Γαυδομελέτη (Gosso-Malta) (for references to Lipsius' edition, Wendt and
Zöckler, in loco), it is not too much to
say that Meleda could not have been
reached without a miracle under the

ὑετὸν τὸν ἐφεστῶτα, καὶ διὰ τὸ ψῦχος. 3. Συστρέψαντος δὲ τοῦ
Παύλου φρυγάνων [1] πλῆθος, καὶ ἐπιθέντος ἐπὶ τὴν πυράν, ἔχιδνα [2] ἐκ

[1] After **φρυγ.** ℵABC 61, Vulg., Tisch., W.H., Weiss, Wendt, Blass add **τι**, but Hilg. omits (so Gig.).

[2] The authorities for **απο** instead of **εκ** are overwhelming, ℵABCHLI, and other authorities above with Hilg. For **εξελ.**, which is strongly supported by ℵABC 61, and so other authorities above, except Hilg., HLP (Meyer, Alford) read **διεξ.**

circumstances of weather described in the narrative, cf. Dean Howson's "Melita," B.D.[1], ii., pp. 315-317, and Zahn (in answer to Mommsen), *Einleitung*, ii., p. 422.
Ver. 2. **βάρβαροι**, *i.e.*, they were not a Greek-speaking population, cf. Rom. i. 14 (not barbarians in the modern sense of rude and uncivilised); they were of Phœnician descent, and came under the Roman dominion in the second Punic War, Livy, xxi., 51. Ramsay, *St. Paul*, p. 343, sees in the title an indication that the writer was himself of Greek nationality. For the use of the term in classical Greek, and by Philo and Josephus, see "Barbarian" (F. C. Conybeare), Hastings' B.D., Grimm-Thayer, *sub v.*, and Mr. Page's note. (In 2 Macc. ii. 21 the writer describes Judas Maccabæus as chasing "barbarous multitudes," **τὰ βάρβαρα πλήθη**, retorting on the Greeks the epithet habitually applied by them to all nations not their own, *Speaker's Commentary*.) See further the evidence of coins and inscriptions in Zahn, *Einleitung*, ii., 422, proving as against Mommsen that the Phœnician tongue had not died out in the island, and cf. above, Introd., p. 8.—**οὐ τὴν τυχ.**, cf. xix. 11, "no common kindness," R.V. (and so A.V. in xix. 11).—**φιλαν.** : see note on xxvii. 3. The word is found in LXX, Esther viii. 13, 2 Macc. vi. 22, xiv. 9, 3 Macc. iii. 15, 18, and in classical Greek, but it was a word which a physician would be very likely to employ, for Hippocrates speaks of "philanthropy" in a physician as ever accompanying a real love of his profession. Galen distinguishes between those who healed through "philanthropy" and those who healed merely for gain, and even a more generous diet for the sick was called **φιλανθρωποτέρα τροφή**, Hobart, p. 296. The word is used here only and in Tit. iii. 4 in N.T.—**ἀνάψ. γὰρ πυράν**, Luke xii. 49, James iii. 5 ; if we read the simple verb (see critical note) we have it three times with **λύχνον** in Luke viii. 16, xi. 33, xv. 8, and nowhere else

in N.T. (except with meaning "to touch"). **πυράν** : only here and in ver. 3 in N.T., cf. Judith vii. 5, 1 Macc. xii. 28, 2 Macc. i. 22, x. 36 (see H. and R.), and similar phrases in classical Greek. —**προσελάβοντο**, cf. xvii. 5, xviii. 26 for similar use, and five times by St. Paul ; cf. 2 Macc. x. 15, see critical note. —**ἐφεστῶτα**, cf. Polyb., xviii. 3, 7 ; in N.T. 2 Tim. iv. 6, only in Luke and Paul, *præsentem*, Wetstein, "present," A. and R.V. Weiss and De Wette take it as meaning that the rain suddenly came upon them.—**ψῦχος** : this and the mention of the rain prove that St. Paul's ship could not have encountered a sirocco wind, *i.e.*, from the south-east, for this only blows for two or three days, and even in November is hot and sultry (Hackett). W.H. read **ψύχος**, but Weiss, Wendt, Blass as above, see Winer-Schmiedel, p. 68.
Ver. 3. **συστρέψαντος** : here only in Acts, but cf. xi. 27, xvi. 39, in β text ; = exemplum **αὐτουργίας**, Bengel. *Cf.* Matt. xvii. 22, W.H., R.V. margin ; of collecting men, 2 Macc. xiv. 30. — **φρυγάνων** : brushwood, copse ; the furze still growing near St. Paul's Bay would well afford material for a fire (Lewin), and it may be quite true that wood is found nowhere else but in a place at a distance from the Bay ; in classical Greek used in plural for dry sticks, especially firewood ; here only in N.T., but several times in LXX, for straw, stubble, and bramble.—**τι** before **πλῆθος**, see critical note : implying as much as he could carry, Weiss ; **πλ.** used elsewhere of persons.—**ἔχιδνα** : the objection that no poisonous serpents are found to-day in Malta, like that based on the absence of wood in ver. 2, may well be dismissed as "too trivial to deserve notice ; such changes are natural and probable in a small island, populous and long civilised," Ramsay, *St. Paul*, p. 343, Breusing, p. 191, Vars, p. 243 ; so too J. Smith, p. 151, 4th edition, refers to the gradual disappearance of the viper in Arran as the island became more frequented, and *cf.*

τῆς θέρμης ἐξελθοῦσα καθῆψε τῆς χειρὸς αὐτοῦ. 4. ὡς δὲ εἶδον
οἱ βάρβαροι κρεμάμενον τὸ θηρίον ἐκ τῆς χειρὸς αὐτοῦ, ἔλεγον πρὸς
ἀλλήλους, Πάντως φονεύς ἐστιν ὁ ἄνθρωπος οὗτος, ὃν διασωθέντα
ἐκ τῆς θαλάσσης ἡ δίκη ζῆν οὐκ εἴασεν. 5. ὁ μὲν οὖν ἀποτινάξας
τὸ θηρίον εἰς τὸ πῦρ, ἔπαθεν οὐδὲν κακόν. 6. οἱ δὲ προσεδόκων
αὐτὸν μέλλειν[1] πίμπρασθαι ἢ καταπίπτειν ἄφνω νεκρόν· ἐπὶ πολὺ
δὲ αὐτῶν προσδοκώντων, καὶ θεωρούντων μηδὲν ἄτοπον εἰς αὐτὸν

---

[1] πίμπρασθαι אcBHLP, Chrys., so Lach., W.H., Weiss, Wendt, Blass, Hilg.;
Tisch. has εμπιπρασ. with א*; πιπρασθ. A.

Hackett's note for similar proof. Mr.
Lewin, as late as 1853, believed that he
saw a viper near St. Paul's Bay, *St.
Paul*, ii., 208.—ἐκ: "out of," but if ἀπό
"by reason of," R.V. margin, "from the
heat," the viper numbed by the cold felt
the sudden heat, and was restored to
activity, *cf.* on its habits (Hackett), ἀπό
"in causæ significatu sæpe apud Græcos,"
Grotius, Bengel. *Cf.* xx. 9, and Luke xxi.
26.—ἐξελθοῦσα, see critical note. διεξ.
supported by Meyer and Alford, as if the
serpent glided out *through* the sticks.—
θέρμης: only in Luke in N.T., but in
classics and in LXX, Job vi. 17, Ps.
xviii. (xix.) 6, Eccl. iv. 11, Ecclus.
xxxviii. 28; often used in medical writers
instead of θερμότης (Hobart), but the
latter is also used in Hipp.—καθῆψε:
only here in N.T., but frequent in classical Greek, and usually in middle, although
not found in LXX, *cf.* however Symm.,
καθάπτεσθαι, Cant. i. 6, *cf.* Epict., *Diss.*,
iii., 20, 10, *i.e.*, τοῦ τραχήλου: (Grimm):
Blass, Page, Felten render "bit," *momor-
dit.* So Nösgen and Zöckler, who think
that this is evidently meant from the context, although not necessarily contained
in the verb itself; Dioscorides used it of
poisonous matter introduced into the
body (Hobart, p. 288). Blass thus expresses the force of the aorist, "momento
temporis hoc factum est, priusquam P.
manum retraxisset".

Ver. 4. τὸ θηρίον: "the beast,"
R.V. Although this is the meaning of
the Greek word, it is to be noted that
St. Luke uses it here exactly as the medical writers, who applied it to venomous
serpents—in particular, to the viper,
ἔχιδνα (so Aristotle), and an antidote
made chiefly from the flesh of vipers
went by the name ἡ θηριακή (Hobart,
Zahn, Knabenbauer), and those bitten
by a viper were called θηριόδηκτοι.—
κρεμ. ἐκ: "hanging from," R.V., it
clung by its mouth to the hand of Paul,
construction as in classical Greek, *cf.*

2 Macc. vi. 10.—πάντως: only in Luke
and Paul, expressing strong affirmation,
cf. xxi. 22, and Luke iv. 23; *cf.* Tob.
xiv. 8, 2 Macc. iii. 13.—φονεύς, a murderer, and therefore justice demands his
life, death for death; they saw that he
was a prisoner perhaps from his chains
(Bengel); at all events the solders would
have guarded him, as we may infer from
xxvii. 42.—ἡ Δίκη: "justice," R.V.,
cf. Hesiod, *Theog.*, 902; so in Soph.,
Ant., 544; *Œd. Col.*, 1384; for the
personification *cf.* Wisdom i. 8, xi.
20, and several instances in 4 Macc., see
Grimm-Thayer, *sub v.* The Maltese
may have heard the name from the
Greeks or Romans, or they may have
honoured a goddess of their own, whose
name Luke here represents by ἡ Δ.,
"debile lumen naturæ . . . nec quis sit
ὁ Δίκαιος *Justus Ultor* norunt," Bengel.—διασωθέντα, see on xxvii. 43.—
οὐκ εἴασεν: "hath not suffered," they
thought of him as already dead, as if
the deadly bite had already done its
work; not *sinit*, as Vulgate, but *sivit*.

Ver. 5. ἀποτ.: only in Luke, Luke
ix. 5, in parallel in Matt. and Mark,
ἐκτ., *cf.* Lam. ii. 7, and in classical
Greek, Eur., *Bacch.*, 253. — ἔπαθεν
οὐδὲν κακόν, *cf.* Mark xvi. 18, Luke
x. 19.

Ver. 6. οἱ δέ . . .: Paul shook off the
viper—the natives looked for a fatal result. They knew the deadly nature of
the bite, and their subsequent conduct
shows that they regarded it as nothing
short of miraculous that Paul escaped.
So St. Luke evidently wishes to describe
the action, see on μὲν οὖν, ver. 5, and
δέ, Rendall, *Acts*, p. 161, Appendix.—
προσεδόκων, see below.—πίμπρασθαι,
from the form πίμπρημι, present infinitive passive, see critical note, and Winer-
Schmiedel, p. 122; *cf.* in LXX, Numb.
v. 21, 22, 27, πρήθειν, H. and R., of parts
of the body becoming swollen. In classical Greek πίμπρασθαι means "to take

γινόμενον,[1] μεταβαλλόμενοι ἔλεγον θεὸν αὐτὸν εἶναι. 7. Ἐν δὲ τοῖς περὶ τὸν τόπον ἐκεῖνον ὑπῆρχε χωρία τῷ πρώτῳ τῆς νήσου, ὀνόματι Ποπλίῳ, ὃς ἀναδεξάμενος ἡμᾶς τρεῖς ἡμέρας[2] φιλοφρόνως ἐξένισεν.

[1] Instead of μεταβαλλ. (אHL, so Tisch., Hilg.) ABP have the aorist μεταβαλ., so W.H., Weiss, Blass, Wendt.

[2] After ημερας τρεις Hilg. adds εν τη οικια αυτου, but not Blass.

fire," and πρήθειν "to cause to swell," and those two ideas are combined, as in the word πρηστήρ, "a venomous snake, the bite of which caused both inflammation and swelling " (Page, *in loco*), cf. Lucan, ix., 790. In the N.T. the verb is peculiar to St. Luke, and it is the usual medical word for inflammation (Hobart, Zahn) in Hipp., Aret., Galen.—καταπίπτειν: only in Luke in N.T., cf. Luke viii. 6, Acts xxvi. 14, it was used by medical writers of persons falling down suddenly from wounds, or in epileptic fits ; Hipp., Galen (Hobart, Zahn), cf. the asp-bitten Charmian in *Ant. and Cleo.* (Shakespeare), Act v., Scene 2.—ἄφνω: only in Acts ii. 2, xvi. 26.—προσδ. . . . ἄτοπον: the two words are described by Hobart as exactly those which a medical man would use (so too Zahn), and he gives two instances of the latter word from Galen, in speaking of the bite of a rabid dog, or of poison, p. 289. The word is used elsewhere in N.T. of something morally amiss ; cf. Luke xxiii. 41, Acts xxv. 5, 2 Thess. iii. 2, but here evidently of something amiss physically. In R.V. it is rendered in each passage "amiss ". The word in N.T. is confined to Luke and Paul, but it is found several times in LXX in an ethical sense (as in N.T., except *in loco*), cf. Job iv. 8, xi. 11, xxvii. 6, xxxiv. 12, xxxv. 13, Prov. xxiv. 55 (xxx. 20), cf. 2 Macc. xiv. 23 ; so too in Thucydides, Josephus, Plutarch, etc. ; but it is used of any harm happening to a person as here, cf. Jos., *Ant.*, viii., 14, 4 ; xi., 5, 2 ; Herodian, iv., 11. προσδοκία, peculiar to St. Luke in N.T. ; cf. Luke xxi. 26, Acts xii. 11, and προσδοκάω, in Luke six times, in Acts five, was, no doubt, frequently used in medical language (Hobart, Zahn) for the expectation of the result of a disease or paroxysm " when they were long in expectation," R.V.), but in Jos., *Ant.*, viii., 14, 4, we have καὶ μηδὲν τῶν ἀτόπων προσδοκᾶν, and in Herodian, iv., 11, μηδὲν ἄτοπον προσδοκοῦντες · εἰς αὐτὸν γιν., cf. Luke iv. 23 (Klostermann, Weiss).— μεταβαλλόμενοι, so frequently in classics without τὴν γνώμην, cf. Jos., *B. J.*, v., 9, 3.

—θεὸν αὐτὸν εἶναι : it is perhaps fanciful to suppose with Grotius and Wetstein that they compared him to the infant Hercules, or to Æsculapius represented with the serpent, but the latter is undoubtedly right in adding, "eleganter autem hic describitur vulgi inconstantia" ; we naturally compare with Chrysostom the startling change in the people of Lystra, xiv., 11, 19, "Aut latro inquiunt aut deus . . . datur tertium : homo Dei" (Bengel).

Ver. 7. χωρία : "lands," R.V. Vulgate, *prædia*. In this passage τόπος and χωρίον occur together, and whilst the former is used of place indefinitely, the latter is used of a definite portion of space enclosed or complete in itself ; cf. John iv. 5 ; Grimm-Thayer's *Syn., sub v.*, τόπος. — τῷ πρώτῳ : an official title technically correct in Malta, Ramsay, *St. Paul*, p. 343, *honoraria appellatio*, so too Schmiedel, *Encycl. Bibl.*, i., 47, 1899 ; as his father was alive, he would not have been called from his estates (see, however, O. Holtzmann, *Neutest. Zeitgeschichte*, p. 106), but the inscriptional authorities confirm the first view, a Greek inscription giving πρῶτος Μελιταίων καὶ Πάτρων, applied to a Roman Knight, Prudens by name, ἱππεὺς Ῥ., so that Publius may well have been of the same rank, and in a Latin inscription we have *municipii Melitensium primus omnium*, see Zahn, *Einleitung*, ii., p. 422 ; Blass, *in loco* ; Zöckler, Holtzmann, Knabenbauer, also Alford, Lewin, Hackett, Renan ; possibly the conjecture may be correct that the Greek and Latin inscriptions give a translation of a title which the Romans already found in vogue in the island. Publius would be naturally the chief authority in the island under the Roman prætor of Sicily, Cic., *Verr.*, iv., 18.— Ποπλίῳ : Greek form for the *prænomen* Publius, "nomen a *populus* derivatum," Blass ; Ramsay, p. 343, thinks that Poplius may = the Greek rendering of the *nomen Popilius*, but that the peasantry may have spoken of him familiarly by his *prænomen* Publius. Tradition makes him bishop of Malta (Felten, Knaben-

8. ἐγένετο δὲ τὸν πατέρα τοῦ Ποπλίου πυρετοῖς καὶ¹ δυσεντερίᾳ
συνεχόμενον κατακεῖσθαι· πρὸς ὃν ὁ Παῦλος εἰσελθὼν καὶ προσευξά-
μενος, ἐπιθεὶς τὰς χεῖρας αὐτῷ, ἰάσατο αὐτόν.   9. τούτου οὖν γενομένου,
καὶ οἱ λοιποὶ οἱ ἔχοντες ἀσθενείας ἐν τῇ νήσῳ προσήρχοντο καὶ

¹ For δυσεντερίῳ 61, Chrys. have the older fem. form, -ια, Winer-Schmiedel,
p. 85.

bauer).—ἀναδεξ.: only here of hospitable reception = ὑποδέχεσθαι, xvii. 7; φιλοφ., 2 Macc. iii. 9, 4 Macc. viii. 5; in the former passage φιλοφ. ἀποδεχθείς, so in Jos., *Ant.*, xiv., 8, 5, φιλοφ. ὑποδέχεσθαι, and instances in Wetstein, see above on ver. 2.—ἡμᾶς: some take the word as referring to Paul and his companions, Luke and Aristarchus (as it seems to lead on to what follows), perhaps including Julius, whilst others point out that he may have entertained the whole crew for the short space of time mentioned, as the ἡμέρας τρεῖς indicates that the entertainment was only provisional; probably he had a large number of slaves (Nösgen, Weiss). Publius may well have been officially responsible for the needs of the Roman soldiers and their prisoners, but φιλοφ. indicates that the duty was performed with generous courtesy.—ἐξένι-σεν: entertained (as his guests), *cf.* x. 6, 23, etc., Heb. xiii. 2. The traditional site was at Civita Vecchia, the old capital of the island, where St. Paul spent the three months, and another tradition places it on the way from St. Paul's Bay to the capital.

Ver. 8. πυρετοῖς: the use of the plural for a fever is peculiar to St. Luke in N.T., and quite medical, Hobart, J. Smith, Zahn (*cf.* Luke iv. 38, 39); although the plural is found in Dem., Lucian in the sense of "intermittent attacks of fever," but Hobart shows that the term was very common in Hipp., and he also quotes from Aretæus and Galen. Each of the other Evangelists uses πυρετός, but in the singular, never in the plural. The disease was common in Malta (J. Smith and C. and H.).—δυσεντερία, see critical note, "dysentery," R.V.; "Lucas medicus morbos accuratius describere solet," Wetstein; another medical term, peculiar to St. Luke in N.T., often joined with πυρετός by Hippocrates (Hobart, Zahn).—συνεχ., *cf.* Luke iv. 38, συνεχομένη πυρετῷ μεγάλῳ, where St. Luke not only speaks of πυρ. μέγας, where Matthew and Mark (viii. 14 and i. 30) have simply πυρετός, but also introduces the term συνεχ. where they have πυρέσ-

σουσα; ἔχεσθαι and συνέχ. are both used by the medical writers as in these passages, although no doubt συνέχεσθαι is sometimes found with a word like νοσήματι in classical Greek (*cf.* Grotius, *in loco*, Hobart, Zahn, Weiss), so in Hippocrates, ὑπὸ δυσεντερίης ἐχομένῳ, and τοῖσιν ὑπὸ τῆς ἡρακλείης νόσου συνεχομένοισιν; nine times in St. Luke, elsewhere only three times in N.T., and once in St. Matt. iv. 24, in a way similar to St. Luke, but joined there not only with νόσοις, but with a word (βασάνοις) which the medical writers (so St. Luke) never employ of bodily disease.—ἰάσατο αὐτόν, *cf.* Mark xvi. 18, the word is more frequently used by the medical writers for "healing" than any other (Hobart), and it occurs in St. Luke's writings fourteen times and once figuratively, in St. Matthew four times and once figuratively, once in St. Mark, three times in St. John, once figuratively, and in the rest of the N.T. three times, but in each case figuratively. In answer to the attempts to regard the miraculous element as an addition to the narrative here, as in the previous chapter, it may be sufficient to quote the remarks of Weizsäcker: "The stormy voyage and shipwreck form the central point of the narrative: to this is appended the residence at Malta. In the former, Paul reveals himself as a prophet; in the latter, as the possessor of miraculous power. We should make a vast mistake, however, if we were to infer from this that the simple travel-record had here been revised by a writer intent upon artificially glorifying the Apostle as a worker of miracles. The narrative is an indivisible whole; it is impossible to disentangle the mere history of travel from it, or to strip away the miraculous additions," *Apostolic Age*, ii., p. 126, E.T.

Ver. 9. ἐθεραπεύοντο: "were cured," R.V. Lekebusch, pp. 382, 393, and Holtzmann, *in loco*, think that the medical skill of St. Luke may also have been instrumental in effecting these cures, and this is urged on the ground that ἡμᾶς, ver. 10, intimates that not only St. Paul received honour in return for the cures

ἐθεραπεύοντο· 10. οἳ καὶ πολλαῖς τιμαῖς ἐτίμησαν ἡμᾶς, καὶ ἀναγο-
μένοις ἐπέθεντο τὰ πρὸς [1] τὴν χρείαν.

11. Μετὰ δὲ τρεῖς μῆνας ἀνήχθημεν ἐν πλοίῳ παρακεχειμακότι ἐν
τῇ νήσῳ, Ἀλεξανδρινῷ,[2] παρασήμῳ Διοσκούροις· 12. καὶ καταχθέντες

---

[1] For the sing. την χρ. אABI 13, 40, 137 have the plural, so Tisch., W.H., R.V.,
Blass, Weiss, Wendt, Hilg.

[2] Blass reads ῳ ην παρασημον Διοσκουρων (Vulg., Syr. P., Gig.).

---

effected. But such a conjecture must
remain quite uncertain, although it is
no doubt quite possible that as we have
here a verb which properly denotes medical treatment (cf. θεραπεία, Luke ix. 11)
for the restoration of health, the care
(cura) of medical skill was freely added
by St. Luke, and enhanced the debt
which the sick owed.
Ver. 10. πολλαῖς τιμαῖς: "with
many honours," A. and R.V., used quite
generally, so in Vulgate, "multis honori-
bus"; even in the expression "honos
habendus medico," Cic., Ad Div., xvi., 9,
we need not limit the word to the
honorarium; so in 1 Tim. v. 17 τιμῆς is
used quite generally, and in Ecclus.
xxxviii. 1 it is very doubtful whether in
the expression "honour a physician,"
τίμα ἰατρόν, the verb refers to payment.
There is therefore no need to take the
word as referring to a physician's fee
in money, as Wordsworth, Humphry,
Plumptre, although the word may have
been so used by a physician; but it was
scarcely likely that St. Paul would have
received such a reward for his services,
to say nothing of the fact that it was contrary to Christ's commands, Matt. x. 8.—
καὶ ἀναγ. ἐπέθεντο: "and when we
sailed they put on board," R.V., so Ramsay, ἀναγ., technical term, xxvii. 2, 3.—
τὰ πρὸς τὴν χ., see critical note, frequently in Luke and Paul, both in
singular and plural, and often in LXX,
cf. Acts xx. 34, Rom. xii. 13, used here
quite generally; it may have included
money, but no doubt things needful,
post naufragium, Bengel.
Ver. 11. τρεῖς μῆνας: no account is
given of St. Paul's doings in Malta, or
of his preaching or founding a Church,
but the writer's interest is centred on the
Apostle's journey to Rome, and what
immediately concerns it. — ἀνήχ., see
above on xiii. 13; in the earlier part of
February, as the shipwreck took place
probably before the middle of November
(Ramsay), but Blass thinks March, as he
places the shipwreck about the commencement of December, but with a

favourable wind the ship would risk the
voyage, even before the regular sailing
season commenced (so Wendt and Ramsay).—Ἀλεξ.: very likely a corn ship,
driven for refuge by the same gale; on
the accent here and in xxvii. 6 see
Winer-Schmiedel, p. 73. — παρακεχειμακότι: only in Luke and Paul in N.T.,
cf. xxvii. 12, 1 Cor. xvi. 6, Tit. iii. 12,
and in classical Greek. — παρασήμῳ
Διοσκ.: "whose sign was the Twin
Brothers," R.V., i.e., Castor and Pollux;
or perhaps in a ship "marked with the
image or figure of the Dioscuri," or the
latter word in the dative may be a dedicatory inscription—marked "To the Dioscuri," i.e., in honour of them, so Wendt,
Holtzmann, Grimm-Thayer. Others take
παρασ. as a noun, so Alford, Page, quoting from an inscription found near Lutro
and given by J. Smith, in which reference
is made to a Dionysius of Alexandria as
gubernator navis parasemo Isopharia.
Phryn. prefers the form Διόσκοροι.
Blass has ῳ ἦν παράσημον Διοσκούρων,
see critical note and Blass, in loco; cf.
for the word 3 Macc. ii. 29. Castor and
Pollux were best known as the tutelary
gods of sailors, and probably at this date
they were both the insigne and the tutela
of the ship. St. Cyril of Alexandria tells
us that it was always the Alexandrian
method to ornament each side of the
prow with the figures of deities, probably
in this case Castor and Pollux, one on
each side of the vessel; and we may
further note that the twin brothers were
specially honoured in the district of
Cyrenaica, not far from Alexandria (Schol.,
Pind., Pyth., v., 6). For other classical
notices cf. Hor., Od., i., 3, 2; iii., 29, 64;
Catull., iv., 27; lxviii., 65; Eur., Helen.,
1663, and "Castor and Pollux," B.D.[2],
and "Dioscuri," Hastings' B.D. The
mention of the ship's sign shows the
minuteness of the information of an eye-
witness, and the fact that an Alexandrian
ship thus wintered in the island is a
strong piece of incidental evidence in
favour of the identification of the island
with Malta; the latter would be a natural

εἰς Συρακούσας, ἐπεμείναμεν ἡμέρας τρεῖς · 13. ὅθεν[1] περιελθόντες
κατηντήσαμεν εἰς Ῥήγιον, καὶ μετὰ μίαν ἡμέραν ἐπιγενομένου νότου

[1] For περιελθ. R.V. marg. has περιελοντες with ℵ*B (Gig. *tulimus*), and so W.H.,
but Weiss, Wendt, Hilg. follow T.R. ; Weiss maintains with Wendt that περιελοντες
is simply a mistake, Θ having fallen out before Ο, but see below.   J. Smith,
p. 156, follows T.R.   Blass in β has και εκειθεν αραντες.

harbour for a ship of Alexandria on the
way to Italy, but Meleda would be altogether out of the course (see J. Smith, p.
278, fourth edit.).

Ver. 12. καταχ. : "touching at," R.V.,
Ramsay, *cf.* xxvii. 3.   We are not told that
St. Paul landed, but the local tradition
makes him the founder of the Sicilian
Church, C. and H., p. 663, small edit.—
Συρ. : (*Siragosa*) about 100 miles distant
from Malta, the capital of Sicily, and
a Roman colony; in a mercantile city St.
Paul would find countrymen and Jewish
proselytes; it was moreover a city of
great historical interest, and a usual
stopping - place for Alexandrian ships
on their voyage to Italy;   see C.
and H., p. 662, *u. s.*, and notices in
Strabo, vi., p. 270 (but see also Grimm-
Thayer, *sub v*., Συρ.) ; Cicero, *Verr.*, iv.,
53 ; Pliny, *N.H.*, iii., 8, and B.D., *sub v.*
For accentuation *cf.* also Grimm-Thayer.
—τρεῖς ἡμέρας : probably to wait for a
favouring breeze from the south.—ἐπεμείναμεν : with accusative of time, *cf.* x. 48,
xxi. 4, 10, ver. 14 below, 1 Cor. xvi. 7.

Ver. 13. περιελθόντες : so A. and
R.V., but latter in margin περιελόντες,
see critical note.   Ramsay also following
T.R. points out that the latter reading
could hardly signify more than "cast off"
("cast loose," margin, R.V.), unnecessary here although important information
in xxvii. 40, where τὰς ἀγκ. is added,
and the meaning is evidently different.
Ramsay renders "by tacking" (the verb
referring to the frequent alteration of the
ship's course); they worked up to Rhegium by good seamanship as they could
not go straight across, J. Smith, C. and
H., p. 663, small edit.   Mr. Lewin, *St.
Paul*, ii., p. 736, takes a different view,
and thinks that they were obliged to
stand out to sea to fill their sails, and so
to come to Rhegium by a circuitous
sweep.   R.V. renders simply "made a
circuit," so Grimm-Thayer.   W.H., ii.,
p. 226, explain their rendering "weighed
anchor" by the use of the verb in xxvii.
40 (but see Blass above), the elliptic employment of transitive verbs being common in Greek nautical language as in
English, and by the opinion that the run

from Syracuse to Rhegium could not be
described as circuitous, unless the ship
was thrown out by contrary winds (but
see above); Mr. Rendall supports W.H.,
Mr. Page the opposite, following T.R.,
so Smith, p. 156, fourth edit., and see
critical note above, and Wendt (1899),
p. 418.   A.V. "fetched a compass," so
Tyndale, which formerly meant that they
made a circuit, but the phrase is now
obsolete, *cf.* 2 Sam. v. 23, 2 Kings iii. 9,
same Greek verb in LXX.—Ῥήγιον :
Reggio, Titus put in here on his way
from Judæa to Puteoli bound for Rome,
Suet., *Tit.*, 5 ; and we learn from Jos.,
Ant., xix., 2, 5, that Caligula began to
construct a harbour for the corn-ships
of Egypt, although he never finished it.
The place was situated at the southern
entrance to the Straits of Messina, here
little more than a few miles in breadth
between it and the city Messina (on its
name from ῥήγνυμι, because Sicily was
at this point rent away from Italy, see
Grimm-Thayer, *sub v*., and Wetstein).
St. Paul was said to have visited Messina,
and to have given the Christians a bishop,
Acta Petri, *Acta Pauli*, Lipsius, p. ix.
(Zöckler).   The coins show us that here
too the Dioscuri were the patron deities.
—κατην. only in Luke and Paul, see
xvi. 1, *cf.* 2 Macc. iv. 44.—ἐπιγ. : "a
south wind sprang up," R.V., here only
in N.T., *cf.* Thuc., iii., 74, iv., 30; Xen.,
Hell., iii., 2, 17, *oborto Austro*, Blass, or
it may mean coming after or in succession to, ἐπί, the previous adverse wind.
—δευτεραῖοι, *cf.* πεμπταῖοι, xx. 6, Blass
in β, John xi. 39, Phil. iii. 5, so in classical Greek.   The distance is about 180
miles, and J. Smith, p. 217, 4th edit.,
points out that if we suppose the ship to
sail at seven knots an hour the voyage
would take about twenty-six hours, and
St. Luke's account is shown to be very
accurate; see also Ramsay and Hackett
for examples of the ancient rate of sailing
quite in accordance with the facts before
us. — Ποτιόλους (*Pozzuoli*), in earlier
days Dicaearchia; its new name was
Latin, probably from the mineral springs
in the neighbourhood *a puteis*, or perhaps *a putendo* (C. and H.).   It was

δευτεραῖοι ἤλθομεν εἰς Ποτιόλους. 14. οὗ εὑρόντες ἀδελφούς,
παρεκλήθημεν [1] ἐπ᾽ αὐτοῖς ἐπιμεῖναι ἡμέρας ἑπτά· καὶ οὕτως εἰς τὴν

[1] For ἐπ᾽ ℵABI Tisch., W.H., R.V., Blass, Wendt have παρ᾽, Hilg. retains ἐπ᾽.
Instead of ἐπιμειναι H 3, 33, 68, 95*, 137, Syr. H., Gig., Theoph. have ἐπιμει-
ναντες, so Blass, Hilg., Ramsay (Wendt admits as possible), and the meaning will
then be "we were comforted among them (xx. 12) while we remained among them
for seven days".

not only a great landing-place for travellers from the East, but the great
harbour for Alexandrian corn-ships, as
also for the trade from Syria and Spain
(Renan, Saint Paul, p. 558). Seneca,
Epist., 77, gives us a vivid description
of the interest taken in the arrival of the
corn-ships, since the people of Rome
depended so much upon this cargo for
food. The importance gained by the
place is shown by the fact that it gave its
name to the bay, once the Bay of Cumæ,
now the Bay of Naples, but in St. Paul's
day Sinus Puteolanus. Here St. Ignatius desired to land that he might follow
the footsteps of St. Paul to Rome (Martyr., v.), see further Jos., Ant., xvii., 12,
1, xviii., 7, 2; Strabo, xvii., 1, 7, and
Wetstein's references. For modern
writers cf. also Lewin, St. Paul, ii., 218,
and Farrar, ii., 386; their description
shows how the Apostle's eyes now rested
upon "one of the loveliest of earthly
scenes".

Ver. 14. ἀδελφούς, see on i. 15,
they may have been from Alexandria,
as the commerce between it and Puteoli
was so considerable; the absence of the
article indicates that the writer knew
nothing of their presence previously, but
at all events Blass is right when he says,
"non magis mirum est Puteolis Christianos ante Paulum fuisse quam Romæ".
Probably after Rome itself Puteoli was the
most ancient Jewish community in Italy.
Jews were there as early as B.C. 4, after
the death of Herod the Great, Jos., Ant.,
xvii., 12, 1; B. J., ii., 7, 1, and Schürer
accepts the notice of the existence of a
Christian Church as in the text, Jewish
People, div. ii., vol. ii., p. 241, E.T., so
too O. Holtzmann, Neutest. Zeitgeschichte, p. 108; see also Lightfoot,
Philippians, p. 26. Rhegium and Puteoli
are the only two Italian towns mentioned in the N.T. (except, of course,
Rome itself), and when we consider that
Puteoli was the most important port, not
only for ships from Alexandria, but also
from Syria, there is nothing surprising in
the fact that Christianity found an early
and an easy entrance; at Pompeii, not

far from Puteoli, Christianity had made
its way, and before 79 A.D. it was discussed by the gossiping loungers in the
street (Ramsay).— παρεκ.: "we were
entreated to tarry," R.V. Ramsay (so
Blass), rendering "we were consoled
among them, remaining seven days" (see
critical note), thinks that R.V., although
strongly supported, is irreconcilable with
St. Paul's situation as a prisoner. Julius
was a Roman officer, and discipline was
natural to him, however friendly he was
towards Paul. Blass compares xx. 12,
and Zöckler also prefers the inferior
reading on account of this more usual
meaning of παρακαλεῖν. Probably the
seven days' delay was needful for Julius
to report his arrival at Rome, and to
receive further orders from the capital,
perhaps with regard to the disposal of
the prisoners, but St. Paul must have
been rejoiced at the opportunity of cele-
brating a Sunday with the little Christian
Church at Puteoli, cf. xx. 6, xxi. 4.—καὶ
οὕτως: "and so we came to Rome,"
about 140 miles, cf. xxvii. 25, "destinatum itineris terminum," Blass, cf. the
article before 'Ρ., Blass, Gram., p. 149,
so Bengel (but see Page's note). Others
take οὕτως as simply = after the stay of
seven days, a notice which leads on to
ver. 15, and makes us to understand how
the brethren came to meet us, since news
would easily have reached Rome, and a
deputation of the brethren have arrived at
Appii Forum. On the former view the
writer marks the conclusion and the aim
of the long journey (cf. εἰς τὴν 'Ρ. before
the verb; in vv. 12, 13, names of places
follow the verb without any article,
Weiss), and there is a kind of triumph in
the words: like an emperor who has
fought a naval battle and overcome, Paul
entered into that most imperial city; he
was nearer now to his crown; Rome received him bound, and saw him crowned
and proclaimed conqueror: cf. Chrys.
Others take ἦλθ. as = ἐπορευόμεθα, the
actual end of the journey following in
ver. 16 (see on the other hand Wendt, in
loco, 1888). But ver. 15 may possibly be
taken as adding an episode which com-

Ῥώμην ἤλθομεν. 15. κἀκεῖθεν οἱ ἀδελφοὶ ἀκούσαντες τὰ περὶ ἡμῶν,
ἐξῆλθον[1] εἰς ἀπάντησιν ἡμῖν ἄχρις Ἀππίου Φόρου καὶ Τριῶν Ταβερνῶν ·
οὓς ἰδὼν ὁ Παῦλος, εὐχαριστήσας τῷ Θεῷ, ἔλαβε θάρσος.

[1] For εξηλθον (so Hilg.) A 17, 40, 61, R.V. have ηλθον; אBI so Tisch., W.H.,
Blass, Wendt have ηλθαν.

mences, as it were, a new section of the
Apostle's work in the meeting with the
brethren from Rome, the journey itself
being regarded as completed in ver. 14
(Nösgen). If we read εἰσήλθομεν in ver.
16, see critical note, the word emphasises apparently the actual entry into
the city, "and when we entered into,"
R.V., or it may simply take up the conclusion of ver. 14 (so Wendt, who sees no
difficulty in the words). Ramsay, however, draws another distinction between
vv. 14 and 16 (to which Wendt (1899)
refers, without endorsing it), and thinks
that the double expression of arrival is
due to the double meaning which the
name of a city-state bears in Greek (*St.
Paul*, pp. 111, 347, and *Expositor*, Jan.,
1899); thus Rome might be restricted to
the walls and buildings, or it might include the whole *ager Romanus*, and so in
ver. 14, "we reached the State Rome,"
we passed through two points in the
ager Romanus, ver. 15, and in ver. 16,
"we entered the (walls of) Rome".
Ver. 15. κἀκεῖθεν, see on xiv. 26.
—τὰ περὶ ἡμῶν: phrase only in Luke
and Paul, see above on p. 481. The
natural supposition is that there were
two companies; one met them in advance
at Appii Forum, and the other nearer
Rome at the Tres Tabernæ.—εἰς ἀπάντησιν, cf. 1 Thess. iv. 17, Matt. xxv. 6,
xxvii. 32 (W.H. margin), frequent in
LXX, cf. Polyb., v., 26, 8. See Plumptre's note on the meeting of Cicero on
this same road on his return from exile,
Senate and people going out to meet
him; for St. Paul's friends in Rome see
Lightfoot, *Philippians*, Introd., and p.
171 ff.; Sanday and Headlam, *Romans*,
xviii., xxvii., xxxiv., xl., etc., Godet,
L'Épître aux Romains, ii., 599 ff. Aquila
and Priscilla would be amongst them.—
Ἀππίου Φόρου: situated on the great
Appian Way, near the modern *Treponti*,
43 miles from Rome, Cic., *Ad Att.*, ii.,
10; Hor., *Sat.*, i., 5, 3, and for the
distance, *Itin. Ant.*, p. 107, *Itin. Hier.*,
p. 611 (see however on this point *Encycl.
Bibl.*, p. 267, 1899). Probably its name
was due to Appius Claudius as the con-
structor of this part of the road, Livy, ix.,
29, and even in the time of St. Paul it

seems to have been connected in some
way with the Appian family. It was
situated at the northern end of a canal
which ran thither from a few miles
apparently above Terracina through the
district of the Pomptine Marshes. The
boatmen of whom Horace speaks in his
lively description, *u. s.*, were employed
in conveying passengers in boats towed
by mules along this canal. The Appian
Way itself was parallel with the canal,
so that the centurion and the Apostle
might have travelled by either, and
this uncertainty as to the route no
doubt made the Roman Christians wait
at Appii Forum. Night travellers apparently preferred the boat. The R.V.
renders "The Market of Appius" (really
the Greek is a transliteration of the
Latin Appii forum, as the words stood
in 1611, "forum" (not Forum), Hastings'
B.D.). The word apparently implied what
we should call a borough or assize town,
cf. Forum Julium, etc. The picture drawn
by Horace suggests a sharp contrast
between the holy joy of the Christian
meeting and the coarse vice and
rude revelry which so often filled the
wretched little town (Plumptre, C. and
H.).—Τριῶν Ταβ.: *Tres Tabernæ*, frequent halting-place, *deversorium*, about
33 miles from Rome on the Via Appia,
probably at the point where the road
from Antium crosses it, near the modern
Cisterna. At this time it was a place of
some importance, cf. Cic., *Ad Att.*, ii.,
12. The Latin *tabernæ* = a shop of
any kind, and would require an adjective
like *deversoria* (*sc. taberna*) to be equivalent to a tavern in the modern sense,
Lewin, *Saint Paul*, ii., 224.—εὐχ. τῷ Θεῷ
ἔλαβε θάρσος, cf. Job xvii. 9, whether
Ramsay is correct in connecting this encouragement with the chronic disorder of
the Apostle, which would often occasion
fits of depression, it is evident that St.
Paul, who was so full of sympathy, "the
heart of the world," and craved for sympathy from others, may well have felt that
he was still a prisoner, and the recent
perilous voyage may also have left its
mark upon him. Anyhow, the meeting
with Christian friends, and the thought
that these Christians were not ashamed

16. ῞ΟΤΕ δὲ [1] ἤλθομεν εἰς [2] ῾Ρώμην, ὁ ἑκατόνταρχος παρέδωκε τοὺς
δεσμίους τῷ στρατοπεδάρχῃ · τῷ δὲ Παύλῳ ἐπετράπη μένειν καθ'
ἑαυτόν, σὺν τῷ φυλάσσοντι αὐτὸν στρατιώτῃ.[3] 17. Ἐγένετο δὲ μετὰ
ἡμέρας τρεῖς συγκαλέσασθαι τὸν Παῦλον τοὺς ὄντας τῶν Ἰουδαίων
πρώτους · συνελθόντων δὲ αὐτῶν, ἔλεγε πρὸς αὐτούς, Ἄνδρες ἀδελφοί,
ἐγὼ οὐδὲν ἐναντίον ποιήσας τῷ λαῷ ἢ τοῖς ἔθεσι τοῖς πατρῴοις,
δέσμιος ἐξ Ἱεροσολύμων παρεδόθην εἰς τὰς χεῖρας τῶν ῾Ρωμαίων·

[1] For ηλθ. (so Hilg.) אBI, Tisch., R.V., Blass, Weiss have εισηλθομεν; A so
W.H. εισηλθαμεν. Before ῾Ρ. א*L, Tisch., Hilg. read την.

[2] After ῾Ρ. T.R. adds ο εκατονταρχος παρεδωκε τους δεσμιους τω στρατοπεδαρχη.
R.V. om. in text, not marg. The words are supported by HLP 137, Syr. H. c*,
Gig., Par. Prov., Blass in β, Hilg., Zöckler. They are om. by אABI 13, 40, 61,
Vulg., Syr. P., Syr. H. text, Boh., Arm., Chrys., Tisch., W.H., Weiss, Wendt
(read simply επετραπη τω Π., if words are omitted); see further below.

[3] Before συν τω φυλασσ. κ.τ.λ. 137 Gig., Par., Prov read εξω της παρεμβολης;
Blass in β, Hilg. (see Wendt's note, p. 420, 1899).

either of the Gospel of Christ, or of Paul
the prisoner, even in Rome, may well
have endued his soul with much strength.
Bishop Lightfoot, *Phil.*, pp. 16, 17 (so too
Hort, *Judaistic Christianity*, p. 113),
thinks that the words may intimate that
it was a relief to St. Paul to find that
some members at least of the Roman
Church were favourably disposed towards
him ; but, as Zöckler points out, there is
certainly no proof here, at least, that
the Church was composed preponderat-
ingly of Jewish Christians, or that Paul
was glad that he received a welcome in
a Church so composed, and we have no
direct evidence of the existence of an
anti-Pauline Jewish party among the
Roman Christians ; but in the presence
of the brethren St. Paul would see a
proof that this love was not merely in
word or in letter, but in deed and in
truth : "videbat Christum etiam Romæ
esse," Bengel.

Ver. 16.—ἤλθομεν, see critical note.
They would enter by the Porta Capena.
On the words which follow see critical
note. They are retained by Blass and
Ramsay, although these writers differ as
to their interpretation, while Lightfoot,
Phil., pp. 7, 8, admitting that the balance
of existing authorities is against them,
inclines to see in the words a genuine
tradition, even if no part of the original
text. For Ramsay's view see above on
xxvii. 1. Blass takes the expression τῷ
στρατ. to refer to Afranius Burrus (and
to this identification Lightfoot attaches
much probability). It is striking that
both before and after Burrus there were
two "prefects," Tac., *Ann.*, xii., 42, xiv.,

51, whereas Luke writes τῷ στρατ., "*the*
captain of the guard"; but on the other
hand we can scarcely draw any decisive
argument from this, because the writer
may refer merely to the "prefect" in
charge of this particular case, whether
he had a colleague or not.—καθ' ἑαυτόν,
see critical note for addition in β text.
Not only the goodwill of the centurion,
and the services which St. Paul had
rendered, but also the terms in which
Festus had reported the case in the
elogium, would combine to secure this
favour. The words do not imply that
Paul was kept in prison in the camp
apart from the other prisoners, but, as in
vv. 23, 30, that he was allowed to have
a house or lodging in the city (Ramsay) ;
he could scarcely have summoned the
Jews to the camp, ver. 17 (Bethge), see
also Lightfoot, *Phil.*, p. 103.—τῷ φυλάσσοντι αὐτὸν στρατ.: *custodia militaris*,
he was still bound to a soldier by a
light chain, so that he could not go
in and out as he pleased, but the form
which his custody took has been well
compared to that which Herod Agrippa
underwent, who was confined at one
time in Rome, Jos., *Ant.*, xviii., 6, 5, at
first in the camp, and afterwards on the
accession of Gaius in a house of his own,
although still under military custody, *cf.*
xxiv. 27.

Ver. 17. The whole section vv. 17-
28 is referred by Hilgenfeld to the
"author to Theophilus". In ver. 20 the
Paul bound for the hope of Israel belongs
only to the "author to Theophilus," *cf.*
xxiii. 6, xxvi. 6 ; it is only the same
author who still supposes him to bear

18. οἵτινες ἀνακρίναντές με ἐβούλοντο ἀπολῦσαι, διὰ τὸ μηδεμίαν αἰτίαν θανάτου ὑπάρχειν ἐν ἐμοί. 19. ἀντιλεγόντων δὲ τῶν Ἰουδαίων,[1] ἠναγκάσθην ἐπικαλέσασθαι Καίσαρα, οὐχ ὡς τοῦ ἔθνους μου ἔχων τι

[1] After Ιουδαιων 137, Syr. H. c*, add και επικραζοντων· αιρε τον εχθρον ημων (cf. xxi. 36, xxii. 22, xxv. 24), so Blass in β, Hilg., Zöckler; and after κατηγορειν (אAB) the same authorities with Gig., Par., Prov. add αλλ' ινα λυτρωσωμαι τ. ψυχην μου εκ θανατου.

the chain, xxvi. 29, which according to xxii. 29, 30, had been long removed. A reference to the passages in question is sufficient to show the unreasonableness of this criticism. In this same section Clemen can only see his two redactors, Judaicus and Antijudaicus, at work again, the latter in vv. 25-28, and the former in vv. 16-24. But it will be noticed that Wendt (1899) still allows that an historical kernel lies at the foundation of the narrative, and although he does not speak so unhesitatingly as in 1888, he still allows that it is not inconceivable that Paul soon after his arrival in Rome should seek to enter into relations with the Jews there, to convince them if possible of his innocence, and to prevent any unfavourable influences on their part upon his trial.—μετὰ ἡμέρας τρεῖς: an intimation of Paul's continuous energy, the previous days may well have been employed in receiving his own friends, and in making his summons known.—τῶν Ἰου.: the edict of Claudius, cf. xviii. 2, had evidently been very transient in its effects, and the Jews soon returned; possibly they may only have emigrated to the neighbourhood, e.g., to Aricia (Schürer).—πρώτους, cf. xiii. 50, xxv. 2, Luke xix. 47, here including the ἀρχισυνάγωγοι, the γερουσιάρχαι, the ἄρχοντες and others, Sanday and Headlam, Romans, p. xxiii., or the word may perhaps be used of social distinction, including the officers named. The Jews in Rome were divided into no less than seven synagogues. It does not of course follow that all came in answer to the Apostle's characteristic summons, as he always turned to his countrymen first. Rendall renders "those that were of the Jews first," as if Paul invited first the members of the synagogues who were Jews, intending to reserve the devout Gentiles for the second place; see R.V. renderings in loco.—συνελθ.: it was natural that Paul should thus assemble them, and that he should then endeavour to show that although a prisoner he was guiltless of any offence against the Jewish nation; otherwise he could not

expect the representatives of his people to listen to his message; so far it would be difficult to find an intimation of anything unhistorical (see Blass, in loco).—ἐγὼ: the word probably occurring first, W.H., R.V. Weiss, seems to indicate from its emphatic position that the Apostle's chief concern on this occasion was to vindicate himself.—ἔλεγε: imperfect, "quia expectatur responsum," Blass, see note on iii. 3.—ἀδελφοὶ . . . λαῷ . . . πατρῴοις: all indicate the same conciliatory spirit: "mira certe Pauli mansuetudo" (Calvin).—ποιήσας: "though I had done," R.V., i.e., at the time he was taken prisoner there had been nothing done by him to merit such treatment.—τῷ λαῷ, cf. xxi. 28. The man who could write Rom. ix. 1 ff. and 1 Cor. vii. 18 (cf. ix. 21) might justly use such words. — παρεδόθην, cf. xxi. 11. The words ascribe primarily to the Jews a share in the imprisonment of which they appear as only the indirect cause, cf. xxi. 33, but Paul summarises the chief points and does not enter into minute details; moreover his words were strictly true, for he would have been freed by the Romans in Jerusalem had not the outcry of the Jews stamped him as a malefactor. For similar instances of a main summary cf. ii. 23, xiii. 29, xxi. 11, xxiii. 27.

Ver. 18. ἀνακ., cf. xxiv. 8, xxv. 6, 26, referring here to the judicial inquiries of Felix and Festus.

Ver. 19. ἀντιλ.: the word is a mild one to describe the bitter enmity of the Jews ("clementer dicit," Bengel); they are not actually represented as speaking against Paul's acquittal, although they are evidently presupposed as doing so by the proposal of Festus, xxv. 9, and by the belief that sooner or later he would fall a victim to their plots the Apostle was no doubt compelled (ἠναγκάσθην) to appeal. Holtzmann seems to forget the part played by the Jews, and their bitter enmity, when he says that in reality Paul was compelled to appeal not by the Jews, but by Festus; see also critical note.— τοῦ ἔθνους μου: they were still his nation,

κατηγορῆσαι. 20. διὰ ταύτην οὖν τὴν αἰτίαν παρεκάλεσα ὑμᾶς ἰδεῖν καὶ προσλαλῆσαι¹· ἔνεκεν γὰρ τῆς ἐλπίδος τοῦ Ἰσραὴλ τὴν ἅλυσιν ταύτην περίκειμαι. 21. οἱ δὲ πρὸς αὐτὸν εἶπον, Ἡμεῖς οὔτε γράμματα περὶ σοῦ ἐδεξάμεθα ἀπὸ τῆς Ἰουδαίας, οὔτε παραγενόμενός τις² τῶν ἀδελφῶν ἀπήγγειλεν ἢ ἐλάλησέ τι περὶ σοῦ πονηρόν. 22. ἀξιοῦμεν δὲ παρὰ σοῦ ἀκοῦσαι ἃ φρονεῖς. περὶ μὲν γὰρ τῆς αἱρέσεως

¹ εινεκεν the Ionic form is supported by ℵ*A, W.H., Weiss, Blass.
² After τις Blass in β, so Hilg. add απο ιεροσολυμων with Gig., Syr. Pesh.

and he was not ashamed to call them so, as a true patriot, when he stood before a foreign tribunal; cf. xxiv. 17, xxvi. 4, " see what friendliness of expression, he does not hold them in odium," Chrysostom. Ver. 20. διὰ ταύτην . . . προσλαλῆσαι: "for this cause therefore did I intreat you to see and to speak with me," R.V. text; in margin a comma is placed after ὑμᾶς, "call for you, to see and to speak with you": but the former seems the more likely, for as a prisoner St. Paul would hardly go out into the synagogue. —ἔνεκεν, see critical note; if εἵνεκεν, the word is only used by St. Luke amongst the Evangelists; cf. Luke iv. 18 (quotation), xviii. 29, and elsewhere only by St. Paul, 2 Cor. iii. 10; Ionic form (see Winer-Schmiedel, p. 50).—τῆς ἐλπίδος τοῦ Ἰ., cf. xxvi. 6.—περίκειμαι: for construction, Winer-Moulton, xxxii., 5; cf. 4 Macc. xii. 3; Clem. Rom., 2 Cor., i., 6 (bis). Nothing could be more pathetic than this reference to the chain, cf. Ephes. iii. 1, iv. 1, vi. 20; the words might well serve as an introduction to what was to follow, the Christian prisoner and the Jewish leaders all had " one hope of their calling," and in that hope they and he were one. Ver. 21. πρὸς αὐτὸν: the emphatic position of the words may indicate, as Weiss suggests, that as Paul had spoken to them up to this point of a personal matter, so they in reply spoke with a like reference.—οὔτε γράμματα, i.e., no official letters from the Sanhedrim—this was practically impossible, for it is not likely that any ship had left Cæsarea before Paul's departure with such intelligence (so Weiss, Blass, Hackett).— τῶν ἀδελ., i.e., of the Jewish nation, cf. ver. 17. The Jews do not assert that they know nothing of Paul, but only that with reference to the statement which he had just made they had received no report (ἀπήγ., cf. R.V., so iv. 23), or had any of his country-

men spoken evil of him. The aorists point to this limitation of the assertion (Page's note, and Nösgen, in loco), and this view prevents us from seeing any contradiction between vv. 21 and 22, for if the statement in the former verse be taken quite generally of Paul's work, the Jews contradicted themselves in ver. 22, where they evidently include Paul in this sect (ταύτης), of which they knew that it was everywhere spoken against. —πονηρόν: the stress need not be laid on this word, as if the sentence meant that they had heard something about Paul, but nothing evil; it may well have been chosen with reference to the Apostle's own expression, οὐδὲν ἐναντίον. Ver. 22. ἀξιοῦμεν δὲ: "but we think good," cf. xv. 38. They acknowledge that no report had reached them to invalidate the statements which Paul had just made as to the causes of his imprisonment, but (δὲ) they would hear not from others, but from himself (παρὰ σοῦ). —ἃ φρονεῖς: evidently no reference to any special view of Christianity as characterising St. Paul's own teaching, but a reference to his claim to be imprisoned for the hope of Israel.—αἱρ.: Christianity was for them only a sect, and therefore they could not understand the Apostle's identification of it with the Jewish national hope. See note on ver. 17.— γνωστόν . . . ἡμῖν: if the view is correct that the edict of Claudius, see chap. xviii. 2, was occasioned by the early preaching of Christianity in Rome, it is possible that the dislocation of the Jewish community then caused may help at all events to explain why the Christian Church in Rome did not grow out of the Jewish synagogue in the capital to the same context as elsewhere, see Sanday and Headlam, Romans, pp. xxi, xxii. It may no doubt be urged that the Christian Church in Rome was not entirely a heathen-Christian Church, and that, as the names in Rom. xvi. indicate, it contained a Jewish element. But it is quite con-

ταύτης γνωστόν ἐστιν ἡμῖν ὅτι πανταχοῦ ἀντιλέγεται.[1] 23. Ταξάμενοι
δὲ αὐτῷ ἡμέραν,[2] ἧκον πρὸς αὐτὸν εἰς τὴν ξενίαν πλείονες · οἷς ἐξετίθετο διαμαρτυρόμενος τὴν βασιλείαν τοῦ Θεοῦ, πείθων τε αὐτοὺς
τὰ[3] περὶ τοῦ Ἰησοῦ, ἀπό τε τοῦ νόμου Μωσέως καὶ τῶν προφητῶν,
ἀπὸ πρωῒ ἕως ἑσπέρας. 24. καὶ οἱ μὲν ἐπείθοντο τοῖς λεγομένοις,

[1] At the end Blass in β with Gig., Par. adds εν ολη τη οικουμενη.

[2] For ηκον ℵAB (A ηλθαν so W.H.) have ηλθον.

[3] τα before περι om. ℵABH Vulg., Boh., Syr. P. and H., Tisch., W.H., R.V.,
Weiss, Blass, Hilg.

ceivable that in the capital, with its two
million inhabitants, the Jews, who had
only recently returned to the city, should
know nothing beyond what is here indicated in such general terms of a poor and
obscure sect who dwelt no longer in the
Jewish quarter. It is also worthy of consideration that the Jews of Rome, whilst
not guilty of any untruth in what they
had just said as to their knowledge of
the Christian sect, may have expressed
themselves in this guarded manner from
political reasons. If St. Paul's statement
in ver. 18 as to the favourable bearing of
the Roman authorities towards him was
true, it was but natural that the Jews
should wish to refrain from hasty or hostile
action towards a prisoner who was evidently treated with consideration in his
bonds ; they would rather act thus than re-
vive an old quarrel which might again lead
to their own political insecurity, see especially Lightfoot, *Philippians*, pp. 15, 16 ;
Felten, *in loco* ; and, further, Rendall, p.
352. Nothing said by the Jews contradicts the existence of a Christian community in Rome, nor is it said that they
wished to learn the Christian tenets from
Paul, as if they knew nothing of them
from their own knowledge, or as if they
knew nothing of the causes of the opposition to the Christian faith ; motives of
curiosity and of policy might well have
prompted a desire to hear Paul speak for
himself, and with such motives there was
apparently mingled a tone of contempt
for a sect of which they might fairly say,
from the experience of their countrymen,
and from their own experience in Rome,
πανταχοῦ ἀντιλέγεται: ἀντιλ. Lucan-
Pauline ; only once elsewhere ; *cf.* John
xix. 12. See β text above.

Ver. 23. ταξάμενοι: *cf.* Matt. xxviii.
16, and Polyb., xviii., 36, 1, for a similar
phrase ; a mutual arrangement between
the two parties ; only here in the middle
voice in Acts.—τὴν ξενίαν: may = τὸ
μίσθωμα, ver. 30 (Weiss, Holtzmann),

or it may refer to entertainment in the
house of a friend, *cf.* xxi. 16, and
Philem., ver. 22. Lewin urges that
although we can well understand that
Paul's friends would wish to entertain
him, we have no evidence that the strictness of the military guard was thus far
relaxed, and he also presses the fact that
Suidas and Hesychius explain ξενία =
κατάλυμα, καταγώγιον, as if it meant a
place of sojourn for hire ; see especially
for the whole question Lewin, *St. Paul*,
ii., 238 ; but see on the other hand
Lightfoot, *Philippians*, p. 9, who lays
stress on N.T. passages quoted above, and
Grimm-Thayer, *sub v.*—πλείονες: more
than at the first time ; Blass takes it as
= *plurimi*, *cf.* ii. 40, xiii. 31.—ἐξετίθετο,
cf. xi. 4, xviii. 26, and in vii. 21 in
a different sense, nowhere else in
N.T. J. Weiss and Vogel both lay
stress upon the recurrence of the
word in the medical writer Dioscorides ; for other references, Grimm-
Thayer, *sub v.* It is possible that the
middle here, as in xi. 4, gives it a reflexive force, the Apostle vindicates his
own conduct (Rendall).—Μωσέως: from
the law of Moses, whose enemy he was
represented to be, no less than from the
Prophets.—πείθων *suavissime*, Bengel ;
on the conative present participle see
Burton, p. 59, but here the word is used
not simply *de conatu* ; it refers here to
the persuasive power of St. Paul's words,
although it does not say that his words
resulted in conviction.—ἀπὸ πρωῒ ἕως
ἑσπέρας, *cf.* for similar expressions
Exod. xviii. 13, 14 A, Job iv. 20 AS,
and other passages where πρωΐθεν is
similarly used (H. and R.).

Ver. 24. οἱ μὲν . . . οἱ δὲ . ., *cf.*
xiv. 4, xvii. 32, whether the verb means
simply listened to what was said (Rendall), or simply denotes an attitude of
receptivity (Nösgen), the fact that Paul
addresses to both classes his final words
indicates that the degree of belief to

οἱ δὲ ἠπίστουν. 25.[1] ἀσύμφωνοι δὲ ὄντες πρὸς ἀλλήλους ἀπελύοντο,
εἰπόντος τοῦ Παύλου ῥῆμα ἕν, "Ὅτι καλῶς τὸ Πνεῦμα τὸ Ἅγιον
ἐλάλησε διὰ Ἡσαΐου τοῦ προφήτου πρὸς τοὺς πατέρας[2] ἡμῶν, λέγον,
26. "Πορεύθητι πρὸς τὸν λαὸν τοῦτον καὶ εἰπέ, Ἀκοῇ ἀκούσετε, καὶ

---

[1] After ασυμ. ℵ*, Vulg., Syr. Pesh. read τε, so Tisch., but Lach., W.H., Weiss,
Blass, Hilg. follow T.R. (Wendt doubtful).

[2] For ημων ℵAB Syr. Pesh., Tisch., W.H., R.V., Blass in β, Hilg., Weiss,
Wendt read υμων. Instead of λεγον (so Blass, Hilg.) ℵBLP, Tisch., W.H.,
Weiss, Wendt have λεγων.

---

which they attained was not sufficient to
convince even the well-disposed Jews
to throw in their lot with Paul. Perhaps
it is best to remember that the tenses are
in the imperfect: "some were being
persuaded of the things, etc.," and this
also keeps up the reference to the previous πείθων, *persuadere studens* (Blass,
Plumptre).—οἱ δὲ ἠπίσ.: "and some
disbelieved," R.V., or "continued in
their disbelief". The verb only here in
Acts, but cf. Luke xxiv. 11, 41, Mark
xvi. 11, 16, 1 Pet. ii. 7, Wisd. x. 7, xii.
17, xviii. 13 (see H. and R.), etc.—
Ver. 25. ἀσύμφωνοι, cf. Wisd. xviii.
19 and Dan., LXX, Bel., ver. 15; cf. for
the phrase Diod. Sic., iv., 1, the word is
found in Josephus, but also in classical
Greek.—δέ: the best attested reading
marks sharply and emphatically the turn
of affairs; there may have been Pharisees
among the well-disposed Jews, and to
these Paul may have made an appeal
when the hope of Israel, now as formerly,
was in question, cf. xxiii. 6; but if so, they
would not decide to rank themselves
amongst "the Pharisees that believed"
however imperfectly, and of them as
well of the unbelievers the writer can
only say ἀπελύοντο, cf. for middle Exod.
xxxiii. 11, and so Polyb., iii., 34, 12.—
εἰπόντος τοῦ Π.: the words do not mean
that they departed because Paul so spoke,
but almost = ἀπολυομένων εἶπεν (so
Blass, Nösgen). It may be that Paul's
words of censure were partly directed
against the spirit which prompted the
Jews to depart all together; in other
words to suppress the differences which
had evidently arisen amongst them, for
the sake of an outward show of fellowship, lest they should again be charged
as *tumultuantes* (Nösgen); but beyond
all this, in their absence of brotherly
love for one who still claimed them as
his ἀδελφοί, in the unbelief of some,
in the want of the courage of their
convictions in others, St. Paul saw
a fulfilment of that hardness and dulness

of heart of which the prophet had spoken.
—ῥῆμα ἕν: "*one* word," emphatically
drawing attention to the prophetical
utterance which followed; it was evening,
the night was drawing on, and (ver. 23)
so too for the disbelieving nation: the
day was far spent, the night was at hand
(Bethge).—καλῶς, cf. Matt. xv. 7, Mark
vii. 6, 9 (as in these two passages placed
first with strong indignation, Page), xii.
28, Luke xx. 39, the word often occurs
in St. Paul's Epistles. It is remarkable
that the same prophetic quotation with
which the Christ had opened His teaching by parables, which is cited in all
four of the Evangelists, should thus form
the solemn close of the historical books
of the N.T. See above on Matt. xiii. 14,
Mark iv. 12, Luke viii. 10, and John xii.
40, where the same words are quoted by
St. John to explain the rejection of
Christ's own teaching, just as here by St.
Paul to explain the rejection of the teaching about Christ. "Est hoc extremum
dictum Pauli in Actis, neque fortuito esse
videtur; totius enim fere libri summam
continet ad gentis evangelium a Judæis
jam translatum esse, quippe spretum ab
eis" (Blass), cf. the course of events in
Antioch, Corinth, Ephesus, xiii. 42, xviii.
6, xix. 9.—τὸ Π. τὸ Ἅ.: the solemnity
of the words is intensified by thus introducing the Holy Ghost, rather than
merely the human agent, as Himself
speaking (see also critical note); and not
only so, but by thus intimating that
they were resisting not man but God, cf.
vii. 51.—ἡμῶν: if we read ὑμῶν the word
indicates that St. Paul would not identify
himself with the unbelieving Jews, cf.
vii. 52, the indignant words of St.
Stephen, which the speaker had himself
heard.
Ver. 26. πορεύθητι . . . εἰπέ: the
quotation is accurately taken from the
LXX, Isai. vi. 9, 10, and the first line
is additional to the words otherwise given
in full by St. Matthew; as the speaker is
the messenger to the Jews who condemns

οὐ μὴ συνῆτε· καὶ βλέποντες βλέψετε, καὶ οὐ μὴ ἴδητε.   27. ἐπα-
χύνθη γὰρ ἡ καρδία τοῦ λαοῦ τούτου, καὶ τοῖς ὡσὶ βαρέως ἤκουσαν,
καὶ τοὺς ὀφθαλμοὺς αὐτῶν ἐκάμμυσαν· μήποτε ἴδωσι τοῖς ὀφθαλμοῖς,
καὶ τοῖς ὡσὶν ἀκούσωσι, καὶ τῇ καρδίᾳ συνῶσι καὶ ἐπιστρέψωσι, καὶ
ἰάσωμαι[1] αὐτούς."   28. γνωστὸν οὖν ἔστω ὑμῖν, ὅτι τοῖς ἔθνεσιν
ἀπεστάλη[2] τὸ σωτήριον τοῦ Θεοῦ, αὐτοὶ καὶ ἀκούσονται.[3]   29. καὶ
ταῦτα αὐτοῦ εἰπόντος, ἀπῆλθον οἱ Ἰουδαῖοι, πολλὴν ἔχοντες ἐν
ἑαυτοῖς συζήτησιν.

---

[1] For ιασωμαι (so Lach.) ℵABHLP, Sev. Theophl., so Tisch., Weiss, W.H.,
Wendt, Blass, Hilg. read ιασομαι.

[2] After απεσταλη ℵ*AB Vulg., Syr. P. and H., Aeth[PP], Tisch., W.H., R.V.,
Blass, Weiss, Wendt, Hilg. read τουτο.

[3] The whole of the verse is wanting in ℵABE 13, 40, 61, 68, so in W.H., Weiss,
but retained by Blass in β, Hilg., with HLP, Syr. H. c*, Vulg.[Clem.], Gig.,
Par. Wendt describes it as an interpolation, cf. ver. 25, see also Lightfoot On a
Fresh Revision, etc., p. 29; Blass, Phil. of the Gospels, p. 92.

---

this hardness of heart, he applies to himself the word πορ.

Ver. 27. ἰάσωμαι, see critical note;
the indicative future as in R.V. adds to the
force and vigour of the passage; after μή
it represents the action of the verb as more
vividly realised as possible and probable
than is the case when the subjunctive is
used (Page), see also Winer-Moulton,
lvi., 2a; Bethge, p. 331; cf. Luke xii. 58,
Acts xxi. 24 (Blass).   It is significant
that Luke the physician should thus
cite as almost the last words of his
record a prophecy ending with ἰάσομαι
(Plummer, St. Luke, Introd., p. lxvi).

Ver. 28. γνωστὸν οὖν: for the word
similarly used cf. ii. 14, iv. 10; xiii. 38.—
τοῦτο τὸ σωτ., see critical note; cf. LXX,
Ps. lxvi. 2, xcvii. 2, 3.   σωτ., adjective,
neuter of σωτήριος, used substantively
(as in classical Greek), so often in LXX
of the Messianic salvation; cf. Luke ii.
30, iii. 6, Ephes. vi. 17, and Clem. Rom.,
Cor., xxxv., 12, xxxvi., 1.   The word is
used only by St. Luke and St. Paul, see
Plummer, note on Luke iii. 6.   For
the whole expression here cf. xiii. 26,
where words very similar are used by
Paul, and with very similar results,
ver. 46. τοῦτο, emphatic this, the very
message of God's salvation, this is
what I am declaring to you.—αὐτοὶ καὶ
ἀκούσονται: "they will also hear,"
R.V.   The words thus rendered may not
convey so plainly a reproach to the Jews
as in A.V., but at the same time they express something more than the mere fact
that Gentiles as well as Jews will now
hear the message; that message will not

only be sent (ἀπεστάλη), but also heard;
the καί may well indicate that whilst the
Jews will hear with the ear only as distinct from the understanding, the Gentiles
will not only hear, but really (καί) listen
(see Rendall and Weiss, in loco).   At the
same time we must remember that as a
background to what the Apostle here says
we have his words in Rom. ix.-xi., and
the thought which he had expressed to
the Roman Church that God had not
really cast away His people, but whilst
through their unbelief the Gentiles had
been called, yet that inclusion of the
heathen in the Messianic kingdom would
rouse the Jews to jealousy, and that
thus all Israel would be saved, Rom. xi.
11; cf. x. 19; Sanday and Headlam,
Romans, p. 341 ff.   We can scarcely
doubt that the words are uttered not
merely to condemn, but to lead to repentance; at all events it would not be
possible to find stronger words against
his own countrymen than those written
by St. Paul in his earliest Epistle, 1
Thess. ii. 15, 16; and yet we know
how St. Paul, for those same countrymen,
could wish himself accused; so Bethge, as
against Overbeck, who can only see that
in Acts the belief of the Gentiles results not in a noble jealousy, but in the
bitter envy of the Jews.   But there
blends with the tone of sadness a note of
triumph in the words αὐτοὶ καὶ ἀκούσονται, the future of their message is assured, and we may borrow two words as
an inscription for these closing pages of
St. Luke's second treatise—the last word
of the Apostle, and the last of the historian

30.[1] Ἔμεινε δὲ ὁ Παῦλος διετίαν ὅλην ἐν ἰδίῳ μισθώματι, καὶ ἀπεδέχετο πάντας τοὺς εἰσπορευομένους [2] πρὸς αὐτόν, 31. κηρύσσων

[1] For εμεινε (Lach., Blass, Hilg.) ℵ*B 13, 61, Tisch., W.H., R.V., Wendt, Weiss have ενεμεινε; Blass in β has μενων with Par. ο Π. om. W.H., R.V., Weiss (not Blass, Hilg.), cf. αυτον for τον Π. in ver. 17, R.V., W.H.

[2] After προς αυτον 137 Syr. H. c*, Gig., Par. add ιουδαιους τε και Ελληνας explanatory of παντας, so Blass in β text, Hilg.; Blass also adds και διελεγετο προς before the inserted words just mentioned, with Gig., Par. Χριστου om. by Tisch., Hilg., with ℵ* Syr. H.

—ἀκούσονται . . . ἀκωλύτως—the word of God was heard and welcomed, and that word was not bound, see the suggestive remarks of Bethge, p. 335, and Zöckler on ver. 31.   Ver. 29. See critical note.—συζήτησιν, rixa, Blass; possibly this may have helped to delay the Apostle's trial, as apparently some of the Jews would not have moved in the matter.   Ver. 30. ἔμεινε δὲ: Blass (so also Hackett, Lekebusch) makes the important remark that the aorist shows that Paul's condition was changed after the two years, cf. ἐκάθισε, xviii. 11 (see also Burton, pp. 19, 20). When, therefore, Luke wrote his history, the inference is that the Apostle had been liberated either from prison or by death. Blass indicates another change, viz., that he may have been removed into the prætorium, and that his trial was just coming on.—ἰδίῳ μισθ., see above on ver. 23. That the Apostle should have been able to hire a house at his own expense receives confirmation from the coincidence with Phil. iv. 10, 14, 18; others have suggested (Wendt, 1899, Knabenbauer) that he may have gained the means of hiring it by his own work. See in this connection Rendel Harris, Four Lectures, etc., pp. 50, 51, and the extract from the Armenian Version of Ephrem's Commentary on the Acts. It would seem that Ephrem imagined that the rent of the lodging was paid by the proceeds of the cloak and books (2 Tim. iv. 13). Lightfoot, Philippians, p. 9, holds that ἰδίῳ certainly distinguishes the μίσθωμα here from the ξενία above, see his note, and Grimm-Thayer, in loco. It is quite true that μίσθωμα is not used in this sense of a hired house elsewhere (indeed it is used especially of the wages of hire in a bad sense, Deut. xxiii. 18, Mic. i. 7, Ezek. xvi. 31), but Lightfoot admits that it may be used here exceptionally as a translation of the Latin conductum, meaning here a suite of apartments only, not the whole house (Lewin), the Latin

meritoria (sc. loca) seems to be used very much in this same double sense of μίσθωμα.—διετίαν ὅλην, cf. xxiv. 27, only in Luke, not in classical Greek, but in Philo (see also Grimm-Thayer, and Deissmann, Neue Bibelstudien, p. 86), so too τριετίαν only in Luke; see on xx. 31. The two years were spent not only in preaching, but in writing, as we may fairly believe, Ephesians, Colossians, Philemon, and Philippians.—ἀπεδέχετο, see above, xv. 4, xxi. 7, apparently greater freedom than in Cæsarea, xxiv. 23; if it was not for the notice in Phil. i. 13, 17, we might almost suppose that the Apostle was liberated on security or on bail; cf. the account of the imprisonment of Agrippa I. in Rome; see p. 486. — πάντας: all, both Jews and Gentiles; not only the latter, as Bengel thought: "neminem excludebat Dei exemplo," Grotius.—εἰσπορ., see on ix. 28, most frequent in Luke, Friedrich, p. 7; see critical note.   Ver. 31. τὰ περὶ: on the phrase see p. 481. — τοῦ Κ. Ἰ. Χ., see critical note, and cf. xi. 17, xv. 26, the full phrase corresponds with the solemn conclusion of the book.—μετὰ π. παρρ.: the phrase with or without πάσης four times in Acts, and nowhere else in N.T., see on p. 128. In Jerusalem by the Twelve, iv. 29, and in Rome no less than in Jerusalem by St. Paul, the witness was given "with all boldness," cf. Phil. i. 14; and so the promise in the vision vouchsafed to the Apostle of the Gentiles was verified, xxiii. 11, and the aim of the Gentile historian fulfilled when the Gospel was thus preached boldly and openly, ἕως ἐσχ. τῆς γῆς, see note on i. 8.—ἀκωλύτως: "eadem plane dicuntur in ep. ad Phil. Roma data, i. 12 sqq.," Blass, and the word of God had free course and was glorified. The adverb is found in Plato, Epict., Herodian, and also in Josephus. In LXX the adjective is found in Wisd. vii. 22, and the adverb is used by Symm., Job xxxiv. 31.   There is a note of triumph in the word, Bengel, Zöckler,

τὴν βασιλείαν τοῦ Θεοῦ,[1] καὶ διδάσκων τὰ περὶ τοῦ Κυρίου Ἰησοῦ
Χριστοῦ, μετὰ πάσης παρρησίας ἀκωλύτως.

[1] Blass with Syr. H., demid. tol., Par., Wern., Prov. reconstructs β text after
του Θεου: διισχυριζομενος και λεγων ακωλυτως, οτι ουτος εστιν ο Χ. ο υιος του
Θεου, δι' ου μελλει πας ο κοσμος κρινεσθαι, and cf. Hilg. with variations in former
part, but identical after ακωλ.

and we may note with Wordsworth
and Page the cadence of these concluding words, μετα π. π. ἀκωλ. But
all this does not forbid the view that the
writer intended to give a third book
to complete his work. This latter view
is strongly insisted upon by Prof. Ramsay, St. Paul, p. 23 ff., while Bishop
Lightfoot, B.D.², i., 27, can see no conceivable plea for any third treatise, if the
purpose of the narrative is completed by
Paul coming to Rome and there delivering
his message, so, although less strongly,
Harnack, Chron., i., p. 248, see note on i.
8. But Prof. Ramsay has received the
strong support not only of Zöckler, and
curiously enough of Spitta, Apostelgeschichte, p. 318, but still more recently
amongst English writers of Rendall, and
in Germany of Dr. Zahn. Just as in
St. Luke's Gospel xxiv. 44 forms not
merely a starting - point for, but an
anticipation of, the succeeding history,
or just as xxiv. 44-53 contain in a
summary what is afterwards related in
greater detail, Acts i. and ii., so in vv. 30,
31 of Acts xxviii. we have, as it were, a
brief sketch of what succeeded the events
hitherto recorded, and an anticipation of
what followed upon them. This probability remains quite apart from the
additional force which is given to it if
Ramsay is right in regarding πρῶτος,
Acts i. 1, as signifying not simply πρότερος, but the first of a series, a view
strongly supported by Zahn, Einleitung,
ii., p. 371. Certainly the aorist, ver. 30
(see above), and the expression διετίαν
ὅλην seem to show that some fact was
known to the writer which followed the
close of the two years, and we can therefore hardly say that he wrote no more
because he knew no more, unless we also
suppose that he wrote his history at the
conclusion and not during the course of
the two years. This he may have done
while the result of St. Paul's first trial
was still unknown, although Phil. i. 25-
27, ii. 24, Philem. ver. 22, show us plainly
with what confidence the Apostle awaited
the issue. At all events almost any conjecture seems more probable than that
the writer should have concluded so

abruptly if he had nothing more to
chronicle than the immediate and tragic
death of his hero! Zöckler, Apostelgeschichte, p. 162, Spitta, Zur Geschichte
und Litteratur des Urchristentums, I.,
15, 16. To say with Jülicher, Einleitung,
p. 27, that he refrained from doing this
because in such an event he would
chronicle not the triumph but the defeat
of the Gospel is certainly a strange argument, and no one has given a better
answer to it than Harnack by asking,
Since when did the early Christians regard martyrdom as a defeat? Is the
death of Christ, or of Stephen, in the
mind of the author of Acts a defeat? is it
not rather a triumph? Chron., i., 247.
The elaborate discussion of the abrupt conclusion in Acts by Wendt, 1899, pp. 31,
32, is entirely based upon the assumption
that Luke was not the author of Acts,
and that therefore this author, whoever
he was, wrote no more because his information failed him, and he knew no
more. This could not have been so in
the case of Luke, who was with the
Apostle at Rome, as we have from undoubted testimony quite apart from Acts.
See further Introd. For the release of St.
Paul, his subsequent journeys to Spain
and to the East, and his second imprisonment, see in support, Zahn, Einleitung, i., p. 435 ff., Harnack, Chron., i.,
239, Spitta, u. s., Salmon, Introd., p. 403
ff., Die zweite römische Gefangenschaft
des Apostels Paulus, Steinmeyer (1897),
and Critical Review (July), 1898.
There were many possible reasons why
the hearing of St. Paul's appeal was so
long delayed. The record of the previous proceedings forwarded by Festus
may have been lost in the wreck, and it
was therefore necessary to wait for fresh
official information, as the prisoner's
accusers had not arrived. And when
they arrived, it is very possible that they
may have been glad to interpose fresh
obstacles, and that they would be content
to keep Paul bound as before; as evidence was probably wanted, not only
from Jerusalem, but from various parts
of the empire, the interposition of these
fresh delays was easy. St. Paul had

himself suggested that the Jews in Asia ought to be summoned, or to be present, xxiv. 19. That such delays would not be unusual we may learn from Tacitus, *e.g.*, *Ann.*, xiii., 43 ; *cf.* Suet., *Nero*, 15. When we remember how long a delay occurred in the case of the Jewish priests, the friends of Josephus, *Vita*, 3, who were sent to Rome by Felix to plead their cause, it ceases to be surprising that St. Paul was detained so long without a trial ; see on the whole question Lewin, *St. Paul*, ii., 277 ff. ; Lightfoot, *Phil.*, p. 4 ; Knabenbauer, *Actus Apostolorum*, pp. 453, 454, 1899.

ST. PAUL'S EPISTLE

TO THE

ROMANS

INTRODUCTION.

CHAPTER I.

ORIGIN OF THE CHURCH AT ROME.

OF the beginnings of Christianity in Rome nothing whatever is known on direct evidence. The tradition which assigns the founding of the Church there to Peter cannot possibly be maintained. In one form it assumes that Peter, on the occasion referred to in Acts xii. 17, travelled to Rome, and there propagated the Church from the synagogue as a centre. As this departure of Peter from Jerusalem took place, on the usual reckoning, about 42 A.D., there would be time for his twenty-five years' episcopate of Rome, which was once the accepted Romish idea, though now given up even by Romish scholars. But it is clear from the book of Acts (chap. xv.) that Peter was in Jerusalem ten years after this, and it is equally clear from the Epistle to the Romans that he had not been in Rome when this letter was written, seven years later still. In face of a passage like chap. xv. 20 it is impossible to suppose that the Church of Rome had already been the scene of another Apostle's labours. Three years later, when Paul at length arrived in Rome, it had still been unvisited by Peter, to judge from what we read in Acts xxviii.; and even when he wrote the Epistle to the Philippians, towards the close of his first imprisonment, there is no indication that his brother Apostle had yet seen the capital. The earliest tradition represents Peter and Paul as in Rome together, and, indeed, as suffering together, in the Neronian persecution. All the evidence for this will be found in Euseb., *Hist. Eccl.*, II., xxv. What the worth of it is, it is not easy to say. It is not incredible that Peter may have been in Rome about the date in question, especially if Babylon in 1 Peter v. 13 means Rome, as it does in the Apocalypse. But in any case Peter can have had no direct part in founding the Church. In Iren., iii., 1, 2, Peter and Paul are spoken of as "preaching the Gospel in Rome, and founding the Church," at the time that Matthew published his gospel.

That Christianity was there long before this time is indubitable, but the Roman Christians, it has been suggested (see Harvey's note on Iren. *ad loc.*), " appear neither to have had an ecclesiastical polity nor to have been under the regular regimen of the Church. . . . Several expressions in the epistle seem to indicate a crude, unsettled state of things there. . . . They are spoken of as depending rather upon mutual exhortation and instruction than upon any more authoritative communication of evangelical truth (xv. 14) . . . and the Apostle expresses his intention to visit them, according to a purpose entertained ἀπὸ πολλῶν ἐτῶν [ἱκανῶν is the true reading] with the hope that he might come ἐν πληρώματι εὐλογίας (τοῦ εὐαγγελίου) τοῦ Χριστοῦ, *i.e.*, in the collation of spiritual gifts which as yet they had not, and in the establishment of that Apostolical order and government among them which should complete their incorporation with the Body Catholic of Christ's Church." It is quite true that the epistle reveals nothing of the organisation of the Church at Rome, but it reveals just as little of any intention on Paul's part to bestow on the Church the supposed benefits of " Apostolical order and government ". The assumption underlying this expression is quite unhistorical. There was no uniform legal organisation of the Church in the apostolic age; and the Christians in Rome not only depended upon mutual exhortation and instruction, but, as Paul acknowledges, were well able to do so. They had χαρίσματα differing according to the grace given to them, and if they had no legal organisation, they had a vital and spiritual differentiation of organs and functions, for which the other is but a makeshift (chap. xii. 3-8). Sanday and Headlam think that though the Church did not, in the strict sense, owe its origin to Peter and Paul, it may well have owed to them its first existence as an organised whole (Commentary, p. xxxv.). This may be, for it was Paul's habit to appoint elders in all the churches he planted (Acts xiv. 23, Tit. i. 5); but, as the gospel was known at Rome, and believers were baptised there, and no doubt observed the Lord's Supper, it is clear that no particular organisation was wanted either to ensure or to perfect their standing as Christians.

Where tradition fails, we can only fall back on conjecture— conjecture to be verified by its coherence with what the epistle itself reveals. In this connection it has long been customary to refer to Acts ii. 10 (οἱ ἐπιδημοῦντες Ῥωμαῖοι). There were Roman Jews in Jerusalem on the day of Pentecost, and even if they were domiciled there and did not return to Rome, there must have been many visitors who did. The Jews in Rome were numbered by thousands; they occupied a large ward of the city, beyond the

Tiber, by themselves, and they had ceaseless communications with Jerusalem. Hence many have supposed that Christianity came to Rome by some such channel as this. If it did, we should expect it to have originated in the synagogues, the existence of nine of which is definitely attested (Sanday and Headlam, p. xxiv.). The epistle itself gives no direct evidence of any such connection : if the Church originated in the synagogue at Rome, the connection had been completely severed by the time Paul wrote. It has been supposed that the well-known sentence in Suetonius, *Claud.*, 25 (" Iudaeos impulsore Chresto assidue tumultuantes Roma expulit " : see also Acts xviii. 2) refers to conflicts which arose in the synagogues over the alleged Messiahship of Jesus, and that the separation of the Church and the synagogue, and even a change in the prevailing complexion of the Church, which from Jewish-Christian became mainly Gentile-Christian, date from this event ; but no stress can be laid on this. It is clear from Acts xxviii. 17-22 that when Paul came to Rome the leaders of the synagogue either knew nothing or affected to know nothing about the new sect which was growing up beside them. This makes it at least improbable, whatever its actual origin, that the Christian Church at Rome can have had strongly Jewish sympathies. Besides, even if the Church had originated in the synagogue, it is practically certain, from the analogy of other places whose history is known, that the mass of the members would not be Jews by birth, but of the class of proselytes (εὐσεβεῖς, φοβούμενοι τὸν θεόν), whose attachment to Judaism was less rigid, and whose spiritual receptivity was as a rule greater.

Many scholars, impressed by these considerations, have sought rather a Gentile-Christian origin for the Church. Communication, they point out, was constant, not only between Rome and Jerusalem, but between Rome and all the East, and especially all the great towns. There was constant coming and going between Rome and such cities as Antioch, Corinth and Ephesus, not to mention others which had been the scene of Paul's labours. Early Christianity, too, was largely self-propagating. " They that were scattered abroad went everywhere preaching the word " (Acts viii. 4). Hort (*Romans and Ephesians*, p. 9) speaks of " a process of quiet and as it were fortuitous filtration " ; and it was probably by such a process, initiated, suspended, and renewed on different occasions, that the new religion was introduced to Rome. To conceive the matter in this way is no doubt to conceive it very indefinitely, but it is hardly possible to go further. Attempts have been made to do so. Assuming, for instance, that chap. xvi. is in its right place, and really formed part of the Epistle to the Romans, it has been argued that the large number of friends and acquaintances Paul had in the Church, and especially the conspicuous place given to his old associates Prisca and Aquila, prove that the Christianity of the Romans was essentially of the Pauline type, and that the Church therefore owed its origin and its character, indirectly no doubt, to him. The epistle certainly does not bear this on its face ; Paul never says a word which implies that the Romans owed anything, even remotely, to him ; there is rather an impression of regret that they did not. Besides, it is a mistake to assume that all Paul's friends were necessarily " Paulinists " —an expression which neither he nor they could have understood. Among those at Rome, and among the most important, as we should judge by the honourable terms in which they are mentioned (xvi. 7), were some who had been Christians longer than he ; and " the quiet and as it were fortuitous filtration " was that of Christianity, undoubtedly of some universal type, but not distinctively of Paulinism.

CHAPTER II.

CHARACTER OF THE CHURCH AT ROME.

HARDLY any question in New Testament criticism has been more elaborately discussed than this. The traditional opinion was that the Church consisted of Gentile Christians. The idea that it consisted of Jewish Christians, first broached apparently by Koppe in 1824, gained currency through Baur, and for a generation after his essay (1836) commanded wide assent among critics. A strong protest in favour of the old opinion was kept up all the time, but it was not till 1876 that Weizsäcker produced a decisive reaction in its favour. The great mass of the Church, he argued, must have been Gentile-Christian, though there was no doubt a Jewish-Christian minority. An attempt to construct a theory answering more closely to the facts presented by the epistle is that of Beyschlag. He supposes that the Church consisted mainly of proselytes—that is, of persons who were Gentiles by birth, but had passed through the Jews' religion. This would explain the great difficulty of the epistle, that Paul addresses his readers as if they were Gentiles, but argues with them as if they were Jews. Schürer, again, conceives of the Church as non-Jewish, and at the same time non-Pauline; the Hellenistic Jews of the *diaspora* would make Christians comparatively free in their relations to the ceremonial law, but with no adequate comprehension of the Pauline freedom, in principle, from law in every sense; it is an audience like this Paul is trying to elevate to his own standpoint. That such an audience could be found is not to be denied; whether it is to be found here we can only ascertain by comparing this theory with the facts of the epistle. Finally, Holtzmann gives up the attempt to realise the character of the Church. St. Paul had never been in Rome, did not really know the situation there, and has no distinct idea of his audience. When he finds it necessary to explain why he writes to them at all he thinks of them as Gentiles; when their previous culture and spiritual history, their sympathies, antipathies, and mode of reacting toward the Gospel generally, are in question, they are Jews. All this shows that the problem is a complex one; and there is no means of doing anything to solve it but to examine the facts once more. They are all contained in the epistle itself, and it will be convenient to adduce the evidence (1) for the Gentile-Christian character of the readers; (2) for the Jewish-Christian character; and then to ask what conception covers and combines all the facts.

1. Evidence for the Gentile-Christian character of the Church.

(a) Chap. i. 5 f. Paul writes: "We received grace and Apostleship, with a view to obedience of faith ἐν πᾶσιν τοῖς ἔθνεσιν . . . ἐν οἷς ἐστε καὶ ὑμεῖς". Paul's conception of himself as Apostle of the Gentiles (Gal. ii. 8), and his appeal to this vocation in the salutation of his letter, put it beyond doubt that ἔθνη here means Gentiles, as opposed to Israel, and not nations generally. He is exercising his calling as Apostle to the Gentiles in writing to the Romans; for they, too, are in that class. Those who take the Jewish-Christian view argue that Paul would have had no need to tell a Church consisting of Romans by birth that they were included within the scope of his calling as Apostle to the Gentiles. But surely the Apostle's expression is perfectly natural; whereas if ἐν πᾶσιν τοῖς ἔθνεσιν means "among all the nations," it becomes perfectly meaningless.

(b) Chap. i. 13. "I purposed often to come to you, . . . ἵνα τινὰ καρπὸν σχῶ καὶ ἐν ὑμῖν καθὼς καὶ ἐν τοῖς λοιποῖς ἔθνεσιν." This case is quite unambiguous. The Roman Christians are put on a level with the rest of the ἔθνη, and it agrees with this that the distinction of classes in ver. 14 (Greek and barbarian, wise and unintelligent) belongs to the pagan world.

Of course it is not meant here that Paul was Apostle of the Gentiles in such a sense that he would not have preached the Gospel to the Jews; but as far as he has a special vocation—and it is on a special vocation, and not on the duty of preaching the Gospel to every creature, that he bases his right to address the Romans—it is to the Gentile world. The Roman Church, therefore, belonged to that world.

(c) Chap. xi. 13. ὑμῖν δὲ λέγω τοῖς ἔθνεσιν. Here the whole Church is addressed in its character as Gentile. To this it has been replied that the whole Church is not addressed here; with ὑμῖν δὲ Paul expressly turns aside to address only a part of the Church. If the words stood alone, this might be maintained, but the context is decisive in favour of the former meaning. In the continuation of the passage (see especially xi. 25-28) the Church as a whole is warned against contempt for the Jews; it is addressed in the second person (xi. 25, 28, 30 f.), without any suggestion of distinctions in it, whereas the

Jews are spoken of throughout in the third. Further, when Paul speaks of the Jews in chaps. ix.-xi., it is as *"my* brethren," *"my* kinsmen according to the flesh," not *ours* nor *yours*, as would have been the case had the bulk of the Church been of Jewish origin.

(*d*) Chap. xv. 15 f. τολμηροτέρως δὲ ἔγραψα ὑμῖν κ.τ.λ. Here Paul justifies himself, in closing, for writing as he has done—especially, perhaps, for writing so decidedly in chap. xiv.-xv. 13 — to the Romans. The reason he gives is unmistakable. He is a minister of Jesus Christ, a priest in the service of the Gospel; the offering he has to lay on the altar is the Gentiles, and he writes to the Romans because they are Gentiles, to further them in their faith, that when they are presented to God it may be an acceptable offering, sanctified in the Holy Spirit. There is no evading this argument; to say that in vers. 17-20 Paul's justification of this presentation of himself as minister of Jesus Christ εἰς τὰ ἔθνη is directed against Jewish-Christian suspicions and insinuations (*cf*. 2 Cor. x. 12-18, xii. 11, 12) may or may not be true, but is quite irrelevant; even if there were such suspicions, and even if they had begun to find acceptance in Rome, the Gentile character of the Church at Rome as a whole is here put beyond question.

(*e*) Less stress can be laid on passages like vi. 17 f. (ἦτε δοῦλοι τῆς ἁμαρτίας), though they have undoubtedly something which recalls the ἐξ ἐθνῶν ἁμαρτωλοὶ of Gal. ii. 15. By the time he has reached chap. vi. Paul is quite entitled to assume that his readers were once slaves of sin, without suggesting anything about their nationality. Neither do the suggestions of particular sins (*e.g.*, in vi. 12-14) throw any real light on the question. All kinds of bad things are done both by Gentiles and Jews. But discounting weak and uncertain arguments, there is a plain and solid case for maintaining that the great bulk of the Church at Rome was of Gentile origin.

2. Evidence for the Jewish-Christian character of the Church.

(*a*) There are passages in which Paul includes himself and his readers in the first person plural; now no one, it is to be observed, is included with him in the superscription, so that "we" must mean "you and I". Thus iii. 9 προεχόμεθα; are we (Jews) surpassed? But it is very natural to suppose that Paul here, as is his rule, allows his opponents (real or imaginary) to state their own objections in their own person, the "we" neither including himself nor his readers; or if he speaks in his own person, it is the *national* consciousness of the Jew, which Paul of course shared, and not the *joint* consciousness of Paul and his readers, which is conveyed by the plural. Another passage of the same kind is iv. 1 : Ἀβραὰμ τὸν προπάτορα ἡμῶν κατὰ σάρκα. Here also the explanation is the same. Paul says "our" forefather because he has no choice. He could speak of his fellow-countrymen as "*my* kinsmen according to the flesh"; but it would have been obviously absurd for him to speak of Abraham as "my" forefather. It is only through his relation to the nation that he can claim a connection with Abraham, and hence the "our" in iv. 1 is national, not individual, and has nothing to do with the Romans. *Cf.* the precisely similar case in ix. 10 (Isaac *our* father). The same use of the first person plural is found in 1 Cor. x. 1 (All *our* fathers were under the cloud), which no one doubts was written to a thoroughly Gentile Church. As far therefore as passages like these are concerned, they do not invalidate in the least the evidence adduced for the Gentile character of the Church at Rome.

(*b*) Not so simple are those passages which speak either in the first or second person plural of the relation of the readers, or of Paul and his readers alike, to the law. The most important of these is chap. vii. 1-6. Paul here speaks to his readers as persons γινώσκουσι νόμον, knowing what law is. Even if we admit—which is not necessary, nor I believe right—that the reference is to the Mosaic law, it does not follow that the readers were Jews. Indeed the explicit recalling of the law to mind, while he assumes it to be known, might plausibly be alleged as an argument against a Jewish origin. But to pass that by, does not vii. 4, it is argued—So then, my brethren, *ye also were made dead to the law* by the body of Christ—imply that the persons addressed had lived under the law as well as the writer?—in other words, that they were Jews? And is this not confirmed, when we read in ver. 5 f., "When we were in the flesh, the sinful passions, which were *through the law*, wrought in our members to bring forth fruit unto death. But now *we have been discharged from the law*"? Have we not here, in relation to the law, an experience common to Paul and those whom he addressed, and does not this imply that antecedent to their conversion they and he had lived under the law—that is, were Jews by birth? It is natural, at first sight, to think so, but it is certainly wrong. There *is* an experience common to Paul and to all Christians, whatever their birth; if it were not so, they would not be Christians. It is possible also for him to describe that experience in relation to the law; once *all* Christians were under it, now they are so no more. *All* Christians were under it, for all were under sin, and to the Apostle sin and law are correlative terms. The law, indeed, did not take precisely the same form for Jew and Gentile; the one had an objective revelation, the other had a substitute, if not an equivalent for this, written on his heart; but in both it wrought to the same issues. There is nothing in the world less Jewish, there is nothing more human, than Rom. vii. 7-24; but that is Paul's description of life under the law, and of the working of the law in that life. We understand it only too well, though we are not Jews; and so, no doubt, did those to whom it was first addressed. Hence Paul could quite well say to a Gentile Church: Ye were made dead to the law through the body of Christ; and could associate himself with them to say, We were discharged from the law by dying to that in which we were held. A perfectly clear case of this is to be found in Gal. iii. 13-iv. 9. No one imagines that the Galatians were Jews, yet Paul vindicates for them the very thing which he says of the Romans here. God sent forth His Son, he writes, made of a woman, made under law, *to redeem those that are under law*, that *we* might receive the adoption of sons. And because *ye* are sons, God sent forth the spirit of His Son into *our* hearts, etc. The alternation of the first and second persons here shows how Paul could conceive of Jew and Gentile alike as under law in their pre-Christian days, and how in their emancipation from this in Jesus Christ one experience was common to them all. In truth, " sin," " the law," " the curse of the law," " death," are names for something which belongs not to the Jewish but to the human conscience; and it is only because this is so that the Gospel of Paul is also a Gospel for us. Before Christ came and redeemed the world, all men were at bottom on the same footing: Pharisaism, legalism, moralism, or whatever it is called, it is in the last resort the attempt to be good without God, to achieve a righteousness of our own without an initial all-inclusive immeasurable debt to Him; in other words, without submitting, as sinful men must submit, to be justified by faith apart from works of our own, and to find in that justification, and in that only, the spring and impulse of all good. It was because Paul's Jewish experience was digested into a purely and perfectly human experience that he was able to transcend his Judaism, and to preach a universal gospel; and the use of such expressions as we have in vii. 1-6 is no proof that those to whom they applied were Jews too. They apply to us.

(*c*) The character of the argumentation in the epistle has been adduced in support of the Jewish origin of the readers. It is quite true that in the dialectical development of his gospel in Romans Paul often states and answers such objections as would naturally occur to one representing the historical and legal standpoint of the Jews' religion. *Cf*. iii. 1 (What advantage then hath the Jew?), vi. 1 (Are we to continue in sin that grace may abound?), vi. 15

(Are we to sin, because we are not under law, but under grace ?), vii. 7 (What shall we say then ? Is the law sin ?), xi. 1 (I say then, Hath God cast off His people ?). There are two obvious reasons why Paul should have developed his gospel by this dialectical process apart from the assumption that he is meeting the anticipated objections of his readers. One is, that he was a Jew himself, and justified his gospel instinctively, as he went along, against the *primâ facie* objections to it which arose in his own mind. Here, again, however, we must remember that though Paul was a Jew he was a man ; and it does not strike one as rigorously historical, but as somewhat absurd, to characterise as Jewish or as Jewish-Christian the criticism of grace which comes natural to every human being. The other reason is, that Paul had heard already in other places most of the objections to his gospel which he answers in this epistle. There is only one express reference to this, in iii. 8 (As we are slandered, and as some affirm that we say, Let us do evil that good may come : for τινες here, *cf*. 2 Cor. iii. 1, Gal. ii. 12) ; but that Paul's gospel was assiduously and energetically counterworked we know quite well, and he may have heard (through some of his friends in the city) that his adversaries were forestalling him at Rome. These reasons fully explain the nature of his arguments ; and in view of the direct evidence for the Gentile character of the Church they prove nothing on the other side.

(*d*) Great stress was laid by Baur on chaps. ix.-xi. in this connection. These, it was argued, were the real kernel of the epistle— the part for the sake of which it was really written, and by relation to which the rest has to be explained ; and these, moreover, have no interest, or none worth speaking of, for a Gentile Church. It was only to a Jewish-Christian consciousness that this vindication of God's wonderful ways in the history of redemption required to be or could be addressed. Plausible as this may sound, the facts are against it. For whatever reason, it is precisely and unambiguously to the Gentiles that all this section is addressed. In ix. 1 f., x. 1 f. Paul speaks of the Jews in the third person (my prayer to God for *them*, etc.). He calls them *my* kinsmen, not *yours* or *ours*. He quotes himself, but not his readers (xi. 1), as proof that God has not cast off His people, which he would hardly have done had they also been Christian Jews (but see note on this verse). He uses the fate of the Jews, the natural branches, to warn his readers, grafted into the tree of life contrary to nature, against contempt, pride, and unbelief. Whatever the motive of these chapters may have been, it cannot have been that the bulk of the Romish Church was Jewish in origin, or strongly Jewish in sympathy. The apostle's own application of their teaching in xi. 17-24 proves exactly the reverse.

(*e*) Still less can anything be made of an appeal to xiii. 1-7. The Jews were certainly a rebellious and turbulent race, and inherited theocratic ideas which might make them doubt the lawfulness of paying tribute to Cæsar (Deut. xvii. 15, Mark xii. 13-17) ; but Christianity too in all its forms is an idealism which necessarily raises the question of the relation of God's Kingdom to the kingdoms of this world, and so gives occasion to such explanations as those of Paul in chap. xiii. 1-7. It has been pointed out, too, that echoes of this passage occur in the public prayer of the Roman Church in Clem., *ad. Cor.*, I., lxi., at a period when the Gentile character of the Church is not questioned.

(*f*) As for the use of the Old Testament in this epistle, it has no bearing whatever on the nationality of the readers. To all the New Testament writers the Old Testament was revelation, and in a sense Christian revelation ; and they used it in the same way no matter to whom they wrote.

None of these passages is sufficient to prove that the Church as a whole was Jewish-Christian, or even that it was strongly influenced by Jewish ideas. On the other hand, the passages quoted under 1 prove conclusively that the bulk of the Church was Gentile, so that one writing to it as a body thought of it as a Gentile Church. This, of course, would not preclude the existence in it of a minority of Jewish origin. We can hardly conceive, in the lifetime of the Apostles, a Church without such an element. The Apostles themselves were all Jews, and it was their rule—it was even Paul's rule—to preach to the Jew first. But apart from this general presumption, we have a distinct indication in the epistle itself that there was in the Roman Church a Jewish-Christian element. In chap. xiv. Paul speaks of dissensions between "the strong" and "the weak," and though it would be wrong simply to identify these with Gentile and Jewish Christians, it is a safe inference from xv. 7-13, taken in connection with what precedes, that the difference between "strong" and "weak" was not unrelated to that between Gentile and Jew (see notes *ad loc.*). Hence the prevailing tendency of scholars is to recognise that the Church was Gentile as a whole, but had a minority of Jewish origin. To what extent the Gentile mass was influenced by Jewish ideas—how far the Gentile members of the Church had been originally proselytes, and were therefore appreciative of the Jewish-Christian consciousness or in sympathy with it—is another question. As we have seen above, under 2, *b*, *c*, no special assumption of this kind is needed to explain the manner in which Paul vindicates his gospel to them.

CHAPTER III.

CHARACTER OF THE EPISTLE—ITS OCCASION AND PURPOSE.

THE character of the epistle has been a subject of as much discussion as the character of the readers, and the discussion is less likely ever to be closed. A writing of such vitality, which is always being in part lost, and always rediscovered in new power—a writing of such comprehensive scope and such infinite variety of application—a writing at once so personal and historical, and so universal and eternal, is not easily reduced to a formula which leaves nothing to be desired. The definitions of its purpose which have been given by scholars strike one rather as all right than as all wrong. But before entering on an examination of these it will be proper to investigate the occasion of the letter, as it may have some bearing on its purpose.

Paul's intention to visit Rome is first mentioned in Acts xix. 21, and, as Hort remarks, it is expressed with curious emphasis. " After these things were ended, Paul *purposed in the spirit* (ἔθετο ἐν τῷ πνεύματι), when he had passed through Macedonia, and Achaia, to go to Jerusalem, saying, After I have been there, I must also see Rome." He passed through Macedonia and Achaia, as he proposed, and it was during his stay in Corinth (which, according to the usual chronology, was in the winter of 58-59), and towards the close of it, that he wrote this letter. This is a point on which all scholars are agreed. When he wrote, he was on the point of starting, or perhaps had started, on his journey to Jerusalem, with the collection for the poor saints there which had been made in the Churches of Galatia, Macedonia and Achaia (chap. xv. 25 ff., 1 Cor. xvi. 1-4, 2 Cor. viii. ix.). He had with him Timothy and Sosipater, or Sopater (chap. xvi. 21), whom we know otherwise to have been in his company (Acts xx. 4), when he started on that journey. Gaius, his host at the moment (xvi. 23), is probably the same as the Gaius whom he had himself baptised at Corinth (1 Cor. i. 14). The time and place, therefore, at which the Epistle to the Romans was written are beyond question. But we ought to notice these not only formally, as points of geography and chronology, but in their significance in Paul's life. The time was one at which he felt that his work in the

East was done. From Jerusalem and round about unto Illyricum he had fully preached the gospel of Christ. He had no more place in these parts (xv. 19, 23). His eye was turned westward, and rested inevitably on Rome. He had wished to visit it for a good many years (xv. 23), perhaps ever since he had first met Prisca and Aquila in Corinth (Acts xviii. 2), and he had often formed the purpose, though it had been as often disappointed (i. 13). But now it had a definiteness which it had never had before. He did not indeed look on Rome as the goal of his journey ; he meant only to stay there till he had been somewhat satisfied with the Church's fellowship, and then to be convoyed by them toward Spain (xv. 24). But he was a Roman citizen, and must have been conscious, as an expression in i. 8 shows ("Your faith is proclaimed in all the world"), of the supreme importance of the Church which had its seat in the capital of the empire. He would not only wish a point of support there for his further operations in the West ; he must have been more than commonly anxious that Christianity there should appear as what it truly was, and that the Romans should be firmly established in it. If Paul was going to write to the Romans at all, no matter from what immediate impulse—though it should only have been to announce his approaching visit—it would be natural that his communication, in proportion as he realized the place and coming importance of the Church at Rome, should assume a catholic and comprehensive character. We can hardly imagine the man who was conscious of his own vocation as Apostle of the Gentiles, and conscious at the same time of the central significance of this Church, writing anything of a merely formal character to such a community. When *he* introduced himself to *them*, it was a great occasion, and the epistle is the best evidence that he was sensible of its greatness.

There are other considerations which would tell on Paul's mind in the same direction. When he wrote, he was setting out on a journey the issue of which was doubtful and perilous. At the very outset he had to change his course, because of a plot formed against him by the Jews (Acts xx. 3). He dreaded what these same relentless enemies might do in Judæa ; he was not sure that even the Christians in Jerusalem would receive graciously the offering which his love and zeal had raised among the Gentiles on their behalf (chap. xv. 31). He was setting out in readiness not only to be bound, but to die at Jerusalem for the name of the Lord Jesus (Acts xxi. 13). In a sense, therefore, this epistle might be called his testament (Weiss). He puts into it, not merely what is suggested to him by special circumstances of which he is aware in the Church at Rome—*e.g.*, the discussion of the relations between "the strong" and "the weak"—but all that his own situation and that of the Church, looking at both in the largest aspect, determine to be of interest. He has achieved a great work in the East. By carrying the charity of the Gentile Christians to Jerusalem, and fraternising once more with the primitive Church, he hopes to secure and perfect that work, and to effect a more cordial union between the two great branches of Christendom, which so imperfectly understood each other. He has passed through great conflicts, but his mind has only been made clearer by them, and established in firmer possession of the fundamental principles of the Christian life ; he can define it without misgiving in relation to all previous modes of human experience and all earlier stages of religion, whether in Greek or Jew. His heart is set on further labours, but he is profoundly conscious of the uncertainties of the future. Such are the outward and the spiritual conditions under which Paul writes. Is it not manifest that when we give them all the historical definiteness of which they are capable, there is something in them which rises above the casualness of time and place, something which might easily give the epistle not an accidental or occasional character, but the character of an exposition of principles ? Be the immediate motive what it may, it is not incredible that the epistle should have something in it which is rather eternal than historical, and that it should require for its interpretation, not a minute acquaintance with opinion in the apostolic age, but some sense of God and man.

The various opinions as to the purpose of the letter have been classified by almost all writers on Introduction under similar heads : it is only necessary to premise that such opinions do not in fact (whatever their authors may think) necessarily exclude one another.

1. The purpose of the letter, according to some, is *dogmatic*. It is a systematic and formal exposition of the Gospel according to Paul. It is a doctrinal treatise, to which only accident gave the form of a letter ; in other circumstances it might have been a book. This was the opinion which ruled at the time of the Reformation. Luther calls the epistle *absolutissima epitome evangelii*. Melanchthon calls it *doctrinæ Christianæ compendium*. No one can say that these descriptions are inept. Luther did find the Gospel in Romans, and found it in a power which made him the greatest conductor of spiritual force since Paul, which directly regenerated one half of Christendom, and indirectly did much to reform the other half. Melanchthon made the epistle the basis of his Loci. He was delighted to find a theology which did not philosophise about the mysteries of the Trinity, or the modes of incarnation, or active and passive creation ; but through sin and law and grace gave the know-

ledge of Christ and His benefits. The dogmatic conception of the epistle has held its ground even in modern times, and among writers who pride themselves in giving the historical its due. Thus Hausrath describes it as "the essential content of what he otherwise preached by word of mouth". Hilgenfeld calls it "a complete presentation of the Gospel which Paul preaches among the Gentiles". Pfleiderer, more dogmatically still, speaks of it as "an objective development of the truth of the Gospel, drawn from the nature of the Gospel itself". And certainly, whatever the writer's motive may have been, the letter *has* a systematic character. There is no analogy in any other of his epistles to the connected train of thought which runs from i. 16 to viii. 39 or even to xi. 36. There is indeed a break between chaps. viii. and ix., but there is no unbridgeable gulf. Holtzmann gives, as specimens of the way in which they can be connected, the opinions of Mangold (in i.-viii. Paul justifies his doctrine of salvation, in ix.-xi. his action as a missionary), of Holsten (in i.-viii. he justifies the content, in ix.-xi. the result, of his preaching), and of Pfleiderer (in i.-viii. there is the dogmatic, in ix.-xi. the historical aspect of his gospel). This last agrees pretty much with Godet, who makes the subject of the whole eleven chapters salvation by faith, chaps. i.-viii. treating this in relation to the individual, and chaps. ix.-xi. in relation to its development in history. The systematic character of this part, therefore, is beyond doubt. Those who insist upon it are not of course blind to the parts of the epistle (chaps. xiv. and xv.) in which incidental matters affecting the Church at Rome are touched upon; but it is not in these, they would say, but in the formal presentation of the truth in chaps. i.-xi. that the purpose of the letter is revealed. Granting this, however, the question arises whether the systematic character of the epistle is equivalent to a dogmatic character. In other words, is Paul simply expounding, in a neutral, unprejudiced, objective fashion, the whole scope and contents of his gospel, or is he expounding it in relation to something present to his mind, and to the mind of his readers, which gives the exposition a peculiar character?

2. The latter alternative is affirmed by those who hold that the purpose of the epistle is *controversial*. It is an exposition of Paul's gospel indeed, but not a purely dogmatic one, which in an epistle would be gratuitous and out of place. The exposition is throughout conducted with reference to an attack such as would be made on Pauline Christianity from the point of view of Judaism, or even of Jewish Christianity. It is not so much an exposition as a defence and a vindication. Practically this idea governs many interpretations, *e.g.*, that of Lipsius. That there is

an element of truth in it is not to be denied. Paul does not write
in vacuo, in no concrete relations at all. In iii. 8 there is a hint of
actual adversaries and their criticisms on the Pauline gospel ; in
xvi. 17-20 there is another hint of at least possible ones. It may be,
as has been noticed above (p. 566), that Jews or Jewish Christians
were attempting to create prejudice against the Apostle in Rome ;
but we cannot, on the ground that this is a letter, and must therefore have its character explained by the circumstances of the readers,
conclude for certain (with Weizsäcker), that this was the case. In
expounding his gospel systematically to the Romans, Paul defines it,
not necessarily against enemies who were forestalling him in Rome,
but against the criticism which had followed him all through his
missionary work. And we must remember, as has also been referred
to already, that part of that criticism was not so much Jewish as
human. It is not the Jewish or Jewish-Christian consciousness in
particular—it is the consciousness of the natural man at a certain
stage of moral development—which thinks that forgiveness is an
immoral doctrine, and is shocked at the idea of a God " who justifies
the ungodly," or on the other hand, indulges the idea that pardon
procures licence to sin. Though the opposition Paul encountered
everywhere was headed by Jews or by Christians of Jewish birth,
what it represented was by no means exclusively Jewish ; and in an
epistle of this unique character, standing where it stands in the
Apostle's life, and making so little express reference to actual Jewish
adversaries (contrast it in this respect with Galatians or 2 Cor. x.-
xiii.), we must not limit too narrowly the kind of opposition he has in
view. He is stating the case of gospel against law—against all that
is pre-Christian, infra-Christian, and anti-Christian ; and his polemic
has not a temporary but a permanent significance. It is addressed
not to Jews of the first century, but to men, and to Christians, of all
time. Nothing so conclusively proves its necessity as the fact that
it so soon ceased to be understood. It is not easy to live at the
spiritual height at which Paul lived. It is not easy to realise that
religion begins absolutely on God's side ; that it begins with a
demonstration of God's love to the sinful, which man has done
nothing and can do nothing to merit ; and that the assurance of
God's love is not the goal to be reached by our own efforts, but the
only point from which any human effort can start. It is not easy
to realise that justification, in the sense of an initial assurance of
God's love, extending over all our life, is the indispensable pre-
supposition of everything which can be called Christianity. It is
not easy to realise that in the atoning death of Christ and the gift
of the Holy Ghost there are the only and the adequate securities

for Christian morality ; that the only good man is the forgiven man, and that he is good, not because he is under law, but because he is not under law but under grace. There must have been many men who were practically Christian, and that, too, in the broad sense, which gave no advantage to the Jew over the Gentile, but who were far from realising their Christianity in principle like Paul. In his heroic sense, indeed, Christianity hardly survived him ; it was recovered in something like its native power, attested even by a recrudescence of its original perils, at the time of the Reformation ; and it always requires to be rediscovered again. But this is only another way of saying that the polemic of the Epistle to the Romans is not narrowly anti-Jewish ; it is anti-legal ; and whenever legalism establishes itself in the Church anew, whether as mere custom, or as a dogmatic tradition, or as a clerical order claiming to be essential to the constitution of the Church, the Christian conscience will find in this polemic the sword of the spirit to strike it down. We admit, therefore, that the epistle has a controversial aspect; but probably the controversy is not so much with definite adversaries at work in Rome as with those principles and instincts in human nature which long experience as a preacher had made familiar to St. Paul.

3. A third view of the epistle defines its purpose as *conciliatory*. This, again, by no means excludes either of the views already commented on. Even controversy may be conducted in a conciliatory tone, and with a conciliatory purpose. When Paul wrote, he was extremely anxious about the unity of Jew and Gentile in the Church. His journey to Jerusalem had mainly that in view. In the epistle, while there is much that is trenchant in argument, there is nothing that is personal in feeling. There is no contemptuous irony, such as we have in 2 Cor. x.-xiii. ; no uncontrolled passion such as flashes out here and there in Galatians. Although the law works wrath and stimulates sin, he describes it as holy, spiritual, and ordained unto life. He speaks with passionate affection of the Jews (ix. 1 ff.), always recognises their historical prerogatives (iii. 1 ff., ix. 1 ff.), warns the Gentiles against self-exaltation over them, and anticipates the salvation of Israel as a whole. In chaps. xiv.-xv. also his generosity to " the weak," though his judgment is unequivocally with the strong, may be regarded in the same light ; the weak are certainly connected with the Jews, and his aim in the whole passage is the peace and unity of the Church. All this confirms us in thinking that the controversial aspect of the epistle should not be urged with special severity against Jewish Christians, or their modes of thought: Paul has no desire to exasperate any one, but in the position in which he stands, " the greatest moving power in the enlargement

and building up of the universal Church " (Hort), about to visit Jerusalem at once, and Rome, if he can, immediately afterwards, his desire is to win and to unite all.

From this point of view it is possible to form a conception of the purpose of the epistle which will do something like justice to it as a whole. It is an epistle, not a book. Paul wrote to Rome, not simply to clear up his own mind, not as a modern writer might do, addressing the world at large ; he wrote to this particular community, and under a particular impulse. He knew something about the Church, as chaps. xiv. and xv. show ; and while he might have acquired such information from members of it whom he met in Corinth, Ephesus, or elsewhere, it is quite probable, from chap. xvi., that he had friends and correspondents at Rome itself. He wrote to the Roman Christians because it was in his mind to visit them ; but the nature of his letter is determined, not simply by consideration of their necessities, but by consideration of his own position. The letter is " occasional," in the sense that it had a historical motive—to intimate and prepare for the coming visit ; but it is not occasional in the sense in which the first Epistle to the Corinthians is so. It is not a series of answers to questions which the Romans had propounded ; it is not a discussion, relevant to them only, of points either in doctrine or practice which had incidentally come to be of critical importance in Rome. Its character, in relation to St. Paul's mind, is far more central and absolute than this would imply. It is in a real sense a systematic exposition of what he distinctively calls " my gospel " (ii. 16), such an exposition as makes him thoroughly known to a community which he foresaw would have a decisive importance in the history of Christianity. It is not an impromptu note, nor a series of unconnected remarks, each with a motive of its own ; it is the manifesto of his gospel, by means of which the Apostle of the Gentiles, at a great crisis and turning point in his life, establishes relations with the Christian community in the capital of the Gentile world. It can be dated, of course, but no writing in the New Testament is less casual ; none more catholic and eternal. It is quite true that in expounding his gospel Paul proceeds by a certain dialectical process ; he advances step by step, and at every step defines the Christian truth as against some false or defective, some anti-Christian or infra-Christian view ; in this sense it is controversial. But we have seen already the limitations under which alone a controversial character can be ascribed to it ; Paul is not so much controverting anybody in particular as vindicating the truth he expounds against the assaults and misconstructions to which he had found it give rise. There is no animosity against the

Jews in it ; no sentence such as 1 Thess. ii. 15 f. or Gal. v. 12. It is an establishment of principles he aims at ; except in iii. 8, xvi. 17-20 there is no reference to persons. Even in chaps. ix.-xi. (see the introduction at chap. ix.) the whole tone is conciliatory ; the one thing which tries our faith in them is Paul's assurance of the future of his own people. But as an interpretation of the actual working out in human history of that method of salvation which he has expounded in the first eight chapters—as an exhibition of the process through which the rejection of the Jews and the calling of the Gentiles alike contribute eventually to the universality of the Gospel—these chapters are an essential part of the epistle. They are mainly but not exclusively apologetic : they belong to that whole conception of the Gospel, and of the mode in which it becomes the inheritance of the world, which was of one substance with the mind of St. Paul. No one who read the first eleven chapters of the epistle could meet the Apostle as a stranger on anything essential in Christianity as he understood it. No doubt, as Grafe has remarked, it does not contain an eschatology like 1 Cor. xv. or 2 Cor. v., nor a Christology like Col. i. But it establishes that which is fundamental beyond the possibility of misconception. It vindicates once for all the central facts, truths and experiences, without which Christianity cannot exist. It vindicates them at once in their relation to the whole past of mankind, and in their absolute newness, originality and self-sufficiency. It is an utter misapprehension to say that "just the most fundamental doctrines—the Divine Lordship of Christ, the value of His death, the nature of the Sacraments—are assumed rather than stated or proved " (Sanday and Headlam, p. xli.). There can be only one fundamental doctrine, and that doctrine for Paul is the doctrine of justification by faith. That is not part of his gospel, it is the whole of it : there Luther is his true interpreter. If legalists or moralists object, Paul's answer is that justification regenerates, and that nothing else does. By its consistency with this fundamental doctrine, we test everything else that is put forward as Christian. It is only as we hold this, on principle, with the clearness with which Paul held it, that we can know what Christian liberty is in the sense of the New Testament— that liberty in which the will of God is done from the heart, and in which no commandments or ordinances of men, no definitions or traditions, no customs or " orders," have any legal authority for the conscience. And in the only legitimate sense of the word this liberty does not make void, but establishes the law. That is the paradox in the true religion which perpetually baffles those who would reduce it to an institution or a code.

CHAPTER IV.

INTEGRITY OF THE EPISTLE.

The integrity of the Epistle to the Romans has been called in question mainly in connection with chaps. xv. and xvi. Partly on the ground of textual phenomena, partly on internal grounds, the authenticity of these chapters has been denied, in whole or in part; and even among those who recognise chap. xvi. as Pauline, many are unable to recognise Rome as the place to which it was addressed. It will be convenient to consider (1) the questions raised by the position of the doxology, and the various endings; (2) questions raised by the internal character of chap. xv.; and (3) questions connected with the character and destination of chap. xvi.

1. The position of the doxology, and the various endings. The facts in regard to the doxology are as follows:—

(*a*) It is given at xvi. 25-27, and there only, by ℵBCDE, Vulgate, Syriac, Memphitic, Aethiopic and Latin Fathers. This is by far the best attested position for it, and that which, owing to the respect of Erasmus for the Vulgate, it occupies in the received text.

(*b*) At xiv. 23, and there only, it is found in L, most cursives, Greek lectionaries, and Greek commentators except Origen. Possibly the lectionaries explain its appearance at this point. The matter in chaps. xv. and xvi. being of a more personal or temporary interest was not likely to be chosen for reading in church. But in order that the great doxology, which was too short for a lesson by itself, might not be lost in public worship, it was appended to the last lesson before chap. xv.

(*c*) It is found both after xiv. 23 and at xvi. 25-27 in AP 17 arm.

(*d*) It is omitted in both places in FG, but F has space left after xvi. 24, in which f (the Latin of this bi-lingual MS.) has the doxology, while G has space left between chaps. xiv. and xv.

Besides this variety of MS. attestation, there are certain other facts to take into consideration. (*a*) There is the evidence of Origen (in his translator Rufinus) to the text in his time. It runs as follows (ed. Lommatzsch, vii., p. 453): *Caput hoc Marcion, a quo*

Scripturæ evangelicæ et apostolicæ interpolatæ sunt, de hac epistola penitus abstulit; et non solum hoc sed et ab eo loco, ubi scriptum est : omne autem quod non est ex fide peccatum est : *usque ad finem cuncta dissecuit. In aliis vero exemplaribus, id est, in his quae non sunt a Marcione temerata, hoc ipsum caput diverse positum invenimus; in nonnullis etenim codicibus post eum locum quem supra diximus hoc est :* omne autem quod non est ex fide peccatum est : *statim cohærens habetur :* ei autem qui potens est vos confirmare. *Alii vero codices in fine id, ut nunc est positum, continent.* This remark is made at xvi. 25, and *caput hoc* means, of course, this passage, *i.e.*, the doxology. Marcion wholly omitted it there. But what do the following words mean ? What strikes one at first is that he not only omitted it there, but omitted everything standing after " whatsoever is not of faith is sin "—in other words, not only the doxology, but the whole of chaps. xv. and xvi. But Dr. Hort (*vide* Appendix, p. 112), who reads (with what he says seems to be the best MS.) *in eo loco* instead of *ab eo loco,* and changes *hoc* into *hic,* only finds the statement that Marcion cut off the whole of the doxology at xiv. 23, as well as at xvi. 25. But *usque ad finem cuncta dissecuit* is a very misleading way to express this to readers whose copies of the epistle would all contain chaps. xv. and xvi., and it is hardly open to doubt that the first impression of the meaning is the correct one, and that Marcion ended his Epistle to the Romans at xiv. 23. Thus, as Gifford puts it, " we have evidence of a *diversity of position* before Origen's time, and regarded by him as independent of Marcion's mutilated copies. But we have no evidence of *omission* before Marcion, who was at Rome propagating his views about A.D. 138-140."

(*b*) There is the evidence of the " capitulations," or division of the epistle into sections, in some MSS. of the Latin Bible, especially the two best codices of the Vulgate, Codex Amiatinus and Codex Fuldensis, both sixth century MSS. In Codex Amiatinus there are fifty-one sections. The fiftieth, entitled *De periculo contristante fratrem suum esca sua, et quod non sit regnum Dei esca et potus sed justitia et pax et gaudium in Spiritu Sancto,* evidently answers to chap. xiv. 15-23 ; the fifty-first, which is entitled *De mysterio Domini ante passionem in silentio habito, post passionem vero ipsius revelato,* as plainly corresponds to the doxology. The capitulations therefore were drawn up for a Latin MS. which omitted chaps. xv. and xvi. In another way the capitulations in Codex Fuldensis point to the same conclusion.

(*c*) There is the appearance, at least, of different endings. 1. When the doxology stands at xiv. 23, it indicates an ending at that point, though otherwise it is a very unnatural one, as the subject and sense of chap. xiv. run on unbroken to xv. 13. 2. There is at xv. 33 what has sometimes been taken as another ending : " The God of peace be with you all. Amen." 3. There is the benediction at xvi. 20 : " The grace of our Lord Jesus Christ be with you ". This is genuine, and is an ordinary Pauline formula at the close of a letter. 4. There is the benediction at xvi. 24 : " The grace of our Lord Jesus Christ be with you all. Amen." Most editors regard this as spurious ; it has been transferred in Western texts from verse 20 to this place, and finally established itself in both. Gifford, however, regards it as genuine in both places. 5. There is the doxology at xvi. 25-27.

(d) In G all mention of Rome is wanting : see critical note on i. 7, 15.

This complicated combination of facts has not yet been clearly explained, and perhaps never will be. Renan's theory was that Romans is really a circular letter, and that it was sent in various directions, with different endings, which were afterwards combined. Lightfoot thought the facts adduced amounted to irresistible evidence that in early times shorter copies of the epistle existed, containing only chaps. i.-xiv., with or without the doxology ; and the theory by which he explained these facts was this, that " St. Paul, at a later period of his life, reissued the epistle in a shorter form with a view to general circulation, omitting the last two chapters, obliterating the mention of Romans in the first chapter, and adding the doxology, which was no part of the original epistle ". This tempting theory was expounded in the *Journal of Philology*, 1871, in a review of M. Renan ; and this review, along with a minute criticism of Dr. Hort, and a reply by Lightfoot, can be studied in Lightfoot's *Biblical Essays*, pp. 285-374. An acute statement of the objections to it is also given by Gifford in the introduction to his commentary (p. 23 f.) ; yet when all is said, it remains the most satisfying hypothesis that has yet been suggested for the colligation of the facts. Sanday and Headlam think that Paul could not possibly have made the break at xiv. 23—he must have been too conscious that the sense ran on unbroken to xv. 13 ; it was probably to Marcion, therefore, to whom the references to the Jews and the Old Testament in xv. 1-13 were objectionable, that the imperfect copies of the epistle owed their existence. This is hardly convincing. If there is not a break at xiv. 23, there is at least a pause in the thought, and Paul may as easily have made a division there as the author of our present division into chapters. Besides, as Gifford points out (see above,

p. 577), there is evidence that the doxology stood in different positions
(at xiv. 23 for one) before Origen's time, and independently of Marcion's mutilated copies.   Hence some one must have felt that xiv. 23
was not an impossible place to stop at, and that for other than
Marcion's reasons ; and if some one, why not Paul himself ?   But
in the absence of any direct evidence as to how the textual phenomena originated, it is very improbable that any certainty on the
subject will ever be attained.

2. Questions raised by the internal character of chap. xv.

The Tübingen school, or at least some of its more vigorous adherents, followed Baur in finding chap. xv. too moderate in tone for Paul.
Baur regarded the last two chapters as the work of some one " writing in the spirit of the Acts of the Apostles, seeking to soothe the
Judaists and to promote the cause of unity, and therefore tempering
the keen anti-Judaism of Paul with a milder and more conciliatory
conclusion to the epistle ".   An argument like this rests on a general
impression of what it was possible for Paul to write, and can only
be met by another general impression of a different sort.   It is sufficient to say that later scholars are practically at one in finding that
there is nothing in the chapter inconsistent with Pauline authorship.
The Paul by whom Baur measured all things in the epistles is really
not the Paul of history, but of a more or less arbitrary theory ; and
his picture has to be corrected by taking into account precisely such
revelations of his true attitude to the questions of his time as are
found in this chapter.   Lipsius, who thinks the fifteenth chapter as a
whole genuine, nevertheless holds that it has been interpolated.   He
omits the latter part of verse 19—ὥστε με ἀπὸ Ἰερουσαλὴμ καὶ κύκλῳ μέχρι
τοῦ Ἰλλυρικοῦ πεπληρωκέναι τὸ εὐαγγέλιον τοῦ Χριστοῦ—as inconsistent
with Gal. i. 18-24, and unsupported by any accredited historical
evidence.   But he admits that it is supported by Acts ix. 28 f. ; and
if we compare i. 8, Col. i. 23, and remember that what we have before
us is not sworn evidence but a broad rhetorical description of the
Apostle's missionary labours, we shall probably think the expression
characteristically Pauline rather than the reverse.   In verse 20
Lipsius omits οὐχ ὅπου ὠνομάσθη Χριστός, ἵνα μὴ ἐπ᾽ ἀλλότριον θεμέλιον
οἰκοδομῶ, ἀλλά.   The words, he argues, are suggested by 2 Cor. x.
15 ; but the purpose expressed in them, of not preaching the Gospel
in Rome, because Rome is a mission-field belonging to others (who
have introduced Christianity there already), is incompatible with
i. 5, 13-15, xii. 3, xv. 15.   It is enough to answer that the purpose of
not preaching the Gospel at Rome is not expressed here at all.
Paul tells the principle on which he has always acted—the principle

of breaking new ground. It is the principle on which he will act still, for he takes Rome only *en route* for Spain ; but that is not inconsistent with anything he purposes to do at Rome in the way of Christian work, nor with anything he does in this epistle. On the same principle Lipsius omits also verses 23 and 24 ; but with equal groundlessness. The very facts to which he refers, that the plan of travel announced in these verses is nowhere else referred to either in Acts or in the Epistles, and that it was (as he thinks) never carried out, are conclusive evidence of the genuineness of the passage. What motive could a late interpolator have for putting into Paul's mind a projected voyage, of which there was no purpose on record, and which was never actually made ? The unanimous testimony of all sources guarantees the integrity of the text ; and there is no reason whatever to doubt that it is Paul's.

3. Questions connected with the character and destination of chap. xvi.

When we come to this chapter the situation is changed. It is not its genuineness, but its destination, that is called in question. Since 1829, when David Schulz suggested that it was a fragment of an epistle to the Ephesians, this opinion has been widely received. The exact extent of the fragment, indeed, is disputed. Schulz made it consist of verses 1-20 ; Weizsäcker says verses 1-23 ; others, verses 3-20, or 1-15, or 1-16 and 21-23, or 3-16 only. Whatever its limits, the arguments on behalf of it can only be estimated by going over the chapter, and considering them as they emerge.

(*a*) The suggestion is made that Phoebe, sailing from Cenchreæ, would naturally have Ephesus rather than Rome as her goal. But there is no reason to believe that she was sailing from Cenchreæ, though she lived there. Paul may have met her in Corinth on her way to Rome.

(*b*) At first sight there may seem more reason to believe that Aquila and Priscilla point to Ephesus. They had gone thither with Paul at an earlier date (Acts xviii. 19), and they had a church in their house there, which joined them in a greeting to Corinth, when Paul wrote his first Epistle to the Corinthians (1 Cor. xvi. 19) ; and they were there also some years later (2 Tim. iv. 19). The question is whether these facts, in the circumstances, outweigh the fact that the greeting is found here in a letter addressed to Rome. If we look at the whole situation, this is at least doubtful. As fellow-workers of Paul, it is plain that they shared to a large extent his wandering life, and we know that they had originally a connection with Rome (Acts xviii. 2). There is nothing in the least improbable in the idea that though they were in Ephesus, say in 54 and 57 A.D., and again say in 66, they should have been in Rome in 58. Paul must have had his information about the Church in Rome from some one ; and nothing is so likely as that he had it from his old and intimate associates, Aquila and Priscilla, who had themselves a connection of old standing with the capital.

(*c*) There remains the case of Epænetus, who is described as the first fruits of Asia unto Christ. The received text has Achaia, but that is an error. One fails to see, however, why this Epænetus, though the first Christian convert in the province of Asia, should be bound to remain there always. There is no difficulty in supposing that he was at Rome, and that Paul, who knew him, was aware of the fact, and introduced his name to multiply for himself points of contact with the Roman Church.

These are the only definite matters of fact on which the theory of an Ephesian destination of the chapter has been based. They do not amount to anything against the weight of all the external evidence which makes them part of a letter to Rome. Nor is their weight increased by pointing out in the verses which follow the large number of persons with whom Paul had been in personal relations — persons whom he calls " my beloved," " my fellow-labourers," " my fellow-captives " ; " who bestowed much labour on us " ; " his mother and mine ". Paul's life as a missionary brought him into contact with persons in all the great towns of the East, and though he had not yet visited Rome, it cannot be doubted that many of those with whom in the course of his twenty years' ministry he had established such relations as are referred to here, had for one cause or other found their way to the great city. Paul would naturally, in preparing for his own visit, make all that he could of such points of attachment with the Roman Church as he had. It is, as Gifford points out, a very strong, indeed a conclusive argument for the Roman destination of the letter, that of the twenty-two persons named in verses 6-15, not one can be shown to have been at Ephesus ; while (1) Urbanus, Rufus, Ampliatus, Julia and Junia are specifically Roman names, and (2) besides the first four of these names, " ten others, Stachys, Apelles, Tryphaena, Tryphosa, Hermes, Hermas, Patrobas (or Patrobius), Philologus, Julia, Nereus are found in the sepulchral inscriptions on the Appian Way as the names of persons connected with ' Cæsar's household ' (Phil. iv. 22), and contemporary with St. Paul ". Hence, in spite of the difficulty of Paul's knowing so many people in a Church he had never visited, and the equally great difficulty that none of all these people are mentioned in the letters the Apostle afterwards wrote from Rome (see Col. iv. 10 f.), scholars like Lightfoot, Gifford and Sanday find no reason to give up the historical tradition which makes this chapter an integral part of the epistle addressed to Rome. There is really more reason to question verses 17-20 than any other part of the chapter. Words like those in verse 19—ἐφ᾽ ὑμῖν οὖν χαίρω, θέλω δὲ ὑμᾶς κ.τ.λ.—certainly strike one as in better keeping if addressed to a Church with which Paul had had such previous relations as entitled him to take a personal tone than if addressed to strangers. But we cannot tell *a priori* how the consciousness of an Apostle towards a Christian community he had never yet seen was determined; it may, with all the disclaiming of titles to interfere, have involved precisely that authoritativeness and sense of responsibility to and for the Church which is expressed in this passage.

As for the doxology, it stands by itself. Lightfoot thought it no part of the original epistle. Neither did Alford. " Probably," says the latter, " on reperusing his work either at the time, or, as the altered style seems to import, in after years at Rome, he subjoins the fervid and characteristic doxology with which it closes." Opinions on the genuineness of the doxology vary in part (but not exclusively) as opinions vary on the genuineness of the pastoral epistles. In spite of the vindication of the style word by word, the impression it leaves on the mind is hardly Pauline. It seems artificial rather than inspired. It is defended by Gifford, Hort, and Sanday and Headlam ; by Weiss (who thinks Paul may have added it with his own hand), Godet, and many others: rejected by Delitzsch, Pfleiderer, Schultz and Lipsius. In substance it recapitulates the main ideas of the epistle.

Text.

The text printed in this commentary is the *Textus Receptus*, but that which is commented upon is practically that of Westcott and Hort. Various readings, of any importance, have been carefully noted in the *apparatus criticus*, with such an indication of the authorities for them as will be sufficient for those who do not aspire to be experts in this department : care has been taken to give the evidence for those readings in which critical editors depart from the received text. It is impossible here to do more than note the MSS. and other authorities which have been cited; information as to their characteristics and value must be sought from such sources as the *Prolegomena* to Tischendorf's *Novum Testamentum Graecum*, or Scrivener's *Introduction to the Textual Criticism of the New Testament*, or Westcott and Hort's *Introduction*, vol. ii. An easier book to begin with is Hammond's *Textual Criticism applied to the New Testament*. In Sanday and Headlam's Commentary (pp. lxiii.-lxxiv.), there is a lucid account of the chief sources of evidence for the text of Romans, and of their relations to one another; while B. Weiss, in his great work, *Das Neue Testament : Textkritische Untersuchungen und Textherstellung*, gives weight to considerations of a kind that more purely "diplomatic" constructors of texts are apt to overlook.

The principal MSS. of Romans are those which also contain the gospels, *viz.*, אABC. א and B belong to the fourth century, A and C to the fifth. The MSS. next in importance, DEFG, are different from those which are called by the same names in the gospels: they are all Graeco-Latin MSS. D is the Codex Claromontanus which Tischendorf assigns to the sixth century. It wants Romans i. 1-7, 27-30. Tregelles describes it as "one of the most valuable MSS. extant". E is the Codex Sangermanensis, now at St. Petersburg. It is probably not older than the ninth or tenth century, and is described by Sanday and Headlam as "nothing more than a faulty copy of D". F is the Codex Augiensis, now in the library of Trinity College, Cambridge. It is of the ninth century, and wants Romans i. 1-iii. 19 ἐν τῷ νό[μῳ]. G is the Codex Boernerianus, now in Dresden, and is a little later than F. It wants Romans i. 1 ἀφωρισμένος . . . i. 5 πίστεως, and ii. 16 τὰ κρυπτὰ . . . ii. 25 νόμου ἧς. These four all belong to the type of text which Westcott and Hort call Western. Other uncials of less importance are K, Codex Mosquensis; L, Codex Angelicus; and P, Codex Porphyrianus, all of about the same age, *i.e.*, the ninth century. Of cursive MSS. those quoted in this work are 17 (the same as 33 in the Gospels, and 13 in Acts), "the queen of cursives"; 47, of the eleventh or twelfth century, now in the Bodleian Library; and 67, of the eleventh century, now at Vienna. The marginal corrector of this MS., quoted as 67**, gives many peculiar and ancient readings. The versions referred to are the Latin Vulgate, especially as given in Codex Amiatinus *circa* 514 A.D. and Codex Fuldensis, also of sixth century; the old Latin contained in DEFG (see above); the Syriac versions, one of which (the Peshitto) was "certainly current much in its present form early in the fourth century" (Sanday and Headlam), while the other dates from the sixth: an occasional reference is also made to the Egyptian versions, and to the Armenian: the last was made in the fifth century.

To estimate the value of any reading it is necessary to consider the relations to each other of the authorities which support it. In the Epistle to the Romans, as elsewhere in the New Testament, these authorities tend to fall into groups. Thus ℵB form one; DEFG a second; and ℵACLP a third. ℵB form what Westcott and Hort describe as "neutral" authorities; DEFG are "Western"; ℵACLP include what they call "Alexandrian," but are not identical with it. Sanday and Headlam, after giving an account of the authorities for the text, define the "specific characteristics of the textual apparatus of Romans" as these: (i.) the general inferiority in boldness and originality of the Western text; (ii.) the fact that there is a distinct Western element in B, which therefore when it is combined with authorities of the Western type is diminished in value; (iii.) the consequent rise in importance of the group ℵAC; (iv.) the existence of a few scattered readings either of B alone or of B in combination with one or two other authorities which have considerable intrinsic probability, and may be right. By a little practice on the readings for which the authority is given in the *apparatus criticus*, the student can familiarise himself with the facts, and exercise his own judgment on them.

In the notes, Winer means Moulton's edition of Winer's Grammar; W. and H. stands for Westcott and Hort; S. and H. for Sanday and Headlam's Commentary on Romans.

ΠΑΥΛΟΥ ΤΟΥ ΑΠΟΣΤΟΛΟΥ

Η ΠΡΟΣ

ΡΩΜΑΙΟΥΣ ΕΠΙΣΤΟΛΗ.

I. 1. ΠΑΥΛΟΣ δοῦλος Ἰησοῦ Χριστοῦ,ᵃ κλητὸς ἀπόστολος, ἀφωρισμένος a 1 Cor. i. 1, 2.
εἰς εὐαγγέλιον Θεοῦ, 2. (ὃ προεπηγγείλατο διὰ τῶν προφητῶν αὐτοῦ

CHAPTER I.—Vv. 1-7. The usual salutation of the Apostle is expanded, as is natural in writing to persons whom he has not seen, into a description both of himself and of his Gospel. Both, so to speak, need a fuller introduction than if he had been writing to a Church he had himself founded. The central idea of the passage is that of the whole epistle, that the Gospel, as preached by Paul to the Gentiles, was not inconsistent with, but the fulfilment of, God's promises to Israel.

Ver. 1. Paul's description of himself. δοῦλος Ἰ. Χ. The use of the same expression in James, Jude, 2 Pet., shows how universal in the Church was the sense of being under an obligation to Christ which could never be discharged. It is this sense of obligation which makes the δουλεία, here referred to, perfect freedom. κλητὸς ἀπόστολος is an Apostle by vocation. No one can take this honour to himself, any more than that of a saint (ver. 7), unless he is called by God. In the N.T. it is always *God* who calls. It is as an Apostle—*i.e.*, with the sense of his vocation as giving him a title to do so—that Paul writes to the Romans. ἀπόστολος is here used in the narrower sense, which includes only Paul and the twelve, see on xvi. 7. ἀφωρισμένος εἰς εὐαγγέλιον Θεοῦ: for καλεῖν and ἀφορίζειν similarly combined, see Gal. i. 15. The separation is here regarded (as in Gal.) as God's act, though, as far as it had reference to the Gentile mission, it was carried out by an act of the Church at Antioch (Acts xiii. 2, ἀφορίσατε δή

μοι κ.τ.λ.). What it means is "this one thing I do". εὐαγγέλιον θεοῦ is the Gospel which comes from God, the glad tidings of which He is the source and author. As a name for the Christian religion, or the proclamation of it, it had a great fascination for an evangelist like Paul, who uses it out of all proportion oftener than any other N.T. writer.

Ver. 2. ὃ προεπηγγείλατο. The Gospel is not in principle a new thing, a subversion of the true religion as it has hitherto been known to the people of God. On the contrary, God promised it before, through his prophets in the Holy Scriptures. It is the fulfilment of hopes which God Himself inspired. διὰ τῶν προφητῶν does not restrict the reference to the prophets in the strict sense of the word. The O.T., as a whole, is prophetic of the New, and it is in the law (Abraham) and the Psalms (David), as much as in the prophets (Isaiah, Hosea), that Paul finds anticipations and promises of the Gospel: see chap. iv. The omission of the article with ἐν γραφαῖς ἁγίαις (*cf.* xvi. 26) is probably significant, for as against these two passages there are over forty in which αἱ γραφαὶ or ἡ γραφὴ occurs: it emphasises the Divine character of these as opposed to other writings. That is ἅγιον which belongs to God, or is connected with Him: ἅγιαι γραφαὶ is the O.T. as God's book.

Ver. 3 f. περὶ τοῦ υἱοῦ αὐτοῦ: the subject of the Gospel of God is His Son. For the same conception, see 2 Cor. i. 19: ὁ τοῦ θεοῦ γὰρ υἱὸς Χ. Ἰ. ὁ ἐν ὑμῖν δι' ἡμῶν κηρυχθείς. Taken

ἐν γραφαῖς ἁγίαις, 3. περὶ τοῦ υἱοῦ αὐτοῦ, (τοῦ γενομένου ἐκ σπέρματος Δαβὶδ κατὰ σάρκα, 4. τοῦ ὁρισθέντος υἱοῦ Θεοῦ ἐν δυνάμει,
κατὰ πνεῦμα ἁγιωσύνης, ἐξ ἀναστάσεως νεκρῶν,) Ἰησοῦ Χριστοῦ τοῦ
Κυρίου ἡμῶν, 5. (δι᾽ οὗ ἐλάβομεν χάριν καὶ ἀποστολὴν ᶜ εἰς ὑπακοὴν

b Ch. ix. 5.
c Acts i. 25;
1 Cor. ix.
2; Gal. ii.
8.

by itself, "the Son of God" is, in the first instance, a title rather than a name. It goes back to Ps. ii. 7; the person to whom it is applied is conceived as the chosen object of the Divine love, God's instrument for accomplishing the salvation of His people. (Weiss.) The description which follows does not enable us to answer all the questions it raises, yet it is sufficiently clear. "The Son of God" was born of the seed of David according to the flesh. For γενομένου, cf. Gal. iv. 4; for David, 2 Tim. ii. 8, where, as here, the Davidic descent is an essential part of the Pauline Gospel. That it was generally preached and recognised in the primitive Church is proved by these passages, as well as by Heb. vii. 14 and the genealogies in Matthew and Luke; yet it seems a fair inference from our Lord's question in Mk. xii. 35 ff. that for Him it had no real importance. Those who did not directly see in Jesus one transcendently greater than David would not recognise in Him the Saviour by being convinced of His Davidic descent. This person, of royal lineage, was "declared Son of God, with power, according to the spirit of holiness, in virtue of resurrection from the dead". The word ὁρισθέντος is ambiguous; in Acts x. 42, xvii. 31, it is used to describe the appointment of Christ to judge the living and the dead, and is rendered in A.V. "ordained". If to be Son of God were merely an office or a dignity, like that of judge of the world, this meaning might be defended here. There is an approximation to such an idea in Acts xiii. 33, where also Paul is the speaker. "God," he says, "has fulfilled His promise by raising up Jesus; as it is written also in the second Psalm, Thou art My Son, this day have I begotten Thee." Here the resurrection day, strictly speaking, is the birthday of the Son of God; sonship is a dignity to which He is exalted after death. But in view of passages like Gal. iv. 4, 2 Cor. viii. 9, Phil. ii. 5 f., it is impossible to suppose that Paul limited his use of Son of God in this way; even while Jesus lived on earth there was that in Him which no connection with David could explain, but which rested on a relation to God; the resurrection only declared Him to be what He truly was—just as in the Psalm, for that matter, the bold words, This day have I begotten Thee, may be said to refer, not to the right and title, but to the coronation of the King. In virtue of His resurrection, which is here conceived, not as *from* the dead (ἐκ νεκρῶν), but of the dead (ἀναστάσεως νεκρῶν—a resurrection exemplifying, and so guaranteeing, that of others), Christ is established in that dignity which is His, and which answers to His nature. The expression κατὰ πνεῦμα ἁγιωσύνης characterises, Christ ethically, as κατὰ σάρκα does physically. Not that it makes the sonship in question "ethical" as opposed to "metaphysical": no such distinctions were in the Apostle's thought. But the sonship, which was declared by the resurrection, answered to (κατὰ) the spirit of holiness which was the inmost and deepest reality in the Person and life of Jesus. The sense that there is that in Christ which is explained by his connection with mankind, and that also which can only be explained by some peculiar relation to God, is no doubt conveyed in this description, and is the basis of the orthodox doctrine of the two natures in the one Person of the Lord; but it is a mistake to say that that doctrine is formulated here. The connection of the words ἐν δυνάμει is doubtful. They have been joined to ὁρισθέντος (cf. 2 Cor. xiii. 4: ζῇ ἐκ δυνάμεως θεοῦ): declared to be Son of God "by a miracle," a mighty work wrought by God; and also with υἱοῦ θεοῦ = Son of God, not in humiliation, but "in power," a power demonstrated by the gift of the Spirit and its operations in the Church. "Jesus, Messiah, Our Lord," summarises all this. "Our Lord" is the most compendious expression of the Christian consciousness. (A. B. Bruce, *Apologetics*, 398 ff.) "The whole Gospel of Paul is comprehended in this historical Jesus, who has appeared in flesh, but who, on the ground of the πνεῦμα ἁγιωσύνης, which constitutes His essence, has been exalted as Christ and Lord." (Lipsius.)

Ver. 5. Through Christ Paul received χάριν κ. ἀποστολήν. The plural, ἐλάβομεν, may mean no more than the

^d πίστεως ἐν πᾶσι τοῖς ἔθνεσιν, ὑπὲρ τοῦ ὀνόματος ^e αὐτοῦ, 6. ἐν οἷς ^d Ch. xvi.
26 ; Acts
ἐστε καὶ ὑμεῖς, κλητοὶ Ἰησοῦ Χριστοῦ·) 7. πᾶσι τοῖς οὖσιν ἐν Ῥώμῃ, vi. 7.
ἀγαπητοῖς Θεοῦ,¹ κλητοῖς ἁγίοις, χάρις ὑμῖν καὶ εἰρήνη ἀπὸ Θεοῦ ^e Acts v. 41,
ix. 16, xv.
πατρὸς ἡμῶν καὶ Κυρίου Ἰησοῦ Χριστοῦ. 26.

8. Πρῶτον μὲν εὐχαριστῶ τῷ Θεῷ μου διὰ Ἰησοῦ Χριστοῦ ὑπὲρ ²
πάντων ὑμῶν, ὅτι ἡ πίστις ὑμῶν καταγγέλλεται ἐν ὅλῳ τῷ ^f κόσμῳ. ^f 1 Thess. i.
8.

¹ For πασιν τοις ουσιν εν Ρωμη αγαπητοις θεου G reads πασι τοις ουσιν εν
αγαπη θεου. The same MS. also omits τοις εν Ρωμη in ver. 17. This is part of
the evidence on which Lightfoot relied to show that Paul had issued chaps. i.-xiv.
of this Epistle as a circular letter with all local allusions (such as these, and the
many in chaps. xv. and xvi.) omitted. See Introduction, p. 578.

² For υπερ read περι with ℵBACD¹, etc.

singular, or may proceed from the latent consciousness that the writer is not the only person entitled to say this ; it is not expressly meant to include others. χάρις, grace, is common to all Christians ; ἀποστολὴ rests upon a specialised χάρις and implies competence as well as vocation. But in the N.T. these are hardly distinguished ; it is a man's χάρισμα which constitutes his "call" to any particular service in the Church. εἰς ὑπακοὴν πίστεως : the object of the apostleship received through Christ is obedience of faith, i.e., the obedience which consists in faith (but cf. Acts vi. 7) among all the Gentiles. Cf. chap. x. 16, 2 Thess. i. 8. The meaning of ἔθνεσιν (Gentiles, not nations) is fixed by ver. 13 and by Paul's conception of his own vocation, Gal. i. 16, ii. 8, Eph. iii. 1 ff. ὑπὲρ τοῦ ὀνόματος αὐτοῦ : the final purpose of his vocation is that Christ's name may be above every name.

Ver. 6. The Romans, as well as others, are included among the Gentiles, and described as Jesus Christ's called. They belong to Him, because they have heard and obeyed the Gospel. "Calling" in Paul always includes obedience as well as hearing. It is effectual calling, the κλητοὶ being those who have accepted the Divine invitation.

Ver. 7. The salutation proper. It is addressed to all who are in Rome, etc., to include Christians of Jewish as well as Gentile origin. They are ἀγαπητοὶ θεοῦ, God's beloved, because they have had experience of His redeeming love in Jesus Christ ; and they are κλητοὶ ἅγιοι, saints, in virtue of His calling. See on κλητὸς ἀπόστολος above. The word ἅγιος did not originally describe character, but only a certain relation to God ; the ἅγιοι are God's people. What this means depends of course on what God

is ; it is assumed in scripture that the character of God's people will answer to their relation to Him. It is worth mentioning that, as a synonym for Christian, it is never applied in the N.T. to an individual : no person is called ἅγιος. Phil. iv. 21 (ἀσπάσασθε πάντα ἅγιον ἐν Χ. Ἰ.) is not an exception. The ideal of God's people cannot be adequately realised in, and ought not to be presumptuously claimed by, any single person. (Hort's Christian Ecclesia, 56.) Paul wishes the Romans grace and peace (the source and the sum of all Christian blessings) from God our Father, and from the Lord Jesus Christ. The greeting is followed by a thanksgiving, which passes over insensibly into an introduction of a more personal character, in which Paul explains his desire to visit the Romans and to work among them (vers. 8-15).

Ver. 8. πρῶτον μέν. Nothing can take precedence of thanksgiving, when Paul thinks of the Romans, or indeed of any Christian Church in normal health. πρῶτον μὲν suggests that something is to follow, but what it is we are not told ; Paul's mind unconsciously leaves the track on which it started, at least so far as the linguistic following out of it is concerned. Perhaps the next thing was to be the prayer referred to in ver. 10. (Weiss.) διὰ Ἰ. Χ. Jesus Christ must be conceived here as the mediator through whom all our approaches to God are made (Eph. ii. 18), not as He through whom the blessings come for which Paul gives thanks. περὶ πάντων ὑμῶν : the "all" may have a certain emphasis when we remember the divisions to which reference is made in chap. xiv. ἡ πίστις ὑμῶν is "the fact that you are Christians". The very existence of a Church at Rome was

g Phil. iii. 3. 9. μάρτυς γάρ μου ἐστιν ὁ Θεός, ᾧ ᵍλατρεύω ἐν τῷ πνεύματί μου ἐν

τῷ εὐαγγελίῳ τοῦ υἱοῦ αὐτοῖ, ὡς ἀδιαλείπτως μνείαν ὑμῶν ποιοῦμαι,

h Eph. i. 16; πάντοτε ἐπὶ τῶν ʰπροσευχῶν μου δεόμενος, 10. εἴ πως ἤδη ποτὲ
1 Thess.
i. 2.   εὐοδωθήσομαι ἐν τῷ θελήματι τοῦ Θεοῦ, ἐλθεῖν πρὸς ὑμᾶς · 11.

i 1 Thess. ἐπιποθῶ γὰρ ἰδεῖν ὑμᾶς, ἵνα τι ⁱμεταδῶ χάρισμα ὑμῖν ᵏπνευματικόν,
ii. 8.

k 1 Cor. xii. εἰς τὸ στηριχθῆναι ὑμᾶς, 12. τοῦτο δέ ἐστι, συμπαρακληθῆναι ἐν ὑμῖν
1, 4   διὰ τῆς ἐν ἀλλήλοις πίστεως ὑμῶν τε καὶ ἐμοῦ. 13. οὐ θέλω δὲ ὑμᾶς

l ἄχρι τ. δ. ἀγνοεῖν, ἀδελφοί, ὅτι πολλάκις προεθέμην ἐλθεῖν πρὸς ὑμᾶς, (καὶ
here only.
m Phil. i. 22. ἐκωλύθην ἄχρι τοῦ ˡδεῦρο,) ἵνα ᵐκαρπόν τινα σχῶ καὶ ἐν ὑμῖν, καθὼς

something to be thankful for. ἐν ὅλῳ τῷ κόσμῳ is, of course, hyperbole, but a Church in Rome was like "a city set on a hill".

Ver. 9 f. μάρτυς γάρ μού ἐστιν ὁ θεός (Phil. i. 8): at a distance the Apostle cannot directly prove his love, but he appeals to God, who hears his ceaseless prayers for the Romans, as a witness of it. λατρεύω in the LXX is always used of religious service—worship, whether of the true God or of idols. ἐν τῷ πνεύματί μου: Paul's ministry is spiritual and rendered with his spirit—not like that of the ministers in the ἅγιον κοσμικὸν at Jerusalem. ἐν τῷ εὐαγγελίῳ: in preaching the glad tidings of His Son. ὡς ἀδιαλείπτως: the ὡς may either be "how" or "that": looking to 1 Thess. ii. 10, "how" seems more probable. μνείαν ὑμῶν ποιοῦμαι: I remember you. Cf. Job xiv. 13 (O that Thou wouldst appoint me χρόνον ἐν ᾧ μνείαν μου ποιήσῃ). ἐπὶ τῶν προσευχῶν μου: at my prayers. (Winer, p. 470.) For εἴ πως, see Acts xxvii. 12 and Burton, Moods and Tenses, § 276. ἤδη is "now at length," "now, after all this waiting". (S. and H.) The ποτὲ, which can hardly be conveyed in English, marks the indefiniteness which even yet attaches in the writer's mind to the fulfilment of this hope. εὐοδωθήσομαι: the R.V. gives "I may be prospered"; the A.V. "I might have a prosperous journey". The latter brings in the idea of the ὁδὸς, which was no doubt present to consciousness when the word εὐοδοῦσθαι was first used; but it is questionable whether any feeling for the etymology remained in the current employment of the word. The other N.T. examples (1 Cor. xvi. 2, 3 John ver. 2), as well as the LXX, suggest the contrary. Hence the R.V. is probably right. ἐν τῷ θελήματι τοῦ θεοῦ: his long cherished and often disappointed hope had taught Paul to say, "if the Lord will" (Jas. iv. 15).

Ver. 11. ἵνα τι μεταδῶ χάρισμα πνευματικόν. The χαρ. πν. may be understood by reference to 1 Cor. chaps. xii.-xiv. or Rom. chap. xii. No doubt, in substance, Paul imparts his spiritual gift through this epistle: what he wished to do for the Romans was to further their comprehension of the purpose of God in Jesus Christ—a purpose the breadth and bearings of which were yet but imperfectly understood.

Ver. 12. τοῦτο δέ ἐστιν: an explanatory correction. Paul disclaims being in a position in which all the giving must be on his side. When he is among them (ἐν ὑμῖν) his desire is that he may be cheered and strengthened with them (the subject of συνπαρακληθῆναι must be ἐμὲ in the first instance, though widening, as the sentence goes on, into ἡμᾶς) by the faith which both they and he possess (ὑμῶν τε καὶ ἐμοῦ), and which each recognises in the other (ἐν ἀλλήλοις). The ἐν here is to be taken as in 2 Tim. i. 5.

Ver. 13. οὐ θέλω δὲ ὑμᾶς ἀγνοεῖν: a phrase of constant recurrence in Paul, and always with ἀδελφοί (1 Thess. iv. 13, 1 Cor. x. 1, xii. 1, 2 Cor. i. 8). Some emphasis is laid by it on the idea that his desire or purpose to visit them was no passing whim. It was grounded in his vocation as Apostle of the Gentiles, and though it had been often frustrated he had never given it up. ἐκωλύθην ἄχρι τοῦ δεῦρο: probably the main obstacle was evangelistic work which had to be done elsewhere. Cf. chap. xv. 22 f. The purpose of his visit is expressed in ἵνα τινὰ καρπὸν σχῶ: that I may obtain some fruit among you also. καρπὸς denotes the result of labour: it might either mean new converts or the furtherance of the Christians in their new life. καθὼς καὶ ἐν τοῖς λοιποῖς ἔθνεσιν: nothing could indicate more clearly that the Church at Rome, as a whole, was Gentile.

καὶ ἐν τοῖς λοιποῖς ἔθνεσιν.   14. Ἕλλησί τε καὶ βαρβάροις, σοφοῖς
τε καὶ ἀνοήτοις ὀφειλέτης εἰμί·   15. ᵇοὕτω τὸ κατ' ἐμὲ πρόθυμον καὶ   ᵇ Rev. iii. 16.
ὑμῖν τοῖς ἐν Ῥώμῃ ¹ εὐαγγελίσασθαι.   16. Οὐ γὰρ ἐπαισχύνομαι τὸ
εὐαγγέλιον τοῦ Χριστοῦ ² · ᶜδύναμις γὰρ Θεοῦ ἐστιν εἰς σωτηρίαν παντὶ   ᶜ 1 Cor. i. 18, 24.

¹ τοις εν Ρωμη om. G ; see on ver. 7.

² του Χριστου om. אABCD, etc.   πρωτον is omitted here in BG g and Tert.   It
is inserted in אACDKL.   The combination of B with "Western" authorities lessens
its weight in Paul's epp., where B itself has an infusion of Western readings to
which this omission may belong; possibly it may be due to Marcion, who is known
to have omitted both πρωτον and the quotation in ver. 17.   Weiss retains it; W. and
H. bracket.

Ver. 14 f. These verses are naturally taken as an expansion of the
thought contained in the preceding.
Paul's desire to win fruit at Rome, as
among the rest of the Gentiles, arises
out of the obligation (for so he feels it)
to preach the Gospel to all men without
distinction of language or culture. If it
depended only on him, he would be
exercising his ministry at Rome. The
Romans are evidently conceived as
Gentiles, but Paul does not indicate
where they would stand in the broad
classification of ver. 14. It is gratuitous,
and probably mistaken, to argue with
Weiss that he meant to describe them as
βάρβαροι, when we know that the early
Roman Church was Greek speaking. In
τὸ κατ' ἐμὲ πρόθυμον, the simplest construction is to make τὸ κατ' ἐμὲ subject
and πρόθυμον predicate, supplying ἐστι:
all that depends on me is eager, i.e., for
my part, I am all readiness. But it is
possible to take τὸ κατ' ἐμὲ πρόθυμον
together, and to translate: the readiness, so far as I am concerned, (is) to
preach the Gospel to you also who are
in Rome. The contrast implied is that
between willing (which Paul for his part
is equal to) and carrying out the will
(which depends on God (ver. 10)).
With this Paul introduces the great
subject of the epistle, and, in a sense,
of the Gospel—that which he here
designates δικαιοσύνη θεοῦ. The connection is peculiar. He has professed
his readiness to preach the Gospel, even
at Rome. Anywhere, no doubt, one
might have misgivings about identifying
himself with a message which had for
its subject a person who had been put to
death as a criminal; anywhere, the Cross
was to Jews a stumbling block and to
Greeks foolishness. But at Rome, of all
places, where the whole effective force
of humanity seemed to be gathered up,
one might be ashamed to stand forth

as the representative of an apparently
impotent and ineffective thing. But
this the Gospel is not; it is the very
reverse of this, and therefore the Apostle
is proud to identify himself with it. "I
am not ashamed of the Gospel; for it is
a power of God unto salvation to every
one that believeth. It is such because
there is revealed in it δικαιοσύνη θεοῦ—
the very thing men need to ensure salvation; and that in such a manner—from
faith to faith—as to make it accessible to
all. And this, again, only answers to
what stands in the O.T.—It is written,
the righteous shall live by faith."
Ver. 16 f. δύναμις γὰρ θεοῦ ἐστιν : for
it is a power of God. It does no injustice
to render "a Divine power". The conception of the Gospel as a force pervades the epistles to the Corinthians;
its proof, so to speak, is dynamical, not
logical. It is demonstrated, not by
argument, but by what it does; and,
looking to what it can do, Paul is proud
to preach it anywhere. εἰς σωτηρίαν :
σωτηρία is one of a class of words (to
which ζωή, δόξα, κληρονομία belong)
used by Paul to denote the last result of
the acceptance of the Gospel. It is the
most negative of them all, and conceives
of the Gospel as a means for rescuing
men from the ἀπώλεια which awaits
sinners at the last judgment. In παντὶ
τῷ πιστεύοντι Ἰουδαίῳ τε πρῶτον καὶ
Ἕλληνι another of the main interests of
the writer in this epistle is brought
forward; the Gospel is for all, the same
Gospel and on the same terms, but
without prejudice to the historical prerogative of the Jew. Ver. 17 shows how
the Gospel is a Divine saving power.
It is such because there is revealed in it
δικαιοσύνη θεοῦ. Plainly, δικαιοσύνη
θεοῦ is something without which a sinful
man cannot be saved; but what is it?
The expression itself is of the utmost
generality, and the various definite

τῷ πιστεύοντι, Ἰουδαίῳ τε πρῶτον καὶ Ἕλληνι. 17. δικαιοσύνη γὰρ [p] Θεοῦ ἐν αὐτῷ [q] ἀποκαλύπτεται ἐκ πίστεως εἰς πίστιν, καθὼς γέγραπται, "Ὁ δὲ δίκαιος ἐκ πίστεως [r] ζήσεται."

p 2 Cor. v. 21.
q Ch. xvi. 25 f.
r Hab. ii. 4.

meanings which have been assigned to it attempt to justify themselves as relevant, or inevitable, by connecting themselves with the context as a whole. There can be no doubt that the fundamental religious problem for the Apostle—that which made a Gospel necessary, that the solution of which could alone *be* Gospel—was, How shall a sinful man be righteous before God? To Luther, who had instinctive experimental sympathy with the Pauline standpoint, this suggested that **δικαιοσύνη θεοῦ** meant a righteousness valid before God, of which a man can become possessed through faith; for such a righteousness (as the condition of salvation) is the first and last need of the sinful soul. In support of this view reference has been made to ver. 18, where **ἀσέβεια** and **ἀδικία ἀνθρώπων** are represented as the actual existing conditions which the **δικ. θεοῦ** has to replace. No one can deny that a righteousness valid before God is essential to salvation, or that such a righteousness is revealed in the Gospel; but it is another question whether **δικ. θεοῦ** is a natural expression for it. The general sense of scholars seems to have decided against it; but it seems quite credible to me that Paul used **δικ. θεοῦ** broadly to mean "a Divine righteousness," and that the particular shade of meaning which Luther made prominent can be legitimately associated even with these words. Until lately, scholars of the most opposite schools had agreed in finding the key to the expression **δικ. θεοῦ** in two other Pauline passages, where it is contrasted with something else. Thus in chap. x. 3 **δικ. θεοῦ** is opposed to man's **ἰδία δικαιοσύνη**; and in Phil. iii. 9 the opposition is more precisely defined: **μὴ ἔχων ἐμὴν δικαιοσύνην τὴν ἐκ νόμου, ἀλλὰ τὴν διὰ πίστεως Χριστοῦ, τὴν ἐκ θεοῦ δικαιοσύνην ἐπὶ τῇ πίστει.** If this contrast were allowed to tell here, the righteousness of which Paul speaks would be one of which God is the source or author; we do not bring it to Him, He reveals it for our acceptance. And this also, of course, answers to the facts: Gospel righteousness *is* a gift, not an achievement. But then, it is said, there is nothing in the passage to suggest such a contrast; there is not any emphasis whatever on **θεοῦ** to bring before the mind the idea of a righteousness *not* due to God, but a work of man's own. To this it may fairly be answered that the contrast did not *need* to be specially suggested; if it had not presented itself instinctively to those to whom Paul wrote, they would not only have missed the point of this expression, they would not have understood three lines anywhere. We must assume, upon the whole, in the recipients of Paul's epistles, a way of conceiving the Gospel answering broadly to his own; the invisible context, which we have to reproduce as best we can, may be more important sometimes than what we have in black and white. The broad sense of "a Divine righteousness" covers this second, which may be called the historical Protestant interpretation, as well as Luther's; and the fact seems to me an argument for that broader rendering. In view, however, of the undoubted difficulty of the phrase, new light would be welcome, and this has been sought in the O.T. use of **δικαιοσύνη** (צְדָקָה), especially in the Psalms and in Is. xl.-lxvi. See, *e.g.*, Ps. xxxv. 24, 28, li. 14; Is. lvi. 1, lxii. 1; Ps. xcviii. 2. In the last of these passages we have a striking analogy to the one before us: **ἐγνώρισε κύριος τὸ σωτήριον αὐτοῦ, ἐναντίον τῶν ἐθνῶν ἀπεκάλυψε τὴν δικαιοσύνην αὐτοῦ**; and in others we cannot but be struck with the parallelism of "righteousness" and "salvation," sometimes as things which belong to God (Ps. xcviii. 2), sometimes as things which belong to His people. On the strength of facts like these, Theod. Häring, in a stupendous programme entitled **Δικ. θεοῦ** *bei Paulus* (Tübingen, 1896), argues that **δικαιοσύνη θεοῦ** means the judicial action of God in which He justifies His people and accomplishes their salvation. This fits into the context well enough. Put as Paul puts it—how shall man be just with God?—the religious problem is a judicial one, and its solution must be judicial. If the Gospel shows how God justifies (for of course it must be God, the only Judge of all, who does it), it shows everything: salvation is included in God's sentence of justification. Häring himself admits that this interpretation is

18. ᾿ΑΠΟΚΑΛΥΠΤΕΤΑΙ γὰρ ὀργὴ Θεοῦ ἀπ᾿ οὐρανοῦ ἐπὶ πᾶσαν ἀσέβειαν καὶ ἀδικίαν ἀνθρώπων τῶν τὴν ἀλήθειαν ἐν ἀδικίᾳ ˢκατεχόν-

s 2 Thess. ii.
6, 7.

rather of philological than of religious import; this "rechtfertigendes Walten Gottes" cannot but have as its consequence "the justification of man, a righteousness which proceeds from God and is valid before God" (Δικ. θεοῦ bei Paulus, S. 68); that is, this meaning leads by immediate inference to the other two. But it can by no means be carried through (any more than either of the other two) in all places where the phrase occurs; in iii. 5, e.g., Häring himself admits this; in iii. 25, 26, where he insists on the same sense as in i. 17, he does not so much as refer to the clause διὰ τὴν πάρεσιν τῶν προγεγονότων ἁμαρτημάτων ἐν τῇ ἀνοχῇ αὐτοῦ, which, it is not too much to say, necessitates a different shade of meaning for δικαιοσύνη θεοῦ there: see note. The advantage of his rendering is not so much that it simplifies the grammar, as that it revives the sense of a connection (which existed for the Apostle) between the Gospel he preached, and even the language he preached it in, and the anticipations of that Gospel in the O.T., and that it gives prominence to the saving character of God's justifying action. In substance all these three views are Biblical, Pauline and true to experience, whichever is to be vindicated on philological grounds. But the same cannot be said of another, according to which righteousness is here an attribute, or even the character, of God. That the Gospel is the supreme revelation of the character of God, and that the character of God is the source of the Gospel, no one can question. Certainly Paul would not have questioned it. But whether Paul conceived the righteousness which is an eternal attribute of God (cf. iii. 5) as essentially self-communicative—whether he would have said that God justifies (δικαιοῖ) the ungodly because he is himself δίκαιος— is another matter. The righteousness of God, conceived as a Divine attribute, may have appeared to Paul the great difficulty in the way of the justification of sinful man. God's righteousness in this sense is the sinner's condemnation, and no one will succeed in making him find in it the ground of his hope. What is wanted (always in consistency with God's righteousness as one of His inviolable attributes—the great point elaborated in chap. iii. 24-26) is a righteousness which, as man cannot produce it, must be from

God, and which, once received, shall be valid before God; and this is what the Apostle (on the ground of Christ's death for sin) announces. But it introduces confusion to identify with this the conception of an eternal and necessarily self-imparting righteousness of God. The Apostle, in chap. iii. and chap. v., takes our minds along another route. See Barmby in Expositor for August, 1896, and S. and H. ad loc. ἀποκαλύπτεται intimates in a new way that the Divine righteousness spoken of is from God: man would never have known or conceived it but for the act of God in revealing it. Till this ἀποκαλύπτειν it was a μυστήριον: cf. xvi. 25 f. ἐκ πίστεως εἰς πίστιν. Precise definitions of this (e.g., Weiss's: the revelation of the δικ. θεοῦ presupposes faith in the sense of believing acceptance of the Gospel, i.e., it is ἐκ πίστεως; and it leads to faith in the sense of saving reliance on Christ, i.e., it is εἰς πίστιν) strike one as arbitrary. The broad sense seems to be that in the revelation of God's righteousness for man's salvation everything is of faith from first to last. Cf. 2 Cor. ii. 16, iii. 18. This N.T. doctrine the Apostle finds announced before in Hab. ii. 14. ἐκ πίστεως in the quotation is probably to be construed with ζήσεται. To take it with δίκαιος (he who is righteous by faith) would imply a contrast to another mode of being righteous (viz., by works) which there is nothing in the text to suggest. The righteous who trusted in Jehovah were brought by that trust safe through the impending judgment in Habakkuk's time; and as the subjective side of religion, the attitude of the soul to God, never varies, it is the same trust which is the condition of salvation still.

The Gospel of God's righteousness is necessary, because the human race has no righteousness of its own. This is proved of the whole race (i. 18-iii. 20), but in these verses (18-32) first of the heathen. The emphasis lies throughout on the fact that they have sinned against light.

Ver. 18 f. The revelation of the righteousness of God (ver. 17) is needed in view of the revelation of His wrath, from which only δικ. θεοῦ (whether it be His justifying sentence or the righteousness which He bestows on man) can deliver. ὀργὴ in the N.T. is usually

t Neuter in των.   19. διότι τὸ ᵗγνωστὸν τοῦ Θεοῦ φανερόν ἐστιν ἐν αὐτοῖς· ὁ γὰρ
N.T. here
and in   Θεὸς αὐτοῖς ἐφανέρωσε· 20. τὰ γὰρ ἀόρατα αὐτοῦ ἀπὸ κτίσεως
Acts only
(11 times). κόσμου τοῖς ποιήμασι νοούμενα καθορᾶται, ἥ τε ᵘ ἀΐδιος αὐτοῦ δύναμις
u Only here
and Jude καὶ ᵛθειότης, εἰς τὸ εἶναι αὐτοὺς ἀναπολογήτους. 21. διότι γνόντες
vers. 6.
v Here only τὸν Θεόν, οὐχ ὡς Θεὸν ἐδόξασαν ἢ εὐχαρίστησαν, ἀλλ' ἐματαιώθησαν
in N.T.
w 1 Cor. iii. ἐν τοῖς ʷδιαλογισμοῖς αὐτῶν, καὶ ἐσκοτίσθη ἡ ἀσύνετος αὐτῶν καρδία·
20.
x 1 Cor. i. 20. 22. φάσκοντες εἶναι σοφοὶ ˣἐμωράνθησαν, 23. καὶ ἤλλαξαν τὴν δόξαν
τοῦ ἀφθάρτου Θεοῦ ἐν ὁμοιώματι εἰκόνος φθαρτοῦ ἀνθρώπου καὶ

eschatological, but in 1 Thess. ii. 16 it refers to some historical judgment, and in John iii. 36 it is the condemnation of the sinner by God, with all that it involves, present and to come. The revelation of wrath here probably refers mainly to the final judgment : the primary character of Jesus in Paul's Gospel being ὁ ῥυόμενος ἡμᾶς ἐκ τῆς ὀργῆς τῆς ἐρχομένης, 1 Thess. i. 10, Rom. v. 9 ; but it is not forcing it here to make it include God's condemnation uttered in conscience, and attested (ver. 24) in the judicial abandonment of the world. The revelation of the righteousness of God has to match this situation, and reverse it. ἀσέβεια is " positive and active irreligion " : see Trench, Syn., § lxvi. τῶν τὴν ἀλήθειαν ἐν ἀδικίᾳ κατεχόντων may mean (1) who possess the truth, yet live in unrighteousness ; or (2) who suppress the truth by, or in, an unrighteous life. In the N.T. ἀλήθεια is moral rather than speculative ; it is truth of a sort which is held only as it is acted on : cf. the Johannine expression ποιεῖν τὴν ἀλήθειαν. Hence the latter sense is to be preferred (see Wendt, Lehre Jesu, II., S. 203 Anm.). διότι τὸ γνωστὸν τοῦ θεοῦ κ.τ.λ. There is no indisputable way of deciding whether γνωστὸν here means " known " (the usual N.T. sense) or " knowable " (the usual classic sense). Cremer (who compares Phil. iii. 8 τὸ ὑπερέχον τῆς γνώσεως, Heb. vi. 17 τὸ ἀμετάθετον τῆς βουλῆς, Rom. ii. 4 τὸ χρηστὸν τοῦ θεοῦ, and makes τοῦ θεοῦ in the passage before us also gen. poss.) favours the latter. What is meant in either case is the knowledge of God which is independent of such a special revelation as had been given to the Jews. Under this come (ver. 20) His eternal power, and in a word His (eternal) divinity, things inaccessible indeed to sense (ἀόρατα), but clear to intelligence (νοούμενα), ever since creation (ἀπὸ κτίσεως κόσμου : for ἀπὸ thus used, see Winer, 463),

by the things that are made. God's power, and the totality of the Divine attributes constituting the Divine nature, are inevitably impressed on the mind by nature (or, to use the scripture word, by creation). There is that within man which so catches the meaning of all that is without as to issue in an instinctive knowledge of God. (See the magnificent illustration of this in Illingworth's Divine Immanence, chap. ii., on The religious influence of the material world.) This knowledge involves duties, and men are without excuse because, when in possession of it, they did not perform these duties ; that is, did not glorify as God the God whom they thus knew.

Ver. 21 ff. εἰς τὸ εἶναι αὐτοὺς ἀναπολογήτους would naturally express purpose : to make men inexcusable is one, though not the only or the ultimate, intention of God in giving this revelation. But the διότι almost forces us to take the εἰς τὸ as expressing result : so that they are inexcusable, because, etc. (see Burton's Moods and Tenses, § 411). In vers. 21-23 the wrong course taken by humanity is described. Nature shows us that God is to be glorified and thanked, i.e., nature reveals Him to be great and good. But men were not content to accept the impression made on them by nature ; they fell to reasoning upon it, and in their reasonings (διαλογισμοί, " perverse self-willed reasonings or speculations," S. and H.) were made vain (ἐματαιώθησαν) ; the result stultified the process ; their instinctive perception of God became confused and uncertain ; their unintelligent heart, the seat of the moral consciousness, was darkened. In asserting their wisdom they became fools, and showed it conspicuously in their idolatries. They resigned the glory of the incorruptible God (i.e., the incorruptible God, all glorious as He was, and as He was seen in nature to be), and took instead

πετεινῶν καὶ τετραπόδων καὶ ἑρπετῶν. 24. διὸ καὶ [1] παρέδωκεν y Eph.iv.19.
αὐτοὺς ὁ Θεὸς ἐν ταῖς ἐπιθυμίαις τῶν καρδιῶν αὐτῶν εἰς ἀκαθαρσίαν,
τοῦ ἀτιμάζεσθαι τὰ σώματα αὐτῶν ἐν ἑαυτοῖς· 25. οἵτινες μετήλλαξαν
τὴν ἀλήθειαν τοῦ Θεοῦ ἐν τῷ ψεύδει, καὶ [2] ἐσεβάσθησαν καὶ ἐλάτρευσαν z Here only,
τῇ κτίσει παρὰ τὸν κτίσαντα, ὅς ἐστιν εὐλογητὸς εἰς τοὺς αἰῶνας. cf. Acts
                                                                   xvii. 23;
ἀμήν. 26. διὰ τοῦτο παρέδωκεν αὐτοὺς ὁ Θεὸς εἰς πάθη ἀτιμίας· 2 Thess.
                                                                   ii. 4
αἵ τε γὰρ θήλειαι αὐτῶν μετήλλαξαν τὴν φυσικὴν χρῆσιν εἰς τὴν
παρὰ φύσιν· 27. ὁμοίως τε [2] καὶ οἱ ἄρσενες, ἀφέντες τὴν φυσικὴν
χρῆσιν τῆς θηλείας, ἐξεκαύθησαν ἐν τῇ ὀρέξει αὐτῶν εἰς ἀλλήλους,
ἄρσενες ἐν ἄρσεσι τὴν ἀσχημοσύνην κατεργαζόμενοι, καὶ τὴν [a] ἀντι- a 2 Cor. vi.
                                                                    13.
μισθίαν ἣν ἔδει τῆς πλάνης αὐτῶν ἐν ἑαυτοῖς ἀπολαμβάνοντες.
28. Καὶ καθὼς οὐκ ἐδοκίμασαν τὸν Θεὸν ἔχειν ἐν ἐπιγνώσει, παρέδωκεν αὐτοὺς ὁ Θεὸς εἰς ἀδόκιμον νοῦν, ποιεῖν τὰ μὴ [b] καθήκοντα, b Acts xxii.
                                                                   22.

---

[1] διο και: om. και אABC; insert DGKL. εαυτοις D³EGK; αυτοις אABC [1].

[2] For τε which is found in אBD³KL, δε is read by AD¹G ; C has neither.

---

of Him some image of a corruptible,
even of a vile creature. The expression
ἤλλαξαν τὴν δόξαν κ.τ.λ. is borrowed in
part from Ps. cv. 20 (LXX): ἠλλάξαντο
τὴν δόξαν αὐτῶν ἐν ὁμοιώματι μόσχου
ἔσθοντος χόρτον. The reduplication of
the same idea in ἐν ὁμοιώματι εἰκόνος
shows the indignant contempt with
which the Apostle looked on this empty
and abject religion in which God had
been lost. The birds, quadrupeds and
reptiles could all be illustrated from
Egypt.

With ver. 24 the Apostle turns from
this sin to its punishment. Because of
it (διὸ) God gave them up. To lose God
is to lose everything: to lose the connection with Him involved in constantly
glorifying and giving Him thanks, is to
sink into an abyss of darkness, intellectual and moral. It is to become fitted
for wrath at last, under the pressure of
wrath all the time. Such, in idea, is the
history of humanity to Paul, as interpreted by its issue in the moral condition
of the pagan world when he wrote. Exceptions are allowed for (ii. 10), but this
is the position as a whole. παρέδωκεν in
all three places (ver. 24, εἰς ἀκαθαρσίαν ;
ver. 26, εἰς πάθη ἀτιμίας ; ver. 28, εἰς
ἀδόκιμον νοῦν) expresses the judicial
action of God. The sensual impurity
of religions in which the incorruptible
God had been resigned for the image of
an animal, that could not but creep into
the imagination of the worshippers and
debase it, was a Divine judgment. τοῦ
ἀτιμάζεσθαι τὰ σώματα αὐτῶν ἐν αὐτοῖς,

in accordance with the conception of a
judicial act, expresses the Divine purpose
—that their bodies might be dishonoured
among them. For gen. of purpose, see
Winer, 408 ff. (where, however, a
different construction is given for this
passage, τοῦ ἀτιμάζεσθαι being made to
depend immediately on ἀκαθαρσίαν).

Ver. 25. οἵτινες μετήλλαξαν κ.τ.λ.:
being as they were persons who exchanged the truth of God for the lie.
"The truth of God" (cf. ver. 23, "the
glory of God") is the same thing as God
in His truth, or the true God as He had
actually revealed Himself to man. τὸ
ψεῦδος, abstract for concrete, is the
idol or false God. The ἐν (cf. ver. 23)
answers to Hebrew בְּ. παρὰ τὸν
κτίσαντα : to the passing by, i.e.,
disregard or contempt of the Creator.
For this use of παρὰ, see Winer, 503 f.
ὅς ἐστιν εὐλογητός : the doxology relieves the writer's feelings as he contemplates such horrors.

Ver. 26 f. With the second παρέδωκεν
the Apostle proceeds to a further stage
in this judicial abandonment of men,
which is at the same time a revelation
of the wrath of God from heaven against
them. It issues not merely like the first
in sensuality, but in sensuality which
perverts nature as well as disregards
God. The πλάνη, error or going astray
(ver. 27), is probably still the original
one of idolatry ; the ignoring or degrading of God is the first fatal step out of
the way, which ends in this slough.

29. πεπληρωμένους πάσῃ ἀδικίᾳ, πορνείᾳ,[1] πονηρίᾳ, πλεονεξίᾳ, κακίᾳ· μεστοὺς φθόνου, φόνου, ἔριδος, δόλου, κακοηθείας· 30. ψιθυριστὰς, καταλάλους, θεοστυγεῖς, ὑβριστὰς, ὑπερηφάνους, ἀλαζόνας, ἐφευρετὰς κακῶν, γονεῦσιν ἀπειθεῖς, 31. ἀσυνέτους, ἀσυνθέτους, ἀστόργους, ἀσ-

c Ch. ii. 26; πόνδους,[2] ἀνελεήμονας· 32. οἵτινες τὸ ᶜ δικαίωμα τοῦ Θεοῦ ἐπιγνόντες,
Luke i. 6.

ὅτι οἱ τὰ τοιαῦτα πράσσοντες ἄξιοι θανάτου εἰσίν, οὐ μόνον αὐτὰ
d Acts viii.
1, xxii. 20. ποιοῦσιν, ἀλλὰ καὶ ᵈ συνευδοκοῦσι τοῖς πράσσουσι.[3]

[1] πορνεια om. with ℵABCK.

[2] ασπονδους CD³KL, vulg., Syr., is omitted by ℵ¹ABD¹G fuld.¹ Probably a gloss on ασυνθετους.

[3] Westcott and Hort suppose some primitive error probable here; see their *N. T.*, vol. 2, Appendix, p. 108. For ποιουσιν . . . συνευδοκουσιν B reads ποιουντες . . . συνευδοκουντες; and the construction is then completed by various additions, such as ουκ ενοησαν D, ουκ εγνωσαν G, *non intellexerunt* Orig. int.

Ver. 28 ff. In vers. 28-30 we have the third and last παρέδωκεν expanded. As they did not think fit, after trial made (ἐδοκίμασαν), to keep God in their knowledge, God gave them up to a mind which cannot stand trial (ἀδόκιμον). The one thing answers to the other. Virtually, they pronounced the true God ἀδόκιμος, and would have none of Him; and He in turn gave them up to a νοῦς ἀδόκιμος, a mind which is no mind and cannot discharge the functions of one, a mind in which the Divine distinctions of right and wrong are confused and lost, so that God's condemnation cannot but fall on it at last. νοῦς is not only reason, but conscience; when this is perverted, as in the people of whom Paul speaks, or in the Caananites, who did their abominations *unto their Gods*, the last deep of evil has been reached. Most of the words which follow describe sins of malignity or inhumanity rather than sensuality, but they cannot be classified. τὰ μὴ καθήκοντα covers all. καθήκοντα is the Stoic word which Cicero renders *officia*. κακοηθία, the tendency to put the worst construction on everything (Arist. Rh. ii. 13), and κακία are examined in Trench's *Synonyms*, § xi., and ὑβριστής, ὑπερήφανος, ἀλάζων in § xxix. θεοστυγεῖς appears to be always passive in the classics, not God hating, but God hated: *Deo odibiles*, Vulg. The characters are summed up, so to speak, in ver. 32: οἵτινες τὸ δικαίωμα τοῦ θεοῦ ἐπιγνόντες κ.τ.λ.: such persons as, though they know the sentence of God, that those who practise such things are worthy of death, not only do them, but give a whole-hearted complacent assent to those who follow the same practice.

τὸ δικαίωμα τοῦ θεοῦ is that which God has pronounced to be the right, and has thereby established as the proper moral order of the world. θάνατος is death, not as a natural period to life, but as a Divine sentence executed on sin: it is not to be defined as physical, or spiritual, or eternal; by all such abstract analysis it is robbed of part of its meaning, which is as wide as that of life or the soul. ἀλλὰ καὶ συνευδοκοῦσιν: to be guilty of such things oneself, under the impulse of passion, is bad; but it is a more malignant badness to give a cordial and disinterested approval to them in others.

It is a mistake to read these verses as if they were a scientific contribution to comparative religion, but equally a mistake to ignore their weight. Paul is face to face with a world in which the vices he enumerates are rampant, and it is his deliberate judgment that these vices have a real connection with the pagan religions. Who will deny that he was both a competent observer and a competent judge? Religion and morality in the great scale hang together, and morality in the long run is determined by religion. Minds which accepted the religious ideas of Phenicia, of Egypt or of Greece (as represented in the popular mythologies) could not be pure. Their morality, or rather their immorality, is conceived as a Divine judgment upon their religion; and as for their religion, nature itself, the Apostle argues, should have saved them from such ignorance of God, and such misconceptions of Him, as deformed every type of heathenism. A converted pagan (as much as Paul) would be filled with horror as he re-

II. 1. ΔΙΟ [a] ἀναπολόγητος εἶ, ὦ ἄνθρωπε πᾶς ὁ κρίνων· ἐν ᾧ γὰρ a Ch. i. 20.
κρίνεις τὸν ἕτερον, σεαυτὸν κατακρίνεις· τὰ γὰρ αὐτὰ πράσσεις ὁ
κρίνων. 2. οἴδαμεν δὲ [1] ὅτι τὸ κρίμα τοῦ Θεοῦ ἐστι κατὰ ἀλήθειαν
ἐπὶ τοὺς τὰ τοιαῦτα πράσσοντας. 3. Λογίζῃ δὲ τοῦτο, ὦ ἄνθρωπε
ὁ κρίνων τοὺς τὰ τοιαῦτα πράσσοντας καὶ ποιῶν αὐτά, ὅτι σὺ ἐκφεύξῃ b Ch. ix. 23,
τὸ κρίμα τοῦ Θεοῦ ; 4. ἢ τοῦ [b] πλούτου τῆς χρηστότητος αὐτοῦ καὶ xi. 33.
τῆς ἀνοχῆς καὶ τῆς μακροθυμίας καταφρονεῖς, ἀγνοῶν ὅτι τὸ χρηστὸν
τοῦ Θεοῦ εἰς μετάνοιάν σε ἄγει ; 5. κατὰ δὲ τὴν [c] σκληρότητά σου καὶ c Here only.
ἀμετανόητον καρδίαν θησαυρίζεις σεαυτῷ ὀργὴν ἐν ἡμέρᾳ ὀργῆς καὶ

[1] δὲ ABDGKL, γὰρ NC d, vulg. A full statement of the evidence in S. and H.
whose verdict is : " an even balance of authorities, both sides drawing their evidence
from varied quarters ".

flected on the way in which he had once
thought of God ; he would feel in himself that he ought to have known better,
and that everything in the world cried
shame upon him. Now to recognise
this fact is to accept the premises of the
Apostle's argument, and the use to which
he puts it. " Once we went after dumb
idols ; our very worship led us into sin,
and sometimes even consecrated it ; now
we can only see in this our own blindness
and guilt, and God's judgment upon
them "—so we can fancy the converted
pagan speaking. Such a world, then, as
the Apostle describes in this chapter,
with this terrible principle of degenera-
tion at work in it, and no power of self-
regeneration, is a world which waits for
a righteousness of God.

For an interesting attempt to show
Paul's indebtedness for some of the ideas
and arguments of vers. 18-32 to the book
of Wisdom, see S. and H., p. 51 f.

CHAPTER II.—Vers. 1-16. The Apostle
has now to prove that the righteousness
of God is as necessary to the Jew as to
the pagan ; it is the Jew who is really
addressed in this chapter from the beginning, though he is not named till
ver. 9. In vers. 1-10 Paul explains
the principle on which God judges all
men, without distinction.

Ver. 1. διό : The Jew is ready enough
to judge the Gentile. But he forgets
that the same principle on which the
Gentile is condemned, viz., that he does
evil in spite of better knowledge (i. 32),
condemns himself also. His very assent
to the impeachment in chap. i. 18-32 is
his own condemnation. This is the force
of διό : therefore. ἐν ᾧ = in that in which.
τὰ αὐτὰ πράσσεις, not, you do the
identical actions, but your conduct is
the same, i.e., you sin against light.

The sin of the Jews was the same, but
their sins were not.

Ver. 2. κατὰ ἀλήθειαν is predicate :
God's judgment squares with the facts—
this is the whole rule of it. τοὺς τὰ
τοιαῦτα πράσσοντας : those whose conduct is such as has been described. For
the text, see critical note.

Ver. 3. σὺ has strong emphasis. The
Jew certainly thought, in many cases,
that the privilege of his birth would of
itself ensure his entrance into the kingdom (Mt. iii. 8, 9) : this was his practical
conviction, whatever be his proper
creed. Yet the σὺ indicates that of all
men the Jew, so distinguished by special
revelation, should least have fallen into
such an error. He is " the servant who
knew his Lord's will," and whose judgment will be most rigorous if it is
neglected.

Ver. 4. ἢ states the alternative. Either
he thinks he will escape, or he despises,
etc. χρηστότης is the kindliness which
disposes one to do good ; ἀνοχὴ (in N.T.
only here and in iii. 26) is the forbearance
which suspends punishment ; μακροθυμία
is patience, which waits long before it
actively interposes. τὸ χρηστὸν τοῦ
Θεοῦ summarises all three in the concrete. It amounts to contempt of God's
goodness if a man does not know (rather,
ignores : cf. Acts xiii. 27, 1 Cor. xiv. 38,
Rom. x. 3) that its end is, not to approve
of his sins, but to lead him to repentance.

Ver. 5. The δὲ contrasts what happens
with what God designs. θησαυρίζεις
σεαυτῷ ὀργήν : contrast our Lord's many
sayings about " treasure in heaven " (Mt.
vi. 19 ff., xix. 21). ἐν ἡμέρᾳ ὀργῆς = in
the day of wrath. The conception was
quite definite : there was only one day
in view, what is elsewhere called " the
day of the Lord " (2 Cor. i. 14), " the

^{d Here only.} ἀποκαλύψεως ^dδικαιοκρισίας τοῦ Θεοῦ, 6. ὃς ἀποδώσει ἑκάστῳ κατὰ

τὰ ἔργα αὐτοῦ · 7. τοῖς μὲν καθ' ὑπομονὴν ἔργου ἀγαθοῦ δόξαν καὶ

^{e I Cor. xv. 42; 2 Tim.} τιμὴν καὶ ^eἀφθαρσίαν ζητοῦσι, ζωὴν αἰώνιον · 8. τοῖς δὲ ἐξ ^fἐριθείας,

^{i. 10. f Phil. ii. 3;} καὶ ἀπειθοῦσι μὲν ¹ τῇ ἀληθείᾳ, πειθομένοις δὲ τῇ ἀδικίᾳ, θυμὸς καὶ

^{Jas. iii. 14, 16.} ὀργή, 9. θλίψις καὶ στενοχωρία, ἐπὶ πᾶσαν ψυχὴν ἀνθρώπου τοῦ

κατεργαζομένου τὸ κακόν, Ἰουδαίου τε πρῶτον καὶ Ἕλληνος · 10.

δόξα δὲ καὶ τιμὴ καὶ εἰρήνη παντὶ τῷ ἐργαζομένῳ τὸ ἀγαθὸν,

¹ απειθουσι μεν AD³KLN³; om. μεν א¹BDG¹.

day of judgment" (Mt. xi. 22), "the last day" (John vi. 39), "the day of God" (2 Pet. iii. 12), "that day" (2 Tim. i. 12), even simply "the day" (1 Cor. iii. 13, Heb. x. 25). This great day is so defined in the Apostle's imagination that the article can be dispensed with. But see Ps. cx. 5. (cix. LXX.) It is a day when God is revealed as a righteous judge, in the sense of Psalm lxi. 13 (LXX).

Ver. 6. The law enunciated in the Psalm, that God will render to every one according to his works, is valid within the sphere of redemption as well as independent of it. Paul the Christian recognises its validity as unreservedly as Saul the Pharisee would have done. The application of it may lead to very different results in the two cases, but the universal moral conscience, be it in bondage to evil, or emancipated by Christ, accepts it without demur. Paul had no feeling that it contradicted his doctrine of justification by faith, and therefore we are safe to assert that it did not contradict it. It seems a mistake to argue with Weiss that Paul is here speaking of the *Urnorm* of the Divine righteousness, *i.e.*, of the way in which the destiny of men would be determined *if there were no Gospel*. The Gospel does not mean that God denies Himself; He acts in it according to His eternal nature; and though Paul is speaking to men as under the law, the truth which he is insisting upon is one which is equally true whether men are under the law or under grace. It is not a little piece of the leaven of a Jewish or Pharisaic conception of God, not yet purged out, that is found here; but an eternal law of God's relation to man.

Ver. 7. καθ' ὑπομονὴν ἔργου ἀγαθοῦ: *cf.* the collective ἔργον—"life-work": S. and H.—in ver. 15: "by way of stedfastness in well-doing". δόξαν = the glory of the future life, as revealed in the Risen Saviour. τιμήν = honour with

God. ἀφθαρσίαν "proves that the goal of effort is nothing earthly" (Lipsius). ζωὴ αἰώνιος comprehends all these three: as its counterpart, θάνατος in ver. 31, involves the loss of all. ζωὴν is governed by ἀποδώσει.

Ver. 8. τοῖς δὲ ἐξ ἐριθείας: for the use of ἐκ, *cf.* iii. 26, τὸν ἐκ πίστεως Ἰησοῦ; Gal. iii. 7, οἱ ἐκ πίστεως; Ch. iv. 14, οἱ ἐκ νόμου. Lightfoot suggests that it is better to supply πράσσουσιν, and to construe ἐξ ἐριθείας with the participle, as in Phil. i. 17 it is construed with καταγγέλλουσιν: but it is simpler not to supply anything. By "those who are of faction" or "factiousness" (Gal. v. 20, 2 Cor. xii. 20, Phil. i. 16 f., ii. 3, Jas. iii. 14, 16) the Apostle probably means men of a self-willed temper, using all arts to assert themselves against God. The result of this temper—the temper of the party man carried into the spiritual world—is seen in disobedience to the truth and obedience to unrighteousness. See note on ἀλήθεια, i. 18. The moral import of the word is shown by its use as the counterpart of ἀδικία. *Cf.* the same contrast in 1 Cor. xiii. 6. To those who pursue this course there accrues indignation and wrath, etc.

Ver. 9. ὀργὴ is wrath within; θυμός wrath as it overflows. θλίψις and στενοχωρία, according to Trench, *Synonyms*, § 55, express very nearly the same thing, under different images: the former taking the image of pressure, the latter that of confinement in a narrow space. But to draw a distinction between them, based on etymology, would be very misleading. In both pairs of words the same idea is expressed, only intensified by the reduplication. Supply ἔσται for the changed construction. κατεργαζομένου τὸ κακόν: who works at evil and works it out or accomplishes it. The Jew is put first, because as possessor of an express law this is conspicuously true of him.

Ver. 10 f. εἰρήνη is probably =

Ἰουδαίῳ τε πρῶτον καὶ Ἕλληνι· 11. οὐ γάρ ἐστι προσωποληψία παρὰ τῷ Θεῷ. 12. ὅσοι γὰρ ἀνόμως ἥμαρτον, ἀνόμως καὶ ἀπολοῦνται· καὶ ὅσοι ἐν νόμῳ ἥμαρτον, διὰ νόμου κριθήσονται, 13. (οὐ γὰρ οἱ ᵍἀκροαταὶ τοῦ νόμου ¹ δίκαιοι παρὰ τῷ Θεῷ, ἀλλ᾽ οἱ ποιηταὶ τοῦ νόμου δικαιωθήσονται. 14. Ὅταν γὰρ ἔθνη τὰ μὴ νόμον ἔχοντα ʰ φύσει τὰ τοῦ νόμου ποιῇ,² οὗτοι νόμον μὴ ἔχοντες ἑαυτοῖς εἰσι νόμος· 15. οἵτινες ἐνδείκνυνται τὸ ἔργον τοῦ νόμου ⁱγραπτὸν ἐν ταῖς καρδίαις αὐτῶν, συμμαρτυρούσης αὐτῶν τῆς συνειδήσεως, καὶ μεταξὺ ἀλλήλων

g Jas. i. 22 f., 25, iv. 11.

h Gal. ii. 15, iv. 8; Eph. ii. 3.

i Here only in N.T.

¹ ἀκροαται του νομου KL 17, other cursives, Marcion ; om. του ℵABDG. παρα τῳ θεῳ ℵAD³GKL ; om. τῳ BD¹. W. and H. bracket τῳ. ποιηται του νομου D³KL 17, other cursives, Marcion ; om. του ℵABD¹G.

² For ποιη D² (a grammatical correction) ποιωσιν is found in ℵAB.

שָׁלוֹם, a comprehensive term, rather = salvation, than peace in any narrower sense. The Jew still comes first, but it is only order that is involved: the same principle underlies the judgment for Jew and Gentile. It would amount to προσωπολημψία in God, if He made a difference in the Jew's favour because of his birth, or because he possessed the law. This is expanded in vers. 12-16: mere possession of the law does not count. Men are judged according to their works, whether they have or have not had such a special revelation of the Divine will as was given to Israel.

Ver. 12. ἀνόμως means "without law," not necessarily "without the law". In point of fact, no doubt, there was only one law given by God, the Mosaic, and Paul is arguing against those who imagined that the mere possession of it put them in a position of privilege as compared with those to whom it was not given ; but he expresses himself with a generality which would meet the case of more such revelations of God's will having been made to man. As many as sin "without law" shall also perish "without law". Sin and perdition are correlative in Paul. ἀπώλεια (ix. 22, Phil. i. 28, iii. 19) answers to ζωὴ αἰώνιος : it is final exclusion from the blessedness implied in this expression; having no part in the kingdom of God. Similarly, as many as sin "in law" shall be judged "by law". The expression would cover any law, whatever it might be ; really, the Mosaic law is the only one that has to be dealt with. The use of the aorist ἥμαρτον is difficult. Weiss says it is used as though the writer were looking back from the judgment day, when sin is simply past.

Burton compares iii. 23 and calls it a "collective historical aorist" : in either case the English idiom requires the perfect : " all who have sinned ".

Ver. 13. This is the principle of judgment, for not the hearers of law (the Mosaic or any other) are just with God, but the law doers shall be justified. ἀκροαταὶ tends to mean " pupils," constant hearers, who are educated in the law: see ver. 18. But no degree of familiarity with the law avails if it is not done. The forensic sense of δικαιοῦσθαι is apparent in this verse, where it is synonymous with δίκαιοι εἶναι παρὰ τῷ θεῷ : the latter obviously being the opposite of " to be condemned ". Whether there are persons who perfectly keep the law, is a question not raised here. The futures ἀπολοῦνται, κριθήσονται, δικαιωθήσονται all refer to the day of final judgment.

Ver. 14. There is, indeed, when we look closely, no such thing as a man absolutely without the knowledge of God's will, and therefore such a judgment as the Apostle has described is legitimate. Gentiles, " such as have not law " in any special shape, when they do by nature " the things of the law "—i.e., the things required by the law given to Israel, the only one known to the Apostle —are in spite of not having law (as is the supposition here) a law to themselves. ἔθνη is not " the Gentiles," but " Gentiles as such "—persons who can be characterised as " without law ". The supposition made in τὰ μὴ νόμον ἔχοντα is that of the Jews ; and the Apostle's argument is designed to show that though formally, it is not substantially true.

Ver. 15. οἵτινες ἐνδείκνυνται: the relative is qualitative : " inasmuch as

τῶν λογισμῶν κατηγορούντων ἢ καὶ ἀπολογουμένων,) 16. ἐν ἡμέρᾳ
k Ch. xvi 25; ὅτε ¹ κρινεῖ ὁ Θεὸς τὰ κρυπτὰ τῶν ἀνθρώπων, κατὰ τὸ εὐαγγέλιόν ᵏ μου,
2 Tim. ii. 8. διὰ Ἰησοῦ Χριστοῦ.

¹ ἐν ἡμέρᾳ οτε ℵDGKL, vulg., Syr. ἐν ῃ ημερᾳ B (this is one of the cases in
which W. and H. suppose that B unsupported has preserved the true reading,
though they give a place in their margin both to ἐν ημερᾳ οτε and to ἐν ημερᾳ ῃ,
which is found in A and the Memph. (Egyptian) version).

they shew". τὸ ἔργον τοῦ νόμου is the work which the law prescribes, collectively. "Written on their hearts," when contrasted with the law written on the tables of stone, is equal to "unwritten"; the Apostle refers to what the Greeks called ἄγραφος νόμος. To the Greeks, however, this was something greater and more sacred than any statute, or civil constitution; to the Apostle it was less than the great revelation of God's will, which had been made and interpreted to Israel, but nevertheless a true moral authority. There is a triple proof that Gentiles, who are regarded as not having law, are a law to themselves. (1) The appeal to their conduct: as interpreted by the Apostle, their conduct evinces, at least in some, the possession of a law written on the heart; (2) the action of conscience: it joins its testimony, though it be only an inward one, to the outward testimony borne by their conduct; and (3) their thoughts. Their thoughts bear witness to the existence of a law in them, inasmuch as in their mutual intercourse (μεταξὺ ἀλλήλων) these thoughts are busy bringing accusations, or in rarer cases (ἢ καί) putting forward defences, i.e., in any case, exercising moral functions which imply the recognition of a law. This seems to me the only simple and natural explanation of a rather perplexed phrase. We need not ask for what Paul does not give, the object to κατηγορούντων or ἀπολογουμένων: it may be any person, act or situation, which calls into exercise that power of moral judgment which shows that the Gentiles, though without the law of Moses, are not in a condition which makes it impossible to judge them according to their works. The construction in ix. 1 suggests that the συν views the witness of conscience, reflecting on conduct, as something added to the first instinctive consciousness of the nature of an action. συνείδησις does not occur in the Gospels except in John viii. 9; twice only in Acts, xxiii. 1, xxiv. 16, both times in speeches of St. Paul; twenty times in the Pauline epistles. It

occurs in the O.T. only in Ecc. x. 20 (curse not the King, ἐν συνειδήσει σου = ne in cogitatione quidem tua): the ordinary sense is found, for the first time in Biblical Greek, in Sap. xvii. 11. It is a quasi-philosophical word, much used by the Stoics, and belonging rather to the Greek than the Hebrew inheritance of Paul.

Ver. 16. The day meant here is the same as that in ver. 5. Westcott and Hort only put a comma after ἀπολογουμένων, but a longer pause is necessary, unless we are to suppose that only the day of judgment wakes the conscience and the thoughts of man into the moral activity described in ver. 15. This supposition may have some truth in it, but it is not what the Apostle's argument requires. The proof he gives that Gentiles are "a law to themselves" must be capable of verification now, not only at the last day. Hence ver. 16 is really to be taken with the main verbs of the whole paragraph, ἀπολοῦνται, κριθήσονται, δικαιωθήσονται: the great principle of ver. 6—ἀποδώσει ἑκάστῳ κατὰ τὰ ἔργα αὐτοῦ—will be exhibited in action on the day on which God judges the secret things of men through Christ Jesus. A final judgment belonged to Jewish theology, and perhaps, though this is open to question, one in which the Messiah acted as God's representative; but what Paul teaches here does not rest merely on the transference of a Jewish Messianic function to Jesus. If there is anything certain in the N.T. it is that this representation of Jesus as judge of the world rests on the words of our Lord Himself (Mt. vii. 22 f., xxv. 31 ff.). To assert it was an essential part of the Gospel as preached by Paul: cf. Acts xvii. 31. (Baldensperger, *Das Selbstbewusstsein Jesu*, S. 85 f., thinks that in the circles of Jewish Pietism, in the century before Christ, the Messiah was already spoken of as the Divine judge, and as sharing the titles and attributes of Jehovah.)

In vers. 17-24 the Apostle brings to a point the argument for which he has been clearing the way in vers. 1-16.

17. Ἴδε[1] σὺ Ἰουδαῖος [1]ἐπονομάζῃ, καὶ ἐπαναπαύῃ τῷ νόμῳ, καὶ [1] Here only in N.T.

καυχᾶσαι ἐν Θεῷ, 18. καὶ γινώσκεις τὸ θέλημα, καὶ δοκιμάζεις τὰ

[m] διαφέροντα, [n] κατηχούμενος ἐκ τοῦ νόμου · 19. πέποιθάς τε σεαυτὸν [m] Phil. i. 10.
[n] 1 Cor. xiv.

ὁδηγὸν εἶναι τυφλῶν, φῶς τῶν ἐν σκότει, 20. [o]παιδευτὴν ἀφρόνων, [19.]

διδάσκαλον νηπίων, ἔχοντα τὴν μόρφωσιν τῆς γνώσεως καὶ τῆς [o] Heb. xii. 9.

---

[1] ει δε ℵABD[1]K ; ιδε D[3]L Syr.   ει δε has probably been changed into ιδε (Alford) to avoid the anacoluthon.   επαναπαυη τω νομω D[3]KL 17 ; om. τω ℵABD[1].

The Jew makes much of the possession of the law, but when we pass from possession to practice, he is not a whit better than the " lawless " Gentile. The construction is not quite regular, but the meaning is clear. The natural order would be : If thou bearest the name of Jew, and restest upon the law, *and yet in thy conduct settest the law at nought*, art not thou equally under condemnation with sinners of the Gentiles ? But the construction is interrupted at the end of ver. 20, and what ought in logic to be part of the protasis—*if in thy conduct thou settest the law at nought*—is made a sort of apodosis, at least grammatically and rhetorically : *dost thou, in spite of all these privileges, nevertheless set the law at nought ?* The real conclusion, which Paul needs for his argument, Art not thou then in the same condemnation with the Gentiles ? is left for conscience to supply.

Ver. 17. Ἰουδαῖος ἐπονομάζῃ : bearest the name of " Jew ". The ἐπὶ in the compound verb does not denote addition, but direction : Ἰουδαῖος is not conceived as a surname, but a name which has been imposed. Of course it is implied in the context that the name is an honourable one. It is not found in the LXX, and in other places where Paul wishes to indicate the same distinction, and the same pride in it, he says Ἰσραηλεῖται (ix. 4, 2 Cor. xi. 22). The terms must have had a tendency to coalesce in import, though Ἰουδαῖος is national, and Ἰσραηλείτης religious ; for the religion was national. ἐπαναπαύῃ νόμῳ : grammatically νόμῳ is law ; really, it is the Mosaic law. The Jew said, We have a law, and the mere possession of it gave him confidence. *Cf.* Mic. iii. 11, ἐπὶ τὸν Κύριον ἐπανεπαύοντο. καυχᾶσαι ἐν θεῷ : boastest in God, as the covenant God of the Jews, who are His peculiar people. καυχᾶσαι = καυχᾷ : the longer form is the usual one in the κοινή.

Ver. 18. τὸ θέλημα is God's will. Lipsius compares the absolute use of ὁδός, θύρα and ὄνομα. *Cf.* Acts ix. 2, xix. 9, 23, xiv. 27, v. 41. Also 1 Cor. xvi. 12, where God's will is meant, not the will of Apollos. The words δοκιμάζεις τὰ διαφέροντα κατηχούμενος ἐκ τοῦ νόμου are to be taken together. In virtue of being taught out of the law (in the synagogue and the schools) the Jew possesses moral discernment : he does not sink to the νοῦς ἀδόκιμος, the mind which has lost all moral capacity (i. 28). But a certain ambiguity remains in δοκιμάζειν τὰ διαφέροντα : it may mean either (1) to distinguish, by testing, between things which differ—*i.e.*, to discriminate experimentally between good and evil ; or (2) to approve, after testing, the things which are more excellent. There are no grounds on which we can decide positively for either.

Ver. 19 f. πέποιθάς τε κ.τ.λ. The τε indicates that this confidence is the immediate and natural result of what precedes : it is not right, in view of all the N.T. examples, to say that πέποιθας suggests an unjustifiable confidence, though in some cases, as in the present, it is so. *Cf.* 2 Cor. x. 7, Lk. xviii. 9. The blind, those in darkness, the foolish, the babes, are all names for the heathen : the Jew is confident that the Gentiles must come to school to him. παιδευτὴς has reference to moral as well as intellectual discipline : and ἄφρονες are, as in the O.T. (Ps. xiii. 1, LXX), persons without moral intelligence. For the other figures in this verse, *cf.* Mt. xv. 14, Is. xlix. 6, 9, xlii. 6. The confidence of the Jew is based on the fact that he possesses in the law " the outline of knowledge and truth ". Lipsius puts a strong sense upon μόρφωσιν—die leibhaftige Verkörperung : as if the Jew conceived that in the Mosaic law the knowledge and the truth of God were incorporated bodily. Possibly he did, and in a sense it was so, for the Mosaic law was a true revelation of God and His will : but the only other instance of μόρφωσις in the N.T. (2 Tim. iii. 5 :

ἀληθείας ἐν τῷ νόμῳ. 21. ὁ οὖν διδάσκων ἕτερον, σεαυτὸν οὐ
διδάσκεις; ὁ κηρύσσων μὴ κλέπτειν, κλέπτεις; 22. ὁ λέγων μὴ
μοιχεύειν, μοιχεύεις; ὁ βδελυσσόμενος τὰ εἴδωλα, ἱεροσυλεῖς; 23.
ὃς ἐν νόμῳ καυχᾶσαι, διὰ τῆς παραβάσεως τοῦ νόμου τὸν Θεὸν
ἀτιμάζεις; 24. "τὸ γὰρ ὄνομα τοῦ Θεοῦ δι' ὑμᾶς βλασφημεῖται
ἐν τοῖς ἔθνεσι," καθὼς ᵖ γέγραπται. 25. Περιτομὴ μὲν γὰρ ὠφελεῖ,
ἐὰν νόμον πράσσῃς· ἐὰν δὲ παραβάτης νόμου ᾖς, ἡ περιτομή σου

p Is. lii. 5.

ἔχοντες μόρφωσιν εὐσεβείας) rather suggests the same disparaging note which here belongs to πέποιθας. The μόρφωσις τῆς γνώσεως is in point of fact only a form: valuable as the outline or definition of truth was, which the Jew possessed in the law, it was in reality ineffective, so far as the practical authority of the law in the Jew's conduct was concerned.

Ver. 21. Here the grammatical apodosis begins, the οὖν resuming all that has been said in vers. 17-20. κηρύσσων and λέγων are virtually verbs of command: hence the infinitives. The rhetorical question implies that the Jew does *not* teach himself, and that he *does* break the law he would enforce on others.

Ver. 22. βδελυσσόμενος properly expresses physical repulsion: thou that shrinkest in horror from idols. *Cf.* Dan. ix. 27, Mk. xiii. 14. ἱεροσυλεῖς: dost thou rob temples, and so, for the sake of gain, come in contact with abominations without misgiving? This is the meaning, and not, Dost thou rob the temple, by keeping back the temple dues? as has been suggested. The crime of ἱεροσυλία is referred to in Acts xix. 37, and according to Josephus, *Ant.*, iv., 8, 10, it was expressly forbidden to the Jews: μὴ συλᾶν ἱερὰ ξενικά, μηδ' ἂν ἐπωνομασμένον ᾖ τινὶ θεῷ κειμήλιον λαμβάνειν.

Ver. 23. Here again the construction is changed, and probably the use of the relative instead of the participle suggests that the sentence is to be read, not as interrogative, but as declaratory. "Thou who makest it thy boast that thou possessest a law, by the transgressing of that law dishonourest God: that is the sum of the whole matter, and thy sole distinction in contrast with the heathen."

Ver. 24. And this is only what Scripture bids us expect. The Scripture quoted is Is. lii. 5, LXX. The LXX interpret the Hebrew by inserting δι' ὑμᾶς and ἐν τοῖς ἔθνεσιν. Both insertions are in the line of the original

meaning. It was owing to the misery and helplessness of the people of God, in exile among the nations, that the heathen scoffed at the Divine name. " The God of Israel is not able to deliver His people : He is no God." Paul here gives the words quite another turn. God, he says, is now blasphemed among the nations because of the inconsistency between the pretensions of the Jews and their behaviour. As if the heathen were saying : " Like God, like people ; what a Divinity the patron of this odious race must be ". It is surely not right to argue (with Sanday and Headlam) that the throwing of the formula of quotation to the end shows that Paul is conscious of quoting freely : " it is almost as if it were an after-thought that the language he has just used is a quotation at all ". The quotation is as relevant as most that the Apostle uses. He never cares for the context or the original application. When he can express himself in Scripture language he feels that he has the Word of God on his side, and all through this epistle he nails his arguments so, and insists on the confirmation they thus obtain. What the closing of the sentence with καθὼς γέγραπται suggests is not that it occurred to Paul after he had finished that he had almost unconsciously been using Scripture: it is rather that there is a challenge in the words, as if he had said, Let him impugn this who dare contest the Word of God.

In vers. 25-29 another Jewish plea for preferential treatment in the judgment is considered. The μὲν in ver. 25 (περιτομὴ μὲν γὰρ ὠφελεῖ) implies that this plea has no doubt something in it, but it suggests that there are considerations on the other side which in point of fact make it inapplicable or invalid here. It is these considerations which the Apostle proceeds to explain, with a view to clenching the argument that the wrath of God revealed from heaven impends over Jew and Gentile alike.

Ver. 25. περιτομή : the absence of the article suggests that the argument may

ἀκροβυστία γέγονεν. 26. ἐὰν οὖν ἡ ἀκροβυστία τὰ δικαιώματα τοῦ
νόμου φυλάσσῃ, οὐχὶ ἡ ἀκροβυστία αὐτοῦ εἰς περιτομὴν λογισθήσεται; 27. καὶ κρινεῖ ἡ ἐκ φύσεως ἀκροβυστία τὸν νόμον q τελοῦσα q Jas. ii. 8.
σὲ τὸν r διὰ γράμματος καὶ περιτομῆς παραβάτην νόμου. 28. οὐ γὰρ r Ch. iv. 11,
ὁ ἐν τῷ φανερῷ Ἰουδαῖός ἐστιν, οὐδὲ ἡ ἐν τῷ φανερῷ ἐν σαρκὶ xiv. 20.
περιτομή· 29. ἀλλ' ὁ ἐν τῷ κρυπτῷ Ἰουδαῖος, καὶ περιτομὴ καρδίας
ἐν πνεύματι, οὐ γράμματι. οὗ ὁ s ἔπαινος οὐκ ἐξ ἀνθρώπων, ἀλλ' ἐκ s 1 Cor. iv. 5.

be extended to everything of the same
character as circumcision. ὠφελεῖ: Circumcision was the seal of the covenant,
and as such an assurance given to the
circumcised man that he belonged to the
race which was the heir of God's promises. That was undeniably a great
advantage, just as it is an advantage
now to be born a Christian; but if the
actual inheriting of the promises has any
moral conditions attached to it (as
Paul proceeds to show that it has), then
the advantage of circumcision lapses unless these are fulfilled. Now the persons
contemplated here have not fulfilled
them. ἐὰν νόμον πράσσῃς: the habitual
practice of the law is involved in this expression: as Vaughan says, it is almost
like a compound word, "if thou be a law
doer". Similarly παραβάτης νόμου a
law-transgressor. The law, of course,
is the Mosaic one, but it is regarded
simply in its character as law, not as
being definitely this law: hence the absence of the article. γέγονε: by the
very fact becomes and remains.

Ver. 26 f. Here the inference is drawn
from the principle laid down in ver. 25.
This being so, Paul argues, if the uncircumcision maintain the just requirements of the law, shall not his uncircumcision be accounted circumcision, sc.,
because it has really done what circumcision pledged the Jew to do? Cf. Gal.
v. 3. ἡ ἀκροβυστία at the beginning of
the verse is equivalent to the Gentiles
(ἔθνη of ver. 14), the abstract being put
for the concrete: in ἡ ἀκροβυστία αὐτοῦ,
the αὐτοῦ individualises a person who is
conceived as keeping the law, though
not circumcised. As he has done what
circumcision bound the Jew to do, he
will be treated as if in the Jew's position:
his uncircumcision will be reckoned as
circumcision. λογισθήσεται may be
merely a logical future, but like the
other futures in vers. 12-16 it is probably more correct to refer it to what
will take place at the last judgment. The
order of the words in ver. 27 indicates
that the question is not continued: "and

thus the uncircumcision shall judge thee,"
etc. κρινεῖ is emphatic by position: the
Jew, in the case supposed, is so far from
being able to assert a superiority to the
Gentile that the Gentile himself will be
his condemnation. Cf. Mt. xii. 41 f.
ἡ ἐκ φύσεως ἀκροβυστία should properly
convey one idea—"those who are by
nature uncircumcised". But why
should nature be mentioned at all in this
connection? It seems arbitrary to say
with Hofmann that it is referred to in
order to suggest that uncircumcision is
what the Gentile is born in, and therefore involves no guilt. As far as that
goes, Jew and Gentile are alike. Hence
in spite of the grammatical irregularity,
which in any case is not too great for a
nervous writer like Paul, I prefer to
connect ἐκ φύσεως, as Burton does
(Moods and Tenses, § 427), with τελοῦσα,
and to render: "the uncircumcision
which by nature fulfils the law": cf.
ver. 14. τὸν διὰ γράμματος καὶ περιτομῆς παραβάτην νόμου. The διὰ is
that which describes the circumstances
under which, or the accompaniment to
which, anything is done. The Jew is a
law-transgressor, in spite of the facts
that he possesses a written revelation of
God's will, and bears the seal of the
covenant, obliging him to the performance of the law, upon his body. He
has an outward standard, which does not
vary with his moral condition, like the
law written in the pagan's heart; he has
an outward pledge that he belongs to the
people of God, to encourage him when he
is tempted to indolence or despair; in
both these respects he has an immense
advantage over the Gentile, yet both are
neutralised by this—he is a law-transgressor.

Ver. 28 f. The argument of the foregoing verses assumes what is stated
here, and what no one will dispute, that
what constitutes the Jew in the true
sense of the term, and gives the name
of Jew its proper content and dignity, is
not anything outward and visible, but
something inward and spiritual. And

τοῦ Θεοῦ. III. 1. Τί οὖν τὸ περισσὸν τοῦ Ἰουδαίου, ἢ τίς ἡ ὠφέλεια τῆς περιτομῆς; 2. πολὺ, κατὰ πάντα τρόπον. πρῶτον μὲν γὰρ [1] ὅτι

[1] γὰρ om. BD¹G vulg.; ins. אAD³KL Syr. It is bracketed by Westcott and Hort, omitted by Lachmann and Tregelles, inserted by Tischdf.

the same remark applies to circumcision itself. The most natural way to read the Greek seems to me to be this. " Not he who is so outwardly (ὁ ἐν τῷ φανερῷ) is a Jew (in the true sense), nor is that which is outward, in flesh, the true circumcision; but he who is inwardly a Jew (is the true Jew), and heart circumcision, in spirit, not in letter (is the true circumcision)." Thus in the first pair of clauses there is not anything, strictly speaking, to be supplied; the subject is in each case involved in the article. But in the second pair the predicate has in both cases to be supplied from the first— in the one case, Ἰουδαῖος ; in the other, περιτομή. Heart circumcision is an idea already familiar to the O.T. From the Book of Deuteronomy (x. 16, for the meaning comp. xxx. 6) it passed to the prophetic writings : Jer. iv. 4. The contrary expression—uncircumcised in heart and in flesh—is also found: Jer. ix. 26, Ez. xliv. 7. A difficulty is created by the expression ἐν πνεύματι οὐ γράμματι. After ver. 28 we rather expect ἐν πνεύματι οὐ σαρκί: the circumcision being conceived as in one and not another part of man's nature. Practically it is in this sense most commentators take the words : thus Gifford explains them by " a circumcision which does not stop short at outward conformity to the law, but extends to the sphere of the inner life ". But there is no real correspondence here, such as there is in ἐν πνεύματι οὐ σαρκί ; and a comparison of 2 Cor. iii., a chapter pervaded by the contrast of πνεῦμα and γράμμα, suggests a different rendering. πνεῦμα and γράμμα are not the elements in which, but the powers by which, the circumcision is conceived to be effected. " Heart circumcision," without any qualifying words, expresses completely that contrast to circumcision in the flesh, which is in Paul's mind ; and what he adds in the new words, ἐν πνεύματι οὐ γράμματι is the new idea that heart circumcision, which alone deserves the name of circumcision, is achieved by the Spirit of God, not by the written law. Whether there is such a thing as this heart circumcision, wrought by the Spirit, among the Jews, is not explicitly considered ; but it is not

a refutation of this interpretation to point out that πνεῦμα in 2 Cor. is characteristically the gift of the New Covenant. For the very conclusion to which Paul wishes to lead is that the New Covenant is as necessary for the Jew as for the Gentile. οὗ ὁ ἔπαινος κ.τ.λ. The οὗ is masculine, and refers to the ideal Jew. The name Ἰουδαῖος (from Judah = praise, Gen. xxix. 35) probably suggested this remark. οὐκ ἐξ ἀνθρώπων : the love of praise from each other, and religious vanity, are Jewish characteristics strongly commented on by our Lord (John v. 44, xii. 42 f.).

CHAPTER III.—Vers. 1-8. It might easily seem, at this point, as if the Apostle's argument had proved too much. He has shown that the mere possession of the law does not exempt the Jew from judgment, but that God requires its fulfilment ; he has shown that circumcision in the flesh, seal though it be of the covenant and pledge of its promises, is only of value if it represent inward heart circumcision ; he has, it may be argued, reduced the Jew to a position of entire equality with the Gentile. But the consciousness of the Jewish race must protest against such a conclusion. " Salvation is of the Jews " is a word of Christ Himself, and the Apostle is obliged to meet this instinctive protest of the ancient people of God. The whole of the difficulties it raises are more elaborately considered in chaps. ix.-xi. ; here it is only discussed so far as to make plain that it does not invalidate the arguments of chap. ii., nor bar the development of the Apostle's theology. The advantage of the Jew is admitted ; it is admitted that his unbelief may even act as a foil to God's faithfulness, setting it in more glorious relief ; but it is insisted, that if God's character as righteous judge of the world is to be maintained—as it must be —these admissions do not exempt the Jew from that liability to judgment which has just been demonstrated. The details of the interpretation, especially in ver. 7 f., are somewhat perplexed.

Ver. 1 f. τὸ περισσὸν τοῦ Ἰουδαίου is that which the Jew has " over and above " the Gentile. τίς ἡ ὠφέλεια τῆς

ἐπιστεύθησαν τὰ ᵃλόγια τοῦ Θεοῦ.   3. τί γάρ, εἰ ἠπίστησάν τινες ; a Acts vii.
μὴ ἡ ἀπιστία αὐτῶν τὴν πίστιν τοῦ Θεοῦ καταργήσει ;   4. μὴ γένοιτο ·   48; Heb. v. 12; 1
γινέσθω δὲ ὁ Θεὸς ἀληθής, πᾶς δὲ ἄνθρωπος ψεύστης, καθὼς¹ γέγραπ-   Pet. iv.11.
ται, "Ὅπως ἂν δικαιωθῇς ἐν τοῖς λόγοις σου, καὶ νικήσῃς ἐν τῷ

¹ For **καθὼς** ℵB read **καθαπερ**.   **νικησῃς** BGKL, etc., **νικησεις** ℵADE.   For the distribution of authorities here, see note on **πρωτον**, page 589, note². The combination of B with such later Western authorities as G here also lessens its weight ; its reading is probably part of that Western element which it contains, i.e., B and G here represent practically one authority.   But the other group of MSS. represents at least two groups of witnesses, the "neutral" in ℵA, and the Western in D, and its reading is therefore to be preferred.   Weiss, however (*Textkritik der paulinischen Briefe*, S. 46), would reject the indicative both here and in 2 Cor. xii. 21.   The change of **εἰ** and **η** he regards as accidental ; in KLP it occurs some sixty times.

περιτομῆς ; = "What good does his circumcision do him ? " **πολὺ** goes with **τὸ περισσόν**. **κατὰ πάντα τρόπον** : however you choose to view the position. **πρῶτον μὲν** suggests that such an enumeration of Jewish prerogatives might have been made here as is given at length in ix. 4 f. In point of fact, Paul mentions one only, in which the whole force of the Jewish objection to the arguments of chap. ii. is contained, and after disposing of it feels that he has settled the question, and passes on. The first, most weighty, and most far-reaching advantage of the Jews, is that "they were entrusted with the oracles of God". They were made in His grace the depositaries and guardians of revelation. **τὰ λόγια τοῦ θεοῦ** must be regarded as the contents of revelation, having God as their author, and at the time when Paul wrote, identical with the O.T. Scriptures. In the LXX the word **λόγιον** occurs mainly as the equivalent of אִמְרָה, which in various passages (e.g., Ps. cxix. 38) has the sense of "promise" ; in ordinary Greek it means "oracle," the Divine word given at a shrine, and usually referring to the future ; hence it would be natural in using it to think of the prophetic rather than the statutory element in the O.T., and this is what is required here. The O.T. as a whole, and as a revelation of God, has a forward look ; it anticipates completion and excites hope ; and it is not too much to say that this is suggested by describing it as **τὰ λόγια τοῦ θεοῦ**. The sum of it was that God had promised to His people "a future and a hope" (Jer. xxix. 11 : see margin, R.V.), and this promise seemed threatened by the argument of the last chapter.

Ver. 3 f. **τί γάρ;** For how ? i.e.,

Well then, how stands the case ? *Cf.* Phil. i. 18. **εἰ ἠπίστησάν τινες** = if some *did* disbelieve. It is not necessary to render this, with reference to **ἐπιστεύθησαν** in ver. 2, "if some proved faithless to their trust". What is in Paul's mind is that "the oracles of God" have had their fulfilment in Christ, and that those to whom they were entrusted have in some cases (whether few or many he does not here consider) refused their faith to that fulfilment. Surely it is no proper inference that their unbelief must make God's faithfulness of no effect. *He* has kept His promise, and as far as it lay with Him has maintained the original advantage of the Jews, as depositaries and first inheritors of that promise, whatever reception they may have given to its fulfilment. Away with the thought of any reflection upon Him ! When the case is stated between God and man there can only be one conclusion : let God come out (**γινέσθω**) true, and every man a liar ; let Him be just, and every man condemned. This agrees with the words of Scripture itself in Ps. li. (l.) 6, which Paul quotes exactly after the LXX : the Hebrew is distinctly different, but neither it nor the original context are regarded. **ἐν τοῖς λόγοις σου** is a translation of Hebrew words which mean "when Thou speakest," i.e., apparently, when Thou pronouncest sentence upon man ; here the sense must be, "that Thou mayest be pronounced just in respect of what Thou hast spoken," i.e., the **λόγια**, the oracles or promises entrusted to Israel. **νικήσεις** : win thy case (see note on text). Burton, *Moods and Tenses*, §§ 198, 199. **ἐν τῷ κρίνεσθαί σε** : Probably the infinitive is passive: "when thou art judged" ; not middle, "when thou submittest thy case to the

b Ch. v. 8; κρίνεσθαί σε ". 5. εἰ δὲ ἡ ἀδικία ἡμῶν Θεοῦ δικαιοσύνην ᵇ συνίστησι,
2 Cor. vi.
4, vii. 11; τί ἐροῦμεν ; μὴ ἄδικος ὁ Θεὸς ὁ ἐπιφέρων τὴν ὀργήν ; κατὰ ἄνθρωπον
Gal. ii. 18.
λέγω. 6. μὴ γένοιτο· ἐπεὶ πῶς κρινεῖ ὁ Θεὸς τὸν κόσμον ; 7. εἰ
γὰρ ¹ ἡ ἀλήθεια τοῦ Θεοῦ ἐν τῷ ἐμῷ ψεύσματι ἐπερίσσευσεν εἰς τὴν
δόξαν αὐτοῦ, τί ἔτι κἀγὼ ὡς ἁμαρτωλὸς κρίνομαι ; 8. καὶ μὴ καθὼς
c 1 Cor. x. 30. ᶜ βλασφημούμεθα, καὶ ² καθώς φασί τινες ἡμᾶς λέγειν, Ὅτι ποιήσωμεν
τὰ κακὰ ἵνα ἔλθῃ τὰ ἀγαθά ; ὧν τὸ κρίμα ἔνδικόν ἐστι.

¹ εἰ γαρ BDEGKLP, etc. ; εἰ δε ℵA vulg. (some MSS., though others si enim).
This case is to be decided by the same considerations as the last. Tischdf. and W.
and H. put εἰ δε in their text ; W. and H. put εἰ γαρ in marg. On the strange but
frequent exchange of δε and γαρ see Weiss, Textkritik, 66 f.

² και καθως ; om. και BK. W. and H. bracket.

judge ". The quotation from Ps. cxvi. 12, πᾶς ἄνθρωπος ψεύστης, is not important: the main thing, as the formal quotation which follows shows, is the vindication of God from the charge of breach of faith with the Jews in making Christianity the fulfilment of His promises to them.

Ver. 5 f. Here another attempt is made to invalidate the conclusion of chap. ii., that the Jew is to be judged "according to his works," exactly like the Gentile. If the argument of ver. 3 f. is correct, the unbelief of the Jews actually serves to set off the faithfulness of God : it makes it all the more conspicuous ; how then can it leave them exposed to judgment ? This argument is generalised in ver. 5 and answered in ver. 6. "If our unrighteousness" (in the widest sense, ἀδικία being generalised from ἀπιστία, ver. 3) demonstrates (cf. v. 8) God's righteousness (also in the widest sense, δικαιοσύνη being generalised from πίστις, ver. 3), what shall we say ? i.e., what inference shall we draw ? Surely not that God, He who inflicts the wrath due to unrighteousness at the last day (i. 18), is Himself unrighteous, to speak as men speak. Away with the thought ! If this were so, how should God judge the world ? That God does judge the world at last is a fixed point both for Paul and those with whom he argues ; hence every inference which conflicts with it must be summarily set aside. God could not judge at all if He were unjust ; therefore, since He does judge, He is not unjust, not even in judging men whose unrighteousness may have served as a foil to His righteousness. It is not thus that the conclusions of chap. ii. can be evaded by the Jew. ὁ ἐπιφέρων τὴν ὀργήν: the "attributive participle equivalent to a relative clause,

may, like a relative clause, convey a subsidiary idea of cause, purpose, condition or concession " (Burton, Moods and Tenses, § 428, who renders here : is God unrighteous, who (because He) visiteth with wrath ?). κατὰ ἄνθρωπον λέγω : cf. Gal. iii. 15, Rom. vi. 19, 1 Cor. ix. 8. There is always something apologetic in the use of such expressions. Men forget the difference between God and themselves when they contemplate such a situation as that God should be unrighteous ; obviously it is not to be taken seriously. Still, in human language such suppositions are made, and Paul begs that in his lips they may not be taken for more than they really mean.

Ver. 7 f. These verses are extremely difficult, and are interpreted variously according to the force assigned to the τί ἔτι κἀγὼ of ver. 7. Who or what supplies the contrast to this emphatic " I also " ? Some commentators, Gifford, for instance, find it in God, and God's interest in the judgment. If my lie sets in relief the truth of God, and so magnifies His glory, is not that enough ? Why, after God has had this satisfaction from my sin, " why further am I also on my side brought to judgment as a sinner ? " It is a serious, if not a final objection to this, that it merely repeats the argument of ver. 5, which the Apostle has already refuted. Its very generality, too—for any man, as Gifford himself says, may thus protest against being judged,—lessens its relevance : for Paul is discussing not human evasions of God's judgment, but Jewish objections to his previous arguments. Lipsius finds the contrast to κἀγὼ in the Gentile world. A Jew is the speaker, or at all events the Apostle speaks in the character of one : " if my unbelief does magnify His faithfulness,

9. Τί οὖν; προεχόμεθα; οὐ πάντως· προῃτιασάμεθα γὰρ Ἰουδαίους d Ch. vi. 14,
τε καὶ Ἕλληνας πάντας ᵈ ὑφ᾽ ἁμαρτίαν εἶναι, καθὼς γέγραπται, 10. 15; Gal.
iii. 10.

is not that all that is required? Why
am I, too, like the rest of the world,
whose relation to God is so different, and
whose judgment is so necessary, still
brought into judgment?" This would
be legitimate enough, probably, if it
were not for what follows. But the
slander of ver. 8, which forms part of the
same question as τί ἔτι κἀγὼ κ.τ.λ., and
to which reference is made again in chap.
vi. 1, 15, had not the Jews, but the
Apostle in his Christian character, for
its object; hence it seems preferable to
take the κἀγὼ as referring strictly to
himself. That *Paul* would come into
judgment, in spite of the fact that *his*
faithlessness in becoming a Christian
had only set off the faithfulness of God
to Israel, no unbelieving Jew questioned:
and Paul turns this conviction of theirs
(with which, of course, he agrees, so far
as it asserts that he will be judged)
against themselves. If he, for his part,
cannot evade judgment, on the ground
that his sin (as they think it) has been a
foil to God's righteousness, no more can
they on their part: they and he are in
one position, and must be judged together: to condemn him is to expose
themselves to condemnation; that is his
point. The argument of ver. 7 is both
an *argumentum ad hominem* and an *argumentum ad rem*: Paul borrows from his
opponents the premises that he himself
is to be judged as a sinner, and that his lie
has set off God's truth: there is enough
in these premises to serve his purpose,
which is to show that these two propositions which do not exclude each other in
his case do not do so in their case either.
But, of course, he would interpret the
second in a very different way from them.
The question is continued in ver. 8,
though the construction is changed by
the introduction of the parentheses with
καθὼς and the attachment to λέγειν ὅτι
of the clause which would naturally
have gone with τί μή; If judgment
could be evaded by sinning to the glory
of God, so Paul argues, he and other
Christians like him might naturally act
on the principle which slander imputed
to them—that of doing evil that good
might come. No doubt the slander was
of Jewish origin. The doctrine that
righteousness is a gift of God, not to be
won by works of law, but by faith in
Jesus Christ, can always be misrepresented as immoral: "sin the more, it

will only the more magnify grace".
Paul does not stoop to discuss it. The
judgment that comes on those who
by such perversions of reason and conscience seek to evade all judgment is
just. This is all he has to say.

Vers. 9-20. In these verses the
Apostle completes his proof of the universality of sin, and of the liability of all
men, without exception, to judgment.
The τί οὖν of ver. 9 brings back the argument from the digression of vers. 1-8.
In those verses he has shown that the
historical prerogative of the Jews, as the
race entrusted with the oracles of God,
real and great as it is, does not exempt
them from the universal rule that God
will reward every man according to his
works (ii. 6): here, according to the
most probable interpretation of προεχόμεθα, he puts himself in the place of his
fellow-countrymen, and imagines them
asking, "Are we *surpassed*? Is it the
Gentiles who have the advantage of us,
instead of our having the advantage of
them?"

Ver. 9. Τί οὖν; What then? *i.e.*,
how, then, are we to understand the
situation? It is necessary to take these
words by themselves, and make προεχόμεθα a separate question: the answer to
τί could not be οὐ, but must be οὐδέν.
The meaning of προεχόμεθα has been
much discussed. The active προέχειν
means to excel or surpass. Many have
taken προεχόμεθα as middle in the same
sense: So the Vulg. *praecellimus eos*?
and the A.V. "Are we better than
they?" But this use, except in interpreters of this verse, cannot be proved.
The ordinary meaning of the middle
would be "to put forward on one's own
account, as an excuse, or defence".
This is the rendering in the margin of
the R.V. "Do we excuse ourselves?"
If τί οὖν προεχόμεθα could be taken together, it might certainly be rendered,
What then is our plea? but it is impossible to take προεχόμεθα in this sense
without an object, and impossible, as
already explained, to make this combination. The only alternative is to regard προεχόμεθα as passive: What
then? are we excelled? This is the
meaning adopted in the R.V. "Are we
in worse case than they?" It is supported by Lightfoot. Wetstein quotes
one example from Plut. *de Stoic.contrad.*,
1038 D.: τοῖς ἀγαθοῖς πᾶσι προσήκει,

"Ὅτι οὐκ ἔστι δίκαιος οὐδὲ εἷς· 11. οὐκ ἔστιν ὁ συνιῶν,¹ οὐκ ἔστιν
ὁ ἐκζητῶν τὸν Θεόν. 12. πάντες ἐξέκλιναν, ἅμα ἠχρειώθησαν²· οὐκ

¹ ο συνιων; om. ο ABG vulg.; ins. אDKL. The ο before εκζητων is also omitted
BG, and in both places, in text though not in marg., by W. and H. (marg., ο
ζητων). This ζητων is the reading in B.

² ηχρεωθησαν אAB¹D¹G. ουκ εστιν ποιων, so ABG; but אD have ο ποιων.
W. and H. put the former in text, the latter in marg. The second ουκ εστιν is om.
in B 67² and in the marg. of W. and H.

κατ᾽ οὐδὲν προεχομένοις ὑπὸ τοῦ Διός:
"who are in nothing surpassed by
Zeus". The word would thus express
the surprise of the Jew at seeing his prerogatives disappear; "if this line of argument be carried further," he may be
supposed to say, "the relative positions
of Jew and Gentile will turn out to be
the very reverse of what we have believed". This is the idea which is negatived in οὐ πάντως. Strictly speaking,
the οὐ should modify πάντως, and the
meaning be "not in every respect": in
some respects (for instance, the one referred to in ver. 2), a certain superiority
would still belong to the Jew. But to
allude to this seems irrelevant, and there
is no difficulty in taking the words to
mean, "No: not in any way". See
Winer, p. 693 f. "We are not surpassed at all, we who are Jews, for we
have already brought against Jews and
Greeks alike the charge of being all
under sin." ὑπὸ ἁμαρτίαν, cf. vii. 14,
Gal. iii. 22. The idea is that of being
under the power of sin, as well as
simply sinful: men are both guilty and
unable to escape from that condition.
Ver. 10. The long series of quotations, beginning with this verse, has
many points of interest. The καθὼς
γέγραπται with which it is introduced,
shows that the assertion of indiscrim-
inate sinfulness which the Apostle has
just made, corresponds with Scripture
testimony. It is as if he had said, I can
express my opinion in inspired words, and
therefore it has God upon its side. The
quotations themselves are taken from
various parts of the O.T. without distinction; no indication is given when the
writer passes from one book to another.
Thus vv. 10-12 are from Ps. xiv. 1-3;
ver. 13 gives the LXX of Ps. v. 9; ver.
14 corresponds best to Ps. x. 7; in vv.
15-17 there is a condensation of Is. lix.
7 f.; and in ver. 18 we have part of the
first verse of Ps. xxxvi. No attention
whatever is paid to the context. The
value of the quotations for the Apostle's
purpose has been disputed. It has been

pointed out that in Ps. xiv., for instance,
there is mention of a people of God, "a
generation of the righteous," as well as
of the godless world; and that in other
passages only the contemporaries of the
writer, or some of them, and not all men
in all times, are described. Perhaps if we
admit that there is no possibility of an
empirical proof of the universality of sin,
it covers the truth there is in such comments. Paul does not rest his case on
these words of Scripture, interpreted as
modern exegetical science would interpret them. He has brought the charge
of sin against all men in chap. i. 17, in
announcing righteousness as the gift of
the Gospel; in chap. i. 18-32 he has
referred to the facts which bring the
charge home to Gentile consciences; in
chap. ii. he has come to close quarters
with evasions which would naturally
suggest themselves to Jews: and in
both cases he has counted upon finding
in conscience a sure ally. Hence we do
not need to lay too heavy a burden of
proof on these quotations: it is enough
if they show that Scripture points with
unmistakable emphasis in the direction
in which the Apostle is leading his
readers. And there can be no doubt
that it does so. As Gifford well says on
ver. 18: "In the deep inner sense which
St. Paul gives to the passage, 'the
generation of the righteous' would be
the first to acknowledge that they form
no exception to the universal sinfulness
asserted in the opening verses of the
Psalm".
Ver. 10. Οὐκ ἔστιν δίκαιος οὐδὲ εἷς.
There is something to be said for the
idea that this is Paul's thesis, rather
than a quotation of Ps. xiv. 3. Ps. xiv. 3
is correctly quoted in ver. 12, and the
Apostle would hardly quote it twice:
δίκαιος, too, seems chosen to express
exactly the conclusion to which he means
to come in ver. 20. Still, the words
come after καθὼς γέγραπται: hence
they must be Scripture, and there is
nothing they resemble so much as a free
rendering of Ps. xiv. 3.

ἔστι ποιῶν χρηστότητα, οὐκ ἔστιν ἕως ἑνός." 13. "τάφος ἀνεῳγμένος ὁ λάρυγξ αὐτῶν, ταῖς γλώσσαις αὐτῶν ἐδολιοῦσαν" · "ἰὸς ἀσπίδων ὑπὸ τὰ χείλη αὐτῶν". 14. "ὧν τὸ στόμα ¹ ἀρᾶς καὶ πικρίας γέμει." 15. "ὀξεῖς οἱ πόδες αὐτῶν ἐκχέαι αἷμα. 16. σύντριμμα καὶ ταλαιπωρία ἐν ταῖς ὁδοῖς αὐτῶν· 17. καὶ ὁδὸν ᵉ εἰρήνης οὐκ ᵉ Luke i. ἔγνωσαν." 18. "οὐκ ἔστι φόβος Θεοῦ ἀπέναντι τῶν ὀφθαλμῶν ⁷⁹· αὐτῶν." 19. οἴδαμεν δὲ ὅτι ὅσα ὁ νόμος λέγει, τοῖς ᶠ ἐν τῷ νόμῳ ᶠ Ch. iv. 10. λαλεῖ· ἵνα πᾶν στόμα ᵍ φραγῇ, καὶ ʰ ὑπόδικος γένηται πᾶς ὁ κόσμος ᵍ Heb. xi. 33. ʰ Here only.

---

¹ στόμα; after στόμα B 17 read αυτων. This Hebr. idiom may be right, and W. and H. put αυτων in marg.

Ver. 11. οὐκ ἔστιν συνίων. For the form (συνίων or συνιῶν), see Winer, p. 97. If we read ὁ συνίων the meaning is, There is no one to understand: if the article (as in the LXX) be omitted, There is no one who has sense.

Ver. 12. ἠχρεώθησαν is the LXX rendering of נֶאֱלָחוּ, which means "to become sour," "to turn" (of milk): one and all they have become good for nothing. χρηστότητα usually signifies kindness, and so it is rendered in 2 Cor. vi. 6, Eph. ii. 7, Col. iii. 12, Tit. iii. 4 (cf. Rom. ii. 4, xi. 22: goodness): here it answers to Hebrew טוֹב and means "good". οὐκ ἔστιν ἕως ἑνός, non est usque ad unum (Vulg.), which may be even more exactly given in the Scottish idiom: there is not the length of one.

Ver. 13. τάφος . . . ἐδολιοῦσαν is an exact quotation of Ps. v. 10 (LXX). The original seems to describe foreign enemies whose false and treacherous language threatened ruin to Israel. For the form ἐδολιοῦσαν, see Winer, p. 91 (f.). The termination is common in the LXX: Wetstein quotes one grammarian who calls it Boeotian and another Chalcidic; it was apparently widely diffused. The last clause, ἰὸς ἀσπίδων κ.τ.λ., is Ps. cxxxix. 4, LXX.

Ver. 14. Ps. ix. 28, LXX, freely quoted: (Ps. x. 7, A.V.). αὐτῶν after στόμα (W. and H., margin) is a Hebrew idiom which the LXX has in this passage, only in the singular: οὗ τὸ στόμα αὐτοῦ.

Vers. 15-17. These verses are rather a free extract from, than a quotation of, Is. lix. 7, 8. They describe the moral corruption of Israel in the age of the prophet. According to Lipsius, σύντριμμα καὶ ταλαιπωρία refer to the spiritual misery which comes upon the Jews in the path of self-righteousness. But it is much more natural to suppose that the Apostle is pointing to the destruction and misery which human wickedness inflicts on others, than to any such spiritual results of it. It is as if he had said, " Wherever they go, you can trace them by the ruin and distress they leave behind ". The same consideration applies to ver. 17. It does not mean, " They have failed to discover the way of salvation," but " they tread continually in paths of violence ".

Ver. 18. Ps. xxxv. 2, LXX, with αὐτῶν for αὐτοῦ. This verse at once sums up and explains the universal corruption of mankind.

Ver. 19. At this point the first great division of the epistle closes, that which began with chap. i. 18, and has been occupied with asserting the universal prevalence of sin. "We know that whatever the law says, it says to those who are in the law," i.e., to the Jews. For the distinction of λέγειν (in which the object is the main thing) and λαλεῖν (in which the speaker and the mode of utterance are made prominent), see Trench, Synonyms, § lxxvi., and commentary on John viii. 43. It is most natural to suppose that by " the things the law says " Paul means the words he has just quoted from the O.T. These words cannot be evaded by the very persons to whom the O.T. was given, and who have in it, so to speak, the spiritual environment of their life. In this case, ὁ νόμος is used in the wider sense of the old revelation generally, not specifically the Pentateuch, or even the statutory part of Scripture. For this use of the word, cf. 1 Cor. xiv. 21, where ἐν τῷ νόμῳ introduces a quotation from Is. xxviii. 11: and John x. 34 (your law), xv. 25 (their law), both prefacing quota-

τῷ Θεῷ. 20. διότι ἐξ ἔργων νόμου οὐ δικαιωθήσεται πᾶσα σὰρξ ἐνώπιον αὐτοῦ · διὰ γὰρ νόμου ἐπίγνωσις ἁμαρτίας.

tions from Psalms (lxxxii. 6, xxxv. 19). At first sight there seems a disparity between the two parts of the verse. How does the fact that those who are under the law are impeached and condemned by such utterances of the law as those just quoted subserve the Divine intention to stop *every* mouth and make *all the world* answerable to God? We must suppose that all other men—that is, the Gentiles, who are not under the law—are convicted already; and that what is needed to prepare the way for the universal Gospel of grace is that those who have been under law should admit concerning themselves, what they are prompt enough to assert of all others ("sinners of the Gentiles": Gal. ii. 15), that they have not a word to say, and are liable to God's judgment. ὑπόδικος is a classical word, found here only in the N.T. Sanday and Headlam remark its "forensic" character.

Ver. 20. διότι means "because," not "therefore," as in A.V. The rendering "therefore" is perhaps due to the difficulty which the translators had in putting an intelligible meaning into "because". The sense seems to be: Every mouth must be stopped, and all the world shown to be liable to God's judgment, because by works of law no flesh shall be justified before Him. This last proposition—that no flesh shall be justified in this way—is virtually an axiom with the Apostle: it is a first principle in all his spiritual thinking, and hence everything must be true which can be deduced from it, and everything must take place which is required to support it. *Because* this is the fundamental certainty of the case, every mouth *must* be stopped, and the strong words quoted from the law stand where they do to secure this end. The explanation of this axiom is to be found in its principal terms—flesh and law. Flesh primarily denotes human nature in its frailty: to attain to the righteousness of God is a task which no flesh has strength to accomplish. But flesh in Paul has a moral rather than a natural meaning; it is not its weakness in this case, but its strength, which puts justification out of the question; to justify is the very thing which the law cannot do, and it cannot do it because it is weak owing to the flesh (*cf.* viii. 3). But the explanation of the axiom lies not only in "flesh," but in "law". "By the law

comes the full knowledge of sin." (ἐπίγνωσις, a favourite Pauline word: fifteen times used in his epistles.) This is its proper, and indeed its exclusive function. There is no law given with power to give life, and therefore there are no works of law by which men can be justified. The law has served its purpose when it has made men feel to the full how sinful they are; it brings them down to this point, but it is not for it to lift them up. The best exposition of the passage is given by the Apostle himself in Gal. ii. 15 f., where the same quotation is made from Ps. cxliii. 2, and proof given again that it applies to Jew and Gentile alike. In ἐξ ἔργων νόμου, νόμος, of course, is primarily the Mosaic law. As Lipsius remarks, no distinction is drawn by the Apostle between the ritual and the moral elements of it, though the former are in the foreground in the epistle to the Galatians, and the latter in that to the Romans. But the truth would hold of every legal dispensation, and it is perhaps to express this generality, rather than because νόμος is a technical term, that the article is omitted. Under no system of statutes, the Mosaic or any other, will flesh ever succeed in finding acceptance with God. Let mortal man, clothed in works of law, present himself before the Most High, and His verdict must always be: Unrighteous.

Vers. 21-26. The universal need of a Gospel has now been demonstrated, and the Apostle proceeds with his exposition of this Gospel itself. It brings what all men need, a righteousness of God (see on i. 17); and it brings it in such a way as to make it accessible to all. Law contributes nothing to it, though it is attested by the law and the prophets; it is a righteousness which is all of grace. Grace, however, does not signify that moral distinctions are ignored in God's procedure: the righteousness which is held out in the Gospel is held out on the basis of the redemption which is in Christ Jesus. It is put within the sinner's reach at a great cost. It could never be offered to him—it could never be manifested, or indeed have any real existence—but for the propitiatory virtue of the blood of Christ. Christ a propitiation is the inmost soul of the Gospel for sinful men. If God had not set Him forth in this character, not only must we

21. Νυνὶ δὲ χωρὶς νόμου δικαιοσύνη Θεοῦ πεφανέρωται, μαρτυρου- i Matt.v. 17;
μένη ὑπὸ τοῦ νόμου καὶ τῶν ¹προφητῶν· 22. δικαιοσύνη δὲ Θεοῦ διὰ Acts xiii.
15.
πίστεως Ἰησοῦ Χριστοῦ, εἰς πάντας καὶ ἐπὶ πάντας ¹ τοὺς πιστεύοντας· k Ch. x. 12;
1 Cor.xiv.
οὐ γάρ ἐστι ᵏ διαστολή. 23. πάντες γὰρ ἥμαρτον, καὶ ὑστεροῦνται 7.

¹ και επι παντας; so א³DFGKL, but om. א¹ABC. The words are omitted by
Lachm., Tischdf., Tregelles, W. and H., but retained by Weiss, who explains the
omission by homœoteleuton. As επι παντας alone is found in very good MSS. of
the vulg. and in John of Damascus, the received text may be a combination of this
and the true reading.

despair for ever of attaining to a Divine
righteousness; all our attempts to read the
story of the world in any consistency with
the character of God must be baffled.
Past sins God seemed simply to ignore:
He treated them apparently as if they
were not. But the Cross is "the Divine
theodicy for the past history of the world"
(Tholuck); we see in it how seriously God
deals with the sins which for the time
He seemed to pass by. It is a demonstration of His righteousness—that is, in
the widest sense, of His consistency with
His own character,—which would have
been violated by indifference to sin. And
that demonstration is, by God's grace,
given in such a way that it is possible
for Him to be (as He intends to be) at
once just Himself, and the justifier of
those who believe in Jesus. The propitiatory death of Jesus, in other words,
is at once the vindication of God and the
salvation of man. That is why it is central and fundamental in the Apostolic
Gospel. It meets the requirements, at
the same time, of the righteousness of
God and of the sin of man.

Ver. 21. νυνὶ δὲ: but now. All time
is divided for Paul into "now" and
"then". Cf. Eph. ii. 12 f., τῷ καιρῷ
ἐκείνῳ . . . νυνὶ δέ; 2 Cor. v. 16, ἀπὸ
τοῦ νῦν: the reception of the Gospel
means the coming of a new world. χωρὶς
νόμου: legal obedience contributes nothing to evangelic righteousness. It is
plain that in this expression νόμος does
not signify the O.T. revelation or religion
as such, but that religion, or any other,
conceived as embodied in statutes. It is
statutory obedience which (as Paul has
learned by experience) cannot justify.
Hence νόμος has not exactly the same
sense here as in the next clause, ὑπὸ τοῦ
νόμου κ. τῶν προφητῶν, where the whole
expression is equal to the O.T., and the
meaning is that the Gospel is not alien
to the religion of Israel, but really finds
attestation there. This is worth remark-
ing, because there is a similar variation

in the meaning of δικαιοσύνη between
vv. 21 and 25, and in that of ἡ δόξα τοῦ
Θεοῦ between iii. 23 and v. 2. To deny
that words which mean so much, and are
applied so variously, can convey different
shades of meaning, even within the
narrow limits of a few verses, is to
deny that language shares in the life
and subtlety of the mind. πεφανέρωται:
once for all the righteousness of God has
been revealed in the Gospel. Cf. xvi.
26, Col. i. 26, 2 Tim. i. 10, 1 Peter i. 20,
Heb. ix. 8, 26.

Ver. 22. δικαιοσύνη δὲ θεοῦ. The
δὲ is explicative: "a righteousness of
God (see in chap. i. 17) [ver. 21],
and that a righteousness of God
through faith in Jesus Christ". In the
Epistle to the Hebrews Jesus Christ is
undoubtedly set forth as a pattern of
faith: ἀφορῶντες εἰς τὸν τῆς πίστεως
ἀρχηγὸν καὶ τελειωτὴν Ἰησοῦν, Heb. xii.
2. Cf. Heb. ii. 13; but such a thought
is irrelevant here. It is the constant
teaching of Paul that we are justified
(not by sharing Jesus' faith in God, as
some interpreters would take it here, but)
by believing in that manifestation and
offer of God's righteousness which are
made in the propitiatory death of Jesus.
εἰς πάντας καὶ ἐπὶ πάντας: the last
three words are omitted by א ABC and
most edd. If genuine, they add no new
idea to εἰς πάντας; see Winer, p. 521.
For διαστολή, cf. x. 12. The righteousness of God comes to all on the terms of
faith, for all alike need it, and can receive
it only so.

Ver. 23. ἥμαρτον must be rendered
in English "have sinned"; see Burton,
Moods and Tenses, § 54. ὑστεροῦνται
expresses the consequence=and so come
short of the glory of God. To emphasise
the middle, and render "they come short,
and feel that they do so," though suggested
by the comparison of Mt. xix. 20 with Lk.
xv. 14 (Gifford), is not borne out by the
use of the N.T. as a whole. The most
one could say is that sibi is latent in

τῆς δόξης τοῦ Θεοῦ, 24. δικαιούμενοι ¹ δωρεὰν τῇ αὐτοῦ χάριτι, διὰ τῆς ἀπολυτρώσεως τῆς ἐν Χριστῷ Ἰησοῦ, 25. ὃν προέθετο ὁ Θεὸς

the middle : to their loss (not necessarily to their sensible or conscious loss) they come short. The present tense implies that but for sin men might be in enjoyment of " ἡ δόξα τοῦ θεοῦ ". Clearly this cannot be the same as the future heavenly glory of God spoken of in v. 2 : as in John v. 44, xii. 43, it must be the approbation or praise of God. This sense of δόξα is easily derived from that of "reputation," resting on the praise or approval of others. Of course the approbation which God would give to the sinless, and of which sinners fall short, would be identical with justification.

Ver. 24. δικαιούμενοι : grammatically, the word is intractable. If we force a connection with what immediately precedes, we may say with Lipsius that just as Paul has proved the universality of grace through the universality of sin, so here, conversely, he proves the universal absence of merit in men by showing that they are justified freely by God's grace. Westcott and Hort's punctuation (comma after τοῦ θεοῦ) favours this connection, but it is forced and fanciful. In sense δικαιούμενοι refers to πάντας τοὺς πιστεύοντας, and the use of the nominative to resume the main idea after an interruption like that of ver. 23 is rather characteristic than otherwise of the Apostle. δωρεὰν is used in a similar connection in Gal. ii. 21. It signifies " for nothing ". Justification, we are told here, costs the sinner nothing ; in Galatians we are told that if it comes through law, then Christ died " for nothing ". Christ is all in it (1 Cor. i. 30) : hence its absolute freeness. τῇ αὐτοῦ χάριτι repeats the same thing : as δωρεὰν signifies that we contribute nothing, τῇ αὐτοῦ χάριτι signifies that the whole charge is freely supplied by God. αὐτοῦ in this position has a certain emphasis. διὰ τῆς ἀπολυτρώσεως τῆς ἐν Χ. Ἰ. The justification of the sinful, or the coming to them of that righteousness of God which is manifested in the Gospel, takes effect through the redemption that is in Christ Jesus. Perhaps " liberation " would be a fairer word than " redemption " to translate ἀπολύτρωσις. In Eph. i. 7, Col. i. 14, Heb. ix. 15, it is equal to forgiveness. Ἀπολύτρωσις itself is rare ; in the LXX there is but one instance, Dan. iv. 29, in which ὁ χρόνος μου τῆς ἀπολυτρώσεως signifies

the time of Nebuchadnezzar's recovery from his madness. There is here no suggestion of price or cost. Neither is there in the common use of the verb λυτροῦσθαι, which in LXX represents גָּאַל and פָּדָה, the words employed to describe God's liberation of Israel from Egypt (Is. xliii. 3 does not count). On the other hand, the classical examples favour the idea that a reference to the cost of liberation is involved in the word. Thus Jos., Ant., xii. 2, 3 : πλειόνων δὲ ἢ τετρακοσίων ταλάντων τὰ τῆς ἀπολυτρώσεως γενήσεσθαι φαμένων κ.τ.λ. ; and Philo, Quod omnis probus liber, § 17 (of a Spartan boy taken prisoner in war) ἀπογνοὺς ἀπολύτρωσιν ἄσμενος ἑαυτὸν διεχρήσατο, where it is at least most natural to translate " having given up hope of being held to ransom ". In the N.T., too, the cost of man's liberation is often emphasised : 1 Cor. vi. 20, vii. 23, 1 Pet. i. 18 f., and that especially where the cognate words λύτρον and ἀντίλυτρον are employed : Mc. x. 45, 1 Tim. ii. 6. The idea of liberation as the end in view may often have prevailed over that of the particular means employed, but that some means — and especially some cost, toil or sacrifice— were involved, was always understood. It is implied in the use of the word here that justification is a liberation ; the man who receives the righteousness of God is set free by it from some condition of bondage or peril. From what ? The answer is to be sought in the connection of i. 17 and i. 18 : he is set free from a condition in which he was exposed to the wrath of God revealed from heaven against sin. In Eph. i. 7, Col. i. 14, ἀπολύτρωσις is plainly defined as remission of sins : in Eph. i. 14, Rom. viii. 23, 1 Cor. i. 30, it is eschatological.

Ver. 25 f. But the question whether the word ἀπολύτρωσις involves of itself a reference to the cost at which the thing is accomplished is after all of minor consequence : that cost is brought out unambiguously in ver. 25. The ἀπολύτρωσις is in Christ Jesus, and it is in Him as One whom God set forth in propitiatory power, through faith (or, reading διὰ τῆς πίστεως, through the faith referred to), in His blood. προέθετο in Eph. i. 9 (cf. Rom. i. 13) is " purposed " ; but here the other meaning, " set forth " (Vulg. proposuit) suits the context much

ἱλαστήριον διὰ τῆς πίστεως [1] ἐν τῷ αὐτοῦ αἵματι, εἰς [m] ἔνδειξιν τῆς δικαιοσύνης αὐτοῦ, διὰ τὴν πάρεσιν τῶν προγεγονότων ἁμαρτημάτων

m 2 Cor. viii. 24; Phil. i 28.

[1] διὰ τῆς πιστεως; so BC³D³KL 17, but om. της NC¹D¹F, Origen. Most critical edd. omit, but W. and H. give it a place in marg. Weiss puts it in text, and emphasises it with ref. to ver. 22.

better. ἱλαστήριον has been taken in various ways. (1) In the LXX it is the rendering of כַּפֹּרֶת, (A.V.) "mercy-seat". In one passage at least, Ex. xxv. 16, כַּפֹּרֶת is rendered ἱλαστήριον ἐπίθεμα, which is possibly a combination of two translations—a literal one, a "lid" or "covering"; and a figurative or spiritual one, "a propitiatory". Many scholars argue that Paul's use must follow that of the LXX, familiarity with which on the part of his readers is everywhere assumed. But the necessity is not quite apparent; and not to mention the incongruities which are introduced if Jesus is conceived as the mercy-seat upon which the sacrificial blood—His own blood—is sprinkled, there are grammatical reasons against this rendering. Paul must have written, to be clear, τὸ ἱλαστήριον ἡμῶν, or some equivalent phrase. Cf. 1 Cor. v. 8 (Christ our passover). A "mercy-seat" is not such a self-evident, self-interpreting idea, that the Apostle could lay it at the heart of his gospel without a word of explanation. Consequently (2) many take ἱλαστήριον as an adjective. Of those who so take it, some supply θῦμα or ἱερεῖον, making the idea of sacrifice explicit. But it is simpler, and there is no valid objection, to make it masculine, in agreement with ὅν: "whom God set forth in propitiatory power". This use of the word is sufficiently guaranteed by Jos., Ant., xvi. 7, 1: περίφοβος δ' αὐτὸς ἐξῄει καὶ τοῦ δέους ἱλαστήριον μνῆμα . . . κατεσκευάσατο. The passage in 4 Macc. xvii. 22 (καὶ διὰ τοῦ αἵματος τῶν εὐσεβῶν ἐκείνων καὶ τοῦ ἱλαστηρίου [τοῦ] θανάτου αὐτῶν ἡ θεία πρόνοια τὸν Ἰσραὴλ προκακωθέντα διέσωσεν) is indecisive, owing to the doubtful reading.* Perhaps the grammatical question is insoluble; but there is no question that Christ is conceived as endued with propitiatory power, in virtue of His death. He is set forth as ἱλαστήριος(ν) ἐν τῷ αὐτοῦ αἵματι. It is His blood that covers sin. It seems a mere whim of rigour to deny, as Weiss does, that the death of Christ is here conceived as sacrificial. It is in His blood that Christ is endued with propitiatory power; and there is no propitiatory power of blood known to Scripture unless the blood be that of sacrifice. It is not necessary to assume that any particular sacrifice—say the sin offering—is in view; neither is it necessary, in order to find the idea of sacrifice here, to make ἱλαστήριον neuter, and supply θῦμα; it is enough to say that for the Apostle the ideas of blood with propitiatory virtue, and sacrificial blood, must have been the same. The precise connection and purpose of διὰ (τῆς) πίστεως is not at once clear. Grammatically, it might be construed with ἐν τῷ αὐτοῦ αἵματι; cf. Eph. i. 15, Gal. iii. 26 (?), Mk. i. 15; but this lessens the emphasis due to the last words. It seems to be inserted, almost parenthetically, to resume and continue the idea of ver. 22, that the righteousness of God which comes in this way,—namely, in Christ, whom God has set forth in propitiatory power in virtue of His death—comes only to those who believe. Men are saved freely, and it is all God's work, not in the very least their own; yet that work does not avail for any one who does not by faith accept it. What God has given to the world in Christ, infinitely great and absolutely free as it is, is literally nothing unless it is

---

* Seeberg, *Der Tod Christi*, S. 185, adduces it with the reading τοῦ θανάτου, to support the view that in ἱλαστήριον (as a substantive) Paul is thinking not of the concrete *Kapporeth*, but only of that on account of which this sacred article received its name; in other words, of a covering by which that is hidden from God's eyes on account of which He would be obliged to be angry with men. It is possible to take ἱλαστήριον as a substantive = a means of propitiation (as this passage from 4 Macc. shows, if we read τοῦ θανάτου), without special allusion to the כַּפֹּרֶת. But see Deissmann, *Bibelstudien*, S. 121 ff.

ἐν τῇ ἀνοχῇ τοῦ Θεοῦ, 26. πρὸς ἔνδειξιν τῆς δικαιοσύνης αὐτοῦ ἐν

n Ch.viii.18,
xi. 5.   τῷ νῦν ⁿ καιρῷ, εἰς τὸ εἶναι αὐτὸν δίκαιον καὶ δικαιοῦντα τὸν ἐκ πίστεως

taken. Faith must have its place, there-fore, in the profoundest statement of the Gospel, as the correlative of grace. Thus διὰ (τῆς) πίστεως, though parenthetic, is of the last importance. With εἰς ἔνδειξιν τῆς δικαιοσύνης αὐτοῦ κ.τ.λ. we are shown God's purpose in setting forth Christ as a propitiation in His blood. It is done with a view to demonstrate His righteousness, owing to the passing by of the sins previously committed in the forbearance of God. God's righteousness in this place is ob-viously an attribute of God, on which the sin of the world, as hitherto treated by Him, has cast a shadow. Up till now, God has "passed by" sin. He has "winked at" (Acts xvii. 30) the transgres-sions of men perpetrated before Christ came (προ-γεγονότων), ἐν τῇ ἀνοχῇ αὐτοῦ. The last words may be either temporal or causal: while God exercised forbear-ance, or because He exercised it, men sinned, so to speak, with impunity, and God's character was compromised. The underlying thought is the same as in Ps. l. 21: "These things hast Thou done, and I kept silence: *Thou thoughtest that I was altogether such an one as Thyself*". Such had been the course of Providence that God, owing to His forbearance in suspending serious dealing with sin, lay under the imputation of being indifferent to it. But the time had now come to remove this imputation, and vindicate the Divine character. If it was possible once, it was no longer possible now, with Christ set forth in His blood as a propitiation, to maintain that sin was a thing which God regarded with indiffer-ence. Paul does not say in so many words what it is in Christ crucified which constitutes Him a propitiation, and so clears God's character of the charge that He does not care for sin: He lays stress, however, on the fact that an essential element in a propitiation is that it should vindicate the Divine righteousness. It should proclaim with unmistakable clearness that with sin God can hold no terms. (The distinction be-tween πάρεσις, the suspension, and ἄφεσις, the revocation, of punishment, is borne out, according to Lightfoot, *Notes on Epp. of St. Paul*, p. 273, by classical usage, and is essential here.) In ver. 26 this idea is restated, and the significance of a propitiation more fully brought out. "Yes, God set Him forth in this charac-

ter with a view to demonstrate His righteousness, that He might be right-eous Himself, and accept as righteous him who believes in Jesus." The words ἐν τῷ νῦν καιρῷ refer to the Gospel Age, the time in which believers live, in contrast to the time when God exercised forbearance, and men were tempted to accuse Him of indifference to righteous-ness. πρὸς, as distinguished from εἰς, makes us think rather of the person contemplating the end than of the end contemplated; but there is no essential difference. τὴν ἔνδειξιν: the article means "the ἔνδειξις already mentioned in ver. 25". But the last clause, εἰς τὸ εἶναι αὐτὸν κ.τ.λ., is the most important. It makes explicit the whole intention of God in dealing with sin by means of a propitiation. God's righteousness, compromised as it seemed by His forbearance, might have been vindicated in another way; if He had executed judgment upon sin, it would have been a kind of vindication. He would have secured the first object of ver. 26: "that He might be righteous Himself". But part of God's object was to justify the ungodly (chap. iv. 5), upon certain conditions; and *this* could not be attained by the execution of judg-ment upon sin. To combine both objects, and at once vindicate His own righteousness, and put righteousness within reach of the sinful, it was neces-sary that instead of executing judgment God should provide a propitiation. This He did when He set forth Jesus in His blood for the acceptance of faith. (Häring takes the ἔνδειξις of God's righteousness here to be the same as the "revelation" of δικαιοσύνη θεοῦ in i. 17, or the "manifestation" of it in iii. 21; but this is only possible if with him we completely ignore the context, and especially the decisive words, διὰ τὴν πάρεσιν τῶν προγεγονότων ἁμαρτη-μάτων.) The question has been raised whether the righteousness of God, here spoken of as demonstrated at the Cross, is His judicial (Weiss) or His penal righteousness (Meyer). This seems to me an unreal question; the righteous-ness of God is the whole character of God so far as it must be conceived as inconsistent with any indifference about sin. It is a more serious question if we ask what it is in Christ set forth by God in His blood which at once vindicates

'Ιησοῦ. 27. Ποῦ οὖν ἡ καύχησις; ἐξεκλείσθη. διὰ °ποίου νόμου; ο Acts iv. 7.
τῶν ἔργων; οὐχὶ, ἀλλὰ διὰ νόμου πίστεως. 28. λογιζόμεθα οὖν [1]

[1] ουν; so BCD³KL 17, but γαρ ℵAD¹F, Origen-interp. The division of authorities here is like that in ver. 25, and the edd. decide in the same way. W. and H. put γαρ in text, ουν in marg. Weiss puts ουν in text. πιστει δικαιουσθαι ℵ³KL 17, but δικαιουσθαι πιστει ℵ¹ABCD.

God's character and makes it possible for Him to justify those who believe. The passage itself contains nothing explicit—except in the words ἐν τῷ αὐτοῦ αἵματι. It is pedantic and inept to argue that since God could have demonstrated His righteousness *either* by punishment *or* by propitiation, therefore punishment and propitiation have no relation to each other. Christ was a propitiation *in virtue of His death ;* and however a modern mind may construe it, *death* to Paul *was the doom of sin.* To say that God set forth Christ as a propitiation *in His blood* is the same thing as to say that God *made Him to be sin* for us. God's righteousness, therefore, is demonstrated at the Cross, because there, in Christ's death, it is made once for all apparent that He does not palter with sin ; the doom of sin falls by His appointment on the Redeemer. And it is possible, at the same time, to accept as righteous those who by faith unite themselves to Christ upon the Cross, and identify themselves with Him in His death : for in doing so they submit in Him to the Divine sentence upon sin, and at bottom become right with God. It is misleading to render εἰς τὸ εἶναι αὐτὸν δίκαιον κ. δικαιοῦντα, "that He might be just and *yet* the justifier," etc. : the Apostle only means that the two ends have equally to be secured, not that there is necessarily an antagonism between them. But it is more than misleading to render "that He might be just *and therefore* the justifier " : there is no conception of righteousness, capable of being clearly carried out, *and connected with the Cross*, which makes such language intelligible. (See Dorner, *System of Christian Doctrine*, iv., 14, English Translation.) It is the love of God, according to the consistent teaching of the New Testament, which provides the propitiation, by which God's righteousness is vindicated and the justification of the ungodly made possible. τὸν ἐκ πίστεως 'Ιησοῦ is every one who is properly and sufficiently characterised as a believer in Jesus. There is no

difficulty whatever in regarding 'Ιησοῦ as objective genitive, as the use of πιστεύειν throughout the N.T. (Gal. ii. 16, *e.g.*) requires us to do : such expressions as τῷ ἐκ πίστεως 'Αβραάμ (iv. 16) are not in the least a reason to the contrary : they only illustrate the flexibility of the Greek language. See on ver. 22 above.

Vers. 27-31. In these verses the positive exposition of the righteousness of God as offered to faith through the redemption in Christ Jesus, is concluded. The Apostle points out two inferences which can be drawn from it, and which go to commend it to religious minds. The first is, that it excludes boasting. A religious constitution under which men could make claims, or assume anything, in the presence of God, must necessarily be false ; it is at least one mark of truth in the Christian doctrine of justification that by it such presumption is made impossible. The second is, that in its universality and its sameness for all men, it is consistent with (as indeed it flows from) the unity of God. There can be no step-children in the family of God : a system which teaches that there are, like that current among the Jews, must be wrong ; a system like the Christian, which excludes such an idea, is at least so far right. In ver. 31 an objection is raised. The whole system just expounded may be said to make Law void—to stultify and disannul all that has ever been regarded as in possession of Divine moral authority in the world. In reality, the Apostle answers in a word, its effect is precisely the reverse : it establishes law.

Ver. 27. ποῦ οὖν; where, since this is the case, is boasting ? ἐξεκλείσθη : for the use of the tense, *cf.* ἐβλήθη and ἐξηράνθη in John xv. 6 ; it is equivalent to, " is peremptorily, or once for all, shut out ". διὰ ποίου νόμου; By what kind of law ? In other words, How is the " law," the divinely appointed spiritual order, or constitution, which excludes boasting, to be characterised ? Is it by " the works " which it prescribes, and which those who live under it per-

πίστει δικαιοῦσθαι ἄνθρωπον, χωρὶς ἔργων νόμου. 29. ἢ Ἰουδαίων
ὁ Θεὸς μόνον¹; οὐχὶ δὲ καὶ ἐθνῶν; ναὶ, καὶ ἐθνῶν· 30. ἐπείπερ² εἷς
ᵖ ¹ Tim. ii. ὁ ᵖ Θεὸς, ὃς δικαιώσει περιτομὴν ἐκ πίστεως, καὶ ἀκροβυστίαν διὰ τῆς
4 ff.
πίστεως. 31. νόμον οὖν καταργοῦμεν διὰ τῆς πίστεως; μὴ γένοιτο·
ἀλλὰ νόμον ἱστῶμεν.³

¹ μονον ℵACFKL 17; μονων B (W. and H. marg.). δε om. ℵABCDFK.

² For επειπερ ℵ¹ABCD² read ειπερ, and so most editors; but Weiss regards
επειπερ (which is not found elsewhere in the N.T.) as the true reading.

³ For ιστωμεν, ℵ¹ABCD²F, etc., read ιστανομεν.

form? No: its character is given when we call it a constitution or law of "faith". Νόμος in these brief questions is evidently used in a wide sense to denote the religious order or system under which men live, regarded as established by God, and having His authority; the O.T. religion and the N.T. religion, unlike, and in some ways opposed, as they are, are alike νόμος—divine institutes.

Ver. 28. λογιζόμεθα γάρ: see critical note. In λογιζόμεθα there is no idea of an uncertain conclusion: it rather suggests the confident self-consciousness of the reasoner. ἄνθρωπον is not "any human being," as if beings of another sort could be justified otherwise: it is like the German "man" or "one". Cf. 1 Cor. iv. 1, vii. 1, xi. 28, Gal. ii. 16. The sharp distinction drawn between faith and works of law, as characterising two different religious systems, shows that faith must not itself be interpreted as a work of law. In principle it is a renunciation of all such confidence as legal obedience inspires.

Ver. 29 f. ἢ Ἰουδαίων ὁ Θεὸς μόνον; The only way to evade the conclusion of ver. 28 would be to suppose—as is here presented by way of alternative—that God is a God of Jews only. But the supposition is impossible: there is only one God, and therefore He must be God of all, of Gentiles and Jews alike. This is assumed as an axiom by the Apostle. εἴπερ is the best attested reading, but the argument seems to require that it should "approximate to the sense of ἐπείπερ" (Simcox, Language of the N.T., p. 171), which is a variant: "if, as is the fact".* It is simplest to read ver. 30 as explaining and confirming what precedes: He is God of the Gentiles also, if as is the fact God is

one; and (consequently) He will justify the circumcision on the ground of faith and the uncircumcision by means of faith. δικαιώσει is probably logical, rather than temporal, whether the reference be made to the last judgment, or to each case, as it arises, in which God justifies. Lightfoot insists on drawing a distinction between ἐκ πίστεως and διὰ τῆς πίστεως in this passage. "The difference," he says, "will perhaps best be seen by substituting their opposites, οὐ δικαιώσει περιτομὴν ἐκ νόμου, οὐδὲ ἀκροβυστίαν διὰ τοῦ νόμου: when, in the case of the Jews, the falsity of their starting-point, in the case of the Gentiles, the needlessness of a new instrumentality, would be insisted on." (Notes on Epistles of St. Paul, p. 274.) But a comparison of ii. 26, v. 1, ix. 30, Gal. iii. 8 (Weiss), shows that Paul does not construe the prepositions so rigorously: and in point of fact, what he does insist upon here is that justification is to be conceived in precisely the same way for Jew and Gentile. The ἐκ πίστεως and διὰ τῆς πίστεως serve no purpose but to vary the expression.

Ver. 31. νόμον οὖν καταργοῦμεν διὰ τῆς πίστεως; Do we then annul "law" through the faith we have been discussing? Perhaps if Law were written with a capital letter, it would suggest the true meaning. The Apostle speaks as from the consciousness of a Jewish objector: is all that we have ever called Law—the whole Jewish religion—that divinely established order, and everything of the same nature—made void by faith? God forbid, he answers: on the contrary, Law is set upon a secure footing; for the first time it gets its rights. To prove this was one of the main tasks lying upon the Apostle of the New Covenant. One species of proof is given in chap iv.,

---

* But εἴπερ = if God is indeed one (which no Jew, the supposed interlocutor, would deny).

IV. 1. ΤΙ οὖν ἐροῦμεν Ἀβραὰμ τὸν πατέρα ἡμῶν εὑρηκέναι κατὰ σάρκα[1]; 2. εἰ γὰρ Ἀβραὰμ ἐξ ἔργων ἐδικαιώθη, ἔχει καύχημα, ἀλλ᾽ οὐ πρὸς τὸν Θεόν.[2] 3. τί γὰρ ἡ γραφὴ λέγει; "Ἐπίστευσε δὲ Ἀβραὰμ τῷ Θεῷ, καὶ ἐλογίσθη αὐτῷ εἰς δικαιοσύνην. 4. τῷ δὲ ἐργαζομένῳ ὁ μισθὸς οὐ λογίζεται κατὰ [a]χάριν, ἀλλὰ κατὰ τὸ ὀφεί- a Ver. 16.

[1] The T.R. Αβρααμ τον πατερα ημων ευρηκεναι is found in KLP, Theodoret and later fathers. For πατερα, προπατορα is read in אּ[1]ABC[1], etc. ευρηκεναι stands before Αβρααμ in אּACDFG lat. and Egypt. versions, etc. In B 47[1] ευρηκεναι is omitted. The omission (see commentary) gives the easiest and most suitable text. W. and H. omit it from their text but put it in marg. after ερουμεν. The R.V. omits it in marg., inserting it in text. Weiss retains it.

[2] προς τον θεον; om. τον אּABCD[1]F.

where he shows that representative saints under the Old Dispensation, like Abraham, were justified by faith. That is the Divine order still, and it is securer than ever under the Gospel. Another kind of proof is given in chaps. vi.-viii., where the new life of the Christian is unfolded, and we are shown that "the just demands of the law" are fulfilled in believers, and in believers only. The claim which the Apostle makes here, and establishes in these two passages, is the same as that in our Lord's words: I came not to destroy (the law or the prophets), but to fulfil.

CHAPTER IV.—Vers. 1-8. The justification of Abraham, considered in relation to the doctrine just expounded in iii. 21-31. The point to be made out is that the justification of Abraham does not traverse but illustrates the Pauline doctrine.

Ver. 1 The force of οὖν seems to be that the case of Abraham, as commonly understood, has at least the appearance of inconsistency with the Pauline doctrine. "What, then, i.e., on the supposition that vers. 21-31 in chap. iii. are a true exposition of God's method, shall we say of Abraham, our forefather according to the flesh? Does not his case present a difficulty? For if he was justified by works (as one may assume), he has ground for boasting (whereas boasting, according to the previous argument, iii. 27, is excluded)." This seems to me by far the simplest interpretation of the passage. The speaker is a Jewish Christian, or the Apostle putting himself in the place of one. κατὰ σάρκα goes with τὸν προπάτορα ἡμῶν, because the contrast with another kind of fatherhood belonging to Abraham is already in the Apostle's thoughts: see ver. 11. If the reading

εὑρηκέναι be adopted (see critical note), no change is necessary in the interpretation. To take κατὰ σάρκα with εὑρηκέναι, as though the question were : What shall we say that our forefather Abraham found in the way of natural human effort, as opposed to the way of grace and faith? is to put a sense on κατὰ σάρκα which is both forced and irrelevant. The whole question is, What do you make of Abraham, with such a theory as that just described?

Ver. 2 f. With ἀλλ᾽ οὐ πρὸς τὸν Θεόν the Apostle summarily repels the objection. "You say he has ground of boasting? On the contrary, he has no ground of boasting in relation to God, For what does the Scripture say? Abraham *believed* God, and it was imputed to Him for righteousness." The quotation is from Gen. xv. 6, and is exactly as in the LXX, except that Paul writes ἐπίστευσεν δὲ τῷ θεῷ instead of καὶ ἐπίστευσεν τῷ θεῷ, which serves partly to bring out the contrast between the real mode of Abraham's justification, and the mode suggested in ver. 2, partly to give prominence to *faith*, as that on which his argument turned. The reading ἐπίστευσεν δὲ is also found in Jas. i. 23, Philo i., 605 (Mangey), as well as Clem. Rom., I., x., 6, and Just. Martyr, *Dial.*, 92 : so that it was probably current, and not introduced by Paul. It is assumed that something not in itself righteousness was reckoned to Abraham as righteousness; only on this assumption is boasting in his case excluded.

Ver. 4 f. The faith of Abraham, in whatever way it may be more precisely determined by relation to its object, agrees with Christian faith in the essential characteristic, that it is not a work. To him who works—der mit Werken umgehet : Luther—the reward

b Ver. 24; λημα· 5. τῷ δὲ μὴ ἐργαζομένῳ, πιστεύοντι δὲ ᵇ ἐπὶ τὸν δικαιοῦντα
Acts ix.
42. τὸν ἀσεβῆ, ¹ λογίζεται ἡ πίστις αὐτοῦ εἰς ᶜ δικαιοσύνην. 6. καθάπερ
c Ch. ii. 26,
ix. 8. καὶ Δαβὶδ λέγει τὸν μακαρισμὸν τοῦ ἀνθρώπου, ᾧ ὁ Θεὸς λογίζεται
δικαιοσύνην, χωρὶς ἔργων, 7. "Μακάριοι ὧν ἀφέθησαν αἱ ἀνομίαι,
καὶ ὧν ἐπεκαλύφθησαν αἱ ἁμαρτίαι. 8. μακάριος ἀνὴρ ᾧ ² οὐ μὴ

¹ ασεβη; for this ℵD¹FG have the form ασεβην, on which see Winer, p. 76.

² For φ ℵ³ACD³FKL ου is found in ℵ¹BD¹G (so LXX in ℵ¹AB). W. and H.
put ου in text, φ in marg. ου is the better supported reading, but φ "naturally
established itself as the more euphonious" (S. and H.).

is reckoned, not by way of grace (as in Abraham's case), but by way of debt. But to him who does *not* work, *i.e.*, who does not make works his ground of hope toward God—but believes on Him who justifies the ungodly, his *faith* is reckoned for righteousness. Ver. 5 describes the category under which Abraham falls, but is not a generalisation from his case. The ἀσεβὴς (Gen. xviii. 23, Prov. xi. 31, chap. v. 6) is a person who has no *claim* to justification: if he is justified, it must be not on the ground of works, but freely, by God's grace, on which he relies through faith. Of course to believe in this grace of God is to do something; in that sense it is a work; but it is to do something which involves a complete renunciation of hope in anything we can do without God. It excludes merit, boasting, justification ἐξ ἔργων. *Cf.* Philo, i., 486 (quoted in Mayor on Jas. i. 21): δίκαιον γὰρ οὕτως οὐδὲν ὡς ἀκράτῳ καὶ ἀμιγεῖ τῇ πρὸς θεὸν μόνον πίστει κεχρῆσθαι . . . τὸ ἐπὶ μόνῳ τῷ ὄντι βεβαίως καὶ ἀκλινῶς ὁρμεῖν . . . δικαιοσύνης μόνον ἔργον. The whole Pauline gospel could be summed up in this one word—God who justifies the ungodly. Under that device, what room is there for any pretensions or claims of man? It is sometimes argued (on the ground that all God's actions must be "ethical") that God can only pronounce just, or treat as just, those who actually are just; but if this were so, what Gospel would there be for sinful men? This "ethical" gospel is identical with the Pharisaism in which Paul lived before he knew what Christ and faith were, and it led him to despair. It leads all men either to despair or to a temper which is that of the Pharisee rather than the publican of Luke xviii. What it can never beget is the temper of the Gospel. The paradoxical phrase, Him that justifieth the ungodly, does not suggest that justification is a fiction, whether legal or of any other sort, but that it is a miracle. It is a thing that only God can achieve, and that calls into act and manifestation all the resources of the Divine nature. It is achieved through an unparalleled revelation of the judgment and the mercy of God. The miracle of the Gospel is that God comes to the ungodly, with a mercy which is righteous altogether, and enables them through faith, in spite of what they are, to enter into a new relation to Himself, in which goodness becomes possible for them. There can be no spiritual life at all for a sinful man unless he can get an *initial assurance* of an unchanging love of God deeper than sin, and he gets this at the Cross. He gets it by believing in Jesus, and it is justification by faith. The whole secret of New Testament Christianity, and of every revival of religion and reformation of the Church is in that *laetum et ingens paradoxon*, θεὸς ὁ δικαιῶν τὸν ἀσεβῆ.

Ver. 6 ff. καθάπερ καὶ Δαβὶδ: David is not a new illustration of this doctrine, but a new witness to it. The argument just based on Gen. xv. 6 is in agreement with what he says in the 32nd Psalm. The quotation exactly reproduces the LXX. λέγει τὸν μακαρισμὸν τοῦ ἀνθρώπου: "pronounceth blessing upon the man," etc. (R.V.): or, speaks the felicitation of the man. He does so in the exclamation with which the Psalm opens. Obviously to impute righteousness without works, and freely to forgive sins, are to Paul one and the same thing. Yet the former is not a merely negative idea: there is in it an actual bestowment of grace, an actual acceptance with God, as unlike as possible to the establishment of an unprejudiced neutrality between God and man, to which the forgiveness of sins is sometimes reduced.

Vers. 9-12. In these verses the justification of Abraham appears in a new light. In virtue of its ground in his faith, he is not only a forefather κατὰ

λογίσηται Κύριος ἁμαρτίαν." 9. Ὁ ᵈ μακαρισμὸς οὖν οὗτος, ἐπὶ τὴν ᵈ Gal. iv.15.
περιτομὴν, ἢ καὶ ἐπὶ τὴν ἀκροβυστίαν; λέγομεν γὰρ ὅτι ἐλογίσθη
τῷ Ἀβραὰμ ἡ πίστις εἰς δικαιοσύνην. 10. πῶς οὖν ἐλογίσθη; ἐν
περιτομῇ ὄντι, ἢ ἐν ἀκροβυστίᾳ; οὐκ ἐν περιτομῇ, ἀλλ᾽ ἐν ἀκρο-
βυστίᾳ · 11. καὶ σημεῖον ἔλαβε περιτομῆς,[1] ᵉσφραγῖδα τῆς δικαιοσύνης ᵉ 2 Cor. i.22;
τῆς πίστεως τῆς ἐν τῇ ἀκροβυστίᾳ · εἰς τὸ εἶναι αὐτὸν πατέρα πάντων   Eph. i. 13,
                                                                            iv. 30.
τῶν πιστευόντων ᶠδι᾽ ἀκροβυστίας, εἰς τὸ λογισθῆναι καὶ αὐτοῖς τὴν ᶠ Ch. ii. 27.

[1] περιτομης ℵBC²DFKL, etc.; περιτομην AC¹, etc.

σάρκα (i.e., the natural ancestor of the Jews), but he is the spiritual ancestor of all believers. The faith which was imputed to him for righteousness constitutes him such; it is the same in essence as Christian faith; and so it is a vital bond between him and all who believe, whether they be Jews or Gentiles. God's method has been the same through all history.

Ver. 9. ὁ μακαρισμὸς οὖν οὗτος: This felicitation, then, what is its extent? Does it apply to the circumcision only, or to the uncircumcision also? Just as vers. 1-8 correspond to iii. 27 f., so do vers. 9-12 correspond to iii. 29-31. God is not the God of the Jews only, but of the Gentiles also, and the Apostle's purpose here is to show that the felicitation of the justified in Ps. xxxii. is not limited by circumcision. λέγομεν γὰρ κ.τ.λ.: for our proposition is, that his faith was reckoned, etc.

Ver. 10. πῶς οὖν ἐλογίσθη; To say that his faith was reckoned as righteousness, without mentioning circumcision, suggests that the latter was at least not indispensable; still it is not decisive, and so the further question must be asked, How—i.e., under what conditions—was his faith thus reckoned to him? Was it when he was circumcised or when he was uncircumcised? History enables Paul to answer, Not when he was circumcised, but when he was uncircumcised. Abraham's justification is narrated in Gen. xv., his circumcision not till Gen. xvii., some fourteen years later: hence it was not his circumcision on which he depended for acceptance with God.

Ver. 11 f. On the contrary, he received a sign in circumcision, a seal of the righteousness of the faith which he had while uncircumcised. Both sign (אוֹת) and seal (חוֹתָם) are frequently used by Rabbinical writers to

describe circumcision as a symbol or pledge that one is in covenant with God. So even of heathens: "Og was circumcised, and Moses feared אוֹת מִפְּנֵי בְּרִית שֶׁלּוֹ, propter signum foederis ejus". But usually of Jews: "Jonah shewed Leviathan sigillum (חוֹתָמוֹ) Abrahami patris nostri". See Schoettgen, Wetstein, or Delitzsch, ad loc. περιτομῆς (for which W. and H. have in margin περιτομὴν) must be a genitive of apposition. With εἰς τὸ εἶναι the Divine purpose in this relation of circumcision to justification in the case of Abraham is explained. Things were ordered as has been described that he might be father of all that believe while uncircumcised (as he himself did)—that the righteousness in question might be imputed to them; and father of circumcision (i.e., of persons circumcised) in the case of those who are not only circumcised, but also walk in the steps of the faith which he had while not circumcised. It was God's intention that Abraham should be the representative and typical believer, in whom all believers without distinction should recognise their spiritual father; the Divine method of justification was to be inaugurated and illustrated in him, as it should hold good for all who were to be justified: accordingly the whole process took place antecedent to his circumcision, and in no circumstances has circumcision any essential relation to this great blessing. For its true meaning and advantage see on ii. 25. On οὐκ ἐκ περιτομῆς μόνον, see Simcox, Language of the N.T., 184. The grammar in ver. 12 is faulty, and Westcott and Hort suspect a primitive error. Either τοῖς before στοιχοῦσιν must be omitted, or it must be changed, as Hort suggests, into αὐτοῖς, if we are to express the meaning correctly. The sense required by the context is not open to doubt. For

δικαιοσύνην· 12. καὶ πατέρα περιτομῆς τοῖς οὐκ ἐκ περιτομῆς μόνον,
ἀλλὰ καὶ τοῖς στοιχοῦσι¹ τοῖς ἴχνεσι τῆς ἐν τῇ ἀκροβυστίᾳ πίστεως

g Ch. ix. 4; τοῦ πατρὸς ἡμῶν Ἀβραάμ.   13. Οὐ γὰρ διὰ νόμου ἡ ᵍ ἐπαγγελία τῷ
Gal. iii.
17 ff.;   Ἀβραὰμ ἢ τῷ σπέρματι αὐτοῦ, τὸ κληρονόμον αὐτὸν εἶναι τοῦ² κόσμου,
Eph.ii.12;
iii. 6.   ἀλλὰ διὰ δικαιοσύνης πίστεως.   14. εἰ γὰρ οἱ ἐκ νόμου κληρονόμοι,
κεκένωται ἡ πίστις, καὶ κατήργηται ἡ ἐπαγγελία· 15. ὁ γὰρ νόμος

¹ τοῖς στοιχοῦσιν is found in all MSS. but cannot be right; see note in commentary below.   Om. τῇ before ἀκροβυστίᾳ ℵABCD¹F.

² Om. τοῦ before κόσμου ℵABCD, etc.

δι' ἀκροβυστίας cf. ii. 27. For the dative τοῖς ἴχνεσιν see Philipp. iii. 16, Gal. v. 16, 25. But cf. also Winer, p. 274.

Vers. 13-15. The argument of vers. 9-12 is reiterated and confirmed here in other terms. Abraham is the father of all believers: for it is not through law that the promise is given to him or his seed, that he should be heir of the world—a condition which would limit the inheritance to the Jews, but through the righteousness of faith—a condition which extends it to all who believe. We might have expected a quasi-historical proof of this proposition, similar to the proof given in 10 f. that Abraham's justification did not depend on circumcision. But the Apostle takes another and more speculative line. Instead of arguing from the O.T. narrative, as he does in Gal. iii. 14-17, that the promise was given to a justified man before the (Mosaic) law was heard of, and therefore must be fulfilled to all independently of law, he argues that law and promise are mutually exclusive ideas. For (ver. 14) if those who are of law, i.e., Jews only, as partisans of law, are heirs, then faith (the correlative of promise) has been made vain, and the promise of no effect. And this incompatibility of law and promise in idea is supported by the actual effect of the law in human experience. For the law works wrath—the very opposite of promise. But where there is not law, there is not even transgression, still less the wrath which transgression provokes. Here, then, the other series of conceptions finds its sphere : the world is ruled by grace, promise and faith. This is the world in which Abraham lived, and in which all believers live ; and as its typical citizen, he is father of them all.

Ver. 13. ἡ ἐπαγγελία is the Divine promise, which is identical with salvation in the widest sense. The word implies that the promise is held out by God of his own motion. The peculiar content here assigned to the promise, that Abraham should be heir of the world, is not found in so many words in the O.T. Schoettgen, on ver. 3, quotes Mechilta, fol. 25, 2. "Sic quoque de Abrahamo legimus, quod mundum hunc et mundum futurum non nisi ea de causa consecutus sit, quia in Deum credidit, q.d., Gen. xv. 6. And Wetstein, Tanchuma, 165, 1: Abrahamo patri meo Deus possidendum dedit cælum et terram. These passages prove that the idea was not unfamiliar, and it may be regarded as an extension of the promises contained in Gen. xii. 7, xvii. 8, xxii. 17. But what precisely did it mean ? Possibly participation in the sovereignty of the Messiah. Abraham and his seed would then be heirs of the world in the sense of 1 Cor. vi. 2, 2 Tim. ii. 12. So Meyer and many others. In the connection in which the words stand, however, this seems strained ; and the "rationalising" interpretation, which makes the world Abraham's inheritance through the spread of Abraham's faith, and the multiplication of his spiritual children, is probably to be preferred. The religion which is conquering the world is descended from him, its power lies in that faith which he also had, and in proportion as it spreads he inherits the world. τῷ σπέρματι αὐτοῦ : not Christ, as in Gal. iii. 16, but Abraham's descendants in the widest sense. διὰ δικαιοσύνης πίστεως : it was not as one under law, but as one justified by faith, that Abraham had the promise given to him. In the narrative, indeed, the promise (Gen. xii. 7) antedates the justification (Gen. xv. 6), but it is repeated at later periods (see above): and as ver. 14 argues, promise, faith and justification are parts of one spiritual whole.

Ver. 14. κεκένωται cf. 1 Cor. i. 17, ix. 15, 2 Cor. ix. 3. κατήργηται : a

ὀργὴν κατεργάζεται · οὗ γὰρ [1] οὐκ ἔστι νόμος, οὐδὲ παράβασις.   16.

διὰ τοῦτο ἐκ πίστεως, ἵνα κατὰ [h] χάριν, εἰς τὸ εἶναι βεβαίαν τὴν ἐπαγ- h Ver. 4.

γελίαν παντὶ τῷ σπέρματι, οὐ τῷ ἐκ τοῦ νόμου μόνον, ἀλλὰ καὶ

τῷ ἐκ πίστεως Ἀβραάμ, ὅς ἐστι πατὴρ πάντων ἡμῶν, 17. (καθὼς i Gen. xvii.

[i] γέγραπται, "Ὅτι πατέρα πολλῶν ἐθνῶν τέθεικά σε,") κατέναντι οὗ k Ch. viii.

ἐπίστευσε Θεοῦ, τοῦ [k] ζωοποιοῦντος τοὺς νεκροὺς, καὶ καλοῦντος τὰ vi. 13.

[1] ου γαρ; so א³DFKLP, but א¹ABC ου δε.

favourite word of Paul, who uses it twenty-five times.

Ver. 15. ὀργήν: wrath, *i.e.*, the wrath of God. See on i. 18. Under a legal dispensation sin is stimulated, and brought into clear consciousness : men come under the wrath of God, and know that they do. This is the whole and sole result of "the law," and hence law cannot be the means through which God administers His grace, and makes man the heir of all things. On the contrary, to attain this inheritance man must live under a regime of faith. οὖ δὲ : δὲ is the true reading (see critical note), not γάρ : *but* where law is not, neither is there παράβασις. It would not have been true to say οὐδὲ ἁμαρτία, for Paul in chap. ii. recognises the existence and guilt of sin even where men live ἀνόμως ; but in comparison with the deliberate and conscious transgression of those who live ἐν νόμῳ, such sin is comparatively insignificant and venial, and is here left out of account. The alternative systems are reduced to two, Law and Grace (or Promise).

Vers. 16-22. The Apostle can now develop, without further interruption or digression, his idea of the representative (and therefore universal) character of Abraham's justification. The New Testament cannot be said to subvert the Old if the method of justification is the same under both. Nay, it establishes the Old (iii. 31). This is the point which is enforced in the closing verses of chap. iv.

Ver. 16 f. Διὰ τοῦτο : because of the nature of law, and its inability to work anything but wrath. ἐκ πίστεως : the subject is the promise, considered in reference to the mode of its fulfilment. ἵνα κατὰ χάριν : χάρις on God's part is the correlative of πίστις on man's. εἰς τὸ εἶναι βεβαίαν κ.τ.λ. This is the Divine purpose in instituting the spiritual order of grace and faith : it is the only one consistent with universalism in religion. οὐ τῷ ἐκ τοῦ νόμου μόνον ἀλλὰ καὶ τῷ ἐκ πίστεως Ἀβραάμ : there seems

to be some inexactness in expression here. The seed which is "of the Law" ought to mean the Jews, as partisans of law in distinction from faith : then the seed which is "of the faith of Abraham" would mean the Gentiles. But the promise did not belong at all to the seed which was "of the law," *i.e.*, to the Jews, as Abraham's natural descendants ; even in them, faith was required. And the seed which is "of the faith" of Abraham is not quite appropriate to describe Gentile believers exclusively ; the very point of the argument in the passage is that the faith of Abraham is reproduced in all the justified, whether Gentile or Jew. Still there seems no doubt that the persons meant to be contrasted in the two clauses are Jewish and Gentile believers (Meyer), not Jews and Christians (Fritzsche, who supplies σπέρματι before Ἀβραάμ) : the difficulty is that the words do not exactly suit either meaning. ὅς ἐστιν πατὴρ πάντων ἡμῶν. The πάντων is emphatic, and ἡμῶν expresses the consciousness of one who has seen in Abraham the spiritual ancestor of the new Christian community, living (as it does), and inheriting the promise, by faith. *Opponuntur haec verba Judaeis, qui Abrahamum non nominant nisi cum adjecto* אבינו *pater noster* (Schoettgen).

When Paul speaks out of his Jewish consciousness, he shares this pride ("whose are the fathers," ix. 5) ; when he speaks as a Christian, to whom the Church is "the Israel of God" (Gal. vi. 16), and who can even say "*we* are the circumcision," he claims all the Jews boasted of as in reality the property of believers : it is Christians, and not Jews by birth, who can truly say "We have Abraham to our father". The earliest indication (an indirect one) of the Jewish pride in Abraham is perhaps seen in Is. lxiii. 16. That Abraham is the father of us all agrees with Scripture : Gen. xvii. 5 LXX. The ὅτι belongs to the quotation. If there is any parenthesis, it should only

μὴ ὄντα ὡς ὄντα.   18. Ὃς παρ' ἐλπίδα ἐπ' ἐλπίδι ἐπίστευσεν, εἰς
τὸ γενέσθαι αὐτὸν πατέρα πολλῶν ἐθνῶν, κατὰ τὸ εἰρημένον, "Οὕτως

l Here only ἔσται τὸ σπέρμα σου" ·   19. καὶ μὴ ἀσθενήσας τῇ πίστει, [1]οὐ[1] κατε-
in Paul.
m Heb. xi. νόησε τὸ ἑαυτοῦ σῶμα ἤδη [m]νενεκρωμένον, ἑκατονταέτης που ὑπάρχων,
12.
καὶ τὴν νέκρωσιν τῆς μήτρας Σάρρας ·   20. εἰς δὲ τὴν ἐπαγγελίαν
n Eph. vi. 10; τοῦ Θεοῦ οὐ διεκρίθη τῇ ἀπιστίᾳ, ἀλλ' [n]ἐνεδυναμώθη τῇ πίστει, δοὺς
2 Tim. ii.
1; Heb.
xi. 34. δόξαν τῷ Θεῷ,   21. καὶ πληροφορηθεὶς ὅτι ὃ ἐπήγγελται, δυνατός

[1] ου κατενοησεν; so DFKLP, Syr. and lat. Om. ου ℵABC, best MSS. of vulg.,
etc. All the critical edd. omit ου, though both readings are widely and early attested ;
though the sense is quite good either way, the authorities for the omission are undoubtedly stronger. ηδη ℵACDKLP; om. BF 47, etc. W. and H. bracket.
Weiss omits.

be from καθὼς to σέ. As Abraham has
this character in Scripture, so he has it
before God: the two things are one and
the same ; it is his true, historical, Divine
standing, that he is father of all believers.
The attraction in κατέναντι οὗ ἐπίστευσεν θεοῦ is most simply resolved into
κ. θεοῦ ᾧ ἐπίστευσε : but see Winer, p.
204, 206. In characterising the God
whom Abraham believed, the Apostle
brings out further the correspondence
between the patriarch's faith and that of
Christians. He is "God who makes the
dead alive and calls things that are not
as though they were". Such a reference
to Isaac as we find in Heb. xi. 19 (λογισά-
μενος ὅτι καὶ ἐκ νεκρῶν ἐγείρειν δυνατὸς
ὁ θεός) is not suggested here (yet see
ver. 24), and hence it is better to take
ζωοπ. τοὺς νεκροὺς of restoring vitality
to Abraham, whose body was as good as
dead. In the application, the things
that are not are the unborn multitudes
of Abraham's spiritual children. God
speaks of them (hardly, issues his summons to them) as if they had a being.
Faith in a God who is thus conceived
comes nearer than anything else in
Paul to the definition given in Heb xi.
1. On τὰ μὴ ὄντα, see Winer, p. 608.
Ver. 18 ff. Abraham's faith described.
It was both contrary to hope (as far as
nature could give hope), and rested on
hope (that God could do what nature
could not). εἰς τὸ γενέσθαι αὐτὸν πατέρα
κ.τ.λ. (cf. ver. 11) is most properly taken
to express the Divine purpose—that he
might become father, etc. (see Moulton's
note in Winer, p. 414) ; not result—so
that he became. κατὰ τὸ εἰρημένον,
Οὕτως κ.τ.λ., Gen. xv. 5 : the passage
is familiar, and the οὕτως is supposed to
suggest its own interpretation—the stars
of the heaven.

μὴ ἀσθενήσας . . . κατενόησεν, without becoming weak in faith, he considered his own body. "The participle
ἀσθενήσας, though preceding the verb,
is most naturally interpreted as referring
to a (conceived) result of the action denoted by κατενόησεν." Burton, Moods
and Tenses, § 145. This remark holds
good only with the reading κατενόησεν :
if we read οὐ κατ. the meaning is, He
considered not his body quippe qui non
esset imbecillis (Winer, p. 610). ἑκατονταέτης που (circiter) ὑπάρχων : his great
age was the primary and fundamental
fact in the situation : this seems to be
the suggestion of ὑπάρχων as distinct
from ὤν. In ver. 20 (εἰς δὲ τὴν ἐπαγγελίαν) the δὲ contrasts with becoming
weak, as he considered his body, the
actual conduct of Abraham. "He did
not waver in relation to the promise,
in unbelief; on the contrary, he was
strengthened in faith." On διεκρίθη, cf.
Mt. xxi. 21, Jas. i. 6, Rom. xiv. 23. τῇ
ἀπιστίᾳ : instrum. dative ; because of
unbelief. It is simplest to take τῇ
πίστει as dative of respect, though Heb.
xi. 11 can be adduced by those who
would render : "he became strong, recovered his bodily vigour, by faith".
The participles in ver. 21 are loosely
attached to the principal verbs, and are
really equivalent to co-ordinate clauses
with καί. In his whole conduct on this
occasion Abraham glorified God, and demonstrated his own assurance of His
power. See Burton, § 145. δοὺς δόξαν
τῷ θεῷ : for this Hebraism see Josh. vii.
19, Jer. xiii. 16, John ix. 24, Acts xii. 23.
For πληροφορηθείς xiv. 5, Col. iv. 12.
Ver. 22. διὸ : because of this signal
faith, evinced so triumphantly in spite
of all there was to quell it. ἐλογίσθη :
i.e., his faith was reckoned to him as

ἐστι καὶ ποιῆσαι. 22. διὸ καὶ ἐλογίσθη αὐτῷ εἰς δικαιοσύνην.
23. Οὐκ ἐγράφη δὲ δι' αὐτὸν μόνον, ὅτι ἐλογίσθη αὐτῷ. 24. ἀλλὰ
καὶ δι' ἡμᾶς, οἷς μέλλει λογίζεσθαι, τοῖς πιστεύουσιν ἐπὶ τὸν ἐγεί-

righteousness. That which needs to be reckoned as righteousness is not in itself righteousness — on this the Apostle's argument rests in vers. 1-8; yet it is not arbitrarily that faith is so reckoned. The spiritual attitude of a man, who is conscious that in himself he has no strength, and no hope of a future, and who nevertheless casts himself upon, and lives by, the word of God which assures him of a future, is the necessarily and eternally right attitude of all souls to God. He whose attitude it is, is at bottom right with God. Now this was the attitude of Abraham to God, and it is the attitude of all sinners who believe in God through Christ; and to him and them alike it is reckoned by God for righteousness. The Gospel does not subvert the religious order under which Abraham lived; it illustrates, extends, and confirms it.

Vers. 23-25. Conclusion of the argument. Οὐκ ἐγράφη δὲ δι' αὐτὸν μόνον: cf. xiv. 4, 1 Cor. ix. 10, x. 6, 11, Gal. iii. 8. The formula for quoting Scripture is not ἐγράφη but γέγραπται: i.e., Scripture conveys not a historical truth, relating to one person (as here, to Abraham), but a present eternal truth, with some universal application. δι' ἡμᾶς: to show the mode of our justification. οἷς μέλλει λογίζεσθαι: to whom it (the act of believing) is to be imputed as righteousness. μέλλει conveys the idea of a Divine order under which things proceed so. τοῖς πιστεύουσιν is in apposition to οἷς: "believing as we do". (Weiss.) The object of the Christian's faith is the same as that of Abraham's, God that giveth life to the dead. Only in this case it is specifically God as He who raised Jesus our Lord. Cf. 1 Pet. i. 21, where Christians are described as those who through Christ believe in God who raised Him from the dead. In Abraham's case, "God that quickeneth the dead" is merely a synonym for God Omnipotent, who can do what man cannot. In Paul, on the other hand, while omnipotence is included in the description of God—for in Eph. i. 19, in order to give an idea of the greatest conceivable power, the Apostle can do no more than say that it is according to that working of the strength of God's might which He wrought in Christ

when He raised Him from the dead— omnipotence is not the sole object of the Christian's faith. His spiritual attitude toward God is the same as Abraham's, but God is revealed to him, and offered to his faith, in a character in which Abraham did not yet know Him. This is conveyed in the description of the Person in relation to whom the Omnipotence of God has been displayed to Christians. That Person is "Jesus our Lord, who was delivered up for our offences, and raised for our justification". The Resurrection *of Jesus our Lord* entitles us to conceive of God's Omnipotence not as mere unqualified power, but as *power no less than infinite engaged in the work of man's salvation from sin*. In the Resurrection of Jesus, omnipotence is exhibited as *redeeming* power: and in this omnipotence we, like Abraham, believe. παρεδόθη is used in LXX, Is. liii. 12, and its N.T. use, whether God or Christ be the subject of the παραδιδόναι (Rom. viii. 32: Gal. ii. 20, Eph. v. 2), may be derived thence. There is considerable difficulty with the parallel clauses διὰ τὰ παραπτώματα ἡμῶν, and διὰ τὴν δικαίωσιν ἡμῶν. It is safe to assert that Paul did not make an abstract separation between Christ's Death and His Resurrection, as if the Death and the Resurrection either had different motives, or served ends separable from each other. There is a sort of mannerism in the expression here, as there is in xiv. 9, which puts us on our guard against overprecision. This granted, it seems simplest and best to adopt such an interpretation as maintains the same meaning for διὰ in both clauses. This has been done in two ways. (1) The διὰ has been taken retrospectively. "He was delivered up because we had sinned, and raised because we were justified"— sc. by His death. But though Paul writes in v. 9, δικαιωθέντες νῦν ἐν τῷ αἵματι αὐτοῦ, it is impossible to believe that he would have written—as this interpretation requires him to do—that we were justified by Christ's death, and that Christ was *therefore* raised from the dead by God. Justification is not only an act of God, but a spiritual experience; it is dependent upon faith (iii. 25); and it is realised in men as one by one, in

ραντα Ἰησοῦν τὸν Κύριον ἡμῶν ἐκ νεκρῶν, 25. ὃς παρεδόθη διὰ τὰ
o Ch. v. 18. παραπτώματα ἡμῶν, καὶ ἠγέρθη διὰ τὴν °δικαίωσιν ἡμῶν.

the time determined by Providence, they receive the Gospel. Hence διὰ τὴν δικαίωσιν ἡμῶν at least must be prospective.* (2) The διὰ has been taken in both clauses prospectively. "He was delivered up on account of our offences—to make atonement for them; and he was raised on account of our justification—that it might become an accomplished fact." That this interpretation is legitimate, so far as the language goes, cannot be questioned; and if we avoid unreal separations between things that really form one whole, it is thoroughly Pauline. Paul does ascribe expiatory value to the death or the blood of Christ; in that sense it is true the work of Christ was finished on the Cross. But Paul never thought of that by itself; *he knew Christ only as the Risen One who had died, and who had the virtue of His atoning death ever in Him;* this Christ was One, in all that He did and suffered—the Christ who had evoked in him the faith by which he was justified, the only Christ through faith in whom sinful men ever could be justified; and it is natural, therefore, that he should conceive Him as raised with a view to our justification. But it would have been equally legitimate to say that He died for our justification. It is only another way of expressing what every Christian understands—that we believe in a living Saviour, and that it is faith in Him which justifies. But then it is faith in Him as One who not only lives, but was delivered up to death to atone for our offences. He both died and was raised for our justification; the work is one and its end is one. And it is a mistake to argue, as Beyschlag does (*Neutest. Theologie*, ii., 164), that this reference of faith to the Risen Christ who died is inconsistent with the vicarious nature of His expiatory sufferings. That His sufferings had this character is established on independent grounds; and to believe in the Risen Christ is to believe in One in whom the power of that propitiatory vicarious suffering abides for ever. It is indeed solely because the virtue of that suffering is in Him that faith in the Risen Lord does justify. For an exposition of the passage, in which the retrospective force

is given to διὰ, see Candlish in *Expositor*, Dec., 1893. See also Bruce, *St. Paul's Conception of Christianity*, p. 160 ff. The identity in principle of Abrahamic and Christian faith is seen in this, that both are faith in God. But Abraham's is faith in a Divine promise, which only omnipotence could make good; the Christian's is faith in the character of God as revealed in the work of redemption wrought by Christ. That, too, however, involves omnipotence. It was the greatest display of power ever made to man when God raised Christ from the dead, and set Him at His own right hand in the heavenly places; and the Christ so raised was one who had been delivered to death for our offences. That is only another way of saying that the ultimate power in the world—the omnipotence of God—is in the service of a love which provides at infinite cost for the expiation of sin. The only right attitude for any human being in presence of this power is utter self-renunciation, utter abandonment of self to God. This is faith, and it is this which is imputed to men in all ages and under all dispensations for righteousness.

CHAP. V.—Vers. 1-11. The blessings of Justification. The first section of the epistle (chap. i. 18-iii. 20) has proved man's need of the righteousness of God; the second (chap. iii. 21-30) has shown how that righteousness comes, and how it is appropriated; the third (chap. iii. 31-iv. 25) has shown, by the example of Abraham, and the testimony of David, that it does not upset, but establishes the spiritual order revealed in the O.T. The Apostle now, like David, enlarges on the felicity of the justified, and especially on their assurance of God's love and of future blessedness. We may describe the contents of vers. 1-11 in the words which he himself applies (iv. 6) to the 32nd psalm: λέγει τὸν μακαρισμὸν τοῦ ἀνθρώπου ᾧ ὁ θεὸς λογίζεται δικαιοσύνην χωρὶς ἔργων.

Ver. 1. δικαιωθέντες takes up emphatically the δικαίωσιν of iv. 25: Christ's death and resurrection have not been in vain: there are those who have actually been justified in consequence.

* This, however, does not prevent us from conceiving of the resurrection of Christ as His public vindication, and the sign of God's acceptance of the work which He achieved in His death: in a certain sense, therefore, as His justification.

V. 1. ΔΙΚΑΙΩΘΕΝΤΕΣ οὖν ἐκ πίστεως, εἰρήνην ἔχομεν[1] πρὸς τὸν
Θεὸν διὰ τοῦ Κυρίου ἡμῶν Ἰησοῦ Χριστοῦ, 2. δι' οὗ καὶ τὴν προσα-
γωγὴν ἐσχήκαμεν τῇ πίστει[2] εἰς τὴν χάριν ταύτην ἐν ᾗ ἑστήκαμεν·

[1] εχομεν is found in correctors of א and B, in FG (not in the Latin of these
bilingual MSS.) and many cursives; εχωμεν in א¹AB¹CDKL cursives, vulg., Syr.,
etc. The authority for the latter seems therefore overwhelming; but besides the
exegetical reasons which have led interpreters to prefer the former, and which are
noticed in the commentary, we have to consider the frequency with which ο and ω
are confused even in the best MSS. Thus Weiss (*Textkritik*, S. 44 f.) gives the
following instances in which ω is certainly wrong, and is not adopted by any editor:
αφωρισας, Gal. i. 15 in B; ην ως αγκυραν εχωμεν, Heb. vi. 19 in DE; δι' ης
εγγιζωμεν, Heb. vii. 19 in A 31; διαταξωμαι, 1 Cor. xi. 34 in ADEFG 37, 44, 47;
προεχωμεθα, Rom. iii. 9 in AL; θερισωμεν, 1 Cor. ix. 11 in CDEFGLP and many
cursives; αιρησωμαι, Phil. i. 22 in B; εισερχωμεθα, Heb. iv. 3 in AC 17, 37;
συνβασιλευσωμεν, 2 Tim. ii. 12 in ACLP 109; θερισωμεν, Gal. vi. 9 in אCFGLP
cursives. These are only samples, and though the attestation is more divided in
these and similar cases than in Rom. v. 1, they are quite enough to show that in a
variation of this kind no degree of MS. authority could support a reading against a
solid exegetical reason for changing ω into ο. That such solid reason can be given
here I agree with the expositors named below.

[2] τη πιστει א¹CKLP, vulg., Syr. Om. BDF old lat. W. and H. bracket.

Having, therefore, been justified (the
Apostle says), εἰρήνην ἔχομεν πρὸς τὸν
θεόν. The MSS. evidence is overwhelmingly in favour of ἔχωμεν, so much so
that W. and H. notice no other reading,
and Tischdf. says "ἔχωμεν cannot be
rejected unless it is altogether inappropriate, and inappropriate it seemingly is
not". But this last statement is at least
open to dispute. There is no indication
that the Apostle has finished his dogmatic exposition, and is proceeding to
exhortation. To read ἔχωμεν, and then
to take καυχώμεθα as subjunctive both in
ver. 2 and ver. 3 (as the R.V.), is not only
awkward, but inconsistent with οὐ μόνον
δὲ, ver. 3. If the hortative purpose
dominated the passage throughout, the
Apostle must have written μὴ: see
Gifford, p. 122. It is better (reading
ἔχωμεν) to take καυχώμεθα in ver. 2
with δι' οὗ, and co-ordinate it with τὴν
προσαγωγήν: "through whom we have
had our access, and rejoice, etc". Then
the οὐ μόνον is in place. But the unin-
terrupted series of indicatives afterwards, the inappropriateness of the verb
ἔχειν to express "let us realise, let us
make our own," the strong tendency to
give a paraenetic turn to a passage often
read in church, the natural emphasis on
εἰρήνη, and the logic of the situation, are
all in favour of ἔχομεν, which is accordingly adopted by Meyer, Weiss, Lipsius,
Godet and others, in spite of the MSS.,
see critical note. The justified have
peace with God: *i.e.*, His wrath (i. 18)

no longer threatens them; they are accepted in Christ. It is not a change in
their feelings which is indicated, but a
change in God's relation to them.
Ver. 2. δι' οὗ καί: through whom
also. To the fact that we have peace
with God through our Lord Jesus Christ
corresponds this *other* fact, that through
Him we have had (and have) our access
into this grace, etc. προσαγωγὴ has a
certain touch of formality. Christ has
"introduced" us to our standing as
Christians: *cf.* Eph. ii. 18, 1 Pet. iii. 18.
τῇ πίστει: by the faith referred to in
ver. 1. Not to be construed with εἰς τὴν
χάριν ταύτην: which would be without
analogy in the N.T. The grace is substantially one with justification: it is the
new spiritual atmosphere in which the
believer lives as reconciled to God.
καυχώμεθα, which always implies the *expression* of feeling, is to be co-ordinated
with ἔχομεν. ἐπ' ἐλπίδι τῆς δόξης τοῦ
θεοῦ: on the basis of hope in the glory
of God, *i.e.*, of partaking in the glory of
the heavenly kingdom. For ἐπ' ἐλπίδι,
cf. iv. 18: the construction is not elsewhere found with καυχᾶσθαι.
Ver. 3. οὐ μόνον δὲ ἀλλὰ καὶ καυχώμεθα: and not only (do we glory on that
footing), but we also glory in tribulations. *Cf.* Jas. i. 2 ff. ἐν ταῖς θλίψεσιν
does not simply mean "when we are in
tribulations," but also "because we are":
the tribulations being the ground of the
glorying: see ii. 17, 23, v. 11, 1 Cor. iii.
21, 2 Cor. xii. 9, Gal. vi. 14.

a Ch.viii.18, καὶ καυχώμεθα ἐπ᾽ ἐλπίδι τῆς ᵃδόξης τοῦ Θεοῦ.   3. οὐ μόνον δὲ,
21.
      ἀλλὰ καὶ καυχώμεθα ¹ ἐν ταῖς θλίψεσιν, εἰδότες ὅτι ἡ θλίψις ὑπομονὴν

b 2 Cor. ii.9, κατεργάζεται, 4. ἡ δὲ ὑπομονὴ ᵇδοκιμήν, ἡ δὲ δοκιμὴ ἐλπίδα, 5. ἡ
 xiii 3;
Phil.ii.22; δὲ ἐλπὶς οὐ καταισχύνει, ὅτι ἡ ἀγάπη τοῦ Θεοῦ ᶜἐκκέχυται ἐν ταῖς
c Acts ii. 17
f., 33, x.45. καρδίαις ἡμῶν διὰ Πνεύματος Ἁγίου τοῦ δοθέντος ἡμῖν.   6. Ἔτι
dMatt.xxvi.
41.   γὰρ ² Χριστὸς ὄντων ἡμῶν ᵈἀσθενῶν, κατὰ καιρὸν ὑπὲρ ἀσεβῶν ἀπέθανε.

¹ καυχώμεθα אADFKP; καυχωμενοι BC, Origen (twice). The participle is hardly
open to suspicion on the ground of being conformed to ver. 11 (S. and H.) ; it is
much rather the indicative (subjunctive ?) that is open to suspicion as a "mechanical
repetition" (Alford) from the preceding verse. W. and H. put καυχώμεθα in text,
καυχωμενοι in marg. By the rule *proclivi lectioni praestat ardua* Alf. and Treg.
are rather justified for putting καυχωμενοι in the text.

² ετι γαρ אACD¹⁻³KP; εις τι γαρ D²F; *ut quid enim* lat. Iren.-interp.; ει δε L
Syr.; ει γε B. For a full discussion of the readings here, see S. and H. *ad loc.*,
or W. and H., Appendix, p. 108. W. and H. suspect some primitive error ; while
holding the text of B to give a more probable sense than any of the other variants,
Hort thinks ειπερ would better explain all the variations and be equally appropriate.
ετι after ασθενων אABCD¹F.

Ver. 4. ὑπομονὴν κατεργάζεται : has
as its fruit, or effect, endurance. ὑπομονὴ
has more of the sense of bravery and
effort than the English "patience": it is
not so passive. ἡ δὲ ὑπομονὴ δοκιμήν :
endurance produces approvedness—its
result is a spiritual state which has shown
itself proof under trial. *Cf.* Jas. i. 12
(δόκιμος γενόμενος = when he has shown
himself proof). Perhaps the best English equivalent of δοκιμή would be *character*. This in its turn results again in
hope : the experience of what God can
do, or rather of what He does, for the
justified amid the tribulations of this life,
animates into new vigour the hope with
which the life of faith begins.
Ver. 5. ἡ δὲ ἐλπὶς οὐ καταισχύνει :
and hope, *i.e.*, the hope which has not
been extinguished, but confirmed under
trial, does not put to shame. Ps. xxii. 6.
Spes erit res (Bengel). Here the *aurea
catena* comes to an end, and the Apostle
points to that on which it is ultimately
dependent. All these Christian experiences and hopes rest upon an assurance
of the love of God. ὅτι ἡ ἀγάπη τοῦ
Θεοῦ κ.τ.λ. That the love of God to us
is meant, not our love to Him, is obvious
from ver. 6 and the whole connection :
it is the evidence of God's love to us
which the Apostle proceeds to set forth.
ἐκκέχυται ἐν ταῖς καρδίαις ἡμῶν (*cf.*
Joel iii. 1, ii. 28, LXX, Acts x. 45) : has
been poured out in, and still floods, our
hearts. διὰ πνεύματος ἁγίου τοῦ δοθέντος
ἡμῖν : the aorist τοῦ δοθέντος can hardly
refer to Pentecost, in which case ἡμῖν
would express the consciousness of the
Christian community : the spirit was
given to Christians in virtue of their
faith (Gal. iii. 2), and normally on occasion of their baptism (1 Cor. xii. 13, Acts
xix. 1 ff.) : and it is this experience, possibly this event, to which the participle
definitely refers. What the spirit, given
(in baptism) to faith, does, is to flood
the heart with God's love, and with the
assurance of it.
Ver. 6. The reading εἴ γε is well supported, and yields a good sense ("so
surely as": Evans), though the suggestion is made in W. and H. that it may
be a primitive error for εἴ περ (see note
on iii. 30). The assurance we have of
the love of God is no doubt conditioned,
but the condition may be expressed with
the utmost force, as it is with εἴ γε, for
there is no doubt that what it puts as a
hypothesis has actually taken place, *viz.*,
Christ's death for the ungodly. Although
he says εἴ γε, the objective fact which
follows is in no sense open to question :
it is to the Apostle the first of certainties.
Cf. the use of εἴ γε in Eph. iii. 2, iv. 21,
and Ellicott's note on the former.
ἀσθενῶν : the weakness of men who had
not yet received the Spirit is conceived
as appealing to the love of God. ἔτι
goes with ὄντων ἡμ. ἀσθενῶν : the persons concerned were no longer weak,
when Paul wrote, but strong in their new
relation to God. κατὰ καιρὸν has been
taken with ὄντων ἡ. ἀ. ἔτι : "while we
were yet without strength, as the pre-
Christian era implied or required": but
this meaning is remote, and must have
been more clearly suggested. The anal-

7. ᵉ μόλις γὰρ ὑπὲρ δικαίου τις ἀποθανεῖται · ὑπὲρ γὰρ τοῦ ἀγαθοῦ ᵉ Acts xxvii.
¹ τάχα τις καὶ τολμᾷ ἀποθανεῖν · 8. συνίστησι δὲ τὴν ἑαυτοῦ ἀγάπην ⁷ f., 16; 1
Pet. iv.18.
εἰς ἡμᾶς ὁ Θεός,¹ ὅτι ἔτι ἁμαρτωλῶν ὄντων ἡμῶν Χριστὸς ὑπὲρ ἡμῶν ¹⁵. f Philem.
ἀπέθανε. 9. πολλῷ οὖν μᾶλλον, δικαιωθέντες νῦν ἐν τῷ αἵματι

¹ ο θεος om. B.

ogy of Gal. iv. 4, Eph. i. 10, supports the ordinary rendering, "in due time," i.e., at the time determined by the Providence of God and the history of man as the proper time, Christ died. ὑπέρ: in the interest of, not equivalent to ἀντί, instead of : whether the interest of the ungodly is secured by the fact that Christ's death has a substitutionary character, or in some other way, is a question which ὑπέρ does not touch.

Ver. 7. Christ's death for the ungodly assures us of God's love ; for the utmost that human love will do is far less. ὑπὲρ δικαίου: for a righteous man. Some make both δικαίου and τοῦ ἀγαθοῦ neuter : some who take δικαίου as masculine take τοῦ ἀγαθοῦ as neuter (so Weiss and Godet—" pour un juste, pour le bien ") : but as Jowett says, the notion of dying for an abstract idea is entirely unlike the N.T., or the age in which the N.T. was written, while the opposition to Christ's dying for sinful persons requires that persons should be in question here also. The absence of the article with δικαίου corresponds to the virtually negative character of the clause : it is inserted before ἀγαθοῦ because the exceptional case is definitely conceived as happening. ἀποθανεῖται, gnomic ; see Burton, § 69. Unless ἀγαθός is meant to suggest a certain advance upon δίκαιος, it is impossible to see in what respect the second clause adds anything to the first. Of course the words are broadly synonymous, so that often they are both applied to the same person or thing (Lk. xxiii. 50, Rom. vii. 12) ; still there is a difference, and it answers to their application here ; it is *difficult* to die for a just man, it has been found *possible* (one may venture to affirm) to die for a good man. The difference is like that between "just" and "good" in English : the latter is the more generous and inspiring type of character. *Cf.* the Gnostic contrast between the "just" God of the O.T. and the "good" God of the N.T., and the passages quoted in Cremer, *s.v.* ἀγαθός. καὶ τολμᾷ : even prevails upon himself, wins it from himself.

Ver. 8. How greatly is this utmost love of man surpassed by the love of God. He commends, or rather makes good, presents in its true and unmistakable character (for συνίστησιν, *cf.* iii. 5, 2 Cor. vi. 4, vii. 11 ; Gal. ii. 18), His own love toward us, in that while we were yet sinners, etc. ἑαυτοῦ is an emphatic *His :* His, not as opposed to Christ's (as some have strangely taken it), but as opposed to anything that we can point to as love among men : His spontaneous and characteristic love. ἔτι ἁμαρτωλῶν ὄντων ἡμῶν : they are no longer such, but justified, and it is on this the next step in the argument depends.

Ver. 9 f. πολλῷ οὖν μᾶλλον : The argument is from the greater to the less. The supreme difficulty to be overcome in the relations of man and God is the initial one : How can God demonstrate His love to the sinner, and bestow on him a Divine righteousness ? In comparison with this, everything else is easy. Now the Apostle has already shown (iii. 21-30) how the Gospel meets this difficulty : we obtain the righteousness required by believing in Jesus, whom God has set forth as a propitiation through faith in His blood. If such grace was shown us *then*, when we were in sin, much more, justified as we have now been by His blood, shall we be saved from wrath through Him. ἀπὸ τῆς ὀργῆς : the wrath to come : see note on i. 18. This deliverance from wrath does not exhaust Paul's conception of the future (see ver. 2), but it is an important aspect of it, and implies the rest. Verse 10 rather repeats, than grounds anew, the argument of ver. 9. εἰ γὰρ ἐχθροὶ ὄντες : this is practically equivalent to ἔτι ἁμαρτωλῶν ὄντων ἡμῶν. The state of sin was that in which we were ἐχθροί, and the whole connection of ideas in the passage requires us to give ἐχθροί the passive meaning which it undoubtedly has in xi. 28, where it is opposed to ἀγαπητοί. We were in a real sense objects of the Divine hostility. As sinners, we lay under the condemnation of God, and His wrath hung over us. This was the situation which had to be faced : Was

g 1 Thess. i. αὐτοῦ, σωθησόμεθα δι᾽ αὐτοῦ ἀπὸ τῆς ᵍὀργῆς.   10. εἰ γὰρ ἐχθροὶ
10.
ὄντες κατηλλάγημεν τῷ Θεῷ διὰ τοῦ θανάτου τοῦ υἱοῦ αὐτοῦ, πολλῷ
μᾶλλον καταλλαγέντες σωθησόμεθα ἐν τῇ ζωῇ αὐτοῦ · 11. οὐ μόνον
h 1Cor. i. 31. δὲ, ἀλλὰ καὶ καυχώμενοι ἐν τῷ ʰΘεῷ διὰ τοῦ Κυρίου ἡμῶν Ἰησοῦ
i 2 Cor. v. 18
f.   Χριστοῦ, δι᾽ οὗ νῦν τὴν ⁱκαταλλαγὴν ἐλάβομεν.

there love in God equal to it? Yes, when we were enemies we were reconciled to God by the death of His Son. κατηλλάγημεν is a real passive: "we" are the objects, not the subjects, of the reconciliation: the subject is God, 2 Cor. v. 19-21. Compare ver. 11: τὴν καταλλαγὴν ἐλάβομεν. To represent κατηλλάγημεν by an active form, e.g., "we laid aside our hostility to God," or by what is virtually one, e.g., "we were won to lay aside our hostility," is to miss the point of the whole passage. Paul is demonstrating *the love of God*, and he can only do it by pointing to what *God* has done, not to what *we* have done. That we on our part are hostile to God before the reconciliation, and that we afterwards lay aside our enmity, is no doubt true; but here it is entirely irrelevant. The Apostle's thought is simply this: "if, when we lay under the Divine condemnation, the work of our reconciliation to God was achieved by Him through the death of His Son, much more shall the love which wrought so incredibly for us in our extremity carry out our salvation to the end". The subjective side of the truth is here completely, *and intentionally*, left out of sight; the laying aside of *our* hostility adds nothing to God's love, throws no light upon it; hence in an exposition of the love of God it can be ignored. To say that the reconciliation is "mutual," is true in point of fact; it is true, also, to all the suggestions of the English word; but it is not true to the meaning of κατηλλάγημεν, nor to the argument of this passage, which does not prove anything about the Christian, but exhibits the love of God at its height in the Cross, and argues from that to what are comparatively smaller demonstrations of that love. ἐν τῇ ζωῇ αὐτοῦ: the ἐν is instrumental: *cf.* ver. 9 ἐν τῷ αἵματι αὐτοῦ. The Living Lord, in virtue of His life, will save us to the uttermost. *Cf.* John xiv. 19.

Ver. 11. καυχώμενοι is the best attested reading, but hard to construe. It is awkward (with Meyer) to supply καταλλαγέντες with οὐ μόνον δὲ, and retain σωθησόμεθα as the principal verb:

and not only (as reconciled shall we be saved), but also rejoicing, etc. There is no proportion between the things thus co-ordinated, and it is better to assume an inexact construction, and regard καυχώμενοι as adding an independent idea which would have been more properly expressed by the indicative (καυχώμεθα). But see Winer, 441. The Christian glories in God; for though "boasting is excluded" from the true religion (iii. 27); yet to make one's boast *in God* is the perfection of that religion. Yet the believer could not thus glory, but for the Lord Jesus Christ; it is in Him, "clothed in the Gospel," that he obtains that knowledge of God's character which enables him to exult. δι᾽ οὗ νῦν τὴν καταλλαγὴν ἐλάβομεν. Nothing could show more unmistakably that the καταλλαγή is not a change in our disposition toward God, but a change in His attitude toward us. We do not *give* it (by laying aside enmity, distrust, or fear); we *receive* it, by believing in Christ Jesus, whom God has set forth as a propitiation through faith in His blood. We take it as God's unspeakable gift. *Cf.* 2 Macc. ii. 50. ὁ καταλειφθεὶς ἐν τῇ τοῦ παντοκράτορος ὀργῇ πάλιν ἐν τῇ τοῦ μεγάλου δεσπότου καταλλαγῇ μετὰ πάσης δόξης ἐπανωρθώθη. For an examination of the Pauline idea of reconciliation, see especially Schmiedel on 2 Cor. v. 21, *Excursus*.

Vers. 12-21. The treatment of the righteousness of God, as a Divine gift to sinners in Jesus Christ, is now complete, and the Apostle might have passed on to his treatment of the new life (chaps. vi.-viii.). But he introduces at this point a digression in which a comparison—which in most points is rather a contrast—is made between Adam and Christ. Up to this point he has spoken of Christ alone, and the truth of what he has said rests upon its own evidence; it is not affected in the least by any difficulty we may have in adapting what he says of Adam to our knowledge or ignorance of human origins. The general truth he teaches here is that there is a real unity of the human race, on the one hand in sin and

12. Διὰ τοῦτο ὥσπερ δι᾽ ἑνὸς ἀνθρώπου ἡ ἁμαρτία εἰς τὸν κόσμον
εἰσῆλθε, καὶ διὰ τῆς ἁμαρτίας ὁ θάνατος, καὶ οὕτως εἰς πάντας

death, on the other in righteousness and life; in the former aspect the race is summed up in Adam; in the latter, in Christ. It is a distinction, apparently, between the two, that the unity in Adam is natural, having a physical basis in the organic connection of all men through all generations; whereas the unity in Christ is spiritual, being dependent upon faith. Yet this distinction is not specially in view in the passage, which rather treats Adam and Christ in an objective way, the transition (morally) from Adam's doom to that of man being only mediated by the words πάντες ἥμαρτον in ver. 12, and the connection between Christ and the new humanity by οἱ τὴν περισσείαν τῆς χάριτος λαμβάνοντες in ver. 17.

Ver. 12. διὰ τοῦτο refers to that whole conception of Christ's relation to the human race which is expounded in chaps. iii. 21-v. 11. But as this is summed up in v. 1-11, and even in the last words of v. 11 (through Him we received the reconciliation) the grammatical reference may be to these words only. ὥσπερ: the sentence beginning thus is not finished; cf. Mt. xxv. 14. There is a virtual apodosis in the last clause of ver. 14: ὅς ἐστιν τύπος τοῦ μέλλοντος; the natural conclusion would have been, "so also by one man righteousness entered into the world, and life by righteousness". Cf. Winer, p. 712 f. By the entrance of sin into the world is not meant that sin began to be, but that sin as a power entered into that sphere in which man lives. Sin, by Divine appointment, brought death in its train, also as an objective power; the two things were inseparably connected, and consequently death extended over all men (for διῆλθεν, cf. Ps. lxxxvii. 17, Ez. v. 17) ἐφ᾽ ᾧ πάντες ἥμαρτον. The connection of sin and death was a commonplace of Jewish teaching, resting apparently on a literal interpretation of Gen. iii. Cf. Sap. ii. 23 f. ὁ θεὸς ἔκτισεν τὸν ἄνθρωπον ἐπ᾽ ἀφθαρσίᾳ . . . φθόνῳ δὲ διαβόλου θάνατος εἰσῆλθεν εἰς τὸν κόσμον. Cf. also Sir. xxv. 24, Rom. vi. 23, 1 Cor. xv. 56. Paul no doubt uses death to convey various shades of meaning in different places, but he does not explicitly distinguish different senses of the word; and it is probably misleading rather than helpful to say that in one sentence (here, for example) "physical" death is meant, and in another (chap. vii. 24, e.g.) "spiritual" death. The analysis is foreign to his mode of thinking. All that "death" conveys to the mind entered into the world through sin. The words ἐφ᾽ ᾧ πάντες ἥμαρτον, in which the πάντες resumes πάντας of the preceding clause, give the explanation of the universality of death: it rests upon the universality of sin. ἐφ᾽ ᾧ means propterea quod as in 2 Cor. v. 4 and perhaps in Phil. iii. 12. Winer, 491. But in what sense is the universality of sin to be understood? In other words, what precisely is meant by πάντες ἥμαρτον? Many interpreters take the aorist rigorously, and render: because all sinned, i.e., in the sin of Adam. Omnes peccarunt, Adamo peccante (Bengel). This is supported by an appeal to 2 Cor. v. 14, εἰς ὑπὲρ πάντων ἀπέθανεν· ἄρα οἱ πάντες ἀπέθανον: the death of one was the death of all; so here, the sin of one was the sin of all. It seems to me a final objection to this (grammatically quite sound) interpretation, that it really makes the words ἐφ᾽ ᾧ πάντες ἥμαρτον meaningless. They are evidently meant to explain how the death which came into the world through Adam's sin obtained its universal sway, and the reason is that the sin of which death is the consequence was also universally prevalent. The sense in which this was so has been already proved in chap. iii., and the aorist is therefore to be taken as in iii. 23: see note there. Because all men were, in point of fact, sinners, the death which is inseparable from sin extended over all. To drag in the case of infants to refute this, on the ground that πάντες ἥμαρτον does not apply to them (unless in the sense that they sinned in Adam) is to misconceive the situation: to Paul's mind the world consists of persons capable of sinning and of being saved. The case of those in whom the moral consciousness, or indeed any consciousness whatever, has not yet awakened, is simply to be disregarded. We know, and can know, nothing about it. Nothing has been more pernicious in theology than the determination to define sin in such a way that in all its damning import the definition should be applicable to "infants"; it is to this we owe the moral atrocities that have disfigured most

ἀνθρώπους ὁ θάνατος διῆλθεν, ἐφ᾽ ᾧ πάντες ἥμαρτον.   13. ἄχρι
γὰρ νόμου ἁμαρτία ἦν ἐν κόσμῳ· ἁμαρτία δὲ οὐκ ᵏἐλλογεῖται, μὴ
ὄντος νόμου.   14. ἀλλ᾽ ¹ἐβασίλευσεν ὁ θάνατος ἀπὸ Ἀδὰμ μέχρι
Μωσέως καὶ ἐπὶ τοὺς μὴ ἁμαρτήσαντας ¹ ἐπὶ τῷ ὁμοιώματι τῆς

k Philem.
18.
l Vv. 17, 21;
Ch. vi. 12.

---

¹ τοὺς μη αμαρτησαντας, so ℵABCD²G³K²L²; the μη was wanting in some MSS.
known to Origen and in "most Latin MSS." known to Augustine: see W. and H.,
Appendix.   However the omission may have originated, μη is undoubtedly the true
text.

---

creeds, and in great part the idea of
baptismal regeneration, which is an
irrational unethical miracle, invented
by men to get over a puzzle of their
own making.

Ver. 13 f. These two verses are rather
obscure, but must be intended (γὰρ) to
prove what has been asserted in ver. 12.
ἄχρι γὰρ νόμου = ἀπὸ Ἀδὰμ μέχρι
Μωσέως, ver. 14, the law meant being
the Mosaic. The sin which was in the
world before the law is not the guilt of
Adam's fall imputed to the race as fallen
in him, but the actual sin which individuals had committed. Now if law has
no existence, sin is not imputed. Cf. iv.
15. The natural inference would seem
to be that the sins committed during
this period could not be punished. But
what was the case ? The very opposite
of this. Death reigned all through this
period. This unrestrained tyranny of
death (observe the emphatic position
of ἐβασίλευσεν) over persons whose
sins cannot be imputed to them,
seems at variance with the explanation just adopted of πάντες ἥμαρτον.
Indeed Meyer and others use it to
refute that explanation. The reign of
death, apart from imputable individual
sin, implies, they argue, a corresponding
objective reign of sin, apart from individual acts : in other words, justifies the
interpretation of ἐφ᾽ ᾧ πάντες ἥμαρτον
according to which all men sinned in
Adam's sin, and so (and only so) became
subject to death. But the empirical
meaning of ἥμαρτον is decidedly to be
preferred, and we must rather fill out the
argument thus : "all sinned. For there
was sin in the world before Moses; and
though sin is not imputed where there is
no law, and though therefore no particular penalty—death or another—could
be expected for the sins here in question,
yet all that time death reigned, for in the
act of Adam sin and death had been
inseparably and for ever conjoined."
καὶ ἐπὶ τοὺς μὴ ἁμαρτήσαντας ἐπὶ τῷ
ὁμοιώματι κ.τ.λ.—even over those who

did not sin after the likeness of Adam's
transgression. For ἐπὶ, cf. Winer, p. 492.
This describes not some, but all of those
who lived during the period from Adam
to Moses. None of them had like Adam
violated an express prohibition sanctioned
by the death penalty. Yet they all died,
for they all sinned, and in their first
father sin and death had been indis-
solubly united. And this Adam is τύπος
τοῦ μέλλοντος sc. Ἀδάμ. In the coming
Adam and his relations to the race there
will be something on the same pattern
as this. 1 Cor. x. 6, 11, Heb. ix. 14,
1 Cor. xv. 22, 45, 49. Parallels of this
sort between Adam and the Messiah are
common in Rabbinical writings : e.g.,
Schöttgen quotes Neve Schalom, f. 160-
2. "Quemadmodum homo primus fuit
unus in peccato, sic Messias erit postremus, ad auferendum peccatum penitus;" and 9, 9 has "Adamus postremus
est Messias". Cf. Delitzsch : Brief an die
Römer, p. 82 f. The extent to which
the thoughts of this passage on sin and
death, and on the consequences of
Adam's sin to his descendants, can be
traced in Jewish writers, is not quite
clear. As a rule (see above on ver. 12)
they admit the dependence of death on
sin, though Schöttgen quotes a Rabbi
Samuel ben David as saying, "Etiamsi
Adamus primus non peccasset, tamen
mors fuisset". On the unity and solidarity of the race in sin and its consequences, they are not perfectly explicit.
Weber (Die Lehren des Talmud, p. 217)
gives the following summary : "There is
an inherited guilt, but not an inherited
sin ; the fall of Adam has brought death
upon the whole race, not however sinfulness in the sense of a necessity to commit sin ; sin is the result of each individual's decision ; it is, as far as experience goes, universal, yet in itself
even after the Fall not absolutely necessary". This seems to agree very
closely with the Apostle's teaching as
interpreted above. It is the appeal to
experience in Paul (πάντες ἥμαρτον),

παραβάσεως Ἀδάμ, ὅς ἐστι τύπος τοῦ μέλλοντος. 15. Ἀλλ' οὐχ ὡς τὸ παράπτωμα, οὕτω καὶ τὸ χάρισμα. εἰ γὰρ τῷ τοῦ ἑνὸς παραπτώματι οἱ πολλοὶ ἀπέθανον, πολλῷ μᾶλλον ἡ χάρις τοῦ Θεοῦ καὶ ἡ ᵐ δωρεὰ ἐν χάριτι τῇ τοῦ ἑνὸς ἀνθρώπου Ἰησοῦ ⁿ Χριστοῦ εἰς τοὺς πολλοὺς ἐπερίσσευσε. 16. καὶ οὐχ ὡς δι' ἑνὸς ἁμαρτήσαντος, τὸ δώρημα· τὸ μὲν γὰρ κρίμα ἐξ ἑνὸς εἰς κατάκριμα, τὸ δὲ χάρισμα ἐκ πολλῶν παραπτωμάτων εἰς δικαίωμα. 17. εἰ γὰρ τῷ τοῦ ἑνὸς ¹ παραπτώματι ὁ θάνατος ἐβασίλευσε διὰ τοῦ ἑνός, πολλῷ μᾶλλον οἱ τὴν ᵒ περισσείαν τῆς χάριτος καὶ τῆς δωρεᾶς τῆς δικαιοσύνης λαμβά-

m John iv. 10; Eph. iii. 7, iv. 7; n 1 Tim. ii. 5.

o 2 Cor. viii. 2; Jas. i. 21.

---

¹ τω του ενος אBCKLPD lat.; εν τω ενι D-gr.; ἐν ἑνὸς 47, W. and H. marg.; εν ενι παραπτωματι AFG and Weiss. της δωρεας om. B 49, Origen twice; W. and H. bracket. Ιησου Χριστου; but X. I. in B, Origen.

---

crossing with a transcendent view of the unity of the race in Adam, which gives rise to all the difficulties of interpretation; but without this appeal to experience (which many like Bengel, Meyer and Gifford reject) the whole passage would hang in the air, unreal. There must be something which involves the individual in Adam's fate; that something comes into view in πάντες ἥμαρτον, and there only; and without it our interest dies. A sin which we commit in Adam (and which never becomes ours otherwise) is a mere fancy to which one has nothing serious to say. Ver. 15. At this point the parallel of Adam and Christ becomes a contrast: not as the παράπτωμα (the word implies the Fall), so also is the χάρισμα (the gift which is freely provided for sinners in the Gospel, i.e., a Divine righteousness and life). οἱ πολλοὶ means "all," but presents the "all" as a great number. πολλῷ μᾶλλον: the idea underlying the inference is that God delights in mercy; if under His administration one man's offence could have such far-reaching consequences, much more reasonably may we feel sure of the universal influence of one Man's righteous achievement. This idea is the keynote of the whole chapter: see vers. 9, 10, 17. ἡ δωρεὰ ἐν χάριτι is to be construed together: to repeat the article before ἐν χάριτι is not essential, and ἡ δωρεὰ is awkward standing alone. God's χάρις is shown in the gift of His Son, Christ's in His undertaking in obedience to the Father the painful work of our salvation. εἰς τοὺς πολλοὺς like οἱ πολλοὶ is not opposed to "all," but to "one": it is indeed equivalent to "all," and signifies that the "all" are not few. The world

is the subject of redemption; if the race suffered through the first Adam, much more may we argue that what has been done by the Second will benefit the race. ἐπερίσσευσεν: the word is prompted by Paul's own experience: the blessedness of the Christian life far outwent the misery of the life under condemnation. Ver. 16. A fresh point of contrast. That which God bestows (for δώρημα, see Mayor on James i. 17) is not as through one that sinned: the analogy with Adam breaks down here. For the Divine judgment (κρίμα neutral) starting from one (person) resulted in condemnation (for all); whereas the free gift, starting from many offences (which appealed to the mercy of God), has resulted in a sentence of justification (for all). This abstract way of looking at the matter disregards what the Apostle insists on elsewhere, that this "sentence of justification" only takes effect for the individual on the condition of faith. The ἐκ πολλῶν παραπτωμάτων in this verse is a decisive argument for the meaning given above to πάντες ἥμαρτον: redemption is not inspired merely by the fall of the race in Adam, but by its actual and multiplied offences, and this is its glory. ἐξ ἑνός: ἑνὸς is masculine, resuming the ἑνὸς ἁμαρτήσαντος of the previous clause; not neuter, with παραπτώματος anticipated from the following clause. Ver. 17. This verse confirms the preceding. The argument is the same in kind as in ver. 15. The effects of the Fall are indubitable: still less open to doubt are the effects of the work of Christ. With οἱ τὴν περισσείαν τῆς χάριτος καὶ [τῆς δωρεᾶς] τῆς δικαιοσύνης λαμβάνοντες we again touch experience, and an empirical condition is attached

νοντες ἐν ζωῇ βασιλεύσουσι διὰ τοῦ ἑνὸς Ἰησοῦ Χριστοῦ. 18. Ἄρα
οὖν ὡς δι ἑνὸς παραπτώματος, εἰς πάντας ἀνθρώπους, εἰς κατάκριμα·
p Ch. iv. 25. οὕτω καὶ δι᾽ ἑνὸς δικαιώματος, εἰς πάντας ἀνθρώπους, εἰς ᵖ δικαίωσιν
ζωῆς. 19. ὥσπερ γὰρ διὰ τῆς παρακοῆς τοῦ ἑνὸς ἀνθρώπου ἁμαρ-
q Heb. v. 8. τωλοὶ κατεστάθησαν οἱ πολλοί, οὕτω καὶ διὰ τῆς �q ὑπακοῆς τοῦ ἑνὸς

to the abstract universality suggested by
ver. 12. The abundance of the grace
and of (the gift which consists in) righteousness has to be received by faith.
But when by faith a connection is formed
with Christ, the consequences of that
connection, as more agreeable to what
we know of God's nature, can be more
surely counted upon than the consequences of our natural connection with
Adam. Part of the contrast is marked
by the change from "death reigned" to
"*we* shall reign *in life*," not "life shall
reign in or over us". The future in
βασιλεύσουσιν is no doubt logical, but
it refers nevertheless to the consummation of redemption in the Messianic
kingdom in the world to come. *Cf.*
viii. 17, 21, Col. iii. 3 f., 2 Tim. ii. 12.
Ver. 18. With ἄρα οὖν (*cf*. vii. 3,
25, and often in Paul) the conclusion
of the argument is introduced. It is
simplest to take ἑνὸς in both clauses as
neuter. "As through one offence the
result for all men is condemnation, so
also through one righteous act the result
for all men is justification of life." The
result in both cases is mediated; in the
former, by men's actual sin; in the
latter, by their faith in Christ. It has
been questioned whether δικαίωμα can
mean a "righteous act,"—that which
Christ achieved in His death, conceived
as one thing commanding the approval
of God. This sense seems to be required
by the contrast with παράπτωμα, but
Meyer and others argue that, as in ver.
16, the meaning must be "a sentence of
justification". "Through one justifying
sentence (pronounced over the world
because of Christ's death) the result for
all men is justification of life." But this
justifying sentence *in vacuo* is alien to
the realism of Paul's thinking, and no
strain is put upon δικαίωμα (especially
when we observe its correspondence with
παράπτωμα) in making it signify Christ's
work as a thing in which righteousness
is, so to speak, embodied. Lightfoot
(*Notes on Epistles of St. Paul*, p. 292)
adopts this meaning, "a righteous deed,"
and quotes Arist., *Rhet*., i., 13, τὰ ἀδική-
ματα πάντα καὶ τὰ δικαιώματα, and
Eth. Nic., v., 7 (10): καλεῖται δὲ μᾶλλον

δικαιοπράγημα τὸ κοινόν: δικαίωμα δὲ
τὸ ἐπανόρθωμα τοῦ ἀδικήματος. This
sense of an act by which an injustice
is rectified is exactly suitable here.
Through this the result for all men is
δικαίωσις ζωῆς: for the genitive, see
Winer, p. 235. Simcox, *Language of
the N.T.*, 85. When God justifies the
sinner, he enters into and inherits life.
But Lightfoot makes it *gen. appos.*
Ver. 19. The sense of this verse has
been determined by what precedes. The
γὰρ connects it closely with the last
words of verse 18: "justification of *life*;
for, as through, etc.". ἁμαρτωλοὶ κατεστάθησαν: "were constituted sinners".
For the word κατεστ. *cf*. Jas. iv. 4, 2 Pet.
i. 8. It has the same ambiguity as the
English word "constituted" (S. and H.);
but we cannot say, from the word itself,
whether the many constituted sinners,
through the one person's disobedience,
are so constituted immediately and unconditionally, or mediately through their
own sin (to be traced back, of course, to
him); this last, as has been argued above,
is the Apostle's meaning. οὕτως καὶ διὰ
τῆς ὑπακοῆς τοῦ ἑνός: the application
of τῆς ὑπακοῆς has been disputed. By
some (Hofmann, Lechler) it is taken to
cover the whole life and work of Jesus
conceived as the carrying out of the
Father's will: *cf*. Phil. ii. 8. By others
(Meyer) it is limited to Christ's death as
the one great act of obedience on which
the possibility of justification depended:
cf. chap. iii. 25, v. 9. Both ideas are
Pauline, but the last seems most congruous to the context and the contrast
which pervades it. δίκαιοι κατασταθήσονται: "shall be constituted righteous";
the future shows again that Paul is dealing with experience, or at least with
possible experience; the logic which
finds the key to the passage in Bengel's
formula, *Omnes peccarunt Adamo peccante*, would have written here also
δίκαιοι κατεστάθησαν. It is because
Paul conceives of this justification as
conditioned in the case of each of the
πολλοί by faith, and as in process or
taking place in one after another that
he uses the future. A reference to the
Judgment Day (Meyer) is forced: it is

δίκαιοι κατασταθήσονται οἱ πολλοί. 20. Νόμος δὲ παρεισῆλθεν,
ἵνα πλεονάσῃ τὸ παράπτωμα. οὗ δὲ ἐπλεόνασεν ἡ ἁμαρτία, ὑπερεπερίσσευσεν ἡ χάρις· 21. ἵνα ὥσπερ ἐβασίλευσεν ἡ ἁμαρτία ἐν
τῷ θανάτῳ, οὕτω καὶ ἡ χάρις βασιλεύσῃ διὰ δικαιοσύνης εἰς ζωὴν
αἰώνιον, διὰ Ἰησοῦ Χριστοῦ τοῦ Κυρίου ἡμῶν.

not then, but when they believe in Christ,
that men are constituted δίκαιοι.

Ver. 20 f. "The comparison between
Adam and Christ is closed. But in the
middle, between the two, stood the law"
(Meyer). Paul must refer to it in such
a way as to indicate the place it holds
in the order of Providence, and especially
to show that it does not frustrate, but
further, the end contemplated in the
work of Christ. παρεισῆλθεν: see ver.
12 above. Sin entered into the world;
the Law entered into the situation thus
created as an accessory or subordinate
thing; it has not the decisive signficance
in history which the objective power of
sin has. Words in which the same prepositions have a similar force are
παρεισάγω, 2 Pet. ii. 1; παρεισδύνω,
Jude 4; παρεισφέρω, 2 Pet. i. 5: cf.
Gal. ii. 4. There is often in such words,
though not necessarily, the idea of
stealth or secrecy: we might render
"the law slipped in". ἵνα πλεονάσῃ
τὸ παράπτωμα: the purpose expressed
by ἵνα is God's: Winer, p. 575. The
offence is multiplied because the law,
encountering the flesh, evokes its natural
antagonism to God, and so stimulates it
into disobedience. Cf. Gal. iii. 19 ff., and
the development of this idea in chap. vii.
7 ff. As the offence multiplied, the need
of redemption, and the sense of that
need were intensified. οὗ δὲ ἐπλεόνασεν
ἡ ἁμαρτία: ἁμαρτία seems used here,
not παράπτωμα, because more proper
to express the sum total of evil, made up
of repeated acts of disobedience to the
law. "Sin" bulked larger, as "offence"
was added to "offence". οὗ might seem
to refer to Israel only, for it was there
that the law had its seat; but there is
something analogous to this law and its
effects everywhere; and everywhere as
the need of redemption becomes more
pressing grace rises in higher power to
meet it. ὑπερεπερίσσευσεν: "the ἐπλεόνασεν had to be surpassed" (Meyer).
Cf. 2 Cor. vii. 4. Paul is excessively
fond of compounds with ὑπέρ. The
purpose of this abounding manifestation
of grace is, "that as sin reigned in
death, so also should grace reign through
righteousness unto eternal life through

Jesus Christ our Lord". ἐν τῷ θανάτῳ:
it is more natural to oppose this to ζωὴ
αἰώνιος, and regard death as "a province
which sin had won, and in which it
exercised its dominion" (Gifford), than
to make it parallel (with Meyer) to διὰ
δικαιοσύνης, and render "in virtue of
death" (dat. instr.). Grace has not yet
attained to its full sovereignty; it comes
to this sovereignty as it imparts to men
the gift of God's righteousness (διὰ
δικαιοσύνης); its goal, its limit which
is yet no limit, is eternal life. Some,
however, construe εἰς ζωὴν αἰώνιον with
διὰ δικαιοσύνης: through a righteousness which ends in eternal life: cf. εἰς
δικαίωσιν ζωῆς, ver. 18. διὰ Ἰ. Χ. τοῦ
κυρίου ἡμῶν: this full rhetorical close
has almost the value of a doxology.

CHAPTER VI.—Vers. 1-14. In the fifth
chapter, Paul has concluded his exposition of the "righteousness of God"
which is revealed in the Gospel. But
the exposition leaves something to be
desired—something hinted at in iii. 8
("Let us do evil that good may come")
and recalled in v. 20 f. ("Where sin
abounded, grace did superabound"). It
seems, after all, as if the gospel did "make
void the law" (iii. 31) in a bad sense; and
Paul has now to demonstrate that it does
not. It is giving an unreal precision to
his words to say with Lipsius that he
has now to justify his gospel to the
moral consciousness of the Jewish
Christian; it is not Jewish Christians,
obviously, who are addressed in vi. 19 ff.,
and it is not the Jewish-Christian moral
consciousness, but the moral consciousness of all men, which raises the questions
to which he here addresses himself. He
has to show that those who have "received the reconciliation" (v. 11), who
"receive the abundance of the grace and
of the gift of righteousness" (v. 17), are
the very persons in whom "the righteous
requirement of the law" is fulfilled (viii.
4). The libertine argument is rather
Gentile than Jewish, though when Paul
speaks of the new religion as establishing
Law, it is naturally the Mosaic law of
which he thinks. It was the one definite
embodiment of the concept. The justification, to the moral consciousness, of the

a Ch. xi. 22
f.; Col. i.
23; 1
Tim. iv.
16.

b Col. ii. 12.

VI. 1. Τί οὖν ἐροῦμεν; ᵃἐπιμενοῦμεν[1] τῇ ἁμαρτίᾳ, ἵνα ἡ χάρις πλεονάσῃ; 2. μὴ γένοιτο. οἵτινες ἀπεθάνομεν τῇ ἁμαρτίᾳ, πῶς ἔτι ζήσομεν ἐν αὐτῇ; 3. ἢ ἀγνοεῖτε ὅτι ὅσοι ἐβαπτίσθημεν εἰς Χριστὸν Ἰησοῦν,[2] εἰς τὸν θάνατον αὐτοῦ ἐβαπτίσθημεν; 4. ᵇσυνετάφημεν οὖν αὐτῷ διὰ τοῦ βαπτίσματος εἰς τὸν θάνατον· ἵνα, ὥσπερ ἠγέρθη Χριστὸς ἐκ νεκρῶν διὰ τῆς δόξης τοῦ πατρός, οὕτω καὶ ὑμεῖς ἐν

[1] For επιμενουμεν read επιμενωμεν with ABCDF.

[2] Ἰησουν om. B and some cursives; W. and H. bracket. But this kind of omission is frequent; see Weiss, *Textkritik*, S. 88.

Gospel in which a Divine righteousness is freely held out in Jesus Christ to the sinner's faith, fills the next three chapters. In chap. vi. it is shown that the Christian, in baptism, dies to sin; in chap. vii., that by death he is freed from the law, which in point of fact, owing to the corruption of his nature, perpetually stimulates sin; in chap. viii., that the Spirit imparted to believers breaks the power of the flesh, and enables them to live to God.

Ver. 1. Τί οὖν ἐροῦμεν; What inference then shall we draw, *i.e.*, from the relations of sin and grace expounded in v. 20 f.? Are we to continue in sin (*cf.* xi. 22 f.) that grace may abound? Lightfoot suggests "*the* sin" and "*the* grace" just referred to. The question was one sure to be asked by some one; Paul recognises it as a natural question in view of his doctrine, and asks it himself. But he answers it with an indignant negative.

Ver. 2. μὴ γένοιτο, *cf.* iii. 4. οἵτινες ἀπεθάνομεν τῇ ἁμαρτίᾳ: the relative is qualitative: "we, being as we are persons who died to sin". For the dative, see vers. 10, 11, and Winer, p. 263. To have died to sin is to be utterly and for ever out of any relation to it. πῶς ἔτι ζήσομεν; how after that shall we live in it? impossible.

Ver. 3. But this death to sin, on which the whole argument turns, raises a question. It is introduced here quite abruptly; there has been no mention of it hitherto. *When*, it may be asked, did this all-important death take place? The answer is: It is involved in baptism. ἢ ἀγνοεῖτε ὅτι κ.τ.λ.: the only alternative to accepting this argument is to confess ignorance of the meaning of the rite in which they had been received into the Church. ὅσοι ἐβαπτίσθημεν: we all, who were baptised into Christ Jesus, were baptised into His death. The ὅσοι is not partitive but distributive: there is

no argument in the passage at all, unless all Christians were baptised. The expression βαπτισθῆναι εἰς Χριστὸν does not necessarily mean to be baptised into Christ; it may only mean to be baptised Christward, *i.e.*, with Christ in view as the object of faith. *Cf.* 1 Cor. x. 2, and the expression βαπτισθῆναι εἰς τὸ ὄνομα τοῦ Κυρίου Ἰησοῦ. In the same way βαπτισθῆναι εἰς τὸν θάνατον αὐτοῦ might certainly mean to be baptised with Christ's death in view as the object of faith. This is the interpretation of Lipsius. But it falls short of the argumentative requirements of the passage, which demand the idea of an actual union to, or incorporation in, Christ. This is more than Lipsius means, but it does not exclude what he means. The baptism in which we are united to Christ and to His death is one in which we confess our faith, looking to Him and His death. To say that faith justifies but baptism regenerates, breaking the Christian life into two unrelated pieces, as Weiss does—one spiritual and the other magical—is to throw away the Apostle's case. His whole point is that no such division *can* be made. Unless there is a *necessary* connection between justification by faith and the new life, Paul fails to prove that faith establishes the law. The real argument which unites chaps. iii., iv. and v. to chaps. vi., vii. and viii., and repels the charge of antinomianism, is this: justifying faith, looking to Christ and His death, really unites us to Him who died and rose again, as the symbolism of baptism shows to every Christian.

Ver. 4. This symbolism interpreted. συνετάφημεν οὖν αὐτῷ κ.τ.λ.: Therefore we were buried with Him (in the act of immersion) through that baptism into His death—burial being regarded as the natural sequence of death, and a kind of seal set to its reality. *Cf.* 1 Cor. xv. 3 f. It introduces a false abstraction to say

καινότητι ζωῆς περιπατήσωμεν. 5. Εἰ γὰρ °σύμφυτοι γεγόναμεν c Here only,
τῷ ᵈ ὁμοιώματι τοῦ θανάτου αὐτοῦ, ἀλλὰ καὶ τῆς ἀναστάσεως ἐσόμεθα · cf. Luke
viii. 7.
6. τοῦτο γινώσκοντες, ὅτι ὁ παλαιὸς ἡμῶν °ἄνθρωπος συνεσταυρώθη, d Ch. i. 23,
v. 14, viii.
ἵνα καταργηθῇ τὸ σῶμα τῆς ἁμαρτίας, τοῦ μηκέτι δουλεύειν ἡμᾶς τῇ 3; Phil. ii.
7; Rev.
ἁμαρτίᾳ. 7. ὁ γὰρ ἀποθανὼν δεδικαίωται ᶠ ἀπὸ τῆς ἁμαρτίας. 8. e Eph. iv.22;
ix. 7.
Εἰ δὲ ἀπεθάνομεν σὺν Χριστῷ, πιστεύομεν ὅτι καὶ συζήσομεν αὐτῷ· Col. iii. 9.
f Acts xiii.
9. εἰδότες ὅτι Χριστὸς ἐγερθεὶς ἐκ νεκρῶν οὐκ ἔτι ἀποθνήσκει · θάνα- 39.

(with Meyer) that εἰς τὸν θάνατον means
"unto death," not "unto His death":
death in the whole context is perfectly
definite. διὰ τῆς δόξης τοῦ πατρός: in
nothing was the splendour of God's
power revealed so much as in the resurrection of Jesus, Eph. i. 19 f. ἐν
καινότητι ζωῆς: in life of a new quality;
cf. vii. 6, 1 Tim. vi. 17: the construction
makes the new quality of the life prominent. Winer, p. 296.

Ver. 5. This verse proves the legitimacy of the reference to a new life in the
preceding one: union with Christ at one
point (His death) is union with Him
altogether (and therefore in His resurrection). εἰ γὰρ σύμφυτοι γεγόναμεν τῷ
ὁμοιώματι τοῦ θανάτου αὐτοῦ: it is simplest to take συμφ. and τῷ ὁμοιώματι
together—if we have become vitally one
with the likeness of His death; i.e., if
the baptism, which is a similitude of
Christ's death, has had a reality answering to its obvious import, so that we
have really died in it as Christ died, then
we shall have a corresponding experience
of resurrection. τῆς ἀναστάσεως is also
dependent on ὁμοιώματι: baptism, inasmuch as one emerges from the water
after being immersed, is a ὁμοίωμα of
resurrection as well as of death. It does
not seem a real question to ask whether
the ἀνάστασις is ethical or transcendent:
one cannot imagine Paul drawing the
distinction here. (On the word ὁμοίωμα,
see Cremer.)

Ver. 6. All this can be asserted,
knowing as we do that "our old man"
= our old self, what we were before we
became Christians—was crucified with
Him. Paul says συνεσταυρώθη simply
because Christ died on the cross, and we
are baptised into that death, not because
"our old man" is the basest of criminals
for whom crucifixion is the proper penalty.
The object of this crucifixion of the old
man was "that the body of sin might
be brought to nought". τὸ σῶμα τῆς
ἁμαρτίας is the body in which we live:
apart from the crucifixion of the old self
it can be characterised as "a body of

sin". It may be wrong to say that it is
necessarily and essentially sinful—the
body, as such, can have no moral predicate attached to it; it would be as wrong
to deny that it is invariably and persist-
ently a seat and source of sin. The
genitive is perhaps qualitative rather than
possessive, though "the body of which
sin has taken possession" (S. and H.) is a
good paraphrase. See Winer, p. 235, 768.
This body is to be reduced to impotence
τοῦ μηκέτι δουλεύειν ἡμᾶς κ.τ.λ. "that
we may no longer be slaves to sin". The
body is the instrument we use in the
service of sin, and if it is disabled the
service must cease. For the gen. inf.,
see Burton, § 397.

Ver. 7. ὁ γὰρ ἀποθανὼν κ.τ.λ. Here
we have the general principle on which
the foregoing argument rests: death
annuls all obligations, breaks all ties,
cancels all old scores. The difficulty is
that by the words ἀπὸ τῆς ἁμαρτίας
Paul introduces one particular application
of the principle—the one he is concerned
with here—as if it were identical with
the principle itself. "Death clears men
of all claims, especially (to come to the
case before us) it clears us, who have
died with Christ, of the claim of sin, our
old master, to rule over us still." Weiss
would reject the introduction into this
clause of the idea of dying with Christ,
on the ground that the words σὺν Χριστῷ
bring it in as a new idea in the following
verse. But it is no new idea; it is the
idea of the whole passage; and unless
we bring it in here, the quittance from
sin (and not from any obligation in
general) remains inexplicable. Weiss, in
fact, gives it up.

Ver. 8. The Apostle now resumes his
main thought. συνζήσομεν: see note on
ἀνάστασις ver. 5: there is no conscious
separation of ethical and transcendent
life with Christ—to Paul it is one life.

Ver. 9. εἰδότες ... οὐκέτι ἀποθνήσκει:
The new life with Christ will be the same
which Christ Himself lives, a life inaccessible to death. The post-resurrection life of Jesus was not His old life over

τος αὐτοῦ οὐκ ἔτι κυριεύει. 10. ὃ γὰρ ἀπέθανε, τῇ ἁμαρτίᾳ ἀπέθανεν
ἐφάπαξ· ὃ δὲ ζῇ, ζῇ τῷ Θεῷ. 11. οὕτω καὶ ὑμεῖς λογίζεσθε ἑαυτοὺς
νεκροὺς μὲν εἶναι [1] τῇ ἁμαρτίᾳ, ζῶντας δὲ τῷ Θεῷ, ἐν Χριστῷ Ἰησοῦ
τῷ Κυρίῳ ἡμῶν.[2] 12. Μὴ οὖν βασιλευέτω ἡ ἁμαρτία ἐν τῷ θνητῷ

[1] νεκρους μεν ειναι ℵ³KLP; ειναι νεκρους μεν ℵ¹BC; om. ADF 17.
[2] τω κυριω ημων; om. ABDF, and edd.; ins. ℵCKLP.

again; in that life death had dominion over Him, because He made Himself one with us in all the consequences of sin; but now the dominion of death has expired. The principle of ver. 7 can be applied to Christ also: He has died, and the powers which in the old relations had claims upon Him—death, e.g.—have such claims no more.

Ver. 10. This is expanded in ver. 10. ὃ γὰρ ἀπέθανε, τῇ ἁμαρτίᾳ ἀπέθανεν ἐφάπαξ: the δ is 'cognate' accus. Winer, p. 209. "The death that He died, He died to sin once for all." The dative τῇ ἁμαρτίᾳ must be grammatically the same here as in vers. 2, 11, but the interpretation required seems different. While He lived, Christ had undoubtedly relations to sin, though sin was foreign to His will and conscience (2 Cor. v. 21); but after He died these relations ceased; sin could never make Him its victim again as at the Cross. Similarly while we lived (i.e., before we died with Christ), we also had relations to sin; and these relations likewise, different as they were from His, must cease with that death. The difference in the reference of the dative is no doubt an objection to this interpretation, and accordingly the attempt has been made to give the same meaning to dying to sin in Christ's case as in ours, and indeed to make our dying to sin the effect and reproduction of His. "The language of the Apostle seems to imply that there was something in the mind of Christ in dying for us that was the moral equivalent [italics ours] to that death to sin which takes place in us when we believe in Him, something in its very nature fitted to produce the change in us." Somerville, St. Paul's Conception of Christ, p. 100 f. He died, in short, rather than sin— laid down His life rather than violate the will of God; in this sense, which is an ethical one, and points to an experience which can be reproduced in others under His influence, He died to sin. "His death on the Cross was the final triumph of His holiness over all those desires of the flesh that furnish to man unregenerate the motive power of His life." But though this gives an ethical meaning to the words in both cases, it does not give exactly the same ethical meaning; a certain disparity remains. It is more in the line of all Paul's thoughts to say with Holtzmann (N. T. Theol., ii., 118), that Christ by dying paid to sin that tribute to which in virtue of a Divine sentence (κρίμα, v. 16) it could lay claim, and that those therefore who share His death are like Himself absolved from all claims of sin for the future. For ἐφάπαξ, see Heb. vii. 27, ix. 12, x. 10. The very idea of death is that of a summary, decisive, never-to-be-repeated end. ὃ δὲ ζῇ κ.τ.λ. "The life that He lives He lives to God".

Ver. 11. In this verse the application is made of all that precedes. The death with Christ, the life with Christ, are real, yet to be realised. The truth of being a Christian is contained in them, yet the calling of the Christian is to live up to them. We may forget what we should be; we may also (and this is how Paul puts it) forget what we are. We are dead to sin in Christ's death; we are alive to God in Christ's resurrection; let us regard ourselves as such in Christ Jesus. The essence of our faith is a union to Him in which His experience becomes ours. This is the theological reply to antinomianism.

Ver. 12 f. Practical enforcement of vers. 1-11. The inner life is in union with Christ, and the outer (bodily) life must not be inconsistent with it (Weiss). ἐν τῷ θνητῷ ὑμῶν σώματι: the suggestion of θνητὸς is rather that the frail body should be protected against the tyranny of sin, than that sin leads to the death of the body. μηδὲ παριστάνετε . . . ἀλλὰ παραστήσατε: and do not go on, as you have been doing, putting your members at the service of sin, but put them once for all at the service of God. For the difference between pres. and aor. imper., see Winer, p. 393 f. ὅπλα ἀδικίας: the gen. is of quality, cf. Luke xvi. 8, 9. ὅπλα in the N.T. seems always to mean weapons, not instruments: see

ὑμῶν [g] σώματι, εἰς τὸ ὑπακούειν αὐτῇ ἐν[1] ταῖς ἐπιθυμίαις αὐτοῦ · 13. g Ch.viii.11.
μηδὲ παριστάνετε τὰ μέλη ὑμῶν ὅπλα ἀδικίας τῇ ἁμαρτίᾳ · ἀλλὰ
παραστήσατε ἑαυτοὺς τῷ Θεῷ ὡς[2] ἐκ νεκρῶν ζῶντας, καὶ τὰ μέλη
ὑμῶν ὅπλα [h] δικαιοσύνης τῷ Θεῷ. 14. ἁμαρτία γὰρ ὑμῶν οὐ κυριεύσει · h Ch.xiii.12.
οὐ γάρ ἐστε ὑπὸ νόμον, ἀλλ᾽ ὑπὸ χάριν.

15. Τί οὖν; ἁμαρτήσομεν,[3] ὅτι οὐκ ἐσμὲν ὑπὸ [1]νόμον, ἀλλ᾽ ὑπὸ i 1 Cor ix.
χάριν; μὴ γένοιτο.   16. οὐκ οἴδατε ὅτι ᾧ παριστάνετε ἑαυτοὺς   20.
δούλους εἰς ὑπακοὴν, δοῦλοί ἐστε ᾧ ὑπακούετε, ἤτοι ἁμαρτίας εἰς
θάνατον, ἢ ὑπακοῆς εἰς δικαιοσύνην; 17. χάρις δὲ τῷ Θεῷ, ὅτι ἦτε

[1] αυτη εν C³KLP ; om. ℵABC¹ 47, vulg. ; αυτη only, DF, Orig.-inter. The
received reading is apparently an attempt to combine the other two.

[2] ως DFKLP 17 ; but ωσει ℵABC 47.

[3] For αμαρτησομεν ℵABCDKLP read αμαρτησωμεν.

2 Cor. x. 4, 6, 7, and cf. ὀψώνια, ver. 23.
ὡσεὶ ἐκ νεκρῶν ζῶντας: they were *really*
such ; the ὡσεὶ signifies that they are to
think of themselves *as* such, and to act
accordingly.

Ver. 14. They can obey these exhortations, for sin will not be their tyrant
now, since they are not under law, but
under grace. It is not restraint, but
inspiration, which liberates from sin:
not Mount Sinai but Mount Calvary
which makes saints. But this very way
of putting the truth (which will be expanded in chaps. vii. and viii.) seems to
raise the old difficulty of iii. 8, vi. 1
again. The Apostle states it himself,
and proceeds to a final refutation of it.

Ver. 15. ἁμαρτήσωμεν; deliberative:
are we to sin because our life is not ruled
by statutes, but inspired by the sense of
what we owe to that free pardoning
mercy of God? Are we to sin because
God justifies the ungodly at the Cross?

Ver. 16. οὐκ οἴδατε: It is excluded
by the elementary principle that no man
can serve two masters (Matt. vi. 24).
The δούλους is the exclusive property of
one, and he belongs to that one εἰς
ὑπακοὴν, with obedience in view; nothing
else than obedience to his master alone
is contemplated. The masters here are
ἁμαρτία whose service ends in death,
and ὑπακοὴ (*cf.* v. 19) whose service ends
in righteousness. δικαιοσύνη here cannot
be "justification," but righteousness in
the sense of the character which God
approves. ἤτοι here only in N.T. = *of
course* these are the *only* alternatives.

Ver. 17. Paul thanks God that his
readers have already made their choice,
and made it for obedience. ὅτι ἦτε . . .
ὑπηκούσατε δὲ: the co-ordination seems

to imply that Paul is grateful (1) that
their servitude to sin is *past*—ἦτε having
the emphasis ; (2) that they have received
the Gospel. Yet the two things are one,
and it would have been more natural to
subordinate the first: "that though ye
were slaves of sin, ye obeyed," etc.
ὑπηκούσατε εἰς ὃν παρεδόθητε τύπον
διδαχῆς must be resolved into ὑ. τῷ
τύπῳ τῆς διδαχῆς εἰς ὃν παρεδόθητε.
The alternative is εἰς τὸν τύπον τῆς
διδαχῆς ὃς παρεδόθη ὑμῖν (Kypke). But
ὑπακούειν εἴς τι only means to be
obedient with respect to something, not
to be obedient *to* some one, or some
thing, which is the sense required here.
A true parallel is Cyril of Jerus. Catechet.
lect. iv., § iii.: πρὸ δὲ τῆς εἰς τὴν
πίστιν παραδόσεως; the catechumens
were handed over to the faith. But
what is the τύπος διδαχῆς to which the
converts at Rome were handed over?
Many, in the line of these words of
Cyril, conceive of it as a "type of doctrine," a special mode of presenting the
Gospel, which had as catchwords, *e.g.*,
"not under law but under grace," or
"free from sin and slaves to righteousness," or more probably, "dying with
Christ and rising with Him". In other
words, Paulinism as modern theology
conceives it. But this is an anachronism.
It is only modern eyes that see distinct
doctrinal types in the N.T., and Paul,
as far as he knew (1 Cor. xv. 3-11),
preached the same Gospel as the other
Apostles. It is unnecessary, also, to the
argument. In whatever form the Gospel
won the obedience of men, it was inconsistent with their continuance in sin.
Hence it seems nearer the truth to take
τύπος διδαχῆς in a more general sense ;

δοῦλοι τῆς ἁμαρτίας, ὑπηκούσατε δὲ ἐκ καρδίας εἰς ὃν παρεδόθητε
τύπον διδαχῆς. 18. ἐλευθερωθέντες δὲ ἀπὸ τῆς ἁμαρτίας, ἐδουλώθητε
τῇ δικαιοσύνῃ. 19. Ἀνθρώπινον λέγω διὰ τὴν ἀσθένειαν τῆς σαρκὸς

k Matt.
xxvi. 41. ᵏ ὑμῶν. ὥσπερ γὰρ παρεστήσατε τὰ μέλη ὑμῶν δοῦλα τῇ ἀκαθαρσίᾳ
καὶ τῇ ἀνομίᾳ εἰς τὴν ἀνομίαν, οὕτω νῦν παραστήσατε τὰ μέλη ὑμῶν

l 1 Thess. δοῦλα τῇ δικαιοσύνῃ εἰς ¹ ἁγιασμόν. 20. ὅτε γὰρ δοῦλοι ἦτε τῆς
iv. 3 f., 7;
Heb. xii. ἁμαρτίας, ἐλεύθεροι ἦτε τῇ δικαιοσύνῃ. 21. τίνα οὖν καρπὸν εἴχετε
14.
τότε, ἐφ᾽ οἷς νῦν ἐπαισχύνεσθε; τὸ γὰρ τέλος ¹ ἐκείνων θάνατος. 22.

m Luke iii. νυνὶ δὲ ἐλευθερωθέντες ἀπὸ τῆς ἁμαρτίας, δουλωθέντες δὲ τῷ Θεῷ,
14; 1 Cor.
ix. 7; 2 ἔχετε τὸν καρπὸν ὑμῶν εἰς ἁγιασμόν, τὸ δὲ τέλος ζωὴν αἰώνιον.
Cor. xi. 8. 23. τὰ γὰρ ᵐ ὀψώνια τῆς ἁμαρτίας θάνατος· τὸ δὲ χάρισμα τοῦ

¹ το γαρ τελος ℵ¹ACD³KLP; το μεν γαρ τελος ℵ³BD¹F, Syr. As the reasons
for omitting are obvious—the art. is already separated from the substantive, and
there is really nothing to balance it—the μεν is probably original, and is retained
by Lachmann, Weiss, and Tregelles (marg.), though omitted by W. and H.

it is teaching, of course in a definite
form, but regarded chiefly in its ethical
requirements; when received, or when
men were handed over to it, it became a
moral authority. *Cf.* Hort, *Romans and
Ephesians*, p. 32 f. What is the time
referred to in the aorists ὑπηκούσατε
and παρεδόθητε? It is the time when
they became Christians, a time really
fixed by their acceptance of the Gospel
in faith, and outwardly marked by baptism. Baptism is the visible point of
separation between the two servitudes—
to sin and to God.

Ver. 18. There is no absolute independence for man; our nature requires
us to serve *some* master.

Ver. 19. ἀνθρώπινον λέγω διὰ τὴν
ἀσθένειαν τῆς σαρκὸς ὑμῶν. *Cf.* iii. 5,
Gal. iii. 15. Paul apologises for using
this human figure of the relation of slave
to master to convey spiritual truths.
But what is "the weakness of the flesh"
which makes him have recourse to such
figures? Weiss makes it moral. The
Apostle speaks with this unmistakable
plainness and emphasis because he is
writing to morally weak persons whose
nature and past life really made them
liable to temptations to libertinism. This
seems to me confirmed by the reference,
which immediately follows, to the character of their pre-Christian life. Others
make the weakness rather intellectual
than ethical, as if Paul said: "I condescend to your want of spiritual intelligence in using such figures". But this
is not a natural meaning for "the weakness of your flesh," and does not yield
so good a connection with what follows.

δοῦλα τῇ ἀκαθαρσίᾳ καὶ τῇ ἀνομίᾳ:
ἀκαθαρσία defiling the sinner, ἀνομία
disregarding the will of God. If εἰς τὴν
ἀνομίαν should remain in the text, it may
suggest that this bad life never gets beyond itself. On the other hand, to present the members as slaves to righteousness has ἁγιασμός in view, which is a
higher thing. ἁγιασμὸς is sanctification,
primarily as an act or process, eventually
as a result. It is unreal to ask whether
the process or the result is meant here:
they have no meaning apart.

Ver. 20. In every state in which man
lives, there is a bondage and a liberty.
In the old state, it was bondage to sin,
and liberty in relation to righteousness.
For τῇ δικαιοσύνῃ see Winer, 263.

Ver. 21 f. To decide which of the two
lives, or of the two freedoms, is the true,
Paul appeals to their fruits. The marked
contrast between τότε and νῦν is in favour
of those who put the mark of interrogation after τότε. "What fruit therefore
had you *then?* Things of which you are
now ashamed." The construction ἐφ᾽
οἷς ἐπαισχύνεσθε is found also in Isa. i.
29: ᾐσχύνθησαν ἐπὶ τοῖς κήποις. If
the point of interrogation is put after
ἐπαισχύνεσθε, the answer "none" must
be interpolated: and ἐκείνων supplied as
antecedent to ἐφ᾽ οἷς. νυνὶ δέ: But *now*,
now that the situation is reversed, and
you have been freed from sin and made
slaves to God, you have your fruit εἰς
ἁγιασμόν. He does not say what the
fruit is, but we know what the things
are which contribute to and result in
ἁγιασμός: see ver. 19.

Ver. 23. The γὰρ introduces the

Θεοῦ ζωὴ αἰώνιος ἐν Χριστῷ Ἰησοῦ τῷ Κυρίῳ ἡμῶν. VII. 1. Ἢ
ἀγνοεῖτε, ἀδελφοί (γινώσκουσι γὰρ νόμον λαλῶ,) ὅτι ὁ νόμος κυριεύει
τοῦ ἀνθρώπου ἐφ᾽ ὅσον χρόνον ζῇ; 2. ἡ γὰρ ὕπανδρος γυνὴ τῷ ζῶντι
ἀνδρὶ δέδεται νόμῳ· ἐὰν δὲ ἀποθάνῃ ὁ ἀνήρ, κατήργηται ἀπὸ τοῦ
ἀνδρός. 3. ἄρα οὖν ζῶντος τοῦ ἀνδρὸς μοιχαλὶς χρηματίσει, ἐὰν
γένηται ἀνδρὶ ἑτέρῳ· ἐὰν δὲ ἀποθάνῃ ὁ ἀνήρ, ἐλευθέρα ἐστὶν ἀπὸ
τοῦ νόμου, τοῦ μὴ εἶναι αὐτὴν μοιχαλίδα, γενομένην ἀνδρὶ ἑτέρῳ.
4. ὥστε, ἀδελφοί μου, καὶ ὑμεῖς ἐθανατώθητε τῷ νόμῳ διὰ τοῦ
σώματος τοῦ Χριστοῦ, εἰς τὸ γενέσθαι ὑμᾶς ἑτέρῳ, τῷ ἐκ νεκρῶν

general truth of which what has been said of the Romans in ver. 21 f. is an illustration. "All this is normal and natural, for the wages of sin is death," etc. ὀψώνια 1 Macc. iii. 28, xiv. 32. The idea of a warfare (see ὅπλα, ver. 13) is continued. The soldier's pay who enlists in the service of sin is death. τὸ δὲ χάρισμα: but the free gift, etc. The end in God's service is not of debt, but of grace. Tertullian (quoted in S. and H.) renders χάρισμα here *donativum* (the largess given by the emperor to soldiers on a New Year's Day or birthday), keeping on the military association; but Paul could hardly use what is almost a technical expression with himself in a technical sense quite remote from his own. On ζωὴ αἰώνιος ἐν Χ. Ἰ. τῷ κυρίῳ ἡμῶν, see on v. 21.

CHAPTER VII. The subject of chap. vi. is continued. The Apostle shows how by death the Christian is freed from the law, which, good as it is in itself and in the Divine intention, nevertheless, owing to the corruption of man's nature, instead of helping to make him good, perpetually stimulates sin. Vers. 1-6 describe the liberation from the law; vers. 7-13, the actual working of the law; in vers. 14-25 we are shown that this working of the law is due not to anything in itself, but to the power of sin in the flesh.

Vers. 1-6. For ἢ ἀγνοεῖτε, *cf.* vi. 3. Chap. vi. contains the argument which is illustrated in these verses, and the question alludes to it: not to accept the argument that the Christian is free from all legal obligations leaves no alternative but to suppose the persons to whom it is addressed ignorant of the principle by which the duration of all legal obligations is determined. This they cannot be, for Paul speaks γινώσκουσι νόμον = to people who know what law is. Neither Roman nor Mosaic law is specially referred to: the argument rests on the nature of law in general. Even in

ὁ νόμος, though in applying the principle Paul would think first of the Mosaic law, it is not exclusively referred to.

Ver. 2 f. An illustration of the principle. It is the only illustration in which death liberates a person who yet remains alive and can enter into new relations. Of course there is an inexactness, for in the argument the Christian is freed by his own death, and in the illustration the wife is freed by the husband's death; but we must discount that. Paul required an illustration in which both death and a new life appeared. κατήργηται ἀπό: *cf.* ver. 6, Gal. v. 4: she is once for all discharged (or as R.V. in Gal. "severed") from the law of the husband: for the genitive τοῦ ἀνδρός, see Winer, 235. χρηματίσει = she shall be publicly designated: *cf.* Acts xi. 26. τοῦ μὴ εἶναι αὐτὴν μοιχαλίδα κ.τ.λ.: grammatically this may either mean (1) *that she may not be* an adulteress, though married to another man; or (2) *so that she is not*, etc. Meyer prefers the first; and it may be argued that in this place, at all events, the idea of forming another connection is essential: *cf.* εἰς τὸ γενέσθαι ὑμᾶς ἑτέρῳ, ver. 4 (Gifford); but it is difficult to conceive of innocent remarriage as being formally the purpose of the law in question, and the second meaning is therefore to be preferred. *Cf.* Burton, *Moods and Tenses*, § 398.

Ver. 4. ὥστε καὶ ὑμεῖς ἐθανατώθητε τῷ νόμῳ: the inference is drawn rather from the principle than from the example, but καὶ ὑμεῖς means "you as well as the woman in the illustration," not "you Gentiles as well as I a Jew". The last, which is Weiss's interpretation, introduces a violent contrast of which there is not the faintest hint in the context. The meaning of ἐθανατώθητε is fixed by reference to chap. vi. 3-6. The aorist refers to the definite time at which in their baptism the old life (and with it all its legal obligations)

a Matt. xiii.
23; Col. i.
6, 10.
b Gal. v. 24.
ἐγερθέντι, ἵνα [b]καρποφορήσωμεν τῷ Θεῷ. 5. ὅτε γὰρ ἦμεν ἐν τῇ
σαρκὶ, τὰ [b]παθήματα τῶν ἁμαρτιῶν τὰ διὰ τοῦ νόμου ἐνηργεῖτο ἐν
τοῖς μέλεσιν ἡμῶν, εἰς τὸ καρποφορῆσαι τῷ θανάτῳ· 6. νυνὶ δὲ
κατηργήθημεν ἀπὸ τοῦ νόμου, ἀποθανόντες ἐν ᾧ κατειχόμεθα, ὥστε
δουλεύειν ἡμᾶς[1] ἐν καινότητι πνεύματος, καὶ οὐ παλαιότητι γράμματος.

7. Τί οὖν ἐροῦμεν; ὁ νόμος ἁμαρτία; μὴ γένοιτο· ἀλλὰ τὴν
ἁμαρτίαν οὐκ ἔγνων, εἰ μὴ διὰ νόμου· τήν τε γὰρ ἐπιθυμίαν οὐκ

[1] ημας om. BFG. Most edd. (W. and H., Lachm., and Treg.) bracket it; Weiss
omits, but allows that the case is disputable.

came to an end. διὰ τοῦ σώματος τοῦ
Χτοῦ: Weiss rejects as opposed to the
context the "dogmatic" reference to
the sacrificial death of Christ as a satisfaction for sin; all the words imply,
according to him, is that the Christian,
in baptism, experiences a ὁμοίωμα of
Christ's death, or as it is put in vi. 6 is
crucified with Him, and so liberated from
every relation to the law. But if Christ's
death had no spiritual content—if it
were not a death "for our sins" (1 Cor.
xv. 3), a death having the sacrificial
character and atoning virtue described
in iii. 25 f.—there would be no reason
why a sinful man should be baptised into
Christ and His death at all, and in point
of fact no one *would* be baptised. It is
because Christ's death is what it is, a
sin-expiating death, that it draws men
to Him, and spiritually reproduces in
them a reflex or counterpart of His death,
with which all their old relations and
obligations terminate. The object of
this is that they may belong to another,
a different person. Paul does not say
ἑτέρῳ ἀνδρί: the marriage metaphor is
dropped. He is speaking of the experience of Christians one by one, and
though Christ is sometimes spoken of as
the husband or bridegroom of the Church,
there is no Scripture authority for using
this metaphor of His relation to the
individual soul. Neither is this interpretation favoured by the use of καρποφορήσωμεν; to interpret this of the fruit
of the new marriage is both needless and
grotesque. The word is used frequently
in the N.T. for the outcome of the
Christian life, but never with this association; and a reference to vi. 21
shows how natural it is to the Apostle
without any such prompting. Even the
change from the second person (ἐθανατώθητε) to the first (καρποφορήσωμεν)
shows that he is contemplating the end
of the Christian life quite apart from the
suggestions of the metaphor. Christ is

described as τῷ ἐκ νεκρῶν ἐγερθέντι,
because we can only belong to a living
person. τῷ θεῷ is *dat. comm.* God is
the person interested in this result.

Ver. 5. Contrast of the earlier life.
"ἐν τῇ σαρκὶ" is materially the same
as "ὑπὸ τὸν νόμον"; the same state of
the soul is described more from within and
more from without. The opposite would
be ἐν τῷ πνεύματι, or ὑπὸ χάριν. τὰ παθήματα τῶν ἁμαρτιῶν are the passions from
which acts of sin proceed: Gal. v. 24.
τὰ διὰ τοῦ νόμου: it is through the law
that these passions become actualised:
we would never know them for what they
are, if it were not for the law. εἰς τὸ
καρποφορῆσαι τῷ θανάτῳ: there is no
allusion to marriage here any more than
in ver. 4. Death is personified here as
in v. 17: this tyrant of the human race
is the only one who profits by the fruits
of the sinful life.

Ver. 6. νυνὶ δὲ but as things stand, considering what we are as Christians. κατηργήθημεν: *cf.* ver. 2. We are discharged
from the law, by our death to that in which
we were held. But what is this? Most
expositors say the law; Philippi even
makes τοῦ νόμου the antecedent of ἐν ᾧ,
rendering, we have been delivered, by
dying, from the law in which we were
held. This construction is too artificial
to be true; and if we supply τούτῳ with
ἀποθανόντες, something vaguer than the
law, though involving and involved by it
(the old life in the flesh, for instance)
must be meant. ὥστε δουλεύειν κ.τ.λ.:
"enabling us to serve" (S. and H.): for
ὥστε with inf. in N.T., see Blass,
Gramm. des N.T. Griech., § 219. ἐν
καινότητι πνεύματος κ.τ.λ. = in a new
way, which only the possession of the
spirit makes possible, not in the old way
which alone was possible when we were
under the letter of the law. For the
Pauline contrast of πνεῦμα and γράμμα,
see 2 Cor. iii.; for οὐ in this expression,
see Burton, § 481.

ᾔδειν, εἰ μὴ ὁ νόμος ἔλεγεν, "Οὐκ ἐπιθυμήσεις". 8. ᵉἀφορμὴν ᶜ 2 Cor. xi.
δὲ λαβοῦσα ἡ ἁμαρτία διὰ τῆς ἐντολῆς κατειργάσατο ¹ ἐν ἐμοὶ πᾶσαν 12; Gal.
                                                 v. 13; 1
                                                 Tim. v.14.

¹ κατειργασατο ℵACFGKL ; κατηργασατο B¹DP. In chap. xv. 18 all editors
with ℵABCP read κατειργασατο, and this is preferred here by Lachm., W. and H.,
and by Weiss in all places ; but here Tischdf., Treg. and Alford read κατηργασατο.
Variations in the treatment of the augment are very frequent in the MSS.

Vers. 7-13. The actual working of the law. A very close connection between the law and sin is implied in all that has preceded : especially in vi. 14, and in such an expression as τὰ παθήματα τῶν ἁμαρτιῶν τὰ διὰ τοῦ νόμου in vii. 5. This connection has to be examined more closely. The object of the Apostle, according to Weiss, is not to answer a false inference from his teaching, *viz.*, that the law is sin, but to conciliate for his own mind the idea of liberation from the law with the recognition of the O.T. revelation. But the difficulty of conciliating these two things is not peculiar to the Apostle ; it is because we all feel it in some form that the passage is so real to us. *Our* experience of law has been as tragic as his, and we too ask how this comports with the idea of its Divine origin. The much discussed question, whether the subject of this passage (vers. 7-24) is the unregenerate or the regenerate self, or whether in particular vers. 7-13 refer to the unregenerate, and vers. 14-24 to the regenerate, is hardly real. The distinction in its absolute form belongs to doctrine, not to experience. No one could have written the passage but a Christian : it is the experience of the unregenerate, we may say, but seen through regenerate eyes, interpreted in a regenerate mind. It is the Apostle's spiritual history, but universalised ; a history in which one stage is not extinguished by the next, but which is present as a whole to his consciousness, each stage all the time determining and determined by all the rest. We cannot date the things of the spirit as simply as if they were mere historical incidents. τί οὖν ἐροῦμεν, *cf.* vi. 1 : What inference then shall we draw ? *sc.* from the relations of sin and law just suggested. Is the law sin ? Paul repels the thought with horror. ἀλλὰ τὴν ἁμαρτίαν οὐκ ἔγνων : ἀλλὰ may continue the protest = On the contrary, I should not have known sin, etc. ; or it may be restrictive, abating the completeness of the negation involved in the protest. The law is not sin—God forbid ; but, for all that, there is a connection : I should not have known sin but by the law. The last suits the context better : see ver. 21. On οὐκ ἔγνων without ἄν, see Winer, 383 : it is possible, however (Gifford), to render simply, I did not know sin except through the law ; and so also with οὐκ ᾔδειν. διὰ νόμου : of course he thinks of the Mosaic law, but the absence of the article shows that it is the legal, not the Mosaic, character of it which is in view ; and it is this which enables *us* to understand the experience in question. τήν τε γὰρ ἐπιθυμίαν κ.τ.λ. : the desire for what is forbidden is the first conscious form of sin. For the force of τε here see Winer, p. 561. Simcox, *Language of the N.T.*, p. 160. In the very similar construction in 2 Cor. x. 8 Winer suggests an anacoluthon : possibly Paul meant here also to introduce something which would have balanced the τε (I should *both* have been ignorant of lust, unless the law had said, Thou shalt not lust, *and* ignorant of other forms of sin unless the law had prohibited them). But the one instance, as he works it out, suffices him. It seems impossible to deny the reference to the tenth commandment (Exod. xx. 17) when the words οὐκ ἐπιθυμήσεις are quoted from "the law " ; but the special modes of ἐπιθυμία prohibited are of no consequence, and it is beside the mark to argue that Paul's escape from pharisaism began with the discovery that a feeling, not an outward act only, might be sinful. All he says is that the consciousness of sin awoke in him in the shape of a conflict with a prohibitive law, and to illustrate this he quotes the tenth commandment. Its generality made it the most appropriate to quote.

Ver. 8. ἀφορμὴν λαβοῦσα means "having received," not "having taken" occasion. ἡ ἁμαρτία is sin as a power dwelling in man, of the presence of which he is as yet unaware. How it "receives occasion" is not stated ; it must be by coming face to face with something which appeals to ἐπιθυμία ; but when it has received it, it avails itself of the commandment (*viz.*, the one prohibiting ἐπιθυμία) to work in us ἐπιθυμία of

ἐπιθυμίαν· χωρὶς γὰρ νόμου ἁμαρτία νεκρά· 9. ἐγὼ δὲ ἔζων χωρὶς

d Luke xv.
24, 32. νόμου ποτέ· ἐλθούσης δὲ τῆς ἐντολῆς, ἡ ἁμαρτία ^dἀνέζησεν, 10. ἐγὼ

δὲ ἀπέθανον· καὶ εὑρέθη μοι ἡ ἐντολὴ ἡ εἰς ζωὴν, αὕτη εἰς θάνατον.

e Ver. 8. 11. ἡ γὰρ ἁμαρτία ^eἀφορμὴν λαβοῦσα διὰ τῆς ἐντολῆς ἐξηπάτησέ

με, καὶ δι᾽ αὐτῆς ἀπέκτεινεν. 12. ὥστε ὁ μὲν νόμος ἅγιος, καὶ ἡ

ἐντολὴ ἁγία καὶ δικαία καὶ ἀγαθή. 13. Τὸ οὖν ἀγαθὸν ἐμοὶ γέγονε¹

θάνατος; μὴ γένοιτο· ἀλλὰ ἡ ἁμαρτία, ἵνα φανῇ ἁμαρτία, διὰ τοῦ

f 1 Cor. xii.
31; 2 Cor.
i. 8; iv.
17; Gal. i.
13. ἀγαθοῦ μοι κατεργαζομένη θάνατον, ἵνα γένηται καθ᾽ ^fὑπερβολὴν

ἁμαρτωλὸς ἡ ἁμαρτία διὰ τῆς ἐντολῆς. 14. Οἴδαμεν γὰρ² ὅτι ὁ

νόμος πνευματικός ἐστιν· ἐγὼ δὲ σαρκικός³ εἰμι, πεπραμένος ὑπὸ

---

¹ γεγονε KL; εγενετο אABCD.

² γαρ אBCFK; δε AD (Greek) L. See note ¹ page 604.

³ σαρκικος א³LP; but σαρκινος אABCDF. The two words are constantly confused (Alford), but the change may have been made intentionally here with the idea that an ethical word was wanted.

---

every sort. It really *is* the commandment which it uses, for without law sin is dead. *Cf.* iv. 15, v. 13: but especially 1 Cor. xv. 56. Apart from the law we have no experience either of its character or of its vitality.

Ver. 9. ἐγὼ δὲ ἔζων χωρὶς νόμου ποτέ: this is ideal biography. There is not really a period in life to which one can look back as the happy time when he had no conscience; the lost paradise in the infancy of men or nations only serves as a foil to the moral conflicts and disorder of maturer years, of which we are clearly conscious. ἐλθούσης δὲ τῆς ἐντολῆς κ.τ.λ. In these words, on the other hand, the most intensely real experience is vividly reproduced. When the commandment came, sin "came to life again"; its dormant energies woke, and "I died". "There is a deep tragic pathos in the brief and simple statement; it seems to point to some definite period full of painful recollections" (Gifford). To say that "death" here means the loss of immortality (bodily death without the hope of resurrection), as Lipsius, or that it means only "spiritual" death, is to lose touch with the Apostle's mode of thought. It is an indivisible thing, all doom and despair, too simply felt to be a subject for analysis.

Ver. 10. The result is that the commandment defeats its own intention; it has life in view, but it ends in death. Here also analysis only misleads. Life and death are indivisible wholes.

Ver. 11. Yet this result is not due to the commandment in itself. It is in-

dwelling sin, inherited from Adam, which, when it has found a base of operations, employs the commandment to deceive (*cf.* Gen. iii. 13) and to kill. "Sin here takes the place of the Tempter" in Genesis (S. and H.).

Ver. 12. The conclusion is that the law is holy (this is the answer to the question with which the discussion started in ver. 7: ὁ νόμος ἁμαρτία;), and the commandment, which is the law in operation, holy and just and good. ἁγία means that it belongs to God and has a character corresponding; δικαία that its requirements are those which answer to the relations in which man stands to God and his fellow-creatures; ἀγαθή that in its nature and aim it is beneficent; man's weal, not his woe, is its natural end. There is no formal contrast to ὁ μὲν νόμος, such as was perhaps in the Apostle's mind when he began the sentence, and might have been introduced by ἡ δὲ ἁμαρτία; but a real contrast is given in ver. 13.

Ver. 13. The description of the commandment as "good" raises the problem of ver. 7 in a new form. Can the good issue in evil? Did that which is good turn out to be death to me? This also is denied, or rather repelled. It was not the good law, but sin, which became death to the Apostle. And in this there was a Divine intention, *viz.*, that sin might appear sin, might come out in its true colours, by working death for man through that which is good. Sin turns God's intended blessing into a curse; nothing could more clearly show what it

τὴν ἁμαρτίαν. 15. ὃ γὰρ κατεργάζομαι, οὐ γινώσκω· οὐ γὰρ ὃ
θέλω, τοῦτο πράσσω· ἀλλ' ὃ μισῶ, τοῦτο ποιῶ. 16. εἰ δὲ ὃ οὐ
θέλω, τοῦτο ποιῶ, g σύμφημι τῷ νόμῳ ὅτι καλός. 17. νυνὶ δὲ οὐκ- gHere only.

is, or excite a stronger desire for deliverance from it. The second clause with ἵνα
(ἵνα γένηται καθ' ὑπερβολὴν ἁμαρτωλὸς
ἡ ἁμαρτία) seems co-ordinate with the
first, yet intensifies it: personified sin
not only appears, but actually turns out
to be, beyond measure sinful through its
perversion of the commandment.

Vers. 14-25. The last section of the
chapter confirms the argument in which
Paul has vindicated the law, by exhibiting the power of sin in the flesh. It is
this which makes the law weak, and
defeats its good intention. "Hitherto
he had contrasted himself, in respect of
his whole being, with the Divine law;
now, however, he begins to describe a
discord which exists within himself"
(Tholuck).

Ver. 14. ὁ νόμος πνευματικός: the
law comes from God who is Spirit, and
it shares His nature: its affinities are
Divine, not human. ἐγὼ δὲ σάρκινός
εἰμι, πεπραμένος ὑπὸ τὴν ἁμαρτίαν: I,
as opposed to the law, am a creature of
flesh, sold under sin. σάρκινος is properly material = carneus, consisting of
flesh, as opposed to σαρκικός, which is
ethical = carnalis. Paul uses it because
he is thinking of human nature, rather
than of human character, as in opposition
to the Divine law. He does not mean
that there is no higher element in human
nature having affinity to the law (against
this see vers. 22-25), but that such higher
elements are so depressed and impotent
that no injustice is done in describing
human nature as in his own person he
describes it here. Flesh has such an
exclusive preponderance that man can
only be regarded as a being who has no
affinity for the spiritual law of God, and
necessarily kicks against it. Not that
this is to be regarded as his essential
nature. It describes him only as πεπραμένος ὑπὸ τὴν ἁμαρτίαν: the slave of sin.
To speak of man as "flesh" is to speak
of him as distinguished from God who is
"Spirit"; but owing to the diffusion of
sin in humanity, and the ascendency it
has acquired, this mere distinction becomes an antagonism, and the mind of
"the flesh" is enmity against God. In
σάρκινος there is the sense of man's
weakness, and pity for it; σαρκικός
would only have expressed condemnation, perhaps a shade of disgust or con-

tempt. Weiss rightly remarks that the
present tense εἰμι is determined simply
by the ἐστιν preceding. Paul is contrasting the law of God and human
nature, of course on the basis of his own
experience; but the contrast is worked
out ideally, or timelessly, as we might
say, all the tenses being present; it is
obvious, however, on reflection, that the
experience described is essentially that
of his pre-Christian days. It is the unregenerate man's experience, surviving
at least in memory into regenerate days,
and read with regenerate eyes.

Ver. 15. Only the hypothesis of
slavery explains his acts. For what I
do οὐ γινώσκω, i.e., I do not recognise it
as my own, as a thing for which I am
responsible and which I can approve:
my act is that of a slave who is but the
instrument of another's will. οὐ γὰρ ὃ
θέλω κ.τ.λ. There is "an incomprehensible contradiction in his action".
κατεργάζεσθαι is to effect, to bring about
by one's own work; πράσσειν is to work
at, to busy oneself with, a thing, with
or without success, but with purpose;
ποιεῖν is simply to make or produce.

Ver. 16. ὃ οὐ θέλω takes up ὃ μισῶ:
the negative expression is strong enough
for the argument. In doing what he
hates, i.e., in doing evil against his will,
he will agrees with the law, that it is
good. καλός suggests the moral beauty
or nobility of the law, not like ἀγαθή
(ver. 12) its beneficial purpose.

Ver. 17. Νυνὶ δὲ οὐκέτι ἐγὼ κατεργάζομαι αὐτό. ἐγὼ is the true I, and emphatic. As things are, in view of the
facts just explained, it is not the true
self which is responsible for this line of
conduct, but the sin which has its abode
in the man: contrast viii. 11 τὸ ἐνοικοῦν
αὐτοῦ πνεῦμα ἐν ὑμῖν. "Paul said, 'It
is no more I that do it, but sin that
dwelleth in me,' and 'I live, yet not I,
but Christ that liveth in me'; and both
these sayings of his touch on the unsay-
able" (Dr. John Duncan). To be saved
from sin, a man must at the same time
own it and disown it; it is this practical
paradox which is reflected in this verse.
It is safe for a Christian like Paul—
it is not safe for everybody—to explain
his failings by the watchword, Not I,
but indwelling sin. That might be antinomian, or manichean, as well as evan-

ἔτι ἐγὼ κατεργάζομαι αὐτό, ἀλλ᾽ ἡ οἰκοῦσα¹ ἐν ἐμοὶ ἁμαρτία. 18.

Οἶδα γὰρ ὅτι οὐκ οἰκεῖ ἐν ἐμοὶ (τουτέστιν ἐν τῇ σαρκί μου,) ἀγαθόν·

h Only here τὸ γὰρ θέλειν ʰπαράκειταί μοι, τὸ δὲ κατεργάζεσθαι τὸ καλὸν οὐχ
and ver.
21.   εὑρίσκω.² 19. οὐ γὰρ ὃ θέλω ποιῶ ἀγαθόν· ἀλλ᾽ ὃ οὐ θέλω κακόν,

τοῦτο πράσσω. 20. εἰ δὲ ὃ οὐ θέλω ἐγὼ,³ τοῦτο ποιῶ, οὐκ ἔτι ἐγὼ

κατεργάζομαι αὐτό, ἀλλ᾽ ἡ οἰκοῦσα ἐν ἐμοὶ ἁμαρτία. 21. Εὑρίσκω

ἄρα τὸν νόμον τῷ θέλοντι ἐμοὶ ποιεῖν τὸ καλόν, ὅτι ἐμοὶ τὸ κακὸν

i Here only. παράκειται. 22. ⁱσυνήδομαι γὰρ τῷ νόμῳ τοῦ Θεοῦ κατὰ τὸν ἔσω

---

¹ For οικουσα אB read ενοικουσα, which is right.

² ουχ ευρισκω DFKLP ; ου alone without ευρισκω אABC.

³ θελω εγω אAKLP, Syr.; om. εγω BCDEFG. W. and H. omit εγω from text
but put it in marg. Weiss thinks if it had been inserted after the apodosis had been
written it would have been before ου θελω, and as it might easily be omitted to
conform to ver. 16, the first clause of which is verbally the same, he counts it genuine,
though admitting that the case is difficult.

---

gelical. A true saint may say it in a
moment of passion, but a sinner had
better not make it a principle.

Ver. 18. It is sin, and nothing but
sin, that has to be taken account of in
this connection, for " I know that in me,
that is in my flesh, there dwells no
good ". For τοῦτ᾽ ἔστιν see on i. 12. ἐν
ἐμοὶ = ἐν τῇ σαρκί μου = in me, regarded
as a creature of flesh, apart from any
relation to or affinity for God and His
spirit. This, of course, is not a complete
view of what man is at any stage of his
life. τὸ γὰρ θέλειν παράκειταί μοι :
θέλειν is rather wish than will : the
want of will is the very thing lamented.
An inclination to the good is at his
hand, within the limit of his resources,
but not the actual effecting of the good.

Ver. 19. In this verse there is a repetition of verse 15, but what was there
an abstract contrast between inclination
and action is here sharpened into the
moral contrast between good inclination
and bad action.

Ver. 20. The same conclusion as in
ver. 17. If the first ἐγὼ is right, it
must go with οὐ θέλω : Paul distinguishes
himself sharply, as a person whose inclination is violated by his actions, from
the indwelling sin which is really responsible for them.

Vers. 21-23 summarise the argument.
εὑρίσκω ἄρα τὸν νόμον . . . ὅτι : most
commentators hold that the clause introduced by ὅτι is the explanation of
τὸν νόμον. The law, in short, which
Paul has discovered by experience, is
the constant fact that when his inclination is to do good, evil is present with
him. This sense of law approximates

very closely to the modern sense which
the word bears in physical science—so
closely that its very modernness may
be made an objection to it. Possibly
Paul meant, in using the word, to convey at the same time the idea of an
outward compulsion put on him by sin,
which expressed itself in this constant
incapacity to do the good he inclined
to—authority or constraint as well as
normality being included in his idea of
the word. But ὁ νόμος in Paul always
seems to have much more definitely the
suggestion of something with legislative
authority : it is questionable whether the
first meaning given above would have
occurred, or would have seemed natural,
except to a reader familiar with the
phraseology of modern science. Besides,
the subject of the whole paragraph is
the relation of " the law " to sin, and the
form of the sentence is quite analogous
to that of ver. 10, in which a preliminary
conclusion has been come to on the
question. Hence I agree with those who
make τὸν νόμον the Mosaic law. The
construction is not intolerable, if we
observe that εὑρίσκω ἄρα τὸν νόμον τῷ
θέλοντι ἐμοὶ κ.τ.λ. is equivalent to
εὑρίσκεται ἄρα ὁ νόμος τῷ θέλοντι ἐμοὶ
κ.τ.λ. " This is what I find the law—
or life under the law—to come to in
experience : when I wish to do good, evil
is present with me." This is the answer
he has already given in ver. 7 to the
question, Is the law sin ? No, it is not
sin, but nevertheless sin is most closely
connected with it. The repeated ἐμοί
has something tragic in it : me, who am
so anxious to do otherwise.

Ver. 22 f. Further explanation : the

ᵏ ἄνθρωπον· 23. βλέπω δὲ ἕτερον νόμον ἐν τοῖς μέλεσί μου ἀντιστρα- ᵏ 2 Cor. iv.
τευόμενον τῷ νόμῳ τοῦ νοός μου, καὶ ¹αἰχμαλωτίζοντά με ¹ τῷ νόμῳ 16; Eph.
iii. 16.
τῆς ἁμαρτίας τῷ ὄντι ἐν τοῖς μέλεσί μου. 24. ταλαίπωρος ἐγὼ 1 2 Cor. x. 5.
2 Tim. iii.
ἄνθρωπος· τίς με ῥύσεται ἐκ τοῦ σώματος τοῦ θανάτου τούτου; 6.
25. εὐχαριστῶ² τῷ Θεῷ διὰ Ἰησοῦ Χριστοῦ τοῦ Κυρίου ἡμῶν. ἄρα
οὖν αὐτὸς ἐγὼ τῷ μὲν νοῖ³ δουλεύω νόμῳ Θεοῦ· τῇ δὲ σαρκὶ νόμῳ

---

¹ αιχμαλωτιζοντα με εν τω νομω ℵBDFKP; om. εν ACL, most cursives, Syr.
and many fathers. The omission, according to Weiss, is manifestly made to simplify
the expression. Lachm. omits; W. and H. bracket.

² ευχαριστω ℵAKLP, most cursives and fathers; W. and H. in marg. χαρις
B., Sah., Orig. 1. This is the reading adopted in all the crit. edd. as the one from
which the variants are most easily deduced (e.g., η χαρις του θεου D, vulg.; η χ. τ.
κυριου F; χαρις δε τω θεω ℵ¹C²).

³ τω μεν νοι, om. μεν ℵ¹FG, vulg., and Lat. fathers. The omission must be
accidental, and all edd. except Tischdf. keep μεν.

---

incongruity between inclination and
action has its roots in a division within
man's nature. The law of God legislates
for him, and in the inner man (Eph. iii.
16) he delights in it. The inner man is
not equivalent to the new or regenerate
man; it is that side of every man's
nature which is akin to God, and is the
point of attachment, so to speak, for the
regenerating spirit. It is called inward
because it is not seen. What *is* seen is
described in ver. 23. Here also νόμος is
not used in the modern physical sense,
but imaginatively: "I see that a power
to legislate, of a different kind (different
from the law of God), asserts itself in my
members, making war on the law of my
mind". The law of my mind is practically identical with the law of God in
ver. 22: and the νοῦς itself, if not
identical with ὁ ἔσω ἄνθρωπος, is its
chief organ. Paul does not see in his
nature two normal modes in which
certain forces operate; he sees two
authorities saying to him, Do this, and the
higher succumbing to the lower. As the
lower prevails, it leads him captive to the
law of Sin which is in his members, or in
other words to itself: "of whom a man
is overcome, of the same is he brought
in bondage". The end therefore is that
man, as a creature of flesh, living under
law, does what Sin enjoins. It is the law
of Sin to which he gives obedience.
Ver. 24. ταλαίπωρος ἐγὼ ἄνθρωπος·
τίς με ῥύσεται; "a wail of anguish and
a cry for help". The words are not
those of the Apostle's heart as he writes;
they are the words which he knows are
wrung from the heart of the man who
realises that he is himself in the state

just described. Paul has reproduced
this vividly from his own experience, but
ταλαίπωρος ἐγὼ ἄνθρωπος is not the cry
of the Christian Paul, but of the man
whom sin and law have brought to
despair. ἐκ τοῦ σώματος τοῦ θανάτου
τούτου: "*This* death" is the death of
which man is acutely conscious in the
condition described: it is the same as
the death of ver. 9, but intensely realised
through the experience of captivity to
sin. "The body of this death" is therefore the same as "the body of sin" in
chap. vi. 6: it is the body which, as the
instrument if not the seat of sin, is involved in its doom. Salvation must include deliverance from the body so far
as the body has this character and
destiny.
Ver. 25. The exclamation of thanksgiving shows that the longed-for deliverance has actually been achieved. The
regenerate man's ideal contemplation of
his pre-Christian state rises with sudden
joy into a declaration of his actual emancipation as a Christian. διὰ Ἰ. Χ. τοῦ
Κυρίου ἡμῶν: Christ is regarded as the
mediator through whom the thanksgiving
ascends to God, not as the author of the
deliverance for which thanks are given.
With ἄρα οὖν αὐτὸς ἐγώ the Apostle
introduces the conclusion of this whole
discussion. "So then I myself—that is,
I, leaving Jesus Christ our Lord out of
the question—can get no further than
this: with the mind, or in the inner man,
I serve a law of God (a Divine law), but
with the flesh, or in my actual outward
life, a law of sin." We might say *the*
law of God, or of sin; but the absence
of the definite article emphasises the

ἁμαρτίας. VIII. 1. Οὐδὲν ἄρα νῦν κατάκριμα τοῖς ἐν Χριστῷ Ἰησοῦ
a John viii.
32-36; Ch. μὴ κατὰ σάρκα περιπατοῦσιν, ἀλλὰ κατὰ πνεῦμα.[1] 2. ὁ γὰρ νόμος
vi. 18, 22;
Gal. v. 1. τοῦ πνεύματος τῆς ζωῆς ἐν Χριστῷ Ἰησοῦ ᵃἠλευθέρωσέ με[2] ἀπὸ τοῦ

[1] μη κατα σαρκα περιπατουσιν αλλα κατα πνευμα om. ℵ[1]BCD[1]F 47, Egypt. and
Ethiopic versions, Orig. and Athan. and all crit. edd. The first part of the addition,
μη . . . περιπατουσιν, is found in AD², vulg., Syr.; the rest, αλλα κατα πνευμα,
in ℵ³D³KLP and most later authorities.

[2] ηλευθερωσεν με ACDKLP, vulg., Syr. For με, σε is found ℵBFG, and also in
Latin and Syriac authorities. ημας is supported by Egypt. and Aeth. versions.
The case is a very difficult one. σε is the harder reading, and Weiss, who adopts
it, argues that it was changed into με under the influence of the preceding paragraphs in which the first person rules. Sanday and Headlam think σε can hardly
be right because it is nowhere suggested in the context. W. and H. suspect a
primitive error. "The distribution of documents, combined with internal evidence,
favours the omission of both pronouns, which is supported by some MSS. of
Arm(enian version), and perhaps by Orig. loc., Ruf. com.; σε, a very unlikely
reading, is probably only an early repetition of -σε" (Appendix to N.T., p. 108).

character of law. αὐτὸς ἐγώ: see 2
Cor. x. 1, xii. 13.

CHAPTER VIII. For the place of this
chapter in the argument see chap. vi.,
ad init. The general subject is the life
in the spirit, by which the power of sin
is broken, and the believer enabled to
live to God. It falls into three parts (1)
vers. 1-11, in which the spirit as opposed
to the flesh is described as the principle
of righteousness and life; (2) vers. 12-
27, in which it is regarded as a spirit of
adoption, the first fruits of a heavenly
inheritance for the children of God; and
(3) vers. 28-39, in which Paul concludes
the argument, glorying in the assurance
of God's immutable love in Jesus Christ.
(1) Vers. 1-11. The Spirit as the
principle of righteousness and life.
Ver. 1. οὐδὲν ἄρα νῦν κατάκριμα τοῖς
ἐν X. Ἰ. The οὐδὲν is emphatic: condemnation is in every sense out of the
question. νῦν is temporal: it distinguishes the Christian from the pre-
Christian period of life. The bold assertion is an inference (ἄρα) from what is
implied in the thanksgiving to God
through Jesus Christ (vii. 25). The description of Christians as "those who
are in Christ Jesus" goes back to the
words of Jesus Himself in John xv.
Ver. 2. There is no condemnation,
for all ground for it has been removed.
"The law of the spirit of the life which
is in Christ Jesus made me [thee] free
from the law of sin and death." It is
subjection to the law of sin and death
which involves condemnation; emancipation from it leaves no place for condemnation. For the meaning of "the
law" see on vii. 23. The spirit which

brings to the believer the life which is
in Christ Jesus brings with it also the
Divine law for the believer's life; but it
is now, as Paul says in Gal. iii. 21, a
"νόμος ὁ δυνάμενος ζωοποιῆσαι," not an
impotent law written on tables of stone,
and hence righteousness comes by it;
it proves more than a match for the
authority exercised over man by the
forces of sin and death. Paul would
not have called the Divine law (even as
a series of statutes) a law of sin and
death, though he says τὸ γράμμα ἀπο-
κτείνει; Sin and Death are conceived
objectively as powers which impose
their own law on unredeemed men.
Ver. 3. He now explains how this
was done. It was not done by the law:
that is the first point. If τὸ ἀδύνατον is
active (= "the inability" of the law) we
must suppose that Paul meant to finish
the sentence, "was overcome," or "was
removed" by God. If it is passive (=
"that which is impossible" for the law),
we must suppose he meant to finish it,
"was achieved" or "accomplished" by
God. There is really no way of deciding whether ἀδύνατον is active or passive,
and the anacoluthon makes it impossible
to tell what construction Paul had in his
mind, i.e., whether ἀδύνατον is nominative or accusative. For the best examination of the grammar see S. and H. ἐν
ᾧ probably refers to ἀδύνατον: the point
at which the law was impotent, in which
it was weak through the flesh. This is
better than to render ἐν ᾧ "in that," or
"because". For the meaning cf. vii. 18.
What the law could not do, God did by
sending τὸν ἑαυτοῦ υἱὸν His own Son.
With the coming of so great a Person,

νόμου τῆς ἁμαρτίας καὶ τοῦ θανάτου. 3. Τὸ γὰρ ἀδύνατον τοῦ νόμου, ἐν ᾧ ἠσθένει διὰ τῆς σαρκός, ὁ Θεὸς τὸν ἑαυτοῦ υἱὸν πέμψας ἐν ᵇὁμοιώματι σαρκὸς ἁμαρτίας καὶ περὶ ἁμαρτίας κατέκρινε τὴν ᵇ See Ch. vi. v.

uniquely related to God (for this is implied both here and in ver. 32, as contrasted with ver. 14), a new saving power entered the world. God sent His Son ἐν ὁμοιώματι σαρκὸς ἁμαρτίας. The connection implies that sending Him thus was in some way related to the end to be secured. But what do the words mean? ὁμοίωμα occurs in Rom. i. 23, v. 14, vi. 5, and also in Phil. ii. 7. This last passage, in which Christ is described as ἐν ὁμοιώματι ἀνθρώπων γενόμενος, is the one which is most akin to Rom. viii. 3, and most easily illustrates it. There must have been a reason why Paul wrote in Philippians ἐν ὁμοιώματι ἀνθ. γενόμενος instead of ἄνθρωπος γενόμενος, and it may well have been the same reason which made him write here ἐν ὁμοιώματι σαρκὸς ἁμαρτίας instead of ἐν σαρκὶ ἁμαρτίας. He wishes to indicate not that Christ was not really man, or that His flesh was not really what in us is σάρξ ἁμαρτίας, but that what for ordinary men is their natural condition is for this Person only an assumed condition (Holtzmann, N.T. Theol., ii., 74). But the emphasis in ὁμοίωμα is on Christ's likeness to us, not His unlikeness; "flesh of sin" is one idea to the Apostle, and what he means by it is that God sent His Son in that nature which in us is identified with sin. This was the "form" (and "form" rather than "likeness" is what ὁμοίωμα signifies) in which Christ appeared among men. It does not prejudice Christ's sinlessness, which is a fixed point with the Apostle ab initio; and if any one says that it involves a contradiction to maintain that Christ was sinless, and that He came in a nature which in us is identified with sin, it may be pointed out that this identification does not belong to the essence of our nature, but to its corruption, and that the uniform teaching of the N.T. is that Christ is one with us—short of sin. The likeness and the limitation of it (though the former is the point here urged) are equally essential in the Redeemer. But God sent His Son not only ἐν ὁμ. σ. ἁ. but καὶ περὶ ἁμαρτίας. These words indicate the aim of the mission. Christ was sent in our nature "in connection with sin". The R.V. renders "as an offering for sin". This is legitimate, for περὶ ἁμαρτίας is used

both in the LXX (Lev. iv. 33 and passim, Ps. xl. 6, 2 Chr. xxix. 24) and in the N.T. (Heb. x. 6, 8) in the sense of "sin-offering" (usually answering to Heb. חַטָּאת, but in Isa. liii. 10 to אָשָׁם); but it is not formally necessary. But when the question is asked, In what sense did God send His Son "in connection with sin"? there is only one answer possible. He sent Him to expiate sin by His sacrificial death. This is the centre and foundation of Paul's gospel (iii. 25 ff.), and to ignore it here is really to assume that he used the words καὶ περὶ ἁμαρτίας (which have at least sacrificial associations) either with no meaning in particular, or with a meaning alien to his constant and dearest thoughts. Weiss says it is impossible to think here of expiating sin, because only the removal of the power of sin belongs to the context. But we cannot thus set the end against the means; the Apostle's doctrine is that the power of sin cannot be broken except by expiating it, and that is the very thing he teaches here. This fixes the meaning and the reference of κατέκρινεν. It is sometimes interpreted as if Christ were the subject: "Christ by His sinless life in our nature condemned sin in that nature," i.e., showed that it was not inevitable, and in so doing gave us hope; and this sense of "condemned" is supported by reference to Mt. xii. 41 f. But the true argument (especially according to the analogy of that passage) would rather be, "Christ by His sinless life in our nature condemned our sinful lives, and left us inexcusable and without hope". The truth is, we get on to a wrong track if we ignore the force of περὶ ἁμαρτίας, or fail to see that God, not Christ, is the subject of κατέκρινεν. God's condemnation of sin is expressed in His sending His Son in our nature, and in such a connection with sin that He died for it—i.e., took its condemnation upon Himself. Christ's death exhibits God's condemnation of sin in the flesh. ἐν τῇ σαρκὶ is to be construed with κατέκρινεν: the flesh—that in which sin had reigned—was also that in which God's condemnation of sin was executed. But Paul does not mean that by His sinless life in our nature Christ had broken the power of

c Ch. ii. 26., ἁμαρτίαν ἐν τῇ σαρκὶ. 4. ἵνα τὸ δικαίωμα τοῦ ᵉ νόμου πληρωθῇ ἐν ἡμῖν, τοῖς μὴ κατὰ σάρκα περιπατοῦσιν, ἀλλὰ κατὰ πνεῦμα. 5. Οἱ

d Ch. xii. 3, γὰρ κατὰ σάρκα ὄντες τὰ τῆς σαρκὸς ᵈ φρονοῦσιν· οἱ δὲ κατὰ πνεῦμα,
16; Phil.
ii. 5; Col. τὰ τοῦ πνεύματος. 6. τὸ γὰρ ᵉ φρόνημα τῆς σαρκὸς θάνατος· τὸ δὲ
iii. 2.

e Only in φρόνημα τοῦ πνεύματος ζωὴ καὶ εἰρήνη. 7. διότι τὸ φρόνημα τῆς
this ch. σαρκὸς ἔχθρα εἰς Θεόν· τῷ γὰρ νόμῳ τοῦ Θεοῦ οὐχ ὑποτάσσεται,

f 1 Thess. οὐδὲ γὰρ δύναται· 8. οἱ δὲ ἐν σαρκὶ ὄντες Θεῷ ᶠ ἀρέσαι οὐ δύνανται.
ii.4; iv. 1;
Gal. i. 10. 9. Ὑμεῖς δὲ οὐκ ἐστὲ ἐν σαρκί, ἀλλ᾽ ἐν πνεύματι, εἴπερ πνεῦμα

g 1 Cor. vii. Θεοῦ οἰκεῖ ἐν ὑμῖν. εἰ δέ τις πνεῦμα Χριστοῦ οὐκ ᵍ ἔχει, οὗτος οὐκ
40. ἔστιν αὐτοῦ. 10. εἰ δὲ Χριστὸς ἐν ὑμῖν, τὸ μὲν σῶμα νεκρὸν δι᾽

sin at one point for the human race; he means that in the death of His own Son, who had come in our nature to make atonement for sin, God had pronounced the doom of sin, and brought its claims and its authority over man to an end. This is the only interpretation which does not introduce elements quite alien to the Apostle's mode of thought.

Ver. 4. All this was done ἵνα τὸ δικ. τοῦ νόμου πληρωθῇ ἐν ἡμῖν: that the just requirement of the law (i.e., a righteous life) might be fulfilled in us. See note on iii. 31. ἐν ἡμῖν (not ὑφ᾽ ἡμῶν), for it is not our doing, though done in us (Weiss). τοῖς μὴ κατὰ σάρκα κ.τ.λ. = inasmuch as we walk not, etc. This is the condition under which the Divine purpose is fulfilled: there is no physical necessity in it. κατὰ σάρκα: the flesh meant is our corrupt human nature. κατὰ πνεῦμα: the spirit is the Divine spirit which is given to those who are in Christ Jesus. It is in them "both law and impulse".

Ver. 5. The meaning of the sentence "is not contained in the repetitions of γὰρ by which it is hooked together" (Jowett). οἱ κατὰ σάρκα ὄντες are those whose nature is determined simply by the flesh; their "mind," i.e., their moral interest, their thought and study, is upon τὰ τῆς σαρκός: for which see Gal. v. 19 f. οἱ κατὰ πνεῦμα are those whose nature is determined by the spirit: for τὰ τοῦ πνεύματος see Gal. v. 22.

Ver. 6. τὸ γὰρ φρόνημα τῆς σαρκὸς θάνατος: this does not so much mean that a man living after the flesh is without the life of God, as that death is the end of this line of conduct, chap. vi. 23, Gal. vi. 8. ζωὴ καὶ εἰρήνη: these on the other hand are conceived as present results involved in "the mind of the spirit". It is not arbitrary to distinguish thus: θάνατος in Paul is essentially the

doom awaiting a certain life, ζωὴ and εἰρήνη possessions and experiences of the believer.

Ver. 7 f. The reason why the mind of the flesh terminates so fatally: it is hostility to God, the fountain of life. Alienation from Him is necessarily fatal. It is the flesh which does not (for indeed it cannot) submit itself to God; as the seat of indwelling sin it is in permanent revolt, and those who are in it (a stronger expression, yet substantially identically with those who are after it, ver. 5) cannot please God.

Ver. 9. Paul applies to his readers what he has said in vers. 5-8. ὑμεῖς is emphatic. You can please God, for you are not in the flesh, etc. εἴπερ has its proper force: "if, as is the fact": cf. iii. 30, viii. 17; and the excellent examination of other N.T. instances in Simcox, Language of the N.T., 171 f. Yet the possibility of the fact being otherwise in isolated cases, is admitted when he goes on: εἰ δέ τις πνεῦμα Χριστοῦ οὐκ ἔχει κ.τ.λ. For εἰ followed by οὐ see Winer, 599 f. οὗτος οὐκ ἔστιν αὐτοῦ: only the indwelling of Christ's spirit proves a real relation to Him.

Ver. 10. Consequences of this indwelling of Christ in the Christian. In one respect, they are not yet so complete as might be expected. τὸ μὲν σῶμα νεκρὸν: the body, it cannot be denied, is dead because of sin: the experience we call death is inevitable for it. τὸ δὲ πνεῦμα ζωή: but the spirit (i.e., the human spirit, as is shown by the contrast with σῶμα) is life, God-begotten, God-sustained life, and therefore beyond the reach of death. As death is due to sin, so is this life to δικαιοσύνη. It is probably not real to distinguish here between "justification" and "moral righteousness of life," and to say that the word means either to the exclusion of the other. The

ἁμαρτίαν, τὸ δὲ πνεῦμα ζωὴ διὰ δικαιοσύνην.   11. εἰ δὲ τὸ πνεῦμα
τοῦ ἐγείραντος Ἰησοῦν [1] ἐκ νεκρῶν οἰκεῖ ἐν ὑμῖν, ὁ ἐγείρας τὸν Χριστὸν
ἐκ νεκρῶν [h] ζωοποιήσει καὶ τὰ θνητὰ σώματα ὑμῶν, διὰ τοῦ ἐνοικοῦντος   h Ch. iv. 17.
αὐτοῦ πνεύματος ἐν ὑμῖν.

12. Ἄρα οὖν, ἀδελφοί, ὀφειλέται ἐσμὲν οὐ τῇ σαρκί, τοῦ κατὰ
σάρκα ζῆν· 13. εἰ γὰρ κατὰ σάρκα ζῆτε, μέλλετε ἀποθνήσκειν·   i Col. iii. 9.
εἰ δὲ πνεύματι τὰς [i]πράξεις τοῦ σώματος θανατοῦτε, ζήσεσθε.   14. [l] Ver. 19; k Gal. v. 18.
Ὅσοι γὰρ πνεύματι Θεοῦ [k] ἄγονται, οὗτοί εἰσιν υἱοὶ [l]Θεοῦ.[2]   15. οὐ   Gal. iii. 26, iv. 6 f.

[1] Ιησουν א[3]CDFKLP. τον Ιησουν א[1]AB, W. and H., Weiss, Tdf., etc. τον
before Χριστον is om. in א[1]ABCD[1], [2]F and all edd. Χριστον is the reading of
BD[3]FKLP, but Χριστον Ιησουν is found in אAD 31, 47, and many fathers, and
is adopted by W. and H., not by Weiss. ζωοποιησει και; om. και א A 47; W. and
H. bracket; Treg. brackets it in marg. δια το ενοικουν αυτου πνευμα BDEFGKLP
it. vg. δια του ενοικουντος αυτου πνευματος אAC, many cursives, Copt., Arm.,
Aeth. This is a very old variant; Clem. Alex. has the gen., Iren., Tert. and Orig.
the accus. The genitive (according to Weiss) probably owes its wide diffusion,
though not its origin, to the interest taken in it by the orthodox in connection with
the Macedonian controversy. It may have originated in an emendation conforming
the structure to that of vi. 4 (δια της δοξης του πατρος). Edd. are divided. Lachm.,
Treg., and Weiss adopt the accusative, Tischdf. and W. and H. the genitive, but
W. and H. put accusative in marg.

[2] For εισιν υιοι θεου אACD read υιοι θεου εισιν.

whole argument of chaps. vi.-viii. is that
neither can exist without the other. No
man can begin to be good till he is justified freely by God's grace in Christ Jesus,
and no one has been so justified who
has not begun to live the good life in the
spirit.

Ver. 11. But though the present results of the indwelling of the spirit are
not all we might desire, the future is
sure. The indwelling spirit is that of
Him who raised Jesus from the dead,
and as such it is the guarantee that our
mortal bodies also (as well as our spirits)
shall share in immortality. The same
argument, in effect, is used in Eph. i.
18-20. "The power that worketh in us"
is the same with which "God wrought
in Christ when He raised Him from the
dead and set Him at His own right hand
in the heavenly places"; and it will work
to the same issue in us as in Him. The
reading in the last clause is very doubtful, but whether we take the accus.
(according to which the indwelling of
the spirit is the ground on which God
raises our mortal bodies to undying life)
or the genit. (according to which the
spirit is itself the agent in this resurrection—a conception not found elsewhere
in Scripture), in either case a share in the
Christian resurrection is conditioned by
the possession of the Spirit of Christ. It
is clear from the alternation of πνεῦμα

θεοῦ and πνεῦμα χριστοῦ in ver. 9 that
the Spirit of Christ is the same as the
Spirit of God, and the use of χριστὸς
alone in the next verse shows that this
same spirit is the alter ego of Christ.
Cf. Phil. i. 19; Gal. iv. 6; Eph. iii. 17.
This is one of the passages in which the
presuppositions of the Trinitarian conception of God come out most clearly.

(2) Vers. 12-27. The Spirit as a spirit
of adoption, the first-fruits of the inheritance of the children of God.

Ver. 12 f. The blessed condition and
hopes of Christians, as described in these
last verses, lay them under obligations:
to whom, or to what? Not (ver. 12) to
the flesh, to live according to it; to it
they owe nothing. If they live after the
flesh they are destined to die—the final
doom in which there is no hope; but if
by the spirit (i.e., God's Spirit) they put
to death the doings of the body, they
shall live—the life against which death is
powerless. We might have expected τῆς
σαρκὸς instead of τοῦ σώματος, but in
the absence of the spirit the body in all
it does is only the tool of the flesh: the
two are morally equivalent.

Ver. 14. Ye shall live, for as many as
are led by God's Spirit are God's sons,
and life is congruous to such a dignity.
υἱὸς suggests the rank and privileges of
the persons in question; τέκνον (in ver.
16 f.) their kinship in nature to God. Yet

γὰρ ἐλάβετε πνεῦμα δουλείας πάλιν εἰς φόβον, ἀλλ' ἐλάβετε πνεῦμα
m Ver. 23; m υἱοθεσίας, ἐν ᾧ κράζομεν, 'Αββᾶ, ὁ πατήρ. 16. αὐτὸ τὸ πνεῦμα
Gal. iv. 5;
Eph. i. 5 n συμμαρτυρεῖ τῷ πνεύματι ἡμῶν, ὅτι ἐσμὲν τέκνα Θεοῦ. 17. εἰ δὲ
(ch. ix. 4).
n Ch. ii. 15; τέκνα, καὶ κληρονόμοι· κληρονόμοι μὲν Θεοῦ, συγκληρονόμοι δὲ
ix. i.
o 2 Tim. ii. Χριστοῦ· εἴπερ συμπάσχομεν, ἵνα καὶ ° συνδοξασθῶμεν. 18. Λογί-
11 f.
p Ch. iii. 26. ζομαι γὰρ ὅτι οὐκ ἄξια τὰ παθήματα τοῦ νῦν p καιροῦ πρὸς τὴν

this cannot everywhere be urged in the
N.T.

Ver. 15. Sons, οὐ γὰρ ἐλάβετε πνεῦμα
δουλείας. The aorist refers to the time
of their baptism, when they received the
Spirit. It was not the Spirit proper to
slaves, leading them again to shrink from
God in fear as they had done when
under the law of sin and death, but
πνεῦμα υἱοθεσίας, a spirit proper to those
who were being translated from the
servile to the filial relation to God. υἱοθεσία is a word used in the N.T. by Paul
only, but "no word is more common in
Greek inscriptions of the Hellenistic
time: the idea, like the word, is native
Greek" (E. L. Hicks, quoted in S. and H.),
see Gal. iv. 5, Eph. i. 5. The word
serves to distinguish those who are made
sons by an act of grace from the only-
begotten Son of God: τὸν ἑαυτοῦ υἱὸν
ver. 3, τοῦ ἰδίου υἱοῦ ver. 32. But the
act of grace is not one which makes only
an outward difference in our position ; it
is accomplished in the giving of a spirit
which creates in us a new nature. In
the spirit of adoption we cry Abba,
Father. We have not only the status,
but the heart of sons. κράζομεν (often
with φωνῇ μεγάλῃ) is a strong word : it
denotes the loud irrepressible cry with
which the consciousness of sonship
breaks from the Christian heart in prayer.
The change to the first person marks
Paul's inclusion of himself in the number of those who have and utter this
consciousness ; and it is probably this
inclusion of himself, as a person whose
native language was "Hebrew" (Acts
xxi. 40), to which is due the double form
'Αββᾶ ὁ πατήρ. The last word certainly
interprets the first, but it is not thought of
as doing so : "we cry, Father, Father".
Ver. 16. The punctuation in W. and
H. margin deserves notice. "In that
we cry, Abba, Father, the Spirit itself
beareth witness with our spirit," etc.
Our own spirit tells us we are God's
children, but the voice with which it
speaks is, as we know, prompted and
inspired by the Divine Spirit itself. For
similar distinctions Gifford compares ii.
15 and ix. 1. τέκνα Θεοῦ: τέκνα, not υἱοὶ,

is used with strict propriety here, as it
is the reality of the filial nature, not the
legitimacy of the filial position, which is
being proved.

Ver. 17. Yet this last is involved, for
"if children, also heirs". Cf. Gal. iv. 7
where κληρονόμος is relative to υἱὸς ;
and all the passages in which the Spirit
is regarded as "the earnest" of an
inheritance : 2 Cor. i. 22, v. 5, Eph. i.
14. It is from God the inheritance
comes, and we share in it with Christ
(Mark. xii. 7). For what it is, see 1
Cor. ii. 9 f. The inheritance attached
to Divine sonship is attained only on the
condition expressed in the clause εἴπερ
συμπάσχομεν ἵνα καὶ συνδοξασθῶμεν.
On εἴπερ, see ver. 9. "Rom. viii. 17 gains
in pathos, when we see that the share of
the disciples in the Master's sufferings
was felt to be a fact of which there was
no question." Simcox, Language of
N.T., p. 171. Paul was sure of it in his
own case, and took it for granted in that
of others. Those who share Christ's
sufferings now will share His glory hereafter ; and in order to share His glory
hereafter it is necessary to begin by
sharing His sufferings here.

Ver. 18. The passage extending from
this verse to ver. 27 is described by
Lipsius as a "threefold testimony to the
future transfiguration which awaits suffering believers". In vers. 19-22 there
is the first testimony—the sighing of
creation ; in vers. 23-25 the second, the
yearning hope of Christians themselves,
related as it is to the possession of the
first fruits of the Spirit ; and in vers. 26 f.
the third, the intercession of the Spirit
which helps us in our prayers, and lends
words to our longing. λογιζόμεθα γὰρ
κ.τ.λ. λογίζομαι is a favourite word
with Paul : the instance most like this
is the one in iii. 28. It does not suggest a
more or less dubious result of calculation ;
rather by litotes does it express the
strongest assurance. The insignificance
of present suffering compared with future
glory was a fixed idea with the Apostle,
2 Cor. iv. 17 f. For οὐκ ἄξια . . . πρὸς
see Winer, 505 (d). With τὴν μέλλουσαν
δόξαν ἀποκαλυφθῆναι cf. in Gal. iii. 23

μέλλουσαν δόξαν ἀποκαλυφθῆναι εἰς ἡμᾶς. 19. Ἡ γὰρ ἀποκαραδοκία τῆς κτίσεως τὴν ἀποκάλυψιν τῶν υἱῶν τοῦ ᵍΘεοῦ ἀπεκδέχεται. 20. q Ver. 14
τῇ γὰρ ʳματαιότητι ἡ κτίσις ὑπετάγη, οὐχ ἑκοῦσα, ἀλλὰ διὰ τὸν ὑπο- r Eph. iv. 17.
τάξαντα, ἐπ᾽ ἐλπίδι,¹ 21. ὅτι ² καὶ αὐτὴ ἡ κτίσις ἐλευθερωθήσεται ἀπὸ
τῆς δουλείας τῆς φθορᾶς εἰς τὴν ἐλευθερίαν τῆς δόξης τῶν τέκνων τοῦ

¹ επ ελπιδι. In ℵBDFG we find εφ ελπιδι, and this is printed by Tischdf. and
W. and H. The same mistake (?) occurs Rom. iv. 18 in CDFG, Rom. v. 2 in DFG,
and Tit. i. 2 in D; cf. also αφηλπικοτες in FG Eph. iv. 19. In these circumstances
it seems doubtful whether εφ᾽ ελπιδι should be put in the text.

² For οτι ℵDFG read διοτι. The δι may easily have been omitted after ελπιδι,
and therefore Tischdf. and Weiss read διοτι, though most edd. οτι.

τὴν μέλλ. πίστιν ἀποκαλ. The unusual
order emphasises the futurity. εἰς ἡμᾶς
= toward and upon us. The glory
comes from without, to transfigure them.
It is revealed at the ἀποκάλυψις (1 Cor.
i. 7, 2 Th. i. 7, 1 Pet. i. 7, 13, iv. 13),
the glorious second coming, of Christ,
and is indeed His glory of which they
are made partakers.

Ver. 19. First testimony to this glorious
future : creation sighs for it. In some
sense the hope and promise of it is
involved in the present constitution of
the world. For a fine speculative interpretation see E. Caird's *Evolution of
Religion*, ii., 124 f. In Paul, however,
the spirit of the passage is rather poetic
than philosophical. Its affinities are
with Gen. iii. 17, where the ground is
cursed for man's sake : he conceives of
all creation as involved in the fortunes
of humanity. But this, if creation be
personified, naturally leads to the idea of
a mysterious sympathy between the
world and man, and this is what the
Apostle expresses. Creation is not inert,
utterly unspiritual, alien to our life and
its hopes. It is the natural ally of our
souls. What rises from it is the music
of humanity—not apparently so still and
sad to Paul as to Wordsworth, but
with a note of hope in it rising triumphantly above all the pain of conflict.
ἀποκαραδοκία (Phil. i. 20) denotes absorbed, persistent expectation—waiting,
as it were, with uplifted head. ἡ κτίσις
is the world and all that it contains,
animate and inanimate, as distinguished
from man. τὴν ἀποκ. τῶν υἱῶν τοῦ θεοῦ :
cf. 1 John iii. 2. With the revelation of
the sons of God humanity would attain
its end, and nature too.

Ver. 20. For creation was subjected
to vanity, etc. ματαιότης is not classical, but is often used in the LXX, especially for הֶבֶל. The idea is that of look-

ing for what one does not find—hence
of futility, frustration, disappointment.
ματαιότης ματαιοτήτων is the "vanity
of vanities " in Eccl., the complaint of the
utter resultlessness of life. Sin brought
this doom on creation ; it made a pessi-
mistic view of the universe inevitable.
ὑπετάγη : the precise time denoted is
that of the Fall, when God pronounced
the ground cursed for man's sake. Creation came under this doom οὐχ ἑκοῦσα
ἀλλὰ διὰ τὸν ὑποτάξαντα : the last words
seem best referred to God : it was on
account of Him—that His righteousness
might be shown in the punishment of
sin—that the sentence fell upon man,
carrying consequences which extended
to the whole realm intended originally
for his dominion. The sentence on man,
however, was not hopeless, and creation
shared in his hope as in his doom.
When the curse is completely removed
from man, as it will be when the sons of
God are revealed, it will pass from creation also ; and for this creation sighs. It
was made subject to vanity on the footing
of this hope ; the hope is latent, so to
speak, in the constitution of nature, and
comes out, in its sighing, to a sympathetic ear.

Ver. 21. Contents of the hope. It
makes no difference in meaning, whether
we read ὅτι or διότι. αὐτὴ ἡ κτίσις :
creation as well as man. ἡ δουλεία τῆς
φθορᾶς : a system in which nothing continues in one stay, in which death claims
everything, in which there is not even an
analogy to immortality, is a system of
slavery—in subjection to "vanity," with
no high eternal worth of its own. From
such a condition creation is to be emancipated ; it is to share in the liberty which
belongs to the glory of the children of
God. When man's redemption is complete, he will find himself in a new world
matching with his new condition (Isa.
lxv. 17, 2 Pet. iii. 13, Rev. xxi. 1) : this is

s Mark xvi. 15; Col. i. 15, 23.
Θεοῦ. 22. οἴδαμεν γὰρ ὅτι πᾶσα ἡ *κτίσις συστενάζει καὶ συνωδίνει
ἄχρι τοῦ νῦν· 23. οὐ μόνον δὲ, ἀλλὰ καὶ αὐτοὶ τὴν ἀπαρχὴν τοῦ
Πνεύματος ἔχοντες, καὶ ἡμεῖς [1] αὐτοὶ ἐν ἑαυτοῖς στενάζομεν, υἱοθεσίαν

t 1 Cor. i. 7; Gal. v. 5; Phil. iii. 20; Heb. ix. 28.
ἀπεκδεχόμενοι τὴν ἀπολύτρωσιν τοῦ σώματος ἡμῶν. 24. τῇ γὰρ
ἐλπίδι ἐσώθημεν. ἐλπὶς δὲ βλεπομένη οὐκ ἔστιν ἐλπίς· ὁ γὰρ
βλέπει τις, τί καὶ ἐλπίζει [2]; 25. εἰ δὲ ὃ οὐ βλέπομεν ἐλπίζομεν,

---

[1] ἡμεῖς om. B 31, 73, 93, vulg. The rec. text is that of DFKLP. In ℵAC 47 the order of the words is εχοντες ημεις και αυτοι. This is followed by Tischdf. Lachm., Treg. and W. and H. bracket ημεις in this position; Weiss omits it altogether.

[2] The reading of B is ο γαρ βλεπει τις ελπιζει. This is adopted by W. and H., Weiss. Of the received text—ο γαρ βλεπει τις τι και ελπιζει—τι is wanting in ℵ, and και in DFG, vulg., Pesh. The reading of B is difficult, and seems to have been partially amended in different ways which are combined in the received text. For ελπιζει ℵ[1]A 47, marg., have υπομενει, and W. and H. give a place to this, as well as to the received text, in their margin.

Paul's faith, and the sighing of creation attests it.

Ver. 22. οἴδαμεν γὰρ κ.τ.λ.: How Christians know this Paul does not say. Perhaps we may say that the Christian consciousness of sin and redemption is in contact with the ultimate realities of the universe, and that no interpretation of nature can be true but one which, like this, is in essential harmony with it. The force of the preposition in συστενάζει and συνωδίνει is not that *we* sigh and are in pain, and creation along with us; but that the whole frame of creation, all its parts together, *unite* in sighing and in pain. Weiss is right in saying that there is no reference to the *dolores Messiae*; but in συνωδίνει there is the suggestion of the travail out of which the new world is to be born. ἄχρι τοῦ νῦν means up till now, without stopping, ever since the moment of ὑπετάγη.

Ver. 23. Second testimony to the glorious future. οὐ μόνον δὲ *sc.* ἡ κτίσις—not only all creation, but we Christians: we ourselves, τὴν ἀπαρχὴν τοῦ πνεύματος ἔχοντες. τοῦ πνεύματος is gen. of apposition: the spirit which Christians have received is itself the first fruits (elsewhere, the earnest: see on ver. 17) of this glory; and *because* we have it (not *although*: it is the foretaste of heaven, the heaven begun in the Christian, which intensifies his yearning, and makes him more vehemently than nature long for complete redemption), we also sigh in ourselves υἱοθεσίαν ἀπεκδεχόμενοι, τὴν ἀπολύτρωσιν τοῦ σώματος ἡμῶν. The key to these words is found in i. 4. Christ was Son of God always, but was only declared to be so in power ἐξ ἀναστάσεως νεκρῶν, and so it is with

believers. They have already received adoption, and as led by the spirit are sons of God; but only when their mortal bodies have been quickened, and the corruptible has put on incorruption, will they possess all that sonship involves. For this they wait and sigh, and the inextinguishable hope, born of the spirit dwelling in them, guarantees its own fulfilment. *Cf.* Phil. iii. 21; 1 Cor. xv. 51; 2 Cor. v. 2; and for ἀπολύτρωσις in this sense, 1 Cor. i. 30.

Ver. 24 f. This sentence explains why Paul can speak of Christians as *waiting* for adoption, while they are nevertheless in the enjoyment of sonship. It is because salvation is essentially related to the future. "We wait for it: for we were saved *in hope*." The dat. τῇ ἐλπίδι is that of mode or respect. Our salvation was qualified from the beginning by reference to a good yet to be. Weiss argues that the sense of ἐλπὶς in the second clause (*res sperata*) makes it "absolutely necessary" to take it so in the first, and that this leaves no alternative but to make τῇ ἐλπίδι *dat. comm.* and translate: "for, for this object of hope—eternal life and glory—were we delivered from eternal destruction". But the "absolute necessity" is imaginary; a word with the nuances of ἐλπίς in a mind with the speed of Paul's need not be treated so rigorously, especially as the resulting construction is in itself extremely dubious. Hope, the Apostle argues, is an essential characteristic of our salvation; but hope turned sight is hope no more, for who hopes for what he sees? We do *not* see all the Gospel held out to us, but it is the object of our Christian hope nevertheless; it is as true

δι' ὑπομονῆς ἀπεκδεχόμεθα. 26. Ὡσαύτως δὲ καὶ τὸ Πνεῦμα
ᵘσυναντιλαμβάνεται ταῖς ἀσθενείαις ¹ ἡμῶν· τὸ γὰρ τί προσευξώμεθα ᵤ Luke x.40.
καθὸ δεῖ, οὐκ οἴδαμεν, ἀλλ' αὐτὸ τὸ Πνεῦμα ᵛὑπερεντυγχάνει ὑπὲρ ᵥ Here only
ἡμῶν στεναγμοῖς ἀλαλήτοις· 27. ὁ δὲ ἐρευνῶν τὰς καρδίας οἶδε τί in N.T.
τὸ φρόνημα τοῦ πνεύματος, ὅτι κατὰ Θεὸν ἐντυγχάνει ὑπὲρ ἁγίων.
28. Οἴδαμεν δὲ ὅτι τοῖς ἀγαπῶσι τὸν Θεὸν πάντα συνεργεῖ ² εἰς ἀγαθόν,

¹ For ταις ασθενειαις ℵABCD have τη ασθενεια. υπερ ημων CKLP; but om.
ℵABDF.
² After συνεργει, ο θεος is found in AB. W. and H. bracket it, but Lachm. and
Weiss regard it as the true text. It was omitted as cumbrous and unnecessary.
Cf. i. 28, where ο θεος is omitted in ℵA in much the same way; here it is wanting in
ℵACDFKL.

and sure as the love of God which in Christ
Jesus reconciled us to Himself and gave
us the spirit of adoption, and therefore
we wait for it in patience. For διὰ cf.
ii. 27. ὑπομονή: in 1 Thess. i. 3 we
have ἡ ὑπομονὴ τῆς ἐλπίδος ὑμῶν used of
a suffering but steadfast Church: ὑπομονὴ
is the constancy which belongs to and
characterises hope in dark days. In the
pastoral epistles (1 Tim. vi. 10; Tit. ii.
2) instead of the πίστις, ἀγάπη, ἐλπίς,
of earlier letters, Paul writes πίστις,
ἀγάπη, ὑπομονή, as if he had discovered
by experience that in this life "hope"
has mainly to be shown in the form of
"patience".
Ver. 26. Third testimony to the glorious
future: the sighing of creation, our own
sighing, and this action of the Spirit,
point consistently to one conclusion.
συναντιλαμβάνεται, cf. Luke x. 40. The
weakness which the Spirit helps is that
due to our ignorance: τὸ γὰρ τί προσευξώμεθα καθὸ δεῖ οὐκ οἴδαμεν. The
article makes the whole clause object
of οἴδαμεν: Winer, p. 644. Broadly
speaking, we do know what we are to
pray for—the perfecting of salvation;
but we do not know what we are to
pray for καθὸ δεῖ—according as the need
is at the moment; we know the end, which
is common to all prayers, but not what is
necessary at each crisis of need in order
to enable us to attain this end. ἀλλὰ
αὐτὸ τὸ πνεῦμα ὑπερεντυγχάνει στεναγμοῖς ἀλαλήτοις. ὑπερεντυγχάνει is
found here only in N.T., but ἐντυγχάνειν
in this sense in vers. 27, 34, Heb. vii. 25.
In Rom. xi. 2 with κατὰ = to make
intercession against. ἀλαλήτοις does
not mean "unspoken" but "unutterable". The στεναγμοὶ of believers find
expression, adequate or inadequate, in
their prayers, and in such utterances as
this very passage of Romans, but there

is a testimony to the glory awaiting them
more profound and passionate than even
this. It is the intercession of the Spirit
with στεναγμοὶ ἀλάλητοι—groanings (or
sighs) that baffle words, αὐτὸ τὸ πνεῦμα
is undoubtedly God's Spirit as distinguished from ours, yet what is here
affirmed must fall within Christian experience, for Paul says in the next
verse that He Who searches the hearts
knows what is the mind of the Spirit in
this unutterable intercession. It is in
the heart, therefore, that it takes place.
"The whole passage illustrates in even
a startling manner the truth and reality
of the 'coming' of the Holy Ghost—
the extent to which, if I may venture to
say it, He has separated Himself—as
Christ did at His Incarnation—from His
eternal glory and blessedness, and entered
into the life of man. . . . His intercession
for us—so intimately does He share all
the evils of our condition—is a kind of
agony" (R. W. Dale, Christian Doctrine,
p. 140 f.).
Ver. 27. This intercession, with which
our heart goes, though it is deeper than
words, the Heart Searcher understands.
τί τὸ φρόν. τοῦ πνεύματος: what the
Spirit is set upon, the whole object of its
thought and endeavour. ὅτι, viz., that
He intercedes κατὰ θεόν in agreement
with God's will, see 2 Cor. vii. 9-11.
ὑπὲρ ἁγίων on behalf of those who are
God's. Both the intercession of Christ
and the intercession of the Spirit are
represented in the N.T. as made on behalf of those who are in Christ—saints,
the Church, not mankind in general.
Vers. 28-39. Conclusion of the argument: the Apostle glories in the
assurance of God's eternal and un-
changeable love in Jesus Christ.
οἴδαμεν δὲ = further, we know: in a
sense this is one ground more for be-

w Eph. i. 5,
11; 1 Cor.
ii. 7.
x Phil. iii.
21 (10).

τοῖς κατὰ πρόθεσιν κλητοῖς οὖσιν. 29. ὅτι οὓς προέγνω, καὶ ʷ προώρισε ˣ συμμόρφους τῆς εἰκόνος τοῦ υἱοῦ αὐτοῦ, εἰς τὸ εἶναι αὐτὸν πρωτότοκον ἐν πολλοῖς ἀδελφοῖς· 30. οὓς δὲ προώρισε, τούτους καὶ ἐκάλεσε· καὶ οὓς ἐκάλεσε, τούτους καὶ ἐδικαίωσεν· οὓς δὲ ἐδικαίωσε, τούτους καὶ ἐδόξασε. 31. Τί οὖν ἐροῦμεν πρὸς ταῦτα; εἰ ὁ Θεὸς ὑπὲρ

lieving in the glorious future: God is ever with us, and will not abandon us at last. πάντα συνεργεῖ (ὁ θεός): συνεργεῖ is naturally neuter, and if ὁ θεός is the true reading, it is probably best to render "God co-operates for good in all things (πάντα accus. of ref. as in 1 Cor. ix. 25, x. 33) with those," etc. τοῖς ἀγαπ. τὸν θεόν describes the persons in question from the human side; τοῖς κατὰ πρόθεσιν κλητοῖς οὖσιν describes them from the Divine side. It is in pursuance of a purpose of God (for πρόθεσις with reference to the eternal purpose of redemption, see ix. 11, Eph. i. 11, iii. 11, 2 Tim. i. 9) that they are called. "Calling" in Paul never means "invitation"; it is always "effectual calling".

Ver. 29 f. These verses give the proof that God in all things co-operates for good with the called. They show how His gracious purpose, beginning with foreknowledge and foreordination perfects all that concerns them on to the final glory. οὓς προέγνω: those whom He foreknew—in what sense? as persons who would answer His love with love? This is at least irrelevant, and alien to Paul's general mode of thought. That salvation begins with God, and begins in eternity, are fundamental ideas with him, which he here applies to Christians, without raising any of the problems involved in the relation of the human will to the Divine. He comes upon these in chap. ix., but not here. Yet we may be sure that προέγνω has the pregnant sense that γιγνώσκω (יָדַע) often has in Scripture: e.g., in Ps. i. 6, Amos iii. 2: hence we may render, "those of whom God took knowledge from eternity" (Eph. i. 4). καὶ προώρισεν κ.τ.λ., "he also foreordained to be conformed to the image of His Son". This conformity is the last stage in salvation, as προέγνω is the first. The image is in import not merely spiritual but eschatological. The Son of God is the Lord who appeared to Paul by Damascus: to be conformed to His image is to share His glory as well as His holiness. The Pauline Gospel is hopelessly distorted when this is forgotten. εἰς τὸ

εἶναι αὐτὸν πρωτότοκον ἐν πολλοῖς ἀδελφοῖς: the end, and in all this is the exaltation of Christ. It is implied in πρωτότοκον that He also is regarded as only having attained the fulness of His Sonship through the resurrection (cf. i. 4, and Col. i. 18 πρωτότοκος ἐκ τῶν νεκρῶν). The idea of Christ's dignity as firstborn among many brethren who all owe their salvation to Him is sublimely interpreted in Heb. ii. 10-13. The Apostle now resumes the series of the Divine acts in our salvation. οὓς δὲ προώρισεν, τούτους καὶ ἐκάλεσεν. The eternal foreordination appears in time as "calling," of course as effectual calling: where salvation is contemplated as the work of God alone (as here) there can be no breakdown in its processes. The next stages are summarily indicated. ἐδικαίωσεν: God in Jesus Christ forgave our sins, and accepted us as righteous in His sight; ungodly as we had been, He put us right with Himself. In that, everything else is included. The whole argument of chaps. vi.-viii. has been that justification and the new life of holiness in the Spirit are inseparable experiences. Hence Paul can take one step to the end, and write οὓς δὲ ἐδικαίωσεν, τούτους καὶ ἐδόξασεν. Yet the tense in the last word is amazing. It is the most daring anticipation of faith that even the N.T. contains: the life is not to be taken out of it by the philosophical consideration that with God there is neither before nor after.

Ver. 31. τί οὖν ἐροῦμεν πρὸς ταῦτα; the idea underlying all that precedes is that of the suffering to be endured by those who would share Christ's glory (ver. 17). The Apostle has disparaged the suffering in comparison with the glory (ver. 18); he has interpreted it (vers. 19-27) as in a manner prophetic of the glory; he has in these last verses asserted the presence through all the Christian's life of an eternal victorious purpose of love: all this is included in ταῦτα. For ὑπὲρ and κατὰ, cf. 2 Cor. xiii. 8.

Ver. 32. The Christian's faith in providence is an inference from redemption. The same God who did not spare His own Son will freely give us all things.

ἡμῶν, τίς καθ᾽ ἡμῶν; 32. ὅς γε τοῦ ἰδίου υἱοῦ οὐκ ἐφείσατο, ἀλλ᾽
ὑπὲρ ἡμῶν πάντων παρέδωκεν αὐτόν, πῶς οὐχὶ καὶ σὺν αὐτῷ τὰ
πάντα ἡμῖν ʸ χαρίσεται; 33. τίς ἐγκαλέσει κατὰ ἐκλεκτῶν Θεοῦ; y ι Cor. ii.
Θεὸς ὁ δικαιῶν· 34. τίς ὁ κατακρίνων; Χριστὸς[1] ὁ ἀποθανών, iii. 18.
μᾶλλον δὲ καὶ ἐγερθείς, ὃς καὶ ἔστιν ἐν δεξιᾷ τοῦ Θεοῦ, ὃς καὶ

[1] Χριστός alone BDEK, most cursives, and Treg. Χριστὸς Ἰησοῦς ℵACFL 17,
vulg., etc. Weiss puts X. I. in text, thinking the omission in B, etc., accidental;
W. and H., and Lachm. bracket Ἰησοῦς. The καὶ before ἐγερθεὶς is wanting in
ℵABC. The καὶ before ἐστιν is wanting in ℵAC but is found in ℵ³BDFKL. It
is omitted by W. and H., and Tischdf., bracketed by Lachm., but retained by Weiss.
After ἐγερθεὶς ℵ¹AC insert ἐκ νεκρων; W. and H. bracket this, but all other crit. edd.
omit, with ℵ²BDFGKL, etc.

οὐκ ἐφείσατο, cf. Gen. xxii. 12, οὐκ ἐφείσω
τοῦ υἱοῦ σου τοῦ ἀγαπητοῦ δι᾽ ἐμέ. It
vivifies the impression of God's love
through the sense of the sacrifice it made.
ὑπὲρ πάντων ἡμῶν: none were worthy of
such a sacrifice (Weiss). παρέδωκεν sc.
to death: iv. 25. πῶς οὐχὶ καί: the
argument of selfishness is that he who
has done so much need do no more;
that of love, that he who has done so
much is certain to do more. σὺν αὐτῷ
τὰ πάντα: τὰ πάντα has a collective
force. It is usually taken to mean the
whole of what furthers the Christian's
life, the whole of what contributes to the
perfecting of his salvation; all this will
be freely given to him by God. But
why should it not mean "all things"
without any such qualification? When
God gives us His Son He gives us the
world; there is nothing which does not
work together for our good; all things
are ours. Cf. ι Cor. iii. 22 f.
Ver. 33 f. The punctuation here is a
very difficult problem: see the text and
margin of R.V. The reminiscence of
Is. l. 8 f. in verse 33 makes it more
difficult; for it suggests that the normal
structure is that of an affirmation followed by a question, whereas Paul
begins with a question to which the
affirmation (with at least a trace of
Isaiah's language in it) is an answer. It
is even possible to read every clause
interrogatively, though that is less effective. τίς ἐγκαλέσει κατὰ ἐκλεκτῶν θεοῦ;
who shall bring a charge against persons
who are God's chosen? The absence of
the article (cf. ὑπὲρ ἀγίων, ver. 27) brings
out the character in which the persons in
question figure, not their individual personality. For the word see Col. iii.
12; 2 Tim. ii. 10; Tit. i. 1; for the thing
cf. ι Thess. i. 4; Eph. i. 4; John xv. 16.
It describes Christians as persons who
owe their standing as such to the act of

God's grace. All Christians are conscious that this is the truth about their
position: they belong to God, because
He has taken them for His own. To
say that the word designates "not those
who are destined for final salvation, but
those who are 'summoned' or 'selected'
for the privilege of serving God and
carrying out His will" (S. and H.), is to
leave the rails of the Apostle's thought
altogether. There is nothing here (vers.
28-30) about the privilege of serving God
and carrying out His will; the one thing
Paul is concerned with is the security
given by the eternal love of God that the
work of salvation will be carried through,
in spite of all impediments, from foreknowledge to final glory. The ἐκλεκτοὶ
θεοῦ are those who ought to have such
security: they should have a faith and
an assurance proportioned to the love of
God. Paul is one of them, and because
he is, he is sure, not that he is called to
serve God, but that nothing can ever
separate him from God's love in Christ.
The question τίς ἐγκαλέσει is best answered by taking both the following
clauses together: "It is God that justifieth: who is he that shall condemn?"
(cf. Is. l. 8 f.). But many make τίς ὁ
κατακρινῶν a new question, and find the
answer in verse 34: Χριστὸς [Ἰησοῦς] ὁ
ἀποθανών = the only person who can
condemn is the Judge, viz., Christ, but
He is so far from condemning that His
has done everything to deliver us from
condemnation. What Christian, Paul
seems to ask, can speak of κατάκριμα
with his eye on Christ, who died for our
sins? μᾶλλον δὲ ἐγερθεὶς [ἐκ νεκρων]:
cf. Gal. iv. 9; and chap. iv. 25. The
correction in μᾶλλον is formal (Weiss):
Paul does not mean that the resurrection
is more important than the cross; he
improves upon an expression which has
not conveyed all that was in his mind.

z Ver. 27;
Heb. vii.
25.

^zἐντυγχάνει ὑπὲρ ἡμῶν· 35. τίς ἡμᾶς χωρίσει ἀπὸ τῆς ἀγάπης
τοῦ Χριστοῦ [1]; θλίψις, ἢ στενοχωρία, ἢ διωγμός, ἢ λιμός, ἢ γυμνό-
της, ἢ κίνδυνος, ἢ μάχαιρα; 36. (καθὼς γέγραπται, "Ὅτι ἕνεκά
σου θανατούμεθα ὅλην τὴν ἡμέραν· ἐλογίσθημεν ὡς πρόβατα σφα-

[1] τοῦ Χριστοῦ; so most MSS. But ‭‮אB, with some cursives and fathers, have
τοῦ θεοῦ. This is usually regarded as a change made to agree with ver. 39, because
B, after τοῦ θεοῦ, adds τῆς ἐν Χριστῳ Ἰησου. But this may have been added, as
Weiss remarks, for the very reason that B already read τοῦ θεοῦ; and as ‭‮א has τοῦ
θεοῦ without this addition, and it was very natural to change it (with an eye to vv.
34 and 37) into τοῦ Χριστοῦ, it seems probable that τοῦ θεοῦ is the original reading.
Weiss adopts it, and W. and H. put it in marg.

Our position depends upon Jesus Christ
who died, nay rather, over whom death
no more has dominion (vi. 9), who is at
God's right hand (this phrase, which
describes Christ's exaltation as a sharing
in the universal sovereignty of God, is
borrowed from Ps. cx. 1, and is oftener
used in the N.T. than any other words
of the Old), who also makes intercession
on our behalf. ὃς καὶ ἐντυγχάνει: a
solemn climax is marked by the repetition
of ὅς, and by the καὶ which deliberately
adds the intercession to all that has gone
before. The Christian consciousness,
even in an apostle, cannot transcend this.
This is Paul's final security—the last
ground of his triumphant assurance:
Jesus Christ, at God's right hand, with
the virtue of His atoning death in Him,
pleads His people's cause. Cf. Heb. ix.
24, vii. 25, 1 John ii. 1 f.

Ver. 35 f. τίς ἡμᾶς χωρίσει ἀπὸ τῆς
ἀγάπης τοῦ Χριστοῦ; If this verse is to
be most closely connected with ver. 34,
τοῦ Χριστοῦ will appear the more probable reading, for there Christ is the
subject throughout; but at vers. 28, 31,
39 the love of God is the determining
idea, and at this point it seems to be
caught up again in view of the conclusion—facts which favour the reading τοῦ
θεοῦ. In any case it is the Divine love
for us which is meant. With the list of
troubles cf. 2 Cor. vi. 4-10, xi. 26 f., xii.
10. They were those which had befallen
Paul himself, and he knew that the love
of God in Jesus Christ could reach and
sustain the heart through them all. The
quotation from Ps. xliv. 23 is peculiar.
It exactly reproduces the LXX, even the
ὅτι being simply transferred. The καθὼς
implies that such experiences as those
named in ver. 35 are in agreement with
what Scripture holds out as the fortune
of God's people. Possibly the mention
of the sword recalled to the Apostle's
memory the θανατούμεθα of the psalm,

and suggested the quotation. The point
of it, both in the psalm and in the epistle,
lies in ἕνεκεν σοῦ. This is what the
Psalmist could not understand. That
men should suffer for sin, for infidelity to
God, was intelligible enough; but he and
his countrymen were suffering because of
their faithfulness, and the psalm is his
despairing expostulation with God. But
the Apostle understood it. To suffer for
Christ's sake was to enter into the fellowship of Christ's sufferings, and that is
the very situation in which the love of
Christ is most real, near, and sure to the
soul. Cf. chap. v. 3, 2 Cor. i. 5, Col. i.
24. Instead of despairing, he glories in
tribulations.

Ver. 37. ὑπερνικῶμεν: a word probably coined by Paul, who loves compounds with ὑπέρ. The Vulg. gives
superamus, with which Lipsius agrees
(obsiegen, like over-power): but Cyprian
supervincimus. Later Greek writers
distinguish νικᾶν and ὑπερνικᾶν (see
Grimm, s.v.), and justify the happy rendering "we are more than conquerors".
Perhaps it is a mistake to define in what
the "more" consists; but if we do, the
answer must be sought on the line indicated in the note on ἕνεκεν σοῦ: these
trials not only do not cut us off from
Christ's love, they actually give us more
intimate and thrilling experiences of it.
διὰ τοῦ ἀγαπήσαντος ἡμᾶς: the aorist
points to Christ's death as the great
demonstration of His love: cf. Gal. ii.
20, also Rev. xii. 11.

Ver. 38 f. The Apostle's personal
conviction given in confirmation of all
that has been said, especially of ver. 37.
πέπεισμαι cf. 2 Tim. i. 12. οὔτε θάνατος
οὔτε ζωὴ: death is mentioned first, either
with ver. 36 in mind, or as the most tremendous enemy the Apostle could conceive. If Christ's love can hold us in
and through death, what is left for us to
fear? Much of the N.T. bears on this

γῆς ‧ ’’) 37. ἀλλ’ ἐν τούτοις πᾶσιν ὑπερνικῶμεν διὰ τοῦ ἀγαπήσαντος
ἡμᾶς.   38. πέπεισμαι γὰρ ὅτι οὔτε θάνατος οὔτε ζωή, οὔτε ἄγγελοι
οὔτε ἀρχαὶ οὔτε δυνάμεις, οὔτε ἐνεστῶτα οὔτε μέλλοντα, 39. οὔτε
ὕψωμα οὔτε βάθος, οὔτε τις κτίσις ἑτέρα δυνήσεται ἡμᾶς χωρίσαι
ἀπὸ τῆς ἀγάπης τοῦ Θεοῦ, τῆς ἐν Χριστῷ Ἰησοῦ τῷ Κυρίῳ ἡμῶν.

very point, cf. John viii. 51, x. 28, xi. 25
f., 1 Thess. iv. 13-18, 1 Cor. xv., 2 Cor.
iv. 16-v. 5, Rom. xiv. 8, Heb. ii. 14 f.
The blank horror of dying is annihilated
by the love of Christ. Neither death nor
life is to be explained: explanations
" only limit the flight of the Apostle's
thoughts just when they would soar
above all limitation " (Gifford). οὔτε
ἄγγελοι οὔτε ἀρχαὶ: this, according to
the best authorities, forms a second pair
of forces conceivably hostile to the
Christian. As in every pair there is a
kind of contrast, some have sought one
here also: either making ἄγγελοι good
and ἀρχαὶ evil powers, though both
spiritual ; or ἄγγελοι heavenly, and
ἀρχαὶ (as in Lc. xii. 11, Tit. iii. 1)
earthly powers, in which case either
might be either good or bad. But this
is arbitrary: and a comparison of 1 Cor.
xv. 24, Eph. i. 21 favours a suggestion in
S. and H. that possibly in a very early
copy οὔτε δυνάμεις had been accidentally
omitted after οὔτε ἀρχαὶ, and then added
in the margin, but reinserted in a wrong
place. The T.R. "neither angels nor
principalities nor powers " brings together all the conceptions with which
the Apostle peopled the invisible spiritual
world, whatever their character, and declares their inability to come between us
and the love of Christ. οὔτε ἐνεστῶτα
οὔτε μέλλοντα: cf. 1 Cor. iii. 22. οὔτε
ὕψωμα οὔτε βάθος: no dimensions of
space. Whether these words pictured
something to Paul's imagination we
cannot tell ; the patristic attempts to give
them definiteness are not happy. οὔτε
τις κτίσις ἑτέρα: nor any created thing
of different kind. All the things Paul
has mentioned come under the head of
κτίσις ; if there is anything of a different
kind which comes under the same head,
he includes it too. The suggestions of
" another world," or of "aspects of
reality out of relation to our faculties,"
and therefore as yet unknown to us, are
toys, remote from the seriousness and
passion of the Apostle's mind. Nothing
that God has made, whatever be its
nature, shall be able to separate us ἀπὸ
τῆς ἀγάπης τοῦ θεοῦ τῆς ἐν Χ. Ἰ. τοῦ κ.
ἡμῶν. The love of Christ is God's love,

manifested to us in Him ; and it is only
in Him that a Divine love is manifested
which can inspire the triumphant assurance of this verse.

CHAPTERS IX.-XI. With the eighth
chapter Paul concludes the positive
exposition of his gospel. Starting with
the theme of i. 16 f., he showed in i. 18-
iii. 20 the universal sinfulness of men
—Gentile and Jew ; in iii. 21-v. 21 he
explained, illustrated and glorified the
gospel of justification by faith in Christ,
set forth by God as a propitiation for
sin ; in vi. 1-viii. 39 he has vindicated
this gospel from the charge of moral
inefficiency, by showing that justification
by faith is inseparably connected with a
new life in the Spirit, a life over which
sin has no dominion and in which the
just demands of God's law are fulfilled.
He has even carried this spiritual life
on, in hope, to its consummation in
glory : and no more remains to be said.
With chap. ix. a new subject is introduced. There is no formal link of
connection with what precedes. Struc-
turally, the new division of the epistle
stands quite apart from the earlier ; it
might have been written, and probably
was written, after a break. But though
no logical relation between the parts is
expressed, a psychological connection
between them is not hard to discover.
The new section deals with a problem
which presented great difficulty to the
early Church, and especially to men of
Jewish birth, a problem which haunted
the Apostle's own mind and was no
doubt thrust on his attention by his
unbelieving countrymen, a problem all
the more painful to him as he realised
more completely the greatness and glory
of the Christian salvation. This was the
problem constituted by the fact that the
Jews as a whole did not receive the
Gospel. They were God's chosen people,
but if the Christian Gospel brought
salvation they had no share in it. The
Messiah was to spring from them, but if
Jesus was the Messiah this privilege
meant not redemption but condemnation,
for they rejected Him almost with one
consent. In short, if the birth of the
Christian Church and the gathering of

IX. 1. ᾽ΑΛΗΘΕΙΑΝ λέγω ἐν Χριστῷ, οὐ ᵃ ψεύδομαι, συμμαρτυρούσης μοι τῆς συνειδήσεώς μου ἐν Πνεύματι ῾Αγίῳ, 2. ὅτι λύπη μοι ἐστὶ

Gentiles into it represented the carrying out of God's purpose to bless and save men, God must have turned His back upon Himself; He must have broken His promise to Israel, and cast off His chosen people. But as this must seem impossible, the Jewish inference would be that the Gospel preached by Paul could not be of God, nor the Gentile Churches, as Paul asserted, God's true Israel. This is the situation to which the Apostle addresses himself in the ninth and the two following chapters. It is a historical problem, in the first instance, he has to deal with, not a dogmatic one; and it is necessary to keep the historical situation in view, if we are to avoid illegitimate inferences from the arguments or illustrations of the Apostle. After the introductory statement (ix. 1-5), which shows how deeply his heart is pledged to his brethren after the flesh, he works out a solution of the problem —or an interpretation of the position —along three lines. In each of these there are many incidental points of view, but they can be broadly discriminated. (1) In the first, chap. ix. 6-29, Paul asserts the absolute freedom and sovereignty of God as against any claim, made as of right, on the part of man. The Jewish objection to the Gospel, to which reference is made above, really means that the Jewish nation had a claim of right upon God, giving them a title to salvation, which God must acknowledge; Paul argues that all God's action, as exhibited in Scripture, and especially in the history of Israel itself— to say nothing of the essential relations of Creator and creature—refutes such a claim. (2) In the second, chap. ix. 30- x. 21, Paul turns from this more speculative aspect of the situation to its moral character, and points out that the explanation of the present rejection of the Jews is to be found in the fact that they have wilfully and stubbornly rejected the Gospel. Their minds have been set on a righteousness of their own, and they have refused to submit themselves to the righteousness of God. (3) In the third, chap. xi., he rises again to an absolute or speculative point of view. The present unbelief of the Jews and incoming of the Gentiles are no doubt, to a Jew, disconcerting events; yet in spite of them, or rather—which is more wonderful still —by means of them, God's promises to

the fathers will be fulfilled, and all Israel saved. Gentile Christianity will provoke the unbelieving Jews to jealousy, and they too will enter the Messianic Kingdom. In the very events which seem to throw the pious Jewish mind out of its reckoning, there is a gracious providence, a depth of riches and wisdom and knowledge which no words can express. The present situation, which at the first glance is heart-breaking (ix. 2), is only one incident in the working out of a purpose which when completed reveals the whole glory of God's mercy, and evokes the loftiest and most heartfelt praise. "He shut up all unto disobedience that He might have mercy on all. . . . Of Him and through Him and to Him are all things. Unto Him be glory for ever." Since Baur's time several scholars have held that the mass of the Roman Church was Jewish-Christian, and that these three chapters, with their apologetic aim, are specially addressed to that community, as one which naturally felt the pressure of the difficulty with which they deal. But the Roman Church, as these very chapters show (cf. ix. 3, my kinsmen, not our; xi. 13, ὑμῖν δὲ λέγω τοῖς ἔθνεσιν), was certainly Gentile, whatever influence Jewish modes of thought and practice may have had in it; and it was quite natural for the Apostle, in writing what he evidently meant from the first should be both a systematic and a circular letter, to include in it a statement of his thoughts on one of the most difficult and importunate questions of the time. The extraordinary daring of chap. xi. ad fin. is not unrelated to the extraordinary passion of chap. ix. ad init. The whole discussion is a magnificent illustration of the aphorism, that great thoughts come from the heart.

CHAPTER IX.—Vv. 1-5. The intense pain with which Paul contemplates the unbelief of his countrymen. Ver. 1. ἀλήθειαν λέγω ἐν Χριστῷ, οὐ ψεύδομαι. The solemn asseveration is meant to clear him of the suspicion that in preaching to the Gentiles he is animated by hostility or even indifference to the Jews. Yet cf. 2 Cor. xi. 31, Gal. i. 20. ἐν Χριστῷ means that he speaks in fellowship with Christ, so that falsehood is impossible. For συμμαρτ. cf. ii. 15, viii. 16. The μοι is governed by συν: conscience attests what he says, and that ἐν πνεύματι ἁγίῳ—the spirit of

μεγάλη, καὶ ἀδιάλειπτος [b] ὀδύνη [c] τῇ καρδίᾳ μου, 3. ηὐχόμην γὰρ [b 2 Tim. i. 3.] [c 1 Tim. vi.] αὐτὸς ἐγὼ ἀνάθεμα εἶναι [1] ἀπὸ τοῦ Χριστοῦ ὑπὲρ τῶν ἀδελφῶν μου, [10.] [d Gal. iv. 24;] τῶν συγγενῶν μου κατὰ σάρκα · 4. οἵτινές εἰσιν Ἰσραηλῖται, ὧν ἡ [Eph. ii. 12.] [e Cf. Heb.] υἱοθεσία, καὶ ἡ δόξα, καὶ αἱ διαθῆκαι,[2] [d] καὶ ἡ νομοθεσία,[e] καὶ ἡ λατ- [vii. 11,] [viii. 6.]

[1] αυτος εγω αναθεμα ειναι, so CKL ; but in ℵABDF αναθεμα ειναι αυτος εγω.

[2] αι διαθηκαι ℵCK and versions; η διαθηκη BDF ; see note [2] (on πρῶτον), page 589. The plural is no doubt right here, and was mechanically changed as standing between two singulars. At the end of the verse DEFG also read η επαγγελια instead of αι επαγγελιαι.

God, in which all the functions of the Christian life are carried on: so that assurance is made doubly and trebly sure.

Ver. 2. The fact of Paul's sorrow is stated here; the cause of it is revealed in ver. 3. Weiss remarks on the triple climax: λύπη being intensified in ὀδύνη, μεγάλη in ἀδιάλειπτος, and μοι in τῇ καρδίᾳ μου. Paul cannot find words strong enough to convey his feeling.

Ver. 3. ηὐχόμην γὰρ ἀνάθεμα εἶναι κ.τ.λ. For I could wish that I myself were anathema, etc. For the omission of ἄν see Acts xxv. 22, Gal. iv. 20. Paul could wish this if it were a wish that could be realised for the good of Israel. The form of expression implies that the wish had actually been conceived, but in such sentences "the context alone implies what the present state of mind is" (Burton, Moods and Tenses, § 33). ἀνάθεμα is to be construed with ἀπὸ τοῦ Χριστοῦ: the idea of separation from Christ, final and fatal separation, is conveyed. For the construction cf. Gal. v. 4 (κατηργήθητε ἀπὸ Χριστοῦ). ἀνάθεμα Gal. i. 8 f., 1 Cor. xii. 3, xvi. 22 is the equivalent of the Hebrew חֵרֶם, Deut. vii. 26, Josh. vii. 12—that which is put under the ban, and irrevocably devoted to destruction. It is beside the mark to speak of such an utterance as this as unethical. Rather might we call it with Dorner "a spark from the fire of Christ's substitutionary love". There is a passion in it more profound than that of Moses' prayer in Ex. xxxii. 32. Moses identifies himself with his people, and if they cannot be saved would perish with them; Paul could find it in his heart, were it possible, to perish for them. τῶν συγγενῶν μου κατὰ σάρκα distinguishes these from his Christian brethren.

Ver. 4 f. The intensity of Paul's distress, and of his longing for the salvation of his countrymen, is partly explained in this verse. It is the greatness of his people, their unique place of privilege in God's providence, the splendour of the inheritance and of the hopes which they forfeit by unbelief, that make their unbelief at once so painful, and so perplexing. οἵτινές εἰσιν Ἰσραηλεῖται: being, as they are, Israelites. Israelites is not the national but the theocratic name; it expresses the spiritual prerogative of the nation, cf. 2 Cor. xi. 22, Gal. vi. 16. ὧν ἡ υἱοθεσία: this is not the Christian sonship, but that which is referred to in such passages as Ex. iv. 22, Hos. xi. 1. Yet it may be wrong to speak of it as if it were merely national; it seems to be distributed and applied to the individual members of the nation in Deut. xiv. 1, Hos. i. 10 (ii. 1 Heb.). ἡ δόξα: the glory must refer to something definite, like the pillar of cloud and fire, the כְּבוֹד יהוה of the O.T., the שְׁכִינָה of later Jewish theology; there is probably reference to it in Acts vii. 2, Heb. ix. 5. αἱ διαθῆκαι: in other places Paul speaks of the O.T. religion as one covenant, one (legal) administration of the relations between God and man (e.g., in 2 Cor. iii.): here, where αἱ διαθῆκαι is expressly distinguished from ἡ νομοθεσία (the great Sinaitic legislation: 2 Macc. vi. 23), the various covenants God made with the patriarchs must be meant. Cf. Wisd. xviii. 22, Sir. xliv. 11, 2 Macc. viii. 15. ἡ λατρεία is the cultus of the tabernacle and the temple, the only legitimate cultus in the world. αἱ ἐπαγγελίαι are the Messianic promises: in the Israelitish religion "the best was yet to be," as all the highest minds knew. Ver. 5. ὧν οἱ πατέρες: Abraham, Isaac and Jacob. The greatness of its ancestry ennobled Israel, and made its position in Paul's time harder to understand and to endure. Who could think without the keenest pain of the sons of such fathers forfeiting everything for which the fathers had been called?

f Ch. xii. 1. ρεία,ᶠ καὶ αἱ ἐπαγγελίαι,ᵍ 5. ὧν οἱ πατέρες,ʰ καὶ ἐξ ὧν ὁ Χριστὸς τὸ
g Ch. xv. 8;
Gal. iii.16, κατὰ σάρκα, ὁ ὢν ἐπὶ πάντων Θεὸς εὐλογητὸς ⁱ εἰς τοὺς αἰῶνας. ἀμήν.
21; Heb.
vi. 12.   h Ch. xi. 28.   i Ch. i. 23; 2 Cor. xi. 31.

But the supreme distinction of Israel has yet to be mentioned. ἐξ ὧν ὁ Χριστὸς τὸ κατὰ σάρκα, ὁ ὢν ἐπὶ πάντων θεὸς εὐλογητὸς εἰς τοὺς αἰῶνας. Ἀμήν. The only point in the interpretation of this verse, in which it can be said that interpreters are wholly at one, is the statement that of Israel the Messiah came, according to the flesh. The words τὸ κατὰ σάρκα define the extent to which the Messiah can be explained by His descent from Israel; for anything going beyond σάρξ, or ordinary humanity, the explanation must be sought elsewhere. The limitation suggests an antithesis, and one in which the spiritual or Divine side of the Messiah's nature should find expression, this being the natural counterpart of σάρξ: and such an antithesis has been sought and found in the words which follow. He who, according to the flesh, is of Israel, is at the same time over all, God blessed for ever. This interpretation, which refers the whole of the words after ἐξ ὧν to ὁ Χριστὸς, is adopted by many of the best scholars: Gifford, Sanday, Westcott (see *N.T.*, vol. ii., app., p. 110), Weiss, etc., and has much in its favour. (1) It *does* supply the complementary antithesis which τὸ κατὰ σάρκα suggests. (2) Grammatically it is simple, for ὁ ὢν naturally applies to what precedes: the person who is over all is naturally the person just mentioned, unless there is decisive reason to the contrary. (3) If we adopt another punctuation, and make the words ὁ ὢν ἐπὶ πάντων θεὸς εὐλογητὸς εἰς τοὺς αἰῶνας a doxology—"God Who is over all be blessed for ever"—there are grammatical objections. These are (*a*) the use of ὤν, which is at least abnormal. "God Who is over all" would naturally be expressed by ὁ ἐπὶ πάντων θεὸς without ὤν: the ὤν suggests the reference to Christ. (*b*) The position of εὐλογητὸς is unparalleled in a doxology; it ought, as in Eph. i. 3 and the LXX., to stand first in the sentence. But these reasons are not decisive. As for (1), though a complementary antithesis to τὸ κατὰ σάρκα is suggested, it is not imperatively demanded here, as in i. 3 f. The greatness reflected upon Israel by the origin of the person in question is sufficiently conveyed by ὁ Χριστός, without any expansion. As for (2), it is true to say that ὁ ὢν naturally refers to what precedes: the only question is, whether

the natural reference may not in any given case be precluded. Many scholars think it is precluded here. Meyer, for instance, argues that "Paul has *never* used the express θεὸς of Christ, since he has not adopted, like John, the Alexandrian form of conceiving and setting forth the Divine essence of Christ, but has adhered to the popular concrete, strictly monotheistic terminology, not modified by philosophical speculation even for the designation of Christ; and he always accurately distinguishes God and Christ". To this he adds the more dubious reasons that in the genuine apostolic writings (he excludes 2 Tim. iv. 18, 2 Pet. iii. 18, Heb. xiii. 21, and Rev.) there is no doxology to Christ in the form usual in doxologies referring to God, and that by ἐπὶ πάντων the Son's subordination is denied. To these last arguments it may be answered that if the words in question do apply to Christ they are not a doxology at all (Gifford), but a declaration of deity, like 2 Cor. xi. 31, and that Christ's subordination is not affected by His being described as ὁ ὢν ἐπὶ πάντων any more than by His own claim to have all authority in heaven and on earth. But the first of Meyer's arguments has a weight which it is impossible not to feel, and it becomes the more decisive the more we realise Paul's whole habit of thought and speech. To say with Dr. Gifford, "When we review the history of the interpretation it cannot but be regarded as a remarkable fact that every objection urged against the ancient interpretation rests ultimately on dogmatic presuppositions," hardly covers such a position as Meyer represents. For the "dogmatic presuppositions" are not arbitrary, but merely sum up the whole impression made on the mind by the study of Paul's writings, an impression by which we cannot but be influenced, especially in deciding delicate and dubious questions like this. If we ask ourselves point blank, whether Paul, as we know his mind from his epistles, would express his sense of Christ's greatness by calling Him God blessed for ever, it seems to me almost impossible to answer in the affirmative. Such an assertion is not on the same plane with the conception of Christ which meets us everywhere in the Apostle's writings; and though there is some irregularity in the grammar, and perhaps some

6. Οὐχ οἷον δὲ ὅτι ἐκπέπτωκεν[k] ὁ λόγος τοῦ Θεοῦ. οὐ γὰρ πάντες [k Here only; Jas. i. 11; 1 Pet. i. 24.] οἱ ἐξ Ἰσραήλ, οὗτοι Ἰσραήλ· 7. οὐδ᾽ ὅτι εἰσὶ σπέρμα[l] Ἀβραάμ, [l 1 Ch. xi. 1; 2 Cor. xi. 22; John viii. 33, 37.] πάντες τέκνα, ἀλλ᾽ " ἐν Ἰσαὰκ κληθήσεταί σοι σπέρμα". 8. τοῦτ᾽ ἔστιν, οὐ τὰ τέκνα τῆς σαρκός, ταῦτα τέκνα τοῦ Θεοῦ· ἀλλὰ τὰ τέκνα τῆς ἐπαγγελίας[m] λογίζεται εἰς σπέρμα. 9. ἐπαγγελίας γὰρ [m Gal. iv. 28.] ὁ λόγος οὗτος, "Κατὰ τὸν καιρὸν τοῦτον[n] ἐλεύσομαι, καὶ ἔσται τῇ [n Gen. xviii. 10.]

difficulty in seeing the point of a doxology, I agree with those who would put a colon or a period at σάρκα, and make the words that follow refer not to Christ but to the Father. This is the punctuation given in the margin by W. and H., and " alone seems adequate to account for the whole of the language employed, more especially when considered in relation to the context" (Hort, *N.T.*, vol. ii., app., p. 110). The doxology is, indeed, somewhat hard to comprehend; it seems at the first glance without a motive, and no psychological explanation of it yet offered is very satisfying. It is as if Paul, having carried the privileges of Israel to a climax by mentioning the origin of the Messiah as far as regards His humanity, suddenly felt himself face to face with the problem of the time, how to reconcile these extraordinary privileges with the rejection of the Jews; and before addressing himself to any study or solution of it expressed in this way his devout and adoring faith, even under the pressure of such a perplexity, in the sovereign providence of God. The use of ὤν, which is in itself unnecessary, emphasises ἐπὶ πάντων; and this emphasis is "fully justified if St. Paul's purpose is to suggest that the tragic apostasy of the Jews (vers. 2, 3) is itself part of the dispensations of Him Who is God over all, over Jew and Gentile alike, over past, present and future alike; so that the ascription of blessing to Him is a homage to His Divine purpose and power of bringing good out of evil in the course of the ages (xi. 13-16, 25-36)": W. and H., ii., app., p. 110. Full discussions of the passage are given in Meyer, S. and H., and Gifford; also by Dr. Ezra Abbot in the *Journal of the Society of Biblical Exegesis*, 1883. With this preface Paul proceeds to justify the ways of God to men: see the introductory remarks above. The first section of his argument (ix. 6-29) is in the narrower sense a theodicy—a vindication of God's right in dealing as He has dealt with Israel. In the first part of this (vers. 6-13) he shows that the rejection of the mass of Israel from the Messianic Kingdom involves no breach

or failure of the Divine promise. The promise is not given to all the natural descendants of Abraham, but only to a chosen seed, the Israel of God.

Ver. 6. οὐχ οἷον δὲ ὅτι: this unique expression is explained by Buttmann (*Grammar*, p. 372, Thayer's Transl.) as a blending of two formulas—οὐχ οἷον followed by a finite verb, and οὐχ ὅτι, which is common in the N.T. The meaning is, But, in spite of my grief, I do not mean to say any such thing as that the Word of God has come to nothing. For not all they that are of Israel, *i.e.*, born of the patriarch, are Israel, *i.e.*, the people of God. This is merely an application of our Lord's words, That which is born of the flesh is flesh. It is not what we get from our fathers and mothers that ensures our place in the family of God. For the use of οὗτοι in this verse to resume and define the subject see Gal. iii. 7.

Ver. 7. Nor because they are Abraham's seed, are they all τέκνα, *i.e.*, children in the sense which entitles them to the inheritance, iv. 11, viii. 17. God from the very first made a distinction here, and definitely announced that the seed of Abraham to which the promise belonged should come in the line of Isaac—not of Ishmael, though he also could call Abraham father. Ἐν Ἰσαὰκ κληθήσεταί σοι σπέρμα = Gen. xxi. 12, LXX. The words literally mean that in the line of Isaac Abraham should have the posterity which would properly bear his name, and inherit the promises made to him by God. Isaac's descendants are the true Abrahamidae.

Ver. 8 f. τοῦτ᾽ ἔστιν: the meaning of this action of God is now made clear. It signifies that not mere bodily descent from Abraham makes one a child of God —that was never the case, not even in Abraham's time; it is the children of the promise who are reckoned a seed to Abraham, for the word in virtue of which Isaac, the true son and heir, was born, was a word of promise. He was born, to use the language of the Gospel, from above; and something analogous to this is necessary, whenever a man (even a

Σάῤῥᾳ υἱός ".[o] 10. οὐ μόνον δέ, ἀλλὰ καὶ Ῥεβέκκα ἐξ ἑνὸς κοίτην[p]
ἔχουσα, Ἰσαὰκ τοῦ πατρὸς ἡμῶν· 11. μήπω γὰρ γεννηθέντων, μηδὲ
πραξάντων τι ἀγαθὸν ἢ κακόν,[1] ἵνα ἡ κατ᾽ ἐκλογὴν[q] τοῦ Θεοῦ πρόθεσις
μένῃ, οὐκ ἐξ ἔργων, ἀλλ᾽ ἐκ τοῦ καλοῦντος,[r] 12. ἐῤῥήθη αὐτῇ, "Ὅτι

o Gen. xviii. 10.
p Ch. xiii. 13; Heb. xiii. 4; Luke xi. 7.
q Ch. xi. 5, 7, 28; Acts ix. 15; 1 Th. i. 4.
r Gal. v. 8.

[1] **κακον** DFKL; **φαυλον** ℵAB. **του θεου προθεσις**; all the best MSS., ℵABDFKL and edd. read **προθεσις του θεου.**

descendant of Abraham) claims to be a child of God and an heir of His kingdom. From Gal. iv. 28 (Now we, brethren, like Isaac, are children of promise) we see that the relation to God in question here is one open to Gentiles as well as Jews: if we are Christ's, then we too are Abraham's seed, and heirs according to promise. The argumentative suggestion in vers. 6-9 is that just as God discriminated at the first between the children of Abraham, so He is discriminating still; the fact that many do not receive the Gospel no more proves that the promise has failed than the fact that God chose Isaac only and set aside Ishmael.

Ver. 10 ff. But the argument can be made more decisive. A Jewish opponent might say, "Ishmael was an illegitimate child, who naturally had no rights as against Isaac; we are the legitimate descendants of the patriarch, and our right to the inheritance is indefeasible". To this the Apostle replies in vers. 10-13. Not only did God make the distinction already referred to, but in the case of *Isaac's* children, where there seemed no ground for making any distinction whatever, He distinguished again, and said, The elder shall serve the younger. Jacob and Esau had one father, one mother, and were twin sons; the only ground on which either could have been preferred was that of priority of birth, and this was disregarded by God; Esau, the elder, was rejected, and Jacob, the younger, was made heir of the promises. Further, this was done by God of His sovereign freedom: the decisive word was spoken to their mother while they were as yet unborn and had achieved neither good nor evil. Claims as of right, therefore, made against God, are futile, whether they are based on descent or on works. There is no way in which they can be established; and, as we have just seen, God acts in entire disregard of them. God's purpose to save men, and make them heirs of His kingdom—a purpose which is characterised as **κατ' ἐκλογήν,** or involving a choice—is not determined at all by consideration of such claims as the Jews put forward. In forming it, and carrying it out, God acts with perfect freedom. In the case in question His action in regard to Jacob and Esau agrees with His word in the prophet Malachi: Jacob I loved but Esau I hated; and further than this we cannot go. To avoid misapprehending this, however, it is necessary to keep the Apostle's purpose in view. He wishes to show that God's promise has not broken down, though many of the children of Abraham have no part in its fulfilment in Christ. He does so by showing that there has always been a distinction, among the descendants of the patriarchs, between those who have merely the natural connection to boast of, and those who are the Israel of God; and, as against Jewish pretensions, he shows at the same time that this distinction can be traced to nothing but God's sovereignty. It is not of works, but of Him Who effectually calls men. We may say, if we please, that sovereignty in this sense is "just a name for what is *unrevealed* of God" (T. Erskine, *The Brazen Serpent*, p. 259), but though it is unrevealed we must not conceive of it as arbitrary—*i.e.*, as non-rational or non-moral. It is the sovereignty of *God*, and God is not *exlex;* He is a law to Himself—a law all love and holiness and truth—in all His purposes towards men. So Calvin: "ubi mentionem gloriæ Dei audis, illic justitiam cogita". Paul has mentioned in an earlier chapter, among the notes of true religion, the exclusion of boasting (iii. 27); and in substance that is the argument he is using here. No Jewish birth, no legal works, can give a man a claim which God is bound to honour; and no man urging such claims can say that God's word has become of no effect though his claims are disallowed, and he gets no part in the inheritance of God's people.

οὐ μόνον δέ: *cf.* v. 11, viii. 23 = Not only is this so, but a more striking and convincing illustration can be given. **ἀλλὰ καὶ Ῥεβέκκα**: the sentence thus begun is never finished, but the sense is

ὁ μείζων δουλεύσει τῷ ἐλάσσονι·" 13. καθὼς¹ γέγραπται, "Τὸν
Ἰακὼβ ἠγάπησα, τὸν δὲ Ἠσαῦ ἐμίσησα".

14. Τί οὖν ἐροῦμεν; μὴ ἀδικία παρὰ τῷ Θεῷ;ˢ μὴ γένοιτο.   15. s Ch. ii. 11.
τῷ γὰρ Μωσῇ λέγει, "Ἐλεήσω ὃν ἂν ἐλεῶ, καὶ οἰκτειρήσω ὃν ἂν

¹ καθαπερ B, Orig. 1 (instead of καθως) is read by Weiss and W. and H., though
the latter put καθως in marg. *Cf.* iii. 4, xi. 8, and 1 Cor. x. 10.

continued in ver. 12. Ἰσαὰκ τοῦ πατρὸς
ἡμῶν: Paul speaks here out of his own
consciousness as a Jew, addressing himself to a problem which greatly exercised
other Jews; and calls Isaac "father" as
the person from whom the inheritance
was to come. Ver. 11. μήπω γὰρ γεννηθέντων μηδὲ πραξάντων: "the conditional
negatives (μήπω, μηδὲ) represent the circumstances not as mere facts of history,
but as conditions entering into God's
counsel and plan. The time of the prediction was thus chosen, in order to make it
clear that He Who calls men to be heirs of
His salvation makes free choice of whom
He will, unfettered by any claims of birth
or merit" (Gifford). πρόθεσις in this theological sense is a specially Pauline word.
The purpose it describes is universal in
its bearings, for it is the purpose of One
who works all things according to the
counsel of His will, Eph. i. 11; it is
eternal, a πρόθεσις τῶν αἰώνων, Eph. iii.
11; it is God's ἰδία πρόθεσις, 2 Tim. i. 9,
a purpose, the meaning, contents, and
end of which find their explanation in
God alone; it is a purpose κατ᾽ ἐκλογήν,
i.e., the carrying of it out involves choice
and discrimination between man and
man, and between race and race; and
in spite of the side of mystery which
belongs to such a conception, it is a perfectly intelligible purpose, for it is described as πρόθεσις ἣν ἐποίησεν ἐν
Χριστῷ Ἰησοῦ, and what God means by
Christ Jesus no one can doubt. God's
eternal purpose, the purpose carried out
κατ᾽ ἐκλογήν, yet embracing the universe,
is clearly revealed in His Son. The permanent determining element, wherever
this purpose is concerned, is not the
works of men, but the will and call of
God; and to make this plain was the
intention of God in speaking as He did,
and when He did, to Rebecca about her
children. If we look to Gen. xxv. 23, it
is indisputably the nations of Israel and
Edom that are referred to: "Two nations
are in thy womb, and two manner of
peoples shall be separated from thy
bowels; and the one people shall be
stronger than the other people, and the
elder shall serve the younger". The

same is true also of Mal. i. 2: "I loved
Jacob, but Esau I hated, and made his
mountains a desolation," etc. Yet it
would not be right to say that Paul is here
considering merely the parts assigned
by God to nations in the drama of providence; He is obviously thinking of Jacob
and Esau as individuals, whose own relation to God's promise and inheritance
(involving no doubt that of their posterity) was determined by God before
they were born or had done either good
or ill. On the other hand, it would not
be right to say that Paul here refers the
eternal salvation or perdition of individuals to an absolute decree of God
which has no relation to what they are
or do, but rests simply on His inscrutable will. He is engaged in precluding
the idea that man can have claims of
right against God, and with it the idea
that the exclusion of the mass of Israel
from the Messiah's kingdom convicts
God of breach of faith toward the children of Abraham; and this He can do
quite effectually, on the lines indicated,
without consciously facing this tremendous hypothesis.

Vv. 14-21. In the second part of his
theodicy Paul meets the objection that
this sovereign freedom of God is essentially unjust.

Ver. 14. τί οὖν ἐροῦμεν; *cf.* vi. 1,
vii. 7, viii. 31. It is Paul who speaks,
anticipating, as he cannot help doing,
the objection which is sure to rise, not
only in Jewish minds, though it is with
them he is directly concerned, but in the
mind of every human being who reads
his words. Yet he states the objection
as one in itself incredible. μὴ ἀδικία
παρὰ τῷ θεῷ; surely we cannot say that
there is unrighteousness with God? This
is the force of the μὴ, and Paul can
answer at once μὴ γένοιτο: away with
the thought! God says Himself that He
shows mercy with that sovereign freedom
which Paul has ascribed to Him; and the
principle of action which God announces
as His own cannot be unjust.

Ver. 15. τῷ Μωυσεῖ γὰρ λέγει. τῷ
Μωυσεῖ is emphatic by position: the
person to whom this declaration was

t Gal. v. 7. οἰκτείρω". 16. ἄρα οὖν οὐ τοῦ θέλοντος, οὐδὲ τοῦ τρέχοντος,ᵗ ἀλλὰ
τοῦ ἐλεοῦντος ¹ Θεοῦ. 17. λέγει γὰρ ἡ γραφὴ τῷ Φαραὼ, "Ὅτι εἰς
u 1 Tim. i. αὐτὸ τοῦτο ἐξήγειρά σε, ὅπως ἐνδείξωμαιᵘ ἐν σοὶ τὴν δύναμίν μου,
16.
v Luke ix. καὶ ὅπως διαγγελῇ ᵛ τὸ ὄνομά μου ἐν πάσῃ τῇ γῇ". 18. ἄρα οὖν ὃν
60; Acts
xxi. 26. θέλει, |ἐλεεῖ · ὃν δὲ θέλει, σκληρύνει. 19. Ἐρεῖς οὖν μοι,² Τί ἔτι

¹ For ἐλεουντος read ἐλεωντος with ℵAB¹DF.

² For ουν μοι ℵABP 47 read μοι ουν. τι ετι μεμφεται ℵAKLP, but τι ουν ετι
μεμφεται BDFG, Orig.-inter. This ουν is inserted by Lachm. and Weiss, bracketed
in marg. by Treg., simply omitted (on the principle of judging referred to in note ²,
page 589) by W. and H.

made, as well as the voice which made
it, render it peculiarly significant to a
Jew. The words (exactly as LXX, Exod.
xxxiii. 19) occur in the answer to a prayer
of Moses, and may have been regarded
by Paul as having special reference to
him; as if the point of the quotation
were, Even one who had deserved so
well as Moses experienced God's mercy
solely because God willed that He
should. But that is not necessary, and
is not what the original means. The
emphasis is on ὃν ἂν, and the point is
that in showing mercy God is determined
by nothing outside of His mercy itself.
οἰκτείρειν is stronger than ἐλεεῖν; it
suggests more strongly the emotion
attendant on pity, and even its expression in voice or gesture.

Ver. 16. Conclusion from this word of
God. It (namely, the experience of God's
mercy) does not depend on man's resolve
or effort (for τρέχειν cf. 1 Cor. ix. 24 ff.),
but on God's merciful act. This, of
course, merely repeats vers. 12, 13,
buttressing the principle of God's sovereign freedom in the exercise of mercy
by reference to His own word in Exod.
xxxiii. 19.

Ver. 17 f. But Paul goes further, and
explains the contrary phenomenon—that
of a man who does not and cannot
receive mercy—in the same way. λέγει
γὰρ ἡ γραφή: it is on Scripture the
burden of proof is laid here and at ver.
15. A Jew might answer the arguments
Paul uses here if they were the Apostle's
own; to Scripture he can make no reply;
it must silence, even where it does not
convince. τῷ Φαραὼ: All men, and not
those only who are the objects of His
mercy, come within the scope of God's
sovereignty. Pharaoh as well as Moses
can be quoted to illustrate it. He was
the open adversary of God, an avowed,
implacable adversary; yet a Divine purpose was fulfilled in his life, and that

purpose and nothing else is the explanation of his very being. εἰς αὐτὸ τοῦτο
ἐξήγειρά σε. The LXX in Exod. ix.
16 read: καὶ ἕνεκεν τούτου διετηρήθης,
the last word, answering to the Hebrew
הֶעֱמַדְתִּיךָ, being used in the sense
of "thou wast kept alive"—the sense
adopted by Dillmann for the Hebrew;
probably Paul changed it intentionally
to give the meaning, "for this reason
I brought thee on the stage of history":
cf. Hab. i. 6, Zec. xi. 16, Jer. xxvii.
41 (S. and H.). The purpose Pharaoh
was designed to serve, and actually did
serve, on this stage, was certainly not his
own; as certainly it was God's. God's
power was shown in the penal miracles
by which Pharaoh and Egypt were
visited, and his name is proclaimed to
this day wherever the story of the Exodus
is told.

Ver. 18. From the two instances just
quoted Paul draws the comprehensive
conclusion: So then on whom He will
He has mercy, and whom He will He
hardens. The whole emphasis is on
θέλει. The two modes in which God
acts upon man are showing mercy and
hardening, and it depends upon God's
will in which of these two modes He
actually does act. The word σκληρύνει
is borrowed from the history of Pharaoh,
Ex. vii. 3, 22; viii. 19; ix. 12; xiv. 17.
What precisely the hardening means,
and in what relation God's hardening of
Pharaoh's heart stood to Pharaoh's own
hardening of it against God, are not
unimportant questions, but they are
questions which Paul does not here
raise. He has one aim always in view
here—to show that man has no claim as
of right against God; and he finds a
decisive proof of this (at least for a Jew)
in the opposite examples of Moses and
Pharaoh, interpreted as these are by
unmistakable words of God Himself.

μέμφεται *; τῷ γὰρ βουλήματι ˣ αὐτοῦ τίς ἀνθέστηκε; 20. μενοῦνγε, ὦ ʷ Heb. viii. 8.
ἄνθρωπε,¹ ʸ σὺ τίς εἶ ὁ ἀνταποκρινόμενος ᶻ τῷ Θεῷ; μὴ ἐρεῖ τὸ πλάσμα ˣ Acts xxvii.
τῷ πλάσαντι, Τί με ἐποίησας οὕτως; 21. ἢ οὐκ ἔχει ἐξουσίαν ὁ ⁱᵛ· 3.
κεραμεὺς ᵃ τοῦ πηλοῦ, ἐκ τοῦ αὐτοῦ φυράματος ποιῆσαι ὃ μὲν εἰς ᶻ Luke xiv.
6.
a Jer. c. 18; Isaiah xlv. 9; Sir. xxxvi. (xxxiii.) 13; Sap. xv. 7.

¹ ω ανθρωπε stands before μενουνγε in א¹AB (B omits γε), and so in all crit. edd.

It was through God, in the last resort, that Moses and Pharaoh were what they were, signal instances of the Divine mercy and the Divine wrath.

Ver. 19 ff. But human nature is not so easily silenced. This interpretation of all human life, with all its diversities of character and experience, through the will of God alone, as if that will by itself explained everything, is not adequate to the facts. If Moses and Pharaoh alike are to be explained by reference to that will—that is, are to be explained in precisely the same way—then the difference between Moses and Pharaoh disappears. The moral interpretation of the world is annulled by the religious one. If God is equally behind the most opposite moral phenomena, then it is open to any one to say, what Paul here anticipates will be said, τί ἔτι μέμφεται; why does he still find fault? For who withstands his resolve? To this objection there is really no answer, and it ought to be frankly admitted that the Apostle does not answer it. The attempt to understand the relation between the human will and the Divine seems to lead of necessity to an antinomy which thought has not as yet succeeded in transcending. To assert the absoluteness of God in the unexplained unqualified sense of verse 18 makes the moral life unintelligible; but to explain the moral life by ascribing to man a freedom which makes him stand in independence over against God reduces the universe to anarchy. Up to this point Paul has been insisting on the former point of view, and he insists on it still as against the human presumption which would plead its rights against God; but in the very act of doing so he passes over (in ver. 22) to an intermediate standpoint, showing that God has not in point of fact acted arbitrarily, in a freedom uncontrolled by moral law; and from that again he advances in the following chapter to do full justice to the other side of the antinomy—the liberty and responsibility of man. The act of Israel, as well as the will of God, lies behind the painful situation he is trying to understand.

Ver. 20. ὦ ἄνθρωπε is not used contemptuously, but it is set intentionally over against τῷ Θεῷ: the objector is reminded emphatically of what he is, and of the person to whom he is speaking. It is not for a man to adopt this tone toward God. For μενοῦνγε cf. x. 18, Phil. iii. 8: the idea is, So far from your having the right to raise such objections, it is rather for me to ask, Who art thou? etc. Paul, as has been observed above, does not refute, but repels the objection. It is inconsistent, he urges, with the relation of the creature to the Creator. μὴ ἐρεῖ κ.τ.λ. Surely the thing formed shall not say, etc. The first words of the quotation are from Isa. xxix. 16: μὴ ἐρεῖ τὸ πλάσμα τῷ πλάσαντι αὐτό Οὐ σύ με ἔπλασας; ἢ τὸ ποίημα τῷ ποιήσαντι Οὐ συνετῶς με ἐποίησας; The fact that the words originally refer to Israel as a nation, and to God's shaping of its destiny, does not prove in the least that Paul is dealing with nations, and not with individuals, here. He never pays any attention to the original application of the O.T. words he uses; and neither Moses nor Pharaoh nor the person addressed as ὦ ἄνθρωπε is a nation. The person addressed is one who feels that the principle enunciated in ver. 18 must be qualified somehow, and so he makes the protest against it which Paul attempts in this summary fashion to repress. A man is not a thing, and if the whole explanation of his destiny is to be sought in the bare will of God, he *will* say, Why didst Thou make me thus? and not even the authority of Paul will silence him.

Ver. 21. ἢ οὐκ ἔχει ἐξουσίαν ὁ κεραμεὺς τοῦ πηλοῦ κ.τ.λ. The ἢ puts this as the alternative. *Either* you must recognise this absoluteness of God in silence, *or* you must make the preposterous assertion that the potter has not power over the clay, etc. The power of the potter over the clay is of course undoubted: he takes the same lump, and makes one vessel for noble and another for ignoble uses; it is not the quality of the clay, but the will of the potter, that decides to what use each part of the lump is to be put. True, the objector might say, but irrelevant. For man is

b 2 Tim. ii. τιμὴν σκεῦος, ὃ δὲ εἰς ἀτιμίαν; ᵇ 22. εἰ δὲ θέλων ὁ Θεὸς ἐνδείξασθαι ᶜ
20 f.
c Verse 17. τὴν ὀργήν, καὶ γνωρίσαι τὸ δυνατὸν ᵈ αὐτοῦ, ἤνεγκεν ᵉ ἐν πολλῇ μακρο-
d Here
only; cf. θυμίᾳ σκεύη ὀργῆς κατηρτισμένα εἰς ἀπώλειαν · ᶠ 23. καὶ ¹ ἵνα γνωρίσῃ
ch. viii. 3.
e Heb. xii. τὸν πλοῦτον τῆς δόξης αὐτοῦ ἐπὶ σκεύη ἐλέους, ἃ προητοίμασεν ᵍ εἰς
20.
f Matt. vii. 13; John xvii. 12; Phil. iii. 19. g Eph. ii. 10.

¹ και ινα γνωριση; the και is omitted by W. and H. following B 37, 39, 47, vulg.,
Copt., etc. Treg. brackets it in marg. Weiss thinks it was omitted because the
transcriber could not see the point of it, and felt it easy to connect ινα with the
principal verb.

not clay, and the relation of God to man
is not that of the potter to dead matter.
To say that it is, is just to concede the
objector's point—the moral significance
is taken out of life, and God has no
room any longer to pronounce moral
judgments, or to speak of man in terms
of praise or blame.

Vv. 22-29. Paul's argument, to speak
plainly, has got into an *impasse*. He
is not able to carry it through, and
to maintain the sovereign freedom of
God as the whole and sole explanation
of human destiny, whether in men or
nations. He does, indeed, assert that
freedom to the last, against the pre-
sumptuousness of man; but in this third
section of his theodicy, he begins to
withdraw from the ground of speculation
to that of fact, and to exhibit God's
action, not as a bare unintelligible exercise of will, which inevitably provokes
rebellion, but as an exercise of will of
such a character that man can have
nothing to urge against it. εἰ δὲ: the
δὲ marks the transition to the new point
of view. It is as if Paul said: You
may find this abstract presentation of
God's relations to man a hard doctrine,
but if His actual treatment of men, even
of those who are σκεύη ὀργῆς κατ. εἰς
ἀπώλειαν, is distinguished by longsuffering and patience, what can you say
against that? θέλων has been rendered
(1) because it is His will; (2) although it
is His will. In the former case, God
bears long with the vessels of wrath in
order that the display of His wrath and
power may be more tremendous at last.
But (a) such an idea is inconsistent with
the contrast implied in δέ: it is an aggravation of the very difficulty from which the
Apostle is making his escape; (b) it is inconsistent with the words ἐν πολλῇ μακροθυμίᾳ; it is not longsuffering if the end
in view is a more awful display of wrath;
there is no real longsuffering unless the
end in view is to give the sinner place
for repentance. Hence the other view
(2) is substantially right. Although it is

God's will to display His wrath and to
show what He can do, still He does not
proceed precipitately, but gives ample
opportunity to the sinner to repent and
escape. We are entitled to say "the
sinner," though Paul does not say so
explicitly, for ἡ ὀργή, the wrath of God,
is relative to sin, and to nothing else:
except as against sin, there is no such
thing as wrath in God. In σκεύη ὀργῆς
the word σκεύη is perhaps prompted by
the previous verse, but the whole associations of the potter and the clay are not
to be carried over: they are expressly precluded by ἤνεγκεν ἐν πολλῇ μακροθυμίᾳ.
Paul does not say how the σκεύη
ὀργῆς came to be what they are, the
objects upon which the wrath and power
of God are to be revealed; he only says
that such as they are, God has shown
great patience with them. It seems a
mistake in W. and H. to print σκεύη ὀργῆς
as a quotation from Jer. l. (LXX xxvii.)
25; for there the words mean "the instruments *by* which God executes His
wrath," *les armes de sa colère* (Reuss).
κατηρτισμένα εἰς ἀπώλειαν: ἀπώλεια
(Phil. i. 28, iii. 19) means perdition, final
ruin; by what agency the persons referred to have been fitted for it Paul
does not say; what he does say is, that
fitted for such a doom as they are, God
has nevertheless endured them in much
longsuffering, so that they at least cannot say, Why dost thou find fault? For
κατηρτισμένος = perfected, made quite
fit or ripe, see Luke vi. 40, 1 Cor. i. 10:
cf. also 2 Tim. iii. 17.

Ver. 23 f. The sentence beginning
with εἰ δὲ θέλων is not grammatically
completed, but ver. 23 is an irregular
parallel to ver. 22. God's purpose is
regarded as twofold. It is on the one
hand to show His wrath and make
known His power; it is on the other
hand to make known the riches of His
glory (*cf.* Eph. iii. 16). The first part of
it is carried out on those who are σκεύη
ὀργῆς, the latter on those who are σκεύη
ἐλέους; but, in carrying out both parts

δόξαν· 24. οὓς καὶ ἐκάλεσεν ἡμᾶς οὐ μόνον ἐξ Ἰουδαίων, ἀλλὰ καὶ
ἐξ ἐθνῶν· 25. (ὡς καὶ ἐν τῷ Ὡσηὲ λέγει, "Καλέσω τὸν οὐ λαόν μου,
λαόν μου· καὶ τὴν οὐκ ἠγαπημένην, ἠγαπημένην". 26. "Καὶ
ἔσται, ἐν τῷ τόπῳ οὗ ἐρρήθη αὐτοῖς,[1] Οὐ λαός μου ὑμεῖς, ἐκεῖ κληθή-
σονται υἱοὶ Θεοῦ ζῶντος." 27. Ἡσαΐας [h] δὲ κράζει ὑπὲρ [i] τοῦ Ἰσραήλ,   h Is. x. 22 f.
"Ἐὰν ᾖ ὁ ἀριθμὸς τῶν υἱῶν Ἰσραὴλ ὡς ἡ ἄμμος τῆς θαλάσσης, τὸ   i 2 Cor. i. 6 (end).

[1] αυτοις is wanting in BFG and the best MSS. of the vulg. As no reason can be
suggested for its omission, if it were original, Weiss supposes it was added in conformity with the LXX. He therefore omits it altogether; W. and H. bracket.

alike, God acts in a way which is so far
from giving man room to complain that
it commands his wonder and adoration;
for the σκεύη ὀργῆς there is much longsuffering, for the σκεύη ἐλέους a preparation and a calling in which God's free
unmerited mercy is conspicuous. καὶ
ἵνα γνωρίσῃ : This is mentioned as a
principal purpose of God. ἐπὶ σκεύη
ἐλέους : the glory is conceived as something shed upon the persons concerned ;
they are irradiated with the Divine
brightness. Cf. 2 Thess. i. 10. δόξα
in such connections has usually a super-
sensible eschatological meaning ; its
content was fixed for Paul by his vision
of Christ as Lord of Glory. The end of
God's ways with the vessels of mercy
is to conform them to the image of His
exalted Son. ἃ προητοίμασεν εἰς δόξαν :
Paul does not shrink from introducing God
as subject here. The vessels of mercy, in
whom the Divine glory is to be revealed,
are such as God prepared before for that
destiny. That Paul is not speaking here
abstractly, as in his discussion of the
relations of creature and Creator in ver.
21 f., but on the basis of experience, is
shown by the words which immediately
follow : οὓς καὶ ἐκάλεσεν ἡμᾶς = whom
he also called in us. The σκεύη ἐλέους,
in other words, are not a mere theological
conception = "God's elect " : they are
the actual members of the Christian
Church, Jew and Gentile ; and it is not
a deduction from the necessities of the
Divine nature, but an account of real
experiences of God's goodness, which is
given both in προητοίμασεν and in
ἐκάλεσεν. How much is covered by
προητοίμασεν is not clear, but the text
presents no ground whatever for importing into it the idea of an unconditional
eternal decree. Those who are called
know that the antecedents of their calling, the processes which lead up to and
prepare for it, are of God. They know
that in all these processes, even in the

remote initial stages of them, to the
significance of which they were blind at
the time, glory was in view. The fact
that both Jews and Gentiles are called
shows that this preparation is not limited
to any one nation ; the fact that the
called are from among both Jews and
Gentiles shows that no one can claim
God's mercy as a right in virtue of his
birth in some particular race.
Ver. 25 f. This result of God's ways
with man—His calling not only from the
Jews but from the Gentiles—agrees with
His own declarations in Scripture. Ver.
25 answers roughly to Hos. ii. 23, LXX :
I will love her who was not beloved, and
will say to that which was not My people,
Thou art My people. Not My people
(= Lo-ammi) and Not beloved (= Lo-
ruhamah) were the names of a son and
a daughter of Hosea, who symbolised
the kingdom of Israel, rejected of God
but destined to share again in His favour.
Paul here applies to the calling of the
Gentiles words which spoke originally of
the restoration of Israel—an instance
which shows how misleading it may be
to press the context of the other passages
quoted in this chapter. Ver. 26 is also a
quotation from Hos. i. 10 (LXX) : the
ἐκεῖ is supplied by Paul. The application of it is similar to that of ver. 25. In
Hosea the promise is that the Israelites
who had lost their standing as God's
people should have it given back to them,
in all its dignity. This also Paul reads
of the calling of the Gentiles. They
were once no people of God's, but now
have their part in the adoption. But
what is the meaning of "in the place
where . . . there shall they be called " ?
It is not certain that in Hosea there is
any reference to a place at all (see margin
of R.V.), and it is not easy to see what
Paul can mean by the emphatic ἐκεῖ.
The ordinary explanation—the Gentile
lands—is as good as any, but seems
hardly equal to the stress laid on ἐκεῖ.

k Here only
(and so
also of
ὑπόλειμ-
μα).
l Mark xiii.
4; Luke
iv. 2, 13.
m Here only in N. T.

κατάλειμμα [1] [k] σωθήσεται · 28. λόγον γὰρ συντελῶν [1] καὶ συντέμνων [m] ἐν δικαιοσύνη · ὅτι λόγον συντετμημένον [2] ποιήσει Κύριος ἐπὶ τῆς γῆς ". 29. Καὶ καθὼς προείρηκεν Ἡσαίας, " Εἰ μὴ Κύριος Σαβαὼθ ἐγκατέλιπεν ἡμῖν σπέρμα, ὡς Σόδομα ἂν ἐγενήθημεν, καὶ ὡς Γόμορρα ἂν

[1] For καταλειμμα (which is the reading of the LXX) DFKLP, read with ℵ¹AB υπολειμμα.

[2] εν δικαιοσυνη οτι λογον συντετμημενον om. ℵ¹AB 47. "Western and Syrian " authorities have the words, in agreement with the LXX. But the γαρ after the first λογον makes the whole sentence, in this case, untranslatable ; and though Weiss and Alford defend the received text, and Treg. brackets the words in question in marg., most edd. omit them.

Ver. 27 f. From the calling of the Gentiles, as foretold in prophecy, Paul passes now to the partial, but only partial, calling of Israel, as announced by the same authority. The Jews cannot quarrel with the situation in which they find themselves when it answers so exactly to the Word of God. ὑπὲρ is here indistinguishable from περί: it is not a loud intercession on Israel's behalf, but a solemn declaration concerning Israel, that the prophet makes ; see Grimm, s.v., i., 5. The quotation in ver. 27 is from Isa. x. 22 f., but the opening words are modified by recollection of Hos. i. 10 just quoted. The LXX reads καὶ ἐὰν γένηται ὁ λαὸς Ἰσραὴλ ὡς ἡ ἄμμος τῆς θαλάσσης, τὸ κατάλειμμα αὐτῶν σωθήσεται. λόγον συντελῶν καὶ συντέμνων [ἐν δικαιοσύνῃ, ὅτι λόγον συντετμημένον] κύριος ποιήσει ἐν τῇ οἰκουμένῃ ὅλῃ. The words bracketed are omitted by most editors, but the sense is not affected. τὸ ὑπόλειμμα has the emphasis: *only* the remnant shall be saved. This doctrine Paul apparently finds confirmed by the words λόγον γὰρ συντελῶν καὶ συντέμνων ποιήσει κύριος ἐπὶ τῆς γῆς. It is doubtful whether any one could assign meaning to these words unless he had an idea beforehand of what they ought to or must mean. Cheyne renders the Hebrew to which they answer, " For a final work and a decisive doth the Lord execute within all the land "; and there is the same general idea in Sanday and Headlam's version of Paul: " For a word, accomplishing and abridging it, that is, a sentence conclusive and concise, will the Lord do upon the earth ". Weiss, who retains the words bracketed, makes λόγον = God's promise : God fulfils it indeed (συντελῶν), but He at the same time limits or contracts it (συντέμνων), i.e., fulfils it to some of Israel, not to all. This, no doubt, is the sense required, but can any

one say that the words convey it ? We should rather say that Paul put his own thought into the words of the LXX, in which a difficult passage of Isaiah was translated almost at haphazard, and in doing so lent them a meaning which they could not be said to have of themselves.

Ver. 29. But his last quotation is in verbal agreement with the LXX Isa. i. 9, and transparently clear. The σπέρμα or seed which God leaves is the same as the ὑπόλειμμα. The figure is not to be pressed. The remnant is not the germ of a new people ; Paul expects Israel as a whole to be restored.

With this the theodicy proper closes. The unbelief of the Jews was a great problem to the Apostolic age, and one which easily led to scepticism concerning the Gospel. The chosen people without a part in the kingdom of God —impossible. This chapter is Paul's attempt to explain this situation as one not involving any unrighteousness or breach of faith on the part of God. It is not necessary to resume the various stages of the argument as they have been elucidated in the notes. The point of greatest difficulty is no doubt that presented by vers. 22 and 23. Many good scholars, Meyer and Lipsius for example, hold that Paul in these verses is not withdrawing from, but carrying through, the argument from God's absoluteness stated so emphatically in ver. 21. They hold that the σκεύη ὀργῆς κατηρτισμένα εἰς ἀπώλειαν would not be σκεύη ὀργῆς at all, if their repentance and amendment were conceivable ; and although God bears long with them—that is, defers their destruction—it is only in order that He may have time and opportunity to manifest the riches of His glory on the vessels of mercy. But the answer to this is plain. It assumes that human life, in its relation to God, *can* be inter-

ὡμοιώθημεν ".) 30. Τί οὖν ἐροῦμεν; ὅτι ἔθνη τὰ μὴ ⁿ διώκοντα δικαιοσύνην κατέλαβε ^p δικαιοσύνην, δικαιοσύνην δὲ τὴν ἐκ πίστεως · 31. Ἰσραὴλ δὲ διώκων νόμον δικαιοσύνης εἰς νόμον δικαιοσύνης ¹ οὐκ ἔφθασε.^q 32. διατί; ὅτι οὐκ ἐκ πίστεως, ἀλλ' ὡς ^r ἐξ ἔργων νόμου ².

o n Ch. ii. 14.
o Ch. xii. 13, xiv. 19; 1 Cor. xiv. 1; 1 Tim. vi. 11; 2 Tim. ii.22.
p 1 Cor. ix. 24; Phil. iii. 12, 17. q Phil. iii. 16. r Philem. ver. 14.

¹ Om. second **δικαιοσυνης** א¹ABDG, all edd.

² νομου om. א¹ABF 47, vulg., and most edd. Alf. is doubtful.

preted by the analogy of clay in its relation to the potter; in other words, that moral and spiritual experiences can be construed and made intelligible through what are merely physical categories. But this is not the case. And if it be said that justice is not done, by the interpretation given in this commentary, to the expression **σκεύη ὀργῆς**, it may also be said that justice is not done, by the interpretation of Meyer and Lipsius, to the expression **ἐν πολλῇ μακροθυμίᾳ**. Each of these allegations may be said to neutralise the other—that is, neither is decisive for the interpretation of the passage; and the Apostle's meaning remains to be determined by the general movement of his thought. In spite of the great difficulties of the section as a whole, I cannot hesitate to read it as above.

CHAPTER IX.—Ver. 30-X. 21. We come now to the second main division of that part of the epistle in which Paul discusses the problem raised by the relation of the Jews to the Gospel. He has shown in chap. ix. 6-29 that they have no claim as of right to salvation: their whole history, as recorded and interpreted in the Scriptures, exhibited God acting on quite a different principle; he now proceeds to show more definitely that it was owing to their own guilt that they were rejected. They followed, and persisted in following, a path on which salvation was not to be found; and they were inexcusable in doing so, inasmuch as God had made *His* way of salvation plain and accessible to all.

Ver. 30 f. **τί οὖν ἐροῦμεν;** usually, as in ver. 14, this question is followed by another, but here by an assertion. The conclusion of the foregoing discussion is—not that God has been faithless or unjust, but—this paradoxical position: Gentiles (**ἔθνη**, not **τὰ ἔθνη**) that did not follow after righteousness attained righteousness, the righteousness which comes of faith; while Israel, which followed after a law of righteousness, did not attain that law. **διώκειν** and **καταλαμβάνειν** are correlative terms: see

Wetstein. The repetition of **δικαιοσύνη** is striking: it is the one fundamental conception on which Paul's gospel rests; the questions at issue between him and the Jews were questions as to what it was, and how it was to be attained. **τὰ μὴ διώκοντα δικαιοσύνην** is not an unfair description of the pagan races as contrasted with the Jews; how to be right with God was not their main interest. **δικαιοσύνην δὲ τὴν ἐκ πίστεως**: for the form of the explanatory clause with **δὲ** *cf.* iii. 22, 1 Cor. ii. 6. It is not surprising that a righteousness of this sort should be found even by those who are not in quest of it; its nature is that it is brought and offered to men, and faith is simply the act of appropriating it. **Ἰσραὴλ δὲ κ.τ.λ.**: this is the astonishing thing which does need explanation. **διώκων νόμον δικαιοσύνης.** The idea is not that Israel was in quest of a law of righteousness, in the sense of a rule by the observance of which righteousness would be attained: every Israelite believed himself to be, and already was, in possession of such a law. It must rather be that Israel aimed incessantly at bringing its conduct up to the standard of a law in which righteousness was certainly held out, but was never able to achieve its purpose. The **νόμος δικαιοσύνης**, the unattained goal of Israel's efforts, is of course the Mosaic law; but it is referred to, not definitely, but in its characteristic qualities, as law, and as exhibiting and enjoining (not bestowing) righteousness. **εἰς νόμον οὐκ ἔφθασεν**: did not attain to, arrive at, that law—it remained out of their reach. Legal religion proved a failure.

Ver. 32. **διὰ τί;** Why? A result so confounding needs explanation. **ὅτι οὐκ ἐκ πίστεως ἀλλ' ὡς ἐξ ἔργων**: it seems too precise to supply with Weiss **ἐδίωξεν νόμον δικαιοσύνης.** The reason of Israel's religious failure was that its whole religious effort and attitude was not of faith, but (so they conceived the case) of works. By inserting **ὡς** Paul dissociates himself from this conception, and leaves it to Israel; he does not believe (having

προσέκοψαν γὰρ ¹ τῷ λίθῳ τοῦ προσκόμματος, 33. καθὼς γέγραπται,
" Ἰδού, τίθημι ἐν Σιὼν λίθον προσκόμματος, καὶ πέτραν σκανδάλου ·
καὶ πᾶς ² ὁ πιστεύων ἐπ᾽ αὐτῷ οὐ καταισχυνθήσεται".

¹ γαρ ℵ³D³KLP ; om. ℵ¹ABD¹F.   ² πας om. ℵABDF 47 and all edd.

learned the contrary by bitter experience)
that there is any outlet along this road.
Everything in religion depends on the
nature of the start. You may start
ἐκ πίστεως, from an utter abandonment
to God, and an entire dependence on
Him, and in this case a righteousness is
possible which you will recognise as
δικαιοσύνη θεοῦ, God's own gift and
work in you ; or you may start ἐξ ἔργων,
which really means in independence of
God, and try to work out, without coming
under obligation to God, a righteousness
of your own, for which you may subsequently claim His approval, and in this
case, like the Jews, all your efforts will
be baffled. Your starting-point is unreal,
impossible ; it is not truly ἐξ ἔργων, but
only ὡς ἐξ ἔργων ; it is an idea of your
own, not a truth on which life can be
carried out, that you are in any sense
independent of God. Such an idea,
however, rooted in the mind, may
effectually pervert and wreck the soul,
by making the Divine way of attaining
righteousness and life offensive to it ;
and this is what happened to the Jews.
Because of that profoundly false relation
to God προσέκοψαν τῷ λίθῳ τοῦ προσκόμματος. The stone on which they
stumbled was Christ, and especially His
Cross. The σκάνδαλον of the Cross, at
which they stumbled, is not simply the
fact that it *is* a cross, whereas they expected a Messianic throne ; the Cross
offended them because, as interpreted by
Paul, it summoned them to begin
their religious life, from the very beginning, at the foot of the Crucified, and
with the sense upon their hearts of an
infinite debt to Him, which no "works"
could ever repay.

Ver. 33. Yet paradoxical as this may
seem, it agrees with the words of Scripture. The quotation is a mixture of
Isa. xxviii. 16 and viii. 14: and it is
interesting to remark that the same
passages are quoted in conjunction,
though they are not mixed as here, in
1 Pet. ii. 6-8. The original reference of
them is not exactly Messianic. The
stone laid in Zion (Isa. xxviii. 16) is
indeed interpreted by Delitzsch of the
kingdom of promise as identified with
its Sovereign Head, but the stone of

stumbling (Isa. viii. 14) is unequivocally
God Himself : all who do not give Him
honour are broken against His government as on a stone, or caught in it as
in a snare. Paul inserts ἐπ᾽ αὐτῷ after
ὁ πιστεύων (as Peter also does), and
applies the figure of the stone in both
cases to Christ, and to the contrary
relations which men may assume to Him.
Some stumble over Him (as the Jews,
for the reasons just given) ; others build
on Him and find Him a sure foundation,
or (without a figure) put their trust in
Him and are not put to shame. *Cf.* Ps.
cxviii. 22, Mt. xxi. 42, 1 Cor. iii. 11,
Acts. iv. 12, Eph. ii. 20.

CHAPTER X.—Ver. 1. The Apostle
cannot enlarge on this melancholy situation without expressing once more the
deep grief which it causes him. Since
the Jews are referred to in the third
person (ὑπὲρ αὐτῶν) it is clear that the
persons addressed are a Gentile Church.
ἀδελφοί : Paul's heart seems drawn to
his spiritual kindred as he feels the
deep gulf which separates him meanwhile from his kinsmen according to the
flesh. ἡ μὲν εὐδοκία τῆς ἐμῆς καρδίας :
the meaning of εὐδοκία must be gathered
from such examples as Mt. xi. 26, Eph. i.
5, 9, Phil. i. 15, ii. 13, 2 Thess. i. 11.
His heart's εὐδοκία is that in which his
heart could rest with complacency ; that
which would be a perfect satisfaction to
it. This is virtually the same as "desire," and an "Etymologicum ineditum"
quoted in Schleusner explains it by
βούλημα, γνώμη, προαίρεσις, ἐπιθυμία.
His inmost desire and his supplication
to God are in their interest, with a view
to their salvation. The μὲν has no corresponding δέ ; the sad reality which
answers to it does not need again to be
expressed.

Ver. 2. Their good qualities compel
his affection. ζῆλον θεοῦ ἔχουσιν : they
have a zeal for God, are intensely
(though mistakenly) religious. *Cf.* Gal.
i. 14. An unbelieving Jew could interpret his opposition to the lawless gospel
of Paul as zeal for the divinely-given
rule of life, and his opposition to the
crucified Messiah as zeal for the divinely-
given promises. It was God's honour
for which he stood in refusing the Gos-

X. 1. ΑΔΕΛΦΟΙ, ἡ μὲν εὐδοκία τῆς ἐμῆς καρδίας, καὶ ἡ δέησις ἡ [1 a 2 Cor. xi. 2.] πρὸς τὸν Θεὸν ὑπὲρ τοῦ Ἰσραήλ ἐστιν εἰς σωτηρίαν. 2. μαρτυρῶ [b Acts xvii. 23; 1 Tim. i. 13.] γὰρ αὐτοῖς ὅτι ζῆλον Θεοῦ[a] ἔχουσιν, ἀλλ᾽ οὐ κατ᾽ ἐπίγνωσιν. 3. [c Gal. vi. 5.] ἀγνοοῦντες[b] γὰρ τὴν τοῦ Θεοῦ δικαιοσύνην, καὶ τὴν ἰδίαν[c] δικαιοσύνην [2 d Phil. iii. 9. e Mark iii.] ζητοῦντες στῆσαι, τῇ δικαιοσύνῃ τοῦ Θεοῦ οὐχ ὑπετάγησαν. 4. τέλος[e] [26; Heb. vii. 3.]

[1] η before προς τον θεον om. ℵABDF. For του Ισραηλ εστιν read αυτων with ℵABDFP 47, etc.

[2] την ιδιαν δικαιοσυνην ℵFGKL and most cursives, is adopted by Tischdf., but most edd. with ABDP 47, vulg. omit δικαιοσυνην.

pel. ἀλλ᾽ οὐ κατ᾽ ἐπίγνωσιν: this religious earnestness is not regulated by adequate knowledge. For ἐπίγνωσις see Eph. iv. 13, Phil. i. 9, Col. i. 9, 10, ii. 2, 1 Tim. ii. 4, 2 Tim. ii. 25; it is especially used of religious knowledge, and suggests attainment in it (ἄρτι γινώσκω ἐκ μέρους, τότε δὲ ἐπιγνώσομαι, 1 Cor. xiii. 12).

Ver. 3. This verse goes to the root of the matter, and explains the failure of the Gospel among the Jews. It was due to their ignorance of the righteousness of God. All men need and crave righteousness, and the Jews, in their ignorance of God's, sought to establish a righteousness of their own. *Their own* is the key to the situation. Their idea was that they could be good men without becoming God's debtors, or owing anything at all to Him. Such an idea, of course, shows complete ignorance of the essential relations of God and man, and when acted on fatally perverts life. It did so with the Jews. When the Gospel came, revealing the righteousness of God—that for which man must be absolutely indebted to God's grace, and which he can never boast of as "his own"—it cut right across all the habits and prejudices of the Jews, and they did not submit themselves to it. Paul interprets the position of his nation through the recollection of his own experience as a Pharisee—no doubt rightly on the whole. For ὑπετάγησαν in middle sense see viii. 7, xiii. 1, Heb. xii. 9, Jas. iv. 7, 1 Pet. ii. 13.

Ver. 4. Further proof that the pursuit of a righteousness of one's own by legal observances is a mistake, the act of men "in ignorance". τέλος γὰρ νόμου χριστὸς εἰς δικαιοσύνην παντὶ τῷ πιστεύοντι: For Christ is law's end, etc. The sense required—a sense which the words very naturally yield—is that with Christ in the field law as a means of attaining righteousness has ceased and

determined. The moment a man sees Christ and understands what He is and what He has done, he feels that legal religion is a thing of the past: the way to righteousness is not the observance of statutes, no matter though they have been promulgated by God Himself; it is faith, the abandonment of the soul to the redeeming judgment and mercy of God in His Son. The meaning is virtually the same as that of our Lord's words in Luke xvi. 16. νόμου without the article is "law" in the widest sense; the Mosaic law is only one of the most important instances which come under this description; and it, with all statutory conceptions of religion, ends when Christ appears. It is quite true to say that Christ consummates or fulfils the law (hence Calvin would prefer *complementum* or *perfectio* to *finis* as a rendering of τέλος); quite true also that He is the goal of the O.T. dispensation, and that it is designed to lead to Him (*cf.* Mt. v. 17, Gal. iii. 24); but though both true and Pauline, these ideas are irrelevant here, where Paul is insisting, not on the connection, but on the incompatibility, of law and faith, of one's own righteousness and the righteousness of God. Besides, in limiting νόμος to the Mosaic O.T. law, this interpretation does less than justice to the language, and misses the point of παντὶ τῷ πιστεύοντι: there is *no* believer, *Gentile or Jew*, for whom law, *Mosaic or other*, retains validity or significance as a way to δικαιοσύνη, after the revelation of the righteousness of God in Christ.

In ver. 5 ff. Paul describes more fully, and in O.T. terms, the two ways of attaining δικαιοσύνη—law and faith. His aim is to show that they are mutually exclusive, but that the latter is open and accessible to all.

Ver. 5. Μωυσῆς γὰρ γράφει: Moses' authority is unimpeachable on this point. The righteousness that comes from law

γὰρ νόμου Χριστὸς εἰς δικαιοσύνην παντὶ τῷ πιστεύοντι. 5. Μωσῆς
γὰρ γράφει τὴν δικαιοσύνην τὴν ἐκ τοῦ νόμου,[1] "Ὅτι ὁ ποιήσας αὐτὰ
f Ch. ix. 30; ἄνθρωπος ζήσεται ἐν αὐτοῖς". 6. ἡ δὲ ἐκ [f] πίστεως δικαιοσύνη οὕτω
Gal. iii. 8.
g Cf. Eph. λέγει, "Μὴ εἴπῃς ἐν τῇ καρδίᾳ σου, Τίς ἀναβήσεται [g] εἰς τὸν οὐρανόν;"
iv. 8 f.
h Ch. ix. 8. τοῦτ᾽ ἔστι [h] Χριστὸν καταγαγεῖν· 7. "ἤ, Τίς καταβήσεται εἰς τὴν

[1] τὴν εκ του νομου DFKLP; om. του ℵB (A). οτι stands after γραφει, not before
ὁ ποιησας, in ℵ[1]AD[1] 17, vulg. It stands as in the received text in ℵ[3]BD[3]FGKL,
etc. Most edd. put it after γραφει, but not Weiss, who argues that it was removed
from its proper place after νομου in order to provide an object for ποιησας after αυτα
had been dropped. He reads Μ. γαρ γραφει την δ. τ. εκ νομου οτι ο π. αυτα α. ζ.
εν αυτη. According to W. and H. the original text was οτι την δικαιοσυνην την εκ
νομου ο ποιησας ανθρωπος ζησεται εν αυτη. Possibly this best explains the variants,
but it strikes one as too artificially grammatical for Paul. αυτα om. ℵ[1]AD-gr., vulg.
For εν αυτοις (from LXX), which is found in DFKLP, ℵ[1]AB 17, 47, vulg. read εν
αυτη; and so all edd.

must be an achievement: the man who
has *done* it shall live in it, Lev. xviii. 5.
Paul writes ἐν αὐτῇ with reference to
δικαιοσύνην: the ἐν αὐτοῖς of the LXX
refers to πάντα τὰ κρίματα which precedes. Moses, of course, in writing
thus did not mock his people; the O.T.
religion, though an imperfect, was a real
religion, under which men could be right
with God. To keep the law of God and
live by doing so (Mt. xix. 17) was the
natural aim and hope of a true Israelite;
only, in this case, the law was not a
collection of statutes, but a revelation of
God's character and will, and he who
sought to keep it did so not alone, but in
conscious dependence on God whose
grace was shown above all things else
by His gift of such a revelation. Paul,
however, is writing with Pharisees and
legalists in his eye, and with the remembrance of his own experience as a Pharisee in his heart; and *his* idea no doubt is
that this road leads nowhere. *Cf.* Gal.
iii. 10-12. To keep the law thus is an
impossibility.
Ver. 6 f. ἡ δὲ ἐκ πίστεως δικαιοσύνη
οὕτως λέγει. It is remarkable that Paul
does not make Moses his authority here,
though he is about to express himself in
words which certainly go back to Deut.
xxx. 12-14. It is the righteousness of
faith itself which speaks, describing its
own character and accessibility in words
with a fine flavour of inspiration about
them. But it is not so much a quotation we find here, as a free reproduction
and still freer application of a very
familiar passage of the O.T. It is irrelevant to point out that what the writer in
Deuteronomy means is that the law (ἡ
ἐντολὴ αὕτη ἣν ἐγὼ ἐντέλλομαί σοι
σήμερον) is not oppressive nor imprac-

ticable (as Paul in ver. 5 tacitly assumes
it to be); the Apostle is not thinking in
the least what the writer of Deuteronomy meant; as the representative of
the righteousness of faith, he is putting
his own thoughts—his inspired conviction and experience of the Gospel—into
a free reproduction of these ancient inspired words. μὴ εἴπῃς ἐν τῇ καρδίᾳ
σου: = do not think, especially thoughts
you would be ashamed to utter. τίς
ἀναβήσεται εἰς τὸν οὐρανόν; . . . ἢ τίς
καταβήσεται εἰς τὴν ἄβυσσον; There
is no impossible preliminary to be accomplished before the true religion is
got under way; we have neither to scale
heaven nor descend into the abyss.
ἄβυσσος (in N.T.) only in Lc. viii. 31
and seven times in Rev. But *cf.*
Ps. cvi. 26, lxx. 20. The passage in
Deuteronomy has εἰς τὸ πέραν τῆς
θαλάσσης. These two indefinite proverbial expressions for the impossible are
interpreted by Paul. With τοῦτ᾽ ἔστιν
(vers. 6, 7), he introduces a *midrash*
upon each. The first means (in his
mind) bringing Christ down; the second,
bringing Christ up from the dead. Evidently the righteousness of faith is concerned with a Christ of whom both these
things are true—a descent from heaven,
and a rising from the dead, Incarnation
and Resurrection. We could not bring
about either by any effort, but we do not
need to; Christ incarnate and risen is
here already, God's gift to faith.
Ver. 8. ἐγγύς σου τὸ ῥῆμά ἐστιν . . .
τοῦτ᾽ ἔστιν τὸ ῥῆμα τῆς πίστεως ὃ
κηρύσσομεν. What is in the lips of the
preacher is near to all who hear. In
Deut. the word is of course the Mosaic
law; here it is the Gospel, the word
which deals with that πίστις on which

ἄβυσσον; " τοῦτ' ἔστι Χριστὸν ἐκ νεκρῶν ἀναγαγεῖν.[1] 8. ἀλλὰ τί [i] Heb. xiii. 20.

λέγει; "Ἐγγύς σου τὸ ῥῆμά [k] ἐστιν, ἐν τῷ στόματί σου καὶ ἐν τῇ [k] Acts x. 37; verse 17;

καρδίᾳ σου · " τοῦτ' ἔστι τὸ ῥῆμα [l] τῆς πίστεως ὃ κηρύσσομεν · 9. ὅτι [l] Eph. v. 26, vi. 17.

ἐὰν ὁμολογήσῃς ἐν τῷ στόματί σου Κύριον Ἰησοῦν,[1] καὶ πιστεύσῃς ἐν [l] Acts x. 37; 1 Pet. i. 25.

τῇ καρδίᾳ σου ὅτι ὁ Θεὸς αὐτὸν ἤγειρεν ἐκ νεκρῶν, σωθήσῃ · 10.

καρδίᾳ γὰρ πιστεύεται εἰς δικαιοσύνην, στόματι δὲ ὁμολογεῖται εἰς

σωτηρίαν. 11. λέγει γὰρ ἡ γραφή, "Πᾶς ὁ πιστεύων ἐπ' αὐτῷ οὐ

---

[1] ὁμολογήσῃς εν τω στοματι σου Κυριον Ιησουν: this is the reading of most MSS., and is retained by Weiss and on the marg. by W. and H. For Κυριον Ιησουν B and Clem. Alex. have οτι Κυριος Ιησους, which W. and H. put in their text, and Lachm. and Treg. on margin. But B. and Clem. Alex. also insert το ρημα before εν τω στοματι σου, and this also W. and H. put in text. Weiss regards it as a thoughtless repetition from ver. 8, to give an object to ομολογησης; whether the further change of Κυριον Ιησουν into οτι Κυριος Ιησους (to conform to the parallel clause) took place before or after this can hardly be decided.

---

the righteousness of God depends. τῆς πίστεως is objt. gen. The whole idea of the verses is that righteousness has not to be achieved, but only appropriated.

Ver. 9. Apparently this verse gives the content of what the Apostle describes as "the word of faith which we preach". ὅτι = viz. The reference both to heart and mouth in Deut. suits his purpose, and he utilises it; the closing words in the LXX (καὶ ἐν ταῖς χερσί σου ποιεῖν αὐτό) he disregards. ἐὰν ὁμολογήσῃς τὸ ῥῆμα . . . ὅτι Κύριος Ἰησοῦς: the putting of the confession before the faith which inspires it, and of which it is the confession, seems to be due simply to the fact that in the O.T. passage present to the Apostle's mind ἐν τῷ στόματί σου precedes ἐν τῇ καρδίᾳ σου. τὸ ῥῆμα is virtually = the Gospel, as God's word concerning His Son and faith in Him. We confess it when we say, Jesus is Lord. Cf. 1 Cor. xii. 3, Phil. ii. 11. The exaltation of Jesus is the fundamental Christian confession, and presupposes the resurrection; and it is this exaltation which here (as in the other passages referred to) is meant by His Lordship. It is mechanical to say that the first part of ver. 9 (Jesus is Lord) refers to the doubting question in ver. 6, and therefore means a confession of the incarnation; and the second part of it (God raised Him from the dead) to the doubting question of ver. 7. Paul nowhere connects the Lordship of Christ with His incarnation, and there is certainly no reference to His Divine nature here. The confession of the first part of the verse answers to the faith in the second; he who believes in his heart that God raised Christ from the dead can

confess with his mouth (on that ground and in that sense) that Jesus is Lord. On the basis of such mutually interpreting faith and confession he is saved. This does not deprive the death of Christ of the significance which Paul ascribes to it elsewhere. Christ could not be raised unless He had first died, and when He is raised it is with the virtue of His sin-atoning death in Him. His exaltation is that of one who has borne our sins, and the sense of this gives passion to the love with which believers confess Him Lord.

Ver. 10. καρδίᾳ γὰρ πιστεύεται εἰς δικαιοσύνην, στόματι δὲ ὁμολογεῖται εἰς σωτηρίαν. The parallelism is like that in the previous verse, though the order of the clauses is reversed. To be saved one must attain δικαιοσύνη, and this depends on heart-faith; such faith, again, leading to salvation, must confess itself. To separate the two clauses, and look for an independent meaning in each, is a mistake; a heart believing unto righteousness, and a mouth making confession unto salvation, are not really two things, but two sides of the same thing. The formalism which seems to contrast them is merely a mental (perhaps only a literary) idiosyncrasy of the writer. It is true to say that such a confession as is meant here was made at baptism; but to limit it to baptism, or to use this verse to prove baptism essential to salvation, is, as Weiss says, *unerhörter Dogmatismus*.

Ver. 11. This verse proves from Scripture the main idea in the preceding, *viz.*, that faith saves. It is a quotation from Is. xxviii. 16 (see ix. 33) with the addition of πᾶς, to which nothing corre-

m Ch. iii.22. καταισχυνθήσεται ". 12. οὐ γάρ ἐστι διαστολὴ ᵐ Ἰουδαίου τε καὶ
1 Cor. xiv.
7. ῞Ελληνος · ὁ γὰρ αὐτὸς Κύριος πάντων, πλουτῶν εἰς πάντας τοὺς
ἐπικαλουμένους αὐτόν. 13. "Πᾶς γὰρ ὃς ἂν ἐπικαλέσηται τὸ ὄνομα
Κυρίου, σωθήσεται." 14. Πῶς οὖν ἐπικαλέσονται ¹ εἰς ὃν οὐκ ἐπίστευσαν ; πῶς δὲ πιστεύσουσιν οὗ οὐκ ἤκουσαν ; πῶς δὲ ἀκούσουσι

¹ ἐπικαλεσονται KLP ; ἐπικαλεσωνται אABDF, all edd. So for πιστευσουσιν
AKL, read πιστευσωσιν with אBDF. The received ακουσουσι of L has been
corrected into the classical ακουσονται in א¹DFK ; the true reading ακουσωσι is
preserved only in B (with correctors of א and A) and some cursives.

sponds either in Hebr. or LXX. Yet
oddly enough it is on this πᾶς that the
rest of the Apostle's argument turns.
The way of righteousness and salvation
by faith, he goes on to show, is meant
for all.

Ver. 12. οὐ γάρ ἐστι διαστολὴ
Ἰουδαίου τε καὶ ῞Ελληνος : this has been
proved in one sense in chap. iii.—there is
no distinction between them in point of
sin ; it is now asserted in another sense
—there is no distinction between them in
that the same Lord is waiting to save all
on the same conditions. κύριος πάντων
is best taken as predicate : the same Lord
is Lord of all : cf. Acts x. 36, Phil. ii. 10
f. Christ is undoubtedly meant : in His
presence, in view of His work and His
present relation to men, all differences
disappear ; there can be only one religion. πλουτῶν εἰς πάντας : abounding
in wealth toward all. Christ can impart
to all men what all men need—the
righteousness of God. Cf. v. 15-17, Eph.
iii. 8, τὸ ἀνεξιχνίαστον πλοῦτος τοῦ
Χριστοῦ. τοὺς ἐπικαλουμένους αὐτόν :
cf. 1 C. i. 2 where Christians are described as οἱ ἐπικαλούμενοι τὸ ὄνομα τ.
Κ. ἡμῶν Ἰ. Χ. The formula, as the next
verse shows, is borrowed from the Old
Testament ; and as Weiss remarks, verse
13 sets aside every idea of a distinction
between the invocation of God and that
of Christ. To a Christian, as Paul conceives him, Christ has at least the religious value of God ; the Christian soul
has that adoring attitude to Christ which
(when shown in relation to Jehovah) was
characteristic of O.T. religion. See Acts
ix. 14, 21, Acts xxii. 16 (Paul's conversion),
2 Tim. ii. 22. It is a fair paraphrase of
the words to say that salvation depends
on this : whether a sinful man will make
appeal for it to Christ in prayer, as to
One in whom all God's saving judgment
and mercy dwell bodily. It rests with
Christ, so appealed to, to make a man
partaker in the righteousness of God and
eternal life.

Ver. 13. For every one who invokes
the name of the Lord shall be saved.
The words are from Joel iii. 5 (= ii. 32
LXX). "The Lord" in the original is
Jehovah ; here, manifestly, Christ—a
proof how completely Christ stands in
God's place in all that concerns salva-
tion.

Ver. 14 f. It is difficult to trace very
clearly the line of the Apostle's thought
here. Many scholars (including W. and
H. and Lipsius) connect vers. 14 and 15
closely with what precedes, and mark a
break between ver. 15 and ver. 16. It
is as if Paul were expanding the πᾶς
of ver. 13 and justifying that universal
preaching of the Gospel which was itself
a stumbling block to the Jews. Every
one who invokes the name of the Lord
shall be saved, and therefore the conditions of such invocation must be put
within reach of every one. It is no
argument against this interpretation that
the ideas it introduces are not essential
to the main purpose of the chapter, which
is to prove the culpability of the Jews :
the eager fulness of Paul's mind often
carries him on thus. Others read vers.
14-21 continuously, and mark a break at
ver. 13 (e.g., Weiss, Sanday and Headlam). They lay stress on the οὖν in ver.
14 (cf. ix. 14, ix. 30, xi. 1, 11) as indicating
that a paragraph has ended, and that the
writer is facing the consequences which
flow from it, the objections which can
be made to it, etc. In this case the
connection would be something like this.
Salvation depends upon invoking Christ ;
but to invoke Christ depends upon certain
conditions which the Jews may say it
has been beyond their power to fulfil ;
let us inquire into the conditions, and
see whether such a plea holds good. The
first of these connections seems to me
much the simpler, and it has the advantage of covering the second. For if
the invocation of Christ, which is the
sole and universal condition of salvation,
has been made possible for all men, it

χωρὶς κηρύσσοντος ; 15. πῶς δὲ κηρύξουσιν,[1] ἐὰν μὴ ἀποσταλῶσι ;
καθὼς γέγραπται, " Ὡς ὡραῖοι οἱ πόδες τῶν εὐαγγελιζομένων εἰρήνην,[2]
τῶν εὐαγγελιζομένων τὰ ἀγαθά ". 16. Ἀλλ᾽ οὐ πάντες [n] ὑπήκουσαν n Acts vi. 7.
τῷ εὐαγγελίῳ· Ἡσαΐας γὰρ λέγει, " Κύριε, τίς ἐπίστευσε τῇ [o] ἀκοῇ o 1 Thess.ii.
ἡμῶν ; " 17. ἄρα ἡ πίστις ἐξ ἀκοῆς, ἡ δὲ ἀκοὴ διὰ ῥήματος Θεοῦ.[3] 13; Heb. iv. 2.

[1] For κηρυξουσιν read κηρυξωσιν with אABDKLP. For καθως read καθαπερ
with B. See note [1], page 598.

[2] ευαγγελιζομενων ειρηνην των om. א1ABC 47 ; ins. א3DFKLP. The omission
may be due to homœoteleuton. Weiss thinks it is, and keeps these words in the
text ; Treg. thinks it possible, and brackets them in margin. On the other hand,
they may have been inserted to make the quotation agree better (it does not even
then agree closely) with the LXX. The MSS. authority by itself is decisive for the
omission. τα αγαθα א1D2,3KL ; om. τα א3ABCD1F (and LXX). W. and H. read
ως ωραιοι οι ποδες των ευαγγελιζομενων αγαθα.

[3] θεου AD2,3 (gr.) KL ; Χριστου א1BCD 47 and all edd.

has been made possible for the Jews.
The special application to them, in which
the argument of the chapter is clinched,
is not made till ver. 19 ; here they are
only involved with the rest of the world
which has heard the Gospel. πῶς οὖν
ἐπικαλέσωνται : sc. τοῦτον. πῶς δὲ
πιστεύσωσιν οὗ οὐκ ἤκουσαν ; It is
simplest to render, How are they to
believe on Him *Whom* they have not
heard ? identifying the voice of the
preachers with that of Christ. Winer, p.
249. Cf. Eph. ii. 17. The rendering,
Him *of Whom* they have not heard,
would be legitimate in poetry. πῶς δὲ
ἀκούσωσιν : this deliberative form is in
all probability right : see critical note
and Blass, *Gramm. des Neut. Griech.*,
205. ἐὰν μὴ ἀποσταλῶσιν : viz., by
the Lord Whom they preach, and Who
is heard speaking when they speak.
Cf. 1 Cor. i. 17, ἀπέστειλέν με Χριστὸς
. . . εὐαγγελίζεσθαι. To find here the
idea of an official ministry, as something
belonging essentially to the constitution
of the Church, is grotesque. " St. Paul
argues back from effect to cause, through
the series of Prayer, Faith, Hearing,
Preaching, Sending ; thus the last link
in his argument must be the first in the
realisation from which the rest follow ;
this one therefore he confirms by the
prophetic announcement in Isa. lii. 7 "
(Gifford). ὡς ὡραῖοι : the true text of
Romans greatly abbreviates the prophet's
words, but the joy with which the deliverance from Babylon was foreseen is
in keeping with that with which Paul
contemplates the universal preaching of
the Gospel.
Ver. 16. The fact remains, however,
in spite of this universal preaching, that

there has not been a universal surrender
to the Gospel. οὐ πάντες : the Jews are
present to the writer's mind here, though
the words might apply more widely ;
hence the compassionate mode of statement. Cf. iii. 3 : εἰ ἠπίστησάν τινες.
Yet this quantum of unbelief does not
discomfit the Apostle ; for it also, as
well as the proclamation of the Gospel,
is included in the prophecy. τίς ἐπίστευσεν τῇ ἀκοῇ ἡμῶν is a lament over
practically universal unbelief. ἡ ἀκοὴ
ἡμῶν in Isaiah means " that which we
heard," but who the " we " are is not
clear. If a representative prophet speaks,
ἀκοὴ will mean that which he and other
prophets heard from God : = Who hath
believed the revelation made to us ? Cf.
Isa. xxviii. 9, 19. If a representative of
repenting Israel speaks, ἀκοὴ will mean
that which he and his countrymen have
heard from the prophets : = Who hath
believed the message delivered to us ?
Assuming that Paul as a preacher instinctively used the words to express
his own thought and experience in his
vocation, they will mean here, Who has
believed the message delivered by us
Apostles ?
Ver. 17. This verse is really parenthetic : Paul's logical mind cannot let
slip the chance of showing how this
quotation confirms the connection of
ideas in ver. 14. ἄρα suits a rapid
passing inference better than the more
deliberate ἄρα οὖν which is much more
frequent in Romans. Cf. 1 Cor. xv. 18,
2 Cor. v. 14, Gal. ii. 17. So then faith
comes from a message (that which is
received by the hearer of the Gospel),
and the message διὰ ῥήματος Χριστοῦ
through the Word concerning Christ.

18. ἀλλὰ λέγω, Μὴ οὐκ ἤκουσαν; μενοῦνγε "εἰς πᾶσαν τὴν γῆν

ἐξῆλθεν ὁ φθόγγος αὐτῶν, καὶ εἰς τὰ πέρατα τῆς οἰκουμένης τὰ

p Ch. xi. 14; ῥήματα αὐτῶν". 19. Ἀλλὰ λέγω, Μὴ οὐκ ἔγνω Ἰσραήλ[1]; πρῶτος
1 Cor. x.
22.　　Μωσῆς λέγει, "Ἐγὼ ᵖπαραζηλώσω ὑμᾶς ἐπ' οὐκ ἔθνει, ἐπὶ ἔθνει

[1] Ισραηλ before ουκ εγνω אABCD[1,3]F.

That which when heard is ἀκοή is when spoken ῥῆμα, and it is the condition of faith. The construction in ῥῆμα Χριστοῦ is the same as in τὸ ῥῆμα τῆς πίστεως in ver. 8. The words could not signify Christ's command.

Ver. 18. The process of convicting the Jews is now under way, and ἀλλὰ λέγω introduces a plea on their behalf. It is Paul who speaks: hence the form of the question μὴ οὐκ ἤκουσαν suggests *his* opinion as to the answer. To *hear* is necessary in order to believe; you do not mean to say they did *not* hear? *Cf.* 1 Cor. ix. 4, 5, xi. 22. μενοῦνγε is *immo vero*. The contrary is so clearly the case that there is a touch of derision in the word with which Paul introduces the proof of it. *Cf.* ix. 20. The Gospel has been preached in all the world: the words of Ps. xix. 4 (exactly as in LXX) are at once the expression and the proof of this. Of course they refer to the revelation of God in nature, but their use will seem legitimate enough if we remember that Paul *knew* the extent to which the Gospel had been proclaimed in his day. *Cf.* Col. i. 6, 23. It was as widely diffused as the Diaspora, and the poetic inspired expression for this had a charm of its own.

Ver. 19. ἀλλὰ λέγω: another attempt to introduce a plea on behalf of Israel. You cannot say, "they did not hear"; surely you do not mean to say, then, *Israel did not understand?* At first sight there seems an unnatural emphasis here on *Israel*, but this is not the case. The generality of the argument must be abandoned now, for the passages next to be quoted, which are already present to Paul's mind, contrast Israel with the Gentiles, and so bring it into prominence; and it is in the case of Israel, of all nations, that the plea of not understanding is most out of place. Above all nations Israel ought to have understood a message from God: Israel, and in-

ability to understand God's Word, ought to be incompatible ideas. πρῶτος Μωυσῆς λέγει, Deut. xxxii. 21. πρῶτος suggests the beginning of a line of witnesses to this effect: virtually it means, even Moses, at the very beginning of their history. The point of the citation is not very clear. Like the passages quoted in ix. 25, 26, it might have been adduced by Paul as a proof that the Gentiles were to be called into God's kingdom, and called in order to rouse the Jews to jealousy; but to be in place here, there must be also the latent idea that if peoples beyond the covenant (who were not peoples at all), and unintelligent peoples (*i.e.*, idol worshippers) could understand the Gospel, a privileged and religiously gifted people like the Jews was surely inexcusable if it failed to understand it. The same idea seems to be enforced again in ver. 20. Ἡσαίας δὲ ἀποτολμᾷ: "breaks out boldly" (Gifford). It was an act of great daring to speak thus to a nation with the exclusive temper of Israel, and Paul who needed the same courage in carrying the Gospel to the Gentiles was the man to see this. οἱ ἐμὲ μὴ ἐπερωτῶντες means those who put no question to me, *sc.*, about the way of salvation. In Isa. lxv. 1 the clauses occur in reverse order. What the prophet has in view is God's spontaneous unmerited goodness, which takes the initiative, unsolicited, in showing mercy to faithless Jews who made no appeal to Him and never sought Him; the Apostle applies this, like the similar passages in ix. 25 f., to the reception of the Gospel by the Gentiles.* If God was found and recognised in His character and purposes, where all the conditions seemed so much against it, surely Israel must be inexcusable if it has missed the meaning of the Gospel. The very calling of the Gentiles, predicted and interpreted as it is in the passages quoted, should itself

---

* The part of Isa. lxv. 1 which is not quoted here (I said, Behold Me, behold Me, unto a nation that was not called by My name) is meant, as usually pointed, to refer to the Gentiles, and this tradition of its application Paul may have learned from Gamaliel (Cheyne); but the pointing is wrong: *see* Cheyne.

ἀσυνέτῳ παροργιῶ ὑμᾶς ". 20. Ἡσαΐας δὲ ᵠ ἀποτολμᾷ καὶ λέγει, ᵠ Here only.
" Εὑρέθην τοῖς ¹ ἐμὲ μὴ ζητοῦσιν, ἐμφανὴς ἐγενόμην τοῖς ἐμὲ μὴ
ἐπερωτῶσι ". 21. πρὸς δὲ τὸν Ἰσραὴλ λέγει, " Ὅλην τὴν ἡμέραν ʳ Luke ii.
34; Acts
ἐξεπέτασα τὰς χεῖράς μου πρὸς λαὸν ἀπειθοῦντα καὶ ʳ ἀντιλέγοντα ". xiii. 45;
xxviii. 22.

¹ ευρεθην τοις ℵACD²⁻³LP ; but εν τοις BD¹FG. Sanday and Headlam call this
"a Western reading which has found its way into B ". W. and H. put εν in marg.

have been a message to the Jews, which
they could not misunderstand ; it should
have opened their eyes as with a lightning flash to the position in which they
stood—that of men who had forfeited
their place among the people of God—
and provoked them, out of jealousy, to
vie with these outsiders in welcoming
the righteousness of faith.
Ver. 21. πρὸς δὲ τὸν Ἰσραὴλ λέγει :
That is what he says of the Gentiles, but
as for Israel, he says, etc., Isa. lxv. 2. For
πρὸς = with reference to, see Heb. i. 7
f., Luke xii. 41. The arms outstretched
all the day long are the symbol of that
incessant pleading love which Israel
through all its history has consistently
despised. It is not want of knowledge,
then, nor want of intelligence, but wilful
and stubborn disobedience, that explains
the exclusion of Israel (meanwhile) from
the Kingdom of Christ and all its blessings. This is not inconsistent with ver.
3, if we go to the root of the matter.
For the ignorance there spoken of is one
which has its root in the will, in the
pride of a heart which is determined to
have a righteousness of its own without
coming under any obligation to God for
it, and which therefore cannot assume the
attitude to which the Gospel becomes
credibly Divine ; while the ignorance
suggested as a plea for unbelief is that
of men to whom the Gospel has never
been presented at all. The latter ignorance might annul responsibility ; the
former gives its full significance to guilt.
CHAPTER XI. On the place of this
chapter in the argument, see introduction to chap. ix. above. Briefly, the
ninth chapter means, God is sovereign,
and the tenth chapter means, Israel has
sinned. Both of these are presented in
relative independence as explanations of
the perplexing fact which confronted the
Apostle, namely, that the Jews did not
receive the Gospel, while the Gentiles
did ; in this chapter, the two are brought
into relation to each other, and we are
shown (to some extent) how in the
sovereign providence of God even the
sin of Israel is made to contribute to the

working out of a universal purpose of redemption—a redemption in which Israel
also shares, in accordance with the inviolable promise of God. The chapter
can be naturally divided into three
sections : (1) vers. 1-10, in which the
question immediately arising out of
chap. x. is discussed, viz., whether the
unbelief of which Israel as a whole has
been convicted involves God's rejection
of the chosen people ; (2) vers. 11-24, in
which the result to be attained by the
partial and temporary exclusion of the
Jews from the Messianic kingdom is enlarged upon, and the Gentiles warned
against self-exaltation ; and (3) vers. 25-
36, in which Paul magnifies the unsearchable wisdom, love and faithfulness
of God, as revealed in securing by a
common method the salvation alike of
Israel and the Gentiles.
(1) Vv. 1-10. λέγω οὖν : the οὖν intimates that it is with the conclusion
reached in chap. x. before his mind that
Paul puts the following question : the
unbelief of Israel naturally suggested it.
μὴ ἀπώσατο ὁ θεὸς τὸν λαὸν αὐτοῦ ;
For the words, cf. Ps. xciv. 14 (xciii. LXX),
I Sam. xii. 22. In both places the promise is given οὐκ ἀπώσεται ὁ Κ. τ. λ.
αὐτοῦ, and the familiar words give the
effect of asking, Has God broken His
express and repeated promise ? μὴ suggests the negative answer, which is expressed more passionately in μὴ γένοιτο.
Cf. iii. 6, ix. 14. Israel may be faithless
to Him, but He abides faithful. καὶ γὰρ
ἐγὼ Ἰσραηλίτης εἰμί : This is often
read as if it were an argument in favour
of the negative answer ; as if Paul meant,
God has not cast off His people, I myself am a living proof to the contrary.
But this is hardly conciliatory, to say
the least ; and it is better to take the
words as explaining why Paul puts the
question with μή (suggesting the negative answer), and why he then gives the
denial with such vehemence. "I, too,
am an Israelite, to whom the very idea
of God's rejection of His people is an
impious and incredible idea, to be repelled with horror." ἐκ σπέρ. Ἀβραάμ :

XI. 1. ΛΕΓΩ οὖν, Μὴ ἀπώσατο ὁ Θεὸς τὸν λαὸν αὐτοῦ ; μὴ γένοιτο ·
a Phil. iii. 5. καὶ γὰρ ἐγὼ Ἰσραηλίτης εἰμὶ, ἐκ σπέρματος Ἀβραὰμ, φυλῆς ª Βενιαμίν.
2. οὐκ ἀπώσατο ὁ Θεὸς τὸν λαὸν αὐτοῦ, ὃν προέγνω. ἢ οὐκ οἴδατε
ἐν Ἠλίᾳ τί λέγει ἡ γραφή ; ὡς ἐντυγχάνει τῷ Θεῷ κατὰ τοῦ Ἰσραὴλ,
λέγων,[1] 3. "Κύριε, τοὺς προφήτας σου ἀπέκτειναν, καὶ [2] τὰ θυσιασ-
τήριά σου κατέσκαψαν · κἀγὼ ὑπελείφθην μόνος, καὶ ζητοῦσι τὴν
ψυχήν μου ". 4. ἀλλὰ τί λέγει αὐτῷ ὁ χρηματισμός ; "Κατέλιπον
ἐμαυτῷ ἑπτακισχιλίους ἄνδρας, οἵτινες οὐκ ἔκαμψαν γόνυ τῇ Βάαλ."
b Ch. iii. 26.
c Ch. ix. 11. 5. οὕτως οὖν καὶ ἐν τῷ νῦν ᵇ καιρῷ λεῖμμα κατ᾽ ᶜ ἐκλογὴν χάριτος

<hr>

[1] λέγων אּ¹L ; om. אּ³ABCDF.

[2] καὶ before τα θυσιαστηρια אּ³DL ; om. אּ¹ABCF 17.

<hr>

no proselyte. **φυλῆς Βενιαμείν**: the one tribe which with Judah mainly represented the post-exilic theocratic people. Ver. 2 f. **οὐκ ἀπώσατο**: formal denial of what the heart has indignantly protested against in ver. 1. **ὃν προέγνω** must contain a reason which makes the rejection incredible or impossible. This excludes the interpretation of Weiss, who thinks that Paul means to say that God *knew* what Israel was *before* He chose it, and therefore cannot cast it off as if its unbelief had disappointed Him ; He knew from the first what it would be. To plead thus for God is too paltry. We must take **προέγνω** as in viii. 29 : the meaning is, Israel stood before God's eyes from eternity as His people, and in the immutableness of the sovereign love with which He made it His lies the impossibility of its rejection. The idea is the same as in ver. 29 below. **ἢ οὐκ οἴδατε**: this is the alternative. He who says, God *has* cast off Israel, must be ignorant of what Scripture says **ἐν Ἠλίᾳ** in the passage which gives the history of Elijah. The sections of the Bible were designated, not as now by chapter and verse, but by some descriptive phrase: *cf.* **ἐπὶ τῆς βάτου**, Mark xii. 26 : and in Philo **ἐν ταῖς ἀραῖς** = Gen. iii. 15. Many references are made in this form by Hebrew writers. For **ἐντυγχάνειν κατὰ** *cf.* 1 Macc. viii. 32 : it means to plead (not intercede) with God against Israel. **τὰ θυσιαστήρια** is one of the indications that in Elijah's time there was no law requiring only one altar for Jehovah. The words are quoted from 1 Kings xix. ver. 10 or 14. In Elijah's mood, Paul might have said something similar of his own time, for their circumstances were not alike. The Apostle, like the prophet, was lonely and perse-

cuted, and Israel as a whole seemed to have abandoned God or been abandoned by Him. But he understands God's way (and His faithfulness) better. Ver. 4. **ὁ χρηματισμός**: the word is related to **χρηματίζω** (Mt. ii. 12, 22, Acts x. 22, Heb. viii. 5) as **χρησμὸς** to **χράω**: it means the oracle, or answer of God. Here only in N.T., but see 2 Macc. ii. 4, xi. 17. The quotation is from 1 Kings xix. 18 with **ἐμαυτῷ** added, by which Paul suggests God's interest in this remnant, and the fact that He has a purpose of His own identified with them. *God* has reserved the seven thousand ; He has reserved them for *Himself*; it is on this the proof depends that He has not cast off His people. The seven thousand are Israel to Him. Yet His unchanging faithfulness in keeping a people is not represented as a merely unconditional decree, having no relation to anything but His own will, for the seven thousand are described by their character : **οἵτινες οὐκ ἔκαμψαν γόνυ τῇ Βάαλ**. **οἵτινες** is qualitative : *such* were those whom God reserved for Himself, men who never bowed knee to Baal. **Βάαλ** takes the fem. art. because it was often replaced in reading by בשֶׁת (LXX **αἰσχύνη**). Ver. 5. Application of the principle of ver. 4 to the present. **ὁ νῦν καιρὸς** is the present regarded not merely as a date, but as in some sense a crisis. **λεῖμμα γέγονεν**: a remnant has come to be—this is the fact which has emerged from the general unbelief of Israel. **κατ᾽ ἐκλογὴν χάριτος**: on these words the emphasis lies. The existence of the remnant is due to an election of grace, a choice on the part of God the motive of which is to be sought in His unmerited

γέγονεν. 6. εἰ δὲ χάριτι, οὐκ ἔτι ἐξ ἔργων· ἐπεὶ ἡ χάρις οὐκ ἔτι γίνεται χάρις. εἰ δὲ ἐξ ἔργων, οὐκ ἔτι ἐστὶ χάρις· ἐπεὶ τὸ ἔργον οὐκ ἔτι ἐστὶν ἔργον.[1] 7. Τί οὖν; ὃ ἐπιζητεῖ Ἰσραήλ, τούτου[2] οὐκ ἐπέτυχεν, ἡ δὲ ἐκλογὴ ἐπέτυχεν· οἱ δὲ λοιποὶ ἐπωρώθησαν 8. (καθὼς[3] γέγραπται, "Ἔδωκεν αὐτοῖς ὁ Θεὸς πνεῦμα κατανύξεως, ὀφθαλμοὺς τοῦ μὴ βλέπειν, καὶ ὦτα τοῦ μὴ ἀκούειν"), ἕως τῆς σήμερον[d] ἡμέρας. 9. καὶ Δαβὶδ λέγει, "Γενηθήτω ἡ τράπεζα αὐτῶν εἰς παγίδα καὶ εἰς

d 2 Cor. iii. 14.

[1] ει δε εξ εργων ουκ ετι εστι χαρις επει το εργον ουκ ετι εστιν εργον. All this is omitted in ℵ[1]ACDEFG, vulg., Egypt. verss., Orig. lat. and Latin fathers; inserted with some variations (for the last εργον B has χαρις, by a slip, surely) in ℵ[3]BL and later MSS. According to Sanday and Headlam, there can be no doubt that the addition is a gloss; B is not sufficient to justify a Western addition of this kind against such preponderating authority. The words are omitted by most edd., but Alf. brackets them, and Weiss retains them in the text; the χαρις in B for εργον at end only makes the omission by homœot. easier.

[2] For τουτου read τουτο with ℵABCDFL.

[3] καθως; read with ℵB καθαπερ. See note [1], page 673.

love alone. The idea is the same as in chap. ix. 6-13: but cf. note on ver. 4.

Ver. 6. Expansion of χάριτος in ver. 5: grace and works are mutually exclusive. Nothing a man can do gives him a claim as of right against God to be included in the remnant. ἐπεί: otherwise. Cf. ver. 22, iii. 6. *Gratia nisi gratis sit gratia non est.* Aug. The fact that there is a remnant, and one owing its existence to God's grace, is the proof that (in spite of the wholesale defection of Israel) God has not cast off His people.

Ver. 7. τί οὖν; What then? How are we to describe the present situation, if not in the painful language of verse 1? Thus: ὃ ἐπιζητεῖ Ἰσραήλ κ.τ.λ. What Israel is in quest of is δικαιοσύνη: the present conveys more sympathetically than the impft. of some MSS. the Apostle's sense of the ceaseless and noble (though misdirected)efforts of his countrymen. ἐπέτυχεν: Jas. iv. 2, Heb. vi. 15. ἡ δὲ ἐκλογή = οἱ ἐκλεκτοί = τὸ λεῖμμα. ἐπωρώθησαν: were hardened, 2 Cor. iii. 14, John xii. 40, Mc. vi. 52, viii. 17. Paul does not say how they were hardened or by whom: there is the same indefiniteness here as in κατηρτισμένα εἰς ἀπώλειαν in ix. 22. It may be quite possible to give a true sense to the assertion that they were hardened *by God* (cf. the following verse), although the hardening in this case is always regarded as a punishment for sin, that is, as a confirming in an obduracy which originally was *not* of God, but their own; as if the idea were, first they would not, and then, in

God's just reaction against their sin, they could not; but it is a mistake to import into the text a definiteness which does not belong to it. It is rather essential to Paul's argument that he should not be bound down to one-sided interpretations of what he has intentionally left vague.

Ver. 8 ff. This hardening (at the present day ver. 5) agrees with God's action toward Israel in the past, as exhibited in Scripture. The words from the O.T. can hardly be called a quotation; Deut. xxix. 4, Is. xxix. 10, Is. vi. 9, 10, all contributed something to them. The πνεῦμα κατανύξεως is from Is. xxix. 10, and answers to the Heb. רוּחַ תַּרְדֵּמָה, a spirit of deep sleep or torpor. Virtually it is defined by what follows—unseeing eyes, unhearing ears: a spirit which produces a condition of insensibility, to which every appeal is vain. κατάνυξις only occurs in LXX, Is. xxix. 10, Ps. lix. 4 (οἶνον κατανύξεως); but the verb κατανύσσομαι is used by Theod. in Dan. x. 15 to translate נִרְדָּם (cognate to תַּרְדֵּמָה), and in other places of any overpowering emotion: see Fritzsche *ad loc.* Winer, p. 117. It *is* God Who sends this spirit of stupor, but He does not send it arbitrarily nor at random: it is always a judgment. ἕως τῆς σήμερον ἡμέρας: in Deut. xxix. 4 ἕως τῆς ἡ. ταύτης. The change emphasises the fact that what Israel had been from the beginning it was when Paul wrote,

θήραν, καὶ εἰς σκάνδαλον καὶ εἰς ἀνταπόδομα αὐτοῖς· 10. σκοτισ-
θήτωσαν οἱ ὀφθαλμοὶ αὐτῶν τοῦ μὴ βλέπειν, καὶ τὸν νῶτον αὐτῶν
e Ps. lxviii. δια παντὸς ᵉσύγκαμψον". 11. Λέγω οὖν, Μὴ ἔπταισαν ἵνα πέσωσι;
22 f.
(LXX).   μὴ γένοιτο· ἀλλὰ τῷ αὐτῶν ᶠπαραπτώματι ἡ σωτηρία τοῖς ἔθνεσιν,
f Ch. iv. 25.
g Ch. x. 19. εἰς τὸ ᵍ παραζηλῶσαι αὐτούς. 12. εἰ δὲ τὸ παράπτωμα αὐτῶν πλοῦτος
κόσμου, καὶ τὸ ἥττημα αὐτῶν πλοῦτος ἐθνῶν, πόσῳ μᾶλλον τὸ πλή-

and that God had acted toward it from
the beginning on the same principle on
which He was acting then. *Cf.* Acts
vii. 51 f. **καὶ Δαυεὶδ λέγει**: another
proof of **ἐπωρώθησαν**, though strictly
speaking a wish or an imprecation cannot
prove anything, unless it be assumed that
it has been fulfilled, and so can be taken
as the description of a fact. Paul takes
it for granted that the doom invoked in
these words has come upon the Jews.
γενηθήτω ἡ τράπεζα αὐτῶν κ.τ.λ. Their
table in the psalm is that in which they
delight, and it is this which is to prove
their ruin. **παγίς, θήρα**, and **σκάνδαλον**
are all variations of the same idea, that
of snare or trap—*i.e.*, sudden destruction.
What the Jews delighted in was the law,
and the law misunderstood proved their
ruin. In seeking a righteousness of their
own based upon it they missed and forfeited the righteousness of God which
is given to faith in Christ. **καὶ εἰς
ἀνταπόδομα αὐτοῖς**: this does not exactly
reproduce either the Heb. or the LXX, but
it involves the idea that the fate of the
Jews is the recompense of their sin—not
a result to be simply referred to a decree
of God. Their perverse attitude to the
law is avenged in their incapacity to
understand and receive the Gospel. **τοῦ
μὴ βλέπειν**: for this Gen. both in ver.
8 and ver. 10, see Buttmann, *Gram. of
N.T. Greek*, p. 267 (E. tr.). **τὸν νῶτον
αὐτῶν διὰ παντὸς σύγκαμψον**: keep them
continually in spiritual bondage, stoop-
ing under a load too heavy to be borne:
cf. Acts xv. 10.

This is the condition in which by God's
act, requiting their own sins, and especially their self-righteous adherence to the
law as a way of salvation, the Jews find
themselves. It is a condition so grievous,
and so remote from what one anticipates
for a people chosen by God, that it confronts Paul again with the difficulty of
ver. 1, and obliges him to state it once
more—this time in a way which mitigates
its severity, and hints that the fall of
Israel is not the last thing concerning
them to be taken into account. What if
God's purpose includes and uses their
fall? What if it is not final? It is

with new ideas of this sort, introduced
to take the edge from the stern utterances of vers. 8-10, that Paul deals in
vers. 11-24.

Ver. 11. **λέγω οὖν**: I say then, taking
up the problem again. **μὴ ἔπταισαν ἵνα
πέσωσιν**; surely they did not stumble so
as to fall? The subject is the mass of
the Jewish nation, all but the elect remnant. The contrast here between stumbling and falling shows that the latter is
meant of an irremediable fall, from which
there is no rising. This is one of the
cases in which **ἵνα** is loosely used; it
cannot possibly be translated "in order
that". For similar examples *cf.* 1 Thess.
v. 4, 1 Cor. vii. 29, Gal. v. 17. **ἀλλὰ**:
on the contrary, by their (moral) fall
salvation has come to the Gentiles to
provoke them (the unbelieving Israelites)
to jealousy. The fact stated here is
illustrated at every point in Paul's own
ministry; he turned to the Gentiles
because the Jews would not hear him.
See Acts xiii. 46 ff., xviii. 6, xxviii. 25-28.
The end in view in it (*cf.* x. 19) is his
proof that the stumbling of the Jews is
not to be interpreted in the sense of a
final fall. A recovery is in prospect.

Ver. 12. Both **ἥττημα** and **πλήρωμα**
are difficult words, but it is not necessary
to suppose that they answer mathematic-
ally to one another, though Wetstein
explains them by − and +. **ἥττημα** may
mean (as in Is. xxxi. 8) defeat, or (as in
1 Cor. vi. 7) loss; it can hardly mean
diminutio eorum, or *paucitas Judæorum
credentium;* **τὸ πλήρωμα αὐτῶν** must
mean the making up of them to their
full numbers. There is an exhaustive
study of the word **πλήρωμα** by Prof. J.
Armitage Robinson in *The Expositor*,
April, 1898. His paraphrase of this verse
is very good. "If the Gentiles have
been enriched in a sense through the
very miscarriage and disaster of Israel,
what wealth is in store for them in the
great Return, when all Israel shall be
saved—'when God hath made the pile
complete!'" The enrichment referred
to is in both cases that which comes
through participating in the blessings of
the Gospel.

ρωμα αὐτῶν; 13. Ὑμῖν γὰρ [1] λέγω τοῖς ἔθνεσιν· ἐφ' ὅσον μέν εἰμι
ἐγὼ ἐθνῶν ἀπόστολος, τὴν διακονίαν μου δοξάζω, 14. εἴ πως παρα-
ζηλώσω μου τὴν σάρκα, καὶ σώσω τινὰς ἐξ αὐτῶν. 15. εἰ γὰρ ἡ
[h] ἀποβολὴ αὐτῶν καταλλαγὴ κόσμου, τίς ἡ [i] πρόσληψις, εἰ μὴ ζωὴ ἐκ h Acts xxvii. 22.
νεκρῶν; 16. εἰ δὲ ἡ ἀπαρχὴ ἁγία, καὶ τὸ φύραμα· καὶ εἰ ἡ ῥίζα i Ch. xiv. 3.

---

[1] υμιν γαρ DFL; υμιν ουν C; υμιν δε ℵABP 47, all edd. εφ οσον μεν L, vulg.,
D³ lat. For μεν ℵABCP have μεν ουν, and so all edd.

Ver. 13 f. ὑμῖν δὲ λέγω τοῖς ἔθνεσιν.
Paul does not here address a new class
of readers. He has been speaking all
along to a Gentile church, and speaking
to it in that character (see above, pp.
561 ff.); and he feels it necessary to show
the relevance, in such circumstances, of
bestowing so much attention on the condition and prospects of the Jews. His
mission to the Gentiles has an indirect
bearing on his own countrymen; the
more successful he can make it, the
greater is the prospect that some of the
Jews also may be provoked to jealousy
and saved. Every Jew, again, who is
saved, goes to make up the πλήρωμα of
ver. 12, and so to bring on a time of
unimaginable blessing for the Gentile
world. ἐφ' ὅσον Mt. xxv. 40. μὲν οὖν
is printed in all the critical editions, but
Sanday and Headlam would read μενοῦν
as one word, and discount the restrictive
force of the μέν, which suggests that
apostleship to Gentiles was but one part
of Paul's mission. ἐγὼ: the pronoun
expresses not merely a noble consciousness of vocation, but Paul's feeling that
in his particular case at all events a
mission to the Gentiles could not but
include that ulterior reference to the Jews.
His devotion, accordingly, to his Gentile
ministry, never let them fall out of view.
"As far then as apostleship to Gentiles
is represented by *me* (as no doubt it is)
I glorify my ministry (by faithful discharge of it), if by any means I may save
some of the Jews." For the interpretation
of δοξάζω see 2 Thess. iii. 1, John xvii.
4. For εἴ πως see Buttmann, p. 255 f.
τινὰς ἐξ αὐτῶν: disenchanting experience
taught him to speak thus. *Cf.* 1 Cor.
ix. 22.
Ver. 15 f. From the personal explanation of ver. 13 f., which interrupts the
argument, Paul reverts to the ideas of
ver. 12. To save *any* Jew was a great
object, even with an apostle of the Gentiles: εἰ γὰρ ἡ ἀποβολὴ αὐτῶν κ.τ.λ.
Their ἀποβολὴ is their rejection by God
on the ground of unbelief. καταλλαγὴ
κόσμου: a world's reconciliation. In 2

Cor. v. 19 the world's reconciliation is the
act of God in Christ; but it was an act
which for the mass of mankind only took
effect when Jewish unbelief diverted the
Gospel to the Gentiles. ἡ πρόσλημψις:
the assumption of the Jews into God's
favour. ζωὴ ἐκ νεκρῶν. Modern expositors almost all find in these words a
reference to the resurrection; the restoration of the Jews at once brings on the
end; the dead are raised, and the
Messiah's kingdom is set up, glorious
and incorruptible. It is quite true that
in Jewish apocalyptic literature the resurrection introduces the new era, and
that Paul shared in the apocalyptic
ideas current in his time; but it does not
follow that he was thinking of the resurrection here. ζωὴ ἐκ νεκρῶν would
certainly be a singular way to describe
it, and it is not enough to say with Weiss
that Paul used this expression instead
of ἀνάστασις in order to carry the mind
beyond the fact of resurrection to the
state which it introduced. It seems
better to leave it undefined (*cf.* ἄπειρα
ἀγαθά Theophyl.), and to regard it as
an ordinary English reader regards "life
from the dead," as a description of unimaginable blessing. This is more impressive than to bind the original and
daring speculation of a passage like this
by reference to apocalyptic ideas, with
which Paul was no doubt familiar, but
which are not suggested here, and could
least of all control his thoughts when
they were working on a line so entirely
his own. "Words fail him, and he
employs the strongest he can find, thinking rather of their general force than of
their precise signification" (Jowett). εἰ
δὲ ἡ ἀπαρχὴ ἁγία, καὶ τὸ φύραμα. This
explains Paul's assurance that Israel has
a future. For ἀπ. and φύρ. see Num.
xv. 19-21. By the offering of the first
fruits the whole mass, and the whole
produce of the land, were consecrated.
Both this figure, and that of the root and
the branches, signify the same thing. As
the application in ver. 28 proves, what
is presented in both is the relation of the

ἁγία, καὶ οἱ κλάδοι. 17. εἰ δέ τινες τῶν κλάδων ἐξεκλάσθησαν, σὺ
δὲ ᵏ ἀγριέλαιος ὢν ¹ἐνεκεντρίσθης ἐν αὐτοῖς, καὶ συγκοινωνὸς τῆς ῥίζης
καὶ τῆς πιότητος ¹ τῆς ἐλαίας ἐγένου, 18. μὴ ᵐ κατακαυχῶ τῶν κλάδων·
εἰ δὲ κατακαυχᾶσαι, οὐ σὺ τὴν ῥίζαν βαστάζεις, ἀλλ᾽ ἡ ῥίζα σέ.
19. Ἐρεῖς οὖν, Ἐξεκλάσθησαν οἱ ² κλάδοι, ἵνα ἐγὼ"ἐγκεντρισθῶ. 20.
καλῶς· τῇ ἀπιστίᾳ ἐξεκλάσθησαν,³ σὺ δὲ τῇ πίστει ἕστηκας. μὴ

k Ver. 24
only in
N.T.
l Sep. xvi.
11.
m Jas. ii. 13,
iii. 14.

¹ και της πιοτητος א³ALD²˒³P; om. και א¹BCD¹F. It is om. by W. and H.,
Weiss, Alf. and Tischdf.

² Om. οι before κλαδοι with אABCD³FLP.

³ εξεκλασθησαν אACD³LP; εκλασθησαν BD¹F. Lachm. and Treg. prefer the
latter, but all other edd. the former. Weiss (*Textkritik*, S. 34) gives many similar
examples in which the preposition in compounds is dropped by oversight. For
υψηλοφρονει אAB read υψηλα φρονει; and so most edd.

patriarchs to the people as a whole. As
chosen by God, the fathers were ἅγιοι,
i.e., God's people, and this standing (in
spite of the arguments in chap. ix., and in
spite of the hard facts of the situation
when Paul wrote) belongs inalienably to
their children. They are God's, and it
will yet become apparent that they are.
Vers. 17-24. In these verses, which
in a sense are a long parenthesis,
Paul anticipates an objection which
Gentile readers might take to his use
of the last figure, the root and the
branches; and he draws from it two
special lessons—one, of humility, for the
objectors; the other, of hope, for Israel.
Ver. 17. A Gentile Christian might
feel that the very fact that Jews were rejected and Gentiles accepted qualified
the assurance with which Paul had just
spoken of the future of Israel. It is the
disposition to think so, and to presume
on one's own favoured position, which
the Apostle rebukes in μὴ κατακαυχῶ
τῶν κλάδων. εἰ δέ τινες τῶν κ. ἐξεκλάσθησαν: τινες puts the case mildly: *cf.*
iii. 3. ἐξεκλάσθησαν, *sc.*, as fruitless. σὺ
δὲ ἀγριέλαιος ὤν: σὺ is the presumptuous individual before the Apostle's mind,
not the Gentile Church collectively. The
ἀγριέλαιος is the olive in its natural
uncultivated state. ἐνεκεντρίσθης ἐν
αὐτοῖς, *sc.*, among the native branches of
the cultivated olive. The process here
supposed is one that in horticulture is
never performed. The cultivated branch
is always engrafted upon the wild stock,
and not *vice versâ*. This Paul knew
quite well (see παρὰ φύσιν, ver. 24), and
the force of his reproof to the presuming
Gentile turns on the fact that the process
was an unnatural one. [*Ordine com-
mutato res magis causis quam causas*

rebus aptavit (Origen).] It gave the
Gentile no room to boast over the rejected Jews. συνκοινωνὸς τῆς ῥίζης τῆς
πιότ. τῆς ἐλαίας: there is an argument
in συν. At the best, the Gentile only
shares with Jews in the virtues of a root
which is not Gentile, but Jewish: he
has his part in the consecration of the
patriarchs, the one historical root of the
people of God, and in the blessings God
attached to it. For πιότης *cf.* Jud. ix.
7. The accumulation of genitives is
apparently an imitation of such Hebrew
constructions as Isa. xxviii. 1, 16: the
meaning is, a partaker in the root of the
fat olive tree.
Ver. 18. μὴ κατακαυχῶ τῶν κλάδων:
for the genitive see Buttm., 185. Between "if thou boastest," and "thou
bearest not the root," there is no formal
connection: for such breviloquence,
which requires us to supply "consider"
or "remember," see Winer, p. 773. The
sense is, You owe all you are proud of
to an (artificially formed) relation to the
race you would despise.
Ver. 19. ἐρεῖς οὖν: the presumptuous
Gentile persists. "It is not to the root
I compare myself, but branches were
broken off that I might be engrafted:
that surely involves some superiority in
me."
Ver. 20. καλῶς: "a form of partial
and often ironical assent" (Gifford).
Paul does not think it worth while to
dispute the assertion of ver. 19, though
as it stands it is by no means indisputable; he prefers to point out what it
overlooks—the moral conditions of being
broken off and of standing secure—and
to urge them on the conscience. τῇ
ἀπιστίᾳ: an account of unbelief, *cf.*
Gal. vi. 12, Winer, p. 270. τῇ πίστει

ὑψηλοφρόνει, ἀλλὰ φοβοῦ · 21. εἰ γὰρ ὁ Θεὸς τῶν κατὰ φύσιν κλάδων
οὐκ ἐφείσατο · μή πως[1] οὐδὲ σοῦ φείσηται. 22. Ἴδε οὖν χρηστότητα
καὶ ⁿἀποτομίαν Θεοῦ · ἐπὶ μὲν τοὺς πεσόντας ἀποτομίαν · ἐπὶ δὲ σὲ n Here only in N.T.
χρηστότητα,[2] ἐὰν ἐπιμείνῃς τῇ χρηστότητι · ἐπεὶ καὶ σὺ ἐκκοπήσῃ ·
23. καὶ ἐκεῖνοι δὲ, ἐὰν μὴ ἐπιμείνωσι[3] τῇ ἀπιστίᾳ, ἐγκεντρισθήσονται ·
δυνατὸς γάρ ἐστιν ὁ Θεὸς πάλιν ἐγκεντρίσαι αὐτούς. 24. εἰ γὰρ σὺ
ἐκ τῆς κατὰ φύσιν ἐξεκόπης ἀγριελαίου, καὶ παρὰ ᵒφύσιν ἔνεκεν- o Ch. i. 26.
τρίσθης εἰς ᵖκαλλιέλαιον, πόσῳ μᾶλλον οὗτοι οἱ κατὰ φύσιν ἐγκεν- p Here only.

[1] Om. μηπως ℵABCP 47. For φεισηται ℵBCDFL read φεισεται. All crit.
edd. read φεισεται, but while most edd. omit μηπως it is retained by Weiss (with
DEFGL, most majusc. and fathers) and bracketed by Alford. Weiss finds it impossible to regard it as an insertion, since it makes an easy text irregular and
difficult ; but its omission, he thinks, need not have been intentional ; it may be a
mere overlook of the transcriber's.

[2] χρηστοτητα the second time D³FL ; but χρηστοτης θεου ABCD¹, and so all
edd. For επιμεινης ℵBD¹ read επιμενης, and so most edd. but not Alf.

[3] For επιμεινωσιν ℵ¹BD¹ read επιμενωσιν ; see also last verse.

ἔστηκας : the security of the Gentiles
depended on faith, and it is the most
elementary principle of a religion of
faith (iii. 27) that it excludes boasting.
μὴ ὑψηλὰ φρόνει : cf. xii. 16. 1 Tim. vi.
17 has μὴ ὑψηλοφρονεῖν. Neither is
classical. φοβοῦ : consistent with πίστις.
Timor opponitur non fiduciæ sed super-
cilio et securitati (Bengel).
Ver. 21. As far as comparisons can
be made at all in such things, the Jews
had been more securely invested in the
kingdom than the Gentiles. They were,
in the language of the figure, not artificially grafted, but native branches, on
the tree of God's people ; yet even that
did not prevent Him from cutting off
those who did not believe. And if He
did not spare them, He will not spare
Gentiles either, if in pride they fall from
faith. On εἰ . . . οὐκ ἐφείσατο see
Winer, 599 f. The true reading of the
last word is φείσεται (not φείσηται), but
Weiss would retain μήπως (see crit. note)
even with this future, and supply the
missing link of thought from φοβοῦ : one
may fear that he will not, etc. The ironical reserve of this (though the future
makes the thing to be feared as certain
as possible) is quite Pauline, and the
μήπως (DFGL) may be genuine.
Ver. 22. Behold then God's goodness
and severity, sc., in the case of the Gentiles and Jews as now before us. ἀπο-
τομία : here only in N.T. The moral
idea is that of peremptoriness, inexor-
ableness ; in Greek writers it is contrasted
with ἡμερότης, τὸ ἐπιεικές, πρᾳότης.

Cf. 2 Cor. xiii. 10. ἐὰν ἐπιμένῃς τῇ
χρηστότητι : if you remain on in the
goodness, i.e., continue to be indebted to
it, and to it alone, for your religious
position. This excludes presumption,
and in general all such temper as is betrayed in taking an attitude of superiority
to the Jews. The Jews lost their standing because they had come to believe
that it was indefectible, and independent
of moral conditions ; and if the Gentiles
commit the same mistake they will incur
the same doom. It is not to Israel only
God may say, The kingdom is taken
from you, and given to a nation bringing
forth the fruits thereof. ἐπεὶ, otherwise :
see ver. 6.
Ver. 23. κἀκεῖνοι δέ : and they too,
they on the other hand, viz., the unbelieving Jews. ἐὰν μὴ κ.τ.λ., unless
they remain on in their unbelief. It is
assumed that they need not do this. The
hardening spoken of in vers. 7-10, though
it is a judgment upon sin, and may seem
from the nature of the case to be irremediable, is not to be so absolutely
taken. Even in the most hardened re-
jector of the Gospel we are not to limit
either the resources of God's power, or
the possibilities of change in a self-con-
scious, self-determining creature. All
things are possible to him that believeth,
and we are not to say that in this man
or that, Jew or Gentile, unbelief is final,
and belief an impossibility. If the Jews
give up their unbelief ἐγκεντρισθήσονται
they will be incorporated again in the
true people of God. δυνατὸς γάρ ἐστιν

τρισθήσονται τῇ ἰδίᾳ ἐλαίᾳ; 25. Οὐ γὰρ θέλω ὑμᾶς ἀγνοεῖν,
q Ch. xv. 15, ἀδελφοί, τὸ μυστήριον τοῦτο (ἵνα μὴ ἦτε παρ᾽ ἑαυτοῖς¹ φρόνιμοι), ὅτι
24; 2 Cor.
i. 14; ii. 5. πώρωσις ἀπὸ q μέρους τῷ Ἰσραὴλ γέγονεν, ἄχρις οὗ τὸ πλήρωμα τῶν

¹ παρ᾽ ἑαυτοῖς ℵCDL; ἐν ἑαυτοῖς AB. Weiss, W. and H., Treg. and Alf.
put ἐν in text, apparently on the ground that παρ᾽ has been conformed to xii. 16;
but W. and H. give παρ᾽ a place in marg.

ὁ θεός κ.τ.λ. The phrase implies not
only the possibility but the difficulty of
the operation. Cf. xiv. 4. With man it
is impossible, but not with God. Nothing less than the thought of God could
keep Paul from despairing of the future
of Israel.

Ver. 24. God's power to engraft the
Jews again into the stock of His people
proved a fortiori by comparison with
what He has done for the Gentiles. To
restore His own is more natural, conceivable, and one may even say easy,
than to call those who are not His own.
The Gentile Christian (1) was cut ἐκ τῆς
κατὰ φύσιν ἀγριελαίου, from what is in
its own nature an uncultivated olive,
with no suitableness for the uses which
the olive is intended to subserve, and (2)
παρὰ φύσιν in violation of nature was
engrafted into a good olive; in comparison with this doubly unnatural process
one may well argue πόσῳ μᾶλλον κ.τ.λ.
how much more shall these, the Jews
who κατὰ φύσιν (in their own nature)
belong to the good tree, have their connection with it re-established? Weiss
takes ἐγκεντρισθήσονται as a logical
future, and it may be so; but Paul believes
in his logic, and has probably in view in
the word that actual restoration of the
Jews of which he now proceeds to speak.

Vv. 25-32. In this concluding section
Paul abandons the ground of argument
for that of revelation. He has discussed
the problems arising out of the rejection
of Israel and the calling of the Gentiles,
when taken in connection with the promises of God to His people; and he has
tried to make it clear that in all His
dealings with His people, God has acted
righteously, that for all that has befallen
them the Jews have full responsibility,
and that a Divine purpose, with blessing
in it to both Jew and Gentile, has indirectly been getting itself carried into
effect through this perplexing history.
The rejection of the Jews has led to the
calling of the Gentiles, and the calling
of the Gentiles, by provoking the Jews
to jealousy, is eventually to lead to their
conversion too. All this, it may be said,
is matter of argument; it is more or less

convincing as the argument appeals with
less or greater force to our minds. It is
Paul's construction and interpretation of
the facts before him, and his anticipation
of the result in which they are likely to
issue; but it has no greater authority
than the reasoning by which he supports
it, or the motives which suggest one
line of reasoning upon the facts rather
than another. We can understand how
patriotism, and religious faith in God's
promise, and insight into the psychological influences which determine human
conduct, all contribute some weight to
his argument; but he is not content to
rest upon argument alone the central
truth he has been expounding—that
the hardening of Israel is temporary as
well as partial, and that when "the
fulness of the Gentiles" has come in
the hardening will cease, and all Israel
be saved. He expressly puts this truth
forward as a revelation (μυστήριον,
ver. 25). What this means psycho-
logically we cannot tell, but it is clear
that for Paul it was an essential part of
the true religion, so far as he could make
out the manner of its working in the
world. He might try to lead the mind
up to it along various lines of argument,
or to confirm it by considerations of
various kinds; but for him it had a
Divine authority, antecedent to argument and independent of it. He sought
arguments to make it credible and intelligible, not for his own sake, but for
the sake of others. How much a revelation of this kind will weigh with the
modern reader depends on the extent to
which on general grounds he can recognise in Paul an inspired interpreter of
Christianity. History, it must be admitted, throws no light on his words.
The Gentiles are not fully gathered in;
the time to say whether Israel as a whole
is to have any distinct or decisive place
in the final fulfilment of God's gracious
purpose is therefore not yet. One feels
as if the nationalism of the passage fell
short of Paul's great word, There is
neither Greek nor Jew; but there the
Jews are, a problem to unbelief as well
as to faith; think what we will of it, it is

ἐθνῶν εἰσέλθη· 26. καὶ οὕτω πᾶς Ἰσραὴλ σωθήσεται, καθὼς γέγραπται, "Ἥξει ἐκ Σιὼν ὁ ῥυόμενος, καὶ¹ ἀποστρέψει ἀσεβείας ἀπὸ

¹ καὶ before αποστρεψει om. ℵABCD¹F.

of them salvation comes; and it is at
least as credible as the reverse (without
considering Paul's arguments at all) that
Providence is not preserving them for
nothing, and that in some such way as
is here indicated there is a close connection between their salvation and the salvation of the world.

Ver. 25. οὐ γὰρ θέλω ὑμᾶς ἀγνοεῖν:
cf. i. 13, 1 Cor. x. 1, xii. 1, 2 Cor. i. 8,
but especially 1 Thess. iv. 13, where
as here it is used to introduce a revelation. An often-repeated phrase tends
to be formal, but the thing of which
Paul would not have his readers ignorant
is usually important. As the phrase
is invariably followed by ἀδελφοί, the
latter also tends to be formal: it is at
least a mistake to see anything of
peculiar intimacy or affection in it in
such connections. As ver. 28 and ver.
30 prove, in which they are contrasted with the Jews, the ἀδελφοί are
Gentiles, and they are practically identical with the Roman Church. τὸ μυστήριον τοῦτο: the word μυστήριον only
occurs once in the Synoptical Gospels
(Mark iv. 11 and parallels) and not at all
in John; but Paul uses it often (twenty-
one times, including two in 1 Tim.). It
always refers to something which though
once hidden, or in its nature a secret, is
now revealed. In some passages it is
applied to the Christian revelation as a
whole (e.g., in Rom. xvi. 25, 1 Cor. ii. 1,
Eph. i. 9, Col. ii. 2: in the last it is
identified simpliciter with Christ). In
others it is applied to the Christian
revelation as a whole, but with some
special aspect of it in view: thus in Eph.
iii. 3 the special aspect of "revelation"
or "mystery"—for it is all one—in the
Gospel is the destined inclusion of the
Gentiles among the people of God, while
in Col. i. 26 f. it is the indwelling Christ,
as the pledge of immortality. In others,
again, any particular element in the great
revelation is called a "mystery". Thus
in 1 Cor. xv. 51 the truth communicated
about those who live to see the second
advent is described by this name, and it
might have been used in the similar
passage in 1 Thess. iv. 15, where Paul
says instead that he speaks ἐν λόγῳ
κυρίου. This is merely to claim for
his words the authority of revelation in

another way. The passage before us
comes under this last head. It is a
piece of revelation — something which
has been communicated to Paul ἐν
ἀποκαλύψει for the good of the Church
—that hardening in part has come upon
Israel until the fulness of the Gentiles
has come in. The new ideas in this
revelation are the limits in extent (ἀπὸ
μέρους) and in time (ἄχρι οὗ). ἵνα μὴ
ἦτε ἐν ἑαυτοῖς φρόνιμοι: it would tend
to self-conceit if the Gentiles in ignorance of this Divine appointment concluded off-hand that the Jews could
never be converted as a whole, and that
they themselves therefore were in a place
of permanent and exclusive privilege.
For ἐν ἑαυτοῖς (AB) παρ' ἑαυτοῖς is
found in ℵCDL, etc. Both occur in
LXX but the former is much more
likely to have been changed. τὸ πλήρωμα τῶν ἐθνῶν = the full number, totality, of the Gentiles. It does not mean
a number pre-determined beforehand,
which has to be made up, whether to
answer to the blanks in Israel or to the
demands of a Divine decree, but the
Gentiles in their full strength. When
the Gentiles in their full strength have
come in, the power which is to provoke
Israel to jealousy will be fully felt, with
the result described in ver. 26.

Ver. 26. καὶ οὕτως = and thus; not
merely temporal, but = under the influence of the jealousy so excited—under
the impression produced on the Jews by
the sight of the Gentiles in their fulness
peopling the kingdom—all Israel shall be
saved. This is an independent sentence.
For πᾶς Ἰσραὴλ see 1 Kings xii. 1, 2
Chron. xii. 1. It means Israel as a
whole. Paul is thinking of the historical
people, as the contrast with Gentiles
shows, but he is not thinking of them
one by one. Israel a Christian nation,
Israel as a nation a part of the Messianic
kingdom, is the content of his thought.
To make πᾶς Ἰσραὴλ refer to a "spiritual" Israel, or to the elect, is to miss
the mark: it foretells a "conversion of
the Jews so universal that the separation
into an 'elect remnant' and 'the rest who
were hardened' shall disappear" (Gifford).
καθὼς γέγραπται Isa. lix. 20 f., but the
last words ὅταν ἀφέλωμαι κ.τ.λ. from
Isa. xxvii. 9. The prophet says ἕνεκεν

Ἰακώβ · 27. καὶ αὕτη αὐτοῖς ἡ παρ' ἐμοῦ διαθήκη, ὅταν ἀφέλωμαι
r Ch. v. 10. τὰς ἁμαρτίας αὐτῶν". 28. Κατὰ μὲν τὸ εὐαγγέλιον, ʳ ἐχθροὶ δι'
s Ch. ix. 5. ὑμᾶς · κατὰ δὲ τὴν ἐκλογὴν, ἀγαπητοὶ διὰ τοὺς ˢ πατέρας. 29.
ἀμεταμέλητα γὰρ τὰ χαρίσματα καὶ ἡ κλῆσις τοῦ Θεοῦ. 30. Ὥσπερ
γὰρ καὶ ¹ ὑμεῖς ποτε ἠπειθήσατε τῷ Θεῷ, νῦν δὲ ἠλεήθητε τῇ τούτων

¹ καὶ before ὑμεῖς om. ℵcorr.ABCD¹F. For νυν, which is found in ACDEFGL,
νυνι is read in B. W. and H. put νυν in text, νυνι in marg. Weiss puts νυνι in
text, thinking that the double νυν in ver. 31 may have induced the dropping of the ι.
For other cases, see *Textkritik*, S. 62.

Σιών : Paul's ἐκ Σιὼν is probably a lapse
of memory, due to the impression of
passages like Ps. xiv. 7, liii. 7, Isa. ii. 3,
though Philippi thinks it intentional—the
object being to emphasise the title of the
Jews, as against the Gentiles, to a share
in the kingdom. It is then as if he said :
Salvation is of the Jews, and surely therefore *for* them. It is impossible to say
that ἥξει refers to the first or to the
second advent : the distinction is not
present to Paul's mind as he writes; all
he is concerned with is the fact that
in prophetic scripture language is used
which implies that Israel as a people is
to inherit the Messianic salvation. ὁ
ῥυόμενος, Hebrew גֹּאֵל is the Messiah.
ἀποστρέψει ἀσεβείας. Cf. Bar. iii. 7,
1 Macc. iv. 58.
Ver. 27. καὶ αὕτη κ.τ.λ. This is My
covenant with them = this is the constitution which I give them to live under.
Weiss interprets this by what follows,
making the αὕτη prospective, but this is
somewhat forced. The διαθήκη is not
equivalent to the removal of sins, though
it is based upon it : it covers the whole
condition introduced by that removal.
Cf. Jer. xxxi. 31 ff. The deliverance
referred to in vers. 26 and 27, though
promised to Israel as a whole, is a religious and ethical one. It has no
political significance, and nothing to do
with any assumed restoration of the
Jews to Canaan. This is obvious even
apart from the argument of Weiss that
the deliverance in question is to be immediately followed by the resurrection;
an argument which depends on a doubtful interpretation of ζωὴ ἐκ νεκρῶν ver.
15.
Ver. 28. κατὰ μὲν τὸ εὐαγγέλιον. In
both clauses κατὰ defines the rule by
which God's relation to Israel is determined. When He looks at the Gospel,
which they have rejected, they are ἐχθροὶ,
objects of His hostility, and that δι' ὑμᾶς,
for the sake of the Gentiles, to whom the
Gospel in this way comes; when He
looks at the ἐκλογὴ, the choice which
He made of Israel to be His people, they
are ἀγαπητοὶ, objects of His love, and
that διὰ τοὺς πατέρας, on account of
Abraham, Isaac and Jacob, with whom
He made an everlasting covenant (*cf.*
Gen. xvii. 19, Luke i. 54 f.). The passive
meaning of ἐχθροὶ is fixed by the contrast with ἀγαπητοὶ, as well as by the
logic of the passage : *cf.* v. 10.
Ver. 29. Proof that the Israelites, in
virtue of their relation to the fathers, are
objects of God's love. ἀμεταμέλητα *cf.*
2 Cor. vii. 10 : it may mean either what is
not or what cannot be repented of : here
the latter. God's gifts of grace, and His
calling, are things upon which there is
no going back. The χαρίσματα are not
the moral and intellectual qualifications
with which Israel was endowed for its
mission in the world (Godet), but the
privileges of grace enumerated in chap.
ix. 4 f. Neither is the κλῆσις of God
a "calling" in the modern sense of a
vocation or career assigned to any one
by Him; it is His authoritative invitation to a part in the Messianic kingdom.
From Israel these things can never be
withdrawn.
Vv. 30-32. There is the less need,
too, that they should be withdrawn,
because God makes the very misuse of
them contribute to the working out
of His universal purpose of redemption. The past unbelief of the Gentiles
and the mercy they presently enjoy,
the present unbelief of the Jews and
the mercy they are destined to enjoy
in the future—these things not only
correspond to each other, but they are
interwoven with each other; they are
parts of a system which God controls,
and in which every element conditions
and is conditioned by all the rest : there
is a Divine necessity pervading and controlling all the freedom of men—a Divine
purpose mastering all the random activity
of human wills; a purpose which is read

ἀπειθείᾳ· 31. οὕτω καὶ οὗτοι νῦν ἠπείθησαν, τῷ ὑμετέρῳ ἐλέει ἵνα
καὶ αὐτοὶ¹ ἐλεηθῶσι· 32. συνέκλεισε γὰρ ὁ Θεὸς τοὺς πάντας εἰς
ἀπείθειαν, ἵνα τοὺς πάντας ἐλεήσῃ.   33. Ὦ βάθος πλούτου καὶ
σοφίας καὶ γνώσεως Θεοῦ! ὡς ἀνεξερεύνητα τὰ κρίματα αὐτοῦ, καὶ

---

¹ After αυτοι ℵBD¹ ins. νυν ; and so Tischdf. and W. and H., not Weiss, who
regards it as a mere mechanical repetition.   Some cursives have ὕστερον.

---

out by the Apostle in verse 32 : God shut
them all up into disobedience that He
might have mercy upon them all. Ver.
30. ποτὲ : once, in the past, chap. i. 18-32.
τῇ τούτων ἀπειθείᾳ = owing to their disobedience. *Cf.* vers. 11, 15. Ver. 31. τῷ
ὑμετέρῳ ἐλέει is to be construed with ἵνα
καὶ αὐτοὶ νῦν ἐλεηθῶσιν. For the order
cf. Gal. ii. 10, 2 Cor. xii. 7. It seems
pedantic to make the construction strictly
parallel to τῇ τούτων ἀπειθίᾳ, and to
translate : "that owing to the mercy
shown to you—*i.e.*, owing to the jealousy
to which the Jews would be stirred at
seeing the Gentiles the objects of Divine
mercy—they also may obtain mercy";
the simpler construction is to take the
dative as explanatory of the verb, and to
translate : "that they may be made the
objects of the very same mercy which
has been shown to you". This is really
the point which the Apostle wishes to be
at; though the idea brought out in the
former rendering is essential in the
passage, it is not essential, nor obvious,
in these particular words. The second
νῦν (wanting in AD**FGL) is probably
genuine (ℵB), but cannot be forced to
mean more than "now in their turn".
The imminence of the result is not in view.
Ver. 32. συνέκλεισεν γὰρ ὁ Θεὸς τοὺς
πάντας εἰς ἀπειθιαν : this is the nearest
approach made in the N.T. to putting
the sin of man into a direct and positive
relation to the act and purpose of God.
But it would be a mistake to draw inferences from the concrete historical
problem before the Apostle—*viz.*, God's
dealings with Jew and Gentile, and the
mutual relations and influence of Jew
and Gentile in the evolution of God's
purpose—and to apply them to the general
abstract question of the relation of the
human will to the Divine. Paul is not
thinking of this question at all, and his
authority could not be claimed for such
inferences. Salvation, he sees, as he
looks at the world before him, is to come
to Jew and Gentile alike by the way of
free grace ; and it answers to this, that
in the providence of God, Jew and Gentile
alike have been made to feel the need of
grace by being shut up under disobedience. It is within Paul's thought to
say that the sin of Jews and Gentiles,
to whom he preached the Gospel, did not
lie outside the control, or outside the
redeeming purpose, of God ; but it does
not seem to me to be within his thought
to say that God ordains sin in general
for the sake of, or with a view to, redemption. This is a fancy question
which an apostle would hardly discuss.
God subordinates sin to His purpose, but
it is not a subordinate element in His
purpose. The same order of considerations ought to guide us in the interpretation of τοὺς πάντας. "Them all"
certainly refers in the first instance to
Jews and Gentiles. It is not the same
as τοὺς ἀμφοτέρους, "both parties";
but it differs from it in its present connection only by giving emphasis to the
fact that both parties consist of numbers,
to all of whom the truth here stated
applies. To find here a doctrine of universal salvation—a dogmatic assertion
that every man will at last receive mercy
—is simply to desert the ground on which
the Apostle is standing. It is to leave
off thinking about the concrete problem
before his mind, and to start thinking
about something quite different. It is
gratuitous to contrast, as, *e.g.*, is done by
Lipsius, this passage with others in which
Paul speaks of ἀπολλύμενοι as well as
σωζόμενοι, and to say that they represent
irreconcilable view-points—the Apostle
speaking in the present instance from the
standpoint of Divine teleology ; in the
other, from that of actual experience.
The truth is, as Weiss puts it, there is
not a word here to show how far, when
the history of man has reached its term,
Paul conceived God's saving purpose to
be realised. συνέκλεισεν answering to

הִסְגִּיר is frequent in LXX : the συν
does not refer to the fact that Jews and
Gentiles are shut up *together*, but indicates that those who are shut up are
shut up on all sides, so that they cannot
escape : *cf.* con-*cludo* and examples in
Gal. iii. 22, Ps. xxx. 9 LXX. ἐλεήσῃ :

t Eph. iii. 8. ᵗἀνεξιχνίαστοι αἱ ὁδοὶ αὐτοῦ. 34. "τίς γὰρ ἔγνω νοῦν Κυρίου; ἢ τίς σύμβουλος αὐτοῦ ἐγένετο;" 35. ἢ "τίς προέδωκεν αὐτῷ, καὶ ἀνταποδοθήσεται αὐτῷ;" 36. ὅτι ἐξ αὐτοῦ καὶ δι' αὐτοῦ καὶ εἰς αὐτὸν τὰ πάντα· αὐτῷ ἡ δόξα εἰς τοὺς αἰῶνας. ἀμήν.

"to have mercy upon" means "to make partakers of that 'common salvation' (Jude 3) which is emphatically a dispensation of mercy" (Gifford).

Ver. 33. ὦ βάθος πλούτου κ.τ.λ. In ver. 32 the content of the chapter is no doubt condensed, but it is more natural to regard the doxology as prompted by the view of God's Providence which pervades the whole discussion than by the one sentence in which it is summed up. βάθος: a universal figure for what is immeasurable or incalculable: cf. 1 Cor. ii. 10, Apoc. ii. 24, Eph. iii. 18. The genitives πλούτου, σοφίας and γνώσεως are most simply construed as co-ordinate. For πλοῦτος used thus absolutely see Eph. iii. 8, Phil. iv. 19. Perhaps the key to the meaning here is to be found in x. 12: what Paul adores is the unsearchable wealth of love that enables God to meet and far more than meet the appalling necessities of the world; love less deep would soon be bankrupt at the task. In σοφία and γνῶσις the intellectual resources are brought into view with which God has ordered, disposed and controlled all the forces of the world and of man's history so as to make them subservient to His love. The world, with its conflict of races, religions, passions and even vices, may seem to be a realm of chaos; but when we see it in the light of God as Paul did, we see the signs of wisdom and knowledge, of a conscious purpose transcending human thought, and calling forth adoring praise. For the distinction of σοφία and γνῶσις, which especially in relation to God is to be felt rather than defined, see Trench, N.T. Synonyms, § lxxv. τὰ κρίματα αὐτοῦ: except 1 Cor. vi. 7 which is different, this is the only example of κρίματα (plural) in the N.T. It is probably used not in the narrower sense (which would be illustrated by reference, e.g., to the "hardening" of Israel), but in the wider sense of the Hebrew מִשְׁפָּטִים, to which it often answers in the LXX. In Ps. xxxvi. 6 we have τὰ κρίματά σου ἄβυσσος πολλή: where Cheyne's note is, "Thy judgments—in their various effects of destruction and salvation". This is Paul's thought; hence τὰ κρίματα αὐτοῦ and αἱ ὁδοὶ αὐτοῦ are prac-

tically the same. As Moses says (Deut. xxxii. 4), All His ways are judgment.

Ver. 34. Proof from Scripture of the unsearchableness of God's ways: He has had no confidant. Isa. xl. 13, 1 Cor. ii. 16. It is mere pedantry to refer half the verse to σοφία and the other half to γνῶσις.

Ver. 35. ἢ τίς προέδωκεν αὐτῷ, καὶ ἀνταποδοθήσεται αὐτῷ; see Job xli. 11 (A.V.). The translation of Job xli. 3, Hebrew, is perhaps Paul's own, as the LXX is entirely different and wrong. The point of the quotation has been variously explained. If it continues the proof of ver. 33, the underlying assumption is that God's ways would be finite and comprehensible if they were determined by what men had done, so as merely to requite that. It seems better, however, to read the words in the largest sense, and then they express the fundamental truth of religion as Paul understood it—viz., that the initiative in religion belongs to God; or as he puts it elsewhere, that we have nothing we did not receive, and that boasting is excluded. The relation of man to God in these conditions is one which naturally expresses itself in doxology.

Ver. 36. ὅτι ἐξ αὐτοῦ κ.τ.λ. Strictly speaking, the ὅτι confirms the last truth—man's absolute dependence on God—by making it part of a wider generalisation. ἐξ αὐτοῦ: from Him, as their source; δι' αὐτοῦ: through Him, as the power by whose continuous energy the world is sustained and ruled; εἰς αὐτὸν: unto Him, as their goal, for whose glory they exist. A reference of any kind to the Trinity is out of the question. It is a question, however, whether τὰ πάντα means "all things" in the sense of the universe (cf. 1 Cor. viii. 6, Col. i. 16, Heb. ii. 10) or whether it is not limited by the article to all the things which have just been in contemplation, the whole marvellous action of God's riches and wisdom and knowledge, as interpreted by the Apostle in regard to the work of redemption (for an example of τὰ πάντα in this sense see 2 Cor. v. 18). I incline to the last view. The universe of grace, with all that goes on in it for the common salvation of Jew and Gentile, is of God and through God and to

XII. 1. ΠΑΡΑΚΑΛΩ οὖν ὑμᾶς, ἀδελφοί, ᵃ διὰ τῶν οἰκτιρμῶν τοῦ ᵃ Ch. xv.30;
Θεοῦ, παραστῆσαι τὰ σώματα ὑμῶν θυσίαν ζῶσαν, ἁγίαν, εὐάρεστον   2 Cor. x. 1.

God. To Him be the glory which such a display of wisdom and love demands.

CHAPTER XII. The distinction of doctrinal and practical is not one that can be pressed anywhere in the N.T., and as little in Paul as in any other writer. It is under practical compulsion of some kind that he develops most of his characteristic doctrines, and he has no doctrines which do not imply a corresponding practice. Yet the distinction does exist, and the remainder of this epistle, especially chaps. xii. 1-xv. 13, may be properly described as the practical part of it. Not that it is independent of the other. On the contrary, it is nothing but the application of it. (οὖν ver. 1.) Christian ethics are relative to the Christian revelation. It is the relations in which we stand that determine our duties, and the new relations in which we are set both to God and to other men by faith in Jesus Christ have a new morality corresponding to them. There is such a thing as a Christian ethic with a range, a delicacy, a flavour, all its own. There is no formal exposition of it here, though perhaps the nearest approach to such a thing that we have in the N.T., but a comprehensive illustration of it in a variety of bearings. Paul starts (xii. 1 f.) with a general exhortation, covering the whole Christian life. From this he proceeds to the spirit and temper which ought to characterise Christians as members of the same society, dwelling especially on the graces of humility and love (xii. 3-21). In the following chapter he discusses the duties of the individual to his legal superiors (xiii. 1-7); his duties to his neighbour, as comprehended in the love which fulfils the law (xiii. 8-10); and the urgent duty of sanctification in view of the Parousia. With chap. xiv. he comes to a different subject, and one apparently of peculiar interest in Rome at the time. It is one of those questions in which the claim of Christian liberty has to accommodate itself to the social necessity created by the weakness of brethren, and the discussion of it extends from xiv. 1-xv. 13, and concludes the "practical" part of the epistle.

Ver. 1. παρακαλῶ οὖν: the reference is to all that has been said since i. 16, but especially to what more closely precedes. Cf. Eph. iv. 1, 1 Tim. ii. 1, 1 Cor. iv. 16. The οὖν connects the two parts of the epistle, not formally but really, and shows the dependence of the "practical" upon the "doctrinal". It is the new world of realities to which the soul is introduced by the Christian revelation on which Christian morality depends. It is relative to that world, and would become unreal along with it. διὰ τῶν οἰκτιρμῶν: for the substantive see 2 Cor. i. 3 (= רַחֲמִים, which has no singular). διὰ in such expressions (cf. 1 Cor. i. 10, 2 Cor. x. 1) indicates that in which the motive is found: Winer, p. 477. The mercies are those which God has shown in the work of redemption through Christ. παραστῆσαι is not per se sacrificial: in chap. vi. 13, 16, 19 it is used of putting the body at the disposal of God or of sin: see also 2 Cor. iv. 14, xi. 2, Col. i. 22, 28, Eph. v. 27. τὰ σώματα ὑμῶν is not exactly the same as ὑμᾶς αὐτούς, yet no stress is to be laid on the words as though Paul were requiring the sanctification of the body as opposed to the spirit: the body is in view here as the instrument by which all human service is rendered to God, and the service which it does render, in the manner supposed, is not a bodily but a spiritual service. θυσίαν ζῶσαν: "living," as opposed to the slain animals offered by the Jews. This seems to be the only case in which the new life as a whole is spoken of by Paul as a sacrifice —a thank offering—to God. A more limited use of the idea of θυσία is seen in Phil. ii. 17, iv. 18; cf. also Heb. xiii. 15 f., 1 Pet. ii. 5. ἁγίαν: contrast i. 24. εὐάρεστον according to all analogy (see concordance) should go with τῷ θεῷ, and this is secured by the order of the words in A𝕏 vulg. τὴν λογικὴν λατρείαν ὑμῶν: in apposition not to τὰ σώματα ὑμῶν but to the presenting of the body as a living sacrifice. For other examples see Winer, 669. λατρεία (ix. 4, Heb. ix. 1, 6, John xvi. 2) is cultus, ritual service, worship; and such a presentation of the body, as the organ of all moral action, to God, is the only thing that can be characterised as λογικὴ λατρεία, spiritual worship. Any other worship, any retention of Jewish or pagan rites, anything coming under the description of opus operatum, is foreign to the Christian θυσία; it is λατρεία which is not λογική, not appropriate to a being whose essence is λόγος, i.e., reason or spirit.

b 1 Pet. ii. 1. τῷ Θεῷ,¹ τὴν ᵇ λογικὴν ᶜ λατρείαν ὑμῶν · 2. καὶ μὴ συσχηματίζεσθε τῷ
c Ch. ix. 4.
d Matt. xvii. αἰῶνι τούτῳ, ἀλλὰ ᵈ μεταμορφοῦσθε ² τῇ ἀνακαινώσει τοῦ νοὸς ὑμῶν, εἰς
2; 2 Cor.
iii. 18.　τὸ δοκιμάζειν ὑμᾶς τί τὸ θέλημα τοῦ Θεοῦ τὸ ἀγαθὸν καὶ εὐάρεστον

καὶ τέλειον. 3. Λέγω γὰρ, διὰ τῆς χάριτος τῆς δοθείσης μοι, παντὶ

τῷ ὄντι ἐν ὑμῖν, μὴ ὑπερφρονεῖν παρ' ὃ δεῖ φρονεῖν, ἀλλὰ φρονεῖν εἰς

---

¹ τω θεω before ευαρεστον ℵ¹AP, vulg. So W. and H. text, but marg. as rec.
Weiss. on the ground that τω θεω is to be construed with παραστησαι, keeps
these words to the end.

² συνσχηματιζεσθε . . . μεταμορφουσθε; so BLP, W. and H. text; but συνσχη-
ματιζεσθαι and μεταμορφουσθαι in AB²D¹ (gr.) F. The infin. is read by Lachm.
and in marg. by Treg. and W. and H., but is obviously an alteration of the imperative to have it construed with παρακαλω (Weiss). υμων after νοος is om. by
ABD¹ (gr.) F 47 and all edd.

Ver. 2. καὶ μὴ συνσχηματίζεσθε:
the imperative is better supported (BLP)
than the infinitive (ADFG). For the word
cf. 1 Pet. i. 14. The distinctions that
have been drawn between συνσχηματίζεσθε and μεταμορφοῦσθε—on the ground
of other distinctions assumed between
σχῆμα and μορφή—though supported by
distinguished scholars, remind one of the
shrewd remark of Jowett, that there is
a more dangerous deficiency for the
commentator than ignorance of Greek,
namely, ignorance of language. In the
face of such examples as are quoted
by Weiss (Plut., Mor., p. 719 B: τὸ
μεμορφωμένον καὶ ἐσχηματισμένον: Eur.,
Iph. T., 292, μορφῆς σχήματα) and
Wetstein (Sext. Emp., ἢ μένει μὲν ἐν τῇ
οἰκείᾳ ὑποστάσει, εἰς ἄλλο δὲ εἶδος ἀντ'
ἄλλου μεταλαμβάνον γεννᾶται, ὡς ὁ
μετασχηματιζόμενος κηρός, καὶ ἄλλοτε
ἄλλην μορφὴν ἀναδεχόμενος) it is impossible not to regard the distinctions in
question as very arbitrary. For the best
supported and most relevant, reflected in
Sanday and Headlam's paraphrase ("do
not adopt the external and fleeting fashion
of this world, but be ye transformed in
your inmost nature"), see Lightfoot on
Phil. ii. 7, or Gifford on the same passage
(The Incarnation, pp. 22 ff., 88 ff.). τῷ
αἰῶνι τούτῳ: "This world" or "age"
is opposed to that which is to come; it
is an evil world (Gal. i. 4) of which Satan
is the God (2 Cor. iv. 4). Even apparent
or superficial conformity to a system controlled by such a spirit, much more an
actual accommodation to its ways, would
be fatal to the Christian life. By nature,
the Christian is at home in this world
(cf. Eph. ii. 2); such as it is, its life and
his life are one; and his deliverance is
accomplished as he is transformed τῇ
ἀνακαινώσει τοῦ νοός, by the renewing

of his mind. νοῦς in the Apostle's usage
(see chap. vii.) is both intellectual and
moral—the practical reason, or moral
consciousness. This is corrupted and
atrophied in the natural man, and renewed by the action of the Holy Spirit.
The process would in modern language
be described rather as sanctification than
regeneration, but regeneration is assumed
(Tit. iii. 5). εἰς τὸ δοκιμάζειν: this is
the purpose of the transforming renewal
of the mind. It is that Christians may
prove, i.e., discern in their experience,
what the will of God is. Cf. ii. 18. An
unrenewed mind cannot do this; it is
destitute of moral discernment—has no
proper moral faculty. τὸ ἀγαθὸν καὶ
εὐάρεστον καὶ τέλειον: these words may
either qualify τὸ θέλημα τοῦ Θεοῦ as in
A.V., or be in apposition to it, as in
R.V. margin. The last agrees better
with the rhythm of the sentence. The
will of God is identified with what is
ἀγαθόν, good in the moral sense; εὐάρεστον well pleasing, sc., to God (so in all the
nine cases of the adjective and three of
the verb εὐαρεστεῖν which are found in the
N.T.); and τέλειον ethically adequate or
complete: Dt. xviii. 13, Mt. v. 48. No
one discovers the line of action which
from possessing these characteristics can
be identified as the will of God unless
he is transformed from his native affinity
to the world by the renewing of his mind
by the Holy Spirit.

Vers. 3-8. The duties of members of
the Church as such: avoidance of self-
exaltation, and mutual service in the
measure of the gift bestowed on each.
λέγω γάρ: the γὰρ indicates that "humility is the immediate effect of self-sur-
render to God" (Gifford). διὰ τῆς
χάριτος κ.τ.λ. Paul illustrates in his
own person, in giving this advice, the

τὸ ⁰σωφρονεῖν, ἑκάστῳ ὡς ὁ Θεὸς ἐμέρισε ᶠ μέτρον πίστεως. 4. Καθάπερ e 2 Cor. v.13;
γὰρ ἐν ἑνὶ σώματι μέλη πολλὰ ¹ ἔχομεν, τὰ δὲ μέλη πάντα οὐ τὴν f Eph. iv, 7,
αὐτὴν ἔχει πρᾶξιν · 5. οὕτως οἱ πολλοὶ ἓν σῶμά ἐσμεν ἐν Χριστῷ,
ὁ ² δὲ καθ᾽ εἷς ἀλλήλων μέλη, 6. ἔχοντες δὲ χαρίσματα κατὰ τὴν
χάριν τὴν δοθεῖσαν ἡμῖν διάφορα · εἴτε προφητείαν, κατὰ τὴν

¹ For μελη πολλα ALP read πολλα μελη with ℵBDF latt. and most edd ; but
W. and H. give μελη πολλα a place in marg.

² For ο δε (altered to agree with εις ?) read το δε ℵABD¹F gr. P. 47.

rule he is laying down for the Church.
He speaks "through the grace given
him," and therefore without presumption ;
but he does speak, and so puts his
wisdom and love at the service of the
Church. παντὶ τῷ ὄντι ἐν ὑμῖν : everybody in the Church needed this word.
To himself, every man is in a sense the
most important person in the world, and
it always needs much grace to see what
other people are, and to keep a sense
of moral proportion. μὴ ὑπερφρονεῖν :
ὑπερφρονεῖν here only in N.T., but a
common word. παρ᾽ ὃ δεῖ φρονεῖν :
beyond the mind or habit of thought
one ought to have. For this use of
παρά see xiv. 5, Lc. xiii. 2, Heb. i. 9.
φρονεῖν εἰς τὸ σωφρονεῖν : to cherish a
habit of thought tending to sobriety of
mind. σωφροσύνη is described by Jos.,
Macc. 2 f., as giving man dominion not
only over bodily ἐπιθυμίαι but also over
those of the soul, such as φιλαρχία,
κενοδοξία, ἀλαζονεία, μεγαλαυχία, βασ-
κανία. These are precisely the qualities
to which Paul opposes it here. φρονεῖν
and its cognates are favourite words with
Paul : what they all suggest is the importance to character, especially to Christian
character, of the prevailing mood of the
mind—the moral temper, as it might be
called. It should always tend to sobriety ;
but he gives a special rule for it in
ἑκάστῳ ὡς ὁ Θεὸς ἐμέρισεν μέτρον
πίστεως. ἑκάστῳ is governed by ἐμέρισεν : its place makes it emphatic. Cf.
1 Cor. iii. 5. Whatever the characteristic of any individual may be, it is due
to the discriminating act of God in
measuring out faith to him in greater or
less degree. Taken in connection with
what precedes, the idea seems to be :
There are *various* degrees of self-estimation proper, for God gives one more and
another less ; but all are fundamentally
regulated by humility, for no one has
anything that he has not received. 1
Cor. iv. 7.

Ver. 4 f. καθάπερ γὰρ : For language
and figure *cf.* 1 Cor. xii. 12. Also Eph.
iv. 15 f., Col. i. 18. The comparison of
the community to a body—the social
organism—is very common in classical
writers : see Wetstein and Jowett here.
πρᾶξιν : viii. 13. It is that at which the
member works—in modern language, its
function. Every member has its gift, but
it is limited by the fact that it is no more
than a member : it is not the whole body.
1 Cor. xii. 17. οἱ πολλοὶ ἓν σῶμά ἐσμεν
ἐν Χριστῷ : many as we are, we are one
body in Christ ; it is the common relation to Him which unites us. In the
later passages in which Paul uses this
figure (Eph., Col.), Christ is spoken of
as the Head of the body ; but both
here and in 1 Cor. xii. it would agree
better with our instinctive use of the
figure to speak of Him as its soul. His
own figure of the vine and the branches
combines the advantages of both. τὸ δὲ
καθ᾽ εἷς ἀλλήλων μέλη : this qualifies the
unity asserted in ἓν σῶμά ἐσμεν. It is
not a unity in which individuality is
lost ; on the contrary, the individuals
retain their value, only not as independent wholes, but as members one of
another. Each and all exist only in each
other. 1 Cor. xii. 27. For τὸ καθ᾽ εἷς
see Winer, 312.

Ver. 6 ff. At this point an application,
apparently, is made of what has been
said in vers. 4 and 5, but the grammar is
very difficult. Both A.V. and R.V. supply
what is needed in order to read the verses
as an exhortation ; thus in ver. 6, "*let
us prophesy*" ; in ver. 7, "*let us wait*" ;
and in ver. 8, answering to the change
of construction in the Greek, "*let him
do it*". This is the simplest way out of
the difficulty, and is followed by many
scholars (Meyer, Lipsius, Gifford). But
it is not beyond doubt, and there is something to say for the more rigorous construction adopted by Weiss and others,
who put only a comma after μέλη at the
end of ver. 5, and construe ἔχοντες with
ἐσμεν. In either case, there is an apo-

g Here only. ^gἀναλογίαν τῆς πίστεως· 7. εἴτε διακονίαν, ἐν τῇ διακονίᾳ. εἴτε ὁ διδάσκων, ἐν τῇ διδασκαλίᾳ· 8. εἴτε ὁ παρακαλῶν, ἐν τῇ παρακλήσει· ὁ μεταδιδοὺς, ἐν ἁπλότητι· ὁ προϊστάμενος, ἐν σπουδῇ· ὁ ἐλεῶν, ἐν ἱλαρότητι.

dosis to be supplied; but while in the former case it is hinted at in the second half of every clause (as is seen in our English Bibles), in the latter it is simply forgotten. It is as if Paul had said, "We are members one of another, and have gifts differing according to the grace given to us; our gift may be prophecy, prophecy in the proportion of our faith; it may be διακονία in the sphere appropriate for that; another instance would be that of the teacher in *his* department, or of the exhorter in *his*; or again you may have the distributor, whose gift is in the form of ἁπλότης; or the ruler, who is divinely qualified for his function by the gift of σπουδή, moral earnestness; or the man who to show mercy is endowed with a cheerful disposition". All this *requires* an apodosis, but partly because of its length, partly because of the changes in construction as the Apostle proceeds, the apodosis is overlooked. Its import, however, would not vary, as in the A.V., from clause to clause, but would be the same for all the clauses together. Even with the ordinary punctuation, which puts a period at the end of ver. 5, I prefer this reading of the passage. The varying apodoses supplied in the English Bible to the separate clauses are really irrelevant; what is wanted is a common apodosis to the whole conception. "Now having gifts differing according to the grace given to us—as one may see by glancing at the phenomena of church life—let us use them with humility (remembering that they *are* gifts) and with love (inasmuch as we are members one of another)." It is easier to suppose that the construction was suspended, and gradually changed, with some general conclusion like this before the mind from the beginning, than that it broke down, so to speak, as soon as it began; which we must suppose if we insert προφητεύωμεν in ver. 6. But it is not a question which can be infallibly decided. It ought to be observed that there is no hint of anything official in this passage; *all* ministry is a function of membership in the body, and *every* member has the function of ministry to some intent or other. χαρίσματα: i. 11, 1 Cor. i. 7, xii. 4, 9, 31, 1 P. iv. 10.

With the exception of 1 P. iv. 10 (which is not without relation to this passage) Paul alone uses χάρισμα in the N.T. Every χάρισμα is a gift of the Holy Spirit given to the believer for the good of the Church. Some were supernatural (gifts of healings, etc.), others spiritual in the narrower sense: this passage is the best illustration of the word. τὴν δοθεῖσαν, sc., when we believed. προφητείαν κατὰ τὴν ἀναλογίαν τῆς πίστεως. προφητεία is the highest of χαρίσματα, 1 Cor. xiv. 1 ff. When one has it, he has it κατὰ τὴν ἀναλογ. τῆς πίστεως = in the proportion of his faith. The faith meant is that referred to in ver. 3, the measure of which is assigned by God: and since this is the case, it is obviously absurd for a man to give himself airs—ὑπερφρονεῖν—on the strength of being a προφήτης: this would amount to forgetting that in whatever degree he has the gift, he owes it absolutely to God. The expression προφητείαν κατὰ τὴν ἀναλογίαν τῆς πίστεως implies that the more faith one has—the more completely Christian he is — the greater the prophetic endowment will be. [In theology, "the analogy of the faith" is used in quite a different sense, though it was supposed to be justified by this passage. To interpret Scripture, *e.g.*, according to the analogy of the faith meant to interpret the parts, especially difficult or obscure parts, in consistency with the whole. The scope of the whole, again, was supposed to be represented in the creed or rule of faith; and to interpret κατὰ τ. ἀ. τ. πίστεως meant simply not to run counter to the creed. In the passage before us this is an anachronism as well as an irrelevance. There was no rule of faith when the Apostle was thinking out the original interpretation of Christianity contained in this epistle; and there is no exhortation or warning, but only a description of fact, in the words.] διακονία as opposed to προφητεία and the other functions mentioned here probably refers to such services as were material rather than spiritual: they were spiritual however (though connected only with helping the poor, or with the place or forms of worship) because prompted by the Spirit and done in it. One who has this

9. Ἡ ἀγάπη [h] ἀνυπόκριτος. ἀποστυγοῦντες τὸ πονηρὸν, κολλώμενοι h 2 Cor. vi.
τῷ ἀγαθῷ· 10. τῇ φιλαδελφίᾳ εἰς ἀλλήλους φιλόστοργοι. τῇ τιμῇ 6; 1 Tim.
i. 5; Jas.
iii. 17.

gift has it ἐν τῇ διακονίᾳ, i.e., in the qualities and in the sphere proper to it: it is in its own nature limited; it is what it is, and nothing else, and fits a man for this function and no other. This is not "otiose," and it provides a good meaning without importing anything. ὁ διδάσκων ἐν τῇ διδασκαλίᾳ: it is in his teaching that the διδάσκαλος possesses the gift peculiar to him: 1 Cor. xiv. 26. ὁ παρακαλῶν ἐν τῇ παρακλήσει: so again with the exhorter, the man who speaks words of encouragement: cf. xv. 4, 5; Acts iv. 36, ix. 31, xiii. 15. It is in his παράκλησις, and not in something else, that his χάρισμα lies. Thus far Paul has not defined the quality of the χαρίσματα, or shown in what they consist; the functionary is merely said to have his gift in his function—teaching, exhorting, or service. But in the cases which follow, he tells us what the gift, proper to the special functions in view, is; in other words, what is the spiritual quality which, when divinely bestowed, capacitates a man to do this or that for the Church. Thus there is ὁ μεταδιδούς (cf. Eph. iv. 28, Luc. iii. 11), the man who imparts of his means to those who need; he has his χάρισμα in ἁπλότης. Cf. 2 Cor. ix. 11, 13; James i. 5. It is not exactly "liberality," though in these passages it approaches that sense: it is the quality of a mind which has no arrière-pensée in what it does; when it gives, it does so because it sees and feels the need, and for no other reason; this is the sort of mind which *is* liberal, and God assigns a man the function of μεταδιδόναι when He bestows this mind on him by His Spirit. ὁ προϊστάμενος is the person who takes the lead in any way. He might or might not be an official (1 Thess. v. 12, 1 Tim. v. 17, 1 Tim. iii. 4, 5, 12: cf. also πρόστατις xvi. 2, and Hort, *The Christian Ecclesia*, p. 126 f.); but in any case he had the χάρισμα which fitted him for his special function in σπουδή, moral earnestness or vigour. A serious masculine type of character is the pre-supposition for this gift. Finally ὁ ἐλεῶν, he who does deeds of kindness, has his *charisma* in ἱλαρότης. A person of a grudging or despondent mood has not the endowment for showing mercy. He who is to visit the poor, the sick, the sorrowful, will be marked out by God for His special ministry by this endowment

of brightness and good cheer. *Cf.* 2 Cor. ix. 7 = Prov. xxii. 8 and Sir. xxxii. (xxxv.) 11: ἐν πάσῃ δόσει ἱλάρωσον τὸ πρόσωπόν σου, καὶ ἐν εὐφροσύνῃ ἁγίασον δεκάτην.

Vv. 9-21. As far as any single idea pervades the rest of the chapter it is that of the first words in ver. 9: ἡ ἀγάπη ἀνυπόκριτος. The passage as a whole has a strong affinity to 1 Cor. xiii., and along with what may be a reminiscence of our Lord's words, it has something intensely and characteristically Christian. Whatever the grammatical construction may be—and all through the chapter Paul displays an indifference in this respect which is singular even in him—the intention must be supposed to be hortatory, so that it is most natural to supply imperatives (ἔστω or ἐστέ) with the numerous participles.

Ver. 9. ἡ ἀγάπη ἀνυπόκριτος: see 2 Cor. vi. 6, 1 Pet. i. 22. Probably the following clauses ἀποστυγοῦντες . . . κολλώμενοι κ.τ.λ. are meant to explain this. Love is undissembled, it is the unaffected Christian grace, when it shrinks, as with a physical horror, from that which is evil (even in those whom it loves), and cleaves to that which is good. στυγεῖν according to Eustath. in *Il.* a, p. 58 (quoted by Wetstein) adds the idea of φρίσσειν to that of μισεῖν: the ἀπο intensifies the idea of aversion or repulsion. Love is not a principle of mutual indulgence; in the Gospel it is a moral principle, and like Christ Who is the only perfect example of love, it has always something inexorable about it. *He* never condoned evil. τῷ ἀγαθῷ is neuter, like τὸ πονηρόν, though κολλᾶσθαι can be used of persons (1 Cor. vi. 16 f.) as well as things.

Ver. 10. τῇ φιλαδελφίᾳ = in point of brotherly love, *i.e.*, your love to each other as children in the one family of God. Cf. 1 Thess. iv. 9, Heb. xiii. 9, 1 Pet. i. 22, 2 Pet. i. 7, 1 Pet. iii. 8. ἀδελφὸς in the apostolic writings does not mean fellow-man, but fellow-Christian; and φιλαδελφία is the mutual affection of the members of the Christian community. In this they are to be φιλόστοργοι, "tenderly affectioned". The moral purity required in ver. 9 is not to be the only mark of Christian love; since they are members of one family, their love is to have the characters of strong natural

i Here only.
k Matt. xxv.
26.
ἀλλήλους [i]προηγούμενοι· 11. τῇ σπουδῇ μὴ [k]ὀκνηροί, τῷ πνεύματι ζέοντες, τῷ Κυρίῳ [1] δουλεύοντες· 12. τῇ ἐλπίδι χαίροντες, τῇ θλίψει ὑπομένοντες, τῇ προσευχῇ προσκαρτεροῦντες· 13. ταῖς χρείαις [2] τῶν

[1] For κυριω ℵABD[2,3]LP, etc., some Western authorities (D[1]F gr. G lat.) read καιρω, and this appears in the received text, though not in the A.V. The confusion may have arisen from a contraction of the one word being mistaken for that of the other; but was "probably supported by a sense of the difficulty of so comprehensive a clause as τῳ κυριῳ δουλευοντες in the midst of a series of clauses of limited sense" (W. and H., Appendix, p. 110).

[2] ταις χρειαις ℵABD[3]LP is no doubt the correct reading, but there is a curious variant ταις μνειαις in DFG, some MSS. known to Theod. Mops., and in the Lat. transl. of Origen, where, after usibus (= χρειαις) sanctorum communicantes, we read Memini in latinis exemplaribus magis haberi, memoriis sanctorum communicantes. Evidently, as S. and H. remark, this must have arisen at a time when the αγιοι were no longer the members of the community and fellow-Christians whose bodily wants required to be relieved, but the "saints" of the past whose lives were to be commemorated.

affection (στοργή); it is to be warm, spontaneous, constant. τῇ τιμῇ ἀλλήλους προηγούμενοι: "in honour preferring one another". This, which is the rendering of both our English versions, is a good Pauline idea (Phil. ii. 3), but gives προηγούμενοι a meaning not found elsewhere. Hence others render: "in showing honour—i.e., to those whose χαρίσματα entitle them to respect in the Church—giving each other a lead": each, so to speak, being readier than the other to recognise and honour God's gifts in a brother. In this sense, however, προηγούμενοι would rather take the genitive (see Liddell and Scott, who seem, nevertheless, to adopt this rendering); and probably the former, which involves only a natural extension of the meaning of the word, is to be preferred.

Ver. 11. τῇ σπουδῇ μὴ ὀκνηροί: σπουδή occurs twelve times in the N.T., and is translated in our A.V. seven different ways. It denotes the moral earnestness with which one should give himself to his vocation. In this Christians are not to be backward: Acts ix. 38. τῷ πνεύματι ζέοντες: the same figure is frequent in the classics, and we still speak of the blood "boiling". The spiritual temperature is to be high in the Christian community: cf. 1 Thess. v. 20, Acts xviii. 25. If we are to distinguish at all, the πνεῦμα meant is the Spirit of God, though it is that spirit as bestowed upon man. τῷ κυρίῳ δουλεύοντες: we can point to no special connection for this clause. Perhaps the thought is on the same lines as in 1 Cor. xii. 4 f.: there are spiritual gifts of all kinds, but one service in which they are all ex-

hausted—the service of Christ—and in that we must be constantly engaged.

Ver. 12. τῇ ἐλπίδι χαίροντες: the hope in which they are to rejoice is that of Christians: cf. v. 2. The meaning is practically the same as in that passage, but the mental representation is not. τῇ ἐλπίδι is not = ἐπ' ἐλπίδι there, but in a line with the other datives here: in point of hope, rejoicing. τῇ θλίψει ὑπομένοντες: ὑπομ. might have been construed with the accusative (τὴν θλῖψιν), but the absolute use of it, as here, is common (see Mt. x. 22, Jas. v. 11, 1 Pet. ii. 20), and its employment in this instance enables the writer to conform the clause grammatically to the others. τῇ προσευχῇ προσκαρτεροῦντες: cf. Col. iv. 2, Acts i. 14, ii. 42. The strong word suggests not only the constancy with which they are to pray, but the effort that is needed to maintain a habit so much above nature.

Ver. 13. ταῖς χρείαις τῶν ἁγίων κοινωνοῦντες: "the saints" as in viii. 27, 1 Tim. v. 10 are Christians generally. The curious variant ταῖς μνείαις— "taking part in the commemorations of the saints"—dates from an age at which "the saints" were no longer Christians in general, but a select few, as a rule martyrs or confessors in the technical sense. Weiss asserts that the active sense of κοινωνεῖν, to communicate or impart, is foreign to the N.T., but it is difficult to maintain this if we look to such examples as this and Gal. vi. 6, and also to the use of κοινωνία in 2 Cor. ix. 13 (where ἁπλότητι τῆς κοινωνίας εἰς αὐτοὺς means the liberality of your contribution to them), and Heb. xiii. 16, where κοινωνία is a synonym of εὐποιία,

ἁγίων κοινωνοῦντες, τὴν φιλοξενίαν διώκοντες. 14. εὐλογεῖτε τοὺς
διώκοντας ὑμᾶς· εὐλογεῖτε, καὶ μὴ [1] καταρᾶσθε. 15. Χαίρειν μετὰ [1 Luke vi. 28.]
χαιρόντων, καὶ [1] κλαίειν μετὰ κλαιόντων. 16. τὸ αὐτὸ εἰς ἀλλήλους
φρονοῦντες· μὴ τὰ ὑψηλὰ φρονοῦντες, ἀλλὰ τοῖς ταπεινοῖς συναπαγόμενοι. μὴ γίνεσθε φρόνιμοι παρ' ἑαυτοῖς· 17. μηδενὶ κακὸν ἀντὶ
κακοῦ ἀποδιδόντες. προνοούμενοι καλὰ ἐνώπιον πάντων ἀνθρώπων·

---

[1] και before κλαιειν om. ℵBD¹F; ins. AD³LP 47. W. and H. put in marg.;
Weiss in text, regarding its omission as merely accidental.

and certainly active. **τὴν φιλοξενίαν
διώκοντες**: to devote oneself to enter-
taining them when they were strangers
was one chief way of distributing to the
needs of the saints. Hospitality, in the
sense of the N.T. (Heb. xiii. 2, 1 Pet. iv.
9), is not akin to "keeping company,"
or "open house"; it is a form of charity
much needed by travelling, exiled, or
persecuted Christians. The terms in
which it is spoken of in Clem. Rom.
(quoted in S. and H.: **διὰ πίστιν καὶ
φιλοξενίαν ἐδόθη αὐτῷ**—i.e., Abraham—
υἱὸς ἐν γήρᾳ: or, **διὰ φιλοξενίαν καὶ
εὐσέβειαν Λὼτ ἐσώθη**) may seem ex-
travagant; but the key to them, and to
all the apostolic emphasis on the subject,
is to be found in Matt. xxv. 34-36.
Ver. 14. **εὐλογεῖτε τοὺς διώκοντας,
εὐλ. κ. μὴ καταρᾶσθε**: not a quotation
of Mt. v. 44, but probably a reminiscence
of the same saying of Jesus. The change
in construction from participle to imperative, the participle being resumed in the
next sentence, suggests that the form of
the sentence was *given* to Paul—i.e., he
was consciously using borrowed words
without modifying them to suit the
sentence he had begun on his own
account. It may be that when Paul
said **διώκοντες** in ver. 13, the other
sense of the word passed through his
mind and prompted ver. 14; but even
if we could be sure of this (which we
cannot) we should not understand either
verse a whit better.
Ver. 15. **χαίρειν μετὰ χαιρόντων
κ.τ.λ.** The infinites give the expression
the character of a watchword (see Hofmann in Weiss). For the grammar see
Winer, 397, n. 6. To weep with those that
weep is easier than to rejoice with those
who rejoice. Those who rejoice neither
need, expect, nor feel grateful for sympathy in the same degree as those who
weep.
Ver. 16. **τὸ αὐτὸ εἰς ἀλλήλους
φρονοῦντες**: here the Apostle returns
to his own grammar (or disregard of

grammar), and holds to it till ver. 19,
when he changes to the imperative (**μὴ
δότε**) with which he concludes (ver. 21
μὴ νικῶ, νίκα). **τὸ αὐτὸ φρονεῖν**, xv. 5,
is a favourite expression, best explained
by reference to Phil. ii. 2, iv. 2, 2 Cor.
xiii. 11. The idea is that of loving unanimity, and the **εἰς ἀλλήλους** points to
the active manifestation of this temper
in all the mutual relations of Christians.
"Let each so enter into the feelings and
desires of the other as to be of one mind
with him" (Gifford). It is a more
abstract expression of the Golden Rule,
Mt. vii. 12. The negatives which follow
introduce explanatory clauses: they forbid what would destroy the unanimity of
love. **μὴ τὰ ὑψηλὰ φρονοῦντες**: see on
ver. 3 above and xi. 21. Selfish ambition in the Church is fatal to perfect
mutual consideration. **τοῖς ταπεινοῖς
συναπαγόμενοι**. Elsewhere in the N.T.
(seven times) **ταπεινὸς** is only found in
the masculine, and so some would render
it here: condescend to *men* of low estate;
let yourself be carried along in the line of
their interests, not counting such people
beneath you. *Cf*. Gal. ii. 13, 2 Pet. iii. 17.
The bad connotation of **συναπάγεσθαι** in
both these places is due not to itself, but
to the context. The contrast with **τὰ
ὑψηλὰ** leads others to take **τοῖς ταπεινοῖς**
as neuter: and so the R.V. has it, condescend to things that are lowly. Certainty on such points must always be
personal rather than scientific; the first
of the two alternatives impresses me as
much more in harmony with the nature
of the words used than the other. For the
idea *cf*. Wordsworth's sonnet addressed
to Milton . . . "and yet thy heart the
lowliest duties on herself did lay". **μὴ
γίνεσθε φρόνιμοι κ.τ.λ.** Prov. iii. 7. Be
not men of mind in your own conceit.
It is difficult to put our judgment into
a common stock, and estimate another's
as impartially as our own; but love requires it, and without it there is no such
thing as **τὸ αὐτὸ εἰς ἀλλήλους φρονεῖν**.

m Matt.
xxiv. 24;
Gal. iv.15.

18. εἰ ^mδυνατόν, τὸ ἐξ ὑμῶν, μετὰ πάντων ἀνθρώπων εἰρηνεύοντες.

19. Μὴ ἑαυτοὺς ἐκδικοῦντες, ἀγαπητοί, ἀλλὰ δότε τόπον τῇ ὀργῇ·

γέγραπται γάρ, "'Εμοὶ ἐκδίκησις, ἐγὼ ἀνταποδώσω, λέγει Κύριος".

20. ἐὰν οὖν¹ πεινᾷ ὁ ἐχθρός σου, ψώμιζε αὐτόν. ἐὰν διψᾷ, πότιζε

n 2 Tim. iii.
6.

αὐτόν· τοῦτο γὰρ ποιῶν, ἄνθρακας πυρὸς ⁿσωρεύσεις ἐπὶ τὴν κεφαλὴν

αὐτοῦ. 21. μὴ νικῶ ὑπὸ τοῦ κακοῦ, ἀλλὰ νίκα ἐν τῷ ἀγαθῷ τὸ κακόν.

---

¹ εαν ουν D³ gr. L, etc.; εαν alone D¹FD³ lat.; αλλα εαν ℵABP vulg. and all edd.
For την κεφαλην Weiss would read with B alone της κεφαλης.

Ver. 17. From this point the subject treated is chiefly the Christian's attitude to enemies. μηδενὶ κακὸν ἀντὶ κακοῦ ἀποδ. μηδενὶ is emphatic: to no one, Christian or un-Christian. Nothing can ever justify revenge. Cf. 1 Pet. iii. 9, but especially Matt. v. 38-48. προνοούμενοι καλὰ ἐνώπιον κ.τ.λ. Prov. iii. 4, LXX. 2 Cor. viii. 21. What the words mean in Prov. iii. 4 is not clear; they are not a translation of the Hebrew. In 2 Cor. viii. 21 the idea is that of taking precautions to obviate possible slanders; here it is apparently that of living in such a way as not to provoke enmity, or give any occasion for breach of peace. ἐνώπιον: construed with καλά. πάντων has the same kind of emphasis as μηδενί: Requite evil to *no* one; let your conduct be such as *all* must approve.

Ver. 18. εἰ δυνατόν: cf. Matt. xxiv. 24. τὸ ἐξ ὑμῶν: for what depends on you. Cf. i. 15. Over others' conduct we have no control; but the initiative in disturbing the peace is never to lie with the Christian.

Ver. 19. μὴ ἑαυτοὺς ἐκδικοῦντες, ἀγαπητοί. Even when the Christian has been wronged he is not to take the law into his own hand, and right or vindicate himself. For ἐκδικεῖν see Lc. xviii. 3, 5. ἀγαπητοί is striking, and must have some reason: either the extreme difficulty, of which Paul was sensible, of living up to this rule; or possibly some condition of affairs in the Church at Rome, which made the exhortation peculiarly pertinent to the readers, and therefore craved this affectionate address to deprecate, as it were, the "wild justice" with which the natural man is always ready to plead his cause. ἀλλὰ δότε τόπον τῇ ὀργῇ: the wrath spoken of, as the following words show, is that of God; to give place to God's wrath means to leave room for it, not to take God's proper work out of His hands. For the expression cf. Lc. xiv. 9, Sir. xiii. 22, xix. 17, xxxviii. 12, Eph. iv. 27.

For ἡ ὀργὴ used thus absolutely of God's wrath cf. v. 9, 1 Thess. ii. 16. The idea is not that instead of executing vengeance ourselves we are to abandon the offender to the more tremendous vengeance of God; but this—that God, not injured men or those who believe themselves such, is the maintainer of moral order in the world, and that the righting of wrong is to be committed to Him. Cf. especially 1 Pet. ii. 23. γέγραπται γάρ: Deut. xxxii. 35. Paul gives the sense of the Hebrew, not at all that of the LXX, though his language is reminiscent of the latter (ἐν ἡμέρα ἐκδικήσεως ἀνταποδώσω). It is singular that Heb. x. 30 has the quotation in exactly the same form as Paul. So has the Targum of Onkelos; but whether there is any mutual dependence of these three, or whether, independent of all, the verse was current in this form, we cannot tell. The λέγει κύριος (cf. xiv. 11) is supplied by Paul.

Ver. 20. ἀλλά: On the contrary, as opposed to self-avenging, and even to the merely passive resignation of one's case to God. ἐὰν πεινᾷ κ.τ.λ. Prov. xxv. 21 f. exactly as in LXX. The meaning of "heaping burning coals on his head" is hardly open to doubt. It must refer to the burning pain of shame and remorse which the man feels whose hostility is repaid by love. This is the only kind of vengeance the Christian is at liberty to contemplate. Many, however, have referred to 4 Esdr. xvi. 54 (*Non dicat peccator se non peccasse; quoniam carbones ignis comburet super caput ejus, qui dicit: non peccavi coram Domino Deo et gloria ipsius*), and argued that the coals of fire are the Divine judgments which the sinner will bring on himself unless he repents under the constraint of such love. But (1) there is nothing said here about the essential condition, "unless he repents"; this is simply imported; and (2) the aim of the Christian's love to his enemy is thus

XIII. 1. ΠΑΣΑ ψυχὴ ἐξουσίαις ὑπερεχούσαις ὑποτασσέσθω. οὐ
γάρ ἐστιν ἐξουσία εἰ μὴ ἀπὸ¹ Θεοῦ· αἱ δὲ οὖσαι ἐξουσίαι ὑπὸ τοῦ

¹ ει μη απο θεου D¹F, Orig. For απο ℵABD³LP read υπο; and so all edd.
εξουσιαι after ουσαι om. ℵABD¹F and all edd.   υπο του θεου; om. του ℵ¹ADFP
and all edd.

made to be the bringing down of Divine
judgment on him — which is not only
absurd in itself, but in direct antagonism
to the spirit of the passage.

Ver. 21. μὴ νικῶ: the absence of any
connecting particle gives the last verse
the character of a summary: in a word,
be not overcome by evil. ὑπὸ τοῦ κακοῦ
= by the evil your enemy inflicts. The
Christian would be overcome by evil if it
were able to compel him to avenge himself by repaying it in kind. Wrong is
not defeated but doubly victorious when
it is repelled with its own weapons; we
can only overcome it ἐν τῷ ἀγαθῷ through
the good we do to our adversary, turning
him so from an enemy into a friend.
Vincit malos, says Seneca, pertinax
bonitas: Wetst. accumulates similar examples from classical writers. The ἐν
in ἐν τῷ ἀγαθῷ is probably = ב: it might
be explained as instrumental, or rendered
"at the cost of".

CHAPTER XIII. There is not a word
to indicate how the transition is made
from the discussion of the duties of
Christians as members of one body, especially the duties of humility and love
in chap. xii., to the special subject which
meets us in chap. xiii. — the duty of
Christians in relation to the civil
authorities. There is nothing exactly like
vers. 1-7 elsewhere in Paul's epistles,
and it is difficult not to believe that he
had some particular reason for treating
the question here. The Christians in
Rome, though mainly Gentile, as this
epistle proves, were closely connected
with the Jews, and the Jews were no-
toriously bad subjects. Many of them
held, on the ground of Deut. xvii. 15,
that to acknowledge a Gentile ruler
was itself sinful; and the spirit which
prompted Pharisees to ask, Is it lawful
to give tribute to Cæsar or not? Shall
we give or shall we not give? (Mark xii.
14) had no doubt its representatives in
Rome also. As believers in the Messiah,
"in another King, one Jesus" (Acts xvii.
7), even Christians of Gentile origin may
have been open to the impulses of this
same spirit; and unbalanced minds, then
as in all ages, might be disposed to find

in the loyalty which was due to Christ
alone, an emancipation from all subjection to inferior powers. There is here an
apparent point of contact between Christianity and anarchism, and it may have
been the knowledge of some such movement of mind in the Church at Rome
that made Paul write as he did. There
is perhaps nothing in the passage which
is not already given in our Lord's word,
"Render to Cæsar the things that are
Cæsar's, and to God the things that are
God's"; yet nothing can be more worthy
of admiration than the soberness with
which a Christian idealist like Paul lays
down the Divine right of the state. The
use made of the passage to prove the
duty of "passive obedience," or "the
right divine of kings to govern wrong,"
is beside the mark; the Apostle was not
thinking of such things at all. What is
in his mind is that the organisation of
human society, with its distinction of
higher and lower ranks, is essential for
the preservation of moral order, and
therefore, one might add, for the existence of the Kingdom of God itself; so
that no Christian is at liberty to revolt
against that organisation. The state is
of God, and the Christian has to recognise its Divine right in the persons and
requirements in which it is presented
to him: that is all. Whether in any
given case—say in England in 1642—
the true representative of the State was
to be found in the king or in the Com-
mons, Paul, of course, does not enable
us to say. Neither does he say anything bearing on the Divine right of
insurrection. When he wrote, no doubt,
Nero had not yet begun to rage against
the Christians, and the imperial authorities had usually protected the Apostle
himself against popular violence, whether
Jewish or pagan; but even of this we
must not suppose him to be taking any
special account. He had, indeed, had
other experiences (Acts xvi. 37, 2 Cor.
xi. 25 ff.). But the whole discussion presupposes normal conditions: law and its
representatives are of God, and as such
are entitled to all honour and obedience
from Christians.

Ver. 1. πᾶσα ψυχὴ is a Hebraism:

Θεοῦ τεταγμέναι εἰσίν. 2. ὥστε ὁ ἀντιτασσόμενος τῇ ἐξουσίᾳ, τῇ
a Acts vii.   τοῦ Θεοῦ ᵃ διαταγῇ ἀνθέστηκεν· οἱ δὲ ἀνθεστηκότες, ἑαυτοῖς κρίμα
53.   λήψονται. 3. οἱ γὰρ ἄρχοντες οὐκ εἰσὶ φόβος τῶν ἀγαθῶν ἔργων,
ἀλλὰ τῶν κακῶν.[1] θέλεις δὲ μὴ φοβεῖσθαι τὴν ἐξουσίαν; τὸ ἀγαθὸν
ποίει, καὶ ἕξεις ἔπαινον ἐξ αὐτῆς· 4. Θεοῦ γὰρ διάκονός ἐστι σοὶ
εἰς τὸ ἀγαθόν. ἐὰν δὲ τὸ κακὸν ποιῇς, φοβοῦ· οὐ γὰρ εἰκῆ τὴν
μάχαιραν φορεῖ· Θεοῦ γὰρ διάκονός ἐστιν, ἔκδικος εἰς ὀργὴν τῷ τὸ

---

[1] των αγαθων εργων αλλα των κακων D³ gr. L, etc.; τω αγαθω εργω α. τω κακω
ℵABD¹F. The vulg. and lat. fathers have *non sunt timori boni operis*, from which
W. and H. deduce another reading του αγαθου εργου. They suspect a primitive
error, and Hort favours the correction τῷ αγαθοεργῳ, comparing 1 Tim. vi. 18.

cf. Acts ii. 43, iii. 23, and chap. ii. 9.
For ἐξουσίαις *cf.* Luke xii. 11: it is
exactly like "authorities" in English—
abstract for concrete. ὑπερεχούσαις describes the authorities as being actually
in a position of superiority. *Cf.* 1 P.
ii. 13, and 2 Macc. iii. 11 (ἀνδρὸς ἐν
ὑπεροχῇ κειμένου). οὐ γὰρ ἔστιν ἐξουσία
εἰ μὴ ὑπὸ θεοῦ: ὑπὸ is the correct reading (ℵAB), not ἀπό. Weiss compares
Bar. iv. 27. ἔσται γὰρ ὑμῶν ὑπὸ τοῦ
ἐπάγοντος μνεία. It is by God's act
and will alone that there is such a
thing as an authority, or magistrate;
and those that actually exist have
been appointed—set in their place—by
Him. With αἱ δὲ οὖσαι the Apostle
passes from the abstract to the concrete;
the persons and institutions in which for
the time authority had its seat, are before
his mind—in other words, the Empire
with all its grades of officials from the
Emperor down. In itself, and quite apart
from its relation to the Church, this
system had a Divine right to be. It did
not need to be legitimated by any special
relation to the Church; quite as truly as
the Church it existed *Dei gratia*.
Ver. 2. ὥστε *cf.* vii. 4, 12. The
conclusion is that he who sets himself
against the authorities withstands what
has been instituted by God: διαταγῇ
(Acts vii. 53) recalls τεταγμέναι, ver. 1.
The κρίμα, *i.e.*, the judgment or condemnation which those who offer such
resistance shall receive, is of course a
Divine one—that is the nerve of the
whole passage; but most commentators
seem to regard it as coming through the
human authority resisted. This is by no
means clear; even a successful defiance
of authority, which involved no human
κρίμα, would according to Paul ensure
punishment from God. For λήψονται
κρίμα *cf.* Mark xii. 40, Jas. iii. 1:
where also God's judgment alone is in

view. But to say that it is God's judgment only is not to say that it is eternal
damnation. There are many ways in
which God's condemnation of sin is
expressed and executed.
Ver. 3. οἱ γὰρ ἄρχοντες κ.τ.λ. The
γὰρ can only be connected in a forced
and artificial way with the clause which
immediately precedes: it really introduces the reason for a frank and unreserved acceptance of that view of
"authorities" which the Apostle is laying down. It is as if he said: Recognise
the Divine right of the State, for its
representatives are not a terror—an object of dread—to the good work, but to
the bad. φόβος as in Isa. viii. 13. It
is implied that those to whom he speaks
will always be identified with the good
work, and so have the authorities on
their side: it is taken for granted also
that the State will not act in violation of
its own idea, and identify itself with the
bad. θέλεις δὲ μὴ φοβεῖσθαι κ.τ.λ. This
is most expressive when read as an interrogation, though some prefer to take
it as an assertion: that is, to regard
Paul as assuming that the reader does
not want to be afraid of the magistrate,
rather than as inquiring whether he does
or not. To escape fear, τὸ ἀγαθὸν ποίει:
do what is (legally and morally) good.
Ver. 4. Θεοῦ γὰρ διάκονός ἐστιν σοὶ
εἰς τὸ ἀγαθόν. διάκονός is feminine
agreeing with ἐξουσία, which is "almost
personified" (Sanday and Headlam).
The σοὶ is not immediately dependent
on διάκονός, as if the State were conceived as directly serving the person;
the State serves God, with good in view
as the end to be secured by its ministry,
viz., the maintenance of the moral order
in society; and this situation is one the
benefit of which redounds to the individual. ἐὰν δὲ τὸ κακὸν ποιῇς, φοβοῦ:
only when the individual does that which

κακὸν πράσσοντι. 5. διὸ ἀνάγκη ὑποτάσσεσθαι, οὐ μόνον διὰ τὴν
ὀργήν, ἀλλὰ καὶ διὰ τὴν [b] συνείδησιν. 6. διὰ τοῦτο γὰρ καὶ φόρους b 1 Cor. x.
τελεῖτε · λειτουργοὶ γὰρ Θεοῦ εἰσιν, εἰς αὐτὸ τοῦτο προσκαρτεροῦντες.   25, 27; 1
Pet. ii. 19.
7. ἀπόδοτε οὖν [1] πᾶσι τὰς ὀφειλάς · τῷ τὸν φόρον, τὸν φόρον. τῷ

[1] αποδοτε ουν ℵ³D³FLP ; om. ουν ℵ¹ABD¹ and all edd.

is contrary to the end set before the State by God—commits τὸ κακὸν, which frustrates τὸ ἀγαθὸν—need he fear : but then he must fear. οὐ γὰρ εἰκῆ : for not for nothing, but for serious use, does the ruler wear the sword. For εἰκῆ cf. 1 Cor. xv. 2, Gal. iii. 4. φορεῖ is wear, rather than bear : the sword was carried habitually, if not by, then before the higher magistrates, and symbolised the power of life and death which they had in their hands. "The Apostle in this passage," says Gifford, "expressly vindicates the right of capital punishment as divinely entrusted to the magistrate". But "expressly" is perhaps too much, and Paul could not deliberately vindicate what no one had assailed. He did, indeed, on a memorable occasion (later than this) express his readiness to die if his life had been forfeited to the law (Acts xxv. 11) ; but to know that if an individual sets himself to subvert the moral order of the world, its representatives can proceed to extremities against him (on the ground, apparently, that it, as of God's institution, is of priceless value to mankind, whereas he in his opposition to it is of no moral worth at all) is not to vindicate capital punishment as it exists in the law or practice of any given society. When the words θεοῦ γὰρ διάκονός ἐστιν are repeated, it is the punitive ministry of the magistrate which is alone in view. ἔκδικος εἰς ὀργὴν : an avenger for wrath. ὀργὴ in the N.T. almost always (as here) means the wrath of God. It occurs eleven times in Romans : always so. The exceptions are Eph. iv. 31, Col. iii. 8, 1 Tim. ii. 8, Jas. i. 19 f. τῷ τὸ κακὸν πράσσοντι = to him who works at evil. The process is presented in πράσσειν rather than the result. Cf. i. 32.

Ver. 5 f. διὸ ἀνάγκη ὑποτάσσεσθαι : there is a twofold necessity for submission—an external one, in the wrath of God which comes on resistance ; an internal one, in conscience. Even apart from the consequences of disobedience conscience recognises the Divine right and function of the ἐξουσία and freely submits to it. διὰ τοῦτο γὰρ καὶ φόρους

τελεῖτε. διὰ τοῦτο seems to refer to the moral necessity to which appeal has been already made in διὰ τὴν συνείδησιν. It is because conscience recognises the moral value of the State as an ordinance of God that we pay taxes. φόρος is often used of the tribute paid by a subject nation : Neh. v. 4, 1 Macc. viii. 4, Lc. xx. 22 ; but here is probably used indefinitely of any imposts made for the support of the Government. λειτουργοὶ γὰρ θεοῦ εἰσίν : the use of λειτουργοί here instead of διάκονοι emphasises *the official character* of the service which they render. In the LXX λειτουργεῖν is the regular rendering of שֵׁרֵת, and therefore refers frequently to the service of the priests and Levites, a usage the influence of which is seen in chap. xv. 16 and Phil. ii. 17 ; but this was by no means exclusively the case in the O.T. (2 Sam. xiii. 18, 2 Kings x. 5) nor is it so in the New (chap. xv. 27, Phil. ii. 25, 30). It is not a priestly character that the word assigns to the magistracy, but only an official character ; they are in their place by God's appointment for the public good. εἰς αὐτὸ τοῦτο means "to this very end"—the end described in vers. 3 and 4. As προσκαρτεροῦντες is elsewhere construed with the dative (Acts i. 14, vi. 4, chap. xii. 12) it seems necessary here to take εἰς τὸ αὐτὸ with what precedes, and προσκ. by itself as, *e.g.*, in Num. xiii. 21 : spending all their time on the work.

Ver. 7. At this point Weiss begins a new paragraph, but W. and H. make ver. 7 the conclusion of the first part of this chapter. In view of the close connection between vers. 7 and 8 (*cf.* ὀφειλάς, ὀφείλετε) it is better not to make too decided a break at either place. All the words in ver. 7, φόρος, τέλος, φόβος, τιμή, do indeed imply duties to superiors, and seem therefore to continue and to sum up the content of vers. 1-6 ; but ver. 8, in which μηδενὶ μηδὲν ὀφείλετε seems expressly written as the negative counterpart to ἀπόδοτε πᾶσι τὰς ὀφειλάς in ver. 7, introduces at the same time a wider subject—that of the duties of all

c Matt. xvii.
25.
τὸ ᶜτέλος, τὸ τέλος· τῷ τὸν φόβον, τὸν φόβον· τῷ τὴν τιμὴν, τὴν τιμήν. 8. Μηδενὶ μηδὲν ὀφείλετε,[1] εἰ μὴ τὸ ἀγαπᾶν ἀλλήλους· ὁ γὰρ ἀγαπῶν τὸν ἕτερον, νόμον πεπλήρωκε. 9. τὸ γὰρ, "Οὐ μοι-

d Ch. xv. 2;
Gal. v. 14;
Eph. iv.
25.
χεύσεις, οὐ φονεύσεις, οὐ κλέψεις, οὐ ψευδομαρτυρήσεις,[2] οὐκ ἐπι-θυμήσεις," καὶ εἴ τις ἑτέρα ἐντολή, ἐν τούτῳ τῷ λόγῳ ἀνακεφαλαιοῦται, ἐν τῷ, "Ἀγαπήσεις τὸν ᵈπλησίον σου ὡς ἑαυτόν". 10. ἡ ἀγάπη τῷ

e Ch. xi.
12, 25.
πλησίον κακὸν οὐκ ἐργάζεται· ᵉπλήρωμα οὖν νόμου ἡ ἀγάπη.

[1] οφειλετε seems the only possible reading, yet is not given by any authority. οφειλητε ℵ³; οφειλοντες ℵ¹, Orig.; οφιλειτε B. For αγαπαν αλληλους ℵABDFP read αλληλους αγαπαν; so all edd.

[2] ου ψευδομαρτυρησεις om. ABDFL and all edd. The insertion is made by ℵP, etc., to complete the reference to the decalogue. εν τω before αγαπησεις is ins. by ℵADLP; om. by BF latt., Orig.-interp. It is bracketed by Lachm., Treg., Alf., and W. and H.; omitted entirely by Weiss. Instead of εαυτον FLP read σεαυτον with ℵABD.

individuals toward each other. τῷ τὸν φόρον τὸν φόρον : this is quite intelligible, but nothing can make it grammatical : see Winer, p. 737. For the distinction of φόρος and τέλος see Trench, *Syn.*, p. 392. For φόβος and τιμή 1 Pet. ii. 17.

Ver. 8. εἰ μὴ τὸ ἀλλήλους ἀγαπᾶν = except mutual love. This is the *debitum immortale* of Bengel; *hoc enim et quotidie solvere et semper debere expedit nobis* (Origen). ὁ γὰρ ἀγαπῶν τὸν ἕτερον : he who loves his neighbour, the other with whom he has to do. *Cf.* ii. 1, 21 (Weiss). νόμον πεπλήρωκεν = has done all that law requires. From what follows it is clear that Paul is thinking of the Mosaic law; it was virtually the only thing in the world to which he could apply the word νόμος, or which he could use to illustrate that word. The relation of chaps. xii. and xiii. to the Gospels makes it very credible that Paul had here in his mind the words of our Lord in Matt. xxii. 34 ff.

Ver. 9. τὸ γὰρ Οὐ μοιχεύσεις. *Cf.* viii. 26. The order of the commandments here is different from that in Exod. xx. or Deut. v. (Hebrew), but it is the same as in Luke xviii. 20, and (so far) in James ii. 11. This order is also found in Cod. B. of the LXX in Deut. v. καὶ εἴ τις ἑτέρα ἐντολή : this shows that the enumeration does not aim at completeness, and that the insertion in some MSS. of οὐ ψευδομαρτυρήσεις, to complete the second table, is beside the mark. ἀνακεφαλαιοῦται : it is summed up—the scattered particulars are resumed and brought to one. The only other instance of this word in the N.T. (Eph. i. 10) illustrates the present one, though

the meaning is not exactly the same. ἀγαπήσεις τὸν πλησίον σου κ.τ.λ. In Lev. xix. 18 this is given as a summary of various laws, mostly precepts enjoining humanity, in various relations; by our Lord (in Matt. xxii. 39) and by Paul (here and in Gal. v. 14) an ampler, indeed an unlimited range, is given to it. Its supreme position too seems to be what is indicated in James ii. 8 by calling it νόμος βασιλικός.

Ver. 10. ἡ ἀγάπη . . . κακὸν οὐκ ἐργάζεται. This is all that is formally required by the law as quoted above (οὐ μοιχεύσεις, etc.) : therefore love is πλήρωμα νόμου, law's fulfilment. Of course love is an inspiration rather than a restraint, and transcends law as embodied in merely negative commandments; but the form in which the law actually existed determines the form in which the Apostle expresses himself. It is apparent once more that νόμος is the Mosaic law, and not law in general; it is from it the prohibitions are derived on the ground of which the Apostle argues, and to it therefore we must apply his conclusion, πλήρωμα οὖν νόμου ἡ ἀγάπη.

Vv. 11-14. In the closing verses of the chapter Paul enforces this exhortation to mutual love as the fulfilling of the law by reference to the approaching Parousia. We must all appear (and who can tell how soon ?) before the judgment-seat of Christ, that every one may receive the things done in the body : if the awe and the inspiration of that great truth descend upon our hearts, we shall feel how urgent the Apostle's exhortation is. καὶ τοῦτο : *cf.* 1 Cor. vi. 6, 8. In classical writers καὶ ταῦτα is commoner. It

11. ΚΑΙ τοῦτο, εἰδότες τὸν καιρὸν, ὅτι ὥρα ἡμᾶς[1] ἤδη ἐξ ὕπνου
ἐγερθῆναι. νῦν γὰρ ἐγγύτερον ἡμῶν ἡ σωτηρία, ἢ ὅτε ἐπιστεύσαμεν.
12. ἡ νὺξ προέκοψεν, ἡ δὲ ἡμέρα ἤγγικεν· ἀποθώμεθα οὖν τὰ ἔργα
τοῦ [f]σκότους, καὶ ἐνδυσώμεθα[2] τὰ ὅπλα τοῦ [g]φωτός. 13. ὡς ἐν ἡμέρᾳ,
εὐσχημόνως περιπατήσωμεν, μὴ κώμοις καὶ μέθαις, μὴ κοίταις καὶ
ἀσελγείαις, μὴ ἔριδι καὶ ζήλῳ· 14. ἀλλ᾽ ἐνδύσασθε τὸν Κύριον Ἰησοῦν
Χριστὸν,[3] καὶ τῆς σαρκὸς [h]πρόνοιαν μὴ ποιεῖσθε εἰς ἐπιθυμίας.

[f] 1 Cor iv.
5; Eph.
v. 8, 11;
vi. 12; 1
Thess. v.
4 f.
[g] Eph. v.
8 f.; 13.
[h] Acts xxiv.
2.

[1] ημας DEFGL; but א¹ABCP give υμας. υμας is put in text by Weiss, W. and
H., and Tischdf.; and by W. and H. and Treg. in margin. All put ηδη with
אABC before the pronoun.

[2] For και ενδυσωμεθα read ενδυσωμεθα δε with ABC¹D¹P. W. and H. bracket δε;
א¹ and a MS. of Sah. have neither και nor δε. For οπλα AD read εργα. μη εριδι
και ζηλω; B reads the plural ερισι κ. ζηλοις, which W. and H. put in margin, but
it is probably a case of conforming instinctively to the other clauses; cf. the converse
change of plural (αι διαθηκαι) into singular in note [2], page 657 (also in B).

[3] For κυριον I. X. B and Clem. give Χριστον Ιησουν without κυριον, which W.
and H. print in margin, keeping κ. I. X. in text.

sums up all that precedes, but especially vers. 8-10. εἰδότες τὸν καιρόν: ὁ καιρός is not "the time" abstractly, but the time they lived in with its moral import, its critical place in the working out of God's designs. It is their time regarded as having a character of its own, full of significance for them. This is unfolded in ὅτι ὥρα ἤδη κ.τ.λ. ἤδη (without waiting longer) is to be construed with ἐγερθῆναι: "it is time for you at once to awake" (Gifford). No Christian should be asleep, yet the ordinary life of all is but drowsy compared with what it should be, and with what it would be, if the Christian hope were perpetually present to us. νῦν γὰρ ἐγγύτερον ἡμῶν ἡ σωτηρία: for now is salvation nearer us than when we believed. ἡ σωτηρία has here the transcendent eschatological sense: it is the final and complete deliverance from sin and death, and the reception into the heavenly kingdom of our Lord Jesus Christ. This salvation was always near, to the faith of the Apostles; and with the lapse of time it became, of course, nearer. Yet it has often been remarked that in his later epistles Paul seems to contemplate not merely the possibility, but the probability, that he himself would not live to see it. See 2 Cor. v. 1-10, Phil. i. 23. ὅτε ἐπιστεύσαμεν: when we became Christians, 1 Cor. iii. 5, xv. 2, Gal. ii. 16.

Ver. 12. ἡ νὺξ προέκοψεν: the true day dawns only when Christ appears; at present it is night, though a night that has run much of its course. ἀποθώμεθα οὖν τὰ ἔργα τοῦ σκότους. Things that can only be done in the dark—that cannot bear the light of day—are therefore to be put away by the Christian. For ἀποθώμεθα (properly of dress) cf. Jas. i. 21, 1 Pet. ii. 1, Heb. xii. 1. τὰ ὅπλα τοῦ φωτός: for τὰ ὅπλα see on chap. vi. 13, Eph. vi. 11, 1 Thess. v. 8. The idea is that the Christian's life is not a sleep, but a battle. τὰ ὅπλα τοῦ φωτός does not mean "shining armour"; but (on the analogy of τὰ ἔργα τοῦ σκότους) such armour as one can wear when the great day dawns, and we would appear on the Lord's side in the fight. An allusion to the last great battle against the armies of anti-Christ is too remote, and at variance with Paul's use of the figure elsewhere.

Ver. 13. ὡς ἐν ἡμέρᾳ: as one walks in the day, so let us walk εὐσχημόνως. The same adverb is found with the same verb in 1 Thess. iv. 2: A.V. in both places "honestly". The meaning is rather "in seemly fashion," "becomingly"; in 1 Cor. xiv. 40 it is rendered "decently," where also regard for decorum (the æsthetic side of morality) is in view. κῶμοι and μέθαι are again found conjoined in Gal. v. 21; ἔρις and ζῆλος in Gal. v. 20 and 1 Cor. iii. 3. W. and H. following B. put ἔρισι καὶ ζήλοις in margin; the plurals in this case as in the others would indicate the various acts or manifestations of excess, whether in self-indulgence or self-will.

Ver. 14. ἀλλὰ ἐνδύσασθε τὸν Κ. Ἰ. Χριστὸν. ἀλλὰ emphasises the contrast between the true Christian life and that

a Acts xviii.
26; Ch.
xv. 7;
Philemon
v. 12, 17.   b Ch. i. 21.

XIV. 1. ΤΟΝ δὲ ἀσθενοῦντα τῇ πίστει ᵃ προσλαμβάνεσθε, μὴ εἰς διακρίσεις ᵇ διαλογισμῶν.   2. Ὃς μὲν πιστεύει φαγεῖν πάντα, ὁ δὲ

which has just been described. The Christian puts on the Lord Jesus Christ, according to Paul's teaching, in baptism (cf. Gal. iii. 27), as the solemn deliberate act in which he identifies himself, by faith, with Christ in His death and resurrection (chap. vi. 3). But the Christian life is not exhausted in this act, which is rather the starting-point for a putting on of Christ in the ethical sense, a "clothing of the soul in the moral disposition and habits of Christ" (Gifford); or as the Apostle himself puts it in vi. 11, a *reckoning* of ourselves to be dead to sin but alive to God in Christ Jesus. Every time we perform an ethical act of this kind we put on the Lord Jesus Christ more fully. But the principle of all such acts is the Spirit of Christ dwelling in us (chaps. vi.-viii.), and it is the essential antagonism of the spirit to the flesh which determines the form of the last words: καὶ τῆς σαρκὸς πρόνοιαν μὴ ποιεῖσθε εἰς ἐπιθυμίας. It is to inquire too curiously if we inquire whether σάρξ here is used in the physiological sense = the body, or in the moral sense = *libidinosa caro* (as Fritzsche argues): the significance of the word in Paul depends on the fact that in experience these two meanings are indubitably if not inseparably related. Taking the flesh as it is, forethought or provision for it—an interest in it which consults for it, and makes it an object—can only have one end, *viz.*, its ἐπιθυμίαι. All such interest therefore is forbidden as inconsistent with putting on the Lord Jesus Christ in the power of the Holy Spirit.

Chapter XIV. 1-XV. 13. One subject is before the Apostle's mind throughout the whole of this section—the relations of "the strong" and "the weak" in the Church at Rome. It is connected in a variety of ways, which are felt rather than expressed, with what precedes. Thus it is pervaded by the same sense of the supreme importance of mutual love among Christians which characterises chaps. xii. and xiii. It makes use, in much the same way as chap. xiii. 11-14, of the impending judgment (xiv. 10), to quicken the sense of individual and personal responsibility. Possibly, too, there is a more formal connection with chap. xiii. Paul has been warning against the indulgence of the flesh (xiii. 14), and this prompts him, by contrast,

to speak of those who by an inadequate appreciation of Christian liberty were practising an "over-scrupulous asceticism". There has been much discussion as to who "the weak" and "the strong" respectively were. The weakness is weakness in respect of faith; the weak man is one who does not fully appreciate what his Christianity means; in particular, he does not see that the soul which has committed itself to Christ for salvation is emancipated from all law but that which is involved in its responsibility to Him. Hence his conscience is fettered by scruples in regard to customs dating from pre-Christian days. The scruples in question here were connected with the use of flesh and wine, and with the religious observance of certain days (whether as fasts or feasts is open to question). Possibly the persons indulging such scruples were Jewish Christians, but they need not have been. They were certainly not legalists in principle, making the observance of the Jewish law or any part of it an essential condition of the Christian salvation; otherwise Paul, as the Epistle to the Galatians shows, would have addressed them in a different tone. Further, the Jewish law does not prescribe abstinence from wine or from animal food; and there is no suggestion here, as in 1 Cor. 8, that the difficulty was about food that had been offered in sacrifice to false gods. Hence the influence at work in the Roman Church in producing this scrupulosity of conscience was probably of Essene origin, and akin to that which Paul subsequently treats with greater severity at Colossae (Col. ii. 16). At Rome the scruples were only scruples, and though there was danger in them because they rested on a defective apprehension of Christianity, they could be tenderly dealt with; at Colossae they had grown into or adapted themselves to a philosophy of religion which was fatal to Christianity; hence the change of tone. But though "the weak" need not have been Jews, the scruples in which their weakness was expressed, had so far Jewish connections and Jewish affinities; and it is probable, from the way in which (chap. xv. 7-13) the discussion of the relations of the weak and the strong passes over into an exhortation to unity between Jew and Gentile in the Church, that the two classifications had a

ἀσθενῶν λάχανα ἐσθίει. 3. ὁ ἐσθίων τὸν μὴ ἐσθίοντα μὴ ᶜ ἐξουθενείτω, c 1 Cor. i.
καὶ ὁ μὴ [1] ἐσθίων τὸν ἐσθίοντα μὴ κρινέτω· ὁ Θεὸς γὰρ αὐτὸν προ- 28; vi. 4;
σελάβετο. 4. σὺ τίς εἶ ὁ κρίνων ἀλλότριον οἰκέτην; τῷ ἰδίῳ κυρίῳ
στήκει ἢ πίπτει· σταθήσεται δέ· δυνατὸς γάρ ἐστιν [2] ὁ Θεὸς στῆσαι
αὐτόν. 5. Ὃς μὲν κρίνει [3] ἡμέραν παρ᾽ ἡμέραν, ὃς δὲ κρίνει πᾶσαν

[1] For και ο μη אᵃᴰ³LP, read with א¹ABCD¹ ο δε μη.

[2] For δυνατος γαρ εστιν אABCD¹F and all edd. read δυνατει γαρ. ο θεος DFL;
but אABCP (and all edd.) ο κυριος.

[3] ος μεν κρινει א³BDFL; ος μεν γαρ κρινει א¹ACP latt. Weiss regards the γαρ
as a mere interpolation (cf. the case in note [1], page 602); Tischdf. inserts; W. and
H. bracket.

general correspondence; the weak would
be Jews or persons under Jewish influence; the strong would be Gentiles,
or persons at least who understood the
Gospel as it was preached to the Gentiles
by Paul.

Ver. 1. τὸν δὲ ἀσθενοῦντα: as Godet
points out, the part. as opposed to
ἀσθενῇ, denotes one who is for the time
feeble, but who may become strong. τῇ
πίστει: in respect of faith, i.e.—in Paul's
sense of the word — in respect of his
saving reliance on Christ and all that it
involves: see above. One is weak in
respect of faith who does not understand
that salvation is of faith from first to last,
and that faith is secured by its own en-
tireness and intensity, not by a timorous
scrupulosity of conscience. προσλαμβά-
νεσθαι is often used of God's gracious
acceptance of men, but also of men
welcoming other men to their society
and friendship, 2 Macc. viii. 1, x. 15.
μὴ εἰς διακρίσεις διαλογισμῶν: not with
a view to deciding (or passing sentence
on) his doubts. The διαλογισμοί are
the movements of thought in the weak
man, whose anxious mind will not be at
peace; no censure of any kind is implied
by the word. The strong, who welcome
him to the fellowship of the Church, are
to do so unreservedly, not with the
purpose of judging and ruling his mind
by their own. For διάκρισεις see 1 Cor.
xii. 10, Heb. v. 14.

Ver. 2. ὃς μέν: cf. ver. 5, ix. 21.
πιστεύει φαγεῖν πάντα: has confidence
to eat all things. See Winer, p. 405.
Gifford quotes Demosthenes, p. 88:
προέσθαι δὲ τὴν προῖκ᾽ οὐκ ἐπίστευσεν:
"he had not confidence, i.e., was too
cautious, to give up the dowry". This
use of πιστεύειν shows that πίστις to
Paul was essentially an ethical principle;
the man who was strong in it had moral
independence, courage, and originality.

ὁ δὲ ἀσθενῶν λάχανα ἐσθίει: it is impossible to suppose that Paul here is "writing quite generally"; he must have had
a motive for saying what he does, and it
can only be found in the fact that he
knew there were Christians in Rome who
abstained from the use of flesh.

Ver. 3. ὁ ἐσθίων . . . μὴ ἐξουθενείτω
κ.τ.λ. Paul passes no sentence on either
party, but warns both of the temptations
to which they are exposed. He who
eats will be inclined to contempt — to
sneer at the scruples of the weak as mere
prejudice or obscurantism; he who does
not eat will be inclined to censoriousness
—to pronounce the strong, who uses his
liberty, no better than he should be.
This censoriousness is forbidden, because
God (ὁ θεὸς is emphatic by position) has
received the strong into the Church, and
therefore his place in it is not to be
questioned.

Ver. 4. σὺ τίς εἶ ὁ κρίνων ἀλλότριον
οἰκέτην; the sharpness of this rebuke (cf.
ix. 20) shows that Paul, with all his love
and consideration for the weak, was alive
to the possibility of a tyranny of the
weak, and repressed it in its beginnings.
It is easy to lapse from scrupulousness
about one's own conduct into Pharisaism
about that of others. οἰκέτης is rare
in the N.T. Paul has no other example,
and may have used it here for the suggestion (which δοῦλος has not) that the
person referred to belonged to the house.
τῷ ἰδίῳ κυρίῳ στήκει ἢ πίπτει: for the
verbs in the moral sense see 1 Cor. x.
12. The dative is dat. comm. It is his
own Lord who is concerned—it is His
interest which is involved and to Him
(not to you) he must answer—as he
stands or falls. σταθήσεται δέ: but he
shall be made to stand, i.e., shall be preserved in the integrity of his Christian
character. δυνατεῖ γὰρ ὁ Κύριος στῆσαι
αὐτόν: for the Lord has power to keep

d Ch. viii.
5.

ἡμέραν. ἕκαστος ἐν τῷ ἰδίῳ νοῒ πληροφορείσθω. 6. ὁ ᵈ φρονῶν τὴν
ἡμέραν Κυρίῳ φρονεῖ, καὶ ὁ μὴ φρονῶν τὴν ἡμέραν Κυρίῳ οὐ φρονεῖ.¹
ὁ ἐσθίων Κυρίῳ ἐσθίει, εὐχαριστεῖ γὰρ τῷ Θεῷ· καὶ ὁ μὴ ἐσθίων
Κυρίῳ οὐκ ἐσθίει, καὶ εὐχαριστεῖ τῷ Θεῷ. 7. οὐδεὶς γὰρ ἡμῶν

---

¹ και ο μη φρονων την ημεραν Κυριω ου φρονει om. ℵABC¹DF, vulg., Copt., etc.
Almost all crit. edd. follow these authorities and omit; but Alf. only brackets the
words, holding that the omission may be due to homœoteleuton. The clause is
found in C³LP, Syr., Chrys., Thdrt. There are other instances of homœoteleuton
in the attestation of this passage, as Alf. points out. Thus 66¹ omits from ημεραν
to ημεραν, 71 from εσθιει to εσθιει, and L from τω θεω to τω θεω. Insert και before
ο εσθιων with ℵABCDFL.

---

him upright. Paul does not contemplate
the strong man falling and being set up
again by Christ; but in spite of the perils
which liberty brings in its train—and the
Apostle is as conscious of them as the
most timid and scrupulous Christian
could be—he is confident that *Christian*
liberty, through the grace and power of
Christ, will prove a triumphant moral
success.

Ver. 5. The Apostle passes from the
question of food to one of essentially
the same kind—the religious observance
of days. This is generally regarded
as quite independent of the other; but
Weiss argues from ver. 6, where the text
which he adopts in common with most
editors seems to contrast "him who *observes the day*" with "him who *eats*,"
that what we have here is really a sub-
division of the same general subject. In
other words, among those who abstained
from flesh and wine, some did so always,
others only on certain days. "To observe the day" might in itself mean to
observe it by fasting—this would be the
case if one's ordinary custom were to
use flesh and wine; or it might mean to
observe it by feasting—this would be the
case if one ordinarily abstained. Practically, it makes no difference whether
this reading of the passage is correct or
not: Paul argues the question of the distinction of days as if it were an independent question, much as he does in Col.
ii. It is not probable that there is any
reference either to the Jewish Sabbath or
to the Lord's Day, though the principle
on which the Apostle argues defines the
Christian attitude to both. Nothing
whatever in the Christian religion is
legal or statutory, not even the religious
observance of the first day of the week;
that observance originated in faith, and
is not what it should be except as it is
freely maintained by faith. For ὃς μὲν
see ver. 2. κρίνει ἡμ. παρ᾽ ἡμέραν means

judges one day "in comparison with,"
or "to the passing by of" another: *cf.*
i. 25, Winer, 503 f. Side by side with
this, κρίνει πᾶσαν ἡμέραν can only mean,
makes no distinction between days,
counts all alike. In such questions the
important thing is not that the decision
should be this or that, but that each man
should have an intelligent assurance as
to his own conduct: it is, indeed, by
having to take the responsibility of deciding for oneself, without the constraint
of law, that an intelligent Christian conscience is developed. For πληροφορείσθω *cf.* iv. 21, and Lightfoot's note on
Col. iv. 12. νοῦς (vii. 23) is the moral
intelligence, or practical reason; by
means of this, enlightened by the Spirit,
the Christian becomes a law to himself.

Ver. 6. The indifference of the questions at issue, from the religious point of
view, is shown by the fact that *both*
parties, by the line of action they choose,
have the same end in view—*viz.*, the
interest of the Lord. ὁ φρονῶν τὴν
ἡμέραν *cf.* Col. iii. 2. The setting of
the mind upon the day implies of course
some distinction between it and others.
The clause καὶ ὁ μὴ φρονῶν . . . οὐ
φρονεῖ is omitted by most editors, but
its absence from most MSS. might still
be due to homœoteleuton. εὐχαριστεῖ:
thanksgiving to God consecrates *every*
meal, whether it be the ascetic one of
him who abstains from wine and flesh
(ὁ μὴ ἐσθίων), or the more generous one
of him who uses both (ὁ ἐσθίων): *cf.*
Acts xxvii. 35, 1 Cor. x. 30, 1 Tim. iv. 3-
5. The thanksgiving shows that in either
case the Christian is acting εἰς δόξαν
θεοῦ (1 Cor. x. 31), and therefore that
the Lord's interest is safe.

Ver. 7 f. οὐδεὶς γὰρ ἡμῶν ἑαυτῷ ζῇ
κ.τ.λ. The truth which has been
affirmed in regard to the Christian's use
of food, and observance or non-observ-
ance of days, is here based on a larger

ἑαυτῷ ζῇ, καὶ οὐδεὶς ἑαυτῷ ἀποθνήσκει. 8. ἐάν τε γὰρ ζῶμεν,
τῷ Κυρίῳ ζῶμεν· ἐάν τε ἀποθνήσκωμεν, τῷ Κυρίῳ ἀποθνήσκομεν.
ἐάν τε οὖν ζῶμεν, ἐάν τε ἀποθνήσκωμεν, τοῦ Κυρίου ᵉ ἐσμέν.   9. εἰς e Ch. viii.
τοῦτο γὰρ Χριστὸς καὶ ¹ ἀπέθανε καὶ ἀνέστη καὶ ἀνέζησεν, ἵνα καὶ 9; I Cor. iii. 23.
νεκρῶν καὶ ζώντων κυριεύσῃ.   10. Σὺ δὲ τί κρίνεις τὸν ἀδελφόν σου ;
ἢ καὶ σὺ τί ἐξουθενεῖς τὸν ἀδελφόν σου ; πάντες γὰρ ᶠ παραστησόμεθα f Acts
τῷ βήματι τοῦ Χριστοῦ.²   11. γέγραπται γὰρ, " Ζῶ ἐγὼ, λέγει Κύριος, xxvii. 24.
ὅτι ἐμοὶ κάμψει πᾶν γόνυ, καὶ πᾶσα γλῶσσα ἐξομολογήσεται ³ τῷ

¹ Om. και before απεθανε with א¹ABC¹D¹FP.   For ανεστη και ανεζησεν read
only εζησεν with אABCDLP and all edd.

² του Χριστου א³C²LP : του θεου א¹ABC¹DF and all edd.

³ εξομολογησεται πασα γλωσσα BD¹⁻³F (and A of LXX) ; but πασα γλωσσα
εξομολογησεται אACD²LP.   The latter order is followed by Weiss, W. and H.,
and Tischdf.   Probably the verb was put first in BF, etc., to conform to the parallel
clause.

truth of which it is a part.   His whole
life belongs not to himself, but to his
Lord.   " No one of us liveth to himself,"
does not mean, " every man's conduct
affects others for better or worse, whether
he will or not " ; it means, " no Christian
is his own end in life ; what is always
present to his mind, as the rule of his
conduct, is the will and the interest of
his Lord ".   The same holds of his dying.
He does not choose either the time or
the mode of it, like a Roman Stoic, to
please himself.   He dies when the Lord
will, as the Lord will, and even by his
death glorifies God.   In ver. 14 ff. Paul
comes to speak of the influence of conduct
upon others ; but here there is no such
thing in view ; the prominence given to
τῷ κυρίῳ (τοῦ κυρίου) three times in
ver. 8 shows that the one truth present
to his mind is the all-determining significance, for Christian conduct, of the relation to Christ.   This (ideally) determines
everything, alike in life and death ; and
all that is determined by it is right.
Ver. 9.   εἰς τοῦτο γὰρ . . . ἵνα: cf.
2 Cor. ii. 9.   ἔζησεν refers to the resurrection, as is shown by the order of the
words, the connection elsewhere in Paul
of Lordship with the resurrection (cf.
Phil. ii. 9 ff.), and the aorist tense which
describes an act, and not the continued
existence of Christ on earth (Sanday and
Headlam) : cf. Rev. ii. 8 (ὃς ἐγένετο νεκρὸς
κ. ἔζησεν), xx. 4 f.   ἵνα denotes God's
purpose in subjecting His Son to this
experience.   We must not suppose that
ἀπέθανεν is specially connected with
νεκρῶν and ἔζησεν with ζώντων ; there
is the same mannerism as in iv. 25.
Rather is it through Christ's resurrection

that His lordship over the realm of death
is established, so that not even in that
dark world do those who are His cease
to stand in their old relation to Him.
τοῦ κυρίου ἐσμὲν holds alike in the seen
and the unseen.
Ver. 10.   Σὺ δὲ: thou, in contrast with
the one Lord and Judge of all.   In face
of our common responsibility to Him,
how dare we judge each other ?   τὸν
ἀδελφόν σου : another reason for not
judging : it is inconsistent with a recognition of the brotherhood of believers.
ἢ καὶ σὺ τί ἐξουθενεῖς κ.τ.λ.   Or thou,
again, why despisest thou ? etc.   This is
addressed to the strong and free thinking, as the first question is to the weak
and scrupulous Christian.   Censoriousness and contempt are never anything
but sins, not to be practised but shunned,
and that all the more when we remember
that we shall all stand at one bar.
παραστησόμεθα τῷ βήματι τοῦ θεοῦ :
God is the universal Judge.   In 2 Cor.
v. 10 we have τῷ βήματι τοῦ Χριστοῦ,
but here τοῦ θεοῦ is the correct reading.
We cannot suppose that by τοῦ θεοῦ
here Paul means Christ in His Divine
nature ; the true way to mediate between
the two expressions is seen in chap. ii.
16, Acts xvii. 31.   When we all stand at
that bar—and it should be part of our
spiritual environment always—no one
will look at his brother with either
censoriousness or contempt.
Ver. 11.   γέγραπται γάρ: the universal judgment proved from Scripture,
Is. lv. 23.   Paul follows the LXX,
but very freely.   For ζῶ ἐγὼ λέγει κύριος
the LXX has κατ' ἐμαυτοῦ ὀμνύω.   The
same passage is quoted more freely still

Θεῷ". 12. ἄρα οὖν[1] ἕκαστος ἡμῶν περὶ ἑαυτοῦ λόγον δώσει τῷ

Θεῷ. 13. Μηκέτι οὖν ἀλλήλους κρίνωμεν· ἀλλὰ τοῦτο κρίνατε

g Matt. xvi. μᾶλλον, τὸ μὴ τιθέναι πρόσκομμα τῷ ἀδελφῷ ἢ ᵍσκάνδαλον.[2] 14.
23; xviii.
7; Ch. οἶδα καὶ πέπεισμαι ἐν Κυρίῳ Ἰησοῦ, ὅτι οὐδὲν κοινὸν δι᾽ ἑαυτοῦ·[3] εἰ
xvi. 17;
Rev. ii. μὴ τῷ λογιζομένῳ τι κοινὸν εἶναι, ἐκείνῳ κοινόν· 15. εἰ δὲ[4] διὰ βρῶμα
14.
ὁ ἀδελφός σου λυπεῖται, οὐκ ἔτι κατὰ ἀγάπην περιπατεῖς. μὴ τῷ

[1] ουν ℵACEL, all cursives, is put in text by Tdf. and bracketed by Alf. and W. and H. It is omitted in BD¹FP¹, Syr. and by Weiss, who thinks it much more natural that the common Pauline formula **αρα ουν** should have been completed than mutilated. The authorities are divided in the same way between **δωσει** and **απο-δωσει**: BDF supporting the latter, which is adopted by Weiss, and ℵAC the former, which is adopted by W. and H. So also Weiss omits **τω θεω** with BF; but W. and H. bracket it, as it is found in ℵACDLP.

[2] το μη τιθεναι προσκομμα τω αδελφω η σκανδαλον. **προσκομμα** and **η** are both om. by B, Syr., Arm. Weiss thinks this gives the true reading, **το μη τιθεναι τω αδελφω σκανδαλον**, and W. and H. put it in margin.

[3] δι εαυτου ℵBC, followed by W. and H., Weiss, Alf.; **δι αυτου** ADEFGL, and of edd. Lachm. and Treg.

[4] For **ει δε** read **ει γαρ** with ℵABCDFP and all edd.

in Phil. ii. 10 f. to describe the exaltation of Christ. In Isaiah it refers to the coming of God's kingdom, when all nations shall worship Him. **ἐξομολογή-σεται τῷ θεῷ** = shall give thanks or praise to God: xv. 9, Mt. xi. 25, and often in LXX = יְהוָֹה. In the sense of "confess" it takes the accusative.

Ver. 12. **ἄρα (οὖν)**: So then — conclusion of *this* aspect of the subject: *cf.* v. 18, vii. 25. Every word in this sentence is emphatic: **ἕκαστος, περὶ ἑαυτοῦ, λόγον δώσει, τῷ θεῷ.** For **λόγον** in this sense see 1 Pet. iv. 5, Heb. xiii. 17, Matt. xii. 36, Acts xix. 40.

Vv. 13-23. The Apostle now proceeds to argue the question of Christian conduct in things indifferent from another point of view — that of the influence which our conduct may have on others, and of the consideration which is due to them. **μηκέτι οὖν ἀλλήλους κρίνωμεν**: thus much follows from what has been said already, and **κρίνωμεν** therefore forbids both the censorious and the contemptuous estimate of others. **ἀλλὰ τοῦτο κρίνατε μᾶλλον**: be this your judgment rather. *Cf.* 1 Cor. ii. 2, vii. 37. **τὸ μὴ τιθέναι πρόσκομμα τῷ ἀδελφῷ**: this is of course addressed to the liberal party. For **πρόσκομμα** see 1 Cor. viii. 9. The word does not occur in the Gospels, but it is a remarkable fact that in most of our Lord's express teaching about sin, it is sin in the character of **σκάνδαλον**, a snare or stumbling-block to others, with

which He deals. Paul develops his ideas quite freely from his conception of faith, but in all probability he was familiar with what Jesus taught (Matt. xviii.).

Ver. 14. In principle, the Apostle sides with the strong. He has no scruples about meats or drinks or days. **ἐν Κυρίῳ Ἰησοῦ**: it is as a Christian, not as a libertine, that Paul has this conviction; in Christ Jesus he is sure that there is nothing in the world essentially unclean; all things can be consecrated and Christianised by Christian use. **κοινόν**: *cf.* Acts x. 14, 28, Rev. xxi. 27. It is the opposite of **ἅγιον**, and signifies that which is not and cannot be brought into relation to God. **εἰ μὴ τῷ λογιζομένῳ κ.τ.λ.** Though there is nothing which in itself has this character, some things may have it subjectively, *i.e.*, in the judgment of a particular person who cannot help (from some imperfection of conscience) regarding them so; to *him* (**ἐκείνῳ** emphatic) they are what his conscience makes them; and his conscience (unenlightened as it is) is entitled to respect. For **εἰ μὴ** *cf.* Matt. xii. 14, Gal. ii. 16.

Ver. 15. Many expositors here supply something; *e.g.*, "You must have respect therefore for his scruples, although you may not share them, for if," etc. (Sanday and Headlam); but it seems simpler to connect the **γὰρ** with the leading idea in the writer's mind, Put no stumbling-block before a brother, for, etc. **διὰ βρῶμα** is contemptuous: "for the sake of food"

βρώματί σου ἐκεῖνον ἀπόλλυε, ὑπὲρ οὗ Χριστὸς ἀπέθανε. 16. Μὴ ᵸ Ch. iii. 8.
ᵸ βλασφημείσθω οὖν ὑμῶν τὸ ἀγαθόν. 17. οὐ γάρ ἐστιν ἡ βασιλεία ᶦ 1 Cor. iv.
τοῦ ᶦ Θεοῦ βρῶσις καὶ πόσις, ἀλλὰ δικαιοσύνη καὶ εἰρήνη καὶ χαρὰ 20.
ᵏ Matt. vi.
ἐν Πνεύματι Ἁγίῳ· 18. ὁ γὰρ ἐν τούτοις ᶦ ᵏ δουλεύων τῷ Χριστῷ 24; Ch.
xvi. 18;
Eph. vi.
7; Col. iii.
24.

¹ For ἐν τούτοις א³D³L read ἐν τούτῳ with א¹ABCD¹F and all edd.

thy brother is grieved. βρῶμα is the food which the strong eats in spite of his brother's scruples. λυπεῖται need not imply that the weak is induced, against his conscience, to eat also (though that is contemplated as following); it may quite well express the uneasiness and distress with which the weak sees the strong pursue a line of conduct which his conscience cannot approve. Even to cause such pain as this is a violation of the law of Christ. He who does it has ceased to walk κατὰ ἀγάπην, according to love, which is the supreme Christian rule. In the sense of this, and at the same time aware that the weak in these circumstances may easily be cajoled or overborne into doing what his conscience disapproves, the Apostle exclaims abruptly, μὴ τῷ βρώματί σου ἐκεῖνον ἀπόλλυε ὑπὲρ οὗ Χριστὸς ἀπέθανεν. To tamper with conscience, it is here implied, is *ruin*: and the selfish man who so uses his Christian liberty as to lead a weak brother to tamper with his conscience is art and part in that ruin. The wanton contempt such liberty shows for the spirit and example of Christ is emphasised both here and in 1 Cor. viii. 11 f. *Ne pluris feceris tuum cibum quam Christus vitam suam.*

Ver. 16. μὴ βλασφημείσθω οὖν ὑμῶν τὸ ἀγαθόν. τὸ ἀγαθόν is somewhat indefinite. It has been taken (1) as the good common to all Christians — the Messianic salvation—which will be blasphemed by the non-Christian, when they see the wantonness with which Christians rob each other of it by such conduct as Paul reprobates in ver. 15; and (2) as Christian liberty, the freedom of conscience which has been won by Christ, but which will inevitably get a bad name if it is exercised in an inconsiderate loveless fashion. The latter meaning alone seems relevant. For βλασφ. see 1 Cor. x. 30.

Ver. 17. Insistence and strife on such matters are inconsistent with Christianity: οὐ γάρ ἐστιν κ.τ.λ. Usually in Paul ἡ βασιλεία τοῦ θεοῦ is transcendent; the kingdom is that which comes with the second advent, and is the inheritance of believers; it is essentially (as it is called

in 2 Tim. iv. 18) a βασ. ἐπουράνιον. See 1 Thess. ii. 12, 2 Thess. i. 5, 1 Cor. vi. 9 f., xv. 50, Gal. v. 21. This use of the expression, however, does not exclude another, which is more akin to what we find in the Gospels, and regards the Kingdom of God as in some sense also present: we have examples of this here, and in 1 Cor. iv. 20: perhaps also in Acts xx. 25. No doubt for Paul the transcendent associations would always cling to the name, so that we should lose a great deal of what it meant for him if we translated it by "the Christian religion" or any such form of words. It always included the reference to the glory to be revealed. βρῶσις κ. πόσις: eating and drinking—the acts, as opposed to βρῶμα, ver. 15, the thing eaten. ἀλλὰ δικαιοσύνη κ. εἰρήνη κ. χαρὰ ἐν πνεύματι ἁγίῳ: are these words ethical or religious? Does δικ. denote "justification," the right relation of man to God? or "righteousness," in the sense of just dealing? Is εἰρήνη peace with God, the result of justification (as in v. 1), or peace among the members of the Church, the result of consideration for each other? The true answer must be that Paul did not thus distinguish ethical and religious: the words are religious primarily, but the ethical meaning is so far from being excluded by the religious that it is secured by it, and by it alone. That the religious import ought to be put in the forefront is shown by χαρὰ ἐν πν. ἁγ. which is a grace, not a virtue. In comparison with these great spiritual blessings, what Christian could trouble the Church about eating or drinking? For their sake, no self-denial is too great.

Ver. 18. ἐν τούτῳ: "on the principle implied by these virtues" (Sanday and Headlam). One may serve Christ either eating or abstaining, but no one can serve Him whose conduct exhibits indifference to righteousness, peace and joy in the Holy Spirit. δόκιμος τοῖς ἀνθρώποις: so that there can be no occasion given to any one to blaspheme. *Cf.* xvi. 10, 2 Tim. ii. 15, Jas. i. 12. A sound Christian character wins even the world's approval.

VOL. II. 45

εὐάρεστος τῷ Θεῷ, καὶ δόκιμος τοῖς ἀνθρώποις. 19. ἄρα οὖν τὰ

l Ch. xii.
13 ; 1 Cor.
xiv. 1 ; 1
Thess. v.
15.
m Tit. i. 15.
n 1 Cor.
viii. 13.

τῆς εἰρήνης ¹διώκωμεν,¹ καὶ τὰ τῆς οἰκοδομῆς τῆς εἰς ἀλλήλους. 20. Μὴ ἕνεκεν βρώματος κατάλυε τὸ ἔργον τοῦ Θεοῦ. πάντα μὲν ᵐκαθαρά, ἀλλὰ κακὸν τῷ ἀνθρώπῳ τῷ διὰ προσκόμματος ἐσθίοντι. 21. καλὸν τὸ μὴ φαγεῖν ⁿκρέα, μηδὲ πιεῖν οἶνον, μηδὲ ἐν ᾧ ὁ ἀδελφός

¹ διώκωμεν CDE, latt. ; διώκομεν ℵABFLP. According to S. and H. διώκομεν is a "somewhat obvious correction," and less expressive than διώκωμεν. This is also the view of Weiss and Tischdf. But W. and H. put διώκωμεν in text and διώκομεν in marg.

Ver. 19. ἄρα οὖν : see ver. 12. τὰ τῆς εἰρήνης is not materially different from τὴν εἰρήνην : all that belongs to, makes for, peace : we cannot argue from its use here that the word must have exactly the same shade of meaning in ver. 17. διώκωμεν : the indicative διώκομεν is very strongly supported, and would indicate the actual pursuit of all true Christians : "Our aim is peace," and τὰ τῆς οἰκοδομῆς τῆς εἰς ἀλλήλους = mutual upbuilding. Cf. 1 Thess. v. 11, 1 Cor. xiv. 26. The practical rule implied here is that, when anything is morally indifferent to me, before I act on that conviction, I must ask how such action will affect the peace of the Church, and the Christian growth of others.

Ver. 20. Paul repeats the rule of ver. 15. μὴ κατάλυε : the opposite of οἰκοδομεῖν. See Matt. xxvi. 61, Gal. ii. 18. τὸ ἔργον τοῦ θεοῦ (1 Cor. iii. 9) what God has wrought, i.e., the Christian Church (which is destroyed by such wanton conduct) or the Christian character and standing of an individual (which may be ruined in the same way). πάντα μὲν καθαρά : this is the principle of the strong, which Paul concedes (μὲν) ; the difficulty is to get the enlightened to understand that an abstract principle can never be the rule of Christian conduct. The Christian, of course, admits the principle, but he must act from love. To know that all things are clean does not (as is often assumed) settle what the Christian has to do in any given case. It does not define his duty, but only makes clear his responsibility. Acknowledging that principle, and looking with love at other Christians, and the effect of any given line of conduct on them, he has to define his duty for himself. All meat is clean, but not all eating. On the contrary (ἀλλὰ), κακὸν τῷ ἀνθρώπῳ τῷ διὰ προσκόμματος ἐσθίοντι ; sin is involved in the case of the man who eats with offence. Some take this as a warning to the weak ; but the whole

tone of the passage, which is rather a warning to the strong, and the verse immediately following, which surely continues the meaning and is also addressed to the strong, decide against this. The man who eats with offence is therefore the man by whose eating another is made to stumble. For διὰ προσκόμματος see ii. 27, Winer, p. 475.

Ver. 21. A maxim for the strong. For καλὸν cf. Mark xiv. 6. Abstinence in order that others may not be made to stumble is morally noble. ἐν ᾧ : usually προσκόπτειν takes the Dat., ix. 32, 1 Pet. ii. 8. That there were those in the Church at Rome who had scruples as to the use of flesh and wine, see on ver. 2. Paul would not have written the chapter at all unless there had been scruples of some kind ; and he would not have taken these examples if the scruples had concerned something quite different.

Ver. 22. The true text is σὺ πίστιν ἣν ἔχεις : "the faith that thou hast, have thou to thyself in the sight of God ". The verse is still addressed to the strong. The faith he has is the enlightened faith which enables him to see that all things are clean ; such faith does not lose its value though it is not flaunted in reckless action. On κατὰ σεαυτὸν Wetstein quotes Heliod. vii. 16 : κατὰ σαυτὸν ἔχε καὶ μηδενὶ φράζε. Cf. 1 Cor. xiv. 28 (ἑαυτῷ δὲ λαλείτω καὶ τῷ θεῷ). ἐνώπιον τοῦ θεοῦ reminds the strong once more (ver. 10) that the fullest freedom must be balanced by the fullest sense of responsibility to God. In another sense than that of 1 Cor. ix. 21 the Christian made free by faith must feel himself μὴ ἄνομος θεοῦ ἀλλ' ἔννομος Χριστοῦ. μακάριος ὁ μὴ κρίνων ἑαυτὸν ἐν ᾧ δοκιμάζει : "a motive to charitable self-restraint addressed to the strong in faith" (Gifford). It is a rare felicity (this is always what μακάριος denotes) to have a conscience untroubled by scruples—in Paul's words, not to judge oneself in the matter which one approves (sc., by his own practice) ;

σου προσκόπτει ἢ σκανδαλίζεται ἢ ἀσθενεῖ.[1] 22. σὺ πίστιν[2] ἔχεις ;
κατὰ σεαυτὸν ἔχε ἐνώπιον τοῦ Θεοῦ· μακάριος ὁ μὴ κρίνων ἑαυτὸν
ἐν ᾧ °δοκιμάζει. 23. ὁ δὲ διακρινόμενος, ἐὰν φάγῃ, κατακέκριται, ο ι Cor.
ὅτι οὐκ ἐκ πίστεως· πᾶν δὲ ὃ οὐκ ἐκ πίστεως, ἁμαρτία ἐστίν.[3]   xvi. 3.

[1] η σκανδαλιζεται η ασθενει om. ℵ[1]AC, Syr., Copt., Aeth. ; ins. ℵ[3]BDFLP, vulg.,
Sah. S. and H. call this a very clear instance of a Western reading in B, and
therefore justify the omission with W. and H. and Tischdf. ; but Weiss, who thinks
η ασθενει is too difficult to be explained as a gloss, retains the words.

[2] After πιστιν ins. ην ℵABC ; so most edd., omitting the mark of interrogation
after εχεις. For σαυτον read σεαυτον with ℵABCDKLP, etc.

[3] After αμαρτια εστιν the great doxology of chap. xvi. 25-27 is inserted by ALP
and most other MSS., though some, including AP, have it in both places ; om. here
ℵBCD[1], vulg., Syr.

and he who has this felicity should ask
no more. In particular, he should not
run the risk of injuring a brother's conscience, merely for the sake of exercising
in a special way the spiritual freedom
which he has the happiness to possess
—whether he exercises it in that way or
not.

Ver. 23. ὁ δὲ διακρινόμενος ἐὰν φάγῃ
κατακέκριται: such, on the other hand,
is the unhappy situation of the weak—a
new motive for charity. For διακριν.
cf. iv. 20, Jas. i. 6, Mark xi. 23. The
weak Christian cannot be clear in his
own mind that it is permissible to do as
the strong does ; it may be, he thinks
one moment, and the next, it may not be ;
and if he follows the strong and eats in
this state of mind, κατακέκριται he is
condemned. The condemnation is absolute : it is not only that his own conscience pronounces clearly against him
after the act, but that such action incurs
the condemnation of God. It is inconsistent with that conscientiousness
through which alone man can be trained
in goodness ; the moral life would become
chaotic and irredeemable if conscience
were always to be treated so. ὅτι οὐκ
ἐκ πίστεως, sc., ἔφαγεν. The man is
condemned because he did not eat ἐκ
πίστεως : and this is generalised in the
last clause πᾶν δὲ ὃ οὐκ ἐκ πίστεως
ἁμαρτία ἐστίν. All that is not of faith is
sin ; and therefore this eating, as not of
faith, is sin. It is impossible to give πίστις
here a narrower sense than Christianity :
see ver. 1. Everything a Christian man
does that cannot justify itself to him on
the ground of his relation to Christ is
sin. It is too indefinite to render omne
quod non est ex fide as Thomas Aquinas
does by omne quod est contra conscientiam : it would need to be contra

Christianam conscientiam. All a man
cannot do remembering that he is Christ's
—all he cannot do with the judgment-
seat (ver. 10) and the Cross (ver. 15) and
all their restraints and inspirations
present to his mind—is sin. Of course
this is addressed to Christians, and there
is no rule in it for judging the character
or conduct of those who do not know
Christ. To argue from it that works
done before justification are sin, or that
the virtues of the heathen are glittering
vices, is to misapply it altogether.

CHAPTER XV.—Vv. 1-13. The fourteenth chapter has a certain completeness
in itself, and we can understand that if
the Epistle to the Romans was sent as a
circular letter to different churches, some
copies of it might have ended with xiv.
23 : to which the doxology, xvi. 25-27,
might be loosely appended, as it is in A.
L. and many other MSS. But it is
manifestly the same subject which is
continued in xv. 1-13. The Apostle still
treats of the relations of the weak and
the strong, though with a less precise
reference to the problems of the Roman
Church at the time than in chap. xiv.
His argument widens into a plea for
patience and forbearance (enforced by
the example of Christ) and for the union
of all Christians, Jew and Gentile, in
common praise. It seems natural to infer from this that the distinction between
weak and strong had some relation to
that between Jew and Gentile ; the prejudices and scruples of the weak were
probably of Jewish origin.

Ver. 1. ὀφείλομεν δὲ : what constitutes
the obligation is seen in chap. xiv. It
arises out of our relation to others in
Christ. Looking at them in the light of
what He has done for them as well as for
us, and in the light of our responsibility

XV. 1. Ὀφείλομεν δὲ ἡμεῖς οἱ δυνατοὶ τὰ ἀσθενήματα τῶν ᵃ ἀδυνάτων βαστάζειν, καὶ μὴ ἑαυτοῖς ἀρέσκειν· 2. ἕκαστος γὰρ ¹ ἡμῶν τῷ πλησίον ἀρεσκέτω εἰς τὸ ἀγαθὸν πρὸς οἰκοδομήν. 3. καὶ γὰρ ὁ Χριστὸς οὐχ ἑαυτῷ ἤρεσεν, ἀλλὰ, καθὼς γέγραπται, "Οἱ ὀνειδισμοὶ τῶν ὀνειδιζόντων σε ἐπέπεσον ἐπ᾽ ἐμέ". 4. ὅσα γὰρ προεγράφη,² εἰς τὴν ἡμετέραν διδασκαλίαν προεγράφη· ἵνα διὰ τῆς ὑπομονῆς καὶ

¹ Om. γαρ with ℵABCDFLP.

² οσα γαρ προεγραφη ℵACD³LP; so most edd. B, latt., Aeth. give εγραφη. D¹ and F have προσεγραφη, which confirms the reading of ℵAC. προεγραφη ινα ℵ³ALP; but εγραφη ℵ¹BCDF, vulg. and all edd. After και ins. δια ℵABCL. After εχωμεν B adds της παρακλησεως, which W. and H. put in marg.; but the addition is as inept as that of λογων in the same MS. at ver. 18, and to be explained in the same way (an anticipation of a later word).

to the Judge of all, we cannot question that this is our duty. ἡμεῖς οἱ δυνατοί: Paul classes himself with the strong, and makes the obligation his own. δυνατοί is of course used as in chap. xiv.: not as in 1 Cor. i. 26. τὰ ἀσθενήματα τῶν ἀδυνάτων: the things in which their infirmity comes out, its manifestations: here only in N.T. Paul says "bear" their infirmities: because the restrictions and limitations laid by this charity on the liberty of the strong are a burden to them. For the word βαστάζειν and the idea see Matt. viii. 17, Gal. vi. 2, 5, 17. μὴ ἑαυτοῖς ἀρέσκειν: it is very easy for self-pleasing and mere wilfulness to shelter themselves under the disguise of Christian *principle*. But there is only one Christian principle which has no qualification—love.

Ver. 2. τῷ πλησίον ἀρεσκέτω: this rule is qualified by εἰς τὸ ἀγαθὸν πρὸς οἰκοδομήν. Without such qualification it is "men-pleasing" (Gal. i. 10) and inconsistent with fidelity to Christ. *Cf.* 1 Cor. x. 33, where Paul presents himself as an example of the conduct he here commends. For εἰς and πρὸς in this verse *cf.* chap. iii. 25 f. According to Gifford εἰς marks the "aim"—the advantage or benefit of our neighbour—πρὸς the standard of reference; the only "good" for a Christian is to be "built up" in his Christian character.

Ver. 3. καὶ γὰρ ὁ Χριστὸς κ.τ.λ. The duty of not pleasing ourselves is enforced by the example of Christ: He did not please Himself either. If this required proof, we might have expected Paul to prove it by adducing some incident in Christ's life; but this is not what he does. He appeals to a psalm, which is in many places in the N.T. treated as having some reference to Christ (*e.g.*,

John ii. 17 = Ps. lxix. 9, John xv. 25 = Ps. lxix. 4, Matt. xxvii. 27-30 = Ps. lxix. 12, Matt. xxvii. 34 = Ps. lxix. 21, Rom. xi. 9 = Ps. lxix. 22, Acts i. 20 = Ps. lxix. 25: see Perowne, *The Psalms*, i., p. 561 f.); and the words he quotes from it— words spoken as it were by Christ Himself—describe our Lord's experiences in a way which shows that He was no self-pleaser. If He had been, He would never have given Himself up willingly, as He did, to such a fate. It is hardly conceivable that σε in Paul's quotation indicates the man whom Christ is supposed to address: it can quite well be God, as in the psalm. Some have argued from this indirect proof of Christ's character that Paul had no acquaintance with the facts of His life; but the inference is unsound. It would condemn all the N.T. writers of the same ignorance, for they never appeal to incidents in Christ's life; and this summary of the whole character of Christ, possessing as it did for Paul and his readers the authority of inspiration, was more impressive than any isolated example of non-selfpleasing could have been.

Ver. 4. Here Paul justifies his use of the O.T. ὅσα γὰρ προεγράφη = the whole O.T. εἰς τὴν ἡμετέραν διδασκαλίαν ἐγράφη: was written to teach us, and therefore has abiding value. 2 Tim. iii. 16. ἵνα introduces God's purpose, which is wider than the immediate purpose of the Apostle. Paul meant to speak only of bearing the infirmities of the weak, but with the quotation of Ps. lxix. 9 there came in the idea of the Christian's sufferings generally, and it is amid them that God's purpose is to be fulfilled. διὰ τῆς ὑπομ. κ. τῆς παρακλ. τῶν γραφῶν κ.τ.λ.: "that through the patience and the comfort wrought by the

τῆς παρακλήσεως τῶν γραφῶν τὴν ἐλπίδα ἔχωμεν. 5. ὁ δὲ Θεὸς
τῆς ὑπομονῆς καὶ τῆς ᵇπαρακλήσεως δῴη ὑμῖν τὸ αὐτὸ φρονεῖν ἐν
ἀλλήλοις κατὰ Χριστὸν Ἰησοῦν· 6. ἵνα ὁμοθυμαδὸν ἐν ἑνὶ στόματι
δοξάζητε τὸν Θεὸν καὶ πατέρα τοῦ Κυρίου ἡμῶν Ἰησοῦ Χριστοῦ.
7. Διὸ ᶜπροσλαμβάνεσθε ἀλλήλους, καθὼς καὶ ὁ Χριστὸς προσελάβετο ἡμᾶς ¹ εἰς δόξαν Θεοῦ. 8. λέγω δέ, Ἰησοῦν Χριστὸν ² ᵈδιάκονον
γεγενῆσθαι περιτομῆς ᵉὑπὲρ ἀληθείας Θεοῦ, εἰς τὸ βεβαιῶσαι τὰς

b 2 Cor. i. 3-
7; Heb.
vi. 18;
xii. 5.

c Ch. xiv. 1.
d Gal. ii. 17.
e Ch. i. 5;
Phil. ii.
13.

¹ ημας, so BDP cursives; adopted by Weiss, W. and H. text. But υμας is put
in marg. by W. and H., and by many edd. in text. It really seems to have arisen
from ημας being changed to agree with the preceding context in which the readers
are directly addressed. Yet it is strongly supported אACD²∙³FL. Ins. του before
θεου אABCDFP.

² For δε Ιησουν Χριστον read γαρ Χριστον with אABC and all edd. γεγενησθαι
אAELP; γενεσθαι BCDF. The edd. are divided. Tischdf., W. and H., and Treg.
marg. read γεγενησθαι; but W. and H. put γενεσθαι in marg., while Lachm. and
Treg. have it in text. Weiss thinks the case can only be settled by analogy; and
as א, which is the strongest support of γεγενησθαι, quite arbitrarily changes
γενεσθαι in Phil. i. 13 into γεγονεναι, he allows that to discredit it here, and reads
γενεσθαι.

Scriptures we may have our hope".
τὴν ἐλπίδα is the Christian hope, the
hope of the glory of God; and the
Christian has it as he is able, through
the help of God's Word in the Scriptures, to maintain a brave and cheerful
spirit amid all the sufferings and reproaches of life. Cf. v. 2-5. This is, if
not a digression, at least an expansion
of his original idea, and at

Ver. 5 Paul returns to his point in a
prayer: the God of the patience and
comfort just spoken of grant unto you,
etc. τὸ αὐτὸ φρονεῖν ἐν ἀλλήλοις κατὰ
Χριστὸν Ἰησοῦν: cf. xii. 16, where, however, τὸ αὐτὸ φρονεῖν with εἰς ἀλλήλους
is not quite the same. Paul wishes here
that the minds of his readers — their
moral judgment and temper—may all be
determined by Jesus Christ (for κατὰ, expressing the rule according to which, see
chap. viii. 27): in this case there will be
the harmony which the disputes of chap.
xiv. disturbed.

Ver. 6. ἵνα introduces the ultimate
aim of this unanimity. ὁμοθυμαδόν
here only in Paul, but eleven times in
Acts. ἐν ἑνὶ στόματι: in Greek writers
usually ἐξ ἑνὸς στόματος. τὸν Θεὸν καὶ
πατέρα τοῦ Κ. ἡμῶν Ἰ. Χ. The A.V.
renders, "God, even the Father of our
Lord Jesus Christ," making τοῦ Κυρίου
depend on πατέρα only. This rendering
does not make God the God of Christ,
but defines the only true God as the
Father of Christ. It is defended by
Weiss, who appeals to the passages in
which "God and Father" is found with

no genitive: 1 Cor. xv. 24, Eph. v. 20,
Col. iii. 17, Jas. i. 27, iii. 9. The argument is not convincing, especially in
view of Eph. i. 17 (ὁ θεὸς τοῦ Κ. ἡμῶν
Ἰ. Χ., ὁ πατὴρ τῆς δόξης) and John xx.
17: hence the R.V. is probably right
("the God and Father of our Lord").
When the Church glorifies such a God
with one heart and one mouth it will
have transcended all the troubles of chap.
xiv. It is this accordant praise of all
Christians which is the ruling idea in
vers. 7-13.

Ver. 7. διὸ προσλαμβάνεσθε ἀλλήλους: διὸ = that such praise may be
possible. For προσλαμβ. see xiv. 1-3.
καθὼς καὶ ὁ Χριστὸς προσελάβετο ὑμᾶς.
ὑμᾶς covers both parties in the Church,
however they are to be distinguished; if
Christ received both, they are bound to
receive each other. The last words, εἰς
δόξαν τοῦ θεοῦ, are probably to be construed with προσλαμβάνεσθε ἀλλήλους;
they resume the idea of ver. 6 (ἵνα . . .
δοξάζητε); the διὸ with which ver. 7
begins starts from that idea of glorifying
God, and looks on to it as the end to
be attained when all Christians in love
receive each other. But the clause has
of course a meaning even if attached to
what immediately precedes: ὁ Χριστὸς
προσελ. ὑμᾶς. Cf. Phil. ii. 11, Eph. i.
12-14. Christ's reception of the Jews
led to God's being glorified for His faithfulness; His reception of the Gentiles to
God's being glorified for His mercy. So
Weiss, who argues that in what follows
we have the expansion and proof of the

ἐπαγγελίας τῶν πατέρων· 9. τὰ δὲ ἔθνη ὑπὲρ ἐλέους δοξάσαι τὸν
Θεὸν, καθὼς γέγραπται, "Διὰ τοῦτο ᶠ ἐξομολογήσομαί σοι ἐν ἔθνεσι,
καὶ τῷ ὀνόματί σου ψαλῶ". 10. καὶ πάλιν λέγει, "Εὐφράνθητε,
ἔθνη, μετὰ τοῦ λαοῦ αὐτοῦ". 11. καὶ πάλιν, "Αἰνεῖτε τὸν Κύριον,
πάντα τὰ ἔθνη,¹ καὶ ἐπαινέσατε αὐτὸν, πάντες οἱ λαοί". 12. καὶ
πάλιν Ἡσαΐας λέγει, "Ἔσται ἡ ῥίζα τοῦ Ἰεσσαὶ, καὶ ὁ ἀνιστάμενος
ἄρχειν ἐθνῶν, ἐπ᾽ αὐτῷ ἔθνη ἐλπιοῦσιν". 13. ὁ δὲ Θεὸς τῆς ἐλπίδος
πληρῶσαι ὑμᾶς πάσης χαρᾶς καὶ εἰρήνης² ἐν τῷ πιστεύειν, εἰς τὸ
περισσεύειν ὑμᾶς ἐν τῇ ἐλπίδι, ἐν δυνάμει Πνεύματος Ἁγίου.

ᶠ Ch. xiv.
11.

¹ For τον κυριον παντα τα εθνη (so LXX), read παντα τα εθνη τον Κυριον ℵABDP
and all edd. For επαινεσατε (so LXX, B) FLP read επαινεσατωσαν (LXX, A)
ℵABCD.

² Against all edd., who keep the received text, Weiss finds himself compelled,
instead of πληρωσαι υμας πασης χαρας και ειρηνης, to read πληροφορησαι υμας εν
παση χαρα κ. ειρηνη. This is the reading of B, and is found with only the omission
of εν in FG; Weiss thinks it quite inexplicable except as the original; πληροφ. has
a point of attachment in xiv. 5, and the double εν (εν παση χαρα . . . εν τω πιστευειν)
in this clause answers exactly to that in the next (εν τη ελπιδι, εν δυναμει πν. αγιου).
The other reading is supported by ℵACDLP.

idea that God's glory (the glory of His
faithfulness and of His mercy) is the end
contemplated by Christ's reception alike
of Jew and Gentile.

Ver. 8. λέγω γὰρ Χριστὸν διάκονον
γεγενῆσθαι περιτομῆς = what I mean is
this—Christ has been made, etc. διάκονον περιτομῆς is usually understood
as "a minister to the Jews, to circumcised people" (cf. iii. 30, iv. 9), and this
seems to me the only intelligible explanation. In exercising this ministry (and
He exercised directly no other: Matt.
xv. 24) Christ was of course circumcised
Himself and set from His birth (Gal. iv.
4 f.) in the same relation to the law as
all who belonged to the old covenant;
but though this is involved in the fact
that Christ was sent to the Jews, it is
not what is meant by calling Him διάκονον περιτομῆς. ὑπὲρ ἀληθείας θεοῦ:
in the interest of God's truth (cf. i. 5:
ὑπὲρ τοῦ ὀνόματος αὐτοῦ). The truth
of God, as the giver of the promises to
the fathers, was vindicated by Christ's
ministry; for in Him they were all fulfilled, 2 Cor. i. 20. τὰς ἐπαγγ. τῶν
πατέρων: the promises belonged to the
fathers, because they were originally
made to them.

Ver. 9. τὰ δὲ ἔθνη ὑπὲρ ἐλέους δοξάσαι
τὸν θεόν: Some expositors make this
depend directly on λέγω, as if Paul had
meant: "I say Christ has become a
minister of circumcision, in the interest
of the truth of God . . . and that the
Gentiles have glorified God for His

mercy," the only contrast being that between God's faithfulness, as shown to
the descendants of Abraham, and His
mercy as shown to those without the old
covenant. But if τὰ δὲ ἔθνη κ.τ.λ. is
made to depend on εἰς τὸ, as in the A.V.,
there is a double contrast brought out:
that of faithfulness and mercy being no
more emphatic than that of the fathers
and the Gentiles. Indeed, from the passages quoted, it is clear that Paul is pre-
occupied rather with the latter of these
two contrasts than with the former; for
all the passages concern the place of the
Gentiles in the Church. At the same
time it is made clear—even to the Gentiles—that the salvation which they enjoy
is "of the Jews". Hence the Gentiles
must not be contemptuous of scruples or
infirmities, especially such as rise out of
any associations with the old covenant;
nor should the Jews be censorious of a
Gentile liberty which has its vindication
in the free grace of God. καθὼς γέγραπται: the contemplated glorification of
God answers to what we find in Ps. xviii.
50, LXX. Christ is assumed to be the
speaker, and we may say that He gives
thanks to God among the Gentiles when
the Gentiles give thanks to God through
Him (Heb. ii. 12).

Ver. 10. καὶ πάλιν λέγει: Deut. xxxii.
43, LXX. The Hebrew is different.

Ver. 11. καὶ πάλιν, αἰνεῖτε: Ps. cxvii.
1, LXX—only the order of the words
varying.

Ver. 12. καὶ πάλιν Ἡσαΐας λέγει: Isa.

ἐθνῶν, λόγῳ καὶ ἔργῳ, 19. ἐν δυνάμει σημείων καὶ τεράτων, ἐν δυνάμει Πνεύματος Θεοῦ · [1] ὥστε με ἀπὸ Ἰερουσαλὴμ καὶ κύκλῳ μέχρι τοῦ Ἰλλυρικοῦ πεπληρωκέναι τὸ εὐαγγέλιον τοῦ Χριστοῦ. 20. οὕτω δὲ φιλοτιμούμενον [2] [1] εὐαγγελίζεσθαι, οὐχ ὅπου ὠνομάσθη Χριστὸς, ἵνα μὴ ἐπ᾽ ἀλλότριον θεμέλιον οἰκοδομῶ · 21. ἀλλὰ, καθὼς γέγραπται, " Οἷς οὐκ ἀνηγγέλη περὶ αὐτοῦ, ὄψονται · [3] καὶ οἳ οὐκ ἀκηκόασι, συνήσουσι ".

1 Cor. i.
17; ix. 16,
18; 2 Cor.
x. 16.

[1] θεου ℵD²LP ; αγιου ACD¹⁻³ ; om. B. B certainly seems right here, though W. and H. put [αγιου] in text. Both θεου and αγιου seem interpolations to complete the expression.

[2] φιλοτιμουμενον ℵACD²,³L, Orig.; φιλοτιμουμαι BD¹ (gr.) FP. Edd. seem to regard the latter as a change made to simplify the construction, and the case is one of those in which the value of B may be lessened by Western influence ; hence they prefer, as a rule, the former reading. But Weiss reads φιλοτιμουμαι because it is exegetically necessary, and says he is not aware of any such arbitrary change of a participle into a finite verb.

[3] οψονται before οις B ; and so W. and H. and Weiss. The order in received text conforms to the LXX and the next clause.

regarded as counterfeiting that of Christ. τέρας is always rendered " wonder " in the A.V., and, as though the word were unequal to the phenomenon, it is never used alone : in all the places in which it occurs σημεῖον is also found. The latter emphasises the significance of the miracle; it is not merely a sight to stare at, but is suggestive of an actor and a purpose. In this passage, " the power " of signs and wonders seems to mean the power with which they impressed the beholders : more or less it is an interpretation of ἔργῳ. So " the power " of the Holy Ghost means the influence with which the Holy Spirit accompanied the preaching of the Gospel : more or less it answers to λόγῳ : see 1 Thess. i. 5 and cf. the ἀπόδειξει πνεύματος κ. δυνάμεως, 1 Cor. ii. 4. ὥστε με κ.τ.λ. "The result of Christ's working through His Apostle is here stated as if the preceding sentence had been affirmative in form as well as sense " (Gifford). ἀπὸ Ἰερουσαλήμ : this agrees with Acts ix. 26-29, but this, of course, does not prove that it was borrowed from that passage. Even if Paul began his ministry at Damascus, he might quite well speak as he does here, for it is not its chronology, but its range, he is describing ; and to his mind Jerusalem (to which, if let alone, he would have devoted himself, see Acts xxii. 18-22) was its point of departure. καὶ κύκλῳ : most modern commentators have rendered this as if it were τοῦ κύκλῳ— from Jerusalem and its vicinity, by which they mean Syria (though some would include Arabia, Gal. i. 17) : for this use of κύκλῳ see Gen. xxxv. 5, Judith i. 2.

But most Greek commentators render as in the A.V.—" and round about unto Illyricum ". This is the interpretation taken by Hofmann and by S. and H., and is illustrated by Xen., Anab., vii., i., 14 (quoted by the latter) : πότερα διὰ τοῦ ἱεροῦ ὄρους δέοι πορεύεσθαι, ἢ κύκλῳ διὰ μέσης τῆς Θράκης. μέχρι τοῦ Ἰλλυρικοῦ can (so far as μέχρι is concerned) either exclude or include Illyricum. Part of the country so called may have been traversed by Paul in the journey alluded to in Acts xx. 1 f. (διελθὼν δὲ τὰ μέρη ἐκεῖνα), but the language would be satisfied if he had come in sight of Illyricum as he would do in his westward journey through Macedonia. πεπληρωκέναι τὸ εὐαγγ. τοῦ Χριστοῦ : have fulfilled (fully preached) the Gospel of Christ. Cf. Col. i. 25. Paul had done this in the sense in which it was required of an Apostle, whose vocation (to judge from Paul's practice) was to lay the foundation of a church in the chief centres of population, and as soon as the new community was capable of self-propagation, to move on.

Ver. 20. οὕτω δὲ φιλοτιμούμενον (1 Thess. iv. 11, 2 Cor. v. 9) : making it my ambition, however, thus to preach the Gospel, etc. This limits πεπληρωκέναι : he had never sought to preach where Christianity was already established. A point of honour, but not rivalry, is involved in φιλοτιμούμενον. ὠνομάσθη : cf. 2 Tim. ii. 19 and Isa. xxvi. 13, Amos vi. 10. To name the name of the Lord is to confess Him to be what He is to the faith of His people. ἵνα μὴ ἐπ᾽ ἀλλότριον θεμέλιον κ.τ.λ. The duty of an

22. Διὸ καὶ ἐνεκοπτόμην τὰ πολλὰ [1] τοῦ ἐλθεῖν πρὸς ὑμᾶς, 23. νυνὶ δὲ
μηκέτι τόπον ἔχων ἐν τοῖς κλίμασι τούτοις, ἐπιποθίαν δὲ ἔχων τοῦ
ἐλθεῖν πρὸς ὑμᾶς [m] ἀπὸ πολλῶν [2] ἐτῶν, 24. ὡς ἐὰν [3] πορεύωμαι εἰς τὴν
Σπανίαν, ἐλεύσομαι πρὸς ὑμᾶς · ἐλπίζω γὰρ διαπορευόμενος θεάσα-
σθαι ὑμᾶς, καὶ ὑφ᾽ ὑμῶν προπεμφθῆναι ἐκεῖ, ἐὰν ὑμῶν πρῶτον ἀπὸ
μέρους [o] ἐμπλησθῶ. 25. Νυνὶ δὲ πορεύομαι εἰς Ἰερουσαλήμ, διακονῶν

m Luke viii. 43.

n Ver. 15.

o Luke i. 53; vi. 25.

[1] τα πολλα אACLP; πολλακις BDF.

[2] For πολλων אADFL read ικανων with BCP, Weiss, W. and H., Alford.

[3] For ως εαν read ως αν with אABC. Om. ελευσομαι προς υμας אABCDF and all edd.

Apostle was with the foundation, not the superstructure. 1 Cor. iii. 10. The same confidence in his vocation, and the same pride in limiting that confidence, and not boasting of what Christ had done through others, or intruding his operations into their sphere, pervades the tenth chapter of 2 Cor.

Ver. 21. **ἀλλὰ καθὼς γέγραπται**: Paul's actual procedure corresponded with, and indeed led to the fulfilment of, a famous O.T. prophecy. Isa. lii. 11 exactly as in LXX. It is absurd to argue with Fritzsche that Paul found a prediction of his own personal ministry (and of the principles on which he discharged it), in Isaiah, and equally beside the mark to argue that his use of the passage is "quite in accordance with the spirit of the original". The LXX is quite different from the Hebrew, and Paul quotes it because he liked to be able to express his own opinion or practice in Scripture language. It seemed to him to get a Divine confirmation in this way; but an examination of various passages shows that he cared very little for the original meaning or application.

Vv. 22-33. The Apostle's programme. He is at present on his way to Jerusalem with the gifts which his Gentile churches have made for the relief of the poor Christians there. The issue of this visit is dubious, and he begs their prayers for its success. After it is over, he means to proceed to Spain, and on the way he hopes to pay his long deferred visit to Rome.

Ver. 22. **διὸ καὶ ἐνεκοπτόμην**: the work which detained the Apostle in the East also hindered him from visiting Rome. For another **ἐγκόπτειν** see 1 Thess. ii. 18. **τὰ πολλὰ** is more than **πολλάκις** in i. 13: it is distinguished in Greek writers both from **ἐνίοτε** (sometimes) and **ἀεὶ** (always) and is rightly rendered in Vulg. *plerumque*. As a rule,

it was his work which kept Paul from visiting Rome, but he may have had the desire to do so (*e.g.*, when he was in Corinth) and have been prevented by some other cause. The rendering of R.V. "these many times" (apparently, all the definite times included in **πολλά-κις** i. 13) is unsupported by examples.

Ver. 23. **νυνὶ δὲ**: but now — the sentence thus begun is interrupted by **ἐλπίζω γὰρ** and never finished, for the words **ἐλεύσομαι πρὸς ὑμᾶς** in T.R. are an interpolation. **μηκέτι τόπον ἔχων**: not that every soul was converted, but that the Apostolic function of laying foundations had been sufficiently discharged over the area in question. **κλίμα** is only found in the plural in N.T. 2 Cor. xi. 10, Gal. i. 21. **ἐπιπόθειαν**: here only in N.T. **ἀπὸ ἱκανῶν ἐτῶν**: the desire dated "from a good many years back". *Cf.* **ἀπὸ κτίσεως κόσμου**, i. 20, Acts xv. 7.

Ver. 24. **ὡς ἂν πορεύωμαι εἰς τὴν Σπανίαν**: it is here the apodosis begins, which being broken in on by **ἐλπίζω** is never formally resumed, though the sense is taken up again in ver. 28 f. **ὡς ἂν** is temporal = *simulatque*: *cf.* 1 Cor. xi. 34, Phil. ii. 23: Buttmann, p. 232. The principle which Paul has just laid down as regulating his Apostolic work (ver. 20) forbids him to think of Rome as a proper sphere for it; great as is his interest in the capital of the world, he can only pay it a passing visit on the way to another field. **ὑφ᾽ ὑμῶν προπεμφθῆναι ἐκεῖ**: it has been said that Paul expected or claimed "*quasi pro jure suo*" to be escorted all the way to Spain (by sea) by members of the Roman Church; but this is not included in **προπεμφθῆναι**. Practical illustrations are seen in Acts xx. 35, xxi. 5: similar anticipations in 1 Cor. xvi. 6, 11. For **πρῶτον** see Mt. vii. 5, viii. 21. **ἀπὸ μέρους** indicates that no such stay would be equal to the Apostle's longing

τοῖς ἁγίοις. 26. εὐδόκησαν γὰρ Μακεδονία καὶ Ἀχαΐα ᵖ κοινωνίαν p Heb. xiii.
τινὰ ποιήσασθαι εἰς τοὺς πτωχοὺς τῶν ἁγίων τῶν ἐν Ἱερουσαλήμ· 16.
27. εὐδόκησαν γάρ, καὶ ὀφειλέται αὐτῶν εἰσιν. εἰ γὰρ τοῖς πνευματικοῖς αὐτῶν ἐκοινώνησαν τὰ ἔθνη, ὀφείλουσι καὶ ἐν τοῖς σαρκικοῖς
�q λειτουργῆσαι αὐτοῖς. 28. τοῦτο οὖν ἐπιτελέσας, καὶ σφραγισάμενος q 2 Cor. ix.
αὐτοῖς τὸν καρπὸν τοῦτον, ἀπελεύσομαι δι' ὑμῶν εἰς τὴν Σπανίαν. 12.

for fellowship with the Romans, but it would be at least a partial satisfaction of it.

Ver. 25. νυνὶ δὲ is not a resumption of νυνὶ δὲ in ver. 23: there is an entire break in the construction, and Paul begins again, returning from the Spanish journey, which lies in a remote and uncertain future, to the present moment. "But at this moment I am on the way to Jerusalem, ministering to the saints." διακονῶν does not represent this journey as part of his *apostolic ministry*, which might legitimately defer his visit once more (Weiss); it refers to the service rendered to the poor by the money he brought (see 2 Cor. viii. 4). For whatever reason, Paul seems to have used "the saints" (a name applicable to all Christians) with a certain predilection to describe the Jerusalem Church. *Cf.* ver. 31, 1 Cor. xvi. 1, 2 Cor. viii. 4, ix. 1, ix. 12: all in this connection.

Ver. 26. εὐδόκησαν γὰρ Μακεδονία καὶ Ἀχαΐα: Macedonia and Achaia would include all the Pauline Churches in Europe, and we know from 1 Cor. xvi. 1 that a similar contribution was being made in Galatia. εὐδόκησαν expresses the formal *resolution* of the churches in question, but here as in many places with the idea that it was a spontaneous and cordial resolution (though it had been suggested by Paul): see chap. x. 1 (Fritzsche's note there), Luke xii. 32, Gal. i. 15, 1 Cor. i. 21, 1 Thess. ii. 8, iii. 1. κοινωνίαν τινὰ: τινὰ marks the indefiniteness of the collection. It was no assessment to raise a prescribed amount, but "some contribution," more or less according to will and circumstances. For κοινωνίαν in this sense see 2 Cor. viii. 4, ix. 13: where the whole subject is discussed. εἰς τοὺς πτωχοὺς τῶν ἁγίων: from the partitive genitive it is clear that not all the saints in Jerusalem were poor. But Gal. ii. 10, Acts vi. show that the community at least included many poor, towards whom it assumed a responsibility so burdensome that it was unable to discharge it unaided.

Ver. 27. εὐδόκησαν γάρ: they have resolved, I say. Paul felt bound to let

this resolution affect his own conduct, even to the extent of delaying his journey westward. Indeed he explains in 2 Cor., chaps. viii. and ix., that he expected great spiritual results, in the way of a better understanding between Jewish and Gentile Christianity, from this notable act of Gentile charity; hence his desire to see it accomplished, and the necessity laid on him to go once more to Jerusalem. ὀφειλέται: *cf.* i. 14, viii. 12. The resolve of the Gentile Churches to help the poor Jewish Christians, though generous, was not unmotived; in a sense it was the payment of a debt. τοῖς πνευματικοῖς αὐτῶν: the spiritual things belonging to the Jews in which the Gentiles shared are the Gospel and all its blessings— "salvation is of the Jews". All the gifts of Christianity are gifts of the Holy Spirit. ἐν τοῖς σαρκικοῖς: the carnal things of the Gentiles, in which they minister to the Jews, are those which belong to the natural life of man, as a creature of flesh—the universal symbol of these is money. There is the same idea in a similar connection (the support of the Gospel ministry) in 1 Cor. ix. 11. In neither place has σαρκικὰ any ethical connotation. λειτουργῆσαι is simply "to minister to": no official, much less sacerdotal association. *Cf.* Phil. ii. 30.

Ver. 28. τοῦτο οὖν ἐπιτελέσας: having brought this business to a close. It is a mistake to find in Paul's use of ἐπιτελεῖν any reference to the performance of a religious rite: see 2 Cor. viii. 6, 11, Gal. iii. 3, Phil. i. 6. σφραγισάμενος αὐτοῖς τὸν καρπὸν τοῦτον. "This fruit" is, of course, the collection; it is one of the gracious results of the reception of the Gospel by the Gentiles, and Paul loves to conceive and to speak of it spiritually rather than materially. Thus in 2 Cor. viii. and ix. he calls it a χάρις, a διακονία, a κοινωνία, a ἁδρότης, a εὐλογία: never money. The point of the figure in σφραγισάμενος cannot be said to be clear. It may possibly suggest that Paul, in handing over the money to the saints, *authenticates* it to them as the fruit of their πνευματικά, which have been sown among the Gentiles (so S.

r Gal. iii.
14; Eph.
i. 3; Heb.
vi. 7; 1
Pet. iii. 9.

s John iii.
36; Acts
xiv. 2;
xvii. 5.

29. οἶδα δὲ ὅτι, ἐρχόμενος πρὸς ὑμᾶς, ἐν πληρώματι ʳ εὐλογίας τοῦ εὐαγγελίου τοῦ ¹ Χριστοῦ ἐλεύσομαι. 30. Παρακαλῶ δὲ ὑμᾶς, ἀδελφοὶ, διὰ τοῦ Κυρίου ἡμῶν Ἰησοῦ Χριστοῦ, καὶ διὰ τῆς ἀγάπης τοῦ Πνεύματος, συναγωνίσασθαί μοι ἐν ταῖς προσευχαῖς ὑπὲρ ἐμοῦ πρὸς τὸν Θεόν· 31. ἵνα ῥυσθῶ ἀπὸ τῶν ˢ ἀπειθούντων ἐν τῇ Ἰουδαίᾳ, καὶ ἵνα ² ἡ διακονία μου ἡ εἰς Ἱερουσαλὴμ εὐπρόσδεκτος γένηται τοῖς ἁγίοις· 32. ἵνα ἐν χαρᾷ ἔλθω ³ πρὸς ὑμᾶς διὰ θελήματος Θεοῦ, καὶ συναναπαύσωμαι ὑμῖν. 33. ὁ δὲ Θεὸς τῆς εἰρήνης μετὰ πάντων ὑμῶν. ἀμήν.⁴

¹ Om. του ευαγγελιου του ℵABCDF and all edd.

² After και om. ινα with ℵ¹ABCD¹. διακονια ℵACD², ³L; δωροφορια BD¹F. W. and H. regard δωροφορια as a Western reading which belongs to the inferior element in B, and therefore adopt διακονια; so Tischdf. But Weiss thinks διακονια obviously suggested by its use in 2 Cor. viii. 4, ix. 1, 12 f., and puts δωροφορια, which occurs nowhere else in the N.T., in his text. The change of it to διακονια induced, he believes, the further change of εν before Ιερουσαλημ (which is also the reading of BD¹F) into εις (which is found like διακονια in ℵACD³L). This argument seems to have real weight, even though BDF is not always a strong combination of authorities.

³ εν χαρᾳ ελθω. This is the reading of BDEFGLP, and is retained by Weiss. It has the critical advantage of making it possible to understand how B could have come to omit the clause και συναναπαυσωμαι υμιν, and the exegetical advantage of properly defining the end aimed at in the prayer, which was that Paul might come with joy to Rome, not that he might refresh himself after that. W. and H. put the received text in margin, but read in text ινα ... ελθων ... θεου συναναπαυσωμαι υμιν. ελθων is the reading of ℵ¹AC, and these MSS. also omit και. For θεου B has κυριου Ιησου; D¹F Χριστου Ιησου; alii aliter. Possibly the original reading was θεληματος alone (cf. 1 Cor. xvi. 12), which has been variously supplemented.

⁴ αμην om. AF; ins. ℵBCDLP and all edd.

and H.); or it may only mean "when I have *secured* this fruit to them *as their property*" (so Meyer). The ideas of "property," "security," "formality," "solemnity," "finality," are all associated with σφραγίς and σφραγίζω in different passages of the N.T., and it is impossible to say which preponderated in Paul's mind as he wrote these words. *Cf.* John iii. 33, vi. 27. ἀπελεύσομαι is simply *abibo*: the idea of *departing* from Jerusalem is included in it, which is not brought out in the R.V., "I will go on". δι' ὑμῶν: *cf.* 2 Cor. i. 16. εἰς Σπανίαν: there is no evidence that this intention was ever carried out except the well-known passage in Clem. Rom. I. 5 which speaks of Paul as having come ἐπὶ τὸ τέρμα τῆς δύσεως: an expression which, especially if the writer was a Jew, may as well mean Rome as Spain. But all the more if it was not carried out is this passage in Romans assuredly genuine; a second-century writer would not gratuitously ascribe to an apostle

intentions which he must have known were never accomplished. Ver. 29. For ἐρχόμενος ... ἐλεύσομαι *cf.* 1 Cor. ii. 1. ἐν πληρώματι εὐλογίας Χριστοῦ. Paul's desire was to impart to the Romans χάρισμά τι πνευματικόν (i. 11), and he is sure it will be satisfied to the full. When he comes he will bring blessing from Christ to which nothing will be lacking. On πλήρωμα see xi. 12. Ver. 30. παρακαλῶ δὲ ὑμᾶς. In spite of the confident tone of ver. 29, Paul is very conscious of the uncertainties and perils which lie ahead of him, and with the δὲ he turns to this aspect of his situation. ἀδελφοὶ (which W. H. bracket) is an appeal to their Christian sympathy. διὰ τοῦ κυρίου ἡμῶν Ἰ. Χ. For διὰ in this sense see xii. 1. The Romans and Paul were alike servants of this Lord, and His name was a motive to the Romans to sympathise with Paul in all that he had to encounter in Christ's service. διὰ τῆς ἀγάπης τοῦ πνεύματος:

XVI. 1. ΣΥΝΙΣΤΗΜΙ δὲ ὑμῖν Φοίβην τὴν ἀδελφὴν ἡμῶν, οὖσαν [1] a 1 Tim. iii. 8, 12.
ᵃδιάκονον τῆς ἐκκλησίας τῆς ἐν Κεγχρεαῖς· 2. ἵνα αὐτὴν ᵇπροσδέξησθε [2] b Phil. ii. 29.
ἐν Κυρίῳ ἀξίως τῶν ἁγίων, καὶ παραστῆτε αὐτῇ ἐν ᾧ ἂν ὑμῶν χρῄζῃ
πράγματι· καὶ γὰρ αὕτη ᶜπροστάτις πολλῶν ἐγενήθη, καὶ αὐτοῦ c Here only in N.T.

[1] After ουσαν ins. και אᵃBC¹; so Weiss. W. and H. bracket.

[2] αυτην προσδεξησθε אALP; αυτην after προσδ. BCDF. For αυτου εμου read εμου αυτου with ABCL.

the love wrought in Christian hearts by the Spirit of God (Gal. v. 22) is another motive of the same kind. συναγωνίσασθαί μοι, ἐν ταῖς προσευχαῖς. συναγωνίζομαι is found here only in the N.T., but ἀγὼν and ἀγωνίζομαι in a spiritual sense are found in each of the groups into which the Pauline epistles are usually divided. What Paul asks is that they should join him in striving with all their might—in wrestling as it were—against the hostile forces which would frustrate his apostolic work. Cf. Just. Mart., Apol., ii., 13: καὶ εὐχόμενος καὶ παμμάχως ἀγωνιζόμενος. ἀγωνία in Lc. xxii. 44 seems to denote awful fear rather than intense striving. πρὸς τὸν θεόν is not otiose: Paul felt how much it was worth to have God appealed to on his behalf.

Ver. 31 f. ἵνα ῥυσθῶ ἀπὸ τῶν ἀπειθούντων: from the disobedient, i.e., from the Jews who had not received the Gospel, 2 Thess. i. 8, chap. xi. 30. καὶ ἡ διακονία μου κ.τ.λ. It was not the unbelieving Jews only who hated Paul. To them he was an apostate, who had disappointed all their hopes; but even Christian Jews in many cases regarded him as false to the nation's prerogative, and especially to the law. There was a real danger that the contribution he brought from the Gentile Churches might not be graciously accepted, even accepted at all; it might be regarded as a bribe, in return for which Paul's opposition to the law was to be condoned, and the equal standing of his upstart churches in the Kingdom of God acknowledged. It was by no means certain that it would be taken as what it was—a pledge of brotherly love; and God alone could dispose "the saints" to take it as simply as it was offered. Paul's state of mind as seen here is exactly that which is revealed in Acts xx. 17-38, xxi. 13, etc. ἵνα ἐν χαρᾷ ἐλθών . . . συναναπαύσωμαι ὑμῖν. συναναπ. here only in N.T. but cf. συνπαρακληθῆναι, i. 12, and συναγωνίσασθαι ver. 30. "Rest after the personal danger and after the ecclesiastical crisis of which the personal danger formed

a part" (Hort). The ἵνα here seems to be subordinate to, not co-ordinate with, the preceding one. Paul looks forward to a time of joy and rest beyond these anxieties and dangers, as the ultimate end to be secured by their prayers. διὰ θελήματος θεοῦ: it depends on this whether Paul is to return or how. He did reach Rome, by the will of God (i. 10), but hardly in the conditions anticipated here.

Ver. 33. ὁ δὲ θεὸς τῆς εἰρήνης: there is an appropriateness in this designation after ver. 31, but "peace" is one of the ruling ideas in Paul's mind always, and needs no special explanation in a benediction: 2 Cor. xiii. 11, Phil. iv. 9, 1 Thess. v. 23.

CHAPTER XVI. On this chapter see introduction. It consists of five distinct parts: (1) The recommendation of Phœbe to the Church, vers. 1 and 2; (2) a series of greetings from Paul himself, vers. 3-16; (3) a warning against false teachers, vers. 17-20; (4) a series of greetings from companions of Paul, vers. 21-23; (5) a doxology.

Ver. 1 f. Συνίστημι δὲ ὑμῖν Φοίβην. συνίστημι is the technical word for this kind of recommendation, which is equivalent to a certificate of church membership. Paul uses it with especial frequency in 2 Cor., both in this technical sense (iii. 1, v. 12), and in a kindred but wider one (iv. 2, vi. 4, vii. 11, x. 12, 18). τὴν ἀδελφὴν ἡμῶν: our (Christian) sister, 1 Cor. vii. 15, ix. 5. The spiritual kinship thus asserted was a recommendation of itself, but in Phœbe's case Paul can add another. οὖσαν καὶ διάκονον τῆς ἐκκλησίας τῆς ἐν Κεγχρεαῖς: who is also a servant of the Church in Cenchreæ. It is not easy to translate διάκονος, for "servant" is too vague, and "deaconess" is more technical than the original. Διακονία was really a function of membership in the Church, and Phœbe might naturally be described as she is here if like the house of Stephanas at Corinth (1 Cor. xvi. 15) she had given herself εἰς διακονίαν τοῖς ἁγίοις. That

ἐμοῦ. 3. Ἀσπάσασθε Πρίσκιλλαν [1] καὶ Ἀκύλαν τοὺς συνεργούς μου ἐν Χριστῷ Ἰησοῦ, 4. (οἵτινες ὑπὲρ τῆς ψυχῆς μου τὸν ἑαυτῶν τράχηλον ὑπέθηκαν· οἷς οὐκ ἐγὼ μόνος εὐχαριστῶ, ἀλλὰ καὶ πᾶσαι αἱ ἐκκλησίαι τῶν ἐθνῶν·) καὶ τὴν κατ᾽ οἶκον αὐτῶν ἐκκλησίαν. 5. ἀσπάσασθε Ἐπαίνετον τὸν ἀγαπητόν μου, ὅς ἐστιν ἀπαρχὴ τῆς Ἀχαίας [2] εἰς Χρι-

[1] For Πρισκιλλαν (corrected by Acts xviii. 2) read Πρισκαν אABCDFL.

[2] For της Αχαιας LP, read της Ασιας with אABCD¹F. The wrong reading is due to 1 Cor. xvi. 15.

is, a life of habitual charity and hospitality, quite apart from any official position, would justify the name διάκονος. On the other hand it must be remembered that the growth of the Church, under the conditions of ancient society, soon produced "deaconesses" in the official sense, and Phœbe may have had some recognised function of διακονία assigned to her. Cenchreæ was on the Saronic gulf, nine miles E. of Corinth: as the port for Asia and the East, many Christians would pass through it, and a Christian woman who gave herself to hospitality (xii. 13) might have her hands full. ἐν Κυρίῳ: no mere reception of Phœbe into their houses satisfies this —their Christian life was to be open for her to share in it; she was no alien to be debarred from spiritual intimacy. ἀξίως τῶν ἁγίων: with such kindness as it becomes Christians to show. καὶ παραστῆτε αὐτῇ (Jer. xv. 11): after the Christian welcome is assured, Paul bespeaks their help for Phœbe in whatever affair she may require it. He speaks indefinitely, but his language suggests that she was going to Rome on business in which they could assist her. καὶ γὰρ αὐτὴ: in complying with this request they will only be doing for Phœbe what she has done for others, and especially for Paul himself. προστάτις (feminine of προστάτης) is suggested by παραστῆτε. Paul might have said παραστάτις, but uses the more honourable word. προστάτης (patronus) was the title of a citizen in Athens who took charge of the interests of μέτοικοι and persons without civic rights; the corresponding feminine here may suggest that Phœbe was a woman of good position who could render valuable services to such a community as a primitive Christian Church usually was. When she helped Paul we cannot tell. Dr. Gifford suggests the occasion of Acts xviii. 18. Paul's vow "seems to point to a deliverance from danger or sickness," in which she may have ministered to him. It is generally assumed that Phœbe was the bearer of this epistle, and many even of those who regard vers. 3-16 as addressed to Ephesus still hold that vers. 1 and 2 were meant for Rome.

Ver. 3 f. Greeting to Prisca and Aquila. ἀσπάσασθε: only here does Paul commission the whole Church to greet individual members of it (Weiss). For the persons here named see Acts xviii. 2. Paul met them first in Corinth, and according to Meyer converted them there. Here as in Acts xviii. 18, 26 and 1 Tim. iv. 19 the wife is put first, probably as the more distinguished in Christian character and service; in 1 Cor. xvi. 19, where they *send* greetings, the husband naturally gets his precedence. τοὺς συνεργούς μου ἐν Χριστῷ Ἰησοῦ: on first acquaintance they had been fellow-workers, not in Christ Jesus, but in tent-making: they were ὁμότεχνοι, Acts xviii. 3. οἵτινες: *quippe qui*. τὸν ἑαυτῶν τράχηλον: the singular (as Gifford points out) shows that the expression is figurative. To save Paul's life Prisca and Aquila incurred some great danger themselves; what, we cannot tell. They were in his company both in Corinth and Ephesus, at times when he was in extreme peril (Acts xviii. 12, xix. 30 f.), and the recipients of the letter would understand the allusion. The technical sense of ὑποθεῖναι, to give as a pledge, cannot be pressed here, as though Prisca and Aquila had given their personal security (though it involved the hazard of their lives) for Paul's good behaviour. οἷς οὐκ ἐγὼ μόνος εὐχαριστῶ κ.τ.λ. The language implies that the incident referred to had occurred long enough ago for all the Gentile Churches to be aware of it, but yet so recently that both they and the Apostle himself retained a lively feeling of gratitude to his brave friends. καὶ τὴν κατ᾽ οἶκον αὐτῶν ἐκκλησίαν: these words do not mean "their Christian household," nor do they imply that the

στόν. 6. ἀσπάσασθε Μαριάμ,[1] ἥτις πολλὰ [d] ἐκοπίασεν εἰς ἡμᾶς. d Ver. 12.

7. ἀσπάσασθε Ἀνδρόνικον καὶ Ἰουνίαν τοὺς συγγενεῖς μου καὶ
[e] συναιχμαλώτους μου, οἵτινές εἰσιν [f] ἐπίσημοι ἐν τοῖς ἀποστόλοις, e Col. iv.10.
οἳ καὶ πρὸ ἐμοῦ γεγόνασιν[2] ἐν Χριστῷ. 8. ἀσπάσασθε Ἀμπλίαν[3] Philemon 23.
τὸν ἀγαπητόν μου ἐν Κυρίῳ. 9. ἀσπάσασθε Οὐρβανὸν τὸν συνεργὸν f Matt. xxvii. 16.

[1] Μαριαμ ℵDFL; Μαριαν ABCP, and so most edd. For ημας read υμας ℵABC[1]P.

[2] For γεγονασιν read γεγοναν with ℵAB.

[3] For Αμπλιαν read Αμπλιατον with ℵAB[1]F.

whole Christian community (in Rome or in Ephesus) met in the house of Prisca and Aquila. They signify the body of believers meeting for worship there, a body which would only be part of the local Christian community. Cf. 1 Cor. xvi. 19, Col. iv. 15, Philemon 2, Acts xii. 12. "There is no clear example of a separate building set apart for Christian worship within the limits of the Roman Empire before the third century, though apartments in private houses might be specially devoted to this purpose" (Lightfoot on Col. iv. 15). ἀσπάσασθε Ἐπαίνετον τὸν ἀγαπητόν μου: after Priscilla and Aquila, not a single person is known of all those to whom Paul sends greetings in vv. 3-16. ἀπαρχὴ τῆς Ἀσίας: Epænetus was the first convert in Asia (the Roman province of that name). Cf. 1 Cor. xvi. 15. There is no difficulty in supposing that the first Christian of Asia was at this time—temporarily or permanently—in Rome: but the discovery of an Ephesian Epænetus on a Roman inscription (quoted by Sanday and Headlam) is very interesting.

Ver. 6. It is not certain whether Μαριάμ (which is Jewish) or Μαρίαν (Roman) is the true reading. ἥτις πολλὰ ἐκοπίασεν: the much labour she had bestowed is made the ground (ἥτις) of a special greeting. εἰς ὑμᾶς is much better supported than εἰς ἡμᾶς: there is something finer in Paul's appreciation of services rendered to others than if they had been rendered to himself. Cf. Gal. iv. 11.

Ver. 7. Andronicus is a Greek name, which, like most names in this chapter, can be illustrated from inscriptions. Ἰουνίαν may be masculine (from Ἰουνίας, or Ἰουνιᾶς contraction of Junianus), or feminine (from Ἰουνία): probably the former. τοὺς συγγενεῖς μου: i.e., Jews. Cf. ix. 3. It is hardly possible that so many people in the Church addressed (see vv. 11, 21) should be more closely connected with Paul than by the bond of

nationality. But it was natural for him, in writing to a mainly Gentile Church, to distinguish those with whom he had this point of contact. Cf. Col. iv. 11. συναιχμαλώτους μου: this naturally means that on some occasion they had shared Paul's imprisonment: it is doubtful whether it would be satisfied by the idea that they, like him, had also been imprisoned for Christ's sake. The αἰχμάλωτος is a prisoner of war: Paul and his friends were all Salvation Army men. The phrase ἐπίσημοι ἐν τοῖς ἀποστόλοις, men of mark among the Apostles, has the same ambiguity in Greek as in English. It might mean, well-known to the apostolic circle, or distinguished as Apostles. The latter sense is that in which it is taken by "all patristic commentators" (Sanday and Headlam), whose instinct for what words meant in a case of this kind must have been surer than that of a modern reader. It implies, of course, a wide sense of the word Apostle: for justification of which reference may be made to Lightfoot's essay on the name and office of an Apostle (Galatians, 92 ff.) and Harnack, Lehre der zwölf Apostel, S. 111-118. On the other hand, Paul's use of the word Apostle is not such as to make it easy to believe that he thought of a large class of persons who might be so designated, a class so large that two otherwise unknown persons like Andronicus and Junias might be conspicuous in it. Hence scholars like Weiss and Gifford hold that what is meant here is that Andronicus and Junias were honourably known to the Twelve. οἳ καὶ πρὸ ἐμοῦ γέγοναν ἐν Χριστῷ: they had evidently been converted very early, and, like Mnason the Cypriot, were ἀρχαῖοι μαθηταί, Acts xxi. 16. On γέγοναν see Burton, Moods and Tenses, § 82. The English idiom does not allow of a perfect translation, but "were" is more idiomatic than "have been".

Ver. 8. Ἀμπλιᾶτον: "a common Roman slave name". Sanday and Head-

ἡμῶν ἐν Χριστῷ, καὶ Στάχυν τὸν ἀγαπητόν μου. 10. ἀσπάσασθε Ἀπελλῆν τὸν δόκιμον ἐν Χριστῷ. ἀσπάσασθε τοὺς ἐκ τῶν Ἀριστοβούλου. 11. ἀσπάσασθε Ἡρωδίωνα τὸν συγγενῆ μου. ἀσπάσασθε τοὺς ἐκ τῶν Ναρκίσσου, τοὺς ὄντας ἐν Κυρίῳ. 12. ἀσπάσασθε Τρύφαιναν καὶ Τρυφῶσαν τὰς κοπιώσας ἐν Κυρίῳ. ἀσπάσασθε Περσίδα τὴν ἀγαπητήν, ἥτις πολλὰ ἐκοπίασεν ἐν Κυρίῳ. 13. ἀσπάσασθε Ῥοῦφον τὸν ἐκλεκτὸν ἐν Κυρίῳ, καὶ τὴν μητέρα αὐτοῦ καὶ ἐμοῦ.

lam give inscriptions from the cemetery of Domitilla, which make it probable that a person of this name was conspicuous in the earliest Roman Church, and may have been the means of introducing Christianity to a great Roman house. τὸν ἀγαπητόν μου ἐν Κυρίῳ: Paul has none but *Christian* relations to this man.

Ver. 9. Οὐρβανὸν: also a common slave name, "found, as here, in juxtaposition with Ampliatus, in a list of imperial freedmen, on an inscription A.D. 115" (Gifford). τὸν συνεργὸν ἡμῶν: the ἡμῶν (as opposed to μου, ver. 3) seems to suggest that all Christian workers had a common helper in Urbanus. Of Stachys nothing is known but that he was dear to Paul. The name is Greek; but, like the others, has been found in inscriptions connected with the Imperial household.

Ver. 10. Ἀπελλῆν τὸν δόκιμον ἐν Χριστῷ: Apelles, that approved Christian. In some conspicuous way the Christian character of Apelles had been tried and found proof: see Jas. i. 12, 2 Tim. ii. 15. The name is a familiar one, and sometimes Jewish: *Credat Judæus Apella*, Hor., *Sat.*, I., v., 100. By τοὺς ἐκ τῶν Ἀριστοβούλου are meant Christians belonging to the household of Aristobulus. Lightfoot, in his essay on Cæsar's Household (*Philippians*, 171 ff.), makes Aristobulus the grandson of Herod the Great. He was educated in Rome, and probably died there. "Now it seems not improbable, considering the intimate relations between Claudius and Aristobulus, that at the death of the latter his servants, wholly or in part, should be transferred to the palace. In this case they would be designated *Aristobuliani*, for which I suppose St. Paul's οἱ ἐκ τῶν Ἀριστοβούλου to be an equivalent. It is at least not an obvious phrase, and demands explanation" (*Philippians*, 175).

Ver. 11. Ἡρωδίωνα τὸν συγγενῆ μου. This agrees very well with the interpretation just given to τοὺς ἐκ τῶν Ἀριστοβούλου. In the household of Herod's grandson there might naturally be a Jew with a name of this type, whom Paul, for some cause or other, could single out for a special greeting. τοὺς ἐκ τῶν Ναρκίσσου τοὺς ὄντας ἐν Κυρίῳ: the last words may suggest that, though only the Christians in this household have a greeting sent to them, there were other members of it with whom the Church had relations. The Narcissus meant is probably the notorious freedman of Claudius, who was put to death shortly after the accession of Nero (Tac., *Ann.*, xiii., 1), and therefore two or three years before this epistle was written. His slaves would probably pass into the emperor's hands, and increase "Cæsar's househould" as Narcissiani (Lightfoot, *loc. cit.*).

Ver. 12. Τρύφαιναν καὶ Τρυφῶσαν: "It was usual to designate members of the same family by derivatives of the same root" (Lightfoot): hence these two women were probably sisters. The names, which might be rendered "Dainty" and "Disdain" (see Jas. v. 5, Is. lxvi. 11) are characteristically pagan, and unlike the description τὰς κοπιώσας, "who toil in the Lord". They are still at work, but the "much toil" of Persis, the beloved, belongs to some occasion in the past. τὴν ἀγαπητήν: Paul does not here add μου as with the men's names in vv. 8 and 9. Persis was dear to the whole Church.

Ver. 13. Ῥοῦφον τὸν ἐκλεκτὸν ἐν Κυρίῳ: for the name see Mark xv. 21. If Mark wrote his gospel at Rome, as there is ground to believe, this may be the person to whom he refers. In the gospel he is assumed to be well known, and here he is described as "that choice Christian". ἐκλεκτὸν cannot refer simply to the fact of his election to be a Christian, since in whatever sense this is true, it is true of all Christians alike; whereas here it evidently expresses some distinction of Rufus. He was a noble specimen of a Christian. καὶ τὴν μητέρα αὐτοῦ κ. ἐμοῦ: where she had "mothered" Paul we do not know. For the idea *cf.* Mark x. 30.

14. ἀσπάσασθε Ἀσύγκριτον, Φλέγοντα, Ἑρμᾶν, Πατρόβαν, Ἑρμῆν,[1] καὶ τοὺς σὺν αὐτοῖς ἀδελφούς. 15. ἀσπάσασθε Φιλόλογον καὶ Ἰουλίαν, Νηρέα καὶ τὴν ἀδελφὴν αὐτοῦ, καὶ Ὀλυμπᾶν, καὶ τοὺς σὺν αὐτοῖς πάντας ἁγίους. 16. ἀσπάσασθε ἀλλήλους ἐν φιλήματι ἁγίῳ. ἀσπάζονται ὑμᾶς αἱ ἐκκλησίαι[2] τοῦ Χριστοῦ· 17. Παρακαλῶ δὲ ὑμᾶς, ἀδελφοὶ, σκοπεῖν τοὺς τὰς [g] διχοστασίας καὶ τὰ σκάνδαλα, παρὰ τὴν διδαχὴν ἣν ὑμεῖς ἐμάθετε, ποιοῦντας· καὶ ἐκκλίνατε[3] ἀπ' αὐτῶν.

[g] 1 Cor. iii. 3; Gal. v 20.

[1] Here אABCD¹FP and all edd. transpose Ερμαν and Ερμην.
[2] After εκκλησιαι ins. πασαι אABCLP and all edd.
[3] For εκκλινατε read εκκλινετε with א¹BC, Weiss, W. and H., Tischdf.

Ver. 14. Of Asyncritus, Phlegon and Hermes nothing is known. Patrobas (or Patrobius) may have been a dependant of a famous freedman of the same name in Nero's time, who was put to death by Galba (Tac., *Hist.*, i., 49, ii., 95). Hermas has often been identified with the author of The Shepherd, but though the identification goes back to Origen, it is a mistake. "Pastorem vero *nuperrime temporibus nostris* in urbe Roma Herma conscripsit *sedente cathedra urbis Romæ ecclesiæ Pio eps. fratre ejus*": these words of the Canon of Muratori forbid the identification. τοὺς σὺν αὐτοῖς ἀδελφούς indicates that the persons named, and some others designated in this phrase, formed a little community by themselves—perhaps an ἐκκλησία κατ' οἶκόν τινος.

Ver. 15. Philologus and Julia, as connected here, were probably husband and wife; or, as in the next pair, brother and sister. Both, especially the latter, are among the commonest slave names. There are Acts of Nereus and Achilleus in the Acta Sanctorum connected with the early Roman Church. "The sister's name is not given, but one Nereis was a member of the [imperial] household about this time, as appears from an inscription already quoted" (Lightfoot, *loc. cit.*, p. 177). Olympas is a contraction of Olympiodorus. τοὺς σὺν αὐτοῖς πάντας ἁγίους : see on last verse. The πάντας may suggest that a larger number of persons is to be included here.

Ver. 16. ἀλλήλους. When the epistle is read in the Church the Christians are to greet each other, and seal their mutual salutations ἐν φιλήματι ἁγίῳ. In 1 Thess. v. 26 the προϊστάμενοι apparently are to salute the members of the Church so. In 1 Cor. xvi. 20, 2 Cor. xiii. 12, exactly the same form is used as here. The custom of combining greeting and kiss was oriental, and especially Jewish, and in this way became Christian. In 1 Pet. v. 14 the kiss is called φίλημα ἀγάπης ; in Apost. Const., ii., 57, 12, τὸ ἐν Κυρίῳ φίλημα ; in Tert. de Orat., xiv., *osculum pacis.* By ἅγιον the kiss is distinguished from an ordinary greeting of natural affection or friendship ; it belongs to God and the new society of His children ; it is specifically *Christian.* αἱ ἐκκλησίαι πᾶσαι τοῦ Χριστοῦ : "this phrase is unique in the N.T." (Sanday and Headlam). The ordinary form is "the Church" or "the Churches of God" : but in Matt. xvi. 18 Christ says "*my* Church": *cf.* also Acts xx. 28, where τὴν ἐκκλησίαν τοῦ Κυρίου is found in many good authorities. For "all the Community *cf.* ver. 4, 1 Cor. vii. 17, xiv. 33, 2 Cor. viii. 18, xi. 28. Probably Paul was commissioned by some, and he took it on him to speak for the rest. If the faith of the Romans were published in all the world (chap. i. 8), the Churches everywhere would have sufficient interest in them to ratify this courtesy. "Quoniam cognovit omnium erga Romanos studium, omnium nomine salutat."

Vv. 17-20. Warning against false teachers. This comes in very abruptly in the middle of the greetings, and as it stands has the character of an afterthought. The false teachers referred to are quite definitely described, but it is clear that they had not yet appeared in Rome, nor begun to work there. Paul is only warning the Roman Church against a danger which he has seen in other places. There is a very similar passage in Phil. iii. 18 f., which Lightfoot connects with this, arguing that the persons denounced are not Judaising teachers, but antinomian reactionists. It is easier to see grounds for this opinion in Philippians than here : but chap. vi. 1-23 may be quoted in support of it.

h Ch. xiv. 18. οἱ γὰρ τοιοῦτοι τῷ Κυρίῳ ἡμῶν Ἰησοῦ [1] Χριστῷ οὐ [h] δουλεύουσιν,
18.
i Here only ἀλλὰ τῇ ἑαυτῶν κοιλίᾳ· καὶ διὰ τῆς [i] χρηστολογίας καὶ εὐλογίας
in N.T.
ἐξαπατῶσι τὰς καρδίας τῶν ἀκάκων. 19. ἡ γὰρ ὑμῶν ὑπακοὴ εἰς
πάντας ἀφίκετο· χαίρω οὖν τὸ ἐφ' ὑμῖν· [2] θέλω δὲ ὑμᾶς σοφοὺς μὲν
εἶναι εἰς τὸ ἀγαθόν, ἀκεραίους δὲ εἰς τὸ κακόν. 20. ὁ δὲ Θεὸς τῆς
k Rev. ii. 27. εἰρήνης [k] συντρίψει τὸν Σατανᾶν ὑπὸ τοὺς πόδας ὑμῶν ἐν τάχει. ἡ

[1] Ιησου om. ℵABCDFP and all edd.

[2] χαιρω ουν το εφ υμιν ℵ³DF; but ℵ¹ABCLP and all edd. εφ' υμιν ουν χαιρω.
μεν after σοφους ℵACP; om. BDFL. Most edd. omit, but W. and H. bracket.

Ver. 17. σκοπεῖν: to keep your eye upon, either as an example to be followed (Phil. iii. 17), or (as in this case) as a peril to be avoided. τοὺς τὰς διχοστασίας καὶ τὰ σκάνδαλα ποιοῦντας: both the persons and their conduct are supposed to be known; "the divisions" and "the scandals," which had been occasioned in other Churches, are assumed to be familiar to the Romans. τὰ σκάνδαλα refers more naturally to conduct which would create a moral prejudice against the Gospel, and so prevent men from accepting it, than to any ordinary result of Jewish legal teaching. But if the latter caused dissension and generated bad tempers in the Church, it also might give outsiders cause to blaspheme, and to stumble at the Gospel (xiv. 13, 16). παρὰ τὴν διδαχὴν ἣν ὑμεῖς ἐμάθετε: ὑμεῖς is emphatic, and implies that they at least are as yet untouched by the false teaching. By "the teaching which you received" is meant not "Paulinism," but Christianity, though the words of course imply that the Roman Church was not anti-Pauline. ἐκκλίνετε with ἀπὸ in 1 Pet. iii. 11, Prov. iv. 15.

Ver. 18. οἱ γὰρ τοιοῦτοι κ.τ.λ. Christians must not associate with those who do not serve the one Lord. τῷ Κυρίῳ ἡμῶν Χριστῷ: this combination occurs here only in N.T. τῇ ἑαυτῶν κοιλίᾳ: cf. Phil. iii. 19, ὧν ὁ θεὸς ἡ κοιλία. The words need not mean that the teachers in question were mere sensualists, or that they taught Epicurean or antinomian doctrines: the sense must partly be defined by the contrast—it is not our Lord Christ whom they serve; on the contrary, it is base interests of their own. It is a bitter contemptuous way of describing a self-seeking spirit, rather than an allusion to any particular cast of doctrine. διὰ τῆς χρηστολογίας καὶ εὐλογίας: according to Grimm, χρηστολογία refers to the insinuating tone, εὐλογία to the fine style, of the false teachers. Ex-

amples from profane Greek bear out this distinction (εὔαρχός ἐστιν ὁ λόγος καὶ πολλὴν τὴν εὐλογίαν ἐπιδεικνύμενος καὶ εὔλεξις), but as εὐλογία in Biblical Greek, and in Philo and Josephus invariably has a religious sense, Cremer prefers to take it so here also: "pious talk". ἐξαπατῶσι: vii. 11, 1 Cor. iii. 18, 2 Th. ii. 2. ἀκάκων: all the English versions, except Gen. and A.V., render "of the innocent" (Gifford). See Heb. vii. 26. In this place "guileless" is rather the idea: suspecting no evil, and therefore liable to be deceived.

Ver. 19. ἡ γὰρ ὑμῶν ὑπακοὴ: What is the connection? "I give this exhortation, separating you altogether from the false teachers, and from those who are liable to be misled by them; for your obedience (ὑμῶν emphasised by position) has come abroad to all men. (Cf. i. 8.) Over you therefore I rejoice, but," etc. He expresses his confidence in them, but at the same time conveys the feeling of his anxiety. For χαίρειν ἐπὶ see 1 Cor. xiii. 6, xvi. 17. σοφοὺς μὲν εἶναι εἰς τὸ ἀγαθόν, ἀκεραίους δὲ εἰς τὸ κακόν. For ἀκέραιος see Matt. x. 16, Phil. ii. 15, and Trench, Syn., § lvi., where there is a full discussion and comparison with ἄκακος. The fundamental idea of the word is that of freedom from alien or disturbing elements. What Paul here wishes for the Romans—moral intelligence, not impaired in the least by any dealings with evil—does suggest that antinomianism was the peril to be guarded against. Integrity of the moral nature is the best security: the seductive teaching is instinctively repelled.

Ver. 20. ὁ δὲ θεὸς τῆς εἰρήνης: used here with special reference to αἱ διχοστασίαι. Cf. 1 Cor. xiv. 33. συντρίψει τὸν Σατανᾶν: divisions in the Church are Satan's work, and the suppression of them by the God of peace is a victory over Satan. Cf. 2 Cor. xi. 14 f. There is an allusion to Gen iii. 15, though it is

χάρις τοῦ Κυρίου ἡμῶν Ἰησοῦ Χριστοῦ [1] μεθ᾽ ὑμῶν. ἀμήν. 21.
Ἀσπάζονται [2] ὑμᾶς Τιμόθεος ὁ συνεργός μου, καὶ Λούκιος καὶ Ἰάσων
καὶ Σωσίπατρος οἱ συγγενεῖς μου. 22. ἀσπάζομαι ὑμᾶς ἐγὼ
Τέρτιος ὁ γράψας τὴν ἐπιστολὴν ἐν Κυρίῳ. 23. ἀσπάζεται ὑμᾶς
Γάϊος ὁ ξένος μου καὶ τῆς ἐκκλησίας ὅλης. ἀσπάζεται ὑμᾶς Ἔρασ-
τος ὁ οἰκονόμος τῆς πόλεως, καὶ Κούαρτος ὁ ἀδελφός.

[1] Χριστου om. אB, edd.

[2] For ασπαζονται read ασπαζεται אABCD¹F. Om. first μου B 67; W. and H.
bracket.

doubtful whether Paul found anything
there answering to συντρίψει. The LXX
has τηρήσει. ἐν τάχει: cf. Ez. xxix. 5;
Deut. xxviii. 20. The false teachers may
come and cause dissension, but it will
not be long till peace is restored. ἡ
χάρις κ.τ.λ. This benediction can
hardly be supposed to belong only to
vv. 17-20. It rather suggests that some
copies of the epistle ended here; possibly that vv. 1-20 (for there is another
benediction at xiv. 33) were originally an
independent epistle.

Vv. 21-23. Greetings of Paul's companions.

Ver. 21. Τιμόθεος. In many of the
epistles Timothy's name is associated
with Paul's in the opening salutation
(1 and 2 Thess., 2 Cor., Phil., Col.,
Philemon). Perhaps when Paul began
this letter he was absent, but had come
back in time to send his greeting at the
close. He was with Paul (Acts xx. 4 f.)
when he started on the journey to Jerusalem mentioned in xv. 25. Lucius,
Jason and Sosipater are all Jews, but
none of them can be identified. For the
names (which may or may not be those
of the same persons) see Acts xiii. 1,
xvii. 5, xx. 4.

Ver. 22. ἐγὼ Τέρτιος ὁ γράψας τὴν
ἐπιστολήν: the use of the first person
is a striking indication of Paul's courtesy.
To have sent the greeting of his amanuensis in the third person would have been
to treat him as a mere machine (Godet).
ἐν Κυρίῳ goes with ἀσπάζομαι: it is as
a Christian, not in virtue of any other relation he has to the Romans, that Tertius
salutes them.

Ver. 23. Γάϊος ὁ ξένος μου κ. ὅλης
τῆς ἐκκλησίας: As the Epistle to the
Romans was written from Corinth this
hospitable Christian is probably the
same who is mentioned in 1 Cor. i. 14.
Three other persons (apparently) of the
same name are mentioned in Acts xix.
29, xx. 4, and 3 John. By ὁ ξένος μου

is meant that Gaius was Paul's host in
Corinth; ὁ ξένος ὅλης τῆς ἐκκλησίας
might either mean that the whole Christian community met in his house (cf. vv.
5, 14, 15), or that he made all Christians
who came to Corinth welcome. Ἔραστος
ὁ οἰκονόμος τῆς πόλεως. We cannot be
sure that this is the Erastus of Acts xix.
22, 2 Tim. iv. 20: the latter seems to
have been at Paul's disposal in connection with his work. But they may be
the same, and Paul may here be designating Erastus by an office which he had
once held, but held no longer. The city
treasurer (arcarius civitatis) would be an
important person in a poor community
(1 Cor. i. 26 ff.), and he and Gaius
(whose boundless hospitality implies
means) are probably mentioned here as
representing the Corinthian Church.
Κούαρτος ὁ ἀδελφός: Quartus, known to
Paul only as a Christian, had perhaps
some connection with Rome which entitled him to have his salutation inserted.

Ver. 24. The attestation of this verse
is quite insufficient, and it is omitted by
all critical editors.

Vv. 25-27. The doxology. St. Paul's
letters, as a rule, terminate with a benediction, and even apart from the questions
of textual criticism, connected with it,
this doxology has given rise to much
discussion. The closest analogies to it
are found in the doxology at the end of
Ephes., chap. iii., and in Jude (vv. 24 and
25); there is something similar in the
last chapter of Hebrews (xiii. 20 f.),
though not quite at the end; Pauline
doxologies as a rule are briefer (i. 25,
ix. 5, xi. 36, Phil. iv. 20), and more closely
related to what immediately precedes.
This one, in which all the leading ideas
of the Epistle to the Romans may be
discovered, though in a style which reminds one uncomfortably of the Pastoral
Epistles rather than of that to which it is
appended, would seem more in place if it
stood where AL and an immense num-

24. Ἡ χάρις τοῦ Κυρίου ἡμῶν Ἰησοῦ Χριστοῦ μετὰ πάντων ὑμῶν.

Gal. i. 12;   ἀμήν.[1]   25. Τῷ δὲ δυναμένῳ ὑμᾶς στηρίξαι κατὰ τὸ εὐαγγέλιόν μου
Eph. iii.   καὶ τὸ κήρυγμα Ἰησοῦ Χριστοῦ, κατὰ [1] ἀποκάλυψιν μυστηρίου χρόνοις
3.   αἰωνίοις ᵐ σεσιγημένου, 26. φανερωθέντος δὲ νῦν, διά τε γραφῶν προ-
m Here
only in
N.T.   φητικῶν, κατ᾽ ἐπιταγὴν τοῦ αἰωνίου Θεοῦ, εἰς ὑπακοὴν πίστεως εἰς

---

[1] This verse is wanting in אABC; ins. in DFL.   See Introduction, p. 578.

ber of MSS. place it—after xiv. 23. It may represent the first emergence and conscious apprehension of thoughts which were afterwards to become familiar; but it cannot be denied that the many distinct points of contact with later writings give it, in spite of all it has of imposing, a somewhat artificial character, and it may not belong to the Epistle to the Romans any more than the doxology in Matt. vi. belongs to the Lord's Prayer.

Ver. 25 f. τῷ δὲ δυναμένῳ: cf. Eph. iii. 20, Jude v. 24. στηρίξαι: this word takes us back to the beginning of the epistle (i. 11.) Paul wished to impart to them some spiritual gift, to the end that they might be established; but only God is able (cf. xiv. 4) to effect this result. The stablishing is to take place κατὰ τὸ εὐαγγέλιόν μου: in agreement with the gospel Paul preached. When it is achieved, the Romans will be settled and confirmed in Christianity as it was understood by the Apostle. For τὸ εὐαγγέλιόν μου cf. ii. 16, 2 Tim. ii. 8: also 1 Tim. i. 11, τὸ εὐαγγέλιον . . . ὃ ἐπιστεύθην ἐγώ. The expression implies not only that Paul's gospel was his own, in the sense that he was not taught it by any man (Gal. i. 11 f.), but also that it had something characteristic of himself about it. The characteristic feature, to judge by this epistle, was his sense of the absolute freeness of salvation (justification by faith, apart from works of law), and of its absolute universality (for every one that believeth, Jew first, then Greek). τὸ κήρυγμα Ἰησοῦ Χριστοῦ is practically the same as τὸ εὐαγγέλιόν μου. It was in a preaching (1 Cor. ii. 4, xv. 14, Tit. i. 3) of which Jesus Christ was the object that Paul declared the characteristic truths of his gospel: and this preaching, as well as the gospel, may be said to be the rule according to which the Romans are to be established as Christians. κατὰ ἀποκάλυψιν μυστηρίου . . . γνωρισθέντος. This passage "goes not with στηρίξαι, but with κήρυγμα" (Sanday and Headlam). This is the simplest construction: the gospel Paul preaches, the

gospel in accordance with which he would have them established, is itself in accordance with—we may even say identical with—the revelation of a mystery, etc. The μυστήριον here referred to is God's world-embracing purpose of redemption, as it has been set out conspicuously in this epistle. One aspect of this—one element of the mystery—is referred to where μυστήριον is used in xi. 25; but the conception of the Gospel as a μυστήριον revealed in the fulness of the time dominates later epistles, especially Ephesians (cf. Eph. i. 9, iii., 3, 4, 9, vi. 19). The Gospel as Paul understood it was a μυστήριον, because it could never have been known except through Divine revelation: μυστήριον and ἀποκάλυψις are correlative terms. χρόνοις αἰωνίοις: the dative expresses duration. Winer, p. 273; cf. 2 Tim. i. 9, Tit. i. 2. For φανερωθέντος δὲ νῦν cf. iii. 21. The aorist refers to Christ's appearing, though the significance of this had to be made clear by revelation (Weiss). διά τε γραφῶν προφητικῶν . . . γνωρισθέντος: for τε cf. ii. 16. The connection is meant to be as close as possible: the γνωρίζειν follows the φανεροῦν as a matter of course. The γραφαὶ προφητικαί are the O.T. Scriptures of which Paul made constant use in preaching his gospel (cf. κατὰ τὰς γραφὰς in 1 Cor. xv. 3, 4). For him the O.T. was essentially a Christian book. His gospel was witnessed to by the law and the prophets (i. 2, iii. 21, iv., passim), and in that sense the mystery was made known through them. But their significance only came out for one who had the Christian key to them—the knowledge of Christ which revelation had given to Paul. κατ᾽ ἐπιταγὴν τοῦ αἰωνίου θεοῦ: cf. 1 Tim. i. 1, Tit. i. 3. The idea is that only an express command of the Eternal God could justify the promulgation of the secret He had kept so long. For the "Eternal God" cf. Gen. xxi. 33, 1 Tim. i. 17 (τῷ βασιλεῖ τῶν αἰώνων). εἰς ὑπακοὴν πίστεως: cf. i. 5. εἰς πάντα τὰ ἔθνη: in i. 5 it is ἐν

πάντα τὰ ἔθνη γνωρισθέντος, 27. μόνῳ σοφῷ [n] Θεῷ, διὰ Ἰησοῦ Χριστοῦ, n Jude v. 25.
ᾧ [1] ἡ δόξα εἰς τοὺς αἰῶνας. ἀμήν.

Πρὸς Ῥωμαίους ἐγράφη ἀπὸ Κορίνθου διὰ Φοίβης τῆς διακόνου
τῆς ἐν Κεγχρεαῖς ἐκκλησίας.[2]

[1] ω is wanting in B, in F-lat., Orig.-interp., Syr., and is bracketed by W. and H. But whether this is to be explained as an intentional correction to simplify the construction, or a mere oversight (of which Weiss gives examples, *Textkritik*, S. 93), it can hardly be right. Neither can αυτω, which is found in P, be original; it is too natural a correction. Hence edd. are practically unanimous in keeping ω. After τους αιωνας ℵADP add των αιωνων, but W. and H., with BCL and cursives, omit it. Weiss prints the addition in his text, yet argues for its omission (*Textkritik*, 89).

[2] προς ρωμαιους only, in ℵABCD.

πᾶσι τοῖς ἔθνεσιν: for εἰς in this sense see iii. 22. It is very difficult to believe that such mosaic work is the original composition of Paul.

Ver. 27. μόνῳ σοφῷ θεῷ: this description of God suits all that has just been said about His great purpose in human history, and the hiding and revealing of it in due time. The true text in 1 Tim. i. 17 has no σοφῷ. The absence of the article here indicates that it is in virtue of having this character that God is able to stablish the Romans according to Paul's Gospel. ᾧ ἡ δόξα: it is impossible to be sure of the reading here. If ᾧ be omitted, there is no grammatical difficulty whatever: glory is ascribed to God through Jesus Christ, through Whom the eternal purpose of the world's redemption has in God's wisdom been wrought out. But its omission is almost certainly a correction made for simplifi-cation's sake. If it be retained, to whom does it refer? (1) Some say, to Jesus Christ; and this is grammatically the obvious way to take it. But it seems inconsistent with the fact that in τῷ δὲ δυναμένῳ and μόνῳ σοφῷ θεῷ Paul wishes unequivocally to ascribe the glory to God. And though it saves the grammar of the last clause, it sacrifices that of the whole sentence. Hence (2) it seems necessary to refer it to God, and we may suppose, with Sanday and Headlam, that the structure of the sentence being lost amid the heavily-loaded clauses of the doxology, the writer concludes with a well-known formula of praise, ᾧ ἡ δόξα κ.τ.λ. (Gal. i. 15, 2 Tim. iv. 18, Heb. xiii. 21). This might be indicated by putting a dash after Ἰησοῦ Χριστοῦ. The thread is lost, and the writer appends his solemn conclusion as best he can.

THE FIRST EPISTLE OF PAUL

TO THE

CORINTHIANS

INTRODUCTION.

CHAPTER I.

THE CHURCH OF GOD IN CORINTH.

THE establishment of the Church of Corinth was the crowning work of Paul's second missionary journey, and one of the greatest achievements of his life. By repeated interventions crossing his plans of travel, the hand of God had compelled him to enter Europe, through the gate of Macedonia; thence Jewish persecution drove him onwards to Achaia, and prevented his returning to the work left unfinished in the northern province (1 Thess. ii. 14 ff., cf. Acts xvii. 5-15). At Athens, where he first touched Greek soil, the Apostle met with scant success; he arrived at Corinth dispirited and out of health (1 Cor. ii. 3, cf. 1 Thess. iii. 7), with little expectation of the harvest awaiting him. Loneliness aggravated the other causes of the "weakness and fear and trembling" that shook Christ's bold ambassador. His appearance and bearing conveyed an impression of feebleness which acted long afterwards to his prejudice (1 Cor. iv. 10, 2 Cor. x. 1-11, xii. 5, etc.). The new friendship of Aquila and Priscilla proved, however, a cordial to him (Acts xviii. 2 f., cf. Rom. xvi. 3 f.); and the return of Silas and Timothy with good news from Macedonia revived the confidence and vigour of their leader (Acts xviii. 5, cf. 1 Thess. iii. 6-9). Free from the anxiety which had distracted him, and rising above his late defeat, "Paul was *constrained by the word* [cf. for this verb 2 Cor. v. 14, and see Blass' *Acta Apostol., ad loc.*], testifying to the Jews that Jesus is the Christ". The decision with which he now spoke brought about a speedy rupture. The Jews were affronted by the doctrine of a crucified Messiah, which Paul pressed with unsparing rigour (Acts xviii. 5 f., 1 Cor. i. 17, 23, ii. 2). In this crisis the Apostle showed neither weakness nor fear; shaking off the dust of the synagogue, he established a rival *ecclesia* hard by at the house of the proselyte

Titius Justus, marked by his name as a Roman citizen of the *colonia*, who could offer a secure and honourable refuge. The seceders included the Synagogue-chief Crispus and his family, with some other persons of importance. A vision in the following night assured Paul of success and personal safety at Corinth; accordingly "he sat down,"[1] resolved to make full proof of his ministry (Acts xviii. 9-11, *cf.* 2 Cor. i. 18 f.) and staying at least eighteen months in the city—a period much longer than he had spent in any place since first setting out from Antioch. The assault of the Jews miscarried through the firmness and impartiality of the proconsul Gallio. The Apostle found in the Roman Government "the restrainer" of the lawless violence which would have crushed his infant Churches (2 Thess. ii. 6 f.). At Corinth popular feeling ran against the Jews, and their futile attack favourably advertised Paul's work. The murderous plot formed against him some years later (Acts xx. 3) shows how fiercely he was hated by his compatriots in Corinth. He tells us that his success in Macedonia had excited public attention in many quarters, and prepared for his message an interested hearing (1 Thess. i. 8 f.). Outside of Corinth the Gospel was preached with effect throughout Achaia (2 Cor. i. 1); in Cenchreæ, *e.g.*, a regularly constituted Church was formed (Rom. xvi. 1). At his departure (Acts xviii. 18) the Apostle left behind him in this province a Christian community comparatively strong in numbers and conspicuous in the talent and activity of its members (1 Cor. i. 4-8, xiv. 26 ff.), consisting mainly of Gentiles, but with a considerable Jewish infusion (i. 12, vii. 18, xii. 13).

This city, the capital of Roman Greece and the fourth perhaps in size in the empire, was a focus of pagan civilisation, a mirror of the life and society of the age. The centre of a vast commerce, Corinth attracted a crowd of foreigners from East and West, who mingled with the native Greeks and adopted their language and manners. Though not a University town like Athens, Corinth nevertheless prided herself on her culture, and offered a mart to the vendors of all kinds of wisdom. "Not many wise, not many mighty, not many high-born" joined the disciples of the Crucified; but some of Paul's converts came under this description. There were marked social differences and contrasts of wealth and poverty in the Church (1 Cor. vii. 20-24, xi. 21 f., 2 Cor. viii. 12 ff., ix. 6 ff.). Along with slaves, a crowd of artisans and nondescript people, engaged in the petty handicrafts of a great emporium, entered the new society;

---

[1] ἐκάθισεν (Acts xviii. 11): the expression indicates that Paul had been up to this point unsettled, and made up his mind to remain; *cf.* Luke xxiv. 49.

" the foolish things of the world," its " weak" and " baseborn," formed the majority of its constituency (1 Cor. i. 27 ff.)—amongst them many who had been steeped in pagan vice (vi. 9 ff.).

The moral transformation effected in this corrupt material was accompanied by a notable mental quickening. The Hellenic intellect awoke at the touch of spiritual faith. This first Christian society planted upon Greek soil exhibited the characteristic qualities of the race—qualities however of Greece in her decadence rather than her prime. Amongst so many freshly awakened and eager but undisciplined minds, the Greek intellectualism took on a crude and shallow form; it betrayed a childish conceit and fondness for rhetoric and philosophical jargon (i. 17, ii. 1-5, etc.), and allied itself with the factiousness that was the inveterate curse of Greece. The Corinthian talent in matters of " word and knowledge" ran into emulation and frivolous disputes. " The habit of seeming to know all about most things, and of being able to talk glibly about most things, would naturally tend to an excess of individuality, and a diminished sense of corporate responsibilities. This fact supplies, under many different forms, the main drift of 1 Corinthians" (Hort, *Ecclesia*, p. 129). Even the gifts of the Holy Spirit were abused for purposes of display, edification being often the last thing thought of in their exercise (xii., xiv.). The excesses which profaned the Lord's Table (xi. 20 ff.), and the unseemly conduct of women in the Church meetings (xi. 3 ff., xiv. 34 ff.), were symptoms of the lawless self-assertion that marred the excellencies of this Church, and turned the abilities of many of its members into an injury rather than a furtherance to its welfare.

Still graver mischief arose from the influence of heathen society. For men breathing the moral atmosphere of Corinth, and whose earlier habits and notions had been formed in this environment, to conceive and maintain a Christian moral ideal was difficult in the extreme. Deplorable relapses occurred when the fervour of conversion had abated, and the Church proved shamefully tolerant towards sins of impurity (1 Cor. v., 2 Cor. xii. 20 f.). The acuteness of the Greek mind showed itself in antinomian sophistry; the " liberty" from Jewish ceremonial restrictions claimed by Paul for Gentile Christians was by some construed into a general licence, and carried to a length which shocked not merely the scruples of fellow-believers but the common moral instincts (vi. 12 ff., viii. 9-13, x. 23 ff., xi. 13 *b*). The social festivities of Corinth, bound up as they were with idolatry and its impurities, exposed the Church to severe temptation. To draw a hard and fast line in such questions and to forbid all participation in *idolothyta*, after the precedent of Acts xv., would have been the simplest course to take; but Paul feels it necessary to ground the matter on fundamental principles. He will not acknowledge any dominion of the idol over "the earth and its fulness" (x. 26); nor, on the other hand, is it right to prevent neighbourly intercourse between Christians and unbelievers (x. 27 ff.). But where the feast is held under the auspices of a heathen god and as the sequel to his sacrifice the case is altered; participation under these circumstances becomes an act of apostasy, and the feaster identifies himself with the idol as distinctly as in the Lord's Supper he identifies himself with Christ (x. 16 ff.).

The working of the old leaven is patent in the denial of *the resurrection of the dead* made by some Corinthian Christians (xv.). Here the radical scepticism of the age opposed itself to the fact of the resurrection of Jesus Christ, upon which the whole weight of Christian faith and hope, and the entire Christian conception of the world and of destiny, rest as upon their fulcrum and rock of certainty. The disbelief in bodily resurrection and the indifference to bodily sin manifested at Corinth had a common root. They may be traced to the false spiritualism, the contempt for physical nature, characteristic of the theosophy of the times, which gave rise a few years later to the Colossian heresy and was a chief factor in the development of Gnosticism. The teaching of chap. vi., that "your bodies are limbs of Christ," and the command to "glorify God in your bodies," are aimed against the same philosophical assumptions that are combated in chap. xv.; the demand for bodily purity finds in the doctrine of the resurrection its indispensable support and counterpart.

No reference is made in the Epistle to Church officers of any kind. Submission to "the house of Stephanas," and to others rendering like service, is enjoined in xvi. 15 f., but by way of voluntary deference. So early as the first missionary journey in South Galatia Paul had assisted in the "appointing of elders in every Church" (Acts xiv. 23; *cf.* Acts xx. 17, 1 Thess. v. 12, Rom. xii. 8, Phil. i. 1). He had refrained from this step at Corinth for some specific reason—a reason lying, it may be supposed, in the democratic spirit of the Church, which might have ill brooked official control. In xii. 28 the Apostle alludes, however, to "governments" as amongst the things which "God set [*as part of a plan*, Hort] in the Church"; and his promise to "set in order other things" (beside the Lord's Supper) when he comes (xi. 34) may cover the intention to remedy this defect, the consequences of which are painfully apparent (xiv. 26-33, etc.).

This Epistle discloses the interior life of an apostolic Church; hence its surpassing historical interest. We must not, indeed, apply its data without qualification to contemporary Christian societies, even those of Gentile origin. The Corinthian Church presented material of uncommon richness, but intractable to the founder's hand. Its turbulence and party heat are unparalleled in the N.T. records. But while the Church life here portrayed was exceptional in some features, and Paul's Church policy at Corinth may have differed from that pursued elsewhere, this Epistle is peculiarly full in its teaching on the nature and rights of the Church, and in the light it throws upon the conditions under which the first Gentile-Christian communities were moulded. Chaps. xii. and xiii. are the true centre of the Epistle. The very formlessness of this Church, its rudimentary and protoplasmic state, reveals the essence of the Christian society, its substratum and vital tissue, as these can hardly be seen in a more developed and furnished condition. The Apostle Paul is contending for the *bare life* of the Church of God in Corinth.

Corinth now became the advanced post and gateway for Christianity in its westward march. The *new* Corinth, in which Paul laboured, dates from the year 46 B.C., when the city was refounded by Julius Cæsar under the name *Colonia Julia Corinthus* (or *Laus Julii Corinthus*). Just a century earlier the old Corinth had been razed to the ground by Lucius Mummius, upon the defeat of the Achæan league which, with Corinth for its fortress, made a last despairing effort to retrieve the liberties of Greece. Corinth and Carthage fell and rose again simultaneously, marking the epochs at which republican Rome completed the destruction of the old world and imperial Rome began the construction of the new. The fame of ancient Corinth, reaching back to heroic times (see the *Iliad*, ii., 570; Pindar, *Olymp.*, 13)—where " the sweetly breathing Muse" and " death-dealing Ares" flourished side by side—and her later prowess as the bulwark of the Peloponnese and the maritime rival of Athens, were traditions with little interest or meaning for Paul and his disciples. The geographical position of Corinth gave to it enduring importance, and explains the fact that on its restoration the city sprang at once into the foremost rank. Corinth occupies one of the finest sites in Europe. With the Acrocorinthus (nearly 2,000 feet high) and the Oneion range shielding it on the south, it commands the narrow plain of the isthmus, and looks down, eastwards and westwards, upon the Saronic and Corinthian gulfs, which furnished the main artery of commerce between the Ægean and the Euxine seas on the one hand, and the Western Mediterranean upon the other. (See the descriptions in Stanley's *Epp. to the Cor.*, p. 4, also article "Corinth" in Hastings' *Bib. Dict.*; and more at large, Leake's *Morea*, iii., 229-304, Curtius' *Peloponnesus*, ii., 514 f.; and for the antiquities, Pausanias, II., i., 2; Strabo, VIII., vi., 20-24; Dio Chrys., *Orat.*, 37; Ælius Arist., *Ad Poseid.*) The western port, Lechæum, 1½ mile distant, was linked by double walls to the city; Cenchreæ lay 8½ miles eastwards; and a shipway, running north of Corinth, connected the two harbours.

The presiding deities of this maritime city were the sea-god Poseidon, under whose patronage the famous Isthmian games were held (see ix. 24 ff. and notes), and Aphrodité, whose temple crowned the Acrocorinthus. The cultus of Aphrodité (worshipped in her debasing form as *Aphr. Pandemos*) dates back, it is supposed, to prehistoric Phœnician times; its features were more Oriental than Greek—especially the institution of the ἱερόδουλοι, or priestess-courtesans, of whom more than a thousand were attached to the shrine of the goddess. Temples of Serapis and Isis were also conspicuous at Corinth, representing the powerful leaven of Egyptian superstition that helped to demoralise the empire. The luxury and refinement of the elder Corinth were associated with its vice; so notorious was its debauchery that κορινθιάζεσθαι was a euphemism for whoredom; in our own literature "a Corinthian" still means a polished rake. By all accounts, the new Corinth more than rivalled the old in wickedness. Here the Apostle drew, from life, the lurid portraiture of Gentile sin that darkens the first page of his Epistle to the Romans. Within this stronghold of paganism and focus of Greek corruption Paul planted the cross of his Redeemer, rising out of his weakness and fear to a boundless courage. He confronted the world's glory and infamy with the sight of "Jesus Christ and Him crucified," confident that in the word of the cross which he preached there lay a spell to subdue the pride and cleanse the foulness of Corinthian life, a force which would prove to Gentile society in this place of its utter corruption the wisdom and power of God unto salvation. In "the Church of God in Corinth," with all its defects and follies, this redeeming power was lodged.

CHAPTER II.

PAUL'S COMMUNICATIONS WITH CORINTH.

ASSUMING 49 A.D. as the date of the conference in Jerusalem (Acts xv.), 57 as that of Paul's last voyage to the Holy City,[1] we calculate that he arrived at Corinth first in the latter part of the year 50, closing his mission in 52. He was engaged in the interval, until the spring of 56, mainly in the evangelisation of the province of Asia (Acts xix. 10, 22, xx. 1 ff.). When he writes this letter the Apostle is still at Ephesus, intending to remain until Pentecost, and with Passover approaching (xvi. 8 f., v. 7 f. : see notes). Paul's departure from Ephesus was hastened by the riot (Acts xix. 23-xx. 1); and we may take it that this Epistle was despatched in the early spring of 56, very shortly before Paul left Ephesus for Troas in the course of his third missionary journey.

The Apostle had previously sent Timothy and Erastus forward to Corinth, by way of Macedonia, to prepare for his arrival, in pursuance of the plan now sketched in his mind for completing his work in these regions with a view to advancing upon Rome and the further west (Acts xix. 21 f., *cf.* Rom. xv. 16-25). Timothy is likely to arrive soon after this letter, and will be able to enforce its prescriptions (iv. 17; see also xvi. 10 f., and notes). Apollos, who had migrated to Corinth fresh from the instructions of Priscilla and Aquila in Ephesus and had "watered" there what Paul had "planted" (iii. 6, Acts xviii. 27 f.), is back again at Ephesus in the Apostle's company (xvi. 12); he is clear of complicity in the party quarrels with which his name was associated in Corinth (i. 12, iii. 4-8, iv. 6). Quite recently "the people of Chloë" have brought an alarming report of these "strifes" (i. 11); and the Apostle learns from general rumour of the case of incest polluting the Church

---

[1] See article "Chronology of the N.T." in Hastings' *Bib. Dict.*; and for the latter date, article "Paul," i., 5. It is now generally recognised that the dates assigned to Pauline events by Wieseler and Lightfoot are, from 49 onwards, at least a couple of years too late.

(v. 1).   More agreeable tidings have come with Stephanas and his companions (xvi. 17 f.), who bear a dutiful letter of inquiry addressed to Paul, which he answers in chap. vii. ff.   Through their lips, as well as from the Church letter, he receives the assurances of the general loyalty and goodwill of the Corinthian believers.   From all these sources occasion is drawn and material furnished for the writing before us.

This Epistle is not the first which Paul had addressed to Corinth. In chap. v. 9 the writer refers to *an earlier letter* forbidding intercourse with immoral persons.   The terms of this admonition had raised debate.   Some read it as though all dealings with vicious men were inhibited—a restriction that was as good as to tell Corinthian Christians to "go out of the world"!   They could not imagine Paul to mean this; but his words allowed of this construction, and thus opened the door for discussion and for temporising.   The tenor of the lost Epistle probably resembled that of 2 Cor. vi. 14-vii. 1 (see this Comm., *ad loc.*).   This letter had arrived some months previously to our Epistle; for the Church had had time to consider and reply to it, and the condition of things to which it relates has undergone some changes.   It may be referred as far back as the previous autumn (55 A.D.).   Inasmuch as the Church-letter touched on "the collection for the saints" (xvi. 1: see note), it seems likely that the Apostle had made some appeal in the lost Epistle on this subject, eliciting a favourable reply (*cf.* 2 Cor. viii. 10, ix. 2), but with a request for directions as to the mode of gathering the money.

There is reason to believe that *Paul had himself visited Corinth* not very long before writing the aforesaid letter.   The allusions of 2 Cor. ii. 1, xii. 14, 20—xiii. 2 (see notes), imply that he had been *twice* in Corinth before the Second Epistle.   If with Clemen (*Chronol. d. Paulin. Briefe*), Schmiedel (*Handcomm.*, 1 and 2 Kor., *Einleitung*), and Krenkel (*Beiträge z. Aufhellung d. Paul. Briefe*, vi.) we could spread the composition of 1 and 2 Cor. over two years, space would be found for interposing such a visit between them, but at the cost of creating fresh and insuperable chronological difficulties.   In 2 Cor. i. 15 ff. the Apostle defends himself for having *failed* to come recently to Corinth; he had sent Titus, and with him a letter (2 Cor. ii. 4, vii. 8)— distinct, as the present writer holds, from 1 Cor. (a *second lost letter* of Paul to Corinth: see Hastings' *Bib. Dict.*, article "Paul," i. *d.*), and occasioned by an emergency that arose subsequently to its despatch —which gave a new turn to the Apostle's relations with the Church. Meanwhile he has himself left Ephesus (as contemplated in 1 Cor. xvi.), has pushed forward to Macedonia (2 Cor. ii. 12 f.), where at last Titus meets him with the cheering news reflected in 2 Cor. i.-vii. As already shown, a space of but a few weeks elapsed between Paul's writing 1 Cor. and leaving Ephesus for Troas.

We have traced Paul's steps through the months separating the two Epistles, and neither time nor occasion is found for an interjected trip to Corinth. We are thrown back upon the period *before* the first Epistle. Yet 1 Cor. makes no express reference to any recent visit; and its silence, *primâ facie*, negatives the supposition of any such occurrence. There are circumstances however which relieve this adverse presumption. For one thing, the *lost letter* had intervened; this other Epistle, not our 1 Cor., was the sequel of the visit in question. The main thing that occupied Paul's mind on that occasion, and which caused the "grief" referred to in 2 Cor. ii. 1, had been the impurity of life manifest within the Church. Against this he had given solemn warning, while forbearing discipline (2 Cor. xiii. 2). It was with a moral situation of this kind that the missing letter dealt (1 Cor. v. 9-12); the alarm it expressed is still felt in 1 Cor. vi., x., xv. 33 f. Meantime, the horrible case of incest has eclipsed previous transgressions; and while Paul reaffirms the general directions already sent and prompted (*ex hypothesi*) by personal observation, he fastens his attention upon the new criminality just brought to his ears. That previous meeting had been so unhappy for both parties that Paul might well avoid allusion to it; it was an experience he was resolved never to repeat (2 Cor. ii. 1, xii. 20). If he comes again under like conditions, it will be "rod" in hand (1 Cor. iv. 21, 2 Cor. xiii. 2). His forbearance had been misconstrued; some of the offenders were emboldened to defy him, and his Judaistic supplanters subsequently contrasted the severity of his letters with his timidity in face of the mutineers (2 Cor. x. 6, xiii. 1-7)—a taunt which drags from him the allusions of the second Epistle. After all, 1 Cor. is not without traces of the second visit. Nothing so well accounts for the doubts of Paul's disciplinary power hinted in 1 Cor. iv. 18-21 as the encounter supposed. When after his threat, and while the plague grows in virulence (1 Cor. v.) and his opponents challenge him to come (iv. 18)—still more, when he has announced, while fulminating anathemas on paper (v. 4 f., xvi. 22), that his return is postponed, without any imperative reason given for delay (xvi. 5 ff.)—after all this, it is no wonder that even his friends felt themselves aggrieved, and that the most damaging constructions were put upon the Apostle's changes of plan (2 Cor. i. 15 ff., x. 9 ff., xiii. 3 ff.). At last he explains, in 2 Cor., that the postponement is due to his continued desire to "spare" instead of striking. If, notwithstanding these

apprehensions, Paul speaks in 2 Cor. i. 15 of the double visit that
had been for a while intended (a *third* and *fourth* from the beginning)
as "a second joy" (or "grace"), he is probably quoting words of
the Church letter.   Further, one detects in 1 Cor. iv. 1-10 a sharp
note of personal feeling that indicates some recent contact between
writer and readers, and ocular observation on the Apostle's part of
the altered bearing of his spoilt children at Corinth.   This Epistle
manifests a mastery of the situation and a vivid realisation of its
detailed circumstances such as we can best account for on the
supposition that Paul had taken a personal survey of the development of the Church since his first departure, and that behind all he
has heard latterly from others and seen through their eyes, he is
also judging upon the strength of what he has himself witnessed
and knows at first hand.

CHAPTER III.

THE TEACHING OF THE EPISTLE.

WHILE the doctrine of the companion Epistles to the Galatians and Romans lies upon the surface, the theology of this Epistle has to be disentangled from a coil of knotty practical questions. The Apostle writes under constraint, unable to count on the full sympathy of his readers or to say all that is in his mind (ii. 6, iii. 1). Instead of giving free play to his own reflexions, he is compelled through the greater part of the letter to wait upon the caprices of this flighty young Greek Church. At first sight one fails to observe any continuous teaching in the Epistle; a doctrinal analysis of its contents seems out of place. But closer attention discovers a real coherence behind this disconnectedness of form. While Paul comments on the sad news from Corinth and answers seriatim the questions addressed to him, his genius grasps the situation, and the leaven of the Gospel all the while assimilates the discordant mass. The Pauline standpoint is firmly maintained. The Christian principle shows itself master of the Gentile no less than the Jewish field, and gives earnest of its power to meet the changeful and multiplying demands that will be created by its expansion through the world. There is a unity of thought in this letter as real as that stamped upon the Epistle to the Romans, a unity the more impressive because of the baffling conditions under which it is realised.

Paul's Gospel stands here on its defence against the pretensions of worldly wisdom and the corruptions of the fleshly mind; from the height of the Cross it sends its piercing rays into the abyss of pagan sin disclosed at Corinth in its turpitude and demonic force. Amongst the four Evangelical Epistles, this is *the epistle of the cross in its social application*. It bears throughout a realistic stamp. "The Church of God that exists in Corinth," the men and women that compose it, are constantly present to the writer's mind—their diverse states and relationships, their debasing antecedents and surroundings, their crude ideas and conflicting tempers and keen ambitions, their high religious enthusiasm and their low moral sensibilities, their demonstrative but fickle affections and unsteady resolutions. Two things he strives to bring into full contact—Christ crucified and these half-Christianised Corinthian natures. What Romans does for the Gospel in the field of theological exposition, and Galatians in that of doctrinal polemic, and 2 Corinthians in that of personal experience and ministerial vocation, this 1 Corinthians has done in respect of its bearing upon human intercourse and the life of the community.

The foundation upon which Paul had built at Corinth is "Jesus Christ"—*i.e.*, "Jesus Christ crucified" (iii. 11, i. 17 f., ii. 2, xv. 1-3). He does not, any more than in 1 Thessalonians, enter into an exposition of his λόγος τοῦ σταύρου. Not yet, in Corinth at least, had the legalists openly contested Paul's doctrine of salvation through the death of Christ; the first sketch of its argumentative defence appears in 2 Cor. v. 14 ff. The chief peril comes from the opposite quarter, from the dissolving influences of Hellenic scepticism and demoralisation. The form, rather than the contents, of Paul's message is just now in question; he is reproached with the μωρία τοῦ κηρύγματος (i. 18-25). But the form of presentation is determined by the substance of the truth presented; the cross of Christ cannot appear draped in the robes of Greek philosophy. The mere fact that it is "the word of *the cross*" convicts the Gospel of folly in the eyes of the Greek lover of wisdom, as of weakness before the Jewish believer in "signs". A "wise" world that knows not God (i. 21, ii. 6, 14, *cf.* Rom. i. 19-23) will not understand His message, until it learns its ignorance.

1. To *the source of the Gospel* must therefore be traced that scorn of the Corinthian world which so much troubles the Church. It was "the testimony of God" that Paul had first announced (ii. 1); the Corinthian believers are "*of Him* in Christ Jesus," and have learnt to worship God as "Father of us and of our Lord Jesus Christ" (i. 3, 26-31: observe the emphasis thrown in vv. 18-31 upon ὁ Θεὸς in contrast with ὁ κόσμος). Impotent and even absurd "the preaching of the cross" may appear to the Corinthian public; "to the saved" it is "the wisdom" and "the power of God".

(1) The λόγος τοῦ σταύρου is *God's power* at work in its most characteristic and sovereign energy, destined to shatter all adverse potencies (i. 27 ff., xv. 24 ff.). Veiled under a guise of weakness, it thus ensnares the world and exposes its folly (i. 19-21, ii. 6-8, iii. 19); it chooses for its instruments feeble and ignoble things to overthrow the mightiest. The power of God acting in this λόγος is administered by "our Lord Jesus Christ"—His mediator in the universe, and specifically in the Church (viii. 6)—whom the world crucified (ii. 8);

so that it is in effect *the power of Christ*, and " in Christ Jesus " men " come to be of God ". God has made Him unto us " righteousness and sanctification and redemption " (i. 30, *cf.* vi. 11) ; with the " price " of His blood He " bought " us, the body not excepted, for God's property (i. 2, iii. 16, vi. 19 f.) ; from " the strength of sin " and the reign of death Christians are consciously delivered through the death, crowned by the resurrection, of the Lord Jesus and through faith in His name (xv. 1-4, 11, 17 f., 56 f.).

The Holy Spirit constitutes this mysterious power of God in operation. His " demonstration and power " attended Paul's mission to Corinth, giving it an efficacy otherwise unaccountable (ii. 1-6) ; all Christian revelations come by this channel (ii. 11-16). Only " in the Holy Spirit " does any man truly say, " Jesus is Lord " (xii. 3) ; " in the name of the Lord Jesus Christ, and in the Spirit of our God," the foulest sinners of Corinth had been " washed " and " sanctified " (vi. 11). The gifts possessed by this favoured Church are of the Spirit's " distribution," while of God's omnipresent " working" and held under Christ's dominion (xii. 4-11). The manifestations of the Spirit in the Gospel and in the Church differ from all forms of power the world has known ; they reveal a kingdom rich in blessings such as " eye hath not seen nor ear heard, nor man's heart conceived " (ii. 9 f.).

(2) The word of the cross discloses, to those who can understand, *God's wisdom* hitherto shrouded " in mystery," whose manifestation was determined for this epoch from the world's beginning (ii. 6-9). By it the pretentious " wisdom of the age " will be overthrown. The world scorns to be saved by a crucified Messiah, and " the natural man cannot receive the things of the Spirit of God " ; but wisdom is justified of her children. Bringing such a message, the Apostle discards adornments and plausibilities of speech ; his word must speak by its inherent truth and force (ii. 1 ff.). As Christian men advance, the revelation of God increasingly approves itself to them ; it discloses its σοφία τοῖς τελείοις. No longer does the opinion of the world sway them nor its temper cleave to them, they become " men of the Spirit," who " judge all things " and are " judged of none " (ii. 6-iii. 3). One day they shall " judge the world " (vi. 2).

From the standpoint thus gained, in view of the operation of God in whatever belongs to the Gospel, the Apostle defines in chaps. iii. and iv. the position of Christ's ministers : " We are God's fellow-workers " ; Paul the planter, Apollos the waterer—they are nothing ; God " gives the increase ". " Assistants of Christ, stewards of God's mysteries," their qualifications are fidelity and

the possession of the Master's mind (ii. 10, 16, vii. 25, 40).   To
their Lord, not to their fellow-servants, they are answerable.   By
His "call" and "compulsion" they serve the Gospel (i. 1, ix. 16 f.,
xii. 28).   How presumptuous for the Corinthians to be " puffed up
for one against the other " of God's servants !   All alike are theirs,
while they are Christ's and Christ is God's (iii. 4 f., 21-iv. 6).   Let
men look above the stewards to the Master, above the instruments
to God who " worketh all things in all " (xii. 4 ff.).   The Christian
teachers are God's temple-builders ; heavy their loss, if they build
amiss ; terrible their ruin, if instead of strengthening they destroy
the fabric (iii. 10-17).   Their maintenance is not bestowed by the
Church as wages by an employer, but enjoined on the Church by
the Lord's ordinance, upon the same principle of justice which
allows the threshing ox to feed from the corn (ix. 7-12).

The readers must learn what it means to belong to " the Church
of God ".   Despite their presumed knowledge (viii.), " ignorance of
God" is at the root of their errors (xv. 34).   Newly emancipated
from heathenism, they are slow to realise the character and claims
of the God revealed to them in Christ.   The first four chapters seek
at every point to correct this ignorance ; indeed, this underlying vein
runs through the Epistle (*cf.* in this respect 1 Thess. *passim*).
Πάντα εἰς δόξαν Θεοῦ is the maxim that Paul dictates to his readers
(x. 31), and that governs his mind throughout the letter.

2. *The nature of the Christian community* is the subject of chaps.
xii. and xiv., but it pervades the Epistle no less than that of the
sovereign claims of God : "to *the Church* of God in Corinth" the
Apostle writes.

The Græco-Roman cities at this time were honey-combed, in all
grades of life, with private associations—trade-guilds, burial clubs
and friendly societies, religious confraternities ; their existence supplied a great social need, and formed a partial substitute for the
political activity suppressed by the levelling Roman empire.   These
organisations prepared heathen society for Church life ; and Christianity upon Gentile soil largely adopted the forms of combination
in popular use, borrowing from the Greek club almost as much as
from the Jewish synagogue.   But it transformed what it borrowed.
In the Churches of God established in Thessalonica and Corinth the
first stones were laid of the Christian structure of society.   New
conceptions of duty and kinship are unfolded in this Epistle, which
have yet to receive full development.   Paul's sociology naturally
met with resistance from men reared in Paganism ; human nature
is still against it.   The Corinthians brought into the Church their

Greek contentiousness, their lack of loyalty and public spirit. The mental stimulus and large freedom of the new faith, where reverence and self-control were wanting, resulted for the time in greater turbulence rather than in a nobler and happier order.

(1) As we have seen, the Apostle insists above all that the Christian community is *the building of God*. Injury to this "temple of God" is the worst sacrilege (iii. 16 f.). The Church consists of those whom God has "called into the communion of His Son Jesus Christ" (i. 9); who "were, in one Spirit, all baptised into one body . . . and all were made to drink of one Spirit"—"the Spirit that is from God" (ii. 12, xii. 13). This creative, informing Presence determines the nature, constitution and destiny of the Church.

(2) In relation to each other, Christian men form *a brotherhood*. Paul addresses his readers as "brethren" not by way of courtesy or personal friendliness, but to enforce upon them mutual devotion. Each Christian looks upon his fellow as "the brother for whom Christ died"; to "sin against the brethren" is "to sin against Christ" (viii. 11 ff.). By communion of faith and worship in Christ a union of hearts is created more intimate and tender than the world had ever seen. Christians are to each other as eye to ear and hand to foot (xii. 14 ff.). Each has his honourable place in the body, fixed by God; each is necessary to all, all to each (xii. 21-31). The rapturous outburst of chap. xiii. is a song to the praise of Love as the law of Christian brotherhood. Knowledge, faith, miracles are useless or unreal unless yoked to love, which points out the "way" to the right employment of every faculty (xii. 31). "The collection for the saints" of Jerusalem (xvi. 1) was dictated by the affection that binds the scattered parts of the Church of God.

(3) The relations of Christians to God the Father, and to their believing brethren, alike centre in their relationship to Christ: *the Church is His body*—"a κοινωνία of the Son of God" (i. 9). The whole consciousness of the new life—personal or corporate—is grounded there; ἐν Χριστῷ, ἐν Χριστῷ Ἰησοῦ, ἐν Κυρίῳ, is the Apostle's standing definition of Christian states and relations. To use Paul's strong expression (vi. 17), "he who is *cemented to the Lord*, is one spirit". By the fact that they severally inhere in Him, men are constituted "a body of Christ, and *members individually*" (xii. 27). No man in Christ is self-complete; the eye finds its mate in the hand, the head in the foot. This reciprocal subordination dictates the law of the life in Christ Jesus and controls all its movements. The Apostle claims to be himself ἔννομος Χριστοῦ, because he "seeks not his own profit but that of the many" (x. 21 ff.). The question of i. 13,

μεμέρισται ὁ Χριστός; reveals the radical mischief at work in Corinth. The Church was in the eyes of some of its members a kind of debating club or philosophical school, in which αἱρέσεις and σχίσματα were matters of course; to others it was a benefit society, to be used so far as suited inclination and convenience. Against all such debased notions of social life, and selfish abuse of Church privilege, this Epistle is a sustained protest.

This fellowship of Christ is symbolised and sealed by the bread and cup of the Lord's Supper (x. 16 ff.)—the "one loaf" and "one cup" in which all participate, since it is a "*communion* of the body of Christ" and "of the blood of Christ". The "word of the cross" is made by this ordinance a binding "covenant in Christ's blood". The Christian Society is thus known as the fraternity of the Crucified; evermore it "proclaims the Lord's death, till He come" (xi. 26). Such fellowship in Christ, appropriating the whole man, the body with the spirit (vi. 15, 19), excludes *ipso facto* all intercourse with "the demons" and feasting at their "table" (x. 20 ff.); their communion is abhorrent and morally impossible to those who have truly partaken with Christ (*cf.* 2 Cor. vi. 14 ff.).

The introductory thanksgiving signally connects the κοινωνία τοῦ Χριστοῦ with His παρουσία. Hope is a uniting principle, along with faith and love (xiii. 13, *cf.* Eph. iv. 4). The Church of God is no mere temporal fabric. The "gold, silver, precious stones" of its construction will brave the judgment fires (iii. 12-15). "Those who are Christ's, at His coming," form the nucleus of the eternal kingdom of God (xv. 23-28). "The day" which reveals the completed work of Christ "will declare every man's work, of what sort it is"; each of Christ's helpers will then receive his meed of "praise from God," and the approved "saints," as Christ's assessors, will "judge the world" and "angels" (iii. 13, iv. 5, vi. 2 f.).

(4) The regulation of *the charismata*, the wealth and the embarrassment of this Church, is deduced from the above principles. These powers, however manifold, are manifestations of "the same Spirit," who inhabits the entire body of Christ and whose "will" determines the various endowments of its several members (xii. 7-11). They are distributed, as the bodily functions are assigned to their proper organs, for the service of the whole frame. The possessor of one cannot dispense with, and must not despise, his differently gifted brother (xii. 14 ff.). Yet there is a gradation in the charisms; it is right to covet "the greater" among them. Love supplies the criterion; the most *edifying* gifts are the most desirable (xii. 31-xiv. 19). Self-restraint must be exercised by gifted persons, and

order enforced by the community, so that individual talents may be combined for the common good (xiv. 26-33). To the direction of these matters a manly practical sense must be applied ; "the understanding" aids the service of "the spirit" (xiv. 14-20).

This charismatic ministry, diffused through the body of Christ, is the basis of all Christian agency. As yet there are only "functions, not formal offices" (Hort) ; the function is anterior to the office, and may exist without it. Each man in the Church of Corinth spontaneously speaks, sings, serves in whatever fashion (xiv. 26), in virtue of his χάρισμα,—the particular form which the common χάρις assumes in him for the benefit of others. The realisation of the life of Christ in the Christian Society is the aim imposed on each Christian by the Spirit whose indwelling makes him such.

3. The teaching of the Epistle takes a wide outlook in its consideration of *the relations of the Christian to the world*. This relationship is exhibited mainly on its negative side. The believer in Christ, " elect " and " sanctified " (i. 2, 27), built on the foundation of Jesus Christ into God's temple, is separated from the world. The Spirit he has from God makes him a πνευματικός ; he has new faculties, and lives in a changed order of things. There are two worlds—a new world of the Spirit formed within the old κόσμος but utterly distinct from it, unintelligible to it, and destined soon to overthrow and displace it (i. 25-29, ii. 6-14, iii. 18 f., vii. 31).

(1) With the world's *sin* the Church of God holds truceless war. Living in the world, Christians cannot avoid contact with its " fornicators, extortioners," and the rest ; but it can and must keep them out of its ranks (v. 9-13) ; the old leaven is to be " cleansed out " of the " new kneading," since Christ is our paschal lamb (v. 6-8). The sin of the world culminates in its idolatry ; from this the Corinthians, unconditionally, must " flee " (x. 1-14).

(2) The Apostle recognises *the natural order of life* as one who sees through and beyond it. He cherishes, up to this date, the hope of his Lord's speedy return (xv. 51 f.). Hence the provisional character of his advices respecting marriage in chap. vii. He writes at a juncture of suspense, when men should keep themselves free from needless ties. He admits the necessity of marriage in the case of many Corinthians, and applies the law of Christ carefully to the mixed unions so troublesome at Corinth. He fears for his disciples the burdens imposed by domestic cares in times so uncertain, and in a society at war with the world. Christians may not " go out of the world," nor cease to " use " it ; but they must hold it lightly and refrain from " using it to the full ".

In discussing the question of the *idolothyta* Paul gives a glance to the more positive side of the Christian's relations with external nature. He recalls the attitude of the Old Testament towards earthly blessings by quoting, "The earth is the Lord's, and the fulness thereof" (x. 28). The idols have no power to usurp God's creatures, nor to limit His children's use of them. An enlightened conscience will not scruple at the enjoyment of food sacrificed to an idol, though circumstances will often make this inexpedient (viii., x. 23 ff.). The Jewish distinctions of meat are obsolete (vi. 12 f.) ; it was in this sense that Paul had enunciated the much-abused maxim, "All things are lawful to me". The σαρκικά of life he enlists in the service of its πνευματικά ; they serve to multiply and strengthen the bonds of mutual necessity arising from our kinship in Christ (ix. 7-12, *cf.* Rom. xv. 27, Gal. vi.).

In the relationship of man and woman the Apostle sees the natural and spiritual order blended ; he passes from the one to the other with perfect congruity, and appeals to the teaching of "nature," expressed in secular customs of dress, as an exponent of the Divine will (xi. 1-15). While censuring the greed and arrogance displayed by the rich (xi. 17 ff.), he leaves distinctions of wealth and rank uncondemned ; from the analogy applied in chap. xii. 13 ff. we infer that he viewed these as a part of "the fashion of this world," necessary but transient.

(3) *Death*, like sin which gives to it its "sting," belongs to the system of the present evil world. Since the resurrection of Christ, death is in principle "abolished" for those who are His (xv. 26, 55 ff.). The resurrection is no mere immortality of the spirit, such as philosophers conceived ; it is the reversal of death, the recovery of the entire man from its power. Christ's people, to be sure, will not be reclad in mortal habiliments, nor resume the corpse that was laid in the grave. The new frame will differ from the old as the plant from its perished seed. Heavenly bodies must surpass earthly in unimaginable ways. Adam and Christ are types of two modes of being : in our present "natural body" we "wear the image" of the former ; our future body will be "spiritual" after the image of God's Son (xv. 35-57).

This glorious and inconceivable change will supervene—for Christians living or departed alike (xv. 51 f.)—at "the revelation of our Lord Jesus Christ," which the Corinthian Christians are awaiting (i. 7). This is "the end" of the course of revelation and of God's dealings with mankind—when Christ's redemption is complete, when His enemies throughout creation are overcome, and He is able to lay at the Father's feet an empire wholly subdued and everywhere accordant with the Creator's will. Then "the Son Himself" will give the crowning example of submission, "that God may be all in all" (xv. 28). In this sublime issue the teaching of the Epistle culminates. The relation of the Church of Corinth to God, though marred upon its part yet real and sanctifying, which gave the Apostle his starting-point, has been unfolded in ever-widening circles, until it is seen to embrace the universe ; there is formed within it the beginning of a Divine realm that stretches on into unknown worlds, and will bring all finite powers and beings under its sway.

Through this entire development of thought and life Christ is all things. His presence and lordship, the redeeming power of His cross, extend over every field within our view. They cover alike the relations of the individual man to God, of man to man within society, and of man, individually and collectively, to the world around him in the present and before him in the future. Christ is all in all, that through Him finally God may be all in all.

CHAPTER IV.

THE LANGUAGE, TEXT, HISTORY, AND CRITICISM OF THE EPISTLE.

1. LANGUAGE. " The dialect of these Epistles (1 and 2 Cor.) is not Hebraistic, but moves upon the lines of Hellenistic Greek. It finds its analogue, in a multitude of characteristics, in the language of Polybius, the classic of Hellenism, in Epictetus, in Plutarch, in Dionysius of Halicarnassus and others, in such a way as to imply for it and them *a common life-sphere*" (Heinrici). Paul has become in this Epistle, more than elsewhere, τοῖς Ἕλλησιν ὡς Ἕλλην. Its atmosphere and colouring and movement are distinctively *Greek of the period*,—when compared, *e.g.*, with the style of Romans or 2 Thessalonians. While Old Testament references are numerous in 1 Cor., they are employed by way of illustration rather than of proof, and in a Hellenistic not a Rabbinical manner.

The Epistle has a rich vocabulary. Out of the 5,594 Greek words of the New Testament it employs 963—103 peculiar to itself. In the *hapax legomena* one expects the idiosyncrasy of the Epistle to manifest itself. Sixty-eight of these—about two-thirds—are classical, occurring in Attic writers earlier than Aristotle ; twenty-two belong to post-classical authors of the κοινή, or to the Greek of the contemporary inscriptions and papyri. In the residue there is one specifically Septuagint term, εἰδωλεῖον (viii. 10, see note) ; and the Aramæan sentence, μαρὰν ἀθά. Eleven words are left, so far unknown from other documents, or used only by Christian writers after Paul— διερμηνεία, -ευτής, εὐπάρεδρος, ὀλοθρευτής, πιθός (ii. 4), περίψημα, συνζητητής, τυπικῶς, ὑπέρακμος, χοϊκός, χρηστεύομαι ; but every one of these has close kindred or analogues in common Greek ; it is likely enough that all were current in the speech of Corinth : εὐπάρεδρος however, with its transparent sense, has the look of a Pauline coinage. The forty-two additional words of 1 Corinthians (24 if the Pastorals be excluded) limited in their N.T. range to the Pauline Epistles— *Pauline, but not First-Corinthian, h. lgg.*—yield a similar analysis.

Out of the 150 words enumerated by Kennedy in his useful *Sources of N.T. Greek* (pp. 88-91) as " strictly peculiar to the LXX

or N.T.," with the forty or fifty added to this list by including
Philo Judæus, twenty-five occur in this Epistle; but apart from
Hebrew loan-words (such as πάσχα), and excluding near relations
and correlates of recognised classical or post-classical words, there
remains, after the researches of Deissmann (in his *Bibelstudien* and
Neue Bibelstudien) and other students of the Greek inscriptions
and papyri, only a handful, perhaps half a dozen of the twenty-five,
that can be called properly and exclusively " Biblical "—a scanty
residue which further discovery may diminish. So far as 1 Corinthians is concerned, we may dismiss, with Deissmann, "the *legend*
of a Biblical Greek". What is said of the Greek character of the
vocabulary holds good in general of the grammar of this Epistle.
The idioms of Paul's epistolary style form a distinct subject, on
which it is not necessary to enter here.

2. TEXT. The Greek Text of this Epistle stands on the same
footing as that of the rest—all usually contained in the collected
volume entitled Ο ΑΠΟΣΤΟΛΟΣ. Eighteen of the twenty-three known
Pauline uncial Codices belong to 1 Cor.: אB₁AD₂E₃L₂ are complete; CF₂G₃K₂P₂, approximately complete; S₂ contains half, and
ℶH₃I₂M₂Q₂Fᵃ fragments of the Epistle. אBAC were Codices of the
whole New Testament; ℶKLPS included the Acts and Catholic
Epp., P the Apocalypse also. In point of date, Bא belong to the
fourth century; ℶACIQ to the fifth century; DH to the sixth
century; Fᵃ to the seventh century; the rest to the ninth century.
Amongst the numerous correctors of א, אᶜ, of the seventh century,
is important here as elsewhere. ℶ (a palimpsest in the Vatican
Library) and S₂ (Athous Lauræ) are not yet critically edited
or collated: see on these MSS., and for full details respecting
the textual material, C. R. Gregory's *Prolegomena* to Tischendorf's
N.T. Græce, ed. major. Out of the 480 catalogued minuscule
(or cursive) MSS. of Paul few deserve attention. "The ancient
elements" found in them "appear with extreme irregularity in
different places of the Epistles," and Western readings in a remarkably small proportion (Westcott and Hort, *Introd. to the N.T.
in Greek*, § 212). The most notable, and those oftenest cited below,
are 17 (same as 33 of Gospels and 18 of Acts), 37 (Gospels 69, Acts
31, Rev. 14), 47 (Gospels 49)—all extending to viii. 10; and 67 **
(Acts 66, Rev. 34)—the marginal corrections of an ordinary cursive,
which "include a relatively large number of very ancient readings,"
akin to those of M₂(W.H.); 71; 109 (Acts 96). The 265 numbered
Lectionaries containing Acts and Epistles are but partially explored;
none as yet appear of sufficient value to be regularly cited.

The ancient Versions are of fairly uniform character through the N.T. The most valuable are all available here, except the Curetonian Syriac confined to the Gospels.

From the fourth century onwards Patristic references to 1 Corinthians become numerous and full, and afford the critic greater help than in some other Epistles. But the definite and certain aid forthcoming from this quarter is less than might have been expected.

Considering the length of the Epistle, it contains few conspicuous textual difficulties, none of grave exegetical importance. Its text has been from the first carefully preserved. In the following conspectus of various readings all Greek words are *spaced* in which the Textus Receptus is emended by the note. Where the reading is doubtful, a *query* follows the alternative reading supplied in the notes—a query *after the spacing* indicating a reading more likely than not, a query *without the spacing* indicating a possible but less probable reading. Orthographical corrections occurring *passim*, which belong to the N.T. written dialect as this is represented by the five great uncials and exhibited in the standard N.T. Grammars, must be taken for granted throughout.

Excluding the numberless corrections of the kind just noticed and those concerning only points of grammar or the *ordo verborum*, there are more than 200 emendations which affect the sense of the Epistle. Chapters vii. 29, 33 f., xv. 51 are instances of special complication. The restoration of the true text in iii. 1, 4, iv. 2, vii. 3, xi. 29, xv. 47 brings out the finer edge of Paul's style. The Received Text of vi. 20 and vii. 5 contains ecclesiastical glosses ; in iv. 6 and ix. 15 it has helped out Paul's anacolutha ; its habit of extending the shorter names of Christ blunts his meaning—notably in ix. 1 and xvi. 22. The group of (liturgical ?) additions to the genuine text in xi. 24 ff. deserves particular attention. Συνηθεία (viii. 7) and ἱερόθυτον (x. 28) are interesting words restored by criticism. A few readings are noted in the digest which have little or no intrinsic worth, but are of interest in their bearing on the history of the text, especially where they illustrate the peculiarities of the " Western " tradition. One *conjectural emendation* is adopted, *viz.*, that of Westcott and Hort in ch. xii. 2.

3. HISTORY OF THE EPISTLE. This is the first N.T. writing to be cited by name in Christian literature. " Take up," says Clement of Rome to the Corinthians (1 Ep., xlvii.), " the letter of the blessed Paul the Apostle. What was the first thing he wrote to you in the beginning of the Gospel ? Of a truth he wrote to you in the Spirit

touching himself and Cephas and Apollos, because even then you had formed factions." Like other post-apostolic writers, Clement shows an imperfect grasp of Pauline teaching, but his Salutation, with §§ xxiv., xxxiv. 8, xxxvii., xlix., and lxv. 2, bears unmistakable impressions of this Epistle. The Epistle of Barnabas (iv. 9-11, v. 6, vi. 5, xvi. 7-10 ; Hermas, *Mand.* iv. 4 (*cf.* 1 Cor. vii. 39) ; Ignatius, *Ad Eph.*, xvi., xviii., *Ad Rom.*, iv. 3, v. 1, ix. 2 ; Polycarp, *Ad Phil.*, x. 2, *Ad Diognetum*, xii. 5 ; the *Didaché*, i. 5, iii. 3, iv. 3, x. 6, etc., attest the use of this writing in primitive Christian times. From Irenæus onwards it is quoted as Holy Scripture. The Gnostics used it with predilection. The testimony of early Christianity to its Pauline authorship and Apostolic authority is unequivocal and full.

But our Epistle did not at first take a leading place among N.T. writings. Its influence has been " broken and fitful ". It had little to say directly upon the questions (except that of the Resurrection) which chiefly interested the ante-Nicene Church. Tertullian, however, expounded it in his *Adv. Marcionem ;* and Origen wrote annotations, partly preserved in Cramer's *Catena*. In the fourth century, when "controversies on Church discipline and morals began to sway the minds of thoughtful men, this Epistle came to the front " (Edwards). Many of the Church leaders of that time wrote upon 1 Corinthians. Only fragments of the Greek commentators earlier than John Chrysostom (+ 407 A.D.) are extant ; later expositors— the most notable, Theodoret (420 A.D.), Oecumenius (*c.* 950), Theophylact (1078)—built upon him ; his versatile powers shine in the exposition of this Epistle. The Latin commentaries of Pelagius (for long ascribed to Jerome) and of Ambrosiaster (Hilary of Rome ?) testify to the wide use of this Scripture in the West in the fourth and fifth centuries. To Thomas Aquinas we owe the only interpretation of value bequeathed by the Middle Ages. Though subordinated, like all mediæval exegesis, to scholastic theology, his exposition contains fresh and vigorous thought.

Colet's Oxford Lectures on this Epistle (A.D. 1496), and the N.T. *Paraphrase* of Erasmus (1519), breathe the new spirit of the Reformation, which brought 1 Corinthians to the front again, along with Romans and Galatians. The adjustment of liberty and order, the application of evangelical faith to secular life, the reconstitution of the Church with its sacraments and ministry started a multitude of problems calling for its aid. Calvin excelled himself in his interpretation of this Epistle, offending many of his followers by his breadth and candour. Estius, his Romanist contemporary, is no mean rival. Amongst the German Reformers, Melanchthon, W. Musculus, Bullinger handled this Epistle with effect.   Beza's *Annotationes,* and especially his Latin translation, are always worth consulting.   The illustrious Grotius—Arminian, humanistic, practical—found here a congenial subject.   In the seventeenth century 1 Corinthians suffered another eclipse ; no Commentary upon it of any mark appeared between the time of Grotius and Bengel.   All later interpreters are Bengel's disciples.

This Epistle at present suffers no lack of attention.   Beside the larger critical N.T. Commentaries of Germany—those of De Wette, Meyer (re-written, in 1 and 2 Cor., by Heinrici), v. Hofmann, the *Handcommentar* (Schmiedel), and the *Kurtzgefasster* (Schnedermann) —and Alford's great work in this country, the following are of special value : Billroth's *Vorlesungen z. d. Briefen an d. Kor.* (1833), Rückert's *Der 1 Br. Pauli an d. Kor.* (1836), Neander's *Auslegung d. beiden Br. an d. Kor.* (1859),—above all, Heinrici's *Das erste Sendschreiben d. Ap. Paulus an d. Kor.* (1880), a work rich in illustration of Greek thought and manners, and throwing new light on the social development of primitive Christianity.   Godet's *Commentaire sur la prem. ép. aux Corinthiens* (1887 : transl. in Clarks' *F. T. Libr.*), though not his most successful exposition, is marked by his fine spiritual and literary qualities, and is full of instructive matter.

English scholars have addressed themselves zealously to 1 Corinthians, which interests them by its relations to the ethical and social questions of the time.   A. P. Stanley (*The Epistles of Paul to the Corinthians,* 1855) has illuminated the historical and picturesque aspects of the Epistle, C. Hodge (American, 1857) its theological side.   Beet tracks the thought of the Apostle with exceeding closeness, and presents it with concise force (*Epistles to the Corinthians,* 1882).   Freshness and vivacity, with strokes of keen grammatical insight, distinguish the work of T. S. Evans in the *Speaker's Commentary.*   Ellicott's interpretation (1887) is a model of exact and delicate verbal elucidation ; no better book can be placed in the hands of a working Greek Testament student.   The posthumous " Notes " of Lightfoot on chaps. i.-vii. (1895) are written with his ripe knowledge, balanced judgment, and sure touch.   Edwards' *Commentary on the First Epistle to the Corinthians* (1885) ranks with Heinrici's and Ellicott's as a classical piece of exegesis ; it is strong both on the linguistic and philosophical side, and shows a rare power of luminous statement.   M. Dods supplies, in *The Expositor's Bible,* a genial and masterly homiletic application.   Hort's *Christian Ecclesia* and Knowling's *Witness of the Epistles to Christ* exhibit, in the use they make of this document, its decisive bearing on questions of early Church History and Apologetics.

4. CRITICISM. Until quite recently the authenticity and integrity of 1 Corinthians were never doubted. The criticism of F. C. Baur and the Tübingen School left it standing as one of the " four undisputed Epistles " ; Bruno Bauer's attack (*Kritik d. Paul. Briefe*, 1851) was quite isolated. In Holland, however, a more radical criticism has arisen—whose exponents are Loman (*Theologisch Tijdschrift*, 1882-86), Pierson and Naber (*Verisimilia*, 1886), van Manen (*Paulus*, i., ii., 1890-91 ; and *Prot. Kirchenzeitung*, 1882-86), Meyboom (*Theol. Tijdschr.*, 1889-91) ; aided by Steck (*Gal.-Brief*, 1888) in Germany, and " Edwin Johnson " (*Antiqua Mater*, 1887) in England—which sweeps away these four with the rest, leaving nothing but morsels surviving of the genuine Paul. These scholars premise a slow development, along a single line, in early Christian thought. They claim to be the uniformitarians, as against the catastrophists, of Biblical science. The universalism with which Paul is credited, they set down as the final issue, reached in the second century, of the continued interaction of Judaic and Hellenic thought. In support of this view they point out numerous alleged contradictions within the four Epistles and the traces of various tendencies and times affording evidence of compilation, so reducing them to a many-coloured patchwork, the product of a century of conflict and hardly won progress. They attempt to prove the literary dependence of the four on post-Pauline writings, both within and without the New Testament. This theory presents no consistent shape in the hands of its advocates, and has been subjected to a destructive examination by Holtzmann and Jülicher in their N.T. *Einleitungen* (recent editions), by Lipsius (Romans) and Schmiedel (1 and 2 Corinthians) in the *Handcommentar ;* also by Knowling in chap. iii. of his " Witness of the Epistles ". A sound exegesis is the best refutation of extravagances which are, in effect, the *reductio ad absurdum* of the Baurian method.

Another group of critics, maintaining the genuineness of the Corinthian Epistles in substance, desire *to redistribute their contents*. Hagge (*Jahrbuch für prot. Theologie*, 1876) finds *four* older documents behind the two ; Völter (*Theol. Tijdschrift*, 1889) discovers *three*, making considerable excisions besides ; Clemen, who discusses all the schemes of rearrangement in his *Einheitlichkeit d. paul. Briefe* (II., *Die Corintherbr. : cf.* Schmiedel in the *Handcom., an d. Kor., Einleitung*, ii.), dissects the canonical Epistles into *five* originals. These re-combinations are highly ingenious ; Clemen's scheme, which is really plausible, substitutes a carefully marshalled topical order for the spontaneity and discursiveness of the true epistle. The hypotheses of reconstruction have no historical basis, no external evidence in their favour ; their sole appeal is to internal probability. The actual 1 Corinthians vindicates its unity to the sympathetic reader who transports himself into the situation.

Other critics, again, who regard the reconstruction of the Epistle as needless or impracticable, see reason to eliminate certain passages as *interpolations*. Holsten (*Das Evang. d. Paulus*, I., i., 1880), Baljon (*De Tekst d. Brieven aan de Rom., Cor., en Gal.*, 1884), Bois (*Adversaria critica de I. ad Cor.* : Toulouse, 1887), are fertile in suggestions of this kind. Heinrici will not exclude the supposition of " improvements in detail, attempts [made by the first editors] to smooth over or supplement rough or defective passages of the Apostle, which criticism may be able to detect ". Such insertions he finds in the Ἐγὼ δὲ Χριστοῦ of i. 12, and in xv. 56 : so Schmiedel and Clemen in the latter place. We do not deny the abstract possibility of the Epistle having been " touched up " in this way ; glosses such as those the Codices reveal in ii. 4, iv. 6, vii. 3, etc., for aught we know may have crept in *before*, as well as after the divergence of our extant witnesses. None, however, of the alleged " primitive corruptions " are made out convincingly,—except perhaps the transcriptional error which W.H. have detected in xii. 2. Some of these conjectures there will be occasion to notice in the course of the exposition.

Analysis. After the *Introduction* (i. 1-9), the body of the Epistle falls into six principal divisions, as follows : Div. I., *The Corinthian Parties and the Gospel Ministry*, i. 10-iv. 21 ; Div. II., *Questions of Social Morals*, v.-vii. ; Div. III., *Contact with Idolatry*, viii.-xi. 1 ; Div. IV., *Disorders in Worship and Church Life*, xi. 2-xiv. ; Div. V., *The Resurrection of the Body*, xv. ; Div. VI., *Business, News, and Greetings*, xvi. Within these main Divisions, the matter is broken up for clearer elucidation into sixty short Sections, each furnished with a heading and prefatory outline.

ABBREVIATIONS USED IN THE EXPOSITION.

acc. = accusative case.
act. = active voice.
adj. = adjective.
ad loc. = *ad locum*, on this passage.
adv., advl. = adverb, adverbial.
Al. = Alford's *Greek Testament*.

aor. = aorist tense.

art. = grammatical article.

Aug. = Augustine.

Bg. = Bengel's *Gnomon Novi Testamenti*.

Bm. = A. Buttmann's *Grammar of the N.T. Greek* (Eng. Trans., 1873).

Bn. = E. Burton's *Syntax of the Moods and Tenses in the N.T.* (1894).

Bt. = J. A. Beet's *St. Paul's Epp. to the Corinthians* (1882).

Bz. = Beza's *Nov. Testamentum : Interpretatio et Annotationes* (Cantab., 1642).

cl. = classical.

Cm. = John Chrysostom's *Homiliæ* († 407).

comm. = commentary, commentator.

constr. = construction.

Cor. = Corinth, Corinthian or Corinthians.

Cr. = Cremer's *Biblico - Theological Lexicon of N.T. Greek* (Eng. Trans.).

Cv. = Calvin's *In Nov. Testamentum Commentarii*.

dat. = dative case.

Did. = Διδαχὴ τῶν δωδέκα ἀποστόλων.

diff. = difference, different, differently.

D.W. = De Wette's *Handbuch z. N. T.*

eccl. = ecclesiastical.

Ed. = T. C. Edwards' *Commentary on the First Ep. to the Corinthians*.[2]

El. = C. J. Ellicott's *St. Paul's First Epistle to the Corinthians*.

Er. = Erasmus' *In N.T. Annotationes*.

E.V. = English Version.

Ev. = T. S. Evans in *Speaker's Commentary*.

ex. = example.

exc. = except.

Ff. = Fathers.

fut. = future tense.

Gd. = F. Godet's *Commentaire sur la prem. Ép. aux Corinthiens* (Eng. Trans.).

gen. = genitive case.

Gm. = Grimm-Thayer's *Greek-English Lexicon of the N.T.*

Gr. = Greek, or Grotius' *Annotationes in N.T.*

Heb. = Hebrew.

Hf. = J. C. K. von Hofmann's *Die heilige Schrift N.T. untersucht*, ii. 2 (2te Auflage, 1874).

h.l. = *hapax legomenon*, a solitary expression.

Hn. = C. F. G. Heinrici's *Erklärung der Korintherbriefe* (1880), or 1 *Korinther* in Meyer's *krit.-exegetisches Kommentar* (1896).

impf. = imperfect tense.

impv. = imperative mood.

ind. = indicative mood.

indir. = indirect.

inf. = infinitive mood.

interr. = interrogative.

Jer. = Jerome, Hieronymus.

Lidd. = Liddell and Scott's *Greek-English Lexicon*.

e vii. 14; ἐν Κορίνθῳ,[1] e ἡγιασμένοις c ἐν Χριστῷ Ἰησοῦ, a κλητοῖς f ἁγίοις, g σὺν
Rom. xv.
16; Heb.x. g πᾶσι τοῖς h ἐπικαλουμένοις τὸ h ὄνομα τοῦ Κυρίου ἡμῶν Ἰησοῦ Χριστοῦ
10, 29; Jo.
xvii. 17.

f 2 Cor., Eph., Ph., Col., Acts ix. 13, etc.   g 2 Cor.; 2 Tim. ii. 22.   h Acts ii. 21, ix. 14, 21, xxii.
16; Rom. x. 13; Gen. iv. 26, etc.; Ps. cxvi. 4; Joel ii. 32; Zech. xiii. 9.

[1] BD*G, followed by Al., Tr., Tisch.[7], place τῃ . . . Κορινθῳ after ηγιασμ. . . .
Ιησ.: probably a Western deviation.

viii. 29 f.), not distinguished as in Matt.
xx. 16. The thought of the "call" of
God as assigning to each Christian man
his status is prominent in this ep.: see
vv. 9, 24 ff., vii. 17-24.—Σωσθένης ὁ
ἀδελφὸς is a party to the Letter, which
notwithstanding runs in first pers. sing.,
as in Gal. after οἱ σὺν ἐμοὶ πάντες ἀδελφοὶ of i. 2; otherwise in 2 Cor. and
1 and 2 Thess.: Sosthenes (only named
here by P.) shares in this ep. not
as joint-composer, but as witness and
approver. He would scarcely be introduced at this point as amanuensis
(cf. Rom. xvi. 22). S. is a person
known to and honoured by the Cor.,
but now with the Ap. at Ephesus and
in his confidence. He may, or may
not, have been the Sosthenes of Acts
xviii. 17—the name was fairly common.
One ἀρχισυνάγωγος (Crispus) had been
converted at Cor., why not another afterwards? P. would delight to make of a
persecutor an ally. His former position
would give an ex-Synagogue-leader
weight, especially with Jewish Christians; and his subsequent conversion
may account for Luke's exceptionally
preserving Sosthenes' name as Paul's
assailant (see M. Dods on the point, in
Exp. Bib.). Eusebius (Hist. Eccles., i.
12) makes S. one of the Seventy of
Luke x. 17 — "a worthless tradition"
(Lt.).

Ver. 2. τῇ ἐκκλησίᾳ τοῦ Θεοῦ (in
salutation of 1 and 2 Cor. only) gives
supreme dignity to the assembly of
Cor. addressed by the Ap. of Christ
Jesus—the assembled citizens of God's
kingdom and commonwealth (Eph. ii. 12,
19; cf. Tit. ii. 14, 1 Peter ii. 9 f.). τῇ
οὔσῃ ἐν Κορ., "that exists in Corinth"—
lætum et ingens paradoxon (Bg.): so far
the Gospel has reached (2 Cor. x. 13 f.);
in so foul a place it flourishes! (vi. 9 ff.).
Not as earlier, "the assembly of Thessalonians," etc.: the conception of the
ecclesia widens; the local Christian
gathering is part of one extended "congregation of God," existing in this place
or that (see last clause). To τῇ ἐκκλησίᾳ τ. Θεοῦ is apposed, by way of pre-

dicative definition (hence anarthrous),
ἡγιασμένοις ἐν Χριστῷ Ἰησοῦ, "the
Church of God (consisting of men)
sanctified in Christ Jesus": Church
status is grounded on personal relationship to God in Christ. Now this relationship began with God's call, which
summoned each to a holy life within
the Christian fellowship; hence the
further apposition, κλητοῖς ἁγίοις (see
note on 1, and Rom. i. 7; cf. Acts xviii.
10, λαός ἐστίν μοι πολύς κ.τ.λ.). The
pf. pass. ptp. expresses a determinate
state: once for all the Cor. readers
have been devoted to God, by His call
and their consent. This initial sanctification is synchronous with justification
(vi. 11), and is the positive as that is the
negative side of salvation: ἐλευθερωθέντες
ἀπὸ τ. ἁμαρτίας, ἐδουλώθητε τ. δικαιοσύνῃ (Rom. vi. 16-19). "Sanctified in
Christ Jesus" (="living to God in
Christ Jesus," Rom. vi. 11) imports
union with Christ (vi. 17, 19, xii. 11,
Rom. viii. 9 f.) as well as salvation
through Christ. His past work is the
objective ground, His present heavenly
being (implied by the name "Christ
Jesus," as in this order) the active
spring of this ζῆν τῷ Θεῷ: cf. ver. 30
and note. The repeated ref. to the
holiness of the readers recalls them to
their vocation; low practice calls for
the reassertion of high ideals; admonet
Corinthios majestatis ipsorum (Bg.). Cv.
draws a diff. yet consistent inference: "Locus diligenter observandus,
ne requiramus in hoc mundo Ecclesiam
omni ruga et macula carentem". The
adjunct σὺν πᾶσιν . . . τόπῳ may
qualify ἡγιασμένοις κ.τ.λ. (so some
moderns), or the main predicate (Gr.
Ff.): i.e., the Church shares (a) in its
Christian sanctity, or (b) in the Apostle's
good wishes, "with all that call upon
the name," etc. (b) gives a better
balanced sentence, and a true Pauline
sentiment: cf. Eph. vi. 24, also the
Benediction of Clem. Rom. ad Cor., lxv.
—ἐν παντὶ τόπῳ, an expression indefinitely large (see parls.), approaching "in
all the world" of Rom. i. 8, Col. i. 6;

[i]ἐν [i]παντὶ [i]τόπῳ, [k]αὐτῶν τε [l]καὶ [k]ἡμῶν· 3. [l]χάρις ὑμῖν καὶ [l]εἰρήνη [i]2 Cor. ii. 14; 1 Th. ἀπὸ Θεοῦ πατρὸς ἡμῶν καὶ Κυρίου Ἰησοῦ Χριστοῦ.

i. 8; 1 Tim. ii. 8;

4. [m]Εὐχαριστῶ τῷ [m]Θεῷ μου [2]πάντοτε περὶ ὑμῶν, ἐπὶ τῇ [n]χάριτι

Mal. i. 11. [k]Cf. Rom.

τοῦ Θεοῦ τῇ [n]δοθείσῃ ὑμῖν ἐν Χριστῷ Ἰησοῦ· 5. ὅτι ἐν παντὶ

xvi. 13; Eph. vi. 9. 1 Rom. i. 7,

and other Pauline Salutations; cf., however, 1 and 2 Tim., 1 and 2 Pet. Ph. i. 3; Col. i. 3; 1 Th. i. 2; Phm. 4. m xiv. 18; Rom. i. 8; n Twelve times in P.; in Jas. iv. 6 besides.

[1]αυτων και ημων, without τε; so ℵ*A* (seemingly) BD*G, latt. vg. syrsch. cop., Or., Dam. τε a Syrian editorial insertion for smoother reading.

[2]ℵ*B, æth. omit μου: harmonistic insertion from parls.

there is nothing here to indicate the limit given in 2 Cor. i. 1. The readers belong to a *widespread* as well as a holy community; Paul insists on this in the sequel, pointing in reproof to "other churches". To "call on the name of the Lord Jesus Christ"—to invoke Him in prayer as "Lord"—is the mark of the Christian, by which Saul, *e.g.*, once recognised his victims (see parls.), the index of saving faith (xii. 3, Rom. x. 12 ff.). The afterthought αὐτῶν καὶ ἡμῶν, correcting the previous ἡμῶν (Cm., Cv., Gd., Sm.), heightens the sense of wide fellowship given by the previous clause; "one Lord" (viii. 6; Rom. x. 12, xiv. 9, Eph. iv. 5) unites all hearts in the obedience of faith. To attach these pronouns to τόπῳ (*in omni loco ipsorum et nostro*, Vg.) gives a sense strained in various ways: "their place and ours,"—belonging to us equally with them (Mr., El., Ed.); "illorum (prope Cor.), nostro (ubi P. et Sosth. versabantur," Bg.); in non-Pauline and Pauline Churches (Hn.); and so on.

Ver. 3. χάρις ὑμῖν καὶ εἰρήνη ἀπὸ Θεοῦ κ.τ.λ.: Paul's customary greeting; see note on Rom. i. 7. "The occurrence of the peculiar phrase 'grace and peace' in Paul, John, and Peter intimates that we have here the earliest Christian password or *symbolum*" (Ed.). κυρίου might grammatically be parl. to ἡμῶν, both depending upon πατρός, as in 2 Cor. i. 3, etc.; but 1 and 2 Thess. i. 1 (Θεῷ πατρὶ κ. Κυρίῳ Ἰ. Χ.) prove *Father* and *Lord* in this formula to be parl.: *cf.* viii. 6, 2 Cor. xiii. 13; nowhere does P. speak (as in John xx. 17) of God as Father *of Christ and of men* co-ordinately, and for ἡμῶν to come first in such connexion would be incongruous. "The union of" Θεοῦ and Κυρίου "under the vinculum of a common prp. is one of the numberless hints scattered through St. Paul's epp. of the con-

sciously felt and recognised co-ordination" of the Father and Christ (El.).

§ 2. THE THANKSGIVING, i. 4-9. The Pauline thanksgiving holds the place of the *captatio benevolentiæ* in ancient speeches, with the diff. that it is in solemn sincerity addressed to *God*. The Ap. thanks God (1) for *the past grace* given the Cor. in Christ, ver. 4; (2) for *the rich intellectual development of that grace*, according with the sure evidence upon which they had received the Gospel, and attended by an eager anticipation of Christ's advent, vv. 5-7; (3) for *the certainty that they will be perfected in grace* and found unimpeached at Christ's return—a hope founded on God's fidelity to His own signal call, vv. 8 f. Paul reflects gratefully on the past, hopefully on the future of this Church; he is significantly silent respecting its present condition: contrast with this the Thess. and Phil. Thanksgivings. He extracts from a disquieting situation all the comfort possible.

Ver. 4. On εὐχαριστῶ κ.τ.λ., and the form of Paul's introductory thanksgivings, see Rom. i. 8. ἐπὶ τῇ χάριτι κ.τ.λ. —ἐπί (at), of the *occasioning* cause; *cf.* xiii. 6, xiv. 16, etc. τ. δοθείσῃ ὑμῖν (aor. ptp.)—"the grace that was given you," *sc.* at conversion (see 6); contrast the pr. ptp. of continuous bestowment in xv. 57, and the pf. of abiding result in 2 Cor. viii. 1. For ἐν Χριστῷ Ἰησοῦ, see note on ver. 2. P. refers not to the general objective gift of grace in Christ (as in Rom. viii. 32), nor to its eternal bestowment in the thought of God (as in 2 Tim. i. 9), but to its actual conferment at the time when the Cor. became God's κλητοὶ ἅγιοι (2).

Ver. 5. ὅτι κ.τ.λ. stands in explicative apposition to the foregoing τ. χάριτι τ. δοθείσῃ, bringing out the matter of thanksgiving eminent in the conversion of the Cor.—"(I mean), that in every-

o 2 Cor. vi.   ° ἐπλουτίσθητε ἐν αὐτῷ, ἐν παντὶ ᴾ λόγῳ καὶ πάσῃ �q γνώσει, 6. καθὼς
10, ix. 11
only;   τὸ ʳ μαρτύριον τοῦ Χριστοῦ¹ ˢ ἐβεβαιώθη ἐν ὑμῖν· 7. ὥστε ὑμᾶς μὴ
12 times
in LXX.   ᵗ ὑστερεῖσθαι ἐν μηδενὶ ᵘ χαρίσματι, ᵛ ἀπεκδεχομένους τὴν ᵂ ἀποκά-
Gen. xiv.
23, etc.   λυψιν τοῦ ᵂ κυρίου ἡμῶν ᵂ Ἰησοῦ Χριστοῦ· 8. ὃς καὶ ˢ βεβαιώσει
p (In this
sense) 17, ὑμᾶς ˣ ἕως ˣ τέλους ʸ ἀνεγκλήτους ἐν τῇ ᶻ ἡμέρᾳ² τοῦ ᶻ Κυρίου ἡμῶν
ii. 1, 4, iv.
19 f., xii. 8, and nine times besides in P.   q viii. 1 ff., xii. 3, xiii. 2, 8, xiv. 6; thrice (so) in 2 Cor.;
twice in Rom.; Eph. iii. 19; Col. ii 3; 1 Tim. vi. 20; 2 Pet. i. 5 f.; Lk. xi. 52.   r ii. 1; 2 Th. i.
10; 1 Tim. ii. 6; 2 Tim. i. 8; μαρτυρία in John, exc. Rev. xv. 5.   s 2 Cor. i. 21; Rom. xv. 8; Ph.
i. 7; Col. ii. 7; twice in Heb.; Mk. xvi. 20.   t viii. 8, xii. 24, xvi. 17; thrice besides in P.; Heb.
xi. 37; Lk. xv. 14.   u vii. 7, xii. 4 ff.; 2 Cor. i. 11; four times in Rom.; 1 Tim. iv. 14; 1 Pet. iv.
10.   v Rom. viii. 19 ff.; Gal. v. 5; Ph. iii. 20; Heb. ix. 28; 1 Pet. iii. 20 only.   w 2 Th. i. 7;
thrice in 1 Pet.; cf. Gal. i. 12, 16; Rom. viii. 19.   x 2 Cor. i. 13 only.   αχρι τ., Heb. vi. 11; Rev. ii.
26.   μεχρι τ., Heb. iii. 6, 14.   εις τελος, 1 Th. ii. 16.   y Col. i. 22; 1 Tim. iii. 10; Tit. i. 6 f. only.
z iii. 13, iv. 3, v. 5; 2 Cor. i. 14; 10 times besides in P.; Acts ii. 20; Joel iii. 31, etc.

¹ Θεου in B*G, a few minuscc., arm.

² The Western reading is παρουσια: DG, etc. Ambrst., Pelagius, with vg., read
in die adventus (conflate).

thing you were enriched," etc. For this
defining ὅτι after a vbl. noun, cf. ver. 26
and 2 Cor. i. 8. The *affluence* of endowment conferred on the Cor. stirred
the Apostle's deep gratitude (cf. 7, 2 Cor.
viii. 9): this wealth appears in another
light in iv. 6-10, v. 2, viii. 1-3; see also
Introd., p. 730 f. The Church doubtless
dwelt upon this distinction in its recent
letter, to which P. is replying. ἐν παντὶ
is defined, and virtually limited, by ἐν
παντὶ λόγῳ καὶ πάσῃ γνώσει (kindred
gifts, linked by the single prp.): the
exuberance of grace in the Cor. shone
"in all (manner of) utterance and all
(manner of) knowledge". λόγος in this
connexion signifies not *the thing said*
(as in 18), but *the saying of it, loquendi
facultas* (Bz.). "Relatively to γνῶσις,
λόγος is the ability and readiness to *say*
what one understands; γν. the power and
ability to *understand*" (Hn.). "Knowledge" would naturally precede; but the
Cor. excelled and delighted in "speech"
above all: see ii. 1-4, 13, iv. 19 f., xiii. 1.
   Ver. 6. τοῦ Χριστοῦ is objective gen.
to τὸ μαρτύριον—"the witness to Christ,"
—coming from both God and man (xv.
3-11, 2 Thess. i. 10); otherwise in ii. 1;
cf. Rom. i. 2, "the good news of God
about His Son". μαρτύριον indicates
the well-established truth of the message
(see, *e.g.*, xv. 15), εὐαγγέλιον its *beneficial
and welcome nature* (see Rom. i. 16 f.).—
ἐβεβαιώθη ἐν ὑμῖν, "(the witness about
Christ) was made sure among you"; its
reality was verified. By outward demonstration—miracles, etc.; or by the
inner persuasion of a firm faith, "interna
Spiritus virtus" (Cv.)? The latter certainly, in Pauline usage (see parls.: but
not to the exclusion of the former); cf. ii.

4 f., and notes; xii. 10, ἐνεργήματα
δυνάμεων; also 1 Thess. i. 5 f., ii. 13,
Gal. iii. 5; the two went together
—πολλῶν θαυμάτων, ἀφάτου χάριτος
(Cm.). At first discouraged, Paul
preached at Cor. with signal power, and
his message awakened a decided and
energetic faith; see ii. 1-5, xv. 1, 11;
Acts xviii. 5-11.
   Ver. 7 describes the result of the firm
establishment of the Gospel: ὥστε ὑμᾶς
μὴ ὑστερεῖσθαι κ.τ.λ. (ὥστε with inf. of
contemplated result: see Bn. §§ 369 ff.),
"causing you not to feel behindhand in
any gift of grace"; the mid. ὑστερεῖσθαι
implies *subjective reflexion*, the consciousness of inferiority (Ev.): similarly
in Rom. iii. 23, "*find themselves short* of
the glory of God" (Sanday and Headl.);
and in Luke xv. 14, "he began *to feel his
destitution*". The pr. inf. and ptp. of the
vbs. bear no ref. to the time of writing;
their time is given by the governing
ἐβεβαιώθη: the strong assurance with
which the Cor. embraced the Gospel
was followed by a shower of spiritual
energies, of which they had a lively
sense. A χάρισμα (see parls.) is χάρις
in some concrete result (see Cr. *s. v.*),—
a specific *endowment of (God's) grace*,
whether the fundamental charism, embracing all others, of salvation in Christ
(Rom. v. 16), or, *e.g.*, the special and individual charism of continence (vii. 7).
No church excelled the Cor. in the
variety of its endowments and the satisfaction felt in them. Chaps. xii.-xiv.
enumerate and discuss the chief Cor.
χαρίσματα, setting ἀγάπη in their
midst; ethical qualities are included
under this term, vv. 8 f.—ἀπεκδεχομένους τ. ἀποκάλυψιν κ.τ.λ, "while you

Ἰησοῦ Χριστοῦ[1] · 9. [a]πιστὸς ὁ [a]Θεὸς, δι' οὗ [b]ἐκλήθητε εἰς [c]κοινω- [a] x. 13; 2
νίαν τοῦ υἱοῦ αὐτοῦ Ἰησοῦ Χριστοῦ τοῦ Κυρίου ἡμῶν.

Cor. i. 18;
1 Th. v. 24;
2 Th. iii. 3;
2 Tim. ii.

13; Heb. x. 23, xi. 11; Deut. vii. 9; Isa. xlix. 7.   b Ver. 26, vii. 15 ff.; 10 times besides in P.;
1 Pet. i. 15, ii. 9, v. 10; 2 Pet. i. 3.   c x. 16; 2 Cor. vi. 14 f.; Ph. iii. 10; 1 Jo. i. 3; cf. Heb. ii. 14,
iii. 14.

[1] B om. Χριστου, bracketed by W.H. as doubtful ; cf. 2 Cor. i. 14.

eagerly awaited (or eagerly awaiting, as you did) the coming of our Lord Jesus Christ". The vb. is one of P.'s characteristic intensive compounds (see parls.). The anarthrous pr. ptp. implies a continuous state conditioning that of the foregoing clause: the unstinted plenty of Divine gifts continued while the recipients fixed their thought upon the day of Christ; xv. 12, 33 f. show that this expectation had been in many instances relaxed. Rom. viii. and Col. iii. (also 1 John ii. 28-iii. 3) illustrate the bearing of faith in the παρουσία on Christian character; cf. Matt. xxv., Luke xii. 32 ff., etc. It is an ἀποκάλυψις, an "unveiling" of Christ that the Cor. looked for; since although they are "in Christ," still he is hidden (Col. iii. 3 f.); His presence is a mystery (Col. i. 27, Eph. v. 32). "Παρουσία denotes the fact of Christ's (future) presence, ἐπιφάνεια its visibility" and splendour, "ἀποκάλυψις its inner meaning" (Ed.); φανέρωσις (it might be added: Col. iii. 4) its open display. The Cor. were richly blessed with present good, while expecting a good far exceeding it: "a tacit warning against fancied satisfaction in the present" (Gd.: cf. iv. 8).

Ver. 8. ὃς καὶ βεβαιώσει ὑμᾶς echoes ἐβεβαιώθη (6); cf. the thanksgiving of Phil. i. 6. ἕως τέλους (see parls.) points to a consummation, not a mere termination of the present order; cf. Rom. vi. 21 f. ἀνεγκλήτους, "unimpeached," synonymous with ἀμέμπτους (unblamed), but judicial in significance,—in view of the ἡμέρα τοῦ Κυρίου: "free from charge when the day of the Lord shall come"; cf. Rom. viii. 33, τίς ἐγκαλέσει;—ὅς refers to the foregoing κύριος Ἰ. Χ., not to the distant Θεὸς of ver. 4; the Saviour "who will make sure" the innocence of the Cor. on that day is the Judge who will pronounce upon it (cf. Col. i. 22, Eph. v. 27, where Christ is to "present" the Church "unblemished and unimpeached" before Himself): He will then confirm them and vindicate their character, as they have confirmed the testimony about Him (cf. Luke ix. 26). P. does not say the Cor. are ἀνέγκλητοι now; he hopes

that they will prove so then. "The day of our Lord Jesus Christ" (cf. note on iii. 13) is the O.T. "day of Jehovah" (LXX, τ. Κυρίου), translated into the "day of Christ," since God has revealed His purpose to "judge through Jesus Christ" (Rom. ii. 16, Acts xvii. 31).—ἐν τ. ἡμέρᾳ=ἐν τ. παρουσίᾳ τ. κυρ. Ἰ. Χ. (1 Thess. v. 23, etc.), with the added connotation of judgment, to which the ἀποκάλυψις of ver. 7 leads up: for this connexion of thought, see Rom. ii. 5, 2 Thess. i. 7 ff. P. does not say "His day," though ὅς recalls ὁ κύρ. Ἰ. Χ.: Christ's name is repeated ten times in the first ten vv.—six times, as here, in full style—with sustained solemnity of emphasis (cf. the repetition of "God" in 20-29); "P. thus prepares for his exhortations these Cor., who were disposed to treat Christianity as a matter of human choice and personal liking, under the sense that in a Christian Church Christ is the one thing and everything" (Hf.).

Ver. 9. The ground of Paul's hope for the ultimate welfare of the Cor. is God's fidelity. His gifts are bestowed on a wise and settled plan (21, Rom. viii. 28 ff., xi. 29); His word, with it His character, is pledged to the salvation of those who believe in His Son: πιστὸς ὁ Θεὸς δι' οὗ ἐκλήθητε = πιστὸς ὁ καλῶν of 1 Thess. v. 23 f.; the formula πιστὸς ὁ λόγος of the Past. Epp. is not very different. δι' οὗ is "through (older Eng., by) whom you were called"; cf. διὰ θελήματος Θεοῦ (1, see note), and δι' οὗ . . . τὰ πάντα (of God, Rom. xi. 36); similarly in Gal. iv. 7: God had manifestly interposed to bring the Cor. into the communion of Christ (see, further, 26-28); His voice sounded in the ears of the Cor. when the Gospel summons reached them (cf. 1 Thess. ii. 13). Christ (8) and God are both therefore security for the perfecting of their Christian life. —God's accepted call has brought the readers εἰς κοινωνίαν τοῦ υἱοῦ αὐτοῦ Ἰησοῦ Χριστοῦ τοῦ κυρίου ἡμῶν—i.e., not "into a communion (or partnership) with His Son Jesus Christ our Lord" (nowhere else has this noun an objective

d iv. 16, xvi.　10. ᵈ Παρακαλῶ δὲ ὑμᾶς, ἀδελφοί, ᵉ διὰ τοῦ ᵉ ὀνόματος τοῦ Κυρίου
15 ; fre-
quent in
this sense　Ἰησοῦ Χριστοῦ, ἵνα ᶠ τὸ ᶠ αὐτὸ λέγητε πάντες καὶ μὴ ᾖ ἐν ὑμῖν ᵍ σχίσ-
in P. ; also
　　Heb. xiii. 19, 22 ; 1 Pet. ; Jude 3.　e Acts iv. 30, x. 43.　f xii. 25 ; 2 Cor. xiii. 11 ; Rom. xii. 16, xv.
　　5 ; Ph. ii. 2, iv. 2.　g xi. 18, xii. 25 ; Jo. vii. 43, ix. 16, x. 19.

gen. of the *person :* see parls.), but "into
a communion belonging to (and named
after) God's Son," of which *He* is founder,
centre and sum. In this fellowship the
Cor. partake "with all those that call on
the name of our Lord Jesus Christ" (2) ;
κοινωνία denotes *collective participation.*
The κοινωνία τ. υἱοῦ is the same, both in
content and constituency, as the κοινωνία
τ. πνεύματος (see xii. 13, 2 Cor. xiii. 13,
Phil. ii. 1, Eph. iv. 4-6). Its content—
that which the Cor. share in—is *sonship
to God,* since it is "a communion of His
Son," with Christ for "first-born among
many brethren" (Rom. viii. 29 f. ; *cf.*
Heb. ii. 10-16), and consequent *heirship
to God* (Rom. viii. 17, Gal. iii. 26-iv. 7).
The title "our Lord," added to "His
Son Jesus Christ," invests the Christian
communion with present grandeur and
certifies its hope of glory ; Christ's glory
lies in His full manifestation as *Lord*
(xv. 25, Phil. ii. 11), and its glorification
is wrapped up in His (2 Thess. i. 12, ii.
14 ; also 1 Thess. ii. 12). Ver. 9 sustains
and crowns the hope expressed in ver. 8.
For κοινωνία, see further the notes on x.
16 f.

DIVISION I. THE CORINTHIAN PARTIES
AND THE GOSPEL MINISTRY, i. 10-iv.
21. Paul could not honestly give thanks
for the actual condition of the Cor.
Church. The reason for this omission
at once appears. The Church is
rent with factions, which ranged themselves under the names of the leading
Christian teachers. On the causes of
these divisions see *Introduction*, Chap. i.
Out of their crude and childish experience
(iii. 1-4) the Cor. are constructing prematurely a γνῶσις of their own (viii. 1,
see note), a σοφία resembling that "wisdom of the world" which is "foolishness
with God" (18 ff., 30, iii. 18 f., iv. 9 f.) ;
they think themselves already above the
mere λόγος τοῦ σταυροῦ brought by the
Ap., wherein, simple as it appeared,
there lay the wisdom and the power of
God. This conceit had been stimulated,
unwittingly on his part, by the preaching
of Apollos. Ch. iii. 3-7 shows that it
is the Apollonian faction which most
exercises Paul's thoughts at present ; the
irony of i. 18-31 and iv. 6-13 is aimed at
the partisans of Ap., who exalted his
ὑπεροχὴ λόγου κ. σοφίας in disparage-

ment of Paul's unadorned κήρυγμα τοῦ
σταυρου. Mistaking the nature of the
Gospel, the Cor. mistook the office of its
ministers : on the former subject they are
corrected in i. 18-ii. 5 showing in what
sense and why the Gospel *is not*, and in
ii. 6-iii. 2 showing in what sense and to
whom the Gospel *is* a σοφία ; the latter
misconception is rectified in iii. 3-iv. 21,
where, with express reference to Ap. and
P., Christian teachers are shown to be no
competing leaders of human schools but
"fellow-workmen of God" and "servants of Christ," co-operative and complementary instruments of His sovereign
work in the building of the Church.
The four chapters constitute an *apologia*
for the Apostle's teaching and office, parl.
to those of 2 Cor. x.-xiii. and Gal. i.-iii. ;
but the line of defence adopted here is
quite distinct. Here Paul pleads against
Hellenising lovers of wisdom, there
against Judaising lovers of tradition.
Both parties stumbled at the cross ; both
judged of the Ap. κατὰ σάρκα, and fastened upon his defects in visible prestige
and presence. The existence of the
legalist party at Cor. is intimated by the
cry, "I am of Cephas," and by Paul's
words of self-vindication in ix. 1 f. ; but
this faction had as yet reached no considerable head ; it developed rapidly in
the interval between 1 and 2 Cor.

§ 3. THE REPORT ABOUT THE PAR-
TIES, AND PAUL'S EXPOSTULATION,
i. 10-17ᵃ. Without further preface,
the Apostle warns the Cor. solemnly
against their schisms (10), stating the
testimony on which his admonition is
based (11). The four parties are defined
out of the mouths of the Cor. (12) ; and
the Ap. protests esp. against the use
of Christ's name and of his own in
this connexion (13). In founding the
Church he had avoided all self-exaltation,
bent only on fulfilling his mission of
preaching the good news (14-17ᵃ).

Ver. 10. " But I exhort (appeal to)
you, brothers : " the reproof to be given
stands in painful contrast (δέ) with
the Thanksgiving. It is administered
" through the name of our Lord Jesus
Christ," which the Ap. has invoked so
often (see note on 8) ; all the authority
and grace of the Name reinforce his
appeal, " that you say the same thing,

ματα, ἦτε δὲ [h] κατηρτισμένοι ἐν [f] τῷ [f] αὐτῷ [i] νοῒ καὶ ἐν [f] τῇ [f] αὐτῇ [k] γνώμῃ · 11. [l] ἐδηλώθη γάρ μοι περὶ ὑμῶν, ἀδελφοί μου, ὑπὸ [m] τῶν Χλόης ὅτι [n] ἔριδες ἐν ὑμῖν εἰσί · 12. [o] λέγω δὲ τοῦτο, ὅτι ἕκαστος ὑμῶν λέγει, "Ἐγὼ μέν εἰμι [p] Παύλου," "Ἐγὼ δὲ [p] Ἀπολλώ," "Ἐγὼ δὲ

h In ethical sense, 2 Cor. xiii. 11; Gal. vi. 1; Heb. xiii. 21; 1 Pet. v. 10; Lk. vi. 40; Ps. xvi. 5.

i ii. 16, xiv. 14 ff.; 14 times besides in P.; thrice besides in N.T.   k vii. 25, 40; 2 Cor. viii. 10; Phm. 14; Acts xx. 3; Rev. xvii. 13, 17 only; Wisd. vii. 16; 2 Macc. iv. 39, etc.   l iii. 13; Col. i. 8; Heb. ix. 8, xii. 27; 1 Pet. i. 11; 2 Pet. i. 14; Ex. vi. 3, etc.   m Art. thus used, Rom. xvi. 10 f.   n Pl., 2 Cor. xii. 20; Tit. iii. 9.   Sing., iii. 3; Rom. i. 29, xiii. 13; Gal. v. 20; Ph. i. 15.   o In this sense, x. 29; Gal. iii. 17.   p Same gen., iii. 23, xv. 23; Rom. xiv. 8; Acts ix. 2, etc.

all (of you)," instead of "saying, each of you, I am of Paul," etc. (12).—Τὸ αὐτὸ λέγειν, "a strictly classical expression used of political communities which are free from factions, or of diff. states which entertain friendly relations with each other" (Lt.). Τὸ αὐτὸ φρονεῖν, in 2 Cor. xiii. 11, etc., is matter of temper and disposition; τὸ αὐτὸ λέγειν, of attitude and declaration: the former is opposed to self-interest, the latter to party zeal. On the weakened use of ἵνα after παρακαλῶ (purpose passing into purport) see Wr., pp. 420 ff.: more frequently in P., as in cl. usage, this vb. is construed with the inf.; so always in Acts; with ἵνα regularly in Synoptics. For the meanings of παρακαλῶ see iv. 13.

"And (that) there be not amongst you σχίσματα (clefts, splits)," defines negatively the ἵνα τὸ αὐτὸ λέγητε πάντες. The schism (see parls.) is a party division within the Church, not yet, as in eccl. usage, a culpable separation from it; ἔριδες (11) signifies the personal contentions, due to whatever cause, which lead to σχίσματα; αἱρέσεις (xi. 18 f.: see note) are divisions of opinion, or sects founded thereupon (Acts v. 17, etc.), implying a disagreement of principle. The schism is a rent in the Church, an injury to the fabric (cf. iii. 17, xii. 25); hence the further appeal, reverting to the positive form of expression,—"but that you be well and surely (pf. ptp.) adjusted" (coagmentati, Bg.)—"the exact word for the healing or repairing of the breaches caused by the σχίσματα" (Al.). καταρτίζω has a like political sense in cl. Gr. (Herod., iv. 161; v. 28, in opp. to στάσις); "the marked classical colouring of such passages as this leaves a much stronger impression of St. Paul's acquaintance with cl. writers than the rare occasional quotations which occur in his writings" (Lt.). "In the same discernment (νοΐ), and in the same judgment (γνώμῃ)": "νοῦς geht auf die Einsicht, γνώμη auf das Urtheil" (Hn.); gnomé is the application of nous in prac-

tical judgment (see parls.). P. desiderates that ὁμονοεῖν and ὁμογνωμεῖν (see Thucyd., ii. 97, viii. 75; Aristot., Polit., v. 6, 10; Demosth., 281. 21) in Christian matters, should enable the Church to act as one body and to pursue Christ's work with undivided strength.

Ver. 11. The appeal above made implies a serious charge; now the authority for it: "For it has been signified to me about you, my brothers, by the (people) of Chloë".—ἐδηλώθη (see parls.) implies definite information, the disclosure of facts.—οἱ Χλόης, "persons of Chloë's household"—children, companions, or possibly slaves (cf. Rom. xvi. 10): there is nothing further to identify them. "Chloë is usually considered a Cor. Christian, whose people had come to Eph.; but it is more in harmony with St. Paul's discretion to suppose that she was an Ephesian known to the Cor., whose people had been at Cor. and returned to Eph." (Ev., Hf.). "Chloë's people" are distinct from the Cor. deputies of xvi. 17, or Paul would have named the latter here; besides, Stephanas was himself the head of a household.—Χλόη (Verdure) was an epithet of the goddess Demeter, as Φοίβη of Artemis (Rom. xvi. 1): such names were often given to slaves, and C. may have been a freedwoman of property (Lt.). "That strifes exist among you" (cf. iii. 3, 2 Cor. xii. 20) was the information given; these ἔριδες, the next ver. explains, were generating the σχίσματα (see note on 10).

Ver. 12. "But I mean this (τοῦτο δὲ λέγω), that each one of you is saying (instead of your all saying the same thing, 10), 'I am of Paul (am Paul's man),'—'But I of Apollos,'—'But I of Cephas,'—'But I of Christ'!"—ἕκαστος, distributive, as in xiv. 26: each is saying one or other of these things; the party cries are quoted as from successive speakers challenging each other.
The question of the FOUR COR. PARTIES is one of the standing pro-

q In this sense, vii. 34; Mt. xii. 25 f.; 3 Kings xvi. 21.

[p] Κηφᾶ," "Ἐγὼ δὲ [p] Χριστοῦ". 13. [q] μεμέρισται ὁ Χριστός; [1] μὴ Παῦλος ἐσταυρώθη ὑπὲρ [2] ὑμῶν, ἢ [r] εἰς τὸ ὄνομα Παύλου [r] ἐβαπτίσ-

r x. 2; Gal. iii. 27; Mt. xxviii. 19; Acts viii. 16, xix. 3 f.

[1] Thd. 168, *ad loc.*: **τουτο τινες αποφαντικως ανεγνωσαν, εγω δε αυτο κατ' ερωτησιν κεισθαι νομιζω.** Ambrst. interprets *affirmatively*; so Lachm. and W.H. *text*, R.V. *marg.* See note below.

[2] **περι** in BD* (hence W.H. *marg.*); all other Codd. **υπερ.**

blems of N.T. criticism. It is fully examined, and the judgments of different critics are digested, by Gd. *ad loc.*; see also Mr.-Hn., *Einleitung*, § 3; Weiss' *Manual of Introd. to the N.T.*, § 19. After all, this was only a brief phase of Church life at Cor.; P. had just heard of it when he wrote, by the time of 2 Cor. a new situation has arisen. The three first parties are easy to account for: (1) The body of the Ch., converted under P.'s ministry, adhered to its own apostle; P. valued this loyalty and appeals to it, while he condemns its combative expression, — the disposition of men "more Pauline than Paul himself" (Dods) to exalt him to the disparagement of other leaders, and even to the detriment of Christ's glory. (2) Apollos (*cf.* Acts xviii. 24 ff.) had preached at Cor., in the interval since Paul's first departure, with brilliant effect. He possessed Alexandrian culture and a graceful style, whereas P. was deemed at Cor. **ἰδιώτης τῷ λόγῳ** (2 Cor. xi. 6). Some personal converts Ap. had made; others were taken with his genial method, and welcomed his teaching as more advanced than P.'s plain gospel-message. Beside the more cultured Greeks, there would be a sprinkling of liberally-minded Jews, men of speculative bias imbued with Greek letters, who might prefer to say **Ἐγὼ Ἀπολλώ.** Judging from this Ep., the Pauline and Apollonian sections included at present the bulk of the Church, divided between its "planter" and "waterer". **Ἀπολλώς,** of Attic 2nd decl., is probably short for **Ἀπολλώνιος.** (3) In a Judæo-Gentile Church the cry "I am of Paul," or "I am of Apollos," was certain to be met with the retort, "But I of Kephas!" Conservative Jewish believers, when conflict was afoot, rallied to the name of the preacher of Pentecost and the hero of the Church's earliest victories. The use of **Κηφᾶς,** the Aramaic original of **Πέτρος,** indicates that this party affected Palestinian traditions. Some of them may, possibly, have been Peter's converts in Judæa. Had Peter visited Cor., as Dionysius of Cor. supposed (Euseb., *Hist. Eccles.*, ii. 125: Weiss and Harnack favour the tradition), the event would surely have left some trace in these Epp. Judging from the tenor of the two Letters, this faction was of small account in Cor. until the arrival of the Judæan emissaries denounced in 2 Cor., who found a ground of vantage ready in those that shouted "I am of Kephas". In both Epp. P. avoids every appearance of conflict with Peter (*cf.* ix. 5, xv. 5). (4) *The Christ party* forms the crux of the passage:—(*a*) After F. C. Baur, **οἱ Χριστοῦ** has been commonly interpreted by 2 Cor. x. 7: "If any one is confident on his own part that he is Christ's (**Χριστοῦ εἶναι**), let him take this into account with himself, that just as he is Christ's, so also are we". Now P.'s opponents of 2 Cor. were ultra-Judaists; so, it is inferred, these **οἱ Χριστοῦ** must have been. But the Judaisers of 2 Cor. presumed to be "of Christ" as His *ministers*, *apostles* (xi. 13, 23), deriving their commission (as they maintained P. did not) from the fountain-head; whereas the Christ-party of this place plumed themselves, at most, on being His *disciples* (rather than P.'s, etc.): the coincidence is verbal rather than real. Upon Baur's theory, there were *two* parties at Cor., as everywhere else in the Church, diametrically opposed—a Gentile-Christian party, divided here into Pauline and Apollonian sections, and a Jewish-Christian party naming itself from Kephas or Christ as occasion served. Later scholars following Baur's line of interpretation, distinguish variously the Petrine and Christine Judaists: (**α**) Weizsäcker associates the latter with *James*; (**β**) Reuss and Beyschlag see in them strict *followers of the example and maxims of Jesus* as the **διάκονος περιτομῆς,** from which Peter in certain respects deviated; (**γ**) Hilgenfeld, Holsten, Hausrath, Sm., think they had been *in personal relations with Jesus* (it is quite possible that amongst the "five hundred" of xv. 5 some had wandered to Cor.); (**δ**) Gd. strangely conjectures that

θητε; 14. ⁵εὐχαριστῶ τῷ Θεῷ¹ ὅτι οὐδένα ὑμῶν ἐβάπτισα, εἰ μὴ ⁵ See i. 4.
ᵗ iv. 2, vii.
Κρίσπον καὶ Γάϊον, 15. ἵνα μή τις εἴπῃ ὅτι ʳεἰς τὸ ἐμὸν ὄνομα 29; six
times be-
ʳἐβάπτισα² · 16. ἐβάπτισα³ δὲ καὶ τὸν Στεφανᾶ οἶκον · ᵗλοιπὸν sides in
P.; Heb.
x. 13.

¹ א*B, 67**, with Chr. and Dam. (in comment.), *om.* τῳ Θεῳ. A strong group
of witnesses; parls. suggested to copyists the inserted words.

² אABC*, 67**, and several good minuscc., read εβαπτισθητε; instead
of εβαπτισα, as in CᶜDGLP, etc.,—Western and Syrian reading, conformed to context.

³ βεβαπτικα replaces first εβαπτισα in D*G, and second also in D*.

"they were *Gnostics before Gnosticism*, who formulated their title οἱ Χριστοῦ, after the fashion of Cerinthus, *in opp.* not merely to the names of the apostles, but even *to that of Jesus!*" He identifies them with the men who cried "Jesus is anathema" (xii. 2: see note). This notion is an anachronism, and has no real basis in the Epp.

(*b*) 1 Cor. iii. 22 f. (see notes, *ad loc.*) supplies a nearer and safer clue to the interpretation; this is the Apostle's decisive correction of the rivalries of i. 12. The human leaders pitted against each other all belong to the Church (not this teacher or that to this section or that), while *it belongs without distinction to Christ*, and Christ, with all that is His, *to God*. The catholic Ὑμεῖς Χριστοῦ swallows up the self-assertive and sectarian Ἐγὼ δὲ Χριστοῦ. Those who used this cry arrogated the common watchword as their peculium; they erred by despising, as others by glorying in men. "Ἐγὼ Χριστοῦ ad eos pertinet qui in contrariam partem peccabant; *i.e.*, qui sese unius Christi ita dicebant, ut interim iis per quos quos Deus loquitur nihil tribuerent" (Bz.); similarly Aug., Bg., Mr., Hf., El., Bt.

(*c*) The Gr. Ff., followed by Cv., Bleek, Pfleiderer, Räbiger, and others, saw in the Ἐγὼ δὲ Χριστοῦ *the true formula which P. approves*, or even which he utters *propriâ personâ*. But the context subjects all four classes to the same reproach. It is a sufficient condemnation for the fourth party that they said "I am of Christ," in rejoinder to the partisans of Paul and the rest, lowering His name to this competition.

(*d*) Hn., finding the riddle of the "Christus-partei" insoluble, *eliminates it from the text;* "we are driven," he says, "to explain the Ἐγὼ δὲ Χριστοῦ as a gloss, which some reader of the original codex inscribed in the margin, borrowing it from iii. 23 as a counter-confession to the Ἐγὼ μὲν Παύλου κ.τ.λ.".

Ver. 13. In his expostulation P. uses, with telling contrast, the first and last only of the party names: "Is *the Christ* divided? Was *Paul* crucified on your behalf? or into the name of *Paul* were you baptised?" Lachmann, W.H., Mr., Bt., read μεμέρισται ὁ X. as an exclamation: "The Christ (then) has been divided!"—torn in pieces by your strife. But μερίζω (here in pf. of resultful fact) denotes *distribution*, not dismemberment (see parls.): the Christian who asserts "I am Christ's" in distinction from others, claims an *exclusive* part in Him, whereas the one and whole Christ belongs to every limb of His manifold body (see xii. 12; also xi. 3, Rom. x. 12, xiv. 7-9, Eph. iv. 3 ff., Col. ii. 19). A divided Church means a Christ *parcelled out*, appropriated κατὰ μέρος. ὁ Χριστὸς is *the Christ*, in the fulness of all that His title signifies (see xii. 12, etc.).—While μεμέρισται ὁ X.; is Paul's abrupt and indignant question to himself, μὴ Παῦλος ἐσταυρώθη; (aor. of historical event) interrogates the readers—"Is it *Paul* that was crucified for you?" From *the cross* the Ap. draws his first reproof, the point of which vi. 20 makes clear, "You were *bought* at a price": the Cor. therefore were not Paul's or Kephas', nor some of them Christ's and some of them Paul's men, but only Christ's and all Christ's alike.

The cross was the ground of κοινωνία Χριστοῦ (9, x. 16); *baptism*, signalising personal union with Him by faith, its attestation (Rom. vi. 3); to this P. appeals asking, ἢ εἰς τὸ ὄνομα Παύλου ἐβαπτίσθητε; His converts will remember how *Christ's name* was then sealed upon them, and Paul's ignored. What was true of his practice, he tacitly assumes for the other chiefs. The readers had been baptised *as Christians*, not Pauline, Apollonian, or Petrine Christians. Paul's horror at the thought of baptising in *his* name shows how truly Christ's was to him "the name above every name" (Phil. ii. 9; *cf.* 2 Cor. iv. 5).

u vii. 16; Jo. οὐκ ᵘ οἶδα ᵘ εἴ τινα ἄλλον ἐβάπτισα¹·   17a. οὐ γὰρ ᵛ ἀπέστειλέ με
ix. 25;
Acts x. 18, Χριστὸς ² βαπτίζειν, ἀλλ' ʷ εὐαγγελίζεσθαι.³
xix. 2.
v ix. 1 f.;   17b. Οὐκ ἐν ˣ σοφίᾳ ˣ λόγου, ἵνα μὴ ʸ κενωθῇ ὁ ᶻ σταυρὸς τοῦ
Rom. x.
15; Acts
xxii. 21, xxvi. 17; Jo. xvii. 18, xx. 21; with inf., Lk. i. 19, iv. 18, etc.   w Without obj., ix. 16, xv.
2; Rom. i. 15, xv. 20; 2 Cor. x. 16; Gal. iv. 13; Lk. iv. 18 (Isa. lxi. 1), ix. 6, xx. 1; Acts xiv. 7;
Nahum i. 15, etc.   x ii. 1, 4, 13, xii. 8; Col. ii. 23, iii. 16.   y ix. 15; 2 Cor. ix. 3; Rom. iv. 14;
Ph. ii. 7 only.   z Gal. v. 11, vi. 12, 14; Ph. iii. 18.

¹ βεβάπτικα replaces first ἐβάπτισα in D*G, and second also in D*.

² ο Χριστος (for Χριστος), in BG—an instance of the faulty readings that mark
B, or BD, in company of G.

³ B, ευαγγελισασθαι.

Vv. 14-16. In fact, P. had himself baptised very few of the Cor. He sees a providence in this; otherwise he might have seemed wishful to stamp his own name upon his converts, and some colour would have been lent to the action of the Paulinists—"lest any one should say that you were baptised into *my* name". For βαπτίζω εἰς τὸ ὄνομα, *cf.* Matt. xxviii. 19 and other parls.; also βαπτίζω εἰς, x. 2; it corresponds to πιστεύω εἰς, and has the like pregnant force. "The name" connotes the nature and authority of the bearer, and His relationship to those who speak of Him by it. *Crispus* and *Gaius*: both Roman names (see *Introd.*, p. 733); the former a cognomen (*Curly*), the latter an exceedingly common præ-nomen. These two were amongst Paul's earliest converts (Acts xviii. 8, Rom. xvi. 23), the former a Synagogue-ruler. On second thoughts ("he was reminded by his amanuensis," Lt.; or by Steph. himself), P. remembers that he had "baptised the house of Stephanas" (see xvi. 15, and note), the first family here won to Christ. Στεφανᾶς (perhaps short for Στεφανηφόρος), like Κηφᾶς, takes the Doric gen. in -ᾶ usual with proper names in -ᾶς, whether of native or foreign origin (see Bm., p. 20).—λοιπὸν οὐκ οἶδα εἴ τινα κ.τ.λ.: P. cannot recall any other instance of baptism by his own hands at Cor.; this was a slight matter, which left no clear mark in his memory. λοιπόν (more regularly, τὸ λοιπόν), "for the rest"—in point of *time* (vii. 29), or *number*—a somewhat frequent idiom with Paul (*cf.* iv. 2). In οὐκ οἶδα εἰ (*haud scio an*), the conjunction is indir. interr., as in vii. 16.
Ver. 17a justifies Paul's thanking God that he had baptised so few: "For Christ did not send me to baptise, but *to evangelise*". The infs. (*cf.* ii. 1 f., ix. 16, xv. 11; Rom. xv. 17-21) are epexe-getical (of *purpose*); and pres., of continued action (*function*). οὐκ . . . ἀλλά —no qualified, but an absolute denial that Baptism was the Apostle's proper work. For the terms of Paul's commission see Gal. i. 15 f., Eph. iii. 7-9, 1 Tim. ii. 7; also Acts ix. 15, and parls. Baptism was the necessary sequel of preaching, and P. did not suppose his commission narrower than that of the Twelve (Matt. xxviii. 19 f.); but baptising might be performed vicariously, not so preaching. "To *evangelise* is to cast the net—the true apostolic work; to *baptise* is to gather the fish already caught and to put them into vessels" (Gd.). It never occurred to P. that a Christian minister's essential function was to administer sacraments. The Ap. dwells on this matter so much as to suggest (Cv.) that he tacitly contrasts himself with some preachers who made a point of baptising their own converts, as though to vindicate a special interest in them; *cf.* the action of Peter (Acts x. 48), and of Jesus (John iv. 1 f.).
§ 4. The True Power of the Gospel, i. 17b-25. To "preach the gospel" meant, above all, to proclaim the cross of Christ (17b). In Cor. "the wisdom of the world" scouted this message as sheer folly (18). To use "wisdom of word" in meeting such antagonism would have been for P. to fight the world with its own weapons and to betray his cause, the strength of which lay in the Divine power and wisdom embodied in Christ, a force destined, because it was God's, to bring to shame the world's vaunting wisdom (19-25).
Ver. 17b. οὐκ ἐν σοφίᾳ λόγου is grammatical adjunct to ἀλλὰ (ἀπέστ. με Χρ.) εὐαγγελίζεσθαι; but the phrase opens a new vein of thought, and supplies the theme of the subsequent argument up to ii. 6. In vv. 14, 17a Paul

Χριστοῦ.   18. ὁ ᵃλόγος γὰρ ὁ τοῦ ᶻσταύρου ᵇτοῖς μὲν ᵇἀπολλυμένοις   ᵃ In this sense, six times more in P.; Heb. v. 13; Jas. i. 18; Acts

ᶜμωρία ἐστί, ᵇτοῖς δὲ ᵇσωζομένοις, ἡμῖν, ᵈδύναμις ᵈΘεοῦ ἐστί· 19.

γέγραπται γάρ, "ᵉἈπολῶ τὴν σοφίαν τῶν σοφῶν καὶ τὴν ᶠσύνεσιν

xiii. 26, xiv. 3, xx. 32.   b 2 Cor. ii. 15, iv. 3; Acts ii. 47; Lk. xiii. 23.   c Vv. 21, 23, ii. 14, iii. 19 only.   d Ver. 24, ii. 5; 2 Cor. vi. 7, xiii. 4; Rom. i. 16; 2 Tim. i. 8; 1 Pet. i. 5; Mt. xxii. 29; Acts viii. 10.   e Isa. xxix. 14.   f Eph. iii. 4; Col. i. 9, ii. 2; 2 Tim. ii. 7; Mk. xii. 33; Lk. ii. 47 only.

asserted that Christ sent him *not to baptise, but to preach;* further, what he has to preach is *not a philosophy to be discussed, but a message of God to be believed:* " L'évangile n'est pas une sagesse, c'est un salut" (Gd.). In this transition the Ap. silently directs his reproof from the Pauline to the Apollonian party.—In σοφία λόγου (see ii. 1-4, 13; *cf.* the opp. combination in xii. 8) the stress lies on *wisdom* (called in vv. 19 f. "the wisdom of the world")— *sc.* "wisdom" in the common acceptation, as the world understood it and as the Cor. expected it from public teachers: "in wisdom of word" = *in philosophical style.* "To tell good *news* in *wisdom* of word" is an implicit contradiction; "news" only needs and admits of plain, straightforward *telling.* To dress out the story of Calvary in specious rhetoric, or wrap it up in fine-spun theorems, would have been to "empty (**κενώθη**) the cross of Christ," to *eviscerate* the Gospel. The "power of God" lies in the facts and not in any man's presentment of them: "to substitute a system of notions, however true and ennobling, for the fact of Christ's death, is like confounding the theory of gravitation with gravitation itself" (Ed.).—For **κενόω**, factitive of **κενός** (*cf.* xv. 14), see parls.; the commoner syn., **καταργέω** (28, etc.), means *to deprive of activity, make impotent* (in effect), **κενόω** *to deprive of content, make unreal* (in fact).

Ver. 18. What P. asserted in ver. 17 as intrinsically true, he supports by experience (18) and by Scripture (19), combining their testimony in ver. 20.—ὁ λόγος γάρ, ὁ τοῦ σταύρου, "For the word, namely that of the cross". ὁ λόγος (distinguish from the anarthrous λόγος above) takes its sense from **εὐαγγελίζεσθαι** (17); it is "the tale" rather than "the doctrine of the cross," synonymous with **μαρτύριον** (6) and **κήρυγμα** (21).—τοῖς μὲν ἀπολλυμένοις . . . τοῖς δὲ σωζομένοις, the two classes into which P. sees his hearers divide themselves (see parls.). The ptps. are strictly pr.—not expressing *certain expectation* (Mr.), nor *fixed predestination* (Bz.); the rejectors and receivers of "the word" are *in course*

of perishing and *being saved* respectively (*cf.* xv. 2; contrast the aor. of σώζω in Rom. viii. 24, and the pf. in Eph. ii. 5). " In the language of the N.T. salvation is a thing of the past, a thing of the present, and a thing of the future. . . . The divorce of morality and religion is fostered by failing to note this, and so laying the whole stress either on the past or on the future—on the first call or on the final change" (Lt.). Paul paints the situation before his eyes: one set of men deride the story of the cross—these are manifestly perishing; to another set the same story is "God's power unto salvation". The appended pers. pron. (τ. σωζομένοις) ἡμῖν, "to the saved, viz., ourselves," speaks from and to experience: "You and I know that the cross is God's saving power". *Cf.* with the whole expression Rom. i. 16, also John iii. 14-17.—The antithesis to μωρία is not, in the first instance, σοφία, but δύναμις Θεοῦ—a *practical* vindication against false theory; saved men are the Gospel's apology. Yet because it is δύναμις, the word of the cross is, after all, the truest σοφία (see 30, ii. 6 ff.). The double ἐστὶν emphasises the *actuality* of the contrasted results.

Ver. 19. As concerns "the perishing," the above sentence agrees with God's ways of judgment as revealed in Scripture: γέγραπται γάρ κ.τ.λ. The quotation Ἀπολῶ κ.τ.λ. (suggested by τ. ἀπολλυμένοις) belongs to the cycle of Isaiah's prophecies against the worldly-wise politicians of Jerus. in Assyrian times (xxviii.-xxxii.), who despised the word of Jehovah, relying on their shallow and dishonest statecraft; their policy of alliance with Egypt will lead to a shameful overthrow, out of which God will find the means of vindicating His wisdom and saving His people and city. The O.T. and N.T. situations are analogous: Gentile and Jewish wisdom, united in rejection of the Gospel, are coming to a like breakdown; and P. draws a powerful warning from the sacred history.—ἀθετήσω (a reminiscence, perhaps, of Ps. xxxiii. 10) displaces the less pointed κρύψω: otherwise the LXX text of Isa. is followed; in the Heb. the

g Mt. xi. 25;
Lk. x. 21;
Acts xiii.
7 only; Isa.
v. 21; Jer
xviii. 18,
xlix. 6.
h Gal. ii. 21,
iii. 15; 1
Tim. v. 12;
Heb. x. 28;

τῶν [g]συνετῶν [h]ἀθετήσω". 20. [i]ποῦ σοφός; [i]ποῦ [k]γραμματεύς;
[i]ποῦ [l]συζητητὴς [l] τοῦ [m]αἰῶνος [m]τούτου; οὐχὶ [n]ἐμώρανεν ὁ Θεὸς
τὴν σοφίαν τοῦ κόσμου τούτου[2]; 21. ἐπειδὴ γὰρ ἐν τῇ [o]σοφίᾳ τοῦ
[o]Θεοῦ οὐκ [p]ἔγνω ὁ κόσμος διὰ τῆς σοφίας τὸν [p]Θεόν, [q]εὐδόκησεν[3]
ὁ [q]Θεὸς[4] διὰ τῆς [r]μωρίας τοῦ [s]κηρύγματος [t]σῶσαι τοὺς [t]πιστεύοντας·

Jude 8; Mk. vii. 9; Lk. vii. 30.   i In this manner, xii. 17, 19, xv. 55; Rom. iii. 27; Gal. iv. 15; Isa. xxxiii. 18.   k Epp., here only. Syn. Gospp., passim; Ezra vii. 6.   l Here only; -τειν, Lk. xxii. 23, xxiv. 15; Acts vi. 9, ix. 29; six times in Mk; -τησις, Acts xxviii. 29.   m ii. 6 f., iii. 18; eight times besides in P.; Lk. xvi. 8, xx. 34; Mt. xii. 32.   n Rom. i. 22; Mt. v. 13; Isa. xix. 11; Jer. x. 14.   o Ver. 24; Rom. xi. 33; Eph. iii. 10; Lk. xi. 49.   p xv. 34; Rom. i. 21; Gal. iv. 9; 2 Th. i. 8; Tit. i. 16; 1 Jo. iv. 6 ff.; Jo. xiv. 7; Heb. viii. 11 (from Jer.).   q Gal. i. 15; Col. i. 19; Lk. xii. 32.   r See ver. 18.   s ii. 4, xv. 14; Rom. xvi. 25; 2 Tim. iv. 17; Tit. i. 3; Mt. xii. 41. t xv. 2; Rom. x. 9; Eph. ii. 8; Jas. ii. 14, v. 15; Mt. ix. 22; Mk. x. 52, xvi. 16; 5 times in Lk.; Acts xiv. 9, xv. 11, xvi. 31.

[1] συνζητητης: all uncc. exc. LP. The unassimilated form of prp. in such compounds prevails in oldest MSS.

[2] τουτου wanting in א*ABC*D*gr.P. Added in אcC³DcGL, syrr. cop. latt. vg.; the addition is late Western and Syrian. Cf. τ. αιωνος τουτου above, and iii. 19.

[3] ηυδοκησεν: C, Athan.; a characteristic Alexandrian emendation.

[4] For ο Θ., τῳ Θεῳ in G, latt. vg. (placuit Deo),—a Latinism.

vbs. are pass., "the wisdom . . . shall perish," etc. Isa. xxix. is rich in matter for N.T. use: vv. 13, 18 gave our Lord texts, in Matt. xv. 8 f., xi. 5 respectively; the Ap. quotes the chap. twice elsewhere, and ch. xxviii. thrice.

Ver. 20. ποῦ σοφός; ποῦ γραμματεύς; and (possibly) ἐμώρανεν . . . τὴν σοφίαν, are also Isaianic allusions—to Isa. xix. 11 f. (mocking the vain wisdom of Pharaoh's counsellors), and xxxiii. 18 (predicting the disappearance of Sennacherib's revenue clerks and army scouts, as a sign of his defeat). The LXX γραμματικὸς becomes γραμματεύς, in consistence with the sophēr of the latter passage; συνζητητής (cf. ζητοῦσιν, 22), in the third question, is Paul's addition. — γραμματεὺς unmistakably points, in the application, to the Jewish Scribe (cf. our Lord's denunciation in Matt. xxiii.); of the parl. terms, σοφὸς is supposed by most moderns to be general, comprehending Jewish and Gr. wise men together, συνζητητὴς to be specific to the Gr. philosopher—a distinction better reversed, as by Lt. after the Gr. Ff. συνζητέω, with its cognates, is employed in the N.T. of Jewish discussions (Acts vi. 9, xxviii. 29, etc.), and the adjunct τ. αἰῶνος τούτου gives to the term its widest scope, whereas σοφός, esp. at Cor., marks the Gr. intellectual pride; καλεῖ σοφὸν τὸν τῇ Ἑλληνικῇ στωμυλίᾳ κοσμούμενον (Thd.; cf. Rom. i. 23).—ποῦ σοφός (not ὁ σοφός); κ.τ.λ.: "Where is a wise man? where a scribe?

where a disputer of this age?" These orders of men are swept from the field; all such pretensions disappear (cf. 29)—"Did not God make foolish the wisdom of the world?" The world and God are at issue; each counts the other's wisdom folly (cf. 18, 25, 30). But God actually turned to foolishness (infatuavit, Bz.: cf. Rom. i. 21 f., for μωραίνω; also Isa. xliv. 25) the world's imagined wisdom: how, vv. 21-25 proceed to show. On αἰὼν see parls., and Ed.'s note; also Trench's Synon., lix., and Gm., for the distinction between αἰὼν and κόσμος; "αἰών, like sæculum, refers to the prevailing ideas and feelings of the present life, κόσμος to its gross, material character" (Lt.).

Vv. 21-25. The ἐπειδὴ of ver. 21 and that of vv. 22-25 are parl., the second restating and expanding the first (cf. the double ὅταν in xv. 24, and in xv. 27 f.: see notes), rather than proving it; together they justify the assertion implied in ver. 20ᵇ, which virtually repeats ver. 18.

Ver. 21. ἐπειδὴ γάρ (quoniam enim, Cv.) introduces the when and how of God's stultifying the world's wisdom by the λόγος τοῦ σταυροῦ: "For since, in the wisdom of God, the world through its wisdom did not know God, God was pleased," etc.—οὐκ ἔγνω . . . διὰ τ. σοφίας τ. Θεὸν records Paul's experience, e.g., at Athens, in disclosing the ἄγνωστον Θεὸν to philosophers. Of the emphatic adjunct, ἐν τῇ σοφίᾳ τοῦ Θεοῦ,

22. ἐπειδὴ καὶ Ἰουδαῖοι ᵘσημεῖον ¹ ᵘαἰτοῦσι, καὶ Ἕλληνες ᵛσοφίαν ᵛζητοῦσιν· 23. ἡμεῖς δὲ ᵂκηρύσσομεν ᵂˣΧριστὸν ˣἐσταυρωμένον,

ᵘ Mt. xii. 38 f., xvi. 1, xxiv. 3; Lk. xxiii. 8; 7 times in Jo.; Acts iv. 30.   v Prov. ii. 4, xiv. 6; Eccl. vii. 26.   w xv. 12; 2 Cor. i. 19, xi. 4; Ph. i. 15; 1 Tim. iii. 16; Acts viii. 5, ix. 20, xix. 13.   x ii. 2; Gal. iii. 1; Mt. xxviii. 5.

¹ σημεια: all uncc. (with anc. verss.) exc. L.   T.R. conforms to Gosp. parls.

there are two explanations, following the line of Rom. i. 19 f. or Rom. xi. 32 f.: on the former view, the clause qualifies ἔγνω—"the world did not come to know God in His wisdom," evidenced in creation and Providence — so most interpreters ("amid the wisdom of God," Bt.; *in media luce*, Cv.; *in nature and Scripture*, addressed to Gentile and Jew, Bg.; Mr.); on the other hand, Rückert, Reuss, Al., Lt., Ev. attach the clause to οὐκ ἔγνω,—*in God's wise plan* of the world's government, the world's wisdom failed to win the knowledge of Him. The latter is the sounder explanation, being (a) in accord with Paul's reff. elsewhere to σοφία Θεοῦ, (b) presenting a pointed antithesis to σοφία κόσμου, and (c) harmonising with Paul's theory of the education of mankind for Christ, expounded in Gal. iii. 10-iv. 5 and Rom. v. 20 f., vii. 7-25, xi. "Through its (Greek) wisdom the world *knew not* God," as through its (Jewish) righteousness it *pleased not* God; both results were brought about "in the wisdom of God" —according to that "plan of the ages," leading up to "the fulness of the seasons," which embraced the Gentile "times of ignorance" (Acts xvii. 26-31) no less than the Jewish dispensations of covenant and law. "It is part of God's wise providence that He will not be apprehended by intellectual speculation, by 'dry light'" (Ev.). The intellectual was as signal as the moral defeat; the followers of Plato were "shut up," along with those of Moses, εἰς τ. μέλλουσαν πίστιν (Gal. iii. 22 f.).

Now that God's wisdom has reduced the self-wise world to ignorance, εὐδόκησεν σῶσαι: man's extremity, God's opportunity. "It was God's good will" (*placuit Deo:* see parls. for the vb.); εὐδοκία P. associates with θέλημα, βουλὴ on the one hand, and with χάρις, ἀγαθωσύνη on the other: God's sovereign grace rescues man's bankrupt wisdom. διὰ τ. μωρίας τ. κηρύγματος states the *means*, τοὺς πιστεύοντας defines the *qualified objects* of this deliverance. "Through the folly (as the wise world calls it, 18) of the κήρυγμα"—which last term signifies not the act of proclamation

(κήρυξις), but *the message proclaimed* by God's herald (κῆρυξ, see parls.: *the heralding* suggests thoughts of *the kingdom; cf.* Acts xx. 25, Luke viii. 1, etc.). P. designates Christians by the act which makes them such — "those that believe" (see parls.). God saves by *faith.* Faith here stands opposed to Greek knowledge, as in Rom. to Jewish lawworks.

Vv. 22-25 open out the thought of ver. 21: "the world" is parted into "Jews" and "Greeks"; μωρία becomes σκάνδαλον and μωρία; the κήρυγμα is defined as that of Χριστὸς ἐσταυρωμένος; and the πιστεύοντες reappear as the κλητοί. Both Mr. and Al. make this a new sentence, detached from vv. 20 f., and complete in itself, with ἐπειδὴ καί κ.τ.λ. for protasis, and ἡμεῖς δέ κ.τ.λ. for apodosis,—as though the mistaken aims of the world *supplied Paul's motive for preaching Christ;* the point is rather (in accordance with 20) that his "foolish" message, in contrast with (δέ, 23) the desiderated "signs" and "wisdom," *convicts the world of folly* (20); thus the whole of vv. 22-24 falls under the regimen of the 2nd ἐπειδή, which with its καί, emphatically resumes the first ἐπειδή (21)—"since indeed". God turned the world's wise men into fools (20) by bestowing salvation through faith on a ground that they deem folly (21)—in other words, by revealing His power and wisdom in the person of a crucified Messiah, whom Jews and Greeks unite to despise (22-24).

Ver. 22. Ἰουδαῖοι . . . Ἕλληνες— anarthrous; "Jews" *qua* Jews, etc.: in this "asking" and "seeking" the characteristics of each race are "hit off to perfection" (Ed.: see his interesting note); αἰτεῖν expresses "the importunity of the Jews," ζητεῖν "the curious, speculative turn of the Greeks" (Lt.). For the *Jewish* requirement, *cf.* parls. in the case of Jesus; the app., doubtless, were challenged in the same way—P. perhaps publicly at Cor.: "non reperias Corinthi signum editum esse per Paulum, Acta xviii." (Bg.). Respecting this demand, see Lt., *Biblical Essays*, pp. 150 ff. Such dictation Christ never allowed;

y Rom. ix. 'Ιουδαίοις μὲν ᵞ σκάνδαλον, Ἕλλησι ¹ δὲ ʳ μωρίαν, 24. αὐτοῖς δὲ τοῖς
33; Gal. v.
11; 1 Pet. ᶻ κλητοῖς, 'Ιουδαίοις τε καὶ Ἕλλησι, Χριστὸν ᵃ Θεοῦ ᵃ δύναμιν καὶ
ii. 8.
x See ver. 1. ° Θεοῦ ° σοφίαν. 25. ὅτι ᵇ τὸ ᵇ μωρὸν τοῦ Θεοῦ σοφώτερον τῶν
a See ver.18.
b Ver. 27, ° ἀνθρώπων ἐστί, καὶ ᵈ τὸ ᵈ ἀσθενὲς τοῦ Θεοῦ ᵉ ἰσχυρότερον τῶν
iii. 18, iv.
10; 2 Tim. ° ἀνθρώπων ἐστί.²
ii. 23; Tit.
iii. 9. For
neuter idiom, Rom. ii. 4, viii. 3; 2 Cor. iv. 17, viii. 8.   c For constr., Mt. v. 20; Jo. v. 36; 1 Jo.
ii. 2.   d Ver. 27, iv. 10, xii. 22; 2 Cor. x. 10; Gal. iv. 9; Heb. vii. 18; Wisd. ii. 11, xiii. 18. For
constr., see b.   e Ver. 27, iv. 10, x. 22; Mt. iii. 11; Lk. xi. 22; Mic. iv. 3.

¹ ε θ ν ε σ ι ν: all uncc. exc. C³Dᶜ, all verss. exc. arm.   Ελλησιν (as in context): all
minuscc. exc. (about) twelve.

² ε σ τ ι *wanting* in ℵB 17, 67**.   ℵᶜACLP, etc. (Alex. and Syr.) insert at end;
DG (Western), before τ. ανθρωπων.

His miracles were expressions of pity,
not concessions to unbelief, a part of the
Gospel and not external buttresses to it.
Of the Hellenic σοφίαν ζητεῖν Philosophy is itself a monument; *cf.*, amongst
many cl. parls., Herod., iv., 77, Ἕλληνες
πάντας ἀσχόλους εἶναι πρὸς πᾶσαν
σοφίην; also Ælian, *Var. Hist.*, xii., 25;
Juvenal, *Sat.*, I., ii., 58 f.
Ver. 23. Instead of working miracles
to satisfy the Jews, or propounding a
philosophy to entertain the Greeks, "we,
on the other hand, proclaim a crucified
Christ"—Χριστὸν ἐσταυρωμένον, *i.e.*,
Christ as crucified (predicative adjunct),
not "Christ the crucified," nor, strictly,
"Christ crucified"; *cf.*, for the construction, 2 Cor. iv. 5, κηρύσσομεν Χ. 'Ι.
κύριον, "We preach (not ourselves but)
Christ Jesus as Lord". Not a warrior
Messiah, flashing His signs from the
sky, breaking the heathen yoke, but a
Messiah dying in impotence and shame
(see 2 Cor. iv. 10, xiii. 4: *hattalúy*, Deut.
xxi. 23—*the hanged*—He is styled in the
Talmud) is what the app. preach for
their good news! "To Jews indeed a
σκάνδαλον": this word (cl. σκανδάληθρον) signified first the *trap-stick*, then
any obstacle over which one stumbles to
one's injury, an "offence" (syn. with
προσκοπή, πρόσκομμα: see viii. 9, 13),
a moral hindrance presented to the perverse or the weak (see parls.).—τοῖς δὲ
ἔθνεσιν μωρίαν: for the "folly" of offering the *infelix lignum* to cultured Gentiles, see Cicero, *pro Rabirio*, v.: " Nomen
ipsum crucis absit non modo a corpore
civium Romanorum, sed etiam a cogitatione, oculis, auribus"; and Lucian, *De
morte Peregrini*, 13, who mocks at those
who worship τὸν ἀνεσκολοπισμένον τὸν
σοφιστήν,—"that gibbeted sophist!"
For reff. in the early Apologists see
Justin M., *Tryph.*, lxix., and *Apol.*, i.,

13; Tertull., *adv. Jud.*, § 10; Aristo of
Pella, in Routh's *Rel. Sacr.*, i., 95; and
the graffito of the *gibbeted ass* discovered on the wall of the Pædagogium
in the Palatine. To Jews the λόγος τοῦ
σταυροῦ announced the shameful reversal
of their most cherished hopes; to Greeks
and Romans it offered for Saviour and
Lord a man branded throughout the Empire as amongst the basest of criminals;
it was "outrageous," and "absurd".
Ver. 24. αὐτοῖς δὲ τοῖς κλητοῖς, *ipsis
autem vocatis* (Vg.): for the emphatic
prefixed αὐτοῖς, *cf.* 2 Cor. xi. 14, 1 Thess.
16, etc.; it "marks off those alluded to
from the classes to which they nation-
ally belonged" (El.)—"to the called however upon their part, both Jews and
Greeks"—*cf.* the οὐ . . . διαστολὴ of
Rom. iii. 9, 22 ff. "(We proclaim) a
Christ (to these) God's power and God's
wisdom." *Of God* reiterated four times,
with triumphant emphasis, in the stately
march of vv. 24 f. Θεοῦ δύν., Θεοῦ σοφ.
are predicative, in antithesis to ἐσταυρωμένον (23): the app. "preach as power
and wisdom" One who wears to the
world the aspect of utter powerlessness
and folly.—Δύναμις and Σοφία Θεοῦ
were synonyms of the Λόγος in the Alex-
andrian-Jewish speculations, in which
Apollos was probably versed; these surpassing titles Paul appropriates for the
Crucified.—Θεοῦ δύναμιν reaffirms, after
explanation, the δύναμις Θεοῦ of ver.
18; now Θεοῦ σοφίαν is added to it, for
"power" proves "wisdom" here (see
note on 30); the universal efficacy of
the Gospel demonstrates its inner truth,
and faith is finally justified by reason.—
δύναμιν matches the σημεῖον of ver. 22
(see, *e.g.*, 2 Thess. ii. 9); believing Jews
found, after all, in the cross the mightiest
miracle, while Greeks found the deepest
wisdom. The "wisdom of God," secretly

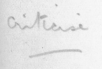

26. ᶠΒλέπετε γὰρ τὴν ᵍκλῆσιν ὑμῶν, ἀδελφοί, ὅτι ʰοὐ ʰπολλοὶ ᶠx. 18; Rev.
vi. 1.
σοφοὶ ⁱκατὰ ⁱσάρκα, ʰοὐ ʰπολλοὶ ᵏδυνατοί, ʰοὐ ʰπολλοὶ ˡεὐγενεῖς· Impv.
otherwise
in iii. 10,
etc.　g vii. 20; Rom. xi. 29; Eph. iv. 1, 4; Ph. iii. 14; 2 Th. i. 11; 2 Tim. i. 9; Heb. iii. 1; 2 Pet.
i. 10.　h iv. 15; Acts i. 5, xxvii. 14.　i x. 18; 17 times besides in P.; cf. Jo. viii. 15.　k Acts
xxv. 5.　l Lk. xix. 12; Acts xvii. 11 (another sense) only; Job i. 3; 2 Macc. x. 13.

working in the times of preparation (20), is thus at length brought to human recognition in Christ. On κλητοῖς see note to ver. 2 : this term is preferable to οἱ σωζόμενοι, or οἱ πιστεύοντες, where the stress rests upon God's initiative in the work of individual salvation; cf. vv. 9, 26, Rom. viii. 28 ff.

Ver. 25. What has been proved in point of fact, viz., the stultification by the cross of man's wisdom, the Ap. (as in Rom. iii. 30, xi. 29, Gal. ii. 6) grounds upon an axiomatic religious principle, that of the absolute superiority of the Divine to the human. That God should thus confound the world one might expect: "because the foolishness of God is wiser than men, and the weakness of God is stronger than men". Granted that the λόγος τ. σταυροῦ is folly and weakness, it is God's folly, God's weakness : will men dare to match themselves with that? (cf. Rom. ix. 20).—τὸ μωρόν (not μωρία as before), τὸ ἀσθενές are concrete terms—the foolish, weak policy of God (cf. τὸ χρηστόν, Rom. ii. 4), the folly and weakness embodied in the cross.—ἰσχυρός (ἰσχύς) implies intrinsic strength; δύναμις is ability, as relative to the task in view.

§ 5. The Objects of the Gospel Call, i. 26-31. § 4 has shown that the Gospel does not come ἐν σοφίᾳ λόγου (17b) by the method of its operation : this will further be evidenced by the status of its recipients. If it were, humanly speaking, a σοφία, it would have addressed itself to σοφοί, and won their adherence; but the case is far otherwise.

Ver. 26. Βλέπετε γὰρ τὴν κλῆσιν ὑμῶν, ἀδελφοί,—"For look at your calling, brothers": God has called you into the fellowship of His Son (9); if His Gospel had been a grand philosophy, would He have addressed it to fools, weaklings, base-born, like most of you? P.'s experience in this respect resembled his Master's (Matt. xi. 25, John vii. 47-49, Acts iv. 13). This argument cuts two ways: it lowers the conceit of the readers (cf. vi. 9-11, and the scathing irony of iv. 7-13), while it discloses the true mission of the Gospel. On κλῆσιν see the note to κλητοῖς (2), also on vii. 20: it signifies not one's temporal voca-

tion in the order of Providence, but one's summons to enter the kingdom of Grace; ὑμῶν is objective gen. For τ. κλῆσιν ὅτι, see note on ὅτι, ver. 5.—οὐ πολλοί (thrice repeated) suggests at least a few of each class amongst the readers: see Introd., p. 730.—οὐ πολλοὶ σοφοί : "hinc Athenis numero tam exiguo lucrifacti sunt homines" (Bg.).—σοφοὶ is qualified by κατὰ σάρκα (see parls., and cf. σοφία σαρκική, 2 Cor. i. 12), in view of the distinction worked out in § 4 between the world's and God's wisdom: the contrast implied resembles that between ἡ κατὰ Θεὸν λύπη and ἡ τοῦ κόσμου λύπη in 2 Cor. vii. 9 ff. The "wise after the flesh" include not only philosophers (20), "but educated men in general, the πεπαιδευμένοι as opposed to the ἰδιῶται. The δυνατοὶ were men of rank and political influence, opp. to δῆμος. The εὐγενεῖς meant, in the aristocratic ages of Greece, men of high descent;" but in later degenerate times "men whose ancestors were virtuous and wealthy, the honesti as opposed to the humiliores of the Empire. Few intellectual men, few politicians, few of the better class of free citizens embraced Christianity" (Ed.). In a Roman colony and capital, the εὐγενεῖς would chiefly be men of hereditary citizenship, like P. himself; the δυνατοί, persons associated with Government and in a position to influence affairs; the former word is applied in an ethical sense to the Berœan Jews in Acts xvii. 11. "That the majority of the first converts from heathenism were either slaves or freedmen, appears from their names" (Lt.); the inscriptions of the Catacombs confirm this. The low social status of the early Christians was the standing reproach of hostile critics, and the boast of Apologists: see the famous passage in Tacitus' Annals, xv., 44; Justin M., Apol., ii., 9; Origen, contra Celsum, ii., 79; Minuc. Felix, vii., 12 (indocti, impoliti, rudes, agrestes). As time went on and Christianity penetrated the higher ranks of society, these words became less strictly true: see Pliny's Ep. ad Trajanum, x., 97, and the cases of Flavius Clemens and Domitilla, cousins of the emperor Domitian (Ed.).

m See ver. 25. 27. ἀλλὰ τὰ ᵐμωρὰ τοῦ κόσμου ⁿἐξελέξατο¹ ὁ Θεός,¹ ἵνα °καταισ-

n Eph. i. 4; Ja. ii. 5; χύνη² τοὺς σοφούς²· καὶ τὰ ᵈἀσθενῆ τοῦ κόσμου ⁿἐξελέξατο ὁ Θεός,

Acts i. 2, 24, xiii.17, ἵνα °καταισχύνη τὰ °ἰσχυρά· 28. καὶ τὰ ᵖἀγενῆ τοῦ κόσμου καὶ τὰ

xv. 7; Mk. xiii. 20; ᑫἐξουθενημένα ⁿἐξελέξατο¹ ὁ Θεός,¹ καὶ ³ τὰ ʳμὴ ʳὄντα, ἵνα τὰ ὄντα

Lk. ix. 35;

Jo. vi. 70, xiii. 18, xv. 16.   o xi. 4 f., 22; 2 Cor. vii. 4, ix. 4; thrice in Rom.; 1 Pet. ii. 6, iii. 16;
Lk. xiii. 17; frequent in O.T.   p N.T. h.l.; in cl. Gr. commonly αγεννης.   q vi. 4, xvi. 11;
2 Cor. x. 10; Rom. xiv. 3, 10; Gal. iv. 14; 1 Th. v. 20; four times besides.   r Rom. iv. 17.

¹ AG, with above 15 minuscc., following some common (? Western) exemplar, jump from εξελεξατο ο Θεος in ver. 27 to the same words in ver. 28, omitting all between. Similar omissions occur in other individual MSS. in this context, where there is much repetition.

² τους σοφους καταισχυνη: all uncc. The T.R. rests on minuscc. only.

³ ℵAC*D*G, 17, om. και; ins. by B and Syrian Codd. W.H. bracket the conj.

The ellipsis of predicate to οὐ πολλοί κ.τ.λ. is commonly filled up by understanding ἐκλήθησαν, as implied in κλῆσιν: "not many wise, etc. (were called)". Mr., Bt., and others, supply εἰσίν, or preferably ἐστέ: "(there are) not many wise, etc. (among you)," or "not many (of you are) wise, etc."; the omission of ὑμεῖς courteously veils the disparagement.

Vv. 27-28. "Nay, but (ἀλλά, the but of exclusion) the foolish . . . the weak . . . the base-born things of the world God did choose out (when He chose you)."—ἐξελέξατο (selected, picked out for Himself) is equivalent to ἐκάλεσεν (2, 9, 26), εὐδόκησεν . . . σῶσαι (21), τὴν χάριν ἔδωκεν ἐν Χ. Ἰ. (4); this word indicates the relation in which the saved are put both to God and to the world, out of (ἐξ) which they were taken (see parls.); nothing here suggests, as in Eph. i. 4, the idea of eternal election. —ἐξελέξατο ὁ Θεός: the astonishing fact thrice repeated, with solemn emphasis of assurance. The objects of God's saving choice and the means of their salvation match each other; by His τὸ μωρὸν and τὸ ἀσθενές (25) He saves τὰ μωρά and τὰ ἀσθενῆ: "the world laughs at our beggarly selves, as it laughs at our beggarly Gospel!" The neut. adj. of vv. 27 f. mark the category to which the selected belong; their very foolishness, weakness, ignobility determine God's choice (cf. Matt. ix. 13, Luke x. 21, etc.).—τοῦ κόσμου is partitive gen.: out of all the world contained, God chose its (actually) foolish, weak, base things—making "fæx urbis lux orbis!" In this God acted deliberately, pursuing the course maintained through previous ages, ἐν τῇ σοφίᾳ τοῦ Θεοῦ (see note, 21): He "selected the foolish

things of the world, that He might shame its wise men (τοὺς σοφούς) . . . the weak things of the world, that He might shame its strong things (τὰ ἰσχυρά), and the base-born things of the world and the things made absolutely nothing of . . . the things non-existent, that He might bring the things existent to naught". In the first instance a class of persons, immediately present to Paul's mind (cf. 20), is to be "put to shame"; in the two latter P. thinks, more at large, of worldly forces and institutions (cf. vii. 31, 2 Cor. x. 4-6). The pride of the cultured and ruling classes of paganism was to be confounded by the powers which Christianity conferred upon its social outcasts; as, e.g., Hindoo Brahminism is shamed by the moral and intellectual superiority acquired by Christian Pariahs.—τὰ ἀγενῆ τοῦ κόσμου, third of the categories of disparagement, is reinforced by τὰ ἐξουθενημένα (from ἐξ and οὐδέν, pf. pass.: things set down as of no account whatever), then capped by the abruptly apposed τὰ μὴ ὄντα, to which is attached the crowning final clause, ἵνα τὰ ὄντα καταργήσῃ. For καταργέω (ut enervaret, Bz.), see note on κενόω (17), and parls.; the scornful world-powers are not merely to be robbed of their glory (as in the two former predictions), but of their power and being, as indeed befell in the end the existing social and political fabric. In τὰ μὴ ὄντα, "μὴ implies that the non-existence is not absolute but estimative" (Al.); the classes to which Christianity appealed were non-entities for philosophers and statesmen, cyphers in their reckoning: contrast οὐκ ὤν, of objective matter of fact, in John x. 12, Acts vii. 5; also Eurip., Troad., 600.— τὰ ὄντα connotes more than bare ex-

ᵃκαταργήσῃ· 29. ὅπως ᵘμὴ ᵗκαυχήσηται ᵘπᾶσα σὰρξ ᵛἐνώπιον ˢii. 6, vi. 15,
αὐτοῦ.¹ 30. ʷἐξ αὐτοῦ δὲ ὑμεῖς ἐστε ˣἐν Χριστῷ Ἰησοῦ, ὃς ἐγενήθη
ἡμῖν ² σοφία ² ʸἀπὸ Θεοῦ, ᶻδικαιοσύνη τε καὶ ᵃἁγιασμὸς καὶ ᵇἀπο-
λύτρωσις· 31. ἵνα, ᶜκαθὼς ᶜγέγραπται, "Ὁ ᵗκαυχώμενος, ἐν Κυρίῳ
ᵗκαυχάσθω".

iv. 21, 23, v. 5, vi. 8.   t iii. 21, iv. 7, xiii. 3; 2 Cor., *passim*; nine times elsewhere in P.; only Jas. i.
9, iv. 16 besides.   Rare and poetical in cl. Gr.   u Hebraistic (or ου . . . πας), lo' . . . *khol*: Rom.
iii. 20; Eph. iv. 29, v. 5; 2 Pet. i. 20; frequent in Epp. of Jo. and Rev.; Mt. xxiv. 22.   v Frequent
in P., Lk., and Rev.; never in Mt. or Mk.   w viii. 6; 2 Cor. v. 18; Rom. xi. 36; Jo. viii. 23,
42, etc.   x 2 Cor. v. 17, xii. 2; Rom. viii. 1, xvi. 7, 11; Gal. i. 22, iii. 28, etc.   y Ver. 3, iv. 5,
vi. 19, etc.   z Rom. i. 17, iii. 21, 25; 2 Cor. v. 21.   a Rom. vi. 19, 22; 1 Th. iv. 4, 7; 2 Th. ii. 13;
1 Tim. ii. 15.   Only Heb. xii. 14; 1 Pet. i. 2 besides   b Rom. iii. 24, viii. 23; Eph. i. 7, 14, iv. 30;
Col. i. 14.   Only Heb. ix. 15, xi. 35; Lk. xxi. 28 besides   c ii. 9; Rom. *passim*; 2 Cor. viii. 15,
ix. 9; Acts vii. 1, 2, xv. 15; Mt. xxvi. 24; Mk. i. 2, ix. 13, xiv. 21; Lk. ii. 23.

¹ ενωπιον του Θεου: all uncc. exc. C*, which is followed by minuscc., vg.,
both syrr., in reading αυτου (to avoid repetition).

² σοφια ημιν (in this order): pre-Syrian uncials.

istence; "ipsum verbum εἶναι eam vim
habet ut significet in aliquo numero
esse, rebus secundis florere" (Pflugk, on
Eurip., *Hecuba*, 284, quoted by Mr.); it is
τὰ ὄντα κατ' ἐξοχήν: *cf.* the adv. ὄντως
in 1 Tim. vi. 19.

Ver. 29. God's purposes in choosing
the refuse of society are gathered up
into the general and salutary design,
revealed in Scripture (see parls.), "that
so no flesh may glory in God's
presence" (a condensed quotation) =
πάντα εἰς δόξαν Θεοῦ (x. 31). For
ὅπως, which carries to larger issue the
intentions stated in the previous clauses,
cf. 2 Cor. viii. 14, 2 Thess. i. 12. Two
Hebraisms, characteristic of the LXX,
here: μὴ . . . πᾶσα (*khōl* . . . *lo'*), for
μηδεμία; and σάρξ (*bāsār*), for *humanity*
in its mortality or sinfulness. *Cf.*, for
this rule of Divine action, 2 Cor. xii.
9 f.; also Plato, *Ion*, 534 E, ἵνα μὴ
διστάζωμεν ὅτι οὐκ ἀνθρώπινά ἐστι τὰ
καλὰ ταῦτα ποιήματα οὐδὲ ἀνθρώπων,
ἀλλὰ θεῖα καὶ θεῶν . . . ὁ θεὸς ἐξεπί-
τηδες διὰ τοῦ φαυλοτάτου ποιητοῦ τὸ
κάλλιστον μέλος ᾖσεν.

Ver. 30. ἐξ αὐτοῦ δὲ ὑμεῖς ἐστε ἐν
Χριστῷ Ἰησοῦ: is ἐν Χ. Ἰησοῦ or ἐξ
αὐτοῦ (*sc.* τοῦ Θεοῦ) the predicate to
ἐστέ?   Does P. mean, "It comes of
Him (God) that you are in Christ Jesus"
—*i.e.*, "Your Christian status is due to
God" (so Mr., Hn., Bt., Ed., Gd., El.)?
or, "It is in Christ Jesus that you are of
Him"—"Your new life derived from
God is grounded in Christ" (Gr. Ff.,
Cv., Bz., Rückert, Hf., Lt.)?   The
latter interpretation suits the order of
words and the trend of thought (see
Lt.): "*You*, whom the world counts as

nothing (26 ff.: note the contrastive δέ),
are *of Him* before whom all human glory
vanishes (29); *in Christ* this Divine
standing is yours".   Thus Paul exalts
those whom he had abased.   The conception of the Christian estate as "of
God," if Johannine, is Pauline too (*cf.*
viii. 6, x. 12, xii. 6, 2 Cor. iv. 6, v. 18,
etc.), and lies in Paul's fundamental
appropriation, after Jesus, of God as
πατὴρ ἡμῶν (i. 4, and *passim*), and in the
correlative doctrine of the υἱοθεσία; the
whole passage (18-29) is dominated by
the thought of the Divine initiative in
salvation.   This derivation from God is
not further defined, as in Gal. iii. 26;
enough to state the grand fact, and to
ground it "in Christ Jesus" (see note, 4).

The relative clause, "who was made
wisdom," etc., unfolds the content of the
life communicated "to us from God" in
Christ.   Of the four defining comple-
ments to ἐγενήθη ἡμῖν, σοφία stands by
itself, with the other three attached by
way of definition—"wisdom from God,
viz., both righteousness, etc."; Mr., Al.,
Gd., however, read the four as co-
ordinate.   On σοφία the whole debate,
from ver. 17 onwards, hinges: we have
seen how God turned the world's wisdom to folly (20-25); now He did this
not for the pleasure of it, but for our
salvation—to establish His own wisdom
(24), and to bestow it upon us in Christ
("us" means Christians collectively—*cf.*
17—while "you" meant the despised
Cor. Christians, 26).   This wisdom (how
diff. from the other! see 17, 19; Jas. iii.
15 ff.) comes as sent "from God" (ἀπὸ
of ultimate source: ἐξ of direct derivation).   It is a vitalising moral force—

a 1 Tim. ii.
2 only.
In LXX,
1 Ki. ii. 3;
2 Macc.
iii. 11, etc.
with τ. Θεοῦ only here.

II. 1. Κἀγὼ ἐλθὼν πρὸς ὑμᾶς, ἀδελφοί, ἦλθον οὐ καθ᾽ ᵃ ὑπεροχὴν λόγου ἢ σοφίας, ᵇ καταγγέλλων ὑμῖν τὸ ᶜ μαρτύριον ¹ τοῦ Θεοῦ. 2. οὐ

b ix. 14, xi. 26; Rom. i. 8; Ph. i. 17 f.; Col. i. 28; often in Acts.   c See i. 6;

¹ μαρτυριον: אᶜBDGLP, vg. sah. syrᵖ., Gr. Ff.; W.H. *mg.*, R.V. *mg.*, Tisch., Tr. μυστηριον: א*AC, cop. syrˢᶜʰ., Lat. Ff.; W.H. *txt.*, R.V. *txt.* The former is the Western and Syrian reading, the latter Alexandrian; the Neutral txt. is doubtful. μυστ. has rather the look of an Alex. harmonistic correction, due to ver. 7 (*cf.* iv. 1, Col. ii. 2, Rev. x. 7). μαρτ. suits better καταγγελλων: see note below.

δύναμις καὶ σοφία (24) — taking the shape of δικαιοσύνη τε καὶ ἁγιασμός, and signally contrasted in its spiritual reality and regenerating energy with the σοφία λόγου and σοφία τ. κόσμου, after which the Cor. hankered. Righteousness and Sanctification are allied "by their theological affinity" (El.): *cf.* note on vi. 11, and Rom. vi. *passim*—hence the double copula τε . . . καί; καὶ ἀπολύτρωσις follows at a little distance (so Lt., Hn., Ed.; who adduce numerous cl. parls. to this use of the Gr. conjunctions): "who was made wisdom to us from God—*viz.*, both righteousness and sanctification, and redemption".—δικαιοσύνη carries with it, implicitly, the Pauline doctrine of Justification by faith in the dying, risen Christ (see vi. 11, and other parls.; esp., for Paul's teaching at Cor., 2 Cor. v. 21). With the *righteousness* of the believer justified in Christ *sanctification* (or *consecration*) is concomitant (see note on the kindred terms in 2); the connexion of chh. v. and vi. in Rom. expounds this τε . . . καί; all δικαιοσύνη ἐν Χριστῷ is εἰς ἁγιασμόν. (Vbl. nouns in -μός denote primarily a process, then the resulting state.)—Ἀπολύτρωσις (based on the λύτρον of Matt. xx. 28, 1 Tim. ii. 6, with ἀπὸ of *separation, release*), *deliverance by ransom*, is the widest term of the three—"primum Christi donum quod inchoatur in nobis, et ultimum quod perficitur" (Cv.); it looks backward to the cross (18), by whose blood we "were bought" for God (vi. 19), so furnishing the ground both of justification (Rom. iii. 24) and sanctification (Heb. x. 10), and forward to the resurrection and glorification of the saints, whereby Christ secures His full purchased rights in them (Rom. viii. 23; Eph. i. 14, iv. 30); thus Redemption covers the entire work of salvation, indicating the essential and just means of its accomplishment (see Cr. on λύτρον and derivatives).

Ver. 31. "In order that, as it stands

written, he who glories, *in the Lord* let him glory;" by "the Lord" the readers could only understand *Christ*, already five times thus titled; so, manifestly, in 2 Cor. x. 17 f., where the citation reappears. Paul quotes the passage as a general Scriptural principle, which eminently applies to the relations of Christians to Christ; ἐν Κυρίῳ belongs to his adaptation of the original: God will have no flesh (see note, 29) exult in his wisdom, strength, high birth (*cf.* the objects of false glorying in Jer.) before Him; He *will* have men exult in "the Lord of glory" (ii. 8; *cf.* Phil. ii. 9 ff.), whom He sent as His own "wisdom" and "power unto salvation" (24, 30). What grieves the Ap. most and appears most fatal in the party strifes of Cor., is the extolling of human names by the side of Christ's and at his expense (see notes on 12-15; also iii. 5, 21-23, and 2 Cor. iv. 5, Gal. vi. 14). Christians are specifically οἱ καυχώμενοι ἐν Χ. Ἰ., Phil. iii. 3. The irregularity of mood after ἵνα — καυχάσθω for subj. καυχᾶται—is accounted for in two ways: either as an *anacoluthon*, the impv. of the original being transplanted in lively quotation (*cf.* Rom. xv. 3, 21); or as an *ellipsis*, with γένηται or πληρωθῇ mentally supplied (*cf.* Rom. iv. 16, Gal. ii. 9, 2 Cor. viii. 13)—explanations not materially different. Clem. Rom. (§ 13) quotes the text with the same peculiarity.

§ 6. PAUL'S CORINTHIAN MISSION, ii. 1-5. Paul has justified his refusing to preach ἐν σοφίᾳ λόγου on two grounds: (1) the nature of the Gospel, (2) the constituency of the Church of Cor.; *it* was no philosophy, and *they* were no philosophers. This refusal he continues to make, in pursuance of *the course adopted from the outset.* So he returns to his starting-point, *viz.*, that "Christ sent" him "to bring good tidings," such as neither required nor admitted of "wisdom of word" (i. 17).

Ver. 1. Κἀγὼ ἐλθὼν . . . ἦλθον:

γὰρ ᵈἔκρινα τοῦ¹ εἰδέναι¹ τι¹ ἐν ὑμῖν, εἰ μὴ Ἰησοῦν ᶠΧριστὸν ᵉκαὶ ᵈIn this sense, vii. 37; 2 Cor. ii. 1, v. 14; Tit. iii.12;
ᵉτοῦτον ᶠἐσταυρωμένον· 3. καὶ ἐγὼ ⁱἐν ᵍἀσθενείᾳ καὶ ⁱἐν ʰφόβῳ

Lk. vii. 43, xii. 57; Acts. iii. 13, etc.   e vi. 6, 8; Rom. xiii. 11; Eph. ii. 8; Ph. i. 28; 3 Jo. 5.
f See i. 23.   g xv. 43; five times in 2 Cor.; Rom. viii. 26; Gal. iv. 13; 1 Tim. v. 23; see also i. 25,
viii. 11.   h 2 Cor. vii. 15; Eph. vi. 5; Ph. ii. 12; Gen. ix. 2; Exod. xv. 16; Ps. liv. 6, etc.

¹τι εἰδέναι (om. του), BD*CP 17, 37; ειδέναι τι, ℵAG; του ειδέναι τι, DᵇL and most others. The two other readings are successive grammatical emendations of the first; cf. Acts xxvii. 1, and the T.R. of vii. 37 below.

" And I at my coming . . . came " : the repeated vb. draws attention to Paul's *arrival*,—to the circumstances and character of his original work at Cor. The emphasis of κἀγώ—"And *I* "—may lie in the correspondence between the message and the messenger—*both* " foolish " and " weak " (i. 25 : so Ed.) ; but the form of the sentence rather suggests allusion to the nearer i. 26—" As it was with you, brothers, to whom I conveyed God's call, so with myself who conveyed it ; you were not wise nor mighty according to flesh, and I came to you as one without wisdom or strength ". Message, hearers, preacher matched each other for folly and feebleness ! " I came not in the way of excellence—καθ᾽ ὑπεροχήν, *cum eminentia* (Bz.)—of word or wisdom,"—not with the bearing of a man distinguished for these accomplishments, and relying upon them for his success : this clause is best attached to the emphatic ἦλθον, which requires a descriptive adjunct (so Or., Cv., Bz., Hf. : *cf.* 3) ; others make it a qualification of καταγγέλλων. Paul's humble mien and plain address presented a striking contrast to the pretensions usual in itinerant professors of wisdom, such as he was taken for at Athens.—ὑπεροχή, from ὑπερέχω (Phil. ii. 3, iii. 8, iv. 7), *to overtop, outdo*. For λόγου ἢ σοφίας, see note on σοφία λόγου (i. 17).

The manner of Paul's preaching was determined by its *matter ;* with such a commission he could not adopt the arts of a rhetorican nor the airs of a philosopher : " I came not like a man eminent in speech or wisdom, in proclaiming to you the testimony of God".—τ. μαρτύριον τ. Θεοῦ (subjective gen. : *cf.* note on i. 6) = τ. εὐαγγέλιον τ. Θεοῦ (Rom. i. 2, 1 Thess. ii. 2, 13, etc. ; *cf.* 1 John v. 9 f.), with the connotation of solemnly attested truth (*cf.* 2 Cor. i. 18 f.) ; P. spoke as one through whom *God* was witnessing. ✓ κηρύσσω (i. 23), denoting official declaration, gives place to καταγγέλλω, signifying full and clear proclamation

(see parls.).—καταγγέλλων, pr. ptp., " in the course of preaching " ; *cf.* 2 Cor. x. 14.

Ver. 2. οὐ γὰρ ἔκρινά τι (or ἔκρινα τὶ) εἰδέναι κ.τ.λ.: "For I did not determine (judge it fit) to know anything (*or*, know something) among you, except (*or*, only) Jesus Christ, and Him crucified ". This explains Paul's unadorned and matter-of-fact delivery.—οὐ negatives ἔκρινα, not εἰδέναι (the rendering " I determined not to know " contravenes the order of words) ; nor is there any instance of οὐ coalescing with κρίνω as in οὔ φημι (*nego*) and the like—these interpretations miss the point: had P. chosen another subject, he might have aimed at a higher style ; he avoided the latter, " for " he did not entertain the former notion. His failure at Athens may have emphasised, but did not originate the Apostle's resolution to know nothing but the cross : *cf.* Gal. iii. 1, 1 Thess. iv. 14, v. 9 f., Acts xiii. 38 f., relating to earlier preaching. For the use of ἔκρινα (*statui*, Bz.) as denoting a practical moral judgment or resolution, *cf.* vii. 37, 2 Cor. ii. 1. Ev. renders τὶ εἰδέναι (thus accented), " to be a know-something " (*aliquid scire*)—to play the philosopher—according to the well-known Attic idiom of Plato's *Apol.*, § 6, and *passim*, where οἴεται τὶ εἰδέναι = δοκεῖ σοφὸς εἶναι ; *cf.* viii. 2, and the emphatic εἶναι τὶς (τὶ) ; also iii. 7, Gal. ii. 6, vi. 3, Acts v. 36. This rendering accounts well for εἰδέναι, and gives additional point to the ὑπεροχὴ of ver. 1 : P. brought with him to Cor. none of the prestige of the professional teachers, who claimed to "know something" ; *Christ and the cross*—this was all he knew. For εἰ μὴ in the corrective sense "only," demanded by this interpretation, see vii. 17. —εἰδέναι is *to possess knowledge*, to be a master ; γινώσκειν (i. 21), *to acquire knowledge*, to be a learner. On ἐσταυρωμένον (pf. ptp., of pregnant fact), *cf.* notes to i. 17, 23.

Vv. 1, 2 say how P. *did not come*, vv. 3-5 how he actually *did come*, to Cor.

i xv. 10; 2 Cor. iii. 7; Rom. xvi. 7; Ph. ii. 7; 1 Th. ii. 5; 1 Tim. ii. 14; Lk. xxii. 44; Acts xii. 11; Rev. i. 10, iv. 2. καὶ ⁱ ἐν ʰ τρόμῳ πολλῷ ⁱ ἐγενόμην πρὸς ὑμᾶς· 4. καὶ ὁ λόγος μου καὶ τὸ ᵏ κήρυγμά μου οὐκ ἐν ¹ πειθοῖς ¹ ἀνθρωπίνης ² σοφίας λόγοις,¹ k See i. 21. 1 H.l.; cl. Gr. πιθανός.

¹ πειθοι . . . λογων, or . . . λογου, in several minuscc., latt. am. (persuasione sapientiæ verbi), sah.: a translator's error due to the adj. being h.l. W.H. follow AD*P, and analogy, in spelling πιθοις (see Gm.).

² Om. ανθρωπινης ℵBDG 17, latt. am. syrsch. Borrowed from ver 13.

Ver. 3. "In weakness": cf. i. 25, 27; also 2 Cor. x. 10, and xiii. 3 f. This condition was bodily—the Cor. had received an impression of Paul's physical feebleness; but the phrase expresses, more broadly, his conscious want of resources for the task before him (cf. 2 Cor. ii. 16, iii. 5). Hence he continues, "and in fear and in much trembling"—the inward emotion and its visible expression (see parls.). P. stood before the Cor. at first a timid, shaken man: on the causes see Introd., ch. i.

For γίνομαι ἐν (versari in), to be in a state of, cf. parls.—πρὸς ὑμᾶς qualifies the whole foregoing sentence: "I was weak, timid, trembling before you (when I addressed you)": ἐγενόμην . . . πρὸς ὑμᾶς might be construed together, ἐγενόμην becoming a vb. of motion—"I came to (and was amongst) you in weakness," etc. (Ed., as in xvi. 10); this would, however, needlessly repeat ver. 1.

Ver. 4. "And my word and my message:" λόγος recalls i. 18; κήρυγμα, i. 21, 23 (see notes). The former includes all that Paul says in proclaiming the Gospel, the latter the specific announcement of God's will and call therein.

οὐκ ἐκ πιθοῖς σοφίας λόγοις, "not in persuasive words of wisdom": the adj. πιθός (= πιθανός, see txtl. note), from πείθομαι, analogous to φιδός from φείδομαι. "Words of wisdom," substantially = "wisdom of word" (i. 17); that expression accentuating the matter, this the manner of teaching—"exquisita eloquutio, quæ artificio magis quam veritate nitatur et pugnet" (Cv.). For the unfavourable nuance of πιθός, see Col. ii. 4 (πιθανολογία), also Gal. i. 10, Matt. xxviii. 14. Eusebius excellently paraphrases (Praep. Ev., i., 3), τὰς μὲν ἀπατηλὰς κ. σοφιστικὰς πιθανολογίας παραιτούμενος). "With a contemptuous touch of irony that reminds one of Socrates in the Gorgias and Apology [cf. Ev., as previously cited, on τὶ εἰδέναι], he disclaims all skill in rhetoric, the spurious art of persuading without in-

structing, held nevertheless in high repute in Cor. But when the Ap. speaks of the demonstration of the Spirit, he soars into a region of which Socrates knew nothing. Socr. sets σοφία against πειθώ; the Ap. regards both as being on well-nigh a common level, from the higher altitude of the Spirit" (Ed.); since the time of Socrates, however, Philosophy had sunk into a πιθανολογία. —ἀπόδειξις, "the technical term for a proof drawn from facts or documents, as opposed to theoretical reasoning; in common use with the Stoics in this sense" (Hn.); see Plato, Theæt., 162 E, and Arist., Eth. Nic., i., 1; ii., 4, for the like antithesis (Ed.).

ἀποδ. πνεύματος καὶ σοφίας gathers up the force of the δύναμιν Θεοῦ of i. 24, and ἐγένετο σοφία κ.τ.λ. of i. 30 (see notes); the proof of the Gospel at Cor. was experimental and ethical, found in the new consciousness and changed lives that attended its proclamation: cf. vi. 11, ix. 1, 2 Cor. iii. 1 ff., 1 Thess. ii. 13 (λόγος Θεοῦ, ὃς κ. ἐνεργεῖται ἐν ὑμῖν τ. πιστεύουσιν).—πνεύματος καὶ δυνάμεως are not objective gen. (in ostendendo Spiritum, etc.), but subjective: the Spirit, with His power, gives the demonstration (similarly in xii. 7, see note); cf. vv. 10, 12, 2 Cor. iii. 3-18, Rom. viii. 16, xv. 19, for Paul's thoughts on the testimonium Spiritus sancti; also John xv. 26, 1 John v. 6 f.—Δύναμις, specially associated with Πνεῦμα after Luke xxiv. 49 (see reff. for P.), is certainly the spiritual power that operates as implied in i. 30, vi. 11, but not to the exclusion of the supernatural physical "powers" which accompanied Apostolic preaching (see note on ἐβεβαιώθη, i. 6; also xii. 1, 7-11, and the combination of Rom. xv. 17 ff.): "latius accipio, nempe pro manu Dei potente omnibus modis per apostolum se exserente" (Cv.). The art. is wanting with πνεύματος, though personal, after the anarthrous ἀποδείξει, according to "the law of correlation" (Wr., p. 175: contrast this with xii. 7, also the double

ἀλλ' ἐν ᵐ ἀποδείξει ⁿ Πνεύματος καὶ ᵒ δυνάμεως· 5. ἵνα ἡ πίστις
ὑμῶν μὴ ᾖ ἐν σοφίᾳ ἀνθρώπων, ἀλλ' ἐν ᵖ δυνάμει ᵖ Θεοῦ.
6. Σοφίαν δὲ λαλοῦμεν ἐν τοῖς ᑫ τελείοις· σοφίαν δὲ οὐ τοῦ
ʳ αἰῶνος ʳ τούτου, οὐδὲ τῶν ˢ ἀρχόντων τοῦ ʳˢ αἰῶνος ʳ τούτου τῶν

m H.l. in N.T. See vb. in iv.9
n In ver. 13, vii. 40; 2 Cor. iii. 3, 6; Rom. viii. 9, 13-15, and
p See

often in P., πν. is anarthrous in like connexion.   o In combination with πν., xii. 10; Rom. i. 4,
xv. 13, 19; 1 Th. i. 5; 2 Tim. i. 7; Heb. ii. 4; Lk. i. 17, iv. 14, xxiv. 49; Acts i. 8, x. 38.   p See
i. 18.   q xiii. 10, xiv. 20; Eph. iv. 13; Ph. iii. 15; Col. i. 28, iv. 12; Heb. v. 14; Jas. i. 4; Mt. v.
48, xix. 21.   r See i. 20.   s Jo. xii. 31, xiv. 30, xvi. 11, with κοσμου; in pl. h.l.; cf. Eph. ii. 2,
vi. 12.   οι αρχοντες, Rom. xiii. 3; Mt. xx. 25; Lk. xxiii. 13, 35, xxiv. 20; Acts iii. 17, and six other
places; Jo. vii. 26, 48, xii. 42.

art. of 1 with the anarthrous phrase of
i. 18). The prpl. clause affirms not the
agency *by* which, but the sphere of
action *in* which, Paul's word operated.
Supply to this verse ἐγένετο from the
ἐγενόμην of ver. 3.

Ver. 5. The Apostle's purpose in dis-
carding the orator's and the sophist's arts
was this: "that your faith might not
rest in wisdom of men, but in (the)
power of God". The κἀγὼ ἦλθον of
ver. 1 dominates the paragraph; P. lives
over again the experience of his early
days in Cor.; this purpose then filled
his breast: so Hf., Gd., with the older
interpreters; most moderns read into the
ἵνα the *Divine* purpose suggested by
i. 27-31. Paul was God's mouthpiece in
declaring the Gospel; he therefore sought
the very end of God Himself, *viz.*, that
God alone should be glorified in the
faith of his hearers (i. 31; *cf.* i. 15).
Had he persuaded the Cor. by clever
reasonings and grounded Christianity
upon their Greek philosophy, his work
would have perished with the wisdom of
the age (see 6, also i. 19, iii. 19 f.).
The disowned σοφία ἀνθρώπων is the
σοφ. τ. κόσμου of i. 10 (see note) in its
moral character, a σοφ. σαρκική (2 Cor. i.
12)—"wisdom of men" as opposed to
that of God,—ἀνθρωπίνη, ver. 13. Yet not
God's *wisdom*, but primarily His *power*
(see notes on i. 18, 24, 30) supplied the
ground on which P. planted his hearers'
faith. All through, he opposes the practical to the speculative, the reality of God's
work to the speciousness of men's talk.
The last ἵνα clause of this long passage
corresponds to the first, ἵνα μὴ κενωθῇ
ὁ σταυρὸς τ. Χριστοῦ (i. 17). ἐν should
be construed with ᾖ (*consistat in*, Bz.)
rather than πίστις, pointing not to the
object of faith but to its substratum: for
this predicative ἐν—"should be (a faith)
in," etc.—*cf.* iv. 20, Eph. v. 18, Acts iv. 12.
SUMMARY. Thus the Apostle's first
ministry at Cor., in respect of his *bearing* (ver. 1), *theme* (2), *temper* (3), *method*

(4), *governing aim* (5), illustrated and
accorded with the Gospel, as that is a
message from God through which His
power works to the confounding of
human wisdom by the seeming impotence of a crucified Messiah (i. 17 *b*-31).

§ 7. THE GOSPEL CONSIDERED AS
WISDOM, ii. 6-9. So far Paul has been
maintaining that his message is a "folly,"
with which "wisdom of word" is out of
keeping; yet all the while he makes it
felt that it is wisdom in the truest sense
—"*God's* wisdom," convicting in its
turn the world of folly. If relatively the
Gospel is not wisdom, absolutely it is
so,—*to persons qualified to understand it.*
This P. now proceeds to show (ii. 6-iii.
2: *cf. Introd.* to Div. II.). The message
of the cross is wisdom to the right people
(§ 7), qualified to comprehend it (§ 8).

Ver. 6. Σοφίαν δὲ λαλοῦμεν κ.τ.λ.:
"(there is) a wisdom, however, (that) we
speak amongst the full-grown". The
anarthrous, predicative σοφίαν asserts
that to be "wisdom" which in ironical
deference to the world has been styled
"folly" (i. 21 ff.). ἐν τοῖς τελείοις, the
mature, the initiates (opp. to νήπιοι,
παιδία, iii. 1, xiv. 20; see parls.) = πνευματικοὶ in contrast with the relatively
σάρκινοι (iii. 1; *cf.* note on μυστήριον,
ver. 7). "The curtain must be lifted
with a caution measured by the spiritual
intelligence of the spectators, ἐπόπται"
(Ev.). This τελειότης the Cor. had by
no means reached; hence they failed to
see where the real wisdom of the Gospel
lay, and estimated its ministers by worldly
standards. ἐν signifies not *to*, nor *in
relation to*, but *amongst* the qualified
hearers—*in such a circle* P. freely expounded deeper truths. λαλέω (*cf.* 7,
13), *to utter, speak out*: P. uses the pl.
not thinking of Sosthenes in particular
(i. 1), but of his fellow-preachers generally,
including Apollos (i. 23, and xv. 11, etc.;
iii. 6, iv. 6).

The "wisdom" uttered in such company is defined first *negatively*: "but a

t See i. 28. ᵗκαταργουμένων · 7. ἀλλὰ λαλοῦμεν ᵘσοφίαν¹ ᵘΘεοῦ¹ ἐν ᵛμυστηρίῳ,
u See i. 21.
v iv. 1; Eph. τὴν ʷἀποκεκρυμμένην, ἣν ˣπροώρισεν ὁ Θεὸς ʸπρὸ τῶν ʸαἰώνων
i. 9, iii. 4;
Col. ii. 2,
iv. 3; Rev. x. 7; Mt. xiii. 11.   w Eph. iii. 9; Col. i. 26; Lk. x. 21; cf. Rom. xvi. 25.   x Rom.
viii. 29 f.; Eph. i. 5, 11; Acts iv. 28.   y H.l.; cf. 2 Tim. i. 9; Tit. i. 2; also Eph. i. 4; 1 Pet.
i. 20; Jo. xvii. 24; see x. 11 below.

¹Θεου σοφιαν: אABCDGP, 15 minuscc. σοφιαν Θ., L, etc.; a Syrian emendation; cf. ver. 6.

wisdom not of this age, nor of the rulers of this age, that are being brought to nought". For **αἰών**, see note to i. 20; it connotes the transitory nature of the world-powers (i. 19, 28; cf. vii. 31, 2 Cor. iv. 18; also 1 John ii. 17, 1 Peter i. 24 ff.). The **ἄρχοντες τ. αἰῶνος τούτου** were taken by Marcion, Or., and other ancients, to be the *angelic, or demonic* (Satanic), rulers of the nations—*sc.* the "princes" of Dan. x.-xii., and Jewish angelology, the **κοσμοκράτορες τ. σκότους τούτου** of Eph. vi. 12 (cf. 2 Cor. iv. 4, Eph. ii. 2, John xii. 31, xiv. 30, xvi. 11—where **ἄρχων** is applied to *Satan*; also Gal. iii. 19, Acts vii. 53, touching the office of *angels* in the Lawgiving): so Sm., after F. C. Baur—"the angels who preside over the various departments of the world, the Law in particular, but possess no perfect insight into the counsels of God, and lose their dominion—from which they take their name of **ἀρχαί** (= **ἄρχοντες**)—with the end of the world (xv. 24)"; see also, at length, Everling, *Die Paulin. Angelologie u. Dämonologie*, pp. 11 ff. But these super-terrestrial potentates could not, without explanation, be charged with the crucifixion of Christ (8); on the other hand, i. 27 ff. shows P. to be thinking in this connexion of *human* powers. Unless otherwise defined, **οἱ ἄρχοντες** denotes "the rulers" of common speech, those, *e.g.*, of Rom. xiii. 3, Luke xxiii. 35. On **τῶν καταργουμένων**, see note to i. 17 (**κενόω**), 28, xv. 24, and other parls. The *Jewish* rulers, whose overthrow is certain and near (1 Thess. ii. 16, Rom. ix. 22, xi.), are aimed at, as being primarily answerable for the death of Jesus (cf. Acts xiii. 27 f.); but P. foresaw the supersession of all existing world-powers by the Messianic kingdom (xv. 24; cf. Rom. xi. 15, Acts xvii. 7); the pr. ptp., perhaps, implies a "gradual nullification of their potency brought about by the Gospel" (El.). P. cannot have meant by **οἱ ἄρχοντες** *the leaders of thought* (as Thd., Thp., Neander suppose), because of the association with **σοφία**); he held a broad, practical

conception of wisdom (sagacity) as shown in *power;* the secular rulers, wise in their own way but not in God's, must come to nought. Statecraft, equally with philosophy, failed when tested by the cross.

Ver. 7. "(We speak . . . a wisdom not of this world . . .) but (**ἀλλά**, of diametrical opposition) a wisdom of God, in (shape of) a mystery."—**ἐν μυστηρίῳ** qualifies **λαλοῦμεν**, rather than **σοφίαν** (as Hn., Ev., Lt. read it—"couched in mystery"), indicating how it is that the App. do not speak in terms of worldly wisdom, and express themselves fully to the **τέλειοι** alone: their message is a Divine secret, that the Spirit of God reveals (10 f.), while "the age" possesses only "the spirit of the world" (12). Hence to the age God's wisdom is uttered "in a mystery" and remains "the hidden (wisdom)"; cf. 2 Cor. iv. 4; also Matt. xiii. 13 ff. (**ἐν παραβολαῖς . . . λαλῶ**), Luke x. 21 f.: **λαλῶ ἐν μυστηρίῳ = ἀποκρύπτω**.—**μυστήριον** (cf. xv. 51) has "its usual meaning in St. Paul's Epp.,—something not comprehensible by unassisted human reason" (El.; for a full account see Ed., or Bt., on the term). The Hellenic "mysteries," which flourished at this time, were practised at night in an imposing dramatic form; and peculiar doctrines were taught in them, which the initiated were sworn to keep secret. This popular notion of "mystery," as a sacred knowledge disclosed to fit persons, on their subjecting themselves to prescribed conditions, is appropriated and adapted in Bibl. Gr. to Divine revelation. The world at large does not perceive God's wisdom in the cross, being wholly disqualified; the Cor. believers apprehend it but partially, since they have imperfectly received the revealing Spirit and are "babes in Christ" (iii. 1 ff.); to the App., and those like them (10 ff.), a full disclosure is made. When he "speaks wisdom among the ripe," P. is not setting forth esoteric doctrines diff. from those preached to beginners, but the same "word of the cross"—for he knows nothing greater or higher (Gal.

ᶻ εἰς ᶻ δόξαν ᶻ ἡμῶν. 8. ἦν οὐδεὶς τῶν ᵃ ἀρχόντων τοῦ ᴵᵃ αἰῶνος ᴵ τούτου   ᶻ xv. 43; 2 Cor.iii.18;
ἔγνωκεν, εἰ γὰρ ἔγνωσαν, οὐκ ἂν τὸν ᵃ Κύριον τῆς ᵃ δόξης ᵇ ἐσταύρω-   iv. 17; 10 times in P.besides;

cf. Heb. ii. 10; 1 Pet. v. 1, 4, 10; Jo. xvii. 22.   a Jas. ii. 1; similarly, Acts vii. 2 (Ps. xxviii. 3, xxiii. 7, 9); Eph. i. 17; cf. Heb. ix. 5.   b See i. 23; cf. Mt. xx. 19, xxvi. 2; Lk. xxiii. 33; Jo. xix. 18; Acts ii. 36, iv. 10.

vi. 14)—in its recondite meaning and larger implications,—as, e.g., in xv. 20-27 of this Ep. (where he relents from the implied threat of iii. 1 ff.), in Rom. v. 12-21, and xi. 25 ff., or Col. i. 15 ff., Eph. v. 22-32.—τὴν ἀποκεκρυμμένην expands the idea of ἐν μυστηρίῳ (see parls.): P. utters, beneath his plain Gospel tale, the deepest truths "in a guise of mystery"—"that (wisdom) hidden away (ἀπὸ τ. αἰώνων, Col. i. 26), which God predetermined before the ages unto (εἰς, aiming at) our glory". That the Gospel is a veiled mystery to many accords with past history and with God's established purpose respecting it; "est occulta antequam expromitur: et quum expromitur, tamen occulta manet multis, imperfectis" (Bg.). The "wisdom of God" now revealed, was destined eternally "for us"—"the believers" (i. 21), "the called" (i. 24), "the elect" (i. 27 ff.), "those that received the Spirit of God" (10 ff.), as men who fulfil the ethical conditions of the case and whom "it has been God's good pleasure to save" (i. 21); see the same thought in Eph. i. 4 ff. This δόξα is not the heavenly glory of the saints; the entire "ministry of the Spirit" is ἐν δόξῃ and carries its subjects on ἀπὸ δόξης εἰς δόξαν (2 Cor. iii. 8-18); His ἀπαρχὴ effects a glorious transformation, by which the base things of the world put to shame its mighty (i. 27 ff.), and "our glory" overthrows "the rulers of this world" (6), "increasing as theirs wanes" (Lt.), cf. Rom. viii. 30. This present (moral) glory is an "earnest" of "that which shall be revealed" (Rom. viii. 18 f.). For προώρισεν, marked out beforehand, see parls., and notes to Rom. viii. 29 f.

Ver. 8. ἦν οὐδεὶς κ.τ.λ.: "which (wisdom) none of the rulers of this age has perceived"—all blind to the significance of the rise of Christianity.—ἔγνωκεν, a pf., approaching the pr. sense (novi) which οἶδα had reached, but implying, as that does not, a process—has come to know, won the knowledge of.—οἱ ἄρχοντες κ.τ.λ., repeated with emphasis from ver. 6—sc. "the rulers of this (great) age," of the world in its length of history and fulness of experience (see x. 11, and note; cf. Eph. i.

10, iii. 5, Rom. xvi. 25 f.). The leaders of the time showed themselves miserably ignorant of God's plans and ways in dealing with the world they ruled; "for if they had known, they would not have crucified the Lord of glory". The Lord of glory is He in whom "our glory" (7) has its manifestation and guarantee—first in His earthly, then in His heavenly estate (cf. xv. 43, 49).—τῆς δόξης, gen. of characterising quality (cf. Eph. i. 17, Acts vii. 2). This glory of the Son of God the disciples saw (John i. 14); of it believers now partake (Rom. viii. 29 f.), and will partake in full hereafter (2 Cor. iii. 18, Phil. iii. 21, etc.), when it culminates in a universal dominion (xv. 23-29, Phil. ii. 9 ff., Heb. i.). Paul's view of Christ always shone with "the glory of that light" in which he first saw Him on the road to Damascus (Acts xxii. 11). Caiaphas and the Sanhedrin, Pilate and the Roman court (cf. Acts xiii. 27 f., 1 Tim. vi. 13) saw nothing of the splendour clothing the Lord Jesus as He stood before them; so knowing, they could not have crucified Him. The expression κύριος τῆς δόξης is no syn. for Christ's Godhead; it signifies the entire grandeur of the incarnate Lord, whom the world's wise and great sentenced to the cross. Their ignorance was a partial excuse (see Luke xxiii. 34, Acts xiii. 27); but it was guilty, like that of Rom. i. 18 f. The crucifiers fairly represented worldly governments. Mark the paradox, resembling Peter's in Acts iii. 15: "Crux servorum supplicium—eo Dominum gloriæ affecerunt" (Bg.). The levity of philosophers in rejecting the cross of Christ was only surpassed by the stupidity of politicians in inflicting it; in both acts the wise of the age proved themselves fools, and God thereby brought them to ruin (i. 28). For εἰ . . . ἄν, stating a hypothesis contrary to past fact (the modus tollens of logic), see Bn. § 248; and cf. xi. 31.

Ver. 9 confirms by the language of Scripture (καθὼς γέγραπται) what has just been said. The verse is open to three different constructions: (1) It seems best to treat the relatives, ἅ, ὅσα, as in apposition to the foregoing ἦν clauses of vv. 7, 8 (the form of the pro-

c See i. 31.
d Isa. lxiv. 4
and lxv. 16
(see note
below).
e Rom. xi.
8 (Deut.
xxix. 4);
Mt. xiii.

σαν· 9. ἀλλὰ ᶜκαθὼς ᶜγέγραπται, ᵈ“ᵃᾺ ᵉὀφθαλμὸς οὐκ εἶδε καὶ ᵉοὖς οὐκ ἤκουσε καὶ ᶠἐπὶ ᶠκαρδίαν ἀνθρώπου οὐκ ᶠἀνέβη, ἃ¹ ἡτοίμασεν ὁ Θεὸς τοῖς ᵍἀγαπῶσιν ᵍαὐτόν”.

10. Ἡμῖν δὲ² ὁ Θεὸς³ ʰἀπεκάλυψε³ ⁱδιὰ τοῦ ⁱΠνεύματος αὐτοῦ⁴·

13, Acts xxviii. 27 (Is. vi. 10). f Hebraism: Acts vii. 23; Is. lxv. 17; Jer. iii. 16. With εν, Lk.
xxiv. 38. g viii. 3; Rom. viii. 28; Mt. xxii. 37 and Lk. x. 27 (Deut. vi. 5); 1 Jo. iv. 20 f., v. 2;
Lk. xi. 42; Jo. v. 42. h iii. 13, xiv. 30; Rom. i. 17; Gal. i. 16, iii. 23; Eph. iii. 5; Mt. xi. 25, xiii.
11. i Rom. v. 5, viii. 11; Eph. iii. 16; Ph. i. 19; 2 Tim. i. 14; Tit. iii. 5; Acts i. 2, xxi. 4.

¹ οσα, ABC, Clem. Rom., Cyr., Hier. α, אDGLP, etc., with many Ff.; Western and Syrian. οσα is easily corrupted into α, not *vice versâ*; and the simple relative in parl. clauses would make against οσα in copying.

² γαρ, B, 37 and seven minuscc., sah. cop., Clem., Bas., Euthal.; W.H., Tr. *mg.* δε, אACDGLP, etc., latt. vg. syrr., Or., Ath., Did., etc.; Tisch., Tr. *txt.* δε is superficially easier; γαρ intrinsically better.

³ απεκαλυψεν ο Θ.: all uncc. exc. L; all oldest verss. exc. sah.

⁴ *Om.* αυτου א*ABC. Add αυτου אᶜDGL, etc.; Western and Syrian.

---

noun being dictated by the LXX original), and thus supplying a further obj. to the emphatically repeated λαλοῦμεν of vv. 6, 7: "but (we speak), as it is written, things which eye," etc. (so Er., Mr., Hn., Al., Ed., El., Bt.). (2) Hf., Ev., after Lachmann, prefix the whole sentence to ἀπεκάλυψεν of ver. 10; but this subordination requires the doubtful reading δέ (for γάρ) in ver. 10, to which it improperly extends the ref. of the formula καθὼς γέγραπται, while it breaks the continuity between the quotation and the foregoing assertions (*cf.* i. 19, 31). (3) Bg., D.W., Gd., Lt., and others, see an anacoluthon here, and supply ἐστίν, *factum est*, or the like, as a peg for the ver. to hang upon, as in Rom. xv. 3— "But, as it is written, (there have come to pass) things which eye," etc. This, however, seems needless after the prominent λαλοῦμεν, and weakens the concatenation of vv. 6-9. The ἀλλὰ follows on the οὐδεὶς of ver. 8, as ἀλλὰ in ver. 7 (see note) on the οὐ of ver. 6. The entire sentence may be thus arranged:—

λαλοῦμεν Θεοῦ σοφίαν . . . τ. ἀποκεκρυμμένην,
 ἣν προώρισεν ὁ Θεὸς κ.τ.λ.,
 ἣν οὐδεὶς τ. ἀρχόντων . . .
 ἔγνωκεν κ.τ.λ.·
ἀλλὰ . . . ἃ ὀφθαλμὸς οὐκ εἶδεν . . .
 ὅσα ἡτοίμασεν ὁ Θεὸς τ. ἀγαπῶσιν αὐτόν.

The words cited do not appear, connectedly, in the O.T. Of the four clauses, the 1st, 2nd, and 4th recall Isai. lxiv. 4 f. (Heb., 3 f.)—after the Hebrew text; the 3rd occurs in a similar strain in Isai. lxv. 17 (LXX, 16); see other parls. In

thought, as Hf. and Bt. point out, this passage corresponds to Isai. lxiv.: in P. God does, as in Isaiah He is besought to do, things unlooked for by the world, to the confusion of its unbelief; in each case these things are done for fit persons—Isaiah's "him that waiteth for Him," etc., being translated into Paul's "those that love Him"; ἐποίησεν is changed to ἡτοίμασεν, in conformity with προώρισεν (7). A further analogy appears between the "terrible things in righteousness" which the prophet foresees in the coming theophany, and the καταργεῖν that P. announces for "the rulers of this world". Clement of Rome (*ad Cor.*, xxxiv. 8) cites the text briefly as a Christian saying, but reverts from Paul's τ. ἀγαπῶσιν to the Isaianic τ. ὑπομένουσιν αὐτόν, manifestly identifying the O. and N.T. sayings.

Or. wrote (on Matt. xxvii. 9), "In nullo regulari libro hoc positum invenitur, nisi in *Secretis Eliæ prophetæ*"—a lost Apocryphum; Jerome found the words both in the *Ascension of Isaiah* and the *Apocalypse of Elias*, but denies Paul's indebtedness to these sources; and Lt. makes out (see note, *ad loc.*) that these books were *later* than Paul. Origen's suggestion has been adopted by many expositors, but is really needless; this is only an extreme example of the Apostle's freedom in adopting and combining O.T. sayings whose substance he desires to use. The Gnostics quoted the passage in favour of their method of esoteric teaching.

ὅσα, of the last clause, is a climax to ἃ of the first—"so many things as God prepared for those that love Him": *cf.* 2 Cor. i. 20, Phil. iv. 8, for the pronomi-

τὸ γὰρ Πνεῦμα πάντα ᵏ ἐρευνᾷ,[1] καὶ τὰ [l]βάθη τοῦ Θεοῦ. 11. τίς γὰρ
οἶδεν ἀνθρώπων τὰ ᵐτοῦ ᵐἀνθρώπου, εἰ μὴ τὸ ⁿπνεῦμα ᵐτοῦ ᵐⁿἀνθρώ-
που τὸ ἐν αὐτῷ; οὕτω καὶ τὰ τοῦ Θεοῦ οὐδεὶς οἶδεν[2] εἰ μὴ τὸ Πνεῦμα

k Rom. viii.
27; 1 Pet.
i. 11; Jo.
v. 39, vii.
52; Rev.
ii. 23.
l Rom. xi. 33;

Eph. iii. 18, in this connexion; Rev. ii. 24, only other inst. of plural. *Cf.* Judith viii. 14. m With
generic art. in sing., Mt. xv. 11 ff., and in the expression ο υιος του ανθρωπου. n v. 3 f., xiv. 14;
Rom. i. 9, viii. 16, xii. 11; somewhat frequently in P. of human spirit; also Acts xvii. 16, xix. 21;
Lk. i. 47; Jo. xiii. 21.

[1] ε ρ α υ ν α, ℵAB*C. So elsewhere in N.T.

[2] ε γ ν ω κ ε ν, ℵABCDP, Euthal., Bas. (G εγνω). οιδεν, L, etc., conforming to
first clause of the verse.

nal idiom.—In ἡτοίμασεν κ.τ.λ. Paul is
not thinking so much of the heavenly
glory (see note on δόξα, 7), as of the
magnificence of blessing, undreamed of
in former ages, which comes already to
believers in Christ (*cf.* i. 5-7).—τ. ἀγαπ.
αὐτὸν affirms the moral precondition for
this full blessedness (*cf.* John xiv. 23)—a
further designation of the ἅγιοι, πιστεύοντες, κλητοί, ἐκλεκτοὶ of chap. i.

§ 8. THE REVEALING SPIRIT, ii. 10-
iii. 2. The world's rulers committed the
frightful crime of "crucifying the Lord
of glory," because in fact they have only
"the spirit of the world," whereas "the
Spirit *of God*" informs His messengers
(10-12), who communicate the things of
His grace in language taught them by
His Spirit and intelligible to the spiritual
(13-16). For the like reason the Cor.
are at fault in their Christian views, being
as yet but half-spiritual men (iii. 1-3).

Ver. 10. The true reading, ἡμῖν γάρ
(*cf.* i. 26), links this ver. to the foregoing
by way of illustration: "For to *us* (being
of those that love Him) God revealed
(them), through the Spirit": *cf.* i. 18,
viii. 3, xiii. 2, 1 John iv. 7; also ἀπεκα-
λύφθη τ. ἁγίοις ἀποστόλοις κ.τ.λ., Eph.
iii. 5, indicating the like ethical receptivity. ἀπεκάλυψεν echoes ἐν μυστηρίῳ
and τ. ἀποκεκρυμμένην (7), signifying a
supernatural disclosure (see notes on i.
7, xiv. 6); *cf.* esp. Rom. xvi. 25, κατὰ
ἀποκάλυψιν μυστηρίου, and Eph. i. 17
in connexion with vv. 6 f. above. The
tense (aor.) points to the *advent* of
Christianity, "the revelation given to
Christians as an event that began a new
epoch in the world's history" (Ed.).—
The Spirit reveals,—"for the Spirit in-
vestigates everything (πάντα ἐραυνᾷ),
even the depths of God": He discloses,
for He first *discovers*—οὐκ ἀγνοίας, ἀλλ'
ἀκριβοῦς γνώσεως τὸ ἐρευνᾶν δεικτικόν
(Cm.). The phrase describes an Intelligence everywhere active, everywhere
penetrating (*cf.* Ps. cxxxix. 1-7). For

the complementary truth concerning the
relation of Father and Spirit, see Rom.
viii. 27. The Spirit is the organ of
mutual understanding between man and
God. P. conceives of Him as internal
to the inspired man, working with and
through, though immeasurably above his
faculties (see iii. 16, Rom. viii. 16, 26,
etc.). τὰ βάθη (pl. of noun βάθος) are
those inscrutable regions, below all that
"the eye sees" and that "comes up
into the heart of a man" (9), where
God's plans for mankind are developed:
cf. Rom. xi. 33 ff., Eph. i. 9 ff., iii. 18,
and by contrast Rev. ii. 24. These deep-
laid counsels centre in Christ, and are
shared by Him (Matt. xi. 27, John v. 20,
xvii. 10, 25); so that it is one thing to
have the Spirit who "sounds the deeps
of God" and to "have the mind of
Christ" (16). The like profound insight
is claimed, in virtue of his possessing
the Holy Spirit, by the writer of the
Wisdom of Solomon (vii.), but in a ὑπεροχὴ
λόγου καὶ σοφίας that goes to discredit
the assumption; *cf.* also Sirach xlii. 18.
The attributes there assigned to the
half-personified "Wisdom," N.T. theology divides between Christ and the
Spirit in their several offices towards
man. The "Spirit" is apprehended in
Wisdom under physical rather than, as
by Paul, under psychological analogies.

Ver. 11. "For amongst men, who
knows (οἶδεν) the things of the man,
except the spirit of the man that is
within him? So also the things of God
none has perceived (ἔγνωκεν), except the
Spirit of God." Far from being otiose,
ἀνθρώπων is emphatic: P. argues from
human to Divine personality; each heart
of man has its secrets (τὰ τοῦ ἀνθρώπου);
"nor even the dearest soul, and next our
own, knows half the reasons why we
smile or sigh"; there is a corresponding
region of inner personal consciousness
with *God* (τὰ τοῦ Θεοῦ). As the man's
own spirit lifts the veil and lights the

o Rom. viii.
15; Acts
viii. 15 ff.,
x. 47, xix.
2; Jo. xx.
22; cf. 2
Tim. i. 7.

τοῦ Θεοῦ. 12. ἡμεῖς δὲ οὐ τὸ °πνεῦμα τοῦ κόσμου °ἐλάβομεν, ἀλλὰ τὸ ᵖΠνεῦμα τὸ ᵖἐκ τοῦ ᵖΘεοῦ, ἵνα εἰδῶμεν τὰ ὑπὸ τοῦ Θεοῦ ᑫχαρισθέντα ἡμῖν· 13. ἃ καὶ λαλοῦμεν, οὐκ ἐν ʳδιδακτοῖς ˢἀνθρωπίνης σοφίας λόγοις, ἀλλ᾽ ἐν ʳδιδακτοῖς ᵗΠνεύματος Ἁγίου,¹ ᵘπνευ-

το πν. του
κοσμου,
h.l.; cf. Eph. ii. 2.   p Rev. xi. 11; απο in same connexion, vi. 19; παρα, Jo. xv. 26.   q Passive,
Ph. i. 29; Phm. 22; Acts iii. 14; cf. Rom. viii. 32; Gal. iii. 18; Ph. ii. 9; Acts xxvii. 24.   r Jo.
vi. 45 (Isa. liv. 13); cf. 1 Th. iv. 9.   s iv. 3, x. 13; Rom. vi. 19; Jas. iii. 7; 1 Pet. ii. 13; Num. v. 6.
t See ver. 4.   u iii. 1, xiv. 37; Gal. iv. 1.

¹ Om. αγιον all uncc. but DcLP.   The insertion is a Syrian emendation.

recesses penetrable by no reasoning from without, so God's Spirit must communicate His thoughts,—or we shall never know them. This reserve belongs to the rights of self-hood. Paul's axiomatic saying assumes the personality of God, and man's affinity to God grounded therein. P. does not in this analogy limit the Ἅγιον Πνεῦμα by human conditions, nor reduce Him to a mere Divine self-consciousness (τὸ ἐκ τοῦ Θεοῦ, 12, guards us against this); the argument is *a minori ad majus* (as in Gal. iii. 15, Rom. v. 7, Luke xi. 13), and valid for the point in question. The Ap. ascribes to a man a natural πνεῦμα (cf. v. 5, 1 Thess. v. 23), which manifests itself in νοῦς and συνείδησις (Rom. ii. 15, vii. 25, etc.; see Cr. on these terms), akin to and receptive of the Πνεῦμα Θεοῦ; but not till quickened by the latter is the πνεῦμα ἀνθρώπου regnant in him, so that the man can be called πνευματικός (see note on 15).—On οἶδεν, as diff. from ἔγνωκεν, see note to ver. 8: "while οἶδα is simple and absolute, γινώσκω is relative, involving more or less the idea of a process of examination" (Lt.): "no one *has got to know* τὰ τοῦ Θεοῦ"—has by *searching* (10) found Him out (Job xi. 7, xxiii. 9, etc.; John xvii. 25)—only His own Spirit *knows*, and therefore reveals Him.

Ver. 12. ἡμεῖς δέ, "But *we*": cf. the emphatic ἡμῖν of ver. 10 (see note), and the ἡμεῖς δὲ of i. 23, standing in contrast with the σοφοὶ and δυνατοὶ of the world. The κόσμος whose "spirit" the App. "did *not* receive," is that whose "wisdom God has reduced to folly" (i. 20 f.), whose "rulers crucified the Lord" (8); its spirit is broadly conceived as the power animating the world in its antipathy to God (cf. 2 Cor. iv. 4, Eph. ii. 2, John xii. 31, etc., 1 John iv. 1-6). Others (Est., Cv., Bz., Hn., Sm.) read the phrase in a more abstract —perhaps too modern—sense, "sapientia mundana et sæcularis," or "the world-consciousness" (Hf.), or "l'esprit

de l'humanité . . . ce que les Païens appellent *la muse* et qui se concentre dans les génies" (Gd.). — "(Not the spirit of the world we received), but the Spirit which is from (issues from: ἐκ, antitheton ἐν, Bg.) God" (compare ὡς ἐκ Θεοῦ, 2 Cor. ii. 17); the phrase recalls the teaching of Jesus in John xiv. 26, xv. 26; see also Rom. v. 5, Gal. iv. 6. "The spirit of the world" breathes in men who are a part of the world; "the Spirit that is from God" visits us from another sphere, bringing knowledge of things removed from natural apprehension (see Isa. lv. 9). ἐλάβομεν implies actual, objective receiving (*taking*), as in iii. 8, xi. 23, etc.—ἵνα εἰδῶμεν κ.τ.λ. (see note on οἶδα, 11; and cf. the emphatic οἶδα of 2 Cor. v. 1, 2 Tim. i. 12) —a bold word here—"that we may *know* (*certo scire*, Cv.) the things that by God were bestowed in His grace upon us". τὰ χαρισθέντα, aor. ptp., points to the historic gifts of God to men in Christ, which would have been idle boons without the Spirit enabling us to "know" them: cf. Eph. i. 17 ff., ἵνα δώῃ . . . πνεῦμα . . . εἰς τ. εἰδέναι. χαρίζομαι (*to deal in* χάρις: see note on χάρισμα, i. 7), *to grant by way of grace, in unmerited favour* (cf. esp. Rom. viii. 32, Gal. iii. 18).

Ver. 13. ἃ καὶ λαλοῦμεν—the vb. of 6, 7 (see note): there opposed to μυστήριον, here to εἰδῶμεν (cf. John iii. 11)—"which things indeed we speak out"; knowing these great things of God, we *tell* them (cf. John xviii. 20; also 2 Cor. iv. 2 ff., Luke xii. 2 f., Acts xxvi. 16). P. has no esoteric doctrines, to be whispered to a select circle; if the τέλειοι and πνευματικοὶ alone comprehend his Gospel, that is not due to reserve on his part. "The καὶ λαλοῦμεν makes it clear that P. does not mean (in 6 and iii. 1 f.) to distinguish two sorts of Gospel; his preaching has always the entire truth for its content, but expressed suitably to the growth of his hearers" (Hn.).

ματικοῖς [1] ᵛπνευματικὰ ᵂσυγκρίνοντες. 14. ˣψυχικὸς δὲ ἄνθρωπος ᵛ ix. 11, x. 3
οὐ ᵞδέχεται τὰ τοῦ Πνεύματος τοῦ Θεοῦ · ᶻμωρία γὰρ αὐτῷ ἐστι, f., xiv.1 ff.;
Rom.i. 11,
vii. 14, xv.
27; Eph.

i. 3, v. 19, vi. 12; Col. i. 9, iii. 16; 1 Pet. ii. 5. w 2 Cor. x. 12; see note below. x xv. 44, 46;
Jas. iii. 15; Jude 19; four times in Lk. and Acts in this sense. y Thrice in 2 Cor., and in 1
and 2 Th. z See i. 18.

[1] πνευματικῶς : B, 17; so W.H. *mg.* A good binary group.

The *mode of utterance* agrees with
the character of the revealing Spirit:
οὐκ ἐν διδακτοῖς ἀνθρωπίνης σοφίας
λόγοις, ἀλλ' ἐν διδακτοῖς κ.τ.λ. " (which
things we speak out), not in human-
wisdom-taught words, but in (words)
Spirit-taught" — *verba rem sequuntur*
(Wetstein). The opposed gens. depend
on διδακτοῖς, denoting *agent* with vbl.
adj.—a construction somewhat rare, but
cl. (so in John vi. 45, Isa. liv. 13 ; diff. in
1 Macc. iv. 7, διδακτοὶ πολέμου) ; they
are anarthrous, signifying opposite *kinds*
of wisdom.—διδακτὸς in earlier Gr.
meant *what can or ought to be taught;*
later, *what is taught* (*cf.* γνωστός, Rom.
i. 19). Paul affirms that his *words* in
matters of revelation, as well as thoughts,
were taught him by the Spirit; he
claims, in some sense, verbal inspiration. In an honest mind thought and
language are one, and whatever determines the former must mould the latter.
Cor. critics complained both of the imperfection of Paul's dialect (2 Cor. x. 10:
see 1 above) and of the poverty of his
ideas; here is his rejoinder. We arrive
thus at the explanation of the obscure
clause, πνευματικοῖς πνευματικὰ συγ-
κρίνοντες,—*combining spiritual things
with spiritual,* wedding kindred speech
to thought (for the ptp. qualifies λαλοῦμεν) : so Er., Cv., Bz., D.W., Mr., Hn.,
Lt., El., Bt. ; "with spiritual phrase
matching spiritual truth" (Ev.). Ver.
13 asserts the correspondence of Apostolic *utterance and thought;* in ver. 14
P. passes to the correspondence of *men
and things.* Other meanings are found
for συγκρίνω, and πνευματικοῖς may be
masc. as well as neut. ; thus the following variant renderings are deduced : (1)
comparing sp. things with *sp.* (Vg., E.V.,
Ed.)—forming them into a correlated
system ; (2) *interpreting,* or *proving, sp.
things by sp.*—sc. O.T. types by N.T.
fulfilments (Cm. and Ff.); (3) *adapting,*
or *appropriating, sp. things to sp. men*
(Est., Olshausen, Gd.), with some strain
upon the vb. ; (4) *interpreting sp. things
to sp. men* (Bg., Rückert, Hf., Stanley,
Al., Sm.). The last explanation is
plausible, in view of the sequel; but it

misses the real point of ver. 13, and is
not clearly supported by the usage of
συνκρίνω, which "means properly to
combine, as διακρίνω to separate" (Lt.).
Ver. 14. With the App. all is *spiritual*
—words and thoughts; for this very
reason men of the world reject their
teaching : "But a natural man does not
accept the things of the Spirit of God"
(*cf.* Rom. viii. 5 ; John xv. 18-21, 1 John
iv. 5).—Of the vbs. for *receiving,* λαμβάνω
(12) regards the object, δέχομαι the
manner and spirit of the act—*to welcome*
(see parls.) ; there is *no receptivity*—
"non vult admittere" (Bg.). Ψυχικός,
in all N.T. instances, has a disparaging
sense, being opposed to πνευματικός (as
ψυχή is not to πνεῦμα), and almost syn.
with σάρκινος or σαρκικός (iii. 1 f.).
The term is in effect *privative*—ὁ μόνην
τ. ἔμφυτον καὶ ἀνθρωπίνην σύνεσιν ἔχων
(Cm.), "quemlibet hominem solis naturæ
facultatibus præditum" (Cv.),—positive
evil being implied by consequence.
Adam's body was ψυχικόν, as not yet
charged, like that of Christ, with the
Divine πνεῦμα (xv. 44-49: syn. with
χοϊκός, and contrasted with ἐπουράνιος).
"The word was coined by Aristotle
(*Eth. Nic.,* III., x., 2) to distinguish the
pleasures of the soul, such as ambition
and desire for knowledge, from those of
the body (ἡδοναὶ σωματικαί)." "Similarly Polybius, and Plutarch (*de Plac.
Phil.,* i., 9 : ψυχικαὶ χαραί, σωματικαὶ
ἡδοναί). "Contrasted with the ἀκρατής,
the ψυχικὸς is the noblest of men. But
to the πνευματικὸς he is related as the
natural to the supernatural" (Ed. : see
Cr., *s. v.*). This epithet, therefore, describes to the Cor. the unregenerate
nature *at its best,* the man commended
in philosophy, actuated by the higher
thoughts and aims of the natural life—
not the sensual man (the *animalis* of the
Vg.), who is ruled by bodily impulse.
Yet the ψυχικός, μὴ ἔχων πνεῦμα (Jude
19), may be lower than the σαρκικός,
where the latter, as in iii. 3 and Gal. v.
17, 25, is already touched but not fully
assimilated by the life-giving Πνεῦμα.—
μωρία γὰρ αὐτῷ κ.τ.λ., rendered by
Krenkel (*Beiträge,* pp. 379 ff.), "For

a Rev. xi. 8.
b iv. 3 f., ix.
3, x. 25,27,
xiv. 24;
Lk. xxiii.
14, and
five times
in Acts.   c Is. xl. 13; Rom. xi. 34; *cf.* Wisd. ix. 13.   d Eph. iv. 16; Col. ii. 2, 19; Acts ix. 22, xvi. 10, xix. 33.

καὶ οὐ δύναται γνῶναι, ὅτι ^aπνευματικῶς ^bἀνακρίνεται· 15.¹ ὁ δὲ ^uπνευματικὸς ^bἀνακρίνει μὲν ² πάντα,³ αὐτὸς δὲ ὑπ' οὐδενὸς ^bἀνακρίνεται.   16. ^cτίς γὰρ ἔγνω νοῦν Κυρίου, ὃς ^dσυμβιβάσει αὐτόν;

¹ Ver. 15 om^d in ℵ* and harl.*, by *homoeoteleuton*, ἀνακρινεται being repeated in vv. 14 and 15 (*cf.* txtl. note on i. 27).

² Om. μεν ACDG; ℵaBLP, etc., insert it. The foregoing δε would condemn it with stylists.

³ τα παντα: ACD*P, 17; W.H. *mg.* (bracketed). παντα, ℵaBGL, etc. The chief copies that omit μεν, substitute for it τα before παντα.

folly belongs (cleaves) to him, and he cannot perceive that he is spiritually searched" (*cf.* xiv. 24 ff., ἀνακρίνεται)—an ingenious and grammatically possible translation, but not consistent with the emphatic ref. of μωρία in ch. i. to *the world's judgment on the Gospel*, nor with the fact that "the things of God" (σοφία Θεοῦ, πνευματικά) are the all-commanding topic of this paragraph. We adhere therefore to the common rendering: "For to him they are folly; and he cannot perceive (them), for (it is) spiritually (that) they are tried"—and he is unspiritual. For γνῶναι, see note on ἔγνωκεν (8).—Ἀνακρίνω must be distinguished from κρίνω, *to judge, deliver a verdict;* and from διακρίνω, *to discern, distinguish* diff. things; it signifies *to examine, inquire into*, being syn. on the one side with ἐραυνάω of ver. 10, and on the other with δοκιμάζω of 1 Thess. v. 21 (see parls.; also Lt. *ad loc.*, and in his *Fresh Revision*³, pp. 69 ff.): "ἀνάκρισις was an Athenian law-term for a preliminary investigation—corresponding *mutatis mutandis* to the part taken in English law-proceedings by the Grand Jury" (*cf.* Acts xxv. 26). The Gospel appears on its trial before the ψυχικοί; like the Athenian philosophers, they give it a first hearing, but they have no organon to test it by. The inquiry is stultified, *ab initio*, by the incompetence of the jury. The unspiritual are out of court as religious critics; they are deaf men judging music.

Ver. 15. "But the spiritual man tries (tests) everything"—a maxim resembling, perhaps designedly, the Stoic dicta concerning "the wise man". Paul sees "in the Πνεῦμα, the Divine power creatively working in the man and imparted to him, the κριτήριον for the right estimate of persons and things, Divine and human. The Stoa on its part was intently con-

cerned 'to know the standard according to which man is judged by man' (Arrian-Epictetus, II., xiii., 16) . . . it found this criterion in *the moral use of Reason*. . . . The Christian believer and the Stoic philosopher both practise an ἀνακρίνειν; both are conscious of standing superior to all judgment from without; but the ground of this superiority, and the inferences drawn from it, are equally opposed in the two cases. The Stoic's judgment on the world leads him, under given conditions, to suicide ('The door stands open,' Epict.): the Christian's judgment on the world leads to the realisation of the victory of the children of God" (Hn.).—πάντα (not *every one*, but neut. pl.) is quite general—*everything; cf.*, for the scope of this faculty, vi. 2 f., x. 15, 1 Thess. v. 21, 1 John ii. 20 f., iv. 1, Rev. ii. 2. Aristotle (*Eth. Nic.*, III., iv.) says of ὁ σπουδαῖος (the man of character), ἕκαστα κρίνει ὀρθῶς, καὶ ἐν ἑκάστοις τἀληθὲς αὐτῷ φαίνεται . . . ὥσπερ κανὼν καὶ μέτρον αὐτῶν ὤν; Plato, *De Rep.*, iii., 409 D (quoted by Ed.), ascribes the same universally critical power to ἡ ἀρετή. Paul's πνευματικὸς judges in virtue of a Divine, all-searching Presence within him; Aristotle's σπουδαῖος, in virtue of his personal qualities and attainments. Paul admirably displays in this Ep. the powers of the πνευματικὸς as ὁ ἀνακρίνων πάντα. There are, of course, limits to the exercise of the ἀνακρίνειν, in the position and opportunities of the individual.

αὐτὸς δὲ ὑπ' οὐδένος ἀνακρίνεται, "while he himself is put on trial by none,"—since none other possesses the probe of truth furnished by the Πνεῦμα τὸ ἐκ τοῦ Θεοῦ; the πνευματικὸς stands on a height from which he overlooks the world, and is overlooked only by God. The statement is ideal, holding good of "the spiritual man" as, and so far as, he

ἡμεῖς δὲ νοῦν Χριστοῦ[1] ἔχομεν. III. 1. Καὶ[2] ἐγώ,[2] ἀδελφοί, οὐκ ᵃ σαρκί-
ἠδυνήθην λαλῆσαι ὑμῖν ὡς ᵘ πνευματικοῖς, ἀλλ᾽ ὡς ᵃσαρκικοῖς,[3] ὡς

ᵃ σαρκί-
νοις, 2
Cor. iii. 3;
Rom. vii.
14; Heb.
vii. 16; in LXX, 2 Chr. xxxii. 8; Ezek. xi. 19, xxxvi. 26

---

[1] κυριου, BD*G (an untrustworthy group): conformed to parl. sentence.

[2] καγω: all uncc. but the Syrian L.

[3] σαρκινοις, אBC*D*, 17, 67**.　　σαρκικοις, DᶜGLP; late Western and
Syrian. Cf. Rom. vii. 14, Heb. vii. 16.

---

is such. Where a Christian is σάρκινος (iii. 1), his spiritual judgment is vitiated; to that extent he puts himself within the measure of the ψυχικός (cf. 1 John iii. 1, iv. 5). If μέν, after ἀνακρίνει, be genuine, it throws into stronger relief the superiority of the man of the Spirit to unspiritual judgment: he holds the touchstone and is the world's trier, not the world his. This exemption P. will claim for himself, on further grounds, in iv. 3 ff.—Ἀνακρίνω, used by P. nine times in this Ep., and in no other, was probably a favourite expression with the overweening Cor.—like "criticism" to-day. Ver. 16. Of the three clauses of Isa. xl. 13, P. adopts in Rom. xi. 34 the 1st and 2nd, here the 1st and 3rd; in both instances from the LXX (which renders the Heb. freely), in both instances without the καθὼς γέγραπται of formal quotation.—ὃς συνβιβάσει αὐτόν (qui instructurus sit eum, Bz.: on the rel. pron. with fut. ind. of contemplated result, see Krüger's Gr. Sprachl., I., § 53, 7, Anm. 8; Bn., § 318) indicates the Divine superiority to creaturely correction, which justifies the enormous claim of ver. 15b. —Συνβιβάζω means (1) to bring together, combine (Col. ii. 2, etc.); (2) to compare, gather, prove by putting things together (Acts xvi. 10); (3) widened in later Gr. to the sense to teach, instruct. The prophet pointed in evidence of God's incomparable wisdom and power to the vastness of creation, wherein lie unimaginable resources for Israel's redemption, that forbid despair. Here too the νοῦς in question is God's infinite wisdom, directing man's salvation through inscrutable ways (6-9); but the Apostle's contention is that this "mind" inspires the organs of revelation (10 ff.), and its superiority to the judgment of the world is relatively also theirs (14 ff.). Paul translates the νοῦν Κυρίου of Isaiah into his own νοῦν Χριστοῦ; to him these minds are identical (cf. Matt. xi. 27, John v. 20, etc.). Such interchanges betray his "innermost conviction of the Godhead of Christ"

(El.).—νοῦς serves his turn better than the literal πνεῦμα of the original (ruach); the intellectual side of the πνεῦμα is concerned, the θεῖον ὄμμα (see note on νοῦς, i. 10). For the emphatic ἡμεῖς, cf. vv. 10, 12, and notes; for the anarthrous nouns, note on ver. 4; νοῦν X. is quasi-predicative—"it is Christ's mind—no other—that we have".—ἔχομεν is not to be softened into perspectam habemus, novimus (Gr.): Christ lives and thinks in the πνευματικός (vi. 17, 2 Cor. xiii. 3 ff., etc.; John xv. 1-8); the unio mystica is the heart of Paul's experience.

CHAPTER III.—Ver. 1. Κἀγώ, ἀδελφοί: The Ap. returns to the strain of ii. 1-5, speaking now not in general terms of ἡμεῖς, οἱ τέλειοι, etc.; but definitely of the Cor. and himself. They demonstrate, unhappily, the incapacity of the unspiritual for spiritual things. The καὶ carries us back to ii. 14: "A natural man does not receive the things of God . . ., and I (accordingly) could not utter (them) to you as to spiritual (men), but as to men of flesh". Yet the Cor. were not ψυχικοί (see note, ii. 14). For λαλῆσαι, see ii. 6; and on the receptivity of the πνευματικός, ii. 13 ff. Cf. Rom. viii. 5-9: οἱ κατὰ πνεῦμα ὄντες τὰ τοῦ Πνεύματος φρονοῦσιν.—(οὐκ . . . ὡς πνευματικοῖς), ἀλλ᾽ ὡς σαρκίνοις: "on the contrary, (I was obliged to speak to you) as to men of flesh"—grammatical zeugma, as well as breviloquence: the affirmative "I was able," carried over from the negative clause οὐκ ἠδυνήθην, passes into the kindred "I was obliged," that is necessarily understood (cf. Eph. iv. 29); ver. 7, vii. 19, x. 24, are similarly expressed, without the zeugma.—Σάρκινος (see parls.) differs from σαρκικός (3, ix. 11, etc.) as carneus from carnalis, fleischern from fleischlich (as leathern from leathery) —ινος implying nature and constitution (ἐν σαρκὶ εἶναι), -ικὸς tendency or character (κατὰ σάρκα εἶναι). So σάρκινος is associated with νηπιότης, σαρκικὸς with ζῆλος καὶ ἔρις: see Trench, Syn., § lxx. The distinction

b xiii. 11,   ᵇνηπίοις ἐν Χριστῷ·   2. ᶜγάλα ὑμᾶς ᵈἐπότισα, καὶ¹ οὐ ᵉβρῶμα·
xiv. 20
(νηπιαζω); οὔπω γὰρ ἠδύνασθε.²
Rom. ii.
20; Gal.   3. ᶠ᾽Αλλ᾽ ᶠοὔτε³ ἔτι⁴ νῦν δύνασθε, ἔτι γὰρ ᵍσαρκικοί⁵ ἐστε·
iv. 1, 3;
Eph. iv.   ʰὅπου γὰρ ἐν ὑμῖν ⁱζῆλος καὶ ⁱἔρις καὶ⁶ διχοστασίαι,⁶ οὐχὶ ⁱσαρκι-
14; 1 Th.
ii. 7; Heb.
v. 13; Mt. xi. 25, xxi. 16; Lk. x. 21; Ps. xviii. 8.   c ix. 7; Heb. v. 12 f.; 1 Pet. ii. 2.   d xii. 13,
Rom. xii. 20; Rev. xiv. 8; Mt. x. 42.   e In sing., viii. 8, 13, x. 3; Rom. xiv. 15, 20; Jo. iv. 34.
f (αλλ᾽ ουδε), iv. 3; 2 Cor. vii. 12; Gal. ii. 3; Acts xix. 2; Lk. xxiii. 15.   g In this sense, 2 Cor. i.
12, x. 4; 1 Pet. ii. 11.   h In the like sense, Col. iii. 11; Heb. ix. 16, x. 18; Ja. iii. 16; 2 Pet. ii. 11.
i Rom. xiii. 13; 2 Cor. xii. 20; Gal. v. 20; Sir. xl. 5. ζηλος alone, in this use, Acts v. 17, xiii. 45; Ja.
iii. 14, 16. ερις, see i. 11.

¹ Om. καὶ ℵABGP, 17, vg. syr. cop. Ins. καὶ DGL, etc.: Western interpolation.
² εδυνασθε: all uncc. but DL. Yet all but C have ηδυνηθην in ver. 1.
³ ουδε: all uncc. but L.   ⁴ B om. ετι, bracketed by Lachm. and W.H.
⁵ D*G read σαρκινοι (twice), in conformity with ver. 1; G reads, perversely,
σαρκικοις there: instances of Western license.
⁶ Om. καὶ διχοστασιαι all uncc. but DGL. Harmonistic importation from
Gal. v. 20.

is one of standpoint, not of degree: in
the σάρκινος the original "flesh" remains (a sort of excuse, as in Rom. vii.
14); the σαρκικὸς manifests its disposition. Both words may, or may not (ix.
11, 2 Cor. iii. 3), connote the sinful, according to the σὰρξ in question.

The apposed ὡς νηπίοις ἐν Χριστῷ
softens, almost tenderly, the censure: the
Cor. are "in Christ"; they possess, in
a measure, His Spirit; but they are
"babes in Christ," not fairly grown out
of "the flesh" (cf. Gal. v. 13-18); the
new nature in them is still confronted
with the old. The νήπιοι are the opp.
of the τέλειοι (ii. 6; see other parls.).
"I could not" suggests that Paul had
attempted to carry his Cor. converts
further, but had failed.

Ver. 2. "(Since you were babes), I
gave you milk to drink, not meat:" a
common figure for the simpler and more
solid forms of instruction contrasted (see
parls.). The teaching of 1 Thess. (see ii.
7 f.) is γάλα as compared with the
βρῶμα of Rom. or Coloss.; so the Synoptics, in comparison with the Fourth
Gospel. The zeugma ἐπότισα . . .
βρῶμα is natural in Paul's conversational
style; see ix. 7, per contra.—οὔπω γὰρ
ἐδύνασθε: "for not yet (while I was
with you) were you equal to it". This
absolute use of δύναμαι (= δυνατός εἰμι)
is cl., but h.l. for the N.T.; the tense
impf., of continued state.

§ 9. God's Rights in the Church,
iii. 3-9. One idea runs through this
chapter and into the next,—that of God's
Church, God's temple at Corinth, in whose
construction so many various builders

are engaged (5-17). For this building's
sake, and because it is His, God beats
down the pride of human craft, making
all things, persons, times, serve His
people, while they serve Christ, as Christ
serves God (18-23). To God His servants are responsible; it is His to judge
and commend them (iv. 1-5). Thus the
thought that the Gospel is "God's power,
God's wisdom," pursued since i. 18, is
brought to bear upon the situation in
Corinth. God who sends the message of
the cross, admitting in its communication no mixture of human wisdom (ch. i.),
chose and inspired His own instruments
for its impartation (ch. ii.). What presumption in the Cor. parties to appropriate the diff. Christian leaders, and
inscribe their names upon rival banners!

Ver. 3. ᾽Αλλ᾽ οὐδὲ ἔτι νῦν δύνασθε:
"Nay, but not even yet (after this further
interval), at the present time, are you
strong enough (immo ne nunc quidem
adhuc potestis, Bz.), for you are yet
carnal". For ἔτι, cf. xv. 17, Gal. i. 10,
v. 11; for σαρκικοί, see note on σάρκινοι
(1). The Cor. are weak (otherwise than
in x. 28) just where they think themselves
strong (viii. 1), viz., in spiritual apprehension; their gifts of "word and knowledge" are a source of weakness, through
the conceit and strife they engender.
The ἀλλ᾽ οὐδὲ clause, with its strong
disjunctives, is better joined to ver. 3 (Al.,
W.H., Sm.) than to ver. 2. The foregoing
οὔπω γὰρ ἐδύνασθε sufficiently explained
the οὐκ ἠδυνήθην of Paul's previous ministry (1); οὐδὲ ἔτι νῦν δύνασθε describes the
present condition of the Cor. (3 f.). It is
reluctantly and with misgiving that the

κοί¹ ἐστε καὶ ᵏ¹κατὰ ¹ἄνθρωπον ᵏπεριπατεῖτε; 4. ὅταν γὰρ λέγῃ   ᵏ 2 Cor. x. 2
ᵐ τις, "Ἐγὼ μέν εἰμι ⁿΠαύλου," ᵐἕτερος δέ, "Ἐγὼ ⁿ᾿Απολλώ,"   f.; Rom.
vi. 4, viii.
οὐχὶ² °σαρκικοί³ ἐστε;   5. τίς⁴ οὖν ἐστι Παῦλος,⁵ τίς⁴ δὲ⁶   4, xiv. 15;
Eph. ii. 2;
᾿Απολλώς,⁵ ἀλλ᾿ ἢ⁷ ᵖδιάκονοι δι᾿ ὧν ᑫἐπιστεύσατε, καὶ ἑκάστῳ   2 Jo. 6.
i ix. 8, xv.
32; Gal. i.
11, iii. 15;

Rom. iii. 5, vii. 22.   m Lk. ix. 57, 59, 61; xi. 15 f.   n See i. 12.   o ανθρωποι, ver. 21, i. 25,
etc.; frequent in P. in such disparaging use; Heb. vii. 28; Acts xiv. 11; Jo. iii. 19; Mt. x. 17, xv.
9 (Isa. xxix. 13); Gen. vi. 5 f.; Isa. ii. 22, etc.   p In this sense, 2 Cor. iii. 6, vi. 4, xi. 15, 23; Eph.
iii. 7; Col. i. 7, 23, 25; 1 Tim. iv. 6.   q See i. 21; also, in absolute use, 2 Cor. iv. 13; Acts viii.
13, xiii. 12, 48, xiv. 1, xv. 7, xvii. 12, 34, xviii. 8.

¹ D*G read σαρκινοι (twice), in conformity with ver. 1; G reads, perversely, σαρκικοις there: instances of Western license.

² ου κ (before ανθρ.), ℵ*ABC, 17. ουχι, DLP; Western and Syrian: parl. to ver. 3.

³ ανθρωποι: all uncc. but ℵᶜLP (Syrian) with syrᵘᵗʳ·, which carry over σαρκικοι from ver. 3.

⁴ τι (twice), ℵ*AB, 17, latt. vg. æth., Lat. Ff. τις, CDGLP, syrᵘᵗʳ· cop., Chr., etc.; seemingly a Western emendation, but not followed by Lat. cdd.

⁵ Απολλως . . . Παυλος, in this order, all uncc. but DbL, which are followed by the bulk of minuscc. and syrᵘᵗʳ·, reversing the order to guard P.'s dignity.

⁶ τι δε εστιν: ℵABCP, 17. Western and Syrian txts. om. εστιν.

⁷ All uncc., but DbᶜLP, om. αλλ᾿ η,—a Syrian insertion.

Apostle later in the Ep. enters into deep doctrine (βρῶμα, cf. note on ii. 6).—ὅπου γὰρ ἐν ὑμῖν κ.τ.λ., "for where (not when, nor whereas—Vg. cum, Mr. quandoquidem) amongst you there is jealousy and strife": this seems to limit the censure (cf. xv. 12, 34); the use of party-names was universal (i. 12), but not due in all cases to ζῆλος καὶ ἔρις. Otherwise the ὅπου clause must be read as a general principle applied to the Cor. = ὅπου γὰρ ζῆλος καὶ ἔρις, ὡς ἐν ὑμῖν—a construction inconsistent with the position of ἐν ὑμῖν. So far as these evils exist, the readers are σαρκικοί, not πνευματικοί. For ἔρις, see note to i. 11; ζῆλος is the emulation, then envy, which is a chief cause of ἔρις. These are companion "works of the flesh" in Gal. v. 20: for the honourable sense of ζῆλος, prevailing in cl. Gr., see 2 Cor. vii. 7, etc.; also Trench, Syn., § xxvi.; zealous and jealous reproduce the diff.

Paul seems to hear the Cor. denying the allegation made in 3a, Ἔτι σαρκικοί ἐστε, and so puts it to them again as a question prefaced by the reason (and limitation), ὅπου ἐν ὑμῖν ζῆλος, κ.τ.λ., and with the further challenge, οὐχὶ . . . καὶ κατὰ ἄνθρωπον περιπατεῖτε; To "walk according to man" (non secundum Deum, humano more, Bg.) is to behave as men are apt to do—the σάρκινοι, the ψυχικοί. This Pauline phrase (confined to the epp. of this group) has κατὰ Θεόν for its tacit anti-

thesis (cf. 4b); Mr.-Hn. quote the parl. καθ᾿ υἱοὺς τ. ἀνθρώπων εἶναι, Sir. xxxvi. 28 (Vg. 25; E.V. 23); also Soph., Ajax, 747, 764, κατ᾿ ἄνθρωπον φρονεῖν.

Ver. 4 is parl. to ver. 3. The protasis, ὅταν γὰρ κ.τ.λ., restates in concreto the charge made in ὅπου γὰρ κ.τ.λ.; while the interr. apodosis, οὐκ ἄνθρωποί ἐστε; gathers into a word the reproach of the foregoing οὐχὶ σαρκικοί ἐστε κ.τ.λ.: where and when the Cor. act in the manner stated, they justify P. in treating them as "carnal". To say "Are you not men?" is at once to accuse and to excuse: see parls.; also 'adâm (mere man) as distinguished from 'îsh (Isa. ii. 9, etc.); cf. Xenoph., Anab., vi., 1. 26, Ἐγώ, ὦ ἄνδρες, ἥδομαι μὲν ὑπὸ ὑμῶν τιμώμενος, εἴπερ ἄνθρωπός εἰμι; Cyrop., vii., 2. 4; and the familiar saying, Humanum est errare.—ὅταν γὰρ λέγῃ τις: "For whenever any one says" (pr. sbj. of recurring contingency); every such utterance shows you to be men. On Ἐγὼ . . . Παύλου, see note to i. 12. The Ap. refers to the Pauline and Apollonian parties only: (1) Because they suffice, by way of example, to make good his point; (2) the main cause of strife, viz., the craving for λόγος σοφίας, lay between these two parties; (3) P. avoided bringing Cephas' name into controversy, while he deals freely with that of his friend and disciple, Apollos, now with him (xvi. 12).

Ver. 5. The Cor. Christians were

r Mt. xv. 13, ὡς ὁ Κύριος ἔδωκεν; 6. ἐγὼ ʳ ἐφύτευσα, Ἀπολλὼς ᵈ ἐπότισεν, ἀλλ᾽
figura-
tively as ὁ Θεὸς ˢ ηὔξανεν· 7. ὥστε οὔτε ὁ ʳ φυτεύων ἐστί τι οὔτε ὁ ᵈ ποτίζων,
here. See
ix. 7.   ἀλλ᾽ ὁ ˢ αὐξάνων Θεός. 8. ὁ ʳ φυτεύων δὲ καὶ ὁ ᵈ ποτίζων ᵗ ἕν εἰσιν·
s Transi-
tively, 2 ἕκαστος δὲ τὸν ᵘ ἴδιον ᵛ μισθὸν λήψεται κατὰ τὸν ᵘ ἴδιον ʷ κόπον.
Cor. ix.
10 only;
see also 2 Cor. x. 15; Eph. ii. 21; Col. i. 10, ii. 19; Acts vi. 7, xii. 24, xix. 20.   t Neut., in this
collective sense, xii. 12; Eph. ii. 14; Jo. x. 30, xvii. 11, 21 ff.   u vii. 7, xv. 23, 38; Gal. vi. 5, 9;
Rom. viii. 32, x. 3; Lk. vi. 44; Jo. i. 11, v. 18, viii. 44, xiii. 1.   v ix. 17 f.; Rom. iv. 41; 1 Tim.
v. 18; 2 Jo. 8; Mt. v. 12, 46, vi. 1 ff.; x. 41 f., xx. 8; Mk. ix. 41; Jo. iv. 36.   w xv. 58, and eight
times in P.; Jo. iv. 38; Rev. ii. 2, xiv. 13.

quarrelling *over the claims of their teachers*, as though the Church were the creature of men: "What therefore (I am compelled to ask) is Apollos? what, on the other side (δέ), is Paul?" —τί is more emphatic than τίς; it breathes *disdain*; "as though Apollos or Paul were anything!" (Lt.). *Apollos* precedes, in continuation of ver. 4. For *both*, the question is answered in one word—διάκονοι, "non autores fidei vestræ, sed ministri duntaxat" (Er.); *cf.* 2 Cor. i. 24, iv. 5.: ὁ Κύριος in the next clause is its antithesis. Paul calls himself διάκονος in view of specific service rendered (2 Cor. iii. 6, vi. 4, etc.), but δοῦλος in his personal relation to Christ (Gal. i. 10, etc.). "Through whose ministration you believed:" *per quos, non in quos* (Bg.: *cf.* i. 15). To "believe" is the decisive act which makes a Christian (see i. 21); for the relation of saving faith to the Apostolic testimony, *cf.* xv. 1-11; 2 Cor. i. 18-22, etc. Some Cor. had been converted through Apollos.

The above-named are servants, each with his specific gift: καὶ ἑκάστῳ ὡς ὁ Κύρ. κ.τ.λ., "and in each case, (servants in such sort) as the Lord bestowed (on him)".— ἑκάστῳ is emphatically projected before the ὡς; *cf.* vii. 17, Rom. xii. 3. The various disposition of Divine gifts in and for the Church is the topic of ch. xii. "The Lord" is surely Christ, as regularly in Paul's dialect, "through whom are all things" (viii. 6, xii. 5; Eph. iv. 7-12, etc.)—the sovereign Dispenser in the House of God; from "Jesus our Lord" (ix. 1) P. received his own commission; the Apostolic preachers are alike "ministers of Christ" (iv. 1): so Thp., Rückert, Bt., Gd. However, Cm., and most modern exegetes, see *God* in ὁ Κύριος on account of vv. 6-9; but the relation of this ver. to the sequel is just that of the δι᾽ αὐτοῦ to the ἐξ αὐτοῦ τὰ πάντα of viii. 6; *cf.* note on ἐξ αὐτοῦ, i. 30; and for the general principle, Matt. xxv. 14 ff.

Vv. 6, 7. The grammatical obj. of this sentence has been given by the foregoing context, *viz.*, the Cor. Church of believers (*cf.* iv. 15).—Φυτεύω Paul uses besides only in ix. 7; his regular metaphor in this connexion is that of ver. 10. "Planting" and "watering" happily picture the relative services of P. and Ap. Ποτίζω, *to give drink, to irrigate*, may have for obj. men (2, xii. 13, etc.), animals (Luke xiii. 15), or plants. In ver. 2, *Paul* was the ποτίζων γάλα. The vb. takes a double acc., of person and thing (Wr., p. 284).—The ἀλλὰ of the last clause goes beyond a mere contrast (δέ) between God and men in their several parts, *excluding* the latter from the essential part: "but *God*—He only, and no other—made it to grow". The planting and watering of Christ's servants were occasions for the exercise of God's vitalising energy. While the former vbs. are aor., gathering up the work of the two ministers into single successive acts, ηὔξανεν is impf. of continued activity: "God was (all the while) making it to grow." Several of the Ff.—Aug. *e.g.*—saw in ποτίζειν the baptism, in φυτεύειν the instruction of catechumens,—"illustrating a general fault of patristic exegesis, the endeavour to attach a technical sense to words in the N.T. which had not yet acquired this meaning" (Lt.).— ὥστε, *itaque* (*and so, so then*), with ind. (*cf.* vii. 38, xi. 27, xiv. 22), points out a result immediately flowing from what has been said: "the planter" and "the waterer," in comparison with "the Lord" who dispensed their powers and "God" who makes their plants to grow, are reduced to nothing; "God who gives the growth" (*qui dat vim crescendi*, Bz.) alone remains. To the subject, ὁ αὐξάνων Θεός, the predicate τὰ πάντα ἐστὶν is tacitly supplied from the negative clauses foregoing.—For ἐστίν τι (*anything of moment*), *cf.* Gal. ii. 6, vi. 3, Acts v. 36, and note on τὶ εἰδέναι, ii. 2. The pr. ptp. with ὁ becomes, virtually a (timeless) substantive—*the planter waterer, Increaser* (Wr., p. 444).

9. ˣΘεοῦ γάρ ἐσμεν ˣσυνεργοί· Θεοῦ ʸγεώργιον, Θεοῦ ᶻοἰκοδομή
ἐστε.

10. Κατὰ τὴν ᵃχάριν τοῦ Θεοῦ τὴν ᵃδοθεῖσάν μοι, ὡς ᵇσοφὸς
ᵉἀρχιτέκτων ᵈθεμέλιον ᵈτέθεικα,[1] ἄλλος δὲ ᵉἐποικοδομεῖ· ἕκαστος

ˣ 1 Th. iii.
2; 2 Cor.
vi. 1;
συνεργος
more
generally;
nine
times in
P.; 3 Jo. 8.

y H.l. in N.T.; Prov. xxiv. 5, xxx. i. 16; γεωργος, Jo. xv. 1; -γειν, Heb. vi. 7.   z In this sense (concrete), Eph. ii. 21; also Mt. xxiv. 1.   a See i. 4.   b In such connexion, here only in N.T.; cf. Exod. xxxv. 10.   c H.l. in N.T.; cf. Isa. iii. 3; Sir. xxxviii. 27; 2 Macc. ii. 29.   d Lk. vi. 48, xiv. 29. For θεμ., see also Rom. xv. 20; Eph. ii. 20; 1 Tim. vi. 19; 2 Tim. ii. 19; Heb. vi. 1.   e Eph. ii. 20; Col. ii. 7; Jude 20; cf. Rom. xv. 20.

[1] εθηκαα, ℵ*ABC*, 17: Neutral and Alexandrian.

Ver. 8. In comparison with God, Ap. and P. are simply nothing (7): in relation to each other they are not rivals, as their Cor. favourers would make them (4): "But the planter and the waterer are *one*" (ἕν, *one thing*)—with one interest and aim, *viz.*, the growth of the Church; *cf.* xii. 12, 20; also John x. 30. Their functions are complementary, not competitive: a further answer to the question, τί οὖν ἐστὶν Ἀπολλώς κ.τ.λ.; The servants of God are nothing before Him, "one thing" before His Church: vanity and variance are alike impossible.

While one in aim, they are distinct in responsibility and reward: "But each will get his own (proper) wage, according to his own toil".—ἴδιος, *appropriate, specific* (*cf.* vii. 7, xv. 23, 28): "congruens iteratio, antitheton ad *unum*" (Bg.).—ἔργον (13-15) denotes *the work achieved*, κόπος *the exertion put forth* (see parls., and κοπιάω, xv. 10, etc.): τί γὰρ εἰ ἔργον οὐκ ἐτέλεσεν; —ἐκοπίασεν δέ (Thp.). The contrast ἕν εἰσιν . . . ἕκαστος δέ, between collective and individual relationships, is characteristic of Paul: *cf.* xii. 5-11, 27, xv. 10 f., Gal. vi. 2-5, Rom. xiv. 7-10. He forbids the man either to assert himself against the community or to merge himself in it. The fixed ratio between present labour in Christ's service and final reward is set forth, diff. but consistently, in the two parables of the Talents and Pounds, Matt. xxv. 14-30, Luke xix. 11-28.

Ver. 9. Θεοῦ . . . συνεργοί sums up in two words, and grounds upon a broad principle (γάρ), what vv. 6 ff. have set out in detail: "we are *God's* fellow-workmen"—employed upon *His* field, *His* building; and "we are God's *fellow-*workmen"—labouring jointly at the same task. The συν- of συνεργοί takes up the ἕν εἰσιν of ver. 8; the context (*cf.* xii. 6) forbids our referring it to the dependent gen. (*cf.* also 2 Cor. i. 24, vi. 1, Phil. iii. 17, 3 John 8), as though P. meant "fellow-

workers *with God*" : "the work (Arbeit) of the διάκονος would be improperly conceived as a *Mit-arbeit* in relation to God; moreover the metaphors which follow exclude the thought of such a fellow-working" (Hn.); also Bg., "operarii Dei, et co-operarii invicem".

As in regard to the labourers, so with the objects of their toil, *God* is all and in all: Θεοῦ γεώργιον, Θεοῦ οἰκοδομή ἐστε, "God's tilth (*arvum, land for tillage*, Ed.), God's building you are". For God as γεωργῶν, *cf.* John xv. 1; as οἰκοδομῶν, Heb. iii. 4, xi. 10. "Of the two images, γεωργ. implies the organic growth of the Church, οἰκοδ. the mutual adaptation of its parts" (Lt.); the one looks backward to vv. 6 ff., the other forward to vv. 10 ff.—Οἰκοδομή displaces οἰκοδόμημα in later Gr.—Θεοῦ, anarthrous by correlation (see note on ἀποδ. Πν., ii. 4): the three gens. are alike gens. of *possession*—"God's workmen, employed on God's field-tillage and God's house-building". Realising God's all-comprehending rights in His Church, the too human Cor. (3 f.) will come to think justly of His ministers.

§ 10. The Responsibility of the Human Builders, iii. 10-17. After the long digression on Wisdom (i. 17-iii. 2), occasioned by the Hellenic misconception of the Gospel underlying the Cor. divisions, the Ap. returned in vv. 3 ff. to the divisions themselves, dealing particularly with the rent between Apollonians and Paulinists. His first business was to reduce the Church leaders to their subordinate place, as *fellow-servants* of the one Divine cause (§ 9). They are *temple-workmen*—not himself and Apollos alone, but all who are labouring on the foundation which he has laid down —and must therefore take heed to the quality of their individual work, which will undergo a searching and fiery test.

Ver. 10. Κατὰ τὴν χάριν κ.τ.λ.: while "the grace of God" has been

f Eph. v. 15; δὲ ᶠ βλεπέτω ᶠ πῶς ᵉ ἐποικοδομεῖ · 11. ᵈ θεμέλιον γὰρ ᵍ ἄλλον οὐδεὶς
Lk. viii.
18. For δύναται ᵈ θεῖναι ᵍ παρὰ τὸν ʰ κείμενον, ὅς ἐστιν Ἰησοῦς ¹ ὁ ¹ Χριστός.¹
βλεπω
(impv.),
viii. 9, x.   12. εἰ δέ τις ἐποικοδομεῖ ἐπὶ τὸν ᵈ θεμέλιον τοῦτον ² ⁱ ᵏ χρυσόν,³
12, xvi.10,
and frequently.   g παρα = η, Lk. iii. 13 ; Heb. i. 4, xi. 4. See note below.   h Mt. v. 14;
Rev. iv. 2, xxi. 16.   i Acts iii. 6, xx. 33 ; 1 Pet. i. 18. For χρυσ., 1 Tim. ii. 9; Heb. ix. 4 ; 1 Pet.
i. 7; Rev. xxi. 18, 21.   k Rev. xvii. 4, xviii. 12, 16. For λιθ. τιμ., Rev. xxi. 11, 19.

¹ Ιησ. Χρ., אABLP, above fifty minn., syrsch. sah. cop. Χρ. Ιησ., C³D, some
minn., latt. vg. syrᵖ· (Western). Χρ., C*. Ιησ. ο. Χρ. (T.R.), a few minn.

² Om. τουτον א*ABC*—a Western and Syrian addition, as in אcC³DLP.

³ χρυσιον, αργυριον: אB (C in latter inst., defective in former), 73, Clem.,
Or., Bas. B, æth. ins. και; so W.H. mg.

given to all Christians, constituting them such (see i. 4), to the Ap. a special and singular " grace was given," " according to" which he " laid a foundation," whereon the Church at Cor. rests : see the like contrast in Eph. iii. 2-9, iv. 7-16; and for Paul's specific gift as founder, xv. 10, 2 Cor. iii. 5 ff., Rom. i. 1-5, xv. 15 ff. The office of the founder is his own, and incommunicable : " you have not many fathers " (iv. 15).

σοφὸς is a correct attributive to ἀρχι-τέκτων : see σοφία (τ. ἀρχόντων), ii. 6, and note ; so in the LXX, Exod. xxxv. 31, Isa. iii. 3, it characterizes the craftsman's skill ; in Arist., Eth. Nic., σοφία is the ἀρετὴ τέχνης—indeed this was its primitive sense (see Ed.). The Church architect (Christ, in the first instance, Matt. xvi. 18) is endowed with the σοφία τοῦ Θεοῦ, the νοῦς Χριστοῦ (ii. 6-16 ; cf. 2 Cor. iii. 4-6, Rom. xv. 16-20). The Gr. ἀρχιτέκτων was not a designer of plans on paper ; he was like the old cathedral builders, the master-mason, developing his ideas in the material. " As a wise master-builder, I laid a foundation (θεμέλιον ἔθηκα), but another builds thereupon" (ἄλλος δὲ ἐποικοδομεῖ) : P. knew that by God's grace his part was done wisely ; let his successors see to theirs. Not " the foundation "—that will be defined immediately (11b) : P. contrasts himself as foundation-layer with later workmen ; hence the vbs. are respectively past and pr. The θεμέλιον, laid out once for all by the ἀρχιτέκτων, determines the site and ground-plan of the edifice (cf. Eph. ii. 20).—With the distributive ἄλλος cf. ἕκαστος (11) : if Apollos, by himself, were intended, ἐποικοδομεῖ would have to be read as impf. (for ἐπῳκ., was building : cf. aor., 14), since he is not now at Cor. Many Christian teachers are busy there (iv. 15). For this indef. ἄλλος, cf. xii. 8 ff., xv. 39 ; and for ἐγώ . . . ἄλλος

δέ, Luke ix. 19, John iv. 37, xiv. 16, xxi. 18. For the compound vb., see parls. ; ἐπ- points to the basis, which gives the standard and measure to all subsequent work.—Hence the warning, ἕκαστος δὲ βλεπέτω πῶς κ.τ.λ. : " But let each man see (to it) how he is building thereupon ! " Working upon the foundation, he must follow the lines laid down ; he must use fit material. Not " how he is to build " (as in vii. 32, aor. sbj.), but " how he is a-building " (pr. ind.)—the work is going on. For the moods of the Indirect Question, see Wr., pp. 373 ff., Bn., §§ 341-356.

Ver. 11 is a parenthetical comment on θεμέλιον : As to the foundation, that is settled ; the workman has to build upon it, not to shift it, nor add to it.—θεμέλιον γὰρ ἄλλον οὐδεὶς δύναται θεῖναι παρὰ κ.τ.λ. : " For another foundation none can lay, beside (other than : παρά, possibly suggesting also in competition with ; or contrary to) that which is laid down, which is JESUS CHRIST ; " other builders there are beside the architect, but no other ground for them to build upon.—κεῖμαι serves as pf. pass. to τίθημι (Phil. i. 16, etc.), connoting fixity of situation (positum est), and so of destination, as in Luke ii. 34. The work of the Apostolic founders is done, once and for ever ; so long as the Church lasts, men will build on what they laid down.—θεμέλιον, here masc. (read as adj., sc. λίθον), as in 2 Tim. ii. 19, Heb. xi. 10, Rev. xxi. 14, 19, and sometimes in LXX ; neut. in Acts xvi. 26, as in the κοινή, and commonly in LXX.—ὅς ἐστιν—continuative, rather than definitive (as in 5) : " There is but one foundation, and it is Jesus Christ " ; cf. ii. 2, xv. 1-11, etc.—Ἰησοῦς Χριστός (not Χ. Ἰ., nor ὁ Χ.), the actual historical person, not any doctrine or argument about Him — " Jesus " revealed and known as " Christ " : see Acts ii. 22, 36, xvii. 3, etc., for the formation of the

ἄργυρον,[1] ᵏλίθους ᵏτιμίους—ˡξύλα, ᵐχόρτον, ⁿκαλάμην—13. ἕκασ- | [l] N.T.,*h.l.*; Ezra v. 8.
του τὸ ἔργον °φανερὸν °γενήσεται · ἡ γὰρ ᵖἡμέρα qδηλώσει, ὅτι ἐν | [m] Elsewhere "grass," Mt. vi. 30, etc.
ʳπυρὶ ˢἀποκαλύπτεται · καὶ ἑκάστου τὸ ἔργον ᵗὁποῖόν ἐστι τὸ |

[n] N.T., *h.l.*; Exod. v. 12, xv. 7; Isa. v. 24.   [o] xi. 19, xiv. 25; Ph. i. 13; Mk. vi. 14; Lk. viii. 17; Acts vii. 13.   [p] See i. 8.   [q] See i. 11.   [r] In like connexion, 2 Th. i. 8; Heb. x. 27, xii. 29; 1 Pet. i. 7; 2 Pet. iii. 7; Jude 7; frequent in Rev. and Mt.; Mk. ix. 43, 48 f.; Jo. xv. 6.   [s] See ii. 10. [t] Gal. ii. 6; 1 Th. i. 9; Acts xxvi. 29; Ja. i. 24.

[1] χρυσιον, αργυριον: אB (C in latter inst., defective in former), 73, Clem., Or., Bas. B, æth. ins. και; so W.H. *mg.*

name; and for this, with Paul the rarer, order, *cf.* ii. 2, Rom. v. 15, xvi. 25, etc.,— also Heb. xiii. 8; in each instance *Jesus Christ* connotes the recognised facts as to His life, death, etc. (*cf.* note on i. 2).

Ver. 12. After the interjected caution to let the *foundation* alone, P. turns to the *superstructure*, to which the work of his coadjutors belongs; δὲ indicates this transition.—εἰ δέ τις ἐποικοδομεῖ, εἰ with ind. (as in 14 f. etc.),—a supposition in matter of fact, while ἐὰν with sbj. (as in iv. 15) denotes a likely contingency. The doubled prp. ἐπί (with acc.)—an idiom characterising later Gr., which loves emphasis—implies growth by way of *accession*: "if any one is building-on,—onto the foundation"; contrast ἐπὶ with dat. in Eph. ii. 20. The material superimposed by the present Cor. builders is of two opposite kinds, rich and durable or paltry and perishing: "gold, silver, costly stones—wood, hay, straw,"—thrown together "in lively ἀσύνδετον" (Mr.). The latter might serve for poor frail huts, but not for the temple of God (17). —λίθοι τίμιοι, the marbles, etc., used in rearing noble houses; but possibly Isa. liv. 11 f. (*cf.* Rev. xxi. 18-21) is in the writer's mind. The figure has been interpreted as relating (*a*) to the diff. sorts of *persons* brought into the Church (Pelagius, Bg., Hf.), since the Cor. believers constitute the Θεοῦ οἰκοδομή (9), the ναὸς Θεοῦ (16)—"my work *are you* in the Lord" (ix. i.; *cf.* Eph. ii. 20 ff., 2 Tim. ii. 19 ff., 1 Peter ii. 4 f.; also the striking parl. in Mal. iii. 1 ff., iv. 1); (*b*) to *the moral fruits* resulting from the labours of various teachers, the character of Church members, this being the specific object of the final judgment (2 Cor. v. 10, Rom. ii. 5-11; *cf.* 1 Cor. xiii. 13) and that which measures the work of their ministers (1 Thess. ii. 19 ff., etc.) —so Or., Cm., Aug., lately Osiander and Gd.; (*c*) to the *doctrines* of the diff. teachers, since for this they are primarily answerable and here lay the point of

present divergence (*cf.* viii. 10 f., Rom. xiv. 15; 2 Cor. xi. 1 ff., 13 ff., Gal. i. 7, etc.)—so Clem. Al., and most moderns. The three views are not really discrepant: teaching shapes character, works express faith; unsound preaching attracts the bad hearer and makes him worse, sound preaching wins and improves the good (see i. 18, 24; 2 Tim. iv. 3; John iii. 18 ff., x. 26 f.). "The materials of this house may denote *doctrines moulding persons*," or "even *persons moulded by doctrines*" (Ev.),—"the doctrine exhibited in a concrete form" (Lt.).

Ver. 13. "The work of each (ἑκάστου resuming the ἕκαστος of 10) will become manifest:" while the Wheat and Tares are in early growth (Matt. xiii. 24 ff.), they are indistinguishable; one man's work is mixed up with another's—"for the Day will disclose (it)".—Ἡ ἡμέρα can only mean *Christ's Judgment Day*: see parls., esp. i. 8, iv. 3 ff., and notes; also Rom. ii. 16, Acts xvii. 31, Matt. xxv. 19. "The day" suggests (*cf.* 1 Thess. v. 2 ff., Rom. xiii. 11 ff.) the hope of *daylight* upon dark problems of human responsibility. But this searching is figured as the scrutiny of *fire*, which at once detects and destroys useless matter: ὅτι ἐν πυρὶ ἀποκαλύπτεται, "because it (the Day) is revealed in fire". For ἀποκαλύπτεται (pr., implying *certainty*, perhaps *nearness*), see notes on i. 7, ii. 10— a supernatural, unprecedented "day," dawning not like our mild familiar sunrise, but "in" splendour of judgment "fire": *cf.* 2 Thess. i. 8. This image comes from the O.T. pictures of a Theophany: Dan. vii. 9 f., Mal. iv. 1, Isa. xxx. 27, lxiv. 1 ff., etc.—καὶ ἑκάστου τὸ ἔργον ὁποῖόν ἐστι κ.τ.λ.: "and each man's work, of what kind it is,—the fire will prove it". The pleonastic αὐτὸ is due to a slight anacoluthon: the sentence begins as though it were to end, "the fire will *show*"; φανερώσει is, however, replaced by the stronger δοκιμάσει suitable to πῦρ, and this

u xi. 28; 2
Cor. viii.

8, xiii. 5;
1 Th.v.21;

Lk.xiv.19;
1 Pet. i. 7;

Zech. xiii.
11.

v xiii. 13; 2

ʳ πῦρ ¹ ᵘ δοκιμάσει · 14. εἴ τινος τὸ ἔργον ᵛ μένει ² ὃ ᵉ ἐπῳκοδόμησε,³ ʷ μισθὸν λήψεται · 15. εἴ τινος τὸ ἔργον ˣ κατακαήσεται, ʸ ζημιωθή- σεται, αὐτὸς δὲ σωθήσεται, ᶻ οὕτω δὲ ᵛ ὡς διὰ ʳ πυρός. 16. ᵃ οὐκ ᵃ οἴδατε ὅτι ᵇ ναὸς Θεοῦ ἐστε καὶ τὸ Πνεῦμα τοῦ Θεοῦ ᶜ οἰκεῖ ⁴ ᶜ ἐν ⁴

Cor. iii. 11, ix. 9; Rom. ix. 11; Heb. x. 34, xii. 27, xiii. 1, 14; Jo. iii. 36, vi. 27, ix. 41.   w Ver. 8.
x Mt. iii. 12, xiii. 30, 40; 2 Pet. iii. 10; Jo. xv. 6.   y Mt. xvi. 26 and parls., for this sense; cf. 2
Cor. vii. 9; Ph. iii. 8.   z iv. 1, ix. 26; Eph. v. 28, 33; Ph. iii. 17; 1 Th. ii. 4; Jas. ii. 12; Lk. xxiv.
24.   a Ten times in this Ep.—v. 6, etc.; Rom. vi. 16; Jas. iv. 4.   b vi. 19; 2 Cor. vi. 16; cf.
Eph. ii. 21 f.; also 2 Th. ii. 4; Rev. iii. 12, xi. i; Jo. ii. 19; Mt. xxvi. 61.   c Rom. vii. 18, 20, viii.
9, 11; 1 Tim. vi. 16.

¹ το πυρ αυτο δοκιμ.: ABCP, 17, 37, 73, other minn., syrˢᶜʰ. Om. αυτο ℵDL, etc., latt. vg. sah. cop.: Western.

² μενεῖ: latt. (manserit), Aug., Ambrst., sah. cop. So Lachm., Tisch., Al., El., W.H., and nearly all modern edd.

³ εποικοδομησεν: all uncc. but B³C. See Wr., p. 84.

⁴ εν υμιν οικει (?) BP, 17 (a good group); preferred by W.H. in txt.

altered vb. requires with it αὐτό, to re-call the object τὸ ἔργον. Mr. and El. attach the pronoun to τὸ πῦρ, "the fire itself," but with pointless emphasis. Others avoid the pleonasm by construing ἑκάστου τὸ ἔργον at the beginning as a nominativus pendens ("as to each man's work"), resembling that of John xv. 2; but the qualification that follows, ὁποῖόν ἐστιν, makes this unlikely: cf. Gal. ii. 6, for the interpolated interr. clause.—δοκι-μάζω is to assay (see LXX parls.),—suggested by the "gold, silver" above: "probabit, non purgabit. Hic locus ignem purgatorium non modo non fovet, sed plane extinguit" (Bg.).—Ἕκαστος, thrice repeated in vv. 10-13, with solemn individualising emphasis.

Vv. 14, 15. The opp. issues of the fiery assay are stated under parl. hypo-theses: εἴ τινος τὸ ἔργον . . . μενεῖ . . . εἴ τινος τὸ ἔργον κατακαήσεται, "If any one's work shall abide . . . shall be burned up". The double ind. with εἰ balances the contrasted suppositions, without signifying likelihood either way: for the opposed vbs., cf. xiii. 8, 13; μενεῖ recalls ὑπομενεῖ of Mal. iii. 2.—δ ἐποικο-δόμησεν (wanting augment: usage varies in this vb.; Wr., p. 83) reminds us that the work examined was built on the one foundation (10 ff.).—μισθὸν λήμψεται and ζημιωθήσεται are the cor-responding apodoses,—μισθὸν being car-ried over to the second of the parl. clauses (Mr., Gd., Lt., Ed.): "He will get a reward . . . will be mulcted (of it)".—ζημιόω retains in pass. its acc. of thing, as a vb. taking double acc.; de-rived from ζημία (opp. of κέρδος: cf. Phil. iii. 7), it signifies to fine, inflict forfeit (in pass., suffer forfeit) of what one pos-sessed, or might have possessed. "αὐτὸς δέ—opposed to μισθός: his reward shall be lost, but his person saved" (Lt.); αὐτὸς is nearly syn. with the ψυχὴ of Matt. xvi. 25 f., etc. The man built on the foundation, though his work proves culpably defective: σωθήσεται promises him the σωτηρία of Christ's heavenly kingdom (see i. 18, and other parls.). Such a minister saves himself, but not his hearers: the opp. result to that of ix. 27, etc. αὐτὸς δὲ σωθήσεται, οὕτως δὲ ὡς διὰ πυρός (δὲ correcting δέ, as in ii. 6)—"yet so (saved) as through fire,"—like Lot fleeing from Sodom; his salva-tion is reduced to a minimum: "He rushes out through the flame, leaving behind the ruin of his work . . . for which, proved to be worthless, he re-ceives no pay" (Bt.), getting through "scorched and with the marks of the flame" upon him (Lt.); "s'il est sauvé, ce ne peut être qu'en échappant à travers les flammes, et grâce à la solidité du fondement" (Gd.); to change the figure, "ut naufragus mercator, amissa merce et lucro, servatus per undas" (Bg.). For the prp., in local sense, see Gm., and Wr., p. 473; διὰ πυρός, proverbial for a hairbreadth escape (see Lt. ad loc.; Eurip., Andr., 487; Elec., 1182, and LXX parls.). The διὰ has been read instru-mentally, "by means of fire,"—sc. the fire of purgatory (see Lt.); an idea foreign to this scene. Cm., by a dreadful in-version of the meaning, reads the διὰ as ἐν πυρί—"will be preserved in fire!" (σώζω nowhere has this sense of τηρέω): εἰπὼν Σωθήσεται, οὐδὲν ἕτερον ἢ τὴν ἐπίτασιν τῆς τιμωρίας ἠνίξατο. For other interpretations, see Mr.

Vv. 16, 17. However poor his work,

ὑμῖν[1]; 17. εἴ τις τὸν ᵇναὸν τοῦ Θεοῦ ᵈφθείρει, ᵈφθερεῖ τοῦτον[2] ὁ ᵈ xv. 33; 2
Θεός· ὁ γὰρ ᵇναὸς τοῦ Θεοῦ ἅγιός ἐστιν, ᵉοἵτινές ἐστε ὑμεῖς.

18. Μηδεὶς ἑαυτὸν ᶠἐξαπατάτω· εἴ τις ᵍδοκεῖ σοφὸς εἶναι ἐν ὑμῖν,

Cor. vii.2,
xi. 3; Eph.
iv. 22; 2
Pet. ii. 12;
Jude 10.
e 2 Cor. viii.

10; Rom. vi. 2; Gal. v. 4; Jas. iv. 14; Acts vii. 53.   f 2 Cor. xi. 3; Rom. vii. 11, xvi. 18; 2 Th. ii.
3; 1 Tim. ii. 14.   g In this sense, viii. 2, xiv. 37; Gal. vi. 3; Ph. iii. 4; Jas. i. 26.

[1] εν υμιν οικει (?), BP, 17 (a good group); preferred by W.H. in *txt*.
[2] αυτον, ADG (Western).

the workman of ver. 15 built upon Christ. There are cases worse than his, and to the εἴ τινος τὸ ἔργον alternatives of vv. 14 f. the Ap. has a third to add in the εἴ τις . . . φθείρει of ver. 17. Beside the good and ill builders, who will gain or lose reward, there are *destroyers* of the house, whom God will *destroy* : the climax of the βλεπέτω πῶς, ver. 10. Gd. well explains the absence of connecting particles between vv. 15 and 16,—a "brusque transition" due to the emotion which seizes the Apostle's heart at the sight of "workmen who even destroy what has been already built"; hence the lively apostrophe and the heightened tone of the passage.—The challenge οὐκ οἴδατε; is characteristic of this Ep. (see parls.), addressed to a Church of superior knowledge (i. 5, viii. 1). For the form οἴδατε, of the κοινή, see Wr., pp. 102 f. —The expression ναὸς Θεοῦ (see parls.) accentuates the Θεοῦ οἰκοδομή, expounded since ver. 9: "Do you not know that you are (a building no less sacred than) *God's temple?*" Not "a temple of God," as one of several; to P. the Church was the spiritual counterpart of the Jewish Temple, and every Church embodied this ideal. For the anarthrous (predicative) phrase, *cf.* Θεοῦ βασιλείαν, vi. 9, and see note on ii. 4.—Ναός (see parls.) denotes the *shrine*, where the Deity resides; ἱερόν (ix. 13, etc.), the *sanctuary*, the temple at large, with its precincts.—ὅτι is not repeated with the second half of the question, καὶ τὸ Πνεῦμα τοῦ Θεοῦ ἐν ὑμῖν οἰκεῖ, the two propositions being virtually one; God's temple in Christian men is constituted by the indwelling of His Spirit: "and (that) the Spirit of God dwells in you?" *cf.* Eph. ii. 21, also 1 Peter ii. 5. The same relationship is expressed by other figures in xii. 5, Eph. iv. 4, etc. So the O.T. congregation of the Lord had for its centre the Shekinah in the Holy Place: Isa. vi., Ezek. xxxvii. 27; *cf.* 2 Cor. vi. 16 ff. This truth is applied to the Christian person in vi. 19.

" If any one destroys the temple of God, God will destroy him "—*talione justissima* (Bg.). On the form of hypothesis, see ver. 14.—φθείρω signifies *to corrupt morally, deprave* (injure in *character*), xv. 33, 2 Cor. xi. 3, as well as *to waste, damage* (injure in *being*: see parls.)— mutually implied in a spiritual building. This Church was menaced with destruction from the immoralities exposed in chh. v., vi., and from its party schisms (i.-iii.), *both* evils fostered by corrupt teaching. The figure is not that of Levitical defilement (φθείρω nowhere means to *pollute* a holy place); this φθορὰ is a structural injury, to be requited in kind. —ὁ Θεὸς closes the warning, with awful emphasis (*cf.* 1 Thess. iv. 6, Rom. xii. 19); God is bound to protect His temple (*cf.* Ps. xlvi., xlviii., lxxiv., Isa. xxvii. 3, lxiv. 10 ff.).—The injury is a *desecration*: " for the temple of God is holy,—which (is what) *you* are ". The added clause οἵτινές ἐστε ὑμεῖς reminds the Cor. at once of the obligations their sanctity imposes (see notes on ἡγιασμένοις, κλητοῖς, ἁγίοις, i. 2; *cf.* 1 Peter ii. 5), and of the protection it guarantees (2 Cor. vi. 14 ff., 2 Thess. ii. 13; John x. 29; Isa. xliii. 1-4, etc., Zech. ii. 8).—οἵτινες, the qualitative relative, refers to ἅγιος more than to ναός, and is predicate (see Wr., pp. 206 f.) with ὑμεῖς for subject.

§ 11. The Church and the World, iii. 18-23. Affectation of philosophy, —" the wisdom of the world," which P. has repudiated on behalf of the Gospel (i., ii.)—was at the bottom of the Cor. troubles. Those who follow human wisdom exalt human masters at the expense of God's glory, and there are teachers who lend themselves to this error and thus build unworthily on the Christian foundation—some who are even destroying, under a show of building, the temple of God (iii. 3-17). That the warnings P. has given to his fellowlabourers bear on the popular λόγος σοφίας is apparent from the manner in which he reverts to the topic at this

ἐν τῷ [h] αἰῶνι τούτῳ [i] μωρὸς γενέσθω, ἵνα γένηται σοφός· 19. ἡ γὰρ
σοφία τοῦ [k] κόσμου [k] τούτου [l] μωρία [m] παρὰ τῷ [1] [m] Θεῷ ἐστί· γέγραπται
γάρ, [n] "Ὁ [o] δρασσόμενος τοὺς σοφοὺς ἐν τῇ [p] πανουργίᾳ αὐτῶν".
20. καὶ πάλιν, "Κύριος γινώσκει τοὺς [q] διαλογισμοὺς τῶν σοφῶν,[2]
ὅτι εἰσὶ [r] μάταιοι". 21. ὥστε μηδεὶς [s] καυχάσθω [s] ἐν ἀνθρώποις·

h See i. 20.
i See i. 25.
k v. 10, vii. 31; Eph. ii. 2; 1 Jo. iv. 17; six times in Jo.
l See i. 18.
m In this sense, Rom. ii. 11, 13; Gal. iii. 11; Eph. vi. 9; 2 Th. i. 6; Jas. i. 27; 1 Pet. ii. 4; Mt. vi. 1; Lk. i. 30, ii. 52; Acts xxvi. 8.
n Job v. 13; see note below.
o N.T. *h.l.*; Lev. ii. 2, v. 12; Num. v. 26; Ps. ii. 12.
p 2 Cor. iv. 2, xi. 3; Eph. iv. 14; Lk. xx. 23; Jos. ix. 10; *πανουργος*, 2 Cor. xii. 16.
q In this sense, Rom. i. 21; Ph. ii. 14; 1 Tim. ii. 8; Jas. ii. 4; Mt. xv. 19, etc.; Lk. ix. 46 f., xxiv. 38; Ps. xciii. 11.
r xv. 17; Tit. iii. 9; Jas. i. 26; 1 Pet. i. 18; Acts xiv. 15; Exod. xx. 7; Ezek. xi. 2.
s See i. 31.

[1] Om. **τῳ** CDG.

[2] **ανθρωπων,** some eight minuscc., am., arm., Marcion as quoted by Epiph., Hier. (in free quot.), LXX.

point. § 11 resumes the strain of §§ 4-8, impressing on teachers and taught alike the true relationship of things human and Divine.

Ver. 18. Accordingly, the **Μηδεὶς ἑαυτὸν ἐξαπατάτω** looks forward, not backward: one may "deceive himself" about the mixing of man's wisdom with God's, but scarcely about the truth of the threatening of ver. 17. "If any one thinks to be wise amongst you, in this age (**αἰῶνι,** *world-period:* see parls.) let him become foolish, that he may become wise."—**δοκεῖ** not *videtur* (Vg., A.V.), but *putat*—"*seemeth to himself*, the usual (though perhaps not universal) sense of **δοκεῖν** in St. Paul" (Lt.: see parls., esp. xiv. 37): the danger is that of *self*-deception (*cf.* the irony in iv. 10, viii. 1 ff.), a danger natural in the case of teachers, esp. if intellectual and cultured—there were a few such at Cor. (i. 26); *cf.* the exhortations of James iii. 1, 13-18.—**ἐν τῷ αἰῶνι τούτῳ** is antithetical to **ἐν ὑμῖν** (put the comma between them), "amongst *you*"—God's temple, Christ's property (17, 23, etc.)—in accordance with ii. 6, 13, and with the contrast between the two wisdoms that dominates this whole Division. Men must not think to be wise in both spheres; the Church's wise are the world's fools, and *vice versâ*. The cross is **μωρία** to the world, and he who espouses it a **μωρὸς** in its opinion—a *fool* with a *criminal* for his Master; and one can only be a Christian sage—wise after the manner of ii. 8 ff.—upon condition of bearing this reproach (so Or., Cm., Luther, Hf., Gd., Hn.). Paul was crazy in the eyes of the world (iv. 10, 2 Cor. v. 13; Acts xxvi. 24), but how wise *amongst us! Cf.* Christ's paradox of *losing the soul to gain it*.

Ver. 19*a* gives the reason why the philosophy of the times must be renounced by the aspirant to Christian wisdom: "For the wisdom of the world is folly with God" (= i. 20); and since it is folly with *God*, it must be counted folly, and not wisdom, *amongst you* (18). *God's* judgment is decisive for His Church.—**παρὰ Θεῷ,** *apud Deum*, *judice Deo* (see parls.).

Vv. 19*b*, 20. That the above *is* God's judgment appears from two sayings of Scripture, bearing on the two classes of worldly wise—the men of affairs (such as the **ἄρχοντες** of ii. 6) and the philosophers (i. 20), distinguished respectively by **πανουργία** and **διαλογισμοί.** In the first text (the *only* N.T. quotation from Job: Phil. i. 19, perhaps an allusion), Paul improves on the LXX, possibly from another version, substituting the vivid **ὁ δρασσόμενος** (*He that grips: cf.* **δραξάμενος φάρυγγος,** Theocritus, xxiv. 28) for **ὁ καταλαμβάνων,** and **πανουργίᾳ αὐτῶν** for **φρονήσει,**—both nearer to the Heb. (LXX reads **πανουργίαν** in ver. 12). The words (from Eliphaz) are "appropriated because of their inherent truth" (Lt.); they reassert the anticipation expressed in ii. 6. For **πανουργία,** see parls.; note its deterioration of meaning, as in Eng. *craft*. When the world's schemers think themselves cleverest, Providence catches them in their own toils.—The second text P. adapts by turning **ἀνθρώπων** into **σοφῶν**: what is true of the vanity of human thoughts generally (*machsh'both 'ādām*) he applies *par excellence* to "the reasonings of *the wise*".—**διαλογισμοί,** signifying in Plutarch's later Gr. *debates*, *arguings* (see parls.), recalls i. 19 f. above, echoing the quotation of that passage. On **μάταιοι,** *futile*, see note to xv. 14 (**κενός**).

Ver. 21*a*. **ὥστε μηδεὶς καυχάσθω ἐν**

22. πάντα γὰρ †ὑμῶν ἐστιν, ᵘεἴτε Παῦλος ᵘεἴτε Ἀπολλὼς ᵘεἴτε †For this gen.,see i. 12, and ver. 4 above.
Κηφᾶς, εἴτε κόσμος εἴτε ᵛζωὴ εἴτε ᵛθάνατος, εἴτε ᵛʷἐνεστῶτα
εἴτε ᵛˣμέλλοντα· πάντα †ὑμῶν ἐστιν¹· 23. ὑμεῖς δὲ †Χριστοῦ, ᵘIn ex-tended enumera-tions, x.
Χριστὸς δὲ †Θεοῦ.

31, xii. 13, xiii. 8; Rom. xii. 6 ff.; Col. i. 16. Rom. viii. 6; Ph. i. 20; 1 Jo. iii. 14; Jo. v. 24. Heb. ix. 11, x. 1.

v Rom. viii. 38. ζωη, θαν. alone, 2 Cor. iv. 12; w vii. 26; Gal. i. 4; Heb. ix. 9. x Col. ii. 17;

¹ Om. 2nd εστιν all uncc. but DbcL.

ἀνθρώποις: "And so let no one glory in men".—ὥστε often, with P., introduces the impv. at the point where argument or explanation passes into exhortation; cf. note on ver. 7, and see iv. 5, v. 8, etc.—ἐν ἀνθρώποις states the forbidden ground of boasting (see parls.), supplying the negative counterpart of i. 31. Paul condemns alike the self-laudation of clever teachers, hinted at in ver. 18, and the admiration rendered to them, along with all partisan applause.

Vv. 21b-23 form an unbroken chain, linking the Cor. and their teachers to the throne of God. Not till the last words of ver. 23 do we find the full justifica-tion (sustaining the initial γάρ) for the prohibition of ver. 21a; "only when the other side to the πάντα ὑμῶν has been expressed, is the object presented in which alone the Church ought to glory" (Hf.); standing by itself, "All things are yours" would be a reason in favour of, rather than against, glorying in human power. The saying of ver. 21b is, very possibly, taken from the lips of the Cor. δοκοῦντες (18), who talked in the high-flown Stoic style, affirming like Zeno (in Diog. Laert., vii., 1. 25), τῶν σοφῶν πάντα εἶναι, or daring with Seneca (de Benef., vii., 2 f.) "emittere hanc vocem, Haec omnia mea esse!" similarly the Stoic in Horace (Sat. I., iii., 125-133; Ep. I., i., 106 ff.): "Sapiens uno minor est Jove, dives, liber, honoratus, pulcher, rex denique regum!" Some such pre-tentious vein is hinted at in iv. 7-10, vi. 12 and x. 22 f., vii. 31. (οἱ χρώμενοι τ. κόσμον: see notes); the affecters of philosophy at Cor. made a "liberal" use of the world. As in vi. 12 and x. 22 f., the Ap. adopts their motto, giving to it a grander scope than its authors dreamed of (22), but only to check and balance it, reproving the conceit of its vaunters by the contrasted principle (δέ) of the Divine dominion in Christ, which absorbs all human proprietorship (23).

First amongst the "all things" that the Cor. may legitimately boast, there stand —suggested by ἀνθρώποις, 21 — "Paul,

Apollos, Cephas," the figureheads of the Church factions (i. 12),—enumerated with εἴτε . . . εἴτε (whether P. or Ap. or Ceph.), since these chiefs belong to the Church alike, not P. to this section, Ap. to that, and so on. Christ (i. 12) is not named in this series of "men"; a diff. place is His (23).—From "Cephas" the enumeration passes per saltum to "the world" (εἴτε κόσμος—anarthrous, as thought of qualitatively; cf. Gal. vi. 14), understood in its largest sense,—the existing order of material things; cf. note on i. 20. The right to use worldly goods, asserted broadly by Greek Chris-tians at Cor. (vi. 12, vii. 31, x. 23 f.: see notes), is frankly admitted; the Church (represented by its three leaders) and the world both exist for "you," —are bound to serve you (cf. 1 Tim. ii. 2-4, iv. 8, vi. 17; Ps. viii., etc.); the Messianic kingdom makes the saints even the world's judges (vi. 2, Rom. iv. 13; Rev. v. 10, etc.).—εἴτε ζωὴ εἴτε θάνατος, by another bold and sudden sweep, carries the Christian empire into the unseen. Not Life alone, but Death —king of fears to a sinful world (Rom. v. 17, 21, Heb. ii. 15)—is the saints' servant (xv. 26, etc.). They hold a con-dominium (Rom. viii. 17, 1 Thess. v. 10) with Him who is "Lord of living and dead" (Rom. xiv. 9, etc.; Eph. iv. 9 f., Rev. i. 18); cf. ἐμοὶ τὸ ζῆν Χριστός, καὶ τὸ ἀποθανεῖν κέρδος, Phil. i. 21.—ζωὴ and θάνατος extend the Christian's estate over all states of being; εἴτε ἐνεστῶτα, εἴτε μέλλοντα, stretch it to all periods and possibilities of time. The former of these ptps. (pf. intransitive of ἐνίστημι) denotes what has come to stand there (instans),—is on the spot, in evidence; the latter what exists in intention,—to be evolved out of the present: see the two pairs of antitheses in Rom. viii. 38 f.; these things cannot hurt the beloved of God (Rom.), nay, must help and serve them (1 Cor.). See other parls. for "things present" (esp. Gal. i. 4) and "to come" (esp. Rom. viii. 17-25).

The Apostle repeats triumphantly his

a See iii. 15.
b In similar constr., Rom. viii. 36, ix. 8;

IV. 1. [a] Οὕτως ἡμᾶς [b] λογιζέσθω [c] ἄνθρωπος [a] ὡς [d] ὑπηρέτας Χριστοῦ, καὶ [e] οἰκονόμους [f] μυστηρίων Θεοῦ. 2. [g] ὃ [1] δὲ [1] [h] λοιπόν,

2 Cor. x. 2; Ph. iii. 13; Acts xix. 27; Mk. xv. 28 (Isa. liii. 12). c xi. 28; 2 Cor. xii. 4; Rom. ii. 1, vii. 24, ix. 20; Gal. vi. 1, 7. d Acts xiii. 5, xxvi. 16; Lk. i. 2; Jo. xviii. 36. e Tit. i. 7; 1 Pet. iv. 10; Lk. xii. 42 (πιστος). f See ii. 7. g ὧδε, similarly in Heb. vii. 8; Rev. xiii. 10, 18, xiv. 12, xvii. 9. h See i. 16.

[1] ὡδε, all uncc. but DᶜEL; also oldest verss. ο δε, however, in Chr. and Gr. Comm. Lachm., following the bulk of minuscc., placed the full stop *after* ωδε.

πάντα ὑμῶν, having gathered into it the totality of finite existence, to *reverse* it by the words ὑμεῖς δὲ Χριστοῦ, "but (not *and*) you are Christ's!" (*cf.* vi. 20, Rom. xii. 1 f., 2 Cor. v. 15). The Cor. readers, exalted to a height outsoaring Stoic pride, are in a moment laid low at the feet of Christ: "Lords of the universe—you are His bondmen, your vast heritage in the present and future you gather as *factors for Him*". P. endorses the doctrine of the kingship of the spiritual man, dilating on it with an eloquence surpassing that of Stoicism; "but," he reminds him, his wealth is that of *a steward*. Our property is immense, but *we* are Another's; we rule, to be ruled. A man cannot own too much, provided that *he recognises his Owner*.

Finally, Christ who demands our subordination, supplies in Himself its grand example: Χριστὸς δὲ Θεοῦ, "but Christ is God's". We are masters of everything, but Christ's servants; *He* Master of us, but God's Servant (*cf.* Acts iii. 13, etc.). For His filial submission, see xi. 3, xv. 22 ff., Rom. vi. 10, and notes; also John viii. 29, x. 29, etc. We cannot accept Cv.'s dilution of the sense, "Hæc subjectio ad Christi *humanitatem* refertur"; for the ὑμεῖς Χριστοῦ, just affirmed, raises Christ high over men. It is enough to say with Thd., Χριστὸς Θεοῦ οὐχ ὡς κτίσμα Θεοῦ, ἀλλ' ὡς Ὑιὸς τοῦ Θεοῦ: *cf.* Heb. v. 8. The sovereignty of the Father is the corner-stone of authority in the universe (xi. 3, xv. 28).

The Ap. has now vindicated God's rights in His Church (see *Introd.* to § 10), and recalled the Cor. from their carnal strife and pursuit of worldly wisdom to the unity, sanctity, and grandeur of their Christian calling, which makes them servants of God through Christ, and in His right the heirs of all things.

§ 12. CHRIST'S SERVANTS ANSWERABLE TO HIMSELF, iv. 1-5. The Ap. has shown his readers their own true position —so high and yet so lowly (§ 11); Paul, Apollos, Cephas are but part of a universe of ministry that waits upon them. But more is to be said about the Christian *leaders*, whose names are so much abused at Cor. If the Church is to understand its proper character, it must reverence theirs. They are its servants; it is not their master. They are its property, because they are *Christ's* property; and His instruments first of all. P. thus resumes the train of thought opened in § 10, where the work of Church-builders was discriminated in relation to *the building;* now it is viewed in its relation to *God the Householder.* Here lies another and the final ground of accusation against the Cor. parties: those who maintained them, in applauding this chief and censuring that, were putting themselves into Christ's judgment-seat, from which the Apostle thrusts them down.

Ver. 1. "In this way let a man take account of us, *viz.,* as servants of Christ," etc." Οὕτως draws attention to the coming ὡς: the vb. λογιζέσθω implies a *reasonable* estimate, drawn from admitted principles (*cf.* Rom. vi. 11; xii. 1, λογικήν), the pr. impv. an *habitual* estimate. The use of ἄνθρωπος for τις (xi. 28, etc.), occasional in cl. Gr., occurs "where a *gravior dicendi formula* is required" (El.). Ὑπηρέτης (only here in Epp.: see parls.) agrees with οἰκέτης (Rom. xiv. 4, *domestic*) in *associating* servant and master, whereas διάκονος rather contrasts them (iii. 5, see note; Mark ix. 35): see Trench, *Syn.,* § 9.—ὡς ὑπηρ. Χριστοῦ κ. οἰκονόμους κ.τ.λ., "as Christ's assistants, and stewards of God's mysteries"—in these relations Jesus set the App. to Himself and God: see Matt. xiii. 11, 52. With P. the Church is the οἶκος (1 Tim. iii. 15), God the οἰκοδεσπότης, its members the οἰκεῖοι (Gal. vi. 10, Eph. ii. 19), and its ministers—the App. in chief—the οἰκονόμοι (ix. 17, Col. i. 25, etc.). The figure of iii. 9 ff. is kept up: those who were ἀρχιτέκτων and ἐποικοδομοῦντες in the rearing of the house, become ὑπηρέται and οἰκονόμοι in its internal economy. The οἰκονόμος was a confidential housekeeper or overseer, commonly a slave, charged with pro-

ⁱ ζητεῖται ^l ἐν τοῖς ^e οἰκονόμοις, ἵνα ^k πιστός τις ^l εὑρέθῃ.   3. ἐμοὶ δὲ ^m εἰς ^m ἐλάχιστόν ἐστιν ἵνα ὑφ' ὑμῶν ⁿ ἀνακριθῶ ἢ ὑπὸ ^o ἀνθρωπίνης ^p ἡμέρας, ^q ἀλλ' ^q οὐδὲ ἐμαυτὸν ⁿ ἀνακρίνω· 4. οὐδὲν γὰρ ἐμαυτῷ ^r σύνοιδα, ἀλλ' οὐκ ^s ἐν τούτῳ ^s δεδικαίωμαι, ὁ δὲ ⁿ ἀνακρίνων με

i In this sense, 2 Cor. xiii. 3; Lk. xii. 6 f.; Mk. viii. 11 f.
k Ver. 17, vii. 25, in this sense; nine times besides in P.; also in Mt., Lk., Heb., 1 Pet., Rev.   l Of moral judgments, xv. 15; 2 Cor. xi. 12, xii. 20; Gal. ii. 17; Ph. iii. 9; 1 Pet. i. 7; six times in Rev.; Acts xxiv. 5.
m Cf. Acts xix. 27. Εἰμι εἰς, h.l. in this sense.   n See ii. 14.   o See ii. 13.   p See i. 8.
q iii. 2; Acts xix. 2.   r Acts v. 2, xii. 12, xiv. 6 only; Lev. v. 1; Job xxvii. 6; 1 Macc. iv. 21; 2 Macc. iv. 41, etc.   See note below.   s vi. 11; Rom. iii. 4 (Ps. l. 6), v. 9; Gal. ii. 17, iii. 11, 24, v. 4; 1 Tit. iii. 16; Acts xiii. 39.

¹ ζητεῖτε, אACDgr.Ggr.P: adopted in many minuscc. ζητεῖται, BL and most minuscc.; so latt. vg. cop. syrr. Doubtful whether the -τε (imperative) is a grammatical emendation, or a mere itacism; neither a clear Western nor Alexandrian reading, DG and AC, in each case, being deserted by their companion verss.

visioning the establishment. Responsible not to his fellows, but to "the Lord," his high trust demands a strict account (Luke xii. 41-48).—On μυστ. Θεοῦ, see notes to ii. 7, 9 f.: the phrase implies not secrets of the master kept from other servants, but secrets *revealed* to them through God's dispensers, to whose judgment and fidelity the disclosure is committed (*cf.* ii. 6, iii. 1).

Ver. 2. ὧδε λοιπὸν (*proinde igitur*) ζητεῖται, ἐν τοῖς οἰκονόμοις κ.τ.λ.: "In such case, it is further sought in stewards (to be sure) that one be found faithful". ὧδε gathers up the position given to "us" in ver. 1; ἐν τοῖς οἰκονόμοις is therefore pleonastic, but repeated for distinctness and by reference to the well-understood rule for *stewards* (Luke xii. 48). λοιπὸν brings in the supplement to an imperfect representation: it is not enough to be *steward*—a *faithful* steward is looked for (an echo of Luke xii. 42 f.). ζητεῖται . . . ἵνα resembles παρακαλῶ ἵνα, i. 10 (see note): the telic force of the conj. has not disappeared; one "seeks" a thing *in order to* "find" it.

Ver. 3. ἐμοὶ δὲ εἰς ἐλάχιστόν ἐστιν ἵνα κ.τ.λ.: "For myself however it amounts to a very small thing that by *you* I should be put to trial, or by a human day (of judgment)." Fidelity is required of stewards: yes, but (δέ) *who is the judge of that fidelity?* Not *you* Cor., nor even my own good conscience, but the Lord only (4: *cf.* Rom. xiv. 4); P. corrects the false inference that might be drawn from iii. 22. ἐμοὶ δὲ takes up the general truth just stated, to apply it as a matter between *me* and *you*. P. is being put on his trial at Cor.—his talents appraised, his motives scrutinised, his administration canvassed with unbecoming presumption. For εἰς in this somewhat

rare, but not necessarily Hebraistic sense, *cf.* vi. 16, Acts xix. 27; see Wr., p. 229. ἵνα . . . ἀνακριθῶ (construction more unclassical than in 1) equals τὸ ἀνακριθῆναι—unless the clause should be rendered, "that I should *have myself tried* by you,"—as though P. might have challenged the judgment of the Cor. (see ix. 2, 2 Cor. iii. 1, xii. 11) but dismissed the thought. Ἀνακρίνω (see note, ii. 15) speaks not of the *final judgment* (κρίνω, 5, v. 12, etc.), but of an *examination*, *investigation* preliminary to it. The "human (ἀνθρωπίνης, *cf.* ii. 13) day," of which P. thinks lightly, is *man's* judgment—that of any man, or all men together; he reserves his case for "*the* day (of the Lord": see i. 8).—ἀλλ' οὐδὲ ἐμαυτὸν ἀνακρίνω: "nay, I do not even try myself!" The ἀλλ' οὐδέ (*cf.* iii. 3) brings forward another suggestion, contrary to that just rejected (ἵνα ὑφ' ὑμῶν ἀνακρ.), to be rejected in its turn. In another sense P. enjoins self-judgment, in xi. 28-32; and in ii. 16 he credited the "spiritual man" with power "to try all things". Ὁ ἑαυτὸν ἀνακρίνων, the self-trier, is one who knows no higher or surer tribunal than his own conscience; Christ's Ap. stands in a very diff. position from this. This transition from Cor. judgment to self-judgment shows that no formal trial was in question, such as Weizsäcker supposes had been mooted at Cor.; arraigned before the bar of public opinion, P. wishes to say that he rates its estimate εἰς ἐλάχιστὸν in comparison with that of his heavenly Master.

Ver. 4. The negative clauses, οὐδὲν γὰρ . . . ἀλλ' οὐκ, together explain, parenthetically, Paul's meaning in ver. 3: "For I am conscious of nothing against myself" (in my conduct as Christ's minister to you: *cf.* 10, 18; 2 Cor. i. 12-

t Mt. viii.29 only. Sir. Κύριός ἐστιν. 5. ὥστε μὴ ᵗπρὸ ᵗκαιροῦ τι κρίνετε, ἕως ἂν ἔλθῃ ὁ
xxx, 24, xlvi. 28, Κύριος, ὃς ¹ καὶ ᵘφωτίσει τὰ ᵛκρυπτὰ τοῦ ʷσκότους καὶ ˣφανερώσει
li. 38. u In this use,2Tim. τὰς ʸβουλὰς τῶν ʸκαρδιῶν· καὶ τότε ὁ ᶻἔπαινος γενήσεται ἑκάστῳ
ᶻ ἀπὸ τοῦ ᶻΘεοῦ.

i. 10; cf.
Jo. i. 9;
Eph. i. 18; Heb. vi. 4, x. 32.   v xiv. 25; 2 Cor. iv. 2; Rom. ii. 16, 29; 1 Pet. iii. 4; Mt. x. 26.
w Rom. xiii. 12; eight times besides in P. in the ethical sense; 1 Pet. ii. 9; 1 Jo. i. 6; Mt. vi. 23;
Jo. iii. 19; Acts xxvi. 18.   x In this connexion, 2 Cor. v. 10 f.; Eph. v. 13; 1 Jo. ii. 19, iii. 2; Rev.
iii. 18; Mk. iv. 22; Jo. iii. 21.   y Of human βουλή, Lk. xxiii. 51; Acts xix. 1 (some texts), xxvii.
12, 42. In pl., N.T. h.l. βουλην καρδιας, Sir. xxxvii. 13.   z Rom. ii. 29; επαινος (with man for
obj.) generally, 2 Cor. viii. 18; Rom. xiii. 3; Ph. iv. 8; 1 Pet. i. 7, ii. 14.

¹ DG, Aug., om. ος: a Western variant.

17)—nothing that calls for judicial inquiry on your part or misgiving on my own—"but not on this ground (οὐκ ἐν τούτῳ) have I been justified". Σύνοιδα with reflexive pron. (h. l. in N.T.) has this connotation, of a guilty conscience, occasionally in cl. Gr. (see Lidd.); cf. the Horatian "Nil conscire sibi, nulla pallescere culpa" (Al.). "By" signifies "against" in Bible Eng. (see New Eng. Dict. s. v., 26 d; cf. Deut. xxvii. 16, Ezek. xxii. 7); "I know no harm by him" is current in the Midland counties (Al.).—For δικαιόω ἐν, see parls. The pf. pass. δεδικαίωμαι defines an act of God complete in the past and determining the writer's present state. P. has been and continues justified—not on the sentence of his conscience as a man self-acquitted ("not of works of righteousness, which we had done," Tit. iii. 5 f.), but as an ill-deserving sinner counted righteous for Christ's sake (i. 30, vi. 11, xv. 17; 2 Cor. v. 17-21, Rom. iii. 23 ff., iv. 25, vii. 24-viii. 1, etc.). This past "justification" is the ground of his whole standing before God (Rom. v. 1 ff.); it forbids presuming on the witness of his own conscience now. A good conscience is worth much; but, after P.'s experience, he cannot rely on its verdict apart from Christ's. Paul looks for his appraisement at the end (5), to the source from which he received his justification at the beginning. Accordingly for the present, he refers to Christ the testing of his daily course: ὁ δὲ ἀνακρίνων με Κύριός ἐστιν, "but he that does try (examine) me is the Lord"—not you, nor my own conscience; I am searched by a purer and a loftier eye. "The Lord is alone qualified for this office" (cf. v. 3 ff., and notes; Rev. ii., iii., John v. 22, etc.). The Lord's present ἀνάκρισις prepares for his final κρίσις (5). The above interpretation, which maintains the Pauline use of δικαιόω, is that of Calovius,

Rückert, Mr., Hn., Bt., and others. Cm., Cv., Est., Bg., Al., Ev., Ed., Gd., Sm., etc., insist on taking the term "in a meaning entirely diff. from its ordinary dogmatic sense" (Gd.), referring it in spite of the tense, on account of ver. 5, to the future judgment; but this brings confusion into Paul's settled language, and abandons the rock of his personal standing before God and men (cf. Gal. ii. 15 ff.). Since P. accepted justification by faith in Christ, not his innocence, but his Saviour's merit has become his fixed ground of assurance.

Ver. 5. The practical conclusion of the statement respecting Christ's servants (see note on ὥστε, iii. 21): "So then do not before the time be passing any judgment". τι, the cognate acc. = κρίσιν τινά, as in John vii. 24. πρὸ καιροῦ (the fit time, not the set time) signifies prematurely (so Æsch., Eumen., 367), as ἐν καιρῷ seasonably (Luke xii. 42). Our Lord gives another reason for not judging, in Matt. vii. 1 ff.; this prohibition, like that, points to His tribunal, bidding men hold back their verdicts on each other in deference to His (cf. Rom. xiv. 10). "Until the Lord come:" ἕως ἂν indicates contingency in the time, not the event itself; for this uncertainty, cf. 1 Thess. v. 2, Matt. xxv. 13, Luke xii. 39, Acts i. 7, etc. His coming is the ἀποκάλυψις toward which the hope of this Church was directed from the first (i. 7: see note); it will reveal with perfect evidence the matters on which the Cor. are officiously and ignorantly pronouncing.—ὃς καὶ φωτίσει κ.τ.λ.: "who shall also illuminate the hidden things of darkness". φωτίζω points to the cause, as φανερόω to the result, and ἀποκαλύπτω (ii. 10) to the mode of Divine disclosures. Christ's presence of itself illuminates (cf. 2 Cor. iv. 6, and other parls.); His Parousia is light as well as fire (iii. 13)—both instruments of judgment. τὰ κρυπτὰ

6. Ταῦτα δὲ, ἀδελφοί, ᵃμετεσχημάτισα εἰς ἐμαυτὸν καὶ Ἀπολλὼ ¹ᵃ 2 Cor. xi.
δι' ὑμᾶς, ἵνα ᵇ ἐν ἡμῖν ᵇ μάθητε τὸ μὴ ᶜὑπὲρ ᶜ ὃ ² γέγραπται φρονεῖν, ³

13 ff.; Ph.
iii. 21; 4
Macc. ix.
22. Also

Joseph., *Ant.*, vii., 10. 5; Philo, *Leg. ad. Gai.*, § 11; Plato, *Leges*, x. 903 E.   b *Cf.* Jo. xiii. 35;
Gen. xlii. 33.   c x. 13; 2 Cor. xii. 6.

¹ Απολλων, ℵ*AB*.   See W.H., *Notes on Selected Readings*, p. 157.   B³, by a
curious blunder, απο πολλων.

² (υπερ) a, ℵABCP 17, 31, 73.   Referring to Scripture at large.

³ *Om.* φρονειν ℵ*ABD*G, latt. vg., Or., Aug., Ambrst.
ℵcCDcLP cop. syrr., Cyr. insert (? Alexandrian); Ath., φυσιουσθαι.

τοῦ σκότους, "the secrets hidden in the
darkness" (*res tenebris occultatas*, Bz.)
—not necessarily *evil* things (see Rom.
ii. 16, 2 Cor. iv. 6), but things impene-
trable to present light.—Chief amongst
these, "the Lord will make manifest
(φανερώσει) *the counsels of the hearts*".
These God (and with Him Christ, ὁ
ἀνακρίνων: 4) already searches out (Rom.
viii. 27; Ps. cxxxix., etc.); then He will
make plain to men, about themselves and
each other, what was dark before.   The
καρδία is the real self, the "hidden,"
"inward man" (Eph. iii. 16 f., 1 Pet.
iii. 4, and other parls.), known absolutely
to God alone (*cor hominis crypta est*, Bz.);
its "counsels" are those self-communings
and purposings which determine action
and belong to the essence of character.—
"And *then* (not before) the (due) praise
will come (ὁ ἔπαινος γενήσεται) to each
from God (not from human lips)."   ἀπὸ
τ. Θεοῦ for it is on *God's* behalf that
Christ will judge; His commendation is
alone of value (Rom. ii. 29; John v. 44).
The Church is *God's* field and temple
(iii. 9 ff.); all work wrought in it awaits
His approval.   ἑκάστῳ recalls the lesson
of iii. 8, 11-13, respecting the discriminating and individual character of Divine
rewards.   "Praise" ambitious Gr. teachers
coveted: let them seek it from God.
"Praise" the Cor. partisans lavished on
their admired leaders: this is God's prerogative, let them check their imperti-
nent eulogies.   Enough was said in iii.
15, 17, of *condemned* work; P. is thinking
here of his true συνεργοί (1 f.), who with
himself labour and hope for approval at
the Day of Christ; little need they reck
of the criticisms of the hour.

§ 13. DISCIPLES ABOVE THEIR MASTER,
iv. 6-13.   What the Ap. has written,
from iii. 3 onwards, turns on the relations
between himself and Apollos; but it has
a wide application to the state of feeling
within the Church (6 f.).   To such ex-
travagance of self-satisfaction and con-

ceit in their new teachers have the Cor.
been carried, that one would think they
had dispensed with the App., and entered
already on the Messianic reign (8).   In
comparison with them, P. and his comrades present a sorry figure, as victims
marked for the world's sport—famished,
beaten, loaded with disgrace, while their
disciples flourish!   (9-13.)

Ver. 6.   Ταῦτα δὲ κ.τ.λ. (δὲ *metabatikon*, of transition): "Now these
things I have adapted (in the way I have
put them) to myself and Apollos".—
μετα-σχηματίζω (see parls.), to *change
the dress*, or *form of presentment* (σχῆμα),
of anything.   P. has put in a specific
personal way—speaking *in concreto*, *ex-
empli gratia*—what he might have expressed more generally; he has done
this δι' ὑμᾶς, "for *your* better instruction,"—not because *he and Ap.* needed
the admonition.   The rendering "I have
in a figure *transferred*" (E.V.), suggests
that the argument of iii. 3-iv. 5 had no
real connexion with P. and A., and was
aimed at others than their partisans—an
erroneous implication: see *Introd.* to
Div. I.   P. writes in the σχῆμα κατ'
ἐξοχήν, aiming through the Apollonian
party at all the warring factions, and at
the factious spirit in the Church; his
reproaches fall on the "puffed up" followers, not upon their unconsenting chiefs
(4).   We found certain *other teachers*,
active at Cor. in the absence of P. and
A., rebuked in iii. 11-17; the Cor. will
easily read between the lines.   This
μετασχηματισμὸς is "id genus in quo
per quandam suspicionem quod non
dicimus accipi volumus" (Quintilian, *In-
stit.*, ix., 2).—Ἀπολλών, the preferable
reading here and in Tit. iii. 13, like the
gen. of i. 12, iii. 4, is acc. of Attic 2nd
decl.; Ἀπολλώ (3rd) is attested in Acts
xix. 1.

ἵνα ἐν ἡμῖν μάθητε τὸ Μὴ ὑπὲρ ἃ
γέγραπται: "that in our case you may
learn the (rule), *Not beyond the things*

d 1 Th. v.   ἵνα μὴ ᵈ εἷς ὑπὲρ τοῦ ᵈ ἑνὸς ᵉ φυσιοῦσθε κατὰ ᶠ τοῦ ᶠ ἑτέρου. 7. τίς
11; cf. x.
17; Gal.   γάρ σε ᵍ διακρίνει; τί δὲ ἔχεις ὃ οὐκ ἔλαβες; ʰ εἰ δὲ καὶ ἔλαβες, ʰτί
iv. 22;
Eph. iv.   ʰ καυχᾶσαι ὡς μὴ λαβών; 8. ἤδη ⁱ κεκορεσμένοι ἐστέ, ἤδη ᵏ ἐπλου-
4 f.
e 18 f., v. 2,   τήσατε, χωρὶς ἡμῶν ˡ ἐβασιλεύσατε· καὶ ᵐ ὄφελόν γε ˡ ἐβασιλεύσατε,
viii. 1,
xiii. 4;

Col. ii. 18; -ωσις, 2 Cor. xii. 20.   f vi. 1, x. 24, 29, xiv. 17; Ro. ii. 1, xiii. 8; Gal. vi. 4; Phil. ii. 4.
g H.l. with pers. obj.; cf. vi. 5; Acts xv. 9; Jude 22.   h For interr. after εἰ, xii. 17. See i. 29.
i Acts xxvii. 38; Deut. xxxi. 20.   k 2 Cor. viii. 9; Rom. x. 12; 1 Tim. vi. 9, 18; 5 times in Rev.;
Lk. i. 53, xii. 21.   l xv. 25; Rom. v. 14, 17, 21, vi. 12; 1 Tim. vi. 15; Rev. v. 10, etc.   m 2 Cor.
xi. 1; Gal. v. 12; Rev. iii. 15.

that are written" : cf. the cl. **Μηδὲν ἄγαν.**
The art. **τὸ** seizes the **Μὴ ὑπὲρ** clause
for the obj. of **μάθητε**; for the construction, cf. Gal. v. 14, Luke xxii. 37, and
see Wr., pp. 135, 644; the elliptical
form ("Not" for "Do not go," or the
like) marks the saying as proverbial,
though only here extant. Ewald suggests
that it was a Rabbinical adage—as much
as to say, *Keep to the rule of Scripture,
Not a step beyond the written word!*
"**γέγραπται** in his libris semper ad V.
T. refertur" (Grotius); but in a general
maxim it is superfluous to look for particular passages intended. In iii. 19 f.,
and indirectly in vv. 4 f. above, P. has
shown the Cor. how to keep their thoughts
about men within the lines marked out
in Scripture.—The 1st **ἵνα** is definitely
applied by the second, apposed **ἵνα**:
"that you be not puffed up, each for his
individual (teacher) against the other".
Scripture teaches the Cor. both not to
"glory in men" and not to "judge" them
(iii. 21, iv. 4 f.).—**φυσιοῦσθε** (**φυσιόω,**
older Gr. **φυσάω** or **φυσιάω,** *to inflate*)
is best explained as irreg. pr. *sbj.* (*cf.*
ζηλοῦτε, Gal. iv. 17); John xvii. 3 is the
only clear ex. of **ἵνα** with ind. in N.T.—
see however Wr., pp. 362 f. Mr. obviates the difficulty by rendering **ἵνα**
where, against Bibl. and later Gr. use.
Fritzsche read **ὃ** (T. R.) for **ἅ** in the
previous clause; then, by a double
itacism, **ἵνα** for **ἵνα** and **φυσιοῦσθαι** for
φυσιοῦσθε, thus getting ingeniously an
inf. clause in 6*c*, standing in apposition
to the **ὃ** of 6*b*—"Not beyond what is
written,—*i.e.*, that one be not puffed up
for the one," etc.).—**εἷς ὑπὲρ τ. ἑνός,** a
reciprocal phrase (*cf.* 1 Thess. v. 11),
"one for the one (teacher), another for
the other " (see i. 12),—zeal "for the
one" admired master generating an
animus "against the other" (**κατὰ τοῦ
ἑτέρου,** *the second*) correspondingly despised. Those who cried up Apollos
cried down Paul, and *vice versâ.*
Ver. 7. **τίς γάρ σε διακρίνει;** "for
who marks thee off?" (or "separates thee?

—*discernit,* Vg.")—what warrant for thy
boasting, "I am of Paul," etc., for rang-
ing thyself in this coterie or that? "The
διάκρισις was self-made" (El.). The
other rendering, "Who makes thee to
differ?" (to be superior : *eximie distinguit,*
Bg.)—*sc.* "who but *God?*"—suits the
vb. **διακρίνω,** but is hardly relevant.
This question stigmatises the partisan
conceit of the Cor. as *presumptuous;*
those that follow, **τί δὲ . . . εἰ δὲ καὶ
. . .** marks it as *ungrateful;* both ways
it is egotistic.—**τί δὲ ἔχεις κ.τ.λ.:** "what
moreover hast thou that thou didst not
receive?"—*i.e., from God* (i. 4 f., 30, iii.
5, 10, xii. 6, etc.). For this pregnant sense
of **λαμβάνω,** *cf.* Acts xx. 35.—"But if
indeed thou didst receive (it), why glory
as one that had not received?" The
receiver may boast of the Giver (i. 31),
not of anything *as his own.* **καὶ** lends
actuality to the vb.; "**εἰ καί,** de re quam
ita esse ut dicitur significamus" (Hermann); *cf.* 2 Cor. iv. 3. **καυχᾶσαι,** a
rare form of 2nd sing. ind. mid.; Wr.,
p. 90. For **ὡς** with ptp., of *point of view*
(*perinde ac*), see Bm., p. 307; *cf.* ver. 3.
Ver. 8 depicts the unjustifiable "glorying" of the readers with an abruptness
due to excited feeling (*cf.* the *asyndeton*
of iii. 16): "How much you have received, and how you boast of it!—So soon
you are satiated!" etc. The three first
clauses—**ἤδη, ἤδη, χωρὶς κ.τ.λ.**—are ex-
clamations rather than questions (W.H.).
Distinguish **ἤδη,** *jam, by this time;* **νῦν,**
nunc, at this time (iii. 2, etc.); **ἄρτι,** *in
præsenti, modo, just now* or *then, at the
moment* (xiii. 12, etc.). **κεκορεσμένοι
ἐστέ** (**κορέννυμι,** *to glut, feed full;* in cl.
Gr. poetical, becoming prose in **κοινή;** for
tense-form, *cf.* i. 10, **ἦτε κατηρτ.:** "So
soon you have had your fill (are quite
satisfied)!" The Cor. reported themselves, in the Church Letter (?), so well
fed by Paul's successors, so furnished in
talent and grace, that they desired nothing
more.—**ἤδη ἐπλουτήσατε** (aor., not pf.
as before): "So soon you grew rich!"
The Thanksgiving (i. 5) and the list of

ἵνα καὶ ἡμεῖς σὺν ὑμῖν ⁿσυμβασιλεύσωμεν. 9. δοκῶ γὰρ ὅτι ¹ ὁ ⁿ 2 Tim. ii.
12.
Θεὸς ἡμᾶς τοὺς ἀποστόλους ᵖἐσχάτους ᑫἀπέδειξεν ὡς ʳἐπιθανατίους, ο See iii. 18,
and note
ὅτι ˢθέατρον ἐγενήθημεν τῷ κόσμῳ, καὶ ἀγγέλοις καὶ ἀνθρώποις· below.
p In this
10. ἡμεῖς ᵗμωροὶ διὰ Χριστόν, ὑμεῖς δὲ ᵘφρόνιμοι ἐν Χριστῷ· ἡμεῖς sense, xv.
8; Matt.
ᵛἀσθενεῖς, ὑμεῖς δὲ ᵛἰσχυροί· ὑμεῖς ʷἔνδοξοι, ἡμεῖς δὲ ˣἄτιμοι· xix. 30;
Mk. ix.
35; Luke

xiv. 9 f.; Jo. viii. 9.   q 2 Th. ii. 4; Acts ii. 22, xxv. 7. -ξις, ii. 4.   r H.l.   s N.T. h.l. in this
sense; see Acts xix. 29, 31.   t See i. 25.   u x. 15; 2 Cor. xi. 19; Rom. xi. 25, xii. 16; Matt. vii.
24, x. 16, xxv. 2 ff.; Lk. xvi. 8.   v See i. 25.   w Eph. v. 27; Luke vii. 25, xiii. 17; LXX passim.
x xii. 23; Mt. xiii. 57; Mk. vi. 4; Isa. liii. 3.

¹δοκω γαρ, ο Θεος, *without* οτι: all pre-Syrian uncc.

charisms in xii. appear to justify this consciousness of wealth; but ostentation corrupted Cor. riches; spiritual satiety is a sign of arrested growth: contrast Phil. iii. 10-14, and *cf.* Rev. iii. 17, "Thou *sayest*, ὅτι Πλούσιός εἰμί καὶ πεπλούτηκα". The climax of this sad irony is χωρὶς ἡμῶν ἐβασιλεύσατε (*aor.* again), "Without us (without our help) you have come to your kingdom!"—"Gradatio: *saturi, divites, reges*" (Bg.). Paul was given to understand, by some Cor., that they had outgrown his teaching: "Then," he says, "you have surely entered the promised kingdom and secured its treasures, if God's stewards have nothing more to impart to you!—*I only wish you had!*" so he continues in the words καὶ ὄφελόν γε κ.τ.λ., "Ay, I would indeed that you had entered the kingdom, that we too might share it with you!" It is Paul's sigh for the end.—Βασιλεύω (see parls.) can only relate to the βασιλεία Θεοῦ, the Messianic reign (20, vi. 9 f., xv. 50; N.T. *passim; cf.* Luke xxii. 28 ff.; vi. 2 f. below; the *judicial* assumptions of the Cor., in 3 ff., square with this); and the aor. in vbs. of "state" is *inceptive* (Br. § 41)—not "you reigned," but "became kings" (ἐβασιλεύσατε). This, of course, can only come about *when Christ returns* (see i. 7, 9, and notes); *then* His saints will share His glory (2 Tim. ii. 10).—ὄφελον (losing its augm.) is in N.T. and later Gr. practically an adv.; it marks, with following ind. past, an impracticable wish (Wr., p. 377); γε (*to be sure*) accentuates the personal feeling. Πλουτέω, βασιλεύω remind us again of Stoic pretensions; see note, iii. 22.

Ver. 9 gives reason in Paul's sorrowful state for the wish that has escaped him. δοκῶ γὰρ ὁ Θεὸς κ.τ.λ. (ὅτι wanting after δοκῶ, as in vii. 40; so in Eng.): "For, methinks, God has exhibited (*spectandos proposuit*, Bz.)

us, the apostles, last"—at the end of the show, in the meanest place (for the use of ἔσχατος, *cf.* Mark ix. 35; for the sentiment, xv. 19 below)—"as (men) doomed to death". One imagines a grand procession, on some day of public festival; in its rear march the criminals on their way to the arena, where the populace will be regaled with their sufferings. Paul's experience in Ephesus suggests the picture (*cf.* xv. 32); that of 2 Cor. ii. 14 is not dissimilar. "The app." (*cf.* ix. 1, xv. 5 ff.), not P. alone, are set in this disgrace: Acts i.-xii. illustrates what is said; possibly recent (unrecorded) sufferings of prominent missionaries gave added point to the comparison. Ἀπο-δείκνυμι (*to show-off*) takes its disparaging sense from the connexion, like δειγματίζω in Col. ii. 15. ἐπιθανατίους (later Gr.) = ἐπὶ τ. θάνατον ὄντας.—ὅτι θέατρον ἐγενήθημεν τῷ κόσμῳ does not give the *reason* for the above ἀπόδειξις, but *re-affirms the fact* with a view to bring forward the spectators; this clause apposed to the foregoing, in which ὅτι was implicit: "Methinks God has set forth us the app. last, as sentenced to death,—that we have been made a spectacle to the world," etc. Hf. would read ὅ,τι θέατρον, "which spectacle," etc.—a tempting constr., suiting the lively style of the passage; but ὅστις occurs as adj. nowhere in the N.T. (unless, possibly, in Heb. ix. 9), and rarely at all in Gr. θέατρον "may mean the *place, spectators, actors,* or *spectacle:* the last meaning is the one used here, and the rarest" (Lt.). "To the world:" so Peter, *e.g.*, at Jerus., Paul in the great Gentile capitals. "*Both to angels* and men" extends the ring to include those invisible watchers—"καί singles them out for special attention" (Lt.)—of whose presence the Ap. was aware (see xi. 10, and other parls.); *angels,* as such, in contrast with *men,*—not the good or bad

y xi. 26, xv. 11. ᵞἄχρι ˣτῆς ˣἄρτι ὥρας καὶ ᵃπεινῶμεν καὶ ᵃᵇδιψῶμεν καὶ
25; 11
times be- ᶜγυμνητεύομεν,¹ καὶ ᵈκολαφιζόμεθα, καὶ ᵉἀστατοῦμεν, 12. καὶ
sides in
P.; freq. ᶠκοπιῶμεν ᵍἐργαζόμενοι ταῖς ἰδίαις ᵍχερσί · ʰλοιδορούμενοι ¹εὐλο-
in Acts
and Rev.

z Art. with αρτι, h.l. Cf. εως αρτι, 13; also ο νυν καιρος, Rom. iii. 26, etc.   a xi. 21, 34; Phil. iv.
12; Lk. i. 53, vi. 21, 25. πειν. κ. διψ, Rom. xii. 20; Matt. v. 6, xxv. 35 ff.; Rev. vii. 16; Jo. vi. 35.
b διψαω (alone), Jo. xix. 28. λιμος κ. διψος, 2 Cor. xi. 27.   c H.l.; Dio Chrys. xxv. 3.   d 2 Cor.
xii. 7; 1 Pet. ii. 20; Matt. xxvi. 67.   e H.l. αστατος in Arist. and later Gr.   f In lit. use.
Eph. iv. 28; 2 Tim. ii. 6; Acts xx. 35; Matt. vi. 28; Luke v. 5.   g Eph. iv. 28; 1 Thess. iv. 11;
Wisd. xv. 17; εργαζομαι (absolute) is fairly common.   h 1 Pet. ii. 23; Acts xxiii. 4; Jo. ix. 28.
i Absolutely, xiv. 16; Rom. xii. 14; 1 Pet. iii. 9.

¹ γυμνιτευομεν: all uncc. but L (B*D* -νειτ-).   From γυμνιτης, Wr., p. 114.

angels specifically (cf. note on vi. 3).
Eph. iii. 10 f. intimates that the heavenly
Intelligences *learn* while they watch.
Ver. 10 represents the contrasted case
of the App. and the Cor. Christians, as
they appear in the estimate of the two
parties. "We" are μωροί, ἀσθενεῖς, ἄτιμοι (cf. i. 18-27, iii. 18, and notes; with
ii. 3, for ἀσθ.); "you," φρόνιμοι, ἰσχυ-
ροί, ἔνδοξοι—the last adj. in heightened
contrast to ἄτιμοι; not merely *honoured*
(ἔντιμοι, Phil. ii. 29), but *glorious*—P.
reflects on the relatively "splendid"
(Luke vii. 25) worldly condition of the
Cor. as compared with his own. μωροὶ
διὰ Χριστόν, "fools because of Christ"
(cf. Matt. v. 11)—who *makes* us so, sends
us with a "foolish" message (i. 23).
Distinguish διά (ix. 23, 2 Cor. iv. 11,
etc.) from ὑπὲρ Χριστοῦ, which means
"on Christ's behalf," as representing Him
(2 Cor. v. 20, etc.). The Ap. does not
call the Cor. σοφοί (see iii. 18), but, with
a fine discrimination, φρόνιμοι ἐν Χριστῷ
(*prudentes in Christo*); he appeals to
them as such in x. 15, 2 Cor. xi. 19—the
epithet was one they affected; writing at
Cor., he is perhaps thinking of *them* in
Rom. xi. 25, xii. 16. The φρόνιμος is
the *man of sense*—no fanatic, rushing to
extremes and affronting the world needlessly: this Church is on dangerously
good terms with the world (viii. 10, x.
14-33, cf. 2 Cor. vi. 14-vii. 1); see *Introd.*,
pp. 731 f.; "Christum et prudentiam carnis
miscere vellent" (Cv.). They deem
themselves "strong" in contrast with
the "feeble in faith" (Rom. xiv. 1), with
whom P. associates himself (ix. 22, etc.),
able to "use the world" (vii. 31) and
not hampered by weak-minded scruples
(vi. 12, x. 23, viii.; see note on iii. 22).
In the third clause P. reverses the order
of prons. (*you . . . we*), returning to
the description of his own mode of life.
The ἀγενής (i. 28) is without the birth
qualifying for public respect, the ἄτιμος
(see parls.) is one actually deprived of
respect—in cl. Gr., *disfranchised.*

Vv. 11, 12a. ἄχρι τῆς ἄρτι ὥρας . . .
ταῖς ἰδίαις χερσὶν describes the ἄτιμοι,
reduced to this position by the world's
contempt and with no means of winning
its respect—a life at the farthest remove
from that of the Gr. gentleman. The
despicableness of his condition touches
the Ap. New features are added to this
picture in 2 Cor. xi. 23-33. On ἄρτι, see
note to ἤδη, ver. 8; cf. ver. 13.—*Hunger,
thirst, ill-clothing*—the common accompaniments of poverty; *blows, homeless-
ness, manual toil*—specific hardships of
Paul's mission. The sentences are pl.:
all Christian missionaries (9) shared in
these sufferings, P. beyond others (xv.
10).—γυμνιτεύω (later Gr.) denotes *light
clothing* or *armour*; cf. γυμνός, Matt.
xxv. 36, Jas. ii. 15 (*ill-clad*).—κολαφίζω
(see parls.), *to fisticuff*, extended to physical violence generally—sometimes lit. true
in Paul's case.—ἀστατέω, *to be unsettled,
with no fixed home*—to Paul's affectionate nature the greatest of privations,
and always suspicious in public repute—
to be a vagrant. On ἐργαζ. τ. ἰδ. χερσίν
—at Eph. now (Acts xx. 34), at Cor.
formerly (Acts xviii. 3)—see note, ix. 6;
manual labour was particularly despised
amongst the ancients: "Non modo
labore meo victum comparo, sed
manuario labore et sordido" (Cv.).

Vv. 12b, 13. Beside their abject condition (11, 12a), the world saw in the
meekness of the App. the marks of *an
abject spirit*, shown in the three particulars of λοιδορούμενοι . . . παρακαλοῦμεν: "id mundus spretum putat"
(Bg.).—λοιδορ. (*reviled to our faces*) implies insulting abuse, δυσφημούμενοι
(*defamed*) injurious abuse: for the former,
cf. 1 Peter ii. 23.—διωκόμενοι ἀνεχόμεθα,
"persecuted, we bear with (lit. *put-up*
with) it"—implying *patience*, while ὑπο-
μένω (xiii. 7, etc.) implies *courage* in the
sufferer. The series of ptps. is pr., denoting habitual treatment—not "when"
but "while we are reviled," etc.—εὐλογοῦμεν . . . παρακαλοῦμεν: to revilings

γούμεν, ᵏ διωκόμενοι ¹ ἀνεχόμεθα, 13. ᵐ βλασφημούμενοι ¹ ⁿ παρα-
καλοῦμεν· ὡς ° περικαθάρματα ² τοῦ κόσμου ἐγενήθημεν, πάντων
ᵖ περίψημα, ۹ ἕως ۹ ἄρτι.

14. Οὐκ ʳ ἐντρέπων ὑμᾶς γράφω ταῦτα, ἀλλ' ὡς τέκνα μου

ᵏ xv. 9; 2
Cor. iv. 9;
Rom. xii.
14; Gal. i.
13; Phil.
iii. 6; 2
Tim. iii.
12; Rev.
xii. 13;

Acts vii. 52, etc.; Matt. v. 10, etc.   l Absol., 2 Cor. xi. 4, 20.   m δυσφ., N.T. *h.l.*; 1 Macc.
vii. 41. δυσφημια, 2 Cor. vi. 8.   n Absol., 2 Cor. v. 20; Rom. xii. 8; 2 Tim. iv. 2; Tit. i. 9; Luke
iii. 18.   o *H.l.*; Prov. xxi. 18.   p *H.l.*; Tobit v. 19; Ignatius *ad Eph.* viii. 1, xviii. 1.   q viii.
7, xv. 6; Mt. xi. 12; four times in John.   r Active, *h.l.*; *cf.* 2 Thess. iii. 14; Tit. ii. 8; Heb. xii.
9, etc. εντροπη, see vi. 5.   s 17, x. 14, xv. 58, and frequently in P.; Heb. vi. 19; Jas. i. 16,
etc.; 1 Jo., *passim*; 1 Pet. ii. 11, iv. 12; 2 Pet. iii. and Jude, αγαπ. For τεκνα, in P., 2 Cor. vi.
13; Gal. iv. 19; Phil. ii. 22; 1 Thess. ii. 7, 11; 1 Tim. i. 2, 18; 2 Tim. ii. 1; Tit. i. 4; Phm. 10.

¹ δυσφημουμενοι, ℵ*ACP 17.
βλασφημ., ℵᶜBDG, etc., latt. vg.—Western and Syrian emendation.
² ωσπερει καθαρματα, G and six minuscc.

they retort with *blessings*, to calumnies
with benevolent *exhortation;* "they beg
men not to be wicked, to return to a
better mind, to be converted to Christ"
(Gd.); *cf.* the instructions of Luke vi.
27 ff. "It is on this its positive side
that" Christian meekness "surpasses the
abstention from retaliation urged by
Plato" (*Crit.*, p. 49: Ed.).—ὡς περικαθάρματα τοῦ κόσμου . . . πάντων περίψημα
(from περι-καθαίρω, -ψάω respectively,
to cleanse, wipe all round, with -μα of
result): the *ne plus ultra* of degradation;
they became "as *rinsings* of the world,—
a *scraping* of all things" (*purgamenta et
ramentum*, Bz.),—the filth that one gets
rid of through the sink and the gutter.
    The above terms may have a further
significance: "the Ap. is carrying on the
metaphor of ἐπιθανατίους above. Both
περικαθ. and περίψ. were used esp. of
those condemned criminals of the lowest
class who were sacrificed as expiatory
offerings, as scapegoats in effect, because
of their degraded life. It was the custom at Athens to reserve certain worthless persons who in case of plague, famine,
or other visitations from heaven, might
be thrown into the sea, in the belief that
they would 'cleanse away,' or 'wipe off,'
the guilt of the nation" (Lt.). περι-
κάθαρμα (for the earlier κάθαρμα occurs
in this sense in Arr.-Epict., III., xxii., 78;
also in Prov. xxi. 11 (LXX): this view
is supported by Hesychius, Luther, Bg.,
Hn., Ed.; rejected, as inappropriate, by
Er., Est., Cv., Bz., Mr., Gd., El. Certainly P. does not look on his sufferings
as a *piaculum;* but he is expressing the
estimate of "the world," which deemed
its vilest fittest to devote to the anger of
the Gods. Possibly some cry of this
sort, anticipating the "Christiani ad
leones" of the martyrdoms, had been

raised against P. by the Ephesian populace (*cf.* xv. 32; also Acts xxii. 22).—ἕως
ἄρτι, repeated with emphasis from ver.
11, shows P. to be writing under the
smart of recent outrage. With his temper, Paul keenly felt personal indignities.
    § 14. PAUL'S FATHERLY DISCIPLINE,
iv. 14-21. All has now been said that
can be concerning the Divisions at Cor.
—the causes underlying them, and the
spirit they manifest and foster in the
Church. In their self-complacent, ungrateful thoughts, the Cor. have raised
themselves quite above the despised and
painful condition of the App. of Christ;
"imitabantur filios qui illustrati parum
curant humiles parentes—ex saturitate
fastidium habebant, ex opulentia in-
solentiam, ex regno superbiam" (Bg.).
The delineation of Paul's state and theirs
in the last Section is, in truth, a bitter
sarcasm upon the behaviour of the
readers; yet P. wishes to admonish, not
to rebuke them (14). He states, in a
softened tone, the measures he is taking
to rectify the evils complained of. His
severity springs from the anxious heart
of a father (14 f.). Yet in the father's
hand, before the paragraph ends, we see
again *the rod* (21).
    Ver. 14. Οὐκ ἐντρέπων κ.τ.λ.: "Not
(by way of) shaming you do I write this,
but admonishing (you) as my children
beloved". It is in *chiding* that the Ap.
addresses both the Cor. and Gal. as his
"children" (2 Cor. vi. 13, xii. 14, Gal. iv.
19); τέκνον ἀγαπητὸν he applies besides
only to *Timothy* (ver. 17 and 2 Tim. i. 2).
Not intentionally here, but in vi. 5 and
xv. 34 he *does* speak πρὸς ἐντροπήν.—τὸ
νουθετεῖν (= ἐν νῷ τιθέναι) is the part of
a *father* (Eph. vi. 4), or *brother* (2 Thess.
iii. 15); "the vb. has a lighter meaning
than ἐντρέπειν or ἐπιτιμᾶν, and implies

t Rom. xv.
14; Col. i.   ᵃ ἀγαπητὰ ᵗ νουθετῶ.¹   15. ἐὰν γὰρ ᵘμυρίους ᵛπαιδαγωγοὺς ἔχητε
28, iii. 16; ἐν Χριστῷ, ἀλλ' οὐ πολλοὺς πατέρας · ἐν γὰρ Χριστῷ 'Ιησοῦ ² διὰ
1 Thess. v.
12, 14; 2   τοῦ εὐαγγελίου ἐγὼ ὑμᾶς ᵂἐγέννησα · 16. ˣπαρακαλῶ οὖν ὑμᾶς,
Thess. iii.
15; Acts   ʸμιμηταί μου γίνεσθε.   17. διὰ τοῦτο ³ ᶻἔπεμψα ᶻὑμῖν Τιμόθεον,
xx. 31.
u xiv. 19;   ὅς ἐστι ˢτέκνον ⁴ μου ⁴ ˢἀγαπητὸν καὶ ᵃπιστὸν ᵃἐν ᵃΚυρίῳ, ὃς ὑμᾶς
Matt.
xviii. 24.   ᵇ ἀναμνήσει τὰς ᶜὁδούς μου τὰς ἐν Χριστῷ,⁵ καθὼς ᵈπανταχοῦ ἐν ᵈπάσῃ
v Gal. iii.
24 f.

w Phm. 10; cf. Gal. iv. 19; 1 Thess. ii. 7 f., 11.   x See i. 10.   y xi. 1; Eph. v. 1; 1 Thess. i. 6,
ii. 14; Heb. vi. 12. For the vb., 2 Thess. iii. 7, 9.   z Phil. ii. 19; Acts xi. 29; dat. commodi.
a Eph. i. 1; Col. i. 2; Acts xvi. 15. πιστος, see ver. 2.   b 2 Cor. vii. 15; 2 Tim. i. 6; Heb. x. 32;
Mk. xi. 21, xiv. 72. -σις, xi. 24.   c Pl., Rom. iii. 16, xi. 33; Heb. iii. 10; James i. 8; Rev. xv. 3;
Acts ii. 28, xiii. 10; xiv. 16; freq. in O.T.   d Acts xvii. 30, xxiv. 3.

¹ νουθετων (?): so ℵACP 17 (Alexandrian, and perhaps Neutral), followed by
Tisch., W.H., Tr. marg., Nestle.
νουθετω BDGL, etc., latt. vg.—Western and Syrian.

² B om. Ιησου, with several Ff.

³ (δια τουτο) αυτο (?) ins. ℵ*AP 17, syrᴾ·, Euthal. ; so Tisch., W.H. marg.
Om. αυτο ℵᶜBCDGL, etc., syrsch. ; W.H. txt., Al., Tr., Nestle. The double
pronoun is characteristic of Paul; αυτο might easily be lost through homœoteleuton.

⁴ μου τεκνον, ℵABCP 17, 37, Euthal.

⁵ Χριστω Ιησου, ℵCDᵇ 17, 37, cop. syrᴾ· Euthal.—Alexandrian.
κυριω Ιησου (om. Χριστω): D*G—Western.
Χριστω, ABDᶜLP, etc., syrsch.—Neutral and Syrian.

a monitory appeal to the νοῦς rather
than a direct rebuke or censure" (El.).
Ver. 15. Reason for this lighter reproof, where stern censure was due—
"For if you should have ten thousand
tutors in Christ, yet (you have) not many
fathers!" The relation of the ἐποικοδομοῦντες to the θεμέλιον τιθείς (iii. 10) is
exchanged for that of the παιδαγωγοὶ to
the πατήρ. The παιδαγωγός (boy-leader)
was not the schoolmaster, but the home-
tutor—a kind of nursery-governor—who
had charge of the child from tender
years, looking after his food and dress,
speech and manners, and when he was
old enough taking him to and from school
(see Lt. on Gal. iii. 24). This epithet
has a touch of disparagement for the
readers (cf. Gal. iii. 25); as Or. says
(Catena), referring to iii. 1 f., οὐδεὶς
ἀνὴρ παιδαγωγεῖται, ἀλλ' εἴ τις νήπιος
καὶ ἀτελής.—μυρίους (xiv. 19) indicates
the very many—probably too many—
teachers busy in this Church (cf. Jas.
iii. 1, and iii. 18 above), in whose guidance
the Cor. felt themselves "rich" and Apostolic direction superfluous (8).—ἀλλά (at
certe) introduces an apodosis in salient
contrast with its protasis: "You may
have ever so many nurses, but only one
father!" From this relationship "non
solum Apollos excluditur, successor; sed
etiam comites, Silas et Timotheus" (Bg.):

ἐγώ (I and no other) ἐγέννησα ὑμᾶς (cf.
Philem. 10, Gal. iv. 19); in the Rabbinical treatise Sanhedrin, f., xix. 2, the like
sentiment occurs, "Whoever teaches the
son of his friend the law, it is as if he
had begotten him"; similarly Philo, de
Virtute, p. 1000.—διὰ τ. εὐαγγελίου: cf.
1 Peter i. 23 ; also i. 18 above, 1 Thess.
i. 5, ii. 19; John vi. 63, etc.
Ver. 16. "I beseech you therefore (as
your father), be imitators of me." γίνεσθε
(pr. impr.) signifies, in moral exhortations,
be in effect, show yourselves (cf. Eph. iv.
32, v. 17). μιμηταὶ γίνεσθε demands,
beyond μιμεῖσθε, a character formed on
the given model. Imitation is the law
of the child's life; cf. Eph. v. 1; and
for the highest illustration, John v. 17-
20. It is one thing to say "I am of
Paul" (i. 12), another to tread in Paul's
steps. The imitation would embrace, in
effect, much of what was described in vv.
9 ff.
Ver. 17. "For this reason"—viz., to
help you to imitate me as your father—
"I sent to you Timothy, who is a beloved child of mine, and faithful in the
Lord". Timothy had left P. before this
letter was written, having been sent forward along with Erastus (possibly a Cor.,
Rom. xvi. 23) to Macedonia (Acts xix. 22),
but with instructions, as it now appears,
to go forward to Cor.; respecting his

ἐκκλησίᾳ ᵉδιδάσκω. 18. ὡς μὴ ἐρχομένου δέ μου πρὸς ὑμᾶς
ᶠἐφυσιώθησάν ᵍτινες· 19. ἐλεύσομαι δὲ ταχέως πρὸς ὑμᾶς, ʰἐὰν ὁ
ʰΚύριος ʰθελήσῃ, καὶ ⁱγνώσομαι οὐ τὸν ᵏλόγον τῶν ᶠπεφυσιωμένων
ἀλλὰ τὴν ᵏˡδύναμιν· 20. οὐ γὰρ ἐν ᵏλόγῳ ἡ ᵐβασιλεία τοῦ ᵐΘεοῦ
ἀλλ᾽ ˡἐν ᵏˡδύναμει. 21. τί θέλετε; ⁿἐν ⁿῥάβδῳ ἔλθω πρὸς ὑμᾶς, ἢ
ἐν ἀγάπῃ ᵒπνεύματί τε ᵖπραότητος¹;

e Of Christian doctrine, Rom. xii. 7; eight times besides in P.; Heb. v. 12; 1 Jo. ii. 27; Gospp. and Acts, passim.

f See ver. 6 above.   g In this sense, 2 Cor. iii. 1, x. 2; Gal. i. 7, ii. 12; 1 Tim. i. 6; 7 times in
Pastt.; 2 Pet. iii. 9, 16; Jude 4.   h James iv. 15; Sir. xxxix. 6.   i 2 Cor. ii. 9, xiii. 6; Rom.
vii. 7; Gal. ii. 9; Phil. ii. 22, iii. 10; 1 Th. iii. 5; 1 Jo. iii. 16; Rev. ii. 23, etc.   k 1 Thess. i. 5;
in similar contrasts, 2 Cor. x. 11; Rom. xv. 18; Col. iii. 17; 1 John iii. 18.   l See i. 18; 10 times
besides in like use in P.   For ἐν δυναμει, xv. 43; 2 Cor. vi. 7; Rom. i. 4, xv. 13, 19; Col. i. 11, 29;
2 Th. i. 11, ii. 9; Mk ix. 1, etc.   m vii. 9 f., xv. 50; Rom. xiv. 17; Gal. v. 21; Eph. v. 5; Col. iv.
11; 1 Th. ii. 12; 2 Th. i. 5; Rev. xii. 10; Mark, Luke, Acts, passim.   n Rev. ii. 27, xii. 5, xix. 15;
Isa. x. 24.   o In like use, 2 Cor. iv. 13; Rom. viii. 15, xi. 8 (Isa. xxix. 10); Gal. vi. 1; Eph. i. 17,
etc.   p 2 Cor. x. 1; six times besides in P.; James i. 21, iii. 13; 1 Pet. iii. 15; Ps. xliv. 4.

¹ πραυτητος, ABC 17.   So commonly, in oldest copies; see Wr., p. 48.

visit, see notes to xvi. 10 f. The Cor. had heard already (through Erastus?) of Timothy's coming; P. does not *announce* the fact, he explains it: "This is why I have sent T. to you"; to the τέκνα ἀγαπητά (14) P. sends a τέκνον ἀγαπητόν (see Phil. ii. 19-22), adding καὶ πιστὸν ἐν Κυρ., since it was a *trusty* agent, one "faithful in the Lord"—in the sphere of Christian duty—that the commission required. For ἐν Κυρίῳ, see parls., esp. Eph. vi. 21, Col. iv. 7; πιστὸς τῷ Κυρίῳ (Acts xvi. 15) denotes a right relationship to Christ, πιστὸς ἐν Κυρίῳ includes responsibility for others.—"Who will remind you of my ways, that are in Christ" (τὰς ὁδούς μου τὰς ἐν Χριστῷ); the adjunct is made a definition by the repeated art. ἀναμιμνήσκω with double acc., like ὑπομιμν. in John xiv. 26, combines our *remind* (a person) and *recall* (a thing). Paul's "ways" had been familiar in Cor. (cf. Acts xx. 31-35; also 2 Cor. i. 12 ff.), but seemed forgotten; the παιδαγωγοὶ had crowded out of mind the πατήρ. He means by ὁδοί μου *habits of life* to be copied (16)—the ἀγωγὴ of 2 Tim. iii. 10 f.—not doctrines to be learnt; see further ix. 19-27, x. 33-xi. 1, 2 Cor. vi. 4-10, x. 1. For ἐν Χριστῷ, see note on ἐν Χ. Ἰ., i. 2. In Paul's gentler qualities Tim. would strongly recall him to the Cor., by conduct even more than words.—"According as" (not *how*) "I teach"—in accordance with my teaching. Paul's *ways* and *teaching* are not the same thing; but the former are regulated by the latter; they will find the same consistency in Tim. "(As I teach) everywhere, in every Church:" the "ways" P. and Tim. observe, and to which the Cor. must be recalled, are

those inculcated uniformly in the Gentile mission; see i. 2 (σὺν πᾶσι ... ἐν παντὶ τόπῳ, and notes), also xi. 16, xiv. 33.

Vv. 18, 19. ὡς μὴ ἐρχομένου δέ μου πρὸς ὑμᾶς ἐφυσιώθησάν τινες: "Some however have been puffed up, under the idea that I am not coming to (visit) you". The contrastive δὲ points to a group of inflated persons (cf. 6, v. 2, viii. 2) hostile to Paul's "ways". The wish was father to the thought, which was suggested to "some" by the fact of *Timothy's* coming. They bore themselves more insolently as not fearing correction;—or did they imagine that Paul is *afraid* of them! Amongst these, presumably, were mischievous teachers (iii. 11-17) who had swelled into importance in Paul's absence, partisans who magnified others to his damage and talked as though the Church could now fairly dispense with him (3, 6, 8, 15). On ὡς with ptp., see Bn. § 440 f., or Goodwin's *Syntax*, or *Grammar*, *ad rem*; cf. note on ὡς μὴ λαβών, ver. 7, also 2 Cor. v. 20, 2 Pet. i. 3: "because (as they suppose) I am not coming". The aor. ἐφυσιώθησαν points to the moment when they heard, to their relief, of *Timothy's* coming. δὲ is postponed in the order of the sentence to avoid separating the closely linked opening words (Wr., pp. 698 f.)—"But (despite their presumption) I shall come speedily, if the Lord will". They say, "He is not coming; he sends Tim. instead!" he replies, "Come I will, and that soon" (see xvi. 8, and note).—ἐὰν ὁ Κύριος θελήσῃ (see parls.), varied to ἐπιτρέψῃ in xvi. 7; the *aor.* sbj. refers the "willing" to the (indeterminate) time of the visit. "The Lord" is *Christ;* that θέλω and θέλημα (see note

a vi. 7, xv. 29; Matt. v. 34.
b Mk. ii. 1; see note below.

V. 1. ᵃ῞Ολως ᵇ ἀκούεται ἐν ὑμῖν ᶜπορνεία, καὶ ᵈτοιαύτη πορνεία ᵈἥτις οὐδὲ ᵉἐν τοῖς ᵉἔθνεσιν ὀνομάζεται,[1] ὥστε ᶠγυναῖκά τινα τοῦ

c In like connexion, Matt. v. 34; Gen. xxxviii. 24; see vi. 13, 18.   d Cf. Heb. ii. 3.
e Rom. i. 13, ii. 24; Gal. i. 16, ii. 2; Col. i. 27; 1 Tim. iii. 16; 1 Pet. ii. 12; Acts xv. 12, xxi. 19.
f vii. 2, 29; Mt. xiv. 4, xxii. 28; Deut. xxviii. 30.

[1] Om. ονομαζεται all uncc. but אᶜLP, and all oldest verss. but syrr.—Added by Syrian emendation.

on xii. 11) are elsewhere referred by P. to God (Mr.) is no sufficient reason for diverting ὁ Κύρ. from its distinctive sense (cf. 17 above, and note on i. 31). Christ determines the movements of His servants (1; cf. 1 Thess. iii. 11, Acts xvi. 7, xviii. 9, etc.).

"And I shall know (take cognisance of) not the word of those that are puffed up (pf. pass. ptp., of settled state), but their power." "γνώσομαι: verbum judiciale; paternam ostendit potestatem" (Bg.). High-flown pretensions P. ignores; he will test their "power," and estimate each man (he is thinking mainly of the ἐποικοδομοῦντες of chap. iii.) by what he can do, not say. The "power" in question is that belonging to "the kingdom of God" (i. 18, 24, ii. 4).

Ver. 20. "For not in word (lies) the kingdom of God, but in power:" another of Paul's religious maxims (see note on i. 29), repeated in many forms: cf. 2 Cor. x. 11, xiii. 3 f., etc. The βασιλεία τοῦ Θεοῦ always (even in Rom. xiv. 17) bears ref. to the final Messianic rule (see vi. 9 f., xv. 24, 50); the "power of God" called it into being and operates in every man who truly serves it. That Divine realm is not built up by windy words (v). To the same test P. offers himself in 2 Cor. xiii. 1-10. For εἶναι (understood) ἐν, see ii. 5 and note.

Ver. 21. τί θέλετε; "What is your will?"—what would you have? τί a sharper πότερον; the latter only once (John vii. 17) in N.T.—"With a rod am I to come to you? or in love and a spirit of meekness?" ἐν ῥάβδῳ (= ἐν κολάσει, ἐν τιμωρίᾳ, Cm.) is sound Gr. for "armed with a rod" (cf. Sir. xlvii. 4, ἐν λίθῳ; Lucian, Dial. Mort., xxiii. 3, καθικόμενος ἐν τ. ῥάβδῳ; add Heb. ix. 25, 1 John v. 6) —the implement of paternal discipline (14) called for by the behaviour of "some" (18). There is reason, however, in the stern note of this question, for connecting it with ch. v. 1 (so Oec., Cv., Bz., Hf.). P. is approaching the subject of the following Section, which already stirs his wrath. For the sbj. of the dubitative

question, ἔλθω, see Wr., p. 356: ἐν ὑμῖν τὸ πρᾶγμα κεῖται (Cm.).—ἐν ἀγάπῃ κ.τ.λ. (ἔλθω); cf. 2 Cor. ii. 1; the constr. of ii. 3 above is somewhat diff. (see note). πνεύματί τε πραΰτητος defines the particular expression of love in which P. desires to come: cf. xiii. 6 f. The Ap. does not mean the Holy Spirit here specifically, though the thought of Him is latent in every ref. to the "spirit" of a Christian man. Πραΰτης (cf. 2 Cor. x. 1) is the disposition most opposed to, and exercised by, the spirit of the conceited and insubordinate τινὲς at Cor.

DIVISION II. QUESTIONS OF SOCIAL MORALS, v.-vii. The Ap. has done with the subject of the Parties, which had claimed attention first because they sprung from a radical misconception of Christianity. But in this typical Hellenic community, social corruptions had arisen which, if not so universal, were still more malignant in their effect. The heathen converts of Cor., but lately washed from the foulest vice (vi. 9 ff.), were some of them slipping back into the mire (2 Cor. xii. 21). An offence of incredible turpitude had just come to the Apostle's ears, to the shame of which the Church appeared indifferent (v). This case, demanding instant judicial action (1-5), leads the Ap. to define more clearly the relation of Christians to men of immoral life, as they may be found within or without the Church (6-13). From sins of uncleanness he passes in ch. vi. to acts of injustice committed in this Church, which, in one instance at least, had been scandalously dragged before the heathen law-courts (1-8). In vi. 12-20 P. returns to the prevalent social evil of Cor., and launches his solemn interdict against fornication, which was, seemingly, sheltered under the pretext of Christian liberty! It is just here, and in the light of the principles now developed, that P. takes up the question of marriage or celibacy, discussed at large in ch. vii. The fact that the Ap. turns at this juncture to the topics raised in the Church Letter, and that ch. vii. is headed with the

πατρὸς ᶠἔχειν· 2. καὶ ὑμεῖς ᵍπεφυσιωμένοι ἐστέ; καὶ οὐχὶ μᾶλλον ᵍSee iv. 6.
ʰἐπενθήσατε, ἵνα ⁱἐξαρθῇ¹ ᵏἐκ ᵏμέσου ὑμῶν ὁ τὸ ˡἔργον τοῦτο
ποιήσας²; 3. ἐγὼ ᵐμὲν ᵐγὰρ ὡς³ ⁿἀπὼν τῷ ᵒσώματι, ⁿπαρὼν δὲ
τῷ ᵒπνεύματι, ἤδη ᵖκέκρικα ὡς ⁿπαρὼν τὸν οὕτω τοῦτο ᑫκατερ-

ʰ2 Cor. xii.
21; James
iv.9; Rev.
xviii. 11
ff.; Mt.
v. 4, ix.
15; Mk.
xvi. 10;

Lk. vi. 25. i Col. ii. 14; Mk. xiii. 15; Jo. xvii. 15, xxi. f. k 2 Cor. vi. 17 (Isa. lii. 11); Col. ii. 14;
2 Thess. ii. 7; Acts xvii. 33, xxiii. 10; Mt. xiii. 49. l In this sense, Mt. xxiii. 3; Lk. xi. 48; Jo.
viii. 41. m See xi. 18. n 2 Cor. x. 1 f., 11, xiii. 2, 10; Phil. i. 27; Col. ii. 5. o vii. 34; Rom.
viii. 10; Eph. iv. 4; 1 Thess. v. 23. p Pf., vii. 37. See ii. 2. q In like sense, Rom.i. 27, ii. 9,
vii. 8 ff.

¹ α ρ θ η : all uncc. but L.

² π ρ α ξ α ς (?), ℵAC, several good minn.; so Tisch., W.H., Nestle. Latt. gessit.
ποιησας, BDGLP, etc. (vg. fecit)—probably Western and Syrian. So Treg., El.,
R.V.

³ Om. ω ς (απων) ℵABCD*P 17, 37, vg., syrsch. cop.

formula Περὶ δὲ ὧν ἐγράψατέ μοι, must
not be allowed to break the strong links
of subject-matter and thought binding it
to chh. v. and vi. Its connexion with
the foregoing context is essential, with
the following comparatively accidental.
§ 15. THE CASE OF INCEST, v. 1-8.
About the party-strifes at Cor. P. has
been informed by the members of a particular family (i. 11); the monstrous case
of incest, to which he turns abruptly
and without any preface (cf. i. 10), is
notorious.
Ver. 1. Ὅλως ἀκούεται κ.τ.λ.: "There
is actually fornication heard of amongst
you!" No wonder that the father of the
Church is compelled to show the "rod"
(iv. 21). Not ἀκούω, as in xi. 18, but
the impersonal ἀκούεται (cf. ἠκούσθη,
Mark ii. 1), indicating common report in the
Church (ἐν ὑμῖν),—and (ὅλως: see parls.)
undoubted fact. — Πορνεία signifies any
immoral sexual relation, whether including (as in Matt. v. 32) or distinguished
from (Matt. xv. 19) μοιχεία.
The sin is branded as of unparalleled
blackness by the description, καὶ τοιαύτη
πορνεία ἥτις κ.τ.λ.: "Yes, and a fornication of such sort"—the καὶ climactic—
"as (there is) not even among the
Gentiles!" While mere πορνεία was excused—not to say approved—in heathen
society, even by strict moralists, such
foulness was abominated. Of this crime
the loose Catullus says (76. 4): "Nam
nihil est quidquam sceleris quo prodeat
ultra"; and Cicero, pro Cluent., 6, 15:
"scelus incredibile, et præter hanc unam
in omni vita inauditum"; Euripides' Hip-
polytus speaks for Gr. sentiment. Greek
and Roman law both stamped it with
infamy; for Jewish law, see Lev. xviii.
7 f., Deut. xxii. 30, also Gen. xlix. 4.—

ἥτις, of quality (as in iii. 17), in place
of the regular correlative οἵα (xv. 48).
Neither ὀνομάζεται (T.R.) nor ἀκούεται
is understood in the ellipsis, simply ἐστίν
—"such as does not exist"; the exceptional heathen instances are such as to
prove the rule. The actual sin is finally
stated: ὥστε γυναῖκά τινα κ.τ.λ., "as
that one (or a certain one) should have a
wife of his father".—ἥτις defines the
quality, ὥστε (with inf.) the content and
extent of the πορνεία.—γυν. τοῦ πατρός
(instead of μητρυίαν) is the term of Lev.
xviii. 8. ἔχειν indicates a continued association, whether in the way of formal
marriage or not; nor does ἔργον (2), nor
κατεργασάμενον (3), make clear this latter
point. That "the father" was living is
not proved by the ἀδικηθεὶς of 2 Cor. vii.
12; P. can hardly have referred to this
foul immorality in the language of 2 Cor.
ii. 5-11, vii. 8-12; the "grief" and
"wrong" of those passages are probably
quite diff. The woman was not a Christian, for Paul passes no sentence upon
her; see ver. 13.
Ver. 2. What are the Cor. doing
under this deep disgrace? Not even
grieving. Καὶ ὑμεῖς πεφυσιωμένοι ἐστέ;
κ.τ.λ.: "And are you (still) puffed up?
and did you not rather mourn?" For
the grammatical force of πεφυσ. ἐστέ,
see parls. in i. 10, iv. 8; and for the vb.,
note to iv. 6. P. confronts the pride of
the Cor. Church with this crushing fact;
no intellectual brilliance, no religious enthusiasm, can cover this hideous blot:
"argumentatur a contrario, ubi enim
luctus est, cessit gloria" (Cv.). The ver.
is best read interrogatively, in view of
the οὐχὶ in 2nd clause (cf. i. 20), and in
Paul's expostulatory style (cf. iv. 7 f.).—
ἐπενθήσατε (see parls.) connotes funeral

r *H.l.* for
Epp.; in
Gospp.
and Acts,
passim.
s With
pron., xiv.
14, xvi.
18; 2 Cor.

γασάμενον, 4. ἐν τῷ ὀνόματι τοῦ Κυρίου ἡμῶν [1] Ἰησοῦ Χριστοῦ,[2] r συναχθέντων ὑμῶν καὶ τοῦ s ἐμοῦ s πνεύματος σὺν τῇ t δυνάμει τοῦ t Κυρίου ἡμῶν Ἰησοῦ Χριστοῦ,[3] 5. u παραδοῦναι v τὸν v τοιοῦτον τῷ u w Σατανᾷ εἰς x ὄλεθρον τῆς y σαρκός, ἵνα τὸ y πνεῦμα σωθῇ ἐν τῇ

ii. 13, vii. 13; Rom. i. 9; Gal. vi. 18; Phil. iv. 23; Phm. 25; 2 Tim. iv. 22; Mk. ii. 8, viii. 12; Luke i. 47, viii. 55. t 2 Cor. xii. 9; 2 Pet. i. 16; Lk. v. 17. u In this sense, 1 Tim. i. 20. v Ver. 11, vii. 15, 28, xvi. 16, 18; 12 times besides in P.; 3 Jo. 8; Mt. xix. 14; Ac. xxii. 22. w vii. 5; 2 Cor. ii. 11, xi. 14, xii. 7; Rom. xvi. 20; 1 Th. ii. 18; 2 Th. ii. 9; 1 Tim. i. 20, v. 15; Gospp. and Rev., *passim.* x 1 Th. v. 3; 2 Th. i. 9; 1 Tim. vi. 9; Prov. xxi. 7. y 2 Cor. vii. 1; Rom. i. 3 f.; Col. ii. 5; 1 Tim. iii. 16; Heb. xii. 9; Mt. xxvi. 41.

[1] *Om.* ημων all uncc. but P.

[2] *Om.* Χριστου ABD*; most critical edd. Copyists are apt to complete *the name.*

[3] *Om.* Χριστου ℵABDP 46.

mourning—over "a brother dead to God, by sin, alas! undone;" the *tense* signifies "*going* into mourning"—"breaking out in grief" (Ev.) when you heard of it. Of such grief the fit sequel is expressed by ἵνα ἀρθῇ ἐκ μέσου ὑμῶν, "that he should be removed from your midst, who so perpetrated this deed". This is the later Gr. "sub-final" ἵνα, of the *desired result*: see Wr., p. 420; Bm., p. 237; *cf.* xiv. 12 f.—πράξας, as distinguished from ποιήσας (T.R.), implies *quality* in the action (see parls.).

Vv. 3-5. The *removal* of the culprit is, in any case, a settled matter: ἐγὼ μὲν γάρ, "For *I* at least" . . . ἤδη κέκρικα, "have already decided"—without waiting till you should act or till I could come. For ἤδη see note, iv. 8; κέκρικα, pf. of judgment that has determinate effect.—μέν *solitarium*—"I indeed (whatever you may do)".—ἀπὼν τῷ σώματι παρὼν δὲ τῷ πνεύματι, "while absent in the body yet present in the spirit": by absence the Ap. might seem disqualified for judging (*cf.* 2 Cor. xii. 20-xiii. 2); he declares that he is *spiritually present*, so present to his inmost consciousness are the facts of the case; *cf.* Col. ii. 5. "St. Paul's spirit, illumined and vivified, as it unquestionably was, by the Divine Spirit, must have been endowed on certain occasions with a more than ordinary insight into the state of a Church at a distance" (Ev.; *cf.* John i. 48; 2 Kings v. 26): "I have already passed sentence, as one present, on him that has so wrought this thing". ὡς παρὼν means "as being present," not "as though present"—which rendering virtually surrenders the previous ἀπὼν . . . παρὼν δέ. —κατεργάζομαι, *to work out, consummate* (see parls.); the qualifying οὕτως probably refers to the man's being a Chris-

tian (*cf.* 12 f.)—"under these conditions" (*cf.* iii. 16 f., vi. 15).

The judgment already determined in the Apostle's mind is delivered in ver. 5, supplying a further obj. (*of the thing*; *cf.* for the construction, Acts xv. 38) to κέκρικα: "I have already judged him . . . (have given sentence), in the name of our Lord Jesus, to deliver him that is such (τὸν τοιοῦτον) to Satan for destruction of his flesh, that his spirit may be saved in the day of the Lord Jesus". The clauses of ver. 4, with their solemn, rounded terms, make fit way for this awful sentence; "graviter suspensa manet et vibrat oratio usque ad ver. 5" (Bg.). The prp. phrases ἐν τῷ ὀνόματι τ. κυρ. Ἰ., σὺν τ. δυνάμει τ. κυρ. ἡμῶν Ἰ., may be connected, either of them or both, with παραδοῦναι or with the subordinate συναχθέντων; and the four combinations thus grammatically possible have each found advocates. The order of words and balance of clauses, as well as intrinsic fitness of connexion, speak for the attachment of the former adjunct to παραδ. Σατ., the latter to συναχθ. ὑμῶν: so Luther, Bg., Mr., Al., Ev., Bt., El. "In the name of the Lord Jesus" every Church act is done, every word of blessing or banning uttered; that Name must be formally used when doom is pronounced in the assembly (see parls.). The gen. abs. clause is parenthetic, supplying the occasion and condition precedent (*aor. ptp.*) of the public sentence; all the responsible parties must be concurrent: "when you have assembled together, and my spirit, along with the power of our Lord Jesus". Along with the gathered assembly, under Paul's unseen directing influence, a *third Supreme Presence* is necessary to make the sentence valid; the Church associates itself

ᶻἡμέρᾳ τοῦ ᶻΚυρίου¹ ᶻʼΙησοῦ.¹ 6. οὐ ᵃκαλὸν τὸ ᵇκαύχημα ὑμῶν · ᶻ See i. 8.
ᵉοὐκ ᶜοἴδατε ὅτι ᵈμικρὰ ᵈᵉζύμη ᵈὅλον τὸ ᵈᵉφύραμα ᵈᵉζυμοῖ ; ᵃ In like sense, ix. 15 ; seven
7. ᶠἐκκαθάρατε οὖν² τὴν ᵍπαλαιὰν ᵉζύμην, ἵνα ἦτε νέον ᵉφύραμα, times be- sides in
καθώς ἐστε ʰἄζυμοι· καὶ γὰρ τὸ ¹πάσχα ἡμῶν ὑπὲρ ἡμῶν ⁱᵏἐτύθη P. ; Jas. ii. 7 ; 1 Pet.
ii. 12 ; Mt.

xv. 26, xxvi. 10 ; Lk. xxi. 5.   b ix. 15 f. ; 7 times besides in P. ; Heb. iii. 6.   c See iii. 16.
d Gal. v. 9. μικρος, cf. Jas. iii. 5 ; Mt. xiii. 32.   e Mt. xiii. 33, xvi. 6 ff., and parls. For φυραμα,
Rom. ix. 21, xi. 16.   f 2 Tim. ii. 21 ; Deut. xxvi. 13 ; Judges vii. 4.   g In like sense, Rom. vi. 6 ;
Eph. iv. 22 ; Col. iii. 9.   h Mt. xxvi. 17, and parls. ; Acts xii. 3, xx. 6 ; Lev. ii. 4, etc.   i Mt.
xxvi. 2, etc. From LXX (Heb. *pesach*) ; in 2 Chron. φασεκ. πασχα θυω, Mk. xiv. 12 ; Lk. xxii. 7.
k x. 20 ; Acts xiv. 13, 18.

¹ τ. κυρ. ημων Ιησου Χριστου, ACP, minuscc.¹⁵, syrr. cop., many Ff.
τ. κυρ. Ι. Χριστου, D Ambrst. *Cf.* ver. 4, i. 8, and 1 Thess. for Pauline usage.

² *Om.* ουν all uncc. but ℵᶜCLP ; all critical edd.

"with the power" of its Head. Realis- ing that it is clothed therewith, the Cor. Church will deliver the appalling sen- tence inspired by the absent Ap.—σὺν τῇ δυνάμει κ.τ.λ. is a *h.l.* ; ἐν δυνάμει (ii. 5, etc.) is frequent in P. "Our Lord Jesus" is Christ the *Judge* (see i. 8).

"Delivering to Satan," in the view of many (including Aug., Cv., Bz., and latterly Hn.), is a synonym for *excom- munication*,—a thrusting out of the con- demned into "the kingdom of darkness," where "the god of this world" holds sway (2 Cor. iv. 4, Eph. ii. 2, vi. 12, Col. i. 13, etc.) ; similarly in 1 Tim. i. 20. But there is no proof that such a formula of excommunication existed either in the Synagogue or the early Church ; and the added words, εἰς ὄλεθρον τῆς σαρκός κ.τ.λ., point to some *physically punitive* and spiritually remedial visitation of the sinner. The σάρξ to be destroyed, it is replied, lies in the man's sinful passions ; but these would, presumably, be strength- ened rather than destroyed by sending him back to the world. "The flesh," as antithetical to "the spirit" (see parls.), is rather the man's *bodily nature ;* and physical maladies, even death, are ascribed in the N.T. to Satan (2 Cor. xii. 7, Luke xiii. 16, John viii. 44, Heb. ii. 14), while on the other hand affliction is made an instrument of spiritual benefit (ix. 27, xi. 30 ff., 2 Cor. iv. 16 f., xii. 7, 1 Peter iv. 1 f.) ; moreover, the App. did occasion- ally, as in the cases of Ananias and Elymas (Acts v., xiii.), pronounce penal sentences in the physical sphere, which took immediate effect on the condemned. It appears certain that P. imposed in this case *a severe physical infliction*—indeed, if ὄλεθρος is to be pressed (see parls.), *a mortal stroke*—as the only means of marking the gravity of the crime and saving the criminal. "Il ne faut pas en

douter, c'est une condamnation à mort que Paul prononce" (Renan) ; not how- ever a sudden death, rather "a slow con- sumption, giving the sinner time to re- pent" (Gd.). The *ejection* of the culprit the Church of itself could and must effect (2, 13) ; for the aggravated chastisement the presence of the Apostle's "spirit," allied "with the power of the Lord Jesus," was necessary.—ὁ Σατανᾶς (Heb. *hassatān*, Aram. *s'tanā :* see parls.), "the Adversary," *sc.* of God and man, to whom every such opportunity is welcome (John viii. 44). That Satan's malignity should be (as one may say) overreached by God's wisdom and mercy (*cf.* iii. 19) is nothing very wonderful (see 2 Cor. xii. 7, Luke xxii. 31 f., also the tempta- tion of our Lord, and of Job) ; hate is proverbially blind. On "*the day of the Lord*," when the ultimate salvation or perdition of each is fixed, see i. 8, Rom. ii. 5-16. That some Cor. afterwards sought *proof* of Paul's supernatural power goes to show, not that this sentence proved abortive, but rather that the offender averted it by prompt repentance.

Ver. 6. "Your vaunt is not good:" καύχημα, *materies gloriandi* (*cf.* αἰσχρὸν κλέος, Eurip., *Helena*, 135 : Mr.), found in the state of the Church, of which the Cor. were proud (iv. 6 ff.) when they ought to have been ashamed.—καλόν, *good* in the sense of *seemly, of fine quality ; cf.* 2 Cor. viii. 21, John x. 32, etc. For οὐκ οἴδατε . . . ; see iii. 16. —The Cor. might reply that the offence, however shameful, was the sin of one man and therefore a little thing ; P. re- torts, that it is "a little *leaven*," enough to "leaven the whole kneading" : *cf.* the Parables of Matt. xiii. 33 and Luke xii. 1. A sin so virulent held an indefinite power of corruption ; it tainted the en- tire community. The φύραμα (φυράω,

1 *H.l.*for vb. Χριστός· 8. ὥστε ¹ ἑορτάζωμεν,¹ μὴ ἐν ° ζύμῃ ᵍ παλαιᾷ μηδὲ ἐν
εορτη,
Col. ii. 16; ᵉ ζύμῃ ᵐ κακίας καὶ ᵐ πονηρίας, ἀλλ' ἐν ʰ ἀζύμοις ⁿ εἰλικρινείας καὶ
passim in
Gospp.   ° ἀληθείας.
m Rom. i.29.

κακια, xiv.
20; Eph. iv. 31; Col. iii. 8; Tit. iii. 3; Jas. i. 21; 1 Pet. ii. 1,16; Acts viii. 22; Mt. vi. 34. πονηρια,
Eph. vi. 12; Acts iii. 26; Mt. xxii. 18; Mk. vii. 22; Lk. xi. 39.   n 2 Cor. i. 12, ii. 17; -νης, Phil.
i. 10.   o In this sense, 2 Cor. vii. 14, xii. 6; Rom. ix. 1; Eph. iv. 25; Phil. i. 18; 2 Jo. 1; 3 Jo. 1;
Acts xxvi. 25; Mk. v. 33.

¹ εορταζομεν, ADP, minuscc. ²⁰; by itacism.

to mix) is the lump of dough kneaded for
a single batch of bread : see parls.

Ver. 7. **ἐκκαθάρατε,** "Cleanse out"
—the aor. implying a *summary*, and **ἐκ-**
a *complete* removal (see parls. ; for simple
καθαίρω, John xv. 2), leaving the Church
"clean": an allusion to the pre-Paschal
removal of leaven (Exod. xii. 15 ff., xiii.
7). For τ. **παλαιὰν ζύμην,** *cf.* Ignatius,
ad Magn., 10, τ. κακὴν ζύμην τ. παλαιω-
θεῖσαν κ. ἐνοξίσασαν, applying, however,
to Judaism what here relates to Gentile
vice. The "old leaven" (denoting not
persons—the incestuous and his like—
but influences : see 8) must be cleansed
away, "in order that you may be a fresh
kneading". **νέον,** *new in point of time*
(see parls.)—the mass of dough, with
the evil ferment removed, kneaded over
again. The Cor. are to be clear of the
παλαιὰ ζύμη "in accordance with the
fact that" (**καθώς**) they "are **ἄζυμοι,**" a
term not used literally—as though the
Church was at this (*sc.* Paschal) season
eating unleavened bread : such a **παρα-
τήρησις** of Jewish law by Gentiles P.
would hardly have encouraged (see Gal.
iv. 9 ff.)—but *morally*, in consistency
with the allegorical strain of the passage;
"in the purpose and command of God,
and in their own profession, they are
separated from all sin, which is to them
what, during the passover week, leaven
was to the Jews. This objective use of
unleavened corresponds to that of *sanctified* in i. 2" (Bt.). *Cf.* the ἤδη καθαροί
ἐστε of John xv. 3; and for the general
principle, i. 30, vi. 11, Rom. vi. 1-11, etc.

Ver. 8 explains the symbolical **ἄζυμοι.**
Participation in the sacrifice of Christ
presumes unleavenedness in the participants; the unleavened bread and the
passover are related (objectively) as repentance and faith (subjectively) : "For
indeed our Lamb *has been slain*, even
Christ". τὸ **πάσχα** . . . ἐτύθη (aor.,
of historical fact)—the Passover Lamb
killed, and leaven not yet cast out : what
a contradiction! The Law prescribed
no exact time, but usage required every

scrap of leaven to be got rid of from the
house at the beginning (eve) of the day,
Nisan 14, on which the Lamb was slain.
πάσχα stands for the Paschal *Lamb*, the
sacrifice of which legally constituted the
Passover (Mark xiv. 12, *cf.* John i. 29).
"Our (Christian) passover," *cf.* Heb.
xiii. 10; and for Paul's appropriation to
the Church of the things of the Old
Covenant, Rom. xi. 17, Gal. iv. 26, vi.
16, Phil. iii. 3. This identification of
Christ crucified with the Paschal Lamb
lends some support to the view that
Jesus died, as the Fourth Gospel appears
to represent, *on the 14th Nisan;* but the
precise coincidence is not essential to
his interpretation. The Pascha (Aram.
pascha = Heb. *pesach*)—in O.T. "Jehovah's Passover"—was the sacrificial
covenant-feast of the kingdom of God in
Israel. It contained three essential elements : (1) *the blood* of the victim,
sprinkled at the exodus on each house-
door, afterwards on the national altar, as
an expiation to God (*cf.* Rom. iii. 25),
who "passes over" when He "sees the
blood"; (2) *the flesh* of the lamb, supplying the food of redeemed Israel as it
sets out to the Holy Mount and the
Promised Land (see x. 16 f., John vi. 32,
51); (3) *the continued feast*, an act of
fellowship, grounded on redemption, between Jehovah and Israel and amongst
the Israelites; *cf.* x. 16-22, xi. 20, and
notes.

With the leaven removed and the Passover Lamb slain, "let us keep the feast"
(ἑορτάζωμεν, pr. sbj. of *continued action*)
—this term again allegorical not literal
(see ἄζυμοι, 7), "a figurative characterisation of the whole Christian conduct
of life" (Mr.). ἅπας ὁ βίος αὐτοῦ
πανήγυρις ἄγια (Clem. Al., *Strom.*, viii.,
quoted by Ed.); to the same effect Cm.,
δείκνυσιν ὅτι πᾶς ὁ χρόνος ἑορτῆς ἐστι
καιρὸς τ. Χριστιανοῖς διὰ τ. ὑπερβολὴν
τ. ἀγαθῶν αὐτοῖς δοθέντων. διὰ τοῦτο
γὰρ ὁ υἱὸς τ. Θεοῦ ἄνθρωπος γέγονε καὶ
ἐτύθη, ἵνα σε ἑορτάζειν ποιήσῃ; *cf.*,
earlier than P., Philo's interpretation of

9. Ἔγραψα ὑμῖν ἐν ᵖτῇ ᵖἐπιστολῇ μὴ ᑫσυναναμίγνυσθαι ʳπόρνοις · ᵖ 2 Cor. vii.
8 ; Rom.
10. καὶ¹ οὐ ˢπάντως τοῖς πόρνοις τοῦ κόσμου τούτου, ἢ τοῖς ᵗπλεο- xvi. 22 ;
etc.
νέκταις ἢ² ᵘἅρπαξιν ἢ ᵛεἰδωλολάτραις, ʷἐπεὶ ˣὀφείλετε³ ʷἄρα ᑫ 2 Th. iii.
14.
r vi. 9; Eph.

v. 5 ; 1 Tim. i. 10 ; twice in Heb., and in Rev.   s ix. 10, 22, xvi. 12 ; Rom. iii. 9 ; 4 times in Acts
and Lk.   t vi. 10 ; Eph. v. 5 ; -τεω, 2 Cor. ii. 11, vii. 2, xii. 17 f., 1 Th. iv. 6.   u vi. 10 ; Mt. vii.
15 ; Lk. xviii. 11 ; -γη, Mt. xxiii. 25 ; Heb. x. 34.   v vi. 9, x. 7 ; Eph. v. 5 ; Rev. xxi. 8, xxii. 15.
w vii. 14.   x In this tense and sense (ωφειλ), 2 Cor. xii. 11 ; Heb. ii. 17 ; Lk. xvii. 10.

¹ *Om.* κα ι all uncc. but אᶜDᶜLP.

² και (not η before αρπ.), all uncc. but אᶜDᵇᶜL.

³ ωφειλετε, all uncc. but D³P.

the Feast, *De migr. Abrah.*, 16 ; *De congr.*
quærend. erudit. gratia, 28.   For ὥστε
with impv., see note on iv. 5.—The ἄζυμα
(unleavened cakes), to be partaken of by
the ἄζυμοι (7), are described by the
attributes εἰλικρινίας καὶ ἀληθείας, "of
sincerity and truth"—a sound inward
disposition, and a right position in accord
with the reality of things.   To the forbidden ἐν ζύμῃ παλαιᾷ (see note, 7) is
added, by way of closer specification,
μηδὲ ἐν ζύμῃ κακίας κ. πονηρίας (*malitiæ*
et nequitiæ)—"κακία the vicious disposition, πονηρία the active exercise of it"
(Lt.) ; see Trench, *Syn.*, § 11.   The
associations of approaching Easter, probably, suggested this train of thought (*cf.*
xv. 23, ἀπαρχή) ; nowhere else does P.
call Christ "the Pascha".

§ 16.   A PREVIOUS LETTER MISREAD,
v. 9-13.   The Cor. Church were taking
no action against the offender of § 15 ; in
this neglect they disregarded the Apostle's
instructions conveyed by some recent
letter.   These instructions they appear
to have misunderstood, reading them as
though Paul forbade Christians to have
any dealings with immoral persons, and
asking for further explanation.   Not im-
probably, they were making their uncertainty on the general question an
excuse for hesitation in this urgent and
flagrant case.   Accordingly the Ap., after
giving sentence upon the πόρνος of vv.
1 f., repeats with all possible distinctness
his direction *to excommunicate persons*
of openly immoral life from the Church.
Profligates of the world must be left to
God's sole judgment.   P. felt that there
was an evasion, prompted by the disposition to palter with sin, in the misunderstanding reported to him ; hence the
closing words of the last Section, condemning the "leaven of badness and
wickedness" and commending the "unleavened bread of sincerity and truth".
On the nature and occasion of *the lost*
letter, see *Introd.*, chap. ii.

Ver. 9.   "I wrote to you in the (my)
letter"—the last the Cor. had received
from P., which is recalled by the matter
just discussed.   The Ff., except Ambrosiaster (? Hilary of Rome, prob.
Isaac, a converted Jew), referred the
ἔγραψα *to this Ep.*, reading the vb. as
epistolary aorist (as in 11 ; see Bn. § 44) ;
but there is nothing in 1 Cor. to sustain
the ref., and ἐν τῇ ἐπιστολῇ seems
"added expressly to guard against this
interpretation" (Ed.).   Modern expositors, from Cv. downwards, find the traces
here of a lost Ep. antecedent to our First ;
2 Cor. x. 10 f. intimates that the Cor.
had received several letters from P. before
the canonical Second.   Some have found
in 2 Cor. vi. 14-vii. 1 a stray leaf of the
missing document ; that par. is certainly
germane to its purpose (see Hilgenfeld,
Einleit. in das N.T., p. 287 ; Whitelaw,
in *Classical Review*, 1890, pp. 12, 317 f.).
The ambiguity lay in the word συναναμίγνυσθαι (*to mix oneself up with*), which
forbids social intimacy, while those who
wished to misunderstand took it as a
prohibition of all intercourse.

Ver. 10 gives the needful definition of
the above injunction.   οὐ πάντως is best
understood as by Er. (*non omnino*), Cv.
(*neque in universum*), Mr., Bt., Ed., El.,
as *not absolutely, not altogether*, οὐ negativing πάντως and making the inhibition a qualified one : "I did not altogether
forbid your holding intercourse with the
fornicators of this world".   To make the
πάντως emphasise the οὐ (as in Rom.
iii. 9)—"Assuredly I did not mean to
forbid association with fornicators outside
the Church" (Lt.)—is to lend the passage the air of *recommending* association
with unconverted profligates !—What
applies to one sort of immorality applies
to others : ἢ τ. πλεονέκταις καὶ ἅρπαξιν
ἢ εἰδωλολάτραις, "or with the covetous
and rapacious, or with idolaters".   The
πλεονεκται (from πλέον and ἔχω : see
parls.) are *the self-aggrandising* in general ;

y Eph. i. 21,   ἐκ τοῦ κόσμου ἐξελθεῖν.   11. νυνὶ [1] δὲ ἔγραψα ὑμῖν μὴ [q] συναναμίγ-
iii. 15;
Mk.iii. 14. νυσθαι ἐάν τις ἀδελφὸς [y] ὀνομαζόμενος ᾖ [r] πόρνος ἢ [t] πλεονέκτης ἢ
z vi. 10;
-ρειν, iv. [v] εἰδωλολάτρης ἢ [z] λοίδορος ἢ [a] μέθυσος ἢ [u] ἅρπαξ, [b] τῷ [b] τοιούτῳ
12; 1 Pet.
ii. 23;   μηδὲ [c] συνεσθίειν·   12. τί γάρ μοι καὶ [2] [d] τοὺς [d] ἔξω κρίνειν; οὐχὶ
-ρια, 1
Tim. v.   [e] τοὺς [e] ἔσω ὑμεῖς κρίνετε, [d] τοὺς δὲ [d] ἔξω ὁ Θεὸς κρίνει; 13. καὶ [3]
14; 1 Pet.
iii.9; Prov. [f] ἐξαρεῖτε [4] τὸν πονηρὸν ἐξ ὑμῶν αὐτῶν.
xxvi. 21;
Sir. xxiii.
8.   a vi. 10; twice in Prov., and in Sir.   b See ver. 5.   c Gal. ii. 12; Acts x. 41, xi. 3; Lk.
xv. 2; Gen. xliii. 32; Ps. c. 5.   d Col. iv. 5; 1 Th. iv. 12; Mk. iv. 11; Prol. to Sirach (ἐκτος).
e H.l.; cf. 2 Cor. iv. 16; Rom. vii. 22; Eph. iii. 16.   f N.T. h.l., Deut. xvii. 7, 12, xxiv. 7.

[1] νυν, ℵ︎ᶜABDᶜGLP; Treg.; W.H., Nestle. νυνι, ℵ︎*CD*ᵇ; Tisch.

[2] Om. και all uncc. but DL.

[3] Om. και all uncc. but D³L.

[4] εξαρατε: all uncc. but D³L (εξαρειτε); see Deut. (parl.).

ἅρπαγες, those who *seize with violence*; sins of greed are frequent in commercial cities. "Idolaters" (the first appearance of the word in literature: cf. notes on viii. 1 and x. 19) included the entire pagan world; Cor. idolatry was specially associated with sensual sin.—ἐπεὶ ... ἄρα κ.τ.λ., "since in that case"—the logical consequence of absolute non-intercourse—"you were bound to go out of the world!" — ἑτέραν οἰκουμένην ὠφείλετε ζητῆσαι (Thp.). One could not pursue any avocation at Cor. without daily contact with such sinners. ὠφείλετε, in the impf. tense of the *unfulfilled condition* (implied in ἄρα); for the omission, common with vbs. of this nature, of the ἂν of contingency, see Wr., p. 382, and cf. Heb. ix. 26. For the principle implied—as against the *cloister*—see John xvii. 14-19.

Ver. 11. νῦν δὲ ἔγραψα, "But now I have written"—in contrast to the Ἔγραψα ... ἐν τῇ ἐπιστ. of ver. 9: "If any one doubted the purport of the former letter, it shall be impossible to mistake my meaning now". The *logical* (not temporal) sense of νῦν (or νυνὶ) is preferred by some interpreters: "But now—*after this, as things now appear*—(you must understand that) I wrote," etc., this ἔγραψα thus repeating the former. Νυνὶ δὲ bears the like emphatic temporal sense in 2 Cor. viii. 11, Eph. ii. 13.—ἐάν τις ἀδελφὸς ὀνομαζόμενος, "if any one bearing the name of *brother*"—the point of the amended rule, which P. in writing before had apparently left to the common-sense of his readers, but is compelled to make explicit. So the μὴ συναναμίγνυσθαι clearly signifies *not to hold fraternal, friendly commerce* with vicious men: cf. xv. 33. Such a one

may be "named," but is not, "a brother"; cf. Rev. iii. 1.—Among the kinds of sinners proscribed P. now inserts the λοίδορος (see note on iv. 12), the "railer," "reviler"—the foul-mouthed abuser of others; and the μέθυσος, "drunkard"—a word bearing in earlier Gr. a comic sense, *tipsy*, afterwards seriously used (Lt.): these sins are companions; cf. vi. 10.—τῷ τοιούτῳ μηδὲ συνεσθίειν: "with him that is such (I bid you) not even to eat". The inf. is *pr.*—of usage, practice; cf. Gal. ii. 12. "Eating together is a sign of friendliness; business transactions are not. If the ref. be restricted to *Christian* fellowship (*sc.* the Agapé), the emphatic *not even* is out of place" (Ed.). To forbid intercourse to this extent implies expulsion from the Church, *and more*; cf. 2 Thess. iii. 14 f. (milder treatment), Mt. xviii. 17. That it should be possible for an actual "idolater"—not merely one who "sits in an idol's house" (viii. 10) as a place indifferent, or who still in some sort believes in its power (viii. 7)—to be in the Church is evidence of the laxity of Cor. Christianity. That this was really the case, and that some Cor., perhaps of philosophical, semi-pantheistic tendencies, wished to combine the worship of the heathen temple with that of the Christian Church, appears likely from x. 14-22; the same syncretism is found in India now; cf. the case of Naaman, 2 Kings v. 17 f.

Vv. 12, 13. τί γάρ μοι τοὺς ἔξω κ.τ.λ.; "For what business of mine is it (*Quid mea refert?* Cv.) to judge those that are outside? (Is it) not those within (that) you judge, while those without God judges?" By these questions P. justifies his excluding the impure ἀδελφὸς ὀνομαζ. from the communion and social courtesies of

VI. 1. ᵃΤολμᾷ τις ὑμῶν ᵇπρᾶγμα ᵇἔχων ᵇπρὸς ᶜτὸν ᶜἕτερον
ᵈκρίνεσθαι ᵉἐπὶ τῶν ᶠἀδίκων, καὶ οὐχὶ ᵉἐπὶ ᵍτῶν ᵍἁγίων; 2. ʰοὐκ ¹

a Rom. v. 7;
2 Cor. x.
12; Acts
v. 13;
Esth. vii.

5; Job xv. 12. b *H.l.;* Thuc. i. 128; Xen. *Mem.* ii. 9. 1. c See iv. 6. d In this sense, Rom.
iii. 4 (Ps. l. 6); Mt. v. 40; Gen. xxvi. 21; Job xiii. 19, xxxix. 34. e Acts xxiii. 30, xxiv. 19, xxv. 9;
Mt. xxviii. 14. f In this sense, ver. 9; *cf.* αμαρτωλοι, Gal. ii. 15, etc.; απιστοι, ver. 6 below.
g In this comprehensive use, xiv. 33, xvi. 1, 15; 2 Cor. viii. 4; Rom. xii. 13, xvi. 15; about 12 times
besides in P.; Heb. vi. 10; Jude 3. h See ver. 6.

¹ η ουκ: all uncc. but D³L. Η perhaps lost by confusion with final Ν of
εγενηθημεν; hence Syrian text.

the Church. He holds jurisdiction over
those *within* its pale; of their conduct
the Church (ὑμεῖς) is bound to take note;
the world outside must be left to the
judgment of God: "cives judicate, ne
alienos" (Bg.). The Ap. places himself
and the Cor. on the one side (*cf.* 4; also
xii. 25 f.), in contrast with God who
judges τοὺς ἔξω. "Within" and "without" denoted in Synagogue usage members and non-members of the sacred
community (see parls.): οἱ ἔσω = οἱ ἅγιοι,
οἱ οἰκεῖοι τῆς πίστεως, οἱ τοῦ Χριστοῦ,
etc. Yet this mutual judgment of Christians by each other has great limitations
(Rom. xiv. 4-10; Matt. vii. 1 ff.); its
sphere lies in vital matters of character
essential to Church life; and there it is
subject to the final Court of Appeal (see
iv. 3 ff.).—ὁ Θεὸς κρίνει (not κρινεῖ): P.
is not anticipating the Last Judgment,
but laying down the principle that God
is *the world's* Judge; see Rom. ii. 16, iii.
6, Heb. xii. 23, etc.—The interrog. οὐχὶ
holds under its regimen the two clauses
linked by the contrastive δέ; El. however
reads τοὺς δὲ ἔξω κ.τ.λ. assertively, as a
concluding "grave enunciation".

From his digression to the lost Ep.
and the general social problem, the Ap.
returns, with vehement emphasis, to the
offender of vv. 1 f. and demands his
expulsion in the solemn words of the
Deuteronomic law. τὸν πονηρὸν is not
Satan ("scelerum omnium principem,"
Cv.), nor "the wicked" in general
—each case as it arises (Hf.); but
"istum improbum" (Bz.), the case of
notorious and extreme guilt which gave
rise to the whole discussion.—ἐξάρατε
(*cf.* ἐκκαθάρατε, 7) takes up again the ἵνα
ἀρθῇ of ver. 2, with the added thought
(ἐξ- . . . ἐξ ὑμῶν αὐτῶν) of the *riddance*
effected by his removal. The terrible
sentence of vv. 3 ff. had not, in so many
words, prescribed ejection, though implying it; and P. needed to be very explicit: see note on ver. 9. The formal
expulsion must proceed from the Cor.,—
ὑμεῖς κρίνετε; the Church is a self-
governing body.

§ 17. LAW-SUITS IN HEATHEN COURTS,
vi. 1-6. Beside the πόρνος, amongst
those to be excommunicated at Cor.,
stood the πλεονέκτης (v. 11); fraud
and robbery were only less rife than
licentiousness; and this element of corruption, along with the other, had reap-
peared within the Church (8). Instead
of being repressed by timely correction,
the evil had grown rank; in several instances aggrieved Christian parties had
carried their complaints before the civil
Courts, to the scandal of the Church and
to Paul's high indignation. Two links
of thought connect chh. v. and vi.: (1)
the kindred nature of *sins of impurity
and of covetousness,* both prevalent at
Cor., both destructive of society; (2) the
lamentable *lack of Church discipline* (v.
12), which enabled these mischiefs to
gather head.

Ver. 1. Τολμᾷ τις ὑμῶν κ.τ.λ.; "Does
any one of you dare?" etc.—"notatur
læsa majestas Christianorum" (Bg.):
τολμᾶν, *sustinere, non erubescere.* This
also was matter of common knowledge,
like the crime of v. 1. The abrupt
interrog. marks the outburst of indignant
feeling. You treat the Church, the seat
of the Holy Spirit (iii. 16 f.), as though
it were without authority or wisdom;
you take your case from the highest
court to the lowest! So the *appellant* is
first censured; in ver. 4 the whole Church
comes in for blame.—Πρᾶγμα (*res, negotium*), κρίνεσθαι (mid.; see parls.), ἐπὶ
with gen., ἐν (2), κριτήριον (2), καθίζω
(4), and perhaps ἥττημα (7), are all in this
passage technical legal expressions.—Οἱ
ἄδικοι—the term applied by the Jews (*cf.*
Gal. ii. 15), and then by Christians, to
the heathen—marks the action censured
as *self-stultifying*—to seek for right from
"the unrighteous"! P. himself appealed
to Roman justice, but never in matters
"between brother and brother," nor in
the way of accusing his injurers (Acts
xxviii. 19); only in defence of his work.
—Οἱ ἅγιοι indicates by contrast the
moral dignity of Christians (see i. 2, and
note), a judicial attribute; *cf. sanctitas*

i Rom. iii. 6; [h] οἴδατε ὅτι [g] οἱ [g] ἅγιοι τὸν [i] κόσμον [i] κρινοῦσι; καὶ εἰ [k] ἐν ὑμῖν
Acts xvii.
31 (οικου- [i][k] κρίνεται ὁ [i] κόσμος, [l] ἀνάξιοί ἐστε [m] κριτηρίων ἐλαχίστων; 3. [h] οὐκ
μενην); 4
times in
John.   k Acts xvii. 31; Lk. xi. 15.   l H.l.; -ιως, xi. 27; ουκ αξιους, Acts xiii. 46.   m Jas. ii. 6;
Judges v. 10; 3 Kings vii. 7 (44); Dan. vii. 10.

fori (Quintilian, xi., 3. 58). There exists a similar Rabbinical inhibition: "It is forbidden to bring a matter of right before idolatrous judges. . . . Whosoever goeth before them with a law-suit is impious, and does the same as though he blasphemed and cursed; and hath lifted his hand against the law of Moses our Teacher,—blessed be he!" (*Shulchan aruch, Choshen hammishpat*, 29). The Roman Government allowed the Jews liberty of internal jurisdiction; the Beth-din (*house of judgment*) was as regular a part of the Israelite economy as the Beth-keneseth (*synagogue*). In Rom. xiii. 1 ff. P. regards the power of the State from a diff. point of view.

Ver. 2. ἢ οὐκ οἴδατε κ.τ.λ.; "Or (is it that) you do not know?" etc. If the appeal to non-Christian tribunals is not made in *insolence* (τολμᾷ) towards the Church, it must be made in *ignorance* of its matchless prerogative. That "the saints will judge the world" is involved in the conception of the Messianic kingdom (Dan. vii. 22; *cf*. Matt. xx. 21); Israel, with its Christ, is to rule, and therefore judge, the nations (Acts i. 6, etc.: *cf*. Gal. vi. 16). See Wisd. iii. 7 f., where participation in this Messianic power is asserted for "the souls of the righteous" in their future state. After the manner of Jesus, the Ap. carried over to the new Israel of God the promises of dominion claimed under the Old Covenant, transforming in transferring them (2 Tim. ii. 12; Rev. xx. 4, xxii. 5, etc.). Paul reminds his readers of a truth they should have known, since it belongs to the nature of "the kingdom of God" (9) and to the glory they look for at "the unveiling of Christ" (i. 7 ff.; *cf*. iv. 8, Rom. viii. 17, etc.). Cm. and others see here a *virtual* judgment of the world, lying in the faith of the saints as contrasted with its unbelief (*cf*. Luke xi. 31, John iii. 18 ff., Rom. viii. 3),—a thought irrelevant here. Ver. 3, moreover, carries the judgment in question into a region far beyond that of *Christian magistrates*, whose appointment some prosaic interpreters see here predicted. The Ap. argues *à majori ad minus*, from the grand and celestial to earthly commonplace. The early Church ascribed this dignity esp. to *the martyrs*: τοῦ Χριστοῦ πάρεδροι

. . . καὶ μέτοχοι τῆς κρίσεως αὐτοῦ καὶ συνδικάζοντες (Euseb., *H.E.*, vi., 42; see Ed.).—ἐν ὑμῖν, *in consessu vestro*—picturing Christ and His saints in session, with "the world" brought in for trial before them. "It is absurd in itself, and quite inconsistent with the Divine idea and counsel, that any of you should now appear at *their* bar, who shall some day appear at *yours*" (Ev.).—κρίνεται, pr. tense, of faith's *certainty* (*cf*. v. 13).—κριτήριον (see 4) signifies *place* rather than *matter* of judgment (see parls.); for the latter sense lexical warrant is wanting. The question *is*: "Are you unworthy of (sitting on) the smallest tribunals?" of forming courts to deal with trifling affairs of secular property?—*cf*. our "petty sessions". Cm. reads the sentence as affirmative, ἀνάξιοι as *nimis digni*, and τ. κριτηρ. ἐλαχ. as the *heathen* tribunals: "It is beneath your dignity to appear before these contemptible courts!" But this does not square with ver. 4.

Ver. 3. The question of ver. 2 urged to its climax: "Know you not that we shall judge *angels?*" Paul already does this, hypothetically, in Gal. i. 8. *Instructed* through the Church (Eph. iii. 10), the heavenly powers will be subject to final *correction* from the same quarter. The angels were identified, in later Jewish thought, with the forces of nature and the destiny of nations (Ps. civ. 4; Dan. x. 13, xii. 1); they must be affected by any judgment embracing the κόσμος. "There is, it seems, a solidarity between the Princes of the nations (*cf*. Paul's ἀρχαὶ κ. ἐξουσίαι, xv. 24, etc.) and the nations directed by them; according to *Shir rabba*, 27 *b*, God does not punish a people until He has first humbled its Angel-prince in the higher world, and according to *Tanchuma, Beshallach*, 13, He will hereafter judge the nations only when He has first judged their Angel-princes" (Weber, *Altsynag. paläst. Théologie*, p. 165); Satan is κατ' ἐξοχὴν "the god of this world" (2 Cor. iv. 4; *cf*. John xiv. 30, Luke iv. 6), and has his "angels" whom P. styles "world-rulers" (Eph. vi. 12, Matt. xxv. 41). On the throne of world-judgment Christ will sit (Acts xvii. 31, Matt. xxv. 31 f.), and "the saints"—*sc*. after their own acquittal—as His assessors. — κρινοῦσιν in this context

[h] οἴδατε ὅτι [n] ἀγγέλους [1] κρινοῦμεν; [o] μήτι [o] γε [p] βιωτικά · 4. [p] βιωτικὰ
μὲν οὖν [m] κριτήρια, ἐὰν ἔχητε τοὺς [q] ἐξουθενημένους ἐν τῇ ἐκκλησίᾳ,
τούτους [r] καθίζετε · 5. πρὸς [s] ἐντροπὴν ὑμῖν λέγω. [t] οὕτως οὐκ
ἔστιν [1] ἐν ὑμῖν σοφὸς [2] οὐδὲ [2] εἷς, [2] ὃς δυνήσεται [u] διακρῖναι [v] ἀνὰ

[n] In like connexion, Rom. viii. 38;
Gal. i. 8; 2 Pet. ii. 4; Jude 6;
Job iv. 18.
[o] H.l.; class.

[p] Lk. xxi. 34; Aristot., Polyb., Philo. Al.   [q] See i. 28.   [r] Transit., Eph. i. 20; Acts ii. 30.
[s] xv. 34; Job xx. 3; Ps. xxxiv. 26, etc. *Cf.* iv. 14.   [t] Gal. iii. 3; Mt. xxvi. 40; Mk. vii. 18; Jo.
xviii. 22.   [u] N.T. *h.l.*, in this sense. *Cf.* iv. 7; xi. 29.   [v] Mt. xiii. 25; Mk. vii. 31; Rev. vii.
17; Ex. xi. 7; Isa. lvii. 5.

[1] εν ι, ℵBCLP, minn. [70] or more (*cf.* Gal. iii. 28, Col. iii. 11).
εστιν, DG 37, etc.: Western correction.

[2] ουδεις σοφος, ℵBC 17, 46, 73; so crit. edd.
ουδε εις σοφος, GP 37, Aug., Ambrst. (*quisquam sapiens*),—later Western; σοφος
simply, D*, earlier Western (?); σοφος ουδε εις, D³L, etc.,—Syrian.

qualifies its objects as *culpable; cf.* ἵνα καταργήσῃ in xv. 24; also v. 12 above, and other parls. The anarthrous ἀγγέλους signifies beings of this order, in contrast with *men* (*cf.* iv. 9; also Jude 6); "P. does not wish to mark out this or that class of angels, but to awaken in the Church the sense of its competence and dignity by reminding it that beings of this lofty nature will one day be subject to its jurisdiction" (Gd.; also El.).—μήτιγε βιωτικά (*nedum quidem :* not surely a continued interrog., as W.H. punctuate) —in sharp contrast to "angels"—"(to say) nothing verily of secular matters!".—μήτιγε (*sc.* λέγωμεν) is a N.T. *h.l.*, —a sound cl. idiom (see Lidd. on μήτις, also El. *ad. loc.*),—negative syn. for πόσῳ μᾶλλον (Rom. xi. 12, 24); for the γε, *cf.* iv. 8.—βιωτικός, of later Gr. (after Aristotle), denotes matters relating to βίος (one's "living"), which differs from ζωὴ as *vita quam* from *vita qua vivimus* —"quae ad hujus vitæ usum pertinent" (Bz.), or "ad victum pertinentia" (Cv.); see Lt. *ad loc.*, and Trench, *Syn.*, § 27.

Vv. 4, 5a. Ver. 4 is rendered in three diff. ways, as (*a*) τ. ἐξουθενημένους ἐν τ. ἐκκλησίᾳ is taken to mean *the heathen judges*, the ἄδικοι of ver. 1 whom the Church could not respect (ἐν, *in the eyes of; cf.* xiv. 11); then τούτους καθίζετε becomes an indignant question—"Do you set up *these* (as your judges)?" so Mr., Hn., Tisch., W.H., R.V. *text*. The position of καθίζετε and the strain put upon its meaning speak against this view—the Cor. Christians did not *appoint* the city magistrates; also the unlikelihood of Paul's using language calculated to excite contempt toward heathen rulers. (*b*) The prevalent construction (Vg., Syr., Bz., Cv., Bg., Ed., El., Lt., A.V., R.V. *marg.*) understands τ. ἐξουθ. ἐν τ. ἐκκλ. as the despised *of the Church itself*

(καυχᾶσθαι ἐν ἀνθρ., iii. 21, iv. 6 ff., implies such a counterpart); then καθίζετε is read as impv., and P. says in sarcasm, "If you have lawsuits in secular affairs, set up the lowest amongst you (for judges of these low matters)!" κριτήρια however (see note on 2, and R.V. *marg.*) signifies not *trials*, nor *matters of trial*, but *tribunals*, and is therefore an unsuitable obj. to ἐὰν ἔχητε: βιωτικὰ κριτήρια are the things *wanting* to the Church, which P. is advising them to set on foot. Moreover, Paul would hardly speak of Christians as "despised" among their fellows, without some touch of blame for their despisers. (*c*) For these reasons, it is better, as Hf. suggests, to put the comma *before*, instead of after, ἐὰν ἔχητε, attaching τοὺς ἐξουθ. to this vb. and reading βιωτ. κριτ. as a *nom.* (or *acc.*) *pendens* to the sentence (*cf.* Rom. viii. 3, Heb. viii. 1; and Bm., pp. 379 ff.): we thus translate, "Well then, for secular tribunals—if you have men that are made of no account in the Church, set these on the bench!" That this prideful Church *has* such persons is undoubted; P. puts the fact hypothetically, as a thing one does not like to assume. μὲν οὖν throws into relief, by way of emphatic resumption, the βιωτικά . . . κριτήρια.—πρὸς ἐντροπὴν ὑμῖν λέγω, "Unto your shame (*lit.* for a shame to you) I say (it)": this relates to the foregoing sentence (*cf.* xv. 34); it is a shame the Cor. Church should have members looked on with utter contempt (*cf.* xii. 21-25); but since it has, it is fitting that they should be its judges in things contemptible! P. writes with anger, whereas he did not, though he might seem to do, in iv. 14.

Ver. 5*b*. Laying aside sarcasm, the Ap. asks most gravely: "(Is it) so (that) there is no wise man found amongst you, who will be able to decide between his

w Job ix. 3　ᵛμέσον τοῦ ἀδελφοῦ αὐτοῦ; 6. ἀλλὰ ἀδελφὸς ᵂμετὰ ἀδελφοῦ
(or dat.).
x Rom. xiii. ᵈᵂκρίνεται, ˣκαὶ ˣτοῦτο ᵉἐπὶ ʸἀπίστων.
11; Eph.
ii. 8; Phil.　7. Ἤδη μὲν οὖν¹ ᶻὅλως ᵃἥττημα ἐν² ὑμῖν ἐστιν ὅτι ᵇκρίματα
i. 28; 3 Jo.
5:　ἔχετε μεθ᾿ ἑαυτῶν· ᶜδιατί³ οὐχὶ μᾶλλον ᵈἀδικεῖσθε; ᶜδιατί³ οὐχὶ
y vii. 12 ff.,
x. 27, xiv.　μᾶλλον ᵉἀποστερεῖσθε; 8. ἀλλὰ ὑμεῖς ᵈἀδικεῖτε καὶ ᵉἀποστερεῖτε,
22 ff.; 2
Cor. vi. 14
f.; 1 Tim. v. 8.　z See v. 1.　a Rom. xi. 12; Isa. xxxi. 8; -αομαι, 2 Cor. xii. 13; 2 Pet. ii. 19 f.
b N.T. h.l.; Ex. xviii. 22.　c 2 Cor. xi. 11; Rom. ix. 32; Rev. xvii. 7; Acts v. 3; oftener in Gospp.
d Pass. (or mid.), 2 Cor. vii. 12; 2 Pet. ii. 12; Acts vii. 24; Rev. ii. 11. For act., 2 Cor. vii. 2; Gal. iv.
12; Col. iii. 25; Phm. 18, etc.　e vii. 5; 1 Tim. vi. 5; Mk. x. 19.

¹ Om. ουν ℵ*D* 17, latt. vg. cop.　So Tisch.; not W.H.
² Om. εν all uncc.; all critical edd.
³ δια τι: critical edd., except Tisch.

brothers?" οὖτως intensifies the question (cf. Gal. iii. 3)—τοσαύτη σπάνις (Cm.)—"so utter a lack of men of sense amongst you Cor., with all your talent and pretensions?" (i. 5, iii. 18, iv. 10). ἐνί, prp. with ellipsis of ἐστίν (Wr., p. 96)—there exists, is found (see parls.). —ἀνὰ μέσον (Hebraistic prpl. phrase) τοῦ ἀδελφοῦ αὐτοῦ—lit. "between his brother"—a defective expression, as though due to confusion of τῶν ἀδελφῶν with the more Hebraistic ἀδελφοῦ καὶ ἀδελφοῦ: an example of the laxity of Paul's conversational Gr.; unless, as Sm. conjectures, there is a "primitive error," and τοῦ ἀδελφοῦ should be corrected to τῶν ἀδελφῶν.

Ver. 6. "Nay, but brother goes to law with brother—this too before unbelievers!" This is an answer to the question of ver. 5, not a continuation of it. The litigation shows that there is no man in the Church wise enough to settle such matters privately; or he would surely have been called in. The ἄδικοι of ver. 1 here figure as ἄπιστοι; see parls.; contrast with οἱ πιστεύοντες (i. 21).

§ 18. WARNING TO IMMORAL CHRISTIANS, vi. 7-11. Behind the scandal of the law-suits there lay a deeper mischief in their cause. They were immediately due to unchristian resentment on the part of the aggrieved; but the chief guilt lay with the aggressors. The defrauders of their brethren, and all doers of wrong, are warned that they forfeit their place in God's kingdom (9 f.), and reminded that the sins they thus commit belong to their unregenerate state (11).

Ver. 7. Ἤδη μὲν οὖν, "Indeed then, to begin with": on ἤδη (already, i.e. before litigation), see note to iv. 8. μὲν here, otherwise than in ver. 4, suggests a suppressed δέ: "but ye aggra-

vate matters by going before the heathen" (Lt.).—ὅλως (see v. 1) ἥττημα (cl. ἥττα): "it is absolutely a failure on your part" —not a mere defect, nor a loss (sc. of the Messianic glory: so Mr., in view of 9), but a moral defeat (see parls.). Ἡττάομαι (see Lidd., s. v., I. 3) signifies to be worsted, beaten in a suit (Lat. causa cadere); this sense excellently suits the context and Paul's epigrammatic style: "Indeed then it is already an unmistakable defeat for you that you have law-suits"—you are beaten before you enter court, by the mere fact that such quarrels arise and reach this pitch.—κρίμα is the πρᾶγμα (1) ripened into an actual case at law. μεθ᾿ ἑαυτῶν, for μετ᾿ ἀλλήλων, implies intestine strife; the 3rd pl. reflexive pron. frequently serves all three persons (Jelf's Gr. Gram., § 654, 2 b).—ἀδικεῖσθε, ἀποστερεῖσθε, mid. voice: "injuriam accipitis, fraudem patimini" (Vg.)—"Why do you not rather submit to wrong, to robbery?" (see Wr., p. 218). Paul reproduces the teaching of Jesus in Luke vi. 27 ff., etc., which applies more strictly as the relationships of life are closer; cf. His own example (1 Pet. ii. 23), and that of the Ap. (iv. 12 f., 16). οὐχὶ μᾶλλον, as in v. 2.

Ver. 8. ἀλλὰ ὑμεῖς κ.τ.λ.: "Nay, but you commit wrong and robbery—this too (cf. 6) upon your brothers!" Mr. reads this, like the parl. ἀλλὰ clause of ver. 6, as a further question; it is the answer to the question of ver. 7—the sad fact contrasted with the duty of the Christian. The spiritual kinship which heightens the duty of submission to wrong, aggravates its commission.

Vv. 9, 10. On ἢ οὐκ οἴδατε; see note to ver. 2. The wrongers of their brethren are surely unaware of the fact that "wrong-doers (ἄδικοι) will not inherit

˟ καὶ ˟ταῦτα ¹ ἀδελφούς. 9. ᵗἢ ᶠοὐκ ᵗοἴδατε ὅτι ᵍἄδικοι ʰⁱβασιλείαν ² ᶠ See iii. 16.
With ἢ,
ᵏΘεοῦ² οὐ ⁱκληρονομήσουσι; ᵏμὴ ᵏπλανᾶσθε· οὔτε ³ ˡπόρνοι οὔτε ³ ver. 2
above.
ᵐεἰδωλολάτραι οὔτε ³ ⁿμοιχοὶ οὔτε ³ ᵒμαλακοὶ οὔτε ³ ᵖἀρσενοκοῖται ᵍ See ver. 1.
ʰ See iv. 20.
10. οὔτε ³ ᵠκλέπται, οὔτε ³ ʳπλεονέκται, οὔτε ³ ˢμέθυσοι, οὐ ³ ᵗλοίδοροι, i xv. 50; Gal.
v. 21; Mt.
οὐχ ³ ᵘἅρπαγες ʰⁱβασιλείαν ʰΘεοῦ οὐ ⁴ ⁱκληρονομήσουσιν. 11. καὶ xxv. 34.
κληρον.,
ᵛταῦτά τινες ἦτε· ἀλλὰ ʷἀπελούσασθε, ἀλλὰ ˟ἡγιάσθητε, ἀλλ' Gal. iv.
30 (Gen.
xxi. 10);

Heb. i. 14, vi. 12; Rev. xxi. 7; Mt. v. 5, xix. 29, etc. (ζωην αιων.). k xv. 33; Gal. vi. 7; Jas. i. 16;
Isa. xli. 10. l See v. 9. m See v. 10. n Heb. xiii. 4; Lk. xviii. 11; Job xxiv. 15; -ενω more
freq. o H.l., of persons; Prov. xxv. 15, xxvi. 22. See note below. p 1 Tim. i. 10. See Lev.
xviii. 22. q 1 Pet. iv. 15; Jo. xii. 6, etc.; ο κλεπτων, Eph. iv. 28. r See v. 11. s See v. 11.
t See v. 11. u See v. 11. v As if for τουτο, Jo. xv. 17; 3 Jo. 4. w Acts xxii. 16; Job ix. 30; cf.
Jo. xiii. 10; Rev. i. 5 (λουω); Eph. v. 26 and Tit. iii. 5 (λουτρον). x See i. 2.

¹ τουτο, all uncc. but L.

² Θεου βασιλειαν (in this order: cf. ver. 10): all uncc. but L.

³ ουτε seven times (πορνοι . . . πλεονεκται), then ου (μεθυσοι), ου, ουχ: ℵACP.
BL, and Syrian text, read ουτε eight times, then ου, ουχ.
D*, ουδε seven times, ουτε twice, then ουχ.

⁴ Om. ου all uncc. but LP (Syrian); cf. ver. 9.

God's kingdom" (which nevertheless they profess to seek, i. 7 ff.)—an axiom of revelation, indeed of conscience, but the over-clever sometimes forget elementary moral principles; hence the μὴ πλανᾶσθε. Their conduct puts them on a level with the heathen (οἱ ἄδικοι, 1). Θεοῦ βασιλείαν (doubly anarthrous; see note on ii. 5), "God's kingdom"—the expression indicating the region and nature of the realm from which unrighteousness excludes; "the kingdom of God is righteousness" (Rom. xiv. 17; cf. Matt. v. 10, xiii. 43, Luke xiv. 14, Rev. i. 18, ii. 8 f., etc.). The deception taking place on this fundamental point springs from the frivolity of the Hellenic nature; it had a specific cause in the libertinism deduced from the gospel of Free Grace and the abrogation of the Mosaic Law (12 f., see notes; cf. Rom. vi. 1, 15, Gal. v. 13).—In vv. 9b, 10 the general warning is carried into detail. Ten classes of sinners are distinguished, uncleanness and greed furnishing the prevailing categories (cf. v. 9-11): "neither fornicators (the conspicuous sin of Cor.: v. 1, etc.; vii. 2) . . . neither covetous men—no drunkards, no railers, no plunderers (see txtl. note) will inherit," etc. Idolaters are ranged between fornicators and adulterers—an association belonging to the cultus of Aphrodité Pandemos at Cor. μαλακοί, soft, voluptuous, appears in this connexion to signify general addiction to sins of the flesh; lexical ground is wanting for the sense of pathici, suggested to some interpreters by the following word

and by the use of molles in Latin. For ἀρσενοκοῖται (cl. παιδερασταί), whose sin of Sodom was widely and shamelessly practised by the Greeks; cf. Rom. i. 24 ff., written from Cor. The three detached classes appended by οὐ to the οὔτε list were specified in v. 11; see notes.

Ver. 11. καὶ ταῦτά τινες ἦτε: "And these things you were, some (of you)". The neuter ταῦτα is contemptuous—"such abominations!" τινὲς softens the aspersion; the majority of Cor. Christians had not been guilty of extreme vice. The stress lies on the tense of ἦτε; "you were"—a thing of the past, cf. Rom. vi. 19, Eph. ii. 11 f.—"But you washed yourselves! but you were sanctified; but you were justified!"—ἀλλὰ thrice repeated, with joyful emphasis, as in 2 Cor. ii. 17, vii. 11. The first of the three vbs. is mid., the other two pass. in voice. ἀπελούσασθε refers to baptism (cf. Acts xxii. 16, Col. ii. 11 f., Eph. v. 26 f., 1 Pet. iii. 21; see i. 13 for its signal importance), in its spiritual meaning; the form of the vb. calls attention to the initiative of the Cor. in getting rid, at the call of God, of the filth of their old life; in baptism their penitent faith took deliberate and formal expression, with this effect. But behind their action in submitting to baptism, there was the action of God, operating to the effect described by the terms ἡγιάσθητε, ἐδικαιώθητε. These twin conceptions of the Christian state in its beginning appear commonly in the reverse order (see i. 30, Rom. vi. 19, etc.); in Rom. v.,

y See iv. 4. ᵞ ἐδικαιώθητε ᵞ ἐν τῷ ὀνόματι τοῦ Κυρίου ¹ Ἰησοῦ ² καὶ ᵞ ἐν τῷ
z x. 23 (same
contrast); πνεύματι τοῦ Θεοῦ ἡμῶν.
2 Cor. xii.
4; freq. in   12. Πάντα μοι ᶻ ἔξεστιν, ἀλλ᾽ οὐ πάντα ᶻᵃ συμφέρει· πάντα μοι
Gospp.
and Acts.

a x. 23, xii. 7; 2 Cor. viii. 10, xii. 1; Heb. xii. 10; Mt. v. 29 f., xviii. 6, xix. 10; Jo. xi. 50, xvi. 7, xviii.
24; Acts xix. 19, xx. 20.

¹ (Κυρ.) η μ ω ν (?), BCP, 17, 37, 73, vg., syrr., cop. ; W.H. *bracket*.
² *Add* Χ ρ ι σ τ ο υ all uncc. but ADᶜL ; all crit. edd.

vi. they are seen to be related as the
resurrection and death of Christ, and in
Rom. vi. to be figured respectively in the
ἀνάδυσις and κατάδυσις which formed
the two movements of baptism ; see notes
ad locc., also Tit. iii. 5 ff. The order
of the words does not justify Calovius, Lipsius, and Mr., with Romanist interpreters,
in finding here "the ethical *continuatio
justificationis*,"—an explanation contrary
to the uniform Pauline signification of
δικαιόω ; the Ap. is thinking (in contrast
with vv. 9 f.) of the status attained by his
readers as ἅγιοι (i. 2, iii. 17, vi. 1),
behind which lay the fundamental fact of
their δικαίωσις. The qualifying prpl.
phrases both belong to the three closely
linked vbs. Baptism is received "in the
name of our Lord Jesus Christ" (quoted
with formal solemnity : *cf.* note on i. 2) :
"in the Spirit of our God" it is validated
and brings its appropriate blessings (*cf.*
John iii. 5-8 : *water* is the formal, *the Sp.*
the essential source of the new birth).

Βαπτίζειν ἐν Πν. ἁγίῳ was the distinctive work of Jesus Christ (Matt. iii. 11,
etc.) ; to be ἐν Πνεύματι (Θεοῦ, Χριστοῦ)
is the distinctive state of a Christian,
including every element of the new life
(19, ii. 12, iii. 16, 2 Cor. i. 21 f., Rom.
v. 5, viii. 2, 9, etc.). *Sanctification* esp.
is grounded in the *Holy* Spirit ; but He
is an agent in *justification* too, for His
witness to sonship implies the assurance
of forgiveness (Rom. viii. 15 ff.). *The
name of our Lord Jesus Christ* sums up
the baptismal confession (*cf.* Rom. x.
8 ff.) ; *the Spirit of our God* constitutes
the power by which that confession is
inspired, and the regeneration effectuated
which makes it good : the two factors
are identified in xii. 3 (see note). "Our
God," in emphatic distinction from the
gods in whose service the Cor. had been
defiled (see viii. 4 ff., 2 Cor. iv. 4, Eph.
ii. 2 ; *cf.* Ps. xcix. 9).

§ 19. THE SANCTITY OF THE BODY,
vi. 12-20. The laxity of morals distinguishing the Cor. Church was in some
instances defended, or half-excused, by
appealing to the principle of *Christian*

liberty, which P. had himself enunciated
in asserting the freedom of Gentile Christians from the Mosaic ceremonial restrictions. From his lips the libertarians
took their motto, Πάντα μοι ἔξεστιν.
The Ap. does not retract this sentence,
but he guards it from abuse : (1) by
setting over against it the balancing
principle of *expediency*, οὐ πάντα συμφέρει ; (2) by defining, in the twofold
example of ver. 13, the sphere within
which it applies, *distinguishing liberty
from licence*. This leads up to a reiterated
prohibition of fornication, grounded on
its nature as a sin against the body itself,
and an act which flagrantly contradicts
the sanctity of its limbs, as they belong
to Christ, being purchased by Him for
the service of God (15-20).

Ver. 12. Πάντα μοι ἔξεστιν stands
twice here, and twice in x. 23 ; P. harps
on the saying in a way to indicate that it
was a watchword with some Cor. party
—perhaps amongst both Paulinists and
Apollonians ; his μοι endorses the declaration (*cf.* viii. 8 f., x. 23 f., Rom. xiv.
14, 20). Very likely it had been quoted
in the Church Letter. This sentence,
like those of ii. 14, iii. 21, iv. 1 (see
notes), recalls the attributes of the Stoic
ideal σοφός, to whom it belongs ἐξεῖναι
ὡς βουλόμεθα διεξάγειν (Arr.-Epict., II.,
i., 21-28; see Hn. *ad loc.*).—ἀλλ᾽ οὐ
πάντα συμφέρει : "Yes, but not all
things are advantageous". — Συμφέρει
(*conducunt*) signifies *contributing* to some
one's benefit—here *one's own*, in x. 24
one's neighbour's.—Parl. to the former
ἀλλ᾽ οὐ, is ἀλλ᾽ οὐκ ἐγὼ ἐξουσιασθήσομαι
κ.τ.λ. : "All things are in my domain ;
yes, but *I* will not be dominated by anything". That is "unprofitable" to a
man which "gets the mastery" over him.
"Such and such a thing is in my power ;
I will take care that it does not get me
into its power. I will never by abuse of
my liberty forfeit that liberty in its noblest
part." This gives the *self-regarding*, as
x. 23 f. the *other-regarding* rule of Christian temperance in the use of things lawful. *Cf.* the instructive chapter Περὶ

ˣ ἔξεστιν, ἀλλ' οὐκ ἐγὼ ᵇ ἐξουσιασθήσομαι ὑπό τινος. 13. τὰ ᵇ vii. 4; Lk.
xxii. 25;
˓ βρώματα τῇ ᵈ κοιλίᾳ καὶ ἡ ᵈ κοιλία τοῖς ᶜ βρώμασιν, ὁ δὲ Θεὸς Eccl. ix.
17.
καὶ ᵉ ταύτην καὶ ᵉ ταῦτα ᶠ καταργήσει· τὸ δὲ σῶμα οὐ τῇ ᵍ πορνείᾳ, ᶜ 1 Tim. iv.
3; Heb.
ἀλλὰ τῷ Κυρίῳ καὶ ὁ Κύριος τῷ σώματι· 14. ὁ δὲ Θεὸς καὶ τὸν ix. 10, xiii.
9; Mt. xiv.
Κύριον ʰ ἤγειρεν, καὶ ἡμᾶς ˡ ἐξεγερεῖ ˡ διὰ τῆς ᵏ δυνάμεως ᵏ αὐτοῦ. 15; Mk.
vii. 19;
15. ˡ οὐκ ˡ οἴδατε ὅτι τὰ σώματα ὑμῶν ² ᵐ μέλη Χριστοῦ ἐστιν; Lk. iii. 11.
ᵈ In this
sense,

Phil. iii. 19; Mt. xv. 17; Rev. x. 9 f.   e For repetition, cf. vii. 7.   f See i. 28.   g See v. 1.
h xv. 4 ff., 2 Cor. i. 9, iv. 14, v. 15; Rom. passim; Gal. i. 1; Eph. i. 20; Col. ii. 12; 1 Th. i. 10; 2 Tim.
ii. 8; Heb. xi. 19; 1 Pet. i. 21, etc.   i Rom. ix. 17 (Exod. ix. 16), in diff. sense.   k See i. 18.
l See iii. 16, vi. 2.   m In like sense, xii. 12 ff.; Rom. xii. 4 f.; Eph. iv. 16, 25, v. 30.

¹ εξεγερει, אCD³KL, etc., syrr., cop., many Ff. ; εξεγειρει, AD*PQ 37.

εξηγειρεν (?), B 67** (a group preserving some valuable readings), cod. amiatinus
of vg. ; W.H. marg.   Beza and Elzevir read υμας, with no certain MS. authority.

² ημων, א*A.

ἐλευθερίας in Arr.-Epict., IV., i. For
the play on ἔξεστιν, cf. ii. 15. The emphatic οὐκ ἐγὼ is the jealous self-assertion
of the spiritual freeman, fearful of falling
again under the dominion of the flesh :
cf. ix. 26 f., Gal. v. 13, 16.

Ver. 13. The maxim "All things are
lawful to me" has been guarded within
its province ; now it must be limited to
its province : "Foods (are) for the belly,
and the belly for its foods".—τὰ βρώματα, the different kinds of food—about
which Jewish law, ascetic practice (Rom.
xiv. 1 ff.), and the supposed defilement
of the idolothyta (viii., x. 25 ff.) caused
many embarrassments. The Ap., adopting the profound principle of Jesus (Mark
vii. 15-23), cuts through these knotty
questions at a stroke : the βρώματα are
morally indifferent ; for they belong to
the κοιλία, not the καρδία (cf. Rom. xiv.
17). Food and the stomach are appropriated to each other ; the main question
about the former is whether or no it suits
the latter.—A second reason for the
moral indifference of matters of the table
lies in their perishing nature ; κοιλία and
βρώματα play a large and troublesome
part in the existing order, "but God will
abolish both this and these". For the
somewhat rare antithetic repetition of
οὖτος, cf. vii. 7, also Josh. viii. 22 (LXX).
The nutritive system forms no part of
the permanent self ; it belongs to the
passing σχῆμα τ. κόσμου τούτου (vii.
31), to the constitution of "flesh and
blood" (xv. 50) and the σῶμα ψυχικόν ;
hence the indifference of foods (viii. 8) :
"quæ destruentur, per se liberum habent
usum" (Bg.; cf. Col. ii. 20 f.).—"But
the body" has relations more vital and
influential than those concerned with its
perishing sustenance—it "is not for for-

nication, but for the Lord and the Lord
for the body" : the same double dat.
clause of mutual appropriation links τὸ
σῶμα with ὁ Κύριος as τὰ βρώματα with
ἡ κοιλία ; each is made for the other and
requires the other. "The body"—regarded as a whole, in contrast with its
temporary apparatus—is fashioned for
the Lord's use ; to yield it to harlotry is
to traverse Christ's rights in it and dis-
qualify oneself for a part in His resurrection (14). The Lord Jesus and πορνεία
contested for the bodies of Christian
men ; loyal to Him they must renounce
that, yielding to that they renounce Him.
In Gr. philosophical ethics the distinction drawn in this ver. had no place ; the
two appetites concerned were treated on
the same footing, as matters of physical
function, the higher ethical considerations attaching to sexual passion being
ignored. Hence the degradation of
woman and the decay of family life,
which brought Greek civilisation to a
shameful end.

Ver. 14 is parl. to ver. 13b ("God" the
agent in both), as ver. 13c to ver. 13a :
the previous δὲ contrasted the several
natures of βρώματα and σῶμα ; this the
opp. issues, καταργήσει and ἐξεγερεῖ. ὁ
Κύριος is the determining factor of both
contrasts. "God will abolish both the
belly and its foods . . . but God both
raised up the Lord, and will raise up us
also through His power." P. substitutes
"us," in the antithesis, for "our bodies,"
since the man, including his body (see xv.
35, 49), is the subject of resurrection.
The saying ἀπαρχὴ Χριστός, of xv. 23,
supplies the nexus between τ. Κύριον
ἤγειρεν and ἡμ. ἐξεγερεῖ ; cf. also 2 Cor.
iv. 14, Rom. viii. 11, xiv. 9, Col. iii. 1,
Phil. iii. 21 ; John v. 20-30, xiv. 2 ff., etc.

n See v. 2.
o Heb. xi.   ⁿ ἄρας ¹ οὖν τὰ ᵐ μέλη τοῦ Χριστοῦ ποιήσω ᵒ πόρνης ᵐ μέλη ; μὴ
31 ; Jas. ii.   γένοιτο · 16. ¹ ἢ ¹ οὐκ ¹ οἴδατε ὅτι ὁ ᵖ κολλώμενος τῇ ᵒ πόρνῃ ἐν
25 ; Rev.
xvii. 1 ff.;   σῶμά ἐστιν ; "Ἔσονται γάρ," ᑫ φησίν, "οἱ δύο εἰς σάρκα μίαν ·"
Mt. xxi.
31 f.; Lk.   17. ὁ δὲ ᵖ κολλώμενος τῷ Κυρίῳ ἓν πνεῦμά ἐστι. 18. ʳ φεύγετε
xv. 30.
p Rom. xii.

9; Acts v. 13, etc.; Lk. x. 11, xv. 15; esp. Mt. xix. 5 (Gen. ii. 24).   q 2 Cor. x. 10; Heb. viii. 5, in parenthetic use.   r x. 14; 1 Tim. vi. 11; 2 Tim. ii. 22; Sir. xxi. 2.

¹ αρα ουν, CP, and several minuscc.   Final σ of αρας easily lost in following ο ; and αρα ουν is plausibly Pauline (G, η αρα ουν).

The prefix in ἐξ-εγερεῖ is local—*out of* (*sc.* the grave; *cf.* ἐξ-ανάστασις, Phil. iii. 11) ; not *de massa dormientium* (Bg.). The raising of Christ (*cf.* Eph. i. 19 ff.), then of Christians, from the dead is the supreme exhibition of God's supernatural "power" (see Rom. iv. 17-24, Matt. xxii. 29, Acts xxvi. 8, etc.). Christ is raised as "Lord," and will rule our life yon side of death more completely than on this (Acts ii. 36, Col. i. 18, Phil. iii. 20 f.).

Vv. 15-17 unfold in its repulsiveness, by vivid concrete presentment, the opposition between the two claimants for bodily service already contrasted: the rival of Christ is ἡ πόρνη ! "Or (if what I have said is not sufficient) do you not know that your bodies are *Christ's limbs*? Should I then take away the limbs of Christ and make them *a harlot's limbs*? Far be it !"—Αἴρω is *to remove, carry off*, as in v. 2 (see parls.), Vg. *tollens*, implying "a voluntary and determined act" (Ed.) ; for the introductory aor. ptp., see Bn., §§ 132, 138. ποιήσω, either (deliberative) aor. sbj. or fut. ind.—"Am I to make, etc.?" or, "Am I going to make?" The former idiom suits an act of *choice* ; this question the tempted Cor. Christian must put to himself : *cf.* the interrog. form of Rom. vi. 1, 15 (-ωμεν).

What is true of Christian men individually, that they are μέλη Χριστοῦ and parts of the σῶμα Χριστοῦ, is true specifically of the physical frame of each ; similarly in vv. 19 f. Paul applies to the Christian man's *body* the glorious truth stated respecting the Christian society in iii. 16 f. In the Hellenic view, the body was the perishing envelope of the man ; in the Scriptural view, it is the abiding vehicle of his spirit. To devote the body to a harlot, one must first withdraw it from Christ's possession : to do *that*, and *for such a purpose*—the bare statement shows the infamy of the proposal. The Biblical formula of deprecation, μὴ γένοιτο, is frequent also in Epictetus ; *cf. Odyssey*, vii., 316, μὴ τοῦτο φίλον Διὶ πατρὶ γένοιτο.

Ver. 16 justifies the strong expression πόρνης μέλη (15), implying that the alliance is a kind of incorporation : "Or (if you object to my putting it in this way), do you not know that he who cleaves to the harlot is one body (with her) ?" ὁ κολλώμενος (see parls.), *qui agglutinatur scorto* (Bz.), indicates that sexual union constitutes a permanent bond between the parties. What has been done lives, morally, in both ; neither is henceforth free of the other. The Divine sentence (uttered prophetically by Adam) which the Ap. quotes to this effect was pronounced upon the first wedded pair, and holds of every such union, whether lawful or unlawful—honourably true (vii. 4, Heb. xiii. 4), or shamefully. In Eph. v. 31 the same Scripture is cited at length, where the Ap. is making out the correspondence between wedlock and Christ's union with the Church : in that place the spiritual union is treated as parl. to the natural union, where this follows the Divine order ; here it stands out as prohibitory to a natural union which violates that order. Here only Paul uses the parenthetical φησίν ("says he," *sc. God*) in citing Scripture ; it is common in Philo, and in the Ep. of Barnabas.—ἔσονται . . . εἰς (Hebraism) = γενήσονται.

Ver. 17. ὁ δὲ κολλώμενος τῳ Κυρίῳ κ.τ.λ.: "But he who cleaves to the Lord is one spirit (with Him)". Adhesion by the act of faith (i. 21, etc.) to Christ (as *Lord, cf.* xii. 3, etc.) establishes a spiritual communion of the man with Him as real and close as the other, bodily communion ("tam arcte quam conjuges sunt unum corpus," Bg.), and as much more influential and enduring as the spirit is above the flesh. "*The* Spirit" is the uniting bond (iii. 16, Rom. viii. 8 f., etc.), but the Ap. is thinking of the *nature* and *sphere* of this union ; hence the anarthrous, generic πνεῦμα, contrasted with σάρξ (16). In 2 Cor. iii. 17 "the Lord" is identified with "the Spirit," and believers are repeatedly said

τὴν ˢπορνείαν. πᾶν ᵗᵘἁμάρτημα ὃ ἐὰν ᵘποιήσῃ ᵛἄνθρωπος, ᵂἐκτὸς ˢ See v. 1.
τοῦ σώματός ἐστιν· ὁ δὲ ˣπορνεύων ʸεἰς τὸ ἴδιον σῶμα ʸἁμαρτάνει.
19. ˡἢ ˡοὐκ ˡοἴδατε ὅτι τὸ ˡ σῶμα ˡ ὑμῶν ᶻναὸς τοῦ ἐν ὑμῖν ʿΑγίου ²
Πνεύματός ² ἐστιν, οὗ ἔχετε ἀπὸ Θεοῦ, καὶ οὐκ ἐστὲ ᵃἑαυτῶν; 20. ᵘ
ᵇἠγοράσθητε γὰρ ᵇᶜτιμῆς. ᵈδοξάσατε ᵉδὴ τὸν ᵈΘεὸν ἐν τῷ σώματι
ὑμῶν καὶ ³ ἐν τῷ πνεύματι ὑμῶν, ἅτινά ἐστι τοῦ Θεοῦ.³

t Rom. iii.
25; Mk.
iii. 28 f.;
Isa. lviii.
1.
u 2 Cor. xi.
7; Jo. viii.
34; 1 Jo.
iii. 4, 8 f.;
Jas. v. 15;
1 Pet. ii.
22.

v See iii. 4. w Prep., xv. 27; 2 Cor. xii. 2. x x. 8; Rev. ii. 14, 20, xvii. 2, xviii. 3, 9; Mk. x. 19;
Ps. lxxii. 27. y viii. 12; Mt. xviii. 15; Lk. xv. 18, 21; Gen. xx. 6, 9. z See iii. 16. a Genitive, see i. 12. b In this sense, vii. 23; 2 Pet. ii. 1; Rev. v. 9, xiv. 3 f.; εξαγορ., Gal. iii. 13, iv. 5.
c In this sense, Mt. xxvii. 6, 9; Acts iv. 34, v. 2 f., vii. 16, xix. 19. d 2 Cor. ix. 13; Rom. i. 21, xv.
6, 9; Gal. i. 24; 1 Pet. ii. 12, iv. 11, 16; Lk. passim, etc. e H.l. in P.; Heb. ii. 16; 4 times in
Acts and Lk.

¹ τα σωματα, A²L, and minuscc. ⁴⁵, cop. ; cf. ver. 15.

² πνευματος αγιου (?) : B 120, f. vg. So W.H. marg.

³ Om. και . . . Θεου all pre-Syrian uncc. The vg. (after the old lat.) reads,
glorificate (clarificate, Cypr., Ambrst.) deum et portate (tollite, Tert.) in corpore
vestro : portate (scil. Deum) is probably due to the corruption of αρα γε (found
in Methodius before δοξασατε) into αρατε. This error was widely spread ; there are
traces of it in Chrysostom. See W.H., Notes on Selected Readings, p. 114.

to be ἐν Πνεύματι ; so that between them
and Christ there exists a κοινωνία Πνεύματος (i. 9, 2 Cor. xiii. 13 ; John xvi. 14,
etc.). For the intimacy of this association of members with the Head, see Gal.
ii. 20, Eph. ii. 5 f., iii. 16 f., Col. ii. 10, iii.
1 ff., John xv. 1 ff., xvii. 23 ff., etc.

Ver. 18. With vehement abruptness
P. turns from exposition to exhortation.
"Flee fornication"—other sins may be
combated ; this must be fled, as by
Joseph in Potiphar's house. φεύγετε
the opposite of κολλᾶσθαι (16). The
parl. φεύγετε ἀπὸ τ. εἰδωλολατρείας of
x. 14 shows "the connexion in Cor.
between impurity and idolatry" (Ed. :
cf. the lists of sins in 9 and v. 11.)—Ἡ
πορνεία contradicts Christ's rights in the
body (13-17) and severs the committer
from Him ; P. has now to say that this
is a sin against the nature of the human
body : "Every act of sin (ἁμάρτημα)
which a man may possibly do, is outside
of the body ; but the fornicator (ὁ
πορνεύων) sins against his own body".
The point of this saying lies in the
contrasted prepositions ἐκτὸς and εἰς :
all bodily sins "defile the flesh" (2 Cor.
vii. 1), but other vices—those of the
κοιλία, e.g.—look outside the body ; this
in its whole essence lies within our
physical nature, so that, while it appropriates the person of another (16), it is
a self-violation. Hence transgressions
of the Seventh Commandment are "sins
of the flesh" and "of the passions" par
éminence. They engage and debauch the
whole person ; they "enter into the

heart," for "they proceed out of the
heart" and touch the springs of being ;
in the highest degree they "defile the
man" (Mark vii. 20 ff.). That inchastity
is extreme dishonour is realised in the
one sex ; Christianity makes it equally so
in the other.

Vv. 19, 20. What a deadly sin, an act
of high treason, this is for the Christian,
Paul's final appeal shows : "Or (if you
do not yet realise the heinousness of
fornication), do you not know that your
body is the temple of the Holy Spirit
within you, which you have (οὗ ἔχετε, gen.
by attraction to Πνεύματος) from God ? "
The Holy Spirit dwells in the readers :
how but in their body, since they are in
the body ? (iii. 16, cf. Rom. viii. 11 ; also
John ii. 21) : there is the same tacit
inference from whole to part as in ver.
15 ; the same assumption that the body
is essential to the man, which underlies
the doctrine of the Resurrection (xv.).
The Christian estimate of πορνεία is thus
categorically opposed to the heathen
estimate. In the temple of Aphrodité
prostitutes were priestesses, and commerce with them was counted a consecration ; it is an absolute desecration of
God's true temple in the man himself.—
"And (that) you are not your own ? "
This too P. asks his readers if they "do
not know ? " The possessor is God,
who has occupied them by His Spirit,
having first purchased them with His
Son's blood : cf. i. 30, iii. 23 ; Rom. viii.
32, 2 Cor. v. 18 ff., Acts xx. 28. "For
you were bought at a price!"—the τιμὴ

a vv. 8, 26;
Rom. xiv.
21; 1 Tim.
ii. 3; Mt.
xviii. 8;
Gen. ii. 18.   b In this connection, Mt. xix. 5, 10 (Gen. ii. 24).   c In this sense, N.T. *h.l.*; Gen. xx. 6; Prov. vi. 29.   d See v. 1; Mt. xv. 19; Mk. vii. 21.

VII. 1. Περὶ δὲ ὧν ἐγράψατέ μοι [1] · ᵃΚαλὸν ᵇἀνθρώπῳ γυναικὸς ᶜἅπτεσθαι · 2. διὰ δὲ τὰς [2] ᵈπορνείας [2] ἕκαστος τὴν ἑαυτοῦ

[1] *Om.* μοι אBC 17, 46, am. fu.*, Tert. So crit. edd.
[2] τὴν πορνειαν : G, vg. syrutr., Tert., Ambrst.

P. does not need to state; it was τίμιον αἷμα (1 Pet. i. 18 f.; Eph. i. 7, Matt. xx. 28, Rev. v. 9). Ἀγοράζω, *to purchase*, syn. with (ἀπο)λυτρόομαι, *to ransom* (i. 30, Tit. ii. 14) : the latter points to the means of redemption, the former to the proprietorship which it creates (*cf.* περιεποιήσατο, Acts xx. 28); both ideas meet in Eph. i. 14. The gen. of price, τιμῆς, indicates the value at which God *rates* His purchase.—δοξάσατε δὴ κ.τ.λ. : " Now glorify God *in your body* "—*sc.* by a chaste life (contrast Rom. ii. 23). δή (rare in N.T. ; *h. l.* in P.), kindred to the temporal ἤδη, makes the command peremptory, breaking off discussion (*cf.* Acts xiii. 2). ἐν, *in*, not *with*, your *body*— the temple wherein each man serves as priest; here the ναός, in Rom. xii. 2 the θυσία.—καὶ ἐν τ. πνεύματι κ.τ.λ., of the T.R., is a Syrian gloss, added as if to complete the sense; *cf.* vii. 34.

§ 20. Marriage or Celibacy? vii. 1-9. At this point the Ap. takes up the questions addressed to him by the Cor. Church (see *Introd.*, chap. ii.). In replying to Paul's previous letter, they had asked for clearer instructions to regulate their intercourse with men living in heathen sins (v.); this request led up to the inquiries respecting the desirability of *marriage*, respecting the duties of married Christians, and the lawfulness of divorce for a Christian married to a heathen, with which ch. vii. is occupied. The headings of vv. 1, 25, chh. viii., xi., xvi., indicate various matters on which the Cor. had consulted their Ap. The local impress and temporary aim of the directions here given on the subject of marriage must be borne in mind; otherwise Paul's treatment will appear to be narrow and unsympathetic, and out of keeping with the exalted sense of its spiritual import disclosed in Eph. v. Indeed, ch. xi. 3-15 of this Ep. show that P. had larger conception on the relations of man and woman than are here unfolded. The obscurity of expression attaching to several passages betrays the writer's embarrassment; this was due partly to the low moral sensibility of the

Cor., and partly to the uncertain continuance of the existing order of life (26-31), which weighed with the Ap. at the time of writing and led him to discourage the formation of domestic ties. In later Epistles, when the present economy had opened out into a larger perspective, the ethics of marriage and the Christian household are worthily developed (see Col. and Eph.).

Ver. 1. Περὶ δὲ ὧν ἐγράψατε : " Now about the things on which you wrote (to me) ".—Περὶ ὧν = περὶ τούτων περὶ ὧν (not ἅ); *cf.* the constructions of rel. pron. in ver. 39, x. 30; see Wr., p. 198.— δὲ *metabatikon* leads to a new topic, in orderly transition from the last : " Now I proceed to deal with the matters of your letter to me "; the questions proposed about marriage are discussed on the ground prepared by the teaching of chh. v. and vi. They form a part of the wide social conflict between Christian and Pagan life at Corinth : see *Introd.* to Div. II. P. answers at once, affirmatively, the question of principle put to him : " It is *right* (καλόν, *honourable*, *morally befitting* —*pulchrum*, *conveniens*, Bg. ; see note on v. 6) for one (ἀνθρώπῳ, *homini*: not ἀνδρί, *man* distinctively, *viro*) not to touch a woman " (to live in strict celibacy).—καλὸν contradicts the οὐ καλὸν ἀνθρώπῳ present in the minds of some of the questioners, influenced by the sensuous atmosphere of Cor. Paul is not disparaging marriage, as though he meant καλλίον μὴ ἅπτ., but *defending celibacy* against those who thought it inhuman.

Ver. 2 : a single life is good in itself, " but " is not generally expedient at Cor. —διὰ τὰς πορνείας, " because of the (prevalent) fornications " (the unusual pl. indicating the variety and extent of profligacy : *cf.* 2 Cor. xii. 21); for this reason marriage, as a rule, is advisable here.—It must be *Christian* marriage, as opposed to heathen libertinism and Jewish polygamy : " let each (man) have his own wife, and each (woman) her proper husband ". The pr. impv., ἐχέτω (*sc. directive*, not permissive), signifies " have and keep to " (*cf.* 2 Tim. i. 13).

[e] **γυναῖκα** [e] **ἐχέτω, καὶ**[1] **ἑκάστη τὸν ἴδιον ἄνδρα ἐχέτω.**[1] 3. **τῇ**
γυναικὶ ὁ ἀνὴρ τὴν [f] **ὀφειλομένην**[2] **εὔνοιαν**[2] [fg] **ἀποδιδότω·** [h] **ὁμοίως**
[h] **δὲ** [h] **καὶ ἡ γυνὴ τῷ ἀνδρί·** 4. **ἡ γυνὴ τοῦ ἰδίου σώματος οὐκ**
[i] **ἐξουσιάζει, ἀλλ' ὁ ἀνήρ·** [h] **ὁμοίως** [h] **δὲ** [h] **καὶ ὁ ἀνὴρ τοῦ ἰδίου σώματος**
οὐκ [i] **ἐξουσιάζει, ἀλλ' ἡ γυνή·** 5. **μὴ** [k] **ἀποστερεῖτε ἀλλήλους,** [l] **εἰ** [l] **μή**
[l] **τι ἂν**[3] [m] **ἐκ** [m] **συμφώνου** [n] **πρὸς** [n] **καιρόν, ἵνα** [o] **σχολάζητε**[4] **τῇ νηστείᾳ**[5]
καὶ[5] **τῇ** [p] **προσευχῇ καὶ πάλιν** [q] **ἐπὶ τὸ** [q] **αὐτὸ** [q] **συνέρχησθε,**[6] **ἵνα μὴ**

e See v. 1.
f *οφειλην*, Rom. xiii. 7; Mt. xviii. 32.
g Rom. xii. 17; 1 Th. v. 15; 1 Tim. v. 4; Rev. xviii. 6; Mt. xviii. 28 ff., xxii. 21; Lk. x. 35.
h Jas. ii. 25; Mt. xxvii. 41; Lk. v. 10, x. 32.
i See vi. 12.
k See vi. 7 f. In this sense, Ex. xxi. 10.
l 2 Cor. xiii. 5; Lk. ix. 13.
m *H.l.* *συμφωνως*, Eccl. vii. 15; *-νειν*, Acts v. 9, xv. 15, etc.; *-νησις*, 2 Cor. vi. 15.
n 1 Th. ii. 17; Lk. viii. 13; Wisd. iv. 4.
o Mt. xii. 44; Ex. v. 8, 17; Ps. xlv. 10.
p In sing., absol., Rom. xii. 12; Col. iv. 2; Acts i. 4.
q (*ητε*) xi. 20, xiv. 23; Acts i. 15, ii. 47; Lk. xvii. 35.

[1] Om. **και εκαστη . . . εχετω**: G, Tert.; by homœoteleuton.
[2] **οφειλην**: all pre-Syrian uncc., 17, 46, 67**, vg. cop. **οφειλ. ευνοι.**: a gloss.
[3] *Om.* **αν** (?) B, Dam., Clem.; W.H. *bracket.* A copyist's grammatical addition (?).
[4] **σχολασητε,** all pre-Syrian uncc. (see note below).
[5] *Om.* **τη νηστειᾳ και** pre-Syrian uncc. and verss. An ecclesiastical gloss.
[6] **ητε,** all uncc. but KLP. Verss. render freely.

The variation **ἑαυτοῦ γυν. . . . ἴδιον ἄνδρα** distinguishes the husband as head and principal (xi. 3); "if this passage stood alone, it would be unsafe to build upon it, but this diff. of expression pervades the whole of the Epp." (Lt.: *cf.* xiv. 35; Eph. v. 22, etc.; Tit. ii. 5; 1 Peter iii. 1, 5). Throughout the passage there is a careful balancing of the terms relating to man and wife, bringing out the equality of the Christian law.—P. does not lay down here the *ground* of marriage, as though it were "ordained for a remedy against sin," but gives a special reason why those should marry at Cor. who might otherwise have remained single: see note on **δέ**, ver. 1.

Vv. 3, 4. Within the bonds of wedlock, "the due" should be yielded (3) by each for the satisfaction and according to the rights of the other (4). This dictum defends marital intercourse against rigorists, as that of ver. 1 commends celibacy against sensualists. The word **ὀφειλὴ** guards, both positively and negatively, the **κοίτη ἀμίαντος** (Heb. xiii. 4); what is due to one alone must be given to one alone (**τῇ γυναικί, τῷ ἀνδρί**). The gloss of the T.R., as old as the Syriac Version, is a piece of mistaken delicacy.—The precise repetition of **ὁμοίως δὲ καὶ** corrects the onesidedness of common sentiment and of public law,—both Greek and Jewish: *she* is as much the mistress of his person, as *he* the master of hers.—**ἐξουσιάζω** (= **ἐξουσίαν ἔχω**) implies *moral* power, *authority* (*cf.* vi. 12). **τοῦ ἰδίου . . . οὐκ ἐξουσιάζει,** "elegans paradoxon" (Bg.)—his (her) own is not his (her) own.

Ver. 5. **μὴ ἀποστερεῖτε κ.τ.λ.**: "Do not rob one another"—*sc.* of the **ὀφειλή**; the deprivation is an injustice (same vb. as in vi. 7 f.); "congruit hoc verbum cum verbo *debendi*" (Bg.). This also, with ver. 4, against the rigorists. The impvs. of this context are *pr.*, relating to habits of life.—**εἰ μὴ κ.τ.λ.** qualifies the command not to rob, by stating an exception: this exception, however, the Ap. "valde limitat" (Bg.), first by **τι** (*in some measure, somehow*), next by **ἄν** (*haply, if the case should arise*), thirdly by **ἐκ συμφώνου** (*of consent:* making the separation no longer robbery), lastly by **πρὸς καιρόν** (*for a season*). Such separation may be made for specific religious ends—"that you may be disengaged for prayer" (*vacetis orationi*, Vg.), and with a view to renewed intercourse (**καὶ πάλιν ἐπὶ τὸ αὐτὸ ἦτε**). So fearful was the Ap. of putting a strain on the ill-disciplined Cor. nature, with sensual incitements rife in the atmosphere: "lest Satan be tempting you because of your want of self-control".—**ἀκρασία**, later Gr. for **ἀκράτεια** (opp. of **ἐγκράτεια,** *cf.* ix. 25), signifies *non-mastery* of appetite.—**Σχολάζω** (here in *aor.*, of particular occasion; **πειράζητε,** *pr.*, of constant possibility), construed with dat. or **πρός τι,** in cl. Gr. often denotes leisure from ordinary for higher pursuits—*e.g.*, **σχολάζειν μουσικῇ, φιλοσοφίᾳ**; also used of scholars who "devote themselves" to a master: a negative condition of **προσκαρτερεῖσ-**

r 1 Th. iii. 5 ʳ πειράζῃ ὑμᾶς ὁ ʳˢ Σατανᾶς διὰ τὴν ᵗ ἀκρασίαν ὑμῶν.¹   6. τοῦτο δὲ
(πειραζ. ο
πειραζων), λέγω κατὰ ᵘ συγγνώμην, οὐ κατ᾽ ᵛ ἐπιταγήν·   7. θέλω γὰρ ² πάντας
Mt. iv. 1,
3; also x. ἀνθρώπους εἶναι ὡς καὶ ἐμαυτόν, ἀλλ᾽ ἕκαστος ἴδιον ᵂ χάρισμα ˣ
13 below.
Jas. i. 13; ἔχει ³ ἐκ Θεοῦ, ὃς ⁴ μὲν ˣ οὕτως ὃς ⁴ δὲ ˣ οὕτως.   8. λέγω δὲ τοῖς
Gen. xxii.
1; 3 Kings ʸ ἀγάμοις καὶ ταῖς ᶻ χήραις, ᵃ Καλὸν αὐτοῖς ἐστιν ⁵ ἐὰν μείνωσιν ὡς
x. 1, etc.
s See v. 5. κἀγώ.   9. ᵇεἰ ᵇδὲ ᵇοὐκ ᶜἐγκρατεύονται, ᵈγαμησάτωσαν· ᵉκρεῖσσον ⁶
t Mt. xxiii.
25; freq. γάρ ἐστι ᵈ γαμῆσαι ⁷ ἢ ᶠ πυροῦσθαι.
in cl. Gr.;
-της, 2

Tim. iii. 3. Antonym of εγκρατεια, Gal. v. 23, etc.   u N.T. h.l.; Sir. iii. 13.   v ver. 25; 2 Cor.
viii. 8; 1 Tim. i. 1; Tit. i. 3, ii. 15; Wisd. xiv. 16 (τυραννων επιταγαις).   w See i. 7.   x Cf. vi. 13.
y vv. 11, 32, 34. Of the man, Iliad iii. 40; of woman (rarely), Eurip. Hel. 690.   z 1 Tim. v. 3 ff.;
Acts vi. 1, ix. 41; Jas. i. 27, etc.   a See ver. 1.   b ix. 2, xi. 6, xv. 13 ff. (δε), xvi. 22; Rom. viii. 9
(δε), xi. 21; 2 Th. iii. 10, 14 (δε); 1 Tim. iii. 5 (δε), v. 8 (δε); etc.   c ix. 25; Gen. xliii. 31; 1 Kings
xiii. 12; -της, Tit. i. 8; -τεια, Gal. v. 23; Acts xxiv. 25; 2 Pet. i. 6. See ακρασια, ver. 5.   d vv. 10,
28 f., etc.; 1 Tim. iv. 3, v. 11, 14; etc.   e Phil. i. 23; 1 Pet. iii. 17; 2 Pet. ii. 21; Prov. iii. 14; cf.
ver. 38 below, xi. 17; Heb. i. 4, etc.   f 2 Cor. xi. 29; Eph. vi. 16; 2 Pet. iii. 12; Rev. i. 15, iii. 18.
H.J., in this sense.

¹ B, Method. om. υμων (?); bracketed by W.H.   May be a copyist's addition,—
a case for the maxim, Brevior lectio præferenda.

² δε (?): ℵ*ACD*G 17, 46, latt. am. fu. cop., Or., Cyr., Dam., Cyp. (Western and Alexandrian).   So Tisch., Tr., W.H., R.V., El., Nestle.
γαρ : B and Syrian uncc., syrr.

³ εχει χαρισμα : all pre-Syrian uncc.

⁴ ο (μεν) . . . ο (δε) : all pre-Syrian uncc.

⁵ Om. εστιν all pre-Syrian uncc.

⁶ κρειττον, ℵBD ; κρεισσον, ACGLP, etc.

⁷ γαμειν (?), ℵ*AC 17, 46.   So Tisch., Tr. marg., W.H. text, Nestle.
γαμησαι, BDGKLP, etc.   W.H. marg., R.V.

θαι τῇ προσευχῇ (Rom. xii. 12, Col.
iv. 2).

Vv. 6, 7. τοῦτο δὲ λέγω points to the
leading direction given in ver. 2, from
which vv. 3-5 digressed : "I advise you
to be married (though I think celibacy
good, 1), κατὰ συγγνώμην," secundum
indulgentiam (Vg.)—i.e., συγκαταβαίνων
τ. ἀσθενείᾳ ὑμῶν (Thp.); οὐ κατ᾽ ἐπιταγήν,
—ex concessione, non ex imperio (Bz.).
The rendering "permission" is somewhat
misleading; συγγνώμη is quite distinct
from the γνώμη opposed to ἐπιταγή in
ver. 25; it signifies either pardon (venia,
excuse for a fault), or, as here, allowance,
regard for circumstances and temperament.—In θέλω δὲ κ.τ.λ. the Ap. states
his personal bent, which he had set aside
in the recommendation just given : "But
I would have all men to be as indeed
myself," sc. cælibem—and contentedly so
(cf. Acts xxvi. 29). ὡς καὶ ἐμαυτόν,
paratactic acc. (attracted to πάντας ἀνθρώπους) = ὡς καὶ αὐτός εἰμι; καὶ emphasises the assertion that the writer is
what he would like others to be. It is
manifest (see also ix. 5) that the Ap. was
unmarried, although Clem. Alex. and
some moderns have inferred otherwise

from Phil. iv. 3. That he had never been
married is by no means certain. Two
things, however, are clear : that if P.
had known the married state, it was
before his apostleship—"wife and children are never hinted at, he goes about
entirely free from such ties " (Lt.) ; further,
that if in early life he had entered this
state, it was not δι᾽ ἀκρασίαν ; he possessed the "grace-gift" (χάρισμα) of
undisquieted continence (opposed to
πυροῦσθαι, 9; cf. Matt. xix. 12), which
was in his case an adjunct of his χάρις
ἀποστολῆς. — "However (= I cannot
have every one like myself, but) each
has a charism of his own from God, the
one in this shape and the other in that."
ὁ δὲ οὕτως does not refer to the married
Christian, as though his state were in
itself a charism, but to any special endowment for service in Christ's kingdom
other than that stated. On χάρισμα
see i. 7 ; and cf. xii. 4-11.
Vv. 8, 9 re-state the answer given in
vv. 1, 2 to the question concerning celibacy v. marriage. "But I say to the
unmarried and the widows, it is right
(καλόν; cf. 1) for them if they remain as
indeed I (am)." The Ap. extends the

10. Τοῖς δὲ ᵈγεγαμηκόσι ᵍπαραγγέλλω, οὐκ ἐγὼ ἀλλ᾽ ὁ Κύριος, ᵍ xi. 17; 10
γυναῖκα ἀπὸ ἀνδρὸς μὴ ʰχωρισθῆναι · ¹ 11. ἐὰν δὲ καὶ ʰχωρισθῇ, sides in
μενέτω ʸἄγαμος ἢ τῷ ἀνδρὶ ⁱκαταλλαγήτω · καὶ ἄνδρα γυναῖκα μὴ in Acts;
                                                                          8 times
                                                                          in Syn.

Gospp.   h In this sense, Mt. xix. 6; Judges iv. 11.   i 2 Cor. v. 18 ff.; Rom. v. 10; ἀποκαταλλ.,
Eph. ii. 16; Col. i. 20 f.; διαλλ., Mt. v. 24.

¹ χωριζεσθαι, ADG (Western).

reassurance given in ver. 1, and fortifies it by his own example, so that those out of wedlock who were under no constraint to enter its bonds might be free from misgiving and reproach. τοῖς ἀγάμοις, in contrast to τοῖς γεγαμηκόσιν, ver. 10: the term is *masc.*—"to unmarried men"; the case of "maidens" is discussed later (25 ff.). "The widows," who would frequently have the disposal of themselves, are included here —they are advised again to the like effect in vv. 39 f. Holsten omits καὶ ταῖς χήραις as out of place; Bois ingeniously suggests that this may be a primitive corruption for καὶ τοῖς χήροις, "the widowers". — As the πορνεῖαι without (2), so ἀκρασία within (5) might make abstention from marriage perilous; hence the qualification added in ver. 9: "But if they have not self-control, let them marry; for better it is to marry than to burn on (with desire)".—πυροῦσθαι, pr. of continued state — "occulta flamma concupiscentiae vastari" (Aug.); the vb. is used of any consuming passion, as in 2 Cor. xi. 29. Not "*better* in so far as marriage is sinless, burning is sinful (Matt. v. 28),"—so Mr.; if marriage and parenthood are holy (14), the fire which burns toward that end surely may be so —"the sacred lowe o' weel-placed love"; but "better" as the unsatisfied craving is a continual temptation, and according to the rule of ver. 35. Better to marry than to burn; but if marriage is impossible, better infinitely to burn than to *sin.*

§ 21. PROHIBITION OF DIVORCE, vii. 10-16. Pagan sentiment and law, while condoning fornication, were exceedingly lax in permitting *divorce* (see Hermann-Stark, *Griech. Privat-alterthümer*, §§ 30. 15, 17), as Jewish practice was on the side of the husband (Matt. v. 31 f., xix. 7 ff.); and marriages were often contracted without affection. Unfit unions became irksome in the extreme, with the stricter ethics and high ideal of the new faith; in many cases one of the partners remained a heathen (12 f.). It was asked whether Christians were really "bound" (δεδουλωμένοι, 15) by the ties of the old

life formed under unholy conditions, and whether it was right for man and wife to live together while one was in the kingdom of God and the other in that of Satan. These questions, propounded in the letter from Cor., Paul has now to answer—(a) as respects Christian couples (10 f.), (b) as respects married pairs divided in religion (12-16).

Vv. 10, 11. "But in the case of those that have married (τ. γεγαμηκόσιν, pf. of settled fact), I charge . . . wife not to separate from husband . . . and husband not to send away (*or* let go) wife." The parenthesis, "not I but the Lord" (it is *His* command, not mine), refers to the indissolubility of marriage to *the authority of Christ.* The exceptional cause of divorce allowed by Jesus, παρεκτὸς λόγου πορνείας (Matt. v. 32, xix. 9; also unmentioned in Mark x. 11, Luke xvi. 18), is not contemplated in the instance of wedded Christians (Paul is addressing *both* partners at once). The Apostle's tone is changed (*cf.* 6 ff.); he is *laying down the law,* and on Supreme Authority. He cites Christ's words in distinction from his own (12), not as though his word was insufficient (see, to the contrary, 40, ii. 16, v. 3 f., xiv. 37, etc.), but inasmuch as this was a principle upon which "the Lord" had pronounced categorically.—It is noticeable that the case of the *woman* seeking separation comes first and is dwelt upon; Christianity had powerfully stirred the feminine mind at Cor. (see xi. 5 ff., xiv. 34 f.). In some cases, not so much incompatibility as ascetic aversion (*cf.* 3 f.) caused the wish to separate.—The γυναῖκα μὴ χωρισθῆναι is qualified by the parenthesis ἐὰν δὲ καὶ χωρισθῇ: "but if indeed she have separated, let her remain unmarried, or be reconciled to her husband". P. is not allowing exceptions from the rule of Christ, but advising in cases where the mischief was done; the aor. sbj., χωρισθῇ, is timeless, taking its occasion from the context: see Bn., § 98. Her remaining unmarried is virtually included in the law of Christ (Matt. v. 32, xix. 9). καταλλαγήτω, pass., "let

k In this
sense, *h.l.*;
cf. Mt.
xix. 29;
Mk. i. 20;
Lk. xviii.
28; Jo.
xiv. 18;
Herod.
v. 39;
Jos. *Ant.*
xv. 7, 10.
l 2 Cor.

k ἀφιέναι. 12. ¹τοῖς δὲ ¹λοιποῖς ἐγὼ¹ λέγω,¹ οὐχ ὁ Κύριος, εἴ τις ἀδελφὸς γυναῖκα ἔχει ᵐἄπιστον καὶ αὐτὴ² ⁿσυνευδοκεῖ °οἰκεῖν °μετ' αὐτοῦ, μὴ ᵏἀφιέτω αὐτήν· 13. καὶ γυνὴ ἥτις³ ἔχει ἄνδρα ᵐἄπιστον καὶ αὐτὸς⁴ ⁿσυνευδοκεῖ⁵ °οἰκεῖν °μετ' αὐτῆς, μὴ ᵏἀφιέτω αὐτόν· 14. ᵖἡγίασται γὰρ ὁ ἀνὴρ ὁ ᵐἄπιστος ἐν τῇ γυναικί,⁶ καὶ ᵖἡγίασται ἡ γυνὴ ἡ ᵐἄπιστος ἐν τῷ ἀνδρί⁷· qἐπεὶ qἄρα τὰ τέκνα ὑμῶν ʳἀκά-

xiii. 2; Rom. xi. 7; 1 Th. iv. 13, v. 6; 1 Tim. v. 20; same idiom in Rev., Acts, and Syn. Gospp.
m See vi. 6. n Rom. i. 32; Lk. xi. 48; Acts viii. 1, xxii. 20; *cf.* ευδοκ. with inf., i. 21. o *H.l.* in
N.T.; Gen. xxvii. 44. p See i. 2. q See v. 10. r 2 Cor. vi. 17 (Isa. lii. 11); Eph. v. 5; freq.
in Syn. Gospp., Acts, and Rev., of πνευματα; also Acts x. 14; Rev. xvii. 4.

¹ λεγω εγω : אABCP (pre-Syrian and non-Western).

² αὕτη, latt. vg., Tert. ; crit. edd. : see ουτος, ver. 13. In uncc. no distinction.

³ ει τις : אD*GP, latt. vg., Chr., Ambrst., Aug., Dam. (Western).

⁴ ουτος, all uncc. but DcKL.

⁵ ευδοκει, B.

⁶ DG add τη πιστη.

⁷ αδελφω, all pre-Syrian uncc. ; vg. and syrr., ανδρι.

her get herself reconciled": the vb. indicates the fact of alienation or dissension, but not the side on which it exists (*cf.* the theological use of **καταλλάσσω** in Rom. v. 10 f.) ; if the husband disallows her return, she must remain **ἄγαμος**.—Romanists have inferred from the text, after Aug., and notwithstanding Matt. v. 32, that even adultery leaves the marriage-vow binding on the wronged partner ; but this question is not in view here (see Ed. *in loc.*).

Vv. 12, 13. "But to the rest"—as distinguished from Christian couples (10) —"say I, not the Lord": this is *my* word, not His. On the problem of mixed marriages, which Jesus had no occasion to regulate, the Ap. delivers his own sentence. Not that he *exhorts*, whereas the Lord commands (Cm.)— **λέγω** is a word of authority (virtually repeating **παραγγέλλω**, 10), as in xiv. 34, 37, xv. 51, 2 Cor. vi. 13, Rom. xii. 3 ; much less, that he *disclaims inspiration* upon this point (Or., Tert., Milton), or betrays *a doubt of his competence* (Baur) : he quoted the dictum of Jesus where it was available, and on the fundamental matter, and indicates frankly that in this further case he is proceeding on his personal judgment. The Christian spouse is forbidden to cast off the non-Christian in terms identical for husband and wife, only **γυνὴ ἥτις** (or **εἴ τις** : 13) standing over against **εἴ τις ἀδελφός** (12). **Ἀφίημι**, used of the **ἀνὴρ** specifically in ver. 11, is now applied to *both* parties : cl. Gr. uses **ἀποπέμπειν** or **ἀπολύειν** (Matt. v.

31) of the husband as *dismissing* the wife, **ἀπολείπειν** of the wife as *deserting* the husband ; "in the structure of the two verses, with their solemn repetition, the equal footing of man and wife is indicated" (Hn. ; *cf.* notes on 2-4 above). **συν-ευδοκεῖ**, "is *jointly* well-pleased,"— implying that the **ἄπιστος** agrees with the Christian spouse in deprecating separation, which the latter (after 10 f.) must needs desire to avoid ; *cf.*, for the force of **συν-**, Luke xi. 48, Acts viii. 1.

Ver. 14 obviates the objection which the Christian wife or husband (for the *order*, see note on 10 f.) might feel to continued union with an unbeliever (*cf.* Paul's own warning in 2 Cor. vi. 14 ff.) : "Will not the saint," some one asks, "be defiled, and the 'limbs of Christ' (vi. 15) be desecrated by intercourse with a heathen?" To such a protest **ἡγίασται γὰρ κ.τ.λ.** replies : "For the husband that is an unbeliever, *has been sanctified* in his wife," and *vice versâ*. **ἡγίασται . . . ὁ ἄπιστος** is a paradox : it does not affirm a conversion in the unbeliever remaining such—whether *incipient* or *prospective* (D.W., and some others)— the pf. tense signifies a relationship *established* for the non-Christian *in the past*,—*sc.* at the conversion of the believing spouse ; but man and wife are part of each other, in such a sense (*cf.* vi. 16 f., by contrast) that the sanctification of the one includes the other so far as their wedlock is concerned. The married believer in offering her- (or him-) self to God could not but present hus-

θαρτά ἐστι, νῦν δὲ ἅγιά ἐστιν. 15. εἰ δὲ ὁ ᵐἄπιστος ʰχωρίζεται, ⁵ ix. 19; Rom. vi. 18, 22; Gal. iv. 3; Tit. ii. 3; 2 Pet. ii. 19; Acts vii. 6. ᵗNeut., ᵛHere only.

ʰχωριζέσθω· οὐ ˢδεδούλωται ὁ ἀδελφὸς ἢ ἡ¹ ἀδελφὴ ἐν ᵗτοῖς ᵗτοιούτοις. ᵘἐν δὲ εἰρήνῃ ᵘᶻκέκληκεν ἡμᾶς² ὁ ᶻΘεός· 16. ᵛτί γὰρ ᵛʷοἶδας, γύναι, ʷεἰ τὸν ἄνδρα σώσεις; ἢ ᵛτί ᵛʷοἶδας, ἄνερ,

Rom. i. 32, ii. 2 f.; Gal. v. 21, 23; Eph. v. 27.   u Gal. i. 6; Eph. iv. 4; 1 Th. iv. 7.
w Cf. Acts x. 18, xix. 2; Jo. ix. 25; Jer. xxxvii. 6.

¹ אGP om. second η.

² υμας (?) : א*ACK 46, 73, cop. (Alexandrian) ; so Tisch., W.H. txt., Nestle, R.V. marg.

ημας : BDGL, latt. vg., syrr. (Western) ; Treg., Al., W.H. marg., R.V. txt., El.

band (or wife) in the same act—"sanctified in the wife, brother," respectively—and treats him (or her) henceforth as sacred. "Whatever the husband may be in himself, in the wife's thought and feeling he is a holy object. . . . Similarly the Christian's friends, abilities, wealth, time, are, or should be, holy" (Bt.). Marriage with an unbeliever after conversion is barred in 2 Cor. vi. 14.

The (relative) sanctity of the unconverted spouse is made more evident by the analogous case of children : "Else one must suppose that your children are unclean ; but as it is, they are holy !" P. appeals to the instinct of the religious parent ; the Christian father or mother cannot look on children, given by God through marriage, as things unclean. Offspring are holy as bound up with the holy parent ; and this principle of family solidarity holds good of the conjugal tie no less than of the filial derived therefrom. See the full discussion of this text in Ed. ; it has played no small part in Christian jurisprudence, and in the doctrine of Infant Baptism ; it "enunciates the principle which leads to Infant Baptism, viz. that the child of Christian parents shall be treated as a Christian" (Lt.).—On ἐπεὶ ἄρα, alioqui certe, si res se aliter haberet, see v. 10 and parls. ; νῦν δέ, as in v. 11, is both temporal and logical (cf. xv. 20, Rom. vi. 22).

Ver. 15a. The Christian wife or husband is not to seek divorce from the non-Christian (12-14) ; but if the latter insists on separation, it is not to be refused : "But if the unbeliever separates, he may separate "—let the separation take its course (χωριζέσθω, pr. impv.) : for this impv. of consent, cf. ver. 36, xiv. 38.—οὐ δεδούλωται (pf. of fixed condition), "the brother or the sister in such circumstances is not kept in bondage" ; cf. ver. 39—the stronger vb. of this passage implies that for the repudiated party to

continue bound to the repudiator would be slavery. Christ's law forbids putting away (10 ff.), but does not forbid the one put away to accept dismissal. Whether the freedom of the innocent divorced extends to remarriage, does not appear : the Roman Church takes the negative view—though contrary to the Canon Law (see Wordsworth, in loc.) ; the Lutheran Church the affirmative, allowing remarriage on desertio malitiosa ; "in view of ver. 11, the inference that the divorced should remain unmarried is the safer" (so Hn., against Mr.). If, however, the repudiator forms a new union, cutting off the hope of restoration, the case appears then to come under the exception made in Matt. v. 31. With ἐν τοιούτοις, neut., cf. ἐν τούτοις, Rom. viii. 37 ; and ἐν οἷς, Phil. iv. 11.

Vv. 15b, 16. ἐν δὲ εἰρήνῃ ὁ Θεός . . . σώσεις ; The Christian spouse forsaken by the heathen is free from the former yoke ; but such freedom is undesirable. Two considerations make against it : Peace is better for a Christian than disruption (15b) ; and there is the possibility of saving the unbeliever by remaining with him, or her (16). Thus P. reverts, by the contrastive δέ, to his prevailing thought, that the marriage tie, once formed, should in every way possible be maintained. On this view of the connexion, the full stop should be set at ἐν τοιούτοις, and the colon at ὁ Θεός. "In peace," etc.—opposed to χωριζέσθω, like καταλλαγήτω in ver. 11—appeals to the ruling temper of the Christian life, determined once for all by God's call in the Gospel, "ex quo consequitur retinendum esse nobis infidelem, ac omnibus officiis demerendum ; nedum ut vel eum ipsi deseramus, vel ad nos deserendos provocemus" (Bz.) ; cf. Rom. xii. 18, for the general thought. For the construction of ἐν εἰρήνῃ, cf. 1 Thess. iv. 7, Gal. i. 6, Eph. iv. 4.—Ver. 16 follows up the

x Gal. i. 7, 19; see note below.
y In this sense, 2 Cor. x. 13; Heb. vii. 2; Mk. vi. 41; Lk. xii. 13; Josh. xiii. 7. *Cf.* i. 13. z See i. 9 (God the caller). a See iii. 3.

ᵂ εἰ τὴν γυναῖκα σώσεις¹; 17. ˣ εἰ ˣ μὴ ἑκάστῳ ὡς ʸ ἐμέρισεν² ὁ Θεός,³ ἕκαστον ὡς ᶻ κέκληκεν ὁ ᶻ Κύριος,⁴ οὕτω ᵃ περιπατείτω · καὶ

¹ Add η μη (for ει μη of ver. 17) a few minn., hcl.-syr. marg., and Chr.; by itacism.

² μεμερικεν, ℵ*B. So most crit. edd.; see, however, El. in favour of the aorist. Possibly Rom. xii. 3 has influenced the copyists.

³ (μεμερ.) ο Κυριος: all pre-Syrian uncc.

⁴ (κεκληκ.) ο Θεος: as above (ver. 15). See parls.

appeal to Christian principle, by a challenge addressed in turn to the wifely and the manly heart: "(Keep the peace, if you can, with the unconverted spouse), for how do you know, O wife, that you will not *save* your husband? or how do you know, O husband, that you will not *save* your wife?" That εἰ in this connexion (see parls.), after τί οἶδας implying a *fear*, may mean "that . . . not" in English idiom (as though it were: "How do you know? it may be you will save, etc.!") is admitted by Hn. and Ed., though they reject the above interpretation, which is that of the ancient commentt. from Cm. down to Lyra, of Cv. and Bz., and of Ev. and Lt. amongst moderns: see the convincing notes of the two last-named; "Confirmatio est superioris sententiæ: non cur discedente infideli liberetur fidelis; sed contra, cur ita sit utendum hac libertate, ut infidelem, si fieri potest, retineat fidelis ac Christo lucrificet" (Bz.).—τί οἶδας; connotes "not the manner in which the knowledge is to be obtained, but the extent of it" (Ed.)—"what do you know as to the question whether, etc.?"

The above sentences are curiously ambiguous; taken by themselves, they may be read as reasons either *against* or *for* separation. The latter interpretation is adopted, as to ver. 15b by most, and as to ver. 16 by nearly all recent exegetes (including Bg., Mr., Hf., Hn., Al., Bt., Ed., Gd., El.): "God has called us in peace (and peace is only possible through separation); for how do you know, wife or husband, that you will save the other?" As much as to say, "Why cling to him, or her, on so ill-founded a hope?" Grammatical considerations being fairly balanced, the tenor of the previous context determines the Apostle's meaning. In the favourite modern exposition, the essential thought has to be read between the lines. It should also be observed that the Cor., with their lax moral notions, needed dissuasives from rather

than encouragements to divorce; and on the other hand, that to discountenance the hope of a soul's salvation is strangely unlike the Ap. (*cf.* x. 33). On the construction here adopted, P. returns at the close of the Section to the thought with which it opened—μὴ χωρισθῆναι.

§ 22. GOD'S CALLING AND ONE'S EARTHLY STATION, vii. 17-24. In treating of questions relating to marriage, the Apostle's general advice—admitting of large exceptions (2, 9, 15)—had been that each, whether single or married, should be content with his present state (1, 8, 10-14, 27). The Christian revolution had excited in some minds a morbid restlessness and eagerness for change, which disturbed domestic relations (*cf.* Matt. x. 36), but was not confined thereto. This wider tendency the Ap. combats in the ensuing paragraph; he urges his readers to acquiesce in their position in life and to turn it to account as Christians. In Thessalonica a similar excitement had led men to abandon daily work and throw their support upon the Church (1 Thess. iv. 11 f., 2 Thess. iii. 6-15). Hn., in Meyer's *Comm.*, p. 229, points out the close resemblance, both in form and matter, between this section and certain passages in Epictetus (*Dissert.*, I., xix., 47 ff.; II., ix., 19 f.). *The freedom of the inner man* and *loyal acceptance of the providence of God* are inculcated by both the Stoic and the Christian philosopher, from their differing standpoints.

Ver. 17. "Only, in each case as the Lord has apportioned to him, in each case as God has called him, so let him (the believer) walk." Under this general rule the exceptional and guarded permission of divorce in ver. 15 was to be understood. For εἰ μὴ in this *exceptive* sense (= πλήν), *cf.* Rom. xiv. 14, Gal. i. 7, 19; see Bm., p. 359. The repeated distributive ἕκαστος extends the principle pointedly to *every* situation in life; *cf.* vv. 20, 24, iii. 5, 8-13. On μεμέρικεν,

οὕτως ἐν ᵇταῖς ᵇἐκκλησίαις πάσαις ᶜδιατάσσομαι.¹ 18. ᵈπεριτετ- ᵇ Pl., xi. 16,
μημένος τις ᶻἐκλήθη; μὴ ᵉἐπισπάσθω· ᶠἐν ᶠἀκροβυστίᾳ τις² xiv. 33 f.,
ᶻἐκλήθη²; μὴ ᵈπεριτεμνέσθω· 19. ἡ ᵍπεριτομὴ ʰοὐδέν ἐστι, καὶ xvi. 1, 19;
7 times in
2 Cor.; 5
times be-
sides in

P.; Rev. i. 4 ff., xxii. 16; Acts xv. 41, xvi. 5. c Mid., xi. 34; Tit. i. 5; Acts vii. 44, xx. 13, xxiv. 23.
In this connexion, xvi. 1. d Gal. ii. 3, v. 2 f., vi. 12 f.; Col. ii. 11; cf. Acts xv. 1, 5, xvi. 3, xxi. 21.
e HJ.; Isa. v. 18. See note below. f Rom. iv. 10 ff. ἀκροβ. freq. in P.; Acts xi. 3. g Rom. ii.
25-29; often in P.; Jo. vii. 22 f., Acts vii. 8, x. 45, xi. 2. h xiii. 2; 2 Cor. xii. 11; Mt. xxiii. 16,
18; Jo. viii. 54.

¹ διδασκω, D*G, latt. vg. (doceo). Cf. iv. 17.

² κεκληται τις: ℵABP 17, 37, 46. τις κεκληται: D*G, Dam. (Western).
τις εκληθη (as in parl. clause), DᶜKL, etc. (Syrian).

see ver. 33 and i. 12 : the Christian's secular status is a μέρος which "the Lord," the Disposer of men's affairs, has assigned him (cf. Matt. xxv. 14 f.).— ὡς κέκληκεν, on the other hand, refers not to the secular "vocation" but, as always (see 15, 18, 21 f., i. 9, 26, etc.), to the "call" of God's grace in the Gospel, which came to the individual readers under these circumstances or those.— οὕτως περιπατείτω enjoins the *pursuance* of the Christian life in harmony with the conditions thus determined at its outset. P. does not mean to stereotype a Christian's secular employment from the time of his conversion, but forbids his renouncing this under a false notion of spiritual freedom, or in contempt of secular things as though there were no will of God for him in their disposition. The last clause of the ver. shows that the tendency here reproved was widespread ; cf. i. 2, xi. 16, xiv. 33, 36.

Vv. 18, 19. The rule of ver. 17 applied to the most prominent and critical distinction in the Church, that between *Jew and Gentile* : περιτετμημένος τις ἐκλήθη κ.τ.λ.; "Was any one called (as) a *circumcised* man ? let him not have the mark effaced".—ἐπισπάσθω alludes to a surgical operation (ἐπισπάω, *to draw over*) by which renegade Jews effaced the Covenant sign: see 1 Macc. i. 11 ff., Joseph., *Ant.*, xii., 5, 1; Celsus, vii., 25. 5 ; also Schürer, *Hist. of Jewish People*, I., i., p. 203, and Wetstein *ad loc.* Such apostates were called *m'shūkim, recutiti* (Buxtorf's *Lexic.*, p. 1274).—On the opp. direction to the Gentile, μὴ περιτεμνέσθω, the Ep. to the Gal. is a powerful commentary ; here the negative reasons against the change suffice (17, 19).—The variation in tense and order of words in the two questions is noticeable : "Was any one a circumcised man at the time of his call (ἐκλήθη) ? . . . Has any one been called (κέκληται) though in uncir-

cumcision ? "—To clinch the matter (cf. i. 31, iii. 7) P. applies one of his great axioms : "Circumcision is nothing, and uncircumcision is nothing ; but keeping of God's commands "—that is everything. In Gal. v. 6, vi. 15 this maxim reappears, with πίστις δι' ἀγάπης ἐνεργουμένη and καινὴ κτίσις respectively in the antithesis : this text puts the condition of acceptance *objectively*, as it lies in a right attitude toward God (cf. Rom. ii. 25 ff.) ; those other texts supply the *subjective* criterion, lying in a right disposition of the man. In Gal. v., οὐκ ἰσχύει—opposed to ἐνεργουμένη—signalises the *impotence* of external states, the other two passages their *nothingness* as religious qualifications.—"Those who would contrast the teaching of St. Paul with that of St. James, or exaggerate his doctrine of justification by faith, should reflect on this τήρησις ἐντολῶν Θεοῦ" (Lt.).

Ver. 20. Diff. views are taken of this ver., as κλῆσις is referred to the religious *call* or secular *calling* of the man ; and as ᾗ is accordingly rendered "wherewith" (instrum. dat. : cf. Eph. iv. 1, 2 Tim. i. 9), or "wherein" (governed by the foregoing ἐν : cf. 15, 18, 24 ; see Wr., pp. 524 f.). The latter interpretation is negatived by the fact that it destroys the unity of sense between κλῆσις and ἐκλήθη (see note on 18: does κλῆσις in Gr. anywhere mean *avocation ?*). Besides, "circumcision" and "uncircumcision" are not "callings". Yet P. is manifestly referring to outward conditions affecting the religious call. The stress of the sentence lies on μενέτω (cf. 24) ; and Gal. iii. 2 f., v. 2-6, give the clue to the Apostle's meaning. A change of secular condition adopted under the idea that circumcision or uncircumcision is "something," that it makes a diff. in the eyes of God, would be a change ot religious princple, *an abandonment of the basis of our call* to salvation by grace and through faith ; cf. Gal. ii. 11-21.

ᵢ τηρ. (cf. Acts iv. 3, v. 18) ἐντ. N.T. h.l.; Sir. xxxii. 23; Wisd. vi. 18 (νομων). τηρειν ἐντ., Mt. xix. 17; Jo. xiv. 21, xv. 10;

ᾗ ᵗἀκροβυστία ʰοὐδέν ἐστιν, ἀλλὰ ⁱτήρησις ⁱἐντολῶν ⁱΘεοῦ. 20. ἕκαστος ᵘἐν τῇ ᵏκλήσει ᾗ ᵏᵃᶻἐκλήθη, ἐν ταύτῃ μενέτω· 21. δοῦλος ᶻἐκλήθης; μή σοι ⁱμελέτω· ἀλλ' εἰ καὶ δύνασαι ἐλεύθερος γενέσθαι, μᾶλλον ᵐχρῆσαι. 22. ὁ γὰρ ἐν Κυρίῳ ᶻκληθεὶς δοῦλος, ⁿἀπελεύ-θερος Κυρίου ἐστιν· °ὁμοίως καὶ ˡὁ ἐλεύθερος ᶻκληθείς, ᵖδοῦλός ἐστι ᵖΧριστοῦ. 23. ᑫτιμῆς ᑫἠγοράσθητε· μὴ γίνεσθε δοῦλοι ʳἀνθρώ-

Acts xv. 5 (νομον); 1 Jo. ii. 3 f., iii. 22, 24, v. 3; Rev. xiv. 12. εντολ. Θε., Mt. xv. 3; Rev. xii. 17, xiv. 12; Ezra x. 3; cf. Κυρ. εντ., xiv. 37.   k See i. 26.   l ix. 9; 1 Pet. v. 7; Acts xviii. 17; 5 times in Gospp.   m ver. 31, ix. 12, 15; 1 Tim. i. 8, v. 23; Acts xxvii. 17.   n H.l.; see note below.   o See ver. 3.   p Rom. i. 1, etc.; Gal. i. 10; Eph. vi. 6; Col. iii. 21, iv. 12; Ja. i. 1; 2 Pet. i. 1.   q See vi. 20.   r Cf. Gal. i. 10; Eph. vi. 6; Col. iii. 22 f.

¹ Om. και ℵABP 17, 46, vg. syrr.   δε και, DG 37.   και only, KL, etc.

The Gentile who embraced circumcision in order to fulfil the law of God was severing himself from Christ and falling from grace. The "abide" of 1 Cor. is parl. to the "stand fast" of Gal.

Ver. 21. From the chief religious, the Ap. passes to the chief *social* distinction of the times: *cf.* Gal. iii. 28, Col. iii. 11. This contrast is developed only on one side—no freeman wished to become a slave, as Gentiles wished to be Jews; but the slaves, numerous in this Church (i. 26 ff.), sighed for liberty; their conversion stimulated this longing. The advice to the slave is read in two opposite ways: (a) "In slavery wast thou called? never mind (μή σοι μελέτω)! But still if thou canst also become free, rather make use of it (than not)"—so Ev. excellently renders, with Cv., Bz., Gr., Hf., Bt., Gd., Lt., supplying τῇ ἐλευθερίᾳ for complement to μᾶλλον χρῆσαι; while (b) Est., Bg., D.W., Mr., Hn., Weiss, Weizsäcker, Al., El., Sm. supply τῇ δου-λείᾳ, and suppose P. to recommend the slave, with liberty offered, to "make use rather" of his servile condition. εἰ καὶ may either mean (a) "if verily" (Luke xi. 18; so ἐὰν καὶ in xi. 28, Gal. vi. 1), or (b) "although" (Phil. ii. 17, Luke xi. 8, etc.). The ancient commentators differed on this text, with a leaning to (b). The advocates of (b) exaggerate the sense of vv. 20, 24, which condemns change not *per se* but, as in the case of circumcision, because it compromises Christian faith and standing. "Freedom" is the object proximately suggested to "rather use" by "free" just above; and the sense of χράομαι in ver. 31, ix. 12, 15—to "avail oneself of an opportunity of good" (Lt.)—speaks in favour of (a). The οὐ δεδούλωται of ver. 15 and the μὴ γίνεσθε δοῦλοι ἀνθρώπων of ver. 23 indicate Paul's feeling for free-

dom; and the δύνασθαι ἐλεύθερος γενέσ-θαι was to the Christian slave a precious item in his providential μέρος (17).

Upon this view, ἀλλὰ . . . χρῆσαι forms a parenthesis, resembling in its connexion the οὐ δεδούλ. clause of ver. 15, by which P. intimates that in urging contentment with a slave's lot he does not preclude his embracing liberty, should it be offered. Having said this by the way, he supports his μή σοι μελέτω by the comforting reflexion of ver. 22a, which is completed in ver. 22b by the corresponding truth for the freeman.

Ver. 22. The two sentences, balanced by ὁμοίως (cf. 3 f.), do not precisely match: ὁ ἐν Κυρίῳ κληθεὶς δοῦλος is "the slave that was called in the Lord" (i.e., under Christ's authority), but ὁ ἐλεύ-θερος κληθεὶς is rather "the freeman, in that he was called"; his *call* has made the latter Christ's slave, while the former, *though a slave*, is the Lord's freedman. —ἀπελεύθερος, *libertus* (the prp. imply-ing severance as in ἀπολύτρωσις, i. 30) —*freedman of a Lord;* "Christ buys us from our old master, sin, and then sets us free; but a service is still due from the *libertus* to the *patronus*" (Lt.); *cf.* Rom. vi. 17 f.; also ἔννομος Χριστοῦ, ix. 21, with the same gen. of possession. Ignatius makes a touching allusion to this passage, *ad Rom.*, 4: "I am till the present time a slave; but if I suffer I shall be Jesus Christ's freeman, and I shall rise up [in the resurrection] free!"

Ver. 23. τιμῆς ἠγοράσθητε (see note on vi. 20) explains the position both of the δοῦλος ἀπελεύθερος and the ἐλεύθ. δοῦλος by the same act of purchase: the slave has been liberated from sin, and the freeman bound to a new Lord. The point of the appended exhortation, μὴ γίνεσθε δοῦλ. ἀνθρ., is not obvious: we can scarcely imagine *free Christians selling*

πων. 24. ἕκαστος ἐν ᾧ ᵘᶻἐκλήθη, ἀδελφοί, ἐν τούτῳ μενέτω ⁸παρὰ τῷ¹ Θεῷ.

25. Περὶ δὲ τῶν ᵗπαρθένων ᵘἐπιταγὴν Κυρίου οὐκ ἔχω· ᵛγνώμην δὲ ᵛδίδωμι, ὡς ʷἠλεημένος ʷὑπὸ ʷΚυρίου ˣπιστὸς εἶναι. 26. νομίζω οὖν τοῦτο ʸκαλὸν ὑπάρχειν διὰ τὴν ᶻἐνεστῶσαν ᵃἀνάγκην, ὅτι

s For sense of παρα, cf. Lk. i. 30, ii. 52; 1 Pet. ii.4. t In this ch. and 2 Cor. xi. 2; Mt. i. 23 (Isa. vii. 14), xxv. 1 ff.,

Lk. i. 27; Acts xxi. 9; Rev. xiv. 4. u See ver. 6. v See i. 10; γν. διδ., 2 Cor. viii. 10. w 2 Cor. iv. 1; Ph. ii. 27; 1 Tim. i. 13, 16. The vb., Rom. ix. 15 ff., xi. 30 ff.; Mt. v. 7. x See iv. 2. y See ver. 1. z See iii. 22. a 2 Cor. vi. 4, xii. 10; 1 Th. iii. 7; Lk. xxi. 23; 1 Kings xxii. 2.

¹ Om. τ φ all uncc. but A, which is followed by a considerable minority of minn.

themselves into slavery; and subservience to party leaders (so Mr., Hf., Lt., El.; cf. i. 12, ii. 4, etc.) appears foreign to this context. It is better to take the warning quite generally: as much as to say, "Let no human influence divert you from service to God, or infringe on the devotion due to your Redeemer"; cf. Gal. v. 1, vi. 14. Public opinion and the social pressure of heathenism were too likely to enslave the Corinthians.

Ver. 24 reiterates with urgency, as addressed to "brethren," the fundamental rule laid down in ver. 20. ἐν τῇ κλήσει ᾗ now becomes, abstractly, ἐν ᾧ . . . ἐν τούτῳ—"wherein each was called, in that let him abide in the sight of God"; here as there the Christian vocation is intended, the status of faith and saintship, with which no human power may interfere and which, when duly realised, will of itself control outward relations and circumstances (Gal. ii. 20, Rom. xiv. 23). For παρὰ Θεῷ, cf. iii. 19 and parls.

§ 23. ADVANTAGES OF THE SINGLE STATE, vii. 25-35. Paul's opinion had been asked particularly, in this connexion, about the case of marriageable daughters (25): was it wise for fathers, as things were, to settle their daughters in marriage? He delivers his judgment on this delicate matter, turning aside in vv. 29-31 to a general reflexion upon the posture of Christians towards the perishing world around them; then returning to point out the freedom from care and material engrossment enjoyed by the unwedded (32 ff.), he restates in ver. 36 his advice περὶ τῶν παρθένων.

Ver. 25. Περὶ δὲ τῶν παρθένων: a topic pointedly included in the περὶ ὦν ἐγράψατε of the Church Letter (1). In vv. 1-16 P. had spoken of the conduct of self-directing men and women in regard to marriage; there remains the case of daughters at home, for whose disposal the father was responsible (36 f.). On this point Paul has no "command" to

give, whether proceeding immediately (10, ix. 14) or mediately (xiv. 37) from "the Lord"; he "gives" his γνώμη, his settled and responsible "opinion". He pronounces "as (i.e., feeling myself to be; cf. 29 ff., iv. 7, 18) one ἠλεημένος ὑπὸ Κυρίου πιστὸς εἶναι"—conscious that he is "faithful through the mercy effectually shown" him (pf. pass. ptp.; cf. 1 Tim. i. 13, 16) "by the Lord,"—faithful in this pronouncement to his stewardship under Christ (see iv. 1 f., and ii. 16). His advice is therefore to be trusted. The distinction made is not between higher and lower grades of inspiration or authority (cf. note on 12); but between peremptory rule, and conditional advice requiring the concurrence of those advised. Paul's opinion, qua opinion, as much as his injunction, is that of the Lord's steward and mouthpiece.

Ver. 26. νομίζω οὖν τοῦτο κ.τ.λ.: "I consider therefore"—the formula by which one gives a γνώμη (contrast the παραγγέλλω, διατάσσομαι of 10, 17)—"this to be good because of the present straits": καλὸν ὑπάρχειν, "good in principle" or "in nature" (cf. xi. 7, xii. 22); the existing situation is such as to make the course recommended entirely right and honourable (see note on καλόν, 1, also 8, 38).—The ἀνάγκη—narrowness, "pinching stress" (Ev.)—belongs to the καιρὸς συνεσταλμένος (29), the brief earthly continuance visible for the Church, a period exposed to persecution (28) with its hardships and perils; this "might or might not be the beginning of the ἀνάγκη μεγάλη predicted by Jesus" in Luke xxi. 23 (Lt.). ἐνεστῶσαν signifies "present" rather than "impending" (see iii. 22, Gal. i. 4); the distress of the time, which P. was feeling keenly at Ephesus (iv. 9 ff., xv. 32), portended a speedy crisis.—ὅτι καλὸν ἀνθρώπῳ τὸ οὕτως εἶναι is open to three constructions, as ὅτι is rendered that, because, or which (ὅ,τι): (a) makes

b Ver. 40; ʸκαλὸν ἀνθρώπῳ τὸ ᵇοὕτως εἶναι. 27. ᵉδέδεσαι ᶜγυναικί; μὴ
Jo. iv. 6.
c Ver. 39; ᵈζήτει ᵉλύσιν. ᶠλέλυσαι ἀπὸ γυναικός; μὴ ᵈζήτει γυναῖκα. 28.
Rom. vii.
2. ἐὰν δὲ καὶ ᵍγήμῃς,¹ οὐχ ἥμαρτες· καὶ ἐὰν ˡγήμῃ ἡ ᵗπαρθένος,
d In like
sense, οὐχ ἥμαρτε· ʰθλίψιν δὲ τῇ ⁱσαρκὶ ʰἕξουσιν ᵏοἱ ᵏτοιοῦτοι, ἐγὼ
Rom. ii
7; Col. iii.
1; 1 Pet. iii. 11; Rev. ix. 6; Mt. vi. 33, xiii. 45. e N.T. h.l.; Eccl. viii. 1; Wisd. viii. 8. f Acts
xxii. 30; Jo. xi. 44; Ps. cxlv. 7. g See ver. 9; also note below. h Jc. xvi. 33; Rev. ii. 10; Sir.
li. 3. i For dat., 2 Cor. xii. 7; for use of σαρξ, v. 5. k See v. 5.

¹ γαμησῃς, א(A)BP 17, 37, 46.
γημῃς, KL, etc. λαβῃς γυναικα, DG, latt. vg., Tert.

the clause an expanded restatement of
τοῦτο καλὸν ὑπάρχειν—"I think then
this to be good . . . that it is good (I
say) for a man to remain as he is" (so
Mr., Ed., El., and most); (b) makes it
the ground, lying in the principle stated
in ver. 1, for Paul's specific advice in the
matter of the παρθένοι—"I think this to
be good (in their case) . . . because it
is good for one (ἀνθρώπῳ; see note on
1) to remain as one is," sc. to continue
single (Bz., D.W., Gd.); (c) by attaching
ὅ,τι as relative to the antecedent τοῦτο,
and defining it by the subsequent τ.
οὕτως εἶναι, Hn. gets another rendering
—"I think this to be good (in the case
of maidens) because of the present straits,
which is good (as I have said, 1) for one
generally, viz., to remain unmarried."
(b) and (c), yielding a like sense, avoid
the anacoluthon — the former at the
expense of leaving τοῦτο undefined, the
latter by an artificial arrangement of the
words; both explanations are somewhat
wide of the mark, for διὰ τ. ἐνεστ. ἀνάγκην supplies here the ground of advice,
and ver. 1, on which they are based, is
differently conceived (see note). In giving
his advice "about the maidens," P.
suddenly bethinks himself to widen it to
both sexes (see 27 f.). So he recasts
his sentence, throwing the ὅτι καλόν
κ.τ.λ., with characteristic conversational
freedom (cf. iv. 9), into apposition to
the incomplete inf. clause: "I think this
to be good because of the present straits
—yes, that it is good ἀνθρώπῳ (for any
one, not τ. παρθένοις only) not to change
one's state". οὕτως εἶναι, "to be just
as one is" (see parls.)—a state defined
by the context.
Vv. 27, 28 apply in detail the advice
just given, and first as it bears on men,
then on maidens.—δέδεσαι, λέλυσαι, pf.
pass. of present state determined by the
past; μὴ ζήτει, pr. impv., "do not be
seeking". The two directions of ver. 27
reinforce, from the new point of view,

the instructions of vv. 10-16 and 8 respectively.—λέλυσαι, as opp. of δέδεσαι,
applies either to bachelor or widower.
In ver. 28 the general advice of 27 is
guarded from being overpressed; cf. the
relation of ver. 2 to 1 and ver. 9 to 8.
The punctuation of El. and Nestle best
marks the connexion of thought, closing
ver. 27 with a full stop, each of the parl.
ἐὰν . . . ἥμαρτες (-εν) clauses with a
colon, and separating θλίψιν δὲ and ἐγὼ
δὲ by a comma. In the second supposition (both with ἐὰν and sbj. of probable
contingency) P. reverts to the case of "the
maiden," from which he was diverted in
ver. 26; he makes her, by implication,
responsible for her marriage, although
in 36 ff., later, the action of the father
is alone considered.—γαμέω is used in
the act. here, and in ver. 39, both of man
and woman; cl. Gr. applies it to the
latter in pass.; cf. note on the double
ἀφιέτω in vv. 12 f. ἔγημα and ἐγαμήθην
are the older and later aors.—The aor. in
the apodosis — ἥμαρτες, ἥμαρτεν — is
proleptic (Bn. § 50; Bm., pp. 198 f.,
202), rather than gnomic (Mr., Hn., Ed.),
as though by way of general reflexion:
the Ap. addresses specific instances—
"thou didst not . . . she did not sin"; cf.,
for instance, John xv. 11, Rev. x. 7.
The marriage Paul discourages is no
sin, but will bring suffering from which
he would fain save his friends. "But
affliction for the flesh such (as may
marry) will have, but I am seeking to
spare you." With θλίψις cf. σκόλοψ τῇ
σαρκί (2 Cor. xii. 7; also v. 5 above);
there is some thought, possibly, of recompense to "the flesh" which has had
its way against advice. The affliction
that Paul foresees is aptly indicated by
Photius: "More easily and with small
distress shall we endure if we have no
wives and children to carry along with us
in persecutions and countless miseries".
At such times, for those who have domestic cares, there arises "the terrible

δὲ ὑμῶν ¹φείδομαι. 29. ᵐΤοῦτο δέ ᵐφημι, ἀδελφοί, ὁ ⁿκαιρὸς ¹
ᵒσυνεσταλμένος ². ᵖτὸ ᵖλοιπόν ²ἐστιν ²ἵνα καὶ οἱ ᑫἔχοντες ᑫγυναῖ-
κας ὡς μὴ ᑫἔχοντες ὦσι, 30. καὶ οἱ ʳκλαίοντες ὡς μὴ ʳκλαίοντες,
καὶ οἱ ʳχαίροντες ὡς μὴ ʳχαίροντες, καὶ οἱ ˢἀγοράζοντες ὡς μὴ
ᵗκατέχοντες, 31. καὶ οἱ ᵘχρώμενοι τῷ ³κόσμῳ ³τούτῳ ³ ὡς μὴ
ʳκαταχρώμενοι· ʷπαράγει γὰρ τὸ ˣσχῆμα τοῦ κόσμου τούτου.

1 2 Cor. i.23, xii. 6, xiii. 2; Rom. viii.32, xi. 21; Acts xx. 29; 2 Pet. ii. 4 f. m xv. 50; see vi. 16. Cf. i. 12. n In like sense, 2 Cor. vi.

2; Rom. xiii. 11; Eph. v. 16; Col. iv. 5; 2 Tim. iv. 6; Rev. xii. 12; Lk. xix. 44; Jo. vii. 8. o N.T. h.l. (cf. Acts v. 6); Sir. iv. 31. p See i. 16; τὸ λ., Ph. iii. 1, iv. 8; 2 Th. iii. 1; Heb. x. 13; Mk. xiv. 41. q See v. 1. r 2 Cor. vi. 10; Rom. xii. 15; Jo. xvi. 20. s See vi. 20. t In this sense, 2 Cor. vi. 10; Josh. i. 11. See xi. 2. u See ver. 21. v ix. 18. w Mt. ix. 9, etc.; mid., 1 Jo. ii. 8, 17. x Ph. ii. 8; Isa. iii. 17.

¹ Beza and Elzevir read οτι ο καιρος, after DG and the Western txt.

²συνεσταλμενος εστιν το λοιπον, אABD* (om. το) P 17, 37, 46, and many Ff. With this order of words, the *stop* follows εστιν: so B* (according to Tisch.); see note below. G 67**, latt. vg., Tert., Hier., Aug. write εστιν *twice*. συνεσταλμ. το λοιπον εστιν, DᶜKL, etc.—L, syrr. cop., followed by Elz. and Griesbach, put the stop at εστιν; Stephens, Bz., and most edd. of T.R. placed it before το λοιπον.

³τον κοσμον (om. τουτ.), אAB, cop. DG 17 add τουτον. τω κοσμω τουτω: Syrian uncc., etc.; a grammatical emendation.

alternative, between duty to God and affection to wife and children" (Lt.).—φείδομαι appears to be a *conative present* (see Bn. § 11; cf. Ro. ii. 4, Gal. v. 4).

Vv. 29–31. τοῦτο δέ φημι, ἀδελφοί, κ.τ.λ.: "This moreover I assert, brethren: *The time is cut short*".—φημί, as distinguished from λέγω, "marks the gravity and importance of the statement" (El.).—Συνστέλλω (*to contract, shorten sail*) acquired the meaning *to depress, defeat* (1 Macc. iii. 6, 2 Macc. vi. 12); hence some render συνεσταλμένος by "calamitous," but without lexical warrant.—ὁ καιρός (see parls.) is "the season," the epoch of suspense in which the Church was then placed, looking for Christ's coming (i. 7) and uncertain of its date. The prospect is "contracted"; *short views* must be taken of life.

The connexion of τὸ λοιπὸν and ἵνα ... ὦσιν with the foregoing affords a signal example of the grammatical looseness which mars Paul's style. (*a*) As to τὸ λοιπόν: (1) Cm., the Gr. Ff., Bz., Al., Ev., Hn., Gd., Ed., R.V. *mg.* attach it to συνεστ. ἐστίν, in a manner "contrary to its usual position in Paul's epp. and diluting the force of the solemn ὁ καιρός ... ἐστίν" (El.). (2) The Vg. and Lat. Ff., Est., Cv., A.V. read τὸ λοιπὸν as predicate to ἐστὶν understood, thus commencing a new sentence,—"reliquum est ut," etc.; this is well enough in Latin, but scarcely tolerable Greek. (3) Mr., Hf., Bt., El., Lt., W.H., R.V.

txt. subordinate τὸ λοιπόν, thrown forward with emphasis, to the ἵνα clause (cf. Gal. ii. 10, Rom. xi. 31)—"so that henceforth indeed those that have wives may be as without them," etc.; this gives compactness to the whole sentence, and proper relevance to the adv. Those who realise the import of the pending crisis will *from this time* sit loose to mundane interests. (*b*) As to the connexion of ἵνα ... ὦσιν: this clause may define either *the Apostle's purpose*, as attached to φημί (so Bz., Hf., Ed.), or *the Divine purpose* implied in συνεστ. ἐστίν (so most interpreters). Both explanations give a fitting sense: *the Ap. urges*, or *God has determined*, the limitation of the temporal horizon, in order to call off Christians from secular absorption. In this solemn connexion the latter is, presumably, Paul's uppermost thought.

Vv. 29b, 30 are "the picture of spiritual detachment in the various situations in life" (Gd.). Home with its joys and griefs, business, the use of the world, must be carried on as under notice to quit, by men prepared to cast loose from the shores of time (cf. Luke xii. 29–36; by contrast, Luke xiv. 18 ff.). From wedlock the Ap. turns, as in vv. 17–24, to other earthly conditions—there considered as *stations* not to be wilfully changed, here as *engagements* not to be allowed to cumber the soul. Ed. observes that the Stoic condemned the interaction, here recognised, between "the

y Mt. xxviii. 14; Wisd. vi. 16, vii. 23. μεριμνα, Mt. xiii. 22, etc. z See ver. 8. a xii. 25; Ph. ii. 20, iv. 6; Mt. vi. 25 ff., x. 19.

32. θέλω δὲ ὑμᾶς ʸἀμερίμνους εἶναι. ὁ ᶻἄγαμος ᵃμεριμνᾷ τὰ τοῦ Κυρίου, πῶς ᵇἀρέσει¹ τῷ Κυρίῳ / 33. ὁ δὲ ᶜγαμήσας ᵃμεριμνᾷ τὰ τοῦ κόσμου, πῶς ᵇἀρέσει¹ τῇ γυναικί.² 34. ᵈμεμέρισται² ἡ γυνὴ² καὶ ἡ ᵉπαρθένος². ἡ ᶻἄγαμος ᵃμεριμνᾷ τὰ τοῦ Κυρίου, ἵνα ᾖ ἁγία καὶ³ ᶠσώματι⁴ καὶ ᶠπνεύματι⁴· τ̔ δὲ ᶜγαμήσασα ᵃμεριμνᾷ τὰ τοῦ

b x. 33; Rom. viii. 8, xv. i. ff.; Gal. i. 10; 1 Th. ii. 4, 15, iv. 1; 2 Tim. ii. 4.
c See ver. 9, and note on ver. 28.   d In this sense, see i. 13; diff. in ver. 17.   e See ver. 25.
f See v. 3.

¹ αρεση (thrice) : all pre-Syrian uncc.

² A perplexed *varia lectio* :—

(1) και (μεμερισται), ℵABDgr.P 17, vg. syrsch. cop.   Om. και DcGKL, etc. (later Western and Syrian).

(2) και (η γυνη): all uncc. but D*E, and most minn.   Om. και D*, etc., codd. mentioned by Hier., syrsch. cop.

(3) η γυνη η αγαμος και η παρθενος (μεριμνα), BP 46, 73, four other minn., vg. cop., Eus., Amb., Hier., Pel. So Tr., W.H., R.V. *marg.*

η γυνη και η παρθενος η αγαμος (μεριμνα), ℵADGKL, etc., latt. syrr. (? Western and Syrian). [ℵAFb 17 write η αγαμος after both γυνη and παρθενος.] So Tisch., R.V. *txt.*, El., Nestle. See, on punctuation, note below.

The text here adopted reads : (33) μεριμνα τα του κοσμου, πως αρεση τω κοσμω, και μεμερισται.   (34) και η γυνη η αγαμος και η παρθενος μεριμνα τα του κυριου κ.τ.λ. See Heinrici's conjecture, stated below.

³ Om. και ADI²P 17, 37, syrsch. cop.   ⁴ τω (σωμ., πν.), ℵABP 17, 37, 46.

soul's emotions and external conditions; the latter he would have described as a thing indifferent, the former as a defect : πᾶν μὲν γὰρ πάθος ἁμαρτία" (Plut., *Virt. Mor.*, 10). "Summa est, Christiani hominis animum rebus terrenis non debere occupari, nec in illis conquiescere : sic enim vivere nos oportet, quasi singulis momentis migrandum sit e vita" (Cv.).—ὡς μὴ ἔχοντες κ.τ.λ, not *like, in the manner of*, but "*with the feeling of* those who have not," etc., ὡς with ptp. implying subjective attitude—a limitation "proceeding from the mind of the speaking or acting subject" (Bm., p. 307) ; *cf.* ver. 25 and note. —ἀγοράζοντες (*marketing*) gives place in the negative to κατέχοντες, *possessing, holding fast* (*cf.* 2 Cor. vi. 10).—Χράομαι governs acc. occasionally in late Gr.; the case of τὸν κόσμον may be influenced by καταχρώμενοι, with which cl. authors admit the acc. The second vb. (with dat. in ix. 18) is the intensive of the first —*to use to the full* (*use up*) ; not *to misuse*—a meaning lexically valid, but inappropriate here. "Abuse" had both meanings in older Eng., like the Lat. *abutor ;* it appears in Cranmer's Bible with the former sense in Col. ii. 22. A reason for sparing use of the world lies in its *transitory form*, 31b—a sentence kindred to the declaration of ver. 29a.—

σχῆμα (*cf.* iv. 6, and other parls.) denotes phenomenal guise — *habitus, fashion* — as distinguished from μορφή, proper and essential shape : see the two words in Phil. ii. 6 ff., with the discussions of Lt. and Gifford *ad loc.* "The world" has a dress suited to its fleeting existence. —παράγει affirms "not so much the present actual fact, as the inevitable issue ; the σχῆμα of the world has no enduring character" (El.) ; "its fascination is that of the theatre" (Ed.) ; *cf.* 1 John ii. 17. The Ap. is thinking not of the fabric of nature, but of mundane human life—the world of marryings and marketings, of feasts and funerals.

Then what this world to thee, my heart?
Its gifts nor feed thee nor can bless.
Thou hast no owner's part in all its fleetingness.
—J. H. Newman.

Vv. 32-34. θέλω δὲ ὑμᾶς κ.τ.λ. (*cf.* 7) : " But I want you to be unanxious (ἀμερίμνους) ;" *cf.* φείδομαι, ver. 28. This is the reason why P. labours the advice of this section ; see our Lord's dehortations from ἡ μέριμνα τοῦ αἰῶνος in Matt. vi. 25-34 and xiii. 22.—Vv. 32b-34 describe, not without a touch of humour, the exemption in this respect of the unmarried : *he* "is anxious in respect of the things of the Lord "—not "of the world, as to how he should please his wife !" After bidding the readers to be ἀμέριμνοι, P. writes μεριμνᾷ τ. τοῦ Κυρίου, with a

κόσμου, πῶς ^bἀρέσει ^lτῷ ἀνδρί. 35. τοῦτο δὲ πρὸς τὸ ὑμῶν αὐτῶν ^gσυμφο-
^gσυμφέρον ²λέγω· οὐχ ἵνα ^hβρόχον ὑμῖν ⁱἐπιβάλω, ἀλλὰ πρὸς τὸ
^kεὔσχημον καὶ ^lεὐπρόσεδρον ³τῷ Κυρίῳ ^mἀπερισπάστως.

ρον, x. 33
Eccl. ii. 3;
(Symmachus).
h N.T. h.l.;
Prov.vi.5,

vii. 21, xxii. 25.   i With dat., Mk. xi. 7, xiv. 46; Acts iv. 3; Prov. xx. 26.   k xii. 24; Acts xiii. 50,
xvii. 12; Mk. xv. 43. Cf. xii. 23, xiv. 40.   l ευπαρεδρον, h.l. Cf. ix. 13; Prov. viii. 3 (παρεδρευω);
Wisd. vi. 15, ix. 4 (-εδρος).   m H.l.; -στος, Wisd. xvi. 11; Lk. x. 40; Sir. xli. 2 (περισπασθαι).

---

¹ α ρ ε σ η (thrice): all pre-Syrian uncc.   ² σ υ μ φ ο ρ ο ν, ℵ*ABD* 17.

³ ε υ π α ρ ε δ ρ ο ν: all uncc. but KL.

---

certain *catechresis* in the vb., for the sake of the antithesis. The accs. are of *limitation* rather than of transitive obj. πῶς ἀρέσῃ is indirect question, retaining the deliberative sbj.—"is anxious . . . (asking) how he should please," etc. For the supreme motive, "pleasing *the Lord*," *cf*. iv. 1-5, 2 Cor. v. 9, etc. ὁ γαμήσας, aor. of the *event* (pf. in 10: *cf*. note), which brought a new care.— Accepting the reading καὶ μεμέρισται. καὶ ἡ γυνὴ ἡ ἄγαμος, with the stop at μεμέρ. (the only possible punctuation with ἡ ἄγαμος in this position: see txtl. note), then it is added about the married Christian, that "he has been (since his marriage) divided,"—*parcelled out* (see note on i. 12): part of him is assigned to the Lord, part to the world. Lt. says that this rendering (R.V. *mg*.) "throws sense and parallelism into confusion, for καὶ μεμέρισται is not wanted with ver. 33, which is complete in itself": nay, the addition is made just because the parl. would be untrue if not so qualified; the married Christian does not care *simply* for "the things of the world" as the unmarried for "the things of the Lord," he cares for *both* "and is divided," giving but half his mind to Christ (so Ewald, Hf., Hn., Ed.). The attachment of καὶ μεμέρισται to ver. 34, with the Western reading (see txtl. note), retained by Mr., Bt., El., Lt., Sm., A.V., and R.V. *txt*., in accordance with most of the older commentt., gives to μερίζω a meaning doubtful in itself and without N.T. parl.: "And *there is a distinction between* the wife and the maiden". Gd. escapes this objection by reading μεμέρισται κ. ἡ γυνὴ as a sentence by itself, "the wife also is divided"—then continuing, "And the unwedded maiden cares for," etc.; an awkward and improbable construction as the text stands (but see Hn. below). Txtl. criticism and exegesis concur in making καὶ μεμέρισται a further assertion about ὁ γαμήσας, revealing his full disadvantage.

Hn., by a very tempting conjecture, proposes to insert a second μεμέρισται after the first: πῶς ἀρέσῃ τ. γυναικί, καὶ μεμέρισται· μεμέρισται καὶ ἡ γυνή. ἡ ἄγαμος καὶ ἡ παρθένος μεριμνᾷ κ.τ.λ.— "He that has married is anxious in regard to the things of the world, how he may please his wife, and is divided; divided also is the wife. The unmarried (woman), with the maiden, is anxious as to the things of the Lord." This would account for the double καί, which embarrasses the critical text; it gives a fuller and more balanced sense, in harmony moreover with Paul's principle of putting husband and wife on equal terms (2 ff., 11-16); and nothing was easier than for a doubled word, in the unpunctuated and unspaced early copies, to fall out in transcription. Placing the full stop at μεμέρισται, without the aid of Hn.'s emendation, ἡ γυνὴ ἡ ἄγαμος καὶ ἡ παρθένος are made the combined subject of μεριμνᾷ (34), "the unmarried woman" being the general category, within which "the maiden," whose case raised this discussion (25), is specially noted; the two subjects forming one idea, take a sing. verb.

The purpose ἵνα ἡ ἁγία κ.τ.λ. is the subjective counterpart of the question πῶς ἀρέσῃ of ver. 32; note the similar combination in Rom. xii. 1, also 1 Thess. iv. 3; and see notes on ἁγίοις, ἡγιασμένοις, i. 2. Holiness τῷ σώματι (dat. of *sphere*; see Wr., p. 270) comes first in this connexion (*cf*. 4; vi. 20), and τῷ πνεύματι is added to make up the entire person and to mark the inner region of sanctification; "the spirit" which animates the body, being akin to God (John iv. 24) and communicating with His Spirit (Rom. viii. 16), is the basis and organ of our sanctification (*cf*. 1 Thess. v. 23, 2 Thess. ii. 13).—Of ἡ γαμήσασα, "she that has married," on the contrary, the same must be said as of ὁ γαμήσας (33); she studies to "please her husband" as well as "the Lord".

Ver. 35. A third time P. declares that

n xiii. 5;
Deut.xxv.
3; Ezek.
xvi. 7 f.
-ων, xii.
23;
-οσυνη,
Rom.i.27.

o With
inf., Acts
viii. 20; 2

36. Εἰ δέ τις ⁿἀσχημονεῖν ἐπὶ τὴν παρθένον αὐτοῦ °νομίζει, ἐὰν· ᾖ
ᵖὑπέρακμος, καὶ οὕτως ᵠὀφείλει γίνεσθαι, ὃ θέλει ποιείτω· οὐχ
ἁμαρτάνει· ʳγαμείτωσαν.¹   37. ὃς δὲ ἕστηκεν ˢἑδραῖος² ἐν τῇ
καρδίᾳ,² μὴ ᵗἔχων ᵗἀνάγκην, ᵘἐξουσίαν δὲ ᵘἔχει περὶ τοῦ ἰδίου
ᵛθελήματος, καὶ τοῦτο ʷκέκρικεν ἐν τῇ⁸ καρδίᾳ αὐτοῦ³ τοῦ⁴ ˣτηρεῖν

Macc. vii. 19; cl. Gr.   p H.l.; παρακμαζω, Sir. xlii. 9.   q Pres., in this sense, ix. 10, xi. 7,
10; 2 Cor. xii. 14; Rom. xv. 1; Eph. v. 28; 2 Th. i. 3, ii. 13; Heb. v. 3, 12, etc.   r See ver. 9.
s xv. 58; Col. i. 23.   t Heb. vii. 27; Lk. xiv. 18; Jude 3.   u Rom. ix. 21; 2 Th. iii. 9; Acts ix. 14;
Lk. xii. 5, xix. 17; Mt. vii. 29, ix. 6; Mk. iii. 15; Jo. x. 18, xix. 10, 11; h.l. with περι.   v Of human
will, xvi. 12; Eph. ii. 3; 2 Pet. i. 21; Lk. xxiii. 25; Jo. i. 13; 3 Ki. v. 8.   w See ver. 3.   x 2 Cor.
xi. 9; 1 Th. v. 23; 1 Tim. v. 22, vi. 14; Jas. i. 27; Jude 21.

¹ γαμειτω, DG syrˢᶜʰ., Epiph., Aug.; non peccat si nubat, latt. vg., Ambrst.

² εν τη καρδια εδραιος: so pre-Syrian uncc.

³ εν τη ιδια καρδια (om. αυτου), אABP 31, 46.

⁴ Om. του אABP, minn.²⁰.   Ins. του DGKL (Western and Syrian).

he is consulting for the welfare of his
readers (cf. 28b, 32a), not insisting on
his own preference nor laying down an
absolute rule: "looking to (πρός) your
advantage I say (it)". τὸ σύμφορον is
the abstract of συμφέρει (vi. 12, x. 23).—
The βρόχος is the noose or lasso by which
a wild creature is snared: P. does not
wish by what he says to deprive the Cor.
of any liberty,—to capture his readers
and shut them up to celibacy—"not that
I may throw a snare over you". He
aims at what is socially εὔσχημον, "of
honourable guise," as belonging to the
Christian decorum of life (see parls.);
and at what is religiously εὐπάρεδρον τῷ
Κυρίῳ, "promotive-of-fit-waiting on the
Lord".—ἀπερισπάστως recalls the περιε-
σπᾶτο used of Martha in Luke x. 38-42,
and suggests that the Ap. had this story
in his mind, esp. as μεριμνάω, his leading
expression in this Section, is the word of
reproof used by Jesus there. Epictetus'
dissuasive from marriage, in his Dissertt.,
III., xxii., 67 ff., curiously resembles
Paul's: τοιαύτης οὔσης καταστάσεως
οἵα νῦν ἐστιν, ὡς ἐν παρατάξει, μή ποτ'
ἀπερίσπαστον εἶναι δεῖ τ. Κυνικὸν ὅλον
πρὸς τῇ διακονίᾳ τοῦ Θεοῦ, ἐπιφοιτᾶν
ἀνθρώποις δυνάμενον, οὐ προσδεδεμένον
καθήκουσιν ἰδιωτικοῖς οὐδ' ἐμπεπλεγ-
μένον (cf. 2 Tim. ii. 4) σχέσεσιν, ἃς
παραβαίνων οὐκέτι σώσει τὸ τοῦ καλοῦ
καὶ ἀγαθοῦ πρόσωπον, τηρῶν δ' ἀπολεῖ
τὸν ἄγγελον κ. κατάσκοπον κ. κήρυκα
τῶν θεῶν; (69).

§ 24. FREEDOM TO MARRY, vii. 36-40.
The question of the marriage of Cor.
Christian maidens Paul has discussed on
grounds of expediency. The narrow
earthly horizon, the perils of the Christian

lot, the division between religious and
domestic duty esp. probable under these
conditions, render the married state undesirable (28-34). The Ap. does not on
these grounds forbid marriage,—to do so
would entangle some of his readers
perilously; he recommends what appears
to him the course generally fitting, and
advantageous for their spiritual interests
(35 f.). If the parent's judgment points
the other way, or if circumstances are
such as to enforce consent, then so let it
be (36). But where the father can thus
decide without misgiving, he will do well
to keep his daughter at home (37 f.).
Similarly in the case of the Christian
widow: she is free to marry "in the Lord";
but, in Paul's decided opinion, she will be
happier to refrain (39 f.).   The Ap. gives
inspired advice, and the bias of his own
mind is clearly seen; but he finds no sin
in marriage; he guards sensitively the
rights of individual feeling and conscience, and leaves the decision in each
case to the responsible parties.

Ver. 36. By a contrastive δὲ P. passes
from the εὔσχημον at which his dissuasive
was aimed, to the ἀσχημονεῖν that
might be thought to result in some cases
from following it.—The vb. (= ἀσχήμων
εἶναι) signifies either to act unbecomingly
(xiii. 5), or to suffer disgrace, turpem
videri (Vg.); the antithesis, and the adjunct ἐπὶ τὴν παρθένον, dictate the former
sense, which is post-classical.—On νομίζει
(is of opinion), see ver. 26.   It was socially
discreditable, both amongst Greeks and
Jews (cf. Sirach xlii. 9), to keep one's
daughter at home, without obvious reason, for any long period beyond adult
age; a Christian father might feel this

τὴν ἑαυτοῦ παρθένον, [y]καλῶς [y]ποιεῖ.[1] 38. ὥστε καὶ ὁ [x]ἐκγαμίζων [23] [y] Ph. iv. 14; Acts x.33;
[y]καλῶς [y]ποιεῖ,[3] ὁ δὲ[4] μὴ [z]ἐκγαμίζων[5] [ya]κρεῖσσον [y]ποιεῖ.[6] 39. Jas. ii. 8, 19; 2 Pet.
γυνὴ [b]δέδεται νόμῳ[7] [c]ἐφ᾽ [c]ὅσον [c]χρόνον ζῇ ὁ ἀνὴρ αὐτῆς· ἐὰν δὲ i. 19; 3 Jo. 6; 3
[d]κοιμηθῇ ὁ ἀνὴρ αὐτῆς,[8] [e]ἐλευθέρα ἐστὶν ᾧ θέλει [f]γαμηθῆναι, Ki.viii.18. [z] Mt. xxii.
μόνον [f]ἐν [f]Κυρίῳ. 40. [g]μακαριωτέρα δέ ἐστιν ἐὰν [h]οὕτω μείνῃ, 30, xxiv. 38; Lk.
[i]κατὰ τὴν ἐμὴν [i]γνώμην· [k]δοκῶ δὲ[9] κἀγὼ [l]πνεῦμα Θεοῦ [l]ἔχειν. xvii. 27, xx. 35.
a See ver. 9.

b See ver. 27.   c Rom. vii. 1; Gal. iv. 1; cf. Mk. ii. 19; 2 Pet. i. 13.   d xi. 30, xv. 6 ff.; 1 Th. iv. 13 ff.; 2 Pet. iii. 4; Jo. xi. 11 f., etc.   e ix. 19; Rom. vi. 20, vii. 3; h.l. with inf.   f xi. 11, etc., characteristic and peculiar to P.; cf. ἐν Χρ.   g Of (human) persons, Rom. iv. 7 f. (from LXX), xiv. 22; Jas. i. 12, 25; 1 Pet. iii. 14, iv. 14; Rev. i. 3, etc.; Mt. v. 3 ff., etc. Compar. h.l.   h See ver. 26.   i See ver. 6.   k See iii. 18.   l Rom. viii. 9; Jude 19. Cf. ii. 12.

[1] ποιησει, אAB 17, 46, 67**, cop.   [2] γαμιζων, אABD 17, 46.

[3] γαμιζων την εαυτου παρθενον: אABDP 17, 37, 46, latt. vg. syrr.; BD put εαυτου after παρθενον (?).

[4] και ο μη: א*ABDG 17, 37, 46.   [5] γαμιζων, א*ABDG 17, 37, 46.

[6] ποιησει, א*AB 17, 37, 46, 67**, cop., Bas.
Minn. 3 and 114 om. ver. 38 in consequence of the homœoteleuton ποιει (vv. 37 f.); through same mistake G and several other copies om. ver. 38a, ωστε . . . ποιει.

[7] Om. νομῳ (derived from Rom. vii. 2) א*ABD* 17, 67**, the oldest copies of vg., Clem., Or., Athan., Tert.

[8] Om. αυτης אABKP, more than seventy minn.

[9] δοκω γαρ (?): B 17, 37, 67**, Cyr., Amb., Ambrst.   Preferred by W.H.

discredit for his religion's sake (cf. x. 32), and might be reproached as doing his child and society a wrong. — ἐὰν ᾖ ὑπέρακμος, "if she be past the bloom (of youth)"—the μέτριος χρόνος ἀκμῆς, fixed by Plato (Rep., vi., 460 E) at twenty, the ætas nubilis.—καὶ οὕτως ὀφείλει (see parls.) γίνεσθαι—"and so matters ought to proceed" (pr. inf.)—states a further presumable reason for consent: duty may require it—where, e.g., the girl has been promised, or is so situated that a continued veto may give rise to peril or scandal (cf. 2). In such circumstances the father's course is clear: "let him do what he wills" (θέλει); cf. ver. 35. γαμείτωσαν — i.e., the daughter and her suitor, the claim of the latter being hinted at in the previous ὀφείλει: pr. impv.; "Let the marriage take its course". Ver. 37. For the opposite resolution, adopted by a father who "keeps his own virgin (daughter)" instead of "marrying" her (38), four conditions are laid down: (1) unshaken firmness in his own mind (ἕστηκεν ἐν τῇ καρδίᾳ ἑδραῖος, cf. Rom. xiv. 5, 23), as against social pressure; (2) the absence of constraint (μὴ ἔχων ἀνάγκην) arising from previous engagement or irresistible circumstances; (3) his full authority to act as he will

(ἐξουσίαν δὲ ἔχει κ.τ.λ.) — slaves, on the other hand, could not dispose of their children, and the unqualified patria potestas belonged only to Roman citizens (see Ed. in loc.); ἐξουσία, however, signifies moral power, which reaches in the household far beyond civil right; (4) a judgment deliberately and independently formed to this effect (τοῦτο κέκρικεν ἐν τῇ ἰδίᾳ καρδίᾳ). Granting all this, the father who "has decided to keep his own maiden, does well"—καλῶς, rightly, honourably well (see note on καλόν, 1). The repeated καρδία (the mind, the seat of thought and will, rather than the heart with its modern emotional connotation; cf. ii. 9, iv. 5, and notes), and the phrase περὶ τοῦ ἰδίου θελήματος, press on the father the necessity of using his judgment and acting on his personal responsibility; as in vv. 6 f., 28, 35, the Ap. is jealous of allowing his own authority or inclination to overbear the conscience of his disciples; cf. Rom. xiv. 4-10, 22 f.—This ἀνάγκη urges in the opp. direction to that of ver. 26; in both cases the word signifies compulsion, dictating action other than that one would independently have taken.—ἐξουσίαν . . . περὶ κ.τ.λ. is "power as touching his own resolve," the right to act as one will—in other

838 ΠΡΟΣ ΚΟΡΙΝΘΙΟΥΣ Ā VIII.

xv. 29,
xxi. 25;
Rev. ii.
14, 20.
b In this disparaging sense, xiii. 2, 8; Rom. ii. 20; 1 Tim. vi. 20; see also i. 5.   c See iv. 6.   d In
this sense, x. 23, xiv. 4, 17; 1 Th. v. 11; Acts ix. 31, xx. 32; Mt. xvi. 18.

VIII. 1. Περὶ δὲ τῶν ᵃεἰδωλοθύτων· οἴδαμεν, ὅτι πάντες ᵇγνῶσιν ἔχομεν. ἡ ᵇγνῶσις ᶜφυσιοῖ, ἡ δὲ ἀγάπη ᵈοἰκοδομεῖ.   2. εἰ δέ¹

¹ Om. δε ℵABP 17, 46, 73, vg. (older codd.), cop.

words, mastery of the situation.—The obj., τ. παρθένον, suggests the tacit complement to τηρεῖν (see parls.) : "to *keep intact*, in what he believes to be the best state " for the Lord's service (Ed.). " The will of the maiden is left wholly out of court " (Hn.) ; social custom ignored this factor in marriage ; for all that, it might constitute the opposed ἀνάγκη, and might, in some circumstances, practically limit the paternal ἐξουσία ; see ver. 28b, and note.

Ver. 38, the sum of the matter : either to marry one's daughter or refuse her in marriage is, abstractly viewed, an honourable course ; the latter, in Paul's judgment, and for Christians in the present posture of things, is *better*. " Ce bien et mieux résument tout le chapitre " (Gd.).

Vv. 39, 40 dispose, by way of appendix to the case of the maiden and to the like effect, of the question of *the remarriage of Christian widows*. Ver. 39 is repeated in almost identical terms, for another purpose, in Rom. vii. 2.—On δέδεται and γαμηθῆναι (cl. γαμεθῆναι), see vv. 27 f. ; κοιμηθῇ, the term for Christian death (see parls.).—" She is free to be married to whom she will," while the maiden is disposed of by her father's will (36 f.) ; μόνον ἐν Κυρίῳ (*cf.* 2 Cor. vi. 14 ff., 1 Thess. iv. 3 ff.) forbids union with a heathen ; it also forbids any union formed with un-Christian motives and otherwise than under Christ's sanction (*cf.* Thess. iv. 4 f.).—" But more blessed she is " (μακαριωτέρα δέ : see parls.)— not merely happier by exemption from trouble (26 ff.), but *religiously* happier in her undivided devotion to the Lord (32 ff.)—"if she abide as she is ". This advice was largely followed in the Pauline Churches, so that before long widows came to be regularly enrolled for Church service (1 Tim. v. 3-16).—κατὰ τὴν ἐμὴν γνώμην (see note on 26) : Paul's *advice*, not command.—δοκῶ δὲ κἀγώ κ.τ.λ. : " However I think, for my own part (however others may deem of me), that Ӏ have (an inspiration of) God's Spirit " (the anarthrous πνεῦμα Θεοῦ : *cf.* xii. 3, etc.) ; see for Paul's claim to Divine guidance, extending to his *opinions* as

well as commands, ver. 25, ii. 10-16, iv. 1, ix. 2, xiv. 37.—On δοκῶ, see note to iv. 9 ; it is the language of modesty, not misgiving. The Ap. commends his advice in all these matters, conscious that it proceeds from the highest source and is not the outcome of mere human prudence or personal inclination.

DIVISION III. CONTACT WITH IDOLATRY, viii.-x. We have traced in the previous chapters the disastrous reaction of the old leaven upon the new Christian kneading at Cor. But Christian society had its *external* as well as its internal problems—a fact already evident in the discussion of ch. vi. respecting the carrying of disputes to the heathen law-courts. A much larger difficulty, involving the whole problem of social intercourse between Christians and their heathen neighbours, had been raised by the Church Letter—the question περὶ τῶν εἰδωλοθύτων (viii. 1). *Was it lawful for a Christian to eat flesh that had been offered in sacrifice to an idol?* Social festivities commonly partook of a religious character, being conducted under the auspices of some deity, to whom libations were poured or to whom the animals consumed had been dedicated in sacrifice. The "idol's house" (viii. 10) was a rendezvous for banquets. Much of the meat on sale in the markets and found on ordinary tables came from the temples ; and without inquiry it was impossible to discriminate (x. 25-28). Jewish rule was uncompromisingly strict upon this point ; and the letter of the Jerusalem Council, addressed to the Churches of Antioch, Syria, and Cilicia, had directed "the brethren from among the Gentiles " to "abstain from *idolothyta* " (Acts xv. 29). The Cor. Church, in consulting Paul, had expressed its own leaning towards liberty in this matter (viii.) ; what will the Ap. say? It is a real dilemma for him. He has to vindicate the broad principles of spiritual religion ; at the same time he must avoid wounding Jewish feeling, and must guard Gentile weakness against the seductions of heathen feasts and against the peril of relapsing into idolatry through inter-

τις ᵉδοκεῖ ᶠεἰδέναι ¹ ᶠτι, οὐδέπω ² οὐδὲν ³ ἔγνωκε ⁴ ᵍκαθὼς ᵍδεῖ ᵉ See iii. 18.
γνῶναι· 3. εἰ δέ τις ʰἀγαπᾷ τὸν ʰΘεόν, οὗτος ⁱἔγνωσται ὑπ⁵ κεναι, see

                                                         ᶠ ἐγνω-
                                                          ii. 8.
                                                         ᵍ Cf. Rom.

viii. 26; Eph. vi. 20; Col. iv. 4, 6; 1 Th. iv. 1; 2 Th. iii. 7; 1 Tim. iii. 15.   h Rom. viii. 28; Mt.
xxii. 37; Lk. x. 27 (Deut. vi. 5); 1 Jo. iv. 20 f., v. 2.   i Gal. iv. 9; 2 Tim. ii. 19 (Nu. xvi. 5); Mt.
vii. 23, xxv. 12.

¹ ἐγνωκεναι, all pre-Syrian uncc., 17, 46, many Ff.

² ουπω, ℵABP 17, 46, 73.   ουδεπω, Western and Syrian.

³ *Om.* ουδεν all pre-Syrian uncc.—T.R. a grammatical emendation.

⁴ εγνω, all pre-Syrian uncc.   The -κε a doubling of the following κα-.

⁵ Om. υπ' αυτου ℵ* 17, Clem.

course with unconverted kindred and neighbours. In theory Paul is for *freedom*, but in practice for great *restrictions* upon the use of idolothyta. (1) He admits that the question is decided in principle by the fundamental truth of religion, *viz.*, that *God is one*, from which it follows that *the sacrifice to the idol is an invalid transaction* (viii. 1 ff.; x. 19, 26). But (2) many have not grasped this inference, being still in some sense under the spell of the idol; for them to eat would be sin, and *for their sake stronger-minded brethren should abstain* (viii. 7-13; x. 23-30). To this effect (3) P. sets forth *his own example*, (a) in *the abridgment of* his personal *liberty for the good of others* (ix. 1-22; x. 33-xi. 1), and (b) in *the jealous discipline of bodily appetite* (ix. 23 ff.). The last consideration leads (4) to a solemn warning against *contamination by idolatry*, drawn (a) from *the early history of Israel*, and further (b) from *the communion of the Lord's Table*, which utterly forbids participation in "the table of demons" (x. 1-22). These instances show in a manner evident to the good sense of the readers (x. 15), that to take part in a heathen sacrificial feast is in effect a recognition of idolatry and an apostasy from Christ.

§ 25. KNOWLEDGE OF THE ONE GOD AND ONE LORD, viii. 1-6. In inquiring from their Ap. "about the εἰδωλόθυτα," the Cor. had intimated their "knowledge" of the falsity of the entire system of idolatry. Here Paul checks them at the outset. The pretension betrays their one-sided intellectualism. Such matters are never settled by knowledge; *love* is the true arbiter (2 f.). After this caution, he takes up the statement of the Cor. creed made in the Church Letter, with its implications respecting idolatry (4 ff.).

Ver. 1a. Περὶ δὲ τῶν εἰδωλοθύτων: another topic of the Church Letter, to which the Apostle continues his reply

(see note on vii. 1; also *Introd.*, chap. ii.). The word εἰδωλόθυτον (see parls.), "the *idol*-sacrifice," substituted for the ἱερόθυτον (x. 28) of the heathen vocabulary, conveys an implicit judgment on the question in hand; see note on εἴδωλον, ver. 4, and on x. 19 f.; also Acts xv. 20, τὰ ἀλισγήματα τῶν εἰδώλων. — οἴδαμεν —ὅτι πάντες γνῶσιν ἔχομεν: the common rendering, "We know *that* we all have knowledge" yields a weak tautology, and misses the irony of the passage; otherwise than in οἴδαμεν ὅτι of ver. 4, this is the *causal* ὅτι (so Bg., Hn., Ed.). The Cor. in making their inquiry virtually answered it themselves; they wrote Οἴδαμεν ὅτι οὐδὲν εἴδωλον ἐν τῷ κόσμῳ (4); and P. takes them up at the first word with his arresting comment: "'We know' (say you?) because 'we all have knowledge'!—Knowledge puffs up," etc. —For γνῶσιν ἔχομεν, *cf.* ver. 10; the phrase breathes the pride of the Cor. illuminati; in γνῶσις this Church felt itself rich (i. 5, iv. 10); its wealth was its peril.

Ver. 1b. The Ap. gives to Cor. vanity a sudden, sharp rebuke by his epigram, Ἡ γνῶσις φυσιοῖ, ἡ δὲ ἀγάπη οἰκοδομεῖ: "Knowledge puffs up, but Love builds up". Hn. aptly compares Aristotle's axiom, Τὸ τέλος οὐ γνῶσις, ἀλλὰ πρᾶξις (*Nic. Eth.*, i., 1). For φυσιόω, *to inflate*, see note on iv. 6. The appeal of the Church to Knowledge as decisive in the controversy about "meats" disclosed the great flaw in its character—its poverty of love (xiii. 1 ff.). The tacit obj. of οἰκοδομεῖ is the Church, the Θεοῦ οἰκοδομή (iii. 9, 16); Eph. iv. 15 f. describes the *edifying* power of love; see also Matt. xxii. 37-40, 1 John iv. 16-21. For the Biblical use of ἀγάπη, see note to xiii. 1. The divisive question at issue Love would turn into a means of strengthening the bonds of Church life; Knowledge operating alone makes it an engine of destruction (11 f.).

Vv. 2, 3. Loveless knowledge is *ruinous*

k 2 Cor. ix.   αὐτοῦ.¹   4. περὶ ² τῆς ᵏ βρώσεως ² οὖν τῶν ⁿ εἰδωλοθύτων · ¹ οἴδαμεν
10; Rom.
xiv. 17;   ¹ ὅτι οὐδὲν ᵐ εἴδωλον ἐν κόσμῳ, καὶ ὅτι οὐδεὶς Θεὸς ἕτερος ³ ⁿ εἰ ⁿ μὴ
Col. ii.
16; Heb.
xii. 16.   l iii. 16, vi. 2 f., etc. ; diff., ver. 1.   m x. 19, xii. 2; 2 Cor. vi. 16; Rom. ii. 22; 1 Th. i. 9;
1 Jo. v. 21; Rev. ix. 20; Acts vii. 41, xv. 20; see also ver. 1, v. 10. In LXX *passim*, for Heb. *'elilim*,
and *gillulim*.   n For this use, see i. 14.

¹ Om. υπ' αυτου ℵ* 17, Clem. Alex.

² περι δε της γνωσεως, D*ᵍʳ.; περι της γνωσεως ουν, P 121.

³ Om. ετερος all pre-Syrian uncc.

(1*b*); more than that, it is *self-stultifying*. The contrasted hypotheses—εἴ τις
δοκεῖ ἐγνωκέναι τι (= δοκεῖ σοφὸς εἶναι,
iii. 18) and εἴ τις ἀγαπᾷ τὸν Θεόν—define
the position of men who build upon their
own mental acquirements, or who make
love to God the basis of life. For emphatic
δοκεῖ, *cf*. iii. 18, vii. 40; it implies an
opinion, well- or ill-founded, and confidence in that opinion. The pf. ἐγνωκέναι
signifies *knowledge acquired* (for which,
therefore, one might claim credit), while
the aors. ἔγνω and γνῶναι denote the *acquisition of* (right) *knowledge*, rendered
impossible by self-conceit—" he has never
yet learnt as he ought to do ". For τι
—probably τὶ in this connexion, *something* emphatically, *something great*—*cf*.
note on τὶ εἰδέναι, ii. 2. The *Enchiridion*
of Epictetus supplies a parl. to ver. 2:
" Prefer to seem to know nothing ; and if
to any thou shouldst seem to be somebody, distrust thyself " ; similarly Socrates, in Plato's *Apology*, 23.

Ver. 3 is one of Paul's John-like
sayings. In the apodosis he substitutes,
by an adroit turn, " is known (ἔγνωσται :
pf. pass. of *abiding effect* upon the obj.)
by God " for " hath come to know God,"
the expected consequence—see the like
correction in Gal. iv. 9 ; *cf*. Phil. ii. 12 f.,
iii. 12; John xv. 16; 1 John iv. 10. Paul
would ascribe nothing to human acquisition; religion is a bestowment, not an
achievement; our love or knowledge is
the reflex of the divine love and knowledge directed toward us. Philo, quoted by
Ed., has the same thought : γνωριζόμεθα
μᾶλλον ἢ γνωρίζομεν (*De Cherub*., § 32).
—οὗτος ἔγνωσται ὑπ' αὐτοῦ (*sc*. τοῦ Θεοῦ),
" *he* (and not the other) is known by Him ".
Ev. reverses the ref. of the prons. : " He
(God) hath been known by him (the man
loving Him) "—an unlikely use of οὗτος.

Ver. 4. After his thrust at Cor. γνῶσις,
P. resumes, with οὖν (*cf*. xi. 17-20), from
ver. 1 the question " About the eating of
idolothyta," repeating the " we know "
at which he had interrupted his correspondents. For οἴδαμεν in a *confessio

fidei*, *cf*. 1 John v. 18 ff. That the theological statement given in vv. 4 ff. *comes
from the mouth of the Corinthians* seems
probable from the following considerations : (*a*) the repeated οἴδαμεν (*h.l.* in
this Ep. ; *cf*. the frequent interrog. οὐκ
οἴδατε ; of chh. iii., v., vi. ; also xii. 2),
by which P. *associates himself with the
readers*, who are men of knowledge (i. 5,
x. 15, etc.) ; (*b*) *the solemn rhythm* of vv.
4*b* and 6, resembling a confessional formula (*cf*. Eph. iv. 4 ff., 1 Tim. iii. 16)—
ver. 5 may be an interjected comment of
the Church Letter upon its creed ; (*c*) the
expression " gods many and lords many "
applied to heathen divinities, which is
foreign to Pauline as to Jewish phraseology, but natural *on the lips of old
polytheists ;* (*d*) the aptness with which
ἀλλ' οὐκ ἐν πᾶσιν ἡ γνῶσις (7) fits in
with this explanation, being understood as
Paul's reply to his readers' declaration of
their enlightened faith. See, on this question, W. Lock in *Expositor*, V., vi., 65.
The articles of belief cited from the Cor.
in vv. 4*b* and 6 had probably been formulated first by P., like the Πάντα μοι
ἔξεστιν of vi. 12, and so would be fitly
quoted to him.—οὐδὲν εἴδωλον ἐν κόσμῳ
(*cf*. x. 19), being parl. to οὐδεὶς Θεὸς
κ.τ.λ., should be rendered not " An idol
is nothing," etc., but " There is no idol in
the world " (so R.V. virtually, Mr., Hf.,
Bt., Ed., Sm.). Existence is denied to the
idol not absolutely (see 5, x. 19 f.), but
relatively; it has no real place ἐν κόσμῳ,
no power over the elements of nature;
" the earth is the Lord's," etc. (x. 26) ;
there is no Zeus in the sky, nor Poseidon
ruling the sea, but " one God and Father "
everywhere,—a faith emancipating enlightened Christians from every heathen-
ish superstition.—οὐδὲν εἴδωλον κ.τ.λ.
forms the polemic counterpart to οὐδεὶς
Θεὸς εἰ μὴ εἷς (see parls.),—the corner-
stone of Jehovism, which Christ has
made the world's creed.—εἴδωλον (*sc*. a
thing possessing εἶδος, *form* only), *semblance, phantasm*, renders in the LXX
several Hebrew words for false gods—

εἷς · 5. καὶ γὰρ εἴπερ εἰσὶ ᵒλεγόμενοι Θεοί, εἴτε ἐν οὐρανῳ εἴτε
ἐπὶ τῆς ¹ γῆς, ὥσπερ εἰσὶ θεοὶ πολλοὶ καὶ ᴾκύριοι πολλοί,
6. ἀλλ᾽ ² ἡμῖν εἷς Θεὸς ὁ πατήρ, ᑫἐξ ᑫοὗ τὰ πάντα καὶ ἡμεῖς ʳ εἰς
ʳαὐτόν · καὶ εἷς Κύριος Ἰησοῦς Χριστός, ˢδι᾽ ˢοὗ ³ τὰ πάντα καὶ
ἡμεῖς ˢδι᾽ ˢαὐτοῦ.⁴

ᵒ Eph. ii. 11;
2 Th. ii. 4.
ᴾ Cf. Acts
xxv. 26;
1 Tim. vi.
15; Lk.
xvi. 13;
Rev. xvii.
14.
ᑫ See i. 30.
ʳ Rom. xi.

36; Eph. i. 5; cf. Col. i. 16.   s Rom. xi. 36; Col. i. 16; Heb. i. 2; Jo. i. 3, etc. Cf. xv. 57; 1 Tim.
ii. 5; Rom. i. 5, v. 1 f., 17, 21; Gal. i. 1; Eph. i. 5, ii. 18; 1 Th. v. 9; Tit. iii. 6; 1 Jo. iv. 9.

¹ Om. τηs all uncc. and many minn.

² Om. αλλ᾽ (?) B, basm., Irint., Eus. ; Lachm. and W.H. bracket.
ημιν δε, 17, cop., Cyrhier., Epiph.

³ ον (?) B, æth., Epiph. ; W.H. marg.

⁴ The minn. 55, 72**, 109, 178, supported by Gregory of Nazianzus orat. 39, 12,
Basil in several passages, Cyr., Dam., make the addition και εν πνευμα αγιον εν ω
τα παντα—a Trinitarian gloss.   Chrysostom ²⁰² expressly controverts this reading.

—esp. 'elīlīm, nothings, and hebhel, empti-
ness ; the term was applied first to the
images, then to the (supposed) godships
they represent, branding them as shams
and shows : see 1 Thess. i. 9, Acts xiv.
15, Ps. xcvi. 5.   The κόσμος reveals the
being and power of the One God (Rom.
i. 20); idolaters have no living God, but
are ἄθεοι ἐν τῷ κόσμῳ (Eph. ii. 12).
Ver. 5 : a comment of the Cor. on their
confession of faith, showing their "knowledge" of its bearing.—καὶ γὰρ εἴπερ
εἰσίν κ.τ.λ.: "For indeed, granting the
existence of so-called gods, whether in
heaven or upon earth, as indeed there
are many (such) gods and lords, yet to
us," etc.   The -περ of εἴπερ and ὥσπερ
enhances the supposition (see El., ad
loc.), allowing its utmost possibility.—
εἴπερ κ.τ.λ. admits their existence (in
some sense) as reputed deities ; ὥσπερ
κ.τ.λ. points to their astonishing multitude, while distinguishing them, in a
manner parl. to the distinction between ὁ
Θεὸς and ὁ Κύριος, as "gods" in their
assumed deity and "lords" in their
assumed dominion.   The repeated εἰσὶν
asserts an actual being of some sort behind the εἴδωλον (see x. 19-22), but the
θεότης or κυριότης is merely λεγομένη ;
for the force of this ptp., cf. 2 Thess. ii.
4, Eph. ii. 11.   With πολλοὶ cf. κατείδωλον πόλιν, Acts xvii. 16, and the Gr.
saying, Πάντα θεῶν πλέα.—Κύριος is a
title given to gods in Gr. inscriptions ; a h.l. for Bib. Gr. : cf., however,
'adonīm in Isa. xxvi. 13 ; also Deut. x. 17 ;
Ps. cxxxvi. 2 f.—In heaven, on earth : the
two great domains of God's kingdom
(Matt. vi. 10), usurped by the false gods.
Ver. 6 affirms in positive Christian

terms, as ver. 4b stated negatively and
retrospectively, the creed of the Cor. believers.   The "one God" of O.T. monotheism is "to us one God the Father".
"Of whom are all things, and we for
Him :" the universe issues from God,
and "we," His sons in Christ, are
destined therein for His use and glory—
He would reap in "us" His glory, as a
father in the children of his house ; see,
on this latter purpose, Eph. i. 5, 10 ff.,
18b, iii. 9 ff. ; also 1 Peter ii. 9, Jas. i.
18, John xvii. 9 f., etc. ; cf. Aug., "Fecisti
nos ad Te".   In the emphatic ἡμεῖς εἰς
αὐτὸν there speaks the joyful consciousness of Gentiles called to know and serve
the true God ; cf. xii. 2 f., Eph. ii.
11 ff.—The "one Lord Jesus Christ" is
Mediator, as in 1 Tim. ii. 5—"through
whom are all things, and we through
Him" ; again ἡμεῖς stands out with high
distinction from the dim background of
τὰ πάντα.   The contrasted ἐξ οὗ, εἰς
αὐτὸν of the previous clause is replaced
by the doubled διὰ of this : God is
the source of all nature, but the end
specifically of redeemed humanity ; Christ
is equally the Mediator—and in this
capacity the Lord (xv. 24-28)—of nature
and of men.   The universe is of God
through Christ (Heb. i. 2, John i. 3) : we
are for God through Christ (2 Cor. v. 18,
Eph. i. 5, etc.).   Col. i. 15 ff. unfolds
this doctrine of the double Lordship of
Christ, basing His redemptional upon
His creational headship.—It is an exegetical violence to limit the second τὰ πάντα,
as Grotius and Baur have done, to "the
ethical new creation" ; in 2 Cor. v. 18
the context gives this limitation, which
in our passage it excludes.   The inferior

t See ver. 1.
u συνηθεια,
xi. 16; Jo.
xviii. 39.
See note
below.
v See iv. 13.
w See ver. 1.
x With sub-

7. Ἀλλ᾽ οὐκ ἐν πᾶσιν ἡ [t] γνῶσις, τινὲς δὲ τῇ [u] συνειδήσει[1] τοῦ[2] [m] εἰδώλου[2] [v] ἕως[2] [v] ἄρτι[2] ὡς [w] εἰδωλόθυτον ἐσθίουσι, καὶ ἡ [x] συνείδησις αὐτῶν [y] ἀσθενὴς οὖσα [z] μολύνεται. 8. [a] βρῶμα δὲ ἡμᾶς οὐ [b] παρίστησι[3] τῷ Θεῷ· οὔτε γὰρ[4] ἐὰν[5] φάγωμεν [c] περισσεύομεν,[5]

jective gen., x. 29; 2 Cor. i. 12, iv. 2, v. 11; Rom. ii. 15, ix. 1; Tit. i. 15, etc.   y The adj., in this
sense, h.l. (see ver. 12, and Rom. xiv. 1 for -εω).   For other sense of adj., i. 25, iv. 10.   z Rev. iii.
4, xiv. 4; -υσμος, 2 Cor. vii. 1.   a See iii. 2.   b 2 Cor. iv. 14, xi. 2; 5 times in Rom.; 4 times
besides in P.; also in Acts, Lk., Mt. xxvi. 53.   c xiv. 12, xv. 58; freq. in P.; also in GG. and Acts.

[1] συνηθεια, ℵ*ABP 17, 46, 67**, cop., Euthal., Dam.   συνειδησει, DGL, etc.

[2] συνηθεια εως αρτι του ειδωλου (in this order): all uncc. but ALP.

[3] παραστησει, ℵ*AB 17, 46, 67**, cop. basm.

[4] Om. γαρ ℵAB, am. tol. cop. basm.
Ins. γαρ DGLP, etc.—Western and Syrian.

[5] εαν μη φαγ. υστερουμεθα . . . εαν φαγ. περισσευομεν (in this
order): A*B 17*, 46, oldest vg. cop. basm.; so Tr., Al., W.H., Nestle, El., R.V.
The order of T.R. is that of Western and Syrian uncc., the minn., latt. and
syrr.; ℵ and A** read εαν μη φαγ. περισσευομεν . . . εαν φαγ. υστερουμεθα:
so Lachm.   Tr. further follows B in reading περισσευομεθα for -ομεν.

reading δι᾽ ὅν (for οὗ: see txtl. note),
"because of whom are all things," would
consist with a lower doctrine of Christ's
Person, representing Him as preconceived
object, while with δι᾽ οὗ He is pre-
existent medium of creation. The full
Christology of the 3rd group of the Epp.
is latent here. The faith which refers all
things to the one God our Father as
their spring, and subordinates all things
to the one Lord our Redeemer, leaves no
smallest spot in the universe for other
deities; intelligent Christians justly inferred that the material of the idolothyta
was unaffected by the hollow rites of
heathen sacrifice.

§ 26. THE WEAK CONSCIENCE OF
THE OLD IDOLATER, viii. 7-13. The
knowledge of the one Father and Lord
upon which the Cor. Church prided itself,
had not released all its members from
fears respecting the idolothyta; in some
the intellect outran the heart, in others it
lagged behind. With the latter, through
weakness of understanding or force of
habit, the influence of the heathen god
still attached to objects associated with
his worship (7). For á man in this state
of mind to partake of the consecrated
flesh would be an act of compliance with
heathenism ; and if the example of some
less scrupulous brother should lead him
thus to violate his conscience and to fall
into idolatry, heavy blame will lie at the
door of his virtual tempter (10-12). Such
blame P. declares that he will himself on
no account incur (13).

Ver. 7. "But not in all is there the

knowledge" (ἡ γνῶσις) which you and I
claim to have (1, 10), expressed just now
in the terms of the Church confession
(4 ff.).—τῇ συνηθείᾳ ἕως ἄρτι τοῦ εἰδώλου, "by reason of their habitation up
till now to the idol": for this dat. of
defining cause, cf. Eph. ii. 1.—ἕως ἄρτι
(cf. iv. 13, 11) qualifies the quasi-vbl. noun
συνηθεία, actively used, which, as in 4
Macc. xiii. 21 and cl. Gr., signifies with
the objective gen. (= συνηθεία πρὸς or
μετά) intercourse, familiarity with ; the
other, passive sense is seen in xi. 16.
The Western reading, συνειδήσει, preferred by some critics as the lectio ardua,
gives the sense, "through relation of
conscience to the idol" (Hf., Hn.).—ὡς
εἰδωλόθυτον ἐσθίουσι, "as an idol-sacri-
fice eat (the meat in question)"—under
the consciousness that it is such, with
the sense haunting them that what they
eat belongs to the idol and associates
them with it; cf. x. 18 ff. and notes.
"And their conscience, since it is weak
(unable to get rid of this feeling), is
soiled" (opp. of the καθαρὰ συνείδησις
of 1 Tim. iii. 9, 2 Tim. i. 3). The consciousness of sharing in idol-worship is
defiling to the spirit of a Christian ; to
taste knowingly of idolothyta, under any
circumstances, thus affects converts from
heathenism who have not the full faith
that the earth is the Lord's and the fulness thereof; now, "whatsoever is not of
faith is sin" (Rom. xiv. 23).

Ver. 8. βρῶμα δέ κ.τ.λ.: "But food
will not present us to God," non exhibebit
nos Deo (Mr.): that on the ground of

οὔτε ἐὰν μὴ[1] φάγωμεν [d]ὑστερούμεθα.[1]   9. [e]βλέπετε δὲ [e]μήπως [d]See i. 7;
ἡ [f]ἐξουσία ὑμῶν αὕτη [g]πρόσκομμα γένηται τοῖς [y]ἀσθενοῦσιν.[2]   also xvi.
10. ἐὰν γάρ τις ἴδῃ σε,[3] τὸν ἔχοντα [t]γνῶσιν, ἐν [h]εἰδωλείῳ [i]κατα-   ii.,-ησις.
κείμενον, οὐχὶ ἡ [x]συνείδησις αὐτοῦ [y]ἀσθενοῦς[4] ὄντος[4] [k]οἰκοδομηθή-

17, -ημα;
Phil. iv.
e x. 12; Gal.
v. 15; Col.
ii. 8; Heb.
iii. 12, xii.

25; Acts xiii. 40; Lk. xxi. 8. *Cf.* iii. 10, and reff.   f See vii. 37; also vi. 12.   g Rom. ix.
32 f. (Isa. viii. 14), xiv. 13, 20; 1 Pet. ii. 8; *cf.* -κοπτω, Rom. xiv. 21; εγκοπη, ix. 12 below.
h N.T. *h.l.*; 1 Esdr. ii. 9; 1 Macc. i. 47, x. 83.   i In this sense, Mk. ii. 15, xiv. 3; Lk. vii. 37.
= ανακειμ.   k See ver. 1; here only ironical. See note below.

[1] εαν μη φαγ. υστερουμεθα . . . εαν φαγ. περισσευομεν (in this
order): A*B 17*, 46, oldest vg. cop. basm.; so Tr., Al., W.H., Nestle, El., R.V.
The order of T.R. is that of Western and Syrian uncc., the minn., latt. and
syrr.; ℵ and A** read εαν μη φαγ. περισσευομεν . . . εαν φαγ. υστερουμεθα:
so Lachm. Tr. further follows B in reading περισσευομεθα for -ομεν.

[2] ασθενεσιν, all uncc. but L.

[3] BG, vg., Aug., Ambrst. om. σε; *bracketed* by Lachm. and W.H.

[4] Many Latin interpp., including vg., read *cum sit infirma*, as if for ασθενης ουσα.

which the verdict turns may be said to
"present" one to the judge. To "commend" is συν-, not παρίστημι (see parls.);
for the *fut.* (see txtl. note), *cf.* Rom. xiv.
10, 2 Cor. iv. 14, Col. i. 28.—βρώματα
do not enter into our permanent being
(vi. 13; see note); *they* will not be the
criteria of the approaching Judgment.—
The alternative οὔτε clauses negative the
two opposite ways in which "food"
might have been supposed to "present us
to God": "neither if we do not eat, are
we the worse off (ὑστερούμεθα: see note
on i. 7); nor if we eat, are we the better
off (περισσεύομεν: do we abound, exceed others)". The latter predicate is
appropriate to the "strong," who deemed
themselves in a superior position, on a
higher ground of faith.—Ver. 8, like vv.
4-6, represents the *pro* in the question
περὶ βρώσεως, as vv. 7, 8-13 the *contra*.
Chap. viii. is virtually a dialogue; the
double (challenging and rebutting) δὲ of
vv. 8 f., with the words "*your right*" of
ver. 9, in accordance with Paul's dialectical style (*cf.* Rom. iii. 1-8), compels us
to read this ver., like vv. 1, 4-6, as *from
the mouth of the Cor.*, possibly from the
Church Letter; "hic alter erat, vel esse
poterat, Corinthiorum prætextus" (Cv.).
At the word μολύνεται P. hears some of
his readers interject: "The conscience
of the weak brother is *defiled*, you say,
by eating after my example. But (δέ)
how so? You have taught us that God
will not judge us by these trifling ex-
ternals; abstinence or use of 'meats'
makes no difference to our intrinsic
state." This Paul admits, to set against
it the caution βλέπετε δὲ μὴ κ.τ.λ., on
which the rest of the paragraph hangs.

Ver. 9. "Beware, however, lest this
right of yours"—*sc.* to eat the idolothyta,
for which many of the Cor. are contending, and probably in the Church Letter
(1). For ἐξουσία in this use, *cf.* ix. 4 ff.,
12, also ἔξεστιν in vi. 12, x. 23. The
Jerus. Council (Acts xv. 29), to whose
decree P. was a party, had not denied *in
principle* the lawfulness of using idolothyta; it forbade such use to the mixed
Judæo-Gentile Churches within a certain
area, in deference to Jewish feeling. Paul
comes in effect to the same conclusion,
though he *advises* instead of commanding. The πρόσκομμα is an obstacle
thrown in the way of "the weak," over
which they may stumble into a moral fall,
not having the strength either to overcome their scruples or to disregard an
example contrary to their conscience.

Ver. 10 enforces (γάρ) the above warning.—σὲ τὸν ἔχοντα γνῶσιν, "thee, the
man that has knowledge" (see 1): the
Cor. pretension to superior enlightenment, shown in vv. 2 f. to be faulty in
Christian theory, now discloses its practical mischief. The behaviour of the
Christian man of knowledge who "re-
clines (at table) in an idol's temple," is
represented as a sort of bravado—a thing
done to show his "knowledge," his complete freedom from superstition about the
idol. This act is censured because of its
effect upon the mind of others; in x. 18-22
it will be condemned on its own account.
The form εἰδωλίον (or -εῖον) occurs in
the Apocrypha; it follows the formation
of Gr. temple names—'Απολλωνεῖον, etc.
—οὐχὶ ἡ συνείδησις αὐτοῦ, ἀσθενοῦς
ὄντος κ.τ.λ.; "will not his conscience,
weak as he is, be 'edified' unto eating

l See i. 18.
m Rom. iv.   σεται εἰς τὸ τὰ ^wεἰδωλόθυτα ἐσθίειν; 11. καὶ ^l ^lἀπολεῖται ^l ὁ
19, xiv. 1   ^mἀσθενῶν ² ἀδελφὸς ² ἐπὶ ³ τῇ σῇ ^tγνώσει,² δι' ὃν ⁿΧριστὸς ⁿἀπέθανεν.
f., 21, in
figur.   12. οὕτω δὲ ^oἁμαρτάνοντες ^oεἰς τοὺς ἀδελφοὺς καὶ ^pτύπτοντες
sense.
See ver. 7. αὐτῶν τὴν ^xσυνείδησιν ^mἀσθενοῦσαν, ^oεἰς Χριστὸν ^oἁμαρτάνετε.
n xv. 3; 2
Cor. v. 15; 13. ^qδιόπερ εἰ ^aβρῶμα ^rσκανδαλίζει τὸν ἀδελφόν μου, οὐ μὴ φάγω
Rom. v. 6
ff., vi. 8 ff., ^sκρέα εἰς τὸν αἰῶνα, ἵνα μὴ τὸν ἀδελφόν μου ^{4 r}σκανδαλίσω.
viii. 34,
xiv. 9;
Gal. ii. 21; 1 Th. iv. 14, v. 10; 1 Pet. iii. 18; Jo. xi. 50 ff.   o See vi. 18.   p N.T. h.l.; cf. 1 Kings
i. 8; Prov. xxvi. 22.   q x. 14.   διο, see xii. 3.   r Rom. xiv. 21; Mt. xv. 12, xvii. 27; Sir. ix. 5,
xxiii. 8, xxxii. (xxxv.) 15.   s Rom. xiv. 21, pl.

¹ ἀπολλυται γαρ : אּ*B 17, cop. basm., Clem.; απολλυται ουν, AP.
και απολλυται : אּcD*b 46, 67**, Bas.   και απολειται : DcGL, etc., vg. syrr.
(late Western and Syrian).

² ο ασθενων εν τη ση γνωσει, ο αδελφος δι' ον κ.τ.λ. (in this
order): all pre-Syrian uncc.

³ εν, all uncc. but L.

⁴ The Western texts om. the second μου.

the foods offered to idols ? "—not *because*
he is weak (as though overpowered by a
stronger mind), but *while* he is still weak,
as under the lingering belief that the idol
is "something in the world" (7): "his
verbis exprimitur horror infirmi, tamen
edentis" (Bg.).—Thus eating unpersuaded
"in his own mind" (Rom. xiv. 5), he sins
(Rom. xiv. 23), and therefore "is perishing" (11). The vb. "edified"—instead
of "persuaded" or the like—is used in
sad irony (cf. Tert., "ædificatur ad
ruinam," *De Præscr. Hæretic.*, 3); P. probably takes up the word in this connexion from the Church Letter: the eaters
of idolothyta thought their practice "edifying" to less advanced brethren—"*edifying*, forsooth!—to what end?"
Ver. 11. "For the weak man [whom
you talk of building up!] *is being destroyed* through thy knowledge — the
brother, on whose account Christ died!"
(Rom. xiv. 15). This affirms, with terrible emphasis, the issue implied by ver.
10: "est ædificatio ruinosa" (Cv.).—ὁ
ἀσθενῶν means (more than ὁ ἀσθενής)
the man in a continued state of weakness.—ἐν τῇ σῇ γνώσει, "on the ground
(*or* in the sphere) of thy knowledge";
in this atmosphere the weak faith of the
other cannot live (cf. ἐν in ii. 4 ; Eph. iv.
16, ἐν ἀγάπῃ). His "knowledge" leaves
the tempter inexcusable. "Notice the
threefold darkness of the picture: there
perishes, thy brother, for whom Christ
died" (Bt.). Paul appeals to the strongest
feelings of a Christian—brotherly love
and loyalty to Christ. For the prospective δι' ὅν, cf. Rom. iv. 25 ; Christ's death

is thus frustrated of its dear object (cf.
Gal. ii. 21) by thy heartless folly!
Ver. 12. In such case, not only the
weak brother sins by yielding, but the
strong who tempted him; and the latter
sins directly "against Christ" (for the
construction, cf. vi. 18): "But sinning in
this way against the brethren, and inflicting a blow on their conscience while
it is weak, you sin against Christ".—τὴν
συνείδησιν ἀσθενοῦσαν, not "their weak
conscience" (τὴν ἀσθεν.), but "their conscience weak as it is": how base to
strike the weak!—τύπτω describes as
the violent wrong of the injurer, what is a
μόλυσμα and πρόσκομμα (7, 9) in its
effect upon the injured. A *blow* on the
conscience shocks and deranges it.—For
the bearing of such an act on *Christ*, see
Matt. xviii. 6 ff., xxv. 40, 45 ; also Zech.
ii. 8, etc. The principle of union with
Christ, which forbids sin against oneself
(vi. 15), forbids sin against one's brother.
Ver. 13 sums up the debate in the
language of personal conviction: "Wherefore verily"—for this last reason above
all—"if (a matter of) food (βρῶμα, indef.)
is stumbling my brother, I will eat no
flesh-meats for evermore, that I may not
stumble my brother".—κρέα (pl. of κρέας)
signifies the kinds of βρῶμα in question,
including probably beside the idolothyta
other animal foods which might scandalise
men of narrow views, such as the vege-
tarians of Rom. xiv. 13-21 (see notes *ad
loc.*).—Four times in vv. 11-13 P. repeats
the word ἀδελφός, seeking to elicit the
love which was needed to control Cor.
knowledge (cf. 2 f.).—For "σκανδαλίζω,

IX. 1. Οὐκ εἰμὶ ἀπόστολος [1]; οὐκ εἰμὶ [a]ἐλεύθερος [1]; οὐχὶ Ἰησοῦν [2] ᾰ ver. 19;
Χριστὸν [2] τὸν [b]Κύριον ἡμῶν [b]ἑώρακα [3]; οὐ τὸ [c]ἔργον μου ὑμεῖς ἐστε
ἐν Κυρίῳ; 2. [d]εἰ ἄλλοις οὐκ εἰμὶ ἀπόστολος, [d]ἀλλά [d]γε ὑμῖν εἰμι·
ἡ γὰρ [e]σφραγὶς τῆς [4] ἐμῆς [4] [f]ἀποστολῆς ὑμεῖς ἐστε ἐν Κυρίῳ.

Rom. vii.
3; Gal. iv.
22 ff.; 1
Pet. ii. 16.
b Jo. xx. 18,
25; Acts
xxii. 14 f.
c iii. 13 ff.,

xv. 58, xvi. 10; Rom. xiv. 20; Phil. i. 22, ii. 30; 2 Tim. iv. 5; Acts xiii. 2, xiv. 26.   d Lk. xxiv.
21; cf. Phil. iii. 8.   For αλλα after hypoth., see iv. 15, viii. 6; 2 Cor. xi. 6, xiii. 4; Rom. vi. 5.
e Rom. iv. 11; 2 Tim. ii. 19; Rev. v. 1, etc. -ιζομαι, 2 Cor. i. 22; Rom. xv. 28; Eph. i. 13, iv. 30;
Rev. vii. 3, etc.   f Rom. i. 5; Gal. ii. 8; Acts i. 25; Deut. xxii. 7.

[1] . . . ελευθερος; . . . αποστολος; (in this order): ℵABP 17, 37, 46, vg. syrsch. cop.

[2] Ιησουν (without Χριστον), ℵAB 46, oldest vg. sah. basm.
Χριστον Ιησουν, G, Tert., Aug., Pelag.; Ιησουν Χριστον, DKLP, etc., syrsch.
cop.   Cf. note on ver. 4.

[3] εορακα, ℵB*DcGP; so Tisch., W.H., Nestle.   See Wr., p. 108.

[4] σφραγις μου της αποστολης: ℵBP 17, 46.

to put a σκάνδαλον (cl. σκανδάληθρον, trap-stick = πρόσκομμα, 9) in another's way," cf. Rom. xiv. 21 and parls. The strong negation οὐ μή ("no fear lest": see Wr., p. 634 ff.) is further heightened by εἰς τὸν αἰῶνα, "to eternity". The rendering "while the world standeth" is based on the use of αἰῶν (perpetuity) in such passages as i. 20, where the context narrows its meaning; in this phrase the noun has its full sense, but used rhetorically.

§ 27. Paul's Apostolic Status, ix. 1-6. The Ap. is ready to forego his right to use the idolothyta, wherever this claim hurts the susceptibilities of any brother (viii. 13). He is "free" as any man in Cor. in such respects; more than this, he is "an apostle" (ix. 1), and the Church of Cor. is witness to the fact, being itself his answer to all challengers (2 f.). If so, he has the right to look to his Churches for maintenance, and that in the ordinary comfort of married life—a claim unquestioned in the case of his colleagues in the apostleship (4-6).

Ver. 1. οὐκ εἰμὶ ἐλεύθερος; This question, arising out of the foregoing §, properly comes first. The freedom supposed is that of principle; in ver. 19 it will take a personal complexion. P. is no longer bound by Mosaic restrictions in the matters under dispute (cf. ver. 21, x. 29, Gal. ii. 4, iv. 12, v. 1); he holds the right belonging to every emancipated Christian.—Far beyond this reaches the question, οὐκ εἰμὶ ἀπόστολος; which P. answers by putting two other questions, one to his own consciousness, the other to that of his readers: "Have I not seen Jesus our Lord? Are not you my work in the Lord?"—Ἰησοῦν . . . ἑόρακα (cf.

Acts vii. 55, ix. 5, 17, xxii. 8, xxvi. 15) is a unique expression with P.; it describes not a spiritual apprehension, the γνῶναι Χριστὸν of the believer, nor the ecstatic visions which he had sometimes enjoyed in a state of trance (2 Cor. xii. 1 ff.), but that actual beholding of the human and glorified Redeemer which befell him on the way to Damascus; from this dated both his faith and his mission (Acts ix. 1-32, Gal. i. 10-17). Paul seldom uses "Jesus" as the name of our Lord distinctively, always with specific ref. to the historical Person (cf. xii. 3, 1, 1 Thess. iv. 14; Eph. iv. 21; Phil. ii. 10; 2 Cor. iv. 10-14). The visible and glorious man who then appeared, declared Himself as "Jesus"; from that instant Saul knew that he had seen the crucified Jesus risen and reigning. Asking of his new-found Lord, "What wilt Thou have me to do?" he received the command out of which his commission unfolded itself. Personal knowledge of the Lord and a "word from His mouth" (Acts xxii. 14) were necessary to constitute an Apostle in the primary sense, the immediate "emissary" of Jesus (cf. Mark iii. 13, Acts i. 21 f.); in virtue of this experience, P. classes himself with "the other App." (xv. 7 ff., Gal. i. 16 f.); his right to do so was in due time acknowledged by them (Gal. ii. 6-9). The great interview, in its full import, was Paul's own secret; his Apostolic power, derived therefrom, was manifest to the whole world (2 Cor. iii. 1 ff., xii. 12), the Cor. Church supplying a conspicuous proof.

Vv. 2, 3. If not at Corinth amongst those who cried "I am of Cephas," elsewhere Paul's apostleship was denied by the Judaistic party, against whom he

g 2 Cor. vii.
11; Phil.
i. 7, 16; 2
Tim. iv.
16; 1 Pet.
iii. 15
(with

3. ἡ ἐμὴ ᵍἀπολογία τοῖς ἐμὲ ʰἀνακρίνουσιν αὕτη ¹ ἐστί · **4.** ¹μὴ ¹οὐκ ᵏἔχομεν ᵏἐξουσίαν φαγεῖν καὶ πιεῖν ² ; **5.** ¹μὴ ¹οὐκ ᵏἔχομεν ᵏἐξουσίαν ἀδελφὴν ³ γυναῖκα ³ ¹περιάγειν, ὡς καὶ οἱ λοιποὶ ᵐἀπό-

dat.); Acts xxii. 1, xxv. 16. h See ii. 14. i xi. 22; Rom. x. 18 f. k See vii. 37. l Trans.,
N.T. *h.l.*; Ezek. xxxvii. 2. *Cf.* Acts xiii. 11; Mt. iv. 23, etc. m In this sense, xii. 28 f., xv. 7,
9; 2 Cor. xi. 5 (?); Gal. i. 17, 19; Eph. ii. 20, iii. 5, iv. 11; 1 Th. ii. 6; 2 Pet. iii. 2; Gospp. and
Acts, *passim*.

¹ εστιν αυτη (in this order) : ℵABP 17, 37, 46.

² πειν, B*; or πιν, ℵ*D*G. See Wr., p. 112.

³ Clem. Al., Hier., Aug., Hil., with the arm. vers., read γυναικας or αδελφας
γυναικας, conforming the obj. to εχομεν.

had afterwards to write 2 Cor. x. ff. In this trial he counts on the Cor. standing by him: "If to others I am no apostle, at any rate (ἀλλά γε, *at certe*, Bz.) I am *to you*". He does not say "*of* others," as though distinguishing two fields of jurisdiction in the sense of Gal. ii. 8, rather "*in the eyes of* others"; *cf.* the dat. of viii. 6. For ἀλλά γε, *cf.* Plato, *Gorg.*, 470 D., εἰ δὲ μὴ (δρῶ), ἀλλ' ἀκούω γε.—γε throws its emphasis on ὑμῖν; so P. continues: "The seal of my apostleship *you* are, in the Lord"; *cf.* Rom. iv. 11, 2 Cor. i. 22. This seal came from the hand of the Lord, affixed by the Master to His servant's work (*cf.* 2 Cor. iii. 1 ff.). Despite its imperfections, the Cor. Church was a shining evidence of Paul's commission; it was probably the largest Church as yet raised in his independent ministry. For ἐν Κυρίῳ, see note on iv. 15, and vii. 22.—"*This*"—referring to vv. 1, 2—"is my answer to those that put me on my defence": I point them to you!—ἀπολογία (see parls.) is a *self-exculpation*. For ἀνακρίνω, *cf.* notes on ii. 14 f., iv. 4.—It is Paul's ἀποστολή, not the ἐξουσία of vv. 4 ff., that is called in question; hence the vein of self-defence pervading the Epp. of this period. Granted the *apostleship* (and this the readers cannot deny), the *right* followed as a matter of course: this needed no "apology".

Vv. 4-6. The rights P. vindicates for himself and his fellow-labourers in the Gospel, are (*a*) the right *to maintenance*; (*b*) *to marriage*; (*c*) *to release from manual labour*.—(*a*) μὴ οὐκ ἔχομεν; "Is it that we have not?"—ironical question, as in xi. 22—"Of course we have". P. writes in pl. *collegas includens* (Bg.), the ἀποστολή suggesting οἱ λοιποὶ mentioned in the next ver.—ἐξουσίαν φαγεῖν καὶ πεῖν (later Gr. for πιεῖν), "right to eat and drink,"—*sc.* as guests of the Church: see

Mark vi. 10, Luke x. 7, xxii. 30. The added καὶ πεῖν, and the illustrations of vv. 7 and 13, show that the obj. of the two vbs. is not the idolothyta, but the material provision for Christ's apostles, supplied by those they serve (11); this ἐξουσία is analogous to, not parl. with, that of viii. 9, belonging not to the ἐλεύθερος as such, but to the ἀπόστολος; *cf.* the *Didaché*, 13, "Every true prophet is worthy of his food". George Fox characteristically notes the moderation of the demand: "The Ap. said 'Have I not power to eat and to drink?' But he did not say, 'to take tithes, Easter reckonings, Midsummer dues, augmentations, and great sums of money'." ἐξουσίαν, as a verbal noun, governs the bare inf., like ἔξεστιν.—(*b*) Paul claims, in order to renounce, the ἐξουσίαν ἀδελφὴν γυναῖκα περιάγειν—the "right to take about (with us) a sister as wife"—*i.e.*, a Christian wife: brachyology for "to have a Christian sister to wife, and take her about with us".—ἀδελφὴν is obj., γυναῖκα objective complement to περιάγειν, on which the stress lies; "non ex habendo, sed ex circumducendo sumtus afferebatur ecclesiis" (Bg.). The Clementine Vg. rendering, *mulierem sororem circumducendi* (as though from γυν. ἀδελφ.), gives a sense at variance both with grammar and decorum, not to be justified by Luke viii. 2 f. This misinterpreted text was used in defence of the scandalous practice of priests and monks keeping as "sisters" γυναῖκες συνεισακτοί, which was condemned by the Nicene Council, and often subsequently; so Jerome (Ep. 23, *ad Eustoch.*), "Agapetarum pestis . . . sine nuptiis aliud nomen uxorum . . . novum concubinarum genus" (see Suicer's *Thesaurus, s. vv.* Ἀγαπητή, Ἀδελφή).—From the ὡς καὶ clause it appears that "the rest of the App.," generally speaking, were married, and their wives often travelled

στολοι καὶ οἱ ⁿ ἀδελφοὶ τοῦ ⁿ Κυρίου καὶ ° Κηφᾶς; 6. ἢ μόνος ἐγὼ ⁿ Gal. i. 19; Acts i. 14; Mt. xii. 46 ff., xiii. 55; Jo. ii. 12, vii. 3, 5, 10. ° 12, iii. 22, xv. 5; Gal.

καὶ Βαρνάβας, οὐκ ᵏ ἔχομεν ᵏ ἐξουσίαν τοῦ¹ μὴ ᵖ ἐργάζεσθαι;

7. Τίς ᑫ στρατεύεται ἰδίοις ʳ ὀψωνίοις ˢ ποτέ; τίς ᵗ φυτεύει ᵗᵘ ἀμπε-

λῶνα καὶ ἐκ² τοῦ² καρποῦ² αὐτοῦ οὐκ ἐσθίει; ἢ³ τίς ᵛ ποιμαίνει

▨i. 18, ii. 9 ff., Jo. i. 43. p In this usage, Rom. iv. 4 f.; 1 Th. ii. 9; 2 Th. iii. 8 ff.; see iv. 12. qᵒ2 Cor. x. 3; 1 Tim. i. 18; 2 Tim. ii. 4; Jas. iv. 1; 1 Pet. ii. 11; Lk. iii. 14; Isa. xxix. 7. r 2 Cor. xi. ▨8; Rom. vi. 23; Lk. iii. 14; 1 Esdr. iv. 56; 1 Macc. iii. 28, xiv. 32. s In this use, Heb. i. 5, 13; ▨cf. Eph. v. 29. t See iii. 6; with αμπ., Deut. xx. 6. u Mt. xx. 1 ff., xxi. 28 ff.; Lk. xiii. 6; Isa. ▨v. 1 ff., etc. v Vb., 1 Pet. v. 2 and Acts xx. 28 (ποιμνιον); Jude 12; Rev. ii. 27, etc., vii. 17; Jo. ▨xxi. 16; Mt. ii. 6; Lk. xvii. 7 (with αροτριοω); 1 Ki. xxv. 16. Noun, Mt. xxvi. 31; Lk. ii. 8; Jo. x. ▨16; Gen. xxxii. 16.

¹ Om. τ ο υ all pre-Syrian uncc.

² τ ο ν κ α ρ π ο ν: all pre-Syrian uncc. εκ των καρπων, C³, Dam.

³ Om. η (?) BC²DG, latt. vg. sah. Tr., W.H., and Nestle bracket. η retained by ℵAC*KLP, cop. BDG is a suspicious group (W.H.).

with them; the "forsaking" of Luke xviii. 28-30 was not final (in the parl. Matt. xix. 28 f., Mark x. 28 ff., γυνὴ does not appear); according to tradition, John however was celibate. "The brothers of the Lord" were also orthodox Jews in this respect (on their relationship to Jesus, see Lt., *Essay* in Comm. on Galatians); indeed, they came near to founding a kind of Christian dynasty in Jerus. "And Cephas," separately mentioned as the most eminent instance of the married Christian missionary. The association of the ἀδελφοὶ τ. Κυρ. with the ἀπόστολοι does not prove that they were counted amongst these, or bore this title of office; while distinguished from the latter by their specific name (*cf.* Gal. i. 19), they are linked with them as persons of like eminence; see the position of James in Acts.—(*c*) The third ἐξουσία, μὴ ἐργάζεσθαι, Paul and his old comrade Barnabas had laid aside. Barn. had stripped himself of property at Jerus. in the early days (Acts iv. 36 f.); and he and P. together, in the pioneer mission of Acts xiii. f., worked their way as handicraftsmen. Now separated, they both continued this practice, which was exceptional—μόνος ἐγὼ κ. Βαρνάβας. The allusion implies wide-spread knowledge of the career of Barn., which ends for us at Acts xv. 39. Notwithstanding the παροξυσμὸς in which they parted, the two great missionaries remained in friendly alliance; *cf.* Paul's reff. to Mark, Barnabas' cousin, in Col. iv. 10, 2 Tim. iv. 11. For ἐργάζομαι, as denoting *manual* labour, see parls.; a cl. usage, like that of Eng. *workmen*. This third ἐξουσία was the negative side of the first (*cf.* 1 Thess. ii. 9, also 2 Cor. xi. 9, and ἀδάπανον θήσω of 18 below).—The three

rights in fact amount to the *one* which Paul argues for in the sequel: he might justly have imposed his personal support, and that in the more expensive character of a married man, upon the Christian communities for which he laboured, thus sparing himself the disadvantages and hardships of manual toil.

§ 28. The Claim of Ministers to Public Maintenance, ix. 7-15*a*. Paul asserts his right to live at the charge of the Christian community, in order to show the Cor. how he has waived this prerogative (15*b*, etc.). But before doing this, he will further vindicate the right; for it was sure to be disputed, and his renunciation might be used to the disadvantage of other servants of Christ. He therefore formally establishes the claim: (*a*) on grounds of natural analogy (7); (*b*) by proof from Scripture (8-10); (*c*) by the intrinsic justice of the case (11); (*d*) by comparison with O.T. practice (13); finally (*e*) by ref. to the express commandment of the Lord (14). In ver. 12 he indicates, by the way, that "others" of inferior standing are making themselves chargeable on the Cor. Church.

Ver. 7 puts the question under three figures—virtual arguments from nature—drawn from the *camp*, the *vineyard*, the *flock*. These figures had been similarly used by our Lord: (1) in Luke xi. 21 f., xiv. 31; (2) in Matt. xx. 1 ff., xxi. 28 ff.; (3) in Luke xii. 32, John x., and xxi. 15 ff. *Cf.* in Paul for (1) xiv. 8, Eph. vi. 10 ff., 1 Thess. v. 8; (2) iii. 6 ff.; (3) Acts xx. 28, Eph. iv. 11. On ὀψωνίοις, see Gm.: it denotes primarily "rations" served out in lieu of pay; then military "stipends" of any kind; then "wages" generally; see parls.—ἰδίοις ὀψων., not

w See iii. 3. ᵛποίμνην καὶ ἐκ τοῦ γάλακτος τῆς ᵛποίμνης οὐκ ἐσθίει; 8. μὴ
x η και, xvi.
6 (?); 2   ᵂκατὰ ᵂἄνθρωπον ταῦτα λαλῶ,¹ ˣἢ οὐχὶ² ˣκαὶ ὁ νόμος ταῦτα
Cor. i. 13;
Rom. ii.   λέγει²; 9. ἐν γὰρ τῷ Μωσέως³ νόμῳ γέγραπται,⁴ "Οὐ ᵞφιμώσεις⁵
15; Lk. xi.
11 f., xviii. βοῦν ᶻἀλοῶντα· μὴ ᵃτῶν βοῶν ᵃμέλει τῷ Θεῷ, 10. ἢ δι' ἡμᾶς
11. In-
terrog.   ᵇπάντως λέγει; δι' ἡμᾶς γὰρ ἐγράφη, ὅτι ᵈἐπ' ᵈἐλπίδι⁶ ᶜὀφείλει⁶
as here,
Rom. iv.
9; Lk. xii. 41.   y κημωσεις, if genuine, h.l. φιμωσεις. Deut. xxv. 4; so 1 Tim. v. 18; 1 Pet. ii. 15;
Mt. xxii. 12, 34; Mk. i. 25, etc. See txtl. and exegetical notes.   z 1 Tim. v. 18 (Deut. xxv. 4);
1 Chron. xxi. 20.   a See vii. 21. With gen., N.T. h.l.; usually περι, Mt. xxii. 16, etc.   b See v. 10.
c See vii. 36.   d Rom. iv. 18, v. 2, viii. 20; Tit. i. 2; Acts ii. 26 (Psa. xvi. 9), xxvi. 6.

¹ λεγω, DG—characteristic Western alteration.

² η και ο νομος ταυτα ου λεγει; ℵABCD 46.
η ει και ο νομος ταυτα λεγει; G, arm. T.R. in KLP, etc.

³ Μωϋσεως: all uncc. but A. So passim.

⁴ γεγραπται γαρ (om. rest of clause): DG, Hil., etc.—Western emendation.

⁵ κημωσεις (?), B*D*G, Chr., Thdrt., Cyr. So Tisch., Tr., Al., El., Nestle, W.H.
marg. See note 3 on last p.; on the other hand, κημ. is h.l., and φιμ. might
easily be borrowed from Deut.
φιμωσεις, ℵAB³CDᵇᶜKLP, etc. So Lachm., W.H. txt., and R.V.

⁶ οφειλει επ' ελπιδι (in this order): pre-Syrian non-Western uncc.

"at his proper pay," but "at his private
(as distinguished from public) charges":
cf. xi. 21, Gal. ii. 2. The use of ποτὲ
to widen negative, interr. (virtually negative), and hypothetical propositions, common in cl. Greek, is infrequent in N.T.
—In the third question, a partitive ἐκ with
gen. replaces the acc., the image suggesting a share: "the shepherd is still
remunerated in the East by a share of
the milk" (Mr.); or is P. thinking of the
solid food (ἐσθίει) which comes "out of
the milk"? For the cognate acc., ποιμαίνει ποίμνην, cf. 1 Peter v. 2, also
John x. 16.

Vv. 8-10a. μὴ κατὰ ἄνθρωπον κ.τ.λ.;
"Am I saying these things as any man
might do"—in accordance with human
practice (as just seen in 7)?—κατὰ ἄνθρ.,
in contrast with what ὁ νόμος λέγει; cf.
Gal. iii. 15 ff. This dialectic use of μή, ἢ
or ἢ καί, in a train of questions, is very
Pauline; ἢ καὶ recommends the second
alternative; cf. Rom. iv. 9, Luke xii. 41.
—"The law" is abolished as a means of
obtaining salvation (Rom iii. 19 ff., etc.);
it remains a revelation of truth and right
(Rom. vii. 12 ff.), and P. draws from it
guidance for Christian conduct; cf. xiv.
34, Rom. xiii. 8 ff., and (comprehensively)
Rom. viii. 4. The ethics of the N.T. are
those of the Old, enhanced by Christ (see
Matt. v. 17 ff.). Paul speaks however
here, somewhat distantly, of the "law of
Moses" (cf. vv. 20 f., x. 2); but of "the
law of Christ" in Gal. vi. 2 (cf. John i.
17, viii. 17, x. 34, xv. 25).—Οὐ φιμώσεις
κ.τ.λ., "Thou shalt not muzzle a thresh-

ing ox," cited to the same effect in 1
Tim. v. 18,—οὐ with fut. reproducing the
Heb. lo' with impf. of emphatic prohibition. Deut. xxv. 4, detached where it
stands, belongs to a series of Mosaic
commands enjoining humane treatment
of animals, regarded as being in some
sense a part of the sacred community:
cf. Exod. xx. 10, xxiii. 12, 19, Deut. xxii.
4, 6 f., 10. Corn was threshed either by
the feet of cattle (Mic. iv. 12 f.), or by a
sledge driven over the threshing-floor (2
Sam xxiv. 22).—μὴ τῶν βοῶν μέλει τῷ
Θεῷ κ.τ.λ.; "Is it for the oxen that God
cares, or on our account, by all means,
does He say (it)?" The argumentative
πάντως (cf. Rom. iii. 9, Luke iv. 23), "on
every ground"—slightly diff. in ver. 22,
more so in v. 10: not that "God is concerned wholly (exclusively) for us" in this
rule; but on every account a provision
made for the beasts in man's service must
hold good, à fortiori, for God's proper
servants; cf. Matt. vi. 26 ff., also x. 31,
xii. 12. δι' ἡμᾶς, emphatically repeated,
signifies not men as against oxen, but nos
evangelii ministros (Est.) in analogy to
oxen; the right of Christ's ministers "to
eat and drink" is safeguarded by the
principle that gives the ox his provender
out of the corn he treads. Paul's method
in such interpretations is radically diff.
from that of Philo, who says, Οὐ ὑπὲρ
τῶν ἀλόγων ὁ νόμος, ἀλλ' ὑπὲρ τῶν νοῦν
κ. λόγον ἐχόντων, De Victim. offer., § 1:
Philo destroys the historical sense; Paul
extracts its moral principle.

Ver. 10b. δι' ἡμᾶς γάρ (cf. 1 Thess.

ὁ ᵉἀροτριῶν ᵉἀροτριᾷ, καὶ ὁ ᶻἀλοῶν τῆς¹ ἐλπίδος¹ αὐτοῦ¹ ᶠμετέχειν ᵉ Lk. xvii. 7
ᵈἐπ' ᵈἐλπίδι.¹ 11. εἰ ἡμεῖς ὑμῖν τὰ ᵍπνευματικὰ ʰἐσπείραμεν, (see note v); Deut. xxii. 10.
ⁱμέγα ⁱεἰ ἡμεῖς ὑμῶν τὰ ᵍσαρκικὰ ᵏθερίσομεν²; 12a. εἰ ἄλλοι τῆς ᶠx. 17 ff.; Heb. ii.
ˡἐξουσίας³ ˡὑμῶν³ᶠμετέχουσιν, οὐ μᾶλλον ἡμεῖς; 12b. ἀλλ' οὐκ ᵐἐχρη- 14, v. 13, vii. 13;
σάμεθα τῇ ˡἐξουσίᾳ ταύτῃ · ἀλλὰ πάντα ⁿστέγομεν, ἵνα μὴ ᵒᵖἐγκο- Prov. i. 18, etc.
g In this

contrast, iii. 1; Rom. vii. 14 (σαρκίνος), xv. 27; cf. Eph. vi. 12, etc.   h In this sense, 2 Cor. ix. 6,
10; Gal. vi. 7 f.; Jas. iii. 18.   i 2 Cor. xi. 15; Gen. xlv. 28; Isa. xlix. 6.   k 2 Cor. ix. 6; Mt. xxv.
24, 26; Jo. iv. 36; Ps. cxxv. 5.   l With obj. gen., Rom. ix. 21; Mt. x. 1; Jo. xvii. 2; Sir. x. 4, xvii. 2.
m See vii. 21.   n xiii. 7; 1 Th. iii. 1, 5; Sir. viii. 17. ¦Only Pauline in N.T.   o N.T. h.l. -πτω,
Rom. xv. 22; Gal. v. 7; 1 Th. ii. 18; 1 Pet. iii. 7; Acts xxiv. 4.   p προσκ. διδ., 2 Cor. vi. 3.

¹ ἐπ' ελπιδι του μετεχειν: א*A (εφ') BCP 17, syrr. sah. cop., Or., Eus.,
Cyr., Aug.; in spe fructus percipiendi, vg., Pelag.
της ελπιδος αυτου μετεχειν: DG.
T.R. a conflate (Syrian) reading, combining the Western and non-Western texts.
² θερισωμεν, CDGLP, above thirty minn.; metamus, latt. vg., Latt. Ff.: by itacism.
³ της υμων εξουσιας (in this order): all uncc. but KL.

ii. 20, for γὰρ in affirm. reply) κ.τ.λ.:
"Yes, it was written on our account (cf.
Rom. iv. 23 f.)—(to wit), that the plough-
ing (ox) ought to plough in hope, and the
threshing (ox) in hope of partaking"
(ἐπ' ἐλπίδι τοῦ μετέχειν). The explanatory ὅτι clause (cf. i. 5, 26, iv. 9 and
note) restates and amplifies the previous
quotation. The Ap. is not explaining
how the command came to be given
("because," E.V.), but unfolding the
principle that lies in it.—The right of
the ox in threshing also belongs in equity
to the ox at the plough; all contributors
to the harvest are included, whether at
an earlier or later stage.—ὀφείλει, emphatic—debet (Vg.): the hope of participation in the fruit is due to the labourer
—beast or man. The moral, as applied
to Christian teachers, is obvious; it embraces the successive stages of the common work (cf. iii. 9, John iv. 36).—
ἀροτριᾶν (sometimes "to sow"; so El.
and some others here) contains the root
of the Lat. aro and older Eng. ear.

Vv. 11, 12a appeal to the sense of
justice in the Cor.; τὸ δίκαιον δείκνυσιν
τοῦ πράγματος (Thp.): cf. Gal. vi. 6.—
μέγα εἰ . . .; "Is it a great thing if
. . . ?" = "Is it a great thing to ask (or
look for) that . . . ?" cf. 2 Cor. xi. 15; the
construction is akin to that of θαυμάζω εἰ
(see Gm., s.v. Εἰ, i., 4)—a kind of litotes,
suggesting where one might have vigor-
ously asserted. The repeated collocation ἡμεῖς ὑμῖν, ἡμεῖς ὑμῶν, brings
out the personal nature of this claim:
"We sowed for you the things of the
Spirit; should not we reap from you the
(needed) carnal things?"—τὰ πνευματικὰ
(cf. ii. 12, xii. 1-13, Rom. viii. 2, 5 f., Gal.

v. 22, etc.) include all the distinctive boons
of the Christian faith; "the carnal
things" embrace, besides food and drink
(4), all suitable bodily "goods" (Gal. vi.
6).—The question of ver. 12a assumes that
other Christian teachers received maintenance from the Cor. Church; the claim
of Paul and his fellow-missioners was
paramount (cf. iv. 15; also 2 Cor. x.
12-18, xi. 12 ff., 20, where this comparison comes up in a new form).—ὑμῶν is
surely gen. of object, as in Matt. x. 1
(= ἐξουσίαν ἐπὶ, Luke ix. 1), John xvii.
2,—"the claim upon you". Ev. and Ed.
read the pron. as subjective gen.,—the
latter basing the phrase on iii. 22 f.—sc.
"if others share in your domain," instead of "in dominion over you"; this
rendering is sound in grammar, and has
a basis in iv. 7-12, but lies outside the
scope of ἐξουσία in this context. The
expression "others participate" suggests
a right belonging to these "others"
in a lesser degree (cf. μετέχω in 10): the
πατὴρ should be first honoured, then the
παιδαγωγοί (iv. 15).

Ver. 12b. "But we did not use this
right"—i.e., P. and his comrades in the
Cor. mission (2 Cor. i. 19).—ἀλλὰ πάντα
στέγομεν: "Nay, we put up with everything (omnia sustinemus, Vg.), lest we
should cause any (kind of) hindrance to
the good news about Christ".—στέγω
(see parls.), syn. in later Gr. with ὑπο-
μένω, βαστάζω, "marks the patient and
enduring spirit with which the Ap. puts
up with all the consequences naturally
resulting from" his policy of abstinence
(El.). What this involved we have partly
seen in iv. 11 ff.; cf. 2 Cor. xi. 27, Acts
xx. 34.—The ἐνκοπὴ he sought to obviate

πήν [1] τινα [1] [p] δῶμεν τῷ εὐαγγελίῳ τοῦ Χριστοῦ. 13. [q] οὐκ [q] οἴδατε ὅτι οἱ τὰ [r] ἱερὰ [r] ἐργαζόμενοι ἐκ [2] τοῦ ἱεροῦ ἐσθίουσιν, οἱ τῷ [s] θυσιαστηρίῳ [t] προσεδρεύοντες [3] τῷ [s] θυσιαστηρίῳ [u] συμμερίζονται;
14. οὕτω καὶ ὁ Κύριος [v] διέταξε τοῖς τὸ εὐαγγέλιον [w] καταγγέλλουσιν [x] ἐκ τοῦ εὐαγγελίου [v x] ζῆν. 15a. ἐγὼ δὲ οὐδενὶ [4] [m] ἐχρησάμην [4] τούτων.

q See iii. 16.
r *H.l.* *Adj.*, 2 Tim. iii. 15; Josh. vi. 7; 2 Macc. v. 16, etc. *Vb.*, in this use, Jer. xxxvii. 9.
s x. 18; Rom. xi. 3 (3 Kings xix. 10); Heb. vii. 13, xiii. 10; Mt. v. 23, etc.; Rev. vi. 9, etc.
t παρεδρ., N.T. *h.l.*; *cf.* vii. 35; Prov. i. 21.
u *H.l.*
v With dat., xvi. 1; Tit. i. 5; Mt. xi. 1; Acts xxiii. 31, xxiv. 23. With inf., Lk. viii. 55; Acts xviii. 2, xxiv. 23. With dat. and inf., thus, *h.l.*
w See ii. 1.
x Rom. i. 17 and Heb. x. 31 (Hab. ii. 4); *cf.* Mt. iv. 4 (Deut. viii. 3).

[1] **τινα εγκοπην** (in this order): ℵABC 17, 46. **εκκοπην**, ℵD*L; Tisch. **ενκοπην**, BG; W.H., Nestle.

[2] **τα εκ**: ℵBD*G 46. Om. **τα** ACD[bc]KLP (Alex. and Syrian).

[3] **παρεδρευοντες**: all uncc. but ℵ[c]KL.

[4] **ου κεχρημαι ουδενι**: all uncc. but K.

(military term of later Gr., from **ἐνκόπτω**, *to cut into*, *break up*, a road, so *to hinder* a march) lay (*a*) in the reproach of venality, as old as Socrates and the Sophists, attaching to the acceptance of remuneration by a wandering teacher, which his enemies desired to fasten on Paul (1 Thess. ii. 3 ff., 2 Cor. xi. 7 ff., xii. 13 ff.); and (*b*) in the fact that P. would have shackled his movements by taking wages from particular Churches (19), so giving them a lien upon his ministrations. For the Hebraistic phrase **ἐνκοπὴν δίδωμι** (= **ἐνκόπτω**), *cf.* xiv. 7, 2 Thess. i. 8.—**τοῦ Χριστοῦ** is always *obj.* gen. after **εὐαγγέλιον**; see Rom. i. 2 f., also **μαρτύριον τ. Χριστοῦ**, i. 6 above.

Vv. 13, 14. After the personal "aside" of vv. 11 f., Paul returns to his main proof, deriving a further reason for the disputed **ἐξουσία** from the Temple service. "Do you not know"—you men of knowledge (*cf.* iii. 16)—**ὅτι οἱ τὰ ἱερὰ ἐργαζόμενοι ἐκ τοῦ ἱεροῦ ἐσθίουσιν**; "that those employed in the sacred offices eat what comes from the sacred place (the Temple)?"—"qui sacris operantur, ex sacrario edunt" (Cv.): see the rules *ad hoc* in Lev. vi. 8-vii. 38 and Num. xviii. 8-19. For **ἐργάζομαι** (of *business*, *employment*), *cf.* iv. 12, Acts xviii. 3, etc.—"Those that are assiduous at the altar," *qui altari assident* (Bz.)—*i.e.*, the priests engaged in the higher ritual functions—are distinguished from other Temple ministers; the position of Paul and his colleagues is analogous to that of these chief dignitaries.—**παρεδρεύω**, *to have one's seat beside*; *cf.* **εὐπάρεδρον**, vii. 35. P. argues by analogy from the Jewish priest to the Christian minister in respect of *the claim to maintenance*; we cannot infer from this *an identity of function*, any more than in the previous comparison with "the threshing ox".—**τ. θυσιαστηρίῳ συνμερίζονται**, "have their portion with the altar," *i.e.*, share with it in the sacrifices—"altaris esse socios in dividendo victimas" (Bz.); parts of these were consumed in the altar-fire, and parts reserved for the priests (Lev. x. 12-15). Some refer the first half of ver. 13 to Gentile and the last to Israelite practice; but "with the Ap., **τὸ ἱερὸν** is only *the sanctuary* of the God of Israel, **τὸ θυσιαστήριον** only *the altar* on which sacrifice is made to Him" (Hf.): *cf.* Acts xxii. 17, etc., and the Gospels *passim*, as to **ἱερόν**; x. 18, as to **θυσιαστήριον**; *cf.* x. 1-12, for the use in this Ep. of O.T. analogies.—"So also (in accordance with this precedent) did the Lord appoint for those that preach the good tidings to live of the good tidings."—**ἐκ τ. εὐαγγ.** in ver. 14 matches **ἐκ τ. ἱεροῦ**, ver. 13; **τοῖς . . . καταγγέλλουσιν, τοῖς . . . ἐργαζομένοις**: *cf.* **ἱερουργοῦντα τ. εὐαγγ. τ. Θεοῦ**, Rom. xv. 16.—For the "ordinance" of "the Lord" (*sc.* Jesus), see parls.; the allusion speaks for detailed knowledge of the sayings of Jesus, on the part of writer and readers; *cf.* vii. 10, xi. 23 ff., and notes.—**διατάσσω**, act., as in vii. 17, xi. 34; mid. in xvi. 1.—**ζῆν ἐκ**, of source of livelihood (*ex quo quod evangelium prædicant*, Bz.), in cl. Gr. often **ζῆν ἀπὸ** (see parls.). For **καταγγέλλω**, see note on ii. 1.

Ver. 15*a*. "But for my part, I have used none of these things:" does Paul mean "none of the privileges" included in the above **ἐξουσία**? or "none of the

15b. Οὐκ ἔγραψα δὲ ταῦτα ἵνα οὕτω γένηται [y] ἐν ἐμοί· [za] καλὸν [y] So used,
γάρ μοι [a] μᾶλλον ἀποθανεῖν ἢ τὸ [b] καύχημά μου ἵνα [1] τις [1] [c] κενώσῃ.[2]   Mt. xvii.
16. ἐὰν γὰρ [d] εὐαγγελίζωμαι, οὐκ ἔστι μοι [b] καύχημα· [e] ἀνάγκη γάρ   12; Lk.
                                                                          xxii. 37,
μοι [ef] ἐπίκειται, [g] οὐαὶ δέ μοι [g] ἐστὶν ἐὰν μὴ [d] εὐαγγελίζωμαι.[3]   xxiii. 31;
                                                                          Jo. xiv.30;
                                                                          1 Jo. iv.9.
                                                                          z See vii. 1.
Acts xx. 35; cf. Phil. i. 23.   b See v. 6.   c See i. 17.   d See i. 17, for absol. use.   a Mk. ix. 42;
37. *Iliad*, vi. 458, κρατερὴ δ' ἐπεκείσετ' ἀνάγκη.   f Heb. ix. 10; Acts xxvii. 20;   e See vii.
g Jude 11; Syn. Gospp., Rev., *passim*; with εστιν, N.T. *h.l.*; Hos. ix. 12.   Jo. xi. 35.

[1] ουδεις, א*BD* 17, sah. basm., Tert., Ambrst. ουθεις μη, A.
τις (interr.), G 26. ινα τις : אcCDbcKLP, etc., vg., Bas., Chr., Hier., Aug.

[2] κενωσει, all uncc. but K.

[3] ευαγγελισωμαι (?), BCDG, vg., Aug., Ambrst. So Tr., W.H. *txt.*, Nestle.
ευαγγελιζωμαι, אAK (LP, -ζομαι), etc.; Tisch., W.H. *marg.*
The Westerns (DG, etc.) have -ισωμαι *twice* in this ver.

reasons" by which they have been enforced (so Hf., Hn., the former with exclusive ref. to 13 f.)? The parl. sentence
of ver. 12, and the οὕτως γένηται of the
next clause, are decisive for the former
view. "The authority" in question included a number of rights (4 ff.), *all* of
which P. has foregone.—ἐγὼ emphasises,
in preparation for the sequel, and in distinction from the broader statement of
ver. 12, etc., Paul's individual position in
the matter; and the pf. κέχρημαι (replacing the historical aor. of 12) affirms a
settled position; the refusal has become
a rule. From this point to the end of
the ch. the Ap. writes in the 1st sing.,
revealing his inner thoughts respecting
the conduct of his own ministry.

§ 30. PAUL'S RENOUNCEMENT OF
RIGHT FOR THE GOSPEL'S SAKE, ix.
15b-23. The Ap. has been insisting all
this time on the right of Christ's ministers
to material support from those they serve,
in order that for his own part he may
explicitly renounce it. This renunciation
is his "boast," and his "reward"; of his
office he cannot boast, nor seek reward
for it, since it was imposed upon him
(15-18). In this abnegation P. finds his
freedom, which he uses to make himself
impartially the slave of all; untrammelled
by any particular ties, he is able to adapt
himself to every condition and class of
men, and thus to win for the Gospel
larger gains (19-22). For himself, his
best hope is to partake in its salvation
with those he strives to save (23).

Ver. 15b. "Now I have not written
this (4-14) in order that it should be so
done (*viz.*, provision made for 'living of
the gospel') in my case." The epistolary ἔγραψα may refer either to a whole
letter now completed (Rom. xv. 15), or
to words just written (Wr., p. 347; *cf.*

v. 11).—ἐν ἐμοί (the sphere of application), "in the range of my work and responsibility," not "to me" (dat. of person
advantaged, as in vv. 20 ff.); *cf.* iv. 2, 6.
—On the best-attested reading, καλὸν
γάρ μοι μᾶλλον ἀποθανεῖν ἤ—τὸ καύχημά
μου οὐδεὶς κενώσει, the sentence is interrupted at ἤ: "For it is well for me
rather to die than"—P. breaks off, im-
patient of the very thought of pecuniary
dependence (*cf.* 2 Cor. xi. 10), and instead of completing the comparison by
the words "that any one should make
void my boast," he exclaims vehemently,
"My boast no one shall make void!" (so
Al., Ed.). μᾶλλον ἤ qualifies the whole
clause, not καλὸν alone. This anacoluthon, or aposiopesis, if it has no exact
parl. in the N.T., is only an extreme
instance of Pauline *oratio variata* (such as
appears, *e.g.*, in Gal. ii. 4 f. and again
in ver. 6, and in Rom. v. 12-15), where an
extended sentence forgets its beginning,
throwing itself suddenly into a new
shape; this occurred in a smaller way in
vii. 37 above. Strong feeling (*cf.* 2 Cor.
xi. 9 ff., on the same point) is apt to disorder Paul's grammar in this way. He
began to say that he *would rather die
than be dependent* on Cor. pay; he ends
by saying, absolutely, he *will never be so
dependent*. The T.R. attempts to patch
the rent.—Other explanations of the older
txt. are given : (*a*) Lachmann puts a stop
after καύχ. μου—"Better for me to die
than my boast; no one shall make it
void!" (*b*) Mr. and Bt. make ἤ disjunctive, despite the μᾶλλον : "Better for me
to die—or (*sc.* if I live) no one shall make
void my boast!" (*c*) Ev. and El. read
οὐδεὶς κενώσει as equivalent to ἵνα τις
κενώσει, supposing ἵνα to be understood
and the οὐ to be pleonastic—expedients
for which there is a precarious grammati-

h Rom. viii.
20; Exod.
xxi. 13.
i See iii. 8.
With εχω,
Mt. vi. 1
ff.; cf. 2
Jo. 8.

17. εἰ γὰρ ᵸἑκὼν τοῦτο πράσσω, ⁱμισθὸν ⁱἔχω· εἰ δὲ ᵏἄκων, ¹οἰκονομίαν ᵐπεπίστευμαι· 18. τίς οὖν μοι¹ ἐστὶν² ὁ ¹μισθός; ἵνα ᵈεὐαγγελιζόμενος ⁿἀδάπανον ᵒθήσω τὸ εὐαγγέλιον τοῦ³ Χριστοῦ,ᵃ

k N.T. h.l.; Job xiv. 17.   l Eph. i. 10, iii. 2, 9; Col. i. 25; 1 Tim. i. 4; Lk. xvi. 2 ff.;
Isa. xxii. 19, 21. Cf. iv. 1 ff.   m In this sense, Gal. ii. 7; Rom. iii. 2; 1 Th. ii. 4; 1 Tim. i. 11;
Tit. i. 3; Lk. xvi. 11; Jo. ii. 24.   n H.l.   o In this usage, Rom. iv. 17 (Gen. xvii. 5); Mt. xxii.
44 (Ps. cix. 1); Gen. xxxii. 12; Wisd. x. 21. Poetical in cl. Gr.

¹ μου, א*ACK 17, 46, vg. syrsch. sah. cop., Cyr., Hier.
μοι, BD*GLP, etc., Chr., Aug. Seemingly Western.

² εσται μοι: D*G.

³ Om. του Χριστου אABCD* 17, 46, vg. sah. cop.

cal analogy. (d) Lachmann also conjectured ἀποθανεῖν νὴ for ἀποθανεῖν ἤ, Michelsen and Baljon adding the easy insertion of ὃ before οὐδείς : "It is good for me rather to die ! Yea, by my glorying (cf. xv. 31), which no one shall make void." (e) Hf., Gd., and others, in despair fall back on the T.R.

Vv. 16-18. Paul goes on to explain, by two contrasted suppositions (in actual and conceivable matter), that this is a point of honour with him. Forced as he had been into the service of the Gospel, in a manner so diff. from the other App., unless he might serve gratuitously his position would be too humiliating.

Ver. 16. The fact of his preaching supplies in itself no καύχημα: "For if I be preaching the good news (εὐαγγελίζωμαι), it is no (matter of) boasting to me; for necessity is imposed on me". For ἀνάγκη, see notes on vii. 26, 37 ; also Philem. 14, where it contrasts with κατὰ ἐκούσιον as with ἑκὼν here.—'Επίκειμαι is virtually pass. to ἐπιτίθημι (see parls.), "to lay" a task, by authority, "upon" some one : P. was, in the Apostolic ranks, a pressed man, not a volunteer,—"laid hold of" (Phil. iii. 12) against his previous will; he entered Christ's service as a captive enemy (cf. xv. 8, 2 Cor. ii. 14). While a gift of Divine mercy (vii. 25, 2 Cor. iv. 1, etc.), his commission was a determination of the Divine sovereignty (i. 1, etc.). For service rendered upon this footing there can never be any boasting; cf. Luke xvii. 10.—That all glorying in this direction was excluded, is sustained by the exclamation, "For woe is to me if I should not preach the Gospel !" ὅπου τὸ Οὐαὶ παράκειται ἐὰν μὴ ποιῇ, οὐκ ἔχει καύχημα (Or.). —ἐὰν μὴ εὐαγγελίσωμαι (contrast the pr. εὐαγγελίζωμαι, of former clause), aor. sbj., of comprehensive fut. ref., from the standpoint of the original "necessity imposed"; cf., for the con-

struction, viii. 8, xv. 36. The interjection οὐαὶ is here a quasi-substantive, as in Rev. ix. 12. Had P. disobeyed the call of God, his course from that time onwards must have been one of condemnation and misery. To fight against "Necessity" the Greeks conceived as ruin; their 'Ανάγκη was a blind, cruel Fate, Paul's ἀνάγκη is the compulsion of Sovereign Grace.

Ver. 17 completes a chain of four explanatory γάρs (cf. i. 17-21). To make his position clearer, P. puts two further contrasted hypotheses, the former imaginary, the latter suggesting the fact : (a) "For if I am engaged on this (work) of my own free will (ἑκών), I have reward (mercedem habeo)"—sc. the supposed καύχημα of ver. 16, the right to credit his work to himself (cf. Rom. iv. 2, 4); not the future Messianic reward (so Mr. and others), for ἔχω implies attained possession (see parls.), much as ἀπέχω in Matt. vi. 2, etc. For πράσσω, see note on v. 2. (b) "But"—the contrasted matter of fact— "if against my will (ἄκων = ἀνάγκη, 16), with a stewardship I have been entrusted"; cf. iv. 1 f., 1 Tim. i. 12, etc.— The οἰκονόμος (see note, iv. 1), however highly placed, is a slave whose work is chosen for him and whose one merit is faithful obedience. In Paul's consciousness of stewardship there mingled submission to God, gratitude for the trust bestowed, and independence of human control (cf. 19, iv. 3).—The use of πιστεύω in pass. with personal subject and acc. of thing (imitating vbs. of double acc.), is confined to Paul in N.T.; see Wr., pp. 287, 326. Τὸ οἰκονομίαν πεπίστευμαι one tacitly adds, from the contrasted clause, καὶ μισθὸν οὐκ ἔχω: "Christ's bondman, I claim no hire for my stewardship; God's trust is enough for me".

Ver. 18. Yet, after all, Paul has his reward: "What then (οὖν, things being so) is my reward?"—ὁ μισθός, "the

εἰς τὸ μὴ ᵖκαταχρήσασθαι τῇ ᵍἐξουσίᾳ μου ἐν τῷ εὐαγγελίῳ. 19. ᵖ See vii.31.
ᵍ See vii. 37.
ʳἐλεύθερος γὰρ ὢν ʳἐκ πάντων, πᾶσιν ἐμαυτὸν ˢἐδούλωσα, ἵνα ᵗτοὺς ʳ N.T. *h.l.*
With απο,
ᵗπλείονας ᵘκερδήσω· 20. καὶ ἐγενόμην τοῖς Ἰουδαίοις ὡς Ἰουδαῖος, Rom. vi.
18, 22, vii.
3, viii. 2,

21; commonly bare gen. in cl. Gr.   s See vii. 15.   t x. 5, xv. 6; 2 Cor. ii. 6, iv. 15, ix. 2; Phil.
i. 14; Heb. vii. 23; Acts xix. 32, xxvii. 12; Lk. vii. 43; Exod. xxiii. 2.   u 1 Pet. iii. 1 and Mt.
xviii. 15, of *persons*.

reward" proper to such a case, is simply to take no pay : "that, while I preach the good news, I may make the good news free of charge" (ἀδάπανον θήσω, *gratuitum constituam*, Bz.). No thought of *future* (deferred) *pay*, nor of *supererogatory work* beyond the strict duty of the οἰκονόμος, but only of the satisfaction felt by a generous mind in rendering unpaid service (*cf.* Acts xx. 33 ff.). The Ap. plays on the word μισθός—first denied, then asserted, much as on σοφία in ii. 1-8; he repudiates "reward" in the mercenary sense, to claim it in the larger ethical sense. He "boasts" that the Cor. spend nothing on him, while he spends himself on them (*cf.* 2 Cor. xi. 9-12, xii. 14 f.).—ἵνα replaces the inf. in apposition to μισθός, "marking the purposive result involved" (El.)—*to make, as I intended, the Gospel costless.*—θήσω is *fut.*, intimating assurance of the purpose, as in Gal. ii. 4 (see Wr., p. 361).—τίθημι with objective complement, a construction of cl. Gr. poetry and later prose, which Heb. idiom demands frequently in LXX; *cf.* xii. 28, xv. 25.—"So that I might not use to the full (εἰς τ. μὴ καταχρήσασθαι: see vii. 31) my right in the gospel"—*sc.* that maintained in the former part of the ch.: a further purpose of Paul's preaching gratuitously, involved in that just stated, and bearing on *himself* as the ἀδάπ. θήσω bore upon the readers.—Ἐξουσία ἐν τ. εὐαγγελίῳ is "a right (involved) in (proclaiming) the good news," belonging to the εὐαγγελιζόμενος (14). P. was resolved to keep well within his rights, in handling the Gospel (*cf.* Matt. x. 8; also vi. 7b, 8a above). This sentiment applies to every kind of "right in *the gospel*" of gratuitous salvation; it reappears, with another bearing, in 2 Cor. xiii. 3-10.
Ver. 19. ἐλεύθερος γὰρ ὢν κ.τ.λ. serves further to explain, not εἰς τ. μὴ καταχρήσ. (the impropriety of a grasping use of such right is manifest), but Paul's general policy of self-abnegation (15-18). The real aim of this long discussion of ministerial ἐξουσία comes into view; the Ap. shows himself to the Cor. as *an example of superior privilege held upon trust for the community*, of *liberty asserted*

with a view to self-abnegation: "For, being free from all, to all I enslaved myself, that I might gain the more".—πάντων is masc., like the antithetical πᾶσιν (*cf.* τ. πᾶσιν, 22); ἐλεύθερος ἐκ—a rare construction (commonly ἀπό)—implies *extrication*, escape from danger (*cf.* Luke i. 71, 2 Tim. ii. 26). In ver. 1 ἐλεύθερος signified freedom from needless and burdensome scruple, here freedom *from entangling dependence.* Paul freed himself from everybody, just that he might be everybody's servant; had he been bound as a salaried minister to any particular Church, his services would in that degree have been limited. For the motive of this δουλεία, *cf.* Gal. v. 13; and for Paul's aim, in its widest bearing, Rom. i. 14, xv. 1; also John xiii. 12 ff., Luke xxii. 24 ff.—τοὺς πλείονας, "the more" —not "the greater part" (as in x. 5; so Mr. and others), nor *quam plurimos* (Bg.), but "so much more" than could otherwise have been gained (*cf.* 2 Cor. iv. 15, Luke vii. 43; so Ed.). The expression κερδήσω is used for σώσω (22), in allusion to the charge of *gain-seeking* to which P. was exposed (2 Cor. xi. 12, xii. 17 f., 1 Thess. ii. 5; *cf.* Tit. i. 7, 11); "gain I did seek," he says, "and greedily —the gain of winning all sorts of men for Christ" (*cf.* Matt. iv. 19).
Vv. 20-22. This gain of his calling P. sought (1) *among the Jews, and those* who with them were *under law* (20); (2) amongst the body of *the Gentiles, without law* (21); (3) amongst *the weak believers*, who were imperilled by the inconsiderate use of liberty on the part of the stronger (22a). Each of these classes the Ap. saves by identifying himself with it in turn; and this plan he could only follow by keeping clear of sectional obligations (19). Ed., coupling vv. 20b and 21, distinguishes three points of view—"race, religion, conscience".—"I *became* to the Jews as a Jew," for Paul was no longer such in the common acceptation: see note on ἐλεύθερος (1), also Gal. ii. 4, iv. 12; for evidence of his Jewish conformity, see Acts xvi. 3, xviii. 18, xxi. 23 ff.; also the speeches in Acts xiii. 16 ff., xxii. 1 ff., xxvi. 2 ff.; and Rom. i. 16, ix. 1 ff., xi. 1, xv. 8, for his warm patriotism.—τοῖς ὑπὸ

ᵛ Rom. vi. 14 f.; Gal. iv. 4 f., 21. ᵂ In this exact meaning, Acts ii. 23; also Wisd. xvii. 2. -ως, Rom. ii. 12.

ἵνα Ἰουδαίους ᵘ κερδήσω· τοῖς ᵛ ὑπὸ ᵛ νόμον ὡς ᵛ ὑπὸ ᵛ νόμον,[1] ἵνα τοὺς ᵛ ὑπὸ ᵛ νόμον ᵘ κερδήσω· 21. τοῖς ᵂ ἀνόμοις ὡς ᵂ ἄνομος, μὴ ὢν ᵂ ἄνομος Θεῷ[2] ἀλλ᾽ ˣ ἔννομος Χριστῷ,[2] ἵνα ᵘ κερδήσω[3] ᵂ ἀνόμους·[4] 22a. ἐγενόμην τοῖς ʸ ἀσθενέσιν ὡς[5] ʸ ἀσθενής, ἵνα τοὺς ʸ ἀσθενεῖς ᵘ κερδήσω· 22b. ᶻτοῖς ᶻ πᾶσι γέγονα τὰ[6] πάντα, ἵνα ᵃ πάντως[7] τινὰς[7]

x Acts xix. 39; "law-abiding" in cl. Gr.   y See i. 25 and iv. 10.   z x. 17; 2 Cor. v. 10, 15; Rom. xi. 32; Eph. iv. 13; Phil. ii. 21; Mk. xiv. 64.   a See v. 10.

[1] *Insert* μη ων αυτος υπο νομον all uncc. but K, and many minn., latt. vg. sah. syrᴾ·, Or., Cyr., Dam., Aug.—lost through homœoteleuton (repeated υπο νομον).

[2] Θεου . . . Χριστου: all uncc. but DᶜKL.

[3] κερδανω, all uncc. but ℵᶜDKL. The same MSS., κερδησω in context.

[4] τους ανομους: all uncc. but ℵᶜGKL.

[5] *Om.* ως ℵ*AB d e vg., Or., Cyp., Amb., Ambrst.

[6] *Om.* τα all pre-Syrian uncc.

[7] παντας (for παντως τινας), the Westerns, including vg.: *ut omnes facerem salvos.*

νόμον enlarges the category τ. Ἰουδαίοις by including circumcised proselytes (see Gal. v. 1-3); and ὡς ὑπὸ νόμον defines Paul's Judaism as subjection, by way of accommodation, to legal observance, to which the ptpl. phrase (wanting in the T.R.), μὴ ὢν αὐτὸς ὑπὸ νόμον, intimates that he is no longer bound in principle —μὴ with ptp. implying subjective stand-point ("not being in my view"), and αὐτὸς denoting *on my part, of and for myself* (*cf.* Rom. vii. 25). P.'s self-denying conform-ity to legal environment brought on him the reproach of "still preaching circum-cision" (Gal. v. 11).—In relation to Gen-tiles also he takes an attitude open to misunderstanding and which he wishes to guard: "to those out-of-law (τ. ἀνό-μοις) as out-of-law—though I am not out-of-law in respect of God, but in-law (ἔννομος) in respect of Christ". ἄνομος was the Jewish designation for all be-yond the pale of Mosaism (see Rom. ii. 9-16, etc.): Paul became this to Gentiles (Gal. iv. 12), abandoning his natural position, in that he did not practise the law of Moses amongst them nor make it the basis or aim of his preaching to them; see Acts xiv. 15 ff., xvii. 22 ff. He was ἄνομος therefore, in the narrow Jewish sense; not so in the true religious sense —"in relation to God"; indeed P. is now *more than* ὑπὸ νόμον, he is ἔννομος Χριστοῦ (= ἐν νόμῳ Χριστοῦ; *cf.* Gal. vi. 2, Rom. iii. 27, 31, viii. 2)—*non ex-istens exlex Deo, sed inlex Christo* (Est.). The Christian stands within the law as entering into its spirit and becoming one with it in nature; he is "in the law of Christ" as he is "in Christ" (*cf.* Gal. ii.

20, 2 Cor. v. 17). This νόμος Χριστοῦ P. expounds in Rom. xii., xiii. (esp. 10), Col. iii., Eph. iv. 20-v. 9, after John xiii. 34, Matt. v.-vii., etc. Its fulfilment is guaranteed by the fact that it is "the law of the Spirit of life in Christ Jesus" (Rom. viii. 1 ff.), who "dwells in" the Christian (iii. 16), operating not as an outward yoke but an implanted life.—ἵνα κερδάνω τ. ἀνόμους follows τ. ἀνόμοις ὡς ἄνομος, after the μὴ ὢν parenthesis, in the manner of the two ἵνα clauses of ver. 20 (κερδάνω and κερδήσω are the Attic and non-Attic forms of the 1st aor. sbj.). —Describing the third of his self-adapta-tions, P. resumes the ἐγενόμην of the first, coming home to the situation of his readers: "I became to the weak (not *as weak*, but actually) *weak* (see txtl. note), that I might gain the weak". So well did he enter into the scruples of the timid and half-enlightened (see *e.g.* viii. 7, 10, Rom. xiv. 1 f.), that he forgot his own strength (viii. 4, Rom. xv. 1) and felt himself "weak" with them: *cf.* 2 Cor. xi. 29, τίς ἀσθενεῖ, καὶ οὐκ ἀσθενῶ;

Ver. 22b sums up (in the pf. γέγονα of abiding fact replacing the historical ἐγενόμην, and with the objective σώσω for the subjective κερδήσω) the Apostle's conduct in the various relations of his ministry: "To all men I have become all things, that by all means I might save some".—On πάντως, which varies in sense according to its position and con-text, see ver. 10, v. 10; here it is adv. of manner to σώσω, *omni quovis modo.* "That in all this description of his οἰκονομία or συγκατάβασις P. sets forth no unchristian compliance with men, but

^bσώσω. 23. τοῦτο¹ δὲ ποιῶ διὰ τὸ εὐαγγέλιον, ἵνα ^cσυγκοινωνὸς ^b Of *human*
αὐτοῦ γένωμαι.

24. ^dΟὐκ ^dοἴδατε ὅτι οἱ ἐν ^eσταδίῳ τρέχοντες πάντες μὲν τρέχουσιν, εἷς δὲ λαμβάνει τὸ ^fβραβεῖον; οὕτω τρέχετε ἵνα ^gκαταλάβητε.
25. πᾶς δὲ ὁ ^hἀγωνιζόμενος πάντα ⁱἐγκρατεύεται· ἐκεῖνοι μὲν οὖν

b Of *human* action, Rom. xi. 14; 1 Tim. iv. 16; Jas. v. 15, 20; c Rom. xi. 17; Phil. i. 7; Rev. i. 9. -*νειν*,

Eph. v. 11. d See iii. 16. e In this sense, N.T. *h.l.*; *cf.* Lk. xxiv. 13, etc. See Herod. v. 22, ἀγωνιζεσθαι σταδιον. f Phil. iii. 14; -*ενω*, Col. ii. 18, iii. 15. g In this sense, Rom. ix. 30; Phil. iii. 12 f.; Exod. xv. 9. h Col. i. 29, iv. 12; 1 Tim. iv. 10, vi. 12; 2 Tim. iv. 7; Lk. xiii. 24; Jo. xviii. 36; Sir. iv. 28, etc. i See vii. 9.

¹ παντα, all uncc. but KL, and all anc. verss. but syr. and go.

the practical wisdom of true Christian love and self-denial in the exercise of his office, this he expects will be self-evident to his readers, so well acquainted with his character (2 Cor. i. 12 ff., v. 11). This kind of wisdom is so much more manifestly the fruit in P. of experience under the discipline of the Spirit, as his temper was the more fiery and uncompromising " (Mr.); "non mentientis actus, sed compatientis affectus" (Aug.). This behaviour appeared to his enemies timeserving and duplicity (2 Cor. i. 12, iv. 2, xii. 16, Gal. i. 10).

Ver. 23. Paul's course in its chameleon-like changes is governed by a simple practical aim: "But all things I do for the gospel's sake". His one purpose is to fulfil his Gospel stewardship (17, iv. 1 ff., etc., Acts xx. 24); Phil. iii. 7-14 presents the inner side of the "one thing" he pursues. The intensity with which this end is sought accounts for the variety of means; the most resolute, in a complicated situation, becomes the most versatile of men. **διὰ τὸ εὐαγγέλιον,** "on the gospel's account", with a view to spread the good news most widely and carry it into effect most completely: for **διὰ** of the end as a ground of action, *cf.* iv. 17, viii. 11, Rom. iv. 25. For himself Paul's sole ambition is "that I may be joint-partaker in it (with those I save) "—that he may win its salvation along with many others, the fruit of his ministry (*cf.* 1 Thess. ii. 19 f.; also John xiv. 3, xvii. 24).

§ 30. PAUL'S ASCETICISM, ix. 24-27. The last words of § 29 indicate that the writer feels his own salvation to be bound up in his mission to his fellowmen. The self-denial practised for the latter of these objects is necessary, in point of fact, *for both*. His example should teach the Cor. the need of stern self-discipline on their personal account, as well as in the interests of weaker brethren. From ix. 24 onwards to x. 22 P. pursues this line of

warning, addressed to men who were imperilling their own souls by self-indulgence and worldly conformity. Of the danger of missing the prize of life through indiscipline P. is keenly sensible in his own case; he conveys his apprehension under the picture, so familiar to the Cor., of the Isthmian Games.

Ver. 24. **Οὐκ οἴδατε . . .**; *cf.* ver. 13, etc. **οἱ ἐν σταδίῳ τρέχοντες, πάντες μὲν τρέχουσιν, εἷς δὲ κ.τ.λ.**: "Those that run in the stadium, run *all* (of them), but *one* receives the prize ". As much as to say, "Entering the race is not winning it; do not be satisfied with running, but make sure of winning—*So run that you may secure (the prize)*!" The art. is wanting with **σταδίῳ**, as often after prps., esp. when the noun is quasi-proper; *cf.* our "at court," "in church." The *stadion* was the race-course, always a fixed length of 600 Gr., or 606¾ Eng. ft.; hence a measure of distance, as in Matt. xiv. 24—*a furlong.*—For the antithesis of **πάντες** and **εἷς**, conveying the point of the warning, *cf.* the emphatic **πάντες** of x. 1-4 (see note); also vi. 12, x. 23.—**οὕτως** may point backward to **εἷς** ("run like that one": *cf.* 14, ii. 11), or forward to **ἵνα (καταλάβ.**)—a particle substituted for the regular correlative, **ὥστε** (*cf.* Acts xiv. 1, John iii. 16), where the result is an *aim* to be achieved; the latter connexion is more probable, since the following vv. dilate on the conditions of success.

Ver. 25. **πᾶς δὲ ὁ ἀγωνιζόμενος κ.τ.λ.**: "But every combatant is temperate in everything—they, to be sure, that they may win a perishable garland; but we an imperishable." The stress in the first clause lies on **πᾶς**, **πάντα**—no competitor can afford to be self-indulgent in anything; in the second on **ἐκεῖνοι**, **ἡμεῖς**—if *they* are so abstinent for so poor a prize, what should *we* be? For ten months before the contest in the Great Games, the athletes were required, under

k xv. 53 f.; ἵνα ᵏ φθαρτὸν ¹στέφανον λάβωσιν, ἡμεῖς δὲ ᵐ ἄφθαρτον · 26. ἐγὼ
Rom. i.
23; 1 Pet. ⁿ τοίνυν ᵒ οὕτω τρέχω, ᵒ ὡς οὐκ ᵖ ἀδήλως · ᵒ οὕτω πυκτεύω, ᵒ ὡς οὐκ
i. 18, 23.
l Phil. iv. 1; q ἀέρα ʳ δέρων · 27. ἀλλ᾽ ˢ ὑπωπιάζω μου τὸ σῶμα καὶ ᵗ δουλαγωγῶ,
1 Th. ii.
19; 2 Tim. ᵘ μήπως ἄλλοις ᵛ κηρύξας αὐτὸς ʷ ἀδόκιμος γένωμαι.
iv. 8; Jas.
i. 12; 1
Pet. v. 4; Rev. ii. 10, iii. 11, etc.; Mt. xxvii. 29, etc. -ow, 2 Tim. ii. 5.   m xv. 52; Rom. i. 23; 1 Pet.
i. 4, 23, iii. 4.   n H.l. in Paul; Heb. xiii. 13; Lk. xx. 25; Isa. iii. 10, v. 13.   o Cf. iii. 15.
p H.l.; -λος, xiv. 8; -oτης, 1 Tim. vi. 17.   q xiv. 9; Eph. ii. 4; 1 Th. iv. 17; Acts xxii. 23; Rev. ix.
2, xvi. 17; Wisd. v. 11 f.   r 2 Cor. xi. 20; Acts v. 40, vi. 37, xxii. 19; Mt. xxi. 35, etc.   s Lk. xviii.
5; -πιον, Prov. xx. 30.   t N.T. h.l.; Diodorus, and Longinus.   u See viii. 9.   v See i. 23.
Absol., xv. 11; Rom. x. 14 f.; 1 Pet. iii. 19; similarly in Syn. Gospp.   w 2 Cor. xiii. 5 ff.; Rom. i.
28; 2 Tim. iii. 8; Tit. i. 16; Heb. vi. 8.

oath, to follow a prescribed diet (ἀναγ-κοφαγία) and regimen (ἄσκησις): Pausanias V. 24. 9; Philostratus De Gymn., p. 4; Arrian-Epict., III. xv. 3, xxiii. 2; Xenoph. Symp. viii. 37; Horace, Ars Poet. 412 ff., "Qui studet optatam cursu contingere metam, Multa tulit fecitque puer, sudavit et alsit, Abstinuit venere et vino." ἐγκρατεύεται (see vii. 9) implies temperance in a positive degree—not mere abstinence, but vigorous control of appetite and passion; πάντα is acc. of specification. The "garland" of the victor in the Isthmian Games was of pine-leaves, at an earlier time of parsley, in the Olympian Games of wild-olive; yet these were the most coveted honours in the whole Greek world.—φθαρτὸν and ἄφθαρτον are again contrasted in xv. 53.

Vv. 26, 27. "Therefore I so run, in no uncertain fashion; so I ply my fists, not like one that beats the air." "So—as the context describes, and as you see me (cf. xv. 32)"; the Ap. feels himself, while he writes, to be straining every nerve like the racer, striking home like the trained pugilist: for this graphic οὕτως, cf. xv. 11, Gal. i. 6, 2 Thess. iii. 17; the adv. would be otiose as mere antecedent to ὡς.—τοίνυν (similarly τοίγαρ in 1 Thess. iv. 8) brings in the prompt, emphatic inference drawn from the last clause: "We are fighting for the immortal crown—I as a leader and exemplar; surely then I make no false step in the course, I strike no random blows." ἀδήλως is susceptible both of the objective sense prevailing in cl. Gr., obscure, inconspicuous (preferred by Mr. and Gd. here, as though P. meant, "not keeping out of sight, in the ruck"; cf. xiv. 8); and (preferably) of the subjective sense, unsure, without certain aim (Thuc., I. 2. 1; Plato, Symp. 181 D; Polybius)—"ut non in incertum" (Bz.); "scio quod petam et quomodo" (Bg.); πρὸς σκοπόν τινα βλέπων, οὐκ εἰκῆ καὶ μάτην (Cm.): cf. Phil. iii. 14. The image of the race suggests that of pugilism (πυκτεύω),

another exercise of the Pentathlon of the arena: the former a familiar N.T. metaphor, the latter h.l.—ὡς οὐκ ἀέρα δέρων, "ut non aerem cædens" (Bz.), "smiting something more solid than air" (οὐκ negatives ἀέρα, not δέρων),—esp. my own body (27); cf. Virgil's "verberat ictibus auras" (Æn. v. 377). P.'s are no blows of a clumsy fighter that fail to land—struck in's Blaue hinein. Bg., Hf., Ed. suppose him to be thinking of the σκιομαχία, sham-fight, practised in training or by way of prelude, without an antagonist. δέρω means to flay, then beat severely, smite; cf. our vulgar hiding.

Ver. 27. The fully-attested reading ὑπωπιάζω (from ὑπὸ and ὤψ, to hit under the eye) continues the pugilistic metaphor and suits Paul's vehemence; "contundo corpus meum" (Bz.), "lividum facio" (Cod. Claromontanus), "I beat my body black and blue": a vivid picture of the corporal discipline to which P. subjects himself in the prosecution of his work (cf. iv. 11—esp. κολαφιζόμεθα; 2 Cor. xi. 23 ff., Gal. vi. 17, 2 Tim. ii. 4). ὑποπιάζω (ὑπὸ + πιέζω; cf. 2 Cor. xi. 32, etc.)—preferred by Hf. and Hn., after Clem. Alex.—giving the milder sense, to force under, subdue, subigo (Cv.), is almost syn. with δουλαγωγῶ.

P.'s severe bodily suffering, entailed by the circumstances of his ministry, he accepts as needful for his own sanctification (cf. 2 Cor. xii. 7),—a physical castigation which tames the flesh for the uses of the spirit (cf. 1 Pet. iv. 1 f.; also, for the principle involved, Rom. viii. 13, Col. iii. 5). The practices of the Middle-Age Flagellants and similar self-torturers have been justified by this text; but Paul's discipline was not arbitrary and self-inflicted, it was dictated by his calling (12b, 23)—a cross laid on him by the hand of God, and borne for the Gospel's and the Church's sake (cf. Col. i. 24). In Col. ii. 23 he guards against the ascetic extravagances which this passage, perhaps even in his life-time, was used

X. 1. ᵃΟὐ ᵃθέλω δὲ¹ ὑμᾶς ᵃἀγνοεῖν, ἀδελφοί, ὅτι οἱ ᵇπατέρες ᵇἡμῶν πάντες ᶜὑπὸ τὴν νεφέλην ᶜἦσαν καὶ πάντες ᵈδιὰ τῆς θαλάσσης ᵈδιῆλθον, 2. καὶ πάντες ᵉεἰς τὸν Μωσῆν² ᵉἐβαπτίσαντο³ ἐν τῇ

ᵃ 2 Cor. i. 8; Rom. i. 13; 1 Th. iv. 13.
ᵇ Freq. in Acts; Jo. iv.20,vi.31.

ᶜ ix. 20; Gal. iv. 21, v. 18; Acts iv. 12; Jo. i. 49.　　ᵈ 2 Cor. i. 16; Acts ix. 32; Mt. xii. 43; Lev. xxvi. 5; elsewhere with acc.　　ᵉ Rom. vi. 3; Gal. iii. 27; Acts viii. 16. Cf. i. 13 and xii. 13. Mid. voice, here only; Mk. vii. 4 (?); Acts xxii. 16.

¹ γαρ, all uncc. but אᶜKL, all anc. verss. but syr.

² Μωυσην: see note on ix. 9.

³ εβαπτισθησαν (?), אACDG 17, 46 (Western and Alexandrian); so Tisch., Tr. marg., W.H. marg., Nestle. εβαπτισαντο, BKLP, etc. (Neutral and Syrian); so Tr. txt., W.H. txt., El.—the more difficult reading : see note below.

to support.—This "buffeting" of his physical frame enabled P. to "lead (his body) about as a slave,"—as one might do a bullying antagonist after a sound beating. Paul's physical temperament, it appears, had stood in the way of his success as a minister of Christ; and the hindrance was providentially overcome by the terrible hardships through which he passed in pursuit of his ministry. This experience he commends to the Cor. He had felt the fear, from which the above course of rigorous self-abnegation in the interest of others has saved him, "lest haply, after preaching to others, I myself should prove reprobate" (ἀδόκιμος γένωμαι) : the opp. result to that of ver. 23.—For κηρύσσω, see i. 23 ; the κῆρυξ at the Games summoned the competitors and announced the rules of the contest. With ἀδόκιμος, rejectaneus, cf. δοκιμάζω, iii. 13, and note ; see 2 Cor. xiii. 5 ff., and other parls.—On the Gr. Games, see the Dict. of Gr. and Rom. Antiq. (Isthmia, Stadium) ; Hermann, Lehrbuch d. gottesdienstl. Alterthümer, § 50; also the supplementary Note on Greek Athletic Festivals in Bt.

§ 31. THE BACKSLIDING OF ANCIENT ISRAEL, x. 1-5. The Apostle has just confessed, in warning others, his own fear of reprobation. That this is no idle fear the history of the O.T. Church plainly proves. All the Israelite fathers were rescued from Egypt, and sealed with the ancient sacraments, and virtually partook of Christ in the wilderness ; but, alas, how few of those first redeemed entered the Promised Land !

Vv. 1, 2. The phrase οὐ θέλω ὑμᾶς ἀγνοεῖν (see parls.) calls attention to something not altogether within the range of the reader's knowledge (contrast οὐκ οἴδατε ; ix. 24, etc.); γὰρ attaches the paragraph, by way of enforcement, to the foregoing ἀδόκιμος. "Our fathers" is not written inadver-

tently to Gentile "brethren," out of P.'s "national consciousness" (Mr.) ; the phrase identifies the N.T. Church with "Israel" (cf. Rom. iv. 1, 11 ff., xi. 17 f., Gal. iii. 7, 29, Phil. iii. 3 ; also Clem. ad Cor. 4) ; the fate of the fathers admonishes the children (Ps. lxxviii. 8, xcv. 9, etc. ; Matt. xxiii. 29 ff., Heb. iii., iv.). The point of the warning lies in the five-times repeated πάντες : "All our fathers escaped by miracle from the house of bondage ; all received the tokens of the Mosaic covenant ; all participated under its forms in Christ ; and yet most of them perished ! (5)"; cf. the πάντες μέν . . . εἰς δὲ of ix. 24, and note.—For ὑπὸ τὴν νεφέλην, διὰ τῆς θαλάσσης, cf. Ps. cv. 39, cvi. 11 ; also Wisd. x. 17, xix. 7. "The cloud" shading and guiding the Israelites from above, and "the sea" making a path for them through its midst and drowning their enemies behind them, were glorious signs to "our fathers" of God's salvation ; together they formed a λοῦτρον παλινγενεσίας (Tit. iii. 5), inaugurating the national covenant life ; as it trode the miraculous path between upper and nether waters, Israel was born into its Divine estate. Thus "they all received their baptism unto Moses in the cloud and in the sea," since in this act they committed themselves to the guidance of Moses, entering through him into acknowledged fellowship with God ; even so the Cor. in the use of the same symbolic element had been "baptized unto Christ" (cf. Rom. vi. 3 f., Gal. iii. 27). For the parl. between Moses and Christ, see Heb. iii. Paul sees a baptism in the waters of the Exodus, as Peter in the waters of the Deluge (1 Pet. iii. 20 f.).—ἐβαπτίσαντο, mid. voice (see parls.), implies consent of the subjects—"had themselves baptised" (cf. ἀπελούσασθε, vi. 11)—aggravating their apostasy.

Vv. 3, 4. After deliverance came the question of sustenance. This was effected

f See iii. 2.
g See ii. 13.
h Heb. ix.
10; Ps. ci.
9; Dan.
i. 16
(Theod.).

νεφέλῃ καὶ ἐν τῇ θαλάσσῃ, 3. καὶ πάντες τὸ[1] αὐτὸ[1] [f]βρῶμα[2] [g]πνευματικὸν[2] ἔφαγον 4a. καὶ πάντες τὸ[3] αὐτὸ[3] [h]πόμα[4] [g]πνευματικὸν[4] ἔπιον[4] · 4b. ἔπινον γὰρ ἐκ [g]πνευματικῆς ἀκολουθούσης[i]πέτρας·

i Rom. ix. 33 (Isa. viii. 14); 1 Pet. ii. 8; Mt. vii. 24, xvi. 18, etc.

[1] το αυτο om. א*, æth.; A 46 om. αυτο.

[2] πνευματικον βρωμα εφαγον (in this order): א*BC²P. πνευμ. εφ. βρ.: A 17, Mcion. βρ. πνευμ. εφ.: אᶜDGKL, etc.; Western and Syrian.

[3] æth., Chr. om. το αυτο. A 46 om. αυτο.

[4] πνευματικον επιον πομα (in this order): all non-Western pre-Syrian uncc.

in the desert by means no less miraculous and symbolic: "and they all ate the same spiritual food, and all drank the same spiritual drink"—the manna of Exod. xvi. 13 ff., etc., and the stream drawn from the rocks of Rephidim (Exod. xvii.) and Kadesh (Num. xx.).—The epithet πνευματικὸν does not negative the materiality of the βρῶμα and πόμα, any more than the corporeality of the ripe Christian man described in ii. 15; it ascribes to these nutriments a higher virtue—such as, e.g., the bread of Christ's miracles had for intelligent partakers—a spiritual meaning and influence: for the bread, see Deut. viii. 2 f. (cf. Matt. iv. 3 f., John vi. 31 ff., Ps. lxxviii. 23 ff.); for the water, Exod. xvii. 7, Num. xx. 13, Ps. cv. 41, Isa. xxxv. 6.—In drinking from the smitten rock the Israelites "were drinking" at the same time "of a spiritual rock"—and that not supplying them once alone, but "following" them throughout their history. Ver. 4b explains 4a (γὰρ): P. justifies his calling the miraculous water "spiritual," not by saying that the rock from which it issued was a spiritual (and no material) rock, but that there was "a spiritual rock accompanying" God's people; from this they drank in spirit, while their bodies drank from the water flowing at their feet. The lesson is strictly parl. to that of Deut. viii. 3 f. respecting the manna. In truth, another rock was there beside the visible cliff of Rephidim: "Now this rock (ἡ πέτρα δέ) was the Christ!" The "meat" and "drink" are the actual desert food—"the same" for "all," but endowed for all with a "spiritual" grace; the "spiritual rock" which imparted this virtue is distinguished as "following" the people, being superior to local limitations—a rock not symbolic of Christ, but identical with Him. This identification our Lord virtually made in the words of John vii. 37. The impf.

ἔπινον (4b), exchanged for ἔπιον (4a), indicates the continuous aid drawn from this "following rock".

Baur, Al., and others suppose P. to be adopting the Rabbinical legend that the water-bearing Rephidim rock journeyed onwards with the Israelites (see Bammidbar Rabba, s. 1; Eisenmenger, Entd. Judenthum, I. 312, 467, II. 876 f.). Philo allegorized this fable in application to the Logos (Leg. alleg. II. §§ 21 f.; Quod det. pot. insid. solet, § 30). This may have suggested Paul's conception, but the predicate πνευματικῆς emphatically discards the prodigy; "we must not disgrace P. by making him say that the pre-incarnate Christ followed the march of Israel in the shape of a lump of rock!" (Hf.). ὁ Χριστός—not the doctrine, nor the hope of the Christ, but Himself—assumes that Christ existed in Israelite times and was spiritually present with the O.T. Church, and that the grace attending its ordinances was mediated by Him. "The spiritual homogeneity of the two covenants"—which gives to the Apostle's warning its real cogency—"rests on the identity of the Divine Head of both. The practical consequence saute aux yeux: Christ lived already in the midst of the ancient people, and that people has perished! How can you suppose, you Christians, that you are secured from the same fate!" (Gd.).

Holsten rejects the parenthetical ἡ πέτρα δέ clause as a theological gloss; but it is necessary to explain the previous ἐκ πνευμ. ἀκολ. πέτρας, and is covered doctrinally by the δι' οὗ τὰ πάντα of viii. 6 (see note). Already Jewish theology had referred to the hypostatized "Wisdom" (see Wisd. x.), or "the Logos" (Philo passim), the protection and sustenance of ancient Israel. The O.T. saw the spiritual "rock of Israel" in Jehovah (Deut. xxxii., 2 Sam. xxiii. 3, Isa. xvii. 10, xxvi. 4, etc.), whose offices

ῐ̔ δὲ¹ πέτρα¹ ᵏ ἦν ὁ Χριστός. 5. ἀλλ' οὐκ ¹ἐν ᵐ τοῖς ᵐ πλείοσιν ᵏ ειμι in
αὐτῶν ¹ⁿ εὐδόκησεν² ὁ ⁿ Θεός· ᵒ κατεστρώθησαν γὰρ ἐν τῇ ἐρήμῳ. Mt. xiii.
37, xxvi.
6. Ταῦτα δὲ ᵖ τύποι ἡμῶν ἐγενήθησαν, ᑫ εἰς ᑫ τὸ ᑫ μὴ εἶναι ἡμᾶς 26; Jo.
xv. 1;
ἐπιθυμητὰς κακῶν, καθὼς κἀκεῖνοι ˢ ἐπεθύμησαν· 7. μηδὲ ᵗ εἰδω- Gen. xli.
26 f.; Ex.
xii. 11;

Ezek. xxxvii. 11.   1 2 Cor. xii. 10; Mt. iii. 17, and parls.; Jer. xiv. 12.   m See ix. 19.   n i. 21;
Gal. i. 15; Col. i. 19; Mt. iii. 17, etc.; Lk. xii. 32.   Cf. ευδοκια, Eph. i. 5, 9; Ph. ii. 13; Mt. xi. 26;
Lk. ii. 14, x. 21.   o Numb. xiv. 16.   p In this sense, Rom. v. 14; diff. in Rom. vi. 17, etc.
q 2 Cor. iv. 4; 2 Th. ii. 2; 1 Pet. iii. 7; Acts vii. 19.   r N.T. h.l.; Numb. xi. 34. A cl. word.
s Absol., Rom. vii. 7, xiii. 9 (Ex. xx. 17); Gal. v. 17; Ja. iv. 2.   t See ver. 10.

¹ η πετρα δε: ℵBD*c—irregular order.
² ηυδοκησεν, AB*C. On the augment, see Wr., p. 83.

of grace, in the N.T. view of things, devolve on Christ.—The Ap. does not in so many words associate the "spiritual food" and "drink" of vv. 3 f. with the Lord's Supper, as he did the crossing of the Red Sea with Baptism; but the second analogy is suggested by the first, and by the reference to the Eucharist in vv. 15 ff. In no other place in the N. T. are the two Sacraments collocated.

Ver. 5. "But not with the greater part (of them)"—a "tragic litotes: only Joshua and Caleb reached the Promised Land" (Num. xiv. 30: Mr.). The result negatives what one expects from the antecedents; hence the strong adversative ἀλλ' οὐκ.—τοῖς πλείοσιν—"the majority" of the πάντες so highly favoured; cf. xv. 6. ηὐδόκησεν ἐν (after the LXX), Heb. chaphets b'; the ἐν resembles that of ix. 15; see Wr., p. 291.—κατεστρώθησαν γὰρ κ.τ.λ., "For they (their bodies) were laid prostrate in the wilderness," gives graphic proof, in words borrowed from the O.T. narrative, of God's displeasure; sooner or later this doom overtook nearly all the witnesses of the Exodus (cf. Heb. iii. 17). "What a spectacle for the eyes of the self-satisfied Cor.: all these bodies, full-fed with miraculous nourishment, strewing the soil of the desert!" (Gd.).

§ 32. The Moral Contagion of Idolatry, x. 6-14. The fall of the Israel of the Exodus was due to the very temptations now surrounding the Cor. Church —to the allurements of idolatry and its attendant impurity (6 ff.), and to the cherishing of discontent and presumption (9 f.). Their fate may prove our salvation, if we lay it to heart; the present trial, manifestly, is nothing new; and God who appoints it will keep it within our strength, and will provide us with means of escape (11 ff.). The whole is summed up in one word, "Flee from idolatry!" (14).

Ver. 6. ταῦτα τύποι ἡμῶν ἐγενήθησαν may mean (a) "These things have been made our examples," typi nobis (Cv.)— sc. exx. for our use; (b) "In these things (acc. of specification) they proved types of us"—figuræ nostri (Vg., Bz., Mr., Bt., R.V. marg.); or (c) "As types of us they became such" (so Hf.: cf. ταῦτα . . . ἦτε, vi. 11)—a construction clashing with that of the parl. ver. 11. (a) best suits the application of ταῦτα in the sequel (cf. 1 Pet. v. 3); to make the fallen Israelites prophetic "types" of the Cor. would be to presume the ruin of the latter!—ἐγενήθησαν is pl. despite the neut. pl. subject ταῦτα, through the attraction of the predicate: so πάντα ταῦτα κακουργίαι ἦσαν in Xenophon; the incidents included are distinctly viewed. For the deterrent "example," cf. Heb. iv. 11.—With ἐπιθυμ. κακῶν cf. ἐφευρετὰς κακῶν, Rom. i. 30: the double ἐπιθυμητὰς . . . ἐπεθύμησαν recalls Num. xi. 4 (LXX); in alluding to the old "lusting" for the diet of Egypt, the Ap. hints at the attraction of the Cor. idol-feasts; but his dehortation applies to all κακά (cf. 2 Cor. xiii. 7, 1 Thess. v. 15, etc.). The general admonition is specialised in four particulars, with repeated μηδὲ—idolatry, fornication, tempting of the Lord, murmuring—based on the analogy furnished by vv. 1-5.

Ver. 7. μηδὲ εἰδωλολάτραι γίνεσθε, "And do not become idolaters": in apposition to the εἰς τὸ μὴ clause of ver. 6, the dependent sentence of purpose passing into a direct impv.; for the like conversational freedom, cf. i. 31, iv. 16, vii. 37, ix. 15, and notes. The repetition of this warning in ver. 14 shows its urgency. Even where eating of the εἰδωλόθυτα was innocent, it might be a stepping-stone to εἰδωλολατρεία.—Enforcing his appeal by ref. to the calf-worship at Sinai, the Ap. dwells on the accompaniments of this apostasy; here

u Exod.
xxxii. 6;
intrans.
passim.
v In this
sense,
opp. to
καθίζω or
the like,
Acts ix. 6,
34, xii. 7,
etc.; Mk.
ix. 27; Lk.
iv. 29, v. 25, etc.; Jo. xi. 31.   w N.T. *h.l.; cf.* Judg. xvi. 25; 2 Ki. vi. 5; Jer. xxxviii. 4.   x See
vi. 18.   y Of *persons*, Rom. xi. 11, 22, xiv. 4; Heb. iv. 11; Rev. ii. 5; Lk. xxi. 24.   z Lk. iv. 12
(Deut. vi. 16), x. 25; Ps. lxxvii. 18.   a Exod. xvii. 2, 7; Acts v. 9, xv. 10; Heb. iii. 9; (Jo.) viii. 6.
Cf. vii. 5.   b Numb. xxi. 6; Mk. xvi. 18; Lk. x. 19; *cf.* Jo. iii. 14.   c Exod. xvi. 7; Numb. xiv.
29; Mt. xx. 11; Lk. v. 30; four times in Jo.

λολάτραι γίνεσθε καθώς τινες αὐτῶν, ὡς[1] γέγραπται, "[u]Ἐκάθισεν
ὁ λαὸς φαγεῖν καὶ πιεῖν[2] καὶ [v]ἀνέστησαν [w]παίζειν"·   8. μηδὲ
[x]πορνεύωμεν, καθώς τινες αὐτῶν [x]ἐπόρνευσαν καὶ [y]ἔπεσον[3] ἐν[4]
μίᾳ ἡμέρᾳ εἰκοσιτρεῖς χιλιάδες·   9. μηδὲ [z]ἐκπειράζωμεν τὸν Χριστόν,[5] καθὼς καί τινες αὐτῶν [a]ἐπείρασαν[6] καὶ ὑπὸ τῶν [b]ὄφεων
ἀπώλοντο·[7]   10. μηδὲ [c]γογγύζετε,[8] καθὼς[9] καί[10] τινες αὐτῶν

[1] ωσπερ, אABDᶜL, many minn.: unusual in this connexion.   ως, CD*KL, etc.

[2] πειν, א (πιν) B*D*G; see note on ix. 4.

[3] επεσαν: all pre-Syrian uncc. So *passim*; see Wr., pp. 86 f.

[4] *Om.* εν א*BD*G (Neutral and Western). Ins. εν: Alexandrian and Syrian.

[5] τον Κυριον, אBCP 17, 46, 73, syrᵖ·ᵐᵍ· cop., Epiph.   τον Θεον A 2, Euthal.
τον Χριστον DGKL, etc., latt. vg. syrˢᶜʰ· sah., Mcion. (Western and Syrian).

[6] εξεπειρασαν (?), אCD*GP 17, 46, 73—assimilated to previous vb.
επειρασαν, ABDᶜKL, etc.; so W.H. *txt.*, Nestle, El.

[7] απωλλυντο, אAB: *h.l.* for the impf.

[8] γογγυζωμεν, אDG (Western)—assimilated to context.

[9] καθαπερ, אBP, Or., Bas.

[10] *Om.* και all uncc. but KL.

lay the peril of his readers who, when
released from the superstition of the old
religion (viii. 4), were still attracted by
its feasting and gaiety: "The people sat
down to eat and drink, and rose up to
sport" (following the LXX precisely).
This παίζειν, as in idolatrous festivals
commonly, included singing and dancing
round the calf (Exod. xxxii. 18 f.); there
is no need to imagine a darker meaning.
It was a scene of wild, careless merri-
ment, shocking under the circumstances
and most perilous, that Moses witnessed
as he descended bearing the Tables of
the Law.—πεῖν, *cf.* ix. 4 and note.

Ver. 8. μηδὲ πορνεύωμεν: here P.
comes closer to his readers, adopting the
communicative 1st pl. For the prevalence of this vice at Cor. and its connexion with Cor. idolatry, see vii. 2, vi. 11,
and *Introd.*, p. 734 (*cf.* Num. xxv., 1 f. also
Rev. ii. 14); for its existence in the Cor.
Church, ch. v. above, and 2 Cor. xii. 21.
Wisd. xiv. 12 affirms, of idolatry at large,
ἀρχὴ πορνείας ἐπίνοια εἰδώλων; see the
connexion of Rom. i. 24 with the foregoing context.—"23,000" is a curious
variation from the figure given in Num.
xxv. 9 for the slain of Baal-Peor, which
is followed by other Jewish authorities,
viz., 24,000. It is more respectful to

credit the Ap. with a trifling inadvertence
than to suppose, with Gd., that he makes
a deliberate understatement to be within
the mark. Ev. gives no evidence for his
alleged "Jewish tradition" in support of
the reduced estimate. Possibly, a primitive error of the copyist, substituting γ′
for δ′ (Hn.).

Vv. 9, 10. The sins condemned in vv.
7, 8 are sins of *sensuality*; these, of *unbelief* (Ed.)—which takes two forms: of
presumption, daring God's judgments;
or of *despair*, doubting His goodness.
The whole wilderness history, with its
crucial events of Massah and Meribah, is
represented as a "trying of the Lord"
in Ps. xcv. 8 ff. (*cf.* Num. xiv. 22), a
δοκιμασία (Heb. iii. 7-12); this process
culminated in the insolence of Num. xxi.
4 f., which was punished by the infliction
of the "fiery serpents". The like sin,
of presuming on the Divine forbearance,
the Cor. would commit if they trifled
with idolatry (*cf.* 22) and "sinned wilfully
after receiving the knowledge of the
truth" (Heb. x. 26; Rom. vi. 1); *cf.*
Deut. vi. 16 (Matt. iv. 7), Ps. lxxviii. 17
ff., for this trait of the Israelite character.
ἐκ-πειράζω is to *try thoroughly, to the
utmost*—as though one would see how far
God's indulgence will go. The graphic

[c] ἐγόγγυσαν καὶ ἀπώλοντο ὑπὸ τοῦ [d] ὀλοθρευτοῦ. 11. ταῦτα [1] δὲ
πάντα [1] [e] τύποι [2] [f] συνέβαινον [3] ἐκείνοις, ἐγράφη δὲ [g] πρὸς [h] νουθε-
σίαν ἡμῶν, [l] εἰς οὓς τὰ [i] τέλη τῶν [k] αἰώνων [l] κατήντησεν.[4] 12. ὥστε
ὁ [m] δοκῶν [n] ἑστάναι [o] βλεπέτω μὴ [y] πέσῃ. 13. [p] πειρασμὸς ὑμᾶς
οὐκ [q] εἴληφεν [5] εἰ μὴ [r] ἀνθρώπινος· [s] πιστὸς δὲ ὁ [s] Θεός, ὃς οὐκ

d *H.l.*; -ευω, Heb. xi. 28 (Exod. xii. 23); -ευσις, Josh. xvii. 13.
e τυπικως, *h.l.*; -κος, in Plutarch.

f 1 Pet. iv. 12; 2 Pet. ii. 22; four times in Lk. and Acts; once in Mt. g In this use, vi. 5, vii. 35, xii. 7, etc. h Eph. vi. 4; Tit. iii. 10; Judith vii. 27; Wisd. xvi. 6; -ετειν, see iv. 14. i In this sense, *h.l.* *Cf.* Mt. xiii. 39; Heb. ix. 26; also Rom. x. 4; 1 Pet. i. 9. k Pl., in like sense, ii. 7; Eph. iii. 9, 11; Col. i. 26; 1 Tim. i. 17; Heb. i. 8, xi. 3. l xiv. 36; Eph. iv. 13; Ph. iii. 11; Acts xxvi. 7. In lit. sense, Acts xvi. 1, etc. m See iii. 18. n In this tense and sense, 2 Cor. i. 24; Rom. v. 2, xi. 20; 2 Tim. ii. 19. Same inf. in Acts xii. 14; Lk. xiii. 25. o See viii. 9. p Gal. iv. 14; 1 Tim. vi. 9; Heb. iii. 8 (Ps. xciv. 8); Jas. i. 2, 12; 1 Pet. i. 6; Mt. vi. 13, etc. q λαμβανω with like subject, Lk. v. 26, vii. 16; Exod. xv. 15. r See ii. 13. s See i. 9.

[1] *Om.* **παντα** AB 17, sah., Mcion., Tert., Or., Cyr., Bas. **ταυτα δε παντα**: CKLP, etc., vg. syrr. cop. (Alexandrian); **παντα δε ταυτα**: ℵDG 46, Aug. (Western).

[2] **τυπικως**: all uncc. but DGL, which assimilate to ver. 6.

[3] **συνεβαινεν**, ℵBCK, twelve minn., Mcion., Or., Bas., Cyr. **συνεβαινον**, ADG, etc. (Western).

[4] **κατηντηκεν**, ℵBD*G, Bas., Euthal., Cyr. **κατηντησεν**, ACDᶜKL, etc.—Alexandrian and Syrian.

[5] **ου** (*sic*) **καταλαβῃ**: G, latt. vg. (*non apprehendat*), Latt. Ff.

impf., **ἀπώλλυντο**, "lay a-perishing," transports us to the scene of misery resulting from this experiment upon God!—**ὑπὸ** of *agent* after **ἀπόλλυμι**—a cl. idiom, *h.l.* for N.T.—elsewhere construed with dat., or **ἐν** and dat., of *cause* or *ground* of destruction (viii. 11, Rom. xiv. 15, etc.).—The "murmuring" also occurred repeatedly in the wilderness; but P. alludes specifically to the rebellion of Korah and its punishment—the only instance of violent death overtaking this sin (Num. xvi. 41). The **ὀλοθρευτὴς** in such supernatural chastisement is conceived as the "destroying angel" (2 Sam. xxiv. 16, Isa. xxxvii. 36), called **ὁ ὀλοθρεύων** in Exod. xii. 23, Heb. xi. 28 (*cf.* Wisd. xviii. 25); in later Jewish theology, *Sammael*, or the Angel of Death (Weber, *Altsyn. Théologie*, p. 244). The O.T. analogy suggests that P. had in view the murmurings of jealous partisans and unworthy teachers at Cor. (i. 12, iii. 6, iv. 6, 18 ff.); at this point he reverts to the impv. of 2nd. pers., **γογγύζετε.—τινες** (*quidam*), used throughout of the Israelite offenders, may mean *many* or *few*, anything short of "all" (1-4); *cf.* ver. 5, also ix. 22, viii. 7, Rom. iii. 3.

Ver. 11. "Now these things befel them by way of example" (**τυπικῶς**)—or "typically," "prefiguratively," if the other rendering of **τύποι** in ver. 6 be preferred ("in figura contingebant illis," Vg.); the adv. became current in the latter sense in eccl. Gr. The judgments quoted were *exemplary* in their nature; the story of them serves as a lesson for all time—"they were written with a view to (**πρὸς**) our admonition".—**συνέβαινον**, *impf.*, of the train of events; **ἐγράφη**, *aor.*, of the act of record summing them up. For the admonitory purpose of O.T. writers, see Isa. viii. 16, xxx. 8 ff., Hab. ii. 2 f., Deut. xxxi. 19 ff.—"Unto whom the ends of the ages have reached" (**κατήντηκεν**, *devenerunt*, Vg.)—"whom they have overtaken". **καταντάω** signifies reaching a mark, "arriving at" a definite point, whether the ultimate goal or not (see parls.). **τὰ τέλη τῶν αἰώνων** is syn. with **ἡ συντέλεια τ. αἰώνων** (Matt. xiii. 40, etc.) and other eschatological expressions (*cf.* 1 Peter i. 20, Heb. i. 2; also Gal. iv. 4, Eph. i. 10); the pl. indicates the *manifold* issues culminating in the Christian Church. "World-ages" (**αἰῶνες**) do not simply follow each other, but proceed side by side; so in particular the age of Israel and that of the Gentiles" (Hf.); "the ends" of Jewish and Pagan history alike are disclosed in Christianity; both streams converged, under God's direction (*cf.* Acts xv. 15 ff., xvii. 26 ff.), upon the Gentile Churches (**τέλος** has the double sense of *conclusion* and *aim*). The Church is the heir of the spiritual training of mankind; *cf.*, for the general idea, John iv. 37 f., 2 Tim. iii. 16 f., Gal. iii. 29, Eph. i. 9 ff.

Vv. 12, 13. The "examples" just set forth are full of warning (*a*), but with an

t With inf., ^t ἐάσει ¹ ὑμᾶς ^u πειρασθῆναι ^v ὑπὲρ ^v ὃ ² δύνασθε, ἀλλὰ ποιήσει σὺν
Mt. xxiv.
43; Lk. τῷ ^p πειρασμῷ καὶ τὴν ^w ἔκβασιν τοῦ δύνασθαι ὑμᾶς ^{3 x} ὑπενεγκεῖν.
iv. 41; 4
times in 14. ^y διόπερ, ^z ἀγαπητοί ^z μου, ^a φεύγετε ^a ἀπὸ τῆς ^b εἰδωλολατρείας.
Acts.
u See ver. 9
above. v See iv. 6. w Heb. xiii. 7; Wisd. ii. 17, viii. 10, xi. 14. x 2 Tim. iii. 11; 1 Pet. ii.
19; Job ii. 10; Ps. liv. 12; Prov. vi. 33. y See viii. 13. z Ph. ii. 12; 2 Pet. i. 17; Mt. xii. 18 (Isa.
xlii. 1). a See vi. 18. b Gal. v. 20; Col. iii. 5; 1 Pet. iv. 3; -τρης, ver. 7 above.

¹ αφησει DG—Western emendation.

² G and several latt. insert ου (*super id quod non*).

³ *Om.* υμας all uncc. but אcDcK.

aspect of (*b*) encouragement besides. (*a*) "So then"—ὥστε with impv., as in iii. 21 (see note)—"he that thinks (ὁ δοκῶν: see note, iii. 18) that he stands, let him take heed (βλεπέτω) lest he fall!" For "such *thinking*, as it leads to trust in one-self, is the beginning of a perilous se-curity" (Hf.); this vanity was precisely the danger of the Cor. (see iv. 6 ff., v. 2, etc.). For the pf. ἑστάναι, in this em-phatic sense (*to stand fast*), see parls. A moral "fall" is apprehended, involving personal ruin (5, 8; Rom. xi. 11, 22).— (*b*) The example which alarms the self-confident, may give hope to the despon-dent; it shows that the present trials are not unprecedented: πειρασμὸς ὑμᾶς οὐκ εἴληφεν εἰ μὴ ἀνθρώπινος, "It is only *human* temptation that has come upon you"—such as men have been through before. Ver. 13 follows sharply on ver. 12, ἀσυνδέτως, correcting a depressing fear that would arise in some minds.— εἴληφεν (see parls.) describes a situation which "has seized" and holds one in its grasp (pf.).—ἀνθρώπινος connotes both *quod hominibus solet* (Cv.) and *homini superabilis* (Bg.), *such as man can bear* (R.V.),—σύμμετρος τῇ φύσει (Thd.). Some give an objective turn to the adj., reading the clause as one of *further warning*: "It is only *trial from men* that has overtaken you" (so, with varia-tions, Chr., Est., Gr., Bg.—*opponitur tentatio demoniaca*). But the sequel im-plies a temptation measured by the strength of the tempted; moreover, as El. says, P. would have written οὔπω ἔλαβεν, rather than οὐκ εἴληφεν, if fore-boding worse trial in store; nor did he conceive the actual trials of the Cor., any more than those of the Thess. or Asian Churches (1 Thess. iii. 5, Eph. vi. 10 ff.), as without diabolical elements (see 20 ff., vii. 5, 2 Cor. xi. 3, 14).—εἰ μὴ is attached to ἀνθρώπινος alone: lit. "temptation has not seized you, except a human (temptation)"—*i.e.*, "otherwise than hu-man".—πιστὸς δὲ ὁ Θεός contrasts the

human and Divine; for the natural trial a supernatural Providence guarantees sufficient aid (see parls.). ὅς = ὅτι οὗτος (*cf.* 2 Cor. i. 18): "God is faithful in that (*or* so that) He etc.". Paul ascribes to God not the origination, but the *con-trol* of temptation (*cf.* Matt. vi. 13, Luke xxii. 31 f., James i. 12 ff.): the πειρασμὸς is inevitable, lying in the conditions of human nature; God limits it, and supplies along with it the ἔκβασις.—For the el-lipsis in (ὑπὲρ ὃ) δύνασθε, *cf.* iii. 2.—The art. in ὁ πειρασμός, τὴν ἔκβασιν, is indi-vidualising: "the temptation" and "the egress" match each other, the latter pro-vided for the former; hence καί, "also," *indivulso nexu* (Bg.). *Issue* is a sense of ἔκβασις in later Gr.; in cl. Gr. *disem-barkation*, then *exit, escape*. In τοῦ δύνασθαι ὑπενεγκεῖν (for gen. inf. of *purpose*, see Wr., p. 408) the subject is not expressed; as coming under God's general dealing with men, it is conceived inde-finitely—"that one may be able to bear". Shut into a *cul de sac*, a man de-spairs; but let him see a door open for his exit, and he will struggle on with his load. ἔκβασις signifies *getting clear* away *from* the struggle; ὑπενεγκεῖν, *holding up under* it, the latter made possible by the hope of the former. How different all this from the Stoic consolation of sui-cide: "The door stands open"! In the Cor. "temptation" we must include both the allurements of idolatry and the persecution which its abandonment en-tailed.

Ver. 14 gives the final point to all that has been urged, from ver. 1 onwards: the sad fate of the Israelite fathers, the correspondence between their trials and those of the Cor. readers, the possibility of effectual resistance, and the certain relief to which the Divine fidelity is pledged—these considerations combine to enforce the appeal, *Flee from idolatry*; *cf.* vi. 18*a*, and note.—διόπερ, as in viii. 13 (see note), points with emphatic finger along the line of past history; ἀγαπητοί

15. ᶜ Ὡς ᵈ φρονίμοις · ᶜ λέγω κρίνατε ὑμεῖς ὅ ᵉ φημι · 16. τὸ ᶜ 2 Cor. vi.
13; *cf.*
ᶠ ποτήριον τῆς ᵍ εὐλογίας ὃ ʰ εὐλογοῦμεν, οὐχὶ ⁱ κοινωνία τοῦ ˡ Acts xvii.
22.
ᵏ αἵματος ˡ τοῦ ᵏ Χριστοῦ ˡ ἐστιν ˡ ; τὸν ˡ ἄρτον ὃν ᵐ κλῶμεν, οὐχὶ ᵈ See iv. 10.
e See vii.29.
f xi. 25 ff.;

Mt. xxvi. 27 (*cf.* 39), and parls.; see also Mt. xx. 22 f.; Rev. xiv. 10, etc. For position of noun, Jo.
xviii. 11; Mt. xxi. 42, etc. g Gal. iii. 14; Jas. iii. 10; Rev. v. 12 f., vii. 12; Gen. xxviii. 4.
h Mt. xxvi. 26; Mk. xi. 10, xiv. 22; Lk. xxiv. 30. Here only of *things*. See also iv. 12. i With obj.
gen., Ph. iii. 10. See also i. 9, and note on construction. k xi. 25, 27; Eph. ii. 13; Heb. ix. 12,
14; 1 Pet. i. 2; Jo. i. 7; Rev. i. 5, v. 9, vii. 14, etc.; Mt. xxvi. 28, etc.; Jo. vi. 53 ff. l xi. 23 ff.;
Acts ii. 42, 46, xx. 7, 11, xxvii. 35; Mt. xxvi. 26, etc.; Jo. vi. 35 ff., xiii. 18, xxi. 13. m xi. 24; Acts
ii. 46, etc.; Mt. xxvi. 26, etc., xiv. 19, xv. 36; Lk. xxiv. 30.

¹ κοινωνια εστιν του αιματος του Χριστου (in this order) : ABP. So
Tr., W.H.—diff. from parl. clause. A has εστιν after κοινωνια in second clause also.

μου (*cf.* iv. 14) reinforces admonition with entreaty.

§ 33. THE COMMUNION OF THE LORD, AND OF DEMONS, x. 15-24. A further warning the Ap. will give against dalliance with idolatry, based on Christian practice as the former was based on Israelite history. He points to *the table of the Lord's Supper*, and asks the Cor. to judge as men of sense whether it is possible to take of Christ's *cup* and *loaf*, and then to sit at a table where in reality one communicates with demons! What can be more revolting than such conduct? what more insulting towards the Lord?

Ver. 15. Ὡς φρονίμοις λέγω · κρίνατε ὑμεῖς ὅ φημι : "As to men of sense I speak ; be yourselves the judges of what I affirm." With this prefatory appeal to the intelligence of the readers *cf.* the introductory phrases of Rom. vi. 19, Gal. iii. 15 ; the ground of admonition in this § lies entirely within the judgment of the Cor., as that of the last § did not (1). The Cor. are φρόνιμοι, intellectually clever and shrewd, not σοφοί (as some of them thought themselves to be, iii. 18); this compliment is consistent with the censure of iii. 1 ff. ; see parls., also Trench *Syn.*, § lxxv. "The new conception of the πνευματικὸς caused the word φρόνιμος to sink to a much lower level in the N.T. than it occupied in Plato or Aristotle" (Ed.). Philo disparages φρόνησις, defining it as μέση πανουργίας κ. μωρίας (*Quod Deus immut.*, § 35) ; he says, σοφία μὲν γὰρ πρὸς θεραπείαν Θεοῦ, φρόνησις δὲ πρὸς ἀνθρώπινον βίον διοίκησιν (*De præm. et pæn.* § 14).—On φημί (again in 19), *cf.* vii. 29, and note. For like appeals, see Luke xii. 57, Acts iv. 19. The questions that follow, the readers will easily answer from their knowledge of religious custom and feeling.

Ver. 16. κοινωνία is the key-word of this passage (see parls.) ; the Lord's Supper constitutes a "communion" centring in Christ, as the Jewish festal rites centred in "the altar" (18), and as "the demons," the unseen objects of idolatrous worship, supply their basis of communion in idolatrous feasts (21 f.). Such fellowship involves (1) *the ground of communion*, the sacred object celebrated in common ; (2) *the association* established amongst the celebrants, separating them from all others : "The word *communion* denotes the fellowship of persons with persons in one and the same object" (Ev.). These two ideas take expression in vv. 16, 17 in turn; their joint force lies behind the protest of vv. 20 ff.—Appealing to the Eucharist—or *Eulogia*, as it was also called—P. begins with "the cup" (*cf.* the order of Luke xxii. 17 ff., and *Didaché* ix. 2 f.), the prominent object in the sacrificial meal (21), containing, as one may say, the essence of the feast (*cf.* Ps. xxiii. 5). τ. εὐλογίας is attributive gen. (like "cup of salvation" in Ps. cxvi. 13 ; see other parls., for both words) ; so Cv., "destinatus ad mysticam eulogiam," and Hn. (see his note). Christ blessed this cup, making it thus for ever a "cup of blessing" ; *cf.* the early sacramental phrases, οἱ τῆς εὐλογίας Ἰησοῦ ἄρτοι in Or. on Matt. x. 25, and τὰς εὐλογίας τ. Χριστοῦ ἐσθίειν from the Catacombs (X. Kraus, *Roma sotteranea*, 217), cited by Hn. On this view, ὁ εὐλογοῦμεν is no repetition of τῆς εὐλογίας, but is antithetical to it in the manner of Eph. i. 3 : *sc.* "the cup which gives blessing, for which we give blessing to God". The prevalent interpretation of τ. ποτήρ. τ. εὐλογίας makes the phrase a rendering of *kōs habb'rakah*, the *third* cup of the Passover meal, over which a specific blessing was pronounced (often identified with that of the Eucharist) ; or, as Ed. thinks (referring to Luke xxii. 20), the *fourth*, which closed the meal and was attended with the singing of the

n xi. 24 ff.; ¹κοινωνία τοῦ ⁿσώματος τοῦ ⁿΧριστοῦ ἐστιν; 17. ὅτι εἷς ἄρτος,
26; Rom.
vii. 4; Ph. ἓν σῶμα °οἱ °πολλοί ἐσμεν, ᴾοἱ γὰρ ᴾπάντες ἐκ τοῦ ἑνὸς ἄρτου
iii. 21;
Col. i. 22; Heb. x. 10; 1 Pet. ii. 24.   o Ver. 33; 2 Cor. ii. 17; Rom. v. 15, 19, xii. 5; Heb. xii. 15;
Mt. xxiv. 12; Mk. vi. 2.   p See ix. 22.

Hallel. Such a technical Hebraism would scarcely be obvious to the Cor., and the gen. so construed is artificial in point of Gr. idiom ; whereas the former construction is natural, and gives a sense in keeping with the readers' experience.—τὸ ποτήριον, τὸν ἄρτον are acc. by *inverse relative attraction*, a constr. not unknown, though rare, in cl. Gr. (see Wr., p. 204). Hf. thinks that, with the merging of these nouns in the rel. clause, the *act of blessing* the cup and *breaking* the bread becomes the real subject of κοινωνία in each instance—as though P. wrote, "when we bless the cup, break the bread, is it not a communion, etc. ? " In any case, the "communion" looks beyond the bare ποτήριον and ἄρτος to the whole sacred action, the *usus poculi,* etc. (Bg.), of which they form the centre. " The bread " is " blessed " equally with " the cup," but in its case the prominent symbolic act is that of *breaking* (see parls.), which connotes the distribution to "many" of the "one loaf." Thus " the sacramental bread came to be known as the κλασμός: so *Did.,* § 9 " (Ed.).—On the pl. εὐλογοῦμεν, κλῶμεν, Mr. observes : " *Whose* was it to officiate in this consecration ? At this date, when the order of public worship in the Church was far from being settled, *any Christian man was competent.* By the time of Justin (*Apol.* i. 65) the function was reserved for the προεστώς, but on the understanding that he represented the community and acted in communion with it (see Ritschl, *Altkath. Kirche,*² pp. 365 f.). The pls. of our passage speak out of the consciousness of the Christian fellowship, in which it is matter of indifference who may be, in this instance or that, its administrative organ."—οὐχὶ κοινωνία τοῦ αἵματος, τοῦ σώματος, τοῦ Χριστοῦ; " Is it not a communion of (or in) the blood, the body, of Christ ? " (*cf.,* for the gen. after κοινωνία, note on i. 9) —not "a communion *with* the blood, etc." The stress lies on τοῦ Χριστοῦ in both questions : through the cup and loaf believers participate together in *Christ,* in the sacrifice of His blood offered to God (Rom. iii. 25, Eph. i. 7, Heb. ix. 11 ff., 24 ff.), and in the whole redemption wrought through His bodily life and death and resurrection. τὸ σῶμα τοῦ Χριστοῦ

carries our thoughts from the incarnation (Phil. ii. 7), through the crucifixion (Col. i. 22), on to the heavenly glory of the Redeemer (Phil. iii. 21). The cup and bread are here styled " a *communion* in Christ's blood and body " ; in His own words (xi. 25), " the *new covenant* in My blood,"—a communion on the basis of the covenant established by the sacrifice of the Cross.

Ver. 17 unfolds the assertion virtually contained in the question just asked : " Seeing that (ὅτι) there is one bread, we, the many, are one body " ; so Vg., " Quoniam unus panis, unum corpus multi sumus," Cv., Bz., Bg., Hf., Bt., Hn., Gd., El., R.V. marg. ; *cf.* the mutually supporting unities of Eph. iv. 4 ff. The saying is aphoristic : *One bread makes one body* (Hn.)—a maxim of hospitality (equally true of "the cup ") that applies to all associations cemented by a common feast. " The bread " suggests the further, kindred idea of *a common nourishment* sustaining an identical life, the loaf on the table symbolising the ἀληθινὸς ἄρτος of John vi., which feeds the Church in every limb (xii. 13).—" For (γὰρ of explanation) we all partake from (partitive ἐκ, *cf.* ix. 7) the one bread"; eating from the common loaf attests and seals the *union* of the participants in Christ.

Ver. 17 is parenthetical, but no interpolation as Sm. thinks ; it is necessary to develop the idea of κοινωνία in ver. 16, showing how vital to the Church is the fellowship of the Lord's Table, that was being violated by attendance at idol-feasts.—The elliptical ὅτι . . . ἐσμεν is often construed as a continued dependent clause under the regimen of ὅτι: either (*a*) " Since we, who are many, are one bread (loaf), one body " (A.V., R.V. txt., with several ancient Verss., Est., Al., Sm.) ; or (*b*) " Since there (is) one bread, (and) we, the many, are one body" (D.W., Mr.)—these renderings making the two statements a double reason for the κοινωνία of ver. 16, instead of seeing in the εἷς ἄρτος an evidence of the ἓν σῶμα. But (*a*) confuses two distinct figures, and identifies unsuitably "the bread" with the Church itself. (*b*) escapes this error by reading into the first clause the ἐστὶν required to match ἐσμὲν in the second ; but the copulative "and " is

ᵠμετέχομεν. 18. ᶜβλέπετε τὸν Ἰσραὴλ ˢκατὰ ˢσάρκα· οὐχὶ¹ οἱ ᵠ See ix. 10.
ἐσθίοντες τὰς θυσίας ᵗκοινωνοὶ τοῦ ⁿθυσιαστηρίου εἰσί; 19. τί ˢSee i. 26.
οὖν ᵉφημι; ὅτι ʷεἴδωλόν² τί ἐστιν, ἢ ὅτι ᵛεἰδωλόθυτον² τί ἐστιν; viii. 23;
20. ἀλλ᾽ ὅτι ἃ ˣθύει³ τὰ⁴ ʸἔθνη,⁴ ᶻδαιμονίοις ˣθύει³ καὶ οὐ Θεῷ⁵· Heb.x.33;

Mt. xxiii. 30; Lk. v. 10.   u See ix. 13.   v See viii. 1.   w See viii. 4.   x Absol., Acts xiv. 13,
18 (with dat., as here); Exod. xxiii. 18.   See v. 7.   y See i. 23, v. 1, τ. ἐθνη.   z Deut. xxxii. 17;
1 Tim. iv. 1; Acts xvii. 18; Jas. ii.19; Rev. ix. 20, xvi. 14; Gospp. passim.

¹ ο υ χ, אACD*G.   ουχι, B and Syrians; so W.H. marg.

² ε ι δ ω λ ο θ υ τ ο ν . . . ε ι δ ω λ ο ν (in this order): אaBC**DP 46, 73, latt. vg.
sah. cop., Aug., Ambrst.   א*AC* om. η οτι ειδωλον τι εστιν, by homœoleuton—a
circumstance tending to prove a common (Alexandrian?) ancestor. Similarly 17,
71 om. οτι ειδωλοθυτον κ.τ.λ.—a reading indicated also by Tert. and Aug.

³ θ υ ο υ σ ι ν (twice), all uncc. but KL.

⁴ Om. τα εθνη (?) BDG, Mcion., Tert.   Lachm., Tisch., Al. om.; W.H. and Nestle
bracket the words.

⁵ κ α ι ο υ Θ ε ῳ θ υ ο υ σ ι ν (in this order): אABCP 17, 37, 46.

artificially supplied; moreover, Mr.'s interpretation reverses the contextual relation of the ἄρτος and σῶμα, making the
latter the ground of the former, whereas
Paul argues that the bread assures the
oneness of the body; through loaf and
cup we realise our communion in Christ.
Ver. 18. "For look at Israel after the
flesh: are not those that eat the sacrifice
communicants of the altar?"—i.e., participation in the sacrificial feast constitutes fellowship in the sacrifice.—τὸν
Ἰσραὴλ κατὰ σάρκα, in contrast with
Ἰσρ. κατὰ πνεῦμα (Rom. ii. 28 f., Gal. iv.
29, vi. 16, etc.; see note on οἱ πατ. ἡμῶν,
1). The Ap. is not thinking of the priests
specifically, as in ix. 13 (Hn.), nor of the
people as sharing with them (Al.), but of
the festal communion of Israelites as
such—e.g., at the Passover, the sacrificial
meal κατ᾽ ἐξοχήν: see Lev. vii. 11-34,
Deut. xii. 11-28, 1 Sam. ix. 12 ff. The
altar furnishes the table at which Jehovah's guests enjoy their covenant
fellowship in the gifts of His salvation.
The feasters are thus κοινωνοὶ τ. θυσιασ-
τηρίου, recognising the altar as their
common altar and mutually pledging
themselves to its service.
Vv. 19, 20. Paul's appeal to the meaning of the Lord's Supper is leading up to
a prohibition of attendance at the idol-
feasts. Against this veto the men of
"knowledge" will argue that idolatry is
illusion (viii. 4 ff.), its rites having no such
ground in reality as belongs to Christian
observances; the festival has no religious
meaning to them, and does not touch
their conscience (contrast viii. 7); if
friendship or social feeling invites their

presence, why should they not go? Paul
admits the non-reality of the idol in
itself; but he discerns other terrible pre-
sences behind the image—"demons"
are virtually worshipped at the idol-feast,
and with these the celebrants are brought
into contact. "What then do I affirm
(the φημὶ of 15 resumed)? that an idol-
sacrifice is anything (has reality)? or that
an idol is anything? (to say this would
be to contradict viii. 4). No, but that
(ἀλλ᾽ ὅτι) what the Gentiles sacrifice they
sacrifice to demons, and not to God; and
I would not that you should be communicants of the demons!" How could the
Cor., as "men of sense, judge" of a situation like this? The riot and debauch
attending heathen festivals showed that
foul spirits of evil presided over them: cf.
vv. 6 ff., referring to the worship of Baal-
Peor, with which the allusion here made
to Deut. xxxii. 17 (cf. Ps. cvi. 37 f.) is in
keeping. "That the worship of heathen
cults was offered quoad eventum—not
indeed quoad intentionem—to devils was,
consistently with their strict monotheism,
the general view of later Jews" (Mr.).
Heathenism P. regarded as the domain
of Satan (2 Cor. iv. 4, Eph. ii. 2, vi. 12;
cf. Luke iv. 6, 1 John v. 19), under whose
rule the demons serve as the angels under
that of God (2 Cor. xii. 7, 1 Tim. iv. 1;
cf. Matt. xii. 24, xxv. 41, etc.); idolatry
was, above everything, inspired by Satan.
δαιμόνιον (=δαίμων, of which it is neut.
adj.) was primarily synon. with θεῖον—
"δαίμων is related to θεὸς as numen to
persona divina" (Cr.); τὸ δαιμόνιον
οὐδέν ἐστιν ἀλλ᾽ ἢ θεὸς ἢ θεοῦ ἔργον
(Arist., Rhet., ii., 23. 8); hence Socrates

a (Nolo), xvi. 7; 2 Cor. xii. 20; Rom. vii. 16; 2 Th. iii. 10; 3 Jo. 13; Rev. ii. 21; freq.

οὐ ^aθέλω δὲ ὑμᾶς ^tκοινωνοὺς τῶν ^zδαιμονίων γίνεσθαι· 21. οὐ δύνασθε ^fποτήριον Κυρίου πίνειν καὶ ^fποτήριον ^zδαιμονίων, οὐ δύνασθε ^bτραπέζης Κυρίου ^qμετέχειν καὶ ^bτραπέζης ^{zb}δαιμονίων· 22. ἢ ^cπαραζηλοῦμεν τὸν Κύριον; μὴ ^dἰσχυρότεροι αὐτοῦ ἐσμεν;

in Gospp.; cf. x. 1.   b Rom. xi. 9; Ps. lxxvii. 20; also Mt. xv. 27; Lk. xvi. 21, xxii. 21, 30. For τρ. δαιμ, cf. Isa. lxv. 11.   c Rom. x. 19 (Deut. xxxii. 21), xi. 11, 14.   d See i. 25.

called the mysterious guiding voice within him δαιμόνιόν τι. Ed. observes a tendency, beginning with Eurip. and Plato and accentuated in the Stoics, " to use the word in a depreciatory sense"; already in Homer it often suggested the *uncanny*, the supernatural as an object of dread. The word was ready to hand for the LXX translators, who used it to render various Heb. epithets for heathen gods. Later Judaism, which peopled the unseen with good and evil spirits, made δαιμόνια a general term for the latter, apart from any specific refer. to idols (see, already, Tob. iii. 8, etc.); hence its prominence in the Gospels, and the origin of the word *demoniac* (ὁ δαιμονιζόμενος): on the whole subject, see Cr. *s.v.*, also Everling's *Paulinische Angelologie u. Dämonologie*. For κοινωνοὶ τ. δαιμονίων, *cf.* Isa. xliv. 11, where the "fellows" of the idol signify a kind of religious guild, brought into mystic union with their god through the sacrificial meal (see Cheyne *ad loc.*); also Isa. lxv. 11. Ver. 20c is calculated to bring home to the Cor. the fearful danger of trifling with idolatry.

Vv. 21, 22. This lively apostrophe sets in the strongest light the inconsistency of Cor. Christians who conform to idolatry, the untenability of their position. "You cannot drink the Lord's cup and the cup of *demons*"—the two together! "You cannot partake of the Lord's table and the table of *demons!*" Cf. the τίς μετοχή, κοινωνία, κ.τ.λ.; of. 2 Cor. vi. 14 ff., and other parls. The nouns forming the obj. are anarthrous as being qualitative, the impossibility lying in the *kind* of the two cups; *cf.* note on ii. 5. "The *Lord's* cup" is that received at His direction and signifying allegiance to Him; in ver. 16, "the cup of (His) blessing."—Possibly, P. alludes here to Mal. i. 7, 12, where 'the table" signifies "the altar of Jehovah"; but the expression is borrowed without this identification. In this context table and altar are essentially distinguished; the altar *supplies* the table (*cf.* Heb. xiii. 10). "S. Coena convivium, non sacrificium; in mensa, non in altari" (Bg.). The τράπεζα includes the ποτήριον and

ἄρτος of ver. 16 together. This passage gives its name of "the Lord's Table" to the Eucharist.—"Or (is it that) we provoke the Lord to jealousy?"—is this what we mean by eating at both tables? Paul includes himself in this question; such conduct is conceivable in his case, since he had no scruple against the idolothyta on their own account (see viii., ix. 1). Deut. xxxii. 21 (neighbouring the previous allusion of 20) sufficiently indicates the result of such insolence: see other O.T. parls. For this argumentative ἢ in Paul's questions, *cf.* vi. 9, etc., ix. 6.—If the Cor. *are* daring Christ's sovereign displeasure by coquetting with idolatry, they must suppose themselves "stronger than He"! As sensible and prudent men they must see the absurdity, as well as the awful peril, of such double-dealing: *cf.* Deut. xxxii. 6, 28 f. ἰσχυρός (i. 25) implies inherent, personal strength. Of the δύναμις τ. κυρ. Ἰησοῦ P. had given a solemn impression in ch. v. 4 f.; *cf.* 2 Cor. xiii. 3 f.

§ 34. LIBERTY AND ITS LIMITS, x. 23-xi. 1. The maxim "All things are lawful" was pleaded in defence of the use of the idolothyta, as of other Cor. laxities; so the Ap. has to discuss it a second time (*cf.* vi. 12). In ch. vi. he bade his readers guard the application of this principle for their own sake, now for the sake of others; there in the interests of purity, here of charity (23 f.). When buying meat in the market, or when dining at an unbeliever's table, the Christian need not enquire whether the flesh offered him is sacrificial or not; but if the fact is pointedly brought to his notice, he should abstain, to avoid giving scandal (25-30). Above all such regulations stands the supreme and comprehensive rule of *doing everything to God's glory* (31). Let the Cor. follow Paul as he himself follows Christ, in living for the highest good of others (32-xi. 1).

Ver. 23. On πάντα ἔξεστιν κ.τ.λ., see notes to vi. 12. The form of that ver. seems to be purposely repeated here (μοι only omitted), with the effect of bringing out the *altruistic* as complementary to the *self-regarding* side of Christian ex-

23. ᵉΠάντα μοι ¹ ᵉἔξεστιν, ἀλλ᾽ ᵉοὐ πάντα ᵉσυμφέρει· ᵉπάντα   e See vi. 1e.
μοι ¹ ᵉἔξεστιν, ἀλλ᾽ οὐ πάντα ᶠοἰκοδομεῖ· 24. μηδεὶς ᵍτὸ ᵍἑαυτοῦ   f See viii.10.
ʰζητείτω, ἀλλὰ ⁱτὸ τοῦ ⁱἑτέρου ἕκαστος.² 25. πᾶν τὸ ἐν ᵏμακέλλῳ   g xiii. 5;
ˡπωλούμενον ἐσθίετε, μηδὲν ᵐἀνακρίνοντες διὰ τὴν ⁿσυνείδησιν,
26. ᵒτοῦ γὰρ ³ Κυρίου ³ ἡ γῆ καὶ τὸ ᵖπλήρωμα αὐτῆς· 27. εἰ δέ⁴

Ph. ii. 4,
21; cf.Mt.
xvi. 23.
h Ver. 33,
xiii. 5; 2
Cor. xii.
14; Ph. ii.
21; Neh.

ii. 10. See i. 22.   i Ph. ii. 21.   o ετερος, see iv. 6.   k H.l.; see note below.   l Mt. x. 29, etc.;
h.l. in Epp.   m See ii. 14.   n See viii. 10.   o Ps. xxiii. 1, xlix. 12.   p In this sense, Mk. vi.
43, viii. 20.

¹ Om. μοι (supplied from vi. 12) all pre-Syrian uncc.

² Om. εκαστος pre-Syrian uncc. and verss.

³ του Κυριου γαρ (in this order): all uncc. but AHKLP.

⁴ Om. δε pre-Syrian uncc. and verss.

pediency. On Paul's dialectical use of the words of opponents, cf. viii. 1 ff. and notes. Closing his discussion about the sacrificial meats, P. returns to the point from which he set out in ch. viii., viz., *the supremacy of love* in Church life—there commended as superior to *knowledge*, here as supplying the guard of *liberty;* in both passages, it is the principle of *edification.*—The tacit obj. of οἰκοδομεῖ (see viii. 1, iii. 9-17) is "the Church of God" (32). Edification, in its proper meaning, is always relative to the community; P. is safe-guarding not the particular interests of "the weak brother" so much as the welfare of the Church, when he says, "Not all things edify".

Ver. 24. With μηδεὶς τ. ἑαυτοῦ κ.τ.λ. cf. xiii. 5, Rom. xiv. 7, xv. 2, Gal. vi. 2, Phil. ii. 1 ff. After ἀλλὰ understand ἕκαστος, from the previous μηδείς: cf. the ellipsis in iii. 1, 7, vii. 19 (Bm., p. 392). For ὁ ἔτερος (= ὁ πλησίον, Rom. xv. 2), wider than ὁ ἀδελφός (viii. 11; cf. 27 f.)—"the other" in contrast with oneself—see parls.; Gr. idiom prefers "the other" where we say "others".—τὸ ἑαυτοῦ, τὸ τοῦ ἑτέρου, implies some definite good—"his own, the other's interest": a N.T. h. l.; the pl. elsewhere in such connexion (cf. Matt. xxii. 21).

Vv. 25, 26. The above rule is now applied in the concrete. πᾶν τὸ ἐν μακέλλῳ πωλούμενον κ.τ.λ., "Anything that is on sale in the meat-market eat, not asking any question of conscience". μάκελλον is a term of late Gr., borrowed from Latin (*macellum*): possibly a local word, introduced by the *colonia;* for the anarthrous ἐν μακ., cf. note on ἐν σταδίῳ (ix. 24).—μηδὲν ἀνακρίνοντες διὰ συνείδησιν might mean "for conscience' sake (to avoid embarrassment of conscience) making no enquiry" (Cm.,

Er., Hf., El., Holsten), as though addressed to men of weak conscience—Bg. however, "propter conscientiam alienam" (referring to 29); or, "because of your (*sc.* strong) conscience making no enquiry"—since you are not troubled with scruples (Est., Mr., Ed.); or, "making no enquiry on the ground of conscience," the adv. phrase simply defining the kind of question deprecated (so Bz., Hn., Bt., Gd., Ev.): the last interpretation best suits the generality of the terms, and the connexion with ver. 26. For ἀνακρίνω, see ii. 14, iv. 3, ix. 3, and notes; it signifies enquiry with a view to judgment at the bar of conscience.—μηδέν, acc. of *definition*, as in Acts x. 20, xi. 12; Sm. baldly renders it as transitive obj., "examining nothing"—*kein Fleischstück untersuchend!* For μὴ in ptpl. clause, see Wr., p. 606.—The citation from Ps. xxiv. 1, recalling the argument of viii. 4 ff., quiets the buyer's conscience: consecration to an idol cannot deprive the Lord of anything that belongs to "the earth and its fulness," and which His providence supplies for His servants' need; cf. Rom. xiv. 6b, 14, 1 Tim. iv. 4.—πλήρωμα, in its primary sense, *id quo res impletur* (cf. Lt., *Colossians*, pp. 257 ff.); "terra si arboribus, herbis, animalibus etc., careret, esset tanquam domus supellectile et omnibus instrumentis vacua" (Cv.).

Ver. 27: a case parl. to that of vv. 25 f., attached therefore asyndetically; cf. the two clauses of ver. 16. When one buys for himself, the question arises at the *shop;* when he is the guest of another, it arises at the *table.* "If some one invites you, of the unbelievers, and you determine to go."—τῶν ἀπίστων is emphatic by position: in a non-Christian house sacrificial meat was likely to be used, and here the Christian's conduct

q Mt. xxii. 3 ff.; Lk. vii. 39, xiv. 7 ff.; Jo. ii. 2; Esth. v. 12.
r See vi. 6.
s Lk. x. 8; Mk. vi. 41; Acts xvi. 34; Gen. xliii. 31 f.
t ιεροθυτον, *h.l.*; see txtl. and exeg. notes.
u Lk. xx. 37; Acts xxiii. 30; Jo. xi. 57; 2 Macc. iii. 7, vi. 11, xiv. 37.
v In this sense, see i. 12.
w Mt. ix. 4, xxvii. 46; Lk. xiii. 7; Acts iv. 25, vii. 26.

τις [q] καλεῖ ὑμᾶς τῶν [r] ἀπίστων[1] καὶ θέλετε πορεύεσθαι, πᾶν τὸ [s] παρατιθέμενον ὑμῖν ἐσθίετε, μηδὲν [m] ἀνακρίνοντες διὰ τὴν [n] συνείδησιν· 28. ἐὰν δέ τις ὑμῖν[2] εἴπῃ, "Τοῦτο [t] εἰδωλόθυτόν[3] ἐστι," μὴ ἐσθίετε, δι' ἐκεῖνον τὸν [u] μηνύσαντα καὶ τὴν [n] συνείδησιν, [o] τοῦ[4] γὰρ Κυρίου[4] ἡ γῆ[4] καὶ τὸ [p] πλήρωμα αὐτῆς[4]· 29. [n] συνείδησιν δὲ [v] λέγω οὐχὶ τὴν ἑαυτοῦ,[5] ἀλλὰ [i] τὴν τοῦ [i] ἑτέρου· [w] ἱνατί γὰρ ἡ

[1] Add **εις δειπνον** DG, latt., some codd. of vg. sah.: a characteristic Western gloss.

[2] Om. **υμιν** G, latt. vg.

[3] **ιεροθυτον,** ℵABH, sah., some latt. codd., Julian (as instanced in Cyr.[229]), also Cyr.[233]. A Biblical *h.l.*; see note below.

[4] *Om.* **του γαρ Κυρ. . . . αυτης** all pre-Syrian uncc. and verss. (including vg.),—repeated from ver. 26; C[3] adds it to ver. 31 instead.

[5] For **εαυτου** D* has the correction **σεαυτου**; H and some others, **εμαυτου.**

would be narrowly watched.—**θέλετε** in N.T., as in cl. Gr. (see Lidd., under **βούλομαι,** as against Gm. under **θέλω**: *cf.* note on xii. 11), signifies *will*, *active purpose*, not mere *wish* ("are disposed to go," E.V.); the invited make up their mind to go, are *bent* on it (P. "non valde probat," Bg.; "a hint that it would be wise to keep away," El.); the next clause discovers them there, with the viands before them. P. assumes social intercourse of Christians with heathen—not with false Christians (v. 10 f.); there can be no question, after vv. 20 ff., of attending an idol-feast or **κατακεῖσθαι ἐν εἰδωλίῳ** (viii. 10).—**τ. παρατιθέμενον** replaces **τ. πωλούμενον** of ver. 25; the rest is a repetition: no more need to raise the question of conscience in the one case than in the other.

Vv. 28, 29*a*. **ἐὰν δὲ . . . εἴπῃ,** "But if any one say to you"—a probable contingency, as **εἴ τις καλεῖ κ.τ.λ.** (27) was an assumed fact; see Bn. on the forms of the Condit. Sentence, §§ 242 ff.—**δὲ** confronts this contingency with *both* the situations described in vv. 25 and 27. The information, "This is sacrificial meat," might be volunteered to the Christian purchaser in the market (by the salesman, or a by-stander), or to the Christian guest at the unbeliever's table (by the host, or by a fellow-guest), the communication being prompted by civility and the wish to spare the supposed susceptibilities of the Christian, or by the desire to embarrass him; whatever its occasion or motive, it alters the situation. The genuine reading, **ἱερόθυτον** (*slain-as-sacred*, i.e., *in sacrifice*), takes the statement as from the mouth of unbelievers; a Jew or Christian would presumably say **εἰδωλόθυτον,** as above and here in T.R.: Reuss and El. suppose the informant to be "a Christian converted from heathenism" using the inoffensive term "at the table of a heathen host"; but **τ. ἀπίστων** suggests *heathen* company, and **μηνύσαντα** *private* information. "Forbear eating (**μὴ ἐσθίετε,** revoking the permission of 25 ff.) for the sake of him that informed (you), and for conscience' sake."—**Μηνύω** (see parls.), *to disclose* what does not appear on the surface or is imparted secretly. The informant expects the Christian to be shocked; with his **συνήθεια τ. εἰδώλου** (viii. 7), he looks on the flesh of the sacrifice as having acquired a religious character (it is **ἱερόθυτον**); by saying **Τοῦτο ἱερόθυτον,** he calls conscience into play—*whose* conscience the next clause shows.—**διὰ τὸν μηνύσαντα καὶ τὴν συνείδησιν** form one idea, being governed by the same prp., **καὶ** adding an explanation; from regard to the *conscience* of the **μηνύσας**—not his possible contempt or ill-will—the Christian should decline the offered flesh or stop eating it.—**συνείδησιν δὲ λέγω, οὐ τὴν ἑαυτοῦ κ.τ.λ.,** "Conscience however I mean, not one's own, but that of the other". Ver. 29*a* explains the **διὰ τ. συνείδησιν** of ver. 28, and reconciles its instruction with that of vv. 25, 27, while it brings the matter under the governing rule laid down in vv. 23 f. By contrast with "the other," the 2nd pl. of ver. 28 becomes here 2nd sing. reflexive.

Vv. 29*b*, 30 justify, in two rhetorical questions, the Christian's deference to

[x] ἐλευθερία μου κρίνεται ὑπὸ [y] ἄλλης [n] συνειδήσεως; 30. [b] εἰ δὲ [1] ἐγὼ
[z] χάριτι [a] μετέχω, [b] τί [b] βλασφημοῦμαι [c] ὑπὲρ [c] οὗ ἐγὼ [d] εὐχαριστῶ;
31. εἴτε οὖν ἐσθίετε εἴτε πίνετε, εἴτε τι ποιεῖτε, πάντα [e] εἰς [e] δόξαν
Θεοῦ ποιεῖτε. 32. [f] ἀπρόσκοποι γίνεσθε [2] καὶ [2] [g] Ἰουδαίοις [2] καὶ
[g] Ἕλλησι καὶ τῇ [h] ἐκκλησίᾳ τοῦ [h] Θεοῦ · 33. καθὼς κἀγὼ πάντα
πᾶσιν [i] ἀρέσκω, μὴ [k] ζητῶν τὸ ἐμαυτοῦ [l] συμφέρον [3] ἀλλὰ τὸ [m] τῶν

x 2 Cor. iii.
17; Rom.
viii. 21;
Gal. ii. 5,
v. 1, 13;
Jas. i. 25,
ii. 12; 1
Pet. ii.16;
2 Pet. ii.
19.
y H.l. in
this use;
cf. Job
xix. 27.　　z In this sense, xv. 57; 5 times more in P.; Lk. vi. 32 ff.　　a See ix. 12.　　b With
human obj., Rom. iii. 8, xiv. 16; Tit. iii. 2; 1 Pet. iv. 4. For interr. after εἰ, see xii. 17.　　c For
the ellipsis, cf. vii. 1, etc.　　d Absol., xi. 24, xiv. 17; 1 Th. v. 18; see i. 4.　　e See ii. 7.　　f Ph.
i. 10; Acts xxiv. 16; Sir. xxxv. (xxxii.) 21.　　g In this antithesis, i. 24; Rom. i. 16, ii. 9 f., iii. 9, x.
12; Gal. iii. 28; Col. iii. 11; Acts xiv. 1, xviii. 4, xix. 10, 17, xx. 21.　　h See i. 2.　　i See vii. 32.
k See ver. 24.　　l συμφορον, see vii. 35.　　m See ver. 17.

[1] *Om.* δε all but a few minuscc., with Thd. and Oec.

[2] καὶ Ἰουδαίοις γίνεσθε (in this order): ℵ*ABC, 17, 37, 73.

[3] συμφορον, ℵ*ABC.

the conscience of another: (*a*) ἵνα τί
γὰρ κ.τ.λ.; "For to what purpose is my
liberty judged by another conscience?"
i.e. "What good end will be served by
my eating under these circumstances,
and exposing my freedom to the censure
of an unsympathetic conscience?" *cf.* ii.
15, Matt. vii. 6. ἵνα τί (γένηται); *ut
quid?* (Vg.), signifies *purpose*, not *ground*
as Mr. and others take it; there is *nothing to be gained* by the exercise of
liberty in this case. For κρίνω in adverse
sense, see parls. For the previous
συνείδ. τὴν τοῦ ἑτέρου (*alterius*), ἄλλης
(*alienæ*) συνειδήσεως is substituted (*cf.*
xv. 29, 2 Cor. xi. 4), indicating a distinction not merely in the persons but in
the *consciences* severally possessed. The
Ap. says here of Liberty what he says of
Faith in Rom. xiv. 22: κατὰ σεαυτὸν
ἔχε ἐνώπιον τοῦ Θεοῦ.—Question (*b*) intimates that, instead of any benefit resulting from the assertion of liberty in face
of conscientious condemnation, positive
harm results—thanksgiving leads to *blasphemy!* "If I with thanks (*or* by grace)
partake, why am I blasphemed over (that
for) which I give thanks?" The τί is
prospective, as in xv. 29 f. = εἰς τί or ἵνα
τί; The bare χάριτι can scarcely mean
here "by (the) grace (of God)"—esp. in
view of εὐχαριστῶ; *cf.* Rom. xiv. 6 and
16 (for βλασφημοῦμαι). Men of heathen
conscience, seeing the Christian give
thanks knowingly over food devoted to
the idol, will regard his act as one of
sacrilegious indulgence and denounce it
accordingly; it seems to them a revolting
hypocrisy; "*Quelle religion est celle-là?*
devaient dire les païens" (Gd.)—a grievous πρόσκομμα both to Jews and Greeks
(32); *cf.* Rom. ii. 24.—ὑπὲρ οὗ absorbs

the dem. pron. governed by the same
prp.; *cf.* vii. 39, 2 Cor. ii. 3. The repeated emphatic ἐγὼ points to the Christian as devout on his own part, yet in-
curring the scandal of gross irreverence.

Vv. 31, 32 conclude the matter with
two solemn, comprehensive rules, introduced by the collective οὖν (*cf.* Rom. v.
9, xi. 22), relating to *God's glory* and to
man's salvation. The supreme maxim of
duty, πάντα εἰς δόξαν Θεοῦ ποιεῖτε,
applies to all that Christians "eat or
drink" (including the idolothyta),—indeed to whatever they "do"; *cf.* Rom. xiv.
20 ff., Col. iii. 17.—A second general rule
emerges from the discussion: "Offence-
less prove yourselves, both to Jews and
to Greeks and to the church of God".
ἀπρόσκοποι here act., as in Sir. xxxv. 21,
not causing to stumble; elsewhere pass.
in sense. For γίνεσθε, see note on vii. 23.
The three classes named make up Paul's
world of men: "Jews" and "Greeks"
embrace all outside the Church (i. 22, ix.
20 f.); Christian believers alone form
"the Church of God" (*cf.* i. 2, and note;
also Gal. vi. 16). This text and xii. 28
afford the first ex. in P. of the comprehensive use of ἐκκλησία, as transcending
local ref. "The church of God" is
bound up with His glory (31); its sacredness supplies a new deterrent from self-
indulgence. It contains "the weak"
who are liable to injury (viii. 9, ix. 22).

Ver. 33, xi. 1. Paul's personal example
played a large part in his argument (ix.);
it is fitting he should refer to it in
summing up. The negative ἀπρόσκοποι
γίνεσθε, in 2nd person, now becomes
the positive ἐγὼ πάντα πᾶσιν ἀρέσκω in
the 1st: "As I also in all things please
all." ἀρέσκω is *to comply with, accom-*

a See iv. 16.
b Vv. 17, 22;
Rom. xv.
11; Lk.
xvi. 8;
-νος, iv. 5.
c In this

ᵐ πολλῶν, ἵνα σωθῶσι · XI. 1. ᵃ μιμηταί μου γίνεσθε, καθὼς κἀγὼ Χριστοῦ.

2. ᵇ Ἐπαινῶ δὲ ὑμᾶς, ἀδελφοί,¹ ὅτι πάντα μου ᶜ μέμνησθε, καὶ

tense, 2 Tim. i. 4.   *Cf.* iv. 17.   μνημονεύω common in this sense.

¹ *Om.* α δ ε λ φ ο ι ℵABCP, 46, 73, sah. cop.—a Western addition.

modate oneself to, not *give enjoyment to* (*cf.* Rom. xv. 1, 3)—no need to speak of a "conative present," resembling ζητῶ ἀρέσκειν. Paul's universal compliance is qualified by its *purpose*, ἵνα σωθῶσιν, in the light of which the verbal contradiction with Gal. i. 10, 1 Thess. ii. 4, is removed; there is nothing in his power that P. will not do for any man, to help his salvation (*cf.* ix. 22*b*).—Between the ἀρέσκω and its purpose lies the μὴ ζητῶν clause, in which the Ap. professes for himself the rule commended to the Cor. in ver. 27. The "self-advantage" which P. sets aside, touches his highest welfare (*cf.* Rom. ix. 3); P. sacrificed what seemed to be his spiritual as well as material gain—spending, *e.g.*, weary hours in tent-making that might have been given to pious study—to secure spiritual gain for others; thus "losing himself," he "found himself unto life eternal." "The many," in contrast with the single self; *cf.* ver. 17, Rom. v. 15 ff. —Through his own pattern P. points the readers to that of his Master and theirs: "Show yourselves (γίνεσθε, see 32, vii. 23) imitators of me, as I also (am) of Christ". P. does not point his readers *backward* to the historical model ("of Jesus," or "Jesus Christ," as in Eph. iv. 21), but *upward* to the actual "Christ," whose existence is evermore devoted to God (Rom. vi. 10 f.) and to men His brethren (Rom. viii. 34 f., i. 30), "in" whom the Cor. believers "are" (i. 2, 30). Paul's *imitatio Christi* turns on the great acts of Christ's redeeming work (Eph. v. 2, Phil. ii. 5-11), rather than on the incidents of His earthly course.

DIVISION IV. DISORDERS IN WORSHIP AND CHURCH LIFE, xi.-xiv. The Ap. returns to the internal affairs of the Church, which occupied him in Div. I., dealing however not as at the outset with the relations of the Cor. Church to its ministry, but with the mutual relations and behaviour of its members within the society. The questions arising under this head are bound up with the moral and social problems of Divs. II. and III., and several leading topics of former

chaps. reappear in a new connexion— *e.g.*, the Christian relationship of the sexes (common to v., vi., and xi.), the Lord's Supper (x. and xi.), the superiority of Love to Knowledge (viii. and xiii.). The matters treated in these chaps. are well defined: (1) *the unveiling of the head by women* in public worship, xi. 2-16; (2) *profanation of the Lord's Table*, 17-34; (3) *the exercise of spiritual gifts*, xii. 1-11 and xiv.—.a subject which leads the Ap. into two digressions: (*a*) on *the corporate nature of the Church*, xii. 12-31; (*b*) on *the supremacy of love*, xiii. As in the earlier parts of the letter, the train of thought is objectively dictated; the matters taken up arise from the faulty state of the Cor. Church, and were supplied to the writer partly, as in chh. vii.-x., by the Church Letter, and partly by information conveyed in other ways (see xi. 18, and *Introd.*, chap. ii.), which indicated the existence of disorders and scandals within the community of the gravity of which it was unaware.

§ 35. THE WOMAN'S VEIL, xi. 2-6. P. is glad to believe that the Church at Cor. is loyal to his instructions (2); he interrupts his censures by a word of praise. This commendation, however, he proceeds to qualify. First, in respect of a matter whose underlying principles his readers had not grasped: he hears that some women speak in Church-meetings, and that bareheaded! For a woman to discard the veil means to cast off masculine authority, which is a fixed part of the Divine order, like man's subordination to Christ (3 f.). She who so acts disgraces her own head, and only needs to go a step further to rank herself with the degraded of her sex (5 f.).

Ver. 2. The praise here given is so little suggested by the context, and to little accords with the tone of the Ep., esp. with what was said in the like connexion in iv. 16 f., that one conjectures the Ap. to be quoting *professions made in the Letter from Cor.* rather than writing simply out of his own mind: "Now I praise you that [as you say] 'in all things you remember me, and hold fast the in-

καθὼς ^dπαρέδωκα ὑμῖν τὰς ^eπαραδόσεις κατέχετε. 3. ^fθέλω δὲ ^d In this sense,
ὑμᾶς ^fεἰδέναι ὅτι παντὸς ἀνδρὸς ἡ κεφαλὴ ὁ¹ Χριστός ἐστι, κεφαλὴ ver. 23,
δὲ ^gγυναικὸς ὁ ^gἀνήρ, κεφαλὴ δὲ ^hΧριστοῦ² ὁ ^hΘεός. 4. πᾶς xv. 3; Lk. i. 2; Acts xvi. 4.
ἀνὴρ ⁱπροσευχόμενος ἢ ^kπροφητεύων, ^lκατὰ ^lκεφαλῆς ἔχων, ^mκα- e Gal. i. 14;
Col. ii. 8;
2 Th. ii.

15, iii. 6; Mt. xv. 2, etc.   f Col. ii. 1; *cf.* x. 1 above.   g For the contrast, vii. 3 ff.; Rom. vii.
2; Eph. v. 22; Col. iii. 18 f.; 1 Tim. ii. 12-15; 1 Pet. iii. 1; Mk. x. 2 ff.   h i. 24, iii. 23, xv. 24-28,
57; 2 Cor. i. 19, iv. 6, v. 18 f.; Eph. i. 17, 20, iii. 21; Ph. ii. 5-11; Col. i. 15, 19; 1 Tim. ii. 5; Tit.
iii. 6; Heb. i., iii. 6, etc.; 1 Pet. iv. 11; Jo. i. 1 f., xvii. 3 f., etc.; 1 Jo. iv. 9 f., etc.   i Absol., xiv.
14 f.; Eph. vi. 18; 1 Th. v. 17; 1 Tim. ii. 8, etc.   k xiii. 9, xiv. 1 ff.; Acts ii. 17 f., etc.; Mt. vii.
22; Lk. i. 67.   l Esth. vi. 12.   m See i. 27.

¹ Om. o B*D*G; so W.H. *marg.*

² του Χριστου, אABD, 17, 37, 46, Clem.   CGKLP om. του.   See note below.

structions as I delivered them to you'". For such adoption by P. of the words of his readers, see notes on viii. 1 ff. Self-esteem characterised this Church (iv. 8 ff., v. 2); the declaration was sincere, and contained a measure of truth; P. accepts it for what it is worth.—δέ, introducing the new topic, marks also the connexion between vv. 1 and 2: "I bid you imitate me—but I am glad to know (from your letter) that you do".—πάντα, acc. of *definition* (not obj.), as in ix. 25, x. 33; the vb. regularly governs a gen. in N.T.: μέμνησθε, like *memini*, a pf. pres.—"you have been kept in remembrance of me".—παρά-δοσις, a "giving-over" (without the associations of our *tradition*), applies to historical fact, teaching, or rules of practice delivered, through whatever means, to the keeping of others: for reference to *fact* and *usage*, see ver. 23; to *fact* and *doctrine*, xv. 1; to the three combined, as here, 2 Thess. ii. 15; for its currency in Jewish Schools, Matt. xv. 2 ff., etc.—κατέχετε, as in xv. 2; κρατεῖτε, 2 Thess. ii. 15. καθὼς κ.τ.λ. implies maintenance in *form* as well as substance, observance of the τύπος διδαχῆς (Rom. vi. 17).

Ver. 3. θέλω δὲ ὑμᾶς εἰδέναι (= οὐ θέλω κ.τ.λ. of x. 1; see note): "But I would have you know"—the previous commendation throws into relief the coming censure. The indecorum in question offends against a foundation principle, *viz.*, that of *subordination under the Divine government*; this the Cor., with all their knowledge, cannot "know," or they would not have allowed their women to throw off the ἐξουσία ἐπὶ τῆς κεφαλῆς (10). The violated principle is thus stated: "Of every man the Christ is the head, while the man is head of woman, and God is head of Christ". As to the wording of this sentence: παντὸς ἀνδρὸς bears emphasis in the 1st

clause asserting, like the parl. 2nd clause, a universal truth which holds of the man (*vir*) as such; the predicate of the 1st clause is distinguished by the def. art.,— "Christ is the (proper, essential) head," etc. (*cf.* ἡ εἰρήνη, Eph. ii. 14, and see Bm., pp. 124 f.); ὁ Χριστός, in 1st and 3rd clauses, means "the Christ" in the wide scope of His offices (*cf.* x. 4, xii. 12, xv. 22); for anarthrous κεφαλὴ γυναικός, *cf.* note on ii. 5. That Christ is "every man's" true head is an application of the revealed truth that He is the "one Lord" of created nature (viii. 6; Col. i. 15 f.), combined with the palpable fact that the ἀνὴρ has no (intervening) lord in creation (*cf.* 9); he stands forth in worship, amidst his family, with no visible superior, holding headship direct from his Maker, and brought by his manhood into direct responsibility to Him "through whom are all things". Ed., following Cm. and Mr. (not Hn.), limits this manly subordination to the Christian order of life; "the man is head of the woman in virtue of the marriage union, Christ of the man in virtue of union with Him through faith": but faith is common to the sexes, on this footing οὐκ ἔνι ἄρσεν καὶ θῆλυ (Gal. iii. 28); on the other hand, in Pauline theology, the law of marriage and the social order are grounded in Christ. Paul's argument has no force unless the parl. assertions rest on a common basis. The question is one that touches the fundamental proprieties of life (8-15); and the three headships enumerated belong to the hierarchy of nature.—"The Christ" of the 3rd clause is "the Christ" of the 1st, without distinction made of natures or states; He who is "every man's head," the Lord of nature, presents the pattern of loyalty in His perfect obedience to the Father (xv. 28, Gal. iv. 4; Heb. v. 5, 8, etc.); *cf.* iii. 22 f., where

n N.T. *h.l.*;
Lev. xiii.
45;
o xii. 11.
p Acts xxi.
24; Numb.
vi. 9.
q N.T. *h.l.*;
Gen.
xxxviii.
15, etc.
r Acts viii. 32, xviii. 18; 2 Ki. xiv. 26.   s xiv. 35; Eph. v. 12; Tit. i. 11; Gen. xli. 3, etc.

ταισχύνει τὴν κεφαλὴν αὐτοῦ · 5. πᾶσα δὲ γυνὴ ¹προσευχομένη ἢ ᵏπροφητεύουσα ⁿἀκατακαλύπτῳ τῇ κεφαλῇ, ᵐκαταισχύνει τὴν κεφαλὴν ἑαυτῆς,¹ °ἓν γάρ ἐστι καὶ τὸ °αὐτὸ τῇ ᵖἐξυρημένῃ · 6. εἰ γὰρ οὐ ᑫκατακαλύπτεται γυνή, καὶ ʳκειράσθω · εἰ δὲ ˢαἰσχρὸν γυναικὶ τὸ ʳκείρασθαι ἢ ᵖξυρᾶσθαι, ᑫκατακαλυπτέσθω.

¹ αυτης (?) all uncc. but BDᶜK, in conformity with ver. 4.   W.H. place εαυτης in *marg*.   The reading αυτης has the appearance of a harmonistic emendation.

with the same δέ . . . δὲ a chain of subordinate *possession* is drawn out, corresponding to this subordination of *rule*. Submission in office, whether of woman to man or Christ to God, consists with equality of nature.

Vv. 4, 5: the high doctrine just asserted applied to the matter of feminine attire. Since man *qua* man has no head but Christ, before. whom they worship in common, while woman has man to own for her head, *he must not and she must be veiled*. The regulation is not limited to those of either sex who "pray or prophesy"; but such activity called attention to the apparel, and doubtless it was amongst the more demonstrative women that the impropriety occurred; in the excitement of public speaking the shawl might unconsciously be thrown back. προσευχόμενος κ.τ.λ., "when he (she) prays or prophesies,"—in the act of so doing.—κατὰ κεφαλῆς ἔχων, "wearing *down from* the head (a veil": κάλυμμα understood), the practice being for the woman in going out of the house to throw the upper fold or lappet of her robe over her head so as to cover the brow: see Peplos in the *Dict. of Antiq*. ἀκατακαλ. τ. κεφαλῇ, "with the head uncovered," dat. of manner, as χάριτι in x. 30.—Is it the *literal* or *figurative* "head" that is meant as obj. to καταισχύνει? Ver. 3 requires the latter sense, while the sequel suggests the former; Al. and Ed. think *both* are intended at once. Hf. is probably right in abiding by the reading ἑαυτῆς (see txtl. note); he supposes that the Ap. purposely broke off the parallelism at the end of ver. 5, thus sharpening his reproof: the man who wears a veil "puts to shame his head" —*i.e.* Christ, whose lordship he represents (7); the woman who discards it "puts to shame *her own head*"—the dishonour done to the dominant sex falls upon herself. That the shame comes home to *her* is shown by the supporting

sentence: ἓν γάρ ἐστιν καὶ τὸ αὐτό (*cf*. iii. 8) τῇ ἐξυρημένῃ, "for she is one and the same thing with her that is shaven" (Mr., Ev., Bt., Ed., El.); "It is one and the same thing," etc. (E.V.), would require τῷ ἐξυρῆσθαι. Amongst Greeks only the *hetæræ*, so numerous in Cor., went about unveiled; slave-women wore the shaven head—also a punishment of the adulteress (see Wetstein *in loc*., and *cf*. Num. v. 18); with these the Christian woman who emancipates herself from becoming restraints of dress, is in effect identified. To shave the head is to carry out thoroughly its unveiling, to remove nature's as well as fashion's covering (15).

Ver. 6, with a second γάρ, presses the above identity; the Ap. bids the woman who discards the veil carry her defiance a step further: "For if a woman is not veiled, let her also crop (her head); but if it is a disgrace for a woman to crop (it) or to keep (it) shaven, let her retain the veil" (καλυπτέσθω, pr. impv., *continuous*). P. uses the *modus tollens* of the hypothetical syllogism: "If a woman prefers a bare head, she should remove her hair; womanly feeling forbids the latter, then it should forbid the former, for the like shame attaches to both." The argument appeals to Gr. and Eastern sentiment; "physical barefacedness led to the inference of moral, in a city like Corinth" (Ev.). κειράσθω and κείρασθαι, aor. mid., denote a single act on the woman's part, "to cut off her locks"; ξυρᾶσθαι, pres. mid.,—a shaven condition; the single art. comprises the infs. in one view.—Paul's directions do not agree precisely with current practice. Jewish men covered their heads at prayers with the Tallith (*cf*. the allusion of 2 Cor. iii. 14 ff.)—this custom, retained probably by some Jews at Christian meetings (4), P. corrects without censure; women were both veiled and kept behind a screen. Amongst the Greeks,

7. Ἀνὴρ μὲν γὰρ οὐκ ᵗὀφείλει ᑫκατακαλύπτεσθαι τὴν κεφαλήν, ᵘεἰκὼν καὶ ᵛδόξα ᵛΘεοῦ ʷὑπάρχων, γυνὴ ¹ δὲ ᵛδόξα ἀνδρός ἐστιν· 8. οὐ γάρ ἐστιν ἀνὴρ ἐκ γυναικός, ἀλλὰ γυνὴ ἐξ ἀνδρός· 9. καὶ γὰρ οὐκ ˣἐκτίσθη ἀνὴρ διὰ τὴν γυναῖκα, ἀλλὰ γυνὴ διὰ τὸν ἄνδρα·

t See vii. 36.
u Gen. i. 26 f.; cf. xv. 49; 2 Cor. iv. 4; Rom. i.23, viii. 29; Col. i. 15, iii. 10.
x Rom. i.

v Cf. 2 Cor. iv. 6; Ph. i. 11; Heb. i. 3; Jo. i. 14, xvii. 22; Ps. xviii. 1.   w See vii. 26.
25; Col. i. 16, iii. 10; 1 Tim. iv. 11; Mt. xix. 4; Mk. xiii. 19.

¹ ἡ γυνὴ δε: ℵcABD*G.

both sexes worshipped with *uncovered* head, although women covered their heads at other times (see Hermann, *Gottesdienstl. Alterthümer*, § 36, 18 f.; Plato, *Phædo*, 89B, C), while Roman men and women alike *covered* their heads during religious rites (Servius *ad Æn.*, iii., 407). The usage here prescribed seems to be an adaptation of Gr. custom to Christian conceptions. With us the diff. of sex is more strongly marked in the general attire than with the ancients; but the draped head has still its appropriateness, and the distinction laid down in this passage has been universally observed.—The woman is recognised by the side of the man as "praying" and "prophesying" (see note on xii. 10); there is no ground in the text for limiting the ref. in her case to the exercise of these gifts *in domestic and private circles* (thus Hf., Bt., and some others); on the contradiction with xiv. 34, see note *ad loc.* Under the Old Covenant women were at times signally endued with supernatural powers, and the prophetess occasionally played a leading public part (*e.g.* Deborah and Huldah); in the Christian dispensation, from Acts i. 14 onwards, they receive a more equal share in the powers of the Spirit (see Acts ii. 17 f., Gal. iii. 28). But in the point of ἐξουσία there lies an ineffaceable distinction.

§ 36. MAN AND WOMAN IN THE LORD, xi. 7-16. The Ap. has insisted on the woman's retaining the veil in token of the Divine order pervading the universe, which Christ exhibits in His subordination to the Father. But he has some further observations to make on the relative position of the sexes. In the first place, he bases what he has said of the headship of man on *the story of creation*, exhibiting man as the direct reflexion of God, woman as derived and auxiliary (7-9); in this connexion the ref. to "the angels" must be understood (10). At the same time, man and woman are *necessary each to the other* and *derive alike from God* (11 f.). Having thus grounded

the matter upon Christian principle, P. appeals in confirmation to *natural feeling* (13-15), and finally to *the unbroken custom of the Church* (16).

Ver. 7. ἀνὴρ (not ὁ ἀνὴρ) μὲν γὰρ κ.τ.λ.: "For *man* indeed (being man) ought not to have his head veiled" (καλύπτεσθαι, pr. inf. of *custom*), in contrast with woman who *ought* (5, 10)—this is as wrong on his part as it is right on hers; οὐκ negatives the whole sentence, as in ver. 1. ὀφείλει, like δεῖ (19), denotes moral or rational necessity, the former vb. in a more personal, the latter in a more abstract way. For *him* to veil his head would be to veil the "image and glory of God"; Christ, *the image of* God, became ἄνθρωπος as ἀνήρ.—ὑπάρχων (see parls.), "being constituted" so. To accompany εἰκών, P. substitutes for the ὁμοίωσις (*d'muth*) of Gen. the more expressive δόξα—by which the LXX renders the synonymous *t'munah* of Ps. xvii. 15—God's "glory" being His likeness in visible splendour; *cf.* Heb. i. 3. P. conceives Gen. i. 26 to apply to Adam as ἀνήρ primarily, although in ver. 27 it stands, "God created man in His own image . . . *male and female* created He them".—ἡ γυνὴ δὲ κ.τ.λ. presents a shortened antithesis to the μὲν clause; logically completed it reads, "But the woman (ought to have her head veiled, for she) is the glory of the man"—δόξα ἀνδρός—not of the race (ἀνθρώπου), but of the stronger sex. Paul omits εἰκών, which does not hold here; she is not man's reflexion, but his counterpart—not "like to like, but like in difference," wedded as "perfect music unto noble words"; she partakes, through him, in the εἰκὼν Θεοῦ (Gen. i. 27). That which in our common nature is most admirable —faith, purity, beauty—man sees more excellently and proportionately shown in hers. It follows that he who degrades a woman sullies his manhood, and is the worst enemy of his race; the respect shown to women is the measure and safeguard of human dignity.

y Cf. vii.37;
see note
below.
z Rev. xiv.
14. ἐπὶ
in like
connec-
tion, Jo.
xx. 7;

Rev. i. 20, vii. 3, etc., xii. 1, etc.
31; Mk. xiii. 27; Lk. xvi. 22.
passim; Lam. iii. 3.

10. διὰ τοῦτο ᵗὀφείλει ἡ γυνὴ ʸἐξουσίαν ᶻἔχειν ᶻἐπὶ τῆς κεφαλῆς, διὰ τοὺς ᵃἀγγέλους. 11. ᵇπλὴν οὔτε ἀνὴρ¹ χωρὶς γυναικός,¹ οὔτε γυνὴ¹ χωρὶς ἀνδρὸς¹ ἐν Κυρίῳ· 12. ὥσπερ γὰρ ἡ γυνὴ ἐκ τοῦ ἀνδρός, οὕτω καὶ ὁ ἀνὴρ διὰ τῆς γυναικός· τὰ δὲ πάντα ἐκ τοῦ

a In pl. abs., with art., xiii. 1; Heb. i. 4 ff.; Mt. xiii. 49, xxv.
b Eph. v. 33; Ph. i. 18, iii. 16, iv. 14; Rev. ii. 25; Mt., Lk.,

¹ γυνη χωρις ανδρος . . . ανηρ χωρις γυναικος (in this order): all uncc. but DᵇKL, all anc. verss. but syrr. and vg.

Vv. 8, 9 add two more to the chain of *for's* extending from ver. 6: a double reason for asserting that woman is man's glory appears in the revelation of the origin of mankind made by Scripture (Gen. ii. 18-25: the *second* narrative of Creation, J of the critics), where Eve is represented as framed from a rib taken out of Adam's body to be his "help-mate". Woman originates *from* (ἐστὶν ἐκ), and was created *for* (because of, ἐκτίσθη διὰ) man, not *vice versa*.—"ἐκ-τίσθη differs from ἐστὶν as purpose from fact," (Ed.).—καὶ γάρ, "For *also*" (9) —the second statement goes to explain the first: Man was there already; and Woman was fashioned out of him for his need. Whether the story of the extracted rib is read as poetry or prosaic fact, the relationship set forth is the same.

Ver. 10 is the counterstatement to ver. 7a, undeveloped there: "*For this reason* the woman is bound to wear authority upon her head"—*sc.*, the reason made out in vv. 7b-9, that her nature is derived and auxiliary. The ἐξουσία (= σημεῖον ἐξουσίας) that she "has (wears)," is that to which she submits, with the veil "upon her head" for its symbol; *cf.* xii. 23, where τιμή = σημεῖον τιμῆς. So the soldier under the Queen's colours might be said to "have authority over his head". Ev. quotes Shakesp., *Macb.*, iii. 4, "Present him *eminence* both with eye and tongue," as a parl. expression for the authority of another pictured in one-self.—διὰ τοὺς ἀγγέλους suggests, by way of after-thought, a supplementary motive for the decent veil, which the Ap. merely hints, leaving a crux for his interpreters. In iv. 9 he adduced the "angels" as interested spectators of the conduct of Christ's servants, and in vi. 3 he spoke of certain of them as to be judged by the saints (see notes); in manifold ways these exalted beings are associated with God's earthly kingdom (see Luke ii. 13, xii. 8, xv. 10, Acts i. 10, etc.; Heb. i. 14, xii. 22 f.; Rev. *passim*);

in accordance with Jewish belief, they appear as agents of the Lawgiving in Gal. iii. 19 (Acts vii. 53), and in Heb. i. 7 are identified with the forces of nature. The same line of thought connects the angels here with *the maintenance of the laws and limits imposed at Creation* (*cf.* Job. xxxviii. 7), reverence for which P. expresses in his own style by this allusion; see Hn., Ed., and Gd. *in loc.* With this general view the interpretation is consistent which regards the angels as *present in Divine worship and offended by irreverence and misconduct* (see 1 Tim. v. 21), as (possibly) edified too by good behaviour (see Eph. iii. 10); *cf.* the ancient words of the Liturgy, "Therefore with Angels and Archangels, etc." A familiar thought with the Ff.; thus Cm. *ad loc.*, "Open the eyes of faith, and thou shalt behold a multitude of angels; if the air is filled with angels, much more the Church"; and Thp., τοῖς ἀγγέλοις αἰδουμένη. Similarly Hooker, "The house of prayer is a Court beautified with the presence of Celestial powers; there we stand, we sing, we sound forth hymns to God, having His angels intermingled as our associates; with reference hereunto the Ap. doth require so great care to be taken of decency for the Angels' sake" (*Eccl. Pol.*, v. 25. 2). P. cannot mean *evil* angels subject to sensual temptation, as many, after Tert., have read the passage, basing it on a precarious interpretation of Gen. vi. 4 (see Everling, *Die paul. Angelologie u.s.w.*, pp. 32 ff.)—an explanation far-fetched and grossly improbable. Others have seen in these ἄγγελοι *pious men, prophets, Church-officers*, even *match-makers!* Others have proposed emendations of the text, substituting διὰ τοὺς ἀγελαίους or τὰς ἀγέλας, or διὰ τῆς ἀγγελίας (*during the preaching!*). Baur, Sm., and others would delete the troublesome words as a primitive *gloss*.

Vv. 11, 12. πλὴν κ.τ.λ. modifies and guards the foregoing; this conj. lies

Θεοῦ. 13. ἐν[1] ᶜὑμῖν ᵉαὐτοῖς[1] ᵉκρίνατε · ᵈπρέπον ἐστὶ γυναῖκα ᶜ Cf. Lk.
ⁿἀκατακάλυπτον τῷ Θεῷ προσεύχεσθαι ; 14. ἢ[2] οὐδὲ αὐτὴ[3] ἡ xii. 57.
ᵉφύσις[3] διδάσκει ὑμᾶς ὅτι ἀνὴρ μὲν ἐὰν ᶠκομᾷ, ᵍἀτιμία αὐτῷ ἐστι · κρίνατε, x. 15 ; Acts iv. 19 ; Jo.
15. γυνὴ δὲ ἐὰν ᶠκομᾷ, δόξα αὐτῇ ἐστιν ; ὅτι ἡ ʰκόμη ⁱἀντὶ vii. 24. d Mt. iii. 15 ; I Macc.

xii. 11. -πει, Eph. v. 3 ; I Tim. ii. 10 ; Tit. ii. 1 ; Heb. ii. 10, vii. 26 ; Ps. lxiv. 1. e Rom. i. 26, ii. 14, 27, xi. 24 ; Gal. ii. 15, iv. 8 ; Eph. ii. 3. f H.l. in Bib. Gr. g xv. 43 ; Rom. i. 26, etc. -μος, see iv. 10. -αζω, see Rom. i. 24, etc. h N.T. h.l. ; Numb. vi. 5. i Lk. xi. 11 ; Jas. iv. 15.

[1] D latt. vg., Ambrst., Pelag. (Western) read υμεις αυτοι for εν υμιν αυτοις.

[2] Om. η all uncc. but DᶜKL.

[3] η φυσις αυτη (in this order) : pre-Syrian uncc.

between δὲ and ἀλλά in its force—*but besides, howbeit.* What has been said in vv. 3-10 must not be overpressed : woman is subordinate, not inferior ; the sexes are alike, and inseparably necessary to the Christian order (11) ; and if man is the fountain, woman is the channel of the race's life (12). οὔτε γυνὴ . . . οὔτε ἀνὴρ κ.τ.λ. : "Neither is there woman apart from man, nor man apart from woman in the Lord." Here Tennyson is the best commentator : "Either sex alone is half itself . . . each fulfils defect in each, and always thought in thought, purpose in purpose, will in will, they grow . . . the two-celled heart beating, with one full stroke, life ". ἐν Κυρίῳ (cf. vii. 39, etc.), i.e. *under the rule of Christ,* where woman's rights are realised as nowhere in heathenism (cf. Gal. iii. 28, Eph. v. 28 ; also the wording of vii. 3 f. above). For the contrast of ἐκ and διά, see viii. 6 ; "the woman has an equivalent in the Divine order of nature, that as man is the *initial* cause of being to the woman, so woman is the *instrumental* cause of being to the man " (Ev.). But the ἀνήρ is only a relative source ; God is absolute Father—τὰ δὲ πάντα ἐκ τοῦ Θεοῦ (cf. viii. 6, i. 30 and note, Rom. xi. 36). To Him man and woman owe one reverence.

Ver. 13. There is a constitutional feeling which supports the above inference in favour of the woman's veil ; it was implied already in the καταισχύνει and αἰσχρόν of vv. 5 f., and is now explicitly stated : "Amongst yourselves (*inter* rather than *intra vos ipsos*) judge ye ; is it seemly for a woman unveiled to be engaged in prayer (pr. inf.) to God ? "—an appeal to social sentiment (cf. Rom. ii. 15, μεταξὺ ἀλλήλων), recalling the κρίνατε ὑμεῖς of x. 15. πρέπον (neut. ptp. : see parls.), as distinguished from ὀφείλω or δεῖ (7, 19), denotes *befittingness,* suita-

bility to nature or character. τῷ Θεῷ lends solemnity to προσεύχεσθαι.

Vv. 14, 15. The question οὐδὲ ἡ φύσις αὐτὴ κ.τ.λ.; summons *personal instinct* to the aid of social sentiment : "Does not even nature of herself teach you that, etc. ? " For ἡ φύσις, see Rom. ii. 14 ; in this connexion it points to man's *moral constitution* rather than to external regulations ; Hf. and El. however, taking φύσις in the latter sense, reverse the order of thought in vv. 13 f., seeing in the former ver. individual instinct (they render ἐν ἑαυτοῖς *within yourselves*), and in this ver. social rule.—Hf. and Hn., by a strained constr. of διδάσκει, render ὅτι "because," and draw the obj. of "teach" from ver. 13, seeing in ὅτι κ.τ.λ. the *ground* of the affirmative answer tacitly given to both questions : "Does not nature of herself teach (this) ? (Yes), for if a man have long hair, etc." The common rendering is preferable ; the teaching of nature is expressed in a double sentence, which gathers the *consensus gentium* on the subject : "that in a man's case, if he wear long hair (*vir quidem si comam nutriat,* Vg.), it is a dishonour to him ; but in a woman's, if she wear long hair, it is a glory to her ". ἀνήρ, γυνὴ stand in conspicuous antithesis preceding the conj. : what is discreditable in the one is delightful in the other. Homer's warriors, it is true, wore long hair (καρηκομῶντες Ἀχαιοί), a fashion retained at Sparta ; but the Athenian youth cropped his head at 18, and it was a mark of foppery or effeminacy (a legal ἀτιμία), except for the aristocratic Knights, to let the hair afterwards grow long. This feeling prevailed in ancient as it does in modern manners (cf. the case of Absalom). In the rule of the Nazirites natural instinct was set aside by an exceptional religious vocation. The woman's κόμη is not merely

k Heb. i. 12 k **περιβολαίου δέδοται** [1] **αὐτῇ.** [1] 16. εἰ δέ τις [1] δοκεῖ m **φιλόνεικος**
(Ps. ci.
26); Exod. **εἶναι, ἡμεῖς τοιαύτην** n **συνήθειαν οὐκ ἔχομεν οὐδὲ αἱ** o **ἐκκλησίαι**
xxii. 27;
Job xxvi. **τοῦ** o **Θεοῦ.**
6; Ps.
ciii. 6. 17. Τοῦτο δὲ p **παραγγέλλων** [2] οὐκ q **ἐπαινῶ,** [2] ὅτι οὐκ εἰς τὸ
l See iii. 18.
m N.T. h.l.;

Ezek. iii. 7. -κια, Lk. xxii. 24. -κειν, Prov. x. 12.   n See viii. 7.   o See i. 2; full expression,
N.T. h.l. in pl. For pl. εκκλ., see vii. 17.   p See vii. 10.   q See ver. 2.

[1] αυτη δεδοται : CHP, 37, 46.   Om. αυτη DG (Western).   T.R., as in ℵAB, etc.

[2] παραγγελλων ουκ επαινω: ℵC³DcGKLP, etc. ; some latt. cop.   So Tisch., W.H.
txt., R.V., El., Nestle.   External evidence fairly balanced.

παραγγελλω ουκ επαινων: AC*G, 17, 46, 67**, vg. syrsch.   So Lachm., Tr., Al.,
W.H. marg.   Both verbs in -ων: D*gr., 137 ; both in -ω: B.   See note below.

---

no ἀτιμία, but a positive δόξα ; herself the δόξα ἀνδρός, her beauty has in this its crown and ensign. And this " glory " is grounded upon her humility : " because her hair to serve as a hood (ἀντὶ περιβολαίου) has been given her "—not as a substitute for head-dress (this would be to stultify Paul's contention), but in the nature of a covering, thus to match the veil (en guise de voile, Gd.) ; cf. χάριν ἀντὶ χάριτος, John i. 16 ; ἀντὶ κασιγνήτου ξεῖνος . . . τέτευκται, Odyss. viii. 456. δέδοται (pf. pass.) connotes a permanent boon (see 2 Cor. viii. 1, 1 John iii. 1, etc.). περιβόλαιον (from περιβάλλω), a wrapper, mantle, is here exceptionally used of head-gear.

Ver. 16 closes the discussion sharply, with its appeal to established Christian rule. If, after all that the Ap. has advanced in maintenance of the modest distinction between the sexes, any one is still minded to debate, he must be put down by authority—that of P. himself and his colleagues (ἡμεῖς), supported by universal Christendom ; cf. xiv. 33, 37 ff.—δοκεῖ φιλόνεικος εἶναι, not " seems," but " thinks (presumes ; see parls.) to be contentious " ; εἴ τις takes ind. of the case supposed (as in x. 27), and too likely in quarrelsome Cor. φιλόνεικος, not amans victoriæ (Est.) as if from νική, but avidus litium (from νεῖκος),—a disputer for disputation's sake.—ἡμεῖς, in contrast with αἱ ἐκκλησίαι, means not " I and those likeminded " (Mr.), but " I and my fellowministers " or " I and the Apostles generally " (cf. iv. 6-13, xv. 11, 2 Cor. i. 19, iv. 13, etc.).—τοιαύτην συνήθειαν, the custom described in vv. 4 f. above, which gave rise to the whole discussion ; not, as many understand it, the custom of being contentious (a temper, surely, rather than a custom) : no one could think of the App. (ἡμεῖς) indulging such a habit ! The advocates of feminine emancipation

may have supposed that P., the champion of liberty, was himself on their side, and that the rejection of the veil was in vogue elsewhere ; he denies both. For συνήθεια, Lat. con-suetudo, see viii. 7 ; for αἱ ἐκκλησίαι τοῦ Θεοῦ, i. 2, iv. 17, the pl. conveying the idea of unanimity amongst many. Those who explain " such a custom " as that of " being contentious," usually link this ver. with vv. 17 ff. It is true that the σχίσματα of the sequel, like the ἔριδες of i. 11, tended to φιλόνεικία ; in truth the disputatiousness of the Cor. ran into everything—a woman's shawl, or the merits of the Arch-apostles !

§ 37. THE CHURCH MEETING FOR THE WORSE, xi. 17-22. The Cor. Church had written self-complacently, expecting the Apostle's commendation upon its report (2). In reply P. has just pointed out one serious irregularity, which might indeed be put down to ignorance (3, 16). No such excuse is possible in regard to the disorders he has now to speak of, which are reported to him on evidence that he cannot discredit (18)—viz., the divisions apparent in the Church meetings (19), and the gross selfishness and sensuality displayed at the common meals (20 ff.). Such behaviour he certainly cannot praise (17, 22).

Ver. 17. If the T.R. be correct, τοῦτο (repeated in 22b) points to the instruction about to be given respecting the Lord's Supper : " Moreover (δέ), in giving you this charge I do not praise (you), seeing that, etc.": so Cm. and Gr. Ff., Er., Est., Bg., Hf., Hn., Sm. In vv. 3 ff. P. rectified an error, now he must censure a glaring fault ; " le ton devient celui du blâme positif " (Gd.) ; vv. 3 and 17 both detract, in different degrees, from the " praise " of ver. 2. τοῦτο παραγγέλλων has to wait long for its explanation ; P. lingers over his preliminary rehearsal of

ʳ κρεῖττον¹ ἀλλ᾽ εἰς τὸ ˢ ἧττον¹ ᵗ συνέρχεσθε. 18. ᵘ πρῶτον ᵘᵛ μὲν ʳ See vii. 9.
ᵛ γάρ, ᵗ συνερχομένων ὑμῶν ἐν τῇ² ἐκκλησίᾳ, ἀκούω ʷ σχίσματα ἐν ˢ N.T. *h.l.*;
Isa.xxiii.8.
ὑμῖν ˣ ὑπάρχειν, καὶ ʸ μέρος ʸ τι πιστεύω · 19. ᶻ δεῖ γὰρ καὶ ᵃ αἱρέσεις Adv. in 2
Cor. xii.
ἐν ὑμῖν εἶναι, ἵνα³ οἱ ᵇ δόκιμοι ᶜ φανεροὶ ᵈ γένωνται ἐν ὑμῖν. 20. 15; *cf.* vi.
7 above.
ᵗᵈ συνερχομένων οὖν ὑμῶν ᵈ ἐπὶ τὸ ᵈ αὐτό, οὐκ ἔστι ᵉ Κυριακὸν ᶠ δεῖπ- ᵗ Vv. 33 f.,
xiv. 23,26;
Acts i. 6,
etc.; Mk.

iii. 20, etc. u Rom. i. 8, iii. 2; Heb. vii. 2; Jas. iii. 17; without μεν, xii. 28, xv. 46, etc. v v. 3;
2 Cor. ix. 1, xi. 4; Rom. ii. 25, iii. 2; Heb. vii. 18, xii. 10; Acts xxviii. 22. w See i. 10. x See
vii. 26. y Bibl., *h.l.*; Thuc. iv. 30; Xen., *Eq.*, i. 12, etc. z See viii. 2. a Gal. v. 20; 2 Pet.
ii. 1; five times (sing.) in Acts. b 2 Cor. x. 18, xiii. 7; Rom. xiv. 18,xvi. 10; 2 Tim. ii. 15; Jas.
i. 12. αδοκ., ix. 27. c See iii. 13. d xiv. 23; with ειμι, vii. 5. e Rev. i. 10. See note below.
f Jo. xiii. 2, 4; Rev. xix. 9, 17; Lk. xiv. 12 ff.

¹ κρεισσον ... ησσον: all pre-Syrian uncc.
² *Om.* τη all uncc. and many minn.
³ ινα και (?): BD*, 37, 71, vg. sah., Ambrst. So Treg., Lachm.; W.H., Nestle
bracket και.

the founding of the Lord's Supper, and
the "charge" is held in suspense; its
gist becomes evident in vv. 20 f. Neither
the feminine indecorum censured in the
last § (to which τοῦτο is referred by Mr.,
Bt., Gd., El., etc.), nor *the contentiousness*
glanced at in ver. 16 (by which Ev. and
Ed. explain it), has been, strictly speaking,
matter of a *charge;* moreover, the backward ref. of τοῦτο involves the awk-
wardness of associating ἐπαινῶ and its
introductory ptp. with disconnected objects; these interpretations better fit the
other reading, παραγγέλλω ... ἐπαινῶν.
With certain specific and solemn injunctions respecting the Eucharist in view,
P. says, "I do not praise (you), in that
not for the better but for the worse you
come together".—ὅτι, with the like broad
sense as in i. 5, ix. 10, gives at once the
content and *ground* of dispraise. The
general profitlessness of the Church assemblies reached its climax in the desecration of the Lord's Supper, their
hallowing bond (x. 16 f.).

Ver. 18. The severe reproach, εἰς τὸ
ἧσσον συνέρχεσθε, is justified by vv.
18-22, which lead round to the intended
παραγγελία.—πρῶτον μὲν requires an
ἔπειτα δέ, that is not forthcoming (*cf.*
Rom. i. 8): the complement appears to
lie in xii.-xiv.—*viz., the abuse of spiritual
gifts,* a further and prominent ground of
disapproval (Mr., Hn., El.). Bt. and Ed.
find the antithesis in τὰ λοιπά, ver. 34*b*.
Hf. renders πρῶτον "chiefly," dispensing with any complement, but μὲν supposes a mental δέ. Ver. 20 gives no
contrasted ground of censure, it stands
upon *the same ground.*—συνερχομένων
ὑμῶν ἐν ἐκκλησίᾳ (not τῇ ἐκκλ., *in the
Church*): "as often as you come together

in assembly"—ptp. pr. of *repeated* occurrence; the σχίσματα in Church meetings
were chronic. For ἀκούω σχίσματα, see
i. 10 f.; the pr. "I am hearing" suggests
(in contrast with ἐδηλώθη above) *continued* information from various quarters
(*cf.* v. 1, ἀκούεται): hence the qualifying
μέρος τι (acc. of *definition*) πιστεύω,
wanting in ch. i.; P. does not "believe"
everything reported to him, but so much
as is stated he does credit.—ὑπάρχειν
(see parls.) implies not the bare fact, but
a *characteristic fact,* a *proprium* of this
Church—"have their place (are there)
amongst you": *cf.* Acts xxviii. 18.

Ver. 19. Paul is prepared to believe
what he thus hears; these divisions were
inevitable: "For indeed parties must
needs exist among you".—δεῖ affirms a
necessity lying in the moral conditions
of the case (see note on ὀφείλω, 7).—
αἵρεσις (see parls., and note on i. 11;
from αἱρέομαι, *to choose*) is more specific
than σχίσμα, implying *mental tendency*
—in philosophy a *school, Richtung,* then
a *sect* or *party formed on a basis of
opinion:* see Cr., *s.v.;* also Trench, *Syn.*
§ 4; "Heresy is theoretical schism,
schism practical heresy". These words
designate, as yet, parties within the
Church; in Tit. iii. 10, 2 Peter ii. 1, they
verge toward their ecclesiastical use.
—Now there is a true purpose of God
fulfilled in these unhappy divisions; they
serve to sift the loyal from the disloyal:
"in order that also the approved may
become manifest among you". These
αἱρέσεις are a magnet attracting unsound
and unsettled minds, and leaving genuine
believers to stand out "approved" by
their constancy; see 2 Thess. ii. 11 f.,
where the same thought is differently

νον φαγεῖν· 21. ἕκαστος γὰρ τὸ ἴδιον [f] δεῖπνον [g] προλαμβάνει [1] ἐν [2] τῷ φαγεῖν, καὶ [h] ὃς μὲν [i] πεινᾷ [h] ὃς δὲ [k] μεθύει· 22. [l] μὴ γὰρ οἰκίας [l] οὐκ ἔχετε εἰς τὸ ἐσθίειν καὶ πίνειν; [m] ἢ τῆς [n] ἐκκλησίας τοῦ [n] Θεοῦ [o] καταφρονεῖτε, καὶ [p] καταισχύνετε τοὺς [q] μὴ [q] ἔχοντας; τί ὑμῖν [3] εἴπω [3]; [r] ἐπαινέσω [4] ὑμᾶς; ἐν τούτῳ οὐκ [r] ἐπαινῶ.

g Gal. vi. 1 (in diff. sense); Mk. xiv. 8; Wisd. xvii. 16.
h xii. 8, 28; 2 Cor. ii. 16; Rom. ix. 21, xiv. 2, 5; 2 Tim. ii. 20; Jude 22; once in Acts, nine times in Syn. GG.
i See iv. 11.
k 1 Th. v. 7; Acts ii. 15; Mt. xxiv. 49; Jo. ii. 10.
l See ix. 4.
m For η in double interrogg., *cf.* i. 13, ix. 8, 10, x. 19, xiv. 36.
n See i. 2.
o Rom. ii. 4; 1 Tim. iv. 12, vi. 2; Heb. xii. 2; 2 Pet. ii. 10; thrice in GG.
p See i. 27.
q Lk. iii. 11, xxii. 36.
r See ver. 2.

[1] **προσλαμβανει,** A, some 20 minn. **προ** and **προς** often confused in comp. vbs.
[2] **επι τῳ φαγειν**: DG, vg. (*ad manducandum*).
[3] **ειπω υμιν** (in this order): all uncc. but KL.
[4] **επαινω,** BG, vg., Latt. Ff. For position of the *interrog.*, see note below.

applied; also Rom. v. 4, **ἡ ὑπομονὴ κατεργάζεται δοκιμήν,** 1 Peter i. 7; also Tert., *De Præscr. Hæret.*, 4, "ut fides habendo tentationem habeat etiam probationem". For **δόκιμος,** *accepted on proof*, see parls., esp. ix. 27; those approved with God thus "become manifest" to men; "l'effet est de manifester au grand jour les membres de l'église sérieux et de bon aloi" (Gd.). "Dominus talibus experimentis probat constantiam suorum. Pulchra consolatio!" (Cv.).

Vv. 20, 21 resume with emphasis the circumstantial clause of ver. 18 and draw out, by **οὖν,** the disastrous issue of the **σχίσματα**: they produce *a visible separation at the common meal of the Church, destroying the reality of the Lord's Supper*. Ch. i. 12, iii. 3 f., iv. 6, showed that the Cor. divisions were of a *partisan* character, and i. 19 that *intellectual* differences entered into them (*cf.* viii. 1-7); but *distinctions of wealth* contributed to the same effect. The two latter influences conspired, the richer and more cultivated Cor. Christians leaning to a self-indulgence which they justified on the ground of enlightenment; the **αἱρέσεις** sloped down toward **κραιπάλη καὶ μέθη.—ἐπὶ τὸ αὐτό,** "to the same (spot)".—**οὐκ ἔστιν κ.τ.λ.** can hardly mean, "it is not to eat the Lord's Supper" (so Al. and others)—for the Cor. *intended* this, but by unworthy behaviour (26 f.) neutralised their purpose: P. says either "it (*sc.* your feast) is not an eating of the Lord's Supper" (A.V., Bz., Est., D.W., Bt., Hn., El., Gd.: "ce n'est pas là manger, etc."); or, "it is not (possible) to eat the Lord's Supper" (R.V., Bg., Mr., Hf., Ed., Ev.)—such eating *is out of the question*. Ver. 21 bears out the last interpretation, since it describes a state of things not merely nullifying but *repugnant to* any true **κυριακὸν δεῖπνον**; **οὐκ ἔστιν** carries this strong sense, negativing the *idea* as well as fact, in Heb. ix. 5, and often in cl. Gr.—The adj. **κυριακὸν** (=**τοῦ Κυρίου**) stands in emphatic contrast with **ἴδιον,** the termination **-κὸς** signifying *kind* or *nature*: "It is impossible to eat a supper *of the Lord*, for each man is in haste to get (**προλαμβάνει**—*præoccupat*, Bz.) *his own* supper when he eats,"—or "during the meal" (Ev.; **ἐν τῷ φαγεῖν,** *in edendo*, Bz.; not *ad manducandum*, as in Vg.). Instead of waiting for one another (33), the Cor., as they entered the assembly-room bringing their provisions, sat down at once to consume each his own supply, like private diners at a restaurant; **προ-** suggests, in view of ver. 22, that the rich even *hurried* to do this, so as to avoid sharing with slaves and low people at a common dish (22).—The **κυρ. δεῖπνον** was a kind of club-supper, with which the evening meeting of the Church commenced (18*a*, 20*a*), taking place at least once a week on the Lord's Day (*cf.* Acts xx. 7 ff.). This Church-supper, afterwards called the Agapé (see *Dict. of Christian Antiq. s.v.*; also Ed. *ad loc.*) was analogous to the **συσσίτια** and **ἔρανοι** held by the guilds and friendly societies then rife amongst the Greeks. Originating as a kind of enlarged family meal in the Church of Jerus. (Acts ii. 46), the practice of the common supper accorded so well with social custom that it was universal amongst Christians in the first century (see Weizsäcker's *Apost. Age*, vol. ii., pp. 279-286). Gradually the Eucharist was separated from the Agapé for greater decorum, and the latter degenerated and became ex-

23. Ἐγὼ γὰρ ˢπαρέλαβον ἀπὸ τοῦ Κυρίου, ὃ καὶ ᵗπαρέδωκα ὑμῖν, ὅτι ὁ Κύριος Ἰησοῦς ἐν τῇ νυκτὶ ᾗ ᵘπαρεδίδοτο ¹ ᵛἔλαβεν ᵛἄρτον, 24. καὶ ʷεὐχαριστήσας ˣἔκλασε καὶ εἶπε, "Λάβετε,² φάγετε² τοῦτό μου ʸἐστὶ τὸ σῶμα ᶻτὸ ᶻὑπὲρ ὑμῶν κλώμενον³· τοῦτο ποιεῖτε

ˢ In this sense, xv. 1, 3; seven times besides in P.
t See ver. 2.
u Of persons, v. 5; 12 times besides in P.; in this connexion, Mt. x. 21, xvii. 22, xxvi. 2, 45 ff., etc.   v Mt. xiv. 19, xv. 26, 36, xvi. 5, 7, xxvi. 26; Lk. vi. 4; Jo. xxi. 13; Acts xxvii. 35.   w See i. 4.   x See x. 16.   y See x. 4.   z The ellipsis (without κλωμ.), h.l.

¹ παρεδίδετο, all uncc. but B³LP.   See Bm., p. 47.
² Om. λαβετε, φαγετε (from Mt. xxvi. 26) all uncc. but C³KLP.
³ Om. κλωμενον ℵ*ABC*, 17, 67**, Cyr.

Add κλωμενον ℵcC³Db, cGKLP, latt. syrr.; θρυπτομενον, D*; διδομενον (Lk.), sah. cop. vg., Cyp.   The three ptps. are various attempts to fill up a seeming ellipsis.

tinct; here they are one, as in the Last Supper itself. The table was provisioned at Cor. not from a general fund (as was usual in the ἔρανοι or *collegia*), but by each guest bringing his contribution in kind, a practice not uncommon in private parties, which had the disadvantage of accentuating social differences. While the poor brought little or nothing to the feast and might be ashamed to show his fare, the rich man exhibited a loaded basket out of which he could feed to repletion. All κοινωνία was destroyed; such vulgarity would have disgraced a heathen guild - feast. The *Lord*, the common Host, was forgotten at His table. ὃς μὲν πεινᾷ—sc. the poor man, whose small store was insufficient, or who arriving late (for his time was not his own) found the table cleared (*cf.* προλαμβάνει). ὃς δὲ μεθύει, "but another is drunk!" or in the lighter sense suggested by πεινᾷ, plus *satis bibit* (Gr., Hn.), "drinks to the full" (*cf.* John ii. 10); the scene of sensual greed and pride might well culminate in drunkenness. Of all imaginable schisms the most shocking: hunger and intoxication side by side, at what is supposed to be the Table of the Lord! This is indeed "meeting for the worse".—For the demonstr. use of the rel. pron. with μὲν and δέ, see Wr., p. 130.

Ver. 22. μὴ γὰρ οἰκίας οὐκ ἔχετε κ.τ.λ.; "For is it that you have not houses to eat and drink in?" See ver. 34, and note. The γὰρ brings in an ironical excuse: "For I suppose you act thus because you are houseless, and must satisfy your appetite at church!" *cf.* πῶς γάρ; Acts viii. 31.—If this voracity cannot be excused by a physical need which the offenders had no other means of supplying—if, that is to say, their

action is *deliberate*—they must intend to pour scorn on the Church and to insult their humbler brethren: "Or do you despise the church of God, and cast shame on those that are without means?" For ἡ ἐκκλησία τοῦ Θεοῦ, an expression of awful dignity, see i. 2, x. 32. τοὺς μὴ ἔχοντας, "the have-nots" (*cf.* 2 Cor. viii. 12)—οἱ ἔχοντες in cl. Gr. signifies "the men of property"; μή (of the *point of view*) rather than οὐ (of the *fact*), for the poor with their beggarly rations are shamed by the full-fed on this very account. What could show coarser contempt for the Church assembly?—P. shows a fine self-restraint in the *litotes* of the last sentence: τί εἴπω ὑμῖν; κ.τ.λ.: "What am I to say to you? Should I praise (you)? In this matter I praise you not". ἐπαινέσω, deliberative aor. sbj., like εἴπω, for the question refers not to the future, but to the situation depicted (see Wr., p. 356). ἐν τούτῳ has great point and emphasis when attached to the following οὐκ ἐπαινῶ (so R.V. marg., after early Verss., Bz., Est., Hn., Gd., Bt., El., Ed.); thus also ἐπαινέσω better matches εἴπω, and the last clause prepares for the important ἐγὼ δὲ παρέλαβον of the ensuing ver.

§ 38. Unworthy Participants of the Lord's Bread and Cup, xi. 23-34. The behaviour of the wealthier Cor. at the Church Supper is scandalous in itself; viewed in the light of the institution and meaning of the Eucharistic ordinance, their culpability is extreme (23-27). The sense of this should set the readers on self-examination (28 f.). The sickness and mortality rife amongst them are a sign of the Lord's displeasure in this very matter, and a loud call to amendment (30-32). Two practical directions are finally given: that the members of the

a For εἰς   ª εἰς τὴν ἐμὴν ᵇ ἀνάμνησιν". 25. ᵉ ὡσαύτως καὶ τὸ ᵈ ποτήριον μετὰ
with vbl.
noun, cf.   τὸ ᵉ δειπνῆσαι, λέγων, "Τοῦτο τὸ ᵈ ποτήριον ἡ ᶠ καινὴ ᶠ διαθήκη
Mk. i. 4,
xiv. 9. ι ἐστὶν ᵍ ἐν τῷ ἐμῷ ¹ ᵍ αἵματι ¹ · τοῦτο ποιεῖτε, ʰ ὁσάκις ἂν ² πίνητε,
Th. iv. 17
and Mt.
viii. 34 are Hebraistic.   b Lk. xxii. 19; Heb. x. 3; Lev. xxiv. 7.   c Lk. xxii. 20; Rom. viii. 26;
Mt. xxi. 30; Lk. xx. 31; Prov. xxvii. 15.   d See x. 16.   e Lk. xxii. 20, xvii. 8; Rev. iii. 20;
Prov. xxiii. 1; Tob. viii. 1.   f 2 Cor. iii. 6; Heb. viii. 8 (Jer. xxxviii. 31), ix. 15.   g Heb. ix. 22,
25; x. 19; 1 Jo. v. 6; Zech. ix. 11.   h Rev. xi. 6.

¹ αἱματι μου (Lk.) : ACP, 17, 37, 46.   ² εαν, ℵBC, 17. See Wr., p. 390.

Church should wait until all are gathered
before commencing supper; and that
where hunger forbids delay, food should
first be taken at home (33 f.).

Vv. 23, 24. Amongst the things the
Ap. had "delivered" to his readers, that
they professed to be "holding fast" (2),
was the story of the Last Supper of the
Lord Jesus, which the Church perpetu-
ates in its communion-feast.—ἐγώ, antithetical to ὑμῖν: I the imparter, you the
receivers, of these solemn facts.—ἀπὸ
neither excludes, nor suggests (cf. i. 30,
xiv. 36, etc.) as παρὰ might have done
(Gal. i. 12, 1 Thess. ii. 13), independent
impartation to P.; "it marks the whence
of the communication, in a wide and
general sense" (El.); the Ap. vouches
for it that what he related came authenti-
cally from the Lord. παραλαμβάνω denotes "receiving a deposit or trust"
(Ed.). "The Lord Jesus," see i. 8.
—The allusion to "the night in which He
was betrayed" (graphic impf., "while
the betrayal went on"), is no mere note
of time; it throws into relief the fidelity
of Jesus in the covenant (25) thus made
with His people, and enhances the holy
pathos of the recollection; behind the
Saviour lurks the Traitor. Incidentally,
it shows how detailed and matter-of-fact
was the account of the Passion given to
Paul's converts. For the irreg. impf.,
παρεδίδετο, see Wr., p. 95, note 3.—
ἔλαβεν ἄρτον, "took a loaf" (ein Brod:
cf. the εἶς ἄρτος of x. 17)—one of the flat
and brittle unleavened cakes of the Passover Table.—καὶ εὐχαριστήσας ἔκλασεν
κ.τ.λ., "and after pronouncing the blessing, broke it and said, etc." This
εὐχαριστία was apparently the blessing
inaugurating the meal, which was followed by the symbolic bread-breaking,
whereas "the cup" was administered
μετὰ τὸ δειπνῆσαι (25); cf. Luke xxii.
17 ff. (see notes ad loc. in vol. i.), whose
account is nearly the same as Paul's, differing in some important particulars from
that of Matt. and Mark. Luke, however,
introduces a preparatory cup of renuncia-

tion on the part of Jesus, "prolusio
cœnæ" (Bg.). The fractio panis, the
sign of the commencement of a household or social meal (Luke xxiv. 30; Acts
ii. 42), is prominent in each narrative;
this act supplied another name for the
Sacrament.—Regarding the words pronounced over the broken loaf, we bear in
mind (1) that Jesus said of the bread
"This is my body," Himself sitting there
in His visible person, when the identification of substance could not occur to any
one; (2) that the parl. saying concerning
"the cup" expounds by the word "covenant" (covenant in my blood, in Luke and
P.; my blood of the covenant, in Matt.
and Mark) the connexion of symbol and
thing symbolised, linking the cup and
blood, and by analogy the loaf and body,
as one not by confusion of substance but
by correspondence of relation: what the
blood effects, the cup sets forth and seals.
The bread, standing for the body, "is
the body" representatively; broken for
Christ's disciples, it serves materially in
the Supper the part which His slain body
is about to serve spiritually "for the life
of the world". Our Lord thus puts into
an acted parable the doctrine taught by
figurative speech in John vi. 48 ff.
"ἐστὶν is here the copula of symbolic
being; otherwise the identity of subject and predicate would form a conception equally impossible to Speaker and
hearers" (Mr.).—τὸ ὑπὲρ ὑμῶν (κλώμενον
an early gloss), "that is for you"—in all
its relations subsisting for men; for our
advantage He wore the σῶμα σαρκός
(2 Cor. viii. 9, Phil. ii. 7, Heb. ii. 14 ff.,
etc.). The τοῦτο ποιεῖτε clause is peculiar to Luke and Paul: their witness is
good evidence that the words are ἀπὸ
τοῦ Κυρίου (23). The sacrificial sense
put on ποιεῖτε by many "Catholic" exegetes (as though syn. with the Homeric
ῥέζειν, and 'asah of Exod. xxix. 39,
etc.) is without lexical warrant, and
"plane præter mentem Scripturæ" as
the R.C. Estius honestly says; see also
El. ad loc.—εἰς τὴν ἐμὴν (cf. ὑμετέραν,

^aεἰς τὴν ἐμὴν ^bἀνάμνησιν". 26. ^hὁσάκις γὰρ ἂν¹ ἐσθίητε τὸνⁱ Rom. v.
10, vi. 3, 5;
ἄρτον τοῦτον καὶ τὸ ποτήριον τοῦτο² πίνητε, τὸν ⁱθάνατον τοῦ ⁱΚυρίου Phil. iii.
10; cf. viii.
^kκαταγγέλλετε, ^lἄχρις ^lοῦ ἂν³ ἔλθῃ. 27. ὥστε ὃς ἂν ἐσθίῃ τὸν 11, xv. 3;
2 Cor. v.
ἄρτον τοῦτον² ἢ πίνῃ τὸ ^mποτήριον τοῦ ^mΚυρίου^{4 n}ἀναξίως,^{4 o}ἔνοχος 15; Rom.
v. 6 ff., vi.
10, etc.

k See ii. 1. l xv. 25; Rom. xi. 25; Gal. iii. 19, etc. m x. 21. n N.T. h.l.; 2 Macc. xiv. 22.
-ιος, see vi. 2. o Heb. ii. 15; Jas. ii. 10 (same constr.; also in Isa. liv. 17); Mk. iii. 29, xiv. 64.
With dat., Mt. v. 21 f.; Deut. xix. 10.

¹εαν, ℵBC, 17. See Wr., p. 390.

²Om. τουτο and τοῦτον all pre-Syrian codd.

³Om. αν all pre-Syrian uncc., and many minn.

⁴αναξιως του Κυριου, ℵDᶜL, above 20 minn., and seemingly Or. in one place.

xv. 31) ἀνάμνησιν, in mei memoriam (Cv.); Ed. reads it "My commemoration" in contrast to that of Moses (x. 2), making τ. ἐμὴν correspond to καινὴν of ver. 25.

Ver. 25. ὡσαύτως καὶ τὸ ποτήριον: "In the same fashion also (He gave) the cup". The two ritual actions correspond, and form one covenant.—μετὰ τὸ δειπνῆσαι (as in Luke)—"postquam cœnaverunt" (Cv.), or better "cœnatum est" (Rom. Liturgy)—is studiously added to "emphasise the distinction between the Lord's Supper and an ordinary evening meal; cf. vv. 20 f.—The eating of the bread originally formed part of the common meal (consider Matt. xxvi. 26, Mark xiv. 22, ἐσθιόντων αὐτῶν), and may still have so continued, but the cup was certainly afterwards" (El.)—a solemn close to the κυριακὸν δεῖπνον.—" This cup is (see note 24: ἐστὶν wanting in Luke) the new covenant, in my blood"; cf. notes on x. 16 f. for τὸ ποτ., and the relation of διαθήκη to κοινωνία. The cup, given by the Lord's hand and tasted by each disciple in turn, is a virtual covenant for all concerned; in His blood it becomes so (ἐν τ. αἵμ. is made by its position a further predicate, not a mere adjunct of διαθ.: cf. Rom. iii. 25), since that is the ground on which God grants and man accepts the covenant. For διαθήκη, see Cr., s.v.; this term, in distinction from συνθήκη, indicates the initiative of God as Disposer in the great agreement. For P.'s interpretation of ἐν τ. αἵματι, see Rom. iii. 23 ff., Eph. i. 7, ii. 13 ff., Col. i. 20; also parls. in Ep. to Heb., Rev. i. 5, 1 John i. 7, 1 Pet. i. 18 f. For "new covenant," see parls.: καινός, new in nature, contents, as securing complete forgiveness and spiritual renovation (Jer. xxxi. 31 ff., etc.).—" This do . . . for the commemoration of Me": see ver. 24b; τοῦτο includes, beside the

act, the accompanying words, without which the ἀνάμνησις is imperfect. ὁσάκις ἐὰν (late Gr. for ἄν) πίνητε: "so many times as (quotiescunque) you drink (it)"—the cup of the context; not "so often as you drink" (Hf.), sc. at any table where Christians meet. Our Lord prescribed no set times; P. assumes that celebration will be frequent, for he directs that, however frequent, it must be guided by the Lord's instructions, so as to keep the remembrance of Him unimpaired.

Ver. 26. Familiarity helped to blunt in the Cor. their reverence for the Eucharist; hence the repeated ὁσάκις ἐάν: "for so many times as you eat this bread and drink the cup, you are proclaiming the Lord's death, until He come". γὰρ has its proper explicative force: Christ bade His disciples thus perpetually commemorate Him (24 f.: ποιεῖτε, "go on to do"—sustained action), "for it is thus that you publish His death, and in this form the testimony will continue till He comes again." καταγγέλλετε (see parls.), on this view ind., is the active expression of ἀνάμνησις: "Christus de beneficio mortis suae nos admonet, et nos coram hominibus id recognovimus" (Cv.). The ordinance is a verbum visibile, a "preaching" of the entire Church in silent ministry: "Christi sanguis scripturarum omnium sacramento ac testimonio effusus prædicatur" (Cyprian, quoted by Ed.). ἄχρι οῦ ἔλθῃ states the terminus ad quem, given in the words of Jesus at the Table, Luke xxii. 18, Matt. xxvi. 29. The rite looks forward as well as backward; a rehearsal of the Passion Supper, a foretaste of the Marriage Supper of the Lamb. Paul thus "associates with the καταγγέλλειν of the celebrants the fear and trembling that belong to the Maranatha of xvi. 22" (Mr.). The pathos and the glory of the Table of the Lord were alike lost on the Corinthians.

ἔσται ° τοῦ [p] σώματος καὶ [1] [p] αἵματος τοῦ [p] Κυρίου. 28. [q] δοκιμαζέτω
δὲ [r] ἄνθρωπος [2] ἑαυτὸν,[2] καὶ [s] οὕτως ἐκ τοῦ ἄρτου ἐσθιέτω καὶ ἐκ τοῦ
ποτηρίου πινέτω· 29. ὁ γὰρ ἐσθίων καὶ πίνων ἀναξίως,[3] [t] κρίμα
ἑαυτῷ ἐσθίει καὶ πίνει, μὴ [u] διακρίνων τὸ [p] σῶμα τοῦ [4] Κυρίου.[4]

p See x. 16. q See iii. 13. r See iv. 1. s In this sense, xiv. 25; Rom. v. 12, xi. 26; Acts vii. 8, xvii. 33, xxviii. 14. t 8 times besides in P.; 1 Pet. iv. 17; 2 Pet. ii. 3; Jude 4; Acts xxiv. 25; thrice in Rev., six times in GG. u Acts xv. 9; Jas. ii. 4; Job. xii. 11. *Cf.* iv. 7.

[1] **του αιματος**: all uncc., above 40 minn., and many Ff.

[2] **εαυτον ανθρωπος** (in this order): CDGP.

[3] *Om.* **αναξιως** ℵ*ABC*, 17, sah.,—a Western popular gloss; current in Ff.

[4] *Om.* **του Κυριου** ℵ*ABC*, 17, 67**, am.* fu.*.

Ver. 27 draws the practical consequence of vv. 20-26, stating the judgement upon Cor. behaviour at the Supper that a right estimate of the covenant-cup and bread demands: "So then, whoever eats the bread or drinks the cup of the Lord unworthily, will be held guilty (**ἔνοχος ἔσται**; *reus tenetur*, Bz.; rather, *tenebitur*) of the body and blood of the Lord"; it is *this* that he ignores or insults; *cf.* ver. 29. On **ὥστε** with ind., see note to iii. 7. What "unworthily" means is patent from vv. 20 ff.—The *or*, for *and*, between **ἐσθίῃ** and **πίνῃ** supplies the single text adducible for the R.C. practice of *lay communion in one kind*: "non leve argumentum," says Est., "non enim sic loqueretur Ap., si non sentiret unam speciem sine altera sumi posse". But *and* appeared in just the same connexion in ver. 26, and reappears in vv. 28 f.; "or" replaces "and" when one is thinking of the parl. acts distinctly, and the same communicant might behave unworthily in *either* act, esp. as the breaking of the bread and taking of the cup at this time came in probably at the beginning and end respectively of the Church Supper, and were separated by an interval of time; see notes on **εὐχαριστήσας** and **μετὰ τ. δειπν.** (24 f.). **ἔνοχος** (from **ἐν-έχω**, *to hold in* some liability) acquires in late Gr., like **αἴτιος**, a gen. of *person against whom* offence is committed; see Ed. *in loc.* To outrage the emblem is to outrage its original—as if one should mock at the Queen's picture or at his country's flag. Except **ἔλθῃ**, the vbs. throughout this passage are pr. in tense, relating to habit.

Ver. 28. "But (in contrast with the guilt described, and in order to escape it) let a man put himself to proof, and so from the bread let him eat and from the cup let him drink." **ἄνθρωπος**, replacing **ὃς ἄν** (27), is *qualitative*, "containing the ideas of infirmity and responsibility" (Gd.); *cf.* iii. 4, x. 13. On **δοκιμάζω**, see iii. 13, and parls.; it signifies not *judicial examination* (**ἀνακρίνω**, iv. 3, etc.), nor *discriminative* estimate (**διακρίνω**, 31), but *self-probing* (*probet se ipsum*, Vg.; not *exploret se*, Bz.) with a view to fit partaking; any serious attempt at this would make the scene of vv. 20 ff. impossible: the impv. is *pr.*, enjoining a practice; the communicant must test himself habitually by the great realities with which he is confronted, asking himself, *e.g.*, whether he "discerns the Lord's body" (29).—**καὶ οὕτως**: scarcely *sic demum* (Bg.), but *hoc cum animo; cf.* Phil. iv. 1. **ἐκ . . . ἐσθιέτω, ἐκ . . . πινέτω**—a solemn fulness of expression, in keeping with the temper of mind required; the prp. implies participation with others (*cf.* ix. 7, 13, x. 17).

Ver. 29. Participation in the bread and cup is itself a **δοκιμασία**: "For he that eats and drinks, a judgment for himself (sentence on himself) he eats and drinks". The single art. of **ὁ ἐσθίων καὶ πίνων**, combining the acts, negatives the R.C. inference from the **ἢ** of ver. 27 (see note). Contact with Christ in this ordinance probes each man to the depths (*cf.* John iii. 18 f., ix. 39); it is true of the Lord's *verbum visibile*, as of His *verbum audibile*, that he who receives it **ἔχει τὸν κρίνοντα αὐτόν** (John xii. 48). His attitude toward the Lord at His table revealed with shocking evidence the spiritual condition of many a Cor. Christian—his carnality and blindness as one "not distinguishing the body".—The two senses given by interpreters to **διακρίνω** are, as Hn. says, somewhat blended here ("Beruht jedes Urtheilen auf *Ent*scheiden und *Unter*scheiden"), as in *dijudicans* (Vg.): one "discerns (judges clearly and rightly of) the (Lord's) body" in the sacrament, and therein "discriminates"

30. διὰ τοῦτο ἐν ὑμῖν πολλοὶ ᵛἀσθενεῖς καὶ ᵂἄρρωστοι, καὶ ˣκοιμῶν- ᵛ 2 Cor. x.
ται ʸἱκανοί· 31. εἰ γὰρ¹ ἑαυτοὺς ᵘδιεκρίνομεν, οὐκ ἂν ᵃἐκρινόμεθα· 10; Mt.
xxv. 43;
32. ᵃκρινόμενοι δέ, ὑπὸ Κυρίου ² ᶻπαιδευόμεθα, ἵνα μὴ σὺν τῷ κόσμῳ Lk. x. 9;
Acts iv. 9,
ᵃκατακριθῶμεν. 33. ὥστε, ἀδελφοί μου, ᵇσυνερχόμενοι εἰς τὸ ᵂ v. 15 f.
Mt. xiv.
14; Mk.
vi. 5, 13,

xvi. 18; Mal. i. 8; Sir. vii. 35. -τειν, 2 Kings xii. 15; -τημα, Sir. x. 10; -τια, Ps. xl. 3.   x See vii.
39.   y Acts xii. 12, xiv. 21, xix. 19; Lk. vii. 11, viii. 32.   z 2 Cor. vi. 9; Tit. ii. 12; Heb. xii. 6;
Rev. iii. 19; Prov. iii. 11.   a Rom. ii. 1 (cf. xiv. 23); also 2 Pet. ii. 6; Rom. iii. 6; Acts xvii. 31;
Jo. iil. 17.   b See ver. 18.

¹ δε, א*ABDG, 17, 46, latt. vg.
γαρ, CאcCKLP, sah. cop., Bas., Cyr.; Alexandrian and Syrian.
² του Κυριου: אBC, 17, 37.   Om. του ADGKLP, etc. (Western and Syrian).

the rite from all other eating and drinking—precisely what the Cor. failed to do
(20 ff.). They did not descry the signified in the sign, the Incarnate and Crucified in His memorial loaf and cup, and
their Supper became a mere vulgar matter
of meat and drink. This ordinance exposed them for what they were—σαρκικοί
(iii. 3).—τὸ σῶμα (cf. 24 ff.)—a reverent
aposiopesis, resembling ἡ ἡμέρα in iii.
13 (see note); the explanation of some
Lutherans, that τὸ σῶμα means "the substance" underlying the material element,
is foreign to the context and to Apostolic
times. On "the serious doctrinal question" as to what the unfaithful receive
in the sacrament, see El. ad loc. Distinguish κρίμα (unhappily rendered "damnation" in A.V.), a judicial sentence of
any kind, from κατάκριμα, the final
condemnation of the sinner (32; Rom. v.
16).

Ver. 30. In evidence of the "judgment" which profanation of the Lord's
Table entails, the Ap. points to the sad
fact that "amongst you many are sick
and weakly, and not a few are sleeping".
—ἀσθενεῖς applies to maladies of any
kind, ἄρρωστοι to cases of debility and
continued ill-health—ægroti et valetudi-
narii (Bz.). The added κοιμῶνται (the
Christian syn. for ἀποθνήσκουσιν) shows
that P. is speaking not figuratively of
low spiritual conditions, but literally of
physical inflictions which he knows to be
their consequence (διὰ τοῦτο). We must
be careful not to generalise from this
single instance (see John ix. 3). The
mere coincidence of such afflictions with
the desecration of the Eucharist could
not have justified P. in making this
statement; he must have been conscious
of some specific revelation to this effect.
For ἱκανοί (a sufficient number—something like our "plenty of you"), see
parls.; "something less than πολλοί,

though sufficiently numerous to arouse
serious attention" (El.). The "sleepers"
had died in the Lord, or this term would
not have been used of them; it does not
appear that this visitation had singled
out the profaners of the Sacrament; the
community is suffering, for widely-spread
offence. Both in the removal and infliction of physical evil, the inauguration of
the New Covenant, as of the Old, was
marked by displays of supernatural power.

Vv. 31, 32. Such chastisements may
be averted; when they come, it is for our
salvation: "If however we discerned (or
discriminated: dijudicaremus, Vg.) ourselves, we should not be judged".—
διακρίνω is taken up from ver. 29 (see
note); it is distinguished from κρίνω,
which in turn is contrasted with κατα-
κρίνω (32).—τῷ κόσμῳ in the sequel explains the bearing of διακρίνω here: it
expresses a discriminating judgment, by
which the Christian rightly appreciates
his own status and calling, and realises
his distinctive character, even as the
διακρίνων of ver. 29 realises the diff. between the κυριακὸν δεῖπνον and a common
δεῖπνον. The alliterative play on κρίνω
and its compounds is untranslatable; cf.
ii. 13 ff., iv. 3 ff. For the form of hypothesis, see ii. 8; for the pers. of ἑαυτοὺς,
vi. 7.—κρινόμενοι δὲ assumes, from ver.
30, as a fact the consequence hypothetically denied in the last sentence: "But
under judgment as we are, we are being
chastised by the Lord, in order that we
may not with the world be condemned"
(κατακριθῶμεν, judged-against, to our
ruin). Thus hope is extracted from a
sorrowful situation; cf. Heb. xii. 6 f.,
Rev. iii. 19; νουθεσίας μᾶλλόν ἐστιν ἢ
καταδίκης τὸ γινόμενον (Cm.). On παιδεύω, to treat as a boy, see Trench, Syn.,
§ 32. Plato describes παιδεία as δύναμις
θεραπευτικὴ τῇ ψυχῇ; cf. the proverb,
παθήματα μαθήματα. Ch. v. 5 is the

c xvi. 11;
Acts xvii. φαγεῖν, ἀλλήλους ᵉἐκδέχεσθε· 34. εἰ δέ¹ τις ᵈπεινᾷ, ᵉἐν ᵍοἴκῳ
16; Jas. v.
7; Heb. x. ἐσθιέτω· ἵνα μὴ εἰς ᵗκρίμα ᵇσυνέρχησθε. τὰ δὲ λοιπά, ᶠὡς ᶠἂν
13, xi. 10. ἔλθω, ᵍδιατάξομαι.²
d See iv. 11.
e xiv. 35;
Mk. ii. 1; Deut. xi. 19 f. f Rom. xv. 24; Phil. ii. 23; cf. xii. 2 below. g See vii. 17.

¹ Om. δε pre-Syrian uncc., latt. vg. cop. ² διαταξωμαι, ADG, 37.

extreme case of such "chastening" unto
salvation; cf. Ps. cxix. 67, etc.—κρινό-
μενα (pr.), a disciplinary *proceeding;*
κατακριθῶμεν (aor.), a definitive *pronouncement;* cf. Acts xvii. 31, etc. P. associates himself, by 1st pers. pl., with the
readers, sharing his Churches' troubles
(2 Cor. xi. 28 f.).

Vv. 33, 34a. The "charge" (17) proceeds from inward to outward, from
self-examination (28) to *mutual accommodation* respecting the Lord's Supper.
Religious decorum depends on two conditions,—*a becoming spirit* associated
with *fitting external arrangements*, such
as good sense and reverence dictate:
"And so, my brothers, when you meet
for the meal, *wait for one another*".—
ἀδελφοί μου adds a touch of affection to
what has been severely said.—συνερχό-
μενοι carries us back to vv. 17, 20; the
same train of admonition throughout.—
τὸ φαγεῖν embraces the entire Church
Supper; see notes on vv. 20 f.; the
order ἀλλήλους ἐκδέχεσθε (*invicem ex-
pectate*, Vg.) forbids the hasty and schis-
matic τὸ ἴδιον δεῖπνον προλαβεῖν (21);
no one must begin supper till the Church
is gathered, so that all may commence
together and share alike. To *wait for*
others presumes *waiting to feast with
them.*—ἐκδέχομαι never means *excipio*
(*receive:* so Hf., and a few others), but
always *exspecto* in the N.T.; with the
former sense in cl. Gr., it signifies *to receive* (a person) *from* some particular
quarter.—Some might object that hunger
is pressing, and they cannot wait; to
these Paul says, "If any one is hungry,
let him eat *at home*"—staying his appetite before he comes to the meeting;
cf. vv. 21, 22a. The Church Supper is
for good-fellowship, not for bodily need;
to eat there like a famished man, absorbed in one's food—if nothing worse
happen—is to exclude Christian and religious thoughts.—ἐν οἴκῳ, not ἐν ἐκκλησίᾳ (18: note the absence of the
art.).—"Coming together εἰς κρίμα"
(for a judgment) defines the "coming together εἰς ἧσσον" of ver. 17 in terms of
vv. 29-32. συνέρχησθε, pr. sbj., of the

stated meetings, as in ver. 18, etc. This
warning (ἵνα μή) closes the παραγγελία
introduced in ver. 17. For a clear and im-
partial account of the various doctrines
of the Lord's Supper connected with this
passage, see Bt., pp. 206 ff.

Ver. 34b. τὰ λοιπά, an *etcetera* appended to the charge—"other matters,"
probably of detail connected with the
Church Supper and the κοινωνία. Ed.
takes this as the antithesis to the πρῶτον
μὲν of ver. 18 (see note), and supposes
λοιπὰ to refer to other *different* matters,
of which P. would postpone discussion
till his arrival—addressing himself notwithstanding to one of the principal of
these λοιπὰ in xii. 1 ff.—ὡς ἂν ἔλθω,
"according as I may come": the Ap. is
uncertain *when and under what circumstances* he may next visit Cor. (cf. xvi.
5-9); his intention to set matters in order
is subject to this contingency.—διατάξομαι (see parls.) refers, presumably, to
points of *external* order, such as those
just dealt with. Romanists (see Est.)
justify by this text their alleged unwritten
apostolic traditions respecting the Eucharist; *fasting communion, e.g.,* is
placed amongst the unspecified λοιπά.

§ 39. THE VARIOUS CHARISMS OF THE
ONE SPIRIT, xii. 1-11. In treating of the
questions of Church order discussed in
this Div. of the Ep., the Ap. penetrates
from the outward and visible to that
which is innermost and divinest in the
Christian Society: (1) the question of
the woman's veil, a matter of social decorum; (2) the observance of *the Lord's
Supper*, a matter of Church communion;
and now (3) the operation of *the Spirit of
God* in the Church, wherein lies the very
mystery of its life. The words διαιρέσεις
in ver. 4 and πάντα ταῦτα in ver. 11 give
the clue to Paul's intent in this §. Many
Cor. took a low and half superstitious
view of the Holy Spirit's influence, seeing
in such charisms as the "tongues"—
phenomena analogous to, though far surpassing, pagan manifestations (2)—the
proper evidence of His working, while
they underrated endowments of a less
striking but more vital and serviceable

XII. 1. Περὶ δὲ τῶν [a]πνευματικῶν, ἀδελφοί, [b]οὐ [b]θέλω ὑμᾶς   a See x. 3 f.
  b See x. 1.
[b]ἀγνοεῖν. 2. οἴδατε ὅτι [1] ἔθνη ἦτε, πρὸς τὰ [c]εἴδωλα τὰ [d]ἄφωνα,   c See viii. 4.
  d xiv. 10; 2
ὡς [e]ἂν ἤγεσθε, [f]ἀπαγόμενοι · 3. διὸ [g]γνωρίζω ὑμῖν ὅτι οὐδεὶς [h]ἐν   Pet. ii. 16;
  Acts viii.
[h]πνεύματι Θεοῦ λαλῶν λέγει [i]ἀνάθεμα Ἰησοῦν,[2] καὶ οὐδεὶς δύναται   32 (Isa.
  liii. 7).
  e With

impf. in rel. clause, Mk. vi. 56; Acts ii. 45, iv. 35; Gen. ii. 19.   f In trans. use, Mt. xxvi. 57, etc.;
Lk. xxi. 12; Acts xii. 19, xxiii. 17, xxiv. 7.   g xv. 1; 2 Cor. viii. 1; Rom. ix. 22 f., xvi. 26; Gal. i.
11; 11 times in Eph., Col., Phil.; 2 Pet. i. 16; 4 times in Lk. and Acts; Jo. xv. 15, xvii. 26.
h Eph. vi. 18; Rev. i. 10; Jude 20; Mt. xxii. 43; Lk. ii. 27, iv. 1; Mic. iii. 8.   i xvi. 22; Rom. ix.
1; Gal. i. f.; Acts xxiii. 14.

[1] ο τ ι ο τ ε (?): all uncc. but Ggr.Kmg.; K*, a few minn., and Ff., read οτε alone.
W.H. conjecture οτι οτε to be a primitive error for ο τ ι π ο τ ε (?); cf. Eph. ii. 11,
and the use of ποτε in Rom. xi. 30; Col. i. 21; 1 Pet. ii. 10. The confusion of π
with τι is a common scribe's error; and in the old continuous writing (οτιποτε), it
is likely enough that the copyist's eye, in some primitive MS., skipped the π, esp.
as no immediate countersense resulted to warn him of the oversight.

[2] Ι η σ ο υ ς, ℵABC, 17*, 46*, cop. syrr. (seemingly), Euthal.
Ιησου, F, 17**, vg. (anathema Jesu), Ath., Hil. Ιησουν, DGKLP, sah.,—Western
and Syrian. See note below.

nature (31, xiii. 8, 13, xiv. 12). For the
moment, Paul's object is twofold: first,
to lay down a general criterion of the
presence of Christ's Spirit (3), and then
to show the wide manifoldness of His
working in the community of believers
(4-11).
Ver. 1. For the heading of the new
topic, which runs on to the end of ch.
xiv., see note on vii. 1. τῶν πνευματικῶν
is neut.—"concerning spiritual things
(gifts, powers)," as in xiv. 1 (cf. πνευμάτων, 12) and viii. 1; not "spiritual
persons" (xiv. 37, ii. 15), as Hf. and
some others would take it: not the
status of the persons spiritually endowed,
but the operations of the Spirit who en-
dows them are in question. "δὲ is transitional, with a shade of antithesis to τὰ
λοιπὰ . . . διατάξομαι: 'Whatever subject I postpone, I must not delay to
explain the nature of spiritual gifts'"
(Ed.). On οὐ θέλω ἀγνοεῖν, cf. note to
x. 1: the Ap. has something to explain
not quite obvious and highly important.
Ver. 2. On the critical reading,
οἴδατε ὅτι ὅτε ἔθνη ἦτε . . . ὡς ἂν
ἤγεσθε ἀπαγόμενοι, there are two plausible constructions: (a) that of Bg., Bm.
(pp. 383 f.), Ed., who regard ὡς as a
resumption of the ὅτι, after the parenthetical ὅτε clause, and thus translate: "You
know that, when you were Gentiles,—
how you were always led to those voiceless idols, being carried away". There
are two reasons against this construction
—(1) the improbability of ὅτι being forgotten after so short an interruption; (2)
the inversion of the proper relation between ὡς ἂν ἤγεσθε and ἀπαγόμενοι, the

former of which is naturally construed as
subordinate and adverbial to the latter,
the "leading to idols" supplying the condition under which the "carrying off"
took place. (b) We are driven back upon
the alternative construction, adopted by
Est., Mr., Hn., Ev., Bt., Gd., El. (see his
note, and Krüger's Sprachl., § 354 b,
Anm. 1 f., for similar instances), who
regard ἀπαγόμενοι as chief predicate after
ὅτι, and complete the ptp. by ἦτε, which
is mentally taken up from the interposed
temporal clause: "You know that, when
you were Gentiles, to those voiceless
idols, however you might be led, (you
were) carried away". Since οἶδα with
ptpl. complement occurs but once besides
in N.T. (2 Cor. xii. 2, and there with
acc. ptp., not nom. as here), the confusion between the ptpl. construction
and the ὅτι construction after οἶδα, by
which Mr. accounts for the grammatical
irregularity, is not very probable. The
emendation of W.H. (see txtl. note) is
most tempting, in view of Eph. ii. 11;
it wholly obviates the difficulty of grammar: "You know that once (ὅτι ποτέ)
you were Gentiles, carried off to those
dumb idols, howsoever you might be
led".—The Cor., now belonging to the
λαὸς Θεοῦ, distinguish themselves from
the ἔθνη (see v. 1, x. 20); to be "led
away to the (worship of the) idols" is
the characteristic of Gentiles (viii. 7).
ἀπάγω implies force rather than charm
in the ἀπάγων; P. is not thinking of any
earlier truth from which the heathen
were enticed, but of the overwhelming
current by which they were "carried
off" (abreptos, Bz.), cf. 2 Cor. iv. 4, 2

k N.T. *h.l.*; εἰπεῖν Κύριον [1] Ἰησοῦν [1] εἰ μὴ [h] ἐν [h] Πνεύματι Ἁγίῳ. 4. [k] διαιρέσεις
1 Chron.
xxvi. 1; [2] δὲ [1] χαρισμάτων εἰσί, τὸ δὲ αὐτὸ Πνεῦμα · 5. καὶ [k] διαιρέσεις [m] δια-
Chron.
viii. 14; κονίων εἰσί, καὶ ὁ αὐτὸς Κύριος · 6. καὶ [k] διαιρέσεις [n] ἐνεργημάτων
Ezra vi.
18; -ρειν, εἰσίν, ὁ δὲ [2] αὐτός [2] ἐστι [3] Θεὸς ὁ [o] ἐνεργῶν [p] τὰ [pq] πάντα [q] ἐν [q] πᾶσιν.
ver. 11.
l See i. 7.
Pl. only in this ch., Rom. xi. 29, xii. 6.   m Pl. *h.l.*; xvi. 15, 2 Cor. *passim*, eight times more in P.;
Heb. i. 14; Rev. ii. 19; 8 times in Acts; also Lk. x. 40.   n *H.l.*   o 2 Cor. i. 6, iv. 12; Rom. vii.
5; Gal. ii. 8, iii. 5, v. 6; 8 times more in P.; also Jas. v. 16; Mt. xiv. 2; Mk. vi. 14.   p See viii. 6.
q xv. 28; Eph. i. 23; Col. iii. 11.

[1] **Κυριος Ιησους**: ℵABC, 17, 46, 67**, 73, vg. syr^sch.
Κυριον Ιησουν: DGKLP, etc.   See note below.

[2] **και ο αυτος** (?): BC, 37, 46 ; W.H. *txt*.   **ο δε αυτος** : ℵAKLP, vg. syrr.   **ο**
αυτος δε : DG.

[3] *Om.* **εστι** ℵ*ACDGP, vg.   Add after **αυτος** ℵcKL, etc. ; after **ενεργων**, B.

Tim. ii. 26, Matt. xii. 29. With this agrees the qualifying ὡς ἄν ἤγεσθε (not ἀνήγεσθε, as Hf. and Hn. read; this gives an irrelevant sense—"led up," "led in sacrifice"), indicating the uncertainty and caprice of the directing powers—"pro nutu ducentium" (Est.). For the right sort of ἄγεσθαι, see Rom. viii. 14, Gal. v. 18.—On the εἴδωλα, *cf.* viii. 4; the *voicelessness* of the idol is part of its nothingness (*cf.* Ps. cxv. 4-7, etc.); the Pagans were led by no intelligent, conscious guidance, but by an occult power behind the idol (x. 19 ff.).

Ver. 3. Their old experience of the spells of heathenism had not prepared the Cor. to understand the workings of God's Spirit and the notes of His presence. On this subject they had asked (1), and P. now gives instruction: "Wherefore I inform you". They knew how men could be "carried away" by supernatural influences; they wanted a criterion for distinguishing those truly Divine. The test P. supplies is that of *loyalty to Jesus Christ*. "No one speaking in the Spirit of God says ΑΝΑΘΕΜΑ ΙΗΣΟΥΣ, and no one can say ΚΥΡΙΟΣ ΙΗΣΟΥΣ except in the Holy Spirit." *Jesus is anathema, Jesus is Lord*, are the battle-cries of the spirits of error and of truth contending at Cor. The second watchword is obvious, its *inclusiveness* is the point of interest; it certificates *all* true Christians, with whatever διαιρέσεις χαρισμάτων (4 ff.), as possessors of the Holy Spirit, since He inspires the confession of their Master's name which makes them such (see i. 2, Rom. x. 9, Phil. ii. 11, etc.). Not a mystical "tongue," but the clear intelligent confession "Jesus is Lord" marks out the genuine πνευματικός; *cf.* the parl. cry Ἀββᾶ ὁ πατήρ, of Gal. iv. 6. "He shall glorify *Me*," said

Jesus (John xvi. 14) of the coming Spirit: this is the infallible proof of His indwelling.—But who were those who might say at Cor., "Jesus is *anathema*"? *Faciebant gentes*, says Bg., *sed magis Judæi*. Ἀνάθεμα (see parls.) is Hebraistic in Biblical use, denoting that which is *cherem, vowed to God for destruction as under His curse*, like Achan in Joshua's camp. So the High Priest and the Jewish people treated Jesus (John xi. 49 f., Gal. iii. 13), using perhaps these very words of execration (*cf.* Heb. vi. 6), which Saul of Tarsus himself had doubtless uttered in blaspheming the Nazarene (1 Tim. i. 13); this cry, so apt to Jewish lips, resounded in the Synagogue in response to apostolic preaching. Christian assemblies, in the midst of their praises of the Lord Jesus, would sometimes be startled by a fierce Jew screaming out like a man possessed, "Jesus is anathema!"—for unbelievers on some occasions had access to Christian meetings (xiv. 24). Such frenzied shouts, heard in moments of devotion, affected susceptible natures as with the presence of an unearthly power; hence the contrast which Paul draws. This watchword of hostile Jews would be taken up by the Gentile mobs which they roused against the Nazarenes; see Acts xiii. 45, xviii. 6, where βλασφημοῦντες may well include λέγοντες Ἀνάθεμα Ἰησοῦς. Gd., *ad loc.*, and W. F. Slater (*Faith and Life of the Early Church*, pp. 348 f.) suppose *both* cries to originate in the Church; they ascribe the anathema to *heretics* resembling Cerinthus and the Ophites, who separated *Jesus* from *Christ* (*cf.* 1 John ii. 18 ff., iv. 1-6); but this identification is foreign to the situation and context, and is surely an anachronism.—The distinction between λαλέω and λέγω is well

7. ἑκάστῳ δὲ δίδοται ἡ ʳφανέρωσις τοῦ Πνεύματος πρὸς τὸ ˢσυμφέρον· ^r 2 Cor. iv.
2; -οω, see
8. ᵗ ᾧ μὲν γὰρ διὰ τοῦ Πνεύματος δίδοται ᵘλόγος ᵘ ᵛσοφίας, ᵗἄλλῳ δὲ   iv. 5.
^s Ptp., 2
ᵘλόγος ᵘ ᵛγνώσεως, κατὰ τὸ ʷαὐτὸ ʷΠνεῦμα· 9. ᵗἑτέρῳ δὲ ¹πίστις ἐν   Cor. xii.
1; Heb.
xii. 10;

Acts xx. 20; see also vi. 12 and vii. 35.   t For normal use of ος μεν, see xi. 21.   ος μεν . . . αλλος
δε, Mt. xiii. 4 f.; Mk. iv. 4.   αλλος . . . ετερος, Mt. xvi. 14; Heb. xi. 35 f.; cf. Gal. i. 6.   ετερος, see
iii. 4.   αλλος . . . αλλος, xv. 39, 41; Jo. iv. 37.   u See i. 5; λογ. σοφ., ii. 13.   v Rom. xi. 33;
Col. ii. 3; Eccl. i. 16, 18, ii. 26.   σοφια, i. 17; γνωσις, i. 5.   w ver. 11, 2 Cor. iv. 13, xii. 18. ἐν. πν.,
vv. 13 f.; Eph. ii. 18, iv. 4.

¹ Om. δε ℵ*BDG, 67**, vg. syrsch.   A, with the Syrian codd., inserts.

exemplified here: λαλεῖν ἐν is "to speak in the element and sphere of, under the influence of" the Holy Spirit.

Vv. 4-6. "But," while the Spirit prompts in all Christians the simultaneous confession *Jesus is Lord*, this unity of faith bears multiform fruit in "distributions of grace-gifts, services, workings". These are not separate classes of πνευματικά, but varied designations of the πνευματικὰ collectively—a *trinity* of blessing associating its possessors in turn with *the Spirit, the Lord*, and *God* the fountain of all. What is a χάρισμα (see i. 7) in respect of its quality and ground, is a διακονία in view of its usefulness (see 21-25), and an ἐνέργημα in virtue of the power operative therein. The identity of the first and second of the syns. rests on that of "the Lord" and "the Spirit" (*cf.* 2 Cor. iii. 17 f.), and that of the second and third upon the relation of Christ to the Father (see John v. 17 ff., xiv. 8-14). For the Trinitarian structure of the passage, *cf.* 2 Cor. xiii. 13, Eph. iv. 4 ff.—Κύριος and διακονία are correlative; all Church-ministry is directed by "the Lord" and rendered primarily to Him (iv. 1, vii. 12, viii. 6, Rom. xii. 11, xiv. 4-9, Matt. xxv. 40, etc.). διακονία embraces every "work of ministration" (Eph. iv. 12): gradually the term narrowed to official and esp. bodily ministrations, to the duties of the διάκονος (Phil. i. 1, etc.); see xvi. 15, and *cf.* Rom. xv. 31 with xi. 13 for the twofold use.—ἐνέργημα (*effectus*, rather than *operatio*, Vg.)—the result of ἐνεργέω; this favourite Pauline vb. signifies an *effective*, and with ἐν an *immanent* activity. —τὰ πάντα covers the whole sphere in which spiritual charisms operate: *cf.* Eph. iv. 6. Ver. 11 refers the same πάντα ἐνεργεῖν to "the Spirit," who is God indwelling; Power, in its largest, ultimate sense, "belongeth unto God" (*cf.* Eph. i. 11, etc., Phil. ii. 13)—"the same God, who works . . . in all" (Rom. iii. 29 f.), knowing no respect of persons

and operative in the doings of every Christian man; *cf.* i. 30a, and note.— διαιρέσεις appears to be act., *dividings, distributings*, rather than pass., *differences, varieties*; see ver. 11. The pl. points to the constantly repeated *dealings out* of the Spirit's store of gifts to the members of Christ's body.

Ver. 7. ἑκάστῳ δὲ κ.τ.λ.—distributive in contrast with the collective τ. πᾶσιν of ver. 6; *cf.* Eph. iv. 6 f., and the emphatic ἔκαστος of iii. 5-13: "But to *each* there is being given the manifestation of the Spirit with a view to profiting"; *cf.* Eph. iv. 7-16, where the δωρεὰ τ. Χριστοῦ is similarly portioned out amongst the members of Christ, for manifold and reciprocal service to His body. The thought of mutual benefit, there amply expressed, is here slightly indicated by πρὸς τὸ συμφέρον (*ad utilitatem*, Vg.): see vi. 12, x. 23, 33, on this word.—δίδοται, *datur* (not *datum est*), indicates continuous bestowment; so in vv. 8 ff.: these charisms, blossoming out in rich, changeful variety, disclose the potencies of the Spirit ever dwelling in the Church.— φανέρωσις (opp. of κρύψις) governs τ. Πνεύματος in obj. gen.: to each is granted some personal gift in which he *shows forth* the Spirit by whose inspiration he calls Jesus Lord (3); for the constr., *cf.* 2 Cor., iv. 2. For the general idea, Matt. v. 14 ff., Luke xii. 1 f., 1 Peter ii. 9.

Vv. 8-10 exhibit by way of example (γάρ) *nine* chief manifestations in which the Holy Spirit was displayed: *word of wisdom, word of knowledge, faith, healings, powers, prophecy, discernings of spirits, kinds of tongues, interpreting of tongues*. The *fourth* and *fifth* are specially marked as χαρίσματα and ἐνεργήματα respectively; the *first* is said to be given "through," the *second* "according to," the *third* and *fourth* "in the same" (or "the one) Spirit," whose operation in the whole is collectively reaffirmed in ver. 12. In distinguishing the recipients, P. begins with

x vv. 28, 30; τῷ ᵂαὐτῷ ᵂ Πνεύματι, ᵗ ἄλλῳ δὲ ¹ χαρίσματα ˣ ἰαμάτων ἐν τῷ ᵂ αὐτῷ ¹
Jer. xl. 6. -σις, Acts ᵂ Πνεύματι, 10. ᵗ ἄλλῳ δὲ ⁿ ἐνεργήματα ʸ δυνάμεων, ᵗ ἄλλῳ δὲ ² ᶻ προ-
iv. 22;
-αομαι, φητεία, ᵗ ἄλλῳ δὲ ² ᵃ διακρίσεις πνευμάτων· ᵗ ἑτέρῳ ³ δὲ ³ ᵇ γένη
freq. in
GG. and

Acts. y Pl. in this sense, vv. 28 f.; 2 Cor. xii. 12; Gal. iii. 5 (virtually); 2 Th. ii. 9; Heb. ii. 4,
vi. 5; Acts ii. 22, viii. 13, xix. 11; GG. passim. z xiii. 2, 8, xiv. 6, 22; Rom. xii. 6; 1 Th. v. 20; 1
Tim. i. 18, iv. 14; Rev. i. 3, etc.; Mt. xiii. 14. -ευω, see xi. 4; -της, ver. 28. a Rom. xiv. 1;
Heb. v. 14; Job xxxvii. 16. -νειν, see vi. 5. b γεν. γλ., ver. 28; xiv. 10; Mt. xiii. 47, xvii. 21;
Gen. i. 11, etc.

¹ ἐνι, AB, 17, 67**, latt. vg. So crit. edd.
αυτῳ, ℵDGKLP (Western and Syrian): harmonistic correction.

² BDG om. δε twice, after αλλῳ.

³ Om. δε (after ετερῳ) ℵ*BDGP, latt. vg.
Add δε ACKL, syrr. cop.—Alexandrian and Syrian; cf. ver. 9.

the colourless ᾧ μέν (for the rel. pr. in this use, cf. xi. 21); but in continuation ἄλλῳ δέ (to another) is varied with ἑτέρῳ (to some one else); the latter seems to mark a more specific, qualitative difference: cf. the interchange in xv. 39 ff., also in 2 Cor. xi. 4, and ἕτερος in xiv. 21, Rom. vii. 23; ἕτερος moreover dispenses with the contrastive δέ, as conveying its own antithesis (Hn. however, against Mr., takes the prons. to be used indifferently). Accordingly, the third (faith) and eighth (tongues) in the chain of gifts indicate points of transition, in the writer's thought, from one sort of endowment to another; and the nine thus fall into three divisions, of two, five, and two members respectively, with λόγος, πίστις, γλῶσσαι for their titles, the first of which exhibits the Πνεῦμα working through the νοῦς, the second in distinction from the νοῦς, and the third in supersession of the νοῦς: for this basis of discrimination, cf. xiv. 14-20; also xiii. 8, where the like threefold distinction appears in another order. The above arrangement is that of Mr.; Ed. gives a more elaborate and somewhat diff. analysis.—(a) λόγος σοφίας and γνώσεως were the charisms most abounding at Cor.: see i. 5, and the relevant notes on i. 17, 30, ii. 1, 4. "Wisdom" is the larger acquisition,—the truth of God wrought into the man; "knowledge" is that truth intellectually apprehended and objectified: see Ed. ad loc., who says, "The παρέκβασις of σοφία is mysticism, of γνώσεως is rationalism". Expressed in λόγος, both gifts serve the Church πρὸς τὸ συμφέρον (7); they are the qualifications of pastor and teacher respectively. "The Spirit" is the channel (διά) conveying Wisdom; "the same Spirit" is the standard (κατά) regulating Knowledge.—(b) πίστις impresses its character on the whole second series;

standing alone, with emphasis, it implies an energy and demonstrativeness of faith (cf. πᾶσα πίστις, xiii. 2), ein Glaubens-heroismus (Mr.): ἰάματα and δυνάμεις are operations of such faith in the material sphere, by way of miracle; προφητεία and διάκρισις πνευμάτων, in the purely spiritual sphere, by way of revelation. Faith however may be exhibited in conspicuous degree apart from these particular demonstrations (cf. Matt. xvii. 20, xxi. 21, Mark xvi. 17 f.). The first two of the five are imparted "in (i.e., grounded upon, exercised in the sphere of) the same (the one) Spirit"; what is said of these is understood of the other three (cf. ἐν in ver. 3): "in the same Spirit" dwell the endowments of a fruitful understanding and of a potent faith; "in the one Spirit" —in His power and bestowment alone— all "gifts of healings" lie (cf. Mark iii. 28 ff.). The ἰάματα (acts of healing; see parls.) are χαρίσματα by eminence— gracious acts (cf. Luke vii. 21, ἐχαρί-σατο): the δυνάμεις (powers; see parls.) display strength rather than grace, e.g., in the sentence of v. 5 above, or that contemplated in 2 Cor. xiii. 2 ff., 10; they are "acts of energy".—Προφητεία, as an edifying gift of speech, is akin to the λόγος graces of (a); it is contrasted with γλῶσσαι (c) in xiv., as being an intelligent exercise. But prophecy, while employing the νοῦς, has a deeper seat; it is no branch of σοφία or γνῶσις as though coming by rational insight, but an ἀποκάλυψις of hidden things of God realised through a peculiar clearness and intensity of faith (2 Cor. iv. 13 f.; Heb. xi. 1, 13; Luke x. 21 f., etc.), and is in line therefore with the miraculous powers preceding; hence "the prophet" is regularly distinguished from "the teacher".
—"Discernment of spirits" is the counter-part and safeguard of "prophesying,"

ᵇ°γλωσσῶν, ᵗἄλλῳ δὲ ᵈἑρμηνεία °γλωσσῶν· 11. πάντα δὲ ταῦτα ᶜ In this sense, vv. 28, 30, xiii., xiv. *passim*; Acts ii. 3 f., 11, x. 46, xix. 6; Mk.
°ἐνεργεῖ τὸ °ἓν καὶ τὸ °αὐτὸ Πνεῦμα, ᶠδιαιροῦν ᵍἰδίᾳ ἑκάστῳ
καθὼς ʰβούλεται.

12. ᶦΚαθάπερ γὰρ τὸ σῶμα ἕν ἐστι καὶ ᵏμέλη ἔχει ¹ πολλά,¹

xvi. 17. d xiv. 26; Sir. *prologue*, xlvii. 17. -ευτης, xiv. 28; -ευω, Heb. vii. 2. e See xi. 5. ἐν πν, and αυτ., see ver. 9. f Lk. xv. 12; Josh. xviii. 5. -σις, ver. 4 above. g N.T. *h.l.*; 2 Macc. iv. 34. h Of *God*, Heb. vi. 17; Jas. i. 18; 2 Pet. iii. 9; 1 Kings ii. 25. -ημα, Rom. ix. 19. i See x. 10. k See vi. 15.

¹ πολλα εχει (in this order): non-Western and pre-Syrian uncc.

demanding the like super-rational penetration; the true critic may not have originative faculty, but his mind moves in the same region with that of the originator and tracks his steps. διακρίσεις, pl., for this gift had many and various occasions of exercise: see parls., also for διακρίνω, vi. 5, etc.; as to the power itself and the need for its exercise, *cf.* 1 Thess. v. 20 ff., 2 Thess. ii. 2, 9 ff., 1 John ii. 18 ff., iv. 1-6, Matt. xxiv. 11 f. P. exhibits this διάκρισις admirably in ver. 3 above; it displays itself in Acts xiii. 8 ff., along with the ἐνέργημα δυνάμεως; *cf.* Acts v. 1-11.—(c) The "kinds of tongues," with their attendant "interpretation," constitute the third order of specific charisms; in this exercise the intelligence of the speaker is suspended. The γλῶσσαι, ranked first by the Cor. because of their sensational character, P. enumerates last in regard of "profiting" (7); ch. xiv. will justify this relative depreciation. The "tongues" of this Ep. cannot have signified the power to speak strange languages in missionary preaching, as many have inferred from the terms used in the account of the manifestation of the Day of Pentecost; see notes on Acts ii. 4-11. γένη implies that this ecstatic phenomenon was far from uniform; the *"new* tongues" of Mark xvi. 17, together with the indications of ch. xiii. 1 and xiv. of this Ep., point to the breaking out of an exalted and mystical utterance differing from all recognised human speech; this utterance varied at diff. times and places in its mode and attendant conditions, and in the impression it produced on the hearers; it is regularly spoken of in the pl. The necessity of ἑρμηνεία for the extraction of any benefit to the Church from the Tongues will be shown in ch. xiv.; sometimes the possessor of the Tongue became interpreter also (xiv. 13). On the γλῶσσαι generally, see Ed., *ad loc.*; also Hn.

Ver. 11 sums up the last par. (4-10), impressing on the Cor. with redoubled emphasis the *variety in unity* of the "gifts," and vindicating the sanctity of each: "But all these things worketh the one and the same Spirit" (*cf.* 9). In the qualifying clause, "dividing separately (*seorsim*) as He wills," διαιροῦν takes up the διαιρέσεις of vv. 4-6; ἑκάστῳ is resumed from ver. 7; ἰδίᾳ adds the thought that the Spirit deals with each recipient by himself, *individually* and *appropriately* (*cf.* vii. 7, iii. 8, xv. 23); while καθὼς βούλεται signifies that He acts in the distribution upon His *choice and judgment*, where lies the hidden reason for the giving or withholding of each particular gift.—For βούλομαι, see parls.; and for its difference from ἐθέλω, *cf.* ver. 18; also iv. 19, 21, and parls. Eurip., *Hippol.*, 1329 f., supplies a good example of the distinction, οὐδεὶς ἀπαντᾶν βούλεται προθυμίᾳ τῇ τοῦ θέλοντος, ἀλλ' ἀφιστάμεθ' ἀεί: "None of us *likes* to cross the purpose of one that *is* bent on anything, but we always stand aside". No predicate could more strongly imply *personality* than does βούλεται.

§ 40. THE ONE BODY, OF MANY MEMBERS, xii. 12-20. The manifold graces, ministries, workings (4 ff.), that proceed from the action of the Holy Spirit in the Christian community, stand not only in common dependence upon Him (§ 39), but are mutually bound to each other. The Church of Christ is "the body" for the Spirit of God; and these operations are its correlated functional activities (12 f.). Differentiation is of the essence of bodily life. The unity of the Church is not that of inorganic nature,—a monotonous aggregation of similars, as in a pool of water or a heap of stones; it is the oneness of a living organism, no member of which exercises the same faculty as another. Without "many members," contrasted as foot with hand or sight with smell (14-17), there would be no body at all, but only a single monstrous limb (19). In God's creative plan, it is the integration and

l Mt. iii. 11; πάντα δὲ τὰ ᵏμέλη τοῦ σώματος τοῦ¹ ἑνὸς¹ πολλὰ ὄντα ἕν ἐστι
Acts i. 5,
xi. 16. σῶμα, οὕτω καὶ ὁ Χριστός· 13. καὶ γὰρ ¹ἐν ᵐἑνὶ ᵐΠνεύματι
m See vv.
9, 11; ἐν ἡμεῖς πάντες ⁿεἰς ᵐἓν ᵐσῶμα ᵐⁿἐβαπτίσθημεν, εἴτε °Ἰουδαῖοι
πν., ἐν
σωμ., εἴτε °ᵠἝλληνες, εἴτε ᴾδοῦλοι εἴτε ᴾἐλεύθεροι, καὶ πάντες ᵠεἰς² ἓν
Eph. iv. 4.
n See x. 2. Πνεῦμα ³ᵠἐποτίσθημεν.⁴ 14. καὶ γὰρ τὸ σῶμα οὐκ ἐστὶν ἓν ᵏμέλος
o See x. 32.
p Eph. vi. 18
(with εἴτε); Gal. iii. 28; Col. iii. 11; Rev. vi. 15, xiii. 16, xix. 18. εἴτε ... εἴτε, see iii. 22.   q See
iii. 2. For acc. with pass. (without εἰς), 2 Th. ii. 15; Heb. vi. 9; Rev. xvi. 9; Mk. x. 38; Lk. xii. 47.

¹ Om. του ενος all uncc. but ℵcD, Hil., Ambrst. (ex uno corpore).

² Om. εις all uncc. but DcKL.

² εις εν πομα : a number of minn., with Macarius and (virtually) Clem. Al.

⁴ εφωτισθημεν, L, and several minn.; A, εσμεν.

reciprocity of a multitude of distinct organs that makes up the physical and the social frame (18 ff.).

Ver. 12. "The one Spirit," the leading thought of § 39, suggests the similitude of "the body" for the Church (called in ch. iii. the *tillage, building, temple* of God), since this is the seat of His multifarious energies. In the Eph. and Col. Epp. τὸ σῶμα becomes a fixed title for the Christian community, setting forth its relation both to the inhabiting Spirit and to the sovereign Head; as yet it remains a plastic figure. Aristotle had applied this image to the State, the *body politic;* and the idea was a Gr. commonplace. The Ap. is still insisting on the breadth of the Holy Spirit's working, as against Cor. partisanship and predilection for miraculous endowments; hence the reiterated ἐν and πολλά, also the emphatic πάντα of the second clause: "but *all* the members of the body, many as they are (πολλὰ ὄντα), are *one* body". In applying the comparison, Paul writes not as one expects, οὕτως ἡ ἐκκλησία or οὕτως ἡμεῖς, but with heightened solemnity οὕτως καὶ ὁ Χριστός, "so also is the Christ!" "Christ stands by metonomy for the community united through Him and grounded in Him" (Hn.). This substitution shows how realistic was P.'s conception of believers as subsisting "in Christ," and raises the idea of Church-unity to its highest point; "all the members are instinct with one personality" (Ed.): *cf.* Gal. ii. 20, 2 Cor. xiii. 3, 5, for this identification in the case of the individual Christian. The later representation of Christ and the Church as Head and Body is implicit in this phrase. For Χριστὸς with art., *cf.* i. 12, x. 4, etc.; also Eph. v. 23 ff.

Ver. 13. καὶ γὰρ ἐν ἑνὶ Πνεύματι κ.τ.λ.: "For indeed in *one* Spirit we *all*

into *one* body were baptized—whether Jews or Greeks, whether bondmen or freemen—and we *all* of *one* Spirit were made to drink,"—*were drenched* (Ev.). An appeal to experience (*cf.* Gal. iii. 2 ff., iv. 6; also Acts xix. 2-6): at their baptism the Cor. believers, differing in race and rank, were consciously made one; *one* Spirit flooded their souls with the love and joy of a common faith in Christ.—For βαπτίζω ἐν and εἰς, see parls.: ἐν defines the *element* and *ruling influence* of the baptism, εἰς the *relationship* to which it introduces. P. refers to actual Christian baptism, the essence of which lay in the regenerating influence of the Holy Spirit (John iii. 5 ff., Tit. iii. 5 f.); baptism represents the entire process of personal salvation which it seals and attests (Eph. i. 13, Gal. iii. 26 ff., Rom. vi. 2 ff.), as the Queen's coronation imports her whole investiture with royalty. That Jews and Greeks, slaves and freemen, had received at the outset an identical Spirit, shows that they were intended to form a single body, and that this body was designed to have a wide variety of members (11 f.).—ἐποτίσθημεν (see parls.) has been referred by Cm., Aug., Cv., Est., and latterly by Hn., to the ποτήριον of the *Lord's Supper* (x. 16, xi. 25), as though καὶ coupled the two consecutive Sacraments (*cf.* x. 2 f., and notes); but the *tense*, parl. to ἐβαπτίσθημεν (otherwise in x. 16, etc.), points to *a past event*, not a repeated act; and it is "the blood of Christ," not the Holy Spirit, that fills (symbolically) the Eucharistic cup. The two aors. describe the same primary experience under opposite figures (the former of which is *acted* in baptism), as an outward affusion and an inward absorption; the Cor. were at once *immersed in* (*cf.* συνετάφημεν, Rom. vi. 4) and *saturated with* the Spirit; the

ἀλλὰ πολλά· 15. ἐὰν εἴπῃ ὁ πούς, "Ὅτι οὐκ εἰμὶ χείρ, οὐκ ʳεἰμὶ ʳἐκ τοῦ σώματος," οὐ ˢπαρὰ τοῦτο οὐκ ʳἐστὶν ʳἐκ τοῦ σώματος¹· 16. καὶ ἐὰν εἴπῃ τὸ οὖς, "Ὅτι οὐκ εἰμὶ ὁ ὀφθαλμός, οὐκ ʳεἰμὶ ʳἐκ τοῦ σώματος," οὐ ˢπαρὰ τοῦτο οὐκ ʳἐστὶν ʳἐκ τοῦ σώματος¹· 17. ᵗεἰ ὅλον τὸ σῶμα ὀφθαλμός, ᵗποῦ ἡ ᵘἀκοή; ᵗεἰ ὅλον ᵘἀκοή, ᵗποῦ ἡ ᵛὄσφρησις; 18. ʷνυνὶ² δὲ ὁ Θεὸς ˣἔθετο τὰ ᵏμέλη, ʸἓν ʸἕκαστον αὐτῶν, ἐν τῷ σώματι ᶻκαθὼς ᶻἠθέλησεν·

ʳ Of *things*, *h.l.* in N.T. Of *persons*, see i. 30; partitive, as here, Mt. xxvi. 73; Acts xxi. 8, etc.; Obad. 11.   ˢ N.T. *h.l.*, in this sense; cl.

Gr., Lidd. *s.v.* I. 6; syn. with διᾰ, Philo, I. 263.   ᵗ που, see i. 20.   Interrog. after εἰ, iv. 7, x. 30, xv. 12, 32; 8 times more in P.; etc.   ᵘ 2 Pet. ii. 8.   For other uses, see Rom. x. 16 f.; Gal. iii. 2, etc.   ᵛ *H.l.*   ʷ Logical, vii. 14, xiii. 13, xiv. 6, xv. 20, etc.   ˣ ver. 28; Rom. iv. 17; 1 Th. v. 9; 1 Tim. i. 12, ii. 7; 2 Tim. i. 11; Heb. i. 2; Acts xx. 28; Gen. xvii. 5.   ʸ Six times more in P.; freq. in Lk. and Acts; Rev. xxi. 21.   ᶻ Of *God*, xv. 38; without καθως, iv. 19; Rom. ix. 18, 22; Col. i. 27; 1 Tim. ii. 4; 1 Pet. iii. 10; Jas. iv. 15; Mt. xxvi. 39.   *Cf.* θελημα Θε., i. 1 and parls.

¹ Pointed interrog. by Tr., as in T.R.; affirm. by other crit. edd.   See note below.

² νυν (?) ABDG.   So Tr., W.H. *txt.*, R.V., El., Nestle.

νυνι, אCDᵇᶜKLP.   So Tisch., W.H. *marg.*

second figure supplements the first: *cf.* Rom. v. 5, Tit. iii. 5, 6.—ποτίζω, which takes double acc. (iii. 2), retains that of the thing in the passive.

Ver. 14 recalls, under the analogy of the σῶμα, the reason given in ver. 12 for the diversity of spiritual powers displayed in the Church: it is not "one member," but "many" that constitute the "body". This thesis the rest of thè § illustrates.

Vv. 15, 16 represent with lively fancy the *foot* and *ear* in turn—organs of activity and intelligence—as disclaiming their part in the body, because they have not the powers of the *hand* and *eye*: an image of jealous or discouraged Cor. Christians, emulous of the shining gifts of their fellows. In each case it is the lowlier but kindred organ that desponds, *pars de parte quam simillima loquens* (Bg.): *cf.* ver. 21.—οὐκ εἰμὶ ἐκ τοῦ σώματος, "I am not of the body"—not a mere partitive expression; it signifies *dependence* (*pendens ab*: *cf.* Gal. iii. 10, Tit. i. 10, etc.; Wr., p. 461), hence *derived status* or *character*.—Paul contradicts, in identical terms, the self-disparagement of the two chagrined members: οὐ παρὰ τοῦτο κ.τ.λ. must be read as a statement—"it is not therefore not of the body" (R.V., Bg., Mr., Hn., Hf., Ed., El., Bt., Sm.); not a question (A.V., Cv., Bz., Est., D.W., Al., Gd.), which would require μὴ instead of οὐ—"Is it for this reason not of the body?" For παρὰ with acc. of *reason* (*along of this*), see parls.: "in accordance with this," *viz.*, the disclaimer just made (so Mr., Hn., Hf., Ev., El., Er.—*deplorans sortem suam*). The foot or ear does not sever itself from the body by distinguish-

ing itself from hand or eye; its pettish argument (ἐὰν εἴπῃ κ.τ.λ.) leaves it where it was. Gd., Ed., and others, less aptly refer τοῦτο not to the *saying* of the foot, etc., but to the *fact* that it is not hand, etc. For double οὐ, *cf.* 2 Thess. iii. 9.

Ver. 17 expostulates in the vein of vv. 15 f. with those who exalt one order of gifts (either as possessing it themselves or envying it in their neighbours) to the contempt of others; the despised function is as needful as the admired to make up the body: "If all the body (were) eye, where the hearing? if all (were) hearing, where the smelling?" The senses are set in order of dignity; the ear wishes to be the eye (16), but then its indispensable service of *hearing* would be undischarged; so the nose might desire promotion to the rank of an ear, leaving the body impotent to *smell*. The discontent of the lower members and the scornfulness of the higher are alike signs of a selfish individualism, indifferent to the welfare of the body ecclesiastic.—ἦν (*cf.* ver. 9) is understood here.—Ἡ ὄσφρησις is "the sense of smell"—not *odor*, but *odoratus* (Vg.).

Ver. 18. "But now (argumentative νῦν, 'as things are': see v. 11) God has appointed the members, each single one of them, in the body as He willed." It is *God's will* that has ranged the physical organs—and by analogy the members of the Church—in their several places and offices (*cf.* i. 1, iii. 5). Dissatisfaction with one's particular charism, or contempt for that of another, is disloyalty towards *Him* and distrust of His wisdom. This is Paul's *ultima ratio*: ὦ ἄνθρωπε, σὺ τίς εἶ κ.τ.λ.; Rom. ix. 20.—

a Eph. iv.
28; 1 Th. 19. εἰ δὲ ἦν τὰ¹ πάντα ἓν ᵏμέλος, ᵗποῦ τὸ σῶμα; 20. ʷνῦν²ʷδὲ
i. 8, iv. 9,
12, v. 1; πολλὰ μὲν³ ᵏμέλη, ἓν δὲ σῶμα.
Heb. v.12,
x. 36; 21. Οὐ δύναται δὲ⁴ ὀφθαλμὸς⁴ εἰπεῖν τῇ χειρί, "ᵃΧρείαν σου οὐκ
thrice in ᵃἔχω·" ἢ πάλιν ἡ κεφαλὴ τοῖς ποσί, "ᵃΧρείαν ὑμῶν οὐκ ᵃἔχω·"
Rev.;
Acts ii.45, 22. ἀλλὰ ᵇπολλῷ ᵇμᾶλλον τὰ ᶜδοκοῦντα ᵈμέλη τοῦ ᵈσώματος
iv. 35;
freq. in
GG. b 2 Cor. iii. 9, 11; Rom. v. 9 ff.; Phil. i. 23, ii. 12; Mt. vi. 30; Mk. x. 48; Lk. xviii. 39.
c In first sense, 2 Cor. x. 9; Gal. ii. 2, 6, 9; Mt. xvii. 25, etc. For second, see iii. 18. d See vv. 12
ff., vi. 15.

¹ Om. τα (?) BG, 17; Lach., Tr., W.H. *bracket.*

² νυνι, GP; see ver. 18.

³ *Om.* μεν (?) BD, 73, Aug. So W.H. *txt.;* Lachm., Tr. *brackets.*

⁴ ο οφθαλμος: all uncc. but K, and many minuscc.
Om. δε ACGP, 17, 37, syrsch. cop. (Alex. and late Western); ℵBDKL, vg.
retain.

For τίθημι in mid. voice, *cf.* ver. 28 and
other parls.; the *tense* refers the Divine
appointment constituting the body to past
time generally—"has set" rather than
"set". The prefixed ἓν *singles out* the
individual for the Divine regard, distributed by ἕκαστον; each limb by itself
has its part assigned by God.—ἠθέλησεν
signifies determining *will,* as βούλεται
(11, note) discriminating *choice.*

Vv. 19, 20 rehearse the doctrine of
vv. 12-14, now vividly illustrated by vv.
15 ff., viz., that *a manifold variety of
organs* is indispensable for the existence
of the Church. First the principle is
suggested by a rhetorical question, in the
strain of ver. 17: "But if all were one
member, where (were) the body?" Secondly, it is *affirmed,* with grave conclu-
siveness: "But as the case stands (νῦν
δέ)—*Many members, yet one body*".—
Πολλὰ μέλη, ἓν δὲ σῶμα sums up the
whole exposition in a concise epigram,
which was perhaps already proverbial (*cf.*
ix. 24).—ἐστὶν hardly needs to be supplied. *Cf.,* for the thought, x. 17, and
notes on vv. 12, 14 above.

§ 41. THE MUTUAL DEPENDENCE OF
THE BODY'S MEMBERS, xii. 21-31*a.* Mul-
tiformity, it has been shown, is of the
essence of organic life. But the variously
endowed members, being needful to the
body, are consequently *necessary to each
other*—those that seem "weaker" sometimes the more so (21 f.), while the less
honoured have a dignity of their own;
thus all the members cherish mutual respect and fellow-feeling (23-26). This
holds good of the Church, with its
numerous grades of personal calling and
endowment (27 f.). No one charism belongs to all Christians (29 f.). There is
choice and purpose in God's distributive

appointments, which leave, moreover,
room for man's personal effort. We
should desire *the best* of His gifts (31).

Ver. 21 personifies again the physical
members, in the fashion of vv. 15 f.:
there the inferior disparaged itself as
though it were no part of the body at
all; here the superior disparages its fellow, affecting independence. "The eye
(might wish to say but) cannot say to
the hand, I have no need of thee! or the
head in turn to the feet, I have no need
of you!" The *eye* and *head* are imagined
looking superciliously on their companions; in vv. 15 f. the *ear* and *foot*
play the part of discontented rivals.—οὐ
δύναται—a moral and practical impossibility (*cf.* x. 21): at every turn the eye
wants the hand, or the head calls on the
foot, in order to reach its ends; the keen
eye and scheming head of the *paralytic*
—what a picture of impotence! The
famous Roman fable of *the Belly and the
Members* is recalled by the Apostle's
apologue. There is no such thing in the
physical, nor in the social, fabric as independence.—πάλιν (*cf.* iii. 20, 2 Cor. x.
7, Rom. xv. 10), *vicissim* (Hn.), rather
than *iterum* (Vg.) or *rursum* (Bz.), adduces another instance of the same kind
as the former.

Vv. 22-24*a.* "On the contrary" (ἀλλά),
instead of the more powerful and dignified (23) bodily parts dispensing with the
humbler (21), it is "much more" the
case that these latter—"the weaker" or
"less honourable as they may seem to
be" (τὰ δοκοῦντα . . . ἀσθενέστερα
ὑπάρχειν)—"are necessary" in themselves (22), and treated with "more abundant honour" in our care of the body.
By πολλῷ μᾶλλον (*cf.* Plato, *Phædo,*
80 E, ἀλλὰ πολλῷ μᾶλλον), *multo potius*

ᵉἀσθενέστερα ᶠὑπάρχειν ᵍἀναγκαῖά ἐστι· 23. καὶ ἃ ᶜδοκοῦμεν
ʰἀτιμότερα εἶναι τοῦ σώματος, τούτοις ⁱτιμὴν ᵏπερισσοτέραν ⁱ¹περι-
τίθεμεν· καὶ τὰ ᵐἀσχήμονα ἡμῶν ⁿεὐσχημοσύνην ᵏπερισσοτέραν
ἔχει, 24. τὰ δὲ ⁿεὐσχήμονα ἡμῶν οὐ ᵃχρείαν ᵃἔχει· ἀλλ᾽ ὁ Θεὸς
ᵒσυνεκέρασεν τὸ σῶμα, τῷ ᵖὑστερουμένῳ ᵏπερισσοτέραν δοὺς
ⁱτιμήν, 25. ἵνα μὴ ᾖ ᑫσχίσμα² ἐν τῷ σώματι, ἀλλὰ τὸ αὐτὸ ʳὑπὲρ
ἀλλήλων ʳμεριμνῶσι τὰ ᵈμέλη· 26. καὶ ˢεἴτε³ πάσχει ἓν μέλος,

e See i. 27.
f See vii. 26.
g 2 Cor. ix.
5; Ph. i.
24, ii. 25;
Tit. iii.14;
Heb. viii.
3; Acts x.
24, xiii.46.
h See iv. 10.
i Esth. i. 20.
For τιμη.,
Rom. ix.
21, xii. 10,
xiii. 7; 1

Th. iv. 4; 1 Tim. v. 17, vi. 1; 2 Tim. ii. 20 f.; 1 Pet. iii. 7.   k Compar., xv. 10; 2 Cor. ii. 7, x. 8;
Heb. vi. 17, vii. 15; 9 times in GG.   l In this sense, Mt. xxvii. 28, Mk. xv. 17; cf. Mt. xxi. 33,
xxvii. 48; Ruth iii. 3. -σις, 1 Pet. iii. 3.   m N.T. h.l.; Deut. xxiv. 1; cf. -συνη, Rom. i. 27; Rev.
xvi. 15, vii. 36.   n N.T. h.l.; in Plato, Xen. -ων, see vii. 35; -ονως, xiv. 40.   o Heb. iv. 2.
p See i. 7.   q See i. 10.   r See vii. 32. With υπερ, N.T. h.l.; Ps. xxxvii. 18.   s See iii. 22.

¹ ὑστερουντι, אcDGKL, etc.—Western and Syrian.

² σχισματα, א*DGL, above 30 minuscc.—Western. So Tisch.⁸, Treg. marg.;
other edd. σχισμα: cf. i. 10, xi. 18.

³ ειτι (?) BG, some latt. vg. (et si quid), Ambrst. (Western). So Lachm., Treg.
Favoured by its dissidence from the parl. ειτε. A omits altogether.

(Bz.) or a fortiori (Ev.), the position of
ver. 21 is more than negatived; the inferior members are not merely shielded
from contempt, but guarded with exceptional respect. By the "weaker" and
"ignobler" parts P. cannot mean the
hands or feet spoken of in ver. 21, for
these are strong and usually uncovered
(see περιτίθεμεν, 23); but members in
appearance quite subordinate and actually feeble—viz., the more delicate vital
organs. Amongst these the ἀσχήμονα
signify definitely τὰ αἰδοῖα, quæ in-
honesta sunt (Vg.); cf. Rev. xvi. 15, τὴν
ἀσχημοσύνην.—The ἀσθενέστερα and
ἀτιμότερα, the "comparatively weak"
and "feeble" (comparativus molliens,
Bg.), are wide categories applicable to
the same members from diff. points of
view. Weakness, in the case, e.g., of the
heart, is compensated by needfulness;
ignobility, as in the viscera, by careful
tendance shown in ample clothing—"we
put about them (clothe them with) a more
abundant honour" (for the use of τιμή,
cf. ἐξουσία in xi. 10). The unseemliness
(indecency) attaching to certain organs,
always guarded from sight, "brings with
it (ἔχει, cf. Heb. x. 35) a more abundant
seemliness". Against most commentt.
(Gd., e.g., thinks only of "les soins de la
toilette"!), Ed. maintains that εὐσχημοσύνη (23) has a moral sense, looking beyond the honour of apparel; "the greater
comeliness relates rather to function".
Is any office more responsible than that
of parenthood, anything more sacred
than the mother's womb and mother's
breast? (cf. Luke xi. 27; also Heb. xiii.

4).—τὰ δὲ εὐσχήμονα κ.τ.λ.: "But our
seemly parts"—head and face, e.g. (the
human face divine)—"have no need,"
their distinction being conspicuous; see
xi. 7a, where this visible, but also moral,
εὐσχημοσύνη is raised to its highest
grade. From this text Bg. inferred the
impiety of patches!—On ὑπάρχειν, see
note to xi. 7; δοκέω has in vv. 22 f. its
two meanings—non-personal and personal—of seem and suppose; like methinks
and I think, Germ., dünken and denken.
Vv. 24b, 25. "But God compounded
(συν-εκέρασεν, mixed together; Vg. con-
temperavit) the body." The assertion of
God's workmanship in the structure of
the physical organs (cf. 18) was necessary, when many thinkers affirmed the evil
of matter and regarded physical appetites
as degrading (cf. 1 Tim. iv. 3, Col. ii.
23; also vi. 13, 18 ff. above). This accounts for the adversative ἀλλά—"Nay
but": P. tacitly contradicts those who
saw nothing but ἀτιμία and ἀσχημοσύνη
in vital bodily functions. For ὁ Θεὸς
συνεκέρασεν, cf. Ps. cxxxix. 13-16 (where
the womb is "God's laboratory," Delitzsch), Eccl. xi. 5, Job x. 8-11. Ed.
reads the assertion as directed against
philosophy; "where Aristotle says 'nature,' P. says 'God'".—τῷ ὑστερουμένῳ
περισσοτέραν δοὺς τιμήν, "to the part
which suffers lack (opus habenti, Cv.: cf.
note, i. 7) having assigned more abundant honour"; so that the human instinct respecting the ignobler organs of
the body (ver. 23) is the reflex of a Divine
ordinance: cf. xi. 14 f., to the like effect.—
"That there may not be division (σχίσμα:

t Rom. viii. ᵗσυμπάσχει πάντα τὰ μέλη· ˢεἴτε ᵘδοξάζεται ἐν¹ μέλος, ᵛσυγ-
17.
ᵘ With   χαίρει πάντα τὰ μέλη.   27. ὑμεῖς δέ ἐστε ᵂσῶμα ᵂΧριστοῦ, καὶ
human
obj., 2   ᵈμέλη ˣἐκ ˣμέρους²· 28. καὶ ʸοὓς μὲν ᶻἔθετο ὁ ᶻΘεὸς ἐν τῇ
Cor. iii.
10; Rom. ᵃἐκκλησίᾳ ᵇπρῶτον ᶜἀποστόλους, ᵇδεύτερον ᵈπροφήτας, ᵇτρίτον
viii. 30, xi.
13; Rev. ᵉδιδασκάλους, ᵇἔπειτα ᶠδυνάμεις, ᵉεἶτα³ χαρίσματα ᵍἰαμάτων,
xviii. 7;
Lk. iv. 15.
Cf. vi. 20; h.l. of body.   v xiii. 6; Ph. ii. 17 f.; Lk. i. 58, xv. 6, 9.   w Eph. iv. 12, v. 30.   Cf. vv.
12 ff.; Rom. xii. 4 f.   x xiii. 9 f., 12; 1 Kings xxiii. 26.   απο μερ., Rom. xi. 25, etc.; μερος τι, xi. 18.
y See ver. 8.   z See ver. 18.   a See i. 2.   Earliest instance of η εκκλ. absol., in supra-local sense;
cf. Eph. i. 22, etc.; Col. i. 18, etc.; Mt. xvi. 18, xviii. 17.   b πρ. . . δευτ., Heb. x. 9; Mt. xxi. 28,
30, xxii. 25 f. (τριτος), 38; Lk. xix. 16, 18; Rev. iv. 7 (τριτ.), etc.; δευτ. . . . τριτ., Lk. xii. 38.   πρωτ.
. . . επειτα or ειτα (ειτεν), xv. 46; 1 Th. iv. 16 f.; 1 Tim. iii. 10; Heb. vii. 2; Jas. iii. 17; Mk. iv. 28.
c Pl., see iv. 9.   d Pl., thus, xiv. 29, 32; Eph. ii. 20, iii. 5, iv. 11; Acts xi. 27, xiii. 1, xv. 32.   e Pl.,
in this sense, Eph. iv. 11 (with αποστ., προφ.); 2 Tim. iv. 3; Heb. v. 12; Jas. iii. 1; Acts xiii. 1 (with
προφ.).   f See ver. 10.   g See ver. 9.

¹ *Om.* εν ℵ*AB, Thdrt.   So the crit. edd.

² μελους, D*, latt. vg. (*membra de membro*), syrp., and many Ff. (ουκ ειπεν μελη
εκ μελων, αλλα μελη πολλα εκ μελους ενος· μελος γαρ η κεφαλη του ολου σωματος:
Severian, in *Catena*).   A characteristic Western variant.

³ επειτα, all uncc. but KL.   DG, Hil., Amb. omit.

see parls.) in the body "—the manifestation of the jealousy or scorn depicted in
vv. 16 and 21, which have their counterpart at present in the Cor. Church (i.
10 ff., iv. 6, etc.).—The opposite state of
things (ἀλλά), so desirable in the spiritual
organism, is realised by Divine art in the
natural: "God tempered the body together" in this way, "that . . . the
members might have the same solicitude for one another". The physical
members are obliged, by the structure of
the frame, to care for one another; the
hand is as anxious to guard the eye or
the stomach, to help the mouth or the
foot, as to serve itself; the eye is watch-
man for every other organ; each feels
its own usefulness and cherishes its fellows; all "have the same care," since
they have the same interest—that of "the
one body". This *societas membrorum*
makes the physical order both a parable
of and a basis for the spiritual. For τὸ
αὐτό, cf. i. 10, 2 Cor. xiii. 11, Phil. ii. 2,
etc.—μεριμνῶσιν (see esp. vii. 32 ff., for
this shade of meaning) is in pr. sbj., of
habitual feeling; in pl., despite neut.
subject, since the μέλη have been individually personified (15 f., 21).
Ver. 26 illustrates the unselfish solicitude of the bodily organs; the nervous
connexion makes it a veritable συμπά-
θεια (συμπάσχει).   Plato applies the
same analogy to the State in a striking
passage in his *Politicus*, 462C; see also
Cm., *ad loc.*—δοξάζεται (*glorificatur*,
Cv.; not *gloriatur*, Vg.) goes beyond
nervous sympathy; "δόξα is more than
εὐεξία" (Ed.): for δοξάζω, applied to the

body, cf. xv. 40 ff., Phil. iii. 21. Cm.
says finely, "When the head is crowned,
the whole man feels itself glorified;
when the mouth speaks, the eyes laugh
and are filled with gladness".
Ver. 27. The figure of *the body*, developed from ver. 14 to 26 with deliberation and completeness, is now applied in
detail to the Church, where the same
solidarity of manifold parts and powers
obtains (4 ff.): "Now you are (ὑμεῖς δέ
ἐστε) a *body* of (in relation to) Christ,
and members severally"—scarcely "*the*
body of Christ" specifically (El.), as if
P. might have written τὸ σῶμα τοῦ
Χριστοῦ (as in Eph. iv. 12, etc.); this
has not yet become the recognised title
of the Church (see note on 12 above);
nor is the anarthrous σῶμα to be read
distributively, as though the Cor. Church
were thought of as one amongst many
σώματα. P. is interpreting his parable:
the Cor. are, in their relation to Christ,
what the body is to the man.—Χριστοῦ
is anarthrous by correlation (cf. note on
Θεοῦ σοφίαν, ii. 7).—ἐκ μέρους signifies
the *partial* by contrast, not as in xiii. 9
with the *perfect*, but with the *whole*
(body)—*particulatim* (Bz.): ἐκ *of the
point of view*—"*from* (and so according
to) the *part* (allotted to each)"; see ver.
11; cf. also μερίζομαι in vii. 17, etc.;
similarly, ἐκ μέτρου in John iii. 34, ἐξ
ἰσότητος in 2 Cor. viii. 13.
Ver. 28 expounds the μέλη ἐκ μέρους.
—οὓς μὲν (cf. 8 ff.) should be followed by
οὓς δέ; but πρῶτον intervening suggests
δεύτερον, τρίτον in the sequel—"instead
of a mere enumeration P. prefers an ar-

ʰ ἀντιλήψεις, ⁱ κυβερνήσεις, ᵏ γένη ᵏ γλωσσῶν· 29. μὴ πάντες
ᶜ ἀπόστολοι; μὴ πάντες ᵈ προφῆται; μὴ πάντες ᵉ διδάσκαλοι;
μὴ πάντες ᶠ δυνάμεις; 30. μὴ πάντες ᵍ χαρίσματα ἔχουσιν ᵍ ἰαμάτων; μὴ πάντες ᵏ γλώσσαις ᵏ λαλοῦσι; μὴ πάντες ˡ διερμηνεύουσι;
31a. ᵐ ζηλοῦτε δὲ τὰ ᵍ χαρίσματα τὰ ⁿ κρείττονα.⁹

h N.T. h.l.;
Ps. xxi.
20; Sir.xi.
12; 2
Macc.viii.
19. -λαμ-
βάνεσθαι,
Acts xx.
35.

i N.T. h.l.;
Prov. i. 5,

xi. 14, xxiv. 6. -της, Acts xxvii. 11; Rev. xviii. 17.   k See ver. 10; xiii. 1.   l xiv. 5, 13, 27;
Acts ix. 36; Lk. xxiv. 27; 2 Macc. i. 36; -της, xiv. 28.   m In this sense, xiv. 1, 39; Sir. li. 18;
-της, see xiv. 12.   n μειζονα, xiii. 13, xiv. 5; Jas. iv. 6; Mt. xxiii. 17, 19.

⁹ μ ε ι ζ ο ν α, ℵABC, 17, 37, 67**, cod. am. (of vg.), many Gr. Ff.
κρειττονα (DG, κρεισσονα) is Western and Syrian.

rangement in order of rank" (Wr., pp. 710 f.); and this mode of distinction in turn gives place to ἔπειτα, at the point where with δυνάμεις abstract categories (as in 8 ff.) are substituted for the concrete—a striking instance of P.'s mobility of style; the last three of the series are appended asyndetically.—The nine functions of vv. 8 ff. are replaced by *eight*, which may be thus classified: (1) three *teaching* orders, (2) two kinds of *miraculous*, and (3) two of *administrative* functions, with (4) the one notable *ecstatic* gift. Three are identical in each list —*viz.*, δυνάμεις, χαρίσματα ἰαμάτων, and γένη γλωσσῶν, taking much the same position in both enumerations (see the earlier notes). The *apostles, prophets, teachers* (ranged in order of the *importance*, rather than the affinity of their powers) exercise amongst them the *word of wisdom, prophecy*, and *word of knowledge*—"the Apostles" possessing a rich measure of many gifts; these three will be expanded into the *five* of Eph. iv. 11. The ἑρμηνία γλωσσῶν (10), omitted at this point, appears in the sequel (30); and the διάκρισις πνευμάτων (10) is tacitly understood as the companion of προφη-τεία, while the πίστις of ver. 9 pervades other charisms. Nothing is really wanting here that belonged to the χαρίσματα of § 39, while ἀντιλήμψεις and κυβερνή-σεις—"helpings, governings"—enrich that previous catalogue; "helpings" stands in apt connexion with "healings". The two added offices became the special functions of the διάκονος and ἐπίσκοπος of a somewhat later time (Phil. i. 1; *cf.* Rom. xii. 7 f.).—No trace as yet appears of definite Church organisation at Cor.; but the charisms here introduced were necessary to the equipment of the Christian Society, and the appointment of officers charged with their systematic exercise was only a question of time (see *Introd.*, chap. i., p. 732; ii. 2.

4). A sort of unofficial ἀντίλημψις and κυβέρνησις is assigned to Stephanas and his family in xvi. 15 f. These vbl. nouns, from ἀντιλαμβάνομαι and κυβερ-νάω, mean by etymology *taking hold of (to help)* and *steering, piloting*, respectively. The figurative use of the latter is rare outside of poetry; so κυβέρνησις πολίων in Pindar, *Pyth.*, x., 112, and in the newly discovered Bacchylides, xiii., 152. "Government" of the Church implies a share of the "word of wisdom" and "knowledge" (8); see 1 Tim. v. 17, 2 Tim. ii. 2, Tit. i. 9.—For ἔθετο ὁ Θεός, *cf.* ver. 18: "God appointed (set for Himself) *in the church*"—meaning *the entire Christian Society*, with all its "apostles" and the rest. The earliest N.T. example of ἐκκλησία in its ecumenical sense; see however Matt. xvi. 18, and note on i. 2 above.

Vv. 29, 30. In this string of rhetorical questions P. recapitulates once more the charisms, in the terms of ver. 28. He adds now to the γλώσσαις λαλεῖν its complementary διερμηνεύειν (see 10, and xiv. 13, etc.: διὰ in this vb. imports *translation*); and omits ἀντιλήμ-ψεις and κυβερνήσεις, for these functions had not taken articulate shape at Cor.: the eight are thus reduced to *seven*. The stress of these interrogations rests on the seven times repeated *all;* let prophet, teacher, healer, and the rest, fulfil each contentedly his μέρος in the commonwealth of grace, without trenching upon or envying the prerogative of another; "non omnia possumus omnes". Thus by fit division of labour the efficiency of the whole body of Christ will be secured and all Church functions duly discharged.—δυνάμεις may be nom. (Bg., Hf., Hn., Al., Bt., Gd., El.), in the vein of the foregoing questions—"are all powers?" (*cf.* xv. 24, Rom. viii. 38, etc., for the personification—applied elsewhere, however, to *supernatural* Powers); but

o 2 Cor. i. 8, iv. 17;   31*b*. Καὶ ἔτι ᵒκαθ᾽ ᵒὑπερβολὴν ᴾὁδὸν ὑμῖν δείκνυμι. XIII. 1.

Rom. vii. 13; Gal. i. 13.   ἐὰν ταῖς ᵇᶜγλώσσαις τῶν ᵃἀνθρώπων ᵇλαλῶ καὶ τῶν ᵃᶜἀγγέλων

p See iv. 17. a See iv. 9.   ἀγάπην δὲ μὴ ἔχω, ᵈγέγονα ᵉχαλκὸς ᶠἠχῶν ἢ ᵍκύμβαλον ʰἀλαλάζον·

b xii. 30, xiv. *passim*; Mk. xvi. 17; Acts ii. 4 ff., x. 46, xix. 6 (καὶ προφητ.).   c Acts vii. 38, viii. 26, xii. 8, xxiii. 9, xxvii. 23 f.; Rev. v. 2, 11, etc.; Mt. i. 20, etc., xxviii. 5 ff., etc.; Lk. i. 13, ii. 9 ff.; Zech. i. 13 f., etc.   d ver. 11; 2 Cor. xii. 11.   e Mk. vi. 8; Rev. xviii. 12; Gen. iv. 22.   f N.T. *h.l.*; Jer. xxvii. 42; ηχος, Acts ii. 2; Lk. xxi. 25.   g N.T. *h.l.*; 1 Chron. xiii. 8, etc.; Ps. cl. 5.   h Mk. v. 38; Josh. vi. 20.

these " powers " are in vv. 28 and 8 ff. so decidedly separated from the *teaching* and associated with the *healing* gifts, that δυνάμεις appears to look forward, and to be obj. (prospectively) to ἔχουσιν along with χαρίσματα ἰαμάτων : " do *all* possess powers ? *all* grace-gifts of healings ? " (so Bz., Mr., Ed.). For δύναμιν ἔχω, see Rev. iii. 8; also Luke ix. 1, Acts i. 8, Matt. xiv. 2.

Ver. 31*a* corrects the inference which an indolent nature or weak judgment might draw from vv. 29 f., supposing that God's sovereign ordination super-sedes man's effort. Our striving has a part to play, along with God's bestow-ment, in spiritual acquisitions; hence the contrastive δέ. " But (for all that) be zealous after the *greater* gifts." A man must not, *e.g.*, be content to " speak with tongues " when he might " pro-phesy " (xiv. 1 ff.), nor to work miracles when beside that he might teach in the " word of wisdom ".—ζηλόω (see parls.) implies in its good sense an *ardent*, in its bad sense (xiii. 4) an *emulous* pursuit. The *greater* (μείζονα) gifts are those in-trinsically greater, or more beneficial (xiv. 5)—conditions usually coincident.

§ 42. The Way to Christian Emi-nence, xii. 31*b*-xiii. 3. Carefully and luminously Paul has set forth the mani-foldness of the Holy Spirit's gifts that contribute to common life of the Church. *All* are necessary, *all* honourable in their proper use; *all* are of God's ordination. Some of the charisms are, however, more desirable than others. But if these " greater gifts " be sought in selfish emulation (as the ζηλοῦτε of ver. 31*a*, taken by itself, might suggest), their true purpose and blessing will be missed; gifts *of grace* (χαρίσματα) are not for men actuated by the ζῆλος of party spirit and ambition (*cf.* 4 f., iii. 3; 2 Cor. xii. 20, Gal. v. 20). While encouraging the Cor. to seek larger spiritual powers, the Ap. must " besides point out " the " way " to this end (31*b*), the way to escape the perils besetting their progress (4 ff.) and to win the goal of the Christian life (8-13). *Love* is the path to power in the

Church; all loveless abilities, endow-ments, sacrifices are, from the Christian point of view, simply *good for nothing* (1-3).

Ver. 31*b*. Καὶ ἔτι κ.τ.λ. (*cf.* ἔτι τε καί, Luke xiv. 26)—" And besides "—adds to the exhortation just given (31*a*) an indication of the *way* to carry it out; the ζῆλος which aims at the μείζονα χαρίσματα must be that of ἀγάπη. This clause introduces and properly belongs to ch. xiii. (W.H.). καθ᾽ ὑπερβολήν (see parls.) is superlative, not compar.; P. is not pointing out " a *more* excellent way " than that of seeking and using the charisms of ch. xii. (with such a mean-ing he should have written Ἔτι δέ : *cf.* Luke xxiv. 41, etc.), but " a *super-ex-cellent* way " (*une voie souverainement excellente*, Gd.) to win them (*cf.* viii. 1 *b*, 1 Jo. iv. 7). Δείκνυμι is " to point out " as with the finger.

Ver. 1. This *way* will be described in vv. 4-7, but first its *necessity* must be proved: this is shown by the five parl. hypotheses of vv. 1 ff., — respecting *tongues, prophecy, knowledge*, and *de-votion of goods* or *of person*. The first supposition takes up the charism last mentioned (xii. 30) and most valued at Cor.: ἐὰν τ. γλώσσαις . . . λαλῶ, ἀγάπην δὲ μὴ ἔχω (form of probable hypothesis—*too* prob. at Cor.), " If with the tongues of men I be speaking, and of angels, but am without love,"—in that case, " I have become a sounding brass or a clanging cymbal "—I have gained by this admired endowment the power of making *so much senseless noise* (*cf.* xiv. 6-11, 23, 27 f.). With love in the speaker, his γλωσσολαλία would be kept within the bounds of edification (xiv. 6, 12-19, 27), and would possess a tone and pathos far different from that described. —" Tongues *of men* " does not signify *foreign languages* (so Or., Hf., Al., Thiersch), such as are supposed to have been spoken on the Day of Pentecost (see note on xii. 10); they are, in this whole context, ecstatic and inarticulate forms of speech, such as " men " do some-times exercise : " tongues of angels " (καὶ

2. καὶ[1] ἐὰν[1] ἔχω [i]προφητείαν καὶ εἰδῶ τὰ [k]μυστήρια πάντα καὶ
πᾶσαν τὴν [kl]γνῶσιν, καὶ[1] ἐὰν[1] [m]ἔχω πᾶσαν τὴν [m]πίστιν ὥστε
[n]ὄρη [no]μεθιστάνειν,[2] ἀγάπην δὲ μὴ ἔχω, [p]οὐδέν[3] εἰμι· 3. καὶ[1]
ἐὰν[1] [q]ψωμίσω πάντα τὰ [r]ὑπάρχοντά μου, καὶ[1] ἐὰν[1] [s]παραδῶ τὸ
σῶμά μου ἵνα [t]καυθήσωμαι,[4] ἀγάπην δὲ μὴ ἔχω, οὐδὲν[3] [u]ὠφελοῦμαι.

[i] See xii. 10.
[k] See iv. 1.
μυστ. and
γνωσ.,
Rom. xi.
25; Eph.
i. 9, iii. 3
f., vi. 19;
Col. ii. 2;
Mt. xiii.
11.

l See i. 5.   m Rom. xiv. 22; 1 Tim. i. 19; Acts xiv. 9; Jas. ii. 1, 18; Mt. xvii. 20, xxi. 21; Mk. iv.
40, xi. 22.   n Isa. liv. 10.   o Col. i. 13; Lk. xvi. 4; Acts xiii. 22, xix. 26.   p See vii. 19.   q Rom.
xii. 20 (Prov. xxv. 21); Numb. xi. 4, 18, etc.; -ιον, Jo. xiii. 26 ff.   r Heb. x. 34; Acts iv. 32; thrice
in Mt.; 8 times in Lk.   s Cf. Acts xv. 26. For like sense, 2 Cor. iv. 11; Rom. iv. 25, and parls.;
Dan. iii. 28.   t καυχησ., see i. 29.   u Mk. v. 26; Mt. xvi. 26; Prov. x. 2. Cf. xiv. 6, and parls.

[1] Of the 4 instances of καὶ εαν (T.R.), καν is given in (1) by AC, 17; in (2) by AB,
17; in (3) by ABC, 17; in (4) by AC.   Al., W.H. read καν (?) throughout; Tisch.,
El., Nestle adhere to καὶ εαν; Lachm. and Tr. vary.   After εαν, καὶ εαν is more
likely: see vii. 28, xii. 15 f.; Mk. iii. 24 f.; Lk. xvii. 3 f. Nowhere else is καν well
attested in such connexion.

[2] μεθιστᾰναι (?), אBDG, 17.   So Lachm., Tr., Tisch., El., Nestle.
μεθιστᾰνειν, ACKL, etc. (? Alexandrian and Syrian),—the rarer form; but -ανω
forms of ιστημι and compounds are not infrequent in P.   See Wr., pp. 94, 106.

[3] ουθεν (1): all non-Western uncc., accepted by crit. edd.; so Stephens (1550).
ουθεν (2): אA, 17.   Tisch. adopts this in both.   See Wr., p. 48.

[4] καυχησωμαι, אAB, 17, cop. sah., Hier. (ob similitudinem verbi, qua apud
Græcos "ardeam" et "glorier" una litteræ parte distinguitur, apud nostros
error inolevit.   Sed et apud Græcos exemplaria sunt diversa).   Lachm., R.V. marg.,
and W.H. adopt this reading, against other edd.   See Note of the last-named,
vol. ii., pp. 116 f., where Clem. Rom., Clem. Al., Or., are claimed on this side.
καυθησομαι, DGL (-ωμαι, CK), latt. vg. syrutr., and the bulk of Ff.—suspiciously
like a Western emendation.   See note below.

of the climax: "aye, and of angels!")
describes this mystic utterance at its
highest (cf. λαλεῖ Θεῷ, xiv. 2)—a mode
of expression above this world. Possibly
P. associated the supernatural γλῶσσαι,
by which he was himself distinguished
(xiv. 18), with the ἄρρητα ῥήματα heard
by him "in paradise" (2 Cor. xii. 4);
cf. the "song" (Rev. xiv. 2 f.) which
only those redeemed out of the earth"
understand. The Rabbis held Hebrew to
be the language of the angels.—χαλκὸς
denotes any instrument of brass; κύμ-
βαλον, the particular loud and shrill
instrument which the sound of the
"tongues" resembled.

Ver. 2. Prophecy in its widest range,
and faith at its utmost stretch—in those
lacking love, both amount to "nothing!" (ἐὰν) εἰδῶ τὰ μυστήρια πάντα
κ.τ.λ., "If I know all the mysteries (of
revelation) and all the knowledge (relating
thereto)," explains καὶ ἐὰν ἔχω προφητείαν
by stating the source, or resources, from
which "prophecy" is drawn: πᾶσαν τ.
γνῶσιν (attached somewhat awkwardly
to εἰδῶ), combined with τ. μυστ., posits
a mental grasp of the contents of revelation added to the supernatural insight
which discovers them (see notes on λόγος

γνώσεως and προφητεία, xii. 8 ff.), as
e.g. in the case of Isaiah. Hn. supplies
ἔχω, instead of the nearer εἰδῶ, before
τ. γνῶσιν (cf. viii. 1, 10), reading "if I
have all knowledge" as a second, distinct assumption following on "if I know
all mysteries," on account of the incongruity of Prophecy and Knowledge;
but the point of P.'s extreme supposition
lies in this unusual combination—the
intellect of a philosopher joined to the
inspiration of a seer.—For μυστήρια, see
note on ii. 1 (see note on xii.
9) ὥστε μεθιστάνειν ὄρη—an allusion to
the hyperbolical sayings of Jesus ad rem
(Matt. xvii. 20, xxi. 21; see notes in vol.
i.); in the pr. (continuous) inf.—"to remove mountain after mountain" (Ed.).
Whatever God may be pleased to accomplish through such a man (cf. iii. 9), he
is personally worthless. On the form
οὐδέν, see Wr., p. 48; for the thought,
cf. iii. 18, 2 Cor. xii. 11, Gal. vi. 3.

Ver. 3. The suppositions of these
three vv. cover three principal forms of
activity in the Church—the spheres, viz.,
of supernatural manifestation, of spiritual
influence, of material aid (3); loveless
men who show conspicuous power in
these several respects, in the first in-

v For *both*,
cf. 2 Cor.
vi. 6;
Rom. ii. 4;
Gal. v. 22.
μακροθ., 1
Th. v. 14;
Heb. vi.
15; Jas. v.
7 f.; Mt.
xviii. 26,

4. Ἡ ἀγάπη ᵛμακροθυμεῖ, ᵛʷχρηστεύεται· ἡ ἀγάπη οὐ ˣζηλοῖ, ἡ ἀγάπη ¹ οὐ ʸπερπερεύεται· οὐ ᶻφυσιοῦται, 5. οὐκ ᵃἀσχημονεῖ· οὐ ᵇζητεῖ ᵇτὰ ² ᵇἑαυτῆς, οὐ ᶜπαροξύνεται· οὐ ᵈλογίζεται ᵉτὸ ᵉκακόν, 6. οὐ ᶠχαίρει ᶠἐπὶ τῇ ἀδικίᾳ ᵍσυγχαίρει δὲ ʰτῇ ʰἀληθείᾳ· 7. πάντα ⁱστέγει, πάντα πιστεύει· πάντα ἐλπίζει, πάντα ᵏὑπομένει.

29; Lk. xviii. 7; Prov. xix. 11. -μια, 10 times in P.; 4 in other Epp.; -μως, Acts xxvi. 3. w H.l. in Gr. x In this sense, Acts vii. 9, xvii. 5; Jas. iv. 2. Diff. in xii. 31, etc.; diff. again in Gal. iv. 17 f. y H.l. See note below. z See iv. 6. a See vii. 36. b See x. 24. c Acts xvii. 16. -σμος, Acts xv. 39; Heb. x. 24. d In this sense (act.), Rom. iv. 6, 8 (Ps. xxxi. 2); 2 Cor. v. 19; diff. in iv. 1, ver. 11 below. e Five times in Rom.; Jo. xviii. 23; 3 Jo. 11. f xvi. 17; 2 Cor. vii. 13; Acts xv. 31; Lk. i. 14; Mt. xviii. 13; Prov. xxiv. 19. g See xii. 26. h In this sense, 16 times more in P.; Heb. x. 26; Jas. v. 19; 1 Pet. i. 22; 2 Pet. i. 12, ii. 2; Jo. *passim*. i See ix. 12. k With acc., Rom. viii. 24; 2 Tim. ii. 10 (παντα); Heb. x. 32, xii. 2 f.; Jas. i. 12; Wisd. xvi. 22.

¹ *Om.* η αγαπη (?) B, 17, and a few other minn., f. vg. cop., and a number of Ff. So W.H., Tr.,; Nestle *brackets*. Tisch. reads η αγαπη thrice, but attaches the second to χρηστ., and the third to ζηλοι.

² το μη εαυτης: B, Clem. The best codd. may contain a vicious reading.

stance are *sound signifying nothing;* in the second, they *are nothing;* in the third, they *gain nothing.* Those who make sacrifices to benefit others *without love,* must have some hidden selfish recompense that they count upon; but they will cheat themselves.—ἐὰν ψωμίσω κ.τ.λ., "If I should dole out all my property". The vb. (derived from ψωμός —ψωμίον, John xiii. 26 ff.—a *bit* or *crumb*) takes acc. of *person* in Rom. xii. 20 (LXX), here of *thing*—both regular: "Si distribuero in cibos pauperum" (Vg.), "Si insumam alendis egenis" (Bz.).—The sacrifice of *property* rises to its climax in that of *bodily life: cf.* Job ii. 4 f., Dan. iii. 28, Gal. ii. 20, etc.; John x. 11, xv. 13.—But in either case, *ex hypothesi,* the devotion is vitiated by its motive—ἵνα καυχήσωμαι, "that I may make a boast" (*cf.* Matt. vi. 1 ff.); it is prompted by ambition, not love. So the self-immolator forfeits the end he seeks; his glorifying becomes κενοδοξία (Gal. v. 26, Phil. ii. 3; *cf.* John v. 44). οὐδὲν ὠφελοῦμαι signifies loss of *final* benefit (*cf.* Gal. v. 2, Rom. ii. 25, Luke ix. 25). This entire train of supposition P. puts in the 1st pers., so avoiding the appearance of censure: *cf.,* for the *usus loquendi,* xiv. 14-19, viii. 13, ix. 26 f.—κανθήσωμαι is a grammatical *monstrum,*—a reading that cannot well be explained except as a corruption of καυχήσωμαι; it was favoured by the thought of the Christian martyrdoms, and perhaps by the influence of Dan. iii. 28. Hn., Gd., Ed., El., amongst critical comment., are in favour of the T.R., which is supported by the story, told in Josephus (*B.J.,* vii. 8. 7), of a Buddhist fakir who about this time immolated himself by fire at Athens.

§ 43. The Qualities of Christian Love, xiii. 4-13. The previous vv. have justified the καθ' ὑπερβολὴν of xii. 31. The loftiest human faculties of man are seen to be frustrate without love; by its aid alone are they brought to their proper excellence and just use. But this "way" of Christian attainment has still to be "described," and the promise of xii. 31b fulfilled. So while vv. 1-3 have proved the *necessity,* the rest of the chap. shows the *nature and working* of the indispensable ἀγάπη. The Cor. may see in this description the mirror of what they ought to be and are not; they will learn how childish are the superiorities on which they plume themselves. (*a*) The *behaviour* of Love is delineated in fifteen exquisite aphorisms (4-7); (*b*) its *permanence,* in contrast with the transitory and partial character of the prized χαρίσματα (8-13).

Vv. 4-7. In vv. 1-3 Paul's utterance began to rise with the elevation of his theme into the Hebraic rhythm (observe the recurrent ἀγάπην δὲ μὴ ἔχω, and the repeated οὐδέν) which marks his more impassioned passages (see *e.g.,* Rom. viii. 31 ff., Eph. i. 8 ff.; on a smaller scale, iii. 22 f. above). Here this rhythm dominates the structure of his sentences: they run in seven couplets, arranged as *one* (affirm.), *four* (neg.), and *two* (aff.) verse-lines, with the subject (ἡ ἀγάπη) repeated at the head of the 2nd line. The ver. which closes the middle, longer movement becomes a triplet, making a pause in the chant by the antithetical

8. ἡ ἀγάπη οὐδέποτε ¹ἐκπίπτει¹· ᵐεἴτε δὲ² ᵐπροφητεῖαι,³ ¹ πιπτει, of *things*,
ⁿκαταργηθήσονται²· ᵐεἴτε ᵒγλῶσσαι, ᵖπαύσονται· ᵐεἴτε ᑫγνω- Lk. xvi. 17; 1 Kings iii.

19. *Cf.* Rom. ix. 6; Acts xii. 7; Jas. i. 11. Of *persons*, see x. 8.   m Rom. xii. 6. For ειτε, ειτε, see iii. 22. προφητ., see xii. 10.   n See i. 28.   o See xii. 10.   p In this sense, Acts xx. 1; Exod. ix. 33 f.   q See i. 5.

¹ πιπτει, ℵABC, 17, 67**. εκπιπτει, Western and Syrian.
² Om. δε C*D*GKP, latt. vg. cop. Tr. *brackets*. Required to effect transition from η αγαπη; easily dropped by copyist after ειτε.
³ προφητεια, καταργηθησεται (?): B A (-εια, -σονται). So W.H. *marg.*

repetition of the second clause. The par. then reads as follows:—

" Love suffers long, shows kindness.
    Love envies not, makes no self-display;
    Is not puffed up, behaves not unseemly;
    Seeks not her advantage, is not embittered;
    Imputes not evil, rejoices not at wrong,
        but shares in the joy of the truth.
All things she tolerates, all things she believes;
All things she hopes for, all things she endures."

The first line supples the general theme, defining the two fundamental excellencies of Love—her patience towards evil, and kindly activity in good. In the negative movement, the first half-lines set forth Love's *attitude*—free from jealousy, arrogance (*cf.* iv. 6*b*), avarice, grudge-bearing; while the second member in each case sets forth her *temper*—modest, refined in feeling, placable, having her joy in goodness. The third movement reverts to the opening note, on which it descants.—For the individual words: μακροθυμέω is *to be long-tempered* (*longanimis est*, Er.)—a characteristic of God (Rom. ii. 4, etc.)—patient towards injurious or provoking *persons;* this includes οὐ παροξύνεται, οὐ λογίζεται τὸ κακόν, πάντα στέγει; whereas ὑπομένει, closing the list, signifies patience in respect of adverse and afflictive *circumstances;* the two unite in Col. i. 11: see Trench, *Syn.*, § liii.—χρηστεύεται—a vb. perhaps of Paul's coining—*plays the part of a* χρηστός (*benignus*), one who renders gracious, well-disposed service to others (Trench, *Syn.*, § lxiii): P. associates μακροθυμία and χρηστότης repeatedly (see parls.).—οὐ ζηλοῖ qualifies the ζηλοῦτε of xii. 31: directed towards right *objects*, ζῆλος is laudable ambition; directed towards *persons*, it is base envy; desire for excellencies manifest in others should stimulate not ill-will but admiring love.—The vb. περπερεύεται (parl. in form to χρηστεύεται) occurs only in Marc. Anton., v., 5 besides, where it is rendered *ostentare se* (the Vg. *perperam se agit* rests on mistaken resemblance), to

show oneself off : πέρπερος, used by Polybius and Epictetus, signifies *braggart, boastful* (see Gm., *s.v.*), its sense here.—He who is *envious* (ζηλ.) of superiority in others is commonly *ostentatious* (περπ.) of superiority assumed in himself, and *arrogant* (φυσ.) towards inferiors. Such φυσιοῦσθαι is a mark of bad taste—a *moral indecency*, from which Love is clear (οὐκ ἀσχημονεῖ: see parls.); she has the instinct for the seemly; Love imparts a delicacy of feeling beyond the rules of politeness.—The absence of *pride* is the burden of the two former of the negative couplets, the absence of *greed* of the two latter. For οὐ ζητεῖ κ.τ.λ., *cf.* parls.; 2 Cor. xii. 13 ff. supplies a fine illustration in the writer. Selfishness generates the *irritability* denied concerning Love in οὐ παροξύνεται; intent on one's own advantage, one is incessantly angered to find the world at cross purposes with him. Except Heb. x. 24, the only other N.T. parls. (Acts xv. 39, xvii. 16) ascribe to *P. himself* the παροξυσμὸς which he now condemns; as in the case of ζῆλος (see iii. 3), there is a bad and a good *exasperation;* anger *may* be holy, though commonly a sin. To "rejoice at iniquity," when seeing it in others, is a sign of deep debasement (Rom. i. 32); Love, on the contrary, finds her joy in the joy of " the Truth" (personified: *cf.* Rom. vii. 22, Ps. lxxxv. 10 f., 3 John 8, 12)—she rejoices in the progress and vindication of the Gospel, which is "the truth" of God (*cf.* Phil. i. 7, Col. i. 3-6; 3 John 4): ἀδικία and ἀλήθεια are similarly contrasted in 2 Thess. ii. 10, 12.—The four πάντα clauses form a chiasmus: the first and fourth relating to the bearing of ill, the second and third to expectation of good in others; the first pair belong to the present, the last to the future. For στέγει, see parls.; Bz. and a few others render the clause " omnia *tegit*," in accordance with the radical sense of the vb.; but *suffert* (Vg.) is its Pauline, and also prevalent cl. sense.—Πίστις appears

r Cf. xii. 27.
s See xi. 4.

t H.l. For
the adj.,
see ii. 6;
of things,
Rom. xii.
2; Heb.
ix. 11; Jas.
i. 4, 17, 25;
1 Jo. iv. 18.

u See iii. 1.
1 Pet. v. 12; Jo. xi. 50. Abs., here only.

σις, ⁿκαταργηθήσεται· 9. ʳἐκ ʳμέρους γὰρ γινώσκομεν καὶ ʳἐκ ʳμέρους ⁸προφητεύομεν· 10. ὅταν δὲ ἔλθῃ ᵗτὸ ᵗτέλειον, τότε¹ τὸ ʳἐκ ʳμέρους ⁿκαταργηθήσεται. 11. ὅτε ἤμην ᵘνήπιος, ὡς ᵘνήπιος ἐλάλουν,² ὡς ᵘνήπιος ᵛἐφρόνουν,² ὡς ᵘνήπιος ᵂἐλογιζόμην²· ὅτε δὲ³ ˣγέγονα ʸἀνήρ, ⁿκατήργηκα τὰ τοῦ ᵘνηπίου. 12. ᶻβλέπομεν

v Abs., N.T. h.l.; Isa. xliv. 18.   w In this sense, 8 times more in P.; Heb. xi. 19;
x See ver. 1.   y In contrast with νήπιος, cf. xiv. 20;
Gal. iv. 1-5; Eph. iv. 13.   z 2 Cor. x. 7, xii. 6; Rom. vii. 23, viii. 24 f.; Heb. ii. 9, iii. 19; Jas. ii.
22; Acts i. 9, ix. 8; Mt. vi. 4, vii. 3, xiii. 13, etc., xv. 31; Lk. x. 23 f., etc.

¹ Om. τοτε all uncc. but DcKL.

² ελαλουν ως νηπιος, εφρονουν ως νηπ., ελογιζομην ως νηπ. (in this order): ℵAB, 17. All crit. edd.

³ Om. δε ℵABD*, 67**. Here δε weakens the antithesis. Cf. note 8 above.

to bear in Gal. v. 22 the meaning of *faith in men* belonging to πιστεύει here. *Hope* animates and is nourished by *endurance:* ὑπομένει (*sustinet*, not *patitur*), the active patience of the stout-hearted soldier; see Trench, *Syn.*, § liii., and N.T. parls.

Ver. 8. Love, that bears, also *outwears everything:* "Love never faileth". That πίπτει denotes "falling" in the sense of cessation, dropping out of existence (*cf.* x. 8, Luke xvi. 17), not moral failure (as in x. 12, etc.), is manifest from the parl. clauses and from ver. 13. The charisms of chh. xii. and xiv. are bestowed *on the way* and serve the wayfaring Church, they cease each of them at a determined point; but the Way of Love leads indefinitely beyond them; οὐ διασφάλλεται, ἀλλ' ἀεὶ μένει βεβαία καὶ ἀκίνητος (Thd.). — "Prophesyings, tongues, and knowledge"—faculties inspired, ecstatic, intellectual—are the three typical forms of Christian expression. The abolition of Prophecies and Knowledge is explained in vv. 9 ff. as the superseding of the partial by the perfect; they "will be done away" by a completer realisation of the objects they seek, —viz., by *intuition* into the now hidden things of God and of man (xiv. 24 f.), and by adequate *comprehension* of the things revealed (see note on 12). Of the Tongues it is simply said that "they will *stop*" (παύσονται), having like other miracles a temporary significance (*cf.* xiv. 22); not giving place to any higher development of the like kind, they lapse and terminate (*desinent*, Bg.).

Vv. 9, 10: reasons why *Prophecy* and *Knowledge* must be abolished. Though amongst the μείζονα (xii. 31) and rich in edification (xiv. 6), these charisms are partial in scope, and therefore temporary: the fragmentary gives place to the com-

plete.—ἐκ μέρους (see note, xii. 27, and parls.): coming *of a part*, our knowledge and prophesying are limited by the limiting conditions of their origin. For the conscious imperfection of *Prophecy*, *cf.* 1 Peter i. 10 f.; this text has some bearing on the much-discussed "inerrancy" of Scripture.—ὅταν δὲ ἔλθῃ τὸ τέλειον, τὸ ἐκ μέρους καταργηθήσεται, "But when there comes *the perfect* (*full-grown, mature;* see note on ii. 6), the 'in part' will be abolished": *cf.* Eph. iv. 13 f., where τέλειος is contrasted with νήπιος as here; also Phil. iii. 11 ff. This τελείωσις is brought about at the παρουσία—it "comes" with the Lord from heaven (xv. 47; *cf.* 1 Thess. i. 10, and i. 7 above); that of Eph. iv. is some what earlier.

Ver. 11 illustrates the abolition of the partial by the perfect through the transition from *the child to the man*—in speech (ἐλάλουν), in disposition and aim (ἐφρόνουν), and in mental activity (ἐλογιζόμην). These three points of diff. can hardly be identified with the γλῶσσαι, προφητεία, and γνῶσις respectively; though "spake as a babe" may allude to the childish fondness of the Cor. for γλωσσολαλία (*cf.* xiv. 18 ff.), and "to reason" to the distinction of γνῶσις. On the later-Gr. mid. form ἤμην, see Wr., pp. 95 f.—ὅταν with sbj. is the *when* of future contingency, ὅτε with ind. the *when* of past or present fact.—ὅτε γέγονα ἀνὴρ κατήργηκα κ.τ.λ.: "now that (*ex quo*) I have become a man (*vir factus sum: cf.* ἀνὴρ τέλειος in Eph. iv. 12), I have abolished the things of the child". Such is the κατάργησις which Prophecy and Knowledge (Scripture and Theology), as at present known, must undergo through the approaching "revelation" (i. 7). "Non dicit, *Quum abolevi puerilia, factus*

γὰρ [1] ᵃ ἄρτι δι᾽ ᵇ ἐσόπτρου ἐν ᶜ αἰνίγματι, ᵃ τότε δὲ ᵈ πρόσωπον ᵈ πρὸς ᵃ See iv. 13.
ᵈ πρόσωπον · ᵃ ἄρτι γινώσκω ʳ ἐκ ʳ μέρους, ᵃ τότε δὲ ᵉ ἐπιγνώσομαι
καθὼς καὶ ᵉ ἐπεγνώσθην. 13. ᶠ νυνὶ ᶠ δὲ μένει πίστις, ἐλπίς, ἀγάπη,
τὰ τρία ταῦτα · ᵍ μείζων δὲ τούτων ἡ ἀγάπη.

ᵃ See iv. 13.
ἄρτι . . .
τότε, 2
Th. ii. 7 f.
ᵇ Jas. i. 23;
Wisd. vii.
26; Sir.
xii. 11.
See note

below.   c N.T. *h.l.;* Numb. xii. 8; Sir. xxxix. 3.   d N.T. *h.l.;* Gen. xxxii. 30.   *Cf.* 2 Jo. 12;
3 Jo. 14; Numb. xii. 8; also 2 Cor. iii. 18.   e xiv. 37, xvi. 18; 8 times more in P.; 2 Pet. ii. 21;
many times in Syn. GG. and Acts. For the antith., *cf.* viii. 2 f.; Gal. iv. 9.   f See xii. 18.
g See xii. 31. For compar. with παντων, xv. 19; Mt. xiii. 32; Lk. ix. 46.

[1] DG, latt. vg., Latt. Ff. om. **γαρ.**

sum vir. Hiems non affert ver; sed ver
pellit hiemem: sic est in anima et ecclesia" (Bg.).—**γέγονα** and **κατήργηκα,**
in pf. of *abiding result;* for **καταργέω,** *cf.*
i. 28 and parls.

Ver. 12 figures in another way the
contrast between the present partial and
the coming perfect Christian state, in
respect particularly of *knowledge:* it is
the diff. between discernment by broken
reflexion and by immediate intuition.
"For we see now through a mirror, in
(the fashion of) a riddle; but then face
to face."—**βλέπω,** as distinguished from
ὁράω, points to the fact and manner of
seeing rather than the object seen (see
parls.). On **ἄρτι,** see note to iv. 11; it
fastens on the *immediate* present.—**δι᾽**
ἐσόπτρου, "by means of a mirror":
ancient mirrors made of burnished metal
—a specialty of Cor.—were poor re-
flectors; the art of silvering glass was
discovered in the 13th century.—**ἔσοπ-**
τρον = **κάτοπτρον** (2 Cor. iii. 18), or
ἔνοπτρον (cl. Gr.); not **διόπτρα,** *specu-*
lare, the semi-transparent *window* of talc
(the *lapis specularis* of the ancients), as
some have explained the term. *Cf.* Philo,
De Decal., § 21, "As by a mirror, the
reason discerns images of God acting
and making the world and administering
the universe"; also Plato's celebrated
representation (*Repub.,* vii., 514) of the
world of sense as a train of shadows
imaging the real. Mr., Hf., Gd., Al., El.
adopt the local sense of **διά,** "*through* a
mirror," in allusion to the appearance of
the imaged object as *behind* the reflector:
but it is the *dimness,* not the displace-
ment, of the image that P. is thinking of.
—Such a sight of the Divine realities,
in blurred reflexions, presents them **ἐν**
αἰνίγματι, *enigmatically*—"in (the shape
of) a riddle" rather than a full intelligible
view. Divine revelation opens up fresh
mysteries; advanced knowledge raises
vaster problems. With our defective
earthly powers, this is inevitable.—**πρόσ-**
ωπον πρὸς πρόσωπον, Heb. *panīm 'el-*
panīm (see parls.), with a reminiscence of

Num. xii. 8, **στόμα κατὰ στόμα . . . καὶ οὐ**
δι᾽ αἰνιγμάτων (referring to the converse of
God with Moses): the "face" *to* which
ours will be turned, is *God's. God* is the
tacit obj. of ver. 12*b,* which interprets the
above figure: "Now I know (**γινώσκω,**
a *learner's* knowledge: see i. 21, etc.;
contrast **οἶδα,** 2 above and ii. 11) partially; but then I shall know-well (**ἐπι-**
γνώσομαι, as also I was well-known".
God has formed a perfect apprehension
of the believing soul (viii. 3); He possesses an immediate, full, and interested
discernment of its conditions (Rom. viii.
27, etc.); its future knowledge will match,
in some sense, His present knowledge of
it, the searching effect of which it has
realised (Gal. iv. 9, etc.).

Ver. 13. **νυνὶ δὲ μένει κ.τ.λ.**—final
conclusion of the matter, **μένει** being
antithetical to **πίπτει κ.τ.λ.** of the foregoing: "But as it is (*nunc autem*), there
abides faith, hope, love—these three!"
they stay; the others pass (8 ff.). Faith
and Hope are elements of the perfect and
permanent state; new objects of trust
and desire will come into sight in the
widening visions of the life eternal. But
Love, both now and then, surpasses its
companions, being the character of God
(viii. 3, 1 John iv. 8, 16); in Love is the
fruition of Faith's efforts (Gal. v. 6) and
Hope's anticipations; it alone gives worth
to every human power (1-3). The popular
interpretation, since Cm., has read **νυνὶ**
as *temporal* instead of logical, identifying
it with the **ἄρτι** of ver. 12, as though the
Ap. meant that *for the present* Faith and
Hope "abide" with Love, but Love
alone "abides" for ever. But P. puts
the three on the same footing in respect
of enduringness—"these three" in comparison with the other three of ver. 8—
pointedly adding Faith and Hope to share
and support the "abiding" of Love;
"love is *greater* among these," not more
lasting.—For **μείζων** with partitive gen.,
cf. Matt. xxiii. 11, and see Wr., p. 303.
For the pregnant, absolute **μένει,** *cf.* iii.
14, 1 John ii. 6, 2 John 2.

a Rom. ix.
30, xii. 13,
xiv. 19;
Ph. iii.
12, 14; 1
Th. v. 15;
Isa. li. 1;
Sir. xxvii.
8.

XIV. 1. ᵃΔιώκετε τὴν ἀγάπην· ᵇζηλοῦτε δὲ τὰ ᶜπνευματικά, μᾶλλον δὲ ἵνα ᵈπροφητεύητε. 2. ὁ γὰρ ᵉλαλῶν ᵉγλώσσῃ, οὐκ ᶠἀνθρώποις λαλεῖ ἀλλὰ τῷ¹ ᶠΘεῷ· οὐδεὶς γὰρ ἀκούει, ᵍπνεύματι δὲ λαλεῖ ʰμυστήρια· 3. ὁ δὲ ᵈπροφητεύων, ᶠἀνθρώποις λαλεῖ

b See xii. 31.   c See xii. 1.   d See xi. 4.   e See xiii. 1.   f See i. 25.   g vv. 14 f.; Acts xvii.
16.   h See ii. 7.

¹ Om. τ ῳ the pre-Syrian uncc.

§ 44. THE GIFTS OF TONGUES AND OF PROPHECY, xiv. 1-6. The digression upon ἡ ἀγάπη has not diverted us from the subject of this Div.; Love has shown the way (xii. 31b) in which all τὰ πνευματικά (xii. 1, xiv. 1) are to be sought, the animating principle and ulterior aim that should govern their exercise. But the principle of Love supplies, further, a criterion by which the charisms are to be relatively estimated—*their use in edification* (3 ff., 12, 19, 26). Thus P. at length answers the question addressed to him from Cor. as to the worth of the several "spiritual powers," and in particular as to the relative value of Tongues and Prophesying. He has led up to this answer by his exposition of the general Christian truths bearing upon the matter —*viz.* the office of the Holy Spirit as the distributor of God's gifts (xii. 3-11), the organic nature of the Church (12-31), and the sovereignty of love in the Christian life (xiii.).

Ver. 1. "Pursue love"—follow intently this καθ' ὑπερβολὴν ὁδόν (xii. 31b: see note): διώκω (see parls.: pr. impr.) signifies to prosecute to its goal (xiii. 13) a course on which one has entered. ζηλοῦτε δὲ τὰ πνευματικά, "but (continue to) covet the spiritual (gifts)": P. resumes xii. 31 (see note, also on xii. 1). Love is exalted in the interest of the charisms, not to their disparagement; it is not to be pursued by forgetting everything else, but opens the true way to everything else: "Sectamini charitatem, affectate spiritualia" (Cv.).—"But rather (in preference to other gifts) that you may prophesy": this is chief amongst "the greater charisms" of xii. 31. Perhaps the Cor. had asked specifically which of the two, Tongues or Prophecy, was to be preferred. ἵνα προφητεύητε (*cf.* θέλω . . . μᾶλλον ἵνα, 5) differs from τὸ προφητεύειν by making the object distinctly an *aim:* in striving after the charisms, Prophecy is to be set highest and to control the rest. For the use of ἵνα, *cf.* note on i. 10, also Bm., pp. 235 ff.

Vv. 2, 3. The reason for preferring Prophecy, on the principles laid down, is that one's fellows receive no benefit from the Tongues: except *God,* "no one hears" the latter—*i.e.* hears understandingly (*cf.* Eph. i. 13, iv. 29, etc.). There was *sound* enough in the glossolalia (xiii. 1), but no sense (23). πνεύματι δὲ λαλεῖ κ.τ.λ., "but in spirit he is speaking mysteries"; δὲ points a contrast to the οὐδεὶς . . . ἀκούει: there is something worth hearing—deep things muttered by those quivering lips, that should be rationally spoken. For μυστήριον, see note on ii. 7, and Cr. *s.v.*: *mystery* in Scripture is the correlate of *revelation;* here it stops short of disclosure, tantalizing the Church, which hears and hears not. πνεύματι, dat. of manner or instr.,—"with the spirit," but without the "understanding" (νοῦς: 14 ff.; *cf.* note to xii. 8).—"But he who prophesies *does speak to men*—edification and exhortation and comfort." παράκλησις and παραμυθία are distinct from οἰκοδομή: prophetic speech serves for (a) "the further upbuilding of the Christian life, (b) the stimulation of the Christian will, (c) the strengthening of the Christian spirit" (Hf.). παραμυθία has ref. to sorrow or fear (see parls.); παράκλησις (far commoner) to duty; οἰκοδομή, in the widest sense, to knowledge and character and the progress of the Church: this last stands alone in the sequel.

Ver. 4. "He that speaks with a tongue edifies himself, but he that prophesies edifies a church (assembly)"— not one but many persons, not himself but a whole community. The impression made on the γλωσσολαλῶν by his utterance, since it was delivered in a rapture and without clear conception (12 ff.), must have been vague; but it powerfully confirmed his faith, since it left an abiding sense of possession by the Spirit of God (*cf.* 2 Cor. xii. 1-10). Our deepest feelings frequently enter the mind below the surface consciousness.

Ver. 5. Notwithstanding the above drawback, the Tongues are a real and desirable charism; the better is preferred

ⁱοἰκοδομὴν καὶ ^kπαράκλησιν καὶ ^lπαραμυθίαν. 4. ὁ ^eλαλῶν ^eγλώσσῃ ἑαυτὸν ^mοἰκοδομεῖ, ὁ δὲ ^dπροφητεύων ⁿἐκκλησίαν ^mοἰκοδομεῖ. 5. θέλω δὲ πάντας ὑμᾶς ^eλαλεῖν ^eγλώσσαις, μᾶλλον δὲ ἵνα ^dπροφητεύητε· ^oμείζων γὰρ¹ ὁ ^dπροφητεύων ἢ ὁ ^eλαλῶν ^eγλώσσαις, ^pἐκτὸς ^pεἰ μὴ ^qδιερμηνεύῃ, ἵνα ἡ ἐκκλησία ⁱοἰκοδομὴν λάβῃ. 6. ^rνῦνι² ^rδέ, ἀδελφοί, ἐὰν ἔλθω πρὸς ὑμᾶς ^eγλώσσαις ^eλαλῶν, ^sτί ὑμᾶς ὠφελήσω, ἐὰν μὴ ὑμῖν λαλήσω ἢ³ ἐν^t ἀποκαλύψει ἢ ἐν ^uγνώσει, ἢ ἐν ^{v w}προφητείᾳ ἢ ἐν⁴ ^wδιδαχῇ;

i vv. 12, 26; 2 Cor. x. 8, xii. 19, xiii. 10; Rom. xiv. 19, xv. 2; Eph. iv. 12, 16, 29. see ver. 4, -μεω. k Freq. in P.; thrice in Heb.; 6 times in Lk., Acts.

l N.T. *h.l.*; Wisd. xix. 12. -ιον, Phil. ii. 1; -εισθαι, 1 Th. ii. 11.   m See viii. 1.   n Naruse, anarthrous, see xi. 18.   o See xii. 31.   p xv. 2; 1 Tim. v. 19. For ἐκτος, *cf.* vi. 18.   q See xii. 30. r See xii. 18.   s Mt. xvi. 26; Mk. viii. 36; also xiii. 3; Rom. ii. 25; Gal. v. 2. *Cf.* xv. 32; Rom. iii. 1; Jas. ii. 14.   t See i. 7. Abs., ver. 26; Gal. ii. 2; Eph. i. 17, iii. 3.   u See i. 5.   v See xii. 10. w ver. 26; *cf.* xii. 29. διδαχη., Rom. vi. 17, xvi. 17; 2 Tim. iv. 2; Tit. i. 9; Heb. vi. 2, xiii. 9; 2 Jo. 9, 10; thrice in Rev.; 4 times in Acts; 11 in GG.

¹ δε, ℵABP, cop. γαρ, DGKL, etc., latt. vg. syrr. (Western and Syrian).

² νυν all pre-Syrian uncc. *Cf.* xii. 18.

³ Om. η (first) ℵ, 17, 67**, cop.

⁴ Om. εν (last) ℵDgr.Ggr. So Tisch.; Tr. *brackets.*

to *the good :* "Yet I would have you all speak with tongues,—but rather that you might prophesy." μᾶλλον ἵνα προφητεύητε is repeated from ver. 1 : what the Ap. bids his readers prefer, he prefers for them—not to the exclusion of the Tongues, for the two gifts might be held at once (6, 18), but as looking beyond them.—θέλω ἵνα occurs several times in the Gospels without any marked telic force (Matt. vii. 12, Mark vi. 25, ix. 30, John xvii. 24), but only here in P.; its substitution for the inf. (λαλεῖν) of the coordinate clause is significant.—"Moreover he who prophesies is greater than he who speaks with tongues"—attached by the part. δὲ where one expected γάρ (T.R.); P. is not justifying *his own* preference just stated, but giving a further reason why *the Cor.* should covet Prophecy more than Tongues : the main reason lies in the eminent usefulness of this charism (2-4); besides that (δέ), its possessor is a "greater" person (μείζων : *cf.* xii. 31) "than the speaker with tongues —except in the case that he interprets (his ecstatic utterance), that the Church may get edification". The power to interpret *superadded* to the glossolalia (see 13, 26 ff., xii. 10) puts the mystic speaker on a level with the prophet : first "uttering mysteries" (2) and then making them plain to his hearers, he accomplishes in two acts what the prophet does in one. ἐκτὸς εἰ μὴ is a Pauline pleonasm (see parls.), consisting of ἐκτὸς εἰ (*except if*) and εἰ μή (*unless*) run together; "with this exception,—unless

he interpret" (Wr., p. 756). For εἰ with sbj., in distinction from ἐάν, see Wr., p. 368; it "represents that the event will decide the point" (El.). To supply τις with διερμην., supposing *another* interpreter meant, is ungrammatical; the *identity* of speaker and interpreter is the essential point. He interprets with the express intention that the Church may be edified (ἵνα . . . οἰκοδομὴν λάβῃ).

Ver. 6. What the Ap. has said touching the criterion of *edification*, he applies to his own approaching visit (iv. 18 ff., xvi. 5 ff.) : "But at the present time, brothers,"—νῦν δέ, *temporal*, as in v. 11, etc.; not *logical*, as in vii. 14, xiii. 13, etc. (see Hf., against most interpreters). It is *the situation at Cor.* which gives point to this ref. : what help could the Ap. bring to his readers in their troubled state, if he were to offer them nothing but confused mutterings and ravings? (*cf.* 7-11)—an appeal to common sense. —The hypotheses are parl. (expressing by ἐὰν actual possibility, *cf.* 18; not mere conceivability)—the second the negative of the first : "if I should come to you speaking with tongues, wherein shall I profit you—if I do not speak in (the way of) revelation or knowledge, or prophesying or teaching?" In the four ἢ clauses, the second pair matches the first : revelation comes through the prophet, knowledge through the teacher (*cf.* xii. 8, 10, 28, etc.). For ἔρχομαι with ptp. of the *character* or *capacity* in which one comes—"a (mere) speaker with tongues," unable to interpret (see 5)

x Gal. iii.
15; Jo.
xii. 42; 2
Macc. xv.
5.
y N.T. h.l.;
Wisd.
xiii. 17,
xiv. 29.
z Mt. xxiv.
29; Isa.
xiii. 10.

7. Ὅμως τὰ ᵞἄψυχα ᶻφωνὴν ᶻδιδόντα, ᵃεἴτε ᵇαὐλὸς ᵃεἴτε ᶜκιθάρα, ἐὰν ᵈδιαστολὴν τοῖς ᵉφθόγγοις μὴ ᶻδῷ, πῶς γνωσθήσεται τὸ ᶠαὐλούμενον ἢ τὸ ᶠκιθαριζόμενον; 8. καὶ γὰρ ἐὰν ᵍἄδηλον ᶻφωνὴν ¹ ʰσάλπιγξ ¹ ᶻδῷ, τίς ⁱπαρασκευάσεται εἰς πόλεμον; 9. οὕτω καὶ ὑμεῖς διὰ τῆς γλώσσης ἐὰν μὴ ᵏεὔσημον λόγον ᶻδῶτε, πῶς γνωσθήσεται τὸ λαλούμενον; ἔσεσθε γὰρ εἰς ¹ἀέρα λαλοῦντες.

ηχω δι-
δοῦσα θορυβον, Eurip., *Hec.*, 1093.　　a See iii. 22.　　b N.T. *h.l.*; -λητης, Mt. ix. 23.　　c Rev. i.
8, xiv. 2, xv. 2; Gen. iv. 21, etc.　d Rom. iii. 22, x. 12; Exod. viii. 23.　　e Rom. x. 18 (Ps. xviii.
4); Wisd. xix. 18.　f Mt. xi. 17, αυλ.; κιθαρ, Rev. xiv. 2; Isa. xxiii. 16.　g Lk. xi. 44.　See iii.
26.　h Mt. xxiv. 31; Rev. i. 10, viii. 13; Exod. xix. 16, 19. See xv. 52.　i 2 Cor. ix. 2 f.; Acts
x. 10; Jer. xii. 5.　k N.T. *h.l.*; Ps. lxxx. 3.　See note below.　l See ix. 26.

¹ σαλπιγξ φωνην, ℵAP. So Tisch., W.H. *txt.*, Nestle.
φων. σαλπ. : BDGKL. So Tr., Al., W.H. *marg.*, El.

—*cf.* Acts xix. 18, Matt. xi. 18 f., Mark i. 39, Luke xiii. 7.

§ 45. Utterance Useless without Clear Sense, xiv. 7-13. P. has just asked what the Cor. would think of him, if in their present need he came exhibiting his power as a speaker with Tongues, but without a word of prophetic inspiration or wise teaching to offer. Such speech would be a mockery to the hearers. This holds good of sound universally, when considered as a means of communication—in the case, *e.g.*, of lifeless instruments, the flute and lyre with their modulated notes, or the military trumpet with its varied signals (7 f.); so with articulate speech, in its numberless dialects. To the instructed ear every syllable carries a meaning; to the foreigner it is gibberish (10 f.). Just as useless are the Tongues in the Church without interpretation (9, 12 f.).

Ver. 7. Ὅμως τὰ ἄψυχα, "Quin et inanima" (Cv.); as in Gal. iii. 15, the part. emphasises the word immediately following, not φωνὴν διδόντα ("though giving sound") in contrast to ἐὰν διαστολὴν . . . μὴ δῷ (so however Wr., Gm., Mr., Sm.: "yet unless they give a distinction, etc."). The argument is *a minori ad majus*, from dead instruments to living speech: "Yet even in the case of lifeless things (τὰ ἄψυχα, generic art.) when they give sound, unless they give a distinction in their notes" (so Hf., Ed., Gd., El.).—φθόγγος denotes a measured, harmonious sound, whether of voice (Rom. x. 18) or instrument; see Plato, *Tim.* 80.—διαστολὴ is referred by Lidd., and by Ev. *ad loc.*, to the *pause* between notes; by most others (after Plato, *Phileb.*, 17C; *cf.* Oec. *ad loc.*) to the *interval* (= διάστημα) or distinction of pitch; possibly (so Cv., El.) it includes

both in untechnical fashion—whatever in fact distinguishes the φθόγγοι.—πῶς γνωσθήσεται κ.τ.λ.; "How will that which is being piped or harped be discerned?"—how will the air be made out, if the notes run confusedly into one another? The double art., τὸ αὐλ. . . . τὸ κιθαρ., separates the two sorts of music. This comparison used applies to *inarticulate* γλωσσολαλία, not to foreign languages.

Ver. 8. To the *pipe* and *harp*, adornments of peace, P. adds for further illustration (καὶ γάρ) the warlike *trumpet*. This ruder instrument furnishes a stronger example: varied signals can be given by its simple note, provided there is an understanding between trumpeter and hearers; "unius tubæ cantus alius ad alia vocat milites" (Bg.). Without such agreement, or with a wavering, indistinct sound, the loudest blast utters nothing to purpose: "For if the trumpet also gives an uncertain voice, who will prepare for battle?" How disastrous, at the critical moment, to doubt whether the trumpet sounds Advance or Retreat!

Ver. 9 enforces the twofold illustration of vv. 7 f.: "So also in your case (οὕτως καὶ ὑμεῖς), if through the tongue you do not give a word of clear signification (εὔσημον λόγον), how will that which is spoken be discerned?"—εὔ-σημος (from εὖ and σῆμα, *a sign*) implies *a meaning* in the word, and *a meaning good to make out; cf.* Sophocles, *Antig.*, 1004, 1021.—πῶς γνωσθήσεται κ.τ.λ.; is an echo from ver. 7; and "the tongue" (διὰ τῆς γλώσσης: *cf.* iii. 5, vi. 4, vii. 17), as the means of *living* speech, is thrust before the ἐὰν in emphatic contrast to "the lifeless" pipe, etc. P. does not therefore refer in this sentence (as Est., Gd., Ed. would have it) to the supernatural Tongue

10. τοσαῦτα, ᵐ εἰ ᵐ τύχοι, ⁿ γένη φωνῶν ἐστιν¹ ἐν κόσμῳ καὶ οὐδὲν ᵐ xv. 37 only, in
αὐτῶν² ᵒ ἄφωνον· 11. ἐὰν οὖν μὴ εἰδῶ³ τὴν ᵖ δύναμιν τῆς φωνῆς, N.T.; cf. xvi. 6,
ἔσομαι τῷ λαλοῦντι ᑫ βάρβαρος, καὶ ὁ λαλῶν ʳ ἐν⁴ ἐμοὶ ᑫ βάρβαρος· ᵗᵘᵡᵒᵛ. n See xii.
12. οὕτω καὶ ὑμεῖς, ἐπεὶ ˢ ζηλωταί ἐστε ᵗ πνευμάτων, πρὸς τὴν ᵒ H.l. in this

sense; cf. xii. 2.   p N.T. h.l. in this sense; Numb. vi. 21; Plat., Crat., 394B, etc.   q Rom.
i. 14; Col. iii. 11; Acts xxviii. 2, 4.   r Cf. vi. 2; Rom. xi. 25 (?). See Wr., p. 481.   s Gal. i. 14;
Tit. ii. 14; 1 Pet. iii. 13; four times in Lk. and Acts; cf. -οω, xii. 36.   t Pl., see xii. 10.

¹ εισιν: all uncc. but KL.   ² Om. αυτων all pre-Syrian uncc.
³ ιδω, by itacism, AD*L, 17, 46.   G, γινωσκω.
⁴ Om. εν DG, 67**, latt. vg. syrutr. cop.

(elsewhere, moreover, expressed by the anarthrous γλῶσσα: otherwise here), for it is precisely his objection to this charism that it gives an ἄσημον instead of a εὔσημον λόγον (16, 19, 23); he means to say: "As inanimate instruments by due modulation, and by the fixed meaning attached to their notes, become expressive, so it is in a higher degree with the human tongue; its vocables convey a meaning just in so far as they are ordered, articulate, and conformed to usage". Now this is what the Cor. Glossolalia *was not*: "for you will be (otherwise) speaking into the air "—the issue of uninterpreted Tongue-speaking (cf. 2, 17, etc.).—εἰς ἀέρα λαλεῖν, a proverbial expression (cf. ix. 26) for ineffectual speech, like our "talking to the wind"; in Philo, ἀερομυθεῖν.

Ver. 10. Speaking of vocal utterance, the Ap. is reminded of the *multitude* of human dialects; this suggests a further proof of his contention, that there must be a settled and well-observed connexion between sound and sense. "Ever so many kinds of voices, it may chance, exist in the world."—On εἰ τύχοι (*if it should hap* = τυχόν, xvi. 6), which removes all known limit from the τοσαῦτα, see note of El. For the anarthrous ἐν κόσμῳ, cf. 2 Cor. v. 19; "in the *world*" —a sphere so wide.—καὶ οὐδὲν (sc. τῶν γενῶν) ἄφωνον, "and none (of them) voiceless": not tautologous, but asserting for every "kind of voice" the real nature of a voice, *viz.*, that *it means something to somebody;* "nullum genus vocum vocis expers" (Est.); "aucune langue n'est une non-langue"; the Greeks love these paradoxical expressions—cf. βίος ἀβίωτος, χάρις ἄχαρις (Gd., Hn.). The Vg. and Bz. miss the point in rendering, "nihil est mutum".
Ver. 11. "If then I know not the meaning of the voice" (τὴν δύναμιν τῆς φωνῆς, *vim* or *virtutem vocis*)—for every voice *has* a meaning (10b); on this very

possible hypothesis, "I shall be a barbarian to the speaker, and the speaker a barbarian in relation to me" (ἐν ἐμοί, cf. Matt. xxi. 42, and perhaps ii. 6 above), or "in my ear". By this illustration of the futility of the uninterpreted Tongues, Paul implicitly distinguishes them from natural foreign languages; there is a μετάβασις εἰς ἄλλο γένος in the comparison, just as in the previous comparison with harp and trumpet; one does not *compare* things identical. The second figure goes beyond the first; since the foreign speech, like the mysterious γλῶσσαι (2), may hide a precious meaning, and is the more provoking on that account, as the repeated βάρβαρος intimates.

Ver. 12. οὕτως καὶ ὑμεῖς is parl. to ver. 9; but the application is now turned into an exhortation. P. leaves the last comparison to speak for itself, and hastens to enforce his lesson: "So also with yourselves; since you are coveters of spirits (ζηλωταί ἐστε πνευμάτων), seek that you may abound (in them) with a view to the edifying of the church"— or "for the edifying of the church seek (them), that you may abound (therein)". The latter rendering, preferred by Cv., Mr., Al., Hf., Sm., is truer to the order of the words, and reproduces the emphasis of πρὸς τὴν οἰκοδομ. τῆς ἐκκλ. ζητεῖτε has its object supplied beforehand in the previous clause, and ἵνα (περισσεύητε) bears its ordinary sense as conj. of *purpose*. Spiritual powers are indeed *to be sought* (cf. 1, xii. 31), provided that they be sought for the religious profiting of others, *with a view to abound in service* to the Church. The ἵνα clause is thus parl. to πρὸς τ. οἰκοδομήν (cf. vii. 35, 2 Tim. iii. 16); cf. John x. 10, and other parls. for περισσεύω.—ζηλωταί, zealots, *enthusiasts after spirits* (Ev.),—used perhaps with a touch of irony (Hn.). The Cor. have already the eagerness that P. commends in ver. 1;

u See ver. 3. u οἰκοδομὴν τῆς ἐκκλησίας ζητεῖτε, ἵνα ᵛπερισσεύητε · 13. διόπερ ¹
v See viii. 8.
w See xiii. ὁ ʷλαλῶν ʷγλώσσῃ ˣπροσευχέσθω ˣἵνα ʸδιερμηνεύῃ.
ι.
x ινα, Phil. 14. Ἐὰν γὰρ² προσεύχωμαι γλώσσῃ, τὸ ᶻπνεῦμά μου προσεύχεται
i. 9; Col. i.
9, iv. 3; ²ὁ δὲ νοῦς μου ᵃἄκαρπός ἐστι. 15. ᵇτί ᵇοὖν ᵇἐστι; προσεύξομαι³
Th. i. 11,
iii. 1; Mt. τῷ ᶜπνεύματι, προσεύξομαι³ δὲ καὶ⁴ τῷ ᵈνοΐ· ᵉψαλῶ τῷ ᶜπνεύματι,
xxiv. 20;
Mk. xiv.
35; οπως, Acts viii. 15. y See xii. 30. z|See ii. 11. a Eph. v. 11; Tit. iii. 14; 2 Pet. i. 8;
Jude 12; Mt. xiii. 22; Jer. ii. 6; Wisd. xv. 4. — b Ver. 26; Acts xxi. 22. c See ii. 11. Instrum.
dat., ver. 2; Rom. viii. 13; Gal. iii. 3, v. 16, 25; 1 Pet. iii. 18, iv. 6. d Rom. vii. 25. e Rom.
xv. 9 (Ps. xvii. 49); Eph. v. 19; Jas. v. 13; Pss. *passim*.

¹ διο, all uncc. but אcKL.

² Om. γαρ (?) BG, 17, sah. Hence Lachm. and W.H. *bracket*.

³ προσευξωμαι (twice), ADGP, 46; א, -ωμαι, -ομαι.

⁴ Om. και GKP, latt. vg. sah.—Western variant.

but it is not prompted by the best motives, nor directed to the most useful end: this word was common amongst Greeks as describing the ardent votaries of a school or party, or those jealous for the honour of some particular master (*cf.* Gal. i. 14).—πνεύματα differs somewhat from τὰ πνευματικά (1), signifying not "the (proper) spiritual" powers, but *unseen forces* generally (see xii. 10, διακρίσεις πνευμάτων, 1 John iv. 1, and the warning of xii. 3; *cf.* the notes); "the Cor. sought supernatural endowments, no matter what their nature might be" (Ed.)—at any rate, they thought too little of the true source and use of the charisms, but too much and too emulously of their outward impression and prestige (see πνευμάτων, 32).—Everling (*Die paul. Angel. u. Dämonologie*, pp. 40 ff.) infers from this passage, along with Rev. xxii. 6, the conception of a *number* of Divine "spirits" that may possess men; but he overpresses the turn of a single phrase, in contradiction to the context, which knows only "the one and the self-same Spirit" as from God (xii. 11).

Ver. 13. "Wherefore (since thus only can the γλώσσαις λαλῶν edify the church) let him who speaks with a tongue pray that he may interpret": *cf.* ver. 5. It appears that the speaker with Tongues in some instances could recall, on recovery, what he had uttered in his trance-ecstasy, so as to render it into rational speech. The three vbs. are *pr.*, regulating current procedure.—The ἵνα clause, after προσευχέσθω, gives the *purport* of the prayer, as in Phil. i. 9; *cf.* i. 10 above, xvi. 12; Luke ix. 40, etc. Mr., El., and others, prefer to borrow γλώσσῃ from the next ver., and render thus: "Let him that speaks (with a tongue)

pray (therewith), in order that he may interpret"; but this strains the construction, and γλώσσῃ appears to be added in ver. 14 just because the vb. προσεύχομαι had not been so understood before.

§ 46. The ΝΟΥΣ the needed ally of the ΠΝΕΥΜΑ, xiv. 14-20. In § 44 the Ap. has insisted on *edification* as the end and mark of God's gifts to His Church, and in § 45 on *intelligibility* as a condition necessary thereto. Now the faculty of intelligence is the νοῦς; and we are thus brought to see that for a profitable conduct of worship, and for a sane and sound Church life (14, 17 ff., 23), the understanding must be in exercise: it is a vehicle indispensable (14 f.) to the energies of the spirit. On this point P. is at one with the men of Gnosis at Cor.; he discountenances all assumptions made in the name of "the Spirit" that offend against sober judgment (20). This passage, in a sense, counterbalances i. 18-ii. 5; it shows how far the Ap. is from approving a blind fanaticism or irrational mysticism, when he exalts the Gospel at the expense of "the wisdom of the world".

Ver. 14. The Tongue has been marked out as an inferior charism, because it *does not edify others*; it is less desirable also because *it does not turn to account the man's own intelligence*: "If I pray with a tongue, my spirit prays, but my understanding (νοῦς) is unfruitful". The introductory γάρ (see txtl. note) seems hardly needed; if genuine, it attaches this ver. to ver. 13, as giving a further reason why the γλωσσολαλῶν should desire to interpret—*viz.*, that his own mind may partake fruitfully in his prayers. In any case, the consideration here

^e ψαλῶ δὲ ¹ καὶ τῷ ^d νοΐ. · 16. ἐπεὶ ἐὰν εὐλογήσῃς ² τῷ ^{3 c} πνεύματι,   f See x. 16.
ὁ ^g ἀναπληρῶν τὸν ^h τόπον τοῦ ⁱ ἰδιώτου πῶς ^k ἐρεῖ ^k τὸ ^k ἀμὴν ^l ἐπὶ τῇ   g Precisely thus, Bibl. h.l.
σῇ ^m εὐχαριστίᾳ, ⁿ ἐπειδὴ τί λέγεις οὐκ οἶδε; 17. σὺ μὲν γὰρ   See xvi. 17.
^o καλῶς ^p εὐχαριστεῖς, ἀλλ᾽ ^q ὁ ^q ἕτερος ⁴ οὐκ ^r οἰκοδομεῖται. 18.   Found in Joseph.
^p εὐχαριστῶ τῷ Θεῷ μου,⁵ πάντων ὑμῶν ^s γλώσσαις ^{6 s} λαλῶν ⁷.   and Philo.
   h N.T. h.l.

in this sense, Sir. xii. 12; cf. Lk. xiv. 9 f.   i Ver. 23 f.; 2 Cor. xi. 6; Acts iv. 13; Prov. vi. 8. See note below.   k 2 Cor. i. 20; λεγ. αμην, Rev. v. 14, etc.   l 2 Cor. xii. 21; Heb. viii. 1; Acts xi. 19.   m 12 times in P.; Acts xxiv. 3; Rev. iv. 9, vii. 12; -τος, Col. iii. 15; -τεω, passim in P. n See i. 21.   o See vii. 37.   p See i. 4, and m above. Absol., see xi. 24.   q See iv. 6.   r See viii. 1.   s See xiii. 1.

¹ Om. δε (?) BG, 46. Lachm. om.; Tr. and W.H. bracket.

² ευλογης, all uncc. but GKL.

³ εν πνευματι (?): אcBDP, 73, cop. sah. W.H. bracket.

πνευματι (?), א*AG, 17, latt. vg. syrr. So Tisch., Tr., W.H. txt., R.V., Nestle. τω πνευματι: KL, etc., Chr., Thdrt.—as in ver. 15.

⁴ εταιρος, G, syrsch.—an obvious itacism; see Mt. xi. 16.

⁵ Om. μου all pre-Syrian witnesses.

⁶ γλωσση (?), אADG, 17, latt. vg. So Lachm., Tr., Tisch., W.H. marg., Nestle —perhaps borrowed from vv. 13 and 19 (? Western).

γλωσσαις (?), BKLP, etc., cop. syrr. So W.H. txt.

⁷ λαλω, all uncc. but KL. The ptp. a grammatical emendation.

brought in opens a new point of view. " The *fruit* of the speaker is found in the profit of the hearer" (Thd.).—" The **νοῦς** is here, as distinguished from the **πνεῦμα**, the reflective and so-called discursive faculty, *pars intellectiva*, the human **πνεῦμα** *quatenus cogitat et intelligit*" (El.): see Beck's *Bibl. Psychology*, or Laidlaw's *Bib. Doctrine of Man*, *s.vv.*; and cf. notes on i. 10, ii. 16 above; also on Rom. vii. 23, 25. Religious feelings and activities—prayer in chief (Phil. iii. 3, Rom. i. 9, etc.)—take their rise in the spirit; normally, they pass upward into conception and expression through the intellect.

Ver. 15. It is the part of *nous* to share in and aid the exercises of *pneuma*: " What is (the case) then? I will pray with the spirit; but I will also pray with the understanding: I will sing with the spirit; but I will also sing with the understanding".—τί οὖν ἐστιν; " How then stands the matter?" (*Quid ergo est?* Vg.): one of the lively phrases of Greek dialogue; it " calls attention, with some little alacrity, to the upshot of what has just been said" (El.).—ψάλλω denoted, first, *playing on strings*, then *singing* to such accompaniment; Eph. v. 19 distinguishes this vb. from ᾄδω. Ed. thinks that instrumentation is implied; unless forbidden, Gr. Christians would be sure to grace their songs with music. Through its LXX use, esp. in the title

Ψαλμοί, t'hillīm (Heb.), the word came to signify *the singing of praise to God*; but the connexion indicates a larger ref. than to the singing of the O.T. Psalms; it included the " improvised psalms which were sung in the Glossolalia, and could only be made intelligible by interpretation" (Mr.). Ecstatic utterance commonly falls into a kind of chant or rhapsody, without articulate words.

Ver. 16. " Since if thou bless (God) in spirit": πνεύματι, anarthrous—" in *spirit*" only, without understanding; cf. ἐὰν προσεύχ. γλώσσῃ, ver. 14.—Εὐλογέω (cf. x. 16, Matt. xiv. 19) is used elliptically, of *praise to God*, like εὐχαριστέω (17, xi. 24); it bears ref. to the *form*, as εὐχ. to the *matter* of thanksgiving; possibly P. alludes to the solemn act of praise at the Eucharist, this ellipsis being peculiar to blessing at *meals*.—ἐπεί (cf. v. 10, vii. 14) has its " usual causal and retrospective force, introducing the alternative" (El.; so *quandoquidem*, Bz.; *alioqui*, Cv.).—ὁ ἀναπληρῶν τὸν τόπον τοῦ ἰδιώτου, πῶς ἐρεῖ κ.τ.λ.; " he who fills the position of the unlearned, how will he say the Amen at thy thanksgiving?" P. does not here speak of ὁ ἰδιώτης simply (cf. 24), as meaning one unversed in Christianity; nor can this word, at so early a date, signify the *lay* Christian specifically (as the Ff. mostly read it); the man supposed " *holds the place* of one unversed " in the matter in question

t See xi. 18;
also ver. 4
above.
u θελω η
(malo),
N.T. h.l.;
2 Macc.
xiv. 42.
" A com-

19. ἀλλ' ᵗἐν ᵗἐκκλησίᾳ ᵘθέλω πέντε λόγους διὰ¹ τοῦ ᵈνοός¹ μου λαλῆσαι, ἵνα καὶ ἄλλους ᵛκατηχήσω, ᵘἢ ᵂμυρίους λόγους ἐν γλώσσῃ. 20. ἀδελφοί, μὴ ˣπαιδία γίνεσθε ταῖς ʸφρεσίν· ἀλλὰ τῇ ᶻκακίᾳ ᵃᵇνηπιάζετε, ταῖς δὲ ʸφρεσὶ ᵇτέλειοι γίνεσθε.

mon formula" in cl. Gr., Wr., p. 302. *Cf.* Lk. xv. 7, xvii. 2; Mt. xviii. 9. Numb. xxii. 6; Tob. iii. 6, etc., LXX.   v Rom. ii. 18; Gal. vi. 6; Lk. i. 4; Acts xviii. 25, xxi. 21, 24.   w See iv. 15. x In like sense, Mt. xi. 16. See νηπιος, iii. 6, xiii. 11.   y N.T. *h.l.;* Prov. xviii. 2.   z See v. 8. a *H.l.;* see xiii. 11; in Homer, νηπιαχεύω.   b See ii. 6; for the contrast, iii. 1.

¹τῳ νοι μου: all uncc. but KL. *Cf.* ver. 15.

being an ἰδιώτης γλώσσῃ (*cf.* 2 Cor. xi. 6): Thd. rightly paraphrases by ἀμύητος, *uninitiated.* In cl. Gr., ἰδιώτης means a *private person* in distinction from the State and its officers, then a *layman* as distinguished from the expert or professional man. The ptp. ἀναπληρῶν, *filling up* (see parls.), represents the ἰδιώτης as a necessary complement of the γλωσσολαλῶν (xii. 30). Hn. and others insist on the literal (local) sense of τόπος, as equivalent to ἕδρα not τάξις, supposing that the ἰδιῶται occupied a separate part of the assembly room; but this is surely to pre-date later usage.—The united "Amen" seals the thanksgiving pronounced by a single voice, making it the act of the Church—"*the* Amen," since this was the familiar formula taken over from Synagogue worship; *cf.* 2 Cor. i. 18 ff. On its ecclesiastical use, see El. *ad loc.,* and *Dict. of Christian Antiq. s.v.*—ἐπειδὴ τί λέγεις οὐκ οἶδεν = the οὐδεὶς ἀκούει of ver. 2. El. observes, "From this ver. it would seem to follow that at least some portions of early Christian worship were extempore": indeed, it is plain that extempore utterance prevailed in the Cor. Church (*cf.* 14 f.).

Ver. 17. "For thou indeed givest thanks well"—admirably, finely (καλῶς: *cf.* Luke xx. 39, James ii. 19): words *légèrement ironiques* (Gd.).—εὐχαριστεῖς = εὐλογεῖς (16: see note, also on i. 4).—ὁ ἕτερος, *i.e.,* the ἰδιώτης of ver. 16 signifies, as in iv. 6, x. 29; the pron. a distinct or even opposite person. P. estimates the devotions of the Church by a spiritually utilitarian standard; the abstractly beautiful is subordinated to the practically edifying: the like test is applied to a diff. matter in x. 23, 33.

Vv. 18, 19. Again (*cf.* 6, iv. 6, ix.) the Ap. uses *himself* for an instance in point. Even at Cor., where this charism was abundant, no one "speaks with tongues" (mark the pl. γλώσσαις) so largely as P. does on occasion; far from thinking lightly of the gift, he "thanks

God" that he excels in it. 2 Cor. v. 13 and xii. 1-4 show that P. was rich in ecstatic experiences; *cf.* Gal. ii. 2, Acts ix. 12, xvi. 9, xxii. 17, xxvii. 23 f., etc.— The omission of ὅτι after εὐχαριστῶ is exceptional, but scarcely irregular; it belongs to conversational liveliness, and occurs occasionally after a number of the *verba declarandi* in cl. Gr.: *cf.* note on δοκῶ κ.τ.λ., iv. 9; and see Wr., p. 683. The Vg., omitting μᾶλλον, reads *omnium vestrum lingua loquor,* making P. thank God that he could speak in every tongue used at Cor.; Jerome, in his Notes, refers the μᾶλλον *to the other App.,* as though P. exulted in being a better linguist than any of the Twelve! —ἀλλὰ ἐν ἐκκλησίᾳ κ.τ.λ.: "but in church-assembly (*cf.* note on ver. 4) I would (rather) utter five words with my understanding, that I might indeed instruct others, than ten thousand words in a tongue!"—ἀλλὰ contradicts the seeming implication of ver. 18—"but for all that": one might have supposed that P. would make much of a power in which he excels; on the contrary, he puts it aside and prefers to use every-day speech, as being *the more serviceable; cf.* for the sentiment, ix. 19-23, 2 Cor. i. 24, iv. 5, 12, 15, xi. 7, xiii. 9, 1 Thess. ii. 6 ff. With his Tongue P. might speak in solitude, "to himself and to God" (2, 28, 2 Cor. v. 13); amongst his brethren, his one thought is, how best to help and benefit *them.*—For νοῦς in contrast with πνεῦμα, see note on ver. 14; for its declension, *cf.* i. 10.—κατηχέω (see parls.) differs from διδάσκω as it connotes, usually at least, *oral* impartation ("ut alios *voce instituam,*" Bz.), including here prophecy or doctrine (6). On θέλω . . . ἤ, dispensing with μᾶλλον, see parls.; *malim . . . quam,* Bz. For the rhetorical μυρίους, *cf.* iv. 15.

Ver. 20. P. has argued the superiority of intelligible speech, as a man of practical sense; he finally appeals to the good sense of his readers: "Brethren, be not

21. Ἐν τῷ νόμῳ γέγραπται, "῞Οτι ἐν ᵉἑτερογλώσσοις¹ καὶ ἐν ᶜ Isa. xxviii.
ᵈχείλεσιν ᵉἑτέροις² λαλήσω τῷ λαῷ τούτῳ, ᶠκαὶ οὐδ᾽ ᶠοὕτως ᵍεἰσα- 11 f.; Ps.
cxiii. 1
κούσονταί μου, λέγει Κύριος". 22. ὥστε αἱ ʰγλῶσσαι ⁱεἰς ᵈ Rom. iii. (Aquila).
13; Heb.
ⁱσημεῖόν εἰσιν οὐ τοῖς πιστεύουσιν, ἀλλὰ ᵏτοῖς ᵏἀπίστοις· ἡ δὲ xiii. 15; 1
Pet. iii.
10; Mt.

xv. 8 (Isa. xxix. 13).   e Cf. Acts ii. 4; Exod. xxx. 9.   For gen. ετερων, cf. 2 Cor. viii. 8.   f See
xi. 28.   g Heb. v. 7; Mt. vi. 7; Lk. i. 13; Acts x. 31; Deut. i. 43.   h See xii. 10.   i In like
sense, Rom. iv. 11; Rev. xii. 1, 3, xv. 1; Mt. xxiv. 30; Lk. ii. 12, 34. εις σημ., Gen. ix. 13; Isa.
xix. 20, lv. 13; Ezek. xx. 12.   k See vi. 6.

¹ ετεραις γλωσσαις: G latt. vg. (in aliis linguis et labiis aliis) and Latt. Ff.

² ετερων: ℵAB, 17, 67**, 73.   So crit. edd.

children in mind" (see parls.)—"in judgment" (Ed.), "the reasoning power on
its reflective and discriminating side"
(El.); φρένες differs from νοῦς much as
φρόνιμος from σοφός (see notes to iv.
10, x. 15). Emulation and love of display were betraying this Church into a
childishness the very opposite of that
broad intelligence and enlightenment on
which it plumed itself (i. 5, iv. 10, viii. 1,
x. 15, etc.). "It is characteristic of the
child to prefer the amusing to the useful,
the shining to the solid" (Gd.). This
is a keen reproof, softened, however, by the
kindly ἀδελφοί ("suavem vim habet,"
Bg.).—γίνεσθε, "be in effect," "show
yourselves"; cf. xi. 1, etc. "In malice,
however, be babes (act the babe); but in
mind show yourselves full-grown (men)".
—For the force of the ending in νηπι-
άζω, cf. πυρρ-άζω, to redden, Matt. xvi.
2; the vb. is based on νήπιος, a kind of
superlative to παιδίον—"be (not boyish,
but actually) childish" (Ed.), or "in-
fantile, in malice". For the antithesis of
τέλειος (= ἀνήρ) and νήπιος, see ii. 6,
xiii. 9 ff., and parls. For κακία, cf. note
on v. 8: P. desiderates the affection of
the little child (see Eph. iv. 32 f., for the
qualities opp. to κακία), as Jesus (in
Matt. xviii. 1 ff.) its simplicity and hum-
bleness. Gd. excellently paraphrases this
ver.: "Si vous voulez être des enfants,
à la bonne heure, pourvu que ce soit
quant à la malice; mais, quant à l'intelligence, avancez de plus en plus vers la
maturité complète".

§ 47. The Strange Tongues an Occasion of Unbelief, xiv. 21-25. The
Ap. has striven to wean the Cor. from
their childish admiration of the Tongues
by showing how unedifying they are in
comparison with Prophecy. The Scripture quoted to confirm his argument (21)
ascribes to this kind of manifestation a
punitive character. Through an alien
voice the Lord speaks to those refusing

to hear, by way of "sign to the unbelieving" (22). These abnormal utterances neither instruct the Church nor
convert the world. The unconverted see
in them the symptoms of madness (23).
Prophecy has an effect far different; it
searches every heart, and compels the
most prejudiced to acknowledge the presence of God in the Christian assembly
(24 f.).

Ver. 21. This O.T. citation is adduced not by way of Scriptural proof,
but in solemn asseveration of what P. has
intimated, to his readers' surprise, respecting the inferiority of the Glossolalia;
cf. the manner of quotation in i. 19, ii. 9,
iii. 19. The passage of Isaiah reveals a
principle applying to all such modes of
speech on God's part. The title ὁ νόμος
Jewish usage extended to Scripture
at large; see Rom. iii. 19, John x. 34.
P. shows here his independence of the
LXX: the first clause, ὅτι . . . τούτῳ,
follows the Heb., only turning the prophet's third person ("He will speak")
into the first, thus appropriating the
words to God (λέγει Κύριος); Origen's
Hexapla and Aquila's Gr. Version run in
almost the same terms (El.). Paul's
second clause, καὶ οὐδ᾽ οὕτως εἰσακού-
σονταί μου, is based on the latter clause
of ver. 12 (translated precisely in the
LXX, καὶ οὐκ ἠθέλησαν ἀκούειν), but
with a new turn of meaning drawn from
the general context: he omits as irrelevant the former part of ver. 12. The
original is therefore condensed, and somewhat adapted. Hf. and Ed. discuss at
length the Pauline application of Isaiah's
thought. According to the true interpretation of Isa. xxviii. 9 ff. (see Cheyne,
Delitzsch, or Dillmann ad loc.), the
drunken Israelites are mocking in their
cups the teaching of God through His
prophet, as though it were only fit for
an infant school; in anger therefore He
threatens to give His lessons through

[l] προφητεία οὐ [k] τοῖς [k] ἀπίστοις, ἀλλὰ τοῖς πιστεύουσιν.
23. ἐὰν οὖν [m] συνέλθῃ[1] [n] ἡ [n] ἐκκλησία [n] ὅλη [m] ἐπὶ τὸ [m] αὐτὸ καὶ πάντες [h] γλώσσαις[2] [h] λαλῶσιν,[2] εἰσέλθωσι δὲ [o] ἰδιῶται ἢ [k] ἄπιστοι, οὐκ ἐροῦσιν ὅτι [p] μαίνεσθε;
24. ἐὰν δὲ πάντες [q] προφητεύωσιν, εἰσέλθῃ δέ τις [k] ἄπιστος ἢ [o] ἰδιώτης, [r] ἐλέγχεται ὑπὸ πάντων, [s] ἀνακρίνεται

l See xii. 10. m See xi. 20. n Rom. xvi. 23; Acts v. 11, xv. 22. o See ver. 16. p Acts xii. 15, xxvi. 24 f.; Jo. x. 20; Jer. xxxvi. 26; Wisd. xiv. 28. q See xi. 5. r Eph. v. 11, 13; five times in Pastt.; Jo. iii. 20, viii. 46, xvi. 8, etc.; -γμος, 2 Tim. iii. 16. s See ii. 14.

[1] **ελθῃ**: BGgr. **συν** easily lost in foregoing **ουν.**

[2] **λαλωσιν γλωσσαις** (in this order): all uncc. but DKL. G has **λαλησωσιν.** D puts **παντες** last.

the lips of foreign conquerors (11), in whose speech the despisers of the mild, plain teaching of His servants (12) shall painfully spell out their ruin. The **ὅτι** (*kī*) is part of the citation: "For in men of alien tongue and in lips of aliens I will speak to this people; and not even thus will they hearken to me, saith the Lord". God spoke to Israel through the strange Assyrian tongue *in retribution*, not to confirm their faith but to consummate their unbelief. The Glossolalia may serve a similar melancholy purpose in the Church. This analogy does not support, any more than that of vv. 10 f. (see notes), the notion that the Tongues of Corinth were foreign languages.—**εἰσακούω,** *to hear with attention*, *effect*, shares the meaning of **ὑπακούω** (*obedio*) in the LXX and in cl. Gr.

Ver. 22. The real point of the above citation from Isaiah comes out in **ὥστε αἱ γλῶσσαι εἰς σημεῖόν κ.τ.λ.,** "And so the tongues are for a sign not to the believing, but to the unbelievers"—*sc.* to "those who will not hear," who having rejected other modes of instruction find their unbelief confirmed, and even justified (23*b*), by this phenomenon. This interpretation (*cf.* Matt. xvi. 4; and for **εἰς σημεῖον** in the judicial sense, Is. viii. 18) is dictated by the logical connexion of vv. 21, 22, which forbids the thought of *a convincing and saving sign*, read into this passage by Cm. and many others. P. desires to quench rather than stimulate the Cor. ardour for Tongues.—**ἡ δὲ προφητεία κ.τ.λ.,** "while prophecy on the other hand" (**δέ**) serves the opposite purpose—it "(is for a sign) not to the unbelievers, but to the believing". **οἱ πιστεύοντες** implies the act continued into a habit (*cf.* i. 21); **οἱ ἄπιστοι,** the determinate character. For **ὥστε** with ind., see note on iii. 7.

Ver. 23 shows the disastrous impression which the exercise of the Tongues, carried to its full extent, must make upon men outside—a result that follows (**οὖν**) from the aforesaid intention of the gift (22): "If then the entire Church should assemble together and all should be speaking with tongues, but there should enter uninstructed persons or unbelievers, will they not say that *you are mad!*" If the Tongues are, as many Cor. think, the highest manifestation of the Spirit, then to have the whole Church simultaneously so speaking would be the *ne plus ultra* of spiritual power; but, in fact, the Church would then resemble nothing so much as a congregation of lunatics! A *reductio ad absurdum* for the fanatical coveters of Tongues.—The **ἰδιῶται** (here unqualified: otherwise in 16; *cf.* note) are persons *unacquainted with Christianity* (altogether uninitiated) and receiving their first impression of it in this way, whereas the **ἄπιστοι** are rejectors of the faith. The impression made upon either party will be the same. The effect here imagined is altogether diff. from that of the Day of Pentecost, when the "other tongues" spoke intelligibly to those religiously susceptible amongst non-believers (Acts ii. 11 ff.). The imputation of *madness* from men of the world P. earnestly deprecates (Acts xxvi. 24 f.).—Ed. renders **ἰδιῶται** "separatists"—unattached Christians; but this interpretation wants lexical support, and is out of keeping with ver. 16: did any such class of Christians then exist?

Vv. 24, 25. How diff. (**δέ**) and how blessed the result, "if all should be prophesying and there should enter some unbeliever or stranger to Christianity (**ἰδιώτης**: see previous note), he is convicted by all, he is searched by all, the secret things of his heart become manifest; and so he will fall on his face and worship God, reporting that verily God is among you!" This brings out two further notes of eminence in the charism of

ὑπὸ πάντων· 25. καὶ¹ οὕτω¹ ᵗτὰ ᵗκρυπτὰ τῆς ᵗκαρδίας αὐτοῦ
ᵘφανερὰ ᵘγίνεται· καὶ ᵛοὕτω ʷπεσὼν ʷἐπὶ ʷπρόσωπον ˣπροσκυνή-
σει τῷ Θεῷ, ʸἀπαγγέλλων ὅτι ὁ Θεὸς ¹ᶻὄντως² ἐν ὑμῖν ἐστι.
26. ᵃΤί ᵃοὖν ἐστιν, ἀδελφοί; ὅταν ᵇσυνέρχησθε, ἕκαστος ὑμῶν³
ᵉψαλμὸν ἔχει, ᵈδιδαχὴν ἔχει, ᵉγλῶσσαν⁴ ἔχει, ᵈἀποκάλυψιν⁴ ἔχει,

t See iv. 5.
With
καρδ., 1
Pet. iii. 4.
u See xi. 19.
v See xi. 28;
ver. 21
above.
w Mt. xvii.
6, xxvi.
39; Lk. v.

12, xvii. 16; Rev. xi. 16; Numb. xvi. 4, xx. 6.   x *H.l.* in P., with Acts xxiv. 11. Freq. in GG.
and Rev.   y 1 Th. i. 9; Heb. ii. 12; 1 Jo. i. 2 f.; GG. and Acts, *passim*; Gen. xiv. 13.   z Gal.
iii. 21; four times in 1 Tim.; four in GG.   a See ver. 15.   b See xi. 18.   c Eph. v. 19; Col.
iii. 16; Isa. lxvi. 20. βιβλ. ψ., Lk. xx. 42, xxiv. 44; Acts i. 20, xiii. 33. *Cf.* ver. 15.   d See ver.
6.   e See xii. 10. *Cf.* ερμηνευτης, ver. 28.

¹ *Om.* καὶ οὕτω all pre-Syrian witnesses, including vg.

² ὄντως ὁ Θεός (in this order): all pre-Syrian uncc. *Om.* ὁ ℵ*D*G: so
Tisch., but not other edd.: probably a Western error: the ο easily lost between ς
and θ in uncial script.

³ *Om.* υμων ℵ*AB, 17, cop. So crit. edd. Obvious grammatical addition.

⁴ ἀποκαλυψιν . . . γλωσσαν (in this order): all uncc. but L. K and many
minn. om. γλωσσ. εχει, a few copies om. αποκαλ. εχει, by homœoteleuton.

Prophecy when compared with Tongues:
(1) The former edifies the Church (3 ff.);
(2) it employs a man's rational powers
(14-19); (3) it can be exercised safely *by
the whole Church*, and (4) *to the conversion of sinners*. That "all" should
"prophesy" is a part of the Messianic
ideal, the earnest of which was given in
the descent of the Spirit at Pentecost:
see Num. xi. 23-29, Joel ii. 28, Acts. ii.
4, 15 ff.; the speaking of Pentecost
Peter *identifies* with prophesying, whereas P. emphatically *distinguishes* the Cor.
Glossolalia therefrom. Prophecy is an
inspired utterance proceeding from a
supernatural intuition, which penetrates
"the things of the man," "the secrets of
his heart," no less than "the things of
God" (ii. 10 ff.): the light of heart-
searching knowledge and speech, proceeding from every believer, is concentrated
on the unconverted man as he enters the
assembly. His conscience is probed on
all sides; he is pierced and overwhelmed
with the sense of his sin (*cf.* John iv. 29,
also i. 48, viii. 9, Acts viii. 18 ff., xxiv.
25). This form of Prophecy abides in
the Church, as the normal instrument for
"convicting the world of sin" (John xvi.
8 ff.); it belongs potentially to "all"
Christians, and is in fact the reaction of
the Spirit of Christ in them upon the unregenerate (*cf.* John xx. 22 f.); ἐλέγχεται
is the precise word of John xvi. 8.—
Ἀνακρίνω (see ii. 14 and parls.) denotes not *to judge*, but *to put on trial,
to sift judicially*. God alone, through
Christ, is the judge of "the heart's
secrets" (iv. 5, Rom. ii. 16); but the
God-taught word of man throws a search-

ing light into these recesses. In ver. 24
the ἄπιστος precedes the ἰδιώτης (*cf.* 23),
since in his case the arresting effect of
Prophecy is the more signal.—προσ-
κυνήσει and ὄντως ὁ Θεὸς κ.τ.λ. are a
reminiscence of Is. xlv. 14, following the
Heb. txt. rather than the LXX (*cf.* note
on 21).—ἀπ-αγγέλλων, "taking word
away," *reporting, proclaiming abroad* (*cf.*
parls.), thus diffusing the impression he
has received (*cf.* John iv. 29).—ὄντως
(*revera*, Cv.), *really, in very deed*—contradicts denials of God's working in
Christianity, such as the ἄπιστος himself formerly had made.—πεσών (aor.
ptp., of an act leading up to that of
principal vb. and forming part of the
same movement) indicates the prostra-
tion of a soul suddenly overpowered by
the Divine presence. To convince men
that "God is in the midst of her" is the
true success of the Church.

§ 48. SELF-CONTROL IN RELIGIOUS
EXERCISES, xiv. 26-33. The enquiry of
the Cor. as to whether Tongues or Prophecy is the charism more to be coveted
is now disposed of. P. supplements his
answer by giving in the two last paragraphs of this chap. certain directions of
a more general bearing relative to the
conduct of Church meetings, which arise
from the whole teaching of chh. xi.-xiv.:
see the *Introd.* to Div. iv.

Ver. 26. τί οὖν ἐστίν (*cf.* 15), ἀδελφοί;
"How then stands the case, brothers?"
οὖν is widely resumptive, taking in the
whole state of the Cor. Church as now
reviewed, with esp. ref. to its abundance
of charisms, amongst which Tongues
and Prophecy are conspicuous; *edifica-*

f Ver. 12.
For προς,
Jo. xi. 3;
1 Pet.
iv. 12.
g See ver. 3.
h Single,

^{e} ἑρμηνείαν ^{1} ἔχει· πάντα ^{f} πρὸς ^{fg} οἰκοδομὴν γενέσθω.^{2} 27. ^{h} εἴτε γλώσσῃ τις λαλεῖ, ^{i} κατὰ δύο ἢ ^{k} τὸ ^{k} πλεῖστον τρεῖς καὶ ^{l} ἀνὰ μέρος, καὶ εἷς ^{m} διερμηνευέτω· 28. ἐὰν δὲ μὴ ᾖ ^{n} διερμηνευτής,^{3}

h.l.; completed by προφ. δε, in oratio variata.   i Distrib. with numb., Mk. vi. 40; cf. ver. 31.
So ανα, Lk. ix. 3, x. 1; John ii. 6.   k The phrase, h.l.; πλειστος, Mt. xi. 20, xxi. 8; Mk. iv. 1.
l H.l.; ανα μερος αδειν, Polyb. iv. 20. 10.   Diff. from εκ μερους, xiii. 9; and απο μερους, Rom. xi. 25.
m See xii. 30.   n H.l.   See txtl. note.

^{1} DG, διερμην[ε]ιαν; ADL, -ιαν for -ειαν, a common itacism.
^{2} γινεσθω: all uncc., and all but a few minn.
^{3} ερμηνευτης: B, with DG (which prefix ο).   So Lachm., Tr., W.H. marg.
διερμηνευτης: אADb,c KL, etc., Chr., Euthal., etc.; "vox apud antiquos Græcos non usitata" (Tisch.).

tion must once more be insisted on as the true aim of them all.—ὅταν συνέρχησθε, "whensoever you assemble" (cf. xi. 18 ff.): here pr.; the aor. of ver. 23 referred to particular occasions.—"Each has a psalm (to sing)—a teaching, a revelation (to impart)—a tongue, an interpretation (to give)." The succession of the objects of ἔχει perhaps reflects the order commonly pursued in the Church meetings. For ἕκαστος, cf. i. 12, etc.: every Cor. Christian has his faculty; there is no lack of gifts for utterance or readiness to use them; cf. i. 5, also iv. 6 ff. This exuberance made the difficulty; all wanted to speak at once—women as well as men (34); ἔχει, in promptu habet (Mr.)—"iteratum, eleganter exprimit divisam donorum copiam" (Bg.). The ψαλμὸς might be an original song (though not chanted unintelligibly, ἐν γλώσσῃ—the latter is enumerated distinctly: see note on ψαλῶ, 15), or an O.T. Psalm Christianly interpreted (see parls.); similarly Philo, De Vita Cont., § 10, describing the Therapeutæ, ὁ ἀναστὰς ὑμῶν ὕμνον ᾄδει εἰς τ. Θεόν, ἢ καινὸν αὐτὸς πεποιηκώς, ἢ ἀρχαῖόν τινα τῶν πάλαι ποιητῶν. For N.T. psalms, see Luke i., ii., Rev. iv. 11, v. 9 f., 12 f., xv. 3 f.—διδαχὴ and ἀποκάλυψις (see 6 above; xii. 28 f.), the two leading forms of Christian edification. Beside the γλῶσσα is set the complementary ἑρμηνία, by which it is utilised for the Church: cf. xii. 10, 30; and vv. 1-19 passim.—πάντα πρὸς τὴν οἰκοδομὴν γινέσθω (pr. impv.), "Let everything be carried on with a view to edification".

Vv. 27, 28. The maxim πρὸς τ. οἰκοδομὴν κ.τ.λ. is applied to Tongues and Prophecy, as the two main competing gifts: "Whether any one speaks with a tongue (let them speak: sc. λαλείτωσαν) to the number of two (κατὰ δύο), or at the most three" (at one meeting)—"fiat

per binos, aut ad plurimum ternos" (Bz.).—καὶ ἀνὰ μέρος, "and in turn," idque vicissim (Cv.)—not all confusedly speaking at once. Ed. ingeniously renders the κατὰ and ἀνὰ clauses "by two, or at most three together, and in turns" (antiphonally), as though the Tongues could be combined in a duet—"the beginning of Church music and antiphonal singing amongst Christians": but this does not comport with the ecstatic nature of the Glossolalia; moreover, the sense thus given to the second clause would be properly expressed by ἐν μέρει, not ἀνὰ μέρος (Hn.).—"And let one person interpret": whether one of the γλωσσολαλοῦντες (13),or some one else present (ἄλλος, xii. 10); the use of several interpreters at the same meeting might occasion delay or confusion. "If however there be no interpreter (present), let him (the speaker with the Tongue) keep silence in the Church, but let him talk to himself and to God": unless his utterance can be translated, he must refrain in public, and be content to enjoy his charism in solitude and in secret converse with God (cf. 2 ff.); the instruction to "speak in his heart, noiselessly" (so Cm., Est., Hf.) would be contrary to λαλεῖν, and indeed to the nature of a tongue. "ᾖ for cl. παρῇ, sit for adsit; cf. Luke v. 17; Iliad ix. 688" (Ed.).

Vv. 29, 30. προφῆται δὲ δύο ἢ τρεῖς κ.τ.λ.: "But in the case of prophets, let two or three speak, and let the others discern" (dijudicent, Vg.). In form this sentence varies from the parl. clause respecting the Tongues (27); see Wr., p. 709, on the frequency of oratio variata in P., due to his vivacity and conversational freedom; the anarthrous προφῆται is quasi-hypothetical, in contrast with γλώσσῃ τις λαλεῖ—not "the prophets," but "supposing they (the speakers) be prophets, let them speak, etc." The

° σιγάτω ᵖ ἐν ᵖ ἐκκλησίᾳ, ἑαυτῷ δὲ λαλείτω καὶ τῷ Θεῷ. 29. ᑫ προφῆται δὲ δύο ἢ τρεῖς λαλείτωσαν, καὶ οἱ ἄλλοι ¹ ʳ διακρινέτωσαν·
30. ἐὰν δὲ ἄλλῳ ˢ ἀποκαλυφθῇ καθημένῳ, ὁ πρῶτος ° σιγάτω· 31.
δύνασθε γὰρ ᵗ καθ᾽ ᵗ ἕνα πάντες ᵘ προφητεύειν, ἵνα πάντες ᵛ μανθάνωσι
καὶ πάντες ʷ παρακαλῶνται· 32. καὶ ˣ πνεύματα ² ᑫˣ προφητῶν

° Rom. xvi. 25; six times in Lk. and Acts. For change of subject, see Wr., p. 787.
p See xi. 18.
q See xii. 29.
r See vi. 5.   s See ii. 10.   t See ver. 27. For καθ᾽ ενα, add Eph. v. 33; Jo. xxi. 25; καθ᾽ εἰς, Rom. xii. 5; Mk. xiv. 19; Jo. viii. 9.   u See xi. 5.   v Absol., Col. i. 7; 1 Tim. ii. 11; 2 Tim. iii. 7; Mt. xi. 29; Jo. vi. 45.   w Frequent throughout P.; in Acts rarely; in GG., only Lk. iii. 18 with this sense.   x Rev. xxii. 6. πνευματα, see xii. 10.

¹ Om. οι αλλοι D*GL—an example of Western license.
² πνευμα, DG, 67**, latt. (not vg.), syrˢᶜʰ., Epiph., Latt. Ff.

number to prophesy at any meeting is limited to "two or three," like that of the Tongue-speakers; the condition ἀνὰ μέρος (27) is self-evident, where edification is consciously intended (3, etc.). "The others" are the other *prophets* present, who were competent to speak (31); these silent prophets may employ themselves in the necessary "discernment of spirits" (see xii. 10)—διακρινέτωσαν, acting as critics of the revelations given through their brethren. The powers of προφητεία and διάκρισις appear to have been frequently combined, like those of artist and art-critic. It is noticed that in the *Didaché* a contrary instruction to this (and to 1 Thess. v. 20 f.) is given: πάντα προφήτην λαλοῦντα ἐν πνεύματι οὐ πειράσετε οὐδὲ διακρινεῖτε.— The above regulation implies pre-arrangement amongst the speakers; but this must not hinder the free movement of the Spirit; if a communication be made *ex tempore* to a silent prophet, the speaker should give way to him: "But if anything be revealed to another seated" (the prophesier *stood*, as in Synagogue reading and exhortation: Luke iv. 1, Acts xiii. 16), "let the first be silent". σιγάτω does not command (as σιγησάτω might) an *instant* cessation; "some token would probably be given, by motion or gesture, that an ἀποκάλυψις had been vouchsafed to another of the προφῆται; this would be a sign to the speaker to close his address, and to let the newly illumined succeed to him" (El.). Even inspired prophets might speak too long and require to be stopped!

Ver. 31. By economy of time, every one who has the prophetic gift may exercise it in turn; so the Church will enjoy, in variety of exhortation, the full benefit of the powers of the Spirit conferred on all its members: "For you can (in this way) all prophesy one by one (καθ᾽ ἕνα:

singulatim, Cv.), in order that all may learn and all may be encouraged". Stress lies on the repeated πάντες (cf. xii. 12 f.): let *every* prophet get his turn, and *every* hearer will receive benefit (cf. 26b); even if the Church members were all prophets, as Paul imagined in ver. 24, and thinks desirable (1-5), by due arrangement, and self-suppression on the part of the eloquent, all might be heard.

Ver. 32. The maxim πνεύματα προφητῶν προφήταις ὑποτάσσεται, is coupled by καὶ to ver. 31 under the regimen of γάρ; it gives the *subjective*, as ver. 31 the main *objective*, reason why the prophets should submit to regulation. "How can I prophesy *to order?*" one of them might ask; "how restrain the Spirit's course in me?" The Ap. replies: "(for) also the spirits of the prophets are subject to the prophets"; this Divine gift is put under the control and responsibility of the possessor's will, that it may be exercised with discretion and brotherly love, for its appointed ends. An *unruly prophet* is therefore no genuine prophet; he lacks one of the necessary marks of the Holy Spirit's indwelling (see 33, 37). This kind of subjection could hardly be ascribed to the ecstatic Glossolalia. On the pl. πνεύματα, signifying manifold forms or distributions (xii. 4, 11) of the Spirit's power, see note on xii. 10.— ὑποτάσσεται is the pr. of a general truth: "a Gnomic Present" (Bn., § 12); cf. iii. 13, 2 Cor. ix. 7.

Ver. 33. The apophthegm of ver. 32 exemplifies the universal principle of order in God's works; cf. the deduction drawn in xi. 3. God's gift of the Spirit submits itself to the receiver's will, through whose direction its exercise is brought into regulated and edifying use: "For God is not (a God) of disorder (or *seditionis*, Cv.), but of peace". To suppose that God inspires His prophets

[q] **προφήταις [y] ὑποτάσσεται· 33. οὐ γάρ ἐστιν [z] ἀκαταστασίας ὁ**
[a] Θεὸς ἀλλ' [a] εἰρήνης, ὡς ἐν [b] πάσαις ταῖς [b] ἐκκλησίαις [c] τῶν [c] ἁγίων.[1]
34.[2] Αἱ γυναῖκες ὑμῶν [3] ἐν ταῖς ἐκκλησίαις [o] σιγάτωσαν· οὐ γὰρ
[d] ἐπιτέτραπται [4] αὐταῖς λαλεῖν ἀλλὰ [y] ὑποτάσσεσθαι,[5] καθὼς καὶ

y xv. 27 f., xvi. 16.
15 times besides in P.; thrice in Lk. (*πνευματα υποτασσ.*, x. 20); four exx. in Heb.; one in Jas.; six in 1 Pet.
z 2 Cor. vi. 5, xii. 20; Lk. xxi. 9; Jas. iii. 16; Prov. xxi. 8; Tob. iv. 13. -*τος*, Jas. i. 8.
a 2 Cor. xiii. 11; Rom. xv. 33, xvi. 20; Phil. iv. 9; 1 Th. v. 23; Heb. xiii. 20; 2 Th. iii. 16 (*ὁ κυρ. τ. ειρ.*).
b See vii. 17.
c See vi. 1.
d Impers. pass., Acts xxvi. 1, xxviii. 16. See also xvi. 7; 1 Tim. ii. 12, Acts xxi. 39.

[1] ℵ by its punctuation distinctly attaches **ως . . . αγιων** to ver. 33. So Chr. and Ff.; so also the crit. edd., exc. Tisch., Weiss, W.H. *marg*. See note below.

[2] DG and several Latin authorities read vv. 34, 35 after 40.

[3] *Om.* **υμων** ℵAB, 17, vg. cop., Or., Mcion., Cyp.

[4] **επιτρεπεται**, all uncc. but KL.

[5] **υποτασσεσθωσαν**: ℵAB, 17, 73, syr^sch. cop. basm., Mcion. **υποτασσεσθαι**: DGKL, latt. vg.—a Western emendation.

to speak two or three at a time, to make a tumult in the Church and refuse control, would be to suppose Him the author of confusion, of chaos instead of cosmos.—**ἀκαταστασία** (see parls.) is a word of the LXX and later Gr., denoting civil disorder or mutiny; it recalls the **σχίσματα** and **ἔριδες** of i. 10 f., xi. 18 f., to which emulation in the display of spiritual powers seems to have contributed.—"As it is in all the Churches of the saints": in evidence of the "peace" which God confers on human society, P. can point to the conduct of Church meetings in all other Christian communities—a feature proper to "assemblies *of the saints*". Here is a final and solemn reason why the prophets of Cor. should practise self-control and mutual deference: *cf.* xi. 16; also i. 2*b*, and note; xvi. 1.—On the connexion of the **ὡς** clause, see Ed. or El. W.H. attach it to ver. 31, regarding vv. 32, 33*a* as a parenthesis; but this breaks the continuity of vv. 31, 32; nor does it appear that "all the churches" had the superabundance of prophets that necessitated the restrictions imposed in vv. 29-31. Other leading editors (Tisch., Mr., Hn., Hf., Bt., Gd.) link this qualification to the following context; but it comes in clumsily before the impv. of ver. 34, and the repetition of **ἐν ταῖς ἐκκλησίαις** is particularly awkward. On the other hand, the ref. to the example of the other Churches appropriately concludes the Apostle's appeals on the weighty subject, of universal interest, which has occupied him throughout this chapter.

§ 49. Final Instructions on Church Order, xiv. 34-40. In vv. 34 ff. P. returns to the matter which he first touched upon in reproving the disorderly Church life at Cor., *viz.*, the irregular behaviour of certain Christian women (xi. 2-16): there it was their *dress*, now it is their *tongue* that he briefly reproves. Vv. 37 f., glancing over the injunctions of Div. IV. at large, commend their recognition as a test of the high pretensions to spiritual insight made at Cor. Ver. 39 recapitulates Paul's deliverance on the vexed question of Tongues *versus* Prophecy. Ver. 40 adds the final maxim of *propriety and order*,—a rule of administration as comprehensive and important as the **πάντα πρὸς οἰκοδομὴν** of ver. 26.

Ver. 34. **Αἱ γυναῖκες ἐν ταῖς ἐκκλησίαις σιγάτωσαν**: "Let women (Gr. generic art.) keep silence in the church assemblies, for it is not allowed them to speak"; *cf.* 1 Tim. ii. 12, where the "speaking" of this passage is defined as "teaching, or using authority over a man". The contradiction between this veto and the language of xi. 5, which assumes that women "pray" and "prophesy" in gatherings of Christians and forbids their doing so "with uncovered head," is relieved by supposing (*a*) that in xi. 5 P. refers to *private gatherings* (so Cv., Bg., Mr., Bt., Ev., El.), or means specifically *at home* (Hf.), while here speaking **ἐν ἐκκλησίᾳ** is forbidden (35); but there is nothing in ch. xi. to indicate this distinction, which *ex hyp.* is vital to the matter; moreover, at this early date, the distinction between public and private Christian meetings—in *church* or *house*—was very imperfectly developed. Or (*b*), the instances admitted in xi. 5 were *exceptional*, "où la femme se sentirait

ὁ νόμος λέγει· 35.[1] εἰ δέ τι μαθεῖν[2] θέλουσιν, ᵉἐν ᵒοἴκῳ τοὺς   e See xi. 34.
ἰδίους ἄνδρας ᶠἐπερωτάτωσαν· ᵍαἰσχρὸν γάρ ἐστι γυναιξὶν[3] ʰἐν   f Rom. x.
ʰἐκκλησίᾳ[4] λαλεῖν.[4] 36. ἢ ἀφ᾽ ὑμῶν ὁ ¹λόγος τοῦ ¹Θεοῦ ἐξῆλθεν;   20 (Isa. lxv. 1); in
ἢ ᵏεἰς ὑμᾶς μόνους ᵏκατήντησεν; 37. εἴ τις ¹δοκεῖ ᵐπροφήτης   GG. freq.
εἶναι ἢ ⁿπνευματικός, ᵒἐπιγινωσκέτω ἃ γράφω ὑμῖν, ᵒὅτι τοῦ⁵   g See xi. 6.
   h See xi. 18.
   i 2 Cor. ii.
   17, iv. 2;
   Rom. ix.
   6; Phil. i.

14; Col. i. 25; 1 Th. ii. 13; 1 Tim. iv. 5; 2 Tim. ii. 9; Tit. ii. 5; occasional in other Epp.; freq. in Syn. GG. and Acts. k See x. 11. l See iii. 18. m See xii. 28; sing. thus, Acts xxi. 10; Tit. i. 12 (?). n See ii. 15. o 2 Cor. i. 14, xiii. 5; Acts iii. 10, iv. 13. For vb., see xiii. 12.

[1] DG and several Latin authorities read vv. 34, 35 after 40.

[2] μαθειν: ℵcBDGKL, etc. So all edd. except W.H., who put μανθανειν (?) in txt., following ℵ*A², 17, and a few other minn. with Greg.Nyss., and μαθ. in marg.

[3] γυναικι: ℵAB, 17, 73, vg., cop. basm.

[4] λαλειν εν εκκλησια (in this order): ℵAB, 17.
GL, and a few others, εν εκκλησιαις (cf. ver. 34).

[5] Om. του all but a few minn.; cf. vii. 19.

pressée de donner essor à un élan extraordinaire de l'Esprit " (Gd.): but πᾶσα γυνή (xi. 5) suggests frequent occurrence. (c) Hn. supposes *participation in the ecstatic manifestations* forbidden, as though γλώσσῃ were understood with λαλεῖν. (d) Ed. thinks the tacit *permission* of xi. 5 here *withdrawn*, on maturer consideration. But (e), in view of the words that follow, "but let them *be subject*" and "if they want *to learn*" (contrasted with λαλεῖν by δέ), and on comparison with the more explicit language of 1 Tim. ii. 12, in view moreover of the principle affirmed in ch. xi. 3 ff., it appears probable that P. is thinking of *Church-teaching and authoritative direction* as a rôle unfit for women.—ὑποτασσέσθωσαν is the keynote of Paul's doctrine on the subject (cf. also Eph. v. 22 ff., etc.). This command cannot fairly be set aside as a temporary regulation due to the state of ancient society. If the Ap. was right, there is a ὑποτάσσεσθαι which lies in the nature of the sexes and the plan of creation; but this must be understood with the recollection of what Christian *subjection* is (see Gal. v. 13b, Eph. v. 22 ff.; also note on xi. 3 above).—What "the law says" was evidently in Paul's mind when he grounded his doctrine in ch. xi. on the O.T. story of the creation of Man and Woman. For Jewish sentiment in the matter, see Wetstein *ad loc.*, Vitringa, *Synag.*, p. 724; Schöttgen, *Hor.*, p. 658. For Gr. feeling, cf. Soph., *Ajax*, 293, γυναιξὶ κόσμον ἡ σιγὴ φέρει (Ed.); for Early Church rule, *Const. Apost.*, iii. 6, *Conc. Carthag.*, iv. 99 (quoted by El.).

Ver. 35. εἰ δέ τι θέλουσιν μανθάνειν: "But if they want to *learn* something"

—if this is the motive that prompts them to speak. This plea furnishes an excuse, consistent with the submission enjoined, for women raising their voices in the Church meetings; but even so P. deprecates the liberty. As between μανθάνειν and μαθεῖν after θέλω and the like, El. thus distinguishes: "when attention is directed to the procedure of the action specified, the pr. is commonly used; when simply to the action itself, the aor." —In bidding the Cor. women of enquiring minds to "ask at home of their own husbands," P. is laying down a general rule, not disposing of all cases that might arise; since the impv. of ver. 35 admits of exceptions, so may that of ver. 34: the utterances of Pentecost (Acts ii. 4) proceeded from "all," both men and women (cf. 18 f.); there is also the notable instance of Philip's "four daughters which did prophesy" (Acts. xxi. 9). At Cor. there was a disposition to put men and women on an equal footing in public speaking and Church leadership; this is stigmatized as αἰσχρὸν (*turpe, inhonestum*; cf. xi. 6, 13 ff.); it shocks moral feeling. For ἐν ἐκκλησίᾳ, see xi. 18.

Ver. 36. The Ap. adds the authority of Christian usage to that of natural instinct (cf. the connexion of xi. 14 and 16), in a tone of indignant protest: "Or (is it) from *you* (that) the word of God went out? or to *you only* did it reach?" —*i.e.*, "Neque primi, neque soli estis Christiani" (Est.). The Cor. acted without thinking of any but themselves, as though they were the one Church in the world, or might set the fashion to all the rest (see note on i. 2b; also 33 above, and xi. 16). For the self-sufficiency of this

[p] Κυρίου εἰσὶν [1] [p] ἐντολαί [1]· 38. εἰ δέ τις [q] ἀγνοεῖ, [q] ἀγνοείτω.[2]
39. Ὥστε, ἀδελφοί,[3] [r] ζηλοῦτε τὸ [s] προφητεύειν, καὶ τὸ [t] λαλεῖν [4]
[t] γλώσσαις [5] [u] μὴ [u] κωλύετε.[5] 40. πάντα [6] [v] εὐσχημόνως καὶ κατὰ
[w] τάξιν γινέσθω.

p Lk. i. 6. εντ. Θ., see vii. 19. *Cf.* also ix. 14, vii. 40, ii. 16.
q 2 Cor. vi. 9 (pass.); Rom. ii. 4, vi. 3, vii. 1, x. 3; Gal. i. 22 (pass.); 1 Tim. i. 13. See also x. 1. Six times in N.T. besides (see esp. 2 Pet. ii. 12). Sir. v. 15.
r See xii. 31.
s See xi. 5.
t See xiii. 1.
u Mt. xix. 14, etc. For κωλ. in P., Rom. i. 13; 1 Th. ii. 16; 1 Tim. iv. 3.
v Rom. xiii. 13; 1 Th. iv. 12; -μων, see xii. 24; -οσυνη, xii. 23.
w Col. ii. 5; Lk. i. 8; Heb. v. 6, etc.; Job xxxviii. 12. Contrast *ατακτος*, -ως, 1 Th. v. 14; 2 Th. iii. 6, 11. *Cf.* xv. 23.

[1] **εστιν εντολη**: ℵAB, 17, cop., Aug. (ℵ[c], **εντ. εστ.**). D*G, 14, Or., Hil., Ambrst., **εστιν** simply (Western); so Tisch. **εισιν εντολαι**: Syrian emendation.

[2] **αγνοειται** (?): ℵ*A*D*G, Or., latt. vg., Amb., Ambrst., Hil.; so Lachm., Tr. *marg.*, Tisch., W.H. *txt.*, R.V. *marg.*, Nestle. Possibly a Western corruption.
αγνοειτω (?): ℵ[c]A[2]BD[bc], etc.; retained by Tr. *txt.*, R.V. *txt.*, W.H. *marg.* See note below.

[3] **αδελφοι μου**: ℵAB*, 67**, syrr. cop. Om. **μου** Western and Syrian.

[4] **εν γλωσσαις**: BD*G, cop., Tr. *marg.*

[5] **το λαλειν μη κωλυετε γλωσσαις** (in this order): ℵABP, 17, 73—conformed by Western and Syrian edd. to usual order.

[6] **παντα δε**: all uncc. but KL.

church, *cf.* iv. 6 ff., v. 2. On **καταντάω εἰς,** see x. 11.—**ἢ** links this ver. with the foregoing, "Or (if what I have said is not sufficient), etc."

Vv. 37, 38. **ἃ γράφω ὑμῖν**, in the apodosis, includes, beside the last particular (34 ff.), the other instructions of this Ep.; **προφήτης** and **πνευματικὸς** in the protasis recall esp. the directions of chh. xii.-xiv.: *cf.* xi. 4, xii. 1, xiv. 1.—**δοκεῖ,** as in iii. 18 (see note), is *putat, sibi videtur* (not *videtur* alone, Vg.), denoting self-estimation. The term **πνευματικὸς** includes every one endowed with a special gift of the Spirit; *cf.* the pl. **πνεύματα,** ver. 12. Hf. and Hn. think however that the disjunctive **ἢ** narrows the ref. of "spiritual," by contrast with "prophet," to the sense of "speaker with tongues"; but this is a needless inference from the part.; the Ap. means "a prophet, or a man of the Spirit (in any sense)". The adj. **πνευματικός** (in masc.: see parls.) refers not to spiritual *powers* (**τὰ πνευματικά,** xii. 1, etc.), but to spiritual *character* (= **ὁ κατὰ πνεῦμα, ἐν πνεύματι,** Rom. viii.), which gives insight in matters of revelation (*cf.* John vii. 17, viii. 31 f.). While the true "prophet," having a kindred inspiration (*cf.* 29), will "know well of the things" the Ap. "writes, that they are a commandment of the Lord" (**Κυρίου ἐστὶν ἐντολή,** "are what *the Lord* commands"; *cf.* ii. 10-16, vii. 40, and notes, 2 Cor. xiii. 3), this ability belongs to "the spiritual" generally, who "judge all things" (ii. 15); being "of God," they hear His voice in others (*cf.* John viii. 42 f., etc.; 1 John ii. 20, iv. 6). The "Lord" is Christ, the Head of the Church, who "gives commandment to His Apostles" (*cf.* vii. 10, 25, xi. 23, xii. 3, etc.; Matt. xxviii. 20, etc.).—For **ἐπι-γινωσκέτω,** *cf.* xiii. 12—"judicet atque agnoscat" (Est.); the pr. impv. asks for a continued acknowledgment of Christ's authority in His Apostle.—"But if any one is ignorant (of this), *he is ignored*" (**ἀγνοεῖται**)—a retribution in kind. The professor of Divine knowledge who does not discern Paul's inspiration, proves his ignorance; his character as "prophet" or "spiritual" is not recognised, since he does not recognise the Apostle's character; *cf.* Matt. x. 14 f., 41, John xiii. 20, for this criterion as laid down by Christ; the Ap. John assumes it in 1 iv. 6.—**ἀγοεῖται,** is pr. in tense, *ignoratur* (not *ignorabitur*, Vg.), affirming an actual rejection—*sc. by the Lord*, who says to such despisers of His servants, "I know you not" (*cf.* viii. 3; 2 Tim. ii. 19; John v. 42, etc.); but *by His Apostle* too, who cannot acknowledge for fellow-servants men who repudiate the Lord's authority in him (*cf.* 3 John 9 f.). Christ foretold that He would have to disown "many who had *prophesied*" in His name (Matt. vii. 22 f.). If **ἀγνοείτω** be read (still preferred by Mr., Bt., Ev., Gd., with R.V. txt.), the impv. is *permissive*, as in vii. 15: "sibi suæque ignorantiæ relinquen-

XV. 1. ᵃΓνωρίζω δὲ ὑμῖν, ἀδελφοί, τὸ ᵇεὐαγγέλιον ὃ ᵇεὐηγγελισά-　ᵃ See xii. 3.
μην ὑμῖν, ᵐὃ ᵐ καὶ ᶜπαρελάβετε, ᵈ ἐν ᵐ ᾧ ᵐ καὶ ᵈἑστήκατε, 2. δι' οὗ　ᵇ See i. 17.
καὶ ᵉσώζεσθε · τίνι λόγῳ ᵇεὐηγγελισάμην ὑμῖν, εἰ ᶠκατέχετε, ᵍἐκτὸς
（In this constr., 2 Cor. xi. 7; Lk. i. 19, ii. 10;）

Acts xiii. 32.　c See xi. 23.　d Rom. v. 2; Col. iv. 12; Jo. viii. 44; cf. 2 Cor. i. 24.　e Pr.,
see i. 18; also, beside ptpl. use, Heb. v. 7, vii. 25; 1 Pet. iii. 21, iv. 18; Jude 23; Acts xxvii. 20.
f See xi. 2.　g See xiv. 5.

dos esse censeo" (Est.)—a counsel of despair; contrast 2 Tim. ii. 24 ff.

Vv. 39, 40 restate the advice of ver. 1 in the light of the subsequent discussion, moderating the Church's zeal for demonstrative charisms by insisting on the seemliness and good order which had been violated by their unrestrained exercise (26-33). "And so, my brothers, covet to prophesy": ζηλοῦτε, cf. xii. 31; τὸ προφητεύειν replaces by the regular inf. the telic ἵνα προφητεύητε of ver. 1 (see note).—καὶ τὸ λαλεῖν μὴ κωλύετε γλώσσαις, "and the speaking with tongues do not hinder"; this is to be allowed in the Church, but not encouraged like Prophecy, of course with the proviso that the Tongue has its interpreter (13, 28). For ὥστε with impv., see iv. 5, etc.—πάντα δὲ γινέσθω: "But let all things be carried on, etc.": the δὲ attaches this caution specially to ver. 39; zeal for Prophecy and permission of Glossolalia must be guarded by the observance at all points of decorum and discipline.—εὐσχημόνως (see parls., and note on vii. 35), honeste (Vg.) or decenter; North. Eng. mensefully (cf. Eph. iv. 1, v. 4, and 33 above)—a sort of "ethical enhancement of the more mechanical κατὰ τάξιν" (El.). On the latter expression, opp. of ἀτάκτως, cf. 2 Thess. iii. 6 f., also xi. 34b above: the Cor. would interpret it by P.'s previous instructions—his παραδόσεις, ἐντολαί, ὁδοὶ ἐν Χριστῷ —and those given in this Ep.—εὐσχημόνως demands a right Christian taste and deportment, κατὰ τάξιν a strict Christian method and rule of procedure.

DIVISION V.: THE RESURRECTION OF THE BODY, CHAP. xv. Some members of the Cor. Church denied the resurrection of the dead (12), compelling the Ap. to enter on a systematic defence and exposition of this Christian doctrine. The question was not raised in the Church Letter; nor does Paul indicate the source of his information; the opinion of the τινὲς was openly expressed, and was doubtless matter of common report (cf. v. 1). Their position was incompatible with Christianity; it contravened, in-

ferentially, the whole verity and saving worth of the Gospel (1 f., 13-19). Such scepticism nullified the faith and hope of the Church (11) as effectually as the party-divisions destroyed its love. While standing apart from the practical and personal questions upon which the Ep. turns (and accordingly reserved to the last), this doctrinal controversy has two important points of connexion with them, lying (1) in the differences of opinion prevalent at Cor. (cf. 12, λέγουσιν ἐν ὑμῖν τινες, with ἵνα τὸ αὐτὸ λέγητε πάντες, i. 10), and (2) in the laxity of moral sentiment associated with Cor. unbelief (cf. 32 ff. with v. 2, vi. 8 f., viii. 10, x. 14, 21 f., xi. 21, 29 ff.). This latter trait identifies the doubters of the Resurrection with the men who justified antinomian tendencies by the assumption of superior "knowledge" (see notes on vi. 12 and viii. 1, etc.); affecting "the wisdom of this world," they cherished the rooted prejudice of Greek culture, against the idea of a bodily redemption (see Introd., p. 732). To men of this way of thinking the Resurrection was a folly even more than the Cross; some of those who had overcome the latter offence, still stumbled at the former. Unbelief in the Resurrection was sure to be excited wherever the Gospel spread amongst educated Greeks; the Ap. feels that he must grapple boldly with this difficulty at its first appearance in the Church; he puts forth his full strength to conquer it and to commend the truth that was impugned to the intelligent Corinthians. Sceptics as they are in regard to the general doctrine, the τινὲς do not question the personal resurrection of Jesus Christ (a circumstance of great apologetic value); the Apostle's refutation starts from the assumption of this cardinal fact. They will not admit the recovery of the body as a part of the Christian salvation; they reject it as a principle, and a law of the kingdom of God. It was probably held that Christ's rising from the dead was a unique, symbolical occurrence, bringing about for believers in Him a redemption wholly spiritual, a literal and full deliverance from the

h Rom. xiii. g εἰ μὴ ʰ εἰκῇ ἐπιστεύσατε ; 3. ᵏ παρέδωκα γὰρ ὑμῖν ¹ ἐν ¹ πρώτοις,
4, Gal. iii. 4, iv. 11 ; ᵐ ὅ ᵐ καὶ ᵉπαρέλαβον, ὅτι ⁿ Χριστὸς ⁿἀπέθανεν ᵒ ὑπὲρ τῶν ᵒ ἁμαρτιῶν
Col. ii. 18; Prov.
xxviii. 25.   i See iii. 5.   k See xi. 2.   l N.T. h.l.; Gen. xxxiii. 2.   m Rom. ix. 24; Gal.
ii. 10; 2 Th. i. 11; 1 Pet. ii. 8, iii. 21.   n See viii. 11.   o Gal. i. 4; Heb., 4 times; Ezek. xlv.
22. Cf. περι αμαρτ., Rom. viii. 3, etc.

flesh and the world of matter.—Paul's argument is in two parts: (A) vv. 1-34, concerning *the certainty* ; (B) vv. 35-57, concerning *the nature* of the Resurrection. To establish its certainty (A), P. begins by (a) rehearsing *the historical evidence* of Christ's bodily resurrection, which had been preached by himself ἐν πρώτοις and so received by the readers (1-11); (b) he shows that *to deny the resurrection of the dead is to deny Christ's resurrection*, and so to declare the Gospel witness false and its salvation illusive (12-19); and further, (c) that *the risen Christ is the first-fruit* of a great harvest, whose ingathering is essential to the fulfilment of the kingdom of God (20-28); (d) he closes this part of the case by pointing to the *practical results of faith or unbelief in a future resurrection* (29-34). (B) The nature of the resurrection body is (a) *illustrated* by the difference between *the seed and the perfect plant ;* also by the endless variety of material forms, instanced in animal organisms and in the heavenly bodies, which helps us to understand how there may be a future body of a higher order than the present human frame (35-43). (b) This difference between the σῶμα πνευματικὸν and the σῶμα ψυχικὸν being premised, it is argued that our investiture with the former is as necessary *a consequence of our relation to Christ* as our investiture with the latter is a consequence of our relation to Adam (44-49). (c) Only by this transformation, by *the victory over death and sin* thus achieved, can the promise of God in Scripture be fulfilled, His redeeming purpose effected, and the work of His servants made secure (51-58).—This is the earliest Christian doctrinal essay; in method and argumentative character it is akin to the Ep. to the Romans. Hn. ably defends its integrity against the attempts of Clemen and the Dutch School to make out interpolations and contradictions.

§50. The Facts concerning Christ's Resurrection, xv. 1-11. The doubt which the Ap. combats strikes at the fundamental, probative fact of his Gospel. He must therefore go back to the beginning, and reassert the "first things" he had taught at Cor. (1-4); to establish

the resurrection of Jesus Christ is logically to destroy the theorem, "There is no resurrection of the dead" (12). Six successive appearances of the Risen One are enumerated—the first made to Kephas, and the last to Paul himself—(5-9); the list is not intended as exhaustive, but includes the names most prominent in the Church, the witnesses whose testimony would be best known and most accessible. The Ap. dwells on the astonishing mercy that was in this way vouchsafed to himself (9 f.), insisting finally, on the unbroken agreement of the Apostolic preaching and of the Church's faith in regard to this supremely important event (11).

Vv. 1, 2. "Now I give you to know, brothers" (cf. xii. 3, for γνωρίζω): Paul writes, with a touch of blame, as though *informing* the Cor. of what the staple of his message had been, that on which their whole Christianity is built (cf. 2 Cor. xiii. 5, Rom. vi. 3)—viz., "the good news which," on the one hand, "I proclaimed to you (for cognate noun and vb., emphasising the *benefit* of the news, cf. ix. 18, etc.), which also," on the other hand, "you received; in which also you stand fast (cf. i. 6, xi. 2), through which also you are being saved". Ver. 11 similarly contrasts the correspondent part of proclaimers and receivers in attesting the saving facts (cf. xi. 23). The three relative clauses describe the inception, continuance, and progressive benefits of the faith of this Church.—σώζεσθε affirms a present, continuous salvation (cf. Rom. viii. 24, Eph. ii. 8); but "salvation," with Paul, always looks on to the future (see Rom. v. 9, 1 Thess. v. 8 ff.).—The connection of τίνι λόγῳ εὐηγγελισάμην ὑμῖν; is difficult to seize. The two interpretations of the R.V., txt. and marg. (also A.V.), are those commonly adapted : (a) making the τίνι λόγῳ dependent on γνωρίζω, as appositive to τὸ εὐαγγέλιον κ.τ.λ., "I make known the good news . . . with what word I preached, etc." (so Bg., Hn., Ed.); (b) prefixing the clause, with an inversion of the normal order, to the hypothetical εἰ κατέχετε, which states the condition of σώζεσθε, "(you are saved), if you hold fast by what word I preached (it) to you" (Bz., Mr., Ev.,

ἡμῶν [p]κατὰ τὰς [p]γραφάς· 4. καὶ ὅτι [q]ἐτάφη, καὶ ὅτι [r]ἐγήγερται
τῇ [s]τρίτῃ [1][s]ἡμέρᾳ, [1][p]κατὰ τὰς [p]γραφάς· 5. καὶ ὅτι [t]ὤφθη [u]Κηφᾷ,

[p] Jas. ii. 8.
γραφαι,
Rom. i. 2,
xv. 4; 2
Pet. iii.

16; 14 exx. in GG. and Acts. Scrr. relevant in (1): Ps. xxi., Isa. liii., Zech. xiii. 7, Dan. ix. 24,
etc.; in (2), Ps. xv. 10, Isa. xxv. 7 f., liii. 9 f., Hos. vi. 2; Jonah i. 17 (see Mt. xii. 40), etc.   q Rom.
vi. 4 (συνεταφημεν); Mt. viii. 21 f.; Lk. xvi. 22; Acts ii. 29, v. 6, 9 f.; Gen. xxiii. 4.   r Vv. 13 ff.;
see vi. 14. For pf. pass., outside this ch.; 2 Tim. ii. 8; Mk. vi. 14.   s Mt. xii. 40, xvii. 23, xx.
19, xxvi. 61, xxvii. 40, 63; Lk. xiii. 32, xxiv. 7, 21, 46; John ii. 19 f.   t In this tense, 1 Tim. iii.
16; Rev. xi. 19, xii. 1, 3; freq. in Acts; Mt. xvii. 3; Lk. i. 11, xxii. 43, xxiv. 34. Cf. ix. 1.   u See ix. 5.

¹τη ημερα τη τριτη: ℵABD, 17, 37.

Gd., Bt., El., Sm., Wr., Bm.). There
are convincing objections to both views,
advanced by Mr. and El. against (a), and
by Ed. and Hn. against (b): beside the
harsh inversion it requires, (b) leaves the
interrog. τίνι (the instances of τίς for ὅς,
with ἔχω, adduced in Bm.'s *Grammar* are
not really parl.), and the substitution of
λόγος for εὐαγγέλιον, unexplained. Preferring therefore construction (a), one
feels that at this distance the τίνι λόγῳ
clause practically detaches itself from
γνωρίζω (Hf.); the Ap. restates τὸ εὐαγγέλιον ὃ εὐηγγελισάμην ὑμῖν in the
altered shape of *a challenge to the
memory and faith* of his readers—an
interrogation prompted by the misgiving
expressed directly afterwards in εἰ κατέχετε: "In what word (I ask) did I preach
(it) to you?—(you will remember) if you
are holding (it) fast!—unless you believed
idly!" The λόγος is "the *word* of the
gospel" (Acts xv. 7; *cf.* Eph. i. 13, Col.
i. 5), "the story of the cross," etc. (i. 17),
as *told* by P.—*quo sermone* (Bz.); not
qua ratione (Vg.); nor *quo pacto* (Er.,
Cv.). Can it be that the Cor. have let this
slip? or did they believe it εἰκῇ—not
frustra, in vain (so Vg., and most others,
as in Gal. iii. 4), but in the common cl. sense
of εἰκῇ, *temere* (*cf.* Rom. xiii. 4, Col. ii.
18), *heedlessly, at random*, without serious
apprehension, without realising the facts
involved. The self-contradiction of the
τινὲς (12) shows *levity* of belief. For
ἐκτὸς εἰ μὴ, see xiv. 5.

Vv. 3, 4 answer the question put in
ver. 2, reinforcing the readers: "For I
delivered to you amongst the first things,
that which I also received".—καὶ emphasises the identity of the παραδοθὲν
and παραλημφθέν, involved in the character of a "faithful steward" (iv. 1 f., *cf.*
John xvii. 8, etc.). *How* these matters
had been received—whether by direct
revelation (Gal. i. 12) or through other
contributory channels (*cf.* note on xi. 23
above)—is irrelevant.—ἐν πρώτοις, *in
primis*, in chief (*cf.* 1 Tim. i. 15 f.). The
things thus delivered are "that Christ

died for our sins according to the Scriptures, and that He was buried, and that
He has been raised on the third day
according to the Scriptures". Amongst
the three πρῶτα, the first and third are
πρώτιστα (*cf.* 2 Cor. v. 14 f., Rom. iv. 25,
1 Thess. iv. 14, etc.); the second is the
link between them, signalising at once the
completeness of the death and the reality
of the resurrection (*cf.* Rom. vi. 4, x. 7):
ὅτι ἐτάφη καὶ ὅτι ἐγήγερται is a more
vivid and circumstantial expression for ὅτι
ἐγήγερται ἐκ νεκρῶν (12, etc.).—The two
chiefest facts P. and the other Apostolic
preachers (11) were accustomed to verify,
both separately and jointly, from the Old
Testament, κατὰ τὰς γραφάς (Acts xiii.
32 ff., xvii. 3, xxvi. 22 f., Rom. i. 2 ff.),
after the manner of Jesus (Luke xxii. 37,
xxiv. 25 ff., John iii. 14). But it was the
facts that opened their eyes to the meaning of the Scriptures concerned (*cf.* John
ii. 22, xx. 9). The death and burial are
affirmed in the *aor.* as historical events;
the resurrection is put with emphasis into
the *pf.* tense, as an abiding power (*cf.*
14, 17, 20) = ἐγερθεὶς . . . οὐκέτι ἀποθνήσκει (Rom. vi. 9; *cf.* Heb. vii. 25).—
"For our sins," see parls.—"pro peccatis
nostris abolendis" (Bg.). "P. could not
have said ὑπὲρ τῶν ἁμαρτιῶν ἡμῶν if
Christ's death were only an example of
self-denial, not because ὑπὲρ must be
rendered 'instead of' (*in loco*), but because the ref. to *sin* involves with ὑπὲρ
the notion of expiation" (Ed.); *cf.* the
excellent note of Mr.; see the exposition
of the relation of Christ's death to man's
sin in 2 Cor. v. 18 ff., Rom. iii. 23 ff., v. 6-
11, Gal. iii. 10 ff., with notes in this Comm.
ad locc.; also ver. 56 below, and note. The
definition *on the third day* indicates that
"in His case restoration to life ensued,
instead of the corruption of the corpse
that sets in otherwise after this interval"
(Hf.). Jesus appears to have seen a
Scriptural necessity in the "third day"
(Luke xxiv. 46).

Ver. 5. καὶ ὅτι ὤφθη Κηφᾷ, εἶτα τοῖς
δώδεκα: so much of the *evidence* P.

v Acts vi. 2; εἶτα[1] ᵛτοῖς ᵛδώδεκα[2]· 6. ἔπειτα ᵗὤφθη ᵂἐπάνω πεντακοσίοις
above
twenty ἀδελφοῖς ˣἐφάπαξ, ἐξ ὧν ʸοἱ ʸπλείους[3] ᶻμένουσιν ᵃἕως ᵃἄρτι,
times in
GG.; cf. τινὲς δὲ καὶ[4] ᵇἐκοιμήθησαν· 7. ἔπειτα[5] ᵗὤφθη Ἰακώβῳ, εἶτα[6]
Rev. xxi.
14. τοῖς ἀποστόλοις πᾶσιν· 8. ᶜἔσχατον δὲ ᶜπάντων, ᵈὡσπερεὶ τῷ
w Mk. xiv.
5. See

Wr., p. 313.   x Rom. vi. 10; Heb. vii. 27, ix. 12, x. 10.   See note below.   y See ix. 19.
z In this sense, Phil. i. 25 ; John xxi. 22 f.   a See iv. 13.   b See vii. 39.   c Adv., Mk. xii. 22
(with παντων) ; Num. xxxi. 2. For adj., see ver. 26.   d Bibl. h.l. See note below.

[1] επειτα (?), אA, 17, 37, 46. So Tisch., Tr., and W.H. marg.
εıτα, BDcKLP. μετα ταυτα: D*G.

[2] ενδεκα, DG, latt. vg., and Latt. Ff.,—a characteristic Western emendation.

[3] πλειονες, pre-Syrian uncc.

[4] Om. και pre-Syrian uncc. and verss.

[5] ειτα, D, Cyr.

[6] επειτα (?), א*AGK, 17, 46. So Tisch., Lachm., Tr., W.H. marg.
ειτα, אcBDLP, etc. Cf. note 2.

states as having been formally delivered
to the Cor. along with the facts attested ;
for these two clauses are under the
regimen of παρέδωκα (ver. 3). The
manifold testimony was detailed with
more or less fulness at diff. times ; but
P. seems always to have related *imprimis*
the witness of Kephas and the Twelve,
beside the revelation to himself (8). The
Lord's manifestation to Peter (on the
form *Kephas*, see i. 12) preceded that
given to the body of the Apostles (Luke
xxiv. 34). Peter's evidence, as the witness
of Pentecost and ἀπόστολος τ. περιτομῆς,
was of palmary importance, ἀξιόχρεων
εἰς μαρτυρίαν (Thd.), esp. in view of the
consensus to be asserted in ver. 11 (*cf.* i.
12).—ὤφθη with dat., *appeared* (pass.
aor., in reflexive sense : see Bm., pp. 52,
187), is used of exceptional, supernatural
appearances (see parls.). "The twelve,"
the college of the App., without exact regard to number : actually *ten*, wanting
Judas Iscariot, and Thomas absent on the
first meeting. Luke speaks on this occasion of "the eleven (the Western reading
here) and those with them," xxiv. 33 ;
Paul cites the official witnesses.

Ver. 6 carries forward ὤφθη into a new
sentence, independent of παρέδωκα . . .
ὅτι : the four remaining manifestations
P. recites without indicating whether or
not they formed a part of his original
communication.—ἔπειτα (*cf.* 23, 46, xii.
28) ὤφθη κ.τ.λ. : "After that (*deinde*) He
appeared to above (ἐπάνω, *cf.* Mark xiv.
5) five hundred brethren once for all"
(*semel*, Bz.). Nowhere else has ἐφάπαξ
the meaning *simul*, *at once* (so Vg., and
most interpreters, in violation of usage).
This was the culminating manifestation

of the risen Jesus, made at the general
gathering to which His brethren were
invited by Him *in a body*, as it is related
in Matt. xxviii. 7, 10, Mark xvi. 7 ; the
appearance to "the eleven" described in
Matt. xxviii. 16 ff. is recorded as the
sequel to this summons, and implies the
presence of a larger assembly (see esp.
the words οἱ δὲ ἐδίστασαν in ver. 17),
such as P. alludes to ; the great charge
of Matt. xxviii. 18 ff., closing the First
Gospel, corresponds by its importance to
this ἐφάπαξ.—P. writes a quarter of a
century after the event ; the followers
of Jesus were mostly young in age for
"the majority" (οἱ πλείονες) to have
been still alive. On ἕως ἄρτι, see iv. 13.

Ver. 7. "After that, He appeared to
James"—*sc. James, the brother of the
Lord*, as elsewhere in P. (Gal. i. 19, ii. 9,
12), included in the ἀδελφοὶ τ. Κυρίου of
ix. 5 above (see note) ; associated with P.
in Acts xv. 13, xxi. 18 (see notes). The
manifestation to James—only mentioned
here—the chief of our Lord's formerly
unbelieving brothers (John vii. 5), explains the presence of "His brothers"
amongst the 120 disciples at Jerus. (Acts
i. 14) and James' subsequent leadership
in the mother Church. His high position
at the time of writing accounts for his
citation in this place. Paul made acquaintance with James as well as Peter on his
first visit to the Jerus. Church (Gal. i.
18 f.). The well-known story about the
meeting of Jesus with James told by
Jerome (*De viris illustr.*, 2) implies an
earlier date for this than Paul's narrative
admits of, since ἔπειτα signifies succession in *time ;* succession of *rank* cannot
be intended.—"After that, to all the

ᵉἐκτρώματι, ᵗὤφθη κἀμοί· 9. ἐγὼ γάρ εἰμι ὁ ᶠἐλάχιστος τῶν
ἀποστόλων, ὃς οὐκ εἰμὶ ᵍἱκανὸς καλεῖσθαι ἀπόστολος, διότι ʰἐδίωξα
τὴν ⁱἐκκλησίαν τοῦ ⁱΘεοῦ· 10. ᵏχάριτι δὲ ᵏΘεοῦ εἰμι ὅ εἰμι, καὶ
ἡ ⁱχάρις αὐτοῦ ἡ¹ ⁱεἰς ἐμὲ οὐ ᵐκενὴ² ᵐἐγενήθη, ἀλλὰ ⁿπερισσότερον
πάντων ᵒἐκοπίασα· οὐκ ἐγὼ δέ, ἀλλ᾽ ἡ ᵏχάρις τοῦ ᵏΘεοῦ ἡ³ σὺν

ᵉ N.T. h.l.;
Job iii. 16;
Eccl. vi. 3.
ᶠ Of per-
sons, Mt.
v. 19, xxv.
40, 45.
Cf. Eph.
iii. 8; see
also iv. 3,
vi. 2,

above. g 2 Cor. iii. 5; 2 Tim. ii. 2 and Mt. iii. 11 (with inf.); Ex. iv. 10. h Gal. i. 13, 23, iv.
29; Phil. iii. 6; Acts ix. 4 f., xxii. 4, 7 f., xxvi. 11, 14 f.; Rev. xii. 13; Mt. v. 10 ff., etc. i See i. 2.
k See i. 4. l 1 Pet. i. 10; cf. 2 Cor. ix. 8; Rom. v. 15. m 1 Th. ii. 1, iii. 5 (εἰς κενον). For κενος,
see ver. 14. n Adv., Mk. vii. 36; Heb. vi. 17, vii. 15. For comp. adj., see xii. 23. o Rom. xvi.
6, 12; Ph. ii. 16; Acts xx. 35; Mt. vi. 28; Psa. cxxvi. 1. For κοπος, see iii. 8.

¹ Om. η DG, latt. verss. and Ff.—gratia ejus in me.

² πτωχη ουκ εγενηθη: DG (γεγονεν), some latt., Amb., Ambrst. (pauper, egena).

³ Om. η ℵ*BD*G, latt. vg. So crit. edd., exc. W.H. marg. Cf. note 1.

apostles": in this formal enumeration, ἀπόστολοις bears its strictest sense, and could hardly include James (see Acts i. 13 f.; he is not certainly so styled in Gal. i. 19). Paul was, presumably, aware of the absence of Thomas on the occasion of ver. 5, and his consequent scepticism (John xx. 24 ff.); he therefore says distinctly that *all* participated in this latter sight, which coincides in point of time with Acts i. 6-12, not John xx. 26. The witness of the First App. to the resurrection was complete and unqualified.

Ver. 8. ἔσχατον δὲ πάντων, ὡσπερεὶ τῷ ἐκτρώματι: "But last of all, as it were to the abortion (a creature so unfit and so repulsive), He appeared also *to me*".—ἔσχατον (adv.) πάντων marks the conclusion of a long series; *cf.* iv. 9, also Mark xii. 22.—ὡσπερεί, a frequent cl. conjunction, "nonnihil mitigat—*ut si* [or *quasi*]: docet non debere hoc nimium premi. . . . Articulus vim habet (τῷ ἐκτρώματι). Quod inter liberos est abortus, inquit, id ego sum in apostolis. . . . Ut abortus non est dignus humano nomine, sic apostolus negat se dignum apostoli appellatione" (Bg.; similarly Est., Mr., Al., Ed., Sm.); ἔκτρωμα need not be pressed beyond this figurative and descriptive meaning. However, Cv., Gr., Bt., Gd., and many find in the phrase an indication of *the suddenness and violence* of Paul's birth into Christ; Hn. and El. see pictured in it, more appropriately, *the unripe birth* of one who was changed at a stroke from the persecutor into the Apostle, instead of maturing normally for his work,—" P. describes himself thus in contrast with those who, when Jesus appeared to them, were already brothers or apostles, already born as God's children into the life of faith in Christ" (Hf.). Sm. aptly sug-

gests that τὸ ἔκτρωμα was one of the insulting epithets flung at Paul by the Judaists; in their eyes he was a *wirklich Missgeburt*. He adopts the title—"the abortion, as they call me"—and gives it a deeper meaning. His low stature may have suggested the taunt: *cf.* 2 Cor. x. 10, and *Acta Pauli et Theclae*, 3. An *abortion* is a living, genuine offspring.

Ver. 9. ὁ ἐλάχιστος corresponds to ἔσχατον πάντων (8); "the least" properly comes "last": *cf.* Eph. iii. 8, which enhances this expression; also 1 Tim. i. 15.—ὃς οὐκ εἰμὶ ἱκανὸς καλεῖσθαι κ.τ.λ., "who am not fit to bear the name of apostle".—ἱκανὸς (lit. *reaching up to*, *hinreichend*), as distinguished from ἄξιον (*worthy*: xvi. 4), denotes *adequacy*, *competence* for office or work (*cf.* 2 Cor. iii. 5); the words are interchangeable "where the capacity to act consists in a certain moral condition of mind and heart" (Ed.: *cf.* Matt. iii. 11, and John i. 27).—διότι (*propterea quod*, Bz.) ἐδίωξα κ.τ.λ., "because I persecuted the Church of God"—a remorse which never left the Ap. (*cf.* Gal. i. 13, 1 Tim. i. 13 ff., Acts xxvi. 9 ff.); the prominence of this fact in Luke's narrative is a sign of Paul's hand. The Church of Jerus., whatever opposition to himself might proceed from it, was always to Paul "the church of God" (Gal. i. 13, 22): on this phrase, see note to i. 2. For καλέομαι, in this sense, *cf.* Rom. ix. 25 f., Heb. ii. 11. This ver. explains how P. is "the abortion" among the App.; in respect of *his dwarfishness*, and *the unripeness of his birth* into Apostleship.

Ver. 10. "God's grace," which makes Paul what he *is* (see ix. 1 f.: the double εἰμὶ is firmly assertive—"I am what I verily am"), is the *favour*, utterly undeserved, that summoned Saul of Tarsus

p See iii. 22.
q See i. 23.
r See iii. 5
(ver. 2
above).
s See i. 23.
t Mt. xvii.
9, xiv. 2,
etc. (απο

ἐμοί.   11. ^p εἴτε οὖν ¹ ἐγὼ ^p εἴτε ἐκεῖνοι, οὕτω ^q κηρύσσομεν καὶ οὕτως ^r ἐπιστεύσατε.

12. Εἰ δὲ ^{su} Χριστὸς ^s κηρύσσεται ὅτι ^t ἐκ ^t νεκρῶν ^{tu} ἐγήγερται, ^v πῶς λέγουσί τινες ² ἐν ὑμῖν ² ὅτι ^w ἀνάστασις ^w νεκρῶν οὐκ ἔστιν ;

τ. νεκρ.) ; Mk. vi. 14 ; Lk. ix. 7 ; Jo. ii. 22, xii. 1, 9, 17, xxi. 14 ; Acts iii. 15, iv. 10, xiii. 30 ; 1 Pet. i. 21 ; Heb. xi. 19 ; 8 exx. in Rom. ; 7 in P. elsewhere.   u See ver. 4.   v Rom. vi. 2 ; Gal. ii. 14, iv. 9.   w Rom. i. 4 ; in Acts five times ; Heb. vi. 2 ; 1 Pet. i. 3 ; Mt. xxii. 31 ; Lk. xx. 35.

¹ *Om.* η אּ*BD*G, latt. vg.   So crit. edd., exc. W.H. *marg.*   *Cf.* note 1 (p. 921).

² εν υμιν τινες : אּABP, 17.

from the foremost rank of the persecutors to the foremost rank amongst the servants of the Lord Jesus: *cf.* 1 Tim. i. 14, Eph. iii. 8, ii. 7, Gal. i. 13 ff. The grace of Apostleship implies the antecedent grace of forgiveness and adoption.—**καὶ ἡ χάρις αὐτοῦ ἡ εἰς ἐμὲ κ.τ.λ.,** "and His grace that was extended (*or* went out) unto me, has not proved vain": *cf.* the emphatic **ἐμοὶ** of Eph. iii. 8; the repeated art. marks *me* as the signal object of this grace; for **χάρις εἰς,** *cf.* 1 Peter i. 10.—**κενή** (*cf.* 14) means not *void of result* (that is **ματαία,** 17), but *void of reality*: Paul's Apostleship was no titular office, no mere benevolence towards an unworthy man; the favour brought with it a *labour* quite as extraordinary—"nay, but (**ἀλλ'**) more abundantly than they all did I labour".—**κοπιάω** connotes *exertion, painful* or *exhausting toil;* see note on **κόπος,** iii. 8. So that, if last and least at the outset, and conspicuously unfit for Apostleship, *in execution* P. took the premier place: see 2 Cor. x. 13-18, xi. 23, xii. 11 ff., Rom. xv. 15-21.—**αὐτῶν πάντων,** presumably, *more than all the rest together:* by his single labours P. had extended the kingdom of Christ over a region wider than all the Twelve had traversed up to this date.—From the depth of Paul's self-abasement a new pride is ready to spring, which is corrected instantly by the words, **οὐκ ἐγὼ δέ, ἀλλ' ἡ χάρις τοῦ Θεοῦ σὺν ἐμοί:** "not *I*, however, but the grace of God (working) with me"—this really wrought the work; I was its instrument. See iii. 7 ff., xii. 6, Phil. ii. 12 f., Eph. iii. 20, Col. i. 29; and for the turn of expression, Gal. ii. 20.

Ver. 11 breaks off the comparison between himself and the other App., into which Paul was being drawn, to sum up the statement of fact and evidence concerning Christ's resurrection: "Whether then it were I (8 f.) or they (Kephas, the Twelve, the first disciples, James: 5 ff.),

so we proclaim (3 f.), and *so* you believed (2)". For **εἴτε, εἴτε,** giving alternatives indifferent from the point of view assumed, *cf.* iii. 22, x. 31, etc.—**οὕτως** is emphatic: in the essential matters of vv. 1-4 and the crucial point of the resurrection of Jesus, there is not the least variation in the authoritative testimony; Peter, James, Paul—Jerusalem, Antioch, Corinth—are in perfect accord, preaching, believing, with one mind and one mouth, that the crucified Jesus rose from the dead.—On **κηρύσσω,** see note to i. 23.—This closes the case on the ground of testimony.

§ 51. If Christ is not Risen? xv. 12-19. Paul has intrenched his own position; he advances to demolish that of his opponents. His negative demonstration, taking the form of a destructive hypothetical syllogism, has two branches: he deduces (*a*), in vv. 13-15, from the (supposed) non-existence of the fact of resurrection, *the falsity of the faith* (**κενὴ ἡ πίστις**) accorded to it, and *of the witnesses* attesting it; (*b*), in vv. 17-19, from the non-existence of the fact, *the unreality of the effects* derived from it (**ματαία ἡ πίστις**). Are the sceptics at Cor. prepared to affirm that the App. are liars? and that the new life and hopes of their fellow-Christians are an illusion? In arguing these two points, P. presses on the impugners twice over (13, 16), that their general denial logically and in principle excludes *Christ's* resurrection.

Ver. 12. **δὲ** contrasts with the affirmation of all Christians (11) the contradictory dogma of **τινὲς ἐν ὑμῖν.** For their sake P. made the rehearsal of vv. 1 ff. "But if Christ is preached, (to wit) that He is raised from the dead"—not "it is preached that Christ, etc.": the preaching of Christ *is* the preaching *of His resurrection;* **ἐγηγερμένος** and **ἐσταυρωμένος** (see i. 23 f., ii. 2) are, both of them, predicates inseparable from **Χριστός** (*cf.* Rom. iv. 24 f., viii. 34, x. 9, 2 Cor. v. 15;

13. εἰ¹ δὲ ᵂἀνάστασις ᵂνεκρῶν οὐκ ἔστιν,¹ οὐδὲ ᵘΧριστὸς ᵘἐγήγερται · ^x See ver.
10; also
14. εἰ δὲ ᵘΧριστὸς οὐκ ᵘἐγήγερται, ˣκενὸν ἄρα² τὸ ʸκήρυγμα ἡμῶν, ver. 58;
Eph. v.
ˣκενὴ δὲ³ καὶ ἡ πίστις ὑμῶν⁴· 15. ᶻεὑρισκόμεθα δὲ καὶ ᵃψευδο- 6; Col. ii.
8; Jas. ii.
μάρτυρες τοῦ Θεοῦ, ὅτι ᵇἐμαρτυρήσαμεν ᵇᶜκατὰ τοῦ ᶜΘεοῦ ὅτι 20; Acts
iv. 25.
ᵈἤγειρε τὸν Χριστόν, ὃν οὐκ ᵈἤγειρεν εἴπερ⁵ ἄρα ᵈνεκροὶ οὐκ ᵈἐγεί- ^y See i. 21.
z See iv. 2.
a Mt. xxvi.

60. *Cf.* Acts vi. 13, μαρτ. ψευδεις; -ρειν, Mk. x. 19; -ρια, Mt. xv. 19.   b N.T. *h.l.   Cf.* καταμαρτ.,
Mt. xxvi. 62; also Mk. xiv. 56 f.   For vb., 2 Cor. viii. 3; Rom. iii. 21, x. 2; Gal. iv. 15; Col. iv. 13;
1 Tim. v. 10, vi. 13; in Acts and Heb. freq. in Mt. and Lk. once each; Rev., 4 exx.; Gosp. and Epp.
of Jo. *passim.*   c *Cf.* Acts iv. 26, vi. 13; Mt. xii. 32.   d See vi. 14.   *Cf.* Mt. x. 8, xi. 5; Mk. xii.
26; Lk. vii. 22, x. 37; Jo. v. 21; Acts xxvi. 8.

¹ ℵ*E, with several minn., om. ει ... εστιν, the copyist's eye skipping from ver.
12*b* to ver. 13*a*.   Several such omissions occur, in important ancient copies, in the
duplicated clauses of this context.

² αρα και (?): ℵ*ADgr.GKP, some 25 minn.   So Tisch., Lachm., and Nestle
(*bracket*); Tr. and W.H. *marg.*   See ver. 18.

³ *Om.* δε pre-Syrian uncc. and verss.

⁴ ημων (?): BD*, 17, 67**, sah. basm., Cyr.-Hier., Epiph., Ruf.—witnesses few, but
varied, and forming a strong group.   So W.H. *txt.* and R.V. *marg.*
υμων, as in all other witnesses, R.V. retains in *txt.*, W.H. relegate to *marg.*
Ver. 11 speaks for πιστις υμων.

⁵ ειπερ ... εγειρονται omd. by D, 43, sah. basm. syrsch.; some latt. codd.
ει ... εγειρονται omd. by P, 123, and two chief codd. of vg.   See note 1 above.

Acts xvii. 18, 1 Peter iii. 18, 21, etc.).
For the pf. ἐγήγερται, see ver. 4.—If this
is so, "how (is it that) amongst *you*
some say?"—a crying contradiction,
that Christ is preached as risen and is
so believed by the readers, and yet some
of them say, Ἀνάστασις νεκρῶν οὐκ
ἔστιν, "There is no (such thing as a)
resurrection of dead (men)!" (*cf.* the
modern dogma, "Miracles never happen"),—a sweeping denial of anything of
the kind.   The doctrine of the Sadducees
(Acts xxiii. 8); *cf.*, for the Greeks, out of
countless parls., Æschylus, *Eumen.*, 639,
ἅπαξ θανόντος οὔτις ἐστ' ἀνάστασις.
—The deniers are "some" (not many),
quidam, quos nominare nolo (Mr.: *cf.* 2
Cor. x. 2, etc., Gal. i. 7): "were they
the 'few wise men' of i. 26?" (Ed.).
Their maxim belonged to the current
"wisdom of this age" (i. 20, iii. 19 f.).
—πῶς, of surprised expostulation, as in
Gal. ii. 14; for the emphasis on ἐν ὑμῖν,
cf. John xiv. 9, πῶς σὺ λέγεις;
Ver. 13 opposes (δὲ) the thesis of the
τινὲς by a syllogism in the *modus tollens*
—"sublato genere, tollitur et species"
(Gr.): if bodily resurrection is *per se* impossible, then *there is no risen Christ* (so
Bg., Mr., Al., Bt., Ed., El., etc.); the
abstract universal negative of the deniers
ver. 16 will restate in the concrete.   Hn.
and Gd. (somewhat similarly Cm., Cv.)
hold, on the other hand, that P. is making out the essential connexion between

Christ's rising and that of *the Christian
dead*—in which case he should have
written ἡ ἀνάστασις τῶν νεκρῶν; he
speaks of "the dead *in Christ*" first in
ver. 18.   Hn. and Gd. justly observe
that the τινὲς might have allowed Christ's
resurrection as an exception; but the
point of Paul's argument is that *this is
logically impossible*, that the absolute
philosophical denial of bodily resurrection precludes the raising up of Jesus
Christ; on the other hand, if *He* is risen,
the axiom Ἀνάστασις οὐκ ἔστιν is dis-
proved, the spell of death is broken, and
Christ's rising carries with it that of
those who are "in Christ" (18, 20-23, 1
Thess. iv. 14; *cf.* John xi. 25, Heb. ii. 15).
Vv. 14, 15.   The implicit affirmative
conclusion just intimated P. will develop
afterwards.   He has first to push the
opposing axiom to further consequences:
(1) if the fact is untrue, *the testimony is
untrue*—"But if Christ is not raised, vain
therefore is our proclamation, vain also
your faith".—κενός (see note on οὐ κενή,
10; and *cf.* κενόω, i. 17, etc.) signifies
void, unsubstantial (*inanis*, Vg.)—a hollow witness, a *hollow* belief, while μά-
ταιος (17; see parls.) is "vain" as
ineffectual, frustrate.   For κήρυγμα, see
note on i. 21; on its distinction from
λόγος (2), see ii. 4: ἡμῶν includes P. and
his colleagues (11).   For ἄρα, see v. 10.—
If "the message is empty," declaring a
thing that is not, "the faith is also

e See iii. 20. ρονται¹· 16. εἰ¹ γὰρ ᵈνεκροὶ οὐκ ᵈἐγείρονται,¹ οὐδὲ ᵘΧριστὸς ᵘἐγήγερ-
f Jo. viii. 21.
24, ix. 34. ται· 17. εἰ δὲ ᵘΧριστὸς οὐκ ᵘἐγήγερται, ᵉματαία ἡ πίστις ὑμῶν,² ἔτι³
g See vii. 39.
h 1 Th. iv. ἐστὲ ᶠἐν ταῖς ᶠἁμαρτίαις ὑμῶν· 18. ἄρα καὶ οἱ ᵍʰ κοιμηθέντες ʰ ἐν
16. Cf. i. 2.

¹ ειπερ . . . εγειρονται omd. by D, 43, sah. basm. syrsch.; some latt. cod.
ει . . . εγειρονται omd. by P, 123, and two chief codd. of vg. See note 3 above.

² Ins. εστιν (?): BD*. Lachm. and W.H. *bracket*. If original, easily dropped in
view of ver. 14.

³ και ετι: ℵ*A, 31, sah. basm. syrsch.; vg., *adhuc enim*. οτι ετι, 37, 43, Tert.
τι ετι, d e (*quid adhuc*).

empty," building on the thing that is
not; preaching and faith have no genuine
content; the Gospel is evacuated of all
reality.—For the character of P. and his
fellow-witnesses this conclusion has a
serious aspect: "We are found moreover (to be) false witnesses of God"—
men who have given *lying* testimony,
and that about *God*, "the worst sort of
impostors" (Gd.)! τοῦ Θεοῦ is objective
gen., as the next clause shows; it is
always "God" to whom P. imputes the
raising of Christ, who by this act gave
His verdict concerning Jesus (Rom. i. 4,
Gal. i. 1, Eph. i. 20; Acts ii. 36, xiii.
30-39, xvii. 31).—δὲ καὶ calls emphatic
attention to another and contrasted side
of the matter in hand.—εὑρισκόμεθα approaches the sense of ἐλεγχόμεθα or
ἁλισκόμεθα (see parls.)—"discovered"
in a false and guilty position.—Nothing
can be stronger evidence than this passage to the objective reality, in Paul's
experience, of the risen form of Jesus.
The suspicion of *hallucination*, on his
own part or that of the other witnesses,
was foreign to his mind; the matter
stood on the plain footing of testimony,
given by a large number of intelligent,
sober, and responsible witnesses to a
sensible, concrete, circumstantial fact:
"Either He rose from the grave, or we
lied in affirming it"—the dilemma admits
of no escape.—ὅτι ἐμαρτυρήσαμεν κ.τ.λ.:
"in that we testified against God that
He raised up the Christ—whom He did
not raise, if indeed then (as 'some'
affirm) dead (men) are not raised up".
κατὰ τ. Θεοῦ, *adversus Deum* (Vg., Est.,
Mr., Hn., Gd., Ed., Sm.), as always in
such connexion in N.T. (see iv. 6 and
parls.), not *de Deo* (Er., Bz., Al., El.,
A.V.); the falsehood (*ex hyp*.) would
have *wronged* God, as, *e.g.*, the ascription
of miracles to God traduces Him in the
eyes of Deists.—ἤγειρε τὸν Χριστόν,
"the Messiah," whom "according to
the Scriptures" (3 f.; *cf*. Luke xxiv. 46,
Acts xvii. 3, xxvi. 22 f., etc.) God was

bound to raise from the dead.—εἴπερ
ἄρα, *si videlicet* (Bz.), *supposing to be
sure;* see viii. 5; and v. 10, for ἄρα.

Ver. 16 restates the position of the
τινές (13; see note), in order to press it
to another, even more intolerable conclusion: (1) vv. 14, 15 proved *the witness
untrue*, if the fact is unreal; (2) vv. 17,
18 conclude *the effects unreal*, if the fact
is unreal.

Vv. 17, 18 unfold this latter consequence in a form parl. to the former: εἰ
δὲ . . . ἄρα (14). For ματαία (syn. with
ἀργή, James ii. 20; with ἀνωφελεῖς,
Tit. iii. 9), see note on κενόν (14); a
faith is "frustrate," "null and void,"
which does not *save from sin;* now
"Christ died for our sins" (3), but His
resurrection makes His death valid, pub-
lishing it to men as accepted by God
and availing for redemption (Rom. iv.
25, viii. 33 f., x. 9; Luke xxiv. 46 f.;
Acts xiii. 32-38—observe the γνωστὸν
οὖν ἔστω); it is hereby that "God *gives*
the victory" over both sin and death (57).
In Christ's resurrection is the seal of our
justification, and the spring of our sanctification (Rom. vi. 4-11); both are wanting, if He is still in the grave. The absence
of both is implied in being "yet in your
sins"—unforgiven, unrenewed. Now this
is contrary to experience (i. 30, vi. 11);
the Cor. readers *know* themselves to be
saved men, as Paul and the App. know
themselves to be honest men (15). P.
leaves the inference, which observes the
strict method of the *modus tollens*, to the
consciousness of his readers (*cf*. 20):
"We are true witnesses, you are redeemed believers; on both accounts it
is certain that Christ has risen,—and
therefore that there is a resurrection of
the dead".—A further miserable consequence of the negative dogma emerges
from the last: ἄρα καὶ οἱ κοιμηθέντες . . .
ἀπώλοντο. "Then also those that were
laid to sleep in Christ perished!"—
perished (ptp. and vb. both aor.) when
we laid them to rest, and with the

h Χριστῷ ⁱ ἀπώλοντο· 19. εἰ ἐν τῇ ᵏ ζωῇ ταύτῃ ¹ᵐ ἠλπικότες

ἐσμὲν ¹ ¹ ἐν Χριστῷ ¹ μόνον, ⁿ ἐλεεινότεροι πάντων ἀνθρώπων ἐσμέν.

20. Νυνὶ δὲ ᵒ Χριστὸς ᵒ ἐγήγερται ᵒ ἐκ νεκρῶν, ᵖ ἀπαρχὴ τῶν

l i See viii.
11.
k Phil. i. 20;
Jas. iv. 14;
1 Pet. iii.
10 (Psa.
xxxiii.

12). l Eph. i. 12; 4 Kings xviii. 5; cf. ελπιζ. εις, 2 Cor. i. 10. m Pf., 2 Cor. i. 10; 1 Tim. iv. 10,
v. 5, vi. 17; Jo. v. 45. n Rev. iii. 17; for compar. with παντων, see xiii. 13. o See vv. 4 and 12.
p xvi. 15; Rom. viii. 23, xi. 16, xvi. 5; 2 Th. ii. 13 (?); Jas. i. 18; Rev. xiv. 4; Exod. xxiii. 19, etc.

¹ εν Χριστω ηλπικοτες εσμεν (in this order)|: all pre-Syrian uncc.

"perishing" which befalls those "yet in their sins" (cf. i. 18, viii. 11, Rom. ii. 12, vi. 23, etc.; also John viii. 21, 24). They were "put to sleep *in Christ*" (cf. 1 Thess. iv. 14), as the sense of His presence and the promises of His gospel turned their death into sleep (John xi. 11, etc.). The ματαιότης of being lulled to sleep when falling into utter ruin! They thought "the sting of death" drawn (56), and lay down to rest untroubled: cruelly deceived! For the unclassical position of ἄρα, see Wr., p. 699.

Ver. 19 expresses the infinite bitterness of such a deception. In the right order of words (see txtl. note), μόνον is attached to ἠλπικότες (cf. Luke xxiv. 21): "If in this life we have *only* had *hope* in Christ"—no present deliverance from sin, no future inheritance in heaven— "we are more than all men to be pitied". For a hope without legitimate basis or ultimate fruition, Christians have sacrificed all material good! (cf. 30 ff., iv. 11 ff.; Heb. x. 32-46, Luke xviii. 22, etc.). ἠλπικότες ἐσμὲν = ἠλπίκαμεν (1 Tim. iv. 10), with stress laid on the actual condition of those who have formed this futile hope. ἐν Χριστῷ points to Christ as the *ground* of Christian hope (cf. Phil. ii. 19). ἐν τῇ ζωῇ ταύτῃ brings to mind all that the Christian forfeits here and now—losing "this life" for the vain promise of another, letting earth go in grasping at a fancied heaven; no wonder the world pities us!—Ed. *ad loc.* answers well the censure passed on the Ap., as though he made the worth of goodness depend on its future reward: (1) P. does not say "we are more *worthless*"—a good man may be very "pitiable," and all the more because of his worth; (2) on Paul's hypothesis (17), moral character is undermined, while future happiness is destroyed, by denial of the Resurrection.

§ 52. THE FIRSTFRUIT OF THE RESURRECTION AND THE HARVEST, xv. 20-28. Paul has proved the actuality of Christ's personal resurrection by the abundant and truthful testimony to the fact (5-15), and by the experimental reality of its effects (17). In ver. 20a he therefore affirms it unconditionally, having overthrown the contrary assertion that "there is no resurrection of the dead." But Christ never stands alone; He forms "a body" with "many members" (xii. 12); He is "firstborn among many brothers" (Rom. viii. 29, Col. i. 18, John xv. 5, etc.). His rising shows that bodily resurrection is possible; nay, it is *inevitable* for those who are in Him (18, 20b, 23). In truth, the universal redemption of Christ's people from the grave is *indispensable* for the realisation of human destiny and for the assured triumph of God's kingdom (24-28). The Ap. thus advances from the experimental (§ 51) to the theological proof of his theorem, much as in Rom. v. 1-11, 12-21.

Ver. 20. Νυνὶ δέ (cf. xii. 18) marks the logical point P. has reached by the *reductio ad impossibile* of the negative proposition attacked in ver. 12. Christ has been raised; therefore there is a resurrection of the dead (12-18): "now" the ground is cleared and the foundation laid for the declaration that *the Christian dead shall rise in Him*—"Christ has been raised from the dead, *a firstfruit of them that have fallen asleep*"; He has risen in this character and purpose, "not to remain alone in His estate of glory" (Gd.).—ἀπαρχὴ τῶν κεκοιμημένων (pf. of abiding state: cf. John xi. 11 f., Matt. xxvii. 52) = ἀρχή, πρωτότοκος ἐκ τῶν νεκρῶν and πρωτότοκος τῶν νεκρῶν (Col. i. 18, Rev. i. 5).—Cm. and Bg. are surely right in seeing here an allusion to the first harvest-sheaf (ἀπαρχὴν του θερισμοῦ ὑμῶν, Lev. xxiii. 10: cf. in this connexion Matt. xiii. 39 ff. with John v. 28 f. and Rev. xiv. 14 ff.) of the Passover, which was presented in the Sanctuary on the 16th Nisan, probably the day of the resurrection of Jesus; this allusion is in the Easter strain of v. 6 ff. (see notes). The first ripe sheaf is an earnest and sample of the harvest, consecrated to God and laid up with Him (cf. Rom. vi. 10 f.) in anticipation of the rest. The Resurrection has begun.

Vv. 21, 22 explain the identification of

q See vii. 39.
r See i. 21.
s See ver. 12.
t xi. 12, xvi. 1; 5 exx. in Rom.; Gal. iv. 29; Jas. ii. 26; Jo. v. 21, 26.
u vii. 14; 2 Cor. v. 19; Gal. ii. 17; Eph. i. 4, iii. 11; Acts iv. 2.
v Rom. iv. 17, viii. 11; Jo. v. 21; 4 Ki. v. 7.
w N.T. h.l.; 1 Ki. iv. 10; 2 Ki. xxiii. 13. See -ξις, xiv. 40.

q κεκοιμημένων ἐγένετο.¹ 21. ʳ ἐπειδὴ γὰρ δι᾽ ἀνθρώπου ὁ² θάνατος, καὶ δι᾽ ἀνθρώπου ˢ ἀνάστασις ˢ νεκρῶν· 22. ᵗ ὥσπερ γὰρ ᵘ ἐν τῷ Ἀδὰμ πάντες ἀποθνήσκουσιν, ᵗ οὕτω ᵗ καὶ ᵘ ἐν τῷ Χριστῷ πάντες ᵛ ζωοποιηθήσονται· 23. ἕκαστος δὲ ἐν τῷ ἰδίῳ ʷ τάγματι· ᵖ ἀπαρχὴ

---

¹ Om. ΕΓΕΝΕΤΟ all pre-Syrian witnesses.   ² Om. ο ℵABD*K, 17, 67.**

---

the risen Christ with those sleeping in death, which was assumed by the word ἀπαρχή. It rests on the fact that Christ is the antitype of Adam, the medium of life to the race as Adam was of death. This parl. is resumed in vv. 46 ff., where it is applied to *the nature of the resurrection body*, as here to *the universality of the resurrection*. These two passages form the complement of Rom. v. 12-21; the antithesis of Adam and Christ—who represent *flesh, trespass, death* and *spirit, righteousness, life* respectively—is thus extended over the entire career of the race viewed as a history of sin and redemption.—" For since through man (there is) death, through man also (there is) a resurrection of the dead": δι᾽ ἀνθρώπου, "through a man (*qua* man)"—*through human means* or *mediation*. For ἐπειδὴ, *quandoquidem* (Cv.), see i. 21 f.; the first fact necessitated and shaped the second: *man* was the channel conveying death to his kind (Rom. v. 12), through the same channel the counter current must flow (Rom. v. 15, etc.).—This goes deeper than ἀπαρχή; Christ is the ἀρχή, the principle and root of resurrection-life (Col. i. 18).—"*Through* man" implies that Death is not, as philosophy supposed, a law of finite being or a necessity of fate; it is an event of history, a calamity brought by man upon himself and capable of removal by the like means. —ὥσπερ γὰρ ἐν τῷ Ἀδὰμ κ.τ.λ.: "For just as in the Adam all die, so also in the Christ all will be made alive". The foregoing double δι᾽ ἀνθρώπου opens out into " the (representative) Adam and Christ"—the natural and spiritual, earthly and heavenly counterparts (45 ff.), the two types and founders of humanity, paralleled by ὥσπερ . . . καὶ οὕτως (*cf.* Rom. v. 12 ff.).—The stress of the comparison does not lie on πάντες, as though the Ap. meant to say that "*all* (men)" will rise in Christ as certainly as they die in Adam (so, with variations, Or., Cm., Cv., Mr., Gd., Sm., El., referring

to John v. 28 f., Acts xxiv. 15): as Bt. says, the absence of ἄνθρωποι tells against such ref. to the *race* (contrast Rom. v. 12, 18), also the use of ζωοποιέω (see below). The point is that as death in all cases is *grounded in Adam*, so life in all cases is *grounded in Christ* (*cf.* John vi. 53, xi. 25)—no death without the one, no life without the other (Aug., Bg., Hf., Ed., Hn., Bt.). πάντες = οἱ πολλοί (Rom. v. 18 f.), as set in contrast with ὁ εἷς ἄνθρωπος.—Ζωοποιέω is narrower in extension than ἐγείρω (20), since the latter applies to every one raised from the grave (15 f., 35); wider in intension, as it imports not the mere raising of the body, but restoration to " life " in the full sense of the term (Hf.; *cf.* 45, Rom. vi. 8, viii. 11; John v. 21, vi. 63),—an ἀνάστασιν ζωῆς (John v. 29). A firm and broad basis is now shown to exist for the solidarity between Christ and the holy dead (οἱ κεκοιμημένοι) affirmed in ver. 20.

Ver. 23. But ἀπαρχὴ implies *difference* in agreement, distinction in order along with unity in nature and determining principle. Hence the added qualification, ἕκαστος δὲ ἐν τῷ ἰδίῳ τάγματι, κ.τ.λ.: " But each in his proper rank— Christ (as) firstfruit; thereafter, at His coming, the (people) of Christ ". τάγμα signifies a military *division* (*cf.* xiv. 40). There are two τάγματα (*cf.* Matt. xiii. 8) of the resurrection host; the Captain (ὁ ἀρχηγός, Heb. ii. 10; *cf.* ἀπαρχὴ above), in His solitary glory; and the rest of the army now sleeping, to rise at His trumpet's sound (52, 1 Thess. iv. 16).—It is incongruous to make a third τάγμα out of τὸ τέλος (ver. 24) as Bg. and Mr. would do, paraphrasing this as " the *last act* (of the resurrection),"— *viz.*, the resurrection *of non-Christians*. *Their* introduction is irrelevant: P. has proved the resurrection of Christ, and is now making out that the resurrection of His sleeping ones is bound up with His own. *Christ and Christians* are the participants in the resurrection of life. ἔπειτα, opp. of πρῶτον (*cf.* 46) implied

Χριστός, ἔπειτα ˣοἱ ˣΧριστοῦ¹ ʸἐν τῇ ʸπαρουσίᾳ αὐτοῦ². 24. ˣFor gen.
constr.,
ᶻεἶτα τὸ ᵃτέλος, ὅταν ᵇπαραδῷ³ τὴν ᶜβασιλείαν τῷ ᵈΘεῷ καὶ see i. 12.
ʸ1 Th. ii.
ᵈπατρί, ὅταν ᵉκαταργήσῃ πᾶσαν ᶠἀρχὴν καὶ πᾶσαν ᶠἐξουσίαν καὶ 19, iii. 13,
v. 23; 1
Jo. ii. 28.

The noun freq. with this ref. *Cf.* xvi. 17.   z Single, in temp. sense, Jas. i. 15; Mk. iv. 17, viii.
25; Lk. viii. 12; Jo. xiii. 5, xix. 27, xx. 27.   a 1 Pet. iv. 7; Mt. xxiv. 6, 14. See i. 8.   b *Cf.*
Mt. xi. 27; Lk. iv. 6.   c See iv. 20.   Abs., Acts xx. 25; Lk. xii. 32, xix. 15; Rev. i. 6, v. 10.
d 2 Cor. i. 3, xi. 31; Rom. xv. 6; Gal. i. 4; Eph. i. 3, iii. 14; Col. i. 3; 1 Pet. i. 3; Rev. i. 6.   e See
i. 28.   f All three, Eph. i. 21. αρχ. and εξουσ., Eph. iii. 10, vi. 12; Col. i. 16, ii. 10, 15; Tit. iii. 1.
αρχ. and δυν., Rom. viii. 38. εξουσ. and δυν., 1 Pet. iii. 22; Rev. xvii. 13.

¹ τοῦ Χριστοῦ: all Gr. MSS.   The early printed texts omᵈ. τοῦ by error.

² Ins. ελπισαντες (οι εν τη παρουσια αυτου ελπισαντες): G, with several latt. codd.,
Hil., Ambrst.,—also *qui in adventu ejus crediderunt;* instances of Western license.

³ παραδιδῷ (?), 𝔑ADP, 67**.   Or παραδιδοι (?), BG.; so Lachm. *txt.* and
Tr. *txt.,* Nestle, R.V.   See Wr., p. 360; Bm., p. 46.

in ἀπαρχὴ, is defined by ἐν τῇ παρουσίᾳ. Some attach the latter phrase to οἱ τοῦ Χριστοῦ, referring it to the *first* advent; but Christ's παρουσία in the N.T. always signifies His *future* coming. There is nothing to exclude O.T. saints (see x. 4; Heb. xi. 26, 40, John i. 11), nor even the righteous heathen (Acts x. 35, Matt. xxv. 32, 34, John x. 16), from the τάγμα of "those who are Christ's".

Ver. 24. εἶτα τὸ τέλος: "*Then* (is) the end"—sc., "at His coming". Christ's advent, attended with the resurrection of His redeemed to eternal life, concludes the world's history; then "the harvest" which is "the end of the world" (Matt. xiii. 39 f., 49; *cf.* Rev. xiv. 15 f.), "the end of all things" (1 Pet. iv. 7), the dénoûment of the drama of sin and redemption in which "the Adam" and "the Christ" have played out their respective parts, the limit of the human horizon.—As ἔπειτα was defined by ἐν τῇ παρουσίᾳ, so εἶτα by the two ὅταν clauses: "when He yields up the kingdom to His God and Father, when He has abolished every rule and every authority and power". The two vbs. denote distinct, but connected and complementary acts. παραδιδῷ (the reading παραδιδοῖ is sbj., not opt.: Bm., p. 46) is *pr.* sbj., signifying a proceeding, contingent in its date and manner of occurrence, but concurrent with εἶτα, which again rests upon ἐν τ. παρουσίᾳ. The aor. sbj. καταργήσῃ (Lat. *futurum exactum*) signalises an event lying behind the παραδιδῷ and by its nature antecedent thereto, —"when He shall have done away, etc."; every opposing force has been destroyed, *then* Christ lays at the Father's feet His kingdom. "Cum *tradat* (not *tradiderit:* so Vg., reading παραδῷ) regnum, etc., cum evacuerit omnem princi-

patum, etc."—The title τῷ Θεῷ καὶ πατρί, "to Him who is God and Father," contains the reason for this παράδοσις: Christ's one aim was to glorify the Father (Luke ii. 49, John iv. 34, vi. 38, xvii. 4, etc.); this end was reached proximately at the cross (John xix. 30), and will be so ultimately when our Lord, having "subdued all things to Himself" (Phil. iii. 21), is able to present to the Father a realm dominated by His will and filled with His obedient sons (*cf.* Matt. vi. 9 f.). This is no ceasing of Christ's rule, but the inauguration of *God's* eternal kingdom: παραδιδῷ does not connote the *losing* of anything (see John xvii. 10); it is just the rendering to another of what is designed for Him (*cf.* 3, v. 5, Rom. viii. 32, Luke iv. 6, x. 22, etc.). "The end" does not mean the termination of *Christ's sovereignty,* which in its largest sense began before the world (John i. 1-3, xvii. 5) and is its goal (Col. i. 16); but the termination of *the reign of sin and death* (Rom. v. 21; *cf.* John vi. 37 ff.). At the συντέλεια "the throne of God and of the Lamb," "the kingdom of Christ and of God," fills the N.T. horizon (Eph. v. 5, Rev. xi. 15, xxii. 3).—ἀρχὴν, ἐξουσίαν κ.τ.λ., should not be limited (with Ff. generally, Est., Ed., Gd., El., Sm.; Everling, *Paulin. Angelol. u.s.w.,* p. 44, in view of Eph. i. 21, vi. 12, Col. ii. 15, etc.) to *angelic powers,* or *demons;* nor (as by Cv., Gr.: *cf.* ii. 6) to *earthly rulers:* πᾶσαν ... πᾶσαν ... (see πάντας τοὺς ἐχθροὺς, 25; πάντα ὑπέταξεν, 27; also Rom. viii. 37-39) embraces *all* forces oppugnant to God (Bg., Cr., Hn., Hf., Bt.), on earth or above it, whether they exercise *princely sway* (ἀρχὴν) or *moral authority* (ἐξουσίαν) or *active power* (δύναμιν). Death is a βασιλεὺς amongst these (Rom. v.

g See viii. 2. f δύναμιν· 25. g δεῖ γὰρ αὐτὸν h βασιλεύειν i ἄχρις i οὗ ἂν l k θῇ
h See iv. 8.
i See xi. 26. πάντας τοὺς k ἐχθροὺς 2 ὑπὸ τοὺς πόδας αὐτοῦ· 26.3 ἔσχατος ἐχθρὸς
k Ps. cix. 1 ;
l Acts ii. 35 ; e καταργεῖται ὁ θάνατος.   27. "1 πάντα" γὰρ "ὑπέταξεν ὑπὸ τοὺς
  Heb. i. 13,
x. 13 ; Mt. πόδας αὐτοῦ·" 3 ὅταν δὲ εἴπῃ ὅτι 4 "1 πάντα ὑποτέτακται" (m δῆλον
xxii. 44.
Ps. viii. 6.
In like connexion, Eph. i. 22 ; Phil. iii. 21 ; Heb. ii. 8 ; 1 Pet. iii. 22 ; see xiv. 32.   m Gal. iii. 11.

1 Om. αν all pre-Syrian codd. Cf. xi. 26.

2 Insert αυτου AG, 17, sah. cop. syrsch.

3 א*, 17, om. εσχατος . . . ποδας αυτου (26, 27a), by skipping from the ποδας
αυτου of ver. 25. See notes on vv. 13-16.

4 Om. οτι (?) B d e, vg., and several Ff. Lachm. brackets ; W.H. om. in marg.

14); and behind death Satan (Heb. ii. 14 f.), "the prince" and "god of this world" (2 Cor. iv. 4, John xiv. 30). On καταργέω, see note to i. 28.

Ver. 25 sustains the representation of the τέλος just given by prophetic words of Scripture (cf. 3 f.): "For He must needs reign, until He has put all the enemies underneath His feet". Not till every enemy of God is vanquished can Christ's existing kingdom reach its end. P. is thinking of the culmination, not the cessation, of Christ's kingship (see note on παραδιδῷ, 24).—πάντας is added to the text of the Psalmist, as if to say: "Every one of the foes proscribed in the Messiah's charter must submit, before He can present to His Father a perfect kingdom"; see parls., for other applications of this cardinal O.T. dictum.—On δεῖ, see note to viii. 2.—ἄχρις οὗ—radically "up to," rather than "until, (the time at) which"—in later Gr. takes sbj. of future contingency dispensing with ἄν (Wr., p. 371).—The words of Ps. cx. are freely adapted: θῇ gets its subject from αὐτόν, viz. Christ—not God, as imported by Est., Bz., Bg., Hf., Gd., to suit the Ps.; it is parl. in tense-construction to καταργήσῃ (24, see note).

Ver. 26. ἔσχατος ἐχθρὸς καταργεῖται ὁ θάνατος : "(As) last enemy death is abolished"—in other words, "is abolished last among these enemies".—ἔσχατος is the emphatic part of the predicate; and καταργ. (see i. 28) is in pr. tense, of what is true now in God's determination, in the fixed succession of things (cf. iii. 13). Death personified, as in ver. 55, Isa. xxv. 8, Rev. xx. 14. If all enemies must be subdued, and death is last to fall, then "the end" (24) cannot be until Christ has delivered His own from its power and thus broken Death's sceptre.—This ver. should close with a full stop. Καταργεῖται ὁ θάνατος is the Christian counter-position to the Ἀνάσ-

τασις οὐκ ἔστιν of Cor. philosophy; the τινὲς of ver. 12 say, "There is no resurrection"; P. replies, "There is to be no death". The dogma of unbelief has been confuted in fact by Christ's bodily resurrection (13 ff.); in experience, by the saving effect thereof in Christians (17); and now finally in principle, by its contrariety to the purpose and scope of redemption (21-26), which finds its goal in the death of Death. Hofmann makes τὸ τέλος in ver. 24 adverbial to ver. 26 ("at last," cf. 1 Peter iii. 8), with the ὅταν clauses as its definitions and the γὰρ clause parenthetical: "then finally, when etc., when etc. (for etc.), as last enemy death is abolished". His construction is too artificial to be sustained; but he sees rightly that this ver. is the climax of the Apostle's argument.

Vv. 27, 28 are a supplement to vv. 20-26. They reaffirm, in new words of Scripture, the unlimited dominion assigned to Christ (25-27a), in order to reassert more impressively the truth that only through His absolute victory can the kingdom of God be consummated (24a, 28b). The opening γὰρ adduces, by way of comment, a prophecy parl. to that cited in ver. 25 and specifically applied in ver. 26. Psalm viii. promised to man complete rule over his domain (cf. Heb. ii. 5 ff.); as man Christ here stands forth the countertype of Adam (21 f.) who forfeited our estate, winning for Himself and His own the deliverance from death (Heb. ii. 9, 14 f.) which seals His conquest and sets "all things under His feet". But (δὲ . . . δὲ) this subjection of all things to Christ is no infringement of God's sovereignty nor alienation of His rights; on the contrary, it is the means to their perfect realisation. Such is the purport of the two ὅταν sentences, the second of which repeats in another way, after the interposed δῆλον ὅτι clause, what the first has announced, τότε αὐτὸς

ᵐὅτι ⁿἐκτὸς τοῦ ¹ὑποτάξαντος αὐτῷ τὰ ¹πάντα), 28. ὅταν ¹ δὲ ¹ὑποταγῇ
αὐτῷ τὰ πάντα,¹ τότε καὶ ² αὐτὸς ὁ υἱὸς ¹ὑποταγήσεται τῷ ¹ὑποτά-
ξαντι αὐτῷ τὰ ¹πάντα, ἵνα °ᾖ ὁ Θεὸς τὰ ³ °ᵖπάντα ° ἐν ᵖπᾶσιν.

ⁿ In this sense, Acts xxvi. 22 ; Isa. xxvi. 13. *Cf.* vi. 18, and xiv. 5.

o Col. iii. 11 ; Herod., iii., 157, παντα ην εν τοις Βαβυλωνιοισι Ζωπυρος (Al.).   p See xii. 6.

¹ οταν . . . παντα omd. by א*, and a few others, skipping from τ. παντα of ver. 27.
² Om. και BDG, 17, 67**, latt. vg.   Lachm. and W.H. *bracket ;* Tr. omits.
³ *Om.* τα ABD*, 17.   So Lachm., Tr., W.H., Nestle.   Tisch. retains.

ὁ υἱὸς furnishing their common apodosis
(*cf.* 54) ; so Hf., R.V. marg., after the Vg.
and Lat. interpreters.   The two vv. then
read as follows : "For 'all things did He
put in subjection under His feet'.   But
when He hath said, 'All things are
brought to subjection' (manifestly, with
the exception of Him that put all things
in subjection to Him)—yea, when all
things have become subject to Him, then
shall (also) the Son Himself become subject to Him that made subject to Him all
things, to the end that God may be all
in all".—*God* is the tacit subject of
ὑπέταξεν, as supplied by the familiar Ps.
and brought out by the ptps. in vv. 27*b*,
28*b* ; but *Christ* is subject to εἴπῃ—not
God speaking in Scr., or at the end of
the world (so Mr., Ed., El., etc.), nor ἡ
γραφή (D.W., and others), nor *propheta*
(Bg.).   "All things are subdued!" is the
joyful announcement *by the Son* that the
grand promise recorded in the 8th Psalm
is fulfilled ; "the ὑπέταξεν of God affirms
the purpose, the ὑποτέτακται of Christ
attests its accomplishment" (Hf., Hn.).
Thus ὅταν εἴπῃ is simultaneous with
ὅταν καταργήσῃ (24) and ὅταν θῇ ὑπὸ τ.
πόδας (25) : Christ proclaims the victory
at last achieved ; He reports that, with
the abolition of death, His commission is
ended and the travail of His soul satisfied.   For anticipatory sayings of His,
giving an earnest of this crowning word,
see Matt. xi. 27, xxviii. 18, John iii. 35.—
ὅταν ὑποταγῇ κ.τ.λ. (28) reassumes objectively, as matter of fact, what was
given subjectively in ὅταν εἴπῃ κ.τ.λ. as
the verdict of Christ upon His own
finished work.   Those who read δῆλον
ὅτι κ.τ.λ. as a principal sentence, the
apodosis to the first ὅταν clause (A.V.,
Mr., El., etc.), borrow from the protasis
πάντα ὑποτέτακται—more strictly ὑπο-
τετάξεται or (by zeugma) ἔσται, after
the virtually fut. εἴπῃ (*cf.* 28*b*, 54*b*) ; this,
however, makes a halting sentence :
"But when He [God] says, 'All things
have been made subject,' it is evident
[that this will be, *or* that all things will

be subjected] with the exception of Him,
etc."—an affirmation of quite subsidiary
importance, on which the writer has no
need to dwell.   The non-inclusion of
God in the category of "things subjected" is rather a self-evident assumption made by the way, and serving to
prepare for and throw into relief the real
apodosis, "then shall the Son Himself
also become subject, etc.," to which both
the ὅταν clauses press forward.   The
advl. use of δῆλον ὅτι (perhaps better
written δηλονότι = δηλαδή), signifying
manifestly or *to wit* (*sine dubio*, Vg.), is
familiar in Attic Gr. ; no other certain
instance occurs in the N.T.   The remark
that He who *gave* dominion is not Himself *under* it, reserves behind the Messianic reign the absolute supremacy of
God, to which Christ will conform at the
plenitude of His kingship.—τὰ πάντα
(equivalent to "the universe") gathers
into a totality the πάντα otherwise
separate and diverse : *cf.* Col. i. 17, τὰ
πάντα ἐν αὐτῷ συνέστηκεν.—ὑποταγήσεται (mid. in force, like the 2nd aor.
pass. in Rom. x. 3, in consistency with
the initiative ascribed to Christ throughout) has often been explained away, to
avoid Arian or Sabellian inferences from
the text ; it affirms no other subjection
of the Son than is involved in Sonship
(see note on 24).   This implies no inferiority of nature, no extrusion from
power, but the free submission of love
(αὐτὸς ὁ υἱός, "the Son of His own
accord will subject Himself"—not in
addition to, but in distinction from the
πάντα), which is the essence of the filial
spirit that actuated Christ from first to
last (*cf.* John viii. 29, xii. 27, etc.).
Whatsoever glory He gains is devoted
to the glory and power of the Father
(John xvii. 2, etc.), who glorifies Him
in turn (John xvii. 5 ; Phil. ii. 9 ff.).
ὑποταγήσεται speaks the closing word
of Christ's mission, as Ἰδοὺ ἥκω τοῦ
ποιῆσαι τὸ θέλημά σου was its opening
word (Heb. x. 7).—It is hard to say
whether ἵνα ᾖ ὁ Θεὸς κ.τ.λ. is dependent

q See v. 10.
r Acts xxi.
13; Mk.
xi. 5; Jo.
xi. 47; in
LXX, Jer.
iv. 30, v.
31; Hos. ix. 5.

29. [q] [r]Ἐπεὶ [r]τί [r]ποιήσουσιν οἱ βαπτιζόμενοι[1] ὑπὲρ τῶν νεκρῶν,[1] εἰ [s]ὅλως [t]νεκροὶ οὐκ [t]ἐγείρονται[1]; [u]τί [u]καὶ βαπτίζονται ὑπὲρ τῶν[2] νεκρῶν[2]; 30. [u]τί [u]καὶ ἡμεῖς [v]κινδυνεύομεν [w]πᾶσαν [w]ὥραν;

s See v. 1.　　t See ver. 15.　　　u Here and Rom. viii. 24 (?) only.　　v Acts xix.
27, 40; Lk. viii. 23 (abs. as here); Isa. xxviii. 13; Jonah i. 4; -νος, 2 Cor. xi. 26.　　w N.T. h.l.;
Ex. xviii. 22, 26; Lev. xvi. 2. Cf. Rom. viii. 36.

[1] Lachm., Tisch., Al., W.H., El., Nestle, and others, place the *interrog*. sign *after* νεκρων, attaching εἰ ολως κ.τ.λ. to the following sentence. Tr. puts it as far back as βαπτιζομενοι. See note below.

[2] αυτων, all uncc. but DcL.

on ὁ υἱὸς ὑποταγήσεται (so most commentt.) or on τ. ὑποτάξαντι (so Hf., and some others). This solemn conclusion most fitly attaches to the princ. vb.; it expresses the loyal *purpose of the Son* in His self-subjection, whose submission exhibits the unity of the Godhead (*cf.* John x. 30-36, xvii. 23), and constitutes itself the focus and uniting bond of a universe in which God's will is everywhere regnant and His being everywhere immanent.—πᾶσιν *neuter*, like πάντα.

§ 53. THE EFFECT OF UNBELIEF IN THE RESURRECTION, xv. 29-34. To clinch the argument for the truth and the necessity of the Christian resurrection and to bring it home to the readers, the Ap. points out how futile Christian devotion must be, such as is witnessed in "those baptised for the dead" and in his own daily hazards, if death ends all (29-31); present enjoyment would then appear the highest good (32). The effect of unbelief in the future life is already painfully apparent in the relaxed moral tone of a certain part of the Cor. Church (33 f.).

Vv. 29, 30. There are certain conditions of interpretation bearing on the sense of the much discussed expression οἱ βαπτιζόμενοι ὑπὲρ τῶν νεκρῶν which bar out a large number of attempted explanations: (*a*) οἱ βαπτιζόμενοι, unless otherwise defined, can only mean *the recipients of Christian baptism*, in its well-understood sense as the rite of initiation into the Christian state administered upon confession of faith (i. 13 ff., xii. 13, Rom. vi. 3 f., Gal. iii. 27, etc.). (*b*) ὑπὲρ τῶν νεκρῶν (not ὑπὲρ νεκρῶν, "on behalf of dead persons" as such: *cf*. 12, etc.) points to *a specific class of* "*the dead*" interested in the baptism of the living—presumably to "the (Christian) dead" of the last §, and probably to those amongst them who were connected with "the baptised" in question. (*c*) In following up ver. 29 with the words of

ver. 30 (τί καὶ ἡμεῖς κινδυνεύομεν;) P. *associates himself with the action of* "those baptised for the dead," indicating that they and he are engaged on the same behalf (for καὶ ἡμεῖς associating "we" with persons aforementioned, *cf*. 2 Cor. iv. 13, Gal. ii. 16, iv. 3, Eph. ii. 3, etc.). This last consideration excludes the interpretation, at present widely adopted (Ambrst., Anselm, Grot., Mr., Holsten, Al., Hn., Bt., El., Sm.), that P. alludes to a practice then (it is conjectured) in vogue at Cor., which existed much later amongst the heretical Cerinthians and Marcionites (see Cm. *ad loc.* in Cramer's *Catena; Tert., De Resurr. Carnis*, 48, *adv. Marc.*, v., 10; Epiph., *Hær.*, xxxviii., 6), *viz*., that of the *vicarious baptism* of living Christians as proxies for relatives or friends dying unbaptised. With such a proceeding P. could not have identified himself, even supposing that it existed at this time in the Church (of which there is no evidence), and that he had used it by way of *argumentum ad hominem*. An appeal to such a superstitious *opus operatum* would have laid the Ap. open to a damaging retort. Gd. justly asks, ' A quoi eût servi ce procédé de mauvaise logique et de bonne foi douteuse ? " This objection tells less forcibly against the view, lately suggested, that P. alludes to *some practice of substitutionary baptism observed in the Pagan mysteries*, finding thus a witness to the Resurrection in the heathen conscience, καὶ ἡμεῖς adding thereto the Christian practical testimony; but condition (*a*) forbids this solution. As El. admits, condition (*b*) also bears strongly against the prevalent exposition. (*b*) moreover negatives the idea of Cm. and the Gr. Ff., maintained by Est. and Ev. (see the ingenious *Addit. Note* of the latter), that ὑπὲρ τῶν νεκρῶν means, as Thp. puts it, ὑπὲρ ἀναστάσεως, ἐπὶ προσδοκίᾳ ἀναστάσεως: if P. meant this, why did he not say it? The fol-

31. ˣ καθ᾽ ˣ ἡμέραν ἀποθνῄσκω, ʸ νὴ τὴν ᶻ ὑμετέραν ¹ ᵃ καύχησιν ² ἣν ˣ 2 Cor. xi.
ᵃ ἔχω ᵃ ἐν Χριστῷ Ἰησοῦ τῷ Κυρίῳ ἡμῶν· 32. εἰ ᵇ κατὰ ᵇ ἄνθρωπον

in Heb.;
28; thrice
13 exx. in
Lk. and

Acts; Mt. xxvi. 55.   y N.T. *h.l.*; Gen. xlii. 15 f.   z = obj. gen., Rom. xi. 31; so ἡμετ., Rom.
xv. 4. See note below.   a Rom. xv. 17, For the noun, Rom. iii. 27,; 6 exx. in 2 Cor.; 1 Th.
ii. 19; Jas. iv. 16. -ημα, see v. 6; -αομαι, see i. 29.   b See iii. 3, and note below.

¹ ἡμετέραν: A, and many minn., Or., Thdrt. So Stephens and Beza, but not
Elzevir.

² Ins. αδελφοι ℵABKP, and 15 minn., sah. cop. vg. syrr.
Omᵈ. by the Western and Syrian codd.

lowing ὑπὲρ αὐτῶν indicates that by
ὑπὲρ τῶν νεκρῶν definite (dead) *persons*
are meant. Ed. notices with approval
the rendering of John Edwards (Camb.,
1692), who supposed these "baptized"
to be men *converted* to Christianity *by
the heroism of the martyrs;* somewhat
similarly, Gd. This points in the right
direction, but misses the force of ὑπέρ
(*on behalf of;* not διά, *on account of*),
and narrows the ref. of τῶν νεκρῶν (*cf.*
18, 20, 23); there is no indication in the
ep. of *martyrdoms* at Cor. (see, on the
contrary, iv. 9 f.). P. is referring rather
to a much commoner, indeed a normal
experience, that the death of Christians
leads to the conversion of survivors, who
in the first instance "for the sake of the
dead" (their beloved dead), and in the
hope of reunion, turn to Christ—*e.g.*,
when a dying mother wins her son by
the appeal, "Meet me in heaven!"
Such appeals, and their frequent salutary
effect, give strong and touching evidence
of *faith in the resurrection;* some recent
example of the kind may have suggested
this ref. Paul designates such converts
"*baptised* for the dead," since Baptism
seals the new believer and commits him
to the Christian life (see note, xii. 13)
with all its losses and hazards (*cf.* 30).
The hope of future blessedness, allying
itself with family affections and friendship, was one of the most powerful
factors in the early spread of Christianity.
Mr. objects to this view (expounded by
Köster) that τ. νεκρῶν needs definition
by συγγενῶν καὶ φίλων, or the like, to
bear such meaning; but to each of these
βαπτιζόμενοι those who had thus influenced him would be "*the* dead". The
obscure passage has, upon this explanation, a large, abiding import suitable to
the solemn and elevated context in which
it stands; the words reveal a communion
in Christ between the living and departed (*cf.* Rom. xiv. 9), to which the
hope of the resurrection gives validity
and worth (*cf.* 1 Thess. v. 10, 2 Thess. ii.

1).—For ἐπεί, *since otherwise, else* (alio-
quin, Vg.; Germ. *da sonst*), see note on
v. 10.—τί ποιήσουσιν; (see LXX parls.)
indicates that the hope on which these
baptisms rest will be stultified, without a
resurrection; it will betray them (Rom.
v. 5).—εἰ ὅλως νεκροὶ κ.τ.λ., "If absolutely (*omnino*, Vg.: see note, v. 10)
dead men are not raised" (the axiom of
the unbelievers, 12, 15, etc.), unfolds the
assumption involved in ἐπεί as the protasis of τί καὶ βαπτίζονται ὑπὲρ αὐτῶν;
which repeats, with emphasis on the
pronoun, the former question—"Why
indeed are they baptised *for them?*"
how can *they* be interested in the baptism of survivors, if they have perished
(18)? On this assumption, converts
would have been gained upon *false hopes*
(*cf.* 19), as well as upon *false testimony*
(15).—"Why also do *we* run hazard
every hour?"—further consequent of εἰ
νεκροὶ οὐκ ἐγείρονται: "our case (that
of the App. and other missionaries, brav-
ing death unceasingly: see 11; iv. 9 ff.,
2 Cor. iv. 10 ff., xi. 23 ff.; John xv.
18-xvi. 22) is parl. to theirs; as they, in
love for the dead whom they hope to
meet again, take up the cross of Christian
profession, so we in the same hope face
hourly peril".

Vv. 31, 32*a*. In no slight jeopardy do
P. and his comrades stand; for his part
he declares, "Daily *I am dying;* my life
at Ephesus has been that of a combatant
with wild beasts in the arena—*for what
end,* if there is no resurrection?" With
καθ᾽ ἡμέραν ἀποθνῄσκω *cf.* 2 Cor. iv. 10,
xi. 23, Rom. viii. 36; referring to his
present "affliction in Asia," P. writes in
2 Cor. i. 8 f., "We have had the sentence of death in ourselves". Ed. softens
the expression into "self-denial, dying
to self and the world": better Cv.,
"obsideor assiduis mortibus quotidie";
and Gd., "Not a day, nor an hour of the
day, when they might not expect to be
seized and led out to execution".—P.
had not been in this extreme peril at

e H.l.; see °ἐθηριομάχησα ἐν Ἐφέσῳ, ᵈτί μοι τὸ ᵈὄφελος; εἰ ᵗνεκροὶ οὐκ
note
below. ᵗἐγείρονται, °Φάγωμεν καὶ πίωμεν, ᶠαὔριον γὰρ ἀποθνήσκομεν.
d Jas. ii. 14,
16; Job
xv. 3; cf. xiv. 6, xiii. 3.   e Isa. xxii. 13.   f Adv., Jas. iv. 13; Acts xxiii. 20, xxv. 22; Lk. xii. 28,
xiii. 32 f.; Mt. vi. 30; Exod. viii. 29.

Cor. (see Acts xviii. 9 f.), and his readers might think the description overdrawn; so he exclaims, νὴ τ. ὑμετέραν καύχησιν κ.τ.λ.: "Yea, by the glorying over you, brothers, which I have in Christ Jesus our Lord!" cf. the protests of 2 Cor. i. 18, 23, xi. 10 f., 31, Rom. ix. 1. He protests by this καύχησις as by that which is dearest to him: cf. i. 4 ff., iv. 14, 2 Cor. vii. 3, 14 ff.; similarly in 1 Thess. ii. 19 f., 2 Thess. i. 4, Phil. iv. 1, etc. For this rare use of the pron., cf. xi. 24, τ. ἐμὴν ἀνάμνησιν (and note), 2 Cor. ix. 3. νή (= ναί) with acc. of adjuration, a cl. idiom.—Paul's "glorying" he "holds in Christ Jesus our Lord" (cf. i. 7); it is laid up with Christ as a καύχημα εἰς ἡμέραν X. (Phil. ii. 16; cf. iii. 8, iv. 3 ff. above, 1 Thess. ii. 19, Col. i. 4, etc.).—"If in the manner of men I have fought with wild beasts in Ephesus, what is the profit?" κατὰ ἄνθρωπον bears the stress, "humanitus—spe vitæ præsentis duntaxat" (Bg.: cf. iii. 3 f.); seeking the rewards—applause, money, etc.— for which men risk their lives. Instead of these, P. earns poverty and infamy (iv. 9 ff., Phil. iii. 7 f.); if there is no "day of Christ" when his "glorying" will be realised, he has been befooled (cf. 19 and note, Phil. iii. 14, 2 Tim iv. 8; Matt. xix. 27 ff., Luke xiv. 14, xxii. 28 ff.).—ὄφελος (from ὀφέλλω, to increase; nearly syn. with μισθός, iii. 8, etc.; or κέρδος, Phil. i. 21) signifies the consequent advantage accruing to P. from his fight; that it brings present moral benefit is obvious, but this is not the point (cf. ix. 24-27; see Ed. ad loc., touching the diff. of pagan and Christian morality). — ἐθηριομάχησα is probably figurative, though Gd., Weizsäcker (Apost. Zeitalter², pp. 325 f.), McGiffert (Christianity in the Apost. Age, pp. 280 f.), with some older expositors, take it that P. had been actually a θηριομάχος in the Ephesian amphitheatre, despite his Roman citizenship. But no such experience is recorded in the list of his woes in 2 Cor. xi.; moreover it appears from Acts xix. 31-40 that P. had friends in high quarters at Eph., who would have prevented this outrage if attempted. Ignatius (ad Rom., v.; cf. ad Smyrn., iv.) applies the figure to his guards, borrowing it probably from this place. The metaphor is

in the strain of iv. 9 (see note); cf. also Ps. xxii. 12, 16, etc., and the use of θηρίον in the Rev.—In view of this last parl. and of 2 Tim. iv. 17, Krenkel in his Beiträge, V., finds the "wild beast" of Paul's struggle in the Imperial Power, which K. thinks was already so designated "in the secret language of Christians" (cf. 2 Thess. ii. 5 f.). But nothing in Acts xix. indicates conflict on P.'s part with the magistrates of Eph. (and Lk. habitually traces with care his relations with Roman authorities); it was the city-mob, instigated by the shrine-makers, which attacked him; before the riot he had been probably in danger of assassination from this quarter, as well as from "the Asian Jews," who set upon him afterwards in Jerusalem (Acts xxi. 27 ff.). Bt. observes the climax: κινδυνεύω, ἀποθνήσκω, θηριομαχῶ.

Ver. 32b states in words of Scripture the desperation that ensues upon loss of faith in a future life: "If (the) dead are not raised (the Sadducean dogma repeated a sixth time), 'Let us eat and drink, for to-morrow we die!'" εἰ νεκροὶ κ.τ.λ. is rightly attached by the early Gr. and most modern commentt. to the following clause. Paul is not drawing his own conclusion in these words, nor suggesting that the resurrection supplies the only motive against a sensual life; but he points out (cf. 33 f.) the patent fruit of the unbelief in question. This is just what men were saying on all sides; the words quoted voice the moral recklessness bred by loss of hope beyond death. Gr. and Rom. literature teem with examples of this spirit (see Wisd. ii. 6; Herod., ii., 78, Thuc., ii., 53, and other reff. furnished by Ed. ad loc.); indeed Paul's O.T. citation might have served for the axiom of popular Epicureanism. Hn. describes ancient drinking-cups, recently discovered, ornamented with skeleton figures wreathed in roses and named after famous philosophers, poets, and gourmands, with mottoes attached such as these: τὸ τέλος ἡδονή, τέρπε ζῶν σεαυτόν, σκηνὴ βίος, τοῦτ' ἄνθρωπος (written over a skeleton holding a skull), ζῶν μετάλαβε τὸ γὰρ αὔριον ἄδηλόν ἐστιν. Cf. our own miserable adage, "A short life and a merry one!" Vv. 33, 34 deliver Paul's judgment

33. [g] μὴ [g] πλανᾶσθε· “[h] φθείρουσιν [i] ἤθη [k] χρήσθ’ [1] [l] ὁμιλίαι κακαί”.
34. [m] ἐκνήψατε [n] δικαίως καὶ μὴ ἁμαρτάνετε, [o] ἀγνωσίαν γὰρ [o] Θεοῦ
τινες ἔχουσι· πρὸς [p] ἐντροπὴν ὑμῖν λέγω.[2]
35. [q] Ἀλλ’ [q] ἐρεῖ [q] τις, “Πῶς [r] ἐγείρονται οἱ [r] νεκροί; [s] ποίῳ δὲ

g See vi. 9. h See iii. 17. i N.T. *h.l.*; Sir. xx. 26. k Elsewhere in N.T. *of persons* (*cf.* Jer. xxiv. 2); Rom. ii. 4; Eph. iv. 32, etc. -ευομαι, xiii. 4; -οτης, 2 Cor. vi. 6, and eight times besides in P. l N.T. *h.l.*; Ex. xxi. 10; Prov. vii. 21; Wisd. viii. 18. m N.T. *h.l.*; Gen. ix. 24; 1 Ki. xxv. 37; Joel i. 5, ανανηφω. n 1 Th. ii. 10; Tit. ii. 12; 1 Pet. ii. 23; Lk. xxiii. 41; Deut. xvi. 20. o Wisd. xiii. 1. αγνωσ., 1 Pet. ii. 15; Job xxxv. 16. p See vi. 5. q Jas. ii. 16. r See ver. 15. s Rom. iii. 27; Jas. iv. 14; 1 Pet. i. 11, ii. 20; Rev. iii. 3; oftener in GG. and Acts.

[1] **χρηστα,** all uncc., many minn., and nearly all Ff. Printed **χρησθ’** for sake of metre. Read, doubtless, with elision of the **α.**

[2] **λαλω,** ℵBDP. **λεγω,** AGL, etc. A freq. variation; *cf.* vi. 5.

upon the situation: the disbelief in the Resurrection declared in the Cor. Church is of a piece with its low ethics (iii. 1 ff., iv. 18-v. 2) and its heathen intimacies (viii. 10, x. 14-22, 2 Cor. v. 14-vii. 1); it springs from **ἀγνωσία Θεοῦ,** from a feeble religious consciousness.—**μὴ πλανᾶσθε** (see parls.), “Be not misled (seduced)”: the seduction lay in the specious philosophy under which sceptical tenets were advanced, concealing their demoralising tendency. The line the Ap. quotes (an ordinary senarius of the dialogue in the Attic drama: **χρηστά,** so *written* in the best copies, was probably *read* **χρήσθ’,** Wr., Hn.) is attributed to Menander (322 B.C.), of the New Comedy and an Epicurean, by Tert. and Hier., followed by most others. But this was a proverbial gnomé, and probably current long before Menander. **ὁμιλίαι** bears the narrower sense of *conversations* (A.V.; *colloquia*, Vg.), or the wider sense, more fitting here, of *intercourse*, *companionships* (R.V.).—**ἐκνήψατε δικαίως κ.τ.λ.** (*cf.* 32*b*, xi. 21; and parls. for **ἐκνήφω**): “Rouse up to soberness in righteous fashion, and cease to sin” (the first impv. is *aor.*, of a single action; the second *pr.*, of a course of action)—a startling call, to men fallen as if into a drunken sleep under the seductions of sensualism and heathen society and the fumes of intellectual pride. **δικαίως** signifies the *manner* of the awaking; it is *right* the Cor. should rouse themselves from self-delusion; P. assails their conscience.—**ἀγνωσίαν γὰρ Θεοῦ τινες** (*cf.* 12) **ἔχουσιν,** “For some have (maintain) an ignorance of God” (*cf.* the use of **ἔχω** in 31, viii. 1, Rom. iv. 2, v. 1, respecting *states of mind*); this asserts, beyond **τὸν Θεὸν ἀγνοοῦσιν,** a characteristic, a persistent condition, in which the Cor. **τινὲς** share with the heathen (xii. 2, Rom. i. 19 ff., etc.).—**πρὸς ἐντροπὴν ὑμῖν λαλῶ,** “I say (it) for a shame to you,” otherwise than in iv. 14. “Ignorance of God” is a deeper evil than the ingratitude toward the Ap. which he censured earlier; this can only be remedied by a thorough inward reaction—“ad pudorem vobis incutiendum dico” (Cv.). That these wise Cor. should be taxed with “ignorance,” and “*of God*” on the knowledge of whom they flattered themselves above all (viii. 1, 4), was humiliating indeed.

§ 54. THE MANNER OF THE RESURRECTION, xv. 35-42*a*. We enter on the second part of the Apostle’s argument touching the Resurrection: see the analysis, *Introd.* to Div. V. He has established the truth of the doctrine and the certainty of the event, and proceeds consequently to set forth *the manner of its occurrence* and *the nature of the new body* to be assumed. P. has still in view the unbelieving “some,” and pursues the dialectical and apologetic vein of the foregoing context. The deniers found in *the inconceivability of the process* (35) a further and, in their eyes, decisive objection against the reality of the fact. In vindicating his doctrine upon this side, P. therefore confirms its truth; he traces its analogies in nature, and its harmony with the order of Divine revelation; and the first half of his grand argument culminates in the second. See Edwards’ subtle analysis of vv. 35-44.

Ver. 35. **Ἀλλὰ ἐρεῖ τις**: this form of interlocution belongs to Jewish dialectic (see parls.); *cf.* ver. 12, also **ἐρεῖς μοι,** Rom. ix. 19, and the familiar Pauline challenge, **τί οὖν ἐροῦμεν;**—“How are the dead raised up? With what sort of (**ποίῳ δέ**) body moreover do they come?”—two distinct questions. **δὲ** might indeed introduce the same question in an altered form (Mr., Bt., El., Sm.), but the vbs. and the interr. prons. are both different. The first (*cf.* Luke i. 34, John iii. 9, vi. 52, Heb. ii. 3, 1 John iii. 17)

t Thus in Lk. xi. 40, xii. 20; Ps. xciii. 8; five times in 2 Cor. xi., xii. (ref. to P. σώματι ἔρχονται; " 36. ᵗἄφρον,¹ σὺ ὃ σπείρεις οὐ ᵘζωοποιεῖται ἐὰν μὴ ᵛἀποθάνῃ· 37. καὶ ὃ σπείρεις, οὐ τὸ σῶμα τὸ γενησόμενον σπείρεις, ἀλλὰ ʷγυμνὸν ˣκόκκον, ʸεἰ ʸτύχοι ˣᶻσίτου ἤ τινος ᵃτῶν ᵃλοιπῶν· 38. ὁ δὲ Θεὸς αὐτῷ² δίδωσι² σῶμα ᵇκαθὼς ᵇἠθέλησε,

himself); Rom. ii. 20; Eph. v. 17; 1 Pet. ii. 15.   u See ver. 22.   v Cf. Jo. xii. 24.   w H.l. in this usage. For common use, see 2 Cor. v. 3, etc.   x Jo. xii. 24. κοκ., Mt. xiii. 31, xvii. 20.   y See xiv. 10.   z In like connexion, Mt. xiii. 25, 29 f.; Mk. iv. 28.   a See vii. 12, xi. 34.   b See xii. 18.

² αφρων, all uncc. but KL.

³ διδωσιν αυτω: ℵABP, 17—chief pre-Syrian and non-Western witnesses.

intimates *the impossibility of the thing*, and is answered in ver. 36; the latter, *the inconceivability of the manner*, answered in vv. 37 ff. (so Cm., Cv., D.W., Hf., Ed.). The sceptics advance their second question to justify the first: they say, "The resurrection P. preaches is absurd; how can any one imagine a new body rising out of the perished corpse— a body suitable to the deathless spirit?" The vbs. are *logical* pr., as concerned with general truths (*cf.* 26); "actio rei declaratur absque significatione temporis" (Er.).—ἔρχονται (*cf.* John v. 29; 1 Thess. iv. 14, ὁ Θεὸς ἄξει) graphically represents the difficulty of the objectors: "In what bodily form do we picture the dead coming on the scene?"

Ver. 36. ἄφρων (opposite of φρόνιμοι, iv. 10, x. 15) taxes the propounder of these questions not with moral obliquity, but with mental stupidity (see parls.). Wanting the art. (*cf.* Luke xii. 20), the word is an assertion rather than an exclamation: "Insensé que tu es, toi qui te crois si sage!" (Gd.). Some attach σὺ as subject to ἄφρων, but this weakens the adj., and the pron. is required to give due emphasis to ὃ σπείρεις following. With a little sense, the questioner might answer himself; every time he sows his garden-plot, he assumes the principle denied in regard to man's material form, *viz.*, that *death is the transition to a further life*—"that which thou thyself sowest, is not made alive except it die". This answers πῶς ἐγείρονται; by ref. to the analogy of nature. P. does not explain, any more than Jesus, the *modus operandi* of the Resurrection; what he shows is that the mystery raises no prejudice against the reality, for the same mystery is wrapped up in every vegetating seed.—ἐγείρονται in the question is substituted for ζωοποιεῖται in the answer (see note on 22; *cf.* other parls.), since it is *life* that rises out of the dying seed, and the Resurrection is an evolution, not a reinstatement. Our Lord uses the same figure with the like implication, but another application, in John xii. 23 f.

Vv. 37, 38 make answer to the second branch of the question of ver. 35, by the aid of the same profound analogy.—καὶ ὃ σπείρεις, οὐ τὸ σῶμα τὸ γενησόμενον σπείρεις, "And what thou sowest—not the body that will come to be dost thou sow". It is the object of the sower to realise a new ποιότης in his seed. If any one interrupted him with the question, "What sort of a body can the grain take that you drop in the earth to rot?" the sower would dismiss him as a fool; he has *seen* in this case "the body that is to be". Now the actuality of the lower resurrection vindicates the conceivability of the higher.—τὸ γενησόμενον states not merely a future certainty (*that shall be; quod futurum sit*, Vg.), but a normal process (*oriturum*, Bz.: *quod nascetur*, Cv., Bg.).—ἀλλὰ γυμνὸν κόκκον, "but a naked grain"—unclothed with any body, wanting the appearance and furnishing of life (*cf.* 2 Cor. v. 3, ἐνδυσάμενοι, οὐ γυμνοί).—For εἰ τύχοι ("if it should chance, of wheat"), see note on xiv. 10: the *kind* of grain is indiff.—"or of any of the rest (of the seeds)". The grain of wheat gives to the eye no more promise of the body to spring from it than a grain of sand.—ὁ δὲ Θεὸς stands in opposition to σὺ ὃ σπείρεις—God the life-giver responding to the sower's trustful act. "But God gives it a body, according as He willed" (ἠθέλησεν)—not "as He wills" (according to His choice or liking), but in accordance with His past decree in creation, by which the propagation of life on the earth was determined from the beginning (Gen. i. 11 f.; for the vb., *cf.* note on xii. 18). To allege an impossibility in the case is to impugn the power and resources of the Creator (*cf.* Acts xxvi. 8), manifested in this very way every spring-time. The Divine will is the efficient nexus between seed and plant (*cf.* xii. 6).—"And (He gives) to each of the seeds a body of its own

καὶ ἑκάστῳ τῶν σπερμάτων τὸ [1] ᵉἴδιον σῶμα. 39. οὐ πᾶσα σὰρξ ᶜ Ver. 23.
ἡ αὐτὴ σάρξ· ἀλλὰ ᵈἄλλη ᵈμὲν σὰρξ [2] ἀνθρώπων, ᵈἄλλη ᵈδὲ σὰρξ [3] Anarth-
ᵉκτηνῶν, [4] ᵈἄλλη ᵈδὲ ᵍἰχθύων, [5] ᵈἄλλη ᵈδὲ [6] ᶠπτηνῶν. [5] 40. καὶ rous, Gal.
σώματα ʰἐπουράνια, καὶ σώματα ʰⁱἐπίγεια· ἀλλ' ᵏἑτέρα ᵏμὲν ἡ Tit. i. 3,

vi. 9; 1
Tim. ii. 6,
vi. 15;
12, ii. 19;
2 Pet. i.

20, ii. 16; Acts xxviii. 30; Jo. x. 12.   d Phrase, N.T. *h.l.*   e Lk. x. 34; Acts xxiii. 24; Rev.
xviii. 13; Numb. xx. 4, etc.   f N.T. *h.l.*; Job v. 7. Prose for πετεινος (Rom. i. 23, etc.), which is
poetical in cl. Gr.   g Freq. in GG.; *h.l.* in Epp.   h The antith. in Phil. ii. 10 and Jo. iii. 12.
επουρ., vv. 48 f.; five times in Eph.; 2 Tim. iv. 18; six times in Heb.; Mt. xviii. 35. *Cf.* Eph. i.
10; Mt. vi. 9, etc.   i 2 Cor. v. 1; Phil. iii. 19; Jas. iii. 15. *Cf.* τα επι της γης, Eph. i. 10, etc.
k This form of antith., *h.l.* in N.T. For ετερος, see xii. 9.

[1] *Om.* το all pre-Syrian codd.

[2] *Om.* σαρξ all uncc., and very many minn.

[3] *Om.* σαρξ (before κτηνων): the Western witnesses.

[4] κτηνους, Western. K, 37, 47, om. this clause altogether, skipping to πτηνων,
through homœoteleuton.

[5] πτηνων ... ιχθυων (in this order): all uncc. but GKL; 17, cop. vg. syrsch.

[6] *Ins.* σαρξ (before πτηνων) all uncc. but AKLP. Ver. 39b, corrected, reads:
αλλα αλλη μεν ανθρωπων, αλλη δε σαρξ κτηνων, αλλη δε σαρξ πτηνων, αλλη
δε ιχθυων.

(ἴδιον)". This added clause meets the
finer point of the second question of ver.
35; God will find a *fit* body for man's
redeemed nature, as He does for each of
the numberless seeds vivified in the soil.
"How unintelligent to think, as the
Pharisees did, that the same body that
was buried must be restored, if there is
to be a resurrection! Every wheat-stalk
contradicts thee!" (Mr.)

Ver. 39. The rest of the § goes to
sustain ver. 38b, showing the inexhaustible
variety of organic forms in the Divine
economy of nature and the fitness of
each for the life it clothes. This is
manifest, to begin with, in the varied
types of animal life: οὐ πᾶσα σὰρξ ἡ
αὐτὴ σάρξ, "All flesh is not the same
flesh"—in the zoological realm there is
no uniformity, but endless differentiation.
(Ed. makes πᾶσα σὰρξ predicate—"the
same flesh is not all flesh," *i.e.*, physical assimilation means differentiation—
getting out of the sentence a physiological idea obscure in itself and not very
relevant to the context). Instead of *men,
cattle, birds, fishes,* with their hetero-
geneous natures, being lodged in the
same kind of corporeity, their frame and
organs vary with their inner constitution
and needs. If God can find a body for
beast and fish, in the lower range, no less
than for man, why not, in the higher
range, for man immortal no less than for
man mortal?—κτῆνος (from κτάομαι),
denoting cattle as beasts of *purchase* in
the first instance, is applied to four-footed
beasts at large: *cf.* Gen. i. 25 ff., ii. 20.

Ver. 40. The possibility of a future
body unimaginably diff. from the present
is indicated in the contrast suggested by
the diff. *regions* of the two: "Bodies
also heavenly there are, and bodies
earthly". The σὰρξ of ver. 39 is now
dropped, for it belongs only to the σῶμα
ἐπίγειον. What does P. mean by his
σώματα ἐπουράνια? The previous context and the tenor of the argument lead
us to think of *bodies for celestial inhabitants, sc.* the angels (Luke xx. 36, Matt.
xxviii. 2, etc.), as suitable to their condition as the σώματα ἐπίγεια are for the
forms of terrestrial life just enumerated
(so Mr., D.W., Al., El., Sm.); moreover
σῶμα is never used elsewhere in Bib. Gr.,
and rarely in cl. Gr., of inorganic bodies.
On the other hand, ver. 41 in connexion
with ver. 40b strongly suggests the *sun,
moon,* etc., as the "heavenly bodies" in
Paul's mind (so Bg., Hf., Hn., Ed., Bt.,
Gd., and most moderns). The former
considerations preponderate, esp. when
we find P. in vv. 47 ff. (see notes) resuming the same contrast in the antithesis
between "the earthy man" and "the
heavenly". Paul is thinking of *the risen
Christ* whom he had seen, more than of
the angels, as supplying the type of the
σῶμα ἐπουράνιον; *cf.* Phil. iii. 20 f. Gm.,
Hilgenfeld, Holsten, Everling (*Die paul.
Angelologie u.s.w.,* pp. 46 ff.) combine
the above interpretations by attributing
to P. the belief of Philo and the Jewish
mystics that the stars are animated, and
are to be identified with the O.T. "angels,"
as by the heathen with their gods. This

l Thus in 2 Cor. iii. 7, 18; Lk. ix. 31 f.; Ex. xvi. 10. Cf. ii. 7 above. m Acts ii. 20; Mt. xxiv. 29; Lk. xxi. 25; 4 exx. in Rev.

τῶν ʰἐπουρανίων ˡδόξα, ᵏἑτέρα ᵏδὲ ἡ τῶν ʰⁱἐπιγείων. 41. ἄλλη ˡδόξα ᵐἡλίου, καὶ ἄλλη ˡδόξα ᵐσελήνης, καὶ ἄλλη ˡδόξα ⁿἀστέρων · ⁿἀστὴρ γὰρ ⁿἀστέρος ᵒδιαφέρει ἐν ˡδόξῃ. 42a. οὕτω καὶ ἡ ᵖἀνάστασις τῶν ᵖνεκρῶν.

42b. ᑫΣπείρεται ἐν ʳφθορᾷ, ˢἐγείρεται ἐν ᵗἀφθαρσίᾳ · 43. ᑫσπείρεται ἐν ᵘἀτιμίᾳ, ˢἐγείρεται ἐν ˡδόξῃ · ᑫσπείρεται ἐν ᵛἀσθενείᾳ,

n Jude 13 (fig.); Mt. ii. four times, xxiv. 29; 14 exx. in Rev. o In this use, Gal. iv. 1; Dan. vii. 3 (Theod.). Cf. Rom. ii. 18, etc.; also iv. 7 above. p See ver. 12. q Ver. 36; see note below.
r Ver. 50; Rom. viii. 21; Gal. vi. 8; Col. ii. 22; 2 Pet. i. 4, ii. 12, 19; Jonah ii. 7. s See vi. 14.
t Rom. ii. 7; Eph. vi. 24; 2 Tim. i. 10; Wisd. ii. 23, vi. 18 f. u See xi. 14. v See ii. 3; and for antith., 2 Cor. xii. 9 f., xiii. 4 f., Heb. xi. 34.

notion is wanting in Biblical support. P. asserts that there are "bodies" for *heavenly* beings, just as there are for earthly (*cf.* 49); the adj. ἐπουράνια supplies the ποιότης desiderated in ver. 35. The heavenly and earthly bodies, alike as being "bodies," are far diff. in "glory". —ἀλλὰ ἑτέρα κ.τ.λ. traverses the mistaken inference as to the identity of nature in the two kinds of organism, which might be hastily drawn from ver. 39b: "But the glory of the heavenlies is indeed one (glory), and the (glory) of the earthlies another".—ἑτέρα (*cf.* note on xii. 8 ff.) implies a diff. wider, or at least more salient, than that connoted by the ἄλλη of vv. 39 and 41; where the two are distinguished in cl. Gr., ἄλλος marks a generic, ἕτερος a specific diff. How utterly diff. was the glory of the risen Lord, who appeared to P. (Acts xxvi. 13), from that of any earthly Potentate!

Ver. 41. Even amongst the σώματα ἐπουράνια there are varieties, just as amongst the ἐπίγεια (39), such as are indicated by the diff. of aspect in the visible celestial objects: "There is one glory of sun, and another glory of moon, and another glory of stars—for star differs from star in glory". While these luminous orbs are not to be *identified* with the "heavenly bodies" of ver. 40 (see note), they serve to symbolise the diversity of glory amongst them; all are glorious, but in degrees.—ἄλλη, as in ver. 39 (contrast 40), indicates diff. *within* the same order. The frequent symbolic association of sun and stars with *God*, *the angels*, *the righteous*, and with *the glorified Jesus*, may account for the asyndetic transition from ver. 40b (signifying *persons*) to 41. From the distinctions manifest amid the common glory of the visible heavens we may conjecture corresponding distinctions in the heavenly Intelligences and in the bodies appropriate to them.

Ver. 42a sums up what has been advanced in vv. 36-41, and presents it in six words: οὕτως καὶ ἡ ἀνάστασις τῶν νεκρῶν, "So indeed is the resurrection of the dead". It is as *possible* as that plants of wholly diff. form should shoot from the seed sown by your own hand; and the *form* of each risen body will be determined by God, who finds a suitable organism for every type of earthly life, and can do so equally for every type and grade of heavenly life, in a region where, as sun, moon, and stars nightly show, the universal splendour is graduated and varied infinitely.

§ 55. The First Adam and the Last, xv. 42b-49. The Ap. has now removed à priori objections, and brought his theory of bodily resurrection within the lines of natural analogy and probability of reason. He has at the same time largely expounded it, intimating (1) that *the present is*, in some sense, *the seed of the future body*, and (2) that the two will differ as *the heavenly must needs differ from the earthly*. He goes on to show that this diff. has its basis and pattern in the diff. between *the primitive Adam and the glorified Christ*, who are contrasted in condition (42b, 43), in nature (44 ff.), and in origin (47 ff.).

Vv. 42b, 43. Σπείρεται ἐν φθορᾷ . . . ἐν ἀτιμίᾳ . . . ἐν ἀσθενείᾳ: "The sowing is in corruption (perishableness) . . . in dishonour . . . in weakness". It is better, with Cv., Wr. (p. 656), and Hn., to regard σπείρεται and ἐγείρεται as *impersonal*, since no subject is supplied; the vbs., thrice repeated with emphasis, are contrasted in idea; the antithesis lies between two opp. stages of being (*cf.*, for the mode of expression, Luke xii. 48). σπείρεται recalls, and applies in the most general way, the ὃ σπείρεις and σπέρματα of vv. 36 ff. To interpret this vb. as figuring the act of *burial* ("verbum amœnissimum pro sepultura," Bg.; so Cm., Gr., Mr., Bt., El., and many others) confuses the analogy (the "sowing" is expressly distinguished from the "dying"

ᵃἐγείρεται ʷἐν ᵛʷδυνάμει· 44. ᑫσπείρεται σῶμα ˣψυχικόν, ˢἐγείρεται σῶμα ʸπνευματικόν. ἔστι¹ σῶμα ˣψυχικόν, καὶ² ἔστι²
σῶμα ³ʸπνευματικόν· 45. ᶻοὕτω καὶ ᶻγέγραπται, "ᵃ'Εγένετο ὁ
πρῶτος ἄνθρωπος⁴ 'Αδὰμ ᵃεἰς ψυχὴν ζῶσαν·" ὁ ἔσχατος 'Αδὰμ

w See iv. 20.
x See ii. 14.
y See ii. 15.
z Mt ii. 5;
Lk. xxiv.
46. Cf.
Acts xiii.
47; and ix.
14 above.

a Gen. ii. 7; Rom. xi. 9; 1 Pet. ii. 7; Mt. xxi. 42 and Acts iv. 11 (Ps. cxvii. 22); Acts v. 36; Lk. xiii. 19.

¹ ει εστιν: all pre-Syrian codd., and all ancient verss. exc. syrr.
² εστιν και: all uncc. but KL.   ³ Om. σωμα pre-Syrian codd.
⁴ BK, and several minn., om. ανθρωπος.

of the seed, 36), and jars with ἐν ἀσθενείᾳ (a sick man, not a corpse, is called *weak*), and with ψυχικὸν in ver. 44; *cf.* also vv. 50-54, where ἡ φθορά, τὸ φθαρτόν, τὸ θνητὸν τοῦτο are identified with the *living* ἡμεῖς. Our *present life* is the seed-time (Gal. vi. 7 ff.), and our "mortal bodies" (Rom. viii. 10 f.) are in the germinal state, concluding with death (36), out of which a wholly diff. organism will spring. The attributes φθορά (*cf.* δουλεία τ. φθορᾶς, Rom. viii. 21), ἀτιμία (*cf.* Phil. iii. 21), ἀσθενεία (*cf.* 2 Cor. xiii. 4)—summed up in the θνητὰ σώματα of Rom. viii. 11 and μορφὴ δούλου of Phil. ii. 7—are those that P. is wont to ascribe to man's actual physique, in contrast with the ἀφθαρσία, δόξα, δύναμις of the post-resurrection state: see 2 Cor. iv. 7, 10, 16, v. 1, 4, Rom. i. 4, viii. 18-23. Thus, with variety in detail, Est. ("moritur corpus multis ante mortem miseriis et fœditatibus obnoxium, suscitabitur idem corpus omni ex parte gloriosum"), Cv., Hf., Hn., Ed. Gd. refers the three-fold σπείρεται to the three moments of *burial, mortal life,* and *birth* respectively; van Hengel identifies it with *procreation,* quite unsuitably.

Ver. 44. "There is sown a psychic body; there is raised a spiritual body." This dictum grounds the antithesis un-folded in vv. 42 f. upon its proper basis; the diff. is not a matter of *condition* merely, but of *constitution.* Corruption, dishonour, feebleness are, in great part, penal inflictions (Rom. v. 12 ff.), signalis-ing not a natural defect, but a positive subjection to the power of sin (53-56); man, however, is essentially ψυχὴ under the present order (45), and his body there-fore is essentially ψυχικὸν as determined by that order (*cf.* vi. 13, and note; Col. ii. 20 ff., Matt. xxii. 30, etc.), being fitted to and expressive of the "soul" wherein his earthly being centres; see the note on ψυχικός, ii. 14. Though inadequate, "natural" is the best available rendering of this adj.; it indicates the moulding

of man's body by its environment and its adaptation to existing functions; the same body is χοϊκὸν in respect of its material (47).—ψυχικὸν is only relatively a term of disparagement; the "psychic body" has in it the making of the "spiritual"; "its adaptation for the present service of the soul is the *sowing* of it, that is the initial step in its adapta-tion for the future uses of the spirit. An organism fitted to be the seat of mind, to express emotion, to carry out the be-hests of will, is in process of being adapted for a still nobler ministry" (Ed.): "he that sows to the Spirit (in the natural body), will reap of the Spirit (in the spiritual body)," Gal. vi. 8.—"If there is a psychic body, there is also a spiritual": a frame suited to man's earthly life argues a frame suited to his heavenly life, accord-ing to the principle of ver. 38*b* (*cf.* the argument from lower to higher in Matt. vi. 30); and the σῶμα πν. lies, in some way, germinally hidden in the σῶμα ψ., to be unfolded from it under "the uni-versal law of progress" (Ed.).—ἔστιν (*existit*) bears emphasis in each clause; from the *fact* of sense P. argues to the *fact* of faith. Observe txtl. notes 1-3.

Ver. 45 puts into words of Scripture the law of development affirmed, there-by showing its agreement with the plan of creation and its realisation in the two successive heads of the race. Into his citation of Gen. ii. 7 (LXX) P. introduces πρῶτος and duplicates ἄνθρωπος by 'Αδάμ (*ha'adām*), to prepare for his an-tithetical addition ὁ ἔσχατος 'Αδὰμ εἰς πνεῦμα ζωοποιοῦν. On the principle of ver. 44*b*, the Adam created as ψυχὴ was the crude beginning of humanity (the pred. ψυχὴ ζῶσα is shared by A. with the *animals,* Gen. i. 20, 24)—a "first" requiring a "last" as his complement and explanation. The two types differ here not as the sin-committing and sin-abolishing (Rom. v. 12 ff.), but as the rudimentary and finished man respec-tively, with their physique to match.—

b See ver. 22.   εἰς πνεῦμα ^bζωοποίουν.   46. ἀλλ' οὐ πρῶτον τὸ ^yπνευματικὸν

c Jo. iii. 31, —same antith.   ἀλλὰ τὸ ^xψυχικόν, ἔπειτα τὸ ^yπνευματικόν·   47. ὁ πρῶτος ἄνθρω-

d H.l.; see note below.   πος ^{c e}ἐκ ^cγῆς, ^dχοϊκός· ὁ δεύτερος ἄνθρωπος ὁ Κύριος ^{1 ce}ἐξ

e 2 Cor. v. 2; Gal. i. 8; 1 Th. i. 10; 2 Pet. i. 18; freq. in Rev.; Mt. xxviii. 2; Lk. iii. 22, x. 18, xi. 13; Jo. i. 32, xii. 28; Acts ii. 2.   Ref. to Chr., Jo. iii. 13, etc., vi. 31 ff.

¹ *Om.* ο Κυριος ℵ*BCD*G, 17, 67**, latt. vg. cop., many Ff.
Ins. ο Κυριος ℵcADb,cKLP, and syrr.   Tert. censures this reading in Mcion. An instance of the Syrian readings followed by A, even in Paul.

Ἀδάμ is repeated in the second clause by way of maintaining the humanity of Christ and His genetic relation to the protoplast (*cf.* Luke i. 23-38), essential as the ground of our bodily relationship to Him (48 f.; *cf.* Heb. ii. 14 ff.).—The time of Christ's γενέσθαι εἰς πν. ζωοπ., in view of the context and esp. of vv. 42 ff., can only be *His resurrection from the grave* (Est., Gr., Mr., Hn., Hf., El.), which supplies the hinge of Paul's whole argument (*cf.* Rom. i. 4, vi. 4 ff., x. 9, etc.); not *the incarnation* (Thp., Bz., Baur, Ed.), for His pre-resurrection body was a σῶμα ψυχικόν (Rom. viii. 3, etc.; 2 Cor. xiii. 4, Phil. ii. 7, etc.). By rising from the dead, Christ ἐγενήθη εἰς πνεῦμα—He entered on the spiritual and ultimate form of human existence; and at the same time, ἐγενήθη εἰς πν. ζωοποιοῦν—He entered this state so as to communicate it to His fellows: *cf.* vv. 20-23, Col. i. 18, Rev. i. 5; also Rom. viii. 10 f., 2 Cor. iv. 14; John vi. 33, xi. 25, xiv. 19, etc. The action of Jesus in "breathing" upon His disciples while He said, "Receive the Holy Spirit" (John xx. 22 f.), symbolised the vitalising relationship which at this epoch He assumed towards mankind; this act raised to a higher potency the original "breathing" of God by which man "became a living soul". "Spirit is life-power, having the ground of its vitality in itself, while the soul has only a subject and conditioned life; spirit vitalises that which is outside of itself, soul leads its individual life within the sphere marked out by its environment" (Hf.); *cf.* John iii. 34, iv. 14, v. 25 f.; Heb. vii. 25.—ὁ ἔσχατος ἄνθρωπος recalls the Rabbinical title, *ha'adām ha'acharōn*, given to the Messiah (*Neve Shalom*, ix. 9): Christ is not, however, *the later* or second, but *the last*, the final Adam. The *two Adams* of Philo, based on the duplicate narrative of Gen. i., ii.—the ideal "man after the image of God" and the actual "man of the dust of the earth"—with which Pfleiderer and others identify Paul's πρῶτος and ἔσχατος, χοϊκὸς

and ἐπουράνιος Ἀδάμ, are not to be found here. For (*a*) Philo's *first* is Paul's *last;* (*b*) *both* Paul's Adams are equally concrete; (*c*) the resurrection of Christ distinguishes their respective periods, a crisis the conception of which is foreign to Philo's theology; (*d*) moreover, Gen. i. 26 is referred in xi. 7 above to the *historical*, not the ideal, First Man.

Ver. 46 might have been expressly aimed at the Philonian exegesis; it affirms a development from lower to higher, from the dispensation of ψυχὴ to that of πνεῦμα, the precise opp. of that extracted from Gen. i., ii. by Philo. (ἀλλ' οὐ) "Nay, but not first is the spiritual, but the psychic—after that (ἔπειτα: *cf.* 23) the spiritual". P. states a general law (σῶμα is not to be understood with the adjs.): the ψυχικὸν as such demands the πνευματικὸν to follow it (44); they succeed in this order, not the reverse. "The Ap. does not share the notion, long regarded as orthodox, that humanity was created in a state of moral and physical perfection. . . . Independently of the Fall, there must have been progress from an inferior state, the psychic, which he posits as man's point of departure, to a superior state, the spiritual, foreseen and determined as man's goal from the first" (Gd. *ad loc.:* see the whole passage).

Vv. 47-49 draw another contrast between the two "men," types of the two eras of humanity, which is suggested by the words χοῦν ἀπὸ τῆς γῆς ('*aphar minha'adamāh*) of Gen. ii. 7. The first is ἐκ γῆς, χοϊκός (*terrenus*, Vg.; more literally, *pulvereus*, Bz.); the second is ἐξ οὐρανοῦ (om. ὁ Κύριος). The former epithets, and by antithesis the latter, point to *bodily* origin and substance (*cf.* 40, also 2 Cor. iv. 7, ἐν ὀστρακίνοις σκεύεσιν), but connote the whole quality of the life thus determined.—The expression ἐξ οὐρανοῦ (*e cœlo*, Bz.; not *de cœlo*, Vg.) has led to the identifying of the δεύτερος ἄνθρ. with *the incarnate* Christ (see Ed.), to the confusion of

ᵉᵉ οὐρανοῦ · 48. ᶠ οἷος ὁ ᵈ χοϊκός, ᶠ τοιοῦτοι καὶ οἱ ᵈ χοϊκοί · καὶ ᶠ οἷος ὁ ᵍ ἐπουράνιος, ᶠ τοιοῦτοι καὶ οἱ ᵍ ἐπουράνιοι · 49. καὶ καθὼς ʰ ἐφορέσαμεν τὴν ⁱ εἰκόνα τοῦ ᵈ χοϊκοῦ, ʰ φορέσομεν ¹ καὶ τὴν ⁱ εἰκόνα τοῦ ᵍ ἐπουρανίου.

50. Τοῦτο δέ ² ᵏ φημι, ἀδελφοί, ὅτι ˡ σὰρξ καὶ ˡ αἷμα ᵐ βασιλείαν ᵐ Θεοῦ ᵐ κληρονομῆσαι οὐ ⁿ δύνανται,³ οὐδὲ ἡ ᵒ φθορὰ τὴν ᵖ ἀφθαρσίαν

f In this order, 2 Cor. x. 11; Mt. xiii. 19. οιος besides, 2 Cor. xii. 20; Phil. i. 30; 1 Th. i. 5; 2 Tim. iii. 11; Rev. xvi. 18;

Mk. ix. 3.　　g See ver. 40.　　h Rom. xiii. 4; Mt. xi. 8; Jo. xix. 5; Jas. ii. 3; Prov. xvi. 23.
i See xi. 7.　　k See vii. 29.　　l Eph. vi. 12; Heb. ii. 14; Mt. xvi. 17; Sir. xiv. 18; cf. Lk. xxiv. 39.
m See vi. 9 (with κληρονομ.).　　n δυναται, for the compound subj. and sing. vb., cf. Mt. v. 18; there the pred. precedes.　　N.T. h.l. for such a constr. ad sensum, in this order.　　o, p See ver. 42.

¹ φορεσωμεν, all uncc. but B, with 46, and many minn. W.H. retain -ομεν in marg., R.V. and Weiss in txt., referring -ωμεν to marg.; other crit. edd., -ωμεν.

² γαρ, DG, Tert.　　　　　　　　³ δυναται, אBP, 73, Or.

Paul's argument (cf. note on 45). This phrase is suggested by the antithetical ἐκ γῆς: the form of existence in which the risen Jesus appeared was super-terrestrial and pneumatic (cf. 2 Cor. v. 2); it possessed a life and attributes imparted "from heaven"—by an immediate and sovereign act of God (Rom. i. 4, vi. 4, 2 Cor. xiii. 4, Eph. i. 19 f., 1 Peter i. 21, etc.). This transformation of the body of Jesus was foreshadowed by His Transfiguration, and consummated in His Ascension; P. realised it with the most powerful effect in the revelation to himself of the risen Christ "from heaven". The glorious change attested, indeed, the origin of Christ's personality, but it should not be confused with that origin (Rom. i. 4; cf. Matt. xvii. 5). From His resurrection onwards, Christ became to human faith the ἄνθρωπος ἐπουράνιος (Rom. vi. 9 f., Rev. i. 17 ff.), who was taken previously for a θνητὸς and χοϊκὸς like other men.—Baur, Pfleiderer, Beyschlag (N.T. Theology), Sm., and others, see in the ἄνθρωπος ἐξ οὐρανοῦ the pre-existent Christ, whom they identify with Philo's ideal or "heavenly man" of Gen. i. 26 (see note on 45 above); on this interpretation an entire Christology is based —the theory that Christ in his pre-incarnate state was simply the Urmensch, the prototype of humanity, existing thus, either in fact or in the Divine idea, with God from eternity, and being in this sense the Eternal Son. Doubtless the "second man" is ideally first and reveals the true end and type of humanity, and this conception is, so far, a just inference from Paul's teaching. But what P. actually sets forth is the historical relation of the two Adams in the development of mankind, Christ succeeding and displacing our first father (46, see note; 49), whereas the Baurian Urmensch is antecedent to the earthly Adam.

The above χοϊκὸς and ἐπουράνιος have severally their copies in χοϊκοὶ and ἐπουράνιοι (48). Is this a purely physical distinction, between pre- and post-resurrection states of the same men (cf. 44)? or is there a moral connotation implied, as Hf. and Ed. suggest? The latter seems likely, esp. on comparison of Phil. iii. 18 ff., Col. iii. 1-4, Rom. vi. 4, and in transition to the exhortation of ver. 49. Those who are to be "heavenly" in body hereafter already "sit in heavenly places" (Eph. ii. 6), while those are "earthy" in every sense "whose flesh hath soul to suit," οἱ τὰ ἐπίγεια φρονοῦντες. — Admitting the larger scope of ver. 48, we accept the strongly attested hortatory φορέσωμεν of ver. 49: "Let us wear also the image of the Heavenly One". The εἰκὼν embraces the entire "man"—not the body alone, the σχῆμα and σκεῦος ἀνθρώπου (Phil. ii. 7, 2 Cor. iv. 7, 1 Thess. iv. 4)— in Adam and Christ respectively (cf. xi. 7, 2 Cor. iii. 18, Rom. viii. 29, Col. i. 15, iii. 10); and we are exhorted to "put on Christ" (Rom. xiii. 14, Gal. iii. 27), realising that to wear His moral likeness here carries with it the wearing of His bodily likeness hereafter: see vv. 20-23, Rom. viii. 11; 1 John iii. 2 f.

§ 56. VICTORY OVER DEATH, xv. 50-58. The second part of the argument of this chapter has now reached the same platform as the first (cf. §§ 51 and 54). The Resurrection of the Body, it has been shown, is an essential part of the Divine world-plan and necessary to the fulfilment of God's kingdom through Christ (20-27); and the transformation of the

q See ii. 7. ^m κληρονομεῖ.¹ 51. ἰδοὺ ^q μυστήριον ὑμῖν λέγω· πάντες μὲν² οὐ³
r See vii. 39.
s Rom. i. 23 ^r κοιμηθησόμεθα,³ πάντες δὲ ^s ἀλλαγησόμεθα,³ 52. ἐν ^t ἀτόμῳ, ἐν
(Ps. cv.
20); Gal.
iv. 20; Heb. i. 12 (Ps. ci. 26); Acts vi. 14; Lev. xxvii. 33.   t Bibl. h.l.

¹ κληρονομησει: C*D*G, vg. cop. syrr.   ² Om. μεν BC*D*.

³ παντες ου κοιμηθησομεθα παντες δε αλλαγησομεθα (as in
T.R., om. only μεν): BD_bcKLP, etc., cop. syrr., Or., Cyr., Greg.-Nyss., Chr.,
Thdrt. So Tisch., Tr. *txt.*, Al., R.V., W.H., El., Nestle.

παντες κοιμηθησομεθα ου παντες δε αλλαγησομεθα: ℵ(A)CG, 17, Gr. codd.
mentioned by Hier. and by Aug. So Lachm. and Tr. *marg.* A* reads παντες
κοιμηθ. οι παντες κ.τ.λ., afterwards correcting οι to ου, but then inserting ου
before κοιμηθ. as well.

παντες αναστησομεθα ου παντες δε αλλαγ.: D*, d e f, vg. (*omnes quidem resur-*
gemus [or *resurgimus*], *sed non omnes immutabimur*) ; latt. codd. mentioned by Hier.,
by Aug. and Pelag., Hil.   Hier. writes (*Ep.* 119): " Quæritis quo sensu dictum sit et
quomodo in 1 ad Cor. ep. Pauli apost. sit legendum : *Omnes quidem dormiemus, non*
autem omnes immutabimur, an juxta quædam exemplaria : *Non omnes dormiemus,*
omnes autem immutabimur ; utrumque enim in Græcis codd. invenitur ".   The
Patristic authorities from the 3rd to the 5th century stood in doubt as to the true
reading, and the Gr. MSS. then presented great confusion.   Intrinsic considerations are decisive in favour of the T.R., in adopting which the Syrian edd. showed
excellent judgment.   The unusual position of ου (after παντες), and the fact that ου
κοιμηθησ. appear to express an anticipation that failed of fulfilment, led to the
shifting of the ου.   αναστησομεθα is a bold Western paraphrase.   The reading
of B and the T.R. alone agrees with Paul's situation (*cf.* 1 Th. iv. 15), and with
the tenor of this passage.   See note below.   For full textual evidence and discussion, see Tisch.⁸, *ad loc.*, also W.H., vol. ii., p. 118.

earthly into the heavenly, of the psychic
into the pneumatic form of being, is involved in the present constitution of
things and accords with the lines of development traceable in nature and revelation (36-49). In a word, P. holds the
Christian resurrection to be grounded in
the person and mission of Christ, as He
is on the one hand the Son of God and
mediatorial Head of His kingdom (24-28),
and on the other hand the Second Adam
and Firstborn of a spiritual humanity (22
f., 45-49). He finds the key to this great
controversy, as to so many others, in the
supremacy of Christ, the "one Lord,
through whom are all things and we
through Him" (viii. 6). It remains for
him only to state the practical conclusion
of this reasoning (50), to describe our
anticipated transformation and victory
over death (51-57), and to urge his readers
in this confidence to accomplish worthily
their life's work (58).

Ver. 50. Τοῦτο δέ φημι, ἀδελφοί (see
note, vii. 29) introduces, with a pause, an
emphatic reassertion of the ruling thought
of the previous §—that of the opposition between the psychic body of the
First Adam and the spiritual body of the
Second; manifestly the former is unfit
for God's heavenly kingdom—with the
latter, it is assumed (48b; *cf.* Luke xx.

34 ff., 1 John iii. 2 f.), we must be clothed
to enter that diviner realm: " Flesh and
blood cannot inherit God's kingdom ; nor
indeed doth corruption (perishableness)
inherit incorruption (imperishableness) ".
The second assertion explicates the first :
σὰρξ κ. αἷμα = φθορά (*cf.* 42, and note),
since decay is inherent in our bodily
nature ; ὁ ἔξω ἄνθρωπος διαφθείρεται
(2 Cor. iv. 16; *cf.* Rom. viii. 10 f.).
" Flesh " is the matter and " blood " the
essence and life-vehicle of man's present
corporeity. *Nature* forbids eternal life
in this earthly dress (*cf.* note on 46).
" Inherit " points to the kingdom as the
right of the sons of God (Rom. viii. 17,
etc.; *cf.* Matt. xxv. 34), but a heritage
unrealised during the " bondage of corruption " (see Rom. viii. 21 ff.). Another,
but removeable, disability of " flesh and
blood " appears in Matt. xvi. 17.

Vv. 51, 52. This bodily change, indispensable in view of the incompatibility
just affirmed, is the object of a momentous
revelation communicated to P., to which
he calls our earnest attention : " Lo, I
tell you a mystery ! " On μυστήριον,
see note to ii. 1. P. began by demonstrating *the historical fact* of Christ's
resurrection (1-11); he then *reasoned*
upon it, in its bearings on religion and
nature (12-49); now he adds *a new specific*

ᵘῥιπῇ¹ ὀφθαλμοῦ, ἐν τῇ ἐσχάτῃ ᵛσάλπιγγι· ᵂσαλπίσει γάρ, καὶ
οἱ ˣνεκροὶ ˣἐγερθήσονται² ᵞἄφθαρτοι, καὶ ἡμεῖς ˢἀλλαγησόμεθα.

53. ᶻδεῖ γὰρ τὸ ᵃφθαρτὸν τοῦτο ᵇἐνδύσασθαι ᵖἀφθαρσίαν καὶ τὸ

ᵘ Bibl. h.i.
Eur. Iph.
Tr., 885;
-ιζειν, Jas.
i. 6.
v See xiv. 8.
w Mt. vi. 2 ;

Rev. ten times.   x See ver. 15.   y See ix. 25.   z See viii. 2.   a See ix. 25.   b 2 Cor. v.
3; Rom. xiii. 12, 14; Eph. iv. 24, vi. 11; Col. iii. 10; Ps. cxxxi. 9.

¹ D*G, 67**, and some others, read ροπη. Hier.: "εν ριπη sive εν ροπη
οφθαλμου, utrumque enim legitur, et nostri interpretati sunt *in momento* et in *ictu
oculi*".

² αναστησονται, ADGP.

revelation to crown his teaching. In
doing so, P. challenges his opponents in
the right of his inspiration and authority,
hitherto in the background in this chap.
Ver. 15 only vindicated his *honesty*.

In ver. 51b ἀλλαγησόμεθα (required
by 50 and repeated in 52) bears the
stress ; to it the first πάντες (reiterated
with emphasis) looks forward ; οὐ κοιμηθησόμεθα is parenthetical : "We shall
all — not sleep, but — we shall all be
changed". ἀλλάσσω is interpreted by
ἐνδύομαι of ver. 53 and μετασχηματίζω
of Phil. iii. 21. As much as to say :
"Our perishable flesh and blood, whether
through death or not, must undergo a
change". That such a change is impending for the dead in Christ is evident
from the foregoing argument (see esp.
22 f., 36, 42 f.) ; P. adds to this the declaration that the change will be universal, that *it will extend to those living*
when the Last Trumpet sounds (52),
amongst whom he then hoped that many
of the present generation would be found :
cf. i. 7 ; also 1 Thess. iv. 15 ff., where
the like is affirmed ἐν λόγῳ Κυρίου. This
hope dictates the interjected οὐ κοιμηθησόμεθα, which disturbs the grammar
of the sentence and necessitates the contrastive δὲ attached to the repeated
πάντες (see txtl. note ; Wr., p. 695 ; also
El. *ad loc.*). There is no need to suppose a trajection of οὐ (as if for οὐ πάντες,
or οὐ μὲν πάντες κοιμηθησ.), nor any
diff. between the sense of ἀλλαγησ. in vv.
51 and 52 : the certainty of change in *all*
who shall "inherit incorruption" is declared (51), and the assurance is given
that while this change takes place in
"the dead" who are "raised incorruptible," at the same time "we" (the
assumed living) shall undergo a corresponding change (52 ; *cf.* 2 Cor. v. 2 ff.).
Thus in "all" believers, whether sleeping or waking when Christ's trumpet
sounds, the necessary development will
be effected (53 f.).—The critical moment
is defined by three vivid phrases : ἐν

ἀτόμῳ (cl. Gr., ἐν ἀκαρεῖ), ἐν ῥιπῇ ὀφθαλμοῦ (*in ictu oculi*, Vg. ; *in a twinkling*),
ἐν τῇ ἐσχάτῃ σάλπιγγι—the first two
describing *the instantaneousness*, and the
last (with allusion perhaps to the saying
of Matt. xxiv. 31 : *cf.* 1 Thess. iv. 16) *the
solemn finality* of the transformation.
The former idea is emphasized, possibly,
to preclude the fear of a slow painful
process. The σάλπιγξ was the war-
trumpet, used for signals and commands
(*cf.* ἐν κελεύσματι, 1 Thess. iv. 16) ; and
σαλπίσει (sc. ὁ σαλπιγκτής) is indef. in
subject, according to military idiom (*cf.*
Xen., *Anab.*, I., ii., 17). 1 Thess. iv.
identifies the "trumpet" with the "arch-
angel's voice" : any such description is
of course figurative.

Vv. 52, 53. The necessity for change,
negatively declared in ver. 50, is now reaffirmed positively, as a necessity lying in
the nature and relations of the changed :
"For this corruptible (perishable) is bound
(δεῖ : *cf.* xi. 19) to put on incorruption
(imperishableness), and this mortal to put
on immortality". The double τοῦτο
speaks, as in 2 Cor. v. 2, Rom. vii. 24,
out of P.'s painful self-consciousness : *cf.*
2 Cor. iv. 10, Gal. vi. 17.—τὸ θνητὸν
and τὸ φθαρτόν (*concrete*, of felt necessity : ἡ φθορά, 50, *abstract*, of general
principle) relate, as in vv. 42 ff., to *the
present, living body* of the ἡμεῖς, not to
the dead body deposited in the grave.
The aforesaid "change" is now represented as an *investiture* (ἐνδύσασθαι)
with incorruption and immortality ; the
two ideas are adjusted in 2 Cor. v. 4,
where it is conceived that the living
Christian will "put on" the new, spiritual
body "over" (ἐπ-ενδύσασθαι) his earthly
frame, which will then be "absorbed"
(καταποθῇ) by it.

Ver. 54. This clothing of the saints
with immortality fulfils a notable O.T.
word respecting the Day of the Lord :
"Then will be brought to pass the word
that is written, *Death has been swallowed
up* (κατεπόθη, the vb. adopted in 2 Cor.

c 2 Cor. iv.
11, v. 4 ;
Rom. vi.
12, viii.
11.
d 1 Tim. vi.
16 ; Wisd.
viii. 13,
etc.
e Ver. 28,
xvi. 2 ; 2

^cθνητὸν τοῦτο ^bἐνδύσασθαι ^dἀθανασίαν· 54. ^eὅταν δὲ ¹ τὸ ^aφθαρτὸν τοῦτο ^bἐνδύσηται ^pἀφθαρσίαν καὶ ¹ τὸ ^cθνητὸν τοῦτο ^bἐνδύσηται ^dἀθανασίαν,² ^eτότε ^fγενήσεται ὁ λόγος ὁ γεγραμμένος, "^gΚατεπόθη ὁ θάνατος ^hεἰς ^hνῖκος". 55. ποῦ σου, θάνατε, τὸ ⁱκέντρον³; ποῦ σου, ᾅδη,⁴ τὸ ^hνῖκος³; 56. τὸ δὲ ⁱκέντρον τοῦ θανάτου ἡ ἁμαρτία,

Cor. xii. 10 ; Col. iii. 4 ; 1 Th. v. 3 ; Lk. v. 35 ; Jo. viii. 28.　　f Mt. v. 18 ; Mk. xi. 23.　　g Isa. xxv. 8 (see note below) ; in this sense, 2 Cor. v. 4, also ii. 7 ; Mt. xxiii. 24 ; Heb. xi. 29 ; 1 Pet. v. 8 ; Rev. xii. 16.　　h Mt. xii. 20 ; 2 Ki. ii. 26 ; Job xxxvi. 7.　　i Hos. xiii. 14 ; Acts xxvi. 14 ; Rev. ix. 10.

¹ ℵ*C*IM, cop. vg., and several Ff., om. το φθαρτον . . . και, reducing the two οταν clauses to one—οταν δε το θνητον τουτο κ.τ.λ. G om. the entire double οταν clause, skipping from αθανασιαν in ver. 53 to αθανασιαν in ver. 54.

² την αθανασιαν : ℵAI, 17 ; so I in ver. 53.

³ νικος . . . κεντρον (in this order) : ℵBCIM, 17, cop. vg. (BD*I : νεικος, vv. 54 f.).

⁴ θανατε twice : ℵ*BCDGI, 67**, cop. vg., and many Ff. ; ᾳδη in Hosea.

v. 4 as above) *unto victory !*" ὅταν, with its double clause, recalls the double ὅταν of ver. 24 and of vv. 27 f. (see notes), which are parl. to each other and to this, alike marking the great "when," the epoch of the consummation. The destruction of the "last enemy" secures absolute "victory" for Christ and His own. Paul corrects the LXX txt. of Isa. xxv. 8, which makes Death the victor,— κατέπιεν ὁ θάνατος ἰσχύσας ; he appears to have read the Heb. passively *bulla',* for Massoretic *billa'* : Theodotion's translation is identical with Paul's. *lanetsach (for ever)* is often rendered εἰς νῖκος (later Gr. form of νίκη) by the LXX, according to the Aramaic sense of the noun ; its Heb. sense implies a final and unqualified overthrow of the King of Terrors, and therefore admits of P.'s application. "This is the farthest reaching of all O.T. prophecies ; it bears allusion to Gen. iii." (Dillmann ; see also Delitzsch, on the Isaianic txt.), and reverses the doom there pronounced.

Vv. 55-57. At this climax P. breaks into a song of triumph over Death, in the strain of Hosea's rapturous anticipation of Israel's resurrection from national death. [Many interpreters, however, put the opp. sense on Hos. xiii. 14, as though God were summoning Death and the Grave to ply all their forces for Israel's annihilation, and this accords with the prophet's context ; but violent alterations of mood are characteristic of Hosea : see Nowack *ad loc.* in *Handkom. z. A.T.,* also Orelli's *Minor Prophets,* or Cheyne in *C.B.S.*] The passage has the Hebra-istic lilt of Paul's more exalted passages ; *cf.* xiii. 4 ff., and parls. there noted.

"Where, O Death, is thy victory?
Where, O Death, is thy sting?
Now the sting of Death is Sin, and the strength of Sin is the Law ;
But to God be thanks, who gives to us the victory
Through our Lord Jesus Christ!"

P. freely adapts the words of Hosea, repeating θάνατε in the second line, where Hosea writes *she'ōl* (LXX ᾅδη), since *death* is the enemy he pursues throughout (Ed. notes that ᾅδης never occurs in Paul's Epp.) ; and he substitutes syn. terms for each of the other nouns to suit his own vein, νῖκος being taken up from ver. 54, and κέντρον preparing for the thought of ver. 56.—τὸ δὲ κέντρον κ.τ.λ. throws into an epigram the doctrine of Rom. iv.-viii. and Gal. iii. respecting the inter-relations of Sin, Law, and Death : "Mors aculeum quo pungat non habet nisi peccatum ; et huic aculeo Lex vim mortiferam addit" (Cv.). *Sin* gives to death, as we mortals know it, its poignancy, its penal character and humiliating form, with the entire "bondage of corruption" that attaches to it : see esp. Rom. v. 12, 17, vi. 10, 23, vii. 24, viii. 10, 20 ff., Heb. ii. 14 f. Apart from sin, our present bodily existence must have terminated in the course of nature (44-46) ; but the change would have been effected in a far diff. way, without the horror and anguish of dissolution—as indeed it will be for the redeemed who have the happiness to be alive at the Second Advent (see 51 f., and parls.).

ἡ δὲ δύναμις τῆς ἁμαρτίας ὁ νόμος· 57. τῷ δὲ Θεῷ [k] χάρις τῷ
διδόντι ἡμῖν τὸ [h]νῖκος διὰ τοῦ Κυρίου ἡμῶν Ἰησοῦ Χριστοῦ. 58.
Ὥστε, [l]ἀδελφοί μου [l]ἀγαπητοί, [m]ἑδραῖοι γίνεσθε, [n]ἀμετακίνητοι,
[o]περισσεύοντες ἐν τῷ [p]ἔργῳ τοῦ [p]Κυρίου πάντοτε, εἰδότες ὅτι ὁ[m] See vii.
[q]κόπος ὑμῶν οὐκ ἔστι [r]κενὸς ἐν Κυρίῳ.

k See x. 30.
l As form of
address,
h.l. in P.;
Jas. i. 16,
19, ii. 5.
m See vii.
37.
n H.l.; cf.
Col. i. 23.
o See viii. 8;

in like connection, 2 Cor. viii. 2, 7, ix. 8; Rom. xv. 13; Phil. i. 9; Col. ii. 7; 1 Th. iii. 12, iv. 1, 10.
p xvi. 10; Phil. ii. 30; cf. Rom. xiv. 20 (τ. ἐργ. τ. Θ.).   q See iii. 8.   r See ver. 10.

For those who "fall asleep in Christ" (18, 20; 1 Thess. iv. 14), death, while it is still *death* and naturally feared (οὐ θέλομεν ἐκδύσασθαι, 2 Cor. v. 4), is robbed of its "sting" (*cf.* 1 John iv. 18; also John v. 24, viii. 51 f., xi. 25 f., 2 Tim. i. 10; Rev. xx. 6), *viz.*, the sense of guilt and dread of judgment—"tametsi adhuc nos pungit, non tamen letaliter, quia retusum est ejus acumen, ne in animæ vitalia penetret" (Cv.).—κέντρον is *sting* (as in Rev. ix. 10), not *goad* (as in Acts xxvi. 14); Death is personified as a venomous creature, inflicting poisoned and fatal wounds. Here Death reigns through Sin, as in Rom. v. 17; Rom. v. 21 pictures Sin reigning in Death: the effect through the cause, the cause in the effect.—While Death gets from Sin its *sting*, Sin in turn receives from the Law its *power*. ἡ δύναμις τῆς ἁμαρτίας ὁ νόμος condenses into six words Paul's teaching on the relation of Sin to Law (see Rom. iv. 15, v. 20, vi. 14, vii.; Gal. ii. 16, iii., iv. 21-v. 4)—the view, based on his experience as a Pharisee, that the law of God, imposing on sinful man impossible yet necessary tasks, promising salvation upon terms he can never fulfil and threatening death upon non-fulfilment, in effect exasperates his sin and involves him in hopeless guilt; ἡ ἁμαρτία ... διὰ τ. ἐντολῆς ... με ἀπέκτεινεν (Rom. vii. 11).—The exclamation of relief, "Thanks be to God, etc.," is precisely parl. to Rom. vii. 25a, viii. 1 f.—The believer's "victory" lies in deliverance through Christ's propitiatory death (Rom. iii. 23 f.; *cf.* i. 17 f., 30, vi. 11 above) from the condemnation of the Law, and thereby from "the power of Sin," and thereby from the bitterness of Death. Law, Sin, and Death were bound into a firm chain, only dissoluble by "the word of the cross"—God's *power* to the saved" (i. 18; *cf.* Rom. i. 16 f., viii. 1 ff.). Thus the Ap. finally links his doctrine of the Bodily Resurrection and Transformation of Christians to his fundamental teaching as to Justification and the Forgiveness of Sins; ch. xv. is a part

of the λόγος τ. σταυροῦ which alone P. proclaims at Cor. (ii. 1 f.).—God "*gives to us* the victory," won for us by "our Lord Jesus Christ," which otherwise Sin, strengthened (instead of being broken) by the Law, had given to Death. The pr. ptp. τῷ διδόντι τὸ νῖκος asserts the experience of redemption (*cf.* i. 2, vi. 19; 2 Cor. v. 21, xiii. 5, Rom. v. 1 f., Eph. i. 7); similarly ὑπερνικῶμεν, Rom. viii. 37, declares the continuous triumph of faith: for the sentiment, *cf.* Rom. v. 2-11, 1 Thess. v. 16 ff., Phil. iv. 4, 1 Peter i. 3-9.

Ver. 56 is set aside by Sm., and Clemen (*Die Einheitlichkeit d. paul. Br., ad loc.*), after Straatmann and Völter, as a "marginal note" of some early Paulinist, on the ground that it is out of keeping with the lyrical strain of the passage, and with the absence of the anti-legal polemic from this Ep. But the ideas of this ver. fill the contemporary Rom. and Gal. Epp., and are uppermost there in Paul's highest moods (see Rom. viii. 31 ff., 2 Cor. v. 13-21); they are expressed with an originality and pregnant force unmistakably Pauline, and in a rhythmical, imaginative turn of expression harmonising with the context. In this Ep., which "knows nothing but Jesus Christ and Him crucified," the Ap. was bound to link his theology of the Resurrection to the doctrine of salvation by the Cross: see vv. 17 f., in proof that the λόγος τῆς ἀναστάσεως is one, in Paul's mind, with the λόγος τοῦ σταυροῦ.

Ver. 58 briefly directs the previous teaching against the unsettlement caused by Cor. doubts. This unbelief was taxed in vv. 32 ff. with sensualism and ignorance of God; its *enervating effect on Christian work* is here indicated. For ὥστε with impv., *cf.* iii. 21, iv. 5, etc. —ἑδραῖοι γίνεσθε, "show yourselves steadfast": see note on vii. 23, also x. 32, xi. 1; for the adj., see parls. In Col. i. 23 the combination ἑδραῖοι, ἀμετακίνητοι ("not-to-be-moved") is almost identically repeated; similarly in Aristotle, *Nic. Eth.*, II., iv., 3, τὸ βεβαίως καὶ ἀμετακινήτως ἔχειν is specified as a con-

XVI. 1. Περὶ δὲ τῆς ᵃλογίας¹ τῆς εἰς ᵇτοὺς ᵇἁγίους· ᶜὥσπερ
ᵈδιέταξα ᵉταῖς ᵉἐκκλησίαις τῆς Γαλατίας, ᶜοὕτω καὶ ὑμεῖς ποιήσατε.

¹ λογειας (?) : B*or ** and I.

dition of all right and virtuous doing.
—περισσεύοντες κ.τ.λ. adds the positive
to the foregoing negative side of the injunction : " abounding (overflowing : see
parls.) in the work of the Lord always ".
τ. ἔργον τ. Κυρίου (cf. ix. 1 ; Col. iii. 23
f., Matt. xxi. 28, Mark xiii. 34) is " the
work " which " the Lord " prescribes,
while " the work of God " (Rom. xiv. 20 :
cf. iii. 9 above) is " the work " which
" God " does : contrast xii. 5 and 6 above.
—" Knowing (as you do) that your toil is
not empty in the Lord." εἰδότες implies
assured knowledge, such as springs from
the confirmation of faith given in this
chap. On κόπος, see note to iii. 8 ; and
on κενός, ver. 14 : the " toil " is " empty "
which is spent on illusion ; " ce n'est pas
là une activité d'apparat, accompli dans
le néant, comme si souvent le travail
terrestre, mais un sérieux labeur, accompli dans la sphère de l'éternelle réalité "
(Gd.) ; hence the pr. ἐστὶν rather than
ἔσται.—ἐν Κυρίῳ : in the sphere of Christ's
authority, wrought under His headship,
which supplies the basis of all Christian
relations and duties ; cf. ver. 36, iv. 17,
vii. 22, etc.

DIVISION VI. BUSINESS, NEWS, AND
GREETINGS, xvi. The Ap. has delivered
his mind to the Cor. upon the questions
which prompted this great Ep. He had
reserved to the last the profound and
solemn problem of the Future Life, in
its treatment of which the conceit of
intellect and the moral levity that spoiled
this powerful Greek Church found their
most characteristic expression. To the
defence and exposition of the Christian
hope of the Resurrection of the Body P.
has devoted in chap. xv. all his powers
of dialectic and of theological construction, bringing his argument to the glorious conclusion with which, in § 56, the
thought of the Ep. culminates. He has
thus carried his readers far away from
the Cor. atmosphere of jealousy and
debate, of sensuality and social corruption, infecting their Church, to seat them
in the heavenly places in Christ Jesus.
There remain a few matters of personal
interest, to be disposed of in two or three
paragraphs—concerning *the collection for*

Jerusalem (1-4), *his own and Timothy's
intended visits*, and *the invitation declined
by Apollos* (5-12). These are followed
by an energetic *final exhortation*, into
which is woven *a commendation of
Stephanas and other Cor.* now with P.
(13-18), and by *the epistolary salutations*
which are full and animated, a word of
severe warning being attached to his
own *affectionate greeting* and *autograph
signature* (19-24).

§ 57. CONCERNING THE COLLECTION,
xvi. 1-4. During his Third Missionary
Journey P. was collecting money for the
relief of the Christian poor in Jerusalem.
Two chaps. in the middle of 2 Cor. are
devoted to this business, which, as it
seems, had moved slowly in the interval
between the two Epp. The collection
had been set on foot some time ago in
Galatia (1) ; in Macedonia it had been
warmly taken up (2 Cor. viii. f.) ; from
Acts xx. 4 we learn that " Asians " also
(from Ephesus and the neighbourhood)
accompanied P. in the deputation which
conveyed the Gentile offering to the
mother Church. A little later, in writing
to Rome (xv. 25-32), the Ap. refers to
the collection, with great satisfaction, as
completed. Every province of the Pauline
mission appears to have aided in this
charity, which, while it relieved a dis-
tressing need, was prompted also by
Paul's warm love for his people (Rom. ix.
3), and by his desire to knit together the
Gentile and Jewish sections of the
Church, and to prove to the latter the
true faith and brotherhood of the converts from heathenism (2 Cor. ix. 11-14).
P. had taken part in a similar relief sent
from Antioch many years before (Acts
xi. f.) ; and in the Conference of Jerus.,
when the direction of the Gentile mission
was committed to him, the heads of the
Judæan Church laid on him the injunction to " remember the poor " (Gal. ii.
10). Foreign Jews were accustomed, as
an act of piety, to replenish the poor-
funds of the mother city. The Christian
community of Jerus. suffered from chronic
poverty. With little natural or commercial wealth, the city lived mainly upon
its religious character—on the attrac-
tions of the Temple and the Feasts

2. [f] κατὰ [g] μίαν [h] σαββάτων [1] ἕκαστος ὑμῶν [i] παρ᾽ [i] ἑαυτῷ τιθέτω, [k] θησαυρίζων ὅ,τι ἂν [2] [l] εὐοδῶται [3]· ἵνα μή, [m] ὅταν ἔλθω, [m] τότε

f Distrib., see xiv. 27, xv. 31.
g Acts xx. 7; Mk. xvi.

2; Lk. xxiv. 1; Jo. xx. 1, 19.   h In this sense, Mk. xvi. 9; Lk. xviii. 12.   i Mt. xxi. 25. παρα, cf. 2 Tim. iv. 13; Lk. xix. 7, etc.   k 2 Cor. xii. 14; Rom. ii. 5; Jas. v. 3; 2 Pet. iii. 7; Mt. vi. 19 f.; Lk. xii. 21; 4 Ki. xx. 17.   l Rom. i. 10; 3 Jo. 2; Gen. xxxix. 3, 23.   m See xv. 54.

[1] σαββατου, all uncc. but א* (σαββατω), אᶜKLM.

[2] εαν (?), BIM.   So W.H., uniformly.   [3] ευοδωθη, אᶜACIKM, etc.

thronged by Jews from the whole world; and the Nazarenes, while suffering from the intense bigotry of their compatriots in other ways, would find it esp. difficult to participate in employments connected with religion. 1 Thess. ii. 14 intimates that the Judæan Churches had recently undergone severe persecution.

Ver. 1. "But about the collection that (is made) for the saints" (τῆς εἰς τ. ἁγίους). This clause might be construed as subordinate to the following ὡς διέταξα; it reads more naturally as a detached title to the par.—indicating this, seemingly, as another topic of the Church Letter (cf. vii. 1, viii. 1, xii. 1). The subject is alluded to as one in which the Cor. were already interested (see 2 Cor. ix. 2).—λογία (more correctly spelt λογεία) = cl. Gr. συλλογή, or ἔρανος (club-contribution); elsewhere in Paul χάρις (3), εὐλογία (2 Cor. ix. 5), λειτουργία (2 Cor. ix. 12), κοινωνία (Rom. xv. 26). Till the other day this word counted as a h.l. in Gr. literature; but the Egyptian Gr. papyri furnish instances of it as a business term, denoting, along with λογεύω (from which it should be derived), the collecting of money either in the way of imposts or voluntary assessments: see Deissmann's Bibelstudien, pp. 40 ff., Hn. in Meyer's Kommentar ad loc.—The Cor. understand from previous communications who are meant by "the saints" (cf. Rom. xv. 31): Hf. thinks that the Christians of Jerus. are so called by eminence, but such a distinction is un-Pauline (Gal. iii. 28); rather, the fact that the collection is made for the saints commends it to saints (i. 2: cf. 2 Cor. ix. 12 ff.). Such ministry is part of "the work of the Lord" in which the Cor., a moment ago, were bidden to "abound" (xv. 58). —ὥσπερ διέταξα κ.τ.λ.: "Just as I gave order to the Churches of Galatia, so also do you act". This direction was either given by P. personally on his last visit to Gal. at the outset of the Third Missionary Journey (Acts xviii. 23), more than two years before, or through letter or messengers from Ephesus at a later time. This ref. fairly implies that the arrangement made had been successful in Gal.; the business being completed there some while ago, the Ap. makes no observation upon it in the extant Ep. to the Gal., which was probably contemporary with 1 and 2 Cor. (See Lt., Introd. to Gal.) On the question as to the part of "Galatia" intended, see Introd. to Gal. in this Comm., and notes on the relevant passages in Acts.

Ver. 2 rehearses the rule previously laid down for Galatia: "On every first (day) of the week let each of you by himself (= at home) lay up, making a store (of it), whatever he may be prospered in".—μίαν σαββάτου—'echād shabbāth or bashshabbāth—according to Hebrew idiom (see parls.) for the days of the week, the term κυριακὴ ἡμέρα (Rev. i. 10) not being yet current, while the heathen name (dies solis) is avoided. The earliest mention of this Christian day, going to show that the First Day, not the Sabbath, was already the Sacred Day of the Church (cf. Acts xx. 7), appropriate therefore for deeds of charity (cf. Matt. xii. 10).—παρ᾽ ἑαυτῷ, apud se, chez lui (see parls.).— θησαυρίζων, "making a treasure," describes each householder "paulatim cumulum aliquem faciens" (Gr.), till at the end the accumulated store should be paid over.—εὐοδῶται (from εὖ and ὁδός, to send well on one's way) is pr. sbj., with ἂν of contingency and ὅ, τι in acc. of specification: any little superfluity that Providence might throw in a Cor. Christian's way, he could put into this sacred hoard (cf. 2 Cor. viii. 12). Many in this Church were slaves, without wages or stated income. The Vg. renders, "quod si bene placuerit," as though reading ὅ, τι ἐὰν εὐδοκῇ; and Bg. wrongly, "quod commodum sit".—ἵνα μή, ὅταν ἔλθω, τότε κ.τ.λ.: "that there may not be, when I come, collections going on then". P. would avoid the unseemliness and the difficulty of raising the money suddenly, at the last moment; and he wishes when he comes to be free to devote himself to

n Absol.,
Heb. ix.   [a] λογίαι γίνωνται.   3. ὅταν δὲ [n] παραγένωμαι, οὓς ἐὰν [o] δοκιμάσητε,[1]
11; Acts   [p] δι᾽ [p] ἐπιστολῶν [1] τούτους πέμψω [q] ἀπενεγκεῖν τὴν [r] χάριν ὑμῶν εἰς
passim;
Lk.xii. 51, Ἰερουσαλήμ·   4. ἐὰν δὲ ᾖ [2] [s] ἄξιον [2] τοῦ κἀμὲ πορεύεσθαι, σὺν ἐμοὶ
xix. 16;
Jo. iii. 23; πορεύσονται.
Gen. xiv.
13.
o In this   5. Ἐλεύσομαι δὲ πρὸς ὑμᾶς ὅταν Μακεδονίαν [t] διέλθω, Μακεδονίαν
sense, 2
Cor. viii.   γὰρ [t] διέρχομαι·   6. [e] πρὸς ὑμᾶς δὲ [u] τυχὸν [v,e] παραμενῶ,[3] ἢ καὶ [4]
8; Rom.   [w] παραχειμάσω, ἵνα ὑμεῖς με [x] προπέμψητε οὗ ἐὰν πορεύωμαι·
i. 28, xiv.
22; 1 Th.
ii. 4. _Cf._ iii. 13.   p 2 Cor. x. 11; 2 Th. ii. 2, 15, iii. 14.   q Rev. xvii. 3, xxi. 10; Acts xix. 12;
Lk. xvi. 22; Mk. xv. 1.   r In this sense, 2 Cor. viii. 6 f., 19.   s With gen. of _thing_, Rom. i. 12; 1
Tim. i. 15, iv. 9, v. 18, vi. 1; 11 exx. in Lk. and Acts; Mt. iii. 8.   Here only with inf.; _cf._ Lk. xxiv.
25.   t See x. 1.   u Bibl. _h.l._; cl. idiom; _cf._ xiv. 10.   v _καταμενω_, Acts i. 13; _παραμενω_,
Phil. i. 25; Heb. vii. 23; Jas. i. 25; Gen. xliv. 33.   w Tit. iii. 12; Acts xxvii. 12, xxviii. 11.
x 2 Cor. i. 16; Rom. xv. 24; Tit. iii. 13; 3 Jo. 6; Acts xv. 3, xx. 38, xxi. 5.

[1] Lachm., Tisch., Tr., W.H., R.V. _marg._, _place the comma after_ δι᾽ επισ-
τολην, _attaching this adjunct to_ δοκιμασητε: see note below.

[2] αξιον η: ℵcABCIMP.   So critt. edd., exc. Tisch.

[3] καταμενω (?): BM, 67**. So W.H. and Weiss: παραμ. looks like an assimilation to παραχειμασω; the stronger καταμενω is intrinsically fitting, by contrast
with εν παροδφ: see note below.

[4] _Om._ και (?) BM; W.H. _txt._—και in _marg._

higher matters (_cf._ Acts vi. 2)—"tunc alia
agens" (Bg.).

Vv. 3, 4. The Cor. are to choose delegates to bear their bounty, who will travel
to Jerus. with P., if this be deemed fit.
Acts xx. 1-4 shows that in the event a
large number of representatives of Gentile Churches voyaged with P., doubtless
on this common errand.—δι᾽ ἐπιστολῶν
may qualify either δοκιμάσητε (Bz., Cv.,
Est., A.V. and R.V. txt., Ed.) or πέμψω
(R.V. marg., with Gr. Ff., and most
moderns). Being chosen by the Cor., the
delegates surely must have credentials
from them (_cf._ 2 Cor. iii. 1, and Acts xv.,
for such letters passing from Church to
Church; also 1 Clem. _ad Corinth._). At
the same time, as P. is directing the
whole business, he will "send" the deputies and introduce them at Jerus. On
δοκιμάζω, see note to iii. 13.—ἐὰν δὲ
ἄξιον ᾖ κ.τ.λ., "But if it be worth while
that _I_ should journey too, they shall
journey with me"—a hint that P. would
only take part in presenting the collection if the character of the aid sent made
it creditable; otherwise the delegates
must go alone; he will not associate
himself with a _mean_ charity. The inf.
(in gen. case), τοῦ κἀμὲ πορεύεσθαι, depends on ἄξιον—"worthy of my going,"
"si dignum fuerit ut et ego eam" (Vg.);
it can hardly be softened into "if it be
right (seemly on any ground: as in 2
Thess. i. 3, where ἄξιον is unqualified)
that I should go" (Ed.)—as though

the Ap. deprecated being obtrusive; he
is guarding his self-respect, being scarcely
sure of the liberality of the Cor. "Justa
estimatio sui non est superbia" (Bg.).

§ 58. VISITS TO CORINTH, xvi. 5-12.
The arrangements for the Collection have
led P. to speak of his approaching visit
to Cor., and he explains more definitely
his plans in this respect (5-9). _Timothy's_
coming, though not certain, may be
looked for speedily; and the Ap., with
some solicitude, asks for him considerate
treatment (10 f.). _Apollos_ is not coming
at present, as the Cor. seem to have desired and as Paul had urged upon him;
he prefers to wait until circumstances
are more favourable (12).

Vv. 5, 6. "But I will come to you,
when I have gone through Macedonia."
The Ap. writes from Ephesus some time
before Pentecost (8), probably before
Easter (v. 8; see note); he intends to
traverse Macedonia on his way (διέρχομαι, repeated with emphasis, regularly
denotes in the Acts _an evangelistic tour:_
see xiii. 6, xvi. 6, xx. 25, etc.), completing
the work of his mission, there so abruptly
terminated (Acts xvi. f.). This task will
require considerable time (it occupied the
months of summer and autumn, during
which the Ap. penetrated beyond Mac.
into Illyria; Rom. xv. 19), so that P.
expects to see Cor. not much before
winter (6). He adds therefore in explanation, "For I am going through
Macedonia (_travelling over_ the region:

7. ʸοὐ ʸθέλω γὰρ ὑμᾶς ᶻἄρτι ἐν ᵃπαρόδῳ ἰδεῖν· ἐλπίζω δὲ ¹ χρόνον
τινὰ ᵇᶜἐπιμεῖναι ᶜπρὸς ὑμᾶς, ἐὰν ὁ Κύριος ᵈἐπιτρέπῃ.² 8. ᵇἐπιμενῶ
δὲ ἐν Ἐφέσῳ ἕως τῆς ᵉΠεντηκοστῆς· 9. ᶠθύρα γάρ μοι ᶠἀνέῳγε
μεγάλη καὶ ᵍἐνεργής,³ καὶ ʰἀντικείμενοι πολλοί. 10. ἐὰν δὲ ἔλθῃ
Τιμόθεος,⁴ ⁱβλέπετε ἵνα ᵏἀφόβως ᶜγένηται ᶜπρὸς ὑμᾶς· τὸ γὰρ

y See x. 20.
z See iv. 11.
a N.T. h.l.; Gen.
xxxviii. 14.
b In this sense, Gal. i. 18 (with πρός);

Phil. i. 24; Acts six times.   c See ii. 3; also 1 Th. iii. 4; 1 Jo. i. 2; Jo. i. 1; Mt. xiii. 56.
d See xiv. 34.   e Acts ii. 1, xx. 16; Tob. ii. 1; 2 Macc. xii. 32.   f 2 Cor. ii. 12; Col. iv. 3; Acts
xiv. 27; Rev. iii. 8, 20, iv. 1; Isa. xiv. 1.   For θύρα (fig.), Lk. xiii. 24; Jo. x. 9; Hos. ii. 15.   For
the vb., 2 Cor. vi. 11; Rom. iii. 13; Rev. iii. 7; Mt. vii. 7 f., etc.   g Phm. 6; Heb. iv. 12; -γειν,
-γημα, see xii. 6; -γεια, Eph. i. 19, etc.   h Gal. v. 17; Phil. i. 28; 2 Th. ii. 4; 1 Tim. i. 10, v. 14;
Lk. xiii. 17, xxi. 15; Zech. iii. 1.   i See i. 26.   With ἵνα, Col. iv. 17; πως, see iii. 10.   k Phil.
i. 14; Jude 12; Lk. i. 74; Prov. i. 33; Wisd. xvii. 4.

¹ γαρ, all uncc. but KL, and all anc. verss. but syrp. æth.
² επιτρεψη, ℵABCM (P -ψει); -πη, Western and Syrian.
³ εναργης, some latt. and vg., evidens; no extant Gr. codd.
⁴ Τειμοθεος, a favourite itacism of B*D*.

pr., of imminent purpose); but with you haply I will abide (καταμενῶ, as in Acts i. 13, signifies, by contrast to διέρχομαι, keeping to Cor. instead of touring through the province), or [even] spend the winter". Paul will time his visit, if possible, so as to make his winter-quarters in Cor.; in any case, when he arrives, he will give the Cor. the full benefit of his presence. He did so stay for three months (Acts xx. 3). For πρὸς, in converse with, see vv. 7, 10, ii. 3, and parls.—τυχὸν (acc. abs. of neut. ptp.) = εἰ τύχοι (see parl.)—another of the cl. idioms confined to this Ep.; it indicates the uncertainty of human plans, and is piously replaced by ἐὰν ὁ Κύρ. ἐπιτρέψῃ in ver. 7.—In this plan P. has a further aim, which he mentions to show his dependence on the Cor.: "in order that you may send me forward, wheresoever I may go"—i.e. probably, though not certainly, to Jerus. (4); cf. ver. 11, 2 Cor. i. 16, Rom xv. 24. It would help P., whose infirmities required friendly attentions, to have a good "send-off" on his leaving Europe. A generous "collection for the saints" would be a welcome lift (1, 4).

Ver. 7. "For I would not see you now, in passing; for (γὰρ) I hope to stay some length of time (χρόνον τινὰ) with you, if the Lord permit." P. could have crossed by sea and taken Cor. on his way to Mac. (cf. 2 Cor. i. 15 f.); the Cor. had requested his speedy coming, which might have been so arranged. But such a visit could only have been ἐν παρόδῳ (explaining the ἄρτι), "in the way-by," as the summer must be devoted to Mac.; this flying visit would not be of service; there is much to be done at Cor. (xi. 34, etc.),

and when the Ap. does come he means to stay "some time". His recent short visit had been very unsatisfactory (see Introd., chap. ii.).—For ἄρτι, see note on iv. 11; it is in tacit contrast with the future, as in xiii. 12. For ἐπιμεῖναι, "to stay on" (in time)—distinguished from καταμένω, "to stay fixedly" (in place or condition: 6), see parls.—ἐὰν ὁ Κύρ. κ.τ.λ., see parls., also to iv. 19,—pia conditio (Bg.): Paul's plans have been repeatedly overruled (Acts xvi. 6 f.; 1 Thess. ii. 18). He says "if the Lord permit," thinking of his visit as a pleasure; but "if the Lord will," in the parl. clause, iv. 18 f., viewing it as a painful duty.

Vv. 8, 9. "But I stay on in Ephesus until the Pentecost"—τῆς πεντηκοστῆς (ἡμέρας), "the fiftieth day" from the 16th Nisan in the Passover Feast (see parls.). This suggests that P. is writing not very long before Whitsuntide; v. 6 ff. indicated a date for the Ep. immediately antecedent to Easter. Ver. 9 explains why the Ap. must remain at Eph. some time longer, although required at Cor.: "for a door is open to me, great and effectual, and (there are) many adversaries". This θύρα is defined in Col. iv. 3 (cf. 2 Cor. ii. 12) as a θύρα τοῦ λόγου—a door open to the preacher; in Acts xiv. 27 it is seen from the other side, as θύρα πίστεως—a door for the entrance of the believing hearer; see parls. for kindred applications of the figure. The door is μεγάλη in respect of its width and the region into which it opens, ἐνεργής in respect of the influence gained by entering it.—ἀντικείμενοι πολλοί (cf. xv. 32): an additional reason for not retreating; cf. Phil. i. 28. The terrible riot that shortly

[l] ἔργον [l] Κυρίου [m] ἐργάζεται ὡς καὶ ἐγώ[1]· 11. μή τις οὖν αὐτὸν
[n] ἐξουθενήσῃ· [x] προπέμψατε δὲ αὐτὸν [o] ἐν [o] εἰρήνῃ, ἵνα ἔλθῃ πρός
με· [p] ἐκδέχομαι γὰρ αὐτὸν μετὰ τῶν ἀδελφῶν. 12. Περὶ δὲ Ἀπολλὼ
τοῦ ἀδελφοῦ· [q] πολλὰ[2] [r] παρεκάλεσα αὐτὸν [r] ἵνα ἔλθῃ πρὸς ὑμᾶς
μετὰ τῶν ἀδελφῶν· καὶ [s] πάντως οὐκ [t] ἦν [tu] θέλημα [u] ἵνα νῦν
ἔλθῃ, ἐλεύσεται δὲ ὅταν [v] εὐκαιρήσῃ.

l See xv. 58.
m Acts xiii. 41 (Hab. i. 5); Jo. iii. 21, vi. 28, ix. 4; Mt. xxvi. 10; Ps. xliii. 1.
n See i. 28.
o See vii. 15.
p See xi. 33.
q Adv., ver. 19; Rom. xvi. 6, 12, xv. 22 (τα π.); Jas. iii. 2; ten times in Mk.
r See i. 10.
s See v. 10.
t Mt. xviii. 14.
u Jo. vi. 39 f. *Cf.* θελω ινα, Mt. vii. 12; Mk. vi. 25, x. 35; Lk. vi. 31; Jo. xvii. 24.
v Acts xvii. 21; Mk. vi. 31. -ρος, Heb. iv. 6; Mk. vi. 21; -ρως, 2 Tim. iv. 2; Mk. xiv. 11; -ρια, Lk. xxii. 6.

[1] **καγω**: ℵACKLP, and some minn.: so most crit. edd. **και εγω**: DG, etc. **ε γ ω** (simply): BM. So W.H. *txt*.
The last reading best accounts for the others. It appears to be Neutral; **καγω** Alexandrian, **και εγω** Western and Syrian. The emphasis given by **και** is scarcely in keeping here, while it is perfectly suitable in vii. 8 and x. 33 (which may have suggested **καγω** to copyists here), and in 2 Cor. xi. 12; *cf.* Gal. iv. 12.

[2] ℵ*D*G, with corresponding latt. and some anc. codd. of vg., preface this clause with **δηλω υμιν οτι (πολλα κ.τ.λ.)**—an ex. of Western license.

afterwards drove Paul from Eph. verified this statement (Acts xix.). Evangelism flourishes under fierce opposition; "Sæpe bonum et, contra id, malum simul valde vigent" (Bg.).

Vv. 10, 11. **ἐὰν** (not **ὅταν**) **δὲ ἔλθῃ Τιμόθεος**: "But if Timothy come"—his coming is not *certain*. He and Erastus have been before this sent to Macedonia (Acts xix. 21 f.) in advance of P., with instructions to go forward to Cor. (iv. 17 above); he might be expected to arrive about the same time as this letter. But local circumstances, or even the report of the unfriendly attitude of the Cor. (Ed.), might detain him in Mac. He is found in Mac. with P. when some months later 2 Cor. is written: there is no explicit ref. in that Ep. to Timothy's presence at Cor. in the interval; but *Titus'* visit and report are largely in evidence. Ed. says, "In point of fact he (Tim.) did not come" (*cf.* Lt., *Journal of Sac. and Cl. Philology*, ii., 198 ff.; also El.). But this assertion is too positive. In iv. 17 above P. announced Tim.'s coming definitely and laid stress upon it. Tim. shares in the Address of 2 Cor., and the fact that he is associated by the Ap. with himself in the significant "we" of vii. 2 ff. (*cf.* ii. 5-11) points to his being involved in some way in the "grief" which P. had suffered from Cor. subsequently to the writing of 1 Cor. Very possibly *Timothy* was the **ἀδικηθεὶς** of 2 Cor. vii. 12, in whose person, seeking as he did to carry out the directions of 1 Cor. iv. 17, Paul had been insulted by some prominent Cor. Christian (**ὁ ἀδικήσας**).—If this actually happened, the apprehensions expressed here about the treatment Tim. might receive, proved only too well-founded: "see (to it) that without fear he may be with you" (or *hold converse with you*: **γένηται πρὸς ὑμᾶς,** see ii. 3, and parls.) . . . "let no one then set him at naught". These words point to Timothy's diffidence, as well as to his comparative youth: see 1 Tim. iv. 12, and the vein of exhortation in 2 Tim. ii. 1-13 and iii. 10-iv. 18. Tim. was P.'s complement, as Melanchthon was Luther's—gentle, affectionate, studious, but not of robust or masculine character. The temper of the Cor. Church would be peculiarly trying and discouraging to him. Paul hopes that regard for him will have some restraining effect upon the Cor.—**τὸ γὰρ ἔργον Κυρίου** (*cf.* xv. 58) **κ.τ.λ.** identifies Timothy in the strongest way with P. himself: *cf.* iv. 17, Phil. ii. 20; similarly respecting Titus, in 2 Cor. viii. 23. For **ἐξουθενέω,** see parls.—"But send him forward *in peace*"—for if Tim. attempts the task indicated in iv. 17, a rupture is very possible, such as, we gather from 2 Cor. ii. and vii., actually ensued.—From the following words, "that he may come to me, for I am awaiting him," it appears that P. expects Tim's return before he leaves Eph.: *cf.*, for the vb., xi. 33.—It is doubtful whether **μετὰ τῶν ἀδελφῶν** qualifies the subject—"I with the brethren"—those of vv. 12-18, the Cor. brethren now in Eph. and interested in Tim's success at

13. [w] Γρηγορεῖτε, [x] στήκετε ἐν τῇ πίστει· [y] ἀνδρίζεσθε,[1] [z] κρα-
ταιοῦσθε· 14. [a] πάντα [a] ὑμῶν ἐν ἀγάπῃ [b] γινέσθω. 15. [c] Παρακαλῶ
δὲ ὑμᾶς, ἀδελφοί—[d] οἴδατε τὴν [e] οἰκίαν Στεφανᾶ,[2] [d] ὅτι ἐστὶν [f] ἀπαρχὴ
τῆς Ἀχαΐας καὶ [g] εἰς [h] διακονίαν τοῖς [i] ἁγίοις [g] ἔταξαν ἑαυτοὺς—
16. [c] ἵνα καὶ ὑμεῖς [k] ὑποτάσσησθε [l] τοῖς [l] τοιούτοις, καὶ παντὶ τῷ

w Col. iv. 2; 1 Th. v. 6, 10; Acts xx. 31; 1 Pet. v. 8; thrice in Rev.; 14 exx. in Syn. GG. x In this sense, Rom. xiv. 4; Gal. v. 1; Phil. i. 27, iv. 1; 1 Th. iii. 8; 2 Th. ii. 12; Jo. viii. 44. y N.T. *h.l.*; Josh. i. 6. z Eph. iii. 16; Lk. i. 80, ii. 40; Neh. ii. 18. -αιος, 1 Pet. v. 6. a This constr. of πας, *h.l.* b See ix. 15. c See i. 10; ver. 12. d See iii. 20; with οιδα, 2 Cor. xii. 3 f.; 1 Th. ii. 1. e Phil. iv. 22; Jo. iv. 53; Gen. l. 8. f See xv. 20. g Acts xiii. 48; *cf.* 2 Macc. vi. 21, προς and dat. For vb., Rom. xiii. 1; Acts xv. 2; Mt. viii. 9, etc. h See xii. 5. i See vi. 1. k See xiv. 32. l See v. 5.

[1] Ins. **και** AD, cop. vg. syrsch.

[2] **Στεφανα και Φορτουνατου**: ℵcD and some minn., vg. (oldest codd.), cop., Dam., Ambrst. C*G add **και Αχαϊκου** besides.

Cor., who are delaying their return until he brings his report (so Hf., Gd.); or the object—"I await him with (= and) the brethren," *i.e.* those, including possibly Erastus, whom P. expects to arrive at Eph. from Cor. along with Tim. (so most interpreters). The relevancy of the words on the latter construction is not obvious. On the former view, "the brethren" of vv. 11 and 12 are the same, being the deputies who had brought over the Cor. Church Letter to P., and who are now awaiting Tim's return before they themselves return home. This hints an additional reason why the Cor. should with all speed send Timothy back to Paul "in peace".

Ver. 12. The manner in which the clause **Περὶ δὲ Ἀπολλὼ τοῦ ἀδελφοῦ** is loosely prefixed to the statement of this ver. ("Now about Apollos the brother"—) suggests that Apollos' coming had been mentioned in the Church Letter: *cf.* ver. 1, vii. 1, etc. Respecting *Apollos*, see notes to i. 12, and Acts xviii. 24 ff.—Considering the way in which Ap. had been made a rival to P. in Cor., it shows magnanimity on Paul's side to desire his return, and a modest delicacy on the side of Apollos to decline the request: **καὶ πάντως οὐκ ἦν θέλημα ἵνα κ.τ.λ.**, "And there was no will at all (it was altogether contrary to his will) that he should come now".—**εὐκαιρέω** (see parls.) denotes "to have good opportunity". The present ferment at Cor. affords no **καιρὸς** for Apollos' coming. For **πάντως**, and **θέλημα ἵνα**, see parls.

§ 59. Concluding Homily, xvi. 13-18. According to the Apostle's wont, at the end of his letter he gathers up the burden of his message into a single concise and stirring exhortation (13 f.). *Watchfulness*, *steadfastness*, *manly vigour*, above all *Christian love*, were the qualities in which this Church was lacking. Their "love" they would have a particular opportunity of showing to the family of Stephanas, who had been foremost in works of benevolence (15 f.); for St. is now returning home in charge of this Ep. with his two companions, after they had brought the letter of the Church to P. and cheered him by their society. The deputation has done a timely public service in the best spirit; their kindly offices must be duly acknowledged (17 f.).

Vv. 13, 14. **Γρηγορεῖτε, στήκετε** belong to a class of vbs. peculiar to later Gr.—presents based on older perfects; the former from **ἐγρήγορα (ἐγείρω)**, the latter from **ἕστηκα (ἵστημι)**. The first exhortation recalls xv. 33 f., the second iv. 17, x. 12, xv. 2, 11 ff.—**ἀνδρίζεσθε**, "play the man," *viriliter agite* (Vg.), adds an active element to the passive and defensive attitude implied in the previous impvs.; it looks back to xiii. 11 and xiv. 20 (relating to the *glossolalia*), but exhorts in general to the courageous prosecution of the Christian life by the Cor., who were enfeebled by contact with heathen society (x., 2 Cor. vi. 11 ff.). This word is common in cl. Gr.; *cf.* 1 Macc. ii. 64, **ἰσχύσατε κ. ἀνδρίζεσθε ἐν τῷ νόμῳ**, also the Homeric **ἀνέρες ἐστέ**.—**κραταιοῦσθε** enjoins manful activity, in its most energetic form (see parls.). **κράτος**, from which, through **κραταιός** (1 Peter v. 6), the vb. is derived (cl. Gr. **κρατύνω**), signifies *superior power*, *mastery* (see Col. i. 11, 1 Tim. vi. 16): "be [not merely strong, but] *mighty*". The four impvs. of ver. 13 are directed respectively against the *heedlessness*, *fickleness*, *childishness*, and *moral enervation* of the

m 2 Cor. vi. ^m συνεργοῦντι καὶ ⁿ κοπιῶντι.   17. ° Χαίρω δὲ ° ἐπὶ τῇ ^p παρουσίᾳ
1; Rom.
viii. 28;   Στεφανᾶ καὶ Φουρτουνάτου ¹ καὶ Ἀχαϊκοῦ, ὅτι τὸ ^q ὑμῶν ² ^r ὑστέρημα
Jas. ii. 22;
Mk. xvi.   οὗτοι ³ ^s ἀνεπλήρωσαν· 18. ^t ἀνέπαυσαν γὰρ ⁴ τὸ ἐμὸν ^u πνεῦμα καὶ
20; 1
Esdr. vii.   τὸ ὑμῶν· ^v ἐπιγινώσκετε οὖν ¹ τοὺς ¹ τοιούτους.
2; 1 Macc.
xii. 1.
-γος, see iii. 9.   n See xv. 10.   o See xiii. 6.   p In this use, 2 Cor. vii. 6 f.; Phil. i. 26, ii. 12;
2 Macc. viii. 12, xv. 21. Cf. xv. 23.   q υμετερον, see xv. 31.   r 2 Cor. viii. 13 f., ix. 12, xi. 9;
Phil. ii. 30; Col. i. 24; 1 Th. iii. 10; Lk. xxi. 4; Judg. xviii. 10. -εω, see i. 7.   s See xiv. 16; in
this antith., Phil. ii. 30.   t 2 Cor. vii. 13; Phm. 7, 20; Mt. xi. 28; 1 Chron. xxii. 9, 18. -σις, Mt.
xi. 29, xii. 43; Rev. iv. 8, xiv. 11.   u See xiv. 15.   v 2 Cor. vi. 9; Deut. i. 17, xxxiii. 9. Cf.
1 Th. v. 12.

¹ Φορτουνατου, all uncc. but KMP.

² υμετερον, all uncc. but אAKL.

³ ουτοι, אBCKLP. αυτοι, ADGM, with vg. syrr.; so Lachm., Tr. marg.

⁴ Ins. και DG, latt. vg., Ambrst.

Cor.: the fifth—"All your doings, let them be done (or carried on: γινέσθω) in love"—reiterates the appeal of chh. viii. and xiii. touching the radical fault of this Church; see also ii. 3, iv. 6, vi. 1-8, xi. 21 f., xii. 21, etc.

Vv. 15, 16 urge particular instances of the above ἐν ἀγάπῃ γινέσθω. The ἵνα clause of ver. 16 is complementary to παρακαλῶ (see note on i. 10), and is suspended to make room for the explanatory οἴδατε . . . ἑαυτούς: "you know that the household of Stephanas is the first-fruit of Achaia, and that they set themselves for ministering to the saints".— τὴν οἰκίαν κ.τ.λ., acc. by attraction to οἴδατε, according to the well-known Gr. usage with vbs. of this class (Wr., p. 781). There were earlier individual converts in Achaia (see Acts xvii. 34), but with this family the Gospel took root in the province and the earnest appeared of the subsequent ingathering: cf. Rom. xvi. 5; also i. 16 above, and note. The St. family must have been of independent means; for ἔταξαν ἑαυτοὺς (they arrayed or appointed themselves—made this their business) implies a systematic laying out of themselves for service, such as is possible only to those free to dispose, as they choose, of their persons and their time; see this idiom in Plato, Rep., ii., 371C. —"The saints" can hardly be the Jerus. saints of ver. 1, since εἰς διακονίαν is quite general, and the last words of ver. 16 imply manifold Christian labour; the present commission of St. to Eph. is an instance of "service to the saints".—P. "exhorts" his "brethren . . . that you also (in return for their service to you) submit yourselves to such as these (τ. τοιούτοις, referring to the interpolated οἴδατε κ.τ.λ.), and to every one that

shares in the work and labours". These persons did not constitute a body of Church officers; we find no traces as yet of an official order in the church of Cor.: the Ap. enjoins spontaneous submission to the direction of those able and disposed to lead in good works. The prp. in σύν-εργοῦντι refers not to St. specifically, still less to P., but generally to co-operative labour in the Church, while κοπιῶντι implies labour carried to the point of toil or suffering (see note on κόπος, iii. 8; also xv. 58). Loyal and hard work in the cause of Christ earns willing respect and deference in the Church: cf. 1 Thess. v. 12 f.

Vv. 17, 18. "But I rejoice at the presence (or coming) of Stephanas, and Fortunatus, and Achaïcus." The stress lying on παρουσίᾳ explains the introductory δέ: "You must show respect to such men, when they reach home; but I am glad that just now they are here". —Fortunatus (Lat. name, and common) and Achaïcus (Gr., and rare) are Stephanas' companions in the deputation; the three will speedily return to Cor. Since P. thus commends them at the end of his Ep., written in reply to the Letter they had brought from Cor., perhaps they were to be its bearers also.— On Stephanas, see i. 16. The two latter names are also h.ll. in N.T.; a Fortunatus appears in Clement's list of emissaries from Rom. to Cor. (ad Cor. § 65). Ed. supposes all three to be slaves (Achaïcus, at least, resembles a slave-name), and identifies them with οἱ τ. Χλόης of i. 11; but this does not comport with the position given to Stephanas in vv. 15 f.; see, further, note on i. 11.—("I rejoice at their presence), because the (or my) lack of you these have filled up". ὑμέ-

19. ^wἈσπάζονται ὑμᾶς[1] αἱ ^xἐκκλησίαι τῆς ^{x,y}Ἀσίας· ^wἀσπάζονται[2]
ὑμᾶς ^yἐν ^yΚυρίῳ ^zπολλὰ Ἀκύλας καὶ Πρίσκιλλα,[3] σὺν ^aτῇ ^{a,b}κατ'
^bοἶκον αὐτῶν ^aἐκκλησίᾳ[4]· 20. ^wἀσπάζονται ὑμᾶς οἱ ἀδελφοὶ πάντες.

w Finis of
P.'s Epp.,
exc. Gal.,
Eph., 1
and 2
Tim.;
of other

Epp., exc. 2 Pet., 1 Jo., Jude.   x See ver. 1.   y Rom. xvi. 2 ff.; see vii. 22 above, etc.   z See
ver. 12.   a Rom. xvi. 5; Col. iv. 15; Phm. 2.   b Acts ii. 46, v. 42; cf. εν οικω, xi. 34 above.

[1] CP, syrsch. ins. πασαι.

[2] ασπαζεται, אCDKP. ασπαζονται: BGLM, etc.

[3] Πρισκα, אBMP, 17, vg. (best codd.) cop.   See note below.

[4] DG, latt. vg., Clem., Pelag. add παρ' οις και ξενιζομαι (apud quos et hospitor)—
an ancient gloss, contradicting the απο Φιλιππων of the Subscription.

τερον represents the *objective* gen. (*cf.*
xv. 31): the presence of the three with
P. could not make up any lack in Cor.,
but it made up to P. for *the absence of
the Cor.*, supplying him, representatively,
with their desired society. El. and others
read the poss. pron. *subjectively*—"what
you were lacking in (*i.e.*, your want of
access) towards me": this constr. is
consistent with the usage of ὑστέρημα (see
parls.); but the former suits better the
antithesis to παρουσία (Ed.), and Paul's
fine courtesy.—"For they refreshed my
spirit—and yours." ἀναπαύω (see parls.)
describes the restful effect of friendly
converse and sympathy. Paul adds καὶ
ὑμῶν, realising that the comfort of heart
received by himself will react upon his
friends at Cor.: the Cor. will be cheered
to know that their fellowship, in the
persons of S., F., and A., has so greatly
cheered him at a time of weariness and
heavy trial (*cf.* 2 Cor. ii. 3, vii. 3).

Ver. 18b repeats in another form the
advice of ver. 16: "Acknowledge (know
well) then such men as these". For
τοὺς τοιούτους, see parls., and ver. 16.
—ἐπιγινώσκω (see parls.) denotes strictly
accurate knowledge, of persons or things;
but knowledge of personal qualities implies corresponding *regard to and treatment of* those who possess such qualities:
cf. 1 Thess. v. 12 f.

§ 60. FINAL GREETINGS, xvi. 19-24.
The Ep. closes with three public salutations from the Christians surrounding P.
at Ephesus to their brethren at Cor. (19,
20a), followed by a request to the latter,
such as appears besides in 1 Thess., 2
Cor., Rom., and Phil., to "salute one
another" in token of brotherly union,
and of communion with those who now
send their greetings (20b). The letter is
then sealed with the writer's personal
salutation (21-24) penned by his own
hand, and stamped with a characteristic
double motto peculiar to this Ep., which

expresses the supreme peril and supreme
consolation of the Christian calling (22).

Vv. 19, 20a. Three successive clauses,
headed by ἀσπάζομαι: "There salute
you the Churches of Asia. There saluteth
you in the Lord abundantly Aquila and
Prisca, with the assembly (church) at
their house. There salute you all the
brethren". The pl. expression, αἱ ἐκκλησίαι τῆς Ἀσίας, accords with what
appears elsewhere as to the general diffusion of the Gospel in the province of
Asia during Paul's three years' ministry
at Eph. (Acts xix. 10, 26; Col. i. 6, ii. 1,
iv. 13, 16), and as to the solidarity of the
Asian Churches gathered round Eph., to
which collectively the Revelation of John,
and probably the (so-called) Ep. to the
Ephesians, were addressed. While P.
had not personally visited all these communities (Col. ii. 1), he was in touch
with them and knew their mind towards
their brethren in Greece. Desiring a
more catholic feeling in the Cor. Church
(see note on i. 2), P. makes the most of
these Church greetings.—The second
salutation has a note of personal warmth,
as the first of catholic breadth: Aq. and
Prisca "send much greeting" (πολλά—
cf. 12, etc.—in requests and wishes, implies *frequency* or *intensity*, or *both*);
and "in the Lord"—not as a matter of
ordinary friendship, but in the way of
love and service to Christ. This worthy
pair entertained the Ap. in Cor. when he
first came there (Acts xviii. 1 ff.); on
some occasion (perhaps about this time
at Eph.) they risked their lives for his
(Rom. xvi. 4). They had now migrated
to Eph., where they reappear some years
later in 2 Tim. iv. 19; see notes on Rom.
xvi. 3 ff., for their further history.
Thrice their names figure in the Acts,
and thrice in the Epp.—*Prisca first*
("Priscilla" only in Acts) four times:
see Hort's *Prolegom. to Rom. and Eph.*,
pp. 12 ff., Sand.-Headlam, *Romans*, pp.

c 2 Cor. xiii.
12; Rom.
xvi. 16; 1
Th. v. 26;
1 Pet. v.
ἀσπάσασθε ἀλλήλους ἐν ᶜφιλήματι ᶜἁγίῳ.　21. Ὁ ᵈἀσπασμὸς,
ᵈτῇ ᵉἐμῇ ᵈᵉχειρί, ΠΑΎΛΟΥ·　22. ᶠᵍεἰ ᶠτις ᵍοὐ ʰφιλεῖ τὸν ʰΚύριον

14. φίλημα besides, Lk. vii. 45, xxii. 48; Prov. xxvii. 6; Cant. i. 2. φιλέω in this sense, Mt. xxvi.
48, etc.; καταφιλέω, Acts xx. 37; 5 exx. in GG.　d Col. iv. 18; 2 Th. iii. 17. The noun besides,
Mt. xxiii. 7; Lk. i. 29, etc.　e Gal. vi. 11; Phm. 19.　f 2 Tim. iii. 10; Mt. xvi. 24; Rev. xiv. 11.
g See vii. 9.　h Jo. xxi. 15 ff.　Cf. note c above.

418 ff., also Rom. *ad loc.* above, on the
conjectures associated with this lady's
name. The vb. is sing., the two sending
one greeting.—The "ecclesia at their
house" can scarcely mean the whole
Eph. Church, but some neighbouring
part of it accustomed to gather, more
or less formally, at Aquila's hospitable
hearth. If P. lodged with A. (see txtl.
note), as he had done in Cor., the house
would be a rendezvous for Ephesian
Christians: *cf.* Rom. xvi. 5, Col. iv. 15,
Philem. 2, Acts xii. 12.—οἱ ἀδελφοὶ πάντες comprise the whole body of Ephesian
believers, in distinction from the smaller
circle of Aquila's house, and from the
mass of the Asian Christians.

Ver. 20*b*. ἐν φιλήματι ἁγίῳ = ἐν φιλήματι ἀγάπης (1 Peter v. 14). This Heb.
custom of the sacred kiss is retained, at
Communion, by the Greek and Eastern
Churches; it died out in the West from
the 13th cent., after having been the
subject of many Conciliar limitations,
occasioned by its abuse in the decline of
Christian simplicity. ἁγίῳ by position is predicative—"in a kiss that is
holy". See Art. *Kiss* in *Dict. of Christian Antiquities*.

Vv. 21–24. Paul's autograph salutation, which authenticates the letter (*cf.* 2
Thess. iii. 17), includes the *title* of the
greeting (21), the double *motto* (22), and
the *greeting* proper—in two wishes (23 f.).

Ver. 21. ὁ ἀσπασμὸς τ. ἐμῇ χειρί,—
ΠΑΎΛΟΥ: "the salution, with my own
hand,—of *PAUL* ".—Παύλου apposed to
τῇ ἐμῇ, and inscribed with the distinction
of a personal signature. Up to this
point, the Ep. was presumably written by
another hand (*cf.* Rom. xvi. 22).

Vv. 22, 23. With pen in hand, Paul
must needs give expression, in two words,
to the pent-up feeling under which he has
written—a fiery seal burnt upon the last
leaf of the Letter; ch. vi. 12–17 of Gal.
occupies a like place in that Ep. The
sentiment, or motto, of the ἀσπασμὸς
forms two clauses: (*a*) "If any one loves
not the Lord, let him be anathema".—
οὐ (instead of μή) in hypothetical clauses
may rest upon the vb., constituting it a
negative term—*sc.*, "*hates* the Lord" (so
Ed.: *cf.* vii. 9, xi. 6, xv. 13; and Rom.

vii. 20, where οὐ θέλω = *nolo*); but Wr.
(pp. 599–602) rightly distinguishes such
instances as this and ix. 2 (*cf.* note) from the
above class of combinations, accounting
for the οὐ as contradictory to some tacit
assertion—"if any one does *not* love the
Lord" (as he ought, or pretends, to do):
it is a *spurious* love that is accursed—a
cold, false heart which, knowing the
Lord, does not really love Him (*cf.* viii.
1 ff., xiii. 1 f.). The use of φιλέω for
ἀγαπάω (only in Tit. iii. 15 elsewhere in
P.: *cf.* the interchange in John xxi. 15
ff.) is noticeable: for the distinction, see
Gm., *s.v.* φιλέω; Cr., *s.v.* ἀγαπάω;
Trench, *N.T. Syn.*, § 12.—οὐ φιλεῖ
strikes a deep note of accusation; it is a
charge of *heartlessness*—human affection
to the Master is wanting, to say nothing
of higher feeling, as with Judas and his
traitor kiss (see Mt., xxvi. 47 f.); perhaps
ἐν φιλήματι just above suggested this
φιλεῖ.—Paul's curse on the Lord's false
lovers recalls xii. 3 (see note on ἀνάθεμα):
the haters of Jesus outside the Church,
inspired by Satan, call Him "anathema"
instead of "Lord"; and those who bow
the knee to Him with a feigned heart are
themselves anathema—this cry a retort
to that.—ἤτω for ἔστω (see Wr., p. 85)
prevails in N.T.; it is common in later Gr.

(*b*) The second clause of the motto,
Μαρὰν ἀθά, is Aramaic transliterated into
Gr.; the original cannot be quite certainly
restored.—Μαρὰν, it is fairly certain, represents *Marán* (Syrian) or *Maran'a*
(Aramaic: the final '*a* of the suffixed
noun having coalesced with the initial
'*a* of the vb.), and ἀθά the pf. Peal of
'*atha*', *to come*. But it is doubtful
whether '*atha*' is strictly *past*—"our Lord
hath come" (so Cm. and the ancients,
with the Syriac Vers.; and Kautzsch in
his *Gramm. d. Bib.-Aramäischen*, pp. 12
and 174; see also Field's *Otium Norvic.*,
iii., pp. 110 f.); or whether the pf. should
be rendered *proleptically*—"Our Lord
cometh," "will come," "is at hand,"
after the manner of Phil. iv. 5, 1 Thess.
iv. 14 ff., James v. 7 ff., Rev. i. 7, iii. 11,
xxii. 20. The latter sense accords with
the context, with the strain of ch. xv.,
and with the N.T. attitude towards our
Lord's return: see i. 7, xi. 26, 1 Thess. i.

Ἰησοῦν [1] Χριστόν,[1] [i] ἤτω [k] ἀνάθεμα · [l] Μαρὰν ἀθά.[2] 23. Ἡ [m] χάρις [i] Jas. v. 12; Ps. ciii.
τοῦ [m] Κυρίου [3] Ἰησοῦ Χριστοῦ [4] [m] μεθ' ὑμῶν. ἡ [n] ἀγάπη [n] μου μετὰ 31; 1 Macc. x. 31.
πάντων ὑμῶν ἐν Χριστῷ Ἰησοῦ. ἀμήν.[5] k See xii. 3.
Πρὸς Κορινθίους πρώτη ἐγράφη ἀπὸ Φιλίππων διὰ Στεφανᾶ καὶ l H.l.; see note
Φουρτουνάτου καὶ Ἀχαϊκοῦ καὶ Τιμοθέου.[6] below.
m 2 Cor.xiii. 13; Rom.

xvi. 20, 24; Gal. vi. 18; Phil. iv. 23; 1 Th. v. 28; 2 Th. iii. 18; Phm. 25; Rev. xxii. 21. Without μεθ' ὑμ., 2 Cor. viii. 9; Acts xv. 11. n Subj. gen., Phil. i. 9; Col. i. 8, 13; 1 Th. iii. 6; 2 Th. i. 3; Phm. 5, 7; Rev. ii. 4, 19; Mt. xxiv. 12; Jo. xv. 9 f. H.l. for this form of wish; cf. 2 Cor. xii. 15.

[1] *Om.* Ιησουν Χριστον ℵ*ABC*M, 17. KP, syr^{sch.}, Victorin., Pelag. add ημων to Κυριον. Ιησ. χρ. is a Western and Syrian addition. The arm. vers., one cod. of vg., and a few Ff., add Ιησουν alone.

[2] Some edd. write μαραναθα as a single word.

[3] ALP, many minn., cop. syr^{sch.}, several Ff., ins. ημων.

[4] *Om.* Χριστου ℵ*B, 17, 73, oldest vg. go., Thdrt. So the crit. edd., exc. Lachm. and R.V., who retain Χρ.

[5] *Om.* αμην BFM, 17. So all crit. edd.; only Lachm. *brackets.* A liturgical addition.

[6] The Subscription, as in other Epp., varies much in form. ℵABC* read προς Κορινθιους ᾱ, as at the beginning of the Ep. The received Subscr., due probably to a misunderstanding of ver. 5 (Μακεδονιαν γαρ διερχομαι), appears first in the Syrian uncc. KL. B³P and a few others have, more correctly, εγραφη απο Εφεσου.

10, etc. So most moderns. Bickell, Gd., and a few others, would read *Maran'a tha'*, making the vb. *impv.* — "Our Lord, O come!"—in keeping with Rev. xxii. 20; but this is questionable in grammar, and less appropriate. The exclamation, like Ἀββᾶ (Rom. viii. 15, Gal. iv. 6) and Ἀμήν, was probably caught up by Gentile Christians from the first preachers, who in moments of rapture naturally reverted to their mother tongue; *cf.* Ed. *ad loc.* Such salient and mystic phrases might serve as watch-words, or on occasion as passwords, amongst the early Christians. In *Didaché*, x. 6, Μαρὰν ἀθὰ stands as the closing formula of the Thanksgiving Prayer at the Eucharist, apparently in the sense of xi. 26 above. For other interpretations, numerous and often fanciful, see the digest in Mr.-Hn. *ad loc.*, also N. Schmidt in the *Journal of Bibl. Liter.*, 1894, i., ii., 50 ff.

Vv. 23, 24. Having uttered the great watchword of the waiting Church, Paul has only to add his personal *benediction upon the readers:* (1) in his favourite phrase of farewell, desiring them *Christ's grace*—a wish expanded in 2 Cor. into the Trinitarian blessing of ch. xiii. 13; (2) in the further wish, peculiar to this Ep. and fitting in view of the frequent censures of the letter, which might seem to indicate alienation on the writer's part (*cf.* iv. 14 f., 2 Cor. xi. 11, xii. 15; Gal. iv. 16 ff.)—"*My love* be with you all in Christ Jesus". Many Cor. Christians ranged themselves under other leaders, many criticised and opposed the Ap., some he has been obliged to threaten with the "rod" (iv. 21); nevertheless he desires his love to "all,"—and that abidingly, "*with* you all, *in* Christ *Jesus*," who is the basis and bond of love amongst His people. Mr., Hn., Bt. read the last sentence as a *matter-of-fact*, not a wish, understanding ἐστὶν instead of εἴη—"My love is with you, etc."; but this destroys the parallelism with ver. 23 (see El.). The sentence expresses an *aspiration* rather than an actuality. Paul's "love in Christ Jesus" is not, strictly speaking, *with* those who "love not the Lord" (21), nor with those who "destroy the temple of God" (iii. 17), nor with the culprit of v. 1-5.

The Expositor's Greek Testament

EXTRACTS FROM PRESS NOTICES OF VOL. I.

" Dr. Bruce's commentary on the Synoptics is a notable piece of work. It is cheering and refreshing to find these books, with which our inner life is so closely bound up, treated frankly and honestly, as well as adequately for English readers, and withal in so believing and reverent a spirit that the treatment need not repel the most orthodox. . . . All is set forth with great frankness and admirable common sense, and often in racy language, not without an occasional Scottish flavour."—*Athenæum*.

" Dr. Marcus Dods has produced a fine piece of work. His introduction is clear, careful and decisive in its tone. We have found his notes stimulating and suggestive. They are marked by accurate scholarship and deep reverence."—*Guardian*.

" The first thing that strikes one when he takes up the volume on the Gospels is the uncommon handsomeness of the book. It is a joy to handle it and look into its pages. It is the very book to lure a student into reading. The form is so superb, the paper so choice and so light, the margins so delightfully broad, the type so clear and so tasteful. . . . The two scholars to whom this volume has been committed are the very men for the work. Each is a master of his subject, and each has gone into his task *con amore*. . . . A work worthy of the most cordial appreciation."—*Critical Review*.

" The book may be cordially recommended to students of the Greek Testament, to whom it will unquestionably prove an immense boon. The names of the authors are a guarantee both for accuracy of scholarship and for a treatment of the text at once learned, and popular, reverential and thoroughly up to date."—*Scotsman*.

" It is written with a freshness and ability, and in the sight of the latest results of constructive scholarship."—*Standard*.

" Dr. Nicoll's edition, in its valuable introduction, its critical apparatus and its finely compressed notes on many crucial passages, incorporates a large measure of the results of modern scholarship."
—*Literature*.

" We can cordially congratulate both editor and publishers on this work, and can as cordially recommend it to those for whom it is specially designed."—*Speaker*.

" Dr. Bruce has done a thoroughly original piece of work, and made every man who has to expound the Gospels his debtor. It is not only a good book: one need not hesitate to say that it is the best book on the Synoptics a minister could consult. It can be read through with delight, with exhilaration, with a constant wonder at its freshness, fertility and insight. It is a unique contribution to the interpretation of the mind of Christ."—*British Weekly*.

The Expositor's Bible

EDITED BY THE REV.

W. ROBERTSON NICOLL, M.A., LL.D.

Each Volume may be had separately, price 7s. 6d. Sets may still be obtained at Subscription Terms, as shown below.

* *The Volumes of the different Series are not assorted on Subscription Terms.*

FIRST SERIES.

Subscription Price, 24s. Separate Volumes, 7s. 6d. each.

St. Mark
By the Rt. Rev. G. A. CHADWICK, D.D.
Colossians and Philemon
By the Rev. ALEX. MACLAREN.
Genesis
By the Rev. Prof. MARCUS DODS, D.D.
1st Samuel
By the Rev. Prof. W. G. BLAIKIE, D.D., LL.D.
2nd Samuel
By the Rev. Prof. W. G. BLAIKIE, D.D., LL.D.
Hebrews
By the Rev. Principal T. C. EDWARDS, D.D.

SECOND SERIES.

Subscription Price, 24s. Separate Volumes, 7s. 6d. each.

Galatians
By the Rev. Prof. G. G. FINDLAY, B.A.
Isaiah. Chapters I.-XXXIX.
By the Rev. Prof. G. ADAM SMITH, M.A., D.D.
The Pastoral Epistles
By the Rev. ALFRED PLUMMER, D.D.
The First Epistle to the Corinthians
By the Rev. Prof. MARCUS DODS, D.D.
Epistles of St. John
By the Most Rev. W. ALEXANDER, D.D., Archbishop of Armagh.
Book of Revelation
By the Rev. Prof. W. MILLIGAN, D.D.

THIRD SERIES.

Subscription Price, 24s. Separate Volumes, 7s. 6d. each.

Judges and Ruth
By the Rev. R. A. WATSON, D.D.
The Prophecies of Jeremiah
With a Sketch of his Life and Times. By the Rev. C. J. BALL, M.A.
Exodus
By the Rt. Rev. G. A. CHADWICK, D.D.
St. Matthew
By the Rev. J. MONRO GIBSON, D.D.
St. Luke
By the Rev. HENRY BURTON, M.A.
Isaiah. Chapters XL.-LXVI.
By the Rev. Prof. G. ADAM SMITH, M.A., D.D.

FOURTH SERIES.

Subscription Price, 24s. Separate Volumes, 7s. 6d. each.

Gospel of St. John. Vol. I.
By the Rev. Prof. MARCUS DODS, D.D.
Acts of the Apostles. Vol. I.
By the Rev. Prof. G. T. STOKES, D.D.
Leviticus
By the Rev. S. H. KELLOGG, D.D.
Proverbs
By the Rev. R. F. HORTON, M.A., D.D.
St. James and St. Jude
By the Rev. A. PLUMMER, D.D.
Ecclesiastes
With a New Translation. By the Rev. SAMUEL COX, D.D.

FIFTH SERIES.

Subscription Price, 24s. Separate Volumes, 7s. 6d. each.

Thessalonians
By the Rev. JAMES DENNEY, D.D.
Job
By the Rev. R. A. WATSON, D.D.
The Gospel of St. John. Vol. II.
By Prof. MARCUS DODS, D.D.
Ephesians
By the Rev. Prof. G. G. FINDLAY, B.A.
The Acts of the Apostles. Vol. II.
By the Rev. Prof. G. T. STOKES, D.D.
The Psalms. Vol. I.
By the Rev. ALEXANDER MACLAREN, D.D.

SIXTH SERIES.

Subscription Price, 24s. Separate Volumes, 7s. 6d. each.

Philippians
By the Rev. Principal RAINY, D.D.
1st Kings
By the Very Rev. F. W. FARRAR, D.D., F.R.S.
Ezra, Nehemiah, and Esther
By the Rev. Prof. W. F. ADENEY, M.A.
Joshua
By the Rev. Prof. W. G. BLAIKIE, D.D., LL.D.
The Psalms. Vol. II.
By the Rev. ALEXANDER MACLAREN, D.D.
Epistles of Peter
By the Rev. Prof. LUMBY, D.D.

SEVENTH SERIES.

Subscription Price, 24s. Separate Volumes, 7s. 6d. each.

Romans
By the Rev. HANDLEY C. G. MOULE, M.A., D.D.
2nd Kings
By the Very Rev. F. W. FARRAR, D.D., F.R.S
Chronicles
By the Rev. W H. BENNETT, M.A.
2nd Corinthians
By the Rev. JAMES DENNEY, D.D.
Numbers
By the Rev. R. A. WATSON, D.D.
The Psalms. Vol. III.
By the Rev. ALEXANDER MACLAREN, D.D.

EIGHTH AND FINAL SERIES.

Seven Volumes. Subscription Price, 28s. Separate Volumes, 7s. 6d. each.

Book of Daniel
By the Very Rev. F. W. FARRAR, D.D., F.R S.
Jeremiah
By the Rev. W. H. BENNETT, M.A.
Deuteronomy
By the Rev. Prof. ANDREW HARPER, D.D.
The Song of Solomon and the Lamentations of Jeremiah
By the Rev. W. F. ADENEY, M.A.
Ezekiel
By the Rev. JOHN SKINNER, M.A.
The Book of the Twelve Prophets
By the Rev. Prof. GEORGE ADAM SMITH, D.D. In Two Volumes.

LONDON: HODDER & STOUGHTON, 27 PATERNOSTER ROW.